THE

MENNONITE ENCYCLOPEDIA

THE

Mennonite Encyclopedia

A Comprehensive Reference Work
on the
Anabaptist-Mennonite Movement

VOLUME I

A–C

Mennonite Brethren Publishing House, Hillsboro, Kansas
Mennonite Publication Office, Newton, Kansas
Mennonite Publishing House, Scottdale, Pennsylvania

1955

EDITORS

Cornelius Krahn, Editor
North Newton, Kansas

Melvin Gingerich, Managing Editor
Goshen College, Goshen, Indiana

Orlando Harms, Associate Editor
Hillsboro, Kansas

PREFACE

In view of the fact that the first volume of the *Mennonite Encyclopedia* is out of print, the publishers and editors have agreed to prepare a reprint. It is the present intention to reprint the remaining volumes at intervals of one year. Some corrections have been made based on information gathered in the editorial offices contributed by readers of the *Encyclopedia*. These corrections have been limited to such as can be made without changing the number of lines in the column.

The editors are also charged with the responsibility of planning for a completely revised edition of the *Encyclopedia* when the reprint is exhausted. They solicit suggestions and information for both the reprint and the revised edition.

CORNELIUS KRAHN, Editor
MELVIN GINGERICH, Managing Editor

January, 1969

BOARD OF EDITORS

1955

Editors

Publisher's Preface

The *Mennonite Encyclopedia* is a joint publishing enterprise, in which three North American Mennonite publishing agencies are co-operating. The direct administration of the enterprise is assigned to a Publishing Committee of six, composed of two representatives appointed by each agency. The Publishing Committee appoints the Editorial Board and Editorial Council for the *Encyclopedia*, approves the editorial policies, fixes the format, chooses the printer, and determines the general publication policies. The financial underwriting of the costs of production and the sales distribution of the finished product is handled by the three agencies under an appropriate agreement. Each agency is responsible for the distribution within its own agreed upon Mennonite constituency, but the Mennonite Publishing House handles the general distribution and sales.

The associated publishers with their representatives on the Publishing Committee as of 1954 are as follows: *Mennonite Brethren Publishing House,* Hillsboro, Kansas, for the Mennonite Brethren Church (Orlando Harms, P. E. Schellenberg); *Mennonite Publication Office,* Newton, Kansas, for the General Conference Mennonite Church (H. J. Andres, Abram Wiebe); *Mennonite Publishing House,* Scottdale, Pennsylvania, for the Mennonite Church (Paul Erb, A. J. Metzler).

PAUL ERB, *Chairman, The Publishing Committee*

EDITORIAL COUNCIL

1955

At Large

PREFACE

The *Mennonite Encyclopedia* is designed to give comprehensive and authentic information on a wide range of historical and contemporary topics relating to the Anabaptist-Mennonite movement from the beginning in the early 16th century to the present time.

It attempts an exhaustive coverage in all fields of Anabaptist-Mennonite history, theology, ethics, and life, except in biography where the selection has been limited to the more significant personages, and in family histories where only the larger families have been treated. A serious attempt has been made to supply articles on all known existing and extinct congregations, institutions, ecclesiastical organizations, and church publications, in all countries and in all branches of Anabaptists and Mennonites. At least brief articles are supplied on all known Anabaptist martyrs—Swiss, German, Austrian, and Dutch—over 2,000 in number. Special diligence has been applied to the history of the Mennonites in Russia, Prussia, and Poland, where organized Mennonitism is now apparently extinct; articles are furnished on all former Mennonite settlements and villages, and also as far as possible for all elders in these countries.

Occasionally the most diligent efforts have failed to uncover even the minimum of information on desired topics, either because sources are no longer available or because assigned writers failed to deliver the needed materials. The lack of working scholars for certain areas and fields has been keenly felt. In spite of diligent efforts the editors were not in a position, in view of the limits of time and other duties, to do the research and editing which might well have improved the quality and extended the scope of many articles. They can plead also that in many cases the basic research, and often the evaluation and interpretation of primary data, has not yet been done. It was not possible, for instance, to fully exploit the most recent Anabaptist source publications such as the *Täufer-Akten* volumes for Hesse, Zürich, Baden-Pfalz, etc., which appeared during the course of the preparation of the first volume. To have awaited the results of further research and publication in the vast field covered by the *Encyclopedia* would have unwarrantably delayed publication. An endeavor will be made to correct omissions by adding supplementary articles in Volume IV.

The *Encyclopedia* has leaned heavily for its European articles upon the *Mennonitisches Lexikon*, edited by the late Christian Hege (1869-1943) and Christian Neff (1863-1946) and published in Germany at Frankfurt a.M. and Weierhof (Pfalz). This pioneer effort, whose first installment was published in 1913, had reached the letter "O" by 1942 when the vicissitudes of World War II forced its suspension. After the war publication was resumed in 1951 by the new editors, Ernst Crous of Göttingen, Germany, and Harold S. Bender of Goshen, Indiana. It is hoped that the *Lexikon* will be completed in time for the *Encyclopedia* to take full advantage of its content, with its rich mine of information, particularly on the Anabaptists of the 16th century. The editors of the *Encyclopedia* fully and gratefully acknowledge their indebtedness to the *Lexikon*. Outstanding Anabaptist scholars such as Johann Loserth of Graz,

Austria; Gustav Bossert, Sr., of Horb, Württemberg; and Karel Vos of Middelstum, Holland, were substantial contributors, in addition to editors Hege and Neff themselves who together wrote more than half of the contents. Most of the European material in the *Lexikon* has been used in the *Encyclopedia* with only slight revisions, but some articles have been considerably condensed or enlarged, and some omitted. A few articles have been completely rewritten, and those dealing with contemporary topics have been brought up to date.

Though built basically upon the *Lexikon* for its European materials, the *Encyclopedia* is far from being merely a translation and reprint of the former work. The field of North and South American Mennonitism, which was scarcely touched by the *Lexikon*, has been exhaustively covered by the *Encyclopedia*. Certain other areas of interest which were somewhat neglected by the *Lexikon* have been properly covered in the new work, such as agriculture, business, cultural pursuits, family history, missions, and charities. A considerable number of new theological articles have been added, and reports on ecclesiastical organizations and practices have been greatly expanded. Sociological and cultural aspects have been broadly covered. Many more biographies, and congregational and institutional articles, have been included, the selection of which was made in consultation with the Editorial Council. The number of maps and illustrations has been greatly increased, most of which appear here for the first time.

The editors wish to gratefully acknowledge their indebtedness to the heirs of the late editors-publishers of the *Mennonitisches Lexikon* who generously made available the entire contents of the German publication, including the extant unpublished manuscripts, with all rights. Here should be mentioned Adele Hege of Karlsruhe-Thomashof, Baden, and Hans and Ina Neff, Mrs. Löber, and Mrs. Hirschler, all now of Weierhof. The current editors and publishers of the *Lexikon* have also graciously made available all their materials with full rights. In return the *Encyclopedia* is making all its materials available to the *Lexikon* for use in the publication of a second edition or supplementary volume. This collaboration across the Atlantic is not only a source of scholarly satisfaction but also a symbol of the ties of brotherhood which unite the Mennonite churches across the boundaries of geography, nationality, and language.

The editors also gladly acknowledge their indebtedness to the large number of their associates and collaborators on the Editorial Board and Editorial Council, as well as to the many writers of articles, without whose help the *Encyclopedia* would have been quite impossible. The loss of C. Henry Smith, one of the two original editors, in the very first years of the work, has been deeply felt, although his wisdom, vision, and comprehensive knowledge were available for the planning of the work, which was completed in essence before his late lamented death. Except for the untimely death of C. F. Klassen in 1954, the entire Editorial Board could work together in the completion of Volume I, and of Volume II which is to follow soon. The Editorial Council, to whom many questions and numerous articles have been referred, have rendered a most useful service. The editors gratefully acknowledge outstanding contributions by Assistant Editors N. van der Zijpp (for Holland), Ernst Crous (for Germany), and Robert Friedmann (for the Hutterian Brethren). In particular van der Zijpp did a vast amount of painstaking work in the Dutch articles so that this field has been exhaustively and reliably covered.

The entire translation of the *Mennonitisches Lexikon* materials was the work of Elizabeth Horsch Bender. We are indebted to Mrs. Bender not only for her excellent translations but also for her strong support in the final copy-editing and proofreading in which she shared equally with the editors.

The bibliographies accompanying the articles are chiefly designed to indicate the sources and authorities upon which the articles rest. Only in a few cases are they deliberately exhaustive.

Spellings of book titles and authors' names conform to the forms found in the sources, even though, in accord with the variable spelling practices of the 16th-18th centuries, there are evident inconsistencies. The authoritative modernization of Dutch spelling carried through in recent years, which we have respected for current usage, has contributed to the quantity of the inconsistencies in the Dutch articles. As a general policy the spelling of place names currently obtaining in the country of location has been followed. Exceptions have been made for such familiar forms as Cologne, Munich, Rome, Vienna, Danzig, etc., where the common English form is used. Exceptions have also been made for the Mennonite village and settlement names in Russia such as Chortitza (not Khortitsa) and in former East and West Prussia, where the familiar German forms have been used instead of the official Russian or Polish forms. But for France, Switzerland, Luxembourg, and Belgium the current national forms have been followed instead of the German version, even when the population is still German-speaking. In general the spelling of the foreign place names has been conformed to the published recommendations of the United States Board of Geographic Names and the usage of the standard geographic dictionaries.

Attention should be called to the practice of the *Encyclopedia* in listing personal names of the 16th century as titles of articles. Since family names were not in general use in Holland and Northwest Germany until the second third of the 17th century, the first or given name rather than the second name (which was usually either a patronymic or an occupational or place name) is used as the first word in the article title. For example, the article on Menno Simons appears under *Menno* rather than *Simons,* and the martyr Adriaen Jansz appears under *Adriaen* rather than *Jansz.*

Authors of articles are indicated by their initials (see key on pp. xiii-xvi) except in the case of the major authors in the *Mennonitisches Lexikon* where last names are written out, *viz.,* Hege, Loserth, and Neff. The initials of the *Encyclopedia* editors who have revised these and other *Lexikon* articles are added. However, the work of the editors in revision and enlargement of other articles, which at times was extensive, is not recognized by initials. In general N. van der Zijpp is editorially responsible for all Dutch articles, Ernst Crous for all German articles, Cornelius Krahn for all Russian articles, and Robert Friedmann for all Austrian and European Hutterite articles.

The editors would not fail to acknowledge the patient and generous support accorded them by the publishers in all stages of a rather extensive and expensive publishing venture. They share with the publishers the hope that their common faith may be rewarded in a generous reception of the finished product by the public both within and without the Mennonite brotherhood. It is no merely antiquarian interest which has motivated them, but rather a sincere desire that the riches of the past history and current life of the Anabaptist-Mennonite move-ment be made more generally available.

Harold S. Bender, Editor
Cornelius Krahn, Associate Editor

KEY TO SYMBOLS AND ABBREVIATIONS

A. Symbols Used for the North American Mennonite Bodies

Church of God in Christ, Mennonite (CGC)
Conservative Amish Mennonite (CAM)
Evangelical Mennonite Brethren (EMB)
Evangelical Mennonite Church (EMC)
Evan. Menn. (Kleine Gemeinde) (EMC, KG)
Gen. Conference Mennonite Church (GCM)
Hutterian Brethren (HB)

Krimmer Mennonite Brethren (KMB)
Mennonite Brethren Church (MB)
Mennonite Brethren, in Christ (MBC)
Mennonite Church (MC)
Old Order Amish Mennonite Church (OOA)
Old Order Mennonite Church (OOM)
United Missionary Church (UMC)

B. Geographical Abbreviations

States of the United States of America

Cal.	California	Mo.	Missouri
Col.	Colorado	Mont.	Montana
D.C.	Dist. of Columbia	Neb.	Nebraska
Fla.	Florida	N.D.	North Dakota
Ia.	Iowa	N.Y.	New York
Ida.	Idaho	O.	Ohio
Ill.	Illinois	Okla.	Oklahoma
Ind.	Indiana	Ore.	Oregon
Kan.	Kansas	Pa.	Pennsylvania
Ky.	Kentucky	S.D.	South Dakota
Minn.	Minnesota	Tex.	Texas
Miss.	Mississippi	Va.	Virginia

Countries

Arg.	Argentina
Au.	Austria
Br.	Brazil
Can.	Canada
Fr.	France
Ger.	Germany
Neth.	Netherlands
Par.	Paraguay
P.R.	Puerto Rico
Ru.	Russia
Sw.	Switzerland
Uru.	Uruguay

Provinces of Canada

Alta.	Alberta
B.C.	British Columbia
Man.	Manitoba
Ont.	Ontario
Sask.	Saskatchewan

Other

Co.	County
Twp.	Township

C. Bibliographical Symbols

ADB *Allgemeine Deutsche Biographie* 56v. (Leipzig, 1875-1912).

Beck, Geschichts-Bücher Josef Beck, *Die Geschichts-Bücher der Wiedertäufer in Oesterreich-Ungarn* (Vienna, 1883).

Bender, Two Centuries H. S. Bender, *Two Centuries of American Mennonite Literature, A Bibliography of Mennonitica Americana 1727-1928* (Goshen, 1929).

Bibliographie des Martyrologes F. Vander Haeghen, Th. Arnold, and R. Vanden Berghe, *Bibliographie des Martyrologes Protestants Néerlandais. II. Receuils* (The Hague, 1890).

Biogr. Wb. H. Visscher and L. A. Van Langeraad, *Biographisch Woordenboek von Protestantsche Godgeleerden in Nederland,* A-L (I, Utrecht), later by J. P. de Bie and J. Loosjes (II, III, IV, V, and installment #29, The Hague) 1903-

Blaupot t. C., Friesland Steven Blaupot ten Cate, *Geschiedenis der Doopsgezinden in Friesland* (Leeuwarden, 1839).

Blaupot t. C., Groningen . . . *Groningen, Overijssel en Oost-Friesland,* 2v. (Leeuwarden, 1842).

Blaupot t. C., Holland . . . *Holland, Zeeland, Utrecht en Gelderland,* 2v. (Amsterdam, 1847).

BRN S. Cramer and F. Pijper, *Bibliotheca Reformatoria Neerlandica,* 10v. (The Hague, 1903-14).

Catalogus Amst. *Catalogus der Werken over de Doopsgezinden en hunne Geschiedenis aanwezig in de Bibliotheek der Vereenigde Doopsgezinde Gemeente te Amsterdam* (Amsterdam, 1919).

DB *Doopsgezinde Bijdragen* vv. 1-56 (Amsterdam, 1861-1919).

DJ *Doopsgezind Jaarboekje* vv. 1-48 (Assen, et al., 1901-).

Friesen, Brüderschaft P. M. Friesen, *Die Alt-Evangelische Mennonitische Brüderschaft in Russland (1789-1910) im Rahmen der mennonitischen Gesamtgeschichte* (Halbstadt, 1911).

Gbl. *Gemeindeblatt der Mennoniten* vv. 1-85 (Sinsheim, later Karlsruhe, 1870-).

Gem.-Kal. *Mennonitischer Gemeinde-Kalender* (formerly *Christlicher Gem.-Kal.*) (various places, chiefly Kaiserslautern, Weierhof, Karlsruhe, 1892-).

Gesch. Bl. *Mennonitische Geschichtsblätter. Herausgegeben vom Mennonitischen Geschichtsverein* vv. 1-11 (Frankfurt, later Karlsruhe, 1936-).

Grosheide, Bijdrage Greta Grosheide, *Bijdrage tot de Geschiedenis der Anabaptisten in Amsterdam* (Hilversum, 1938).

Grosheide, Verhooren *Verhooren en Vonissen der Wederdoopers, betrokken bij de aanslagen op Amsterdam in 1534 en 1535,* in *Bijdragen en Mededeelingen van het Historisch Genootschap,* Vol. XLI (Amsterdam, 1920).

HRE: Herzog-Hauck, *Realencyclopädie für Prot. Theol. und Kirche* (3.ed., 24vv., Leipzig, 1896-1913).

Inv. Arch. Amst. J. G. de Hoop Scheffer, *Inventaris der Archiefstukken berustende bij de Vereenigde Doopsgezinde Gemeente te Amsterdam* 2v. (Amsterdam, 1883-84).

Kühler, Geschiedenis I W. J. Kühler, *Geschiedenis der Nederlandsche Doopsgezinden in de Zestiende Eeuw* (Haarlem, 1932).

Kühler, Geschiedenis II,1 *Idem, Geschiedenis van de Doopsgezinden in Nederland II. 1600-1735 Eerste Helft* (Haarlem, 1940).

Kühler, Geschiedenis II,2 *Idem, Geschiedenis van de Doopsgezinden in Nederland: Gemeentelijk Leven 1650-1735* (Haarlem, 1950).

Loserth, Anabaptismus Johann Loserth, *Der Anabaptismus in Tirol* (Vienna, 1892).

Loserth, Communismus J. Loserth, *Der Communismus der Mährischen Wiedertäufer im 16. und 17. Jahrhundert: Beiträge zu ihrer Lehre, Geschichte und Verfassung (Archiv für österreichische Geschichte,* Vol. LXXXI, 1, 1895).

Mart. Mir. D(utch) Tileman Jansz van Braght, *Het Bloedigh Tooneel of Martelaers Spiegel der Doops-gesinde of Weereloose Christenen, Die om 't getuygenis van Jesus haren Salighmaker geleden hebben ende gedood zijn van Christi tijd af tot desen tijd toe. Den Tweeden Druk* (Amsterdam, 1685), Part II.

Mart. Mir. E(nglish) *Idem, The Bloody Theatre or Martyrs' Mirror of the Defenseless Christians Who Baptized Only upon Confession of Faith and Who Suffered and Died for the Testimony of Jesus Their Saviour . . . to the Year A.D. 1660* (Scottdale, Pa., 1951).

Mellink, Wederdopers A. F. Mellink, *De Wederdopers in de Noordelijke Nederlanden 1531-1544* (Groningen, 1954).

Menn. Bl. *Mennonitische Blätter* vv. 1-88 (1854-1941), published variously at Danzig, Hamburg-Altona, and Elbing (W. Prussia).

Menn. Life *Mennonite Life* (North Newton, Kan., 1946-).

ML Christian Hege and Christian Neff, *Mennonitisches Lexikon,* 3v., A-R (Frankfurt and Weierhof, I, 1913; II, 1937; III, 1958; and IV, 1967.

MQR *Mennonite Quarterly Review* (Goshen, Ind., 1927-).

Müller, Berner Täufer Ernst Müller, *Geschichte der Bernischen Täufer* (Frauenfeld, 1895).

Naamlijst *Naamlijst der tegenwoordig in dienst zijnde predikanten der Mennoniten in de vereenigde Nederlanden* (Amsterdam, 1731, 1743, 1755, 1757, 1766, 1769, 1775, 1780, 1782, 1784, 1786, 1787, 1789, 1791, 1793, 1802, 1804, 1806, 1808, 1810, 1815, 1829).

N.N.B.Wb. *Nieuw Nederlandsch Biografisch Woordenboek* vv. 1-10 (Leiden, 1911-37).

Offer *Dit Boec wort genoemt: Het Offer des Herren, om het inhout van sommighe opgheofferde kinderen Godts . . .* (n.p., 1562, 1567, 1570, 1578, 1580, Amsterdam, 1590, n.p., 1591, Amsterdam, 1595, Harlingen, 1599). The 1570 edition is cited as reproduced in BRN II, 51-486. At the end of the volume is found *Een Liedtboecxken, tracterende van den Offer des Heeren* (pp. 499-617).

Reimer, Familiennamen Gustav E. Reimer, *Die Familiennamen der westpreussischen Mennoniten* (Weierhof, 1940).

Rembert, Wiedertäufer Karl Rembert, *Die "Wiedertäufer" im Herzogtum Jülich* (Berlin, 1899).

RGG: *Die Religion in Geschichte und Gegenwart* (2.ed., 5 vv., Tübingen, 1927-32).

TA Baden-Pfalz M. Krebs, *Quellen zur Geschichte der Täufer. IV. Band, Baden und Pfalz* (Gütersloh, 1951).

TA Hessen G. Franz, *Urkundliche Quellen zur hessischen Reformationsgeschichte. Vierter Band, Wiedertäuferakten 1527-1626* (Marburg, 1951).

TA Zürich L. von Muralt und W. Schmid, *Quellen zur Geschichte der Täufer in der Schweiz. Erster Band Zürich* (Zürich, 1952).

Verheyden, Brugge A. L. E. Verheyden, *Het Brugsche Martyrologium (12 October 1527-7 Augustus 1573)* (Brussel, n.d., [1944]).

Verheyden, Courtrai, *Le Martyrologe Courtraisien et la Martyrologe Bruxellois* (Vilvorde, 1950).

Verheyden, Gent *Idem, Het Gentsche Martyrologium (1530-1595)* (Brugge, 1946).

Wackernagel, Kirchenlied Ph. Wackernagel, *Das deutsche Kirchenlied,* 5v. (Leipzig, 1864-77).

Wackernagel, Lieder Philipp Wackernagel, *Lieder der niederländischen Reformierten aus der Zeit der Verfolgung im 16. Jahrhundert* (Frankfurt, 1867).

Wiswedel, Bilder W. Wiswedel, *Bilder und Führergestalten aus dem Täufertum,* 3v. (Kassel, I, 1928; II, 1930; III, 1952).

Wolkan, Geschicht-Buch Rudolf Wolkan, *Geschicht-Buch der Hutterischen Brüder* (Macleod, Alta., and Vienna, 1923).

Wolkan, Lieder *Idem, Die Lieder der Wiedertäufer* (Berlin, 1903).

Zieglschmid, Chronik A. J. F. Zieglschmid, *Die älteste Chronik der Hutterischen Brüder: Ein Sprachdenkmal aus frühneuhochdeutscher Zeit* (Ithaca, 1943).

Zieglschmid, Klein-Geschichtsbuch *Idem, Das Klein-Geschichtsbuch der Hutterischen Brüder* (Philadelphia, 1947).

D. Other Symbols and Abbreviations

A.D.S. Algemeene Doopsgezinde Societeit. **MCC** Mennonite Central Committee.

CPS Civilian Public Service. **KfK** Kommission für kirchliche Angelegenheiten.

q.v. "quod vide," "which see," is a cross-reference indicating that an article on the subject is to be found in the regular alphabetical order.

* signifies deceased. **†** indicates that an illustration will be found at the end of the volume.

MAPS AND ILLUSTRATIONS

The maps listed below will be found in the text next to the articles they serve. Illustrations are grouped at the end of each volume. For a complete list of illustrations in Volume I, see pp. 1 f. of pictorial supplement.

Alphabetical List of Maps, Volumes I—IV

Africa
Alberta
Alexandertal (Samara)
Allen Co., Ohio
Alsace, Upper
Alternative Service Camps
Amish Settlements
Argentina
Austria
Barnaul (Russia)
Belgium
Bern (Canton)
Brazil
British Columbia
Bucks-Montgomery Co., Pa.
California
Canada (all Mennonites)
Caucasus Region
Central Asia
Chaco Mennonite Colonies
Chicago
China
Chortitza (Russia)
Church of God in Christ, Mennonite
Civilian Public Service
Congo
Conservative Amish Mennonite Church
Cottonwood Co., Minn.
Danzig, Free State
East Reserve, Manitoba
Elkhart-Lagrange Co., Ind.
Emmental (Switzerland)
Europe
Evangelical Mennonite Church
Evangelical Mennonite Brethren
(above 2 on one map)
France
Far East
Frazer River Valley (B.C.)
Friesland (Holland)
Galicia
General Conference Mennonite Church
Germany
Groningen (Holland)
Harvey-McPherson-Marion Co., Kan.
Holmes Co., Ohio
Hutterites in North America
Hutterite Bruderhofs in Europe
Idaho (with Washington)
Illinois
India
Indiana
Indonesia
Iowa

Japan
Java Mission
Johnson-Washington Co., Iowa
Kansas
Krimmer Mennonite Brethren
Lancaster Co.
Manitoba
Maryland
Luxembourg
Memrik (Russia)
Menn. Colonies in Mexico
Mennonite Church
Mennonite Brethren Church
Michigan
Mifflin Co., Pa.
Missouri
Molotschna (Russia)
Montana (with Washington)
Nebraska
Netherlands
New York
North America
North Holland Province
Ohio
Oklahoma
Oregon (with Washington)
Orenburg (Russia)
Ontario
Palatinate (Germany)
Paraguay
Pennsylvania
Rockingham Co., Va.
Russia (Europe)
San Joaquin Valley, Cal.
Saskatchewan
South Dakota
Siberia
Somerset Co., Pa.
South America
Switzerland
Tazewell-Woodford-McLean Co., Ill.
Terek (Russia)
Trakt (Russia)
Ukraine
Uruguay (see Argentina)
United States
Virginia
Volga Region (Russia)
Washington, Oregon, Idaho, Montana
Waterloo Co., Ont.
Wayne Co., Ohio
West Reserve, Manitoba
Zagradovka (Russia)

KEY TO SYMBOLS FOR WRITERS IN VOLUME I

Albrecht, E. A., Fortuna, Mo.	E.A.A.
Albrecht, Edwin, Grabill, Ind.	E.A.
Albright, Raymond W., Reading, Pa.	R.W.A.
Amstutz, Ira, Apple Creek, O.	I.A.
Amstutz, J. E., Trenton, O.	J.E.A.
Andres, H. J., Newton, Kan.	H.J.A.
Arnold, Eberhard, Primavera, Alto Par.	E.C.H.A.
Bacon, Gordon, Bremen, Ind.	G.B.
Baerg, H. G., Lustre, Mont.	H.G.B.
Barfoot, Winnifred, Port Hope, Ont.	W.B.
Bargen, Mary, Mt. Lake, Minn.	M.B.
Barley, Percy R., Gormley, Ont.	P.Ba.
*Barthel, H. C., Balk, Neth.	H.C.B.
*Bartsch, Franz (Russia)	F.B.
Basinger, Elmer, Summerfield, Ill.	E.B.
Bauman, Harold, Orrville, O.	H.B.
Bauman, H. R., Champa, India	H.R.B.
Bauman, I. W., Bluffton, O.	I.W.B.
Beachy, Alvin J., Bluffton, O.	A.J.B.
Beachy, Jonas S., Garnett, Kan.	J.S.B.
Bender, Byron W., Martinsburg, Pa.	B.W.B.
Bender, H. S., Goshen, Ind.	H.S.B.
Bender, Mrs. H. S., Goshen, Ind.	E.H.B.
Bender, Paul, Goshen, Ind.	P.Be.
Berg, H. Ford, Scottdale, Pa.	H.F.B.
Berg, P. H., Hillsboro, Kan.	P.H.B.
Bergen, J. I., Chilliwack, B.C.	J.I.B.
Bergen, J. W., Goltry, Okla.	J.W.B.
*Bergmann, Cornelius, Jena, Ger.	C.B.
*Binnerts, A. S., Haarlem, Neth.	A.S.B.
Bittinger, Elmer E., Springs, Pa.	E.E.B.
Bixler, Annie, Kidron, O.	A.Bi.
*Boekenoogen, J. G., Krommenie, Neth.	J.G.B.
Bontrager, David A., Middlebury, Ind.	D.A.B.
Bontrager, Eli J., Shipshewana, Ind.	E.J.B.
Bontrager, John K., Darien, N.Y.	J.B.
Bontrager, Manasseh, Middlebury, Ind.	M.B.
*Brandt, Th., Leipzig, Ger.	Th.B.
Braun, A., Ibersheim, Ger.	A.B.
Braun, B. J., Dinuba, Cal.	B.J.B.
Braun, J. P., Abbotsford, B.C.	J.P.B.
*Braun, Peter, Oberursel, Ger.	P.Br.
Brenneman, T. H., Sarasota, Fla.	T.H.B.
Brown, W. Cecil, Owen Sound, Ont.	W.C.B.
Brunk, George R., Denbigh, Va.	G.R.B.
Brunk, Harry A., Harrisonburg, Va.	H.A.B.
Buckwalter, Paul, Los Angeles, Cal.	P.Bu.
Bueckert, David, Eyebrow, Sask.	D.B.
Bueckert, John P., Gretna, Man.	J.P.Bu.
Buller, P. P., Newton, Kan.	P.P.B.
Burgess, William K., Detroit, Mich.	W.K.B.
Burkholder, D. O., Nappanee, Ind.	D.O.B.
*Burkholder, L. J., Markham, Ont.	L.J.B.
Burkholder, Oscar, Breslau, Ont.	O.B.
*Busé, H. J., Hallum, Neth.	H.J.B.
Byers, Noah E., Bluffton, O.	N.E.B.
Byler, J. N., Akron, Pa.	J.N.B.
*Calcar van, J. D., Beverwijk, Neth.	J.D.vC.
Calhoun, I. R., Chicago, Ill.	I.R.C.
*ten Cate, E. M., Apeldoorn, Neth.	E.M.t.C.
*Claassen, H. Albert, Beatrice, Neb.	H.A.C.
Clemens, J. C., Lansdale, Pa.	J.C.C.
Clemens, James R., Goshen, Ind.	J.R.C.
Coffman, Barbara F., Vineland, Ont.	B.F.C.
Correll, Ernst H., Washington, D.C.	E.H.C.
*Cramer, Samuel, Amsterdam, Neth.	S.C.
Cressman, J. B., Kitchener, Ont.	J.B.C.
Cressman, John A., Preston, Ont.	J.A.C.
Crous, Ernst, Göttingen, Ger.	E.C.
Culp, Emanuel I., Tiskilwa, Ill.	E.I.C.
Dahlenberg, Paul, Cordell, Okla.	P.D.
Dalke, Herbert M., Weatherford, Okla.	H.M.D.
Dean, R. D., Athens, Mich.	R.D.D.
Decker, David, Olivet, S.D.	D.D.
*Delden, J. van, Gronau, Ger.	J.v.D.
Dester, Emil A.	E.A.D.
Dettweiler, Reuben, Elmira, Ont.	R.D.
Dick, A. A., Mountain Lake, Minn.	A.A.D.
Dick, George G., Bloomfield, Mont.	G.G.D.
Dick, Peter J., Chilliwack, B.C.	P.J.D.
Diener, Charles, Canton, Kan.	C.D.
Diener, D. Edward, Clarence, N.Y.	D.E.D.
Diller, Clarence D., Bluffton, O.	C.D.D.
Dollinger, Robert, Weiden, Ger.	R.Do.
*Driedger, A., Heubuden, Ger.	A.D.
Driver, Jos. C., La Junta, Col.	J.C.D.
Dueck, A. H., N. Kildonan, Man.	A.H.D.
Dueck, H. ·H., County Line, B.C.	H.H.D.
Dutcher, Frank, Beech, Ky.	F.D.
Dyck, Cornelius J., Elbing, Kan.	C.J.D.
Dyck, F. K., Whitewater, Man.	F.K.D.
Dyck, P. P., Rosemary, Alta.	P.P.D.
Ebersole, Allen B., Canton, O.	A.B.E.
Eichorn, Annie, Clarence, N.Y.	A.E.
*Ellenberger, H., Ludwigshafen, Ger.	H.E.
Engbrecht, Marvin, Dolton, S.D.	M.E.
Enns, J. H., Winnipeg, Man.	H.J.E.
Enns, John, Lowe Farm, Man.	J.E.
*Ens, Gerhard, Rosthern, Sask.	G.E.
Epp, Arnold A., Burrton, Kan.	A.A.E.
*Epp, David H., Chortitza, Ru.	D.H.E.
Epp, Dietrich H., Rosthern, Sask.	D.E.
Epp, J. H., Hepburn, Sask.	J.H.E.
Erb, Allen H., La Junta, Col.	A.H.E.
Erb, Paul, Scottdale, Pa.	P.E.
Ewert, Benjamin, Winnipeg, Man.	B.E.
*Fast, Bernhard (Russia)	B.F.
Fast, J. W., Blaine, Wash.	J.W.Fa.
Fast, Leander D., Channing, Mich.	L.D.F.
de Fehr, C. A., Winnipeg, Man.	C.A.D.F.
Fisher, Sam, Woodburn, Ind.	S.F.
*Fleischer, F. C., Winterswijk, Neth.	F.C.F.
Foth, Johannes, Friedelsheim, Ger.	J.F.
Foth, Robert	R.Foth
Franz, J. H., Filadelfia, Par.	J.H.Franz
Franzen, Henry, Buhler, Kan.	H.F.
Fretz, Clarence, Harrisonburg, Va.	C.F.
Fretz, J. C., Kitchener, Ont.	J.C.F.
Fretz, J. Herbert, Freeman, S.D.	J.H.F.
Fretz, J. Winfield, N. Newton, Kan.	J.W.F.
Friedmann, Robert, Kalamazoo, Mich.	R.F.
Friesen, Arthur, Clinton, Okla.	A.F.

Lark, James, Hopkins Park, Ill.	J.H.L.	Peters, Jacob H., Langham, Sask.	J.H.P.
Leaman, A. H., Chicago, Ill.	A.H.L.	Pittman, Leonard	L.P.
Leatherman, Quintus, Souderton, Pa.	Q.L.	Plett, C. F., Dinuba, Cal.	C.F.P.
*Leendertz, C. A., Norden, Ger.	C.A.L.	*Pohl, Matthias, Sembach, Ger.	M.P.
Lehman, Leland C., Berne, Ind.	L.C.L.	Pugh, Donald, Alymer, Ont.	D.P.
Lehman, M. M., Butterfield, Minn.	M.M.L.	Quiring, Horst, Stuttgart, Ger.	H.Q.
Lehman, Ralph S., Denver, Col.	R.S.L.	Quiring, Walter, Winnipeg, Man.	W.Q.
Lehman, Rhoda F., Chambersburg, Pa.	R.F.L.	Raber, Frank B., Kansas City, Kan.	F.B.R.
Lehrman, H. H., Aberdeen, Ida.	H.H.L.	Ramseyer, L. L., Bluffton, O.	L.L.R.
Lepp, Henry, Bakersfield, Cal.	H.L.	Rassi, L. L., Elkhart, Ind.	L.L.Ras.
Lichti, Elmer, Deer Creek, Okla.	E.L.	Redekop, H. H., Winkler, Man.	H.H.R.
Litwiller, Nelson, Goshen, Ind.	N.L.	Redekop, J. K., Mountain Lake, Minn.	J.K.R.
Loewen, Jacob G., Creswell, Ore.	J.G.L.	Regehr, Jacob I., Main Centre, Sask.	J.I.R.
Lohrenz, G., Winnipeg, Man.	G.L.	Regier, Elizabeth Linscheid, Newton, Kan.	E.L.R.
Lohrenz, J. H., Hillsboro, Kan.	J.H.Lo.	Regier, P. L.	P.L.R.
*Loosjes, J., Bussum, Neth.	J.L.	Reimer, David P., Giroux, Man.	D.P.R.
*Loserth, J., Graz, Au.	Loserth	Reimer, Gustav, Montevideo, Uru.	G.R.
*Lulofs, S., The Hague, Neth.	S.L.	Reimer, Gustav E., Jr., Montevideo, Uru.	G.R.Jr.
Maarse, J., Hoorn, Neth.	J.M.	*Reinders, L., Berlikum, Neth.	L.R.
Mallott, Floyd E., Chicago, Ill.	F.E.M.	Rembert, Karl, Crefeld, Ger.	K.R.
*Mannhardt, H. G., Danzig, Ger.	H.G.M., also G.M.	Rempel, Heinrich	H.R.
		Rempel, J. G., Rosthern, Sask.	J.G.R.
Massanari, Karl L., Goshen, Ind.	K.L.M.	Rempel, P. A., Altona, Man.	P.A.R.
Mast, C. Z., Elverson, Pa.	C.Z.M.	Riggall, J. H., Staten Island, N.Y.	J.H.R.
Mast, John B., Weatherford, Okla.	J.B.M.	Ringenberg, R., Augsburg, Ger.	R.R.
Miller, Grace, Kalona, Ia.	G.Mi.	*Risser, John D., Hagerstown, Md.	J.D.R.
Miller, Herbert E., Newton, Kan.	H.E.M.	Rogalsky, J. P., Hillsboro, Kan.	J.P.R.
Miller, Ivan J., Grantsville, Md.	I.J.M.	Roth, Paul, Canby, Ore.	P.N.R.
Miller, Jonas B., Grantsville, Md.	J.B.Mi.	Rupp, E. E., Archbold, O.	E.E.R.
Miller, L. A., Arthur, Ill.	L.A.M.	Sauder, Jerry H., Grabill, Ind.	J.H.S.
Miller, Orie A., Peoria, Ill.	O.A.M.	Schantz, Albert, Fronberg bei Schwandorf,	
Miller, Russell M., Goshen, Ind.	R.M.M.	Ger.	A.S.
Miller, Thomas H., Kalona, Ia.	T.H.M.	Schellenberg, B. J., Winnipeg, Man.	B.J.S.
Mohr, W. H., Allentown, Pa.	W.H.M.	Schellenberg, P. E., Hillsboro, Kan.	P.E.S.
Moyer, Grace, Allentown, Pa.	G.Mo.	Schmidt, John F., N. Newton, Kan.	J.F.S.
Müller, Ernst, Prehof, Ger.	E.M.	Schmucker, N. J., Berne, Ind.	N.J.S.
Mumaw, Gladys, Elkhart, Ind.	G.Mu.	Schowalter, Paul, Weierhof, Ger.	P.S.
Mumaw, John R., Harrisonburg, Va.	J.R.M.	Schrock, T. E., Clarksville, Mich.	T.E.S.
Mumaw, Stanford, Dalton, O.	S.M.	Schroeder, G. W., Munich, N.D.	G.W.S.
Musselman, Howard Y., Orrtanna, Pa.	H.M.	Schultz, George P., Chicago, Ill.	G.P.S.
*Neff, Christian, Weierhof, Ger.	Neff	Schulz, J. J., Winnipeg, Man.	J.J.S.
Neil, Mrs. C. A., Levering, Mich.	C.A.N.	Sepp, A. A., Edam, Neth.	A.A.S.
Neuenschwander, A., Grabill, Ind.	A.N.	Shank, Clarence, Marion, Pa.	C.S.
Neuenschwander, A. J., Wadsworth, O.	A.J.N.	Shank, Clarence A., Wakarusa, Ind.	C.A.S.
Neufeld, Cornelius G., Didsbury, Alta.	C.G.N.	Shank, J. R., Versailles, Mo.	J.R.S.
Neufeld, Henry, Winnipeg, Man.	H.N.	Shank, J. W., Harrisonburg, Va.	J.W.S.
Neufeld, I. G., Phoenix, Ariz.	I.G.N.	Shank, J. Ward, Broadway, Va.	J.Wa.S.
Neufeld, Jacob A., Virgil, Ont.	J.A.N., also J.N.	Shank, Lester C., Harrisonburg, Va.	L.C.S.
Neufeld, Peter T., Inman, Kan.	P.T.N.	Shantz, H., Markham, Ont.	H.S.
Neuhouser, J. S., Ft. Wayne, Ind.	J.S.N.	Shantz, Ray, Castor, Alta.	R.S.
Nickel, Ben J., Wolf Point, Mont.	B.J.N.	Shantz, Sidney S., Hanover, Ont.	S.S.S.
Nickel, J. W., Denver, Col.	J.W.N.	Shelly, Paul R., Bluffton, O.	P.R.S.
Niepoth, Wilhelm, Crefeld, Ger.	W.N.	Shelly, Ward W., Coopersburg, Pa.	W.W.S.
Nighswander, Fred L., Stouffville, Ont.	F.L.N.	Shirk, Eli M., Ephrata, Pa.	E.M.S.
*Nijdam, C., Amsterdam, Neth.	C.N.	Short, Reuben, Bluffton, O.	R.Sho.
Nissley, Joseph M., Altoona, Pa.	J.M.N.	Showalter, Timothy, Broadway, Va.	T.S.
Nussbaumer, Hans, Altkirch, Fr.	H.Nu.	Siemens, John K., Hillsboro, Kan.	J.K.S.
*Nussbaumer, Samuel, Basel, Sw.	S.N.	*van Slee, J. C., Deventer, Neth.	J.C.S.
Ortmann, Hellmuth, Munich, N.D.	H.O.	*Smissen, H. van der, Hamburg, Ger.	H.vdS.
Overholt, Fanny, Council Bluffs, Ia.	F.O.	Smith, Abraham, Markham, Ont.	A.Sm.
Oyer, D. S., St. Johns, Mich.	D.S.O.	*Smith, C. Henry, Bluffton, O.	C.H.S.
Pannabecker, S. F., Chicago, Ill.	S.F.P.	Smith, Tilman R., Eureka, Ill.	T.R.S.
Pasma, F. H., Hilversum, Neth.	F.H.P.	Smith, Willard H., Goshen, Ind.	W.H.S.
Pearson, Bruce W., Flint, Mich.	B.W.P.	Smucker, Don. E., Chicago, Ill.	D.E.S.
Penner, D. H., Boyd, Okla.	D.H.P.	Snyder, Elvin V., La Plata, Puerto Rico	E.V.S.
Penner, Walter L., Bakersfield, Cal.	W.L.P.	Snyder, Paul V., Kalona, Ia.	P.V.S.

The Mennonite Encyclopedia

A

Aachen (Fr., Aix-la-Chapelle; Dutch, Aken), an ancient city on the western (Belgian) border of Germany, was already in the 16th century the seat of a thriving Mennonite congregation which was of significance in promoting contacts between the German and Dutch Anabaptists. Through the Anabaptists the doctrines of the Reformation were introduced to Aachen; this occurred in 1530, at the time of the coronation of Ferdinand I, who was to become their bitter enemy. W. Wolf ("Beiträge zu einer Reformationsgeschichte der Stadt Aachen," in *Theologische Arbeiten aus dem Rheinischen Wissenschaftlichen Prediger-Verein,* n.s. 7, 1905, 69-103) stresses the fact that any Protestant movement in Aachen before 1545 can with considerable certainty be claimed as Anabaptist. See "Rechnungsbücher der Aachener Mennonitengemeinde," in *Zeitschrift des Aachener Geschichtsvereins,* VI (1884) 295-338.

Among these early Anabaptists in Aachen was the glazier Wilhelm Stupmann, also called Mottencop or Mottenkoepgen, who preached in Maastricht and Liége, and who, as the Duke of Jülich reported to Bishop Eberhard of Liége on Aug. 16, 1533, had formed in the city a congregation whose members called each other Christian brethren. The council also received a report at about this time of the sermons of the citizen Laurenz Teschenmacher, which though designated as Lutheran, were actually Anabaptist sermons. The initial hearing against him was futile, since Teschenmacher refused to admit anything. The movement grew to such an extent that the council found it expedient to pass four severe measures of repression (Jan. 3, Jan. 20, April 4, and July 20, 1534) threatening non-Catholics with death. Executions and expulsions followed. Nevertheless the Anabaptists gained new adherents in the city, even among the nobility. Until about the middle of the century they were the only Reformation party in the city, during the 40's apparently suffering less oppression. But in February 1550, upon the command of Ferdinand (later emperor), the city council passed a decree prohibiting anyone from holding office or serving on the council, who had not lived in the city for seven successive years.

After the Peace of Augsburg in 1555, which excluded the Anabaptists, a hostile attitude toward them became apparent, which led to bloody persecution. When Hans Raiffer (*q.v.*), a Hutterite missionary from Moravia, stopped in Aachen and held services there, he was arrested by the council on Jan. 9, 1558, with eleven others. One of the prisoners retracted and was released, but the others could not be persuaded to do so either by friendly entreaty or severe torture. Six women were beaten and banished; after long incarceration the men were burned at the stake: Hans Raiffer on Oct. 19, 1558; Heinrich Adams and his brother-in-law Hans Beck on Oct. 22, 1558; Matthew Schmid and Dil-

mann Schneider on Jan. 4, 1559. The magistrates were for some time unable to agree on the death penalty. At length, Dec. 30, 1558, eight of them pledged (the document is in the Aachen archives) that in case any of their fellow magistrates did not appear upon notification to judge imprisoned rebaptized persons, they would not regard them any longer as magistrates, and would close their houses against them and hold no conversation with them; if a lawsuit should arise from this action, they would share the expense.

In 1559 a large number of Protestants from the Netherlands came to Aachen, who designated themselves as Lutheran and Reformed, and hence could not be banished as long as they conducted themselves quietly (as the council replied on May 15 to a letter from Philip II). But against the Mennonites among these immigrants the decree was enforced. Frequently citizens and noblemen were summoned on the charge that they had not had their children baptized and held services in their homes. Midwives were required under oath to report all parents who did not have their children baptized. Banishment followed. In 1573 the preacher Balthasar Marie was banished. When the guilds passed a regulation (July 23, 1574) admitting Protestants to the council, many Mennonites returned. Hans de Ries (*q.v.*) the noted preacher of the Mennonite congregation in Alkmaar, was for a time in Aachen and instituted a disputation on the nature of original sin. About 1580, when the Protestant majority gained control of the city, there was in Aachen a well-organized Mennonite congregation which had its own minister and maintained a school. The stern orders of the Duke of Jülich for the extermination of Anabaptists and Reformed in his territory added to the membership of the Mennonite congregation in the city. Complaints were made by pastors that some Lutherans and Reformed were joining the Mennonites. As long as the Protestants controlled the council no measures were taken against them, but after the re-establishment of a Catholic regime (1598) the mayor prohibited Mennonite preaching and banished the preacher. However, because of the financial embarrassment of the city the council refrained from passing more stringent measures and in return for a payment of 2,000 talers it postponed carrying out the decree of banishment. But in 1601 the Mennonites were compelled to choose between having their children baptized as Catholics and leaving the city, and most of them went to the neighboring town of Burtscheid (*q.v.*). Those who returned during the winter were banished anew in April 1602. The council tried to banish them from Burtscheid as well, and at its instigation, on July 16, 1602, the bailiff of Burtscheid ordered the Mennonites to leave within four days; but these orders were never carried out. The abbess of Burtscheid granted them residence in return for certain fees,

and they were also able to meet in Aachen **again**.
In 1607 there were in three of the nine districts in
Aachen 27 Mennonite families among 300 Catholic,
64 Reformed, and 87 Lutheran households. In a
few years a thriving congregation had been formed.
However, it was short-lived, for in 1614 600 of its
members were banished (mandate of Sept. 16, 1614,
in *Catalogus Amst.*, 101).

Some of those who remained submitted to having
their children baptized; the rest joined the Mennonites of Burtscheid to form a congregation which
those of near-by Vaals (*q.v.*) also joined. They
held their religious services in Vaals, and under
the protection of the Dutch States-General they
preached, baptized, and observed communion freely. But the broken congregation never regained its
former importance. In the middle of the 17th century there were living in Burtscheid 24 Mennonite
families; one hundred years later there were half
that number; by 1800 there were only two families
left. Today there are no Mennonites in Aachen.

In the 18th century, 1711-47, Jan Helgers was
the minister of this congregation, which was then
called Vaals-and-Maastricht; 1747-68, Peter Staal
was its preacher. In 1768 the congregation was
divided into two congregations, known respectively
as Vaals-Burtscheid and Maastricht. Vaals-Burtscheid did not succeed in having a pastor of its
own; the minister of the Maastricht (*q.v.*) congregation preached in Vaals until 1787. After his death
the congregation had no pastor of its own, but was
served twice a year by the Crefeld ministers Wopko
Molenaar, Zino von Abema, and van der Ploeg.
The last families were Loevenich (Leuvenig),
Schorn, Noppenei, de Graf, and Goyen.   HEGE.

Mart. Mir.; J. Fey, *Zur Gesch. Aachens im 16. Jahr.*
(Aachen, 1905); H. Forsthoff, *Rheinische Kirchengesch.*
I: *Die Ref. am Niederrhein* (Essen, 1929): *Aachen,* 365;
J. Hansen, "Die Wiedertäufer in Aachen und in der
Aachener Gegend," in *Ztscht des Aachener Geschichts-
vereins,* 1884; Macco; *Die ref. Bewegungen während des
16. Jahrh. in der Reichsstadt Aachen* (Leipzig, 1900);
H. F. Macco, *Zur Ref.-Gesch. Aachens während des 16.
Jahrh.* (Aachen, 1907); Rembert, *Wiedertäufer; Gedenk-
boek der Ned. Herv. Kerk van Maastricht 1632-1932*
(Maastricht, 1932) 380-82; *Beitr. zur Gesch. rheinischer
Menn.* (Weierhof, 1939); *DB,* 1909, 122; *ML* I, 1 f.

Aalen, county seat (*Kreisstadt*) in the Jagst district
of Württemberg, where the Anabaptist movement
of the Reformation period gained entry in the
domains of the noble families, but was brutally
suppressed by the raids of the Swabian League
(*q.v.*). The best known of these raids was the
attack on Mantelhof, an Ellwangen fief of the
barons of Woellwart, two miles southwest of Aalen.
Here the Anabaptists were meeting for a New
Year's service in 1531. The notorious Berthold
Aichele (*q.v.*), the provost of the Swabian League,
took the entire assembly prisoner and had them
put to death, some by hanging, and others by burning, because they refused to deny their faith. Seventeen Anabaptists met their death on this occasion.
(*Beschreibung des Oberamts Aalen,* Stuttgart, 1854,
321.)   HEGE.

Aalsmeer, a Mennonite congregation in the Dutch
province of North Holland, about ten miles southwest of Amsterdam. The population of the town
was 12,182 in 1947, with 1,230 Mennonites.

There must have been Anabaptists living here
as early as 1534, for on April 10 of that year two
inhabitants of Aalsmeer, both with the name of
Jan Dirks, were among the three Anabaptists who
opened the long series of martyrs in the Netherlands (Kühler, *Geschiedenis* I, 107). They remained steadfast, "going to their death like sheep, so
that it was amazing to see." Presumably these
Anabaptists lived for the most part in safe hiding
places in these swamps and marshes, "out of the
world" (*uit-den-weg:* 'out of the way), of which
the street (Menniste Buurt) is still a reminder.
In March 1597 a resolution of the States-General indicates that they were quite numerous in this region
by that time.

Very early there were here congregations of the
so-called Frisians, Waterlanders, and Flemish. The
Frisians met for worship in a *vermaning* (meetinghouse) at the end of present Uiterweg 378, called
De Vermaning and later *De Oude Vermaning*; the
Waterlanders met in *De Zandberg,* Uiterweg 14;
the Flemish in *De Leeuwenkuil,* Uiterweg 79.

About 1640 a division occurred among the Flemish; the enforcement of *eenvoud* (nonconformity)
had stirred up feeling, so that the *preciezen* (strict)
began to meet in a meetinghouse on the Zijdweg,
while the *rekkelijken* (more liberal) remained in
De Leeuwenkuil. In 1687 the breach between the
Flemish, Old Flemish, and Waterlanders was healed,
and from that time on they were known as
the *Vereenigde Waterlandse en Vlaamse Doopsgezinde Gemeente* and held their meetings at the Zijdweg. The decline in membership was an urgent
factor in this union, for together they had scarcely
57 members. This congregation in 1738 called Jan
de Bleyker of Middelharnis as its first salaried
minister. The church was burned down in 1844,
but was rebuilt in 1845.

The Frisian congregation was larger. It held
strictly to tradition on all points; but not much is
known about its history. Under the leadership of
four preachers chosen by the congregation without
previous discussion with the candidates (*zonder
voorafspraak:* they were not to decline before the
call, for the voice of the congregation was considered as *vox Dei*) they developed a strong spiritual life.

About 1780 this congregation also had a division
for the reason that a *voorafspraak* (previous consultation) was held about the choice of a preacher,
the *preciezen* condemning this step. Then in 1787
the *Nieuwe Vermaning,* Uiterweg 354, was used by
one part of the group, and the congregation funds
were divided. For a long time relations between
the *Oude Vermaning* group and the *Nieuwe Vermaning* group (the groups were known by the
names of their churches) were so strained that it
was forbidden by each group to marry into the
other. Nevertheless both groups observed the old
customs as strictly as possible, even the principle
of the lay ministry. As late as 1861 in choosing a
minister this statement was still used: "We believe
and testify that there is a need of workers in the

vineyard of the Lord, we must not get them from an academy or university, but must choose them by majority vote from the midst of the brotherhood." But on the other hand, it also occurred that a preacher crossed Haarlem Lake with his fishing boat, attended services at Haarlem, and—the next week preached the sermon he heard there to his own congregation. It also happened that young men preferred to remain outside the congregation rather than run the risk of being called to the ministry, because young men had to promise at their baptism to take upon themselves the obligation of the ministry in case they should be chosen.

On June 8, 1866, after a long conference tactfully conducted, the three congregations, the *Oude Vermaning,* the *Nieuwe Vermaning,* and that on the Zijdweg, with a total of about 400 members, united into the *Doopsgezinde Gemeente Aalsmeer* (Mennonite Church of Aalsmeer), having previously, on Oct. 22, 1865, held a joint communion service. Pastor Simon Gorter (*q.v.*) of the congregation on the Zijdweg deserves much of the credit for bringing this union about, although it took place during Brouwer's term. The old churches were unfortunately all torn down and replaced by a new large church (1867).

Now came the golden age of the congregation; in the fifty years after the merger the membership doubled. In 1913 the membership stood at 870, with about 500 catechumens and a total of 2,000 souls. In 1949 these were the figures: 781 members with about 520 households, about 340 catechumens, about 800 boys and girls between 8 and 20, who attend Westhill Sunday-school services, and about 600 nonmember households, who nevertheless maintain contact with the congregation, making an estimated total of about 4,000 souls.

Whence this difference in size? First, the modernist trend (beginning with Pastor L. van Cleeff, 1887-1905) relaxed the bonds with the old tradition. Second, the increased prosperity of the first thirty years of the present century has placed the members, almost exclusively gardeners, more "into the world." Third, an unreligious, though not antireligious socialism obtained a foothold in this congregation. Through these three influences the church received an influx of new members. When the new church was built in 1928 (planned by the architect J. F. Staal), seating room for 600 was considered adequate (the church built in 1867 under van Cleeff was enlarged to provide 800 seats). Although the position of the church "in the world" is much more difficult than formerly ("uit den weg" is still generally felt) it is agreed that it is impossible to move back into the past and that the church must assume and strengthen its position in this situation.

Of importance in accomplishing this purpose is the Westhill (Sunday school) work begun in 1927, which brings boys and girls of 4 to 20 years together in the service of their age group wherever possible. In strong regular growth the Westhill work has increased to 28 divisions with more than 800 girls and boys, with 160 leaders, assistants, organists, and about 30 workers behind the scene. These services are very faithfully attended (80-90 per cent). This work is also of significance for the entire country through a course in leadership and the publication of three periodicals: *De Bloem in Knop* (The Flower in Bud) for the four- to seven-year-olds, *Ontplooiing* (Unfolding) for the eight- to twelve-year-olds, and *Jonge Bloei* (Young Blossom) for the thirteen- to twenty-year-olds and older. In addition the congregation issues a monthly youth periodical, *De Toorts* (The Torch) and a monthly congregational paper, *Levenslicht* (Light of Life). In Aalsmeer-East and Aalsmeer-West districts have been established for religious services which are held once in two weeks. Thus the Aalsmeer congregation has 26 group services on every Sunday from September to June, most of which are conducted by lay members. In the congregation there are further a women's organization, a members' group, four youth groups (total of 110 members), a girls' workshop, and a library.

The history of the congregation has thus far not been written. In the *Doopsgezinde Jaarboekje* of 1920 Rev. Luikinga wrote a good sketch, "Langs een oude Vermaning." On the occasion of the third centennial of the founding of the congregation on the Zijdweg a booklet by D. W. Keesen Az. appeared, containing a brief chronicle of the most important events in the congregation. In this excellent portfolio pictures of the Aalsmeer churches as well as important facts were made available. The ministers who served the congregation after the union were P. Brouwer, 1863-87; L. van Cleeff, 1887-1905; W. Luikinga, 1907-15; H. C. Barthel, 1916-26; R. C. de Lange since 1927.

R. C. DE L.

Inv. Arch. Amst. II, No. 1439-52; II, 2, No. 1-2; Blaupot t. C., *Holland* I and II; *DJ* 1850, 16-21; 88-106; *DB* 1867, 196-98; *ML* I, 3 f.

Aankomelingen, or **aankomende vrienden,** the term used by early Dutch Mennonites for those who were of the age to be received into the brotherhood. After the regular services they received some instruction from the Bible and later from the confession of faith. If necessary, they were first taught to read. (See **Catechism** and **Youth.**) vDZ.

Aarau: see **Aargau.**

Aarburg: see **Aargau.**

Aardenburg, a small town of 3,800 inhabitants in the Dutch province of Zeeland, not far from the Belgian border. Here a Mennonite congregation was founded in 1614 by refugees from Flanders, though it is known that there had been a congregation in Aardenburg and vicinity at an earlier period. The new congregation had a hard time at first; in spite of religious freedom proclaimed by the States-General on May 1, 1615, especially for the Mennonites living here, they were still molested by the city government. The first meetings were held in a private house, and later in a meetinghouse in de Biezen outside the town. In 1636 a church was built in Aardenburg.

In the 17th century the congregation had excellent leaders. Jacques van Maldegem (*q.v.*) was elder until about 1636, Boudewijn de Meyere (*q.v.*) from 1633 to 1681, and Ghijsel Hebberecht (*q.v.*)

from about 1657 to 1680. Under their leadership the grim conflict with the government took place regarding exemption from military service, which, as everywhere in Holland, was finally also granted to the Mennonites of Aardenburg in return for a specified fee. About 1650 the congregation reached its greatest strength. Soon after this many Mennonites moved to Middelburg and the province of Holland. Familiar Mennonite family names, such as van Eeghen, Dobbelaer, Dyserinck, van der Sluys, of families which had come from Belgium and settled here, disappeared from the registers by about 1700.

When the *Lammerenkrijgh* (*q.v.*) divided the Mennonites of Holland into two camps, the Aardenburg congregation joined the Zonists (*q.v.*) after a visit by Samuel Apostool (*q.v.*) in 1665. Sometimes the congregation was called the congregation of Old Flemish. Even before 1691 no suitable lay preacher could be found in their own ranks, and a preacher was therefore called in on a salary. In the 18th century and especially in the first half of the 19th century there was a decline: the membership, which stood at 126 in 1636, and which had increased to more than 160 in 1670, was down to 46 in 1840. In 1952 the number of baptized members is 116, of whom half live in the town and half in the vicinity.

The congregation is a member of the *Zuidhollands-Zeeuwse Ring* (*q.v.*). It has a Sunday school, a youth organization, a women's organization, and a reading club. The members are exempt from payment or have reduced rates for medical and hospital care. The preachers of the congregation during the past century were H. Broese van Groenou, 1852-83; C. P. van Eeghen, Jr., 1883-92; G. Hofstede Gz., 1893-1903; Jacob Koekebakker, 1903-19; J. G. Frerichs, 1921-27; F. van der Wissel, 1927-32; Abr. Mulder, 1932-41; M. J. Nolthenius, 1941-51; and S. A. Vis, 1952-   .

In 1793 the church, which was in a dilapidated state, and was also much too large, was completely remodeled; in 1856 it was improved and in 1872 an organ was added. During September and October 1944 the church and parsonage were severely damaged, but have been rebuilt with the aid of the brotherhood.

Worthy of note is the fact that the Aardenburg congregation has a seal. The old church of 1636 was situated behind a house "where the lamb protruded" (*waar het lammeke uitstak*). And so this lamb was chosen as the symbol. The seal shows the lamb and has the marginal legend, *"de Kerck het Lam tot Aerdenburgh."*   vDZ.

H. Broese van Groenou, "Uit het verleden der Doopsgezinde gemeente te Aardenburg," in *DB* 1876, 1877, 1879, 1883, 1884, 1885; *ML* I, 4.

Aargau. The origins of the Anabaptist movement in the canton of Aargau, Switzerland, go back to 1526. Among its most prominent members were Hans Pfistermeyer (*q.v.*) and Heini Seiler (*q.v.*) the hatter, both of Aarau. The former was won for the movement (1525) by Jakob Gross (*q.v.*) of Waldshut; but on April 19, 1531, in Bern, where

as a prisoner he had to take part in a religious disputation, he rejoined the Reformed Church. The latter was arrested in Bern and after a severe trial involving torture, in which he remained steadfast, he was sentenced to death on April 8. In 1531 he was a fellow prisoner with Pfistermeyer, who urged him to yield on the point of infant baptism, but he refused and was drowned in that year. (The *Martyrs' Mirror* statement that he was executed in 1529 seems incorrect.) Another leader of the Anabaptists was Bernhard Sager of Bremgarten, who likewise was in prison in 1529 but was later released. In 1530 the government at Aarau fined the Anabaptists who had listened to the sermons of the Anabaptist Martin Weniger (*q.v.*) in the region of Solothurn.

Encouraged by the recantation of Hans Pfistermeyer, the government proclaimed a public religious disputation on July 1, 1532, which was held in Zofingen (*q.v.*) in Aargau. It was unsuccessful, however, for the Anabaptist movement (*Täuferunwesen*) continued to spread. One leading Anabaptist, Fridli Iberger of Schwyz, was, to be sure, induced to recant. He was one of the prisoners who had escaped from the Hexenturm in Zürich. After his exile from Zürich he worked successfully for the Anabaptist cause in Basel. Banished from Basel under penalty of death because of his violent attitude, he worked for a time as a cowherd. He was finally arrested in Rüttigen in the district (*Vogtei*) of Biberstein.

Stern measures were undertaken against the Anabaptists. Two of them, Hoegerli (called Hägerley in the *Martyrs' Mirror,* where the date of his death is incorrectly given as 1529) and Schnider (later, in 1535, another considerable number, including a native of Wallis [Valois] mentioned in the *Martyrs' Mirror* as "the young fellow of Wallis"), were taken to Bern and executed with the sword in 1535.

In the district (*Amt*) of Lenzburg the Anabaptist movement appears to have quietly spread. The meeting place was near the border, enabling them to flee quickly in case of pursuit. In a public discussion in 1538 two Anabaptists from this district and two from the district of Aarburg, besides Hans Vogt of Villingen, took part. When after this debate more rigorous measures were adopted, many emigrated to Moravia. By the middle of the 16th century this movement toward Moravia could be observed throughout Aargau. In 1548 Bern issued a decree imposing a fine of five pounds on women and ten pounds on men who attended Anabaptist meetings. Among those thus fined was a Rudolph Müller. Anabaptist books were to be collected and a strict watch kept over the Anabaptists. This led to a widespread emigration to Moravia. Frequently the local pastor was surprised by the departure of entire families. The property of these emigrants was confiscated. In 1578 the citizens were forbidden to purchase the estates of Anabaptists about to leave, in order to make sure that their fortunes would accrue to the state. Thus the state acquired 510 pounds from seven emigrants.

In Baden the two Swiss Brethren leaders Kuenzli and Johannes Kern were active in the Anabaptist cause as early as the 1520's. It is impossible to ascertain whether the movement spread to any considerable extent in this strongly Catholic region. But in the neighboring Protestant regions this must have been the case. This is indicated by the numerous emigrations to Moravia which were organized by Heinrich Müller of Meisterschwanden. From Reinach, to the south, 26 families emigrated. The receipts of the district treasury amounted in 23 years to 10,277 pounds. Most of the emigrants were of the well-to-do peasant class and their departure created a great sensation. All kinds of measures to prevent their going were resorted to. The pastor of the state church exhorted his members to avoid the emigrants to Moravia, calling the Anabaptists insurrectionists. Thereupon Baschi Frey of Menziken arose and asked the preacher whether he could name any insurrectionists. For this interruption he was mildly punished by a fine of ten pounds. Rudolph Schnider, Jakob Kolb, Hans Meyer, and Hans Locher are mentioned as insurrectionists, i.e., Anabaptist preachers, besides Jeremias Läser, who was held as prisoner in the castle March 19-21, 1593, and then taken to Bern.

In the 17th century Kulm became the center of the Swiss Brethren movement in the Wynen Valley. Heinrich Müller had come this far on his journey of propaganda, and persuaded many to emigrate to Moravia. We find familiar names among them and their relatives, such as Hans Haury of Hirschtal (had to pay a fine of 100 pounds for his sister), Hans Uli Widmer of Bottwyl, Hans Schwytzer of Hirschtal, Hans Schumacher of Wynstägen (in the *Martyrs' Mirror* incorrectly said to be from Wünistern), the Müller family in Bonhusen, Hans Luscher of Zofingen, Elsi und Uli Gut with their large family in the hamlet of Hinderswil. Josef Hauser (*q.v.*) of Zofingen, a learned man, originally a clergyman, was appointed as a Hutterite preacher at Neumühle in Moravia on probation; Hans Suter moved in 1587 from Seon to Moravia and had to pay a removal fee of 40 pounds. Hans Rudolph Suter was taken to Bern in 1593 because he was an Anabaptist preacher.

A martyr in the district of Aarburg was Hans Madliger, who was drowned at Hamburg on Feb. 10, 1531. Also from this place many emigrated to Moravia, among them one Hans Riedtmann of Brittnau, who went in 1573. About this time the Anabaptist preacher Andreas Glur of Birrwyl, also called Andreas Birrwyler, was active in the region of Aarburg. He must have been very successful. When he was captured in 1580 there were a surprising number of Anabaptists in the region. Among them were, for instance, in Balzenwyl "the entire village with women and children, and man and maid-servants"; besides, there are 58 persons mentioned in the same document, most of them heads of families or mothers. All of them were summoned for a hearing on Dec. 3, 1585; but persuasion was in vain. They declared that they wanted to remain true to the Gospel and to God, who is truth and life. Fridli Rot, Andreas Beringer, Hans Hofer, and Hans

Myer were the spokesmen. Seven years later (1592) they managed again to present their case skillfully and forcefully. The government, they said, was to punish the evil but not the good whom it was harassing. It was not its task to judge faith. They believed in a universal Christian church, which was present wherever two or three were gathered together in the name of Christ. Finally, they said, a Christian government was not permitted to use the sword. The chancellery of Aarburg was unable to convince them and turned to Bern for counsel. Orders came back to proceed with severe measures to enforce compliance, which was done.

This pressure led to new emigration, but this time the emigrants were largely the younger people. Through pastoral records their names are better known than those of earlier migrations. We meet familiar names, like Hartmann Kuenzli of Egliswyl, Henry Stählin of Birrwyl, Melchior Hunzicker of Leerau, Uli Hegis of the same place, Ulrich Bär of Schoepfland, whom they tried in vain to persuade to recant, Uli Bachmann of Bottenstein. Some of them returned to their homes again, like Peter Hoeggi of Seon, to whom (1624) his fortune of 400 pounds was restored after he promised to "conduct himself obediently." Those who remained were severely dealt with. In 1599 three Anabaptist women were imprisoned; one of them died after a third trial as a result of torture. She was the daughter or daughter-in-law of the above Fridli Iberger. Of those who emigrated to Moravia, three are particularly worthy of mention. One is Heinrich Müller of Meisterschwanden. In Beck's *Geschichts-Bücher* (281) he is called Heinrich Sumer, a miller of Maschwanden. It is recorded of him that with Jakob Mändel he was drowned on Oct. 9, 1582, in Baden. The second is Hans Meyer, banished May 29, 1591, probably one of the elders who on Jan. 1, 1646, signed a new rental contract with Count Kolonitsch. Of Josef Hauser it is recorded that after a long and fruitful activity in Moravia, where he was highly esteemed for his learning (he knew Latin, Greek, Hebrew, French, and German), he died at Prybitz, Sept. 3, 1616.

After the Thirty Years' War only a few traces of the Anabaptist movement are found in Aargau. Among the names recorded are Martin Burger of Burg in Reinach, Rudolph Kuenzy at Muhren, Bernhard Rohr at Uerkheim, Dätwyler in Offringen, Hans Dester, and Jacob Gut, who was banished Sept. 10, 1660. The rest of the Swiss Brethren also left their homeland and emigrated to Alsace and the Palatinate (especially in 1671). Those who remained rallied around the Bachmann family in Bottwyl and the Haury family in Waldgraben. Most of these took part in the great emigration of the Swiss Brethren in 1711 to the Palatinate and the Netherlands. In the region of Zofingen they were found later than anywhere else. As late as 1720, Hans Bachmann went from here to the Palatinate; until his death he received support from his Swiss homeland. There are today no Mennonites in Aargau.

"Not until 1726 can it be officially stated that there was in Aargau no longer an Anabaptist" (Heiz).

NEFF

J. Heiz, *Die Täufer im Aargau* (Aarau, 1902); *Zwingliana* I (1903) 235. Concerning Heiz the *Zwingliana* states that his book is based on Müller, *Berner Täufer*, but is nevertheless an independent study. "Not until now has it been clear to what extent these regions were involved in the Anabaptist movement. The whole is a story of two hundred years of suffering." See also Merz, *Inventar der aargauischen Stadtarchive* I (Aargau, 1917): *Zofingen, Baumgarten, Aarburg, Aarau, Baden, Lenzburg, Mellingen; ML I, 4.*

Aaron Martin group (OOM). Aaron Martin, born Aug. 30, 1918, in Lancaster Co., Pa., joined with the "Jacob Stauffer people" in eastern Snyder Co., Pa., but in 1945 led one of the two-way schisms in that congregation. Martin was ordained to the ministry after this schism, June 4, 1945, and four weeks later bishop. In 1950 the group had 28 members and used the meetinghouse a few miles west of the Susquehanna Trail. Further divisions, a total of four in seven years, have reduced the group to small fractions each with a bishop, minister, and deacon, all using the same meetinghouse at different times. I.D.L.

Aaron Rissler Congregation: see **Rissler Group.**

Abbekerk, a village in the Dutch province of North Holland, about ten miles north of Hoorn, where there was a Mennonite congregation and church building until the middle of the 18th century; some time before 1730 the congregation united with the one at Twisk (*q.v.*) about six miles beyond Hoorn. In the early days there was a *kerkepad* (church path) through the meadows to Twisk, made by the Mennonites going to church. A seat in the church council at Twisk is still occupied by a member living at Abbekerk. The members living in Abbekerk numbered 15 in 1950. (*ML* I, 6.)

vDZ.

Abbeyville Mennonite Church (MC) was located on what is now the western edge of Lancaster, Pa. With the coming of three Hans Brubakers, John Meyers, a Christian and two Andrew Hersheys, Benjamin Road, Peter Swarr, and others, 1717-27, who settled west and northwest of "Lancaster Town," there were too many Mennonites to worship in private homes. By 1750 John Jacob Brubaker and Ulrich Roadt, ministers, received a deed for one acre on the south end of the present Christian B. Herr farm, whereon a meetinghouse was soon erected. The foundation wall can still be struck in plowing and a few Erisman, Binkley, and Hershey tombstones are still intact. Here these people worshiped until 1792, when a larger church called Brubaker's was built a mile north of Rohrerstown. Bishop Benjamin Hershey, Lancaster Mennonite Conference moderator during the American Revolution, worshiped and is buried here. Undoubtedly the first Lancaster conferences were held alternately with the Mellinger and Abbeyville congregations. I.D.L.

Abbotsford is a village of about 1,000 population, located in the center of the fertile lower Fraser River valley, 2½ miles north of the U.S. boundary and about 40 miles east of the Pacific coast, on the Trans-Canada highway, in British Columbia. In the surrounding area the chief occupations are dairying, poultry raising, and berry and fruit growing. In the immediate vicinity are seven Mennonite congregations, each having its own house of worship: four Mennonite Brethren, two General Conference, and one Evangelical Mennonite Brethren, with a total membership of approximately 1,500. There are also two Mennonite Bible schools and one large private Mennonite high school. C.F.K.

Abbotsford Evangelical Mennonite Brethren Church at MacCallum Road, Abbotsford, B.C., is a member of the E.M.B. Conference of North America; the members came to British Columbia mostly from Langham and Dalmeny, Sask. This church was organized in 1946 under the leadership of Abram Dickmann and Abram Warkentin. In the beginning the church had 25 members but now (1950) has 91 members. The first meetinghouse, a cement foundation basement, was erected in 1948 (40 x 70) and is still in use. The leader and pastor (1950) is Cornelius A. Wall and the deacon, Henry Martens.

A.A.T.

Abbotsford Mennonite Brethren Church, Abbotsford, B.C.: see **South Abbotsford** Mennonite Brethren Church and **North Abbotsford** Mennonite Brethren Church.

Abbotsford United Mennonite Church (GCM), near the village of Abbotsford, B.C., had 201 baptized members on Jan. 1, 1948. The first settlers, coming from 1929 to 1932, were J. B. Sawatzky, A. Penner, J. Redekop, P. Heinrichs, E. Kroeker, and J. Kehler. The group increased every year; in November 1936 they organized a church, and in 1937 erected a frame church, which was enlarged in 1946 to seat 600. The members came from several congregations in the prairie provinces, and are of the immigrant groups from Russia of 1874 and 1923. They are farmers, engaged chiefly in poultry raising and berry farming. Trade and industry are a secondary vocation. Church services are conducted in High German; but at home High German, Low German, and English are used. The present (1948) elder is Heinrich M. Epp, and the ministers are H. Neufeld, H. Neudorf, and A. Loewen.

C.G.T.

A-B-C Books, primers called in German *Namenbüchlein,* more recently *Fibel* (which is a derivative of *Bibel*), a collection of religious readings for beginners.

In the education of Anabaptists and Mennonites these booklets have played a vital role almost up to the present. Though the early Mennonites did not care for academic education, they yet wanted everyone to be taught reading and writing in order to be able to study at firsthand the Bible and other devotional material. The A-B-C books of former days were, however, very different from today's primers. The children learned the alphabet and then at once had to read the Lord's Prayer, the Apostles' Creed, the Ten Commandments, and various prayers. The oldest known primer used by the Mennonites is an 18th century Swiss *Namenbüchlein* of 1740 (copy in Goshen College Library. See Friedmann, *Mennonite Piety,* 213 and Plate V).

In the United States Christopher Dock (d. 1771; *q.v.*) was apparently the earliest Mennonite educator who worked in this direction. He wrote several sets of A-B-C rhymes for his pupils in the pious style of his time (Brumbaugh, *Life and Work of Christopher Dock,* 182, 241 f., 263 f.) and otherwise taught, in the same general way as Europeans did, the reading of sacred passages right after mastering the alphabet. Christopher Saur (*q.v.*) in Germantown printed an *A-B-C und Buchstabierbuch, bei allen Religionen ohne billigen Anstoss zu gebrauchen* for the German-speaking Pietists and sectarians, as early as 1738 or 39. Whether it was much used among the Mennonites is not certain.

The first original Mennonite production of this sort was Bishop Benjamin Eby's *Neues Buchstabier- und Lesebuch,* first published in Kitchener (formerly Berlin), Ont., in 1839, which then passed through eight editions up to 1909, and was used primarily among the (old) Mennonites. This book, too, contains spelling drills, prayers, Bible passages, and pious sentences. It was in its time very much used. With such books youngsters were taught High German in Sunday schools when the church at large was more and more shifting to English for its services (H. S. Bender, *Mennonite Sunday School Centennial,* Scottdale, 1940, 40). John F. Funk published an *A-B-C Buchstabier- und Lesebuch* (Elkhart, 1902, 1905, 1912) with similar contents, primarily for the Manitoba Mennonites. Peter Schertz, Trenton, Ohio, published a one-page *Das Goldene A-B-C.*

Only a few copies of the A-B-C books used among the Mennonites in Prussia, Poland, and Russia are extant (Fr. Tr. Harmann; C. S. Weber, Striegau; Trowitzsch, Frankfurt; C. W. Hindemith, Kalisch, etc.). They usually had the alphabet, the Ten Commandments, some prayers, and on the last page the picture of a rooster. The Mennonites of the prairie states used the Liebhart A-B-C book published by the Abingdon Press (Cincinnati and New York), which was reprinted by Welty and Sprunger at Berne, Ind., D. Goerz at Halstead, Kan. (1881), and the Mennonite Publishing House, Scottdale. The Mennonites of Mexico are printing and using a revised abbreviated edition of the Elkhart *A-B-C Buchstabier- und Lesebuch* (of the illustrations only the rooster on the last page remained).

To help bilingual readers the Mennonite Publishing House published the *Englisch-Deutsche Fibel,* based on *Sander's Pictorial Primer,* and the Herald Publishing Co., Newton, published Witter's *Deutsch-Englische Fibel* (since 1925 in many editions). To help the Mennonites of South America in their educational efforts, the Textbook Committee of the Mennonite Central Committee published *Leselust* by Richard Lange in 1948. (R. Friedmann, *Menn. Piety Through the Centuries,* Goshen, 1949.) **R.F., C.K.**

Abeele, Achior van den, from 1712 the preacher of the United Flemish and Frisian Mennonites who regularly assembled on Koningstraat in Haarlem (Dutch province of North Holland) in the first half of the 18th century. He wrote poetry and published the following: *Den weg der vergankelykheyd* (The Way of Transitoriness), (Haarlem, 1717), with a title page engraving by Vincent van der Vinne, 208 pp.; *Eens Jongelings pelgrimagie of wandelweg* (A Youth's Pilgrimage or Way) with reflections on the flood of Dec. 25, 1717; *De Stand van een lydend Christen* (The State of a Suffering Christian), (1718) 112 pp.; *Het Wereldlyk Alarm geestelykerwys toegepast* (The Worldly Alarm Applied Spiritually), (1719) 48 pp.; *Eenige stichtelyke gedachten over de algemeene genadige bezoekingen Gods* (Some Devotional Thoughts on the General Gracious Visitations of God), (1718) 24 pp.; *Den uyterlyken Boogaard* (The Outward Orchard), (1730) 160 pp.; *De Christelyke Huyshouding* (The Christian Household), (1740) 176 pp. In the second book appear verses about the Mennonites Isaak van Kalcker, Cornelis and Evert Mabé (Blaupot t. C., *Holland* I, 345 f.; *ML* I, 6.) **K.V.**

Aberdeen, a town of 1,500, situated in southeastern Idaho, Bingham County, not far from the west shore of the American Falls Reservoir Lake. Approximately 261 Mennonite church members live within shopping distance of Aberdeen. All belong to the General Conference Mennonite congregation, the only one in the area, organized in June 1907. Of these, 43 per cent live in the town. Mennonites have lived in this area since 1906. (*ML* I, 10.) **H.C.W.**

Aberdeen (Idaho) First Mennonite Church (GCM), a member of the Pacific District Conference, was organized on July 4, 1907, with a membership of 36 and the Elder Jacob Hege officiating. The church was erected in 1909, enlarged in 1938, and again in 1947. Its seating capacity is 500. The congregation, with a membership of 357, has twenty-five Sunday-school classes, four Christian Endeavor societies, four mission societies, and one Brotherhood; it has two missionaries on the foreign field. (See **Emmanuel** Mennonite Church, Aberdeen, extinct.) **H.N.H.**

Aberdeen Mennonite Brethren Church, located four miles southeast of Aberdeen in northern Saskatchewan, is a member of the Canadian Conference of the Mennonite Brethren Church. In 1903 a few families gathered in the home of G. J. Sawatzky for their regular services. From 1904 to 1919 they gathered in a schoolhouse near by until they were able to erect their own church building. The church was organized in 1906 with 22 members. At present (1951) the membership stands at 51. The church has been under the leadership of the following ministers: Gerhard Sawatzky, 1903-12; John P. Siemens, 1912-20; H. G. Sawatzky, 1920-31; B. L. Sawatzky, 1931-41; Heinrich W. Niessen, 1941-44, and G. K. Sawatzky, 1945-51. **J.H.Epp.**

Aberli, Heinrich, a baker in Zürich, who joined the Anabaptist movement about 1525, and was soon among the most zealous of Conrad Grebel's followers (Cornelius, 22). He boldly disregarded the regulations concerning fasts, thereby creating a stir. In contemporary reports his conduct is repeatedly described as defiant (R. Stähelin, *Huldreich Zwingli* I, Basel, 1895, 203; L. Keller, *Die Reformation*, Leipzig, 1885, 390). From Waldshut, where he was a voluntary trooper among the Zürich guards who were to defend Waldshut, he wrote an interesting letter to his home city (*Archiv für österreichische Geschichte*, 1877, 101). It was he who sheltered Balthasar Hubmaier in his home when he fled from Waldshut to Zürich, until the city government traced him there and imprisoned him (J. Loserth, *Dr. Balthasar Hubmaier*, Brno, 1893). He was a signatory of the letter written to Thomas Müntzer on Sept. 5, 1524, by the Zürich opponents of infant baptism (Cornelius II, 246 and 248).   Neff

H. S. Bender, *Conrad Grebel 1498-1526, Founder of the Swiss Brethren* (Goshen, 1950); C. A. Cornelius, *Gesch. des Münsterischen Aufruhrs* II (Leipzig, 1860); *ML* I, 11.

Abraham (Abraham van Royen or Abraham van Roey), an Anabaptist martyr, a locksmith by trade, was burned at the stake at Antwerp on Feb. 4, 1556. His name is mentioned in a song, "Aenhoort Godt, hemelsche Vader" (Hear, O God, heavenly Father), which is found as No. 16 in the *Liedtboecxken van den Offer des Heeren* (1563).   vDZ.

Offer, 564; *Mart. Mir.* D 166, E 554; Génard, *Antw. Arch.-Blad* VIII, 428, 431, XIV, 20-21, No. 233; Wolkan, *Lieder*, 63, 72.

Abraham Picolet, an Anabaptist martyr, burned at the stake in Antwerp in 1569. From the trial, as related in the *Martyrs' Mirror,* it appears that Abraham was a young man who four years before had been in Germany. He had not yet received baptism upon confession of his faith. He was seized in the woods of Wilrijck near Antwerp and imprisoned in the Steen at Antwerp (*q.v.*), with Hendrik van Etten (*q.v.*) and another young man, Herman, who later became unfaithful. Abraham was examined three times. Van Braght gives the information that Abraham and Hendrik wrote many letters from prison, which, however, were all lost except one, a rather long letter from Abraham to his sisters, which is included in the *Martyrs' Mirror*. In this letter Abraham calls himself "a prisoner because of God's Word." Abraham and Hendrik were both condemned to death and hanged along the road to Wilrijck. The date of the execution is not known. (*Mart. Mir.* D 475-80, E 818-23.)   vDZ.

Abraham Tancreet (or Tanghereet), an Anabaptist martyr, burned at the stake in Gent, Belgium, Aug. 7, 1559. He was born at Nukerke (Nijpkerke) in Flanders and was a tailor by trade. On the Friday following Whitsunday he was captured with eleven others. The execution took place on the Vrijdagsmarkt in Gent at seven o'clock in the morning. Concerning Abraham and the other eleven brethren and sisters, who all remained steadfast, there is a song: "Ick moet een liet beginnen" (I must begin a song), which appears in the *Liedtboecxken van den Offer des Heeren* of 1563 (No. 14). It is also mentioned by Wolkan.   vDZ.

Offer, 348, 556 ff.; *Mart. Mir.* D 246, E 620-22; Verheyden, *Gent*, No. 62, p. 25; Wolkan, *Lieder*, 62-71.

Abrahamsz, Galenus: see **Galenus Abrahamsz de Haan.**

Abrath. The Old Order Amish Mennonites have a different procedure in holding their regular church services from that of the other branches. In this, as well as in many other practices, they still cling to the practice which their forefathers brought along from Europe. The services are opened by the singing of a hymn from the *Ausbund,* and when the congregation starts singing all of the ministers present retire to a separate room for counsel. This assembly is called *Abrath,* or in the Pennsylvania-German dialect *Abrote,* and may be expressed in English as a "separate council." The purpose of this ministerial council is to give the ministers a chance to discuss any circumstances or needs that any one of them has in mind that require ministerial attention or discussion. Any matter that needs to be brought before the congregation must be first discussed here and a plan for procedure formulated. A full agreement of all ministers present is necessary on all matters of procedure before anything is brought before the congregation.

A further purpose of this ministerial council is to decide who is to conduct the services on this particular day. The one that is farthest in arrears in taking his turn at preaching a sermon in the district is entitled to preach the main sermon, and the one farthest in arrears in opening the services is assigned this task; this is the mode of procedure in all districts. Exceptions are sometimes made where special services are held for a visiting minister and where there is no question as to whose duty it is to conduct the service. Sometimes in such instances no special council is held. These exceptions are rather rare however.   E.J.B.

Abreisskalender, Christlicher, a devotional booklet published in the form of a pad containing daily devotional reading sheets to be torn off as used, arranged to be hung on the wall of a room, edited by J. Kroeker, published by the Mennonite firm *Raduga* at Halbstadt, Russia, beginning with the year 1899 and ceasing publication with the beginning of World War I. It was not particularly Mennonite in character, designed to serve an interdenominational public and widely sold among non-Mennonites, who took over half of the edition of 25,000 copies (in the last years). It was the first German devotional calendar in Russia, and undoubtedly was an imitation of similar calendars in Germany, such as the Neukirchener, which were quite popular among the Mennonites and were pietistic in character. (*ML* I, II.)   H.S.B.

Absolon de Zanger (Absolon van Combe, van Tomme), an Anabaptist martyr, a weaver by trade, was burned at the stake Nov. 20, 1561, at Kortrijk in Flanders, together with Willem van Haverbeke. Van Braght wrongly places this martyrdom in 1558. (*Mart. Mir.* D 200, E 582; Verheyden, *Courtrai-Bruxelles,* No. 12, p. 35.)   vDZ.

Abstinence, a voluntary or self-imposed effort to refrain from indulging in certain harmful practices, especially the use of strong drink or tobacco. Many Mennonite groups believe that it is sinful to indulge in these practices (see Rom. 12:1). In most Mennonite Brethren communities the use of tobacco or strong drink is made a test of church membership. The Church of God in Christ Mennonite, the Krimmer Mennonite Brethren, the Evangelical Mennonite Brethren, and the Kleine Gemeinde take similar positions. In general, smoking and drinking are condemned as twin evils in the General Conference Mennonite Church as well as in the (old) Mennonite Church, although there is variation in local attitudes.

Mennonites, however, have not always had a conscience against the use of these items. Some Mennonites, including Amish, raise tobacco as a cash crop. Lancaster County (Pa.) is the center of the tobacco-growing region, as far as Mennonites are concerned, but other counties of the state, as well as Maryland, southern Ontario, and other regions are involved. Many Mennonites, including some women and ministers, used tobacco extensively in the 19th century.

The coming of the Russian Mennonites of 1874-75, many of whom were abstainers, the Sunday-school movement, the temperance movement, and the anti-tobacco efforts of the late 19th and early 20th centuries helped to change this attitude of acceptance to one of general abstinence. As this conscience developed, many individuals wrote John F. Funk chiding him for his failure to take a stand on drinking and smoking in the *Herald of Truth*. The following excerpt on smoking, taken from the March 1878 issue of this paper, reveals the intensity of this pressure. "We stand between two fires. . . . Among our American Mennonites the use of tobacco prevails. . . . Some are so wedded to the habit that they are offended if anyone speaks against it. . . . Among our Russian Mennonite brethren there are those who stand on the contrary side of this question. . . . They have made it a rule of their church . . . and it is an offense to them when they see anyone use it . . . and there are even among our American Mennonites, members here and there who hold the same views." Many of the (old) Mennonite and Amish congregations gradually developed a conscience against the use of tobacco and alcoholic beverages; however, there are still some within these circles who grow and use tobacco.

The attitude of the Mennonites on abstinence, both in America and in Europe, has been influenced to a considerable extent by the 19th and early 20th century abstinence movements on one hand and on the other by the prevailing mores of the larger community which to a greater or less degree have infiltrated them. Some of the more conservative groups, particularly the Old Colony Mennonites of Mexico, have not yet experienced the impact of the abstinence movement, and among them smoking is more prevalent. In general, there is more of a conscience on the use of liquor in nearly all Mennonite groups, with the possible exception of the

Hutterites, than there is on the use of tobacco (see **Alcohol** and **Tobacco**).　H.J.Stu.

J. W. Fretz, "The Growth and Use of Tobacco Among Mennonites," in *Proceedings of the Seventh Annual Conference on Cultural Problems* (1949) 87-100; H. J. Stucky, "Cultural Interaction Among the Mennonites Since 1870" (M.A. thesis, Northwestern University, Evanston, Ill., 1947) 40 ff.

Acadia Valley Church is a small appointment of the Canadian Northwest Conference of the United Missionary Church, located 20 miles southwest of Alsask, Sask. In 1950 there were about 10 members and the average attendance in Sunday school was 51. Recent pastors have been D. C. Eby, W. M. Redfield, and Peter Dyck. The few members of the Mennonites (MC) in the community worship with the U.M.C. group, but have separate communion services.　E.R.S.

Acronius, Johannes, physician and mathematician, b. in 1520 at Akkrum (Dutch province of Friesland), d. Oct. 18, 1564, at Basel; was a friend of David Joris *(q.v.),* published Joris's ideas in 45 aphorisms and also an account of his life and court trial, titled *Ad N. N. popularem epistola, d.d. 28 Julii 1559.* (*ADB* I, 41; *ML* I, 12.)

Acronius, Johannes, Reformed divine, son of Dominicus Acronius, b. 1565 at Grimersum in East Friesland, d. at Haarlem in 1627, studied in Neustadt a.d.H., Germany (at the Casimirianum), under Ursinus and Franz Junius, in 1584 became a preacher in Eilsum (Dutch province of Friesland), in 1601 in Groningen, and in 1611 in Wesel. In 1614 when Wesel was destroyed, he fled to Deventer. In April 1617 he was made professor at the university in Franeker, in 1618 became preacher in Kampen and delegate to the national synod in Dordrecht (1618-19). From 1619 until his death (Sept. 29, 1627) he was stationed in Haarlem. While at Groningen he was very influential in the provincial synod and was appointed plenipotentiary in Drenthe by William Louis of Nassau. He thrice refused a call to Amsterdam as preacher. In 1602 he was involved in an argument with the Mennonites led by J. C. Rolwagen *(q.v.).* Against him he wrote *Apologia ofte Verandtwordinge des Edicts . . . tegen der Wederdooperen . . .* (Groningen, 1602). (*Biogr. Wb.* I, 19-29; *ML* I, 12.)　K.V.

Acronius, Ruardus, a Reformed divine, date of birth unknown, d. 1611, first a priest, then a preacher in Franeker (1572), Alkmaar (1574), Bolsward (1579), Cornjum (1580) which released him to Leeuwarden (1583-91), where he became involved in disputes with his more moderate colleague Balck. From 1599 until his death he was stationed in Schiedam. In his Frisian period Acronius violently opposed the Mennonites. His hindering their meeting in Cornjum resulted in a public disputation with the Mennonites in Leeuwarden *(q.v.),* whose spokesman was Pieter van Ceulen *(q.v.).* This disputation lasted through 155 sessions from Aug. 16 to Nov. 17, 1596. The proceedings were published in the *Protocol Dat is, De gantsche handelinge des ghesprecx . . .* (Franeker, 1597). One of his other works named by van der Aa in his *Biographisch Woordenboek* (I, 44-45) is *Seer grondighe ende uit Godes Woordt wel ghefondeerde onderrichtinghe tegens de lasteringhe ende het geschrey der Wederdooperen—over het onderholt ende de middelen daer door de dienaren der warer ghemeynte Christi in haren Dienst—ondholden worden* (Franeker, 1599).   K.V.

J. Reitsma, *Honderd jaren uit de Gesch. der herv. in Friesland* (Leeuwarden, 1876) contains a detailed discussion of the dispute; *Biogr. Wb.* I, 29-36; *ML* I, 12.

Adam Foppensz, a Dutch Anabaptist from Amsterdam, was seized in May 1535. He had been rebaptized four years before by Jan Volkertsz Trypmaker *(q.v.);* his wife was not *in't verbond* (a member of the church). After the *Naaktloopers (q.v.)* incident in Amsterdam (February 1535), Adam had left the city and wandered in its environs. He had nothing to do with the revolt of May 10-11, 1535. He possessed a letter from the martyr Baef Claesdochter *(q.v.)* which she had sent him shortly before she went to prison. It is not known whether or in what manner Adam was put to death. (Grosheide, *Verhooren,* 112-16.) vpZ.

Adam Henricx (also called Kistmaeckers), an Anabaptist martyr who is not included in the martyr books, a goldsmith by trade, came from Deventer in the Netherlands, was drowned July 23, 1561, at the Steen prison in Antwerp because he "persisted in the heresy of the Anabaptists." (Génard, *Antw. Arch.-Blad* IX, 123, 133, 137; XIV, 30-31, No. 341.)   vpZ.

Adam Jansz, an Anabaptist martyr, an elder at Leiden in the Dutch province of South Holland, was executed in January 1535. (*DB* 1917, 120, No. 117.)

Adam Pastor, originally called Roelof (Rudolph) Martens or Martin, b. at Dorpen in Westphalia, was a Catholic priest at Aschendorf, gave up the office in 1533 and joined the Anabaptists, probably in Münster. He was one of Jan Bockelson's emissaries, but soon freed himself of Münsterite influence and united with the peaceful Anabaptists. Between 1543 and 1545 (in 1542 according to Vos, p. 102) he was ordained as elder by Menno Simons, took an active part in the conference at Lübeck, opposing Blesdijk *(q.v.),* and was also at the conferences at Emden and Goch in 1547, at which Menno was chairman. At the latter he was banned on the charge of denying the Trinity, but he continued his work as an Anabaptist preacher, especially along the Lower Rhine and in Münster. In Odenkirchen *(q.v.)* he headed a congregation which existed for a long time. In 1552 he had a meeting in Lübeck with Menno Simons where the Deity of Christ and the Trinity were the subjects of a disputation. On this disputation see the second part of his only extant writing (with the exception of his *Een Concordantie oft Register der ganscher Bibel,* 1559), *Underscheit tusschen rechte leer unde valsche leer der twistigen articulen* (published by Samuel Cramer in *BRN* V, 361-581 with an excellent introduction, 317-59). The report of the disputation occupies pages 517-81. Other writings from his pen were: *Disputation mit Dirk Philipps, Von der Barm-*

herzigkeit Gottes, Von Menschengeboten, and *Dit zijn die Articulen van Davidt Jorisz leere . . .* (originally written in Dutch), none of which have survived. He spent his last years wandering. He died between 1560 and 1570 probably in Münster and was buried in Ueberwasser. His followers were known as Adamites.   NEFF, H.S.B.

DB 1900, 105; F. S. Bock, *Historia Antitrinitariorum* (Leipzig, 1784) I, 589-91; *HRE* XIV (Leipzig, 1904) 759 f.; J. Horsch, *Menno Simons* (Scottdale, 1916) 194-203; C. Krahn, *Menno Simons* (Karlsruhe, 1936) 67 ff.; Kühler, *Geschiedenis* I, 279, 284-90 *et passim;* J. H. Ott, *Annales Anabaptistici* (Basel, 1672); Rembert, *Wiedertäufer;* K. Vos, *Menno Simons* (Leiden, 1914) 100 ff. The best discussion of Adam Pastor and his theology is that by S. Cramer in *BRN* V (1909) 317-59; E. M. Wilbur, *A Hist. of Unitarianism* (Cambridge, 1946) 40-48. See *MQR XXII,* 148f.

Adamites (Adamieten), the name given a group of Anabaptists in a book by Azend van Buchell (Buchelius), *Descriptio urbis Rheno-Trajectinae,* written in 1592, published in part in Utrecht in 1801, 53 pages. He was probably referring to the followers of Adam Pastor *(q.v.;* also *Diarium* of Arend van Buchell, published in Amsterdam, 1907, 289). Cornelis Adriaensz (Brother Cornelis, *q.v.),* the fanatical opponent of the Anabaptists in Flanders, also speaks of the Adamites *(Historie en wonderbare Sermonen* II, Brugge, 484-87). The name may also be an epithet of opprobrium in connection with the notorious appearance in the nude of certain misguided Anabaptists in Amsterdam in 1530. (*DB* 1903, 52.)   vpZ.

Adams County, Ind., is located in the east central part of the state. The Mennonites and Amish are located in the southern half of the county. The settlement extends west into the neighboring Wells County. Berne is the center of the community, which also includes the villages of Monroe, Linngrove, and Geneva in Adams County and Vera Cruz and Reiffsburg in Wells County.

There are over 2,000 Mennonites and Amish in the entire community, of whom 1,312 (in 1952) belong to the First Mennonite Church (GCM) in Berne *(q.v.),* the largest Mennonite church in America. The community also has four Old Order Amish Mennonite congregations, usually known as Swiss Amish. There are also two Missionary Church Association congregations, an Evangelical Mennonite Church congregation, a Reformed Amish Christian congregation, and a large Christian Apostolic *(Neutäufer)* church.

The first Mennonites to arrive in the community were Christian and Peter Baumgartner, who settled in 1838 near Vera Cruz, Wells Co., just across the Adams county line; this was the earliest Mennonite settlement in Indiana. The next year their father, David Baumgartner, a minister, arrived and started a church. These settlers and the ones who followed were from the Jura in the canton of Bern, Switzerland. During the 1850's large groups from the Jura came directly to this settlement and purchased land around the present town of Berne. Amish from the Jura and Alsace began to settle here in 1853. The Amish group was divided in 1866, when Henry Egly, a bishop in the church, organized the first Defenseless Mennonite congregation, now known as

Evangelical Mennonite Church. This latter group was further divided by the formation of the Missionary Church Association in 1898.

The *Christlicher Bundesbote* and *The Mennonite,* official publications of the General Conference Mennonite Church, were printed at Berne until 1936. The Mennonite Book Concern is at Berne. D.L.G.

Eva F. Sprunger, *The First Hundred Years, A Hist. of the Menn. Church in Adams Co., Indiana,* 1838-1938 (Berne, 1938).

Adams County (Ind.) Amish settlement was established in 1850, when Henry Egly and family moved there from Butler Co., Ohio. Other early settlers included these men with their families: John Hirshe, Philip Hirshe, Dan Kauffman, Joseph Kauffman, Minister Joseph Schwartz from Stark Co., Ohio, and Deacon John Schwartz from the same place. In 1866 there was a division within the church, Bishop Henry Egly leaving the congregation to form the Defenseless Mennonites (now called Evangelical Mennonites), after which Joseph Schwartz was ordained bishop of the Old Order Amish congregation. There are now three Amish districts in the community, the East, the West, and the North, with a membership of approximately 85 in each district, and respective bishops Samuel Hilty, Peter Girod, and Joseph L. Schwartz. The Reformed Amish Christians *(q.v.)* are a small group which separated from the main body of Amish in this county, but dissolved in 1952. N.Z.

Adams County, Pa., is located in the south central part of the state between populous Mennonite settlements, with York-Lancaster counties on the east, Franklin (Pa.)-Washington (Md.) counties on the west. The Mennonites reside primarily in the western portion near the area of fruit growing and processing in which many are engaged. The three Mennonite churches of the county all have a common origin. The Mummasburg, Pa., congregation, Lancaster Conference, dating back to about 1800, had a membership of 39 in 1953. The Fairfield, Pa., congregation (GCM) was organized in 1927, after a division from the Mummasburg congregation. In January 1950 its membership was 71. The Bethel congregation at Mummasburg, Ohio and E.A.M. Conference (MC), was organized in 1939. In 1953 it had a membership of 62.   H.M.

Adams, Heinrich, a Hutterite martyr, was seized on a journey from Moravia to Holland, in Aachen *(q.v.),* Germany, Jan. 9, 1558, with all his fellow worshipers as he attended a service there. Since he could not be persuaded to recant, he was executed Oct. 22, 1558, with his brother-in-law Hans Weckh *(q.v.).* Adams composed two hymns of 54 and 12 stanzas respectively, probably in prison. The longer one contains in its first 42 stanzas the acrostic, "Heinrich Adam meiner ehelichen Schwester Marien." About him an anonymous poet wrote a song of 105 stanzas, "Fröhlich so will ich heben an," the first 50 stanzas of which are published in the *Zeitschrift des Aachener Geschichts-Vereins,* 1884.

A Hinrich Adam, probably the same person, is the author of four hymns found in *Die Lieder der hutterischen Brüder* (Scottdale, 1914) 611-19. (Wol-

kan, *Lieder,* 210. *Mart. Mir.* D 209-12, E 588-90; *ML* I, 12 f.)   HEGE.

Adelsheim, a Mennonite congregation in northern Baden, Germany, near Wertheim, founded in 1912. Before Adelsheim was chosen as the name and location of the congregation, the scattered Mennonite families of the region met at some central farm home, first at the Fry home called Faustenhof, then for a time in Boedigheim, and later at the Kaufmann home called Selgentalerhof, four miles from the little town of Adelsheim. The earliest known ministers were Philipp Kaufmann, ordained preacher and elder in 1894, Johannes Fellmann of Neidelsbach, ordained preacher in 1894, and Johannes Horsch of Eubigheim, ordained preacher in 1901. At its organization in 1912, the congregation had 54 baptized members. When the services were moved to Adelsheim because the elder had located there, services were held first in the hall of a shoe factory, then in the hall of an elementary school. During World War I, Preacher Christian Schmutz of Heidelberg moved to Adelsheim, serving there until his death in 1921. Further ordinations: Johannes Horsch as elder in 1924, Heinrich Schmutz as preacher in 1924 (d. 1938), Heinrich Kaufmann of Klein-Eicholzheim as preacher in 1927, F. Warkentin as preacher in 1950. Ernst Zimmermann, a preacher in Ueberlingen since 1929 and elder since 1937, moved to the community (Wettersdorf) in 1937, and has since served as elder, Elder Johannes Horsch having moved away to Wagenbach in 1932. In 1950 the congregation had 37 baptized members, with 13 children. Family names are Schmutz, Hege (2), Kaufmann, Hotel, Lichti, Rassy, Zimmermann, and Warkentin, the latter being of Russian Mennonite refugee origin. Most of the families are farmers. In 1928 the small Adelsheim hospital service was taken over by Mennonite nurses, who still carry on and are a part of the congregation. Services are held once a month, with a Bible study also once a month. E.Z.

Adelsheim (Dolinovka), founded in 1869, was a village of the Chortitza *(q.v.)* settlement in South Russia. The railroad station was Chortitza, some 20 miles distant, and the post office was Nikolaipol *(q.v.).* In 1918 the land area of 5,300 acres was occupied by 64 farmers with a population of 334. Most of the inhabitants were members of the Mennonite Church with a church building at Nikolaipol. There was also a Mennonite Brethren congregation.

After the Revolution only a little more than one third of the land was given to the Adelsheim collective. In 1930 the minister of the M.B. congregation, Peter Unger, and another family were exiled as kulaks. The ministers of the Mennonite Church, David Penner and Dietrich Pauls, were silenced. From 1936 to 1939, 17 more men were exiled. In 1941 when the Germans approached, the whole village was to be evacuated to the East, but only seven persons were sent away. Five men had been drafted into the Red army. During the German occupation the economic, cultural, and religious life was revived.

On Oct. 4, 1943, the inhabitants of Adelsheim left their homes on 54 wagons for Apostolovo to proceed by train to Lodz; they left Lodz on Jan. 17, 1945, to escape the approaching Red army. Of the 382 persons from Adelsheim, 198 were sent back to Russia, mostly to Siberia. Most of those who remained in Germany found new homes in Canada.
C.K.

Adige Valley in southern Tirol, Austria (German, Etschtal). The chronicles of the Hutterian Brethren divided the martyrs of Tirol into three groups; viz., those in the Puster Valley, those in the Adige Valley, and those in the Inn, Valley. In the Adige Valley, the towns on the Eisack, namely, Brixen, Klausen, Sterzing, and Guffidaun, witnessed respectively 16, 7, 30, and 19 martyrdoms (see **Brixen**) —an unusually high number. But the Adige Valley itself, beginning with the Malser Haide, was also the scene of an extensive Anabaptist movement, even though the number of martyrs here is not so high as along the Eisack.

The first Anabaptists whom the government dealt with were found in Mals and Glurns in 1527 and had probably been won to the faith by Swiss Brethren evangelists. The government immediately ordered Jakob Trapp, the local administrator, to stamp out the movement. In 1528 there were Anabaptist trials in Bozen and Gargazon, and the archbishop and cardinal of Salzburg were notified that Salzburg Anabaptists were moving into Tirol. Other communities, such as Meran, Bozen, Trient, and Glurns, were informed of the distinctive marks used by the Anabaptists. In Meran there are also lawsuits against them. Here and there they were dealt with leniently. Thus on April 4, 1528, directives were sent to the authorities of Bozen to treat the Anabaptist prisoners with lenience "without injuring their honor" (without applying the Horb penalty) because of their ignorance, and to dismiss them with a suitable fine. In the same year Joerg Zaunring, Hutter's later companion and treasurer, and Kürschner (or Klesinger), who was baptized by him, were active at Leifers and Kaltern. The latter was seized April 25, 1529, in a night meeting at Kitzbühel with six companions.

In Kaltern, as the list of 1581 shows, four Anabaptists were put to death at the stake. But Kürschner was executed on June 2, 1529, at Innsbruck. At the same time the administrator of Petersberg seized five others, who escaped by night. In the region of Bozen the persecution continued; already the officers were showing their aversion to the continued bloodshed, and justifying their disobedience on the ground that these were not ordinary criminals and that some of them came from regions outside their jurisdiction, as from Sarntheim and Wangen.

The Anabaptists found a relatively safe region northeast of Bozen in the many ravines and hamlets of the long Ritten mountain range, where Zaunring served as trustee of their funds. Among those captured there was Hans Gasser, who also met his death at Bozen in 1529. At the same time

Georg Blaurock *(q.v.)*, having fled from Switzerland, arrived here and took over Kürschner's orphaned congregation. In the region of the Eisack and the Adige from Klausen to Neumarkt he found a fertile field. The large crowd gathering to hear him at Voels near Leifers made it inevitable that the authorities would finally find him; he and his companion Hans Langegger were seized and burned at the stake at Klausen on Sept. 6, 1529. The congregation was then led by Benedikt, who was active in Vill and Tramin, until he too was captured and executed.

Incessant persecution drove the Anabaptists out of the northerly parts of Tirol into the region of Trient, though they maintained themselves in many places in the Adige Valley. Early in 1530 seven were captured in the Neumarkt jurisdiction, including the two *Vorsteher,* Martin Nauk of Deutsch-Noffen and Benedikt Campner of Breitenberg. In the following years persecution was sharpened in the valleys of the Adige and Eisack. In Klausen Ulrich Müllner was put to death in October 1531, and in Bozen and Kaltern a number of men and women were executed during July. Nevertheless their numbers increased. In the district of Guffidaun Jakob Hutter led a meeting in which 150 persons took communion. In the days of the severest persecution they were able to find a bare living. In 1533, when persecution reached its height, they turned their eyes toward Moravia, where Jakob Hutter organized his brotherhood.

In Tirol, however, the Anabaptist movement did not die even after Hutter's death; Hans Amon *(q.v.)* and Onophrius Griesinger *(q.v.)* continued his work, the former in Moravia and the latter in Tirol, where they gathered in Lüsen near Brixen. Soon they were found again in Guffidaun, Terlan, and Bozen. With the execution of Griesinger the authorities thought they had given the movement its deathblow, but the Anabaptists appeared again and again in Klausen, Lüsen, Wengen, etc., at the end of 1544 in Meran, in 1554 in Kastelbell, Kortsch, and Schlanders. In Kortsch 50 persons assembled for a meeting. In Schlanders Hans Pürchner *(q.v.)* was beheaded in 1556. "They leaned his back against a post and thus beheaded him; for he was unable to kneel, so miserably had they racked and tortured him." Well-to-do persons were among the Anabaptist emigrés from the Adige; on March 28, 1558, it was reported that two brothers, Remigius and Christoph Heugen, had sold their property at Eyrs and had left 12,000 guilders' worth of possessions behind to go to Moravia. Several leaders appeared repeatedly in Kastelbell, and the property of 19 emigrants was confiscated. In the following year people from Laas followed, and on Nov. 12, 1560, it was reported to the government that recently about 1,000 Anabaptists had met in the district of Schlanders "and led many into this dangerous sect, who were also led away with wife and child and much capital."

Similar information is given in this district three years later: "In general an increase in the sect is noticeable." In 1567 there were Anabaptists in Glurns. Naturally the migration to Moravia grew stronger, as the Anabaptists there were given more freedom of movement. Frequently they simply abandoned their property and left. In 1578 two *Vorsteher* attracted some attention, one of them from Mals. In 1584 there were Anabaptists in Latsch near Schlanders and in Prad, Laubach, and Tschengels. Martin Gruber, who was seized on the Malser Haide on the point of leading a group to Moravia, came from Graun. The Vintschgau was the region where the apostles of that time were most occupied "with catching fish." That Anabaptism was still able to propagate itself along the Adige and in Vintschgau in the 1590's is seen in a letter sent by the government to the authorities on the Adige in 1592, as well as in the orders given three years later to Nanders and Schlanders, stating that some Anabaptists had again been noted in the Vintschgau. Not until the end of the 16th century did the movement become extinct in these parts of Tirol. (J. Loserth, *Der Anabaptismus in Tirol*, Vienna, 1892; *ML* I, 613.) LOSERTH.

Admission into the Church. From the beginning of its history, admission into the membership of the Anabaptist-Mennonite movement (church) has been (1) a matter of the action of the local congregation or its ministers, and (2) the voluntary action of the candidate. In all cases the minimum requirement has been a personal confession of faith followed by water baptism for those never previously baptized, and at times for those baptized by a different mode of baptism, or even for those baptized by any one else except a minister of the group itself. In earlier times infant baptism was never recognized, but in the 19th and 20th centuries gradually some groups or congregations dropped the requirement of rebaptism for those transferring from denominations who practiced infant baptism, requiring only confession of faith and a certificate of previous membership or letter of transfer.

Many groups, depending on circumstances, have added to these minimum requirements others such as probation for a period of months up to two years; a period of instruction by the bishop-elder or a minister, usually on Sundays before or after the regular morning service, lasting from several weeks to a year, either on the basis of a formal catechism or the personal outlines of the minister; a personal free testimony or account of a conversion experience and assurance given either privately before the minister or the church board or a committee of the congregation, or before the entire congregation, usually followed by a vote of acceptance by the congregation; explicit acceptance of a particular official confession of faith; a vow of obedience to the church and loyalty to its discipline and practices. In many groups, especially the more conservative, the final ceremonial act in admission to membership is the giving of the right hand of fellowship by the elder or bishop and the kiss of brotherhood (for women candidates given by the wife of the bishop). In such groups also only the

elder or bishop can receive members into the church.

The age of first admission into the church became traditional and fixed at 15-18 (or even later) in later Anabaptist-Mennonite history everywhere in Europe. In some areas it even became the custom to delay it until just before marriage, and marriage was not permitted until admission into the church had been completed. Usually once a year the elder or minister in charge announced that a class of instruction of candidates for church membership was being formed and invited anyone desiring to join to turn in his name. This instruction was then carried on regularly in connection with the Sunday morning service over a period of months (or even a year) with the reception into membership taking place about Easter. While those traditions were naturally brought along to America by the various immigrant groups and perpetuated here, new influences in the latter part of the 19th and first half of the 20th century, particularly coming from the revivalistic movement, have brought about a substantial lowering of the age of admission into the church, so that now the average age in such a group as the Mennonite Church (MC) is below 15 and in most cases 12 or even 10. By contrast the trend among the Dutch Mennonites has been to delay church membership, often beyond 20. Also, although in most groups where an attested conversion experience is a prerequisite for church membership, the admission through baptism follows closely upon the conversion experience, in the Mennonite Brethren group a period of probation is commonly required and the gap between conversion and baptism may be as much as three to five years. However, in the Mennonite Church (MC), where it is now becoming a rather common practice to have an annual week of "revival" or evangelistic meetings, the annual candidates for church membership are almost exclusively the "converts" produced by the meetings, and these are customarily baptized and received into church membership a few weeks later, with a rather short period of instruction.

The practice in regard to the nature and content of the instruction and the actual responses of the candidate to the questions of the elder or bishop at the time of baptism have varied throughout history and still vary. The use of a catechism came into vogue, probably by imitation of the common Protestant practice of catechetical instruction before confirmation, in the second half of the 17th century in Holland (first printed catechism 1640), in the first half of the 18th century in Germany (first printed German catechism 1664), and in Switzerland much later. The Mennonite Brethren group in Russia initially (founded 1860) rejected the catechism and indeed all pre-baptismal instruction as dangerous formalism, but in recent decades has instituted regular instruction and probation. (See **Catechism**.)

Those transferring from other denominations or Mennonite branches are sometimes accepted on the basis of a public confession of faith, together with a vow of obedience and loyalty, followed by a vote of the church board or congregation, but sometimes solely on the basis of a simple certificate of good standing or letter of recommendation. Such transfers and acceptances are sometimes merely reported by the minister; often, however, they are accepted only on the basis of a personal appearance of the candidate in the congregation at a regular service. Members transferring from other congregations of the same Mennonite group or conference are often treated exactly like those transferring from other denominations, requiring a public appearance, confession of faith, vow of obedience, and vote by the congregation. Excommunicated members or members who have fallen into gross sin are in the more conservative groups readmitted into membership on almost identical terms with those who have never been baptized (except that rebaptism is not required), the candidate being received from his knees in the presence of the congregation at a regular service, on the basis of a public confession of sin, confession of faith, and renewed covenant of obedience and loyalty to Christ and the church.

Some groups and congregations make written records of admission into membership in an official church book, some only in the private record of the bishop, pastor, or deacon, and some not at all.

Some groups will not baptize anyone unless he is at the same time admitted into the membership of the local congregation. Others will baptize without such admission and permit the candidate to join the church of his choice.

The variations in details of requirements and procedures for admission are so numerous and divergent in the various countries, branches, and even congregations as to make it impossible to report them in an encyclopedia article without excessive use of space. See the articles on the individual groups or conferences for further specific information as to current practices.   H.S.B.

Adriaen, an Anabaptist martyr, who according to the *Liedtboecxken van den Offer des Heeren* (*BRN* II, 566) was put to death in 1559 in the Steen prison at Antwerp. He is presumably identical with Adriaen Pan (*q.v.*).   vDZ.

Adriaen Adriaensz of Benschop. Several weeks after an insurrection of revolutionary and fanatical Anabaptists was crushed at Hazerswoude (*q.v.*) near Leiden, Holland, on December 31, 1535, some of the group had come to Poeldijk in the province of South Holland. Among them was Adriaen Adriaensz, who considered himself a man of God, and his followers proclaimed him as "die Coninck van Yserahel" (the King of Israel). He frequently stayed at the house of Jutte Eeuwouts (*q.v.*), where he announced that God would punish the world for shedding the blood of the saints. This group was imprisoned during the night of March 8, 1536, at Poeldijk, and shortly afterwards executed at The Hague; but Adriaen was not with the company at this time, and may perhaps have escaped. We do not hear further of him. He had previously been at Amsterdam instigating the Anabaptist revolt

there on May 10 and 11, 1535, and had also been active in Groningen.   vDZ.

E. van Bergen, "De Wederdoopers in het Westland," *Bijdr. v. d. Gesch. v. h. Bisdom Haarlem* (1903) 269-88; Grosheide, *Verhooren,* 60-61.

Adriaen Aersen, a Dutch Anabaptist martyr, a weaver by trade. He lived for some years in Schiedam (Dutch province of South Holland), had been rebaptized by Gerrit van Benschop, and took into his house many Anabaptist "leeraars en herdoopers" (ministers and rebaptizers). He was beheaded in Zierikzee, Dutch province of Zeeland, on May 8, 1535. (J. W. te Water, *Ref. van Zeeland,* 1766, 7.)   vDZ.

Adriaen Brael, an Anabaptist martyr of Wincle, Belgium, was captured in 1561 at a meeting in Brugge, Flanders, with 15 others. At their arrest, when the police demanded the surrender of their books and arms, they replied that they were non-resistant. En route to the prison, three escaped; the others endured captivity willingly and cheerfully, rejoicing in their approaching martyrdom. Twice they were haled before the authorities and openly confessed their faith. They were therefore condemned to die and were burned at the stake. Adriaen died on Dec. 10, 1561; on the same day Marin Eeuwout (Marijntgen Aelmeers), Andries Viblarre (Andries de Molenaar), Nicasius Aelmaere (Nikasen Amare), and Lucas Heindricx were also executed. The rest were put to death on the next day. A number of these martyrs are found in the song, "Genade en Vrede moet godvresende zijn" (Mercy and peace must be God-fearing), from the old Dutch hymnbook, *Veelderhande Liedekens* (1569); also included in Wackernagel, *Lieder,* 130. (*Mart. Mir.* D 288, E 655; Verheyden, *Brugge,* No. 34, p. 48; *ML* I, 252.)   vDZ.

Adriaen den Burry (or van den Burie), an Anabaptist martyr, a joiner by trade, was taken prisoner at Oudenaerde in Belgium in 1565, and remaining constant in faith was burned there at the stake on July 10, 1565. (*Mart. Mir.* D 324, E 686; *ML* I, 304.)

Adriaen Claesz, an Anabaptist preacher (*leeraar*) in Holland, was beheaded May 16, 1534. (*DB* 1917, 122, No. 150.)   vDZ.

Adriaen Cornelisse was beheaded at Zierikzee in the Dutch province of Zeeland on June 2, 1537. He had "bought and read a book of the Reformer Johannes Pomeranus"; besides this, he had also distributed "heretical books, containing false doctrines on the holy Sacrament," and furthermore lodged some persons "who claimed to be messengers of Christ." This martyr may be presumed to have been an Anabaptist. (J. W. te Water, *Ref. van Zeeland,* 1766, 8.)   vDZ.

Adriaen Cornelisz, an Anabaptist martyr, born at Schoonhoven, Holland, a glazier in Delft, wished to visit several brethren imprisoned in Leiden and tried to persuade the guard to release them, but was himself tricked and arrested. After brutal torture he was strangled on Nov. 24, 1552, and his body burned. With him died two brethren, Henrick Dircksz and Dirc Jansz, and two sisters, Anneken and Mariken. The *Martyrs' Mirror* prints a lengthy prayer, an admonition to his friends, and a "Confession before the authorities and the priests," all by Adriaen Cornelisz. His knowledge of the Bible and his skill in response embarrassed his learned opponents. When, for example, the priest asked whether there had been no children in the household of the Philippian jailer, he answered "No." "How do you know that?" "It is written: The jailor rejoiced with all his house because he believed. Children cannot rejoice over faith, for they have no faith." De Hoop-Scheffer surmises that he is one of the men responsible for the term "Mennisten-streeken," by which the Dutch once designated the effort to tell a truth and to omit a truth, or to tell only a half-truth and create the impression of having told the whole truth, or to indicate the answer to a question, and yet leave the impression on the questioner that the answer was complete (*DB* 1868, 35 ff.).

The *Offer des Heeren* contains a song about Adriaen which begins, "Danct Godt en wilt zijn lof verbreyden, wiens wercken zijn by ons openbaer; Adriaen Cornelisz quam tot Leyden om sin Vrienden te besoecken daer" (Wolkan, 66). The *Liedtboecxken van den Offer des Heeren* contains another song commemorating the four martyrs at Leiden in 1552 which begins, "Ick magh wel droeflyck singen, in desen tijt van noot" (also in Wolkan, *Lieder,* 61). Another song in the *Liedtboecxken* has Cornelisz for its author and begins, "Eylaes ick mach wel suchten dat nu buert so groot ellent." This song is also found in Wackernagel, No. 98.

NEFF, vDZ.

Offer, 195-218; 526-31; 578-80; *Mart. Mir.* D 133-42, E 526-35; *DB* 1899, 96; 1906, 70 ff.; Wackernagel, *Lieder,* 194; Wolkan, *Lieder,* 61, 63, 66; *ML* I, 371.

Adriaen Cornelisz, of Spaarndam near Haarlem, in the Dutch province of Holland, an Anabaptist martyr, was executed on May 15, 1535, at Amsterdam with nine other martyrs. He was baptized by Gerrit Boeckbinder and did not regret this baptism.

vDZ.

Mart. Mir. D 412, E 764; Grosheide, *Verhooren,* 70-72; *ML* I, 371.

Adriaen van Daele, an Anabaptist martyr, not found in the martyr books, was burned at the stake at Antwerp Feb. 17, 1573, together with four others. He was accused of attending forbidden meetings in Antwerp as well as elsewhere. (Génard, *Antw. Arch.-Blad* XIII, 104, 106, 173; XIV, 90-91, No. 1010.)

vDZ.

Adriaen de Goudsmid (Goldsmith), an Anabaptist leader, who baptized at Leiden in the Dutch province of South Holland. (*DB* 1917, 114, No. 45.)

vDZ.

Adriaen van 'sGravenhage, an Anabaptist martyr, a linen weaver by trade, was seized at Vught near 'sHertogenbosch in the Dutch province of North Brabant with eleven other men and women. All of them were poor except the goldsmith Paulus van Druynen, the preacher of the congregation, and his wife. Adriaen and Paulus were burned at the stake together with Michael Stevens van Oosterhout, a potter, and Jan Block of Gent, a weaver, Sept. 9, 1538. Two days later several others were executed, including Jan van Capelle. On Sept. 14, another execution took place. The *Martyrs' Mirror* names the seven judges who sentenced them and the godparents chosen by the court for the forcible baptism of the nine-month-old son of Paulus. Michael was the deacon of the congregation, which was Melchiorite, i.e., followers of Melchior Hofmann (*q.v.*). This is supposedly the first execution in the northern half of the Low Countries at which an attempt was made to prevent the victims from speaking at the site of the execution by gagging them with a knotted rope. (*Mart. Mir.* D 41-42, E 447 f.; *DB* 1917, 186-94; *ML* II, 161.)

K.V.

Adriaen van Hee, an Anabaptist martyr, a cutler by trade, seized with five other brethren at a religious gathering in the forest of Obignies near Doornik (Tournai) in Belgium. They were imprisoned in Doornik for fourteen days, and afterward, because they remained steadfast in the faith, burned at the stake "bij den Bosch op de Henegousche Heerlijkheyd" (near the forest in the Henegou territory) at Obignies. This execution took place in 1558. Other brethren burned to death at the same time with Adriaen were Joos Meeuwens, Willem, Goosen, Egbert de Hoedemaker, and Lambert van Doornik. (*Mart. Mir.* D 203, E 584.)

vDZ.

Adriaen de Hoedemaker (also called Kort-Adriaentgen van Gent: Short Adriaen from Gent), whose official name was Adriaen van den (or der) Zwalme, an Anabaptist martyr, was burned at the stake at Brugge in Belgium, Aug. 7, 1573 (1574 in *Mart. Mir.* is an error). Adriaen, who was a hatter by trade, was baptized about 1572 by the elder (*oudste*) Paulus van Meenen (*q.v.*). Shortly afterwards he was imprisoned at Gent, and after being retained a year in prison, he softened under the repeated trials, and abjured his faith. Having thus become free, he went to Dordrecht in the Dutch province of South Holland. After four months he returned to Flanders, and avoiding Gent, established himself at Brugge, where he joined the congregation. Before long he was recaptured and remained faithful to death. Adriaen was 21 years of age. He was the last martyr in Brugge. (*Mart. Mir.* D 676, E 992, 1095; Verheyden, *Brugge,* No. 72. p. 63.)

vDZ.

Adriaen Jacobs, a Dutch Mennonite martyr, was arrested Aug. 5, 1571, when a Mennonite meeting was surprised by the sheriff at Nieuwvaart, or Klundert (*q.v.*), Dutch province of Brabant. Adriaen was from near-by Dordrecht (*q.v.*); he was 28 years old and married. He was a cloth-shearer by trade, a well-educated and well-to-do man. The martyr Cornelis Cornelisz de Gijselaer (*q.v.*), taken prisoner at the same time, was his uncle. Adriaen was tortured several times and very cruelly. On Aug. 21, after severe torture, he felt very weak and was inclined to recant his convictions, and requested mercy, but the next day, having been tortured again *jusques aux os* (to the bones), he was strong and steadfast in his faith. He confessed that he had been baptized at Dordrecht by a person called Lenartsz, and that he had regularly attended the meetings of the congregation in that town. In his prison he wrote some letters to the "Church of God at Dordrecht." These letters are all lost. A "testament" or farewell letter to his wife never reached the poor woman, because it fell into the hands of the commissioner; in this way it was saved. It has been published in *DB* 1912, 45-48. Adriaen was executed, probably in October 1571, at Klundert. It is rather surprising that van Braght, who circumstantially deals with that surprised meeting of Klundert and its victims (*Mart. Mir.* D 603-5, E 929; the year 1572 there is wrong; it must be 1571), does not mention the martyr Adriaen Jacobs. (*DB* 1912, 29-48.)　　　　　　vdZ.

Adriaen Jacopsen: see **Andries Jacobs.**

Adriaen Jansz, an Anabaptist martyr, a hatter by trade, was burned at the stake in 1571 at Lille (Rijssel) in France, with Jelis de Backer (*q.v.*). While in prison Adriaen wrote two letters to his wife and one to the "brethren and sisters." These letters, which give evidence of a firm faith, were included in the martyr books, the *Martyrs' Mirror* among others. The letters were printed for the first time in 1588. Adriaen says that he wrote them "with tears," and wanted to write more, but the circumstances in the prison were not suitable. Evidently he was confined, as was the case with most of the martyrs, in a dark underground dungeon. He asked that greetings be taken to J. S. (Servaes Jansz, according to Vos). Vos is of the opinion that Adriaen was also a preacher (*prediker*). (*Mart. Mir.* D 549, E 883-85; *ML* II, 322, 389.)　　　　　　vdZ.

Adriaen Jorisse, who is called Pieter Jorisz in the *Martyrs' Mirror,* was beheaded at Zierikzee in the Dutch province of Zeeland, on Sept. 4, 1536, although he was originally from the Dutch town of Brouwershaven. He was rebaptized by Lenaert van Antwerpen a few months before his execution. (J. W. te Water, *Ref. in Zeeland,* 1766, 7-8; *Mart. Mir.* D 38, E 445.)　　　　　　vdZ.

Adriaen Lourysz, an Anabaptist martyr, was beheaded at Haarlem, Holland, on March 26, 1534, with six other martyrs. He was the preacher (*leeraar*) of the congregation at Leiden (Dutch province of South Holland), a tawer by trade. His indictment states that he had been rebaptized, and according to his own testimony had baptized many himself, that he also had an "other opinion" of the Holy Sacrament of the Altar (the Mass) than that of the "Holy Church" (Roman Catholic) and that he did not regret holding this opinion. He was condemned to be led to the scaffold and there "executed with the sword," and his body then placed on a wheel and his head displayed on a pole

as an abhorrent example. The sentence of Adriaen and the six other brethren is fully treated in *DB* 1917, 150-51.

K. Vos writes at length about Adriaen in *DB* 1917, 143-50, and states that he was captured in Haarlem, was also called Adriaen Vermeer (*q.v.*), and was likely the father of the later (Reformed) burgomaster of Leiden, Pieter Adriaensz van der Werff. (*Inv. Arch. Amst.* I, No. 745; *DB* 1917, 143-50; 151-52.)　　　　　　vdZ.

Adriaen Olieu (also called A. Ol, or A. du Rieu), an Anabaptist martyr, put to death in Armentières, France. He came from Halewijn (Halluin) in Flanders and was "of a fitting old age." According to the *Martyrs' Mirror* he was tortured without result and in 1567 burned at the stake. Van Braght also lists the martyr Adriaen Ol, who was likewise executed in Armentières in about 1569. These two names probably refer to the same martyr, the year of whose death has not yet been fully established. Adriaen was a well-known preacher (*leeraar*) in Flanders, for many years a minister in the Armentières congregation. The martyr Jacob de Rore (*q.v.*) addressed his nineteenth letter to him. There is some question as to whether this martyr was actually an Anabaptist. (*DB* 1899, 138.)　　　　　　vdZ.

Mart. Mir. D 345, 475, E 704, 818; see also the letter D 471-73, E 814-18; Vos, *Antwerpen,* 359; *ML* III, 297, 299.

Adriaen Pan (also called A. Peeterssone Pan), an Anabaptist martyr, a native of Driel in the Dutch province of Gelderland, who with his wife Neelken Jacobs (*q.v.*) lived at Nijvel (Nivelles), south of Brussels. Driven by the persecution they fled from Nijvel to Antwerp. Here they were captured on April 25, 1559, and put into the Steen prison; both were condemned to death. Their house furnishings were sold for about 75 guilders. Adriaen was sentenced on June 16 and beheaded on June 18, 1559. The *Offer des Heeren* and later martyr books contain two short letters written by Adriaen, which reveal that he was an ordinary man, who as he himself said, "did not have the gift of writing very well." A song about Adriaen and Neelken, "Duysternis gaet van henen, wanneer dat licht coemt aen" (Darkness goes from hence, whene'er that light arrives), appears in *Het Offer* and is mentioned in Wolkan, *Lieder.*　　　　　　vdZ.

Offer, 342-47; *Mart. Mir.* D 245-46, E 618; Wolkan, *Lieder,* 67; Génard, *Antw. Arch.-Blad* IX, 2, 8, 16; XIV, 26-27, No. 292; *ML* III, 333.

Adriaen Pietersz, an otherwise unknown martyr, also called "Adriaen met een oog" (Adriaen with one eye), of Alkmaar in the Dutch province of North Holland, executed in The Hague on May 12, 1534, because he "really despised the sacrament and held that pilgrimages were useless." It is not certain whether he was a "Sacramentist" (*q.v.*) or an Anabaptist. (Grosheide, *Bijdrage,* 51, 302; *DB* 1917, 181.)　　　　　　vdZ.

Adriaen Pietersz (or A. Pier Trappers), an Anabaptist martyr, lived at Winkel in the Dutch province of North Holland, was burned at the stake in The Hague on July 7, 1558, because he had taken part in Anabaptist meetings and intended to be rebaptized. He was thus not yet a member of the congregation. Waechlink Dirks (*q.v.*) and Maerten Cornelisz (*q.v.*) died with him. (*Inv. Arch. Amst.* I, No. 392; *Mart. Mir.* D 202, E 583.)   VDZ.

Adriaen Pietersz, an Anabaptist martyr, was burned at the stake in 1570 at Haarlem, in the Dutch province of North Holland, for his faith. Details are wanting. (*Mart. Mir.* D 509, E 848.)   VDZ.

Adriaen Reyers, a printer who disseminated Anabaptist literature, was banned from Antwerp in 1536. After this he worked in Delft and other Dutch towns. On Oct. 2, 1542, by a verdict of the court of Holland he was also banned from the district of Holland. No further trace of him has been found. (*Inv. Arch. Amst.* I, No. 248.)   VDZ.

Adriaen Rogiers, an Anabaptist martyr, was born in "Rossem-lant" in the Dutch province of Gelderland, and from about 1560 lived at Gent in Belgium, where he was baptized into the congregation in 1562 or 1563. By trade Adriaen was a hatter. It appears that he was imprisoned for a considerable time. During his imprisonment he wrote three letters to his wife which are included in the *Martyrs' Mirror* as well as in other martyr books. He was burned at the stake in Gent on the Vrijdagsmarkt on Dec. 4, 1572, at the age of 35. Sharing martyrdom with him were Martin van den Straeten, Mattheus Bernaerts, and Dingentgen van Hondschoote (*q.v.*). (*Mart. Mir.* D 623-31, E 947-59; Verheyden, *Gent*, No. 206, p. 59.)   VDZ.

Adriaen Vermeer, an Anabaptist martyr executed at Haarlem in the Dutch province of North Holland in 1537. He was preacher (*leeraar*) of the congregation at Leiden. K. Vos (*DB* 1917, 150) conjectures that he was one of the seven ministers beheaded at Haarlem on March 26, 1534, and claims that he is identical with Adriaen Lourysz. (*DB* 1917, 143-50.)   VDZ.

Adriaen de Wever (Weaver), preacher at Delft in the Dutch province of South Holland, was executed in 1534. Details are lacking. (*DB* 1917, 118, No. 90.)   VDZ.

Adriaen Willemsz, an Anabaptist martyr, beheaded at Vianen in the Dutch province of South Holland on March 22, 1569. He was captured in his house on the night of April 4, 1568. Much effort was made to have Adriaen return to the Roman Church. Repeatedly, and even after he had been sentenced, he was visited in his cell by monks who "sought to rob him of his faith," but Adriaen remained steadfast and died "with a willing heart, retaining his faith." In contrast to most of the martyrs, he was well-treated and did not have to endure any torture. According to tradition, Adriaen, during his imprisonment of nearly a year, produced various writings, which were lost at the time of a flood in February 1571. (*Mart. Mir.* D 366, E 721.)   VDZ.

Adriaen de Wintere, an Anabaptist martyr, born at Rupelmonde, Flanders, a "wageman" (wagoner) by trade, was burned to death and his head placed on a pole at Antwerp, Jan. 20, 1553. He is not mentioned in the martyr books. (Génard, *Antw. Arch.-Blad* VIII, 421-22; XIV, 20-21, No. 221.)   VDZ.

Adriaen Wouterssone, an Anabaptist martyr, of Heusden in Brabant, Holland, who is not found in the martyr books, was burned at the stake and his head placed on a pole at Antwerp, Sept. 23, 1552, together with two other brethren. His wife, Mechtelt Melis, was drowned for her faith on the same day. (Génard, *Antw. Arch.-Blad* VIII, 420, 422; XIV, 20-21, No. 218.)   VDZ.

Adriaenken Jansdochter, an Anabaptist martyr, lived at Molenaarsgraaf, near Dordrecht in the Dutch province of South Holland. She was imprisoned in the Vuylpoort in Dordrecht, and died on March 28, 1572, after being strangled and then burned, along with Jan Woutersz (*q.v.*). When Adriaenken learned about her death sentence she thanked God that she was found worthy to offer up her body to God. Her mouth having been stopped with a wooden plug, she could not speak to the bystanders at her execution, among whom were some fellow believers. The *Martyrs' Mirror* includes a letter which Adriaenken wrote in prison to her husband, J. A. van Dort, as well as his reply written Jan. 18 or 19, 1572. In this letter her husband encourages her to stand true and persevere in her faith. There is also a song concerning Adriaenken and Jan Wouters which begins: "Uut de woestyn roepen wy Heer tot dy, Die ons in alle noot staet by" (From the wilderness we cry to Thee, O Lord, Who in every need art near). (*Mart. Mir.* D 566-569, E 897-900; *ML* II, 390.)   VDZ.

Adrian First Mennonite Church (EM) of Adrian, Mich., was organized Oct. 23, 1949. A basement church was built in 1947 and the superstructure completed in 1953. The 1953 membership was 28.   R.SHO.

Adrian, Heinrich (1851-1936), minister and elder of the Mennonite Brethren Church, b. March 22, 1851, in the village of Rudnerweide, Molotschna Mennonite Colony, South Russia, the third of eight children in the family of Heinrich and Sarah (nee Klassen) **Adrian.**

In boyhood he received an elementary education in the local village school. On Dec. 14, 1871, he married Helena Loewen, after which he established his home in the Mennonite colony in the Crimea. The family migrated to America in 1874 and located on a farm near Parker, S.D. They were the parents of 13 children. In 1904 the family moved to Kansas, living first on a farm near Buhler and after 1916 in Buhler.

After his conversion Heinrich Adrian joined the M.B. Church through baptism on May 21, 1877. The local M.B. church elected him to the ministry, and to the eldership on Oct. 30, 1881. His early ministerial service was chiefly in the M.B. Church at Parker, S.D., and in the congregations of the new settlements in the Dakotas. Coming to Kansas, he had a fruitful ministry in the Ebenezer and

Buhler M.B. churches from 1904 to 1927, being presiding elder from 1907 to 1924. In addition he frequently visited other M.B. churches in Kansas and Oklahoma. He was active in M.B. conference work for many years. Between 1882 and 1900 the conference frequently employed him for part-time home mission work, in which he traveled extensively and conducted many meetings in various churches. He served on the M.B. Foreign Mission Board 1907-12. He died at Buhler on July 9, 1936, and was interred at the local M.B. cemetery.   J.H.L.

Adriana IJsbrantsdochter, an Anabaptist martyr, was drowned at Amsterdam, on May 15, 1535, on account of her faith, along with six other women, while on the same day two men were beheaded. They were accused of departing from the universal Christian faith (Roman Catholic Church), of violating the decrees of the emperor, and of revealing no compunction in regard to their heresy. (*Mart. Mir.* D 413, E 764; Grosheide, *Verhooren,* 58.)
vDZ.

Adriana Jansdochter, an Anabaptist martyr from Benschop, Dutch province of Utrecht, was drowned at Amsterdam on May 21, 1535 (*Martyrs' Mirror* incorrectly records May 15), along with ten other martyrs, all women, because they had been rebaptized, according to the indictment. Adriana was the daughter of Jan van Reenen and Leentgen, who were both Anabaptists. The magistrate sought in vain for Jan van Reenen, and Leentgen died the death of a martyr on the same day as her daughter. Lijsbeth Jansdochter of Benschop, who was executed in Amsterdam six days before, May 15, 1535, was presumably a sister of Adriana. (*Mart. Mir.* D 413, E 764; Grosheide, *Verhooren,* 70; *ML* II, 390.)
vDZ.

Adriana Lambrechts, an Anabaptist martyr, wife of the martyr Henrick Dacho (*q.v.*), born "in de Langestrate," who is not mentioned in the martyr books, was drowned at the Steen prison at Antwerp on March 17 or 19, 1559, because she had been rebaptized, and was "stiff-necked in the doctrine of the Anabaptists." This martyr must be identical with Naentken Leerverkoopster (*q.v.*). (Génard, *Antw. Arch.-Blad* VIII, 460, 472; IX, 17; XIV, 26-27, No. 284.)
vDZ.

Adriane (Naerken) Vyncx, an Anabaptist martyr who is not mentioned in the martyr books, born at West-Vleteren in Flanders, wife of Kaerle de Vos, was baptized in the year 1536. She was connected with the congregation at Gent and probably lived there. She was seized at Brugge, in Belgium, and on Aug. 28, 1536, was burned at the stake there. (Verheyden, *Brugge,* No. 10, p. 33.)
vDZ.

A.D.S., the abbreviation for Algemeene Doopsgezinde Societeit (*q.v.*).

Adshembet, village in the central part of the Crimean peninsula, district of Byten, province of Taurida, Russia. Railroad station, Byuk-Onlar (7 miles distant) on the southern branch of the Kursk-Sevastopol line. Post office, Kurmann-Kemelchi. The village, which comprised some 6,000 acres of arable land and had a population of 80 in 1913, was founded in 1897 on lands owned by Lustig and leased in 1900 to Mennonites. The language used was German. No information was available on its fate between and after the two world wars.
H.R.

Adventists: see **Seventh Day Adventists.**

Aeberli, Lorenz, an Anabaptist martyr of Bern, Switzerland, participant in the religious disputation held at Bern (*q.v.*) in 1538, executed June 3, 1539.

Aecht Jan Middelborchsdochter, an Anabaptist martyr, born at Zwolle, drowned at Utrecht in the Netherlands on June 11, 1539. (*Berigten Hist. Genootschap, Utrecht,* IV, II, 1851, 139.)   vDZ.

Aecht Melis, an Anabaptist martyr, captured at Krommeniedijk in the Dutch province of North Holland, was put to death after horrible torture, presumably in 1534 (1542, the date given in the *Martyrs' Mirror,* is wrong in any case), along with a number of other brethren and sisters, including her husband, Willem. (*Mart. Mir.* D 62, E 465; *DB* 1917, 170; *ML* III, 70.)   vDZ.

Aechtgen Jansdochter, wife of Jan Zijvertszoon, of Amsterdam, was sentenced because she lodged the *Naaktloopers* (*q.v.*) (Anabaptists who walked naked in the streets as a witness). She was a member of the congregation. She was hanged before the door of her own house on June 1, 1535. (Grosheide, *Verhooren,* 148-49.)   vDZ.

Aechtken Joris Adriaensdochter (called simply Aechtken in the *Martyrs' Mirror*), an Anabaptist martyr, of Zierikzee in the Dutch province of Zeeland (she is therefore also called Aechtgen van Zierikzee, or Sirckzee), was drowned together with five other women martyrs at the Steen prison at Antwerp on July 19, 1559. On May 20 of this year the women had been apprehended by the margrave of Antwerp. Aechtken confessed her faith willingly and freely, and therefore was brutally drowned during the night. Aechtken and the other women martyrs are found in two old martyr-songs: in "Een Liedeken van ses vrouwen," beginning "Babels Raets Mandamenten," in which her name is not expressly named, and also in the song "Aenhoort Godt hemelsche Vader" (Een liedeken van 72 vrienden, te Antwerpen gedood tusschen 1555 en 1560). Both songs are in the *Liedtboecxken van den Offer des Heeren,* 1563; they are No. 16 and No. 19 respectively.   vDZ.

Offer, 566, 581 ff.; *Mart. Mir.* D 249-50; E 623; Génard, *Antw. Arch.-Blad* IX, 3, 9; 26-27, No. 298; Wolkan, *Lieder,* 63, 71, 72.

Aeff Peters, widow of Frans Jansz, was drowned June 31 (probably a typographical inversion for 13) 1541, at Utrecht in the Netherlands. She had been rebaptized by the elder Jan Matthijsz van Middelburg (*q.v.*) about six years before, but later she was led astray by the Batenburgers (*q.v.*). This fact is, however, not stated in the verdict. (*Berigten Hist. Genootschap, Utrecht,* IV, II, 1851, 139.)   vDZ.

Aeffgen Lystyncx (Aeff Pietersdochter, wife of Geryt Lystyncx), a native of Amsterdam or perhaps of

Limmen in the Dutch province of North Holland, a very wealthy woman, was won to the Anabaptist cause and played a very active role in the movement. She was repeatedly fined but could not be captured because she was continually in flight (1533, 1536, 1538). Without any doubt she was a member of the congregation and exerted much influence, but it is doubtful that this influence was always the best, for she was drawn more and more into the Münster maelstrom. In the early part of 1535 she resided in Jan van Leiden's New Jerusalem where she was known as a prophetess. Upon the fall of Münster, June 1535, she was imprisoned, yet evidently set free, for in December 1535 she was recaptured at Hazerswoude (*q.v.*) in the Dutch province of South Holland because she participated in the revolt there. She then received pardon but later was again active. In 1538 she was banned perpetually from Holland and her property confiscated. Her husband, evidently not an Anabaptist, protested. After this she disappears from history. She is one of those numerous figures who during this agitated period in the Netherlands sought for spiritual renewing but who never had the satisfaction of arriving at a peaceful and loyal acceptance of the Gospel. (*Inv. Arch. Amst.* I, Nos. 108, 191; *DB* 1917, 116-17; Grosheide, *Bijdrage,* 33, 55-57, 76, 81-82.)   vDZ.

Aefterman, Gillis: see **Jelis Outerman.**

Ael Thomasdochter (or Ael Seelten), a martyr, was drowned in a sack at Delft, in the Dutch province of South Holland, near the school tower, and buried in the gallows-yard. This martyr and the four women executed with her were probably followers of David Joris (*q.v.*). (*Inv. Arch. Amst.* I, No. 749; *DB* 1899, 158-60; 1917, 160-67.)   vDZ.

Aelbert Gerritsz, born at Veldhuizen near Zwolle, was beheaded at Utrecht in the Netherlands on June 21, 1544. He was a Batenburger (*q.v.*). (*Berigten Hist. Genootschap, Utrecht,* IV, II, 1851, 146.)   vDZ.

Aelken Jansdochter, an Anabaptist martyr of The Hague, was married to Simon Diericx, a turner of Middelburg in the Dutch province of Zeeland, and about 37 years of age. She was rebaptized in Middelburg and because she "persisted," that is, would not forsake her faith, she was burned at the stake there in 1569. The exact date is not known, although it was presumably May 2.   vDZ.

K. R. Pekelharing, "Bijdr. v. d. Gesch. der Herv. in Zeeland," in *Archief Zeeuwsch Gen.* VI (1866) 92.

Aeltestenrat, Council of Elders, composed of the elders, ministers, and deacons of the Mennonite churches of Baden (9) and Württemberg (5), five of the eight in Bavaria, and two in the Palatinate. It meets four times annually to deliberate on questions concerning the individual churches and on questions concerning the conference, known as the *Badisch-württembergisch-bayerischer Gemeindeverband* (Union of the congregations of Baden, Württemberg, and Bavaria). The churches are supervised by the *Aeltestenrat* jointly; therefore no one

elder makes important decisions without first hearing the advice of the others, and in a sense all the congregations operate as one united congregation. Actually the elders are chosen by the *Aeltestenrat* to serve the entire group, even though they have primary responsibility locally in one congregation.

In the sessions, which are always preceded by the discussion of a passage of Scripture, all the activities of the individual congregations, as well as the wishes of the members are considered, relations between the congregations regulated, decisions about church discipline made, communion dates set, and measures for the welfare of the congregations passed. The decisions of the *Aeltestenrat* on important issues are usually preceded by an inquiry of the church members. Minutes are kept of all proceedings, which afford an interesting record of the development of the congregations, with primary reference to church discipline. But the record is complete only since 1876; most of the previous minutes have been lost. The *Aeltestenrat* has no permanent president, a different chairman being chosen for each meeting. However, usually one or more of the senior elders carry decisive weight in the deliberations of the group. For many years the meetings have been held in Heilbronn.

There were similar councils of elders (*Aeltesten-Convent*) in Holland, West Prussia, Russia, and America before the organization of the modern church conferences.   HEGE.

Aeltgen van Gent, a button maker, in whose house in Homburger Street in Utrecht, Holland, a Mennonite congregation was accustomed to meet 1560-62. She apparently fled the persecution of 1562. No trial or verdict concerning her has been found. She is mentioned only in the confessions of prisoners. (*DB* 1903, 12, 15, 40.)   vDZ.

Aeltgen (or **Alijdt**) **Gielisdochter** (*Martyrs' Mirror,* Aeltje Gilles), the wife of Jacob Janssen, an Anabaptist martyr of Benschop, Dutch province of Utrecht, was executed at Amsterdam on May 21, 1535 (*Martyrs' Mirror* incorrectly says May 15), along with ten other martyrs, all women. Aeltgen had been baptized at Benschop by Gherijt Ghijsen, and was one of the group who had gone from Amsterdam to Bergklooster (*q.v.*). She refused to forsake her faith. (*Mart. Mir.* D 413, E 764; Grosheide, *Verhooren,* 68, 70.)   vDZ.

Aeltgen (or **Alijdt**) **Wouters,** of Asperen, an Anabaptist martyr, was drowned at Amsterdam on May 21, 1535 (*Martyrs' Mirror* incorrectly says May 15), because she had been rebaptized (by Gherijt Ghijsen of Benschop) and had joined the "sect and heresy of the Anabaptists." On the same day ten other women, along with Aeltgen, were subjected to the cruel death of drowning. Aeltgen was one of the group who had gone from Amsterdam to Bergklooster (*q.v.*). (*Mart. Mir.* D 413, E 764; Grosheide, *Verhooren,* 69, 70, 140.)   vDZ.

Aeltjen Baten, an Anabaptist martyr, drowned in the Maas River at Liége, Belgium, at the end of

October 1593 (*Martyrs' Mirror* says July 24, 1595, which is certainly incorrect). She was an elderly woman who was seized in the summer of 1593 with her husband Quintijn Jacobs and a young woman Maeyken Wouters (*q.v.*) at Zonhoven near Hasselt, where they were living. All three were taken to Liége. Quintijn was released, but the women could not be induced to change their minds. For ten weeks they were kept in prison "in des Officiaels Toren." When they heard their death sentence "they thanked the Lord with laughing mouth." Taken to the Maas bridge by the executioner, Aeltje said, "This is a beautiful city, would that it like Nineveh would repent." Then she was prevented from speaking and was cast into the water. From prison she had sent a greeting to her husband and asked that "he bring up my children in the fear of the Lord." A song about her, beginning: "Voorwaer 't dient niet Versweghen, des weerelts blintheyd groot," is found in *Veelderhande Liedekens* (1559) and later songbooks.   NEFF, VDZ.

Mart. Mir. D 789, E 1091; W. Bax, *Het Prot. in het Bisdom Luik* . . . II (The Hague, 1941) 343-47; *ML* I, 136.

Aemilius, Gerardus, Reformed pastor and also a physician at Oud-Beyerland in the Dutch province of South Holland, had a dispute at this town on Sunday, April 8, 1663, with Tieleman Jansz van Braght (*q.v.*), the Mennonite elder of Dordrecht and the author of the *Martyrs' Mirror.* The debate, which pertained to the question whether or not infant baptism is Scriptural, lasted from six o'clock in the evening until two at night, attended by a large concourse of the people. At this hour, Aemilius broke off the dispute, and was not willing to continue it publicly on the following day. It had been the stipulation of van Braght that it be held "with open doors in the church of the Reformed or the Mennonites." On June 20 of that year Aemilius visited van Braght in Dordrecht and kindly requested that they "no longer dispute quarrelsomely with each other, but debate in friendly discussion." A copy of the document (72 pp.) of the dispute held in Oud-Beyerland is to be found in the Mennonite archives at Amsterdam (*Inv. Arch. Amst.* I, No. 612; see also Blaupot t.C., *Holland* I, 197-99).   VDZ.

Aerdt (Arent) Aerssens, a Dutch Anabaptist martyr of Utrecht, who in the *Martyrs' Mirror* is called Arent Passementwercker, was burned at the stake at Antwerp on Dec. 16, 1558. The *Martyrs' Mirror* states that together with him five other martyrs were executed. This is not quite correct; according to the records compiled by Génard, on Dec. 16 the following martyrs were burned: Aerdt Aerssens (Arent Passementwercker), Peeter Henricx (Pieter in de Vettewarier), Jan Collen (Hans van Borculo), and Geert Franssens (Geraert Passementwercker). Aerdt is also mentioned in the song, "Aenhoort God, hemelsche Vader" (Hear, O God, heavenly Father), No. 16 of the *Liedtboecxken van den Offer des Heeren.*   VDZ.

Offer, 566; *Mart. Mir.* D 202, E 583; *Génard, Antw.*

Arch.-Blad VIII, 454, 466; XIV, 24-25, No. 271; *Wolkan, Lieder,* 63, 72.

Aert (van Gershoven), a native of Tongeren in Brabant, Belgium, an Anabaptist martyr, not in the martyr books, was drowned at Antwerp at the Steen prison on Oct. 17, 1562, together with his brother, Jacob van Gershoven (*q.v.*), because he was rebaptized and persisted in the doctrine of the Anabaptists. (Génard, *Antw. Arch.-Blad* IX, 142, 150, 162; XIV, 32-33, No. 367.)   VDZ.

Aert Claudiuszn Centurio, a native of Brussels, an Anabaptist martyr, beheaded at Utrecht in the Netherlands on June 11, 1535, together with others, including his father, Claudy Centurio (*q.v.*). (*Berigten Hist. Gen. Utrecht,* IV, II, 1851, 139.) VDZ.

Aert de Hane, placed on trial at Antwerp on Sept. 24, 1563, and again on Oct. 8 of the same year. At the trial on Dec. 8, he confessed that he repented. In December 1563 he had to appear a third time before the commissioners, but this time the verdict was "delayed until the following month because of his illness." We do not learn about the outcome of the trial. Perhaps he died in prison. (Génard, *Antw. Arch.-Blad* IX, 152, 156, 157; XIV, 32-33, No. 374.)   VDZ.

Aert Jansz, Dutch martyr, a joiner by trade, of "Osche" (Oss in Brabant?), was decapitated and "the head placed on a stake" at Delft in the Dutch province of South Holland on Jan. 7, 1538, together with ten others, because they had been rebaptized. Probably they were followers of David Joris (*q.v.*). (*Inv. Arch. Amst.* I, No. 749; *DB* 1899, 158-60; 1917, 160-67.)   VDZ.

Aeschliman, Paul R. (1862-1938), pastor First Mennonite Church (GCM), Colfax, Wash., b. Oct. 25, 1862, near Brenets, canton of Neuchâtel, Switzerland, son of Christ Pierre Aeschliman and Julia Roulet-Aeschliman, d. March 19, 1938. He came to Pulaski, Iowa, in 1884 with several brothers. He had six brothers and two sisters. Married Phebe Diefenbach, Pulaski, Aug. 25, 1892; children: (Adp.) Beulah Pearl, b. 1896; Rupert, b. 1901.

He was educated in Switzerland and in the Mennonite Seminary, Halstead, Kan., 1891-92. In November 1886 he moved to Washington Territory, later returning to Kansas for schooling, to Iowa for marriage, and then back to Washington to farm. He was elected minister July 1, 1893, to serve a Mennonite group in Whitman Co., Wash., which had been organized by J. B. Baer, Field Secretary of the G.C. Mennonite Church. He served this church for more than 43 years until 1936, at which time he was made pastor emeritus.

He served in the following capacities: traveling pastor Pac. Dist. Conf., 1896-1908; chmn. Evang. Com., Pac. Dist. Conf. for a number of years beginning in 1908; member G.C. Home Miss. Bd., 1899-1908, G.C. Relief Com., 1911-20, and G.C. Program Com., 1923-32. He was a minister-at-large for the Pacific District for many years.   J.H.LA.

Affirmation, a substitute for the legal oath (*q.v.*).

Afgedeelden (Separated Ones). After the union in 1591 of many High German (*q.v.*) and Frisian (*q.v.*) Mennonite congregations in the Netherlands and the Rhineland on the basis of the Concept of Cologne, many Waterlanders (*q.v.*) also joined them in 1601. This group was known as the *Bevredigde Broederschap* (United Brotherhood). In 1613, however, another split took place. Leenaert Clock (*q.v.*) left this union with most of the High Germans and Frisians; Clock's group was called *Afgedeelden* (they united with the Flemish in 1639). (Kühler, *Geschiedenis* II, 93 f., 193.) vDZ.

Africa. The continent of Africa has been the scene of Mennonite mission activity for more than 50 years. In 1890 Eusebius Hershey of the Mennonite Brethren in Christ Church went on his own to Liberia to engage in missionary work without denominational support. He soon died on the field but his sacrifice inspired others of his church to volunteer for work in Africa. In 1901 workers from his church went to Africa under the Sudan Interior Mission. In 1905 the Mennonite Brethren in Christ Missionary Society for Africa was founded. With the formation of the United Missionary Society (*q.v.*) in 1920 by the Mennonite Brethren in Christ, the work was taken over by the new organization. In 1951 this church had 52 missionaries in Nigeria, 6 in the Belgian Congo, 1 in Egypt, and 1 in the Anglo-Egyptian Sudan.

The Defenseless Mennonite Conference supported missionaries in Africa beginning about 1890 and the Central Conference of Mennonites sent its first missionaries to that continent in 1906. Both churches, however, discontinued their work in 1909 because of the congested condition of the field in which they were working. The two churches then in 1911 organized the United Mennonite Board of Missions, which name was changed to the Congo Inland Mission (*q.v.*) in 1912. By 1950 this organization had 59 missionaries under appointment and on the field. The work was being supported by four conferences, the C.C.M., E.M.C., E.M.B., and G.C.M. As a result of the work of the Congo Inland Mission there are 11,000 Christians in their area (1950).

In 1920 Mennonite Brethren missionaries established an independent mission in the Belgian Congo. The Africa Mission Association later assumed responsibility for the mission. After this organization had operated the mission for more than a decade, the M.B. general conference in 1943 took official charge of the field. By 1950 the M.B. Church had 19 missionaries in the Kwango (*q.v.*) field and 6 in the Kasai (*q.v.*) field. In these two fields were more than 4,000 Christians.

The Eastern Mennonite Board of Missions and Charities (*q.v.*) of the Lancaster Mennonite Conference (MC) opened work in the Tanganyika Territory, Africa, in 1934. Five congregations served by 11 ministers and one bishop had a membership of 864 in 1952. The Eastern Board (*q.v.*) in 1953 began the Somalia (*q.v.*) Mennonite Mission.

The Mennonite Central Committee in its relief program during World War II co-operated with the UNRRA (*q.v.*) in Egypt, furnishing workers and relief supplies for the refugee camps in that area. In 1945 three of these MCC workers were transferred by UNRRA to Ethiopia. During the next few years other workers were sent into this field, and a relief program was operated by the Mennonite Relief Committee (Elkhart). Finally in 1948 the emperor of Ethiopia gave the Mennonites consent to begin mission activity in his country, after which the Eastern Mennonite Board of Missions and Charities opened work 250 miles southeast of Addis Ababa. Twenty-two of their missionaries were serving in this field in 1953.   M.G.

Africa Inland Mission. After stirring messages on African mission work were given to the Defenseless Mennonites and the Central Illinois Conference of Mennonites by representatives of the Africa Inland Mission in 1905, both groups decided to open mission stations under this organization. In April 1906 the Foreign Mission Committee of the Central Illinois Conference sent its first missionaries to Africa and some time later the Defenseless Mennonites sent their first workers to East Africa. Both conferences, however, discontinued their work under the Africa Inland Misson when their missionaries had completed their first term of service. It was felt that it would be advisable to begin an independent Mennonite mission program in Africa and so the Congo Inland Mission (*q.v.*) was organized by the above two conferences.   M.G.

Africa Mennonite Brethren Mission: see Belgian Congo Mennonite Brethren Mission.

Africa Mennonite Mission. The Lancaster Mennonite Conference (MC) opened mission work in Musoma District, Tanganyika Territory, East Africa, on May 26, 1934, when John H. Mosemann, Jr. and wife and Elam Stauffer and wife, the first couples to be sent out, landed at Shirati by dhow. The beginning of the church in East Africa was on Sept. 15, 1935, when 15 persons were baptized and 6 others received into church fellowship. The total membership of the churches in Musoma District grew by 1953 to 864. The five stations were Shirati, Bukiroba, Mugango, Bumangi, and Nyabasi. From the beginning the objective was to build self-supporting, self-propagating, and self-governing churches. No money was brought from America for the native African church. Church buildings and church operation have been supported only by money and labor given in Africa, and self-propagation of the church has been the responsibility of the native members. This was in the form of organized village work. Government of the church while it was small was by counseling all of its members. In 1938 the first steps were taken toward setting up the African General Church Council, when several members were chosen to counsel with the missionaries on matters of church government. The General Church Council is now made up of members chosen biennially by the churches to serve as elders or counselors. In 1948 there were 17 African elders

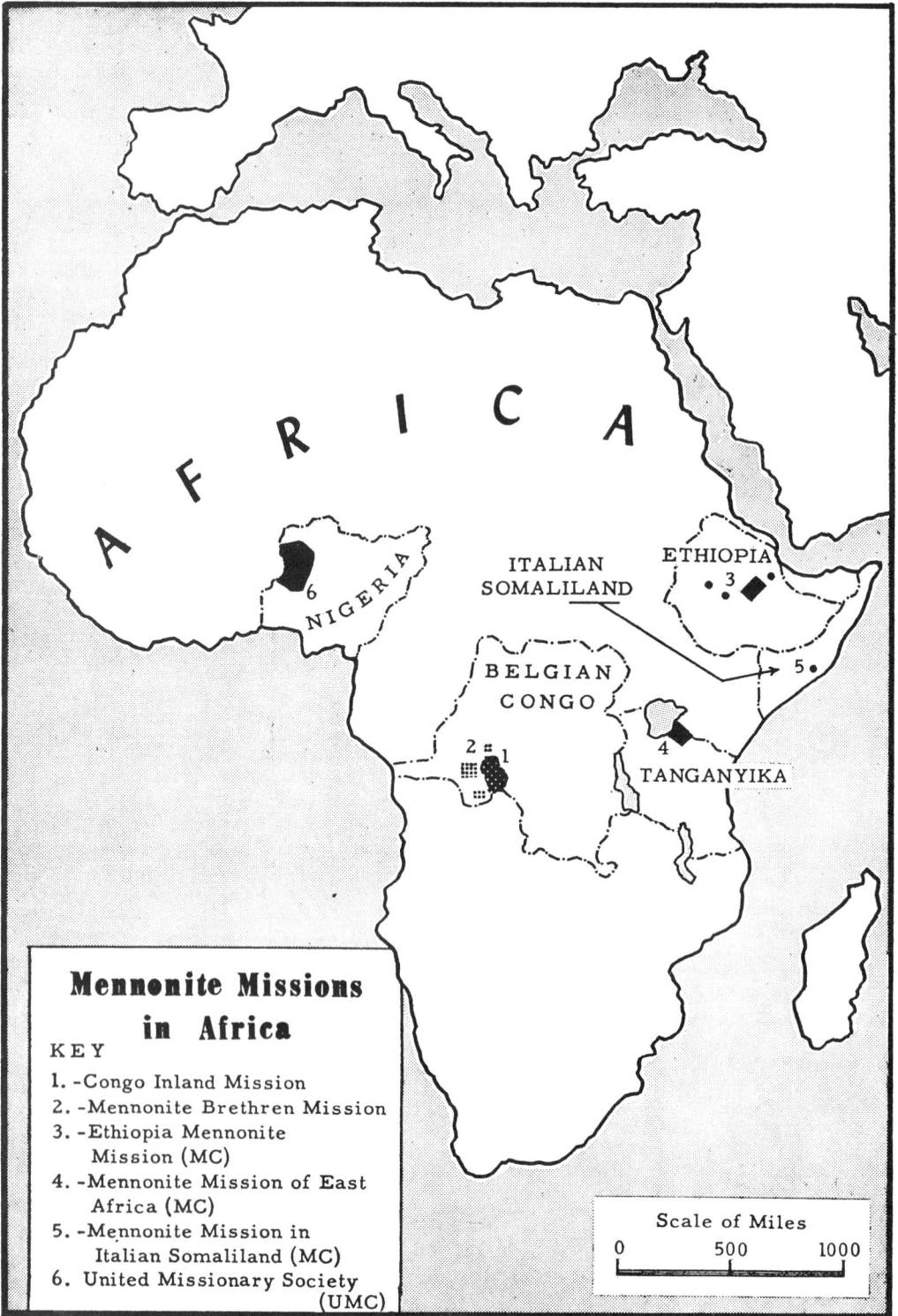

A F R I C A

NIGERIA

ITALIAN
SOMALILAND

ETHIOPIA
3

BELGIAN
CONGO

5

6

2 1

4

TANGANYIKA

Mennonite Missions
in Africa

KEY

1. -Congo Inland Mission
2. -Mennonite Brethren Mission
3. -Ethiopia Mennonite
   Mission (MC)
4. -Mennonite Mission of East
   Africa (MC)
5. -Mennonite Mission in
   Italian Somaliland (MC)
6. United Missionary Society
   (UMC)

Scale of Miles

0   500   1000

who with all ordained missionaries on the field constitute the General Church Council, which acts in an advisory capacity. It was set up to aid in indigenous governing from the beginning. Steps were under way for formal organization of the African church and ordination of African leaders.

Elam Stauffer was ordained bishop for the church in East Africa on Sept. 5, 1938, at Bukiroba by Henry E. Lutz. He had bishop oversight of all of the work in East Africa until April 24, 1941, when W. Ray Wenger was ordained at Mugango to assist Stauffer. He died on June 9, 1945. Since then all the ordained men on the field have assisted Elam Stauffer, awaiting the further development and organization of the African church.   E.W.S.

Agrachan was an intended village in the northeastern part of the Mennonite colony established in 1901 in the Terek (*q.v.*) region on the Caspian Sea in Russia, south of the Agrachan Peninsula and of the camp of Peter I there in 1722. Planned for 33 landless Mennonite families, it was never settled because the salty character of the soil made it unsuitable for agriculture. (*ML* I, 14.)   HEGE.

Agrarian Movement. A part of the series of revolutions taking place in Mexico during the first half of the 20th century involved the rise of the peasant class. The movement affecting the rural classes is referred to as the Agrarian Movement. The central aspect of the Agrarian Movement was the breaking up of large *haciendas* or estates into smaller units with the intention of having groups of Mexican farmers operate them for their own use. It was not a communist movement in the Russian sense, but rather an attempt to put land ownership into the hands of the native peons who for generations had been virtual serfs to large landowners. At times Mennonites who had settled in Mexico became fearful lest the Agrarian Movement encroach on their land holdings. There was, however, small justification for these fears, since the Mexican government at all times scrupulously protected Mennonite land holdings, and at no time were they in danger.   J.W.F.

Agricola, Franciscus, d. 1620, priest at Sittard in the Dutch province of Limburg and a Catholic writer, attacked the Mennonites in his *Ketzer-Brunn oder Grundwurtzel aller Secten* (Cologne, 1583), and *Confutatio Anabaptistorum Germanice.* Karl Rembert (*Wiedertäufer*, 564) quotes an unintentionally favorable comment on the Anabaptists (quoted in translation by John Horsch, *Mennonites in Europe,* Scottdale, 1942, 294) which he attributes to a book by Agricola, *Erster evangelischer Prozess wider allerlei grausame Irrtümer der Wiedertäufer* (Cologne, 1582; 2nd ed. 1591). (*N.N.B.Wb.* III, 14-17.)   vDZ.

Agricola, Stephan, pastor in Augsburg (*q.v.*), Germany, who was appointed with Rhegius, Frosch, and Weller to persuade the Anabaptist preachers imprisoned in the city to recant by a conference with them on Sept. 21 and 25, 1527.   HEGE.

Agricultural Association (*Verein zur fördersamen Verbreitung des Gehölz-, Garten-, Seiden- und Weinbaus*), organized in the Molotschna Mennonite settlement, South Russia, in 1830 and in the Chortitza Mennonite settlement in 1832. It was usually referred to as *Landwirtschaftlicher Verein.* Contenius (*q.v.*) must first have conceived the idea for such an organization in order to promote agriculture. Johann Cornies (*q.v.*), the model farmer of the Molotschna settlement who had attracted the attention not only of the local Russian government, but even in the circles of St. Petersburg, was asked to draw up a constitution for this Agricultural Association. The constitution was approved on Nov. 12, 1830, by General Inzov, the president of the Guardians' Committee (*q.v.*), called the *Fürsorge-Komitee,* a Russian government agency for the supervision of foreign settlements, with headquarters in Odessa. Johann Cornies was appointed lifetime chairman of the Molotschna Agricultural Association. The purpose of the association was an effective propagation of afforestation, horticulture, silk industry, and viniculture. In 1836 all trades of the settlement were included and in 1843 education was also added. The constitution of the Agricultural Association is not available.

The name "Agricultural Association" was later changed to Agricultural Commission. This commission consisted of at least three members, appointed by the Guardians' Committee from a list of six candidates elected by the village meetings of the district. The candidates had to be elected from those farmers who had made the greatest progress in agriculture and stock breeding, and could serve as example to others. The time of service was at least nine years, unless ill health or misconduct prevented the member from discharging his duties. The commission had no part in administration of the district (volost) nor executive power, but its suggestions and recommendations were to be considered by village authorities and individuals as if coming from the district office. The commission was to hold at least three general and two district meetings annually. Its members received no salary, but were exempted from some of the obligations of other citizens of the community. The commission made an annual report to the Guardians' Committee, especially about individuals who had distinguished themselves in any branch of farming and could be awarded premiums of 10-30 roubles. The Chortitza Agricultural Commission was in existence until 1880, while the Molotschna Agricultural Commission continued to the time of the Revolution in 1917.

The chairmen of the Molotschna Agricultural Association served in the following order: Johann Cornies, Philipp Wiebe, David Cornies, Peter Schmidt. After this the Molotschna Agricultural Commission was divided into two parts, the Halbstadt and the Gnadenfeld branches. Chairmen of the Halbstadt branch were, in order: Klaas Wiebe, Heinrich Reimer, Johannes Wiebe, and Peter P. Neufeld; of the Gnadenfeld branch: Peter Schmidt, Gerhard Fast, Heinrich Siebert, Peter Bergmann.

David Unruh, and Abraham Rempel. The Chortitza Agricultural Commission had the following chairmen and outstanding leaders: Jacob Penner, Franz Pauls, Heinrich Hildebrandt, Johann Siemens, David Redekop, David Koop, and Jakob Niebuhr. Probably in no other settlement did the Agricultural Association or Commission contribute so much to the raising of the economic and cultural life of the settlement as in the Molotschna, and without question the most significant era was that of the chairmanship of Johann Cornies. (About the significance of the Agricultural Association see also **Agriculture among the Mennonites of Russia.**)

C.K.

D. G. Rempel, "The Menn. Colonies in New Russia, a Study of Their Settlement and Economic Development from 1789-1914" (unpublished doctoral dissertation at Stanford University, 1933); A. Ehrt, *Das Mennonitentum in Russland von seiner Einwanderung bis zur Gegenwart* (Berlin, 1932).

Agriculture: see Farming.

Agriculture among the Mennonites of Russia. The agricultural activities of the Mennonites of Russia can be divided into three periods: 1789-1860, 1860-1917, and 1917-43.

1789-1860. When the Mennonites came to the Ukraine at the end of the 18th century and the beginning of the 19th century they settled on the barren steppes. Pioneer conditions made large-scale grain raising impossible and the distance to the market made it unprofitable. Thus stock farming, particularly the breeding of sheep, became the chief occupation. Through the Guardians' Committee (*q.v.*) the Chortitza settlement received during the first years 30 merinos for which about 18,200 acres of reserved land were set aside. By 1819 the flock consisted of 1,000 head. The beginning in the Molotschna settlement was very much the same. A severe winter in 1812-13 caused great losses not only of sheep but also of horses and cattle. In 1825 the Guardians' Committee charged Johann Cornies (*q.v.*) with the task of restocking not only the flocks of the Mennonites, but also of the other colonists in the province of Taurida. He purchased sheep from the czar's own flocks and also imported some rams from Saxony. At that time the average Mennonite farm had between 125 and 150 sheep. Wool found a ready market in the mills of Ekaterinoslav and other places. Sheep breeding reached its highest point between 1836 and 1841 and then gradually began to decline because of the increased competition of fine wool from overseas and also the increase of grain production in the Ukraine.

The breeding of cattle was more profitable and of longer duration than that of sheep. The early settlers of Chortitza and Molotschna brought with them a considerable number of East Frisian cattle. Under the leadership of Cornies, the chairman of the Agricultural Association (*q.v.*), the Mennonites adopted a scientific method of crossing their cattle with local breeds in order to hasten the process of acclimatization. The crossing was made with carefully selected specimens of the East Frisian cattle which they had brought along and the Ukrainian gray cattle as well as Kalmuk cattle. The product

of this crossing became known as a Molotschna cow or the German Red cow (*q.v.*). The average annual milk production per cow was upward of 580 gal. and the fat-content was 3.8 to 4 per cent. The breeding of the pure East Frisian cow was also continued. The Mennonites found a good market for butter and cheese in the cities of Berdyansk, Sevastopol, Yevpatoria, Kerch, Taganrog, and Ekaterinoslav. The sale of cattle to outsiders at this time was a very important factor. In 1836, 251 cows were sold in the Molotschna settlement; by 1845 the number had risen to 1,429 and declined again to 840 in 1846.

The horses which the immigrants had brought from West Prussia degenerated during the first decades in Russia. Efforts at improving them were made through the use of stallions of local breeds which were obtained from the Don Cossacks and later from government studs. The product obtained through this crossing was a combination of farm and carriage horse. It was strongly built, of medium height, and usually black or roan in color. With the increase of grain farming, the demand for draft power also increased. In 1836 the number of horses per farm in the Molotschna settlement amounted to 6.2; by 1841 it had increased to 8.4, by 1855 to 10.6.

During the first decades of the settlement the cultivation of land played a minor role. The land in the immediate neighborhood of the village was usually used for grazing purposes only. Wheat, oats, potatoes, flax, and vegetables were raised on distant fields of not more than 14-27 acres per farm. Drought made farming risky. Another handicap was the lack of agricultural machinery.

The greatest change and influence on the agricultural and economic life came through the Agricultural Association and its chairman, Johann Cornies. After Cornies had demonstrated on his estates what progress could be made in the raising of cattle, horses, sheep, and trees, he exercised a tremendous influence on the surrounding Mennonite and non-Mennonite population not only through his example, but also through the Agricultural Association, which was sponsored and supervised by the Guardians' Committee, a government agency. In 1845 he had on two estates 22,000 merinos and in 1847 his herd of horses on one estate alone numbered 500. His sheep, cattle, and horses were sought far and near. Through the introduction of the summer fallow, fall plowing, rotation of crops, and other means, he demonstrated the successful raising of grain on the steppes. Neither of his estates bore a trace of a tree when Cornies acquired them. By 1845 he had some 35 acres of shade trees, about 16 acres of fruit trees, and a large nursery. Thus his estates became an experiment station where the surrounding farmers obtained advice and help and were enabled to improve their stock and farming methods. The Guardians' Committee authorized him to enforce rules and regulations regarding improvements of farming methods and the settlement in general. Under the supervision of the Agricultural Association orchards and shade trees were planted. After 20 years more than 5 million trees had been planted in the 47 villages of the Molotschna. Among the fruit trees grown at this time were grapes and mulberries, the latter for their leaves, which were fed to the silkworms. For a short time the silk industry (*q.v.*) was one of the main sources of income. In 1835 Cornies made it obligatory in the whole Molotschna settlement to summer fallow some land. Simultaneously he introduced the following rotation of crops: summer fallow, barley, wheat, and rye. In 1845 this improvement was also introduced in the Chortitza settlement. Very soon the results of the new methods of farming were evidenced by increased yields.

Cornies exercised great influence among the Mennonites, other colonists, and the surrounding Russians, especially the Dukhobors and the Molokans, as well as the native tribes, such as Kalmuks, Tatars, and others. To all of them he was a friend and adviser, trusted and honored. It has sometimes been said that the Mennonites failed to do mission work among the surrounding population. While this is true of direct evangelism, there is hardly anywhere in the history of the Mennonites an example that exceeds this one in the Ukraine, where the neighboring population was given an opportunity to to watch the demonstration of consecrated Christian living, benefiting by the advice and the help given freely out of Christian love.

By 1860 a complete revolution had taken place in the field of agriculture. The once prospering silk industry and the raising of flax and tobacco gradually disappeared. The breeding of sheep lost its significance and that of cattle also decreased. Around 1850 approximately one third of the land had been plowed and only one third of the crops raised was wheat. Now the great wheat revolution was taking place.

1860-1917. The years around 1860 marked not only a religious but also an economic and agricultural crisis in the history of the Mennonites of Russia. The number of families increased rapidly and it was prohibited to parcel out the normal-sized farm. By 1860 nearly two thirds of the Molotschna families were landless. These landless had no voice in the village and district assemblies. Theoretically any Mennonite who wished to take up farming was entitled to the legal norm of 175 acres of land as long as there was reserve or surplus land. In practice it was, however, different. The Guardians' Committee required that every applicant for land should possess from 1,000 to 2,000 rubles in order to start farming on a regular scale because of the notion that all Mennonite farmers had to be "model farmers." This limited the number of those who were able to start to a very few. Besides, the Guardians' Committee had leased the surplus land to the settlement as grazing land for the community flocks and to large-scale sheep ranchers. Cornies favored the distribution of this land among the landless, but after his death the reactionary element among the colonists obtained control of the district offices. Finally in 1866 through an imperial decree, the Guardians' Committee was instructed to grant the right of voting to all homestead-owning colonists regardless of whether they owned farm land or not and to distribute some of the reserve and surplus land in the Molotschna among the landless. By 1869 some 50,000 acres had been distributed to 1,563 families.

The next step toward the solution of the problem was the creation of a colonization fund. Thus the conflict which had lasted for more than ten years finally resulted in the adoption of a colonization system, subsequently so highly perfected that it could well be called a model system, whereby the younger generations were provided with land on very easy terms. Only because of this could Mennonites establish as many daughter colonies as they did all over the Russian provinces from the Ukraine to the Amur River. This again determined the course of the agricultural and economic life and the status of prosperity they attained. Most of the daughter colonies originated through the purchase of land by the mother colonies of Chortitza and Molotschna. The financial resources were obtained by special land taxes, loans made by banks and private individuals, and the income from communal land. It is estimated that at the outbreak of World War I, Mennonites of Russia owned about 3 million acres of land and the total number of Mennonites was over 100,000. As far as the acquisition and distribution of land were concerned, the owners in the mother colonies owned about two tenths of the total, the large estate owners about three tenths, while about five tenths was owned by the owners in the daughter colonies. Some 384 Mennonite large estate owners possessed about 1 million acres of land, of which a 50,000-acre ranch was the largest.

After 1860 Russian grain came more and more into demand in western European countries. In the early fifties the arable land on all average Mennonite farms of the Molotschna settlement had been about 60 acres, while in 1875 it averaged about 90 acres, and in 1888 it amounted to about 120 acres per farm, and the land prices had increased considerably. The expansion of the area of cultivation had now nearly reached its limit. The 175-acre typical Mennonite farm of the Molotschna settlement was used as follows: for house and garden plot 6 acres, for orchards and other trees about 2½ acres, for pastures and meadows about 46 acres, and for arable land about 120 acres. A similar expansion of grain farming took place in the Chortitza settlement. In the case of the smaller "half-farm" the situation was different.

The added land under cultivation was chiefly used for bread grains to an almost total exclusion of forage crops. Simultaneously grain production on these farms became more and more commercialized, that is, an ever-increasing amount of grain was produced for the market instead of home consumption. By 1880 wheat had become the predominant crop. Originally mostly summer wheat was raised by the Mennonites. Gradually hard winter wheat was introduced and soon became prominent. This was the native variety grown along the coast of the Black Sea and the Sea of Azov. About 1850 the London market began to appreciate the quality of this wheat because of the nutritive content of the flour it produced. A growing demand for this wheat, the concentration of the Mennonites and others on wheat farming, and the opening of ports along the Black Sea and the Sea of Azov soon made the Ukraine the granary of Europe. According to H. D. Seymour the ports of Berdyansk and Mariupol near the Molotschna colony shipped the best quality of wheat. Cornelius Jansen stated that the Mennonites of the Molotschna settlement in 1855 produced about half a million bushels of wheat. The hard red winter wheat variety raised by the Mennonites was known under the name *Krimka*. In America it became known as the Hard Red Turkey variety. It is rust resistant, winter hardy, and very suitable for baking. When the Mennonites coming to Kansas in 1874 brought with them this variety of wheat, Bernhard Warkentin (*q.v.*) and Mark A. Carlton imported it in larger quantities for seed. Thus the prairie states and provinces became the breadbasket of America as the Ukraine had become the breadbasket of Europe.

Parallel to the wheat revolution among the Mennonites of Russia went the birth of a Mennonite industry (*q.v.*) producing chiefly agricultural machinery. The first foundry was opened by Peter Lepp (*q.v.*) in 1860 in Chortitza. Before World War I, the eight largest manufacturing plants had a combined sale of more than 3 million rubles annually. Another result was a rapidly growing milling industry. Outstanding among the millers was Niebuhr and Co., Alexandrovsk, having an annual sale of 3 million rubles. A flourishing commerce and trade also resulted from this development.

Originally the Mennonites used the four-field rotation system, having three fourths of the land under cultivation with grain and the remainder left for summer fallow, part of which was planted with potatoes, corn, sunflowers, watermelons, etc. A typical crop cycle in Chortitza and Molotschna until the 1860's was as follows: summer fallow; barley; wheat; rye and oats. During the seventies and eighties the summer fallow was reduced considerably. One of the common crop cycles now was: summer fallow; winter wheat; barley; spring wheat; rye or oats. At the turn of the century a more balanced system of farming was achieved by putting more acreage under corn, potatoes, watermelons, pumpkins, etc. Hardly any commercial fertilizer was used among the Mennonites. Animal manure, however, was applied on practically every farm.

Because of the enormous expansion of the crop area during this period, the preparation of the soil did not necessarily improve in spite of the fact that better and more machinery could be obtained direct from Mennonite factories. Instead of plowing the land with a single furrow plow some large-scale farmers began to use a multiple share or *bukker* plow. Instead of plowing the land in the fall as had been customary, some began to plow and sow in the spring, using the drill *bukker*. Such prac-

tices were usually temporary and wherever the expansion of the crop area had reached its limit the soil was again worked thoroughly. The summer fallow was worked continually in order to kill all weeds and retain the moisture. The Mennonites used mostly machinery made in their own factories, among them plows, *bukkers,* harrows, drills, *lobogreykas* (mowers), threshing machines, etc. During the last decade prior to World War I American binders replaced the *lobogreyka*. The threshing which had originally been done with a stone roller was later done by threshing machines also produced in the Mennonite factories. Many thousands of seasonal workers of surrounding Russian communities found employment in the Mennonite villages.

With the increased tillage of arable land the breeding of sheep and dairy cattle decreased. Infusions of new blood upon the German Red stock were made. Improvements were obtained through the Wilstermarch strain. The German Red cow became very popular far beyond the Mennonite settlements. It was exported to the Caucasus, Turkestan, Siberia, and even Turkey. The Mennonites of the Trakt or Köppental settlement, Samara, developed their own breed of dairy cattle starting with Dutch cattle they had brought from Prussia and crossing them with the German Red Cow of the Ukraine and other breeds. They produced the so-called Menno Dutch cattle, with an exceptionally good quality and quantity of milk. After the Russian Revolution these cattle were also introduced into other provinces besides Samara.

The expansion of the cultivated area required an increased supply of draft power, which was furnished during the past century exclusively by horses. The horses used by the Mennonites were known as the "colonist horse" which was in quality and appearance superior to the common horse. This breed was improved by crossing it with imported Belgian and Dutch sires; carriage horses were improved chiefly by Russian stock. These improvements were first made on the Mennonite estates, whence the horses found their way into the villages.

1917-43. The following are the phases of Russian Communism which destroyed not only Mennonite agriculture in Russia, but also the Mennonite settlements as a whole. The Revolution of 1917 with the Civil War following it, the nationalization of all land, and the subsequent famine of 1921-22 were only the beginning of the great tragedy. During the New Economic Policy (NEP) perhaps some 25,000 Mennonites took advantage of the opportunity to leave the country and to establish new homes in Canada, while those that remained recuperated somewhat from the first blows and tried to adjust themselves to the new conditions. Improvement of breeds of horses and cattle as well as seed was taken up again and even promoted by the government. The Mennonites were permitted to organize an *Allrussischer Mennonitischer Landwirtschaftlicher Verein* (*q.v.*) as well as to publish a magazine *Der praktische Landwirt* (*q.v.*). But this was only the calm before the storm.

From 1928 to 1933 collectivization (*q.v.*) was rigidly introduced with the subsequent liquidation of kulaks (*q.v.*). Most of the farmers that had been able to retain some signs of prosperity even in these days were sent to Siberia or the north for slave labor, while those remaining were forced into collectives as a final step of the nationalization of all property and the subjugation of the individual to the state. The All-Mennonite Agricultural Association was liquidated in the summer of 1928. Severe new attacks on the traditional way of life followed in 1936-38 during the great purge of the Communist party, which reached down into every collective of the remotest settlement. Among the millions of collective farmers sent into exile were many thousands of Mennonites. At the outbreak of World War II, it was a policy of the Soviet government to remove all citizens of German background to Siberia and many of the Mennonite farmers had to give up their homes and villages. Only some 35,000 Mennonites were still in their homes when the German army occupied the Ukraine in 1941. During the years of 1941 to 1943 the Mennonites were permitted, although under great handicaps, to revive some of their agricultural practices of the past. With the withdrawal of the German army from the Ukraine and the removal of the civilian population into the interior of Germany the history of the Mennonite settlements in Russia came to a tragic end. Those Mennonites that had remained in Russia and those that were forcibly repatriated by the Russians are scattered mostly in Asiatic Russia in slave labor camps, in mines, and in collectives, and no definite information about them is available. C.K.

D. H. Epp, *Die Chortitzer Menn.* (Odessa, 1889); Friesen, *Brüderschaft*; A. Klaus, *Unsere Kolonien* (Odessa, 1887); C. E. Bondar, *Sekta Mennonitov v Rossii* (Petrograd, 1916); A. Ehrt, *Das Mennonitentum in Russland von seiner Einwanderung bis zur Gegenwart* (Berlin, 1932); D. G. Rempel, "The Menn. Colonies in New Russia . . . 1789-1914" (unpublished doctoral dissertation at Stanford University, 1933); C. Krahn, ed., *From the Steppes to the Prairies* (Newton, 1949); F. Isaac, *Die Molotschnaer Menn.* (Halbstadt, 1908); D. H. Epp, *Johann Cornies* (Ekaterinoslav and Berdyansk, 1909) and reprint (Steinbach, Man., 1946).

Ahlefeldt. A branch of this old aristocratic family in the province of Holstein in North Germany was in possession of the domain of Fresenburg (*q.v.*) from 1526 to 1641, where the village of Wüstenfelde (*q.v.*) was located, between Hamburg and Lübeck, Germany. In 1543 the owner, Bartholomäus von Ahlefeldt, permitted the Mennonites to settle there. In his younger years he is said to have given military service in the Netherlands, and there become aware of the peaceable Anabaptists, having witnessed the execution of several of Menno's followers. Convinced that they were not the dangerous insurgents and fanatics they were reputed to be, he opened his lands to them, which until that time had been mostly occupied by serfs. A descendant of B. von Ahlefeldt was one of the first to abandon the practice of serfdom.

The Mennonites had a printshop in Lübeck to distribute Bibles and other books. In 1554 it was moved to Oldesloe where ten tons of books were confiscated and the matter reported to Christian III of Denmark without naming the persons involved. After this the Mennonite printers moved to Fresenburg, where Bartholomäus von Ahlefeldt built a house for them. Since this is about the time that Menno Simons moved to Fresenburg and his books were printed there, there is a possibility that he was involved in this matter. Although King Christian did everything possible to have Ahlefeldt expel the Mennonites, the latter remained their protector. During the Thirty Years' War the Mennonite settlement was destroyed and the Mennonites moved to other places. H.vDS., HEGE, C.K.

G. Roosen, *Unschuld und Gegenbericht* (Ratzeburg, 1902); E. F. Goverts, "Das adelige Gut Fresenburg und die Mennoniten," in *Ztscht der Zentralstelle für Niedersächs. Familiengesch.* (Hamburg, 1925) Heft 3-5; C. Krahn, *Menno Simons* (Karlsruhe, 1936); R. Dollinger, *Gesch. der Menn. in Schleswig-Holstein, Hamburg, und Lübeck* (Neumünster, 1930); J. Schröder, *Topographie des Herzogthums Holstein, des Fürstenthums Lübeck und der freien Städte Hamburg und Lübeck* (Oldenburg, 1841); *ML* I, 14.

Aichele (or Aichelin), **Berthold,** imperial provost and provost of the Swabian League (*q.v.*), who in 1528-31 executed many Anabaptists in Württemberg and Tirol at the command of Ferdinand I (*q.v.*), archduke of Austria. One of his notorious deeds was the attack on Mantelhof near Aalen (*q.v.*), where on Christmas 1531 he captured the peasant owner and his son and had both hanged on a linden tree in Essingen, while he set fire to the buildings, killing all the others who remained true to their faith—17 in all. (According to Friedrich Roth, Aichele was no longer in the employ of the Swabian League in 1531, for in March 1530 he was already serving the *Truchsess* Georg von Waldburg.) The steadfastness of the Anabaptists in execution, particularly that of the Anabaptist missionary Onophrius Griesinger (*q.v.*) in Tirol in 1538, instilled fear into him, so that after Griesinger's death he vowed never again to execute an Anabaptist (Beck, 140). He was the chief agent of the Catholic authorities in suppressing Protestantism as well as Anabaptism and boasted of having hanged 40 Protestant pastors and over 1,200 revolutionaries and heretics (Anabaptists). The report in *Blätter für württembergische Kirchengeschichte* (1892) that he was murdered in the spring of 1534 must be incorrect, since the Hutterite chronicles expressly state that he was present at the execution of Griesinger in 1538. He is the chief character of the historical novel *Der Reichsprofos* (Heilbronn, 1904) by Pastor Stehle of Heilbronn (pseudonym, Philipp Spiesz). HEGE.

J. Beck, *Geschichts-Bücher*, 27, 140; J. Rauscher, *Württemb. Ref.-Gesch.* (1934) 34; Roth, *Beitr. zur bayr. Kirchengesch.* XVIII (1912) 134; *Württemb. Kirchengesch.* (Stuttgart, 1893) 324; *Blätter für Württemb. Kirchengesch.* (1892) 5, and (1897) 22, 35; *ML* I, 14.

Aichhorn, fortress on the Svarcava northwest of Brno, Moravia, where the Hutterites succeeded in maintaining themselves in small groups for several years after their brethren had been banished from Moravia. In 1650 they, too, were driven out. With their withdrawal the last remnant of Anabaptists disappeared from Moravia. (*ML* I, 15.)

HEGE.

Aichner, Hans, a Hutterite martyr, after fourteen weeks' imprisonment was beheaded and then burned Aug. 13, 1585, with two fellow believers, the tailor Wolf Raufer and the potter Jörg Bruckmaier (*q.v.*) in Berkhausen near Ried (Upper Austria, at that time Bavarian). (*Mart. Mir.* D 754, E 1060; *ML* I, 15.)

HEGE.

Aid Plan: see **Amish Aid Plan, Amish Aid Society, Mennonite Aid Plans,** and **Mutual Aid.**

Ainsworth, Henry, b. about 1571 at Swanton, Morley Norfolk, England, d. 1612 at Amsterdam, the leader of the Brownists (*q.v.*) or Free Churchmen. In 1593 he joined this church of Independents at Amsterdam and became their preacher. He cooperated on a friendly basis for many years with Francis Johnson, who was the pastor of the church in Amsterdam from 1597 on. In 1610, however, Ainsworth and a large part of the membership withdrew, evidently on the issue of the maintenance of discipline in the church, a point on which Ainsworth did not agree with Johnson. Ainsworth became the leader of the new group and remained so until his death. The church building was assigned to the Ainsworthians. The Johnsonians removed to Emden, East Frisia. Ainsworth was a very scholarly man, versed in Hebrew and other languages, and wrote many books, especially Bible commentaries and polemic pamphlets. He composed a confession of faith, consisting of 45 articles (English, 1596; Dutch, same year; English reprint, 1598; Dutch reprint, 1680). His complete works were published in 1623, reprinted 1639, and 1870-84.

Ainsworth declined to join the Reformed Church of the Netherlands. In fact he had more sympathy with the Mennonites than with the Reformed, although he rejected Mennonitism, and made the following remark concerning John Smyth (*q.v.*): "God's hand is heavy upon him, in giving him over from error to error and now at last to the abomination of Anabaptism" (de Hoop-Scheffer and Griffis, *History of the Free Churchmen,* 119). Between Ainsworth and the Mennonites there were many common points of agreement: they held the same views on the origin and organization of the church, its absolute autonomy, its order and government ("avoyding the Popishe disorders and ongodly communion of all false Christians, and especiallie of the wicked Preachers and hirelings," Browne had stated). Both the Brownists and Mennonites had unpaid preachers and pastors; in both groups there was a tendency to distinguish themselves from the children of the world by simplicity of dress and purity of morals (*op. cit.,* 31). Ainsworth's grievances regarding the Reformed Church were many, but he could not resolve to join the Mennonites as John Smyth had done.   vDZ.

J. G. de Hoop-Scheffer and W. E. Griffis, *Hist. of the Free Churchmen, called the Brownists, Pilgrim Fathers*

and Baptists in the Dutch Republic, 1581-1701 (Ithaca, 1922).

Aken, Johan Andries van, preacher at Utrecht, b. Jan. 9, 1623, at Rivers near Aachen, Germany, d. May 11, 1706, at Utrecht. He was a son of Frans Andries and Katharina Woestenraad, and perhaps a great-grandson of Gillis van Aken (*q.v.*). Early orphaned, he was reared by his uncle Jelis de Graaf, a manufacturer of shears. He stayed for a time in Leiden and Middelburg, and in 1645 went to Utrecht, where he married Maria Cornelis de Schut in 1646. She died in 1667. In 1668 he married the widow of Denys de Nekker, Josina, nee Wille, who died in 1703. From 1652 on he was a Mennonite preacher at Utrecht. During the dissensions in the congregation from 1660 to 1664 he sided with W. van Maurik (*q.v.*). For more than fifty years he preached and enjoyed the high esteem of his fellow citizens. This is shown by the fact that in 1672 the magistrate of Utrecht sent him to Amsterdam to borrow 100,000 guilders to redeem several citizens who had been taken as hostages by the French. He was wealthy and very benevolent to the poor, regardless of creed. Chr. Tirion preached his funeral sermon, which was printed at Utrecht, 1706 (*Catalogus Amst.,* 251).

K.V.

G. ten Cate, "Iets over Johan Andries van Aken en zijn geslacht," in *DB* 1872, *DB* 1916, 145 ff.; H. B. Berghuys, *Gesch. der Doopsgez. Gem. te Utrecht* (Utrecht, 1925) *passim; ML* I, 15.

Aker, Lambert Klaasz, b. 1616 at Hoorn, d. 1690 in Harlingen, was a preacher of the Old Frisians or Jan Jacobsgezinden, first at Hoorn and later at Harlingen. He held fast to the use of the Biestkens Bible (*q.v.*) whereas the newer *Statenvertaling* (state translation) had been adopted into general use among the Mennonites as well as the Reformed. Specific information about him is lacking. In *Aanhangzel,* the appendix by G. Maatschoen to Schijn's *Geschiedenis der Mennoniten* (Amsterdam, 1745) 432, there is a portrait of Aker in copper etching.   vDZ.

Akerkoopers, a name, otherwise unknown, which Rues (*Tegenwoordige staet der Doopsgezinden,* 1745, 29) used especially for the most conservative Mennonites of Holland. It is possible that these *Akerkoopers* are identical with the *Huiskoopers* (*q.v.*).   vDZ.

Akers (La.) Mennonite Church, situated 40 miles north of New Orleans, La., is a member of the South Central Conference (MC), with a baptized membership of 29 in 1953, none of whom are of Mennonite descent. Their minister was converted at Allemands, La., in 1940 and was ordained to preach at Akers in 1941. The Akers church was built and dedicated in April 1942. The first converts here (11) were baptized in June 1944. The minister Henry J. Tregle, Jr. and wife are of French descent. Nearly all of the families were formerly members of the Roman Catholic Church.

P.H.

Akersloot, a village in the Dutch province of North Holland, not far from Alkmaar. According to Blaupot ten Cate (*Holland* II, 44) there was once a congregation in this village, but there is no further information about it.   vdZ.

Akkrum, a village in the Dutch province of Friesland, south of Leeuwarden, the seat of a Mennonite congregation. Historical information about this congregation is very scarce. Elder Leenaert Bouwens baptized five persons here between 1563 and 1565. The date of the origin of the congregation is uncertain; but by about 1660 there was a church here; perhaps also a church already standing was enlarged in 1677. The congregation, which like most of the congregations in Friesland belonged to the Lamist wing, joined the Friesche Doopsgezinde Sociëteit in 1695 and had at that time 87 members who did not receive support. In the 18th century some difficulties arose, when a Moravian Brethren (Herrnhuter) (*q.v.*) congregation was organized here, whose leaders were the clothier Johann Lorenz 1742-69, and after him Johann Wilhelm Zander, Menno Abels, and Johann Gottlieb Reimann. It attracted some of the members from the Mennonite congregation; the Mennonites complained about this matter in a letter to the Lamist congregation in Amsterdam (letter of 1746 in *Inv. Arch. Amst.* II, No. 1453). About 1797 the Herrnhuter congregation died out; the remaining members united with the Mennonites. During the 18th and 19th centuries the van der Goot and Hylkema families were very numerous in this congregation.

In the 18th century the congregation still had lay preachers, usually three or four at a time; Djurre Sakes (Veenstra) was the last of these; from 1789 to 1825, more than 37 years, he served the congregation, which grew to such an extent that the church had to be enlarged in 1822. After his death the congregation called Sytze K. de Waard, 1826-38, the first preacher who had received a theological education at the seminary in Amsterdam; he was followed by Bartel van Geuns, 1829-30. Then came Steven Blaupot ten Cate (*q.v.*) 1830-39; during his ministry a new church was built in 1835 and the Ring (district) Akkrum organized in 1837. During this century the congregation began to flourish. In 1830 the membership was 209; in 1838 it was 321; 1861 it was 403; in 1898 it reached its high point with 439 members; then it began to decline. In 1950 it had 180 members. Following Blaupot ten Cate the congregation was served by A. A. Hulshoff, 1839-45; S. Hoekstra Bzn., 1845-52; Adr. Loosjes, 1853-54; J. Visscher, 1855-85; S. Wartena, Jr., 1886-97; D. Kossen, 1898-1913; J. Kooiman, 1914-23; A. Keuter, 1925-28; S. I. van der Meulen, 1929-43; G. M. Kosters, 1944-47, and J. Nooter since 1949.

The congregation has organizations for the women and youth and a Sunday school for the children.

There is in Akkrum a home for the aged known as "Coopersburg" (*q.v.*), erected in 1900. The home was the gift of the American Folkert H. Cooper, who emigrated from Akkrum about 1875 and made his fortune in America. He dedicated the building to the memory of his parents Willem Harmens Kuiper and IJtje Rommerts de Vries, who were members of the Mennonite Church of Akkrum. F. H. Cooper died in 1904 and was buried with his wife in the garden behind the home. The home has 22 rooms for Akkrum residents, preferably married couples of the age of 60 or older, who may be admitted without cost. No distinction is made between Mennonites and non-Mennonites. The Mennonite pastor of Akkrum is a member of the board managing the foundation.   vdZ.

Blaupot t.C., *Friesland, passim; DB* 1885, 68, 90; W. Lütjeharms, *Het philadelph.-oecum. streven der Hernhutters in de Nederlanden in de 18e Eeuw* (Zeist, 1935) 64, 83-84; S. I. van der Meulen, *Feestrede 16 Juni 1935; Inv. Arch. Amst.* II, 1453 f.; *ML* I, 15 f.

Akkrum, Ring. The Ring (district) Akkrum is a union of Mennonite congregations in Friesland for the purpose of mutual support in preaching and instruction of baptismal candidates, especially in the case of a vacant pulpit or the illness of a minister. In addition to Ring Akkrum there are in the province also Ring Bolsward (*q.v.*) and Ring Dantumawoude (*q.v.*). Ring Akkrum is the oldest and was begun in 1837 by historian Steven Blaupot ten Cate (*q.v.*), who was the Mennonite minister in Akkrum (*q.v.*) 1830-39.

The first congregations to unite in the Ring were Akkrum, Baard, Gorredijk-Lippenhuizen, Grouw, Irnsum-Poppingawier, Joure, Kromwal, Oldeboorn, Terhorne, Tjalleberd, Warga, and IJlst. After Ring Bolsward was organized Baard, Kromwal (now called IJtens), and IJlst joined the latter. The congregations now in the Akkrum Ring are Akkrum, Grouw, Irnsum-Poppingawier, Warga, Leeuwarden, Drachten, Tjalleberd, Heerenveen, Bovenknijpe, Gorredijk, Terhorne, Joure, and Wolvega. (Blaupot t. C., *Friesland*, 250; *ML* I, 16.)   D.K., vdZ.

Ak-Mechet, a village located eight miles from the city of Khiva in Asiatic Russia, settled April 16, 1884, by a small group of Mennonites under the leadership of Claas Epp (*q.v.*), who had separated from the Köppental-Orloff church (Samara) in 1880 and 1881 primarily for the purpose of avoiding forestry service and also to seek a place of refuge for the time of the great tribulation of the last days. After attempting to settle in Tashkent and later in Bokhara, they came to Khiva where they were joined by some followers of Elder A. Peters (*q.v.*) from the Molotschna.

Their first place of settlement in Khiva was on the bank of the Lausan River, a branch of the Amu-Darya. Since residence here was made impossible by predatory attacks and thefts by Turkomen, they received from the khan of Khiva the park Ak-Mechet which belonged to one of his relatives. Only a small part of the group settled here, the rest migrating to America. Originally the land of Ak-Mechet covered only about thirteen acres; hence, the Mennonites, unable to farm, raised vegetables and made their living in the trades of cabinetmaking and tailoring. The church consisted of about 25 families, who were supporters of Claas Epp, and who owned a church building which also served as a school and residence for the teacher.

Before the death of Claas Epp (Jan. 6, 1913), the majority of the group recognized the errors in his teachings and separated from him, turning to the leadership of W. Penner (*q.v.*). Epp's views gradually disappeared and the religious and economic life of the community improved. Soon they learned to fertilize and irrigate the sandy soil in order to raise rice and cotton.

The group lived undisturbed for approximately 55 years, hardly noticing World War I and the change of government when the Soviets took over. When the local Soviet government in 1925 was about to streamline the cultural, economic, and religious life of the Mennonites according to the Marxian doctrines, the Ak-Mechet group simply sent a delegation to Moscow and received from Kalinin, president of the Soviet Union, a document guaranteeing that they could continue their way of life unmolested. Their Asiatic neighbors, however, were forced to join the collectives. Ten years later in 1935 the Mennonite mayor of Ak-Mechet was again requested by the Soviet authorities of Khiva to organize a collective, but with the document signed by Kalinin the group felt safe and secure. When they refused, ten persons including the mayor and the minister were arrested and publicly tried as counter-revolutionaries. They gave a brilliant testimony which lasted far into the night. Death by shooting was the sentence for each of them and their families were to be exiled.

On the following day the GPU trucks appeared to take the families into exile. All the women of the settlement came out, clustered around the trucks, and piled up in front of the wheels, demanding unitedly that none of them or all be taken. The GPU agents seemed to be overwhelmed and returned to the city of Khiva leaving the trucks. After a few days more trucks came to take the entire group. Thus the Mennonites of Ak-Mechet were compelled to leave the place that had been their refuge for more than half a century. They were taken to the city of Samarkand by truck, ship, and train, whence they proceeded approximately 100 miles southeast into a desert. Here they were forced to pioneer with the few tools which they had brought with them. Whether any of them have survived is unknown.   F.B., C.K.

F. Bartsch, *Unser Auszug nach Mittel-Asien* (North Kildonan, Man., 1948); this reprint of the original 1907 edition published at Halbstadt, Russia, contains a supplement, 83-90, "Auszüge aus der 'Gesch. von Ak-Metschet,' von Alexander Rempel"; *Menn. Bl.*, 1884, 64, 79; 1901, 93; *ML* I, 16.

Akmolinsk, a district in the Kirghiz steppe of West Siberia, 240,000 sq. mi. in area, with about 700,000 inhabitants (1912). Near Omsk (*q.v.*), the capital of the district of Akmolinsk, Mennonites from the Russian provinces of Taurida and Samara settled in 1899, among them the families of John Matthies, Franz Balzer, Julius Dick, Peter Dick from Taurida, and H. Ewert and Gerhard Ewert from Samara. Peter J. Wiens started a business in Omsk in 1897.

These were the first Mennonites to settle in **Siberia.** In the year 1899 the brothers Peter, Nikolai, and Johann Friesen with several other families bought a tract of land 160 miles west of Omsk near the railroad station Tokushi, and founded the settlement of Friesenov. In the following years numerous families settled on both sides of the Siberian railway. They secured their land usually from Russian officers and preferred to settle on individual farms. Some villages were, however, also formed; e.g., Margenau, Alexandrovka, and Hamberg, near the station Gorkoye. The number of Mennonites in the district of Akmolinsk was about 5,000 in 1913.

The settlements in Akmolinsk achieved relative prosperity, whereas the large settlements in the districts of Pavlodar (*q.v.*) and Barnaul (*q.v.*) (province of Tomsk) were very poor. Near Omsk (New Omsk) a four-year continuation school was established in 1910 in connection with the village school, which had a six-year course. It was planned as a teachers' seminary for the Siberian Mennonites. Near Omsk the Mennonites Lepp and Friesen founded (1913) a farm implement factory. (*ML* I, 17.)   A.J.K.

Akron, Mich., Tuscola Co., a village near which an Old Order Mennonite community was established in 1887. Daniel Lehman of Fairgrove, Mich., minister, reported a membership of 13 soon after the turn of the century. It is now extinct.   M.G.

Akron, Lancaster Co., Pa., since 1936 headquarters of the Mennonite Central Committee, located ten miles northeast of the city of Lancaster, was founded in 1833 by people of German descent and was first named New Berlin, in 1880 changed to Akron in order to secure a Federal post office, since there already was a New Berlin within the state. The present population within the borough limits is approximately 2,000, of whom the Mennonites constitute a small minority. Although largely a residential village, there are the following industries: a shoe factory, heel factory, garment factory, pretzel factory, and a city bakery. Three converted residences and one erected office building and archives house the MCC offices.   J.N.B.

Aktatch, a strip of land in the northern part of the Mennonite colony founded in 1901 in the Terek (*q.v.*) region on the Caspian Sea in Russia. It was intended for colonization, but since the land was unsuitable for agriculture, the plan was abandoned. (*ML* I, 17.)   Hege.

Aktatchi: see **Busau-Aktatchi.**

Alabama, one of the southern states, admitted to the Union in 1819, named for the Alibamu Indians. In 1945 the Eastern Mennonite Board of Missions and Charities (Lancaster Conference) opened mission work in Escambia County, near the Florida border, and now (1950) has 4 ministers and 22 members there. The East Brewton mission was first established (in 1945), followed by the Wallace Highway area (1948), the Atmore area and the Appleton area (1949).   J.C.W.

Alard, Nicolas (1644-99), a Lutheran theologian, provost at **Eiderstedt, Schleswig, Germany, from**

1682 until his death, where he became involved in many disputes with the followers of David Joris. (*ADB* I, 173; *ML* I, 17.)

Alaska, a United States Territory, area 586,400 sq. mi., located along the northwestern boundary of Canada and acquired from Russia by purchase in 1867. Its 1950 population was 127,117. Although the Mennonites have established no settlements in the territory, they have been interested in the region as a missionary field. In the 1878 conference session of the General Conference Mennonite Church it was decided that S. S. Haury (*q.v.*) of Summerfield, Ill., should investigate the possibilities of mission work in Alaska, with a view to immediate beginning. In March 1879 Haury, accompanied by J. B. Baer (*q.v.*) left for Alaska. Both men taught school for a time while exploring the situation. After spending two months on Kodiak Island and some time at Cook's Inlet and finding no unoccupied field, they returned to the states. Later it appeared that Sitka might offer an open field but when it became evident that the Presbyterians planned to resume work there, the Mennonite plans were dropped. Haury soon began his missionary work among the Arapahoes of the Indian Territory.

Since that time there has been intermittent interest in Alaska. In 1896 John K. Brubaker (*q.v.*), a minister in the Lancaster Mennonite Conference, accompanied by J. S. Lehman, made a four months' evangelistic trip to Alaska. In 1949 Mahlon Stoltzfus and William Anders flew their plane to Alaska for the purpose of investigating mission opportunities which their church (MC) might enter in that country. Their report suggested that Alaska presented many opportunities for Christian service and evangelism. Recently representatives of the Alberta Saskatchewan (MC) mission board have made trips of investigation. Stoltzfus began work in 1952 at Fortuna Lodge. M.G.

Alba (or Alva), Ferdinand Alvarez de Toledo, Duke of Alba (1508-82). Under Charles V he was the leader of the Spanish troops in the battle of Mühlberg, 1547, and later under the son of Charles, Philip II, was Spanish viceroy in the Netherlands from 1567 to 1573. The ruthlessness with which he attempted to suppress the Protestant movement in the Netherlands has stigmatized his name in history for all time. The Inquisition introduced into the Netherlands by his predecessor, Margaret of Parma, took thousands to execution at the stake and the scaffold. He instituted a tribunal for the suppression of heresy, popularly called the "Council of Blood," to wipe out not only those suspected of Protestant leanings, but also those who were dissatisfied with his ruthless measures. Counts Egmont and Hoorn were executed in 1568.

Thousands of the most highly respected families in Flanders tried to escape Alba by flight. Among these were many Mennonites, some of whom fled to the northern province of Holland and sought refuge there with their brethren. Because of their origin they were later called Flemish, at first to distinguish them from and later to contrast them

with the Waterlanders and Frisians, and for over 200 years constituted a separate branch of Mennonites, although many joined them who were not geographically Flemish in origin. Others fled via Emden to Germany, many of whom settled in Hamburg.

In spite of all his cruelty and hardness—more than 18,000 are said to have been executed by Alba—he did not succeed in suppressing the unrest. On the contrary, under the direction of William of Orange the States-General declared themselves independent, took up arms against the Spanish tyrants in 1568, and won their political independence. (*ML* I, 17.)
H. vDS.

Albany (Ore.) Mennonite Church (MC), three miles north of Albany, is a member of the Pacific Coast Conference. The 1952 membership was 213. This congregation had its beginning in 1898 when several Mennonite families began to meet in schools to worship. Later they obtained a small rural building known as the Geisendorfer church. Here the congregation was organized by Bishop David Garber of Idaho in 1899. From 1909 to 1952 the congregation worshiped in Albany. J. P. Bontrager served this congregation almost continuously since its beginning, first as pastor and later as bishop after his removal to California. The present ministers are M. E. Brenneman, George Kauffman, and Paul Yoder. V.M.K.

Albert (van Meppel), executed as an Anabaptist along with ten others on May 14, 1535, at Amsterdam. He had been involved in the Anabaptist revolt, May 10-11, at Amsterdam. (Grosheide, *Verhooren,* 64; *Bijdrage,* 61, 305.) vdZ.

Albert Pieters Sinckes was executed as an Anabaptist at Alkmaar, Holland, in 1536. He was a Münsterite, had visited Münster, and planned an attack on Alkmaar (*DB* 1909, 16, 19). vdZ.

Albert Reyersz (also called Oldeknecht), an Anabaptist martyr, was beheaded at Amsterdam on April 12, 1537. Contrary to the proclamation of the emperor, he had held meetings of Anabaptists in his house. Albert Reyersz stemmed from Bolsward in the Dutch province of Friesland. Two other brethren were executed with him. (*Inv. Arch. Amst.* I, 182; *Mart. Mir.* D 414, E 420; Grosheide, *Bijdrage,* 307.) vdZ.

Alberta. The most westerly of the three prairie provinces of Canada, Alberta extends 750 miles north of the United States boundary and averages from 250 to 400 miles wide, with an area of 255,000 sq. mi. and a population of 796,169 in 1941. Three fifths of its area is suitable for agriculture. Southern Alberta specializes in grain farming; central Alberta, the most densely populated, in mixed farming; and northern Alberta, the most rapidly growing section, in forestry, farming, and oil and gas. It is the leading coal producer among the provinces and has extensive oil and gas fields. Its Banff and Jasper national parks in the Rocky Mountains are world-famous.

In 1893 Jacob Y. Shantz (*q.v.*) of Ontario selected Didsbury (*q.v.*), Alta., 50 miles north of Calgary,

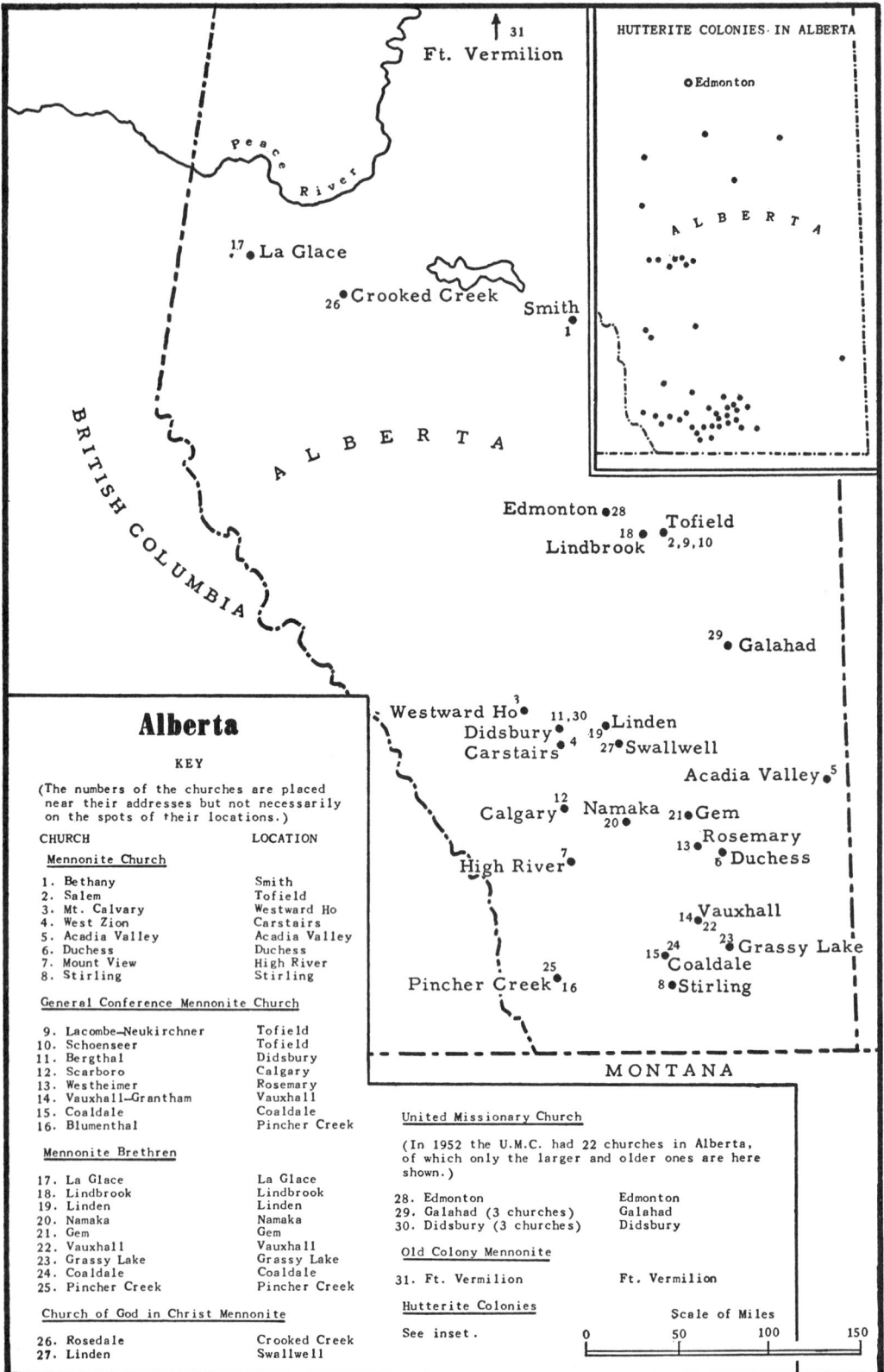

↑ 31
Ft. Vermilion

Peace River

¹⁷• **La Glace**

₂₆• **Crooked Creek**

Smith
1

HUTTERITE COLONIES IN ALBERTA

○ Edmonton

A L B E R T A

B R I T I S H   C O L U M B I A

A L B E R T A

Edmonton •28
18 • **Tofield**
Lindbrook • 2,9,10

²⁹• **Galahad**

Westward Ho •³   11,30
Didsbury •   •**Linden**
Carstairs • 4   19   27•**Swallwell**

Acadia Valley •⁵

Calgary •¹²   **Namaka** 21•**Gem**
20•

13• **Rosemary**
6• **Duchess**

High River •⁷

14•²²**Vauxhall**

15•²⁴   ²³•**Grassy Lake**
Coaldale

Pincher Creek •₁₆   8•**Stirling**

M O N T A N A

Alberta

KEY

(The numbers of the churches are placed
near their addresses but not necessarily
on the spots of their locations.)

CHURCH	LOCATION
Mennonite Church	
1. Bethany	Smith
2. Salem	Tofield
3. Mt. Calvary	Westward Ho
4. West Zion	Carstairs
5. Acadia Valley	Acadia Valley
6. Duchess	Duchess
7. Mount View	High River
8. Stirling	Stirling
General Conference Mennonite Church	
9. Lacombe–Neukirchner	Tofield
10. Schoenseer	Tofield
11. Bergthal	Didsbury
12. Scarboro	Calgary
13. Westheimer	Rosemary
14. Vauxhall–Grantham	Vauxhall
15. Coaldale	Coaldale
16. Blumenthal	Pincher Creek
Mennonite Brethren	
17. La Glace	La Glace
18. Lindbrook	Lindbrook
19. Linden	Linden
20. Namaka	Namaka
21. Gem	Gem
22. Vauxhall	Vauxhall
23. Grassy Lake	Grassy Lake
24. Coaldale	Coaldale
25. Pincher Creek	Pincher Creek
Church of God in Christ Mennonite	
26. Rosedale	Crooked Creek
27. Linden	Swallwell

United Missionary Church

(In 1952 the U.M.C. had 22 churches in Alberta,
of which only the larger and older ones are here
shown.)

28. Edmonton	Edmonton
29. Galahad (3 churches)	Galahad
30. Didsbury (3 churches)	Didsbury

Old Colony Mennonite

31. Ft. Vermilion	Ft. Vermilion

Hutterite Colonies

See inset.

Scale of Miles

0   50   100   150

as a suitable location for a new Mennonite settlement and in the following year established a colony of 34 Waterloo Co., Ont., residents in that area. This pioneer Mennonite (MBC) settlement in Alberta grew in size during the years so that by 1951 there were 24 ministers of that church (now UMC) serving there, with about 500 members.

In April 1901 Mennonite (MC) settlers from Waterloo County joined others of their number in the area of Carstairs-Didsbury so that it was possible in that year to organize the West Zion congregation and build a church. A similar group of settlers organized a congregation in the same year near High River, 40 miles south of Calgary. Mennonites (OOM) from northwestern Iowa settled near Mayton, Alta., in 1901, organizing the Mayton Mennonite Church (MC Conference) in 1903. Other settlers came from Indiana and Michigan in 1910 and a few years later organized the now extinct Clearwater Mennonite (MC) congregation. The Salem Mennonite Church (MC) near Tofield, of Amish Mennonite origin, was established by settlers who came from Iowa and Nebraska from 1910 to 1913. The Duchess Mennonite Church, 100 miles east of Calgary, was established by settlers from Eastern Pennsylvania in 1915. The Alberta District Conference (MC) was organized in 1904 and the Alberta-Saskatchewan Conference (*q.v.*) in 1907. In 1953 eight congregations with a membership of 490 were located in Alberta.

A larger number of Alberta Mennonites are those belonging to the General Conference Mennonite Church (*q.v.*). In 1953 there were 1,174 members in seven congregations: Bergthal at Didsbury; Blumenthal at Pincher Creek; Coaldale at Coaldale; Scarboro, Calgary; Schoensee, Tofield; Vauxhall-Grantham, Vauxhall; Westheim, Rosemary. The first G.C. Mennonite settlers had moved into Alberta from Manitoba as early as 1901. The majority, however, settled in the area after World War I, most being of the newer immigration from Russia 1922-27.

The Mennonite Brethren in 1951 had ten churches in the area with a membership of 1124. These congregations were Vauxhall, Grassy Lake, Namaka, Gem, Coaldale, Lindbrook, Pincher Creek, Linden, Rosemary, and La Glace. Their settlement in Alberta began in 1926 with the establishment of the community at Coaldale, and all of the settlers are of the 1922-27 immigration from Russia.

Other Mennonite groups in Alberta include the two congregations of the Church of God in Christ, Mennonite, Linden (founded 1902) and Rosedale (f. 1928), which have a membership of 436. In 1932 Old Colony Mennonites left Saskatchewan to found a new colony in the Peace River area in northern Alberta. The settlement near Fort Vermillion had grown to a membership of 130 by 1950, with additions of dissatisfied families coming from Mexico. The E.M.B. Conference had two congregations in Alberta, Swalwell and Namaka. Their settlement was begun in Swalwell in 1933, but the two churches have recently joined the M.B. conference.

Since 1918 the Hutterian Brethren have been establishing colonies in Alberta. Their 29 colonies in 1950 had a combined population of 4,200. Most of their Alberta colonies are located in the southwestern part of the province, south and southwest of Lethbridge and MacLeod, although others are scattered north almost to Edmonton.

The total baptized Mennonite membership of Alberta in 1953 was more than 4,000, in addition to the Hutterites and U.M.C. (MBC). (*ML* I, 17.)

M.G.

Alberta Mennonite High School at Coaldale, located in the midst of a large Mennonite settlement, was sponsored by the Alberta Conference of the Mennonite Brethren Church with the purpose of giving its young people an opportunity to get their instruction in a Christian institution from Christian teachers with special emphasis on the ideals of the church in matters of faith and practice.

It is owned and operated by the Alberta Mennonite Educational Society, founded especially for this purpose on March 8, 1946, by 72 members of the conference with 89 shares at $50.00 each. The curriculum of the A.M.H.S. is the same as that prescribed by the Department of Education of the Province of Alberta for all high schools in the province and the school is under the supervision of the government high-school inspector.

The school building is 28 x 84 ft. with three classrooms on the main floor and living quarters for girl students in the basement. There is a kitchen and a dining hall, and also a teacherage for three families. Since the opening of the school in 1946, the enrollment has ranged from 28 to 70, the present (1950-51) enrollment. In 1951 grades seven and eight were added and in 1952 two additional classrooms were built. Principals who have served the school are Henry Thiessen and Peter G. Klassen. The A.M.H.S. is the only Mennonite high school in the province.   B.B.J.

Alberta Provincial Conference of the Mennonite Brethren Church. The first Mennonite Brethren churches in Alberta were established in 1926, when immigrant Mennonites from Russia settled there. A few years later these churches united into a provincial organization known as the Alberta Provincial Conference of the M.B. Church. The purpose was to strengthen the churches and to promote various home mission projects. This conference elects a home mission committee composed of chairman, assistant chairman, and secretary-treasurer, which directs the various phases of home mission work in the province. The following M.B. churches in Alberta constituted this conference in 1949: Coaldale, Grassy Lake, Pincher Creek, Vauxhall, Namaka, Gem, Linden, Rosemary, Lindbrook, and La Glace. The total church membership of the conference was 955.

In all churches annual Bible conferences are conducted under the auspices of the mission committee, in co-operation with other Mennonite churches and in the spirit of mutual love and respect. Two Bible schools, one at Coaldale and one at Gem, serve the constituency. A Mennonite high school at Coaldale is supported by the conference and serves to provide Christian education to the young people. Sunday-school teachers' courses, young people's rallies, ministers' courses, and courses for church choir leaders are held annually if possible.

The following ministers have served in itinerating work and in conducting meetings for a number of years: B. B. Janz, J. J. Siemens, Abram A. Toews, D. Pankratz, P. P. Doerksen, A. G. Martens, J. A. Toews, Sr., J. A. Toews, Jr., H. Kornelson, B. W. Sawatzky, A. P. Willms, and A. A. Toews, Peter Goerz, Franz Friesen, Jac. P. Dyck; Peter Warkentin, H. R. Siemens, H. D. Siemens, Nic. A. Rempel, H. G. Klassen, Dav. Kroeker, Jac. Klassen, Martin Hamm, H. H. Rempel, and David Dyck. A.A.T.

Alberta-Saskatchewan Mennonite Conference (MC) was organized after the opening of free homesteads in the Province of Alberta by the Canadian government brought Mennonite colonists into the great Northwest. In 1902 a number from Ontario settled at Carstairs and High River, Alta. In 1903 the Ontario (old) Mennonite Conference, held at Vineland, commissioned Bishop S. F. Coffman to visit these colonies, ordain ministers, and organize congregations. About this time A. S. Bauman, a minister formerly of the Stauffer Mennonites in Eastern Pennsylvania, with a group of his members from there, settled at Mayton, Alta. In 1904 the Alberta District Conference was organized with A. S. Bauman as temporary bishop, which position he held for a few years. In 1906 another group of settlers emigrated from Ontario to Saskatchewan, having Eli S. Hallman of (Berlin) Kitchener, Ont., as their minister. In the Alberta conference of 1907, the Alberta-Saskatchewan Mennonite Conference was organized, and Hallman was chosen as their overseer. Later he was ordained bishop in Ontario for the new conference. During the following years many groups moved to the West. A group of Amish Mennonites from Nebraska settled at Tofield, Alta., with Bishop N. E. Roth in charge. Another group of Mennonites from Pennsylvania settled at Duchess, Alta., with Henry B. Ramer as their minister. A few families moved from the East to Acadia Valley, Alta., and Herbert, Sask. As the churches grew, other bishops were ordained; namely, Israel R. Shantz, Norman B. Stauffer, Isaac Miller, Moses H. Schmitt, John B. Stauffer, John G. Hochstetler, and Clarence J. Ramer. The last three named are the bishops at present. The Mt. View congregation at Creston, Mont., is affiliated with this conference. In the last few years several new mission posts have been opened in northern Alberta by young mission workers to whom the conference mission board has given charges. In 1949 a small Hutterite group near Stirling joined the conference as a congregation. In 1953 this conference district numbered 4 bishops, 16 ministers, 7 deacons, 10 congregations, and 726 members. M.G.

Alberus, Erasmus, b. in 1500 in Bruchenbrücken in Wetterau, Germany, d. May 5, 1553. As a follower of Luther he attained the office of superintendent of churches in Neu-Brandenburg (Mecklenburg). He wrote *Die Fabeln* (1534), which were re-published in 1892 by Wilhelm Braune in the *Neudrucke deutscher Literaturwerke*, with an introductory biographical sketch. He also wrote: *Dit is een seer schoon Christelijcke onderwijsinghe vanden Doopsel, teghen die Wederdoopers, Papisten* . . . (Oesterhout, n.d.) followed by a short article on the Lord's Supper and a hymn. Of greater importance is his *Wider die verfluchte Lere der Carlstader und alle fürnemste Heubter der Sacramentirer, Rottengeister, Wiedertauffer* . . . (Neu-Brandenburg, 1565). This book is one of the most malicious slanders against the Mennonites, a collection of every kind of vile report. Johannes Mathesius (*q.v.*) used two books by Alberus in his attacks on the Anabaptists in his sermons on Luther. K.V.

Volz, *Die Lutherpredigten des J. Mathesius* (Leipzig, 1930); E. Körner, "Erasmus Alberus, das Kämpferleben eines Gottesgelehrten aus Luthers Schule nach den Quellen dargestellt," in *Quellen und Darstellungen aus der Gesch. des Ref.-Jahrh.* XV (Leipzig, 1910); *Catalogus Amst.,* 98, 175; *ML* I, 18.

Albigenses, a religious group, very numerous in Southern France in the 12th and 13th centuries, generally considered as a part of the Cathars (*q.v.*). The name is derived from the French city of Albi in Languedoc. They were ruthlessly persecuted and finally annihilated in a crusade proclaimed by Innocent III and led by Count Simon de Montfort; the war of extermination lasted twenty years (1209-29), and was marked by the atrocities of religious hatred. Many writers, among them Ernest Müller (*Berner Täufer,* p. 53), list them among the old evangelical movements, therefore related to the Waldenses and Anabaptists. But this assumption is negated by their unscriptural dualistic-Manichaean doctrine. They resembled the Waldenses and similar religious movements in their moral earnestness and their rejection of the priesthood, but held to other erroneous doctrines and practices. (*ML* I, 18.) NEFF.

Albrecht (Allbrecht, Albright), a family name which occurs in Anabaptist and Mennonite circles, both of Swiss-Hutterite and Dutch origin. Michael Albrecht was chosen as a deacon in the Hutterian Brethren group in 1593; Hans Albrecht, a minister of the Hutterian Brethren, died in 1688; and a Jacob Albrecht appears in the records of the Hutterian Brethren in 1763. In the records of the Mennonite Church of Danzig the name appears as early as 1666. From Danzig this family spread to Russia and America. In West Prussia, the name occurred mostly in the "Frisian" congregations. At Danzig the forms Albertz and Alberts also appeared in both the "Frisian" and the "Flemish" congregations in the 17th century. In West Prussia there were in 1776 (without Danzig) 14 families of this name, in 1910 120 persons, in 1935 (without Elbing) 104 persons. Members of the family also migrated to Russia and America.

Two contemporary Mennonite ministers, Abraham Albrecht (1880) and Franz Albrecht (1876) of Kansas and Nebraska respectively, were both born in Russia and emigrated to North America. Erwin Albrecht is a G.C. Mennonite minister in

Missouri, and Edwin Albrecht is a C.A.M. minister in Indiana. The Albrechts of Ontario hold largely to the Old Order Mennonite bodies, although Jacob Albright (1789-1879) was a deacon in the Mennonite Church (MC). The Albrechts of the Mennonites in Illinois are descendants of five brothers and two sisters who came from Bavaria and settled in Illinois in 1837. The most widely known of this group was Henry V. Albrecht (1860-1935), deacon of the Willow Springs congregation (MC) near Tiskilwa.

In the 18th century the name was found among the German-speaking Pennsylvanians, both within and without the Mennonite Church. A publisher named Johann Albrecht of Lancaster issued an edition of Menno Simons' *Fundament Buch* in 1794. Jacob Albrecht (1759-1808) of Lutheran background founded the Evangelical Association in the early years of the 19th century.

G.R., J.C.W.

Albrecht, Margrave of Brandenburg-Ansbach, last grand master of the Teutonic Order and first duke in Prussia, b. May 16, 1490, at Ansbach, Bavaria, d. March 20, 1568. In 1525 he joined the Lutherans after a period of leaning toward Schwenckfeldianism. He offered domicile to the Anabaptists in his country (Prussia), which had been greatly impoverished in the Polish-Prussian war (1519-21), and permitted them to settle in East Prussia near Bardeyn, not far from the town of Preussisch-Holland. But in an otherwise entirely orthodox Lutheran state, this colony was an object of annoyance to the clergy. The duke turned to Martin Luther in 1532 for an exposition of John 6, but received no reply for over a year. Luther finally advised against toleration. On June 12, 1533, he replied to Luther (the letter is found in Th. Kolde). Until 1535 the margrave followed a policy of toleration, but in 1535 exaggerated reports on Münster caused him to have the Anabaptists expelled by an order of Oct. 23, 1535. But the officials, unwilling to weaken the depopulated land, did not carry out the orders very strictly. They persuaded the duke to permit a new settlement of Anabaptists in 1539 in the village of Schönberg in the same vicinity. However, the duke again yielded to the clergy and in 1543 ordered these settlers banished unless they recanted. Also the later immigrant Mennonites from Holland, who settled in Schönberg as early as 1545 and later (1556-58) at Drausensee and Ellerwald, were repeatedly hit by edicts of expulsion, in consequence of which they may have settled in the adjacent Polish territory. (See **East Prussia**.)   HEGE.

E. Randt, *Die Menn. in Ostpreussen und Litauen bis zum Jahre 1772* (Königsberg, 1912); B. Schumacher, *Niederländische Ansiedlungen im Herzogtum Preussen z. Z. Herzog Albrechts* (Leipzig, 1903); Th. Kolde, *Analecta Lutherana* (1883) 137-39: Fr. Thudichum, *Deutsche Ref.* II (Leipzig, 1909) 540; P. Tschackert, *Urkundenbuch zur Ref.-Gesch. des Herzogtums Preussen* II (1890) 202 f., No. 994 and No. 999; S. G. Schultz, *Caspar Schwenckfeld von Ossig* (Norristown, 1948); H. Penner, *Ansiedlung menn. Niederländer im Weichselmündungsgebiet . . .* Weierhof, 1940); *idem,* "Anabaptists and Mennonites of East Prussia," *MQR* XXII (1948) 212-25; *ML* I, 19.

Albrecht V (1528-79), Duke of Bavaria 1550-79, was in many regards similar to his brother-in-law, Emperor Maximilian II; that is, he appeared mildly tolerant to the rising tide of the Lutheran Reformation. He was at first indifferent to religious questions, primarily interested in the arts and sciences. In 1556 he permitted the communion with both emblems (Lutheran) and ordered an investigation of conditions in the Catholic Church (a report of 1558 reveals everywhere gross immorality among the clergy). Naturally, such conditions were relatively favorable for the spread of Anabaptism; the peace, however, was but of short duration. Already in 1556, Emperor Ferdinand I, father-in-law of Albrecht and the most powerful opponent of the Anabaptists, induced the duke to call in the newly created order of the Jesuits who in a short time caused him to change his mind. The aggressive Counter Reformation set in. Stern orders were issued to ferret out Anabaptists, and to eradicate this "sect" with all means wherever found. Thus in the city of Burghausen several Anabaptist martyrs are reported before 1559. The most notable case of persecution, however, is that of the outstanding Hutterite missionary Klaus Felbinger (*q.v.*), who together with his brother-companion was executed in Landshut in 1560, in spite of a most brilliant defense. Unfortunately research on this period is sadly lacking, and the sources have not yet been published which would give a clearer picture of Anabaptist life in Bavaria in the second half of the 16th century. The movement seems to have been less strong than in adjacent Württemberg. In both countries the Hutterites were diligently working as missionaries for their brotherhood. Duke Wilhelm V, the successor of Albrecht, stated in a mandate of 1586 that 600 Anabaptists had left the country, apparently for Moravia. When Albrecht V died in 1579, Bavaria had become another stronghold of Catholicism like Austria, and Anabaptism seems to have been waning. (*ML* I, 18.)   A.K., R.F.

Albrecht Friedrich, the second duke of Prussia 1569-1618, son of Duke Albrecht, born April 29, 1553, at Königsberg, d. Aug. 27, 1618. Since he was imbecile, the regency (1577-1603) of East Prussia was held by Margrave George Frederick. His reign was marked by intolerance toward the Anabaptists, zealously fanned by the Lutheran theologians. The clergy frequently opposed even the physicians "who were recommended and sent to the duke from outside the country, because they claimed to fear they were sometimes Anabaptists or Sacramentarians, sometimes soothsayers and magicians" (*ADB* I, 313). A petition for toleration made by the Anabaptists at the time of George Frederick's appointment to the regency in 1577 was refused on Jan. 8, 1579, on the basis of an old decision by Philip Melanchthon. At the same time it was decided that by May 1, 1579, all Anabaptists or Mennonites were to leave the country. George Frederick, who tried to attain "uniformity in the religion of the Christian faith," frequently issued mandates ordering his subjects under penalty of physical punishment and confiscation of possessions to leave the country or join the state church. Foreign merchants were, however, permitted to do business; thus it was possible for some Mennonites to remain in the country. HEGE.

E. Randt, *Die Menn. in. Ostpreussen und Litauen bis zum Jahre 1772* (Königsberg, 1912); *ML* I, 19.

Albright (Albrecht), **Jacob.** On Sept. 19, 1732, Johannes and Anna Albrecht arrived in the port of Philadelphia from Rotterdam on the *Johnson*. They were very likely emigrants from the Rhineland and of the Lutheran faith with pietistic inclination. Into their home near Pottstown, Pa., a second son, Jacob, was born on May 1, 1759. After brief service in the Revolutionary War he was married to Catherine Cope in 1785, bought a farm, and established a tiling business in Lancaster Co., Pa., near the flourishing Ephrata Cloister.

Dissatisfied with the Lutheran Church in his community, Albright temporarily associated with the Methodists but soon began to preach among his German neighbors and to Germans throughout eastern and central Pennsylvania, Maryland, and Virginia, for whom he believed no adequate religious culture was being provided. By 1800 his followers were so numerous that he established the first classes of the United Brethren denomination and in 1803 held an official conference of his coworkers. He was named a bishop of the church in 1807 and charged with the responsibility of drafting a form of government and order, which he left incomplete at his premature death on May 18, 1808. He lies buried in Kleinfeltersville, Pa., where the Evangelical Church, of which he was the founder, erected a memorial church in 1850. (See **Evangelical United Brethren Church.**) R.W.A.

Raymond W. Albright, *A History of the Evangelical Church* (Harrisburg, 1942, rev. ed., 1945) 21-82.

Alckmaer, J. C. van, Dutch Mennonite author of devotional poems. He wrote *Een nieu Schriftuerlijck Liedtboecxken ghemaeckt uyt den O. ende N.T.; met noch twee Christel. Sendtbrieven* (Hoorn, 1615), second enlarged edition 1630. (*ML* I, 19; *Catalogus Amst.,* 271.) HEGE.

Alcohol. Almost as old in the history of humanity as the use of intoxicating or alcoholic drinks is the attempt by intelligent rulers and leaders to promote or require temperance if not prohibition. In addition to religious teaching against drinking, political and moral reasons have been advanced for the restriction or entire prohibition of the manufacture and use of intoxicants. In medieval Europe the manufacture of wine and beer, the chief fermented liquors, was not sufficiently widespread to permit much intemperance. After the 13th century, however, the increase of wealth led to a heavier consumption of hard liquors (whiskey, brandy, gin, etc.) and a corresponding increase in the evil effects of the use of alcohol.

The Reformation Period. The 16th century was an age of excessive drinking, particularly in Germany. Prof. Blanke in his *Reformation und Alkoholismus,* which is an unusually thorough and valuable study on this question, says that the 16th century was one of drinking and gluttony. ("Das

16. Jahrhundert ist das Sauf- und Fressjahrhundert, wenigstens in deutschen Landen.") All the leading reformers complained about the excessive drinking, and Sebastian Franck's (d. 1543) booklet (tr.) *Concerning the Horrible Vice of Drunkenness* paints a terrible picture of the evil. Both Luther and Franck viewed drunkenness as a sign of the last times, and Franck concluded that only the Judgment Day could cleanse the Kingdom of Christ of this and similar evils. Blanke believes that the coming of the Reformation actually increased drunkenness, and Luther himself complained that the people had misunderstood his teaching of Christian liberty. Various attempts were made by the leaders of church and state to improve conditions, but all failed. Blanke suggests that the only real hope was total abstinence, but no one at that time advocated such a course except Sebastian Franck, the lone prophet on the extreme left, and possibly the Anabaptists.

Probably the very first (and one of the very few) writings against the use of alcoholic liquors was that of 1525 by Ludwig Haetzer (*ca.* 1500-29), an Anabaptist of somewhat uncertain character, entitled *Von dem Evangelischen Zechen und von der Christenred aus heiliger geschrifft 1525 dem Konstanzer Bürger Achatius Froembd gewidmet,* published at Augsburg, whither Haetzer came after his expulsion from Zürich on Jan. 21, and where he laid the foundations for what later became an Anabaptist congregation there. Neff's article on Haetzer (*ML* I, 226-7) analyzes the content of that part of the booklet which deals with *"Zechen"* (drinking liquor) as follows: "He speaks at length of how one must enter through much tribulation into the Kingdom of God. It is one of the tricks of Satan to praise drinking and carousing (*Zechen und Saufen*) as Gospel freedom. They call it 'evangelical drinking' as though it befits the 'evangelicals' to drink. Accordingly he is the most 'evangelical' who carouses and carries on the worst. They say, you can't force young people into narrow confines, you must let water run freely or it will burst out somewhere and do damage. But what does the Gospel say? The first Christians came together to worship God and not to drink. Christ and not Bacchus brought them together. The joy of the Christian is joy in the Holy Ghost. Haetzer continues to expound in detail the seriously Christian, truly evangelical manner of life as taught by the Holy Scriptures. But how shall the evangelical congregations deal with drinkers? They shall excommunicate them as such who are of no value to the church of God, but rather harm."

The Anabaptists and Alcohol. The earliest Anabaptist confession, *The Seven Articles of Schleitheim* (1527), forbade in Article 4 the patronage of drinking places. Capito, the reformer of Strasbourg, states in a contemporary letter that the Anabaptists had undertaken to refrain, among other things, from drinking ("zu meiden das üppige Spielen, Saufen, Fressen, Ehebrechen, Kriegen, Totschlagen"). Bullinger, Zwingli's successor in Zürich, in his 1560 work against the Anabaptists

(*Von der Wiedertaufferen Ursprung*) states that they drank only unfermented sweet cider (*Süssmost*) and water. Anabaptists were often identified as such because they refused in the inns to drink alcoholic liquors to the health of other guests, whereupon they were arrested and executed. An illustration of this is Michael Seifensieder, a preacher of the Hutterites, who with two associates was arrested on Jan. 8, 1536, in an inn in Vienna for the above reason, having been discovered by his refusal to drink, and was finally burned at the stake on March 31, 1536. The Hutterite Peter Riedemann's *Confession of Faith,* written in 1540, says "concerning innkeepers," "neither do we allow any of our number to be a public innkeeper, serving either wine or beer, since this goeth with all that is unchaste, ungodly and decadent, and drunkards and good-for-nothing fellows get there together to carry out their headstrong wills. . . . It is nearly impossible for an innkeeper to keep himself from sin"; and "concerning standing drinks" (standing–setting up), "it is the cause of evil and transgression of the commandments of God . . . , for thereby is the man moved and lured on to drink when he otherwise would not do so. Therefore it is against nature and is sin and evil. . . . Therefore the standing of drinks is evil at the root no matter how it is done. It is an invention of the devil to catch men, drawing them into his net, making them cleave to him and forsake God and leading them into all sins. Therefore, one should flee from it as from the face of a serpent" (1950 English edition, pages 127-29). It may well be assumed that the Swiss Brethren and other Anabaptists followed a similar standard. Menno Simons' writings contain many statements against the use of alcoholic drinks. This does not prove that the early Anabaptists required total abstinence, but does indicate a very sensitive conscience on the question of alcoholic drinks. There is abundant evidence on the other hand that the Hutterite Bruderhofs grew hops and grapes, and manufactured wine and beer, at least for delivery to their feudal overlords. That the modern Hutterites in North America make and drink their own wine would suggest that they drank wine also in their early history.

It appears that the Anabaptists as a whole were not quite so strict in regard to alcohol as some of the Swiss Brethren and Hutterites. While the writings of Menno Simons, Dirk Philips, and others contain many admonitions to a sober life with warnings against drunkenness based upon such passages as I Thess. 5:5-8, they did not call for total abstinence. In the *Martyrs' Mirror* (D 347, 480, E 706, 822) one of the martyrs is reported as drinking a glass of wine. The noted elder Leenaert Bouwens was certainly not a teetotaler, and there is no evidence that the Mennonites of Holland in the 17th and 18th centuries were objectors to alcohol. On the contrary, there were many brewers and especially distillers of brandy among them. However, topers (*droncken-drinckers*) were subject to excommunication.

One of the chief reasons given by the reformers and others against total abstinence was the fear of promoting the idea of works-salvation or legalism, with the thought that by abstinence one could gain merit with God. The Anabaptists had no such fear. They were not afraid to advocate strict ethics and a high standard of Christian living in discipleship even though they were often accused of legalism and moralism on many points. As Blanke points out, the idea of total abstinence as a cure for the drink evil was promoted in the 16th to the 18th centuries by the Free Church movements, not by the state churches. In the 17th century, it was George Fox and the Quakers in England and the Inspirationists in France, Holland, and Germany who advocated complete abstinence from alcoholic liquors. In the 18th century it was John Wesley and the Methodists. In fact even in the 19th century the temperance and abstinence movements were largely the work of Free Church leaders in America and in Europe, but particularly in America.

Meanwhile during this period the Mennonites in Europe lost something of their earlier strictness in the matter, and some seem to have inclined to the drinking customs of their environment. In fact in some areas Mennonites took the lead in the manufacture and dispensing of liquor. (See the end sections of this article.)

The immigrants from Germany, France, and Switzerland to the United States and Canada from 1683 to 1873 had no scruples against moderate drinking and numbers of them brought with them experience and skills in the distilling of alcoholic liquor. Whiskey distilling, and occasionally brewing, on a small scale was fairly common among the settlers in the pioneer communities of colonial and later days, particularly in Pennsylvania and Maryland. Samuel Bechtel, a Mennonite settler of pre-Revolutionary days (before 1776) near Hagerstown, Md., who personally built a Mennonite church on his property, built a self-contained unit including a flour mill, blacksmith shop, and distillery. Abraham Overholt, who was during his whole lifetime (d. 1870) an active member of the Scottdale, Pa., Mennonite congregation and served at different times as a trustee there, and whose brother was a minister and bishop, established at Broadford near by in 1810 a distillery which has developed into a major industry, now a part of the Schenley Distilleries Corporation, which still sells a whiskey labeled "Old Overholt" with a picture of Abraham on the label. (Incidentally, none of Abraham's children became Mennonites, and a grandson was Henry Clay Frick, the steel magnate, worth $100 million at his death.) Isaac, August, and Henry Leisy, all Mennonites and brothers from Friedelsheim, Palatinate, Germany, who came to the United States in 1852, founded the Leisy brewery in Keokuk, Iowa, in 1862. In 1872 the family purchased the brewery of Fred Haltnorth in Cleveland and transferred operations to that city. In 1935 after the repeal of prohibition, the Leisy Brewing Company was reorganized and Herbert F.

Leisy, grandson of Isaac Leisy, became and still is its president. The family has not been Mennonite for several generations.

Movements for temperance and abstinence did not rise among the Mennonites at any place in Europe (except when they were brought in from the outside) and most European Mennonites did not and do not to this day sympathize with or take part in such movements, with some notable exceptions such as the late Elder Michael Horsch of Ingolstadt, Bavaria, and certain French elders as Pierre Sommer, Joseph Muller, and Pierre Widmer. The leading temperance movement of Europe, the Blue Cross Society (*Blaues Kreuz*), a Christian organization for the rescuing of alcoholics through religious renewal and a pledge of total abstinence, grew out of a Swiss temperance society organized in Geneva in 1877, which rapidly became an international movement of considerable strength, reaching Germany in 1885. It requires total abstinence of its members, but does not condemn the moderate use of alcoholic liquors by others, seeking rather to enlist all in an organized movement to rescue alcoholics and promote temperance. Among the French Mennonites there has been more activity in the total abstinence and Blue Cross movements than anywhere else among Mennonites in Europe. Pierre Sommer, editor of the Mennonite paper *Christ Seul* (1907-41), published many articles advocating abstinence, trying vigorously to promote among the French Mennonites a stronger position on the renunciation of alcoholic beverages and influencing many young people. Joseph Muller, Elder of the Toul Mennonite Church, has been a strong leader of the Blue Cross Society in the region of Nancy–Toul, with a high reputation among the French Protestants and others. On his farm "Bois-le-Comte" near Toul, he has received since 1925 many drunkards, many of whom he led to a real conversion, through Christian love, and into the practice of total abstinence. The Toul Mennonite Church has been very greatly influenced by the personality and the work of Joseph Muller, and a number of the members of this church have taken the position of complete abstinence. Muller is a member of the national board of the French Blue Cross Society. Pierre Widmer, the present editor of *Christ Seul,* son-in-law of Pierre Sommer, is a promoter of the movement for total abstinence —and a member of the French Blue Cross Society. As a public school teacher he has continued to promote the cause through *Christ Seul,* as his predecessor had. In Holland a Mennonite group to promote total abstinence was formed in 1924 as a section of the *Gemeentedag* movement under the name *Arbeidsgroep voor Geheelonthouding.* Also some Dutch Mennonite ministers, especially H. C. Barthel (*q.v.*), were permanent members of the Dutch association for total abstinence.

In Russia there were by 1819 several Mennonite brewers in the Chortitza colony and moderate drinking was fairly common in all the Mennonite settlements in Russia, there being drinking houses in a number of the Mennonite villages. However,

as early as 1830 the *Kleine Gemeinde,* a small strict schismatic group, protested vigorously against the use of alcoholic beverages and tobacco. By the middle of the century, a temperance society was founded in the village of Gnadenfeld, which promoted abstinence and whose members signed a lifetime pledge of total abstinence and distributed tracts promoting their ideas. The founders of the Mennonite Brethren Church were vigorous champions of abstinence, and always had prohibition of beverages with a high alcoholic content as one of their principles, although they did not forbid moderate drinking of wine and beer. By 1870 most Russian Mennonites had developed a conscience against drinking hard liquors, although the Mennonite General Conference never adopted any resolution on this question paralleling the Mennonite Brethren.

Meanwhile in the United States and Canada a general temperance movement was developing, beginning in the first decade of the 19th century and rising to a powerful reform movement, carried in general by the Protestant churches, particularly Methodists and Baptists. The first organized temperance society appeared in 1808, the stronger American Temperance Union in 1833, the powerful Woman's Christian Temperance Union in 1874, and the well-organized Anti-Saloon League in 1895. This movement was supported early by the Sunday schools, and when temperance Sundays and temperance lessons were introduced into the International Uniform Lessons in 1881, developing in 1892 into regular quarterly temperance lessons, a powerful impetus was given to the rapidly developing temperance and total abstinence cause. Mennonites gradually came under the influence of this movement, although at first, whether in the older Pennsylvania settlements and their daughter settlements, or in the Russian Mennonite settlements of 1874 f. in Canada, there was opposition to members becoming active participants in temperance organizations and temperance agitation. The resolutions of the Ontario Mennonite Conference in 1842, and the Western District (General Conference) of 1879 illustrate this. However, in the 19th century apparently no Mennonite conferences dared to go further in binding legislation than to forbid members to hold licenses to sell liquor or to go into saloons to drink (see Indiana Mennonite Conference 1875-79, 1884, 1893, Southwestern Pennsylvania Conference 1888, Lancaster Conference of this and earlier years). Gradually by the end of the century resolutions began to appear condemning the "liquor traffic." It is clear that the American temperance and total abstinence movement was beginning to take root in the Mennonite mind as a generation was reared on Sunday-school temperance lessons, and as the vigorous agitation of the Anti-Saloon League and the great temperance unions began to take effect. Kansas, where many Mennonites from Russia settled, was one of the strongest states in prohibition sentiment, with a state-wide complete prohibition law from 1881 to 1950. Oklahoma has also been under a complete prohibition law from its admission to statehood in 1908. By the early 20th century most Mennonites had become total abstainers, even to the extent of using unfermented grape juice instead of wine for the communion service. Notable exceptions were such groups as the Old Order Amish and those communities where there were more recent immigrants, especially from Alsace. The Old Order Amish were never much affected by the temperance movement. Some of the newer Mennonite immigrants from Russia (1873 ff.) were vigorous champions of total abstinence. An outstanding example was the prominent Cornelius Jansen family. The town of Jansen, Neb., founded by this family, had a provision in its charter that no saloons could ever be established within its limits. Jacob Y. Shantz, a prominent lay leader of Kitchener (then Berlin), Ont., was an active temperance worker as early as 1860. P. S. Hartman (1849-1934), a layman near Harrisonburg, Va., was similarly active. J. S. Hartzler, a minister in Elkhart Co., Ind., 1882 ff., did his part. Bishop John Smith (d. 1906) was an early advocate of temperance among the Amish Mennonites of Central Illinois.

In the United States the temperance and prohibition movements grew to be very powerful in the first quarter of the 20th century, with widespread adoption of local option laws permitting local communities to vote out the sale of liquor, state-wide prohibition laws, and finally national prohibition effected through the 18th amendment passed in 1919 and effective in 1920, which was the law of the land until its repeal in 1933. Most Mennonites actively supported this movement and took part in local option elections against the liquor traffic. Numbers of Mennonites voted in local and national elections for the prohibition party which was organized as a national party in 1869 and is still in existence. The traditional opposition of some Mennonites to participation in politics caused some to withhold their vote even in local option elections. In other areas, however, even the most conservative leaders publicly urged their members to go to the polls to vote on the liquor issue. The disillusionment accompanying the breakdown of national prohibition has broken somewhat the spell of the belief that such evils as the drink evil can be cured by legislation and has had repercussions in the attitude of Mennonites toward voting on any issue. It became clear that it is impossible by legislation to enforce high ethical standards upon a population if the majority do not believe in such standards. The realization of this fact has probably promoted a greater withdrawal from politics in general among Mennonites. Meanwhile the pattern of total abstinence has become thoroughly established among American Mennonites of all branches, most of whom today would not knowingly tolerate among their membership the drinking of alcoholic beverages.

The entrance into Europe after 1945 of several hundred American Mennonites, whether as relief workers or visitors, all of them abstaining altogether from the drinking of alcoholic beverages including even light wines and beer, has emphasized the difference between American Mennonites and the European Mennonites, who on the whole have continued their tolerance of moderate drinking and many of whom frequently set on their tables, particularly for festive occasions, alcoholic beverages such as wine or cider or who furnish such beverages to their farmhands as a part of the daily maintenance. It is evident that the descendants of the European Mennonites who came to America have been Americanized also in respect to the alcoholic beverage question. Although America in general, since the breakdown of prohibition, has increased its drinking, particularly of hard liquors, the American Mennonites as a whole are firmly set in their opposition to alcoholic drinking in any form.

Whether the coming of the Russian Mennonites to America 1873-80, with their general and growing conscience against drinking, was an appreciable factor in the promotion of temperance among the earlier immigrants, as claimed by Harley J. Stuckey in his 1947 master's thesis ("Cultural Interaction Among the Mennonites since 1870," Northwestern University, unprinted), is an open question. Although there is probably some truth to this claim, the indigenous American temperance movement was certainly a more powerful factor. It is possible that John F. Funk (1835-1930), the editor and publisher of the *Herald of Truth* (the church paper of the [old] Mennonites and Amish Mennonites, founded in 1864), was himself influenced by the Russian Mennonite attitude and in turn aroused to more vigorous advocacy of the temperance cause in his paper. Certain it is that in the years of the publication of this paper before the coming of the Russian Mennonites nothing was said against either drinking or smoking, and that after 1881 articles of this type appeared regularly. All the church schools established by the Mennonites of all branches, either high school or college, have rules prohibiting the use of strong drink by their students.

In the large Swiss Mennonite community around Berne, Ind., the temperance movement early took root. One of the primary figures was John Christian Rohrer, who had come there in 1885 from Bern, Switzerland, where he had been a charter member of the Blue Cross Society, said to be the first person known to sign a German total abstinence pledge. In 1886 he succeeded in organizing a German temperance society at Berne, all of whose charter members were Mennonites, and which was joined soon after by the pastor of the church, S. F. Sprunger, although the majority of the church members were opposed to it. There were four saloons in the small village of Berne at that time, patronized in part by Mennonites, and the society quietly worked and successfully changed public sentiment in the community in favor of temperance and against saloons. A determined campaign to eliminate the saloons from the city by legal methods was begun in 1902, led by Fred Rohrer, son of the founder of the temperance society. The exciting story of this struggle, which included such outrages as four assaults upon Rohrer's person and a dynamiting of his home, but was finally crowned with success, is told in the book *Saloon Fight at Berne, Indiana*. The Temperance Society at Berne published in 1901 a 16-page booklet by J. G. Ewert of Hillsboro, Kan., *Die Bibel und Enthaltsamkeit*, which was reprinted in an enlarged and revised edition in 1903 with a total issue of 10,000 copies.

H.S.B.

Fritz Blanke, "Reformation und Alcoholismus," *Zwingliana*, 1949, pp. 75-89; *Saloon Fight at Berne, Indiana* (Berne, 1913).

Alcohol Among the Mennonites of Northeast Germany. Among the crafts brought to the Vistula delta from Holland by the Dutch Mennonite refugees, the distilling of brandy and whiskey, i.e., the manufacture of fine liquors from raw brandy, played a by no means insignificant part. Two of these businesses founded by Mennonites reached a more than local importance; indeed they had in a sense a European and even world-wide importance.

Since 1598 there was a distillery in the Breitgasse in Danzig in the house *Zum Lachs* (*Lachs:* salmon) founded by Ambrosius Vermeulen (Ter Meulen, van der Meulen, Vermoelen, Mole), which is still in existence, even though the business was moved out of Danzig in 1945. The firm has been passed down on the female side of the family. In this way it passed into the possession of the Mennonite families Wedling (Isaac Wedling), Hecker (1730 to Dirk Hekker), and Bestvater (1758 to Dirk Bestvater), and later into non-Mennonite possession. This early period of the firm is preserved by the labels on the bottles, depicting the old firm trademark, the salmon, and also the old tavern sign, the six-pointed star, and the inscription "Isaac Wedling Wwe und Eydam Dirck Hekker." The products of this firm were known far beyond the borders of Germany, especially the famous *Danziger Goldwasser* with its floating goldleaf, the *Kurfürstliche Magen,* and the *Krambambuli*. Both Lessing in his *Minna von Barnhelm*, and Heinrich von Kleist in his *Der zerbrochene Krug* mention the liqueurs of the Danziger Lachs. In 1745 Christoph Friedrich Wedekind dedicated a poem to the Krambambuli under the title "Lob-Gedicht über die gebrannten Wasser im Lachs zu Dantzig," with 102 stanzas, the last of which is,

> Nun, Bürger von dem Weichselstrande,
> Ihr Mennonisten habet Danck,
> Es geh euch wohl zu Schiff und Lande,
> Gott segne euren Necktartranck.
> Leb, edles Dantzig, grün und blüh,
> Tusch! Vivat dein Krambambuli.

This poem is the source of the student song "Krambambuli."

In a later period the firm of Peter Stobbe of Tiegenhof in the Grosse Werder was founded, whose *Machandel* (elderberry whiskey) likewise attained a more than local importance, even reaching America, and was sold for more than 200 years up to 1945.

Even though from about the middle of the 18th

century more and more Mennonites in northeastern Germany have engaged in the distilling of brandy as well as in the liquor trade and barkeeping, so that in the city of Danzig the terms "Mennonite" and "tavern" became almost synonymous, this fact cannot be attributed to a particular love of the Mennonites for this trade. A deeper reason for this fact is that all other vocations were closed to them by the constantly more rigorous rulings of the trade guilds. On Nov. 24, 1749, for example, the guild of lace and tapemakers decided "that from now on no Mennonite youth may be enrolled or certified, nor shall any be admitted to the estate of master." Similar decisions were passed by the Danzig city council in November 1749 and in 1755 (*Mennonite Life,* 1951, 36). The consequence for a Danzig family, the Kauenhovens for example, which had between 1656 and 1749 only two distillers but more than twenty lace and braid makers, was that the latter craft now disappeared among them and eighteen Kauenhovens were engaged in the manufacture and sale of alcohol.

The increasing demand for "Branntwein Danziger Art" and the occupational limitations caused many Mennonites of Danzig to settle in other cities of the German Northeast. In 1724 there were already six Mennonite families engaged in distilling in Königsberg in Prussia. Later there were Mennonite distillers also in Pillau, Rastenburg, Tilsit, and Memel. A fairly accurate picture of the participation of the Mennonites in the manufacture and sale of alcohol in northeast Germany is given by the official Mennonite register of 1776, which was published by Gustav E. Reimer. Among a total of 12,603 Mennonites there were 27 engaged in the liquor business in Danzig and its suburbs, 5 in the Grosse Werder district, 13 in Elbing, 3 in Memel, and 4 in Tilsit. For Königsberg the list of citizens shows in the period of 1749-1809 a total of 53 engaged in the liquor business among a total of 109 Mennonites in all vocations. Some of their taverns were known throughout the city; for example, in Danzig-Langfuhr the *Machandeltreppchen,* later *Zum goldenen Löwen* (owner Heinrich Zimmermann, 1787-1845), in Königsberg *Zur goldenen Axt* (owner Heinrich Kauenhowen, 1797-1871), in Memel the "Bunte Bock" (owner Wilhelm Sprunck, 1765-1871), all members of well-known Mennonite families. In 1726 the noted Danzig elder Hans von Steen became a merchant and distiller. Quite a number of the inns, taverns, and distilleries in the area were in Mennonite hands.

After 1800, when the restrictions that prohibited the Mennonites from engaging in other pursuits in the Danzig area were removed, Mennonite participation in the liquor traffic declined rapidly. Julius Zimmermann (1821-98), a noted master millbuilder in Danzig, reported, "When I observe the life of the Mennonite congregation in Danzig I find to my gratification that among the means of livelihood the number of barkeepers among them has decreased in a very conspicuous degree, since, according to investigation made by Loewens, of seventy-four engaged in this business in our youth, there are only four engaged in it now, which goal and success has been attained only by an essentially higher education in comparison to former times." However, as late as 1936 the German Mennonite address book lists four tavern keepers in the city of Danzig and twice as many in the country congregations. There was a saying among the Mennonites even in Berlin, "Anyone who is a genuine Mennonite must be able to hold his drinks." At the meetings of the West Prussian and Danzig church board meetings and conference sessions, neither alcohol nor tobacco was missing.

Thus it is evident that the urban Mennonites of northeast Germany played an important part in the manufacture and distribution of alcohol, however almost exclusively with brandy and liquors. The number of brewers and beer-barkeepers among them is negligible. From a purely economic point of view they greatly benefited their communities; Randt reports that the six Mennonite distillers of Königsberg in the period from 1718 to 1724 paid an excise tax of 29,311 talers. The extent to which the Mennonites of northeast Germany contributed to the misuse of alcohol cannot be ascertained here. They themselves probably had no scruples against the business in which they were engaged, for public opinion of the time saw in brandy and whiskey only their stimulating and healing effect. There is no evidence that the Mennonites of that time had a reputation for inebriety. On the whole the opinion concerning them expressed by Randt was the common one: "In no court records are there complaints or charges of the authorities or other people against the Mennonites on the point of laziness and shiftlessness, but on the contrary they are always praised as quiet and industrious people." K.K.

"Vom 'echten doppelten Lachs,' vom Krambambuli und den Danziger Mennoniten," *Mitt. des Sippenverbandes der Danziger Menn. Familien Epp-Kauenhowen-Zimmermann,* 1940, 181-84; "Tiegenhof, sein Machandel und das Gr. Werder," *ibid.,* 140-42; A. Schmidt, "Ein Stammbuch aus dem 'Lachs,'" *Danziger familiengesch. Beitr.,* 1938, 19-21; P. Kliewer, "Ein zweites Stammbuch aus dem Danziger 'Lachs,'" *Mitt. des Sippenverbandes Danziger Menn. Familien,* 1941, 37-50; G. E. Reimer, "Ein Mennonitenverzeichnis aus dem Jahre 1776," *Danziger familiengesch. Beitr.* (Heft 5, 5-7, 1940-43); E. Randt, *Die Menn. in Ostpreussen und Litauen bis zum Jahre 1771* (Königsberg phil. diss., 1912).

Alcohol Among the Mennonites of Northwest Germany. Among the Mennonites of North Germany beer brewers and brandy distillers were relatively numerous. This may be due in part to the fact that not all professions and trades were open to them. In the region of Lübeck in the 16th and 17th centuries the Roosen family was even engaged in the manufacture of gunpowder.

For Norden Abraham Fast reports (*Die Kulturleistungen der Mennoniten in Ostfriesland und Münsterland 1939-47*): "It was the especial achievement of Privy Councillor Jan ten Doornkaat Koolman to develop the distillery founded by his father into a business of outstanding economic importance for the city and to make the Doornkaat the popular whiskey of East Friesland and beyond. On Jan. 9, 1886, the city of Norden instituted a spectacular torchlight parade for the celebration of the fiftieth anniversary of his business career. In the procession one of the objects of exhibition was an original export flask with the legend, '2,000,000 liters annual production.' From the laudatory addresses of his colleagues on this occasion the following sentences are characteristic: 'It is a day of blessing and of joy not only for Your High Well-Born and your family, but also for the entire city and vicinity. All the world therefore understands the necessity of celebrating the day. (This apology because the honored man was very averse to such publicity of his person.) We have the most immediate cause for doing so. For indeed from this thriving business substantial contributions flow daily to the city coffers, and a population of laborers is created, exemplary in its kind. But we also come with hearts filled with gratitude for all the benevolent deeds which have flowed to the city so richly and amply from your hand from time to time during the last fifty years. We thank you for the faithful devotion with which you have occupied all the posts of honor as senator, *Bürgervorsteher,* deputy to the local parliament and the Reichstag. As a citizen always true and conscientious and with a heart full of love for all your fellow citizens, aiding and supporting where it was a matter of relieving distress and assisting the unfortunate, in all idealistic undertakings co-operating helpfully and actively, you are the unparalleled example of loyal citizenship.'

"Under his successors, Jan and Hildebrand ten Doornkaat Koolman, the company in 1905 consumed 5,803,400 lbs. of grain and paid a distillery tax of 684,049 marks."

Concerning Mennonite distilleries in Leer, Fast gives the following information: "The distillery and yeast factory of the brothers Fritz and Gerhard Brouer was of general importance in that it developed large tracts of formerly unusable moorland. Such reclaiming of the heath was of especial value at a time when the government had not yet subsidized such undertakings and the work was of a pioneering nature. The founder of the business, the 82-year-old Consul F. Brouer, is still living (1946)."

Concerning Friedrichstadt and Eiderstedt we read in Robert Dollinger's *Geschichte der Mennoniten in Schleswig-Holstein* (Hamburg and Lübeck, 1930): In Eiderstedt the merchant Andreas Linnich "furnished the prince with 73 Reichstalers' worth of Hamburg beer during his visit to Toenning in 1659." In Friedrichstadt there were Mennonite brewers and distillers about 1700. "One of the respected brewery owners was Claus Jakob Tetens, who in 1715 in a period of nine months furnished 243 barrels (Tonnen) of beer to the garrison town of Tönning, which was more than one sixth of the total supply. Among his customers were the military, the mayor, and the two Lutheran pastors." In Friedrichstadt Spanish wine was provided for communion in 1668. In 1770 intoxication was made the ground for applying the "small ban." In Eiderstedt the prominent boatowner, merchant, and landowner Adam Teekes of Ameland in West Friesland, had to pay a fine in Westerhever in 1742 for desecrating the Sabbath by immoderate drinking (*Zechen*).   E.C.

Alda, a martyr, killed at Kufstein on the Inn, Tirol, in 1530, otherwise unknown. (*Mart. Mir.* D 31, E 439.)

Aldasy, Antal, author of a treatise on the Anabaptists in Hungary and Transylvania in the 16th and 17th centuries, published in Budapest in 1893, in the Hungarian language. (*ML* I, 20.)   HEGE.

Aldboro, Elgin Co., Ont., bordering Lake Erie, was a preaching place under the Ontario Mennonite (MC) Conference, first recorded in 1874 as meeting every fourth Sunday. Later the meetings were held every two weeks. Two ministers were ordained in the 1870's. In 1880 Aldboro alternated with Mosa in the *Meeting Calendar.* The Aldboro meetings were held in a schoolhouse a mile or two east from Clachan. The regularity of communion services twice a year until 1916 at Mosa indicates that these congregations were active for a quarter of a century.   J.C.F.

Aldegonde, Philips van Marnix, Heer van Sint, b. 1540 at Brussels, d. 1598 at Leiden, educated at the universities of Leiden, Paris, and Dôle. At Dôle he broke with Catholicism in 1558 to become a follower of Calvin. He traveled through Italy and in 1559 came to Geneva, and presumably stayed there until 1562. About this time he came in contact with William of Orange and became an indefatigable fighter in the revolt against the Spanish King Philip II, who also ruled over the Netherlands. He defended the notorious iconoclasm of 1566 (two pamphlets of 1566 and 1567). For these martial followers of Calvin and Beza the uprising was first of all a religious conflict between the Christian truth and Rome. Marnix van St. Aldegonde filled important and responsible positions. He remained a good friend of William of Orange, although later a serious difference of opinion arose between them. Whereas William was inclined toward tolerance toward other creeds, Aldegonde had no tolerance whatever. Though he might have been inclined to tolerate the Roman Catholics politically, he did not take the same attitude toward the Mennonites, calling them fanatics and intolerable in the state (*Ondersoeckinge . . . der Geestdrijuische Leere . . .*, 1595; *Responce Apologétique,* 1598). He considered death a fitting penalty for Anabaptists. He tried to persuade William to take severe measures against them, but was not successful. In a letter of March 31, 1577, to the Reformed preacher Caspar Heidanus at Middelburg, Aldegonde wrote about "the matter of the Anabaptists" whom he calls people "who seek to destroy the bond of all human society." The prince, he continues, will have nothing to do with suppressive measures and will not oppress the Mennonites, both as a matter of principle and of practical statesmanship (G. Brandt, 588-90).

After 1585 Aldegonde retired from politics, devoting himself principally to letters. Among other writings he wrote the Psalms in rhyme and began

a translation of the Bible as a commission from the Dutch States-General, but completed only a small part of it.   vDZ.

A. A. van Schelven, *Marnix van St. Aldegonde* (Utrecht, 1939); W. F. Dankbaar, *Hoogtepunten uit het Ned. Calvinisme in de 16e Eeuw* (Haarlem, 1946), Chap. II, 41-85: "Marnix van St. Aldegonde en zijn betekenis voor de vestiging van de Nederl. Geref. Kerk"; G. Brandt, Hist. der Ref. I (Amsterdam, 1671); *N.N.B.Wb.* I, 1307; *ML* III, 43.

Aldekerk, a village about ten miles northwest of Crefeld, Germany, from which the first Mennonites moved to Crefeld in 1609. For example, Herman op den Graeff (see **Graeff**), from Aldekerk, became a citizen of Kempen in 1605, and from there went to Crefeld. The Crefeld de Greiff family does not come from Aldekerk as is asserted in *ML* I, 20, but from Niedersaulheim.

                                              NEFF.
Rembert, *Wiedertäufer,* 579; Fabricius, *Erläuterung zum gesch. Atlas der Rheinpr.* V, 265; *ML* I, 20.

Alden Conservative Amish Mennonite Church, one mile west of Alden, Erie Co., N.Y., a member of the C.A.M. Conference, was organized in 1925 with about 25 members. In 1922 and soon after, settlers moved into this new section from various states and also from Canada. Services were held in the Millgrove and Town Line Methodist churches. The present meetinghouse was built in 1927. The 1953 membership was 160. Ministers who served this congregation are John Bontrager, John Helmuth, Noah D. Miller, Joseph J. Miller, and David Beachy. In 1934 a branch Sunday school was established near Williamsville, N.Y., where ten years later a new mission building was erected. Here the average attendance is 40, with Preacher Richard Bender in charge. David Beachy is the present Alden bishop, with Joe Miller assistant minister.

                                              J.B.
Aldendorp, Goris Hendriks van, a Mennonite preacher of the Flemish congregation in Utrecht, Holland, 1649-72, who, together with A. van Heuven, Johan Andries van Aken, and Dr. Willem van Maurick, sided with the party of Galenus Abrahamsz de Haan (*q.v.*) in the quarrel at Utrecht. The opposing party was led by Robert van Hoogvelt. The cause of the strife was van Maurick's preaching in the Waterlander congregation in Rotterdam and the idea that the head of each family had the right to serve communion in his own home. The majority were on Aldendorp's side. Their opponents, supported by seventeen outside ministers (van Braght and B. van Weenigem the most outstanding among them), secured the aid of the city authorities and thus won the argument (*Wydtloopiger verhael van de Beklaeglijcke onlusten . . . binnen Utrecht,* Utrecht, 1662). These four preachers published *Een Belijdenisse, aengaende de voornaemste Leerstucken . . .* (Utrecht, 1659). This confession is not entirely trinitarian. C. Gentman, a Reformed preacher, wrote a booklet refuting it, *Eenige Aanteekeningen over een belijdenisse . . .* (1662). Aldendorp wrote *Extract uyt een Brief van Seecker Vriendt . . .* (Leyden, 1662). On Aug. 12, 1661, the civil authorities forbade the four preachers to preach

under penalty of 100 guilders. Their suspension lasted until Aug. 4, 1664; but the next year the congregation of Utrecht was divided into two parts, which met separately, and this division was not healed until 1675, three years after Aldendorp's death. (*DB* 1916, 145-94, *et passim; Catalogus Amst.,* 119, 120; *ML* I, 20.) K.V., vDZ.

Alderfer (Altaffer), a Swiss family name found among the Mennonites of eastern Pennsylvania, in the G.C.M. and M.C. groups. Immigration records indicate that a Frederick Aldorfer arrived in Pennsylvania in 1732, and another Frederick Aldoerfer a year later. At this writing it seems impossible to identify them with certainty. One of them is the ancestor of a large number of Mennonites living chiefly in Montgomery Co., Pa., today. He was a member of the Salford Mennonite congregation of this county in 1739; Mennonites now living in that area are undoubtedly his descendants. One of the well-known members of this family is Dr. Harold F. Alderfer of the faculty of Pennsylvania State College. Three of the ordained members of the Franconia Conference (MC) today bear the name Alderfer. Another prominent member of the Salford Alderfer family was Alvin C. Alderfer (1869-1941), late treasurer of the Eastern District Conference (GC).

The other Alderfer immigrant settled at Quittaphilia Creek, Lebanon County. According to Maurice W. Altaffer, United States Consul General in Bremen, Germany (1950), the family lived in that area for two or three generations; then the consul's ancestors located in the Shenandoah Valley, Virginia, for several generations, after which they settled in Williams County, northwestern Ohio. For many generations this branch of the family has been Reformed, although Mr. Altaffer believes that his Mennonite ancestors migrated from the neighborhood of Zürich, Switzerland, to the Palatinate in the 17th century and later to Lebanon Co., Pa. James Y. Heckler, a historian of Salford Twp., Pa., believed that the 1732 Alderfer immigrant settled in Salford, and that the 1733 immigrant located in Lancaster County. (It must have been Lebanon County.) J.C.W.

Alders, Abraham, b. Oct. 12, 1702, in Goch, Germany, d. Jan. 24, 1774, the son of Govert Alders and Elisabeth Walien (both died in 1709), reared by his uncles Anthony Smits (d. 1715) and Peter Luterbach in Hoorn. After 1720 he lived in Duisburg, where he built a textile factory, which was later moved to Goch. In 1724 he married Katharine ten Cate. In 1729 the Mennonite church in Goch (Elder, Peter Wendelen) chose him as minister. His funeral sermon was preached by Jelle Brouwer of Cleve. (*Lijkreden op Abraham Alders, Leeraar te Goch,* Cleve, 1774; *ML* I, 20.) K.V.

Alecowitz (Alexowitz), a Bruderhof of the Hutterian Brethren near Eibenschitz (*q.v.*) in Moravia, founded about 1552 and existing until 1623. (*ML* I, 20.) HEGE.

Alenson, Hans Arentsz, Dutch Mennonite preacher, born at Hondschoote in Flanders, fled to Holland, lived at Leiden, Amsterdam (after about 1591), Leeuwarden (after 1598), Delft (about 1615), and Haarlem (after about 1625), died at an advanced age in April or May 1644 at Haarlem. At first he belonged to the Flemish Mennonites, but after being banned he joined the Waterlander group. By trade he was at first a grocer and afterwards a weaver. The hypothesis of some art experts, Hofstede de Groot and Valentiner among others, that the two portraits in the Penrhyn Collection in England, painted by Rembrandt in 1634, represent Hans Alenson and his wife, has proved to be false. The pictures in question are those of the English clergyman John Ellison of Norwich and his wife.

Alenson is known only as the author of the very important *Tegen-Bericht op den voorreden van't groote Martelaer-Boeck der Doopsgezinde,* which was published at Haarlem in 1630 from the press of Jan Pietersz Does. The booklet was reprinted in *Bibliotheca Reformatoria Neerlandica* VII (1910), pages 139 to 266. The purpose of the *Tegen-Bericht* is to show (1) that Hans de Ries and the other liberal Waterlander and Flemish compilers of the first edition of the *groote martelaarsboek* had not, as the strictly orthodox Frisian publishers of the third edition of 1626 had charged, falsified the martyrs' confessions and omitted part of the Melchior Hofmann doctrine of the incarnation (*q.v.*); and (2) that Menno and his contemporaries had in many points been more liberal than the unbending Frisians claimed in what they proclaimed in 1626 to be the true teachings of Menno. The value of the booklet lies in all the information which Alenson gives from his personal acquaintance and conversation with several friends of Menno who had outlived him, as well as with various martyrs. S.C., vDZ.

BRN VII, 139-266; H. F. Wijnman, *Jaarboek Amstelodamum,* 1931, 81 ff.; *ML* I, 20.

Aleph Jacobs, an Anabaptist martyr, persisted in his view that all that took place in the Catholic Church was idolatry, and was burned at the stake on June 28, 1553, at Leeuwarden, Dutch province of Friesland, with two other martyrs. vDZ.

Inv. Arch. Amst. I, No. 746; J. Reitsma, *Honderd jaren Kerkherv. in Friesland* (Leeuwarden, 1876) 63.

Alexander, an Anabaptist martyr, a schoolmaster by vocation, also at one time a sexton, leader of the Anabaptists in Thuringia, executed in November 1533 in Frankenhausen, Germany. Wappler (100) calls him "one of the noblest figures in the Anabaptist movement" of Middle Germany and responsible for the vigorous spread of Anabaptism in northern Thuringia and the southern Harz region. He was baptized at the end of 1529, probably by Volkmar Bernhard at Esperstedt, and was continuously active in an itinerant ministry of evangelism until his arrest at Frankenhausen in July 1532. He baptized many in the territory between Fulda and Frankenhausen. Wappler (348-51) presents his "confession" of July 8, 1533, **which**

actually consists of his answers to the court inquisitor and is a valuable account of his activity as well as his methods and teachings.   H.S.B.

W. Wiswedel, *Bilder* I, 88 f.; E. Jakobs, "Die Wiedertäufer im Harz," in *Ztscht des Harz-Vereins für Gesch. . . .* XXXII (1899) 423-536; P. Wappler, *Die Täuferbewegung in Thüringen von 1526-1584* (Jena, 1913) 92-101, 348-52, *et passim.*

Alexander I, Czar of Russia (1801-25), great benefactor of the Mennonites, confirmed the great charter of privileges of his father and predecessor, Paul I, of Sept. 6, 1800, and took a friendly interest in them. To the Molotschna colony he made a gift of 6,000 rubles for a church building. Good evidence of his paternal benevolence are his two visits to the Mennonite colonies on May 21, 1818, and in 1825 shortly before his death (Epp, 208). His benevolent friendly manner in his dealings with the Russian Mennonites and in his acceptance of their simple hospitality, is still remembered in some families. Many Mennonite villages in Russia were named after him or his grandson Alexander II, such as Alexanderkrone, Alexanderfeld, Alexandertal, Alexanderheim.   NEFF.

Friesen, *Brüderschaft;* D. H. Epp, *Johann Cornies, Züge aus seinem Leben und Wirken* (Berdyansk, 1909); *ML* I, 21.

Alexander II, Czar of Russia (1855-81), son of Nicholas I, nephew of Alexander I, very favorable to the Mennonites, confirmed their charter of privileges. For their faithful (nonmilitary) service in the Ukrainian war (1854) and the Turkish war (1877) he presented the Mennonites of Chortitza with a handwritten document expressing his royal thanks. To the Mennonites of the Molotschna he expressed his good wishes "for the praiseworthy manner in their quartering and feeding of 6,000 immigrant Bulgarians." Significant was the position of the czar on the question of the bearing of arms (1871-74), when the Mennonites were to be drafted into armed service upon the passing of the law of universal conscription. He sent his adjutant, Count Totleben, into the colony to prevent their emigration to America, and granted their request for freedom from military service on the condition that their young men of military age serve in forestry (*q.v.*). (*ML* I, 21.)   NEFF.

Alexander de Bode, an Anabaptist martyr, a joiner by trade, who is not in the martyr books, was executed in Antwerp at the Steen prison on Nov. 19, 1558, because he had been rebaptized. We do not know the manner of his execution. This martyr is identical with Sander Hendriksz (*q.v.*). (Génard, *Antw. Arch.-Blad* VIII, 452, 465; XIV, 24 f., No. 269.)   vDZ.

Alexanderfeld, a village in the Mennonite settlement of Zagradovka in the Russian province of Kherson, 70 miles north of the city of Kherson, near the Ingulets, a tributary of the Dnieper, was founded in 1872 by Mennonites from the Molotschna colony. The railroad station was Nikolo-Kozelsk (17 miles distant) and the postal station was Tiege. The population was reduced in 1909 by the emigration of 100 persons to Siberia (Tomsk province, Barnaul district) and in 1913

numbered 220. Half of these belonged to the Mennonite Church (united with the Nikolaifeld Mennonite Church) and half to the Mennonite Brethren (united with the Tiege Mennonite Brethren Church). The inhabitants were almost exclusively engaged in farming and cattle raising. There were two steam mills in Alexanderfeld. The village embraced 3,500 acres of land. In 1908 the population was 411.

During the Russian Revolution of 1917 and especially at the time of the occupation of Zagradovka by Machno (*q.v.*), the Mennonites suffered very severely and some of the villages were completely destroyed.

The collectivization of Alexanderfeld was begun in 1930, and resulted in the exile of many kulaks. Deportation was repeated in 1937-38, when during one night 62 men and 3 women of Alexanderfeld, of a total population of 350, were exiled. During the German invasion of the Ukraine at the beginning of World War II the Soviets first evacuated all men between the ages of 18 and 50 and then the total population. Most of the people, however, fell into the hands of the German army and were returned to their homes. In October 1943 the population of Alexanderfeld left Russia with the others to be settled in the Warthegau, Germany. When Germany collapsed, the Red army sent many of them back to Russia while the remaining have found new homes in Canada and Paraguay. (G. Lohrenz, *Sagradowka,* Rosthern, 1947; *ML* I, 21.)

HEGE, C.K.

Alexanderfeld Church of God in Christ, Mennonite congregation, near Hillsboro, Marion Co., Kan. The first members assembled for worship services in the Gnadenau school, which was later purchased for that purpose. In 1910 the Mennonite Brethren church seating 250 was purchased and moved to the present location. John D. Dueck was the first resident minister, serving 1887-1918. In 1919 his son David H. Dyck was ordained to the ministry and served until 1943. The present minister is Jona Dyck, who followed P. G. Hiebert. Several deacons have been ordained in the history of the church, of whom John M. Jost is now active. Most of the members are of Dutch-North German-Russian descent and many speak the Low German dialect in their homes. The Sunday school was organized in 1913. A sewing circle, started in 1921, helps to support mission stations, hospitals, and MCC relief work. Sunday-school enrollment is 122, and church membership 88 (1953).   P.G.H.

Alexanderfeld (also called Alexandrodar, *q.v.*), a village in the Mennonite district Wohldemfürst-Alexanderfeld, Russia, of the Kuban settlement. (*ML* I, 21.)   HEGE.

Alexanderheim, a village of the Chortitza (Russia) Mennonites on leased land, in which there was after 1889 a subsidiary of the Einlage Mennonite Brethren congregation (Einlage, *q.v.*) in the district of Pavlograd, province of Ekaterinoslav. (Friesen, *Brüderschaft,* 451; *ML* I, 21.)   NEFF.

Alexanderkrone, the name of several Mennonite villages in Russia, a school, and a congregation.

1. A village in the Mennonite settlement of Zagradovka (*q.v.*) in the province of Kherson, not far from the Ingulets, a tributary of the Dnieper. Railroad station Nikolo-Kozelsk (10 miles distant). The village was founded in 1883, numbered (1912) 110 inhabitants, all members of the Tiege (*q.v.*) Mennonite Church and all farmers. (For later developments see **Zagradovka**.) (*ML* I, 21.) HEGE.

2. A village in the southwest part of the Mennonite settlement on the Molotschna (*q.v.*), on the left bank of the Yushanlee River, province Taurida, 65 miles northwest of Berdyansk, one of the latest villages of the Halbstadt district, was founded in 1857 and in 1913 numbered 550 inhabitants, who were mostly engaged in agriculture. To the village belonged some 8,500 acres of land. The soil was fertile, but not suitable for winter wheat. Besides an elementary school, in which two teachers taught 60 children (in 1913), there was in Alexanderkrone after 1906 a three-class Russian business school with about 90 students. The Alexanderkrone Mennonite Church (*q.v.*) had a church building from 1890 on. The village had a tile factory, a steam mill, and two windmills. (Concerning the later developments, see **Molotschna**.) (*ML* I, 21.) HEGE.

3. The Alexanderkrone Mennonite Church, Molotschna settlement, province Taurida, originally a branch of the Margenau Mennonite Church (*q.v.*). In 1890 the congregation became independent and built in the village of Alexanderkrone a spacious church, in which services were held every Sunday. Footwashing was observed with communion. The Alexanderkrone Mennonite Church (in 1913) numbered 1,700, of whom 600 were baptized members. The members, including the inhabitants of the neighboring Kleefeld, Lichtfelde, Steinfeld, Neukirch, and Prangenau, were chiefly farmers. The church participated in mission work and carried on social work. Its ministers were unsalaried. Heinrich Koop (b. Nov. 18, 1844) served as its first elder (after 1901). (For later developments see **Molotschna**.) (*ML* I, 22.) H.K.

Alexanderkrone Business School in the village of that name in the Molotschna settlement, South Russia, was founded by a school union (*Schulverein*) as a Zentralschule in 1906. In spite of great difficulties with the government, the school opened with 3 teachers and 69 students; an increasing student body soon required the engagement of another teacher. A large beautiful building housed the school. In 1916 it was converted into a business college in order to secure more rights. But it did not exist long as such. Soon after the outbreak of the Revolution it passed into communist control and was reorganized to fit their pattern. A series of able teachers served the school, among them I. Regehr, D. P. Enns, G. H. Peters, and H. Neufeld. H.G.

Alexandertal Secondary School was located in the Alexandertal Mennonite settlement (*q.v.*) in the province of Samara, Russia. This school differed somewhat from the pattern of the Zentralschule (see Vol. II, 153). The Zentralschule was a parochial Mennonite Secondary School in Russia supported and controlled by the Mennonite constituency. The Alexandertal Secondary School was supported by government funds, although religious instruction and German were strongly emphasized. C.K.

Alexandertal, the last of the original Mennonite settlements to be founded in Russia, located in the district and province of Samara (today Kuibyshev), on the left bank of the Volga. The distance from the edge of the settlement to the town of Samara was about 85 miles and to the Volga 56 miles. It lay somewhat to the northeast of the intersection of the 54° latitude and 68° longitude on the Kondurtcha, a tributary of the Sok, which flows into the Volga north of Samara (see map of settlement).

The leader of the colony was Claas Epp Sr., who was also one of the founders of the Am Trakt settlement in 1854 in the southern part of the province of Samara, also on the left bank of the Volga, opposite Saratov (father of Claas Epp Jr., *q.v.*, who led a group to Central Asia).

The immigration began on Aug. 20, 1859, and was not finished until about 1870. The Russian government put a tract of some 26,500 acres at the disposal of the settlement, measuring 10 miles from north to south and 8½ miles from east to west.

The settlers were Mennonites of West Prussia, who stemmed from the Grosse Werder district east of Danzig, and from the Graudenz lowlands farther up the Vistula River. The first villages founded were Alexandertal and Neuhoffnung, followed by Mariental, Grotsfelde, Muravyevka. Each settler received a plot of 65 dessiatines (approximately 175 acres). Later came the settlement of the villages of Orloff, Liebental, Schönau, Lindenau, and Marienau. At the turn of the century the last three named united into a single unit under the name of Krasnovka. The later settlers received smaller farms of 32 to 40 dessiatines.

The colloquial language of these settlers was exclusively German; the original immigrants retained their *Plattdeutsch,* but with few exceptions the children were taught High German.

Farms were given only to the Mennonite immigrants. With them had come a number of families of smiths, carpenters, cabinetmakers, shoemakers, and tailors, mostly Lutherans with a few Catholics, who received no land, but were given home sites on the communal land.

The population table of the Alexandertal settlement in 1913, which had in the following years increased, follows:

POPULATION TABLE OF THE ALEXANDERTAL VOLOST AND VICINITY IN 1913

Prepared by M. Fast

Name of Village	Church	Fam.	Souls
1. Alexandertal	Mennonite	41	199
(founded 1859)	Brethren	5	22
	Lutheran	8	29
	Rom. Catholic	1	5
	Total	55	255

Name of Village	Church	Fam.	Souls
2. Neuhoffnung	Mennonite	17	97
(founded 1860)	Brethren	3	20
	Lutheran	5	25
	Total	25	142
3. Mariental	Mennonite	15	77
(founded 1863)	Brethren	6	25
	Lutheran	5	35
	Total	26	137
4. Grotsfelde	Mennonite	7	40
(founded 1863)	Brethren	1	5
	Total	8	45
5. Muravyevka	Mennonite	14	53
(founded 1863)	Lutheran	2	6
	Total	16	59
6. Orloff	Mennonite	11	42
(founded 1867)	Brethren	3	14
	Lutheran	3	17
	Total	17	73
7. Liebental	Mennonite	6	24
(founded 1870)	Brethren	1	4
	Lutheran	4	13
	Total	11	41
8. Krasnovka	Mennonite	22	119
(founded 1870)	Brethren	1	7
	Lutheran	2	6
	Total	25	132
Vicinity	Mennonite	46	246
	Brethren	7	34
	Total	53	280
Summary	Mennonite	79	877
	Brethren	27	131
	Lutheran	29	131
	Catholic	1	5
	Total	236	1144

The lands taken over by these settlers were steppes inhabited by nomad Asiatic tribes: Bashkirs, Kalmucks, and Kirghiz, remnants of the Mongolian invasion of 1240-1480, who retreated back into the trans-Caspian steppes when Ivan III (the Terrible) annexed these regions into the Muscovite empire, whereas the Tatars of the Kazansk hordes settled here. The colonized area rises from the Kondurtcha, along which the meadow of the colony lay, toward the west and forms a rolling hilly landscape crossed by some forests and groves. The soil consists of a layer of humus (black) about 28 inches in depth on a subsoil of red clay. The land is very fertile and has adequate precipitation; all sorts of grain thrive on it: wheat, rye, oats, barley, and millet, as well as potatoes and vegetables.

The climate is continental with very warm summers, so that watermelons thrive, and cold, snowy winters, which are gradually growing milder. The transitions in spring and fall are usually short.

Winter begins in November, and the spring sowing begins April 1-15.

In a wide arc west and north of the Alexandertal settlement were the Lutheran settlements with a sprinkling of Roman Catholics; most of these settlers came after the Polish revolution of 1863. Whereas in the north and south the colonial land bordered immediately upon native Russian villages, and in the east was bounded by the Kondurtcha, in a wider circumference were the villages of new colonists from the southern provinces of Russia, most of them from the Ukraine, and interspersed with them some Baltic settlements. Then there were also the villages of the Mordvinians, Russians, Chuvashes, and Tatars, from which the Mennonites recruited their laborers. In the north, only about 3½ miles from Mariental was the large market town of Koshki (which was also the postal center of Alexandertal), where one could hear seven or eight different languages spoken on the weekly market days.

With few exceptions the Mennonites were farmers. Most of the immigrants brought with them some capital and were able to buy neighboring unsettled land. The farms were isolated as they had been in West Prussia rather than in the village pattern, and about half of the buildings were of massive stone, and the rest of logs. There were no closed villages.

Since the colony was so far removed from distribution centers and also because at the time of settlement Russia was producing an oversupply of agricultural products, land was correspondingly low in price. In the first years of the settlement a farm could be bought for 600-800 rubles ($300-400); at the turn of the century cultivated land sold for nearly ten times that price.

Beginning in 1895 an upward trend was noticed in financial prosperity, brought about by Russian export of grain and the organization of a dairy co-operative by the Mennonites, who engaged experts from Estonia to manage it. Several years later Bernhard von Bergen, one of the members of the co-operative, took over the organization and established on his land another at Mariental, while an Estonian cheesemaker set up dairies in Orloff and Krasnovka. Another factor in producing prosperity was the opening of a railroad line extending to Melekess, a town 35 miles distant from the colony, which made it possible to import seed wheat from Sweden (since the varieties the colonists had tried were not very successful on the soil of the colony) and to organize a profitable business in farm machinery. The native population in a very short time had adopted the methods of the German farmers.

In 1910 the bridge over the Volga was begun, and the railroad line completed from Melekess to Asiatic Russia which passed the colony about three miles away, touching the market village Koshki. Pogruznaya now became the station where the colonists shipped their produce. All of these factors contributed to the financial prosperity of the colonies before World War I. In the wake of prosperity enterprise increased. Mennonites built and prosperously operated power mills in and beyond the colony. Various kinds of shops and factories for the manufacture of farm machinery and soap were established.

In the early 1880's the Mennonite farmers bought the Rettungstal land complex, which bordered on Lindenau. This land had been assigned to Lutheran settlers, but had never been occupied. Individual Mennonites bought farms in Starey Buyam, Kolyzovka, Bessovka, and Alexandrovka, and settled on them. And finally in 1898 a group of young Mennonite farmers took over in hereditary lease with option on purchase, a large tract of steppe land of about 4,900 acres 3 miles from the railroad station Bezenchuk, 40 miles from Alexandertal in the south of the Samara province. Other fields were bought of the Russian natives, until finally about 27,000 were in the hands of Mennonite enterprise, besides the equal amount of land in the mother colony.

The first village school was built in Neuhoffnung by the people of Alexandertal and Neuhoffnung. Similar schools were built in Mariental, Muravyevka, and Krasnovka. These schools were supported and the teachers paid by the villages. At first only German was taught in these schools; under Alexander III (1881-94), however, in the train of the program of Russianization the Russian language became compulsory. Whereas the immigrants could speak very little Russian, their children mastered the language. The secondary school (*Ministerial-Schule*) instituted by the Russian government in Alexandertal also contributed to their mastery of Russian; the teachers were paid by the government, and the buildings were maintained by the colony. In 1917 the colony took entire charge of this school, making it a *Fortbildungsschule* with the program of a *Progymnasium*.

For purposes of insurance the Alexandertal colony was a subsidiary of the Molotschna Mutual Fire Insurance Company (*q.v.*) (fire elder since 1895 was Heinrich Görz). Alexandertal had additional agencies for insurance against hail, theft of horses, hauling, and the replacement of grain lost by fire. In 1907 an agricultural union was formed which maintained experimental fields and worked for the improvement of horse and cattle breeding.

The village of Alexandertal was the center of the settlement. It was the site of the secondary school, the church, and the regional government, since the colony constituted a closed political unit or *volost* and closed community or *Gemeindebezirk*.

In the early days of the settlement religious services were held in a sod hut (*zemlyanka*), then in the Neuhoffnung village school and in a private house in Mariental, until the church was built in Alexandertal in 1866. This congregation had about 1,000 souls including the children. Services were all held in German. Ministers were chosen from the congregations and received no salary. The

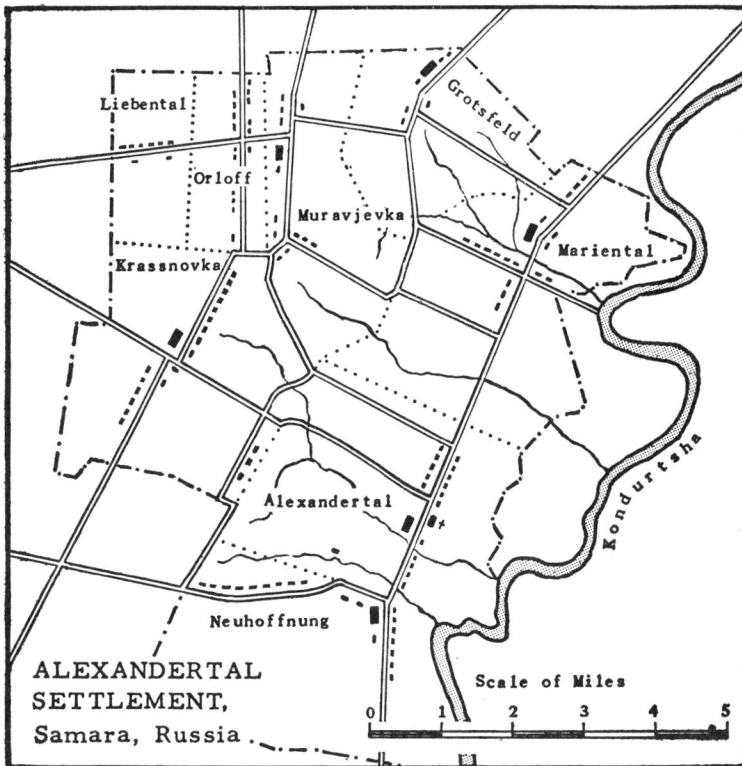

ALEXANDERTAL
SETTLEMENT,
Samara, Russia.

Scale of Miles

first elder was Dietrich Hamm, b. December 12, 1814, in Fürstenwerder in West Prussia, ordained to the ministry at Ladekopp, West Prussia, in 1852, ordained an elder in Alexandertal in 1862. He was followed by Jacob Toews (*q.v.*), Mariental, and at his resignation by Johann Wiebe (*q.v.*), Schoenau, then Jakob Regehr (*q.v.*), Mariental (b. 1841 at Heubuden, West Prussia), who served the congregation until 1918. Then he was succeeded by his son Eduard Regehr, and when Eduard was exiled by the Communist government, by Heinrich Penner (*q.v.*), Alexandertal, who was the last elder of the congregation.

Church discipline was exercised in the congregation. Religious instruction was given in the secondary school by the ministers. The congregation with a member of the *Allgemeine Mennonitische Bundeskonferenz* and was visited by traveling evangelists. It contributed to the support of the school for the deaf in the Molotschna, the mental hospital Bethania, the mission of the Dutch Mennonites in Sumatra and Java, and also did missionary work among the native population of the neighboring villages. The needy of the congregation were cared for by deacons.

In 1877 some of the members joined the Mennonite Brethren (*q.v.*), leaving the Alexandertal church. When their numbers were large enough, this group built a church at Mariental (*q.v.*). But since the Alexandertal church was also the social center, the new group no longer felt at home in the colony, and many emigrated to other settlements.

The Revolution of 1917 caused serious unrest, which could at first be settled by skilled negotiations, but soon threatened the economic and religious life. During the time of the NEP there was a religious revival, in which about half of the losses of membership were regained. But arrests were made more and more frequently by the new government; uneasiness caused some of the colonists to emigrate. In 1929 with the execution of the policy of the "general line," or complete collectivization and liquidation of all private ownership, came the group exile of Alexandertal colonists to the compulsory labor camps along the Arctic, to Siberia and Kazakhstan, where many found a premature death under the most difficult conditions. In the colony area the settlers remaining were forcibly united into collectives. Epidemics and catastrophic starvation snatched many away. During World War II the remnants of the Alexandertal Mennonites were without exception banished to Kazakhstan and other regions, so that the colony has been liquidated and has ceased to exist. (*ML* I, 22 f.)   B.J.H.

Alexandertal, a name of several Mennonite villages in South Russia.

1. A village in the southeast of the Molotschna Mennonite colony, district of Gnadenfeld, province of Taurida (Russia), founded in 1820. It embraced 3,300 acres and (1913) numbered about 400 inhabitants. The village had one steam mill, one windmill, and one store. (For later developments see **Molotschna.**) (*ML* I, 24.)

2. A village in the south of the Mennonite-leased colony in the volost of Verchnerogatchik, district of Melitopol, province of Taurida (Russia), post office Verchnerogatchik, railroad station Nikopol, 20 miles away, located in a valley, founded in 1867, numbered 279 (1911) inhabitants, all Mennonites, and all farmers. In the village there was a school which gave both German and Russian instruction. The Mennonites were members of the Fürstenland Mennonite Church.   HEGE.

Alexanderwohl was the name of a Mennonite village and congregation in the Molotschna settlement, Russia, and is also the name of a Mennonite congregation in Kansas.

1. *Russia.* The Alexanderwohl Mennonite village and congregation originated in 1821 when 21 Mennonite families left their home community near Schwetz and Kulm (*q.v.*) along the Vistula River to settle in the Ukraine. The settlement near Schwetz was known as Przechovka or Kleinsee. At exactly what time this settlement and the congregation here originated is unknown. There is, however, a very old church record in existence which records 1640 as the date of birth of a member. This church record was likely started after the middle of the 17th century and is today in possession of the Alexanderwohl Mennonite Church in Kansas. The title page reads: *Die Erste Stamm Nahmen Unserer Bisher so genante Oude Vlamingen oder Groningersche Mennonisten Societaet alhier in Preusen.* The record begins with a list of names common in the congregation at that time and occasionally states from where the bearer of the name came. Some of the more common names in the church record during the 17th and 18th century are Becker, Buller, Cornels, Decker, Dirks, Funck, Jantz, Isaak, Koehn, Nachtigahl, Pankratz, Penner, Ratzlaff, Richert, Schellenberger, Wedel, Frey, Schmidt, Sperling, Unrau, Voth. It is interesting to note that most of these names are still common in the Alexanderwohl community in Kansas.

From the reference to "Old Flemish" or "Groninger Mennonites" one is not to understand that the congregation came in a body from the Netherlands, but this indicates that it was affiliated with the Flemish, not the Frisian, conference. The "Old" indicates that the congregation originally had very conservative leanings. According to the names, some of the original members must have come from the Netherlands, some from the neighboring Lutherans, and one, Schellenberger, from the Hutterian Brethren.

The first known elder of the congregation was Berend Ratzlaff. Others who served in Prussia were Benjamin Wedel I, 1742-85; Jakob Wedel, 1754-91; Peter Jantz, 1774-1810; Benjamin Wedel II, 1766-1813; Peter Wedel I, 1769-1814?; and Peter Wedel II, 1792-1821. Under the leadership of Peter Wedel the group moved from Prussia to Russia in 1821. Wedel was succeeded by Jakob Buller (1827-1901) who led the congregation from

Russia to America in 1874. Here he was followed by Peter Balzer (1874-1907), Heinrich Banman (1843-1933), P. H. Unruh (1881-1943), and Philip A. Wedel (1897-1967).

From time to time Mennonites left the Schwetz settlement organizing new congregations at different places. In 1765 some families founded the Brenkenhoffswalde-Franztal (q.v.) settlement in Mark Brandenburg. Most of these later went to Russia, establishing such villages as Gnadenfeld (q.v.) and Waldheim (q.v.) on the Molotschna in the neighborhood of Alexanderwohl, with whom they kept in contact.

When Elder Peter Wedel led a group of 21 families of the Schwetz congregation to the Molotschna settlement in 1821, they are said to have been met by Czar Alexander I who wished them well in their undertaking. Hence the name "Alexanderwohl" for the village and congregation established in the heart of the Molotschna settlement. In 1823 a few more families joined them. In 1903 the village had a population of 630 and owned a complex of 6,210 acres of land. In addition to cattle and sheep, wheat was raised in great quantities. Johann Cornies (q.v.) was the benefactor of this community also, aiding it in many cultural and economic gains. The Alexanderwohl Mennonite congregation erected a church building in 1865 after having conducted services in the school building for some time.

After Elder Jakob Buller migrated to America with the Alexanderwohl congregation, the new occupants of the village organized a new Alexanderwohl congregation. However, this congregation was served by the elders of the Margenau Mennonite Church. Before World War II about one third of the village belonged to the Mennonite Brethren Church. During the Revolution Alexanderwohl suffered like the rest of the Molotschna settlement and World War II brought exile and evacuation which spelled the end of Alexanderwohl in Russia.

2. America. When in the 1870's a new conscription law was in preparation in Russia, the Alexanderwohl Mennonite Church became the center of conferences and migration activities. Its elder Jakob Buller (q.v.) served as delegate to both St. Petersburg and America. Upon his return from his inspection trip to America in 1873, almost the entire village and congregation emigrated with him. This is the only case in the Old Colony and Molotschna settlements where an entire village left as a unit. The Alexanderwohl congregation had some members outside its own village. These and some others that joined them left Alexanderwohl July 20, 1874, crossing the ocean on the S.S. Cimbria and S.S. Teutonia. The Cimbria left Hamburg on July 31, 1874, with 303 adults and 172 children and with Jakob Buller as their leader. After arriving in New York on Aug. 15, the group proceeded to Lincoln, Neb., arriving Sept. 22. From Lincoln they went to Topeka, Kan. In that state their leaders purchased 34 sections of land north of Newton in Marion and McPherson counties at an average of $2.50 per acre in cash. Until homes were built the group lived in an immigration house located on section 33 in Menno Township. Following the pattern to which they had been accustomed in Russia, they established the villages of Grünfeld, Emmethal, Gnadenthal, Gnadenfeld, Blumenfeld, Blumenort, Springfield, Schoenthal, and Steinbach. Gradually the village pattern was abandoned and each settler moved onto his own land. Remnants of some villages can still be recognized.

Dietrich Gaeddert, leader of a group of 203 adults and 104 children, arrived in New York on the Teutonia, Aug. 15, 1874. This group, composed of the remainder of the Alexanderwohl congregation and a few others, settled 20 miles west of Alexanderwohl north of the present-day Buhler, Kan., community and organized the Hoffnungsau Mennonite Church (q.v.). The present Buhler and Inman Mennonite churches are daughter congregations of Hoffnungsau and now (1950) have a total membership of nearly a thousand.

Jakob Buller's group organized the Neu-Alexanderwohl Church in 1874 with 265 members. (The "Neu" was soon dropped.) By 1880 the membership had increased to 467 partly through the reception of young members but also through the addition of new immigrants. During the first years the congregation worshiped in the immigration house and in some of the schools in the various villages. In 1878 the congregation joined the General Conference Mennonite Church and in 1886, 1½ miles northeast of present-day Goessel it erected a large meetinghouse, which has been enlarged and remodeled several times. In 1908, when the congregation had grown to a membership of 884, the Tabor Mennonite Church (q.v.), located five miles southeast of the mother church, was organized with some 150 members. P. H. Richert was its first elder. Again in 1920 when the Alexanderwohl membership had reached 958, the Goessel Mennonite Church (q.v.), located in Goessel, was organized with about 180 members, P. P. Buller serving as the first elder. The spread of the community to the north caused the organization of the Lehigh Mennonite Church (q.v.); the spread to the east, the Walton (q.v.) and Burns (q.v.) Mennonite congregations. Families from the Alexanderwohl community moving to western Kansas organized the Meadow Mennonite Church (q.v.). The present Alexanderwohl community extends from Newton 30 miles north to Hillsboro and Lehigh and more than 15 miles from east to west, making it the largest compact Mennonite settlement in Kansas. In 1950 the membership of the Alexanderwohl Mennonite Church was 968 and the combined membership of the daughter congregations was about 1,200, making a total of 2,168.

The following ministers in addition to the elders have served the Alexanderwohl congregation: Peter Voth, Peter Unrau, Heinrich Richert, Heinrich Goertz, Jakob Richert, Heinrich Banman, Peter Pankratz, C. P. Wedel, C. C. Wedel, T. R. Voth, and A. J. Banman. C. H. Wedel, the first president of Bethel College, came from the Alexanderwohl church.

In addition to public schools, the Alexanderwohl community had a number of parochial schools, outstanding among which were the Emmatal school (*q.v.*) and the school of Peter Balzer (*q.v.*). Gradually the parochial schools disappeared. In 1906 the Goessel Preparatory School (*q.v.*) was started with Peter P. Buller, who taught the school for 18 years, as its first principal. Later the present Goessel High School, a state school, replaced this school. Before the end of the past century the Bethesda Hospital (*q.v.*) and the Bethesda Home for the Aged (*q.v.*) were organized at Goessel.

Most of the Alexanderwohl members are farmers raising wheat and other small grain. A few businesses, shops, stores, and a co-operative are located in Goessel (*q.v.*). Although High German is seldom heard and English has become predominant, Low German is still common in the homes and in social intercourse. Some of the sturdy Mennonite qualities of the old country have been better preserved in the Alexanderwohl community than elsewhere.

Until after World War I all services of the congregation were conducted in the German language. By the end of World War II only an occasional German service was held. Footwashing in connection with the observance of the Lord's Supper was practiced until 1950. The silent kneeling prayer of the congregation at the close of the worship service, traditional in Alexanderwohl, was discontinued early in this century. It was at this time that the organ was introduced into the worship service, causing the gradual discontinuation of the *Vorsänger* system. The congregation maintains a church library and has the usual organizations, such as young people's, women's mission societies, Sunday school, etc.† C.K.

Alexanderwohl Church Record; H. Banman, "Gesch. der Alexanderwohler Menn.-Gem. bei Goessel, Kansas," in *Bundesbote-Kal.*, 1926; B. H. Unruh, "Die Menn. in der Neu-Mark," in *Gem.-Kal.*, 1941; *Menn. Life*, October 1949; *From the Steppes to the Prairies*, ed. C. Krahn (Newton, 1949); *ML* I, 25.

Alexandrodar, a name given to villages and congregations in the Russian Caucasus.

1. *Alexandrodar* (also called Alexanderfeld), a village in the Mennonite colony of Wohldemfürst-Alexanderfeld (*q.v.*) in the Kuban River district, railway station Bogoslovskaya, post office Velikoknyazheskoye, founded in 1864, covered 5,400 acres and in 1912 had a population of 950, mostly Mennonites, belonging in part to the Mennonite Church (who built a church here in 1896), in part to the Mennonite Brethren, and in part to the *Jerusalemsfreunde*. In this community there were two schools, attended by about 200 children. Most of the inhabitants were farmers; there were 32 farms of 135 acres each, and several farms of 37 acres. Only Mennonites were permitted to own land. The adherents of other creeds were for the most part employed in the farm machinery factory at Alexandrodar, which had a good market in the Caucasus. To promote farming, a short-loan bank was established.

2. A congregation of the Mennonite Church in the colony of Wohldemfürst-Alexanderfeld (*q.v.*) on the Kuban (*q.v.*) River, Caucasus district, was established in 1886 by the settling of Mennonites from the Molotschna colony (*q.v.*). The Kuban settlement had been started in 1864 by Mennonite Brethren. The government granted them some of the crown lands along the Kuban River for colonization, each family receiving 135 acres. Nevertheless many returned to their old home and their property was taken over by members of the Mennonite congregations. These united in 1886 to form the Mennonite Church of Alexandrodar on the Kuban. Kornelius Dirks, Elder of the Waldheim congregation (province Taurida), was commissioned by the *Allgemeine Bundeskonferenz der Mennoniten* (*q.v.*) to head the work of the church. From 1887 to 1902 he visited the church several times annually, and in 1902 settled among them. At first services were held in private homes and later in a rented hall; in 1896 the congregation acquired a church building. In 1912 the church had 312 souls (including 174 children), most of whom lived in Alexandrodar and Wohldemfürst; s u b s i d i a r y churches arose in Ebenfeld and Hochfeld. Most of the inhabitants were landowners. Social welfare was carried on in providing for widows, orphans, and the poor by means of an assessment of the members; the church had no other assets. A women's sewing circle contributed to foreign missions through its products. Services were conducted every Sunday and holiday. Preachers served without salary. Hege.

3. *Alexandrodar* Mennonite Church of *Jerusalemsfreunde* was organized by those members of the group coming from Gnadenfeld, Molotschna, to the Kuma River, Caucasia, at the Wohldemfürst (*q.v.*) Mennonite settlement. Nikolai Schmidt (*q.v.*), a former minister of the Mennonite Church, was the leader and minister of this group.

Until 1907 the Sunday services were held alternately in the schools of Wohldemfürst and Alexandrodar. In co-operation with the music association made up of members of all branches of Mennonites, a spacious auditorium was built in 1907, with a seating capacity of 300, for the use of all, where services were held. It was located halfway between the two villages. Services were conducted on alternate Sundays for adults and children. Most of the members were farmers, some were businessmen, etc. In 1912 the church had 93 members over 20 years of age and 100 children. Nikolai Schmidt was succeeded as elder by Isaak Fast (*q.v.*).

4. Seat of the Kuban Mennonite Brethren Church (*q.v.*), founded in 1864, numbered about 375 souls in 1912. (*ML* I, 26.) S.F.

Alexandropol, a subsidiary of the Mennonite Brethren Church at Memrik (*q.v.*), in the Bachmut district, province of Ekaterinoslav (Russia), located on purchased land in the village of Alexandropol and vicinity, founded in 1888 by fifteen Mennonite

Brethren families. Since the population was increasing rapidly, a church seating 400 was erected in 1893; it was closed by the police in 1901, but reopened in the same year. Leaders: Franz Goossen and Cornelius Isaak. (D. H. Epp, *Die Memriker Ansiedlung*, Berdyansk, 1910; *ML* I, 26.) NEFF.

Alexandrovka, a frequently used name for Mennonite villages in Russia.

1. A village not far from the railway station of Gorkoye, in the district of Akmolinsk (*q.v.*), Siberia, founded at the beginning of the 20th century by Mennonites from South Russia.

2. A leased colony of the Mennonites of Chortitza in the province of Ekaterinoslav, Verchnednye-provsk district, also called Kuzmitsky, comprised 4,860 acres of arable land, numbered (1911) 200 souls (40 families), who belonged to the Neu-Chortitza Mennonite Church. (Friesen, *Brüderschaft*.)

3. A village in the Memrik settlement (*q.v.*), volost Golytsenov, district Bachmut in the province of Ekaterinoslav, on the right bank of the Volchya River, south of the railway Ekaterinoslav-Taganrog, post office and railroad station Zhelannaya. The village, like the other nine villages of the Memrik settlement, was founded in 1885 by landless Mennonites from the Molotschna settlement in the province of Taurida and numbered 170 inhabitants (37 families) in 1913, who were predominantly farmers, owning 3,000 acres of arable land. There was a steam mill in the village. In the village school instruction was given in both the Russian and German languages. Most of the inhabitants belonged to the Memrik-Kalinov Mennonite Church. (D. H. Epp, *Die Memriker Ansiedlung*, Berdyansk, 1910.)

4. A settlement in the province of Samara, district Stavropol, whose inhabitants belonged to the Mennonite Church at Alexandertal (*q.v.*) and the Mennonite Brethren at Mariental (*q.v.*), some 20 miles distant. The settlement maintained an electric mill. (*ML* I, 26.) HEGE.

Alexberger, Leonhard, an Anabaptist martyr in Upper Austria, was baptized by Hans Hut (*q.v.*) in Steyr. Since he would not recant, he was beheaded on March 30, 1528, with Hans Schützenacker, Sigmund Pentler, Matth. Pürchinger, Hans Muhr (*q.v.*), and Hans Penzenauer, upon order of King Ferdinand, and then burned. HEGE.

J. Jäkel, *Zur Gesch. der Wiedertäufer in Oberösterreich, und speciell in Freistadt* (*Mus. Jahr. Ber.* XLVII, 1889) 31-35; A. Nicoladoni, *Johannes Bünderlin von Linz* (Berlin, 1893) 74-94.

Alexian Brothers Hospital, Chicago, Ill., the location of the first Civilian Public Service hospital unit to be established during World War II. It opened in March 1942 under the Association of Catholic Conscientious Objectors. At least twelve Mennonites served in the unit, mostly as nurses. Since only male patients were accepted, all nursing personnel was male. Some unit members enrolled in a practical nursing course and some specialized in the study of Chinese language and culture to prepare themselves for possible relief work in China. The Brethren Service Committee administered the

unit during the last months up to the time of its close in July 1946. The unit published a 32-page description entitled *Of Human Importance*. M.G.

Alf, Gottfried F., a Baptist preacher and evangelist in Adamov near Warsaw in Russian Poland, tried to bring about a union of the Baptists and the Mennonites at that place. After he had baptized a small number of Mennonites the movement failed, for he rejected footwashing and nonresistance. NEFF.

Friesen, *Brüderschaft*, 244; E. Kupsch, *Gesch. der Baptisten in Polen, 1852-1932* (Zdunska-Wola, 1932).

Alfalfa County, Okla., in the northwestern part of the state, has two Mennonite churches, a General Conference and a Church of God in Christ, Mennonite. Approximately four fifths of the 125 Mennonites in the county belong to the G.C. congregation. The Mennonite settlement extends into Major County. The first Mennonites to settle in this area came in 1905. J.W.B.

Algemeen Doopsgezind Weekblad is a weekly of eight pages which is published by the Algemeene Doopsgezinde Societeit (first issue Oct. 5, 1946) and is sent to all Dutch Mennonite families, with an edition of 22,000 copies, price 3.25 gilders per year. The editor is S. H. N: Gorter of Apeldoorn, who is assisted by an editorial staff. It is printed by the firm of T. Banda, Kollum. Every four weeks a group of neighboring congregations has insert pages put into the paper with local announcements (schedule of services, etc.) for that group. The Amsterdam congregation has an extra page every two weeks.

The *Algemeen Doopsgezind Weekblad* is a postwar development. *De Zondagsbode* (*q.v.*), published by the A.D.S., was ordered to cease publication by the German occupation authorities, the last number being that of June 21, 1942. After the liberation several numbers of a small paper, *De Noodbrug*, were published. It was largely through the efforts of C. Nijdam, at the time chairman of the A.D.S., that the *Weekblad* came into being; its purpose is to form a bond among all the Mennonite congregations in the Netherlands. vDZ.

Algemeen Emeritaatsfonds voor Doopsgezinde Leeraren (General Fund for the Retirement of Mennonite Ministers) was founded Oct. 24, 1848, and began its work Jan. 1, 1849. The instigation came from the Mennonite pastors in the Zaanstreek, a district near Amsterdam, where there have always been many Mennonites and where there are many congregations. The office of the fund therefore was located in Zaandam. The purpose of the fund is to secure a pension to all pastors who are members, to take effect at the age of sixty-five. In case of disability it is paid earlier. For these two distinct types of cases there are two separate funds; besides this there is a reserve fund in Amsterdam that was endowed by members of the Amsterdam church. The annually required funds are secured from interest on the capital and collections taken in the churches. Not only the ministers are members, but in most cases also the congregations. In this case the congregation pays two thirds of the annual assessment and its minister one third. With the exception of the churches in Friesland, which have their own retirement fund, and three other churches, all the Mennonite churches in the Netherlands are members of the *Emeritaatsfonds.* The Mennonite ministers in Friesland are also practically all members, as were also several congregations and ministers in Germany up to World War II. At the end of 1912 the fund had 117 contributing ministers and 18 pensioners; in addition, 80 Mennonite congregations belonged to the organization. The benevolent effect of the fund can be visualized by considering past achievements; in the first fifty years of its existence it was able to pay out 322,071 guilders to 67 retired ministers.   J.G.B.

Notwithstanding the blessing the fund brought, the administration had to contend with continued anxieties because the financial basis was too weak. In 1928 it was evident that the funds in the future would not be adequate for the requirements; therefore it was decided that the pensionable age would be raised from 65 to 67 years, and that the obligations for old-age insurance should be assumed by the *Algemeene Friesche Levensverzekerings-maatschappij.* By means of these measures the fund again became sound, and in 1937 it was possible to change the eligible age back from 67 to 65 years. In 1943 the fund was closed, that is, from that date no new applicants were accepted. Finally, at the meeting of Oct. 5, 1948, at which time the centennial of the organization was commemorated, the members decided to transfer further responsibility for administration to the *Algemeene Pensioenstichting der A.D.S.* The *Zaanse Fonds,* as the *Algemeen Emeritaatsfonds* for Mennonite ministers was usually called, had completed its course.   vDZ.

Handelingen van de Alg. Vergadering, op 5 Oct. 1948 te Zaandam contains the commemorative speech by Ds. F. H. Pasma; *ML* I, 27.

Algemeene Belydenissen is a booklet published in 1665 by Pieter Arentsz in Amsterdam, reprinted in Haarlem in 1700 and at Rotterdam in 1739. The complete title is *De Algemeene Belydenissen der Vereenighde Vlaemsche, Vriesche en Hooghduytsche Doopsgesinde Gemeynte Gods, waer op van haer de Geestelijcke Ghemeynschap aen de eens-geloovige Doops-gesinde aengeboden in Christelijcke Vrede op verscheyde tijden, met verscheyde Volcken gemaeckt en bevestight is.*

Following the introduction (*Aen den Leser,* signed Amsterdam, Sept. 21, 1665, by Tobias Govertsz van den Wyngaert and Isaack van Vreden), the booklet presents the six confessions of faith: *Concept van Ceulen; Van den Eenigen Godt, Vader, Soon ende Heyligen Geest, En van de Mensch-werdinge des Soons Godts* (the confession of Outerman); *Olyf-tacx; Confessie der Vereenighde Vriesen ende Hooghduytschen; De Artijckelen des Christelijcken Geloofs* (the Dordrecht Confession). The Amsterdam copy adds, with separate pagination and signature, the *Oprecht Verbondt van Eenigheydt.*

Shortly before the split between the Lamists and Zonists in Amsterdam, the wish had been ex-pressed in June 1660, at a conference of conservative leaders at Leiden, to have a new and general edition of the accepted confessions of faith published. After the *Lammerenkrijg* (*q.v.*), when the conservative congregations united among themselves as the Zonists, the wish was carried out. In the first place, says the Foreword, in order to show that "we are still standing unchanged in the teaching of the Gospel, accepted by our forefathers"; in the second place, in order to make the basis of the Zonists known; and in the third place, because some confessions have been sold out and are no longer obtainable.

The third edition of the booklet (1739 at Rotterdam) was published by I.P.S. (J. P. Schabaelje), who added: *de Principale Artykelen des Geloofs eeniger Doopsgez. Gemeente, die men noemt Waterlanders, Vlamingen en Duitschen, getrokken uit haar uit gegevene Confessien.* A second edition had appeared at Haarlem in 1700. (*Catalogus Amst.,* 169-71.)   vDZ.

Algemeene Doopsgezinde Societeit (A.D.S.). In the course of the 17th and 18th centuries in the Netherlands various regional Sociëteits (*q.v.*) or conferences had been organized. These were groupings of Mennonite congregations, usually for some practical end. In 1811 the Algemeene Doopsgezinde Sociëteit (General Mennonite Association) was organized. The direct occasion for its founding was as follows: Since 1735 the Lamist congregation at Amsterdam had a seminary for the training of preachers, and this seminary remained when the various congregations in Amsterdam gradually united. But in consequence of the financial decrees of Napoleon in 1810 the income of the Amsterdam Mennonite Church was no longer adequate to bear the expenses alone. Prof. Hesselink (*q.v.*) set up a plan for the organization of a general association for the purpose of supporting the seminary, and after some discussion with neighboring congregations (Haarlem, Zaandam-Nieuwe Huis, and Zaandam-Oostzijde) whereby a misunderstanding which had arisen between Amsterdam and Haarlem was speedily cleared away, invitations were sent to 132 congregations in the Netherlands to take part. Scarcely 50 of them joined the Sociëteit. Several congregations repudiated the plan; many said that in principle they were in harmony with the plan, but were not in a condition to take part on account of financial weakness.

On May 17, 1811, the regulations were drawn up at a meeting in Haarlem. On Aug. 21 and 22, 1811, the delegates of the 50 congregations met as an executive gathering.

The goal of the Sociëteit was twofold: first it served "to promote preaching service" by supporting the seminary, so that "the preaching of God's Word be done by competent and worthy preachers." The second objective was to guarantee a suitable salary for young men who had completed the course at the seminary, by granting a subsidy to congregations who were unable to raise the necessary funds.

The directorate at first consisted of twenty men, chosen by those member congregations who contributed a satisfactory sum to the treasury of the

A.D.S. Not until 1950 was the old system abolished which gave more votes to one congregaton than to another according to the amount contributed. Representation is henceforth in proportion to the membership of the congregation. In the course of time all Dutch Mennonite congregations have become members of the A.D.S., the last joining in 1870, and some of the congregations in northwest Germany also belong to it. The number of congregational representatives (called *bestuurders*) is at present 66. The directors choose an executive board of about ten to fourteen members which transact the current business.

In the first century of its existence the work of the Societeit was mostly of a financial nature, but through the organization of 1923, planned by P. Feenstra Jr. (*q.v.*), the chairman at that time, this has been largely changed. The new constitution, which became effective on Jan. 1, 1924, called for a concentration of effort; the task of the A.D.S. became more inclusive and covered a wider ground. If the objective of the Societeit in 1811 was the promotion of the service of preaching and matters connected with it, that of 1923 reads: "the promotion of the religious, moral, and directly connected with these, the material needs of the Mennonites, first of all the preaching service among them and also its representation outside of the brotherhood." This outside representation includes for example that the A.D.S. in the name of the Dutch Mennonites could and did discuss with the Mennonites of other countries, with the government, and with other denominations what happened during the war period from 1940 to 1945.

The A.D.S. has from the beginning had a number of committees appointed by the directors. First to be named is the College of Curators, which supervise the seminary. Then later came the Committee for the *Proponenten* (ministerial candidates), the Committee for Spiritual Interests, and the Committee for the Archives of the Congregations. Since the reorganization of 1923 all the different kinds of work done in the Dutch Mennonite brotherhood are now included in the work of the A.D.S.: a committee for supervision of the *Zondagsbode* (*q.v.*), a Mennonite weekly (now the *Algemeen Doopsgezind Weekblad, q.v.*); a committee to look after the scattered Mennonites (diaspora), which sends out visiting preachers and looks up Mennonites who live in places where there is no Mennonite congregation, and which stimulates the formation of new congregations. An efficient *Verhuisdenbureau* keeps the addresses of all the members who move out of a congregation. Of great importance is the committee for *Geestelijke belangen* (spiritual interests), a broad committee, in which representatives of all kinds of movements among the Dutch Mennonites sit, and which serves in an advisory capacity to the Executive Committee. A subdivision of this committee was the committee for *Liturgie,* which published a *Kanselboek* (ministers' manual, *q.v.*) in 1948.

During the German occupation of the Netherlands (1940-45) the Societeit (A.D.S.) became to a still greater degree the center of the brotherhood. It maintained contact with other churches in the I.K.O. (*Inter-Kerkelijk Overleg*). From the I.K.O. various messages were issued to the congregations, protesting against the persecution of the Jews, slave labor, deportation to Germany, and other measures of the occupation. When all independent associations in our brotherhood were prohibited by German regulations (*Elspeetse Vereniging, q.v., Zendingsraad, q.v., Jongerenbond, q.v.*), the A.D.S. temporarily took over.

In respect to finances a great change and improvement came about in the formation of a *Pensioenstichting,* through which appropriate pensions can be given to aged or sick ministers and to their widows. Formerly there were seven Mennonite pension organizations. Since the war the salaries of ministers have been raised (1949). For all of this the congregations pay contributions to the A.D.S. in proportion to their membership.

With other churches the A.D.S. co-operates in the ecumenical union, including such things as the broadcasting of religious services and the religious instruction of children in the grades of the public schools.

In 1949 a two-year correspondence course was begun, called the *kadercursus* (basic course), with eight instructors in various fields (including Old and New Testament and Mennonite history), which has as its objective the awakening of a definite Mennonite life by means of imparting information.

Since 1946 the A.D.S. has published a weekly organ which is sent to all the Dutch Mennonites (22,000 copies), the *Algemeen Doopsgezind Weekblad* (*q.v.*). A publication committee looks after the publication of booklets on Mennonite history and doctrine. Through the agency of the A.D.S. a new hymnal was produced (1944) in order to put an end to the multiplicity of hymnals in use.

Since the reorganization of the A.D.S. the chairmen have been: 1924-29, A. Binnerts Szn., Haarlem; 1929-34, P. B. Westerdijk, Amsterdam; 1934-39, A. H. van Drooge, Deventer; 1939-45, F. H. Pasma, Grouw; 1945-46, C. Nijdam, Zeist; 1946-51, W. F. Golterman, Amsterdam, and H. Craandijk, Amsterdam, since October 1951. The present secretary is R. de Zeeuw; the treasurers are G. H. Rahusen and P. F. Kühler.

An annual report of the meetings of the A.D.S. is issued, which contains also the names of the directors, officers, and students. vdZ.

Verslag van den staat . . . der A.D.S. annually 1812-1951; P. van der Meulen, *De wording der Alg. Doopsgez. Soc.* (Wormerveer, 1947); Sam. Muller, *De Gesch. van het ontstaan en de vestiging der A.D.S.* (Amsterdam, 1861); S. Cramer, *Rede, gehouden bij de herdenking van het 100-jarig bestaan der A.D.S.* (Amsterdam, 1911); P. van der Meulen, "Dutch Menn. Unite During Crisis." *Menn. Life* (July 1948) III, 20-22; ML I, 27.

Algerius, a martyr who is known only through the *Martyrs' Mirror,* which states definitely that he was an Anabaptist. He came from the kingdom of Naples and had as a young student in Padua been admitted to the church through baptism by a brother. Soon thereafter he was thrown into prison;

from here he wrote to his brethren a deeply moving letter, joyfully enthusiastic, showing a thorough knowledge of Scripture. He endured all torture steadfastly. He was sent to Venice and there every means was employed to persuade him to recant. It was in vain. Now he was brought to Rome and delivered to the Pope, who tried in vain to convert him and then gave him over to a most terrible death in 1557. The letter mentioned above deserves to be made accessible to all. Van Bracht characterizes it with these words: "In this letter there is such wisdom, such holiness and dignity that we have read it countless times. Thereby our love to God has been rekindled, as also our zeal not only to live with Christ, but also, if necessity required it, to die for Him and for His truth." (*Mart. Mir.* D 185-90, E 570-73; *ML* I, 27 ff.)   Neff.

Aliessovo, a village in the Mennonite settlement in the district and province of Orenburg (*q.v.*), Russia, railway station Platovka. It lies on a plateau that is cut on the east by a gorge, and bordered on the west by a low mountain range. The village was founded in 1895 by three Mennonite families of South Russia, and was increased in the following years by further immigration. Although six families emigrated to Siberia, the number of families in the village rose to twenty-one (1913). In the village there was a Russian-German public school, which, though under the Ministry of Education, was entirely supported by the inhabitants of the village, who were all Mennonites. (*ML* I, 28.) P.D.

Alij(d)t Henrich Rommertsdochter, an Anabaptist martyr of "Gilthuys in't land van Benten," viz., Gildehaus in the district of Bentheim, Germany. She was seized in the house of Lambrecht Duppijns (*q.v.*) in Haarlem (Holland) on May 23, 1539, and after being tortured was drowned there on May 29, 1539. Alijdt was presumably a follower of David Joris (*q.v.*). (*Bijdr. en Meded. Hist. Genootschap, Utrecht,* XLI, 1920, 201, 208-10.)   vDZ.

Alkmaar, a town in the Dutch province of North Holland, population (1947) 34,837, with 665 Mennonites. Shortly after 1530 Alkmaar and the vicinity were already a center of Anabaptist activity. In 1533 two women from here were taken prisoner and put to death on Feb. 5, 1534, in The Hague. There must have been an active and a rather large circle of Anabaptists, many of whom were put to death in the course of time. Most of these victims were under Münsterite influence.

Slowly the congregation came to more peaceful principles. Leenaert Bouwens (*q.v.*) baptized no less than 123 persons here between 1551 and 1578. It is not certain that Menno visited the Alkmaar congregation. At the siege of Alkmaar by the Spaniards in 1573 the Mennonites aided the magistrates in defending the town, but were exempt from bearing arms.

At the end of the 16th century there were three congregations, a Frisian, a Flemish, and a Waterlander. The last one was the largest. Their preacher was the well-known Hans de Ries (*q.v.*), who began his service here in 1597 or 1598. This congregation held its services in a barn at the Koningsweg (enlarged in 1617) on the site of the present Mennonite church. The Flemish, whose history is almost unknown, united with the Waterlanders in 1674.

The Frisians built a simple barn-church in the Ridderstraat in 1616 (remodeled in 1682). From 1738 there was close co-operation between the Ridderstraat and the Koningsweg congregations, although they were independent. The Frisian congregation belonged to the Frisian Sociëteit and also to the Zonist Sociëteit, and the Waterlander congregation belonged to the Rijper (Waterlander) Sociëteit. In 1738 Martin Schagen was called as preacher of both congregations, and henceforth the two congregations had only one pastor. In 1809 the congregations decided on a full union, and the building in the Ridderstraat was sold. This was due in part to the size of the congregations, both being small (in 1807 Ridderstraat had about 40 members, Koningsweg about 70) and not wealthy. The church at the Koningsweg was used by French soldiers in 1795-97; thereby many old archive papers and books were lost. The church was remodeled in the 19th century; an organ was added in 1819. The congregation, which numbered 105 members (other sources say 98 members in November 1809) on Jan. 1, 1809 (when the union took place), had 240 in 1876. Since then the number of members has risen steadily: in 1898, 469; in 1951, 756.

Since the union in 1738 the congregation has been served by the following ministers: Martin Schagen, 1738-41; Rogerus Buitenpost, 1741-47; Jan de Bleyker, 1747-83; Jan ten Kate, 1783-98; Jacobus David Vissering, 1798-1809; Daniel Ysenbeek, 1809-55; Pieter Bruyn, 1855-62; Hermanus de Boer, 1863-97; Pieter Jacob Glasz, 1898-1910; Herman Westra, 1911-32; Frederik Kuiper, 1932-45; Arend Jan van der Sluis since 1946.

In the congregation there are organizations for the women, the men (*Broederkring*), and the young people, a members' club called "Hans de Ries," which arranges for evening meetings, visits the sick, etc., and a choir. A children's church is maintained in co-operation with the *Nederlandse Protestanten Bond.* There is also a children's Sunday school.   vDZ.

DB 1880, 1882, 1883, 1891, 1909; (J. de Lange Czn.), *Beknopte Gesch. der Doopsgez. Gem. te Alkmaar* (1927); *Inv. Arch. Amst.* II, 1455-69; II a, 4-8.

Allart Janszoon, an Anabaptist martyr, burned at the stake on Dec. 13, 1554, at Leeuwarden in the Dutch province of Friesland, because of his faith, together with Anthonis Fockes.   vDZ.

Inv. Arch. Amst. I, No. 746; Reitsma, *Honderd jaren . . . Kerkherv. in Friesland* (Leeuwarden, 1876) 63.

Allebach (Allenbach, Allebaugh), a Swiss Mennonite family strongly represented in the Franconia Mennonite Conference (MC) of Pennsylvania. The ancestor of this family is said to have been Christian Allebach, one of the members of the Salford (MC) congregation in 1739. One of his descendants was Deacon David G. Allebach (1802-88) of the Towamencin (MC) congregation. Another was the nonagenarian, John Allebach (1805-1902), preacher of the Rockhill congregation (MC), who in turn was the father of Christian B. Allebach (1841-1917), preacher of the Towamencin (MC) congregation. Another descendant was Deacon Joseph B. Allebach (1844-1923) of the Rockhill (MC) congregation. Christian B. Allebach was the father of Alpheus K. Allebach, for a time the superintendent of Eastern Mennonite Home for the Aged at Souderton, Pa. Another member of the Allebach family was David K. Allebach, local historian of Hatfield, Pa. Toward the close of the 19th century one of the teachers in the Mennonite mission school among the Arapahoe Indians at Darlington, Okla., was H. G. Allebach.

Among the early settlers in eastern Pennsylvania were also John and Andrew Allebach who came to America in 1734, both without known descendants.   J.C.W.

Allegany County, Md., lies in the mountainous western neck of the state. Formed from Washington County in 1776, it originally included the present Garrett County, which lies to the west. Garrett was formed from Allegany in 1872.

As early as 1800 Amish settlers were seated on lands in the present area of Garrett County and at present Amish and Mennonites are located in this area. (See **Somerset Co.,** Pa. and **Garrett Co., Md.**)

A Mennonite congregation, member of the Southwestern Pennsylvania Mennonite Conference (MC), is located at Pinto, a village eight miles southwest of Cumberland. This congregation, extending into Mineral Co., W. Va., organized Nov. 27, 1927, currently (1951) numbers 130 members.

A mission outpost, with services every fourth Sunday, is maintained at Flintstone, a village 12 miles east of Cumberland, by the Mennonite churches of Washington County.   I.J.M.

Allegheny (Pa.) Mennonite Church (MC), under the Lancaster Mennonite Conference, in Brecknock Twp., Berks Co., Pa., near Alleghenyville. The first Mennonite settler was Jacob Bauman (1722-70), son of Wendel of Pequea, coming in 1745, who was followed by his brothers Christian and Peter in 1751, also by Peter Eshelman and his sons Jacob and Peter in 1749. Benedict Horning came in 1759. The congregation was organized probably in 1760. Christian Bauman (1724-90) was the first minister. In 1802 Joseph Bauman (1766-1849), his son, was ordained a minister. In 1816 before moving to Waterloo Co., Ont., he preached a fitting farewell sermon under a tree near his home a mile east from the Allegheny Mennonite Church. Between 1807 and 1825 probably 30 members of this congregation moved to Ontario. The congregation worshiped in private homes until 1855, when they built the first meetinghouse, which is still in use. The 1948 membership was 10.   A.M.W.

Allemands Mennonite Church at Allemands, La., is located 30 miles west of New Orleans, La., on U.S. Highway 90, "The Old Spanish Trail." It is a member of the South Central Conference (MC), and had a membership of 36 in 1953. A congregation was organized in the spring of 1918 but existed only a few years because nearly all of the members moved away. In the spring of 1936, C. A. Wenger and wife moved back to Allemands. That fall their son and wife and one daughter with her husband moved to Allemands. Shortly after they were established, bishops A. O. Histand, Doylestown, Pa., and E. S. Hallman, Tuleta, Tex., ordained John E. Wenger as minister and Lester Hackman as deacon. With the exception of these two families, all members are natives. Nearly all are of French descent and Catholic background.   P.H.

Allen, an extinct congregation (MC) in Cumberland Co., Pa.   I.D.L.

Allen County, Ind., is located on the far eastern side of the state, about 60 miles south of the Michigan border, county seat, Fort Wayne. The Mennonites and Amish are located in the northeast quarter of the county, the first settlers having come to Allen County about 1850 directly from Germany and France to settle near Leo. According to the 1949 *Mennonite Yearbook* there are in the county 180 Old Order Amish Mennonites, 143 Conservative Amish Mennonites, and 375 Mennonites (MC); there are also two Evangelical Mennonite churches in the county, with a total membership of about 190. The three Mennonite (MC) churches are the Anderson near Huntertown, the First Mennonite (formerly Mennonite Gospel Mission) in Fort Wayne, and the Leo Mennonite in the town of Leo. There is one Conservative Amish church near Harlan. The two Evangelical Mennonite churches are in Grabill and Fort Wayne.   A.B.E.

Allen County (Ind.) Conservative Amish Mennonite Church had its beginning in October 1921 when a group under the leadership of Bishop John Bontrager started church and Sunday school in the Dicky schoolhouse two miles west of Sherwood, Ohio. A year later Bishop Solomon Swartzentruber and Bishop John Troyer reinstated Bishop Bontrager and Deacon John Helmuth, who had been dismissed by the Old Order Amish Church, to their positions of leadership in the congregation. Later when these men moved to New York, Bishop Swartzentruber had charge of the small flock. In 1929 several families from the Allen County Old Order Amish were taken into the congregation. In 1929 the church building, one mile west of Harlan, Ind., was dedicated. In March 1948 a new church was built 1½ miles southwest of Harlan. It is now known as the Cuba Conservative Amish Mennonite Church (*q.v.*). The minister is Edwin Albrecht, the deacon Menno D. Miller.   S.F.

Allen County (Ind.) Old Order Amish settlement, located approximately 12 miles northeast of Fort Wayne, with addresses such as Leo, Grabill, Harlan, and Woodburn, is divided into three groups. The first group was established in 1853, when 52 persons migrated by ox team from Stark Co., Ohio.

Among them were Bishop Peter Graber and his three brothers, Jacob, Christian, and John. In 1882 John Schmucker, son-in-law of Bishop Peter Graber, was ordained bishop. The present bishops are Peter R. Schmucker and Samuel Graber. This group has two congregations known as the North Schmucker and the South Schmucker districts, with approximately 80 families. The second group, the Graber Amish congregation, was started in 1909 by ministers Joseph and John Graber because of dissension in the Schmucker group. Joseph Graber was ordained bishop of the group in 1915 and Eli Wagler is now serving in that office. There are 70 families in the group. The third group, the Lengacher Amish congregation, organized by Bishop Seth H. Byler of Hartville, Ohio, on March 21, 1943, is a division of the Allen County Graber church. There are 62 members, served by Bishop Clarence Lengacher, ordained bishop in 1946, and ministers Jacob and Victor Yoder.   N.Z.

Allen County, Ohio, is located in the northwestern section of the state and was formed in 1820. It consists of fertile farming land, once covered with hardwood forests. Lima, with a population of 50,000, is the county seat. There are two substantial Mennonite communities in the county, a Swiss group in the northeastern part around Bluffton; and another in the southwestern corner in the region of Elida, consisting of three Mennonite (MC) congregations with a membership of about 400, originally immigrants largely from Virginia and Fairfield Co., Ohio. Only two of the four G.C.M. congregations of the Swiss group, Ebenezer and First Mennonite, are located within this county. The other two, St. Johns and Grace in Pandora, are just across the line in Putnam County. In Bluffton also there is a small congregation of the Evangelical Mennonites with a membership of about 50. The Reformed Mennonite congregation, with a small membership, is located several miles west of Bluffton. In Lima are three small Mennonite mission congregations sponsored respectively by the General Conference, the Mennonites (MC), and the United Missionary Church.   C.H.S.

Allensville, Pa., a village located in Menno Township about 8 miles from the southwest end of the Kishacoquillas Valley in Mifflin County in the central part of Pennsylvania. The first settlers in this valley were Scotch-Irish and arrived during the late summer of 1754. The village was laid out in lots in 1806 and was first named Horrelton, for Christopher Horrel, who opened the first store at that place. In 1831 a post office was established there and named Allensville, for a family by that name about which little is known. The present population (1950) is about 350.

The village is located in the center of an Amish settlement made up of Amish Mennonites and Old Order Amish Mennonites. The first Amish Mennonites arrived in this area about 1760, the first church being organized during the latter half of the 18th century. The Allensville Mennonite Meetinghouse serving a membership of 323 is located one mile east of the village. The Old Order Amish

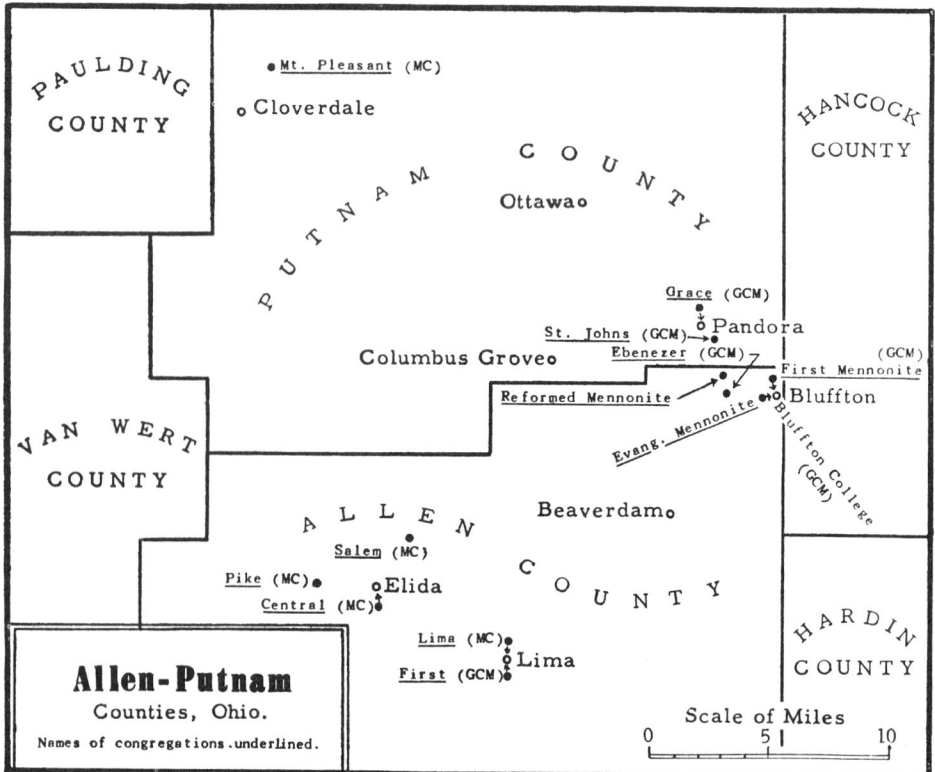

Allen-Putnam Counties, Ohio.
Names of congregations underlined.

Mennonites hold their worship services in private residences. About 15 per cent of the Amish Mennonites live in the village, the total number of Amish and Old Order Amish Mennonites of the settlement being approximately 500. (Samuel W. Peachey, *Amish of Kishacoquillas Valley,* Scottdale, 1930). E.D.Z.

Allensville Mennonite Church (MC), Allensville, Pa., a congregation formerly called Allensville Amish Mennonite Church, was organized in 1861 by Solomon Byler. It later became a member of the Ohio and Eastern A.M. Joint Conference. The first meetinghouse was built a short distance east of Allensville, Pa., in 1869 and rebuilt in 1932. A new building was erected in 1949. The membership in 1953 was 349; bishop, B. R. Peachey; preachers, J. B. Zook, J. E. Hartzler; deacon, U. S. Zook. U.D.H.

Allentown, county seat of Lehigh Co., Pa., population (1950) 106,254. Since the earliest days of the community, Allentown has been a shopping center for a large area, and today shipments of merchandise within a radius of 35 miles are scheduled regularly. Within this area live approximately 6,200 Mennonites, of whom 2,240 are affiliated with the G.C. Mennonite Church, the first having come to the city about 60 years ago. There are several Mennonite Brethren in Christ and (old) Mennonite churches in Allentown and vicinity, among them the Bethel Mennonite Brethren in Christ Church (*q.v.*) in Allentown, but the First Mennonite (*q.v.*) is the only G.C. Mennonite church there. W.H.M.

Allentown First Mennonite Church (GCM), a member of the Eastern District Conference, is located in Allentown, Lehigh Co., Pa. From 1893 to 1902 the Mennonite families who had moved to Allentown met for occasional services in rented halls. On Aug. 3, 1903, they organized a congregation, and purchased a lot, on which they built a small frame meetinghouse, in 1905. The present substantial brick meetinghouse was built in 1915. The membership in 1908 was 69; in 1953 it was 221.

Ministers and their terms of service are: William H. Grubb, 1903-05; W. S. Gottshall, 1905-09; A. M. Fretz supplied 1909-10; S. P. Preheim, 1910-12; A. M. Fretz supplied 1912; Victor B. Boyer, 1913-29; Howard G. Nyce, 1929-48; Maynard Shelly, 1949.

Deacons and their terms of service are: Harvey S. Kummery, 1903-41; Herbert S. Stauffer, 1918-20; Menno Sell, 1921-41; Victor C. Backensto, 1941- ; William H. Mohr, 1941- J.H.F.

"History of the Allentown Congregation," *1906 Mennonite Yearbook and Almanac* (Quakertown, Pa., 1906); "First Mennonite Church, Allentown, Pa.," 1944 *Yearbook of the General Conference* (Newton, 1944); J. C. Wenger, *History of the Mennonites in the Franconia Conference* (Telford, Pa., 1937).

Allentown Mennonite Mission (MC), located at Sixth and Cleveland Streets, Allentown, Pa., is operated by the Franconia Mennonite (MC) Board of Missions and Charities. Efforts in mission work in Allentown were begun as early as 1930 by in-

terested laymen and Preacher David L. Gehman. Evangelistic services conducted by Elias W. Kulp were held at 810 St. John Street in a building rented by the mission board. The work was discontinued within a short time but was revived in 1945. The 1953 membership of 27 was being served by Alvin Detweiler. Q.L.

Allentown State Hospital, Allentown, Pa., was the location of a Mennonite Civilian Public Service mental hospital unit from November 1943 to May 1946. The original group of men were transferred from Camp Downey. At least 36 men served in the unit during its 2½ years. M.G.

Allert Jansz, an Anabaptist martyr, who was seized on April 13, 1570, at Haarlem in the Dutch province of North Holland, and at the same place burned to death on May 6, 1570, after many attempts to make him recant. (*Mart. Mir.* D 506, E 845; *ML* II, 390.) NEFF.

Alles, Derk, b. March 8, 1639, at Meeden, Holland, d. at Groningen, May 12, 1711, was from 1666 to 1679 a preacher and from 1679 to 1711 an elder of the Groninger Old Flemish in the Netherlands. According to his own records he held 307 baptismal services ("*opneming gedaan*") and baptized a total of 1,832 persons on his journeys. In 1699 he ordained his son Alle Derks (*q.v.*) to the ministry, who took the place of elder after his father's death. (Blaupot t.C., *Groningen* I, 158.) vDZ.

Allgemeine Bundeskonferenz der Mennonitengemeinden in Russland (General Conference of the Mennonite Congregations in Russia, from 1888 to 1917 called *Allgemeine Konferenz . . .*) founded in 1883. In the beginning the Mennonite elders of Russia counseled together by meeting in a *Kirchenkonvent* (*q.v.*) similar to their colleagues in South Germany and Pennsylvania who met as an *Aeltestenrat* (*q.v.*). This had also been the tradition in Prussia and Holland. The *Kirchenkonvent* became more official and regular in 1883 when the problems affecting all Mennonites of Russia increased and annual meetings at which minutes were kept became necessary. The founders and early promoters of the conference were the elders Johann Töws and David Hamm (Trakt), Abraham Görz and B. Harder (Molotschna), and Heinrich Epp (Chortitza).

Among the major problems confronting the Mennonites of Russia around 1880 was the matter of alternative service for the young men of military age. On June 14, 1879, the elders of the various Mennonite settlements had met in Neu-Halbstadt and decided to petition the Governor-General von Totleben to insure complete separation of the alternative service from the military machine and to allow for their own supervision of the spiritual and moral welfare of their young men. At this meeting it was also decided to delegate Andreas Voth, president of the Mennonite School Council, to Moscow to mediate in educational matters. These two questions—military conscription and the Russianization of the Mennonite schools—concerned and disturbed all Mennonites alike. On Nov. 17,

1882, some elders met in Halbstadt and decided to organize a conference with annual meetings to bring all congregations closer together to form one body in accordance with Eph. 2:20-22. This would provide a platform to discuss matters of common concern and to have an official representation in dealing with the government. Already at this time ministers were appointed to serve the boys in forestry camps.

The first official meeting of the conference took place on Jan. 24-25, 1883, at Halbstadt, at which Elder David Hamm preached the conference sermon based on I Thess. 5:12-15, proclaiming the conference motto: "In essentials unity; in nonessentials liberty; and in all things charity." The unity of the children of God (John 17) within and without the Mennonite fold, as well as home mission work, Sunday schools, and improved catechetical instruction were strongly emphasized. From the very beginning the founding of a theological seminary and a conference paper were on the agenda and were discussed frequently in the succeeding years. The conference operated without a constitution, although one was adopted at its last session in 1926, which never became operative.

Most of the congregations were represented at the Halbstadt session, with the exception of two small ones in Poland which never joined the conference, and most of the preachers were present, so that the conference grew in size only through the addition of new settlements and through the delegation of lay members. Regular lists of delegates were not kept until 1910, when the conference was placed under government supervision. After that the number of the delegates was about 175, and the number of participating congregations 45 to 52. The Mennonite Brethren and other smaller groups were not originally represented.

The annual conference sessions, lasting two or three days, were held in the largest churches in the provinces of Taurida, Ekaterinoslav, and Kherson. Practical considerations prevented taking the conference to the remoter congregations, as, e.g., to the provinces of Samara and Orenburg, to say nothing of those across the Urals in Siberia.

The activities and problems of the conference can be divided into two periods: 1883-1910 and 1910-26. During the first period the organization dealt predominantly with internal conference matters. During the second, emergency conditions made the conference an organization which embraced all branches of Mennonites, in some respects similar to the present Mennonite Central Committee of North America.

1883-1910. Some of the problems and tasks consistently confronting the conference during its first period were the following: home missions (*Reisepredigt,* evangelism, etc.), philanthropic work (Muntau hospital, *q.v.,* Tiege institution for the deaf, *q.v.,* Bethania hospital, *q.v.,* etc.), religious education (Sunday school, catechetical instruction, supervision of religious instruction in secondary schools, etc.), foreign missions (appointment and training of missionary candidates, support of Dutch Mennonite mission work, etc.), publication (*Ge-*

sangbuch, Choralbuch, uniform catechism, ministers' manual, conference paper, Mennonite history textbook, etc.), forestry service (negotiations with the government, appointment of camp directors and ministers, camp discipline, raising of funds for camps, sending visiting ministers to camps, etc.), congregational practices and discipline (ban, avoidance, election of ministers and elders, Lord's Supper, mode of baptism, nonconformity, marriage among relatives, etc.), and introduction of uniform church records. The delegates to the annual conference sessions signed the resolutions and were expected to present them to their congregations and abide by them, although every congregation maintained its independence and right to deviate where it disagreed, in harmony with the conference motto. Thus the conference was more of an advisory body attempting to find solutions to common problems than an authoritative administrative organization.

In the beginning the chairman of the conference was the elder of the congregation that served as host. A. Görz and B. Harder were the first chairman and secretary respectively. After 1892 a steering committee was elected for three years consisting of the chairman and three assistants, a sort of program committee, checking and arranging suggestions for the conference agenda. Beginning in 1912 the *Kommission für Kirchenangelegenheiten (q.v.,* called *KfK)* was responsible for arranging the programs and obtaining permission to hold the conference. The conference committees and officers were always elected by majority vote. As in the case of the *Kirchenkonvent* the delegates to the conference were composed mostly of elders and ministers of congregations considering themselves members of the conference. Lay representatives began to attend the conference in connection with problems pertaining to forestry service, education, etc., being invited as specialists in their field to report about matters in which decisions had to be reached. A free, active, and equal participation of lay members came about only in the second period of the conference. From 1883 to 1909 the number of representatives varied from 16 to 38, representing from 11 to 37 congregations.

One of the most frequently presented and discussed tasks of the conference was the establishment of a theological seminary, which was unfortunately never realized. Sometimes there was no unanimous feeling of need for such an institution, again no agreement was reached on how to carry it out, or government permission was not granted. At one time a plan was presented by which the seminary would have become a department of a secondary school. This was not approved by a group which felt that it should be a separate institution. Thus efforts along these lines were confined to short term Bible courses for ministers and the training of ministerial and missionary candidates in non-Mennonite schools located mostly in Germany and Switzerland. More and more it became the practice to elect ministers from among the ranks of Mennonite secondary school teachers, especially those teaching religious subjects.

Another project often discussed was that of a

conference organ. The Mennonites of Russia read widely the Mennonite papers of Germany and even of America until finally *Der Botschafter* (*q.v.*), a privately published journal, filled their need for a time. At the end, 1925-28, the conference had its dream fulfilled in publishing *Unser Blatt* (*q.v.*). The publishing of the *Mennonitisches Jahrbuch* (*q.v.*), also a conference project edited by H. Dirks and D. H. Epp, had been realized at a much earlier date. The conference was most successful in publishing songbooks and materials for religious instruction. In 1912 the publication of D. H. Epp's history of the Mennonites for use in secondary schools and at home was approved. Apparently this project was never carried out. Dr. Theodor Ediger lectured at the conference in 1912 and 1913 on the significance and methods of teaching Mennonite history in secondary schools. As a result the conference arranged for a contest granting awards of 500, 300, and 200 rubles as prizes for the best manuscripts submitted, with the intention of publishing the most suitable for use in schools.

The greatest achievement of the conference was probably in the realm of home and foreign missions. It sent elders to newly established settlements and helped them organize congregations. Elders, missionaries, and itinerant ministers did much to unify practices and beliefs among the congregations which had originally come from heterogeneous backgrounds in West Prussia and Poland. The conference was the strongest supporter of the Dutch foreign mission work in Java and Sumatra in both financial contributions and furnishing missionaries. The greatest promoter of this cause was Missionary Heinrich Dirks who had been the first Russian Mennonite missionary to Java, and who reported annually about the mission work at the conference. In 1906 a resolution was passed requesting representation on the Dutch Mennonite mission board, which was granted.

In matters of Christian living and church discipline the conference passed many resolutions, some of which dealt with camp life in forestry service (*q.v.*). It went on record repeatedly as favoring wholesome recreational activities for the youth and opposing dancing, card playing, drinking alcoholic beverages, and the establishment of saloons in Mennonite villages. It favored the establishment of libraries, young people's meetings, song festivals, etc. The ban was considered not a means of punishment, but of reforming the sinner. Ban and avoidance were considered inseparable.

Repeatedly the matter of preparing candidates for baptism as well as the mode of baptism were discussed. According to a letter from Elder Johann Töws in 1886 the conference went on record stating that "a second baptism upon a personal confession of faith is unscriptural" and that a person who has been instructed in school, at home, and by the ministers in the way of salvation and baptized upon confession of faith and then later in life, through the grace of God and the work of the Holy Spirit realized more fully his lost condition and salvation need not be rebaptized, just as a couple is not remarried because they have come to a fuller realization of the significance and duties of married life"; and that there is no Scriptural proof that salvation depends on the outward form of baptism.

An interesting minute in 1888 records a resolution to attempt the initiation of "a general conference of all Mennonite congregations of Europe," which was probably the first official step along the lines of creating a Mennonite world conference. The same conference went on record leaving it up to the local congregations as to whether or not they wished to practice consecration of children.

1910-26. With the year 1910 great changes in the work of the conference were inaugurated. The list of delegates and the program had to be submitted to the Russian government for approval prior to receiving official permission for holding the conference, which was from then on always held in the presence of a government representative. All minutes had to be kept in the Russian language. Only with great difficulty could permission be obtained to conduct the meetings in the German language. During the war years 1914-16 no conference sessions could be held because of the war.

Before World War I the Russian parliament (*Duma*) issued a new law regarding religious groups in Russia by which the Mennonites were stripped of their former privileges and treated as a "sect." This and other matters were dealt with repeatedly and necessitated some changes in the organization of the conference. In 1910 a *Glaubenskommission* was appointed which developed into the *Kommission für Kirchenangelegenheiten* and functioned as a permanent executive committee of the conference.

The new and grave problems confronting all Mennonites of Russia made it desirable for the other groups to join with the General Conference in an attempt to arrive at solutions. Thus the conference gradually included all Mennonite congregations of all branches in Russia. As early as 1906 the minutes stated that the Mennonite Brethren were to be invited to future conferences especially because of the many common interests, such as schools and forestry service. Although some individuals may have followed this invitation at once, the first conference at which the Mennonite Brethren participated officially in large numbers was that at Schönsee in 1910. From here on they were regular participants, but only of those sessions at which common problems were discussed. The conference now began to work on a constitution which was, however, not immediately completed nor ever approved by the czarist government. The autonomous Mennonite congregations were originally quite opposed to such a constitution, fearing that the local congregations would thereby lose their freedom.

The programs of the conferences 1917-19 still followed the traditional pattern, although new problems took much time on the agenda. The conference of 1917 reviewed the matter of education, nonresistance, the spiritual welfare of those in service, creation of Mennonite archives, etc. Addresses were also given on the reorganization of the conference and the proposed constitution. It was decided that the conference was to be a "bond of spiritual unity" for all Mennonites and that the various branches could still hold their separate conferences. Thus in 1917 the conference had actually become the over-all organization of Mennonite branches with equal rights for all groups.

The need for a civil organization parallel to the conference was recognized. Such an organization came into being at a meeting in Ohrloff in 1917 in the *Allgemeiner Mennonitischer Kongress (q.v)*. It was also decided that the *KfK* was to continue, consisting of four members to be elected for three years. The chairman was to devote his full time to the work of the conference with a salary of 3,600 rubles.

During 1920-21 the conference did not meet because of the unsettled conditions in Russia. In 1922 it met in Chortitza. Again there were no meetings 1923-24. The last two meetings took place in Moscow in 1925 and in Melitopol in 1926.

These two conferences, for which again permission had to be obtained under the greatest of difficulties, and at which Communist government representatives participated, made it clear to those present or represented that the situation had become more critical than ever before in the history of the conference. Not only were former privileges taken from the Mennonites, but they now realized that in the Soviet Union there was no place for an organized Christian conference with a program and activities to maintain and build up the religious life of the congregations. Although the programs reveal that the conference was probably more alert and active than ever before, very few of the projects were carried out, and even those already begun, like *Unser Blatt (q.v.)*, had to be discontinued. One of the great concerns was again the establishment of a Mennonite theological seminary or a Bible school, especially now that the Mennonite schools had been taken over by the government. Thus when the conference, after nearly 50 years of existence, was ready to launch large-scale projects, all its activities were forcibly discontinued. The constitution of the conference which had been in preparation for a long time was adopted at the last conference session in Melitopol in 1926 but very likely was never approved by the government. Most of the delegates of the last two conferences perished in exile in a few years. Thus these meetings could again be called "Martyr Synods" like the Augsburg conference during the 16th century. Especially significant during these crucial years was the work of the *KfK*, now functioning as an executive committee, and the work of many faithful ministers and lay members sacrificing in many instances their lives to help in such causes as conscientious objection to war, the freeing of ministers and churches from taxation and in other legal matters, when the confession of Christianity had become a matter of life and death.

The conference met annually until 1913 inclusive.

Because of the war, the next meeting could not be held until 1917, in Halbstadt. In 1918 two conferences were held, the first regularly, in Lichtenau, the second an emergency meeting with fewer delegates at Landskrone. The 1919 (September) conference in Rudnerweide had to be closed early because of bandits in the neighborhood. The next two conferences were held by special permission from Moscow as follows: October 1922, in Chortitza; January 1925, in Moscow. The one of October 1926, in Melitopol, met as an "All-Ukrainian" conference, with permission from the Kharkov Ukrainian government and with the presence of two government representatives. In Landskrone, because of suspension of railroad travel, only 41 delegates representing only 26 congregations were present. The Moscow conference in 1925 had 73 delegates in addition to the *KfK (q.v.)* with representation of all major settlements in the USSR. At Melitopol in 1926, 83 delegates were present representing 22,380 members.

Of the 38 conference sessions, 24 took place in the Molotschna settlement with the town of Halbstadt the most frequent location, five in the Chortitza settlement, and one each at Zagradovka, Memrik, New York, Schönfeld, Berdyansk, Yazekovo, Moscow, and Melitopol. The largest number of delegates was at the Schönsee conference in 1910 with 173 present, representing 52 congregations, and the next largest the Lichtenau conference in 1918, where 19 elders, 139 ministers, and 125 lay members participated.   C.K.

Heinrich Ediger, *Beschlüsse der von den geistlichen und anderen Vertretern der Mennonitengemeinden Russlands abgehaltenen Konferenzen für die Jahre 1879 bis 1913* (Berdyansk, 1914); D. H. Epp, "Zur Geschichte der Bundeskonferenz der russländischen Mennonitengemeinden," *Unser Blatt*, 1926, No. 1, 17-19; No. 2, 39-41; No. 4, 101-4; "Protokoll der Allukrainischen Konferenz der Mennonitengemeinden . . . in Melitopol . . . 1926," *Unser Blatt* II, 2 (Nov. 1926) 47-51; see also minutes of other sessions since 1913; P. M. Friesen, *Konfession oder Sekte?* Friesen, *Brüderschaft*, 527-47; C. Henry Smith, *The Story of the Mennonites* (Newton, Kansas, 1950) 464-68.

Allgemeiner Mennonitischer Kongress was the name of an organization of all Mennonites in Russia to represent their economic and cultural interests. This *Kongress* came into being immediately after the Revolution in 1917 through the efforts of the *Molotschnaer Mennonitische Verein*. The first and only *Kongress* convened in Ohrloff, Molotschna, Aug. 14-18, 1917. A total of 198 delegates took part, representing the various Mennonite settlements, groups, and interests. B. H. Unruh was elected first chairman and J. H. Janzen functioned as recording secretary.

Reports were heard from representatives of the various Mennonite settlements, the young men in alternative service, etc. Lectures were given on matters pertaining to the new provisional government, the ownership of land, agriculture in general, the Mennonite schools, etc. The delegates worked in four sections—political, cultural, legal, and organizational. It was decided to establish a permanent *Allgemeiner Mennonitischer Kongress* which was to regulate and administer the public civic matters of all Mennonite communities similarly to the *Bundeskonferenz* in the spiritual realm. Lawyers, engineers, farmers, and university-trained educators and theologians discussed vital questions of this crucial day on a high level. Approximately 75 per cent of the delegates had secondary school training, of whom 15 per cent had university training. The matter of education, the men in alternative service, and the relationship of the Mennonites to the new Kerensky government were some of the major concerns of the *Kongress*. The *Kongress* would very likely have become the most important organization of the Mennonites of Russia if the political development had not doomed it to a premature death.

The newly founded *Kongress* never convened again for several reasons: the civil war made an all-Russian Mennonite meeting impossible for years; later the *Verband der Bürger Holländischer Herkunft* (q.v.) for the Ukraine and the *Allrussischer Mennonitischer Landwirtschaftlicher Verein* (q.v.) for the rest of Russia were organized; and the radical communistic course of the new government made the *Kongress* impossible. (*Protokoll des Allgemeinen Mennonitischen Kongresses in Ohrloff, Taurien, vom 14.-18. August 1917,* reprinted in *Menn. Warte,* January 1938 ff.). C.K.

Allgyer, Samuel Evans, son of Joseph and Barbara (Zook) Allgyer, was born near McVeytown, Mifflin Co., Pa., March 8, 1859, d. Nov. 15, 1953. His parents moved to Wayne Co., Ohio, and in 1878 settled near West Liberty, Ohio. They were members of the Amish Mennonite Church, with which he also united. On Jan. 18, 1883, he was united in marriage with Priscilla A. Umble, daughter of Jacob and Barbara (Kurtz) Umble, of Gap, Lancaster Co., Pa. They were the parents of eight children: Eva (1883), Barbara (1885), Maud (1887), Roy (1890), Anna Mary (1892), Ruth (1898), Samuel M. (1903), and John M. (1905). He attended the public schools in Pennsylvania and Ohio from 1865 to 1877 and the Smithville, Ohio, Normal School in 1875. From his marriage in 1883 to 1912 he was a farmer, at first renting and later purchasing his father's farm.

As a young man he served as secretary of the Amish Mennonite (German) Sunday school in Champaign Co., Ohio, and later served as superintendent until his ordination to the ministry in 1905. He became deeply interested in the Ohio Sunday School Conference soon after its organization and took an active part in the annual meeting of the conference. He was one of the moving spirits in the organization of the Logan-Champaign Annual Sunday School Conference and Quarterly Mission Meeting. In the early nineties during a revival at the Mt. Tabor M.E. Church near his home he became convinced that his formal connection with the church was not sufficient. As a result of Bible study and prayer he and his wife were converted in their home during the time that the revival meetings were in progress at the church.

After his ordination to the ministry Allgyer devoted himself more and more to the work of the church and spent weeks and even months away from home conducting Bible conferences and evangelistic services (continued meetings). He was interested especially in building up the mission stations east and west and as a result of his countrywide services became one of the most widely known evangelists in the church. As a result of these activities and connections, he was elected the first field worker of the Mennonite Board of Missions and Charities in 1908, and continued in this position until 1940. In 1908 he was ordained bishop of the Oak Grove Church in Champaign County, Ohio, and served as bishop of seven western Ohio churches. He served seven different terms as moderator of the Ohio Mennonite and Eastern A.M. Conference and was moderator of the Mennonite General Conference in 1931. In 1919 the Mennonite Church sent him to Europe as a special delegate to visit the young men engaged in relief work under the Friends Service Committee.

J.S.U.

Alliance, Evangelical, founded in 1846 in London, by representatives of 50 Protestant churches, for the purpose of uniting all Protestant churches of the world which have a common foundation of faith in order to resist hostile influences and to strengthen and further the cause of a Biblical-evangelical Christianity. A confession of faith adopted at London covered nine points, in which belief was expressed in a triune God, justification only by faith, the absolute authority of the Holy Scriptures. At the same conference seven branch unions were decided upon; two of them in Germany, of which one covered North Germany, the other South Germany and Switzerland.

The climax of the alliance movement was reached in Berlin in 1857. This important international meeting was attended by 1,252 participants. Eight Mennonites were present; these were the ministers Roosen of Hamburg-Altona, Molenaar of Monsheim, Risser of Sembach, Quiring of Thiensdorf, Epp of Heubuden, J. Mannhardt of Danzig, the merchant Momber of Danzig, and W. Mannhardt of Berlin. Risser wrote a detailed, enthusiastic report of the conference (*Menn. Bl.,* 1857, 63 ff.). Similar meetings were held in Geneva (1861), Amsterdam (1867), New York (1873), Basel (1879), Copenhagen (1884), Florence (1891), London (1896), Florence (1903), and London (1906).

No later meeting succeeded in stirring up as much enthusiasm as that in Berlin. More and more, partisan attacks by the Alliance element against the *Protestanten-Verein* and against stiff Lutheranism caused trouble. Also, complaints arose against the encroachment and unbrotherly attitude of the Baptists and Methodists, which prevented agreement and hindered co-operation. On the other hand, the practical achievements of the Alliance must be recognized. In 1855 it effectively stood up for the rights of the Baptists of Prussia and Mecklenburg, who were being persecuted by the police; in 1863 it defended Matamoros, who was imprisoned in Spain for his Protestant faith (*Menn. Bl.* 1864, 44); in 1876 it took the part of Russian Protestants; in 1879 it stood up for the rights of retired Hessian pastors; in 1879 in Basel Prof. Christlieb protested openly against Great Britain's disgraceful opium trade.

Interest in the efforts of the Alliance declined steadily. In 1902 the eleventh general conference was to meet in Hamburg. The invitation had been issued. For the local committee Pastor H. van der Smissen of Altona was the secretary (*Menn. Bl.,* 1901, 45). The difficulties mentioned above interfered to some extent, but the chief obstacle was the opposition of non-English circles to the Boer War. Therefore the English committee postponed the conference to 1903 and held it in Florence. The last conference of the Alliance met in 1907 in London.

After 1903 the Alliance became more firmly knit in Germany. The five member groups (Berlin, Hamburg, Saxony, West Germany, and South Germany) formed a committee of ten which met as occasion arose with the chairman. The chairman of the Hamburg group was Pastor H. van der Smissen, who was also a member of the committee of ten.

This alliance is not to be confused with the many unions formed in recent times on an alliance basis; these have no connection with the Evangelical Alliance or any of its branches. Of especial importance among these is the Blankenburg Alliance (*q.v.*) which can be considered as a continuation of the Smith meetings of 1875 (P. Fleisch, *Die moderne Gemeinschaftsbewegung,* 63). German Mennonites actively and constructively participated in all these alliance efforts. The original Evangelical Alliance has declined considerably in significance, particularly since the growth of the later ecumenical movements. The world-wide prayer week is one of its lasting contributions.

NEFF.

"Evangelical Alliance," in the *New Schaff-Herzog Encyclopedia* . . . (Grand Rapids, 1949); "Allianz, Evangelische," in *RGG;* Friesen, *Brüderschaft; ML* I, 35.

Allianz Gemeinden (Alliance Churches), the popular name of two Mennonite congregations in Russia, namely at Lichtfelde and Altonau, whose official name was *Evangelische Mennoniten-Gemeinden* (*q.v.*). These congregations separated from the Mennonite Church because of their position on baptism, communion, and discipline. They practiced only immersion, but did not demand it of members coming from other groups; they refused to take communion with the unconverted, observing it only with believing members of Protestant groups; hence the name "Alliance Churches."

This group tried to serve as a bridge between the Mennonite and Mennonite Brethren groups in Russia. In the emigration to Canada after World War II, however, members of the Alliance Churches did not continue as a separate organization, but joined the Mennonite Brethren. In Paraguay, on the contrary, they continued as a separate group in the immigration of 1930 ff., and in Brazil they joined the General Conference Mennonite Church. The Evangelical Mennonite Brethren (*q.v.*) are in spirit and practice closely related to the *Evangelische Mennoniten-Gemeinden.* (Friesen, *Brüderschaft,* 722; *ML* I, 35.)

NEFF.

All-Mennonite Convention. A series of nine unofficial meetings held from 1913 to 1936 by representatives of various branches of the Mennonite Church in the United States for the purpose of discussing common problems in the hope that such discussions might bring about greater unity among the various groups. The movement had its inception in an editorial by I. A. Sommer, "In What Fundamentals Do Mennonites Agree?" which appeared in *The Mennonite* in 1913. In response to the suggestion of N. E. Byers, then president of Goshen College, for a discussion of common problems, the editor of *The Mennonite* called for a meeting of representatives of the various groups which met with considerable support, and which resulted in the first of the series held at Berne, Ind., the same year. Later sessions were held in Carlock, Ill., 1916; Bluffton, Ohio, 1919; Goshen, Ind., 1922; Nappanee, Ind., 1925; Hillsboro, Kan., 1927; Berne, Ind., 1930; Newton, Kan., 1933; Topeka, Ind., 1936.

Later partly due to the appearance of other cooperative movements among the Mennonites—relief, peace, and cultural—interest in the original All-Mennonite Convention died out, and no sessions were held after 1936. Detailed reports of all the proceedings of these sessions have been published.

C.H.S.

Echoes of the First All-Menn. Conv. in America (Hillsboro, Kan., 1913, also in a German edition); *Report of the Second All-Menn. Conv.* and succeeding reports, 1916, 1919, 1922, 1925, 1927, 1930, 1933, and 1936; P. E. Whitmer, "The All-Mennonite Convention," *Yearbook of the Gen. Conf. of the Menn. Ch. of N. A.,* 1931, 42-3; N. E. Byers, "The All-Menn. Conv.," *Menn. Life* III (July 1948) 7, 8, 10.

Allrussischer Mennonitischer Landwirtschaftlicher Verein (All-Russian Mennonite Agricultural Union). In the time of the "New Economic Policy" (1921-27) the co-operative movement in the Soviet Union was able to show a significant growth. In 1921-22 the country, to be sure, experienced another catastrophic famine, but from that time on the curve of growth of co-operatives rose steadily.

After the Bolshevik Revolution the interests of Mennonite churches had been represented in Moscow by P. F. Froese and C. F. Klassen. Their right to do so was based on the authorization of the congregations and their membership in the "United Council of Religious Brotherhoods and Groups" in Moscow. When this organization was compelled to dissolve, there was thereafter no legal basis for the work of Froese and Klassen. Thereupon the idea arose that it was possible and necessary to call a purely Mennonite organization into being. In October 1922 a meeting of representatives of the eastern Mennonite communities was held in Alexandertal (Alt-Samara), which decided to create an organization for religious and economic purposes and appointed a committee to initiate the organization. This committee met in November 1922 in Alexandertal, and after careful consideration adopted a constitution for an *Allrussischer Mennonitischer Landwirtschaftlicher Verein*. But the idea of a religious and economic union could not be carried out under the laws of Russia, and so the two were separated, with the churches establishing the *Kommission für Kirchliche Angelegenheiten* for religious purposes.

After tedious negotiations the constitution of the A.M.L.V. was confirmed by the office of the All-Russian Central Executive Committee of the Soviets, and in October 1923 the first meeting of representatives took place in Alexandertal. P. F. Froese, C. F. Klassen, and F. F. Isaak were chosen as an executive committee. To pass emergency measures that might be found necessary between sessions of the organization, a council was formed consisting of representatives of all the larger local chapters.

The A.M.L.V. met four times: in Alexandertal in 1923, in Davlekanovo in 1924, and in Moscow in 1925 and 1927. The meetings of representatives as well as the organization as such performed an important function as a bond of union between the various settlements. The A.M.L.V. represented the Mennonite settlements in Samara, Ufa, Orenburg, the German Volga Republic (am Trakt), the northern Caucasus, Crimea, West Siberia, Kazakhstan (near Pavlodar), and Turkestan (at Aulie-Ata and Khiva); in other words, all the settlements with the exception of those in the Ukraine. It consisted of 19 chapters with 56 subchapters. It represented 4,965 family farms, or 80 per cent of all the farms, with about 44,000 persons; this was approximately two fifths of the Mennonites living in the Soviet Union, the remaining three fifths living in the Ukraine. The work of all the chapters dealt primarily with the improvement of seed and of stock. They produced seed of first, second, and third reproduction, as well as select seed. The products of the Mennonite seed associations were highly rated by the government experimental stations. In the field of stock breeding tangible results were also evident. In Siberia it was the German Red cow, on the Volga, the Dutch and Simmental cow, in the steppes of Orenburg the German Red cow. Dairying was also outstandingly successful, especially in the manufacture of cheese. Brick cheese and Dutch cheese were produced in great quantities and placed on the market. There were also notable stations for the purification of grain, as well as tractor stations.

The A.M.L.V. had representatives abroad: A. A. Friesen for North America, B. H. Unruh and A. J. Fast for Germany.

The valuable help given in Russia by the American Mennonite Relief and the significant accomplishments of the network of the A.M.L.V. made it possible for the Mennonites to secure repeated permission in Moscow for the surplus Mennonites from the overcrowded villages to leave the country. This could not be construed as a total "emigration," but only as a taking care of the excess population. For several years the efforts of the representatives in Moscow made it possible for some of the Mennonites to leave the country at a reduced price. In 1925 and 1926 Franz C. Thiessen managed the technical side of the emigration under the auspices of the A.M.L.V. In 1927 Mennonite emigration from Russia was practically stopped. The large eight-room residence which served as headquarters of the A.M.L.V. in Moscow on the Taganskaya Ulitsa became the center for all Mennonites visiting Moscow.

From May 1925 to December 1926 the A.M.L.V. published a periodical, *Der Praktische Landwirt,* with the motto, "In union there is strength."

Other persons besides those mentioned above, who were active in the work of the A.M.L.V., were Joh. W. Ewert of Alexandertal, and later Hermann Fr. Dyck, a former teacher in the business college in Halbstadt.

Throughout its existence the A.M.L.V. was compelled to fight for its permission to function and even for its bare right to exist. It was particularly molested by the German section of the Communist Party in the Soviet Union. But Russian economists also felt it to be a foreign body in the Soviet cooperative movement. One of them proposed that it be dissolved on the following grounds:

1. The A.M.L.V. had nourished the illusion among the Mennonites that they had a right to their own associations and to independent development.

2. The A.M.L.V. had been a hindrance in sovietizing the Mennonite settlements.

3. From the standpoint of the Soviet policy it had been an error on the part of the central government to grant recognition to the A.M.L.V., for it thereby promoted Mennonite separatism, which did not fit into the program of the nationalities policy of the Soviets.

By 1927 it was clear that the Party would not dissolve the A.M.L.V. by administrative methods, but would throttle it financially and tear the local organizations out of the network of the national body. The Association was to be maneuvered into a deficit and thereby compromised in the eyes of its members. A legal trial was initiated against the A.M.L.V., which it, of course, lost.

By 1927 the period of the New Economic Policy was at an end, and the Party had already inaugurated the program of collectivization. The A.M.L.V. could now no longer exist, and in the summer of 1928 the executive committee was compelled to accept the proposal of the central body of the Soviet agricultural co-operatives (*selskossoyus*) to liquidate the A.M.L.V. The year of the great economic revolution, 1929, approached. With it the Mennonite churches faced a new great catastrophe.   P.F.

Allstedt, a village in Thuringia, Germany, where Erhard Polrus or Pulrus, an Anabaptist leader, was executed as a martyr in 1532 after repeated torture. In 1523 Thomas Müntzer (*q.v.*) was the parson of Allstedt.   HEGE.

P. Wappler, *Die Täuferbewegung in Thüringen* (Jena. 1913) 536; W. Wiswedel, *Bilder* I, 89.

Almanacs, yearly publications containing calendars and usually additional information on holidays, beginnings of the seasons, the phases of the moon, etc., as well as religious articles and secular information of value to the home or farm, have been widely used in Mennnonite homes. Both denominational and secular almanacs are used extensively by Mennonites, one of the most popular being Baer's *Agricultural Almanac* published at Lancaster, Pa., since 1825.

In 1870 the *Mennonite Family Almanac,* later known as the *Family Almanac (q.v.),* appeared both in English and German *(Familien-Kalender, q.v.),* coming from the John F. Funk and Brother press. The *Christlicher Familien-Kalender* published by David Goerz, Halstead, Kan., first appeared in 1885 but in 1886 became the *Bundesbote-Kalender (q.v.).* The German *Christlicher Gemeinde-Kalender (q.v.)* first printed in Frankfurt, Germany, appeared in 1892. The *Mennonite Year Book and Almanac (q.v.)* printed by N. S. Stauffer, Quakertown, Pa., had its first issue in 1895. The *Christlicher Familienkalender für die Deutschen in Russland (q.v.)* appeared in 1897. The first *Doopsgezind Jaarboekje (q.v.)* was published in 1901 for the calendar year 1902. The *Mennonite Year-Book and Directory (q.v.)* carried the date 1905 on its first issue. The *Year Book of the Central Conference of Mennonites (q.v.)* appeared in 1922. The Mennonite Brethren published their first *Vorwärts-Kalender (q.v.)* for 1925. The *Neue Amerikanische Calender (q.v.),* privately printed and serving an Old Order Amish Mennonite constituency, was first published in 1930.   M.G.

Clarence S. Brigham, *An Account of American Almanacs and Their Value for Historical Study* (Worcester, Mass., 1925).

Almbruderhof, Triesenberg, in the principality of Liechtenstein *(q.v.),* the site of a community (Bruderhof) of the Hutterian Brethren, a brotherhood founded by Eberhard Arnold *(q.v.)* in Sannerz in the year 1920. It was settled in March 1934 as a result of restrictions imposed by the Nazi government in Germany, which made it necessary to move the education and publication activities of the Rhoenbruderhof *(q.v.)* out of Germany into another country. The school children of the Rhoenbruderhof were cared for in the resort hotel of Silum (elevation 5,000 ft.), and some neighboring Alpine huts; buildings and land were leased. In addition to the school, a bindery and a turner's workshop were set up, and in the course of time more land was rented in the Rhine Valley to provide food for the growing colony. The publishing house *(Buchverlag des Almbruderhofes)* published the books of the *Eberhard-Arnold-Verlag,* and in 1934 *Innenland, Ein Wegweiser in die Seele der Bibel und in den Kampf um die Wirklichkeit* by Eberhard Arnold.

The Almbruderhof was organized in accord with Hutterite tradition, and in connection with the sale of books, writings, and the products of its workshops carried on an intensive propaganda in the adjacent parts of Switzerland. Active connections were also maintained with England; beginning in 1934 an increasing number of English converts joined the brotherhood. The relationship of the Almbruderhof with the mother colony and with the American Hutterites was close and intimate. In 1935, as the Bruderhof increased through the influx of men of military age from Germany, the political community of Triesenberg raised a protest against the increase in size. The objections subsided when the Brethren presented their side of the matter in addresses and articles in the public press, although the government limited the colony to a membership of 80, inclusive of the children. During a journey to Holland, England, and Scotland, Eberhard Arnold won the practical support of friends of the Bruderhof. In 1934 and 1935 the Bruderhof maintained a small station in Zürich, the cradle of Anabaptism, which served as a training station for some young Hutterites, for the sale of their products, and as a missionary outpost. In 1936, when military duty was extended to include Germans living in foreign countries, the brotherhood was compelled to look for a new home for these brethren and their families, since the Liechtenstein government could not give them the right of asylum. Thus it came about that the Cotswold Bruderhof was founded in England in 1936. The Almbruderhof experienced another increase a year later, when the Rhoenbruderhof was dissolved and some of its inmates found a reception there. In the summer of 1937 the Hutterite elders, David Hofer of Manitoba and Michael Waldner of South Dakota, visited the Bruderhof, and from there traveled over Tirol, Moravia, and Hungary, visiting the sites of early Hutterite history. In 1938, when Austria fell under the power of Germany, the brethren of the Almbruderhof moved into the Cotswold Bruderhof. At present the Hutterite way of life is carried on in the Bruderhofs of Primavera, Paraguay, and Wheathill, England.   E.C.H.A.

Almelo, a town in the Dutch province of Overijssel (pop. in 1947 was 40,118, with 241 Mennonites). According to tradition a Mennonite family by the name of Warnaars came here from Flanders about 1550 bringing with them a linen factory. The existence of a congregation here in the early period is surmised, but there is no evidence of its existence before 1601. In 1629 the congregation seems to have belonged to the Flemish *(Inv. Arch. Amst.* I, 571). About 1650 a number of Mennonites from Westphalia came to Almelo. For a time meetings were held in a yarn house— most of the members were weavers; in 1684 a church was built, which was remodeled and enlarged in 1791. (The church still has an interesting clock and two decorative vases, made by the noted clockmaker Hendrik van Heylbron *(q.v.),* physician and also member of the congregation, placed in 1791.) At this time the organ too was added. In 1927 the church was entirely renovated. The parsonage, a characteristic old house, was sold in 1874. The congregation, which was Flemish in the

17th century and united with the Zonist Sociëteit in the 18th, has always been small. In 1730 the membership was 130. In the course of the 18th century the membership decreased markedly, the cause of the decline being no doubt chiefly the internal dissension in the congregation. The very conservative Jacobus Rijsdijk (*q.v.*) was minister of the congregation from 1715 to 1723 and from 1742 to 1744. In 1844 there were only 73 members; since that time the membership has been increasing somewhat; 125 in 1900 and 185 in 1950. Some of the members live in surrounding villages.

Old documents possessed by the congregation are an *Armenboek* with records from 1692, a *Protocolboek* from 1715 to 1771, and a *Kerkeboek* opened in 1754.

Over and over again the congregation had difficulty with the baron of Almelo (Graaf van Regteren): in 1746 regarding the calling of R. Klopper as minister, in 1775 regarding the wife of a member of the Reformed Church who joined the Mennonite congregation, in 1790 regarding an organ that had been put into the church. With the dawn of freedom and equality for the Mennonites in 1795 these unpleasantnesses disappear. In that year the Mennonite minister Gerardus ten Cate delivered an address in the Reformed Church, "Feestrede over de staatkundige toestand."

The ministers since 1746 have been Reinier Klopper, 1746-52; Gerardus ten Cate until 1755; Pieter Beets, 1756-71; Gerardus ten Cate (the second time), 1772-1810; Egbert David ten Cate, 1811-38; Cornelis Cardinaal, Jr., 1838-73; Isaac Molenaar, 1875-76; Anne Willem Huidekoper, 1877-78; August Snellen, 1879-86; Bauke Haga, 1888-91; Wiebe J. van Douwen, 1891-1911; Petrus Marinus Heringa, 1912-20; L. G. Holtz, 1921-27; O. T. Hylkema, 1928-39; N. van der Zijpp, 1940-46; H. Luikinga, 1947-49; S. Gosses Gzn. since 1950.

The congregation belongs to Ring (district) Twenthe. It has an organization for the women, one for the men, one for young people, and a Sunday school. vDZ.

G. Heeringa, *Uit het verleden der Doopsgez. in Twenthe* (Borne, n.d.) 22-29 and 83-85; Blaupot t.C., *Groningen* I and II, *passim; Inv. Arch. Amst.* II, 1470 f.; *ML* I, 35.

Almira Mennonite (MC) Church, near Almira, Markham Township, Ont. What was formerly known as Huber's and Stecklin in the northwest part of Markham Township became extinct with the building of a brick church on the fifth concession of Markham in 1860. Since the schism of 1889-90 this meetinghouse has been used alternately by the Old Order Mennonites and the Mennonites (MC) of the community. The ministers who resided near the church and served it are Adam Wideman, Jacob Wideman, Samuel Wideman, Lewis S. Weber, and Aaron D. Grove. The deacons who have served here and at the near-by Wideman (*q.v.*) church conjointly are Daniel Hoover, Sr., Christian L. Hoover, Manasseh R. Fretz, and Jacob H. Wideman. Revival meetings are occasionally held and other ministers of the county

also serve upon request. The Almira (MC) membership here has never been large, usually about 30. (L. J. Burkholder, *Brief Hist. of Menn. in Ont.*, Markham, 1935.) J.C.F.

Almira Mennonite (OOM) Church, near Almira, Markham Twp., York Co., Ont., is one of the three meetinghouses used by the Markham congregation of the Old Order Mennonite Markham-Waterloo Conference. The meetinghouse was built in or about 1860. Dissension resulted in a division into two factions about 1890, the one continuing with the Ontario Mennonite (MC) Conference, the other becoming the Old Order group. Since then both factions alternate their services in the meetinghouse. The ministerial leadership is identical with that of Reesor's (*q.v.*) and Altona (*q.v.*), Christian Reesor having been the first bishop. Ministers who followed were Christian Burkholder, Christian Gayman, and Levi Grove. The ministers are Thomas Reesor, Abraham Smith (bishop), Fred Nighswander, and Cecil Reesor. The (1953) membership of the three meeting places is approximately 100. A.SM.

Almonde, Hans van, elder of the Mennonite congregation at Danzig from March 14, 1752, to Dec. 27, 1758, the day of his death. He was born in Danzig in 1690, the son of Cornelius van Almonde, whose father presumably emigrated from Holland. The van Almonde family was in the 17th and 18th centuries one of the most respected among the Danzig Mennonites, but at the end of the 18th century they transferred to the Reformed Church. In the 19th century the name died out here, but the Almonde house on Langgarten stood until recently, and probably Allmodengasse derived its name from them. (*ML* I, 36.) G.M.

Almont. As early as 1800, Mennonites living along the Ridge Road near Almont, Bucks Co., Pa., worshiped in a schoolhouse. By 1826 Mennonites joined with Lutherans and Reformed groups in the erection of a union meetinghouse. It appears that Rockhill members living in the Almont area felt the need of a place of worship in their own community. Ministers, chiefly from the Rockhill congregation, were supplied for the Mennonite services at Almont. By 1885 all rights of Mennonites to the church building were released by one of the Mennonite (MC) bishops. The hope for establishment of a Mennonite church at Almont was never realized. The Lutherans and Reformed now alternate services in the Jerusalem church at Almont. Q.L.

Almosenpfleger, designation for deacons in the Mennonite churches of Baden, Germany. As co-directors of the congregation it is their duty to direct the material work of the church. They are to have charge of the offerings of the church, to support the needy with these funds, to be concerned for the widows and orphans, to visit the sick, to assist the elders in carrying out the duties of their office, and to see that members live a Christian life and that the ministers preach the true Word of God. Furthermore, it is their duty to attend the meetings of the elders of the Baden *Gemeindeverband,* to take part in the deliberations, and to see to the execution of their decisions in the churches. In every congregation there is usually an unsalaried deacon, who is elected from the membership. Besides this, the poor fund of the *Gemeindeverband* is in the care of one of the deacons; this fund is made up of alms not needed by the individual congregations and is used according to need for the support of the poor. (See **Mutual Aid, Armendiener, Diener der Notdurft, Deacon.**) (*ML* I, 35.) HEGE.

Alms. By this term (*Almosen*) the Mennonites of South Germany designate gifts of money which are placed in the offering box upon leaving the church at the close of a service. Twice this box is mentioned in the New Testament: Mark 12:41-44 (cf. Luke 21:1-4) and Matt. 27:6. The treasury in the Old Testament (II Chron. 24:6 f.; Neh. 12:44, and 13:4 and 9) was intended to receive gifts for divine worship and particularly for the upkeep of the House of God. According to I Cor. 16:2 the Apostle Paul advised the churches at Galatia and Corinth to gather some gifts of money on each Sabbath, and to lay it aside until he would come to use it for the needy brethren in Jerusalem. Thereby he laid the foundation for Sunday alms in the Christian Church.

We are therefore considering a primitive Christian custom. It most certainly agrees with the mind of Jesus. What He says (Matt. 6:3 and 4) about giving alms in secret is here beautifully fulfilled. It is a different kind of giving than a public donation, which one often gives in order to read his name in the list of receipts. The real purpose of this offering should be constantly kept in mind in all of our churches; the money should not be used to meet general church expenses, or the joy of giving will be lost. Where the collected gifts are used exclusively for alleviation of need among the brethren, this Christian custom is hallowed in a Biblical manner, and can create great blessing in our churches. This does not, of course, mean that other special offerings, such as for missions, cannot be placed in these boxes; these are usually announced beforehand. (*Menn. Bl.* 1886, p. 30; *ML* I, 36.) NEFF.

In Holland it does not seem to have been the original practice to collect alms during worship services, nor were alms boxes found at the meetinghouse door. Sometimes the deacons received gifts before the service. During the middle of the 17th century the alms box at the door was general. At the same time or somewhat later it became the practice in many Mennonite congregations to have the deacons collect alms during the services in a little velvet bag attached to a stick, as was usually done in the Reformed churches. This practice is still found in some of our congregations, but usually the alms are now dropped in boxes at the church door. In a great number of congregations the deacons formerly collected gifts by visiting the members of the congregation in their homes. The alms were and are usually separately managed, but in some congregations they go into the general treasury. (N. van der Zijpp, *Gesch. der Doopsgezinden in Nederland,* Arnhem, 1952, 114-15, 123-25.) vDZ.

In the early Mennonite settlements in Pennsyl-

vania (1683 ff.) and Ontario (1785 ff.) the custom of placing "alms" boxes at the exits of the meetinghouses was continued, and is still followed in the more conservative congregations there to this day. However, it also became the custom in many congregations in these regions and in daughter settlements, as is in general practiced by all congregations of the (old) Mennonites, Amish Mennonites, and related groups, to receive an "alms offering" for the poor of the congregation at each communion service in connection with the observance of the ordinance of footwashing. This fund is traditionally administered by the deacon, who is thought of as the custodian of the "alms" fund.

The use of the alms box at the entrance of the church must have been a very old practice among the Mennonites of Prussia and Russia, dating back to early days in the Netherlands. In many of the Canadian churches the alms box is still to be found, although the use of a collection plate in raising an offering is becoming predominant. H.S.B.

Alpha Mennonite (MC) Church, 3½ miles northwest of Alpha, Jackson Co., Minn., was organized at the time of the dedication of the meetinghouse in May 1898. The first families—among them Snyder, Shearer, Garber, and Herner—came from Cullom, Ill. S. G. Lapp of Roseland, Neb., was the bishop here a number of years, but in the spring of 1916 was drowned in a railroad accident on the way to Alpha. In 1907 he ordained C. J. Garber minister. In 1919 Bishop J. M. Kreider ordained N. E. Landis minister (now bishop) and C. M. Bute deacon. Active workers have gone from this base to 17 different fields including Puerto Rico. The sewing circle (Dorcas Band) was organized April 2, 1902. The present rural membership lives almost entirely north of Alpha and near-by Jackson, while 20 per cent of the membership live in town. Present (1953) membership is 78. C.J.G.

Alpine Street Mennonite Church: see **Seventh Street** Mennonite Church, Upland, Cal.

Alringh, Harmen Berentsz (1710-57), son of Berent Alringh, preacher in Leer, Germany, 1742 until his death on April 12, 1757. On July 4, 1745, he was married to Grietje Waerma, a sister of the minister Hendrik Waerma in Emden, who preached his funeral sermon. He said that in spite of deafness Alringh had managed his office for fifteen years with great energy and zeal. K.V.

H. Waerma, *Lijk-Predikacie op H. B. Alringh, Leeraar te Leer,* delivered at Emden, April 14, 1757, ms. copy in the Amst. Menn. lib.; *ML* I, 36.

Alsace is a French province (German to 1697 and 1871-1919), pop. 1,305,529 (1940) and area 3,437 sq. mi., lying on the west bank of the Rhine between Switzerland and the German Palatinate. It consists of the two departments of Upper (Haut-Rhin) and Lower (Bas-Rhin) Alsace, and since 1945 also the territory of Belfort.

The Anabaptist movement found early entry into Alsace. Its center was Strasbourg (*q.v.*), which offered asylum to those persecuted for their faith and in which such men as Jakob Gross (*q.v.*), Balthasar Hubmaier (*q.v.*), Wilhelm Reublin (*q.v.*), Michael Sattler (*q.v.*), and Hans Denk (*q.v.*) lived

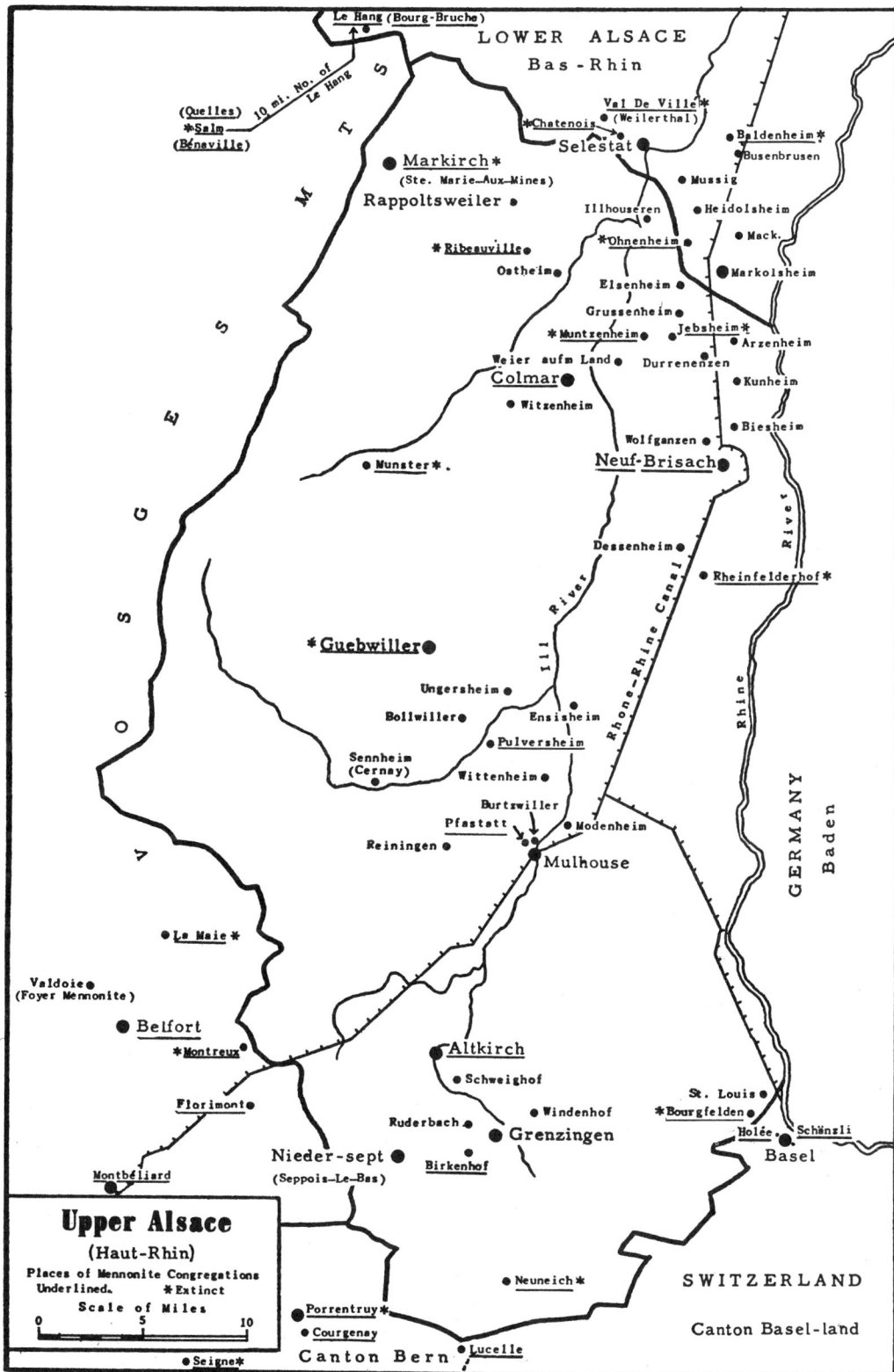

Le Hang (Bourg-Bruche)

LOWER ALSACE
Bas - Rhin

(Quelles)   10 ml. No. of   Le Hang
*Salm
(Bénaville)

M T S

Val De Ville *
(Weilerthal)

*Chatenois
Selestat

*Baldenheim *
*Busenbrusen

Markirch *
(Ste. Marie-Aux-Mines)

Mussig

Rappoltsweiler

Illhouseren

Heidolsheim

Mack.

*Ribeauville

*Ohnenheim

Ostheim

Elsenheim

Markolsheim

Grussenheim

*Muntzenheim

Jebsheim *
Arzenheim

Weier aufm Land

Colmar

Durrenenzen

Kunheim

Witzenheim

Wolfganzen

Biesheim

Munster *

Neuf-Brisach

Ill River

Dessenheim

Rhone-Rhine Canal

Rhine River

*Rheinfelderhof *

*Guebwiller

Rhine

GERMANY
Baden

Ungersheim

Bollwiller

Ensisheim

*Pulversheim

Sennheim
(Cernay)

Wittenheim

Burtzwiller

Pfastatt

Modenheim

Reiningen

Mulhouse

La Maie *

Valdoie
(Foyer Mennonite)

VOSGES MTS

Belfort

*Montreux

Altkirch

Schweighof

St. Louis
*Bourgfelden

Florimont

Ruderbach

Windenhof

Holée
Schönzli

Nieder-sept
(Seppois-Le-Bas)

Birkenhof

Grenzingen

Basel

Montbéliard

Upper Alsace

(Haut-Rhin)

Places of Mennonite Congregations
Underlined.   *Extinct

Scale of Miles

0   5   10

Neuneich *

SWITZERLAND

Canton Basel-land

*Porrentruy *

*Courgenay

Seigne *

Canton Bern

Lucelle

for a while. Melchior Hofmann (*q.v.*) made his first contacts with the Anabaptists here, and here spent his last years in prison. Thus it was inevitable that an Anabaptist congregation should be formed here; it reached its highest development under the leadership of Pilgram Marpeck (*q.v.*) about 1530. But the reformers saw in it a threat to the new Protestant church and attacked it orally and in writing. Bucer (*q.v.*) was especially active in this conflict. The outcome was the edict of the magistrate to expel them from the city (Feb. 16, 1534). It was, however, not strictly enforced, for in 1556 there was an Anabaptist congregation of about 100 in the city, including Peter Novesianus, a professor in the local Gymnasium, who was banished from the city. Many other members of the congregation emigrated with him. But it still remained an important center; a series of conferences was held here in 1555, 1557, 1568, and later. In the 18th and 19th centuries the congregation was small and weak, and finally disbanded in 1875.

From Strasbourg the Anabaptist movement was transplanted into the vicinity and over a large part of Alsace. "Its members used to meet in the forests at Eckbolsheim, Lingolsheim, St. Oswald, and in the region of Schnakenloch." This is the origin of the expression, "the forest church of the Anabaptists" (Röhrich II, 95). There were also Anabaptists at Ruprechtsau, Schiltigheim, Benfeld, Schlettstadt (*q.v.*), and on the Murrhof and Gansau near Strasbourg. Under the pressure of persecution, which did not abate until 1560, they withdrew into the remote parts of the mountains or plains, where they finally earned general respect and found toleration by their simplicity of customs, industry, and cleanliness (Röhrich III, 215). Sebastian of Dingelen, an old basket weaver, was their leader (*Vorsteher*); other members whose names are known were Ott Helfenstein and Jakob Ernst (Röhrich III, 139). In 1533 the citizens of Schlettstadt were forbidden upon penalty of expulsion to admit any Anabaptists. In 1538 the pastor of Rosheim wrote to a citizen of Strasbourg that 25 Anabaptists had been seized in the woods at Epfig, and that 300 Anabaptists had recently held a meeting in the woods. On the day following Easter in 1540, 69 Anabaptists were captured at one time near Illkirch (Röhrich II, 254).

Ensisheim (*q.v.*), south of Strasbourg (near Mulhouse), the seat of the government of the local Austrian lands, was the scene of the bloodiest persecutions. Here alone about 600 Anabaptists were executed. Here King Ferdinand (*q.v.*) issued a severe mandate against the Anabaptists on May 24, 1529, based on the imperial law of April 23, 1529, that the authorities be on the alert for any who did not have their infants baptized or who were refugees on account of rebaptism. The mandate was repeated in sharper form on May 26, 1535, and Dec. 10, 1544.

Nevertheless the Anabaptists maintained themselves in the country. An extraordinarily sharp mandate issued by Ferdinand on July 5, 1561, complains about the negligence and carelessness of his subordinates in pursuing and exterminating the "dangerous and offensive evil." Especially the lead-ers were to be apprehended and executed in accord with the edict of 1529. The authorities should be on their guard and watch those who sold their property, bring them to court and by torture if necessary examine them about their fellow members and leaders, and try to convert them. All children should be baptized early. Those who refuse to have theirs baptized should be considered Anabaptists and should be treated in accord with the mandates. No Anabaptist should be lodged or fed or aided in any possible way. This mandate was to be read to the people by the pastors on several successive Sundays and holidays and also by other officials in public places, so that everybody could be informed and defend himself against such "heretical, damned sect" and avoid the ruin of his soul and body.

This mandate was proclaimed on June 28, 1561, by Count Egenolph at Rappoltstein with the further admonition that the citizens should try to convert anybody they noticed with heretical faith or practice, and in case of obstinacy, report such persons to the court for punishment. Citizens who were negligent in doing so were also to be subject to punishment.

Nevertheless Anabaptism was able to persist for some time longer in Alsace. On July 2, 1572, a notice was proclaimed at Ingersheim near Colmar "on account of Anabaptism," which states that of the 100 citizens in Ingersheim about 30 were infected with Anabaptism. The wealthiest of them was Valentin Mangoldt. He had been warned several times, but was obstinate. The Anabaptists were meeting at three different places: usually on Sunday in the forest above Reichenweier, at Ingersheim in the cave, and in a vineyard and a woods near Winzenheim. Three other persons also used to go there and listen to them. A man and a child were buried in a vineyard. This had been going on for thirty years (records in the archives of Colmar).

Gradually the oppressive measures instituted by the Austrian government at Ensisheim achieved their aim. Only a few Anabaptist remnants were left. But during the Thirty Years' War their numbers were again increased by an influx from Switzerland. A Catholic priest of Ste. Marie-aux-Mines, Jean le Bachelle, wrote on March 12, 1643, to his friend Paul Ferry, the priest in Metz (records of the Colmar archives), that the Anabaptists had been settling in the country for some time. "They used to hold their religious meetings in a forest between Ste. Marie-aux-Mines (*q.v.*) and Schlettstadt. Now they meet in a barn. They have no priests, but one of them reads the Scripture aloud in German, and then they sing psalms according to the translation by Lobwasser. Then anyone who feels led to do so or has anything to say arises and explains the Scripture. If someone wants to be married or baptized upon confession of his faith they have somebody come from Switzerland; he is a man with the same trade as theirs; I have seen such a man; he was dressed in the Swiss manner."

During the "Swedish War" Mennonites "came into the country after Bern and Zürich had subjected their people to Zwinglianism, and France had relaxed its immigration regulations in order to have the land made arable." "They settled especially in the central Vosges, and were farmers and cattle raisers. Their families were usually large, numbering eight or nine children. In the valley of Ste. Marie they were accepted as citizens by contract with the religious and secular authorities, and were exempt from military service in return for an annual fee of 45 livres."

They called themselves Mennonites or Manzites, after one of their most respected martyrs, according to the book written early in the 18th century by a Catholic priest of Mutzig with the title, *Etat et mémoire des anabaptistes d'Alsace*. Another account, *L'Etat du temporale dressé par M. Antoine Rice, prêtre deligué par le duc de Lorraine en 1802*, reported that there were in Ste. Marie three branches of Anabaptists who had no communion with each other. In order to distinguish themselves from one another one group wore long beards and dressed in linen, summer and winter; and the second wore shorter beards and dressed in coarse wool cloth; while the third group looked almost like the Catholics. These Anabaptists had no churches, but met in homes. This report is obviously only partly reliable; there cannot have been more than two branches, the Amish and the "Reistish" or Mennonites. Virtually all the Mennonites of Alsace followed Ammann in 1694-97, and thus should be considered Amish after that date.

Another interesting account of the Mennonites in Alsace is found in the work of Ph. A. Grandidier (*q.v.,* d. 1787) *Oeuvres inédites* (6 vv., Colmar, 1865-68): "The Mennonites always live in the country, on the estates of large landowners, who like to take them as renters because they pay more than others, . . . by the industrious tilling of the soil and their good conduct. They are the most gentle and peace-loving of all people in their trade; they are energetic, alert, moderate, simple, benevolent. They wear beards, their shoes have no ties, their clothes no buttons. They seek to settle in the loneliest parts of the Vosges (mountains). When it is time for the harvest, mowing and threshing, the Swiss Brethren come and help, and when the work is finished they return to the places where they are tolerated or those where they are not known. If a Mennonite needs hired help he employs only members of his faith. In the villages where they live they pay the same fees to the church for marriage or burial as the Catholics, and are obliged to pay the same school fees as the Catholics, although they do not wish to have their children instructed by the schoolmasters. They do not accept infant baptism and assert that no church has the right to say that it is the only true one in contradistinction to the others. The government should be obeyed. Baptism should be imparted at a mature age; baptismal candidates must pass an examination to determine whether they are worthy of being received into the brotherhood. In baptism the elder takes water and pours it on the candidate with the words, 'I baptize you in the name of the Father, Son, and Holy Ghost.' Communion is observed twice a year, usually in the home of the elder, where services are also held. First the Scripture is read in the current language, then one of the ministers preaches on the passage read, and at the close of the address the elder gives each brother some ordinary bread; each one extends his hand and receives it, while the elder recites the words of the institution of the service. The brethren hold the bread in their hands until the preacher says, 'Take, eat'; then they all eat it together. The same elder goes from row to row with the cup and the preacher says, 'Drink in the name of Jesus in commemoration of His death.' All drink from the cup and wait in reverent silence; then the elder explains the effect that this act should have." Grandidier's report was confirmed by the Mennonite preachers Jean Bachmann and Philipp Heggi of Heidolsheim.

This report is supplemented by the formulary of the ordination of an elder of the same period; it was found among some family papers: "A brief essay on how the office of elder is bestowed upon a *völligen Diener*. First after the general voice of the congregation is taken, the candidate is asked whether he still acknowledges his baptismal covenant as he made it on his knees; then he is asked to kneel in the presence of the regular congregation and three elders lay their hands on his uncovered head and one says: In the name of the Lord and His church I commit to you the entire care for the congregation, to instruct the baptismal candidates, and if they are ready, to administer baptism with the consent of the congregation; second, to preach the suffering of Christ and distribute the emblems of communion to those who are ready for it; third, to perform marriage ceremonies for those who are ready, according to Christian regulation, and who are one in faith; fourth, to apply the binding key against those who through vice or disobedience are under censure of the congregation and the preachers; fifth, to apply the loosing key toward those who are reconciled to God and the brotherhood, and with the consent of the brotherhood offer them a hand and receive them; sixth, to aid needy congregations by supplying preachers and elders, ordain elders by the laying on of hands according to the content of the Gospel and to help other congregations by visiting them and to correct all errors and shortcomings with the Word of God, and take with you young or *angesetzte Diener;* seventh, assume the care of widows and orphans, and see that widows are given their due; eighth, to eliminate from the congregation all disorder, abuse of clothing, and whatever is contrary to Scripture, and on the other hand to implant sacred Christian order into the congregation through Jesus Christ, Amen." On Feb. 4, 1660, the Alsatian ministers signed the Dordrecht (Holland) Confession (of 1632) in Ohnenheim; later they also recognized the Flemish confession of Amsterdam of 1681.

Grandidier states that there were 62 Anabaptist families living in 16 villages of the bishopric of Strasbourg; they met in Baldenheim, Ohnenheim, Jebsheim, and Markirch. The places where the Mennonites lived were as follows: Baldenheim with

8 households, Munzenheim 4, Heidolsheim 4, Bessenbiessen 2, Ohnenheim 9, Maggenheim 2, Elsenheim 1, Gurzenheim 1, Jebsheim 7, Artzenheim 1, Kühnheim 4, Dienesheim 4, Weier 3, Ostheim 1, Illkirch 11, and Markirch 10. In addition it was rumored that there were some Mennonites in Neu-Breisach and Strohstadt. The total number was estimated at 496 persons. These figures are obviously incomplete. At the beginning of the 18th century there were five times that number.

To be sure, their numbers were sharply reduced by emigration to America. Repeatedly attempts were made to expel them from their homes in Alsace. About 1673 the abbot of Münster, Charles Marchand, hoped to bring about this expulsion in Ohnenheim (q.v.) through the count palatine of Birkenfeld, the heir of Rappoltstein. He pointed out to the prince that they had been granted permission to settle only on the express condition that they should not practice their religion; but for two years they had been holding public meetings and exercised their religion in the mill (evidently a reference to the conference of 1660). He therefore begged that the evil be eradicated with the roots and that they be expelled, but this never happened. It was the priest of Ohnenheim-Heidolsheim who had denounced the secret meetings, complaining that he had nobody in the church. It seems that the Anabaptists were more strictly dealt with after this, in order to compel them to return to the Catholic Church. In 1686 the Jesuits won an Anabaptist family with seven children in Schlettstadt, but this seems to be an isolated case.

Meanwhile more and more Anabaptists were coming from Switzerland, especially from Bern, particularly from 1671 to 1711. There must have been hundreds of them. Ernst Müller reports (*Berner Täufer*, 198) that a certain Beatus Fischer was interested in their case in Alsace and brought about the settlement of 1671 in Reichenweier.

On Feb. 27, 1696, Jakob Ammann (q.v.) complained in the name of his brethren who had settled two years previously in the valley of Ste. Marie-aux-Mines and of Ulrich Miller, who had lived there longer, that they were compelled to take part in defensive military service and that their children were being drawn into military service (Mathiot, 26). By negotiation they were released from this duty upon the annual payment of 46 French livres. But six years later the Mennonites of Markirch presented another petition to the authorities requesting release from such service, pointing out that the prince of Birkenfeld had previously exempted them from the service upon payment of 15 talers.

This petition was apparently successful. But now the envy of their neighbors was aroused. In 1708 they raised a solemn protest against the Anabaptists who did not bear arms; it was just as right to excuse them from military service as the Anabaptists, who had settled in large numbers in the valley. This led to catastrophe for the Mennonites. An exact list of the Mennonites was demanded and presented in 1704, signed by Hans Zimmermann and Jakob Ammann. It contained 40 familiar names, such as Lugenbühl, Bachmann, Joder, Hochstettler,

Zimmermann, Rupp, Maurer, Gerig, Gerber, Müller, and Roth. A second list required in 1708 contained about 60 names (Mathiot, 28).

The complaints against the Mennonites did not cease. Many of them had through industry and frugality acquired a little wealth, thus arousing general envy. In consequence, the intendant Pelletier de la Houssaye wrote to the court of Louis XIV inquiring what his attitude should be. He received a reply from Voisin, the secretary of the king, Aug. 13, 1712, saying that the king was by no means inclined to tolerate the Mennonites in Alsace. They should be driven out of the country either by a general decree or by special orders of the communities where they were found, with a reference to the treaty of Münster and Osnabrück, which stipulated that only adherents of the Augsburg Confession and the "alleged" Reformed Church should be permitted to live in Alsace. At his request Voisin sent the intendant an express confirmation of the royal opinion, and on Sept. 9, 1712, orders were issued to the officials in Alsace to expel the Mennonites from the country without exception, those who had settled there recently as well as those who had long been living there, and to forbid their settling in any other province of France (Mathiot, 30 f).

This command no doubt evoked consternation among the Mennonites of Alsace. Many emigrated. Some settled in the principality of Montbéliard, others in Germany in Breisgau, Zweibrücken, and the Palatinate, and many moved into near-by Lorraine, which had not yet been incorporated into France and where the border came quite close to Markirch (Hang, Salm, Upper Saar Valley). Most of the emigrants received from the local authorities a certificate that they were leaving the country only on account of their religion. One of these was issued on Nov. 8, 1715 (*Archive Haut-Rhin* E. 2808), reading as follows: "The Anabaptists Nic. Blank, H. Kipfer, Chr. and A. Kropf, David Chertzer and Mich. Maurer have until now lived in very good discipline and order, peace and harmony among the other inhabitants, without having committed anything blameworthy, to say nothing of anything criminal, and that they must leave the land only on account of their Anabaptist religion." Others, a considerable number, remained in Alsace. On Oct. 23, 1727, a list of Mennonites living in Alsace was again required, with data on numbers, place of residence, and occupation. It was forwarded to Versailles on Nov. 24, accompanied probably by a petition. (Mathiot presents the document on pp. 32-35, and comments correctly that it was written in 1727, and not in 1762, as the document is dated.) On June 7, 1728, came the reply of the minister d'Angerillac, who had presented the matter to the king. The king accepted the petition, and would permit the Mennonites to remain, but their children, when grown, must leave the country. It is likely that the duke of Zweibrücken as baron of Rappoltstein intervened in their favor. He called the king's attention to the fact that the Mennonites had settled here more than a century before the country had been united with France, and that they had made a large part of the Rappoltstein arable, that they distinguished themselves in the improvement of stock and that during an epidemic among the cattle their medication prevented the death of many cattle, and that they had restored the valley of Ste. Marie, which had been thoroughly devastated by the Swedes, into a fertile condition; it might therefore be advisable to make permanent settlers of a certain number of Mennonites and grant them toleration. Mathiot says that complaints against the Alsatian Mennonites were received by the court again in 1744, 1766, and 1780; in consequence new reports were required concerning them. Since these reports were favorable to the Mennonites and the landowners granted them protection they were tolerated. It had been reported at one time that many Mennonites had married Calvinists in order to stay in the country. This is probably the reason why the intendant had issued the order in 1715 that only those might stay in the province who would swear to be Calvinists. "This was," says Mathiot, "a clever method of discovering the Mennonites, and a cruel method of dividing families."

It is possible that the Mennonites were aware of the opinion of the duke of Rappoltstein; hence, in spite of the unfriendly royal decree, they turned to the duke de Choiseul with the request that they be treated with more toleration in Alsace, and that they be excused from the usual form of the oath in court. In his reply of April 6, 1766, the court rejected this petition in the curtest form as a shameless desire. It would be their best support to be unknown, so that no one would know who they were and that they were not included in the Peace of Westphalia. In a second letter of Sept. 9, 1766, the duke de Choiseul informed them that the king had not only refused their petition, but had also added that if the Mennonites were so bold as to present another petition and did not remain silent, they would be absolutely expelled.

But the Mennonites did not allow this exchange to intimidate them. "Their loyalty to their law was stronger than their submissiveness." "Their law permits them to reply only Yea to the formula of the oath and forbids them to raise a hand, because they believe they would thereby be challenging God. This they consider ungodly and are of the opinion that a man who must swear is less to be trusted than a man who does not swear." A Mennonite by the name of Jakob Frey, who refused to render the oath at court as a witness on Sept. 7, 1769, was punished by banishment from the country for life and a fine of ten livres, besides the costs of the trial. This verdict was approved by the king and expressed his opinion that the Mennonites "could under no pretext be excused from the performance of the common laws of the land." For a time the Mennonites were apparently without any legal rights in this respect. It was not until 1812 that the legal principle was established that "members of recognized religious associations give in place of the oath a declaration in accord with their religion." Geigel, *Kirchen- und Stiftungsrecht,* says in connection with Alsace-Lorraine (I, 12): "Mennonites are granted a formula of confession in place of the oath." This is confirmed by a regulation of the *Oberlandesgericht* at Strasbourg of March 18, 1881, and a decision of the civil chamber of the *Landgericht* at Colmar on March 17, 1882 (ten Doornkaat Koolman, *Die Verpflichtung der Mennoniten an Eidesstatt,* Berlin, 1893, 45 ff.).

There is little information available on the further development of the Mennonites of Alsace. Their life was rather secluded; they were little in the public eye. Through family papers more is known about the Neuneich (*q.v.*) congregation (now Birkenhof) in the county of Pfirdt and its connections with other congregations. It is not a friendly picture that unfolds before our view. There were quarrels and unpleasantness between elders and preachers that disturbed the peace within the congregation. Outside preachers had to be called in to settle the difficulties, and were not always successful. Sometimes an elder or preacher had to be silenced. But at the same time we admire the great earnestness and the loyalty to the brotherhood that are everywhere evident.

A deep stir was caused by the marriage of a member of the Münsterrol (*q.v.*) congregation with his brother's widow, and also a marriage in the same congregation between cousins. The other congregations, as Markirch, Colmar, Salm, and "from the lower land," declared themselves unanimously against these marriages. A letter also came from a Swiss congregation, signed by Uli Amman, which castigated the "unbiblical" conduct of the elder: it was (1) contrary to the law of Moses, (2) contrary to the Gospel, (3) contrary to apostolic teaching, (4) contrary to the teaching of Dirk Philips, (5) contrary to the articles of our faith, (6) contrary to the *Ordnungsbrief* of Essingen (*q.v.*). The elder of the Münsteroller congregation had to confess his error and express his penitence.

Not seldom were conferences of the Alsatian brethren held, in which an *Ordnungsbrief* was decided upon for the congregations of Alsace, which were read aloud in the congregations and accepted as the norm. Two such *Ordnungsbriefe* have been preserved. One was adopted in Steinselz on April 28, 1752; it says: "We preachers and elders have gathered from many lands and towns to consult with each other first, how we were standing in the faith and have found that we have agreed in articles of faith." The following resolutions were adopted: (1) Married couples who quarrel are to be put out of the congregation; if one partner is penitent and is received back into the brotherhood, but the other will not be converted, but remains in his sins, the former shall for that reason not remain outside the congregation, but shall not marry another so long as the partner lives. (2) When a brother or sister joins or marries a worldly person, but repents and desires to be readmitted into the brotherhood, he shall not be denied acceptance, but only on the condition that he bring the other partner with him; if he cannot do this, he must leave his partner, but provide him with the necessities of life and separate himself for the sake of heaven and earnestly pray that he may be converted and acknowledge the truth. (3) But if a brother or sister is guilty of adultery with a person of the world and penitently returns to the congregation, he shall not be free to marry another as long as the other lives. (4) No brother shall take the liberty of leasing a large farm or making debts, thereby burdening the brotherhood or inflicting shame on it or borrow money for wholesale trade without taking counsel. (5) No brother shall deprive another or a worldly person of a lease, deceive him or raise its cost behind his back. (6) Improper clothing (the wearing of square ties and shoes with high heels), as well as the new manners of smoking or snuffing tobacco, removing the beard with the razor and the like is forbidden and shall, if it is not stopped, be punished with excommunication.

The second *Ordnungsbrief,* adopted at Essingen (*q.v.*) in the Palatinate near Landau on Nov. 22, 1779, is still more explicit. There were 19 congregations represented here by 39 preachers and elders; among them were the Alsatian congregations of Münsteroll (later Belfort and Florimont), Neuneich, Colmar, Markirch, Salm (at that time in Lorraine), Münster, Strasbourg, Struth, Froensburg, Essingen, Hochstatt. The *Ordnungsbrief* contains 16 points. Points 1 and 2 deal with faith, the others with the life in the brotherhood. It says (condensed):

(1) We accept the Dordrecht Confession as in accord with the Word of God, and each should strive to observe the 33 articles and obey them. (2) Concerning the incarnation of Christ we should stay by the Scripture, and acknowledge Him with Paul as the Son of God, and with Peter as the son of David after the flesh, and avoid unnecessary disputation. (3) explains how the unrest caused by several brethren in rebellion against the preachers and elders shall be punished and removed. (4) and (5) describe how the congregations shall be cared for by the preachers and elders. (6) tells how the ministers and elders shall execute their offices. (7) No brother shall become involved in buying, building, or other things connected with large sums of money or usury without the knowledge and counsel of the brethren or elders. (8) Marriage shall take place with the foreknowledge and consent of the preachers or elders and also of the parents in the Lord and not in the world. (9) Avoidance shall be practiced toward those who leave the truth of the Gospel and the brotherhood, whereby the name of God or the congregation may be injured, and members shall withdraw from all who have fallen away with all moderation and modesty on the basis of the apostles. (10) Brethren and sisters shall greet one another with the kiss of the Lord; but those who have not been received shall not be greeted with a kiss, but with the words, "May God come to your aid." (11) requires aid for the poor widows, and orphans. (12-14) repeat the Steinselz stipulations concerning the use of tobacco and immodest dress (the hair on top of the head shall not be cut in the indecent manner of the world). (15) Servants and maids, if they are members of the brotherhood, shall be employed before all others; nor shall they accept employment of non-members. (16) Preachers and elders shall be more careful in teaching and admonishing, in baptism and communion, in Christian discipline and punishment according to the Gospel; if a preacher cannot cope with a situation in his congregation he shall ask other congregations for assistance and this aid is promised him.

A conference of preachers and elders on the Entenfang near Strasbourg on Sept. 6, 1796, stipulated that "those who after fleshly error have married outside the congregation and brotherhood, if they are admitted into the congregation, shall be remarried anew, for the apostle says that this shall take place only in the Lord; and in the days of Noah those fared badly who refused to be punished by God's Spirit."

Great distress was caused the Mennonites in Alsace by the question of military service. As long as France was a republic they were released from military service and guard duty. They were treated considerately by the republican government. The national assembly of June 12, 1790, decided that all active citizens must be registered for guard duty. The Mennonites asked for exemption and were granted it, with the loss of certain rights of citizenship.

Three years later, on Aug. 18, 1793, the division of welfare in Paris, evidently in reply to a petition of the Mennonites personally delivered by delegates sent for that purpose to Paris, reached the decision that they were to be entirely free of military duty, a part of which follows: "The Mennonites of France, citizens, have sent delegates to present to us that their worship and customs forbid their bearing arms and to request that they be used in other branches of service. We have seen in them simple hearts and have therefore thought that a good constitution should use all virtues for the common good. We therefore invite you to exercise the same kindness and gentleness toward them as is their character, and to prevent their being persecuted and to give them the kind of work they desire, such as building fortifications or roads of transportation, or even to perform their service by a monetary payment." It was signed by Couthon, Barrère, Hérault, St. Just, Thuriot, and Robespierre.

It was a very different matter when Napoleon became emperor of France. Now the Mennonites were all drawn into the army. A petition to the emperor was either ignored or answered in the negative. On June 19, 1808, a conference meeting at the Bildhäuserhof below Schlettstadt dealt with this matter. There were 9 congregations present with 22 preachers or elders. It was decided to send two men to Paris who could speak French. Jan. 29, 1809, was set aside as a day of prayer and fasting for the success of the mission. The men sent were Christian Gingerich of Wallenrade in Lorraine and Christian Engel of Jambrot (4 miles west of Avricourt) in the Welschländer congregation. The congregations of the Palatinate and Hesse helped to defray the expenses of this mission: Ibersheimerhof, with 200 doubloons, Donnersberg near Mainz with 16, and Kaiserslautern with 10. A sum of 423 doubloons was collected. But the delegates could accomplish nothing in Paris. Therefore two additional conferences were held, one at Winting on April 22, 1811, the other at Bildhausen on June 2, 1811. Nevertheless the decision stood: "For the sake of his faith nobody may refuse service in the army."

In the Franco-Prussian War (1870-71) the congregations of Wissembourg and Belfort suffered most severely. An offering was held for them, with practical results, and eased their distress.

After a long interval conference activity was resumed at the end of the 19th century. The first conference took place in 1896 at Munzenheim near Colmar. It was decided that the conference should convene annually, but the first regular annual conference was that which met at Pulversheim on May 25, 1907, when several brethren urged the appointment of a traveling evangelist. At the following conference, meeting at Saarburg May 2, 1908, the matter was further discussed, but the conference at Holeestrasse in Basel, Feb. 13, 1909, decided to dispense with a traveling preacher and instead have each of the 13 congregations in the association regularly visit all the other congregations for the purpose of pastoral care and preaching service. At the same time a fund was opened for the conference and traveling ministry. The visits in the homes and congregations were carried out and the institution was still further developed at the conference in Wolfganzen on April 29, 1911. On June 1, 1913, H. Volkmar was appointed as the first traveling minister: he was followed in 1917 by Fritz Goldschmidt of Basel. The conferences of the Mennonites of Alsace-Lorraine were attended by brethren from Baden and the Palatinate. This led to the Alsatian Mennonites' joining the *Konferenz der süddeutschen Mennoniten*. Two brethren from Alsace-Lorraine, Valentin Pelsy of Mückenhof, and J. Peterschmitt of Rheinfelderhof, were made members of the administrative committee of this conference. New life began to stir in all the congregations. Then World War I broke out in 1914. Again the Alsatian brethren suffered severely; and again general aid was given by their brethren. Large relief gifts came from America, and much need was alleviated.

The Treaty of Versailles of 1919 joined Alsace to France, and the union with the South German Mennonites was dissolved. On the other hand, a closer fellowship was formed with the Swiss and with the French-speaking congregations of inner France, with active co-operation in conferences. It was not until 1925, however, that the conference was again officially organized under the name, *Association des Eglises Evangeliques Mennonites de France*. The conference has always included all the German-speaking congregations of both Alsace and Lorraine. In 1901 the congregations of inner France, those using the French language, began to

hold a separate conference, which was formally incorporated in 1907. Suspended until 1927, it was reinstituted in that year, really as a sub-section of the *Association* of 1925. The Alsace-Lorraine Conference, continuing thus until 1939, then suspended until 1946, when it was again organized as an independent conference.

In 1837 the Hochwald congregation was dissolved; the members who did not emigrate to America united with the young Protestant congregation there (*Menn. Bl.*, 1898, 73). One congregation has its seat in Switzerland, namely, Basel-Holeestrasse; Niederrödern und Geisberg were united with Deutschhof (*q.v.*) of the Palatinate until World War II. The other Mennonite congregations in Alsace are Birkenhof, with 51 baptized members, Altkirch 72, Basel-Holee 152 (of whom possibly 102 live in Alsace), Colmar 70, Neuf-Brisach 65, Pfastatt 202, Pulversheim 65, Hang 100, Geisberg 63. The total baptized membership in 1950 was 720, with an additional 250 children, these making a total community of approximately 1,000. NEFF.

The Cultural Significance of the Alsatian Mennonites. The Mennonites aroused the displeasure of their neighbors, as has been said above. If the neighbors were in a favorable position with the authorities and landowners, their influence was often detrimental to the Mennonites. It was then a simple matter to use the religious differences as a shield behind which to get rid of an unwelcome competitor. But about the middle of the 18th century such religious and economic politics ceased. The reason for this turn of attitude was not a change of attitude toward freedom on the part of the authorities; rather, it was the influence of the prominent physiocrats, with their new economic philosophy which arose about the middle of the 18th century. For them the core of the economic life lay in the farming class of society, especially the renters. Only they were considered productive members of society, and with the landowners were contrasted with the sterile, unfruitful class in industry, trade, free vocations, and the servant class. It was the glorification of the feudal system shortly before its destruction by the great French Revolution.

Alsace was the seat of important secular and spiritual lords. They had already previously learned to appreciate the industrious and dependable Mennonites as good renters. To protect the farmers, especially the renters of the large holdings, became a moral obligation and was praised as a law of reason. In 1771 the abbot Baudeau wrote concerning the lot "of those valuable people, who . . . cultivate the property of others," in his *Explication du tableau économique*: "All that oppresses, degrades, wrongs, robs them strikes deep wounds on society. All that elevates them, all that would contribute to their well-being, their contentment, their wealth, is a source of happiness for all classes." This was meant especially for the ears of the landowners. In this economic view, valid at the time, lie the roots of the favor enjoyed by Mennonite renters long before the influences of the French Revolution. Indeed, the interest in these physiocratic ideas and their learned and effective sponsors reached all

the way to the salons of Paris. The literature of
these circles was occupied with this fashion. This
is seen, for instance, in a delicate duodecimo volume
of informal, chatty essays, *Les soirées Helvetiennes,
Alsaciennes, et Fran-Comtoises* (Amsterdam and
Paris, 1772, which also appeared in English translation at the same time). It should not be surprising that these "Evening entertainments in Alsace" speak in long chapters about the "influence
of good morals on agriculture." The book contains a section "On the Anabaptists" (pp. 40 ff.).
Alexander Frederic Jaques Masson, Marquis de
Pezay (1741-77), also presented the salons with
entertaining material on the competent Mennonites
in a colorful series of comic opera, travel reports,
and military writings. In his youth he had been
the military tutor of Louis XVI. His varied talent
brought him great influence, but also foes, who
finally overthrew him. He was then appointed
inspector of the French coast, having previously
been assigned the task of evaluating the state of the
eastern border from the military and economic
point of view. He thus became acquainted with the
Alsatian Mennonites. He is certainly not a religious
fanatic when he presents an interesting and thorough description of their life and work in both the
internal and external aspects. He introduces his
praise of their morality with a comparison with
China's people and country, a popular comparison
at the time, for to the physiocrats China seemed
the model agrarian state. The fields of the Mennonites could be recognized from afar by their better care; they themselves could be recognized by
their clothing without buttons and shoes without
buckles. Then Pezay follows them to the remotest
nooks of the Vosges where they have their straw
huts, "which are as plain as they and intelligently
constructed." "Ancient hospitality" is offered the
traveler in all simplicity but with conspicuous cleanliness, and he lingers on his description of the
charms of the daughters. The Anabaptists (he continued) are the same everywhere: gentle, kindly,
industrious. He quotes the opinion expressed by
the mayor of Amsterdam concerning the Dutch
Mennonites. Then Pezay concludes his song of
praise with the familiar story of the conscientious
Mennonite farmer in Waldeck in the Seven Years'
War. (This story is still found in the readers and
pedagogical writings. See *DB* 1872, p. 94.)

The tenth "evening entertainment" is devoted to
the especial skill of the Mennonites in meadow culture. It is a misfortune for France that there are
so few Anabaptists in inner France and its border
provinces. Pezay praises the freedom offered them
in Montbéliard, where they are permitted to do
much good, although the soil is very poor. They
also show their great competence in the manufacture of equipment. But their particular capability
lies in their irrigation of meadows by means of
skillfully planned ditches. He urgently recommends
imitation of this method; the skill is certainly not
a quality of their particular religion. (See Donnersberg for a discussion of the art of meadow culture
peculiar to the Mennonites.)

Then Pezay deals in detail with a further pecu-
liarity of Mennonite farming methods; they make
the boundary ditches of their fields and woodlots
in such a way that a crop can be raised there too.
This leads him to a detailed discussion of this
method "applied to the rivers and creeks of France."

The entire eleventh "entertainment" is devoted
to this subject. Again and again, especially in his
reflections concerning the river police, he returns
to the example of the Mennonites. Thus all the
meadows of France would be watered and dams
and ditches would be used and planted over the
nation according to their pattern. He declares himself ready to instruct all those living along the rivers and estimates enormous gains for the kingdom,
which would eclipse the yield of the tax collectors.
Nothing in these 400 pages excites him as much as
this example. He remarks ironically at one place
that in view of the "galloping" spirit of enterprise
among high and low, there are in Paris surely
2,000 persons, who, if they found out about the
method of the Mennonites, would compete for the
monopoly of leasing the river dams of France.

The Marquis de Pezay died young. It is not clear
how much improvement resulted from his enthusiastic plans. For us it is of significance to know
that he was a friend of Voltaire's. His rationalistic
point of view toward universal cultural improvement led to his interest in the Mennonites. The
experiences of the marquis among the Alsatian
Mennonites were no doubt known to Voltaire. The
writer of the foreword of the 1776 German edition
of the confession of faith by Cornelis Ris (Hamburg, 1776, p. XXVII), probably a Hamburg Mennonite minister, mentions the "simple manner of
life, the industry of the Mennonite congregations
in Alsace," referring to the *Soirées Helvetiennes* as
his source.

The Alsatian Mennonite as the type of an upright
man, who is capable and skilled in his work, was
also presented by the Alsatian poet and teacher
Gottlieb K. Pfeffel of the 18th century. The renter,
"an intelligent Mennonite," who bravely tells the
truth even to his baron, is an incidental figure with
Pfeffel.

The Marquis de Pezay and his Anabaptist recollections did not pass into oblivion. The feuilleton-
ist of *Le Siècle,* a Paris periodical, found the volume in a secondhand bookstall, and visited the
Mennonites in the Vosges before and after. He
was Alfred Michiels, who wrote in a vein very
similar to Pezay's, and describes the Mennonites in
his book, *Les Anabaptistes des Vosges* (1860). But
his account is not as objective or careful as that of
the marquis; in many instances the book has the
flavor of a novel. Nevertheless his recollections of
the past should be gratefully acknowledged. The
congregation and the people of Salm are brought
to life for the reader in a fluent style. The visit
in the home of the Elder Augsburger is the center
of the narrative. Again the economic example of
the Mennonites in all respects, in household and in
farming, and their marriage customs and also their
attitude to tobacco are broadly described. Michiels'
presentation of the history of the Mennonites and
their martyrs is somewhat dubious, given as it is

in the *feuilleton* spirit of the journalist. True to history is his confirmation of the interest of the Alsatian Mennonites in botany and medicine. Michiels reports that he found books along this line in their homes. He also knows of the Mennonites of the Palatinate, that many of them understand veterinary medicine, which explains their excellent herds of cattle. Family histories tell us that the Alsatian Mennonites in turn took progressive methods of agriculture to the Palatinate (see **Dettweiler**).

After Michiels there was probably no author who wrote about the Mennonites of Alsace on his own observation. *Elsässische Lebensbilder* by Margarete Spörlin (2 v., Basel, 1875) contains a story entitled *Das Waldhaus* which describes a Mennonite family during the French Revolution; it is of slight significance. Werner Wittich, the agrarian historian of Strasbourg, in his *Deutsche und französische Kultur im Elsass* (Strasbourg, 1900), presents a valuable picture of the contrasts in the social attitude of the various creeds in the simplified formula, "Protestant" and Catholic.   E.H.C.

A. Frölich, *Sektentum und Separatismus im jetzigen kirchl. Leben der evan. Bevölkerung Elsass-Lothringens* (Strassburg, 1889) contains a section, 14-23, on the Mennonites in Alsace-Lorraine; C. Gerbert, *Gesch. der Strassburger Sektenbew. z. Z. der Ref.* (Strasbourg, 1889); Ph. Grandidier, *Oeuvres inédites*, 6 v. (Colmar, 1865-68); Louis Hauth, *Les Anabaptistes à Strasbourg au temps de la ref.* (Strasbourg, 1860); A. Hulshoff, *Gesch. van de Doopsgez. te Straatsburg van 1525 tot 1557* (Amsterdam, 1905); Ch. Mathiot, *Recherches hist. sur les Anabaptistes* (Belfort, 1922); A. Michiels, *Les Anabaptistes des Vosges* (Paris, 1860); X. Mosemann, *Les Anabaptistes à Colmar 1534-35;* T. W. Röhrich, *Gesch. der Ref. im Elsass und besonders in Strassburg*, 3 v. (Strasbourg, 1831-33); T. W. Röhrich, *Zur Gesch. der Strassburgischen Wiedertäufer in den Jahren 1527 bis 1534* (Ztscht für hist. Theol., 1860, 3-121); *Les Soirées Helvetiennes, Alsaciennes, et Fran-Comtoises* (Amsterdam and Paris, 1772); A. F. J. Masson (Marquis de Pezay), *Oeuvres agréables et morales ou variétés littéraires précédées d'un discours sur la vie et les ouvrages de l'auteur*, 2 v. (Liége, 1792); *Etat et mémoire des anabaptistes d'Alsace* (written by a priest of Mutzig at the beginning of the 18th c.); *L'Etat du temporale dressé par M. Antoine Rice, prêtre déligué par le duc de Lorraine en 1802;* V. Pelsy and P. Sommer, "Précis d'Histoire des Eglises Mennonites" (Montbéliard, 1914 and 1937); in *Almanach Menn. du Cinquaintenaire* (Montbéliard, 1951); ML I, 553-63.

Alseider, Christian, an Anabaptist martyr, executed in 1533 (not in 1536 as in the *Martyrs' Mirror*) with six brethren: Hans Bekh, Balser Schneider, Waltan Gsäl, Wölfl of Götzenberg, Hans Maurer, and Peter Kranawitter, in the castle of Guffidaun (in the Adige Valley in Austria). To make them recant they were severely tortured. Only Wölfl wavered under the duress, but he repented and then remained steadfast like the rest. In a letter to the congregation in the Adige they stated that there were ten others still in prison, all of whom wished to witness for the Lord with their blood. (Beck, *Geschichts-Bücher*, 108 f.; *Mart. Mir.* D 33, E 444; *ML* I, 36.)   HEGE.

Altar *(altare, altarium)* is since Tertullian and Cyprian in the third century A.D. the name given the table at which communion is served ("Lord's table," I Cor. 11:23). The celebration of the love feast *(Agape)* and the Lord's Supper connected with it required a table. Jesus observed the first Lord's Supper with the disciples at a table and thus the disciples later presumably also observed it. When the Christian worship service was transferred from private homes to a special building, the exclusive use of tables for communion services continued. Usually the table was covered with a linen cloth.

Later in the Roman Catholic Church altars were made coffin- and box-shaped, since they also served as storing places for the sacred relics. Then roofs and canopies supported on pillars were placed above the altars for ornamental purposes, topped at their highest point by a golden crown, while crosses, crucifixes, and candles were placed on the altar surface. The altar cloths, especially the front panel, were fashioned of costly material. The table altar thus became a sacrificial altar. Instead of the one altar in a church, several were set up. The Middle Ages brought the Gothic altars, which were provided with increasingly elaborate carvings and ornamentation.

All this the Reformation radically changed in Protestant churches. While the Reformed churches replaced the altar with a firm and movable table, the Lutheran and Anglican churches removed only the additions that had made an altar of the Lord's table, keeping the fixed altar. In the order of Reformation of Homburg, Hessen, of November or December 1536 it was stipulated that all altars should be removed from the churches except the one from which the emblems of the Lord's Supper were dispensed. This altar was henceforth to be called a table rather than an altar, since the communion service is not a sacrifice but the commemoration of the sacrifice which Christ made once for all. The altars were removed because the heathen, Jews, and Roman Catholics understood an altar to be a place of sacrifice. (Fr. Thudichum, *Die deutsche Ref.* II, 1909.)

The Mennonite churches in the Netherlands for the most part use a table, which is placed before the pulpit, from which the bread and wine are served. This table is set there only during the communion service (whereas in the Reformed churches the table is usually not removed).

In America none of the more conservative or traditional groups, whether of German, Swiss, or Russian background, use the communion table. This is true without exception among the (old) Mennonites and the Mennonite Brethren. In the General Conference Mennonite Church, however, particularly in the city churches, the majority now use the communion table from which the bread and wine are served. In some cases even candles have been placed upon the table. (*ML* I, 37.)
                                                            NEFF.

Altdiakon (elder deacon), an honorary office of the two former churches of Schleswig-Holstein. When a deacon had for a number of years rendered especially useful service, he could, upon the request of the church council, be chosen by the congregation as "elder deacon." This office lasted for life, whereas deacons were chosen only for a number of years.

A few Dutch congregations also have a similar office, as for instance in Rotterdam. After a member has served on the church council for five years he is transferred into the *oude dienst*. The members of the *oude dienst* meet twice a year with the council, especially to give advice in financial and spiritual matters (see **Almosenpfleger**). (*ML* I, 38.)

H.vdS., vdZ.

Alte Kolonie (Old Colony). This term was originally used to distinguish the Chortitza (*q.v.*) Mennonite settlement of Russia (founded in 1789) from the later Molotschna (*q.v.*) settlement (founded in 1803). When in 1874-80 the Mennonites from the Chortitza and Fürstenland (*q.v.*) settlements established their homes on the West Reserve in Manitoba, and the Bergthal (*q.v.*) on the East Reserve, the latter were usually referred to as *Bergthaler* and the former as *Altkolonier* (Old Colonists), since they had come from the Old Colony (Chortitza) in Russia. Although the official name of the Old Colony group is "Reinland Mennonite Church" (*q.v.*), it has generally become known as the Old Colony Mennonite Church (*q.v.*), and the people are referred to as Old Colonists. This group can be found in Manitoba, Saskatchewan, and Mexico, and represents the most conservative wing of the Russo-German Mennonites, comparing with the Old Order Amish and the Hutterites in their beliefs and practices, especially in matters pertaining to nonconformity to the world. (*ML* I, 38.)   C.K.

Altenheim (Home for the Aged) of the Bergthal Mennonite Church in Gretna, Man., was started in July 1918 and continued in operation until July 1938. During its existence it was under the supervision of Deacon John Buhr, Gretna. Five or six appointed persons served the institution at various times. The number of inmates varied from 10 to 25. Since July 1938, the building, which is still the property of the Bergthal Church, has been occupied as a girls' dormitory of the Mennonite Collegiate Institute of Gretna. (See **Homes for the Aged**.)   B.E.

Altenmarkt, a community (Bruderhof) of Hutterian Brethren in Moravia, founded in 1545, who built tanneries and leather factories there. From 1553 on, Altenmarkt was one of their chief centers. On July 28, 1605, and again on Sept. 20, 1619, the house was burned down by soldiers. In October 1622 the Anabaptists had to leave Altenmarkt, abandoning all their goods, whereupon they settled in Hungary. (*ML* I, 39.)   HEGE.

Alternative Service Work Camps. In June 1941 the Canadian government informed the Committee on Military Problems of the Conference of Historic Peace Churches (Ontario) that alternative service was to be provided for conscientious objectors to war. The C.O.'s were to serve for four months in Alternative Service camps operated by the Department of Mines and Resources. Later the time was extended for the duration of the war. The government agreed to provide maintenance and traveling expenses to and from camp, and to pay the men 50 cents a day. The churches were also allowed to appoint religious advisers.

The first camp was located at Chalk River, 625 miles northwest of Toronto and 83 miles northwest of Sault Ste. Marie, Mich., at the point where the

Montreal River empties into Lake Superior. The place had formerly been a lumber camp. The first campers arrived there in July 1941, and during the first summer there were as many as 165 there at one time. J. Harold Sherk served as the religious adviser of the camp, but during the winter Harold D. Groh substituted for a three-month period. The men were employed by the Department of Highways in the construction of the joining link of the Trans-Canada route. Most of the men worked in the gravel pits or at clearing the bushlands.

In May 1942 the British Columbia Forest Service concluded an agreement with the Dominion Government to give alternative service work to hundreds of conscientious objectors. Their work was to consist of snag falling, road building, erecting telephone lines, fire fighting, and reforestation. Under the arrangement the Dominion Government paid the Forest Service $2.50 per day per man. Of this amount, the camper was paid 50 cents and the rest was used to take care of his board, lodging, and medical attention. The lease expired with the end of the government year but it was renewed for a twelve-month period, as the military authorities feared a bombing of the west coast that might produce a forest fire hazard.

In the spring of 1942, forestry camps were opened in British Columbia, and during the summer the men from Camp Montreal River were transferred west to the new camps. *The Beacon,* which was the mimeographed publication carrying news from the British Columbia camps, in July 1943 listed 19 for the province. Fourteen of these were on Vancouver Island and five on the mainland in western British Columbia. They were designated by such terms as C-1, Q-3, and GT-5 but also carried names such as Hill 60 camp, Campbell Lake camp, and Seymour Mountain camp. A camp engaged in road building was located in Saskatchewan.

By April 1943 17 of the British Columbia camps were working on forest protection and two on national park projects. Five national park camps were operated in Alberta, one in Saskatchewan, and one in Manitoba. The national park camps were under the Department of Mines and Resources. Two camps in Ontario under this department, the Montreal River camp and the Chalk River camp, were, however, engaged in highway construction.

At the same time, a shortage of farm labor developed in Canada. *The Beacon* reported in April 1943 that in the previous autumn a sizable portion of the Alberta harvest had remained in the fields because of the shortage of farm labor. An Order in Council effective May 1, 1943, transferred the Alternative Service System from the Canadian Selective Service System and military control to the Ministry of Labor, a civilian agency, and opened the way for the use of conscientious objectors on farms and in factories.

The increasing problem of dependency had also been a factor in bringing about the new program of gradual withdrawal of the men from the camps and their individual assignments to farms and factories. Under the new arrangement, farmers paid conscientious objectors $25 per month plus room and board. The rest of the wages were turned over to the Canadian Red Cross. Those working in factories or where maintenance could not be supplied by the employers were given $38 a month in addition and the balance was given to the Red Cross. Up to June 1944 over $300,000 had been contributed to the Red Cross under this plan. In addition, a varying scale of from $10 to $20 a month was provided for dependents. All men were covered by compensation laws. If the Alternative Service officer approved, the cost of medical emergencies could be subtracted from the Red Cross contributions. The men in the camps, however, continued receiving only 50 cents a day plus board, lodging, compensation insurance, and medical and dental care. Dependents of men in camp, however, could receive help from the provinces or municipalities in which they resided. If such help was given, the Ministry of Labor reimbursed the government unit making the payment.

The men who were assigned to their own farms were under the control of the Alternative Service Officer, regarding working conditions, assignments, transfers, dismissals, and wages. In theory men could have been assigned to defense plants or also to foreign service, teaching, or social service. The government, although interested in placing each man where he could contribute most to the nation, took his preference into account. Only a few were placed in teaching positions, among the Indians, Japanese, and Eskimos, where public sentiment did not prevent them from serving.

Whenever men were placed on farms or in industry, a contract was made. When the first contracts expired in 1944, the chairman and secretary of the Mennonite Military Problems Committee in Ontario were asked to spend eleven days sitting with the Alternative Service officials in Division A reviewing and renewing the contracts. Later the two men attended eight regional meetings in Division B. In both areas they brought up problems and grievances that might have received no consideration had they not been present. In spite of these safeguards the contracts differed in many details, as seemed necessary in the judgment of the Alternative Service officers. This lack of equality among C.O. workers often led to dissatisfaction, but an attempt was made by the Mennonite Military Problems Committee in Ontario to explain the differing contracts and to show the people how difficult it was to obtain perfect justice for everyone in a war period.

The Alternative Service program was administered by a chief Alternative Service officer, with headquarters in Ottawa. There were 13 mobilization districts in the Dominion, each with an Alternative Service officer and a staff of eight or more persons. In 1944 and 1945 those between 18 and 38 were registered, but men were not called up until they had reached 18½ years of age.

When a medical notice was received from the Mobilization Board, the man reported to a doctor for a physical examination. Within eight days after the notice for a physical examination was received, the man filled in an application signed by his pastor, requesting a C.O. status. This was sent to the Mobilization Board. Mennonites of the 1874-80 migration and Dukhobors were given automatic postponement as conscientious objectors upon certification by their pastors or leaders. After the Mobilization Board declared a man to be a conscientious objector, they presented the name to the district Alternative Service officer, who then placed the man in a camp, in a factory, or on a farm. The officer, after investigating the needs of the man and the job he was to be given, used his discretion in drawing up a suitable contract, which provided for the wages and other compensations mentioned above as well as the regular payments to the Canadian Red Cross.

After the Ministry of Labor took charge of the conscientious objectors, a decreasing number were sent to the camps. In March 1944 the British Columbia Forest Service camps were closed and the men sent back to their home provinces where they were placed in agriculture or industry. Other camps were closed, too, so that by June 1944 only seven remained. These were Chalk River, Ont.; Riddy Mountain, Man.; Banff and Seebe, Alta.; Radium Hot Springs, B.C.; a small road camp in Saskatchewan; and the Montreal River camp.

Most of the men in camps at the late date were those who had refused the work assigned them or had refused work of any kind. They were sentenced to the camps in a Magistrate's Court and taken to the camps by police escort. There was no appeal from the decision of any of the 13 Mobilization Boards. The boards had the privilege of calling upon the justice of the peace of a man's home community to interview him when they questioned his sincerity, but when they denied him his C.O. status there was nothing he could do. These men were escorted to the military barracks by the Royal Canadian Mounted Police, where the army attempted to persuade them to accept military service. When they refused, they were given one, two, or three fourteen-day courts-martial in the guardhouse. "In the majority of these cases, the military authorities recommend to the Mobilization Boards that these men be given the status of postponed C.O.'s. Official figures indicate that about 300 men have been involved in this group during the five years that Canada has been at war." It should be added that most of these 300 were Jehovah's Witnesses.

In the early spring of 1945, there were approximately 6,000 C.O.'s under contract in Canada. A report as of March 31, 1944, stated that there were 8,932 conscientious objectors who were given postponement of military service in Canada. "Of these, 245 have offered their services in the armed forces and 122 have volunteered as noncombatants in the medical and dental corps. Of the others, 3,188 were placed in agriculture and 1,295 in other employment."

A table in *Erfahrungen der Mennoniten in Canada während des zweiten Weltkrieges* lists the following number of conscientious objectors for all of Canada during the entire war.

Prince Edward Island	3
Nova Scotia	29
New Brunswick	2
Quebec	28
Ontario	2,602
Manitoba	2,948
Saskatchewan	2,320
Alberta	1,157
British Columbia	1,611
Total	10,700

Of the approximately 9,000 in March 1944, about 2,000 were Dukhobors. Of the total, approximately 63 per cent were Mennonites, 20 per cent Dukhobors, 10 per cent Plymouth Brethren, Christadelphians, and Pentecostal groups, and 3 per cent Jehovah's Witnesses. A partial list of churches represented in the camps included 30 denominations. Manitoba, the home of thousands of Russian Mennonites and Dukhobors, furnished the largest number of objectors of all of the Canadian provinces.

On Aug. 15, 1946, the government of Canada revoked the Order in Council P.C. 3030 and all C.O.'s returned to civilian life. Up to that date over 5,000 Mennonite young men of Canada had been classed as C.O.'s and had served in camps or in other areas under a system of conscription. What effect had this experience upon them? J. W. Nickel, a young Canadian Mennonite minister who preached in many of their camps, declared that camp life among other results "taught those, who because of previous isolated church life held the members of another denomination in narrow esteem, to respect and love their brother." (For a map of the A.S. camps see **Civilian Public Service**.)

M.G.

M. Gingerich, *Service for Peace, A Hist. of Menn. Civilian Public Service* (Akron, Pa., 1949); *Erfahrungen der Menn. in Canada während des zweiten Weltkrieges, 1939-1945* (Steinbach, Man., 1948); P. L. Storms, "Forest Service in B. C. Service Work Camps," *Christian Monitor* (Oct. 1943); J. W. Nickel, "The Canadian Conscientious Objector," *Menn. Life* (Jan. 1948) 24-28.

Alt-Evangelische Mennonitische Brüderschaft in Russland (1789-1910), *im Rahmen der Mennonitischen Gesamtgeschichte, Die,* an important historical work by Peter M. Friesen, published at Halbstadt, South Russia, in 1911 by the Mennonite publishing firm *Raduga,* of which 776 pages deal with the Mennonites of Russia and 154 with the Mennonites of America. In two introductory chapters Friesen briefly sketches the history of the Mennonites prior to their migration to Russia, followed by a chapter dealing with the Mennonites in Russia from 1789 to 1860. The next chapter, containing more than 400 pages, is devoted to the origin and development of the Mennonite Brethren Church. Successive chapters are devoted to nonresistance, patriotism, doctrines, practices, missions, education, mutual aid, the spread of the Mennonites, industry, business, and statistics pertaining to the development of the Mennonites in Russia. The portion of the book presenting the Mennonites in America has chapters on the Mennonite Brethren, the General Conference Mennonites, and the (old) Mennonites. The preface is most informative about the origin of the book, the author's attitudes, and the religious and cultural situation of the Mennonites in Russia before World War I.

In 1887 P. M. Friesen (*q.v.*), a member of the Mennonite Brethren Church, was given the assignment of writing the history of the first twenty-five years of his church, which had been established in 1860. Visiting churches and archives, "continually looking, listening, and gathering material," he completed his task after twenty-five years. The nearly 1,000-page volume contained much more in scope and content than he had been asked to write. His continual addition of new materials, chapters, and documents to his manuscript has caused a certain lack of organization in the composition of the book, making it somewhat difficult to locate specific information in the bulky volume.

While at work the author became so enchanted by the total history of the Mennonites that he soon gave up his original plan of presenting only the first twenty-five years of the history of the Mennonite Brethren Church, and gave a fairly objective picture of the whole. As a university-trained educator who had lived and taught in non-Mennonite communities, and who had become a Russian patriot and lover of the Russian language and literature, and who had above all attained an appreciation of his own Mennonite people from a distance, he freely criticized the weaknesses of all groups within the brotherhood. In his evaluation of traditional Mennonitism in comparison to the more recent pietistic influences he is probably a little prejudiced in favor of the latter and in his attitude toward those who left Russia in 1874-80 for conscience' sake he is somewhat blinded by his Russian patriotism. Although the book does not present an integrated story of the Mennonites of Russia, it is an indispensable illustrated collection of historical material, especially now that the documents in Russia are no longer available, and will remain a mine of information in this field.

C.K.

Altevangelische Wehrlose Taufgesinnten-Gemeinden, the name the Swiss Mennonites once gave themselves. In a petition to the government in 1810 the Langnau congregation emphasized the right to the use of this name in that they traced their derivation to the time when the Christian Church became a state religion and had forsaken its apostolic character and become worldly, from which time on there had been "old Evangelicals" who remained true to the apostolic church in spite of all persecution. Later the Swiss Mennonites may have clung to the name the more tenaciously because of the rise of a new church founded by Samuel Fröhlich about 1832 called the *Neutäufer* (New Anabaptists; see **Apostolic Christian Church**). The conference of the Swiss Mennonites now (since 1910) bears the name *Konferenz der altevangelischen Taufgesinnten Gemeinden der Schweiz.* The *Neutäufer* call themselves in Switzerland *Gemeinschaft evangelisch Taufgesinnter.*

The yearbook which H. G. Mannhardt of Danzig published in 1888 carried the title, *Jahrbuch der altevangelischen Taufgesinnten oder Mennoniten-Gemeinden.* According to the author, he had no particular purpose in this use of the name, but it was only an incidental introduction of Swiss usage (*Menn. Bl.*, 1888, 21 and 25). In the second (1891) edition of her book, *Ursprung, Entwicklung und Schicksale der Taufgesinnten oder Mennoniten* (Soltau, 1888), Anna Brons added the word *altevangelische* to the title. In like manner P. M. Friesen put it into the title of his book, *Die Alt-Evangelische Mennonitische Brüderschaft in Russland* (Halbstadt, 1911). Johannes Bartsch's use of it in his *Geschichte der Gemeinde Jesu Christi, das heisst: der Altevangelischen- und Mennoniten-Gemeinden* (Elkhart, 1898) is the only known use in an American book and is distinctly an imitation of Keller, Brons, and Mannhardt. John Horsch had used the term once in 1891 in a series of three articles in the *Herold der Wahrheit* (Elkhart), *"Die Altevangelischen Taufgesinnten und die Münsterischen Wiedertäufer,"* during the period when he was under Keller's influence, but he did not continue its use.

Actually the introduction of the term *Alt-Evangelisch* and its corresponding historical concept into the literature and usage of the German Mennonites after 1885 was largely due to the influence of the noted archivist, historian, and defender of the Anabaptists, Ludwig Keller, of Münster, Germany. Keller developed the theory that there was a succession of true evangelical groups down through history, outside the Roman Church, and that the Anabaptists of the Reformation period were a continuation or revival of these groups. In his Berlin lecture of 1887 (*Zur Geschichte der Altevangelischen Gemeinden,* Berlin, 1889) he pressed his point vigorously and told (p. 41) how he was led to use this name, having found it in use among the Swiss Mennonites. He used the term extensively for the first time in his book, *Die Reformation und die älteren Reformparteien* (Leipzig, 1885), making it the carrying symbol of his historical construction. At this time also he advocated its use in his articles in the *Mennonitische Blätter,* where it appeared for the first time in February 1885 in his article, *Die "altevangelischen Taufgesinnten" und der Urprung dieses Namens,* reprinted from the January 1885 *Zionspilger* of Langnau, Switzerland. For a time some German Mennonites used the term, being deeply influenced by their powerful friend, but they never adopted the term *altevangelisch* as a part of their official name. The newly founded (April 1886) *Vereinigung der Mennoniten-Gemeinden im deutschen Reich* chose rather the name "Mennoniten," much to Keller's disappointment. (*Menn. Bl.* XXXIII, 1886, 33-34; *ML* I, 41.)

H.S.B.

Althamer, Andreas, a Lutheran divine, b. about 1500 in Brenz near Bundelfingen, Württemberg, Germany, d. 1539 as pastor in Ansbach. According to the *Allgemeine deutsche Biographie* the year of his death is uncertain: "According to one, he died about 1540, according to another he was still in Ansbach in 1544, and then went to the Silesian principality of the margrave of Brandenburg, where he died in Jägersdorf in 1564 as the leading pastor." He was a zealous Lutheran and as such took part in the disputation of 1528 in Bern, Switzerland, and there defended the Lutheran doctrine of the Lord's Supper. While pastor in Eltersdorf near Erlangen he wrote a refutation of Hans Denk's booklet, *Wer die Warhait warlich lieb hat, mag sich hierinn brüfen in erkandtnuss seines Glaubens auf das sich nyemandt in im selbs erhebe, sonder wisse, von wem man weisshait bitten und entphahen soll.* In this booklet Denk collected 40 apparently contradictory passages of Scripture. Althamer's booklet bears the title: *Dialloge hoc est, conciliatio locorum scripturae, qui prima facie inter se pugnare videntur* (Nürnberg, 1527). According to Kolde (*HRE,* 3d ed., I, 413) this is one of Althamer's most widely read writings, which later, greatly enlarged, was published in many editions and was at once translated into German at Althamer's request by his good friend, Sebastian Franck of Wörth. Althamer was very likely the author of the anonymous booklet with the very similar title: *Conciliationes scripturae, qui specie tenus inter se pugnare videntur, Centuriae duae* (Nürnberg, 1534), with an original foreword and additions of his own. At that time Franck was still the Lutheran pastor in Gustenfelden (Middle Franconia) and an opponent of the Anabaptists. But by 1531 Franck had become the first historiographer of the Anabaptists in the *Chronica, Zeitbuch oder Geschichtbibel* and is considered their private friend. In the later edition of 1534 Althamer omitted the polemics against the Anabaptists, as Franck had already done.

As a determined enemy of the Anabaptists Althamer revealed himself in two other writings, also apparently written in Eltersdorf, before he went as deacon to the St. Sebaldus Church in Nürnberg. (The second of these two writings is not mentioned in the best-known accounts of Althamer's life.) They are:

1. *Von der Erbsund das sye der Christen kynder gleich als wol verdamb als der heyden. Und von dem heyligen Tauff ob er die Erbsund hynweg nem* (Nürnberg, 1527).

2. *Ein kurtze Unterricht den Pfarrherrn und Predigern in meiner gnedigen Herrn der Markgrafen zu Brandenburg etc., Fürstenthumben und Landes hieniden in Francken und auf dem Gebirg verordnet, wes sie das Volk wider etliche verführische lere der widertauffer an den Feyertagen auff der Canntzel zum getreulichsten und besten aus göttlicher schrifft vermanen und unterrichten sollen.* A copy is to be found in the city library of Frankfurt, which was reprinted in Will's *Beiträge.*

The former writing presents in detail the Lutheran doctrine of original sin, which is treated throughout in a responsible sense. If it is responsible, it is also damnable, and the necessity of baptism as the "bath of regeneration" follows. The entire content of the booklet follows this line of thought, with many Bible references. On the last pages the author presents a clever refutation—from his point of view—of arguments against infant baptism.

The second booklet was printed, according to the foreword, upon the wish and direction of Margrave George of Brandenburg, who in his own name and that of his nephew, Margrave Albrecht, had it distributed to all the pastors and preachers in his domain, "for faithful use, in order that their parishioners be not misled by Anabaptist teaching." In this writing Althamer tried to prove the doctrine of infant baptism from the Old Testament. What circumcision was, viz., a sign of the divine covenant and grace, that baptism is in the New Covenant. As the former was performed on children at eight days, so must baptism also be performed. Also from the command to baptize it follows that little children must be baptized; they are included in the term "all nations," etc. The conclusion of the booklet deals directly with the community of goods of the Anabaptists, which is rejected as a devilish doctrine that stirs up rebellion.

One other booklet of his must also be mentioned: *Das unser Christus Jesus warer Gott sey, Zeugnüss der heyligen geschrifft, Wider die newen Juden und Arrianer unter christlichem Namen, welche die Gottheyt Christi verleugnen* (Nürnberg, 1526).

On April 16, 1531, Althamer, together with the local pastor Sigmund Schneeweiss (*q.v.*) and Joh. Rurer (*q.v.*), cross-examined the Anabaptist prisoners Bernhard Weith (Weickmann, *q.v.*) and Julius Lober (*q.v.*) in Ansbach. Althamer and Rurer in 1530 delivered an official opinion concerning the confession of Johann Hechtlein, who had become an Anabaptist for the second time. (See **Brandenburg-Ansbach**.)   NEFF.

K. Schornbaum, *Quellen zur Gesch. der Wiedertäufer* II: *Markgraftum Brandenburg* (Leipzig, 1934; *Bavaria*, first division) in the index of persons, p. 366 under "Hechtlein, Hans," and pp. 205-8; E. Teufel, "Der Täuferprozess des Pfarrers Joh. Hechtlein in Schalkhausen bei Ansbach 1529-30," in *Ztschr für Bayr. Kirchengesch.*, 1949, No. 2, 88-97; G. A. Will, "Althamers Unterricht," in *Beiträge zur Gesch. des Antibaptismus in Frankenland* (Nürnberg, 1773) 115; *idem*, *Beiträge zur Fränkischen Kirchenhist.* (Nürnberg, 1770) 321-68; Th. Kolde, *Andreas Althamer, der Humanist und Reformator in Brandenburg-Ansbach* (Erlangen, 1895); *ML* I, 41-2.

Alting, Menso (1541-1612), a Calvinist divine, educated at Heidelberg, worked at first in the Palatinate (after 1566) and 1574-1612 as preacher in Emden, where he promoted the spread of Calvinism at the cost of Lutheranism and Anabaptism. Before the religious disputation at Emden in 1578, in which he was the speaker on the Reformed side, he published a book against the Mennonites.   HEGE.

H. Klugkist, *Menso Alting, eine Gestalt aus der Kampfzeit der calvinistischen Kirche* (Berlin, 1928); *Protocol Dat is, Alle Handelinghe des Ghesprecx tot Embden . . .* (Emden, 1579); *ML* I, 42.

Altkirch, a Mennonite congregation in Upper Alsace. Its members live in the vicinity of the town of Altkirch, and are for the most part descendants of Mennonite immigrants from Switzerland to France and Alsace. Whether they settled at Altkirch in the 17th century soon after the close of the Thirty Years' War (1650), or whether they came from other Alsatian Mennonite communities is not clear. Probably the latter is the case. The Altkirch congregation (for a time known as Altkirch-Dammerkirch and then Altkirch-Birkenhof) has existed since about 1825. Its first minister, Joseph Hirschi, was born in Sigolsheim (district of Col-

mar) and died about 1865 in Hirsingen near Altkirch.

Services were at first held in private homes; since 1846 (renovated in 1928) the congregation has had a meetinghouse in Birkenhof, and since 1825 a cemetery. The meetinghouse in Altkirch was built in 1926. In 1912 Altkirch had 115 baptized members, and in 1950 it had 72, with 51 at Birkenhof, most of them farmers; they live scattered in 12 villages. For instruction of youth the Dordrecht Confession is used; for congregational singing the German hymnal of the General Conference Mennonite Church of America is used (previously the *Ausbund*). The Birkenhof families are of Amish origin and the congregation observes footwashing with communion. It is one of two churches in Europe which still do so. Altkirch is not Amish. During the past 50 years some families have migrated to this neighborhood from Switzerland. The congregation belongs to the *Konferenz der elsasslothringischen Mennonitengemeinden*. The ministers are unsalaried. The congregation has biweekly meetings, with Sunday school for the children and annual Bible instruction meetings. In 1926 a church was built near the Samuel Nussbaumer farm. The first young people's institute for the French and Alsatian youth took place in Altkirch in 1949. The present elder, who serves both Altkirch and Birkenhof, is Hans Nussbaumer, preceded for many years by Jacques Graber. Three additional young ministers assist: Hans Richard, Jacques Graber, and Samuel Nussbaumer. Family names at Altkirch are Amstutz, Goldschmidt, Gyger, Graber, Kaufmann, Roth, Oberli, Nussbaumer, Richard, Rich, Weiss; at Birkenhof one finds Amstutz, Hirschi, Ramseyer, Richard, Neuschwander, Sommer, Wenger. (*ML* I, 48.)   H.Nu.

Altkirchliche Mennoniten: see Kirchliche Mennoniten.

Alt-Kronsweide, Russia, originally Kronsweide, was one of the first villages of the Chortitza Mennonite colony, located on the banks of the Dnieper. In 1833 the major part of the village was moved to a site three miles away, where Neu-Kronsweide was established, leaving only six farmers in Alt-Kronsweide. The rest of the settlement was sold in 1910 to the *Allgemeine Mennonitische Konferenz* (General Mennonite Conference), which built a mental hospital here called Bethania (*q.v.*). (D. H. Epp, *Die Chortitzer Menn.*, Odessa, 1889; Friesen, *Brüderschaft*, 675; *ML* I, 42.)   NEFF.

Altleiningen, a Mennonite congregation in the Palatinate (Germany), in existence since the 17th century. At first the members, who lived chiefly on farms and mills in the vicinity of Grünstadt, met in the village of Rodenbach, where they owned a cemetery which they used until the middle of the 19th century, but which is today unknown. In 1790 the meeting place was changed to Weissmühle near Eisenberg. Thus it came about that in the Ibersheim Resolutions of 1803 it is called the Eisenberg church, for which David Herstein signed as minister. Near Altleiningen in the village of Höningen services were also held. In 1811 a trim, friendly little church was built in Altleiningen; the beautiful stone pillars of the entry, of real artistic merit, are said to have come from the old monastery at Höningen. Now the church met every Sunday in its own building. There were about 120 baptized members. For a long time Johannes Goebel of Hertlingshausen, a patriarch of the congregation, and J. Hertzler of Stauf, served them as preachers. Also Johannes Stauffer of Friedelsheim and Jakob Rings of Battenberg are mentioned as preachers. Pastor Schiller of Westheim, an extraordinary Palatinate parson, preached once upon request in this little church, and relates in the *Pfälzer Memorabile* how he lost the text of his sermon (*Gem.-Kal.* 1893 and 1914).

After the Franco-Prussian War of 1870-71 the church was served from Weierhof by H. Risser, a theological student and teacher in the school at Weierhof, and later by Preacher Th. Löwenberg; but the membership decreased sharply. Emigration to America and into other congregations was the chief cause. Finally the church was completely empty. Then the *Vereinigung der Mennoniten-Gemeinden im Deutschen Reich* (Union of Mennonite Congregations in Germany) provided for seven regular services per year. When in 1900 the registration of land was carried out in the Palatinate, and there was no clear title to the church and its bit of land, the remaining members gave their right in it to the *Vereinigung* in gratitude for its service to the congregation. In 1912 the membership was scarcely 15 or 20, living in Altleiningen and Höningen. In the two decades between the two world wars the membership of the Altleiningen congregation doubled through influx of families from the outside and by natural increase. The church was renovated and equipped with a reed organ to accompany congregational singing. In 1935 the congregation was made a branch of the Sembach (*q.v.*) congregation, and has been served since by the Sembach minister. In 1939 the first baptismal service in fifty years was observed in Altleiningen with six baptismal candidates; in 1943, 1946, 1948, and 1951 baptismal services were again held. Communion is celebrated twice a year; regular services are held once or twice a month. In 1951 the number of souls was 40, including children. (*ML* I, 42.) HEGE.

Altona, a city in Germany, population 170,000, adjacent to and since 1937 part of Hamburg, with which it is the seat of the Hamburg-Altona (*q.v.*) Mennonite congregation.

Altona was a village in the Mennonite colony of Zagradovka (*q.v.*), province of Kherson, Russia, 80 miles north of the city of Kherson, in the valley of the Ingulets, a tributary of the Dnieper, founded in 1873 by Mennonites from the Molotschna colony. The original settlement was made on the right bank of the Ingulets; in 1876 and 1877 the village was moved to the near-by hills because of frequent floods on the original site. The postal station was Tiege. In 1900, 95 Mennonites emigrated from here to Siberia and settled near Barnaul (*q.v.*), province of Tomsk. Altona embraced about 2,700 acres with 36 farms; it had

180 inhabitants, most of them farmers. There were also windmills and electric mills, cabinetmaking, tile manufacture, coral agate quarrying. With few exceptions all the families were Mennonites, equally divided among the Nikolaifeld Mennonite Church (*q.v.*), the Tiege Mennonite Brethren Church (*q.v.*), and the Altonau Evangelical Mennonite Church (*q.v.*), which arose here in 1907. Altona had a German elementary school. (G. Lohrenz, *Sagradowka,* Rosthern, 1947; *ML* I, 48.) HEGE.

Altona, a southern Manitoba town, located approximately 70 miles south of Winnipeg and 7 miles from the U.S. border, founded in 1895. It is the seat of Rhineland municipality, which has a population of about 10,000. The Altona village population is 1,231 (1950 census), of whom 95 per cent are Mennonites. The Mennonite congregations in the area are: Bergthal, Sommerfeld, and Rudnerweide, one in Altona and two in the close vicinity.

The soil in the Altona district, predominantly a heavy black loam, is admirably suited to diversified farming. Sugar beets, sunflowers, corn, and soybeans as well as the normal grain crops, play a vital role in production. The Altona area is noted for its high quality poultry flocks. One third of the approved flocks in the province are located in Rhineland municipality. There are also several herds of registered Holstein and Shorthorn cattle in the district. This diversification has proved highly beneficial to the economic stability of the area.

Present industries include Co-operative Vegetable Oils Ltd., producing sunflower seed oil, oil-cake, Pres-to-logs (hulls for fuel), feed, Safflo, soybean oil and meal; Rhineland Co-op Hatchery-Chicks; Altona Farm Machine Shop, making custom built farm machinery and attachments; D. W. Friesen & Sons Ltd., commercial printing and stationery; Altona Feed Service Mill, poultry, hog and cattle feed; Manitoba Dairy and Poultry Co-op, eggs and poultry; and a puffed wheat company.

Its service industries include four grocery stores, three general stores, eleven garages and implement dealers, two barbers, one druggist, four fuel dealers, two jewelers, two lumber dealers, two beauty shops, three shoe repair shops, two clothing shops, four confectionery, two blacksmiths, two restaurants, one bakery, one bus depot, one theater, one bookstore, one dairy, and two lawyers.

The educational facilities of Altona include Elim Bible School, one three-room elementary school, and a good, modern senior high school. The total school enrollment is over 300. There are seven elementary and three high-school teachers. Manitoba Dept. of Agriculture extension service, has an agricultural school representative stationed in town. An agricultural school is operated during the winter months together with a home economics course under the auspices of the local agricultural society and the extension service.

The 30-bed capacity Altona Hospital was completed May 31, 1948. It will hold 60 beds in an emergency. Four doctors serve the area. *The Altona Echo,* editor D. K. Friesen, has a circulation of about 1,900. Its service organizations are the Altona Chamber of Commerce; Rhineland Agricultural Society; Rhineland Branch Canadian Legion, B.E.S.L.; Altona Women's Institute; Altona and District Community Club; Federation of Southern Manitoba Co-operatives; and the Red River Mutual Fire Insurance Co. (all-Mennonite and incorporated).   H.H.H.

Altona Hospital is located in Altona, the heart of the Mennonite community of the West Reserve, southern Manitoba. The first hospital in Altona, Bethania Hospital, was organized in 1936 as an independent institution and supported by private contributions from individuals and community groups, coming into being when the Rural Municipality of Rhineland donated for hospital purposes a whole block of land with the large residence thereon. It was soon filled beyond capacity and larger premises were needed. In 1946, under the Dominion-Provincial-Municipal Health Plan, various municipal councils adjoining Altona submitted the matter of erecting a new and larger hospital under the said plan to a vote of the taxpayers residing within the prescribed hospital area, to be paid through tax levies for a 30-year period on debentures. The vote was overwhelmingly affirmative.

The normal 30-bed capacity of the new Altona Hospital, classified as Unit No. 24 in the Do-Pro-Mun. H. Plan, completed in May 1948, can be extended to a maximum capacity of 60 beds in case of emergencies. The total construction costs were $227,500, including remodeling of the old hospital for a Nurses' Home. Outstanding features are the modern and complete X-ray facilities, the up-to-date operating room and equipment, together with the best ward equipment, private or semi-private, furnished free by various community organizations, enabling the Altona Hospital Unit No. 24 to render a hospital service which sets a high standard for the rest of the province of Manitoba.   H.H.H.

Altona (Manitoba) Mennonite Brethren Church dates back to the years 1927-31. After Mennonite Brethren moved into the little town, a house was occasionally rented for holding church meetings. Teachers and students of the Winkler Bible School and others conducted evangelistic meetings. In 1931 the church was organized under the leadership of Johann Andres with about 15 members. A house was rented and dedicated Oct. 4, 1931. In 1937 a small frame building near the station was bought. The 1949 membership was 14 with George A. Braun serving as leader.   H.H.R.

Altona Mennonite Church (MC), an extinct congregation of the Ontario Mennonite Conference which met in the Altona Mennonite meetinghouse, situated on the Pickering-Uxbridge town line, Ontario County, three miles east of the village of Stouffville. The Stouffers came to this village 1804. Barkeys, Hoovers, Nighswanders, Lehmans, and several other families spread into this area from Markham. Daniel Kreider was minister in 1825. In 1852 the present brick building was erected, although a schoolhouse on this site was used for preaching

many years before. Altona is listed in the meeting calendar for 1854 for a meeting every four weeks. In 1858 the ministers' conference ordained a minister and a deacon for the district. Daniel Lehman became deacon in 1851, followed by Jacob R. Reesor, Samuel G. Reesor, and Isaiah Hoover, who became deacon in 1913. Samuel Hoover was ordained minister in 1873 and served 20 years. He was followed by John G. Hoover. In the spring of 1920 the work was relinquished to the Old Order Mennonite faction and the remaining members transferred to the Wideman (*q.v.*) congregation, Markham.   J.C.F.

Altona Mennonite (OOM) Meetinghouse, of Altona, Pickering Twp., Ontario Co., Ont., is one of three meetinghouses used by the Markham congregation of the Markham-Waterloo Old Order Mennonite Conference, the ministerial leadership being identical with Reesor's and Almira. The early history of the congregation is uncertain, but the first grave in the cemetery is dated 1835. Services were held in a schoolhouse until 1852 when the present house was built. From 1890, when the group separated from the Ontario Mennonite Conference (MC), to 1919 approximately, services alternated with the Mennonite Church (MC), but since then only with Reesor's and Almira. Combined membership of the three places is about 100.   F.L.N.

Altona (Ontario) United Missionary Church was organized July 5, 1875, under the leadership of Daniel Barkey, Mennon Nighswander, and Abraham Ressor. In 1949 the membership was 40 with H. S. Hallman serving as pastor.   E.R.S.

Altonau (also called Altenau and Altona), southwesternmost village of the Mennonite colony on the Molotschna, was founded in 1804, the last Mennonite village to be established on the left bank of the Molotschna River, and therefore among the oldest settlements of the Halbstadt volost, district Berdyansk, Taurida province in South Russia, ten miles from the railroad station Feodorovka, and six miles south of Lichtenau, a station on a railway line. Altonau had a post office after 1908. The village embraced about 4,800 acres of arable soil, part of it sandy, part of it black. There were 22 full-sized farms and the same number of small farms. In 1912 Altonau had a population of 800, almost all Mennonites, most of whom belonged to the congregations at Lichtenau, Ohrloff, Rückenau, and Lichtfelde. The two-class elementary school, in which two teachers gave instruction in German and Russian, was attended by 60 pupils. Most of the inhabitants were engaged in agriculture. There were also a tile factory, a soap factory, a blacksmith shop, a vinegar factory, and some mills. (See **Molotschna**.) (*ML* I, 47.)   D.W.

Altonau Evangelical Mennonite Church (post office, Tiege), Orloff, province of Kherson, South Russia. This congregation came into existence May 14, 1907. Elder Franz Martins and the majority of the ministers of the Nikolaifeld Mennonite Church believed that in the practice of baptism, communion, and discipline in general, the church had greatly deviated from its confession of faith and the Word of God. Believing that the majority of the members were unwilling to return to a church practice as visualized by Menno Simons and the early fathers of the Mennonite Church, they left the Nikolaifeld Mennonite Church and organized the Altonau Evangelical Mennonite Church with 57 members. This group adhered to the confession of faith of the Mennonite Church but had the following special characteristics: (1) They admitted as members only those who professed to have accepted Christ as their personal Saviour. (2) They baptized by immersion only, but did not insist on a rebaptism of those wishing to join. (3) They admitted non-members to communion, provided such visitors professed to be reborn. (4) They performed marriage for non-baptized persons when there were no other reasons against such act. (5) Members marrying unregenerated partners were excommunicated.

At first meetings were held in a private building. In 1914 a modern church with a seating capacity of about 450 was erected in the village of Orloff. In 1922 this congregation had 214 members. The first elder was Franz Martins (1907-24); his successor was Jakob Janzen (1924-?). (Friesen, *Brüderschaft;* G. Lohrenz, *Sagradowka,* Rosthern, 1947; *ML* I, 47.) G.L.

Altoona (Pa.) Mennonite Gospel Mission was established in 1910, under the Southwestern Pennsylvania Mennonite (MC) Conference. In 1926 a meetinghouse was built at 2504 Fourth Avenue and named the First Mennonite Church. About one half of the congregation of 68 members in 1949 lived in the city which has a population of 80,000. With the exception of the staff of workers, all the members are converts of the mission. J. M. Nissley was superintendent and pastor 1919-49.
J.M.N.

Altoona (Pa.) Church (MBC) was a former city mission of the Gospel Workers' Society of the Mennonite Brethren in Christ of Pennsylvania, opened April 24, 1900, but was closed some years later.
E.R.S.

Altsamara, another name for the Alexandertal (*q.v.*) Mennonite settlement in the province of Samara, Russia.

Alt-Schöppen (also called Schöpen and Sköpen), an estate in Lithuania, which together with Neu-Schöppen and Neusorge were once given in hereditary tenure for thirty years to Mennonites from the region of Culm by Frederick William I (*q.v.*). Since the plague of 1711 had taken most of the population of this territory, Frederick William I invited farmers of the Vistula Delta to settle here. The Mennonites who would settle in Prussian Lithuania were promised full religious freedom and exemption from any military obligations, which guarantees were given to them in writing, dated at Königsberg, March 1, 1713. As a result some 42 Mennonite families settled on these three estates. Because the promises regarding the military exemption were not kept, the settlement was dissolved after eleven years. C.K.

W. Mannhardt, *Die Wehrfreiheit der Altpreussischen Menn.* (Danzig, 1863) 116 ff.; *ML* I, 48.

Alt-Täufer, a designation often used for the Mennonites in Switzerland to distinguish them from the *Neutäufer* (*q.v.*), a church founded in 1832 by Samuel Fröhlich (*q.v.*), which included some former members of the Emmental Mennonite congregation. (*ML* I, 48.) NEFF.

Alumni Journal, the official organ of the Mennonite Collegiate Alumni Association (Mennonite Collegiate Institute of Gretna, Man.), was published only four times from December 1935 to April 1937 at Gretna. It was an eight-page magazine using both German and English with a circulation of approximately 500, mostly ex-students of the Mennonite Collegiate Institute. J. K. Friesen served as editor.
G.E.

Alwinz, a town in Transylvania (then Austria, now Rumania) where in 1621 a Hutterite Bruderhof composed of refugees from Slovakia was established, which existed up to 1767. When the Hutterites were hard pressed by the rising power of the Catholic estates in Austria, Moravia, and Hungary, Bethlen Gabor (*q.v.*), Prince of Transylvania, offered 183 homeless Brethren a refuge in his principality. In the charter (*Hausbrief*) of the Alwinz settlement of 1622, he says, "As I was made aware that the Brethren have been driven from their homes, I have received them as competent workers and craftsmen who could teach others, and I assign to them fields and vineyards." In 1623 another group of exiled Hutterites from Maskowitz in Moravia were settled in Alwinz (Beck, 416). Here they began anew to establish their customary community of goods on the Bruderhof. Then came war, and Turk and Tatar alike burned and plundered the settlement (1658-61), so that the residents had to take refuge in the fortress of near-by Hermannstadt. After that time the group never was able to develop successfully. By the middle of the 18th century the number of Brethren who were still loyal to the old ways had dwindled to about 50, and when as the final test, the new type of persecution by the Jesuits came upon them in the mid-seventeen hundreds, not more than 19 persons stood the trial. The rest were gradually converted to Catholicism.

At this critical juncture, a stream of fresh blood came into the brotherhood from a totally unexpected side. Lutheran transmigrants from Carinthia (*q.v.*) arrived in Transylvania in 1755 and 1756, and a few of their men found work in and around Alwinz. Andreas Wurz and Georg Waldner (father of Johannes Waldner, *q.v.*, the author of the *Klein-Geschichtsbuch*) were among them. While these newcomers got into great difficulties with authorities and nobles, the small Hutterite flock at Alwinz (among them the courageous and strong Joseph Kuhr, *q.v.*) received them in a brotherly way. The Carinthians listened. Here were new sounds never heard before. Here was the true Gospel spirit, and a living concern for one's neighbor. They now stopped going to the Lutheran worship, began reading Hutterite books (Riedemann's *Rechenschaft*), and soon were convinced that the Hutterite way was the right way for earnest Christians. This came to pass in spite of the fact that the old

Alwinz Hutterite group was but a shadow of the great past, and the communistic organization of the Bruderhof had long been given up. As the chronicles state, the brotherhood was dying out (*im Verfliessen*). It is of interest to note that preacher Roth corresponded with Peter Weber, preacher of Hardenburg in the Palatinate. In 1761 the Carinthian "New" Hutterites began to establish a brotherhood in near-by Creutz, as reported in Johannes Waldner's chronicle (*Denkwürdigkeiten*), now published as *Klein-Geschichtsbuch der Hutterischen Brüder*. In 1762 Hans Kleinsasser (formerly from Carinthia) was elected *Vorsteher* or bishop of the new brotherhood, and was ordained in Alwinz by the laying on of hands by the *Vorsteher* of the "Old Alwinz" group, Märtl Roth (who himself was soon to turn Catholic). In 1762 new and severe persecutions and oppressions set in, guided in the main by the notorious Jesuit Delpini (*q.v.*). Brethren were put into prison, and the seizure of their children was threatened. There could no longer be any doubt that the government planned their total eradication, and it became clear that there was no chance to survive in Transylvania. After much praying, counseling, and hesitation, and after two Brethren, Joseph Kuhr and Johannes Stahl, had explored new possibilities in Wallachia beyond the Carpathian Mountains, the brotherhood in Alwinz decided to risk the new venture. With unheard of hardships they escaped from Transylvania, young and old, healthy and sick, crossing a rugged mountain pass, until they reached their new, and yet only temporary destination, the fertile plains of Wallachia. That was in 1767. Several Brethren from Alwinz who at this time lay in chains in a Hermannstadt jail, joined them later after liberation. The brotherhood was saved from extinction, and a new life began. After further migration in 1782 into the Ukraine, where Count Romanzov settled them at Vishenka (*q.v.*), even the traditional community of goods was re-established.

The Dutch *Naamlijst* of 1755 names Mertil Both as elder of the Alwinz Bruderhof after 1742, and Joseph Gor (Kuhr) as minister after 1747. Deknatel (*q.v.*), an Amsterdam preacher, carried on a correspondence with the Alwinz Bruderhof and sent it money contributed by the Dutch Mennonites. (See **Carinthia, Transylvania, Joseph Kuhr, Johannes Stahl, Johannes Waldner.**) R.F.

Klein-Geschichtsbuch (ed. Zieglschmid) 1947, 239-57; Beck, *Geschichts-Bücher;* J. Loserth, "Decline and Revival of the Hutterites," *MQR* IV (April 1930) 93-112; J. Horsch, *The Hutterian Brethren 1528-1931* (Goshen, 1931) 89-95; W. Schmidt, *Die Stiftung des katholischen theresianischen Waisenhauses zu Hermannstadt im Jahre 1767* (n.d., hitherto unknown) contains an important appendix on the conversion of the Hutterian Brethren to Catholicism. This book and the archives of the former official state university in Hermannstadt contain further significant material, especially on the cross-examinations of the Hutterites and Carinthians, e.g., Michael Hofer; R. Friedmann, in *Archiv für Ref.-Gesch.*, XXVI (1929) 181; Julius Bieltz, "Eine Habaner Töpfersiedlung in Siebenbürgen (Alwintz)," in *Wiener Ztschr für Volkskunde* XXXII (1927); *ML* I, 48.

Alzey, county seat of the Hessian province of Rheinhessen, Germany, where the teachings of the Anabaptists had already at the beginning of the Reformation found numerous adherents. The violent attempt of Dietrich von Schönberg (burgrave of Alzey 1520-32) to suppress the Anabaptist movement caused a great stir and induced Pastor Johann Odenbach (*q.v.*) at Moscheln in the adjacent territory of Zweibrücken to make a powerful appeal on their behalf to the judge at Alzey. The document, one of the few writings of the Reformation period which opposed the use of force in matters concerning faith, appeared in print the same year with the title, *Ein Sendbrieff und Ratschlag an verordnete Richter über die armen gefangenen zu Altzey, so man nennet Wiederteuffer.* (A copy is in the State Library in München.) The judges refused to sentence them, since there had been no infraction of the law; but the prisoners were later executed without sentence, the nine men beheaded and the women drowned. The burgrave dealt in like fashion with all the Anabaptists who fell into his hands; he had them taken from their homes and like beasts of slaughter led to the place of execution. Cheerfully, says the Hutterite chronicle, they went to their death. While the Brethren were being executed or drowned, the survivors sang hymns of praise (Beck, *Geschichts-Bücher,* 30). In his official opinion to the council of Nürnberg, Dr. Scheurl asserted that the mass executions had taken place before July 1528. The sorrows of these martyrs are depicted in a song of 41 stanzas: "Herr Gott, in Deinem Reich," found in *Die Lieder der Hutterischen Brüder* (Scottdale, 1914) 40-45.

It is not clear from the incomplete archival records how many Anabaptists were executed. The only official document which states the number of prisoners, viz., the statement of Chancellor Venningen, had already been completed before the proclamation of the electoral mandate of March 5, 1528. It names 20 prisoners, no women being among them. The author remarks that 20 women were suspected of Anabaptism, but they had not been arrested nor examined by the inquisitor (Krebs, 573). Meanwhile the high reward offered in the electoral mandate had resulted in an increase in the number of prisoners. Now there were no longer only the 20 Anabaptists of the chancellor's statement, for it is mentioned that a new judgment would now have to be arrived at concerning the new prisoners. The Hutterite chronicle places the number executed in the Palatinate at 350, basing this on the testimony of refugees who later came to Moravia from the Palatinate and who had witnessed how the Anabaptists there had been seized in their homes "and brought to the place of judgment like sheep to the slaughter." They reported that those who recanted had their fingers cut off or a cross branded on their foreheads with a red-hot iron (Beck, 30 f.). The latter statements are also confirmed in an extant official document. Those who recanted had to leave the country, and were threatened with the death penalty in case they should return to the Palatinate or backslide again into Anabaptism (Hege, 65).

The number 350 as given by the Hutterite chronicle for the martyrs of Alzey has been questioned by certain historians, since a list of martyrs which was found on the person of Julius Lober at the time of his arrest (which, to be sure, makes no claim to completeness) mentions only 14 executions at Alzey, 3 at Heidelberg, and 5 at Bruchsal (Beck, 311; see also G. Bossert, "Beiträge zur badisch-pfälzischen Ref.-Gesch." in *Ztscht für die Gesch. des Oberrheins* LIX, 1905, 82). Since further documentary evidence is lacking, the exact number of the martyrs can no longer be determined. It is worth while to note in this connection, however, the statements of Philipp Rupp of Nussloch near Heidelberg, who on May 1, 1529, was asked by the judge where "the great mass of Anabaptists" might be, and replied, "It is not to be known. There were formerly more but they have been destroyed by murder" (Hege, 62). The reports in the Hutterite chronicle that the elector suffered great remorse on account of the many executions also suggest that there must have been a large number of martyrs. These reports add that the authorities did not soon again take the life of an Anabaptist "although they persecute, exile, and do not tolerate us until the present day" (Beck, 32). These statements are confirmed by the fact that after 1529, in spite of imperial mandates and the decrees of the Reichstag, so far as is known, no further executions of Anabaptists took place in the Palatinate.

By this barbarous method the Anabaptist movement was temporarily suppressed in the region of Alzey, but thirty years later it reappeared, when Hutterite missionaries labored here and induced their adherents to emigrate to Moravia. Again the authorities opposed them. In the fall of 1567 Missionary Leonhard Dax (*q.v.*) was arrested with his wife and several fellow believers, and imprisoned in the castle at Alzey, the ruins of which are still standing. Dax had to answer repeatedly to the superintendent. An excerpt from the proceedings was published in Schnellhorn's *Sammlung für die Geschichte, vornehmlich zur Kirchen- und Gelehrtengeschichte* (Nördlingen, 1779) 380-99. Also extant are letters of consolation to the prisoners at Alzey written by Kaspar Braitmichel (*q.v.*) and Peter Walpot (*q.v.*); they are in the possession of the Hutterian Brethren at Frankfort, S.D. Dax was released Feb. 25, 1568; his writing of 1567, *Ein Bekanntnuss und Rechenschaft*, in which he explains that the defensive arguments of the Anabaptists had not received adequate attention, was a factor in inducing Frederick III, elector Palatine, to arrange for the disputation of May 28 to June 19, 1571, at Frankenthal. In spite of repeated orders of banishment, the Anabaptists succeeded in maintaining themselves in the region of Alzey until near the close of the 16th century. But finally they, like all the other Anabaptists of the Palatinate, had to yield to government pressure and emigrate to Moravia, the only country where they could at that time exercise their faith unmolested.

After the Thirty Years' War (1648) Anabaptists found toleration in the Palatinate. The elector Karl Ludwig offered them protection since he needed laborers to rebuild his devastated land. Here Anabaptist exiles from Switzerland, the Mennonites of today, found refuge. A government report of Jan. 14, 1686, counted in Alzey 147 families with 280 children. Then the desolation of the war of Louis XIV of France came over the Palatinate, and the great emigrations to America began. In 1697 the reports (Karlsruhe General State Archives) record 64 families, in 1717 only 19. Then the number rose again. In 1743 there were 287 persons, in 1739, 575 persons (85 families), and in 1773, 635 persons.

The district of Alzey, since 1815 reduced in size and incorporated in Rheinhessen, included in Reformation times a large part of the present-day province of Rheinhessen; and a number of the localities listed then as having Anabaptists, have Mennonites today, though no longer in the modern district (Kreis) of Alzey. These Mennonites belong to the congregations of Ibersheim (*q.v.*), Monsheim (*q.v.*), Weierhof (*q.v.*), and Uffhofen (*q.v.*). The now extinct congregations of Oberflörsheim (*q.v.*), Erbesbüdesheim (*q.v.*), and Spiesheim-Wallertheim (*q.v.*) were in the old Alzey district. Today only Uffhofen (*q.v.*), with about 60 members in the village and neighborhood, is in Alzey. It is, however, the successor to the former Erbesbüdesheim and Spiesheim-Wallertheim congregations. HEGE.

W. Wiswedel, *Bilder* II, 23; Manfred Krebs, "Die Wiedertäufer am Oberrhein," in *Ztscht für Gesch. des Oberrheins* XLIV (1931); Manfred Krebs, *Quellen zur Gesch. der Täufer* IV: "Baden und Pfalz" (Gütersloh, 1951) contains all the archival materials relating to Alzey Anabaptists in the chapter "Kurpfalz," including the statement by Chancellor Venningen, the "Denkschrift" by Odenbach, the statement by Otther, the mandate of March 5, 1528, and the record of the examination of the accused at Nussloch; C. Hege, *Die Täufer in der Kurpfalz* (Frankfurt, 1908); *ML* I, 49.

Amadore (Mich.) Mennonite Brethren in Christ Church, now extinct, was established in 1900. In the early years of this century, it had a membership of 16. M.G.

Aman, Burkhard, "a pious man," according to the *Martyrs' Mirror* (D 814, E 1113), "who lived on the Lake of Zürich," and was imprisoned for his faith for 1½ years. He escaped unexpectedly and without the knowledge of the government (1639), but died soon after as a result of the imprisonment. (*ML* I, 49.) NEFF.

Amare, Nicasen: see Nicasen van Aelmeers.

Ameland, Dutch North Sea island (pop. in 1947 was 2,258 with 311 Mennonites), on which the Anabaptist movement doubtless early found many adherents. It is certain that in the first half of the 16 century several Anabaptist congregations arose there. The baptismal list of the Elder Leenaert Bouwens (*q.v.*) states that he was on Ameland eight times between 1551 and 1582 to serve the churches there with baptism. He baptized not fewer than 99 persons: 47 at Hollum, 49 at Ballum. and 3 in Nes.

About this time, in 1556, the division between the Waterlanders on one side and the stricter Frisians and Flemish on the other took place in the province of Holland which probably soon affected Ameland. In Nes, where the attitude has always been less strict than in the other villages of this island, a Waterlander congregation separated from the main body. This may explain why Leenaert

Bouwens baptized only three at Nes, and these on his first trip. In Hollum too the Waterlander group found followers in the course of time and built a church there. It is odd that the Waterlander meetinghouse here, as also in Harlingen, was called the "blue barn."

After the division the mother church was called the Flemish brotherhood, and retained its original strictness. In 1599 and later, when Jan Jacobsz (q.v.) of Harlingen tried to sharpen the regulations concerning the ban, the Flemish congregation on Ameland sided with him and called itself the Jan Jacobsz congregation, which name it retained until 1855. It had adherents in all three villages. In the 17th century, perhaps early and perhaps not until after 1664, for some unknown reason, the Foppe Ones (q.v.) or Laus Ooms group separated from them and later joined the Humsterland (q.v.) Flemish Sociëteit in Groningen and secured adherents in all three villages.

The three congregations, the Waterlanders, Jan Jacobsgezinden, and the Foppe Ones group, existed side by side on Ameland until the beginning of the 19th century. Besides their greater leniency, the Waterlanders differed from the others also in employing salaried, trained ministers after 1761. The preachers of the Jan Jacobsz and Foppe Ones congregations were untrained and unsalaried, although they received considerable compensation in the form of voluntary gifts on occasions such as the communion service, funerals, and other services. The Jan Jacobsz church always distinguished between preachers (leeraars, proef-dienaaren), from whose ranks elders were chosen, and elders, of whom there were always two at the head of the church.

The congregation owes much to Kornelis Pietersz Sorgdrager (q.v.), who was its elder 1793-1826. Jacob Jobs, his predecessor and co-elder (elder 1769-1804), had also, although changing times demanded different methods, held obstinately to the old customs; but Sorgdrager realized that old principles could be retained even if forms were changed. Gradually he introduced the necessary changes. The form of church services used everywhere else was adopted; namely, the reading of a passage of Scripture at every church service and instead of silent prayer the audible prayer of the preacher. Likewise the Biestkens Bible (q.v.) was replaced by the better state translation, and the antiquated De Geestelijke Goudschaale (q.v.) by the Reformed hymnal. Sorgdrager also entered zealously into the spiritual preparation of candidates for baptism by introducing regular instruction. Previously, when new members were received, the articles of a Mennonite confession of faith were read and those who desired baptism were merely asked whether they agreed with them.

In the 19th century the three churches combined, first the two conservative groups in 1804, which took the name of the Jan Jacobsz church. In 1815 union with the Waterlander group was considered, but failed. Nevertheless, a feeling of need developed for the kind of preaching and instruction provided in almost all Mennonite churches in Holland by trained ministers, and the simplest way of securing this would have been union with the Waterlander group, who in Costers had such a pastor; but unfortunately his manner of life was an obstacle. Then the Jan Jacobsz church turned in 1850 to the Algemeene Doopsgezinde Sociëteit in Amsterdam, which provided two theological candidates to serve the church in succession. In 1852, in conjunction with the Frisian Sociëteit they made it possible for the church to call its own minister, K. S. Gorter.

In 1854 Costers of the Waterlander congregation retired, and then on Jan. 1, 1855, the Jan Jacobsz church joined the Waterlander group. The newly formed church took the name "Mennonite Church of Ameland," and was to be served by two ministers, one at Nes, the other at Hollum. But for many years Gorter alone had charge of all the church services on Ameland. In 1883 it was decided to form a separate congregation in each of the three villages. The smallest is that at Ballum. At present (1951) there is only one minister for the three congregations, who resides in Hollum.

The number of Mennonites on Ameland has steadily decreased. In 1627 the Catholic priest van der Heyden wrote as an eyewitness in his book entitled *Verrichtingen der Jesuiten in Friesland*, "In Ameland the inclination in matters of faith is in general toward the doctrine of the Mennonites." In 1812 about half the population, or 1,023 souls, was Mennonite; in 1838 the number had suddenly decreased to 690. In 1859 there were 591; in 1889, 549; in 1899, 535; in 1909, 521; and in 1947, 311 souls. The decline was thus most pronounced in the first half of the 19th century. It is possible to follow the decline in the number of baptized members exactly by means of reports. In 1804 the combined Jan Jacobsz and Foppe Ones churches had 531 members; the Waterlander group had 70, making a total of 601. In 1838 there were in the former 270, in the latter 50, a total of 320. In 1855 the number in the united church was 304. In 1913 Hollum had 157 members, Ballum 47, and Nes 68, making a total of 272 members. In 1950 the corresponding figures were: Hollum 127, Ballum 46, and Nes 48, making a total of 221.

J.L.

K. S. Gorter, "Uit de vroegere Gesch. der Doopsgez. gem. op Ameland" DB 1889, 1-50 and 1890, 1-38; Blaupot t.C., Friesland; H. J. de Jongh, Jubelrede wegens 50-jariger Predikdienst in de Oude Vl Doopsgez. gem. te Ameland 17 Julij 1842 (Amsterdam, 1850, Catalogus Amst., 320); Archief Eerediensten 1806-13, Portefeuille 109 (National archives in The Hague); Inv. Arch. Amst. II, 1472-1521; II, 2, Nos. 9-11; ML I, 50.

Ameldonck, Thomas, d. 1689, was the first preacher of the Mennonite congregation at Nijmegen (Netherlands). He came from Goch to Nijmegen in 1672, and did much for the welfare of the congregation (DB 1893, 32). His son Jan Ameldonck Leeuw was chosen preacher of this congregation in 1690 (DB 1874, 26). The Ameldoncks stemmed from the Rhine region. By 1566 an Ameldonck was already an elder in Cologne (DB 1893, 32).

vDZ.

America (Argentina) Mennonite (MC) Church,

located in the town of America (6,000 inhabitants), county seat of Rivadavia County, on the Bragado-Pico branch of the Ferro-Carril Oeste (Western Railroad) in the province of Buenos Aires, Argentina, was organized in March 1928, and in 1953 had a membership of 21. The work here was started by J. L. Rutt, missionary from Elizabethtown, Pa.; continued by E. V. Snyder of Breslau, Ont.; carried on under the direction of Agustin Darino, who is a graduate of the Mennonite Bible Institute of Bragado, Argentina, and in 1950 directed by Daniel W. Miller. The seating capacity of the hall is 180 and the services are conducted entirely in the Spanish language. The members are of Spanish, Italian, and mixed European with Indian blood.   E.V.S.

American. Proper usage restricts this designation to the United States, excluding Canada. North American, South American, and Central American are self-explanatory.

American Fork, Utah, the location of Mennonite Civilian Public Service Unit No. 127, which was established at the Utah Training School in January 1944 and closed in February 1946. It housed 650 children on a 600-acre farm. The 15 men of the unit worked mainly on the farm, doing diversified tasks, including the maintaining of the grounds and the plant. A few spent most of their time doing attendant work with children. M.G.

American Friends Service Committee was organized in 1917 by Friends who were deeply concerned for the spiritual values endangered by the World War. Young Friends and others desirous of making a constructive, nonmilitary contribution to the world through relief and reconstruction activities in devastated war areas offered their services to the committee. Among the 600 men and women who were engaged in this kind of activity in France during and after World War I were a considerable number of Mennonites, who either were released from military service for this activity or volunteered directly for it. (See **Reconstruction Work** in France.)

Mennonite relief work in Spain, 1937-40, under the Mennonite Relief Committee (Elkhart), and in France 1939-41 under the Mennonite Central Committee, was carried on through the good offices and administrative channels of the A.F.S.C. who gave the workers technical A.F.S.C. appointments and handled all shipping of goods and supplies as well as the transfer of funds.

Between the two wars, Mennonite co-operation with the Friends was continued through meetings of the Conference of Pacifist Churches (*q.v.*) and later through the sessions of the Conference of Historic Peace Churches (*q.v.*). With the coming of the military draft preceding World War II, the American Friends Service Committee, the Brethren Service Committee, and the Mennonite Central Committee (*q.v.*) assumed the leadership in organizing the National Service Board for Religious Objectors (*q.v.*). Although later the Friends withdrew from active support of the NSBRO, co-operation between the Mennonites and the A.F.S.C., particularly in matters pertaining to the draft of

conscientious objectors and the planning of relief projects, has continued.   M.G.

Twenty-Five Years Under the Red and Black Star (Philadelphia, 1942); M. Gingerich, *Service for Peace* (Akron, 1949); G. F. Hershberger, *The Mennonite Church in the Second World War* (Scottdale, 1951).

American Mennonite Aid Committee was founded on April 4, 1884, in Newton, Kan., to aid Mennonites in Aulie Ata (*q.v.*) and Khiva (*q.v.*), Central Asia, to come to America. The officers elected were B. Regier, president; David Goerz, secretary; A. Sudermann, treasurer; members were Chr. Krehbiel, D. Gaeddert, H. Richert and Wm. Ewert. The minutes of this meeting and an appeal for contributions were printed in *Christlicher Bundesbote* (April 15, 1884). It is stated that some $10,000 were needed to help about 26 families to come to America. The following issues of the paper carried reports about the need, help given and the coming of these families to America. In Beatrice, Neb., where a large number of the families settled, a special Nebraska Aid Committee functioned. After the settling of the families the American Mennonite Aid Committee was discontinued.   C.K.

American Mennonite Relief. In his letter to Russian officials on Sept. 9, 1921, A. J. Miller, director of American Mennonite Relief, explained the nature and purpose of the organization. Miller stated that the A.M.R. "is an unofficial, volunteer, American organization for social service. It maintains a base at Constantinople where relief supplies are ready for prompt shipment to Russia to be received and distributed by the American Mennonite Relief organization."

The A.M.R. was a special organization set up under the Mennonite Central Committee to distribute relief in Russia. It operated during the entire Russian famine period, working under its agreement of Oct. 1, 1921, with the Moscow government and under the agreement with the Soviet Republic obtained by the A.R.A. (*q.v.*), with which and under which organization A.M.R. carried on its relief activities up to the time of the closing of the A.R.A. in 1923. A resolution of the MCC on Aug. 1, 1925, called for the closing of the work of the A.M.R. on Oct. 1, but the organization was not disbanded until 1926.

The agreement between the A.M.R. and the Soviet Republic contained 19 points. Point one stated that the A.M.R., within the limits of its resources and facilities, would supply "food, clothing, and medical relief to the needy civilian population, especially women and children and the sick, regardless of race, religion, or social or political status." Although the preamble of the agreement had expressed the desire of the American Mennonites to give impartial aid "in the regions where their co-religionists are suffering from the effects of the famine" and although most of the aid was given in the Mennonite settlements of southern Russia, the purpose of A.M.R. was to give relief wherever it was needed.

The total disbursements made by the MCC for Russian relief during the years of the A.M.R. amounted to $1,292,825.65. Among the American

Mennonites who participated in the work of the A.M.R. in Russia were A. J. Miller, Clayton Kratz (*q.v.*), P. C. Hiebert, O. O. Miller, Arthur Slagel, C. E. Krehbiel, G. G. Hiebert, Mr. and Mrs. D. M. Hofer, P. H. Unruh, H. C. Yoder, and Dan Schroeder. A. J. Miller was director of the A.M.R. throughout its history.   M.G.

P. C. Hiebert and O. O. Miller, *Feeding the Hungry, Russian Famine 1919-1925* (Akron, Pa., 1929).

American Relief Administration (A.R.A.), under the chairmanship of Herbert Hoover, was an unofficial volunteer American charitable organization that conducted relief work in Europe after World War I. It was estimated that more than 90 per cent of all foreign relief given to Russia in 1921-23 during the famine in that country, was handled through the A.R.A. The Mennonite Central Committee was affiliated with the A.R.A. in its Russian relief program and experienced cordial and helpful relations with it during the entire period of A.R.A. relief work in that country.   M.G.

P. C. Hiebert and O. O. Miller, *Feeding the Hungry, Russian Famine 1919-1925* (Akron, 1929); H. H. Fisher, *The American Relief Administration in Russia, 1921-1923* (Russel Sage Foundation, 1943).

American Sunday School Union, a national religious association in the United States founded in Philadelphia in 1824 (successor to Sunday and Adult School Union of Philadelphia, founded in 1817), having for its object the organization and support of Sunday schools in needy communities not otherwise provided with Sunday schools, and the publication and circulation of moral and religious literature, particularly for Sunday-school teachers and pupils. Anyone who contributes $300 annually and is approved by its board of directors is eligible for membership.

The Union has in its time had a tremendous influence in American religious life, and no little influence on the American Mennonites. It early undertook a great campaign to establish a Sunday school in every new community on the western frontier and sent out a large number of Sunday-school missionaries. It introduced the "Uniform Lessons" in 1826 (used until 1872, when the new "International Uniform Lessons" were introduced) and soon thereafter a series of widely used "Union Question Books," which were used in many early Mennonite Sunday schools and without doubt were the models for John H. Oberholtzer's *Das unparteiische biblische Fragenbuch* . . . (Milford Square, Pa., 1859), and for the Sunday-school question books edited by John F. Funk and published from 1880 on by the Mennonite Publishing Company of Elkhart, Ind. It published an enormous amount of juvenile literature and Sunday-school lesson helps and papers, which once had a wide circulation in many Mennonite communities, particularly those in which the young people began to use the English language in 1830-90. Early Mennonite Sunday-school libraries contained many of these books.   H.S.B.

American Tract Society, founded in New York City, 1825, a merger of some fifty local and sectarian societies, interdenominational and international in its work, for the purpose of publishing and circulating "whatever would best diffuse a knowledge of Christ as the Redeemer and promote the interests of true religion and sound morality." In 1841 it inaugurated a missionary colportage program. In recent years its emphasis has been strong in reaching foreign language groups among American immigrants. Its publications were once widely used in Mennonite Sunday schools in America, and found their way into many Mennonite homes, especially before the inauguration of denominational publishing programs. The Society is still active. It depends for support upon voluntary contributions from individuals and churches.   H.S.B.

Amersfoort, a city in the Dutch province of Utrecht (population in 1947 was 55,996, with 348 Mennonites), where Leenaert Bouwens baptized 30 persons in the mid 16th century, 4 in 1558. There was at this time a congregation of about 30 members, which used to meet in the house of Lubbert Gerrits (*q.v.*), who in that year (1559) fled from Amersfoort to Hoorn. In 1569 14 persons were punished here by the confiscation of their possessions and exile as a penalty for attending meetings of the Anabaptists (*Wederdoopers*); Steven Pietersz (*q.v.*), in whose house the congregation had worshiped, was put to death. Beyond this very little is known about this congregation. It was frequently without a preacher; the last one whose name is known was Salomo Stenfurt, who was still serving the congregation in 1702. At any rate the congregation was no longer in existence in 1731.

In 1903 the Mennonites living in Amersfoort organized as a group (*Kring*); E. M. ten Cate, at Apeldoorn since 1904, came regularly to give catechetical instruction and to preach for them in the Lutheran church. The first baptism was performed in 1905 (*DB* 1905, 193). In 1913 the group was able to build its own church, and in 1923 it became a congregation. In 1924 it called F. Kuiper as its minister (1924-28); he was succeeded by T. O. M. H. Hylkema, 1928-36; W. F. Golterman, 1936-42; S. Gosses Gzn, 1942-50, and A. G. van Gilse since 1951.

The congregation is a member of Ring Utrecht-Gooi. It has a women's organization, men's organization, youth organization, and a choir; work with the young people is carried on in co-operation with other groups of the locality. The membership was 240 in 1950, and 247 in 1927, with 32 catechumens.   vDZ.

J. Kleyntjes, "Onderzoek naar de Herdoopers in Amersfoort," in *Archief v. d. Gesch. v. h. Aartsbisdom Utrecht* LXI (1937) 648-51; *DB* 1868, 94 f.; 1875, 87; 1918, 119-37; *Inv. Arch. Amst.* II, No. 1522; *ML* I, 55.

Ames, William, one of the first Quakers who went from England to Holland in 1655 with John Stubbs and William Caton. He made a deep impression and had great influence especially among the Mennonites. From there Ames went to the Palatinate, but remained only a short time. Upon his return to Amsterdam he was notified to leave the city within twenty-four hours. He did not comply and with another Quaker was imprisoned for six days and then led outside the gate. On the following day they were again inside the city, and were tolerated until Ames left voluntarily. Among the Mennonites he won for his church were Cornelis Roelofs and Jacob van Buylaert, who appeared at the meeting of the Mennonites at Harlingen in 1670 (Aug. 3) and tried to win them to the Quakers, though without success. In Gouda and Rotterdam he also succeeded in persuading Mennonites to join the Quakers. At a conference held in Rotterdam in 1657 by delegates of the Flemish congregations, and at Gouda in 1659, the Quaker question was discussed. Here an earnest admonition was issued to all preachers, "as much as possible to resist the Quakers and faithfully to protect their flocks."

In the same year, 1659, Ames went to Germany again. He received a friendly reception from the elector Palatine and his pious sister Elizabeth. With Caton and Higgins he founded the Quaker church at Kriegsheim, whose members had been Mennonites (*Menn. Bl.,* 1912, 11). In 1659 Ames also went to Hamburg and successfully established contacts with the Mennonites; a considerable number of their members, including some of the most prominent such as Berend Roelofs, joined them. His presence created great unrest in the strictly Lutheran city. On June 24, 1660, the council issued a mandate that all Quakers were to leave the city and vicinity within four days. Ames apparently turned to Friedrichstadt, where a Quaker congregation composed chiefly of former Mennonites was soon established. From Holstein Ames went to Bohemia and then turned north to Prussia, where some Mennonites followed his teaching. At the end of June 1661 Ames entered Danzig. In July he was brought before the court. Here he stated that he had met none of his faith there, but had once been in a Mennonite church; he had wanted to ask them a question, but they had refused to allow it. He was not the same as they, but wished that they would live better, and more honestly. Ames had to leave the city, but his doctrine spread nevertheless. In 1663 several Quakers were brought to court and imprisoned.

Ames had returned to Holland and traveled through the provinces of Gelderland and Overijssel, where he visited most of the Mennonite churches, but without success. With Caton he seems to have been more successful in Friesland. Mennonites, Socinians, and others arranged Quakerlike meetings, causing much dissension. In 1662 the government of Friesland passed a law forbidding Quakers and Socinians to enter the province. Any who were found were to be imprisoned in the workhouse and held to steady work. Anyone giving information about one of them would receive a reward of 25 Frisian guilders. From this time on nothing further is heard about Quakers in the Dutch provinces. Nor is there any further trace of Ames (*Menn. Bl.,* 1854, 42 ff.).

The library of the Amsterdam Mennonite Church contains two works by Ames; *Het Ligt dat in de duisternisse schijnt, beweesen den Weg tot God te sijn* (Amsterdam, 1660), and *De Verborgentheden van het Rijke Godts ende de werckinge, leydinge*

en bestieringe van Gods Geest verklaart, in tegenstellinge van de letterlijcke oeffeningen voorgestelt als de ware Godtsdienst door Galenus Abrahamsz . . . (Amsterdam, 1661). Pieter Balling wrote against Ames (*Catalogus Amst.,* 118).   NEFF.

W. Hubben, *Die Quäker in der deutschen Vergangenheit* (Leipzig, 1929); W. Hull, *The Rise of Quakerism in Amsterdam 1658-1668* (Swarthmore College Monographs on Quaker History, No. 4, 1938) contains an extensive biography of William Ames, the only one yet written; C. B. Hylkema, *Reformateurs,* 2v. (Haarlem, 1900 and 1902); *ML* I, 55.

Amish Aid Plans. The Old Order Amish Mennonites in almost all of their communities have formulated agreements covering the sharing of losses resulting from fire and lightning. In most areas damage by storm or tornado is also covered.

The Amish Aid Plan in effect in Indiana covers the 11 counties in which they reside as well as 4 counties in Michigan. Their printed statement declares: "This Plan is used in lieu of insuring our property with the old line or mutual insurance companies, and to avoid the unequal yoke spoken of by Paul in II Cor. 6:14 and of paying of losses on property, which we, as a God-fearing people, claim to be inconsistent with our established faith and belief in the doctrines of Christ." In the Indiana Plan, disinterested brethren chosen from various church districts estimate the extent of the loss and award the loser a sum equal to three fourths of the estimated loss or damage, this sum being obtained by a property assessment of all of the members of the 15 counties.

The exact date of the formation of the original Indiana Plan is not known, although there was a brief outline of the system, written in German, previous to 1915. During the depression years of the thirties the Federal Land Bank at Louisville, Ken., requested that the plan be placed in print in order to make possible federal loans to Amish farmers. This was done in December 1934, at which time the Indiana Plan was officially entitled "The Amish Aid Plan."

The Amish community around Arthur, Ill., has a similar plan, while the settlements in Iowa and Wisconsin are combined for assessments. The Kansas, Oklahoma, and Oregon Amish are united in one aid plan. The Old Order Amish aid plan area in Ohio covering the Holmes-Tuscarawas-Wayne settlement, Stark County, Coshocton, Geauga County, Madison County, and Defiance County in 1949 covered property worth more than $6,800,-000. See also **Amish Aid Society** of Lancaster Co., Pa., which includes Lancaster and adjoining counties as well as St. Marys Co., Md.   M.G.

Amish Aid Society of Lancaster Co., Pa., an unchartered organization of the Old Order Amish Mennonites of the county, started in the early 1890's with Benjamin Beiler as the first secretary and Jonas Fisher as the first treasurer. At present, Benjamin Beiler's son Christ and John F. Stoltzfus, both of Bird-in-Hand, are the secretaries, and the first treasurer's son, John M. Fisher, Gordonville, the treasurer. In addition to the three, there is a trustee in each of the other districts, of which there are approximately 20. The members assess their own buildings, subject to the final decisions of the secretaries, with no building above $10,000. All of the trustees in May of each year divide the annual losses pro rata among the trustees. Lebanon County, the Kishacoquillas Valley in Mifflin County, and St. Marys Co., Md., are also in the Society in addition to the local and Chester County groups. The insurance carried amounts to about $12,000,000. When there are no serious losses a levy of 1 or 1½ mills per year is sufficient to meet the liabilities of the organization.   I.D.L.

Amish Division, the most serious and only major schism which occurred in the South German Anabaptist-Mennonite groups, when a considerable minority under the leadership of Elder Jakob Ammann (*q.v.*) of Erlenbach, canton of Bern, Switzerland, in 1693-97 divided from the main body. The proper name for the new groups is Amish Mennonite although frequently they are referred to simply as Amish. Not all the descendants have retained the name and the principles of the original group—none at all in Europe, all of them having reunited with the main body. However, there are still in the United States (20,000) and in Canada (3,000) those who retain the name in some form, and whose existence and history therefore is directly related to this schism.

From the original documents which have been preserved, it is clear that Jakob Ammann's attempt to force the elders in the Emmental (canton of Bern) to accept the *Meidung,* i.e., the shunning or avoidance of excommunicated persons, was the chief if not full cause of the division, although several minor issues were mentioned. The following account by Milton Gascho (*MQR,* Oct. 1937) is authoritative.

"Uli Ammann, possibly a brother of Jakob Ammann, mentions three issues on which Hans Reist, the leader of the opposing side, would not agree with them, namely: *Meidung,* the excommunication of a woman who had admitted speaking a falsehood, and saying that true or true-hearted persons (*treuherzige*) would be saved. Of course, he tried to show that Reist was to blame for not believing in *Meidung,* for not excommunicating the woman, and for, as the Amish accused, saying that all true-hearted persons would be saved. Jakob Ammann in his letter of Nov. 22, 1693, accused Reist and his group of having forsaken the doctrines of Christ and the apostles by their attitude to these three issues. In another letter Ammann asked all persons to report to him how they believed on these three issues. (He did not specify the case of the woman who admitted speaking a falsehood but spoke of disciplining falsehood in general.) He actually excommunicated preachers Niklaus Moser, Peter Giger, and some others on the charge of falsehood because they had once said they believed in *Meidung* and then when they saw that Reist and Ammann disagreed on the interpretation of the teaching, they refused to accept the doctrine with

Ammann's emphasis. In the letter written by Peter Giger we see that before the question of *Meidung* had caused much trouble, Hans Reist had a controversy in his congregation because Ammann had started holding the communion service twice a year. There is, however, no indication that this question had any large part in the controversy. The practice of footwashing must also have been introduced by Ammann and practiced by the Amish during the time of the controversy, but there is no evidence in the letters written at the time that this practice had any part in causing the division. It is interesting to note that the letter written by Christian Blank was written for the express purpose of proving that neither *Meidung* nor footwashing was the cause of the division. But this in itself is evidence that footwashing as well as *Meidung* was practiced by the Amish and not by the other group at the time the letter was written. C. H. Smith says, 'The Swiss church had never adopted the practice. But Ammann now also introduced the first form of its observance among his followers.' Even though we have no evidence that footwashing had any part in starting the controversy, we know that it had a part before the trouble was over, for Uli Ammann accuses the other side of making it an issue when the Amish sought a reconciliation, and again in a letter written Jan. 21, 1711, we find that the Amish in another attempt at reconciliation wished to continue the practice.

."One of the other things for which Ammann contended was uniformity in dress, which included the style of hats, garments for the body, shoes and stockings. He also taught against the trimming of the beard and attending services in the state church. In fact he excommunicated a number of persons in the congregation at Markirch because they would not confess with him that it was wrong to attend services at the state church. Some of the other disputes that arose during the course of the controversy concerned to which side a meetinghouse belonged and who had the higher authority, Reist or Ammann. Smith says, 'There seems to have been some dispute also regarding the use of tobacco,' but there is no mention of tobacco in any of the documents in the three printed collections. The main issues of the controversy were the first three mentioned, namely: (1) *Meidung,* (2) whether those who speak falsehoods should be excommunicated, (3) and whether one could say that true-hearted persons would be saved.

"Some of those on the other side thought *Meidung* as Ammann would have it was unscriptural, others thought that it had a certain amount of good in it, but that the practice should not be forced on those who did not believe in it. Another point which those on the Reist side questioned was Ammann's method of excommunicating those who did not believe as he did. Of all these various things, *Meidung* seems to be the subject of most of the doctrinal contention."

The specific order of events of the division, which occurred in late July or early August 1693, is as follows. Elder Jakob Ammann of Erlenbach had started to hold the communion services twice a year instead of only once as had been the practice in Switzerland. Two elders, Hans Reist and Benedict Schneider, opposed this innovation although it was decided to permit it. Ammann and Reist thus became the leaders of opposing factions on this issue. Shortly, however, the main issue of the controversy between the two men shifted rapidly to the *Meidung* question by Ammann's asking two preachers (Niklaus Moser and Peter Giger), who were called by Reist to help settle the communion controversy in his own congregation, to ask Reist what he believed concerning the *Meidung*. Learning that Reist opposed it Ammann took three ministers (Uli Ammann, Christian Blank, and Niklaus Augspurger) with him on a tour of the churches to find out what the ministers in Switzerland believed about the *Meidung*. Discovering that only a few of them agreed with him, Ammann decided to call a meeting of all the Swiss ministers in Niklaus Moser's barn near Friedersmatt, to which however not all the ministers came. Among the absentees was Hans Reist. Since the meeting was inconclusive, a second meeting was called for two weeks later. This meeting was fairly large, but again Hans Reist did not appear, although Ammann had twice requested him through intermediaries to indicate his stand on the *Meidung*. (Reist did write a letter rejecting the *Meidung* and asking his readers not to pay too much attention to Ammann.) The controversy hastened to a climax. Ammann laid before the meeting a letter listing six charges against Hans Reist, and when he had read the charges declared Hans Reist to be excommunicated. After further controversial discussion Ammann excommunicated Niklaus Moser and Peter Giger and shortly thereafter Peter Habegger, Jacob Schwartz, and Peter im Gul (Ingold) after all these men had refused to accept the *Meidung*. At this Peter Zimmermann said, "There you have it," and the meeting broke up, the Ammann party leaving the building without shaking hands. A little later seven of the "Amish" held a meeting near by which can be viewed as the first Amish party gathering. Shortly after this Ammann expelled by letter Benedict Schneider and Hans im Wiler, who refused to accept the *Meidung*. Niklaus Baltzli was expelled personally on the ground of teaching that true-hearted persons would be saved. Either shortly before his tour through Switzerland or shortly thereafter, Ammann expelled a number of the members of the church at Markirch in Alsace because they did not admit that attending services in the state church was wrong.

Various attempts were made by both ministers and lay members to persuade Jakob Ammann to recall his hasty action of excommunication, but to all he turned a deaf ear. Soon some persons from the Emmental wrote to the brotherhood in the Palatinate describing what happened and asking for help. On Oct. 16, 1693, some of the Palatine ministers wrote to the Amish asking them to seek

a reconciliation. The Palatine ministers also at this time wrote a letter to the ministers in Alsace who had written them about the troubles at Markirch, advising the Alsace ministers not to pay too much attention to Jakob Ammann and his new teaching. On Nov. 22, 1693, Ammann answered the letter from the Palatinate with the approval of a number of ministers in Alsace where he was at that time staying. The signatures on the letter are, besides Ammann, Jakob Kleiner, Jakob Kauffman, Hans Moyer, Peter Zimmermann, Hans Bachman, Hans Neuhauser, Felix Hager, Nigli Ausperger, Heinrich Gerei, Christle Steiner, Ully Oswalt, Uli Ammann. About this time also Ammann sent out his *Warnungsschrift,* a letter or broadside in which he asked all church members either to report to him that they accepted his view on the three controversial issues or to prove to him that he was wrong. They were asked to report before Feb. 20, 1694, and were to be excommunicated if they did not do so by March 7.

A major attempt at a reconciliation was made in the second week in March 1694 at a meeting called at Ohnenheim in Alsace at the request of the ministers of the Palatinate, at which both sides were to be represented. Ten men came from Switzerland and seven from the Palatinate, but the number of "Amish" present is not known. The Palatines begged the Amish not to continue acting so rashly, but the latter insisted that the opposing side accept the three major points of the controversy. When neither side would yield the Palatines proposed a compromise yielding the two minor points of the controversy, but not surrendering on the *Meidung*. Some minor difficulties were also discussed. When no agreement could be reached, the Amish left the meeting. On the following day the Swiss ministers decided to agree with the Palatines and drafted a joint statement giving the reasons why they could not agree with Jakob Ammann, dated March 13, 1694. The list of signers was as follows: For the Swiss, Hans Reist, Peter Habegger, Ulrich Falb, Niklaus Baltzli, Peter Geiger, Dursch Rohrer, Jakob Schwartz, Daniel Grimmstettler, Ulrich Blatzley; for the Palatines, Jakob Gut, Hans Gut, Peter Zolfinger, Christian Holi, Benedikt Mellinger, Hans Heinrich Bär, Hans Rudi Nägeli.

About this time Ammann placed the opposing Palatine ministers under the ban and also numerous other persons whom he had never seen. This is the climax in the story of the division. Now the entire Mennonite brotherhood in Switzerland. Alsace, and South Germany was divided into factions. A large majority of the churches in the Palatinate and Switzerland were against Ammann, but practically all the Alsatian churches followed him. North Germany was not directly involved although a letter by Elder Gerhard Roosen of Hamburg was sent to a friend in Alsace in 1697 expressing a concern about the outcome of the controversy.

Various attempts at a reconciliation were undertaken between 1694 and 1698, both by correspondence and in meetings, but all failed. The Amish finally decided they had been too rash with their use of the ban, in having acted without the consent of their congregations and accordingly placed themselves under the ban (probably in 1698). When after a time the Amish indicated that they would like to be received into the church again, the other side stated they would receive them, but when the Amish insisted again that the other side agree with them on the *Meidung* and the other issues, negotiations broke down. Later, after the Amish had been received into the church fellowship by ministers who had not participated in the original division, and their several attempts at reconciliation began to bear some fruit, the matter of the literal observance of footwashing as the Amish practiced it became a bone of contention and proved to be a barrier on the road to peace, since the Swiss Mennonites had never practiced this ordinance before. On Feb. 7, 1700, some Amish leaders again decided to put themselves under the ban, but this move failed to produce the desired peace. No other attempts at reconciliation are recorded until 1711. On Jan. 21 of that year a group of Amish from the Palatinate came to Heidelsheim in Alsace desiring to make peace with the brotherhood there provided they would be allowed to practice the *Meidung* and footwashing. The Heidelsheim congregation then wrote to Switzerland for advice, and finally decided, in spite of a negative answer, to receive Uli Ammann and Hans Gerber, two of the petitioners, into fellowship again. This had no effect on the larger division which continued unresolved.

Throughout the controversy, which in essence lasted from 1693 to 1698, Jakob Ammann appears as the leader of the radical party and Hans Reist as the leader of the continuing "regular" group, who refused to follow Ammann, the innovator. For this reason at times the Amish referred to the other party as the "Reistleut." However, this did not persist. It is fair to say that the Amish party was a deviation from the main body inasmuch as they introduced two practices which were foreign to historical Swiss Mennonitism, namely, *Meidung* and footwashing, as well as more rigid regulations on matters of costume. Ammann and his party represent a rigidly conservative point of view which insisted upon sharp discipline and inflexible adherence to the practices which they considered essential to a true Christian church. It is this inflexible conservatism which has marked the Amish ever since and which has resulted in an unchanging perpetuation of forms of worship and church organization as well as costume, customs, and language. To this day the Old Order Amish in North America have continued with little change the Amish way as fixed by Jakob Ammann and his associates about the year 1700. In this sense they constitute a most interesting and valuable reproduction in modern times of Swiss-Alsatian-Palatine Mennonite practices of 250 years ago. See **Amish Mennonites** for a further history of the Amish. H.S.B.

The Letters of the Amish Division of 1693-1711, Translated and edited by John B. Mast, Pub. by Chr. J. Schlabach (Oregon City, 1950) contains among others, Amman's letter of Nov. 22, 1693, to the ministers of the Palatinate, which explains his dealings with his opponents and justifies his position and procedure, also his "Warning Letter" of Nov. 22, 1693, to the brotherhood not yet agreeing with him. All the German printed forms of these letters and other documents related to the Amish schism are listed in full in Milton Gascho's "The Amish Division of 1693-1697 in Switzerland and Alsace," in *MQR* XI (Oct. 1937) 235-66, which contains a full account of the activities of Ammann and the best available account of the division. M. Pohl, "Gesch. Beitr. aus den Menn. Gem.," in *Gem.-Kal.,* 1908, 136-51, and 1909, 133-41, reprints most of the Amish letters with some commentary; *ML* I, 56.

Amish Mennonite Children's Home, near Grantsville, Md., was opened in 1913 and discontinued in 1938 because of the restrictive laws dealing with the interstate movement of children. Sponsored by Minister Jacob S. Miller, the project was first studied by the Conservative Amish Mennonite Conference of 1912. In 1913 the project was started in the private home of Minister Noah Brenneman, Accident, Md., who had been appointed superintendent. In 1916 a brick building accommodating 75 children was erected north of Grantsville. Brenneman continued as superintendent until July 1, 1928, and after that served as assistant until the home was closed. Children from the institution were placed in private homes in New York, Pennsylvania, Ohio, Indiana, Michigan, Iowa, and Delaware. J.B.Mi.

Amish Mennonite Publishing Association is operated under the direction of the Conservative Amish Mennonite Conference and Old Order Amish Mennonite Church members. S. D. Guengerich, Bishop Jacob F. Swartzentruber, Preacher Peter Swartzentruber, Preacher Gideon Yoder, of the Kalona-Wellman, Iowa, community, and Bishop Eli J. Bontreger of Shipshewana, Ind., organized this board in January 1912.

Five members serve on this board for a five-year term. One of the five is annually elected president. The board elects a secretary-treasurer once a year, who is not a board member. The first manager of the Association was S. D. Guengerich (*q.v.*), who was succeeded at his death by L. A. Miller.

The duties of the board are to appoint editors for the different departments of the *Herold der Wahrheit* (*q.v.*) printed at the Mennonite Publishing House, Scottdale, Pa., and to appoint a secretary-treasurer to take care of the incoming and outgoing funds. The board members in 1950 were Walter E. Beachy, Wellman, Iowa, president; and Fred Nisly, Benjamin L. Yoder, Joseph G. Gingerich, and Enos H. Miller, secretary-treasurer, all of Kalona, Iowa. L.A.M.

Amish Mennonite Yearbook and Directory containing the names of the bishops, ministers, and deacons of the Old Order Amish Mennonite, Conservative Amish Mennonite, and Old Order Mennonite churches was printed in 1938 by the Amish Mennonite Publishing Association, Arthur, Ill. The 24-page booklet contained 15 pages of almanac material and 5 pages of names and addresses. War conditions and high costs prevented further publication. L.A.M.

Amish Mennonites, that segment of the Swiss-Alsatian-South German Anabaptist-Mennonites and their descendants in North America who are the offspring of the group who under the leadership of Elder Jakob Ammann (*q.v.*) of Erlenbach, canton of Bern, Switzerland, in 1693-97 separated from the main body in Switzerland.

Since the full story of this division is told elsewhere (see **Amish Division**), it remains only to say that Ammann must have visited the Markirch (Alsace) congregation about the same time, where he excommunicated some members, and that he almost immediately got into a controversy with the ministers of the Palatinate who tried to effect a reconciliation. He found almost united support from the ministers of Alsace, but proceeded to place most of the Palatine ministers under the ban. In a few years Ammann and his associates decided they had been too rash and tried to effect a reconciliation, failing largely because they confessed only to an error in method and spirit while refusing to surrender their demand for the *Meidung*. Thus the division was made permanent because of the intransigence of Ammann. Ammann also held strict views on other points, including the wearing of the untrimmed beard, uniformity in dress, including style of hats, garments for the body, shoes and stockings, and prohibition of attendance at services of the state church. He seems to have held that the *Treuherzigen* (those friends of the Anabaptists who shared many of their views and helped them in times of persecution but for some reason would not join the group openly, perhaps out of fear) will not be saved, meaning that no one will be saved outside the Anabaptist fold. He also introduced footwashing as an ordinance, which was hitherto not practiced by the Swiss Anabaptists, but was practiced in Holland.

The proper name of the followers of Jakob Ammann is "Amish Mennonite" although frequently they are referred to simply as Amish. Not all of the descendants have retained the name and the principles of the original group—none at all in Europe—most of them having reunited with the main body. However, there are still in the United States (20,-000) and in Canada (3,000) those who retain the name in some form. In Europe there have been Amish settlements in Montbéliard, Holland, Bavaria, Galicia, and Volhynia, all of lesser size and significance, but in the United States many large and important Amish communities have been established. Because the Amish have kept few records, are highly traditional, and have produced practically no literature, not even historical, it is difficult to trace their history.

History in Europe. 1. *Switzerland.* Originally there were two groups of Amish in Switzerland—(*a*) a few ministers and members in the Emmental; (*b*) all of the Anabaptists in the Lake Thun settlement. Very early (1696?) some of these emigrated to the Markirch area in Alsace, and soon after others went to the Neuchâtel (Jura) region of Switzerland. When the general emigration from

the canton of Bern to the area of the Bishopric of Basel (Jura-Porrentruy) began, the Amish joined the movement establishing two congregations, La Chaux de Fonds and Neuenburg. By 1750 all the Amish were out of Bernese territory, although when the Bishopric of Basel was incorporated into Bern (1810?) the Amish congregations were still there. They gradually lost their distinctive identity and by the end of the 19th century were no longer considered Amish, being a part of the Swiss Mennonite Conference. A Swiss leader, probably Elder Samuel Baehler of Langnau, writing in 1886 in the *Mennonitische Blätter* (34-35) says: "I may add that there are also two so-called Amish Mennonite congregations here, one in the Neuchâtel Jura [La Chaux de Fonds] and the other in Basel [Holeestrasse]. As far as the Neuchâtel group is concerned they are quite closely related to us [the Swiss Mennonite churches], however they still practice footwashing among themselves." The Basel Amish congregation never associated with the Swiss Mennonite conference since it was actually a part of the Alsatian Amish group. Few Amish emigrants came directly from Switzerland to the United States.

2. *Alsace-France.* When the Amish division occurred there were several Anabaptist-Mennonite congregations in Alsace (at that time not a part of France). All of these followed Ammann's lead and Ammann himself settled in Ste. Marie aux Mines (Markirch) in 1696. When heavy pressure and actual persecution forced emigration from this area (1710-30), a considerable number of families migrated to the territory of Montbéliard (German Mümpelgart), at that time and until its incorporation into France in 1790(?) an enclave belonging to the Protestant duchy of Württemberg in South Germany. Others settled in the region of Birkenhof on the Alsatian-Swiss border. Under pressure some of the Ste. Marie aux Mines group moved across the near-by border into Lorraine. Gradually Amish families migrated to other places until small congregations had been established well into the interior of France proper, and by 1815 a small settlement in Luxembourg. Emigration also took Alsatian Amish families eastward and northward into Germany and after 1815 to North America. Small groups were settled by 1759 in southern Baden across the Rhine in the Breisgau and by 1802 in Southern Bavaria near Ingolstadt, Regensburg, and Munich. Direct emigration from Alsace-Lorraine and Bavaria to the United States and Canada resulted in large Amish communities: in Waterloo Co., Ont. (1824 ff.), Central Illinois (1829 ff.), Stark Co., Ohio (Canton), and Fulton Co., Ohio (Archbold, 1835 ff.). A heavy drain from the Alsace-Lorraine-Montbéliard Amish communities to these North Central states took care of excess population and kept down their further expansion in France. A continuous small trickle of Swiss Mennonite families into southern Alsace from 1880 on gradually diluted the Amish stock, especially around Mulhouse and Altkirch. About 1790 a small number of Montbéliard (and Ibersheim, Germany) Amish

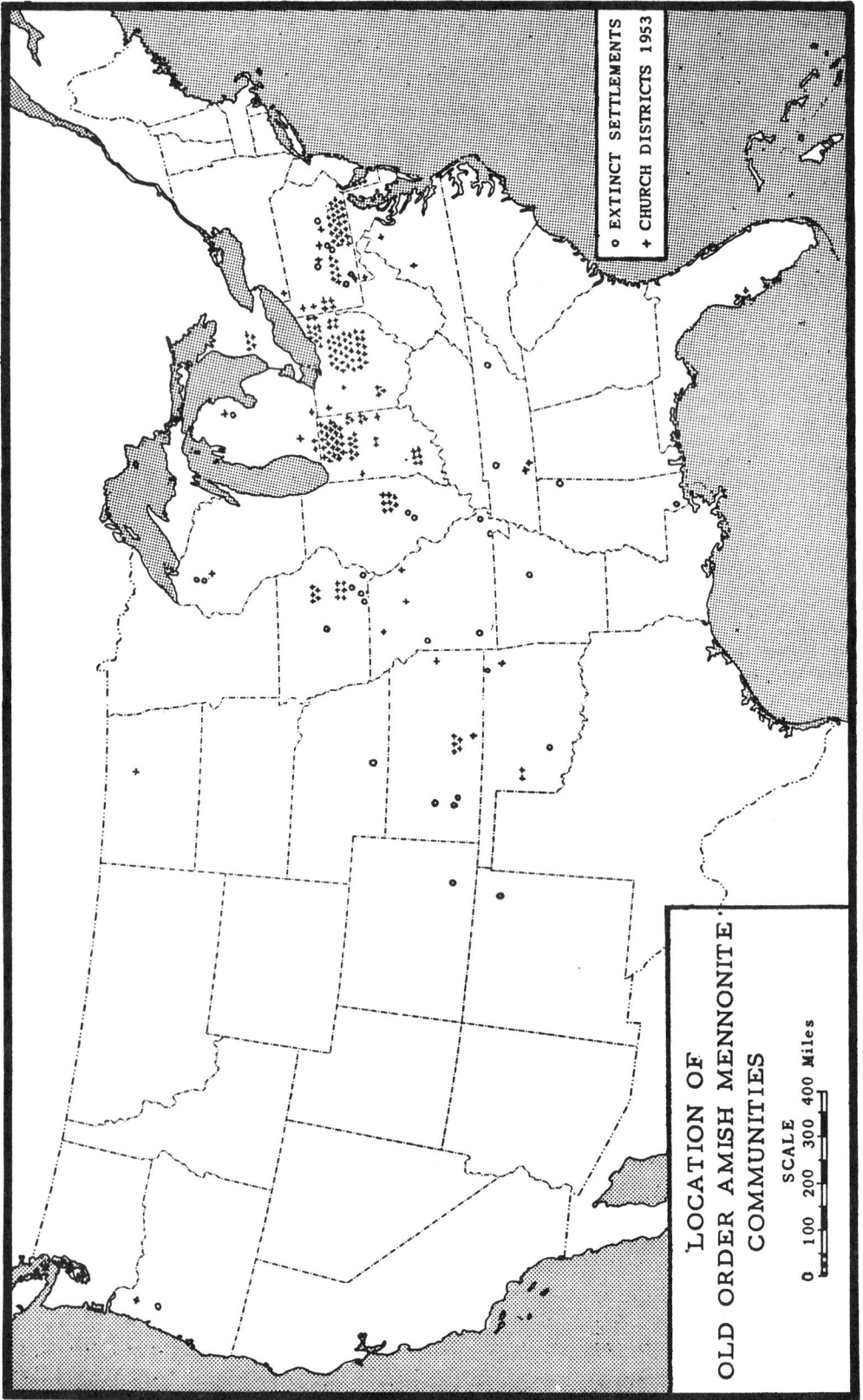

LOCATION OF
OLD ORDER AMISH MENNONITE
COMMUNITIES

SCALE

0 100 200 300 400 Miles

o EXTINCT SETTLEMENTS
+ CHURCH DISTRICTS 1953

families migrated to the Lemberg region in Galicia and from there to Volhynia, Russia, whence they reached Kansas and South Dakota as a part of the great Russian emigration in 1873 ff.

3. *Germany*. Of the Swiss Mennonites living in the Palatinate at the time of the Amish schism only a small number followed Ammann, chiefly in the region of Kaiserslautern. Later a settlement from Alsace was made at Essingen near Landau. The Amish did not expand in the Palatinate but did send out emigrants in three directions (largely supplemented by families from Alsace and Lorraine). The first of these was to middle Germany in the Hesse-Cassel region, where as early as 1730 certain families appeared in Wittgenstein, then Waldeck (by 1750), then in the Lahn Valley near Marburg (by 1800). A small settlement also existed for a time near Neuwied and also in the Eiffel region. By 1830 these groups began to disintegrate by direct emigration to the Amish settlement in Somerset Co., Pa., Garrett Co., Md. (region of Grantsville-Springs), and to the Amish settlement in western Waterloo Co., Ont. An Amish settlement in Hesse north of Wiesbaden sent large numbers of settlers to Butler Co., Ohio, 1817 ff. These are known as the Hessian Amish. All the European Hessian Amish congregations died out by 1900. The second Amish movement from the Palatinate (and from Alsace-Lorraine) was to Bavaria (Ingolstadt, Regensburg, and Munich). The Ingolstadt and Munich groups ultimately became extinct by emigration (to Ontario and Illinois). The Regensburg group continues, however, diluted with Mennonite additions from other places in South Germany, and the Munich congregation was reconstituted with a mixed Amish and Mennonite population from other places. The third emigration was to Galicia and Volhynia 1785 ff. This group emigrated *in toto* to the United States in the great Russian emigration of 1873 ff., settling at two places, viz: Moundridge, Kan., and Freeman, S.D. Meanwhile the remnants of the original Palatinate Amish settlements merged with the Mennonite congregation of Kaiserslautern in 1915.

4. *Russia*. The only Amish settlement was that in Volhynia, made by families who had at first settled near Lemberg in Galicia, founded in 1803, becoming extinct by migration to the United States in 1875.

5. *Holland*. Two Amish congregations were established near Groningen and Kampen by immigration from Switzerland and the Palatinate about 1750. They continued a separate existence there until about 1850 when they were absorbed into the Dutch Mennonite congregations near by.

6. *Amish Conferences and Literature in Europe*. Two Amish general conferences are known to have been called for the purpose of giving guidance in church policies and discipline, with formulated resolutions which have been handed down in manuscript form: at Essingen near Landau, Palatinate (at that time Alsace) in 1759, and at Essingen again in 1779. The Amish churches used the Dordrecht

Confession of Faith (1632, adopted by the Alsatian churches in 1659) together with the Elbing catechism of 1783, reprinted at Waldeck in 1797 and henceforth known as the Waldeck Catechism. They also adopted the *Ernsthafte Christenpflicht* (1739) as their prayerbook and reprinted the Ephrata German *Martyrs' Mirror* at Pirmasens in 1780. No permanent conference of distinctively Amish churches in Europe was ever organized, although after the incorporation of Alsace-Lorraine in Germany in 1870 the churches there affiliated loosely with the *Badische Verband* and organized their own separate conferences in 1901 and 1907. After the reincorporation with France in 1918 two separate conferences were formed, a French-speaking and an Alsatian German-speaking, both of which continue. Distinctive Amish practices and customs persisted until into the 20th century but gradually died out—wearing of the full beard, hooks and eyes and special costume, shunning and footwashing. Two congregations alone, Birkenhof and Diesen, still retain the practice of footwashing. The Luxembourg group retained this practice until 1941 when their aged bishop died. Thus any distinctive contribution of the Amish to European Mennonitism was lost, and the effects of the schism of 1693 were completely overcome by attrition without any conscious formal reunion. The churches at Regensburg and Munich, it is true, never joined the Mennonite conference of this region, known as the *Badische Verband,* although this was due more to personalities than to principles except that these churches do not desire to submerge their autonomy into the rather close corporate government of the *Badische Verband*. They have however joined both the South German Mennonite Conference (formed in 1886) and the all-German *Vereinigung* (in 1908).

North America. 1. *Pennsylvania*. The first scattered Amish settlers arrived in Pennsylvania possibly as early as 1720, and not being able to fellowship with the Mennonites already there, settled in Berks and Chester counties adjoining the Lancaster County settlement in the east, as well as in Lancaster County proper, forming three congregations about 1740-60: one north of Reading which became extinct by 1786 as the result of Indian raids, one in Chester County near Malvern, which died out before 1800, and one near Morgantown which soon developed into a very large settlement and spilled over into Chester County, ultimately extending over a block of 40 miles north and south and 20 miles east and west, which today contains at least 4,000 baptized descendants of the pre-Revolutionary settlers. This group always remained sharply distinct from the larger Lancaster Mennonite Conference group with which it was in the closest geographical proximity. Because of lack of land, all later Amish immigrants passed by this region, except for transient halts, and the surplus population also migrated westward. Direct settlements were established from the Berks-Lancaster-Chester settlement only in Somerset Co. (1767 ff.), Mifflin Co. (Kishacoquillas Valley) 1793 ff., and Union Co., Pa. (Buffalo Valley) 1810, extinct by 1890, and in Fairfield Co., Ohio, 1810 ff., extinct by 1890 also. A few scattered families continued to go west during the next century, but not until 1940 was a true daughter colony established, and then only on a small scale in Arundel Co., Md. The Somerset County settlement was actually populated more by direct immigration from Hesse 1830-60 than from Eastern Pennsylvania, spilling over into adjacent Garrett Co., Md. The Somerset County group was in three distinct locations, north around Johnstown, middle around Berlin, and south around Springs-Grantsville. Only the south settlement survived the 19th century.

2. *Ohio*. The chief daughter colony of the Somerset County settlements was the large Holmes Co., Ohio, colony, begun in 1807, but not flourishing until after the War of 1812, although some Somerset County families moved directly to the Johnson Co., Iowa, settlement 1845 ff. and to Elkhart Co., Ind., about the same time. Yet both these latter settlements were predominantly offshoots of the Holmes County settlements. This Holmes County group gradually expanded into Tuscarawas County eastward and into Wayne County northward, ultimately becoming the largest single settlement of Amish, exceeding even the Berks-Lancaster settlement, with a current baptized population of about 5,000. Daughter settlements from Holmes County are Geauga County (1880), Stark County (Hartville), and Plain City, Ohio, and Arthur, Ill. (1880).

The Fairfield County Amish settlement disintegrated when some families moved to Wayne County, near Smithville, and to the West Liberty, Ohio, settlement, and later largely to Lagrange Co., Ind., near Topeka and Ligonier. However, the Smithville and West Liberty settlements were actually founded directly from Mifflin Co. and Union Co., Pa. (with some Lancaster-Berks additions), in 1810 and 1845 respectively. Daughter colonies from these latter two settlements were those of Cass Co. (Garden City), Mo. (1880) and Hubbard, Ore. (1890).

Direct Alsatian Amish settlements were made in Stark Co. (near Louisville) 1830, Wayne Co. 1830 ff., and Fulton Co., Ohio, 1835 ff. (the latter with a large element from Montbéliard). Some emigration from these settlements helped establish the Washington-Henry Co., Iowa, colony near Wayland (1847) and the Allen Co., Ind. (Leo-Grabill) and Adams Co., Ind. (Berne), both about the same time, although direct immigration from Alsace to both contributed. There was cross-immigration also from the Amish settlement in Ontario to these settlements.

3. *New York*. A single Amish settlement was established in New York State direct from Alsace and Bavaria in 1845 in Lewis County (Croghan) with cross-migration from the Ontario Amish settlement.

4. *Indiana*. There was no substantial original direct Amish immigration from Europe to Indiana. The Allen County-Adams County Alsatian type settlement of 1850 have been mentioned. In Elkhart County immigrants direct from Somerset Co., Pa., established the largest Amish settlement west of Holmes County (with additions from this latter place) in 1842, east of Goshen, and slightly later around Nappanee west of Goshen. Today these two

settlements together (not geographically one) have a baptized population of at least 4,000. The Howard-Miami settlement (north of Kokomo) 1860 and the Daviess County colony southwest of Indianapolis, were both established from Holmes County and never became large.

5. *Illinois*. A large Alsatian Amish settlement was established 1829 ff. in Central Illinois east of Peoria with later outposts at Hopedale, Flanagan, Tiskilwa (the latter chiefly from Bavaria), and Fisher. A small Lancaster-Mifflin County Amish colony was established near Danvers in 1854.

6. *Iowa*. The Iowa Amish came in two groups about the same time (1845) settling in two distinct colonies: the Alsatian Amish in Henry-Washington County, near Wayland (with additions from Ontario), the Holmes County-Somerset County group near Kalona (Johnson County).

7. *Nebraska*. Nebraska received a considerable Alsatian Amish settlement near Milford, largely by way of the Central Illinois, Wayland, Iowa, and Ontario settlements. A daughter settlement was established at Tofield, Alta., north of Edmonton about 1910. Another settlement was established at Albany, Oregon, by way of Thurman, Colorado, in 1894.

8. *Kansas*. In 1888-90 Harper Co. received an Amish migration of the Somerset-Holmes County strain, with some additional contingents from Elkhart Co., Ind., Arthur, Ill., and Johnson Co., Iowa. Earlier in 1875 the Volhynian Amish had come to Moundridge but with connections only with the Russian Mennonites, not with the older American Amish.

9. *South Dakota*. The Volhynian Amish group settled near Freeman in 1875.

10. *Ontario, Canada*. The large Amish settlement in Waterloo County west of Kitchener was established in 1824 ff. by Amish from Bavaria and Alsace-Lorraine. A small outpost of this group was established near Zurich, some 90 miles farther northwest.

Thus gradually in 150 years a large number of Amish settlements were scattered across the United States from Eastern Pennsylvania to Oregon, basically of three major strains: the earliest 18th century immigration from Switzerland and the Palatinate to Eastern Pennsylvania, the 19th century Alsatian-Bavarian-Hessian Amish movement to western Pennsylvania, Ohio, Illinois, and Ontario, and the Volhynian Amish of the 1874 immigration to Kansas and South Daktota.

Of these three the last group had almost lost its Amish character before it came and soon was assimilated almost completely into the Western and Northern District General Conference groups. The Alsatian-Bavarian Amish ultimately all were assimilated into the (old) Mennonite group, with a few exceptions which have broken off in a conservative reaction to remain outside the main stream. The Lancaster-Mifflin-Somerset segment, the first migration with its daughter colonies, has broken up into four phases: (1) the largest which has remained strongly in the original (old) Amish pattern, independent, non-assimilated; (2) a medium-sized progressive phase which has also been assimilated into the (old) Mennonite group along with the Alsatian Amish; (3) and another group of about the same size which has held the middle of the road, remained independent but organized into the Conservative Amish; (4) a still more progressive phase, which in turn has been broken up into two sub-phases, the Central Illinois (Stucky) Amish group now merged with the General Conference, and the smaller (Egli Amish or Defenceless) Evangelical Mennonite group, an independent organized conference.

A large number of the family names among the Amish are unique and characteristic of that group although, since before 1693-97 Swiss and Alsatians were a united group, some family names will be found in the descendants of both groups today. The following list includes all the more numerous and characteristic Amish family names.

1. *Amish Family Names* primarily of the Old Order and Conservative Amish Groups and those descending from the early Pennsylvania Amish settlers and the Hessian Amish:

Beachy—Peachey	Lambright
Bender	Lantz
Blauch—Blough	Lapp
Bontrager—Borntraeger	Mast
Brenneman	Miller
Byler—Beiler	Mullet
Burkholder	Nissley
Christner	Otto
Chupp	Petersheim
Coblentz	Plank
Esch—Eash	*Raber
Gingerich—Guengerich	Schrock
Glick	Shetler
Graber	Slabaugh—Schlappach
Hartzler—Hertzler	Smucker—Schmucker
Helmuth	Stoltzfus
Hershberger	Stutzman
Hooley	Swartzendruber—
Hostetler—Hochstetler	Schwarzentruber
Kanagy—Gnaegi	Troyer
Kauffman	Umble
Keim	*Wagler
King	Yoder
Knepp	Zook—Zug

* More common in the Alsatian group.

2. *Amish Family Names* Primarily of the Alsatian Group and Their Descendants:

Albrecht	Gunden—Gundy
Augsburger	Guth
Bachman	Heiser
Bechler	Imhoff
Beller	Jantzi
Belsley	Kennel
Berkey—Burcki	Kinsinger
Camp—Kemp	Klopfenstein
Conrad	Litwiller
Egli	Nafziger—Noffsinger
Eicher	Oesch—Esch
Fahrney	Oyer—Auer
Flickinger	Raber
Gascho	Ramseyer
Gerig	Rediger

Ringenberg	Strubhar
Ropp—Rupp	Stuckey
Rocke—Roggi	Studer
Roth	Sutter
Ruvenacht	Sweitzer
Schertz	Verkler
Slagel	Wagler
Smith	Wyse
Sommer	Yordy
Springer	Yutzi—Jutzi
Stahley	Zehr

The Amish communities which were settled in America before 1870 experienced a number of serious schisms which broke the unity of the group. Even apart from this the earlier pre-Revolutionary immigrants of the Berks-Lancaster settlement and the latter Alsatian Amish immigrants never really formed a harmonious working relationship although the Amish General conferences 1862-78, called *Diener-Versammlungen* (q.v.), represented a partially successful attempt. The following schisms and resultant branches are to be noted.

1. Old Order versus Progressive 1850-80. The Old Order Amish (q.v.) group resisted change and has continued to this day as unorganized but close-knit group settlements with communion fellowship of about 14,000 baptized members. The progressive element organized three district conferences after 1882: Eastern Amish Mennonite (q.v.), Indiana-Michigan Amish Mennonite (q.v.), and Western District Amish Mennonite (q.v.), all of which later merged with the Mennonite (MC) conferences and are now an integral part of that branch, representing today possibly 15,000 members.

2. An in-between group of congregations which did not accept either the Old Order or the progressive position organized the Conservative Amish Mennonite (q.v.) Conference in 1910, which with allied independent congregations numbers about 4,000 members. More recently over 20 congregations with nearly 1,500 members, standing between the Old Order and the Conservative Amish, have been formed from groups breaking away from the Old Order. They are not yet organized into a conference.

3. On the other hand, two schisms occurred among the Alsatian Amish settlements of Illinois, Indiana, and Ohio 1865-75 which led to the formation of the Evangelical Mennonite Church (q.v.; at first called Defenceless Mennonites, q.v.) with about 1,500 members, and the Central Conference (Ill.) (q.v.), now a member of the General Conference Mennonite Church, with some 3,000 members. In the Defenceless group about 1898 a schism resulted in the formation of the Missionary Church Association with now over 5,000 members. The Volhynian Amish settlement of Freeman, S.D., and Moundridge, Kan., never formed a separate conference but joined the General Conference Mennonite Church as individual congregations.

The characteristic practices, customs, and attitudes known as "Amish" are actually characteristic only of the Old Order Amish today, and are described in the article **Old Order Amish**. H.S.B.

John A. Hostetler, *Annotated Bibl. on the Amish*

8

(Scottdale, 1951), an exhaustive bibliography of publications in North America by or about the Amish of all groups. Practically nothing on the Amish has appeared in Europe.

Amish Mutual Fire Insurance Association of Atglen, Pa., originally known as the Amish Mutual Aid Plan, was organized around 1875 by the Old Order Amish Mennonite churches of Lancaster Co., Pa. Previous to that time freewill offerings had been taken to cover the fire losses of members. Sometimes, however, members did not receive enough to cover their losses while prominent members received more than was required. To equalize this, a company with power to assess and tax was organized. A few years later, when the Millwood and Conestoga Amish Mennonite congregations were organized, they also joined the Mutual Aid Plan.

These churches worked together until January 1923, when the Amish Mennonite and Conservative Amish Mennonite congregations organized the separate company now operating as the Amish Mutual Fire Insurance Association. When in 1928 a Pennsylvania law abolished all insurance companies not carrying a surplus fund and paying a state license, a license was taken out in January 1929, and a surplus fund raised by borrowing $10,000, which was invested in public school bonds. Later this money was raised by assessment and the note was paid. In 1949 the total insurance in force exceeded $8,000,000. The company is now licensed in Pennsylvania, Maryland, and Delaware. The three conferences represented in it are the Ohio and Eastern Amish Mennonite, the Lancaster Mennonite, and the Conservative Amish Mennonite. All types of farm buildings, dwellings, garages, churches, livestock, and farm machinery are covered against fire and storm, and automobiles and trucks are covered against fire and theft. Only members in good standing in non-resistant churches are insured. In charge of the organization is a board of seven directors, none of whom receive salaries, although the secretary and treasurer receive some compensation for their services. I.G.K.

Amman, Hartmann, canon of the Augustinian Order, Gymnasium professor at Brixen in Tirol (b. June 21, 1856), published in the 46th and 47th programs of the *gymnasium* at Brixen (1896 and 1897) a treatise with the title, *Die Wiedertäufer in Michelsberg im Pustertale und deren Urgichten* (124 pp.). In the presentation, the court records preserved in the f.b. court archives at Brixen were used. The confessions extorted from the Anabaptists, often by means of torture, reveal many details about the spread of the Anabaptist movement in Tirol in the second and third quarters of the 16th century. The booklet contains valuable information about the success of Anabaptist leaders such as Jakob Hutter, Hans Amon, Offrus Griesinger, and Leonhard Lanzenstiel. In many points it complements the research of J. Beck (*q.v.*) and J. Loserth (*q.v.*) on the Anabaptist movement in Austria in the 16th century. (*ML* I, 57.) Hege.

Ammann, Jakob, a Mennonite elder, a native of Erlenbach in the Simme Valley south of Thun, canton of Bern, Switzerland, founder of the Amish branch of the Mennonite brotherhood through a schism which he occasioned in 1693 in the Emmental, canton of Bern. It is possible that he is identical with the Jakob Ammann who was born at Erlenbach on Feb. 12, 1644, as the son of Michael and Anna Rupp Ammann, but he was probably not the brother of Ulrich Ammann who was born in 1661 at Oberhofen near Thun and fled to the region of Neuchâtel in 1709, where he was still living in 1733. He was resident in the region of Ste. Marie-aux-Mines (Markirch), Upper Alsace, on Feb. 27, 1696, for on that date he signed a petition in the name of his brethren who had settled there two years previously, against compulsory militia service. In 1704 he with an associate signed a list of 40 familiar Mennonite names, apparently all the heads of families resident in that location, also a similar list of some 60 names in 1708, both lists being required by the authorities. Evidently he was the leader (elder) of the congregation at this place, possibly from 1694 on. No further record of Ammann himself is known, except that Erlenbach records report a daughter baptized in the Reformed Church there as an adult in 1730 and mention her father as having died prior to that time outside the territory. A psalm book which belonged to a son, Baltz Ammann, in 1741 is now in the library of the Swiss Mennonite Church at Jeangisboden near Tramelan in the Bernese Jura.

Jakob Ammann's own account of the tragic "Amish" division of 1693, together with other letters which deal with the same matter, makes it clear that he was directly responsible and that he caused the schism by personally excommunicating all the elders and ministers in Switzerland who would not agree with him to introduce and practice the *Meidung* or shunning of excommunicated members. He made a tour of the Swiss congregations, calling several meetings of elders and ministers, and acting in an ill-considered and harsh manner, as he himself later confessed. Since the full story of this division is told elsewhere (see **Amish Division**), it remains only to say that Ammann must have visited the Markirch (Alsace) congregation about the same time, where he excommunicated some members, and that he almost immediately got into a controversy with the ministers of the Palatinate who tried to effect a reconciliation. He found almost united support from the ministers of Alsace, but proceeded to place most of the Palatine ministers under the ban. In a few years Ammann and his associates decided they had been too rash and tried to effect a reconciliation, failing largely because they confessed only to an error in method and spirit while refusing to surrender their demand for the *Meidung*. Thus the division was made permanent because of the intransigence of Ammann.

Ammann also held strict views on other points, such as the wearing of the untrimmed beard, uniformity in dress, including style of hats, garments, shoes and stockings, and prohibition of attendance at services of the state church. He seems to have held that the *Treuherzigen* (those friends of the Anabaptists who shared many of their views and helped them in times of persecution but for some reason would not join the group openly, perhaps out of fear) would not be saved, meaning that no one would be saved outside the Anabaptist fold. He also introduced footwashing as an ordinance, which had hitherto not been practiced by the Swiss Anabaptists, but was practiced in Holland. (See Half-Anabaptists.)   H.S.B.

The Letters of the Amish Division of 1693-1711, translated and edited by John B. Mast, published by Christian J. Schlabach (Oregon City, 1950) contains Ammann's letter of Nov. 22, 1693, to the ministers of the Palatinate, which explains his dealings with his opponents and justifies his position and procedure; also his "Warning Letter" of Nov. 22, 1693, to the brotherhood not yet agreeing with him. All the German printed forms of these letters and other documents related to the Amish schism are listed in full in Milton Gascho's "The Amish Division of 1693-1697 in Switzerland and Alsace," in MQR (Oct. 1937) 235-66, which contains a full account of the activities of Ammann and the best account of the division. See also D. L. Gratz, "The Home of Jacob Ammannn," MQR XXV (April 1951) 137-39: ML I, 57.

Amnestie-placcaat (Proclamation of Amnesty), issued by Emperor Charles V concerning the Melchiorites or Anabaptists in the Netherlands on Feb. 27, 1534. Though both those who have performed rebaptism and those who have been rebaptized— thus the proclamation—have forfeited life and property, they will receive pardon and be restored to favor if they apply to their confessors within 24 days with a solemn declaration of repentance. On March 20, 1534, after the term was closed, only 15 Anabaptists had reported. (*Inv. Arch. Amst.* I, Nos. 19, 20, 21a, 27; Kühler, *Geschiedenis* I, 93-94.)
                                                      vdZ.

Amnestie-Plakat (Proclamation of Amnesty), issued by the government of Bern (Switzerland) on Feb. 11, 1711, offering the Swiss Brethren "free departure from our lands as well as the complete withdrawal of their goods." The term "amnesty" implies the forgetting and forgiving of guilt, a complete remission of penalty on the part of the state. The nearly two centuries old struggle of the Bernese government with the Swiss Brethren thereby entered its last stage. Not in any previous mandate had free withdrawal been granted. The opening sentences, to be sure, indicate that the government was reluctant to issue this amnesty. This long "present proclamation" begins thus:

We, the mayor, councillors and citizens of the city of Bern, do herewith announce to all: Since we by our wholesome regulations and orders issued from time to time from our paternal care of the canton, have always applied all earnestness and have done our utmost by means of both gentle kindness and also in real application of . . . punishment, to rid our lands and cantons of the so-called sect of the Anabaptists and to cleanse them of these, nevertheless unhappy experience testifies that all the kind and severe means applied . . . against the so-called Anabaptists found from time to time in our land have profited nothing, but that their number has rather increased than decreased.

The government therefore considered it wise to permit "free exit" since they refused to render the oath of allegiance, indeed they "refused to take up arms in case of emergency to defend and protect the dear fatherland." The next question was then: Whither? They noted that there was not yet any country where these people could live freely according to their consciences. The first country considered was the Netherlands. It was therefore decided:

1. It should be permitted the emigrating Anabaptists to go to Prussia, "in order there to be able to exercise their freedom of conscience the better. . . ." Yet Bern would not permit them to stay in Neuchâtel, which had been a Prussian domain since 1707.

2. All Anabaptist persons who had hitherto remained in concealment, those who had been banished by the government, as well as the preachers were not to be included in this "freedom of withdrawal."

3. "We have found it wise that the Anabaptists now in the custody of the state" should be released with security, but should neither hold nor attend meetings in the meantime. All those who could not make use of this amnesty should have the privilege of having other members of their families receive their property.

4. The time of departure had been determined in consultation with Runkel, the Dutch ambassador in Bern, and set for the end of June. By that time each family should have its affairs in order. Each family should make an exact report of its means and property, on penalty of confiscation.

5. The government was not responsible for the traveling expenses; it was enough that in leaving "they were graciously permitted" to take their possessions. Reformed spouses of Anabaptists should likewise have the privilege of free withdrawal.

6. In case of mixed marriages, where not all the children belonged to the Anabaptist sect, the Reformed members of the family should also be permitted to leave, but would thereby lose their citizenship.

In conclusion it is remarked that these measures were necessary for the security of the country. For each Anabaptist who returned to Bern, the sponsors would be obliged to pay 50 doubloons for a preacher, and 10 for an ordinary layman to the *Täufer-Kammer* (q.v.). The Anabaptists who had been expelled should now be more closely watched. Anabaptists and all others who now left the country were no longer to be regarded as citizens. In case "contrary to our better expectations some of these persons belonging to this Anabaptist sect should reject our merciful grace and be so bold as to return to our land," they should be considered as seducers of the people and be punished accordingly. All officials were ordered with all seriousness to read this proclamation aloud from all the pulpits and to post it in public places.   S.G.

Amon, Hans, bishop of the Hutterian Brethren in Moravia, successor of Jakob Hutter (q.v.), cloth weaver by trade, hence frequently called "Tuchmacher." Amon came from Bavaria and was among the eighty persons who had left Kromau (q.v.) in

1529 and settled in Austerlitz (*q.v.*). From 1530 to 1534 he worked with Jakob Hutter in Tirol, when the persecution of the Anabaptists was at its height. In 1535 Hutter transferred to him the leadership of the Hutterite congregations, which he retained for seven years. Before his death he named Leonhard Lanzenstiel (*q.v.*) as his successor. At Candlemas 1542 Amon died at Schäkowitz in Moravia. To his memory Georg Bruckmaier (*q.v.*), who was burned at the stake for his faith at Ried in Upper Austria, dedicated several verses (Beck, 87). Seventeen of Amon's open letters are still extant, preserved (original or copy) in the possession of the Hutterian Brethren in Frankfort, S.D. Copies and some originals are also scattered among Austrian archives. An epistle addressed to the imprisoned Brethren on the sea (galley slaves of Andrea Doria) was published condensed by Beck in *Wiedertäufer in Kärnten* (1867) 123 f. Amon also wrote three hymns: "Der ewig Gott, der mächtig" (32 stanzas); "O, ihr herzlieben Brüder mein" (10 stanzas), and "Unbillig habens ghandelt die bös und gottlos Rott." The assertion of Kripp in *Ein Beitrag zur Geschichte der Wiedertäufer in Tirol* (Innsbruck, 1857), that Amon was captured at Götzenberg in Tirol and executed at Michelsburg with ten brethren is erroneous.

HEGE.

H. Ammann. *Die Wiedertäufer in Michelsburg* im Pusterthale (Brixen, 1896); Beck, *Geschichts-Bücher;* J. Loserth, *Der Anabaptismus in Tirol* (Vienna, 1892); *Lieder der hutterischen Brüder* (Scottdale, 1914) 95-97 and 116-20; J. Horsch, *Kurzgefasste Gesch. der Menn.* (Elkhart, 1890) 127; Zieglschmid, *Chronik; ML* I, 57.

Ampsinck, Johannes Assuerus (*ca.* 1560-1642), a Reformed minister at Ootmarsum and Haarlem, Holland, became an army chaplain and led a dissolute life. He is the author of several works, which severely attack the Mennonites. Of importance is *Eenighe Propositien nopende de kerckelijcke discipline, . . .* (Haarlem, 1590). Pages 129 to 140 deal with the "Tyrannije der Vlaemsche Wederdooperen." On pages 141 to 187 the book contains a "Copie van een geschrift ghesonden van sommighe Vriezen aen den Vlamingen." This letter was lost on the streets of Haarlem by a brother from Franeker (July 1589) and fell into Ampsinck's hands. It contains a number of charges made by the Frisians against the Flemish and therefore served Ampsinck as evidence of "Flemish tyranny." (*Biogr. Wb.* I, 147-53; *Catalogus Amst.,* 175, 182, 185, 187.) vDZ.

A. M. R.: see **American Mennonite Relief.**

Amsdorf, Nicolaus von, b. 1483 in Torgau, Germany, d. May 14, 1565, in Eisenach, the reformer of Magdeburg, was Luther's trusted friend and zealous co-worker, a harsh character, as was shown especially in his controversy with Melchior Hofmann (*q.v.*). It is unlikely that the two met in Wittenberg in 1525 (Krohn, 58). Friedrich Otto zur Linden states in his book, *Melchior Hofmann,* that Hofmann, on his second journey to Wittenberg (1527), looked Amsdorf up in Magdeburg in order to receive from him an oral explanation of his eschatological views, which Amsdorf had already sent him in writing. Following the advice of Luther, Amsdorf gave him

a very unfriendly reception, and after a violent exchange of words showed him the door. At the same time he wrote a coarse polemic against Hofmann: *Eine Vermahnung an die von Magdeburg, dass sie sich vor falschen Propheten zu hüten wissen* (1527). Hofmann replied to his opponent "with all love," although he felt that Amsdorf was to blame for his imprisonment in Magdeburg, on his return from Wittenberg. When Amsdorf replied with a pamphlet filled with new attacks, Hofmann was content to send it to Luther with a complaint.

A year later strife flared up again. In Hamburg Amsdorf became acquainted with Hofmann's chiliastic writings, and turned against him with a pamphlet: *Das Melchior Hoffmann ein falscher Prophet und seine Lehre vom Jüngsten Tag unrecht, falsch und wider Gott ist; an alle Heilige und Gläubige an J. Chr. zu Kiel und im ganzen Holstein* (1528). Hofmann replied with an unusually violent lampoon: *Dass Nicolaus Amsdorf, der Magdeburger Pastor, ein Lügenhafter falscher Nasengeist sei, öffentlich bewiesen durch Melchior Hoffmann, Prediger zu Kiel im Land zu Holstein* (Kiel, 1528). This pamphlet created a great stir. Luther sided with his friend. The latter seems to have answered in similar vein, but there is no trace of the pamphlet. Hofmann's reply, *Dass Nic. Amsdorf, der Magdeburger Pastor, nicht weiss, was er schreiben oder schwätzen soll,* has been preserved.

In the violence of his quarrel, Amsdorf throws the Anabaptists and Zwinglians into one group. In the church regulations of Goslar (1531) drawn up by him he says, "Every pastor shall confess openly that he believes and holds that the Zwinglian and Anabaptist doctrine of the sacrament, an external word and sign, is wrong, false, a lie and heresy; therefore he shall teach and vow never to teach their doctrine, but with all his power to fight, teach, and strive against it" (Richter's *Kirchen-Ordnungen,* 154 ff.). In his *Positiones wider die Wiedertäufer und Sacramentierer* (336), he writes, "The Anabaptists and sacramentalists impress all Germany now with their sanctity, as formerly the monks impressed the whole world; not that they have true sanctity, but vaunt themselves with a pretended one." In a similar vein he expressed himself on Dec. 18, 1532, in a letter to the council of the city of Soest, warning them of Joh. Campanus and Melchior Hofmann (Rembert, *Wiedertäufer,* 191).

NEFF.

Th. Pressel, *Nicolaus von Amsdorf* (Elbing, 1862); N. B. Krohn, *Gesch. der fanatischen und enthusiastischen Wiedertäufer, vornehmlich in Niederdeutschland* (Leipzig, 1758); F. O. z. Linden, *Melchior Hofmann, ein Prophet der Wiedertäufer* (Haarlem, 1885); N. Amsdorf, *Schlussreden wider die Wiedertäufer und Sacramentierer* (Magdeburg, 1535) reprinted in J. G. Walch, *D. M. Luthers sämmtliche Schriften,* XX (St. Louis, 1890), Col. 1742-51; G. Wolf, *Quellenkunde der deutschen Ref.* II, Part 2 (Gotha, 1922) par. 93, p. 12. Numerous writings by Amsdorf are found in the archives in Weimar; *ML* I, 58.

Amssler, Jakob, a delegate of the Hutterian Brethren in Sobotiste (Hungary), on Oct. 8 or 18, 1655, who with Christoph Baumhauer received from Elector Palatine Karl Ludwig permission to colonize the Hutterian Brethren in Mannheim beside the "Rhine gate." Amssler, a smith by trade, had come from Switzerland, and on March 18, 1648, was chosen to serve as preacher in the church at Sobotiste. (Beck, *Geschichts-Bücher,* 477 and 492; *ML* I, 58.)　　　　　　　　　　　　　　HEGE.

Amsterdam (pop. 803,847 in 1947; 8,517 Mennonites). The Mennonite congregation in Amsterdam is the largest in the world. Only since 1801 has there been a united Amsterdam Mennonite church; it was formed by the gradual union of eleven congregations. In spite of many divisions the Mennonites of Amsterdam have always been of central importance to the brotherhood in Holland and beyond. This is shown by the history of the congregation, which can be divided into five periods: (1) 1530-78, the time of its rise; (2) 1578-1664, the golden age; (3) 1664-1801, the decline; (4) the 19th century, restoration and development; (5) the present church.

1. *The Rise of the Church* (1530-78). The origin of the Amsterdam Anabaptist congregation goes back to 1530. At the close of this year Jan Volkertsz Trypmaker, a disciple of Melchior Hofmann, came from Emden to Amsterdam, where he became the head of a church, upon which he, like his teacher, urged peace and obedience to the government. In 1531 Hofmann himself was in Amsterdam and baptized many. In November (Fr. O. zur Linden, *Melchior Hofmann,* Haarlem, 1885) the council of Amsterdam ordered the mayor to persecute the followers of the new doctrine. Trypmaker surrendered voluntarily, and with eight other Anabaptists was taken to The Hague and on Dec. 5, 1531, beheaded.

Jan Matthyszoon, the Haarlem baker, soon appeared in Amsterdam as a prophet and sent out his twelve apostles, among them Jan Beuckelszoon of Leiden and Jacob van Campen (end of 1533). Early in 1534 the summons to go to Münster created a "crusade," which was, however, prevented (see **Bergklooster**). Meanwhile Jacob van Campen succeeded in gathering the peaceful elements and in persuading by letter the assembly of 32 preachers in Sparendam (near Amsterdam), to abandon the plan to storm the city (December 1534). The church in Amsterdam grew day by day. After Pentecost 1534 about 300 new members had joined; their total number is estimated (surely an exaggeration) at 3,500. The government succeeded in stopping a meeting of Anabaptists at the house of Jan Pauw. In February 1535 a group of 12 men and women, madly shouting in the streets at night, "Truth is naked," roused more anger than fear. They paid the death penalty. Meanwhile, however, a leader appeared for the insurgents. He was Jan van Geelen (*q.v.*), who had escaped from Münster in December 1534. With 40 followers he stormed the courthouse during the night of May 10, 1535, where a celebration was taking place. The attack failed; in the scrimmage a burgomaster and several citizens fell. On the following morning the eleven surviving rioters were executed (see **Naaktloopers**).

Now there began for the Anabaptist congregation, though it had had no part in the riot, a time of severe suffering. They had received some of the "crusaders" in their midst, like Hendrik van Maastricht, but they personally had only given warning and resistance to all insurrection; Pieter Koster of Zaandam opposed it with his pen. The government, spurred on by public indignation, delivered all the Anabaptists it could find to the executioner; 46, including many women, were executed in Amsterdam from May 10 to July 28. Jacob van Campen was seized after a long search and cruelly killed (July 10, 1535).

Persecution lasted nearly 40 years. In some years the number of martyrs was unusually high; this was connected with political events, the inauguration of a new mayor (1542), the resumption of authority by the emperor (1552), the Spanish reaction (1567). Sufficient grounds for condemnation were attendance at a meeting or having heard an Anabaptist preacher. Everywhere a spiritual relationship with the insurgents was assumed (see van Braght's correct comment, *Mart. Mir.* D 411, E 763). The list of martyrs is long. In many cases only the name and method of execution are given. The very brevity and monotony of these reports make them shocking. In most cases they had for years not attended a Catholic service. How touching it is to read Clement Hendriks' letters! His greatest grief is the fact that the brethren think he has recanted; he does not tell his parents the tortures he has undergone and consoles them concerning his lot. What courage there was in Pieter Pieterszoon Bekjen, who mounted the stake singing a defiant hymn of faith, and in his friend Willem Janszoon, who upon hearing of his friend's execution, hastened to his side from Waterland in spite of many obstacles in order to cry, "Fight faithfully, dear brother!" It cost him his life. What honor is shown by Ellert Jansz and others, who would not flee, although they could have done so. They were mostly common people, craftsmen from the city, and sailors. Their letters betray piety rather than learning. But there were also respected and wealthy persons among them. In the sentences mention is made that according to an old charter their estates, all but 100 pounds, went to the emperor if they were citizens of Amsterdam; the rest went to the city coffers.

A long visit of Menno Simons about 1542 doubtless contributed a great deal toward strengthening the church. Claas Gerbrantsz of Wormer recalls his preaching ten years later. In Jan Claeszoon Menno found a loyal disciple, who as a bookseller was of great assistance in spreading his writings. The violent persecution of 1543 and 1544 probably drove Menno out of the city; two letters show that he kept up his connections with the congregation at Amsterdam (Menno Simons, *Complete Works,* Part I, 1871, 277-80, 281 f.) The former warns them not to attend Catholic services, and severely criticizes the excuse of the followers of Joris (*q.v.*) and Batenburg (*q.v.*), that one could outwardly remain Catholic. The date of this letter is probably between 1545 and 1550. The second letter was probably written in 1557 or 1558. He urges the brethren to visit the victims of the plague. From the end of 1557 into 1558 while this dread disease ravaged the city, government orders forbade any contact with the victims. Menno says, "The hairs of your head are numbered; death is the door to the better life."

The names of the preachers in this period of suffering are lost. Only of Jan Claeszoon is it said that he was a teacher of the Anabaptists; but many martyrs were baptized by Gillis van Aken, "a head and bishop of the Anabaptists," or heard him preach. Leenaert Bouwens also baptized 218 persons in Amsterdam after 1551. The congregation met for worship in small groups in the homes of friends, in attics and hiding-places, or at night on the gallows field which, according to popular belief, was haunted by evil spirits, or in boats on the water. A *weetdoener* (notifier) informed the members of each meeting to be held. The number of members is estimated at about 2,000.

From 1553 on the Anabaptists had a respite of a few years. During the Spanish rule under Alba the stakes flamed up again; Amsterdam became known as *Moorddam* (Murderdam). To be sure, the character of the Anabaptists was now better known, and the name *Wederdooper* was being replaced by *Mennist;* nevertheless adult baptism was still a capital crime. Deliverance dawned when Prince William I forced the city to surrender in 1578. During these days it was decided to accept Mennonites as citizens without an oath. When the gates were opened, the refugees returned. Of 137 outsiders who became citizens, 26 were Anabaptists. Amsterdam now became the city of refuge for all that were persecuted for their faith.

2. *The Golden Age* (1578-1664). After 1581 the Mennonites in North Holland enjoyed toleration; in Amsterdam they were generously protected by the government. The reason for this was certainly that the Mennonites added to the wealth of the city by their energy and commercial skill, but also the fact that prominent families entered into connections with them. The government soon had occasion to defend the commercial interests of the Anabaptists when London authorities refused to release, without the sworn affidavits of the owners, goods belonging to Mennonites taken from Spanish prize ships. The government was able to refer to the fact that in Amsterdam the simple word of the Mennonites was sufficient. The Reformed, who had recently themselves been persecuted but were now the ruling church, sought to oppress the Anabaptists in Amsterdam and later (1597) to force a disputation with Lubbert Gerritsz; but the council put a stop to it.

Now we hear more about the Mennonites; they are coming out of concealment. In 1578 they regularly met on the Nieuwendyk near the old Haarlem locks in the Emden or Condé quarter; but even as late as 1581 the place of meeting was announced beforehand. Already we meet the leading parties of Mennonites. The oldest and most numerous were the Waterlanders (*q.v.*). In 1581 they held here the first conference, attended by 12 congregations, at which the first church discipline was adopted (*DB* 1877, 80-87). Their most prominent leader was already Hans de Ries (*q.v.*), who later had his residence at Alkmaar. About 1600 the following groups are mentioned: the Waterlanders (*q.v.*) meeting on the Teerketelsteeg and after 1615 on the Singel canal near the Jan Roodenpoortstoren, in *de grote Spyker* (the great warehouse) or *by den Toren* (at the gates); the Flemish (*q.v.*) or *Contrahuiskoopers* (anti-house-buyers) meeting after 1608 on the Singel near a brewery which had a lamb as its gable sign (today Odeon) in a storehouse which Harmen Hendriksz van Warendorp equipped for them as a meetinghouse and which was enlarged in 1639, called *bij't Lam* (Lamist congregation); the Old Flemish (*q.v.*), also known as the Danzig Old Flemish (*q.v.*) on the N. Z. Achterburgwal at the "6 Kruikjes" (in 1620 a group separated from them which met in the Tuinstraat, but returned in 1730). They practiced footwashing only as a service of love for elders and preachers who visited them from the outside. There were also two branches of Frisians: the Jan Jacobsz group (from the province of Friesland) meeting in the Bloemstraat, and the Frisians (from the province of North Holland, led by Lubbert Gerritsz) meeting on the Heerengracht. The meeting place of the *Hoogduitsen* or High German group is not known. A variegated picture of church life!

The early decades of the 17th century were characterized by efforts of the various branches of Mennonites to unite; to do this they had to overcome old prejudices, but they were not immune to new causes for dissension coming from without. They came in contact with the "world" and were influenced by the trends of the time. Amsterdam frequently led in this striving for unity. As early as 1591 the High Germans and the Frisians, represented by Leenaert Clock and Lubbert Gerritsz, united on the basis of the Concept of Cologne. After several years this united group made successful overtures to the Waterlanders. About 1594 the union took place in Amsterdam, in 1601 it was accomplished in most places; they were now called the *Bevredigde Broederschap* (*q.v.*) (Conciliated Brotherhood). They gave up separation from the world and began to call themselves *Doopsgezinde* (Baptism-minded) in preference to "Mennonites." In Amsterdam Lubbert Gerritsz (*q.v.*) was the most influential preacher. After his death some of the High German group separated from them, led by Leenaert Clock (1613).

In 1615 the church was increased in size by the admission of an English congregation under John Smyth (*q.v.*). Smyth belonged to the Brownists (*q.v.*), a church existing in Amsterdam since 1593. To facilitate an understanding with him, Hans de Ries and Lubbert Gerritsz wrote a confession of faith in 1610, frequently called the Confession of Hans de Ries, but regarded by the Waterlanders as a personal confession. The church building of the English group was located in the Engelsche Steeg near the Bakkerstraat; until about 1640 English services were held for them.

After a vain attempt at union between the Waterlanders and the Flemish in 1603, the Amsterdam Flemish in 1626 offered union to many congregations of the Frisians and High Germans on the basis of a confession of faith called *Olyftacxken*

(Olive Branch, *q.v.*). Encouraged by the favorable reception of the idea they issued in 1627 a "letter for preparation of peace" (*brief tot Vredebereiding*), and in 1629 a "peace proposal" (*Vrede-Presentatie*). After a conference in Amsterdam, the Frisians and the High Germans replied by offering the *Hoogduitsche Confessie,* also called the Confession of Jan Cents (1630). On the way to successful solution, the union was postponed for several years, while the Flemish, torn apart by the "house-buying" quarrel, tried to reunite. This Flemish union finally took place in 1632 on the basis of the Dordrecht Confession. Part of the Flemish congregation, *bij den Kruikjes,* transferred to the Lamist congregation. In 1639 the union of the Flemish and the combined Frisians and High German group followed on the basis of the confessions of 1626 and 1632.

With the exception of the three smaller groups, there were now in Amsterdam only the two large groups, the Lamist and the Toren congregations. Their union seemed to be near. In 1647 the Waterlanders tried again for union. Forty-one congregations sent delegates to Amsterdam for the first conference since 1581 (in 1611 a limited number of congregations had met in Amsterdam). In 1647 the old church discipline was revised and union was offered to all the Flemish, not only those in Amsterdam but in all Holland. In order to meet their request for a confession of faith, that of Hans de Ries was given them; but at the same time it was emphatically stated that no confession should be placed over the Scriptures in authority and it should be valid only in so far as it agreed with the Holy Scriptures. This proposal met with little response; the negative answer followed in 1649, signed by Galenus Abrahamsz de Haan.

Meanwhile a division was developing in the Lamist congregation which grew more serious than all the former divisions, involving the entire Dutch brotherhood. The Collegiants (*q.v.* also called Rijnsburgers) and Socinians, who had been spreading in Holland since 1600, entered the Mennonite congregations. In Amsterdam the sharp difference that had been engendered thereby (first among the Waterlanders) found expression in the disputes between Nittert Obbesz, the youngest minister of the Grote Spyker congregation, and Hans de Ries, 1622-26. There were even disturbances in church services. Joost van den Vondel (*q.v.*), the classical poet of Holland, who had recently been a deacon in the Toren congregation, took sides by writing *Antidotum* (*q.v.*) in 1627. The quarrel was not entirely eliminated by the mutual signing of a confession. Nittert Obbesz was not reinstated as a minister.

The greatest effect of the Collegiant and Socinian influence was evident in the discord between Galenus Abrahamsz de Haan and Samuel Apostool in the Flemish Lamist congregation. The Collegiants, a widespread group in Holland with outspokenly antichurch principles, met in free assemblies (colleges) where all were permitted to speak. Baptism was by immersion. They also held the Lord's Supper, but neither ceremony was considered a required ordinance. Their meetings were open to members of all churches. Everywhere they secured sympathizers among the Mennonites. In Amsterdam, where they had been holding their meetings, Galenus joined them and soon became their leader. He had been chosen as minister of the Flemish in 1648 along with David Spruyt, a kindred spirit. Objections raised at their ordination were weakened by their agreement to the *Olyftacxken* Confession, but shortly after 1650 the *Lammerenkrijg* (*q.v.*) broke out, which caused the great division among the Dutch Mennonites. The conservatives held fast to the confession of doctrine as necessary to salvation. The followers of Galenus put all the weight on Christian living. The *Lammerenkrijg,* which developed a deplorable personal bitterness, took place in three periods.

(*a*) In the Amsterdam congregation. The representatives of the *ouderen,* the ministers Tobias Goverts van den Wyngaart, Tileman Tielen, and Dr. de Vries, argued against Galenus and David Spruyt. The latter explained their views in 19 articles not intended for publication; they were however, without their knowledge, published in 1658 with a refutation. Galenus defended himself with an enlarged edition of the articles, refuting his opponents. He won many adherents in the congregation. The conservative members looked for support among outside preachers.

(*b*) The second period began with a meeting in Leiden in June 1660, where the significance of this dispute for the entire brotherhood was keenly felt. Four men, among them the well-known Tieleman Jansz van Braght, were sent to Amsterdam; they were to persuade the Galenus group to submit, or if they did not recant, to lay aside the office of preacher temporarily. Their message was not accepted at all, and when the conservative party tried to draw the visiting mediators before the Amsterdam church for a report and thus bring about a discussion, Galenus cited the rule of the church forbidding unrequested meddling from outside, and had the magistrate of Amsterdam intervene. In 1662 they arrived at a short truce; they were to tolerate each other in doctrine, life, and views. During this time four ministers were chosen, two of them, Samuel Apostool and Isaac van Vreede, of the conservative group. But on Nov. 15, 1662, the strife flared up anew; Apostool and Galenus attacked each other from the pulpit concerning the doctrine of redemption. Now the conservative group appealed to the Reformed for aid.

(*c*) At the instigation of the Reformed, Galenus was charged with Socinian views, but was exonerated by the Court of Holland in 1663. A peace proposal of the conservative party (December 1663) required the recognition of the conservative confessions and doctrines by the younger party; a violent quarrel broke out when the proposal was submitted. Now the magistrate of Amsterdam acted with vigor, and forbade all disputing about difficult questions that savored of Socinianism. In vain. The cleavage was too deep, and when the party of

Galenus was granted the church property, the conservative party separated under the leadership of Samuel Apostool, Tobias van den Wyngaard, and Isaac van Vreede, with about 500 members (May or June 1664). Soon they were called Zonists after their chapel, a former brewery on the Singel, which had a sun for the gable sign. The other party remained in possession of the church *van't Lam* (Lamb); they were called Lamists.

Externally viewed, the dispute was an affair of the ministers, but it had deeply excited the congregation. Not only did members take part in the disputations, but vituperative letters flew back and forth. The intervention of the Amsterdam government is not surprising, as there were occasional tumults on the streets. The government always strove to maintain quiet and religious toleration impartially.

3. *Decline* (1664-1801). About 1664 the Lamists had about 2,000 members. The Waterlanders approached them again; the peace proposal of 1647 was reprinted in 1667; in 1668 the union of the Lamist and Toren congregations took place, the united congregation being called Lamist and Toren group (*van't Lam en bij den Toren*). In 1676 the congregation had 2,369 members; in 1720, 2,000; in 1745, 1,500; and in 1801, before the union with the Zonists, about 800. Urged by the Rotterdam congregation, Galenus began to offer instruction to train young men for the ministry. He did this from 1681 until his death in 1706. In 1725 or 1727 the Frisians of Bloemstraat (Jan Jacobsz group) joined the Lamist and Toren congregation. In 1728 the last 16 members of this combined church handed the church property over; its history was without important events.

The Zonists experienced divisions as well as growth; in 1670 a small group, called the *Kleine Zon*, left them and met in the Prinsenstraat, with an exit facing the Prinsengracht; in 1679, after long, futile negotiations with the Lamists, they returned to the Zonist congregation. A small group had separated from the *Kleine Zon* in 1675; their meeting place, Het Sterretje, was located on the Prinsengracht opposite the Noorderkerk. In 1692 Het Sterretje united with the Old Frisians. The latter had earlier assembled on the Heerengracht, but in 1664 had purchased from the Waterlanders the *Oude Spyker* (old warehouse) on the Teerketelsteeg and in 1702, with the consent of the magistrate, moved to the *Kleine Zon* on the Prinsengracht; the name "Arche Noë" was passed on to each new building. Shortly before their union with the Zonists, Marten Schagen, the famous historian, was their minister (1727-38). On account of lack of preachers and small size of the congregation (in 1745, 150 members) they united with the Zonist congregation. Finally the Old Flemish at the Kruikjes followed, merging in 1788 with the Zonist congregation (in 1745, 65 members; 1788, 41 members). Thus the more conservative churches had all united. The Zonist congregation in 1745 consisted of about 500 members, in 1801 only of about 300. At the close of the 18th century there remained

only two divergent congregations in Amsterdam, the Lamists and the Zonists.

To call this period the time of "collapse" does not do it full justice. To be sure, viewed externally, the great decrease in numbers is obvious. There are many reasons for this. The earlier separation from the "world" had yielded to absorption by the world; the industry of the older generation had greatly increased their prosperity, for the Amsterdam Mennonites took part in all the great commercial enterprises. A certain simplicity still marked them, but wealth became apparent in many cases in costliness of dress and house furnishings. The enjoyment of worldly goods was no longer disparaged. Along the Vecht, a river in the province of Utrecht, many Amsterdam Mennonites had stately country homes; the place was called *Mennisten Hemel* (Mennonite Heaven). All of this led to a decline of interest in religious matters. Furthermore many members who wished to hold state offices transferred to the Reformed Church, as did the great-grandfather of the poet van Lennep (one branch of the van Lenneps remained Mennonite). The movement spread throughout the country; but the Amsterdam church probably suffered most severely.

Meanwhile the attitude of the state to the Mennonites had also changed. In 1672 they were officially recognized. Fifty years earlier (1621) the Amsterdam magistrate had forbidden their ministers to perform marriages in the courthouse. The Mennonites complied; only the Frisians had their marriages first performed by ministers and then confirmed by the state. Besides this, the magistrate in 1714 required the introduction of "children's books," which were at first birth registers, and which were later, after the French period, used by the churches for their own purposes. The government favored the churches in permitting their religious and charitable institutions to remain tax-free.

The Mennonites took as friendly as possible an attitude toward the state. In 1650 they assisted energetically in fortifying Amsterdam, and in 1672, when the Netherlands were threatened by Louis XIV, they offered large sums for the support of the army. The Lamist and Toren congregation contributed 5,000 florins; the gifts of the other congregations are not known. Later the Amsterdam congregations took an active part in the congratulation of William IV as stadholder (1747). When the movement for independence flared up in the Netherlands, the Mennonites sided with the Patriots, the opponents of the stadholder of the House of Orange, and took up arms; the overthrow of the government was celebrated in the churches.

In the 17th and 18th centuries the magistrates of Amsterdam had recognized the importance of the Mennonites in writing (1642) to Zürich on behalf of the persecuted Mennonites of Switzerland; and the repeated efforts of the States-General in favor of the Swiss and Palatine Mennonites were often instigated by Amsterdam Mennonites and supported by the magistrate. This was the case in the intervention of William III in 1694 and 1697 with the Palatine elector. In 1660 the magistrate praised the

Mennonites for their generous gifts to the Waldenses. The Mennonites of Amsterdam had become a power to be reckoned with.

Even though there was a perceptible decline among the Amsterdam Mennonites in church feeling and regard for the religion of their forefathers, a part of the heritage was preserved—a practical Christianity. This was most evident in the generous support of brethren in other countries, in which the Amsterdam congregations took the lead. In the face of want among the brethren, all differences disappeared. The Lamists gave help to the Palatine Mennonites as early as 1672. After the persecutions (1694) the Lamist, Zonist, and Frisian congregations united to aid them, and when Bern (1709) decided upon the complete eradication of the Mennonites, a conference of the Mennonite churches in Holland was held in Amsterdam. In 1710 the *Commissie tot de buitenlandsche nooden* (Commission for Foreign Needs) was appointed, consisting of delegates of the three Amsterdam churches. In 1726 a permanent relief fund was established by the commission. The *Commissie* met for the last time in 1758, and the fund was dissolved in 1803. Though all Dutch Mennonite congregations contributed generously to this work of charity, Amsterdam was the heart of the *Commissie*. In the Amsterdam churches, the Lamist and Toren congregation paid in 1727, 8,470 florins; 1773, 14,500 florins; 1736, 12,000 florins: the Zonist congregation paid 1,824, 4,902, and 2,575 florins: Frisians and the Frisian Sociëteit 3,165, 5,174, and 7,625 florins: the Kruikjes congregation 435, 132, and 3,240 florins (Blaupot t.C., *Holland* II, 117 f., 231 f.).

The inclination toward the practical brought about in the congregations an exemplary system of relief for the poor; the contemporary writers, Rues and especially Wagenaar give detailed descriptions. It is worthy of note that Theodor Fliedner (*q.v.*) received his impulse to found the German deaconess system in his study of poor-relief among the Amsterdam Mennonites. The Amsterdam Mennonites also supported public charitable institutions. Thus the *Maatschappij tot Nut van't Algemeen* (*q.v.*) (Society for the Promotion of the Common Good), the great interdenominational organization for national welfare, founded by the Mennonite minister Jan Nieuwenhuyzen (*q.v.*) of Monnikendam, received the warmest support from the ministers J. A. Hoekstra and A. H. van Gelder; the latter was for years an active director and had charge of disbursements. The Institute for the Deaf in Groningen had the co-operation of the Mennonite Seminary professors Hesselink and R. Koopmans.

The inner life of the Amsterdam churches proceeded smoothly. After the division, when each party found its own field of work, bitterness subsided. Futile attempts at union were made in 1672, 1684, 1685, and 1691 by the Zonists. Until Galenus' death in 1706 his powerful personality dominated the Lamists. Among his successors the influence of the Remonstrants (*q.v.*) was more pronounced, the need for educated ministers and the lack of a seminary of their own favored an approach (see **Amsterdam Seminary**). The Remonstrant

candidate J. Bremer (*q.v.*) served first the Mennonites of Leiden, then in Amsterdam. The most noteworthy evidence of the change is the 17 articles which were presented to J. Stinstra (*q.v.*) when he was called to become the minister of the Lamist congregation in 1735. His signature was considered important "because unity in doctrine is the foundation of the peace and edification of the church." The articles were mostly Remonstrant statements and a rejection of Socinianism; only two articles deal with baptism and the oath. Rues thought he was justified in calling the Lamists "Remonstrant Mennonites." Connections with the Collegiants were also loosened; the latter died out, holding their last meeting in Amsterdam in 1791.

The change in congregational life of the Lamist church was also evident in the ability of ministers of different branches to work together harmoniously. Thus Bremer and van Leuvenig (*q.v.*) worked side by side with the pietistic J. Deknatel (*q.v.*). In the latter the Herrnhut group (Moravians), appearing in Holland from 1738 on, found a potent friend and advocate. The focal position of the Amsterdam congregation actually increased during this period. Rues, the diligent and exact observer, frequently pointed this out. "During the time of Galenus the influence of the Lamists asserted itself through the outstanding personality of this man, the wealth of the church, and its love of knowledge." The church acquired a central position, becoming "the focal point for a large proportion of Mennonites." Certainly their open-minded generosity played an important role here. Many small and weak congregations in Holland and elsewhere were supported; but of equal importance was the opening of the seminary by the Lamist congregation in 1735. Here the future ministers received their training, needy students were supported, and many congregations provided with preachers. Just in this period of transition from lay preachers to trained preachers and the consequent lack of preachers, causing congregations to die out, the seminary aided as much as possible. The archives testify to the extensive correspondence between Amsterdam and other congregations in these matters. Well-known ministers of the Amsterdam Lamist congregation were Bartholomeus van Leuvenig, 1712-43; Joannes Deknatel, 1726-57; Johannes Bremer, 1728-57; Gerardus van Heyningen, 1758-1801; Allard Hulshoff, 1759-95; and Willem de Vos, 1762-1814.

The Zonist congregation, which had always had a smaller membership than the Lamist church, had also some prominent ministers, such as Hermannus Schijn in 1690-1727, Gerardus Maatschoen in 1726-50, Pieter Smidt in 1728-81, who also was appointed as a professor for training ministers, and Arend Hendrik van Gelder in 1780-1819. At the end of this period the Zonists again approached the Lamists. Financial conditions in the Zonist congregation made a union desirable. Of the old antipathy nothing was left. In some respects the Lamists were closer to the old tradition than the Zonists. The *Kleine Bundel* (hymnbook), completed in 1791, and in 1793 in use as a hymnal by the Lamists, is much more evangelical than the *Groote Bundel*, adopted in 1796 by the Zonists, which contained hymns of definitely rationalistic character. The attempt at union failed in 1795, but was successful in 1801 (April 22). Everything was peacefully settled (see **Zonists**). A stone was placed in the gable of the Singelkerk building (1949) to commemorate the union between the congregations *bij 't Lam* and *van den Toren* in 1668, and between these and the Zonist congregation in 1801.

4. *The Nineteenth Century.* The significance of the 19th century for the Amsterdam Mennonites can be only roughly sketched. Historical evaluation is not yet possible. There seems to have been a strengthening of the church. In the first place, a concentration of forces took place. The new name of the church, *Vereenigde Doopsgezinde Gemeente* (United Mennonite Church), hardly suggests the old disputes. Outwardly this is shown in many respects. In the composition of the church council and the appointment of preachers complete merging took place. Two ministers of the Zonist congregation were retired; their third minister A. H. van Gelder became a minister of the united church. Three church buildings were, of course, too many for a membership of about 1,100; hence the Zonist church was sold; the Toren church was rented out in 1812 and sold in 1813; the rooms needed for counseling, auditorium, library, etc., which had up to this time been located at the church *bij 't Lam* were remodeled. This church (Singelkerk) was now the only one used by the Mennonites, and was completely remodeled and enlarged in 1840. As hymnals both the *Groote Bundel* and the *Kleine Bundel* were used, besides a version of the Psalms in modern poetic form, published by the Art Union, *Laus Deo salus populo,* which had already been used by the Zonist and Lamist congregations since 1762 and 1791 respectively.

The union of 1801 was of highest significance to the immediate future. After ten years of working together the two groups were so completely merged that they could act as a unit, permitting the Amsterdam congregation to take the initiative in forming the Algemeene Doopsgezinde Sociëteit (*q.v.*). The Amsterdam congregation now co-operated with other congregations in trying to revitalize the brotherhood. Because of its great historic services (entire support of the seminary for 75 years) and its liberal contributions for the formation of the A.D.S., the Amsterdam church was given the leadership; it became to a still greater extent the Mennonite center in Holland.

It was certainly not an insignificant sign, that professors Muller, van Gilse, and de Hoop-Scheffer gave up the office of minister of the Amsterdam church for that of a seminary professor. The most important professors were close to the most important men of the church; reciprocal influence of one upon the other naturally followed. The early professors were obliged to preach for the church several times a year. The pietistic Jan de Liefde (*q.v.*) opposed the predominant position which Amsterdam held in the brotherhood and attacked the power of money, but with no effect. Up to the present Amsterdam has remained the influential center of the Dutch Mennonites.

At the beginning of the 19th century, leadership fortunately lay in strong hands. By 1840 the crisis was past, and from there on, conditions have been slowly improving. The most prominent personality of the first half of the century was undoubtedly Samuel Muller (*q.v.*). In opposition to the trend which was concerned only with "politics, social betterment, and nature study," he demanded a Biblical theology and a Christianity which, though no less remote from dogmatism than that of the preceding century, would address itself to the religious sense rather than the intellect. It was his lifework to raise the Mennonites to a level equal to that of the other Protestant churches; the genuinely Mennonite features were to be emphasized. To that end he labored as a preacher, to that end he taught and did research in Mennonite history. The Dutch Mennonite Missionary Society owes its founding to him (1847); it has always had its seat in Amsterdam, and it has had very active support from a part of the congregation. The congregation acted again in the interest of the public in 1844 when the church council set up a savings bank (*Spaarkas*), then lacking in Amsterdam. The *Zondagsbode* was published in Amsterdam (1887 ff.); it was long edited by P. Feenstra, Jr. (*q.v.*), minister in Amsterdam.

In the second half of the 19th century the tension between the conservatives and the liberals in the Amsterdam congregation became acute. The ministers P. van der Goot, A. Loosjes, and T. Kuiper were to the "right" and a great many of the leaders (*opzieners*) and deacons, on the other hand, were to the "left." Toward the end of the 19th century two of the three vacancies were filled by liberal ministers and only one by an orthodox minister. In view of the fact that a very large proportion of the members of the congregation preferred orthodox leadership, especially for religious instruction, it was decided to call a fourth minister, so that both wings could be equally represented among the ministers. This was followed in principle until 1942, when a fifth minister was chosen who is to occupy an intermediary position between the two. Personal harmony was always well preserved. (From 1892 to 1912 a group of orthodox-pietistic members separated for church services and Sunday school, under the leadership of C. P. van Eeghen Jr., (*q.v.*).

J.ᴛD.K.

5. *The Twentieth Century.* The population of the city increased steadily. By 1947 it had 803,000 inhabitants. The congregation also grew, though at a slower rate, until about 1935, when the membership in the city and vicinity had reached over 6,000. Since 1935 it has declined somewhat. At present, 1950, the membership is 5,522. The city has been divided into four and then into five districts for pastoral visits and catechetical instruction as well as for further spiritual work and for the deacons' work. Each district has its own minister for visitation work, who is assisted by a religious instructor and a district committee. The work of the deacons

in the district is looked after by one of the 20 supervisors (*opzieners*) and deacons, who also have charge of the administration of the church properties and the contributions made by the members and of the upkeep of the buildings. Together with the ministers they constitute the church board that directs the congregation.

In 1904 a second church building was opened, located at Oosterpark 5. Since 1920, Nieuwendam (*q.v.*) with a small frame church built in 1843 is also a part of the city. In 1930 a district house with a chapel was built at Karperweg 5. Plans have been made to build a church in the west end of the city, where a new district for 200,000 inhabitants is in process of building. Temporarily services are held in a hall owned by the city. There are thus five places in Amsterdam where Sunday morning services are regularly held.

The Singelkerk has remained the central point for the entire congregation. There baptisms and quarterly communion services are held. Communion is sometimes also administered in some of the district chapels. The Singelkerk is also the meeting place for the church board, the deaconesses, and twice a year for the 300 workers in the children's clubs, youth work, young people's organizations, women's associations, and other district organizations. In the Singelkerk lectures are held for the seminary students, and in it is located the library and archive room. Also the offices of the A.D.S. are attached to the Singelkerk.

The administration of the work operates at present (1950) through a card system, in which data are given about each family represented in the membership, arranged according to districts and further according to communities containing 20 to 30 members.

Since the union of the Lamists and Zonists in 1801 the Amsterdam congregation has been served by the following ministers: from the Lamists came Willem de Vos, who served until 1814; Hoito Tichelaar until 1810; Binse Koopmans until 1826. From the Zonists came A. H. van Gelder, who served until 1819; other ministers were Sam. Muller, 1814-29; Jan van Geuns, 1814-29; Jan ter Borg, 1818-29; Abr. Doyer, 1828-51; Jan Boeke, 1830-54; Jan van Gilse, 1837-49; J. G. de Hoop-Scheffer, 1849-59; P. van der Goot, 1851-76; A. Loosjes, 1854-93; Taco Kuiper, 1862-91; R. Brouwer, 1876-77; I. J. le Cosquino de Bussy, 1878-84; J. Boetje, 1884-90; W. I. Leendertz, 1890-1912; P. Feenstra, Jr., 1891-1916; I. H. Boeke, 1893-1911; A. K. Kuiper, 1901-30; P. B. Westerdijk, 1911-34; Vinc. Loosjes, 1912-21; F. Dijkema, 1916-42; J. W. van Stuyvenberg, 1921-36; C. Nijdam, 1930-33; J. D. Dozy, 1933- ; O. L. van der Veen, 1935- ; T. O. M. H. Hylkema, 1936-49; G. J. W. den Herder, 1942- ; W. F. Golterman, 1942-46; Fr. Kuiper, 1947- ; Miss C. W. Brugman, 1947- ; H. Bremer, 1949- .

The number of children in Sunday school and of catechumens has sharply decreased. At the time of greatest extent there were approximately 1,800 children; now there are scarcely half that number. The reason for this is in the first place the general indifference to the church and religion, then also the smaller size of the families of the members (seldom more than three, very seldom more than six). The fact that government care of the poor provides for non-church members as well as the church provides for its members has been a contributory factor, since the poor families who are not interested in religion are no longer urged by their children to join a church, as was formerly frequently the case.

Toward the end of the 19th century and in the early 20th the question was warmly debated whether a person baptized as an infant in another denomination could be admitted into the Amsterdam congregation—even though he had in the meantime been admitted into another Mennonite congregation; since 1949 admission is offered to members of any Christian faith (hence also to Roman Catholics). The applicant is, however, examined to determine whether his desire to unite with the Mennonites is genuine. The number of men and women from non-Mennonite circles who are baptized at an advanced age (some at 70 or older) is increasing. A considerable proportion of the members of the Amsterdam congregation is thus of non-Mennonite extraction.

The five deaconesses (*q.v.*) together with several deacons have the management of the *hofjes* (homes for the aged and the poor). The Rijpenhofje was acquired by the Lamist and Toren congregation in 1747 as a gift of the de Rijp-Centen family. In 1912 it was completely renovated; it now comprises 20 free apartments for elderly single women. The Zonshofje at Prinsengracht 159-171 was built in 1765 on the site of the former church known as *De kleine Zon* (later *Arke Noachs*) and was enlarged at the end of the 19th century by the addition of a wing. It has room for 32 unattached elderly women. The home for the aged and the orphanage of the Zonists established in 1667 in Tuinstraat, was discontinued in 1799. The Lamist congregation established a large home for the aged in 1669 at Kerkstraat 312, with a large garden on the Heerengracht. For want of clients this house was closed at the close of the 19th century.

Since 1946 plans have been under consideration for a new charitable home for the Amsterdam congregation. The Lindenhofje founded in 1614 by the Waterlander Toren congregation was sold in 1801. The Huizen de Vogel, Kerkstraat 316-320, provide lodging for nine aged married couples. De Lelie, Bloemstraat 129-131, provides a home for seven elderly married couples and four unattached men.

Orphans were formerly cared for in families by both the Zonists and the Frisians. The Lamist congregation opened an orphanage in 1677 on the Prinsengracht, and later the Huizen de Vogel, in the Kerkstraat, which was discontinued in 1800. The orphans were then transferred to the Collegiant home, De Oranje Appel, which had already been accepting many Mennonite orphans. Since then this orphanage has had exclusively Mennonite directors, some of whom are appointed by the supervisors and deacons of the Amsterdam congregation. Until 1923 it was located at the Heerengracht near the Huidenstraat, and later at De Lairessestraat, since 1930 at Hilversum. At present (1950) there are about 30 orphans, some of them from outside Amsterdam. A number of orphans of Mennonite parentage and several children whose parents were deprived of guardianship have been placed in families under the responsibility of the *Commissie voor de Buitenbestedelingen.*

Since 1894 the *Doopsgezinde Wijkverpleging* (Mennonite district nursing) has had charge of nursing care in the home, with three nurses. The Association for Providing Nourishing Food furnishes needy Mennonite patients with milk, eggs, and meals. Since 1938 the Amsterdam congregation in co-operation with the congregation in Utrecht has been directing the originally non-Mennonite brotherhood house at Bilthoven (*q.v.*).

In addition to Sunday schools in the various districts of Amsterdam several women's organizations are at work, a circle for young people of ages 18 to 35, an organization (the Mennonite Builders) for ages 12 to 18, a youth group *Elfregi* (*q.v.*). There is also a section of the Mennonite Peace Group in the congregation.

The Amsterdam congregation is a member of all the Mennonite organizations in the Netherlands and of the Noordhollandse Ring (district conference).   FR. K.

DB 1861-1912; Blaupot t.C., *Holland* I and II; Anna Brons, *Ursprung, Entwicklung und Schicksale der . . . Menn.* (3rd ed., Emden, 1912); J. G. de Hoop-Scheffer, *De Broederschap der Doopsgez.* (Amsterdam, 1866). For the first period: J. ter Gouw, *Gesch. van Amst.* IV-VII (Amsterdam, 1884-91); J. G. de Hoop-Scheffer, *Gesch. der Kerkherv. in Nederland van haar ontstaan tot 1531* (Amsterdam, 1873), also published in German (Leipzig, 1886); Kühler, *Geschiedenis* I, II, and III; Grosheide, *Verhooren;* Grosheide, *Bijdrage; BRN* II, 78 ff., 478 ff., 654, and VII, 30-45. For the second and third periods: J. Wagenaar, *Amsterdam* I and II (Amsterdam, 1760-65); S. F. Rues, *Tegenwoordige Staet der Doopsgez.,* translated and edited by M. Schagen (Amsterdam, 1745); W. J. Kühler, *Het Socianisme in Nederland* (Leiden, 1912). For the third period: S. Cramer, "De vereeniging der twee amst. gem. in 1801" (*DB* 1898); C. Sepp, *Joh. Stinstra en zijn tijd* I and II (Amsterdam, 1865 f.). For the fourth period: S. Cramer, "De Doopsgez. broederschap in de 19e eeuw" (*DB* 1901); *ML* I, 58-66.

Amsterdam Mennonite Library *(Bibliotheek en Archief van de Vereenigde Doopsgezinde Gemeente te Amsterdam).* The foundation for the very rich collection owned by the congregation at Amsterdam and placed at the service of the seminary students was laid by the preacher of the Lamist congregation and also a doctor of medicine at Amsterdam, J. Reyers, in the gift of his library to the church in 1680. Other contributions followed. In 1801 the library of the Amsterdam Zonist congregation was added, and later the library of the Utrecht congregation which it had received by bequest from the historian Martin Schagen (*q.v.*). In 1833 the library was enriched by a gift by G. J. van Rijswijk containing a number of rare books on Mennonite history. When Samuel Muller became professor of the seminary the library was greatly expanded. The expenses for this were defrayed in part by the sale of the equipment of a physical laboratory of the seminary and by the large contributions made

by the members of the Amsterdam congregation during those years.

The library contains not only Mennonitica. In 1768 P. Fontein, a minister at Amsterdam, bequeathed to the library a valuable collection of books in the field of ancient languages. In 1894 it received as a gift the unique collection of the late minister Loosjes on Pascal and Vinet. In 1946 the late minister C. Nijdam willed to the library a number of works by and about Schleiermacher.

A systematic catalog with a Latin foreword by G. Hesselink was printed in 1793. In 1854 the first part of a new catalog was published, containing titles of general theological works. In 1888 the second part was published, drawn up by J. G. de Hoop-Scheffer. It contained (*a*) *Teleiobaptistica* (*Mennonitica*); (*b*) Greek and Latin classics, philology, and other works. A new catalog of Mennonitica alone appeared in 1919 prepared by J. G. Boekenoogen.

The greatest treasures of the library are the old writings of Menno Simons, David Joris, Dirk Philips, the old martyr literature (an almost complete set of the editions of the *Offer des Heeren*), and a large rare collection of small writings on the *Lammerenkrijg,* a large collection of Mennonite hymnbooks, etc.

A very valuable supplement to the collection of printed works are the archives of the Amsterdam congregation. Besides a number of letters and documents important to Mennonite history there are for instance the membership records of the Waterlander congregation of the period 1612-73, of the Flemish 1625-70; of the Lamist and Toren congregation after the union with the Waterlanders 1668-1829; and of the Zonist congregation 1686-1801. In addition a great number of letters from and to Amsterdam, also the records and documents of the various Sociëteiten and the archives of the *Commissie voor Buitenlandse Nooden* containing a large number of letters and reports concerning the persecution and emigration of the Swiss Mennonites to America. For this archival material a catalog prepared by the archivist de Hoop-Scheffer was published in two parts (1883 and 1884). The entire catalog contains 7,521 numbers. The library is now located at Singel 452, in a house which was bought by the congregation as early as 1633, but the library was not brought here until 1839, after it was reorganized.   vDZ.

Catalogus der Werken over de Doopsgez. en hunne gesch. aanwezig in de Bibl. der Ver. Doopsgez. te Amst. (Amsterdam, 1919); *Inventaris der Archiefstukken berustende bij de Ver Doopsgez. Gem. te Amst.* 2 v. (Amsterdam, 1883, 1884.)

Amsterdam Mennonite Theological Seminary *(Kweekschool).* Until well in the 17th century the Mennonite congregations in Holland were served by lay preachers. In the 17th century an attempt was made to meet the rising educational level and the interest in art and science by choosing the best-educated men possible, usually physicians. But many congregations were not thriving, and many were near extinction. At a meeting of the Waterlander Sociëteit at Haarlem in 1675, Jan van Ranst (*q.v.*)

expressed his grave concern about this serious condition, the church board of the Rotterdam congregation having already written about it to Galenus Abrahamsz de Haan (*q.v.*) in Amsterdam. The congregations of Rotterdam and Leiden were ready to establish a seminary, but Haarlem opposed it, considering scholarly learning superfluous for a preacher. Then the deacons of the Amsterdam Lamist and Toren congregation passed a resolution in 1680 which gave Galenus Abrahamsz de Haan charge of training several young people for the ministry. With modest means and a small library he did the best he could to fulfill his obligation. After his death the students had to continue their studies at the Remonstrant seminary where they had heard lectures before. A far-reaching fraternization resulted, so that finally the Mennonite congregations chose Remonstrant candidates to fill their pulpits, a policy the Remonstrants were compelled to oppose in their own interest.

Then the council of the Amsterdam Lamist and Toren congregation decided to urge the establishment of a seminary of its own. An attempt was made for a union or association of congregations which would be responsible for the new seminary, but there was little interest. Only six congregations were represented at the meeting; the Zonist congregation wanted to bind the professor to a creed, and other congregations had financial doubts. Thereupon the Lamist and Toren congregation of Amsterdam opened the Mennonite seminary at its own expense, furnishing the salary of the professor and scholarships for six to eight students. Tjerk Nieuwenhuis (*q.v.*) was appointed professor (1735-59). In 1753 the Zonist congregation of Amsterdam appointed P. Smidt (*q.v.*), one of its preachers, as a professor to train preachers for its own group, but after his death (1781) no successor could be found. From this time on the preachers for the Zonist congregations were educated either by competent preachers of the group or at the Lamist seminary. This was the status until 1801.

At the Lamist seminary Prof. Nieuwenhuis was succeeded by H. Oosterbaan (*q.v.*) (d. 1807) from 1761 to 1785, and G. Hesselink (*q.v.*) from 1786 to 1811. The Amsterdam church had generously opened its seminary to outside Mennonite students, who were supported by other congregations or supported themselves. Students of other denominations were also admitted, and Mennonite students attended lectures in philosophy and church history at the Remonstrant seminary and at the Amsterdam Athenaeum. A board of curators had the supervision; a regulation of 1737 controlled instruction and contained among others the 18 articles of faith on which the students were examined before they were appointed to the ministry. The first two professors were philosophers rather than theologians; i.e., in line with the current philosophical trend in Holland they taught natural science, especially physics and mathematics (applied philosophy). The church council provided the equipment for a laboratory for their teaching. In 1780 the seminary enjoyed its most flourishing period with 18 students. Under Hesselink, who distinguished himself as

a theologian by his exegetical dictionary of the New Testament, the crisis came. Financially weakened by the French occupation, the Amsterdam combined Lamist and Zonist congregation could no longer support the seminary alone, and appealed to other congregations for aid. In 1811 the Algemeene Doopsgezinde Sociëteit (*q.v.*) was organized, with its main purpose to assume the support and management of the Mennonite seminary, and to assist the poorer congregations by the improvement of salaries for preachers. Without compulsion of any kind it succeeded in bringing all the Dutch congregations into the A.D.S. and in making the transition to a salaried, trained ministry. Hesselink lived to witness the founding of the A.D.S. His successor was R. Koopmans (1812-26) (*q.v*), a thorough scholar, who wore himself out in service for his brethren. After his death a change was made in the plan of instruction. In 1827 S. Muller (d. 1875) (*q.v.*) was chosen professor of dogmatics (1827-57), practical theology, and—an innovation—Mennonite history; and in the same year W. Cnoop Koopmans (*q.v.*), the son of R. Koopmans, was chosen (1827-49) professor of exegesis, general church history, and ethics. An interest in the past awoke, as is shown by the writings of S. Blaupot ten Cate, A. M. Cramer, and S. Muller. Since then there have always been two professors at the seminary. J. van Gilse, 1849-59; S. Hoekstra, 1857-92, and J. G. de Hoop-Scheffer, 1860-90 (d. 1893), were the occupants of the professorships during the heart of the 19th century.

All of these men are honored in the world of scholarship; but they were also potent forces in the advancement of new spiritual life. Under Hoekstra and de Hoop-Scheffer modern theology began its growth in Holland; they were the first professors to teach at the same time at the University of Amsterdam. Until 1871 the seminary professors gave only a part of the general theological instruction; for their study in languages and philosophy the students had to attend the Athenaeum. In 1876 a law was passed requiring a theological department at the University of Amsterdam, the former Athenaeum. Hoekstra was appointed for systematic theology and de Hoop-Scheffer for Semitic languages. Arrangements for instruction were altered to the extent of requiring Mennonite theological students to take university examinations and limiting seminary instruction to dogmatics, ethics, practical theology with practice in preaching and lecturing, cursory reading of the New Testament, and Mennonite history and principles.

Later professors at the university and seminary were S. Cramer, 1890-1912; I. J. le Cosquino de Bussy, 1892-1916; W. J. Kühler, 1912-46; J. G. Appeldoorn, 1916-33; N. Westendorp Boerma, 1935-45; and W. Leendertz since 1948, lecturer since 1933; F. J. de Holl, 1933-34; W. F. Golterman since 1946 and N. van der Zijpp since 1946-65 as instructors at the Mennonite seminary only.

In 1907 women were first admitted as students at the seminary. In 1950, 34 students were enrolled at the seminary (12 of them women). The board of directors of the seminary consists of seven members of the directorate of the Algemeene Doopsgezinde Sociëteit and the professors. The number of students at the seminary, which during the first half of the 19th century scarcely exceeded 20, reached its peak in 1895 with 51 students, and decreased thereafter (1900, 33; 1906, 16; 1939, 33; 1952, 24).

A great aid to study is offered by the library of the Amsterdam Mennonite church (see **Amsterdam Mennonite Library**). The significance of the Mennonite seminary lies in the fact that it trains future ministers for the performance of their office in accordance with the needs of the brotherhood, that it acquaints the students with the Mennonite past, thus strengthening the love for the brotherhood, that it gives them instruction in doctrine, which is under the influence of tradition, and that it—a gain that must not be undervalued—promotes fellowship among the Mennonite students. These are all things that a university cannot offer.

At present there are only very few Dutch congregations that do not have a theologically trained minister. Nearly all ministers have attended the University of Amsterdam (*q.v.*) and the Mennonite Theological Seminary. The co-operation between these two institutions continues to be harmonious. The entrance requirements for each is graduation from a humanistic "gymnasium." The combined theological training at the university and seminary requires at least five years. After having passed the examinations at either institution the student has become a *proponent*—a ministerial candidate—of the A.D.S. Under the sponsorship of the latter he now preaches his trial sermons in various congregations where there are vacancies until he is placed.

In no other country have the Mennonites had a theological seminary of such long standing nor have the ministers received such uniform and thorough theological training as is the case in Holland. A few Mennonites of other countries have attended the Mennonite Seminary of Amsterdam and after World War II some of the Dutch theological students studied in American Mennonite colleges as exchange students.   J. tD.C., vdZ.

S. Muller, "Gesch. van het onderwijs in de theol. bij de Nederlandsche Doopsgez.," *DJ* 1850, 67-197; Blaupot t. C., *Holland* II, 90-117; W. Kühler, "De oprichting van de Amsterdamsche Kweek-school in 1735" (*DB* 1918, 43-84); P. van der Meulen, *De wording der Alg. Doopsgez. Soc.* (Wormerveer, 1947); P. van der Meulen, "Dutch Menn. Unite During Crisis," *Menn. Life* III (July 1948) 20-22; L. Hesta, "Gesch. Notizen über die Vorbildung zum Predigtdienst bei den Menn. in den Niederlanden," *Menn. Bl.* XXXIII (1886) 25, 35-36, 57-60, 81-85, 95-98. *ML* I, 67 f.

Amsterdam University. The University of Amsterdam is, in contrast to the other three universities of the Netherlands, viz., Leiden, Utrecht, and Groningen, which are state universities, an institution of the city of Amsterdam. It grew out of the Athenaeum, which was founded there in 1632. The occasion for its founding was the wish of the citizens of Amsterdam to have their sons educated in their home town, and their love of intellectual liberty, which created a field for scholars of Arminian

belief. The Athenaeum was a university in miniature; in 1732, at the celebration of its centennial, it had only two professors. In 1815 it was recognized as having equal rights with the national universities. At the beginning of the 19th century D. J. van Lennep was its guiding star. But after the law of 1876 was passed which reformed university teaching and gave the Athenaeum the rights of a university, including the right to grant degrees, and the city opened the university in 1877, the school made a sudden, undreamed-of growth, and acquired its five faculties: theology, law, medicine, philology and philosophy, and natural sciences. In the old Athenaeum there had, to be sure, been an occasional chair of theology; usually, however, theology was left to the seminary, which was founded in 1632 by the Remonstrants and transferred to Leiden in 1873 for ecclesiastical reasons. In 1817 the Lutheran seminary was added. The denominational division was sharp; even the professors in the aula were separated from their colleagues by a dividing wall. Genestet wrote a merry little verse about the Lutheran, the Remonstrant, and the two honest Mennonites, who were separated by a wall as if they were antichrists. Since 1946 Reformed theological students also have the opportunity to study at the Amsterdam university through the appointment of two theology professors by the Reformed Church. Since the theology students already hold a diploma of graduation from a gymnasium or have passed the state examination, they take two examinations at the university, the so-called *Propaedeutic* examination that covers Hebrew and philosophy, and the *Candidaatsexamen*, that covers the Old and New Testaments, church history and history of doctrines, comparative history of religion, ethics, and philosophy of religion. After these examinations the students study further at their own seminaries. They may also take the doctoral examination at the university.

The seminary professors may also be professors at the university at the same time; this happens regularly. The Mennonite seminary professors, de Hoop-Scheffer, Hoekstra, Cramer, de Bussy, Kühler, Appeldoorn were also university professors, and in 1950 Leendertz also.

There is a second university at Amsterdam, founded in 1906, called the Free University. It was created by Dr. Abraham Kuyper and is supported by the *Gereformeerde Kerk*, the strongly Calvinistic body which separated from the Dutch state church known as the *Hervormde Kerk* in 1892 under the leadership of Dr. Abraham Kuyper. (*ML* I, 66-68.)

                                              J.tD.K., vdZ.

Amstutz (am Stutz, Am Stutz, Stutz, Amstuz, Amstoutz), a Mennonite family name originating in Sigriswil, in the steep hills on the northern shore of Lake Thun, canton of Bern, Switzerland. The name, which means "on the steep," aptly fits this abrupt terrain. It first appears in the chronicles of that area in the 14th century.

It appears that no members of the Amstutz family were Anabaptists while living at Sigriswil. Members of the family figured in the migration from

German-speaking Switzerland to French-speaking Switzerland, settling in the district of Münster in the Bernese Jura in the first half of the 18th century. Here most of the family became Anabaptist. One Amstutz family has lived in the commune of Chatelat for more than 150 years. In 1743 members of the Amstutz family settled at Massevaux, Alsace. During the following three decades other members of this family located to the south in the commune of Florimont and across the French border in the district of Pruntrut, Switzerland. Another Amstutz family settled in the principality of Montbéliard. It is quite certain that none were Mennonites before arriving in these settlements but most of them joined after their arrival.

Most of the members of the Mennonite branch of the Amstutz family emigrated to America early in the 19th century. The first of this family to emigrate were John B. Amstutz and his sister Anna in 1818, who settled in the Allen-Putnam counties, Ohio, community. Another John Amstutz left the commune of Chatelat near Münster in 1819 and became one of the early settlers of the Sonnenberg Mennonite settlement in Wayne Co., Ohio. Most of his brothers and sisters followed him in the next decade. Two brothers, Ulrich and John Amstutz, from the Florimont Mennonite community, settled in the newly founded Chippewa (now called Crown Hill) Mennonite community in Wayne Co., Ohio, in 1825. Their descendants became leaders in that church. In 1834 another Ulrich Amstutz from the Florimont community came to America with his family, settling in Putnam Co., Ohio. Several Amstutz brothers and sisters emigrated from the Montbéliard Amish community to America. One settled in Fulton Co., Ohio, while others went to Amish communities in Indiana. John settled in Putnam Co., Ohio, where he followed the trade of wagonmaker. In 1842 John M. Amstutz, a minister, left the Jura for America, settling in the Putnam County community, where he died ten years later.

The name Amstutz is one of the most frequent in the Swiss Mennonite settlements of Sonnenberg and Crown Hill in Wayne Co., Ohio, and Bluffton-Pandora, Ohio.

Prominent personalities bearing the family name have been or are:

1. John M. Amstutz (1804-60), minister of the Münsterberg congregation near Münster, canton of Bern; minister of the Putnam County congregation from 1842 until his death in 1860.

2. David C. Amstutz (1842-1924), minister and later bishop of the Crown Hill Mennonite Church, Wayne Co., Ohio.

3. Peter B. Amstutz (1846-1938), farmer and sawmill operator near Bluffton, Ohio, who wrote a history of the Allen-Putnam (counties, Ohio) Swiss Mennonite settlement, entitled *Geschichtliche Ereignisse der Mennoniten-Ansiedlung in Allen and Putnam counties, Ohio* (1925), and *Evangelium und Krieg* (1918), and *Das zweite Kommen Christi* (1925).

4. Noah S. Amstutz (b. 1864), living at Val-

paraiso, Ind.; reared in Crown Hill settlement; made important inventions in connection with photo-telegraphy. (See *Who's Who in America*, 1950-51.)

5. John E. Amstutz (b. 1881), minister at Trenton, Ohio, Mennonite Church for over 30 years.

6. Louis Amstutz (b. 1889), present bishop of Sonnenberg Mennonite Church in Wayne Co., Ohio.

7. H. Clair Amstutz (b. 1909), physician of Goshen, Ind.; frequent contributor to Mennonite periodicals on the topic of Mennonites and health.

8. Daniel Amstutz, missionary in Java many years, at home in the Bernese Jura, Switzerland.

D.L.G.

Amur. The Mennonite settlements on the Amur River near Blagoveshchensk in eastern Asiatic Russia (*q.v.*) were the last to be established voluntarily by the Mennonites of Russia. As early as 1860 the Mennonites of the Ukraine had sent a delegation to investigate land along the Amur which the government was offering for settlement. However, at this time the surplus population of the Mennonite colonies preferred to settle in the Crimea and other near-by places, and after 1874 in America. After the Russo-Japanese war in 1904-5 non-Mennonite German settlers and others began to pioneer in the Amur region, the Mennonites restricting their settlement activities to western Siberia at this time.

After the Russian Revolution of 1917, when the Mennonites became increasingly aware of the anti-religious policy of Communism and were forced into collectives and exile, many of them attempted to leave the country, while some looked for a haven in the Far East. At this time the Soviet government was still interested in settling uninhabited stretches of land along the Amur with people from European Russia on a voluntary basis, offering them 400 roubles per family, 15 acres of land per family member, and reduced freight rates. These privileges were later extended to settlers from western Siberia. The several delegations of Mennonites from western Siberia went to investigate the land near Blagoveshchensk in 1926. The first settlers were Isaak Ewert and Wilhelm Boldt with a group of 42 families, who left Slavgorod March 24, 1927, by train, taking with them their household goods, farm implements, and animals and arrived at Blagoveshchensk April 12. This group, followed by numerous other families, established the Usman settlement, which had a population of 593. Village names included Rosental, Blumenort, Silberfeld, Eichenfeld, and Gnadenfeld. The settlement was located on the banks of the Topkochna River, 20 miles from the Amur River. Other settlements were Savitaya, with a population of 520 persons living in the villages of Pribrezhnoye, Schönsee, Halbstadt, Orechov, and Rheinfeld; Muchino, with 307 persons in the villages Yurgino, Bodanovka, and others; and the settlement of Nevzorovka. The largest settlement was Shumanovka with a population of 867 living in the villages of Shumanovka, Friedensfeld, Kleefeld, New York, Belo Berozovo, Memrik, Grünfeld, and Ebenfeld. Most of the settlers along the Amur River came from western

Siberia, but many of the European Russian settlements were also represented. They had hardly established themselves economically and organized schools and churches when they were also forced to join collectives and give up their former way of life. Their attempts to gain permission to leave the country were in vain. Longingly they began to look across the Amur River to the Little Khingan Mountains in Manchuria.

The account of the adventurous escape of a large part of the Shumanovka settlement is typical. Jakob Siemens, leader of the Shumanovka collective, carefully worked out detailed plans for a mass crossing of the Amur River into China. On Dec. 16, 1930, after less than four years in the Amur settlement, the exodus began. Most of the population of the village of Shumanovka and some individuals from neighboring villages, a total of 217 persons, crossed the river on 60 sleds and in the bitter winter with the help of Chinese guides continued their trip to the city of Harbin, where the group arrived Feb. 12, 1931. Here they met others who had left the Amur settlements in a similar way. Harbin (*q.v.*) gradually became the center of many refugees who finally found new homes in Paraguay, Brazil, and the United States during 1931-34, largely with the help of the Mennonite Central Committee. No information is available concerning those that remained in the Mennonite settlements along the Amur River.   C.K.

A. Loewen and A. Friesen, *Die Flucht über den Amur* (Steinbach, 1946); I. Ewert, "Blumenort, Amurgebiet," *Unser Blatt* III (1928) 89; W. Quiring, *Russlanddeutsche suchen eine Heimat* (Karlsruhe, 1938).

Amusements. With their emphasis upon a life of piety, not conformed to the standards of a sinful society, and upon constant Christian discipleship, Mennonites have throughout their history been known for their disapproval of "worldly amusements." Heinrich Bullinger, successor to Zwingli in Zürich, said of the Anabaptists, "They denounced covetousness, pride, profanity, the lewd conversation and immorality of the world, drinking and gluttony." Other writers of this early period add their witness to the observation that these Anabaptists were not guilty of intemperate eating and drinking but in contrast lived irreproachably among their neighbors, who joined in testifying to the high character of these unusual persons in their society.

That the standards of the average Mennonite regarding acceptable forms of amusements are strict even in the 19th and 20th centuries is proved by the fact that since 1865 more than 120 conference resolutions defining and condemning worldly amusements have been passed by the various (old) Mennonite district conferences. Illustration of the strict position of this church is Point X in a list of standards drawn up by the General Problems Committee of the Mennonite General Conference by order of the conference session of 1939. Point X on "Worldly Amusements" declares, "These are as natural for worldlings as the joy of the Lord is for Christians. . . . All the carnal amusements that appeal to the gratification of the flesh; such as theaters, moving picture shows, circuses, gambling resorts, dances, card playing, popular swimming resorts, and such like are destructive to spiritual life, and should therefore be scrupulously avoided by all Christian people."

Although varying degrees of prohibitions are endorsed by the majority opinion of the various American Mennonite groups, it is safe to say that in the mid-20th century all branches opposed drinking of alcoholic beverages, dancing, gambling, card playing, and indiscriminate attendance at the theater and motion pictures. More strict groups opposed in addition participation in county and state fairs, where much undesirable entertainment was mixed with the educational features; attendance at commercialized athletic activities; participation in and attendance of high-school plays and operettas; and participation in bands and orchestras. Some forbade the use of the radio and television.

The Mennonites of Europe in all countries in their earlier history held similar high standards and practiced restrictions on "worldly amusements" including the theater, the dance, cards, etc. This has continued to be true throughout the history of the Mennonites in Russia, Switzerland, and France to the present day. Some Dutch Mennonite groups, such as the Waterlanders, soon gave up their opposition to the theater. Joost van den Vondel (*q.v.*), the famous writer of tragedies, was a deacon of the Amsterdam Waterlander Church 1616-20, and another member of the same church, Jan Theunis (*q.v.*), kept a kind of amusement place, a combination of museum, theater, and wineshop, which was frequented by many Mennonites. At the end of the 17th century the Lamists (*q.v.*) took full part in the Amsterdam amusements, and at the end of the 18th century the Dutch Mennonites—with only a few exceptions—had fully given up their opposition to the theater. In Northwest Germany, the opposition to the theater disappeared in the 19th century. In West Prussia and the Palatinate a similar gradual change, not complete, took place in the 20th century. In the *Badischer Verband* churches the ban on the theater, etc., is still maintained. (See **Theater.**)

In some very conservative Mennonite groups in America, where young people customarily joined the church at about the age of marriage or in their late teens, strict prohibitions as to amusements were not imposed before baptism. In some of these groups certain types of folk dancing are still practiced among the young people at their "parties."

That Mennonites throughout their four centuries when not subjected to fierce persecution received their share of joy in living no one who knows their history or has observed them closely would deny. Observers have frequently remarked on the poise, serenity, and peace of mind written clearly into the countenances of these people. Possessing an inner peace, the typical Mennonite has not found it necessary to drug a restless spirit by resorting to sensual and ever more exciting amusements.

Mennonites have, however, obtained recreational values from their regular activities. Not separating life into the sacred and secular, they have found religious and spiritual significance and satisfaction in their daily tasks. Having developed a sense of community and brotherhood, through mutual aid they learned how to work and share together as they fellowshiped. Raising a barn for a neighbor, plowing the fields of a sick brother, joining in a quilting party, canning meat for foreign relief, preparing food and clothing for the needy in the city and rural missions, and many other brotherhood activities brought young and old together in work, play, and worship. In recent years the social life of the more seriously minded young people has to an increasing degree revolved around service projects. There is, however, also evidence among some groups that young people tend to participate increasingly in general secular amusements and to patronize various forms of semi-commercialized recreation, such as school athletics, theaters, and motion pictures.

There have always been special occasions, however, when more than the usual emphasis was placed upon social activity. Weddings, singings (*q.v.*), picnics, holiday programs, visits by distant friends or relatives, traveling, public sales, family reunions, brotherhood gatherings, and other events have brought Mennonites together where they have given expression to both their serious and their carefree attitudes in a psychologically satisfying manner.   M.G.

Anabaptist. 1. *Sixteenth Century Usage.* "Anabaptist" is actually a Greek word meaning "rebaptizer," used in church Latin from the 4th century onward, and appearing at least as early as 1532 in the English, seldom used in 16th-century German or Dutch, where the translation *Wiedertäufer* and *Wederdooper* is used from the beginning of Anabaptist history in 1525. It was never used by the Anabaptists themselves but often vigorously objected to by them because of the opprobrium and criminal character attached to the name. Its introduction and constant use by the enemies of the Anabaptists can best be explained by the fact that the imperial law code from Justinian's time (A.D. 529) on, made rebaptism one of the two heresies penalized by death, the other being Anti-Trinitarianism. Thus to classify the Reformation radicals as "Anabaptists" made them at once legally subject to condemnation and execution, although it still remained necessary for each local jurisdiction to implement the basic code. (Thus Zürich did not decree the death penalty for Anabaptists until 1526.) The first imperial mandate (Jan. 4, 1528, Speyer) against the Anabaptists specifically grounds the required suppression on the ancient imperial law as follows: "Since in both ecclesiastical and civil law Anabaptism (*der Widertauf*) is forbidden under severe penalties, and since the imperial code decrees and orders, on pain of the highest penalty of death, that no one shall have himself baptized a second time or baptize another . . . ."

The very first literary attacks on Anabaptism (Zwingli's *Von der Taufe, von der Wiedertaufe, und von der Kindertaufe* of May 1525, and Oecolampadius' *Ein Gespräch etlicher Predicanten zu Basel gehalten mit etlichen Bekennern der Wieder-*tauffe, also of 1525) use the term *Wiedertäufer.* The Latin writings likewise use *Anabaptists* (e.g., Faber's *Adversus Doctorem Balthasarum Pacimontanium, Anabaptistarum Nostri Saeculi, Primum Authorem, Orthodoxae Fidei Catholica Defensio* of 1528). However, in Zwingli's testimony against the local Anabaptists before the Zürich court in March 1525 he uses the term *Täufer* exclusively. Strangely enough, Zwingli uses the term "Catabaptist" in his major attack against the group in 1527, *In Catabaptistarum Strophas Elenchus,* instead of "Anabaptist."

It has sometimes been assumed that the evil connotation of the epithet *Anabaptist* is associated primarily with the dreadful Münster episode of 1534-35. However, the fairly extensive polemic literature of the period before that time, written by Luther, Melanchthon, Zwingli, Bader, Rhegius, Faber, Bugenhagen, Menius, Bullinger, and others, gives abundant evidence that it was a designation of severest reproach and condemnation long before Münster. The Augsburg Confession of 1530 condemns the "Anabaptists" specifically in three articles, though in part based on misinformation. Abundant citations could be given showing that the term "Anabaptist" in all its forms and translations was always essentially one of condemnation as of grievous heresy and crime. More, in his *Confutation of Tindale's Works* (1532), speaks of "pernitious and Anabaptistical opinions." This completely evil connotation of the name, which makes it truly an opprobrious epithet, carried through the 16th century and on down through the following centuries until modern times. It is this sense of condemnation and execration which has made some modern historians, particularly Mennonites, hesitate to use it, but usage is gradually overcoming the objectionable sense.

An illustration of the strong objection by those dubbed Anabaptists to its application to them is the title of Dirk Philips' Dutch tract written in 1545 but first published as the fourth part of his *Enchiridion* in 1564, which reads as follows: *Een Apologia, ofte verantwoordinghe, dat wy (die van de werelt met grooten onrecht Anabaptisten gescholden worden) gheen wederdoopers noch sectemakers en zijn; maer dat wy een zijn met de rechte Ghemeynte Gods die van aenbeginne gheweest is.* (An Apology or Reply, that we who are by the world with great injustice accusingly called Anabaptists are no rebaptizers nor sect-makers, but that we are one with the true church of God which has been from the beginning.)

The original use of "Anabaptist" in the 4th and following centuries was to refer to the rebaptism of those who had been baptized by heretics, or of those who had been baptized by bishops who had temporarily and partially recanted under persecution. There was considerable controversy over both points in North Africa; over the former from Tertullian's time on (A.D. 200) and over the latter in Augustine's time (Donatist controversy). In both cases the Roman bishop's position won out, namely, that rebaptism should not be required nor permitted.

Those who insisted on rebaptism were in effect repudiating therefore the authority of the church.

The Anabaptists of the Reformation period, however, did not repudiate infant baptism because they denied the validity of office of the bishop or the authority of the church (although they did in fact deny both) but rather because they denied the readiness of an infant to receive baptism on New Testament terms. They called for baptism only on confession of faith and commitment to discipleship by the candidate. They denied that infant baptism was baptism at all and hence denied that they were "rebaptizers." However, their real objection to the name '"Anabaptist" was not this minor technical one; it was rather their refusal to be classed as heretics and to be reckoned as not being the true church. Their intensity of feeling on this must be understood in the light of their deep conviction that they were the true church and that the Roman Catholic and Protestant churches were the false churches. Naturally also they did not wish to be classed as heretics subject to the death penalty merely on the basis of an epithetical identification with the Anabaptists of earlier centuries whom the imperial law condemned to death. They wished to stand on their own faith and to have their testimony and doctrine received on its own merits.

Although the meaning put into "Anabaptist" before 1535 was bad enough, additional overtones were added after Münster. Already frightened by the rapid spread as well as obstinate steadfastness and evident spiritual power of the movement, and already firmly believing the Anabaptists to be a threat to the existing order and social stability, the leaders of church and state were now sure of it for the Münsterites were actually militant revolutionaries and perverters of Christian ethics.

Hitherto the Anabaptists had lived irreproachable lives, but now the scandalous behavior of the King of Münster and his henchmen was known to all. So the invective against the Anabaptists now rises to a shrill crescendo. The Protestants in particular were concerned to vindicate themselves of the Catholic charge of complicity in and responsibility for the Anabaptists by going to extreme lengths of condemnation. The epithet "Anabaptist" was thus filled with even more venom than before, if that could be possible. It became the synonym for everything dangerous to church and state, much like "Bolshevik" or "Communist" in contemporary America.

Furthermore, the epithet was used indiscriminately of all types of left-wing groups, whereby the sins of the worst were applied to all. In retrospect Thomas Müntzer, the leader of the Peasants' Revolt in 1525, was now dubbed an Anabaptist and his sins were added to the others. In fact, he came to be thought of as the originator and most typical leader of the movement, even though he never practiced nor taught rebaptism, and had no connection with the true Anabaptist movement.

The Anabaptists themselves used no common name, indeed they were not a unified organized movement throughout, although the Swiss-South German, Dutch-North German, and Hutterite wings were soon separately organized and disciplined. Their most common self-designation was "Brethren." Because of the strong leadership of Jakob Hutter (d. 1535) among the Moravian Anabaptists, who adopted community of goods, this group was soon called "Hutterisch" or the "Hutterian Brethren," while the non-communist group being originally of Swiss origin was called "Swiss Brethren," even though they lived in many places outside of Switzerland such as the lower Rhine region. In Holland after 1545 the group came to be called "Mennists" after their chief leader Menno Simons, a name which gradually developed into "Mennonist" and then "Mennonit," although early in the 17th century "Doopsgezind" (German, "Taufgesinnt") came into use in Holland and ultimately superseded "Mennonit." Thus at least one syllable of the original "Wederdooper" is retained in the modern designation of the descendants of the original Dutch Anabaptists.

The 17th-century English Baptists took the major part of "Anabaptists" for their name and passed it on down to their 10,000,000 modern spiritual descendants. The 19th-century Baptists of Germany however did not take "Täufer," the proper translation, for their name, but instead, "Baptisten." It remained for modern German scholars to adopt the term "Täufer" as the designation for the Anabaptists of the Reformation period, thus taking up Zwingli's early 1525 word instead of "Wiedertäufer."

H.S.B.

2. *Modern Interpretations of "Anabaptist."* The German word *Täufer* has a definite meaning and is applied exclusively today to those evangelical Anabaptists who represent the ancestors of today's Mennonites all over the world. German church historiography has generally abandoned the terms *Anabaptisten* and *Wiedertäufer;* Dutch historians use the terms *Doopers* or *Doopsgezinden* for the German *Täufer.* In English, American, and French church historiography, however, the term *Anabaptist* (Dutch *Wederdooper,* German *Wiedertäufer,* French *Anabaptiste*) is used in a much broader and more inclusive sense to cover all types of radicals of the Reformation period. Basically the word "Anabaptist" indicates nothing more than the rejection of infant baptism (on whatever ground) and the consequent practice of adult baptism or baptism on confession of faith. This general principle was, in the 16th century, held by many different groups which can scarcely be thrown together indiscriminately under the heading "Anabaptist" in the sense that it is used in this ENCYCLOPEDIA (although from the 16th to the 18th centuries it was almost universally so used in Europe). For instance, the Socinian Polish church accepted this principle without belonging to what generally is called Anabaptism. The same is true of scattered groups in England in the 16th century, which sometimes are called Anabaptists, or with scattered individuals of the "enthusiastic" fringe who have only a very

loose connection with the main body of evangelical Anabaptists, or the fanatical revolutionary Münsterites of 1534-35. Professor Bainton of Yale, for instance, almost identifies the term "Anabaptist" with what he calls Left-Wing Protestantism in general, that radical wing of widely varied types which pressed for complete separation of state and church, and at the same time for a believers' or gathered church. (In German church history, mainly through the work of E. Troeltsch, *The Social Teachings of the Christian Churches,* 1931, first German edition, 1912, the term "sect" is used for these groups in general. Unfortunately it is not applicable in English and American church history.) It is quite obvious that this interpretation of the concept of Anabaptism is much too broad to be usefully applied to any one distinct body. Not all Protestant groups which practice adult baptism can be classified as Anabaptists, as can be clearly seen, for instance, in the distinction between Anabaptists and Baptists. But even so, the term still needs a more precise definition whereby a distinction must also be drawn between the *stillen Täufer* or evangelical Anabaptists (see *Church History,* 1940, 362) who accept the principle of nonresistance (*q.v.*), and all other related groups which decline nonresistance (*q.v.*), and accept the "sword" as a positive instrument. To this latter group may be counted the millennialist Münsterites (*q.v.*) and their partisans in Holland and elsewhere. (Troeltsch suggested the term "Taborites" for this type. In English church history the "Fifth Monarchy Men" would fall under this category.)

As a matter of fact, the phenomenon of Anabaptism has been subjected to manifold and widely varying interpretations, and even today, with greatly improved factual knowledge, there is no complete agreement among church historians regarding its understanding and definition.

Anabaptism certainly does not simply mean (*a*) the refusal of infant baptism for whatever reason. Even the reformers themselves, Luther and Zwingli, admitted in the earlier years of their work that infant baptism is without Scriptural basis. (*b*) Nor is Anabaptism the same as fanaticism (*Schwärmertum, Schwarmgeisterei*). This is the traditional confusion mainly among Lutherans (e.g., Karl Holl) because Luther himself called all his opponents *Schwärmer,* i.e., people who have replaced Biblical theology with personal inspiration, special illumination, or private revelations. It is quite obvious that most Anabaptists were far from any such fanaticism (which they hated just as much as did Luther). Their strict Biblicism is beyond doubt; it was at once their strength and their limitation. (*c*) Anabaptism has hardly anything in common with traditional millennialism, even though certain millennialists favored and still favor adult baptism (e.g., the Münsterites, the Fifth Monarchy Men, later some Pietists). Millennialism was for Anabaptists always but a marginal idea. Finally (*d*) Anabaptism should not be confused with Anti-Trinitarianism as has so often been done and still

occasionally is done (Dunin-Borkowski and Wilbur: see **Anti-Trinitarianism**). The Polish Socinians, though practicing adult baptism, declined any connection with western Anabaptism; and yet, Wilbur still considers many early Anabaptists as forerunners of Unitarianism. Thus all these interpretations expanded the term "Anabaptist" into a general concept of Free Church Protestantism, by which the concept of genuine Anabaptism loses its character and its meaningfulness.

We now turn to modern attempts at positive definition or delineation of the concept of Anabaptism.

(1) By way of introduction credit should be given to the work of the German historian Ernst Troeltsch (d. 1923), whose distinction between "church" and "sect," mentioned above, was a great step forward in church historical analysis. The Troeltsch term "sect" corresponds approximately to the English "gathered" or believers' church. Unfortunately, for Troeltsch Anabaptism coincides almost completely with this concept of sectarianism, even though a healthy distinction is presented between the "evangelical" or nonresistant groups and Taborites who accept the "sword." That the concept of "sect" with Troeltsch is too broad can be seen from the fact that he includes also the German Pietists and the English Methodists in this class. The more advanced distinction between an ecclesiastical church type, a denominational church type, and the sect type (J. Wach) was not yet known to Troeltsch. Hence he cannot visualize either the temptation of later Anabaptism (and Mennonitism) to slip away from the original path of brotherhood and to transform itself more and more into a denomination.

(2) Roland H. Bainton (*Journal of Religion* XXI, 1941, 124-34) discusses the main features of the left-wing groups, pointing out a tradition in Protestantism which extols the heretics (*Ketzer*) for being radical, that is, nonconformists. Sebastian Franck (1531) (*q.v.*) uses for the first time this term "heretic" in a positive sense (somewhat concordant to Troeltsch's concept of "sect"); the same is done by Gottfried Arnold (*q.v.*) in his *Kirchen- und Ketzer-Historie* (1699), which is followed by other similar treatments. This approach, though enlightening, is still too comprehensive.

(3) A. Ritschl (d. 1889) construed his church history (*Geschichte des Pietismus,* 1883) rather artificially, without any deeper understanding of Anabaptism. He drew a line of tradition from the Third Order of the Franciscans (Tertiarii) to the Anabaptists and from them to the Pietists, even though no immediate contact between these groups could be demonstrated. To be sure, there are certain similarities and points of contact but the genius of these three movements is radically different so that this construction is of little value. Ritschl erroneously calls the Anabaptists "medieval," due to their emphasis upon what he calls "works" (i.e., practiced discipleship). For similar reasons also K. Holl misinterprets the Anabaptists, taking their practical Christianity as a form of Catholic

works-righteousness (gaining merit through works), which Lutherans strictly abhor. This kind of church historiography with borrowed terms does not lead very far and is more confusing than helpful—though still widely accepted.

(4) Ludwig Keller (*q.v.*) goes further along this line of construed church history but with much richer material at hand and a more sympathetic understanding of the "heretics." He visualized the existence of sect-like "Old-Evangelical Brotherhoods" throughout the centuries which kept a sort of underground contact among themselves, seeing a long line of tradition in church history of such brotherhoods (with similar patterns of life). In particular he ties the Waldenses (*q.v.*) very closely to the early Anabaptists. This still unproved Waldensian origin theory, started in the 17th century by H. Montanus (*q.v.*), was popular for a long time but must be abandoned today in view of the results of modern research. No contact with Waldenses could be found, and, what weighs more, the genius of the two groups is very different. Keller was deceived by certain similarities (such as nonconformity) just as Ritschl and Troeltsch were deceived. Yet it must be admitted that Keller has greatly advanced our understanding of the earlier history of Anabaptism.

(5) Anabaptists were no mystics either, as for instance Rufus M. Jones (*Studies in Mystical Religion,* 2nd ed. 1923) has interpreted them. It is true that in the earliest period of Anabaptism some outstanding leaders manifested mystical traits, but in general the simple Biblicistic life of the Brethren is very different from that of mystically oriented men and women. Even though Anabaptists and Quakers have a number of traits in common (above all their nonresistance), and contacts between the two groups have always been cordial and sometimes close, they are rather different types.

(6) Johannes Kühn (*Toleranz und Offenbarung,* 1923) was perhaps the first to clearly recognize and analyze the independent character of the Anabaptists, and put them on an equal level with related phenomena in church history. He distinguished within "Biblical" Protestantism five major types which he called prophetic (Luther), spiritualistic (Schwenckfeld, Roger Williams), *Täuferische Nachfolge* (combining both Anabaptists and Quakers, the latter corresponding group in England), mystical (D. Joris, J. Boehme), and ethical-rationalistic (Arminians, Spener). The discipleship idea (*imitatio Christi*) is to Kühn the distinguishing feature of the Anabaptists; it implies both brotherly love and *Gelassenheit* (inner surrender, conquest of selfishness, yieldedness). This certainly holds true for Anabaptists as well as for Quakers. What actually distinguishes them most is the theology of martyrdom (*q.v.*) of the Anabaptists which, however, Kühn does not follow up.

(7) Those who have followed the socio-economic interpretation of history have classified the Anabaptists primarily as social revolutionaries of the lower classes, or even as forerunners of modern Socialism or Communism, rather than as a religious movement. See, e.g., Karl Kautsky, *Communism in Central Europe in the Time of the Reformation* (1897).

(8) Max Göbel first (*Geschichte des Christlichen Lebens in der Rheinisch-Westfälisch evangelischen Kirche,* 1848-49), followed by many others, particularly John Horsch, d. 1941, holds that Anabaptism is merely a consistent evangelical Protestantism, seeking to recreate without compromise the original New Testament church, the culmination of the original vision of Luther and Zwingli.

(9) Alfred Hegler and Ernst Troeltsch distinguished the individualistic "Spiritualists" like Hans Denk, Johannes Bünderlin, and others, from the true Anabaptists who were anything but individualists, holding strongly to group discipline and order.

(10) Robert Friedmann attempted a further interpretation of Anabaptism by distinguishing the Protestant types according to their particular interest in different parts of the New Testament which then become decisive for life and thought. The Anabaptists derive a great deal of strength from the study of the synoptic Gospels while mystics incline to lean more heavily upon the Johannine writings. The major Protestant denominations for their part have found their foundation primarily in the Pauline epistles and Pauline theology, and millennialists stress above all the book of Revelation. Some *Schwärmer* finally do not stress the Scriptures too much but rely in the main upon their own inspiration (Müntzer, David Joris, etc.). The simple life of the Anabaptists, their stress upon obedience to the Word of God and His commandments, their idea of discipleship (including possible martyrdom), their lessened interest in formal theology, this all brings them nearer to the spirit of Christ's exemplary life and teachings as recorded above all in the first three Gospels and in the book of Acts.

It is .quite clear that this rapid survey by no means exhausts the problem involved in a delineation of the idea of evangelical Anabaptism. The present analysis has been more negative than positive. It needs, therefore, ample supplementation. H. S. Bender's *Anabaptist Vision* and his analysis of the church concept of the Brethren (*MQR* XVIII, 1944, 67-88, and XIX, 1945, 90-100) might well supply it. (R. Friedmann, "Conception of an Anabaptist," *Church Hist.* IX, 1940, 341-65.)

R.F.

Anabaptist Memorial (*Täufer-Memorial*), a document drawn up by the Reformed clergy, is one of the most important for the history of the Mennonites in Bern. It affords not only a deep insight into the life of the Reformed Church, but is also the best testimonial imaginable for the Anabaptists. This noted court record is found in several copies in the archives of the university of Bern. On Feb. 15, 1693, a government order was issued "to an honorable Convent" (Collegium of the clergy), to determine the reason for this leaven and how to counteract the strong increase of Anabaptism. They were asked to report their findings in written form and send it to the council.

An extensive opinion was worked out by the clergy and presented to the city council. It is called, *Ursachen der je mehr und mehr anwachsenden Widertäufer-Sect, samt beigefügten Mitteln, wie solchem Uebel abzuhelfen* (Reasons for the steadily increasing Anabaptist sect, together with added means for eliminating this evil). The document is proof that the general decline in morals cannot be blamed on the Anabaptists. Finally the church awoke to the fact that the fault might lie on the side of the Reformed Church. The defects causing the decline were found (1) in the governing class; (2) in the life and doctrine of the clergy; and (3) among the subjects.

Quite openly the vices in the life of the ruling class, the clergy, and among the people are pointed out. With the rulers the greatest offense was their use of the office to enrich themselves instead of holding "the honor of God and the welfare of the subjects as their purpose." Without doubt many persons were "enticed by the example of love and kindness that the Anabaptists exercise among themselves," and are thus "led into erroneous faith."

Among the clergy the greatest lack was inadequate teaching, either because they did not have it, or because they did not trouble themselves to preach clearly, for which reason the "power of the Word, the proof of the Spirit, and the desired edification" were lacking. They did not preach "the pure and unadulterated Word of God without mingling it with human wisdom and invention." The Bible was not connectedly or thoroughly explained, to inform the listeners, in order that they "might experience divine truth and the power of the mystery of salvation in the indivisibility of all the articles of faith." It should be a part of the conscientious performance of the office of preaching to follow the example of the apostles in house to house visitation to admonish the fathers and mothers, the children and servants, encourage, and comfort them; to prove by kindly encouragement that the salvation of the listeners was a matter of concern to the preachers. Whereas the Anabaptists carried on such family visits, instruction and friendly encouragement by the so-called preachers, the council found that among the "proper preachers, who must give an account for each lamb in their fold," such efforts were neglected.

A further cause of this distressing situation was to be sought in the life and conduct of the preachers. The example of the Anabaptist-minded made it clear that the evangelical simplicity, humility, gentleness, self-denial, and love of a pious, godly walk is the best sermon to the people. It could not be sufficiently bemoaned that "this so necessary and saving part of their office" is of so little concern to them. Whence among the Anabaptists, "not only offense and annoyance, but also blameworthy and derogatory gossip and belittling of the Reformed preachers and their service follows." Many preachers revealed in the performance of their church service that they did not seek the honor of the Great Shepherd and the edification of the church, but rather their own honor and benefit, instead of performing the office of preaching conscientiously.

It was deplorable and most offensive that some clergymen are found in inns and there "showed themselves properly spiritual neither in words nor in deed."

The third point deals with the "causes to be found among the common people, which are offensive to the Anabaptists." Ruthlessness was prevalent, so "that our preaching is not blessed" and bears no fruit, but is mere letter service. What was most offensive to the Anabaptists was that open sinners were found in the church along with the good and enjoyed communion with them. This was true in spite of the fact that the Reformed doctrine required church discipline. Frivolous swearing or profanity was not only found among the people of all classes, but it was even tolerated. No punishment of any kind was meted out against immoderate eating and drinking and other similar misconduct, desecration of the Sabbath, and lying and deception in trade. Such things could not be found among the Anabaptists in their "apparent piety, simplicity, self-denial, patience, love, kindness, benevolence, strength, and zeal in prayer, worship, and the like." This was the reason why they were held in high regard by the people and "were very strong in winning hearts."

Then the measures to improve the situation are named. A thorough reformation should be made among all classes of people. In order to "lead the people on the right road or keep them in it" it was necessary to remove the causes of offense (Luke 17:1, 2). The church officials should lead exemplary lives and show a fatherly attitude toward their subjects. The preachers should "faithfully admonish to church attendance and hearing the public preaching of the Word of God." The preachers should also take a deeper interest in souls seeking salvation "and instruct them kindly in matters of salvation and their Christian duties, praise their good intentions, industry, and zeal, thank God for them, and pray for His grace and blessing upon them." Teachers and preachers should in all things seek "to prove their service," and live irreproachable and holy lives as examples to the flock.

Church discipline should be more strictly enforced, the prebendaries set up "Reformed and according to the Gospel . . . , so that through reproof, admonition, conviction, and humiliation of the offenders the offenses would be done away with and the sinner brought to true repentance and reform . . . . Otherwise where the preaching and church discipline is not carried out in purity and simplicity, no power or blessing can be hoped for it."

The entire document, which gives a true picture of contemporary conditions in state and church, is at the same time evidence that the clergy were really serious in creating better conditions. But in spite of the recognition of their own weaknesses, they were unable to arrive at Christian toleration. (*Miss. Hist. Helv.* III, 38 in the library of the city and university of Bern.)   S.G.

Anabaptisticum et Enthusiasticum Pantheon Und
Geistliches Rüst-Hausz Wider die Alten Quäcker

Und Neuen Frey-Geister . . . 1702. A strange pamphleteering volume, large folio in size, with over 1,000 pages, compiled by a certain Johann Friedrich Corvinus (Rabe), a Lutheran minister of Hornburg (d. 1724). The volume contains fourteen different pamphlets attacking practically everybody who was not of the strict Lutheran orthodoxy of about 1700. It attacks above all the Quakers, but also Mystics, Pansophists (Rosicrucians), all kinds of Pietists (e.g., Labadie), philosophers such as Descartes, Spinoza and Hobbes, Jews, Cromwell and his Puritans, and, last but not least, the "old and new fanatics of Anabaptist spirit" (pamphlet II). Yet, in the text proper, only Thomas Müntzer is discussed.

To Mennonites the book is of value because it prints in its sixth pamphlet, called *Alte und neue Schwarmgeister Brut und Quaker Greuel,* on pp. 352-61 the full text of the *Confession oder Kurzes und einfältiges Glaubens Bekenntnis derer so man nennet die vereinigten Flämischen, Friesischen und Hochdeutschen Taufgesinnten oder Mennoniten, ausgegeben durch die Gemeinde in Preussen,* 1660, and subsequently on pp. 362-67 the *Kurze Unterweisung aus der Schrift,* 1690 (in full), the oldest known German Prussian catechism, also called the *Fragebüchlein* (see Friedmann, *Menn. Piety,* 119, 129 f.), yet without the prayers usually printed within this otherwise well-known Prussian devotional manual. (The only known copy of this confession and catechism is that in the Amsterdam Mennonite Library.) Remarkably, this print appears only as an appendix to the pamphlet VI and is without commentary, something unusual in this otherwise so venomous book.

In general, the book has value as a collection of original sources and information otherwise not available (see W. Hubben, *Die Quäker in der deutschen Vergangenheit,* 1929, 97). As such it might be compared with the more neutral *Annales Anabaptistici* of 1672 (*q.v.*), and with G. Arnold's *Kirchen- und Ketzerhistorie* of 1699, where the heretics are eulogized. No doubt, the Lutheran orthodoxy was then fighting a hard fight of survival, and the book was a tool in this struggle.

It should be mentioned that pamphlet No. III contains B. Figken's *Historia Fanaticorum* (Danzig, 1701) mainly against the then rather aggressive Quakers. Allegedly this pamphlet is a translation of an English original (London, 1660). No. XII has the long-winded title, *Erschröckliche Brüderschaft der alten und neuen Wiedertäuffer, Quäker, Schwärmer und freigeister mit denen heil- und Gottlosen Juden* (1702). (*ML* I, 69.)   R.F.

Anadol Forestry Service Camp (*Anadoler Forstei*), a camp in the Russian province of Ekaterinoslav, district of Mariupol, which was established for Mennonite young men as an alternative to military service in 1880, about five miles from the railroad station of Gross-Anadol and Volnovacha, and occupied by an average of 170 men. (*ML* I, 70.) A.B.

Ananyevo Forestry Service Camp (*Ananjever Forstei*), a camp in the Russian province of Kherson, established in 1907 on crown lands, three miles

from the railroad and postal station of Sherebkovo, for 74 Mennonite young men, as an alternative to military service. It was supervised by a preacher-manager. In July 1913 the subsidiary unit Baital, ten miles distant, also established for 75 men, was assigned to another forestry service camp, although its personnel was transferred back to the main camp, and the name was changed from Ananyevo to Sherebkovo Forestry Service Camp. (*ML* I, 70.)
G.F.

Anastasius Veluanus, Johannes (Dutch name: Jan Gerrits Versteghe), year of birth unknown, died after 1567 as ecclesiastical superintendent at Bacharach, Germany, was a Dutch reformer. Originally, he had been a priest in the Roman Catholic Church at Garderen in the Dutch province of Gelderland. In 1544 he became an evangelical preacher, and later joined the movement of the *Nationaal-Gereformeerden* (who were opposed to the Calvinist Reformed on the doctrine of predestination and other matters), in which he became a leading figure. He held to a Biblical Humanism after the manner of Zwingli and called himself Zwinglian. Of special importance is the book he published in 1554 (the preface is dated at Strasbourg where he resided at this time), *Der Leken Wechwyser* (The Layman's Guide), which was widely read and turned countless persons to the Reformation, especially among the more educated in the Netherlands.

In *Der Leken Wechwyser* there is frequent reference to the *Wederdopers,* by which Anastasius means the Anabaptists. He is well informed about them. He writes, for example, concerning the Davidians (the followers of David Joris), who say that one may renounce the truth without committing sin (*Der Leken W.* in *BRN* IV, 344) and he knows about the party disputes among the Mennonites (*ibid.,* 314, 333). Although decidedly rejecting their principles he is an exception among contemporary anti-Anabaptist writers in that he correctly distinguishes between the Münsterites and the peaceful Anabaptists, to whom he refers respectively as *enthoesiasten* (fanatics) and *eenfeldighen* (meaning both the innocent ones and the simple ones). These "simple" ones have a "conduct that is irreproachable, and in their lack of wisdom are still peacefully minded," namely, the "best Mennonisten" (*ibid.,* 203). Elsewhere he writes that it is to be greatly deplored that the blind Anabaptists err so grossly, but that many among them live so irreproachably and die so magnificently for things which they think are godly, that it is highly commendable (*ibid.,* 338). With moderation he opposes the doctrine of the incarnation held by Menno Simons and his group (*ibid.,* 138-42); he defends infant baptism with nine arguments (*ibid.,* 193-203), and upholds fulfilling the duty of the magistracy and military service (*ibid.,* 348 ff., 351 ff.). His judgment is extremely moderate and departs widely from the unkind criticism of the later Calvinistic opponents such as Guido de Brèz and others. He firmly opposes the execution of Anabaptists (*ibid.,* 343, 238), and his plea for tolerance regarding them is superb: "The sword of the emperor is to punish those who . . . intentionally perpetrate gross sins against the Ten Commandments. But those who in good faith, unknowingly are deceived . . . these one should not in any fashion put to death. The poor blind Anabaptists are treated very unjustly in Brabant, Holland, and in the district of Utrecht, which no one can deny. If they retain their opinions, then they are burned at the stake; if they fall back again into Catholicism, then they still must die. How shall we answer before the judgment seat of Christ in that we do not live so irreproachably and die as steadfastly for the true doctrine as some of the Anabaptists do for their errors?" "The tyrants have a bitterness beyond all measure against the poor Anabaptists" (*ibid.*, 337). This is a tone seldom found in an opponent who differed fundamentally with the principles of the Mennonites.

vdZ.

W. Moll, "Joh. Veluanus," in *Kerkhist. Archief* I (1857) 1-134; F. Pijper, *BRN* IV, Introduction, 81-121, and reprint of *Der Leken Wechwyser* and other writings, 122-490; *DB* 1916, 111, 117-30.

Anchor Mennonite Church (GCM), Anchor Twp., McLean Co., Ill., was started as a Sunday school at the Rockford schoolhouse, five miles south of Anchor, by a group of about 14 families who had moved there from North Danvers, Ill., in 1884. In 1894 Joseph Stuckey (*q.v.*), who had frequently visited and preached in the community, organized a church, of which Aaron Augspurger was elected pastor, and which joined the Central (Illinois) Conference. A frame building 30 ft. x 40 ft. was erected in 1910. The 1949 membership was 31.   G.Mi.

Ancken, Hans, of Auzeldingen in the canton of Bern, Switzerland, a martyr of whom nothing is known except that he is named among the 40 Anabaptists executed in Bern on Sept. 17, 1543, given in a marginal note in the *Märtyrerspiegel* printed in Ephrata (1748) 138. (*ML* I, 70.)

Neff.

Ancken, Peter, of the Siebetal in the canton of Bern, Switzerland, a martyr who is mentioned only in the *Märtyrerspiegel* (Ephrata, 1748) list, p. 138, as having been executed in Bern on Sept. 17, 1543. (*ML* I, 70.)

Neff.

Anderson County, Kan., Amish settlement. The first Old Order Amish moved to Anderson County from the Haven settlement in Reno Co., Kan., in the spring of 1903. The five families were those of Benedict Mullet, Joe E. G. Yoder, Ammon Miller, Levi L. Knepp, and Rudy D. Bontrager. Seven families from Gibson, Miss., joined them in the spring of 1904, including the family of Preacher Isaac Chupp. Following the death of Chupp, Eli Beachy was ordained preacher in 1904 and Noah J. Yoder in 1905. In 1953 the congregation had a membership of 49, with Jerry J. Yoder serving as preacher. The local address of most of the members was Garnett.   J.S.B.

Anderson Mennonite Church (MC) is located on the Carroll Road, 10 miles northwest of Fort Wayne, Ind. The first Mennonite Sunday school in the area was conducted by Henry Easterday and Lee Sailors of the Fort Wayne Mennonite mission in May 1933. The work was sponsored by the Leo congregation

until its organization as a separate church in 1940. The building used for worship is an abandoned Baptist church.

The present pastor (1953), Jos. S. Neuhouser, has ministered to the spiritual needs of the congregation since its beginning. The membership is 15. The congregation also sponsors a mission Sunday school 15 miles south of Fort Wayne, near Ossian, Ind.

J.S.N.

A.N.D.P.V. (*Algemene Nederlandse Doopsgezinde Predikanten-Vereniging*). From 1913 to 1926 a number of Dutch Mennonite ministers met regularly once a year at Amsterdam to discuss practical questions, in which M. L. Deenik of Leeuwarden and F. Dijkema were leaders. Besides this, in Friesland the *Friesche Doopsgezinde Predikanten-Vergadering* has held yearly meetings at Leeuwarden since 1847. In 1926 A. Binnerts Szn (*q.v.*) took the initiative to found a general Mennonite ministerial association; on April 25, 1927, the first meeting of this *Algemene Nederlandse Doopsgezinde Predikanten-Vereniging* was held in Amsterdam, 65 ministers being present. First members of the board were A. Binnerts Szn, president; J. IJntema, secretary-treasurer; and S. H. N. Gorter. In course of time nearly all Dutch Mennonite ministers joined the association. The A.N.D.P.V. meets twice a year, at Amsterdam in the second week after Easter and in one of several other towns in the second week of September. At each meeting usually two subjects are introduced and discussed, one of a theological nature and the other more practical (problems of catechetical instruction, visitation of the sick, etc.). After the founding of the A.N.D.P.V. the Frisian meetings and those led by Deenik and Dijkema were no longer held. (H. W. Meihuizen, "Een kwart eeuw A.N.D.P.V.," *Stemmen* I, 5, November 1952.)   vdZ.

Andreae, Jacob (1528-90), one of the most influential Lutheran theologians of his time, and one of the most resolute opponents of the Anabaptists in the 16th century. As a general superintendent in Göppingen, Württemberg, he was very active in the work of the Reformation and had also much influence upon the sharp attitude of Duke Christoph toward all "sectarians" in Württemberg. G. Bossert, Jr., claims that it was most likely Andreae who incited the duke against the Anabaptists and gave him the idea that these sectarians "live like beasts without reason" (Bossert, *Quellen*, etc., 137 n.). Together with Brenz (*q.v.*) he took part in the great Anabaptist disputation at Pfeddersheim in the Palatinate (*q.v.*) in August 1557. The *Quellen* (148-61) contain a document, *Contra Anabaptistarum opinionem*, which seems to be a report of this colloquium drawn up most likely by Andreae and presented to the duke. It contains an elaborate refutation of ten articles allegedly defended by the Anabaptists (Swiss or Hutterite). In November 1557 several leading Lutheran theologians convened at Worms on the Rhine to discuss the procedure of dealing uniformly with the Anabaptists. Melanchthon, Brenz, and Andreae were among those present. The result is a pamphlet entitled, *Prozess wie* *es soll gehalten werden mit den Wiedertäufern, durch etliche Gelehrten so zu Worms versammelt gestellt.* The Stuttgart state archives has a document, *Bedenken der Wiedertäufer halber,* of the same year (*Quellen,* 161-68) which is identical with the *Prozess;* most likely Andreae had presented it, too, to the duke. The *Prozess* advocates the death penalty for Anabaptists according to Leviticus 24. The *Bedenken* has the same passage but crossed out. Bossert, Jr. surmises that this was done by Brenz, and he adds characteristically, "Andreae pushed and Brenz put on the brakes." The Hutterites drew up a statement in their defense against the accusations of the Worms document, called *Handbüchlein wider den Prozess der zu Worms am Rhein wider die Brüder so man die Hutterischen nennt ausgangen ist im 1557 Jahr,* etc. (*Klein-Geschichtsbuch der Hutterischen Brüder,* 1947, 274 footnote). It seems that this little book was printed, but no copy is known save some handwritten ones.

In 1558 eventually Duke Christoph issued the long-expected mandate regulating the treatment of all sectarians (Anabaptists, Schwenckfeldians, Sacramentarians, etc.) in Württemberg. The text is published in *Quellen,* 168-71 (an original copy of the mandate is also in Goshen College Library). Most likely Andreae was instrumental also in the drafting of this important document.

In 1562 Andreae was appointed provost of the great Stiftskirche, the cathedral of Tübingen, and he became also professor and chancellor of the university of this city. In 1567 he preached here a series of sermons on the principal divisions of the Christian religion, and in eight sermons subjected the views of the Anabaptists to a critical and unfriendly analysis. The sermons were published in Tübingen in 1568 under the title, *Dreyundreissig Predigen von den fürnembsten Spaltungen in der Christlichen Religion, so sich zwischen den Bäbstischen, Lutherischen, Zwinglischen, Schwenckfeldern, und Wiederteuffern halten* (copy in the library of Goshen College). A second edition appeared in 1573, another one in 1589. In these sermons Andreae gives vent to violent attacks against the Anabaptists, completely misinterpreting their idea of holiness of life (which is so foreign to Lutheran theology). It impresses one as very peculiar that a theologian of Andreae's rank could give his words emphasis in no other way than by ridiculing the simple appearance of an Anabaptist preacher and representing the earnestness of these brethren as hypocrisy and a deception of the devil. Andreae's sermons offer a good insight into the inglorious methods of attack and the hateful tone current among the prominent theologians of the time. This attitude is the more deplorable as Andreae was relatively well informed about the Anabaptists and their teaching. Many times he had come into personal contact with them, and he knew at least some of their literature. In his sermons he expressly quotes two books of Anabaptist origin, (*a*) *Die Rechenschaft unserer Religion, Lehr und Glaubens,* which is of course nothing other than Peter Riedemann's (*q.v.*) well-known Hutterite confession of faith, printed in 1565, and apparently in circulation also

in Württemberg where Hutterites were active in missionary work, and (*b*) *Heut und Gestern,* which has recently been identified as Pilgram Marpeck's outstanding *Testamentserläuterung* (*q.v.*) of 1542-44, also printed, though anonymously. Wiswedel reprints from Andreae's sermon the passage dealing with this book.

That Andreae could not grasp the intentions of the Anabaptists might be taken as indicative of the deep-rooted differences between Lutheran Protestantism, based on a rigid and rational theology (Andreae was instrumental also in the drafting of the Formula of Concord), and the Anabaptist vision based on the untheological and rather existential idea of a committed discipleship.

Johann Valentin Andreae (1586-1654), a grandson of Jakob, an important churchman who insisted on purification of morals, is the author of the complaint, "He who now tries to live an upright life is called a fanatic, a Schwenckfelder, an Anabaptist" (W. Möller, *Lehrbuch der Kirchengesch.,* 3d ed., 1907, III, 418).　　　　　　　　　　　　R.F.

G. Bossert, Sr., in *Blätter für württemb. Kirchengesch.,* 1912, 42 ff.; G. Bossert, Jr., "Aus der nebenkirchlichen religiösen Bewegung der Ref.-Zeit in Württemberg (Wiedertäufer und Schwenckfelder)," in *Blätter für württemb. Kirchengesch.,* 1929, 23 ff.; G. Bossert, Sr., *Quellen zur Gesch. der Wiedertäufer: I, Herzogtum Württemberg* (Leipzig, 1930); Chr. Hege, *Die Täufer in der Kurpfalz* (Frankfurt, 1908) 93 f.; W. Wiswedel, "Die Testamentserläuterung, ein Beitrag zur Täufergesch.," in *Blätter für württemb. Kirchengesch.,* 1937, 66; *HRE,* "Andreae, Jacob"; *ML* I, 71.

Andreas, Johann, b. Sept. 8, 1802, in Klein Mausdorf, West Prussia, Germany, d. Jan. 11, 1877, in Mount Pleasant, Iowa. He became the elder of the Elbing-Ellerwald Mennonite Church in 1846 and served the church in this capacity until 1869.

When on March 3, 1868, the Prussian Cabinet Order was passed according to which Mennonites would have to serve the government in military or alternative service, Johann Andreas was one of the few leaders who were opposed to any form of service. On this matter he was in agreement with the elders and ministers of the Trakt Mennonite settlements who refused to have Christian fellowship with those who would conform to the Cabinet's Order. In a circular letter to his congregation dated Nov. 18, 1869, Elder Andreas pleaded "with those who wished in the future to participate in the Lord's Supper on the ground of the traditional Mennonite confession of faith" that they should notify him before Jan. 1, 1870, and informed those who wished to conform to the Cabinet's Order that they would have to partake of the Lord's Supper separately. Although he urged in his letter "that all members of the congregation should come and none stay away," only a small group remained loyal to the traditional principle of nonresistance.

The pressure from within his congregation forced Andreas to resign his eldership. When he emigrated to America, only a comparatively small group from his congregation followed his example. The rigor of the controversy so severely affected his health that he died within five months after his family reached Mount Pleasant, Iowa. The family had chosen to make their home in Beatrice, Neb., where he was buried.   **H.A.C., C.K.**

Andreas von Neiss, an Anabaptist martyr who was executed with the sword at Neuburg on the Danube in Bavaria. He was an outstandingly successful preacher, who baptized many, but is not mentioned in the *Martyrs' Mirror.* (Wolkan, *Lieder,* 29 f; *ML* I, 70.)   NEFF.

Andreasfeld Mennonite Brethren Church, located in the village of Andreasfeld about 17 miles east of Chortitza, district of Alexandrovsk, province of Ekaterinoslav, South Russia, was organized in 1870 as a branch of the Einlage (*q.v.*) (Kitchkas) M.B. Church, the main congregation of the denomination in the Old Colony (*q.v.*). There were 12 families and a membership of 60. It had its own church edifice, which was also the place of worship of the Einlage congregation for some time. The leased village of Ebenfeld and the landowners of Blumenau belonged to other congregations. A system of local education was under church control. Aron Lepp, elder of the Einlage congregation, and John Siemens, noted evangelist and Bible expositor, were the leading ministers. August Liebig, Baptist evangelist, resided at Andreasfeld in the 1870's. For some time it appeared that the Baptist influence would gain the upper hand in the congregation, since the first ministers were ordained by Baptist preachers; however, under the able leadership of Lepp the church soon steadied itself to a positive evangelical ministry on M.B. principles. As a result the church prospered and exerted a wholesome influence on the other branch churches in the Old Colony. Historically the Andreasfeld church is noted as the site of the first M.B. conference (*Bundeskonferenz*) in 1872 and several thereafter. The resignation of Elder Lepp as leader of the Einlage M.B. Church in 1903, and the subsequent transfer of these headquarters to Einlage, and the emigration of several members, caused a decline in membership and a loss of its importance in the Old Colony group. This church found its end after the withdrawal of the German occupation army from the Ukraine in 1943. (Friesen, *Brüderschaft,* 403; *ML* I, 70.)   **P.H.B.**

Andres auf der Stultzen: see Castelberger, Andreas.

Andres (Andreas, Androes, Andresen), a Mennonite family of West Prussian background, appearing in rural Flemish congregations, first mentioned in 1638 at Schmerblock. In West Prussia 6 families of this name were counted in 1776 (without Danzig), and 56 persons in 1935 (without Elbing). Members of the family also migrated to Russia and America. Leading European members of the family included Cornelius Andres, elder of the Grosswerder congregation, 1736-41; and Johann Andreas (*q.v.*), elder of the Elbing-Ellerwald congregation, 1846-69, who emigrated with a group to Beatrice, Neb., in 1876. The genealogy of the Andres family was compiled by Anna Andres, formerly of Fürstenwerder, West Prussia (in manuscript). H. J. Andres is administrator of the Bethel Deaconess Hospital, Newton, Kan. Members of the Andres family are located also in Nebraska, Manitoba, Ontario,

and Saskatchewan, as well as in other American Mennonite communities. The name also occurred among the Mennonites of Russia.   **G.R.**

Andrew's Bridge, a Negro mission of the Lancaster Mennonite Conference (MC), elevated above the Octoraro in southern Lancaster Co., Pa., was opened Jan. 16, 1938, by the Mellinger congregation. The Lina May Thompson (Colored) home was the center of the work. In 1945 a new commodious meetinghouse was built by the mission board. Israel D. Rohrer, who was since ordained for the ministry to the deaf, was for some years the superintendent. Bernard B. Kautz also served in this position. Jacob K. Mellinger was ordained on June 5, 1946, as the first local minister, and on May 11, 1949, Daniel D. Leaman was ordained his assistant. The 1952 membership was 55. John R. Winey was ordained deacon on July 20, 1952. It is now an organized congregation of both Negro and white, augmented by the influx of overflowing congregations more central, due to high prices of land in the heart of Lancaster County.   **I.D.L.**

Andreyevka (also called Gnadental), a village in the Mennonite colony of Nikolaipol near Aulie-Ata (*q.v.*), Russia, at the foot of the northwest spur of the Tianshan range in Turkestan, about 5,000 ft. above sea level, established in 1882 by Mennonites, chiefly from the Molotschna colony under the leadership of A. Peters (*q.v.*), who hoped to acquire here complete exemption from military service. The village had about 30 families of farmers. The soil was loamy, mixed with stones, and was irrigated with water from the mountain brooks. At first the colonists lived in poverty, but gradually became prosperous. Most of them belonged to the Nikolaipol Mennonite Brethren congregation. The ultimate fate of this settlement is unknown. (*ML* I, 71.)   HEGE.

Andries Claessen (Claeszen, Claesz), an Anabaptist martyr of Dronrijp, a village between Franeker and Leeuwarden in the Dutch province of Friesland. He is said to have been a rather wealthy man who held meetings in his house. Karel Vos' idea that he was a Münsterite is unproved and is not very probable. He was arrested in 1535 by the stadholder Georg Schenk and taken to Leeuwarden. After a three-day imprisonment in the dungeon he was beheaded on March 13, 1535 (not March 16, as the *Martyrs' Mirror* states), and broken on the wheel. He left six young children. Sympathetic friends provided for them, though not without danger to themselves. (*Mart. Mir.* D 37-38, E 444; *DB* 1899, 67, 105, and 109; 1917, 172; *ML* I, 359.)
        O.H., vDZ.

Andries Gherytszoen van Castricum, an Anabaptist martyr, lived at Amsterdam, was beheaded there on May 28, 1534, by decree of the Court of Holland. Details are lacking. (Grosheide, *Bijdrage,* 51, 302.)
        vDZ.

Andries Hermansz (A. Harmanszoon), an Anabaptist martyr of the Dutch province of Gelderland, was beheaded at Amsterdam on April 12, 1537, with two other brethren. He held "conventiculen" (meetings) in his house and preached there.

(*Inv. Arch. Amst.* I, No. 183; *Mart. Mir.* D 414, E 765; Grosheide, *Bijdrage,* 140-41, 307.) vDZ.

Andries Jacobsz (also called Adriaen Jacobsen), a Flemish Anabaptist martyr, son of Jacob Dirksz (*q.v.*) and brother of Hans (Jan) Jacobsz, was burned at the stake together with them on March 17, 1568, at Antwerp. Van Braght relates that he was betrothed at the time he was captured and that his fiancee and also his sister were among the bystanders who witnessed the execution. The father, Jacob Dirksz, had some time previously fled with his family from Utrecht in the Netherlands to Antwerp in order to escape persecution. (*Mart. Mir.* D 370, E 724; Génard, *Antw. Arch.-Blad* X, 14, 68; XIV, 54-55, No. 632.) vDZ.

Andries van Laarbeke, an Anabaptist martyr, seized on July 15, 1558, at Middelburg in the Dutch province of Zeeland, together with Mayken Daniels and Jan Hendricksz. All three had fled from Flanders. Inquiries were made of the dean of the Catholic Church at Roesselaere (Belgium) concerning them by the magistrates of Middelburg. This explains the long duration of their imprisonment. They were put to death on Feb. 21, 1559. Because they "persisted in various errors and unlawful opinions" and would not relinquish their faith, they were subjected to the severest punishment. All three were tied to a stake in the town square at Middelburg, strangled, and then burned to death; afterwards their charred bodies were displayed outside the Noorddampoort. Because the government anticipated popular disturbances at the time of this execution, additional police precautions were taken. vDZ.

K. R. Pekelharing, "Bijdr. v. d. Gesch. der Herv. in Zeeland," *Archief Zeeuwsch Gen.* VI, (1866) 38-40.

Andries Langedul, an Anabaptist martyr, beheaded at Antwerp on Nov. 8, 1559, along with Laurens van der Leyen and Mattheus Pottebakker. Andries was captured while he was reading the Bible. His wife had just been delivered of a child, but could be taken away and thus did not fall into the hands of the persecutors. Andries was born at Ieper in Flanders. He was executed secretly within the Steen prison at Antwerp. Andries' name occurs also in the song, "Aenhoort Godt, hemelsche Vader" (Give ear, O God, heavenly Father), in the *Liedtboecxken van den Offer des Heeren,* No. 16, in which Andries is listed as No. 57; also mentioned by Wolkan, *Lieder.* vDZ.

Offer, 567; *Mart. Mir.* D 262, 269; E 633, 639; Génard, *Antw. Arch.-Blad* IX, 5, 10; XIV, 26-27, No. 303; Wolkan, *Lieder,* 63, 72; ML II, 617.

Andries Meulenaer and **Francijntgen Meulenaers** (Miller), Anabaptist martyrs, who were seized in Brugge in Flanders in 1561 with ten brethren and one sister with whom they were attending a meeting. Though they were repeatedly tried on the rack, they joyfully bore the chains and steadfastly confessed their faith. On Dec. 10, 1561, Andries and four fellow prisoners died at the stake; on the next day Francijntgen endured the same fate with the remaining prisoners. Andries is identical with **Andries Viblarre,** born at Zwevezele. His name is also found in the song, "Genade en Vrede moet Godvresende zijn" (Mercy and peace must be Godfearing), in the Dutch hymnbook *Veelderhande Liedekens,* 1569. NEFF.

Mart. Mir. D 288, E 655; Verheyden, *Brugge,* Nos. 33 and 41, pp. 48 and 50; ML III, 176; Wackernagel, *Lieder,* 130.

Andries N., the name given by the *Martyrs' Mirror* to two martyrs who were executed in 1570. The author explains the initial N. as signifying that they were dead to the world and had devoted themselves to the service of Christ. One of them died in Antwerp with his father and brother after giving a good testimony to his faith and suffering all the torture cheerfully. This martyr is identical with Andries Jacobsz (*q.v.*). The other was imprisoned for his faith and after three hours of cruel torture was burned at the stake. This martyr, concerning whom particulars are lacking, was not executed in Antwerp, as the *Martyrs' Mirror* states, but at Haarlem. (*Mart. Mir.* D 506, E 845; *Bibliographie* II, Nos. 19, 20; ML I, 70.) NEFF, vDZ.

Andries van Niel, who appeared in the Dutch province of Limburg as a reformer, was an Anabaptist, according to Bax. He was burned at the stake on Jan. 19, 1534, at Curingen. (W. Bax, *Het Protest. in het Bisdom Luik,* I, The Hague, 1937, 26.) vDZ.

Andries Smu(e)l, an Anabaptist martyr. The *Martyrs' Mirror* mentions a martyr by this name who was burned at the stake in Amsterdam in 1546 with Dirk Pietersz (Smuel), and also includes from both men an "account and confession of faith," drawn up at Amsterdam for the Commissioners. Andries is, however, not mentioned in the official verdicts, although Dirk Pietersz is; hence the existence of an Andries Smuel is doubtful. (*Mart. Mir.* D 75, E 475.) vDZ.

Andriesz, Pieter: see **Hesseling, Pieter A.**

Anfang, Wastl (also called Schmidt and Sensenschmidt), a Hutterite missionary, chosen preacher at Neumühl in Moravia on Feb. 20, 1581, sent to Tirol in 1584, and later again served as a missionary in Tirol. Against him and Hans Zuckenhammer (*q.v.*) the Bavarian duke Wilhelm V (*q.v.*) issued a mandate on Feb. 27, 1587, offering a reward of 100 guilders for their capture. But they did not fall into the hands of the Bavarian government. Anfang died Dec. 2, 1602, at Nikolsburg, Moravia. HEGE.

Beck, *Geschichts-Bücher,* 275 and 335; Winter, *Gesch. der bayr. Wiedertäufer* (München, 1809); ML I, 71.

Angas, William Henry, d. 1832, English Baptist preacher, who awakened and vitalized a missionary spirit among the Mennonites of Holland and Germany. The Dutch Mennonite Missionary Aid Society owes its origin, May 18, 1821, to his efforts, for (*Mennonitische Blätter,* 1895, 46) it was originally a Dutch branch of the missionary society of the English Baptists at Serampur. In a leaflet printed in Dutch the director of this aid society appealed to all his co-believers for support of foreign mission work. Weydmann (*q.v.*), the Mennonite preacher of Monsheim, translated it into German and sent it to the Palatine Mennonites on Jan. 19, 1824. But nothing more happened. Then Angas, on a tour at his own expense through Prussia, Poland, Bavaria, Switzerland, and France, everywhere visiting Mennonite churches, arrived in the Palatinate. He stayed here about four weeks, visiting all the churches. His zealous efforts brought about a small "conference" of the Palatine-Hessian Mennonites at the Spitalhof, July 13, 1824, the first conference of this group since 1805, on whom he seems to have made a deep and lasting impression. It was here decided to put up a missionary box in every church and to take a missionary offering on the first Sunday of every month, after reports on and prayer for this important cause. The contributions were given to the English Baptist Mission until the founding of the Dutch Mennonite Mission Society (*q.v.*) in the year 1847. Angas also sent two Mennonite youths, at his expense, to the school at Beuggen to study for the position of teacher-preacher in the Mennonite churches.

Angas' work among the Mennonites bore fruit. Conferences were held annually. In mission work a common, unifying task had been found, which led to dealing with other important church problems. A small part of the Palatine Mennonites of course viewed the mission cause with distrust as an innovation. The Amsterdam Mennonite Library possesses a printed letter of Angas in German, dated at Danzig, July 1823 (26 pages), in which he writes about the mission field at Serampore in India, and its stations, also mentioning a number of mission schools and translations of the Bible or parts of the Bible in 42 Indian languages. At the end of the letter he asks for support of this mission work and returns thanks for the love and friendship which the West Prussian Mennonites paid him when visiting their churches. NEFF.

Menn. Bl., 1907, 89; *ML* I, 72; *An die Aeltesten, Lehrer und Mitglieder der sämmtlichen Menn. Gem. in West Preussen* (Danzig, July 1823); F. A. Fox, *Memoirs of H. W. Angas* (London, 1834); *DB* 1862, 13.

Anjum, a village in the northeast of the Dutch province of Friesland, where a Mennonite church once existed. Leenaert Bouwens (*q.v.*) baptized at least 159 persons here, according to his list; there was later here a branch of the Jan Jacobsz group which had a church of its own, but which died out in 1729. J.L.

J. Loosjes, "Jan Jacobsz en de Jan Jacobsgezinden," in *Ned. archief v. Kerkgesch.* XI (The Hague, 1914); Blaupot t.C., *Friesland; Archief der Gem. Terschelling,* in the Mennonite archives at Amsterdam; *ML* I, 72.

Anken (Ancken) Hans, a Swiss Mennonite farmer-preacher and elder in the Emmental, b. 1673 or 1674 in Spiez, canton of Bern, who was deported to Holland July 13, 1711, at the age of 37, with his wife, 30, a son, and two daughters. They were placed in the *Neuenburger* boat, on which he was supervisor with Peter Lehner. He settled with several families near the Dutch town of Groningen (*q.v.*), where he founded a small congregation, and served as their first preacher. When he purchased his house, called the "large monastery," its architecture offended some as being "too ostentatious," which resulted in a division of the

congregation into Old and New Swiss (about 1720). Anken was the head of the *Nieuwe Zwitsers* (*q.v.*). NEFF.

Müller, *Berner Täufer,* 319, 321, 323; J. Huizinga, *Stamboek of Geslachtregister van de Nakomelingen van Samuel Peter (Meihuizen) en Barbara Fry* (Groningen, 1890) 59; *ML* I, 72.

Anklam, Joachim van, from 1722 a deacon of the Lamist congregation at Amsterdam, was an active member of the Dutch *Commissie voor Buitenlandsche Nooden* (Committee for Foreign Needs) 1724-44; he did much in behalf of the oppressed Mennonites in Lithuania and Prussia, and took care of the financial problems of the colonization of the refugees in Wageningen (*q.v.*). (*Inv. Arch. Amst.* I, Nos. 1076, 1237, 1630, 1633; II, 2, Nos. 717, 725, 737a.) He is also called Jochem Hansz van den Eynde; his parents came from Danzig to Amsterdam. Joachim was baptized here Nov. 10, 1690. vDZ.

Anna, the wife of Gerryt Roggens, of Groningen, Holland, an Anabaptist martyr, drowned on June 11, 1535, at Utrecht in the Netherlands. (*Berigten Hist. Genootschap, Utrecht,* IV, II, 1851, 139.) vDZ.

Anna Bueckhorst, born at Halteren, an Anabaptist martyr, drowned at Utrecht in the Netherlands on June 11, 1535. *Berigten Hist. Genootschap, Utrecht,* IV, II, 1851, 139.) vDZ.

Anna Cantiana, an Anabaptist martyr, burned at the stake in 1550 in London. The *Martyrs' Mirror* relates that she, like Johan Knel (*q.v.*), who was executed the same year, held Menno Simons' view on the incarnation; viz., that Christ did not receive His human body from Mary. For this information van Braght refers to the preface of the *Oude Offerboek* of 1615. (*Mart. Mir.* D 99, E 498.) vDZ.

Anna von Freiburg (also Frieburg), an Anabaptist martyr who was drowned at Freiburg (apparently in Switzerland) in 1529. The *Martyrs' Mirror* gives a moving prayer of sincere faith which she spoke before her death. In the *Ausbund* (*q.v.*) a song (No. 36) is attributed to her, which begins, "Ewiger Vater vom Himmelreich, Ich ruf zu Dir gar inniglich," and which is printed in Wackernagel, *Kirchenlied* III, 487. But manuscripts of the Hutterian Brethren make it clear that the author was Ursula Helriglin, who was imprisoned in St. Petersburg in Tirol in 1538, at the age of 17, and not released until 1543. NEFF.

Mart. Mir. D 26, E 434; Beck, *Geschichts-Bücher,* 157; Wolkan, *Lieder,* 178; Wolkan, *Gesch.-Buch,* 194; *ML* I, 72, 696.

Anna Jansdochter and **Geertruydt Jansdochter,** sisters, Anabaptist martyrs in the Netherlands, beheaded at The Hague on Feb. 4, 1534, because they had been rebaptized. They were from Alkmaar in the Dutch province of North Holland. Further information is lacking. (*Inv. Arch. Amst.* I, No. 8, 11; *DB* 1909, 10; *ML* II, 390.) NEFF, vDZ.

Anna (An[ne]le) Malerin and Ursula Ochsentreiberin were among the first Anabaptist martyrs in Tirol. They were both taken captive with some other worshipers on Aug. 15, 1529, at a service on a meadow near Mills, not far from Hall on the Inn, by the judge of Hertenberg. Whereas most of the prisoners signed a recantation and accepted church penance Anna and Ursula remained true to their faith. They were therefore condemned to death in Hall and drowned in the Inn. Their steadfastness in the face of death evoked general admiration. The two women are commemorated in a song, "An unser Frauentag, das geschah," in which their capture is related.   HEGE.

Mart. Mir. D 28, E 437; Beck, Geschichts-Bücher, 90; G. Loesche, Archiv. Beitr. zur Gesch. des Täufertums u. des Prot. in Tirol (Vienna, 1926) 30; J. Loserth, Der Anabaptismus in Tirol (Vienna, 1892) 473; the song is found in Wolkan, Lieder, 14-16, and in Die Lieder der Hutt. Brüder (Scottdale, 1914) 46-47; ML III, 3.

Anna Matijs van Doncksdochter, an Anabaptist martyr, born at Loenen, drowned at Utrecht in the Netherlands on June 11, 1535. (Berigten Hist. Genootschap, Utrecht, IV, II, 1851, 139.)   vDZ.

Anna von Oldenburg, wife of Count Enno I of East Friesland (1528-40); after his death she became the regent (1540-62). She was evidently aware of the great economic advantage of having Mennonite settlements in the country and therefore sought to protect them. In 1543 she received an imperial letter (Charles V) concerning the Anabaptists. In the fall of the same year her brother-in-law, John, duke of East Friesland, brought her another letter from the emperor, in which he asked for information about David Joris (q.v.) and possible measures against the Emden Anabaptists. She apparently paid little attention to it.

In 1544, in a sharp letter from Maria, sister of Charles V, and regent of the Netherlands, to East Friesland, Anna was ostracized and excommunicated as an offender against divine and imperial majesty, because she harbored those who had been declared to be enemies of God and the emperor. This made a deep impression. Immediately the government issued a mandate that all members of any sect, especially Anabaptists, were to leave the country at once, and that on penalty of severe punishment no one should venture to rent them houses and fields, land and goods, or offer them shelter. This mandate created consternation among the Anabaptists. When it appeared that they were on the point of leaving, John a Lasco (q.v.) intervened and procured from the duchess a new order, banishing only chronic agitators and fanatics among the Anabaptists. Nevertheless many peaceful Anabaptists emigrated, including Menno Simons (q.v.). The above-mentioned mandate of 1544 is the first known document to use the term "Mennist."

On April 6, 1549, Anna issued a new edict against the Anabaptists, forbidding, on penalty of corporal punishment and confiscation of goods, any inhabitant of the realm to aid the Anabaptists in any manner. But it was apparently not strictly carried out. When she was charged with offering Anabaptists a friendly reception contrary to imperial instruction, she replied that his Majesty was poorly informed about the Anabaptists. Until her death Anna remained favorable to the Mennonites. (J. P. Müller, Die Menn. in Ostfriesland, Emden, 1887, ML I, 72.)   NEFF.

Anna-Parochie, Sint (St.), a village in the Dutch province of Friesland, northwest of Leeuwarden, formerly also called simply Annakerk. The village is built on land reclaimed from the Middenzee, which was dammed up in 1505 and was called Het Bildt; three villages were built on it, St. Anna-Parochie, St. Jacobi-Parochie, and Lieve-Vrouwen-Parochie. Leenaert Bouwens baptized a total of 197 persons in Het Bildt between 1563 and 1582, many of whom were no doubt residents of St. Anna; hence it is thought that a congregation dates to that time. The congregation was called Het Bildt in the early period; the name St. Annakerk was not used until 1644. For a time there were two congregations. One, which died out between 1757 and 1759, belonged to the Jan Jacobsgezinden group. The other, which had a subsidiary in the neighboring Oudebildtzijl (q.v.), had 18 members about 1700. Nothing is known about the history of this congregation in the 18th century. In 1808 the congregation of St. Anna-Parochie was dissolved; the church was torn down and the few remaining members joined the small but now independent Oudebildtzijl. After 1806 the meetinghouse was used for various purposes. In 1808-12 it lodged a platoon of French soldiers; finally it was torn down in 1869. In 1871, however, a new congregation was founded in St. Anna-Parochie and a church built in the next year. In 1873 the congregation called H. Ens as its first minister. From 1881 to 1896 St. Anna-Parochie was united for preaching service with Berlikum (q.v.).

At the time of the reorganization in 1871 there were 30 members; in 1898 there were 45 with 40 catechumens; in 1950 there were 159 with 50 catechumens. Since its restoration the congregation has been served by the following ministers: H. Ens, 1873-80; J. de Stoppelaar, 1880-81; with Berlikum, R. Kuperus, 1882-84; after a long vacancy P. Oosterbaan, 1898-1901; A. M. Cramer, 1901-4; H. Bakels, 1908-9 and 1911-16; W. H. toe Water, 1916-23; M. J. Kosters Gz, 1923-29; Miss M. T. Gerritsma, 1929-32; Miss C. Boerlage, 1933-41; M. van der Meulen, 1941-46; A. P. van de Water, 1948-50; since then Miss C. Schepman.

The congregation, composed largely of gardeners who are not wealthy, has a Sunday school for children, an organization for women, and one for the young people.   vDZ.

Inv. Arch. Amst. II, 1523; Blaupot t. C., Friesland, passim; DB 1872, 189; 1873, 189; 1874, 141; J. Loosjes, "Jan Jacobsz en de Jan Jacobsgezinden," Ned. Archief v. Kerkgesch. XI (The Hague, 1914) 225-26; H. J. Busé, "De verdwenen Dg gemeenten in Friesland," Vrije Fries XXII (Leeuwarden, 1915) reprint, 4-6; ML I, 73.

Anna Petersdochter, wife of Peter (van) Galen, an Anabaptist martyr, was strangled and hanged as an Anabaptist on May 21, 1535. In the summer of 1534 she was baptized by Gherijt van Benschop, and refused to recant her faith. (Grosheide, Verhooren, 66; Bijdrage, 61, 305.)   vDZ.

Annakerk, the old name for St. Anna-Parochie (q.v.).

Annales Anabaptistici, a scholarly compilation by the Zürich professor of church history Johann Heinrich Ottius (Otte) (*q.v.*), published in Basel, Switzerland, in 1672, still today a valuable source of information about the Anabaptists. That such a relatively dispassionate recording could be published and was also read, may be taken as a sign that toward the end of the 17th century, with the coming of Pietism, a certain lively interest in the story of the "heretics" and their earnest Christianity had arisen among the Protestants. G. Arnold's *Kirchen-und Ketzer-Historie* (1699) was a still stronger expression of this trend. Of course, Ottius' intentions did not yet go quite that far. What he wanted to do was a first presentation (as objective as possible) of the things which then were summarily called "Anabaptist" and which today could perhaps better be described by the collective term "the left wing of the Reformation," including not only the different branches of Anabaptism and Mennonitism, but also the Schwenckfeldians, Anti-Trinitarians, and all the many marginal sects of the first half of the 16th century. (Ottius lists not less than 77 different groups of so-called Anabaptists.) The later parts of the book (after 1550) concentrate more consistently on the Dutch Mennonites, the Swiss Brethren, and the Austrian Hutterites, since the other groups had more or less died out. Ottius presents in his book excerpts from a great number of sources in the form of annals year by year with but little comment of his own. He starts with the year 1521 (Müntzer, Storch, Zwickau Prophets), and ends with 1670-71, when the Dutch burghers interceded in vain with Swiss authorities on behalf of their persecuted brethren in Switzerland, and when Berne issued new edicts against the Anabaptists. The book is written entirely in Latin except for direct quotations from sources. The full title of the book is *Annales Anabaptistici hoc est, Historia Universalis de Anabaptistarum origine, progressu, factionibus & schismatis, paradoxis, tumultibus, colloquiis, pacificationibus, locis & sedibus, scriptis hinc illinc emissis, edictis & judiciis, ac quicquid præterea ad rem facere videtur. His præmissa prolegomena 1. Ad lectorem. 2. de variis Anabaptistarum fectis tractatio duplex. 3. collatio cum veteribus hæreticis. 4. de Donatistis. 5. quomodo tractandi ejusmodi homines; uná cum Indice copioso.*

To judge the reliability of this book, we have to study the sources used. Naturally only a selection can be presented here, but it will suffice to show that very little was available in print to the learned author which can be called favorable to the Anabaptists, or at least objective. This is part of the list: Bullinger (Zürich, 1530-60) (*q.v.*); Guido de Bréz and Austro-Sylvius (Netherlands, 1585) (*q.v.*); Dooreslaer (Netherlands, 1637) (*q.v.*); Chr. Andr. Fischer (the Catholic priest in Moravia, around 1600, archfoe of the Hutterites) (*q.v.*); Hoornbeek (Netherlands, 1653) (*q.v.*); Mehrning (Germany, 1647-48) (*q.v.*); Meshovius (Germany, 1617) (*q.v.*); Joh. Sleidanus (Germany, 1564); F. Spanheim (Netherlands, 1645) (*q.v.*) (one of the worst opponents of the Mennonites, partly responsible for the acts of the Swiss authorities); *Successio Anabaptistica* (Cologne, 1603) (*q.v.*). A few of his sources, however, were of a more positive quality such as the *Ausbund,* the Dutch martyr books of 1615 (Haarlem) and of 1617 (Hoorn), and the Colloquium of Frankenthal, 1571. From these and similar sources Ottius extracted a picture of the Anabaptists through a century and a half as objectively as possible. To a certain extent he actually succeeded in this endeavor in spite of his questionable sources. The book has 360 pages and a good index. It must have found quite wide attention, since it was quoted often by later historians in this field. R.F.

Anneken, the wife of Ydse Gaukes, an Anabaptist martyr, who was taken prisoner with eleven others by the Spaniards in Deventer, Holland, March 11, 1571, and was put into the Noordenberger tower. The other eleven were: her husband Ydse Gaukes, Dirk van Wesel and his wife Janneken, Herman de Verwer (Wever), Bruijn de Wever, Anthonis de Wever, Claes Opreyder, Lijsbeth Somerhuys, Catharina Somerhuys, Lijntgen Joris and her daughter Trijntgen. At first only four of the twelve remained faithful: the women all became unfaithful but afterwards they returned to the faith. On May 24, 1571, some monks came to inform the prisoners that they were to be executed and to warn them; they remained until midnight, trying in vain to persuade them to deny their faith. The next day the execution was to take place, but that day only Anthonis and Bruijn were beheaded. Anneken was burned some time later, but before June 16, together with Dirk, Harmen, Janneken, and the Somerhuys sisters. At that execution suddenly there came about a *swaer gedruysch* (loud crash), as van Braght tells it, as of thunder, so that the onlookers were thrown down and smitten with fear. On June 16 also the last ones of this company, Ydse Gaukes, Claes Opreyder, Lijntgen and her daughter, were burned at the stake; all remained faithful in their great suffering. (*Mart. Mir.* D 552-54, E 885-88; *DB* 1919, 29-37.) vDZ.

Anneken Boens, an Anabaptist martyr, daughter of Matthys Boens of Antwerp, cousin of Truyken Boens (*q.v.*), baptized as was also Truyken, by Gillis van Aken (*q.v.*), was drowned at Amsterdam March 3, 1550. (Vos, *Antwerpen,* 379; Grosheide, *Bijdrage,* 308.)

Anneken Botson, an Anabaptist martyr, was seized with her daughter Janneken and a fellow believer, Maeyken Pieters, at Neustadt, "in the Lutzelburgerland," Luxembourg, in 1585, and taken to St-Veit. Because they refused to recant they soon suffered martyrdom. "But they went like innocent sheep to the place of sacrifice and died undismayed," records the Anabaptist chronicle. These martyrs were not yet in the *Groot Offerboek* of 1613. (*Mart. Mir.* D 753, E 1060; *ML* I, 250.) O.H., vDZ.

Anneken van Brussel, an Anabaptist martyr whose true name was Tanneken Leonets. She was unmarried. Four fellow believers (Jacob de Schoenlapper and his wife, Anneken Walraven, and

Grietge, a widow of Brussels) were burned at the stake with her at Antwerp on Pentecost, May 22, 1575, with screws on their tongues. At the close of the account in the *Martyrs' Mirror* it is said that these witnesses produced many writings in their captivity, which were, however, destroyed in the revolt against the Spanish on Nov. 4, 1576.

NEFF, vDZ.

Mart. Mir. D 693, E 1007; Génard, *Antw. Arch.-Blad* XIII, 193, 202; XIV, 96-97, No. 1083; *ML* I, 73.

Anneke(n) Gerrits (Anna Gherytsdochter van Ast or van Dordrecht), the wife of Ghysbert Jansz van Woerden, an Anabaptist martyr, baptized by Gillis van Aken, was executed at Amsterdam on Jan. 15, 1550, along with Trijntje van Dorsten (*q.v.*). She gave her life for her faith by drowning. (Vos, *Antwerpen*, 387; Grosheide, *Bijdrage*, 157, 308.)

vDZ.

Anneken Hendriks (Anna Heyndriksdochter, also called Anneke de Vlaster), an Anabaptist martyr of Friesland, who was living in Amsterdam. Through treachery she was taken prisoner by the city officials. Because she held fast to her faith, she was severely tortured on Oct. 27, 1571, with the intent of learning from her the names of other Mennonites. But even this ill treatment could not make her recant, and consequently she was put to death on the town square (Dam) on Nov. 10, 1571. The execution took place in an unusually cruel manner. Anneken was tied to a ladder; her mouth was filled with gunpowder, and in this condition she was carried from the city hall to the ignited stake and thrown into the flames. She was 53 years old and an ordinary woman who could neither read nor write. In her sentence she was condemned because "she was married according to Mennonite custom, and at night in a country house." The *Martyrs' Mirror* records that there is a song concerning her, but gives no further information, apparently meaning the song found in the Dutch hymnbook *Veelderhande Liedekens* (1569), which begins "Ick moet u nu gaen verclaren, Watter t'Amsterdam is geschiet" (I must now declare to you, What took place at Amsterdam). (*DB* 1908, 51; *Mart. Mir.* D 537-38, E 872-74; Grosheide, *Bijdrage*, 310; *ML* II, 282.)

vDZ.

Anneken vanden Hove (Anna Emels, also called Anneken uyt-den Hove), an Anabaptist martyr, was a domestic servant for two ladies by the name of Ramparts at Brussels, Belgium. In company with these ladies she attended the Mennonite meetings. In December 1594 all three were imprisoned. Because the two ladies recanted they were set free, but Anneken would not renounce her faith. Finally she was condemned to be buried alive. Van Braght related in detail this horrible execution which took place a mile from Brussels on July 19, 1597. Anneken, who was unmarried and 48 years of age at the time of her execution, was the last victim of the Inquisition in the southern Netherlands (now Belgium). With her the long series of martyrdoms there came to an end. Soon after her execution a song about her martyrdom was published (a copy of this song is extant in the Dutch Royal Library

at the Hague) with the title, *Een nieu Liedeken van een jonge Dochter die binnen Breussel levendich gedolven is, . . .* It begins, "Fij Cain wreet moordadich, Fij Pharo obstinaet" (Fie, cruel and murderous Cain, fie, obstinate Pharaoh), and has 21 stanzas; according to this song Anneken was 33 years old; this, however, is not correct. In 1610 (place and printer unknown) a pamphlet of four pages was published: *Een corte Beschrijvinghe van een jonghe Dochter, die tot Brussel levendich ghedolven is om het Woordt des Heeren int jaer 1597*, which was revision in prose, followed by the song itself. The booklet, published in 1601 at Antwerp by Jérôme Verdussen in the French language: *Brief et Veritable Discours de la Mort d'aucuns Vaillants et glorieux Martyrs . . .*, also speaks of the death of Anneken, though the Roman Catholic author thinks the execution was right. About Anneken's death Jacques van Vivere wrote a song: *De Uyt-spraecke van Anna Uyt Den Hove . . .* (Leiden, 1598). The Reformed martyrbook of Haemstede, *Historie der Martelaren* (edition of 1609) also includes this Anabaptist martyr; its account differs somewhat from that of the Mennonite martyrbooks, including van Braght, *Martyrs' Mirror*. The Haemstede version seems rather to agree with the above song and the prose report. (*Mart. Mir.* D 792-99, E 1093; Verheyden, *Courtrai-Bruxelles*, No. 168, p. 105; *ML* II, 353.)

vDZ.

Anneken Jans, a Dutch Anabaptist martyr, also known as Anneken wt den Briel, because she once lived there, and also called Anneken van Rotterdam, because she suffered death by martyrdom there, was a follower of David Joris (*q.v.*). According to Nippold (*David Joris,* 56), she had greatly influenced this Anabaptist preacher. As heiress of a considerable fortune, she sacrificed everything for her faith, and at the age of 24, as she herself said, was baptized with her husband, Arent Jans, by a Meynert in their home at Brielle in the Dutch province of South Holland. She fled to England in 1536, where her husband died, and in 1538 returned to Holland in order to settle her affairs and to meet David Joris in Delft. Because she was singing a hymn she was arrested in December 1538 at Rotterdam as she was about to step into the boat for Delft together with her traveling companion and sister in the faith, Christina (*q.v.*). She was charged with sectarianism, openly confessed her faith, and at the age of 28 was drowned in Rotterdam on Jan. 24, 1539. The *Martyrs' Mirror* relates that on her way to the place of execution she addressed a petition to the crowd, asking that someone adopt her 15-month-old son Esaias (Isaiah), to whom she would give a full purse. A baker who had six children volunteered. At home he had to endure his wife's displeasure, but was richly blessed with earthly goods and left great possessions to his children. This Esaias de Lind, Anneken's son, became a brewer and mayor of Rotterdam (not Mennonite).

A letter dated 1538 (1536 according to Vos) is also given in the *Martyrs' Mirror*, which Anneken wrote to D. J. (obviously David Joris), urging him with warm, inspiring words to faithful performance of his office. "For as the rain refreshes the earth and the dew refreshes the flowers of the field and gives them a fragrance dear to men, so your admonition, preaching, and instruction gives men life, food, and taste, though it contains no high wisdom, and shows them the way of the perfect wisdom of God, whereby they grow into the stature of a perfect man in Christ Jesus, our Lord. What beauty you have with others, and what goodness above others! Such as these increase in virtue more and more, until they approach God's perfectness and are openly seen with Him in Zion, for which we long with sighs to see the end of our faith." The letter closes with the words, "O thou sanctified of the Lord, be brave, let nothing dismay you; yet a little while, and He will come and show us a sample of His glory, for the judgment of the world, but to His and our glorification."

Still more important is Anneken's will addressed to her son Esaias, which was printed in 1539, the year of Anneken's death, and repeatedly thereafter; it is found in the oldest edition (1562) of the Dutch martyr book, *Het Offer des Heeren,* and in all the following martyr books, including the *Martyrs' Mirror.* The city library of Hamburg has a copy of the first printing in 1539. J. G. de Hoop-Scheffer says of it (in *DB* 1870, 51), "The testament is one of those broadsides and short popular writings which, scattered among the people by the hundreds and thousands after 1520 have in part been destroyed and burned, but often carefully preserved and passed on from generation to generation as a precious heirloom. Some of them, like the above, have been collected by the Amsterdam Mennonite Library and saved from destruction." Nippold judged it to be "one of the most worthy witnesses of the self-denying, sacrificing, steadfast piety of the Anabaptists." We have here, indeed, a glorious confession of faith and evidence of faithful mother love, which deserves to be better known.

An unknown poet worked this confession into a beautiful song which was admitted into the oldest hymnbooks of the Anabaptists, the Dutch *Het Offer des Heeren* and the German *Ausbund,* No. 18. Anneken was the author of a song that appeared early enough to be included in David Joris's *Geestelyck Liedtboecxken* (extant in the Royal Library in The Hague) and afterwards included in other Mennonite songbooks. The song begins: "Ick hoer die Basuene blasen" (I hear the trumpet blow). This remarkable song is an exception in Mennonite martyr literature in that we find here in no mistaken terms the thought of vengeance, especially in the eleventh and twelfth stanzas. The saints are to wash their feet in the blood of the ungodly and are prompted to play a new song on their harps because God "comes to pay" (*kumpt om te betalen*), i.e., to punish the ungodly. This song is printed by Wackernagel, *Lieder,* p. 82, No. 5.   NEFF, vDZ.

Offer, 70-77; *Mart. Mir.* D 48-50, 143-45, E 453; Fr. Nippold, "David Joris von Delft," in *Ztscht für die hist. Theol.,* 1863; K. Vos, "Anneken Jans," in *Rotterdamsch Jaarboekje* (1918) 14-18; Wolkan, *Lieder,* 65, 129; *ML* I, 73.

Anneken Jans, an Anabaptist martyr of Woerden in the Dutch province of South Holland, was living in Middelburg, in the Dutch province of Zeeland, where she was burned at the stake on Dec. 3, 1571, because she had been rebaptized, and notwithstanding the teaching of learned theologians "remained stubborn and obstinate in her error, false opinions, and heresy."   vDZ.

K. R. Pekelharing, "Bijdr. v. d. Gesch. der Herv. in Zeeland," *Archief Zeeuwsch Gen.* VI, 1866, 95.

Anneken van Leiden, "who was put to death with Mariken," is identical with Annetgen Symonsdochter (*q.v.*).

Anneken Ogiers, also known as Anneken Jans and Anneken Boogaerts, an Anabaptist martyr. She was the daughter of Jan Ogiers and the wife of Adriaen Boogaerts, a potter, who lived at Haarlem in the Dutch province of North Holland, *in den Witten Valk* (at the White Falcon). Anneken was baptized about 1553 at Amsterdam; for this reason she was imprisoned and when she was unwilling to forsake her faith, was condemned to be drowned. This sentence was carried out in 1570 (date unknown) in the town hall at Haarlem (thus not in public). (*Mart. Mir.* D 505, E 844; *ML* III, 294.)   vDZ.

Anneken (Tanneken) van Roosbroecke, an Anabaptist martyr, born at Lier in Brabant, Belgium, burned to death Jan. 31, 1551 (not 1550 as recorded in both *Offer des Heeren* and *Martyrs' Mirror*), at Lier, together with Govert (Godevaert Mertens), Gillis (Gielis van Aerde), and Mariken (Marie Vlaminx). Anneken was treated indecently by the executioner. She remained loyal in her faith, and at the strangling-post still sang: "Op U betrou ick, Heere." Concerning Anneken and her three fellow martyrs a song was written by the martyr-to-be, Hans van Overdam (*q.v.*). This song begins: "Alsmen schreef duyst vijfhondert, En daer toe noch vijftich jaer" and was included in the *Veelderhande Liedekens* of 1569, and from 1570 on in the *Liedtboecxken van den Offer des Heeren* (also in Wackernagel, *Lieder,* 126, and in Wolkan, *Lieder,* 63).   vDZ.

Offer, 568-77; *Mart. Mir.* D 96-97, E 494 f.; *Bibliographie,* No. 23; Génard, *Antw. Arch.-Blad* VIII, 393; XIV, 18-19, No. 197; *ML* I, 73.

Anneken van Rotterdam: see **Anneken Jans.**

Annetgen Antheunis was tried on the rack on Feb. 20, 1558, at Rotterdam, because she adhered to the Anabaptist faith. She stated that she was 30 years old and was born at Buren in the Dutch province of Gelderland, and had been baptized in Rotterdam by Leenaert Bouwens. She was given a death sentence, but it is not known that the execution was performed. (*Mart. Mir.* D 191-92, E 574; *DB* 1905, 172; *ML* I, 74-75.)   NEFF, vDZ.

Annetgen Symonsdochter (also called Anneken van Leiden), an Anabaptist martyr, who, according to the Leiden *Sententieboek* (record of sentences), was condemned for heresy on Nov. 24, 1552, and was drowned the same day at Leiden, in the Dutch province of South Holland. In a song composed about her and other martyrs, "Ick mach wel droeflijck singen, In desen tijt van noot" (I well may sing with grief In this time of need) (*Liedtboecx-ken van den Offer des Heeren*, No. 6), it appears that at the time of the trial Annetgen spoke very freely concerning her belief. She was a young woman, unmarried, and not yet baptized. The inquisitors offered to release her if she would obediently return to the Roman fold, but Annetgen refused and spoke scoffingly that she in no sense wanted anything to do with the Catholic Church and its "bread-god" (*brootgodt*). She endured the grim ordeal of martyrdom with courage. (*Offer*, 526, 578; *Mart. Mir.* D 132, E 526; Wolkan, *Lieder*, 61; *ML* I, 73-74.)   NEFF, vDZ.

Annovka, an important and thriving leased village of the Molotschna Mennonites in the Crimea near Kurman-Kemeltchi in Russia, with a combined church building and schoolhouse. The inhabitants were members of the Mennonite Brethren church at Spat-Schöntal in the Crimea. (Friesen, *Brüderschaft*, 470; *ML* I, 74.)   NEFF.

Annweilertal, the beautiful valley of the Queich near Annweiler, a town not far from Landau in the Palatinate, Germany. Ernst Müller's (*Berner Täufer*, 209) list of Mennonite congregations in the Palatinate above Mannheim mentions a Mennonite church at Annweiler, two hours south of Landau, with 20 families. The preachers were Christian Eicher and Steffen Affholter. It is obviously the St. Johann congregation.   NEFF.

Anointing with Oil. It is recorded in Mark 6:13 that the twelve apostles "anointed with oil many that were sick, and healed them." The Epistle of James (5:14, 15) instructs the elder to pray over the sick man who requests help, "anointing him with oil in the name of the Lord: and the prayer of faith shall save the sick, and the Lord shall raise him up; and if he have committed sins, they shall be forgiven him." The only known Anabaptist mention of this anointing is the denial of its identity with the Roman Catholic sacrament of extreme unction (*Mart. Mir.* E 423, 778, 779). The most careful exegetical analyses of the passage in James are those of Henry Alford in his commentary, *The Greek Testament*, and J. A. Bengel in his *Gnomon*. D. L. Moody, the American revivalist, was anointed in his last illness at his request. The Church of the Brethren observes the anointing of the sick with oil.

In several branches of the Mennonite brotherhood, since the 19th century at least, sick members occasionally request the ministers to come to their bedside and pray for their recovery, accompanying the prayer with the symbolical anointing taught in James 5. This is true of the C.A.M., the E.M.B., the C.G.C., the K.M.B., the O.O.A., the O.O.M., the U.M.C., and occasionally in the M.B. group. It was not altogether unknown among some of the Mennonite congregations in Russia, though seldom practiced. The G.C.M. group does not observe this practice.

The rite usually includes most or all of the following: singing of a stanza or two of a hymn; the reading of the relevant passage in James 5; an interpretation of the passage; a discussion of the

meaning of prayer; opportunity for the sick person to give an expression of his faith, or to confess sin, the application of olive oil to the sick person's head; and prayer accompanied by the laying on of hands. The rite is intended to give expression to the sick Christian's faith (he himself is to call for the ceremony) and to stimulate his faith in the healing power of God. The oil is a mere symbol of this healing power. It is normally expected that the ill person has the assurance that God wishes to raise him up, though this is not universally required; it may be merely the expression of a general faith coupled with a resignation to God's will. It is never a mandate to God demanding immediate or ultimate healing. Nor is it intended as a preparation for death. The James passage applies to illness, not bone fractures, congenital abnormalities, loss of limbs or extremities, etc.

Since the Reformed Mennonites, who separated from the Lancaster Conference (MC) in 1812, do not observe the practice, and since the U.M.C. and the O.O.M. bodies, who separated from the M.C. 1870-80, do observe its practice, it is possible that the Old Order Amish and the Mennonites (MC) began to anoint with oil during the 19th century as a result of the renewed interest in Bible study which the brotherhood experienced in that era. There is no record of this practice among any of the Mennonites of Europe.

The administration of the rite in the M.C., O.O.A., C.A.M., and O.O.M. groups is usually reserved for the bishop or for the other ministers by his authorization. In such groups as the E.M.B., M.B., and U.M.C., any minister may anoint.

                                        J.C.W.

H. Alford, *The Greek Testament* (Cambridge, 1903) IV, 327; D. Attwater, *A Catholic Dictionary* (New York, 1942): "Anointing," "Chrism," "Extreme Unction"; J. A. Bengel: *Gnomon* (Philadelphia and New York, 1864) II, 722; Geo. R. Brunk, *Ready Scripture Reasons* (Scottdale, 1926) 102-7; Vergilius Ferm, *An Encycl. of Rel.* (New York, 1945): "Anointing," "Chrism," "Oils"; Daniel Kauffman, *Bible Doctrine* (Scottdale, 1914) 433-8; *idem*, *Doctrines of the Bible* (Scottdale, 1928) 424-8; *idem*, *Menn. Cycl. Dictionary* (Scottdale, 1937) 11; W. R. Moody, *The Life of Dwight L. Moody* (Revell, 1900) 551; *Mart. Mir.* E 423, 778, 779; J. C. Wenger, *The Doctrines of the Menn.* (Scottdale, 1950) 28.

Anolaima, Cundinamarca, Colombia, S.A., an evangelistic and educational center of the General Conference Mennonite Mission (GCM), of Colombia, located about 3 miles from Cachipay and about 50 from Bogota. In June 1948 Alice Bachert began evangelistic and social work in this center and soon had gathered around her a loyal group of believers. In January 1949 a day school was begun with the help of a trained teacher and as a result of this educational program as well as much evangelistic work the first group of five believers was able to be baptized on June 26, 1949.   G.S.

Anpleunis vanden Berghe, an Anabaptist martyr, who, according to *ML* I, 74, was a Dutch nobleman, forced to leave his country estate and to wander, because he had permitted the Mennonites to preach on his estate and had lodged some fellow believers. This information is only partly correct, because this martyr was not a nobleman, though he was a rather wealthy man, nor was he from Holland. According to the records he was an *agriculteur* (farmer) born at Zwevegem in Flanders. He was imprisoned at Kortrijk in Flanders and declared that he had been a member of the Anabaptist congregation there for several years. After cruel torture he was burned at the stake at Kortrijk on Dec. 17, 1568 (*Mart. Mir.* wrongly 1569, without exact date). His widow Kalleken (*q.v.*) was put to death on April 30, 1569. (*Mart. Mir.* D 406, E 758; *ML* I, 74; Verheyden, *Courtrai-Bruxelles*, 37, No. 20.)   vDZ.

Anshelm, Valerius, physician and city chronicler of Bern, Switzerland, born in Rottweil in Württemberg, died at Bern about 1545. He came to Bern in 1504, became a schoolmaster there in 1505, and city physician in 1520. Prosecuted by the government for his Lutheran views, he transferred his residence to Rottweil in 1525, but returned to Bern in 1528, and in 1529 received the commission to write the chronicles of the city "from the Burgundian war to this hour." He carried out his assignment with such skill and conscientious industry that his work is considered an outstanding source for the history of the Reformation period. In it he gives a truthful and benevolent judgment and description of the Anabaptists. Müller (*Berner Täufer*) states that Anshelm relates the account of the cruel execution of Michael Sattler in a tone very sympathetic to the Anabaptists, "having himself been a companion in suffering with Sattler while he lay in prison in Rottweil; whether it was Lutheranism he was suspected of, or Anabaptism, he does not say." (Anshelm, V, 185, anno 1527.) Anshelm's chronicles of Bern were published in a new edition by the Historical Society of the canton of Bern in 1884 under the title: *Die Berner-Chronik des Valerius Anshelm.* Vol. V (1896) covers 1523-29. (*ML* I, 74.) NEFF.

Anslo, Cornelis Claesz, b. in Amsterdam in 1592, died there in 1646, fourth son of Claas Claasz Anslo. The latter was born in 1555 in Anslo (now Oslo), Norway, and assumed the name of the city; died in 1632 in Amsterdam, where he settled in 1580; married Geertgen Jans in 1582 and was a preacher of the Waterlander Mennonite congregation. He was a cloth merchant and founded the Anslo-hofje (home for the aged), which still exists. Cornelis Anslo became a Waterlander preacher on July 14, 1617. Schijn calls him a very earnest, pious, upright, and intelligent preacher. His wealth enabled him to give liberally to the poor. In 1625 he became involved in a violent dispute with a fellow preacher, Nittert Obbesz, and published against him the pamphlet, *Dialogus of Zaamenspreekinge tusschen eenen waarheidszoekenden Neutralist genoemd Vrederik en een waterlandschen broeder* (Hoorn, 1626). Among his friends were Joost van den Vondel (*q.v.*), the great Dutch poet, and Rembrandt. Vondel wrote a poem for two weddings in the Anslo family: that of Gerbrand Anslo (son of Cornelis) in 1636 and that of Gerbrand's daughter Alida in 1658. Rembrandt painted several portraits of him. The widely known painting, "The Mennonite Preacher C. C. Anslo and a Widow" (or his wife), was purchased by the Prussian government

10

for a large sum and hangs in the National Gallery of Berlin. An etching of the same subject is in the Chicago Art Institute and one of Anslo alone is in the Fogg Museum of Art at Harvard University. The following verse by Vondel is about Anslo.

Ay, Rembrandt maal Cornelis' stemm!
Het sichtbre deel is 't minst van hem:
't Onsichtbre kent men slechts door d'ooren;
Die Anslo zien wil, moet hem hooren.

("O Rembrandt, draw Cornelis' voice! The visible part is the least of him: the invisible is known only by hearing; he who would see Anslo must hear him.")

Below Anslo's picture in an anteroom of the Singel Mennonite Church in Amsterdam are the following lines (in Dutch) by Andr. Spinniker: "Whoever looks at Anslo's picture, his heart is deeply moved by Anslo's fiery zeal evident in his eyes; yet could a brush make his voice heard, everyone's heart would be converted to virtuous living." K.V.

L. Hesta, "Cornelis Claesz Anslo," in *Gem.-Kal.*, 1898, 82-85 (with reproduction of the Berlin painting); Kühler, *Geschiedenis* II, 1, see Index; J. W. Muller, "De naam Anslo," in *Tijdschr. voor Nederl. Taal en Letterk.* XLVIII, 225-32; H. M. Rotermund, "Rembrandt and the Mennonites," *Menn. Life*, VII (1952) 7-10; DB 1865, 69; *Biogr. Wb.* I, 1937; *ML* I, 74.

Anslo, Reyer, nephew of the above, born in Amsterdam in 1626, died at Perugia, Italy, May 16, 1669, distinguished himself as a poet. He wrote: *155 Bijbelsche Printverbeeldingen; De Parijssche Bruyloft* (a tragedy); *De Martelkroon van Steven; Schilderkroon;* and *De Pest te Napels.* He was baptized by the Waterlanders in 1646, but in 1649 was won over to Catholicism by the Jesuits and went to Rome, where he took holy orders and entered the service of Cardinal Luigi Capponi.   K.V.

N.N.B. Wb. (1911) I, 153 f.; H. H. Knippenberg, *Reyer Anslo* (Amsterdam, 1913); *ML* I, 74.

Anthoenis Courtsen, from "Oerdorp in Friesland" (now Ureterp), was banned from the Dutch province of Friesland for blaspheming the Catholic sacrament. Afterwards he attended Anabaptist meetings including some at Leiden at the house of the Anabaptist preacher (*leeraar*) Adriaen de Goudsmid (*q.v.*), and was seized at Amsterdam at the beginning of May 1552. His trial lasted for months. From these court proceedings we incidentally hear many things concerning Mennonite songs. Anthoenis obtained from a tailor's journeyman in Workum the song, "O Godt, ich moet u claghen" (To Thee, O God, I deplore), and wrote it down in a book. This cannot be the poem concerning the martyrdom of Joost Verbeeck (Antwerp, 1561, *q.v.*) which begins with the same words. Anthoenis also possessed a *geestelick Liedtbouckxen* (book of spiritual songs) which contained many hymns. Which songbook this was, is not gone into further. From these documents it appears that "spiritual songs" were very numerous among the Mennonites, and that many compiled a collection of such hymns for themselves. Anthoenis did not become a martyr. He recanted, but this did not really save him from the executioner. On Jan. 16, 1553, he was beheaded in

Amsterdam. (*Inv. Arch. Amst.* I, No. 372; Grosheide, *Bijdrage,* 159-65, 390.)   vDZ.

Anthoenis Elberts, an Anabaptist martyr, was put to death May 14, 1535, at Amsterdam, along with ten other brethren. This execution was very cruel; before they were beheaded, they were cut open alive and their hearts removed from their bodies, and after the decapitation their corpses were quartered, and as a deterrent example to the people their heads were displayed on the top of poles. This Anthoenis and his fellow martyrs had taken part in an attack on Amsterdam on May 10, 1535. They had been stirred up by Jan van Geelen (*q.v.*), the ambassador of Münster (Grosheide, *Verhooren,* 63-64). The names of these martyrs do not occur in the older martyr books, nor does the *Martyrs' Mirror* include them. It is possible that no recollection remained, especially regarding these oldest martyrs in Amsterdam. Of the approximately 100 martyrs who were seized in Amsterdam and vicinity during the first years, only a very few are included in the martyr books. It is also possible that these persons were intentionally omitted from the martyr books because they were more or less Münsterite, and as such were not to be considered along with the nonresistant Mennonites, although by no means all of them had participated in the Münster atrocities. The martyr books were really not consistent in the inclusion or exclusion of such semi-Münsterites. However, the assertion of K. Vos (*DB* 1917, 170) that the martyrs included by van Braght on pages 412-15 (Dutch ed. of 1685), a total of 19 men and 17 women executed between Dec. 31, 1534, and July 7, 1535, were "without exception Münster-minded," is incorrect.   vDZ.

Anthonie Lacquart, an Anabaptist martyr, also known as Anthonis (Teunis) Keute (*q.v.*).

Anthonie (de) Rocke (or Antoine Rogne), an Anabaptist martyr, executed at Antwerp on June 10, 1558, the husband of the martyr Noëlle Mazille (*q.v.*). He was a weaver by trade. This Anthonie de Rocke is not the man called Anthonis (*q.v.*) by the *Martyrs' Mirror.* (Génard, in *Antw. Arch.-Blad* VIII, 444-47, 464; XIV, 24-25, No. 257.)   vDZ.

Anthonis, a martyr, was executed at Antwerp by the sword for the sake of Christ, together with Hendrik Leerverkooper and Dirck de Schilder in 1558. His name is found in the song, "Aenhoort Godt, hemelsche Vader" (Hear, O God, heavenly Father) (*Liedtboecxken van den Offer des Heeren,* No. 16). This martyr is identical with Antonis van Houtere (*q.v.*). (*Mart. Mir.* D 202, E 583; *Offer,* 565; Wolkan, *Lieder,* 63, 72).   vDZ.

Anthonis van Asselroye, a martyr, a Flemish Anabaptist preacher and elder, was tortured and executed for his faith in 1550. Another martyr, Peter Bruynen, who suffered death in Antwerp in 1551, confessed that he had been baptized by Anthonis van Asselroye upon the confession of his faith. This Anthonis van Asselroye, is identical with the elder, Theunis van Hastenrath (*q.v.*). (*Mart. Mir.* D 100, E 497 f.; *ML* I, 75.)   vDZ.

Anthonis van Cassele (also called Antheunis van Hellegoete or Anthonis van Gent), a cloth-shearer who was burned as a martyr on July 5, 1559. On the first Friday after Pentecost the following persons were taken prisoner in this town: Pieter Coerten, Kaerle Tancreet, Anthonis van Cassele, Hans de Vette, Proentgen, the wife of Kaerle, Jacob Spillebout, Abraham Tancreet, Maeyken Floris, Marcus de Smet, Hans de Smet, Maritgen (also called Miertgen or Mijntgen), the wife of Hans de Vette, and Tanneken, wife of Hans de Smet. All remained faithful and were burned at Gent. On July 5, 1559, the first four mentioned, then on Aug. 7 the next six persons, finally on June 27, 1560, the last two women mentioned were burned. There are two songs about these martyrs, namely, "Een liedeken van XII Vrienden van Gent" (*Liedtboecxken van den Offer des Heeren,* No. 14) and another song that begins with the words, "Een eeuwighe vruecht die niet en vergaat," found in *Veelderhande Liedekens* (1569).   NEFF, vDZ.

Offer, 348, 556-59; *Mart. Mir.* D 246, E 620; Verheyden, *Gent,* No. 58-67 and 73-74, pp. 25-26; *ML* I, 75.

Anthonis Claes (Cleys), an Anabaptist martyr, was drowned in a tub at the Steen prison at Antwerp on Jan. 26, 1560, together with three other brethren. He was from Dordrecht in the Dutch province of South Holland. His name is also found in a song, "Aenhoort Godt, hemelsche Vader" (Hear, O God, heavenly Father), No. 16 of the *Liedtboecxken van den Offer des Heeren.*   vDZ.

Offer, 567; *Mart. Mir.* D 270, E 640; *ML* I, 358; Wolkan, *Lieder,* 63, 72; Génard, *Antw. Arch.-Blad* IX, 6, 10; XIV, 28-29, No. 307.

Anthonis (Anthoon) Fockes, an Anabaptist martyr, executed for his faith at Leeuwarden in the Dutch province of Friesland on Dec. 13, 1554, along with Allart Jansz. He was put to death by drowning. He condemned all that was done by the Roman Catholic Church as idolatry.   vDZ.

Inv. Arch. Amst. I, 746; Reitsma, *Honderd jaren Kerkherv. in Friesland* (Leeuwarden, 1876) 63.

Anthonis Jacobssone, an Anabaptist martyr, not mentioned in martyr books, was burned alive at Antwerp on Jan. 20, 1553. (Génard, *Antw. Arch.-Blad* VIII, 421, 422; XIV, 20-21; No. 222.)   vDZ.

Anthonis (Teunis) Keute, an Anabaptist martyr, burned at the stake at Brugge in Flanders, on Dec. 11, 1561. According to Verheyden, he is to be identified with Anthonie Lacquart, born at Hondschoote in Flanders. (*Mart. Mir.* D 288, E 655; Verheyden, *Brugge,* No. 40, p. 50.)   vDZ.

Anthonis Schoonvelt, also named Thonis (Thuenis) van Waestene, an Anabaptist martyr, strangled and burned on the marketplace at Ieper, Belgium, in 1561. Along with several others he was captured in Ten Hoogensieken, near Ieper, and also remained true to his faith in spite of severe torture. Anthonis and the others spoke very freely and disrespectfully concerning the Roman Catholic Church and the "Sacrament of the Altar," calling the latter an idol. Anthonis occurs in the song, "Geroert ben ick van binnen" (I am moved within), which is to be found in the *Nieu Liedenboeck* of 1562 and in the *Liedt boecxken van den Offer des Heeren* of 1563, No. 23. It is reprinted by Wackernagel. (*Offer*, 605; *Mart. Mir.* D 285, E 652; Wackernagel, *Lieder*, No. 65, p. 141.) vdZ.

Anthonis Welsch, an Anabaptist martyr, journeyed from Germany to Italy with Franciscus van der Sach (*q.v.*) to visit a group of believers there. On the return trip they were apprehended at Capo d' Istria, about 100 miles from Venice, where they were initially examined and then taken by sea to Venice, arriving there on Sept. 1, 1562. Here they remained in prison two years, during which time they were frequently examined. Remaining steadfast in the faith, they were both condemned to death in 1564 and drowned in the sea at Venice. (*Mart. Mir.* D 298 f., E 664.) vdZ.

Anthonis de Wever, an Anabaptist martyr, was seized with eleven fellow believers on March 11, 1571, at Deventer, Holland, by the constables of Duke Alba (*q.v.*), and after severe torture was beheaded on May 25, 1571. See **Anneken**, the wife of Ydse Gaukes. (*Mart. Mir.* D 552-54, E 885; *DB* 1919, 29-37; *ML* I, 75.) Neff.

Anthonis Ysbaarts, an Anabaptist martyr, was burned at the stake for his faith in the year 1573 at Thielt in Flanders. He had previously been in the employ of the chief bailiff of Gent and in this capacity had been present at the execution of many Mennonites. He was later converted and joined the Mennonites. Shortly after his conversion while he was living in Thielt to supervise the affairs of some Mennonites who had emigrated to Friesland, he was taken captive. Efforts were made to divert him from his faith, but he remained steadfast. To a monk, who even after the sentence had been pronounced tried personally to move him to recant, he spoke as follows: "Leave me in peace, my mind is at ease and my departure at hand, for the clock that stands there will not strike more than once before I hope to have made my offering and to be at home with my Saviour, upon whom all my hope and trust rests." (*Mart. Mir.* D 674, E 991.) vdZ.

Anthonisz, Jan (Joannes Antonides): see **Theunis, Jan.**

Anthony, Ebenezer, son of Francis and Isabelle (Fackman) Anthony, b. Nov. 27, 1865, near the village of Kilsyth, Grey Co., Ont., grew up on the farm and attended public school. On Oct. 9, 1889, he married Harriet Alma French, to whom were born four children. He was converted in 1886, and in 1888 he entered the ministry of the Mennonite Brethren in Christ Church (now the United Missionary Church). He was ordained in 1891 and gave 21 years of active service to the ministry, holding pastorates in the Ontario Conference, and also at Brown City, Caledonia, and Greenwood, in the Michigan Conference. In 1895 he was appointed first Presiding Elder of the Michigan Conference, serving in this capacity for two terms of five years each (1895-1900, 1904-9).

He was the first foreign missionary of the Michigan Conference, and leader of the pioneer missionary party sent out by the Mennonite Brethren in Christ to Nigeria in 1901. He was invalided home in 1903, and never fully recovered from the disease which he had contracted. He was greatly used of God to stir up interest in foreign missions, particularly in the Michigan Conference.

He died April 6, 1913, at Brown City, Mich., and was buried in the Brown City cemetery. E.R.S.

Gospel Banner, April 17, 1913, 14; J. A. Huffman, *Hist. of the Menn. Brethren in Christ Church* (New Carlisle, Ohio, 1920) 222; E. R. Storms, *What God Hath Wrought* (1948) Ch. III.

Antidotum, the title of a poem by the Dutch poet Joost van den Vondel (*q.v.*), published in 1626 at Amsterdam, taking the part of Obbesz in the dispute between Hans de Ries (*q.v.*) and Nittert Obbesz (*q.v.*). The complete title is *Antidotum, Tegen het vergift der Geest-drijvers. Tot verdedigingh van 't beschreven woord Gods.* (Concerning the dispute see Kühler, *Geschiedenis* II, 1, pp. 142-75.) vdZ.

Antioch, Idaho: see **Nampa Mennonite Church.**

Antioch Church, located four miles southwest of Decatur, Ind., is a member of the Indiana Conference of the United Missionary Church. The church was organized in 1921 with Jacob Hygema as the first pastor. Since 1947 the minister has been Lloyd Null. In 1950 there were 33 members. E.R.S.

Anti-Trinitarianism, *encounter with Anabaptism and Mennonitism.* Anti-Trinitarianism, Arianism, Socinianism, the Polish or Minor Church, in America, Unitarianism—all these names indicate by and large the same attitude, the rejection of the doctrine of the Trinity (*q.v.*) and doubt or denial of the deity of Christ. It is theological or doctrinal rationalism, readily compatible however with an otherwise ethically strict way of life and serious religious concerns. Since the New Testament writers themselves, not yet using the term "Trinity," frequently use a language which can be construed as not clearly distinguishing between the Persons of the Godhead (*MQR* XII, 1938, 215), a rationalistically-minded student of the Scriptures might be induced to this kind of theological thinking. Like all reform-minded Christians of the 16th century, Anabaptists and Mennonites were also exposed to this temptation, primarily because of their inherent radicalism and their lay Christianity; but both groups consciously resisted this way, partly, at least due to their basic anti-intellectual (or anti-theological) frame of mind. Anti-Trinitarians were (and still are) intellectually ambitious, they like to speculate, i.e., to rely on their own reason, while Anabaptists prefer a simplicity of mind, pressing for genuine discipleship without too much theological reflection which can so easily spoil the readiness to act. R. H. Bainton (*Journal of Religion*, 1941, 124 ff.) calls Anti-Trinitarianism. "Left-Wing theology" which once cut across nearly all groups of the left-wing Reformation, and was even shared in the beginning by Luther and Calvin. Quiet, evangelical Anabaptism of the 16th century had very few brethren who forsook their first loyalties in favor of this type of "liberal" theology. Actually only two cases of such a defection are known: Ludwig Haetzer (*q.v.*) in the South who, however, had never been an Anabaptist in the stricter sense of the term (d. 1528), and Adam Pastor (*q.v.*) in the North who for just this attitude was excommunicated by Dirk Philips in 1547-58, most likely with the tacit consent of Menno Simons (J. Horsch, *Menno Simons*, 198). All other names of so-called Anabaptists, listed by Dunin-Borkowsky (*q.v.*) as "Unitarians before Faustus Socinus," prove faulty: either they were not Anabaptists or they were not Anti-Trinitarians. The case of Hans Denk has not been fully cleared, although there may be some ground for the charge and some modern Unitarian writers have claimed him as a forerunner of this movement (see F. L. Weis, *The Life, Teachings and Works of Johannes Denck*, n.p., 1925, and also his *Life and Teachings of Ludwig Hetzer*, n.p., 1930). As to the contention that Pilgram Marpeck leaned toward this theology, J. C. Wenger proved conclusively the exact opposite (*MQR* XII, 1938, 215 ff.). The fact, however, should readily be admitted that in their numerous doctrinal writings (*q.v.*) the Brethren touched the doctrine of the Trinity but slightly. They did so not because of doubt and rationalistic theology but because of their practical approach even to theological questions. But if we look at the records of their religious disputations (*q.v.*) or of the martyr trials, we immediately discover that the Brethren, when asked, openly and unconditionally professed their belief in the Holy Trinity. Among the hundreds of Dutch Anabaptist and Mennonite martyrs, only Herman van Vlekwijk (*q.v.*), executed at Brugge in 1569, was an Anti-Trinitarian.

The later Doopsgezinden of the Netherlands because of their broad-mindedness and rationalistic leanings were perhaps more exposed to such a deviation than the rural brethren in South Germany and Switzerland. And yet, Socinianism met at first no response whatsoever to its work among the Dutch Mennonites. In 1598, the Socinian (Polish) minister Ch. Ostorrodt visited Hans de Ries (*q.v.*), the outstanding leader of the Waterlanders, but without the slightest result. Kühler (*Geschiedenis* II, 52) explains this fact by the undeniable spiritualistic tendencies in Ries' Christianity which ran strictly counter to Socinian ideas. "Moreover, the ideal of a Christian discipleship was bound to wither away in the cool and sober atmosphere of Socinian teachings." It was almost a life-and-death question for the Doopsgezinden, though not always recognized as such.

It cannot be denied that during the second half of the 17th century the picture changed quite markedly in Holland. Poland, no longer tolerant, outlawed Socinianism and its members had to flee to many lands. A great number of them found a safe refuge and a hearty welcome in the enlightened Netherlands. In the meantime also the Doopsgezinden had softened down their principles, thus making possible a friendly encounter with the group from Poland. After all, in their practical behavior they had quite a bit in common. It was on the neutral ground of the Rijnsburg Collegiants (*q.v.*) that Mennonites and Socinians first met and became

better acquainted with each other. According to E. M. Wilbur (*A History of Unitarianism*, 567) the Collegiants had functioned as the agency through which Socinianism could "permeate" the Mennonite body by the end of the 17th century, at least to a certain extent. Wilbur also claims (585) that the affinity of the Socinians in the Netherlands was, on the intellectual and social side, primarily with the Remonstrants, but on the practical side definitely with the Mennonites. When in 1787 the Collegiants dissolved, most of their adherents joined the Mennonite Church. However, the main body of Dutch Mennonitism rejected Socinianism. (For a fuller treatment of the Socinian relations of the Dutch Mennonites see **Socinianism**.)

In the 19th century through the entry of German Rationalism and higher criticism into the Dutch theological schools where Mennonite pastors got their training, as well as in Dutch theology in general, the intellectual leadership of the Dutch Mennonites gradually abandoned almost completely the Trinitarian position for the Unitarian. With very few exceptions for more than two generations the Dutch Mennonite preachers were solidly Unitarian, holding indeed to extreme modernist positions. The middle of the 20th century finds them, however, in a marked swing back to the Trinitarian evangelical theology, particularly under the influence of Barth and Brunner. To some extent the theologically trained pastors of the northwest German churches at Emden, Crefeld, and connected groups followed identical trends with the Dutch churches with whom they were closely associated. However, nowhere else in Europe or America did Anti-Trinitarianism ever find lodgment or open expression.

The Minor Church in Poland sought also to come into contact with the Hutterite communities in Moravia; such attempts were made in 1568-70, 1590, and 1608-9 (*MQR* XXII, 1948, 155-59). The Poles admired the organization of the Bruderhofs (households or communes) while the Hutterites on their part had but little appreciation for their learned visitors, and remained aloof. Two epistles by Peter Walpot (*q.v.*) to the Polish Brethren (1571) are most revealing regarding the differences between the primitive Christian discipleship and unconditional obedience of the Hutterites on the one side, and the theoretical speculation and argumentation of the Poles on the other side (*Chronik*, ed. Zieglschmid, 440-58). Walpot likes to quote II Cor. 10:5 in defense of his position. Nevertheless, the repeated visits and the ensuing correspondence clearly indicate a continued interest on the part of the Poles in this model experiment of Christian community living. It is well to remember that the Poles, too, stressed strictness in life and nonresistance. But that did not impress the Hutterites who (according to Comenius) called these Unitarians "heathen" with whom they did not wish to have any dealings.

The above-mentioned Unitarian minister Ostorrodt tried also to make contact with the Swiss Brethren in Strasbourg, to which group he directed a long epistle or tract, 16 pages in print (Wotschke in *Arch. f. Ref.-Gesch.,* XII, 1915, 137 ff.). It is a highly interesting plea for his doctrinal position while at the same time fully acknowledging all the other religious and moral teachings of the Gospels. The Brethren then convened at a conference in Strasbourg in 1592, deciding upon the right answer. In a letter to the church in Poland they unequivocally rejected Ostorrodt's arguments. "Believing is not a decision of human reason but the acceptance of that which to reason is incomprehensible" (*MQR* V, 1931, 26, n. 136). That is Anabaptism's answer to the lure of Anti-Trinitarianism. It seems that Ostorrodt had his long epistle later printed, because we know that as late as 1654 Andreas Ehrenpreis, the outstanding Hutterite *Vorsteher* in Slovakia, rejected Ostorrodt's theses once again in a booklet extant only in several Hutterite mss. He seems to have been prompted to this rejoinder by a strange man, Dr. Daniel Zwicker, a Unitarian from Danzig, who for a short time had joined the Hutterite brotherhood. It remained an unsuccessful episode in every regard. No bridge could span the deep gap which separated Anabaptism from Anti-Trinitarianism. (See **Thessalonica, Trinity, Venice, Zwicker.**)   R.F.

R. Friedmann, "The Encounter of Anabaptists and Menn. with Anti-Trinitarianism," *MQR* XXII (1948) 139 ff.; E. M. Wilbur, *A Hist. of Unitarianism; Socinianism and its Antecedents* (Cambridge, 1946); Kühler, *Geschiedenis* I and II; *idem, Het Socinianisme in Nederland* (Leiden, 1912); J. C. van Slee, *De Gesch. van het Socinianisme in de Nederlanden* (Haarlem, 1914); S. Dunin-Borkowski, "Quellenstudien zur Vorgesch. der Unitarier des 16. Jahrh.," in *Stella Matutina* (Feldkirch, 1931); and the *MQR* articles quoted: *ML* I, 76.

Antoine Rogne: see **Anthonie (de) Rocke.**

Antonette Lievens, an Anabaptist, author of a song, "Aansiet, o Heer, onsen strijt groot," which gives her name in acrostic. Nothing else is known about her. The song is found in *Het Tweede Liedeboeck,* published by Nicolaes Biestkens (Amsterdam, 1583). (Wolkan, *Lieder,* 70.)   vDZ.

Antonides, Henricus (Hendrik Anthonieszoon van der Linden), also called Nerdaenus, after Naarden, his birthplace in the Netherlands, b. Feb. 13, 1546, d. March 14, 1614, at Franeker. He was a Roman monk until about 1563, was banned after his abdication, stayed in East Friesland where perhaps in 1573 he became a Reformed pastor at Dijkhuizen, then at Enkhuizen, Holland, in January 1579, and when the university at Franeker opened in 1585, he became a professor in theology there. He was an opponent of the Mennonites. He apparently studied the "heresies" of Menno Simons; in 1587 he had a debate at Loosdrecht with a certain Mennonite preacher called Cornelius. Also in East Friesland he caused the Mennonites trouble. A planned debate with Pieter van Ceulen (*q.v.*) was not held. He incited his students against the Mennonites and attacked them in his lectures and in his university sermons. One of his students was Johannes Bogerman (*q.v.*). Antonides also attacked Mennonites with his pen: in 1576 in his *Elenchus Anabaptisticus,* and in 1589 in three Latin lectures. In 1589 the Reformed Synod of Bolsward commissioned him to publish a new edition of Menno's *Fundamentboek*

and to provide it with comments. However, nothing came of this. (*Biogr. Wb.* VI, 64-71; C. Krahn, "Menno Simons' *Fundament-boek* of 1539-1540," *MQR,* October 1939.)   vDZ.

Antonides, Joannes, usually called Antonides van der Goes, after Goes, Holland, the place of his birth, May 3, 1647, d. Sept. 15, 1684, in Rotterdam. By his contemporaries he was regarded as one of the greatest poets, but that opinion is no longer held. His parents were simple members of the Mennonite congregation at Goes; his father, Anthoni Janssen, also tried to write verse. When Joannis was four years old, his parents moved to Amsterdam, where Joannis attended the Latin school and then worked in an apothecary shop. Later he studied medicine at the university of Utrecht and received his doctor's degree on June 5, 1674, after which he became a physician in Rotterdam. Antonides took no active part in the congregational life. It is not even certain that he joined that church, although Samuel Muller regards him as having been a member (*DJ* 1840, 113; *DB* 1899, 187).   vDZ.

Antonijn de Waele (also called Antheunis Behaghe), an Anabaptist martyr, was burned at the stake at the Vrijdagsmarkt in Gent on Nov. 9, 1563, together with Christiaen van Wetteren. He was born at Bassey (in Artois, France) and was by trade first a shoemaker and later a lacemaker. His name is found in a song of the *Liedtboecxken van den Offer des Heeren* (No. 13), "Alsmen schreef duyst vijfhondert jaer ende twee en 't sestich mede." (Verheyden, *Gent,* p. 30, No. 97; *Mart. Mir.* D 300, E 666; *Offer* I, 651.)   vDZ.

Antonis van Houtere, an Anabaptist martyr, who is not found in the martyr books, was executed at the Steen prison in Antwerp, on Oct. 8, 1558. He came from Weert in Brabant and had been rebaptized. His wife, Geertruydt, was put to death on Dec. 30 of the same year. (Génard, *Antw. Arch.-Blad* VIII, 450, 465, 469; XIV, 24-25, No. 266.)   vDZ.

Antonius (Antonie) Kistemaker was sent with Jacob Kremer, as a *Commissaris* (commissioner) to Münster (*q.v.*) by an assembly of Anabaptists in the Dutch province of Groningen in April 1534. When the two returned as messengers of the notorious Jan van Geelen (*q.v.*) to propagate Rothmann's book *Van den Wraecke* (*q.v.*), a revolt broke out in 't Zandt (*q.v.*) in the province of Groningen. Antonius, a native of Appingedam in the Dutch province of Groningen, soon afterwards went to East Friesland in Germany, where he was imprisoned.   vDZ.

Nicolai's *Inlasschingen,* in Bullinger's *Teghens de Wederdoopers,* in *BRN* VII, 362, 365, 369; Kühler, *Geschiedenis* I, 139, 143, 145; *DB* 1917, 119.

Antonius von Köln, "pious Antonius," one of the earlier Anabaptist leaders, worked from *ca.* 1533 to 1560 in the Lower Rhine region, a dealer in English linen by trade. He was not a brother of the Cologne Anabaptist, Gerhard von Westerburg, whose name was Arnt (C. A. Cornelius, *Berichte der Augenzeugen . . . ,* 293 and J. Habets, *De Wederdoopers* *te Maastricht,* 171). Thus Rembert was mistaken when he considered Antonius a brother of Gerhard von Westerburg (*Wiedertäufer . . .* 44 f., 434 f.). Antonius worked quietly in Jülich, viz., in Bracht, district of Brüggen (C. A. Cornelius, *Geschichte des Münsterischen Aufruhrs* I, 227). Occasionally he made contacts with Dutch Anabaptists. In 1542 he was ordained elder by Menno Simons and Dirk Philips, and took part in the conference at Emden (1547) and at Goch (1547) (Rembert, 500). In a disputation between the Brethren or Christian Brethren (the name assumed by the Anabaptists) and the Calvinists (church inspection committee appointed by the duke of Jülich) a difference on the doctrine of the incarnation became apparent between the Brethren and Antonius.

When the Brethren once more in writing contested Antonius' views, Antonius forwarded the letter to Dirk Philips, and asked for his opinion. Perhaps Antonius had already rejected the views of the Dutch; in any case in 1550 he left them. In 1550 he is mentioned as a leader of the Christian Brethren at Ratheim. (See **Gillis van Aken.**) The church had been permitted to gather there in peace under the protection of Heinrich v. Olmissen, called Mulstroe. Antonius lived in the castle of Mulstroe's widow in 1559; he was known for his "piety and sanctity." These brief notices are not sufficient to form a sketch of his character. Antonius was one of those Anabaptists who traveled over the country preaching and baptizing. He was also in England, probably not for purely business purposes. Dates of birth and death are not known. (The letter of Dirk Philips mentioned above is found in manuscript form in the Amsterdam Mennonite Library *Inv. Arch. Amst.* II, No. 1971 r.) In a Dutch list of elders (Vos, *Menno Simons,* 256) he is Thomas Antonius. **тD.K.**

Rembert, *Wiedertäufer,* 44 f., 434 f.; *BRN* VII, 50 f. (*Successio Anabaptistica*); K. Vos, *Menno Simons* (Leiden, 1914) 94; *ML* I, 76.

Antwerp (*Antwerpen*). In this city there was as early as the late Middle Ages evidence of heresy and opposition to the Roman Church. Since there were in the city many printing presses to spread the new ideas, the Reformation found early entry here. In 1519 Jacob Praepositus, prior of the Augustinian monastery, and Cornelis Grafaeus, the city secretary, promulgated Lutheran doctrine; and two monks from the Augustinian monastery, Hendrik Vos and Joannes van Essen, were burned as martyrs on July 1, 1523, in Brussels. In their memory Luther composed the song beginning, "Ein neuwes Lied wir heben an, Das welt Gott unser Herre."

Anabaptism also soon won adherents here, and by 1534 there was a large group. A proclamation of Feb. 12, 1535, named a number of them. The first Anabaptist to be executed was Jeronimus Pael, beheaded on Feb. 16, 1535. Jan Smeitgen or Smekens (*q.v.*), a preacher who had fled to Antwerp from Maastricht, was burned on May 24, 1537. At this time revolutionary Anabaptism (Münsterites) seems to have had a large following. Jan van Geelen (*q.v.*) visited Antwerp in 1534. The David Jorist

group also had a few adherents. But the peaceful Mennonites soon predominated. The history of the Anabaptists in Antwerp is hard to write. It is the very disturbed history of an extremely important Anabaptist center. Strada reports that the Mennonites had a larger following than the Lutherans, though less than the Calvinists. Morillon estimated the number of Mennonites in 1566 at 2,000. Many of them suffered a martyr's death. Very often torture was applied. In 1559, 15 Mennonites were in prison at the same time; in 1569 again a great number were taken prisoner when a service in Jan Poote's house was surprised. A *Liedeken* sings about no fewer than 72 martyrs put to death between 1550 and 1560 (*Offer,* 563-68). In 1573 the congregation, which was meeting in the house of Jan de Chordis, was overtaken; 35 persons were imprisoned, 28 of whom were executed. The congregation had its own midwife; thus the authorities were not informed what children were born (and remained unbaptized). During the severe persecutions many fled to foreign countries, to England (1552), to Emden, and especially to Holland. The parents of van den Vondel (*q.v.*) fled to Cologne (*q.v.*). The cross-examinations show that many were engaged in the textile industry. That a number of the executed were well-to-do is shown by the proceeds from their confiscated property.

In *Antwerpsch Archievenblad* XIV, P. Génard has compiled a list of persons who were sentenced in this city from 1521 to Aug. 6, 1577, for religious reasons (*ter cause van de religie*), i.e., heresy. In total there were about 1,700 persons, of whom 1,107 are referred to by name. Of the 1,107, at least 431 were Anabaptists. To this group of Anabaptists others may certainly be added, including some whose "heresy" is not defined, and also some whose names are not mentioned. Of the above-mentioned number of 431, who can be referred to definitely as Anabaptists, it is not clear what the results of the court were for 27; 159 escaped out of prison and were banned forever; 248 were put to death (170 men and 78 women).

Probably there were several congregations, which assembled in private homes. For a long time one of the meeting places was in the Kramersstraat near the Schuttersbron. *Weetdoeners* (notifiers) announced to the members where the meetings were to be held. The preacher Jan van de Walle confessed that he had attended a service where there were 50 persons and where 18 or 20 were baptized. They also assembled in the open outside the city. In 1566 a meeting of 300 brethren and sisters was overtaken.

In January 1566 the congregation had at least 16 preachers. Many elders worked here. The best known are Gillis van Aken (*q.v.*), who baptized a large number; Leenaert Bouwens (*q.v.*), who baptized almost 300 persons between 1554 and 1565; Joachim Vermeeren, Joost Verbeeck, Herman Timmerman, Hendrik van Arnhem, Paulus van Meenen, and Hans Busschaert (*q.v.*). Besides the elders there were also some important preachers: Jan van den Walle, Adriaen du Rieu, Hans Symons, Jelis Bernaerts, Jan van Ophoorn; with the exception of the last, all of these died a martyr's death in Antwerp.

Since Antwerp was so important as a Mennonite center in Belgium, it is natural that the preachers of the Flemish congregations, meeting in Gent about 1545, inquired of the' Antwerp group whether an elder might be available (A. L. E. Verheyden, "Mennisme in Vlaanderen," unpublished ms.).

When the conflict between Frisian and Flemish parties (1566-67) occurred in Friesland, whither many Mennonites from Belgium had moved, the elders and preachers from Antwerp repeatedly acted as a mediator—among others Hendrik van Arnhem, Hans Busschaert, and the preachers Hans Symons and Filips Bostijn. The Antwerp congregation was not divided, though not all the members judged the Frisian party with equal severity; but it favored the conservative practice of making any who transferred their membership from a non-Flemish congregation submit to rebaptism. Hans de Ries (q.v.), who was attracted to the Mennonites, did not become a member of the Antwerp congregation (Kühler, Geschiedenis I, 351) for that reason.

In the meantime (the date is unknown) a Waterlander congregation had also formed in Antwerp, in which Albrecht Verspeck (q.v.) was a preacher in 1576, who a little later emigrated to Holland. This congregation (like the one at Gent) was represented at the big Waterlander conference in Amsterdam in 1581. During the brief period when William of Orange was governor of Antwerp, the Mennonites had peace. He exempted them from the oath in 1566 (DB 1875, 96 ff.). After his withdrawal and with the coming of Alba the situation again became very difficult, as the severe persecution of 1573 proves. More and more of the Mennonites moved to the Netherlands, where the bloody persecutions were past. When the Spanish general Parma conquered the city on Aug. 16, 1585, there was a mass exodus, more than 35,000 inhabitants leaving Antwerp. For the most part they were Calvinists, but the last Mennonites also left the city. vDZ.

P. Génard, in Antw. Arch.-Blad VII, VIII, IX, X, XII, XIII, and XIV; K. Vos, De Doopsgezinden te Antwerpen in de sestiende eeuw (Comm. Royale d'Histoire de Belgique (LXXXIV); Bibliographie II, 639 ff., alphabetical list, and 798 (Anvers); DB 1872, 57; 1875, 95, 96-8; 1877, 82, 86, 87; ML I, 76.

Antwerpen, Een Liedeken van LXXII Vrienden Binnen Antwerpen Ghedoot Tusschen Tiaer LV en de LX (A Song about Seventy-two Friends Put to Death in Antwerp between the Years [15]55 and [15]60). This song appears in the Liedtboecxken van den Offer des Heeren as No. 16 (BRN II, 563-68) and begins with the lines: "Aenhoort Godt hemelsche Vader, Ons clagen in deser tijt" (O God, heavenly Father, Hear our pleadings in this time).

Concerning the 72 martyrs referred to here, see Génard, Antwerpsch Archievenblad XIV, 20. In this source most of them are named in reference to their places of birth; the song itself mentions their trades. The song was composed in 1560, and was already included in the second songbook (Een nieu

Liedenboeck) of 1562. This song is also mentioned by Wolkan, Lieder (63, 72). vDZ.

Antwort, Die, Eine Monatsschrift für Jung und Alt. This periodical was published by the Winkler Bible School, Winkler, Man., 1934-36, to give an "answer" to religious and moral questions and to stimulate the Bible schools and churches to blaze new trails in the Sunday schools. It served the ministers ,with exegetical articles and outlines. It was also to serve as a bond of union between the various Bible schools. Unfortunately it did not meet with the necessary response to make possible its continuance, particularly since the editor of the periodical, A. H. Unruh, was unable to devote the necessary time to the paper in addition to his work as a teacher. A.H.U.

Anwald, Hermann, a victim of the Anabaptist persecutions by the Swabian League. He was born in Jettingen, south of Burgau, was a servant of Eitelhans Langenmantel (q.v.) and like his master joined the Anabaptists. He was instructed by Hans Denk (q.v.) and Hans Hut (q.v.) and baptized by Hans Hut at Shrovetide 1527 at Augsburg. When the Anabaptists were arraigned before the magistrates in the fall of 1527, he reported to the council, but was dismissed. With his master, who was released from prison on Oct. 14, he went to Göppingen and from here he cared for Langenmantel's needs. Anwald had only recently been married to a maid of the Langenmantel home, who had also been baptized by Hans Hut (according to the testimony of Burkhard von Ofen). On April 24, 1528, Anwald and his wife Margaret were seized with their master at Leitheim. Although both recanted, they were executed on May 11, 1528, Hermann beheaded, and Margaret drowned. HEGE.

Fr. Roth, "Zur Gesch. der Wiedertäufer in Oberschwaben," in Ztscht des hist. Vereins für Schwaben und Neuburg, 1900; ML I, 76.

Anwil, a congregation of the Swiss Brethren in the canton of Basel (q.v.).

Anwohner, the German name commonly used for the landless (q.v.) Mennonites of South Russia who settled in little shacks on the outskirts of prosperous villages eking out a meager living. The literal meaning of the word is "living adjacent" and it implied the same as "across the tracks." The problem of this Mennonite proletariat arose for the following reasons: families were usually large, government regulations prohibited the subdivision of standard farms, surplus land was either not available or had already been distributed, and additional industries had not been sufficiently developed to absorb this labor. By 1860 nearly two thirds of the Molotschna families were landless or Anwohner. They were forced to become artisans, or farm hands, with a few acres of land for gardens, and had no voice in the conduct of secular government.

The problem of the landless was gradually solved by making all surplus land available to them, by dividing farms, by establishing a mutual aid system through which daughter settlements were established, and the development of industries. Nevertheless, most of the settlements continued to have a surplus population living as *Anwohner*. The Alexanderwohl village may be typical. In 1874 two fifths of the population were landless. At that time the pressure was relieved by a large migration to America. (See also **Agriculture** and **Industry**.)

C.K.

Apeldoorn, a town in the Dutch province of Gelderland (population in 1947 was 83,449, including 636 Mennonites), where there has been a Mennonite congregation since 1896. On Nov. 8, 1895, Joh. Hoekstra, a retired minister, and J. Noe, Gzn, J. C. Dirks, and J. H. Steghers HJzn, Mennonites living at Apeldoorn, decided to organize a congregation, since there were 61 Mennonites living there. On Feb. 6, 1896, the congregation was called into being and a church board appointed; 49 members had joined the congregation. J. P. van der Vegte of Blokzijl was called as minister, preaching his first sermon there on Aug. 23, 1896. The services were at first conducted in the church of the Dutch Protestant Union, but on Dec. 14, 1930, the congregation dedicated its own church.

J. P. van der Vegte served the congregation from 1896 to 1904; he was followed by E. M. ten Cate, 1904-25, who also served the Amersfoort congregation 1919-24; T. J. van der Ploeg, 1926-38; M. van der Meulen, 1939-42; A. P. van de Water 1942-46; S. H. N. Gorter, 1946-51; and R. J. Faber since 1951. In 1896 the membership was 49; in 1904, 109; in 1925, 300; in 1952, 327. The congregation has a women's organization and a youth circle. (*DB* 1896, 209; *Levende Steenen; 50 jaar Doopsg. Gem.,* Apeldoorn, 1946; *ML* I, 77.)

vdZ.

Apocrypha, the name commonly given to a series of Jewish writings composed 200 B.C.-A.D. 100, not included by either the Jews or the Protestants in the canonical (divinely inspired and authoritative) Scriptures of the Old Testament, though considered canonical by the Roman Catholic and Greek Orthodox churches and usually by them printed with and scattered through the Old Testament. In Protestant Bibles the Apocrypha was printed as a separate collection between the Old and New Testaments, appearing in all English Bibles up to 1827 and commonly printed in the Luther Bible (German) until recent times. The 14 books of the Apocrypha are: I Esdras, II Esdras, Tobit, Judith, The Rest of Esther, The Wisdom of Solomon, Ecclesiasticus (often called "Sirach"), Baruch with the Epistle of Jeremiah, The Song of the Three Holy Children, The History of Susanna, Bel and the Dragon, The Prayer of Manasses, I Maccabees, II Maccabees. The term N.T. Apocrypha is sometimes used to refer to early Christian literature produced in imitation of the Gospels, Acts, Epistles, and Revelation, although no exactly defined collection of writings is so recognized by the church.

The Anabaptists, and following them the Mennonites, of all countries in general followed the Reformers and the Protestant churches in denying divine inspiration and authoritative character to the O.T. Apocrypha. Certain books, particularly Sirach, Tobit, and the Wisdom of Solomon, were highly esteemed however, and Neff (*ML* I, 77) claims that Hans Denk cites them, particularly Sirach, as equal in authority with the O.T. books.

Among the Anabaptist martyrs and the leaders like Menno Simons and Dirk Philips we find the apocryphal books of the Old Testament frequently cited, especially *The Wisdom of Solomon* and *Jesus Sirach*. Vos (*Menno Simons,* 194) said that Menno ascribes to the Apocrypha the same authority as to the canonical Scriptures. This is not correct, and is especially not true of Dirk Philips. The attitude of the early Mennonites to the Apocrypha and its relation to the canon can be clearly seen in the conversation of the martyr Jacques d'Auchy (*q.v.*) with the inquisitor Lindanus (*Offer,* 302). Lindanus is trying to prove the Catholic doctrine of purgatory and the Mass for the dead, and to do so refers to I Macc. 12:43. Jaques, who to be sure cites the books of the Apocrypha as edifying literature, refuses to ascribe to them any authority for Christian teaching, saying, "The early Christians used this name [viz., Apocrypha] to designate that they are not authentic books from which a rule or ordinance might be taken." Further he says, "I do not find that Christ and His apostles accepted them [the Apocryphal books] or drew any testimony from them." The opinion of Dr. J. H. Wessel (*Leerst. Strijd tusschen Nederl. Geref. en Doopsgezinden in de zestiende eeuw,* Assen, 1945, 109) seems correct: "It seems to me that we shall not find among the Anabaptists that they put the Apocrypha on a par with the canonical books." (See also *Inv. Arch. Amst.* I, No. 757.)

It is interesting to note that the Old Order Amish in the United States traditionally use the book of Tobit as the basis for the wedding sermon. A manuscript *Amish Ministers Manual* directs the use of Tobit in the wedding service in the following words: "So one turns to the book of Tobit. Although it is an apocryphal book and is not counted among the books of Holy Scripture, it nevertheless gives a beautiful teaching, strengthens the pious and God-fearing ones in the faith, especially in regard to marriage, and leads through all trial and tribulation to the hope that God finally will bring things to a conclusion with joy. So one begins in the book of Tobit . . ." (*MQR* XV, April 1941, 101). A summary of the part of Tobit used in the Amish wedding sermon is printed in Joh. D. Hochstetler's reproduction of an Amish document of 1781, *Ein alter Brief* (Elkhart, 1916) 14-20.

Through the influence of the Pennsylvania Germans some conservative Mennonites, particularly the Old Order Amish, have become quite fond of the strange N.T. apocryphal book known as the *Gospel of Nicodemus* (*Evangelium Nicodemi*) which went through several German editions in Pennsylvania in the 19th century. (*ML* I, 77.)

H.S.B., vdZ.

Apollonia, wife of Leonhard Seyle(r?), an Anabaptist martyr, was captured in 1539 in Tirol (Austria), taken to Brixen, and there condemned to death by drowning. (*Mart. Mir.* D 45, E 450.)

vdZ.

Apollonia Ottes was a sister in the congregation at Leeuwarden in the Dutch province of Friesland, who, when Menno Simons traveled by way of Leeuwarden to Harlingen in the spring of 1557 to resolve the pending difference between Leenaert Bouwens (*q.v.*) and himself regarding the use of the ban and shunning, accompanied him there and at the time of the discussion at Harlingen eavesdropped from behind the door. In her old age she used to relate that Menno Simons, who took a moderate position, was persuaded by threatening on the part of Leenaert Bouwens to take a very strict position, so that henceforth he also consented to the strict use of shunning in marriage. The story of Apollonia appeared for the first time in Hans Alenson's *Tegenbericht* (Counter-Answer) regarding the *Martyrs' Mirror* of 1631 (reprinted in *BRN* VII, 257-59). Vos and Kühler attach great value to the story of Apollonia; Krahn less; Horsch discredits it altogether. It appears to me advisable not to attach too great significance to a story that Apollonia told evidently many years after the incident.   vDZ.

BRN VII, 257-59; K. Vos, Menno Simons (Leiden, 1914) 136-38; Kühler, Geschiedenis I, 319, 321; C. Krahn, Menno Simons (Karlsruhe, 1936) 92-93; John Horsch, "Is Dr. Kühler's Conception of Early Dutch Anabaptism Historically Sound," in MQR VII (1933) 48-60 and 97-126; the Apollonia Ottes story is discussed at length on pp. 111-13.

Apostles' Creed. In its earliest form this confession of faith, also called *Symbolum Apostolicum,* may be traced back to the middle of the second century through several references made to the creed by Irenaeus and Tertullian. Additions were made in the 4th and 7th centuries so that it reached its present form by about A.D. 700. The creed devotes one section to God the Father, one to Jesus Christ, God's Son, and one to the Holy Spirit and the salvation which He brings. It is believed that the creed arose on the foundation of the triune baptismal formula, and was later expanded to give the six saving acts of Christ, and three of the Holy Spirit: these nine together with the three naming each member of the Trinity thus making a total of twelve articles.

It is of interest that the Waldenses, although vigorous opponents of every form of ecclesiasticism, stated in Article I of their ancient confession of faith: "We believe and hold fast all that is contained in the twelve articles of the Apostolic Creed; and regard as error all that differs therefrom and does not agree with said twelve articles" (*Mart. Mir.* E 284). Reinerius, an opponent of the Waldenses, also testifies to their acceptance of every article of the Apostles' Creed (Horsch).

Similarly, the Anabaptists assented to the truth of the Apostles' Creed, although making little or no liturgical use of it. Hubmaier (*q.v.*) wrote an amplification of the creed entitled, *The Twelve Articles of Christian Belief* (Vedder, 178). Hymn No. 2 of the *Ausbund* (*q.v.*) is an expansion of the Apostles' Creed: "Der Christliche Glaube, gesangweise gemacht." In his defense against G. Faber, Menno writes that Christ alone is the foundation of the church and not with the addition of the twelve articles of faith, on which Faber based his argument (*Opera Omnia,* 1681, 321a). (See Krahn, *Menno Simons,* 122.) The martyr Jaques d' Auchy (d. 1559) begins his *Bekenntenisse des Gheloofs* (Confession of Faith) with a statement that is very similar to the twelve articles, and is here and there identical with it. Van Braght in Part I of his *Martyrs' Mirror* (1660 and 1685; E 27) gives the Apostles' Creed and says, "We must believe it with our hearts and confess it with our mouths." Galenus Abrahamsz de Haan says that the knowledge of the truth embraces only a few points or principal articles, not more than are found in the Symbolum of the apostles (*Korte Grondstellingen,* following his *Verdediging der Christenen,* 1699, 10-11). See also his *Anleyding tot de Kennis van de Chr. Godsdienst* (Amsterdam, 1677) 31-34. Dirk Philips (*q.v.*) wrote a *Confession of our Faith,* found in the English *Enchiridion* (*q.v.*) of 1910 as the first item, which may have been more or less a commentary on the Creed; at least it is trinitarian in both content and organization. Peter Riedemann's (*q.v.*) *Rechenschaft* of 1565, "Confession of our Faith, Teaching and Life," is clearly a commentary on the Creed. In the doctrinal examination given by Roman Catholic theologians to the Danzig Mennonite elder, Georg Hansen (*q.v.*), in 1678, he was expressly asked about the acceptance of the Apostles' Creed. He replied that the Mennonites make no use of it, although they do not reject it but recognize its full value (Hansen, *Fundamentbuch,* p. 45, Q. 46).

In modern times the standing of the Apostles' Creed in Mennonite circles varies according to the country and group. In many congregations of South Germany and West Prussia, says Christian Neff, the Creed is held in high esteem and is employed in catechetical instruction, while the Dutch and North German congregations reject or ignore it. (Some conservative Dutch church leaders, e.g., T. Kuiper, *q.v.,* wished to retain the Apostles' Creed; see *DB* 1880, 150.) An attempt to make the Creed the basis for a union of all the Mennonites of Germany at a conference in Friedelsheim in 1874 failed completely. In America it is recognized as a good summary of the fundamental doctrines of the Christian faith; the American editions of Roosen's *Gemütsgespräch* (*q.v.*) since 1850 give the text of the Creed (first English edition, 1857; first use of the Creed in the German edition of 1868, issued by John F. Funk, *q.v.*).   J.C.W., vDZ.

Ausbund; Mart. Mir. E 27, 284; C. A. Briggs, Theological Symbolics (New York, 1914) 40 ff.; (Georg Hansen) Ein Fundamentbuch der Christlichen Lehre (Elkhart, 1893); Gbl., 1874, 55; J. Horsch, Mennonites in Europe (Scottdale, 1950) 5; Menn. Bl., 1874, 43; Ch. Neff, APOSTOLISCHES GLAUBENSBEKENNTNIS, ML I, 78 f.; D. Philips, Enchiridion or Hand Book . . . (Elkhart, 1910) 9-14; Peter Ridemann, Rechenschaft . . . (Cotswold-Bruderhof, Ashton Keynes, Wilts., England, 1938) 8-44; (Gerrit Roosen) Christian Spiritual Conversation on Saving Faith (Lancaster, 1857) 260; H. C. Vedder, Balthasar Hubmaier . . . (New York, 1905) 178.

Apostolic Mennonite Church, Trenton, Butler Co., Ohio (officially named the "Apostolic Mennonite

Society"), was originally an Amish Mennonite settlement established in 1819 by Christian Augsburger and five other families from Alsace, France, who organized an Amish congregation in 1825. In 1832 a shipload of Mennonites from Hesse settled here. Since the two groups did not get along well together two separate congregations (Amish-Augsburger, and Mennonite-Hessian) were organized, although the first meetinghouses were not built until 1863 and 1864, respectively, by the two congregations. In 1897 the two were merged and in 1907 the present brick church building, with a seating capacity of 250, was erected. A third faction, which did not agree with either the Augsburger or the Hessian group, organized separately at Collinsville in 1835 but the group was never large and dissolved after a generation, the members joining the other two groups.

Historically this settlement is important as the first Alsatian Amish settlement in North America and as the mother colony from which the many first Alsatian Amish settlers went to central Illinois (1829 ff.) and later to eastern Iowa (1840 ff.), to Henry County (Wayland) and Davis County (Pulaski). Joseph Goldsmith, a prominent early Amish bishop, was ordained (1838) here. The Augsburger (Amish) congregation belonged to the Amish General Conference, 1862-78, but never joined the later Eastern Amish Mennonite Conference. In 1892 the Hessian congregation joined the General Conference Mennonites. (W. H. Grubb, *Hist. of the Menn. of Butler Co., Ohio*, Trenton, 1916.)   J.E.A.

Apostolic Christian Church of America. The founder of the Apostolic Christian Church was Samuel Fröhlich, b. July 4, 1803, in Brugg, Switzerland, where he received his early education. From 1820 to 1825 Fröhlich studied theology at several Swiss universities, but with little personal conviction. In 1825 he was converted and changed his life completely and continued to prepare for the ministry. He entered the ministry in 1828 but soon his religious views were questioned by the state church. In 1830 his ministry was recalled and in 1832 Fröhlich was excluded from the state church. He then began to organize a church of his own. His first followers were equally from the Reformed Church and from dissatisfied Mennonites in Switzerland. The first congregation was organized at Langnau in the Emmental under the name of *Gemeinschaft Evangelisch Taufgesinnter*. Because some of the first converts were Mennonites, when the new group settled near Amish communities in America it was sometimes called "New Amish," although there has never been any Amish element or influence in the group. In Switzerland they have been called *Neutäufer* on a similar basis. Without doubt, the Emmental Mennonite Church had considerable influence on Fröhlich's religious views. Christian Gerber, an elder in the Mennonite Church at Emmental, called Fröhlich's attention to the fact that his written statement of belief did not cover military service, and so objection to military service in a combatant capacity became one of the church's

tenets of faith. The difficulties encountered because of a conscience against war caused many to emigrate to America.

The first Apostolic Christian Church in America was organized in 1852 among the Amish Mennonites in Croghan, New York. The Virkler family, the members of which were Mennonites, requested that Fröhlich send an elder to their community; so Benedict Weyeneth was sent from Switzerland in 1847, at which time services were begun. He later ordained Joseph Virkler as minister and organized an Apostolic Christian congregation at that place. Elder Weyeneth then went back to Europe but later came to Woodford Co., Ill., and soon found converts among dissatisfied Amish Mennonites there. Joseph Graybill, an Amish Mennonite, was one of the first converts and the first Apostolic Christian minister in Illinois. He was a very zealous member of the new sect and worked hard, but at first the church grew slowly. Members of the denomination from Switzerland began to settle in Ohio as early as 1848. Heavy migrations from Switzerland and lesser migrations from Germany and Alsace aided a much more rapid growth in later years.

The church has had some divisions. The most widespread has been the defection of a group which is called the Apostolic Christian (Nazarean) in 1907. Many of the Ohio churches are of this group and there are also some strong churches in Illinois of the Nazarene group. In doctrine there is little difference and there is some fellowship between the groups. Numerous efforts have been made to get the two groups together. The division was caused largely because of the main body holding to the German language. The main body has long since given up the German language. Another small conservative group, located chiefly in Central Illinois, separated from the main body in the early 1930's under the leadership of Martin Steidinger of Fairbury, Ill. Some of the New York churches have continued to call themselves locally "Evangelical Baptists," but this does not represent a division. The full official name of the main body is "Apostolic Christian Church of America." Locally, especially in Illinois, they are often called "New Amish," though without any historical justification.

It is difficult to secure accurate statistics for the Apostolic Christians since neither group publishes a yearbook or other informational material, and neither has a church organ. *The U. S. Census of Religious Bodies* for 1936 lists Apostolic Christians of America with 5,841 members in 57 churches (only 1,300 growth since 1906), and the Nazarene branch with 1,663 members in 31 churches. The *1952 Yearbook of American Churches* reports from denominational sources for 1950, for the first group "inclusive membership" 7,300 in 56 churches and 56 "ordained clergy with charges," for the second group similarly 4,500 members in 50 churches with 100 clergy. This would make a total of 11,800 members in 106 churches. There are organized congregations in Illinois, Iowa, Oklahoma, Kansas, Indiana, Michigan, Minnesota, Ohio, Oregon, Connecticut, New Jersey, New York, West Virginia, Alabama, Pennsylvania, Virginia, Washington,

D.C., Arizona, and California. The largest church was at Bluffton, Ind., with approximately 800 members. A number of Illinois congregations had 500 or more members each. In Europe the church has had a substantial growth. It was estimated that there were 70,000 members in the Balkan states, particularly in Hungary and Jugoslavia, where they are called Nazarenes. There are smaller groups in Switzerland, Alsace, and Württemberg (Germany).

Church government is largely congregational in form. There are general meetings of the brethren called periodically for discussing mutual problems; however, these meetings are only advisory. Fröhlich called the first of these at Hauptwil in 1836. In America the "Brotherhood Meetings," as they are called, convene biennially (1953, etc.), with elders' meetings falling in the intervening years.

The Apostolic Christian Church has its own mutual Brotherhood Aid Plan. The system is well organized and very effective. The plan covers both personal property and real estate.

Relief work has been carried on through AID, a relief agency within the church. It is a counterpart of "Hilfe," the European relief society organized in Zürich in 1921. Many European members, particularly in the Balkans, were put into prison during World War II because of military refusal. Relief work has been extensively carried on for these people and others who are not members of the church.

The chief benevolent institutions are old people's homes. The first of these was organized in Europe in 1856 and the aged members of the church are well cared for.

Doctrinally the Apostolic Christian Church is much like the Mennonite Church. Baptism is administered by immersion, but Fröhlich himself was baptized by sprinkling. The women wear a veiling during times of prayer. The members of the church enter only noncombatant service when drafted into the army.

In general, this religious group is very prosperous financially, and in Illinois particularly some very substantial business leaders are members of the Apostolic Christian Church. **T.R.S.**

Hermann Rüegger, Sr., *Aufzeichnungen über Entstehung und Bekenntnis der Gemeinschaft Evangelisch Taufgesinnter* (Zürich, 1948); *Apostolic Christian Church History* I (Chicago, 1949); Henry Michel, *A Historical Sketch of the Apostolic Christian Church* (Lake Bloomington, Ill., 1947); *"Nazarenes" in Jugoslavia* (Syracuse, 1928); *Die Umtriebe der Neutäufer und ihre Lehre von der Kindertaufe* (Bern, 1841); *Glaubensbekenntnisz der Neuen Deutschen Baptisten Gemeinde in den Vereinigten Staaten* (Elkhart, 1880); S. H. Fröhlich, *Baptism, Who Shall and Who Shall Not Be Baptised* (1854 edition translated from the French text into German by Henry Michel, and from the German into English by the publishers, Syracuse, 1929); J. W. Fretz, "The Apostolic Christian Church," *Menn. Life,* Oct. 1951, 19.

Apostolic Succession. The Roman Catholic Church teaches what it calls the *Successio Apostolica.* This doctrine of the Apostolic Succession holds that by an unbroken line of ordinations by proper bishops from the days of the apostles to the present the apostolicity of the church is maintained and guaranteed, thus giving the church the guarantee that it is the true church of Christ by tracing it back to the apostles and from there to Jesus Christ Himself. It teaches that Jesus founded the church, and appointed the apostles and in particular Peter (Matt. 16:18-20; John 21:15-17) to lead it into all truth, and that the apostles ordained their successors, conferring by the laying on of hands the grace to perform this ecclesiastical office, that is, to perform it according to the meaning that Christ had given it. So even today each priest in the Roman Catholic Church, when he performs a church act, can act efficaciously by virtue of the Apostolic Succession. Inherent in the Apostolic Succession are both the transfer of grace and the authority for exercising power.

From the beginning this doctrine has not been without opposition. Many medieval sects such as Arnoldists and Waldenses created powerful opposition. They believed that the bearers of church offices could not act by virtue of a transferred power but only by virtue of direct grace. (Ludwig Keller, who asserted that the Waldenses attached great value to the Apostolic Succession in his *Die Reformation und die älteren Reformparteien* of 1866, was mistaken, as Th. Kolde in *Ztscht f. Kirchengesch.* VII, 1885, has clearly shown.) The Waldenses and others greatly emphasized the apostolic-prophetic element, and this spiritualism we find again in the Anabaptists, but this is not the apostolic succession by ordination.

The break with Rome in the Reformation also means the break with the teaching of the Apostolic Succession. Only the Anglican Church and the Lutheran Church of Sweden have retained it.

The leading reformers themselves rejected the doctrine specifically (although we find a number of inconsistencies among the Lutherans as well as among the Calvinists). Luther did it most radically: for him that which makes a pastor is the ordination by the congregation. *"Wählt die Gemeinde einen Pfarrer, so soll man ihn durch Gebet und Handauflegung der Gesamtheit empfehlen und bestätigen, und fest glauben: a deo gestum et factum esse"* (*Werke, Weimar ed.* XII, 191.). The office is given to the pastor in no other way than for instance to any official or *Amtmann* (*Werke, Weimar ed.* VI, 408). *"Ordinare non est consecrare, damus in virtute verbi quod habemus, auctoritatem praedicandi verbum et dandi sacramenta; hoc est ordinari"* (*Werke, Weimar ed.* XV, 751). (To ordain does not mean to consecrate. We only give by virtue of the command we have, the authority of preaching the Word and administering the sacraments.)

For Calvin the case is somewhat different. The bearers of office, *pastores vel ministri* (pastors), *doctores* (teachers), *presbyteri vel seniores* (elders, bishops), and *diaconi* (deacons), who do not differ from each other in rank, but only in function, together form the *presbyterium* (consistory or vestry), which governs the church, and which is self-perpetuating of itself by co-operation. The congregation does not choose the bearers of church office but merely gives its consent (*consensus et approbatio*).

The fact that the Calvinist practice has developed with some variations in different countries, has no bearing on this. From the closed nature of the consistory one might conclude that Calvin did not fully give up the Apostolic Succession. However, that he did this in principle follows from the statement that at the founding of a congregation, "the people," i.e., the congregation, shall choose the presbyters, who then will regulate the organization of the congregation, first of all by appointing a consistory. Also the Reformation and the churches springing from it retained the laying on of hands in the ordination to church office after Biblical example. This, however, did not mean a transfer of grace, but a petition for grace.

Do the Anabaptists and Mennonites have the doctrine of the Apostolic Succession? De Hoop-Scheffer thinks he finds it in the early Fathers. Kühler (*Zondagsbode,* May 30, 1926) says that this is a legend. However, the case is not so simple as Kühler thinks. It seems that in addition to a spiritual conception of church office (which really is no office, for all members of the congregation are *eo ipso* priests), there continues to exist among Mennonites a view which is not entirely free of the idea of the apostolic succession. In the first congregation in Zürich, to be sure, we do not find it. Grebel, the layman, performed the first (re)baptism, and apparently did not hold the doctrine (Bender, *Conrad Grebel,* Goshen, 1950, 137). It is rather remarkable that it was these Swiss Brethren in particular who later traced their spiritual descent back to the apostles, calling themselves *"Altevangelische."* Among the Dutch Mennonites we find, besides the apostolic-prophetical conception of the spiritualists (Melchior Hoffman, Hans Denk, Jan Matthysz, partly Hans de Ries, later especially Galenus Abrahamsz), also very clearly the opposite line (Obbe Philips until he came under the influence of Seb. Franck, Ebbe Pieters, Jan Jacobsz, and in a later period Laurens Hendriks, Douwe Feddriks, Herman Schijn). In Obbe this is very clear. Later when he had left the brotherhood, he wrote about his ordination by Bartel Boeckbinder: "The laying on of hands we felt very well, and all the words we heard well; but we neither felt nor heard the Holy Spirit." This points to the fact that Obbe then believed and expected that with the laying on of hands the Holy Ghost would pass from the ordainer to the ordained; in other words, that he believed the teaching of the Apostolic Succession.

When Menno and Dirk Philips, both of whom were ordained as elder by Obbe, came to the insight that Obbe's ordination traced back to Jan Matthysz, who was "self-appointed" (that is, he was not ordained officially, there was therefore no continuation) and that thus their apostolic succession was left hanging in thin air, they did not lay down their office. This shows that they accepted at the most the idea, but by no means the consequences of an apostolic succession. In speaking of the offices (see **Ministry**), both Menno and Dirk start from two possibilities; either the bearer of office (minister) is called directly by God, or he is chosen by the congregation; the latter can then be done either directly by the members or indirectly via the elders. However greatly the power of the elders developed about the middle of the 16th century, and however much these people also depreciated the prophetic conception of church office, which is also understandable in the light of the experiences of the fanatics (Münsterites), there is no thought of an apostolic succession in the real sense. They understood that the actual working of the Holy Spirit is not bound to the continuity of ordination from apostolic times. Nor is this the conception of the martyr Hans de Smet, who was executed in 1558 in Aachen, Germany, who when asked about his authority (*sending*) answered: he had not put himself into the office but God and His Spirit in His church (*Mart. Mir.* D 210a, E 588). Menno then also quietly repudiates the accusation of Gellius Faber, that their church (*kerke ofte secte*) is not apostolic and still very young, "hardly sixteen or seventeen years old," and that their teachers are self-appointed (*van zich zelf lopen*) (*Complete Works,* Part II, 1871, 97, 100 f.) Menno looks upon his congregation as being apostolic, although age, antiquity, and continuity of ordination are lacking, because it lives and acts in the spirit of the apostles (see also Krahn, *Menno Simons,* 1936, 120-21). Neither Menno nor Dirk Philips, when speaking about the ordinances (*"Ordonnancien"*) of the congregation, puts the emphasis upon the antiquity of the church, but upon the truth of its teaching and upon the holiness of its servants and members (see *BRN* X, 393-408).

The Mennonite practice of earlier and later times, also in America, of laying on of hands in baptism, and of conducting communion services only by ordained elders, is rather a compliance with the Biblical tradition (I Tim. 4:14; Titus 1:5) than a matter of dogma. Compare the quotation in the *Zondagsbode* of May 26, 1926: "Ordination should take place with the laying on of hands, but without superstition." In the Netherlands a number of instances can be cited even in a rather early time, when baptism was not administered by an elder, but by a deacon, who had not been ordained by the laying on of hands. And when the first congregation in Germantown, Pa., before 1708 requested the congregation in Hamburg to send an elder to them to ordain an elder, the ministers of Hamburg advised the congregation of Germantown to ordain one of their own preachers as an elder or bishop without the service of a bishop, which they did (Smith, *Mennonite Immigration to Pennsylvania,* Norristown, 1929, 104-5).

When in the schism in the Dutch congregations, the extreme conservative groups such as Old Flemish, Jan Jacobsz group, Groninger Old Flemish and later also the Zonists clung to the idea that their church was the true church of God, they occasionally appealed to the continuity of ordination, although hesitatingly and uncertainly, and therefore did conceive it as an apostolic succession in the Roman Catholic sense, even though not going back beyond the Reformation period.

Jacob Pieters van der Meulen (*q.v.*) held a different view. Shortly after 1600 he became involved in a heated pen battle on the Apostolic Succession with Roman Catholic theologians. He wrote a book *Successio Apostolica, dat is Naecominghe oft de Naetredinghe der Apostelen, waerin dat die bestaet, nae dat ghetuyghenisse der H. Schriftueren* (Alkmaar, 1600). He tried to show how wrongly the Roman Catholics interpret the apostolic succession. The true "successors" are not the Roman Catholics, but the Mennonites. "The true succession is that we are bound to no succession of place or person, but to the succession of the teaching of the truth; for the true churches were called apostolic, not on the grounds of succession, but on the grounds of continuation of the true doctrine." It is the same thing as Menno and Dirk Philips meant when they qualified themselves as being apostolic because they taught "the doctrine and usage of the holy apostles and of the first unadulterated church."

To the progressive Lamists (*q.v.*) the Apostolic Succession was no longer a question, for their conception of the church was altogether along the line of Seb. Franck (*q.v.*) and Coornhert (*q.v.*), and according to them the true church is nowhere to be found on the earth. These spiritualists put so much emphasis on the freedom of the Holy Spirit, that there was no place for any apostolic succession. Although they went a long way with Jacob P. van der Meulen, they went beyond him, in regarding any official ordination as being unnecessary or even undesirable.

Influenced by this spiritualism, ordination gradually disappeared among the Dutch Mennonites. Since about 1750 the laying on of hands has seldom been practiced. Only in very recent times have a few ministers been ordained by the laying on of hands. In those cases it was not the doctrine of the Apostolic Succession, but rather a return to Biblical practice, that influenced the action.

The attitude of the Mennonites of Dutch background in West Prussia, Poland, Russia, and America in the matter of apostolic succession has always been very much the same as that of the early Dutch Mennonites who did not attach any significance to the illusory attempt to trace the calling and the appointment of preachers and elders to the apostles. It was not the "office" and its "sacramental" character that guaranteed to them that they were members of a true apostolic church. They compared the whole congregation as such, its faith, spirit, and life, with that of the apostolic church to find the assurance whether or not they were true spiritual successors of the early church as Christ intended it to be.

This attitude, however, did not prevent that, in the later history, at times too much significance was attached to the outward form of selection and ordination to the office, especially of elders. When the first Mennonites settled at Chortitza, Russia, and were without an elder, upon suggestion from their home church in West Prussia, they selected candidates for the ministry and from among these candidates an elder was appointed and installed through correspondence by the elders in Prussia. This unusual procedure caused some difficulties, partly due to the strain of the pioneer conditions. Some objected to ordination by correspondence as not being in harmony with the tradition of laying on of hands. The laying on of hands has always been and still is practiced. The authority and power traditionally attached to the office of an elder and minister has, however, in modern times been somewhat modified. The practice that the elder is a supervisor of a larger district is gradually disappearing, and more and more, each congregation has become independent with its own pastor performing all the functions of the former elder. Accordingly a second ordination to the office of elder is not always performed.

In the North American Mennonite groups of Swiss-South German background, both the concept and practice of ordination only by the laying on of hands by a previously so ordained bishop or elder has been carefully and strictly maintained except in rare emergencies. One of these emergencies was the request of the new settlement near Vineland in Lincoln Co., Ont., in 1801 to have a bishop sent from Bucks Co., Pa., for ordination purposes. The Bucks County church declined to send a bishop, advising the new settlement to proceed without one.

John Herr, the founder of the Herrite or Reformed Mennonites, was never ordained by a bishop, although he himself functioned as one. John Holdeman (*q.v.*), the founder of the Church of God in Christ, Mennonite, in 1856, also was never ordained by a bishop, although he himself practiced all the duties of a bishop. The same is true of the Kleine Gemeinde, the Mennonite Brethren, and others when they organized. (*ML* I, 79.)   vDZ.

Apostolische Brüder (Apostolic Brethren), the popular designation for the Waldenses in the later Middle Ages and in the Reformation period, also at times for the Anabaptists (Keller, *Reformation,* 8, 11, 34, etc.). The apostolic example which they tried to realize in teaching and in life may have led to this designation. J. H. Ottius, *Annales Anabaptistici* (Basel, 1672) Preface 2, states: "They are called apostolic from their apostles or missionaries; according to others, because they claimed to follow the apostles exactly, took the Bible literally, left their possessions, and without shoes, without wallets, without money traveled about everywhere, washed one another's feet, and ordered that all goods should be held in common." It is nevertheless worth noticing that this name was applied anew by Mennonites in Russia in the *Apostolische Brüdergemeinde* (*q.v.*). (*ML* I, 78.)   Neff.

Apostolische Brüdergemeinde (Apostolic Brethren, also known as *Brotbrechergemeinde*) originated during the formative years of the Mennonite Brethren in 1865-66 in the Molotschna settlement, South Russia, and was organized as a separate brotherhood under the leadership of Elder Hermann Peters (*q.v.*). The group, consisting of some 20 families, soon moved to the Crimea, where other Mennonite families joined them. During the years 1900-01 the whole group moved from the Crimea to Siberia, settling north and east of the city of Omsk, near Kiryanovka and Trussovka, and on smaller places and estates. Hermann Peters continued as the elder of the congregation and resided at Kiryanovka.

The group consisted mostly of farmers and a few businessmen. Kiryanovka had a co-operative and produced an especially good quality of butter which was exported to foreign countries. The Trussovka group raised and prepared barley for cereal and sunflowers for oil, which was extracted in its own refineries. Several large flour mills were operated and owned by the members of the congregation.

The Apostolic Brethren Congregation was extremely conservative in retaining Mennonite traditions but was at the same time strongly influenced by the revival movement of the middle of the 19th century. Baptism by immersion was practiced. The group followed a very strict practice of nonconformity to the outside world and church discipline. Instead of the common greetings when friends met or departed they used the words "grace" and "peace." Only the German *Du* was permissible and not the formal *Sie*. No physicians were consulted in cases of sickness in order not to interfere with the will of God. The name *Brotbrecher* (breadbreaker) was a nickname received because of the group's original practice of never using a knife to cut the bread, since "Jesus took the bread and broke it." Later this practice was discontinued and only followed during the commemoration of the Lord's Supper. The group did not observe any festivals such as Christmas or Easter, but practiced fasting. No pictures were allowed anywhere. All prayer was audible and those praying either raised their hands or knelt.

Up until World War I the young men refused to register for government alternative service, and when they were forcibly transported to the forestry camps where other Mennonite men served, they refused to do any work. Yet these families would not leave for America as so many other Mennonites had done. Before World War I the group discontinued the practice of not registering for military service and accepted the alternative service. At this time the name "Apostolic Brethren Congregation" was changed into "Evangelical Mennonite Church of God" (*Evangelische Mennoniten-Gottesgemeinde*). From that time on there was more co-operation between the group and the other Mennonite churches, especially in matters pertaining to military service.

Hermann Peters, the founder, died at the time of the outbreak of World War I and was succeeded by H. J. Warkentin as elder. The total number of members was about 150 with a total population of 400. Under Communism the group was dissolved as were also the other Mennonite congregations.

C.K.

Friesen, *Brüderschaft;* J. J. Hildebrand, *Gesch. der Evangelischen Menn. Gottesgem.*, Part II: *Sibirien* (Winnipeg, 1952) 53-80; *ML* I, 78.

Apostool, a Mennonite family which stems from Flanders. In 1581 Jacob Apostool, a Mennonite, the son of Francois Apostool and Margarete Salme, came to Haarlem with his wife Maaijken Drijvers (a daughter of Andries Drijvers of Meenen). In 1583 a son, Jacob Francois, was born to them. He married Catelijntje van Steenkiste, a native of .Nieuwkerk (or Nipkerke) in Flanders. Some of the outstanding members of the Apostool family were: Samuel Apostool (*q.v.*); Andries Apostool, who was chosen deacon of the Zonist congregation in Amsterdam in 1675; Pieter Apostool (*q.v.*); Andries Apostool (*q.v.*); Pieter Apostool, who was three times chosen deacon of the Zonist congregation in Amsterdam, in 1705, 1714, and 1724. vDZ.

Apostool, Andries, was one of the leaders of the conservative Mennonites in the Netherlands and was four times a deacon in the Zonist congregation in Amsterdam (chosen in 1733, 1743, 1755, 1766). On Oct. 25, 1735, he represented this congregation at the conference called by the Lamist and Toren congregation in Amsterdam to arrange for the founding of a theological seminary (see **Amsterdam Seminary**). He was also present at a meeting of representatives of the *Sociëteit* of Groninger Old Flemish and of the Zonist *Sociëteit* on the matter of forming a union, which, however, did not occur (1766).

Andries Apostool wrote *De Mennoniten of Doopsgezinden verdedigd* (Amsterdam, 1763), directed against Georgius Erhard, the Reformed preacher of Zaandijk. (*N.N.B.Wb.* I, 161.)   vDZ.

Apostool, Pieter, d. 1680, was chosen deacon of the Zonist congregation in Amsterdam in 1670, and preacher in 1672. In 1674 he signed the *Grondsteen van Vrede en Verdraegsaemheijt* (*q.v.*), which united the Zonist congregations into a Sociëteit. He is the author of *Verdedigingh der Vredespresentatie . . . aen Dr. Galenus Abrahamsz en de Seijne gedaan* (Amsterdam, 1664). (*ML* I, 79.)   vDZ.

Apostool, Samuel, b. June 15, 1638, d. April 29, 1699, was a doctor of medicine and a physician by vocation. In March 1662, at the age of nearly 24, he was chosen preacher by the Flemish Lamist congregation at Amsterdam. In this congregation were at the time two parties, one led by Galenus Abrahamsz de Haan (*q.v.*), who was influenced by the Collegiants and did not want to emphasize the significance of any of the existing confessions, and the other, which was conservative and held the group of the Flemish to be the true church of God, and strictly adhered to the confessions of faith. Of this conservative group Samuel Apostool soon became an influential leader. The dispute, known as the *Lammerenkrijg* (*q.v.*), flamed so high that Apostool in May or June 1664 left the congregation with 500 followers; having held their meetings in a rented warehouse in the Oude Teertuinen for a time, they bought a brewery on Sept. 19, 1664, and used it as a meetinghouse. This building had on its gable the sign of the sun, *de Zon,* and was, like the church *bij 't Lam,* situated on the Cingel (Singel). There Apostool's group organized a congregation. After their leader they were sometimes called Apostoolists, but after their church mostly the Zonists (*q.v.*). For a century they remained the strict wing of the Mennonites, and like their founder S. Apostool, adhered to these three doctrines: the eternal deity of Christ, complete justification through the blood of Christ, and the existence of the true church of God on earth.

Apostool contended with Galenus, who had remained leader of the Lamist congregation with 2,000 members, for the possession of the church and church property; but the burgomasters of Amsterdam rejected his claim upon the church because he refused to recognize the Galenists as brethren, whereas Galenus and his followers were quite willing to acknowledge the Apostoolists as such. In 1672 the two congregations came to an agreement for the division of the church property.

In 1664 Apostool signed the *Verbondt van Eenigheydt* (*q.v.*) accepted in Utrecht. In June 1665 Apostool traveled to Zeeland to urge the congregations there to join this union, which later developed into the Zonist Conference (*q.v.*). He had little success, partly on account of the powerful opposition of Adriaen van Eeghen (q.v.), the preacher at Middelburg. Only the congregation of Goes was won for the union.

Apostool was also present at the discussions held in 1684 and 1685 between representatives of the Lamists and Zonists in futile attempts to reach some kind of agreement. He did not speak much there, but at the meeting of Aug. 8, 1684, he declared that the Zonists were not disinclined to acknowledge the Lamists as brethren if no steps would be taken in opposition to the *algemeene gronden der Doopsgezinden,* i.e., the general doctrines of the Mennonites, because he considered unity to be impossible without a common system of doctrine. (*Verhaal van de Onderhandelingen,* . . . Amsterdam, 1685, p. 9. In the copy in my possession there is a note inserted by pen by one of the men present that Apostool was the speaker. vdZ.)

Apostool left no published works with the exception of *Waarheids-Oeffeninge,* a booklet which he wrote in collaboration with his colleague Samuel van Deyl (Amsterdam, 1677, reprinted in 1686, 1730, and 1743). His funeral sermon was preached by Reynsckes Overwijk (*Catalogus Amst.,* 250).†

vDZ.

L. Bidloo, *Onbepaalde verdraagzaamheid* (Amsterdam, 1701); H. Schijn, *Gesch. der Menn.* II (Amsterdam, 1744) 597-606; Blaupot t. C., *Holland, passim;* W. J. Kühler, *Het Socinianisme in Nederland* (Leiden, 1912) 169 ff.; E. M. Wilbur, *A Hist. of Unitarianism* (Cambridge, 1947) 560-62; *ML* I, 79.

Appeldoorn, Jan Gerrit, b. Nov. 12, 1861, at Harlingen, d. Feb. 7, 1945, at Bilthoven, educated at the university and the Mennonite seminary at Amsterdam, and became ministerial candidate in 1888. He was a minister in the Mennonite congregations of Gorredijk-Lippenhuizen (1889-1904) and Emden (1904-16). On Jan. 22, 1903, he received the Th.D. degree with his thesis: *De leer der sympathie bij David Hume en Adam Smith* (The doctrine of sympathy as found in David Hume and Adam Smith). In 1916 he became pro-

fessor at the university and the Mennonite seminary at Amsterdam and gave lectures on philosophy of religion until his retirement at the age of 70 in 1931.

vDZ.

Appelsga, a moorland colony, made arable in the 19th century, in the southern part of the Dutch province of Friesland, where some Mennonites settled and acquired a church and a parsonage. On Nov. 7, 1867, A. H. ten Cate of Gorredijk conducted the first service. From March 12, 1871, to Oct. 26, 1873, H. Boetje filled the office of minister. He was their only minister, for the membership declined rapidly (in 1902 there were seven, and in 1913 only three members), and services were discontinued. The Friesche Doopsgezinde Sociëteit (*q.v.*) took over the church and parsonage, leased the church to the Reformed congregation, and later sold it. (*ML* I, 79.)

K.V.

Appenzell. From the canton of Zürich (*q.v.*) the Anabaptist movement spread into the neighboring canton of Appenzell. Already in 1525 Hippolyt (Eberle) Bolt (*q.v.;* his name was, however, actually Hippolyt Eberle; see Egli, 27; Bolt or Polt was the popular shortened form of the given name) of Lachen won more than 1,500 persons in Appenzell. In Teuffen (canton of Appenzell) the old local pastor was replaced by the St. Gall Anabaptist Joh. Krüsi; but neither Bolt nor Krüsi was able to maintain himself long, for the government was master of the situation. Nevertheless congregations were formed in Herisau, Teuffen, and Gais, but they lost their church discipline for lack of leadership and pressure from without. Verena Baumann of Herisau induced 1,200 persons to stop working, evidently in expectation of the coming of Christ. Hunger and government intervention sobered them, and they also accepted a disputation suggested by the clergy which was held on Oct. 10, 1527, at Teuffen, where about 400 Anabaptists are said to have appeared. The outcome was considered a victory for the established church, and from that time Anabaptist influence waned (1529). Nevertheless Zwingli considered them a threat and asked Zürich to make a protest to Appenzell and Solothurn for their lenient treatment of the Anabaptists. Perhaps this threat of persecution led to the decision of some Anabaptists to emigrate to Moravia in 1528. But they were caught with Wolfgang Ulimann, their leader, in Waldsee (Upper Swabia); ten men were beheaded, the women drowned, and those who recanted sent back to Appenzell; all in the canton who did not recant were threatened with death by the sword or by drowning (1530). An Anabaptist from Chur, who refused to leave, was drowned, probably in 1528. In the spring of 1529 George Blaurock, who had been expelled, returned to Appenzell at the risk of his life, preaching and baptizing. Not until 1579 did a second group succeed in reaching Moravia, of course losing all their possessions.

TH.B.

Joh. Kessler, *Sabbata,* ed. Egli and Schoch (St. Gall, 1902); E. Egli, *Die St. Galler Täufer* (Zürich, 1887); *ML* I, 80.

Appingedam, a city in the Dutch province of Groningen (pop. 7,300, with 35 Mennonites). It is known that there was an Anabaptist center here in the early days of the movement, for in 1537 Obbe Philipps ordained his brother Dirk Philipps as bishop in Den Dam. Leenaert Bouwens in 20 visits between 1551 and 1557 baptized 93 persons; between 1557 and 1563, 5 persons; and between 1563 and 1568, in 5 visits, 31 persons, totaling 129. About 1596 Jan Gerrits van Emden became the preacher here, after he had been living in Appingedam for 20 years. In 1606 he moved to Haarlem, and soon after to Danzig. The congregation at Appingedam, which belonged to the Groninger Old Flemish group, was relatively strong in the 17th century, but declined in the second half of the 18th, at least in part in consequence of the Collegiant disputes. Its membership was in 1710, 50 men; in 1733, 26 men and 33 women; in 1754 only 15 men and 15 women; in 1767, only 14 members. To be sure, it had in 1754 a considerable number of unbaptized older persons, but their treasury for the poor was deeply in debt. At the beginning of the 17th century they held their meetings in a building that was built in 1570 as the town mint. They later met in a building given them by Grietje Hans Blaupot in 1694. When the Blaupot family died out the church became extinct. By 1785 it was no longer mentioned in the reports of the Groninger Old Flemish Sociëteit, and in 1800 there were only 10 Mennonites living here. For at least 50 years after 1707 Jan Symons Blaupot served the congregation as preacher. The present Mennonites at Appingedam belong to the congregation of Leermens-Loppersum (*q.v.*).   K.V., vDZ.

DB 1879, 3; Blaupot t. C., *Groningen* I, II, *passim;* v. d. Aa, *Aardrijkskundig Woordenboek* I (Gorinchem, 1839) 306; *ML* I, 80.

Apple Creek, with a population of 525, is a Wayne Co., Ohio, town, located seven miles southeast of Wooster on Route #250. This East Union Township town is on the western edge of the original Swiss Mennonite settlement of Sonnenberg, Ohio. Hence it is the business and school center of the Mennonites living in East Union Township.   I.A.

Applebachsville. Mennonites helped to build a union church at this place, in Haycock Twp., Bucks Co., Pa., in 1855. In that year it was known as the "German Evangelical Lutheran and Reformed and Mennonite Church." However, there is no record of Mennonites ever having conducted regular services in this church just for their own group. It is probable that the Mennonites were of the Oberholtzer (*q.v.*) group.   Q.L.

Appointment, a term familiarly used in the (old) Mennonite Church, especially in Eastern Pennsylvania and Ontario, to refer to the stated Sunday worship service of a congregation. In these areas most congregations in earlier times (in the Lancaster Conference often at present) usually had Sunday services only every two weeks. It thus became necessary to fix and announce in advance the appointed dates for services, and this was usually done annually for the entire year ahead. These "appointments" were then printed in a pamphlet called a *Calendar,* either a *Meeting Calendar* or *Calendar of Appointments.* By metonymy the meeting places listed in the calendar were also called "appointments." These "appointments" were not identical with the congregations, since they were for designated meetinghouses, and sometimes a congregation might have two or three meetinghouses, and often an appointment might be in a schoolhouse and for a group of worshipers on the fringe of a settlement or in a new settlement when there was as yet no organized congregation. Moreover the attendance at a given appointment might and usually did include worshipers from several congregations in a settlement since not more than half of the meetinghouses were in use on a given Sunday.

The term "appointment" is also used in Eastern Pennsylvania and elsewhere for the special services "appointed" for a visiting minister from a distance, who according to custom is often invited to preach in a series of meetinghouses in succession on Sunday morning and evening and on weekday evenings and whose "appointments" are announced in all the meetinghouses of the district.   H.S.B.

Arapahoe, Nebr., a small town near Republican River in Furnas County. A few Amish Mennonite families from central Illinois settled near Arapahoe in the late 1880's. No congregation was formed. There was no ordained minister in the group. Services were held irregularly in homes. After a few years the families moved back to former home communities.   N.P.S.

Arapahoe Mennonite (GCM) **Mission.** Work among the Arapahoe Indians was begun by S. S. Haury in 1880. When the General Conference Mennonite Church was searching for a mission field, S. S. Haury went to the Indians in Oklahoma in 1877, where he made contact with the Arapahoes. He reported to the Mission Board that he intended to return to them as a missionary for the next year. However, the actual beginning was delayed until 1880 when he was helped by voluntary workers to erect the necessary buildings. A school built in Darlington was destroyed by fire Feb. 19, 1882, and was replaced by a brick building. In 1882 the government transferred all of its buildings except one at Cantonment to this mission. At Christmas 1882 there were 14 workers on the field, among whom were S. S. Haury, H. R. Voth, J. A. Funk, and O. S. Schultz. In the fall of 1883 the schools at both mission stations—Darlington (*q.v.*) and Cantonment (*q.v.*) were opened. G. A. Linscheid taught the Cantonment school from 1895-98 as a missionary.

In 1884 J. J. Kliewer succeeded S. S. Haury and in 1888 the first convert was baptized. In 1896, because the Indians were moving away and the children were required to attend government schools, the Darlington station was abandoned. Gradually the Arapahoes centered around Canton (*q.v.*). In 1926 the church membership was 75 and in 1952 it had risen to 111. The J. J. Kliewers served in the mission field, 1884-97; J. A. Funk, who reduced the Arapahoe language to writing, 1896-1920; the H. T. Neufelds, 1921-27. They were followed by the G. A. Linscheids, and later by the Arthur Friesens. Since April 1947 the Alfred Wiebes have been serving the Arapahoes. C.K.

H. P. Krehbiel, *Hist. of the General Conf. of the Menn. Church* II (Newton, 1938) 13; Ed. G. Kaufman, *Development of the Missionary and Philanthropic Interest Among the Menn. of N. America* (Berne, 1931) 135-40; *Cheyenne and Arapahoe Messenger*, 1930-39; *ML* I, 80.

Arapey, Uruguay. Campamento Arapey is an old deserted army camp in northwestern Uruguay about 375 miles from Montevideo where some 400 Danzig-West Prussian Mennonite immigrants were quartered temporarily on their arrival in Uruguay on Oct. 27, 1948, until the first permanent settlement at El Ombu was made in 1950. It is in an inaccessible part of the country, in the midst of large tracts of cattle and sheep range. The nearest city, Salto, is approximately 55 miles away. W.T.S.

Arbeidsgroep van Doopsgezinden tegen de krijgsdienst (Mennonite Work Group Against Military Service.) Toward the end of the 19th century the old principle of nonresistance had apparently died out among the Dutch Mennonites. When in 1898 compulsory military service was introduced and the possibility of employing a substitute no longer existed, there was no opposition worth mentioning in the Mennonite congregations, and the young Mennonite men who were subsequently called up for military service accepted the situation. There were, however, during World War I some Mennonites who had scruples and there were also some who refused to render military service, who came of Mennonite families. These scruples, however, were based on a Tolstoy-humanistic anti-militarism rather than the principle of Biblical nonresistance once held by the Mennonite brotherhood. The Mennonite objectors met in 1922 and created an *Arbeidsgroep tot trouw aan het beginsel der weerloosheid onder Doopsgezinden* (Work Group for Loyalty to the Principle of Nonresistance among the Dutch Mennonites). This work group, which was a division of the already existing *Gemeentedag-Vereniging* (see **Broederschapswerk**), soon adopted the name *Arbeidsgroep van Doopsgezinden tegen de krijgsdienst*. Their objections were based on the Bible in conjunction with the old tradition of the brotherhood. In 1924 a booklet was published in the name of the group, written by J. M. Leendertz, *Een Doopsgezind getuigenis tegen militair geweld* (a Mennonite witness against military force), 3,000 copies of which were distributed. There was among a large part of the Dutch Mennonite brotherhood deep-seated opposition to the Arbeidsgroep and its ideals, but the group continued its activity to carry into the congregations anew the old principle. It also assisted the conscientious objectors in Mennonite circles, among other things by giving information on the act concerning conscientious objectors passed by the legislature of the Netherlands (*Dienstweigeringswet*,

1925). They also co-operated with organizations having the same goal, such as the *Kerk en Vrede* and the Dutch Quakers. Leading figures in the Arbeidsgroep were J. M. Leendertz, Jan Gleijsteen, H. C. Barthel, F. Kuiper, C. P. Inja, G. J. A. van Staden, Jacob ter Meulen, and others. The membership reached about 300 at its highest point.

During World War II and the German occupation, positive peace work was done. As early as 1939 J. Gleijsteen and C. P. Inja began to organize relief work, at first in co-operation with some Quakers; their aid consisted in gathering money (1939-46 about 80,000 fl), food and clothing for the benefit of severely damaged Rotterdam, for the numerous non-Aryan Christians and for Jewish refugees, and later for the Jewish concentration camp kept by the Germans at Westerbork in Drenthe, while through co-operation with the so-called *Werkgemeenschap van Doopsgezinden en Geestverwanten* (W.D.G.) dozens of children from hungering cities could be sent to the rural congregations. For all this work the W.D.G. had groups in many places in the Netherlands to assist it, and much of the work had to be done in secret.

In 1946 after the end of the war the Arbeidsgroep, though retaining its old purpose, changed its name to *Doopsgezinde Vredesgroep* (q.v.), since this name expresses more positively and more exactly the nature of the organization. Some of the members of the former Arbeidsgroep did not join the new organization, but on the other hand many more new members were received. vDZ.

Arbeiter, Hans, an elder of the Hutterian Brethren, had previously been an elder of the Swiss Brethren at Aachen, Worms, and Kreuznach (Beck, *Geschichts-Bücher,* 268). In 1557, through the work of Hans Schmidt (q.v.), he joined the Hutterites, emigrated to Moravia, and was chosen to the ministry in 1562 (Beck, 213 and 229). In 1568 he was sent as a missionary with Heinrich Schuster into the Rhenish Palatinate. In the bishopric of Speyer, at Hainbach, he was seized on July 18, 1568, and taken to Kirrweiler Castle, where he lay more than a half year and several times disputed with the cathedral preacher, Dr. Lamprecht. The content of these conversations Arbeiter collected in his Confession or *Rechenschaft*. The manuscript has been preserved; the Hutterian Brethren of Frankfort, S.D., have a copy; another is located in the Pressburg Cathedral library. The imprisonment of Hans Arbeiter was used by Hans Gärber as the subject of three songs: "Wollen singen zu dieser Frist," 50 stanzas; "Aber wollen wir heben an," 50 stanzas; "Wollt ihr nun weiter singen," 60 stanzas. They are referred to in the hymnbooks of the Hutterian Brethren as "beautiful songs," though as Beck (268) remarks, they are without a "just claim to this epithet." Before joining the Hutterian Brethren Arbeiter had already been imprisoned at Hainbach; thus his imprisonment in 1568 with Schuster was his second. HEGE.

Beck, *Geschichts-Bücher;* R. Friedmann, "Die Briefe der österr. Täufer," in *Archiv f. Ref.-Gesch.*, 1929, 26 f.;

Wolkan, *Lieder;* Chr. Hege, *Die Täufer in der Kurpfalz* (Frankfurt, 1908); *ML* I, 80.

Arbenz, Emil, professor in St. Gall, in 1886 published a booklet, *Aus dem Briefwechsel Vadians,* in which he lists 25 letters written by Conrad Grebel (*q.v.*) to Vadian in the years 1518 to 1525. Even more valuable is his publication of the entire text of the correspondence of Vadian in the original language, *Vadianische Briefsammlung der Stadtbibliothek St. Gallen* I-VII (*Jahresbericht des historischen Vereins in St. Gallen* 1888-1913). These letters—most of them in Latin, a few in German— offer valuable source material· for the study of the rise of the Anabaptist movement in Zürich and particularly of the career of Conrad Grebel, by presenting his gradual development as leader of the Anabaptist movement. They include 56 letters from Grebel to Vadian, and 2 from others to Grebel. (*ML* I, 81.)   NEFF.

Archbold, a town with a population of 1,200, located in the southwest corner of Fulton County in northwestern Ohio. It is the center of a large (originally Amish) Mennonite settlement of (now) more than 2,200 members, extending eastward 10 miles to Wauseon, the county seat, and westward 7 miles to the town of Stryker in Williams County. The original settlers came from Alsace and Montbéliard in France during the 1830's.

Five congregations of the Mennonite Church (MC), with a total combined membership of 1,700 have meetinghouses in the vicinity of Archbold, but none in the town itself. The Evangelical Mennonite Church has two congregations with a combined membership of 500, one with a meetinghouse in Archbold, and the other in Wauseon. The Reformed Mennonite Church has a small congregation with a meetinghouse northeast of Archbold, and the Church of God in Christ Mennonites have also a small congregation with a meetinghouse in the near-by village of Pettisville. The Archbold community has furnished several foreign and city missionaries. Several of the congregations have mission outposts in suburban Toledo, 40 miles distant.

A unique feature of the Archbold community is the development of a number of small Mennonite industries which serve to absorb the surplus farm labor, so that few of the members find it necessary to go to larger cities for employment. Among these industries are woodworking and furniture factories, a farm machinery factory, and a meat packing plant and livestock sales establishment. G.F.H.

Archbold Evangelical Mennonite Church, located at Archbold, Fulton Co., Ohio, is a member of the Evangelical Mennonite (formerly Defenseless) Conference. The church was organized about the year 1870 as a secession from the main Amish Mennonite group. Worship services in that period were held in the homes of the members. In 1880 a brick church accommodating 200 persons was built 2½ miles east of Archbold. In 1922 this church was razed and made part of a new church erected in town, with a capacity of 450, the membership having grown to 494. Approximately 100 of these members, assisted by the local congregation, erected a church building at Wauseon, Ohio, 10 miles east

of Archbold, and began regular services there in 1949. This church has a seating capacity of 350.

Ministers serving the congregation at Archbold have been Joseph Rupp, John Dietsch, Daniel Rupp, Jos. Egly, Eli Rupp, Ben Rupp, J. C. Miller, Elmer Klopfenstein, E. M. Stagle, Sam Rupp, Reuben Short, and H. E. Bertsche, who is the present pastor. Gordon Zimmerman is the pastor of the new church at Wauseon, Ohio.   E.E.R.

Archbold Reformed Mennonite Church, located five miles northeast of Archbold, Ohio, is also called the Lauber Hill Reformed Mennonite Church. Organized around 1855, its first church was erected in 1864. The present building was constructed in the early 1870's. For a time there was a second meetinghouse south of Archbold where services were held once a month for the benefit of those living at a distance from Lauber Hill. It was discontinued when automobiles came into general use. The first ministers in the congregation were Jacob Binder and Benedict Meister. In 1951 the approximate membership was 75. The origin of this congregation is obscure. The first families came from Wayne Co., Ohio, about 1834. A few families came direct from Canton Bern, Switzerland, and some apparently from the Amish Mennonite Church near by.   A.F.

Architecture. What can be said about "Mennonites and architecture" is related mostly to their retaining accustomed architectural patterns and their creative efforts in adjusting them to new environments. As the Mennonites outside of Holland and Northwest Germany are predominantly a rural folk, the objects in which their architectural patterns found expression are mostly dwelling places, barns, and school and church buildings. Nowhere, however, has any characteristic or distinctive architectural style developed which was created by Mennonites.

There are two major sources of origin and lines of development for Mennonite culture including architectural patterns—the Mennonites of Swiss background who migrated either directly from Switzerland to Pennsylvania or indirectly by way of Germany, during the early 18th century, and accepted the Pennsylvania-German architectural patterns, and the Prusso-German Mennonites of Dutch background who settled in the Vistula River Delta near Danzig and migrated to Russia at the end of the 18th century, whence some came to America in the second half of the 19th century.

Switzerland. The Swiss Mennonites, when leaving home and settling in South Germany, Alsace-Lorraine, Volhynia, Galicia, and America, adhered to their culture and traditions in their respective environments for a long time. In countries like South Germany, Alsace-Lorraine, and Holland a gradual adjustment took place, while in countries with a definitely contrasting culture adjustment was much slower. This was the case in Volhynia, Galicia, and Pennsylvania. And yet the meetinghouses or churches of the Mennonites in South Germany and Alsace-Lorraine even in our day indicate a direct expression of their straightforward Christian belief and practices.

It is of interest to note that in Switzerland, for instance at Langnau and Sonnenberg (Jeangisboden) and quite generally, the meetinghouse is built to look much like a dwelling house, actually inhabited by a family in the first story, with the church room or rooms in the second story. In some places a schoolroom displaces the family quarters on the first floor, as at Moron.

The Swiss and South German Mennonites and Amish who settled in Pennsylvania during the 18th century became an integral part of the developing Pennsylvania-German culture and made their own significant contribution to it. This culture is by background a composite of various South German cultural strains which were transplanted to Eastern Pennsylvania by representatives of the Lutherans, Reformed, Mennonites, Moravians, and some mystic and pietistic groups. Here in the new American environment under pioneer conditions the Pennsylvania-German culture emerged. The architectural patterns which the Pennsylvania-German Mennonites followed are for the most part an integral part of this culture. A visitor to the Pennsylvania-German country is most impressed by the unique barns which he finds not only in Pennsylvania, but wherever these people have moved during the past century in states like Ohio, Indiana, Iowa, and Ontario. The barns (*q.v.*) including the motifs and decorative designs are also of South German background. J. J. Stoudt writes that the designs once had religious meaning, but Alfred L. Shoemaker's *Hex, No!* shows that they no longer have religious significance. According to Shoemaker the painting of barns in Pennsylvania was introduced around 1830. The "plain people" including the Amish and the Mennonites accepted this innovation but were reluctant to make use of symbols and decorative designs on their barns although they used them freely in penmanship and embroidery. In matters pertaining to dwelling places and other structures in the barnyard the Amish and Mennonites have more or less followed the prevailing practices of their respective communities.

In their church architecture, however, the Mennonites in Pennsylvania did not follow the prevailing practices of the "church people" neighbors, but went their own distinctive way. Their meetinghouse has an interesting history. During the 16th to 18th centuries when the Mennonites of Switzerland were outlawed and could not build churches or special buildings for worship purposes the worship had of necessity to be either in private homes or in the forests and deep mountain glens. No meetinghouses were built in Switzerland or neighboring Alsace and France before the second half of the 19th century. The Amish, being a conservative branch of the Mennonites, maintained the practice even in countries where there was no restriction along these lines. The Mennonites of colonial Pennsylvania (1683-1789), however, during pioneer days built log or stone buildings to serve as schools during the week and as churches on Sunday. Gradually separate buildings for each purpose were erected; usually close together, with a whitewashed stone type soon becoming predominant, later replaced by a brick structure. Originally the church building was very plain and similar to the school. As the congregations grew in size the buildings grew in length. The original meetinghouse usually had one entrance at the end or side; later, two—one for men and one for women. A small porch at the entrance was in many cases extended across one entire side and end of the meetinghouse. Originally no paint was applied to the interior woodwork and furniture of the building. Men sat on one side and the women on the other on benches without backs. Hats and bonnets were hung on racks suspended from the ceiling over the benches. The ministers sat around a table at the wall opposite the entrance. Gradually a long pulpit was introduced, from which the sermon was delivered, backed by a long bench on which all the ministers sat during the service. Today the pulpits are largely modernized although the long bench is still commonly in use. In the Eastern Pennsylvania meetinghouses of the more conservative groups, no provision is made for pianos or organs, symbolism or art work, steeples and bells, stained glass windows, etc., even today. In the cemeteries near the meetinghouses small simple headstones bearing the names of the departed are found. Stoves were early placed into meetinghouses but lights only recently with the advent of evening meetings. With the coming of Sunday schools and other activities of the congregations a basement was added.

The origin and development of the Pennsylvania-German Mennonite meetinghouse is most closely related to that of the other plain people such as the Friends, and is most likely patterned directly after the Quaker meetinghouse which was brought from England. This meetinghouse type has spread to Virginia, Ontario, Ohio, and the western states where the architectural patterns underwent some modifications, especially in the Middle West. Smaller groups again under pioneer conditions and joined frequently by newcomers from Europe did not always maintain the structural design of the meetinghouse in its original form. Sometimes it was abandoned altogether and replaced by prevailing styles in the respective communities. Thus there is less uniformity along these lines among the Mennonites of Pennsylvania-German background in the Middle West and prairie states than is the case in Pennsylvania, Ontario, and Virginia. Under the impact of prevailing American architectural styles the more progressive groups of Pennsylvania at present too, are less uniform in traditional meetinghouse structure than they formerly were. Some congregations have broken away completely and others are attempting to retain the good qualities and features in their adjustment to the needs and functions of a Mennonite congregation in our day. (For appearance and developments of the Pennsylvania-German meetinghouse see illustrations.)

It is possible though not likely that the early Mennonite meetinghouse of Pennsylvania was also influenced by practices common among the Mennonites of the Palatinate in South Germany. Until 1750 the Mennonites in the Palatinate had not yet been able to erect special houses for worship, and after this almost no emigrants crossed the Atlantic until after 1815. The first church buildings in the Palatinate were plain one-story structures with rectangular windows that gave little impression of being "churches." Some changes in both the exterior and interior took place during the 19th century. Organs were introduced and sometimes provisions for choirs were made. These changes usually came about in connection with a trained ministry which was gradually introduced from the beginning of the 19th century.

Before presenting the Prusso-Russo-German architectural practices, it is necessary to summarize their background. Mennonite families coming from the various provinces to the Low Countries during the 16th and 17th centuries and settling along the Vistula River merged into a religio-cultural unit that retained its characteristics even after adjustment to the new environment, which practices were also continued on the steppes of Russia, the prairies of North America, the Chaco of Paraguay, and the hills of Mexico, whither migrating groups later came. This perpetuated culture was, however, neither purely Dutch nor German but a composite of the two, based on religious principles adhered to for centuries. The peculiar architectural patterns and practices must be viewed against this background.

Holland. In Holland the Mennonite influence on architecture has been limited to church buildings, since the residences of Mennonites, both in the country and in towns, show no difference from other Dutch houses. But Mennonite meetinghouses in Holland, at least until about 1840, are quite different from other Protestant church buildings. From the origin of Anabaptism until the end of persecution, i.e., from 1530 to about 1570, Anabaptists and Mennonites did not meet in special meetinghouses, but worshiped where they could gather best, in the open air, in the attic of a warehouse, in a cellar, in a granary, or in other hidden places. About 1570, and in the country somewhat earlier, Mennonites began to assemble in the house of one of the members of the congregation. After persecution had ended, they usually rented a room for worshiping. About 1600 most congregations began to rent or to buy a warehouse or a barn, which was adapted for the meetings only by making small transformations. In the second half of the 17th century nearly every congregation had a meetinghouse of its own. The Flemish congregation at Amsterdam secured its meetinghouse *bij't Lam* (now Singelkerk) as early as 1608. About the same time the congregations of Rotterdam, Haarlem, Leeuwarden, and Leiden secured their meetinghouses. Before 1795 Mennonites of Holland, like other dissenters, were allowed to worship only in such meetinghouses as had no towers nor bells, so that no one would be "misled" into attending their services, nor were they allowed to be built on street fronts; hence all the Mennonite churches of this period in the towns of Holland are hidden churches (*schuilkerken*). Good examples of those old hidden churches are today the Mennonite

churches of Amsterdam (*Singelkerk*), Haarlem, and Grouw, Friesland. In the country too the meetinghouses were not allowed to look like churches; mostly they looked like ordinary houses or barns. Especially in the Zaan region of North Holland near Amsterdam many of these barnlike meetinghouses were erected, of which some still exist, e.g., Zaandam-West (built in 1684), Krommenie (1700), Westzaan-Zuid (1731). Typical houselike churches of this period were the meetinghouses of Stroe, on the island Wieringen, which burned down in 1933, the church of Nes on the island of Ameland, those of Zijldijk in Groningen, and the little Menno Simons church at Pingjum, Friesland, restored in 1950. Even a large and important congregation like Harlingen assembled during the 17th and 18th centuries in a barnlike structure called *De Blauwe Schuur* (the blue barn). In the early 17th century all the churches were very simple and unpainted, and the furniture was also plain. There were no chairs or pews, only benches without backs; no pulpit, but on one side a kind of platform on which the ministers and deacons sat on a bench (later on chairs). There was no heating and the building had only a few small windows, mostly placed rather high in the walls. Sometimes one corner of the meeting place was enclosed as a room for the preachers and deacons to meet in before the service began. This kind of meetinghouse, of which the ground plan was a square, or a rectangle, the square ground form being the oldest, continued to be the normal type for the more conservative Mennonites, such as the Groninger Old Flemish Jan-Jacobsz group, until their congregations were dissolved in the 18th and early 19th centuries. Both Lamists and Zonists permitted more convenience and even some luxury. Their meetinghouses had chairs (for the women) instead of only benches, and a pulpit like that of the Reformed churches. Of this group the former church of Rotterdam (burned down 1940) with its oak boarding and its beautifully carved pulpit was a fine example. The exterior of all those churches was very plain, and stained glass windows, with two or three exceptions, were not permitted. The old country church of Irnsum, Friesland, however, had a small painted window by 1684, and Witveen in 1712 (*DB* 1872, 34-35). After 1796, when Mennonites obtained full civil rights, no further restrictions were imposed in the building of Mennonite churches. Henceforth the church buildings could be erected on street fronts, and they could have towers, if so desired. Yet towers on Mennonite churches are very rare; some have a little spire or elevation on the facade, like Enschede, IJtens, Joure, Veenwouden, and Oudebildtzijl, the latter having a bell. Only the church of Wageningen (built 1951) has a real tower. About the middle of the 19th century most of the Dutch Mennonite churches were remodeled and many were built new. With a few exceptions they are of no importance in an artistic sense. They are mostly very plain, yet following the artistic ideas of this period by adapting Renaissance porches and Gothic ogival windows. Of higher artistic merit are some churches built in the last thirty years. Mennonite churches in Holland usually have a balcony, which is also the location of the choir during the service, if there is a choir. They also have rooms for the meetings of the church board, catechetical classes, etc. All Dutch churches now have organs, introduced generally at the end of the 18th century, the first installed in Utrecht in 1765. Some churches also have beautiful stained glass windows, such as for instance Hilversum and Heerlen. Basements are unknown in Holland. vDZ.

The settlement and building practices of the native population in the Vistula Delta differed considerably from those introduced by the Dutch Mennonites who established themselves there. Before the arrival of the Dutch Mennonites it was the custom of the natives to settle in compact villages and to build dwelling places, barns, and sheds as separate units. The Mennonites usually located along a river, each on his own land with dwelling place, barn, and shed under one roof, built at right angles with the street. In this long structure the dwelling place was nearest the street; immediately behind it was the barn and finally the shed. More prosperous farmers occasionally attached the shed to the barn in a triangular fashion. At times another section was added to the shed making the total building assume the shape of a cross (*Kreuzhof*). During the last decades this architectural pattern underwent considerable modification, especially on the larger estates, although the traditional structures could still be found.

Wherever the Mennonites of Prussian background went they took with them their way of life including their architectural traditions, and some of them were preserved in greater purity in isolated settlements in Russia and America than in Prussia. The pattern of the buildings was always the same although different materials were used. In the pioneer stages solid mud walls or adobe brick were used. Later they were replaced by wood or brick. The straw roof was replaced by tiles, tin, or shingles. A deviation from the early Dutch tradition in Prussia was that they settled in compact villages in Russia, and perpetuated the practice in Manitoba, Mexico, and Paraguay. The interior of the house was arranged much as it had been in Prussia and in most

of the homes traditional homemade furniture was found.

The dwelling house, always one story, had two entrances, one at the front and one at the rear, each leading into a room serving as a hall (*Vorderhaus* and *Hinterhaus*). Between these two halls was a kitchen and in the chimney above it the hams and sausages were smoked. The front hall led into the parlor called *Grosse Stube*. From the back hall one could reach the two rooms across from the parlor called *Kleine Stube* and *Eckstube*. Into these three rooms extended a brick stove which was heated from the kitchen with straw, wood, or dried manure. Between the kitchen and the entrance to the barn were two rooms, the *Sommerstube* for the boys and the pantry with steps leading into the basement. The attics of the dwelling place and barn were used for storing grain and feed.

The dwelling house and barn were connected either directly by a door or by a short hallway. One side of the barn was arranged for horses and the other for cows. From the barn one entered directly into a large shed where hay, chaff, straw, and possibly machinery were stored. The threshing machine was quite frequently placed in a separate storage room, and the straw outside. The well was located either in the barn or next to the barn door. In addition to implement sheds there were usually a summer kitchen and possibly a small house for the retired parents. The house was usually surrounded by a large yard with many shade trees, an orchard, and well-kept flower and vegetable gardens. Some characteristics such as the predominance of the tulip bed bore evidence of their Dutch background.

When the Mennonites from Russia, in 1874 and the following years, went to the prairie states and provinces of the United States and Canada, they continued their architectural traditions. In the United States, however, they soon discontinued them, accepting the prevailing American practices. Only a very few Mennonite pioneer buildings can be found in the prairie states today. In Manitoba, however, where the more conservative Mennonites settled, they long retained not only the village pattern but also the architectural practices. Although some villages have disappeared and some modern

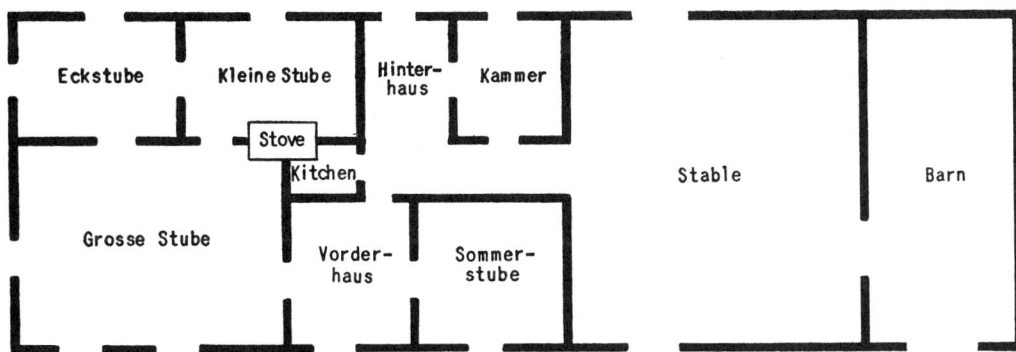

Adaptation of Russian Mennonite house according to J. Toews in A. Klaus, Unsere Kolonien

buildings are found on farms of the original Mennonite settlement, the old villages and the traditional style of buildings are still represented. Some of the houses are neglected but others are kept in good repair and painted. This is especially the case where more recent immigrants from Russia have taken over the farms of the conservative Mennonites who have moved to Mexico or Paraguay. Most of the buildings are wooden structures surrounded by board or lattice fence. When after World War I the conservative Mennonites of Canada moved to Mexico and Paraguay they again transplanted their architectural patterns to an entirely new environment. In Mexico the expected change from the use of adobe or mud to wood has not taken place. One can also detect other instances of conformity and adjustment to the Latin-American environment in spite of the extremely conservative attitude of the settlers. The high roofs and the spacious attics have almost completely disappeared and the traditional wooden fences around the yards have been replaced by high adobe fences which constitute an adjustment to the environment and protection against thievery. In general the buildings are smaller here than they were in Canada and Russia.

As has been stated, the later Russo-German architectural pattern in Prussia had originated with the coming of the Dutch Mennonites in the 16th century. Specialists distinguish in the Low Countries between the Frisian, the Saxon, and the Brabant architecture. A comparison of these styles with those in use by the Mennonites leads to the conclusion that the traditional Mennonite pattern must be of Frisian background, but has been somewhat modified during the various adjustments to new environments. It should be kept in mind, however, that the architectural patterns of the Low Countries and northern Germany have much in common and differ radically from those in South Germany and Switzerland (see illustrations).

In church architecture there is considerable similarity between the Pennsylvania-German meetinghouse and that of the Russo-German Mennonites. Both groups originated in strictly Reformed surroundings in which Catholic ritual was abhorred and only plain whitewashed churches were tolerated.

In Northwest Germany one or two of the older buildings of architectural type have been preserved, the one at Norden being a particularly beautiful 18th-century type.

Among the Prussian Mennonite rural churches, where the first meetinghouse was that of Thiensdorf erected in 1722, the Heubuden church was typical. It was a large wooden structure extremely plain, with little resemblance to a church building, located in an open field. The main floor was for women and the balcony for men, very much like the Singel Church of Amsterdam. The pulpit was located on the long side with an enclosure for ministers and deacons on either side. A pipe organ was added in the 18th century. Similarly constructed were the churches of Fürstenwerder, Schönsee, Rosenort, and others. A definite Lutheran influence was evidenced in the churches of Elbing, Marienburg, Montau, and others which were constructed of brick, and had either steeples or crosses and Gothic or Roman arches. The Danzig Mennonite Church represented an attempt to retain the old pattern with an adjustment to present trends.

The early Mennonite churches of Russia bore a striking similarity with those of Prussia, the Chortitza church closely resembling the Heubuden church. During the pioneer days in many settlements, like early Pennsylvania, the same building was used as a school during the week and for worship on Sunday. Perhaps this is the reason why schools and churches were similar in construction for a long time. The typical church structure before World War I was a long brick building rarely with a steeple but with arched windows still revealing the old pattern. The most extreme adjustment to the Russian environment was the Einlage Mennonite Church built in a sort of Russian baroque surrounded by a very heavy brick fence.

When in 1874 and after, the Mennonites came to the prairie states and provinces from Russia and Prussia, they continued constructing churches along the traditional lines. The First Mennonite Church of Beatrice, Neb.; the Hoffnungsau Mennonite Church near Buhler, Kan.; the Gnadenberg Mennonite Church near Whitewater, Kan.; and the former Kleine Gemeinde Church near Meade, Kan., were some of the examples of this tradition. In the process of replacing the old buildings, most of the congregations gradually imitated surrounding practices with little regard to their own principles and traditions.

The early Mennonites of Manitoba and Saskatchewan continued to build the traditional plain churches to which they were accustomed in Russia, often using the same buildings also for schools. The Old Colony Mennonites, Sommerfelder, and other groups definitely adhered to a uniform pattern similar to that of Mennonites of Pennsylvania, which they are continuing in Mexico and Paraguay. It is interesting to note that the dwelling places in Mexico are made of adobe while some church buildings are still being constructed of imported lumber, an indication that in the realm of religious practices there is greater reluctance to give up traditions.

There are two noticeable extremes among the Mennonites of America regarding church buildings. The ultraconservative groups—the Amish, Hutterites, and others—have developed a principle that no special building is to be provided for worship purposes only. They meet in private homes or school buildings. What was originally a necessity has become a basic principle of their faith. The other extreme is that of those Mennonite congregations who, unaware of their principles, accept almost any architectural patterns found in their respective communities. This has produced some very odd mixtures and contradictions like the towers found on many Mennonite churches of the prairies, which are remnants of fortresses of the Middle Ages. When and how did these towers become the adornment of Mennonite churches and what connection is there between them and a church in which the Gospel of redemption and a nonresistant way of life is proclaimed?

In conclusion it must be said that Mennonites have not developed more of a specific church architecture than have Methodists, Baptists, or some of the other denominations, and yet there have been certain characteristics peculiar to them. Mennonites of Holland, Prussia, Russia, and the eastern United States have at times developed certain characteristics which express simplicity, honesty, and integration of their basic principles.† C.K.

J. H. Gallee, *Das niederländische Bauernhaus und seine Bewohner* (Utrecht, 2v. 1908-09, one vol. text, one vol. illustrations); H. Wiebe, *Das Siedlungswerk niederländischer Mennoniten im Weichseltal zwischen Fordon und Weissenberg b. z. Ausgang des 18. Jahrh.* (Marburg a.d. Lahn, 1952); C. Krahn, "The Ethnic Origin of the Menn. from Russia," in *Menn. Life* III, No. 3 (1948) 45; J. C. Wenger, *History of the Menn. of the Franconia Conf.* (Telford, 1937); R. S. Montgomery, *Home Craft Course in Penn.-German Architecture* (Plymouth Meeting, 1945); M. G. Weaver, *Menn. of Lancaster Conf.* (Scottdale, 1931); G. M. Ludwig, *The Influence of the Penna. Dutch in the Middle West* (Pennsylvania German Folklore Society, 1947); C. G. Bachman, *The Old Order Amish of Lancaster Co.* (Norristown, 1942); *The Menn. Community*, January 1950; C. Henry Smith, *The Menn. Immigration to Penna.* (Norristown, 1929); J. J. Stoudt, *Penna. Folk-Art* (Allentown, 1948); P. Schowalter, "Menn. Churches in South Germany," *Menn. Life* VII (Jan. 1952); *idem*, "Die Kirchen der Mennoniten in Pfalz-Hessen," in *Menn. Jahrbuch*, 1952; E. K. Francis, "The Menn. Farmhouse in Manitoba," *MQR* XXVIII (1954) 56-59.

Archives. Official depositories of documents were almost unknown among the Mennonites of America until recent times. The immigrants of 1683-1873 whose descendants constitute the (old) Mennonite and related branches, coming from Switzerland, South Germany, and France where the congregations kept few if any records, established none in their new home. On the contrary through a strange twist, record-keeping, even of membership lists, was often considered an evidence of pride. Written minutes of the annual and semiannual conference meetings were not kept until quite late, e.g., in the Franconia Conference not before 1905. Sometimes, even after the establishment of general organizations such as boards, few records were preserved, and sometimes secretaries did not pass on record books or files of correspondence to their successors. Much important material has been lost or destroyed —few documents of any sort have been preserved, even letters dating before 1870. A noteworthy exception are the Alms books of the Skippack (1738-) and Franconia (1753-) congregations in Montgomery Co., Pa., of the Franconia Conference. The important records of the Germantown congregation (1708 ff.), the first Mennonite congregation in North America, which were still extant in 1835, have since disappeared.

In 1937 the Mennonite General Conference (MC) established "The Archives of the Mennonite Church" under the administration of its Historical Committee, which employs a trained archivist-librarian. The archives are located (since 1940) in the Goshen College Library building, Goshen, Ind.,

and now contain over 200,000 items. The most important deposits are: the John F. Funk collection, including the records of the Mennonite Publishing Company, certain records of the Mennonite Board of Missions and Charities and the Mennonite Board of Education, the records of certain General Conference committees, as Peace Problems Committee, General S.S. Committee, the Commission for Christian Education and Young People's Work, Inter-Board Committee, also of certain district conferences and congregations, the letters of John Horsch, George Lapp, S. D. Guengerich, J. D. Mininger, M. S. Steiner, Edward Yoder, and the diaries of J. S. Coffman. For a list of contents see "General Catalogue of the Archives of the Mennonite Church" by N. P. Springer in *Mennonite Historical Bulletin* X (January 1949). The archival materials of the Mennonite Central Committee before 1945 and the Corporación Paraguaya are on deposit here also, but the Mennonite Civilian Public Service records (exclusive of government records) together with the MCC records since 1945 are on deposit in the MCC central file at the Akron, Pa., headquarters. The Mennonite Historical Library at Goshen College contains a considerable amount of documentary materials. Most of the district conferences have official historians and a few have historical societies, but little has been done in the collection of documentary materials except by the Ontario Conference, which has a conference archives, located in a room in the Golden Rule Bookstore, Kitchener, Ont.

In the General Conference Mennonite Church, however, due to the fact that the Mennonites of Dutch, Prussian, and Russian background were inclined to keep records, diaries, and copies of correspondence, much valuable historical material has been accumulated and preserved in homes and congregations. Soon after the coming of the Prusso-Russo-German Mennonites to America in 1873 ff., interest in collecting material of this nature was manifested. Since these congregations, formed by Mennonites of the above background, gradually all joined the G.C. Mennonite Church, efforts along these lines coincided with those of this Conference. After some individual efforts at collecting and preserving materials pertaining to the Mennonites, a Mennonite Historical Association (Society) was organized in 1911 at the General Conference session at Bluffton, Ohio, one of whose purposes was the collection of documentary materials. The collection is kept in the vault of the present G.C. Headquarters at Newton, Kan., and Bethel College. Most of the material collected consists of letters, diaries, church records, deeds, photographs, rare periodicals, and some books brought to America by the Mennonites coming from Russia, Poland, and Prussia. In 1920, the Association reported that it had collected more than 10,000 separate items. It proposed the erection of a memorial building to house the conference historical materials, possibly on the Bethel College campus. Although this plan as a conference project did not materialize, a modern, fireproof library with space to house such materials has now been constructed (1953). In

1937, the Mennonite Historical Association was replaced by the present Historical Committee of the G.C. Mennonite Church. The documentary materials of the Mennonite Historical Association were transferred to the Bethel College Historical Library, which collects material for both the school and the conference. In recent years, numerous items and larger collections have been added. Among them were the diaries and collections of L. E. Zimmermann, Leonhard Sudermann, Cornelius Jansen, David Goerz, B. Warkentin, D. Gaeddert, C. H. Wedel, H. P. Krehbiel, C. E. Krehbiel, J. H. Janzen, A. A. Friesen, and a number of church records including some of the Danzig (W. Prussia) Mennonite Church.

The General Conference Headquarters at Newton, Kan., maintains an archival collection. The C. Henry Smith Collection at Bluffton College contains some documentary material, as does the library of the Mennonite Biblical Seminary in Chicago. The Canadian Board of Mennonite Colonization, Saskatoon, has the files pertaining to Mennonite immigration to Canada since World War I. The Historical Committee of the Conference is now working on a project to microfilm all records, diaries, and other items of historical significance found in congregations and private homes. In addition to this, an extensive microfilming program is under way in Europe. It is planned to complete the microfilming of the archives of the Mennonite Church of Amsterdam and the materials on the Anabaptists in Innsbruck and other places in 1954.

In Germany the congregational archives of Danzig, Orlofferfelde, and Heubuden, the only significant ones for West Prussia, were lost or destroyed in 1945. The Hamburg-Altona congregational archives are only in part preserved. The small documentary collection established by Christian Neff at his Weierhof home has been preserved and given to the Mennonite Historical Society (Mennonitische Forschungsstelle, Göttingen) of Germany. It remains at the Weierhof.

The most extensive Mennonite archives anywhere are those of the Dutch Mennonite churches. These have been for the most part concentrated in the archives of the United Mennonite Church in Amsterdam. A catalog of the great collection here was published in 1883-84, under the title *Inventaris der Archiefstukken berustende bij de Vereenigde Doopsgezinde Gemeente te Amsterdam*, by Dr. J. G. de Hoop-Scheffer. Part I (1883), containing material relating to Mennonites in general, occupies 467 pages, with 2,334 numbered items. Part II, Section I, containing (1884) the archives of the Amsterdam Mennonite Church, occupies 496 pages, with 3,320 numbered items. Of this material, pp. 371-420, items 2,571-2,862 contain correspondence with foreign Mennonite churches, chiefly German. Part II, Section II, "Archival Material of Mennonite Churches Outside of Amsterdam," occupies 165 pages with 867 numbered items, plus 24 items of supplementary material belonging to the various parts of the whole catalog. In this section pp. 1-109 and items 1-679 are from Dutch churches, while pp. 109-62,

items 680-867, contain correspondence from foreign Mennonites, all from Germany except three from Switzerland and one from France. Since these catalogs were issued, much additional material has been acquired (about 400 items), of which no printed list is available. Not all the archival materials from the Dutch congregations are desposited in Amsterdam, since many congregations have their own archives. Some congregations have deposited their archives with the municipal Archives, such as Rotterdam, while other congregations had given their valuable documents and books into the safekeeping of the provincial or state Archives. For instance, the archives of Almelo are now in Zwolle, those of Zaandam-West at Haarlem, and those of many congregations at Leeuwarden. Among the important archives are those of Groningen (catalog by A. Pakhuis, 1940), Deventer, Rotterdam (catalog by E. Wiersum, n.d.), and Middelburg (catalog by L. Lasonder, 1906).

The Swiss Mennonite conference has established its official historical collection, including archival materials, in the building of the Sonnenberg Mennonite Church at Jeangisboden near Tramelan in the Bernese Jura.

In Russia each of the two original Mennonite colonies, Chortitza (founded 1789) and Molotschna (founded 1804), had official district (*volost*) archives. Both were destroyed either by bandits or by wanton Russian officials in 1921. The Mennonite Central Archives which was established in 1917 by the General Conference of the Mennonite Churches of Russia, and located in Halbstadt, Ukraine, under the direction of Peter Braun, director of the Halbstadt Zentralschule and the Mennonite Normal School, was hidden in a house which was confiscated by the government in 1929. Whether the archives were saved and transferred to some central Russian archives, such as Moscow, is not known. This was a rich archive containing the records of various official Mennonite organizations as well as private collections of documents. Its contents are listed in the article by Peter Braun, "Archive von Bolschewisten zerstört," in *Mennonitische Geschichtsblätter* I (1936) 32-36, where the story of the destruction or loss of the three archives is told. Only a small portion of the large David H. Epp collection of Chortitza was brought to Canada. The collection fell into the hands of the Red army during the Mennonite flight from Russia in 1943. The records of the Mennonite Central Committee relief work in Russia 1920-25 were deposited in a Mennonite home in the Alexandertal colony in 1925 by Director Alvin J. Miller when he left Russia.

The important Odessa Archives of the Russian governmental *Fürsorge Amt* (Guardians' Committee), which had supervision of matters relating to the Mennonite and other foreign colonies in South Russia (1803 ff.), was brought out to Berlin during World War II by the German army, and deposited in the library of the *Sammlung Georg Leibbrandt*. Its present whereabouts is unknown. Much material on the earlier immigration of the Russian Mennonites to Canada (1873-80) is in the Canadian government archives at Ottawa. Part of this material was published by Ernst H. Correll in the *MQR* 1935-50. In 1945 an attempt was made without much success, to establish a central depository in Canada located in Winnipeg, for Mennonite records rescued from Russia and brought to Canada. A small collection is now located at the Canadian Mennonite Bible College in Winnipeg. The valuable files accumulated in the office of B. H. Unruh of Karlsruhe relating to the emigration from Russia 1920-40, taken for safekeeping to Central Germany along with the library of Karlsruhe Technical University, are apparently lost.

The Hutterian Brethren brought with them from Russia to South Dakota in 1873-75 (now in part in Manitoba and Alberta) much valuable manuscript material, including their two great chronicles, and numerous epistles, doctrinal books, hymnbooks, and constitutions for their religious and economic life. The two chronicles (*q.v.*) have recently been published in America, 1943 and 1945.

Vast amounts of archival material relating to the Mennonites, both in their earlier history (Anabaptist period 1525-1618) and in more recent times, repose in official government archives, throughout Europe. The persecution of the Anabaptists in Switzerland, Germany, Austria, Holland, and elsewhere occasioned multitudinous investigations, trials, and other legal procedures, all of which are duly recorded in government documents, concentrated in the centers of Anabaptist activity, such as Zürich, Basel, Bern, Strasbourg, Augsburg, Münster, Amsterdam, Innsbruck, and Vienna, as well as in countless city, provincial, and state depositories. Numerous Hutterite manuscripts were confiscated from the Bruderhofs and deposited in the archives and libraries of Austria, Hungary, and Moravia during the 17th century and later. A great collection of such materials, assembled by Josef v. Beck (reported in his *Geschichts-Bücher,* 1883), was deposited in the state archives at Brno, Czechoslovakia (described by H. S. Bender in *MQR* XXIII, April 1949, 105-6, "Anabaptist Manuscripts in the Archives at Brno, Czeckoslovakia"). See also Robert Friedmann's "Die Briefe der Oesterreichischen Täufer (Ein Bericht)" in *Archiv für Reformationsgeschichte* XXVI (1929) 30-80, and 161-92.

Only in the last two generations have the great Anabaptist documentary collections been used extensively by scholars—resulting in a great number of scholarly monographs on regional and local Anabaptist history. The great enterprise of publication of all Anabaptist documents in German language countries, begun by the German *Verein für Reformationsgeschichte* in 1925 with a subsidy from the Prussian state, is just now being brought to relative completion (see **Täuferakten**). (*ML* I, 81.) H.S.B.

Arent Block, an Anabaptist martyr from Zevenbergen, Dutch province of North Brabant (not Transylvania as *ML* has it), was one of the seven martyrs who were put to death at Breda (same province) in 1572. The *Martyrs' Mirror* states that Arent, on the way to the place of execution, dropped a note hoping that one of his friends would pick it up. But the letter fell into the hands of his enemies, and Arent and his companion Cornelis de Gyselaar (*q.v.*) were brought back to prison for another severe torture, after which they were burned at the stake. (*Mart. Mir.* D 603, E 929 ff.; *ML* I, 237.)   NEFF, vDZ.

Arent van Essen, an Anabaptist martyr, an elder and schoolteacher, was captured with his wife Ursula, Neeltgen, an old woman, and her daughter Tryntgen, at Maastricht by the bailiffs of Alba, and after the most cruel torture all four were burned at the stake, Jan. 9, 1570.   vDZ.

Mart. Mir. D 502, E 842 f.; W. Bax, *Het. Prot. in het bisdom Luik* II (The Hague, 1941) 306-10; *ML* I, 609.

Arent Jacobssen Keyser (Arend Jacobsz), an Anabaptist martyr of Monnikendam in the Dutch province of North Holland, was beheaded at Amsterdam on March 6, 1535, along with eight other brethren. An excerpt from the death sentence is to be found in the *Martyrs' Mirror.* (*Mart. Mir.* D 412, E 763; Grosheide, *Verhooren,* 52 f.; *ML* II, 386.)   vDZ.

Arent Jacobsz (called Arnold Jacob in the English *Martyrs' Mirror*) an Anabaptist martyr of De Rijp in the Dutch province of North Holland, was brought to Monnikendam along with his wife and oldest son, where all three were drowned in 1539. They were thrown from a boat into the sea with heavy stones tied about their necks. (*Mart. Mir.* D 51, E 455; *ML* I, 86.)   NEFF.

Arent Janssen (Jansz), an Anabaptist martyr, a native of Gorinchem in the Dutch province of South Holland, a thread-twister by trade, was beheaded at Amsterdam on March 6, 1535, along with eight other brethren, among whom was Jan Paeuw (*q.v.*). (*Mart. Mir.* D 412, E 763; *Inv. Arch. Amst.* I, No. 93; Grosheide, *Verhooren,* 52 f.; *ML* II, 391.)   NEFF.

Arent Passementwerker (braid weaver), an Anabaptist martyr, who was executed at Antwerp in 1558. He is identical with Aerdt (Arent) Aerssens (*q.v.*). (*Mart. Mir.* D 202, E 583.)   NEFF.

Arents, Lenart (van Aken), was one of the group of 13 Mennonite and Quaker families of Crefeld, who formed the first permanent German settlement in America, landing on Oct. 6, 1683. He was a descendant of the martyr Lenaert Aerntsz. The family was Mennonite until the coming of the Quakers to Crefeld in 1671; he was one of those who made the transfer to the latter group. His wife was a sister of one Wilhelm Strepers, who also emigrated to America on the *Concord* (*q.v.*), and Jan Strepers, who had bought of William Penn 5,000 acres in Pennsylvania on March 10, 1683. Arents also secured 1,000 acres of William Penn on June 11, 1683; thus he was one of the first six Crefeld purchasers of land in America. He died Dec. 3, 1714, leaving three daughters.   HEGE.

D. K. Cassel, *Gesch. der Menn.* (Philadelphia, 1890) 37; W. Niepoth, *Zur Gesch. der Menn. in Rheydt* (1937) 13 f.; Fr. Nieper, *Die ersten deutschen Auswanderer von Krefeld nach Pennsylvanien* (Mörs, 1940) 89 ff.; W. Hull, *William Penn and the Dutch Quaker Migration to Penna.* (Swarthmore, 1935); *ML* I, 81.

Argentina, a Spanish-speaking republic on the Atlantic side of the Andes in the southern part of South America, with an area of 1,079,965 sq. mi. and a population (1947) of 16,104,929, next to Brazil the largest in South America. Mennonites (MC, North America) first entered the country in 1917 as missionaries (see **Argentine Mennonite Mission**), locating in the territory 50-150 miles west of Buenos Aires, which has become the heart of the Mennonite mission enterprise there. Work was established at Cosquin in the province of Cordoba in 1935, among the Indians in the far north Chaco territory in 1943, and in the capital city of Buenos Aires in 1949. The North American staff of the mission has averaged 20-25 persons in recent years, with a present (1953) church membership of 745. The church organ is *La Voz Menonita* (since 1932).

In 1948 about 150 Russian Mennonites forsook the transport en route from Germany to Paraguay while it was temporarily stalled in Buenos Aires, and settled largely in the city and its environs as day-laborers. Additions to the group from Paraguay since that time have increased the total of Russian Mennonites in the country to over 400. Since the group lacked all church privileges, the Mennonite Central Committee, at the request of the various interested Mennonite mission boards of North America, established a religious and social center in the city in 1949, at first under the direction of Bishop Nelson Litwiller of the Argentine Mennonite Mission, but since 1950 under the direction of the minister Martin Duerksen, formerly of Paraguay.

The Mennonite Bible School at Bragado, F.C.O., the Spanish training school of the Argentine Mennonite Mission, seeks to serve not only the mission's own needs in Argentina, but also the Spanish training needs of the Paraguayan Mennonites. H.S.B.

Argentine Mennonite Conference. This conference (MC) was first organized in 1923 and is composed of all bishops, ministers, missionaries, appointed national workers, one delegate for each congregation up to 19 members and 2 for congregations of 20 or more throughout the Argentine Republic. While the custom had been to hold yearly meetings, this was changed to biennial meetings in 1942, due to the high cost of bringing together the delegates from such widely separated zones and districts. In the alternate years the general young people's institute meets, at which time a pastors' meeting usually is convened to take care of any necessary reorganization or business. All these meetings are held in the splendid eucalyptus campground near Trenque Lauquen.

The convention of this conference is largely a spiritual meeting to which often outstanding speakers from other denominations are invited, but reports are heard from such committees as the following: the Bible Institute, the Old People's Home, the Young People's Institute, the Children's Camp, the Publication Committee, the Historical Committee, Women's Evangelical Society, Pastors' Meeting, Charities and Welfare, and from the following individuals: the general secretary, the delegate to

the Confederation of Evangelical Churches, and from one delegate from each congregation represented, also the president and the treasurer.

Recommendations are made toward the greater efficiency of the work and the witness of the church. In 1953 there were 32 congregations with 745 members in the conference. Serving them were 3 bishops and 14 ministers, of whom 7 were natives of Argentina. The executive committee had as its president Albano Luayza, and two other members of the five-man committee were Argentines. The conference now meets biennially in January and represents the work of the Argentine Mennonite Mission, under the auspices of the Mennonite Board of Missions and Charities, Elkhart, Ind.

E.V.S.

Argentine Mennonite Mission (MC). During the 13 years, 1904 to 1917, the movement developed that gave birth to the Argentine Mennonite Mission. Mennonite youth in Goshen College studied about the neglected South American continent. Churches and wide-awake individuals contributed to a fund for South American missions. The Mennonite Board of Missions and Charities in 1911 sent J. W. Shank as its representative on a six months' tour of investigation in Peru, Bolivia, Chile, Argentina, and Uruguay. Then followed a general solicitation campaign that brought over $20,000 for the new mission. By the late summer of 1917 the four missionaries under appointment, the T. K. Hersheys and J. W. Shanks, sailed to Buenos Aires, arriving on Sept. 11.

The task before these novices was to survey the great Argentine field and choose a strategic region for the proposed mission. After 14 months of language study, during which time also the missionaries made extensive survey trips in the interior, they chose the rich agricultural region some hundreds of miles directly west of the capital. The transfer to Pehuajo, the chosen center for the new mission, was made early in 1919.

The task of evangelism inaugurated in Pehuajo in April 1919 has continued throughout the years with varying degrees of confidence and enthusiasm. At the end of the first decade, seven growing churches were in existence and from these, outstations and branch Sunday schools were being nourished. At the end of the second decade the work had extended into 3 provinces with 14 outstations receiving attention from 8 central churches. At the end of the third decade there were 13 main stations and 25 outstations. During the last part of this decade the mission to the Chaco Indians, 1,000 miles north, was opened.

By 1953 the total membership had reached 650 while the church community attendance at services reached approximately 1,500. During its 35 years of existence the mission acquired 28 properties valued at 480,555 Argentine pesos. Among these properties there are 14 churches, 17 pastoral homes, 2 children's homes, and a Bible school. The working staff in 1952 consisted of 27 missionaries and 20 native Christian workers who gave all their time to religious or educational work.

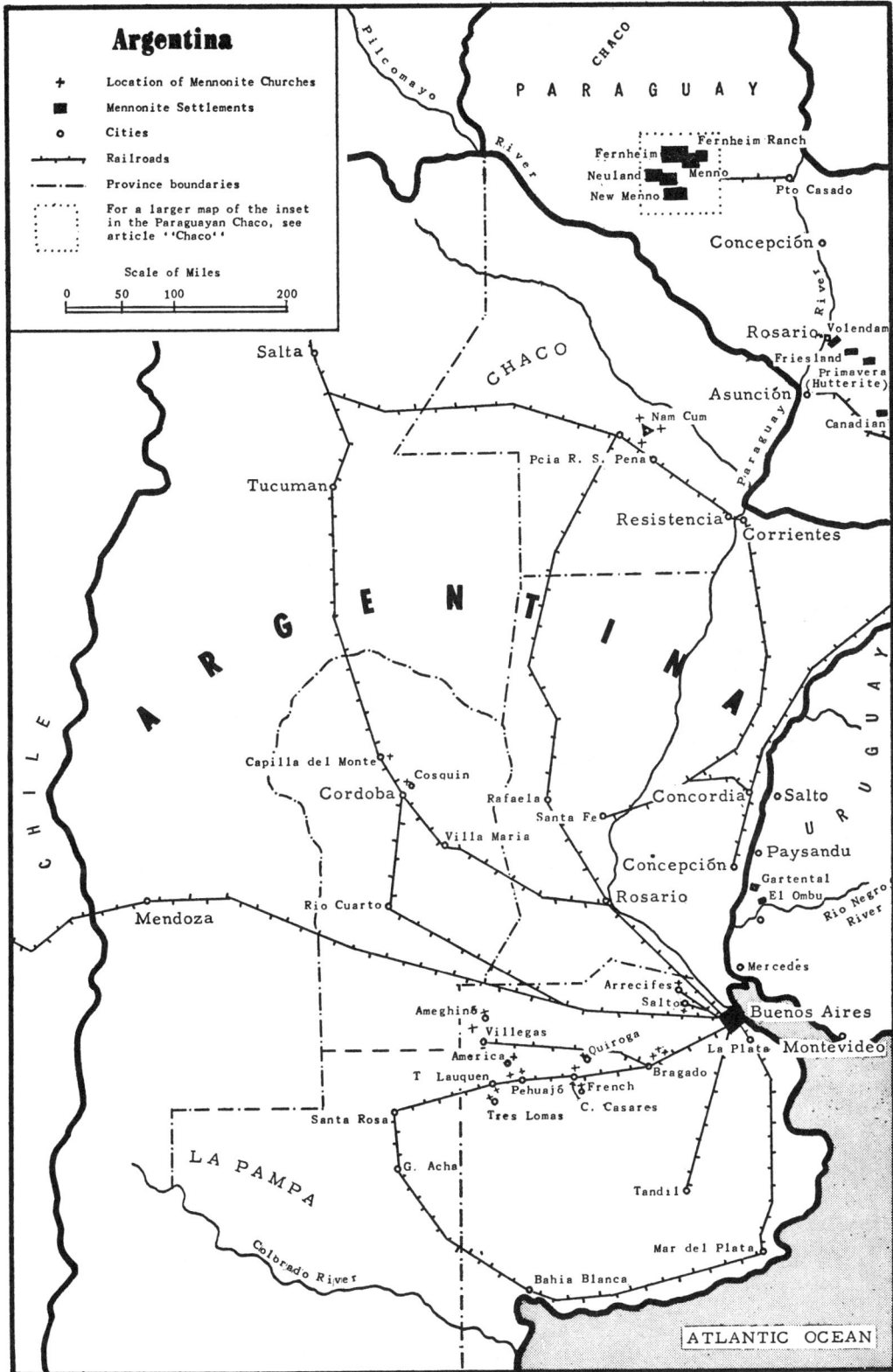

Argentina

+ Location of Mennonite Churches
■ Mennonite Settlements
○ Cities
⊢ Railroads
—·—·— Province boundaries
⸬ For a larger map of the inset
in the Paraguayan Chaco, see
article ''Chaco''

Scale of Miles
0   50   100   200

PARAGUAY

Pilcomayo

CHACO

River

Fernheim Ranch
Fernheim
Neuland   Menno
New Menno
Pto Casado

Concepción

Rosario   Volendam
Friesland
Primavera
(Hutterite)

Asunción
Canadian

Salta

CHACO

Nam Cum
Pcia R. S. Pena

Tucuman

Resistencia   Corrientes

A R G E N T I N A

U R U G U A Y

Capilla del Monte   Cosquin
Cordoba
Rafaela
Santa Fe   Concordia   Salto
Villa Maria
Concepción   Paysandu
Rio Cuarto   Rosario   Gartental
El Ombu   Rio Negro
River
Mendoza

Mercedes

CHILE

Arrecifes   Buenos Aires
Ameghino   Salto
Villegas   La Plata   Montevideo
America   Quiroga
T Lauquen   Bragado
Pehuajó   French
Tres Lomas   C. Casares
Santa Rosa

LA PAMPA

G. Acha

Tandil

Colbrado River

Mar del Plata

Bahia Blanca

ATLANTIC OCEAN

The original policy of the Mission was to evangelize the people of the rural regions and not to seek locations in Buenos Aires. After 25 years, however, it became necessary to form in Buenos Aires a church composed of Mennonite families and individuals who had moved to the great city. With the exception of this one church, all other churches are located in progressive rural towns and villages. Only the Chaco Indian mission is entirely rural.

Not least among the Mission's activities are the institutions that have been founded. The printery has made possible the distribution of hundreds of thousands of tracts, pamphlets, and other literature. The orphanage has for more than 25 years sheltered children, many of whom have grown up and formed Christian homes. The Bible school has produced trained men and women for the ever-extending service of the mission. (J. W. Shank *et al., The Gospel Under the Southern Cross*, Scottdale, 1943.)   J.W.S.

Arians, a designation derived from the name of Arius, who denied the deity of Christ, applied to the Socinians, particularly in Poland, with whom the Mennonites were often identified by their opponents. In the court records of the state archives in Karlsruhe of the period preceding the Thirty Years' War are repeated warnings and suspicions that the Mennonites of the Palatinate maintained connections with the Arians (Socinians) in Poland and agreed with them in doctrine (Chr. Hege, *Die Täufer in der Kurpfalz*). When the "Arians" were banished from Poland and their property confiscated in 1658, and zealous officials and self-seeking important men wished to have this decree applied to the Mennonites as well, King John Casimir protected them by a special ordinance of Nov. 20, 1660, expressly stating that this law must not be used against the "Männisten." At the provincial parliament in Marienburg (later West Prussia) in 1676, the voivode of Pomerellia tried to enforce the "Arian" law upon the Mennonites, but was not successful. He fared no better in his attempt to have the parliament apply it to the Mennonites. Again and again there were friends who defended the Mennonites. This time it was the Lauenburg judge Prebendau who sided with them. He personally persuaded King John Sobieski to destroy the order which had already been drawn up against them and to issue the rescript of 1678 to protect them. In the Landtag of 1696 in Marienburg the Ermland bishop demanded that the Mennonites be excluded from the rights of dissidents and be classed with Jews and Arians; he was not successful. The last attempt to have the Mennonites classed with the Arians, in the parliament of 1699 and 1700, was likewise a failure. (W. Mannhardt, *Die Wehrfreiheit der Altpreussischen Menn.*, Danzig, 1863; *ML* I, 81.)   NEFF.

Arisz, Marcus, preacher in the Norden (Germany) Mennonite Church, b. Sept. 16, 1716, at Amsterdam, received into the church there by baptism Dec. 8, 1737, d. Dec. 4, 1784, at Norden. He was at first engaged in the carpenter's and cabinetmaker's trade, then, "enlightened by the Lord," he devoted him-

self to the study of theology under the well-known Mennonite preacher Jeme Deknatel (*q.v.*) in Amsterdam. On Oct. 27, 1740, he was called to be the preacher of the Waterlander congregation in Norden, and on July 9 was ordained by Cornelis van Kampen, the pastor of the church at Emden. His faithful work through 44 years brought great blessing to his church. Reinhard Rahusen of Leer preached the funeral sermon (*Menn. Bl.,* 1861, 57). Arisz was deeply pious and of great faith, as is shown in his correspondence with Deknatel (*Menn. Bl.,* 1859, 12 and 19). His wife was a Moravian, for which reason he associated much with members of the Moravian congregation in Norden, causing some displeasure in his own church. Under his leadership, after many attempts, the union of the Waterlander congregation with the Ukowallist (so-called Groninger Old Flemish) congregation in Norden was achieved on April 12, 1780. For four years before his death he served the united church, with his fellow preacher Bavinck of Leer. NEFF.

Jan ten Doornkaat Koolman, *Kurze Mitt. aus der Gesch. der Gem. Norden bis 1797* (Norden, 1903); *ML* I, 82.

Arizona. Mennonites first became interested in Arizona in connection with mission work in that state. Peter Stauffer, who was employed in the government Indian service among the Hopi Indians at Keams Canyon, called the attention of the General Conference (GC) mission board to the possibilities of beginning work at that place. In 1893 H. R. Voth (*q.v.*) started the mission work among the Hopi Indians (*q.v.*) at Oraibi (*q.v.*). Soon stations were opened also at Hotevilla (*q.v.*) and Moen Copi (*q.v.*).

No large-scale Mennonite settlements have been made in Arizona. Families live scattered as farmers, businessmen, employees, instructors, etc. In 1918 a number of Mennonite farmers from Oklahoma, Kansas, and Minnesota started a settlement at Sahuarita, 20 miles south of Tucson on irrigation land. Because of complications resulting from the water rights, the settlement was discontinued.

On the extreme northern edge of Phoenix is the community of Sunnyslope where some 75 Mennonites and Amish live. During the winter months they are usually joined by some temporary residents. In February 1946 the Sunnyslope Mennonite (MC) Church (*q.v.*) was organized.

The University of Arizona, Tucson, has a considerable number of Mennonites on its staff. Among them are E. R. Riesen, Dean of the College of Liberal Arts; Oswald Wedel, Head of the Department of History and Political Science; A. B. Schmidt, Business and Public Administration; Emil W. Haury, Head of the Department of Anthropology; F. A. Conrad, Head of the Department of Sociology; and others, mostly graduates and former members of the faculty of Bethel College. There are a number of other families located in Tucson, but no Mennonite congregation has been established. Samuel Burkhard is a member of the faculty at the Arizona State College, Tempe; and

Daniel F. Jantzen, Peoria, Ariz., was very likely the first Mennonite to enter the teaching profession in that state. C.K.

Ed. G. Kaufman, *The Development of the Missionary and Philanthropic Interest Among the Menn. of N.A.* (Berne, 1931); *ML* I, 82.

Arkadak, the name of a new Mennonite colony near the station of the same name in the Russian province of Saratov, district Balashov (lat. 51°, long. 62°), with about 180 Mennonite families, of whom about one sixth belonged to the Mennonite Brethren Church. The land, 9,414 dessiatines (about 25,500 acres), was bought in 1910 by the land commission of Chortitza for the landless of the Chortitza district (*volost*). Several other Mennonite districts of Ekaterinoslav province took part in the purchase; each settler received a farm of 50 dessiatines (135 acres).

Through the colony flows the little Arkadak River, a tributary of the Khopor, which sends its waters southward to the Don. On the left bank of the Arkadak lay the villages of Vladimirovka, Borissopol, Dmitrovka, and Marianovka. They had flat land, the soil slightly mixed with sand. The other three villages, Vyazemskoye, Leonidovka, and Lidyevka, were situated on the right bank of the Arkadak. The land there was rolling, and the soil less sandy than on the other side. The entire settlement had good, fertile land (20 to 28 inches of humus, subsoil mostly clay). Wheat, rye, barley, oats, sunflower, and millet throve best here. The purchase price was about 170 roubles per dessiatine ($32.00 per acre); after three years the value of the land had almost doubled. The villages, each consisting of 24-27 homesteads, were from one to five miles from the station and post office of Arkadak. A number of Mennonites established businesses and industries at Arkadak. The colony was prosperous and a success during the first decade of its existence.

The first—and for one year the only—minister of the colony was Abraham Martens (b. Dec. 6, 1868, in Einlage, Chortitza, d. April 27, 1911, in Arkadak). He was a gifted man, whose delicate physique early succumbed to the threefold burden of pioneer farming, preaching, and teaching school. In 1913 the colony had six ministers of the Mennonite Church: Johann Braun and Gerhard Löwen in Vyazemskoye, Abraham Ens in Leonidovka, Johann Nikkel in Dmitrovka, Johann Bueckert and Johann Nikkel in Borissopol. It had three Mennonite Brethren ministers: Johann Pauls in Vyazemskoye, Heinrich Block in Dmitrovka, and Johann Epp in Marianovka. Baptism and communion were administered in the Mennonite Church by the elders of Chortitza. The ministers were unsalaried and were teachers or farmers by profession.

The main church building of the Mennonite Church was a spacious house built by Prince Vyazemsky for his laborers in the village Vyazemskoye. In the other villages services were held every two weeks in school buildings or homes. From 1912 on church records were kept. The Mennonite Brethren met every Sunday in private homes. Later a church building was secured in Vyazemskoye. For the instruction of candidates for baptism the Mennonites used the *Katechismus der Mennonitengemeinden in Russland*.

For a while a secondary school functioned at Borissopol, Arkadak. In most of the villages there were small choral societies with mixed choruses of more than 80 members. The colony helped to support the home for the mentally ill, *Bethania*, and the foreign missions of the Dutch and Russian Mennonites. The colony had also set up a fund for the traveling expenses of ministers and elders who visited them. The village population was made up of farmers, but near the station there was a settlement of 16 Mennonite families who owned a farm-machinery factory, a steam driven mill, an oil press, a large tile factory, etc. The colony was not organized as an independent district (*volost*) but was attached to the Russian *volost* of Arkadak, near which it was located.

By the time of the Revolution in 1917 most of the settlers had paid for their land which was now nationalized and redistributed according to the size of the family. During the Revolution and immediately thereafter the settlement suffered comparatively little. Some hardships were experienced during the following years of drought. During the NEP (New Economic Policy) period a gradual revival of some economic phases took place.

The Mennonite Church of Arkadak which consisted of some 250 members in 1914 had grown to 350 in 1925, the total population being about 1,500. From 1922 to 1925 the leading minister of the Mennonite Church was Johann Bueckert, although elders from the Old Colony still administered baptism and communion services. In 1926 Dietrich Rempel was elected the first elder. At this time meetings were possible only in private homes in small numbers and possibly at funerals. On August 8, 1925, 156 persons left Arkadak, arriving in Quebec on Sept. 4. They were followed by other families.

Until 1926-27 the use of the traditional textbooks, opening the schools with song and prayer, and Christmas programs had been tolerated. After this the old teachers were dismissed and the communistic program was fully instituted. In 1931 the schools of the first four villages and of the latter three were consolidated into two schools consisting of four grades. A secondary school was established in the church buildings at Vyazemskoye. Only a few of the young people became members of the komsomol (Communist Youth Society).

In 1929 collectivization was forcibly introduced into the villages by various means. Many families joined those in Moscow waiting for permission to leave the country, in which they failed. At this time some 15 men were exiled including Elder Dietrich Rempel. The resistance was broken and thus collectivization was enforced.

Gradually exemption from military service, in which respect Johann Bueckert deserves especially much credit, became impossible. The last young men permitted to do alternative service under the greatest hardships were drafted in 1932. They were treated like criminals. At the time of the battle of Stalingrad the inhabitants of the entire Arkadak settlement were evacuated to Asiatic Russia (Sept. 1941), scattered over a large area of industries and collective farms, and were compelled to eke out a meager living. It is not known what happened to the villages which they left behind. Many of those in exile perished because of the poor living conditions. (*ML* I, 82.)   G.L., C.K.

Arkansas, a south central agricultural state, bounded on the east by the Mississippi River. Amish Mennonites settled near Stuttgart in the east central part of the state in the decade of the 1880's but by 1920 the settlement had become extinct. A new wave of Amish Mennonite migration began in 1925 but in approximately a decade this settlement too had ceased to exist (see **Arkansas County** Amish Mennonites).

In 1883 a small group of Mennonites from Henry Co., Iowa, located a short distance north of Stuttgart near Fairmount and organized a Mennonite Brethren in Christ Church. By 1891 the congregation had approximately 50 members but the church was discontinued in 1899. From 1927 to 1937 there was an old Order Amish community north of Stuttgart. (*ML* I, 83.)   M.G.

Arkansas County Amish Mennonites (Arkansas). Several settlements of Mennonites and Amish were started at various times in this county. The first Amish Mennonite immigration began in 1880. Among the first to move into the vicinity of Stuttgart were the families of Jacob Schulz, Christ and Joe Roth, John and Chris Nofziger, Jacob Yoder, Jonathan Beck, and Jacob Beck, most of them coming from Hickory Co., Mo. The first resident minister was Jonathan Beck who died there in 1891, and the first resident bishop was Jacob Yoder who moved there in 1912. Other family names were Springer, Stutzman, Rich, Stahley, and Sheffle. A meetinghouse was erected about six miles southeast of Stuttgart, known as the Yoder church. The settlement died out, however, by 1920, and the meetinghouse was moved to Pryor, Okla.

In 1925 a new wave of immigration began, this time from Iowa through the efforts of land agents. Those who moved from Kalona, Iowa, were Joe Eimen, Manass Brenneman, Wm. J. Schrock, Simon Gingerich, Solomon C. Ropp, Thomas and Leroy Miller, and Lloyd Knepp. Almon P. Hostetler and John and Noah Smucker came from Indiana. This new group of settlers, attracted by cheap land and to rice farming, was made up of Mennonite, Conservative Amish Mennonite, and Old Order Amish Mennonites. There was no minister in the group, and they formed a union Sunday school. Because of lack of ministerial leadership for many years and unsatisfactory church life, many began to return to their former homes. When the depression came in 1929 most of the settlers left the community.

A number of Old Order Amish families from Michigan moved to a location north of Stuttgart in 1927. Among the group was Noah Bontrager, bishop, and Eli Bontrager, minister. Others among them were the Swartz and Yoder families. This settlement met a number of calamities, however, including the death of their bishop in 1929. The last of the Old Order Amish moved out in April 1937.   J.A.H.

Arke Noachs or *Arke Noë* (Noah's Ark) was the name of the meeting place of the congregation of the Old Frisians in Amsterdam. The oldest church with this name was located on the Nieuwezijds Achterburgwal; it was furnished in 1606 and remained in use until 1664, when the congregation moved to the Teerketelsteeg, where they had bought the Kleine Spyker from the Waterlanders; this building was also named the "Arke Noë." In 1720 the congregation moved again, this time to "Kleine Zon," the church of a splinter group from the Zon located in the Prinsenstraat. This third building was also called Noah's Ark. When the congregation united with the Zonists in 1752 the Arke Noë was rebuilt as the Zonshofje for aged women of the congregation. (*Inv. Arch. Amst.* II, Nos. 82-90.)   vDZ.

Arkona, Middlesex Co., Ont., an extinct Reformed Mennonite congregation. In 1911 its membership of 30 was served by the ministers Elbert Morningstar and George Sitter. (*ML* I, 83.)

Arlington Mennonite Church in Westminster Twp., Reno Co., Kan. (GC), was organized on Nov. 30, 1905, with 25 members. Most of the families were Swiss-Galician Mennonites who had come to Kansas at the end of the past century. In 1907 a house of worship was built near Arlington which was destroyed by fire in October 1924. The present church was dedicated in June 1925. John P. Linscheid served as minister until 1937. Since that time various ministerial students and others have assisted with the services. George Kopper was the second minister. In 1953 John F. Schmidt was serving the congregation of 30 members. (*ML* I, 83.) E.L.R.

Armendiener (in Dutch *Armen-dienaar*) was the title for a deacon used among the Mennonites of Europe everywhere. His duty was to look after the poor, neglected, and afflicted within the congregation and where necessary to assist them with material goods. He was also in some regions the chairman of the congregational business meetings (see **Deacon, Diener der Notdurft,** and **Mutual Aid**).

Armenia, a land known in the Bible as Ararat (Isa. 37:38; II Kings 19:37) and bounded roughly by the Taurus Mountains on the west and Caucasus Mountains on the north. The principal portion lies within Turkish territory in Asia Minor; a second portion lies in Trans-Caucasia, now incorporated as an Armenian Republic in the U.S.S.R.; a third portion lies in the northwest tip of Persia. It is a land of plateaus, mountain peaks, and important river sources. Early inhabitants were replaced about the 6th century B.C. by an invasion of Aryans who became ancestors of the present Armenians. Repeated invasions culminating in the 11th to the 14th centuries destroyed the last vestige of political independence.

Conversion to Christianity occurred under Gregory the Illuminator, an Armenian prince, who won the king in 261. The Armenian church is thus known as the Gregorian Church. With the loss of political existence Armenian nationalism has centered about the Patriarch as head of the church. Both Roman Catholics and Protestants have sought to do missionary work among the Armenians, the former hoping to win the old church to alignment with Rome and the latter to a reformed, revived position. Both were unsuccessful in their primary aim but succeeded in organizing separate Christian groups. Following the terrible massacres of 1894-96 when 88,000 Armenians lost their lives at the hands of the Turks, every effort was made to relieve distress. Among other agencies one Mennonite mission came into being at that time—the United Orphanage and Mission at Hadjin, Turkey. Although the society was organized on an interdenominational basis the Mennonite Brethren in Christ were at all times predominant on its board. About twenty workers from this church served in the mission between 1898 and 1938. Rose Lambert and Anna Gerber were the first to go. The former was the author of *Hadjin and the Armenian Massacres* (Fleming Revell, 1911). Work was carried on in Hadjin and at Everek, but after World War I it was transferred from Armenia to Syria—Alexandretta, Damascus, Kirik Khan, Latakie, Beirut, and Aleppo. By 1938 it was necessary to withdraw the remaining missionaries, but the church continued on an indigenous basis.   S.F.P.

Report of the United Orphanage and Mission of Hadjin and Everek, Turkey, in Asia (Dayton, 1911); Storms, *What God Hath Wrought* (Springfield, Ohio, 1948); ML I, 83.

Armentières, a small town in northern France, close to the Belgian border, where in 1564 the Mennonite martyrs, Daniel Calvaerd and Pieter Florisz, and in 1567, Adriaen Olieux and Karel Halling, were executed. The martyr Claes van Armentières, executed at Antwerp in 1575, came from this place. There must have been a congregation at Armentières, of which mention is made in the *Martyrs' Mirror* (D 345, E 704), where Adriaen Olieux is called a minister of the church at Armentières. According to the letter of the Inquisitor Pierre Titelman (*q.v*), written from Yper (Ieper), Belgium, Nov. 14, 1561, to the Regent Maria of Hungary at Brussels, the Anabaptist congregation at Armentières had so many members that they were forced, in order to keep their meetings secret, "to hold their communion services, or —as they say—their breaking of bread, at various times and places, each meeting consisting of 80 to 100 persons." In the same letter it is stated that many Anabaptists had fled from Yper (*q.v.*) to Armentières.   vdZ.

Armentrout, an extinct Mennonite congregation, established in 1885, at Dry Fork, W. Va., under the Virginia Mennonite (MC) Conference. In the early years of this century, its membership was reported as 23. (*ML* I, 83).   M.G.

Arminianism, a theological system named after the Dutch Reformed theologian, Jacobus Arminius (1560-1609) (*q.v.*), popular Reformed preacher in Amsterdam (1588-1603), professor of theology at Leiden University 1603-9. Arminius rebelled against the more extreme aspects of Calvinistic theology, particularly as they were being taught by Calvin's successors in Switzerland and Holland. He rejected extreme views of predestination and the divine decrees, particularly those under the name of supra-lapsarianism, which claimed that God had to ordain sin in order that man must be lost so that God could save him. Arminius wished to defend the justice of God and the freedom of man's will, taking the position that predestination was based upon foreknowledge. Because of his views, he was bitterly attacked by Gomarus, a fellow theologian at Leiden. The controversy was not settled before the death of Arminius even though the Dutch government directly intervened. Unfortunately the theological issues became confused with political issues, the Arminians being generally in favor of republicanism in Holland, whereas the Gomarists preferred the monarchy. The leaders of the Arminian party after 1609 were Episcopius, Arminius' successor at Leiden, Uyttenbogaart, Limborch, and Grotius, all men of great talent and scholarship. These men set forth their position in the "Five Articles of the Remonstrance" addressed in 1610 to the Dutch government, in which they rejected the five main ideas of classic Calvinism. The followers of Arminius refused to be called Arminians, taking rather the name Remonstrants.

The Arminius-Gomarus controversy was finally settled by the famous Synod of Dordrecht (1618-19) which condemned the Arminian articles, deposed some 200 Arminian preachers, and exiled from the country those who refused to submit. In 1619 the Arminian group organized, under the name "Remonstrant Reformed Brotherhood," in effect a new denomination which at first suffered persecution, but was tolerated from 1632 on and finally officially recognized in 1795. (See **Remonstrants.**) In Holland the movement remained small, but the ideas of Arminius had influence far beyond his native land. Many Lutherans in Germany found them more congenial than confessional Calvinism, and many of the leaders of the Anglican Church in England in the 16th and 17th centuries held substantially the same position. However, the greatest historical influence for Arminian ideas came through the Wesleyan movement in England where John Wesley, John Fletcher, Richard Watson, and other Methodist theologians advocated them wholeheartedly (George Whitefield, however, was a Calvinist). Arminianism thus became the official Methodist theology from the mid-18th century on. The Mennonites of Holland were also basically in sympathy with the position of Arminius, although they did not share those Calvinistic views which he still maintained.

Because of their opposition to the absolutism of Dutch Calvinism, particularly in its persecuting form, the Arminians advocated instead toleration and sympathized with other persecuted Protestant groups. This made for a friendly relation with the Socinians (*q.v.*) when the latter fled from Poland to Holland during the persecution after 1650. Due to Socinianism and other influences the Remonstrants gradually became more liberal in their theological position, departing considerably from the original position of Arminius which was completely evangelical and orthodox and not rationalistic or liberal.

Arminianism as a system can best be described by showing how it differs from the historic five main points of Calvinism, which are: total depravity, unconditional election, limited atonement, irresistible grace, and the perseverance of the saints or eternal security. Arminius taught by contrast that depravity is a state which leaves the will free and man responsible for his own destiny through choice of faith or unbelief, denying the imputation of guilt for Adam's sin, although acknowledging inherited depravity. Election or predestination is conditional, based upon God's foreknowledge and not upon an arbitrary decree. The atonement of Christ is for all, not just for the elect, even though not all accept it and therefore fail to receive its benefits. God's grace is not irresistible, but can be rejected, and persistently, by man in his free will. The possibility of falling from grace is asserted, and the claim that those once in grace will never be lost is rejected. Arminius did strongly believe and teach the necessity of the grace of God for man's redemption, the sinfulness of man, the objective character of the atonement, and the reality of the keeping power of Christ. He did not deny God's omnipotence, but he did not follow the doctrinal development which made God the author of sin and the eternal condemnation of men. He emphasized on the basis of clear expressions of the Bible the need and the importance of faith as the condition for the effective operation of the grace of God.

In essence Arminianism was a mediating position between hyper-Calvinism and Pelagianism with its emphasis on the goodness of man and his ability to save himself. He was more on the side of Luther than that of Calvin and Beza although Luther was also a predestinarian. Unfortunately in the course of the succeeding centuries Arminianism in Holland inclined more and more to Socinianism and Pelagianism, that is, Unitarianism and moralism. This was true in England also. However, the combination which John Wesley made, whereby he joined a vital emphasis upon regeneration and the experience of the sanctifying grace of God with Arminian free will and responsibility made the Methodist teaching a powerful and satisfying evangelical theology. In this form it has had great influence, particularly in North America. It can readily be seen, however, why insistent Calvinists condemn Arminianism and accuse it of being the father of modern liberalism. This charge is, however, historically incorrect, particularly when applied to Arminius himself. The later developments are a deviation from original Arminianism.

Mennonites have been historically Arminian in their theology whether they distinctly espoused the Arminian viewpoint or not. They never accepted Calvinism either in the Swiss-South German branch or in the Dutch-North German wing. Nor did any Mennonite confession of faith in any country teach any of the five points of Calvinism. However, in recent times, particularly in North America, some Mennonites, having come under the influence of certain Bible institutes and the literature produced by this movement and its schools, have adopted the Calvinist doctrine of the perseverance of the saints or "once in grace always in grace." In doing so, they have departed from the historic Arminianism of the Anabaptist-Mennonite movement. To some extent the extreme doctrine of total depravity has also won entrance here and there, although nowhere do the other three Calvinistic articles seem to have won acceptance. It might be mentioned here also that on the other hand some Mennonites, particularly the Mennonite Brethren in Christ, now called United Missionary Church, have also taken over certain ideas from Methodism, particularly the doctrine called "second work of grace," by which is meant a distinct experience of sanctification apart from and subsequent to regeneration.

In Holland the Mennonites came into close and friendly contact with the Arminian movement, both in its Remonstrant organized form, and its Collegiant form. The seminary which the Remonstrants established in 1634 furnished Mennonites the opportunity for a theological training for the ministry before the establishment of the Amsterdam seminary in 1735. Relations between the two groups have always been friendly. When in 1619 the Dutch government prohibited church services of the Remonstrants and banished their leaders, owing to the lack of preachers a movement originated in favor of the lay sermon, which found organized expression in the society of Collegiants (*q.v.*) sometimes called Rijnsburgers, because they had their chief center at Rijnsburg near Leiden. Members of the Reformed, Remonstrant, and Mennonite groups could join a local Collegiant society without forfeiting membership in their own denomination. Since many of the Mennonite ideas, such as adult baptism, rejection of war, simplicity in clothing and life, practical Christian love, etc., were shared by the Collegiants, the contact between the two groups was close, intimate, and continuous. Through this channel also the Mennonites became more familiar with Arminian ideas. Dutch Mennonitism in the late 19th century adopted a modernistic Unitarian theology which went far beyond historical Arminianism. However, the Mennonites of West Prussia, Russia, South Germany, France, Switzerland, and North America have remained on a consistent evangelical Arminian basis, not because they have adopted an official Arminian terminology, but because in essence this is what they have always held from the beginning. So far as is known the writings of Arminius and of the Arminians were never read to any extent by the Mennonites outside of Holland, who remained basically readers of the Bible and of Menno Simons. (A. W. Harrison, *Arminianism*, London, 1937; *ML* I, 83.)   H.S.B.

Arminius, Jacobus (Jakob Hermans), b. Oct. 10, 1560, at Oudewater, South Holland, d. Oct. 19, 1609, at Leiden, a Dutch theologian, was educated in his youth by a Catholic priest Aemilius, who had strong leanings toward Calvinism. In 1575 Arminius went to Marburg, and in 1576 to the newly established University at Leiden to study theology. By 1582 he studied at Geneva with Beza, and stayed for a while in Basel. In 1589 he was made Reformed preacher in Amsterdam, where he worked with great zeal and was soon a man of influence. In 1603 he accepted a theological professorship at Leiden, where the excellence of his instruction made him equally influential. He soon became involved in a quarrel with his colleague Franz Gomarus, a rigid Calvinist. The question at issue was the recognition that should be given to the church teaching on the "recepta doctrina." Practically, Arminius almost rejected Calvin's doctrine of predestination in its full consequence. By his opponents he was accused of being Catholic. In the midst of this quarrel Arminius, the forerunner of the later Remonstrants (*q.v.*), died. (See **Arminianism**.)

It is strange that Arminius, who was accused of unorthodoxy by the strict Calvinists, was asked to attack the Mennonites. The Reformed Synod of North Holland had decided in 1599 that "the arguments of the Anabaptists should be collected in a book and refuted on the basis of Scripture for the instruction of the weak." The synod in South Holland of that year expressed the same wish. Arminius took the task upon himself. Reports on the progress of the book were made at the synod year by year. In 1601 he said he was very busy gathering the "voornaemste stucken" (principal articles). In 1602 he reported that the multiplicity of articles had slowed down the work. In the ensuing years Arminius continued to report that he was busy. In 1605 he asked to be relieved of the task, partly on the ground that he was suspected by some (Gomarists) of unsoundness on several points, and wished to be cleared. The work made no progress, and in 1608 the synod decided once more to urge Arminius to undertake it. He died in the following year. Soon his followers accepted the Mennonite confession of Hans de Ries. (*DB* 1910, 28-32.)

vDZ.

Arnaud, a village located about five miles east and one mile south of Morris, Man., across the Red River on the Soo Line (Canadian Pacific Railway) to Minneapolis, Minn., and about forty miles south of Winnipeg. Population of the village is about 100; within a three-mile radius there is an additional population of mostly (90 per cent) Mennonites who purchased farms from English, Scotch, and Irish settlers in the years 1924-27 incl. The farm land near Arnaud is low-lying but under normal conditions the heavy black loam yields good returns. There are two grain elevators, two implement shops and garages combined, two general stores, two Mennonite churches, the membership of which is about half Mennonite and half Mennonite Brethren,

a public school with primary and grade 11 classes, which takes care of educational requirements, and a railway station and post office.　　H.H.H.

Arnaud Mennonite Brethren Church, of Municipality Franklin, Man., was organized on June 14, 1925. It erected its church in 1935. The 1953 baptized membership was 58. Ten ministers, 3 missionaries, and 21 teachers have come out of this church. It is a member of the Manitoba Provincial and the Canadian District Conferences of the Mennonite Brethren Church. I. I. Toews is the present minister.　　H.N.

Arnaud Mennonite Church (GC) was organized in the summer of 1944 and erected its church building the same year in the village of Arnaud, Man. Most of its members had previously belonged to the Mennonite church near St. Elizabeth, 7 miles away. The church there proved too small by 1944 and since many families lived as far as 12 to 15 miles away, it was decided to organize and build a church at Arnaud. At the present time (1948) about 40 families belong to this congregation, with an active membership of 87. Two ministers are in charge of services at the present time, and all services are conducted in the German language. The year 1949 was the twenty-fifth anniversary of the coming of the first Mennonites from Russia to this district. With Arnaud as center and within a radius of 12 miles, live approximately 100 Mennonite families who belong to three separate congregations of this area.　　P.R.H.

Arndt in gen Eschenbroich, one of the leaders (called *Richter*) of the Anabaptist congregation at Hückelhoven near Erkelenz in Rhenish Prussia; "he founded the congregation in 1532 and was its first preacher." He was pardoned by the government, but nevertheless remained with his church. (Rembert, *Wiedertäufer*, 71 and 436; *ML* I, 85.) Neff.

Arndt, Johann (1555-1621), German Lutheran theologian, churchman, and author of two devotional books of great fame: *Sechs Bücher vom wahren Christentum* (1605), and *Paradiesgärtlein voller Christlicher Tugenden* (1612), which books exerted a far-reaching influence upon the Protestant world. In a sense Arndt may be called the "father of German Pietism," which is the trend toward an inward or subjective Christianity with a strongly emotional tinge. Next to Jakob Boehme and Valentin Weigel he is also considered the most significant mystic in Lutheranism. The "pietistic" in Arndt and his followers consists in a most characteristic shift of emphasis: away from the doctrine of the "Word," that is the teaching of justification by faith alone, and the rational, orthodox theology implied in this doctrine, and toward an experiential sanctification of life, a certain holiness mysticism, which is nonintellectual and untheological. There is no doubt that Arndt helped to soften the rigid Lutheran orthodoxy, and to introduce a mellow devotional element formerly strongly missing. His *Wahres Christentum* is an edifying reader of meditations and prayers of great emotional warmth; in the older editions the book comprises up to 1,500 pages; the *Paradiesgärtlein* has less than half this size.

In Mennonite circles these books were widely used, replacing older, genuinely Mennonite devotional material (which was never very extensive). In fact the *Wahres Christentum* was the most used devotional book in German Mennonite families from about the middle of the 17th century on for possibly two centuries. With the exception of Gottfried Arnold, no Lutheran author had such enduring influence in Mennonite circles as Arndt, working for an unnoticed shift in Mennonite piety toward Pietism. It has not been known until recent times that the *Paradiesgärtlein* served also as a source for the first Swiss-Mennonite prayerbook, the *Ernsthafte Christenpflicht* of 1739. (See Devotional Books.)   R.F.

R. Friedmann, *Menn. Piety Through the Centuries* (Goshen, 1949) 23 ff.; W. Koepp, *Johannes Arndt, eine Untersuchung über die Mystik im Luthertum*, 1912; F. J. Winter, *Johannes Arndt, . . .* (Leipzig, 1911); *ML* I, 85.

Arnhem, capital of the Dutch province of Gelderland (population in 1947 was 97,350 with 725 Mennonites). Presumably there was a congregation here as early as 1539 or 1540, but its existence cannot be proved before 1596. Information about this congregation is very scarce. In 1603 it met in the house of Jan Wints, a smith, and in 1607 at the home of a basket weaver; in the following year in the Turfstraat; and about 1629 in a house on the Ketelstraat. In 1617 the city council decided that the Mennonites should take a more active part in the civil defense and in 1624 Pouwel Huyberts (preacher or elder?) was fined ten guilders for withdrawing from the defense of the city. On April 21, 1632, Cornelis Jansz and Dirk Rendersen of Arnhem signed the Flemish confession at Dordrecht, which indicates that the Arnhem congregation belonged to that wing. In 1664 Arnhem united with the stricter wing of the Zonists. Since then scarce information becomes still scarcer. On Jan. 30, 1715, a house was bought for the Mennonite congregation (intended for a church? It was later called the *Mennisten Erf*). On Feb. 21, 1787, Abraham de Haas said that he was the only remaining member of the congregation. In the early 19th century the Amsterdam congregation had the supervision of the fund called *Mennisten-fonds* or *Mennisten Erf*.

On March 10, 1851, 28 Mennonites living in Arnhem notified the government of their intention to organize a Mennonite congregation there; permission was given on Jan. 20, 1852, and meetings were originally held in a hall in the Bakkerstraat. In 1855 the congregation received a preacher in H. Haga, who served the congregation 1855-87. The later preachers were H. J. Elhorst, 1887-98; B. P. Plantinga, 1898-1901; G. Wuite, 1901-10; P. J. Glasz, 1910-11; D. Pottinga, 1912-25; P. Vis, 1926-38; J. E. Tuininga, 1939-46; and Th. van der Veer since 1946. The first service here was conducted by J. Boeke, the Mennonite minister of Amsterdam, June 13, 1852.

The congregation increased rapidly in membership. In 1861 the number of baptized members was 60, in 1900 it was 390, in 1950 it was 685. On Sept. 8, 1889, the congregation began to hold its services in the present church in Weverstraat. The church was damaged in the war in September 1944.

The congregation is a member of Ring Arnhem. It has a men's organization, a committee to visit newly organized Mennonite congregations, a division of the *Doopsgezinde Zendingsvereeniging*. It supports a Sunday school for the children together with the Remonstrants and the liberal Reformed Church. In Doorwerth near Arnhem stands the Mennonite home for the aged called "Mooiland" (lovely land); another home for the aged is "Avondzon" (evening sun), maintained at Velp near Arnhem in co-operation with the Remonstrants and the Reformed.   vDZ.

Inv. Arch. Amst. II, Nos. 1524-30; II, 2, Nos. 12-25; *DB* 1863, 43-74; *Een eeuw Doopsgezinde Gemeente, Herdenkings-geschrift* (Arnhem, 1952); *Het Archief der Doopsgezinde Gemeente te Arnhem*, 1936; *ML* I, 85.

Arnhem, Ring, a regional organization of Mennonite congregations, which, like Ring Akkrum (*q.v.*), was formed for the purpose of mutual assistance in case of the illness of the minister or a vacancy. Ring Arnhem was founded June 18, 1856. Originally the Ring consisted of the congregations at Arnhem, Deventer, Nijmegen, Winterswijk, and Zutfen, together with three congregations located in Germany: Emmerich, Cleve, and Goch. The German congregations eventually died out, while in the Dutch district several new congregations arose to join the Ring. Consequently the total churches became so large and the district so extended that a decision was reached to divide the area into the Ring Arnhem and the Ring Utrecht-Gooi. To the former now belong the following congregations: Arnhem, Apeldoorn, Deventer, Eindhoven, Nijmegen, Wageningen, Winterswijk, Zutfen, and South-Limburg (Heerlen) and the *Kringen* (fellowships) at Doetichem, 's Hertogenbosch, and Tiel; while Ring Utrecht-Gooi consists of the congregations at Amersfoort, Baarn, Bussum, Hilversum, Utrecht, Zeist, and the fellowship at Bilthoven. (*ML* I, 85.)   vDZ.

Arnold, Eberhard, was born in Königsberg, Germany, July 26, 1883, the son of the Breslau church history professor, C. F. Arnold, and Elizabeth nee Voigt, and died in Darmstadt, Germany, Nov. 22, 1935. He was the founder and Word Leader in the establishment of a new Hutterite Bruderhof in Germany, which continues to live in its daughter colonies in England and in Paraguay. On his mother's side he was of German descent, on his father's American, his father having been born in Williamsfield, Ohio. Under the live impressions of a strongly revivalistic Christianity, Arnold felt keenly the injustices of the distinctions in class and society as he encountered them in his strictly religious parental home and in school, attending a Gymnasium in Breslau, where his father was professor of church history. Arnold studied theology, philosophy, and pedagogy at the universities of Breslau, Halle, and Erlangen. In 1908 he received his doctor's degree with a thesis on *Urchristliches und Antichristliches im Werdegang Friedrich Nietzsches*. After his marriage with Emy von Hollander, by whom he had five children, Emy, Eberhard, Johann, Hans, and Monika, he worked as a free-lance speaker and writer in Leipzig, Halle, and Berlin from 1909 to

1913 in the interests of genuine love of Christ and a renewal of life derived from the power of the Gospel. Then an illness compelled him to retire to southern Tirol, where in the quietness of the mountains he was able to penetrate deeper into the significance and the demands of Jesus. The witness of these years was the book, *Der Krieg, ein Aufruf zur Innerlichkeit,* which was further developed as a first draft of the book, *Innenland, ein Wegweiser in die Seele der Bibel.* It was first Hermann Kutter and later the Christoph Blumhardts, father and son, who led him ever deeper into the central message of the Gospel, namely, the approaching kingdom of God. In his investigation into spiritual movements Arnold very early came across the Anabaptists and in 1916 published the article, "Zur Geschichte des christlichen Liedes; Die ältesten Lieder der Täufergemeinden." Meanwhile he worked as the secretary of the German Christian Student Union and as the literary head of the Furche-Verlag (publishing house) in Berlin (1915-20). After World War I he came into lively contact with the *Jugendbewegung* (youth movement), whose genuine quest for the original impulses of life, and direct contact with nature and community he sought to direct to fulfillment in Christ (see his book, *Die Religiösität der heutigen Jugend,* Berlin, 1919).

Under the influence of this movement and the powerful impression of the Sermon on the Mount, the Arnold family and several others in 1920 initiated communal living in accordance with primitive Christianity and the original Anabaptists, in Sannerz, Hessen-Nassau. Here a brotherhood came into being to which Eberhard Arnold henceforth devoted his entire life in service both within and without the community. The periodical *Das neue Werk* and the books of the Neuwerk-Verlag served this new community. Besides the very intensive literary and publishing work and the care of numerous seeking guests and helpers, the community devoted itself to horticulture and agriculture and social and educational work with children, youth, and adults. The collaboration of this small group with the Neuwerkbewegung ended in 1922, when a division occurred between the Neuwerk, which had become increasingly ecclesiastical in its emphasis, and the circle in Sannerz, with its emphasis upon radical discipleship, requiring that all areas of life, without exception—the economic included —be placed under the unifying leadership of the spirit of Christ. Then Arnold began to publish in his own plant, known as the Gemeinschaftsverlag, and later Eberhard Arnold-Verlag, the *Quellen christlicher Zeugnisse aus allen Jahrhunderten* (Christian Testimonies Throughout the Centuries); the first volume of which, *Die ersten Christen nach dem Tode der Apostel,* was compiled and introduced by him. The periodical *Die Wegwarte,* which was published from 1926 to 1928, contains various articles from Arnold's pen, as do also *Die Furche* and other German magazines.

The Biblical radicalism of the original Anabaptists corresponded completely, in its faith and manner of living, to the experience at Sannerz. Therefore, when the brotherhood moved to the near-by Sparhof in 1926, also called the Rhoenbruderhof, near Fulda, the extended activity of the community was called a "Bruderhof" after the example of the Hutterite communal households. Eberhard Arnold established contact with the Hutterian Brethren in North America in 1928, and he worked persistently for the union of the young circle with the centuries-old brotherhood movement. The republication of Ehrenpreis' *Sendbrief, die brüderliche Gemeinschaft der Liebe betreffend* in the *Wegwarte* and the *Michel-Hasel Buch,* the publication in German of Bertha Clark's study, *The Hutterian Communities,* and the drafting of the "Grundlagen und Ordnungen" (now in mss. in Primavera, Alto-Paraguay) are the literary evidence of this development.

During a trip to and through America in 1930-31, Arnold visited all the Bruderhofs in South Dakota, Manitoba, and Alberta. His adoption into the community of brethren known as the Hutterites and the commission entrusted to him are attested in the following document (in translation):

The Hutterian Brethren   March 20, 1931
Stand-Off Colony, Macleod, Alta.

To the Bruderhofs
Information to the Hutterite congregations.
1. On Dec. 9, 1930, Eberhard Arnold of the German Bruderhof of the church of God, was incorporated into the Brotherhood who are called the Hutterites, at the Stand-Off Colony, with the teaching of Matt. 28, by Elias Walter, Christian Waldner, Johannes Kleinsasser, and Johannes Entz in the presence of the Stand-Off Colony and Joseph Wipf and Jerg Waldner.
2. On Dec. 19, 1930, Eberhard was confirmed in the service of the Word with laying on of hands by the elders Christian Waldner, Elias Walter, Johannes Kleinsasser, and Johannes Entz. It took place in the Stand-Off Colony with the teaching of Titus 1, and was delivered by Johannes Kleinsasser of the Buck Ranch Bruderhof. Thereby the commission of the brotherhood was given to Eberhard Arnold for Germany, there to proclaim the Word of God, gather the zealous, and to establish in the best order the Bruderhof existing in Neuhof (Fulda) in Hesse-Nassau.

(Signed) Elias Walter

With the active support of the North American Bruderhofs, the Rhoenbruderhof was built up, after Arnold's return, as the mission station and gathering place of the zealous. A printing shop was installed to publish the material on the Anabaptist movement collected by Arnold in Europe and America. In co-operation with Professor Johann Loserth of Graz the printing of the *Klein-Geschichtsbuch* was undertaken (though only 64 pages were printed) with annotations in which Arnold incorporated the fruits of years of research. Various articles for periodicals, for the *Mennonitisches Lexikon,* etc., were published. An account of the Hutterian Brethren was also published in English, entitled *The Hutterian Brothers* (Ashton Keynes, 1940). Other articles by Arnold were published in English in the *Plough,* the English organ of the

Hutterite group, and an English translation of *Innenland*, which was published in German in 1936, is about completed. An intensive work in the inner strengthening of the community with deeply stirring guest addresses and public lectures went hand in hand with the external development of the Rhoenbruderhof.

The rise of National Socialism in Germany in 1933 was accompanied by appreciable difficulty and finally a complete termination of the work in Germany in 1937. First the publication work of the *Klein-Geschichtsbuch* had to be stopped. Since the educational work of the colony was interfered with by the Gestapo, a new settlement, the Almbruderhof, was made in 1934 in the principality of Liechtenstein, a task to which Arnold had to devote the major portion of his time. In addition to many petitions to the authorities, in which Arnold stressed the peaceable character of the brotherhood and the comprehensiveness of its task for the kingdom of God, he completely rewrote *Innenland* to present the truth of the Bruderhof against the errors of the time. A journey undertaken in the spring of 1935 to Holland, England, and Scotland in the interests of the development of the Bruderhof brought him in closer contact with the Dutch Mennonites and the English Quakers. From the midst of all these tasks Eberhard Arnold was suddenly called away by death on Nov. 22, 1935.

The fundamental recognition and characteristic of his life was the confident expectation of the coming of the kingdom of God, which would reveal itself in repentance and a radical change in beginning a new life of love and justice in brotherly community and a sincere responsibility for public life. Christ is the decisive new dawn of God in history; His Spirit unites the brotherhood, here and now, in the authorization of the mission in all the world. The practical life of the brotherhood already corresponds everywhere with the character of the coming kingdom wherever Christ is accepted in His entirety, in accordance with the prophetic and apostolic word. Community of goods, baptism by faith, memorial Lord's Supper as a unifying meal of the entire brotherhood, church discipline, church orders in the sense of organic diversity are the counterpart within the community to the mission, the radical testimony of peace and the readiness to suffer outside the community. In all these points the *Artikelbücher*, the *Rechenschaft* by Peter Riedemann, the epistles, *Vorreden*, doctrines, hymns, and orders of the brethren who are called the Hutterites were fundamental and directive.

The work of complete communal living, begun by Eberhard Arnold, was carried forward in the Cotswold and Oaksey Bruderhofs in England after his death and the expulsion of the community from Germany in 1937. Today it still remains on the same foundation in the Wheathill Bruderhof in England and the three Bruderhofs in Primavera, Paraguay.

Arnold's scholarly work in Anabaptist history still awaits publication. His songs have become the living possessions of the Bruderhofs in Paraguay and England. The most important of Arnold's published works are: *Urchristliches und Antichristliches im Werdegang Friedrich Nietzsches* (Eilenberg, 1910); *Innenland, ein Wegweiser in die Seele der Bibel und in den Kampf um die Wirklichkeit* (Almbruderhof, Liechtenstein, 1936); *Die ersten Christen nach dem Tode der Apostel* (Sannerz and Berlin, 1926); an English translation of the introduction titled *The Individual and World Need* (Ashton Keynes, 1938); *The Peace of God* (Ashton Keynes, 1940); hymns in *Sonnenlieder* (Eberhard-Arnold Verlag, Sannerz and Leipzig, 1924); *Sonnenlieder*, Part II (Rhoenbruderhof, 1933).

E.C.H.A.

Arnold, Gottfried (1666-1714), German Pietist, church historian, independent author of devotional books, and from 1704 to his death pastor of a Lutheran church in Brandenburg. As the most prominent mediator between Anabaptism and German Pietism (*q.v.*) he was widely read among the Mennonites of the 18th and 19th centuries, and exerted a tangible influence upon the Mennonite church as a whole toward a more pietistic and "inward" Christianity. In studying Arnold, one must distinguish between the earlier independent author (1696-1704) who opposed the doctrinal and ecclesiastical orthodoxy of his time, and the later church man who found some reconciliation with the established Lutheran theology (1704-14). The influence of J. P. Spener (who died 1705) and rising Pietism is quite obvious in his writings, yet Arnold pursues his own ways and is in a strict sense not a follower of Spener. He might be better characterized as a pietistic separatist who distrusted dogma and ecclesiasticism altogether, and who sought a semi-mystical foundation of his faith in the subjectivity of religious experience, following somewhat the lead of Johann Arndt (*q.v.*, d. 1621) and Valentin Weigel (*q.v.*, d. 1588). In 1696 he published his first major work, *Die erste Liebe, das ist die wahre Abbildung der ersten Christen nach ihrem lebendigen Glauben und Leben*, an almost revolutionary book of the new trend which established his fame and brought him an appointment as professor at the University of Giessen in 1697, which he resigned a year later. This book gives a new picture of the primitive church as the ideal brotherhood to be emulated. Its appeal was tremendous throughout the 18th century (six editions appeared up to 1780, latest European edition 1845) and continued also its value as a favorite devotional reader among the Pennsylvania Germans (numerous editions in America).

Three years later, Arnold published his *opus magnum*, the *Unpartheiische Kirchen- und Ketzer-Historie* (*q.v.*, first edition at Frankfurt a.M., 1699-1700, second edition 1729, an enlarged third edition, edited by others, at Schaffhausen 1740-42 in three large folio volumes). In a sense it was an epoch-making work, being strictly in opposition to official Lutheran church historiography. Following the footsteps of Sebastian Franck (*q.v.*) he arrived at a new and original appreciation of the free church movements which the established churches called "heretical" and stigmatized as "sects." To Arnold, just the opposite is true: "Those who make heretics are the heretics proper, and those who are called heretics are the real God-fearing people" (*"Die Ketzermacher sind die eigentlichen Ketzer, und die Verketzerten sind die wahrhaft Frommen"*). In search for true representatives of an inward Christianity, Arnold found a great number of original sources both of medieval sectarian movements and of Anabaptism of the 16th century. For the latter he could use the recently published *Annales Anabaptistici* (*q.v.*) by J. H. Ottius (Basel, 1672), the *Geistliches Blumengärtlein* (Amsterdam, 1680), and similar volumes. His detailed presentation and appreciation of the Anabaptists and Mennonites fills no less than 250 pages of the 1740 edition (namely, I, 856-99, 1299-1310, 1313-1500; II, 159-67, 1059-65). A large section was devoted also to reprints of the writings of David Joris (*q.v.*).

Arnold manifests a fine knowledge and grasp of Anabaptism (including the Hutterites) and Mennonitism, and his work did much to dispel false prejudices among the general public. In this sense Arnold's *Ketzer-Historie* might well be considered as a real continuation of Sebastian Franck's similar work, the *Chronica* of 1531 (*q.v.*). In the 18th century this type of church historiography greatly expanded and helped to rehabilitate those despised groups (see **Ketzer-Historie**). The influence of Arnold's work upon official church historians toward a more impartial evaluation of independent groups cannot be doubted, though at first the book occasioned a vigorous controversy with orthodox Lutherans, for new editions of the work appeared long after his death, in 1729 and 1740-42.

All told, Arnold wrote about 50 books, mostly of a mystical-devotional character, some of which also found much response among German Mennonites. In 1700 he published *Das Geheimnis der göttlichen Sophia*, a book clearly following the line of the Christian theosophy of Jakob Boehme (d. 1624). In 1704, another popular book was published, *Wahre Abbildung des inwendigen Christentums* (3rd ed., 1733), which found its way into many Mennonite homes of both continents. One of his latest books, *Theologia Experimentalis, oder Geistliche Erfahrungslehre, Erkenntnis und Erfahrung in den vornehmsten Stücken des lebendigen Christentums*, of 1714, was reprinted in Pennsylvania in 1855 by John Oberholtzer (*q.v.*), the leader of the later General Conference Mennonite group, and advertised in the latter's *Der Religiöse Beobachter* as a highly recommended devotional book. It represents again this type of semi-mystical and subjective inward Christianity, not bound to any ecclesiastical body but also not pressing toward radical commitments and witnessing in the world. It is a book of the *Stillen im Lande* (see Friedmann, *Mennonite Piety*, 255 f.).

Arnold was also a successful hymn writer. Some of his hymns such as "So führst Du doch recht selig," "O Durchbrecher aller Banden," "Frag deinen Gott," and several more have found a place in the hymnals of the German Mennonites. R.F.

E. Seeberg, *Gottfried Arnold, die Wissenschaft und Mystik seiner Zeit, Studien zur Historiography und Mystik* (Leipzig, 1923); R. Friedmann, *Menn. Piety Through the Centuries* (Goshen, 1949). Erich Seeberg also edited a new and well-chosen selection of Arnold's works, *Gottfried Arnold in Auswahl herausgegeben* (München, 1934), omitting, however, all passages concerning Anabaptists and Mennonites; *ML* I, 85 f.

Arnold, Jacob: see **Arent Jacobsz.**

Arnold Mennonite Brethren Church is situated nine miles from Yarrow, B.C. Three years after the first settlers had arrived here, a church organizational meeting was held on Nov. 7, 1943, at which time J. P. Braun, who for 12 years had guided the M.B. Church at Morden, Man., was chosen as the leading minister. Besides the leading minister there were four others: I. Toews, I. Goertzen, J. P. Friesen, and John Kliewer. The deacons were H. Falk and Jacob Wiens. Membership in the church had risen to 202 by 1950. J.P.Б.

Arnoudt (Arent) **Jaeghere** (or Jachere), an Anabaptist martyr, one of the first to suffer death by martyrdom on behalf of his faith at Gent, Flanders. Arnoudt, concerning whom further details are lacking, was beheaded in front of the Gravensteen on July 19, 1535. (Verheyden, *Gent*, 2, No. 3.) vdZ.

Arrecifes Mennonite Church (MC) is a congregation located in the city of Arrecifes, population 10,000, on the Buenos Aires-Rosario branch of the Ferro Carril Central Argentino (Central Argentine Railroad) in the county of Arrecifes, Province of Buenos Aires, Argentina. The work was opened here in February 1943 by S. E. Miller and wife, and a congregation was organized in December 1944. The membership in 1952 was 8. The congregation consists of people of Spanish, Italian, and Indo-Argentine descent, the services being conducted in the Spanish language. S. E. Miller was in charge of this work until January 1947, at which time Feliciano Gorjon, a graduate of the Mennonite Bible Institute at Bragado, F.C.O., was placed in charge. E.V.S.

Art. The following treatment of the theme is limited basically to the graphic arts, in particular painting, drawing, and etching. For treatment of other forms of art and related topics, see **Architecture, Fractur, Handicraft, Literature, Music, Needlework, Pottery**. The article is subdivided as follows: (1) The Mennonite Theme in Art, (2) The Mennonite Attitude Toward Art, (3) The Particular Mennonite Contribution to Art, (4) Mennonite Artists.

1. The Mennonite Theme in Art.

(a) Persons. Seldom have major artists used Mennonite themes in any form of great art, although Mennonite subjects were frequently portrayed by able Dutch painters and etchers. The chief instance is the great Dutch master Rembrandt (*q.v.*), who painted, etched, and drew the Amsterdam Mennonite preacher C. C. Anslo (*q.v.*), a Waterlander leader. His oil painting of Anslo and his wife hangs in the Kaiser Friedrich Museum in Berlin; an original copy of the etching is in the Art Institute of Chicago; both were done in 1641. A copy of Rembrandt's etching of Anslo alone is in the Fogg Museum of Art at Harvard University. Rembrandt also painted or etched various other Waterlander Mennonites. His portrait of Trijn Jans, the wife of H. J. Rooleeuw (*q.v.*), made in 1657, is now in the Lord Penrhyn Collection in

England. Several members of the Amsterdam Mennonite Bruyningh family were also painted by Rembrandt, e.g., Nicolaas Bruyningh, whose portrait of 1652 is now in the Gemälde-Galerie at Cassel, Germany. Rembrandt's painting of Lieven Willemsz van Coppenol (*q.v.*) is in the Edward S. Harkness Collection in New York. Van Coppenol was a noted Mennonite teacher. H. F. Wijman has shown that the portrait by Rembrandt once assumed to be Hans Alenson is actually one of the English clergyman John Ellison.

Other outstanding Dutch artists produced portraits of Mennonite preachers, among them being the Mennonite artist M. J. van Mierevelt (d. 1641, *q.v.*), who painted Hans de Ries (d. 1638) (*q.v.*), the great leader of the Waterlanders, and also produced a portrait of the prominent preacher Lubbert Gerritsz (d. 1612) (*q.v.*), which hangs in the University of Amsterdam; and the artist Lambert Jacobsz (*q.v.*, ca. 1598-1636), himself a Waterlander preacher, who painted his fellow preacher, Jeme de Ring (*q.v.*). There is a portrait, formerly ascribed to Rembrandt but actually by his Mennonite pupil Govert Flinck (1614-60) (*q.v.*), of Gozen Centen, a regent (member of the board of directors) of the Amsterdam Mennonite old people's home called Rijpenhofje. Two other Mennonite regents of the Rijpenhofje, Gozewijn Centen (with family) and Job Sieuwerts, were painted by the Dutch artist Christoffel Lubienietzki in the years 1721 and 1713 respectively. Both pictures, though the property of the Amsterdam Mennonite Church, now hang in the Rijksmuseum. The well-known elder, Jan Gerrits van Emden (d. 1617) (*q.v.*), was painted by Rombout Uylenburch. The prominent Mennonite preacher of Amsterdam, Johannes Deknatel (d. 1759) (*q.v.*), also cofounder of the Amsterdam Mennonite Seminary, was painted in a miniature, which is now in the possession of the Mennonite Historical library of Goshen College. A bust of Menno Simons and one of N. C. Hirschy (d. 1916), first president of Bluffton (Ohio) College, both done by the Mennonite artist J. P. Klassen, are in the Bluffton College Library.

Many wealthy Mennonites had their portraits painted by noted Dutch artists. F. Schmidt Degener has made a thorough study of this in his article "Menniste Portretten" in the magazine *Onze Kunst* (1914, I, 1 ff.). Hendrik Sorgh (1611-70) depicted the Jacob Abrahamsz Bierens family in Amsterdam in 1663. Lucas de Clercq and his wife, both Mennonites, had their portraits made by the renowned painter Frans Hals in 1635. Jan van Hoeck, a member of a well-known Amsterdam Mennonite family, had his picture made by Cornelis van der Voort. If one may include the revolutionary Anabaptists here, then it should be noted that Jan van Leyden (d. 1535) (*q.v.*) was painted several times and that H. Aldegrever made a fine copper-engraving of him in 1536. A good oil painting of him by Herman tom Ring now hangs in the Grandducal Museum at Schwerin, Germany. Of David Joris there is a portrait by the Dutch painter Jan van Scorel, now in the *Oeffentliche Kunstsammlung* at Basel, Switzerland. The great-

est Dutch poet, Joost van den Vondel (1587-1679, *q.v.*), who was a Mennonite (for a time deacon) for many years until his conversion to Catholicism, was often pictured, as for instance by Govert Flinck and Philip de Koninck.

Of the various extant portraits of Menno Simons, none historical, possibly only three have much artistic value, the one of 1683 by Jakob Burkhardt of Hamburg-Altona, that by Jan Luiken of 1743, and the etching of 1949 by the gifted contemporary Dutch etcher, Arent Hendriks. (See the authoritative article by G. J. Boekenoogen, "De Portretten van Menno Simons," in *DB* 1916, 33-106, with reproductions of all then extant portraits, also "The Portraits of Menno Simons," by S. Smeding in *Menn. Life,* July 1948, 16-19.) In 1743 a collection of 30 portraits of Dutch Mennonite leaders from Menno Simons on down appeared in book form in Amsterdam under the title *Versaameling van de afbeeldingen van veele voornaame Mannen en leeraaren, die zoo met het begin der Reformatie als ook in laater tijd het leeraars ampt onder de Doopsgezinde Christenen bedient hebben. Alle op nieuws na de originele, door bekwaame meesters in 't koper gebragt.* In 1677 at Middelburg appeared a collection of etchings by C. van Sichem, *Het Tooneel der Hooftketteren bestaande in verscheyde afbeeltsels van valsche Propheten, naekt-loopers,* etc., which included Menno Simons and David Joris among its pictures of archheretics. The 1608 *Historische Beschrijuinge Ende Afbeeldinge der voornaemste Hooft Ketteren* contains 15 large engraved portraits by van Sichem, among them Balthasar Hubmaier, Adam Pastor, Melchior Rinck, Hans Hut, Ludwig Haetzer, Melchior Hofmann, and the Münsterite leaders, but not the van Sichem portrait of Menno Simons, which was printed as a separate sheet already in 1605 or earlier. Most of these were reproduced in smaller size also in 1608 in *Apocalypsis Insignium Aliquot Heresiarcharum.* The larger collection was reproduced in several editions with varying content, finally in the 1677 edition.

It was very common in the 16th and particularly in the 18th century to hang portraits of the regents, usually painted as a group, in the board rooms of Dutch orphanages and old people's homes. Some Mennonite charitable institutions have pictures of their regents, but they are not so common nor of such an early time.

Outside of Holland, Mennonite preachers and wealthy lay members of Emden, Danzig, and Hamburg in North Germany were portrayed in paintings, etchings, or miniatures, none outstanding.

(b) Events, Activities, and Scenes. There are very few pictures of events in Mennonite history. In the old Town Hall of Amsterdam there were once six oil paintings by Doove Barend (*q.v.*), of the *Wederdoperoproer* (assault on the town hall by a group of revolutionary Anabaptists in 1535), but they have disappeared. In a number of old books certain sensational scenes are reproduced from early Anabaptist history, e.g., the story of the *Naaktloopers,* which was depicted again and again. But

these pictures are seldom of artistic value, and generally not authentic but merely fantastic.

The most extensive use of Mennonite themes was by the noted Dutch etcher Jan Luyken (d. 1712) (*q.v.*), who created the 104 copper engravings used in the second Dutch edition of the *Martyrs' Mirror* (1685) later published separately as *Theatre des Martyrs* (Leyden, 1685?). The original copper plates were extant in Munich in 1929 and were examined by the writer. They had been used in the Pirmasens (1780) German edition of the *Martyrs' Mirror*.

Of great interest are a set of copper engravings from about 1735, representing the ceremonies in Dutch Mennonite churches. In volume VI of *The Ceremonies and the Religious Customs of the Various Nations of the Known World* (London, 1733-37), also published in French (1736) and in Dutch (1738), the noted French engraver, Bernard Picart (1673-1733), and his Dutch associates, who did most of their work in Amsterdam, reproduced two scenes from a Dutch Mennonite communion service in the Amsterdam Singel Church, two engravings of a Mennonite baptism, and two engravings of an Amsterdam Mennonite man in costume, all of 1736 or thereabouts. F. ter Meer painted (Crefeld, 1845) *Die Gehetzten,* a scene showing 16th century Crefeld Mennonites worshiping in a barn.

There is a fine engraving of the old Witmarsum church of about 1820, and many good engravings, mostly from the 18th century, of the churches of Amsterdam, Utrecht, Leiden, Zaandam, and others. A symbolic engraving by D. Kerkhoff (1792) bears the title *Monument van de Doopsgezinden.*

The copper engraving of 1782, *The Mennonite Proposal for Marriage,* by the Danzig artist Daniel Chodowiecky (d. 1801), not a Mennonite, portrays a custom of the Mennonites of that city. The Swiss artist, Aurèle Robert (d. 1871), painted a picture of a Swiss Mennonite family of near Tavannes, Bernese Jura, about 1850, which hangs in the Lausanne (Switzerland) Museum (Musée des Beaux-Arts), entitled *L'Anabaptiste ou ferme Bernois.* The Swiss artist Joseph Reinhard (1749-1829) produced a colored etching of a Mennonite couple at the Johannestor in Basel, entitled *Costumes des Anabaptistes Suisses,* which was published in his noted work on Swiss costumes ca. 1824. An 18th century gravure by E. Maaskamp depicts a Mennonite couple on the Dutch island of Kampen. A similar one by Lewicki depicts an Alsatian couple of *ca.* 1815.

In the United States in recent years Amish themes have been used. The contemporary artists Kiehl and Christian Newswanger of near Lancaster, Pa., have produced a number of interesting Pennsylvania Amish portraits, in painting, etching, and drawing, which have been widely exhibited in recent years and are now in the permanent collection of the Library of Congress at Washington, D.C. Benjamin Eicholtz's *Mennonite Woman* (early 19th century) is in the Philadelphia Museum of Art. The Mennonite artist of Goshen, Ind., A. L. Sprunger, has made linoleum cuts of Amish figures. Oliver Wendell Schenk (1903-), himself a Mennonite student in Goshen, Ind., at the time, produced in 1933 a pen and ink sketch of the noted

Mennonite schoolmaster of the Skippack (Pa.), Christopher Dock (d. 1771), at prayer in his schoolroom, as well as a pencil sketch of the Doylestown, Pa., Mennonite meetinghouse and graveyard. Woldemar Neufeld (1909-), a former Mennonite, painted (*ca.* 1930) the Steinman Mennonite meetinghouse near Baden, Ont. Jakob Sudermann painted the Chortitza, Russia, Mennonite church 1932.

If one should include the Münsterites of 1534-35 with the Anabaptists, then reference would have to be made to numerous works portraying episodes, personalities, or scenes from this tragic affair. One of the most notable among these is the series of 30 black and white drawings (one etching and 29 in woodcut style) by the noted modern German artist, Joseph Sattler (1867-1931), published in Berlin in 1895 under the title *Die Wiedertäufer.* Max Geisberg has made a special study of the Münster Anabaptists in art in his *Die münsterischen Wiedertäufer und Aldegrever...* (Strasbourg, 1907).

2. The Mennonite Attitude Toward Art.

(a) In Principle. The Anabaptist-Mennonites, as more closely related to the Zwinglian-Calvinist phase of the Reformation than to the Lutheran, shared with the former their objection to the use of art in religious worship or in religious activity in any form. With their emphasis upon simplicity, sincerity, and humility, art seemed to them artificial and pretentious, often dangerous and wasteful. Whether their negative attitude was based upon the second commandment, "Thou shalt not make unto thee any graven image," as asserted by Neff (*ML* I, 221), is not clear. Later this was in part the case, and there is evidence that in West Prussia, as well as in Switzerland, and among the later descendants of both groups, this attitude prevailed. A striking illustration is the case of the Danzig Mennonite portrait-painter, Enoch Seemann, Sr. (*q.v.*) (b. 1661 in Elbing), who was placed under the ban in 1697 by the Danzig Flemish Mennonite elder Georg Hansen (*q.v.*) specifically on the ground of violating the second commandment by painting portraits, and was reinstated only after promising to limit himself to landscapes and decorations. (The story is told in Seemann's booklet *Offenbahrung und Bestraffung des gergen Hanszens Thorheit,* Stoltzenberg, 1697.) The Danzig Flemish congregation thoroughly supported their elder in this action. Even then, and for some time, at least until after 1850, Mennonites of this area were not permitted to be professional artists, only amateur practice being considered tolerable.

Possibly the rural character of these groups and their cultural isolation may account for some of their negativism toward art. In any case it has persisted through the 19th century among all Mennonite groups except those in Holland, the North German cities, and the Palatinate. It still is rigidly adhered to by the Old Order Amish of the U.S.A. and most conservative groups of Russian background in Manitoba, Mexico, and in Paraguay, all of whom forbid the hanging of any works of art in their homes, and also the taking of photographs. In the 20th century this attitude gradually disappeared in most Mennonite groups. However, in such a long prevailing negative atmosphere it is not surprising that there have been so few Mennonite artists and that those who wanted to be artists were either expelled or forced to leave

It is worthy of note that no real art developed among Mennonites except in those groups where there was a close connection with the national culture and in urban areas such as Holland and North Germany. The art of illumination of manuscripts, which was handed down in the Pennsylvania German communities and among the Mennonites of Prussia and Russia, found a few Mennonite practitioners (e.g., the teacher Christopher Dock [*q.v.*] of Skippack [d. 1771], preacher John Gross of Deep Run [1814-1903]) but this is a very minor art form. In any case, the Mennonites are known to have practiced only the graphic arts; in the plastic arts they are markedly absent except for some silversmiths in Holland, occasional pottery (e.g., the modern Makkum pottery in Holland), and folk art in such forms as samplers and bed quilts, and some wood carving. In North America, as the Mennonites as a whole began to move out of their cultural isolation and out of a purely rural environment, particularly through the influence of the public elementary and high schools as well as the leadership of their church colleges, a positive attitude toward art gradually replaced the former negative one (but not in the more conservative groups). Departments of art were established in the church colleges, and Mennonites became art teachers and artists in their own right, such as J. P. Klassen of Bluffton College and A. L. Sprunger of Goshen College and Goshen High School. The Mennonite Publishing House at Scottdale began to employ its own Mennonite artists for the art work in its publications, as did also the Mennonite Press at North Newton, Kan.

There are those, however, who doubt whether much great art can be produced in a group which has a strict standard of Christian morals and a strong sense of separation from the "world," and a relative isolation from the main stream of the national culture, since this might interfere with the freedom required for creative art. There are also those who hold on the other side that the autonomy of art is a danger to a truly profound religious experience and that one or the other must be sacrificed.

The Dutch Mennonites are a noteworthy exception to the general Mennonite pattern in their attitude toward art. First among the Waterlander Mennonites toward the end of the 16th century and then during the 17th century among most of the other groups except the most conservative, all opposition to art faded away and was replaced by a genuine appreciation for and love of art in various forms. This is evidenced not only by the commissions given for portraits, and by the appearance of many Mennonite artists, including both painters and etchers of the first rank, but also by the collections of paintings and other art objects in the homes of the wealthier Mennonites who were frequently friends and even patrons of artists. There have been several outstanding Dutch Mennonite art critics and historians, among them the noted Carel van Mander (1548-1606) (*q.v.*), whose *Schilderboek* was the first Dutch history of art.

Something of the love of art among the Dutch Mennonites is also evidenced by the fact that some congregations have valuable and very fine communion cups. Generally they were, like the tankards (jugs) and bread-plates, mostly of pewter, although the congregation of Zwolle had silver cups already in the year 1661, the congregation of Koog-Zaandijk also such from the 17th century, Leiden from 1701, Stavoren from 1745, Rotterdam from 1774, Kampen, Giethoorn, and Joure from the same time. Those of Kampen, Joure, and Rotterdam are of a high artistic value.

(b) Art in Mennonite Homes, Especially in Holland; Mennonite Art Collectors. During the so-called Frisian and Flemish quarrels the former accused the latter of giving too much attention and money to the adornment of their houses, and in the year 1659 a meeting of Groninger Old Flemish leaders at Loppersum forbade the use of stained glass windows in the houses and the making of portraits (Blaupot t.C., *Friesland,* 307-8: see also **Nonconformity**) and even S. F. Rues, who visited the Dutch Mennonites in 1742, stated the fact (Rues, *Tegenwoordige Staet,* Amsterdam, 1745, 27) that the so-called Danzig Old Flemish Mennonites excommunicated members who hung oil paintings and other decorations on the walls of their homes, and specially "when they got to the foolishness of having themselves pictured." But the fact that Carel van Mander could be a member even of the very austere Old Flemish congregation of Haarlem and also be a painter, proves indisputably that Mennonites as such were no opponents of art, generally speaking. We find pictures and other kinds of art in Mennonite homes, particularly of those Mennonites in Amsterdam and other cities of the Netherlands who had grown wealthy during the early 16th century. The picture which H. Sorgh made in 1663 of the Bierens home shows pictures on the wall. Surely we must consider this Bierens interior at Amsterdam as an example of Mennonite life at this time. Later on, and especially in the 18th century, Delft pottery and the valuable chinaware, both cups and large plates, decorated the walls of many Mennonite homes. And this was not only the fact in the more luxurious residences of the province of Holland, but also in the country, as is clear from a report by the Reformed pastor Elgersma (of the year 1685) that the Mennonite preacher Foecke Floris (*q.v.*) caused the people to take away from their walls, cups, plates, pictures, etc. (Hylkema, *Reformateurs* II, Haarlem, 1902, 6.)

Though we cannot determine accurately how many art collectors there have been among the Dutch Mennonites, we know that there were some even in the 17th century. From 1625 on Jan Theunisz (*q.v.*) in Amsterdam was the owner of a kind of restaurant, where the men of the world (among whom were many Mennonites!) used to meet and to view his great collection of art objects and curiosities. The Mennonite Hendrik van Uylenburgh was an art dealer and collector about the same time.

Jan Pietersz Bruyningh, who was painted with his wife by Rembrandt in 1636, had a small collection of oil-paintings by Lastman, Flinck, de Coninck, and two or three pictures by Rembrandt. There is reason to suppose that there were at this time many Mennonite art collectors. Of Mennonite art collectors of the 18th century we should mention among many others, Pieter Teyler van der Hulst (1702-78) (*q.v.*) at Haarlem, who gathered a large collection of valuable books, oil-paintings, drawings, coins and medals, etc. In Rotterdam the brothers Pieter and Jan Bisschop, of whom the first mentioned died in 1758 and the latter in 1771, had a fine collection of precious pictures, drawings of old Dutch and foreign masters, antique vases, splendid miniatures, enamels, gold and silver objects, Japan porcelain of the finest quality, lacquered ware from China, rare shells and other curiosities, which were all packed carefully in large cases. Strangers who visited Rotterdam sought the opportunity of looking at the *Kunstcabinet van de oude heer Bisschop.* In 1778 the stadtholder of the Netherlands, William of Orange, and his spouse, admired the Bisschop collection. Mennonite collectors and collections of the 19th century and today need not be further mentioned.

According to Kühler (II, 1, p. 59), Hendrik van Uylenburgh (1584-1660), the leader of a famous school of art and a well-known art dealer, was a Mennonite, a cousin of Rembrandt's first wife Saskia and a close friend of his. His brother Rombout later lived in Danzig and painted the Mennonite preacher Jan Gerrits (*q.v.*) of Emden. His son Gerrit was also an art dealer, though not with the best reputation.   vDZ.

3. *The Particular Mennonite Contribution to Art.* The relationship between Anabaptism-Mennonitism and the Dutch painting of the 16th and 17th centuries (in the broad sense, drawing and etching) will be considered from three aspects: (*a*) whether there is any fundamental mutual influence or conditioning between Mennonitism in Holland and painting; (*b*) whether there is in the case of Dutch painters who were Mennonites evidence that their faith found expression in their work; (*c*) in which of the Dutch painters does one find Mennonites or Mennonite characteristics portrayed.

Does there exist any fundamental influence and limitation between Mennonitism and Dutch painting? One thinks first and usually of Calvinism when one speaks of Dutch Protestantism, but this exclusiveness is by no means correct. The Reformation had numerous adherents in the Netherlands for 40 years before Calvinism from the south in 1566 won its dominant position. This pre-Calvinist period was to a large extent influenced by Anabaptism; indeed the Reformation and Anabaptism were for a time nearly identical in the Netherlands. (J. G. de Hoop-Scheffer, *Geschiedenis der Kerk-hervorming in Nederland,* 1873, 3.) But the point pertinent to our discussion is this: All that Protestantism has contributed to the cultural life of the Netherlands especially with respect to art can be traced in principle and in its essence to this Anabaptistically determined Reformation. In this realm

Calvinism could contribute nothing new; it merely took over. Also in the ensuing period it was true that Calvinism was the sole authoritative representative of Protestantism, however domineering it may have acted and however domineering it may indeed have been upon the state. Even in the later periods an independent Mennonite share in the cultural fruits of Dutch Protestantism can be assumed—at any rate so great a scholar as Johan Huizinga does so (*Die holländische Kultur des 17. Jahrhunderts,* Jena, 1933).

It is therefore proper, whenever the Protestant element in Dutch painting in its Golden Age is to be considered, to see in it an important aspect of Mennonitism. To be sure, we must guard ourselves against the current idea that Dutch painting is as such Protestant, especially in contrast to a Catholic art of Flanders, which remained under the dominion of Spain. In the first place there are areas where such a contrast does not exist and many connections can be traced, even between Rubens and Rembrandt. In the second place, the contrast is based not only on creed, but also on political and social conditions, the contrast between the bourgeois North and the courtly South. In the third place, we find already in the old Dutch "old Flemish" art of the 15th century, and still more in the Flemish art of the peasant Breughel, tendencies (such as the preference for genre painting, still life and landscape) which became important in later Dutch painting. Finally, many of the motifs of Dutch painting (the peasant pictures of Adriaan van Ostade, the genre pictures of Jan Steen, etc.) hardly fit into any category of Protestantism, especially the Dutch type of Protestantism.

We cannot avoid first of all viewing the effect of Protestantism on Dutch painting as a negative force, limiting and impoverishing it, for Protestantism is responsible first of all for what is lacking in Dutch painting as the nature and motif of its creation. Dutch Protestantism was always extremely hostile to furnishing churches with paintings, and that is as true of Calvinism as of Mennonitism. Thus the church drops out of the picture as an art center. Certain types of painting found in the Middle Ages and in the Catholic countries, such as the crucifixion (with exceptions like Rembrandt), the Virgin, and the saints, no longer are wanted. But there is also a lack of allegorical and mythological subjects from antiquity, such as is found in abundance in Italian and Flemish art, chiefly because Protestantism, Calvinistic as well as Mennonite, looked upon the depiction of these acts with suspicion. It is certainly an effect of Protestantism that causes the first great Dutch art historian, Carel van Mander, himself a Mennonite, to lament, "It is our present want and misfortune [about 1600], that so few figurative subjects can be painted in our Netherlands, whereby an opportunity would be given to our young people and to painters to achieve distinction in the presentation of allegory or in the treatment of the nude. For what there is to paint is mostly pictures according to nature" (i.e., portraits).

On the other hand, though it must be granted

that, as Carel van Mander laments, the Protestant influence led to an impoverishment in comparison with the earlier and contemporary work of other countries, nevertheless closer consideration shows that it also had a positive and fruitful effect. With its attitude toward ecclesiastical art, indeed to art in general, Protestantism preserved Dutch painting from becoming a mere appendage to Italian and Flemish art. It made Dutch art independent; renunciation became a gift. It is therefore largely due to Protestantism that portraiture became a fine art among the Dutch, that in Rembrandt it was developed to the point where the man and the man alone stands before his God, strives with God, is reflected in God. But Protestantism, and especially Dutch Protestantism, is a religion of domesticity; even the churches of that time look more like residences than churches. Dutch landscape painting likewise betrays Protestant influence. Its realism presents a sharp contrast to the symbolism of the Middle Ages and the theatrical lightness of contemporary Italian as well as some of the Flemish landscape painting; for the Protestant the world as such is the scene of a reality that is to be taken seriously, with real tasks and duties! When Dutch landscape painting becomes unreal, it becomes dreamy and romantic as with Ruisdael; here too Protestant individualism must not be overlooked!

In short, an examination of Dutch painting reveals many a feature that bears a Protestant stamp. And within the framework of the Mennonite share in the character of Dutch Protestantism, the question concerning a significant influence of Mennonitism upon Dutch art must, upon this evidence, be answered in the affirmative.

But is there evidence in the cases of all the many Dutch Mennonite artists, especially of the 17th century, that their confession has found expression in their creations? The answer is only in part affirmative. These Mennonite painters do not fall out of the general framework of Dutch art. Perhaps a direct influence of their religious attitude may be seen most easily in the Biblical subjects painted by David Joris, Lambert Jacobsz, Govert Flinck, and Rembrandt. The work of Jan Luiken (q.v.) is in sharp dependence upon his religious inclinations—cf. his illustrations for the Martyrs' Mirror of Tielemann van Braght (Dutch edition of 1685 and German edition of 1780). There is a conspicuous absence of genre painting among all these Mennonite painters. Would it be correct to attribute this lack to their Mennonitism, which was characterized by soundness and good manners? At any rate, it seems that the influence of their faith must be sought in their manner of life rather than in their manner of painting. Houbraken, who usually dwells with pleasure and in detail on the scandals in the lives of the Dutch painters, frequently stresses in the case of the Mennonites their morality, good manners, and piety, as in the case of David Joris (q.v.), van Mierevelt, Flinck, van der Heyden, and Luiken. With a few exceptions, however, such as van Mander and Jacobsz, the artists were not active in religious matters. D.K.

4. Mennonite Artists.

(a) Anabaptists. The only artist among the early Anabaptists was David Joris (1501-56), an early Dutch convert baptized and ordained by Obbe Philips in 1535 or 1536 who soon turned radical mystic, left the brotherhood, also was bitterly opposed by Menno Simons, and lived under a pseudonym in Basel as a wealthy merchant the last 12 years of his life. He was a capable glass painter and a sketcher of Biblical scenes; one of his sketches is in the Vienna Albertina Museum. Some of his preliminary drawings for the glass paintings are preserved in England. Other Anabaptist glass-painters (glas-schrijver, glasgraveur) are mentioned among the Dutch martyrs, such as Jan Woutersz van Cuyck who is called schildersartist en glasgraveur, and a certain Rommeken.

(b) Netherlands. A considerable number of the best Dutch artists have been Mennonites, particularly in the golden age of Dutch art, the 17th century, a few of them Mennonite preachers. It has sometimes been asserted that the greatest of all Dutch painters, Rembrandt van Rijn (1606-69), was a Mennonite. Kühler calls him a Mennonite (Geschiedenis II, 1, p. 58), as does Hendrik van Loon in his biography of Rembrandt. However, the best and most recent scholarship hesitates to claim this with finality, holding as to actual church membership only that "it is probable that Rembrandt at the end of the 1650's either belonged to or stood close to a freer circle of Waterlander Mennonites which stood under Collegiant domination" (H. M. Rotermund, Rembrandt und die religiösen Laienbewegungen in den Niederlanden im 17. Jahrhundert, 1952). In any case Rembrandt's religion was in its deepest essence Mennonite, formed by Mennonite influences, and his essential spirit and expression were Mennonite in character. This is asserted not only by Rotermund, but also by other scholars, most recently by L. Venturi in Painting and Painters (N.Y., 1948), and Jacob Rosenberg in Rembrandt (Cambridge, 1948). The great Rembrandt scholar, F. Schmidt-Degener, says that Rembrandt was "the obvious product of a Mennonite environment."

The first Dutch Mennonite painter, coming before the 17th century, was Carel van Mander (1548-1606), of the stricter Old Flemish group. Among the leading Dutch painters of the golden age were Michiel J. van Mierevelt (1567-1641; Lambert Jacobsz (ca. 1598-1636); Jacob Adriaensz Backer (1608-51, q.v.); Rembrandt's close friend and pupil Govert Flinck (1614-60, q.v.); Salomon van Ruysdael (1605-70, q.v.), and his famous nephew Jacob van Ruisdael (1628-82, q.v.); Samuel van Hoogstraten (1624-48, q.v.); Abraham van den Tempel (1622 or 23-72, q.v.), the son of Lambert Jacobsz; and Jan van der Heyden (1637-1712, q.v.). There was also the noted copperplate-engraver Jan Luiken (1649-1712) who was a Mennonite for only a few years, 1673-5. Dutch Mennonite artists of later times include: Anton Mauve (1838-88), Hendrik Willem Mesdag (1831-1915), and Sientje Mesdag-van Houten (1834-1909). Except for Carel van

Mander and Lambert Jacobsz, the Dutch Mennonite artists were not prominent in church life.

(c) *Germany*. In Germany the two Hamburg painters, Jakob called Balthasar Denner (1685-1749) (*q.v.*) and Dominicus van der Smissen (1705-1760) (*q.v.*), contributed a great deal to art; paintings by the former are found in all of the more important European art galleries. Enoch Seemann, Jr. (*q.v.*, b. 1694 in Elbing, d. 1744 in London), a talented painter and engraver, was a member of the Danzig Mennonite Church. In the 19th century Berend Goos (1815-85) won recognition for his paintings of animals and landscapes. The same is true of the sculptor Emil Heinrich Wurtz, who emigrated to America and lost his life in his prime in the wreck of the S.S. *Burgoyne* on July 4, 1898, at the age of 42 (*Christlicher Gemeinde-Kalender* 1905, 45 ff.). There are also the Crefeld painters, Moritz von Beckerath (1836-96), painter of historical scenes, and Willy von Beckerath (1868-   ), painter and art dealer, and the Danzigers Heinrich Zimmermann (1804-45), Richard Loewens (1856-85), and Hans Mekelburger (1884-1915) who fell on the field of battle in Poland in 1915 at the age of 30 at the beginning of a promising career; the Königsbergers Johann Wientz (years 1781-1849) and Franz Theodor Zimmermann (1807-77 ?). South German Mennonites have produced one good artist, Daniel Wohlgemuth (1875-   ) (*q.v.*) of the Weierhof (Palatinate) community now living at Gundersheim near Worms. Of lesser rank is Fritz Mosimann of Mulhouse, Alsace (since 1914 French territory), member of the Pfastatt congregation, who paints local Alsatian landscapes and scenes. The outstanding modern artist of the West Prussian Mennonites, however, is Marie Birckholtz-Bestvater (b. 1888 at Preussisch-Königsdorf, near Danzig, West Prussia) studied in Berlin and Munich 1908-13, and lived in the Danzig-Zoppot area, where she had her studio until 1945. After living in Berlin 1945-47, she emigrated to Buenos Aires in 1947, where she is now employed in the ceramics firm "Tadeco." Mrs. Birckholtz's mediums are oil and watercolor, her themes landscapes (earlier largely West Prussian) and figure sketches. She has had numerous one-man shows. Most of her works have been destroyed or lost in West Prussia during the war, a few taken along to Argentina. Mention should also be made of Wolf von Beckerath (1896-1944) of Crefeld, and the sculptor Heinrich Mekelburger.

(d) *Russia*. Johann Heinrich Janzen (1844-1904), teacher and preacher of Gnadenfeld in the Molotschna, South Russia, was the first able artist among the Russian Mennonites. Although he had no formal training, his drawings and oil paintings were of good quality. His favorite theme was the Molotschna landscape. Six of his oil paintings have been brought to America, the best being: "Peace on the Molotschna" (A Russian Mennonite farmstead) and "The Thunderstorm," both in the possession of the family of his late brother, Elder Jacob H. Janzen (d. 1950) of Waterloo, Ont. One of Janzen's finest products was *Das Märchen vom Weihnachtsmann*, his own version of the Christmas story, richly illustrated in colors with his own

drawings. He also did the illustrations for his brother Jacob H. Janzen's (Zenian), *Denn meine Augen haben Deinen Heiland gesehen* (Homburg, v.d. Höhe, ca. 1924).

Hans Janzen, son of the above Johann, was the outstanding Mennonite artist in Russia. His favorite theme was also the Molotschna landscape, although he painted portraits as well. He was educated in Moscow, and then taught mathematics, physics, and art at the Mennonite Zentralschule at Orloff in the Molotschna colony. Nothing has been heard of him since 1945, when he was still alive in Russia, but twelve of his paintings have been brought to America. Hans Janzen copied in black and white his father's illustrations for a mimeographed edition of *Das Märchen vom Weihnachtsmann*, which was published by his uncle, Elder Jacob H. Janzen, in Canada.

Perhaps a still finer artist of Russian Mennonite background is Woldemar Neufeld, stepson of Elder Jacob Janzen (Waterloo), b. 1909 at Waldheim, Molotschna, who was a student of Hans Janzen in the Orloff school and came to Canada in 1924. He is therefore properly considered an American artist. After study at Waterloo College, Neufeld attended the Cleveland School of Art (1935-39) and has since set up the Neufeld Studios in New York City and New Preston, Conn. (1949). He has held one-man shows in Cleveland, Chicago, New York, Toronto, and elsewhere. He specializes in color prints and in watercolor, and has painted numerous Waterloo County landscapes. The Library of Congress, the New York Public Library, the Cleveland Museum of Public Art, and many private collectors own his color prints. (See *American Artist*, XVI, Jan. 1952, "Presenting Woldemar Neufeld," 48 ff.

John P. Klassen (1888-   ), born in Kronsgarten, Chortitza, received professional art training at the Universities of Berlin and Munich, and taught art in the Chortitza Zentralschule in Russia before coming to the United States in 1924. He has been professor of art at Bluffton College since 1924, his own specialty being small sculpture, including bas-relief and plaques. Among his works are a bust of Menno Simons and one of N. C. Hirschy (d. 1916), first president of Bluffton College.

J. Sudermann, born ca. 1900 in the Chortitza settlement, educated in Russia and Germany, was an outstanding artist, poet, and teacher among the Mennonites of the Ukraine, last heard of in a concentration camp in Siberia. His favorite themes in oil and watercolor were the landscapes and buildings in the Chortitza area, among them the Chortitza Mennonite Church painted in 1932. A number of his works were brought by relatives to Canada 1947 ff. Johann Funk, formerly a teacher in Arkadak, Saratov, since 1930 in Paraguay, deserves passing mention.

Alexander Harder, a son of preacher Bernhard Harder, and brother of novelist Hans Harder, born and reared in the Alexandertal settlement near Samara on the Volga River, Russia, but living in Germany since 1924, now at Hanau near Frankfurt, has painted many Russian scenes and landscapes. He is known also for his oil painting of

Menno Simons, done for the 1936 Mennonite World Conference.

(e) *United States and Canada.* The chief North American Mennonite artists of native stock are Arthur L. Sprunger (1897-   ) of Goshen, Ind., of Swiss background, and Oliver Wendell Schenk (1903-   ) of an old Virginia-Ohio Mennonite family. Of immigrant Russian Mennonite stock are Hans Bartsch (1884-   ) born at Tashkent, Turkestan, immigrated to Newton, Kans., 1893-4, now resident in New York City; J. P. Klassen (1888-   ) born in Kronsgarten, Chortitza, Russia, immigrated to Bluffton, Ohio, 1924 and since then resident there; Woldemar Neufeld (1909-   ) born at Waldheim, Molotschna, immigrated to Waterloo, Ont., in 1924, now resident in New Preston, Conn.; and D. G. Rempel, born in Russia, immigrated to Bluffton, Ohio, in 1922, student of J. P. Klassen at Bluffton, now living in Akron, Ohio, as a designer and manufacturer of toys, known for his fine small sculpture "The Fallen Horseman," now in the Bluffton College Library, relating an incident in the Ukraine in 1919. Elder Johannes Janzen, formerly a teacher in the Turkestan (Russian) Mennonite settlement, resident in the Stoltz Plateau colony in Santa Catharina, Brazil, from 1930 until recently, now located in the new settlement at Witmarsum in Parana, painted numerous scenes in the Krauel Colony (Santa Catharina) in oil.†

H.S.B.

In addition to the literature cited in the text the following should be noted: *ML*, articles *"Bildende Kunst"* (I, 221) by Christian Neff, and *"Niederländische Malerei"* (II, 241-3) by D. Cattepoel; Arnold Houbraken, *De Groote Schouburgh der Nederlantsche Konstschilders en Schilderessen*, 3 vv. (Amsterdam, 1718 and 1719); J. P. Klassen, "Mennonite Ideals in Art," *Proceedings of the Fourth Annual Conf. on Menn. Cultural Problems* (North Newton, 1945) 135-45; *Mitteilungen des Sippenverbandes der Danziger Menn.-Familien Epp-Kauenhoven-Zimmerman*, containing the following articles by Kurt Kauenhoven: "Wie trugen sich unsere mennonitische Vorfahren" (VI, 1940, 62-4 and 94-5); "Die gottesdienstlichen Gebräuche unserer mennonitischen Vorfahren (Aus den Bildern von Bernard Picart)." "Die Abendmahlsfeier" (VI, 98-101); "Die Taufe" (VI, 129-32); "Die erste gedruckte Erwähnung der Danziger Kauenhowen 1697" (VI, 111-16), referring to Enoch Seemann, Sr., with bibliographical references; *Menn. Life* containing the following articles: S. Smeding, "The Portraits of Menno Simons," July 1948, 16-19; K. Kauenhoven, "Mennonite Artists—Danzig and Koenigsberg," July 1949, 17-23; C. Krahn, "Rembrandt, the Bible, and the Mennonites," 1952, 3-6; H. M. Rotermund, "Rembrandt and the Mennonites, 1952, 7-10; A. Sudermann, "Traum und Wirklichkeit" (on J. Sudermann), 1953, 17-23; also R. Gomersall, "A Father and Son Paint" (on the Newswangers and their Amish etchings), *American-German Review* XVII (1950) 10-13.

Two American Mennonite periodicals have given attention to reproducing the work of Mennonite artists, *Die Mennonitische Warte* (Steinbach, Man., 1935-38) and *Mennonite Life* (North Newton, Kans., 1946-   ). The former published a few watercolors and pen-and-ink sketches by the Russian-American artists J. P. Klassen (Bluffton), John Funk (Saskatoon), and Arnold Dyck (Steinbach-Winnipeg). Dyck, who studied art in Munich, though more active as a writer than an artist, has illustrated some of his own writings with human-interest figure sketches. *Mennonite Life* has covered a broad scope in its reproductions. Articles or reproductions have dealt with the following: A. L. Sprunger, J. P. Klassen, Aurèle Robert, J. Sudermann, Alexander Harder, E. Seemann, H. Zimmermann, F. T. Zimmermann, J. Wientz, Rembrandt, A. Hendriks and the earlier Menno Simons portraits, D. Chodowiecky, D. Wohlgemuth, Heinrich Mekelburger, M. Birckholtz-Bestvater.

Arthur, a village of 1,400 inhabitants on the boundary line of Douglas and Moultrie counties in east central Illinois. Three different branches of Mennonites are represented in the community. The Old Order Amish Mennonites have 800 members in 9 congregations or districts. The Arthur Mennonite Church (MC) under the Illinois Mennonite Conference has 241 members and worships in a building on the east side of Arthur. The Conservative Amish Mennonite congregation with 45 members meets in its church building 3 miles south of Arthur, where it also conducts a Christian day school. A congregation of the Western District Amish Mennonite Conference met in a building one mile north of Arthur prior to 1916.   R.J.Y.

Arthur (Ill.) Amish Mennonite congregation (extinct) built its church in 1897. Begun by dissatisfied Old Order Amish of the community, the church also received members from other states. A list of members who contributed money for the church treasury in 1898 contained 31 names. Ministers who served the church included Seth P. Hershberger, Moses J. Helmuth, and Isaac A. Miller. The Western District A.M. Conference minutes for 1916 reported that the church had been sold. The members had previously moved to Michigan, Ohio, and Indiana.   M.G.

Arthur Conservative Amish Mennonite congregation near Arthur, Ill., was organized March 23, 1945, with a membership of eight. Samuel T. Eash, Middlebury, Ind., Nevin Bender, Greenwood, Del., and Elmer G. Swartzendruber, Wellman, Iowa, were the Executive Committee of the C.A.M. Conference in charge of the organization. In the summer of 1945 and again in 1946 Minister Shem Peachey of Springs, Pa., had charge of the congregation; in the winter of 1945-46 Eli Swartzentruber of Greenwood had charge, but on March 2, 1947, Levi M. Miller was ordained and has since served as minister. Bishop oversight is under the jurisdiction of Elmer G. Swartzendruber. The membership in 1953 was 45.   E.G.S.

Arthur Mennonite Church (MC) in Arthur, Ill., had its beginning in October 1936, when a group of workers from the East Bend congregation near Fisher, Ill., began services in the Obie Bontrager home in Arthur. The first series of meetings was also held there in December of the same year by J. A. Heiser. In the fall of 1938 H. J. King and family moved to Arthur from Harper, Kan., and took charge of the work. In the spring of 1948 Richard Yordy and wife came to assist in the work. The group was organized into a congregation in the Illinois Conference of the Mennonite Church on Sept. 15, 1940, by Bishops C. A. Hartzler and J. A. Heiser, with a charter membership of 56. The 1953 membership was 241. A new church was dedicated in May 1949. The group is almost entirely of Old Order Amish background and drawn from the neighboring Amish community. H.J.K.

Arthur (Ill.) Old Order Amish Mennonite community was started by Moses Yoder, Daniel Miller, and Daniel Otto and their families when they arrived in the community on March 3, 1865, coming from Summit Mills, Somerset Co., Pa. Bishop Joseph Keim from near Goshen, Ind., arriving in the summer of 1865, was the first minister. He organized the first Amish church of that region in 1865 and served it as bishop for seven years. Other settlers moved into the community from Indiana, Iowa, Ohio, and Pennsylvania so that by 1888 it was necessary to divide the church into two districts, the Moultrie County or Beachy District and the Douglas County or Plank District. The Douglas County District was further divided on Dec. 7, 1902, into the Plank and Mast districts, and the Moultrie County District on Feb. 4, 1906. The Plank District was divided again in the fall of 1922 and the Mast District on March 7, 1926, thus forming four districts from the original Douglas County District. Later the two Moultrie County districts were both subdivided, forming four districts. There are thus today eight districts with approximately 800 members (1954).

The present Arthur Amish community has Arthur as its center, while the villages of Chesterville, Cadwell, and Fairbanks also are located in the community. On Oct. 11, 1936, a number of Amish members left the church to join the Mennonites and on March 25, 1945, a small number left to organize a Conservative Amish Mennonite congregation. The following bishops have served the Arthur Amish congregations:

Joseph N. Keim	1865—72 (died)
Jonas (Yoni) Kauffman	1873—80 (d. 1907)
Daniel J. Beachy	1885—1933 (died)
David J. Plank	1892—1945 (died)
A. J. Mast	1904—49 (died)
Dan. C. Schlabach	1919—43 (died)
Sam. N. Beachy	1920—to date
Noah B. Shrock	1925—to date
Noah A. Yoder	1938—to date
Jerry S. Otto	1939—to date
Chris. E. Otto	1948—to date
Obed A. Diener	1949—to date
Menno S. Miller	1951—to date L.A.M.

Article Book, Hutterite. A major doctrinal tract of the Hutterites, originating in Moravia around 1547, extant in about 20 manuscript copies of between 1547 and 1655, published in a condensed form only in the Great Chronicle of the Hutterites as *Die Fünf Artikel des Grössten Streites Zwischen Uns und der Welt* (*Die Aelteste Chronik der Huterischen Bruder*, ed. Zieglschmid, 269-316), and in Lydia Müller's *Glaubenszeugnisse Oberdeutscher Taufgesinnter* (Leipzig, 1938, 238-56) from a Hutterite manuscript which contains but a *Kurzer Auszug* (epitome) of the book as such. The term "Article Book" is not the official title though widely used, particularly among the American Hutterites of today. The original manuscript bears the title, *Ein schön lustig Buchlein etliche Hauptartikel unseres Glaubens betreffend*. The *Geistliches Blumengärtlein* (Amsterdam, 1680) contains still another edition of this tract under the title, *Schriftmässiger Bericht und Zeugnis betreffend die rechte christliche Taufe, Abendmahl, Gemeinschaft, Obrigkeit, und Ehestand*. There is no doubt that the Hutterites considered this book (about 300 leaves in ms.) of equal rank with Peter Riedemann's great *Rechenschaft unseres Glaubens* of 1545 (*q.v.*). It was one of their main doctrinal statements, used both within the community and also as a source when dealing with the outside "world" in order to demonstrate the Biblical correctness of their particular teachings. The author of the great Article Book is not named, although one codex with a *Kurzer Auszug* names expressly the Hutterite elder Peter Walpot as the author (*q.v.*), as does also Ottius, *Annales Anabaptistici* (*q.v.*) of 1672, 160. A careful investigation by R. Friedmann (*Archiv für Reformationsgeschichte*, XXVIII, 1931, 94-102) makes it highly plausible that Peter Walpot, *Vorsteher* (elder) of the Hutterite brotherhood 1565-78, was if not its author then at least its redactor, possibly together with Kasper Braitmichel (*q.v.*) and Hans Kräl (*q.v.*). It is not unlikely that Peter Riedemann also gave some advice as to the first draft, for every Hutterite writing was in some sense the work of the entire community (this is what they call the "unity of the Spirit," *Einigkeit des Heiligen Geistes*). The occasion for the writing of such a succinct doctrinal statement of the Hutterite position (differing from Riedemann's larger and elaborate *Rechenschaft* of 1545) might be found in the discussion leading to the readmission of the remnant of the Gabrielite Brethren (*q.v.*) in 1545. The *Geschicht-Buch* (ed. Zieglschmid, 251-57) has a section, *Unterricht, die Hauptartikel betreffend* (instruction concerning the main articles), which was presented to these candidates. It appears to be the prototype of our Article Book, which is an elaboration of much the same material. The presentation of the Article Book is "punkt- und argumentweis" (item by item, with arguments).

The book is in no way a theological tract, but rather like all Anabaptist doctrinal writings a collection of Biblical proof texts topically arranged to show the correctness of the position of the brotherhood with regard to certain selected problems. The title of the larger edition, *A Beautiful and Pleasant Little Book Concerning the Main Articles of our Faith*, is quite colorless; more to the point is the title used in the Great Chronicle, *The Five Articles of the Greatest Conflict Between Us and the World*. It does not pretend to contain a complete system of Anabaptist thought but only a collection of those points and their arguments which distinguish the Brethren from the "world" and justify their particular stand. (The Schleitheim articles, *q.v.*, were of the same kind of Anabaptist doctrinal writings.) The large Article Book comprises in one codex 286 quarto leaves; this size explains the later appearance of a condensed edition, which in print comprises only 18 pages.

The book deals with the following five articles: (1) Concerning true baptism (and how infant baptism contradicts it); (2) Concerning the Lord's Supper (and how the sacrament of the parsons is against it); (3) Concerning the true inner surrender (*Gelassenheit*) and Christian community of goods; (4) That Christians should not go to war nor should they use sword or violence nor secular litigation. Those functioning in such offices (authorities) cannot be considered to be (true) Christians; (5) Concerning divorce between believers and unbelievers. (NB. One codex has as a fifth article, Concerning taking the oath.) The most stimulating article is, of course, the third where community of goods (*q.v.*, *Gütergemeinschaft*) is interpreted as the supreme expression of brotherly love and of true *Gelassenheit*. It closes with the rhyme

Gottes Wort wär nit so schwer
Wenn nur der Eigennutz nit wär.

Gelassenheit means nothing but self-conquest and sharing all earthly goods with one's brother. It is a top concept among the Hutterites.

The text is presented almost like a catechism: statement, proof text, etc. The tension between spirit and letter is resolved in favor of the latter; that is, the Article Book represents a literalistic type of Christianity in simple obedience to God's Word. Remarkable is the documentation of each article by extensive quotation from the Church fathers and other ancient authorities. The knowledge of the history of Christian thought and church history thus revealed is quite amazing, a fact which can be noticed in the study of any Hutterite tract. A major source for this knowledge must have been Sebastian Franck (*q.v.*), whose various books were certainly well known to the Brethren; it was he who supplied the contact between Anabaptism and humanistic studies. Besides Franck the *Ecclesiastical History* of Eusebius (*q.v.*) was rather popular among all Anabaptist groups, likewise Flavius Josephus (*q.v.*). That Balthasar Hubmaier (*q.v.*), too, a scholastic doctor of theology, was of great assistance (through his writings) in this endeavor of proving arguments by old authorities, is quite certain.

The Article Book must have been widely known in its time. Catholics as well as Lutheran polemics against it are known. (See *Archiv für Reformationsgeschichte*, XXIX, 1932, 1-9.) The brethren continued to use and to copy the book at all times. The new Carinthian exiles (*q.v.*) of the eighteenth century who joined the Hutterites in Transylvania, soon became familiar with this book, too, as late codices, now in Canada, prove.   R.F.

R. Friedmann, "Eine dogmatische Hauptschrift der Hutterischen Täufergemeinschaft in Mähren," *Arch. f. Ref.-Gesch.*, 1931 and 1932.

Artikelboek, the name of the confession of faith used by the Groningen Old Flemish Mennonites (*q.v.*).   vDZ.

Arum, a village in the western part of the Dutch province of Friesland near Harlingen, where two Mennonite churches formerly stood, one of them of the Jan Jacobsz group, whose elder, Jacob Claasen, baptized 15 persons here between 1614 and 1638. This congregation became extinct before 1729, and in that year the church was sold. It is not known to which group the other church adhered; in the *Naamlijst* of 1731 it is called the Pingjum-Arum congregation, having united with the Pingjum congregation about 1695. By 1815 it had died out, for in that year its church was torn down.   J.L.

Blaupot t.C., *Friesland;* Archives of the Terschelling congregation in the Amsterdam Mennonite Archives; J. Loosjes, "Jan Jacobsz en de Janjacobsgezinden," in *Ned. arch. v. Kergesch.* XI (1914); *ML* I, 87; H. J. Buse, "De verdwenen Doopsgezinde gemeenten in Friesland," in *De Frije Fries* XXII (1915) reprint, p. 4.

Aschelberger, Stoffel, one of those Hutterites present at a meeting which was suddenly attacked on Dec. 16, 1539, at Steinabrunn in Lower Austria; a group of about 150 were held captive for six weeks in the neighboring castle of Falkenstein, southeast of Nikolsburg. Twenty of them, including Aschelberger, were put into a special cell. All attempts of Catholic priests from Vienna to convert them having been futile, 90 men, after a moving parting from their wives and children, were chained in pairs and shipped to Trieste, to be chained to the galleys of the Doge Andrea Doria. But they managed to escape from the castle where they were imprisoned, by letting themselves down on a rope. Twenty were seized and came to a wretched end on the galleys. The others reached their home in Moravia. Aschelberger wrote a letter to the church at Znaim (Moravia) and three to his wife, which are in the possession of the Hutterian Brethren at Frankfort, S.D. In the hymn composed by the captives in Falkenstein, "Ein Lied von den 20 Brüdern auf Falkenstein," the second verse is credited to Stoffel Aschelberger. (*ML* I, 87.)   NEFF.

Ascherham, Gabriel (also called Kürschner after his trade as a furrier), leader of an early Anabaptist group in Moravia and Silesia, the so-called Gabrielites (*q.v.*). He was born in Nürnberg, Bavaria, and worked in Schärding (then Bavaria, now Austria) where he seems to have come into contact with Anabaptists, most likely with Hans Hut (*q.v.*) and Ambrosius Spittelmayer (*q.v.*). He joined the group and was made preacher. Soon hereafter he moved to Silesia, where he became active around Glogau, Breslau, and Glatz, establishing small brotherhoods. When the first persecutions set in in 1528, he led his followers into Moravia, then the most tolerant country in Central Europe. On a noble's estate at Rossitz they settled, soon joined by like-minded newcomers from Swabia, Hesse, and the Palatinate, whose leader was Philip Plener (*q.v.*), also called Blauärmel or Weber. This Philippite group (*q.v.*) soon moved away from Rossitz to near-by Auspitz where, by chance, also a Tyrolese Anabaptist group under the leadership of Zaunring and Schützinger had found refuge. In 1531 these three groups (about 4,000 baptized members) formed a loose union at the suggestion of Jakob Hutter (*q.v.*). Ascherham was named their *Vorsteher* or bishop. In 1533, Jakob Hutter, who meanwhile had labored in Tyrol, returned and found many things faulty with this group. Thus he insisted upon a stricter and fairer practice of the (in Moravia long established) community of goods. In consequence, a most painful division took place among the Brethren (in Hutterite writings called *die Zerspaltung*), which for a long time reverberates in all Hutterite documents (Wolkan, *Geschicht-Buch*, 76-104). Now there were three groups in Moravia instead of one: the Hutterites, the Philipites, and the Gabrielites, which had little contact with each other but lived in peace side by side. When the first heavy persecution set in also in Moravia in 1535, each group tried to escape it in its own way. The Philipites returned to Southwest Germany (see **Ausbund**), the Hutterites somehow managed to stay in Moravia, while Ascherham and his group turned northward, to Silesia, Poland, and East Prussia (where they perhaps later mingled with the Mennonites). Only a small Gabrielite group remained behind in Moravia establishing several new households on noble estates, yet still disunited with the Hutterites. Gabriel's old grudge against Jakob Hutter and his people prevented any negotiations (much asked for), even after Hutter's death in 1536. In fact, Ascherham attacked the Hutterite group in speeches, writings, songs, and "improper" letters. In 1542 he even published a booklet against the Hutterites (used by Chr. Andreas Fischer, *q.v.*, in his *Taubenkobel*, 1605), to which they replied in a sharp epistle.

Little is known about the Ascherham group in Silesia. W. Wiswedel's statement is apparently correct when he says of Ascherham that he was no real leader, had little gift for organization, and by his spiritualistic teachings easily antagonized people. His abandonment of the practice of community of goods was not opposed by his followers, but when he began to minimize the issue of baptism, that is, when he showed indifference toward infant baptism, many of his (Anabaptist-minded) adherents were estranged, and many left the group and returned to the Hutterites in Moravia.

In order to strengthen the regard of his followers for his vision, Ascherham published in Silesia in 1544 a new polemical-dogmatic book, called, *Vom Unterschied Göttlicher und Menschlicher Weisheit* (only known copy at the *National Bibliothek* in Vienna, Austria), and had it read at all places where his people met. Wiswedel published most of its text in the *Archiv für Reformationsgeschichte* (1937), where it covers about 53 pages. It is a book of remarkable intellectual and spiritual strength (considering that Ascherham was an unlearned man), but it is most ignoble toward his former brethren, the Anabaptists in Moravia. The genius of this work is rather that of a "spiritual reformer" (like Bünderlin, Hans Denk, Franck) than that of the Anabaptists. All the external things became indifferent to Ascherham—the "spirit" alone mattered. The book is well written and Wiswedel praises its style. As a declaration of his whole philosophy Ascherham places at the beginning four brief statements which sound like a challenge: (1) no one has a right to baptize and to establish church ordinances (regulations) unless he be in the Christian church; (2) no one is in the Christian church unless he has the Holy Spirit; (3) neither faith nor spirit can be obtained from the Scriptures; (4) nor is faith the ground and origin of our salvation. Obviously, these are ten-

ets of a non-Anabaptist nature, and the deeper roots of the conflict become visible.

Only those who have the Holy Spirit (or, as often used, the Spirit of Promise, *Geist der Verheissung*) can distinguish between good and evil, and not those who have just the letter of the Bible. That is the real meaning of the title, "Concerning the Distinction Betweeen Divine and Human Wisdom." Those who preach without the Spirit soon become "literalists," and that leads to error and false appearance. The Kingdom of God is inward only. External organization and regulations (or ordinances) are of no value whatsoever toward salvation. "What they [the Hutterites and all those who do not follow Ascherham] do they perform in a 'legalistic' fashion, and not because of an urge of the Holy Spirit. That is, they show but a pretense of monkish appearance (*angenommener mönchischer Schein*). Do not seek your salvation in external things (*elementische Kreatur*) such as baptism, Lord's Supper, and brotherhood, for they do not guarantee salvation."

Of himself Ascherham declared that he had no personal call from God to begin anything new. Thus he was not an apostle. "But I have received mercy through the spirit of divine understanding to build on the ground laid by Christ and the apostles. God has sanctified me that I may serve according to the order of the Holy Spirit. . . . Thus nobody should meddle with Scriptures and regulations (*Ordnung*) unless he have the Spirit of Promise. And it is through this spirit alone that one loses the will to sin."

Concerning *Gemeinschaft* (the word meaning both brotherhood and community of goods) Ascherham's ideas are strangely contradictory, considering that he was the leader of a group himself, in contrast to the radical spiritualists of that time who, by intention, remained isolated individuals. "The apostles," he says, "did not preach anything about *Gemeinschaft*, but only the Gospel of the kingdom of God and Christ. In believing, they received the Holy Spirit which made them think little of earthly goods. . . . The community of goods, however, which is practiced today [by the Hutterites] is quite different. People are pressed to give up their goods, though they do it reluctantly only, on promise of salvation. They are not urged by the love of the Holy Spirit but they rather think to buy the kingdom of God by such an act [which Ascherham calls 'simony']. I tell you if you are not saved outside your *Gemeinschaft* [brotherhood or community of goods], you will never be saved by it. For salvation does not rest in good deeds, but in the grace of God only. And whoever is saved, in him is brotherhood unbidden."

The most provocative section of the entire book deals with Ascherham's interpretation of baptism. "All baptizing that takes place outside the Holy Spirit is of benefit to none. Since baptism cannot bring the Holy Spirit, no one in the Christian church can be made better or worse by it (*wird gebessert oder gebösert*). Therefore it is not right to condemn anyone on account of baptism. Since baptism cannot produce pious men, people should not be compelled to submit to it unless they have [divine] understanding. Baptism is not a law but presupposes liberty, as do all Christian ordinances (*Ordnungen*). Since reason has such liberty, it would be much better to let little children, who cannot even talk, come to this liberty. As they are baptized they have nothing found nor lost . . . yet if anyone asks me if infant baptism is sin, to him I answer, no. But in order to prevent disorder and superstition, it is well to omit infant baptism since so much misuse sprang from it." "Where there is the Holy Spirit, there is also baptism, the remembrance of Christ [Lord's Supper], and a saintly life. The self-styled brethren, however, say, 'This is our order, we insist on it even if it hurts somebody.' This they call Christian zeal and testimony. But the Holy Spirit does not need such external proofs." "It is not possible to die for the sake of baptism, for that means to miss God's grace in Christ Jesus by whom all men are saved through the death of Christ and not through their own death."

And now follow two appended chapters: An Admonition to the Authorities, and Concerning the Lord's Supper, signed by Gabriel as "the least among his brethren and nobody in the kingdom of God." He exhorts the government in so many words "not to judge by the sword the zeal for God of those who do not understand it better. Since the gift of the Spirit is not in the power of the government, we urge thee not to use the sword over those who do not use the sword against thee but rather are obedient . . . . In these times God does not permit killing anybody for the sake of his faith," etc.

With regard to the Lord's Supper he opposes the symbolical interpretation prevalent among Anabaptist groups. He favors more a sacramental viewpoint, not unlike that later taught by Calvin and his church, namely, that at a dignified celebration the believer actually participates in the body and blood of Christ in a spiritual fashion. . . .

As these excerpts show, this was not a book adapted to build a strong brotherhood or a suffering church. Ascherham, who had come to Silesia in or before 1544 to rally his followers, soon found himself "a shepherd without sheep" (Loserth). Apparently they sought more the spirit of genuine Anabaptism than their leader did. Not much is known about Ascherham's predicament and reaction. We only learn that one year later, in 1545, he died in a small city on the Polish-Silesian border. As for the fate of his group, more will be said in the article **Gabrielites** (*q.v.*). Most of them soon joined the Hutterite brotherhoods.　　R.F.

The Hutterite *Geschicht-Buch;* J. Loserth, *Communismus* and his articles in *ML* II, 24 f.; W. Wiswedel, "Gabriel Ascherham und die nach ihm benannte Bewegung," in *Arch. f. Ref.-Gesch.,* 1937 (with the text of Ascherham's book); *ML* I, 88.

Ashland County, Ohio, is located in the north central part of the state, with Ashland as the county seat. This county was once the home of four Mennonite churches, now all extinct—two of Pennsylvanians, one of the Old Order Amish, and one composed of Bavarian-Palatine immigrants, inclined

later toward the General Conference Mennonite Church (though never actually becoming a member)—all founded before the middle of the past century. The county also contains several other of the Historic Peace Churches—Brethren in Christ, and Brethren. Ashland city is the seat of a Brethren church college, and seminary.　　C.H.S.

J. Umble, "Extinct Ohio Mennonite Churches, The Churches in Ashland County," *MQR* XIX (Jan., July 1945) 41-58, 215-37 and XX (Jan. 1946) 4-52.

Ashland Mennonite Mission (GCM) among the Northern Cheyenne Indians is located one mile west of Ashland, Mont., on the eastern side of the Tongue River, on the old road to the Northern Cheyenne Indian Reservation (formerly Tongue River Indian Reservation). A church built in 1917 by P. A. Kliewer served as an outstation from Birney Mission station until in 1921 when it was moved and a parsonage built. In 1924 Mr. and Mrs. Kliewer had to leave the work, and Mr. and Mrs. Valdo Petter then took care of this field. Valdo Petter died May 5, 1935, and since then his widow, Mrs. Laura Petter, has carried on the work.　　A.H.

Ashtabula County Mennonite Church. The Mennonite Church in Ashtabula County, Ohio, was founded near South Windsor by Amish Mennonite settlers in 1907. Officially known as the Maple Grove Church, it was a member of the Eastern Amish Mennonite Conference. On Feb. 12, 1911, Levi Hartzler, of West Liberty, Ohio, was ordained minister by Bishop S. E. Allgyer. After two years of service Hartzler returned to West Liberty, and the little band dispersed. In 1919 settlement began again near East Orwell. H. N. Troyer moved from Harrisonburg, Va., to East Orwell late in 1923 and was elected Sunday-school superintendent in 1924. Later he was licensed to preach and in 1925 was ordained and became resident pastor. Troyer moved away in 1929, and in 1932 the Plainview Church near Aurora, Ohio, was given full charge of the work. All the active workers later moved away, and the church was sold to another denomination.　　J.S.U.

Asia. 1. *Java and Sumatra.* The first Mennonites to enter Asia permanently were representatives of the Dutch Mennonite Mission Board which established work in East Java (*q.v.*) in 1851 which has developed into a Chinese Mennonite church and a Javanese Mennonite church, now independent of the mission board. The Mennonite Central Committee began a relief work in this area in 1948, which is still continuing. In 1869 missionaries of the Dutch Mennonite Mission Board also established a work on Sumatra (*q.v.*), which had to be abandoned after World War I because of lack of support. The present Mennonite membership in Java is about 10,000.

2. *India.* The next Mennonite mission work in Asia was that established in India in 1899-1901 by the Mennonites of North America: (*a*) by the Mennonite Church (MC) in the Central Provinces in 1899, (*b*) by the General Conference Mennonite Church in the same area but 150 miles farther south a year later, 1900-1, (*c*) by the Mennonite

Brethren Church in 1899 in the far south in Hyderabad, the first two being preceded by relief work by each group in the great famine of 1896-99. All three of these missions have developed into large and vigorous enterprises, with well-established indigenous churches with a total membership (1950) of almost 20,000. The Mennonite (MC) mission established a daughter mission in 1940 in Bihar, some 600 miles to the north of the original mission in the Central Provinces. The M.B.C. Church had earlier entered India in 1924 in Bihar. The Mennonite Central Committee carried on relief work in India in 1945-50, chiefly in the great famine of 1946 in the region near Calcutta. An inter-mission relief agency, called the Mennonite Committee for Relief in India, called forth by this effort, is still in existence.

3. *China* had been entered by several American Mennonite mission boards during the first half of the 20th century, but by 1951 all work had been suspended and all missionaries recalled as a result of the intolerable conditions and pressure imposed by the Communist government established in 1949. H. C. Barthel (KMB Church) arrived in China in 1901 and founded in 1904 an independent organization, the China Mennonite Missionary Society, which carried on an extensive work in Shantung. H. J. Brown started work independently in Hopei province in 1909 which was taken over by the G.C. Mennonite Mission Board officially in 1914. The Mennonite Brethren Mission Board in 1919 took over the work in Fukien province which had been established by F. J. Wiens in 1911. The K.M.B. Conference established a work in Mongolia in 1924. The Mennonite (MC) Mission Board entered China after World War II in 1948. The total membership of all the Mennonite churches in China in 1950 was probably less than 10,000.

4. *Japan.* Mennonites did not enter Japan until after World War II. Then in rapid succession the Mennonite Church (MC), 1949, the G.C. Mennonite Church, 1950, and the M.B. Church in 1950 entered. The first Japanese Mennonites (12) were baptized in the M.C. mission in Hokkaido in 1951.

5. *Asiatic Russia.* Meanwhile Mennonites from the older colonies in European Russia began to migrate to Asiatic Russia (*q.v.*). The first group settled in Turkestan (*q.v.*) 150 miles northeast of Tashkent in 1880-81, establishing a colony which lasted at least until 1930. The total number never exceeded 1,500 souls. The migration into what is known as Siberia (*q.v.*) began in 1899 and resulted in the establishment of large and prosperous colonies in the region of Omsk and Slavgorod-Barnaul before World War I. After World War I in 1926 a small colony was established in the Far East on the Amur River border of Manchuria near Blagoveshchensk. Increasing pressure led to the liquidation of most of this colony by flight into Manchuria (Harbin) in 1930, from which ultimately (1931-33) all emigrated either to California (Reedley) or to Paraguay, with a few reaching Brazil. A smaller number fled from western Russia across the Siberian border into Sinkiang province, finally reaching Shanghai and emigrating to California

in 1949. One family of the Sinkiang group crossed the Himalayas into India, joining the Mennonite Brethren mission there. The western Siberian Mennonite colonies still exist in modified form, having apparently suffered the least of any of the Mennonite settlements in Russia.

6. *Mennonite Relief Work in Asia.* The Mennonite Central Committee entered the Far East with its relief work first in India (1944-50), then China (1945-50) with the Hong Kong relief unit operating until 1952, then the Philippines (1946-50), Japan (1948-), Java (1949-), and Formosa (1950-). Far Eastern Headquarters were established at Hong Kong in 1950. The peak number of workers in Asia was in 1949 with an average of 65.

7. *Mennonite Membership in Asia.* The maximum total baptized Mennonite membership in Asia, including both mission churches and Russian Mennonite settlements was probably reached about 1925 with an estimated 60,000 distributed as fellows: Java and Sumatra 10,000, India 20,000, China 10,000, Turkestan and Siberia 20,000. At present the number is probably less than 45,000 because of heavy losses in China and Asiatic Russia. The maximum number of Mennonite missionaries in Asia was reached about 1935 with nearly 150 persons, all but six North Americans.   H.S.B.

Asiatic Russia, including Siberia (*q.v.*). Approximately one third of Asia belongs to Soviet Russia. As early as 1860 the Mennonites of European Russia sent a delegation composed of Bernhard Warkentin and Martin Riediger to investigate land along the Amur River for possible settlement. However, at that time the surplus Mennonite population found an outlet in the Crimea and soon (1873 ff.) in migration to America.

Some of the Mennonites opposed to any form of compulsory state service and influenced by a chiliastic movement of the day sought refuge in Asia, 1880 ff., one group led by Claasz Epp (*q.v.*) of the Köppental-Ohrloff settlement (*Am Trakt*) in the province of Samara and the other by Elder Abraham Peters (*q.v.*) of the Molotschna settlement. Having obtained permission from the government in Moscow to establish a settlement in the Asiatic territory where there was not yet compulsory conscription, and having had the same confirmed by the governor of the province of Turkestan, von Kaufmann, they proceeded in several groups to Central Asia, starting in 1880. The first group, leaving the Trakt settlement July 3, 1880, arrived in Tashkent on Oct. 18, after a very difficult and adventurous trip through the desert. This group was followed by a second one from Samara and a third under the leadership of Elder A. Peters from the Molotschna and finally a group led by Elder Claas Epp arriving in the fall of 1881. Although the expectations of the return of the Lord and of finding a place of complete exemption from military service were not fulfilled, the group of Claas Epp established the settlement Ak-Mechet (*q.v.*) in the vicinity of the city of Khiva in 1884 and the group of Elder Peters settled near the city of Aulie-Ata (*q.v.*), some 150 miles northeast of the city of

13

Tashkent. A considerable number of these settlers later came to America. After the religious and economic difficulties of the pioneer days were overcome, these two settlements obtained a measure of prosperity. All settlers of the Ak-Mechet settlement were exiled under the Soviet regime.

Individual Mennonites settled in Siberia as early as 1897. In 1899 a settlement near the city of Omsk (*q.v.*), which was at that time the capital of Akmolinsk (*q.v.*), originated. Among the early settlers were Johann Matthies, Franz Balzer, Julius Dick, and Peter Dick from the Ukraine and Heinrich and Gerhard Ewert from Samara. During the same year the brothers Peter, Nikolai, and Johann Friesen with some 100 families purchased land some 150 miles west of Omsk, and established the settlement Friesenov. But large-scale settlements did not start before 1907. At this time well-organized settlements were started on both sides of the Siberian railroad by Mennonite settlers coming from Chortitza and Molotschna and their daughter colonies. By 1914 more than 100 villages had been established by some 200 families from Chortitza and some 1,000 from the Molotschna.

In 1926 there were four major settlements in West Siberia. The largest of them was the Slavgorod-Barnaul (*q.v.*) settlement, located in what was at that time the province of Tomsk (*q.v.*), some 10 miles from the city of Slavgorod. Today Tomsk belongs to the Novo-Sibirsk District. In 1925 this settlement had a population of 13,173 in 58 villages. Before the Revolution new settlements consisting of from two to five villages originated in connection with the Slavgorod-Barnaul settlement. They were the following: Agatch, Svistunovo, Tchaystahi, Glyaden, Pashvya (see **Barnaul**). Another settlement composed of 13 villages was located in three groups between Slavgorod and Pavlodar and known under the name Pavlodar (*q.v.*) settlement (Musdekul, Taldekuduk, and Taskuduk). The Pavlodar settlement near Omsk, today a part of Kazakhstan, consisted of two villages located some 40 miles north of the city of Omsk. The district of Omsk is now a part of the RSFSR. West of the city of Omsk was located the settlement Perfileevka-Friesenov (see *Friesenov*), of approximately 11 villages. Two more villages near Omsk formed the settlement Tchunayevka (*q.v.*). In addition numerous estates could be found along the railroad. The fourth settlement located farther east was the one named Minussinsk some 40 miles from the city by that name. It was composed of only two villages. The fifth settlement was located northwest near the city of Tobelsk. Preceding the nationalization of the land the Mennonites owned 1,500,000 acres of land in these territories.

The Amur territory investigated by Mennonite delegates in 1860 again became the object of investigation in 1926, when the Soviet government was offering land for settlement purposes. While many Mennonites migrated to America 1922-26, some, especially those from West Siberia, became interested in the Far East. They were, however, soon joined by Mennonites from the various settlements of the Ukraine. Thus the last voluntary Mennonite settlement originated near Blagoveshchensk on the Amur River (see **Amur**). A large number of these settlers later crossed the Amur River to Harbin in China whence they proceeded to America.

Since the days of the czars Asiatic Russia has been the "charnel house," as Dostoyevski put it, of those elements not desired in European Russia. Revolutionaries, anarchists, and other political offenders were sent to Siberia for 10-20 years or a life term. It was a measure of punishment which was continued under the Soviet government. Soon it was practiced on a gigantic scale thus far unknown in history. Millions of people were exiled to the North and Far East, not merely for punishment, but mostly for exploitation as slave labor. The threat of an attack on Asiatic and northern Russia was one of the reasons for this measure. At the same time the mass exile served as a means to break the resistance of the population and to speed up the industrialization and collectivization of the land. Millions of citizens were deprived of their rights and exiled to these slave labor camps. The Mennonites no doubt were affected by this measure more than the average Russian population. First of all they were people of deep religious convictions; then they belonged to the middle class; and they were of German background and thus suspected of co-operation with the invading enemy. Although the complete history of the exile of the Mennonites of Asiatic Russia is not available it is known that they were sent to all existing slave labor camps, of which a few were Dalylag in the Far East, a concentration camp which uses its man power for fishing, forestry service, and strategic building; Kolyma within the Arctic Circle in the Far East, a gold and silver mining industry, with strategic building and agriculture; Sakhalin Island, off the Pacific coast being exploited for oil and coal. Thousands upon thousands of slave laborers were employed to build by hand the North-Siberian Railroad north of the Baikal Sea to the east coast, near the towns of Kuznetskstroy, Magnitogorsk, and Komsomolsk. How many Mennonites perished, who they were, how they suffered, how their life ended will never be fully known. But one thing is known—many of them kept their testimony even unto death.

Before and after the Revolution a considerable interest in mission work among the native and Russian population along the Ob River (see **Ob Mission**) originated among the Mennonites of Russia, especially in Siberia. Because of the antireligious attitude of the Soviet government the program could not be fully developed and maintained. (For map, see **Siberia**.)   **C.K.**

On Concentration Camps see D. J. Dallin and B. I. Nicolaevsky, *Forced Labor in Soviet Russia* (New Haven, 1947); on Central Asia see F. Bartsch, *Unser Auszug nach Mittel-Asien* (Steinbach, 1948); A. Loewen and A. Friesen, *Die Flucht über den Amur* (Steinbach, 1946); H. Anger, *Die Deutschen in Sibirien, Reise durch die deutschen Dörfer Westsibiriens* (Berlin and Königsberg, 1930); J. J. Hildebrand, *Sibirien* (Winnipeg, 1952); *ML* I, 88 f.

Asov Forestry Service Camp (*Asover Forstei*) in the province of Ekaterinoslav, 13 miles northwest of the seaport Mariupol on the Sea of Asov, the oldest of the 8 forestry services in operation in Russia prior to World War I. It was founded in 1877, when universal military service was introduced in Russia, for Mennonite young men, who were to give forestry service to the state in lieu of military service. The forest preserves covered 4,400 acres, of which 2,700 acres were planted with forest trees by 1909. In the first year 58 men served in the forest; in 1913 there were 143. The Asov Forest contained several nurseries, which annually offered large numbers of fruit and forest trees for sale. In order to improve tree culture, the materials needed for setting out orchards were given without charge to those who were unable to pay. (*ML* I, 89.)   B.F.

Asperen, a town in the Dutch province of South Holland where there was formerly a Mennonite congregation. It is not known whether the congregation existed during the life of the well-known martyr Dirk Willemsz (*q.v.*) of Asperen, who was executed in 1569. The congregation, which always remained very small, belonged to the Flemish in the 17th century; for it was represented at the conference of the Flemish in 1649 at Haarlem. In 1664 it joined the Zonists. In any case it was no longer in existence in 1731.   vDZ.

Aspisheim, a town in Rhenish Hesse, where there were Mennonites as early as 1664. According to the oldest register of Mennonites in the Palatinate (State archives in Karlsruhe), 7 Mennonite families with 34 members, probably Swiss emigrants, had settled there. Their names were Fried, Lenz, Bliem, Bohrn, and Steffens. By 1680 there were only 3 families with 11 children. After 1744 the town is no longer mentioned in the registers. It is not known whether they were a congregation in themselves, or worshiped with the church at Ibersheim. (*ML* I, 89.)   Neff.

Asselijn, Thomas, b. about 1620 at Dieppe (France), d. 1701 at Amsterdam, a Dutch writer of comedies, the best known of which is *Jan Klaasz, of Gewaande Dienstmagd* (1684, 1683, 1709, 1732). This play and *Kraam-bedt of kandeelmaal van Zaartje Jans* (1684, 1716, 1727, 1739), and *Echtscheiding van Jan Klaasz en Saartje Jans* have some significance in the study of Mennonite history. "In the three parts of the Jan Klaasen trilogy we are placed among the Collegiants; to this group belonged many Mennonites, whom Asselijn—incorrectly, however—lumps together with the Quakers" (G. Kalff). The stricter groups of Mennonites are here exposed to view and their bad habits (prudishness, pretense) shown up.   vDZ.

Concerning these bad habits, see the essay by C. N. Wijbrands, *Het Menniste Zusje* (Amsterdam, 1913). Concerning Asselijn and his comedies see G. Kalff, *Gesch. der Nederl. Letterkunde* V (Groningen, 1910) 192-206.

Assen, capital of the Dutch province of Drente (pop. 1947, 22,602, with 115 Mennonites), where on March 15, 1896, a number of Mennonite residents formed a Mennonite group. B. P. Plantinga of Meppel conducted the first service on Sept. 20,

1896, and came regularly to preach and to give catechetical instruction. The group became a congregation on May 28, 1899, but remained united with Meppel (*q.v.*) until 1916. From 1917 to 1948 it was united with Stadskanaal (*q.v.*), and since 1950 again with Meppel. For many years the Assen congregation held its meetings in a rented hall (of the *Nutsgebouw*). In 1908 it acquired a church of its own, dedicated Oct. 10. The membership of the church was 45 in 1900, 51 in 1926, and 95 in 1952.

After B. P. Plantinga removed from Meppel in 1897, Assen was served by the preachers of Meppel: A. Binnertsz Szn, 1897-1902; W. J. Kühler, 1902-5; T. H. van Veen, 1905-16, the latter in Meppel until 1940. In 1917 Assen acquired a minister of its own in S. Spaans, 1917-39, later in combination with Stadskanaal. After him came H. J. de Wilde, 1941-46; Miss M. Knot, 1946-47; since Sept. 1950 the congregation has been served by the minister of Meppel. The congregation has a woman's association and a Sunday school for the children. (*DB* 1896, 204; 1897, 253; 1899, 209; *DJ* 1910, 88-99; *ML* I, 89.)   vDZ.

Assenheim, a village in the Palatinate, belonged to the Grafschaft of Leiningen until the French Revolution. There was once a Mennonite church here, probably established before 1700. On Oct. 28, 1755, a Johann Peter Neff (b. 1717 in Erpolzheim, came to Assenheim in 1737, d. 1790), and on Nov. 23, 1777, his son, Peter Neff, were ordained preachers. The latter, ordained elder in 1786, signed the Ibersheim Resolutions (*q.v*) of 1803, as the representative of the Assenheim congregation. Services were held only in a private room. Not later than 1820, perhaps in 1813, the Mennonites living in Assenheim united with the church at Friedelsheim, since which there has not been a separate congregation. In 1914 there were 23 Mennonites in Assenheim, in 1951, 27, of whom seven were refugees from the Danzig area. (Dutch *Naamlijsten,* 1769-1810; *ML* I, 89.)   J.F.

Associated Sewing Circles of the Lancaster Mennonite Conference (MC). Mary Parmer of the Vine Street Mission, Lancaster, Pa., in 1897 or earlier had a sewing school in connection with city mission endeavor. On Sept. 2, 1897, the Paradise (congregation) Sewing Circle was organized, followed by others. On Sept. 11, 1911, the Associated Sewing Circles were organized with Mary Mellinger as general chairman. Semiannual meetings are held, when in addition to inspirational talks, the needs of the missions, local and foreign, and relief needs, are allocated to the numerous senior and junior circles over the conference. They also direct the conference-wide collections in the fall for the conference clothing center at Ephrata, Pa. The district mission board in 1948 built the Mary Mellinger Cutting Room at Paradise for the Ephrata clothing center. Here in 1952 they cut 35,735 yards of goods and 28,096 garments.   I.D.L.

Association des Eglises Evangeliques-Mennonites de France is the official name adopted in 1925 by the Conference of Mennonites of France. Actually the

French-speaking churches which had earlier (1907-14) had a separate *Association,* in 1927 again formed a separate conference (see **Conference of French-Speaking Mennonites**) and added the phrase *Groupe de Langue Francaise* to the official name, whereas the German-speaking churches commonly refer to their conference as *Konferenz der Mennoniten in Elsass-Lothringen* (see **Conference of the Mennonites in Alsace-Lorraine**), although their official and legal name is the one given at the head of this article. The *Association* is then the legally registered organization for the totality of the Mennonite congregations in France, actually functioning as two structurally distinct conferences. The legal president and secretary of the *Association* are the actual president and secretary of the Alsatian conference, who have been for many years Elder Joseph Widmer of Mulhouse-Modenheim and Elder Hans Nussbaumer of Altkirch-Schweighof, and the legal address (*siege social*) is 22 Rue d'Ingersheim, Colmar (Haut-Rhin).   H.S.B.

Association Fraternelle Mennonite, a nonprofit organization established June 22, 1950, by the Mennonites of France to serve as an instrument in the growing charitable and church work of the French congregations, representing both French- and German-speaking groups. The president is André Graber, elder of the Belfort congregation, secretary-treasurer Pierre Widmer, elder at Montbeliard and editor of *Christ Seul.* The interests of the French Mennonites of Swiss citizenship (many of whom live in France and belong to the Alsatian churches) and of the Mennonite Central Committee (which assisted by supplying one third of the original capital), who as foreigners may not be officers of the association, are represented by the consultative *Conseil de Frères* (Council of Brothers), whose president is Hans Nussbaumer, elder at Altkirch.

The day after its formation the Association acquired its major property, an estate in Valdoie, suburb of Belfort, now known as the *Foyer Mennonite.* This property serves as a children's home, old people's home, and as a center for conferences and youth activities.

In 1951 the Association acquired a second property, the Mont-des-Oiseaux near Wissembourg in northern Alsace. There also the Association operates a children's home through a subsidiary organization, with the continued collaboration of the Mennonite Central Committee. Philip Hege, elder of the Geisberg congregation, is president of the committee responsible for this home.   J.H.Y.

Association of Citizens of Dutch Extraction: see Verband der Bürger holländischer Herkunft.

Assuerus van Gheemont, a silversmith, probably a Mennonite preacher, imprisoned at Antwerp together with Jeronimus Segers and Hendrick Beverts. While the execution of Jeronimus and Hendrick took place on Sept. 1 or 2, 1551, that of Assuerus was delayed until Jan. 22, 1552. On the rack Assuerus revealed the names of many other Mennonites, and apparently for this betrayal his name is not included in the martyr books. By the fact that he died at the stake, we may assume that he remained true to his faith.   vᴅZ.

DB 1864, 100; Génard, *Antw. Arch.-Blad* VIII, 402-8, 415; XIV, 18 f., No. 103; *ML* II, 112; *BRN* II, 152, Note 3, 184.

Assum, a small village in the Dutch province of North Holland, where, according to Blaupot ten Cate, there must have once been a Mennonite congregation, of which, however, all traces have disappeared. (Blaupot t.C., *Holland* II, 44.)   vᴅZ.

Asuncion, with an approximate population of 128,000, is the capital city of Paraguay. It still occupies the original site of settlement of the first Spanish conquerors, who arrived here on Aug. 15, 1537, on their way to discover a route from the La Plata river system to Peru. Asuncion became the center of economic, social, and political life of this whole region and has grown to be the only large city in Paraguay. It is the only capital city in South America which still carries a distinctly colonial face. It has neither a public water system nor a sewer system. Only in recent times, in spite of wars and revolutions, has a building boom begun to modernize the business district. Busses and streetcars carry the main traffic. Its harbor on the Paraguay River is the principal gate into Paraguay for exports, imports, tourists, and immigrants.

During the years 1929-49 approximately 13,000 Mennonite settlers, who now comprise more than one per cent of Paraguay's population, have passed through this city. During the first years only a few Mennonites lived in Asuncion permanently. Some of these established their own businesses while others found employment. With the coming of the refugees in 1947-48 the number of Mennonites staying in Asuncion increased to approximately 250. Among them were members of the Mennonite Brethren and General Conference groups. When difficult times in the rural colonies became too severe, the number of girls and young men who came here to work in order to supplement their parents' meager income increased. At the time of occasional visits by a minister from the colonies these Mennonites would gather for worship in the German Lutheran Church. After the Mennonite Central Committee had organized a Mennonite Home in the city regular visits by colony ministers were supported by the Home Mission Board of the General Conference Mennonite Church. In 1949 a full-time minister took over the work, which led to the organization of a union church in April 1950. Worship services in the rented "Local Evangelico," Sunday school for children, choir, Bible study, prayer meetings, and sewing circles are some of the activities of the group.

In 1950 two teachers from Fernheim, Chaco, Peter Wiens and Heinrich Ratzlaff, came to Asuncion to work for their state teacher's certificate. Five young boys also began their course in the normal school.

The Mennonite Home, owned and operated by the Mennonite Central Committee, has become the center of Mennonite life in Asuncion. The Mennonites of Asuncion gather here on Sunday evenings for a common meal, fellowship, and program.

Here they receive sympathetic hearing and pick up their mail. Mennonites from the colonies lodge in the Home when on business or visiting in the city. Others stay here and find medical help in local hospitals. The Mennonite Home is also the center of the Paraguay MCC unit and houses the central offices of the MCC South American Area, which have been located here since 1947.   Er.H.

Willard and Verna Smith, *Paraguayan Interlude* (Scottdale, 1950); *Menn. Life* (Jan. 1950).

Athens United Missionary Church is located 18 miles from Battle Creek, Mich. The work was begun on Jan. 16, 1949, with Leonard Pittman in charge.   **L.P.**

Athol, Berks Co., Pa., an extinct Mennonite Brethren in Christ congregation. In 1911 its membership of 11 was served by C. H. Brunner. (*ML* I, 89.)

Attestatie, certificate of membership of the Dutch Mennonites, whereby any member moving from one congregation can be a member of another. Such a statement was used very early. The preachers of the Waterlander congregations, assembled at Amsterdam on March 4, 1581, thought a *"goede attestatie of genoegzame kondschap"* (good certificate or adequate information) necessary for admission as a member (*DB* 1877, 84). The certificate, which as used at present is simply a statement that the person concerned is a member and that he became a member by baptism or by transfer from another congregation, formerly also provided a declaration of good conduct; the *attestatien* of the Groninger Old Flemish contained the special clause that the brother or sister in question was also orthodox in his doctrine. The matter of *attestatien* was definitively regulated by a conference held in Amsterdam in 1863 (*DB* 1865, 39, note 1). The corresponding document is called in English "church letter" (*q.v.*) and in German *Gemeindezeugnis.*
       vDZ.

Au, a village in Vorarlberg, Austria, on the Ach, the center of the Anabaptists in the Bregenz Forest (Mountains) from 1580 to 1585. The severely repressive measures of the government caused many Anabaptists of Au to migrate to Moravia. The migration was headed by the apothecary Melchior Platzer, the most important figure in the Anabaptist movement in Vorarlberg. He became a schoolmaster of the Hutterian Brethren, and died as a martyr in 1583 at Feldkirchen in Vorarlberg. Count Hannibal of Hohenembs, the top-ranking official of the four domains of Vorarlberg, a nephew of the pope and brother-in-law of St. Karl Borromäus, had unsuccessfully sought to have Platzer burned at the stake; Platzer was beheaded and then burned (Beck, 283).   HEGE.

J. Bergmann, "Die Wiedertäufer zu Au im inneren Bregenzerwald und ihre Auswanderung nach Mähren 1585," *Sitzungsberichte der Kaiserlichen Akademie der Wissenschaft III* (Vienna, 1848) 248-57; Beck, *Geschichts-Bücher; ML* I, 89.

Auburn, an extinct Mennonite congregation (MC) at Auburn, Fauquier Co., Va., established in 1902, and having a membership of 15 in 1905. It was last reported in the 1923 *Mennonite Year-Book.*
       M.G.

Aucke Broersz, an Anabaptist martyr, burned at the stake for his faith on April 22, 1553, at Leeuwarden in Friesland, with Aucke Tzallincxz. He had been rebaptized and rejected the Mass. Further particulars are lacking.   vDZ.

Inv. Arch. Amst. I, No. 746; Reitsma, *Honderd jaren Kerkherv. in Friesland* (Leeuwarden, 1876) 63.

Aucke Haythiedochter, from Byrdart (Birdaard in Friesland). was drowned on April 15, 1535, at Leeuwarden in the Dutch province of Friesland, together with eight women who were executed on account of implication in the raid on the "Oldeklooster" (*q.v.*) near Bolsward by the Anabaptists, in which this sister was, however, not involved. (*Inv. Arch. Amst.* I, No. 746; K. Vos, *Menno Simons,* Leiden, 1914, 229.)   vDZ.

Aucke Tzallincxz, an Anabaptist martyr, was burned at the stake on April 22, 1553, at Leeuwarden, in the Dutch province of Friesland, with Aucke Broersz, because he "persisted in his faith." vDZ.

Inv. Arch. Amst. I, No. 746; Reitsma, *Honderd jaren Kerkherv. in Friesland* (Leeuwarden, 1876) 63.

Audrain County, Mo., was the location of an Amish Mennonite settlement which lasted 19 years, 1898-1917. The founding leaders were Jacob D. Guengerich (1843-1926), John C. Gingerich (1846-1929), and John B. Miller (1844-1929), all of Johnson Co., Iowa. Over 20 families moved there, mostly from Iowa. Resident ministers were John Zimmerman, Bishop Noah Yoder, and E. C. Beachy. Causes contributing to the dissolution of the settlement included crop failures, deaths, and church problems. A cemetery of 7 graves marks the center of this former settlement, which was near Centralia.
       L.G.G.

Auf dein Wort was a monthly "for personal Christianity," founded in 1901 by Samuel Keller and continued by von Rechenberg and Jacob Kroeker, published by Walter Loepthien, Meiringen, Germany. When Jacob Kroeker (*q.v.*) assumed the responsibility as co-editor in 1930 he became a regular contributor of articles on Biblical subjects. Some chapters from his books appeared here.
       C.K.

Auf zum Werk! was a monthly organ of the *Mennonitisch-Russische Bibelgesellschaft* (*q.v.*) published from August 1921 to January 1923, and edited by Gustav Enss, Moundridge, Kan., a minister in the General Conference Mennonite Church. It was above all designed to be an informational and promotional paper for the Mennonites of America in the interest of evangelism in Russia and other Slavic countries. The *Mennonitisch-Russische Bibelgesellschaft* was closely associated with the missionary organization *Licht dem Osten* (*q.v.*), Wernigerode a.H., Germany.   C.K.

Aufrichtige Nachrichten *von dem Gegenwärtigen Zustande der Mennoniten oder Taufgesinnten wie auch der Collegianten oder Reinsburger, Beyderseits Ansehnlicher Kirchlicher Gesellschaften in den vereinigten Niederlanden. Samt einer Erzehlung Von den Streitigkeiten, In welche dermahlen einige der zuerst benennten verwickelt sind; Nebst* *verschiedenen andern dienlichen Zusätzen, entworfen von M. Simeon Friderich Rues.* (Jena, 1743.)

Rues, a German Lutheran divine, visited the Netherlands where he spent most of his time interviewing various representatives of the many groups of Mennonites, visiting their services and homes, studying their literature, and making a comparative study of all groups, after which he presented his findings in this book. The Dutch Mennonites liked this account so much that they immediately had it translated into Dutch and published under the title: *Tegenwoordige Staet der Doopsgezinden of Mennoniten, in de Vereenigde Nederlanden;* ... *t' Amsterdam,* by F. Houttuyn, 1745. The translator, whose name is not given, but who was Martin Schagen, a Mennonite preacher and scholar of Utrecht, states that he found it necessary to change some statements and add extensive notes, together with some rearrangement, making a total of 330 pages.

Rues divides his German book of 320 pages into five parts: Fine Mennonites or Old Flemish; Coarse Mennonites or Frisians, Flemish, Waterlanders and United; Controversies between Mennonites and Reformed; Collegiants or the Rijnsburgers; and an appendix treating of the government of Friesland and the Reformed and other clergy. Most significant are the first two chapters in which he gives detailed accounts about the Mennonite doctrines, discipline, organization, practices in worship services, efforts to unite, etc. The Old Flemish, Frisians, Waterlanders, United congregations, Lamists, Zonists, and the many subdivisions of that day are treated. *Aufrichtige Nachrichten* is one of the most important and objective sources on the Dutch Mennonites of the 18th century and a gold mine of information for the Mennonite historian, particularly valuable for American Mennonites, since the Dutch Mennonites at that time confronted problems similar to those which American Mennonites have confronted from the 19th century to the present.   C.K.

Aufwärts was a periodical published and edited by K. G. Neufeld, Davlekanovo, Ufa, Russia. It first appeared in 1909 with the subtitle *Blätter für Sänger und Dirigenten und für Liebhaber des Christlichen Gesanges.* A department was especially devoted to young people, but in general the paper was designed to raise the cultural level of the Mennonites of Russia and to aid song leaders and those interested in music. In the second volume (*Zweite Folge*) the approach was broadened and the paper was especially addressed to young people. It contained stories, articles from world history (by P. B. Harder), natural science (signed *ph.*), poems, and a column entitled *Lose Blätter* by Peter Harder (*q.v.*), a sort of fiction dealing with the Russian scene.

After 24 issues had been published, the editor explained the discontinuance of the paper by saying that although there was great need for a youth paper he was not in a position financially to publish it. He expressed the hope that he would be able to start a young people's illustrated monthly, which evidently did not materialize as he hoped.

Kornelius G. Neufeld was born in the Molotschna settlement, attended the theological seminary and University of Basel, Switzerland, in 1895-97, and studied in London in 1905. He was a secondary school teacher and minister in Russia, and came to California in 1914.   C.K.

Augsburg (Bavaria), at the beginning of the second quarter of the 16th century the center of the Anabaptist movement in South Germany. In a single year (1526) the largest Anabaptist congregation in South Germany was formed here and from here the doctrine spread in all directions when persecution set in and scattered the members.

Among the earliest leading figures living here were Ludwig Haetzer (*q.v.*), Hans Denk (*q.v.*), and Hans Hut (*q.v.*). Ludwig Haetzer had been here in the summer of 1524, but had returned to Zürich, where he joined the opponents of infant baptism. In January 1525 he had to leave the city, and returned to Augsburg, obtained a proofreading position with the printer Silvan Othmar (who later printed several editions of the translation of the prophets by Haetzer and Denk), and gathered about him a number of serious-minded men and women who were not satisfied with the conduct of the Protestant preachers. Though he was not baptized, he appears to have prepared the soil for Anabaptist doctrine. He became inconvenient to the Lutheran preachers, and on their instigation was banished from the city near the end of September 1525 ("with consideration of his position as the head of the sectarians, as an unclean, seditious person, hostile to the Gospel").

At this time Hans Denk (*q.v.*) came to Augsburg. In the winter of 1524-25 at the instigation of the Lutheran preacher Osiander he had been banished from Nürnberg, where he had been rector of the church at St. Sebaldus, had stayed in St. Gall from Easter to autumn of 1525, and now tried to earn his living as a private tutor in Augsburg. It is very likely that he had received his education here and had friends in the city. He probably made advances to Haetzer's followers and unified them more closely.

In May and June of 1526, Balthasar Hubmaier (*q.v.*), the reformer of Waldshut, who had been baptized as an Anabaptist by Wilhelm Reublin at Easter 1526, probably stayed here. Hubmaier persuaded Hans Denk to be baptized and probably performed the rite himself. This was the first adult baptism in Augsburg as far as is known. Thereby the foundation was laid for the Anabaptist congregation in Augsburg and for the spread of Anabaptist doctrine on German territory from the Alps to the Danube. Denk now became a propagandist for the group and baptized many. In May 1526 Hans Denk then won Hans Hut (*q.v.*), whom he had met in Nürnberg. Hut was one of the first opponents of infant baptism in the Reformation period. During the three days of Hut's visit to Augsburg, Denk baptized him in his home, a little house near the Heilig-Kreuz gate. Hut now traveled with unequaled success through South Germany and Austria as an evangelist, returning to

Augsburg in February 1527. Meanwhile violent opposition had compelled Denk to give up the leadership of the Augsburg congregation, as he had become inconvenient to the Lutheran preacher Urban Rhegius. Denk had to answer to the assembled preachers of the town, and was challenged to a public disputation, but he did not accept the invitation and left the city. At the end of October 1526 he arrived in Strasbourg.

At this time a group of prominent and earnest men had joined the Anabaptists in Augsburg, who became leaders in the congregation. Among them were Eitelhans Langenmantel (*q.v.*), of an old patrician family, Jacob Dachser (*q.v.*), a priest who had been a teacher in München, and Sigmund Salminger (*q.v.*), a former Franciscan monk. All were baptized by Hut in February 1527. Hut remained in Augsburg only nine or ten days at that time; but in this short time he made new arrangements to strengthen the brotherhood. While a wild carnival was going on in the streets and the inns, he gathered the Anabaptists for the election of a directorate. Through the lot Sigmund Salminger was chosen as leader, and Jakob Dachser as his assistant. Relief of the poor was also organized. Lacemaker Huber was appointed guardian of the poor, and when he resigned, Hans Kissling (*q.v.*), a mason from the neighboring Friedberg, and Gall Fischer (*q.v.*) took over the care of the poor in the congregation and supervision of the poor-funds. The church grew rapidly. Large numbers from all walks of life joined them, constantly augmented by immigrants from other places. An active spiritual life developed. The number of houses in which services could be held and baptisms performed increased. In order to lose the least possible amount of working time the members met for mutual strengthening at night or early in the morning.

In the summer of 1527 the Anabaptist leaders from nearly every country gathered here. On Aug. 20 they held a synod in Augsburg, at which Hans Denk presided. No record has been preserved, and information of any kind is scarce. The differing views of the leaders, who rarely had an opportunity of discussing matters with each other, seem to have been harmonized; the individual subordinated himself to the common goal. Thus Hans Hut declared himself ready, "in order that unity in genuine love might be found, not to speak to anyone except those who thoroughly agreed, about the mysteries of the Judgment Day, of the end of the world, of the resurrection, of the Kingdom of God, of eternal judgment." "Those who know," who already possess the "understanding of mysteries," were to have patience with the "ignorant"; on the other hand, the others were not to be vexed about matters for which they are too immature. The ideas of Denk probably predominated; it was probably due to his personality that the various views were so harmoniously adjusted. The keynote of the resolutions of the synod is expressed in his booklet, *Von der wahren Liebe,* which appeared in Augsburg at that very time. The result of the

synod was the sending out of evangelists to South Germany, Switzerland, and the provinces of Austria. They had been given no other commission, as Hans Hut said in his cross-examination, than to comfort the brethren and to preach. Peter Scheppach (*q.v.*) and Ulrich Trechsel (*q.v.*) were to go to Worms, Leonhard Spoerle (*q.v.*) and Leonhard von Prukh (*q.v.*) to Bavaria, Hänslin Mittermeier (*q.v.*) of Ingolstadt and Leonhard Dorfbrunner (*q.v.*) to Austria (the latter to Linz), Jörg von Passau (*q.v.*) to Franconia, Eucharius Binder (*q.v.*) and Joachim März (*q.v.*) to the Salzburg region, Hans Denk, Gregory Maler (*q.v.*), and Hans Beckenknecht (*q.v.*) to the cantons of Basel and Zürich. Ludwig Haetzer was sent to Meissen by way of Donauwörth. Hans Hut was to stay in Augsburg for the time being. These were hopeful assignments, but they were not to be carried out. It was the last general meeting of the leaders, for in a few years almost all had suffered a martyr's death; the conference is therefore known as the Martyrs' Synod.

In Augsburg the malice and fear of the Lutheran preachers did not permit the new congregation to get settled. The most violent was Urban Rhegius (*q.v.*), whose sermons attracted scarcely any listeners; soon after the Martyrs' Synod a pamphlet of his appeared, entitled *Wider den newen Taufforden, nothwendige Warnung an alle Christgläubigen* (dated Sept. 6, 1527). Meanwhile the council of Augsburg had proceeded with great severity against the Anabaptists. In August 1527 it had a number of them seized and tortured; the jurist Dr. Konrad Peutinger was charged with the conduct of this investigation, for which he received a fee of 100 guilders. One of the first Anabaptists whom he cross-examined under torture was the guardian of the poor, Hans Kiessling; through him the council learned the names of other Anabaptists, who were arrested as soon as their lodgings were discovered. Among these was the assistant director of the group, Jakob Dachser, who was arrested on Aug. 25. On Sept. 15, a Sunday, when a considerable number were meeting in the house of "the bell-ringer at the wall" the police appeared and arrested all the attendants, native and foreign, among them Hans Hut and Jakob Gross (*q.v.*). In the following days further arrests took place; Eitelhans Langenmantel, who was sick at the time, was dragged from his house to the town hall on a cart. The baptized were ordered to vow under oath that they would not sell their property or leave the city without the knowledge and permission of the city council (*"ohne Wissen und Willen des Rats Leib und Gut nicht zu verkehren"*), that they would stay away from Anabaptist sermons, and that they would obey future summons. The prisoners who had not yet been baptized, but had attended religious services of the Anabaptists, had to pledge themselves "not to meet together, to avoid baptism, and to present themselves to the council upon request." Other "suspicious persons" were arrested on Sept. 18 and 19, including the leader Sigmund Salminger. Several of the arrested found it incomprehensible that they should be forbidden to converse with each other about God's Word. That was not entirely forbidden by the council; "two or three" were to be permitted to read God's Word and converse about it, "but they were not to undertake any meetings or crowds." Those who refused the required oath were to be banished from the city with the obligation never to return.

The leaders remained in arrest; they were Hut, Gross, Dachser, and Salminger. The preachers of the city, Rhegius, Frosch, Agricola, and Keller, were to convert them. On Sept. 21 and 25, 1527, they disputed for hours with the prisoners, without success; for their efforts the city preachers each received four guilders per sermon, and Rhegius received an extra guilder for the sermon which he had delivered against the Anabaptists in the church of St. Peter. On Oct. 1 the council had all the Anabaptists called in who had been released after their trial, and demanded of them the confession of their error and a recantation. The four city preachers lectured them on infant baptism and the oath. Burgomaster Rehlinger explained to them the disadvantages of holding to their position and had records read to them of proceedings against Anabaptists in other places. Four persons recanted, but nine remained steadfast, including the future leader Hans Leupold (q.v.) who was at once banished from the city. The rest requested three days to consider, which was granted. After this time 44 persons complied with the demands of the council and were dismissed with the obligation to appear later and receive sentence. The steadfast were banished, among them the future leader Burkhard Braun (q.v.) from Ofen, with wife and child.

A mandate followed on Oct. 11, 1527, commanding that baptism be administered to children, that rebaptism be abandoned, that the people be satisfied with ordinary church sermons, and flee "corner preachers," neither feeding nor lodging them. Anyone who transgressed one of these commands or acted suspiciously was to be "severely punished in body or life or possessions." On Oct. 7 sentence was passed against five Anabaptists held in chains, Eitelhans Langenmantel, Endres Widholz, Gall Fischer, Hans Kiessling, and Peter Scheppach, who confessed rebaptism to be an error; they were banished from the city. Two other Anabaptists, the guild-master Laux Fischer and the scissors-grinder Eckart, were fined. Left in prison were only the leading figures, Hut, Salminger, Gross, and Dachser. Dr. Peutinger had all degrees of torture applied to Hut; while he lay unconscious after an application of torture his foot upset his candle, igniting the straw in his cell with consequent severe burns. Hut died eight days later. Nevertheless the trial was conducted as if he had been alive. The council condemned him to death at the stake; the corpse was burned on Dec. 7, 1527, and the ashes thrown into the Wertach.

Voices were now heard in the council asking the death penalty for the other Anabaptist leaders, but the majority opposed such a course. On Jan. 22, 1528, to make them more tractable, it was decided to hold them imprisoned longer, and to move them from the front prison (examining room) to the back prison (the actual prison or dungeon). Those who had recanted were also to receive sentence now. On Feb. 10, 1528, they were informed that financially independent persons were to be fined the equivalent of a year's tax, the others were to pay 30 pfennigs to the Heilig-Geist hospital. The men had to abstain from voting for council members for five years; anyone holding city office had to resign. Those who would not recant were led out of the city, and any who would not "swear out" were "beaten out" with rods.

In spite of these severe measures the movement in Augsburg was not extinguished. The places of the imprisoned leaders were at once filled by others, and martyrdom won new converts. On the day the mandate was published, the weaver Augustin Bader (q.v.) invited over 20 fellow believers into his house to observe communion, and on the day after the burning of Hut's body a large number of persons were received into the congregation by baptism. Moreover, the church grew through the addition of persecuted refugees from Bavaria, Franconia, and the Austrian regions.

The new Anabaptist preachers were very active. The busiest were Leonhard Dorfbrunner, who had been sent to Linz by the Martyrs' Synod, returned to Augsburg Nov. 10, 1527, and alone baptized about 100, and George Nospitzer, called Jörg von Passau, who had been sent to Franconia and had returned early in February 1528. They conducted a series of meetings, which were in part well attended. Thus on April 14, 1528, about 60 persons met in a cellar to observe communion, led by Hans Leupold and George Nospitzer. At this meeting two leaders were chosen, Hans Schleifer (q.v.) and Peter Ringmacher (q.v.), who were sent to Regensburg (q.v.) to comfort the brethren there. In connection with this meeting, which lasted until five o'clock in the morning, a meeting of the leaders took place in the home of the goldsmith Laux Kreler (q.v.) to instruct the newly elected leaders, in order that neither should introduce any error.

But the days of the congregation were numbered. On April 12, 1528, Easter Sunday, the council struck the fatal blow. To celebrate the resurrection the congregation met at dawn on the Bürgergässchen, in the home of Susanna Doucher, the wife of the noted sculptor Adolf Doucher, who had gone on a journey to Vienna. The meeting was again conducted by Hans Leupold and George Nospitzer. The congregation, about 100 persons, had been warned of imminent danger and Leupold urged the weak to leave while there was time. Some left; 88 remained. Just as the hostess was on the point of serving those from the outside, at about seven o'clock, the police came and led away all the participants, "men and women, old and young, servants and maids, citizens and foreigners," chained in pairs, including the wives of Sigmund Salminger and Jakob Gross. The excitement among the citizenry was intense. The foreigners, 22 women and 22 men, were to swear not to enter the city within a six-year period; they left Augsburg on April 13. A man and three women who would not swear were placed on the whipping post like ordinary criminals and on April 14 whipped out of the city; the council took the same steps on April 15, 16, and 20, with 16 men and 17 women, who had been in Augsburg for a longer time. Anyone who had opened his house for services was burned through the cheeks; this punishment was inflicted on four women and one man. One woman had her tongue cut out, because she had been guilty of "blaspheming the sacrament." The leader Hans Leupold, refusing to recant, was executed on April 15.

All the Anabaptists who were not in prison now left Augsburg, and went especially to Strasbourg, Esslingen, Reutlingen, Kaufbeuren, Regensburg, Württemberg, and Moravia. About 100 Anabaptists who had been banished from Augsburg were living in Strasbourg in the spring of 1529. An indescribable wretchedness overtook many families who had hitherto lived in peace and prosperity. The leaders who had fled or been banished fell into the hands of persecutors in other regions and were executed: George Nospitzer in Bamberg, Leonhard Dorfbrunner and Melchior der Reiter in Passau, Augustin Bader in Stuttgart.

The congregation in Augsburg never recovered from this blow. Assistance from outside the city was almost impossible. Every stranger was asked at the gate what business he had in the city, where he would lodge, whether he had been rebaptized or adhered to an untolerated group. Suspected persons had to stay outside or were put under oath. All inns were ordered not to accept Anabaptists. Anyone who notified the authorities of an infraction of this rule received a reward of one guilder, was exempt from punishment even if he was a partner in crime, and the fact that he had been the informer was kept secret. Anabaptist preachers now avoided the city, for religious services within the city walls were no longer possible. The remnant of the congregation met frequently in the woods of St. Radegundis near Wellenburg, and at one of these meetings about 70 persons, men and women, were present, according to the statement of a prisoner, Zirgkendorfer, in May 1528. They also assembled in a deep gravel pit in the field near Göggingen. In the summer of 1528 they met several times in the open, usually in the meadows near the fowling-floors. In mid-August the remaining brethren decided not to assemble again. The last leaders, George Schachner (*q.v.*) and Hans Greuel (*q.v.*), both from Munich, turned their backs on Augsburg after Philipp Weber (Plener) had once more vainly attempted to hold a meeting.

The leaders who were still imprisoned, Gross, Salminger, and Dachser, remained steadfast for a long time, but finally their powers of resistance were paralyzed. After three and one-half years of confinement in the dungeon, several days before Christmas in 1530, Salminger recanted (his wife recanted on Jan. 17, 1531); on May 15, 1531, after three and three-fourths years in the dungeon, Jakob Dachser recanted, and on June 22, 1531, Jakob Gross.

About Pentecost of 1529 Josef Riemer of Homburg (Hesse) was chosen as leader; meetings were usually held in his house. A nonresident leader who had great influence was Hans Kendtner, a glazier from Haldenwang in Allgäu, who founded an Anabaptist congregation in Täferdingen, a village north of Augsburg. Both leaders appeared openly in Augsburg in 1531. On Sunday, March 5, they preached with inspiring enthusiasm before a large crowd who had gathered in the church of St. Ulrich for regular services. The sermons created a deep impression. Finally the bailiff seized the Anabaptists; they could probably have fled, but refused to do so. Most of the prisoners, about 40, recanted; but Riemer and Kendtner did not do so until after a long imprisonment. In the week before Easter of 1533 the council made some further arrests, and banished the prisoners upon their recantation. The last recantations were made on April 18, 1535.

"The principal battles in this struggle," writes Friedrich Roth (*Augsburger Reformationsgeschichte,* II, 398), "had been fought and won by the city preachers in 1527 and 1528, by summoning all their forces with the aid of the council, which had offered them its powerful arm in its own interest."

There is no evidence of the existence of an Anabaptist congregation in Augsburg after 1535, although there must have been individual Anabaptists resident in the city at various times. Among the latter was the outstanding South German Anabaptist leader Pilgram Marpeck, who resided here 1544-56, serving throughout the time as an engineer in the employ of the city. His presence here unmolested is a mystery. Either the city council must have relaxed its proscription of Anabaptists, or Marpeck refrained from preaching and promoting the Anabaptist cause within the city, or his services as an engineer were so valuable that the authorities winked at his activities. Possibly all three explanations are partly true. On July 16, 1545, he was warned by the burgomaster, George Herwart. On May 6, 1560, on the basis of testimony that Marpeck had published a booklet of Anabaptist doctrine, the council decided to interview him and request a copy of the booklet. Twice more he was warned, once on Sept. 26, 1553, and a year later on Sept. 25, 1554, when the council actually decided that since they had learned that Marpeck was propagating his error, he should be told to earn his bread elsewhere. However, he continued on the pay roll of the city until his death two years later.

The modern Augsburg Mennonite congregation does not have connections with the 16th century Augsburg Anabaptists, being composed of families which moved into the area in the late 19th century from other Mennonite communities. HEGE.

L. Keller, *Ein Apostel der Wiedertäufer* (Leipzig, 1882); Chr. Meyer, "Zur Gesch. der Wiedertäufer in Oberschwaben," in *Ztscht des hist. Vereins für Schwaben und Neuburg* I (1874); Fr. Roth, "Zur Gesch. der Wiedertäufer in Oberschwaben," in *Ztscht des Hist. Vereins f. Schwaben und Neuburg* XXVII f. (1900 and 1901); Fr. Roth, *Augsburger Ref.-Gesch.* (München, 1904); J. Horsch, *Mennonites in Europe* (Scottdale, 1942); J. C. Wenger, "The Life and Work of Pilgram Marpeck," in *MQR* XII (1938) 137-202; *ML* I, 92 ff.

Augsburg Confession (*Confessio Augustana*), a confession of faith written by Melanchthon, with Luther's counsel and assistance, presented to Emperor Charles V at the Diet of Augsburg in 1530, and there solemnly read, which attained great importance and a high regard, becoming the permanent official Lutheran confession. It embraces 28 articles, in four of which the Anabaptists are mentioned. These four are presented below in the English translation published in Philip Schaff's *Creeds of Christendom* III (New York, 1877, 1919), 10, 13, 16-18.

Article V.—Of the Ministry of the Church.

For the obtaining of this faith, the ministry of teaching the Gospel and administering the Sacraments was instituted.

For by the Word and Sacraments, as by instruments, the Holy Spirit is given: who worketh faith, where and when it pleaseth God, in those that hear the Gospel, to wit, that God, not for our merit's sake, but for Christ's sake, doth justify those who believe that they for Christ's sake are received into favor.

They condemn the Anabaptists and others, who imagine that the Holy Spirit is given to men without the outward word, through their own preparation and works.

Article IX.—Of Baptism.

Of baptism they teach that it is necessary to salvation, and that by baptism the grace of God is offered, and that children are to be baptized who by baptism, being offered to God, are received into God's favor.

They condemn the Anabaptists who allow not the baptism of children, and affirm that children are saved without baptism.

Article XVI.—Of Civil Affairs.

Concerning civil affairs, they teach that such civil ordinances as are lawful are good works of God; that Christians may lawfully bear civil office, sit in judgments, determine matters by the imperial laws, and other laws in present force, appoint just punishments, engage in just war, act as soldiers, make legal bargains and contracts, hold property, take an oath when the magistrates require it, marry a wife, or be given in marriage. They condemn the Anabaptists who forbid Christians these civil offices. They condemn also those that place the perfection of the Gospel, not in the fear of God and in faith, but in forsaking civil offices, inasmuch as the Gospel teacheth an everlasting righteousness of the heart.

Article XVII.—Of Christ's Return to Judgment.

Also they teach that, in the consummation of the world (at the last day), Christ shall appear to judge, and shall raise up all the dead, and shall give unto the godly and elect eternal life and everlasting joys; but ungodly men and the devils shall he condemn unto endless torments.

They condemn the Anabaptists who think that to condemned men and the devils shall be an end of torments. (*ML* I, 91.)   H.S.B.

Augsburg Mennonite Church (Bavaria, Germany). It is interesting to note that the first modern settlement of Mennonites in the region of Augsburg, which began in 1805 with the migration of families from Alsace-Lorraine and the Palatinate, occurred in the very same locality (Wellenburg) where in 1528 Anabaptists had held their meetings. The first families, of both Amish and Mennonite connections, were (at Wellenburg) Gingerich, Miller, Augsburger, König; (at Burkwalden) Nafziger, Stalter, Gut; (Scheppacherhof) Augsburger; (Biburg) Stalter; (Siebenbrunn) Hochstettler; all settled as renters. But these families did not organize a congregation in the 19th century. They held their religious services in the various homes and buried their dead in the gardens. The Napoleonic wars had caused emigration from their homeland, and the tolerance of the reigning houses and the noble landowners made possible the settlement in Bavaria. The inspection records (in the Bavarian state archives in Munich) often bore witness to the fact that it was the colonizing ability of the Mennonite farmers and their moral standards that made them the chosen and preferred settlers. However, the main stream of these settlers went to the region probably because it was easier there to provide for the sons of their large families. The author (R. Ringenberg) is the only descendant of this group of settlers presently living in the Augsburg region.

Besides this circle of settlements immediately around Augsburg, there was also a larger settlement not far away at Neuburg, Donauwörth, and in the area called Donaumoos (*q.v.*) at the start of the 19th century. At Maxweiler in Donaumoos, where Mennonite settlers from Baden and the Palatinate worked hard in cultivating the marshy ground, a congregation was formed with preachers Daniel and Heinrich Müller and Elder Heinrich Zeiset of Willenbach. A church was built in 1832, today used as a school. But the income from the land was inadequate for the needs of the 25 families settled there. In 1852 most of them emigrated to America, although some united with the Eichstock congregation near Dachau, while some married into other Mennonite families, and a few were lost to the church. In the Neuburg and Donauwörth areas an active life developed among the several families. There was an unusual number of conversions from non-Mennonites in the Neuburg area, the intellectual center having been for many years at the Forsthof near Gietelhausen (has been sold). (A burial ground now covered by the forest bears witness of these Mennonites.) Only a very few of the present population know anything of the work of these departed Mennonites.

At the end of the 19th century and the beginning of the 20th new settlements were made in the area between Augsburg, Donauwörth, and Höchstädt by Mennonites from Baden, the Palatinate, Württemberg, and Lower Franconia. It was due to this influx that the organization of new congregations was accomplished. In Neuburg (*q.v.*) a congregation of 40 members was formed under Elder Christian Gingerich and preachers Daniel Suttor of Bartlstockschwaige and Josef Ingold of Tempelhof. However, it dissolved in 1913. The Donauwörth congregation was the offspring of the Neuburg congregation, whose last preacher, Daniel Lichti of

Ellgau, served in Donauwörth (ordained elder in 1914). After a short life of 12 years, the meeting place for practical reasons having been moved to Augsburg, the congregation was reorganized as the Augsburg congregation, retaining the same leadership and most of the same members. The elder was Daniel Lichti, preachers Ulrich Hege (Schloss Markt near Biberach, 1914) and David Musselmann (Urfarhof near Donauwörth, 1914), and deacon Eugen Musselmann (Hellmaringen near Lauingen). Thus after almost exactly 400 years an Augsburg congregation was organized to succeed the original one, which had been wiped out by persecution in 1528.

The families of the congregation, with few exceptions farmers, are as follows: Musselmann from the vicinity of Heidelberg (Baden); Hege from near Hasselbach (Baden); Lichti from near Neustadt (Palatinate); Neff from near Heidelberg. These arrived at the turn of the 20th century. The Suttors, Hirschlers, Dettweilers, and Salzmann-Gingerichs are descendants of the original settlers of 1805 who came from the Palatinate and Alsace-Lorraine to Swabia and Upper Bavaria.

After the death of Daniel Lichti (1928) the office of elder became vacant, and has not been filled locally. The meetings were held in the Methodist chapel at Lauterlech 246 every two weeks. During World War II the congregation met in the Protestant Church at St. Ulrich until it was destroyed by the bombings. Increasing difficulties and danger of bombing attacks caused attendance at the meetings to decline, and in 1944 it came to a virtual standstill when Ulrich Hege, after more than 30 years of faithful service as minister, died on March 29, 1944.

As it became possible to travel again after the end of the war the congregational life gradually revived. On March 9, 1948, Philip Hege of Schloss Markt, a son of Ulrich, was ordained to the ministry, and Erich Musselmann, Hellmaringen, the son of Eugen, was chosen deacon. On each first Sunday of the month (until 1950 in the Methodist chapel, since then in the home of the YMCA at Frauentorstrasse 43) regular meetings are again held, and at the same time services are held for the children by Ernst Dettweiler. Until he moved to Mettingen near Würzburg, Peter Löwen often preached. The war and its aftermath have claimed the lives of six members. Fifteen Mennonite refugees from West Prussia have been added to the Augsburg congregations (especially the Wiebe family).

Even though the Augsburg congregation may be one of the smaller (membership c. 60) links in the chain of Mennonite congregations, it was touched more than most by the great brotherly aid of the MCC, and especially by the student exchange and agricultural trainee exchange with the Mennonites of North America, in which three young men have been permitted to take part.   R.R.

Augsburg, Peace of, the designation of the agreement reached at the Imperial Diet of Augsburg on Sept. 25, 1555, among the states of the Holy Roman Empire which granted to adherents of the Augsburg (Lutheran) Confession (*q.v.*) equality of rights with the Catholics. The Reformed, i.e., all followers of Zwingli and Calvin (called Sacramentarians) and the Anabaptists and all the "sects damned" by Recesses of the Imperial Diet were excluded from this "religious peace." It must not be assumed that this document is an expression of freedom of religion or of tolerance in the modern sense. It is far from that. Only to the rulers was freedom granted to decide which one of the "two religions" should be legally established in their lands. Subjects were required to accept the religion of the ruler, but were permitted to leave the country without loss of goods or honor if they differed. But this applied only to Lutherans and Catholics. Thus the reprehensible, disastrous principle of *cuius regio eius religio* was elevated to the rank of imperial law. Especially detrimental to Protestantism was the "ecclesiastical reservation," whereby a Catholic ruler who was also a bishop or other church official would lose his church office and all secular power as well as the income accruing from his land if he transferred to Protestantism. In any case his subjects would remain Catholic.

In the tedious negotiations, lasting almost a year, it is of especial interest to note that the Palatinate demanded that freedom of worship be granted all subjects, except the "condemned sect." Hesse pleaded for the groups related to the Augsburg Confession, whereas the Duke of Württemberg expressly demanded the exclusion of the Sacramentarians and Anabaptists. It is obvious that in this assemblage of princes the idea of giving religious freedom to the Anabaptists could not arise; their condemnation was agreed upon by all.   NEFF.

G. Wolf, *Der Augsburger Religionsfriede* (1890); M. Ritter, "Der Augsburger Religionsfriede," *Hist. Taschenbuch* (Leipzig, 1882) 212; *ML* I, 92.

Augsburg, Recesses (Decrees) of the Imperial Diet of. In the Recess of the Diet of Augsburg in 1530 the "sect of the Anabaptists" was prohibited. The interdiction issued against them at Speyer in 1529 was renewed by Emperor Charles V with the consent of the electors, princes, and estates. It demanded that children everywhere be baptized with the use of the chrism (an oil for anointing, consecrated by the Bishop on Maundy-Thursday for use in the Catholic Church in administering baptism, confirmation, anointing of the sick and consecration of priests) and with the prescribed prayers and ceremonies; for it is "unchristian and terrible to . . . rob the poor children of the way of salvation and of the grace of the Holy Spirit" (II, paragraph 4, p. 308, par. 16, p. 310, par. 40, p. 312).

In 1551 (II, par. 87-94, pp. 623-24) reference is made in the Recess of the Diet of Augsburg to the regulation previously issued against the Anabaptists; in spite of it the "harmful sect and error" was increasing to such an extent that the authorities were anxiously concerned lest "those who join this sect to some extent do not submit to the civil regulations of the government and in part are unwilling to recognize any government at all." In spite of all warnings and in spite of imprisonment they obstinately reject infant baptism. Sometimes the fault lies in the remissness of the judges, against whom penalties are to be applied by fines, imprisonment, and dismissal from office. Recanting Anabaptists are to be pardoned. How to punish the obstinate can be seen from par. 89: "We decree that all and any Anabaptists and rebaptized men and women who are of accountable age, who because of this disobedient, seducing and seditious error and sect refuse to swear honor to the government or to recognize any authority at all, are to be killed with fire, sword, or the like according to convenience, without a trial." All those are to be considered Anabaptists (par. 92) who despise infant baptism; no one may receive fleeing Anabaptists; if the authorities notice that Anabaptists are staying in their territory, they are not to tolerate them on penalty of excommunication (par. 93). In par. 94 the judges were again admonished to observe this point carefully, otherwise the above penalty will be enforced.

Anabaptists are excluded from the Religious Peace of Augsburg in 1555; for par. 17 (III, p. 18) reads: "But all others, who do not belong to these two religions, are not meant in this peace, but are absolutely excluded." "Today we recognize in this a regrettable lack," says Th. Brieger. (*Neue Sammlung der Reichs-Abschiede in 4 Teilen,* Frankfurt, 1741; *ML* I, 91.)   A.K.

Augsburger, a common Mennonite family name with these variant spellings: Augsberger, Augspurger, Oxberger, Augsbourger. Place of origin: Langnau in the Emmental, canton of Bern, Switzerland. The name likely originated in the 15th century with a person or persons from Augsburg, Germany.

Niggli (Nicholas) Augsburger is mentioned in a letter of 1700 as being a co-worker with Jacob Ammann, founder of the Amish Mennonites.

Members of the Augsburger family were found in the Montbéliard Amish community as early as 1715 and near Corgémont in the Bishopric of Basel in 1720. John Augsburger (1783-18—) and wife were in the first party of Mennonite emigrants who left the Jura in the 19th century, leaving in 1817 to settle in northern Pennsylvania for 12 years before moving on to Wayne Co., Ohio, and later to Adams Co., Ind. Some members of this family founded an (old) Mennonite church near Berne, Ind. When this became defunct some of the family moved to Elida, Ohio.

John Augsburger (1801-67) and wife left the Jura in 1834, settled in Wayne Co., Ohio, for 16 years and then moved to near Bluffton, Ohio, where most of their descendants live.

Christian Augspurger (1782-1848) and family came to America in 1817 from near Strasbourg, Alsace, but being discouraged returned to their native land the following year. But in 1819 they again came to America with other Amish Mennonites and founded a settlement in Butler Co., Ohio. The descendants of Christian Augspurger, his brother Joseph and their second cousin Jacob constitute the major part of the Mennonite settlement at that place today. The above Christian Augspurger received from Napoleon the Legion of Honor medal as an expert farmer.

Prominent personalities were Christian Augspurger (1821-1903), minister at Berne, Ind., for 38 years; Christian Augspurger (1782-1848), founder of the Butler Co., Ohio, Amish settlement; Nicholas Augspurger (1811-72), minister of the Augspurger congregation, Butler Co., Ohio, for 45 years; Christian Augspurger (1839-1907), minister of the Augspurger congregation, Butler Co., Ohio, for 40 years; and Joseph Augspurger (1816-96), minister (later bishop) of the Hessian congregation in Butler Co., Ohio, for 32 years.   D.L.G.

P. B. Amstutz, *Gesch. Ereignisse der Menn. Ansiedlung in Allen und Putnam County* (Bluffton, 1925) 33-36; W. H. Grubb, *Hist. of the Menn. of Butler Co., Ohio* (Trenton, Ohio, 1916).

Augspurger, Aaron, was born Dec. 3, 1865, in Butler Co., Ohio. He was a grandson of Bishop Joseph Stuckey, the founder of the Central Conference. When he was only a few months old, his parents moved to McLean Co., Ill., and located in the Danvers community where Aaron grew to manhood. He was ordained to the ministry by his grandfather on June 10, 1894. It was in large measure his persuasion that induced Bishop Stuckey to call the meeting of the ministers which gave birth to the Central Conference of Mennonites. He was always keenly interested in the organization and promotion of the conference and its work, and with his literary ability made a significant contribution to that end by his work in drafting resolutions, documents, etc. He also took leading parts in initiating the work of publication and foreign missions and served for a time as editor of the *Christian Evangel,* in addition to serving as pastor of the church at Anchor, Ill. He was ordained bishop in 1900 and served as president of the Central Conference in 1899 and 1906-11, and as conference secretary for many years. He died Jan. 8, 1950.

R.L.H.

W. B. Weaver, *Hist. of the Central Conf. Menn. Church* (Danvers, Ill., 1926).

August II, King of Poland, 1697-1733, on Sept. 20, 1697, at Cracow confirmed all the privileges previously granted to the Mennonites. He valued the Mennonites as good taxpayers and protected them when a storm of fanatical hostility on the part of some Polish leaders arose in Parliament in 1699 and 1700, demanding that the severe laws against Arians (*q.v.*) be applied against them. These laws would have confiscated their goods and banished them. King August defended them and had a new charter prepared for them in Warsaw, stating that "Mennonites retain all the rights, privileges and freedom in secular as well as in spiritual matters," (Oct. 12, 1732).   NEFF.

W. Mannhardt, *Die Wehrfreiheit der Altpreussischen Menn.* (Danzig, 1863) 98, 91; *ML* I, 96.

August III, King of Poland from 1733 to 1763, confirmed all previous privileges of the Mennonites on April 16, 1736. On Sept. 18, 1750, at Warsaw, he extended the privileges which had been granted to the Werder Mennonites to apply to those in the lowlands at Graudenz (*q.v.*), Culm (*q.v.*), and

Schwetz (*q.v.*). Most important was the complete freedom from military service granted them, for which privilege they paid a high protection fee. From 1741 to 1759 the Mennonites of Danzig (*q.v.*) had to pay 5,000 florins annually to the state treasury for freedom from military service in accord with an express edict of the king. In 1759 this fee was reduced to 2,000 florins, in 1774 to 1,500, in 1782 to 1,200 florins. But the Mennonites were never admitted to full citizenship. A rescript of August III to the Danzig council even demanded that they should no longer be permitted to work at a trade and at business at the same time; they were to buy the materials for their manufactured wares from citizens, they were not to offer their finished products for sale, but were to sell them only to citizens; they were also forbidden to acquire any more land.   NEFF.

W. Mannhardt, *Die Wehrfreiheit der Altpreussischen Menn.* (Danzig, 1863); *ML* I, 96.

Augusta County, Va., was established in 1738 when it and Frederick County were formed out of a part of Orange County, which included at that time the entire Shenandoah Valley of Virginia. As originally constituted Augusta County included what is now Shenandoah, Rockingham, and Page counties which were formed in 1745, 1777, and 1831 respectively. These are all counties in which Mennonites first settled when they came to the Shenandoah Valley of Virginia. Therefore Augusta County is the custodian of many of the early records of these settlements. Augusta County is also important for the history of a thriving Mennonite settlement within its present limits.   H.A.B.

Augustijn de Backer, an Anabaptist martyr, arrested while kneading dough in his bakery at Beverwijk, Dutch province of North Holland, was sentenced to death because he was rebaptized. He suffered a very cruel death, being bound to a ladder and thus thrown into the fire. The exact year of execution is not known, although 1556 is usually accepted. (*Mart. Mir.* D 165, E 553; *ML* I, 96.)   vDZ.

Augustijn de Vuelpere, an Anabaptist martyr of Antwerp, who is not found in the martyr books. He was accused of having frequented forbidden meetings in and out of town, of possessing forbidden books, and of being rebaptized. He was put to death for his faith at Antwerp on Dec. 16, 1575, together with Lambrecht Henricx. (Génard, *Antw. Arch.-Blad* XIII, 197; XIV, 96-97, No. 1101.)
                                                    vDZ.

Auhagen, Brazil, a small Russian Mennonite settlement established under the auspices of the German government in 1930 some 40 miles from Hammonia in the state of Santa Catarina, adjoining the Krauel (*q.v.*) settlement, on land purchased from the Hanseatic Colonization Company (headquarters at Hamburg, Germany). In Mennonite history there have been only a few instances of Mennonites abandoning a settlement they had begun; e.g., Terek (*q.v.*) in Russia and Auhagen in Brazil. (The Krauel colony in Brazil is now also in the process of dissolution.) Whereas in the Caucasus

the move was motivated primarily by the question of local political security, in Auhagen it was in the first place the unfavorable situation of the Stoltz Plateau on which the settlement was located, and in addition, economic conditions, that compelled the Mennonite refugees from Russia to abandon the settlement.

The settlement was founded in 1930, under unfavorable conditions. The immigrants, the last Brazil installment of the group who escaped from Russia in 1929, took it for granted that they would be settled in connection with the near-by Witmarsum settlement which was already established, and they were deeply disappointed when they learned that they were not to settle on the Pinhal River near Witmarsum. The Stoltz Plateau is a high elevation very difficult to reach, which is probably the reason why it had never been settled. By foot the top is reached from the floor of the valley in an hour; but a wagon requires six hours, which adds greatly to the expense of transportation of produce the 40 miles to Hammonia-Ibirama, the nearest market town. When the settlers arrived they were faced by an impenetrable forest, which would, of course, first have to be conquered. The second problem seemed less difficult: what crops should be raised here? The settlers assumed that the corn and aipim, a tuber used like potatoes and in the manufacture of starch, which grew in the neighboring Krauel settlement, would succeed here. But these crops did not thrive on the plateau, and were abandoned as commercial products. The settlers then tried shipping the wood of the forest to Hammonia. But this also failed, for the supply was not adequate on all the farms, and the cost of shipping devoured the income.

Although it gradually became clear also that their land was not worth the price they paid for it, negotiations with the Hanseatic Colonization Company in Hammonia failed to bring about a reduction in price. Likewise the company refused to build a new road to the settlement to reduce the expenses of transportation. In order to ease the scarcity of money the settlers began to let their daughters and then also their young men work in the neighboring towns (Hammonia, Blumenau, Jaraguay, and as far as Sao Paulo and Rio de Janeiro). The money earned was of value to the settlement, but the loss of its youth weakened it.

By 1934 the fate of the settlement was sealed and the settlers decided to look around for other possible sites. They found nothing promising, and the Dutch Mennonites as well as the German government declined further financial help. The report of a committee of experts that it is impossible to raise corn and aipim on the plateau and that the colony would have to change over to dairying, only served to accelerate the dissolution.

Since there were no prospects of a united settlement elsewhere the emigration proceeded without plan. Most of the Auhagen group settled in the outskirts of Curitiba, the capital of Parana, and took jobs as laborers, craftsmen, and merchants, and especially as dairy farmers. They bought and bred cattle and sold the milk in the city. They were soon able to purchase their land and founded the settlements of Bouqueirao and Xaxim.

There is not the least doubt that the settlers were right in abandoning Auhagen. To have consumed their strength there would have denoted indecision and lack of vision, since their problem could be solved at other places in Brazil to far greater advantage. The last families of the 96 (464 souls) in 1934 left at the beginning of World War II. W.Q.

Auhagen, Otto, was the agricultural expert in the German embassy at Moscow in 1929, at the time when thousands of Mennonite refugees were gathering at Moscow in the hope of escaping imminent catastrophe by emigration. Dr. Auhagen took an unselfish interest in these people, aiding them with expert advice, and induced the Soviet government to yield to their request; above all he again and again presented the distress of these refugees to the German embassy and the Berlin government, thus definitely influencing its attitude in this affair.

In gratitude for his aid and interest the "Moscow refugees" who settled in Santa Catarina on the Stolz Plateau in 1930 named their settlement Auhagen. In the Fernheim colony in the Paraguayan Chaco, which was likewise founded by these refugees, village No. 9 was named Auhagen. W.Q.

O. Auhagen, *Die Schicksalswende des russlanddeutschen Bauerntums in den Jahren 1927-1930* (Leipzig, 1942).

Aulie-Ata, a Mennonite settlement in Russia, was located near the city of the same name, approximately 150 miles northeast of Tashkent (*q.v.*), the capital of Turkestan in Central Asia. This settlement was originated by Mennonites from the Trakt settlement (Samara) under the leadership of Claasz Epp (*q.v.*) and from the Molotschna settlements under the leadership of Elder A. Peters (*q.v.*). Both groups were looking for a refuge to escape military service and to meet Christ at His second coming. After their arrival in Tashkent in 1880 they sent a delegation to the region of the Thianshan Mountain Range to find a location suitable for settlement. Near the city of Aulie-Ata they found a valley averaging 10 miles in width and 100 miles long flanked by the Ala-Tau and the Alexander mountain ranges.

Upon the return of the delegation, the Molotschna group under the leadership of Elder Peters chose this location although they had not been granted complete exemption from military service, while the majority of the Samara group followed Claas Epp to Khiva, where they established the Ak-Mechet (*q.v.*) settlement. The Aulie-Ata settlement established in 1882 consisted of the following villages: Gnadental, Gnadenfeld, Nikolaipol, and Köppental. The latter village was settled by those who had come from Samara. Later the villages Ohrloff and Hohendorf were added. Homes and villages were patterned after those the settlers had left, although they had a somewhat oriental appearance. The use of adobe for building was predominant. All land was irrigated. In 1910 the settlement had a population of 1,000 souls.

In 1884 the Romanovka Mennonite Church (*q.v.*)

was organized at Aulie-Ata with A. Peters as elder. He was succeeded by Johann Regehr (*q.v.*) and later Gerhard Kopper. Not only because of its chiliastic views but also because of other peculiarities, this congregation remained somewhat independent. Partly through influences from the Molotschna and Kuban settlements, the Nikolaipol Mennonite Brethren Church (*q.v.*) was organized here in 1887 with Heinrich Kroeker as its first elder. According to a report of 1925 a third congregation existed at that time. Baptism by immersion had become predominant in all congregations. There was good co-operation not only in the affairs of the community but also in evangelistic endeavors in the surrounding communities. The young men took part in forestry service and encountered some difficulties after the Revolution. Before World War I some of the Aulie-Ata Mennonites came to America. The total membership of all congregations in 1925 was 550. Little is known about the fate of the settlement since that time. C.K.

F. Bartsch, *Unser Auszug nach Mittel-Asien* (North Kildonan, Man., 1948, reprint of first edition of 1907); idem, "Meine Reise nach Turkestan," in *Unser Blatt* I (Oct., Nov. 1925) 9-10, 26-27; J. Janzen, "Menn. Colony in Turkestan" in *MQR* IV (Oct. 1930) 182-289.

Aurich, a city in East Friesland, long the capital of East Friesland; the city contains a provincial archives with important documents under the title "Mennonitica." From Aurich a sharp decree of Edzard II was issued to the Emden council against the Anabaptists on Jan. 13, 1577. From here Count Rudolf Christian on May 26, 1628, issued the first letter of protection to the Mennonites, which became a pattern for future attitudes. About that time there was probably an Anabaptist congregation here, concerning which there are only a few bits of information. On Feb. 10, 1644, Ennon Rippers, Hendrik Stralman, Clas Janssen, Sicke Azelts, and Jakob Frerichs, all citizens of Aurich, complained that their preacher had been taken from them and imprisoned, although they were entirely unaware of any wrongdoing; and that they had been surprised by the police on Feb. 1, 1644, in near-by Oldeborg at divine services, and their leading preacher arrested. The Dutch Elder Leenaert Bouwens (*q.v.*) had baptized six persons at Aurich between 1551 and 1554, and seventeen between 1563 and 1565.

From a register dated 1646, listing 21 names (probably names of families) it is seen that there were in Aurich two Mennonite churches, a Flemish and a Waterlander. The little congregation was obviously not able to meet the increasing financial pressure of the government; it seems to have dissolved through the emigration of the members. In a petition of the East Frisian Mennonites in 1709 the statement is made that the church in Aurich "had died out or had perished in some other way."

At the instigation of Prince George Albrecht the two parties (Mennonites and Uckowallists) met in Aurich on May 1, 1723, in order to consider a new government assessment of 3,000 talers. (J. P. Müller, *Die Menn. in Ostfriesland,* Emden, 1887; *ML* I, 96.) NEFF.

Aurora Church (UMC), 28 miles northwest of Eckville, Alta., had around 12 members in 1950.

E.R.S.

Aurora (Neb.) Menn. Church: see **Pleasant View**.

Ausbund, oldest hymnbook of the Swiss Brethren, and still today in use by the Amish in North America. In its final form it comprises more than 800 pages (hence called *Das dicke Buch*). Through the fine research of Rudolf Wolkan (1903) we are well informed regarding its origins. The nucleus of the book (now part II beginning with hymn No. 81) consists of 51 hymns written by a number of Anabaptists (those called Philipites, *q.v.*) in the dungeons of the castle of Passau on the Danube (Bavaria) where they lay imprisoned between 1535 and 1540, many of them later martyred. Twelve of these hymns were written by Hans Betz (*q.v.*) who died in 1537 in prison, and 11 by Michael Schneider (*q.v.*), the leader of the group. (Wolkan was able to identify most of the otherwise unknown writers.) The oldest print of this part, entitled *Etliche schöne christliche Gesäng wie dieselbigen zu Passau von den Schweizer Brüdern in der Gefenknus im Schloss durch göttliche Gnade gedicht und gesungen worden. Ps. 139,* bears the printing year 1564. (Only known copy in Goshen College Library.) This booklet must have had wide circulation since at the Frankental colloquium, 1571, it was quoted by the opponents of the Brethren. In 1583, a much enlarged edition was brought out, again for the Swiss Brethren (most likely those of the Rhineland), which for the first time bears the title *Ausbund* (paragon), *Das ist etliche schöne christenliche Lieder,* etc. *Allen und jeden Christen, welcher Religion sie seien, unpartheyisch fast nützlich.* This edition had 130 hymns, 80 more than the previous edition. Later prints added a few more (up to 137 in Europe, up to 140 in American editions, among these additions also the famous "Haslibacher Lied," *q.v.*). All in all there are 11 known European editions and about 20 editions in America (latest 1949). The earlier European editions point to Cologne, Rhineland, as likely place of publication (16th and 17th centuries), while Basel and Strasbourg become the new centers for the 18th and 19th century publications; the last European edition is signed Basel, 1838. Then the book came into disuse in Europe, to be replaced by more recent hymnals. In America the first edition was printed at Christopher Saur's (*q.v.*) Germantown press in 1742, most likely prompted by Bishop Henry Funck (details in H. S. Bender, *Two Centuries,* and J. C. Wenger's *History of the Franconia Mennonites*). Among the Swiss Mennonites in Pennsylvania the book was in use throughout the 18th century. But the two new hymnals, *Die Kleine Geistliche Harfe* of 1803 (*q.v.*) and the *Unpartheyisches Gesangbuch* of 1804 (*q.v.*), both of Eastern Pennsylvania origin, replaced the *Ausbund* which from now on was exclusively used by the Amish. All editions are nearly identical, thus preserving the old 16th century flavor through the ages. It is undoubtedly the oldest hymnbook in continuous use in any Christian church anywhere in the world.

The hymns, mainly those of the second (older) part, represent very characteristically the spirit of 16th century Anabaptism (Swiss Brethren), namely, the conviction that their church is a "suffering church" in a relentless world, and that martyrdom is the fate of earnest Christians everywhere. The dominant tone is one of great sorrow, deep loneliness, and protest against a world of wickedness. Yet there is no despair but rather a note of triumph: God will not forsake His own. Among the best-known hymns is No. 131: "O Gott Vater, wir loben Dich und deine Güte preisen," still sung today by the Amish at the beginning of every worship service. According to Wolkan, *Lieder,* this hymn goes back to Leenaert Clock (*q.v.*) of Holland, 1625, but it fits beautifully into the context and prevailing spirit.

The first hymn in the collection comes from Sebastian Franck (*q.v.*), who was by no means an Anabaptist but whose song fittingly introduces the whole group: "This first hymn teaches us how the Christians in spirit and truth should sing, pray, and give praise in Psalms." No. 2 is a metrical version of the Athanasian creed; Nos. 5, 6, 7, and 8 were written by Blaurock, F. Manz, M. Sattler, and Hans Hut respectively, all martyred at the very outset of the Anabaptist movement. Other martyr hymns are by Leonhard Schiemer, Hans Schlaffer, George Blaurock, and Hans Leupold, all victims of the first wave of persecution before 1530. Five hymns are by Hans Büchel (*q.v.*), the Swiss brother who was present at the Frankental colloquium. Eleven hymns are of Dutch origin, and another 11 come from North Germany. Five hymns are, strangely enough, borrowed from the Bohemian Brethren. Many hymns contain exposition of some Bible doctrines (baptism, Lord's Supper, footwashing, even Trinity). No. 57 treats of love ("Die Lieb ist kalt jetzt in der Welt"). Naturally the gloomy outlook on life prevails; e.g., No. 46 (Hans Büchel) has the title "A new Christian hymn of the present terrible latter days in which so many different sects, fanatics and false prophets appear as well as blood-thirsty tyrants." But No. 65 opens with a stanza of joy: "Frölich pfleg ich zu singen Wenn ich solche Freud betracht." While it may be true that most of these hymns, written by men with little poetic genius, are not of a high literary quality, they yet make up for this in sincerity of purpose and the depth of religious conviction.

To us today it seems hardly understandable how some of these very long and cumbersome hymns were sung, sung in worship and also at many other social occasions. Every hymn in the *Ausbund* has a headline indicating the tune. The Brethren never used notes but assumed that these (popular) tunes are known to all as true folk tunes are. Research has disclosed that most of these tunes were secular ones current during the 16th century, and some are still older. Sometimes the original tune of the popular folk song seems hardly fitting to so serious a hymn (e.g., the martyr's story of a brother is sung to the tune, "There went a maiden with a jug"), but it was the text rather than the tune which mattered. Thanks to the work done by G. P. Jackson (1945-46) we are now fairly well informed about the originals of most of these tunes, some of which can be dated as early as 1506, 1512, etc. One tune is from the 13th century, another from 1394. The hymn, "O Gott Vater, wir loben Dich," is sung to the tune "Aus tiefer Not schrei ich zu Dir," which is found to correspond to the secular tune, "Es wollt ein Mägdlein Wasser holen," dated 1534. Today, all the songs are sung very slowly (*langsame Weis*) which prompted J. W. Yoder to assume a kinship to the Gregorian chant. It seems, however, that Jackson's interpretation comes nearer to truth that in uncontrolled group singing each tune is dragged out, which leads to all kinds of strange ornamentation foreign to the original tune.

As already suggested the *Ausbund* went through many European editions, all of them without place of publication (until 1809), and naturally without indicating the editors. Hence the subtitle, "Most useful to all Christians of whatever denomination, impartial." Very few copies from the 16th and 17th centuries have been preserved (more in America, fewer in Europe). As late as 1692 the government of Bern, Switzerland, placed the book on the proscribed list and ordered its confiscation when found (Müller, *Berner Täufer*, 104). All American editions are amplified by two appendices containing the *Confessio* of Thomas v. Imbroich (1558) and *Ein wahrhaftiger Bericht*, "The true story of the hardships which the Brethren around Zürich had to suffer for their faith's sake between 1635 and 1645" (a collection of martyr stories). From another old Anabaptist hymn pamphlet of the 17th century, six "Spiritual Songs" were added ("Tobias war ein frommer Mann," etc.). *Ausbund* apparently means a "select" selection.   R.F.

R. Wolkan, *Die Lieder*, 118 ff., whose research is basic both in clearing up the historical background, in identifying the hymn writers, and in evaluating their work. The most thorough discussion in English is found in C. Henry Smith, *The Menn. Immigration to Penna.* (Norristown, Pa., 1929) 331-42, and 255-57 (there also the tune of "O Gott Vater wir loben Dich," 257); Bender's discovery and description of the oldest edition of 1564 is reported in *MQR* III (1929) 145-50. A complete list of the European editions in R. Friedmann, *Menn. Piety Through the Centuries* (Goshen, 1949) 170 f.; the list of the American editions in H. S. Bender's *Two Centuries of American Menn. Lit.* (Goshen, 1929); J. W. Yoder, *Amische Lieder* (Huntingdon, Pa., 1942) is a transcription of 20 tunes; George P. Jackson, *Mus. Quart.* XXXI (July 1945) 275-88, where the tunes are reconstructed and identified; G. P. Jackson, "The American Amish Sing Medieval Folk Tunes Today," *Southern Folklore Quart.*, X (June 1946) 151-57 (see the thorough review by John Umble in *MQR* XIV, Jan. 1950, 91-93); J. Umble, "The Old Order Amish, Their Hymns and Tunes," *Journ. of Am. Folklore* (Jan. 1939); *ML* I, 97 f.

Auspitz, parent congregation of the Hutterian Brethren in Moravia, established about 1529 by Philip Weber (*q.v.*). He had settled here with a number of fellow believers, who had shortly before settled in Rossitz (*q.v.*). Most of them were Anabaptists from Hesse and the Palatinate, where Weber had been engaged for some time as a missionary (Hege, 60).

Early in 1530 a second congregation arose in Auspitz, formed under the leadership of Jörg Zaunring (*q.v.*) by the Tyrolese who had separated from the congregation at Austerlitz (*q.v.*). There were about 150 persons who had been expelled from the brotherhood at Austerlitz. Two preachers from Tirol, Jakob Hutter (*q.v.*) and Sigmund Schützinger (*q.v.*), were chosen to bring about a reconciliation with the Austerlitz congregation, but their efforts were wrecked by the attitude of the latter whose conduct had been reprehensible. They removed the leader Wilhelm Reublin (*q.v.*) from his office; he had been convicted of telling the untruth and appropriating church funds to his personal use. Zaunring then was entrusted with the leadership of the church. He was assisted by David Böhem (*q.v.*), Burkhard von Ofen (*q.v.*), and Adam Schlegel (*q.v.*), but these were also excommunicated "for unattentiveness." Zaunring was soon afterward banned, for having been too lenient in punishing his wife's adultery.

Since the congregation in Tirol was now without a shepherd, Jakob Hutter and Sigmund Schützinger were called in again about Easter in 1531. In Zaunring's place Schützinger was chosen to direct the congregation, which was soon united with the older church in Auspitz, which was still led by Philip Weber, and Gabriel Ascherham's (*q.v.*) church in Rossitz. The two congregations in Auspitz may have numbered about 2,000 adults, that at Rossitz perhaps 1,200 souls. Hutter returned to Tirol. The three churches were soon augmented by large immigrations of fellow believers from the Tirol, Silesia, Swabia, and the Palatinate.

On Aug. 11, 1533, Jakob Hutter also returned; he found much to criticize in the leadership of the congregations, charged the leaders with negligence, and excommunicated Schützinger. Ascherham and Weber sided with Schützinger. Finally the Tyrolese separated again from the Gabrielites and the Philipites and chose Jakob Hutter as their leader. The members of the other two congregations for the most part returned to their homeland or settled in Poland and Prussia in the persecutions of 1535. Those remaining united with the Hutterites, who had to leave Moravia in 1622 and settled in Hungary (*q.v.*).   HEGE.

Beck, *Geschichts-Bücher*; J. Horsch, *The Hutterian Brethren 1528-1931* . . . (Scottdale, 1931) 38; Chr. Hege, *Die Täufer in der Kurpfalz* (Frankfurt, 1908); *ML* I, 98.

Austen School, in Oxford Twp., Kent Co., Ont.: see **Bothwell.**

Austerlitz, a congregation of the Moravian Anabaptists, founded in the spring of 1528 by about 200 members of the nonresistant branch of the congregation at Nikolsburg. Their first preachers were Jakob Widemann and Philip Weber, who did not share the views of the preachers of the lord of Liechtenstein in the Nikolsburg disputation of 1527, which agreed to the use of the sword and the payment of war-levies, and therefore parted from the other Anabaptists in Nikolsburg. They were given the epithets *Kleinhäufler* and *Stäbler* by Hans Spitelmair, the leading preacher of the lord of Liechtenstein, whereupon they called the Liechtenstein branch *Schwertler*. Before the nonresistant minority left, they sold their possessions as well as they could under the circumstances. When they were assembled outside the city for the departure, they spread out a coat, and "everyone willingly laid his fortune down without compulsion or urging for the support of the needy." At the same time deacons (*Brüder der Notdurft*) were ordained. The lord of Liechtenstein pursued them with his knights and urged them to return and be reconciled, but in vain. Reublin (*q.v.*) reported the division to Pilgram Marpeck in Alsace on Jan. 25, 1531 (Jörg, *Revolutionsperiode,* 680 f.).

The lords of Austerlitz, the four brothers Johann, Wenzel, Peter, and Ulrich von Kaunitz, permitted the nonresistant group from Nikolsburg to settle on the *Haffenmarkt*. Austerlitz was soon to become for several years the center of the Anabaptist movement in Moravia, and even for that in Austria and South Germany. The news of the attitude of the members and of the protection granted by landowners spread rapidly wherever Anabaptists lived and were persecuted. Large numbers of them came in from Tirol, Austria, Styria, Bohemia, Silesia, Bavaria, Swabia, Switzerland, and the Palatinate. Many who were soon to become leaders in the Moravian brotherhood were among them, such as Hans Amon (*q.v.*), Leonhard Lanzenstiel, also called Seiler (*q.v.*), and Jakob Hutter (*q.v.*) in 1529.

From Switzerland Wilhelm Reublin (Röubli) had come, who complained that in the absence of Widemann the church was not properly taught and disciplined. The Tyrolese, who had recently arrived under the leadership of Jörg Zaunring (*q.v.*), a former assistant priest in Rattenberg, sided with Reublin, adding that the preaching was not as comforting as in Tirol, and making complaints about the training of children, the marriage of the sisters, etc. Upon his return Widemann presented the matter to the congregation, which now had to choose between him and Reublin. The Tyrolese had to yield (Jan. 8, 1531) and, led by Zaunring, they migrated to Auspitz (*q.v.*), where they established a new church alongside of the one already there, under the leadership of Philip Weber (*q.v.*).

The members remaining in Austerlitz were banished four years later. Some of them went to Slovakia, others toward Krasnikov in Lodomeria, and only a few stayed in Moravia; these were at Bucovic where the Tyrolese Ulrich Stadler (*q.v.*) became their leader. Their former preacher, Jakob Widemann, suffered a martyr's death "for the sake of baptism" with five other brethren in Vienna in 1536. Stadler and his group, as well as the Slovakians, united with the Hutterian Brethren in 1537. In that year they began to resettle in Austerlitz, and in 1538 erected a household on the Hafnermarkt. They found toleration here for 85 years.

In 1589 there were six households in the domain. But in October 1622, on the basis of an imperial letter of Sept. 28, 1622, they were banished with the loss of all their property. They found a new home in Hungary and Transylvania.   HEGE.

Beck, *Geschichts-Bücher;* J. B. Jörg, *Deutschland in der Revolutionsperiode von 1522-26* (Freiburg, 1851) 680 f.; *Archiv f. Ref.-Gesch.* (1933) 197 f. and 182 ff.; J. Horsch, *The Hutterian Brethren 1528-1931* (Scottdale, 1931); *ML* I, 100.

Austerlitz Brethren, the name given to the followers of Jakob Widemann (*q.v.*) by the Anabaptists who migrated from Austerlitz to Auspitz with Reublin and Zaunring. After Widemann's death the remnants of the Austerlitz Brethren united with the Hutterian Brethren ·about 1537. (Beck, *Geschichts-Bücher,* 96 f.; *ML* I, 100.)   HEGE.

Austria (Oesterreich). The term may be understood in five different senses: (1) the house of Habsburg (*q.v.*), the imperial dynasty, with a history from the early Middle Ages; (2) the Austrian Empire 1804-1918 composed of the crown domain (*Erblande*), Bohemia, Hungary, Galicia, etc.; (3) the Austrian republic established in 1918 which contains about 60 per cent of the old crown domain; (4) the Austrian crown domain, composed of the territories or provinces of Austria proper (sense 5), plus Styria, Carinthia, Tirol, Carniola, Trieste, etc., and since 1805 also the former archbishopric of Salzburg; (5) Austria in the narrow sense, viz., the oldest crown territories of the Habsburg house, being subdivided into the two provinces of Lower and Upper Austria (*Nieder-* and *Oberösterreich*). Vienna (Wien), the capital and residence of the Habsburgs, is situated on the Danube at the far eastern end of Lower Austria. Both provinces are archduchies, whence the Austrian line of the Habsburgs got their title of archdukes. (In 1526 they also became the kings of Bohemia and Hungary.) Since most of the territories included under the fourth sense are treated in separate articles, the present article will deal exclusively with Austria in the narrow sense of the fifth definition, namely, the archduchies of Lower and Upper Austria, with Vienna and Linz as their respective capitals. The Danube runs through the entire length of both provinces as their main artery of traffic (important as such particularly in earlier centuries). The population is of German (Bavarian) stock, representing the inhabitants of the old *Ostmark* (Eastern March), the territory protecting the southeastern frontier of the Holy Roman Empire.

As everywhere in German-speaking lands, Anabaptism flourished also in these two provinces, though it was a strong and vital movement only during the short period of 1526-30. While Anabaptism continued in Tirol until the second half of the 16th century, and in Moravia until 1622, it gradually vanished from the two Austrias, Styria and Carinthia at a rather early date, due more to the lack of outstanding leaders than to the severe persecution by the Habsburgs. As is well known, martyrdom was never an effective deterrent for the Anabaptists.

The story of Anabaptism in Lower and Upper

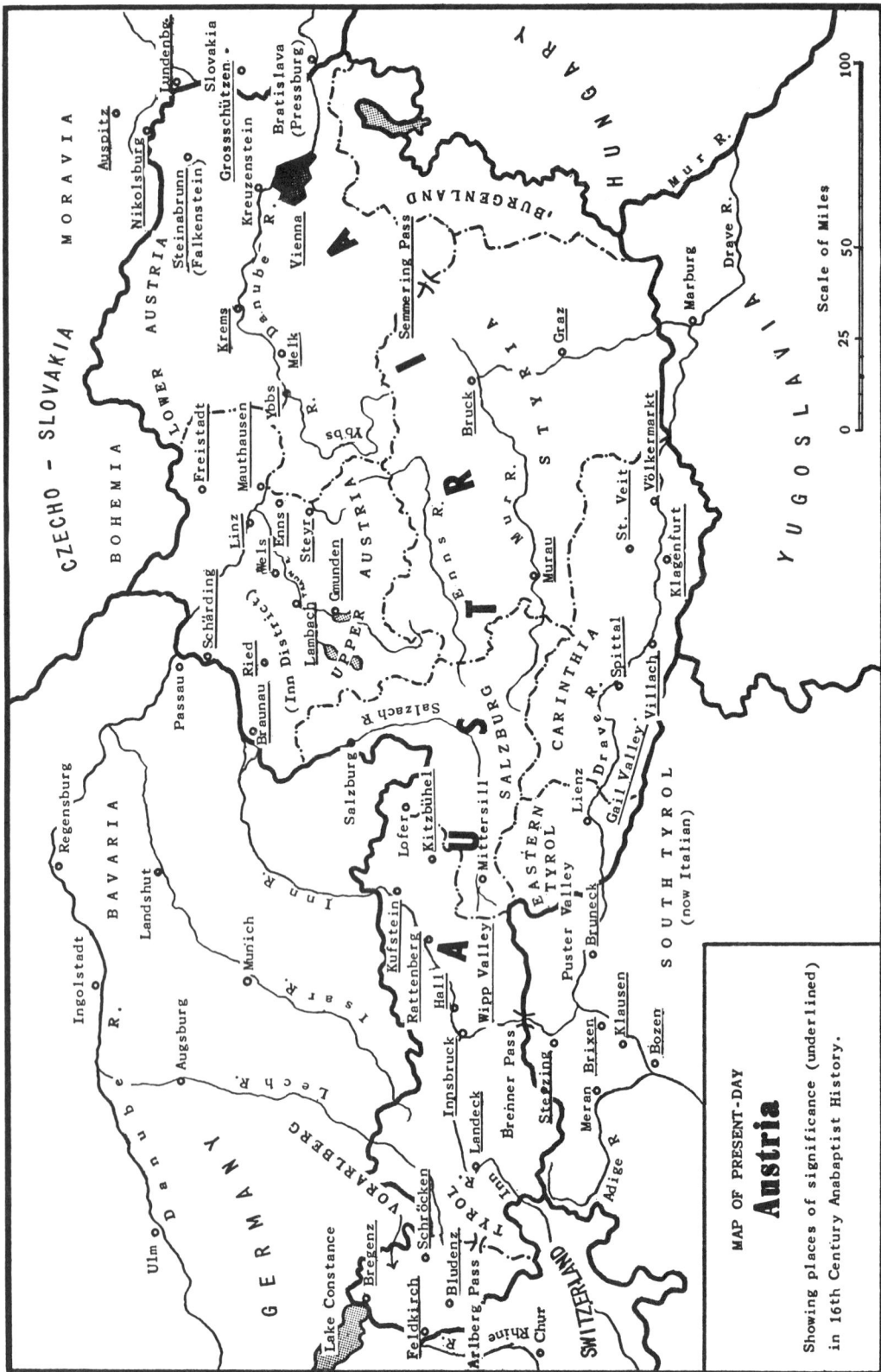

MAP OF PRESENT-DAY

Austria

Showing places of significance (underlined)
in 16th Century Anabaptist History.

Austria has been but little studied. Prof. Johann Loserth published a research paper in 1899, and J. Jäckel published his findings in a few papers between 1889 and 1895. Valuable material was then added by Loserth in his article, **Oesterreich** for the *Mennonitisches Lexikon,* and by Dr. Paul Dedic in his two extensive articles, **Niederösterreich** and **Oberösterreich** also for the *Lexikon.* Dedic based his statements to a great extent upon original, as yet unpublished research in Austrian archives. Since the three articles partly overlap, and in their original form are also too extensive, a condensed summary of them is offered here, with some added viewpoints. For more details, the *Menn. Lexikon* should be consulted. In studying Austrian Anabaptism, a significant distinction must be made between the movement of the 1520's, which stood in the main under the influence of Hans Hut (*q.v.*), and the movement after 1530, dominated by the Hutterian Brethren (*q.v.*) in Moravia, which felt itself responsible for all Anabaptist groups in Austrian lands. While in the 1520's there were some chances for an indigenous Anabaptist movement, particularly in Upper Austria (Steyr), these chances no longer existed when the exceedingly harsh "mandates" of the Habsburgs and the Imperial Diet of Speyer (1529) became operative. From about 1530 onward the two Austrias became a transit area between Tirol or Bavaria on the one side, and Moravia on the other, rather than a place of direct Anabaptist brotherhood activities. No permanent settlement was possible in Austria after 1530, neither could the missionary activities of the Brethren record any major success. Incidentally, the same holds true also for the provinces of Styria, Carinthia, and Salzburg.

1. *Lower Austria.* The most intense activities of Anabaptist leaders fell into the two years, 1527 and 1528. It was then that Hans Hut (*q.v.*), Oswald Glaidt (*q.v.*), and Leonhard Schiemer (*q.v.*) worked so successfully for their new doctrine in Lower and then Upper Austria. Before coming to these countries, these three outstanding missionaries had lived for a while in Nikolsburg (*q.v.*), Moravia, on the estate of the lord of Liechtenstein (*q.v.*), where also Balthasar Hubmaier (*q.v.*) found a refuge and place of activity. Yet not one of these three brethren can be called a follower of Hubmaier even though the latter might have been a strong stimulation and challenge to them. The issue of "the sword" made co-operation with Hubmaier impossible.

The first place of work for Hans Hut was Vienna, where he is said to have baptized more than 50 people (1527), thus establishing a small independent group of brethren. Then he moved on toward Upper Austria where we find him again in the city of Steyr (*q.v.*), active all along his route thither. In the meantime also Oswald Glaidt became active in Vienna, baptizing among others Leonhard Schiemer, a former Barefoot Friar, later one of the outstanding witnesses to the truth among the Anabaptists. He, too, soon moved toward Steyr on the Enns River (Upper Austria), the most important center of Anabaptism at that time. Other places of

Lower Austria besides Vienna mentioned in the records of those early years, were two cities on the river Danube, Krems (*q.v.*) and Melk (*q.v.*), in which latter place Elder Jörg Krautschlögel (*q.v.*) is said to have baptized not less than 400 persons.

The Austrian government soon became alerted. Archduke Ferdinand (since 1526 also king of Bohemia and Hungary, and a generation later emperor of the Holy Roman Empire) was particularly intent on eradicating these "heretics" without, however, comprehending in any way their issues, their spiritual needs, and the reasons for their defection from Catholicism (the conditions of the Catholic Church). From 1527 onward Ferdinand issued one "mandate" after another (details in **Oesterreich,** ML III, 314 ff.) enjoining strictest compliance with his orders to the very last detail. It is well to remember that in his own crown domains Ferdinand held more sway over the nobles than elsewhere, e.g., in Moravia. Hence his comparatively quick success, achieved by the most relentless methods. In this year (1527) the martyrdom of Hubmaier begins. Driven from Nikolsburg, Hubmaier entered Lower Austria where he soon was jailed and finally executed at the stake (March 1528). It was a major event in the history of Anabaptism, even though it had not the consequences which the government had hoped for from this "object lesson." The Anabaptist movement actually gained new followers. The authorities, however, were not slow in proving their determination: the Hutterite *Chronicle* reports for 1528 as many as 91 executions, 28 of them in Vienna alone.

It became obvious that the struggle against this religious "revolt" was harder than anticipated. The government was as yet not as thoroughly organized as in the 17th and 18th centuries, and the administration of the mandates by the local officials was inefficient, though often very brutal. This lack of efficiency was the real opportunity for the spread of the new Anabaptist movement. In spite of ever repeated mandates and "general orders" new groups appeared at many places. The authorities did not understand the movement, but sensed it as dangerous because it challenged the rising princely absolutism ("one prince, one church"). The shortcomings of government and church, however, in allowing all the corruption in the parishes such as absence of priests, and in the dioceses such as absence of bishops, not to speak of the immorality of the clergy at large, were at first not recognized and remedied.

Roving bands of constables on horseback hunted down the Anabaptists but with little success. It became clear that more systematic work was needed. About the time of Hubmaier's execution the government decided to entrust the fight against the new "sect" to a specially appointed "provost" (head of military police) with full authority, Dietrich von Hartitsch (*q.v.*) of ill repute, who thus became the first professional Anabaptist hunter. He was appointed by the King Ferdinand himself. The *Chronicle* of the Hutterites has but this to say about him, "He brought much affliction and grief upon the Brethren. Whenever he caught one in the fields or on the road, he had him beheaded. But those in the villages who refused to give up their faith, he hanged on the door post. That prompted many to emigrate to Nikolsburg, while others fled with wife and children into the mountains, leaving their homes behind. . . ." Many did not know whither to turn, but very few were intimidated. This is confirmed by a government report to the king that "the Anabaptists show no dread but rather a readiness to be arrested. They occasionally denounce themselves to save others. They confess willingly, without fear and without torture. They do not listen to instructors (clergymen). Few backslide, the majority seem to desire death. And even if one recants he cannot be trusted in the long run. Neither teaching nor punishment shows tangible success." And yet, the executions continued with all their senseless brutality. In 1528 the martyrdom of 18 brethren is reported in one place alone, viz., the town of Lengbach (Lembach) in Lower Austria. It was the same at many other places.

Persuasion by good priests might have effected better results, but the government could not find capable clergymen for this work. Moreover, the noble lords did not give much support to this work, for they appreciated the Brethren as most valuable farmers or farmhands whom they disliked to lose. The government had also an eye on the sale of "heretical books" (tracts), which sale was punishable by death. From Hutterite manuscript books we know that a good many Anabaptist tracts must then have circulated all over the country, in spite of all surveillance.

At long last the government received the strongest legal support: the Imperial Diet of Speyer in 1529 published its far-reaching decrees against the Anabaptists with the name "Constitution of Speyer." This gave the legal basis for nation-wide persecution. Attendance at Holy Mass was supervised from now on, and the reception of the Sacrament was ordered and recorded. Whoever stayed away came under suspicion and had to be reported to the authorities. The same held true for the supervision of the confessional.

The Münsterite tragedy of 1534-35 gave the government new impetus and justification for intensified persecutions. Now they claimed to believe that the Austrian Anabaptists taught basically the same doctrine as the Münsterites, hiding it only from the inquisitors. The truth, however, was that at that time the indigenous Anabaptist movement in Lower Austria had already died out. The martyrs whom we will meet from now on are but Hutterite missionaries on their witnessing journeys everywhere. In 1536, three such brethren were caught in the city of Vienna, and soon afterwards executed: Hieronymus Käls (*q.v.*), Hans Oberecker (*q.v.*), and Michel Behem or Seifensieder (*q.v.*). Their story is told in great detail in the *Chronicle* and is worth reading. Two more Hutterite Brethren were caught in this year: Jörg Fasser (*q.v.*) and Leonhard Lanzenstiel (*q.v.*). They soon managed to escape, but in 1537 Fasser was caught again, near Pöggstall in Lower Austria, where he had worked

with great success. He was executed, but his activities led many people to start for Moravia to join the brotherhood.

In December 1539 the provost Hartitsch could finally boast of a major strike. This was the famous attack upon an Anabaptist meeting at Steinabrunn (*q.v.*) in Lower Austria, near the Moravian border. One hundred and thirty-six brethren were captured and were collectively taken into custody in the near-by castle of Falkenstein (*q.v.*). The fate of these brethren is a true epic and deserves wider attention. The Hutterite *Chronicle* as well as Loserth's great study of the Moravian Anabaptists dwell with much detail upon this story. Many of the brethren escaped later on, but a great number of them were still sold as galley slaves to Andrea Doria, Doge of Venice, to serve on his naval vessels in the Mediterranean.

Ever more Brethren turned from the German lands toward Moravia, the "promised land" of Anabaptism. Their route led them along the Danube up to the city of Krems (*q.v.*), whence they turned north. Naturally the authorities became soon alerted and watched all the boats landing in Krems or near by to catch the Anabaptists. Their success, however, seems to have been but moderate when the growth of the Hutterite colonies at this time is considered.

The 1540's brought renewed activities by the authorities, and increased suffering for the Brethren. Vienna was again the scene of pathetic martyrdom—or supreme triumph—by committed disciples. Oswald Glaidt (*q.v.*), Antoni Keim (*q.v.*), and Hans Staudach (*q.v.*) sealed their faith with their blood in 1545. Again it is a story worth retelling, and reference is made here to the articles in this ENCYCLOPEDIA on these cases. It seems that Vienna was still considered by the brethren as a place worth trying to win converts in. In the same year the brother Andreas Kofler (*q.v.*) of Tirol was beheaded for his faith in Ybbs on the Danube (Lower Austria). Also the Carinthian brother Michael Madschidl, his wife and their companion Gurzheim were kept in prison in Vienna for several years. While Gurzheim finally was drowned in the Danube, Madschidl and his wife managed to escape to Moravia. Many more Brethren were lying in chains in Vienna. The *Chronicle* tells us that the women were later freed, but the men were led to the block. They were of good cheer and sang so that the executioner felt sorry for them and carried out his assignment "with a heavy heart."

But Ferdinand was tireless in enjoining strictest compliance to his mandates, calling constantly for greater alertness and energy. The Austrian national archives abound in official correspondence in this matter, and one is amazed at the minute details which found Ferdinand's attention. For instance, he reprimanded certain noble lords for employing Anabaptist farmhands for making hay. Persecution continued, mainly by the ill-famed Dietrich von Hartitsch. The *Chronicle* has this to say about the situation: "They drove the brethren from Moravia to Hungary, from Hungary to

Moravia, from Moravia to Austria, from Austria to Moravia. In summa, God-fearing people have nowhere to go." And yet the brotherhood in Moravia grew (tolerated by the nobles there) and was increased even by many newcomers from Austria.

But eventually the Catholic reform (or Counter Reformation) became more effective. Soon after 1550 the Jesuits came to Austria to undertake its re-catholization. The noble lords were now under still heavier pressure to yield to government orders. Likewise the Catholic Church as a whole began to intensify her reform work, improving the spiritual care of the parishes. Thus Anabaptism in Lower Austria declined and eventually vanished altogether during the second half of the 16th century. In 1622 the Hutterites were expelled from near-by Moravia, and only in Hungary (i.e., Slovakia) did Anabaptism find a precarious refuge up to the 18th century.

2. *Upper Austria.* The story of Anabaptism in Upper Austria is somewhat different from that in its sister province. In Lower Austria, the most important factor in the vicissitudes of Anabaptism was the close proximity of Moravia. From here the Hutterites exerted a noticeable influence, entering the borderland whenever possible. Upper Austria, on the contrary, is rather open toward Bavaria, whence strong Anabaptist forces influenced the life of the neighboring land. In fact, a large part of today's Upper Austria, namely, the Inn district, was in the 16th and 17th centuries a part of Bavaria proper (with the area of the cities of Schärding, *q.v.,* Braunau, and Ried, *q.v.,* all so well known for their Anabaptist activities).

As was mentioned earlier, the outstanding Anabaptist leaders Hans Hut (*q.v.*) and Leonhard Schiemer (*q.v.*), who had come from Nikolsburg to Vienna in 1527, did not stay long in that city. Soon they moved on toward Upper Austria, making the old steel city of Steyr (*q.v.*) on the Enns River the very center of their missionary activities. It is not beyond possibility that this city had been a center of Waldensian activities in the 15th century, thus preparing the soil for later evangelical work. This is at least the contention of Alexander Nicoladoni in his book, *Johannes Bünderlin* (Berlin, 1893), following ideas first proposed by Dr. Ludwig Keller (*q.v.*). Also Hubmaier is said to have preached here in Steyr prior to his coming to Nikolsburg. In 1527 Hans Hut arrived, and soon after him Schiemer, the erstwhile monk, himself a native of Upper Austria. Also the well-known brother Thomas Waldhauser (*q.v.*), a former Catholic priest from Lower Austria, worked for some time in this city before moving on to Moravia (where he was burned at the stake in 1528). As assistants of Hans Hut are named Hieronymus von Mansee and Eucarius Binder (*q.v.*), both of whom had to die at the stake in Salzburg (see **Lang, Matthäus**). Of the "four apostles" chosen by Hut, Schiemer became the most successful missioner in Upper Austria of that time, until he, too, met the

fate of nearly all early leaders—martyrdom (1528). Regarding the Anabaptist activities in Steyr, it is worth noting that they were directed mainly toward urban lower middle class elements such as craftsmen and working men in the steel mills, in contrast to the situation in other countries (Tirol or Switzerland) where Anabaptism found most of its adherents among the rural population, the peasants.

From Steyr Hut went on to Linz (*q.v.*), the provincial capital, where in 1528 he won Ambrosius Spittelmayr (*q.v.*), a man who later became well known as a leader of those brethren who did not renounce the use of the sword (*Schwertler*). Hut did not stay long in Linz but went on to Freistadt (*q.v.*) in northern Upper Austria, where he was particularly successful. A strong Anabaptist group was established there, which caused much concern to the provincial government. Hans Schlaffer (*q.v.*), a Catholic priest in near-by Kefermarkt, was soon won for the cause of Anabaptism. Although an early martyrdom did not leave him much time for "work," he must be counted among the outstanding representatives of Anabaptism of the early period, and his writings, together with those of L. Schiemer, were much read by the Hutterites and are still extant in many of their manuscript books. From Freistadt Hut turned farther west, going through Schärding, Braunau, and Passau into Bavaria (Augsburg) until he, too, met the fate of nearly all the Anabaptist leaders, death as a martyr.

Even before Hut's arrival in Linz, Anabaptist groups must have existed there, for we learn that in 1526 Hans Bünderlin (*q.v.*), the humanistically trained native of this city, had become an active elder of the local brotherhood. But soon he had to flee, and some years later severed his connections with the Brethren altogether. His work was continued by the schoolmaster Leonhard Freisleben, called Eleutherobios (*q.v.*), who is said to have been baptized by Hans Hut. In 1528, he, too, had to flee, joining his brother Christoph Freisleben, former schoolmaster of Wels, Upper Austria, in his exile. The next elder of the brotherhood in Linz was Wolfgang Brandhuber (*q.v.*), the outstanding representative of early Anabaptism in this area. His activities all over Upper Austria and the adjoining bishopric of Passau left deep marks. His assistant was Hans Mittermaier (*q.v.*), in the *Chronicle* called Niedermaier, who had just recently come to Linz from the famous, yet ill-fated martyrs' synod of Augsburg (1527). In 1529, the entire Linz congregation came to a tragic end with the martyrdom of the two elders and 75 brethren.

Persecution set in in Upper Austria at about the same time as in Lower Austria (1527). From government archive records we learn of Anabaptist groups in many places such as Gmunden (*q.v.*), where Peter Riedemann (*q.v.*) lay in chains for three years, Lembach (*q.v.*), Mauthausen (*q.v.*), and Ried (*q.v.*). The story is about the same everywhere: mandates by Ferdinand, decrees by the provincial diet or the Estates, roving bands of constables, trials, executions. And yet the brotherhood groups persisted. The Catholic Church was in a deplorable state, in no way giving spiritual help or guidance to its parishioners; good priests were rare; many parishes had no priests at all or very ignorant ones; the dioceses were without episcopal supervision. Ferdinand again recognized the need for more systematic procedure against the Anabaptists. This time he sent his capable jurist Magister Wolfgang Künigl (*q.v.*) as chief prosecutor to Upper Austria to take care of the Anabaptist trials in the cities of Steyr and Freistadt. (The local judges had been too lenient toward the Brethren.) Among the defendants were craftsmen but also clergymen who had turned away from Catholicism, first to Lutheranism, and then to Anabaptism. The procedure was strictly prescribed, particularly in cases of recantation. Künigl, himself of mild nature, soon understood why the royal mandates were of so little effect. He suggested to Ferdinand certain alleviations of the utterly inhuman and repulsive requirements to be applied in case an Anabaptist was ready to return to the official church. But Ferdinand, narrow in outlook and understanding, was unrelenting and did not allow any softening of the stipulations of his "mercy." J. Loserth (*ML* II, 316) gives a detailed description of this so-called *Horber Busse,* the penance as prescribed for the first time in Horb in Württemberg for those who recanted. For some years Steyr still remained a major center of Anabaptist activities, but the fervor of the 1520's was no longer observable. The great leaders were by now all dead.

From 1528 onward the Hutterite *Chronicle* records a great number of martyrs in nearly all places mentioned above. Peter Riedemann (*q.v.*), the author of the great *Rechenschaft,* was kept as prisoner in Gmunden, Upper Austria, for several years. In his prison cell he drew up the document now known as *Gmundener Rechenschaft.* He escaped from his bonds only through exceptional circumstances (1532). In 1529 the brotherhood of Linz was destroyed as reported above. And so trials and affliction were without bounds. Many lower courts were loath to pass sentence, and tried to evade doing so by many means. But the authorities became ever more intent and stern, urging a "total" solution.

When, in 1535, the great persecution set in also in Moravia, many Brethren began their trek back to their native countries of Bavaria, Württemberg, and the Rhineland. These Brethren took their route along the Danube, and had to pass through the two Austrian archduchies. Among these returning Brethren were also the followers of Philip Plener (*q.v.*), the so-called Philipites (*q.v.*). Some of them stopped their march back in Upper Austria, hoping to be able to carry on their brotherhood in this country. We meet them soon again when Riedemann became interested in them. Others went on, but were caught in the episcopal city of Passau and thrown into a deep dungeon. It was this group which in the dungeon of the castle of Passau composed the oldest hymns of the *Ausbund* (1535-40).

Although the Anabaptist movement gradually died out in the cities it continued for some time in smaller places. Since these brotherhood groups went more and more into hiding, we learn about their life mainly through the Hutterite *Chronicle.* Here we find, for instance, under the year 1537, a lengthy *Sendschreiben an die Brüder im Land ober der Enns,* an epistle to those Philipites who had broken away from their former leader and were now ready for a closer connection with the Hutterites. They had settled down in Upper Austria, but soon found themselves involved in many internal troubles, since strong leadership was lacking. They therefore sent a brother to the communities in Moravia asking for advice about organization and discipline. Peter Riedemann, the *Chronicle* reports, wrote the letter and gave it to the messenger, "to warn the brethren against further damage." In the next year, 1538, Riedemann came personally to Upper Austria to visit these former Philipite settlements, helping them organize their communities along Hutterite patterns. In 1539, he looked them up again while on his way to Hesse. Also the brother Christoph Gschäl from Moravia, engaged on a missionary trip, stopped with these brotherhood groups in 1539 and again in 1541, urging them to join the Hutterite brotherhood in Moravia. It seems that he met with but little success. From the text of the *Chronicle* it becomes obvious that these Upper Austrian (Philipite) groups were a real concern to the Hutterites, who felt themselves in a sense responsible for all Anabaptist groups anywhere in Austria. Some of these former Philipites actually went to Moravia and became Hutterites, while the others "ran away and joined the world" (*die Anderen aber sind verronnen und haben sich der Welt zugesellt*). "In this way," the *Chronicle* continues, "the congregation and meeting in Upper Austria ceased and came to an end."

But individual witnesses to the Anabaptist cause continued to appear in the following period. For instance the brother Hans Blüetl (*q.v.*) was burned at the stake in Ried in the Inn territory in 1545. His story is told in great detail in the *Chronicle* as a great example, for "he went to the place of execution with a laughing mouth." In general, however, the Estates of Upper Austria were right in reporting to the emperor in 1554 that the region "was no more infested with the deceptive sects of Anabaptists, Sacramentalists, and the like." The relentlessness of the Habsburgs and the growing Counter Reformation of the Catholic Church (after 1545) had achieved a full triumph. Anabaptism as a living force had disappeared from the two Austrian provinces.

The archives contain still later records about Anabaptist trials, mainly in Steyr, Schärding, and Ried. In the latter city two brethren were beheaded for their faith even as late as 1605. But all these later victims were, as a rule, but missionaries passing through the country and leaving hardly any local influence. All in all, between 150 and 180 Brethren suffered martyrdom in Upper Austria, of which number about 100 died in the years 1528 to 1530 alone. As for Lower Austria the *Chronicle* reports a sum total of 105 martyrs up to 1542. One may assume that this figure did not essentially increase in the later period. (See **Hapsburg.**)   R.F.

ML III, *"Niederösterreich,"* 243; *"Oberösterreich,"* 285; and *Oesterreich,* 314; the Hutterite *Chronicle* (any edition); G. Loesche, *Gesch. des Prot. in Oesterreich* (Leipzig, 1930); Th. Wiedemann, *Gesch. der Ref. im Lande unter der Enns* (Vienna, 1879); J. Loserth, "Wiedertäufer in Niederösterreich von ihren Anfängen bis zum Tode Hubmaiers," *Bl. für die Landeskunde v. Niederösterreich* (1899) 417-35, and all the other works by Loserth about Hubmaier and the Anabaptists in Moravia; J. Jäkel, *Kirchliche und religiöse Zustände in Freistadt während des Ref.-Zeitalters* (Freistadt, *Jahresbericht des Staatsgymnasiums,* 1889-90); *idem,* "Zur Gesch. der Wiedertäufer in Oberösterreich und speziell in Freistadt," *47te Bericht des Museums Francisco-Carolinum* (Linz, 1889); *idem,* "Zur Frage der Entstehung der Täufergemeinden in Oberösterreich," *Jahresbericht des Staatsgymnasiums zu Freistadt, Ob. Oest.,* 1895; then the literature about Hans Hut, Joh. Bünderlin, and Eleutherobios (see these articles); Prevenhuber, *Annales Styrenses* (Nürnberg, 1740) 233-41; K. Schornbaum, *Quellen zur Gesch. der Wiedertäufer,* II; *Markgraftum Brandenburg* (Leipzig, 1934) contain also some pertinent material.

Austro-Sylvius, P. J. (Dutch: P. J. Semmes van Suyderwoude), year of birth 1575, died 1647, studied theology at the University of Leiden and was afterwards Reformed pastor at Hoogcarspel, Wijdenes, and Venhuizen, all three in the Dutch province of North Holland. Among his numerous writings one book is important for Mennonite History: *Grondige ende clare vertooninghe van het onderscheydt in de voornaemste hooftstucken der Christelijcke religie tusschen de Gereformeerde ende de Wederdooperen* (Enckhuizen, 1637, second edition 1647) (thorough and distinct indication of the differences in the principal points of the Christian religion between the Reformed and the Mennonites).

The motive of this book was as follows: at the (Reformed) synod of North Holland the "blasphemous teachings" of Jacques Outerman (*q.v.*) were brought up for discussion. The synod was of the opinion that those teachings "and the other errors of the Mennonites" should be refuted and charged Austro-Sylvius with the task. When the work made little progress and the author complained that the charge was too difficult for him, the synod decided that Abraham á Dooreslaer (*q.v.*) should assist him. (*Biogr. Wb.* I, 270-74.)   vDZ.

Autonomy of the Congregation, the freedom of the local congregation, without the supervision and overriding control of a general agency of the brotherhood, to manage its own internal affairs such as formulation of a confession of faith, choice of ministers, determination of qualifications for membership, forms of worship, character of discipline, etc., in effect a congregational church polity. Without doubt such local autonomy was characteristic of the Anabaptist movement from the beginning, with certain limitations to be noted later, and has characterized European Mennonitism throughout its history until the present, with the exception of certain small groups. The development of the conference

system everywhere among European Mennonites in the 19th century, in Holland as early as about 1580, has not seriously modified this autonomy. Exceptions are the Mennonite Brethren (founded 1860 in Russia) and the Baden-Württemberg-Bavaria Conference in Germany (organized 1843). The latter conference actually has the most rigid control of its some 20 congregations, considering all to be in effect one large congregation (*Gesamtgemeinde*) and the ministers to be serving the entire group even though with local preaching responsibility. The entire ministerial body of this group meets quarterly and regulates almost everything in the life of the congregation including the discipline of individual members. The Mennonite Brethren Conference in Russia (organized 1872) did not have quite such complete control but was actually a supervening authority, in that local congregational self-government was limited to minor matters. The Hutterian Brotherhood of course had very little autonomy for its individual Bruderhofs.

In America the autonomy of the local congregation has been maintained completely only among the Old Order Amish, the General Conference Mennonite Church, and certain very conservative groups in Manitoba. Elsewhere the development of the conference or synodical system has resulted in varying degrees of control by the conference (either general or district) over the local church. In the Lancaster Conference (MC) for instance there is no local autonomy except in the election of ministers. In the other district conferences of the Mennonite Church (MC) a small and variable amount of congregational autonomy may still exist. An interesting development in Manitoba is the retention of the unified congregational organization for an entire large settlement. Thus the Bergthal Church, with over 3,200 baptized members, 15 meetinghouses, and 20 ministers, larger than all the national or regional Mennonite conferences in Europe except that of the Netherlands, still considers itself to be one congregation with a single ministerial body and one elder, only recently assisted by a co-elder. This actually means no autonomy for any of the local groups. The same is true of the somewhat smaller Rudnerweide and Sommerfeld groups in Manitoba and Saskatchewan.

Local autonomy has however always been in practice limited by (1) powerful overriding common traditions, confessions of faith, and other declarations of principles and practices adopted by special general meetings, the occasional meetings of elders or ministers such as those of Goch (1545), Wismar (1553), Strasbourg (1556), Amsterdam (Waterlanders) (1581), Hofingen (1630), Essingen (1779), Ibersheim (1803), etc., (2) the action of powerful leaders such as Menno Simons, in forcing the discipline or unfrocking of dissident ministers (Adam Pastor, 1550), (3) the withholding of communion fellowship from ministers or members of diverging congregations.

An illustration of how a seemingly complete autonomy can be partially undermined is the actual situation in Holland, where autonomy is a deeply rooted and carefully nourished principle. Here it is in practice (though not legally impossible) almost impossible for a congregation to choose as its minister one who is not a graduate of the Amsterdam Theological Seminary or its equivalent since smaller congregations are dependent upon general conference or church agency sources for necessary subsidies to ministerial salaries, which subsidies are withheld from a lay or insufficiently trained minister, who then is also not welcomed into the ministerial fellowship. For further discussion see **Congregation, Conference, Polity.**   H.S.B.

Aux Convers: see **Les Convers.**

Avoidance, in German *Meidung,* popularized by some American newspapers as the "Mite." Avoidance relates to the break in fellowship, religious and social, which is occasioned by excommunication (*q.v.*) from the brotherhood, and which amounts to almost complete social ostracism. (The term "ban" is properly applied only to the excommunication and not to the ensuing avoidance.) The New Testament places much stress on the intimate life of fellowship and sharing which shall characterize the life of the members of the Christian Church. On such a premise, when anyone grows cold in the Christian life and finally reverts completely to a life of sin, it naturally becomes the duty of the congregation to remove such a person from the fellowship of the church. Avoidance is the name given to the practice of having no fellowship with such excommunicated and impenitent sinners. The New Testament instruction is "not to eat" with such a person, "not to keep company" with him (I Cor. 5:11). The term "avoidance" is taken from Rom. 16:17 where the apostle instructs the believers to "avoid" those who work against the peace of the church. Paul told the Thessalonian Christians to "have no company" with those who disobeyed his epistle (II Thess. 3:14). II John 10 advises not to "receive into the house (neither bid God speed) him that brings not true doctrine."

The man who introduced the practice of strict avoidance or shunning of false or erring brethren into the life of the Anabaptists was Obbe Philips (*q.v.*) of the Netherlands about 1533-35. Obbe had to deal with the hazard of the fanatical Münsterites (*q.v.*), and in order to cope with this danger to his immature flock he instituted a severe practice of avoidance; his followers were to have absolutely nothing to do with the Münster emissaries. When Menno Simons united with the Obbenites in 1536 he also adopted the teaching on avoidance and taught it throughout his life. In his *Loving Admonition* (1541) Menno insisted that all excommunicated persons are to be shunned, "whether it be father or mother, sister or brother, husband or wife, son or daughter, without any respect of persons." Shunning is taught also in the Amsterdam Mennonite Confession of 1627 entitled *Scriptural Instruction,* in the Amsterdam Confession of 1630 written by Jan Cents, in the Thirty-Three Articles of Peter Jans Twisck (*q.v.*) (Article XXIX), and in the Dordrecht Eighteen Articles of 1632 (Article XVII). It should be noted that this doctrine was held in

an effort to be absolutely loyal to every instruction in the Word of God. It was not intended to be a harsh and cold legalistic punishment lacking love and kindness. This is set forth carefully in the Dordrecht Confession of Faith: ". . . such moderation and Christian discretion be used, that such shunning and reproof may not be conducive to his ruin, but serviceable to his amendment. For should he be in need, hungry, thirsty, naked, sick, or visited by some other affliction, we are in duty bound, according to the doctrine and practice of Christ and His apostles, to render him aid and assistance, as necessity may require; otherwise the shunning of him might be rather conducive to his ruin than to his amendment (I Thess. 5:14).

"Therefore we must not treat such offenders as enemies, but exhort them as brethren, in order thereby to bring them to a knowledge of their sins and to repentance; so that they may again become reconciled to God and the church, and be received and admitted into the same—thus exercising love towards them, as is becoming" (II Thess. 3:15).

Menno Simons frequently expressed his concern that avoidance be not carried to harsh extremes. Rather, it was to be observed "with prayer, tears, and a compassionate spirit, out of great love," its purpose being the winning again of the impenitent one. In 1550 Menno wrote: "Such unmerciful, cruel opinion and practice I hate from all my heart . . . . For my heart can not consent to such unmerciful treatment which exceeds the cruelty of the common heathen and Turks . . . . It is contrary to all teaching of the New Testament, and contrary to the Spirit and nature of Christ, according to which all the Scriptures of the New Testament should be judged and understood."

One of the problems which caused difficulty among the early Dutch Mennonites in the practice of shunning was whether or not to require marital avoidance of an excommunicated spouse. Menno Simons was always cautious about trying to enforce marital avoidance. At the height of his powers in 1550 he advocated leniency in this matter in case the parties involved did not feel inclined to practice marital avoidance. A case in point was one Swaen Rutgers, a sister in the Emden congregation who did not feel that she ought to shun her excommunicated husband. There were some who desired to excommunicate her also. Menno objected strenuously, indicating that he would never give his consent to such a course. As late as 1558, three years before his death, Menno was still of the same mind to be lenient in cases where avoidance would involve one's spouse.

In contrast with the Dutch Obbenites and Mennonites, the Swiss Brethren never practiced avoidance in the strict sense. They did seek to obey the passage "not to eat" with an excommunicated sinner, but applied it to the communion table rather than to all social fellowship. This lack of shunning was the chief point of church practice in which the early Swiss Brethren differed from their spiritual cousins in the Low Countries. In Menno's late years (1556) he was visited for two days by two Swiss Brethren ministers of the Rhineland, Zylis and Lemke, who hoped to be able to come to a common understanding with Menno on the subject of avoidance. This common understanding was not reached during the visit. Following their return home the two men wrote to Menno, also on the subject of avoidance. Menno replied with a small book, *Thorough Instruction on Excommunication,* in which he argued eloquently, even appealing to the Latin version of the Scriptures in his desire to show that excommunicated persons should be shunned.

Menno's treatise did not have the desired result, however. Zylis and Lemke decided to by-pass Menno and address themselves directly to the congregations of the Low Countries. In their unfortunate epistle they brought personal charges against Menno, accusing him of being fickle, unfit to be a leader, a man whose writings were self-contradictory. They hoped by this method to wean the Mennonites of the Netherlands away from Menno and his doctrine of shunning, although Menno was fully supported by such other leading elders as Dirk Philips (*q.v.*) and Leenaert Bouwens (*q.v.*). Grieved and aroused, Menno then wrote his last book in January 1559, entitled, *A Thorough Reply to the Slander, Defamation, Backbiting, Unseasoned, and Bitter Words of Zylis and Lemke . . . .* Two years later when Menno died, the difference between the Dutch and the Swiss was still unresolved.

In addition to his writings in the case of Zylis and Lemke, and his incidental discussions on the subject Menno was the author of two specific tracts on avoidance, viz., *A Fundamental Doctrine or an Account of Excommunication, Ban, Exclusion* (1541, found in Engl. ed. of 1871, I, 239-68) and *A Kind Admonition or Instruction from the Word of God . . . Concerning the Shunning and Separation of the Unfaithful Brethren* (1558, in Engl. ed. of 1871, II, 441-49). The first of these was included in all later editions of the *Foundation-Book.*

Dirk Philips (d. 1568) was even more sharp than Menno Simons in his advocacy and practice of avoidance. His *Enchiridion* (first Dutch ed. 1564, many Dutch and German reprints) contains the tract *Een lieffelycke Vermaninghe (van den ban)* first printed in 1558, a most vigorous defense of strict avoidance. A second writing on the subject, *Naeghelaten Schrift van Ban ende Mydinghe,* first published in Dutch in 1602 attached to his *Van die Echt der Christenen,* was also reprinted in both Dutch and German.

Throughout the 16th and 17th centuries the conservative groups among the Dutch Mennonites continued the practice of avoidance. Among the Mennonites of Prussia and Russia it was continued into the 18th and 19th centuries. The Old Colony Mennonites, the Bergthaler, Sommerfelder, and Kleine Gemeinde in Canada, Mexico, and Paraguay, all of direct Prussian-Russian descent, still practice avoidance more or less strictly.

In 1693 trouble arose among the Swiss and Alsatian congregations chiefly over the matter of avoidance. A young elder named Jakob Ammann (*q.v.*) desired to introduce the practice of shunning to Swiss churches. He was supported by some ministers, and opposed by others. The end was a division between the old-line Brethren and the new "Amish." Two and a half centuries later the Old Order Amish of North America still practice the shunning for which Jakob Ammann contended. It is not definitely known where Ammann got his belief in avoidance, but it is probable that he had access to the writings of Menno Simons and was influenced by them. (The first German edition of Menno's *Foundation Book* was in 1575, which contained a tract on avoidance.) Also it should be noted that the elders of the churches of Alsace at a meeting in Ohnenheim in 1660 adopted the Dordrecht Confession of 1632 with its article on shunning. Dirk Philips' *Enchiridion* (first German edition 1715) became very popular among the Amish because of its strong teaching on avoidance.

The most continuous and consistent practice of avoidance is that by the Old Order Amish in the United States, who have continued its rigid practice down to the present day throughout their entire brotherhood, which has over 150 congregations with nearly 15,000 baptized members. The customary practice includes refusal to eat at the same table, even within the family, the refusal of ordinary social intercourse, the refusal to work together in farming operations, etc. The ban is imposed by the bishop with the consent of the congregation, and is applied even to cases where the only "sin" is transfer to another less strict Amish or Mennonite congregation. On the point of avoidance of such members who joined other more liberal Amish or Mennonite groups, before 1900 this practice was confined to the communities east of Ohio and the Swiss Amish of Allen Co. and Adams Co., Ind. More recently this practice has been introduced in some communities west of Pennsylvania, and has caused considerable dissension. In fact the practice of avoidance has been the cause of dissension in many Amish communities at various times, with occasional mutual shunning by factional groups.

From the economic point of view, the "avoidance" amounts to a boycott, and on this ground has several times been challenged in court by excommunicated former Amish members, who have brought legal action claiming damages. The most noted case was that of Yoder vs. Helmuth, Nov. 4-7, 1947, at Wooster, Ohio, which is reported and commented on in full in *MQR* XXIII (April 1949) 76-98. John Holdeman, the founder of the group which now bears the name Church of God in Christ, Mennonite, was once sued at law by an excommunicated member in Williams Co., Ohio. This group still practices avoidance, though not as rigidly as the Old Order Amish.

The Reformed Mennonites, who also still practice avoidance, likewise suffered at least one lawsuit at Chambersburg, Pa.   J.C.W.

Dordrecht Confession of Faith, Art. 17; M. Gascho "The Amish Division of 1693-1697 in Alsace," *MQR* XI (Oct. 1937) 235-66; *Menno Simons' Complete Works* (Elkhart, 1871) I, 239-68; II, 121-37; II, 283-95; Daniel Kauffman, *Mennonite Cyclopedic Dictionary* (Scottdale, 1937): *Shunning;* John Horsch, *Mennonites in Europe*

(Scottdale, 1950) Chap. 38; John B. Mast, *The Letters of the Amish Division* of 1693-1711, Pub. by C. J. Schlabach (Oregon City, 1950); Peter Rideman, *Account of Our Religion, Doctrine and Faith* (1565) (1950) 132; Gerrit Roosen, *Christian Conversation on Saving Faith* (a catechism), Question 128; *Mart. Mir. E. passim* (see Index, 1151); J. H. Yoder, "Caesar and the *Meidung*," *MQR* XXIII (April 1949) 76-98.

Axwyk, a Mennonite church which in the 18th century joined the church at Middelie in the Dutch province of North Holland. Leenaert Bouwens baptized seven persons here. In 1717 Peter Claas Huyberts was preacher (*DB* 1887, 117 f.; *ML* I, 100).

K.V.

Ayers Ranch, a Hutterite Bruderhof at Grass Range, Mont., established in 1944 by the brethren of the Huron (South Dakota) Bruderhof, which was sold. Preacher Johann Stahl with several families settled the Ayers Ranch commune. In 1947 it numbered 53 souls with 20 baptized members. It is a *Darius-Leut* (*q.v.*) colony.

D.D.

Aylmer (Ont.) United Missionary Church was organized in 1900 under the leadership of Sisters Shantz and Ball. The first meetinghouse was built in 1901. In 1950 the congregation, a member of the Ontario United Missionary Church Conference, had 49 members, and Donald Pugh was serving as pastor.

D.P.

B

Baard, a Mennonite congregation in the Dutch province of Friesland, about ten miles southwest of Leeuwarden. The date of its origin is not known. In the 17th century the congregation belonged to the Janjacobsgezinden (*q.v.*) and in 1640 had about 70 members. Of the 18th century the names of two of its elders are known: Hantje Broers, 1714-63, and Broer Eelkes, first as a preacher, and after the death of Hantje as elder, 1743-90. In 1779 the congregation had 60 members. In 1785 it divided with Ameland (*q.v.*) the possessions of the extinct Jan-Jacobsgezinden at Makkum (*q.v.*). It very likely united with the other Mennonites of the locality not long after 1790. The first theologically trained minister of the congregation was J. Y. Veen, 1825-29. In 1821 the Blessum (*q.v.*) congregation of 17 members merged with Baard. In 1861 the membership was 108, in 1898, 101, and in 1950, 57. In 1856 a new church was built because the old one was too small. In 1922 the congregation merged with neighboring IJtens (*q.v.*). The last minister Baard had alone was Miss M. T. Gerritsma, 1917-20. Since the merger the ministers have been living at IJtens: S. I. van Meulen, 1922-29; J. J. van Riemsdijk, 1930-40; G. M. Kosters, 1941-44; T. Hooglag, 1950- . Most of the members are farmers. vDZ.

J. Loosjes, "Jan Jacobsz en de Jan-Jacobsgezinden," *Archief voor Kerkgesch.* XI (The Hague, 1914) 42 f.; *ML* I, 101.

Baarn (pop. 16,434 in 1947, with 200 Mennonites), a beautifully located town in the Dutch province of Utrecht, which has developed rapidly through the influx of residents of Amsterdam (pop. 7,000 in 1914, nearly 17,000 in 1950). A Mennonite circle (*kring*) was formed here on Jan. 20, 1909, with about 50 members (increased to 77 by 1915). The chairman of the executive committee of the circle was a member of the church council of the Hilversum congregation in an advisory capacity. Services were held once a month in the hall of the *Nut* building; first service on June 20, 1909. Catechetical instruction was first given by the Hilversum minister. T. O. Hylkema, then at Amersfoort, was assistant pastor 1931-36; then J. W. van Stuyvenberg, a retired minister of Amsterdam, 1936-43. In 1946 J. E. van Brakel was called as pastor, followed by A. J. Meerdink-van den Ban in 1948.

Meanwhile the circle had organized as a congregation (Jan. 10, 1921) with a membership of about 100; in 1927 it was 140; and in 1950, 163. A church was built in 1927. The congregation has an active Sunday school as well as organizations for the women, men, and young people. Besides the church services there are regular meetings in the homes. In the neighboring Soest, where a number of Mennonites are living, services are held once a month; this subsidiary also has a Sunday school and a women's organization. (*DB* 1908, 206; 1909, 187; *ML* I, 101.) vDZ.

Baburka: see **Burwalde.**

Baccarat is a city of perhaps 10,000 pop., approximately 40 miles southeast of Nancy in the Meurthe Valley of French-speaking Lorraine, known chiefly for its production of crystal and cut-glass. A congregation of Amish Mennonite derivation takes its name from the city, where its meetings have been held since 1882, in a room rented on the property of one of the members in the hamlet of St. Christophe. Before that time meeetings had been held in homes. The date of the organization of the congregation is unknown, but it was probably formed during the first half of the 19th century by members of the congregations of Salm and Hang in the Vosges and Bitsche and Zweibrücken in the Saar Valley. The common family names have been Salzmann, Egli, Sommer, Haury, Kremer, Neuhauser, Ropp, Backer, Rüfenacht (written Riebenacht or Rouvenacht), and Schmoucker. The first known elder of the congregation, Pierre Sommer of Mignéville, died in 1880. The French language was introduced between 1875 and 1880 under the leadership of Jean Sommer, who was also responsible for a re-edition of the catechism booklet (translated from the Zweibrücken catechism) in 1898.

Since its formation in 1907 a branch of this congregation, numbering originally 26, meets quarterly in Gerbéviller for those members living farther west. The membership decreased steadily from 150 in 1888 to 75 in 1930; in 1952 there are approximately 40 members remaining, including children. Meetings are held monthly at St. Christophe, being served chiefly by the traveling ministers of the conference. (Pierre Sommer, "Assemblee de Baccarat," *Christ Seul,* Feb. 1931, 6-9; *ML* I, 101.) J.H.Y.

Bacharach, a district (Oberamt) in the Palatinate, where, according to an edict of Nov. 6, 1588, there were Anabaptists, whom the officials had not found.

W. Rotscheidt, "Wiedertäufer in Bacharach," in *Monatshefte für rheinische Kirchengesch.,* 1909, 218 f.; Chr. Hege, *Die Täufer in der Kurpfalz* (Frankfurt, 1908) 145.

Bachman (Bachmann), a Mennonite family name of Swiss-German origin, mentioned as early as 1672 in a letter written from Freisheim, Germany, which identified the family with Bernese Anabaptists. The family evidently originated at Bottenstein in the canton of Aargau. From Switzerland members of the family moved to the Palatinate. As early as 1742 Andreas Bachmann, together with other Amish immigrants, arrived in eastern Pennsylvania from the Palatinate. The family name became known later in Lebanon Co., Pa., and in near-by areas. A Zürich Bachmann was imprisoned as early as 1640.

It was in the 19th century, however, that the name became common in American Mennonite circles. Of the fourteen leading Amish names introduced among the American Mennonites during that century, C. Henry Smith lists Bachman as fourth in numerical importance. Coming from Alsace during the mid-19th century, the family settled chiefly in central Illinois.

Other members of the family who had emigrated to the Palatinate, moved from there to Galicia, and during the last quarter of the 19th century to the prairie states of America, where the name is found today. Other descendants bearing the name of Bach-mann remained in South Germany, where some are members of the Mennonite Church today.

Andrew Bachman (d. 1864) immigrated to America from Alsace in 1839. During the American Civil War he was a leading bishop in central Illinois, serving the Partridge congregation.

M.G.

P. Bachmann, *Menn. in Kleinpolen, Gedenkbuch zur Erinnerung an die Einwanderung der Menn. nach Kleinpolen (Galizien) vor 150 Jahren* (Lemberg, 1934).

Bachman Mennonite Meetinghouse was located in western Lancaster Co., Pa. Michael Baughman was an early pioneer and land speculator in Lancaster and Lebanon counties. On a large tract in the "Manorland" he gave a lot about 1760 for meeting-house and cemetery purposes. It is now known as Masonville (*q.v.*).

I.D.L.

Bachmann der Schmied (the Blacksmith) took part in the Anabaptist disputation at Wädenswil (*q.v.*) district of Zürich, Switzerland, on Jan. 26, 1613. (Geiser, *Die Taufgesinnten Gemeinden,* Karlsruhe, n.d., 372-74.) Presumably he is identical with Rudolph Bachmann (*q.v.*), who later was put in prison. (*ML* I, 102.)

vDZ.

Bachmann, Elisabeth, an Anabaptist martyr, was seized in Zürich in 1643 with two fellow believers, Elssa Bethezai and Sara Wanry. They remained steadfast in their faith and ended their lives in prison after enduring much want, misery, and wretchedness (*Mart. Mir.* D 822, E 1120; *ML* I, 101 f.).

O.H.

Bachmann, Rudolph, an aged man of Wädenswil, canton of Zürich, Switzerland, was seized in 1640 because of his faith and imprisoned. He remained true to his conviction and was therefore kept in prison to the end of his life (*Mart. Mir.* D 819, E 1118; *ML* I, 102).

O.H.

Bachmans (or Baughmans) Mennonite Church (MC), Virginia Conference, now extinct, located at Lost River, Hardy Co., W. Va. A meetinghouse was built here about 1890, Mennonite services having been held in the area for some time. Services were held there regularly until 1910 or 20 and then intermittently for a number of years. The decline was caused by most of the members moving to other places, particularly the Crest Hill Church near Wardersville, W. Va.

T.S., H.A.B.

Bachmut, a district in the Russian province of Ekaterinoslav, with highly developed industries: rich salt mines, coal mines, a mercury mine, and also factories for the manufacture of railroad ties and cars. In 1889 the Chortitza colony bought in Bachmut 13,019 dessiatines (about 32,000 acres) of Count Ignatyev, upon which seven Mennonite villages were built, viz., New York at the south railway station Zheleznaya, Leonidovka, Ekaterinovka, Romanovka, Alexeyevka, Nikolayevka, and Ignatyevka. The principal occupation of the Mennonites was farming, in which they achieved thriving prosperity. They were also engaged in industry, such as mills, factories, and tile-works, especially in New York (*q.v.*). In 1892 the Mennonites of Chortitza

established the Borissovo colony (*q.v.*) with two villages, Kondratyevka and Nikolaipol, near the south railway station Drushkovka. This land is even better than that in the Ignatyev territory. The church center of both the settlements was in New York, where the elder also resided.

The Memrik (*q.v.*) colonies formed a third settlement in Bachmut, founded in 1885 by independent Mennonite buyers from the province of Taurida. Their principal village was Memrik, about six miles west of station Zhelannaya on the Catherine Railway. The village of Alexandropol, established in 1888, was affiliated with the church at Memrik.

In the district of Bachmut many individual Mennonites owned farms and large holdings not far from the Memrik settlement, also near New York and Bachmut (*ML* I, 102).

D.E.

Backer, Adriaen (*ca.* 1636-84), married Elsje Colijn, was a member of the Waterlander Mennonite congregation at Amsterdam. He was a Dutch painter, a pupil of his uncle Jacob Adriaensz Backer (*q.v.*). For a time he stayed in Rome (1666); upon his return he introduced the baroque style into Holland by imitating Italian masters. The Rijksmuseum at Amsterdam contains four of his paintings. (Thieme-Becker, *Künstlerlexikon; Oud-Holland* XLIII, 1926, 292.)

vDZ.

Backer, Jacob Adriaensz, b. 1608 at Harlingen, Dutch province of Friesland (where his father, Adriaen Tjercksz, a baker, was a deacon of the Waterlander Mennonite Church), d. Aug. 27, 1651, at Amsterdam, was a Dutch painter. He was first a pupil of Lambert Jacobsz (*q.v.*), and later on of Rembrandt, whose way of painting he followed, without reaching the deep penetrating psychology of the master. Yet he was a painter of good reputation and his pictures were in high favor. An "Erection of the Cross" of 1633 is called a masterpiece. He chiefly painted portraits and groups (corporation and civic-guards pictures). He had many pupils, including Adriaen Backer (*q.v.*). After 1650 the quality of his pictures is inferior to his earlier ones. Many of his paintings must have been lost. He also made many drawings. There is a self-portrait of him, now in the museum of Lyons (France). About his life very little is known; likely he was unmarried.

vDZ.

K. Bauch, *Jacob Adriaensz Backer* (Berlin, 1912); *Oud-Holland* XLII (1925) 278; XLIII (1926) 289-92; W. Martin, *De Holl. Schilderkunst in de 17e Eeuw* II (1944, 3d ed.) 112-14.

Backnang, a small town in central Württemberg, Germany, 15 miles northeast of Stuttgart, location of a Mennonite refugee camp 1946-51, and a Mennonite resettlement project 1951-53, where a PAX (*q.v.*) service unit of young voluntary service men from the United States shared in the building of homes. The refugee camp, not exclusively Mennonite, contained at its peak 600 Mennonite refugees from Russia and Poland. The Mennonite Central Committee aided with much food and clothing and had personnel serving there for shorter periods of time, chiefly for processing prospective immigrants to Canada, Paraguay, and Uruguay.

The resettlement project, largely for former Danzig-area Mennonites, was operated by the settlers under German government direction and financing but with a loan from the MCC to each settler family for the necessary down payment. A unit of 10-15 American Mennonite voluntary service workers under MCC direction (Pax Services), supported totally by American Mennonite funds, contributed labor toward the construction of 10 apartment houses, housing 64 families, 1951-54.   H.S.B.

Baczko, Ludwig von, a versatile German author, b. June 8, 1756, at Lyck (East Prussia), d. March 27, 1823, at Königsberg. His father, a Catholic, of a Polish family living in Hungary, was an officer under Frederick the Great and later the owner of an estate in Prussia. He himself was first Lutheran like his mother, then Catholic, was filled with a variety of interests and blessed with a good memory, lost his vision just before completing his formal education. Nevertheless he found opportunity for a many-sided activity in Königsberg, and a permanent residence there. Religious questions occupied him throughout his life; his membership in the Catholic Church in a Protestant community somewhat impeded his progress.

For a livelihood Baczko wrote on many subjects—on history, political economy, besides literary subjects. The Mennonites received his attention in connection with the history of the locality; thus he mentions the church at Königsberg in his *Versuch einer Geschichte und Beschreibung Königsbergs* (Königsberg, 1787, 2nd ed., 1804). An independent work, a family portrait in three acts, *Die Mennoniten* (Königsberg, 1809; also in Dutch, *De Doopsgezinden,* Haarlem, 1809), serves the express purpose of "calling attention to the spirit which animates the adherents of this religious party"; the foreword lays the foundation for the benevolent description by relating several true anecdotes. *Thomas Münzer, dessen Charakter und Schicksale* (Halle and Leipzig)—now antiquated—is a historical inquiry. The travel booklet, *Reise von Posen durch das Königreich Polen und einen Teil von Russland bis an das Meer von Asow,* by Ferdinand von Baczko, published by his father, Ludwig von Baczko (Leipzig, 1821, 2nd ed. 1824), contains a detailed account of the Mennonites from Prussia living on the Molotschna.   E.C.

ADB I, 758 f.; K. Goedeke, *Grundriss der deutschen Dichtung* V (Dresden, 1893) 495 f.; Mannhardt, *Jahrbuch* 1883, 23 f.; *DB* 1884, 127-28; *ML* I, 102.

Bad Axe United Missionary Church, a small appointment of the Michigan Conference located at Bad Axe, Mich. The work was begun as a mission in 1903 and the congregation was organized in 1912. In 1950 there were 18 members and the pastor was M. S. Krake.   E.R.S.

Baden, a state in the German Confederation, where Anabaptism spread as early as the first third of the 16th century. Many Anabaptist leaders were successfully active here, e.g., Balthasar Hubmaier (*q.v.*) in 1525 as pastor in Waldshut. From Staufen near Freiburg came Michael Sattler (*q.v.*). Also in other regions which were added to Baden only in 1803-6,

the doctrines won early adherents, as in the Palatine districts of Heidelberg and Bretten, in the bishopric of Speyer (Bruchsal), in the Kinzig Valley, and in Kraichgau. According to the Baden-Pfalz volume of the *Quellen zur Geschichte der Täufer* (1951), a total of 81 places in Baden appear in the documents as having had one or more Anabaptists 1525-48 in northern (Franconian) Baden, and 33 in southern (Alemannian) Baden, although the number of regularly organized congregations was probably small; most of these Anabaptists came from the peasant classes.

The Anabaptists were also found early in the original duchy of Baden. Their too rapid growth is shown by the mandate of Dec. 15, 1527, of Margrave Philip of Baden, commanding his officials not to tolerate the Anabaptists. "We command you, with especial seriousness, to issue a public order immediately in the city and in all your villages and to proclaim that no one may submit to rebaptism, either to baptize or to be baptized; nor shall anyone adhere to Anabaptism on any other point. Nothing shall be taught or preached about it either privately or publicly. No one shall harbor its adherents (or) offer them refuge, all on penalty of body, of life, and of possessions according to the enormity of the violation of this command, in order that the wicked, erroneous, and wanton act of rebaptism may be erased and removed with its adherents. Moreover we command that all who have themselves or their children rebaptized, or teach and preach publicly shall be seized. The officials shall be told forthwith what punishment is to be applied. And in this you shall not appear careless or negligent" (*Ztscht für Kirchengesch.* XI, 1890, 319).

The rigor with which this decree was carried out is shown by the chronicles of the Hutterian Brethren in Moravia, to whom many refugees from Baden fled. In a report drawn up in 1581 it is shown that in Baden 20 Anabaptists were executed for their faith, in Durlach 12, in Pforzheim 2, and in Bühl 2 (Beck, *Geschichts-Bücher,* 279). On March 19, 1528, Philip requested the imperial viceroy and other councilors of the imperial government at Speyer, as well as the city council of Strasbourg, to investigate the printing of a booklet that had been "compiled for the strengthening of Anabaptism and may result in impropriety and seduction," which was probably printed by Ariase, the servant of Peter Schöffer in Worms (Röhrich, 38).

In spite of these stern measures the new doctrine spread. "The simple people had been perplexed by their church. In Malsch the parson's love of drink drove the people into the arms of the Anabaptists" (Bossert, 78). For their religious services the congregations assembled mostly in the border regions of Baden, the Palatinate, and Speyer, often in outlying homes in the villages; in 1531 and 1532 they met in Neibsheim near Gondelsheim and Flehingen (all in the Bretten district) and in the Hagenmill at Bauerbach (bishopric of Speyer). They also worshiped in the forests, as in Neibsheim, and between Flehingen and Bretten. The old chapel of

Binsheim was very convenient for them (above Grombach and Jöhlingen in the region of Durlach). Here they were surprised at a service in early February 1538 by the butler of the Cathedral Chapter, who arrested the participants. In order to prevent further meetings there, the bishop wanted to have the chapel razed; the chapter refused to do this, however, for it offered shelter from storms to the people of Jöhlingen. The congregations in that region were large; 200-300 persons often attended the meetings. Later, of course, when attendance at religious services was more dangerous, the number was reduced to 10 or 12 (Bossert, 78).

One of their first preachers was Philip Weber (q.v.), who, however, migrated to Moravia early in 1528, and settled in Rossitz. Julius Lober is also named in the court records; he had come from Switzerland and headed the congregation at Bruchsal, which in 1530 had about 500 members. He is probably the Julius who in 1532 baptized the wife of Michael Schneider at Bruchsal. The latter was the leader, and was one of the Anabaptists seized on Sept. 14, 1534, at Passau, who with the hymns they composed in prison laid the foundation for the Ausbund (q.v.) (Wolkan, Lieder, 30). Julius later fled to Ansbach (Beck, Geschichts-Bücher, 71; Bossert, 84). The remnants of the Bruchsal congregation were led to Auspitz (q.v.) in Moravia by Blasius Kuhn (q.v.). About the middle of the 16th century the preachers in Baden were Wendel Metzger of Heidelsheim and Hans Gentner of Sulzfeld; they were said to have baptized the people of Malsch whom the bailiff captured at Bruchrain in 1539 (Bossert, 75). Gentner fled to Moravia, where he died in 1548 at Schäckowitz as "a true evangelical servant of Christ, after many tribulations and many a struggle and battle, which he had to suffer for the sake of the Lord" (Beck, 193).

After the death of Philip (Sept. 17, 1533), his territory was divided by his brothers Bernhard and Ernst. Bernhard became the progenitor of the Baden-Baden line, and Ernst of the Baden-Pfortzheim line, which later, when the residence of the margraves was moved to Durlach (1565), took the name of Baden-Durlach. Bernhard had definitely favored Protestant doctrine. After his death (June 29, 1536) the Reformation was kept out by the strictly Catholic guardians of his minor son; but it made new progress under the rule of Philibert. Not until his death (Oct. 3, 1569) did the Catholic confession come to the fore again, under the guardianship of Duke Albrecht (q.v.) of Bavaria. Albrecht's reign entailed severe persecution for the Anabaptists. The government carried out all the imperial laws against them. In 1571 Hans Geiger of Zell, near Aichelberg in the district of Kirchheim in Württemberg, who had been baptized in Esslingen in 1528, was sentenced to die at the stake; because he recanted, the sentence was moderated to decapitation; he was executed at Bühl (Bossert, 77). Thus the Anabaptists could not be permanent residents in the country; they were exiled as soon as the government learned of their presence.

The Anabaptists in the margravure of Baden-Durlach seem to have fared better. Ernst, the progenitor of the line, tried to settle differences in ecclesiastical matters, and in his later years seriously considered introducing the Reformation. It is worthy of note that in 1544 he read Caspar Schwenckfeld's works and sought personal contact with him. It is therefore probable that Ernst was benevolent to the few Anabaptists remaining in his lands. Official records are lacking; it is known only that there were Anabaptists at Durlach, Knielingen, Eggenstein, and Königsbach, whose leader about 1555 was Hans Schoch of Königsbach (Bossert, 76). In 1556 the Reformation was introduced by Karl II, 1553-77. The co-operation of the superintendent, Jakob Andreae (q.v.) of Göppingen, and the court chaplain of Heidelberg, Michael Diller, who at the colloquy at Worms in 1557 assented to the death penalty for the Anabaptists by signing the document, Prozess, wie es soll gehalten werden mit den Wiedertäufern (q.v.), leads to the conclusion that the Anabaptists were no longer tolerated in Baden-Durlach. In October 1570 Georg Schorich, an influential Jesuit priest of the Munich court, was summoned by Duke Albrecht to assist Count Ottheinrich of Schwarzenberg to recatholicize Baden. He solemnly baptized the child of an Anabaptist on Christmas Day 1570.

Not until the beginning of the 18th century were the Anabaptists permitted to settle in the margravure of Baden-Durlach. Tolerant Karl Wilhelm, 1709-38, the founder of Karlsruhe, on Sept. 15, 1715, promised religious freedom to all who wished to settle in the vicinity of his forest castle, Karlsruhe, and on April 9, 1722, he issued the order to all the clergy of his lands to avoid any harsh attitude toward those of other creeds. The Mennonites of Bern (Switzerland) sought refuge here after the second great emigration (1710). They were for the most part tenant farmers of the estates of baronial landowners, who valued them highly. They settled principally on the estates at Hohenwettersbach near Bretten, at Wangen and Weyer near Emmendingen, and at Hochberg, where they held their meetings in 1747. Because residence was forbidden them by the imperial laws, they were required by a government order of 1755 to pay a protection fee; besides this, a fee was charged in case of death. Their descendants are for the most part members of the present Mennonite congregations in Wössingen (q.v.), Durlach (q.v.), and Heimbronnerhof (q.v.).

Through the addition in 1803 of the portion of the Palatinate (q.v.) on the right bank of the Rhine and in 1806 of the territories of the imperial knights in the Kraichgau to the margravure, the number of Mennonites in Baden was substantially increased. In contrast to former times, the government now showed general appreciation. In the government records the Mennonites are called "good citizens" and "a peaceful and useful religious community." In 1801 Karl Friedrich, the first Baden grand duke of the later period, abolished the old regulations of Baden-Durlach concerning the confiscation of inheritances of Mennonites, and regulated their other legal rights. In an opinion of the provincial government at Mannheim of March 30, 1808, attention is called to the exemplary legal status of the Mennonites in the former Palatinate, where some of them were citizens. "If the state wants them as citizens," the opinion concludes, "and considers them good, then let it also grant them the rights and the confidence of citizens. It is not suitable to secure the guarantee for this from Geneva, Wittenberg, Rome, or Jerusalem." A regulation of April 15, 1809, decreed that henceforth the Mennonites, like all other citizens, must officially record births, weddings, and funerals; they could do this because they were relieved of all state church connections, and were left to their own conscience. Their children were to be excused from attendance at school if the parents engaged regularly tested and recognized private teachers; in the public schools their children had to attend instruction in morals, but were released from instruction in religion if their parents requested it. Because they did not render military service, Mennonites were not to be granted all the rights of citizenship, but only protection.

The military question for the Mennonites in Baden was regulated by a decree of Feb. 13, 1808 (*Kurbadisches Regierungsblatt* No. VII, of March 7, 1808), which stated that the Mennonites should never be required to render actual military service, but only to make a contribution (*Abfindung*). But this arrangement was abolished soon after the death of Karl Friedrich, on account of the "urgency of circumstances" by a decree of June 28, 1812 (*Kurbadisches Regierungsblatt* No. XXIII, of Aug. 1, 1812). The constitution of the grand duchy of Aug. 22, 1818 (*Kurbadisches Regierungsblatt* No. XVIII, of Aug. 29, 1818), stated, "Difference in birth and religion are the basis of . . . no exemption from military duty." Mennonites capable of military service could free themselves of active duty by paying a substitute. At first the churches collected the funds for substitutes as a unit, but before many years some families who had no sons of military age refused to bear the expenses of others. Thus the young men who were subject to military duty, if they had no money, had to choose between accepting military service and emigration (Hunzinger, 129).

After the right of freedom from military duty was abolished by the federal law of Nov. 9, 1867, the Mennonite churches asked the Ministry of War at Karlsruhe to grant their members, like the Mennonites of West Prussia, the privilege of performing their military service without bearing arms. The petition was at first rejected, but was later granted in the following decree on Sept. 15, 1869:

"No. 14,157. Grandducal *Bezirksamt* Sinsheim has been authorized, concerning the decree of Aug. 27, No. 13,271, to inform the elders and leaders of the Mennonite church at Rappenau: Even though it does not seem permissible according to the present military law to grant freedom from military service to Mennonites subject to military duty, consideration of their religious requirements is nevertheless not impossible. We shall therefore as far as possible release Mennonites subject to military duty who request it promptly when conscript-

ed, from direct armed service by assigning them to the transport division or the medical corps, etc., which do not put them into a position which requires them to use arms." (*Gbl.* 1870, 14; 1873, 87, and 1874, No. 6.)

Also on the question of the oath the government met the wishes of the Mennonites. A decree of 1802 granted them the substitution of a solemn vow in place of the oath, using the words, "As truly as I am an honest man." When the law of Dec. 20, 1848, prescribed the formula of affirmation, "I affirm by a solemn vow instead of an oath, that (here follows the statement affirmed) upon my honor and conscience," and demanded of the affirmer that he place his left hand over his heart, the elders on Oct. 16, 1856, requested of the Ministry of Justice that the legal requirements be altered. After the petition had been refused, three elders (Christian Schmutz of Rappenau, Ulrich Hege of Oberbiegelhof, and Heinrich Landes of Ehrstädt) personally presented their petition to the grand duke. Their wish was met by the law of June 5, 1860 (*Regierungsblatt* No. XXX), the first paragraph of which read: ". . . The law of Dec. 20, 1848, concerning the Mennonites is altered as follows: The affirmation of the Mennonites, as valid as an oath, takes place by means of a handclasp and the use of the formula: With this handclasp I affirm in accord with the Word of God in Matthew 5:33-37, that (here follows the statement to be affirmed); or if a written affirmation is permitted, with the formula: I affirm in accord with the Word of God (as above). This affirmation takes the place of the solemn vow in those cases where a solemn vow is legally to be given in place of an oath. In special cases the board can call in a disinterested elder of the Mennonite Church for the affirmation; this must be done if the opposing party requests it. A false solemn vow in place of an oath is subject to the same penalty as perjury." (See *Das von den Gliedern der Mennoniten-Gemeinde im Grossherzogtum Baden an Eidesstatt abzuleistende Handgelübde*, Heilbronn, 1862, and ten Doornkaat-Koolman, *Die Verpflichtung der Mennoniten an Eidesstatt*, Berlin, 1893.)

In the middle of the 19th century two movements had some influence among the Mennonite churches in Baden. About the middle of the century the followers of Johann Michael Hahn, known as the Michelians, won adherents among the Mennonites, which led to a division in 1858. In Dühren and Ursenbacherhof near Sinsheim and also at Heimbronnerhof near Bretten independent congregations with about 140 members altogether were formed, which, however, retained connections with the mother church, and came to be called "Hahnische Mennoniten." In 1845 the *Fröhlichianer* or *Neutäufer* (*q.v.*), who practiced immersion, caused a considerable number of families to leave the Mennonites. They were most successful in the congregation at Streichenberg (*Amt* Sinsheim), which had been in existence since the close of the 17th century, and in the congregation at Willenbach near Jagstfeld, which was founded at the end of the 18th century. These divisions decreased the membership somewhat; but on the other hand they had a stimulating effect on church life. The efforts for revitalizing the church found an ardent promoter in Elder Christian Schmutz (*q.v.*) of Rappenau (1799-1873) (*Gbl.*, 1874, 3-6), in co-operation with two other elders, Ulrich Hege of Oberbiegelhof (1808-72) (*Gbl.*, 1872, 86), and Heinrich Landes of Ehrstädt (1818-86).

Christian Schmutz, who devoted all his energy to the service of the church, stimulated and revived church life in the congregations through personal contact and by writing. An earnest concern of his was the training of young people for the work of the kingdom of God. For the instruction of youth he compiled a catechism entitled *Christliches Lehrbüchlein* (Heilbronn, 1865), which was introduced into many Mennonite churches outside Baden, and into some "free churches" of Switzerland (Göttighofen, Wyl, and Hauptweil in the canton of Thurgau, as well as the neighboring Baptist church in Bischofszell). The founding of the *Gemeindeblatt* in 1870 was also the result of his efforts. The introduction of the office of traveling preacher (*Reiseprediger*) is likewise essentially his work.

The number of Mennonites in Baden changed little in the first half of the 19th century (*Beiträge zur Statistik,* 222), but since then has steadily decreased. The census figures for Baden since 1821 are as follows:

1821	1512	1890	1194
1830	1414	1900	1008
1845	1515	1910	1151
1861	1221	1925	1198
1875	1351		

The Mennonites of Baden for the most part live in the country and are farmers; in 1871 only 63 Mennonites, or 4.64 per cent of the total number, were counted in the five largest cities. Since then the number of Mennonites living in the cities has increased. In 1905 there were 165 Mennonites in the five largest cities; 54 in Mannheim, 41 in Karlsruhe, 27 in Freiburg, 19 in Pforzheim, and 15 in Heidelberg. A tabulation of other places of residence is given in the census of Dec. 1, 1905 (*Beiträge zur Statistik* LXIII, 1911). Statistics of residence of the Mennonites of Baden by districts 1871-1910 are given in the article **Baden,** *ML* I, 106-7.

The decline in membership in Baden was caused in the main by transfer to other confessions through mixed marriages, and by emigration. At the beginning of the 19th century the congregations were still predominantly centered between Heidelberg and Wimpfen. In the course of time many families moved out of the Heidelberg district, for most of the estates, which they had cultivated through generations as tenants of the noble landowners, were now leased to sugar manufacturing plants. Consequently several congregations disappeared, as Baiertal (*q.v.*) and Bruchhausen (*q.v.*). On the other hand, new congregations were formed in the Oberland of Baden, in Württemberg, and in Bavaria, by emigration from the Neckar region of Baden. In Bavaria, where the congregation of Trappstadt in Lower Franconia had been formed in 1770 by immigrants from the Palatinate, the congregations of Würzburg (formerly Rottenbauer) and Giebelstadt were formed by an immigration from Baden beginning in 1805. From 1880 on, Mennonites from Baden settled in South Bavaria (*Menn. Bl.,* 1905, 68 and 75), giving rise to the congregations of Ingolstadt (formerly Däubling and Rottmannshart) and Donauwörth-Augsburg. In Württemberg the congregations at Heilbronn and Möckmühl were formed by Mennonites who moved in from the Heidelberg region. At the Bodensee (Lake Constance) in Baden the church at Ueberlingen (formerly Forsterhof) was begun in 1812 by several families migrating from the Neckar region of Baden.

In 1951 there were in Baden nine Mennonite congregations with membership as follows: Adelsheim, 37; Bretten, 28; Durlach, 110; Hasselbach, 85; Heidelberg, 41; Sinsheim, 85; Schopfheim, 31; Ueberlingen, 67; Wössingen, 67. In addition there were two congregations of Hahnische Mennoniten, Dühren and Heimbronnerhof.

The total population of Mennonites in Baden is more than the 521 baptized members in the nine congregations since some members of the neighboring Württemberg congregations live in Baden, and there are unattached refugees within the border of the province. With the exception of the Hahnisch congregations and Ueberlingen and Schopfheim, all the congregations belong to the *Badisch-Württembergisch-Bayerischer Gemeindeverband* or Conference and to the South German Conference.

HEGE.

Quellen zur Geschichte der Täufer IV, Baden und Pfalz (Gütersloh, 1951); K. F. Reinking, *Die Vormundschaften der Herzoge in Bayern in der Markgrafschaft Baden-Baden im 16. Jahrhundert* (Berlin, 1935) 147; *Kirchenbücher in Baden* published by the *Badische Historische Kommission*, ed. Hermann Franz (2nd ed. 1938) give Anabaptist statistics; T. Röhrich, *Ztscht f. d. hist. Theol.,* 1860; G. Bossert, in *Ztscht f. d. Gesch. d. Oberrheins* LIX (1905); A. Hunzinger, *Das Religions-, Kirchen- und Schulwesen der Mennoniten* (Speyer, 1830); *Beitr. z. Statistik der inneren Verwaltung des Grossherzogtums Baden* (1885); *Die Religionszugehörigkeit in Baden in den letzten 100 Jahren* (n. p. 1927); *ML* I, 103-7.

Baden, a town in the Swiss canton of Aargau (*q.v.*), is known in the history of the Reformation particularly for the religious disputation held there from May 18 to June 8, 1526, in which Johannes Eck, Faber, and Thomas Murner represented the Catholics, and Johann Oecolampadius of Basel and Berchtold Haller of Bern represented the Protestants. Ulrich Zwingli kept himself aloof. Both parties claimed the victory. Most of the priests present, to be sure, voted for Eck (82), whereas Oecolampadius received only ten votes. Nevertheless the skillful and adroit demeanor of Oecolampadius and Haller highly pleased the Protestants in Switzerland.

At the sessions of the Swiss federal parliament at Baden on Nov. 18, 1530, and May 10-16, 1532, it was decided that Anabaptist preachers and all who contributed to their support should be punished by fine or imprisonment. The magistrate should have the Anabaptists instructed by men who knew the Scriptures; those who did not desist he was to drown without further ceremony. But the authorities did not succeed in eradicating the Anabaptists. In 1560 an Anabaptist woman, unwilling to forsake her faith, was drowned. In 1576 Anabaptists from Moravia led many away with all their possessions; their property was therefore confiscated (Müller, *Berner Täufer*, 96). In 1582 two Moravian emissaries, Heinrich Sumer and Jakob Mändel, were captured in Zurzach, brought to Baden and drowned there on Oct. 9 (Beck, *Geschichts-Bücher*, 281).

NEFF.

J. Heiz, "Täufer im Aargau," in *Taschenbuch der historischen Gesellschaft des Kantons Aargau für das Jahr 1902* (Aarau, 1902) 107-205; *ML* I, 107.

Baden, Ont., a police village in Waterloo County, with a population of 690, is noted industrially for linseed oil and Limburger cheese. The first Mennonite (Amish) settlers arrived here in 1824. There are six Mennonite churches within a radius of five miles of the village, two of which are Amish and one Reformed, comprising a total membership of approximately 900, about 15 per cent of whom live within the village. The Baden Mennonite Church originated as a mission built by Peter Mayer in 1913 in an attempt to draw the Mennonites and Amish together.

L.H.W.

Baden Mennonite Church (MC), located in Baden, Waterloo Co., Ont., was started as a mission in 1913 by Peter Moyer, for use by both the Amish and Mennonite conferences of Ontario. The responsibility for Sunday school and preaching was shared by both groups at first; in 1920 the Rural Mission Board of the Ontario Conference appointed four ministers to serve in turn, and this practice continued until 1930, since when one minister has been made responsible for the work. In 1940 it was agreed that the Sunday-school staff should be supplied by the First Mennonite Church of Kitchener. This led to increased growth; Sunday-school attendance, which in the thirties varied from 40 to 20, now increased to 60 and 80. In the autumn of 1945, the congregation was organized and became a member of the Mennonite Conference of Ontario. Membership in 1954 was 62. A summer Bible school was started in 1934, which enrolls over 300. The ministers who have served since 1930 were Noah S. Hunsberger, Newton S. Weber, James Martin, and Urie Bender.

J.C.F.

Bader, Augustin (in most histories erroneously called *Wiedertäuferkönig*, as in the *ADB* I, 760). Bader belonged to the Anabaptists only a short time. He had been a member of the Augsburg congregation, baptized by Jakob Gross (*q.v.*), who had come to Augsburg in the last quarter of 1526. When persecution of Anabaptists in Augsburg set in, he was captured on Sept. 15, 1527, and was released on Oct. 19 upon recanting. His wife, however, who refused to recant, was expelled. He returned to the congregation, accepted the office of leader (*Vorsteher*), and preached and baptized in Augsburg and vicinity.

At the end of February he was appointed to visit the recently established Anabaptist congregation in Kaufbeuren (*q.v.*), which had requested a preacher. He was accompanied by Gall Fischer, his truly devoted friend, in whose house most of the services in Augsburg had been held. They gave the new church a constitution, and helped them elect two leaders and two deacons. But the intervention of the city council brought the organization to a sudden end. Bader and Fischer returned to Augsburg, and the new church was wiped out. The two leaders, the two deacons, and the citizen who had lodged the visitors were beheaded on June 13, 1528; the other members, 30 men and women, were burned through the cheeks or whipped out of the city.

The last meeting in Augsburg attended by Bader was probably the election of leaders on April 2, 1528. He made a radical break with them at the Swiss Anabaptist conference in Teuffen (*q.v.*) because they did not accept his fantastic apocalyptic ideas (see **Krüse, Johannes**). During Passion Week he left the city to visit outside members. On April 9 he held communion services at Stadtbergen, in which Bernhard Zirkendorfer took part, who was executed with Eitelhans Langenmantel (*q.v.*). On the day when the council struck the annihilating blow against the Augsburg congregation (*q.v.*), Bader seems to have been in Mindelheim, probably conducting Easter services in that congregation.

Bader's unstable emotional balance was apparently destroyed by the cruel persecutions which broke in upon the Anabaptists. He saw his fellow preachers die under the executioner's sword, and fellow believers subjected to terrible torture, and was threatened by the same fate. Unstable and fugitive he wandered over the countryside, believing himself to have been called as a prophet. In an arbitrary interpretation of the Book of Ezra he proclaimed a great judgment about to break upon the world at Easter 1530, and the rise of a new kingdom of God on earth, which would be entirely spiritual, dispensing with all earthly instruments, such as baptism, confession, and communion, abolishing images and altars and temporal as well as spiritual government. This would be brought about by the threatening Turkish invasion. He made no revolutionary demands. In the new kingdom, Christ's spirit would reign alone, and Bader considered himself His organ.

Bader's confused ideas had found no response among the Anabaptist congregations he had visited, whether in Moravia, Swabia, Nürnberg, Strasbourg, or Switzerland. Only four men were attracted to his doctrine—Gall Fischer, Oswald Leber, an elderly man who had before the Peasants' War been a preacher in Herbolzheim in the region of Mosbach in Baden and was now filled with hope for the imminent millennium proclaimed by Bader, Hans Köller, a young tailor, and Gastel N., a miller from Bavaria.

In October 1529 the miller rented a shed to Bader at Lautern near Blaubeuren, eight miles west of Ulm, where his four followers settled with their families. After pooling their cash, they had 389 florins in the common fund. Bader informed them of his further revelations; he designated his youngest son, only a few weeks old, as the Messiah and king of the approaching kingdom of God, and himself as his son's representative. The aged Gall Fischer, completely possessed by Bader's hallucinations, imagined one evening that the roof of the shed opened and a golden scepter, a golden crown, a golden sword, and a golden dagger were lowered just in front of Bader. Though the others saw none of this, they were nevertheless convinced that Bader was called to be king. So now they went about procuring royal ornamentation. Köller, a tailor, was to make robes of splendor, and the golden insignia, the sword, chain, crown, dagger, scepter, and ring, were secured from Christoph Gangolf, a goldsmith in Ulm. Bader hoped by means of these insignia to have a magic effect on the converts his four associates were to make.

The farce lasted only a short time. The miller at Lauteren became suspicious and called the village bailiff's attention to the mysterious guests. By an order of the regent at Stuttgart the entire company—five men, three women, and eight children—were arrested at night on Jan. 15, 1530. Officers took possession of the royal insignia. Bader was taken to Stuttgart, Leber and Gastel to Tübingen, Fischer and Köller to Nürtingen. The bailiffs subjected them to several hearings on the rack in the presence of four theologians, including the Tübingen professors, Dr. Gall Müller and Balthasar Käuffelin, to discover Bader's plans. The captives answered willingly. But the government was possessed by a secret fear that Duke Ulrich might have connections with Bader; they hoped to find clues of a secret far-flung conspiracy to throw off Austrian rule. They even supposed that Johann of Saxony, George of Brandenburg-Ansbach, and Philip of Hesse were backing Bader. Margrave George denied these suspicions when rumors reached him in March 1530. Bader's ideas were considered so dangerous that even the Reichstag of Augsburg dealt with them. (The *Confessio Augustana*, Art. XVIII, as well as the *Confutatio* contain an unmistakable condemnation of Bader.)

Although the government should have been convinced by the first hearings that they were dealing with a harmless psychopath, King Ferdinand ordered the cross-examination to be most rigorously continued. Though Leber's arms were torn by the torture applied to force further confessions, no seditious plans could be discovered. All requisites to a plot like that feared by the government were lacking, such as a large following of politically powerful persons, or of such as were inclined to disturbance, as well as the financial resources. None of the captives, with the exception of the youthful Köller, could be persuaded to return to the Catholic Church. On March 30, 1530, Bader was executed at Stuttgart with his own sword after pieces of flesh had been torn from his body with glowing irons.

The executions apparently roused public opinion. To justify the procedure of the government, the Swabian League had the confessions of the victims published by Melchior Ramminger in Augsburg. But they apparently did not have the desired result. Dionysius Dreytwein questioned the justice of the execution, when he wrote in the *Esslinger*

Chronik (1548-64), "Gott ways, ob es ist recht gewesen oder nyt, denn er ist der streng recht richter, der alle Dinge wayst." But the most peculiar ideas were spread by contemporaries. Thus Vadian wrote that Bader had been crowned by the Anabaptists in a village near Tübingen early in April, but that the scheme had failed and the king had been executed. The information given by contemporary historians is of no greater value; they identify the dream-king of Lauteren with the Anabaptists. But it has been demonstrated by recent investigation that this childish play with royal insignia cannot be laid to the charge of the Anabaptists of South Germany.

Wolfgang Capito, the Strasbourg reformer, wanted to marry Bader's widow, Sabina. He desired, as his friend Martin Bucer (*q.v.*) wrote to Ambrosius Blaurer (Jan. 19, 1532), a lowly person as his life-companion, but followed Blaurer's advice and married the widow of Oecolampadius (*q.v.*), who had died on Nov. 24, 1531.   HEGE.

G. Bossert, Sr., "Augustin Bader von Augsburg, der Prophet und König, und seine Genossen nach den Prozessakten von 1530," in *Archiv für Ref.-Gesch.* (1913) 117-75, 209-41, 297-349; XI, 19-64, 103-33, 176-99; Fr. Roth, *Augsb. Ref.-Gesch.* I (1901) 236; *Beiträge zur bayr. Kirchengesch.* XX (1914) 233; *ML* I, 107-9.

Bader, Johannes (1470-1545), the reformer of the city of Landau (Palatinate), in Zweibrücken (*HRE* II, 353). In 1514 he was appointed chaplain in Zweibrücken and at the same time tutor to Prince Louis II; in 1518 he accepted the call to become pastor of the Stiftskirche at Landau. After 1521 he turned more and more definitely toward evangelical doctrine. Repeatedly he was summoned to Speyer to justify himself. But he refused to surrender his evangelical conviction, and was therefore excommunicated on April 17, 1524. He was especially interested in young people.

At Easter 1526 he published the first Protestant catechism entitled *Ein Gesprächbüchlein vom Anfang*, revealing himself as a resolute opponent of Anabaptist doctrine. In 1527 he published his lengthy polemic, *Brüderliche Warnung vor dem neuen abgöttischen Orden der Wiedertäufer*. Hans Denk, banished from Strasbourg, had recently arrived at Landau by way of Bergzabern. Bader's opposition to him brought about a public disputation on Jan. 20, 1527, which dealt chiefly with infant baptism. Bader wrote a justification of the doctrine, and Denk refuted it. Bader published the proceedings in the polemic mentioned above. Nevertheless Denk seems to have made a favorable impression on him.

But the Anabaptists as a whole Bader most resolutely opposed. To that end he engaged the aid of the council, securing from it the order that no citizen or inhabitant of the city be permitted to harbor a person suspected of Anabaptist leanings, or to hold a conversation with him, on penalty of serious punishment. All Anabaptists were banished from the city.

Later Bader became a close associate of Kaspar Schwenckfeld. In an epistle to Bader, Sept. 24,

1531, Schwenckfeld definitely defends the Anabaptists in spite of their error on infant baptism. His influence is evident in Bader's new catechism (1544), especially in the doctrines of baptism and the Lord's Supper. His successor, whom he had himself selected, Joh. Liebmann, a resolute follower of Schwenckfeld, abandoned baptism and the Lord's Supper completely. NEFF.

Chr. Hege, *Die Täufer in der Kurpfalz* (Frankfurt, 1908) 15-21; Gelbert, *Magister Johann Baders Leben und Schriften* (Neustadt a.H., 1868); *ML* I, 109.

Badisch-Württembergisch-Bayerischer Gemeindeverband, the union of eight Mennonite congregations of Baden, five of Württemberg, two of the Palatinate, and four of Bavaria. Originally it probably embraced all the congregations in the former territory of the Palatinate on the right bank of the Rhine, the margravure of Baden-Durlach and the Kraichgau listed by Ernst Müller (*Berner Täufer,* 209-11) as of 1731: Dühren, Hasselbach, Meckesheim, and Wössingen, besides Bockschaft (today Sinsheim), Büchelhof (today Hasselbach), Helmstadt (today Hasselbach), Haschhof (extinct), Hohenhardterhof-Baiertal (extinct) near Wiesloch, Immelhausen (today Sinsheim), Rohrhof (extinct) near Heidelberg, Streichenberg (extinct) near Eppingen, and Zimmerhof (extinct). In the 19th century the Verband was extended to include the churches formed in Württemberg and Bavaria by immigration from Baden. The absence of records makes it impossible to determine the date of its origin. Records of these meetings of the elders, preachers, and deacons were always kept; but most of them have been lost. The oldest record extant, dated Dec. 17, 1840, is a report of the meeting of elders in Hoffenheim at the home of Peter Neff; there are also records of 1841 and 1842, in manuscript form, of meetings of elders. Regular reports on hand begin with 1876. The *Gemeindeblatt* recorded none of the proceedings (*Gbl.* 1896, 93). Important decisions were presented orally to the congregations.

The Verband supervises the affairs of the congregations through the council of elders (*Aeltestenrat, q.v.*). The elders, preachers, and deacons meet four times annually for consultation concerning the welfare of the churches, and agree on matters and methods of church discipline. Theological training is not required for ministers by the churches of the Verband. Preachers are chosen from the congregation, and elders are chosen from the preachers. Every member may vote. Elders, preachers, and deacons perform their duties without salary. Running expenses, such as rent, repairs, heat, traveling expenses, conference expenses, meetings of elders, publications for nurture of congregational life, etc., are defrayed from a special fund, the *Umlagekasse,* established in 1845, toward which each member pays an assessed amount (Ph. Hege, *Rechenschaftsbericht der Umlagekasse des Verbandes der Menn.-Gem. in Baden, Württemberg, und Bayern aus den Jahren 1874 bis inkl. 1899,* Sinsheim, 1900). An additional alms fund (*Almosenkasse*), made up by contributions at regular services, cares for the needs of the poor (see **Almosenpfleger**). In the interests of isolated families, the Verband decided in 1871 to establish the visiting preaching service (*Reisepredigt*); since 1883 there have been two (or one) traveling preachers (*Reiseprediger*), whose salary is met by voluntary contributions. In 1905 the Verband opened deaconess work; by 1915 five nurses had been in service, who received their training in the deaconess home in Karlsruhe. The headquarters for the nursing service in recent years is the Thomashof near Durlach. The organ of the Verband is the *Gemeindeblatt der Mennoniten* (*q.v.*), founded in 1870.

In the Verband churches the communion service is preceded by a preparatory service, which serves to keep the church pure and to reveal and remove hidden faults. In 1907 the questioning of each member before communion in an anteroom ceased. (*Menn. Bl.,* 1908, 3).

The following congregations belonged to the Verband in 1951 (membership figures marked * include unbaptized children): Adelsheim (Baden), 37; Augsburg (Bavaria), 60*; Branchweilerhof (Palatinate), 54; Bretten, 27; Durlach (Baden), 110; Deutschhof (Palatinate), 80; Hasselbach (Baden), 85; Heidelberg (Baden), 41; Heilbronn (Württemberg), 95*; Ingolstadt (Oberbayern), 135*; Möckmühl (Württemberg), 21; Nesselbach (Württemberg), 31; Reutlingen (Württemberg), 130*; Sinsheim (Baden), 95; Stuttgart, 170*; Trappstadt, 55; Wössingen (Baden), 64*; Würzburg-Giebelstadt (Unterfranken), 104.*

The total membership of the Verband was about 1,410 baptized (1,550 souls) in 1951, against about 1,000 in 1900. There were 12 elders and 25 preachers serving the 15 congregations, besides 7 deacons, in 1915; but in 1951, 29 elders, 26 preachers, and 12 deacons serving 18 congregations. Most of the increase in members was due to the addition of postwar refugees from West Prussia and Russia. (*ML* I, 109 f.) HEGE, H.S.B.

Baeck, Ghijsbrecht van, governor (*Drost*) of IJsselstein and Benschop, had the Reformed Hendrik Rol (*q.v.*) in his service as family chaplain (*ca.* 1530). Because Baeck was evidently favorable to the Reformation, and his wife Elsa van Lostadt (*q.v.*) later openly became an Anabaptist, the Anabaptist movement could develop for a time in his territory. (Kühler, *Geschiedenis* I, 99, 175, 208; *ML* I, 110.) NEFF.

Baef Claesd., an Anabaptist martyr, an unmarried woman, was executed for her faith with six other Anabaptist women at Amsterdam on May 15, 1535 (*Mart. Mir.* D 413, E 764; Grosheide, *Verhooren,* 58 f.; *ML* I, 358). VDZ.

Baer (Baehr, Bähr, Bair, Bar, Bare, Barr, Bear, Beare, Behr, Boehr), a Swiss Mennonite family name. One of the earliest records of this name occurs in 1548 when Johannes Bair wrote a letter to the brotherhood in Moravia. This letter is found in the *Martyrs' Mirror.* The name was also found in Bavaria and Franconia. One of the earliest Baer arrivals in America was Jacob who reached Philadelphia Sept. 30, 1727.

The family is found in Lancaster and York counties in Pennsylvania, and also in Maryland, Indiana, Missouri, Kansas, and other western states. Martin Baer of York Co., Pa., moved to Canada in 1800, locating near Hespeler, Ont.

Prominent in this family was Adam Baer (1826-1904), who was born in Lancaster Co., Pa., and later moved to Washington Co., Md., where he was ordained deacon and minister. Martin Baer (-1758) was a pioneer minister and bishop in the Mellinger district of Lancaster Co., Pa. P. J. Boehr was a Mennonite (GCM) missionary in India. John B. Baer (1854-1939) (q.v.) was a prominent minister in the General Conference Mennonite Church, who served as home missionary and field secretary of the General Conference for a period of 15 years.   H.H.H.

Baer, John B., was born at O'Fallon, Ill., May 19, 1854, of Bavarian Mennonite parentage, a member at first of the Summerfield (GCM) congregation. After irregular attendance in the local elementary schools, he attended at various times educational institutions at Lebanon, Ill., Wadsworth, Ohio, Bloomfield, N.J., and was finally graduated in 1887 from the Union Theological Seminary in New York. While in school he engaged in local city mission work in New York, and later worked as colporteur in Canada for the American Tract Society.

In 1879 he accompanied missionary S. S. Haury to Alaska in search of a mission field for the General Conference (GCM). He was ordained to the ministry by A. B. Shelly in 1886, and married to Jennie A. Roberts the same year. For fifteen years he was the home mission and field secretary for the General Conference. In 1894 he moved with his family from Pennsylvania to Bluffton, Ohio, where he served as pastor of the large Swiss congregation, 1900-9. After this he served the Mennonite church at Aberdeen, Idaho, for three years, and his home church at Summerfield, Ill., for six. Because of ill health he retired from the ministry, and spent the remaining years of his life in Los Angeles, Cal., where he died Aug. 23, 1939, at the age of 85 years.
                                                   C.H.S.

Baetken Crauwels, an Anabaptist martyr, wife of Jan Poote (q.v.), was burned at the stake on April 30, 1569, at Antwerp, with Maeyken Christians. She was seized early in February 1569, during a meeting of the congregation in her house. Baetken was 50 years of age and had been married in the congregation eight years before by Joos de Cruysere (q.v.), having been rebaptized shortly before in the woods near Wilrijck, close to Antwerp, by Joachim Vermeeren (q.v.). She was tortured on May 5 but held fast to her baptismal vows, stating that infant baptism was unscriptural. (*Antw. Arch.-Blad* XII, 358, 376, 400; XIV, 64-65, No. 720.)
                                                    vDZ.

Baflo, a village in the northern part of the Dutch province of Groningen, the seat of a former Mennonite church. The Anabaptist movement had found adherents there in 1535; for in a letter of that year the Catholic pastors and deans of several villages of Groningen, including Baflo, are instructed to prosecute the Anabaptists of Münster.

According to Rues this congregation belonged to the Groninger Sociëteit of the Old Flemish, although it is not mentioned in the records of the Sociëteit or in the census. There is, however, a list of members of the Groninger Old Flemish congregations who lost their lives in the great flood of 1717, stating that in the Baflo congregation eight adults and eight children had been drowned. In 1754 the membership was 59.

In the *Naamlijst* (q.v., a register of Mennonite preachers) Baflo is mentioned in 1766, but not in 1773. The congregation must therefore have died out during that period, or perhaps merged with the neighboring Rasquert (q.v.) congregation.
                                                      J.L.

Blaupot t.C., *Friesland; idem, Groningen;* S. F. Rues, *Tegenwoordige Staet der Doopsgezinden* (Amsterdam, 1745); *ML* I, 110 f.

Bagdannen, a former Mennonite congregation near Tilsit, East Prussia, also called "the scattered church of Prussian Lithuania." The Mennonites living here had much to endure from the dragoons of the Prussian King Frederick William I, who finally expelled them from the district. The Mennonite Archives of Amsterdam contain a number of letters and statements from and concerning the congregation of Bagdannen (the first dated Sept. 23, 1723), from which it becomes clear that the Mennonites of the Tilsit Lowland lived in great insecurity, and had to suffer much mistreatment: overnight many brethren had been taken prisoners, and neither letters nor visits, either by the leaders of the congregation itself or by the Dutch Mennonites, had any result. In 1725-26 the congregation was completely expelled from this territory, some emigrating to the Netherlands; most, however, settled in the Kleine Werder and other places of Polish Prussia.

The Dutch Committee of Foreign Needs organized a general offering in May 1726 in behalf of these people, which was taken in all Mennonite churches of Holland, and which brought in more than 30,000 guilders. During this period David Penner was a minister of the church of Bagdannen, whereas Salomon Jantzen seems to have been a deacon. The members of this Lithuanian congregation were mostly of Dutch descent; they had also won some Lutherans for their church, which was taken very ill by the Prussian King. The congregation belonged to the Waterlanders. See also **Dannenberg, Lithunia, Tilsit.** (*Inv. Arch. Amst.* I, Nos. 1571-81; II, 2, Nos. 703-39.)   vDZ.

Bage, a Mennonite settlement in southern Brazil in the State of Rio Grande do Sul, about 25 miles southeast of the city of Bage, and 40 miles north of the Uruguayan border. The Mennonites of Witmarsum in the Krauel Valley of Brazil, facing the difficulties of making a living in that area, in 1945 appointed a committee to investigate new areas for settlement. In 1949 a new resettlement committee was created to serve as official contact agency and negotiator for the Mennonites. For a time it appeared that the government would advance them financial credit for the purpose of helping the Mennonites acquire land and machinery for wheat farming in the State of Rio Grande do Sul, but when this plan did not materialize, Jacob Epp, a leading industrialist of the Witmarsum settlement, rented a 700-acre tract near Bage on a five-year contract. He became the leader of about 70 families who decided to relocate without waiting for government aid or official colony action. In 1949 three families moved to the new area and by the end of 1951 the settlement had grown to 82 families. The colony consists of two agricultural villages plus a small settlement of perhaps a half-dozen families living on land bought privately. Some land purchases are still continuing. The land was purchased largely with the financial aid of the Mennonite Brethren of North America and the settlers are largely Mennonite Brethren. The colony has its own school attended by some 80 Mennonite children, and an organized Mennonite Brethren Church under the leadership of Elder Gerhard Rosenfeld. The teacher of the school (1952) is Lydia Janzen, from Curitiba, the first Mennonite teacher born and educated in Brazil. Efforts are being made to establish a secondary school as well.

The land is rolling and in general suitable for temperate zone farming. The soil is somewhat heavy and sticky. In 1952 a total of 2,500 acres of corn were planted. Wheat is also grown, as well as oats, vegetables, and other common cereals. Farming is done by horses and by tractor. The administration of the colony is in the hands of a committee elected by the settlers. There is no cooperative store, but marketing and purchasing of materials is usually done unitedly. Prices received for their agricultural produce compare somewhat favorably, in general, to those prevalent in the United States.   J.W.F., C.J.D.

Bähler, Samuel, Swiss Mennonite preacher and elder of Langnau, Switzerland, cofounder and editor of the *Zionspilger,* a weekly periodical published since 1881 by the Mennonites in the Emmental (Switzerland), which soon secured a number of faithful subscribers outside Mennonite circles. Bähler was also active in the Sunday school, and as the founder and conductor of the choir of the Emmental congregation, which still functions. This indefatigable man succumbed to lung trouble on Jan. 28, 1890, only 38 years of age, soon after the dedication of the meetinghouse of the congregation (*ML* I, 110).   M.P.

Bahndorf: see Orlovo.

Baiersdorf, today a small market town near Erlangen, once a district government seat in the margravure of Brandenburg. In April 1531 an Anabaptist congregation was broken up there, which had existed since Pentecost of 1530, and numbered about 50 members, in part scattered over the region of Nürnberg and Bamberg. Their beginnings go back to 1525, when they are said to have accepted rebaptism, without outside instigation, because of independently acquired conviction resulting from Bible study. This is the official record sent to the margrave at Ansbach on July 9, 1530, according to which Melchior Kern testified that it was true that he had been baptized again, for he had always heard from the preachers: He who believes and is baptized will be saved. Philip Jakob testified that the Word of God had directed him to rebaptism. Pastor Wolfgang Vogel of Eltersdorf, who was executed in Nürnberg on March 26, 1527, the carpenter Thomas Spiegel at Ostheim, and Johannes von Biberach in Algäu are named as having administered the second baptism before the Peasants' War (*Anzeiger für Kunde der deutschen Vorzeit,* n.F. XV, 294A).

In 1528, 20 brethren were imprisoned at Baiersdorf; they denied all the seditious tendencies of which they were accused. Hans Schmid, Fritz Striegel, and Marx Maier of Uttenreuth (Keller, *Reformation,* 428) were condemned to death on July 6, 1531, and beheaded; the others were whipped and banished from the country.

At their meetings they used to sing Hans Hut's song, "Dank sagen wir dem Herrn der Ehren."
NEFF.

C. A. Cornelius, *Gesch. des Münsterischen Aufruhrs* II (Leipzig, 1860) 47; J. E. Jörg, *Deutschland in der Revolutionsperiode 1526-1528* (Freiburg, 1851); P. Wappler, *Die Täuferbewegung in Thüringen 1526-1584* (Jena, 1913); other material in the city archives of Nürnberg, which have not been thoroughly investigated; *ML* I, 111.

Baiertal, a village in the district of Heidelberg in Baden (Germany), where there was a Mennonite congregation until the beginning of the 20th century. There is evidence of the existence of an Anabaptist congregation here in the Reformation period, in which Philip Weber (*q.v.*) was very active and successful; he had baptized some residents of Nussloch and Leimen, several of whom were summoned for trial on May 1, 1529. The record of the trial, the oldest official account of an Anabaptist trial in the Palatinate, is located in the Karlsruhe state archives. The statements of the captives about the doctrines of their preachers and their Christian view of life are in sharpest contradiction to the slanderous assertions of their opponents. Of the prisoners only Margarete Wilhelm of Nussloch recanted; the others, Hans Wilhelm, Damian Nikot, and Philip Rupp of Nussloch, as well as Henner Schuhmacher of Leimen, would not forsake their faith, and were probably executed on the basis of the Edict of Speyer (*q.v.*), which had been issued a week before the trial, as well as the Palatine mandate of March 5, 1528. No records are left of the sentence. In the later years too the priests had little success in their attempts at conversion; in 1589 these attempts were ruined by the objectionable conduct of the members of the state church, with whom the Anabaptists did not associate. Because of continued oppression most Anabaptists preferred to emigrate to Moravia (Hege, 60-62 and 146-47).

After the Thirty Years' War a new congregation was formed, whose members had come from Switzerland. Their first center was on the Hohenhardterhof; this is the name used for the congregation in a record of 1737 (Müller, *Berner Täufer,* 210; here erroneously called "hohen Eckerhof"). Later it was changed to Schatthausen near Wiesloch (Starck). A register of 1733 notes that the congregation was now called Schatthausen and Baierthal (Hunzinger, 212). The congregation, which after 1840 was called Baiertal, later suffered a sharp decline because of emigration and mixed marriages; in 1867 the church was sold and the proceeds used to cover the cost of printing the *Leitfaden zum Gebrauch bei gottes-dienstlichen Handlungen für die Aeltesten und Prediger der Gesamt-Mennoniten-Gemeinde in Baden* (see **Ministers' Manuals**). After the death of Christian Bachmann (1877) services were conducted by preachers from the neighboring churches. Attendance was, however, so small that services were temporarily suspended in 1879. In 1902 the church became extinct.   HEGE.

Chr. Hege, *Die Täufer in der Kurpfalz* (Frankfurt, 1908); J. A. Starck, *Gesch. der Taufe und der Taufgesinnten* (Leipzig, 1789); A. Hunzinger, *Das Religions-, Kirchen- und Schulwesen der Menn.* (Speyer, 1830); *ML I*, 111 f.

Bair, Johannes, an Anabaptist martyr, was taken prisoner in early November 1528 at Lichtenfels in Franconia (Germany) "for the faith and the divine truth." To the fellow members of his congregation he wrote a short letter in 1548 from the Toren, the prison in Bamberg where he was held, requesting them to send him a Bible. He remained a prisoner in this dungeon for 23 years, never denying his faith. In 1551 he was put to death. (*Mart. Mir.* D 107, E 503; *ML I*, 112.)   HEGE.

Bair Mennonite Meetinghouse (MC) is located three miles east of Hanover, York Co., Pa. On May 14, 1775, Michael Danner, Sr., of Hanover, a York County Commissioner when the county was laid out, obtained from the Penn heirs with preachers John Shenk and Jacob Keagy, deacons John Welty and James Miller, twelve acres for a meetinghouse, schoolhouse, and burying ground. Possibly the Lutherans and Reformed had an interest in the schoolhouse. The first meetinghouse was used until 1860, and the second house until 1908, when the present house was erected. It is a part of the Hostetter-Hanover circuit of the Lancaster Mennonite Conference of which Richard Danner is bishop. The circuit membership is 122.   I.D.L.

Bairs Codorus Mennonite Church (MC) belongs to the Lancaster Conference. It is located in North Codorus Twp., York Co., six miles southwest of York. Henry Newcomer, Ulrich Huber, Peter Hershey, Peter and John Houser, and George Garber were here by 1783. The first church, built after 1800, was razed, and a new brick church was built in 1895. It is part of the Middle York County circuit, with Richard Danner serving as bishop.
                                                   I.D.L.

Baithena, new name for Dhamtari Medical Station (*q.v.*).

Bakels, Herman, b. July 25, 1871, d. July 22, 1952, served as pastor in Warns, 1895-1901, Enkhuizen, 1901-7, and finally in St. Anna-Parochie, 1908-9, and 1911-16. Of his various writings those of greatest interest to us are *Het volk van Menno* (Leiden,

1918), and *Beknopt Bijbelsch Woordenboek* (first ed. Amsterdam, 1917). His modern translation of the New Testament (Amsterdam, 1908) went through many editions (*ML I*, 112).   vDZ.

Baker, Newton Diehl, an American lawyer and public official, was Secretary of War during the administration of President Woodrow Wilson, 1913-21. He was born at Martinsburg, W. Va., in 1871. His term of office in the War Department extended over the period of World War I. His understanding of the Mennonite and Historic Peace Church position on nonresistance and nonparticipation in war was an important factor in securing proper recognition for conscientious objectors during the war; it may have been due in part to the fact that his wife came from a Church of the Brethren background. It was he who outlined to the official delegation consisting of Aaron Loucks, D. D. Miller, and S. G. Shetler, appointed by the Mennonite General Conference, the procedure by which C.O. draftees could finally be segregated from the army and assigned to other services. He rendered the Mennonites a notable and highly appreciated service by his considerate attitude.   S.C.Y.

Bakersfield, Cal., a city which with its suburbs has a population (1953) of over 125,000, situated in the southern part of the San Joaquin Valley, in Kern County. Approximately 500 Mennonites, of whom 90 per cent are Mennonite Brethren, live within shopping distance of the city. About two fifths of this number live in the Rosedale community, approximately 10 miles west of Bakersfield, while the remaining three fifths live in the city. Mennonites have lived in the area since 1909. Two Mennonite churches are located in the area, the Bakersfield M.B. Church (*q.v.*) and the Rosedale M.B. Church (*q.v.*).   H.L.

Bakersfield Mennonite Brethren Church, located at 1230 Monterey St., Bakersfield, Cal., had its beginning as a Sunday school in 1910. The early members mostly came from M.B. congregations in Kansas and Oklahoma, organized into a church by Peter Richert, who was its first minister.

In 1913 B. J. Friesen was called to shepherd this church. He combined this assignment with city mission and extension Sunday-school work in the eastern part of the city. In 1916 the congregation bought a building lot and a hall, moved the hall to this site, and remodeled it into a church. The congregation today has a church 32 x 56 ft. in size.

The congregation gradually increased and in 1924 numbered 150 members. At present (1952) the membership stands at 180, composed of businessmen, laborers, and farmers. The church maintains a very active Sunday school with 200 in attendance, does extension Sunday-school work at East Side Community Chapel, has a Christian Fellowship, a Christian Endeavor, and a very active Ladies' Mission and Sewing Society. B. J. Friesen served the church as pastor from 1913 to 1932. P. N. Hiebert served from 1932 to 1944. He was followed by J. B. Kliewer, Henry Hooge, and Allen Fast. In 1952 the pastors were Arthur Flaming and E. R. Hodel.
                                                   J.H.Lo.

Bakhuizen, a village in the southwest of the Dutch province of Friesland, where there was formerly a Waterlander Mennonite congregation (Kühler, *Geschiedenis* II, I, p. 65). It apparently originated between 1600 and 1620. About 1700 it numbered 40 members. Jan Cornelis, a preacher of this church, who later (1710-50) administered baptism and communion in the neighboring village of Warns as well as in Bakhuizen, reported that he had 43 communicant members there. After 1768 the membership decreased rapidly. In 1799 when the Bakhuizen congregation united with that at Warns, it had only 18 members (9 men and 9 women). The church (*vermaanhuis*) was sold for 150 guilders. (Blaupot t. C., *Friesland; DB* 1874, 87; 1901, 85; 1903, 82; *ML* I, 112.) J.L.

Bakisch, Peter de Lak, a Hungarian noble and landowner, who drew the Anabaptists to his possessions in Unter-Nussdorf. But on May 15, 1548, when the stern mandate of King Ferdinand was issued to the Hungarian landowners "to remove the Anabaptists who had fled to them," Bakisch at once complied. The Anabaptists who had settled on his estate emigrated in part to Moravia where they had come from, and the others to the Rohatetz Forest. (Beck, *Geschichts-Bücher,* 180 and 184; Loserth, *Communismus; ML* I, 112.) NEFF.

Bakker, Gerrit (1789-1871), of Groningen. After studying two years at the university of Groningen and then completing the course at the Amsterdam Mennonite Seminary, he became a *proponent* (ministerial candidate) and began his preaching service in Oldeboorn. During his stay here he brought the Tjalleberd congregation into existence (1817). On March 8, 1818, he began his long term of service in Noordhorn in the province of Groningen (at that time called Terhorne in Humsterland). Under his ministry 1818-71 the congregation prospered, the membership rising from 40 to 90; and in 1838 he managed to get a new church for the congregation, paying a visit to King William I for this purpose.

He was a man of warm, genial piety, an adherent of the so-called Groningen school of theology, which was influenced by Schleiermacher. In the field of social service he was also active; for benefit of the public he founded a department of the *Maatschappij tot Nut van 't Algemeen* (Association for the Promotion of the Common Welfare) in three places. His name lives on especially for his effective part in organizing the *Sociëteit van Doopsgezinde Gemeenten* in Groningen (May 22, 1826), which the congregations in East Friesland also joined in 1878. It was at his instigation that the project was undertaken; he drew up the constitution, and was from the first preliminary meeting chosen as secretary of the organization, holding this important office for 40 years. The Groninger Sociëteit and the *Weduwenfonds* (fund for the support of the widows of ministers) founded by the Sociëteit were also among his chief concerns. vDZ.

Inv. Arch. Amst. I, No. 964; *DB* 1872, 1-10; 1877, 99 f.; K. Vos, *Het 100-jarig bestaan van de Sociëteit van Doopsgez. Gemeenten in Groningen en Oostfriesland* (1926) 16.

Bakker (or Backer), **Johannes de,** became the preacher of the Toren Mennonite church in Amsterdam in 1673. In 1691 he was removed from office, but in 1695 resumed it. His removal from office is discussed in a booklet by H. Bouman, *Korte en klaare aanwijsinge van de proceduren 1691,* and a pamphlet, *Relaas van t'geen is voorgevallen met Dr. J. de Bakker.* He was a physician, zealously defended baptism by pouring, and opposed immersion. He wrote a brief discussion of baptism entitled *Verscheijde redenen, waerom het Overstorten beter voldoet als het onderdompelen* (Several Reasons Why Pouring Is More Satisfactory Than Immersion) (1685, second edition 1687). Also published by him were: in 1707, *Kort onderwijs van de christelijke gebeden waarachter de noodzakelijkheijd van den waterdoop;* in 1712, *Kort onderwijs om wel te prediken;* without date, *De moordenaer voor de Kruijciging bekeert;* and in 1690, *Aanmerkingen over het berigt van den kinderdoop door Balthasar Bekker.* This last writing was directed to Pieter Frenken, preacher in Maastricht. Bakker was doubtless a competent preacher and possessed a well-rounded education. (*Biogr. Wb.* I, 400; *ML* I, 102.) K.V.

Bakker, Paul de (or Paul Backer), participated in the religious disputation of Emden in 1578 as a representative of the Mennonites. (K. Vos, *Menno Simons,* Leiden, 1914, 307.) vDZ.

Baldenheim, an Alsatian village near Schlettstadt, where there was probably a Mennonite congregation in the 17th century. "They met every other Sunday—at most 20 persons. First a preacher spoke about an hour or more, expounding the Gospel. Then another gave testimony to the sermon, as the apostles had done. After the service all fell on their knees in prayer and then sang psalms as is done in the Reformed churches." This is the statement of a Mennonite seized in Basel, Jakob Oberer of Sissach, who had settled in Baldenheim in 1680. Jakob Frick from the canton of Zürich and a Hans from Bern were preachers in this congregation. The Dordrecht Confession of Faith, which was accepted in Ohnenheim in Alsace on Feb. 4, 1660, was signed by Jakob Schnebly of Baldenheim. Ph. A. Grandidier states in his *Oevres historiques inédites* (1865) that Baldenheim was one of the three meeting places of the Alsatian Mennonites; eight families were living there. (P. Burckhardt, *Die Basler Täufer,* 60, 63, and 118; Müller, *Berner Täufer,* 195; *ML* I, 112.) NEFF.

Balen Jansz, Matthijs van, b. Oct. 1, 1611, was a member of the Dordrecht Mennonite congregation. He wrote *Beschrijvinge der Stadt Dordrecht* (Descriptions of the City of Dordrecht), printed in 1677, which is considered a model of contemporary local historiography (*DB* 1862, 106). vDZ.

Balk, a village in the southwest of the Dutch province of Friesland, the seat of the civil community of Gaasterland and also of a Mennonite church, whose members live in several neighboring villages.

The history of this congregation falls into two periods with 1854 as the dividing line. There was probably a church here in the very early time.

Leenaert Bouwens baptized 41 persons here; 32 between 1551 and 1554, 9 between 1557 and 1561. The membership probably never reached 100. Some serious events, now no longer known, caused the membership to decline: by 1720 it was still 70, but by 1763 it was only 10. Then it began a slow increase, maintaining itself at 30 or 35 in the last three years before 1854.

In 1625 the congregation took over a small church, which served until 1863. The congregation belonged to the Old Frisians, specifically to the Pieter Jeltjes (*q.v.*) division, and was one of the last congregations to discard its old Mennonite traditions. It was later also known as an Old Flemish congregation. Until 1854 it had no trained minister, but a lay preacher chosen from its own membership. Anyone chosen for a church office had to accept it. The entire church life was correspondingly simple. The elder who preached stood before a plain lectern. The listeners sat on unpainted, backless benches. Silent prayer was adhered to, but footwashing was abandoned as a general practice. But when a preacher from the outside was received in a home, footwashing and the kiss of peace were observed. The ban was still observed—in 1806 for marrying a non-Mennonite woman—and with it avoidance. At baptism and communion the utensils used were of coarse crockery.

The same simplicity was found in the homes of the members; only the most essential furniture was there, but the bookcase never was missing, which leads to the conclusion that the members were inclined to independent judgment. Clothing was simple; gold and silver were not worn. Of all the traditions that of the clothing was longest preserved. In 1915 an old sister was still living, who had discarded the costume in 1872. (A picture and description of her clothing are found in *DB* 1902.) Tobacco and alcoholic beverages were not used nor offered to others.

To be received into the church, it was not necessary to attend special instruction, but one had to master the *School der Deugd* by Tieleman van Braght (*q.v.*) and the *Onderwijzinge des Christelijken Geloofs* by Boudewijns (*q.v.*). The former was used for the younger persons, the latter for the older. Both these books were reprinted by the "fine Mennonites" in 1824 and 1825. Blaupot ten Cate reports that in 1839 the *Onderwijzinge* of Engel A. van Dooregeest (*q.v.*) was also used in religious instruction. They used the old Biestkens Bible (*q.v.*) and also a Luther translation. Until 1848 their hymnal was the *Kleyn Hoorns Liedtboeck* of 1644 (reprinted 1814). The members voted on the admission of new members.

Military service caused the congregation much difficulty. Several requests were made of the government for exemption, but were not granted. Members helped each other to pay for a substitute; if necessary the church treasury was drawn upon.

Until 1844 the congregation was completely independent. When the A.D.S. was founded, this church asked to be excused from all inquiries and letters concerning the training of ministers, for they had in their own midst enough brethren to serve them with God's Word. For a time they maintained contact with Giethoorn, but longest and closest with Aalsmeer. The preachers of Aalsmeer usually came once a year; that Sunday was a festive day, and on it two sermons were preached. There are still a few letters left from the correspondence with Giethoorn and Aalsmeer, which, together with some old treasurer's accounts, make up all the writings handed down from that period. (This old church, its customs and usages, have been discussed in several volumes of the *DB*, but especially in the issue of 1892. See also Blaupot t. C., *Friesland*, esp. supplement XVIII.)

The situation was radically changed in 1854. Part of the congregation emigrated to America (about 8 miles southwest of Goshen, Ind.) on account of military service. From May 19, 1853, to April 26, 1854, a total of 52 persons emigrated, including 19 members and 2 preachers, R. J. Smits and R. J. Symensma. The elderly Haitje Hantjes Visser was left as the only minister with 14 members. Because he was too old to serve alone, most of these members saw that a change would have to be made. Against the wishes of some, it was decided to call a trained minister. The call was accepted by S. Gorter of Warns and Stavoren. On April 23, 1854, the last lay preacher, H. H. Visser, preached his farewell sermon on Rom. 4:25. Pastor Gorter preached his inaugural sermon on May 7, 1854, on I Cor. 8:1, "Knowledge puffeth up, but charity edifieth." He remained until his death, Aug. 27, 1876.

Evidently some had been waiting for the new order of things, for no fewer than 31 persons from the outside applied for admission and on March 31, 1855, 17 persons were baptized, increasing the membership from 14 to 62. On Feb. 1, 1863, the last sermon was preached in the old church and the present church building was dedicated. The congregation has had the following ministers: S. Gorter, 1854-76; J. J. Honig, 1877-1902; R. van der Veen, 1902-12; H. C. Barthel (*q.v.*), 1912-16; S. J. van der Meulen, 1916-22; B. P. de Vries, 1923-33; W. I. Fleischer, 1933-42; C. F. Brüsewitz, 1943-46; H. J. de Wilde since 1946. All members may vote, and women may hold church office. Services are held every Sunday. The congregation is a member of Ring Bolsward. The membership was 81 in 1898; 100 in 1927; 108 in 1950. The congregation has a Sunday school for children (ages 6-12), a youth's organization and a women's organization. Since 1920 Woudsend (*q.v.*) has joined the Balk congregation for preaching services.   H.C.B.

Gorter's *Doopsgezinde Lectuur*, 1854, 263-98; *DB* 1861, 130 f.; 1887, 86-112; 1892, 46-88; 1902, 26-29; *ML* I, 114.

Balko Mennonite Brethren Church: see **Bethel** Mennonite Brethren Church near Balko, Okla.

Ballum, a village on the Dutch island of Ameland. In 1883 a Mennonite congregation was organized here, which had formerly been a part of the Ameland (*q.v.*) congregation which embraced three villages, each later forming a separate congregation.

Ballum is the smallest of the three; in 1914 it had a membership of 47; in 1950, 40, mostly farmers. They do not have the resources to employ a pastor of their own. The small, simple, but friendly church was dedicated on Oct. 21, 1883, by Pastor Frerichs of Nes with a sermon on Deut. 12. (*DB* 1884, 151; 1889, 1-50; 1890, 1-38; 1912, 133; *ML* I, 114.)   J.L.

Bally, a borough incorporated in 1912 in Berks Co., Pa. It is located in Washington Township (estab. 1832), part of Hereford Township, earlier Colebrookdale, part of "Manatant" (Manatawny). The Hereford area was described as near Cowissioppin, now Goshenhoppen, a name sometimes given the area. Mennonites owned the land and worshiped here prior to 1725; they then were in the "Manatant" congregation, the westernmost of the congregations in the later Franconia Conference (MC), now called the Hereford congregation. Since the division of 1847 there also is located here the Hereford Mennonite (GCM) Church, incorporated in 1893. William H. Bechtel established a post office here named Bally for Father Augustin Bally, priest, 1837-82, in the local Catholic congregation established in 1741.   E.E.S.J.

Balodgahan, a Mennonite (MC) mission station in the village of that name in the Central Provinces of India. The village of 834 acres is situated seven miles southwest of Dhamtari on the Dhamtari-Kanker highway, at the edge of the government-reserved forest. It had previously been considered an outlaw village and because of repeated depredations committed by a criminal band many residents were arrested for crime.

The American Mennonite Mission maintained girls' and boys' orphanages from the time of famine in 1899 and 1900. These boys and girls were growing up and arriving at a marriageable age. To provide homes for those orphans who wished to settle on land, the mission purchased Balodgahan in 1906 at a cost of 8,000 rupees or an equivalent of $2,650.00. The village area consisted of about 600 acres of proprietary forest and agricultural land and more than 200 fields already in possession of resident non-Christian farmers. There were fewer than 350 inhabitants with very few teams and implements, poorly kept homes, and no village improvements.

The mission appointed M. C. Lapp as resident manager to develop the interests of the village, and also authorized the settlement of as many young Christian married couples as could be absorbed into the life of the village. It was soon discovered that the better policy was to sell landholdings to the most industrious and enterprising of our Christian young people in order to build up a self-sustaining Christian community which in the future would also develop into a self-supporting church.

By 1913 about fifty Christian homes had been established on farms of five to ten acres. The mission had constructed a bungalow for the missionary manager and his wife. The girls' orphanage had been moved from Rudri (which had been sold to the government) and cottages built for the girls and also a bungalow for the missionaries in charge of the girls' home.

During the years following, well-constructed primary and middle-school buildings were built. The village congregation which had become organized contributed substantially toward the cost of a house of worship erected in the center of the village. By 1920 the Christian community had outgrown the first church and the construction of a new and larger one was begun. It was of stone and was finished by 1924. It can accommodate nearly a thousand worshipers.

Balodgahan has more than justified the financial investment. In 1949 there were living in the village about 700 Christians including children, and 400 non-Christian residents, totaling 1,100. A widows' home was established with about 50 inmates. The girls' orphanage has become a girls' boarding school. During the school year more than 100 girls were in residence in the institution.

Were double the area available for landholdings, it would soon be taken up by the Indian brethren and sisters who appreciate the value of such investments. Balodgahan has greatly contributed to the self-sufficiency and permanence of the Christian community. (A. Brunk, "A Missionary Administers an Indian Village," *MQR* IV, 1930, 60-67.)
          G.J.L.

Baltasar de Rosieres (Rogiers, Rogieris), an Anabaptist martyr, burned at the stake on the "Big Market" at Antwerp on April 2, 1569, with Jan de Timmerman (*q.v.*) and Jan van Ackeren (*q.v.*). He was born at Doornik (Tournai) in Flanders, was 21 years of age, unmarried and a weaver by trade. He was seized with many others during a meeting of the Antwerp congregation early in February 1569, at the house of Jan Poote (*q.v.*). At his trial he said that he regarded infant baptism as a human institution. He had been rebaptized six months before, but in spite of repeated and extraordinarily painful torture refused to state the name of the person who baptized him or to betray any information concerning the congregation. (*Antw. Arch.-Blad* XII, 350, 370, 399, 439; XIV, 64-65, No. 717.)   vDZ.

Balthasar, an Anabaptist martyr, executed for his faith with two companions at Brno, Moravia, in 1528. No details are known (*Mart. Mir.* D 18, E 428). Another Anabaptist named Balthasar is mentioned in P. Wappler, *Die Täuferbewegung in Thüringen von 1526-1584* (Jena, 1913) p. 110 and 387 (*ML* I, 114).   NEFF.

Balzer (Baltzer), a Mennonite family name of the Frisian group in the Vistula Valley, West Prussia, first mentioned at Montau in 1685. In West Prussia 19 families of this name were counted in 1776, and 27 persons in 1935. Members of this family migrated to Poland, Russia (Molotschna), and America. (See **Heinrich, Peter,** and **J. J. Balzer.**) G.R.

Balzer, Heinrich, a minister of the Kleine Gemeinde (*q.v.*) at Orlov (Molotschna), South Russia, during the 1830's. He is the author of a remarkable tract entitled *Verstand und Vernunft* (Understanding and Reason), written in 1833 (first published by J. G. Stauffer, Quakertown, Pa., in his periodical *Die Kirche unterm Kreuz,* 1886-87). It was re-edited in an English version by Friedmann (in *MQR* XXII, 82-93), together with a discussion of its meaning (*ibid.,* 75-81). The main theme of this semiphilosophical essay regarding the basic principles of Mennonitism is the antithesis of "understanding" and "reason," the difference between a principle appreciated by the "world," namely, natural reason (the intellectual frame of mind), and the other principle that leads the earnest Christian in his search of God's Word, namely, understanding (according to II Tim. 2:7 and similar loci), which can also be called "reason of the heart" (the mind illuminated by the Holy Spirit). It means the faculty to know God and His truth, something inaccessible to natural reason with its science and secular philosophy. Thus Balzer develops most stimulatingly his own theory of the tension between the true Christian and the world, between faith and reason, as a difference of two basic approaches in life. Much depends on whether man chooses understanding or reason as the principle to rely upon. One has to be conscious of this antithesis in order not to fall into the snares of the great enemy. Paul's admonition in II Cor. 10:5, "to bring into captivity every thought to the obedience of Christ" finds here an elaborate apology. "Simplicity is the very element of 'understanding,' but to reason it is obnoxious . . . . Reason, on its part, however, can be led astray through imagination and fancy" (Sect. VI). Balzer warns against any "modernistic" trends in the church tending toward assimilation with the world. This strictly conservative outlook prompted Balzer to part from his former Mennonite affiliation and to join the Kleine Gemeinde, a group not unlike the Reformed Mennonite Church (*q.v.*) in America. In spite of the praise of Biblical simplicity, the essay is unique in the "philosophical" approach to the problem of nonconformity, interpreting the Mennonite position as Balzer saw it, in abstract principles of profound implications. The essay suggests comparison with an old Hutterite letter of 1571 which discusses the similar topic, "Reason and Obedience" (*MQR* XIX, 1945, 27-40). The parallelism of these two Mennonite or Anabaptist documents proves the continuity of one of the main Anabaptist principles up to our time. The implications with regard to learning and other up-to-date problems of church adjustment are obvious.   R.F.

R. Friedmann, "Faith and Reason: The Principles of Mennonitism Reconsidered, in a Treatise of 1833," *MQR* XXII (1948).

Balzer, Jacob J., son of Jacob Balzer and Susanna Ediger, the second child in a family of seven brothers and three sisters, was born Oct. 14, 1860, at Gnadenfeld, Molotschna, South Russia. He came to America with his parents in July 1877, and was married to Susanna Franz, May 5, 1884. To this union was born one son, Jacob S. Balzer. In Russia he attended village school and Zentralschule in Gnadenfeld. He spent one year at Iowa Wesleyan Union College, Mount Pleasant, Iowa.

Balzer was a lifelong member of the Bethel Mennonite (GCM) Church, Mountain Lake, Minn., Sunday-school superintendent for 20 years, minister for 24 years and active in the Northern District of the church, 1889-1927, and then elder, 1927-33. He was also a member of the Home Mission Board and active in Conference work. He was the founder of Mountain Lake Bible School, traveled extensively, and preached in many Mennonite pulpits. He was a lifelong resident of Mountain Lake, Minn., with the exception of four years, when he taught school in Altona, Man. (1909-14). Among his activities was the promotion of mission work and music in the church, organizing weekly *Singstunden* among the young folks. He was an inspiring Bible teacher. Preaching and teaching was his chief work, while traveling and gardening were his avocations. He died in his own home in Mountain Lake, Minn., on Feb. 5, 1946, at the age of 85, and was buried in the Mountain Lake cemetery. An obituary published in the Mountain Lake *Observer,* on Feb. 7, 1946, referred to him as the "grand old citizen."
                    M.B.

Balzer, Peter, was born in Gnadenfeld, a village in the Russian Mennonite colony of Molotschna, Nov. 6, 1847. Losing both his parents in early childhood, his education was provided for by a friend from Steinbach. Under the tutelage of the well-known Mennonite teacher, Heinrich Franz (*q.v.*), he prepared himself for the teaching profession. After teaching for a few years in the village of Liebenau, and after his marriage in 1872 to Sarah Unruh, he joined the Alexanderwohl (*q.v.*) congregation in the emigration to Kansas in 1874, where, in the new Alexanderwohl, he continued to serve the community as a farmer-teacher for 28 years.

In the meantime he also established here a private preparatory school with some encouragement from the Western District Conference (GCM), offering to both local and boarding students from other communities advanced courses for the preparation for the teaching profession. This pioneer preparatory school, which later had many imitators among the western Russian Mennonites, was really the predecessor of the later Emmetal preparatory school in the same community, which later was transplanted to Halstead by the Western Conference and finally developed into Bethel College.

Balzer was ordained to the ministry in the Alexanderwohl (GCM) congregation in 1884 and elected elder in 1896. He was for many years a member of the Foreign Mission Board of the General Conference, and for a time its president; he was president of the directorate of the local Bethesda Hospital (*q.v.*), and a member of the Bethel College Corporation. His first wife having died in 1901, he married the widow of his brother-in-law, Heinrich Richert (*q.v.*), in 1903. He died Dec. 3, 1909.
                    C.H.S.

Mennonite Year Book and Almanac, 1909; H. P. Peters, *History of Education Among the Mennonites in Kansas* (Hillsboro, 1925); *ML* I, 114.

Bamberg, a city in Upper Franconia in Bavaria, the former capital of the bishopric of Bamberg (1007-1802), together with Nürnberg once considered a seat of old-evangelical activity, especially for the Waldenses in Franconia.

Anabaptism also early found entry here, chiefly through Hans Hut (*q.v.*), who baptized many in the region of Bamberg about 1526; also Thomas Spiegel of Ostheim, and Joachim Mertz, a carpenter of Bamberg (Wappler, *Täuferbewegung,* 229 and 315). Weigand, the prince bishop of Redwitz, issued a mandate against the Anabaptists in Bamberg in 1527 and 1528, another in 1529, and a third in 1529 (see **Mandates**). Nineteen Anabaptists were imprisoned in the public jail of the bishop of Bamberg and banished from the country. The bishop's counselors sent a copy of the records of the trial to Kasimir, margrave of Brandenburg, on April 3, 1527. On Jan. 30, 1528, Hans Weissenfelder, a miller of Betzingen, was burned at the stake with four companions, and on the next day Lorenz Reuschlein of Nürnberg was executed with the sword. (Wappler, *Kursachsen,* 45. On page 238 the most peculiar confession of the five martyrs is mentioned; it must have been the result of torture.)

About the same time Jörg, of Passau, a prominent Anabaptist leader, "a well-built young fellow," was also executed (J. E. Jörg, *Deutschland in der Revolutionsperiode 1522-1526*). Johannes Bair (*q.v.*) of Lichtenfels was held a prisoner from Nov. 4, 1528, until his death in 1551 in a tower at Bamberg. George Zaunring (*q.v.*) was beheaded near Bamberg in July 1533 (Wappler, *Kursachsen,* 37). Van Braght (*Mart. Mir.* D 103, E 501) reports the heroic martyr's death of two girls in the bishopric of Bamberg in 1550, which made a deep impression. Thus Anabaptism was widespread in the bishopric before it was wiped out by the brutally violent measures of the government.   NEFF.

H. Haupt, *Die religiösen Sekten in Franken vor der Ref.* (Würzburg, 1882) 26 f.; Keller, *Reformation,* 294-321 (this idea is now thought to be very dubious); S. Berbig, "Die Wiedertäufer im Amt Königsberg in Franken," in *Ztschft f. Kirchengesch.* XIII (1903) 342-50; K. Schottenloher, *Die Buchdrucker-Tätigkeit Georg Erlingers in Bamberg* (Leipzig, 1907) 153; O. Erhard, *Die Ref. der Kirche in Bamberg unter Bischof Weigand 1522-1556, auf Grund archivalischer Beilagen dargestellt* (Erlangen, 1898); P. Wappler, *Die Täuferbewegung in Thüringen 1526-1584* (Jena, 1913); idem, *Die Stellung Kursachsens und des Landgrafen Philipp von Hessen zur Täuferbewegung* (Münster, 1910); *TA* II; *ML* I, 115.

Bämerle, Burkhart, a preacher of the Hutterian Brethren. He was originally an assistant of Philip Weber (*q.v.*) at Auspitz. In 1535, when the Anabaptists were banished from Moravia, he went to Swabia with the Swiss Brethren, and served them as a preacher. In 1542 he returned to Moravia, and became a preacher with the Hutterian Brethren. In 1557 he was seized because of his faith and severely tortured, but was later released. He died in 1567 at Tracht. (Beck, *Geschichts-Bücher,* 72, 151, 152, 252; *ML* I, 115.)   HEGE.

Ban, an instrument of church discipline, which has played an important role in the history of the Mennonites. It is the term used to indicate either exclusion from communion (*kleiner Bann*) or exclusion from membership (*grosser Bann*).

Matt. 18:15-17 is the Biblical foundation of church discipline: "Moreover if thy brother shall trespass against thee, go and tell him his fault between thee and him alone: if he shall hear thee, thou hast gained thy brother. But if he will not hear thee, then take with thee one or two more, that in the mouth of two or three witnesses every word may be established. And if he shall neglect to hear them, tell it unto the church: but if he neglect to hear the church, let him be unto thee as an heathen man and a publican." If Jesus has here expressly pronounced the duty of the church to exercise discipline, He gives the authority in Matt. 16:19, "And I will give unto thee the keys of the kingdom of heaven: and whatsoever thou shalt bind on earth shall be bound in heaven: and whatsoever thou shalt loose on earth shall be loosed in heaven." And in John 20:23 He says to His disciples, "Whose soever sins ye remit, they are remitted unto them; and whose soever sins ye retain, they are retained" (see also I Thess. 5:14; James 5:16).

According to these passages there are three degrees of church discipline; the ban, or excommunication is the third of these. It is, however, not the right of the priest, bishop, or pope to exclude, but alone that of the church, which alone has the authority to pronounce the ban. The ban was practiced thus in the apostolic church (I Cor. 5:3-5); it was managed thus in the old-evangelical groups of the Middle Ages, especially among the Waldenses (Keller, *Reformation,* 56, 57, 109, 224); it was demanded and practiced thus in the Anabaptist churches from their beginning.

The introduction of the ban, i.e., the exclusion of unworthy and corrupt members from the church of Christ, which is to exist as a special community independent of the state, untouched by and unalloyed with the world, was one of the principal demands the Anabaptists made on Zwingli. After a period of wavering, he rejected this demand as he also did on the question of infant baptism (E. Egli, *Analecta Reformatoria* I, 99-149). Punishment of blasphemers by the government (said Zwingli) made the ban unnecessary. Thus Zwingli was in 1525 already strongly in favor of the idea of a state church; but he had prominent opponents in the ranks of his church.

At the Bürgertag of the cities of Zürich, Basel, Bern, Schaffhausen, St. Gall, Mühlhausen, Biel, and Constance on Sept. 27, 1530, Oecolampadius proposed that the ban be introduced again. And a few months later, at the public disputation at St. Gall, Dec. 20-23, 1530, Dominicus Zili defended the ban most vigorously against Zwingli with Scriptural reasons. He was defeated and was forbidden to preach. But the dispute on this question continued for many years in the Reformed Church. Calvinists and Zwinglians were sharply opposed.

The Lutheran Church repeatedly stated the Biblical command to exercise the small and the great ban; but interference by the state and the religious indifference of the individual congregations did not permit a strict and determined application of the Biblical requirement (*HRE* II, 381 ff.).

The position of the Anabaptists on the ban is more consistent and unified. They hold themselves strictly to the word and command of Jesus, Matt. 18. In their concept of the Christian church the use of the ban is implicit. The church is a brotherhood of those who, by their own decision, have obligated themselves in their baptismal vow to a truly pious Christian life as a disciple of Christ. The church must preserve this "pure" character if it is not to suffer dissolution. The wicked and blasphemous have no place in it. The church as the body of Christ must expel them as the human body casts out an unclean ulceration. But the ban may be applied only to coarse, notorious sinners. This was the doctrine and the practice of the early Anabaptists.

In the letter of the Zürich Anabaptists to Thomas Müntzer of Sept. 5, 1524, they say, "Form a Christian church with Christ's help and His rules, as we find them established in Matt. 18 and applied in the Epistles. He who does not correct his faults, is unwilling to believe, and resists the word and act of God and remains so, after Christ and His Word and His rules have been preached to him and he has been admonished with the three witnesses, shall not be killed, but regarded as a heathen and a publican, and left alone."

The seven Articles of Schleitheim (Feb. 24, 1527) state, "The ban shall be used with all those who have yielded themselves to the Lord, to follow in His commands, and with all those who are baptized into one body and permit themselves to be called brethren and sisters, and yet somehow slip and fall into error and sin and have been unwittingly overtaken. These shall be admonished, the second time secretly and the third time be punished openly before the entire church according to Christ's command (Matt. 18). But this shall take place according to the order of the Spirit of God before the breaking of bread, that we may all with one spirit and love break and eat of one bread and drink of one cup."

Especially noteworthy is Balthasar Hubmaier's interpretation of the ban. He does this in two books. One has the title, *Von der brüderlichen Strafe. Wo diese nicht ist, da ist gewisslich auch keine Kirche, obschon die Wassertaufe und das Abendmahl Christi daselbst gehalten werden* (Nikolsburg, 1527). Then he explains: The Christian church is made up of persons who have devoted themselves to God in a new life through baptism. As such they must do the will of Christ. But since human beings remain sinners, a medicine is needed to remove the bad flesh. This medicine is brotherly discipline, without which the church cannot exist. There are two kinds of sins: open sins, which must be punished openly, and secret sins, which must be punished secretly; according to Christ's command, first privately, then before two or three witnesses, and finally before the church. First the brother or sister should have his attention called to his sin in the light of his baptismal vow, and then if he does not hear, and not until then, witnesses shall be called or the church informed. Those who live in strife with each other should be dealt with in the same manner, to lead them to reconciliation. This power of admonition may be exercised by every Christian. Only where the church is a true church, can discipline be exercised properly.

Another pamphlet is directly connected with the above; namely, *Von dem christlichen Bann. Wo derselbe nicht aufgerichtet und gebraucht wird nach dem ordentlichen und ernstlichen Befehl Christi, daselbst regiert nichts denn Sünde, Schande und Laster* (Nikolsburg, 1527). Here he says, "The ban is the public excommunication of a person who is unwilling to desist from a scandalous, open sin. The purpose of the ban is to avoid offending the weak; the second purpose is to cause the sinner to examine himself and reform. The church received the authority to ban from Christ (Matt. 16:19). Christ gave the disciples two keys, one to loose and one to bind. The former is used in baptism; it opens the portals of the church for the forgiving of sins; it is also used with the penitent sinner to receive him again as often as he shows genuine repentance. The second key gives the church the power to excommunicate the sinner." In this connection Hubmaier introduces a formula for the ban with the phrase, "without wishing to encroach upon the liberty of anyone." The church leader points the sinner to his baptismal vow, calls his attention to his sins and the threefold admonition, and then commits him to the devil. It is not permitted to hold intercourse of any kind with him, but neither is it permitted to mistreat or to kill him. Only the government has the power of punishment after as before the excommunication. All deeds of friendship must cease, but in case of need it is permissible to support him. Only members of the church, not those outside the church, may be banned. But all Christians who break their baptismal vow and are unwilling to correct their fault, should be excommunicated, and their names passed on to the other congregations. Whoever sees his sin and asks for pardon shall be received, no matter how often it happens. True penitence is shown by reform of conduct. "But," Hubmaier concludes these explanations, "if the great lords do not want to institute church discipline, no Christian rule will be possible. But to Christians the manger in Bethlehem is a dearer place to linger in than the grand church of the Pharisees; for there he will lose the star that leads to Christ."

It is very interesting and of great significance to note how these instructive statements of Hubmaier's coincide with the practical statements and judgments of the Swiss Brethren. Thus, in the disputation at Zofingen, July 1-9, 1532, the Anabaptists said: "When one is warned once and a second time, and he does not reform, he should be reported to the church, excommunicated, and not received again until he proves himself with the fruits of righteousness. No one shall be banned unless he has committed an open sin which deserves the punishment. These are the abominations that do not inherit the kingdom of God, as Paul points out in Gal. 5. These, if they are known to the church, shall be put out according to the regulation of the ban. The public exercise of the ban is administered by the leader, not without the foreknowledge of the church, but with and in the church, which should hear and judge the affair according to its merits. When one has committed a sin openly, he shall make amends for it openly."

This shows that there was unity among the Swiss and South German Anabaptists in the concept and practice of the ban. Its importance and necessity in the life of the Christian church was everywhere recognized; the churches endeavored to fulfill the Biblical demands earnestly, and yet with love, strictly, and yet with justice. Among some of the Dutch Anabaptists this was not the case. Here a harsh use of the ban was the cause of lamentable quarrels and regrettable divisions. A stricter and a milder branch were formed, a division between the "coarse and the fine," who violently opposed and banned each other. Sebastian Franck must have had this kind of proceedings in mind when he generalized in his *Chronica* (193), "There is much banning in their churches, so that almost every church bans the other, and there is almost as much freedom of belief as in the papacy. Whoever does not say yes to everything, his ears has God stopped, and they begin mournfully to pray for him. If he does not soon turn about, they put him out."

Menno Simons expressed himself at length on the ban in his books. In 1541 he devoted a pamphlet, *A Kind Admonition . . . How a Christian Should Be Disposed; and Concerning the Shunning and Separation of the Unfaithful . . .* (*Complete Works* II, 441), to the question. He demands that believers avoid the company of backslidden members of unclean conduct, in order to make them ashamed of themselves and correct their errors. But this shall be done only after previous admonitions according to Matt. 18 have been disregarded.

Now various opinions arose on the avoidance and the act of excommunication. They concerned principally two questions; namely, whether the ban demanded an avoidance of the banned one by all members including husband or wife, or whether in this instance the requirements could be eased; and whether in all offenses, including coarse carnal sins, a triple warning must precede the ban, and then must be pronounced only if there is no improvement in conduct.

On this question Menno expresses himself in his writing, *A Scriptural Explanation of Excommunication for the Benefit of All Pious and God-fearing Children* (*Complete Works* II, 123) to the effect that the avoidance must extend to worldly relationships, that one may not have dealings with the banned one, nor eat or drink with him, that the avoidance in marriage is not a dissolving of marriage; but the conscience shall herein not be burdened. But if the fallen member yields to the admonition, the ban shall not be applied. He ex-

presses himself similarly in the appendix to his booklet, *Confession of the Triune, Eternal and True God, Father, Son, and Holy Ghost* (*Complete Works* II, 179 ff.). He emphasizes the need for the ban again in his largest work, which is directed against Gellius Faber. In his letters Menno also repeatedly stated his views on the ban. It is his opinion that in the case of coarse carnal sins excommunication must be applied immediately without preliminary admonition. Once more Menno develops his views on the ban in one of his latest works, *An Account of Exclusion or Separation from the Church of Christ* (*Works* II, 239 ff.). Sharply and earnestly he defends avoidance in marriage; he requires Christian moderation and kindness in its application, and especially defends the view that those known to be coarse offenders be put out of the church at once and not after the threefold warning.

The harshest conception of the ban was represented by Leenaert Bouwens (*q.v.*). He demanded an unconditional and universal avoidance in marriage, and in most cases the application of the ban without preliminary admonition and warning. He banned his opponents, who favored a milder view. This led to the first division (1556) of the Anabaptists into Waterlanders and the main Frisian-Flemish group.

A much milder conception of the use of the ban was held by the Swiss Brethren and the Upper German Anabaptists. They were unable to assent to the resolutions of the convention of elders at Wismar in 1554. These resolutions among other things stated: (1) Those who married outside the Anabaptist brotherhood should be excluded, but if they led an upright, Christian life they should be received again. (2) Only in case of absolute necessity was buying or selling permitted with backsliders. (3) Marital avoidance of the backslidden husband or wife should be observed, but not if it violates conscience. Two emissaries of the High German Anabaptists, Zylis and Lemke, personally conferred with Menno Simons, to win him over to a milder view; but they did not succeed. At a large meeting of Anabaptists at Strasbourg in 1557, marital avoidance (*q.v.*) was rejected. Menno and the Dutch were requested by this meeting in a letter not to take an extreme position on the use of the ban, which might lead to division.

Nearly 150 years later it was again the attitude toward the ban that caused a division among the Mennonites. This time it occurred in Switzerland and South Germany. Jakob Ammann (*q.v.*), an elder in a Mennonite congregation in the Bernese Oberland, demanded marital avoidance and refusal to eat with the banned members. Elder Hans Reist of the Emmental and his followers opposed him. This led to the momentous division into Amish and "Reist" Mennonites, which has remained to a large extent even to the present.

The Mennonites clung tenaciously to the requirement of the ban. The Dordrecht Confession of 1632, Art. VII, says, "We confess and believe also a ban . . . . When someone after he has been enlightened and has accepted the knowledge of the truth, and has become a part of the communion of saints, afterwards again falls into coarse sin, he shall not remain in the company of the righteous, but shall be removed as an offensive member and open sinner, and punished before all the members, and scoured out as leaven, and that to his correction and as an example to warn others, and to keep the church pure. In short, that the church must put away him who is evil, whether in doctrine or life, and nobody else." In Article VII the strict avoidance of the banned member is enjoined; only in the case of necessity shall anyone help him or show him brotherly love.

Gerrit Roosen of Hamburg expressed a similar view in *Evangelisches Glaubensbekenntnis der taufgesinnten Christen oder also genannten Mennonisten, wie solches in Altona bei Hamburg öffentlich gelehrt und gepredigt wird,* 1702 (Article VIII). (See *Bekenntnis der preussischen Mennoniten* of 1660.)

The confession of Cornelis Ris of 1773 (Hoorn, Holland) represents the milder concept. It sets up four stages of discipline: (1) the brotherly admonition; (2) earnest admonition and counsel, not to partake of communion until the offense is removed and clear evidence of improvement is shown; (3) open punishment before the church; and (4) excommunication. The avoidance of banned persons should be observed in Christian kindness and love. Between husband and wife this (marital) avoidance (*q.v.*) is not to be observed in any case except for adultery.

In Holland the Waterlanders practiced a mild form of banning, and already in the first half of the 17th century the ban gradually fell into disuse. Both in the Flemish and the Frisian group a division took place in 1586 and 1589 respectively, on the ban. The Old Frisians and Old Flemish were more rigorous in applying the ban than the Young Frisians and the (Soft) Flemish. The latter two groups soon followed the lenient practice of the Waterlanders. After the 18th century the ban was applied only in a few cases and only in the conservative congregations of the Jan Jacobsgezinden and the Old Flemish. Today the Mennonites of Holland as well as in the cities of North Germany have completely given up church discipline. The ban is never exercised. In the Palatine churches only the "small ban" is occasionally applied. The *Formularbuch* of 1852 states, "He who obviously lives in abomination and the works of the flesh and of darkness, cannot belong to Christ, and therefore cannot be a believing member of His body, the Christian church. His evil deeds and sins separate him from God. But since, by the express word of the Lord and His apostles, the holy communion is an exclusive pleasure of the believers, i.e., of those who belong to the Lord as His people, it follows clearly that those who openly live in sin and vice and thereby cause stumbling and offense, can have no part in the holy communion as long as they remain impenitent. Therefore, if there is such a member in a church, who on a Scriptural basis, because of his offensive conduct, cannot be considered worthy of admission to the communion, such

a member, after he has been admonished several times in a brotherly and earnest manner, and still is unwilling to desist from his sinful conduct, shall be excluded from participation in the holy communion by the leaders of the church in question, and not re-admitted until he has expressed genuine penitence in an open confession to the leaders and given evidence of it in his conduct. The exclusion takes place either before the assembled church [which is no longer done, N.] or silently before the leaders of the church."

The Mennonites of Baden and Württemberg hold a much stricter conception and execution of the ban. In their *Leitfaden zum Gebrauch bei gottesdienstlichen Handlungen,* of 1876, the following is said about the ban: "If a member of the church perseveres in his wrongdoing and in his sin in spite of all admonition, then sharing in the communion is denied him. This disciplinary measure (the 'little ban') is to be applied for the lighter offenses. But if a member perseveres in his serious and open sins after repeated admonition, and has not let himself be moved to a change of attitude by exclusion from communion, he is excluded from the church and is no longer considered a member, until he shows a change of attitude and requests admission. Without previous admonition the ban is to be used with members who have fallen into open and flagrant sins . . . and upon marriage with members of the state churches . . . especially when such a member permits his children to be baptized, because he thereby actually disclaims the chief principle of our church, baptism upon confession of faith. Excommunication may be executed only by the elder of the congregation."

The position of the country churches in West Prussia was stated in the confession of faith of 1895: "In the case of flagrant sins which cause offense, an immediate separation from the church is required. This must be done before the church according to I Tim. 5:20. Avoidance of the banned members is connected with the separation according to I Cor. 5 and II Thess. 3. Nevertheless we must take care that hate and enmity do not creep in under the guise of the ban, II Thess. 3:15. But when an excluded member confesses his sins and shows genuine fruits of repentance, then we consider it our duty to receive him again into the church, II Cor. 2:6-10."

Similar regulations concerning the use of the ban are contained in the *Handbuch zum Gebrauch bei gottesdienstlichen Handlungen der Mennoniten-Gemeinden in Russland,* of 1911. The first confession of the Mennonite Brethren of Jan. 6, 1860, states, "Concerning the ban we confess that all wanton and carnally-minded sinners must be put out of the communion of believers, as Paul testifies in II Thess. 3:14 and 15. But if it happens that someone secretly falls into a carnal offense, which may God prevent, and if the Spirit of Christ, who alone is able to create true penitence in us, persuades him to confess and repent, then the church has no power at all to ban such a penitent sinner, because forgiveness of sins is not acquired in or through the ban, but through the merits of Christ.

—An unrepentant sinner, however, may not be admitted into the church until he is sincerely converted to Christ." (This confession is printed only in *Menn. Bl.*, 1863, 11, in article "Die Separatistischen Bewegungen in Süd-Russland.") The Mennonite Brethren Confession of 1902 (*Glaubensbekenntnis der Vereinigten Christlichen Taufgesinnten Mennonitischen Brüdergemeinde in Russland*) takes a similar position, following the earlier edition of 1874.

The Mennonites of North America practice both the forms of the ban, according to their official confessions and disciplines or ministers' manuals, although in some areas of one or two groups the practice has become lax. Avoidance (*q.v.*) is practiced, however, only by the most conservative groups, viz., the Old Order Amish, the Church of God in Christ Mennonite, the Reformed Mennonites, and the Old Colony Mennonites and related groups. The majority of all Mennonites, and all kinds of Amish, in the United States still use the Dordrecht Confession. The General Conference Mennonite Church in its ministers' manual of 1893 took over almost word for word the statements of the Baden *Leitfaden* on the ban. In both theory and practice the Swiss and French Mennonites still practice both forms of the ban, though without the avoidance. NEFF.

Müller, *Berner Täufer;* C. Sachsse, *Dr. Balthasar Hubmaier als Theologe* (Berlin, 1914); C. J. van der Smissen, *Die Glaubenslehre der Mennoniten oder Taufgesinnten, dargestellt von C. Ris* (Hoorn, 1850); E. Troeltsch, *Die Soziallehren der christlichen Kirchen* (Tübingen, 1912); K. Vos, *Menno Simons* (Leiden, 1912); J. Horsch, *Menno Simons* (Scottdale, 1916); C. Krahn, *Menno Simons* (Karlsruhe, 1936); *Allgemeines Formularbuch zum Gebrauch bei dem öffentlichen Gottesdienst in den evangelischen Menn.-Gem.* (Worms, 1852); *Christliches Glaubensbekenntnis der Waffenlosen . . .* (Amsterdam, 1664); *Handbuch für Prediger der Menn.-Gem. in Russland* (1911); *Leitfaden zum Gebrauch bei gottesdienstlichen Handlungen für die Aeltesten und Prediger der Gesamt-Menn.-Gem. in Baden* (Sinsheim, 1876); ML I, 115 ff.; J. Horsch, *Mennonites of Europe* (Scottdale, 1941); J. C. Wenger, *Separated unto God* (Scottdale, 1951); N. van der Zijpp, *Gesch. der Doopsgezinden in Nederland* (Arnhem, 1952) 48 f., 120, 175 f.; ML I, 115-19.

Bandungardjo, seat of a Mennonite congregation on the Indonesian island of Java, in the former territory of the Dutch Mennonite Mission Society. This congregation was organized in 1940 as an independent Javanese church. In 1949 the baptized membership was 64, while 34 children attended the Sunday school. Since 1943 the assistant minister (not ordained) of this congregation has been Mintohardjo. (*Verslag Doopsgez. Zending*, 1949, 15, 16.) vDZ.

Banfield Memorial Church (UMC), located at 439 Vaughan Road, Toronto, Ont., is a member of the Ontario Conference. Organized on Nov. 1, 1897, under the leadership of Noah Detwiler, the congregation first met in rented halls. On April 25, 1948, a new church was dedicated. The membership in 1952 was 107 and F. G. Huson served as pastor. F.G.H.

Bank Mennonite Church (MC) is located 2½ miles west of Dayton, Va., on the bank of Dry River in the Ashby district of Rockingham County. The first church, likely built in 1847, was enlarged in 1870, and served as a place of worship until the 1890's. The church now standing on the grounds was dedicated on Aug. 20, 1893.

The Bank congregation belongs to the Middle District of the Virginia Conference. In 1953 it had a membership of 201 under the leadership of Joseph Heatwole and Melvin Heatwole.

It was in this church that John S. Coffman, the pioneer Mennonite evangelist, was ordained to the ministry on July 18, 1875. This church figured most largely in the Virginia branch of the Wisler (*q.v.*) Mennonite division (Old Order Mennonite) of the Middle District of the Virginia Conference at the close of the 19th century. H.A.B.

Bank Ranch, a Hutterite Bruderhof at Danvers, Mont., founded in 1947 by families from the Wolf Creek Bruderhof at Stirling, Alta. In 1947 it had a population of 54 souls with 20 baptized members. D.D.

Bankroetiers (Defaulters), a small branch of Dutch Mennonites who separated in 1598 from the *Huiskoopers* (*q.v.*) or Old Flemish. Jacob Pieters van der Meulen (*q.v.*), a leader of the *Huiskoopers*, did not think it necessary to excommunicate a brother for bankruptcy. Other leaders, especially Hans Busschaert, held the opposite view. The outcome was that van der Meulen was excommunicated with the debtor and his following. They formed a group known as the *Bankroetiers*. This group was, however, soon dissolved. J.L.

Blaupot t.C., *Friesland;* DB 1876; J. A. Starck, *Gesch. der Taufe und Taufgesinnten* (Leipzig, 1789).

Banman, Heinrich, was born April 19, 1843, in Alexanderwohl, Molotschna Mennonite colony, South Russia, the son of Franz B. and Elizabeth Dalke Banman, both born in the Molotschna. Heinrich was the third child of four. When Heinrich was 14 years old his teacher persuaded the parents to send him to school for three more years to be trained as a teacher. At the age of 20 he began to teach the village school of Hamberg, which he taught for 12 years. On June 12, 1861, he was baptized by Elder Peter Wedel and was received into the Alexanderwohl Mennonite Church (*q.v.*). In 1863 he was married to Helena Buller; this marriage was blessed with nine children, six sons and three daughters. In 1874, at the time of the Mennonite emigration to America, the Banmans too joined the emigrants. For several years he served the Alexanderwohl Mennonite (GCM) Church in Kansas as song leader. In 1884 this church ordained him as minister, in which capacity he served for 40 years. At the death of Elder Peter Balzer he was given the leadership of the church; in 1910 he was elected as elder and served five years. He took an active part in the founding of the Bethesda Hospital and acted as chairman and secretary for 27 years. For 23 years he was the editor of the *Bethesda Herald*. He served on the Western District (GCM) Conference committee of itinerant ministers (*Reiseprediger*) for 23 years and traveled extensively for the conference. A member of the founding group of Bethel College (*q.v.*), he served on the college board of directors for 25 years. He died March 21, 1933, at the age of 89 years and was laid to rest in the Alexanderwohl church cemetery.   C.R.V.

Banning(h), Jacob Pieters, was a preacher in the Waterlander congregation of Wormer and Jisp (in the Dutch province of North Holland). The fact that he did not believe in heaven and hell as finite places in the universe, or in the existence of the devil, caused offense in the congregation. The matter was discussed at a meeting of the congregation on Dec. 8, 1697; here it was apparent that Banning had a following, and a decision could not be arrived at, though he was forbidden to preach. Then the officers of the congregation decided to turn the settlement of the dispute over to certain preachers of the brotherhood. These men, two of whom were Herman Schijn (*q.v.*) and E. A. van Dooregeest (*q.v.*), met on April 2, 1698. When it became apparent that Banning also questioned the resurrection of the body, he was charged with "strange doctrine." Although it was emphatically stated that the committee could not act as judges, and that the congregation alone had the authority to depose him from office—nevertheless he was deprived of his office. It seems that the stirring up of offense and Banning's tactlessness may have turned the scales even more than did the facts of the case. Banning wrote in his own defense: *Eenvoudig Verhaal van de Proceduuren gepleegt in de Waterlandse Doopsgezinde Gemeentens tot Wormer en Jisp, over het doen ophouden van een haarer Leeraaren in zijn Predikdienst . . .* (1698), which was published in two editions in Amsterdam. (*DB* 1898, 78-106; *Catalogus Amst.*, 153.)   vDZ.

Bannmann (Bahnmann, Banman), a Mennonite family name in the Thiensdorf (*q.v.*) Frisian congregation, West Prussia, near Elbing. This family moved to Russia (Molotschna settlement), and some members later to the United States and Canada.   G.R.

Bansterzijl, Dutch province of Groningen, where Leenaert Bouwens (*q.v.*) baptized 18 persons in 1551-54 and another 9 in 1557-61. About a congregation here nothing is known. The members may have joined a congregation in the neighborhood.   vDZ.

Baptism, from the very beginning of Christian history a major ceremony or ordinance (called sacrament by the liturgical churches), instituted by Christ Himself in the Great Commission, the ceremony of initiation into membership in the church.

1. *Meaning.* At the time of the Reformation the Roman Catholic Church taught that baptism was essential to salvation, that it was efficacious for the washing away of original sin and all sins committed up to baptism, that it conveyed divine grace automatically (*ex opere operato*), and that it should be administered to infants at the earliest possible moment, since they are lost without baptism, and that the mode should be pouring or sprinkling. Luther (and the strict Lutherans after him) made but slight change in the meaning of baptism. He denied the *ex opere operato* character of the sacra-

ment, making it conditional upon faith in the recipient, but taught baptismal regeneration. However, since it is obvious that the infant himself cannot exercise faith, he was forced to claim either that the infant had a "sleeping faith" given him by God, or that the godparents (patrons at the baptism) exercised a substitute faith for the infant. Zwingli and Calvin (followed by the Reformed churches generally) held that baptism had no power to convey grace but was only a symbol of acceptance in the church and a pledge to Christian nurture. All forms of Protestantism (Lutheran, Reformed, and Anglican) except Anabaptism, as well as Roman and Greek Catholicism, practiced and required infant baptism for the entire population (usually required by law), thus using it as the necessary and effective instrument to continue or establish and maintain a national or mass church. Regardless of the theological meaning given to it by the church, the mass of the people of that time held infant baptism to be the magical or semi-magical means to salvation, the means of incorporation into the general Christian society, and the solemn religious recognition of the beginning of life. With this great meaning it has remained deeply imbedded in the popular mass mind, both Catholic and Protestant. The tenacity with which state church leaders have clung to infant baptism and vigorously fought all movements for its modification or abolition is abundant proof that it is a necessary pillar of the state church system. Every movement, however, which emphasizes personal belief, commitment, regeneration, and holy living, almost inevitably tends to minimize or nullify the sacramental character of baptism and the baptism of infants, in favor of adult baptism understood as a symbol of regeneration and a pledge to holy living. This was not only true to Anabaptism and its descendants, but is evident in Socinianism, Arminianism, Pietism, and modern Revivalism as well.

The question of the relation of the various Reformation (Catholic, Protestant, Anabaptist) conceptions of the meaning of baptism and the proper subjects of baptism to the original New Testament teaching and the practice of the early church is of course answered differently today by the various groups. This is due in part at least to the lack of explicit N.T. statements on these points. There is no clear-cut case in the N.T. of infant baptism, although the advocates of the latter confidently assert that the report of whole households being baptized must include children, and that the correspondence between baptism and circumcision as the rites of initiation into the people of God under the two covenants strongly implies infant baptism as a parallel to infant circumcision. These arguments were in fact used by the reformers to answer the challenge of the Anabaptists who demanded proof from the Scripture (claimed by the reformers as the sole authority for faith) for infant baptism. Modern scholars have in general agreed that infant baptism cannot be positively proved from the N.T. either theologically or historically, thus granting the Anabaptist claim, and many concede that the logic of the requirement of personal repentance, faith and obedience as called for by Christ and the apostles, requires baptism to be only upon confession of faith, although few go so far as to call for the abandonment of infant baptism. Karl Barth (*Die kirchliche Lehre von der Taufe*, Zürich, 1943) is one of the few (but very influential) who both theologically and practically abandon infant baptism in favor of believers' baptism. Oscar Cullman (*Die Tauflehre des N.T. Erwachsenen- und Kindertaufe*, Zürich, 1948) and Joachim Jeremias (*Hat die älteste Kirche die Kindertaufe geübt?* Göttingen, 1938) take the opposite position. In any case the concept of baptism is closely tied to the conception of the church.

The Anabaptists' insistence upon believers' baptism and upon the meaning of baptism as a symbol and pledge had three roots: first, their Biblicism, second, their concept of the church, and third, their concept of the nature of Christianity. Reading the N.T. and finding everywhere baptism tied to repentance and faith, they concluded that baptism should not be administered to anyone but believers, and that infant baptism was accordingly no baptism at all but only a "water-bath." Since, however, baptism is commanded by Christ, they admitted no one into the churches without it and accordingly "re-"baptized everyone, though not counting it essential to salvation. Their concept of the church as a voluntary fellowship composed only of those who had an experience of conversion and could intelligently commit themselves to discipleship, holy living, and brotherly love, a church to be kept pure from sin and separated from the world, was in direct contrast to the prevailing mass church concept. Adult baptism is, however, essential to the Anabaptist type of church, whereby baptism becomes a distinguishing mark of separation and commitment. Since no compulsion is to be used to force people to belong to the church, to keep them in the church, or to maintain a holy life, voluntary membership with believers' baptism as its outward symbol logically becomes the only admissible procedure of initiation. Finally the Anabaptist concept of discipleship or newness of life in which the Lordship of Christ was to be made to apply to every phase of life, required a type of personal commitment and intelligent discrimination which only adults could have. Believers' baptism thus was essential to Anabaptism, though it was a consequence rather than the foundation of Anabaptist faith.

The evidence of the position of the Anabaptists and Mennonites on baptism from the very beginning to the present is so voluminous, clear, and well known as not to require detailed proof from the sources. A few citations will suffice. Already in 1524 (letter to Müntzer) Conrad Grebel said: "Baptism is described in the Scriptures to mean that the sins of the one to be baptized (who is repenting, and believing both before and after) are washed away through faith and the blood of Christ; that it [further] means that he must be and has become dead to sin and is walking in newness of life and spirit, and [further] that one will assuredly be saved if he lives out the meaning [of baptism] by the inner baptism according to faith." And in December 1524 he (or Mansz?) says in his *Protest and Defense* to the Zürich Council: "Of such passages and their like the entire New Testament Scripture is full: from which I have now clearly learned and know of a surety that baptism is nothing else than a dying to the old man and the putting on of a new; also that Christ commanded to baptize those who had been taught and that the apostles baptized none except those who had been taught, for Christ indeed baptized no one without external evidence of readiness, and certain testimony [of faith] or desire. Whosoever says or teaches other than this does something which he can prove with no Scripture and I should like to listen to anyone who, out of the Scriptures, can prove to me clearly and in truth that John, Christ, or the apostles baptized children or taught that they should be baptized."

The first article of the Schleitheim Confession of 1527 is on baptism and reads as follows: "Observe concerning baptism: Baptism shall be given to all those who have learned repentance and amendment of life, and who believe truly that their sins are taken away by Christ, and to all those who walk in the resurrection of Jesus Christ, and wish to be buried with Him in death, so that they may be resurrected with Him, and to all those who with this significance request it [baptism] of us and demand it for themselves. This excludes all infant baptism, the highest and chief abomination of the pope. In this you have the foundation and testimony of the apostles. Mt. 28, Mk. 16, Acts 2, 8, 16, 19. This we wish to hold simply, yet firmly and with assurance."

Menno Simons speaks often about baptism. Typical quotations are the following: "For however diligently we may search day and night, we yet find but one baptism in the water, pleasing to God, which is expressed and contained in His Word, namely the baptism on the confession of faith, commanded by Christ Jesus, taught and administered by His holy apostles." "The believing receive remission of sins not through baptism, but in baptism, in the following manner: as with their whole heart they believe the precious Gospel of Jesus Christ which has been preached and taught to them, namely the glad tidings of grace, remission of sins, peace, favor, mercy and eternal life through Jesus Christ, our Lord, they experience a change of mind, renounce self, bitterly repent of their old sinful life, and with all diligence give attendance to the Word of the Lord who has shown them such great love; and fulfill all that He has taught and commanded in His holy Gospel. Their confidence is firmly established upon the word of grace promising the remission of sins through the precious blood and the merits of our Lord Jesus Christ. They therefore receive holy baptism as a token of obedience which proceeds from faith, an evidence before God and His church that they firmly believe in the remission of sins through Christ Jesus, as has been preached and taught them from the Word of God" (*Writings*, 244).

Riedemann's *Rechenschaft* (1545) says the following in the section "Concerning the Baptism of Christ and of His Church." "Now because it is a testament of the recognition, knowledge and grace of God, baptism is also, according to the words of Peter, the bond of a good conscience with God, that is, of those who have recognized God. The recognition of God, however, cometh, as hath been said, from hearing the word of the gospel. Therefore we teach that those who have heard the word, believed the same, and have recognized God, should be baptized—and not children."

All the Mennonite confessions and catechisms have clear statements on the meaning and administration of baptism which clearly prove that the original Anabaptist interpretation is still everywhere maintained. There have been periods and places, to be sure, where the actual practice has fallen behind the theory of the confessions, and where baptism at a certain age has become traditional, without a corresponding living experience. In order to overcome this danger some groups have introduced a personal public testimony by the candidate concerning a conversion experience, as well as a careful examination of the candidate either by the bishop or elder, or the ministerial body, or a representative group of members. In Holland the emphasis upon a personal intelligent commitment has led to a very late age for baptism even into the twenties (see **Admission into the Church.**)

2. *Mode and Ritual.* Although baptism by trine immersion was certainly the common practice in the early and medieval church it was discontinued in the course of time (except in the Greek Orthodox Church) so that by the time of the Reformation, pouring was the only mode commonly used. The Reformers continued this mode. The Anabaptists likewise used pouring, which has continued since to be the standard mode among Mennonites except in those groups which have introduced immersion. Conrad Grebel's "Protest and Defense" (1524) specifically uses the phrase "poured over with water" in referring to the baptism at Pentecost: "they were thereafter poured over with water meaning that just as they were cleansed within by the coming of the Holy Spirit, so they also were poured over with water externally to signify for the inner cleansing and dying to sin." Riedemann's *Rechenschaft*, in describing "The Manner of Baptizing, or How One Baptizeth," says, "The Baptizer telleth him to humble himself with bent knees before God and his Church and kneel down, and he taketh pure water and poureth it upon him." K. Vos, in his article on baptism by pouring (*DB* 1911), has assembled numerous citations showing that this was also the method in Holland.

Fortunately a detailed description of the administration of baptism on one of the very first occasions, in Zollikon near Zürich Jan. 25, 1525, has been preserved. It is the baptism of Hans Bruggbach (Brubacher?) by Felix Manz. After Bruggbach had confessed his sins and requested baptism as a sign of his conversion, Blaurock asks Brugg-

bach, "Do you desire the baptism?" to which he replies "Yes." Manz says, "Who will forbid me, that I should not baptize him?" (Acts 10:47), to which Blaurock answers, "No one." Manz then takes a metal dipper (as used in the typical kitchen of that time), pours water from it over the head of the candidate, and says, "I baptize you in the name of God the Father, God the Son, and God the Holy Spirit." It is worth noting that there is record that Grebel, Manz, and Blaurock each performed at least one baptism in the earliest days of the new movement, thus indicating that no particular ordination was as yet required of the one who did the baptizing. The record also shows that baptisms were performed at any time and place, usually in the homes of the candidates or wherever the meeting was being held. However, in St. Gall Grebel baptized a large number (several hundred) in the Sitter River in April 1525, and Wolfgang Ulimann, the St. Gall Anabaptist leader, had been baptized in the Rhine River near Schaffhausen in February. The St. Gall chronicler Kessler describes this latter baptism as follows: "Ulimann . . . ran into Conrad Grebel and was by him so filled with the knowledge of rebaptism that he did not wish only to be poured over with water from a dish, but to be taken altogether naked into the Rhine by Grebel and pressed under and covered over (*undergetruckt und bedeckt werden*)." Remembering that this is only a report by a chronicler of the opposition party written some years afterward and therefore not absolutely reliable, one may conclude that Grebel had intended to follow the customary practice of pouring the baptismal water out of a vessel, but yielded to Ulimann's request for immersion, since they were at the bank of the Rhine. There is no other evidence of the practice of immersion in Anabaptist history anywhere, and the evidence of the uniform practice by pouring is so overwhelming that the Ulimann case must be considered purely exceptional.

Some Baptist historians, in their desire to claim Anabaptist support for their immersion practice, have distorted the Ulimann case and have also claimed that Menno Simons taught and practiced immersion. This is, however, completely in error as has been fully proved by John Horsch, in "Did Menno Simons Practice Baptism by Immersion" (*MQR* I, Jan., 1927, 54-56). In fact Menno speaks at three places about the practice of baptism (*Writings*, 123, 139, 350).

The influence of the Collegiants (*q.v.*) in Holland, who practiced immersion, and with whom many Mennonites had intimate fellowship in the 17th and 18th centuries, led some Dutch Mennonites to adopt immersion. In Leeuwarden Preacher Arrien Jansen at the beginning of the 18th century adopted the position that immersion was the only true baptism and persuaded a part of the church there to practice it. Consequently a large stone baptismal font for immersion was installed in 1715. Although immersion was soon displaced and pouring restored, the stone font remained in the church until 1850. There was also a small faction of the

Hamburg Mennonite Church, known as the Dompelaars (*q.v.*), who separated in 1648-50 and continued for 100 years as a separate group, who practiced immersion, influenced thereto by an English Baptist who had joined the Hamburg congregation. The small group of Mennonites in Baden, Germany, who in 1858 followed Michael Hahn and are known as the "Hahnische" Mennonites also adopted immersion.

However, the chief instance of the entrance of immersion into the Mennonite brotherhood is that of the Mennonite Brethren (*q.v.*), organized in 1860 in South Russia, who adopted immersion as their exclusive mode of baptism at the very outset. From the beginning this group has required those who were baptized by some other mode to be rebaptized by immersion. In view of the fact that Baptist influence was present at the beginning of the M.B. movement, it is probably correct to assume that immersion came from this source. Jacob Reimer, of Gnadenfeld, Molotschna colony, the center of the first M.B. development, in whose home the election of the first ministers in May 1860 had taken place, had already in 1837 become convinced through reading Baptist literature that immersion was the right mode. Abraham Unger, a prominent leader, was very friendly to the Baptists. Baptist leaders August Liebig and Gerhard Oncken of Hamburg were welcome visitors in the 1860's and 1870's, and Unger was in correspondence with Oncken 1859-60. There was also correspondence with the Baptist preacher Alf at Adamov in Polish Russia in 1860. In fact a Mennonite congregation near Adamov, with Peter Ewert as elder, also adopted immersion at this time. The Krimmer Mennonite Brethren Church, which was organized in 1869 in the Crimea as an offshoot of the Kleine Gemeinde there, also adopted immersion under the erroneous impression that Menno Simons baptized by immersion.

The Alliance (Evangelical) Mennonite Church was founded in 1905 in Russia as an offshoot of the Mennonite Church, in part at least to bridge the gap between the Mennonite Brethren, who refused to recognize baptism by any other mode than immersion, and the Mennonite Church, who practiced pouring. This it does by practicing immersion, but recognizing other modes.

In North America immersion was adopted by the Mennonite Brethren in Christ, now called the United Missionary Church (except in the Pennsylvania Conference, where M.B.C. is still used). At first the mode of baptism was left optional with the candidate, but gradually immersion came into favor and by 1896 the conference discipline made immersion the exclusive form. In 1891-96 a division occurred in the Defenseless Mennonite (Egly) Church (now called Evangelical Mennonite), in which immersion was one of the factors, which led to the organization of the Missionary Church Association in 1898 with immersion as the exclusive mode of baptism. The Christian Apostolic Church (New Amish, Neutäufer, Fröhlichianer) organized in 1832 in Switzerland, which was joined by a

minister and a number of members of the Langnau (Emmental) Mennonite Church, also adopted immersion as the mode of baptism. The Brethren in Christ group practiced immersion from its beginning in Lancaster Co., Pa., in 1770. The Evangelical Mennonite Brethren Church, through close association with the M.B. and K.M.B. groups, now permits both modes, pouring and immersion, although formerly immersion was not permitted.

The method of immersion varies. The M.B. group practices single immersion backward, the K.M.B. group trine immersion forward, the M.B.C.-U.M.C. group single immersion forward.

In some periods and regions the matter of baptism in running water (a stream) became an issue, and at times became an accepted practice in some congregations, while others permitted (and still permit) the candidate to have his choice. (This applies to both modes, immersion and pouring.) The usual reason given for this practice has been that Jesus went "into the Jordan" to be baptized. The introduction of the practice of baptizing in the stream was the occasion for serious difficulty among the Amish churches of Ohio and Pennsylvania in the 1850's.

The Church of the Brethren, founded in Schwarzenau, Germany, in 1708 (migrated to Pennsylvania 1719-22), adopted immersion, probably under Dompelaar influence. The aggressiveness of this group, which often settled near Mennonite communities in Pennsylvania, Virginia, Ohio, and Indiana, and its insistent claim that only immersion was baptism, even to the extent at times of teaching that those not immersed cannot be saved, caused much trouble for the Mennonites; and a considerable number of Mennonite families transferred to the Brethren Church. The first book by an American Mennonite author, Heinrich Funck's *Spiegel der Taufe* (Germantown, 1744), was largely a defense of the Mennonite understanding and practice of baptism against the immersionists.

The Mennonite baptismal ritual in all groups and modes is essentially the same. The candidate is asked a series of questions regarding his basic faith, after which he is asked to pledge renunciation of the world and its sin as well as faithful obedience to Christ and His Word, and submission to the rules and regulations of the church which he is about to join. Thereupon the elder or minister baptizes him (in the mode of pouring or sprinkling the candidate kneels during the ceremony), then welcomes him into the fellowship of the church by the right hand of fellowship and, in some groups, by the kiss of brotherhood. In pouring, slightly divergent practices have developed. Some ministers dip the water out of a vessel with two hands (or one hand), which they then pour upon the head of the candidate by opening and inverting the hands. Others have the deacon or assistant minister pour water from a vessel into the cupped hands resting upon the head, where they are then inverted. Still others place the hands already inverted upon the head and have the assistant pour water upon the hands and head, and some simply pour the water directly from the pitcher upon the head.

An 1869 account (*Mitteilungen des Sippenverbandes der Danziger Mennoniten-Familien* . . . III, Göttingen, 1937, pp. 68-69) of a baptism in a West Prussian rural church (Ellerwald) reports a baptism performed by this method. Vos (*DB 1911*) has clearly shown that while the earliest form in Holland was for the elder to dip a handful of water in one hand, as early as 1567 the Old Flemish had the custom of having the elder pour water three times from a stone jug while holding his left hand on the head of the candidate. (He also points out that the Old Flemish rebaptized those transferring to their group from other Mennonite groups.) Vos closes his article (p. 16) with the summarizing comment that the development of the form of baptism among the Dutch Mennonites was from pouring from a dish or jug, to pouring a double handful of water, then to pouring a single handful, and finally in recent times to having the minister moisten his fingers in the baptismal dish and press them gently against the forehead. In West Prussia differences between the various groups in the mode of pouring, carried over from the time when the Flemish and Frisian groups were distinct, persisted to the end in 1945. (See **Infant Baptism.**) H.S.B.

J. Warns, *Die Taufe* . . . (Cassel, 1913, 1922); Friesen, *Brüderschaft*, Chapter XX, "Die Einführung der Tauchtaufe in der M.B.-G. und die formale Gründung der 'Einlager' Gemeinde," 240-66; J. Horsch, *Infant Baptism; Its Origin Among Protestants* . . . (Scottdale, 1917); C. Krahn, *Menno Simons* (Karlsruhe, 1936) 129-38, "Die Taufe auf den Glauben"; J. G. de Hoop Scheffer, "Overzicht der Geschiedenis van den Doop bij Onderdompeling," in *Verslagen en Mededeelingen der Koninklijke Academie van Wetenschappen, Afd. Letterkunde*, 2. reeks, XII, 1883, 119-70; K. Vos, "De Doop bij Overstorting," *DB* 1911, 1-16; M. Barth, *Die Taufe* (Zürich, 1951).

Baptists. One of the largest of the Protestant religious denominations in America. Historians trace the origin of the church back to the European Anabaptists by way of the Mennonites in Amsterdam. Among the various separatist religious groups which developed in the southeastern corner of England during the latter part of the 16th century, either as a result of the presence of Dutch Anabaptist refugees in that area during that period, or because of the return of the Marian exiles from the continent, or perhaps for both reasons, there were among others, two small neighboring Separatist congregations, Scrooby and Gainsboro, the former under the leadership of John Robinson, William Brewster, and William Bradford; and the latter under the leadership of John Smyth. Because of persecution, both fled from England to Amsterdam in 1608, but the Scrooby group soon left for Leiden, later emigrating to America as the Pilgrim Fathers.

Before the close of 1608 John Smyth, convinced that the logical conclusion of separation from the established church involved a renunciation of the chief symbol of initiation into that church, namely, infant baptism, decided to be rebaptized. But not finding at that time in Amsterdam a true church which he considered worthy of administering this rite, he baptized himself, then his chief follower, Thomas Helwys. These two then baptized the rest of the group, some 30 in number.

But before the close of another year (1609) John Smyth had a further change of heart. Having in the meantime become better acquainted with the Mennonites in Amsterdam, he decided that, after all, the Mennonites were a true church, and that he had made a mistake in baptizing himself, since by seeking baptism from the Mennonites he could have retained the line of apostolic succession. With the major part of his congregation, after subscribing to the confession of faith written by Hans de Ries (*q.v.*), which the Mennonites had submitted to him, he now applied for membership with the Waterlander (*q.v.*) Mennonites, the most tolerant wing of the denomination in Amsterdam then.

Thomas Helwys and John Murton, in turn, together with a minority of the group, hesitating to concede that their former baptism had been a mistake, denying the need of apostolic succession, refused to follow Smyth in this venture, withdrew from him, and advised the Mennonites to deny admission of the group to membership. Two years later the Helwys party, deciding that Christians should not try to evade persecution, and no doubt because of their differences with Smyth and his group, returned to London to found the first General or Arminian Baptist Church in England.

The Amsterdam Mennonites hesitated to admit Smyth to their fellowship. In the meantime in 1612 Smyth died, and it was not until 1615, after the group had continued their separate worship in the bakery of Jan Munter, a Waterlander Mennonite, that they were finally admitted to full membership in the Mennonite congregation. But, due to language difficulties, the English branch of the church held their separate worship for some years, until their children learned the Dutch language, when they became an integral part of the congregation.

The London church, in turn, usually known as the General Baptist Church because, like the Mennonites, they espoused the Arminian theology which held that Christ's atonement applied to all mankind, including children, and not only to the elect few as maintained by the Calvinists, developed certain religious practices and beliefs distinct from both their Amsterdam brethren and the other Mennonites. Among other points of difference they declared that the magistracy was a divine institution and that the Christian was not forbidden to take a part in it. They also disagreed with the Mennonite view rejecting the oath and war. Anticipating the later Quakers, they also maintained that a layman, in the absence of the regular pastor, might preach and administer baptism and communion. A lively correspondence, mostly in Latin, was carried on with the Amsterdam Mennonites until well into the middle of the 17th century, asking for closer fellowship between the two churches and suggesting complete union. But the Mennonites, because of these conflicting views mentioned above, refused the union; and so the English Baptists and Dutch Mennonites after this each went their own way.

In the meantime, there had been another independent Baptist movement in England, usually called the Particular Baptists, because, unlike the General Baptists, they had adopted Calvinistic views. In 1616 Henry Jacob, a university graduate, leader of a separatist movement, exiled for a time to Zeeland, Holland, where he may have come in contact with the Dutch Mennonites, returned to London as leader of a small independent church. A division in this group in 1633 led to the formation of another Baptist group, which decided to adopt immersion as the only acceptable mode of baptism. In 1641 this group sent one of their number, Richard Blount, to a Collegiant congregation in Holland, likely Collegiant Mennonite, to receive immersion. Although the two wings of the church, the General and Particular, remained in close fellowship, agreeing in the main on fundamental Baptist doctrines, including immersion, they maintained their independent organizations until their final union in England in 1891.

The growth of the Baptist movement during the first century in England was steady though slow. The first congregation in Wales was organized in 1649, but none in Scotland until near the middle of the following century. During the Commonwealth period, Baptists were among the most influential of the Independent groups, and played a conspicuous role in Cromwell's army. With the Restoration in 1660, at which time they numbered about 20,000, they suffered severe persecution, but under the Toleration Act of 1689 they were granted greater liberty. Like the Quakers and the Mennonites of their day, their insistence upon religious toleration was never popular with the state churches. Among their distinct doctrines were: (1) church membership based on adult confession of faith, and consequent renunciation of infant baptism; (2) separation of church and state; (3) freedom of religious conscience; (4) congregational church government; and (5) immersion as the only Scriptural mode of baptism.

Following the Wesleyan revival at the close of the 18th century, the English Baptists entered upon a period of steady expansion throughout Europe and the non-Christian lands. In 1792 they organized a foreign missionary society and sent William Carey, the pioneer missionary, to India. Soon after, they established the Sunday-school movement, a foreign Bible society, and tract and publication societies. By the middle of the 19th century they had begun congregations in most of the European countries and British colonies, in Germany in 1834, France 1835, Denmark and Sweden 1848, and Italy 1866. About the same time they gained a considerable following among the Russians, mainly among the Stundists (q.v.). Among the prominent English Baptists in history may be mentioned John Bunyan, of *Pilgrim's Progress* fame (1628-88); William Carey, the India missionary (1761-1834); and Charles H. Spurgeon, the famous London preacher (1834-92).

The Baptist Church in America started independently of the English movement, but about the same time. Roger Williams is credited with being the first of the faith in America. Three years after his expulsion from Massachusetts, he sought rebaptism at the hands of a Separatist, Ezekiel Holliman, whom he then in turn baptized, together with several others, thus founding (1639) at Providence, R.I., the first Baptist church in America. Roger Williams did not remain a Baptist, however. Within a few months he deserted his fold to become a "seeker." In 1641 another congregation was formed at Newport, R.I. In 1644 Mark Lukar, a Welsh Baptist immigrant joining the Newport group, introduced immersion, which finally became the accepted form of baptism for the whole American Baptist Church. The movement gradually spread to other colonies, into Massachusetts in 1649; Maine 1682; Pennsylvania 1684; and later into Virginia, North Carolina, and other southern colonies.

Because of their insistence upon complete separation of church and state, the Baptists were extremely unpopular during the Colonial days in those colonies where state churches were well established, especially in New England and Virginia. They were often fined and jailed for their stubborn refusal to conform to the demands of the state church. A conspicuous case is that of Henry Dunster, the first president of Harvard College, who, because he espoused the Baptist doctrines, was expelled from the college, and publicly reprimanded by the ruling authorities for his act. It was only in Baptist Rhode Island and Quaker Pennsylvania that Baptists were granted a measure of religious freedom. With the adoption of the Federal Constitution, Baptists, as well as all other religious groups, were granted complete religious toleration. In the early years American Baptists were inclined to the Arminian theology, but in more recent times they have become largely Calvinistic. In 1845 the slavery question divided the denomination into a northern and a southern division, a cleavage still existing, though on other grounds.

The 19th century was one of steady expansion for American Baptists. Missionary, benevolent, and educational institutions were established, and before the middle of the century a number of theological seminaries, among which were Colgate, 1819; Newton, 1825; and Rochester and Louisville before the Civil War. By 1928 the two Baptist conventions—North and South—controlled 16 theological seminaries and 53 colleges, some of them among the largest in the land. The University of Chicago was originally (1893) a Baptist foundation. Baptist Negroes, too, have their own missionary societies and schools.

In church government the Baptists are strictly congregational and democratic, each congregation free to control its own local affairs. For carrying on their missionary and benevolent work, however, they are united into associations, state and regional, and nationally into conventions. The Baptist World Alliance was founded in 1905.

The total membership of the denomination in the United States (1950), including all twelve of the divisions, totaled about 16,500,000 as follows:

Southern Baptist Convention	7,079,880
Two Negro Conventions	7,091,394
Northern Baptist Convention	1,561,073
American Baptist Association	330,315
All others	425,000
Canadian Baptists, about	100,000
English Baptists, about	255,000
German Baptists, about	70,000

Among the minor groups, perhaps the best known are the Primitive Baptists, though small with a membership of only some 70,000, largely in the South. They compose the extremely conservative wing of the denomination. They oppose Sunday schools, missionary efforts, benevolent associations, instrumental music in church worship, and an educated ministry. They are extremely Calvinistic. They practice laying on of hands, and in some sections footwashing in connection with communion. Extremely individualistic, they are loosely organized, and for that reason are frequently spoken of under such names as Hardshell Baptists, Old School and Anti-Mission Baptists. There is also a Negro Primitive Church of nearly equal numerical strength. Among other minor groups are the General Baptists, United Baptists, Regular Baptists, Free Will Baptists, Separate Baptists, Seventh Day Baptists, Two-Seed-in-the-Spirit Predestinarian Baptists, General Six Principles Baptists.

Because of the similarity of their doctrine of religious toleration, Baptists and Mennonites have occasionally crossed paths in later history. The Dompelaar (*q.v.*) movement in the Hamburg Mennonite Church in the middle of the 17th century was the outcome of a visit to that congregation of a Baptist missionary from London. Baptist missionaries, too, visited the South German Mennonites in the early part of the 19th century, and were partly responsible for the establishment of the first missionary efforts of the German Mennonites (see **Angas**). For a time the Dutch and South German Mennonite missionary gifts were sent to the English Baptist society. During the 1860's and later leading German Baptist ministers visited the newly established Mennonite Brethren Church of Russia, which for a time seriously considered the advisability of affiliation with the Baptists, and did establish communion fellowship with them. Preacher Alf (*q.v.*), leader of the Baptists in Poland, influenced a Mennonite group in Poland (Deutsch-Wymysle) about 1860. The introduction of immersion into the M.B. group was apparently due chiefly to Baptist influence. Many Russian M.B. missionaries served in German Baptist missions, particularly in Kamerun and India. In North America the Mennonite Brethren have had considerable close and sympathetic connections with the Baptists, particularly in the use of Baptist literature and attendance at Baptist theological seminaries. In former years a number have entered the Baptist ministry. (See **Baptists and Mennonites in Russia**.)

Baptists have been conscious of their Anabaptist connections, and have at times emphasized this as a link in their "apostolic succession." Some Mennonites have been influenced by Baptist historiography to construct a Mennonite apostolic succession on a similar basis, though without historical warrant. Because of their historical interest, a series of Baptist historians have rendered notable service in the field of Anabaptist history, among them the two Burrages (*q.v.*) (Henry S., 1837-1926, and Champlin, 1874-), A. H. Newman (*q.v.*) (1852-1933), Henry C. Vedder (1853-1935), and R. J.

Smithson (1880-). Balthasar Hubmaier in particular has become the Baptist hero, no doubt because he alone of the Anabaptists took a position on the magistracy and war which agrees with the Baptist position. G. D. Davidson prepared (1939) an English translation of all of Hubmaier's writings, not yet published. Colgate-Rochester Theological Seminary has a considerable collection of rare early Anabaptist writings, with emphasis on Hubmaier tracts.   C.H.S.

R. Barclay, *The Inner Life of the Religious Societies of the Commonwealth* (London, 1879); C. Burrage, *The Early English Dissenters* (Cambridge, 1912); A. H. Newman, *A History of the Baptist Churches of America* (New York, 1894); R. G. Torbet, *A History of the Baptists* (Philadelphia, 1950); J. G. de Hoop Scheffer, *History of the Free Churchmen Called the Brownists, Pilgrim Fathers, and Baptists in the Dutch Republic 1581-1701*, ed. W. E. Griffis (Ithaca, 1922, first published in Dutch under the title *De Brownisten te Amsterdam*) (*Versl. en Meded., Afd. Letterk.* X, 1881); J. Lehmann, *Gesch. der Deutschen Baptisten* (3d ed., Hamburg, 1922); E. Kupsch, *Gesch. der Baptisten in Polen, 1885-1932;* J. Warns, *Russland und das Evangelium* (Cassel, 1930); M. Kroeker, *Ein reiches Leben* (Jakob Kroeker) (Wüstenrot, Württemb., 1949); *ML* I, 119-24.

Baptists and Mennonites in Russia. The influence of the Baptists on the Mennonites in Russia and the share which the Mennonites had in the origin and spread of the Baptist movement in Russia has not yet been fully investigated. However, that there was a mutual influence is an established fact. The Baptist influence among the Mennonites in Russia coincided with the revival that was started through the work of Eduard Wüst (*q.v.*) and became noticeable when the traditional Mennonite form of baptism was changed on Sept. 23, 1860, by the group which introduced baptism by immersion. When the newly founded Mennonite Brethren Church (*q.v.*) in 1862 made immersion compulsory it adopted a characteristic Baptist practice, which it apparently took over from that group.

P. M. Friesen reports that Jacob Reimer claimed that he had read the life story of the Baptist Anna Judson in 1837, on which occasion he learned that there were some Christians who practiced baptism by immersion. By 1860 other literature had reached the Mennonites in Russia in which baptism by immersion was advocated. During the winter of 1860-61 a correspondence was begun with the Baptist evangelist Gottfried F. Alf (*q.v.*) in Poland and the Mennonite elder Peter Ewert of the Deutsch-Wymysle (*q.v.*) Mennonites who had also just introduced baptism by immersion. The founding and organization of the Einlage Mennonite Brethren Church (*q.v.*) at Chortitza took place in close co-operation with the father of the German Baptist movement, Johann G. Oncken (*q.v.*) of Hamburg. He ordained Abraham Unger as elder of the congregation in 1869. Other Baptist ministers such as K. Benzien (*q.v.*), F. W. Baedeker, and August Liebig (*q.v.*) exerted a very definite influence on the newly organized Mennonite Brethren Church. Although the Baptists did not succeed in achieving an organic union with this Mennonite group, the spiritual ties and spheres of co-operation continued throughout the decades. Some Mennonite Brethren ministers received their training in the Baptist Seminary at Hamburg and many of their missionaries went out to the Baptist mission field in India a part of which was later obtained as a Mennonite Brethren mission field.

On the other hand, the Mennonites and particularly the Mennonite Brethren in Russia had a definite share in the origin and development of the evangelical movement in Russia which resulted in two major groups, the Baptists and Evangelical Christians. Especially the groups which had separated from the Greek Catholic Church, such as the Dukhobors and the Molokans, were a fertile field. The Pietists, Wüst and Bonekämper, introduced into the German settlements of South Russia meetings for devotional purposes called *Stunden* (hours). Those attending these meetings became known as "Stundists." These practices were also accepted by the Mennonites. Gradually some hired Russian helpers attending such meetings were converted. Having observed public baptisms by the Mennonite Brethren, some desired also to be baptized. Thus J. Wieler and his brother G. Wieler baptized the first Russians in 1863. Elder A. Unger of the Einlage M.B. congregation baptized a Yefim Zembal who in turn baptized other Russian Stundists, outstanding among whom was Ivan Ryaboshapka, who became a leading evangelist. Cornelius Jansen of Berdyansk, and the Molotschna Mennonites, helped Scotch Presbyterian evangelist William Melville, who had been working in Russia since 1823, in the distribution of Bibles in Russia, which paved the way for the revival and renewed spread of the Stundist movement which had begun somewhat earlier.

Another source of the Stundist or Evangelical movement originated through the Englishman Lord Radstock, who in St. Petersburg started a tract mission in 1875, primarily among the aristocracy. Outstanding among the leaders were W. A. Pashkov and Korff. Although this movement originally had little to do with the Mennonites, later contacts were established through such men as Jakob Kroeker. After the Bolshevik Revolution in 1917, *Licht im Osten,* Wernigerode a.H., Germany, under the directorship of the Mennonite preacher, Jakob Kroeker (*q.v.*), became the spiritual center of the Russian Baptist and Evangelical Christian refugees in Germany, from which Christian literature was sent to Russia, and where young people were trained for evangelistic work in Slavic countries. Among the leaders and teachers of the institution who had come from Russia in addition to Jakob Kroeker were W. Jack, Wl. Marzinkowskij, B. Harder, J. S. Prochanov.

In Russia itself co-operation between the Mennonites, and the Baptists and Evangelical Christians, continued particularly after the Revolution. To what degree the Mennonites or the followers of Tolstoy are responsible for the fact that many of the Evangelicals and Baptists became conscientious objectors to war is not definitely established. Prior to the severe persecutions under the Soviets, the number of the two groups (Baptists and Evangelicals) was estimated as being above two million.

During the last decade the groups are supposed to have united (according to the *Bolshaya Sovietskaya Encyclopedia*) under the chairmanship of Zhidkov. (For bibliography see **Baptists.**)   E.H., C.K.

Baptists in the Netherlands. In the earliest period a Baptist church existed at Amsterdam under the leadership of John Smyth (*q.v.*) and Thomas Helwys (*q.v.*). Smyth's congregation in 1615 joined that of the Waterlander Mennonites, and in about 1611 Helwys returned to England, upon which the Baptist movement on Dutch soil disappeared for several centuries.

In 1843, J. E. Feisser, the Dutch Reformed pastor at Gasselter-Nijeveen (Drenthe), came to doubt the Scripturalness of infant baptism. In his congregation this became, under his leading, a movement ot reawakening, although in the same year Feisser was excommunicated. He preached for the last time on Dec. 31, 1843. On April 15, 1845, he was rebaptized by immersion along with six brethren and sisters by Julius Koebner, a Baptist preacher from Hamburg who was a representative of Johann Gerhard Oncken (*q.v.*). In this manner a Baptist church again came into existence in the Netherlands. Gradually Baptist congregations arose in Stadskanaal, Weerdingermond, and in other fen colonies in Groningen and Drenthe. On Jan. 26, 1881, the "congregation of baptized Christians," as they called themselves, were united in the Union of Baptist Churches (*Unie van Baptistengemeenten*). They laid great stress, similar to the Mennonites, on voluntary church membership. Baptism, which was executed only by immersion, was performed on the basis of a personal testimony of conversion. No confession of faith was recognized as binding, the revealed truth of the Holy Scriptures being considered sufficient.

The Union is administered by the Union Committee, which is composed of nine members. The congregations are entirely independent and autonomous in the regulation of affairs.

The Union, which in 1927 comprised 31 congregations with 3,212 baptized members, now (1951) consists of 47 congregations with 6,587 members; in addition there are four Baptist congregations with a total of about 400 members who do not belong to the Union. The Baptists in the Netherlands, almost from the beginning, have had their own weekly periodical, *De Christen* (The Christian), and since 1912 an evangelistic paper, *De Zaaier* (The Sower). (G. A. Wumkes, *De opkomst en vestiging van het Baptisme in Nederland,* Sneek, 1912.)   vDZ.

Baraditz, a Bruderhof (*q.v.*) of the Hutterian Brethren in Moravia: see **Paraditz.**

Baratov Mennonite settlement, district of Verknedneprovsk, province of Ekaterinoslav, was established in 1871 by 74 Mennonite families of the Chortitza Mennonite settlement. They established the villages Neu-(Novo) Chortitza and Gnadental on 9,800 acres of land. In 1873 the villages Grünfeld and Steinfeld were added. In 1905 the total population was 2,569. All Mennonites belonged to the Neu-Chortitza Mennonite Church (*q.v.*).

During the confusion following World War I the fiftieth anniversary of its founding was observed. The progress of the first 50 years was gratifying. But the war and the ensuing revolution destroyed much, and the prospects for the future were gloomy, because the victorious Communists were intent upon the forcible execution of their regime. For the progressive Mennonite farmers the new order was a backward step.

The school system of the Baratov settlement was on a relatively high plane. Two well-trained teachers were employed in each village; they were adequately supported by the parents of the pupils. Attendance was satisfactory. In Gnadental there was for a time also a secondary school (Fortbildungsschule) with a special teacher; the school was intended for boys who wished to prepare for higher schools. These who continued their education farther attended the Zentralschule in Chortitza. Particular attention was given religious instruction, and some Mennonite history was taught. The term lasted eight or nine months, and the course eight or nine years. At the conclusion of the course of study the pupils were examined in the subjects they had studied in the Russian language as well as in German and in religion. Those who passed were given two certificates; the one for German and religion was issued by the community leaders and the teacher. For the improvement of instruction, the teachers of the Mennonite villages met in conference about once a month in one of the schools.

Since Communism aimed to exterminate religion and since the Mennonite farmers were opposed to compulsory collectivization, a large part of the Baratov settlement emigrated to Canada in 1923 where they have found a good home.

Those who remained had to undergo much suffering: many of them, especially the more prosperous farmers, perished in exile; church life was violently prevented; in 1929 thousands of Mennonites took flight to emigrate via Moscow, among whom were Baratov settlers. No definite figures are available concerning those that came to Paraguay and Canada. (*ML* I, 124.)   P.A.R.

Barbara, "a prophetess" of the Strasbourg Anabaptists, whose visions and prophecies, chiefly centered around Melchior Hofmann (*q.v.*), created a considerable stir. Barbara was the wife of Hans Kropf and the sister-in-law of Pilgram Marpeck. Hulshof says of her, "Barbara won a great name for herself among the prophetesses." Frans van Hasebroek of Flanders declared in April 1534 at his trial, that he had gone to her house, "had heard of her in the Netherlands, how she performs miracles, therefore he had gone to her." Obbe Philips, in his confession, mentions some of her prophecies.   NEFF.

Ztscht f. d. hist. Theol., 1860, 100; B. N. Krohn, *Gesch. der fanatischen und enthusiastischen Wiedertäufer . . .* (Leipzig, 1758) 273; F. O. zur Linden, *Melchior Hofmann . . .* (Haarlem, 1885) 313; A. Hulshof, *Gesch. van de Doopsgezinden te Straatsburg 1525-1527* (Amsterdam, 1905); *ML* I, 124.

Barbara of Thiers, an Anabaptist martyr, wife of Hans Portzen, was put to death at Fill (*q.v.*) in the Adige (Tirol), Nov. 16, 1529, with Georg

Frick (*q.v.*) and three other brethren and three sisters of her faith. She confessed her faith staunchly, mentioning that she had been baptized by Benedikt von Bruneck, a former people's priest. (Beck, *Geschichts-Bücher*, 89; *Mart. Mir.* D 27, E 435; Wolkan, *Geschicht-Buch*, 53, 55.)   NEFF.

Barbara Jacobsdochter, an Anabaptist martyr of Hazerswoude, Dutch province of South Holland, was drowned on May 15, 1535, at Amsterdam, with six other women, while at the same time three brethren were beheaded. (*Mart. Mir.* D 413, E 764; Grosheide, *Verhooren*, 58-59; *ML* II, 386.)   vDZ.

Barbara Smachscheers, an Anabaptist martyr, was burned at the stake on the Vrijdagsmarkt in Gent, Belgium, on April 13, 1557, together with two other martyrs. Further particulars are lacking (Verheyden, *Gent*, 24, No. 54).   vDZ.

Barbara Thielemans (Tielmans), an Anabaptist martyr, was burned at the stake on March 20, 1549, at Amsterdam, along with seven others. According to the sentence, quoted by van Bright in the *Martyrs' Mirror*, Barbara came from Dordrecht in the Dutch province of South Holland. She was baptized by Gillis van Aken (*q.v.*). Concerning Barbara and her seven companions a song was composed, which begins "Tis nu schier al vervult ons broeders getal" (The number of our brethren, 'tis almost now fulfilled). It appeared in the *Veelderhande Liedekens* of 1556 and afterwards in later songbooks. The song consists of eight stanzas, the first letter of each being the initial of one of the martyrs.   vDZ.

Mart. Mir. D 82, E 483; Grosheide, *Bijdrage*, 155, 308; F. C. Wieder, *Schriftuurlijke Liedekens* (see index on p. 193) (The Hague, 1900).

Barbel, an Anabaptist martyr, who was executed in 1552 at Jülich in Germany. Particulars are lacking (*Mart. Mir.* D 132, E 526).   vDZ.

Barbele Gheerts, an Anabaptist martyr, wife of Henrick van der Borcht, a hatter, born at Geldrop in the Dutch province of Brabant, was drowned together with Neelken Clercx (*q.v.*) in the Schelde at Antwerp on March 16, 1535. (*Antw. Arch.-Blad* VII, 319; XIV, 14-15, No. 141.)   vDZ.

Barbele Peterssens, an Anabaptist martyr of Geldrop in the Dutch province of Brabant, was drowned for the sake of her faith in the Schelde at Antwerp in 1535. (*Antw. Arch.-Blad* VII, 367; XIV, 14-15, No. 145.)   vDZ.

Barbele (Barberken) **Pieters,** an Anabaptist martyr, was executed on July 19, 1576, at Gent in Belgium, with Lippijntgen Roetsaerts (*q.v.*) and Kreupel Sijntgen (*q.v.*). These three women were beheaded rather than drowned, as was the general practice for the execution of women heretics. The reason for changing to this method is not known. These women were not executed in public but inside the Gravenkasteel (castle of the counts). Barbele came from Herten near Weert, Dutch province of Limburg. She had been rebaptized by Jans Heuvebreiere. Van Braght did not possess these details and set the date of her death "about the year 1573." Barbele was married to Michiel Willems (Michiel van Brussel, *q.v.*), who on the same day that his wife was beheaded was burned at the stake in Gent. (*Mart. Mir.* D 643, E 968; Verheyden, *Gent,* 67, No. 239.)   vDZ.

Barbelken Goethals, an Anabaptist martyr, was arrested on a charge of heresy and kept in prison in the monastery of Sint-Pieters in a suburb of Gent, Belgium. She was burned at the stake in this region, together with Saerken (van) Duerhoven (*q.v.*), on Nov. 22 (*Mart. Mir.,* Nov. 21), 1570. (*Mart. Mir.* D 534, E 870; Verheyden, *Gent,* 57, No. 196; *ML* II, 134.)   vDZ.

Barber, Edward, originally belonged to a group of Brownists (*q.v.*), led by Thomas Helwys (*q.v.*) and later by John Murton, who in 1610, while living in Amsterdam, did not wish to unite with the Mennonites there, even though the Brownists too had rejected infant baptism and only baptized adults on confession of faith. Later on he came to the conviction that no baptism except by immersion was Scriptural or valid. He wrote a book, *A Treatise of Baptism or Dipping, Wherein is Clearly Showed, That Our Lord Christ Ordained Dipping and That Sprinkling of Children is not according to Christ's Institutions; and also the Invalidity of Those Arguments, That are Commonly Brought to Justify That Practice* (London, 1641). This book influenced his group to establish baptism by immersion as the only true baptism. This happened after Richard Blount (*q.v.*) had been rebaptized by immersion at Amsterdam or Rijnsburg (*q.v.*). This is the time of the origin of the Baptist Church. "The ties of fellowship with the Dutch Mennonites, whom from that moment they regarded as unbaptized people, were cut off." According to Barclay, however, the practice of baptizing by immersion appears to have been introduced in England as early as Sept. 12, 1633.   vDZ.

J. G. De Hoop Scheffer and W. E. Griffis, *Hist. of the Free Churchmen* (Ithaca, 1922) 180; R. Barclay, *The Inner Life of the Religious Societies of the Commonwealth* (2d ed., London, 1877).

Barber Jans, an Anabaptist martyr, was executed by drowning on Feb. 13, 1570, at Haarlem, Dutch province of North Holland, after which her corpse was burned. Particulars regarding this martyr are not known. (*Mart. Mir.* D 505, E 845; *ML* II, 390.)   vDZ.

Barber Joosten, an Anabaptist martyr, was imprisoned for her faith at Haarlem, Dutch province of North Holland, in 1570. She remained steadfast and was drowned as a heretic. Particulars are lacking. (*Mart. Mir.* D 509, E 848; *ML* II, 432.) vDZ.

Barberken, wife of Michiel van Brussel: see **Barbele Pieters.**

Bardes, Willem, police chief in Amsterdam in 1542, protected the Anabaptists, was consequently imprisoned, and died of the mistreatments he suffered. His son, also named Willem Bardes, likewise assisted the oppressed Anabaptists as far as he was able. According to Brandt, though Willem was not an Anabaptist, his wife was a member of the congregation.   vDZ.

Blaupot t.C., *Holland* I, 31, 32, 183; G. Brandt, *Historie der Reformatie* I (Amsterdam, 1677) 610.

Bardeyn, today Bardehnen, a village in the district of Holland in East Prussia, one of several villages given by Duke Albrecht to a party of Dutch peasants for colonization on Jan. 31, 1527. Bardeyn became the seat of the Dutch settlement, which developed slowly. Not until 1530 was it possible to proceed with the election of a mayor and a pastor. In the same year the colony was augmented by new immigrants from Holland, and although they suffered from repeated attacks of the plague and many moved away, several years later the village was filled again by new settlers.

Religious troubles were added to financial difficulties; in 1543, the Dutch were compelled to send representatives to Schmauch for church inspection, who made a written statement declaring that the concept of baptism and communion held by the settlers was not in accord with the Prussian church rules. They were thereupon ordered to leave the duchy. After several petitions permission to remain was granted those who would recant in Königsberg. Most of the Dutch now left the country. The settlement at Bardeyn died out except for small remnants, which gradually merged with the German and Polish population.

The first settlers were "Sacramentists"; later additions were mostly Anabaptists, who won the native peasants to their doctrine. The church inspection of 1543 revealed that the Dutch of Bardeyn were Anabaptists, and upon this charge they were banished.   F.S.

B. Schumacher, *Niederländische Ansiedlungen im Herzogtum Preussen zur Zeit Herzog Albrechts* (Leipzig, 1903); *ML* I, 124.

Bare (Barre), **Georges:** see **Georges Bare.**

Barent Backer, a citizen of the town of Zwolle in the Dutch province of Overijssel. He was rebaptized at this place by Gerrit Boeckbinder, who also laid on him the office of the ministry (*leeraar*). He read from the Scriptures and preached but did not baptize. After waiting first at Zwolle, he later went to Münster where he was in the service of Jan van Leyden (*q.v.*). He was imprisoned at Amsterdam in June 1535. Just when he had left Münster is not known. He was placed on trial and tortured on July 14 and on July 28, 1535, condemned to be put to death by decapitation and then drawn and quartered. (Grosheide, *Verhooren,* 158-60; *DB* 1917, 119, No. 103.)   vDZ.

Barent Claesz (Claessen) of Zwolle (Dutch province of Overijssel), an Anabaptist martyr, a fuller by trade, was beheaded at Amsterdam on March 6, 1535, with eight others, charged with membership in the Anabaptist brotherhood (*Mart. Mir.* D 412, E 763; Grosheide, *Verhooren,* 52 f.).   vDZ.

Barent Dircksz (called Doove Barent), a Dutch painter, who made six large panels for the old town hall in Amsterdam, representing the revolt of the Anabaptists (*Wederdooper-oproer*) in this city May 10-11, 1535. These pictures were moved to the new town hall in 1655, but shortly after vanished without a trace. A sketch of the pictures is found in the Library of the University of Göttingen, Germany. (*DB* 1919, 127; *Jaarboek Amstelodamum* XXXVIII, 1941, 23.)   vDZ.

Barent Heyndricksz Volkeringksoen, an Anabaptist martyr, was beheaded on Jan. 7, 1539, at Delft, Dutch province of South Holland, with 10 other brethren. He was a native of "Ottensteyn in de Lande van Monster" (Münster in Westphalia?), and likely a follower of David Joris. (*Inv. Arch. Amst.* I, No. 749; *DB* 1899, 158-60; 1917, 160-67.)
vDZ.

Bärg, Wilhelm, a leader in the Karanbosh branch of the Gortchakovka Mennonite Brethren Church of the Davlekanovo Mennonite settlement in Russia. He was known as a deep and independent thinker and as a fearless leader. He was ordained minister in 1887 and chosen leader in 1894.
J.P.R.

Barge, Hermann (b. 1870), a professor at the university of Leipzig, historian, author of the excellent work, *Andreas Bodenstein von Carlstadt* (Leipzig, 1906), which throws much light on the relations and contacts of Karlstadt (*q.v.*) with the Anabaptists, making it very valuable for the student of Mennonite beginnings. In other publications, as in the *Münchener Allgemeinen Zeitung* (Aug. 10, 1900), in an article on "Sozialethische Strömungen des angehenden Mittelalters," he speaks appreciatively of the research of Ludwig Keller, and expresses a very favorable opinion of the old-evangelical church movement. The same attitude is seen in his discussion of Karl Rembert's book, *Die "Wiedertäufer" im Herzogtum Jülich.* In *Studium Lipsiense* (published in honor of Karl Lamprecht, Berlin, 1909), his article, "Der Streit über die Grundlagen der religiösen Erneuerung in der Kontroverse zwischen Luther und Karlstadt, 1524-1525," discloses his fundamental attitude toward research in church history, in which his verdict on A. Ritschl as a historian seems especially important. These writings reveal Barge as one of the modern scholars who approach the history of the Anabaptists with a benevolent, friendly interest and understanding. Another of Barge's important books is *Frühprotestantisches Gemeindechristentum in Wittenberg und Orlamünde* (1909). Barge's works stirred up violent controversy on the part of historians of the Protestant church and of secular history. The literary conflict assumed unpleasant forms. The most important and sharpest of Barge's critics was Karl Müller, professor of Protestant church history at Tübingen, who was, by the way, also a quiet friend of the Mennonites, though he does not express this position as definitely as Ernst Troeltsch. Walther Köhler wrote an analysis of this polemic literature with his own position on the matter in *Göttinger Gelehrten Anzeigen,* 1912. (See *Ztschft f. Kirchengesch.* XXXVII, Nos. 1 and 2, p. 24 f.; *ML* I, 125.)
NEFF.

Bargen, Isaac I., son of Isaac Bargen and Justina Loewen, was the second oldest of four brothers and one sister. He was born Nov. 29, 1857, at Alexanderwohl in the Molotschna settlement in South Russia, and came to America July 4, 1878, settling on a farm east of Mountain Lake, Minn. He married Sara Hiebert, daughter of David Hiebert and Sara Penner, on Dec. 30, 1886. He had five sons and five daughters: Justina, David, Sara, Emma, Mary, William, Walter, Gerhard, Bernhard, and Rosella.

In Russia he attended the Zentralschule at Gnadenfeld and Orloff (*q.v.*); in America he studied four years at Mankato Teachers' College. He was a charter member of First Mennonite Church (*q.v.*) of Mountain Lake, Minn., founder of the Sunday school in his home community, 40 years a Sunday-school teacher, and chairman of church council for eight years. For one year he taught German in St. Paul, Minn. He was a leader in civic affairs, public speaker, superintendent of county schools, 1893-1901; principal of Mountain Lake grade school, 1893-1903; editor and publisher of *Mountain Lake View* and *Unser Besucher,* 1901-14; postmaster of Mountain Lake, 1902-33; founder of Mennonite Aid Society (*q.v.*), 1897; president of this organization until 1925; and then secretary until his death, Aug. 25, 1943.
M.B.

Bärgmann, Johann, was elder of the Nikolayevo Mennonite Church (*q.v.*) of the Orenburg Mennonite settlement (*q.v.*), Russia. Bärgmann was born Dec. 12, 1866, and ordained as minister and leader in 1898.
C.K.

Barickman, a Hutterite Bruderhof, 12 miles west of Headingly, Man. It was founded in 1920 by 12 families of the Maxwell Bruderhof, three miles west of Barickman. The Bruderhof has 2,740 acres of land south of the Assiniboine River. Small grain is the most suitable crop. Other products are honey, fruit, and vegetables. Their first preacher was Samuel Hofer, who died in 1935. In 1931 David Dekker was chosen preacher, and in 1937 David Hofer. In 1941 the Bruderhof numbered 194 souls, 75 being baptized members. In 1941 Preacher David Dekker with 13 families moved to Olivet, Hutchinson Co., S.D.; they bought the Tschetter Bruderhof, which had not been occupied by Hutterites since 1918, when the occupants moved to Alberta, and founded the Rosebud Bruderhof near Rocky Ford. In 1947 the Barickman Bruderhof numbered 135 souls with 54 baptized.
D.D.

Barker Street Amish Mennonite Church, now extinct, established about 1860(?) in St. Joseph Co., Mich., near Vistula, Ind. It is reported that the first settlers who formed this congregation bore the following names: Hartzler, Hooley, King, Kauffman, Plank, Warey, Yoder, and Zook. One of the first ministers, Joseph Kauffman, moved from Barker Street to the Hawpatch congregation, Topeka, Ind., about 1863. Another person who left Barker Street was Deacon Christian Warey (1832-1914); he ultimately settled in Iowa and later became bishop of the East Union congregation there. In 1876 Bishop C. D. Beery of Branch Co., Mich., ordained Harvey Friesner to the ministry to serve Barker Street. The meetinghouse was built in 1893. Ultimately Barker Street was under the joint care of the Indiana-Michigan Mennonite (MC) and Indiana-Michigan Amish Mennonite conferences. The last minister ordained at Barker Street was W. W. Oesch in 1914. Internal difficulties in the congregation in 1923 contributed to its dissolution shortly thereafter.
J.C.W.

D. K. Cassel, *Hist. of the Menn.* (Philadelphia, 1888); J. S. Hartzler and Daniel Kauffman, *Menn. Church Hist.* (Scottdale, 1905); Daniel Kauffman, *Menn. Cyclopedic*

Dictionary (Scottdale, 1937); *Minutes of the Indiana-Michigan Menn. Conf., 1864-1929* (Scottdale, 1929).

Barkman, Peter K. (1826-1917), together with his three sons, Jacob (1848-1935), Peter (1861-1936), Johann (1862-1900), and his two daughters, Mrs. Abr. W. Reimer (1859-   ), and Mrs. Johann S. Friesen (deceased), and his father Jakob J. Barkman (1794-1875) emigrated in 1874 from South Russia to Manitoba. Jakob J. Barkman, who died the following year, had experienced his second emigration, having journeyed some time around 1800 from Prussia to Russia. Peter K. Barkman had been a miller in Russia. In Canada he built and was part owner of the Steinbach flour mill. He was a member of the Kleine Gemeinde (*q.v.*) Mennonite Church.   D.P.R.

Barnaul (also Slavgorod), a Mennonite settlement named after the city of Barnaul on the Ob River in the Altai district of the R.S.F.S.R. in West Siberia, formerly the province of Tomsk. The Barnaul Mennonite settlement was flanked by many other Mennonite settlements located in the vicinity of Omsk (*q.v.*), Slavgorod (*q.v.*), and Pavlodar (*q.v.*). It was some 100 miles south of the great Siberian railroad line between Omsk and Novo-Nikolaievsk (now Novosibirsk), 120 miles north of Pavlodar on the Irtish River and 10 miles from the city of Slavgorod. In later years the city of Barnaul was connected by rail with the main line.

In the beginning of the 20th century this region, known as the Kulundian steppes, was desolate and inhabited only by nomads with herds of cattle.

The first Mennonites in West Siberia were those in Akmolinsk (*q.v.*) near Omsk and Friesenov (*q.v.*) in 1897 ff. In 1906 landless Mennonites of the Orenburg (*q.v.*) Mennonite settlement organized to locate land for settlement purposes in West Siberia. Heinrich Krüger and Jakob Peters were sent as delegates to study land and conditions under which a settlement could be made. They met in West Siberia with delegates from other Mennonite settlements in the Ukraine and together made arrangements with the government to reserve for them some 60,000 dessiatines (162,000 acres) of land near Barnaul. In 1907 the first families from Orenburg arrived to start the Barnaul settlement (some sources set the date as of 1909). Soon various settlers from the Zagradovka, Chortitza, Molotschna, and other Mennonite settlements located in this area. Each male member of the family received from the government 40 acres of land. The Mennonites followed their own method of distributing this land among themselves in farms of equal size. The families without any means received 400 rubles from the settlement funds of the mother colonies. The pioneer conditions were very hard. The crops were fair, but the market was far away and poor.

One of the outstanding early leaders of the Barnaul settlement was Jakob A. Reimer who was its first mayor (*Oberschulze*) 1910-14, and who is said to have been called "the Moses of the Mennonites" by an official in Petersburg. The municipality (*volost*) center was located in the village of Orlov.

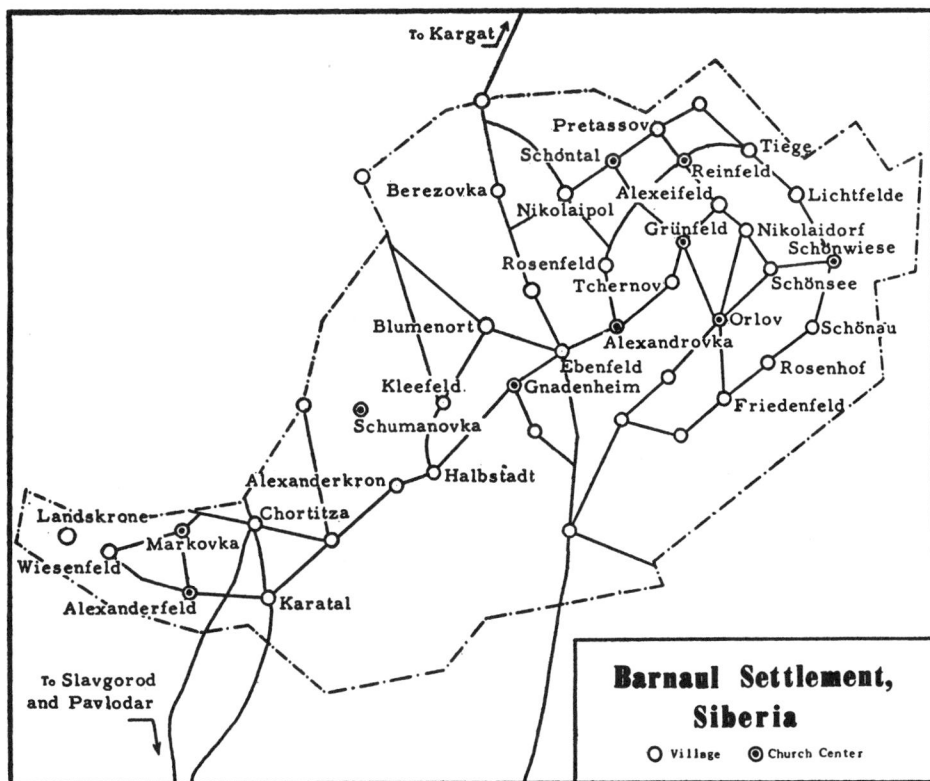

Barnaul Settlement, Siberia

○ Village   ◉ Church Center

In 1917 the municipality was divided, with Chortitza as a second center.

The Barnaul settlement consisted in 1925 of some 58 villages with a population of 13,173. Most of these villages belonged to the Barnaul settlement proper. However, as time went on the families increased and more settlers arrived and numerous smaller settlements sprang up on the fringes of this settlement.

The Orlov municipality of the Barnaul settlement consisted of the following 26 villages: Gnadenfeld, Tiege, Lichtfelde, Schönwiese, Schönau, Schönsee, Nikolaidorf, Alexeyfeld, Reinfeld, Protassov, Schöntal, Grünfeld, Orlov, Rosenhof, Friedensfeld, Alexandrovka, Tchernovka, Rosenwald, Nikolaipol, Berezovka, Hochstädt, Ebenfeld, Blumenort, Gnadenheim, Kleefeld, and Shumanovka. The Chortitza municipality consisted of the following eight villages: Halbstadt, Alexanderkron, Karatal, Chortitza, Markovka, Grieshenka (Alexanderfeld), Stepnoye, and Golenki.

Besides the main Barnaul settlement there were five smaller ones which increased from year to year. About 15 miles to the west was the new settlement Bas Agatch with two villages, Dolinovka and Suvorovka. Svistunovo, 45 miles east of Slavgorod, consisted of two villages, Dolinovka and Tchernyevka. Tchaiatchi with the two villages, Nikolayevka and Tatianovka, was located 42 miles east of Slavgorod. Gliaden, located 72 miles east of Slavgorod, consisted of five villages, while Pashvia was located some 48 miles east of Slavgorod consisting of four villages, Ananyevka, Markovka, Ekaterinovka, and Grigoryevka.

In addition to these little settlements bordering on the Barnaul settlement there were larger ones more distantly located from Barnaul which were not necessarily a part of this settlement. Among them were the Pavlodar (q.v.), the Minussinsk, the Omsk (q.v.), the Friesenov (q.v.), the Tchunayev (q.v.) settlements and others.

About two thirds of the population belonged to the Mennonite Church and most of the others to the Mennonite Brethren. Several families belonged to the *Allianz-Gemeinde* and the Adventists.

The Mennonite Church was divided into five districts averaging 350 baptized members each in 1913: Orlov, Grünfeld, Reinfeld, Shumanovka, and Markovka. The elders in 1913 were Kornelius Harder, Jakob Gerbrandt (graduate of Bethel College), and Kornelius Wienss. Ministers were Anton Löwen, H. Sawatzky, Jakob Enns, and others. The church buildings were located in Schönsee, Grünfeld, Kleefeld, and Markovka. In Orlov the town hall was used for worship services and in some villages private homes.

The Mennonite Brethren were similarly divided into five districts: Schöntal, Schönwiese, Alexandrovka, Gnadenheim, and Alexanderfeld. Elder Jakob Wiens of the Pavlodar settlement served as elder (1913). Ministers were Aaron Reimer, Peter Bärgen, Schmidt, Isaak Braun, and Abram Ratzlaff (1913). Meetinghouses were located in all the villages mentioned as districts and in Alexanderkron.

In all villages elementary schools had been established and the instruction was given in the German and Russian languages. Originally the schoolhouses were primitive and only a few of the teachers had training or experience in teaching. Gradually schools were built in most of the villages and trained teachers were hired. Outstanding among the teachers were Jakob Wedel, Johann D. Friesen, Anton Löwen, and Johann Dyck. Annually two teachers' conferences took place at which lectures were given and common problems were discussed. In 1913 an organization planned and promoted the establishment of a secondary school. It is not known whether it ever materialized.

Most of the village occupants were farmers. The farms averaged 135 acres. Of each farm a few acres were set aside to be rented out. The income formed a fund to be used to buy land for the next generation. There were nine stores, four windmills, two steam mills, one motor mill, and a number of smith and carpenter shops located in the various villages. In Orlov the government erected a hospital and a post office.

During World War I most of the men were drafted, which handicapped the normal development and progress of the new settlement considerably. After the revolution the great poverty of the settlement was somewhat relieved through American Mennonite help. Until 1925 the Mennonites continued private farming and ownership. In 1926 Grünfeld started collective farming. In 1927 other villages began to work most of their land collectively, though each retained some of his property. The government supported this effort by making tractors and threshing machines available. In 1928 radical collectivization was introduced and many of the Mennonite farmers exiled as kulaks. Ministers and churches were taxed to a degree that it was impossible to fulfill the obligations. Religious instruction to young people was prohibited. After 1928 the ministers were gradually exiled and the churches confiscated. Thus collectivization, exile, and the entire religious policy of Communism have broken the Mennonite way of life. However, the settlement has not completely disintegrated as is the case with most of those in European Russia. Hardly any Mennonites from Siberia have been fortunate enough to leave Russia and to come to America since World War II.   C.K.

ML I, 125; J. Quiring, *Die Mundart von Chortitza in Süd-Russland* (Munich, 1928) 39-41; *Bundesbote-Kal.*, 1913, 26-27; *Unser Blatt* II, 182, 210, 277; III, 11-13, 15-16; J. J. Hildebrand, *Sibirien* (Winnipeg, 1952).

Barninge, Sijntgen: see **Sijntgen, Kreupel.**

Barns have held a particularly important place among most Mennonite farmers probably because of their conscientious interest in the stewardship of crops, machinery, and livestock.

From the structural standpoint, one may find three general types of barns in the United States and Canada. First, the large general utility type barn found on farms among those with a Swiss and German Mennonite background. By and large, they are found among the Pennsylvania-German cultural stock. The barns are distinguished by their two stories. The livestock is kept on the first floor and the harvested crops and farm machinery on the second. Usually the second floor contains a wide driveway. Many of these large barns are called bank barns because they are erected with one side against a natural or artificial incline or a hill so as to make it possible to drive with farm wagons and machinery directly onto the second floor. In the eastern United States and Canada farmers generally house their animals during the winter months. Many of them are dairy farmers and make every effort to house their cattle carefully. Therefore larger buildings are needed for livestock, forage, grains, and machinery.

Mennonites in the eastern part of the United States and Canada have often displayed artistic tastes in painting their barns. A wide variety of artistic designs can be found on their barns. A white painted arch over the window of a red painted barn is a common decoration; stars of varying sizes are also frequently painted in central positions on the barn sidings; and other geometric designs are also found. Frequently pictures of a model horse, a cow, or a fowl are painted on a conspicuous place on the barn.

The second general type of barn among Mennonites is found chiefly in the midwestern and western parts of the United States and some parts of Canada. The barns are not as large as those in the east because they are generally not used to provide storage of straw and livestock, but mostly for a kind of temporary shelter for livestock in the more severe winter weather and as a milking shed for those engaged in dairying. The straw and hay are often stacked in the fields or in the barnyards. Machinery is frequently left outdoors throughout the entire year. The high winds and occasional cyclones may account for the fact that barns are lower and smaller in structure. It is noticeable that among these Amish and Mennonites in the Middle West whose parents moved from eastern Pennsylvania communities, the same large, eastern-type barns are found. Mennonites in the Middle West generally paint their barns but artistic designs are seldom found except occasionally on farms of those who have carried over the pattern from their eastern background and Swiss Mennonite heritage.

The third type of barn is common to western Canada, especially Manitoba. It is a single story frame structure, in many ways similar to that found in the midwestern United States, but it is attached directly to the residence and often under one roof with it and the shed to the rear. There is always a direct passage from residence to barn. This type of farmhouse, composed of three structural elements, including the barn, is a Frisian survival transplanted from Russia along with other aspects of European culture. It had been adopted by the Mennonites in Prussia, taken along to Russia and in the early days also to western Canada and, more rarely, the United States. In the original arrangement of the barn, the cows were stabled on both sides of a central feeding alley, while the horses faced the wall next to the residence.

In addition to these general types there are many variations among the scattered Mennonites in various parts of the United States and Canada, such as those in the warmer climates of California and Oklahoma, and the cooler climates of Washington and Minnesota. There is a noticeable variation in the concern exercised for the care and appearance of the barns and accompanying outbuildings. In some areas barns are not painted or well kept up, but in by far the largest number of Mennonite communities, especially in the older settlements, an unpainted and ramshackle barn is a rare exception. In many communities group pressure is exercised against those who do not paint and maintain their barns, and well-kept barns have become a source of community pride. On the other hand, in some areas, such as earlier in Ontario, the unpainted, weathered barn was a folk-custom, which by no means always indicated a careless attitude. (See **Architecture.**) Barns are often used by the Amish for church services, also special occasions such as weddings. J.W.F.

Baron (Barns) im Wald: see Belfort.

Barrville Mennonite Church (GCM), now extinct, organized near Lewistown, Pa., in 1920, was listed under the Eastern District Conference in the *Mennonite Year Book and Almanac* of 1921 for the first time. The record indicated it had 34 members. It was listed for the last time in the 1935 *Year Book,* although the last report of membership was for Jan. 1, 1931, when 30 were reported.　M.G.

Barse, Johannes, a follower of Melchior Hofmann, participant in the disputation at Flensburg, 1529, at the close of which he arose and, according to Bugenhagen, played a comic role. Hofmann's verdict of his conduct is different; it is given in his *Dialogus und gründliche Berichtigung gehaltener Disputation im Lande zu Holstein* . . . .　NEFF.

B. N. Krohn, *Gesch. der fanatischen und enthusiastischen Wiedertäufer* . . . (Leipzig, 1758) 152 and 184, 185; F. O. zur Linden, *Melchior Hofmann* . . . (Haarlem, 1885) 147; *ML I,* 127.

Barsingerhorn (pop. 2,151 in 1947, with 711 Mennonites), a village in the Dutch province of North Holland between Alkmaar and Den Helder, where there is a Mennonite church with parsonage, the center of a widely scattered congregation which until twenty-five years ago was called the congregation of Barsingerhorn, Kolhorn, and Wieringerwaard, but is now called by only the first town. In this "Head of North Holland" there have been Mennonites from the very beginning of the movement. The martyr Willem Wiggersz of Barsingerhorn listed by van Braght (*Mart. Mir.* D 35, E 442) was imprisoned there in 1534. At the same time there were also Anabaptists in the neighboring Kolhorn (*q.v.*). From this time on the existence of congregations here may be assumed. Leenaert Bouwens baptized 41 persons at Barsingerhorn between 1551 and 1561. The history of the congregation or congregations here is obscure for a century, and afterwards data is very scarce; the earliest written document of the congregation dates back only to 1703, and not until 1755-59 and again from 1776 on, are there any minutes or records in the church books. A Flemish congregation was represented at the conference at Haarlem in 1649. There were also delegates of this congregation, which is called Barringhorn and Nieuwe Zijp, at the Flemish Synod of Leiden (*q.v.*) of 1660. The Flemish congregation of Kolhorn probably merged with the Waterlanders later on. According to the *Naamlijst* (*q.v.*) of 1731 there were two congregations: one Waterlander, which was also called Barringhorn and Nieuwe Zijpe, and had a meetinghouse at Barsingerhorn and later also in Nieuwe Zijpe or Wieringerwaard; the other Frisian, also called Barsingerhorn and Kolhorn, which had churches both at Barsingerhorn and Kolhorn. The Frisian church in Barsingerhorn was repaired in 1759; but in 1799, after the English soldiers had used it roughly, it was torn down. The Frisian church in Kolhorn was demolished in 1788 and replaced by a new one in 1790. An unusual fact about this church is that it was built entirely of wood in six hours on Oct. 25, 1790; on the next day the parsonage, also of wood, was put up in three hours. From this time on, this congregation, which in 1784 had only 13 members, had only the one church and parsonage in Kolhorn. The pastor, D. Hovens, had some difficulty with the preacher of the Reformed congregation, because he had given catechetical instruction to a non-Mennonite girl.

The Waterlander congregation, which was also sometimes called Barsingerhorn and Wieringerwaard in the 18th century, was much larger; its membership stood at 230 in 1730, but by 1806 it had dropped to 119. After many fruitless attempts, in 1755, 1781, and 1821, as well as at other times, the union of the two congregations was finally accomplished in 1827, when both congregations happened to be without a preacher at the same time. The united congregation had a membership of 240 in 1840, 300 in 1861, 427 in 1898, and 360 in 1950. Many of the members live in the surrounding villages. The church at Kolhorn was soon abandoned, that in Wieringerwaard in the village of Kreil renovated, and a new one built in Barsingerhorn. A new parsonage was built in 1938.

Since the unification in 1827 the congregation has been served by the following ministers: Benedictus Hoekstra, 1829-83; J. Westerman-Holstijn, 1884-91; P. Zondervan, 1891-92; J. Kooiman, 1893-1911; R. van der Veen, 1912-38; J. Oosterbaan, 1940-50; J. Knot since 1951. Since 1923 the church in Kreil has not been used, all services being held at Barsingerhorn. In 1941 the Barsingerhorn congregation joined the congregations at Noord- and Zuidzijpe for preaching services. The congregation owns much property. Most of the members are engaged in agriculture.

In the congregation there is a women's organization, a youth circle, and a Bible circle; together with the Reformed congregation it supports a Sunday school for children. (*Inv. Arch. Amst.* I, No. 937; II, Nos. 1533-40; *DB* 1880, 81-96; Blaupot t.C., *Holland* I and II *passim*.)   R. vDV., vDZ.

Bartel (Bartels, Barthel, Bartol, Bartelmes, Bartelmeus, Bartholomäus), a Mennonite family name in West Prussia, appearing in the rural Frisian congregations and in the Flemish congregation at Danzig (*q.v.*). It was first mentioned at Montau (*q.v.*) 1639 (Bartel) and at Gross Lubin 1640 (Bartholomäus). Thirty-three families of this name were counted in West Prussia in 1776 (without Danzig), and 171 persons in 1935 (without Elbing). Members of this family migrated to Poland, Russia (Molotschna), and the United States. H. C. Barthel (*q.v.*), of Hillsboro, Kan., was a Mennonite missionary to China. Peter Bartel (*q.v.*), elder of the Gruppe (*q.v.*) congregation West Prussia, was a member of the Mennonite delegation sent to Berlin in 1867 and 1868, to plead for exemption from military service. His report on the work of this delegation was published in *Mennonitische Rundschau* (October 1898).

The Schönsee Mennonite Church (*q.v.*), Prussia, had a number of elders by this name. Elder Peter Bartel of the Gruppe Mennonite Church (*q.v.*) ordained Heinrich Bartel, Culm-Rossgarten, as elder of the Schönsee church in September 1861, who died Sept. 22, 1874. During his time the general conscription law was passed. His strong opposition to military service found much criticism in his own congregation. His son, also Heinrich Bartel, who had been chosen minister in 1887, was ordained on May 4, 1902, and died on March 3, 1905. ("Die Aeltesten der Gemeinde Schönsee seit der Teilung Polens 1773," *Gem.-Kal.* 1941, 80-88.) G.R., C.K.

Bartel, an Anabaptist martyr, who went from Antwerp to Berchem (1550) to comfort Hans van Monster, a brother imprisoned there, was seized, and after brutal torture executed together with Hans van Monster and Old Jacob (*de oude Jacob*). Van Braght records further that Bartel witnessed the execution of Mary van Beckum (*q.v.*) and discussed it with Elder Hendrick van Arnhem (*Mart. Mir.* D 102, E 500; *ML* I, 127).   vDZ.

Bartel (de) Boeckbinder (Bartholomeus van Halle), a bookbinder of 's Hertogenbosch in Brabant, a Dutch Anabaptist, was one of the twelve apostles who were sent out from Amsterdam in 1533 by Jan Matthysz (*q.v.*). Bartel went to Friesland with Dirck Cuyper and baptized four persons in Leeuwarden, among them Obbe Philips; on the next day he ordained Obbe and Hans Scheerder as elders. Bartel, who preached in Sneek and Dordrecht as well as at other places, was obviously an influential man. Later he went to Münster, arriving there on Jan. 5, 1534, in the company of Willem de Cuyper. Although Bartel was not a disciple of the Münster doctrine of violence, he was nevertheless a very confused spirit, a follower of Melchior Hofmann. On March 22, 1534, Bartel de Boeckbinder, Pieter de Houtsager, Willem de Cuyper, and others ran through the streets of Amsterdam with drawn swords in their right hands as a symbol of God's vengeance, loudly crying woe over the city and calling the ungodly to repentance. When the police seized them they did not change their attitude. Bartel and also Pieter and Willem were beheaded about March 26, 1534, at Haarlem.   vDZ.

Inv. Arch. Amst. I, 24, 27; *DB* 1917, 98, 100 f., 125, 151; Kühler, *Geschiedenis* I, 72 f., 75, 105 f.; Grosheide, *Bijdrage*, 25, 51, 302.

Bartel, Hans, an Anabaptist martyr, a weaver by trade, was seized with Hans Wucherer in Bavaria and subjected to a trial on the rack. Seven times the priests came into the prison and tried to turn them from their faith. But they remained steadfast through all the torture inflicted upon them, and were burned at the stake in 1537 at Burghausen a.Inn (*Mart. Mir.* D 41, E 447; *ML* I, 127).

NEFF.

Bartel, Heinrich, of the Deutsch-Kazun Mennonite Church (*q.v.*) was ordained as minister in 1861 and as elder in 1864. He lived in Dt. Czastkov and died on Feb. 27, 1898, at the age of 68.   A. Goertz.

Bartel, Peter, b. March 3, 1813, at Niedergruppe in West Prussia, preacher of the Mennonite congregation Montau-Gruppe near Graudenz (ordained July, 1840). Ordained as elder on Sept. 7, 1856 (*Menn. Bl.*, 1856, 68 and 63), he managed the complete remodeling of the church at Montau in 1859, in spite of opposing elements in the congregation. He met even stronger resistance when he worked for the rebuilding of the church at Gruppe, but perseverance again carried him to his goal. On Oct. 7, 1866, he assisted in the dedication of the new church, which (20,260 marks) was paid for in December 1872. Peter Bartel was also one of the five delegates who brought about a modification of the law demanding universal military duty in favor of the Prussian Mennonites through audiences with King William I, Crown Prince Frederick William, and various ministers. The modification is stated in the cabinet order of the King, of March 3, 1868. Bartel's stern attitude on the military question caused a division in the Montau-Gruppe church. He demanded of the candidates for baptism a pledge that they would not accept military service except in accord with this order, and set up the regulation that any who chose armed military service would no longer be considered members of the church. All who would not sign this regulation would be excommunicated. Ninety-five did not sign, and formed a new congregation in 1871 with its seat at Montau. Peter Bartel died on May 11, 1879 (*ML* I, 127; *Chr. Gem.-Kal.*, 1920, 29, 70-79.)   NEFF.

Bartel, Rudolf, b. April 18, 1875, at Deutsch-Kazun, near Warsaw, Poland, was married to Eleonore Bartel in 1904. He was chosen minister of the Deutsch-Kazun Mennonite Church (*q.v.*) in 1911, and ordained elder the following year. The burdens of the elder during the trying years of World War I and after were heavy. During World War II all male members of the congregation from 17 to 60 years of age were sent by the Poles to the Bereza-Katuska prison. Elder Rudolf Bartel was seized by Polish soldiers on Sept. 7, 1939, and shot. Most of the family were killed by a German bombing attack early in the war. One daughter now lives in Saskatoon, Sask. (Erich Göttner, "Aeltester Rudolf Bartel, Deutsch-Kazun," *Gem.-Kal.* 1941, 89-93.)

C.K.

Bartel, Wilhelm, born at Gnadenfeld in Russia, a zealous follower of the evangelist E. Wüst, through whom he had been converted, took a leading part in the founding of the Mennonite Brethren in Russia. He is a signatory of the declaration of the Brethren at Orlov, March 19, 1860, and took part

in its presentation to the *Fürsorgekomitee* (Guardians' Committee) on Dec. 27, 1860, in which the new church group asserted its Mennonite character and position. For a while he was a Bible colporteur and evangelist in behalf of the Mennonite adherents of Wüst, then he united with the emotional branch, which was founded by the teacher Kappes. As late as 1861 he defended the rapidly growing "happiness" in his letters. But when the most regrettable moral aberrations occurred, into which the movement degenerated in some cases, he detached himself altogether from the movement. But he had no more influence on the further development of the Mennonite Brethren. In the 80's he died in the *Plan* settlement in solitude. (Friesen, *Brüderschaft; ML* I, 128.)   NEFF.

Barthel, Hendrik Christiaan, b. April 19, 1877, d. Dec. 30, 1936, became *proponent* (ministerial candidate) of the A.D.S. in 1902 after completing his studies at the university of Utrecht and the Amsterdam seminary. He served in succession the following congregations: Holwerd, 1902-12; Balk and Woudsend, 1912-16; Aalsmeer, 1916-26; Twisk and Medemblik, 1926-35, in which year he had to resign because of his health. By those who knew him he was honored as a man of simplicity and faithfulness to duty. Through his principles—Christian socialism, total abstinence, nonresistance—he occupied a unique place in the brotherhood. (*De Meerbode* of Aalsmeer, Jan. 5, 1937; *DJ* 1938, 23-27, with portrait.)   VDZ.

Bartholomeus van den Berge, a miller at Dieteren in the Dutch province of Limburg, was baptized in his house in the fall of 1534 by Jan Smeitgen (*q.v.*) in the presence of 10 or 12 persons. Smeitgen took water "from out a small jar" and spoke the old formula for baptism. For reasons of safety, Bartholomeus with his wife, Clementia Heynen, who was also rebaptized, went to Maastricht (Dutch province of Limburg); here, during the night of Jan. 28, 1535, he was captured with 14 other members of the congregation. While all the others recanted, including his wife, Bartholomeus remained steadfast. He was burned to death on Feb. 1, 1535, on the Vrijthof at Maastricht. He is omitted from the martyr books perhaps because he was affected to some extent by the Münster influence. This might be called a kind of naive Münster infection, a kind which is found among many Anabaptists in 1534 and 1535, and especially in the church at Maastricht, where Rothman's book, *Van der Wrake* (Concerning Vengeance), was read. At his trial Bartholomeus said that he had heard "that God will punish the world. That a king would come either from Münster or Amsterdam, and all the brethren would follow him." (W. Bax, *Het Protestantisme in het Bisdom Luik en vooral in Maastricht* I, The Hague, 1941, 70, 72, 113-14.)   VDZ.

Bartholomeus van Halle: see Bartel de Boeckbinder.

Bartholomeus Panten (also called Meeuws or Remeeuws Pantijn), an Anabaptist martyr, was executed by hanging in the Gravenkasteel (castle and prison) at Gent, Belgium, on Sept. 15, 1592, together with Michiel de Widower (Michiel de

Cleercq, *q.v.*). These two men were the last Mennonite martyrs to offer their lives for the sake of Christ in Gent. Bartholomeus was a deacon and the leader of the Gent Mennonite congregation in the last years of its existence. He was born in the Flemish town of Roesselare, had been baptized twenty years before, and was 48 years of age. He was cruelly tortured, but did not divulge the names of his fellow members of the church, nor renounce his faith, but remained loyal and steadfast to the bitter end.

In the *Martyrs' Mirror*, van Braght has included three letters which Bartholomeus wrote while in prison. The first was addressed to his brother Karel Panten, who was living in the Dutch city of Haarlem; the second was addressed to the congregation of believers (to all who love the truth). This second letter had a postscript in which he reports the trial and disputations which he and Michiel had with the Jesuits. The third letter is a "testament" addressed to his daughter, who after his imprisonment had been placed in a Roman Catholic convent.　　　　　　　　　　　　　　　　vDZ.

Offer, 624-25; *Mart. Mir.* D 779-86, E 372; Verheyden, *Gent*, 69, No. 249; *ML* III, 333.

Bartholomeus Potbacker (Bartholomeus Cornelissen), an Anabaptist martyr of Berghen, i.e., Bergen op Zoom, Dutch province of North Brabant, was executed on the market square at Antwerp on Nov. 22, 1555, because he had been rebaptized and persisted in his "wicked opinion." His name is listed in the song, "Aenhoort Godt, hemelsche Vader" (Hear, O God, heavenly Father), No. 16 of the *Liedtboecxken van den Offer des Heeren*. vDZ.

Offer, 564; *Mart. Mir.* D 161, E 550; *Antw. Arch.-Blad* VIII, 427, 429; XIV, 20 f., No. 231.

Barthout Heynricsz, an Anabaptist preacher (*leeraar*), beheaded at Haarlem, Dutch province of North Holland, on March 30, 1534. He was a tailor by trade. (*Inv. Arch. Amst.* I, 745; *DB* 1917, 121, No. 126.)　　　　　　　　　　　　　　　vDZ.

Bartolf, Margarete, an Anabaptist of Niederdorla (in the Erfurt district), a miller's wife, "a stubborn and defiant woman," in a hearing in Niederdorla on Sept. 19, 1564, stated her faith in a confession that testifies beautifully of her experience of salvation. She escaped a martyr's death by flight. (P. Wappler, *Die Täuferbewegung in Thüringen*, Jena, 1913, 506; *ML* I, 128.)　　　　　　　　NEFF.

Bartsch, Franz, a Mennonite preacher in Lysanderhöh in the Russian province of Samara, author of the book, *Unser Auszug nach Mittel-Asien* (Halbstadt, 1907, 2d ed., North Kildonan, Man., 1948), in which he describes the 1880 emigration of Mennonites of the Köppental congregation (Samara) to Khiva (*q.v.*). Bartsch was in the first group of emigrants, but after a few years he returned to Samara (*ML* I, 128).　　　　　　　　　　HEGE.

Bartsch, Johann, one of the two delegates who on Oct. 31, 1786, left their homes in West Prussia to find a suitable location in Russia for a planned colonization. Empress Catherine II had issued a manifesto on July 22, 1763, calling new settlers into her lands and promising them extensive freedoms.

Through her ambassador in Danzig she invited the Mennonites of West Prussia to immigrate to Russia. The document, which promised them complete freedom of religion and freedom from military service, and offered each family 160 acres (65 dessiatines) of land, was signed by George von Trappe (*q.v.*) as the director and curator of the Mennonite colonies (Isaak, *Die Molotschnaer Mennoniten*, 5). It was read to the Flemish congregation in Danzig at an open meeting on Aug. 7, 1786, and was favorably received, though the magistrate of Danzig was much displeased by it.

Nevertheless Johann Bartsch and Jakob Höppner (*q.v.*) left for Russia as deputies of the Russian government and at its expense. They were provided with authorization signed by 60 Mennonites and with a letter of recommendation from von Trappe. At Dubrovna on the Dnieper they were introduced to Prince Potemkin. In the spring of the following year on their journey to Taurida they were also received by the Empress in the presence of her highest dignitaries at Kremenchug. They had to accompany the Empress in her train "out of special favor and grace" to the Crimea. When on their return they were presented to the heir-apparent (later Emperor Paul I), he kissed their cheeks. At the end of the year they returned with von Trappe, the Russian commissar. Their active efforts led to the emigration of 1789.

The two delegates received small thanks for their service. The emigrants were bitterly disappointed at their arrival in Chortitza in 1789; and now all their anger and discontent were heaped upon the two delegates. These placed their authorization and important papers into the hands of the preachers. Soon afterward they were excommunicated from the church. Bartsch was received again upon his request; but a sad fate awaited Höppner. Later a monument was placed on each grave. The monument of Johann Bartsch, a beautiful obelisk of marble, surrounded by a white iron fence, is located in the Rosental colony near Chortitza.　　NEFF.

P. Hildebrandt, *Erste Auswanderung aus dem Danziger Gebiet nach Südrussland* (Halbstadt, 1888); D. H. Epp, *Die Chortitzer Mennoniten* (Odessa, 1889); Johann Bartsch letters (copies at Bethel College Historical Library); C. Henry Smith, *The Story of the Mennonites* (Newton, 1950); F. Isaak, *Die Molotschnaer Mennoniten* (Halbstadt, 1908); *ML* I, 128.

Barvenkovo, a city of about 14,000 inhabitants with (1914) 216 Mennonites on the Torets River in the Russian province of Kharkov, where Mennonites from the Chortitza and Molotschna colonies settled in 1889. The Mennonites in Barvenkovo engaged principally in trade and industry; there were four steam mills, a farm machinery manufacturing plant, and several warehouses in their possession. They maintained an elementary school (attended by 44 pupils in 1913), and together with the Russians also a seven-class business school; in both schools instruction was given in both languages. Barvenkovo formed the center of the Mennonite settlement in the province of Kharkov (*q.v.*). (*ML* I, 129.)　　　　　　　　　　　　　　HEGE.

Bärwalde, a village in the district of Marienburg, West Prussia, in which Mennonites lived from about 1570 to 1945. Bärwalde was originally an estate of the King of Poland, as was also Tiegenhof and its vicinity. The Mennonites living in Bärwalde belonged to the Mennonite congregation of the Grossen Werder which had its center in Tiegenhagen. This church was Flemish, whereas all the Frisian Mennonites in the community were gathered into the Orlofferfeld congregation.

The larger Flemish congregation was supervised by the elder of the Danzig church from 1570 to 1639; from that time on they chose their own elder, who also served the Elbing church. In 1726 Elbing became independent and in 1728 Heubuden also separated as an independent Flemish congregation from the church in the Grossen Werder.

As the latter was still too large, it was divided into four parts about 1740, namely, Rosenort, Tiegenhagen, Ladekopp, and Bärwalde, each of which controlled its own congregational affairs, even though for 20 years they were under one elder. Bärwalde was the first to acquire its own elder in 1809. But because the church built in 1768 stood on Fürstenwerder land, the congregation took the name Fürstenwerder about 1830. The villages of Bärwalde and Fürstenwerder are located close together (*ML I*, 129). H.G.M.

Bas Agatch is the name of a place near Slavgorod, Siberia, near which was located a Mennonite settlement composed of two villages by the name of Dolinovka and Suvorovka. (See also **Barnaul**.)
C.K.

Basel. In August 1525 a small group of Swiss Brethren who met daily in Basel with Michael Schürer, a tailor from Freiburg, was surprised and arrested. Besides the owner of the house and his wife there were present Lorenz Hochrütiner of St. Gall, Ulrich Hugwald of Thurgau, Matthias Graf, a printer, and his wife Katharina Breuner, Elise Müller, and Barbara Grüninger. On Aug. 23 they were released after recanting. Nonresident Anabaptists had to leave the city "forever." The women were threatened with death by drowning, the men by the sword. Hochrütiner and Schürer were banished the second time, their families to be sent after them a week later.

Oecolampadius, the reformer of Basel, was greatly surprised to learn of the existence of the Anabaptist group. In August 1525 he held a disputation with them in his house; he was assisted by Wolfgang Wissenburg, Jakob Immeli (*q.v.*), and Thomas Girfalk (Stähelin, *Basler Reformation,* 123) and also Thomas Leesmeister, an evangelical Augustinian. The proceedings of this debate were printed in three editions: Basel, 1525; Augsburg, 1525; and in Latin, Basel, 1544 (Stähelin, *Briefe* I, 387). It bore the title *Ein Gespräch etlicher Predikanten zu Basel gehalten mit etlichen Bekennern der Wiedertaufe.* (A copy is in the library of the university of Munich; see *Menn. Rundschau,* 1912, July 10, p. 6, note, and Stähelin, *Briefe,* 338. A MS copy is in the Goshen College Library.) The debate centered about infant baptism and the right to separate oneself from the church. The Anabaptists persevered in their Scriptural views and considered themselves the victors. Hubmaier's *Von dem Kindertauf* was a reply to the position of Oecolampadius in this colloquium.

The Anabaptist movement spread. New members were constantly coming in from the neighboring cantons. The *Urfehdebuch,* which records the banishment of imprisoned Anabaptists, mentions the preachers Rudolf Forster, Ulrich Bolt, Friedli Iberger (see **Aargau**), Gabriel Schuhmacher of Aarau, Hans Waldshuter of Zürich, and others.

On June 2, 1526, the first mandate against the Anabaptists was issued in Basel: "Whoever has himself rebaptized is banned with his family from a radius of five miles around .the city." The second mandate, July 24, 1526, forbade Anabaptist meetings in the vicinity of the city (Stähelin, *Basler Reformation,* 130 f.). On July 6 and Aug. 3, 1527, these mandates were repeated, and on March 14, 1528, a heavy fine was fixed for those who attended an Anabaptist sermon or sheltered one of their preachers. The mandates were issued during the parliamentary sessions at Baden, which has for Switzerland a significance similar to that of the Reichstag of Worms for Germany.

At first, however, these mandates were not carried out very strictly. Hans Pfistermeyer (*q.v.*) was repeatedly banished in 1526-27 without further penalty. Felix Manz (*q.v.*) also lived in Basel at this time. This indicates that there was a large congregation of Swiss Brethren. Some of them, Johannes Hausmann, Seckler, and Lorenz Hochrütiner's son Jakob, went to Bern in April 1527, where they were placed in the pillory; the first of these was drowned there in 1528.

In 1527 numerous Anabaptists from Straubing and Augsburg entered Basel; among these were Hans Denk (*q.v.*) who died here, Georg Maler, Ulrich Treschsel, and Hans Beck. Two of them are said to have challenged Oecolampadius after his sermon at St. Martin's to attach himself to their cause, which (they said) he secretly favored. But they were soon recalled by their home congregations to assist in the struggle with the clergy of the established church.

In the same year (1527) a small group of Swiss Brethren meeting in the house of Hans Altenbach were arrested. Pfistermeyer and Ludwig Wolf were among them; they were released with a sharper threat of execution. One of their companions called "Karlin" (perhaps Karl Brennwald, *q.v.*), had the articles of his faith drawn up in written form and on June 30, 1527, presented them to the council. At the request of the council Oecolampadius wrote a refutation, entitled *Unterrichtung von der Wiedertaufe, von der Obrigkeit und von dem Eid auf Karlins N. Wiedertäufers Artikel* (copies in the Goshen College Library and the Library of the University of Basel). The second debate with the Swiss Brethren allegedly held on June 10, 1527, did not take place (Stähelin, *Briefe* II, 78; **Marius**).

Anabaptists from Franconia had also come to Basel, and had worshiped together in the home of Michael Schürer during Lent in 1528. Hans Römer, Christoph Peisker, and Volkmar Fischer are named. Jörg von Passau had likewise wished to come to Basel, where he hoped to find the noblest of the church, in order "to talk to them through the power of God, that the plants may be weeded out which God did not plant, and we may be unified through the Holy Spirit."

Of the other well-known leaders of the Brethren who were temporarily in Basel, Wolfgang Ulimann should be mentioned, who was banished from Basel in August 1528 on penalty of death by drowning; George Blaurock (q.v.) was in prison in Basel in February 1529; his companions were Hans Heide of the canton of Basel and Wolfgang Moser of the Adige Valley. A large number of Anabaptists in flight from the Adige lay imprisoned in Basel.

David Joris (q.v.) lived in Basel from 1544 to 1556 under the pseudonym of Johann von Brügge. Not until three years after his death was his real name discovered; then his corpse was burned and the ashes scattered. In August 1554 Wilhelm Reublin (q.v). appeared, a sick old man, in order to conclude his days in the city where he had begun his theological career as a priest in St. Alban's. The council probably had some doubts about receiving him, for they gave him a sum of 15 pounds for convalescence in Baden in Aargau.

While the Anabaptist movement declined in the city of Basel, it was constantly growing in the canton of Basel. There is evidence of many Swiss Brethren families in Liestal and Lausen. In Liestal we find the names Joder, Walch, Tegerfeld, and Heinimann; in Lausen, Schwytzer and Treyer were the prominent names. Oecolampadius wrote in a letter to Zwingli on July 1, 1528, "Recently over 100 met in the country." Men like Konrad Winkler (executed in Zürich, Jan. 20, 1530) and Bernhard Sager of Bremgarten promoted the new doctrine. Others like Uli Madlinger, Hans Hersberger, and Fridli Schaub supported it.

Now the Basel city council, having introduced the Reformation, resorted to sterner measures. In a Reformation decree of April 1, 1529, paragraph two states, "All Anabaptists, as well as those who have not been rebaptized but who shelter Anabaptists or attend their meetings, shall be kept in prison on *Muss und Brot* with the occasional use of torture reserved, until they recant. Obstinate ones remain in prison until death; those who fall back into Anabaptism shall be executed with the sword."

On Dec. 29, 1529, another disputation was held with eleven imprisoned preachers. This was the third Anabaptist disputation in Basel, but the first ordered by the government. Anabaptism was declared to be a "self-willed, Pharisaic hypocrisy, which pleases itself, condemns everything else, and finally leads to obvious disobedience and sedition." Four Anabaptists made a detailed recantation; the others remained steadfast. This likely angered the council to the extreme, for on Jan. 12, 1530, it had Hans Ludi of Bubendorf beheaded in Basel; Jakob Treyer, one of the debaters in the last disputation, was condemned to death, but was pardoned upon the request of Oecolampadius. Likewise the death sentence pronounced on Hans Hersberger and Uli Madlinger was not carried out.

The congregations at Rothenfluh and Anwil were considered the center of the Anabaptist movement. Forty men from the former and eleven of the latter were seized at the same time early in 1530 and imprisoned in the Basel tower. On Feb. 11 they were released; each was fined the large sum of five pounds. This severe punishment only served to strengthen and increase the movement in this remote region. At the "sand pit" at Lostdorf, 60 men and an equal number of women met for worship.

On Nov. 23, 1530, the council issued a new mandate against the Anabaptists: "All Anabaptists, as well as their adherents and protectors, will be pardoned if they recant when arrested the first time; if they are obstinate they will be banished. Those who fall into the error the second time, and banished persons who return, will be submerged in water and banished again. If those who have been submerged reappear, they shall be drowned without mercy wherever they are found."

The mandate was strictly followed. On Jan. 16, 1531, for the first time, an Anabaptist was "immersed three times according to custom" in the Rhine. The punishment was repeated on others, often in rapid succession. Not seldom the spectators gave voice to their sympathy for the victim. Others were executed. The names of only two persons executed are known to us, Hans Madlinger and Peter Linggscher, who were drowned on Feb. 10, 1531, in a creek near the Homburg castle.

But these ruthless measures did not succeed in crushing the movement. Matthys and Anna Gysin, Bastian and Uli Schmidt, August Buder, Heini Joder, Hans Hersberger and his wife Barbara could not be persuaded to abandon their faith even after years of imprisonment. Jakob Hersberger was placed on the pillory on July 14, 1535, in Basel; the executioner cut out his tongue and two fingers of his right hand as a perjurer.

In 1532 two nonresident Anabaptists were questioned on the rack in Basel, and declared that the Brethren were increasing "splendidly on Lake Geneva; also that there was a congregation at Rappoltsweiler and at Colmar in Alsace. They said they knew nothing of a planned insurrection, which might motivate and justify the terrible executions of the Austrian government in Ensisheim" (J. Horsch, in *Menn. Rundschau,* July 17, 1912).

Anabaptism continued for a long time in the Basel district. The meetings of the congregation "auf dem Blauen" in the 1580's were attended sometimes by 10, sometimes by 30 or 40 of the Swiss Brethren scattered through the community. About 1600 a mason named Peter was their preacher. The congregation was always under suppression. Many were banished. On June 11, 1595, the council, following Zürich's example, sharpened exile by confiscation of property.

About 1616 a small group of Swiss Brethren gathered in the house of Fridli Hersberger in Thürnen. Their preacher was Kaspar Schuhmacher of Safenwyl in Aargau. Others from this place took part in the meetings. They met in Grenzach, or in the "red house" in the Hard or in the woods about Bottmingen. Their preacher was Hans Bürky from the canton of Basel. In Maisprach the Brethren met in the house of Michel Rohrer. In Thürnen the Berchtold family were loyal members of the group.

Many emigrated to Moravia. By 1571 many had already gone there from the canton of Basel: Jakob Riggenbach, his wife and others from Rothenfluh, Heini Schaub and Bastian Buser from Sissach, Werlin Buser from Liestal, Matthias Senn from Tecknau, and others. Thus the old Swiss Brethren families in the Basel region have practically died out. The Brethren who settled in the early 18th century as renters in the canton of Basel, in Läufelfingen, Binningen, and Frenkendorf were immigrants. The dairy-farm Oberbölchen near Eptingen, called the "Anabaptist hut," served as their meeting place about 1722. Others gathered in the "red house" in the Hard or on the Wildenstein; for communion they journeyed to Alsace, as far as Ohnenheim near Colmar.

The prince bishop of Basel, Joh. Konrad, on Feb. 5, 1731, ruled that "Anabaptists and Pietists" were to be banished within six months. Actually only a few were banished. When the French Revolution brought the Swiss Brethren the toleration they had long yearned for, it was revealed that there were many of them in the bishop's Basel and Jura districts, who were henceforth permitted to live according to their faith unmolested (Müller, *Berner Täufer*, 238, 239, and 250).

From the records in the Basel state archives we take the following: on Jan. 9, 1697, three Brethren, Martin Waldner, Martin Moster, and Martin Dettweiler, residents of Langenbrugg, were captured and banished from the canton. On May 3, 1719, Hans Martin of Pratteln was cross-examined "because of his Anabaptist error." He showed a sincere desire to serve God and to live according to the commands of His Word; but he was unable to swear an oath to the government or bear arms, for this would be against his conscience. He was given several months to consider. After 1723 there are no native Anabaptists left in the canton of Basel.

About 60 years later several Swiss Brethren families settled in the canton of Basel. Claus Hirschy of Langnau in the Trachselwald district of the canton of Bern leased the estate of Leonhard Wagner in Alt-Schauenburg and in April 1777 he made half of the estate over to a Hans Schwarz of Schwartnau, Thun district of the canton of Bern, who was a native of Alsace. They held their religious services on the Wildenstein. In 1777 the parson Bleyenstein at Läufelfingen reported that 28 Anabaptists had come to the neighboring dairy-farm and declared that they had acquired tenure of the land. Even the pastor of Bubendorf had accepted an Anabaptist on his estate as a tenant, and a large family had settled in Läufelfingen (in the "Murer-Haus"), who did not attend the state church. The name of the father was Ludwig Plattner, was known in Basel as a linen-weaver, who dealt in sheets. He was afraid that many aberrations and divisions would occur, as had happened through the "Murer" tailor, George Fried; for these

people had been expelled from the bishopric of Basel, and were now trying to get a stronger and stronger footing in the canton of Basel to the greatest harm to religion and the obvious misleading of the people.

This letter was very effective. The church board took energetic steps in the matter. The pastor of Läufelfingen was praised for his vigilance, and he was commissioned to get to the bottom of the affair, by visiting Ludwig Plattner and finding out whether he really fostered this "Anabaptist error," and to take good care that he did not scatter the same, so that they could earnestly prevent the spread of such weeds. The other pastors were asked to keep a watchful eye on the Anabaptists, to apply the most effective methods of correcting such erring ones, and to protect the others from being misled to their errors.

The pastor of Läufelfingen discharged his assigned task with great zeal. He reported that the Anabaptist family had four daughters and three sons; he found the following books: "a large Froschauer Bible in a new reprint of Strasbourg 1748, two New Testaments—a Froschauer and a Lutheran, two books of psalms and hymns, Arndt's *Paradiesgärtlein*, a *Lustgärtlein*, a concordance, a book of confessions of Anabaptist martyrs and similar songs." In the cross-examination the Anabaptist (the report continues) declared that he could not adhere to the established church for conscience' sake, because it permitted too much looseness, swearing, drinking, etc. As an Anabaptist he depended partly on the services he conducted at home with his own family, and partly on meetings of the Anabaptists in the "red house." Their conscience did not permit them to carry or use arms, yet they would probably agree to haul munitions, food, etc., if necessary, to the people. Concerning baptism he said that they leave their children unbaptized until they reach the age of discretion and their own understanding of the faith of their fathers; they were permitted to choose freely between their brotherhood and the established church. The pastor said that he did not fear that this Anabaptist would try to make proselytes, but it was very depressing and dubious to permit people who were so wrong and dangerous in religious matters to gain a footing in the country only because of their supposed industry and conscientiousness, and quiet, retiring habits. . . . He hoped that an exalted government would not grant protection to people who refused it the oath, would not bear arms, and by their example would mislead other subjects to similar disobedience.

Once again the Läufelfingen parson was asked for a report. The church board had heard that the Anabaptists in the canton asserted that Ludwig Plattner was no concern of theirs and was not in their brotherhood; their meetings were not always held in the red house, but alternately in the various homes. They had never had communion services in the canton and did not intend to do so. The parson reported that Ludwig Plattner declared that about 60 years ago there had been a division among their leaders, resulting in two branches which still formed two separate brotherhoods, the upper and the lower. The following differences existed between them:

1. The lower strictly observed the ban; it was not permitted to have any dealings with the banned person, whether he was brother, sister, husband or wife, not even to eat with him.

2. In connection with communion footwashing must be observed according to the example of our Saviour.

3. Communion must be observed twice a year; whereas the upper church considered once a year sufficient, to whom he belonged.

Thus there were in the 18th century two Mennonite congregations in the canton of Basel, an Amish and a "Reist," which had nothing to do with each other. The former assembled for worship in various homes, the latter in the "red house" and on the Wildenstein. Both groups observed communion with the Alsatian brethren. They probably had no elder of their own.

Now the government instituted an exact investigation of the number of Mennonite families. It was shown that seven or eight families had "slipped into" the various communities, totaling about 50 persons. The pastors said that their conduct was quiet and withdrawn, and they observed the Lord's day better than many others, and did not appear before court as a plaintiff or a defendant. In the community of Muttenz, Friedrich Gerig from Lensburg (Aargau), a tenant of the "red house," had been living with his seven children; a brother-in-law lived on the Wildenstein and another on the estate in St. Jakob. In Binningen on the castle estate Michael Stauffer had been a tenant since 1771 and one of his day laborers was Jakob Würgler.

A second list of Anabaptists, compiled in 1783 by the magistrates, gives the following information:

In the district of Hornburg are

1. Johannes Benz, from the canton of Bern, who had come to the "ständigen Alp Divtistberg" in May 1782 and was to remain until May 1786;

2. Christian Bürgy of Emmendingen;

3. David Rohdacher, from near Karlsruhe, both on the Wieland estate at Rothenfluh, whose tenants they had become two and one-half years before for a term of eight years;

4. Ludwig Plattner of Rüderswil, Trachselwald district of the canton of Bern, had entered the canton six years ago, stayed three years in Läufelfingen, and had been on the H. Dietrich estate, called the Wüstmatt, for three of a term of twelve years.

In the Waldenburg district: Jakob Schmucklin with wife and four children, had been on the Arxhof (?) (Arlesheim) as a tenant six years of a term of twelve years. With him lived Peter Neuhäuser with wife and three children, a day laborer.

On the Wildenstein: Christian Freienberger with wife and three children had been in the canton seven years, and his brother-in-law Friedrich Gerig with wife and seven children two years.

In Bubendorf: Christian Müller with wife and three children had been here six years, and Christian Stucky with wife and one child also for six years, a day laborer in the pit.

"They are industrious, economical, submissive, peaceful, withdrawn, and hold their religious services quietly every two weeks, rotating between Schänzli at St. Jakob, the Wildenstein, and the Arxhof."

It is further reported that the tenant on the castle estate at Binningen, who had been there since 1776, had moved away the year before; on the other hand, two Mennonite families had settled at Brüglingen and two "am hohen Stein." In each case the estate was leased to only one, and the other worked for him. The actual tenant at Brüglingen had come from Alsace and had been on the Holdenwand since 1780, and settled here last year; the other came from the margravure. They were between 30 and 40 years old, and had one and two children respectively. The tenant on Hohenstein was from Emmendingen, had two married daughters, and a boy of eight or nine years at home. The other couple was from the Breisgau and had two children of ten or twelve years. On the estate at Liestal there was a Mennonite family which originally came from the canton of Bern, and five years ago came here from Alsace.

On May 6, 1783, the church synod requested a government regulation that the children of Mennonite parents be entered in the church books, so that their age be known, and when Mennonites die, to permit them to be buried in the church cemeteries. They hoped by this measure to bring about a better supervision of the Mennonites; but it was not passed. It seems that after 1845 the Mennonites were permitted to keep their own records of births, deaths, and marriages. In March 1846 Johann Kaufmann, tenant on the Wenkenhof, sought legalization of his signature, since he had been charged by his congregation, which met at the home of its leader at Urchelfelden, to keep the birth and confirmation records in the place of the deceased Schmuggli of Arlesheim. His request was granted.

On May 17, 1783, the regulation was passed that "information should be given about their number, the length of their stay and their moral conduct, and a watchful eye should be kept on them by the local parsons and any objectionable conduct be reported."

From 1805 on, no obstacles of any kind prevented the Mennonites from settling in the canton of Basel. They were to discharge their military duty in the transportation corps (noncombatant).

When in 1798 a Mennonite living on Buneberg refused to swear the civic oath, he was permitted, by an act of the republican government at Aarau, of Sept. 18, 1798, to use the formula, "We promise . . . ."

In 1810, in the regulation concerning the announcing and solemnizing of marriages, the rule was adopted "that all Mennonites living here, who do not form a congregation, be forbidden to have the marriage ceremony performed in any place in the canton, but such persons shall be sent to their homes for the marriage, and shall be tolerated only with properly legalized certificate of citizenship." This regulation was modified by the first decision of the council on Nov. 17, 1821. It granted the request of Johannes Wenger, tenant in Brüglingen, to have his marriage performed according to Mennonite usage. He could, to be sure, give weight to his petition by the fact that his parents had been living in the canton for 40 years, and that he and his brothers had completed their military service in the transportation corps.

On Jan. 5, 1847, the Amish congregation (Binningen, now called Holeestrasse) presented the following petition to the city council: "From olden times to the present the Swiss Brethren living around this city have held their religious services at the homes of the various members.

"Since this constant change causes many inconveniences to all the members, the wish has long arisen among us, that it might be permitted to us to hold our congregational services in a chapel dedicated always and exclusively to this purpose. We have recently agreed on a plan to purchase a plot in the township and to build a very modest chapel on it. We have already selected a very suitable site for it, a field of half an acre belonging to Ziegler Dill in Binningen, on the Hohenletten, near the village Binningen, and now take the liberty to present this respectful petition, that it may be granted us: 1, to buy said piece of land, and 2, to erect a small chapel on it.

"We hope the more confidently for gracious consent, for in France and in several states of Germany similar concessions have been granted our brotherhood, so that there are already several chapels in these countries.

"With sincere gratitude we shall be happy if we are permitted to erect such a chapel, in order to praise the Father of all in our own manner. In the name of the congregation, Johannes Kaufmann, preacher, Wenkenhof."

Upon the declaration of Peter Stucki, tenant of the Wieland estate near St. Johann gate, that Johann Kaufmann on the Wenkenhof had offered to buy it and paid a preliminary sum of 800 fr., the remaining 5,000 fr. of the building costs to be assumed by the congregation, and upon the consent of the church council, the request was granted. This consent is of special interest for its growing spirit of toleration. It says:

"We have unanimously agreed that the request of the Anabaptist brotherhood be granted.

"We are guided by the article of our previous constitution which states: the established church is the Protestant Reformed; the exercise of any other Christian creed is granted under the observance of legal stipulations.

"We are guided also by the fact that permission has been granted to Catholics to use our churches and to the Jews to hold services in private homes.

"It therefore seems so much the less desirable to refuse this right to the Anabaptists, who are essentially Protestant in their faith.

"Nevertheless we do not conceal from ourselves the fact that other sects which might arise here might also make use of this concession, and that namely the sect of the so-called *Neutäufer* (see **Apostolic Christian Church**) who are very active in Switzerland and also in Germany, who are not to be confused with our old Anabaptists, if they should gain a footing in Basel, would not fail to take advantage of this privilege. We therefore thought that the granting of such a privilege could not injure the church any more than the possibility of meeting in any other manner would do.

"Concerning the main point presented by the Anabaptists for the desirability of a chapel, namely that the constant change of meeting-place is fraught with many inconveniences, this is very clear. The number of this division of the Anabaptists (who have footwashing as a distinguishing sign) has increased so greatly in our region, that it is difficult for them to find a room on their farms that is large enough, and the distance between these farms is so great that when it is the turn of an outlying farm to have the meeting, they are unable to be as diligent in attendance as their regulations and also the implanting and preservation of their religion requires, especially in bad weather and on the short winter days.

"Though we do not advise objecting to the granting of the request of these people, it nevertheless seems to us it would be practical to make some regulations, as which we suggest the following:

"1. The Anabaptists are to submit to existing police regulations relating to their services.

"2. They are not to put a bell on their chapel.

"This latter is probably not a rite of these people. Nevertheless it seems to us not beside the point on this first occasion, in which the principles of such regulations are to be set up, to make an express statement.

"Concerning the question as to whether they should be reminded to refrain from proselytizing we were divided. But the majority believed that we should refrain, partly because the Anabaptists in our district have not been engaged in such activity, and partly because it would be in contradiction to other articles of the constitution. The minority wished to have such an article, not because of the group presenting the petition, but because it is now a matter of establishing principles for future cases."

The document was signed on Jan. 14, 1847, by J. Burkhardt.

Thus the time of complete toleration had arrived also for the Mennonites of Basel, and its two congregations could live in accord with their principles in outward peace.

For the further history of the two Basel congregations see **Basel-Schänzli** and **Basel-Holeestrasse.**

In the summer of 1925 the first Mennonite World Conference was held in Basel, in 1952 the fifth.

With the establishment of the European administrative headquarters of the Mennonite Central Committee in Basel in the late fall of 1946 (since December at Arnold Böcklinstr. 11) Basel became more and more a Mennonite center of wider Mennonite significance particularly for the Swiss, Alsatian, French, South German area. Through the initiative of the MCC, the *Basler Glaubenskonferenz* was inaugurated as an annual summer week-end conference in 1947. And in 1951, the *Europäische*

Mennonitische Bibelschule (European Mennonite Bible School) was established here as an annual short-term winter Bible School of 4-6 weeks, which is expected to grow into a significant enterprise. It uses temporarily the MCC headquarters building for classroom purposes. The Fifth Mennonite World Conference was held at St. Chrischona near Basel Aug. 10-15, 1952, with the three near-by conferences (Swiss, Alsatian, and French) serving as hosts. These three conferences also sponsor the *Glaubenskonferenz,* and together with the two South German conferences sponsor the Bible School. Thus Basel is becoming the focal point for inter-conference co-operation and fellowship, a role to which its location at a crossroads of travel as well as a junction point of three countries and two cultures (German and French) ideally adapts it.   NEFF.

P. Burkhardt, *Die Basler Täufer* (Basel, 1898); *idem,* "David Joris und seine Gemeinde in Basel," in *Basler Ztscht f. Gesch. . . . ,* 1949 (also reprint); E. Stähelin, *Briefe und Akten zum Leben Oecolampads* (2 vv., Leipzig, 1927 and 1934); *idem, Das Buch der Basler Reformation* (Basel, 1929); P. Ochs, *Gesch. der Stadt u. Landschaft Basel* (Basel, 1786 ff.) V, 668 ff.; R. H. Bainton, *David Joris, Wiedertäufer und Kämpfer für Toleranz im 16. Jahrhundert* (Leipzig, 1937); E. Teufel, discussion of Bainton's *David Joris,* in *Theol. Rundschau* XIII (1941) 29 ff.; *Sonntagsblatt der Basler Nachrichten,* 1910, Nos. 6-8; *Theol. Jahresbericht* 1911, 645 f.; E. Thurneisen, "Die Basler Täufer," in *Basler Jahrbuch,* 1895 f.; P. Roth, *Die Ref. in Basel* I: *Die Vorbereitungsjahre 1525-1528* (1936) 54; *idem, Aktensammlung zur Gesch. der Basler Ref. . . . 1519-1534* (5 vv., 1937-52); D. Gratz, *Bernese Anabaptists* (Scottdale, 1953); *ML* I, 129.

Basel-Binningen, long the name of a Swiss Mennonite congregation whose meeting place was in Binningen, a district of the city of Basel. The congregation is now called Basel-Holeestrasse (*q.v.*) for the street on which the meetinghouse is located.

H.S.B.

Basel-Holeestrasse, a Mennonite congregation with meetinghouse on the Holeestrasse in Basel, Switzerland, formerly called Basel-Binningen, the Amish congregation mentioned in the article **Basel.** The origins of the congregation go back to the middle of the 18th century, a church book containing records of births, marriages, deaths, and baptisms (probably maintained at the request of the state) having been kept from 1777 on (with an interruption 1880-1910). Throughout its existence a majority of the families of the congregations have lived on the Alsatian side of the near-by border and the congregation has belonged to the Alsatian Conference. In wartime this has caused considerable trouble, particularly in World War II when the Alsatian part of the congregation could not cross the border into Basel and had to meet in near-by Bourgfelden.

The first meetinghouse in the village of Binningen (now incorporated in the city of Basel) was built in 1847 and continued in use until the new meetinghouse was built on the same lot in 1932. The membership has remained fairly constant for several decades, with considerable losses by emigration to the near-by Mulhouse region and to the United States. The 1952 membership was 185 and 50 children. Most common family names have been Roth, Widmer, Wenger, Würgler, and Goldschmidt. Recent elders have been Hans Jacob Schmuckli,

1777-?; Hans Freienberg, 1787-?; Johannes Kaufmann, *ca.* 1800- ?; Fritz Steinbrunner, *ca.* 1830; Hans Steinbrunner, d. *ca.* 1843; Johannes Kaufmann, *ca.* 1845; Hans Schmuckli, *ca.* 1860; Christian Klopfenstein, *ca.* 1870; Joseph Klopfenstein, d. 1878; Jacob Zimmerman; Jacob Widmer, 1874- ? emigrated to America; Michel Widmer, 1893-1924; Christian Roggy, 1896-1904; Daniel Roth, -1927; Jakob Widmer, 1924-42; Fritz Goldschmidt, 1927- ; and Daniel Wenger, 1951- . Services are held every two weeks alternating with Schänzli. The congregation has had an organized chorus since 1896. As late as 1915 it still practiced footwashing. The *Ausbund* was used as hymnal until into the 20th century.   F.G., H.S.B.

Pierre Sommer, "Assemblée de Bale (Holee)" in *Christ Seul* (April, pp. 4-6, and May, pp. 6-9, 1933); *ML* I, 135.

Basel-Schänzli, a Mennonite congregation in the city and canton of Basel, whose beginnings go back to 1790, when Christian Röthlisberger moved from Courtelaryberg (Feuerstein) to Liestal and leased the farm known as the "Schillingsraingütli." He was a preacher, later became elder, and died in 1845, at an age of more than 80 years. Hans Schrag was also a preacher at the same time. Other family names in the church in this early period were Böbli in Oberaesch, Hylti on Homberg near Buckten, Jakob Wagner, Aeschlimann, Schneider, Strohm, and Burkholder. Some families apparently emigrated to America; others died out. In 1850 the church had a membership of only about 30; they were farmers living scattered throughout the canton. Meetings were held on the first Sunday of the month in the homes of the members. In the 1840's several new families settled in the canton of Basel, among them Michael Nussbaumer, born at Lüterkofen in the canton of Solothurn, who had lived for some time in Couroux near Delsberg. He was also a preacher; his descendants today make up a large part of the congregation.

In 1891 David Nussbaumer furnished a room in his house at Schänzli (a suburb of Basel) for meetings, which were held every two weeks. Through the sale of the Schänzli estate the congregation was compelled to find another place for meeting. On Feb. 28, 1902, it decided to build a combined chapel and residence on the road from Basel to Muttenz, for which David Nussbaumer contributed the land. On March 22, 1903, it was dedicated, the name Schänzli having been brought along from the old meeting place. The congregation, in 1914 numbering about 130 members, in 1952 about 150, meets there every two weeks, with Sunday school for the children, introduced in 1948. Church records have been kept since 1900. The seal of the church is an open book with the verses I Cor. 3:11 and I Jno. 5:5, with a cross underneath, around which two hands are clasped, and the words *Altevangelische Taufgesinntengemeinde Schänzli-Basel.* In 1901-44 Samuel Nussbaumer, an outstanding leader among the Swiss Mennonites, served as resident elder. Upon his death Elder Fritz Goldschmitt of the Basel-Holeestrasse congregation was given elder charge of the congregation (*ML* I, 134).   S.N.

Bastiaan Corsz (*alias* Dagge), an Anabaptist martyr. He lived at Oostcapel (Oostkapelle) in the Dutch province of Zeeland, and was about 50 years of age when he was burned at the stake at Middelburg, Zeeland, in 1569, possibly on May 2, having been "rebaptized and persisting in his evil, reprobate opinion." (Pekelharing, *Bijdr. voor de Gesch. der Herv. in Zeeland*, 1886, 92).   vDZ.

Bastiaen, an Anabaptist martyr, remained true to his faith and was put to death on Aug. 15, 1561, at Antwerp, according to the *Martyrs' Mirror*, together with Jan, Hendrik, Hans, Lijntgen, Mariken van Meenen, and Beetken van Brugh. These martyrs are commemorated in the song, "Lieve Broeders, ick groet u met sanghen" (Dear brethren, I greet you with songs), found in the *Tweede Liedtboeck* (1562), and included in Wackernagel, *Lieder.* Génard, *Antw. Arch.-Blad* XIV, 30-33, does not mention him. He did not find a sentence for Aug. 15, 1561. During the years 1561-62 there is listed only one Bastiaen, viz., Bastiaen de Pottere (No. 359), who was executed between June 26 and Sept. 4, 1562, suspected of Anabaptism; but this Bastiaen de Pottere was released. It is hardly possible that this Bastiaen is to be identified with the above martyr. The point is not clear, the more so since the *Martyrs' Mirror* is not correct in the date of the execution; evidently its source is this song, which puts the death of all these martyrs on one day, whereas in fact Jan (Jan van Lyere) was put to death on Sept. 5, 1561; Hendrik (H. van Dale) April 3, 1562; Hans, Oct. 3, 1562; Lijntgen (Lijnken van Dale) Nov. 13, 1562; Mariken van Meenen (Maeyken Eghels) Sept. 4, 1562; and Beetken van Brugh (Betken Laureys) Nov. 13, 1562 (*Mart. Mir.* D 288, E 655; Wackernagel, *Lieder*, 140).   vDZ.

Bastian (*Mart. Mir.,* Bastiaen Glasemaker), an Anabaptist martyr, a glazier by trade, who was beheaded and then burned at Imst in the valley of the Upper Inn (Austria). Van Blargt relates that Bastian and Hans Grünfelder, who shared death by martyrdom with him, addressed a large crowd of spectators (*Mart. Mir.* D 40, E 446).   vDZ.

Bastian, Frederic, of Weiler, in Alsace, France, published in the French language an *Essai sur la vie et les ecrits de Menno Simons* (Strasbourg, 1857). This paper served as a thesis to obtain the bachelor's degree in theology at the Protestant University of Strasbourg (*Catalogus Amst.*, 91; *ML* I, 135.)   vDZ.

Bastian, Hermann, a participant in the religious disputation with Bucer (*q.v.*) in Marburg from Oct. 30 to Nov. 1, 1538 (see **Confirmation**). (W. Diehl, *Zur Gesch. der Konfirmation in Hessen,* Giessen, 1897.)

Batak: see **Batta.**

Batenburg, Jan van, the leader of a group of Münsterite Anabaptists known as the "Batenburgers" or the *Zwaardgeesten* (sword-minded). He was born in 1495, the son of Dirk van Batenburg, who was an illegitimate son of the noble Batenburg family of Gelderland. Jan van Batenburg was the mayor of the city of Steenwijk in Overijssel before he joined the Anabaptists.

The Frisian chronicler Beningha names him as one of the instigators of the notorious attack of 1535 on the Oldeklooster (*q.v.*), a monastery near Bolsward. That he was inclined to violence is shown by the fact that after the capture of Münster in 1535 he won many who had previously been of the same mind as the Anabaptists of Münster as his adherents and thus made himself the head of the *Zwaardgeesten,* who were even more radical than the Münsterites. All who were not converted according to their doctrine, i.e., who would not join their party, could not be pardoned and must be annihilated with the sword. The plundering of churches was permissible. Divorce was obligatory if one party to the marriage was not of their group. "Polygamy was common among them, and, like the early Christians, their goods were the common possession of all." They awaited the imminent return of the Lord, and Batenburg considered himself to be Elijah, who was to appear first. How far this prophet had deviated from the original Anabaptist position can be seen in the fact that he considered baptism unimportant and permitted his followers to attend Catholic services in order to avoid persecution.

Nevertheless some of the other radical Anabaptists tried to reach an understanding with Batenburg. For this purpose a meeting was held in Bocholt (*q.v.*), Westphalia, in 1536 (not 1538 as is sometimes given). At this meeting there were followers of Batenburg, of David Joris, and former Münsterites, although Joris was the only group leader who appeared. Through Joris' influence a compromise was reached, agreeing, among other things, that baptism should no longer be performed. Batenburg's views were accepted to the extent that the use of the sword was declared justifiable in the building of the kingdom of God; but that the time for such use was not yet at hand.

The union achieved in this way was short-lived. Batenburg was able to spread his dangerous doctrine only a short time. In December 1537 he was captured at Vilvoorde in Brabant (Belgium); in prison there he made a confession in February 1538, in which he betrayed many Anabaptists, naming them and telling their places of residence, and confessed that he had lived among them for a time in the province of Groningen. These statements were very significant for the historical events of that time. He exonerated himself as well as he could, presenting himself as having always opposed plundering and the plans for attack on cities such as Amsterdam and Groningen. To no avail; he was executed in 1538.

Batenburg's followers lived scattered throughout the country, and were now severely persecuted. How great their number was can be determined by a thorough examination of the city archives. The archives of Alkmaar, of which Pastor Glass published the most important relevant material (*DB* 1909), reveal that as early as 1537 two women were sentenced for robbing churches, and therefore probably belonged to Batenburg's following; in 1538 again a woman, and in 1541 three women and a man were sentenced. Two of his adherents in Alkmaar were killed in Utrecht in 1541, and others in The Hague in 1544.

The *Zwaardgeesten* probably had a similar following in other places besides Alkmaar, even though it is a known fact that the leaders Zeylmaker, Appelman, and Franz Jansz Mickers stayed there often. For it is known that the leaders of the party lived for a time in and around Kampen (Overijssel), that there were Batenburgers in Deventer and Giethoorn (Overijssel) and in Joure (Friesland), and that a large part of their following lived in the province of Brabant. Also at Leiden some Batenburgers were executed in 1544, and as early as December 1538 the Stadholder Mary had urged the government to caution, because the Anabaptists, "above all the *Zwaardgeesten,* were plotting to surprise the city and certainly had fellow conspirators in the countryside." Peter van Orck, executed in 1544 at Münster, confessed that he had lived in the region of Münster for three or four years. Hence there must have been Batenburgers there too.

After 1544 little is heard of this party. In that year Appelman, their most important leader, was executed at Leiden, after confessing that he had done many evil deeds in the province of Utrecht, and had avenged himself on several Anabaptists by betraying them, as in the case of Jurjen Ketel. There is also a decree of 1549 of Countess Anna of East Friesland, prohibiting the giving of aid to adherents of the Mennonites, Davidites, Obbenites, and of the Batenburg sect. As late as 1552 in Leiden there was still fear of a raid, as well as in 1553 in Kortrijk in Belgium. The Batenburgers did an untold amount of harm to the cause of the peaceful Anabaptists because the government in its fear and hatred of the *Zwaardgeesten* frequently could or would not distinguish the nonresistant Anabaptists from them.   J.L.

Inv. Arch. Amst. I, 188, 189, 269, 351, 352; N. Blesdijk, *Historia Davidis Georgii;* B. N. Krohn, *Gesch. der . . . Wiedertäufer . . . in Niederdeutschland* (Leipzig, 1758); Blaupot t.C., *Friesland; idem, Holland; idem, Groningen;* Hoog, *De Martelaars der Hervorming in Nederland;* H. R. Lambers, *De Kerkherv. op de Veluwe;* C. Sepp, *Geschiedkund. Nasporingen* (Leiden, 1872); A. M. Cramer, *Levensbeschrijving van David Joris* (Leiden, 1845); J. de Hullu, *Beschieden betr. de Hervorming in Overijssel* I: *Deventer, 1522-1546* (1899); *DB* 1864, 1878, 1884, 1894, 1906, 1909; Kühler, *Geschiedenis* I; W. Moller, *Lehrbuch der Kirchengesch.* III: *Ref. und Gegenref.* (ed. G. Kawerau, 1907) 116; R. H. Bainton, *David Joris, . . .* (Leipzig, 1937); *ML* I, 137.

Batta (pl. Battak), a Malay tribe on Sumatra (*q.v.*). The first attempt to convert the Battak to Christianity was made by the English Baptists in 1820. Fourteen years later the Boston Missionary Society sent two missionaries to the Battak, who fell victim to cannibalism. In 1861 the Rhine mission opened its work in the area, spreading to the north; in ten years they had 10 stations with about 2,500 Christians, and in 1914 40 stations with 125,000 baptized members. Toward the south and east the Dutch missions opened their work. In the southernmost province of the Battak area (Mandailing) the Dutch Mennonite mission had its field. The population here is predominantly Mohammedan. The first station was opened in 1871 by Heinrich Dirks

(*q.v.*) at Pakanten (*q.v.*). In the course of time two other stations were established: Penjabungen and Hutagodang (*q.v.*). They had several subsidiary stations, two hospitals, and an orphanage. The Mennonite membership was about 450 in 1914. Pakanten had a hospital and a missionary school. The head nurse, Jonathan Djapangoeloe, worked faithfully here for more than 40 years. P. Nachtigal was a successful missionary at this place from 1911 until his death in 1928. His widow now lives in retirement at Lautenbach, Germany. He established Hutagodang in 1912, and was the only missionary in the station after 1919. In 1925 a migration from the Toba district to Groot-Mandailing opened a new field of work. It was supported by funds raised in Holland by J. E. van Brakel and a generous contribution from the Heubuden Mennonite congregation in East Prussia. After the death of Nachtigal the work was orphaned until 1931, when the Rhine mission took it over. In 1939 the mission congregations joined the Battak church.

N.W., vDZ.

"Land und Leute von Sumatra," in *Gem.-Kal.,* 1909 f.; Joh. Warneck, *Die Religion der Batak* (Die animistischen Religionen des Indischen Archipels, 1909); *idem, 60 Jahre Batak-Mission in Sumatra* (Berlin, 1925); F. Bork, "Die Religion der Batak auf Sumatra," in *Verh. der Gesellschaft deutscher Naturforscher und Aerzte* (82. Versammlung II) 1, 1911; *Jaarverslagen van den Staat en de Verrichtingen der Doopsgezinden Vereeniging tot bevordering der Evangelieverbreiding* (Dutch Mission Society) 1870-1940; *Uit het Verleden en Leden van de Doopsgezinde Zending* (1947); *ML* I, 136.

Bauer (Bower, Bowers, Boer, and de Boer), a Mennonite family name which originated in Switzerland and can be traced back to the 16th century. During the 18th-century persecution, families bearing this name migrated to the Palatinate, Holland, and America. Among the Swiss Mennonites who settled at Sappemeer, Groningen, in 1711 was the Hans Bauer family. Here his descendants changed the name to Boer and de Boer.

Another Hans Bauer migrated from Switzerland to America in 1717 and settled near Bally in what is now Berks Co., Pa. This family later spread to other states including Virginia and Indiana. The name occurs most frequently among Mennonites of the Franconia Conference in Pennsylvania. Prominent was Henry S. Bower (1836-1908) of Chester Co., Pa., who was ordained as Mennonite minister Nov. 30, 1865, and was the author of a family history entitled *A Genealogical Record of the Descendants of Hans Bauer* (Harleysville, Pa., 1897). Among the outstanding Dutch bearers of the name was M. G. de Boer (Baur) born in Groningen (1867), who was professor of history at the University of Amsterdam and editor of *Tijdschrift voor Geschiedenis.* He related his findings in genealogical research in the article, "Vom Thunersee zum Sappemeer; Ein Täufer- und Auswandererschicksal aus drei Jahrhunderten," in *Berner Ztscht für Gesch. und Heimatkunde* (No. I, 1947).

H.H.HAR., C.K.

Bauer, Hans (d. 1749), a native of Switzerland, went with other Mennonites to Pennsylvania between 1711 and 1717, and was one of the first settlers of Hereford Township, Berks County, near

Bally, with many descendants among the American Mennonites of today. His grave, without a monument, can still be identified in the Schwenckfeld cemetery near Clayton, Pa. His wife Anna (d. 1761) is also buried there.   E.E.S.J.

H. S. Bower, *A Genealogical Record of the Descendants of Daniel Stauffer and Hans Bauer and Other Pioneers* (Harleysville, Pa., 1897) 65 ff.; *Schwenkfeldian* VIII, 1941; *ML* I, 137.

Bau(e)r, Hans, b. 1670 or 1671 at Oberhofen in Switzerland, was married to Anna Willener of Sigriswil (b. 1678) on Feb. 19, 1702. Both joined the Mennonites, Hans not until 1711. In 1711 they lived at Courbes above Landeron in the canton of Neuchâtel. They were well-to-do. With their four children they left their native land for the sake of their faith, leaving Basel on July 13, 1711, arriving at Amsterdam Aug. 3, and at Sappemeer in the Dutch province of Groningen at the end of August. At Sappemeer Hans Baur bought 15 acres of land on March 10, 1712, and a house on the Kalkwijk. They belonged to the Amish branch. Hans Bauer died before 1751; his wife, who was still living in 1738, preceded him in death. They were the progenitors of the Groningen Boer or de Boer family.   vdZ.

M. G. de Boer, "Vom Thunersee zum Sappemeer, Ein Täufer- und Auswanderungs-Schicksal aus drei Jahrhunderten," in *Berner Ztscht für Geschichte und Heimatkunde* (1947).

Bauerbach, a village in the Bretten (*q.v.*) district of Baden (Germany), belonged to the bishopric of Speyer in the 16th century. It has been shown that the Anabaptists held meetings in the Hagenmühle near Bauerbach.

G. Bossert, "Beiträge zur badisch-pfälzischen Ref.-Gesch.," in *Ztscht für Kirchengesch. des Oberrheins,* 1904, 35 and 78; 1905, 73, 77.

Bauhin, Johannes (Jean Bouhin, also written Boyn), b. 1509 or 1510 at Amiens in France, d. Jan. 23, 1582, at Basel, a physician by profession, was, while in Paris, converted from Catholicism to the Evangelical faith by reading the works of Erasmus (*q.v.*). In 1540 or 1541 he met David Joris (*q.v.*) in Antwerp. It is not clear if he was already at this time a follower of David. About 1541 Bauhin moved to Basel, where he was a member of the secret David Joris congregation, since this leader and some of his followers had taken residence in Basel (1544). In 1553 or somewhat later trouble arose between David Joris and Bauhin, and the latter probably was banned from the congregation. Bauhin was on friendly terms with Castellio (*q.v.*), who lived in Basel at the same time. (P. Burckhardt, *David Joris und seine Gemeinde in Basel,* 1949, reprint, 9, 37-44, 53, 73, 83.)   vdZ.

Baum, Johann Wilhelm, a professor of theology at the university of Strasbourg, b. Dec. 7, 1809, in Flonheim (Rheinhessen), d. Oct. 28, 1878, author of the classic, *Capito und Butzer, Strassburger Reformatoren* (1860), in which the Anabaptists are also considered, though inadequately and incompletely. Of interest is his opinion: "With some of their views and principles these people were guilty in part of only the one wrong, namely, that they were 300 years too early." The 24 MS quarto vol-

umes of his *Thesaurus epistolicus Reformatorum Alsaticorum,* a collection of about 3,000 copies of documents, which he bequeathed to the library of Strasbourg, have by no means been exhausted with respect to Mennonite history. (J. Ficker, *Thesaurus Baumianus,* 1905; *ML* I, 140.)   NEFF.

Bauman (Baumann, Bowman, Bouman), a Mennonite family name found as early as 1685 in Bern, Switzerland. The name is also found in the Palatine census lists of the following decades. In 1710 Wendell Bauman came to Pennsylvania, settling in what is now Lancaster County. The name is first found in Pennsylvania, and later in Ohio, Ontario, Missouri, Iowa, Illinois, and Virginia. It occurs most commonly in Pennsylvania and Ontario. Among Mennonite leaders bearing the family name was Johannes Bowman (d. 1738), an early minister and bishop of what is now Lancaster Co., Pa., the only bishop from the Conestoga district to attend the first Mennonite conference held in America in 1725. Moses Bowman (1819-98) was a prominent preacher (MC) in Waterloo Co., Ont.

Amos S. Bouman (1854-1911) was born in Ontario and later moved to Iowa, where he was ordained a minister in the Stauffer (*q.v.*) Mennonite Church. He later moved to Alberta and was ordained a bishop there in 1903. Due to some difficulties he left his branch of the church and joined the Mennonite Brethren in Christ. Dr. H. R. Bauman (1897-   ) is a (GCM) missionary stationed at Champa, India. Irvin W. Bauman (1897-   ) is professor of sociology at Bluffton College, Bluffton, Ohio. Dr. Isaiah Bowman (d. 1950), late president of Johns Hopkins University, the outstanding American geographer of recent times, was a grandson of Preacher Moses Bowman (*q.v.*) of Waterloo Co., Ont., himself a native of Waterloo County.

Some of this family emigrated from Switzerland to the Netherlands, settling in the province of Groningen about 1715 (called Bouman or Bouwman).   H.H.HAR.

Baumann, Bernhard, pseudonym of Christian Hohburg (*q.v.*).

Baumann, Christoph, one of the outstanding Anabaptist hymn writers. Nothing is known of his life, except that he lay in prison in Landshut, Bavaria, and probably died there a martyr. The *Ausbund* (*q.v.*) has four songs written by him; but only one of them bears his name as author, viz., "Wo soll ich mich hindrehen" (No. 76). The two songs following this and No. 80 are of his composition; Wolkan proves this by their acrostic form. His songs have considerable poetic value. Their content testifies to a rare strength of faith and deep, hopeful joy. Baumann complains, of course, about the severe trials that men subject him to on account of his faith; but not a word of bitterness passes his lips. He asks God to forgive their sins: "O God, do not reckon it against them unto death; for they are ignorant and blind in everything." (Wolkan, *Lieder,* 146 f., 149; *ML* I, 140.)   NEFF.

Baumann, Georg (Juriaen Bouwman in Dutch *Mart. Mir.*), an Anabaptist martyr, beheaded in 1529 at Bauschlet in Württemburg (Germany), after severe torture, which, however, did not deter him from his faith. (*Mart. Mir.* D 30, E 438; Beck, *Geschichts-Bücher*, 32.) vpZ.

Baumerthof, an estate in Upper Alsace near Altkirch, which was settled probably soon after the Thirty Years' War (1650) by Mennonites from Switzerland. There is evidence that about the middle of the 18th century Daniel and Hans Rich lived there. They were "tenants and milkers." The inhabitants belonged to the church at Neineich, which was represented in the Amish conference at Steinselz in 1752. The *Ordnungsbrief* of the meeting at Essingen in 1779 is signed by Peter Kaufmann as the representative of the congregation. It did not have a meetinghouse, but met at various farms such as Baumerthof, Birkenhof, Blochmund, Liebenstein, Leyhäuserhof, Montigo, and Schweighof. The earliest meeting at Baumerthof took place on June 20, 1790; it was led by Peter Rich of Birkenhof. Peter Rich and Hans Roth of Feldbach were then the elders. On Oct. 28, 1798, Hans Klopfenstein of Buringen and Hans Rich were ordained on the Baumerthof. On Sept. 19 a conference was held here, attended by outside preachers, to settle a dispute between Peter Rich of the Birkenhof and Peter Rich of Liebenstein. It was, however, not settled until at a second meeting at Baumerthof on April 5, 1801. The "peace that was made" was to be entered into the church records. On Jan. 17, 1802, Peter Rich of Baumerthof was ordained as preacher. At a meeting on Dec. 8, 1802, it was forbidden that a member should secure a fellow member's farm through mortgage-foreclosure. (*"Dass keiner dem andern sein gut weglehnen darf bei Bannstrafe."*) On July 24, 1803, another conference gathered there in the "church room." Hans Freienberg of the Basel congregation at St. Jakob and preachers from three other congregations were present. Two preachers were removed from office. At a meeting on Oct. 16, 1803, the *Ordnungsbrief* adopted at St. Jakob near Basel on Aug. 2, 1803, was read and accepted. On Nov. 26, 1803, Peter Rich of the Baumerthof was removed from office and on Dec. 3, 1809, reinstated, after the charge brought against him had been proved false. At a meeting on the Baumerthof on May 21 two brethren were excommunicated because they had "used the sword." They had evidently accepted military service. Two years later this question greatly disturbed the Mennonites of Alsace-Lorraine. They sent two brethren to Paris to assert their nonresistance. On this matter there were many meetings with Palatine Mennonites and many conferences as at Bildhausen near Schlettstadt, at which Peter Rich of Baumerthof represented his church. Mention must also be made of the definite position taken in a conference at Baumerthof on Feb. 17, 1811, against "offensive marriage of cousins." (*ML* I, 14.) NEFF.

Baumgartner (Baumgardner), a Mennonite family name originating in Langnau in the Emmental, canton of Bern, Switzerland. Since the name means literally "tree gardener," it is likely that the name originated in the 15th century with persons who

followed that trade, or perhaps with persons living near a parcel of land called Baumgarten.

The first mention of the family as belonging to the Mennonite faith is in 1608. At this time Fridli Baumgartner died. He had lived on a farm near Langnau called Dürsrütti. His heirs were compelled to relinquish their rights to his estate to the state because the father had been an Anabaptist.

A list made in 1621 of Anabaptists living in the commune of Langnau named five persons with the name of Baumgartner, three of them living at Dürsrütti.

Uli Baumgartner (*q.v.*) of Dürsrütti was an Anabaptist (Swiss Brethren) preacher for many years. In 1629 he was arrested and taken to Trachselwald and later to Bern. After his death, which took place the following year, his property was taken by the government. Two other members of the family were arrested and imprisoned in 1659. The "Dürsrüttilied" tells the pathetic story of their arrest and imprisonment. It was long sung by the Mennonites.

In the documents of the century that followed, frequent mention is made of members of the Baumgartner family who were imprisoned and fined because of their faith. During the decade of 1720 several Baumgartner families left the Emmental and settled at Péry near Corgémont in the Jura Mountains. David Baumgartner (1737-1819) served as a deacon of the congregation there during the latter part of the 18th and early part of the 19th centuries. His son David (1765-1853) was a preacher in the Corgémont congregation. He was ordained in 1789, and emigrated to America in 1837, settling in Wayne Co., Ohio, for two years. He then followed his sons to Wells Co., Ind., where he organized in 1839 the first Mennonite church in that state, sometimes called the Baumgartner congregation, serving it until his death in 1853. Most of the members of the Baumgartner family who were Mennonites in Switzerland migrated to America during the 1830's and settled in Wells and Adams counties, Indiana. Christian Baumgartner (1809-78) was a preacher in the Baumgartner congregation. A few representatives of the family are also found in the Bluffton-Pandora, Ohio, community as well as in Wayne Co., Ohio. D.L.G.

Müller, *Berner Täufer*, 105, 119, 120, 122, 124, 174, 179, 180, 191; S. H. Baumgartner, *Brief Historical Sketches of Seven Generations; Descendants of Deacon David Baumgartner* (Indianapolis, 1908); Eva F. Sprunger, *The First Hundred Years, A History of the Mennonite Church in Adams County, Indiana 1838-1938* (Berne, 1938) 181-88; *ML* I, 141.

Baumgartner, Uli, a preacher of the Swiss Brethren at Dürsrütti near Langnau in the Emmental, canton of Bern, was seized on Sept. 25, 1629, and led to Trachselwald and from there to Bern, where he was cruelly tortured on Nov. 2 to turn him from the error of his faith. He is the subject of the beautiful *Dürsrüttilied* (Müller, *Berner Täufer*, 197, 122). Thirty years later (1659) an Uli Baumgärtner (*Mart. Mir.* D 826 gives his name as Uly Boogaert, and *Mart. Mir.* E 1124 gives his name as Uly Bogart) of Lauperswyl (Rinderspach) with ten fellow believers, preachers, and leaders of the churches, including a Benedict Baumgärtner of Dürsrütti, were held imprisoned in Bern until Sept. 10, 1660, when they were exiled to Holland. The last named returned to his home and was imprisoned again. Nothing further is known about them (Müller, *Berner Täufer*, 174, 179, 191; *ML* I, 141). Neff.

Baumhauer, Christoph, a preacher of the Hutterian Brethren in Sobotiste, Hungary, who, together with Jakob Amssler (*q.v.*) on Oct. 8-18, 1655, received the consent of Elector Karl Ludwig of the Palatinate to establish a settlement of the Hutterian Brethren in Mannheim (*q.v.*); several families settled here; Baumhauer returned to Hungary. After the great destruction brought about in Hungary by war, he was commissioned to seek help from the churches in Holland. With Benjamin Polay, also a preacher, he left for Amsterdam on April 21, 1665, by way of Mannheim, visiting also the churches in Zeeland, Flanders, and Friesland. On Oct. 27 they arrived at home with the Dutch gifts. (A letter of thanks, dated Nov. 24, 1665, to the Dutch churches, is in the archives of the Amsterdam church, No. 2851.) Baumhauer died on Oct. 31, 1681, at Dechtiz, at the age of 60, having served as a preacher for 31 years. (Beck, *Geschichts-Bücher*, 483 f., 492, 520, 537; *ML* I, 141.) Hege.

Bavaria, the second largest state in Germany, in the Reformation period a duchy, which embraced the present provinces of Upper and Lower Bavaria. Here the Anabaptists were most ruthlessly persecuted and most violently suppressed. The reigning dukes were Wilhelm IV and Ludwig, who pronounced the horrifying watchword, "All Anabaptists are to be punished with death. Whoever recants will be beheaded; whoever does not recant will be burned." With inexorable severity this command was carried out. Between 1527 and 1581, 223 Anabaptists were executed in Bavarian territory. Moving hymns relate the valiant martyrdom of the following Anabaptists: Hans Blüetl (*q.v.*), burned at Ried, June 24, 1545; Wolf Rauffer, Jörg Bruckmayer, Hans Aichner, beheaded there, Aug. 13, 1585; Leonhard Sumerauer, beheaded at Burghausen, July 5, 1585; Christian Geiger, beheaded at Munich, Sept. 13, 1586 (*Oesterreichisches Jahrbuch des Protestantismus* XIII, 81). Other names belong to this list of martyrs: Virgil Plattner, beheaded at Schärding in 1529; Hans Mändel and Claus Felbinger (*q.v.*), executed at Landshut in 1560; Wolf Binder at Schärding in 1571; Michael Fischer at Ingolstadt in 1587; Leonhard Boltzinger (*q.v.*) at Julbach near Braunau; Thomas Haan at Freiberg near Braunau, May 12, 1592; and Max Eder at Ried in 1565 (Wolkan, *Lieder*). This is a sad list of martyrs, whose memory lived on among the Anabaptists in the many martyr hymns sung in many congregations.

Vitus Anton Winter reports (*Gesch. der bayrischen Wiedertäufer im 16. Jahrh.*) that as early as 1528 "all Bavaria was full of Anabaptists, preaching in villages and baptizing in barns." Among the Anabaptists expelled from Augsburg, Jan. 12, 1528, were many Bavarians (Riezler, *Gesch. Bayerns* IV, 189); Hans Geraysig of Hochdorf and Diemut of Mammendorf, etc., are named. In Landshut Augustin Würzelburger was active as an Ana-

baptist; he transplanted the movement to Oberhaim near Siesbach with great success. Hans Sedlmayr and Hans Frank, whom he won for the movement, died a few weeks later as martyrs in Landshut. The mandate of Wilhelm IV dated Nov. 15, 1527, against the Anabaptists, opened a veritable hunt for them. Anyone who was in the least suspected was arrested and tried on the rack. Most of them were executed. At the command of Wilhelm, the schoolteacher Georg Wagner (*q.v.*) of Emmering was taken to Munich, placed in the Falkenturm, and burned at the stake, Feb. 18, 1527. Many others followed him. Those who were not beheaded or burned were drowned in the Isar. Anabaptists were also executed in Straubing and Aibling. On Dec. 23, 1527, nine were executed and a woman drowned in Landshut by ducal order. On Jan. 7, 1528, two noblemen, Augustin and Christoph von Perwangen, were executed with the sword at Günzlhofen and Vogach together with a miller from Milstetten in Munich. On Jan. 28 six artisans of Munich were burned in a room. Jakob (or Jörg) Prenner, a laborer of Schmiechen, who had baptized 18 persons, was beheaded at Munich. In other parts of Bavaria many Anabaptists were executed. At Landsberg on May 15, 1528, three were burned and one beheaded (Riezler, *Gesch. Bayerns* IV, 194). The bishop of Regensburg was compelled by the Bavarian dukes by repeated reproaches to execute the imprisoned Augustin Würzelburger on Oct. 10, 1528.

Yet this violence did not succeed in suppressing the movement. On April 27, 1529, the dukes issued a second mandate against the Anabaptists, "that henceforth none of them would escape execution even if he recanted." In the next year the Anabaptists Hans Haschen and Pankratz Wördt were killed. Anabaptists passing through from Moravia to the Palatinate, Hesse, and Switzerland, were seized. On April 22, 1535, Bishop Ernst of Passau issued a mandate forbidding anyone to give shelter to a Moravian Anabaptist. On May 19, 1535, 15 Anabaptists—seven men, five women, and three children—were captured and placed in the Oberhaus, a castle in Passau (*q.v.*) (Wolkan, *Lieder*). On Sept. 14, 1535, 14 additional Moravian Anabaptists were tried on the rack, followed several hours later by another group of 20, including Hans Beck (*q.v.*) of Greding near Eichstätt and his wife Elisabeth. He stated that he had already been previously captured at Eggenburg, but released with 20 others after their cheeks had been burned through with hot irons. On Sept. 24, 1535, again five Anabaptists were seized. None of all these Anabaptists left the prison alive.

In 1559 the news of the existence of an Anabaptist congregation in Schrobenhausen stirred up renewed action. Cardinal Otto of Augsburg called the attention of Duke Albrecht V (*q.v.*) to the presence of Anabaptists there. In haste the duke sent his officers to investigate, but little came of the affair. Hans Lor, the cobbler in whose house the meetings had been held, had fled. Two persons under suspicion were arrested, but their utterances revealed nothing damaging, and they were released.

There was doubtless more truth in the report that Burghausen was an Anabaptist center. As already stated, many died there as martyrs.

Duke Wilhelm V also made it his business to rid the land of Anabaptists. In 1579 he issued a mandate, that "they should be suppressed with all our might." When he learned that Anabaptists were coming from Moravia to win converts, he issued the harsh mandate of Sept. 30, 1584, "to admit no one, to arrest at once all who entered and deliver them to the courts." A reward of 40 to 50 guilders was offered to anyone reporting an Anabaptist to the government. Nevertheless it is reported that they succeeded in winning 600 Bavarians and inducing them to emigrate to Moravia. Some of the most successful secret emissaries of the Anabaptists were Hans Zuckenhammer, a blacksmith and hymn writer, Bastel Segenschmidt, Paul Schuster, Lienhard Vischer, and Hans Körner.

On Feb. 28, 1587, a sharper edict followed, which ordered the officials, on penalty of severe punishment and disfavor, to build a dam that could not be crossed by the intolerable sect of the Anabaptists, which increase day by day in Bavaria, and especially to track down their leaders, Hans Zuckenhammer and Bastel Segenschmidt. For the capture of one of these leaders a reward of 100 florins was offered, and for the capture of an ordinary Anabaptist, 25 to 30 florins. These strong measures were apparently successful, for from now on little is heard of Anabaptists in Bavaria. A few years later the movement seems to have disappeared without a trace.

Approximately 200 years later an elector of Bavaria admitted the Anabaptists back into the country. Those whom his ancestors had most cruelly expelled, he recalled as capable colonists and as good and useful subjects. In 1802, on the invitation of Max Joseph IV, eight Mennonite families left their homes in the Palatinate, and settled between Neuburg and Ingolstadt on the right bank of the Danube. They founded the Mennonite colony of Maxweiler in Donaumoos (*q.v.*). With tremendous effort they worked to turn the marshes into arable and fertile land. On Dec. 9, 1832, they dedicated their newly erected chapel. Twenty years later the congregation was dissolved. In 1855 all of the Mennonites living in Maxweiler sold their property and emigrated to America. Three families remained in Ingolstadt, and others near Neuburg a.d.D. Their descendants belong to the congregations at Ingolstadt and Donauwörth.

A few years after the founding of Maxweiler, a Mennonite congregation was established at Eichstock (*q.v.*) near Munich in Upper Bavaria. In 1818 the first Mennonite families settled here. These came from Alsace; they were joined by others from the Palatinate, Hesse, and Baden. The immigration lasted until 1848; it was strongest in 1820. But very few families settled there permanently. Most of them emigrated to America. (See *Menn. Bl.,* 1886, where the families are enumerated.) The congregation still exists, though very small.

The congregations at Bildhausen and Mönchshof near Schweinfurt in northern Bavaria came into being somewhat earlier than Maxweiler. About 1770 several families emigrating from Baden and Württemberg settled here. The former had a church of their own with an organ, and in 1838 a school. Their first preacher was Christian Stauffer of the Spitalhof near Neustadt a.d.H., who went to America in 1844. In 1856 Bildhausen and Mönchshof numbered 140 communicant members. The congregation is now extinct, their remnant joining the church at Trappstadt (*q.v.*) in Lower Franconia.

The church at Rottenbauer (*q.v.*) near Würzburg arose about 1805. Jakob Bühler and Michael Bähr, who came here from near Heidelberg, are considered its founders. When other families from Baden settled here, the Giebelstadt (*q.v.*) congregation was formed. Since 1804 three Mennonite families had been living on the Hettstädterhof; they had their own services. Their preacher was Michael Musselmann.

The Amish Mennonite settlers who came to the region of Ingolstadt and Regensburg from Alsace and Hesse from 1808 on established two congregations which have been named after these two major centers, although actually no Mennonites lived in these cities until recently, and the Amish meetings were held alternately on the various farms. Regensburg seems to have been the more active group about the middle of the 19th century since in the brief period of 1852-77 six Mennonite publications appeared here: *Neu-Vermehrtes Geistliches Lustgärtlein,* 1852 and 1854; *Die Ernsthafte Christenpflicht,* 1852, a *Gesangbuch,* 1859; a *Christliches Glaubensbekenntnis,* 1876, and a *Katechismus,* 1877. Since 1893 the Regensburg congregation has met in a rented hall in the city. The Amish groups near Ingolstadt died out largely through emigration to America, but were replaced by Mennonite settlers from the Palatinate in the second half of the century, and from Baden and Franconia at the turn of the century and later. In 1891 a congregation was formed at Rottmannshart, which in 1905 was relocated in Ingolstadt, where it built its own meetinghouse in 1951. A similar group of Amish families settled near Munich in the first half of the century, meeting on the farms for worship. Beginning in 1880 Mennonite families from Baden also settled here. In 1892 these two groups merged to form the Munich Mennonite congregation. Munich, Regensburg, and Eichstock have had a joint salaried, trained minister since 1905, quite in contradistinction to the other congregations in Bavaria belonging to the *Badischer Verband,* who have never had a trained salaried minister. These three churches have also, alone in Bavaria, joined the *Vereinigung* (1928).

The membership of the congregations follows:

	1930	1940	1950
Augsburg-Donauwörth	55	75	60
Eichstock	19	22	27
Ingolstadt	----	122	149
Munich	139	168	162
Nürnberg (1947)	----	----	30
Regensburg	100	135	164
Trappstadt	61	70	82
Würzburg	105	59	70
Total	469	651	744

Four congregations, Augsburg, Ingolstadt, Trappstadt, and Würzburg, numbering 361 members, belong to the *Badischer Verband* conference. The three, Eichstock, Munich, and Regensburg, have for years had a joint pastor, and belong to the *Vereinigung*. All the congregations except Ingolstadt, in 1928 formed the Union of Bavarian Congregations (*Vereinigung der Bayerischen Mennoniten-Gemeinden*), which however is only a legal corporation and not a church conference.

In Bavaria the question of nonresistance was decided by the regulation of January 1805, which stated that no creed could release a subject from military duty. But by paying a fee of 185 fl. per man of military age to pay for substitutes from voluntary recruits, they could be released. Since the introduction of universal military conscription, freedom from armed service has been completely eliminated in Bavaria. Mennonites here were not given the privilege granted by the Order of Cabinet of William I of Prussia in 1868.

King Max I (d. 1825) of Bavaria was very favorably inclined toward the Mennonites. He granted them religious freedom and all the rights of citizenship enjoyed by other subjects, and solicited their settlement in Bavaria. The fact that in 1801 the Palatinate, the home of many Mennonites, was added to his dominions, was no doubt the occasion for his action favoring Mennonite settlers. For a full account of the legal provisions made for Mennonites in the 19th century see **Bayern**, ML I, 145-47.

Bavarian Mennonites have furnished some outstanding farmers, who in recent years have been honored with the title of "master farmer." In the person of Elder Michael Horsch (1871-1950) of the Hellmannsberg-Ingolstadt congregation, formerly of Giebelstadt, Bavaria furnished South German Mennonitism one of its outstanding leaders of the 20th century, for a generation the leader of the *Badischer Verband*.

The present (1953) Mennonite congregations in Bavaria are as follows:

Membership (incl. unbaptized children)

Augsburg	60	
Eichstock	25	(5)
Ingolstadt	135	
Munich	165	(45)
Nürnberg	30	(5)
Regensburg	174	(35)
Trappstadt	68	(18)
Würzburg-Giebelstadt	98	
	755	

The Mennonite relief organization known as *Christenpflicht* (*q.v.*) was organized in 1921-22 under the leadership of Michael Horsch, with a board of directors of the Bavarian churches, and has had its seat continuously in Ingolstadt from the beginning. An old people's home was established at Burgweinting near Regensburg in 1931, which had been begun at Niederwinser in 1929.

NEFF, H.S.B.

Riezler, *Geschichte Bayerns* IV; V. A. Winter, *Gesch. der bayrischen Wiedertäufer im 16. Jahrhundert* (Munich, 1809); ML I, 141-47.

Bax, E. Belfort, author of *Rise and Fall of the Anabaptists* (London, 1903), a general description, socialistically tinged; its last chapter is important for its mention of continuations of the movement in Revolution.

Ernst Troeltsch, *The Social Teachings of the Christian Churches and Groups* (New York, 1931).

Bax, Willem, born at Delden, Dutch province of Overijssel, Nov. 20, 1870, died at Maastricht, Dutch province of Limburg, 1950, married Suzanna E. Bakels in 1900, was a Dutch Reformed minister serving last at Maastricht (1914-35). In this city, of which 95.5 per cent of the inhabitants are Roman Catholic, he was an esteemed figure. During the war years (1914-18) he was the spiritual leader for the Protestant German war prisoners who were brought to Maastricht. He took the initiative in publishing a memorial book in 1932 for the tricentennial of the founding of the Reformed congregation there, and in this wrote a number of important historical essays. In regard to Mennonite historical writing, he is of importance because of his exhaustive work, *Het Protestantisme in het Bisdom Luik, en vooral te Maastricht* (Vol. I, 1505-57, The Hague, 1937; Vol. II, 1557-1612, The Hague, 1941). In these works we find material which throws light on the history of the Anabaptists, who were very numerous in this area especially shortly after 1530.   vDZ.

Bay Shore Mennonite Church (MC), located in Sarasota, western Florida, was formally organized as a congregation under the Ohio Mennonite and Eastern A.M. Conference on April 17, 1945, with 20 charter members, in 1953 increased to 120 members. On Feb. 3, 1946, a new church of cement block with a seating capacity of about 250 was dedicated. In the winter of 1947-48 an additional building was erected on the church grounds for Sunday-school classes, young people's activities, and to accommodate the overflowing crowd of the winter tourist season. Mennonites and Amish have been coming to Sarasota for the winter for about 20 years, but there has been an enormous increase since 1945. The increasing number who have located permanently in this vicinity gave rise to the need for a regularly organized congregation.   T.H.B.

Bayle, Pierre, b. Nov. 18, 1647, at Carla in southern France, the son of a Reformed pastor, as a student in Toulouse was persuaded to accept the Catholic faith, but in the next year (1670) returned to the Reformed Church. In 1681 he was made professor of philosophy in Rotterdam, where he died on Dec. 28, 1706, having lost his position in 1693 because of his liberal views and supposed political intrigues. He stood for toleration on the ground that the state could have no jurisdiction in matters of faith, and found both the Catholics and the Reformed authorities opposed to him. His most important work, *Dictionnaire historique et critique* (1695 f.), contains a treatise on the Anabaptists. It shows the current one-sided conception of the origin of the Anabaptists and their development. On the other hand, the unusually copious notes contain a great deal of interesting material important to our history (*Biogr. Wb.* I, 356-59; ML I, 147).   NEFF.

Beachey (Beachy, Beechy, Bitsche, Bitschi, Peachey, Peachy), a Mennonite family name of Swiss origin, almost exclusively Amish since 1697. The name Bitschi is included in John Horsch's *Mennonites in Europe* among the Swiss Mennonite refugees in the Palatinate after 1664 who later came to America. Peter Bitsche, an Amish Mennonite, is said to have come to America from Switzerland, in 1767, settling in what is now Somerset Co., Pa. A family history published in 1892 listed 751 heads of families belonging to this relationship. This family is most numerous in Mifflin and Somerset counties, Pennsylvania, and in parts of Ohio and Indiana, but it is also represented in Illinois, Iowa, Delaware, Maryland, and other states in which there are Old Order Amish or Conservative Amish settlements. Thirty-eight ordained men were listed under the variants of the name in the 1951 lists of Old Order and Conservative Amish ministers. The Peachey variant is common in Mifflin Co., Pa., while the words Beachy and Beechy appear often in various communities. M.G.

Mrs. Harvey Lambright, *Family Record of Samuel J. Beachy and His Descendants* (Millersburg, Ind., 1918); *Memorial History of Peter Bitsche* (1892).

Beachy Amish Churches. The Beachy Amish churches receive their name from Moses M. Beachy (b. 1874) of Salisbury, Pa., who was a bishop of the Old Order Amish settlement known as the Casselman River district from 1916 until his death in 1946. The Beachy Amish churches had their origin in his refusal to pronounce the ban and avoidance upon all who left his congregation to unite with the Conservative Amish Mennonite congregation near Grantsville, Md. Disagreement began as early as 1923, but by 1927 such matters as Sunday school and the use of electricity and automobiles had also become issues. In June 1927 the conservative element of Beachy's congregation withdrew in order to maintain full fellowship with other Old Order Amish congregations.

The Beachy Amish differ from the Old Order Amish in that they allow the use of electrical conveniences, tractors, automobiles, and meetinghouses. They have also instituted Sunday school on alternate Sundays and in a few instances have Sunday evening services. They retain the use of the German language in their worship, except at funerals, the practice of unison singing, and most of the traditional Amish garb.

There were in 1951, 12 Beachy Amish congregations located as follows: three in Pennsylvania, one near Salisbury in Somerset County, and one near Bird-in-Hand in Lancaster County, and one near Hadley in Mercer County; three in Ohio, one near Plain City in Madison County, one at Bunker Hill near Berlin in Holmes County, and one near North Canton in Stark County; four in Indiana, one in Montgomery County, one in Howard and Miami counties near Amboy, and two in Elkhart County, one near Nappanee and one several miles east of Goshen; and two others, one congregation near Norfolk, Va., and one near Kalona, Iowa.

Actually the Beachy Amish are a widespread schism among the Old Order Amish, which is still spreading, and which is called by different names after the leaders in various regions. In Indiana, for instance, they are called the Burkholder Amish after the leader of the Nappanee group. In practice they are between the Old Order Amish and the Conservative Amish, but have no organized conference. In 1953 the group had over 2,000 baptized members. A.J.B.

Beachy congregation of the Casselman River region near Salisbury, Pa., is the oldest congregation of the Beachy Amish (*q.v.*) group. On June 26, 1927, the Old Order Amish Mennonite brotherhood in the Casselman River region of Somerset Co., Pa., suffered a division, resulting in what are locally known as the Yoder (Old Order) and Beachy congregations. These were named after the respective ministers of that date. For more than 26 years each group maintained a one half interest in both the Flag Run (Elk Lick Twp.) and the Summit Mills (Summit Twp.) meetinghouses, each alternately holding regular services at each meetinghouse. But at this date (1953) the Beachy congregation, having sold their one half interest in the above-named meetinghouses to the Old Order group, are building a new meetinghouse named Mountain View, 1½ miles northwest of Salisbury, Pa.

In 1953 the Beachy congregation had 140 members. Bishop Eli D. Tice, Grantsville, Md., and ministers Norman D. Beachy and Noah E. Yoder, Meyersdale, Pa., compose the ministerial body. E.N.H.

Beachy schoolhouse near Bittinger, Md., where Mennonites of the Southwestern Pennsylvania (MC) Conference were holding services at the beginning of the present century. M.G.

Beadle County, S.D., in the northeastern part of the state, has five organized Mennonite congregations, besides the Hutterian Brethren and a mission station in Huron. Approximately 1,300 Mennonites, including about 200 Hutterites, live in the county. The Mennonite settlement extends north into Spink County and northeast into Clark County. Besides the Hutterites, two other branches are represented in the settlement—the General Conference and the Krimmer Mennonite Brethren, the latter being more numerous. The Krimmer M. Brethren arrived in the county in 1902 and soon organized the Bethel (*q.v.*) congregation (KMB), which in 1950 was the largest Mennonite congregation in the area. J.J.K.

Beams of Light, first published Dec. 24, 1905, by the Gospel Witness Company, Scottdale, Pa., was a four-page illustrated paper for children of the home and Sunday school. It contained short articles, stories, and poems, as well as contributions from its young readers. Until June 23, 1907, the inside two pages contained a discussion of the Sunday-school lesson. Except for issues from June 30, 1907, to April 1908, which were 9 x 12 inches, the size of the paper remained 6 x 9 inches until January 1951, when it was enlarged to 8 x 11 inches. Since April 1908 the paper has been published by the Mennonite Publication Board and the Mennonite Publishing House. It has been edited by Daniel Kauffman, D. H. Bender,

A. D. Martin, J. A. Ressler, Lina Z. Ressler, and Betty Weber Springer. The four-page paper contains selected stories and original stories by Mennonite authors, illustrated frequently by Mennonite artists, for the ages from four to eight years. The circulation in 1952 was 20,000. E.D.Z.

Bean Blossom Mennonite Church (MC) is located on State Road 135, eight miles south of Morgantown, Ind., in Bean Blossom, a village in Jackson Twp., Brown Co. The building, which is now (1954) 107 years old, was occupied by the Presbyterian Church until approximately 1941. In May 1945 the Indiana-Michigan Mennonite Mission Board began permanent work there by ordaining and placing there Charles C. Haarer of the Shore congregation, Lagrange Co., Ind. The total baptized membership in 1953 was 34. C.C.H.

Beard. At the time of the beginning of the Swiss Brethren movement (1525) and for several decades later the wearing of the beard was common practice among all classes of society except the Catholic clergy. Hairdressers devised various modes for trimming the beard and the hair. According to Goebel, letting the beard grow was a distinguishing sign of all Anabaptists (M. Goebel, *Gesch. des christl. Lebens in der Rheinisch-Westphälischen Ev. Kirche* I, Coblenz, 1849, 147), although he gives no proof for this, attaching it merely as an additional note to his statement that Thomas Müntzer (1523) required the wearing of the beard according to the example of Christ and as an outward expression of Christian simplicity and discipline. Later Amish base the wearing of the beard upon such Scripture passages as Lev. 19:27 and 21:5, where the trimming of the corners of the beard is forbidden to the men of Israel. It is doubtful, however, that this was the original ground for this regulation.

One of the rules passed at a ministers' conference of the Swiss Brethren held in Strasbourg in 1568 (confirmed at Steinselz in 1752 and at Essingen in 1755) forbade the trimming of the hair or beard according to the worldly fashions. Since the American Old Order Amish of today still follow literally these rules, they wear the beard and the hair of the head according to the plainer 16th-18th century pattern. They usually shave the upper lip but not the neck. Most of them never trim the beard and they wear the hair longer than is done in the current styles. All Amish men are required to let the beard grow as a prerequisite to marriage, and in the strictest groups even unmarried members must wear it. The older Conservative Amish men traditionally wear the beard, but it has never been required by the conference. The Church of God in Christ, Mennonite, requires the beard of all male members, beginning at baptism; usually the full beard (including mustache) is worn. The Hutterian Brethren also require the beard; among the Russian Mennonites, who did not customarily wear the beard, they were called *Bartmennoniten* (Friesen, *Brüderschaft,* 13, note 5). In the Netherlands the Swiss Amish immigrants of the early 18th century who settled in Groningen were called *baardmannen* in contradistinction to the Frisian Mennonites among whom they settled.

Following the French Revolution, Napoleon's soldiers are said to have worn the mustache without the beard to heighten their appearance of fierceness. Apparently at that time the descendants of the Swiss Brethren began wearing the beard without the mustache. But among some of the Amish, those of the Wayland, Iowa, community, for instance, it was not an uncommon practice even as late as the beginning of the present century, to wear a full beard including the hair on the upper lip. European Mennonites in the 19th century gradually dropped all traditional restrictions and regulations regarding the beard, hair, and mustache; the mustache became quite common in the 20th century, especially in Germany and Russia. Among the Mennonites (MC) of North America and related groups the wearing of the lone mustache has always been forbidden. The smooth-shaven face became so common in 20th-century America that Europeans thought of it as typically "American." The general adoption by American Mennonites of the smooth-shaven face is a part of the general cultural accommodation process; the resistance of certain conservative groups to the smooth-shaven face is likewise a part of their resistance to this general accommodation.

During the latter part of the 19th century when certain groups of Amish in America, later called Amish Mennonites, began to depart from the strict rules of the 1568 conference, they began to wear their hair shorter and shorter and also to trim the beard. At first they trimmed the beard so that it was not more than an inch or two long. Finally some began to shave off the side whiskers and still kept the chin whiskers but trimmed them rather short. The Amish who came from Alsace-Lorraine and settled in certain communities in Ohio and Illinois, wore a characteristic pointed chin beard, larger however than a goatee.

Although not quite a typical instance, the Wayne County, Ohio, Amish congregation furnishes an example of the change from the Old Order to what was then known as the "New Order." In the summer of 1889, the congregation, meeting at Pleasant Hill and Oak Grove on alternate Sundays, was threatened with division. Finally a committee of seven laymen was chosen to recommend changes in the discipline. The committee met on Dec. 26 and adopted a number of resolutions. One of these considers as "sinful, the practice of making the hairdress of the men a matter of pride as one often sees." But the resolution goes on to say that since "we find no Scripture against shingling the hair, that is, cutting it short, we are willing to tolerate it if it is done in moderation." This referred, of course, to the men's hairdress. Another resolution relating to the wearing of the beard permitted the young men in the congregation to shave but declared it to be in line with the Scriptural order for brethren as they become older and especially after they enter the marriage state to wear a regular beard, "as always had been the rule and order." The resolution, however, forbade the wearing of a mustache without the beard. Near the close of the 19th century wearing the "lone mustache" was a common practice among young men from Amish families who did not unite with the Amish Church or who for some reason left the church. In order to make the distinction between themselves and their former friends as great as possible, they shaved off the beard and allowed the mustache to grow. They usually were able to cultivate a large heavy mustache and wore it as a sign of their independence.

As time went on and Amish Mennonites associated more with Mennonites, who had discontinued the use of the beard much earlier, the Amish Mennonite beard became smaller and shorter until at last it almost disappeared. As the beard grew smaller the hair of the head was cut shorter and more in the prevailing "barber pattern." In the earlier years in keeping with the Amish practice of making the home the center of activity, the father or the mother had been the family barber, cutting the hair straight across the forehead in front and round at the back of the head.

The beard no longer is a distinguishing feature between Mennonites and the former Amish Mennonites in America who have assumed the name Mennonite. Here and there among the latter one occasionally finds an aged brother still wearing a beard. Some of the Amish Mennonites, who continued to wear the beard well into the present century, gave as reasons that it was one of the distinguishing marks between the sexes and that the wearing of the beard was in conformity with the Scripture prohibiting the members of one sex from copying modes of dress commonly worn by the other. Some have claimed that the smooth-shaven face is effeminate and not "manly."   J.S.U.

For a general discussion of *Beard* see *Encyclopedia Britannica* (1947 ed.) and *Encyclopedia Americana* (1946 ed.). In the article *Beard*, the *Catholic Encyclopedia* (1907 ed.) discusses the religious significance of the beard among the Jews and Catholics. A. H. Leatherman, *Why I Wear a Beard?* (Wadsworth, Ohio, *ca.* 1900), a small privately printed tract.

Beatrice, Neb., a Mennonite community originated in 1877 when a group of Prussian Mennonites coming mostly from the Heubuden and Elbing-Ellerwald Mennonite churches arrived there, after having stopped in Mount Pleasant (*q.v.*), Iowa. A larger group had followed Cornelius Jansen (*q.v.*) to Mount Pleasant, of whom some settled in Kansas. The Beatrice group consisting of 34 families was joined in 1884 by ten families from Khiva (*q.v.*) and other families and individuals.

The city of Beatrice is located in Gage County on the Big Blue River in the southeastern part of the state, 40 miles south of Lincoln, and has a population of about 14,000. It is highly industrialized, manufacturing or processing 42 different products. Approximately 20 per cent of the 520 Mennonites of the community live in the city as businessmen, laborers, or retired farmers. The Mennonite farming community is located mostly west of the city. Beatrice was the residence of Cornelius Jansen and Peter Jansen (*q.v.*).

At present the community is served by two General Conference Mennonite churches, Beatrice Mennonite Church (*q.v.*) in the city and the Beatrice First Mennonite Church (*q.v.*) four miles west of the city. Other institutions include the Mennonite Deaconess Home and Hospital (*q.v.*), the Mennonite Bible Academy (*q.v.*), and a number of convalescent homes owned and operated by Mennonites.   J.T.F.

Beatrice First Mennonite Church (GCM) near Beatrice (*q.v.*), Neb., was organized on Sept. 9, 1877, by 34 families from Prussia with 138 members.

Since 1788 Prussian Mennonites had been migrating to Russia because of religious and economic restrictions. When in the 1870's Russia too introduced general military conscription, Prussian Mennonites began to consider emigration to America. Cornelius Jansen (*q.v.*) of Berdyansk and Wilhelm Ewert (*q.v.*) of Prussia paved the way. Some 30 families of the large Heubuden Mennonite Church (*q.v.*) and a few from the Elbing-Ellerwald Mennonite Church (*q.v.*) under the leadership of Elder Johann Andreas (*q.v.*) who were unwilling to accept noncombatant service, left Germany June 15, 1876, for America, stopping in Mount Pleasant, Iowa (*q.v.*), where Cornelius Jansen temporarily resided. Under his guidance some families went to Beatrice, Neb., arriving there in February 1877, while others followed Peter Dyck to settle near Whitewater (*q.v.*), Elbing (*q.v.*), and Newton (*q.v.*), Kan.

The group at Beatrice was joined by some additional families from Heubuden on June 19, 1877, led by Elder Gerhard Penner (*q.v.*), who died the next year. Elder Johann Andreas had died in Mount Pleasant, Iowa. For a time the newly organized church was served by the elders Isaac Peters of Henderson, Neb., and Leonhard Sudermann of Whitewater, Kan., in addition to its own ministers, Andreas Penner and Heinrich Zimmermann. In 1888 Gerhard Penner, Jr., son of Elder Gerhard Penner, was ordained as minister and elder and served in this capacity until 1920, at which time he was succeeded by Franz Albrecht, 1920-40. From 1940 to 1946 Walter H. Dyck served the congregation as the first full-time minister. He was succeeded by Jacob T. Friesen, 1947- .

For some time the congregation had several meeting places, one in Beatrice (*q.v.*), one four miles west of Beatrice erected in 1879 and patterned after the Heubuden church, and another some ten miles west of the city, which was discontinued. The main sanctuary erected in 1879 was destroyed by fire the first year and immediately rebuilt after the same pattern. It was replaced by a large stone structure in 1951. Customs of worship and social life were continued and changed only with the infiltration of the English language after World War I, which is a partial explanation for the organization of the (Second) Beatrice Mennonite Church (*q.v.*) in 1926. Sunday school, young people's organizations, and missionary interests were started during the first years. In 1892 the congregation joined the Western District Conference, in 1896 the General Conference Mennonite Church. Among the ten families that came from Khiva (*q.v.*) in 1884 were the ministers Johann Jantzen and Johannes K. Penner. The latter became one of the outstanding parochial teachers of the Mennonite community.

The Mennonite Bible Academy (*q.v.*) and the Beatrice Mennonite Deaconess Home and Hospital (*q.v.*) were established by the congregation. The present membership of the congregation is 338 (1953). Numerous families have moved to other communities such as Paso Robles, Cal. (*ML* I, 147.)

C.K.

Beatrice Mennonite Church (GCM), former Second Mennonite Church, Beatrice, Neb., was organized as an independent congregation in 1926 with 75 charter members. The Mennonites who settled in and near Beatrice originally worshiped at different places but constituted one congregation under one elder. Those residing in and near the city at first worshiped in a rented hall. In 1901 a church was built in Beatrice and Sunday school was introduced. The Christian Endeavor society was organized in 1903. Sam D. Ruth conducted a mission Sunday school on Sunday afternoon for over 20 years.

In 1926 the group decided to organize as an independent congregation. By 1953 the membership totaled 174. H. T. Reimer and Jacob Wiebe, elected as lay ministers previous to the organization, served the congregation occasionally after 1926. M. M. Horsch, 1927-39, was elected as the first full-time minister, followed by Reynold Weinbrenner, 1939-42, H. A. Claassen, 1943, E. Koontz, 1944-48, and E. R. Friesen, 1948- . The church was enlarged in 1929 and a full basement added in 1950.

M.G., C.K.

Beatrix Jansdochter, a Dutch Anabaptist martyr of Ter Heide, near The Hague, was drowned with her husband Leenaert Willemsz, on March 17, 1535. There is no mention of the place of execution; likely it was The Hague. (*Inv. Arch. Amst.* I, 744 f.)

vDZ.

Beauillou, a former Mennonite congregation near Chateau-Bêtre, not far from the city of Limoges, France. This congregation of Alsatian descent was still in existence in the early 19th century, but was later dissolved (*DB* 1885, 21).

vDZ.

Beaver Dam Mennonite Church (MC), located near Corry, Erie Co., Pa. In 1940 members of the Britton Run congregation, 15 miles south, organized a Sunday school in the village of Beaver Dam where a group of Mennonites were beginning a settlement on account of soil and atmospheric conditions favorable for growing potatoes. Ivan W. Miller, extensive potato grower from Wayne Co., Ohio, has had a prominent part in the development of the settlement. Lewis Kletzly, formerly of Britton Run, was one of the early workers. Jacob Weirich was the first pastor (until 1951), followed by Kenneth Snyder, 1952- . The 1953 membership was 95.

J.S.U.

Beaver Flats United Missionary Church, six miles southeast of Bingley, Alta., is a small rural appointment of the Canadian N.W. Conference.   E.R.S.

Bebber, Isaac Jacobs van, a son of Jacob Isaacs van Bebber (*q.v.*), a Mennonite of Crefeld, migrated to Germantown in 1684, purchased 1,000 acres of land there of Jacob Telner, moved to Bohemia Manor, Md., in 1704. (For bibliography, see **Bebber, Jacob Isaacs van.**)   H.S.B.

Bebber, Jacob Isaacs van, a member of the Crefeld Mennonite Church, acquired 1,000 acres of land from William Penn through Benjamin Furly on June 11, 1683, and was one of the first six Crefeld land buyers in America. He was temporarily the agent of Dirck Sipman (*q.v.*) of Crefeld, who had on March 10, 1682, bought 5,000 acres of Penn, but did not emigrate. He came to Germantown in 1687, moved to Philadelphia before 1698, and died there ca. 1711.   H.S.B.

D. K. Cassel, *Gesch. der Mennoniten* (Philadelphia, 1890) 37, 41, 77; W. I. Hull, *William Penn and the Dutch Quaker Migrations to Pennsylvania* (Philadelphia, 1935) 187, 215, 243, 253 f., 397, 403, 417; *ML* I, 148.

Bebber, Matthias Jacobs van (d. ca. 1730), one of two sons of Jacob Isaacs van Bebber of the Crefeld group of early Mennonite-Quaker immigrants, is believed to have emigrated to Germantown with a group of Palatinate Mennonites about the year 1687. Little of his background is known except that he is designated as a merchant in several documents pertaining to land grants he made in Pennsylvania in 1703. In 1689 (one report says 1702) he bought the land of Dirk Sipman (*q.v.*) in Pennsylvania (5,000 acres), who had taken over the property (1,000 acres) of Govert Remke (*q.v.*). Both were among the first six Crefeld land buyers in America, but had not emigrated. Van Bebber's property covered the present Perkiomen Township. In 1717 he sold a tract of 100 acres to a group of Mennonite settlers for a nominal sum and specified that it should be set aside as a site for a church and a schoolhouse. About 1725 the first Mennonite church in the Skippack district was erected on this tract; it was the second Mennonite meetinghouse in America. Van Bebber himself, however, never lived in his own township but moved to Cecil County, Md., where he continued his life as a merchant and gentleman and was even a justice of the peace in that community. In 1699 he translated a letter of H. J. van Akon, who wrote to William Penn in Europe asking that the latter plead for more toleration for the Dutch Quakers in the yearly High Dutch proclamation.   J.R.C.

Grund und Lager Buch of Germantown, pp. 189, 277, 289, 306; W. Hull, *William Penn and the Dutch Quaker Migration to Pennsylvania* (Swarthmore College, 1935) 215, 235, 254; S. Pennypacker, *The Settlement of Germantown, Pa., and the Beginning of German Emigration to North America* (Philadelphia, 1899) 141-42; J. C. Wenger, *History of the Mennonites of the Franconia Conference* (Telford, Pa., 1937) 96; D. Cassell, *Gesch. d. Mennoniten* (Philadelphia, 1890) 78, 81-86; S. Pennypacker, *Aantekeningen omtrent het geslacht van Bebber, Catalogus Amst.*, 344; *ML* I, 148.

Bechtel (Bachtel, Bachtell, Bachstel, Bechtold, Böchtel, Baechtold), an old Swiss Mennonite family name. By 1664 Peter Bechtel was listed in the Mennonite census lists of the Palatinate. Jacob Bechtel, also spelled in the immigration lists as Vechtel and Pritel, arrived in Philadelphia Oct. 31, 1737, from the Palatinate. The family first settled in Berks Co., Pa., and later moved to other states, including Ontario and Iowa. Eleven ministers by the name of Bechtel have served in the Franconia (*q.v.*) Conference district.

Prominent in this family was George Bechtel (16?-1759), who came from Mannheim, Germany, to America Aug. 9, 1729, an early leader in the Mennonite Church in Berks Co., Pa.; Andrew S. Bechtel (1874-   ), pastor of the Mennonite church at Hanston, Kan., who served as editor of the *Christian Evangel* (*q.v.*) and also editor of the *Year Book* of the General Conference, 1938-40; and Joseph B. Bechtel (1865-1946), by occupation a watchmaker and jeweler, an influential lay member in the General Conference Mennonite Church. *The Bechtel Family History* written by Joseph Bechtel was published in 1928. (*ML* I, 148.)   H.H.HAR.

Becius, Joannes, b. 1626 at Middelburg (Netherlands), d. after 1687. He studied theology at Utrecht, and about 1652 became pastor of the Kruis Reformed congregation of the Olijfberg in Antwerp. About 1660 he lived in Franeker, and after 1668 was again in his native town of Middelburg. He was no longer a preacher, having apparently made a complete break with the Reformed Church. In 1669 he was a Collegiant. He did not wish to be a "Mennist, Socinian, Calvinist, or Arminian," but a "Christian." For the Mennonites he is of importance in that he came to their aid with his pen in 1670, when they became involved in difficulties with the Reformed Church and the government at Deventer (*q.v.*); he wrote a booklet, *Wederlegginge* . . . in 1670, in which he made a strong plea for liberty of conscience. (*Biogr. Wb.* I, 365-69.) vDZ.

Beck, Charles-Auguste, author of *Essai sur les Mennonites* (Strasbourg, 1855). This little paper, which is of no great importance for our history, though the author thoroughly studied much Dutch Mennonite literature, was a thesis written for the A.B. degree in theology at the Protestant University of Strasbourg, April 29, 1835 (*Catalogus Amst.*, 10).
                                                      vDZ.

Beck, Hans, an Anabaptist martyr, was executed in 1533 at Guffidaun in Tirol (Adige Valley) with B. Schneider, Christian Alseider, Balthasar Gsel, Wolfgang of Götzenberg near Bruneck, Hans Maurer, and Peter Kranenwetter for his Anabaptist faith (*Mart. Mir.* D 41, E 444; Beck, *Geschichts-Bücher*, 108; *ML* I, 148).   NEFF.

Beck, Hans (Beckenknecht in Keller, *Apostel*, 221), from Basel, took part in the Martyrs' Synod at Augsburg (Aug. 20, 1527), with Hans Denk (*q.v.*) and Gregor Maler (*q.v.*) delegated as emissary to the Anabaptists in Basel and Zürich regions. Concerning his personality and work there are no records.
                                                      HEGE.
Röhrich, in *Ztscht f. d. deutsche Theol.*, 1860, 33; L. Keller, *Ein Apostel der Wiedertäufer* (Leipzig, 1882); *ML* I, 148.

Beck, Hans (Beckh), an Anabaptist martyr, was executed with the sword in 1532 at Sterzing on the Eisack in Tirol with five fellow believers (Lambrecht Gruber, Peter Hungerl, Peter Planer, Lorenz Schuster, and Hans Thaler) because they remained true to their faith. From prison they wrote letters to the churches in Moravia, which have been preserved (Beck, *Geschichts-Bücher*, 105; *Mart. Mir.* D 33, E 440; *ML* I, 149).   HEGE.

Beck, Hans (Peckh), from Greding near Eichstätt, Bavaria, was imprisoned with his wife Elisabeth in

the Oberhaus, a castle near Passau (*q.v.*). On Sept. 14, 1535, he was tried with his fellow prisoners and confessed that he had been baptized by Blasy Khumauf (Blasius Kuhn, *q.v.*) of Bruchsal, and that he had been previously imprisoned at Eggenburg in Lower Austria, but released after he and 20 others had been branded by burning through the cheeks (Wolkan, 30). He is evidently identical with Johann Peck (*Mart. Mir.* D I, 401, E 366), who lay in the castle at Passau with 12 others for nine years. Through the intercession of a baron of Jamits, who traveled 36 miles to redeem the prisoners by his pledge for their good behavior, they were released. They probably settled in the village of Pausram in Moravia, where they formed a congregation of Swiss Brethren beside the Hutterites. Three brothers (monks) from the church at Thessalonica (*q.v.*), the present Saloniki in Macedonia, are said to have come to him; through Hans Beck they discussed the articles of faith in Latin, agreed remarkably well, and took communion together. Then they left with the kiss of love and tears in their eyes, and returned to Thessalonica.

Hans Beck is not to be confused with the Hans Peckh (*q.v.*) named in the *Geschichts-Buch* (Wolkan, 105; *ML* I, 149).   NEFF.

Beck, Hans (called Welck and Welkh in the Hutterite chronicles): see **Weckh, Hans.**

Beck, Joseph von (1815-87), Austrian jurist and research scholar in the field of Anabaptism in Austria. His name will always be remembered for his extraordinary first edition of the Hutterite chronicles (1883). He was born in Moravia in a Czech middle-class family, studied law, and soon attained increasingly important positions in various Austrian courts, also as a teacher of law in several law schools. Toward the end of his successful career he was appointed to the Austrian Supreme Court, and two days before his death was knighted by the Emperor Francis Joseph. His law activities allowed him enough leisure time to pursue his real hobby of historical research. While a judge in Bratislava (Pressburg), 1854-66, he discovered in Slovakian and Hungarian archives and libraries a rich and hitherto untapped source: the handwritten manuscripts of the former Hutterian Brethren, Austrian Anabaptists who had spent 200 years here, being expelled from Hungary and migrating eastward to Wallachia and later to Russia. Their precious codices, which had been ruthlessly confiscated upon their expulsion and stored away in many remote places, proved to be a source of first rank. Tirelessly Beck collected this material, in original and transcripts (filling hundreds of boxes today); he traveled through many lands to make this collection as complete as possible, and with his antiquarian interest discovered many an unknown book or document pertaining to the story of the Hutterites. Eventually he put together in a mosaic-like fashion the essential contents of these chronicles and published it as *Die Geschichts-Bücher der Wiedertäufer in Oesterreich-Ungarn* . . . (in *Schriften der Wiener Akademie der Wissenschaften*, F.R.A. 2. 43, Vienna, 1883). It is an exceedingly rich volume, in many regards still unsurpassed. The Introduction is highly illuminating, setting forth the faith of the Brethren (along the line of the famous Schleitheim Articles of 1527), and giving a report of all manuscripts (codices) used—a real mine of information. Also the innumerable footnotes are unsurpassed in details which no research scholar in this field can ever overlook. Unfortunately, Beck never felt prompted to creative historical writing. When he died, his entire collection (the *Nachlass*) was handed over to Johann Loserth (*q.v.*), professor of modern European history at the university of Graz, Austria, to make use of it as he saw fit. A rich series of studies and books by this scholar was the outcome of this unusual scholarly co-operation. When Loserth felt that he had fulfilled this major task he gave the entire collection to the Moravian state archives in Brno, Moravia, where it has been much in demand ever since, and where it is still kept in custody. It was much used by W. Wiswedel for his historical writing on the Anabaptists.

R.F.

See *ML* I, 149, for a detailed biography of Beck by J. Loserth. H. S. Bender describes the Beck collection in *MQR*, April 1949.

Becker (Bekker, Backer), a Mennonite family name in West Prussia, appearing in the Old Flemish congregations and in the Danzig Flemish congregation, was first mentioned at Danzig in 1671. In West Prussia four families of this name were listed in 1776 (without Danzig), six persons in 1935 (without Elbing). Members of this family also emigrated to Russia (Molotschna) and America. The name Becker is not to be confused with Becher, Bächer (1935, 18 persons in West Prussia), etc., a Mennonite family name in the Frisian congregations of Danzig and Montau, nor with Petker, Boettcher, Petcher, etc., a family name of the Frisian Montau (*q.v.*) congregation.

G.R.

Becker, Eduard, author of the history of the Anabaptists of Hesse (*q.v.*), "Zur Geschichte der Wiedertäufer in Oberhessen," published in *Archiv für Hessische Geschichte und Altertumskunde* (Darmstadt, 1914).

Becker, Peter, was the founder of the Anabaptists in Pomerania, and was for this reason deposed from his office in 1556.

Calvary, *Verzeichnis werthvoller und seltener Bücher* (Berlin, 1869); H. Heyden, *Kirchengesch. von Pommern* (Stettin, 1938) 26, 73, 74, 104.

Beckerath, von, an old Crefeld family, came to Crefeld in 1694 as refugees from Rheydt. They had left Gladbach in 1654, where their progenitor Heinrich Jürgens was living in 1618. His son Jürgen Henricks was living in Haarlem in 1658. The sons of his third marriage, Jacob Heinrichs Jürgens and Theiss Heinrichs continued the line in Crefeld and Rheydt. The change from the patronymic form of the name to "von Beckerath" was made about 1700. It is possible that members of the family lived in the village of Beckrath in the Wickrath district for a short time after their expulsion from Gladbach. Members of the family have been prominent in the industrial development of the city, in the life of the Mennonite congregation, and in public affairs. The most famous was Hermann von Beckerath (*q.v.*). (*ML* I, 150.)

W.N.

Beckerath, Hermann von, b. Dec. 13, 1801, in Crefeld, a member of the Mennonite church there, was an outstanding member of the unified Prussian Landtag of 1847, where he made a famous speech for the rights of religious minorities, and with convincing power pointed out to the state its duty to grant constitutional rights (suffrage and eligibility for the Landtag) to all its citizens, including the Jews, regardless of religious creed. This truly liberal address, which testifies to his noble mind, is honored by being presented in full in the book, *Reden und Redner des vereinigten preussischen Landtags* (Kopstadt, 47 f.).

In the following year he entered the German parliament (see **Parliament**) which met in St. Paul's Church at Frankfurt a.M., and was there elected German Minister of Finance, which post he filled from Aug. 5 to Sept. 5, 1848. When King Frederick William IV in a personal letter dated Sept. 19, 1848, tried to induce him to enter the Prussian Cabinet, he declined because the king did not agree with his ideas and suggestions of liberty. Four days later he returned to the federal cabinet with most of his former colleagues. On May 4, 1849, he left it permanently, resigning because he was unable to concur in the acts and decisions to which the majority of the members had agreed. Since this act incurred the anger of his fellow citizens at Crefeld, he spent several weeks in Belgium, and another week in Godesberg, where he had acquired a country home several years later, in order to spend as much of his summer as possible at leisure.

From 1850 to 1853 he was one of the leaders of the liberal party in the Prussian Landtag. Though his health compelled him to give up parliamentary service, his efforts on behalf of his fellow citizens did not cease with his resignation. In 1862 his native city delegated him to represent them at the German trade conference at Munich. He was chosen chairman of the permanent committee of the conference and filled this office with outstanding success. On Nov. 19, 1862, he had a noteworthy audience with King William I, in which the king received him most graciously, conversing with him on political questions; Beckerath expressed his views freely and frankly. He died May 12, 1870, of pneumonia.

It is worth noting that von Beckerath made a speech in the Parliament of 1848 in which he objected to granting any special exemption from military service to groups which had religious scruples against such service, and this even though he was a Mennonite himself, and well knew the historic position of Mennonites against military service and their (at that time) uniform stand in Germany for nonresistance.

NEFF.

H. Kopstadt, *Hermann von Beckerath, Ein Lebensbild* (Braunschweig, 1875); W. Oncken, *Aus dem Leben und den Papieren Hermanns von Beckerath* (Cologne, 1873); M. Siebourg, *Hermann von Beckerath, der Reichsfinanzminister des Jahres 1848* (Crefeld, 1890); *Gem.-Kal.* 1903; W. Oncken, *Hermann von Beckerath* in *ADB* II, 231-35; *Die Heimat*, 1931 and 1940; *ML* I, 150.

Beckh, Blasius, an Anabaptist martyr, was captured with Hans Staudach and Leonhard Schneider of Kaufbeuren (Swabia), and Anthony Keim of Gunzenhausen (Middle Franconia), as they were emigrating to Moravia with their families, and on Aug. 3, 1546, taken to Vienna. The women and children were soon released; but the men were subjected to repeated hearings, and upon threat of death were ordered to turn from their faith; since they refused to do this they were beheaded on Nov. 22, 1546, at Vienna. Moving scenes were enacted before the execution. On the way to the place of execution the four men cheerfully sang hymns. Upon arrival there they knelt and prayed earnestly; one of them blessed the others and comforted them with the remark that they would soon be together in the kingdom of their heavenly Father. This strength of faith deeply impressed the crowd of spectators; even the executioner's assistants were moved, and their superiors said apologetically that it was difficult to have this execution performed, but they had to obey the government. During their imprisonment these martyrs wrote several hymns, which are still extant. (*Mart. Mir.* D 74, E 475; Beck, *Geschichts-Bücher,* 165-67; Wolkan, *Lieder,* 179; *ML* I, 150.)

HEGE.

Beckjen (Bekjen), **Pieter Pietersz:** see **Pieter Pietersz,** called Bekjen.

Beckum, Mary (or Maria) **van,** one of the best-known martyrs among the Dutch Anabaptists. She had joined the followers of David Joris (*q.v.*) and consequently had to leave her mother's house. She found refuge with her brother, the nobleman Jan van Beckum (Beckum is situated in the Dutch province of Overijssel, not far from Delden) of Gelderland, but in May 1544, at the instigation of Goesen van Raesveldt, the bailiff of Twente, a relative and next in line as the heir of the childless Jan van Beckum, she was arrested. The arrest caused great excitement. Ursula, her brother's wife, remained loyally at her side and shared her fate. First the two women were taken to Deventer, and examined there frequently; then they were transferred to Twikkel castle near Delden.

Repeated attempts by priests to deflect them from their faith failed. After a half year's imprisonment the heresy court condemned them both to death. They were burned at the stake on Nov. 13, 1544, at Delden; first Mary, then Ursula. The spectators were deeply moved by their heroic death and their joyful faith. Many wept when the two bade each other farewell. After a prayer revealing her state of mind, Maria, as the chronicle states, went to the stake with indescribable joy.

Their steadfastness made a deep impression. According to legend, the stake to which Mary was bound began to grow green and to blossom, and tradition has it that the Mennonites of Hengelo until well in the 19th century regularly planted a green branch on the site of her execution on the anniversary of her death (Nov. 13). Mary's faith and suffering were commemorated in several hymns that were widely distributed. Wolkan attributes a total of five songs to her, one of which, "Trauren

will ich stehen lassen und singen mit Begier" (43 stanzas), is found in the *Ausbund* (No. 17) and in Wackernagel, *Kirchenlied* (V, 792). This moving song appeared—without place or name of the printer —in 1545 under the title, "Ein new Lied von zweien Jungfrawen vom Adell zu Delden drey meil von Deventer verbranth." Rabus put it into his martyr book: *Historien . . . der Gottes Zeugen . . . und Märtyrern* (Part III, 1559). The song found in the *Offer des Heeren* is a Dutch translation of this German song, and begins with the words, "Droefheyt wil ick nu laten staen en singen met verblijden, van Mary Beckum hef ick aen, die om Gods woort moest lijden."   HEGE, vDZ.

Offer, 509-16; *Mart. Mir.* D 65 (with illustration), E 467; *DB* 1899, 93, 140; 1907, 170-75; *Inv. Arch. Amst.* I, Nos. 282, 291, 305, 322; K. Löffler in *Ztscht für vaterl. Gesch. u. Altertumskunde* LXXI (1913) Part I, 497-99; Wolkan, *Lieder,* 128; *ML* I, 151.

Beckum, Ursula van, nee van Werdum, an Anabaptist martyr, was the oldest daughter of Ulrich van Werdum, an East Frisian captain, and Armgard van Fikensolt of Oldenburg, and was married to Jan van Beckum, a nobleman of Overijssel. Jan's sister, Mary van Beckum (*q.v.*), was received by this couple living at Nyenhues near Deventer or in Beckum (now Bekkum) near Delden, when she had been compelled to flee from her home on account of her adherence to the Anabaptists. In May 1544 Mary was arrested in her brother's house. Ursula accompanied her voluntarily and with her husband's consent to Deventer, where they were frequently cross-examined, and after a half year's imprisonment they were burned at the stake at Delden in the presence of the court, the bailiff Goese van Raesveldt, and an imperial commissar of the court of Gelderland at Arnhem, on Nov. 13, 1544.

Both women faced death resolutely. When the verdict was being carried out on Mary, the priest of Delden tried to spare Ursula the gruesome spectacle, but she said undismayed, "Let me see my sister's end, for I desire to share the glory while she is entering into it." After Mary had been consumed by the flames, the priest tried to induce Ursula to recant, but she steadfastly refused his offer. In mounting the stake she slipped, and said, "I think I am falling." The priest thought she was recanting. "Halt! she wants to fall from her faith," he cried. But Ursula replied, "No, the wood merely slipped; I will not waver in God's Word, but remain steadfast in Christ."

And so, full of the joy of faith, she suffered death in the flames without Jan van Beckum's knowledge. At the end of November he wrote to his brothers-in-law Hicko and Hero van Werdum-Gödens, lamenting that the corpses of the two women were still hanging on the stakes. The execution created great indignation. Ursula's East Frisian relatives, who were not Anabaptists or favorable to them, had Deventer set on fire on Dec. 4, 1546, in revenge. The agents were apprehended and executed. Ursula's brother, Hero van Werdum, was thought to be the instigator. But he could not be convicted, and on July 7, 1551, had the mayor, bailiff, and council of Deventer certify that he had not been

mentioned as a participant at the trial of the arson-
ists.   HEGE, vDZ.

F. Ritter, in *Jahrbuch der Gesellschaft für bildende
Kunst und vaterländische Altertümer zu Emden* XV (1903)
390-410; see also bibliography in preceding article; *ML* I,
151.

Bedenken der Wiedertäufer halber (Nov. 5, 1557),
an official document of Lutheran theologians, now
in the state archives of Stuttgart, Germany, and
identical with a printed pamphlet of the same time
entitled *Prozess, wie es soll gehalten werden mit
den Wiedertäufern, durch etliche Gelehrte so zu
Worms versammelt gewesen, gestellt* (How to proceed against the Anabaptists, drawn up by several
scholars assembled at Worms). The *Bedenken* is
published in full in G. Bossert, *Quellen zur Geschichte der Wiedertäufer I: Herzogtum Württemberg* (1930) 161-68, and may be regarded as the
most concise arguments of the Lutheran theologians
against the Anabaptists, and also as their justification for the application of the death penalty against
them. It is, so to speak, the final statement of the
by then firmly established Lutheran state church.
In the main, it is the work of Philip Melanchthon
(*q.v.*), but the document (in its pamphlet form) is
signed by a number of other leading Lutheran
dignitaries such as Johannes Brenz (*q.v.*) and Jakob
Andreae (*q.v.*), the former more moderate, the latter most radical like Melanchthon. As a whole the
document reveals clearly what these men understood as Anabaptism. It is practically the entire
"left wing" of the Reformation which they attack,
including besides the evangelical Anabaptists (including Hutterites) the anti-Trinitarians, Illuminati
such as David Joris, and other Antinomians. They
all deserve death "by fire or sword," according
to Lev. 24, as their teaching is but "blasphemy."
The subtitle of this document states expressly:
Concerning ecclesiastical judgment and subsequent
ecclesiastical penalty, also concerning corporal punishment of the Anabaptists. For this reason the
document must be considered almost as dangerous
as the decrees of the Imperial Diet (such as, e.g.,
the one of Speyer in 1529). Today it presents to
us in brief the standard accusations raised against
the Anabaptists. "One should know their main
articles," the theologians declare, "in order to recognize their lies and that the Anabaptist sect is not
a Christian church but a devilish seduction." There
are two groups of accusations: (1) public lies
of the Anabaptists which can incite revolt against
the government, and (2) articles though false yet
not directly concerned with secular government.
Among the first articles the *Bedenken* enumerates:
(*a*) that the office of secular princes is sin, and for
that is damned, also that true Christians should
not participate in secular government; (*b*) that
Christians should give all their money and possessions to the Christian community; (*c*) that it is
sinful to take legal action against others in secular
courts; (*d*) that it is sinful to take an oath;
(*e*) that it is right to leave the married spouse
because of the issue of adult baptism. As false
articles under (2) we read the following items:
(*a*) that children are born without original sin;
(*b*) that infant baptism is wrong; (*c*) that God is

but one person as the Jews teach (this argument
turns against the anti-Trinitarians. It is important
to note that Michael Servetus (*q.v.*) was burned at
the stake just four years earlier, in 1553, and that
this was approved by Melanchthon and many others); (*d*) that the sacrament is only a symbol and
not an application of grace (here the Luther-
Zwingli controversy comes in); that the Lord's Supper is but an external sign; (*e*) that man becomes
justified by work and suffering, also by fulfillment
of the Law, and even by special illumination (is
this aimed at David Joris?); (*f*) some also claim
that a reborn man can never fall again into the
wrath of God as he is driven by the Spirit (this
attacks the Antinomians of that age). The Hutterites are later specially attacked because of their
(then novel) common education of the children
(see **Education, Hutterite**). At one place the execution of Servetus is expressly approved (but the
Duke of Württemberg later crossed out this passage). The document declares that according to the
Tables of the Decalogue the authorities are the
custodians of the law in all things pertaining to the
external discipline (*Zucht*) of a country.

Understandably the Brethren were appalled by
these severe denunciations. The well-known Swiss
Brother Hans Büchel (*q.v.*) composed a hymn of
20 stanzas to comfort his people in their new distress. It was later inserted in the *Ausbund* as hymn
46. Also the Hutterites (who had many ties to
Württemberg) felt urged to answer the document;
their rejoinder is contained in a Hutterite codex,
now in Canada (ms copy in the Goshen College
Library), and bears the title: *Handbüchlein wider
den Prozess* . . . (107 leaves). Its author is most
likely Peter Walpot (*q.v.*), the time is about 1558-
59. It is an excellent doctrinal practical statement
of the Anabaptist position, defending among other
things also their school system. "That our children
are dear to us before God and a profound concern,
of this we will give testimony on the Day of
Judgment."

As to the effect of the document no particular
information is available. The official persecutions
continued in their ups and downs according to the
mood of the rulers. (See **Brenz** and **Andreae**.)
                                              R.F.

Chr. Hege, *Die Täufer in der Kurpfalz* (Frankfurt,
1908) footnotes 93-96; R. Friedmann, "Eine dogmatische
Hauptschrift . . .," in *Arch. f. Ref.-Gesch.*, 1931, notes
on pp. 105 and 111; G. Bossert, Sr., in *Blätter f. Württ.
Kirchen-Gesch.*, 1912, 42 f. and G. Bossert, Jr., *ibid.*
(1929) 24 f.

Beech Mennonite Church (MC), formerly called
Buchenland (Beechland), and formerly Amish, is
located near Louisville, Stark Co., Ohio. The first
settlers came from Alsace near the border of Switzerland but seem originally to have emigrated from
the canton of Bern, Switzerland. Original deeds
indicate that John King purchased a farm in 1819.
Michael Schloneger and Jacob Conrad, Jr., purchased farms in 1822. Jacob Conrad, Sr., father of
the above, who had been ordained for the Montbéliard congregation in Alsace, was the first minister. According to tradition the first settlers were
joined in 1823 by others from the canton of Bern.

In 1825 the congregation organized and about 1830 erected a small log meetinghouse. John Schloneger was the first minister ordained by the new congregation and later served as the first resident bishop. Michael Schloneger, a younger brother, was ordained as minister soon after 1860 and a year later as bishop. John Schloneger had died at a comparatively early age. About 1884 the congregation organized a Sunday school under the superintendency of Jacob Schmucker and Michael Maurer, but for some reason this Sunday school was discontinued. The Sunday school effected a permanent organization in 1888 with John Sommers, one of the ministers, and Daniel Schmucker, the deacon, serving as superintendents. Other outstanding Sunday-school workers have been Jacob Meyer, David Schloneger, Harvey H. Sommers, and Mahlon O. Krabill. In 1925 the congregation called Otis N. Johns to serve as bishop. He was a minister at the Canton Mission at that time and was ordained bishop for the Beech congregation before he left. The membership in 1953 was 364.   J.S.U.

Beelthouwer, Johannes Pieterszoon, author of *Antwoort op een Boeckjen, genaemt Mennoos Kerk in en uyt Babel,* . . . (Amsterdam, 1665), written as a reply to and refutation of the book by L. Bidloo (*q.v.*), *Mennoos Kerck in, en uyt Babel, ofte den Aenvang, Voortgang en Reddinge van de Verwarringen der Vlaamsche Doopsgezinden,* . . . (Amsterdam, 1665). Beelthouwer repudiated the "slander" that Galenus Abrahamsz de Haan (*q.v.*) had corrupted Menno's church. Beelthouwer was a (non-Mennonite) Collegiant (*q.v.*). In 1656 he was banished from Enkhuizen as a heretic. (C. B. Hylkema, *Reformateurs* I, Haarlem, 1900, 180 f.; *Catalogus Amst.,* 129.)   vDZ.

Beemster, a Mennonite congregation in the Dutch province of North Holland, 15 miles north of Amsterdam. This region was once the Beemster Lake, which was reclaimed in 1612. Some Mennonites were among the settlers here; they joined the congregation at Oosthuizen (*q.v.*). Nothing is known about the beginning of this congregation; the church book does not begin until 1797. Since about 1787 the congregation has been called Beemster-and-Oosthuizen. It had a church at an early date in Oosthuizen; in 1785 it also acquired one in the village of Midden Beemster, now the only one in the congregation. The congregation was a member of the Frisian Sociëteit in North Holland. In the 18th and 19th centuries the congregation was served for more than a century by many preachers from one family: from 1734 to 1840 Klaas, Jan, Jacob Jansz, and Jan Jacobs Hartog. The last named preached here for 44 years. He was succeeded by the first minister from the Amsterdam seminary, P. Douwes Dekker, 1840-44; after him came J. Sybrandy, 1844-51; H. A. van Cleeff, 1851-85; V. Loosjes, 1886-90; P. A. Vis, 1891-1914; R. Kuipers, 1914-44; since then Miss A. Leistra. Since 1944 the congregation has been combined with Purmerend.

The membership was 36 in 1747; 74 in 1785; 143 in 1819; 200 in 1861; 273 in 1898; 234 in 1927; 190 in 1950. The members live scattered over all of Beemster and some in Oosthuizen, Avenhorn, Schermerhorn, and in Schermer; they are for the most part farmers. The congregation has a Sunday school for children and a women's organization. (Blaupot t. C., *Holland* I and II; *Inv. Arch. Amst.* II, 2, No. 26; *ML* I, 152).   vDZ.

Beerta, a village in the Dutch province of Groningen. There is here a Mennonite congregation, in existence since the 17th century, which together with the Mennonites living in Midwolda formed the Groot or Wold Oldambt congregation. Later it was sometimes called Beerta and sometimes Midwolda. Today the complex is known as the Winschoten congregation. There was in Beerta a church, built about 1700 and used until 1948. Then the church was sold, and since then the 17 members living here attend the church at Winschoten (*q.v.*). (Blaupot t. C., *Groningen* I and II; *ML* I, 152.)   vDZ.

Beetken van Brugh (official name Betken Laureys), an Anabaptist martyr, was put to death on Nov. 13, 1562 (van Braght erroneously has Aug. 15, 1561), with six others at Antwerp. Beetken was drowned. Further particulars are lacking. In the *Tweede Liedboeck* a song is found commemorating these faithful witnesses, which begins with the words, "Lieve broeders, wij groeten u met sangen," published by Wackernagel.   vDZ.

Mart. Mir. D 288, E 655; Wackernagel, *Lieder,* 140; *Antw. Arch.-Blad* IX, 143, 150; XIV, 32 f., No. 371.

Beets, a village in the Dutch province of North Holland, from which the Beets family (*q.v.*) takes its name. Leenaert Bouwens (*q.v.*) baptized 19 persons here between 1563 and 1565, and an additional 10 between 1568 and 1582. Nothing is known concerning a congregation at this place.   vDZ.

Beets, a Dutch family name. Blaupot ten Cate (*Groningen* I, 162) relates that a certain Jan Cornelis, in the persecution of 1570, fled from de Rijp (in the Dutch province of North Holland) to the neighboring village of Beets and hid in a haystack. He then adopted the name of Beets. But this tradition does not seem very acceptable. A. A. Vorsterman van Oijen in 1884 published a *Genealogie van het Geslacht Beets,* from which it appears that there were two Beets families, one Mennonite and the other Reformed, not related. The first Beets of the Mennonite family mentioned here is a Pieter Beets of about 1680, of whom nothing further is known. Pieter Jans Beets was preacher of the Zonist congregation at Amsterdam, 1682-1710. Jan Gerrits Beets was preacher of the Middelie congregation in 1731. In the 18th century the Mennonite Beets family produced many preachers, all of whom belonged to the strictly orthodox wing.   vDZ.

Beets, Cornelis, was a deacon of the Zonist Mennonite congregation at Amsterdam. He was a representative of this congregation on the *Commissie voor Buitenlandsche Nooden,* and was one of the delegates sent to The Hague on March 15, 1710, to plead the cause of the Mennonites of Switzerland before the States-General of Holland. The result of the intervention was, that the States on that very day wrote a letter to the council of Bern. On April

7, 1710, Cornelis Beets was again in The Hague and paid a visit to the Swiss ambassador, Saint-Saphorin, and also to the English ambassador, Lord Townshend. Further particulars of the life of Cornelis Beets, including the dates of his birth and death, are unknown (*DB* 1903, 130, 139). vDZ.

Beets, Gerrit, b. Dec. 21, 1707, ordained as preacher of the congregation of Hamburg-Altona in February 1727, chosen as elder there in 1749, a man of large physique and strong spirit, so eloquent that he was called the Apollo of the church. G. Karsdorp, Jr., writes of him, "His addresses to baptismal candidates and at communion services were especially moving; the Lord was in the temple through the mouth of His servant." On Dec. 9, 1776, a cerebral hemorrhage ended his life in the midst of a sermon. Karsdorp preached his funeral sermon, which was printed in Altona in 1777. His father was Jan Beets, a deacon in Hamburg from 1703 to 1712. The 1710 letter from the Dutch ambassador in Bern to a J. Beets in Hoorn mentioned by Ernst Müller (*Berner Täufer*) may have been addressed to him. Printed works of his are the following: *Lijkrede op H. T. de Jager* (1749); *Lijkrede op G. Karsdorp de Oude* (1750): *De vroolyke gesettheyd eenes Christens tegens de verschrikkingen des doods, . . .* and *Denkmaal in de Harten van Gods Volk* (1749); also *Preek over 1. Cor. 4, 4 en 5,* the sermon in which he was interrupted by the stroke. Neff.

B. C. Roosen, *Gesch. der Menn.-Gem. zu Hamburg-Altona* I, 77; II, 11-13, 25, 51, 59-64; *Catalogus Amst.,* 252; *Menn. Bl.,* 1854, 25; Müller, *Berner Täufer,* 257; *ML* I, 152.

Beets, Jan, b. Sept. 29, 1709, at Hoorn in the Netherlands, d. April 27, 1788. He was the uncle of Pieter Beets (*q.v.*) and the nephew of Gerrit Beets (*q.v.*). On Oct. 11, 1731, he was chosen to the ministry at Hoorn, serving until his death, more than 56 years later. There were during this time five preachers in the congregation, one of them being Cornelis Ris (*q.v.*). Jan Beets belonged to the extremely orthodox wing of the Mennonites. In 1776 he urged that preparations be made for a union with the Reformed Church (in his sermon "Eene Kudde en een herder, dat is de heilige algemeene Christelijke kerk in gemeenschap der Heiligen, opgedragen aan alle ware Zioniten," Hoorn, 1776). Ris also favored this union; for both Ris and Beets were very unhappy about the increasing rationalism among the Mennonites of their day. In his article on them (*ML* I, 152) Neff says that he was a true follower of Zinzendorf. But this is an error. Beets actually opposed the Moravian Brethren (in his *Brief tot Vermaning . . . betr. de Hernhutsche Gemeente,* Hoorn, 1749), but he made contacts with many "who were willing to save orthodoxy," including Tersteegen (letter of Nov. 17, 1750, by Tersteegen to Lauffs in Rheydt; see *Menn. Bl.,* 1891, 102).

Beets wrote much and in great variety. Especially to be mentioned is his *Verklaringe ter proeve opgesteld van eenige hoofdleeringen des geloofs, getrokken uit de geschriften van Menno Simons en*

de *Belijdenissen der Mennoniten* (Hoorn, 1765), a well-known confession of faith. vDZ.

C. Sepp, *Johannes Stinstra en zijn tijd* I (Amsterdam, 1865) 136; II (1866) 99, 188; *Biogr. Wb.* I, 378 f.; *Catalogus Amst.,* 145, 209, 219, 220, 246; *ML* I, 152.

Beets, Pieter, b. 1664 at Hoorn, Dutch province of North Holland, preacher of the Mennonite congregation there from Oct. 24, 1690, to 1707, when he retired, d. Oct. 1, 1710. In collaboration with E. A. van Dooregeest (*q.v.*) and Herman Schijn (*q.v.*) he wrote a brief course of instruction for the oncoming youth, *Kort Onderwijs des Christelijken Geloofs* (first ed. Amsterdam, 1698; it went through eight editions). He wrote also: *Het bereidwillig sterven gesien in de zalige verhuisinge van wijlen Michiel Fortgens,* a funeral oration (Hoorn, 1695). vDZ.

C. Sepp, *Johannes Stinstra en zijn tijd* II (Amsterdam, 1866) 95; *Catalogus Amst.,* 250, 259.

Beets, Pieter, b. March 8, 1729, at Hoorn in Holland, studied at the seminary of the Zonists at Amsterdam, was appointed *proponent* (ministerial candidate) at Medemblik, a few months later ordained as preacher in Middelharnis on the island of Goeree, in 1753 followed a call to the church at Aardenburg, in 1756 became preacher at Almelo in Overijssel, where he worked with his uncle Cornelis Ris (*q.v.*) on the well-known Confession of Faith. In 1764 he was unanimously chosen to the pastorate of Hamburg-Altona, but this he refused in two sincere letters. In 1770 this call was repeated. This time he accepted after a little time for consideration, although his uncle would have preferred to have him accept the call from the large church at Groningen, which he received at the same time, for he would then have been able to use his extensive knowledge and rich gifts in teaching at the university. On June 16, 1771, he delivered his first sermon in Altona, and from then until his untimely death, Aug. 25, 1776, his work there was singularly blessed. G. Karsdorp delivered his funeral oration, "Het character van wylen den Eerw. P. Beets" (Altona, 1776). He was a capable pastor and above all he was a faithful intercessor for his church. He belonged to the strictly orthodox wing of the Mennonites. Through his eloquence he drew so many from other creeds that the balconies of the church had to be supported with iron pillars. He introduced audible prayer, conducted midweek services, and with the consent of the Danish government, re-established the church school in 1774, which had been closed in 1737, and prepared young men for the ministry. Most of his hymns were put into the new hymnal, *Geestelijke Liederen* (Altona, 1777), that was introduced in Hamburg at the beginning of the 19th century. He was one of the Mennonite delegation in Overijssel to greet Prince William V (Orange) in 1766 on his visit in Kampen. His work as an author was outstanding. His printed works are: *Stamboek der Willingen 1591-1761* (Deventer, 1767); *Afscheidsrede te Almelo* (1771); *Intreerede te Hamburg en Altona* (1771); *Schetsen van leerredenen, benevens einige geestelijke liederen* (Altona, 1777); *Dertig predikatiën* (with foreword by C. Ris), 2 vols. (Hoorn, 1778-79), and several other works. His correspondence with Jan Deknatel, the son of the well-known Johannes Deknatel (*q.v.*), is worthy of note (published in *Menn. Bl.,* 1859, 12 and 34), as is also his interesting conception of the custom of infant consecration (*Menn. Bl.,* 1900, 75 f.). He left sketches on Mennonite history, which S. Blaupot ten Cate used in his historical work.   NEFF.

Blaupot t.C., *Groningen,* I, 171 f.; *DB* 1912; *Inv. Arch. Amst.* I, Nos. 757, 758; B. C. Roosen, *Gesch. der Menn. zu Hamburg* II, 50, 60-71; *N.N.B. Wb.* III, 86-87; *Catalogus Amst.,* 246, 249, 250, 278; *ML* I, 152.

Beets Pzn, Pieter (*ca.* 1755-1813), a son of the above Pieter Beets. He was appointed as *proponent* at Altona, and served the congregation of Blokzijl 1782-85. Then he studied two years at the university of Groningen, meanwhile serving the congregation at Leer and Altona. In 1789 he was called to Zaandam-Nieuwe Huis, for the salary —very high for the time—of 1,100 guilders. From 1789 to 1813 he was minister at Zaandam, where he found time in additional to his pastoral work and his duties as supervisor of schools, to train young men for the ministry, especially those who did not like the liberal theology of the Lamist seminary at Amsterdam. He was the author of a number of booklets, especially for young people —*Korte verhalen voor Kinderen* (2 vv.); *De vriendschap der jeugd* (3 vv.); and *Onderwijs in de godsdienst van Jesus Christus.* The *Bibliotheek der theologische letterkunde,* which appeared under his supervision 1803-7, was the first theological journal in the Netherlands; in it he reviewed theological writings that appeared in the Netherlands as well as in other countries. He was one of the founders of the *Nuts-departement* (public welfare) at Zaandam and promoted the organization of a French school there. He was a man of many-sided significance.   VDZ.

Biogr. *Wb.* I, 377-78; Lootsma, *Het Nieuwe Huys 1687-1937,* 76 f., 112, 187; *Catalogus Amst.,* 285, 311, 325.

Begebenheit, Eine, die sich in der Mennoniten-Gemeinde in Deutschland, und in der Schweiz, von 1693 bis 1700 zugetragen hat, a pamphlet of 54 pages, compiled by Joseph Stuckey, of Danvers, Ill. (printed by John F. Funk and Brother, Elkhart, in 1871). It contains four letters regarding the Amish division which took place in Switzerland and Alsace, written by four contemporaries, Jakob Guth, Christian Blanck, Gerhard Roosen, and Uli Ammann. The pamphlet was reprinted (same press) in 1883 and 1906, and was reissued in 1936 by L. A. Miller (A. M. Publishing Association, Arthur, Ill.). This last edition also contains the additional letter of Jakob Ammann, the leader of the Amish division, which appeared in print here for the first time.   C.H.S.

Beghards and **Beguines** are the names of the religious orders of the Middle Ages, who united into convent-like groups for the sake of unselfish activity and a deepening of religious life. The Beghards were the men, the Beguines the women of these free organizations.

Lambert le Begue (d. 1187), a priest of Liége, was formerly considered the founder of these societies, known as beguinages (*HRE* II, 517 ff.). They arose not so much out of the need for homes for impecunious women, as out of the urge for discipleship of Jesus. They were a kind of convent, whose inmates were not required to take the vows of a nun and could freely leave their beguinages. The first beguinage was founded in Cologne in 1230. About 1400 nearly all the cities, and even the small towns had their "houses of God," and they were also found in the countryside as well. In Switzerland they were called Sisters of the Forests.

The number of inmates in a beguinage varied from two to fifty. There was no uniformity in dress; but the greatest simplicity in dress was obligatory. Women who entered gave up all worldly possessions, supporting themselves with the work of their hands. In later times they devoted themselves to social work, especially nursing and the education of girls. In the 14th century they had acquired the character of poorhouses and alms establishments.

The Beghards arose in the 13th century to correspond with the Beguines. They were found in Louvain, Belgium, as early as 1220, and in Antwerp by 1228. Beghard and Beguine are epithets of ridicule probably of Walloon origin. They are also called Lollards, *boni pueri,* or *boni valeti.* Though not so numerous as the Beguines, Beghards were found scattered throughout Germany as far as Poland and the Alps. The earliest Beghards in the Netherlands, where the movement reached its highest development, were principally weavers; later they did much copying and selling of manuscripts. German Beghards were also potters, weavers, etc.; in addition they served as nurses and pallbearers.

In the second half of the 13th century cruel persecution set in. It was assumed that the pantheism of the "Brethren of the Free-Spirit" found its principal support among them, a suspicion which was, for the most part, unfounded. At the Council of Vienna, 1311, it was decided to suppress them because of their heresy. This decree was most brutally enforced. Thousands died at the stake. The male beguinages were transformed into inquisition prisons; the female beguinages were sold and the proceeds used for church purposes. Their most violent opponents were Johann Mülberg, a Dominican of Basel (1400), and Felix Hemmerlin (1440), a Zürich canon.

In Belgium there are still some beguinages, numbering 15 in 1896 with 1,230 members, in 1933 only 11 beguinages. They engage in pious introspection and handwork, chiefly lacemaking, which is an important source of income in the beguinages of Gent. Other occupations are the teaching of children and nursing. Their clothing is usually black, with a white linen headcloth under which they wear close-fitting caps. Two Catholic beguinages have been preserved (1933) in the Netherlands, one at Amsterdam with 13 inmates, and one at Breda with 46.

Ludwig Keller (*Reformation,* 32 ff.) supposes

that the beguinages are identical with the alms-houses of the Waldenses, who erected similar "houses of God" beside their churches where persons not belonging to their brotherhood were given a living. In this way the Waldenses did an enormous amount of social service. Very early the name "Beghard" was applied to the "apostles" they sent out, who founded these almshouses and were the spiritual advisers of the poor. It is a known fact that where the Waldenses were most numerous, there were more beguinages; and that the occupations most frequently found among the Waldenses were also the occupations of the beguinages. In the records of the inquisition in Toulouse, 1306-23, it is at once evident that the heresies confessed by the Waldenses coincide to a surprising degree with those charged against the Beguines.

E. Müller (*Berner Täufer,* 65) agrees with this conclusion, when he says: "The benevolent convents of Beghards and Beguines were the nurseries of Waldensian heresy and are interwoven into Waldensian activities."

Keller finds in the literature of the Beghards and Beguines much that coincides with the writings of the Waldenses and the medieval religious orders related to them. It is, indeed, very likely that there was a certain contact between the Waldensian "friends of God" and the Beghards and Beguines, to whom Nikolaus of Basel (burned in Vienna in 1395) belonged. But this cannot be asserted as a fact, without further investigation. Recent research by Greven, van Mierlo, and Lindeboom has proved that Keller attached too much importance to dubious connections with the Waldenses. The movement of the Beghards and Beguines was rather Roman Catholic and has more to do with the Franciscan Tertiaries than with the Waldenses.

Keller's idea that the Moravian Anabaptists based their communities on the old beguinages is hardly well founded. He assumes that there were connections between them, and that the Anabaptists wrongly forced all of life into this antiquated form, thus degenerating into a stunted sect. Thus he considers it to have been an effect of Beguine tradition, that the Hutterites, in complete misunderstanding of the intentions of their ancestors, applied the beguinage regulations to church life, and were thus led to an exaggerated severity of church discipline, which by means of numerous disputes and divisions weakened them more than the persecutions. This can hardly have been the case. Neff.

J. Greven, *Die Anfänge der Beginen* (Münster, 1912); Keller, *Reformation;* J. van Mierlo, "De bijnaam van Lambertus li Beges en de vroegste beteekenis van het woord begijn," in *Verslag en Meded. der Kon. Vlaamsche Academie,* 1925, 405-47; *idem,* "Lambertus li Beges en verband met de oorsprong der begijnen beweging," *op. cit.,* 1926, 612-60; J. Lindeboom, *Stiefkinderen van het Christendom* (The Hague, 1929) 97-107; *ML* I, 153.

Beginsel (Het) en voortganck der geschillen, scheuringen, en verdeeltheden onder de gene die Doopsgesinden Genoemt worden. *In dese laetste Eeuwe van hondert Jaren herwaerts tot op den Jare 1615. Getrouwelijck beschreven door I.H.V.P.N. Ende nu door J.K.J.H.D.K.F. in 't licht gegeven*

... t' Amsterdam, Gedrukt by Tymon Houthaak, op de Nieuwezijdts Kolk, in de Vogel Struys, A. 1658.

This is the title of a booklet of which Karel van Gent (*q.v.*) was once considered the author. It was completed in 1615, published in 1658, and translated into the German by Christian Joachim Jehring (*q.v.*) and published with other material in Jena, 1720, under the title: *Gründliche Historie von den Begebenheiten, Streitigkeiten und Trennungen, so unter den Taufgesinnten oder Mennonisten von Ihrem Ursprung an bis auf das Jahr 1615 vorgegangen. ...* The Dutch original was edited by Samuel Cramer and published in *Bibliotheca Reformatoria Néerlandica* VII (The Hague, 1910).

Het Beginsel is one of the most valuable sources of information regarding beliefs and practices among the Waterlanders, Frisians, Flemish, and their subdivisions; church discipline, ban, and avoidance; meetings held by Mennonites and discussions between Mennonites and their opponents (Leeuwarden, Emden); the function of elders and ministers; leaders like Menno Simons, Obbe and Dirk Philips, Leenaert Bouwens, Adam Pastor, Gillis van Aken, and especially less-known leaders of the second half of the century such as Pieter van Ceulen, Jan van Ophoorn, Lubbert Gerrits, and others. As an appendix the book presents a part of the *Restitution* of Rothmann in Münster, which was probably added by the publisher. On the other hand, the other supplements, the Confession by Obbe Philips, two letters from Menno Simons to the Brethren at Franeker (1555) and at Emden (1556), as instructions concerning the appointment of Mennonite preachers, had been put in by the author. (See on the contrary: Krohn, *Geschichte,* second index.)

The reliability of the contents of the book has been questioned by men like de Hoop Scheffer, who says that the booklet was inspired by great animosity toward the Mennonites and should therefore be used "with the greatest of caution" (*DB* 1876, 14); and it is true that the booklet was published in 1658 by the opponents of the Mennonites as a weapon against them. However, Cramer states that during the middle of the 19th century the booklet became "one of the primary sources of the history of the 16th century brotherhood" (*BRN* VII, 506). He quotes the Dutch church historian Brandt as saying that the author's objectivity is not questioned by those Mennonites who deplore the numerous divisions of the early Mennonites. Cramer adds that he "sees no reason to deviate from this view" (503). Kühler (*Geschiedenis* I, 365) refers to the author as "the best historian among the Mennonites of his day" and relies heavily on this source. However, de Hoop Scheffer's caution is still valid when it comes to accepting the book's evaluation of all the events and developments presented. Regardless of who the author was, he writes as one who has been disillusioned in some of the basic beliefs and practices of 16th-century Dutch Anabaptism, has been banned, and does not hesitate to let this be known. His case and his booklet can be compared to Obbe Philips and his *Bekentenisse*.

The identity of the author, important as he was, is still a mystery. In his preface the author states that he was born in 1542. He was Catholic by birth and had already decided to become a priest, but by reading the New Testament of the Biestkens (*q.v.*) Bible he arrived at evangelical convictions and joined the adherents of Menno Simons in 1563. At first he belonged to the Frisians, but in October 1568 he was banned, probably because of marriage. Several years later he was admitted by the Flemish, and as one of them he participated in the disputation at Emden in 1578 between the Reformed and the Mennonites. In March 1580 he was also banned by the Flemish for an unknown reason but possibly because he did not agree with their severe application of the ban. Thereafter he did not attach himself to another party, but lived in quiet Mennonite circles, without belonging to any particular branch.

De Hoop-Scheffer considered Carel van Ghendt to be the author of this book (*DB* 1876, 14), as did also G. Brandt (*Hist. der Reformatie*). Samuel Cramer (in his introduction to the edition in *BRN* VII, 492, 496 *et passim*) questioned this assumption. Vos (*Menno Simons*, 307) rejected the assumption completely, and considered Willem Jansen, a Flemish elder, to be the author. No definite conclusion has yet been possible.

Cramer also states (*BRN* VII, 496) that we have a copy of the agreement reached at the Strasbourg Anabaptist conference on Aug. 24, 1565, published by this same I.H.V.P.N. under the title, *Copye, getrouwelyck . . . overgheset . . . in de Nederl. tale door J.H.V.P.N. in Amsterdam Anno 1610 den 2. September.* He was an industrious collector of the writings of Anabaptists and related men, possessing several work of Staupitz, Entfelder, and Denk, and the translation of the Prophets by Denk and Haetzer.   C.K., vDZ.

BRN VII, 489-564; Keller, *Waldenser und die deutschen Bibelübersetzungen* (Leipzig, 1886); B. N. Krohn, *Gesch. der fanatischen und enthusiastischen Wiedertäufer*, . . . (Leipzig, 1758); *Menn. Bl.*, 1911, 85; 1916, 85, 93; K. Vos, *Menno Simons* (Leiden, 1914) 306 f.

Behaghe, Antheunis: see Antonijn de Waele.

Beidler (Beitler, Beutler, Butler, Beudler, Beuthler, Beuttler, Bütler), a Mennonite family name found as early as 1724 in Otterberg, a town in the Palatinate. The name is also found early in Bavaria. Johannes Bütler arrived in Philadelphia from the Palatinate Sept. 1, 1736. John Beutler who was born in Germany July 4, 1792, came to America, and settled in Lancaster Co., Pa. From the eastern part of Pennsylvania the family has spread into the states of Ohio, Indiana, Illinois, Missouri, Iowa, and Kansas.

Prominent in this family was Jacob A. Beutler (1833-86), of Elkhart Co., Ind., who was ordained a minister in 1868 and bishop in 1872. He served in the Holdeman congregation (MC).

A genealogy written by A. J. Fretz entitled *A Genealogical Record of the Descendants of Jacob Beidler* contains the names of several thousand descendants of Jacob Beidler, who was born in Germany in 1708. A genealogical chart is also included.   H.H.HAR.

Beiler, David (1786-1871), son of Christian Beiler and Anna Fischer, great-grandson of immigrant Jakob Beiler who came to Pennsylvania in 1737, a prominent bishop of the Old Order Amish in Lancaster Co., Pa., who lived near Bird-in-Hand. He was one of those leaders who tried to keep the Amish way as conservative and near to old tradition as possible. Thus he represented the genuine spirit of Amish life as it might have existed at the very start of this group (1693). Three writings are known from his pen: (1) *Das Wahre Christentum, eine christliche Betrachtung nach den Lehren der Heiligen Schrift*, written in 1857 when he was aged 71; (2) a letter to Bishop Joseph Schwartzendruber in Iowa, July 3, 1861, dealing with the administration of the ordinances, and (3) his *Memoirs*, written in 1862 (he was then 75), containing besides genealogical notes a comparison of the conditions of his church 60 years ago, and now.

The *Wahre Christentum* (no connection with J. Arndt's book) was published posthumously by J. Baer in Lancaster, Pa., as a 300-page book, one of the few Amish books in existence. It contains Biblical expositions concerning the ordinances, nonresistance, etc., and also several sermons as the Amish service schedule for the year requires. A chapter on "the state of the soul after death" concludes the book. It reveals very well the character of Amish preaching: no emotion, no personal opinions, very little theological speculation, but a compilation of many Biblical texts. "If we have no basis in the Scriptures, then it is merely human opinion" (165). There prevails certainty that God will not abandon people who faithfully keep His commandments.

The letter (*MQR*, 1948, 97-98) repeats somewhat the same ideas concerning ordination, baptism, marriage, etc., emphasizing the strict "old orders" (exactly: regulations) with their simplicity and austerity. The *Memoirs* exist both as manuscript and as a small pamphlet (no date); it reveals Beiler's character very strikingly. He is nostalgic for the good old days 60 years ago when people still used wooden plows and when the primitive forms of former Swiss life (in poverty and oppression) still prevailed, i.e., when the adjustment to American ways of life had not yet begun. Now, in 1862, the "church grows too cold in love." Beiler felt strong misgivings as to the future of his people and the temptation of secularization. He opposes *Hochgelehrsamkeit* (general education) and any ease of conduct of life. The document closes just at the moment when the first of the *Allgemeine Dienerversammlungen* (General Conferences) of the Amish ministers was held in Ohio, June 1862. Beiler is somewhat doubtful whether this really means "the beginning of a reformation" of Amish life and faith. But the fact that 17 years after his death, in 1888, the *Wahres Christentum* was published, proves that his spirit and genius had found actual response.

Beiler was intensely interested in maintaining the older forms of dress, behavior, and worship. At the same time he was deeply distressed because he saw among the brotherhood some who thought it sufficient to manifest lowliness in their outward behavior and to observe the ordinances. In the controversy regarding baptism "in the water," i.e., in a flowing stream, he held to the older method of baptism in the house, but advised ministers under certain conditions to take the counsel of the church. He seems always to have consulted the wishes of the congregation in matters of discipline and general policy. Tradition records that David Beiler and his brother Solomon, Mifflin Co., Pa., an Amish bishop, seldom agreed on vital issues but that David Beiler and Bishop Abraham Pitsche, of Mifflin County, a staunch adherent to the Old Order, were good friends and collaborated in the work of the church.

R.F.

J. Umble, "Memoirs of an Amish Bishop," *MQR* XXII (1948) 94-115; R. Friedmann, *Menn. Piety Through the Centuries* (Goshen, 1949) 245-47; C. Z. Mast, *Annals of the Conestoga Valley* (Elverson, Pa., 1942) 236; *ML* I, 157.

Beiler, Hans (1761-1842), in local circles known as "Hansley," was the first bishop of the Amish church in Kishacoquillas Valley, Mifflin Co., Pa. He was the third son and fifth child of Christopher Beiler and Barbara Yoder, and was born March 1, 1761, probably near Myerstown, Lebanon Co., Pa. He married Mary Detweiler, raised a family of nine children, and was a blacksmith and farmer by trade. He served as bishop of the Mifflin County Amish church from 1806 to his death in 1842. Large numbers of his descendants today are living in Mifflin and Lawrence counties, Pennsylvania. He was buried in the Allensville Mennonite cemetery, Allensville, Pa.

J.A.H.

Beiseker, a Hutterite Bruderhof founded in 1926 by 12 families from the Rosebud Bruderhof near Redland, Alta., with their preacher Paul Stahl, who was chosen to the ministry by the Tschetter Bruderhof in South Dakota in 1901. In 1944 Paul Stahl, Jr., was chosen preacher. In 1947 the Bruderhof had 35 baptized members, and a total population of 70.

D.D.

Beissel, Johann Konrad, b. April 1690, at Eberbach in Baden, Germany, d. July 6, 1768. As a baker's journeyman he devoted himself to an exhaustive study of the Bible and the works of Jakob Böhme. He was converted in 1717. In the late summer of 1720 he emigrated to America (first to Boston) with a group of fellow believers to escape persecution by church and temporal authorities. He was a "man of lively imagination, great energy, and inspiring eloquence, especially when the Spirit came upon him." He went to Germantown, where he learned the weaver's trade for a year under Peter Becker, organizer of the Church of the Brethren, who also baptized him in 1722. He now assumed the name Friedsam Gottrecht. After some time as a hermit at Mill Creek in Lebanon County and as the head of the "newly founded Dunker Church" of Conestoga in Lancaster County, he withdrew to solitude on the Cocalico Creek near Ephrata, and

there established the Ephrata Cloister (*q.v.*) of the Seventh Day Baptists. J. K. Beissel was an outstanding though amateur musician, the composer of over 1,000 hymns, of which 441 were printed.

Beissel rendered great service in the printing of German books in America. The first book printed in America with German letters, by Christopher Saur in Germantown, was Beissel's *Zionitischer Weyrauchs Hügel* (1739). In 1745 he published on his own press in the Ephrata monastery a small extract from the Mennonite *Martyrs' Mirror* with the title, *Das Andenken einiger heiligen Märtyrer oder: die Geschichte etlicher Blutzeugen der Wahrheit . . . Wie solches in dem Blutigen Toneel zu finden. Aus dem Holländischen gründlich und treulich übersetzt. (Durch Theophilum Al. Mack jr.) Drucks der Brüderschaft in Zion.* Anno 1745. Three years later, at the request of the American Mennonites, Beissel undertook the publication of the entire *Martyrs' Mirror* in German. Fourteen brothers of the cloister worked on it three years; six were employed in the paper mill, four as typesetters, and four as printers. The prior of the cloister, the learned Peter Miller of Alsenborn near Kaiserslautern, who had studied theology in Heidelberg, managed the translation from the Dutch into German. Beissel directed the entire undertaking, and thereby earned the gratitude of the Mennonites. The German edition of the *Martyrs' Mirror* is besides the Saur Bible the "most precious German book that was published in the 18th century in the German language in America," and the largest book published in the American colonies before the Revolution.

NEFF.

J. F. Sachse, *The German Sectarians of Pennsylvania, 1708-1800* (Philadelphia, 1899, 1900); Fr. Nieper, *Die ersten deutschen Auswanderer nach Pennsylvanien* (Mörs-Neukirchen, 1940) 137; Heinz Renkewitz, *Hochmann von Hohenau* (Breslau, 1935); W. C. Klein, *Johann Conrad Beissel 1690-1768* (Philadelphia, 1942); *ML* I, 157 (where Beissel is wrongly identified as a member of the Schwarzenau Brethren).

Bekentenisse van beiden Sacramenten Doepe unde Nachtmael der Predicanten tho Munster (Confession concerning the two Sacraments, Baptism and Communion, of the Preachers at Münster) is an old confession of the evangelical ministers of Münster, Westphalia, Germany, before the revolutionary ideas of Jan Matthys reached this city. Author of the detailed tract is Bernhardt Rothmann (*q.v.*). The *Voorrede* dated Oct. 22, 1533, is signed by Bernhardt Rothman, Johan Kloprijs, Herman Staprade, Henrick Roll, Dyonisius Vynnen, and Godfridus Stralen. It was printed in November 1533. Its meager ideas are as follows: Those who have been regenerated by the Holy Spirit, and left off all kinds of unrighteousness and all evil works, should be baptized upon their faith. The communion (*Nachtmael*) is said to be "Eyne leeflyke bykumst unde gemeyn ethen unde drincken der christgeloevigen wo van chrysto tho syner gedechtnysse bevallen" (a fine meeting and common eating and drinking of those who believe in Christ, to which we have been commanded by Christ to His memory). The communion service is a commemoration of what He has done for us and a pledge of what we will do for Him in order to render thanks to Him. A copy of this rare tract is found in the Amsterdam Mennonite Library (*Catalogus Amst.*, 50).   VDZ.

Bekentenisse des Gheloofs, na Godes Woordt: also deselvighe van vele jaren herwaert, ende noch teghenwoordich, by diemen Mennisten noemt, gelooft, geleert ende beleeft wort. This confession is found in the *Historie der warachtighe getuygen Jesu Christi . . . sint het Jaer 1524 tot desen tyt toe,* etc. (Hoorn, 1617). This edition of the martyr-book was a reprint of the 1615 (first) edition, entitled *Historie der Martelaren,* of which the introduction (by Hans de Ries, *q.v.*) was omitted and replaced by an unsigned *Voor-rede* and the *Bekentenisse des Gheloofs,* also unsigned. The confession consists of 33 articles, followed by some extracts from Menno Simons and Dirk Philips concerning the Trinity and the Incarnation. It is strongly orthodox in character. P. J. Twisck (*q.v.*) and Sieuwert Pietersz composed both the *Voor-rede* and the confession (*BRN* VII, 155; *DB* 1870, 72). Though the confession was a private undertaking, not authorized by the church, it had great influence among the Old Frisians, to which group the authors belonged, and it was often considered the official confession of this denomination. It was reprinted in the *Historie van de Vrome Getuygen Jesu Christi* (Hoorn, 1626), and the van Braght *Martyrs' Mirror* in all its Dutch, German, and English editions. A separate edition was published at Hoorn (1620). An English translation was published in 1837 at Winchester, Va., as *The Confession of Faith of the Christians Known by the Name of Mennonites, in Thirty-Three Articles with a Short Extract from their Catechism. Translated from the German, and accompanied with notes.*   VDZ.

Bekentenisse Obbe Philipsz (Confession of Obbe Philips) is the writing of the well-known Dutch Anabaptist elder Obbe Philips (*q.v.*), in which he renounces his office. The full title reads as follows: *Bekentenisse Obbe Philipsz, waer mede hij verclaert sijn Predick-ampt sonder wettelicke beroepinghe gebruyckt te hebben, beclaeght hem dies, en waerschuwet eenen yeders.* In this booklet, supposedly written about 1560, in which he gives many particulars on the original Anabaptist movement in the Netherlands, the author declares that he has left the (Anabaptist) brotherhood ("he left his office and took leave of the brethren") because he could no longer believe that this church or any other visible church was the church of God. The booklet was printed in Amsterdam, 1584, by Cornelis Claesz. The editor, an unknown Calvinist, wrote a lengthy but unimportant preface. A second edition (without year) and a third edition of 1609 appeared in Amsterdam, and in 1658 it was printed in *Beginsel en Voortganck* (*q.v.*). There has also been a French translation, *Obbe Philippe Recognaissance* (Leiden, 1595), but this French edition is lost. Cramer edited a new edition with an important introduction (*BRN* VII, 88-138). In *MQR*, April 1947, 120-22, Leonard Verduin mentions an ancient version of Obbe Philips' Confession.   VDZ.

Bekker, Balthasar, b. 1634 at Metslawier, d. 1698 at Jelsum, 1657-92 Dutch Reformed pastor, author of a number of theological writings, of which *De Betooverde Weereld* (Amsterdam, 1691) had a great influence and was also read by many Mennonites. This book deals with the common opinion of that time concerning devils and ghosts; it attacks superstition in various forms. But the book was not well accepted in the Reformed Church, and a synod, observing some Carthesian philosophy in it, dismissed Bekker from the ministry in 1692. Bekker is also of interest in Mennonite history for his quarrel (1688) with Lieuwe Willems Graaf (*q.v.*), the Mennonite minister of Harlingen (the subject of this quarrel was not at all theological, but merely geographical), and especially for his two books *beright van den kinderdoop* (1689) and *Nader beright over den kinderdoop* (1690) in which he defended infant baptism. The last of these books was a refutation of a writing by Johannes de Bakker (*q.v.*), *Korte en noodige aanmerkingen over het bericht van den kinderdoop* (1689). (*Biogr. Wb.* I, 389-412.)   VDZ.

Bekker, Benjamin, one of the first traveling ministers (*Reiseprediger*) of the Mennonite Brethren in Russia; he took an active part in its founding. He was one of the signatories of the declaration to the Orlov and Halbstadt church leaders on March 19, 1860, and the petition of Dec. 30 to the government. Ordained as traveling evangelist by Elder Heinrich Hübert, he was very successful in this service in 1861 and 1862. At Easter of 1862 he performed in Einlage the first wedding in the Mennonite Brethren Church. He soon joined the extreme "overjoyful" wing, and as their apostle (as he called himself) he exercised a dictatorial authority and banned his fellow preachers who did not share his views, such as J. Reimer and Gerhard Wieler. His influence soon waned. (Friesen, *Brüderschaft,* 199 *et passim; ML* I, 161.)   NEFF.

Bekker (Becker), **Peter** (or Pieter), a preacher of the Mennonites (Groninger Old Flemish) in West Prussia. At the time of the visit of Hendrik Berends Hulshoff (*q.v.*) in 1719 he was living at Przeckowsken on the Vistula. Later he evidently lived at Danzig. In the archives at Amsterdam there are eight letters from him in which he requests help from the Committee for Foreign Needs (*Commissie voor Buitenlandsche Nooden*), because of floods, famine, and persecution. The first letter is dated March 6, 1727, and the last one June 20, 1737 (*Inv. Arch. Amst.* I, Nos. 1088, 1581, 1598, 1610, 1635, 1643, 1645, 1662; II, 2, 738, 740). Whether the Peter Becker who was minister of the congregation at Kleinsee, and who on March 23, 1776, on behalf of this congregation, asked to have their debt canceled (*Inv. Arch. Amst.* I, No. 1713) is the same person, is doubtful. He would then in any case have been very old, for he was a preacher already in 1719.   VDZ.

Bekommerden (Anxious or Grieved), also called *Bekommerde Friezen* or *Bekommerde Mennisten,* the name given a group of Dutch Mennonites who thought the schisms between the Frisians and the

Flemish (1566-67) were unchristian and unnecessary and therefore sided with neither party. We find them at Harlingen, where the preacher Bouwe Lubberts shared their view. Quirijn van der Meulen, an elder at Danzig, also belonged to the *bekommerde Mennisten.* They were excommunicated by the elders Hans Busschaert (*q.v.*) and Jacob Pieters van der Meulen (*q.v.*).   **vDZ.**

(Kühler, *Geschiedenis* I, 428 f.; Vos, *Antwerpen,* 355; *BRN* VII, 70; *Inv. Arch. Amst.* I, Nos. 539, 557, 560-64; II, 1232-41.)

Belfort is a crossroads city of about 50,000 population, lying between upper Alsace and inner France. Though always French in language, the territory belonged to Alsace until the Franco-Prussian War (1871). Formed probably about 1780 as a branch of the Montreux congregation (*q.v.*) ("Münstrollergemeinde"), the Amish Mennonite congregation in this area met first at the farm "La Maie" six miles northeast of Belfort, and was known as the "Lamaenergemeinde." In 1793 this congregation is called Baron im Wald; the elder at this time was Daniel Steiner (*Naamlijst* 1793, 49).

Jacques Klopfenstein, presumably a member of the congregation, began in 1812 the publication of an agricultural almanac, *L'Anabaptiste ou le Cultivateur par Expérience* (*q.v.*). (The Anabaptist or the Experienced Farmer), which took advantage of the Mennonites' general reputation as good farmers, and which continued in publication for over sixty years (though with several changes of printers and publishers, and probably no longer under Mennonite editorship).

In the war of 1870-71 the members suffered considerable losses, and were aided by contributions from other Mennonite churches in Germany.

In 1876 the congregation purchased as a meetinghouse the former Protestant church on Rue Kleber. The city, however, retained its rights to this building and later bought it back. Consequently a chapel, which is still in use, was built at "les Barres" on the edge of the city in 1900.

The following have served as elders of the congregation since 1780: Michel Klopfenstein (ord. 1793), Hans Klopfenstein (ord. *ca.* 1840), David Stoll (ord. *ca.* 1820), Christ Stoll (ord. *ca.* 1840), Jean Stoll (d. 1875 at the age of 90), Jean Rich (went to America in 1884), Pierre Stoll (d. 1887), Christ Graber (ord. 1911, d. 1946), Joseph Roth (ord. 1911, d. 1952), André Graber and Jean Kaufman (ord. 1952). From 1887 to 1911 the congregation was led largely by Pierre Gerig, a lay member, during the period when there was no elder.

The congregation meets biweekly, with a Sunday school for the smaller children. It has a biweekly prayer meeting, and a chorus. Communion is celebrated twice yearly, the practice of footwashing being long since abandoned. The congregation counts somewhat less than the 169 members reported in 1888, in addition to perhaps 30 children, and belongs to the French-language Conference.

                       J.H.Y.

André Kaufmann, "Belfort," congregational history, *Christ Seul, Numero Spécial de Noel,* December 1951, 50-53; Pierre Sommer, *Christ Seul,* July 1930, 8-10; *ML* I, 161.

Belgian Congo Mennonite Brethren Mission was the result of the interest of the M.B. Conference in doing mission work in Africa evidenced by discussions recorded in its Yearbook as early as 1893. In 1896 Peter H. Wedel and H. E. Enns, supported by funds from the M.B. Conference, proceeded to the Cameroons of North Africa to a field of the North American Baptist Mission Society. Unable to withstand the severity of the climate, Mrs. Wedel was soon obliged to leave, her health broken. After seven months Enns died on the field in 1896. Wedel, whose health also failed, planned to go to Europe to seek recovery, but died on the sea Aug. 10, 1897. Mrs. Enns, too, succumbed to the climate, dying Jan. 3, 1898.

In 1912 the Aaron A. Janzens went to the Belgian Congo of Africa, supported by friends of foreign missions within the M.B. Conference. They served on the Congo Inland Mission field from January 1913 to November 1920, when they changed to the Kikwit area of the Kwango district, at first locating at Kikondji, but moving to Kafumba in 1924.

The Kwango district field of the M.B. Conference is some 100 x 110 miles in dimensions. Kikwit is its commercial center. The field operates three main stations. Its population is estimated around 400,000, living in 900 villages. The prominent tribes are the Bampende, Bapinda, Bombala, Bongongo, Bambunda, and Bakwezi.

Kafumba, opened in 1924, is 35 miles south of Kikwit on the Kwilu River. The area it serves is 50 miles square, covering several hundred villages. The station contains an indigenous church, a primary school, a teacher-training school, a Bible school, a hospital, and a printing office. On the mission compound are located five residences for missionaries, two buildings for orphans, seven small buildings for girls' boarding, one large and several small buildings for boys' boarding, fifteen small workers' houses, one church, one new and three old schoolhouses, one new hospital, three old ward huts, and some twenty sheds, storehouses, and workshops. The staff at Kafumba includes the Aaron A. Janzens, Kathryn Willems, the Frank Buschmans, the Irvin L. Friesens, Mathilda Wall, Mary Toews, and Erna Funk. Former workers, now deceased, are Mrs. Ernestina Janzen and Martha Manz.

Matende, opened in 1946, lies 56 miles southeast of Kikwit on an elevated, rolling plateau. Its area is roughly 35 x 35 miles, serving 100 villages with an aggregate population of 50,000. The station has a church, an elementary school, a dispensary, and dormitories for boys and girls. Its buildings are four residences for missionaries, one church, one schoolhouse, one girls' boarding, one boys' boarding, one dispensary, one small ward, one garage and storehouse, six workers' houses, and three sheds and workshops. On the staff at Matende are the A. F. Kroekers, the A. J. Esaus, and Margaret Dyck.

Kipungu, opened in 1948, is some 60 miles southwest of Kikwit. Its area is 56 x 56 miles, containing 200 villages and 200 company posts with a joint population of over 40,000. The station has a church, an elementary school, boys' and girls' dormitories, and does dispensary service. Its buildings are one missionary residence, two houses for native teachers, one provisional church building, one girls' boarding, three boys' boardings, six workers' houses, and two sheds for storage. On the staff are the John B. Kliewers, Anna Enns, and Anna Goertzen.

All three stations promote evangelization in the villages, maintain around 100 village schools taught by national teachers, and dispense medicines when on tour. The Kwango M.B. field has somewhat over 4,000 baptized believers, one ordained minister, nine licensed preachers and evangelists, and up to 100 station and village teachers.   A.E.J.

Belgium. During the reign of Charles V Belgium was the southern part of the Netherlands and was governed in his name by the vice-regent, who resided in Brussels. The influence of the court upon the stadholders in the various provinces was more pronounced in the south than in the north; hence the religious persecutions were also more violent in the southern provinces than in the northern. In the south the powerful nobility remained on the side of the Catholic Church, giving it valuable support. Whereas at the time "heresy" in the northern provinces, and in particular in the provinces along the coast, consisted chiefly of Anabaptist elements, in the south it was more widely distributed over the country and embraced both

Lutherans and Reformed in addition to the Anabaptists. Especially the Reformed made rapid gains under the leadership of Calvin's disciples, after Charles had transferred the crown to his son Philip II in 1555.

But the Anabaptists were also very numerous in Flanders. In organization and structure these congregations differed from those of the north, though the influence of Menno Simons was doubtless strong here too. In Friesland the center of gravity lay in the circle—certainly very small—of elders, and in the south it lay rather in the brotherhood. This difference was the chief cause of the dissension which broke out in Franeker in 1567, and which led to the split between the Flemish and the Frisians. In addition to this difference the northern congregations, especially in Waterland, were more lenient in the application of the ban and avoidance in marriage. A third factor lay in the fact that there were a larger number of well-to-do and respected citizens among the Mennonites, even though most of the members there too were small artisans and craftsmen (members of the guilds). The more elegant dress of many of the refugees from Flanders offended the plainer Frisians. A fourth characteristic was that many of the Belgians, and particularly the Flemish Mennonites, were weavers. The weavers, fullers, and cutters were united in guilds, and this circumstance was doubtless of some significance.

Whereas in the north the followers of Melchior Hofmann were more numerous, there is little

Belgium

16th Century Anabaptist Locations

Underlined cities in Belgium and France, --seats of 16th century Anabaptist congregations.

Underlined cities in Germany, Holland and Luxemburg--current congregations.

Other locations in Belgium--known residences of Anabaptists.

Scale of Miles

0   5   10   20   30

information concerning their activity in the south. It is, however, known that Jan van Geelen preached at Antwerp in 1534. He lived in the home of a certain Jacob van Antwerp in "De Tinnen Pot" (Pewter Jug). David Joris, who was presumably born in Brugge—he at first called himself Johan van Brugge—apparently also had followers in Flanders. Likewise it may be assumed from statements made by the inquisitor Cornelis Adriaensz that there was among others a circle of Nikolaites in Brugge. Also the unitarian ideas of Adam Pastor found reception among some here, as was revealed in the cross-examination of the martyr Herman van Vlekwijk. On the other hand, some martyrs of Belgium did not hold Melchior Hofmann's views on the Incarnation, which Menno adopted.

It is not yet possible to write a connected history of Anabaptism in Flanders. To the present, research in its development is still to be done, and there has not been a single investigation devoted solely to the Belgian Mennonites. One great handicap is the absence of any written church records for any of the Belgian congregations. In the prolonged war against Spain and particularly between 1575 and 1585 these congregations were completely wiped out. Here and there one finds isolated references in Blaupot ten Cate, and the rest must be hunted out of van Braght, from various printed archives, and from chronicles and descriptions of Belgian cities. By this method a mass of material can very likely be assembled; but it will probably never be possible to obtain a complete picture. It may be that at some later time thorough research will reveal new information on the struggles of the Reformation in Belgium.

Among the elders who were in the circle of Menno's chief co-workers three men can be named with certainty: Gillis van Aken (*q.v.*), Hans Busschaert (*q.v.*) or de Wever, and Leenaert Bouwens (*q.v.*). Bouwens baptized 292 persons in Antwerp before 1565, 23 in Brussels, 31 in Doornik, 242 in Gent (this figure may be an error, and should possibly read 116), 13 in Ypres, 25 in Kortrijk, 5 in Mechelen, 47 in Meenen, and 43 in Nijpkercke. Concerning the strength of the Mennonites, Cornelis Adriaens reported that there were 700 Mennonites in Brugge in 1568, and Morillon that there were 2,000 Anabaptists in Antwerp in 1566. These figures seem somewhat questionable, because Cornelis, a monk, is not dependable, and Morillon claims no fewer than 50,000 Calvinists in a population of 86,000. This must be a great exaggeration. We may nevertheless assume that the number of Anabaptists was great, because so many Belgian martyrs are known. As a rule, only small parts of the congregations were imprisoned, and hundreds must have fled to the north after the release of a very sharp edict against the Anabaptists in 1555. Even before this edict, the mandate of Charles V had appeared in Belgium in 1538.

This fugitive type of emigration gradually took place on a larger scale, and many localities were represented, chiefly in Flanders. At the beginning the preachers and elders remained at their post;

but since persecution sought out the leaders in particular and punished them most severely, some of them also took to flight; concerning this Jacob de Roore (or Keersgieter) passed severe judgment. The earliest refugees in many cases settled in East Friesland, especially in Emden. Later refugees settled in the principal towns of Friesland, Holland, and also Twente, introducing the weaving trade there. Even though the majority stemmed from Flanders, there were also Walloons among them; for there was a congregation of Walloons in Leiden, and as late as 1626, when the Mennonites had been totally expelled from Belgium, Virgile de Las had the writings of Menno Simons, Dirk Philips, and Jacques Dosie translated into French for them. Blaupot ten Cate lists a large number of Mennonite families who were descendants of the refugees, among them many with French names; in *De Navorscher* of 1904 are found the names of refugees who had settled in Haarlem.

This general flight is easily understood in the light of the violent persecution raging at the time, which, especially in the south, consigned the captured ones to the stakes. Whereas in the north, according to the report of the inquisitor Lindanus, the Mennonites were generally given a period of from one to six weeks to recant, they were usually executed within a week after capture in the south. The number of executions can no longer be exactly determined, but I estimate it at more than 800. Most of them are named in *Het Offer des Heeren* and in the *Martyrs' Mirror* in alphabetic lists of martyrs and localities, and in the *Bibliographie des Martyrologes Protestants Néerlandais* II. J. Meyhoffer published in the *Martyrologe Protestant des Pays-Bas* (Nessonvaux, 1907) lists from Kortrijk, Rijssel, Doornik, Valenciennes, and Liege. P. Génard had all the archives relating to persecution in Antwerp published in the *Archievenblad* of Antwerp.   vdZ.

K. Vos wrote on Antwerp: "De Doopsgezinden te Antwerpen in de zestiende eeuw" (*Bulletin de la Commission Royale D'Histoire de Belgique* LXXXIV, 1920, 312-90). A. L. E. Verheyden published the documents about martyrs in Brugge, Gent, Kortrijk, Aelst, Doornik, and Nieuwpoort, Brussels, and gave details on Mennonite congregations in these towns (*Het Brugsche Martyrologium*, 1944; *Het Gentsche Martyrologium*, 1946; *Le Martyrologe Courtraisien et le Martyrologe Bruxellois*, 1950. *Le Protestantisme à Nieuwport au XVIe Siècle*, 1951). By the same author: "Mennisme in Vlaanderen" (in *Société d'Histoire du Protestantisme belge* 1942); "De Doopsgezinden te Gent" (in *Bijdragen tot de Gesch. en de Oudheidkunde van Gent*, 1943); and "Introduction to the History of the Mennonites in Flanders" in *MQR* (April 1947) XXI, 51-63. See also W. Bax, *Het Protestantisme in het Bisdom Luik* I (1937), II (1941); and the important work of Edouard de Coussemaker, *Troubles Religieux de XVIe siecle dans la Flandre maritime, 1560-1570* (Brugge, 1877); *ML* I, 161-63.

In November 1945 the Mennonite Relief Committee (Elkhart, Ind.), representing the Mennonite Church (MC), began relief work in Belgium which continued until 1950 and was followed by the inauguration of a direct missionary effort in the autumn of 1950 with the sending of David and Wilma Shank and Orley and Jane Swartzentruber a year later. An MRC reconstruction unit rebuilt numerous houses in the badly ruined village of Bullange in eastern Belgium 1947-48. (Irvin Horst, *A Ministry of Goodwill, A Short Account of Mennonite Relief 1939-1949,* Akron, Pa., 1950, "Belgium," 37-41, and 68-69.)   H.S.B.

Belijdenis, Korte, der Waterlandsche Gemeenten: see **Besluyt der Voornaemste Waterlandsche Leeraren.**

Beliken de Jaghere, an Anabaptist martyr (in *Martyrs' Mirror,* Beliken van der Straten, in the official documents Beelken or Belynken Eyghe(e)re, and also Beelken Jan Stayaertsdochter), was burned at the stake in Gent, Belgium, at the Vrijdagsmarkt at 2 p.m. on March 17, 1573. Beliken was the wife of Martin van der Stra(e)ten (*q.v.*). She was a native of Bommel in the Dutch province of Gelderland but had lived in Gent for seven years. She was 26 years of age and had been married for four years. She had been rebaptized four years before her death in a woods near Gent by a man named Hendrik. Verheyden's suggestion that Beliken de Jaghere is identical with the person who is called Grietgen van Sluys (*q.v.*) in the *Martyrs' Mirror* does not seem tenable. (*Mart. Mir.* D 631, E 954; Verheyden, *Gent,* 61, No. 215.)   vdZ.

Belle (Bailleul), an old town in northern France, which in Reformation times belonged to Flanders, was the scene of the execution of eight Protestant martyrs—five Reformed and three Mennonites. These latter were Maeyken Doornaerts, Francijntgen, and her niece Grietgen, all three burned at the stake in 1556. Many of our martyrs executed in Rijssel, Antwerp, and Brugge were natives of Belle, indicating that there was presumably a congregation here, but there is not a single reference to its existence (*Bibliographie des Martyrologes Protestants Néerlandais*).   vdZ.

Bellerditz, a Hutterian Brethren Bruderhof in Moravia: see **Pellerditz.**

Belleview Mennonite Church (GCM), a Central Conference congregation located near Columbus in southeastern Kansas. Samuel Mishler, who came to Kansas from Illinois in 1880 and who lived about 15 miles south of Columbus, preached for the Mennonites from Illinois who settled near Columbus, and was responsible for the organization of the congregation. In about 1888 Mishler ordained John Nofsinger, a member of the congregation and one of the original settlers, as pastor of the church. The congregation had no conference affiliation until 1920, when it became a member of the Central Conference of Mennonites. Its membership in 1952 was 14.   W.B.W.

Belleville, Pa., is an unincorporated village of about 1,500 inhabitants in the center of Kishacoquillas Valley in Union Township, Mifflin County. Most of the 1,600 Amish and Mennonite residents in the county live within a 10-mile radius of the village. Its main industries are dairy plants, industrial machine works, lumbering, and flour milling. The Kishacoquillas Valley Railroad, called the "K.V. Line," built in 1890 between Belleville and Lewistown, was supported by many Amish and Men-

nonite residents, but was discontinued in 1940. The Maple Grove (*q.v.*) Mennonite Church is located near the town, and many of its members live and work there.   J.A.H.

Belleville (N.Y.) Mennonite Church: see **Lewis County, N.Y.**

Bellevue Mennonite Church, renamed Bellevue Bible Church in 1950, at the western edge of Peoria, Ill., was started in a home by C. Warren Long. Eight months later, on Aug. 6, 1939, a basement building was dedicated. Orie A. Miller became pastor in 1940, and a completed church with parsonage was dedicated on Oct. 11, 1942, at his ordination. The congregation was organized and joined the Illinois Conference in 1943. It withdrew from the conference in 1952. The membership of this independent congregation is 115.   O.A.M.

Belmont Mennonite Church (MC), Elkhart, Ind., was started by the Prairie Street Mennonite Church as a mission outpost on June 23, 1929. The first Sunday-school superintendent was C. W. Leininger and his assistant was John Gingrich. The church was organized as a congregation in January 1949 with 57 charter members. In 1952 the pastor was S. Jay Hostetler and the membership 64.   L.L.H.

Belot, an Anabaptist whom Calvin had arrested in Strasbourg in 1546, and banished because he was selling Anabaptist writings, which were then publicly burned. (Schwarz, *Calvins Briefe* I, 223; *ML* I, 163.)   HEGE.

Belton Camp, a Mennonite Civilian Public Service camp under the National Park Service, was located just inside Glacier National Park and a half mile from Belton, Mont. The camp, No. 55, was opened in September 1942 and closed in September 1946. The principal task of the men was to protect the surrounding forest areas from fire. Their work included the repairing and building of fire trails and bridges. In September 1945 more than 200 men were enrolled in the camp.   M.G.

Bénaville, the principal meeting place of an Amish Mennonite congregation formed in 1924 by former members of the Salm congregation (*q.v.*), one of the oldest congregations in France, formed by immigration from Switzerland 1670-1712. This congregation has also been designated by the names of other meeting places, notably Yquell, Les Quelles, and Fouday (see **Salm**). During the period from 1924 to World War II the congregation numbered at the most ten families with a total of approximately 35 members, and was served chiefly by Henri Volkmar and Jacques Wack, delegated for that purpose by the Alsatian conference. The remaining families now form part of the congregation of Hang (*q.v.*). Current family names have been Augsburger, Beller, Baecher, Gerber, Neuhauser, Lauber, Eymann, and Sommer. (Pierre Sommer, "Assemblée de Salm [suite]," *Christ Seul,* March 1932, 5-7.)   J.H.Y.

Bench. In the early days the Mennonites in the eastern United States seated their ordained men during the Sunday service on a long bench at one side or end of the meetinghouse behind a table. Later, when a pulpit was introduced to replace the table, it was made of sufficient length to completely cover the bench. From this bench (1) the deacon rose to conduct "the opening," i.e., to read a Scripture, offer comment, and lead in prayer; (2) the preacher appointed for the morning rose to preach the sermon; (3) all other ordained men present "gave testimony," seated, in order of seniority. Thus all the men "on the bench" took part in every service. The term "the bench" came to refer to the official ministerial body of the congregation including bishop, preachers, and deacons. To be "on the bench" came to mean to have official responsibility in the congregation, and an ordained man who moved into the congregation was not "on the bench" until officially voted in by the congregation, and might remain "off the bench" all his life. The "bench" is not a formal official term, but only a customary expression. It is, however, still commonly used in the Lancaster, Franconia, and Washington-Franklin (MC) conference districts as well as by the Old Order, Stauffer, and Reformed Mennonites. It is used only in the absence of a one-pastor system.   H.S.B.

Bender, an Amish Mennonite family, first recorded appearance in the Amish community near Waldeck (later near Marburg) in Hesse-Cassel, Germany, about 1790, but probably present earlier in the same group which came to Waldeck about 1730 via Wittgenstein probably from Alsace and originally Switzerland. This group consisted of such families as Guengerich, Schlappach, Otto, Shetler, Schwartzentruber, Yoder, who later settled 1830-60 in Somerset Co., Pa., and ultimately in Johnson Co., Iowa. Bender is not a Swiss name but fairly common in the Middle Rhine region, and apparently entered the group in Germany. Progenitor Daniel (d. about 1842 at Langendorf, Germany) did not come to America, but his second wife and her seven sons did, also one son and daughter by his first marriage, arriving at various times, 1830-51, all but one coming to the region of Springs, Somerset Co., Pa. From these immigrants descended a large number of Old Order Amish, Conservative Amish, and Mennonite families, chiefly located in the original settlement and in Johnson Co., Iowa (Kalona). From this family descend Bishop Daniel H. Bender (*q.v.*), Deacon George L. Bender (*q.v.*), Preacher Harold S. Bender, E. C. Bender, Paul Bender, as well as numerous Amish and Conservative Amish bishops, among them Bishop C. W. Bender and his nephew Bishop Nevin Bender. Another progenitor, Jacob Bender, from the same Hesse community, settled in 1832 in the Amish community west of Kitchener, Ont., where many descendants still live, two of whom were Bishop Jacob M. Bender and Preacher Jacob R. Bender.   H.S.B.

D. M. Bender, *Family Register of Jacob and Magdalena Bender 1832 to 1925* (n.p., n. d.); C. W. Bender, *Descendants of Daniel Bender* (Berlin, Pa., 1948).

Bender, Daniel Henry (1866-1945), outstanding bishop and leader in the organization of church-wide activities of the Mennonite Church (MC), with direct contributions to publication and education, was born near Grantsville, Md., the second son in the family of eight sons and one daughter, of John and Elizabeth (Otto) Bender. The father was a member of the Amish Church and had emigrated from Germany in 1851 because of conscientious objection to military service.

Daniel graduated from the Preparatory and Normal School at Meyersdale, Pa., taught grade schools in his home community for 20 years, and helped to conduct normal schools.

At the age of 21 (1887) he was ordained to the ministry at Springs, Pa. He was ordained bishop in the Hesston, Kan., congregation. In these two capacities he served the church until his resignation in 1930. During his early years he was active in conducting Bible conferences and evangelistic meetings throughout the church.

Early in his church work he became one of a group of leaders who through lifelong activity did much to mold the thought and activities of the church during an important period of awakening and expansion into organized church-wide activities. With his associates he was active in promoting church conferences and the beginnings of the General Conference and of the mission, education, and publication work of the church. He served in important positions on each of these boards, as well as on numerous church committees of various kinds. He was moderator of the Mennonite General Conference in 1915.

His editorial work began with the writing of the *Advanced Sunday School Lesson Quarterly* in 1903, which he continued for nine years. He also inaugurated in 1905 and wrote for 17 years the *Primary Sunday School Quarterly.* The *Lesson Picture Cards* he also began and wrote for some years. In 1904-6 he was editor of the *Herald of Truth,* the church organ, and the *Words of Cheer,* a children's paper, published at Elkhart, Ind. In 1906 he went to Scottdale, Pa., to become office editor of the *Gospel Witness,* and in 1908 of the *Gospel Herald,* merging the two former papers into a new church organ.

His editorship ended in 1909 when the Mennonite Board of Education called him to head a new school at Hesston, Kan. He became principal of Hesston Academy and Bible School, and later president of Hesston College and Bible School when a college department was added, and continued until his retirement in 1930. In this position his influence became widely felt through the molding of the thinking and attitudes of students who were destined to become leaders throughout the church. He was also prominent in colonization activities, and served for years as the president of the Mennonite Board of Colonization, an inter-Mennonite organization with headquarters at Newton, Kan. He retired to spend the last years of his life at Albany, Ore. He was married three times (Ida E. Miller, d. 1902, Sallie Miller, d. 1918, and Anna Kreider). He was the father of seven children, among whom is Paul, professor of physics and registrar at Goshen College.   P.BE.

D. H. Bender, *A Brief Sketch of My Life* (privately printed); *Mennonite Yearbook and Directory* (Scottdale, 1946) 25; Roy H. Umble, "Mennonite Preaching, 1864-1944" (Unpublished doctor's dissertation, Northwestern University).

19

Bender, George Lewis, leader in the missionary movement in the (old) Mennonite Church, b. Feb. 2, 1867, near Grantsville, Md., son of John and Elizabeth (Otto) Bender, d. Jan. 27, 1921, at Elkhart, Ind. Of Amish ancestry, his father coming from the Amish community near Marburg (Hesse, Germany) in 1851 to escape military service, he joined the Mennonite Church in his youth, and lived after 1887 at Elkhart, where he was an ordained deacon from 1907 until his death. First a schoolteacher, then for several years a traveling representative of the Mennonite Publishing Co., and finally clerk in the Elkhart post office, his chief contribution was as treasurer and financial agent of the Mennonite Board of Missions and Charities (organized 1905) and its predecessors from 1892 on. By virtue of his gifts he became in this office the outstanding missionary administrator-leader of the Mennonite Church, 1900-20, as well as the real leader of the Prairie Street Mennonite Church in Elkhart, 1907-20, during a difficult period. He was also cofounder and treasurer of various other church agencies, including the relief agency of the church. Married to Elsie Kolb, he was the father of seven children, the oldest being Harold S., Dean of Goshen College, another Wilbur J., Dean of Harvard College. (John Umble, *Mennonite Pioneers,* Elkhart, 1940, 97-115.) H.S.B.

Benevolent Organization of Mennonites (MC) received its charter from the state of Illinois April 23, 1894, and was evidently taken over by the Mennonite Evangelizing Board in 1896. The charter was signed by M. S. Steiner, John S. Coffman, Abiah R. Zook, Jonas S. Hartzler, and Solomon D. Ebersole. According to its charter, its purpose was "to support, maintain and carry on home and foreign missions, hospitals, orphans' homes, training schools for the education of nurses, deaconesses and Bible students." In a meeting in Chicago, December 1894, the organization assumed responsibility for the Home Mission in Chicago, pledged itself to pay the expenses of an evangelist to be sent to Dickson Co., Tenn., considered establishing an orphans' home, and recommended Elkhart Institute to those who wanted a practical education. That year it elected M. S. Steiner president, J. S. Hartzler vice-president, A. B. Kolb secretary, and A. R. Zook treasurer. M.G.

Beningha, Eggerick (1490-1562), descendant of a noble family of Grimersum in East Friesland, statesman and historian, counselor of Countess Anna (*q.v.*), and the author of the *Ostfriesische Chronik* (1723), an excellent source for the East Frisian Anabaptist movement in the 16th century, which P. Müller used extensively in his *Geschichte der Mennoniten in Ostfriesland.* (*ML* I, 163.) NEFF.

Bennema-Feenstra, Minke, b. Oct. 14, 1873, at Holwerd, Dutch province of Friesland, of an old Mennonite family, was married to Jan Bennema, a dealer in iron, of Groningen. After his death she took over the management of the business for several years. She has a fervent love for the Mennonite brotherhood and in various ways has served the Groningen congregation; among other things, as a member of the church board, and as an active participant in the erection of a rest-home there. For many years she was an executive member of the *Commissie voor Gemeentedagen.* Her spiritual lifework has been the Broederschapshuis at Elspeet (*q.v.*), of which she was chosen an administrative member in 1923 and for which she performed the extensive work of the treasurership 1924-48. She is living at present (1952) at Haarlem. vDZ.

Bennetts Run Schoolhouse Mennonite Church (MC) was a rural mission church two miles west of Bergton, Va., under the Virginia Mennonite Conference. This mission station was carried on in connection with the Valley View Church near Criders, Va. Members from here now worship at the Valley View meetinghouse. The 1948 membership was nine. T.S.

Benrath, Karl (1845-1924), church historian, author of *Geschichte der Reformation in Venedig* (1886) V and special studies entitled "Wiedertäufer in Venetianischen" (*Theol. Studien u. Kritiken,* 1885) which were made use of in the *Mennonitische Lexikon* for articles on the supposed Italian "Anabaptists." He was born Aug. 10, 1845, at Düren, educated at Bonn, Berlin, and Heidelberg, in 187 went on a scientific tour of several years to Italy and England. From 1879 he was professor at Bonn and from 1890 professor of church history at Königsberg.

Benrath's 1885 report on the Anabaptists in the Venice region of North Italy has been authoritatively accepted. However, a 1951 doctoral dissertation at the University of Chicago by Henry A. Dewind, "Relations between Italian Reformers and Anabaptists in the Mid-Sixteenth Century," has proved conclusively that Benrath was wrong in his identification of Italian anti-Trinitarian Protestants as "Anabaptists." This ENCYCLOPEDIA will therefore revise or omit all articles found in the *Mennonitisches Lexikon* on the Italian "Anabaptists," such as **Benedetto, Camillo Renato, Don Pietro, Manelfi,** etc. The article **Italy** will review the entire matter and give the evidence against Benrath's construction. Dewind's basic conclusion is stated in the following words:

"We have learned that an Italian reform movement, which gained a reputation for its rejection of the traditional Christian teachings in the Trinity and in the nature of Christ, and for its open propagation of a variety of other related heretical doctrines, although it was nearly universally denominated 'Anabaptist' both by its members and by its contemporary opponents, shared with the other groups which have also been called 'Anabaptist' only its belief that infant baptism should be supplanted by the performance of that ceremony on willing adults." (*ML* I, 163.) H.S.B.

Benschop, a village in the Dutch province of Utrecht, was soon after 1530 the center of an active Anabaptist movement; Ghijsbrecht van Baec (*q.v.*), the magistrate of IJsselstein, to which Benschop belonged, did not oppose the Anabaptists and his wife, Elsa van Lostadt (*q.v.*), joined them

The Anabaptist movement here was predominantly of a revolutionary character. One of the preachers of the group was Gerrit Ghysen (*DB* 1917, 86). Among the 3,000 who came over the Zuiderzee from Amsterdam on April 27, 1534, on their way to Münster in response to the call of Jan van Leyden, there were at least 150 persons from Benschop. In the next year more than 300 Anabaptists from Benschop appeared to help in the attempt to storm Amsterdam, which was launched by Jan van Feelen (May 10, 1535). After this the movement apparently soon disintegrated. (Kühler, *Geschiedenis* I, 88, 99, 109, 172, 180, 208; *Inv. Arch. Amst.* I, Nos. 156, 159.) vDZ.

Benthem, Heinrich Ludolf, a Lutheran divine, b. Nov. 2, 1661, at Celle in Hannover, d. July 9, 1723, as consistorial councilor in Harburg. He is the author of *Holländischer Kirch- und Schulenstaat* (Frankfurt, 1698), the 19th chapter of which deals with "Anabaptists and Socinians," giving an interesting description of the Dutch Mennonites of his time. Especially noteworthy are his impressions of Galenus Abrahamsz de Haan, derived from personal association. The chapter ends with the complete Dordrecht Confession. (*DB* 1870, 18, note 1; *ML* I, 163.) NEFF.

Bentinus, Michael, one of Hans Denk's (*q.v.*) most intimate friends, Dutch by birth, lived in Basel, where he was an outstanding member of the Erasmian circle. Denk died in his house. (Keller, *Reformation,* 330; *idem, Ein Apostel der Wiedertäufer,* Leipzig, 1882, 253; *ML* I, 163.) NEFF.

Benton Mennonite Church (MC) is located in the village of Benton, Elkhart Co., Ind., a congregation in the Indiana-Michigan Mennonite Conference. It began as a mission Sunday school under the Clinton Frame Mennonite Church. The first service was held on July 9, 1944. On Sept. 5, 1948, it was organized as a separate congregation with a charter membership of 53, in 1951 grown to 63. Galen Johns has been pastor from the start. V.H.

Benzie County (Mich.) Mennonite settlement: see Homestead Mennonite Church.

Benzien, Karl, a deacon of the Baptist Church in Dirschau in West Prussia, left his industrial activities in West Prussia and came to the Chortitza settlement in Russia in 1868 as a farmer. Here he found an open door into the Mennonite Brethren Church in Einlage, where believers of the new evangelical movement were eager to be ministered to by Baptist missionaries, and also to benefit by the exceptional organizational ability of Karl Benzien. On July 10, 1868, he was asked to preside at a meeting and directed their efforts in organizing the Einlage Mennonite Brethren Church, at which time the duties of the various officers of the church were defined. On July 14, 1868, at another business meeting of this new group, Benzien also presided at the election of their first elder, Abraham Unger.

Benzien also took active interest in missionary activities among the native Russians, particularly among the Ostyaks (Khants), who lived under conditions similar to those of the Eskimos in the Omsk district on the northern shores of the Ob River (see **Ob Mission**). With his heart burdened for these natives, he returned repeatedly to the Mennonite circles in Southern Russia to extend the "Macedonian call" in behalf of these needy people. He found a wide-open door for such activities among the Mennonite Brethren and Mennonites. He inspired Johann Peters with his wife and his sister, Helene Peters, as well as Dr. and Mrs. Paul Beer and Johann Keller, to accompany him, beginning the work in the northern Siberian territory of the Ob River among the Ostyaks. He himself continued in this work with evangelistic activities and the distribution of the Bible and Christian literature even as late as 1924. ("Ob Mission," in *Unser Blatt* 3, 24, 216, 242; Friesen, *Brüderschaft,* 776; *ML* I, 164.) J.J.T.

Berbig, Georg, pastor in Coburg, author of the treatises, "Die Wiedertäufer im Amt Königsberg in Franken in den Jahren 1527-28," in *Deutsche Ztscht für Kirchenrecht* XIII (1903) 291-353, and "Wiedertäuferei im Ortslande zu Franken," *ibid.,* XXII (1912) 378-403; also "Die erste kursächsische Visitation im Ortsland Franken," in *Archiv für Ref.-Gesch.* (published by W. Friedensburg) III, IV, and V (1904-9). In the first treatise he published valuable records from the ducal *Haus- und Staatsarchiv zu Coburg* on Anabaptist history, which Wappler corrected in his book, *Die Täuferbewegung in Thüringen, von 1526-1584* (Jena, 1913) 522-24. The second adds supplementary material; Wappler corrects some erroneous readings in it on p. 525. In the third treatise Berbig again produces source material on the Anabaptists in Franconia. On the other hand, his interpretation of the Anabaptist movement, entirely along the lines of the prejudiced, traditional old Lutheran presentation, is less gratifying. He does not succeed in understanding its nature, and cannot give a correct evaluation. Wappler was sharply critical of Berbig's work in Anabaptist history (*Thüringen,* 4 and 525). (*ML* I, 164.) NEFF.

Berchem, Joachim van (*ca.* 1520-74), a well-to-do baronet of Berchem near Antwerp, married Clara, the daughter of David Joris, about 1544, and soon afterward moved with his father-in-law to Basel. Several members of the van Berchem family joined the party: Joachim's mother, Anna van Etten, widow of Johan van Berchem, his brother Renatus (Reinhart), and his sister Anneken. Already in Belgium they had all been ardent followers of David Joris, and in Basel, where, until David's death in 1556, they lived in some luxury, they were faithful members of the secret congregation of David Joris. When it was found out that the wealthy citizen Johann von Bruck was the archheretic David Joris, and when his corpse was exhumed and burned (May 1559), the van Berchems were all imprisoned; they were, however, soon released upon their confession of repentance. (P. Burckhardt, *David Joris und seine Gemeinde in Basel,* 1949, reprint; *Inv. Arch. Amst.* I, No. 286.) vDZ.

Berdichev, town in the province of Volhynia, Russian Poland, is in the vicinity of the former Ostrog (*q.v.*) or Karolswalde (*q.v.*) and Michalin (*q.v.*) Mennonite settlements.   C.K.

Berdyansk, district, city, and Mennonite church. The Berdyansk district is located in the eastern section of Taurida, Russia, in which the Molotschna (*q.v.*) Mennonite settlement was located. The city of Berdyansk, a harbor on the Sea of Azov, had a population of 32,420 in 1910. This town was founded in 1735 and incorporated 100 years later, at which time it grew rapidly because of its strategic location for exporting the produce of the large wheat-producing Mennonite and German settlements.

Among the first Mennonites to move to Berdyansk was Abraham Sudermann, Caldowe, Prussia, in 1845, who built and operated a treadmill there. Being a minister, he started to gather a congregation which was first a subsidiary of the Pordenau Mennonite Church, then independent 1865-76, under Elder Leonhard Sudermann, and later a subsidiary of the Gnadenfeld Mennonite Church, and since 1914 of the Rudnerweide Mennonite Church.

Some of the outstanding members of the congregation were Leonhard Sudermann (*q.v.*), Cornelius Jansen (*q.v.*), and Heinrich Ediger (*q.v.*), printer and mayor. The Mennonites in Berdyansk were mostly businessmen dealing in grain, etc., who formed a "colony" within the city with their own administration and schools. In 1909 there were 109 taxable members, whose property was valued at one million rubles.

The small Mennonite colony of Berdyansk played an important role in the spiritual, cultural, and economic welfare of the surrounding Mennonite settlements. Cornelius Jansen and Leonhard Sudermann were friends of the evangelist Eduard Wüst and Quakers, who visited the Mennonite settlements. Both were also strong promoters and leaders of the great migration of the Mennonites from Russia to the prairie states and provinces in the 1870's. (H. Ediger, *Erinnerungen aus meinem Leben,* Karlsruhe, 1927; *ML* I, 164.)   C.K.

Berea Mennonite Church (MC), Alma, Ont. A Mennonite mission Sunday school was organized on July 13, 1941, in a rural public schoolhouse situated at a place formerly known as Parker, about 3 miles west of Alma, and about 13 miles north of Floradale, Wellington County. Sunday school and preaching services were held each Sunday afternoon, with Reuben Dettwiler of the Floradale congregation in charge. In January 1942 Gordon Schrag began serving as minister, and from then on services were held in the forenoon. On July 27, 1947, it was organized into a congregation of the Ontario Mennonite Conference and was named the Berea congregation. At this time John Garber began serving as minister (ordained bishop in 1951) and Clarence Huber as deacon. In January 1953 the baptized membership was 54, and services were still being held at the schoolhouse.   R.D.

Berea Mennonite Church (MC) near Birch Tree in Shannon Co., Mo., began in 1895 when John I Brubaker moved there with part of the Shelb County congregation of near Cherry Box, Mo. has been a small congregation, often without resident minister, with varying degrees of pro perity and adversity both temporally and spiritua ly. Besides J. L. Brubaker the ministers who hav served in the congregation as resident ministers a J. T. Hamilton, Abraham Unruh, C. B. Drive Leroy Cowan, Noah Ebersole (d. 1952), and present Oney Hathaway. The church now has good attendance and a membership (1952) of 3 Bishops who have served this congregation a Andrew Shenk, Alva Swartzendruber, and W. Hershberger.   J.R.S.

Berea Mennonite Church (MC), located near Mon gomery, Daviess Co., Ind., is affiliated with th Indiana-Michigan Conference. The church w organized March 1, 1921, with 19 members. Th membership (1953) is 224 with many childre young people, and young families. The church w remodeled and enlarged in 1937 and in 1950. Th church administrators of the past have been Am Weldy, deacon, and James Bucher, minister; present they are Edd P. Shrock, bishop, Tobi Slaubaugh, minister, and Paul F. Weldy, deaco The members are of Old Order Amish extractio   E.P.S.

Berean Academy, Elbing, Kan., was founded i September 1946 by the Christian Laymen's Associ tion, later incorporated as "The Berean Christia Laymen's Association." This association was orga ized earlier in that year for the purpose of openir and operating a Mennonite academy in the Ne ton, Whitewater, and Elbing communities. Mer bership in the Association is open to any Me nonite who subscribes to the school's doctrin statement and contributes $25.00 to the support the school annually. A nine-member board of c rectors is elected and entrusted with the respons bility of the affairs of the school.

The academy was located on a 10-acre camp just south of the town of Elbing (*q.v.*). On th property have been placed the following building the administration building in which are locate the school office, study-hall library, and three clas rooms; the auditorium-gymnasium which hous the science classroom, industrial arts shop, dinin room and kitchen, and one classroom; the gir dormitory, which provides room for 14 girls and supervisor; and a teachers' residence. An add tional residence will provide for some boys.

The school was opened for students in Septen ber 1946 with an enrollment of 15 students an two teachers. The work has grown through th early years to 58 students the second year, 54 th third, 71 the fourth, and 76 the fifth year, 1950-5 Six full-time faculty members, a librarian, and cook are employed. Two buses are used to brin the students to school daily, one from south Whitewater, and the other from Newton.

Four years of high-school work, grades 9-1

credited by the Kansas State Department of Instruction, are offered leading to a diploma. Each student is required to take one course in Bible each semester he is enrolled at Berean.

It has been the purpose of the school to maintain a warm evangelistic spirit that, by the gracious blessing of God, may lead the student first to a saving knowledge of the Lord Jesus Christ, and then on to a life of surrender to Him for service wherever He may direct.† W.E.H.

Berean Bible School was opened Sept. 9, 1950, in Allentown, Pa., by the Pennsylvania Mennonite Brethren in Christ. J. E. Hartman served as its first president. The two courses offered are a general Bible course and a pastor's and missionary course. M.G.

Berean Mennonite Brethren in Christ Church, located in Stroudsburg, Monroe Co., Pa., was organized and accepted into the conference in October 1910. In 1914 the first meetinghouse was erected. In 1948 the congregation had 47 members, mostly urban, with W. B. Hottel as pastor. W.B.H.

Berendge (or Beerenthien Beerentsdochter), an Anabaptist martyr, executed at Leeuwarden, Dutch province of Friesland, May 2, 1553, together with Tijs (q.v.). She had poor health and was mostly confined to her bed. But her faith was sound and strong and she refused to recant, but persisted to the bitter end. She was secretly drowned in the town moat, being bound in a sack and thrown from a boat. For Berendge and Tijs a song was composed, "Een nieue liet heb ic gedicht, van twee schaep wtgecoren" (A new song I have made of two chosen sheep), which is found in the Dutch songbook *Veelderhande Liedekens* and is included in Wackernagel. (*Mart. Mir.* D 150, E 539; Wackernagel, *Lieder,* 131; *ML* I, 164.) vdZ.

Berends, Wouter, can be regarded as the progenitor of the Wouters family. His father Beernt Wolters (Wouters) came as a poor man from Westphalia (Germany) about 1670 to Knijpe in the Dutch province of Friesland. He was originally a Roman Catholic, but became a Mennonite and joined the Groninger Old Flemish congregation. His son Wouter Berends, b. 1677, settled as a brushmaker in Joure, and about 1700 as a merchant in Sneek, where he attained great prosperity. He did not unite with the congregation at Sneek, since it belonged to the Waterlander branch, but with the Old Flemish congregation at near-by IJlst. In 1746 on his instigation an Old Flemish congregation was organized (17 members) in Sneek, for which he contributed a warehouse to be used as a church. The date of Wouter Berends' death is not known; he was still living in 1755. There was later much confusion in the adjustment of financial matters between Sneek and IJlst. Wouter Berends had as the last member of the Old Flemish congregation at Joure given the funds of that congregation to it, and now Sneek also laid claim to them. Not until 1767 was the difficulty resolved (*DB* 1890, 102; 1892, 90-98). vdZ.

Berenhout, Claude van, a former soldier, was engaged in 1647 by the Reformed classis of Wal-

cheren to watch that the refugees fleeing from Belgium did not become "infected with the errors of the Anabaptists." Nevertheless many persons coming from Flanders and other places joined the Mennonite congregation at Aardenburg. Although the conclusion of the Peace of Münster in 1648 sharply decreased the number of fugitives from Belgium, Berenhout was still at his post in 1649, when he was examined by the classis preparatory to going to the West Indies as a Reformed preacher. Whether or not his "watches" had any results we do not know (*DB* 1883, 111-13). vdZ.

Berents, Hendrik: see **Hulshoff, Hendrik Berends.**

Berezovka, a village in Russia near the station Davlekanovo in the province of Ufa, where there was a school for the poor from the beginning of the century. It was a 4-class institution with dormitory, founded by Fritz Klassen, who donated 50 dessiatines (135 acres) and a house to the school. Jakob Johannes Martens was made principal; he put his energy and his capital into the cause. (Friesen, *Brüderschaft; ML* I, 164.) NEFF.

Berg (Barg, Baerg, Bark, Barck, Barch), a Mennonite family name in the Flemish congregations of West Prussia, but also mentioned at Gruppe in 1692. In 1776, 16 families of this name were counted in West Prussia (without Danzig), and in 1935, 35 persons (including Elbing). Members of this family emigrated to Russia and America. Peter H. Berg was for many years manager of the M.B. Publishing House, Hillsboro, Kan. The name is found among the M.B. ministers in Alberta, Saskatchewan, Manitoba, Minnesota, Kansas, and Africa. G.R.

Berg, John, minister of the Mennonite Brethren Church, was born in the village of Fürstenwerder, South Russia, March 28, 1849. He was the eighth of nine children in the family of Heinrich and Maria Neumann Berg. His parents struggled in poverty during his childhood days. When he was four, his mother died. On March 2, 1876, he joined the M.B. Church at Orloff, Zagradovka. Soon after this the family emigrated to America, settling at Burrton, Kan.

He felt the call to the Christian ministry at an early age and for a time showed a great desire to become a foreign missionary. In view of preparing for this, he attended a medical school in New York City for one year. Because of sickness he was compelled to discontinue.

On July 11, 1886, he married Anna Wedel. To this union seven children were born. Soon after marriage they went to Rochester, N.Y., where he entered the Baptist Theological Seminary. For some time he was active as traveling evangelist in the M.B. churches. On Pentecost Sunday 1894 he was ordained to the ministry at Marion, Kan. Shortly after this he took pastoral charge of a Baptist church in Anaheim, Cal., where he ministered 14 years.

In 1909 the family established its home at Reedley, Cal., where the M.B. Church elected him as leader. This position he filled for nine years. When, on account of illness, he had to withdraw for some time from the ministry, the family lived for short intervals at Orland, Lodi, and Wasco, Cal. After that they again returned to Reedley and he continued in the ministry.

He was a very active conference worker and served on the Foreign Mission Board of the M.B. Church, 1915-24. In the Pacific District Conference he was an outstanding leader, serving occasionally as moderator. He died at Reedley, Nov. 7, 1941, and was buried at the local M.B. cemetery.

J.H.L.

Berg, Peter, one of the Russian Mennonites who participated in the founding of the Einlage Mennonite Brethren Church in South Russia in 1860 ff. With Abram Unger, Heinrich Neufeld, and Gerhard Wieler he was arrested and put into prison on the charge of involvement in forbidden religious acts; for two weeks they were held there in great distress. Since he was not in agreement with the religious excesses of Neufeld and Wieler, he and others were excluded by some early leaders from the M.B. Church. He emigrated to the Kuban and lived there in quiet seclusion to the end of his life. (Friesen, *Brüderschaft,* 267, 276, 279 f; *ML* I, 164.)

NEFF.

Bergen, a village in the Dutch province of North Holland, where on Nov. 19, 1947, a Mennonite circle (*Kring*) was organized as a branch of the Alkmaar congregation. The circle numbered 80 members in 1953; it is self-directing. Meetings are held periodically in a Reformed church.   vDZ.

Bergen (van Bergen, Bargen, Baergen, van Bargen, von Bargen, von Bergen), a Mennonite family name in the Flemish congregations of West Prussia, was first mentioned 1615. In 1776, 15 families of this name were listed in West Prussia (without Danzig) and in 1935, 52 persons (including Elbing). Members of this family spread to Russia and America. Gerhard van Bargen was the second elder of the Heubuden congregation, 1741-71. Fritz van Bergen (1900-41) founded the van Bergen Family Association and also edited its (mimeographed) periodical. A genealogical periodical, *Der Berg, Sippenzeitung der Familien van Bergen,* appeared from 1934 to 1941, edited by Fritz van Bergen, Frankenau, East Prussia. Isaac I. Bargen (*q.v.*), Mountain Lake, Minn., was for many years secretary of the Mennonite Aid Society at that place. His son Bernhard Bargen is now a professor at Bethel College, North Newton, Kan. The name Bargen is found among Mennonite ministers in British Columbia, Manitoba, Saskatchewan, and Oklahoma.   G.R.

Bergen, Bernhard (according to other sources Peter Bargen or Bergen), b. May 14, 1769, in the Danzig region, d. April 8, 1809, in the Chortitza settlement in the Ukraine, South Russia. He was ordained minister in 1802 (or 1804) and coelder in 1806, both in the Chortitza congregation. The reason for his ordination to the eldership is not clear, since Johann Wiebe was also serving in the office. It was apparently customary in Chortitza to ordain a coelder, who took the place of the elder at his passing. The elder's office was at that time no doubt fraught

with difficulty, for the Chortitza settlement was not yet filled, and there was general dissatisfaction with the plan of settlement and constant friction between the religious and secular leadership in the colony, in addition to a feeling of being forsaken in the desolate steppes, in their separation from the mother church in Prussia.   B.J.S.

Friesen, *Brüderschaft;* D. H. Epp, *Die Chortitzer Mennoniten* (Odessa, 1889); A. Dyck, *Menn. Auslese* (No. 1, 1951).

Bergen United Missionary Church, located two miles west of Bergen, Alta., is a member of the Canadian Northwest Conference. At present (1950) there are nine members and the pastor is P. Dyck.

E.R.S.

Bergey (Bergy, Berke, Berkey, Berki, Berkij, Berky, Birkey, Birki, Birky, Borcki, Borcky, Buerckey, Buercki, Buerge, Buergey, Buergi, Buerki, Burckey, Burcky, Burgey, Burkey, Bürki, Bürky, Burky), a family name among the Swiss Anabaptists in the Emmental during the 17th century and present in the Palatinate Mennonite family census lists of 1672, 1738, 1743, 1752, 1753, 1759, and 1768 (*MQR,* 1940-41). The 1940 census of Mennonite families in South Germany listed 18 families under four variants of the name.

Peter Bürki 1538 and Christen Bürki 1669 appear in the Bernese *Ratsmanual* as Anabaptists. Hans Bürky, a preacher, was exiled in 1710.

As early as 1726 John Ulrich Bergey purchased land in what is now Montgomery Co., Pa. It is believed that he immigrated from Switzerland in 1719. The genealogy of his descendants comprises a book of over 1,000 pages in which more than 600 persons carrying the family name were listed in 1925. The family is found chiefly in eastern Pennsylvania (Franconia Mennonite Conference) and in Ontario, although Mennonite descendants are living in states west of Pennsylvania.

C. H. Smith lists a Christian Buercki, a member of the Amish faith, among the Pennsylvania immigrants of 1737 (*Mennonite Immigration to Pennsylvania,* 228). Six Birkey brothers of the Amish faith settled in Butler Co., Ohio, around 1840 coming from Bavaria, whither their father Christian Bürkey had emigrated from France, Christian's father having come to France from Switzerland. The six brothers moved to Tazewell Co., Ill. only a few years after they had settled in Ohio. Descendants of these brothers are found among the Mennonites of Illinois and in Iowa, Nebraska, and other near-by states. John C. Birky, ordained a bishop in 1890, was for many years a leader in the Western District Amish Mennonite Conference. He served as bishop of the Hopedale, Ill., congregation from 1896 to 1924. His brother Jacob Birky was bishop of the church at Beemer, Neb., for many years but finally moved to Kouts, Ind.

In 1950 at least 12 ministers with variants of the name were serving Mennonite (MC) churches. Eight of these were located west of the Mississippi. E. J. Berkey of Oronogo, Mo., who earlier had engaged extensively in evangelistic meetings, was one of the most widely known members of the family.   M.G.

D. H. Bergey, *The Genealogy of the Bergey Family* (New York, 1925); Harvey Birky, "A Brief History of the Birky Family," *Christian Monitor* (July 1930).

Bergey, David (1845-1932), a prominent leader of the Ontario Mennonites (MC), was the fifth child of Jacob Bergey and Elizabeth Eby, who were of Swiss-German descent, b. July 3, 1845, in Preston, Waterloo Co., Ont., married to Louisa Bowman, daughter of Moses Bowman. Of his seven children, his son Gilbert became secretary of the Ontario Mennonite Conference, following his father's service in the same capacity for a quarter of a century.

Bergey received his education in the public school at Mannheim, the high school at Kitchener, and the normal school in Toronto. In early life he was received as a member of the Mennonite congregation known as Latschar near Mannheim, where he attended until in 1885. He moved to farms west of New Dundee and became deacon of the Blenheim congregation in December 1889. His place of residence was usually on a farm either in Waterloo Township or Wilmot Township. He lived in the town of Waterloo for several years.

He was a gifted man, useful in the communities in various interests. Besides being a schoolteacher, he was a charter member of the Rural Telephone Company; he served on the board of the Mennonite Aid Union; he was the district member for the conference on the Mennonite Evangelizing and Benevolent Board; he was instrumental in organizing Sunday schools at Latschar, at Blenheim, and probably in the rural areas south; he served on the local public school board, in the young people's meeting organization of the church, and as superintendent of the Sunday school. He was also a life member of the British and Foreign Bible Society. J.C.F.

Bergfelder Mennonite Church, Mountain Lake, Minn.: see **Gospel** Mennonite Church.

Berghe, Jan Bosch van, an Anabaptist martyr: see **Jan Durps.**

Bergisches Land, a refugee congregation in the old duchy of Berg, east of Cologne. A group of refugees from the West Prussian congregations at Thiensdorf and Preussisch-Rosengart had held meetings about once a month since Nov. 8, 1947, supported by Pastor Cattepoel, in Niedersessmar-Ahe near Gummersbach. The first communion service was held on March 21, 1948, when the refugees organized a new congregation and elected Fritz Marienfeld (b. March 3, 1889, at Oberkerbsweide, pastor of the Thiensdorf-Pr. Rosengart congregation since 1932) as elder, and Heinrich Pauls (b. Dec. 12, 1906, at Markushof, of the same congregation) as secretary; another Heinrich Pauls (b. Dec. 7, 1906, at Markushof, later lived in Gumbinnen of the same congregation) as deacon, and Karl Hoppe, Hagen, and Hermann Enss, Remscheid, both of the Danzig congregation, as leaders (*Vorsteher*). Marienfeld was ordained to the eldership April 24, 1949, by Rudolf van Beckerath and Pastor Cattepoel of Crefeld, and at Pentecost of that year (July 5) administered the first baptism and communion service. Since July 25, 1948, occa-

sional services have been held in the neighboring Rapperhohn, later Klein Balken, near Overath, and since June 6, 1949, also in Bad Godesberg. Since June 25, 1950, a group in Hagen (Westphalia), since July 23, 1950, a group in Lennep, and since March 4, 1951, a group in Dortmund, and later groups in W. Rondorf, Horrem, Bierth, and Bolsenbach, have been served with preaching service. The congregation now numbers about 250 souls. (*Gem.-Kal.* 1951-53.) E.C.

In the 17th century a number of Mennonites were living in this district, as is indicated in a letter sent from Amsterdam to "the Mennonites in Bergland" (*Inv. Arch. Amst.* I, No. 544). The Mennonites in this territory were aided by the Dutch Fund for Foreign Needs (*Inv. Arch. Amst.* I, Nos. 1193-94). vDZ.

Bergklooster, a half-mile from Hasselt in the Dutch province of Overijssel, is the place designated by the Münsterites as the gathering place where those who wished to go to Münster would assemble on March 24, 1534. Twenty-seven boats from various places crossed the Zuiderzee and sailed on the Swarte Water to land at Bergklooster, with a total of about 3,000 men, women, and children on board, who expected to find a Jeremiah (II Macc. 15) to show them the way to the kingdom of God. The misled crowd, who on orders from Münster probably had weapons with them though they did not use them, fell into the hands of the authorities here. No shot was released and no sword drawn, a fact that shows clearly that though these "innocent people" had indeed given ear to Jan van Leyden's enticing voice, they were by no means revolutionaries. A number of the 3,000 were put to death, especially the leaders, and the rest were sent back home after a short imprisonment. (*Inv. Arch. Amst.* I, Nos. 21-24, 27, 30, 32, 45; Kühler, *Geschiedenis* I, 94-110.) vDZ.

Bergmann (Bergman, Barkmann, Bargmann, Barkman), a Mennonite family name in West Prussia, appearing in the rural Flemish congregations, and since 1685 also mentioned at Danzig (*q.v.*). In 1776 ten families of this name were counted in West Prussia (without Danzig), and in 1935, 83 persons. Members of this family also migrated to Russia and America. The Barkman family name appears among the Mennonite preachers of Manitoba, Kansas, and Nebraska, among them J. F. Barkman (CGC), Steinbach, Man., and J. R. Barkman (EMB), Henderson, Neb. G.R.

Bergmann, Cornelius, a Mennonite historian, b. Jan. 26, 1881, at Neuhoffnung, Samara, d. at Jena, Germany, Oct. 28, 1951. He attended the Zentralschule of Ohrloff in the Molotschna settlement and taught school for five years. In 1907 he graduated from the Gymnasium at Berdyansk, after which he did graduate work at the universities of Leipzig, Berlin, and Zürich, particularly in history, but also in German literature, education, and philosophy. In 1915 he concluded his study and obtained a Ph.D. based on a dissertation which was published under the title *Die Täuferbewegung im Kanton Zürich bis 1660* (Leipzig, 1916). This valuable book is still one of the significant sources pertaining to the early Swiss Anabaptists of Switzerland.

After some teaching at the *Lyzeum* in Zuoz, Switzerland, Bergmann joined the publishing enterprise of Grethlein and Co. of Leipzig as a scholarly editor, after which he became lector of the Eugen Diedrichs Publishing House at Jena, which became his lifework. He published numerous contributions in the realm of literature, culture, and sociology in periodicals, and lectured at the *Volkshochschule* of Jena, etc. Recently he translated Russian classical literature into German in connection with the Slavic Seminar of the University of Jena (Chekhov, Korolenko, etc.), which demonstrated his perfect mastery of both languages. Numerous articles by Bergmann were published in the *Mennonitisches Lexikon* such as **Chortitza** and **Egli, Emil.** More recent was his article, "Ueber das deutsche Schrifttum im Siedlungsraum am Schwarzen Meer und im Wolgagebiet" (*Deutsche Post aus dem Osten,* Berlin, 1943, No. 1, 17-19). He also devoted some time to genealogical research pertaining to the background of his family in Prussia.

K.K.

Bergmann, Hermann A. (1850-1919), was a wealthy Mennonite landlord in southern Russia. Born in West Prussia, he had come to the Ukraine with his parents when he was 12 years old. The father bought a large estate near the village of Solyonoye in the province of Ekaterinoslav. Subsequent purchases by Hermann enlarged the estate to approximately 30,000 acres. Having now joined the ranks of the landed gentry, which class had a virtual monopoly of all important positions in the rural (zemstvo) agencies of government, local political offices of one sort or another fell almost automatically to Hermann Bergmann. For a number of years he was, first, a member of the Ekaterinoslav county governing committee and subsequently a member of this county's assembly. In addition to the above positions, he held other offices at one time or another. Among these the notable ones were that of director of a small-loans society, overseer of the Ekaterinoslav orphanage, and member of the board of directors of the Mennonite high school at Nikolaipol. In 1905 the Bergmann family moved from its estate Bergmannstal, to take up residence in the city of Ekaterinoslav.

Politically Bergmann belonged to the Octobrist Party, which was virtually the only party satisfied with the Manifesto "On the Perfecting of the Order of the State," issued by Nicholas II on Oct. 30, 1905. As implemented by subsequent decrees, this Manifesto established a bicameral legislature—the Council of State and the Duma, the upper and lower legislative chambers respectively. Members of the Duma were elected by a council of electors composed of two colleges of electors chosen respectively by the peasants and by the gentry. When despite this indirect mode of election, the First and Second Dumas (sessions opened on May 10, 1906, and March 5, 1907) manifested a degree of independence, the government decided to reduce to insignificance the voting power of the broad masses of the Russian people. By a most brazen method

of gerrymandering and a peculiar "curial" system of representation, the percentage of peasant representation in subsequent Dumas was reduced from 39 to 19 per cent and that of the gentry increased from 25 to 51 per cent, i.e., where one peasant deputy in 1906 represented about 800,000 peasants, in 1912 he represented 1,700,000 peasants, while a gentry deputy, having in the former year represented 28,000 voters, represented 15,000 voters in 1912. It was to these last two Dumas (Third, 1907-12; Fourth, 1912-17), from which "the people's face" was virtually banned, that Hermann Bergmann and another Mennonite large landowner, Peter Schroeder, were elected. During the winter of 1918-19, when anarchy reigned supreme throughout most of southern Russia, Bergmann, with several close relatives, was brutally murdered by bandits toward the end of January. (*ML* I, 164.)

J.G.R.

Bergthal Mennonite Church (GCM), Corn, Okla. In 1894, two years after the Arapahoe-Cheyenne Reservation in Oklahoma had been opened to settlement, a group of Mennonite families from Pretty Prairie, Hoffnungsau, and Alexanderwohl communities of Kansas moved into this locality. These pioneers had their first meetinghouse near the present site of Shelly schoolhouse, but by 1901 the church had enlarged to such an extent that 3 separate congregations were created—Bergthal, now located 2 miles west and 3 miles north of Corn, and 15 miles southeast of Clinton, and later Herold and Sichar. The 1953 membership was about 86. All of the families from the Pretty Prairie community returned to Kansas so that today most of the members have their connections in the Hoffnungsau and Alexanderwohl communities in Kansas.

H.H.

Bergthal Mennonite Church (GCM) at Didsbury, Alta. Mennonite settlers moved here from Manitoba in 1901 and settled within sight of the Rocky Mountains. During the early years the congregation did not have a resident minister, but the church was served frequently by Gerhard Buhler, Frank Sawatzky, David Toews, and C. F. Sawatzky. Since 1929 the congregation has had its own pastor, the following having served: Wm. Pauls, J. G. Neufeld, and C. G. Neufeld. The 1953 membership was 184. German services are held every Sunday morning. English services are held once a month and young people's meeting once a month in English.

C.G.N.

Bergthal Mennonite Church, Manitoba. In 1874-80 some 1,800 Mennonite families, in all about 8,000 souls, emigrated from southern Russia to Canada, settling in the province of Manitoba. These immigrants came mainly from the following groups or congregations: Bergthal, Chortitza, Fürstenland, and the Kleine Gemeinde. All adhered to the same tenets of faith, used the same catechism, but differed only in some practices.

The Bergthal group in Russia was a daughter colony of Chortitza, and had settled 1836-52 near Mariupol (province of Ekaterinoslav), a little north of the Black Sea. The Bergthal (*q.v.*) Mennonite settlement left Russia as a compact church with its elder, Gerhard Wiebe, and settled in 1874-75 on the east side of the Red River, in Manitoba, 35 to 40 miles south of Winnipeg, in what was known as the East Reserve.

However, in the early 80's about 50 per cent of these original Bergthalers from Russia looked for greener pastures and settled on the west side of the Red River, in what is known as the West Reserve, between Emerson and Rosenfeld. Under the guidance of Bishop Gerhard Wiebe from the East Reserve this settlement soon organized as a self-contained church group, electing their own bishop, Johann Funk, ministers, and deacons, and remains incorporated to this day as the Bergthal Mennonite Church. The group who remained behind in the East Reserve came to be called the Chortitza Church (*q.v.*).

There were progressive-minded members in the Bergthal Church who aimed for higher education among their own people, for better qualified teachers for their own children, and for more active spiritual church life, and who organized Sunday schools, choirs, young people's societies, held prayer meetings, and engaged in foreign mission work. They also felt that contact with other churches of like faith, in exchanging pulpits, would enrich church life. These aims and activities were sanctioned by Bishop Funk and his assistants to a large extent. Strong opposition, however, developed against these activities from the start among the more conservative-minded members and preachers, particularly on the school question, centering around H. H. Ewert (*q.v.*) and the present Gretna Collegiate Institute. The result was a division when these matters came to a head in 1890. A substantial number of this conservative group organized their own congregation, electing Abram Doerksen of the village of Sommerfeld as their bishop; hence this group was and is still known as the Sommerfeld Mennonite Church (see *Sommerfeld Mennonites*).

This division made it necessary that the Bergthal Church choose more ministers, who then applied themselves to accomplish the aims set for spiritual growth. The church grew steadily in membership and widened its activities.

In 1903 the first meeting of the General Conference of Mennonites in Canada was held in the village of Hochstadt, three miles east of Altona. The Bergthal Mennonite Church of Manitoba and the Rosenort Mennonite Church of Saskatchewan were the only groups participating in this conference and are the founders of the Conference of Mennonites in Canada. The annual conference found favor and has seen a steady growth in membership, so that by July 1948 it numbered about 45 congregations. This conference was duly incorporated by the Senate of Canada under Bill "C"—"An Act to incorporate Conference of Mennonites in Canada" —on March 20, 1947. Delegates from Ontario to British Columbia now take part in the annual gatherings. Although most of the Canadian congregations are members of the General Conference Mennonite Church, the Bergthal Church has not joined this conference.

The Bergthal Mennonite Church in 1952 was one of the largest and most influential of the Mennonite churches in Manitoba, numbering about 1,000 families with over 5,000 souls and a membership of 3,500, with one bishop, David Schultz, a cobishop, Jacob M. Pauls, 20 ministers, 10 church buildings, 21 places of worship, 24 Sunday schools, 16 young people's societies, and at least 20 sewing circles. It publishes a journal, *Bergthaler Gemeindeblatt,* and is the chief support of the Elim Bible School (*q.v.*) at Altona and the Gretna Collegiate Institute (see **Gretna.**)   H.H.H.

P. J. Schäfer, *Die Mennoniten in Canada* (Altona, Man.); G. Wiebe, *Ursachen und Gründe der Auswanderung der Mennoniten aus Russland nach Amerika* (Winnipeg, 1900.)

Bergthal Mennonite Church (GCM) and settlement, Pawnee Rock, west-central Kansas, was founded in 1875 by Mennonite immigrants who had come from Poland in 1874. The approximately 30 families establishing the Bergthal Mennonite community were only a few of the families who had come from the Ostrog Mennonite settlement near Zhitomir in the province of Volhynia (*q.v.*). Karolswalde and Antonovka were among the villages of this settlement which had been established by Mennonites coming from the Graudenz (*q.v.*) settlement. Michalin (*q.v.*) was a neighboring settlement. Tobias A. Unruh (*q.v.*) had been elder of the Ostrog or Karolswalde church since 1853 and was a member of the 1873 delegation sent to America to find suitable land for settlement. After his return to Poland he led most of his group to America, where they established the Friedensberg Mennonite Church (*q.v.*) at Avon, S.D., the Canton (*q.v.*), Kan., Mennonite settlement with the present Emmanuel Mennonite Church (*q.v.*) and the congregations of the Church of God in Christ, Mennonite, as well as the Bergthal Mennonite Church near Pawnee Rock.

The Bergthal Mennonite Church and settlement established in 1875 is located in Barton County on land obtained through the Homestead Act and the Santa Fe Railroad. One group lived for a while in a village, the Dundee colony, as they were accustomed to in Russian Poland. They first met in schoolhouses and had 75 members in the newly organized church. During the pioneer days a considerable number joined the local Swedenborg Church. Common names are Schmidt, Unruh, Dirks, and Siebert. The ministers who have served are Abraham Siebert, Jacob Koehn, Tobias Dirks, Peter Dirks, J. B. Schmidt, and J. E. Kaufman. In 1897 the congregation built a church, which was replaced in 1915 by the present brick structure. Sunday school was organized in 1885, followed by such organizations as mission and C.E. societies, choirs, and Bible school. The congregation joined the Western District Conference in 1886. In 1953 the membership was 223.   C.K.

Bergthal Mennonite Church, Sask., is about identical with the Sommerfeld Mennonite Church of Manitoba. When in 1894 the Rosenort Mennonite Church started in Saskatchewan, of whom many members were of the Bergthal Church in Manitoba, a part went off and organized a church of its own, mainly in the Rosthern, Hague, and Osler districts, partly in the Aberdeen district. Today the Bergthal Mennonite Church is spread north in Saskatchewan, though not in dense districts. But in southern Saskatchewan it has some dense settlements, mainly in the Swift Current district. J.G.R.

Bergthal Mennonite settlement and church, near Mariupol, Ekaterinoslav, South Russia, begun in 1836, was the first daughter colony of the Chortitza (*q.v.*) (Old Colony) settlement. The Chortitza settlement, established in 1789, consisted of some 24,000 acres of land with some 20 villages. By 1830 the population had increased so that the surplus land was exhausted and there were many landless people.

In 1836 the government made available a tract of 30,000 acres of arable land approximately 40 miles east of the Molotschna settlement in the district of Mariupol. Some 145 landless Chortitza Mennonite families settled here, establishing five villages—Bergthal, Schönfeld, Schönthal, Heubuden, and Friedrichstal. By 1867 the settlement consisted of some 370 families of whom nearly 100 were again landless or day laborers.

Administratively and ecclesiastically the settlement was independent. The first elder was Jakob Braun, who was succeeded by Gerhard Wiebe (*q.v.*). The administration of the settlement was in the hands of the *Oberschulze*. Because of its distant location the Bergthal settlement had little contact with its mother colony and thus did not keep pace with the developments of the larger settlements. When in the 1870's the educational system of the Mennonites was subjected to the control of the government and a general conscription of young men was in preparation, the leadership of the Bergthal settlement was greatly alarmed. They took part in the delegation to St. Petersburg and in seeking land where they would obtain the lost freedoms. *Oberschulze* Peters and Heinrich Wiebe investigated America for settlement purposes, joining the delegation of 12 in 1873. Elder Gerhard Wiebe writing about the outcome states: "The congregation chose Canada because it is under the protection of the Queen of England and therefore we believe that the principle of nonresistance could be maintained there for a longer period of time and also that the church and school would be under our own administration."

In 1874 the first and largest group left Bergthal via Hamburg for Ontario, arriving in Winnipeg July 31, 1874, on the steamer *International*. From here they proceeded by boat 25 miles south where they established their homes on the East Reserve which had been chosen by their delegates. By 1876 all property of the Bergthal settlement in Russia had been sold and the last of the 500 families consisting of nearly 3,000 persons had left. Only a few families remained in Russia. This was the only Mennonite settlement which migrated as a compact group from Russia to America during that time. Some members of the Kleine Gemeinde joined the Bergthal settlement in Manitoba. Some of the Bergthal group soon moved from the East Reserve to the West Reserve. Those remaining on

the East Reserve later became known as Chortitza Mennonites (*q.v.*), while the majority on the West Reserve were named Sommerfeld Mennonites (*q.v.*) and a more progressive minority retained the name Bergthal Mennonites (see **Bergthal** Mennonite Church).

Although of the same background, the Bergthal and Old Colony Mennonites (coming from Chortitza and Fürstenland in Russia) never united as one congregation. Most of the Old Colony Mennonites later moved to Mexico (*q.v.*) and a considerable number of the Sommerfeld and Chortitza Mennonites migrated to Paraguay (*q.v.*). C.K.

G. Wiebe, *Ursachen und Geschichte der Auswanderung der Mennoniten aus Russland nach Amerika* (Winnipeg, 1900); *ML* I, 165.

Bergthal (Paraguay) **Colony,** 180 miles east of Asuncion, was founded in July 1948, by 740 Old Colony Mennonites from Manitoba (East Reserve) who bought 27,000 acres of forest land at $3 per acre, and established seven villages with Chortitz as center. In 1953, after some return migration, the population was 639 souls in 117 families. H.S.B.

Bergthaler Gemeindeblatt, Das, a four-page German monthly published by the Bergthaler Mennonite Church at Altona, Man. Now (1952) in its seventeenth year, it is edited by David Schulz and H. J. Gerbrandt. M.G.

Bergthold, a Palatine Mennonite family name, transplanted to West Prussia by Jakob Bergthold (*q.v.*), who moved there from Galicia in 1799. Descendants also emigrated to Russia and America. Twenty persons of this name were living in West Prussia in 1935. G.R.

Bergthold, Daniel F., a foreign missionary of the Mennonite Brethren Church, was born at Pyatigorsk, Stavropol, South Russia, on Jan. 12, 1876, the second of seven children. His parents, Heinrich and Alvina (Starke) Bergthold (see **Bergthold, Jakob**), were of Galician German descent, earlier from the Palatinate. After the family had lived in the Kuban settlement in the Russian Caucasus for some time, they emigrated to America about 1877, settling on a farm near Bingham Lake, Minn. After living at Lehigh, Kan., a short time, the family went to Kirk, Col., where their son Daniel grew up, became converted, and joined the M.B. Church in 1890. Daniel attended McPherson College, McPherson, Kan., for one year, and Moody Bible Institute in Chicago for two and one-half years, then he applied to the M.B. Conference for a foreign mission appointment and was accepted as a candidate to India in the fall of 1901. He was, however, first assigned to evangelistic work in the American churches, which he performed for three years. In June 1903 he married Katharina Mandtler of Dalmeny, Sask. In 1904 the family proceeded as missionaries to the M.B. mission field of the Hyderabad state, South India. Six weeks after their arrival Mrs. Bergthold died of smallpox. Bergthold then married Anna Epp on Sept. 17, 1905. On Sept. 5, 1915, Mrs. Bergthold died and on June 20, 1916, Bergthold married Anna Sudermann. He was the father of seven children.

Daniel Bergthold was an outstanding pioneer

foreign missionary. He established a mission station at Nagarkurnool, an important village 80 miles south of Hyderabad, where he did the greater part of his lifework. Having acquired a good command of the Telugu language, he made extensive tours among the villages of that area and preached to many. After some converts had accepted baptism, he established a church which grew and flourished. He spent much time in teaching Scripture, and established a Bible school of which he was principal for seven years. For some time he was business manager of the publication interests of the missions, publishing the vernacular monthly paper, *Suvarthamani,* and for some time also the English paper, *Harvest Field.*

After a period of 41 years' service in the mission, Bergthold returned to America in February 1946. He died at Alhambra, Cal., Oct. 25, 1948, and was buried at the Rosehill Community Cemetery, Whittier, Cal. J.H.L.

Bergthold, Jakob, a Mennonite preacher whose work brought blessing to the Mennonite churches in Galicia and West Prussia. He came from the Palatinate, where his family name is still found in the congregation at Friedelsheim. His grandfather, Jakob Bergthold, was a distiller and a wine merchant in Schifferstadt (Kohlhof), who lived a few years in Herrnhut, where his oldest daughter married a member of the Herrnhut group, then bought a vinegar factory at St. Grethen, near Dürkheim a.d.H., which he operated with success. His oldest son Daniel married Margarete, the daughter of Jakob Lichti, a miller in Harxheim, and there in 1769 acquired a plot of land with a distillery and vinegar distillery.

Here Jakob (II) Bergthold, their oldest son, spent his youth. In 1781 he was baptized in the Mennonite church at Kriegsheim. Four years later his father (Daniel) emigrated with 28 Mennonite families from the Palatinate to Galicia. In response to an invitation of Emperor Joseph II of Austria they settled near the town of Szczerzec south of Lemberg. Jakob II, whose parents lived at Rosenberg, married the sister of Jakob Müller, the elder of the church at Einsiedel. On Dec. 19, 1787, he was chosen preacher, and performed the duties of that office faithfully until 1797, when he migrated to Russia with several brethren and settled in a Hutterite colony at Vishenka on the Desna in the province of Chernigov. But they were unable to adjust themselves to the faith and the conditions among the Hutterian Brethren, and returned to Galicia after a year.

When obstacles were put in the way of Bergthold's staying in Galicia he planned to go to West Prussia. On Nov. 3, 1797, he started out on his journey and visited most of the Prussian churches. Everywhere his bearing and his sermons won him sympathy. Heinrich Donner, the elder at Orlofferfelde, offered him the position of preacher in that church. He accepted and in 1799 moved with his family to Orlofferfelde. Besides preaching he was very active as the corresponding secretary of the *Hauptbibelgesellschaft* in Berlin. "All who knew him," says an obituary, "must truly admit that he was an exceptionally faithful and zealous servant of the Lord, in proclaiming as well as in spreading the saving Word of God" (*Menn. Bl.,* 1867, 29 ff.).

At a time when the various Mennonite groups had no contacts with each other, he, in his capacity of preacher, represented a unique connecting link between the Mennonites of the Palatinate, Galicia, and West Prussia; his equally unusual attempt to make contact with the Hutterian Brethren failed (*ML* I, 166). NEFF.

Bergum, a village in the Dutch province of Friesland. The Mennonites living here, members of the Veenwouden (*q.v.*) congregation, organized a circle (*kring*) on Dec. 19, 1946, but have retained their membership in Veenwouden and attend services there. The circle has 20 members. Since 1947 there has also been a women's circle. vDZ.

Bergzabern, a town of (1944) 4,883 inhabitants in the Palatinate, Germany, foot of the Haardt Mountains, where Hans Denk (*q.v.*), having been banished from Strasbourg, appeared publicly in January 1527 and won considerable influence over the population, especially on Nikolaus Thomae called Sigelspach, the pastor of the church there, who repeatedly expressed Denk's views in letters to Oecolampadius, the Basel reformer, and to Capito and Bucer, the Strasbourg reformers. It was not possible to establish an Anabaptist congregation there; a small circle of Anabaptist-minded men gathered about him for the time being, of whom Sigelspach wrote in 1529 that they were "pious and good men" (Chr. Hege, *Die Täufer in der Kurpfalz,* Frankfurt, 1908, 14). After the Thirty Years' War a number of Swiss Mennonites settled on neighboring estates; they belong to the Deutschhof-Geisberg (*q.v.*) congregation. (*ML* I, 166.) HEGE.

Beringer, Kurt, an Anabaptist(?) from Neunheiligen in Thuringia, Germany, was seized in September 1534 with two companions, a man and a woman, and subjected to a long trial. The "confession" he made there has been published by Paul Wappler in his work, *Die Täuferbewegung in Thüringen von 1526-1584* (Jena, 1913) 361. If this confession is authentic, Beringer was apparently a follower of Thomas Müntzer. The woman who was captured with him is said to have stated that she had been led to the faith by a sermon she had heard Müntzer preach ten years previously at Mühlhausen, whereas Beringer stated that his own spirit had put his faith into him. Finally all three stated that two men from Görmar (near Mühlhausen), one of them called Spann (probably Ludwig Spon, *q.v.*) and the other Moler (Lorenz Moller, *q.v.,* of Görmar), had converted them.

In Beringer's confession he rejects the bodily presence of Christ in the Lord's Supper, and calls infant baptism "nothing but a poor water-bath." Christ died for Himself alone and not for us, and finally "He has no opinion of any Scripture or Gospel except what His Father, rich in mercy, who is in Heaven, has given Him, and has received it from no other than from Jesus Christ, His beloved Son, and through the Holy Ghost."

The Lord's Prayer, which is added, has the form peculiar to the Anabaptists of Thuringia and plays an important role in the court trials. The fourth petition says, "Thy true bread give us, dear Lord: Thy Holy Word is food to our poor soul." Nothing more is known of these Anabaptists. (*ML* I, 166.)

NEFF.

Berislav, city in the Russian province of Kherson, located on the Dnieper River, the center of the region which had been promised by Potemkin to the Mennonites of Danzig in the 1780's for settlement purposes. The land was located on the Konskaya River on the left bank of the Dnieper. Later when a second delegation met Potemkin in Kremenchug in 1789 he informed them that the land was not safe because of the Russo-Turkish war and advised them to settle on the Chortitza River farther north. This change in the settlement became one of the sources of friction between the settlers and the delegates, Höppner and Bartsch (*q.v.*). (D. H. Epp, *Chortitzer Mennoniten,* Rosenthal bei Chortitz, 1889.)

C.K.

Berka, a town on the Werra, in the Eisenach district of Thuringia, Germany, in Reformation times a part of *Amt* Hausbreitenbach (*q.v.*) and the seat of a large Anabaptist congregation. Since Hausbreitenbach was subject to the joint jurisdiction of Saxony and Hesse, which differed in policy on the treatment of Anabaptists, the punishment of Anabaptists was the cause of much controversy between them. Therefore the two councils met in Berka on July 19, 1533, to reach an agreement. They arranged a trial of 18 imprisoned Anabaptists, lasting from July 19 to 21 and sent a comprehensive report, compiled and agreed to by both sides, to their respective rulers. (It is printed in Wappler, *Kursachsen,* 166-76.)

The hearing covered four points: infant baptism, communion, ownership of property, and government. No one, said the Anabaptists, had in the Bible commanded the baptism of infants. They are saved without baptism, since they are by nature pure and by their innocence holy. In the communion they repudiated the bodily presence of Christ; for Christ is in Heaven, whence no man can bring Him down into bread and wine. On the question of possessions, most of them declared that a Christian is obligated to share his goods, since God created all things for the benefit of all human beings. Concerning the government they said that the Christian must be obedient; but he would hardly be able to fill a government office with a clear conscience.

Since the princes of Saxony and Hesse were unable to agree on the punishment, the Anabaptists were released.

On Jan. 7 and 8, 1544, new proceedings were instituted at Berka against the Anabaptists. Sixteen persons were arraigned, of whom seven, including the innkeeper Jobst Isslebe and his wife, openly acknowledged that they had been baptized, and with the exception of Isslebe, who recanted, persisted in their faith; the other nine agreed to remain with the established church and the sacra-

ments. (See the report of these proceedings in Wappler, 216-19.)

Justus Menius (*q.v.*), one of the Lutheran examiners, recommended the death penalty, and won the Elector of Saxony over to his position; but Philip of Hesse did not consent, and the Anabaptists were consequently released. Nothing is known of their subsequent fate.

NEFF.

P. Wappler, *Die Stellung Kursachsens und des Landgrafen Philipp von Hessen zur Täuferbewegung* (Münster, 1910); *ML* I, 167.

Berks County in eastern Pennsylvania, lying between the counties Lancaster on the west, Chester and Montgomery on the south, and Lehigh on the east, is the home of the earliest Amish Mennonite settlements in America, established between Mennonite settlements on three sides.

By 1714 the Yoders from Switzerland had settled in Oley Valley near Pleasantville as the first Amish to settle in America, followed in 1732 and 1737 by the Kauffmans, Fishers, and Beilers. Today there is a flourishing Mennonite church of the Ohio and Eastern A.M. Conference in this area, largely composed of descendants of the early Amish pioneers of this region.

By 1740 the Amish had developed into their first organized congregation in the vicinity of Hamburg and by 1749 they had received their first pastor and leader from Switzerland, Bishop Jacob Hertzler (1703-86), who had been ordained in Switzerland. The congregation was known as Northkill, having derived the name from a creek and a fort built of palisades in that community. In the assaults made (1754-64) by the Delaware Indians in their desperate effort to reclaim the land, some of the Amish fell victim to the tomahawk in 1757. As a result most of the Amish from this area at the foot of the Blue Mountains moved to other parts of the county and province, and the Northkill congregation died out.

They organized congregations at the following places: Maiden Creek near Shillington, now extinct; Tulpehocken near Womelsdorf, now extinct; and a third in the very southern tip of the county in 1760, which became the first permanent Amish congregation in America and is known as the Conestoga Mennonite Church, a member of the Ohio and Eastern A.M. Mennonite Conference. This congregation has founded three other congregations in recent years—the Rock in Caernarvon Township, Zion near Gibraltar, and Oley near Friedensburg.

Refugees from the Northkill congregation had also founded and organized congregations beyond the borders of Berks County. Families by the name of Zug, Lapp, Fisher, and Kauffman founded a flourishing colony near Malvern in Chester County, building the first Amish meetinghouse in America. The church became extinct in 1832, when most of the members moved westward into Lancaster County. Permanent settlements were founded by emigrants from Northkill, Maiden Creek, and Tulpehocken into Somerset and Mifflin counties. One colony was established in Lost Creek

Valley, Juniata County, but it became extinct about 60 years ago.

The first Mennonite meetinghouse in Berks County, known as Hereford (*q.v.*), was built about 1732 in Colebrookdale Township, in the southeastern corner of the county, where the earliest warrants for land were taken out 1720-30 by Stauffers, Beidlers, Wistars, Bechtels, Molls, and Latshaws. At Bally, four miles from Hereford, in Washington Township, near the present site of Boyertown, another meetinghouse was built between 1772 and 1780. Both congregations are active today, and members of the Franconia Mennonite Conference. A General Conference congregation was organized at Hereford in 1848.

Some early Mennonites, comprising at least seven families who had settled in the vicinity of Sinking Springs and Womelsdorf in 1736 upon arrival from Switzerland, never had a pastor of their own. In several instances they had connections by marriage with the Zimmermans in Cocalico Township, Lancaster County. A family burial plot is still in existence with names of Ruchty and Deppen inscribed upon the tombstones. The descendants are now members of the Lutheran or Reformed churches.

A Lancaster Conference mission congregation and a Girls' Home were established in Reading in the late 1920's. The Girls' Home no longer exists, but the original mission has grown into three: Reading Mission established 1922, now with 39 members; Fairview St. Mission established 1932, now 18 members; Seventh St. Mission (colored) established 1938, now with 2 members. C.Z.M.

Berlikum, a village in the Dutch province of Friesland, in existence since 1100, ten miles northwest of Leeuwarden. Centuries ago it was on the shore of the sea (Middelzee) which extended from the north into Friesland. Some peculiar, antique gables indicate the passing of centuries since their building. Now the village, originally a fishing village, is located two hours from the sea and is inhabited by industrious gardeners. Most of the land is owned by nonresidents, and is rented at a high price. With the small size of the fields and the high rate of rent, the inhabitants can, of course, not be very prosperous.

The members of the Mennonite congregation are also, for the most part, gardeners and not well-to-do. The church originated in the 16th century. There are no written records to give information on its history. Leenaert Bouwens baptized no fewer than 255 persons here between 1551 and 1582. In 1695 the membership was about 50. There is only an old account book of 1759 in the archives. Until 1900 there was an old building in the village called the "Oude Vermaning" (old Mennonite meetinghouse). Since the church has very little capital, the A.D.S. and the Friesian Sociëteit give it financial support. After having a vacant pulpit for nearly a half century, it was nearly extinct in 1838, the membership having dropped to 12. Then S. Blaupot ten Cate (*q.v.*) wrote a letter to several congregations asking for contributions "to make the re-establishment of the Berlikum congregation

possible" (*Inv. Arch. Amst.* II, No. 1541), with the result that the congregation again had a preacher in 1839: Sine Hiddes van der Goot, 1839-71. He was followed by I. Molenaar, 1873-74; W. C. Schiff, 1876-77; H. Koekebakker, Jr., 1878-81; R. Kuperus, 1882-84; then after a long vacancy I. Reinders, 1897-1937; E. H. Boer, 1938-41; G. Kater, 1941-46; and since 1946 Miss S. E. Treffers. The present church building dates from 1841.

The membership increased from 12 in 1838 to 67 in 1861, 52 in 1898, and 143 in 1950. The congregation has a Sunday school, a young people's organization, and a women's circle. It is a member of Ring Dantumawoude. L.R., vDZ.

Blaupot t. C., *Friesland,* 88, 189, 206, 246, 247, 306; DB 1872, 189; 1882, 126; *ML* I, 167.

Berlin (Ont.), until 1915 the name of the present city of Kitchener (*q.v.*), the center of the large Mennonite settlement in Waterloo Co., Ont.

Berlin Mennonite Church (MC), Berlin, Ohio, began in 1917 as a mission station or branch of the Martins Creek Church to afford a place of worship for members who did not have transportation to attend the services at Martins Creek during the winter. The Martins Creek congregation purchased a store and apartment house in 1917 and converted it into a church. The first meeting was held in March 1918, in the face of bitter opposition from the people of the community on account of the conscientious objector position of the members. In 1934 a minor division occurred when Earl Miller withdrew with eight or ten members to organize an independent congregation. In 1940 spring and fall communion services were conducted in the Berlin Church for the first time. In 1944 the group was organized as a separate congregation under the Ohio and Eastern A.M. Conference with Simon W. Sommer pastor and D. D. Miller of Martins Creek bishop. The 1953 membership was 157. J.S.U.

Berlin, the former capital of Germany, seat of a Mennonite congregation since 1887. On Oct. 2, 1884, representatives of many Mennonite churches from various parts of Germany met in Hotel Schmidt (*zur Stadtbahn*); this meeting led to the founding in 1886 of the *Vereinigung der Mennoniten-Gemeinden im Deutschen Reich* (*q.v.*). At that time the Mennonites living in Berlin were invited to meet in the hotel, where H. G. Mannhardt, minister of the Danzig congregation, urged them to form a union to prevent their being lost to the church. This gave rise to the *Vereinigung der Berliner Mennoniten,* which at first arranged for social meetings to discuss Mennonite affairs and then through voluntary contributions made it possible for the Berlin Mennonites to have occasional services.

The first service of worship was held on Jan. 16, 1886, in the City Hotel on Dresden Street, where H. van der Smissen, minister of the Hamburg-Altona church, preached on Eph. 2:20-22. But since the use of a hotel room soon created some difficulties, subsequent services were held in the church of the Moravian Brethren. On Jan. 17, 1887, 12 members of the *Vereinigung* with their families met and chose as their board Willy Molenaar, Hermann Wiens, Rudolph Goerke, Gustav Woelcke, and Isaak Brons. The carefully weighed rules were set up in general on the pattern of the constitution of the Danzig church. Male members who paid a fee of at least five marks were entitled to vote at the business meetings, held biannually. The board, which is elected for five years, chooses a chairman, who grants certificates and keeps the books, a secretary, who keeps the records of their monthly meetings, and a treasurer.

Since the congregation did not have adequate funds to employ a preacher, preachers from other churches came on a regular schedule to conduct eleven Sunday services per year in the church of the Moravian Brethren, Wilhelmstrasse 136. The first were H. van der Smissen (Altona), H. G. Mannhardt (Danzig), C. Harder (Elbing), E. Weydmann (Crefeld), J. P. Müller (Emden). After the death of the last three, they were succeeded by A. Siebert (Elbing), G. Kraemer (Crefeld), J. G. Appeldoorn (Emden), and Christian Neff (Weierhof). Baptism and communion were usually administered by van der Smissen and Mannhardt. Since the regular offerings of the members did not suffice to assure these regular services the *Vereinigung der Mennoniten-Gemeinden im Deutschen Reich* contributed 500 marks annually. The Berlin church did not have corporation rights. At first it used the hymnal of the West Prussian churches, but in May 1908 decided to use the new one published by the Danzig church. The church grew steadily. In 1893 it had 80 members; in 1902, 147; in 1910, 248; in 1914, 279. In January 1912 it celebrated its 25th anniversary.   E.H.

In the quarter century 1912-37 World War I and the inflation struck serious wounds in the Berlin congregation, eleven of its members falling in the tragic war. A large new influx of members arrived from the country, especially from the East, from Holland, and many from Russia. And in the city, a city-born generation grew up. Chairmen were Molenaar to 1907, Goerke to 1925, Ernst Harder to 1927, Willy Pauls to 1930, Ernst Crous to 1946. The latter, living in Göttingen, continued the spiritual oversight until 1951. In 1927 the congregation instituted an agency for the care of its youth, in 1929 an organized provision for its poor, in 1934 regular baptismal instruction. In 1931, the year of the great depression, the congregation began to provide for its own services for Christmas, and later also on Good Friday, Easter, and Pentecost; in 1933 a children's celebration was inaugurated for the first Sunday of Advent. In 1935 the first missionary conference took place.

Use was made of theological students in providing preaching services. In 1936 Horst Quiring was engaged as part-time pastor, continuing in this office until he was inducted into military service in 1939, resigning after his return from Russian imprisonment (1947). In lectures and in discussion groups current church matters were discussed.

For some years valuable initiative was furnished by Johannes van Riesen; he later left the congregation, since it was apparently not willing to follow him in every respect. For nine years, 1933-41, it was possible to publish a news leaflet two to four times a year, which kept the members informed on events of the time and also placed historical material at their disposal.

The first half of the third quarter-century was again extremely unsettled. World War II and the currency reform struck wounds again. The minister was called to military service, leaving the congregation to look after itself once more. Connections with the outside remained lively. As representative of the Mennonite Central Committee, M. C. Lehman arrived in 1939; from South Russia some young Mennonite women came to Berlin in 1942; from Holland several Mennonite students came in 1943 to work in the factories. The congregation took an interest in them to the extent of its abilities. The losses on the battlefield and through air attacks within the city mounted. The aged and children were evacuated; men capable of military service were called to the colors. With difficulty the work of the church was carried forward. The chairman of the board (Crous) was transferred to Göttingen in 1944 and was able to come to Berlin only every alternate month; the assistant chairman, Heinrich van Dühren, fell in 1945 in the defense of Berlin. The congregation was threatened with disintegration. Erich Schultz, member of the board since 1944, chairman since 1946, elder since 1949, collected the congregation and gathered in the refugees from the East Zone. The congregation grew to twice its peacetime membership, reaching nearly 1,000 in 1950; several persons from other creeds joined. The congregation has opened its own branch of relief work, and instruction and care of the youth have again been instituted. Since 1947 baptismal and communion services have been held annually, with numerous guests from the East Zone, by Elder Crous.

Since December 1946 the Mennonite Central Committee has had a representative in Berlin, and carried on a program of relief and refugee aid, in co-operation with the Berlin congregation. Ringstrasse 107 was the headquarters and refugee aid center, and it was from here in January 1947 that the notable exodus of over 1,000 Russian Mennonite refugees to Paraguay took place. From here also a package distribution to East Zone Mennonite refugees from Russia and the Danzig area was carried on. Berlin became an important reception and transit point for refugees fleeing from the East en route to Western Germany and overseas. In late 1949 an MCC Nachbarschaftsheim (*q.v.*) was established in the Kreuzberg area at Urbanstrasse 21, which was transferred to Berlin-Lichterfelde-Ost, Promenadenstrasse 15b, in the spring of 1952, when the Ringstrasse center was closed. The new center, now called Mennoheim, also serves the MCC as its refugee aid center, as well as the Berlin congregation as an activity center. The headquarters of CRALOG (Council of Relief Agencies Licensed for Operation in Germany), the channel by which MCC relief supplies were forwarded to Germany, was established in Berlin in March 1946 and continued there until removed to Bremen in the winter of 1950-51. The MCC representative on CRALOG headquarters staff was located in Berlin from the fall of 1946 to the fall of 1947. The continuous presence of the MCC staff in Berlin since the fall of 1946, and the uninterrupted operation of MCC relief, refugee, and neighborhood center work, has been of considerable benefit for the Berlin congregation as an outpost of Mennonitism in the East as well as upon the Mennonites continuing to reside in the East Zone.   E.C.

E. Harder, *Festschrift zur Feier des 25jährigen Bestehens der Berliner Menn.-Gem.* (Berlin, 1912); Ernst Crous, "Karl and Ernst Harder, Ein Nachruf" (Elbing, 1927, from *Menn. Bl.*); Ernst Crous, "Berlin-Göttingen, Erinnerungen an ein bewegtes Jahrzehnt," in *GB1.*, 1949, 31 f.; *Der Mennonit* II (1949) 20; *Berliner Mennoniten-Gemeinde Mitteilungsblatt*, 1937, and *Menn. Bl.* LXXXIV (1937) 13 f.; announcements and annual reports in *Menn. Bl.*, 1928-38; *ML* I, 168.

Bern, in area the second largest canton of Switzerland, and in population (798,294 in 1950) the largest. In the very earliest period Anabaptism obtained a foothold in Bern and has maintained itself to the present in spite of severe persecution. The original home of many of the Mennonite families of South Germany and in turn many families who emigrated to America both in the 18th and 19th centuries is in the Emmental area of Bern. During the Middle Ages Waldenses were found in Bern. In 1399, for example, 130 persons of Waldensian "unbelief" were living in this area. It is possible that they prepared the soil for the rise of Anabaptism; but there is no direct connection.

I. *Beginnings of Anabaptism in Bern.* It is evident from a letter written by Bullinger to Heinrich Simler in Bern that Anabaptists were there already in 1525. Berchtold Haller wrote of the rapid spread of Anabaptism in Bern in his letter to Zwingli dated Nov. 29, 1525. On Jan. 13, 1526, the city council took up the case of a woman who had been rebaptized at Zofingen. And Jakob Gross (*q.v.*) of Waldshut was arrested for Anabaptism in Brugg.

There was much correspondence between the Zürich and Bern reformers on the subject of Anabaptism. In general Haller was a disciple of Zwingli but differed with him on the matter of the persecution of the Anabaptists. Haller felt that the occasion for the spread of Anabaptism was to be found in the low moral and spiritual condition of the masses, and he could not bring himself to favor the death penalty for Anabaptists. Officially the Protestant Reformation was inaugurated in Bern by a mandate dated Feb. 7, 1528. The attempt was made to reform by law. The following regulations are of April 21, 1529: If a man curses he shall throw himself down and kiss the ground, and if anyone refuses to do this, he shall pay a fine of a pound or go to jail. Drinking to one's health was to be punished by a fine of a pound; drunkenness by a day's imprisonment. All gambling was proscribed whether by cards, dice, or otherwise. No dancing on communion days. Irregular customs at weddings shall cease (de Quervain, p. 114). As a whole these regulations accomplished little. Enforcement was lax, and sin persisted in high and low places. In contrast with this, the Anabaptists lived an earnest Christian life, seeking to follow Christ faithfully as His disciples. This manner of life was effective in winning converts to Anabaptism, especially in the rural areas. To stop this the government soon turned to such severe measures as imprisonment and capital punishment.

In 1527 eight Anabaptists came from Basel to Bern. A copy of a confession of faith was taken from them, which Haller sent to Zwingli with the request that he refute it. This was the Schleitheim Confession (*q.v.*), and Zwingli's attempted refutation is found in his *Elenchus*. Six of the eight arrivals were convinced of the errors of Anabaptism, but two remained firm, Hans Hansmann, a treasurer from Basel, and Jakob Hochrüttiner, son of Lorenz Hochrüttiner (*q.v.*), who were then banished.

II. *The First Anabaptist Mandates.* On Aug. 14, 1527, the cantons of Bern, Zürich, and St. Gall issued a combined mandate ordering that the Anabaptists be admonished to desist from the vice (*Laster*) of Anabaptism; those from abroad who disobey shall be banished; if they do not obey this order they shall be drowned. A resident shall be given a double fine if he reverts to Anabaptism. Ministers and those escaping from prison shall be drowned. Since many innocent persons have been misled, the punishments may be lessened on occasion.

The above mandate remained in force until July 31, 1531, when a new one was written. This 1531 mandate required the populace to attend divine services each Sunday in the recognized church of the city or of the near-by village. Each citizen shall receive communion from a regular pastor. Warnings shall follow disobedience, and then banishment on oath or equivalent vow. A second banishment was provided for offenders, but the penalty for a second return was drowning. Those who gave up Anabaptism following banishment were to be received with open hand.

Eight Anabaptists appeared at the great disputation held at Bern Jan. 7-26, 1528, which disputation resulted in the introduction of the Protestant Reformation. The eight were George Blaurock of Chur, Hans Hansmann of Basel, Hans Pfistermeyer and Heini Seiler of Aarau, Ulrich Isler of Bitsch, imprisoned at Basel, Hans Töblinger of Freiburg in Uechtland, Thomas Maler of Mörstadt in the Palatinate, and Vincenz Späting, member of the great senate of Bern. These eight were not admitted to the sessions, however, but were kept in prison and watched carefully. Finally on the 17th day of the disputation they were taken to the city hall where Zwingli interviewed them. Only Späting was persuaded to recant. The others were banished under threat of drowning if they returned.

On May 24, 1529, the first Anabaptist trial was held in Bern. The government representatives were Judge Crispinus Vischer, pastors Berchtold Haller and Caspar Grossmann, and Diebolt von Erlach. The Anabaptists were Heinrich Seiler and wife of Aarau; Veit Oettli of Rheinfelden and his

KEY

Underlined cities : seats of current congregations.

In parenthesis: alternate name for the congregation above.

FRANCE

GERMANY

ZÜRICH

Belfort

Altkirch

Héricourt

Holee

Riehen

Rheinfelden

BASELLAND

Montbéliard

Binningen

BASEL

Muttenz

Brugg

Delle

Schänzli

Liestal

Küttigen

Audincourt

Bonfol

Bubendorf

Lenzburg

Porrentruy

Alle

Laufen

AARAU

Gränichen

Courgenay

Le Mont

Waldenburg

OLTEN

Seon

Lucelle

Terri

Delemont

Aarburg

Bremgarten

St. Ursanne

Bassecourt

Zofingen

Beinwil

St. Hippolyte

Moutier

SOLOTHURN

SOLOTHURN

Roggwil

Langenthal

Boswil

Maïche

Saignelégier

Court

Herzogenbuchsee

Jeangisboden

Moron

Tavannes

Rohrbach

Huttwil

(Sonnenberg)

Tramelan

Cortebert

Büren

Durrenroth

LeNoirmont

Corgemont

Lengnau

Wynigen

Courtelary

Chaux d' Abel (2)

St-Imier

Burgdorf

Wasen

LA CHAUX-DE-FONDS

Biel

Sumiswald

(Bulles)

Lyss

Münchenbuchsee

Trachselwald

Dombresson

Aarberg

Lützelflüh

LUZERN

Zollikofen

Boudry

Lauperswil

Langnau

Trub

BERN

Worb

Signau

Laupen

Köniz

Zaziwil

Neuenegg

Belp

Eggiwil

UNTERWALDEN

Münsingen

FRIBOURG

Wahlern

Oberdiessbach

Schangnau

Schwarzenburg

Heimberg

Steffisburg

THUN

Guggisberg

Sigriswil

Beatenberg

Spiez

Erlenbach

Wimmis

Interlaken

Niesen

Reichenbach

Grindelwald

Frutigen

Kienthal

Zweisimmen

Kandersteg

Adelboden

VAUD

VALAIS

Genève

Canton Bern

SWITZERLAND

Scale of Miles

0   10   20

Basel

BERN

Bern

SWITZERLAND

Geneva

wife Vrena Meyer; Barbli with the wooden leg; and Margareta N. of Sigriswyl. The final sentence for them all was that unless they recanted they should be banished under threat of drowning if they returned.

In spite of various executions the Anabaptist movement spread. (See de Quervain, 125-29.) The senate decided to hold a disputation in an attempt to persuade the Anabaptists to return to the church. The Zofingen disputation (q.v.) took place July 1-9, 1532, with 23 Anabaptists present. The government had the minutes of the disputation printed in booklet form in the hope that this would help suppress Anabaptism. But it had the opposite effect; the Brethren were more active than ever, especially in Sumiswald and Dürrenroth. Consequently the government had to issue fresh orders to deal with the Anabaptists. Those who began to preach were to be imprisoned without mercy.

On March 2, 1533, the Bernese senate issued another mandate, lamenting the continued spread of the Anabaptists, and calling upon them to receive instruction from the official clergy. If they refused to hear the clergy, they were at least to keep quiet and keep their faith to themselves. If they did so, they would be under the care and protection of the government. But if they refused, they would be imprisoned and fed on the income from their property as long as it lasted; thereafter the government would feed them on bread and water until they died or recanted. On April 4, 1533, however, the government began to demand of those who applied for protection that they obey the mandates, that they go to the state church services every Sunday, and that they have their children baptized.

On Nov. 8, 1534, another sharp mandate appeared against "the Anabaptists and the papists." Three times each year, said the mandate, the communion service will be held. Anyone who does not attend for conscience' sake shall report to the pastor or elder. Pastors shall perform all marriages. Those who cannot subscribe to these regulations by oath shall leave the country at once. An appendix was added to this mandate on March 13, 1535, providing that Anabaptists and papists should be imprisoned for eight days in Bern to give them opportunity to consider taking the oath. If they refused, they were to be led to the frontier and threatened with execution if they ever returned, the men with the sword, the women by drowning.

Nevertheless Anabaptism continued to grow. The constable (Weibel) of the Emmental was paid six pounds for locating Anabaptists; in Trachselwald the constable got two pounds, and in Signau eight pounds for "hunting" (jagen) Anabaptists. It was reported that there were 300 Anabaptists in Rued.

III. Executions. The Bernese government spared no means to root out Anabaptism. The Martyrs' Mirror contains a list of 40 Anabaptist executions in Bern (pp. 1129, 1130). Recent research has demonstrated the reliability of this list (Fluri: Berner Heim, 1896; de Quervain, 150-58), which had been questioned by Ernst Müller (Berner Täufer). (See Neff's list of Bernese martyrs, ML I,

171.) Executions were not the only means of coping with the Swiss Brethren, however; the government also employed severe fines, total confiscation of property, long imprisonments, fearful torture, and banishment from the country. The occasion for these extreme measures was not fear of riot or revolution—that is not mentioned. It was rather zeal for the unity of the church. Pastor George Thorman of Lützelflüh describes the Swiss Brethren in his Probierstein . . . des Täufertums (Bern, 1693). He reports that the Anabaptists do not attend the state church services because of the many sinners in the church; they will not participate in the communion services of the state church; they set up their own church; do not baptize their children; refuse all oaths; desist from litigation; do not participate in war; accept no governmental offices; wear no lace collars or ornamentation, which they regard as a sign of pride; speak slowly and sing softly; shun taverns, and baptism and marriage celebrations; go to market but little, and do not trade and barter much . . . . Indeed Thorman upholds the Anabaptists as models of piety and conduct for his own Reformed people to follow.

The Bernese Swiss Brethren were simple believers who accepted the Bible at its face value, although they placed the New Testament above the Old. They held that the true church is separate from the world, and that those who live in sin are to be excluded from the church. Christians must live lives of penitence. No compulsion may be employed in matters of faith. Christians make no use of the police. The church has the right to choose its ministers by voting and the use of the lot, and to ordain them. The model which they strove to follow was the apostolic church, a free church not allied with the state but made up of personal followers of Jesus. The Bernese government, on the other hand, was determined to maintain control over the religious faith and life of its subjects, regulating everything so as to effect the unity of the church and the salvation of the masses. This was the basic reason for compulsory infant baptism, oaths, the emphasis on the sacredness of the state offices, and finally for the persecution of the Anabaptists. Hence the reason for the oppressive measures taken against the Anabaptists was religious, not political.

IV. Disputation and New Mandates. A great disputation between the Reformed and the Anabaptists was held in Bern in March 1538. Many of the participants from the latter group bore names which are still common among the Mennonites: Vogt, Neuenschwander, Salzmann, Aberli, Sutter, Gerber, Hunziker, Schneider (full list, ML I, 172 f.). Thereafter the Anabaptists from outside Bern were to be conducted to the border and threatened with death if they ever returned. A particularly sharp mandate is dated Sept. 6, 1538. In view of the continued increase of the Anabaptists, the elders, preachers, teachers, readers, and ringleaders shall be executed with the sword without mercy. Those in prison who refuse obedience shall be asked "with the rope" (this of men only however, not women). On Nov. 28, 1541, the

Bernese senate was again struggling with the Anabaptist question. A certain magistrate named Hans Franz Nägeli made a lengthy address in which he set forth the major causes for the spread of Anabaptism, namely, the religious indifference of the masses, the unbecoming and stupid conduct of the pastors, and especially the disunity of the church on the doctrine of the Lord's Supper. That very day the senate mitigated the severity of the mandate then in force. Steps were provided for restoration to fellowship in the state church; those who refused were to be punished as thought best.

No new mandates appeared until Feb. 16, 1564, when it was announced that the regulations should be more strictly enforced in the Emmental. A decree was to be read from the pulpits of the districts of Signau, Trachselwald, and Brandis, proclaiming a fine of ten pounds for holding to Anabaptism, and if it was not given up punishment in goods and body would follow. Two years later severer measures were provided by the regulation of April 28, 1566. Anabaptism was punishable by banishment, and those who violated the oath were to be put to death. The citizens were registered, house by house, and were ordered to the church where they had to answer one by one whether they would be obedient to the government. Those who said yes were turned to the right; those refusing, to the left, where the oath of banishment was read to them.

On Dec. 30, 1579, another mandate was issued, threatening further imprisonment and even death for Anabaptists. The public was called on to aid the authorities in the apprehension of the Brethren. Nevertheless the program of persecution failed. Therefore the government decided to appeal to the clergy of the state church for counsel (Blösch I, 306). They advised to cease invoking capital punishment because martyrdom tended to make a favorable impression upon the common people, resulting in the increase rather than the decrease of the sect. The clergy therefore recommended that the preachers or ringleaders should be sentenced to the galleys or condemned to life imprisonment, where they would be supported by the confiscation of Anabaptist property. Stubborn Anabaptists who were not preachers should be banished. The state church clergy also recognized the moral turpitude in their own members and made suggestions as to how to remedy the situation. The date of the recommendations of the clergy was Sept. 3, 1585. The mandate which was then issued first called for improvement in the lives of the members of the state church. The citizens should keep watch for those who do not have their children baptized, and who do not attend the services of the church, and admonish them. If they have no success they shall report them to the authorities. They in turn shall lead the unrepentant to the border; if any return unconverted they shall be punished "in goods and body." Those who associate with the disobedient but are not members of the sect may accompany them out of the country but may not take along their property. Banished preachers who return shall be put to death. He who makes a house or

barn available for Anabaptist meetings shall be fined 100 Bernese pounds (see Blösch I, 107).

The Swiss Brethren submitted a memorandum to the Bernese government on Dec. 18, 1585, containing the following points: (1) The Brethren have the true faith and do not belong to any sect. They desire the Holy Spirit to be their judge. (2) The mandate which has been issued against them is contrary to the mandate of Christ and His Gospel, because no one shall use force upon another person in matters of faith. (3) They want to be obedient to the government as far as their conscience allows; but they want to leave to others the matter of fighting for their fatherland. (4) They reject infant baptism, but not without reason. (5) According to the institution of God they hold to marriage, the ban, and the Lord's Supper, just as Christ commanded, and request that they be allowed to hold to their faith.

Another sharp mandate appeared July 29, 1597, calling attention to the poor attendance at church services, and the declining participation in the Lord's Supper. Civil authorities were called upon to support the clergy in raising the moral level of the clergy. This mandate was issued because of the complaints of the Anabaptists against the clergy for their immoral life.

The persecution of the Anabaptists in Bern led many to emigrate to Moravia in search of peace. This led to a mandate dated April 15, 1592, calling upon the Bernese officials to imprison the Moravian emissaries. The property of those who left Bern was to fall to the government. On April 3, 1610, the senate felt compelled to try to stop the secret exodus to Moravia. On March 6, 1690, the children of Anabaptist marriages which had not been solemnized by the state clergy were declared ineligible to inherit anything from their parents; the estate was to go to the government.

Another measure adopted to suppress Anabaptism was the office of censor. In 1691, for example, a New Testament which the Anabaptists had had published in Basel was confiscated because it was a "falsified and dangerous translation." On Sept. 30, 1692, another mandate reported that a number of Anabaptist books were in circulation, such as one called the *Ausbund,* another, *Confessio* by Thomas Imbroich, and a third, the confession of faith of the Dutch Mennonites (probably the German translation of 1664 or 1691 of the Dordrecht Confession of 1632). The mandate also supposed that a book by Burghausen of Lauperswil, *Wahrhaftige Erscheinung des Engel Gottes* (1562) was an Anabaptist book (it is today unknown).

On Oct. 26, 1641, a mandate called for a stricter enforcement of the law; "looking through the fingers" was to cease. On April 11, 1644, the senate called for the arrest of several Anabaptist preachers by name. The mandate of Dec. 26, 1644, set forth the policy of arresting, imprisoning, and teaching the Anabaptists. Those not accepting instruction were to follow the old mandates: be conducted to the border and made to vow (not swear) never to return under threat of death.

V. *Establishment of the Anabaptist Commission.*

After the Bernese Peasants' War, in which the Anabaptists took absolutely no part, Anabaptism spread rapidly. At a meeting of clergy on May 16, 1654, complaints were made about this spread. On June 6 orders were issued to all officials to ascertain in secret what Anabaptists could be apprehended, who they were, and the names of their preachers and where they lived; they should then report back without delay. The authorities decided to build a penal building or "orphans' house" in Bern to serve as a prison for the Anabaptists. The first victims were imprisoned here on June 27, 1657, before the building was entirely completed. Orders were issued on Dec. 20, 1658, to the officials of Thun, Burgdorf, Langental, and Brugg to arrest the Anabaptist preachers and bring them to Bern to be imprisoned in the orphans' house. The Anabaptist Commission was set up on Feb. 10, 1659. Among the charges listed against the Anabaptists in that year are the following: (1) They preach without the authorization of the government. (2) They baptize without governmental authorization. (3) They exercise church discipline contrary to the statutes of the government. (4) They do not attend the services which are held on Sundays and days of prayer (in the state church).

The mandate of Aug. 9, 1659, was another effort to get all the people lined up for the state church. All officials, state and ecclesiastical, were called upon to live the right kind of life. The government officials were called upon to find and arrest the Anabaptist preachers in valleys, mountains, forests, and desolate places and deliver them up. The clergy were asked to make a house-to-house investigation twice a year to ascertain by name who was and who was not attending the services of the state church and receiving the holy sacraments. A distinction was made between preachers or those who lead astray, and the followers or those who are misled. The leaders were to be brought to the orphans' house at Bern at once, and their goods confiscated. Those not accepting instruction were to be conducted to the border and made to vow that they would never return. If they broke their vow they were to be publicly beaten with rods and again conducted to the border.

VI. *Dutch Intervention.* At this point the Dutch Mennonites made an effort to help their persecuted brethren in Bern. On Oct. 24, 1659, Hans Vlamingh (*q.v.*) of Amsterdam wrote a comprehensive letter to Christoph Lüthard, professor of theology in Bern and a member of the Anabaptist Commission, reporting that he had received letters from the Palatinate, from Alsace, and from other places informing him that the Bernese government had imprisoned eight Mennonites whom he did not hesitate to call brethren. It was also reported, wrote Vlamingh, that these people were not imprisoned for their faith but for disobedience to the government, for assuming the pastoral office by their own will, for holding church services at night, etc. But the charges cannot be sustained, declared Vlamingh. If they choose their ministers and deacons they do so in conformity with the Scriptures. They hold their services at night simply because they are not allowed to hold them by day. And they must obey God rather than men in these matters. Furthermore the Reformed Church in Holland has shed its blood for the principle of freedom of conscience; it is therefore not right to persecute these humble believers in Switzerland. The Mennonites and the Reformed are agreed on the major points of the faith: their difference relates to the swearing of oaths, to the waging of war, and to infant baptism. The first point the Mennonites hold to is simple obedience to Matthew 5, and they keep their Yea as well as others do their oaths. Although they do not go to war they are obedient to their government otherwise. In not baptizing infants they are simply following the New Testament which gives no command or example of infant baptism. Why should anyone persecute such harmless followers of Jesus?

Vlamingh wrote a similar letter to Wilhelm von Diessbach, chairman of the Anabaptist Commission. At the same time Abraham Heidanus, professor of theology in Leiden, at the request of the Dutch Mennonites also wrote a letter to Prof. Lüthard, pleading that the Swiss Mennonites should not be martyred. Also the pastors and elders of the Walloon Church in Amsterdam wrote to their Reformed friends in Bern on Feb. 29, 1660, requesting them to intervene on behalf of the Mennonites with the government of Bern, to stop confiscating their property, etc.

On June 11, 1660, a man named Adolph de Vreede delivered in person a number of letters of intercession to the government in Bern, written by the burgomaster of Amsterdam, by the city of Rotterdam, and by the Dutch States-General (*Mart. Mir.* D 830 ff., E 1132 ff.). De Vreede also submitted six other documents, namely, (1) the decree of Jan. 26, 1577, in which Middelburg granted the Mennonites exemption from the oath; (2) the decree of William of Orange, dated July 16, 1570, granting the Mennonites certain civil liberties; (3) a confirmation of this edict by Maurice of Orange, March 4, 1593; (4) a rebuke given the city of Aardenburg for not giving the Mennonites full religious liberty, May 1, 1615; (5) a repetition of this order, Nov. 16, 1619; (6) a decree from the States-General validating marriages performed by Mennonites as had been the custom for 60 years.

As a whole the intercession was a failure. Bern replied on June 15, 1660, explaining its obligation to maintain the evangelical Reformed faith pure and clear, justifying its efforts to rid the country of its stubborn and unconverted people, etc.

VII. *Banishment from the Country.* Bern at once began to take further measures to cleanse its land of this Anabaptist "weed." De Vreede, however, was given permission to visit the Mennonite prisoners in the orphans' house; but he did not go alone—the Anabaptist Commission accompanied him. He offended both the Commission and the government by his fraternal attitude and by his remarks. On Aug. 27, 1660, since the Mennonites in the orphans' house were still determined to cling to their faith, they were put into a boat, taken to Brugg, and on to the border, whence they were undoubtedly sent to Holland. Bern not only expelled Mennonite leaders from the canton, but made it impossible for them to take along what possessions they had. The Dutch States-General appealed to the Bernese government on this point. On Sept. 10, 1668, a third letter followed in behalf of Swiss refugees. On Dec. 31 Bern replied, rejecting the appeal and stating that the Bernese Mennonites were not to be compared with the Dutch Mennonites. In contrast with the rich Dutch Mennonites, the Swiss Mennonites were poor, tax-free people who refused to take up arms in defense of the fatherland.

All efforts of the Dutch Mennonites and of the Dutch government to help the Swiss Mennonites were futile. Bern continued its relentless persecution. The high point of the oppression was reached in 1671 when the Mennonites were sought out, brought to Bern, and imprisoned there. The ministers were flogged, branded on the back, and sent over the border. The mandate of Sept. 8, 1670, provided for taking the Mennonites from their homes, and notifying them that they had 14 days to get out of the country. Those who did not comply were to be given eight days' time to consider the matter, after which they were to be scourged and led across the border. If anyone returned once, he was to be branded; if he came back a second time, he could expect more severe measures. And these were no idle threats but were carried out fully. Consequently the Bernese prisons were filled with Mennonites. A catalog of the prisoners in the orphans' house on Aug. 31, 1671, reveals that the prisoners there were in three classes: (1) the aged and infirm, 70 or 80 years of age, who were to be kept in jail incommunicado; (2) those who are not yet aged, but who are too poor in health to be sent to the galleys or to be sentenced to other work, who are to be transferred to Tittliger tower; (3) those able physically are to be sent to the galleys at the earliest opportunity. The orphans' house also contained a number of women who held to the Mennonite faith.

VIII. *Emigration to the Palatinate.* Mennonites settled in the Rhenish Palatinate soon after the close of the Thirty Years' War. We learn from a governmental order of the Palatinate, dated July 26, 1651, that there were Mennonites in the country holding secret meetings. Two years later an appeal was sent to Karl Ludwig, the electoral prince, requesting permission to settle in the Palatinate, signed by Hans Mayer and Hans Körber, "together with the Mennonite brethren." In 1653 the Dutch Mennonites also sent aid to their brethren in the Palatinate (Müller, 206). The electoral prince of the Palatinate issued his Mennonite Concession of Aug. 4, 1664, granting limited toleration to the Mennonites whom he allowed to settle in his land. In 1671, the year of climax in persecution in Bern, a steady stream of exiles went down the Rhine to the Palatinate. Jakob Everling of Obersülzen (Palatinate) sent letter after letter to the Dutch Mennonites, reporting the miserable condition of the refugees, arriving as they were with their aged, 70, 80, or 90 years of age, and with

families of children, 8, 10, or 12. On Nov. 2 of that year Everling reported the arrival of almost 700 Bernese Mennonite refugees. On Jan. 1, 1672, Valentine Hüthwohl of Kriegsheim sent to Hans Flamingh a list of all the Mennonites whom he and George Lichti, a preacher formerly of Bern, had been able to register in a four-day journey. The emigration of Bernese Mennonites to the Palatinate continued for many years. Also contacts with the home country of Bern continued. For example, in the years 1762-66 Swiss ministers were called three times to the Palatinate to arbitrate disputes; and when an elder named Jakob Zysset silenced four preachers, an act which led to much dissension in the brotherhood, peace was finally made at Immelhäuserhof near Sinsheim (Baden) in 1782 with the help of the following from Switzerland: Peter Ramseier, Benedict Wälti, Hans Lehmann, Hans Steiner, and David Baumgartner.

The persecution of the Bernese Mennonites meanwhile continued. Fresh mandates were issued in 1691 and 1693. The Bernese government was determined on nothing less than the extermination of Anabaptism, root and branch. Severe measures were taken to assure the removal of the plague of Anabaptism, including threats of the galleys, branding, etc. A mandate of 1695 added that people who were too old to be banished should be imprisoned for life. Additional mandates were issued in 1707, 1708, 1722, and 1729.

IX. *To the Galleys!* In 1616 Bern rejected the galleys as a punishment for the Swiss Brethren, stating this attitude in a letter to Zürich. By 1648, however, Bern was threatening to send a Mennonite named Hans Stentz to the galleys. And on Feb. 25, 1671, Bern finally made the decision to send the "best" Mennonites to the galleys. A dozen Mennonites were confronted with the new policy of galley slavery. Two promised obedience thereafter, and four others promised to quit Bern for good; these were not sent away to the galleys. But six were taken to Italy in the care of a Lieutenant Gerig, where they were put to the oars for a two-year term. Their new masters were kind enough to allow them to wear their beards. In spite of the horror which this severe treatment occasioned in Bern, the government was adamant in continuing the program. In 1714 four more Mennonites were sentenced to the galleys, men 40, 50, even 54 years old. A fifth brother, a preacher from the Palatinate, was also seized on a visit to Bern and received the same sentence. Even the protest of Reformed clergy was of no avail. The protest of the Dutch States-General "on behalf of the Mennonite prisoners and those sold into galley slavery" accomplished more. The Dutch letter was dated June 22, 1714. Bern did not reply until March 27, 1715. Meanwhile the brethren had not yet reached the oars but were being forced to hard labor until spring, when they were to be put on the boats. Strenuous efforts were made by Dutch and Palatine Mennonites as well as non-Mennonite Swiss citizens on their behalf. Indeed a Swiss was actually jailed for his efforts to help the Mennonites, and following his release on the payment of large fines was banished from Bern for life. But the pressure proved too great even for Bern and the government made efforts to have the Brethren released from the galleys. By that time, however, two of them had died. Financial help came from Holland and Crefeld, and even an English archbishop deposited money in a Bernese bank to help in the matter. On Sept. 16, 1715, the three brethren wrote a touching letter of gratitude from Palermo to the brethren in Holland. Once again in 1717 Bern sentenced more Mennonites to galley slavery, but the intervention of the Dutch States-General on this occasion released not only the four sentenced to galley slavery, but the 40 others who had been sentenced to prison. So far as is known, this was the end of galley slavery for the Bernese Mennonites.

X. *A Compulsory Emigration Plan That Failed.* After almost two centuries of struggle with the Bernese Mennonites, the government finally decided to deport the entire group. On May 17, 1699, the senate addressed a letter to the president and directors of the East India Company in Amsterdam informing them of their plan to send the Bernese Mennonites to an East Indian island so that they could not return. Apparently the East India Company did not reply. Meanwhile the Bernese prisons were bulging with ever more Mennonites. A brother from Mannheim managed to slip into a Bernese prison and sent a catalog of the prisoners' names to Amsterdam. A letter of 1709 written by Nicholas Moser to Holland reports the treatment of the Bernese Mennonites. Children were forced to deliver over their parents, and parents the children. A man who hid his Mennonite wife was fined 300 pounds; another who hid his son, 500 pounds. This money went to the "Anabaptist treasury" (*Täufer-Kammer, q.v.*).

Bern next planned to send Mennonites to America. A man named Ritter in Bern who planned to make a trip to America was interested in taking along some poor Bernese families, also some Anabaptists. Bern was prepared to pay him 45 Taler for every Anabaptist he actually got to America. He was to take them to "Carolina." Correspondence was entered into with Great Britain in connection with these plans. All was to be in readiness for the beginning of the journey which was to be made on March 18, 1710. All the necessary passes for the journey down the Rhine had been secured, all except Holland's, that is. And the Dutch were just as firmly decided not to assist in this evil enterprise as the Bernese were determined to carry it out. Bern was told outright that when a man set his foot on Dutch soil he was free. The Bernese ambassador wrote home telling his government how different matters were in Holland from Bern. In Holland, he explained, the Mennonites were influential and beloved. He declared that he would rather fight with all the ministers of the allied powers, England excepted, than with the Mennonites alone. In addition, the States-General addressed a letter to Bern, warmly defending the Mennonites.

Meanwhile the boat with 56 Bernese Mennonites started down the Rhine. Because of sickness and infirmities 32 of them were allowed to disembark at Mannheim. In Nijmegen the remainder left the ship, and turned back to the Palatinate, to Alsace and to Switzerland, to hunt for their wives and children. Travel was difficult for some of them in view of their imprisonment, especially for those whose feet had been in irons during the cold of the previous winter. Nevertheless they were in good spirits. Included in the group were one preacher and two teachers. The men were accustomed to a rough life, wore untrimmed beards, spoke the rough Swiss dialect and understood others with difficulty who did not speak the Swiss. They preferred to sleep on straw, rather than on beds, and since many of them had for a year or two eaten only bread and water, they were not able to eat meat and stronger foods. They desired nothing else than to get back to Mannheim in the Palatinate as soon as possible. They stayed in Cleve over the week end, and one of them preached. The Dutch Mennonites aided them liberally, sending them 1,200 guilders on May 2, 1710.

XI. *Second Major Emigration of the Bernese Mennonites.* The attempt to deport Bernese Mennonites to America evoked repercussions in Bern. The Dutch Mennonites indeed spared no efforts to help the Bernese Mennonites. In vain did the Dutch appeal to the queen of England for help; they also appealed to the English Baptists (Müller, 287). A deputation of eight influential Dutch Mennonites accompanied by four Swiss Mennonites went to The Hague to ask the States-General to renew their efforts on behalf of the Mennonites of Bern. The Bernese ambassador, Saphorin, did all he could to hinder their work, repeatedly calling attention to the refusal of Mennonites to fight for their country. In an attempt to overcome this point the Dutch Mennonites went so far as to offer to furnish troops or to raise funds to compensate for a failure to bear arms. Saphorin replied that Bern had no system of substitute military service or of release for fee, and ventured the prophecy that the Mennonites would never be able to maintain their faith in Switzerland. On two subsequent visits the Mennonite deputation sought in vain to accomplish two aims: (1) to get permission for the wives and children of those who had been sent on the abortive deportation to America, to leave Bern without difficulty; (2) to obtain kind treatment of those recently imprisoned, and permission for them to emigrate; and to put an end to tracking down Mennonites. The Bernese members of the deputation also left a statement vindicating their faith for the archives at Amsterdam. In the end the Dutch Mennonites succeeded in having the States-General ask the Dutch ambassador Runckel in Bern to intercede with Bern for the Mennonites to the end that the severe measures against them be abolished, that they be allowed to worship God undisturbed, and that they be permitted to stay in the country where they had already lived for more than a century. If these requests were not granted, they should at least be given a few years' time to dispose of their property and then be granted the freedom to emigrate.

Runckel pursued his assignment with vigor. But he reported that his obstacles were enormous. No one would admit that an error had been made in dealing with the Mennonites; everything bad about them was believed. The best one could do, thought Runckel, would be to find a refuge for them so that they could all leave Bern as a body. There were opportunities for those Mennonites to locate elsewhere who were artisans and tradesmen, but most of the Mennonites made their living on the farm and with cattle. At this very time 23 Mennonites lay in prison in Bern.

That the Mennonites should leave Bern seemed clear to everyone. But where should they go? King Frederick I of Prussia was willing to take them in with open arms, offering them amazing economic advantages, with the privilege of settling anywhere in his realm, putting at their disposal comfortable homes, farm equipment, etc. But he wanted them all, the rich and the poor, not just the poor. But the Mennonites could not become enthusiastic about the plan; they feared the plague which had broken out there; also the feudal system was still in vogue in Frederick's realm. Runckel proposed settling them all on two large swampy areas of Bern. But the Mennonite leader, Brechbiehl, opposed the plan, and it was dropped when an engineer made an unfavorable report. Other plans were dropped also, so that in the end only one place of refuge remained, the Netherlands. The Dutch Mennonites worked hard to make this possible, and collected 50,000 guilders to help them. They wrote a comforting letter to the imprisoned Mennonites, 52 in number, which the latter answered on Jan. 8, 1711. On Oct. 1, 1710, Runckel reported that the prisoners were being treated tolerably well, they were granted the use of the Bible and a few other books, and they had adequate food and drink, though sleeping accommodations were rather bad. A few weeks later Runckel was able to send a list of 295 additional Mennonites in Bern, apart from those in prison.

On Dec. 10, 1710, Runckel made the following appeal to the Bern government: (1) to give the Swiss Mennonites the choice of Prussia or the Netherlands as their refuge; (2) to publish a general amnesty so that all Mennonites could come out into the open and dispose of their property; (3) to permit them to appoint agents to dispose of any property left behind after their exodus; (4) to release at once those in prison; (5) to permit Reformed partners who were married to Mennonites to emigrate with their spouses and children; (6) to exempt them from the emigration tax which had until then been in force against them.

In response to this appeal the Bern government issued the following amnesty on Feb. 11, 1711: "All efforts up to this time to cleanse the land of Anabaptists have proved fruitless, and the sect has increased. They refuse to swear the civil oath of allegiance, and to bear arms. It appears that the reason for their not leaving the country thus far is that they have been unable to find any country where they would be free to enjoy religious liberty. Therefore through Ambassador Bondeli and through Secretary Runckel we have entered into an agreement with His Majesty in Prussia and with the States-General of the Netherlands respectively to receive these so-called Anabaptist persons into their lands. They will travel to Holland, but if they wish they can locate in Prussia. Free emigration does not apply to those who have already been judicially banished with the confiscation of their goods. Those now in prison will be released on bail. The emigration period with exemption from emigration tax expires the end of June. The trip shall be paid for by those emigrating. Reformed spouses and children may emigrate and take along their property, yet with loss of citizenship. All property taken out of the country must be declared. That which is not declared promptly to the Anabaptist Commission will be confiscated. Meanwhile Anabaptist meetings are forbidden under heavy fines, and the severest penalties will be meted out to those who return to the country after emigration." These concessions were accomplished by the pressure of Prussia and the Dutch States-General. Bern issued a series of mandates in quick succession to expedite the emigration of the Mennonites: Feb. 20, 1711; April 17; April 19; May 11; June 2; June 22; and June 24. The task of leading the emigration was assigned to George Ritter, who was to have led them out the previous year.

Ritter had all kinds of difficulties to overcome. The Ammann-Reist division of 1693 was still so bitterly fresh in the memories of the two groups that they did not want to get into the same ship. One brother, Hans Gerber, refused to emigrate and was sentenced to galley slavery. Others did not want to take the vow never to return to Bern. (Some did return and were sentenced to life imprisonment.)

The date for the departure by ship was set for July 13, 1711. The value of the emigrating Mennonites' property was set at 600,000 pounds. (They had with them 14,000 guilders of their own, plus 18,135 which Runckel had received to give them.) The Anabaptist Commission sent 28,500 guilders to the Dutch Mennonites in payment of the property of the emigrating Mennonites. On the specified date, July 13, boats were loaded with Mennonites at both Bern and Neuchâtel; the boats met at Wangen and continued on their journey to Basel, which they reached three days later. (One Mennonite escaped at Wangen, his vow notwithstanding.) At Basel the party took on two Mennonites who had been given a life sentence for returning to Bern, and who had been released for emigration through the efforts of Runckel. The party, although less than the 50 anticipated, sailed down the Rhine in four boats. Ritter, the leader, was assisted by the Mennonites Daniel Richen and Christian Gäumann (names of passengers in Müller, 307-13). In Mannheim most of the Reist party escaped, many of them to settle in the Palatinate; some to return to Bern, where they were imprisoned for life upon being apprehended.

Finally on Aug. 3 what was left of the original emigrants from Bern, mostly of the Amish Mennonite group, arrived at Amsterdam. For 14 days they were cared for. So eager was the public to visit their quarters that police had to be assigned to the place. Gifts from the public amounted to 1,045 guilders. Of these Bernese Mennonites, mostly Amish, 126 settled in Groningen, 116 in Deventer, 87 in Kampen, and 26 in Harlingen (names listed in Müller, 320-22). The effort to colonize Prussia was for the most part a failure. The Swiss preferred to migrate to America. However, a small settlement was made in Neuchâtel, also in Valagin (*q.v.*), Swiss border regions under Prussian rule.

In Groningen, Sappemeer, and Kampen the immigrants built independent congregations which flourished for a time before becoming merged with the local Mennonites. Most of those who settled in Deventer moved to Kampen (*q.v.*). In Harlingen, where the settlers were mostly of the Reist party, it was decided to return southward and locate in the Palatinate. But the Swiss families who remained in Holland ultimately attained favorable recognition, e.g., the Meihuizen family.

XII. *Anabaptist Bureau (Kammer) and Anabaptist Hunters.* The very fury with which Bern persecuted the Mennonites made friends for them. The masses were moved to sympathy and helpfulness by the severe measures undertaken toward their annihilation. Loserth points out that in Tirol the common people were strongly attracted to the Anabaptists, giving them food, clothing, and shelter; never betraying them to the authorities; warning them of the coming of officers, etc. The same behavior of the common people was to be witnessed in Bern. To carry out its mandates more thoroughly Bern created a special department of state, really a branch of the Commission for Anabaptist Matters, composed of five members (not of the clergy). In the first instance this bureau was charged with caring for the confiscated Mennonite property. But the bureau also was vested with authority to capture, banish, and pardon Anabaptists and in general to see to the enforcement of the Anabaptist mandates. The Anabaptist Bureau was set up in 1699 and dissolved in 1743.

As early as 1663 the government of Bern felt the need of special assistance in hunting out the Mennonites and delivering them over to the authorities. These special officers were to be independent of the sheriff (*Landvogt*) and free to cross cantonal frontiers. Thirty Kreuzer was to be paid for each Anabaptist turned in, the money to come from the possessions of the one arrested, or from confiscated Anabaptist properties, or even from the government itself. For the most part these special officers, later called "Anabaptist hunters," were coarse men, of poor character, and much despised by the better citizens of the land. The Bern government had altercations with local townships (*Gemeinden*) which did not co-operate fully in turning in their Mennonites. A drive for Mennonites (*Täuferjagd*) in the Emmental in 1702

failed through the warnings of the populace, blowing horns, shooting, shouting, and similar signs of the coming of the posse. This happened many times. In 1714 in Sumiswald the Mennonites who were already in the custody of the "hunters" were forcibly released by a mob of 60 or 70 irate citizens. Even disputes between cantons arose as in 1726 when Anabaptist hunters trespassed on Lucerne territory to seize three Mennonite women. Furthermore the local sheriffs were often irritated by the Anabaptist hunters.

Along with all this unhappy spectacle went numerous mandates with their endless penalties; e.g., the mandates of Sept. 30, 1711, and Dec. 11, 1711. The latter stated that any Anabaptist who failed to emigrate, or who returned to Bern, was to be imprisoned either with or without chains until he died or conformed to state church standards. This was made still more severe in the mandate of May 24, 1714, in which the Mennonite preachers were notified that if arrested they would be sent to the galleys or to life imprisonment; this applied also to those who had once been banished and who had returned. The remaining Mennonites were to be again banished, and if they returned, those able to work were to be sent to the galleys, and those too old or feeble were to be given a punishment of similar severity. In an effort to find its Mennonites Bern soon offered a reward of 100 talers for every Mennonite preacher turned in, and 50 talers for everyone who gave testimony in the Mennonite services and for every deacon (*Zeugnisgeber und Almosenpfleger*). The reward for an ordinary lay member was to be 30 Kronen and for women, 15 Kronen.

The service of the book censor was again invoked. A New Testament containing a "Mennonite version," printed in Basel in 1702, was put on the list of forbidden books. Even the Zürich Froschauer Bible was proscribed. Furthermore a list of Mennonite books was to be prepared so that bookbinders could be put on oath not to bind them. Special efforts were also made to prevent the holding of Mennonite church services, and to make it difficult for a Mennonite to secure employment. Since Mennonites married by their own ministers were not legally married, declared Bern, the children have no rights of inheritance. Furthermore, a later mandate provided that if the children of Reformed parents became Mennonites, the parents had the right to disinherit them; but if such children returned to the Reformed Church, they could get their inheritance back, but without interest. The money received from confiscated Anabaptist properties was to be divided into thirds and be assigned to the following three causes: Anabaptist Bureau, city council, and the officials "for their encouragement and their vigilance" (edict of Feb. 19, 1715). This was changed in a mandate of March 17, 1729, which assigned such property to the state church treasury for school and church purposes. (The Mennonite properties were set up as landed properties earning income for the state church, but no money could be spent without the permission of the Anabaptist Bureau.) The Anabaptist Bureau was also responsible to dispose of Mennonite requests for property left behind when they emigrated. In general these requests were denied. In 1720 permission was given for Mennonites to take along their property if they made a solemn affirmation never to return to Bern. If any returned they were to be given life imprisonment. It was decided as early as 1695 not to allow any Mennonite to be buried in a church cemetery or any other recognized burial ground.

One of the chief occasions for tension between Bern and its Mennonites was the matter of their nonresistance. In 1737 plans were made to send these conscientious objectors to the silver mines at Roche, but this was apparently never done. In 1745 a fine of 20 to 30 talers was prescribed. In 1780 the nonresistant Mennonites were threatened with banishment. Other threats were also made. The Mennonites offered to donate a month's labor each year to help build and maintain foot bridges over the Emme, Iflis, and Trub rivers, but the council would not accept this proposal (1786). A milder policy began to be evident in Bern from about 1750, however. The Anabaptist Bureau was abolished in 1743. The Anabaptist hunters also disappeared.

XIII. *Toleration of the Mennonites in Bern.* One of the results of the French Revolution was the abolition of governmental intolerance and the persecution of religious dissenters. Switzerland became a French republic (Helvetic Republic). Article 6 of the Helvetian constitution of April 12, 1798, stated: "Freedom of conscience is unrestricted. However, public statements of opinion on religious matters must not disturb the concord and tranquillity of the people. Every form of divine worship is permitted if it does not disturb the public peace and if it does not demand domination or advantage. Every divine service is under the scrutiny of the police who have the right to ask that the doctrines and duties preached be submitted to them. . . ." The important Edict of Toleration of Feb. 12, 1799, revoked all Swiss laws against religious beliefs and sects. All penalties for religious nonconformity were abolished. All disfranchised Swiss were to be restored to citizenship if they lost it for religious nonconformity. Provision was even made for the banished citizens, or children or grandchildren of banished citizens, to file notice of their banished status on religious grounds, and they were to be welcomed back to their fatherland.

But Bern was not yet ready to stand by this Swiss law. Pressure continued to be exerted against those who would not have their infants baptized. In 1810 a marriage performed by a Mennonite preacher was declared invalid. That same year the Langnau Mennonites petitioned the government for full religious liberty in conformity with the Swiss law of 1799. This petition contained five points: (1) The Mennonites believed in the obligation to show honor to the government so far as conscience allowed. (2) Baptism signifies admission to the church, and faith must precede it. (3) Mennonites observe a holy communion in

their brotherhood and practice the excommunication or church discipline. (4) Mennonites are content to have the state church pastors perform the marriage ceremonies of their unbaptized young people; but their own ministers must marry those who are already church members. (5) Their church has the right to choose and ordain ministers by the laying on of the hands of their elders. To this petition the government replied on Dec. 30, refusing its requests. The law of 1799, said the government, did not apply in this case. Baptism in Switzerland, said they, was not merely a religious symbol but also involved church records of significance in family census data and citizenship records. Similarly weddings have civil significance because of inheritances, etc. The petition of the Mennonites was therefore rejected completely. Furthermore the Mennonites were ordered to bring their children to the state church for baptism, and their marriages were likewise to be performed publicly by state church clergymen. However, since the Mennonites had the testimony of living a quiet life, never disturbing anyone, and made no effort to spread their doctrines, they were not to be disturbed by anyone.

On March 15, 1811, 27 children of Mennonite parentage who had not been baptized since the French Revolution were baptized by force in the Langnau Reformed Church. Mennonite children were also taken to catechetical instruction in the Reformed Church by police force. Parents of children who reached the age of 16 years without being baptized were to suffer the loss of the rights of citizenship.

In 1815 the bishopric of Basel was united with the canton of Bern. This placed the Jura Mennonite congregations under the Bernese government. They therefore appealed to the government for the continuation of the toleration which they had enjoyed before the union. They particularly desired to have their own ministers baptize their converts and perform their weddings, and they wished for continued exemption from the oath and from military service. (Art. 13 of the Articles of Union, dated Nov. 3, 1815, guaranteed the perpetuation of their former rights.) The Emmental Mennonites also wished the same privileges as their Basel brethren. The church council of Bern issued a statement of their attitude on Aug. 3, 1816, in which they proposed that the Mennonites wear a distinguishable garb, that the state church clergyman should at all times have access to their services, and that specimens of all their books of doctrine and edification should be deposited with the superior magistrate (*Oberamt*). On April 19 the church council sent to the Lower Council of Bern the final draft of their proposed Mennonite ordinance. The latter, however, regarded the proposed ordinance as an official recognition of the sect, and in the end no Mennonite ordinance was adopted. An official letter was issued to the superior magistrates of Courtelary, Münster, and Langnau, dated Nov. 22, 1820, stipulating: (1) that every Mennonite register officially with the state church clergyman the birth of his infant child within the first three weeks of its life; (2) that an affirmation (*Gelübde*) was to have the same legal significance as the oath. On Dec. 4, 1824, the church council complained of this "unduly tolerant" official letter which had enhanced materially the standing of the Mennonite sect. They now were able to hold their meetings without interference, they had their own ministers who called themselves servants of the Divine Word, and who were free of every governmental control and inspection! "Up to this point such freedom has never been granted the Pietists, nor the Moravians, nor the Separatists."

Following a number of complaints fresh regulations were made to apply to the Mennonites. An official letter of July 18, 1823, (1) called for a census of all Anabaptists in every district (*Oberamt*); (2) specified that Art. 13 of the Articles of Union between the Bishopric of Basel and Bern applied only to those who then were Mennonites and to their descendants, not to those who had since united with them; (3) demanded a listing of each Anabaptist meeting, giving time and place, to be submitted to the *Oberamt,* who would issue permission for such meetings; (4) provided heavy penalties for winning "proselytes" to the sect, requiring Mennonite preachers to report any persons who wished to unite with them, so that the state officials and the state church clergyman could examine them and dissuade them; (5) declared all future proselytes of the Mennonites liable for military service, etc., as before.

Fear that the Mennonites would multiply and endanger the state kept them from receiving full toleration for a long time. Yet the police interference finally did stop as inconsistent with the then current concept of toleration. Certain difficulties occurred in the Jura in connection with the marriages of excommunicated Mennonites who were required by the state either to return to the Mennonites or to unite with the state church. Mennonite ministers were obligated to report all persons who were partially or wholly excommunicated from their brotherhood, so that such persons could be punished by the police, and so that their children could be provided with religious instruction.

A division occurred in the Emmental Mennonite congregation during the period 1832-35. The new party was led by a young man named Samuel Fröhlich (*q.v.*), founder of the Apostolic Christian Church (*q.v.*), called in Europe "Neutäufer," often known in America by the appellation "New Amish."

The federal government of Switzerland took over the control of the army from the cantonal governments in 1850. The Swiss general assembly immediately passed a law regulating the army and listing categories of persons exempt from military service. The Mennonites were for the first time in the history of the new Confederacy not exempted. They made an official plea, but to no avail. However, no action was taken to induct them and the Mennonites continued free from military service for the next 25 years. In 1874 a new federal constitution was put into effect, which made all Swiss citizens liable to military service. Within the years immediately following, the first Swiss Mennonites found themselves in Swiss army uniform. They have been permitted from that time to the present to serve in the medical corps.

Large numbers of Bernese Mennonites have emigrated to the United States, particularly in the 19th century. During the 18th century only a few scattered families of direct Bernese origin were among the large number who settled in Eastern Pennsylvania, in the Franconia and Lancaster settlements. The first Bernese came to Pennsylvania in 1717 under the leadership of Benedikt Brechbill (*q.v.*). In the 1750's a smaller group followed directly from the Bernese Jura. However, many of the Palatinate Mennonites who came to the Franconia-Lancaster region were of original Bernese origin, having emigrated to the Palatinate 1650-90. The Amish settlers in Eastern Pennsylvania 1738-60 were all of Bernese origin as their names and culture clearly indicate. (See C. H. Smith, *Menn. Immigration to Pennsylvania.*)

During the first half of the 19th century (1817-60) a large number of Bernese Mennonites left their Jura and Emmental homes and settled in Ohio and Indiana. Large congregations composed of the descendants of the immigrants are located in the Sonnenberg (*q.v.*) and Crown Hill (*q.v.*) communities in Wayne Co., Ohio, the Bluffton (*q.v.*)-Pandora community in Allen and Putnam counties, Ohio, the Berne (*q.v.*) community in Adams Co., Ind., the Fortuna (*q.v.*) community in Moniteau Co., Mo., and in the Salem (*q.v.*)-Silverton community in Oregon. Occasional families continued to come until into the 20th century, some settling also in the Wayland (*q.v.*), Iowa, community.

The following is a list of the present-day Mennonite congregations in the canton of Bern (Bulles lies in Bern and Neuchâtel) together with their membership: Bulles, 150; Chaux d'Abel Kapelle, 100; Chaux d' Abelberg, 50; Cortebertberg, 50; Emmental (Langnau), 350; Grosslützel (Courgenay), 100; Kleintal (Moron-Perceux), 250; Pruntrut, 150; Sonnenberg (Jeangisboden-Fürstenberg-Les Mottes), 450; Biel, Emmenholz bei Solothurn, and Reconvilier are not independent congregations; hence their membership is counted elsewhere.

NEFF, J.C.W.

"Acta des gesprächs zwüschenn predicannten Vnnd Tauffbrüderenn Erganngen. Inn der Statt Bernn . . . Im M.D. XXXVIIIten Jar" (ms.); *Berner-Heim,* 1896, 10; E. Blösch, *Gesch. der schweiz.-ref. Kirchen* (2 vv. 1898, 1899); E. H. Correll, *Das Schweizerische Täufermennonitentum* (Tübingen, 1925); A. Fluri, *Beiträge z. Gesch. der bernischen Täufer* (Bern, 1912); *idem, Das Wiedertäufermandat vom 9. August 1659* (reprint from *Blätter für bernische Gesch., Kunst und Altertumskunde.*); S. Geiser and Lerch, *Die Taufgesinnten-Gemeinden* (the only Swiss Mennonite history by Mennonites) (Karlsruhe, 1931); W. Hadorn, *Kirchengesch. der refor. Schweiz* (Zürich, 1907); *idem, Die Refor. in der deutschen Schweiz* (Frauenfeld und Leipzig, 1928); C. L. von Haller, *Gesch. der kirchlichen Revolution oder protestantischen Reform des Kantons Bern* (Luzern, 1836); *Handlung oder Acta der Disputation gehalten zu Zofingen . . . M.D. XXXII im Julio;* G. Joss, *Das Sektenwesen im Kanton Bern* (Bern, 1881); E. Müller, *Geschichte der Bernischen Täufer* (Frauenfeld, 1895); A. H. Newman, *A History of Anti-Pedobaptism . . .* (Philadelphia, 1897); R. Steck und G. Tobler, *Akten-*

sammlung zur Gesch. der Berner Refor. 1521-1532 (Bern, 1923); G. Thormann, Probier-Stein, oder Schrifftmässige und auss dem wahren innerlichen Christenthumb hergenommene gewissenhaffte Prüffung des Täufferthums (Bern, 1693); Th. de Quervain, Kirchliche und soziale Zustände in Bern unmittelbar nach der Einführung der Reformation (Bern, 1906); D. Gratz, Bernese Anabaptists and Their American Descendants (Scottdale, 1953); Inv. Arch. Amst. I, Nos. 1248-1399, 1866-1920; J. Huizinga, Stamboek of Geslachtsregister der nakomelingen van Samuel Peter (Meihuizen) en Barbara Fry (Groningen, 1890); ML I, 168-96.

Berne, Ind., a town of about 2,300, seat of the largest Mennonite congregation in North America, and center of the large Swiss Mennonite settlement, is located in Adams County (*q.v.*) about 35 miles south of Fort Wayne. Approximately 1,800 Mennonites (including children), belonging to the General Conference, Evangelical Mennonites, and various Amish groups, live within the vicinity in all directions from the town, about 35 per cent living in Berne. Swiss Mennonites from the canton of Bern, Switzerland, first settled here in 1838, and gave the town its name. Mennonite churches in this area include the First Mennonite (GCM), in town; Evangelical (Defenseless) Mennonite, in the country; Amish Christian, in the country; and three Old Order Amish groups meeting in homes. The two Missionary Churches in the town and country originally split off from the Defenseless Mennonite group, which in turn was originally Amish from Alsace. The Mennonite Book Concern and many Mennonite business places are located in Berne. The unique things about the community are its Swiss culture, its musical interests, and its religious atmosphere as well as high moral standards. See the article **Berne First Mennonite Church** for an account of the history of the Swiss Mennonite community, and the article **Adams County Amish** for the Amish history.   O.A.K.

Berne Evangelical Mennonite Church is located four miles west and one-half mile north of Berne, Ind. This congregation was the first in the Defenseless Conference to build a church. The church, built in 1871 by Bishop Henry Egly (*q.v.*), the founder of the Defenseless Mennonite Church, was replaced by a larger one in 1881. This building, remodeled in 1937 and again in 1948, has a seating capacity of 350. The membership in 1951 was 250. In 1880 the church experienced a great revival, 75 converts being baptized and added to the church. It observed its seventy-fifth anniversary on Nov. 24, 1946. Pastors who have served the church include Bishop Henry Egly (founder), Joseph Egly, Christ Egly (sons of the founder), Moses Rupp, David Schindler, C. N. Stucky, Eli Lantz, E. M. Becker, Henry Klopfenstein, and N. J. Schmucker, (1951) pastor since 1935.   N.J.S.

Berne First Mennonite Church (GCM), Berne, Adams Co., Ind., is a member of the Middle District Conference. It has 1,320 members (1953).

The background of the majority of the membership is Swiss from the Jura Mountains and the Emmental in the canton of Bern. The first settlers who came to this section were of the Preacher David Baumgartner family, who located in French

Township in 1838. These started the Baumgartner church which united with the Berne church in 1886. Another group of 80 persons, mostly members of the Sprunger family or their relatives by marriage, left the Jura for America in 1852. They cleared trees and drained land around a spot where the town of Berne is now situated. These organized the Berne congregation with Peter S. Lehman as their leader.

In 1856 the Berne group began erecting the first church building, which was completed in 1860. The second meetinghouse was built in 1879, was remodeled in 1886 and again in 1899. The present brick church was started in 1910 and dedicated in 1912, having a seating capacity of 2,000 in the main auditorium and balconies. The church owns a nine-room parsonage, built of brick matching the church. One third of the membership lives in the country and the remainder live in town.

The Bernese Swiss dialect is still spoken in many homes. The church services are in English but there are three German Sunday-school classes. The church does not observe footwashing or separate seating for men and women. Members are disciplined if they do not live according to the Scriptures and rules of the church.

The Sunday school, which was organized in 1874, has a present membership of 1,483 and an average attendance of 1,152 (1952). The Christian Endeavor was organized in 1894. The Women's Missionary Society, organized in 1887, meets once a month. The Girls' Junior and Intermediate Mission Bands also meet monthly. The Christian Temperance Union has charge of the first Sunday evening service of every month. The church also has a library of almost a thousand books.

There has been a strong love for music in the Berne community and as early as 1875 singing schools were instituted with practices held in homes. Out of these grew the choir and choral society which began giving oratorios in 1890. At present the church has several music groups—an adult choir, a young people's choir, a junior choir, and the Choral Society, which gives "The Creation" each June and "The Messiah" each December; also a Men's Chorus of considerable renown, which was organized in 1898, and a Ladies' Chorus organized in 1912.

There were two outstanding leaders in the church whose influence is still felt today. Both were products of the local church and community. One was S. F. Sprunger (*q.v.*), long-time pastor of the church. He fostered a real heart religion with a progressive outlook and promoted education, missions, and conference endeavors. The other was J. F. Lehman, an active layman, influential leader in the Sunday school, Temperance Society, Choral Society, and Christian Endeavor.

In the summer of 1886 a great revival took place in Berne. It was remarkable because there was no outside evangelist with special meetings, special music or publicity as is usually the case. Through the faithful teaching of S. F. Sprunger and the help of J. F. Lehman, a young woman found peace in Christ and soon the spirit spread from one to another until over a hundred persons were converted in about two months.

Ministers who served the Baumgartner congregation in the early days, prior to the merger, were as follows: David Baumgartner, Christian Baumgartner, Ulrich Kipfer, Matthias Strahm, Christian Augsburger, and S. F. Sprunger. Ministers who served the Berne congregation prior to the merger: Peter Lehman, Christian Sprunger, Peter Habegger, Peter M. Neuenschwander, and S. F. Sprunger. Pastors of both of the united churches follow: S. F. Sprunger, 1871-1903; J. W. Kliewer, 1903-11; S. F. Sprunger (Interim), 1911-13; P. R. Schroeder, 1912-28; C. H. Suckau, 1928-43; J. P. Suderman (Interim), 1944-45; and Olin A. Krehbiel, 1945- .

Since the beginning of the church between 60 and 70 members of this congregation have at some time been engaged in various types of Christian service for a shorter or longer period. At present there are 17 members engaged in foreign mission work and 11 in home mission work.

This congregation has entertained the General Conference four times, the last time being in 1947, when over 1,400 delegates and visitors were in attendance.

In 1952 the church gave over $113,098.00 for local support, minister's salary, missions, relief, education, conference, and other causes. (E. Sprunger, *The First Hundred Years*, Berne, 1938.)

O.A.K.

Berne Mennonite Church (MC), Huron Co., Mich., later called Pigeon (*q.v.*).

Berne Witness Company. The first newspaper venture at Berne, Ind., was instituted by a Mennonite enterpriser, Fred Rohrer. Having learned the printer's trade at college, he returned to Berne in 1896, purchased equipment costing less than $600.00, and launched the *Berne Witness*. As an aggressive editor Mr. Rohrer led the legal battle which closed the Berne saloons in 1906. By 1904 the Witness Company was printing ten publications, mainly Mennonite periodicals for the Mennonite Book Concern, the publication agency of the General Conference Mennonite Church. The Witness Company, however, was never a conference institution.

Incorporated in 1906, the firm was long under the management of Clifton H. Sprunger, who died in 1952. Employing 25 persons, the firm continues to publish the *Berne Witness* as a triweekly and does much job printing for both Mennonite and non-Mennonite groups. L.C.L.

Berne Witness VIII, No. 42 (Jan. 22, 1904) 1; ibid., Tenth Anniversary Souvenir Edition (1906) 72 f.; ibid., Thirtieth Anniversary Souvenir Edition (1926) 53-55; L. C. Lehman, "The Economic Development of the Mennonite Community at Berne, Indiana" (unpublished Master's thesis, Ohio State University, 1947).

Berner, Klaus, an Anabaptist martyr of Dorndorf, a village on the Werra near Eisenach, Thuringia, Germany, baptized in 1530 by George von Staffelstein at Herrenhof near Schmalkalden, was seized and imprisoned in Frankenhausen with ten fellow believers in the fall of 1533. He was released through recantation, but soon began again to agitate for Anabaptism. In 1534 he preached in a saw-

mill near Zorge in the South Harz and soon after suffered a martyr's death. NEFF.

P. Wappler, *Die Täuferbewegung in Thüringen* (Jena, 1913) 99; E. Jacobs, *Die Wiedertäufer am Harz* (1899); *ML* I, 197.

Bernhardus, an Anabaptist leader in Franconia, who probably suffered a martyr's death in 1530. In 1524 he was already preaching and baptizing around Coburg. He was apparently well educated. Nothing else is known about him. NEFF.

E. Jacobs, *Die Wiedertäufer am Harz* (1899); *Hefte der Comeniusgesellschaft* (1900) IX, 184; *ML* I, 197.

Bernkopff (Bärnkopf), **Leonhard,** an Anabaptist martyr, was burned at the stake with unusual cruelty in 1542 at Salzburg because he persisted in his faith. (Beck, *Geschichts-Bücher*, 151; *Mart. Mir.* D 62, E 465; Wiswedel, *Bilder* II, 169; *ML* I, 197.)

HEGE.

Bersch, Tobias, an elder of the Hutterian Brethren, a weaver by trade, was chosen as preacher on March 15, 1651, at Sobotiste, Hungary, and ordained on March 16, 1653; appointed as leader (*Vorsteher*) of the Hutterian Brethren in Hungary on Jan. 10, 1694, after the death of Caspar Eglauch (*q.v.*). Only a few details are known about his work. He died in 1701. Matthias Helm was chosen as his successsor. (Beck, *Geschichts-Bücher*, 483, 484, 557, and 563; *ML* I, 197.) HEGE.

Bertel, Hans, a wool weaver who was seized early in 1529 at Strasbourg with the Anabaptists assembled in the house of Claus Bruch. On Tuesday after Palm Sunday he was cross-examined on the rack; when he was asked whether the Anabaptists held their women in common, he denied it. (Röhrich, *Ztscht für die hist. Theol.*, 1860, 48; *ML* I, 197.) HEGE.

Bertie Township, Ont., the center of a now extinct Mennonite (MC) settlement, called the Bertie congregation throughout most of its history. Into this township lying west of Buffalo across the Niagara River in Ontario, Mennonites migrated from eastern Pennsylvania as early as 1788. The main center of worship was a church one mile east of Sherkston. Property deeded in 1828 has from that time served for church building and cemetery purposes. The first church was a log building which served about 30 years. By 1860 the log meetinghouse had been replaced by a brick church, which served during the greater period of strength and decline. In 1916 another church was erected on the same grounds and from it dated a revival of interest and attendance for more than a decade, when decline again set in. In 1931 the Mennonites sold this Bertie church to the Brethren in Christ with burial privileges reserved for the Mennonite families and their descendants.

The first leader of the Bertie congregation was Preacher George Zavitz, son of pioneer Jacob Zavitz who came to Canada in 1788. Other preachers during the succeeding years were John Zavitz (1798-1872), John B. Hershey (1816-1904), Benjamin Hershey (1826-88), Christian Hershey (1768-1845), Nelson Michael (1843-1923), Howard Stevanus, Noah Hunsberger, and Simon Martin. Bishop John

Lapp of Clarence made a definite contribution to the strength and life of this church by his visits and oversight. In 1865 he made a conference-wide appeal in behalf of the ministerial needs of the congregation.

Among the reasons for varying strength and loss was the problem of leadership and the problem of language. Bertie had a few strong leaders able to promote harmony and growth. Others were less capable and a few definitely incapable. Schism had its part and some leaders were interested in other groups and organizations. The General Conference Mennonites had a congregation for a time in the northern part of the township. The United Brethren Church took rise and grew in strength while the Mennonites hesitated on the use of the English language. The Brethren in Christ (Tunker, River Brethren) had their strong leader for Ontario in this area. And so the Mennonite church in its hundred years in Bertie Township experienced more loss than growth, until eventually all Mennonite families have withdrawn, or become absorbed in other local organizations.   J.C.F.

Bertolet Mennonite Church (GCM) of Upper Frederick Twp., Montgomery Co., Pa., was organized about 1846 by several Mennonite families from the Schwenksville congregation living in this area. The meetinghouse still standing was the first and only church erected on this site, although the half-acre lot upon which it stands had been a private burying ground of the Frey family for more than a century before this. The oldest legible marker is dated 1766.

The first meeting in the new meetinghouse was held on May 23, 1847. In the subsequent 1847 conference division, Bertolets sided with the new Eastern Conference, and later the General Conference.

The meetinghouse is located along a historical mile of road. To the north stands the 200-year-old log house of Hans Nice, formerly of Germantown. To the south the Frey-Bertolet-Grubb homestead is found where the late N. B. Grubb was born and reared. In the adjoining barn which had just been built, the famous George Whitefield preached to a great crowd in April 1740. This barn is still in use. Just beyond this is the farmhouse of the famous Henry Antes, the Moravian leader. Here Zinzendorf visited and preached and later General George Washington had headquarters during September 1777.

One of the first Sunday schools in a Mennonite meetinghouse was held at Bertolets in 1848. Regular services were discontinued about 1920 because of small attendance. The remaining members could easily reach the Eden congregation in Schwenksville by automobile and joined there. Some years before this a Bertolets Burial Ground Association had been organized, which has continued to take care of the meetinghouse and grounds as well as the cemetery. About 1950 a group of young people from the Franconia Conference Mennonite Church started a mission Sunday school in the building and have been continuing weekly.   J.H.F.

Bervoets, H., a non-Mennonite physician, was a medical missionary in Java under the Dutch Mennonite missionary board (*Doopsgezinde Vereiniging tot Evangelie-verbreiding*) 1907-30. He and his wife made a very significant contribution to the missionary work there by their great love and devotion to the cause. Dr. Bervoets was the first doctor on the mission field; before his coming, the medical work had been done by the missionaries and nurses. He not only founded several clinics; on Jan. 7, 1915, the central hospital was opened at Kelet (*q.v.*), and on April 30, 1916, the leprosarium at Donorodjo (*q.v.*), on the coast was opened to admit and care for lepers. Dr. Bervoets died July 22, 1933.   vDZ.

Berwangen, a village in the Sinsheim district of Baden, where a Mennonite congregation was formed in the middle of the 19th century, when a division took place in the congregation at Streichenberg near Eppingen as a consequence of the rise of the Fröhlichianer or *Neutäufer* (see **Apostolic Christian Church**). On Sept. 21, 1873, the congregational seat was transferred to Ittlingen (*Gbl.,* 1873, 80) and in 1912 the congregation merged with that at Immelhausen; the combined group was then called the Sinsheim (*q.v.*) congregation. (*ML* I, 200.)   HEGE.

Besluyt der Voornaemste Waterlandsche Leeraren tot Amsterdam, vergadert in den Jare 1626 (Confession of the most prominent Waterlander preachers assembled at Amsterdam 1626). This short confession of 13 articles, signed by 12 church leaders, including Rippert Eenkes (*q.v.*), Hans Alenson (*q.v.*), and Hans de Ries (*q.v.*), was composed during the conflict of the church in Amsterdam with Nittert Obbes (*q.v.*), one of the preachers, who leaned toward Socinianism. It is to be considered as a supplement of the Waterlander Confession of 1610 (*Korte Belijdenis, q.v.*). The *Besluyt* states that there are two kinds of the Word of God, the one being Jesus Christ, the only begotten Son of God, from eternity to all eternity, through whom God the Father created all things; the other being the written Word of God, the Holy Scriptures; both are given to us to save us, but in the strict sense men can be saved only by the Eternal Word of God, which is Jesus Christ. The *Besluyt* was printed at Rotterdam in 1740, under the title: *Korte Belijdenis der Waterlandsche Gemeenten, ten overstaan van Twaalf Leeraars te Amsterdam.*   vDZ.

Bessie Mennonite Brethren Church, Bessie, Okla., was organized Jan. 6, 1905, with 35 members. At first the meetings were conducted in a country school. A church 36 x 26 ft. was built in 1906, and in 1929 the present church 56 x 36 ft. was constructed. Andrew B. P. Schmidt served as the first leader of this group. In 1908 Jacob Reimer was ordained to the ministry and in 1919 as elder. He served the church well as pastor for many years. To 1949 a total of 207 persons have been added to the same by baptism. The 1951 membership was 157 and the pastor, Elmo Warkentin.

The following missionaries have come from this church: Pauline Foote, Mr. and Mrs. P. D. Kiehn,

Mr. and Mrs. Peter Kiehn, all of whom have labored in China; and Mr. and Mrs. Ruben Wedel, who have worked among the Mexicans of South Texas.   J.K.S.

Bestevaer: see **Lucas Lambertsz van Beveren.**

Bestvater (Bestvader), a Mennonite family name in the Frisian congregations of West Prussia, first mentioned at Orlofferfelde (*q.v.*) in 1601. Nineteen families of this name were counted in West Prussia (without Danzig) in 1776, and 28 persons (including Elbing) in 1935. The family also spread to Russia and subsequently to America.   G.R.

Betgen (Betken, Betjen), official name Betgen de Haze, an Anabaptist martyr, a native of Gent, Belgium, and unmarried, was seized at Antwerp for her faith in 1559. She was drowned at the Steen prison in Antwerp on June 28, 1559, together with two other martyrs, Mariken Fransse (*q.v.*) and Neelken Jacobs (*q.v.*). All attempts to make Betgen and her companions forsake their faith failed. A pitiful detail of Betgen's bitter troubles was that her *cleerkens* (garments) had been sold on May 10. Betgen's name is also found in a song of the *Liedtboecxken van den Offer des Heeren* (No. 16): "Aenhoort Godt, hemelsche Vader" (Give ear, O God, heavenly Father). These martyrs were, however, not sisters by birth, as the English *Martyrs' Mirror* seems to indicate.   vDZ.

Offer, 566; *Mart. Mir.* D 244, E 618; *Antw. Arch.-Blad* IX, 3, 8, 16; XIV, 26, 27, No. 294; Wolkan, *Lieder,* 63, 72; *ML* I, 209.

Betgen van Maldeghem (or Betgen Martins), born at Deinze, Flanders, widow of Pieter van Maldeghem, an Anabaptist martyr, was burned at the stake with four companions at Gent, Belgium, on July 21, 1562, confessing her faith without dismay until her death and remaining true to it. Her name and the names of her fellow martyrs are found in a song of the *Liedtboecxken van den Offer des Heeren* (No. 1): "Alsmen schreef duyst vijfhondert jaer Ende twee en tsestich mede" (In the year 1562). (*Offer,* 650; *Mart. Mir.* D 289, E 656; Verheyden, *Gent,* 29, No. 90; *ML* I, 209.)   vDZ.

Bethania, a home for the aged and infirm. This institution was founded in 1946 by the Mennonite Benevolent Society (*q.v.*), 437 Desalaberry St., Winnipeg, Man. The institution is situated 10 miles north of Winnipeg on the banks of the Red River. The patients are cared for in two large houses which have a total capacity of 80 patients. The houses are located on an estate of 110 acres. This land is seeded to vegetables and satisfies the needs of the institution adequately. Pigs, cows, and chickens are also raised and provide the patients with fresh meat, eggs, and dairy products at all times. The executive committee consists of J. J. Schulz, Pres.; H. J. Willms, Secy.-Treas.; J. P. Friesen; and J. J. Klassen, Vice-Pres. The matron of the institution is (1950) Miss Maria Vogt. J.J.S.

Bethania Mennonite Brethren Church near Main Centre, Sask., was organized in 1913 under the leadership of John W. Neufeld, with an initial membership of 44. Neufeld, who moved to Vancouver, B.C., was succeeded by A. R. D. Klassen

and David Berg. The leader in 1951 was Geogre R. Klassen and the membership 41. Bethania belongs to the Herbert district conference.   J.I.R.

Bethania Mennonite Brethren Church, San Diego Co., Cal.: see **Escondido** Mennonite Brethren Church.

Bethania Mental Hospital, established in 1910 on the land of the former village of Alt-Kronsweide, Chortitza settlement, Russia, by the *Allgemeine Bundeskonferenz,* patterned after Bodelschwingh's "Bethel" at Bielefeld, Germany, was the first Mennonite mental hospital and the only one established in Europe. On March 15, 1911, the "Bethel" unit was opened providing room for 16 women, and was followed by the "Salem" unit on Aug. 20, 1911, housing 16 men. Among the 53 patients cared for from Aug. 15, 1911, to Dec. 1, 1912, were 11 acute and 20 chronic mental cases; 8 were epileptic, 12 idiots, and 2 with organic nervous disorders. Of these, 2 were dismissed as healed, 3 as improved, 6 without improvement, and 3 died. Eleven patients had no training, 34 had elementary school, 7 had secondary school, and one was a university graduate. About one third of the patients were admitted free while the others paid 240 rubles per year. The total income (including money for building) by July 1, 1912, was 262,339.90 rubles. The value of Bethania was estimated at this time as being 219,630 rubles.

In March 1911, 22 more beds were added in each division, providing a total of 76 rooms. Of the 88 patients cared for during this year, 2 were under 10 years of age, 19 between 10 and 20, 17 between 20 and 30, 26 between 30 and 40, 8 between 40 and 50; 61 were unmarried, 21 married, and 6 widowed. Almost all Mennonite settlements were represented. Mennonite patients received preference but others were also accepted. Originally the institution had been planned as one sponsored by all Protestant groups in Russia, but this intention could not be accomplished. The conference was the sponsor and owner of Bethania. It was operated by a board of eight directors, most of whom were leading businessmen and industrialists with J. J. Suderman as chairman, and J. G. Lepp as treasurer. Contributions were raised throughout the settlements and congregations. During the second half of 1912 they amounted to 27,600 rubles. However, some of the industrialists and large estate owners contributed up to 40,000 and more. The budget for the year 1912-13 was 37,956.67 rubles. Many of the contributions came in as gifts-in-kind.

The first housefather was Peter Schellenberg, who was succeeded by Jakob K. Janzen (1912-20). Some of the nurses had received training in Bielefeld. The first doctor was W. Stieda, who was later assisted by I. Thiessen.

World War I stopped the rapid development of Bethania and the following Revolution brought it to a gradual end. The report of 1925 summarizes the results of the activities of Bethania during the 15 years of its history. During this time Bethania had had a total of 991 patients, of whom 203 were buried in its own cemetery. Five different doctors, 78 male nurses, 86 female nurses, and 353 additional staff members had served the institution. Of the 204 patients cared for during the year 1925, 101 were Russian, 87 German, and 16 Jewish. After the Revolution the institution was taken over by the province and in 1925 by the federal government. Of the 32,297 rubles received in 1925, 4,868 still came from Mennonite congregations and the rest from the government. The institution still farmed some 200 acres of land. Help in addition to the regular nurses came from the medical school at Halbstadt, Molotschna, which used it for internship.

When in 1927 the village of Einlage (Kitchkas) came under the backwater of the Dneprostroy power dam, Bethania had to be evacuated. At this time Dr. E. Tavonius and Dr. I. Thiessen encouraged the Mennonite constituency to appeal to the government to transfer Bethania to Halbstadt. However, this did not materialize. On May 9, 1927, the patients, among them 33 Mennonites, were transferred to a mental hospital at Igren without the Mennonite personnel. That was the end of Bethania, one of the most successful and generally supported projects among the Mennonites of Russia. Dr. I. Thiessen had been connected with the institution almost throughout the 16 years of its existence. The last housefather was J. P. Wiebe.

C.K.

Friesen, *Brüderschaft,* 660; W. Stieda, "Bethania," *Menn. Jahrbuch,* 1911-12, 92-106; 1913, 154-62; Joh. Wiebe, "Mitteilungen aus 'Bethania' (1925)," *Unser Blatt* I (Feb. 1926) 95; see also *Unser Blatt* II (March 1927) 178; (July 1927) 304; *ML* I, 202.

Bethany Bible Academy, known originally as Bethany Bible School, Munich, N.D., first opened its doors on Oct. 31, 1938, at Alsen, N.D. The next year it was transferred to Munich and until 1943, when a school building was purchased, it was conducted in various buildings. Edward Duerksen, then pastor at Alsen, and H. F. Ortmann of Munich, were instrumental in starting the school and securing the first instructor, J. B. Epp, of Beatrice, Neb. The instructors have all been of the Mennonite faith. The school was originally sponsored by the four Mennonite churches in the community. In 1950 the school was reorganized and incorporated into an interdenominational institution made up of paid up members from all parts of the state of North Dakota. The name was then changed to Bethany Bible Academy. A two-acre plot and a new 40 x 70 ft. building have been added to the original property. The term has also been changed from the five-month winter term to the standard nine-month term. The curriculum offers a standard accredited high-school course with fundamental Bible subjects designed for high-school level young people. The aim of the school is to teach "Faith with Facts" under Christian supervision, companionship, and activity. G. W. Schroeder has been president since 1947.

G.W.S.

Bethany Bible School, located in the town of Hepburn, in northern Saskatchewan, was founded in 1927. For a number of years the school offered a two-year elementary course, increasing it in 1934 to an intensive four-year course. In 1935 it became an active member of the Evangelical Teacher Training Association. A two-year college course was offered 1939-45. Since then it has again offered the regular intensive four-year course in Bible, Christian education, and missions.

At first the school was owned and operated by the Bethany Bible School Association, consisting of members who paid the required fees and who pledged its support, but now the association consists of Mennonite Brethren churches which appoint their representatives on the school board, which guides and directs all the affairs of the school. At present (1949) there are 16 board members representing 9 churches.

In 1948 all property was turned over to the Mennonite Brethren Church of Saskatchewan. It consists of the main school building with four classrooms, an office, a library, and an auditorium; a girls' dormitory with offices, laundry, kitchen and dining-room facilities; a men's dormitory with residence for one teacher and family; two other teacherages; and a campus of approximately six and one-half acres.

The school has had an average attendance of 50-60 students. Most of these come from Mennonite Brethren churches of Saskatchewan, but annually the school has a number of students of other churches, as well as from other provinces.

At least one third of the graduates are active in full-time Christian work and are serving as missionaries in India, Africa, South America, and North America, and as pastors and Bible school teachers.

The school presidents during the years have been D. P. Esau, 1929-34; J. B. Toews, 1934-37; G. W. Peters, 1937-42; G. D. Huebert, 1942-45; J. H. Epp, 1945- .

J.H.E.

Bethany Biblical Seminary, established at Chicago, Ill., in 1905, is the official theological seminary of the Church of the Brethren. In 1945 the General Conference Mennonite Church authorized a school to be known as Mennonite Biblical Seminary and to operate in affiliation with Bethany Biblical Seminary. Each of the affiliated schools has its own directors, constituency, buildings, faculty members, and students. Affiliation is at the level of instruction. Interschool relations are maintained where interests overlap, but at the same time full opportunity is given for attention to individual interest. In the 1951-52 school year the total enrollment in the affiliated schools was 269, of which the Mennonites provided 44.

S.F.P.

Bethany Chapel United Missionary Church, St. Catharines, Lincoln Co., Ont., was organized *ca.* 1908. In 1948 the congregation had 35 members, mostly urban, with W. Cecil Brown serving as pastor.

W.C.B.

Bethany Deaconess Hospital, American Falls, Idaho, was founded by F. B. Wedel of Newton, Kans., in 1909. For the construction cost of the hospital and for maintenance expenses he solicited funds from Mennonite communities and from local sources. The hospital was managed by the founder and by his daughter, Marie, as superintendent for several years. Later the management was carried on by a managing board consisting of ministers and members chosen from two local Mennonite churches at

Aberdeen, Idaho. Because of difficulties in financing operating expenses, the institution was made a county hospital and the name was changed to Schiltz Memorial Hospital. H.C.W.

Bethany Krimmer Mennonite Brethren Church, located in Hillsboro, Marion Co., Kan., had its beginning in 1918 with D. E. Harder as leader and minister. In that year a frame meetinghouse was built with a seating capacity of 150. The church was formally organized with 35 members on Nov. 2, 1927, with P. F. Wall as minister. It was dissolved on Sept. 10, 1936, because of the small membership and the heavy expense of repairing the church, which was then sold. Ministers who served are D. J. S. Mendel, D. W. Tschetter, P. Z. Wiebe, B. C. Willems, D. V. Wiebe, and F. V. Wiebe. C.F.P.

Bethany Mennonite Church (MC), located in the Briery Branch Gap, four miles southwest of Spring Creek, Ashby District, Rockingham Co., Va., is a local mission congregation of the Middle District of the Virginia Conference. Land was purchased for the church in 1913. There are 18 baptized members. H.A.B.

Bethany Mennonite Church (MC) near Elida, Ohio, was the second congregation formed from the Salem-Pike congregation in Allen County between 1924 and 1936. In the latter year when the Salem-Pike congregation withdrew from the Ohio Mennonite and Eastern A.M. Joint Conference after its bishop had been placed under conference censure, 80 members including Preacher J. B. Smith and Deacon Perry Smith, desiring to stay with the conference, formed a separate congregation. They purchased the Dutch Hollow schoolhouse and renamed it Bethany Church. Perry Smith and Sherman Swartz were particularly active in the Sunday school in the early years.

When the Salem-Pike congregation was granted readmission into conference, one of the requirements set up by conference leadership was that the Salem-Pike congregation should transfer title of one of its two church buildings (Pike and Salem) to the Bethany congregation. Salem was turned over to the new group, which in 1941 became Bethany-Salem, and since 1942 has been known as the Salem Mennonite congregation. Membership in 1953 was 108, with Richard Martin serving as pastor. J.S.U.

Bethany Mennonite Church (GCM) of Freeman, S.D., Northern District Mennonite Conference, was founded by members or descendants of Swiss Mennonite and non-colonist Hutterite groups within and surrounding the municipality of Freeman.

The actual organization of the congregation grew out of a concern for the spiritual welfare of Mennonite and Hutterite families living within the town of Freeman, to whom the advantage of congregational fellowship in the surrounding rural churches was not easily accessible. A Sunday-school fellowship had already been functioning in town since about 1896. In the summer of 1898 the first meetinghouse, a frame structure, was built. This group was served from the pulpit alternately

by Christian Kaufman, Christian Mueller, Joseph Kaufman, John L. Wipf, and H. A. Bachman, until Aug. 27, 1905, when the first officers were inducted. The congregation joined the General Conference and Northern District Conference in September 1905 and June 1906 respectively.

The original church was remodeled and enlarged in 1925, and was used until the fire of Sunday morning, Nov. 4, 1945, which destroyed it. The congregation subsequently worshiped in the Freeman Junior College chapel, awaiting a new building, which was completed and dedicated in 1952.

The congregation is now quite cosmopolitan in membership, a part being of non-Mennonite extraction. A majority of the members are townfolk—of various occupations in a town of nearly a thousand population. A few still reside on near-by farms.

The roster of Bethany's full-time and part-time ministers throughout its history includes the names of H. A. Bachman, J. M. Regier, Elmer Basinger, John C. Peters, S. P. Preheim, P. P. Kleinsasser, David E. Harder, P. N. Hiebert, Walter A. Gering, Harold H. Gross, Louis Linscheid, and Hugo Mierau. Lester Hostetler is the present minister; membership (1953) is 287. H.H.G.

Bethany Mennonite Church (MC), southwest of Imlay City, Lapeer Co., Mich., was organized on June 17, 1918, under the Indiana-Michigan Mennonite Conference by Peter Ropp, its first leader. Paul Wittrig, ordained for this congregation in 1938, is the present (1954) minister. In 1953 the membership was 30. P.A.W.

Bethany Mennonite Church (GCM) is located 10 miles southeast of Kingman, Kan., in the Western District Conference. The congregation was organized in 1907 by the first pastor C. J. Voran. The first church was built in 1907, burned in 1930, and a new frame building was built in 1932. Its 1953 membership was 183. H.E.M.

Bethany Mennonite Church (GCM) at Lost River, Sask., belongs to the Conference of Mennonites in Canada. In 1950 the congregation had a membership of 150, with Jacob H. Enns serving as minister. M.G.

Bethany Mennonite Church (MC), now extinct, was located near Neutral, Cherokee Co., Kan., in the southeastern part of the state. The first Mennonite settlers arrived from the east about 1880. Mennonite names in Cherokee County were Miller, Schmidt, Kuhns, Hamilton, Mast, Hooley, Shupe, Imhoff, and Nice. Resident ministers who served the congregation were Samuel Mishler, B. F. Hamilton, Abe Kuhns, Noah Shenk, and Amos Geigley. Samuel Mishler was a bishop, but was expelled from the brotherhood by the Kansas-Nebraska Conference in 1888. A deacon, Samuel Mishler, probably a relative of Bishop Samuel Mishler, also served the congregation. During the earlier period the Mennonites in Cherokee County were somewhat scattered, one group worshiping in the Neutral schoolhouse and another in the Stowel schoolhouse several miles southwest of Neutral. Later the two groups worshiped together and in 1900 built a

church one-half mile east and one-half mile south of Neutral. In 1896 the congregation transferred its membership from the Kansas-Nebraska Conference to the Missouri-Iowa Conference. The Mennonites used the Beasley cemetery, southwest of Neutral. The membership of the congregation was never large. In 1896, 15 members were reported. By 1906 most of the families had relocated. A few remained and were lost to the Mennonite Church.
G.G.Y.

Bethany Mennonite Church (GCM) of Quakertown, Bucks Co., Pa., is a member of the Eastern District Conference. On Dec. 27, 1898, a group of Mennonites living in Quakertown met in St. Paul's Evangelical Church for the purpose of taking preliminary steps toward organizing a congregation. This organization was finally effected at another meeting on Jan. 2, 1899. Services had previously been held occasionally in the St. Paul's church, but action was now taken to have regular services. Later in the same year the above building was purchased and remodeled. The Sunday school, organized in 1895, and the Young People's Society, organized in 1897, antedate the congregation and gave impetus to its organization.

Ministers and their terms of service are A. B. Shelly, 1899-1913; Harvey G. Allebach, 1913-21; P. E. Frantz, 1922-25; Seward M. Rosenberger, 1925-29; Arthur S. Rosenberger, 1930-34; A. J. Neuenschwander, 1939-49; Wilmer B. Denlinger, 1949-   . Deacons and their terms of service are U. S. Stauffer, 1899-1936; Daniel W. Landis, 1899-1925; A. G. Moyer, 1926-34; Milton R. Strunk, 1935-45; John K. Boorse, 1937-   ; Robert M. Landis, 1946-   .

The membership in 1908 was 62, and in 1953 was 156. The common names today are Shelly, Boorse, Landis, Moyer, George, and Martin.
J.H.F.

"History of the Bethany Congregation," in *1902 Mennonite Yearbook and Almanac* (Quakertown); "Bethany Church," in *1926 Mennonite Yearbook and Almanac* (Berne); J. C. Wenger, *Hist. of the Menn. of the Franconia Conference* (Telford, Pa., 1937).

Bethany Mennonite Church, Riverstyx, Ohio, an extinct C.G.C. congregation: see **Riverstyx.**

Bethany Mennonite Church (MC), a member of the Alberta-Saskatchewan Conference, is located near Smith, in northern Alberta. In July 1946, Willis Yoder started work in the district around Smith. As a result, on Oct. 5, 1947, a congregation was organized and 9 persons were baptized, who with the Yoders constituted the 11 charter members, in 1952 increased to 20.
E.S.

Bethany Mennonite Church (GCM) at Watrous, Sask., belonging to the Conference of the Mennonites in Canada. In 1953 the congregation, with Abram Warkentin serving as minister, had a membership of 88.
M.G.

Bethany Mennonite Church (GCM), Woodward Co., Okla., now extinct, had a membership of 37 and a Sunday-school attendance of 40 in 1911.
C.K.

Bethany United Missionary Church, located in Elkton, Mich., was organized in 1903 under the leadership of B. A. Sherk. The first meetinghouse was built in 1907. In 1949 the congregation had 25 members with W. M. William serving as pastor.
R.H.S.

Bethany United Missionary Church, Kitchener, Ont., was organized in 1877. The congregation conducts a branch Sunday school in the city of Kitchener. The 1949 membership was 349, with Arthur Walsh serving as pastor.
A.W.

Bethany (Lincoln Park) United Missionary Church is located in Lincoln Park, Mich.
M.G.

Bethany United Missionary Church, Port Hope, Ont., began as a mission station in June 1940, with M. Dedels and L. Hoover in charge. In May, 1949, the new church was opened and in 1951 the congregation was organized. In 1953 E. Prosser was appointed pastor.
W.B.

Bethany (St. Catharines) United Missionary Church is located at 9 King Street, St. Catharines, Ont.
M.G.

Bethausstreit (controversy concerning a meetinghouse). Johannes Neufeld of Neuhalbstadt, Molotschna settlement, Russia, a member of the Mennonite congregation of Ohrloff-Petershagen, built a large church in Neuhalbstadt in the 1850's almost entirely with his own funds. Afterwards because of the "barley dispute" (*Gerstenstreit*) and other difficulties in the congregation, Neufeld was one of a group which left the congregation. His demand that the newly built church be ceded to his own group led to unedifying dissension. By decision of the board in 1862 the church remained in the possession of the congregation of Ohrloff-Halbstadt (its name since 1848), and two thirds of the building costs were repaid to Neufeld. (Friesen, *Brüderschaft,* 90, notes 204, 221, and 304; *ML* I, 210.)
NEFF.

Beth-Car Mennonite Brethren in Christ Church is located at Staten Island, N.Y. Organized in 1938, the 1953 membership was 51, with Robert W. Smock serving as pastor.
J.H.R.

Bethel Chapel (UMC), Big Valley, Alta., was organized in June 1947. Meetings were held in a building seating 50, and J. W. Cox was appointed pastor in 1951.
J.GA.

Bethel Church of God in Christ Mennonite Church is located two miles west and three miles south of Greensburg, Kiowa Co., Kan. Its first members settled here about 1907, worshiping in schools until 1928, when the present church was built. This congregation had a membership of 81 in 1953, with a staff of two ministers and two deacons, all ordained at this place. Harvey Yost is the minister in charge. All services are in the English language. The services consist of Sunday morning and evening worship, Sunday school, Bible study, and Brotherly Counsel. The congregation observes the ordinance of footwashing at communion, teaches and practices nonconformity to the world, and supports hospitals, rest homes, sewing circles, relief, and missions.
L.J.

Bethel College of the General Conference Mennonite Church is an institution of higher learning located at North Newton, Harvey Co., Kan. It owes its origin to the desire of the Mennonites who emigrated from Russia to Kansas in 1874 and the years following to maintain and perpetuate their special heritage. The preparation of their own teachers and church workers was considered a necessary prerequisite to the achievement of this end. The study of the English language was urged from the very beginning, both as a means of social intercourse with their American neighbors, and as a prerequisite for doing religious work among the English-speaking population. Within three years after the arrival of the first major immigrant groups in this country repeated calls were issued in *Zur Heimath* (*q.v.*) for a conference of school-teachers, religious teachers, and elders to consider school matters. Such a meeting was held on Nov. 15, 1877, in a rural schoolhouse in the Alexander-wohl community about 10 miles north of Newton, Kan. This meeting adopted a set of resolutions the most important of which "recognized the necessity of establishing a Zentralschule in which capable young men . . . could acquire the necessary training for teachers."

The movement resulted in the establishment of the Emmetal school. This was conducted in a private schoolhouse in the Alexanderwohl community during 1882-83 with H. H. Ewert as teacher, under the control of the school committee of the Kansas Mennonite Conference. Thirty students attended the school during the eight-month term. Its purpose was stated to be the preparation of candidates for rural schoolteachers' examinations. However, unsatisfactory housing conditions and a limited curriculum proved serious handicaps. It was evident from the very beginning that, unless more satisfactory facilities could be provided, the future held little promise for the school.

The school was transferred the following year to Halstead, Kan., where a group of brethren, the Halstead College Association, had erected a building which was placed at the disposal of the Kansas Conference rent free for a period of five years. The curriculum was expanded, an additional teacher, P. J. Galle, was employed, and school was opened Sept. 20, 1883. It was officially called "Mennonitische Fortbildungsschule"; its English designation was "The Mennonite Seminary." Seventy-two students attended the school the first year. Its main objectives were: the preparation of rural public school teachers, German parochial school teachers, and church workers. Regarding the third objective, special emphasis was placed upon the preparation of workers for the foreign mission field. As in the case of the Emmetal school, only men students were admitted the first year, but girls were admitted tentatively early in the year and co-education soon became the accepted practice.

The improved facilities attracted a larger attendance and soon proved inadequate, but expansion was impossible, primarily because of the lack of funds. It was then decided to incorporate the Halstead school under the name of Bethel College and to solicit a fund of $100,000. One half of this fund was to be used for endowment, the other half for the erection of suitable buildings.

But while these matters were under considera-

tion the city of Newton made an offer of $15,000 in cash and land valued at $85,000 to the Kansas Mennonite Conference if the school would be located at Newton. A special meeting of the conference, held at Halstead on April 27, 1887, was not ready to accept the Newton offer, but authorized David Goerz, Bernhard Warkentin, and John J. Krehbiel to form a private corporation which could incorporate, build, and control the proposed Bethel College in all details.

Such a corporation was quickly formed. A charter was drawn up which was signed by 33 persons, and approved by the Secretary of State of the State of Kansas on May 23, 1887. The corporation was called "The Bethel College of the Mennonite Church of North America at Newton, Harvey Co., Kansas," and the governing body was defined as a board of nine members, three to be elected annually for a term of three years.

The most important change in the charter to date is the increase in the membership of the board of directors to 13, seven of whom are elected by the corporation from nominations made by the Western District and the Pacific conferences. The bylaws contained specific details pertaining to the board of directors, the faculty, students, curriculum, memberships in the corporation, and relations of the corporation to Mennonite conferences.

The new corporation was given permission to solicit funds within the Mennonite congregations, although the change from conference to corporation (i.e., private) control did not meet with universal approval and the doors were left open for the resumption of conference control. An aggressive financial campaign was undertaken, building operations were begun, the basement was completed, and the cornerstone laid on Oct. 12, 1888. This date has become historic in building operations at Bethel College, and the cornerstones of Science Hall, Memorial Hall, and the new library were laid on the corresponding dates of 1924, 1938, and 1948 respectively. The new building was dedicated on Sept. 19, 1893, and school opened the next day. Five teachers were employed and the total enrollment for the year was 98. No courses of college rank were offered; in fact, much of the work was on the elementary level.

It had been planned originally to continue the Halstead Seminary as a preparatory school for Bethel College, but the new institution took over the teachers and much of the equipment of the Halstead school and the latter was closed permanently on June 7, 1893. The first curriculum of Bethel College consisted of a preparatory course, an academic course, and a prospective college course, each of three years in length. There were no electives.

The new institution was beset with difficulties from the very beginning. The enlarged faculty and the expanded curriculum soon proved inadequate. Library facilities were meager and laboratory facilities were entirely lacking. Extracurricular activities were left entirely to student initiative. There was constant pressure from the student body for further expansion. The curriculum underwent repeated revisions in the effort to meet the needs of both Mennonite youth and the Mennonite Church, and at the same time keep abreast of modern educational trends. The scope of the curriculum has been expanded to include applied arts and sciences. Curricula are now offered leading to the B.A., the B.S., and the Th.B. degrees. The first college degrees were conferred in 1912. Bethel College has also conferred honorary degrees in recognition of distinguished service rendered.

The library now contains more than 30,000 volumes, and receives more than 200 magazines regularly. A new library building was completed in 1952. Alumni Hall, erected by the alumni of Bethel College in 1913, houses the Kauffman Museum, which contains a large and valuable collection of articles covering a wide field and arranged under three major divisions, historical, natural history, and art. Science Hall, erected in 1924-25, provides strictly modern facilities for instruction in the natural sciences. Memorial Hall, dedicated in 1942, provides the facilities for indoor physical training. The kitchen and dining facilities are also located in this building. Its auditorium has a seating capacity of approximately 3,000. The Franz General Shop, erected in 1947, houses the facilities for industrial arts and general shopwork.

Student industries were introduced in 1936. These have assisted many students in acquiring a college education. Scholarships, assistantships, and loan funds provide additional student aid.

Approximately 20 student organizations and activities provide a wide range of extracurricular opportunities to Bethel College students. In the religious field are the Student Christian Association, Student Volunteers for Christian Service, Student Ministers' Fellowship, and the Student Peace Group. Debate, oratory, and dramatics are open to those interested in speech. International Relations Club, Biology Seminar, Cheminar, and other departmental clubs are supported by many students. Both intramural and intercollegiate athletics are stressed. Among the most widely known college organizations is its a cappella choir, The Mennonite Singers. The *Collegian* and the *Graymaroon* are the two student publications. The Memorial Hall Series provides high-class music and lecture numbers not only for the students but also for the constituency within several hours' driving distance from Newton.

The Mennonite Historical Library, established in 1936, is an important center of research for students of Mennonite history. It contains over 7,000 catalogued volumes (1950), some of them rare and extremely valuable, and a large collection of Mennonite periodicals, reports, yearbooks, diaries, letters, photographs, etc. Constant additions are being made to the collections.

The College has published since its beginning annual catalogs, reports, the *School and College Journal* (1898-1902), *Bethel College Monthly* (1903-34), *Mennonite Life* (1946-   ), the *Collegian*, and a number of books mostly printed in the Bethel College Press, which was reorganized in 1949 and known as the Mennonite Press (*q.v.*) owned and operated by the College and the General Conference Mennonite Church.

There was a fairly steady, though somewhat irregular growth in attendance until 1949, since then a decline. The total attendance to date (1949) exceeds 6,700. Of this number, approximately 2,000 have served as public or parochial school teachers and in colleges and universities over wide areas. More than 300 have entered the ministry and the mission field and more than 125 are serving as physicians and nurses. The number entering other specialized fields of service in church, state, or nation exceeds 150. The maximum enrollment was reached in 1938-40, when it totaled 525. The faculty has increased from 5 full-time to more than 40 full- and part-time instructors. The academic status of the faculty has risen steadily and now ranks high among denominational colleges. In 1916 Bethel College was fully accredited by the Kansas State Board of Public Instruction and in 1938 it was admitted to membership in the North Central Association of Colleges and Secondary Schools. The College is also a member of the Kansas Council of Church Colleges, the National Conference of Church-Related Colleges, the Association of American Colleges, and the American Association of Colleges for Teacher Education.

The most difficult problem that has confronted Bethel College during the years has been the finances. But here, too, a gradual change for the better has taken place, especially during the last 15 years. At the opening of Bethel College in 1893, its endowment fund approximated $60,000, its plant value was $43,000, and the net worth of the institution was $103,000 (*Sechster Jahresbericht des Bethel-College-Direktoriums,* 1892-93). In 1952 the endowment fund had reached nearly $654,000, the plant value $870,000, and the net worth exceeded $1,577,000. Bethel has no indebtedness.

A revised statement of the aims and purposes of Bethel College was adopted by the faculty and the Board of Directors in 1936, and in 1942 the college adopted the "Statement of Faith of the Mennonite Church of North America," which the General Conference had adopted in 1941, as its own. These are published in the annual catalog.

In accordance with these aims Bethel College has sought first and foremost to serve the constituency in its most immediate needs, particularly in teaching, the ministry, and the mission field. But Bethel College also aims to foster a love of learning and a spirit of inquiry that will lead to further development of native talents and abilities, and thus enable the individual to serve the larger community and in more specialized fields. Bethel College graduates are taking up graduate work in increasing numbers and are finding their way more and more into highly specialized fields, the different professions, social service, government service, and research.† P.J.W.

Bethel College Bulletin, 1913 ff.; *Erster Jahresbericht des Direktoriums der projectierten Bethel College der Mennonitengemeinschaft von Nord Amerika zu Newton, Kansas,* 1887-88, 3, 6, 15-31, 54; *Erster Katalog von Bethel College zu Newton, Kansas* (1893-94) 3; *First Annual Report of the Board of Directors of Bethel College, 1887-88,* 6-7, 10-15; *Katalog der Mennonitischen Fortbildungsschule* (1892-93) 2; *Gesamt-Protokolle . . . westlichen Distrikt-Konferenz, 1877-1900* (Newton, 1910); 5, 59, 169; H. P. Peters, History and Development of

Education Among the Mennonites in Kansas (Hillsboro, Kan., 1925); *Zur Heimat*, Aug. 15, 1877, Oct. 15, 1877; *School and College Journal*, 1896-1902; *Monatsblätter aus Bethel College*, 1903-17; *Bethel College Monthly*, 1917-35; P. J. Wedel, "History of Bethel College" (1949, ms.); *ML* I, 211.

Bethel College of the United Missionary Church, located at Mishawaka, Ind., is owned and operated by four conferences of the church, Indiana, Michigan, Ohio, and Nebraska, under charter granted by the State of Indiana in 1947. It is a four-year college with two divisions, Liberal Arts College and School of the Bible. It offers a major in Biblical literature and in other regular college fields leading to the B.A. and B.R. degrees. Attendance in 1951-52 was 216, 135 liberal arts, 46 Bible, and 35 special and postgraduate with a faculty of 15 including part-time instructors. The school has a beautiful campus of 40 acres. Its main administration building was completed in 1951.   J.A.Hu.

Bethel College Academy began operations with the opening of Bethel College on Sept. 20, 1893. During the first years the work of Bethel College was confined entirely to the academy and sub-academy level. No courses of college rank were offered. The first curriculum consisted of a two-year preparatory course and a three-year academy course. A Bible course and an evangelists' course were introduced in 1896. These, too, were mostly of academy rank. The preparatory course was discontinued in 1896 and only a few "preparatory branches" were offered as occasion demanded for several years thereafter. The curriculum of the academy was reorganized in 1899 into three separate courses, a German-English, an English, and a normal course each of three years in length, thus allowing students some election.

The academy was reorganized in 1909 on the plan of the four-year public high school. The new curriculum continued the German-English and the English academy courses, expanding them to four years each. The normal course was discontinued and an academy Bible course of five years added. In the same year definite admission requirements were outlined in the catalog for the first time. A four-year normal course was added and the first normal training class organized in 1910. The academy was accredited by the Kansas State Board of Public Instruction in 1910 and by the North Central Association of Colleges and Secondary Schools in 1913. A principal of the normal department was appointed in 1912, but the academy remained under the direct supervision of the president of the College.

In 1915 the purpose of the academy was stated as "(1) to prepare students for college, (2) to give normal training for teaching, and (3) to furnish such instruction as is desired by those who intend to re-enter their community with a general fund of knowledge and a clarified purpose in life." (*Bethel College Bulletin* II, No. 1, May 1915.)

There was much overlapping of college and academy faculty members during these years. College equipment, library, laboratories, etc., were at the disposal of the academy. These were stressed as advantages the academy possessed over the pub-

lic high schools. In 1924 a principal of the academy was appointed, and in 1926 a separate organization of the academy was effected with its own principal and faculty.

The attendance fluctuated considerably but approached 200 at times. But the increasing number of public high schools supported by taxation brought about a rapid decline in attendance, beginning in the early twenties. Free tuition in the high schools weighed heavily against increasing tuition in the academy. The academy became more and more a financial burden to the college and was discontinued at the close of the school year 1926-27.

Its discontinuance was a cause of much regret among the constituency. The academy was a testimony to their interest in education. It had done much to raise the level of culture among the constituency, and to keep it abreast of educational progress in their still relatively new environment. It had fostered adherence to the tenets of the church and had been for years the main source of supply of teachers and church workers so sorely needed in the communities.

The academy was revived for a brief period (1944-46) during World War II under the name "The Mennonite Bible Academy." It had its own separate organization, though under the auspices of the Bethel College Board of Directors. The maximum attendance was 70 with a full- and part-time faculty of 11 members. Because of the increasing number of college students at Bethel College following the close of the war with the resultant heavy demand upon college facilities, the academy at Bethel College was closed again.   P.J.W.

Bethel College Bulletin is the official monthly, four-page periodical of Bethel College, North Newton, Kan. Published since 1914, its purpose has been to furnish friends, alumni, and parents of students with official announcements, news of college functions, progress, and needs, reports of alumni activities, and general articles of educational interest.   J.F.S.

Bethel College Mennonite Church (GCM) at North Newton, Harvey Co., Kan., was organized to meet the needs of a college community, first of all the students and faculty of Bethel College, and also others who were attracted to the services and began attending in increasing numbers. With 22 charter members, the church had its beginning in 1897. C. H. Wedel, Bethel College's first president, was chosen as college pastor, and David Goerz, business manager of the college, as elder. The church became a member of the Western District Conference in 1898 and a year later, 1899, was received into the General Conference.

With the growth of the Newton community and the college, the congregation likewise increased in numbers. The present membership (November 1953) is 530, though nearly one fourth of these may be classified as "non-resident." The resident membership is made up of teachers and other employees of the college, laborers, business and professional people, as well as retired couples living in Newton. Less than 20 families live on farms. There are within the membership at present 23 ordained ministers, some of whom are retired and others of whom are engaged as teachers, missionaries, or administrative workers. The students worship with the congregation and may become associate members.

Services of worship are held every Sunday in the college chapel which has a seating capacity of nearly 600. The need for a separate church building has been felt for some years and in 1950 the erection of a church on the Bethel College campus was begun. The German language was used exclusively until 1912, when provision was made for some English services. Since 1930 all services, with the exception of certain special meetings, have employed only the English language, though the German chorales are still loved and find occasional use.

Since the early ministries of C. H. Wedel and David Goerz, 1897-1912, the church has been served by the following pastors: J. W. Kliewer, 1912-25; H. A. Fast, 1925-30; J. H. Langenwalter (supply), 1931-32; J. W. Kliewer, 1932-35; J. N. Smucker, 1936-42; Lester Hostetler, 1942-52; Harold Buller, 1952- . (*ML* I, 210.)   L.H.

Bethel College Press, North Newton, Kan. In 1902 Bethel College purchased a "Little Model Printing Office," to provide for the printing needs of the college, such as the college paper and blanks for college use and some job printing. An addressograph was added in 1905. In 1906 the press was discontinued because of lack of experienced help.

The matter remained dormant until 1933 when the Bethel College Board of Directors authorized the purchase of a printing press as a part of the new student industries program. More equipment was added from time to time, until the output of the print shop consisted of periodicals, pamphlets, and books in addition to considerable job work. At times it furnished employment to as many as 25 students.

Almost from the beginning of the new venture efforts were made toward co-operation of the College Press with the General Conference Mennonite Board of Publication (GCM). In 1949 an agreement was worked out between the two respective boards which was approved by the executive committee of the General Conference, and accepted by the conference. The printing interests of Bethel College and of the General Conference Board of Publication thus became a joint venture operating under a separate Board of Directors of the Mennonite Press. The Mennonite Press (*q.v.*) is located in the Grattan Building on the Bethel College campus.   P.J.W.

Bethel Deaconess Home and Hospital Society, of Newton, Kan., is a benevolent corporation, chartered March 30, 1903, under the laws of the State of Kansas. The purpose for which this organization was created, as stated in the charter, is the building and maintaining of a deaconess home and hospital, and the establishing and operation of a training school to educate nurses and deaconesses under the auspices of the General Conference Mennonite Church. It was the outgrowth of the deep interest of David Goerz (*q.v.*) in deaconess work among the Mennonites and the need for such work among the Mennonites and in the community. The society was founded by the Board of Directors of Bethel College (*q.v.*) and patterned after the Mennonite deaconess hospitals in Russia.

The society is governed by a board of nine directors. David Goerz, Abraham Ratzlaff, Abraham Baumgartner, H. Banman, Jacob Isaac, J. W. Regier, Bernhard Warkentin, J. J. Krehbiel, and Gustav A. Haury served as members of the first board. The members of the board of directors are elected by the members of the society. Every member, society, congregation, or conference of Mennonites is eligible for membership in the society.

This society established a deaconess program and has maintained a deaconess motherhouse since 1908. The deaconesses attached to this motherhouse have served mainly in the institutions which this society maintains but have also served in other areas. A total of 67 deaconesses have been connected with this motherhouse. At present (1950) the deaconesses number 25.

In addition to the deaconesses, many other workers have been trained to serve in hospitals, homes for aged, and mission fields.

In 1908 the society also built and established the Bethel Deaconess Hospital which has grown into a sizable institution. Affiliated with the hospital is a school of nursing, the purpose of which is to train young women for definite fields of Christian service.

In 1926 the society opened its home for aged which has facilities for 35 guests. At present (1950) plans are in progress to enlarge this institution.

This society has grown consistently through the years and has been of great benefit to the church and community through the services which it has rendered and through the institutions which it maintains.   H.J.A.

Bethel Deaconess Hospital of Newton, Kan., is a 100-bed general hospital owned and operated by the Bethel Deaconess Home and Hospital Society, fully approved by the American College of Surgeons, the American Medical Association, and the Kansas State Board of Health.

The original plant, which had room for 30 patients, was dedicated and opened for service on June 11, 1908, with Sister Frieda Kaufman as the first superintendent. Since that time three additions have been made to the main building and a separate building has been erected for the school of nursing.

The hospital maintains an open medical staff and strives to maintain the best in modern equipment for the diagnosis and treatment of disease. It also strives to render the nursing care to the patient in a spirit of Christian love and devotion. It is the aim and object of the hospital to maintain high professional and ethical standards in its service which is rendered to all regardless of race, creed, color, or of financial standing.

The Bethel Deaconess Hospital School of Nursing is an integral part of the Bethel Deaconess Hospital and was organized in 1908, soon after the hospital was opened. It is accredited and approved by the Board of Nurse Registration and Nursing Education in the State of Kansas. It is the purpose of the school of nursing to select Christian young women with an aptitude for nursing and to assist them to develop this aptitude in an environment that will develop Christian life and character, with special consideration given to those who are preparing for some definite field of Christian service. (*ML* I, 212.)†   H.J.A.

Bethel Girls' Home located in Vancouver, B.C., was founded in 1931 by the Conference of the Mennonite Brethren Churches. The need for such a home was felt particularly during the period of the depression in the early thirties, when Mennonite girls streamed into the city in search of employment. At first about 50 girls visited the home regularly; later this number rose to over 100. For a while the number decreased, but rose again during the new immigration in the later forties. The ministers of the Mennonite Brethren Church (corner Prince Edward St. and 43rd Ave.) provide the girls with spiritual care and guidance, and experienced girls serve as matrons of the home. On Thursday, when the girls have their half-day off, they gather in the home, exchange their experiences, and receive Bible instruction and spiritual care from the ministers. In this manner the Bethel Girls' Home meets a great need. See also **Mary Martha Girls' Home (GCM)** in Vancouver.
                                                J.G.R.

Bethel Home is a home for the aged, an institution of the Church of God in Christ Mennonites located at Montezuma, Gray Co., Kan. The building, constructed in 1948, a modern two-story brick structure 36 x 48, with two wings 36 x 38 each, is built over a full basement. It has a chapel, 25 resident rooms, 4 maternity wards, an office, a waiting room, several soundproof rooms, a fully equipped kitchen, dining-room, laundry, and several other storage rooms. The institution operates on a nonprofit basis. Its initial cost was estimated at $70,000. It is sponsored by the congregations in the United States and built under the direction of the Charitable Institutions Board whose executive officers are G. H. Dyck, Hesston, Kan., chairman; Sam Dirks, Montezuma, Kan., treasurer; and Jacob Wadel, Greensburg, Kan., secretary (1950). A.J.U.

Bethel Home for the Aged, Newton, Kan., is owned and operated by the Bethel Deaconess Home and Hospital Society (*q.v.*) also of Newton, an organization incorporated under the laws of the State of Kansas on March 30, 1903. The object of the society, as stated in the charter, is to establish and maintain a deaconess home and hospital and to build, maintain, and support other benevolent, charitable, or educational undertakings.

The management of the home is delegated to a committee of three, known as the Committee on Management, appointed annually, one member each year, by the board of directors of the society immediately following the annual meeting of the corporation. An Advisory Council of five members is to deliberate and act with the Committee on Management and to help form and develop policies. This council is created as follows: The Bethel

Deaconess Home and Hospital Society elects two men and one woman into the council, one member annually, for a term of three years; the Women's Auxiliary of the hospital elects two members for the council, one member annually, for a term of two years.

The home now provides room for 70 aged people and the persons needed for their care, a wing having been added in 1951-52. Since it opened its doors for service May 9, 1926, it has almost constantly been filled to capacity, giving a home, comfort, and nursing care to its residents.

The home receives life members and temporary residents. Life members pay on the basis of their means and expectancy upon entrance to the home and are assured that all of their needs will be met. They are selected on the basis of need. Temporary residents pay a monthly rate for room, board, and nursing care. Their relationship with the home is not permanent. There are no denominational restrictions for the resident.   H.J.A.

Bethel Hospital at Winkler, Man., is supported by voluntary gifts from Christian friends, and controlled by the Bethel Hospital Society since 1935 when a committee consisting of J. J. Enns, J. A. Kroeker, J. B. Dyck, J. D. Adrian, Dr. A. H. Unruh, C. H. Grunau, secretary, and A. A. Kroeker, chairman, secured the upper floor of the J. B. Dyck residence as a maternity home. The following September the first section of Bethel Hospital was constructed. This provided accommodation for 12 beds. In 1942 the south wing was added, thereby increasing the bed capacity to 36, and in 1946 the north wing was built of fire-resisting materials at a cost of $50,000. This raised the bed capacity to 40 and it also provided two excellent operating rooms as well as space for the installation of modern X-ray diagnostic equipment.

A staff of four registered and nine practical nurses, under Miss Susie Derksen, matron, ministers to the needs of the patients who numbered 354 males, 851 females, and 141 infants in 1948. There were 179 outpatients that year and Dr. C. W. Wiebe and Dr. A. P. Warkentin performed 509 surgical operations.†

(A 24-page booklet entitled *Bethel Hospital, 1936-1949*, was published in 1949.)   P.BR.

Bethel Hospital Association of Mountain Lake, Minn., held its incorporation meeting on Jan. 2, 1905, for the purpose of establishing the Mennonite Hospital of Mountain Lake. The instigator of this movement was Jacob D. Hiebert, who with his brother David had purchased the old village schoolhouse with the intention of converting it into a hospital. By September the hospital was ready for its first patients with Margaretha Friesen as the first nurse.

From 1912 to 1930 the institution was merged with the Bethel Deaconess Hospital of Newton, Kan., the name of the local unit being changed to "Bethel Deaconess Hospital of Mountain Lake." In 1921 a new 20-bed brick hospital was constructed at a cost of about $60,000. The former building was then used as a home for the aged, operated under the same management as the hospital. Since 1911, when the institution was stabilized, superintendents who served a year or more include: Elizabeth Harms, 1911-14; Ida Epp, 1915-27; Clara Schmidt, 1927-28; Agathe Toews, 1929-32; Marie Toews, 1932-34, 1938-46; Marie K. Fast, 1934-37; Elfriede H. Regier, 1947- . Other superintendents served for shorter terms.

By 1947 the service of the Bethel Hospital, as it has been known since it became independent in 1930, had expanded to the point where it cared for a total of 731 patients annually. The capacity of the home for the aged was 20 persons, with every room occupied.

The urgent need for a new and larger home for the aged prompted the construction of a new brick 52-room building at an estimated cost of $240,000, dedicated in 1950.

While the Bethel Hospital Association is organizationally independent of the churches, its constituency is composed almost entirely of Mennonites residing in Mountain Lake and its vicinity. E.W.

Bethel Krimmer Mennonite Brethren Church, located near Hooker, Okla., was organized in April 1907, when a baptism and church dedication service was held, and Klaas D. Willems began to serve as minister. A year later the membership of this group numbered 64 souls. Krimmer Mennonite Brethren had settled here several years earlier, but had worshiped with the Mennonite Brethren at that place. The congregation dissolved early in 1919, scattered by war clouds and depressing experiences as a result of war. The church was sold for use as a Bible academy. H. B. Pauls served as second minister and J. D. Klassen as deacon. C.F.P.

Bethel Krimmer Mennonite Brethren Church, now extinct, was located five miles southwest of Weatherford, Cedar Twp., Custer Co., Okla. The church was organized with 20 members under the guidance of Heinrich and Peter A. Wiebe on Nov. 18, 1897, when a baptismal service was held, and Peter K. Wohlgemuth was elected to serve as first minister. When the mud houses of the members became too small for meeting places, they used a schoolhouse. On Aug. 22, 1904, they dedicated a new church. In 1916 the congregation had a membership of 50. Other ministers who served the congregation are J. M. Friesen and D. E. Harder. The church became extinct in 1937, when the remaining members joined another church and the building was sold. C.F.P.

Bethel (Balko) Mennonite Brethren Church near Balko, Okla., was organized March 2, 1906, with 14 members. S. L. Hodel was chosen as leader and J. H. Neufeld deacon. In December 1906 Gerhard Bartel became presiding minister. Services were held in various homes until 1907, when the first church was built. This was enlarged in 1912. In 1913 Isaac Harms was elected minister and H. P. Kliewer deacon. In 1916 the church was sold and a new one built. From 1916 to 1926 Fred Just served the church as minister. H. H. Martens, elected to the ministry in 1919, assisted for some time.

From 1926 to 1946 H. P. Kliewer served the church as presiding minister. Since then D. H. Penner has led the church. In 1946 the church was rebuilt and enlarged. The 1951 membership was 124. D.H.P.

Bethel (Allentown) Mennonite Brethren in Christ Church is located at 526-530 North 8th Street, Allentown, Pa. In 1952 it was the largest congregation in the denomination, with a membership of 440. M.G.

Bethel (Emmaus) Mennonite Brethren in Christ Church is located at 418-20 Elm Street, Emmaus, Pa. In 1952 it had a membership of 156. M.G.

Bethel Mennonite Brethren in Christ Church, Macungie, Lehigh Co., Pa., was organized in 1901 under the leadership of J. G. Shireman. The 1948 membership was 30 and F. B. Hertzog served as pastor. F.B.H.

Bethel Mennonite Church (MC), near Bothwell, Kent Co., Ont. In 1918 this nearly extinct Mennonite community came up for attention at the annual meeting of the Rural Mission Board of Ontario, with the result that ministers were sent there to conduct services. In 1927 a church was purchased in Bothwell and a resident minister given charge with evening services at Clachan Corners. But the congregation did not revive and the Bothwell property was sold. In 1931 work was resumed as a Sunday school in the Austen school south of Bothwell. A few young people from Waterloo County moved into the community, and a membership was built up from a new circle of families. Arnold Gingrich was ordained and became resident pastor. The Bethel church built a few miles south of Bothwell in 1941 and became the one center of worship, with a membership of 22 in 1953. (See **Aldboro, Austen, Clachan,** and **Mosa.**) J.C.F.

Bethel Mennonite Church (MC), located about eight miles southeast of Canby, Ore., and an equal distance from Hubbard and Aurora, is a member of the Pacific Coast Conference.

Members of the Zion and Hopewell congregations living in this community, five to ten miles from their respective home churches, held Sunday school and preaching services in local schoolhouses while the roads were muddy in the wet season and dusty in the dry season, until 1912, when a church was built for their community. On May 4, 1919, a congregation was organized and a resident minister placed in the community.

Such names as Roth, Mitchell, Strubhar, Nofziger, Bond, Hostetler, Rogie, Yoder, Troyer, Christner, Kropf, Bressler, Schultz, Greenwood, Miller, Kauffman, Good, Snyder, Zook, Schrock, Gingerich, Bontrager, Switzer, Diener, and Birkey are known as being or having been among the worshipers at Bethel. In 1953 the membership was 80. (S. G. Shetler, *Church Hist. of the Pacific Coast Menn. Conf. District,* Scottdale, 1931.) F.J.G.

Bethel Mennonite Church (MC) of Chicago, Ill., is located at 14th Place and Laflin Street. It was started in 1945 as a project among the colored people by the Mission Board of the Illinois Conference. The total membership of Bethel, together with that of Dearborn Street Mission (an outpost at 1808 Dearborn Street), is 53 exclusive of workers, with James H. Lark as pastor (1953). J.H.L.

Bethel Mennonite Church (MC) four miles north of Cootes Store, Rockingham Co., Va., is a member of the Virginia Conference. About 1915 a Sunday school was started by two Baptist girls under a tree near this place. It was later moved to an old store building near by. The Mennonite Church was invited to take the work over and the store building was purchased in 1918 and used for services until around 1925 when it was torn down, moved to its present location, and enlarged. The membership was 110 in 1953 and the pastor was M. D. Emswiler.   T.S.

Bethel Mennonite Church (GCM), located near Dolton in Turner Co., S.D., with a membership of approximately 80, is a member of the Northern District Conference. The first building was dedicated and the congregation organized in December 1892. The present meetinghouse, built in 1920, seats 500. The congregation first had a pastor of its own in 1917, when J. A. Thieszen was appointed. He resigned on Jan. 1, 1950; since that time the congregation has been served by Glenn Epp, Joe Hoffer, H. J. Brown, and Harold Thiessen, who was called on July 1, 1953. One missionary and two pastors have gone out from the congregation to serve in other fields.   J.A.T.

Bethel Mennonite Church (GCM) at Dubois, Clark Co., Idaho, now extinct. In 1912-13 a number of General Conference Mennonite families and some single persons, mostly from central Kansas, moved into this region to take up dry-farm homesteads. During the first several years they met in the various homes for Sunday school and worship. Twice a month one of the ministers from the two Aberdeen, Idaho, G.C.M. churches or P. R. Aschliman from Colfax, Wash., served them.

On Jan. 1, 1916, they met in a schoolhouse and organized the Bethel Mennonite Church, with 40 charter members. Leonard Dirks was in charge of this meeting. Six months later this church joined the Pacific District Conference and in 1917 also the General Conference. The total membership reached about 60. Due to increasing drought and almost total crop failures, more and more families were forced to leave and in 1920 the last Mennonite family left the area. Some moved back to Kansas, some to California, and quite a few to Aberdeen, joining the Mennonite congregation at that place. H.H.L.

Bethel Mennonite Church (MC), located near Elora, Ont., about six miles northeast of Floradale, belongs to the Ontario Mennonite Conference. It was organized on Dec. 21, 1947, with 26 members. The church, a brick structure, formerly owned by the United Church, is situated in a rural district. On Sept. 5, 1948, Henry F. Martin was ordained deacon. On June 19, 1949, Newton L. Gingerich was ordained and is the present (1953) pastor, with 72 members.   R.D.

Bethel Mennonite Church (GCM), near Fortuna, Moniteau Co., Mo., is a member of the Middle District Conference. In April 1866 five families left Wayne Co., Ohio, to become the first Mennonite settlers of this community. Others soon followed and on April 21, 1867, ministers John Schmidt and Jacob Pletscher of Summerfield, Ill., visited the colony to have communion service and organize a church. Nineteen persons took part in this service. The first meetinghouse was built in 1869, enlarged in 1894; it was replaced by a larger church in 1908, with a seating capacity of about 450, which is in use at the present time. The 1952 membership was 137. (*Hist. of Bethel Church, Fortuna, Mo.*)   E.A.A.

Bethel Mennonite Church (MC), located near Garden City in Camp Branch Twp., Cass Co., Mo., was merged with the Sycamore Grove congregation in August 1947. It was a member of the South Central Conference with a membership of 59 at the time of the merger. The congregation was probably organized in 1885 and the church building was built in 1886. It was organized largely through the effort of J. S. Coffman who in his evangelistic efforts in the early eighties gathered up the fragments of the Clearfork congregation in that community and bound them together in the Bethel Mennonite Church. Bishop D. D. Kauffman and Preacher D. F. Driver of the Mt. Zion congregation near Versailles, Mo., helped minister to the spiritual needs of the congregation in its early history. A. D. Wenger served them in the early nineties as resident minister. About this time Preacher L. J. Heatwole came to Missouri and later was to be their first resident bishop. After he moved back to Virginia, Bishop Daniel Kauffman of Versailles served them until the fall of 1912 when Joseph C. Driver, who was serving them at that time as minister, was ordained bishop. During the 60 years or more of the history of this congregation, the ministers who served it besides the bishops were A. D. Wenger, D. Y. Hooley, Daniel Yoder, J. B. Smith, C. S. Houder, W. E. Helmuth, D. S. King, and James Steiner. Bethel's character as a Mennonite congregation alongside the larger Amish Mennonite congregation of Sycamore Grove was its chief reason for existence.   J.C.D.

Bethel Mennonite Church (MC) (formerly called Mummasburg), near Gettysburg, Adams Co., Pa., became a member of the Ohio Mennonite and Eastern Amish Mennonite Conference in May 1947. The total membership in 1953 was 62. It was first organized as a congregation in June 1939, the members having previously belonged to the Mummasburg congregation of the Lancaster Conference. The ministers are A. A. Landis, Ephrata, Pa., and Glen Musselman, Gettysburg.   J.F.K.

Bethel Mennonite Church (GCM), Great Deer, Sask., originated during the 1890's when the Rosthern Mennonite settlement was started and some settlers crossed the North Saskatchewan River. During the first years the church was served by ministers from other congregations. C. F. Sawatzky was minister for 24 years; he was succeeded in 1951 by Isaac J. Nickel. The church building was dedicated by Elder Peter Regier in 1912.   J.G.R.

Bethel Mennonite Church (GCM), located nine miles southeast of Hydro, Caddo Co., Okla., was organized July 10, 1906, as the Bethel Gemeinde, with Gerhard Dick as its first pastor. It is a member of the Western District Conference and in 1952 had a membership of 53. Four ministers have served the congregation, Waldo W. Kaufman being its present pastor.   W.W.K.

Bethel Mennonite Church (GCM), 1½ miles south of Inman, Kan., was organized January 1875 with 35 members and Jacob Klassen as minister. He served as the first elder from 1877 to 1879. Other elders have been Heinrich Toews, 1879 to 1912; Klaas Kroeker, 1912 to 1936; and P. T. Neufeld, 1936 to the present. The church is a member of the General Conference Mennonite Church and of the Western District Conference, with a membership of 313. The first meetinghouse, used until 1897, was an adobe building, erected in 1880 a mile south of the present location. Then a wooden structure was erected at the present location. This was used till 1928, when it was destroyed by lightning. Thereupon a new building was erected, with a seating capacity of about 400. In 1953 the church was again destroyed by fire and a new brick church was built. The church has furnished the following missionaries: H. T. Neufelds, John Thiessens, Frank Ennses, John T. Neufeld, Eva Pauls, Henry Toews, George B. Neufelds, and Arthur Thiessens.
P.T.N.

Bethel Mennonite Church (MC), one mile north of Job in Randolph Co., W. Va., on the west side of the Allegheny Mountains, is under the general direction of the Home Mission Board of the Middle District of the Virginia Conference. It was already in the 1870's a preaching point. In 1907 a church was built, and also a mission home for resident workers, who to a large extent replaced itinerant leaders who had come to the field once or twice a month. The church has a membership of 34.
H.A.B.

Bethel Mennonite Church (GCM) of Lancaster, Pa., is a member of the Eastern District Conference. It was organized in 1946 by a group of interested laymen with the assistance of the Eastern District Home Mission Committee. Don. E. Smucker was its first pastor. The 1952 membership was 65.
A.M.Wi.

Bethel Mennonite Church (GCM), nine miles west and one mile south of Langdon, Cavalier Co., N.D. The congregation was organized in the spring of 1897 and the church was dedicated in the fall of 1900, with Christian Kaufmann, traveling evangelist, present for the services. The membership in 1952 totaled 37, and the pastor was George Hoffman.
G.Ho.

Bethel Mennonite Church (GCM) at Lustre, Mont., began in May 1920 in a little district schoolhouse named Grand View, where the American Sunday School Union organized a Sunday school with approximately 24 pupils, though it was not organized as a congregation until Aug. 2, 1924. In the fall of 1928 a basement was constructed for a meeting place, 2 miles east and 26 miles north of Frazer, Township 31, Range 44, in Valley County. The church, recently completed, seats 250. The congregation is a member of the Northern District Conference. Its 1952 membership was 62. H.G.B.

Bethel Mennonite Church (GCM), Mayfair, Sask., an extinct congregation, was a member of the Conference of Mennonites in Canada.   J.G.R.

Bethel Mennonite Church (GCM), located in Mountain Lake, Minn., formerly called the Mennonite Bethel Church, is a member of the Northern District Conference. Having begun with 47 charter members in 1889, the congregation has grown to an active membership of 698 in 1952. This congregation has built three churches—the first in 1890, the second, an enlargement of the first, in 1894, and the third, a new brick building with a seating capacity of about 970, in 1941.

The members of this congregation are mainly the descendants of Russian Mennonite immigrants from the Molotschna who settled in the vicinity of Mountain Lake, 1873-78. The eight family names which occur most frequently in the present church register are Fast, Peters, Schroeder, Franz, Dick, Friesen, Stoesz, and Penner. The Low German dialect is still commonly spoken in many of the homes. About one half of the members of the congregation live on farms while most of the others reside in Mountain Lake, a village of about 1,900, making their living in business establishments, construction work, domestic and professional services, small industries, day labor, and in various other small-town occupations.

The elders who have served this congregation are: Heinrich H. Regier, 1889-1926; Jacob J. Balzer, 1926-33; John Bartel, 1933-40; Peter R. Schroeder, 1940-41; Peter A. Penner, 1941; Erland Waltner, 1941-49; and Walter Gering, 1950. From 1942 to 1953 Mrs. Peter R. Schroeder was employed as a salaried church worker.   W.G.

Bethel Mennonite Church (GCM), Pekin, Ill., was established through extension work of the East Washington Church in about 1890, when D. D. Augspurger held services at the Railroad schoolhouse, four miles east of Pekin. The congregation was organized in 1905, with Allen Miller as minister. It continued to worship at the Railroad schoolhouse until 1910, when a new church was built about three miles east of Pekin. In 1952 the membership was 70. It is a member of the Central Conference.   G.M.

Bethel (Perkasie) Mennonite Church (GCM) of the Eastern District Conference is located in Perkasie, Bucks Co., Pa. In 1900 a mission of local Mennonite families was started in the Baptist Church. The congregation was organized in June 1905. In 1906 the present site was purchased and in 1911 the present brick church was built. Ministers who have served the church are Harvey W. Shelly, 1905; William H. Grubb, 1905-10; Harvey W. Shelly, 1910-18; Allen M. Fretz, 1918-42; Ward W. Shelly, 1942-51; and Lester Janzen, 1951- . Deacons who have served are Harvey H. Baum,

1905-10; Clayton F. Myers, 1910-45; Ralph N. Lewis, 1946- . The Sunday school was organized in 1905. The membership in 1908 was 35 and in 1952, 63.

J.H.F.

"Bethel Menn. Church," *1913 Mennonite Yearbook and Almanac* (Quakertown); J. C. Wenger, *Hist. of the Menn. of the Franconia Conf.* (Telford, Pa., 1937).

Bethel Mennonite Church (MC), an extinct congregation near Tipton in Moniteau County, Mo. Daniel Brundage (*q.v.*) was ordained bishop of this congregation in 1870.   M.G.

Bethel Mennonite Church (MC), located near Wadsworth, Medina Co., Ohio, had its actual beginning with the half-dozen members who refused to follow their ultraconservative bishop, Abraham Rohrer, during the Wisler controversy about 1870. The original congregation had been made up of settlers from Bucks Co., Pa., in 1829, joined later by others from Lancaster and Lehigh counties in Pennsylvania and from Canada and Maryland. In 1833 they had organized a congregation and erected the Guilford meetinghouse. The first ministers were Jacob Koppes and William Overholt. After the division about 1870 visiting ministers served the progressive group until 1880 when Martin Leatherman was ordained to the ministry. Even then the congregation lacked qualified workers to carry on a Sunday school until several years later. Names that figure prominently in the history of the congregation after 1880 include Kreider, Rohrer, Lind, Newcomer, Stauffer, Kindig, and Detweiler. Until 1930 the congregation worshiped on alternate Sundays at the Guilford meetinghouse which they owned jointly with the Wisler branch and on the intervening Sunday at the Bethel church which they themselves built in 1893. Since 1930 the congregation conducts all of its services at Bethel, remodeled in 1939. The 1953 membership was 129; ministers, Samuel D. Rohrer and J. Robert Kreider. J.S.U.

Bethel Mennonite Church (GCM), located near Waka, Ochiltree Co., Tex., is a member of the Western District Conference. The congregation was organized in April 1922, the first meetings being held in the Jacob B. Wiebe home and later in a schoolhouse. In May 1924 another school was rebuilt into a church, which is still the present meetinghouse with a seating capacity of 100.

H.Wi.

Bethel Mennonite Church (MC), located in Washington Twp., Gratiot Co., Mich., on U.S. Highway No. 27, 10½ miles north of St. Johns, is a member of the Indiana-Michigan Conference. The congregation was organized on July 6, 1920, with 24 charter members, in a schoolhouse three miles east of the present location, with George H. Summer serving as first pastor until his death in 1937. Kore Zook has been minister since 1937, and D. S. Oyer bishop 1942-54. In 1922 a new frame church was built. The present membership (1953) is 137.   D.S.O.

Bethel Mennonite Church (MC), located 3½ miles north of Wayland on the Washington road, in Washington Co., Iowa, was dedicated Jan. 29, 1950. The meetinghouse was built to accommodate the expanding Sugar Creek Church, near Wayland. Four ministers serve it and the Sugar Creek Church jointly. In 1951 the membership attending the Bethel Church totaled 130.   L.B.K.

Bethel Mennonite Church (MC), located in West Liberty, Ohio, had its inception in 1889, when 12 Amish Mennonite young men and women confessed Christ in revival meetings held at the South Union Church by John F. Funk and Daniel J. Johns. The following summer John M. Shenk baptized them in Riley Creek near Bluffton, Ohio. John S. Coffman, John F. Funk, and other visiting Mennonite ministers served the group until 1895 when it built a meetinghouse in West Liberty and David H. Hilty of Bluffton became pastor. The congregation, with English services from the beginning, was the means of saving several scores of Amish Mennonite young people for the Mennonite Church and hastened the change from German to English in the Logan and Champaign County Amish Mennonite congregations. In January 1896 revival meetings by Bishop John Blosser brought 17 young people, chiefly Amish Mennonites, into the congregation. Bethel has provided a church and Sunday-school home for workers and children in the West Liberty Orphans' Home. Ministers who have served the congregation are C. H. Byler, J. B. Smith, John Y. King, Frank Byler (grandson of C. H. Byler), Newton Weber, and Edward Stoltzfus. The congregation has sent out an unusually large number of Christian workers—ministers, missionaries, and teachers. In 1953 it had a membership of 125.   J.S.U.

Bethel Mennonite Church (GCM) of Winton, Merced Co., Cal., under arrangements of the Evangelization Committee of the Pacific District Conference and the Home Mission Board of the General Conference was organized in May 1940 under the leadership of Dillman B. Hess, who served 30 members as their first pastor. J. P. Glanzer followed as leader (1941), using the Koehn church building of which Joel Koehn had been pastor. Koehn was the first Mennonite minister (1920) to serve this community. Now (1953) with 52 members, the church has a permanent home, with John Browning serving as pastor.   M.D.H.

Bethel Mennonite Church (GCM), Wolf Point, Roosevelt Co., Mont., was organized July 27, 1924, after Sunday school had been conducted for a number of years. There were 18 charter members. The basement of the present church was built in June 1929, and the wooden superstructure was dedicated on June 13, 1937. In 1925 this congregation joined the Northern District Conference and in 1926 the General Conference. On March 27, 1947, the congregation was duly incorporated under the laws of the State of Montana. The parsonage was built in 1944. Its 1952 membership was 83.

B.J.N.

Bethel Mennonite Church (KMB), located 13 miles northeast of Yale, Beadle Co., S.D., had its beginning in 1902, when six or seven families who had moved into this locality united to form a congregation with John Z. Kleinsasser as leader. These families met in their homes until 1904, when with a membership of about 30 they built a church with a seating capacity of about 130. This congregation increased, but in the spring of 1910 nine families from this congregation, including the pastor, moved to Dinuba, Cal. The church and lot were then sold, and the members again met in the homes until a new building was dedicated on the present site, with John Tschetter as its pastor. In 1912 the leadership was turned over to J. M. Tschetter. In 1919 a new building was dedicated with the old church serving as an annex. J. M. Tschetter served as pastor until Dec. 12, 1941, when Sam J. R. Hofer took over the leadership, followed by missionary A. K. Wiens in 1944. In April 1947 A. K. Wiens resigned to resume his missionary work in North China, and the congregation called John J. Kleinsasser from Dinuba, a son of the first pastor, to serve as its pastor. J. J. Kleinsasser resigned on June 30, 1952. George Classen accepted the call on June 1, 1953. The church membership was 300 in 1949.   J.J.K.

Bethel Mennonite Mission Church (GCM), corner of Furby Street and Westminster Avenue, Winnipeg, Man., is a member of the Canadian Mennonite Conference. The work began in January 1938, when Benjamin Ewert, itinerant preacher of the Canadian Mennonite Conference, and later minister-at-large, started to hold services in an English Baptist church on Sargent Avenue. For over six years services were held at the corner of Sherbrook Street and Sargent Avenue, but in 1945 the congregation purchased the church which it now used. In 1953 its membership was 210, with many Mennonite students and young people who came to the city for employment attending. During the past two years 50 young people were baptized and received into the fellowship of this church. Most of the services are in English, with a German and an English sermon every Sunday morning. From 1947 to 1949 the Canadian Mennonite Bible College has been located in this church. Benjamin Ewert served the congregation 1938-43, Isaac I. Friesen 1943-51, and David Schroeder since 1951.   B.E.

Bethel Mission, a mission station of the Church of God in Christ Mennonites, is located at Campo 45, 40 miles north of Cuauhtemoc, Chihuahua, Mexico. It was organized in 1933 by John A. Koehn. The first property consisted of a two-acre plot with a three-room house. In 1938 an additional 50 acres of land were added to the property, and again, in 1944, another 1,100 acres of land were purchased together with three sets of buildings, including a church and a two-room school. Jose Francisco Parra was ordained to the ministry in 1938. In 1944 Jacob K. Ensz with his family moved here to take charge as superintendent. The worship services and Sunday school are mainly conducted in the Spanish and English languages. The mission has a regular day school for the children, which is also conducted in the Spanish and English languages. The mission has a modern hospital, grocery store, a number of farmsteads and dwelling houses, voluntary service projects of dairying, poultry raising, and crop experimentation, and several side missions. In 1951 there were 12 workers in the mission and the membership was 34.

J.A.K., H.D.W.

Bethel Publishing Company, now located at 1819 South Main St., Elkhart, Ind., dates back to 1903, when the work of publishing books and the mail-order sale of books and Bibles was begun in New Carlisle, Ohio, by J. A. Huffman, at that time pastor of the New Carlisle United Missionary (then Mennonite Brethren in Christ) Church. The office and book room was at first maintained at the parsonage, and later moved to a business room of the Post Office building of the town. In 1907 the business was moved to Dayton, Ohio, and incorporated as the Bethel Publishing Company. In 1913 when the Dayton flood occurred, destroying all the assets of the Publishing Company except the small printing plant which had been added, which was also damaged, Huffman reorganized the company, sold the printing plant, and moved the business back to New Carlisle. In the meantime, the publication of Huffman's own books had increased, and the Bethel Series of Sunday School Literature had been launched. From this time onward, all printing was let by contract to various printers. In 1920 the business of the Bethel Publishing Company was purchased by the Executive Board of the United Missionary Church, and its management passed into the hands of the church. A few years later the business was moved to its present location, where a suitable building had been erected for it.

The Bethel Publishing Company publishes *The Gospel Banner* (q.v.), the Bethel Series of Sunday School Literature, and books, and engages in ·a general business in church and Sunday-school supplies, including religious books and Bibles. The tithe of the business is devoted to foreign missions.

The Bethel Publishing House is the national headquarters of the United Missionary Church and the United Missionary Society, the overseas arm of the church work. The business, being church-owned, is, by the discipline of the church, under the direction of the Executive Board ·of the United Missionary Church, which board employs an executive agent.

The Executive Board of the United Missionary Church was composed in 1950 of the following persons: R. P. Ditmer, Springfield, Ohio, chairman; W. E. Manges, Elkhart, Ind., vice-chairman; F. B. Hertzog, Emmaus, Pa., secretary; W. E. Manges, Elkhart, Ind., treasurer; E. N. Cassel, Walnutport, Pa.; P. T. Stengle, Allentown, Pa.; T. D. Gehret, Bethlehem, Pa.; J. E. Tuckey, Brown City, Mich.; M. J. Burgess, Pontiac, Mich.; J. A. Huffman, Winona Lake, Ind.; A. Frey, Didsbury, Alta.; P. G. Lehman, Kitchener, Ont.; Ward M. Shantz, Kitchener, Ont.; E. D. Young, Orange, Cal.; A. B. Neufeld, Roy, Wash.   J.A.Hu.

Bethel Springs Mennonite Church (MC) near Culp, Ark., was begun by Maud Buckingham Douglass, who after the death of her first husband at La Junta, Col., finished a nurses' training course there, joined the Mennonite Church there, and then returned to her Arkansas home. A committee of the Missouri-Kansas Conference arranged monthly preaching appointments and a small membership was secured. The first pastor sent was Nelson Histand, and later Frank Horst served the congregation. A church school developed from a one-room grade school with one teacher, into a grade and high school with five teachers, and a building equipped to accommodate the work. Business enterprises for the benefit of the people have been started by Christian investments. The membership has increased from one, when ministers visited the locality in 1935, to upwards of 88 in 1953. Two more churches have been built besides the one at Culp; one in the neighborhood southwest of Mountain Home, called Mountain View; the other southeast of Culp and south of Calico Rock, in the neighborhood of Optimus called Mt. Joy. Other appointments, Sunday school, and summer Bible schools are held at various points.   J.R.S.

Bethel Springs School, Culp, Ark., is a Christian day school in the Ozark Mountains of north central Arkansas. It is directly connected with the mission work in this area and is sponsored by the Mennonite Board of Missions and Charities, Elkhart, Ind.

The necessity of a Christian day school was felt by those burdened with the responsibility for building up the community morally and spiritually. The public schools were not filling the needs of the community educationally. The purpose of the school was, first, to bring every student to a knowledge of Christ and to lead each student to accept Him as Saviour; second, to build strong Christian character; and third, to provide a good educational opportunity for all who wished to avail themselves of it.

It was started as a grade school in 1944 with Dorothea Martin as the first teacher, and had 24 children enrolled. The first three terms were held in the church. A new school building was originally planned as a one-story building with a full basement; but later, after the mission home burned, it was decided to add a second story for additional classroom space and apartments for principal and teachers. This building was completed and school was first held in it in the fall of 1947.

The school now offers twelve grades, having added the four years of high school because of the demand. The total enrollment for 1953-54 was 49.   G.Y.

Bethel United Missionary Church, New Dundee, Waterloo Co., Ont., was organized in 1877. In 1921 a brick building was erected seating 350. In 1948 the membership was 154, with H. Shantz serving as pastor.   H.S.

Bethel United Missionary Church, Petrolia, Lambton Co., Ont., was organized in 1920. In 1948 the membership was 31 and Miss L. Hoover and Miss H. Hill were in charge of the congregation.   L.Hoo.

Bethel United Missionary Church, Roseburg, Mich., was organized by William Graybiel in 1896 in a meetinghouse built the same year and located two miles east and one mile south of Roseburg. The congregation is a member of the Michigan Conference and in 1950 had 34 members with R. D. Dean serving as pastor.   R.D.D.

Bethel United Missionary Church located about seven miles west of Goshen, Ind., was organized in 1873 with 30 charter members. In 1948 the membership was 185, with Russell M. Miller serving as pastor.   R.M.M.

Bethel (Yale) United Missionary Church is located seven miles northeast of Yale, Mich.   M.G.

Bethesda is a small country corners on the 5th Concession of Whitchurch Twp., York Co., Ont. From its earliest records it has been connected with Mennonites. Christian Steckley, born in 1795, who came from Pennsylvania, homesteaded on 1,000 acres extending in a block one and one-fourth miles north and one and one-fourth miles east from this point. The Steckley family consisted of six sons and three daughters. Two of the sons married and joined the Tunker Church. The other sons later became members of the newly organized Mennonite Brethren in Christ group about 1875, John being one of the founders of that church. Church services were held in the Steckley home until the Mennonite church was built on the 5th Concession of Markham, west of Almira, 1860. The appointment was known as Stecklin. J.C.F.

Bethesda Herold, Der, was first published on July 15, 1902, by the Mennonite Bethesda Hospital Society, Goessel, Kan. Appearing on the fifteenth of each month, it is mailed to 700 addresses in approximately a dozen states and Canada. An 8 x 11 in. paper, it regularly has four pages of news items and editorials. The material is mostly in German, except that reports of the hospital and of the directors and the gift lists are in English. The editor is C. C. Wedel, Newton, Kan.   J.J.V.

Bethesda Home, Winkler, Man. In 1919 Mr. and Mrs. Jacob B. Hooge of Winkler, Man., started this old folks' home on their own account for the crippled, blind, aged, and others who sought shelter therein. It was nondenominational, but most of the inmates, 21 at its peak, came from the various Mennonite church groups in the southern part of Manitoba, such as Bergthaler, Sommerfelder, Rudnerweider, Old Colony, and Mennonite Brethren.

The maintenance of most of the inmates was financed by the various church groups named. The Bethesda Home ceased to exist in 1945, and since that time the building has been serving as a dormitory and boardinghouse for men students at the Peniel Bible School, Winkler.   H.H.H.

Bethesda Home for Aged, Goessel, Kan., equipped to take care of 26 guests, is owned and operated by the Mennonite Bethesda Hospital Society of Goessel, a corporation which obtained its charter June 20, 1899. The institution served both as a hospital and home for aged until 1928, when a new hospital was built. The control of the institution is vested in a board of directors consisting of nine members. Its purpose is primarily to serve aged members of the Mennonite church in the immediate community.   H.J.A.

Bethesda Hospital, Goessel, Kan., was established on June 20, 1899, by the Mennonite Bethesda Hospital Society at Goessel. The immediate cause for erecting a hospital was the fact that when Dr. Peter Richert started his practice in the year 1894 at Goessel, he found a well-settled community but no place where difficult cases of illness could be taken care of adequately. He urged the building of a hospital, and after a number of meetings with the local civic leaders, a society was organized and incorporated on June 20, 1899, as the Mennonite Bethesda Hospital Society. Funds were collected and a hospital building was erected. A gift of $10.00 secured a membership with the right to vote at the annual meetings. The first building was a two-story frame structure 30 x 40 ft. over a 15 x 30 ft. basement. Katharine Schellenberg was the first matron and Dr. Charles Henry Kaiser the first physician and surgeon, Dr. Peter Richert having left for California.

The hospital was soon found to be too small for the needs of the community, and so on May 10, 1903, a second 30 x 40 ft. building was completed. These two main buildings were then connected by a passageway which gave room for a kitchen, a dining room, a chapel, and bedrooms for workers. Since a part of the hospital was used as a home for the aged, even this added space did not suffice for long. In 1928-29 a new fireproof two-story brick building was erected across the street from the old hospital. The old building was then used entirely as a home for the aged. The new building opened its doors for service on Oct. 16, 1929, with 15 beds.

Soon after the original Bethesda hospital was established, the need was felt for trained helpers, and so the board of directors decided to open a nurses' training school. The school was established on Dec. 19, 1910, under the direction of Sister Margaret Richert, a deaconess who succeeded Katharina Schellenberg and Mrs. Wilhelmina Schwake as superintendent of nurses. Sister Richert was followed by Sister Anna Schmidt, a deaconess, and Emma Bartel and Tena Heinrichs, all registered nurses. This nurses' school, however, operated under difficulties; most of the students had only grade and parochial schooling which was inadequate. Then too there was only one resident doctor most of the time and he had a practice too large to keep up scheduled classwork. Doctors from neighboring towns helped out and the students received good practical training in bedside nursing but the school did not progress. The course was at first only two years. In 1913 it was made a three-year course and arrangements were made for classwork with other hospitals. In 1912 five students were in training, but only one, Katharina Nikkel, finished the full course. In 1913 Elizabeth L. W. Regier was graduated and in 1916 Helen Neufeld completed the course. Other graduates of the school are Marie Siemens, Sister Anna Schmidt, Mary Duerksen, Agnes Pankratz, and Anna Siemens. Many of the girls that entered the school did not stay to finish the course as the hospital in the beginning always had a department for the aged and it was difficult to interest the girls

in the twofold work. When the requirements for training schools became more difficult to meet, Bethesda's school was discontinued in 1926-27; however, the work of the hospital has gone on progressively. An excellent X-ray apparatus has been installed and the hospital itself is thoroughly modern with up-to-date equipment. The hospital has two good doctors and surgeons and it is to be extended with a new addition to the main building to give more room for hospital beds.   C.C.W.

Bethesda Krimmer Mennonite Brethren Church, located in Huron, S.D., was organized Feb. 15, 1947. In 1953 it had a membership of 53, with Peter G. Hofer serving as minister.   P.G.H.

Bethesda Mennonite Church (GCM) of Henderson, York Co., Neb., is a member of the Northern District Conference, with a membership of 998 (1953). Thirty-five families from the Molotschna Colony, South Russia, had arrived at the immigrant house erected by the Burlington Railroad company one mile east of the present site of Henderson on Oct. 14, 1874. By 1880 the group had grown to about 80 families. A large boulder was erected in 1937 on the original site to mark the place of the immigrant house. Names of the family heads arriving in 1874 were Mrs. Johann Abrahams, Gerhard Abrahams, Peter Abrahams, Heinrich C. Epp, Rev. Heinrich Epp, Johann Epp, Mrs. Johann Fast, Jacob Fast, Jacob Friesen, Johann Friesen, Cornelius Funk, Abraham Heinrichs, Jacob Janzen, Johann Janzen, Peter Lender, Absolom Martins, Benjamin Nachtigal, Jacob Nachtigal, Heinrich Pankratz, Sr., Heinrich Pankratz, Jr., Peter Pankratz, Heinrich Penner, Peter Penner, Gerhard Petker, Benjamin Ratzlaff, Franz Spenst, Mrs. Johann Sperling, Gerhard Toews, Johann Voth, Tobias Voth, Cornelius Wall, Jacob Wall, Peter Wall, Cornelius Warkentin, Peter Wolf.

Two ministers, Heinrich Epp and Benjamin Ratzlaff, came with the first group. Ratzlaff died Oct. 30, 1874. In the spring of 1875 two other ministers, Isaac Peters (q.v.) and Gerhard Epp, arrived. Isaac Peters had been elder of the Mennonite congregation at Pordenau, Molotschna settlement, Russia, from 1867 until 1874, when he emigrated to America with the smaller portion of the Pordenau congregation. Insisting upon stricter requirements for a separated life as an evidence of regeneration than the majority of the membership were willing to agree to, he withdrew in 1880 with a considerable number of members to form the Ebenezer Mennonite Church (q.v.), which (with the Aaron Wall group at Mountain Lake, Minn.) became one of the two founding congregations of the Evangelical Mennonite Brethren Conference (q.v.).

In 1880 a church was built two miles northeast of the present site of Henderson. In 1906 this church was sold and dismantled, and a new one built in Henderson, which was enlarged in 1931, but was destroyed by fire before completion. Immediately the building of a new church was undertaken; it has a seating capacity of about 1,350. It was dedicated March 6, 1932.

Originally footwashing was practiced at the communion service, but was discontinued in 1939. The first reed organ was used about 1915. Discipline for transgression is required by confession. The Sunday-school enrollment is 1105. Young people's meetings, prayer meetings, mission societies, and choirs are organized in the church. German services were discontinued about ten years ago. Ministers who served the church since 1874 are Benjamin Ratzlaff (as far as is known, never served in America, because of illness), Heinrich Epp, Isaac Peters, Gerhard Epp, Jacob Friesen, Peter J. Friesen (he was the first elder to be ordained in America by this group Feb. 25, 1884), Johann Kliewer, Cornelius Wall, Cornelius Regier, Heinrich H. Epp, Peter H. Pankratz, Heinrich D. Epp, Franz G. Pankratz, Johann F. Epp, Abraham W. Friesen. The present (1953) minister is Arnold Nickel.

In 1893 the first Sunday school was held. In 1902 a parochial school was built, which functioned until 1943. In 1904 John H. Epp was ordained as the first missionary from this church to serve among the Indians in Oklahoma. In 1915 Peter J. Boehr was ordained as missionary to China. In 1949 a parsonage was built.   A.W.F.

Bethesda Mennonite Church (GCM) at Langham, Sask., now extinct, was organized in 1906 and discontinued in 1948. The largest membership was 93, in 1943. The congregation was a member of the Canadian District Mennonite Conference.

                                                        J.H.P.

Bethesda Mennonite Church (GCM), located four miles west of Marion Junction, Rosefield Twp., Turner Co., S.D., belongs to the Northern District Conference. The first arrivals to the community came from Russia in the fall of 1874. Since no minister had come along and the winter was unusually severe, no formal worship services were held the first winter; the next summer services were held in the various homes. The first church was built in the fall of 1879. In 1883 a split occurred and the larger group built another church at the present location, which was replaced in 1909 by the present building. Derk P. Tieszen, who was elected to the ministry by the congregation in 1890, had the distinction of serving until Jan. 1, 1939, 48 years in all, 44 years of this time as elder. Abram Willems and Peter T. Unruh also served as ministers in the congregation for more than 30 years.

The Low German language is still commonly used in the homes. Most of the members live on farms, although there is a sprinkling of business and professional people who live in near-by Marion.

The congregation has an active Sunday school, a Christian Endeavor, a women's missionary society, and a choir. There are weekly Sunday morning and evening services but no midweek meetings. The services have become practically all English. Footwashing and communion services are held once a year. The baptized membership on Dec. 1, 1953, was 234, with T. A. van der Smissen as elder.

                                                        J.D.U.

Bethesda, York County, Ont., a Mennonite (MC) meeting place before the Mennonite Brethren in Christ established worship there.   J.C.F.

Bethesda Mental Hospital of the Canadian Mennonite Brethren District Conference is located on a farm near Vineland, Lincoln Co., Ont. It was begun as a private enterprise by Mr. and Mrs. Henry Wiebe who had come to Canada in 1924 and who had formerly worked in the mental hospital Bethania (*q.v.*), Ukraine, Russia. Having an understanding for the lot of the mentally ill, they desired to continue to serve in this field.

In 1932 they took the first patient into their home at Stratford, Ont. To accommodate more patients, they purchased the present farm with large buildings in 1937. The home was supported by voluntary contributions until 1944, when the Ontario Provincial Conference of the M.B. Church bought it. At this time the institution was registered with the government as a private sanitarium. In 1947 the Canadian M.B. District Conference took over the supervision of this institution.

In 1949 this home had 22 patients cared for by a staff of four practical nurses, one orderly, and one part-time registered nurse. Mr. and Mrs. Wiebe were the supervisors. At present only nonviolent patients are admitted. The Conference plans to construct a modern building with the capacity for 30 patients and with facilities for treating more patients.†   I.H.T.

Bethesda United Missionary Church, located four miles northeast of Gormley, Ont., was organized in approximately 1880. The congregation had 31 members in 1948 and Percy R. Barley served as pastor.   P.Ba.

Bethezai, Elisabeth (Elssa), an Anabaptist martyr, was seized in 1643 with Elisabeth Bachmann (*q.v.*) and Sara Wanry (*q.v.*). She died in prison in Zürich (Switzerland). (*Mart. Mir.* D 822, E 1120; *ML* I, 213.)   vDZ.

Bethlehem Mennonite Brethren in Christ Church (UMC), Bethlehem, Pa., one of the largest churches of this branch. In 1887 W. B. Musselman became the first pastor and erected a temporary frame church on Main Street, which was replaced the following year by another on Laurel Street. The present brick church at 1121-25 North Main Street was dedicated Feb. 8, 1920. From 1887 to 1923 there were ten pastors. Since then the ministers have been F. M. Hottel, 1923-32; P. T. Stengele, 1932-45; and N. H. Wolf, since 1945. In 1952 there were 385 members.   E.R.S.

Bethlehem Mennonite Church (GCM), 10 miles northeast of Bloomfield, Dawson Co., Mont., is a member of the Northern District Conference with a membership of 157 (1953). A group of Low-German Mennonites originally from Karolswalde, Poland, coming here from Avon, S.D., in 1906 and a group of Swiss Volhynian Mennonites coming from Freeman, S.D., in 1910, were organized into a church in 1910 by H. A. Bachman of Freeman. A third group from Marion and Dalton, S.D., of

Low-German background, moved into the community in 1910 and joined the congregation in 1911. The present church was dedicated in the spring of 1951. Pastors who have served the church are P. P. Tschetter, 1913-15; John M. Franz, 1916-19 and 1921-23; John Baergen, 1923-26; David D. Schultz (lay minister), 1926-27; Abe P. Unruh, 1927-28; Jacob Sawatzky, 1928-38; Herbert Widmer, 1939-43; and George G. Dick, 1943- . G.G.D.

Bethlen Gabor (1580-1622), of an old line of Hungarian Protestants, was in 1613 chosen prince of Transylvania, and in 1621 king of Hungary, but declined this honor in the treaty of 1622 with Austria. He was a patron of the Moravian Hutterites, whose thoroughness in farming and in handicraft he had learned to know and appreciate, aided the exiles from Moravia, and settled some of them on his estates in Alwinz (*q.v.*). Antal Aldasy, professor at the university of Budapest, published the contract (Latin) between Bethlen Gabor and the Hutterian Brethren settling in Transylvania. (*Archiv für Ref.-Gesch.* XXVIII, 1931, 241; *ML* I, 213.) Neff.

Betken, an Anabaptist martyr: see **Betgen.**

Betken, Doof (deaf), an Anabaptist martyr, was secretly drowned in a tub at the Steen prison in Antwerp on March 16, 1560, together with Betgen van Gent (*q.v.*) and Lysken (*q.v.*) Smits. According to the official records her name was Elisabeth Heuvels, born at Kortrijk or Wervick in Flanders. All three women "persisted in their rebaptism." Their names are found in a song, "Aenhoort Godt, hemelsche Vader" (Give ear, O God, heavenly Father), No. 16 in *Liedtboecxken van den Offer des Heeren.* This song is also mentioned by Wolkan, *Lieder.*   vDZ.

> *Offer*, 567; *Mart. Mir.* D 270, E 640; Wolkan, *Lieder*, 63, 72; *Antw. Arch.-Blad* IX, 7, 11, 17; XIV, 28-29, No. 312; *ML* I, 209.

Betken van Gent, whose actual name was Elisabeth Berents, born at Gent in Belgium, was secretly drowned in a tub in the Steen prison in Antwerp, on March 16, 1560, because she persisted in her faith and refused to recant. Her clothes and furniture had been confiscated and sold on Jan. 4, 1560. By this date she must already have been imprisoned. She was drowned with two other women, Doof Betken (*q.v.*) and Lysken (*q.v.*) Smits. The names of all three women are found in the song, "Aenhoort Godt, hemelsche Vader" (Give ear, O God, heavenly Father), No. 16 in the *Liedtboecxken van den Offer des Heeren,* also mentioned in Wolkan, *Lieder.*   vDZ.

> *Offer*, 567; *Mart. Mir.* D 270, E 640; Wolkan, *Lieder* 63, 72; *Antw. Arch.-Blad* IX, 6, 11; XIV, 28-29, No. 313; *ML* I, 209.

Betken van der Male, an Anabaptist martyr, the widow of Jan van Audelghem. She belonged to the congregation at Kortrijk (Courtrai) in Flanders, having joined in 1566, and attended the meetings held near the city. She was held in prison for 137 days, and was then burned at the stake at Kortrijk on June 4, 1569 (Verheyden, *Courtrai-Bruxelles*, 40, No. 29).   vDZ.

Betrothal. In conformity with general medieval practice Anabaptists expected to supervise and direct the marriage arrangements for their young people. To a medieval European parent the marriage of a son or daughter without his consent was unthinkable. It was not only a piece of folly but in bad taste or even sinful. This view prevailed in many circles till late in the 19th century.

To the Anabaptists, however, marriage like all other human decisions and behavior must conform to the express teachings of the Holy Scriptures. And because no New Testament instance furnished a pattern for the wooing of a wife, some Anabaptist groups accepted the Old Testament example of Abraham's selection of a wife for Isaac to show what is the duty of the parent to his son. Tobit of the Apocrypha still serves the Amish as a model of betrothal and marriage.

The rules of the Frisian Mennonites prescribed that young men and women should not associate too freely. Among the Swiss Anabaptists in the Vosges mountain region of Alsace the wooing of the bride was carried on according to the most literal interpretation of Gen. 24. The deacon known as the "Stecklimann" took the place of the servant who was sent out to win a wife for Isaac. In carrying out his mission the "Stecklimann" mounted a horse even though the prospective bride lived near at hand. Then on his arrival at the home, the details of the Biblical story were followed punctiliously even to offering a drink, presenting gifts, and so on. This procedure with minor variations is still the rule among the Old Order Amish in America. The deacon usually serves as the "Stecklimann." His ordination charge includes the words, "and if there are brethren and sisters who wish to marry, you are to serve them uprightly." One manuscript adds the words, "according to the Christian regulation." He undertakes these duties in great secrecy. He goes to the home of the young woman after all but the parents have retired. After the consent of the young woman and her parents has been obtained and the time for the public announcement decided, the deacon, two weeks before the wedding, announces to the congregation the date of the wedding. Invitations to the wedding are delivered orally and in person by the bridegroom.

Among all Anabaptist-Mennonite groups it was once customary for the preachers or elders to make the marriage proposals. The principal reason for this rule was to insure a "marriage in the Lord," that is, the union of two young people who were members of the church. Anyone who disregarded the rule was subject to church censure. Even such groups as permitted the young people to make their own promise of marriage required them to obtain the consent of their parents. Such practices have now almost universally disappeared in America in favor of the personal proposal by the young man to the chosen one. The change has been due to the general adoption of the American concept of romantic love as the basis for marriage. Among certain of the more conservative groups in Europe, however, the parents still in fact have a large share in selecting a marriage partner.

The Church of God in Christ Mennonites, often called the Holdeman Mennonites, prohibit "dating" for unmarried church members. After he unites with the church a young man cannot see a young woman alone. To go driving with her or to accompany her to the home of a neighbor, he takes several members of her family too. When he wishes to propose he reports to one of the ministers that the Lord has revealed to him that he should take a certain young woman to be his wife. The minister then makes it known to the parents of the girl and secures their consent and hers.

Among the Mennonites of Prussia it was customary into the 19th century for the young man to approach the *Umbitter,* a sort of deacon, who would consult with the parents and the daughter of the house making known the young man's desire. After they had consented the young man would come to the home of the girl and the engagement took place. (Daniel Chodowiecki's painting "Mennonite Proposal for Marriage" illustrates this.) After some visiting among relatives the wedding would take place, usually in two weeks after the engagement. This practice must have been of Dutch Mennonite background and was transplanted from Prussia to Russia and America. The conservative groups in Mexico and Paraguay still adhere to it in some modified form.

In Europe the betrothal is much more serious than in the United States. Everywhere but Holland it is a religious ceremony almost as solemn as the wedding. In Holland it is announced formally in the church paper. J.S.U.

Bettendorf, a noble family in Kraichgau in Baden, Germany, had possessions in Mauer and Gau-Angelloch, on which Mennonites found reception as tenants after their expulsion from the canton of Bern (Switzerland). In the middle of the 19th century through the marriage of Baroness Juliana Friederike of Gau-Angelloch with Johannes Friedrich von Zyllnhardt, Palatine captain and commander at Dillsburg, the possessions passed to the von Zyllnhardt family. The latter also owned Schatthausen, where there was a Mennonite congregation in the 18th century (Baiertal, *Nekrolog der Deutschen* VI, 1828, Part II, 517). In 1742 Eleonore Charlotte van Bettendorf took a warm interest in the Mennonites living on her estates in Altwiesloch, as evidenced in a petition to the Palatine elector (records in the Karlsruhe General Archives). (*ML* I, 213.) HEGE.

Bettingen, a former designation of the Mennonite congregation in the Saarlouis district and in Luxembourg. (Mannhardt, *Jahrbuch,* 1888, 35; *ML* I, 213.)

Betz, Hans, a preacher and author of hymns, which were among those which formed the foundation of the *Ausbund* (*q.v.*). Betz was a weaver of Eger, who joined the Upper German Anabaptists. He was baptized in 1530 above Donauwörth, by Georg Hoffner. There are no details about his work. In August 1535 he went from Eger to Auspitz (*q.v.*) in order to become acquainted with the brotherhood there. On his return he was imprisoned at

Passau with 33 fellow believers, followers of Philip Weber, who were fleeing from Moravia.

In prison he wrote 12 songs (Nos. 81, 92, 104-12, and 122), which are signed "H.B." in the *Ausbund.* Rudolf Wolkan has proved him to be the author (*Lieder,* 32). "In his hymns," says Wolkan (p. 34), "Betz reveals himself, in spite of his honest trade, as a theologically well-trained man. His art of writing poetry, like that of all the Anabaptists, was acquired from the popular folksongs; for he came from their ranks." With the exception of one song (*Ausbund,* No. 112, "Gelobt sei Gott im höchsten Thron"), all of Betz's hymns were published in Wackernagel, *Kirchenlied* V, 1040-54.

An attempt was made to induce Betz to recant, but in vain. "If he could be convinced from Scripture that he erred and a better way be shown him with foundation, he would not resist the truth; so far he had not found a better way to salvation," says the record of his trial (Wolkan, 32). He remained in prison two years longer, until death released him. HEGE.

Wiswedel, *Bilder* II, 105; Beck, *Geschichts-Bücher,* 132 f.; J. Ottius, *Annales Anabaptistici,* 233; V. A. Winter, *Gesch. der bayrischen Wiedertäufer* (1809) 34; Schrödl, *Passanuia Sacra; ML* I, 213.

Betzenhans, an Anabaptist of Ockershausen a.d.L. in the district of Cassel, Germany, was arrested with his wife and two other Anabaptists in March 1543 and cross-examined by Justus Menius (*q.v.*). Whereas he consented to "leave his error," his wife, though she had not been baptized, remained true to her faith and ably defended it before the learned theologian. Nothing else is known about them. NEFF.

P. Wappler, *Die Stellung Kursachsens und des Landgrafen Philipp von Hessen zur Täuferbewegung* (Münster, 1910) 94 f., 213 f.; *ML* I, 213.

Beulah Mennonite Brethren in Christ Church, now extinct, established at Filer, Idaho, in 1907. M.G.

Beulah Mennonite Brethren in Christ Church, Easton, Northampton Co., Pa., was organized in 1912. The 1952 membership was 158 and W. W. Hartman served as pastor. W.W.H.

Beulah Mennonite Church (MC), now extinct, near Westport and Aberdeen, S.D. Several families moved into the area before 1919 and organized a Sunday school May 9, 1920. In 1921 they were organized as the Beulah congregation with 17 members by D. G. Lapp of Nebraska. They were affiliated with the Iowa-Nebraska Conference but in 1922 transferred to the Dakota-Montana (now North Central) under the bishop oversight of I. S. Mast. J. C. Gingerich filled regular appointments except during the summers of 1925 and 1926, when Milo Kauffman served as minister while attending Northern States Teachers' College in Aberdeen. Because of disunity, drought, and depression the group moved away in 1929 except one family, which joined another denomination. F.E.K.

Beulah United Missionary Church is located at Blaine and 9th streets, Elkhart, Ind. In 1952 it was the tenth largest congregation in the denomination with a membership of 209. M.G.

Beutelhans, an Anabaptist martyr, a citizen of Königsberg (*q.v.*) in Franconia, Germany, where he owned a house in the suburbs with vineyards. He was baptized by Hans Hut (*q.v.*), and traveled about the surrounding villages with him, winning many for the Anabaptist movement. On Feb. 8, 1527, he was imprisoned with six fellow believers and soon afterward beheaded (Wappler, 4, note 1). In agony of torture they are reported to have said that their preachers had ordered them to flee to Mülhausen in case the Turks came and there was great want and agitation, and gather there as a Christian group, which would grow to several thousand men (Wappler, 45). It is, however, to be assumed that these statements were forced from them as a consequence of torture, since there was no actual occurrence to confirm them.

The burgomaster and the council of Königsberg gave the imprisoned Anabaptist citizens the testimonial that "they had conducted themselves as citizens," and that "the poor men should be shown mercy and permitted to live."

Still less comprehensible is the reproach of seditious tendencies, when one examines the confession forced from Beutelhans by the repeated, terrible torture (Berbig, 313). The confused statements about Mülhausen and the expected meeting of the "new Christians" there, were obviously suggested to him on the rack. Furthermore, his stress on nonresistance is especially worthy of note. NEFF.

P. Wappler, *Die Stellung Kursachsens und des Landgrafen Philipp von Hessen zur Täuferbewegung* (Münster, 1910); *idem, Die Täuferbewegung in Thüringen* (Jena, 1913); G. Berbig, "Die Wiedertäufer im Amt Königsberg in Franken 1527-28," in *Deutsche Ztscht für Kirchenrecht* XIII (1913); *ML* I, 214.

Beverwijk, a Mennonite congregation in the Dutch province of North Holland, in the beautiful flower bulb district between Haarlem and Alkmaar.

The origin of this congregation can no longer be traced, but already in the earliest times, shortly after 1530, there are traces of Anabaptism here. In June 1535 four Anabaptists of Beverwijk were imprisoned, two of whom died at the stake on July 4, 1535 (Claes Claesz and Cornelis Gijsbertsz), Cornelis Claesz of Beverwijk was executed in 1537 at Alkmaar, and the martyr Augustijn (*q.v.*), executed about 1556, was also from this town. There must soon have been a Waterlander congregation here. The oldest list of members, now in the church archives, dates back to the second half of the 17th century, and begins with the statement that the previous one was lost. In 1668 the congregation bought a house and remodeled it as a church. Although the congregation was small, it contributed 700 guilders in 1727 and 199 guilders in 1736 to the *Fonds voor Buitenlandsche Nooden* (Fund for Foreign Needs), and had a salaried minister as early as the first half of the 18th century; one of these was the former Reformed preacher Anthonius van der Os, who was called in 1758 and paid a salary of 200 guilders, after he had been baptized upon the confession of his faith by the Zaandam Mennonite pastor Cornelis Loosjes Adr.-zn. When van der Os moved to Zaandam-Oost in 1874, ministers of other Mennonite congregations were asked to administer communion, and for other services the members rented pews in the Reformed church. The list of members of this period reveals that several of the members were baptized by immersion in Rijnsburg. The membership, 64 in 1710, had dropped to 4 by 1822.

In the beginning of the 19th century the congregational life became more and more settled. The communion and baptismal services as well as instruction of the youth were given over to the pastor of neighboring Krommenie 1823-65; from 1865 to 1873 the pastor of Westzaan performed this service. Preachers of other congregations were regularly invited in to conduct regular services.

In 1873 the congregation decided to appoint a pastor and called J. Sepp of Witmarsum, and after his death in 1905 J. D. van Calcar 1906-39, and A. Vis since 1939.

In the last 100 years the membership has increased markedly. In 1836 it was 12, in 1898, 114, in 1927, 384, in 1950, 486, and this in spite of the withdrawal of many members who lived in IJmuiden (*q.v.*) to organize a congregation of their own in 1909. The old church was replaced by a larger one in 1912, which has—contrary to the general Mennonite custom in Holland—over its pulpit a statue of Christ, a copy of the noted statue by the Danish sculptor Thorwaldsen. The cost of the building was defrayed by voluntary contributions of the members.

With few exceptions the members belong to the modernistic wing. In 1914 a woman was for the first time chosen to the church directorate. Sunday school is held in conjunction with the Reformed and Lutheran churches. Communion services are held annually on Good Friday. The income derived from the real estate owned by the congregation enables the congregation to provide for its own needs. It has an active youth organization (from 18 to 30 years), a missionary society, choir, women's organization, and Sunday school (*Inv. Arch. Amst.* I, 131, 133, 165, 184, 708, 1128; II, 1544, 1787 f., 1875; *DB* 1864, 172; 1880, 165; 1909, 20; *ML* I, 214).   J.D.vC., vDZ.

Bevredigde Broederschap, the name given a group of Dutch Mennonites about 1600, who formed a union on the basis of the Concept of Cologne (*q.v.*). This group consisted of High Germans, Frisians, and Waterlanders (see **Amsterdam**). In 1613 the newly acquired unity was again destroyed (see **Afgedeelden** and **Clock, Leenaert**).   vDZ.

Beyer, Cornelis, ordained as preacher of the Mennonite congregation in Glückstadt, Holstein, on July 16, 1633, is the author of the *Huishoudingsboeck* of the Frisian church in Friedrichstadt (*ML* I, 215).   NEFF.

Beyerland (Oud), a village in the Dutch province of South Holland where there must once have been two Mennonite churches. According to Elder Hendrik Berents Hulshoff (*q.v.*), one of these belonged to the Danzig Old Flemish (*Bezoekreis*, 35). At the meeting of the United Flemish congregations, held in Haarlem in 1649, and likewise in 1660 and 1664 at Leiden, there were delegates from the united church at Oud-Beyerland. On Sept. 8, 1663, a well-known disputation was held in Oud-Beyerland between the Mennonite preacher Tieleman van Braght (*q.v.*), the author of the *Martyrs' Mirror,* and Gerardus Aemilius (*q.v.*), a Reformed preacher. In the second half of the 18th century the church died out. A letter written by the church council of the Mennonite congregation in Rotterdam on March 13, 1713 (*DB* 1918, 69), says that the Oud-Beyerland congregation was extinct. But there were members living there until the second half of the century. In the neighboring village of Nieuw-Beyerland there were also once Mennonites.

J.L., vDZ.

Inv. Arch. Amst. I, Nos. 445, 612, 896; *DB* 1884, 39; Blaupot t. C., *Holland* I, 330; II, 44; *ML* I, 215.

Beza, Theodorus (Théodore de Bèze), b. June 24, 1519, d. Oct. 13, 1605, successor to Calvin in Geneva, was a violent opponent of the Anabaptists, whereas he warmly defended the persecuted Waldenses and Huguenots in France. In 1557 he undertook a long journey with Guillaume Farel in order to win the Protestant cantons of Switzerland and the Protestant princes of Germany to make a joint intercession to the King of France for the menaced Waldenses in Piedmont. Still more zealously he defended the French Huguenots. On the other hand, he showed no appreciation for the Anabaptist movement. He saw in the Anabaptists only heretics of the worst kind, who "preach community of women, refuse the oath, want to remove the government, and in the face of all that consider themselves sinless." To resist them he advocated the severest penalties, including death. This he stated in his famous booklet, *De hæreticis a civili magistratu puniendis* (Concerning Heretics Who Should Be Punished by the Government), which was published in 1554 and was translated into many languages. Beza called the idea of religious freedom a "devilish dogma," and a "Mohammedan dogma."   NEFF.

H. Hoffmann, *Ref. und Gewissensfreiheit* (1932) 23 and 37; N. Paulus, *Beza im Kampf gegen die Vertreter der Toleranz,* scholarly supplement of *Germania* 1910, Nos. 36 and 37; *ML* I, 215.

Bezenchuk is a station on the Trans-Siberian R.R., about 33 miles from Samara (*q.v.,* now Kuibyshev) and 30 miles from Syzran, near the long bridge over the Volga. In 1897 a group of ten young Mennonites of the Alexandertal colony came to Samara in quest of land, and applied there to the imperial authorities, who accommodatingly granted them a 36-year lease on an area of about 5,400 acres located about five miles from Bezentchuk. At the end of this period they could either purchase it or rent it again. The land was level prairie, with soil suitable for wheat raising. The settlement was begun in 1898. The settlers were Johann Epp, Bernhard Thiessen, Bernhard and Abraham Rahn, Peter Harder, Julius Harder, Gerhard and Heinrich van Riesen, Heinrich Nickel, and Heinrich and Johannes Wiebe. After the difficulties of the pioneer years they built substantial farm buildings, laid out large gardens, in general prospered. The settlement was called Pessotchnoye. A factor in its growth was the government agricultural experi-

mental farm located near Bezenchuk, which imported new varieties of wheat from Sweden. The settlers were thus in a position to distribute the wheat. Pessotchnoye had its own dairy and a German school. The settlers belonged to the Mennonite Church at Alexandertal (*q.v.*) and were served by that church; they also elected a preacher of their own from their own membership. The colony numbered about 15 families with 75 persons. This thriving settlement was liquidated by the Communist government and the settlers banished to the White Sea in the north of Russia. (*ML* I, 200.)   B.H.

Bibel und Pflug, an 8-page semi-monthly German-language journal of the Brazilian Mennonites, edited by Fritz Kliewer, published at Witmarsum; first number, January 1954.   H.S.B.

Bibelstunde (literally "Bible Hour," more accurately "Bible Study Meeting") has been quite common among Mennonite congregations in Germany, Holland, France, and Switzerland, as well as in some areas in Russia, and among North American congregations of more recent immigrant background. *Bibelstunden* are meetings within the congregation apart from the regular services, held sometimes on a weekday evening, or Sunday evening, or on alternate Sunday mornings where regular services are held only biweekly, which have for their purpose a more informal indoctrinating and devotional study of the Bible. They were held before Sunday schools were introduced, and are still held where Sunday schools have not been established. In many American congregations the regular midweek evening meeting often partakes somewhat of the character of a Bible study meeting, although it is more commonly called a prayer meeting.

The origin of the modern *Bibelstunde* is obscure. The very beginnings of the Anabaptist movement, both in Switzerland and Holland, were anchored in Bible study meetings. The little group in Zürich out of which the first Anabaptists came was holding Bible meetings as early as 1522, where Andreas Castelberger (*q.v.*) was an active leader. Conrad Grebel and Felix Manz expounded the Scriptures from the Greek and Hebrew respectively in such meetings. "Bible readings" or Bible study meetings, where lay members were active participants, were characteristic of the early Reformation period in Switzerland and Germany, and no doubt generally. But it was in the Anabaptist movement, with its strong emphasis upon personal religious experience, adult baptism, and every-member participation in the life of the church, where no theological training was possible for the preachers and elders, who had to be chosen directly from the working laity, and where the emphasis upon brotherhood was strong in contrast to the state churches with their clerical emphasis, that Bible study meetings were most common. In fact, it was in these meetings, where every member had the right to ask questions about the Scripture content and to give testimony and exposition, that preachers got their "training." It is probable that in the 16th century these meetings were more characteristic of the Anabaptist movement than formal church services where only an ordained minister preached. In this custom the Anabaptists followed the common practice of earlier dissenting groups such as the medieval Cathari and Waldenses, who also kept alive and promoted their cause through lay meetings for mutual edification, admonition, and encouragement.

The Bible study meetings were continued among the Dutch Mennonites until late in the 18th century. S. F. Rues (*Aufrichtige Nachrichten,* 1743, 130 f.) calls them "Collegia biblica, where each was permitted to express himself," and adds that "thereby many were stimulated to diligence in study of the Word of God and to freedom of expression in order to learn how to speak in church." He reports that the meetings were held weekly at an appointed time in the church, where all who wished could come to discuss Scripture texts and their applications. He says that this had been formerly done in many Mennonite congregations in Holland, and that he found the practice still in use in Groningen and a few other places, although it had ceased in Amsterdam, where those interested in this kind of meeting went to the Collegiant meetings. He adds that it was the kind of meeting now practiced by the Collegiants in Holland and the Pietists in Germany. According to Isaak Peters (in *Menn. Rundschau,* 1906, No. 37), who discusses this question at length, G. J. van Rijswijk, a Dutch Mennonite preacher, as late as 1825 declared that he had been trained for the ministry in the Bible and devotional meetings of the Dutch Mennonites. Peters also cites the noted preacher Hans de Ries (d. 1638) as one who owed his preparation for preaching to these meetings.

While it is clear that the earlier Anabaptists and Dutch Mennonites had their Bible meetings long before the 17th-century Collegiants and Pietists arose, it is nevertheless probable that the modern 19th-20th century practice among the Mennonites of Germany and Russia was a reintroduction due to pietistic influences, for the above-cited Isaak Peters, who emigrated from Russia to the United States in 1874, states that this practice was something new in West Prussia and Russia and was opposed as a novelty when it was reintroduced. Certainly the weekday and Sunday Bible study meetings and prayer meetings were something entirely new when they were introduced among the (old) Mennonites and related American groups in the late 19th and early 20th centuries. Such meetings are still altogether unknown among the conservative groups such as Old Order Amish, Old Order Mennonites (Wisler), Old Colony Mennonites, etc., which is proof that the practice must have died out several centuries ago. The rigid Old Colony custom of having preachers deliver only written sermons copied from sermons of long ago is of course the opposite extreme from the free testimony and Bible exposition by all members of the original Anabaptist *Bibelstunde.*

The Bible study and devotional meetings introduced by Spener in 1675 and characteristic of all pietistic groups since that time apparently have no connection historically with the Anabaptist-Men-

nonite practice. Spener himself in his *Pia Desideria* (1675) specifically calls his meetings a revival of the "old apostolic custom," and cites I Cor. 14 to support his proposal. It is in fact only natural that where there is a revival of lay interest and participation in the life and work of the church there should be a renewed interest in meetings for fellowship and testimony based upon Bible study. Wurster's *Die Bibelstunde* (Stuttgart, 1912), a historical study, fails to even mention the Anabaptists or Mennonites (*ML* I, 216 f.).   H.S.B.

Bible is, besides "Holy Scriptures," the most commonly used name of the Word of God, the collection of the canonical writings in the Old and New Testaments. The word "Bible" is derived from the Greek *biblia,* books; the popular, customary explanation of the word, "book of books," or "the book" is therefore correct.

From the court records of the Anabaptists who were seized at the beginning of the Reformation era it is at once evident that they possessed an amazing knowledge of the Bible. Many see evidence in this fact that they are derived from the Waldenses. In so short a time, it is argued, they would not have been able to acquire it (Müller, *Berner Täufer,* 54); they must have been familiar with the Scriptures from childhood, and this could have been the case only among the Waldenses, for in the Catholic Church it had been forbidden the laity to possess a Bible in the vernacular after the Council of Toulouse in 1229. In order to prevent doctrinal disputes the laity were not permitted to read the Bible; its use was limited to the priests. But among the Waldenses it was considered the right and the duty of all Christians to read the Bible. It was the only norm, the sole rule and guide of faith and life. Every doctrine and every ecclesiastical regulation must be proved from the Bible.

The Anabaptists took the same attitude toward the Bible. For them too it alone was authoritative for doctrine and life, for all worship and activity, for all church regulations and discipline. That all members should read the Bible was to them a self-evident duty, and it was often the only book in the home that was steadily used. Through independent study of the Bible, the members soon acquired an astonishing familiarity with it and a surprising understanding of it. This was characteristic of the Anabaptist-Mennonite movement down until recent times, and is still true to a large extent. The Anabaptists' knowledge of the Bible in the Reformation period is not evidence, however, that they came from the Waldenses; for such knowledge can be acquired in a short time. Examples of new converts in all periods of the Christian church prove this.

Some Anabaptists seem to have given the Apocrypha (*q.v.*) almost equal authority with the canonical books. The Old Order Amish preachers of North America still regularly take the text for the wedding sermon from the apocryphal book of Tobit. To be sure, the printed Bibles of the Reformation period, whether Luther (German), Froschauer (Swiss), Biestkens (Dutch), etc., all included the apocryphal books, and the Roman Catholic Bible has always included the Apocrypha as canonical. The reformers, however, did not rate the apocryphal books as of equal authority with the canonical books.

The principle of the sole authority of the Bible for faith and life was not an exclusive Anabaptist possession, but rather a foundation principle of all Protestantism beginning with Luther himself, and was established against the Roman Catholic principle that the Bible and the tradition of the church together constitute the authoritative norm. The reformers, however, although emphatically proclaiming the principle, were not uniformly consistent in applying it, being led at times by theological and practical considerations to depart from the strict teaching of Scripture. The Anabaptists, being Biblicists and usually unsophisticated readers of the Bible, not trained theologians or scholars, and having made a more complete break with tradition than the reformers, were more radical and consistent in their application of the principle of sole Scriptural authority. They sought to obey the Bible in simple faith, without calculation of consequences for the socio-political or ecclesiastical order.

A striking characteristic of the Anabaptists' attitude toward the Bible is their principle of the supremacy of the New Testament. For them the Old Testament was not binding in the same sense, and in so far as it disagrees with the New it was superseded and abrogated. (See **Old Testament** for a full discussion of this point.)

The Anabaptists and Mennonites have often been described as Biblical literalists. If this means that they tried to obey the commands of Christ and teachings of the New Testament literally, e.g., nonresistance, nonswearing of oaths, footwashing, etc., this is an accurate statement for most of Anabaptist-Mennonite history, though it no longer applies to all modern groups, particularly in Holland and Germany. If by "literalism" is meant a type of naive legalistic and externalistic use of the Bible without regard for its essentially spiritual character, and without finding in it great controlling principles, then that description is not historically valid, although occasionally an extreme and painful literalism has been followed. For a careful discussion of the Anabaptist attitude on this question see the article, **Bible: Inner and Outer Word.**

The doctrine of Scripture was not theoretically expressed in the earlier confessions of faith of the Anabaptists and Mennonites in the first two centuries. The Schleitheim Confession (1527), the Concept of Cologne (1591), the Confession of Hans de Ries and Lubbert Gerrits (1610), the Dordrecht Confession (1632), and all other confessions of this general period have no article on the Bible. Peter Riedemann's *Rechenschaft* (1545), the great Hutterite statement, does not treat the Bible as such, although it deals specifically with the old and new covenants. The first case of a direct article on the Bible is the 1659 Confession drafted by van Aldendorp, van Heuven, Andries, and van Maurik, and printed at Utrecht under the title *Een Belijdenisse.* The Cornelis Ris Confession of 1766 (Hoorn, Holland) contains such an article. Only under the influence of 18th-century German Orthodoxy, which first developed a detailed doctrine of Scripture particularly with regard to inspiration and infallibility, did Mennonite statements of faith begin to become more specific on these points. A second wave of influence in this direction came in the 20th century from the defensive reaction of American evangelical Protestantism against 19th-century liberal theology and Biblical criticism, particularly in the Fundamentalism (*q.v.*) movement. The article on the Bible in the 1921 statement of Christian Fundamentals adopted by the Mennonite Church (MC) of North America is illustrative of this influence.

However, the absence of a theoretical statement on the Scriptures in the earlier Mennonite confessions should not be taken in any sense as evidence of an absence of belief in the authority of the Scriptures. On the contrary, the evidence of the Anabaptist position on this point is overwhelming. While no comprehensive study has been published, several authors have assembled a great amount of evidence, e.g., John Horsch in the chapter on "Authority of the Scriptures" in his *Mennonites in Europe* (1942, pp. 350-58), and Gordon Kaufman in his article, "Some Theological Emphases of the Early Swiss Anabaptists" (*MQR* XXV, 1951, pp. 75-99, section on "The Scriptures," pp. 81-87). See also C. Krahn, "Mennos Christozentrische Schriftverständnis," in his *Menno Simons* (1936, pp. 107-10), and Ellis Graber, "Menno Simons and the Scriptures" (an unpublished manuscript), who states that Menno Simons quotes the Old Testament 290 times, and the New Testament 740 times in the first part (285 pp.) of his *Complete Works.*

The following selections from these two sources will serve to illustrate the evidence.

Conrad Grebel wrote in 1525: "We would ask you to discard the old ordinances of Antichrist and hold to the Word of God alone and be guided by it." The Brethren wrote in 1525 to the Zürich city council: "If it be found then by divine Scripture that we err, we shall gladly accept correction . . . . We desire nothing upon earth but to have these things decided according to the Word of God." Michael Sattler wrote in 1527: "Let no one cause you to depart from the standard that is laid through the letter of Scripture which is sealed by the blood of Christ and of many witnesses of Jesus." At his trial in 1527 Sattler said: "Ye ministers of God, if you have neither heard nor read the Word of God, we would suggest that you send for the most learned men and for the book of the divine Scriptures, and that they with us weigh these things in the light of the Word of God. If they show us from Holy Scripture that we err and are in the wrong, we shall gladly be taught." In the great debates of the Swiss Brethren with the representatives of the Zwinglian state church, held at Zofingen in 1532 and at Bern in 1538, the Brethren speakers continually appealed to the Scriptures and demanded that their opponents abide by it. They said: "We hold that all things should be proven to ascertain what is founded on the holy Word of God, for this will stand when heaven and earth pass away, as Christ Himself said." Pilgram Marpeck wrote concerning the Scriptures and their authority in 1544: "We would sincerely admonish every Christian to be on the alert and personally study the Scriptures, and have a care lest he permit himself to be easily moved and led away from the Scripture and apostolic doctrine by strange teaching and understanding; but let everyone, in accordance with the Scripture and apostolic teaching, strive with great diligence to do God's will, seeing that the Word of truth could not fail us nor mislead us." Menno Simons wrote in 1550: "My dear brethren, I for myself confess that I would rather die than to believe and teach to my brethren a single word concerning the Father, the Son, and the Holy Ghost, at variance with the express testimony of God's Word, as it is so clearly given through the mouth of the prophets, evangelists, and apostles." Again in 1554 Menno said: "But that Gellius appeals to Tertullian, Cyprian, Origen, and Augustine, my reply is, first, if these writers can support their teachings with the Word and command of God, we will admit that they are right. If not, then it is a doctrine of men and accursed according to the Scriptures."

Mennonites have remained throughout their history a people of the Bible, emphasizing "Bible doctrine" rather than theology, except in those places where advanced theological training or higher education has made preacher or people or both more theological and philosophical than Biblical. (See also **Bibles and Bible Translations, Bibelstunden,** and **Gespauwde Klauw.**) (*ML* I, 215.)   H.S.B.

Bible: Inner and Outer Word. The terms "inner Word" and "outer Word" were once used to designate the written and unwritten Word of God. In the place of "inner Word" the terms "illumination" or "inner voice" were often used. These expressions are by no means an invention of the Anabaptists or Spiritualists of the Reformation period. They appear in Augustine's book *Tolle Lege,* from which a Pietist of the 18th century quotes, "The sound of our word strikes your ears, but the Master is within you" (Braun, 97 ff.). Likewise the medieval mystics, Bernhard, Tauler, Thomas à Kempis, Ruysbroeck, Gerhard Groote, Catherine of Siena, etc., heard the inner and immediate voice of God in the stillness. A "Friend of God" called the attention of the "pious, gentle" Tauler, who "possessed a good knowledge of the Bible," to the fact that "he did not yet possess and live by the light of the grace of God and was therefore a Pharisee" (Tränendorf-Metzer, 127). Thomas à Kempis in his *Imitatio* also speaks of "inner illumination," though he does not at all despise the "outer Word." He had the courage, in defiance of the pope, to recommend the Bible as the highest light to those who would be happy. He made four copies of the Bible for distribution (Werner, 127). Bishop Berthold Pirstinger, the author of *Deutsche Theologie* (*q.v.*), also has much to say about "inner illumination" or the "true light," especially in chapters 39-44. Luther rated this booklet very high. Peter

Chelcicky's (*q.v.*) *Net of Faith* speaks of the divine light that is lighted in us through the Holy Spirit: "Faith is a light that God lights in the heart." In this way only does "the birth of God in the depths of the soul" occur. Luther, as Karl Holl remarks, at times stressed the need for the Holy Spirit so strongly that his expressions "seem to approach fanaticism when he says, for instance, 'Everyone shall therefore believe that it is the Word of God when he feels within him that the Bible is true. The heart speaks: this is true, even if I should die one hundred deaths for it.'" It was therefore his idea "that basically every outward authority that seeks to be accepted inwardly needs an inner organ in man that convinces him of the truth of what is offered, the witness of the Holy Spirit" (Holl, 248). Luther bases this concept in part on the verse in the Psalms, "I will hear what God Himself speaks in me." "It could not be comprehended by anyone but such a quiet, reflecting spirit" (*Mitteilungen aus der Studentenbewegung,* 1927-28, No. 1, p. 4). This indicates that for Luther, who was strongly influenced by the mystics on this point, experience is the beginning of the knowledge of the divine character of the Scripture. On the other hand, his opposition to the "enthusiasts," who strongly emphasized the "inner light" or "inner Word," led him to protest against their view that God gives His Spirit in other ways than through the "outer Word." Word and Spirit he put on the same level. God works with man only through the word of Scripture (*Luthers Werke* III, 68 f.; VI, 395). Luther thereby begins the chorus of voices who to our very day have charged that the Anabaptists disavowed the written Word of God, expecting everything of the "inner Word," or that they "want to be sharp judges between the Spirit and the letter," or "they valued the inner Word at the expense of the written Word." Melanchthon says at the close of his *Verlegung etlicher unchristlicher Artikel, welche die Wiedertäufer fürgeben* (1536), "Disregard for the outer Word and the Scripture is blasphemy. . . . Therefore the temporal arm of government shall watch here too and not tolerate this blasphemy, but earnestly resist and punish it." Justus Menius (*q.v.*) in his book, *Der Wiedertäufer Lehre und Geheimnis* (1530), makes a similar statement. The theologians of the university of Marburg asserted that the Anabaptist preacher Melchior Rinck (*q.v.*) held a doctrine of disparagement of the written Word as a spiritless literalism, common to the sectarians (Wappler, 54). The 1527 booklet, *Getreue Warnung der Prediger des Evangeliums zu Strassburg, so Jakob Kautz, Prediger zu Worms, hat ausgehen lassen,* says, "All their teaching leads to the idea that the Scripture is of no account" (Moravian archives at Brno, Beck copy 76, p. 15). Urbanus Rhegius (*q.v.*) in his 1527 book, *Warnung wider den neuen Tauforden* (bl.B), accuses Hans Denk (*q.v.*) and his group of unwillingness to submit to the Scripture: ("thus he lies in the mud. Summa: Anabaptists cannot and will not endure the Scripture"). The *Bedenken der Wiedertäufer halben,* which is identical with *Prozess, wie es soll gehalten werden mit den Widertäufern* (*q.v.*) (1557), says, "Fourth error: God makes Himself known without consideration of the outer Word and without the sacrament." In recent times it was especially Karl Holl, H. Böhmer, and Lydia Müller, who have revived the assertion that the Anabaptists were the spiritual descendants of Thomas Müntzer, that the Spirit rather than the written Word was the highest authority for them, that they believed that revelations in addition to the Scripture are needed and that the spiritual man can therefore dispense with the Bible.

But these charges made against the Anabaptists by no means correspond to the facts of history. The Biblical Anabaptists have never despised the written Word or overemphasized the "inner Word" at the expense of historical revelation. They did not at all desire to be "sharp judges between the spirit and the letter," as Luther charges. This is easy to show from the writings of the Anabaptists. Müntzer and the Münsterites, the Puschhamer and other small groups, do not enter the picture for the Anabaptists kept their distance from them, as many important historians and even the contemporary government of Ulrich of Württemberg recognized (Bossert XI and No. 69, 79). Hubmaier's (*q.v.*) (d. 1528) high estimation of the Scripture is well known. In his *Preislied des göttlichen Wortes* each of the 18 stanzas contains the phrase, "For God's Word will stand forever." The Holy Scripture is for him the touchstone by which all spiritual matters should be decided. God's Word alone should be the judge. "Nothing should be added to or subtracted from the word of Christ." "I consider the Scripture to be a Hercules." "I call upon Heaven and earth to bear witness that I have faithfully said, cursed is he who dissolves the slightest word and does not say amen to it." "The Word of God stands firm as a stone wall." "The Scripture is the friend of God in which Jesus lives, dwells, and rests; there is no spot in it." In his *Christliche Lehrtafel* Hubmaier speaks of the "inner and outer drawing by God." He does not put them side by side independent of each other, but makes the one the result of the other. The "outer drawing" precedes; it takes place through the public proclamation of the written Word. From it comes the "inner drawing": Thus God has enlightened man also inwardly in his soul, "that it may understand the irresistible truth, convinced by the Spirit of God and the spoken Word, so that one must in his own conscience confess that it is true and that it cannot be otherwise." "The Word of God is water to all those who thirst for salvation and is made alive in us through the Spirit of God, without whose work it is only a dead letter." "Do you have Zwingli's word, we want God's Word!" was the cry of the Zürich Anabaptists according to Kessler (Burkhardt, 43). In Augsburg about 60 Anabaptists were sitting together in a cellar, listening to Hans Leupold (*q.v.*) and Jörg von Passau (*q.v.*) read the Bible and explain what they read (Wiswedel II, 62). Hans Schlaffer (*q.v.*), a former priest, declared at his trial, "So I say and swear like Paul: 'God is my

witness in my conscience that . . . I hold the written Gospel of faith in Christ in high esteem'" (Wiswedel II, 194). Veit Grünberger, a Hutterite missionary, remarked in a letter to Peter Walpot, "I hope to be able to learn 100 chapters of the Testament by heart. If I had had the Testament before, I have no doubt that I would know it from memory. Temptation makes one pay attention to the Word" (Codex Michnay, Pressburg, fol. 514). Thomas von Imbroich said in his confession before the court at Cologne (*ca.* 1556), "The Scripture cannot be broken, nor shall anything be added to or subtracted from the Word. It is God's Word, which remains in eternity" (*Mart. Mir.* E 367). Matthias Servaes wrote in prison to a brother asking him to send his wife, who was not yet in prison, a Dutch New Testament, since she was unable to read German (*Mart. Mir.* E 692). Johannes Bair (*q.v.*) of Lichtenfels, who was held in the Bamberg prison 23 years until he died, asked his brethren to send him a Bible, for he had lacked a Bible for many years and had a great thirst for the Word (Wiswedel I, 130). Wolfgang Vogel, a former priest in Eltersdorf near Erlangen, was deprived of his Bible when he was imprisoned in a Nürnberg tower (Wiswedel I, 159). Paul Glock (*q.v.*) passed the time of his 19-year imprisonment in careful Bible study (*Blätter für Württem. Kirchengesch.*, 1929, 29). A familiar statement of Menno Simons was, "Our council (*Konzilium*) is the Scripture."

In the Hutterite catechism in the discussion of the Lord's Prayer we find in the margin no fewer than 131 Biblical references (Wiswedel in *Archiv für Reformationsgesch.*, No. 37, pp. 38 ff.). "Grant us, Lord, to live in Thy Word and to keep Thy covenant," is the prayer of an Anabaptist poet. In a discussion with the Landmarshall in Vienna, the Anabaptists Max and Bernhard Klampferer (*q.v.*) read the Bible to him (Beck, 263). Again and again Anabaptist prisoners made it clear that they would recant if they could be shown something better from the Scriptures (see Wiswedel II, 89, 100, 104). The baptism of infants was rejected by the Anabaptists for the very reason that they found nothing in the New Testament about it, not because an inner voice urged them to do so. The preachers, known as *Diener am Wort,* on their journeys did not tell the people about their dreams and visions, but sought in the simplest way possible to impress the Word of salvation upon their hearts. Their letters, epistles, and confessions are filled with quotations from both the Old and New Testaments, with chapter and verse. In the writings of the shoemaker Peudler as well as in the *Rechenschaft* of Peter Riedemann (*q.v.*) verse after verse is quoted, connected by simple logic and explanation. "The Anabaptists wanted to be Bible Christians and they were precisely that for the most part" (W. Köhler). Also von Muralt confesses frankly that the Swiss Anabaptists were strict Biblicists. "The Anabaptists stand on the platform of the Scripture (*Schriftprinzip*)" (*Zwingliana* 1934, no. 2). Eduard Becker also mentions their "extensive knowledge of the Bible." Likewise Bossert, Jr.: "They are the quiet in the land, they take their direction from the Bible in continuous Bible study" (*Blätter f. Württ. Kirchengesch.*, 1939, 8). To be sure, some modern critics of the Anabaptists, such as Fritz Heyer, have asserted that the Anabaptists used the written Word in a rather legalistic way, but they have not offered proof.

In looking over the total Anabaptist literature, their confessions of faith, catechisms, *Rechenschaften,* letters, and the records of their cross-examinations, we find very little mention of the "inner light." Only a very few were influenced by the ancient mystics. One of these few was Hans Langenmantel (*q.v.*). In his writings we read, "Luther says, he preaches the Gospel of Christ, and with his physical voice he brings Christ into the hearts of his hearers. But I (Langenmantel) say: there must first be something within us that can accept the physical voice inwardly" (Wiswedel II, 74, 75). Ambrosius Spittelmayer declared before his judges, that it was not their intention to instigate revolt, but to learn and desire the divine Word, that all men might be led to the truth . . . and to pray for them that they might be enlightened with the divine light. But Spittelmayer at once explained what he meant by divine light: not by visible visions, but by the Spirit of God Christ leads and teaches His church (Wiswedel II, 14). During the discussions with the Anabaptists imprisoned at Jena, when Melanchthon kept citing Scripture against them, Heinz Kraut (*q.v.*) declared, it was written in his heart as they had been taught by God. The devil could also write. Furthermore, Master Philip killed more people with his dead Scripture than all the hangmen (Wiswedel I, 75 f.). The Anabaptist Umblauft in Regensburg said the Scriptures and the outer Word are merely the witness and lamp of the inner Word of God. Therefore a man can be saved without preaching and Scriptures. Proof: otherwise illiterates could not be saved. We understand God, our Redeemer, not through the dead letter, but through the indwelling of Christ. To the scribes and Pharisees the written Word was not a guide to Christ, but a hindrance and punishment. Furthermore all who did not hear the Word and all who lived before the written Word was given, from Adam to Moses, would be lost. Salvation shall be ascribed alone to the inner Word of God and not be bound to the outer Word, "however useful it may be if God reveals its meaning." The Bible is good for those who use it aright, but its misuse is the source of all heresy and unbelief. Another Anabaptist of Regensburg confessed that knowledge of the truth does not come from human study, . . . it comes only to those to whom it is given by grace through the light of His Spirit (Nestler, 33). Michael Jungemann of Kürnbach in Württemberg considered the office of preaching a good Christian office if the Word is preached pure and unadulterated and if one lives accordingly. A preacher must be blameless. . . . Whatever God admonishes and enlightens him to do, he wants to follow in his life. Michel Humel's widow, 70 years old, was "unteachable" —she declared briefly and finally that she was adequately enlightened. Similar statements were made by a number of other Anabaptists of Württemberg (see Bossert, Index under *Erleuchtung*).

Jakob Kautz (*q.v.*), a former Lutheran preacher, said, "The Word that we speak outwardly with our mouth, hear with our physical ears, write and print with hands, is nothing living, nor the eternal Word of God, but only a witness or indication of the inner Word, so that the inner Word may be rightly understood. Nothing external, be it word, sign, sacrament, or promise, has power to reassure the inner man, comfort him, or make him certain." Scharnschlager (*q.v.*) objected to having the Scriptures called a dead letter, since it was given by the Holy Spirit through holy men of God. As often as he hears or reads it, it is the same as if he heard the Lord and His apostles speak. Furthermore, everyone knows that the letters with which the Scriptures were written are in themselves dead ink and paper, but in the true understanding the Holy Scriptures are not dead ink and letters. If the Holy Scriptures in their meaning and understanding are not opened in the heart by the Holy Ghost, then not only the Holy Scriptures are dead, but Christ Himself with His teaching, His life, suffering, and death, yea even His resurrection are dead; they are of no use to a man to eternal life, even granted that he reads and studies as long as he likes. He could then be called learned in the Scripture, but not taught by the Spirit. "In itself the Scriptures are the Word of God as it is learned, and therefore I should not call them a dead letter, but the Holy Scriptures, as they call themselves" (*Ztscht des Vereins f. d. Gesch. Mährens und Schlesiens,* 1928, 11). Ludwig Haetzer (*q.v.*) remarked, "He who goes only by the Scriptures receives knowledge, but a useless knowledge, which does not reform. No man, no matter how learned he may be, can understand the Scriptures unless he had experienced and learned them in the depth of his soul. Otherwise men speak of the matter like a blind man of color" (Hagen II, 288). In reply to Schwenckfeld's charge that the Anabaptists wanted to make "two words of God," the Swiss Brethren said, "We do not call ink and paper or the perishable part of the books of the Scripture God's Word, Spirit, and life, but we mean the meaning contained in what is composed, spoken, and written." In such a case it is simply a matter of faith, without which God's preached or written Word does not reach the heart and cannot dwell therein to be spirit and life therein, as the Lord says, "The words that I speak are spirit and life, but there are some among you who do not believe." There are not two, but only one Word of God. The external truth is a co-witness and the same truth as the inner truth in the believing heart. When a man hears the Word of God and believes it, in his heart the Holy Spirit makes it life. It is God's fixed ordinance, that He "saves and makes believers by means of external services" (Marpeck's *Antwort auf Schwenckfeld's Beurteilung des Buches der Bundesbezeugung,* 1542, pp. 149 f., 518 f., 521 f., 529 f.). In the booklet, *Prozess, wie es soll gehalten werden mit den Wiedertäufern,* the brethren made an unambiguous reply to the charge that they put the center of gravity on inner illumination and taught that God could make Himself known without the outer Word. They had no pleasure in opposing such defamatory lies, but for the sake of the Word of God one must not neglect to refute them and to put to shame these hairsplitting, sly opponents of the truth. They did not at all believe that God reveals Himself without the hearing of the preached Word, for that would mean an annulment of an ordinance established by Him. They affirmed the word of Paul in I Thess. 2:13 fully and completely. God could indeed have granted the gift of the Holy Spirit to a Saul and to a Cornelius without human mediation, but He considered it good to send them an Ananias and the Apostle Peter and to use their testimony to the end that they should receive the gift of the Holy Spirit. Faith comes from hearing, and Jesus Himself said, "Go ye into all the world." But the outer Word that is preached to the peoples is the image and the instruction in the inner Word, since the believer feels the grace and power of God in his heart and soul, which has been written there by the finger of the divine love of the Holy Spirit. And this is not that which is drawn upon paper or tables of stone, nor is it that which is heard outwardly, because it is not the hearers but the doers of works of piety of a heavenly life as the Scripture says, that are pleasing and acceptable to God (*Handbüchlein*, book 8). The *Geschicht-Buch* of the Hutterian Brethren reports that the brother Benjamin Kempel was expelled from the congregation at Sobotiste because he would not recognize the service of preaching and the daily prayer meetings, and rejected baptism and communion and wished to recognize only teaching through the Holy Spirit. Peter Riedemann's *Rechenschaft* says unequivocally that faith comes from hearing the preaching of the Gospel as is written in Rom. 10:17. When a man yields to the Word, opens his heart, and believes, the Holy Spirit working upon the heart through hearing makes His dwelling in the human heart. "Where the Spirit is not added to the Word, it cannot acquire the uprightness that is valid before God." Likewise Leonhard Schiemer (*q.v.*) declared that if one comes to a knowledge of the truth it takes place not alone through hearing the Word of God outwardly, but he must also have the light of the Holy Spirit in his heart. "For external learning is not sufficient except in so far as it is revealed inwardly in the heart" (Moravian archives at Brno, Beck collection 45, pp. 26-43).

Hans Denk (*q.v.*) discussed the inner and outer Word extensively in three booklets. He did not discard the written Word; the preachers must present and divide Christ and His Word rightly: the Gospel of Christ: His incarnation, life, doctrine, and death, His resurrection, and ascension, the Gospel of His future kingdom and future judgment of His church, etc. Him who is upright God will illuminate and will draw him inwardly and grant him eternal life in His grace. Stadler discussed the same subject in his book, *Vom le-*

bendigen und geschriebenen Wort oder von dem äusserlichen und innerlichen Wort und ihrer Wirkung im Herzen. Unterschied und Bericht. He said that all creation and all creatures including the Holy Scriptures and the spoken and proclaimed Word are good, but they are not the living Word. One must distinguish between the two. The outer Word, as Christ commanded His apostles, is, preach the Gospel to every creature. Here preaching, believing, and baptism are understood and treated purely externally and are only symbols of the living Word, faith, and baptism, which God alone works through His righteousness. A true preacher must accept the true Word of God in the depth of his soul; then it becomes the true Word of God in the depth of the soul. But that which is preached is only the witness or symbol of the true Word. The inner Word is not written, neither upon paper nor upon tables, it is not spoken or preached; man is assured by it through God in the depth of his soul and it becomes engraved in a heart of flesh through the Spirit by the finger of God. The inner Word is witnessed by the outer, as the sign before an inn witnesses the wine in the keg, but the sign is not the wine; thus it is also with the divine order, that always the physical precedes the spiritual: the faith of hearing comes before justification, after which the tested faith grows and works powerfully toward God and all creation. But this does not happen as quickly as the scribes of our day say, who persuade the poor people by saying, "Believe, believe!" Yea, this will soon become evident. Stadler then developed this presentation by Biblical examples. According to the divine plan, the inner Word follows the outer, and the preacher shall admonish through the outer Word, that man should yield himself to God and listen to the inner instructor. One must not make the people depend on the outer Word, or one makes an idol of the preacher, also of the Scriptures and the words. But they are merely an image or a sign or tool. It does no good, and is not sufficient to testify with the mouth, that Christ has come in the flesh; Christ must also become the flesh in us, in the Word and through the Spirit as Paul writes in Gal. 2: "I live, yet not I, but Christ liveth in me." Thus whoever confesses Christ can boast of the living Word and can rightly witness to the truth. "Such preachers we want to expect from God."

We see that from all these Anabaptist writings it is evident that the Anabaptists did not repudiate all historical, objective means of salvation, nor expect everything of "inner light" and the working of the Holy Spirit. But they believed that the working of the Holy Spirit directed upon the human heart must be added to the objective and preached Word. They did not separate the inner Word from the outer Word. The Spirit and the inner Word belong together. Word without Spirit is a dead letter to them. The life-giving Spirit of God turns the written and proclaimed Word into God's Word. The Word of God is the sword of the Holy Spirit; the two belong inseparably together. This was well stated by Wolfgang Vogel (*q.v.*), a former preacher in Eltersdorf: "The spirit clings and hangs alone to the noble, pure, tender, and the holy Word of God through a strong and firm faith." In Marpeck's book we read: "The outer, preached or written Word is one with the inner Word."

Thus the inner Word as used by the Anabaptists is not to be understood in the sense of an inner inspiration, which imparts new truths to man, but as the illuminating work of God. It is of course not to be denied that Denk, Kautz, and also Stadler were inclined to a strong spiritualization. But they were not subject to the danger of pantheism. They were strongly influenced by mysticism and especially by the *Deutsche Theologie* (*q.v.*), as W. Köhler has clearly recognized, "but their speculation was turned toward Biblicism under the influence of Lutheran ideas."

Among the Dutch Mennonites the relation of the outer Word to the inner Word was a point of controversy between Nittert Obbes (*q.v.*) and Hans de Ries (*q.v.*). Nittert Obbes accused de Ries of failing to give the written Word its due in his teaching that there are two kinds of the Word of God, and of attaching greater value to the inner Word than the written Word of God. Ries denied the charge, saying that the inner Word of God was not his imagination but is Christ Himself, who through His Holy Spirit within speaks to, teaches, enlightens, saves, renews, and regenerates us. Jost van den Vondel, the great Dutch poet, who did not have a clear understanding of the dispute, sided with Nittert Obbes in his poem *Antidotum* (*q.v.*). (Kühler, *Geschiedenis* II, 1, 142-75; see also J. H. Maronier, *Het inwendig Woord*, Amsterdam, 1890).   W.W.

Archiv für Refor.-Gesch. XXXVII, No. 1, 38 ff. (article by Wiswedel); Beck, *Geschichts-Bücher*, 263; *Blätter für Württembg. Kirchengesch.*, 1929, 8, 29; G. Bossert, *Quellen zur Gesch. der Wiedertäufer*, I: *Württemberg* (1930) p. XI, and Nos. 69 and 79, Index under *Erleuchtung; Mart. Mir.* (1950); Frido Braun, *Johann Tannhardt* (1934) 97 ff.; P. Burckhardt, *Die Basler Täufer* (Basel, 1898) 43; Wolkan, *Geschicht-Buch*, 630-31; Karl Hagen, *Deutschlands literarische und religiöse Verhältnisse im Reformationszeitalter* II (Erlangen, 1833) 288; *Handbüchlein wider den Prozess, der zu Wurms am Rhein wider die Brüder, so man die Hutterischen nennt ausgegangen ist*, Book VIII; Karl Holl, *Luther und die Schwärmer* (first edition) 248; *Luthers Werke, Volksausgabe* III, 68 f., VI, 395; *Pilgram Marbecks Antwort auf Kaspar Schwenkfelds Beurteilung des Buches der Bundesbezeugung von 1542* (Vienna, 1929) 149-50; 521-22; 529-30; *Mitteilungen aus der Studentenbewegung* (1927-28) No. 1, p. 4; L. von Muralt, *Zwingliana* (1934) No. 2; Hermann Nestler, *Die Wiedertäuferbewegung in Regensburg* (Regensburg, 1926) 33; Friedrich Selle, *Schicksalsbuch der Evang. Kirche in Oesterreich* (1928) 249 f.; Tränendorf-Metzer, *Kirchengeschichtliches Lesebuch* (3d ed.) 127; P. Wappler, *Die Täuferbewegung in Thüringen 1526-1584* (Jena, 1913) 54; Werner, *Die Helden der christlichen Kirche* (Leipzig, 1904) 127; W. Wiswedel, *Bilder* I and II (Kassel, 1928, 1930); *Zeitschrift des Vereins für die Gesch. Mährens und Schlesiens*, 1928, 11.

Bible Conference, a term used only among North American Mennonites in this exact form. Similar terms such as "Bibelkurs" and "Bibelbesprechung" and "Glaubenskonferenz" are used among the Mennonites of Germany, Switzerland, France, and Russia, though with varying application. "Bible Conference," occasionally called "Bible Week," in North America refers primarily to a special series of meetings from one or two days to a week in length, sponsored by a congregation for its own members. "Bibelkurs" is sometimes used in Europe for exactly the same thing, sometimes rather for special meetings for limited groups (age and sex) held at certain centers and amounting to a very short term school. Again "conference" is used in both Europe and North America to refer to large community, regional, or national gatherings for Bible teaching and inspiration. One or more of the above types of Bible conference have become common among Mennonites of most groups in all countries except Holland, having been introduced often through outside (usually pietistic) influence, about the end of the 19th century and become widespread in the first third of the 20th century. Together with the other similar forces (Sunday school, revivalism, etc., in America, *Gemeinschaftsbewegung* in Germany and other countries), they have done much to inculcate a love for the Bible and a warm type of piety, as well as a considerable diffusion of Bible knowledge. They have also at times been the channel for entrance of "new" doctrines, such as Millennialism, "holiness" teachings and even Pentecostalism, "eternal security" teachings, etc. The following discussion will deal first with the Bible conference among the (old) Mennonites of North America, then with the *Bibelkurs* in Central Europe and Russia, and finally with the larger conferences. It is worthy of note that nothing of this sort has apparently ever appeared among the Mennonites of Holland.

1. *Bible Conference,* the name commonly given among the (old) Mennonites of North America to a series of meetings in a local congregation, common in the past two generations, at which visiting ministers delivered addresses on various topics of doctrinal, ethical, and practical character. They were called Bible conferences because the speakers sought to present their material on the basis of a careful study of all the pertinent Scriptures and often used the method of assigning Bible verses to members of the audience to be read by them and then commented upon by the speaker. Sessions were usually held morning, afternoon, and evening, continuing for a week, with two visiting ministers, in effect a sort of Bible school. These Bible conferences were inaugurated about 1890 and soon became very popular, continuing in widespread use until about the time of World War I after which they gradually died out. They usually were held in winter when farmers had only light work and had much time for meetings. They were a powerful influence in the church in the education of the laity in the message of the Bible and indoctrination of the principles of the church. In recent times week-end Bible conferences have been held which use a different method consisting only of addresses by visiting speakers. The Winter Bible School (*q.v.*), which was inaugurated at Goshen College in 1900 as a six weeks' short term school for young people, led gradually to the establishment of similar six weeks' schools in other

parts of the church and ultimately by many still shorter term Bible schools of two and three weeks in length or even one week. (As early as 1902, for instance, the Mennonite church of Roseland, Neb., co-operating with the local Brethren church, held a nine-day Bible school beginning on Dec. 27.) The latter in effect has constituted a revival in slightly different form of the old-fashioned Bible conference, since they are usually held in local congregations and are attended by old as well as young.

In some areas of the church Bible conferences were known as Bible Normals. Under this title meetings were held at least as early as 1902 in Kansas and as early as 1907 and as late as 1930 in Illinois.

2. A similar type of meeting called *Bibelkurs* developed among the Mennonites in Switzerland, South Germany, and France about the same time. The first of these was held in February 1882 in the Swiss congregation of La Chaux de Fonds, in the Bernese Jura region, served by preachers from the Methodist and Baptist churches and the Evangelical Association. It has been continued in this congregation annually and is still held. It was often conducted by the noted non-Mennonite evangelist, Jacob Vetter (*q.v.*). The South German Mennonite preacher and evangelist, Jacob Hege, was invited at this time to conduct a five-day *Bibelkurs* in Langnau and Basel, which proved to have unusual influence and led to a sort of revival and which was repeated in succeeding years. Later similar meetings were held in some of the Baden German Mennonite congregations, which were, however, limited more to one day and were called *Bibelbesprechungen.* In recent years these have been held mostly at the Thomashof, near Durlach, Baden, an institutional center of the South German Mennonites, and at Hellmannsberg near Ingolstadt in Bavaria. In 1907 an annual *Bibelkurs* of two days was instituted in the Palatinate in the Weierhof congregation, which was served by the evangelist Jakob Vetter from 1912 on for many years. Jakob Kroeker (*q.v.*) conducted the *Bibelkurs* for many years; he also served in a similar capacity in Switzerland.

In recent times, practically every congregation in Switzerland and Alsace holds an annual *Bibelkurs,* usually from Thursday to Sunday with morning and evening daily sessions. In a number of congregations these meetings fill the need filled elsewhere by evangelistic services, although they are not quite the same type of meeting. The emphasis in all these meetings is the direct study of the Scriptures in the form of book or chapter study or topical study, but also with emphasis upon the doctrines and practices of the Mennonite Church. Usually they are sponsored by a local congregation which extends an invitation to neighboring congregations to participate. They have come to be a permanently valuable part of the church life in many places. In Russia the Mennonite Brethren began in 1872 an annual *Bibelkurs* (called at first *Missionsschule,* primarily for preachers and candidates), which customarily continued for a month,

introduced and continued by the German Baptist preacher, August Liebig (*q.v.*), but which was something different from the later *Bibelkurs* in Switzerland and Germany. (Liebig later, in the early 20th century, served in Bible conferences among the Mennonite Brethren in the United States.) The Mennonite Church in Russia gradually introduced two-day *Bibelbesprechungen* in various congregations for the better preparation of Christian workers, which again was something different both from Liebig's work and from the congregational *Bibelkurs.* The Bundeskonferenz of 1910 endorsed such meetings in the various congregations for the general public, besides providing for special Bible conferences for preachers and preacher candidates lasting ten days or longer.

3. Quite different from the congregational Bible conference in North America and the *Bibelkurs* in Europe were the large Bible conferences such as the Blankenburg Allianzkonferenz (*q.v.*), founded in 1886, the Gnadau Pfingstkonferenz (founded in 1888, held 1908-21 in Wernigerode), the Glaubens- und Missionskonferenz in Wernigerode sponsored by *Licht im Osten* (1921-43?) with branch conferences at Frankfurt as well as in Switzerland and Holland, and the American conferences such as Niagara, Chautauqua, Winona Lake, Erieside, Estes Park, and similar conferences in the United States which were large annual or biennial national gatherings. Mennonites from Russia were frequent attendants at Blankenburg and Wernigerode, and some American Mennonites attended the similar large conferences in the United States. The influence of these large conferences was not always wholesome and was a frequent source of radical pietistic and millennial (Darbyite) influence. Speakers who became known at the large conferences were sometimes invited to speak at Bible conferences in Mennonite communities or congregations modeled on the pattern of the larger conferences. An illustration of this was E. F. Stroeter, a radical millenarian, active in the Blankenburg conference, who found entrance into Mennonite circles in Russia (and related circles in America) as a Bible conference lecturer. The Newton (Kan.) Mennonite community annual Bible conference has sponsored many non-Mennonite lecturers. Some other congregations and communities have followed a similar pattern. Some kind of annual Bible conference is still fairly common among those G.C.M. congregations who do not have annual evangelistic or revival meetings, as well as among the academies, Bible schools, and colleges of the group, where both student body and public are served. A similar practice is followed widely among the schools of other Mennonite branches. In the schools the term "Bible Lectures" often replaces "Bible Conference." (*ML* I, 216, **Bibelkurse.**)

H.S.B.

Bible Doctrine. *A Treatise on the Great Doctrines of the Bible pertaining to God, Angels, Satan, the Church, and the Salvation, Duties and Destiny of Man.* Compiled by a committee appointed by the Mennonite General Conference, Daniel Kauffman, Editor. Published by Mennonite Publishing House,

Scottdale, Pa., 1914. This volume of 701 pages represents the most extensive effort of the Mennonite Church (MC) in the sphere of Bible doctrine. At the 1911 sessions of Mennonite General Conference (MC) ten writers were appointed to "prepare a work on Christian doctrine, setting forth, from a Scriptural standpoint, those things most commonly believed among us: A. D. Wenger, Fentress, Va.; D. J. Johns, Goshen, Ind.; George R. Brunk, Denbigh, Va.; A. P. Heatwole, Waynesboro, Va.; Noah H. Mack, New Holland, Pa.; D. D. Miller, Middlebury, Ind.; D. H. Bender, Hesston, Kan.; S. E. Allgyer, West Liberty, Ohio; J. E. Hartzler, Goshen, Ind.; Daniel Kauffman, Scottdale, Pa." (from the Preface).

An examination of the work reveals that each of the above except A. P. Heatwole wrote one or more chapters; the following additional men also wrote one or more chapters: J. N. Brubacher, David Burkholder, J. D. Charles, S. F. Coffman, David Garber, J. S. Hartzler, L. J. Heatwole, J. R. Shank, J. B. Smith, and Paul E. Whitmer. The book contains much doctrinal material found in standard Christian theological works, and in addition has sections devoted to "Christian Ordinances" (baptism, communion, footwashing, devotional covering, Christian salutation, anointing with oil, and marriage) and to "Christian Principles" (including discussions on nonconformity to the world, nonresistance, the oath, secret societies, and life insurance). It is a good solid treatise on Bible doctrine as understood by the Mennonite Church, although it is more the codification of a traditional point of view in matters of faith than the fruits of original systematic or exegetical study or of historical research in the Anabaptist-Mennonite faith. Early Christian writers are referred to a number of times (Augustine, Clement, Cyprian, Eusebius, Irenæus, Jerome, Justin, Polycarp, Tertullian), but the several writers betray no acquaintance with Anabaptist writers. Menno's views on baptism, however, are quoted from his writings.

One of the factors which led to the production of a new doctrinal volume, *Doctrines of the Bible,* 1928, Daniel Kauffman, Editor, was the fact that in the old volume some of the material and some of the writers were no longer considered satisfactory. The new book, *Doctrines of the Bible. A Brief Discussion of the Teachings of God's Word* (631 pp.), was completely rewritten and somewhat shortened, but again published by order of the Mennonite General Conference. Daniel Kauffman this time wrote all but two of the 62 chapters, the others being written by D. H. Bender. It went through a second edition in 1929. Both volumes have had a wide circulation and great influence in the Mennonite Church (MC), where they have been considered the standard doctrinal authority for the church.   J.C.W.

Bible Institute, a training school for Christian workers, usually on a lower academic level than that of the college and standard theological seminary, which has sprung up in the United States and Canada in large numbers in the last 50 years as a characteristic and powerful expression of the conservative Protestant movement commonly known as "Fundamentalism." The first such school, the Moody Bible Institute, founded at Chicago in 1886 by D. L. Moody, with the stated purpose "to raise up men and women who will be willing to lay their lives along side the laboring class and the poor, and to bring their gospel to bear upon their lives," was followed by the Bible Institute of Los Angeles founded by R. A. Torrey, former dean at Moody; the Philadelphia School of the Bible founded in 1914 by C. I. Scofield; the Northwestern Bible and Missionary Training School at Minneapolis founded in 1902 by Wm. B. Riley, long-time Fundamentalist leader, and others. Recently academic standards have been raised so that many Bible Institutes now require high-school graduation for entrance and are offering work of college grade. The name is now sometimes being changed to Bible college and advanced work of near seminary character is being added.

In these schools until recently scholastic requirements for matriculation, promotion, and graduation have either not been exacted or else have not been high; any mature person could attend. Thus large numbers of people unable to meet the requirements of college and seminary were able to get one to three years of Bible training. Thousands of students have graduated from these schools to enter the foreign and home mission fields as well as the pastorate in many denominations and in independent churches.

The institutes have also greatly extended their influence through correspondence courses (especially the Moody school), Bible conferences sponsored at widely scattered points throughout the country, and periodical organs such as the *Moody Monthly, King's Business* (Los Angeles), etc. The so-called "Scofield" correspondence course at Moody, and the James M. Gray "Bible Synthesis" course have been taken by thousands, including many Mennonites.

Mennonites early began to attend these schools. When the first Mennonites reached Moody's is not known, but the first (old) Mennonite enrolled in 1893. Large numbers have attended the institutes in Chicago, Los Angeles, Minneapolis, and more recently the Prairie Bible Institute at Three Hills, Alta. The Toronto (Ont.) Bible College has been attended by numerous (old) Mennonites from Ontario. In earlier days a few from this group went to Moody and Los Angeles, but otherwise few (old) Mennonites have attended the Bible institutes, most such students especially in recent decades coming from the General Conference Mennonites, Mennonite Brethren, Evangelical Mennonite Brethren, and other smaller groups of Russian Mennonite background, as well as Mennonite Brethren in Christ. Literally hundreds of young Mennonites have passed through these schools in the past 50 years, possibly several thousand. In the year 1948-49, for instance, a survey revealed that over 200 Mennonite students were attending four Bible institutes in the prairie provinces of Canada: 106 at Three Hills, 72 at Briarcrest. Three fourths of these were Mennonite Brethren.

In 1945, alarmed by the alienation of many young Mennonites from their church and its faith, conservative leaders established Grace Bible Institute (*q.v.*) in Omaha, Neb., as an all-Mennonite Bible Institute, which has grown to considerable size and influence, with General Conference leadership and students predominant. Earlier (1905) the Missionary Church Association (*q.v.*) had established the Fort Wayne Bible Institute, supported and patronized by many M.B.C. (UMC) and Defenseless Mennonites. An early attempt (1903) by the M.B.C. Indiana-Ohio Conference at Elkhart in the former building of the Elkhart (Ind.) Institute (*q.v.*) failed after a short time. In 1944 the Mennonite Brethren established the Pacific Bible Institute at Fresno, Cal., which grew rapidly in size and influence. Actually the Mennonite Brethren Bible College (*q.v.*), established in Winnipeg in 1944, and the Canadian Mennonite Bible College (*q.v.*), established by the General Conference Mennonites at the same place in 1947, are also very similar to Bible institutes, although having a somewhat higher academic standard. The latest Mennonite institution of the institute type is the (MC) Ontario Mennonite Bible Institute (*q.v.*), the enlarged and renamed form of the Ontario Mennonite School, which operates a Bible school (3 months) and a Bible institute (5 months) together, whereas the O.M.B.S. had only a 3-month term. The only European Mennonite school of this type was the Bible school at Tchongrav, Crimea, Russia, conducted by the Mennonite Brethren Conference 1918-24. The Argentine Mennonite Mission has operated a school at Bragado (Pehuajo) since 1926. A school is planned for Montevideo, Uruguay, 1955.

There is no doubt that the Bible institutes have had a marked and in some cases decisive influence in certain Mennonite branches in the U.S.A. and Canada. In some years the total Mennonite attendance at these non-Mennonite institutions must have exceeded 300. Since the Bible institutes commonly are interdenominational, de-emphasizing denominational differences and loyalties, many of their Mennonite graduates have left the church of their fathers to work elsewhere. Also the total absence of teaching on nonresistance and even positive teaching against it, plus at times a surprising amount of militaristic feeling has contributed to a breakdown of nonresistant convictions in some Mennonite circles. Also, since most Bible institutes have a basically Calvinistic theology, teaching "eternal security" and other similar doctrines, these items have been imported into Mennonite churches, in which they were formerly foreign, and have made great inroads into some branches. Premillennialism and Dispensationalism (and even the Postponement Theory of the Kingdom) have been in many cases introduced and promoted largely through Bible institute influence, having practically captured a few branches altogether and become a strong influence in most.

In Europe schools similar to the American Bible institutes have developed, which have also had considerable influence on the Mennonite Church, particularly in Russia, Germany, Switzerland, and France, chiefly through patronage of young Mennonites preparing for the ministry. The oldest of these is St. Chrischona, near Basel, Switzerland, founded in 1840 by C. F. Spitteler, where Heinrich Rappard (d. 1915) was for long years the director. Almost every year since 1900 one or more young Mennonites from Switzerland, Germany, or France have been in attendance, some for a short term, some for the full four-year course. Among them were the late Elder Samuel Nussbaumer (*q.v.*) of Basel, Elder Christian Schnebele and Elder Emanuel Landes of South Germany, Elder Pierre Sommer (*q.v.*) of France, and more recently the Swiss elders Samuel Gerber (Jeangisboden) and Hans Rüfenacht (Langnau). A Mennonite from Russia, Heinrich Braun, taught here for a short time in the 1920's. In France the Institute Biblique de Nogent-sur-Marne (near Paris), a small school of 30-40 students with a three-year course, founded in 1920 by a Reformed pastor, Ruben Saillens, for a time under Baptist control but now independent and interdenominational, has been attended by a total of over 40 young French Mennonites since 1922 (in 1948-49 seven were enrolled). Of considerably less significance have been the French schools in Switzerland—Emmaus at Vennes near Lausanne (leaders De Benoit and René Pache, founded about 1930) and the school of the Action Biblique in Geneva (founded by the Englishman Alexander), likewise the German language Beatenberg School of Mrs. Wasserkrug on Lake Thun.

Germany has had fewer training schools of the Bible institute type. Schools of this character which were attended by Mennonites, chiefly from Russia, were: the Allianz-Bibelschule (*q.v.*) in Berlin (1905-18), founded by the Baptist Karl Mascher, the Englishman Broadbent, and others, and closely related to the Plymouth Brethren, attended by numerous Mennonites from Russia 1907-14, among them A. Braun; the Wiedenest Bibelschule, 1918- , successor to the Berlin school; the Wernigerode school operated by the missionary society *Licht im Osten* (*q.v.*), of which Jakob Kroeker (*q.v.*) was director; the Missionshaus at Barmen; the Missionshaus at Neukirchen, Moers, attended by many Mennonites from Russia; and the Johanneum (founded in 1886 at Bonn, since 1893 at Barmen). Of a higher academic level were the Basel Predigerschule (1876-1914), attended by Emil Händiges among others; the Theologische Schule in Bethel (founded by von Bodelschwingh in 1905 at Bethel near Bielefeld); and the Baptist Predigerseminar at Hamburg-Horn. These schools are more than Bible institutes but less than graduate theological schools of the German university type. German Mennonites preparing for the ministry have usually chosen either the university theological schools or St. Chrischona in Basel in preference.

An honest report of the influence of the Bible institutes must say that the influence has been mixed, sometimes helpful and sometimes harmful. Not having any interest in or responsibility for the historic heritage and particular doctrines and practices of the Mennonites, they have never promoted the Mennonite cause as such, have occasionally been the source of divisive and polemic influence, and have imported some foreign and even dangerous doctrines and emphases. On the other hand, they have often had a good influence in the promotion of spiritual awakening and increased evangelistic and missionary activity. In America they have brought some congregations and even whole branches into the orbit of a "Fundamentalism" which is foreign to the more simple, unpolemic, and untheological character of native Mennonitism.

H.S.B.

Bible Normal: see **Bible Conference.**

Bible School, a name commonly given among Mennonites in America to a more elementary type of school for instruction in the Bible and related subjects, for a shorter or longer term either for the general grounding of young people in Christian faith and experience or for preparation for practical service as lay workers in the local congregation. Some Bible schools are of more advanced character and are called Bible institute (q.v.) or Bible college, while others are designed for children, even of the lowest age level, usually conducted for 2 to 3 weeks in the summer and called summer Bible school (q.v.) or vacation Bible school, while still others are conducted in short terms of 2-6 weeks in the winter season for young people of high-school age and older, and are called winter Bible school (q.v.). In some cases a 1-4 weeks' school is conducted by a local congregation for all its members who may wish to attend and called simply Bible school. The name alone is no evidence of the exact nature of the school, since it is used to cover a wide range of educational operations, including even at times the Sunday school. The present article will deal under the title "Bible School" with schools of 5-9 months' duration primarily for young people of 15-25 years of age.

Such Bible schools are most common among the Mennonites coming to North America from Russia, particularly those of the second great migration (1922-25) to Canada. A list of such schools with denominational affiliation, address, and date of founding follows:

Mennonite Bible Schools in North America arranged in order of establishment

Mountain Lake Bible (Parochial) School	Mountain Lake, Minn.	1886	Inter-Menn.
Buhler Vereinsschule	Buhler, Kan.	1889-1902	GCM
Whitewater Bible School	Whitewater, Kan.	1900-1915	GCM
Hoffnungsau Bible School	Inman, Kan.	1907-1927	GCM
Moundridge Bible School	Moundridge, Kan.	1908-1918	GCM
Gotebo Bible School	Gotebo, Okla.	1910-1917	GCM
Herbert Bible School	Herbert, Sask., Can.	1913	MB
North Enid Bible School	North Enid, Okla.	1921-1938	GCM
Winkler Bible School	Winkler, Man., Can.	1925	MB
Hoffnungsfeld Bible School	Fairview, Okla.	1926-1943	MB
Mountain View Bible College	Didsbury, Alta., Can.	1926	UMC
Immanuel Bible School	Reedley, Cal.	1927	Inter-Menn.
(Reedley Bible School merged in 1941)			
Bethany Bible School and Bible College	Hepburn, Sask., Can.	1927	MB
Lustre Bible School	Frazer, Mont.	1928	Inter-Menn.
Tabor Bible School	Dalmeny, Sask., Can.	1928	MB
Elim Bible School	Altona, Man., Can.	1929	Inter-Menn.
Winnipeg German Bible School	Winnipeg, Man., Can.	1929-1942	MB
Morning Star Bible School	Coaldale, Alta., Can.	1929	MB
Elim Bible School	Yarrow, B.C., Can.	1930	MB
Mennonitische Religionsschule (Disc.)	Winnipeg, Man., Can.	1932	GCM
Rosthern Bible School	Rosthern, Sask., Can.	1932	GCM
Bethesda Bible School	Gem, Alta., Can.	1933	MB
Hoffnungsfeld Bible School (Disc.)	Wembley, Alta., Can.	1933	GCM
La Glace Bible School	La Glace, Alta., Can.	1933-1947	MB
Yarrow Bible School	Yarrow, B.C., Can.	1935	MB
Swift Current Menn. Br. Bible School	Swift Current, Sask., Can.	1936	MB
Dallas Bible School (Disc.)	Dallas, Ore.	1936	Inter-Menn.
Swift Current Bible School	Swift Current, Sask., Can.	1936	GCM
Meade Bible Academy	Meade, Kan.	1936	EMB
Steinbach Bible School	Steinbach, Man., Can.	1936	Inter-Menn.
Dinuba Bible School	Dinuba, Cal.	1937-1941	GCM
Menno Bible Institute	Didsbury, Alta., Can.	1937	GCM
Bethany Bible School (now Academy)	Munich, S.D.	1938-1950	GCM
Bethel Bible Institute	Abbottsford, B.C., Can.	1939	GCM
Emmanuel Bible College	Kitchener, Ont.	1940	UMC
Eden Bible School (now Eden Bible-High School)	Virgil, Ont., Can.	1942	MB
Henderson Bible School	Henderson, Neb.	1942	GCM
Abbottsford M. B. Bible School	Abbottsford, B.C., Can.	1943	MB
Chilliwack M. B. Bible School	Chilliwack, B.C., Can.	1947	MB
Berean Bible School	Allentown, Pa.	1950	UMC

The only one of similar character in the Mennonite Church (MC) is the Ontario Mennonite Bible School at Kitchener, founded in 1907 as a "Winter Bible School" of six weeks, lengthened to three months in 1932, and in 1951 lengthened to five months and rechristened a "Bible Institute" although the three-month curriculum is continued along with the five-month course.

Most of these schools combine some secular high-school subjects with Bible subjects, and a few offer a complete high-school course in addition to a Bible school course. (More recently Mennonite high schools have developed, which offer some Bible subjects along with a regular high-school curriculum.) These schools vary in size from 15 to 175 pupils or students, have a teaching staff of 1-5 teachers, and are supported by donations by local congregations or interested individuals. Some use local church buildings; others have substantial buildings of their own. Some are owned and controlled by conferences, others by congregations or associations of congregations, and some by special societies or associations organized for that purpose. See the articles on each of these schools for detailed information.

The early founding and the rapid growth of these schools among the newer (1922-25) immigrants from Russia in Canada reflects (1) the strong sense of responsibility of these groups for the education of their youth as practiced in Russia, (2) their determination to resist the secularizing influence of the surrounding culture, (3) desire to maintain the German language as long as possible, (4) a desire to retain Mennonitism over against disintegrating influences from the outside, and (5) the evangelistic and experimental emphasis, in part influenced by "Fundamentalistic currents." The latter influence is due in part to the fact that many Bible school teachers have secured their Bible training in fundamentalistic Bible schools since arriving in Canada (they usually could not meet the entrance requirements for regular college or seminary work) and that the textbooks and literature of these fundamentalistic sources were and are widely used by them. It is noteworthy that in the United States few such schools have been established by the much larger Mennonite population, where the influence of the non-Mennonite Bible institutes has been much stronger.

Undoubtedly the Bible schools have had a strong and generally very beneficial influence upon the Mennonites of North America.

In Europe Mennonite Bible schools are almost unknown. Elder Pierre Sommer conducted a small (6-10 pupils) four weeks' school in 1929-1934 at Grand-Charmont and Montbéliard, France. In 1950 the International Mennonite Bible School was established at Basel, Switzerland, under a board of control consisting of representatives of the Mennonite churches of France, Switzerland, and Germany, and the Mennonite Central Committee, with a four-week term, an enrollment of 28 students from five countries, instruction in both German and French, and teachers from five countries. In 1953 the term was made 8 weeks, with Cornelius Wall as principal.

In Russia the Mennonite conference decided in 1887 to establish a theological school for the preparation of preachers, but all attempts throughout the remainder of Mennonite history in Russia to carry out this decision failed. However, other attempts were made. Cornelius Unruh conducted a Bible school in Friedensfeld (Zagradovka colony) from 1907 to his death in 1910. After World War I three "Bible schools" were attempted. One, the Mayak Bible School at Davlekanovo, Ufa (1923-26), was actually in full operation and graduated one class from a three-year course. Similar schools were started in Tchongrav (q.v.) and Orenburg about the same time. The school at Orenburg functioned from 1923 to 1926. An attempt to start such a school in Orloff in the Molotschna Colony about this time was frustrated by refusal of government permission and a later attempt to start the same school privately in Simferopol, Crimea, also failed.

In the Fernheim Mennonite Colony in Paraguay, established in 1930 by refugee settlers from Russia, a private Bible school was established in 1943 in Filadelfia under the leadership of Nikolai Siemens, attended by students from all groups. This is a six-week winter Bible school, usually held in August.

H.S.B.

Friesen, *Brüderschaft*; L. Froese, "Das pädagogische Kultursystem der Menn. Siedlungen in Russland" (unpublished Göttingen Ph.D. dissertation, 1949); M. S. Harder, "Origin, Philosophy, and Development of Education Among the Mennonites" (unpublished U. of Southern Cal. Ph.D. dissertation, 1949); A. Unruh, *Kurze Notizen über Gründung, Bestehen, Bedeutung und Schliessung der mennonitischen Bibelschule zu Tschongraw, Krim, in Russland* (Winkler, Man., n.d., ca. 1925); Peter P. Dyck, *Orenburg am Ural* (Clearbrook, B.C., 1951) 75 ff.

Bible Translations. Mennonites have commonly used the standard Bible translations as used in their countries, German—Martin Luther, English—King James, Netherlands—the *Statenvertaling* (q.v.), etc. They did not use distinctive translations or make or publish their own translations, with certain exceptions as follows:

1. In 1527 Hans Denk and Ludwig Haetzer, spiritualistic Anabaptists, translated the O.T. Prophets out of the Hebrew, first edition 1527 in Worms (12 editions in rapid succession at Worms, Augsburg, and Hagenau) which antedated Luther's O.T. translation and was used by him and the Zürich translators (see **Denk-Haetzer Prophets**).

2. The Zürich complete Bible translation (1524-29) printed by the Zürich firm of Froschauer, originally the Luther text with slight divergence except for the Prophets which used the Denk-Haetzer translation, gradually became more divergent from the Luther Bible and thus more distinctive. Strangely the Froschauer (q.v.) Bibles and New Testaments (q.v.) became very popular with the Swiss Brethren and continued to be used by them after they went out of use in the Swiss Reformed Church. Beginning in 1588 repeated reprints of the older editions were made in Basel

for the Swiss Anabaptists, which became known as *Täufertestamente,* and were even forbidden by the Bernese authorities, who did their best to destroy them and prevent their reprinting. A reprint of the Froschauer New Testament was made in 1787 at Ephrata, Pa., for the Mennonites of that region.

3. The Biestkens Bible (*q.v.*) so called after the Mennonite printer of Emden, Nicolaes Biestkens, though not a Mennonite translation, was actually published for Mennonites beginning in 1560 and up to 1723 reprinted at least 27 times, with 64 N.T. editions, a total of almost 100 editions. Previously in 1556 the Mennonites used, in opposition to the new translation provided by the Reformed Church, the Bible printed by Mierdemans (*q.v.*) and the New Testament of Mattheus Jacobssoon (*q.v.*) of 1556 (reprinted 1558, 1559, 1562). Before 1554 an Anabaptist printer published in Lübeck a Bible which was a combination of the Luther and Dutch translations with a concordance from the Zürich Bible. The printer continued his work at Wüstenfelde (see C. Krahn, *Menno Simons,* Karlsruhe, 1936, 84 ff.). The *Statenvertaling* displaced the Biestkens Bible among the Mennonites in the first half of the 18th century. For the West Prussian Mennonites a special edition of the Biestkens Bible was published in Schottland, a suburb of Danzig, in 1598, called the Schottland Bible (*q.v.*). It was, however, printed in Haarlem, Holland, by Gilles Rooman.

4. Modern Mennonites have not taken part in Bible translation work except in a few cases on mission fields. The greatest of these is the translation of the entire Bible into Javanese (1888-92) on commission of the British and Foreign Bible Society by the Mennonite missionary Pieter Jansz, which has become the most widely used Javanese translation, and resulted in a decoration for Jansz by the Dutch government.

Portions of the New Testament were translated into the Hopi Indian language by General Conference Mennonite missionaries. The entire New Testament, published by the American Bible Society in 1934, and parts of the Old Testament (printed in 1926) were translated into the Cheyenne Indian language by Rodolphe Petter (General Conference Mennonite mission field in Montana). Agnes Sprunger, a Mennonite missionary under the Congo Inland Mission, an American Mennonite Mission Board, translated the New Testament into the Kipende language (a tribe in the Belgian Congo), which was published in 1935. Mennonite missionaries collaborated in the translation of the New Testament into the Kikwango language (a tribe in the Belgian Congo), the major part of this work having been done by Mrs. Aaron A. Janzen (Mennonite Brethren). This translation was published by the American Bible Society in 1950. Missionary G. B. Giesbrecht of the "Light to the Indians" Mission (Mennonite Brethren) in the Paraguayan Chaco, has translated the Gospel of Matthew and portions of other Gospels into the Lengua Indian dialect of that region.

A modern Dutch translation of the New Testament was made by the Mennonite minister G. Vissering (Amsterdam, 1854), of the Psalms and Lamentations by the Mennonite minister J. Dyserinck, but neither has been widely used. The modern translation of the New Testament by H. Bakels (Amsterdam, 1908), however, has gone through three editions. (*ML* I, 217.)   H.S.B., vdZ.

Bibles used by the Anabaptists: see **Biestkens Bible, Froschauer Bible,** and **Schottland Bible.**

Bibliographie des Martyrologes Protestants Néerlandais (Bibliography of the Protestant Martyrs in the Netherlands) is a work in two volumes (La Haye, 1890): I, *Monographies;* II, *Recueils.* It is a publication of the University of Gent and consists of abstracts from the *Bibliotheca Belgica (Bibliographie générale des Pays-Bas)* under the oversight of Ferd. van der Haeghen, Th. J. I. Arnold, and R. van den Berghe. This work is of great significance and value for an understanding of the Protestant martyrs in the Netherlands and Belgium. It describes the publications concerning the martyrs in which the Mennonites, because of their number, occupy the largest place. Of special importance also is the alphabetical list of martyrs in Vol. II, pp. 637-796, where numerous particulars concerning the martyrs are to be found. The Mennonite martyrs in this list are only those included in the *Martyrs' Mirror* of van Braght, and the Reformed martyrs are those included in *De Geschiedenissen der Martelaren* of Adriaan van Haemstede (*q.v.*). The Protestant martyrs listed in the *Bibliographie* total 877.   vdZ.

Bibliographies, Mennonite. Being primarily tools for research, bibliographies are prepared and published only when and where research scholarship is active, or when book collections and libraries have been established. In the Mennonite world scholarship developed first in Holland, and the first bibliographies by Mennonites on Mennonite history and theology developed here, followed by north and west Germany, finally by the United States. Bibliographies on Anabaptist-Mennonite history by non-Mennonites have appeared only when non-Mennonite scholarship became interested in a thorough study of this field, which is only recently. This article will report the significant published bibliographies and library catalogs and literary research reports in chronological order.

1. *Bibliographies before 1900.* The first and only separately published bibliography in the earlier period by Mennonite or non-Mennonite was (the Mennonite scholar) Marten Schagen's 1745 list (*Naamlijst*) of Dutch Mennonite writers and their writings, 1539-1745. A. van der Linde published a bibliography of David Joris in 1867, C. Sepp one of Bernt Rothmann in 1870, and P. Bahlmann published one on the Münsterites in 1894. John Horsch published an extensive bibliography of Anabaptist and Mennonite history in his 1890 booklet, *Kurzgefasste Geschichte der Mennoniten-Gemeinden* listing over 600 published titles and over 100 early

manuscripts. A. H. Newman's *History of Anti-Pedobaptism,* prepared in 1896, but not published until 1902 (Philadelphia), also contains a very valuable and extensive bibliography of 16th-century Anabaptism, containing over 400 titles. C. Sepp's *Bibliotheek van Nederlandsche Kerkgeschiedschrijvers* (Leiden, 1886) contains a small section on "De Doopsgezinden," pp. 386-412.

Several auction-sale catalogs of libraries of Dutch Mennonite scholars approach the character of bibliographies. The important ones are those of G. Maatschoen (Amsterdam, 1752), J. D. Hesselink (Groningen, 1878), and S. Blaupot ten Cate (Groningen, 1885). Occasionally antiquarian booksellers issued special catalogs of Reformation literature containing extensive Anabaptist sections which have considerable bibliographical value. One of the best of these was an 1869 catalog of the Berlin dealer S. Calvary and Co. (*Verzeichniss seltener u. werthvoller Werke: Zur Gesch.- u. Literatur der Wiedertäufer u. der verwandten Secten*). Occasional catalogs of J. Rosenthal (Munich), M. Breslauer (Berlin), and L. Brecher (Brno) are also valuable.

As libraries in Mennonite congregations increased in size and value, occasionally catalogs were published. Such were those of Enschede (Holland) in 1836; Amsterdam in 1854, 1888, and 1919; Danzig in 1869; Hamburg-Altona in 1890. The published (1883) catalog of the archives of the Amsterdam Mennonite Church is also worthy of note. The 1919 Amsterdam catalog with its 357 pages and almost 4,000 titles is in effect a bibliography, and as such is particularly extensive in the field of Dutch Mennonite history and writings by Dutch Mennonites. The handicap of the lack of an index to the Amsterdam catalog was made good by the publication of a mimeographed short title index in 1950 by the Mennonite Historical Society (Goshen, Ind.).

2. *Bibliographies since* 1900.

a. *Bibliographies in Book Form.*

Several independent bibliographies have been published since 1900. H. S. Bender's *Two Centuries of American Mennonite Literature, A Bibliography of Mennonitica Americana 1727-1928* (Goshen, The Mennonite Historical Society, 1929) attempts to list every publication in North America by a Mennonite author, with complete bibliographical data and some annotation, including location of rare items in libraries. K. Kauenhowen's *Das Schrifttum zur Sippenkunde und Geschichte der taufgesinnten Niederländischen Einwanderer (Mennoniten) in Alt-Preussen und ihrer Abzweigungen* (Hamburg, 1939) is the first and only bibliography on the Mennonites of the Danzig area. John A. Hostetler's *Annotated Bibliography on the Amish* (Scottdale, 1951) attempts to list everything written by or about the Old Order Amish, in book, pamphlet, or periodical form, also unpublished theses, dissertations, and papers. Though not printed separately, M. C. Lehman's extensive annotated bibliography on the history of Mennonite relief work in his *History and Principles of Mennonite Relief*

Work, Students' Edition with Syllabus and Annotated Bibliography (Akron, Pa., Mennonite Central Committee, 1945), pp. 52-67 (prepared largely by John Bender and Justus Holsinger), is in effect an exhaustive bibliography in pamphlet form.

b. *Bibliographies in Periodical Articles and Monographs.*

Apart from the bibliographies which have appeared in the past 25 years in monographs in the field of Anabaptist and early Mennonite history in such works as those by Correll, Horsch, Krahn, Smithson, Friedmann, and Bender, in the general works by Smith and Horsch, and the articles in the *Mennonitisches Lexikon,* a number of valuable special bibliographies have been published. These fall into two types, those which merely list titles, with or without brief annotations, and those which give an extended discussion of the major works in essay form, with a running critique and evaluation of the published products of original research or interpretation, indicating the progress achieved by the total forward movement of scholarship.

In the first category the outstanding contributions of recent date are those by Robert Friedmann, Karl Schottenloher, and A. J. F. Zieglschmid. Friedmann gives an exhaustive bibliography on the Austrian Anabaptists, with a section on the Swiss Brethren as connected with the Austrians, in his outstanding bibliographical article, "Die Briefe der Oesterreichischen Täufer IV: Bibliographie," in *Archiv für Reformationsgeschichte* XXVI (1929) 170-87. A. J. F. Zieglschmid attempted the same thing in his two editions of the Hutterite chronicles: *Die älteste Chronik der Hutterischen Brüder* (Philadelphia, 1943) 901-17, and *Das Klein-Geschichtbuch der Hutterischen Brüder* (Philadelphia, 1947) 687-706. The second bibliography includes and enlarges on the first, offering about 400 titles, almost identical in size with Friedmann's list. In fact, it is the Friedmann list supplemented by more recent titles. Schottenloher's monumental *Bibliographie zur deutschen Geschichte im Zeitalter der Glaubensspaltung 1517-1585;* I, *Personen A-L* 1933); II, *Personen M-Z, Orte und Landschaften* (1935); III, *Reich und Kaiser, Territorien und Landesherren* (1936); IV, *Gesamtdarstellungen, Stoffe* (1938); V, *Nachträge und Ergänzungen* (1939); and VI, *Verfasser und Titelverzeichnisse* (1940), covering everything to the end of 1937 (the announced supplementary volume to 1942 has not appeared), gives full recognition to the Anabaptists under *Personen* as well as in Vol. IV, where the heading *Wiedertäufer,* pp. 734-52, contains about 370 titles, with 12 additional titles in *Nachträge* (Vol. V) under the same heading. Schottenloher also attempts to be exhaustive, and his five-volume set is a most valuable work, though not fully exhaustive for Anabaptists. Roland Bainton's section on "Anabaptism and the Spiritual Reformers" in his *Bibliography of the Continental Reformation in English* (New York, 1935) 31-36, gives only English titles. Cornelius Krahn's "Historiography of the Mennonites in the Netherlands" in *MQR* XVIII (1944) 195-224, is selective and goes far beyond the 16th century, while Wilhelm Pauck's "Historiography of the German Reformation During the Past Twenty Years" in *Church History* IX (1940) 305-40, with its section on "Research in the History of the Anabaptists," 335-40, is also selective, but includes all languages. Both Krahn and Pauck are systematic but only slightly annotated. Christian Hege in *Mennonitische Geschichtsblätter*, Vols. II-V (1937-40), attempted an exhaustive coverage of current periodical literature on Anabaptist-Mennonite history (including also in later volumes "kleinere selbständige Veröffentlichungen") arranged by years, beginning with 1936 and continuing to August 1940, without annotations. See the numbers of the *Menn. Geschbl.* for December 1937 (pp. 77-78), December 1938 (pp. 97-99), August 1939 (pp. 59-62), and August 1940 (pp. 60-62). E. Teufel, "Neue Geschichtsliteratur," *Menn. Geschbl.*, May 1951, pp. 58-70, covers 1940-49 by years, giving first periodicals, then books, with annotations. The latest article is that by C. Krahn, "The Anabaptists in Periodical Literature, 1940-50," in *Archiv für Reformationsgeschichte* (1952).

The second type of bibliography, the review-discussion type (*Literaturbericht, Sammelbericht*), is represented by two outstanding extensive contributions by Walter Köhler ("Das Täufertum in der neueren kirchenhistorischen Forschung," in *Archiv für Reformationsgeschichte, 1940-48*) and Eberhard Teufel of Stuttgart-Fellbach ("Täufertum und Quäkertum im Lichte der neueren Forschung") in *Theologische Rundschau, 1941-52*, as well as four earlier discussions: Heinrich Bornkamm, *Mystik, Spiritualismus, und die Anfänge des Pietismus im Luthertum* (Giessen, 1926) 20-22; Chr. Hege, article **Geschichtschreibung** in *ML* II (written in 1926); H. S. Bender, "Recent Progress in Research in Anabaptist History," in *MQR* VIII (1934) pp. 3-17; and Paul Dedic in *Archiv für Reformationsgeschichte* XXXV (1938), "Forschungen zur Geschichte des Oesterreichischen Protestantismus. Sammelbericht über die Epoche 1918-38. Täufertum," pp. 277-81, covering publications on Austrian Anabaptism 1918-38. The discussions by Köhler and Teufel, both masters in the field, deserve a fuller report, both because of their truly extraordinary extent (*ca.* 35,000 words and 65,000 words, respectively) and their exceptionally thorough and critical scholarly character.

It may seem strange that two such similar reports on the same general field should appear virtually parallel in German scholarly literature. However, the organization and approach of the two are somewhat different, and both are essential to the fullest information on current research and publication in the field of Anabaptist history, particularly since World War I. Köhler's report appeared in four installments organized geographically except for the last section, "Die Spiritualisten," XLI (1948), pp. 165-86, which is organized by persons: Sebastian Franck, Dirck Coornhert, Sebastian Castellio, Jacob Acontius, and the Quakers. The three sections on Anabaptism are: "I. Allgemeines, Schweizerische Täufer," XXXVII (1940) 93-107; "II. Das Täufertum in den Niederlanden, England,

Frankreich, Elsass, Thüringen," XXXVIII (1941) 349-64; "III. Württemberg, Bayern, Mähren, Oesterreich, Nord- und Ostseeraum, Russland, Theologie der Täufer," XL (1943) 246-70. Teufel's report appeared in seven installments (the eighth and last covering recent American publications is soon to appear); XIII (1941) 24-57, 103-27, 183-97; XIV (1942) 27-52, 124-54; XV (1943) 56-80, and XVII (1948) 161-81, organized as follows—I. "Die Entwicklung der Forschung seit G. Arnold" (5 pp.); II. "Zur Biographie einzelner Täuferführer" (67 pp.), including David Joris (12), Menno Simons (7), Conrad Grebel (9), Pilgram Marpeck (10), Balthasar Hubmaier (14), and Hans Denk (14); III. "Zur Täufergeschichte einzelner Länder" (80 pp.), including "Schweiz" (16), "Herzogtum Württemberg" (11), "Markgraftum Brandenburg-Anspach-Bayreuth" (19), "Bistümer Eichstätt, Bamberg, Würzburg" (4), "Einzelne heute bayrische Reichsstädte, Augsburg, Regensburg, Rothenburg o.T." (7), "Baden-Kurpfalz" (12), "Rheinland" (7), "Nord- und Ostseeraum" (4). Teufel gives an extensive bibliography at the outset, and at various places throughout adds further briefer topical bibliographical lists, in addition to titles in the text and occasionally in footnotes. Köhler gives no lists, and includes considerably fewer titles, both in the text and in the footnotes, but with most of his titles in the footnotes. Teufel includes several times as many titles as Köhler, but omits the "Spiritualists." (He had earlier reported exhaustively on Sebastian Franck in *Theologische Rundschau*, 1939 and 1940.) Both Köhler and Teufel report at length on certain key books and articles, using these works as the basis for a discussion of basic questions in the historical analysis and interpretation of Anabaptism. Both are fully aware of the American contribution to this field and include English titles as well as Dutch and Swiss in their discussions. Both men are also most sympathetic to the Anabaptist position. Teufel's own 177-page *Literaturbericht* is a remarkably rich, informative, and well-balanced contribution to the field of Anabaptist historiography, probably the most useful ever written.

The *Mennonitisches Lexikon*, in addition to the bibliographies commonly appended to substantial articles, contains a number of extensive bibliographical articles, the chief of which are the following: Neff, **Bekenntnisse des Glaubens** (I, 157-61); Neff, **Gesangbücher** (II, 86-91); Loserth, **Geschichtsbücher der mährischen Täufer** (II, 91-96); Hege, **Geschichtschreibung** (II, 96-101); Neff, **Katechismen** (II, 469-71); **Literatur**, treated in subtopics under German, Dutch, French, and American literature (II, 662-74) by O. Schowalter, H. Jeltes, P. Sommer, and C. H. Smith respectively.

The second part of Robert Friedmann's *Mennonite Piety Through the Centuries* (Goshen, 1949) contains a great amount of bibliographical material, particularly the following chapters, which had also been published in almost identical form in the *MQR* as indicated: II. "Dutch Mennonite Devotional Literature," 105-26 (*MQR*, July 1941); III. "The Devotional Literature of the Mennonites of Danzig and East Prussia to 1800," 127-40 (*MQR*,

July 1944); V. "The Devotional Literature of the Swiss Brethren, 1600-1800," 154-75 (*MQR*, October 1942); and VI. "Mennonite Prayerbooks," 176-202 (*MQR*, October 1943).

The *Mennonite Quarterly Review* (1929-) has published a number of bibliographical articles: H. Jeltes, "Mennonites in Dutch Literature" (XI, April 1937) 142-55; Edward Yoder, "Bibliography of the Writings of John Horsch" (XXI, July 1947) 205-28; H. S. Bender, "Anabaptist Manuscripts in the Archives at Brno, Czechoslovakia" (XXIII, April 1949) 105-7; Nelson Springer, "A Bibliography of the Writings of C. Henry Smith" (XXIII, January 1949) 16-21; Nelson Springer, "The Holdings of the (Goshen) Mennonite Historical Library: Holdings in the Collection Published in the 16th Century" (XXV, October 1951) 313-19, reprinted in enlarged and revised form in 1952. Beginning with its January 1950 number the *MQR* established a regular department of *Bibliographical and Research Notes* designed primarily to give annotated bibliographies and reports on current research in Anabaptist-Mennonite history by countries and subjects. The following have already appeared: H. S. Bender, "Recent Anabaptist Bibliographies" (XXIV, January 1950) 88-93; H. S. Bender, "Publications of the *Mennonitischer Geschichtsverein* 1936-1950" (XXIV, April 1950) 170-73; H. S. Bender, "Mennonite Yearbooks and Almanacs 1940-1950" (XXIV, July 1950) 281-87; Robert Friedmann, "A Comprehensive Review of Research on the Hutterites 1880-1950" (XXIV, October 1950) 353-63; John Umble, "Research on the Amish and Source Materials for the Study of the Amish" (XXV, April 1951) 128-32; Willard H. Smith, "Mennonites in Latin America: An Annotated Bibliography" (XXVI, October 1952) 298-318; H. S. Bender and N. P. Springer, "An Annotated Bibliography of Published Mennonite Sermons" (XXVII, April 1953) 143-57; E. K. Francis, "A Bibliography on the Mennonites of Manitoba" (XXVII, July 1953).

Beginning with 1947 the quarterly *Mennonite Life* (North Newton, Kan.) annually publishes in its April number a "Mennonite Bibliography" compiled by M. Gingerich and C. Krahn, which includes books, pamphlets, and articles (only of non-Mennonite periodicals) of the preceding year dealing with the Anabaptists, Mennonites, and related groups. This journal also annually publishes a report on "Mennonite Research in Progress." The April 1952 issue contained: "Of Hutterite Books" by R. Friedmann; "Pennsylvania Mennonites in Print, 1940-1950" by J. Clemens; "Mennonites in German Literature, 1940-1950" by H. Quiring and C. Krahn; and "Mennonites in Reference Books, 1940-1950" by C. Krahn.

The *Mennonitische Geschichtsblätter* (VI, 1949) published a bibliography of the writings of Christian Neff (pp. 11 ff.) and of Christian Hege (pp. 23 ff.). The *Historische Zeitschrift* in recent years has regularly reported Anabaptist-Mennonite publications in its *Literarbericht* section under "Reformation und Gegenreformation," by the late Walter Köhler and now by H. Bornkamm.

G. J. Honig's *Catalogus der Verzameling "Jacob Honig Jsz. Jr."* in the *Zaanlandsche Oudheidkamer* contains valuable bibliographical information. W. H. Hohmann's *Outlines in Hymnology with Emphasis on Mennonite Hymnology* (North Newton, 1941) contains a chronological check list of Mennonite hymnbooks from the beginning in all languages and countries.

The most complete chronological bibliography of Anabaptist publications is Hans J. Hillerbrand, *A Bibliography of Anabaptism 1520-1630* (Institute of Mennonite Studies, Elkhart, Indiana, 1962). A. Goertz published "Bibliographie zur Geschichte der Mennoniten Altpreussens" in *Kirche im Osten*, 6, 174-90 (Göttingen, 1963). Cornelius Krahn published "Menno Simons Research (1910-1960)" in *No Other Foundation* (North Newton, Kan., 1962).

H.S.B.

Bibliotheca Reformatoria Néerlandica is the title under which a number of important writings from the Reformation period in the Netherlands were published anew, with introductions and notes by Samuel Cramer (*q.v.*), professor at the University of Amsterdam and the Mennonite Seminary of Amsterdam, and F. Pijper, professor at the University of Leiden. The entire series, consisting of ten volumes, of which the first appeared in 1903 and the last three in 1914, was published by Martinus Nijhoff at The Hague. This republication of very rare works is of great value for understanding the history of the church in the 16th century. Of special value to the Mennonites are volumes II, V, VII, and X, which present important writings by or for Mennonites, together with most valuable introductions. Volumes II, V, and VII were edited by Cramer, and X by Pijper, since Cramer had meanwhile died. Pijper began his part with an *In Memoriam*, in which he honored the services of Cramer. A brief summary of the contents of the parts that deal with the Mennonites follows.

Volume II, published in 1904 (683 pages), contains a reprint of *Het Offer des Heeren*, the oldest collection of Anabaptist-Mennonite martyr letters and songs, following the edition of 1570. Further, this volume contains *Een Liedtboecxken, tracterende van den Offer des Heeren*, following the edition of 1570, including the letters and hymns by and about the martyrs, which are found in other editions of *Het Offer des Heeren* with the *Liedtboecxken*, but are missing in the edition of 1570. Volume V, published in 1909 (664 pages), presents Dutch anabaptistica. (1) *Die Slotel van dat Secreet des Nachtmaels. Geschreven door eynen Henrick Rol. Item, eyne rechte Bedijnckung, hoe dat em Liechaem Christi van onsen lichaem tho underscheyden isz;* (2) *Die Ordonnantie Godts*, and *Verclaringe van den gevangenen ende vrien wil*, both by Melchior Hofmann; (3) *Handelinge van der disputacie in Synodo tot Straesburch teghen Melchior Hofmann door die predicanten derselver Stadt;* (4) Two works by Adam Pastor: *Underscheit tusschen rechte leer unde valsche leer, dorch A. P.*, and *Disputation van der Godtheit des Vaders, des Soens unde des hilligen Geistes;* (5) A reprint of a collection published in 1560: *Broederlicke vereeninge van sommighe Kinderen Gods.* This collection comprises (a) *Broederlicke vereeninge aengaende seven articulen;* (b) *Eenen Sendtbrief van Michiel Satler aen de Ghemeynte Gods tot Horb;* (c) *Van der genoechdoeninghe Christi;* (d) *Van der echtscheydinghe;* (e) *Van tweederley gehoorsaemheyd;* (f) *Van hooringhe der valscher propheten;* (g) *Van boose Voorstanders;* (h) *Einen Sendtbrief van Melchior Rinck ende Antonius Jacobsz;* (i) *Van de Sentencie tegen Michiel Satler.*

Volume VII, published in 1910 (587 pages), is called *Zeventiende-eeuwsche schrijvers over de geschiedenis der oudste Doopsgezinden hier te lande* (17th-century writers about the history of the oldest Mennonites in this country), and includes (1) *Successio Anabaptistica, Dat is Babel der Wederdopers door V.P.* (MDCIII); (2) *Bekentenisse Obbe Philipsz,* 1584; (3) *Tegen-Bericht op de voor-Reden vant groot Martelaer Boeck, door Hans Alenson* (1630); (4) Nicolai's *Inlasschingen in Bullingers "Teghens de Wederdoopers"* (MDLXIX); (5) (Carel van Ghendt) *Het beginsel der scheuringen onder de Doop-gesinden* (1658).

Volume X, published in 1914 (723 pages), with the title, *De Geschriften van Dirk Philipsz,* gives a reprint of all the extant writings of this elder, namely: (1) *Enchiridion oft Hantboecxken van de Christelijcke Leere ende Religion, in corte somma begrepen, ten dienste van alle Liefhebbers der waerheit wt der Heyliger Schrift ghemaect, nu nieus gecorrigeert ende vermeerdert door D.P. int Jaer onser Heeren MDLXIIII;* (2) *Verantwoordinghe ende Refutation op twee Sendtbrieven Sebastiani Franck (door) D.P.;* (3) *Sendtbrief, uyt reynder Broederlycker Liefde, aen de vier St(eden) gheschreven, (door) D.P. (1567) 1619;* (4) *Cort, doch grondtlick verhael van den twistigen handel ende onschriftmatigen Ordeel, dat in Fr(iesland) ouer sommighen, die men de Vlamingen noemt, ghegheven is;* (5) *Een Appendix aen ons Boecxken vanden twistigen handel in Vr(iesland) tusschen die Vr(iesen) ende Vl(amingen);* (6) *Van de Echt der Christenen door D.P., 1569;* (7) *Naeghelaten Schrift Van den Euangelischen Ban ende Mijdinghe, door S.G. Diereck Philips. Wt den Fransoyschen vertaelt door C. V. M.,* 1602; (8) Letters and songs of Dirk Philips.   vDZ.

Bibliotheek en Archief der Verenigde Doopsgezinde Gemeente te Amsterdam: see **Amsterdam Mennonite Library.**

Bichsel, a Mennonite family name: see **Bixel.**

Bichsel, Ulrich, an Anabaptist martyr, was executed with six fellow believers in Bern, Aug. 28, 1537. Details are not known.   NEFF.

A. Fluri, *Beitr. z. Gesch. d. bernischen Täufer* I (Bern, 1916) 14; Th. de Quervain, *Kirchliche und soziale Zustände in Bern* (Bern, 1906) 149; *ML* I, 219.

Bidloo, Govert, b. March 12, 1649, at Amsterdam, d. March 30, 1713, at Leiden, well-known physician and professor at the university of Leiden, was a Mennonite, the younger brother of Lambert Bidloo (*q.v.*). After having been first a surgeon at Amster-

dam, he studied medicine at Franeker, where he graduated in 1682. His anatomic atlas, *Anatomia humani corporis* (Amsterdam, 1685, Dutch translation in 1690), was highly esteemed in those days. In 1694 he was appointed professor of medicine and the healing arts at Leiden, and in 1701 he became the chief physician to Stadholder William III. At the same time he was a playwright, and his tragedy, *Karel, erfprins van Spanje* (1679), was very popular. But he more particularly was known as the author of the poem, *Brieven der Gemartelde Apostelen* (The Letters of the Martyred Apostles) (Amsterdam, 1675, reprinted 1698, 1712, 1748).   vDZ.

G. Kalff, *Gesch. der Nederl. Letterkunde* V (Groningen, 1910); Banga, *Gesch. van de Geneeskunde* II (1868); *Catalogus Amst.,* 234.

Bidloo, Lambert, b. Aug. 30, 1638, at Amsterdam; d. there June 11, 1724, a brother of the above. He was a very accomplished man, having mastered many languages, both ancient and modern; by profession an apothecary. During his old age he wrote several books of rather mediocre verse. He wrote in Latin a treatise on botany.

Bidloo belonged to the conservative Mennonites, was a member of the Zonist congregation at Amsterdam, and a deacon at this church after 1700. The growing progressiveness and particularly Mennonite contacts with the Collegiants (*q.v.*) was for him an occasion to present a warning against excessive toleration. In 1701 at Amsterdam (reprinted in 1742) appeared *Onbepaalde verdraagzaamheyd de verwoesting der Doopsgezinden* (Unlimited Toleration the Ruination of the Mennonites). Though the book was published anonymously, everyone knew who the author was. In this book Bidloo admonishes the Mennonites to remain loyal to the doctrine found in the old confessions of faith. This book is a kind of history of the Mennonites in the 17th century, and is significant for an understanding of the conflict between the Zonists (*q.v.*) and the Lamists or Galenists (*q.v.*). When Kornelis van Hoek (*q.v.*) replied in *De Christelijke verdraagzaamheit verdedigt tegens Herman Schijn en L. Bidloo* (Christian Toleration Defended against Herman Schijn and L. Bidloo) (Amsterdam, 1701), Bidloo wrote *Ongebonden licentie de grondslag der Rijnsburgsche Vergadering* (Unrestrained License the Basis of the Rhynsburger group) (Amsterdam, 1702). Schijn also wrote an answer. To these replies van Hoek was provoked to a later defense in *Nader verdediging* (Further Defense).

Bidloo had earlier taken sides in the *Lammerenkrijg* (*q.v.*) in his book: *Mennoos Kerck, in en uyt Babel, ofte den Aenvang, Voortgang en redderinge der Verwarringen der Vlaemsche Doopsgezinden, . . .* (Amsterdam, 1665). (*N.N.B.Wb.* IV, 146-47; *Catalogus Amst.,* 129, 134, 166, 207, II, 144; *ML* I, 219.)   vDZ.

Bidloo, Nicolaas, b. about 1670 at Amsterdam, son of Lambert Bidloo (*q.v.*), was a versatile man. He was a doctor of medicine and at the same time an active artist (especially painted portraits). Later in life he became the personal physician of Peter the Great and the first director of the first medical school in Moscow. (*Menn. Bl.,* 1908, 11; *N.N.B.Wb.* II, 144; *ML* I, 219.) vdZ.

Biehn Mennonite Church (MC) is located about four miles from New Hamburg, Waterloo Co., Ont. This congregation of the Ontario Mennonite Conference took rise about 1865. Early family names found here were Biehn, Cassel, Bechtel, Cressman, Nahrgang, Stauffer, Christner, and others. At first the meetings were held in Green's schoolhouse south of the present site of the church. In 1870 John Biehn gave land for church purposes and a building was erected. In 1900 a plot of land was added to the grounds for cemetery purposes. A few years later the church was rebuilt. Ministers who have served here are Menno Cressman, Ozias Cressman, and Curtis C. Cressman, the present bishop. Those who served in the office of deacon were Menno Cressman, John Nahrgang, Moses Cressman, Jeremiah Good, and Abner Cressman.

Sunday school was first conducted in 1871 with some 40 in attendance. Young people's Bible meetings have been regular since 1911 and have alternated with those of the neighboring Geiger congregation. This church has been definitely missionary in its interests and activity over the years. In 1924 with the coming of Mennonite refugees from Russia a considerable number of families were provided for in the homes of this congregation. Revival meetings, Bible conferences, and summer Bible schools have become regular features among the activities of this church. The membership of the church remained close to the hundred mark. L. J. Burkholder, *Brief History of Menn. in Ontario* (Toronto, 1935.) J.C.F.

Biel, an important city (pop. 48,401) in the canton of Bern (Switzerland) at the foot of the Jura chain, was a thriving town in the age of the Reformation. Thomas Wyttenbach was the reformer of the city. As early as 1505 he attacked certain Catholic doctrines, such as indulgences. As professor of theology at the university of Bern he influenced Zwingli, who was his student. In 1519 Wyttenbach returned to Biel and until his death (1526) he promoted the Reformation there in the face of great obstacles. The Reformation was, however, not successfully introduced into Biel until 1528.

In 1528 some Swiss Brethren leaders came to Biel, among them Blaurock (*q.v.*). It is thought that there was a considerable Swiss Brethren congregation in Biel at that time. Füsslin reports, "the Anabaptists have also slipped into Biel and these named ones are reported: Bernhart Sager of Bremgarten, Thomas Schmär of Neustadt in Franconia, Hanssman Seckler of Basel, Hans Meyer called Pfister-Meyer of Aarau, Hans Toblinger of Freiburg in Uechtland, Ulrich Uller of Brunnen, Georg vom Hause Jakob of Chur, Ulrich Hänger of Bern. These met secretly in the oak woods near the 'Big Stone.' When they were expelled they withdrew to the Bittenberg. On March 9, 1528, the rule was passed concerning them, that if they came back they should be expelled from the canton. It was publicly announced in the churches that nobody

should lodge Anabaptists or detain them in any way on penalty of a severe fine."

Soon the traces of Anabaptists in Biel disappear; they are then found later in the adjoining Jura district. In the 18th century there were several small congregations a few miles north of Biel, e.g., in Plagne (Plentsch), where Niklaus Knör, a preacher expelled in 1757 from Bucheggberg (canton of Solothurn), served his brethren in isolated mountain farms until his death in 1773. Not far from Biel is the village of Pery (Büderich), where Peter Burkhalter, ordained elder in 1766, lived. Büderichgraben was also the home of Jakob Marti and David Baumgartner. At the beginning of the 19th century the congregation, now extinct, numbered 89 members. Täufer-Bänz must also have lived not far from Biel in the 18th century. It is very probable that the stately home of this preacher, who earned his bread by farming a little land and weaving, is the subject of the painting by Aurèle Robert, "L' Anabaptiste ou La Ferme bernoise," now found in the museum at Lausanne.

Biel has been an important market center for the Mennonites in the southern Jura since the 19th century. A number of Mennonite families have in recent years settled in Biel for business reasons. In 1950 there were about 50 members of Mennonite congregations living there. The group meets monthly in the home of the Gruber-Geiser family and is served by elders Samuel Geiser and Jakob Lehmann, both resident in Brügg near Biel.

The *Neutäufer* (*q.v.*) or *Fröhlichianer* are found in considerable numbers in Biel and vicinity. They have a church on Neumarkt Street. S.G.

J. C. Füsslin, *Beiträge zur Erläuterung der Kirchen-Reformations-Geschichten* (Zürich, 1741); S. Geiser, *Die Taufgesinnten-Gemeinden* (Karlsruhe, 1931).

Bierck, Wilhelm von, an Anabaptist martyr, executed in 1552 at Blankenburg (in the Harz?) together with two other brethren. They were put to death by beheading. (*Mart. Mir.* D 132, where the name is spelled Willem van Bierk, E 526.) vdZ.

Bierens, Abraham Dirks, was for 28 years one of the preachers of the United Flemish Lamist congregation in Amsterdam. The dates of his birth and death are not known, but were probably 1591 and 1646 respectively. He died of a cerebral hemorrhage in the pulpit in Dordrecht at the age of 55 years. In 1646 he became the father-in-law of the famous Galenus Abrahamsz de Haan (*q.v.*). He became a preacher in 1617. In 1626 he signed the confession which J. Outerman (*q.v.*) presented to the government. He was also one of the preachers who signed an agreement for the union of the Flemish and Frisians in 1627, to put an end to the divisions among the Mennonites. To this end the confession of faith called the *Olijftacxken* (*q.v.*) (Olive Branch) was compiled. A second attempt at union was made in 1630. There is a picture of Bierens and a formulary for the ordination of preachers and elders written by him in G. Maatschoen's *Aanhangsel op de Geschiedenis der Mennoniten* (Amsterdam, 1745). He is the progenitor of the Bierens de Haan family. (*Inv. Arch. Amst.* I, Nos. 566, 570, 574, 599; *ML* I, 219.) K.V.

Bierens de Haan, Jacob, b. Sept. 2, 1835, and d. Aug. 7, 1911, for many years the treasurer of the *Doopsgezinde Zendings-Vereniging* (*q.v.*) in Amsterdam, an office he filled with outstanding success. Through his faithful and untiring activity in the cause of foreign missions, he was a very well-known and beloved figure among Mennonite friends of missions. He served his congregation at Amsterdam through three terms as leader and deacon and is gratefully remembered there. (*ML* I, 220.)   NEFF.

Bierum, a village in the northeastern part of the Dutch province of Groningen, where there was once a Mennonite congregation belonging to the Groninger Old Flemish. It was always quite small. They had no meetinghouse, but held services in the room of a house. In 1710 there were about 30 members, in 1755, 10, and in 1767 only 4. The so-called Martini flood of 1686 and a second severe flood in 1717 caused heavy losses to the village of Bierum and to the members of the congregation, all of whom were engaged in agriculture. Jan Kriens, an influential elder of the Groninger Old Flemish, lived in Bierum. After 1769 the congregation is no longer listed in the register of Mennonite preachers. (Blaupot t.C., *Groningen* I, 127, 140, 201; *DB* 1879, 3.)   vDZ.

Biessovka, a small Mennonite colony in the Russian province of Samara, settled by emigrants from the Alexandertal church (Altsamara). It was founded in 1890 by the private purchase of an estate of about 1,500 hectares (4,000 acres) and in 1915 numbered 6 farms and families with 35 persons. After 1903 it had its own school. It belonged to the congregation of the mother colony, about 10 miles distant.   C.B.

Biestkens Bible, the designation of the Bible printed by Nikolaes Biestkens, printer of Emden and member of the Mennonite congregation there, which was for many years the Bible commonly used by the Dutch Mennonites, therefore also known as the *Dooperbibel* (Keller, *Waldenser,* 155).

Before 1560 the Mennonites of Holland, like the Reformed and Lutherans, used a Low German Bible, which was based on the old Cologne translation from the Vulgate, and was published by the famous printer, Jacobus van Liesveldt (*q.v.*), in Antwerp in 1526. Menno Simons and his co-workers apparently used the East Frisian edition of the Luther translation prepared by Bugenhagen (1545); in addition they consulted the Erasmus translation of the New Testament (published in Delft in 1524) and the High German Strasbourg and Zürich edition (see S. Muller in *DJ* 1837, 64 ff.).

In 1556 and again in 1559 a new Dutch translation of the Bible was issued by the Reformed Church in Emden; this translation was made by J. N. Utenhove, and was approved by the Reformed Synod in 1562. This translation was not used by the Mennonites, who usually used the New Testament published in 1557 by Mattheus Jacobszoon and reprinted a number of times (1558, 1559, 1562) without naming the place of publication. The Mennonites also used the translation which appeared in

1556, also in Emden, in the house of Steven Mierdemann and Jan Gheylliaert, a translation which closely follows the Old Testament of the Liesveldt Bible and the New Testament of the Froschauer Bible. (See also C. Krahn, *Menno Simons,* 84 ff.)

In 1560 Nikolaes Biestkens printed the entire Bible at Emden for the use of his fellow believers. It is generally known by the name "Biestkens Bible," and went through an extraordinary number of printings, mostly at Amsterdam, but also at Leeuwarden and Harlingen. Keller says (p. 154) that according to le Long there were 7 editions between 1562 and 1565, 24 between 1567 and 1600, and 24 between 1602 and 1650; from 1650 to the end of the century there were 4 editions; the last one was dated 1723. Muller mentions (p. 56) nearly 100 editions; viz., 16 of the entire Bible in folio, 10 in quarto, and one in octavo; of the New Testament there were 13 in quarto, 17 in octavo, 15 in duodecimo, and 19 in sedecimo. This is an indication not only of the size and number of Mennonite churches in Holland at that time, but also of their effectual zeal for the spread and use of the Word of God among them.

For the Dutch-speaking Mennonites in West Prussia a special edition was published in Schottland near Danzig (*HRE* II, 122), but printed in Haarlem. According to Muller (p. 57) this edition with artistic lettering was sold in 1598 by Crijn Vermeulen, a tradesman in Schottland, and gave exact information about the differences between this Bible and that of the Reformed of 1559-90.

Of vital interest is the question of what translation was used as the basis of the Biestkens Bible. Muller says it is exactly Luther's translation, except that in the later editions certain words pertaining to the oath, etc., were changed and some passages, such as Acts 2:30 and Rom. 1 and 3, were given a different form for reasons of dogma. Keller calls attention to the fact that the Biestkens Bible contains not only the Apocrypha, but also the Laodicean Epistle with the heading, "The Epistle of Paul to the Laodiceans, which is found in the oldest Bible printed at Worms." But the text does not follow that of the Worms Bible of 1529, but the Tepler Codex, which leads Keller to the conclusion that in the translation of the Biestkens Bible, not only the Lutheran, but also the Waldensian version was used (see **Bible Translations**). There is, however, no positive proof for this surmise. De Hoop Scheffer has shown (*DB* 1890, 64) that the Biestkens Bible is an improved new edition of the Liesveldt Bible, though the Mierdemann Bible mentioned above was also used.

The Biestkens Bible is the first Dutch edition divided into verses. In this respect it became the model for all later Dutch versions. Its use was continued longest in the Old Flemish churches. It was still in use in the congregations at Aalsmeer and Balk in 1837, for public services as well as family worship. In the other congregations it had been probably everywhere replaced by the superior state translation (*Statenvertaling*) by the close of the 18th century. Some copies of the Biestkens Bible were taken along when the Mennonites went from Prussia to Russia and later to America. At least two copies (one in Bethel College Library) exist. Copies of the first edition are in Mennonite libraries at Amsterdam and Goshen. NEFF.

S. Muller, "Het Ontstaan en het Gebruik van Bijbelvertalingen," in *DB* 1837, 51-65; *HRE* III, "Bibelübersetzungen": "German Translations," 65-84, and "Dutch Translations," 120-24; L. Keller, *Die Waldenser und die deutschen Bibelübersetzungen* (Berlin, 1886); *Menn. Bl.*, 1887; F. Dijkema, "De Doopsgez. en de Statenvertaling," in *De Statenvertaling 1837-1937* (Haarlem, 1937) 86-92; *BRN* V, 587; VII, 263, 493, 509; *ML* I, 220.

Biestkens, Nikolaes, of Diest, Flanders, a printer and editor (1517) at Hoorn, a Mennonite, rendered great service by printing and publishing Mennonite books. He died at Amsterdam in 1585. Of his publications the best known is the Bible he printed in 1560 for the use of the Mennonites, known as the Biestkens Bible (*q.v.*). Two years later he probably published the Dutch martyr- and hymnbook, *Het Offer des Heeren*. He may also have printed the third (1567), the fourth (1570), and the fifth (1578) editions of this book. Then he perhaps moved to Amsterdam, where he printed in 1582 or 1583 the fourth enlarged edition of the oldest Dutch hymnary, entitled, *Het tweede Liedeboek, van vele diversche Liedekens, ghemaect wt den ouden ende nieuwen Testamente, waer af sommighe eertijts in Druck uutghegaen, ende sommige noyt in Druck gheweest hebbende, daer by ghevoecht.* VDZ.

Offer, 8 ff., 20; *Catalogus Amst.,* 211, 266; *ML* I, 220; Wolkan, *Lieder,* 70; *DJ* 1837, 55 ff.; *DB* 1882, 53; 1890, 64; 1918, 107.

Biezen, de, a polder southeast of Aardenburg (*q.v.*), Dutch province of Zeeland, district of Zeeuwsch Vlaanderen, near the Belgian border. About 1615-30 a number of Mennonites from the Flemish territories of Kortrijk, Oudenaerde, and the vicinity of Gent settled here and turned the swamp into a fertile polder by throwing up dikes, one of which is still called *Doopersdijk* (Mennonite dike). Among the Mennonite settlers were the families of Bybau, Claeys, Coppens, Hebberecht, and van der Sluys. They were mostly farmers and rather well-to-do. One of them was Jacques van Maldegem (*q.v.*), a farmer-preacher. De Biezen was at that time not only a Mennonite settlement. A letter of Nov. 8, 1630, from the Council of Flanders to Isabella, Queen of Spain, states that many Mennonites from the vicinity of Gent, Tielt, and other Belgian towns regularly traveled to de Biezen to hold their meetings safely and undisturbed on Dutch territory just across the border, going at night, with blue sacks as marks of recognition, and returning the next night. Soon the Mennonites of de Biezen joined the church of Aardenburg, of which Jacques van Maldegem and later Ghijsel Hebberecht became the ministers. VDZ.

DB 1876, 94-108; the letter to Isabella is found in French in H. Q. Janssen and J. H. van Dale, *Bijdr. tot de Oudheidkunde en Gesch. inz. van Zeeuwsch-Vlaanderen,* VI, 196 ff.

Bifel, Christoph, as yet unknown, but named erroneously as the author of No. 50 in the *Ausbund,* "O Gott, Schöpfer, Heiliger Geist, zu Lob und Preis dir allermeist," which was written by Michael Weisse. (*ML* I, 221.)

Big Ben, a Hutterite Bruderhof near Wolford, Alta., founded in 1922 by members of the New Elm Springs Bruderhof of Ethan, S.D., with their preacher Johann Entz, who had been chosen to the ministry in 1911 at the New Elm Springs Bruderhof. Jacob J. Entz was chosen preacher in 1940. In 1947 the Bruderhof numbered 135 souls, with 52 baptized members. D.D.

Big Valley United Missionary Church is located in Big Valley, Alta.

Bihar Mennonite Mission. Bihar is a province of approximately 70,000 square miles in northeastern India. In January 1940 the Mennonite Board of Missions and Charities (MC) located its first missionaries in this field, when the S. J. Hostetler family arrived in Kodarma. The mission area covers 4,200 square miles and has a population of 1,000,000. Two regions are now occupied by the Mennonites—the Kodarma field and the Palamau field.

During the first ten years of this mission, the following missionary families have worked in this area: John E. Beachy, Henry D. Becker, S. Jay Hostetler, Paul Kniss, S. Allen Shirk, and Milton C. Vogt. By 1952 the mission had 6 congregations with 60 members. (S. J. Hostetler, *We Enter Bihar,* Elkhart, 1951.) M.G.

Bijdragen, Doopsgezinde: see **Doopsgezinde Bijdragen.**

Bijl, a Dutch Mennonite family, descending from Pieter Hansz Bille, b. 1668, at Ribe, Denmark, a Lutheran who settled in Amsterdam. One of his descendants, Pieter Bijl, b. 1807 at Hoorn, d. 1855 at Amsterdam, became a member of the Mennonite Church and married Maartje Hartog, daughter of Jan Hartog, Mennonite minister at Beemster (*q.v.*). Two of their sons were Mennonite ministers: Adrianus Jan Bijl (1837-1904) served the congregations of Wormerveer-Noord and Steenwijk, and Pieter Kornelis Bijl (1852-94) those of Staveren, Edam, Wormerveer-Zuid, and Leeuwarden. Jan Adrianus Pieter Bijl, b. 1882 at Steenwijk, son of Adrianus Jan Bijl, was also a Mennonite minister and served the congregations of den Horn (1914-26) and Nes op Ameland (1926-30). In this year he retired because of mental illness. Many members of this family too are found in the records of the Mennonite churches of Amsterdam, Haarlem, Leiden, and Assen, serving as deacons. VDZ.

Bijler, Gerrit van, an Anabaptist martyr: see **Gerrit van Bijler.**

Bilach, Henslein von, author of the lamentation, "Eins mals spaziert ich hin und her," which appeared in the *Ausbund* (No. 48) and was reprinted in Wackernagel, *Kirchenlied* III, 533. Nothing more is known about him. (*ML* I, 221.) HEGE.

Bilder aus der Kirchengeschichte für Mennonitische Gemeindeschulen (Bethel College, 1899) was the first in a series of books written by C. H. Wedel (*q.v.*), then president of Bethel College, on the subject of church and Mennonite history for use in parochial schools. This little volume of 86 pages has, judging by the number of editions, become not only the most popular book of the author but also of all general Mennonite books published on this subject. An enlarged edition followed in 1904. The sixth edition appeared in 1937. In 1920 the Western District Conference published an English edition translated by Gustav A. Haury (*Sketches from Church History for Mennonite Schools*) which was followed by a second revised edition published by the Herald Book and Printing Company in 1932. In 1951 the seventh German edition in which the second part was completely revised and enlarged by Cornelius Krahn was published by the Herald Book and Printing Company, the publisher of the last editions.

The book is now mostly used by the German-speaking Mennonites of Canada and South America. It is divided into four customary parts (early, medieval, Reformation, and modern) depicting the high lights from church history with a special emphasis upon those events of interest to Mennonites. The last part of the book gives a brief summary of Mennonite history and activities in all countries up to the year of publication.   C.K.

Bildhausen, a former Cistercian monastery, five miles northeast of Münnerstadt in Lower Franconia, Germany, was in the 19th century the seat of a Mennonite congregation, whose members had come from Baden and Württemberg. The first Mennonites settled in the region in the last quarter of the 18th century, where the Anabaptists had in the 15th century had a large following. Peter Neuschwanger is named as the first settler; he arrived in 1770 (*Menn. Bl.,* 1856, 80). Other families soon followed. Services were at first held at various places, and were later transferred to Bildhausen and the adjacent monastery.

The monastery, which had existed since 1156 and was secularized in 1803, was purchased by two barons of Meiningen. The Mennonite Muselmann family bought half the estate in 1818 for 85,000 guilders. The chapel of the monastery, in a state of collapse, was restored and used by the Mennonites as a church. In 1838 the congregation established a school and supported a teacher, Christian Stauffer of the Branchweilerhof near Neustadt a.H., who, however, soon emigrated to America. On April 3, 1897, the estate and the Rindhof located to the east, which had also long been occupied by Mennonites, was bought by a Catholic order in order to build an institution for cretins and idiots (*Bote von Grabfeld,* April 7, 1897). Since the monastery was sold, Mennonite religious services have been held in Trappstadt (*q.v.*). (*ML* I, 221.)   HEGE.

Bildt, Het, a district of the Dutch province of Friesland, reclaimed from the old Middenzee and dammed up in 1505. In this territory Leenaert Bouwens (*q.v.*) baptized between 1563 and 1582 a total of 197 persons. Later on congregations are found in the villages of St. Anna-Parochie (*q.v.*) and Oudebildtzijl (*q.v.*).   VDZ.

Billaerts, Nicolaas and his wife **Tanneken van Pilcken,** members of the Flemish congregation of Den Blok at Haarlem, Dutch province of North Holland, were the founders of an orphanage on the Klein Heiligland near the old people's home called the Blokshofje. Particulars concerning these benefactors are lacking.   VDZ.

De weeshuizen der Doopsgezinden te Haarlem 1634-1934 (Haarlem, 1934) 13-14, 16-17.

Billau, August, born in 1847 at Darmstadt, Germany, studied theology for three years in Bonn; in 1869, at the age of 24, he was chosen as Mennonite minister at Neuwied in place of C. Harder, who had been called to Elbing, and was ordained on March 8, 1871, by Weydmann of Crefeld. For 21 years he faithfully filled the office. He took great pains to gather the small, scattered congregation. Through liberal gifts from the Dutch and North German Mennonite churches, amounting to 4,887 marks, he was able to make extensive repairs in the church and the parsonage. A gift of 1,500 marks, given by a woman in grateful recognition of his pastoral service to her, made it possible to procure a new organ. His influence, borne by his love for the church, extended far beyond his congregation. He frequently participated in the conferences of the Palatine and Hessian Mennonites. In 1880 he preached an anniversary sermon in Monsheim. He took active part in the formation of the *Vereinigung der Mennoniten-Gemeinden im Deutschen Reich.* At the preliminary meeting in Neuwied in 1885 he presided as chairman (*Menn. Bl.,* 1885, 108 f.; also 60). He died July 24, 1892, not quite 45 years of age (*Menn. Bl.,* 1892, 121). (*ML* I, 222.)   NEFF.

Billmeyer. In 1777 the British destroyed the Germantown (Pa.) printing establishment of the Brethren (Dunkard) printer, Christopher Saur, Jr. (*q.v.*). Six years later Peter Leibert, a Brethren minister, and Michael Billmeyer, his Lutheran son-in-law, bought what was usable of the Saur equipment, and set up shop in Germantown, being more or less the successors of the younger Saur. This partnership continued for about three years, after which Billmeyer continued alone, and Leibert started a new printing business. In 1785 the Billmeyer press issued a reprint of the *Ausbund* (*q.v.*), and a polemic from a onetime Franconia Mennonite bishop, *Ein Aufsatz oder Vertheidigung von Christian Funk.* In 1790 it reprinted Roosen's *Christliches Gemütsgespräch.* In 1803 Billmeyer printed the new Franconia Conference hymnbook, *Die kleine geistliche Harfe der Kinder Zions,* and reprinted it in 1820. In 1805 he issued the fourth edition of *Die Wandelnde Seele* by J. P. Schabalie. He was thus in effect for a generation the printer for the Franconia Mennonites.   J.C.W.

Bender: *Two Centuries;* J. S. Flory, *Literary Activity of the German Baptist Brethren in the Eighteenth Century* (Elgin, Ill., 1908) 157-60, 321-27.

Billmyer Mennonite Mission (MC), in Lancaster Co., Pa., was conducted in a chapel on the Baker lime quarries tract along the Susquehanna between Marietta and Bainbridge. It was in charge of the Elizabethtown ministers and served the colored residents of the area in the period 1929-34, after which it was discontinued.   I.D.L.

Billowitz, a Bruderhof of the Hutterian Brethren in Moravia, founded in 1545; on Aug. 28, 1619, the

Hauerhaus was burned down by soldiery. (Beck, *Geschichts-Bücher,* 164, 173; *ML* I, 222.)

Bilt (or Biltius), **Johannes,** preacher of the Reformed Church at Workum in the Dutch province of Friesland, probably the student of Antonides van der Linden who was a violent opponent of the Mennonites, fell into a doctrinal dispute with Rippert Eenkes (*q.v.*), the preacher of the Mennonite church at Workum, which grew so violent that the government intervened and on May 20, 1605, ordered them to carry it on in writing. Both sides were to present their arguments to each other on June 24, and the replies were to be exchanged on July 25. At the appointed time Bilt presented his arguments; but Rippert Eenkes did not present his until November 1606, and then not in Workum, but to the government in Leeuwarden. The magistrate of Workum therefore felt it necessary to send two delegates to Leeuwarden; one of them was Johannes Bilt. He had just published an answer to Eenkes' reply. The government granted them a half year to carry on their pen dispute. Long after the term had expired Bilt handed in a very detailed presentation of the entire controversy, containing 1,483 paragraphs. He apparently achieved his purpose. The government took an unfriendly attitude toward the Mennonites. In the following year (1608) the building of new Mennonite churches was prohibited. (*DB* 1873, 83, 90 ff; *ML* I, 222.)   Neff.

Bilthoven, a village in the Dutch province of Utrecht, where a Mennonite conference center or broederschapshuis (*q.v.*) is located, where Mennonites and others may stay for longer or shorter periods of vacation and also where conferences may be held. The center, which is open throughout the year, was acquired in 1936 in operating condition by the Amsterdam and Utrecht congregations.

In Bilthoven there is also a Mennonite fellowship (*kring*), a subsidiary of the Utrecht congregation, organized in 1932. Since Dec. 11, 1949, the regular worship services have been held in this broederschapshuis; before this time annual communion services had been held in this building, except during the war, when the center was occupied by the German military authorities, and communion services were held in a private home. The membership of the fellowship totals about 115 (1953).   vDZ.

Binder, Eucharius (also called Carius or Eukarius Kellermann, as in Wappler, *Thüringen*), an Anabaptist martyr, was one of the first evangelists of the South German Anabaptists. He came from Coburg, where he was engaged in cabinetmaking, joined the Anabaptists in Thuringia, and was baptized by Hans Hut (*q.v.*) in 1526 in a village near Coburg, as was also his wife, Ursula Nospitzer (Meyer, 248). He accompanied Hans Hut on his journeys and seems to have brought about Hut's entry into Königsberg in Franconia (Berbig, *Königsberg,* 315). In the records published by Berbig his full name is not given; but there is no doubt that he is identical with the Eucharius Tischler of Coburg, who, as Wolf Schreiner of Königsberg says, stated under torture that his brother-in-law Eucharius with three other men, including Johannes von Bibra (Hans Hut), had come to him; after his sermon he had been baptized and soon afterwards all the others present from Königsberg and vicinity had followed his example (Berbig, 315). Wappler reports similar statements by other Anabaptists, e.g., Thoman Spiegel, Hans Weichsenfelder (234, 243-45, 279, 281).

From Königsberg Binder went to Nürnberg and Augsburg. In Augsburg he was present at the baptism of Eitelhans Langenmantel (*q.v.*) in February 1527. He seems to have been influential in Upper Austria later on. In Styria he assisted Hans Hut in sending out four apostles: Hieronymus von Mannsee, Leopold Schiemer, Jakob Portner, and Joachim of Nürnberg (Nicoladoni, *Bünderlin,* 27). According to a statement by Hans Weichsenfelder (Wappler, 231) he was also in Moravia.

In the summer of 1527 we find Binder in Augsburg again, participating in the Martyrs' Synod (Aug. 20, 1527) and at the suggestion of Hut (Meyer, 248) was sent into the region of Salzburg as an evangelist. Here he fell into the hands of the catchpolls. After a brief imprisonment and several trials, in which he courageously defended his faith, a cruel verdict was pronounced on him and his fellow prisoners. With 37 fellow believers, among them the preachers Hieronymus von Mannsee, Joachim März, and Wolfgang Wimmer, he was locked into a house, Oct. 27, 1527, which was then set on fire; all perished in the flames (Beck, *Geschichts-Bücher,* 57). Dr. Johann Eck, the well-known enemy of the Reformation, reported the execution on Nov. 26, 1527, to Duke George of Saxony (Seidemann, 152, appendix 43b). Binder had left his wife in Augsburg; she stayed there with his brother-in-law, Thoman Baur, a day laborer, but spent some time in Laugingen (Roth, 16, 18, and 47). On April 12, 1528, she attended the Easter service, at which all present were arrested (see **Augsburg**).

A hymn of Binder's is still extant, "Wir danken Gott von Herzen," which points out that only suffering and pain open the gates of heaven. It consists of eleven stanzas, and was at first distributed as a leaflet (K. Goedecke, 241). In two of the Hutterian hymnals Binder is named as the author (Beck, 57). In the *Ausbund* it is No. 35, where, however, it is erroneously attributed to Jörg Steinmetzen, who was beheaded in Pforzheim in 1530. Wackernagel reprinted it in *Kirchenlied* (III, 540). The mass execution at Salzburg is mentioned in the song, "Ach Gott im Himmelreich" (*Ausbund,* No. 27), which Wackernagel also included (V, 788).   Hege.

A. Nicoladoni, *Johannes Bünderlin von Linz* (Berlin, 1893); P. Wappler, *Die Täuferbewegung in Thüringen* (Jena, 1913); G. Berbig, "Die Wiedertäufer im Amt Königsberg," in *Deutsche Ztschft für Kirchenrecht* XIII (1903) 315; C. Meyer, in *Ztschft des hist. Vereins für Schwaben und Neuburg* I; K. Goedecke, *Grundriss zur Gesch. der deutschen Dichtung* II (2nd ed.); Seidemann, *Thomas Münzer* (Leipzig, 1842); Fr. Roth, in *Ztschft des hist. Vereins für Schwaben und Neuburg* XXVIII (1901); *ML* I, 222.

Binder, Matthias, a preacher of the Hutterian Brethren in Moravia, ordained Jan. 9, 1569, and sent out as a missionary with Paul Pretten to Württemberg, his former home. His field was the region of Frickenhausen. On April 15, 1573, he was captured at Neuffen (today under the *Oberamt* Nürtingen). In Stuttgart and later in Maulbronn the clergy and the magistrates subjected him to repeated trials on the rack. Since all attempts to persuade him to abandon his faith were futile, he was imprisoned in the Hohenwittlingen (*q.v.*) castle near Urach, where another Hutterite, Paul Glock (*q.v.*), had already been languishing for 17 years. In a fire which broke out in 1576 and burned the castle, they zealously assisted in extinguishing the flames when the prison doors were opened; this so impressed the manager of the prison that he released them. Early in January 1577 they reached the church in Moravia. Binder died Sept. 21, 1593, at Altenmarkt (Beck, *Geschichts-Bücher* 253, 264, and 319; *Mart. Mir.* D 714, E 1026).

Binder, like his fellow prisoner Glock, wrote some poems. He is the author of three hymns: "So wollen wir jetzt heben an," 12 stanzas; "Mein Gott in deinem höchsten Thron," 13 stanzas; and "Wie lieblich ist geziert," 22 stanzas. The hymn, "Merk auf, du wahre Christgemein" (46 stanzas, of which stanzas 1-34 form an acrostic on the names of Matthias Binder, Paul Glock, Veit Urmacher), describes Binder's three-year imprisonment in Württemberg (reprinted in *Die Lieder der Hutterischen Brüder,* Scottdale, 1914, 723-26, 734, 737; see also K. Steiff and G. Mehring, *Geschichtliche Lieder und Sprüche Württembergs,* Stuttgart, 1912, 409-12; Wolkan, *Lieder,* 233). Four of his letters are also extant, dated Neuffen 1574, Maulbronn 1574 and 1575, and Wittlingen 1576, addressed to Peter Walpot and the church in Moravia, which describe his experiences (Beck, 265). (*ML* I, 223.)   HEGE.

Binder, Oswald, an Anabaptist martyr, a preacher, was beheaded in Munich in 1528 (Beck, *Geschichts-Bücher,* 29). No details are known about him. (*ML* I, 223.)   HEGE.

Binder, Wolf, a Hutterite martyr, was seized in the summer of 1570 at Schärding on the Inn and taken to Burghausen (Bavaria), where, after several trials, he was so severely tortured that he was unable to stand. Since he refused to recant, he was beheaded at Schärding in February 1571 (Beck, *Geschichts-Bücher,* 257). An unknown author sang of his martyrdom in the song, "Ach Gott wir tun dies klagen" (30 stanzas; reprinted in *Die Lieder der Hutterischen Brüder,* Scottdale, 1914, 691-93; see Wolkan, *Lieder,* 234; *ML* I, 223).   HEGE.

Bingley (Alberta) United Missionary Church is a member of the Canadian Northwest Conference. It has only a small membership.   E.R.S.

Binkhorst, Pieter van, an otherwise unknown Dutch Anabaptist martyr, who was executed in 1536 at Hazerswoude or Leiden, province of South Holland. Whereas most Anabaptists belonged to the craft guilds or were even quite poor, Pieter van Binkhorst was a man of high rank and very wealthy. (*Inv. Arch. Amst.* I, No. 152.)   VDZ.

Binnerts, Szn., Arjen, b. Aug. 29, 1865, at Witmarsum, where his father was a Mennonite minister, d. July 14, 1932, at Haarlem. He was robust in appearance, with a manly character, a cheerful faith, and a gentle spirit; a sunny person. He was educated for the ministry at the university and the Mennonite seminary in Amsterdam; in September 1891 he became a ministerial candidate and in January 1892 he preached his sermon of acceptance at the IJtens congregation (1892-97), where he found much time for study in addition to his pastoral work (he was interested especially in scientific and social questions). From 1897 to 1902 he served at Meppel and Assen, 1902-7 at Rotterdam, 1907-33 at Haarlem.

For many years he was a director of the Algemeene Doopsgezinde Sociëteit and after its reorganization he served as chairman 1923-28. After that he was appointed chairman of the board of directors of the seminary.

He did not limit his services to the Mennonite brotherhood. He was on the executive committee of the Dutch Protestant Union, and for many years held a leading position in the Central Committee for Liberal Protestantism.

In the Mennonite brotherhood and far beyond it Binnerts, in the course of years, became a man of note and importance. He was not only in contact with the Protestant groups in the Netherlands, in which connection the religious instruction of youth was his great concern, but he also sought connections with the Mennonites of other countries. In May 1911 he attended the anniversary meeting of the German Mennonites in Crefeld, and formed many a friendship there. In the next year he visited the German brethren in West Prussia. Through these contacts he became the appropriate man to be appointed chairman of the newly reorganized (1921) *Commissie voor buitenlandse Noden* (Committee for Foreign Needs), which was later able to do so much for the brethren in Russia.

For those who knew Binnerts, especially as a pastor and preacher, with his cheerful piety, which never became superficial—how he wrestled with the question of war—he was a source of great strength. Albert Schweitzer relates that a meeting with Binnerts in 1928 was for him an unforgettable experience. Binnerts' humor banished all false sentimentality. Binnerts was a liberal and remained one. But gradually a change took place in him. To extreme rational Modernism he was always averse. Spiritual inclination and study led him to the side of the so-called conservative liberalism (*rechts-modernisme*). More and more he became engrossed by the Gospel; he observed "that the Gospel has little to bring those who do not deeply realize that they are sinners before God." This emphasis on the Gospel as the happy message of the forgiveness of sins gave his preaching force.

In 1902 Binnerts together with the publisher L. Hansma founded the *Doopsgezind Jaarboekje,* serving as its editor until 1926, and writing many articles for it with his own hand. A collection of sermons under the title *Het eene noodige* (the one thing needful) was published in 1932. About his trip to West Prussia he reported in *DJ* 1913, 100-117. (Biographical sketch by H. Hulshof with picture *DJ* 1933, 23-36.)   VDZ.

Binnerts, Halbe, b. Oct. 26, 1842, at Heerenveen, where his father was a notary, d. Jan. 5, 1922, at Voorburg, was baptized at Leeuwarden in 1862, studied law at the university of Leiden and received his degree in 1867 with *summa cum laude.* He opened a law practice in Heerenveen. Here he married Magdalena Hermanna Greidanus in 1870. He was very active in affairs pertaining to social welfare; among other things he founded a savings bank. He was a member of the States of Friesland. In 1899 he was made vice-president of the court at Leeuwarden (until 1911) and in 1916 a member of the upper chamber of the States-General. From 1899 to 1911 he lived in Leeuwarden, and found time to devote to the general welfare in addition to his legal work. He was an active and honored member of the Masonic lodge, serving as its chairman after 1909.

In various functions Binnerts served the Mennonite brotherhood. In Heerenveen and also in Leeuwarden he was a member of the church council. He served as treasurer of the Friesche Doopsgezinde Sociëteit (*q.v.*) 1902-11, and on the executive committee of the Algemeene Doopsgezinde Sociëteit 1882-1911, and as its chairman in 1892. He was active on all sorts of Mennonite committees and organizations. The existence of the *Dienstjarenfonds* is due to his efforts. His friend M. L. Deenik wrote a biographical sketch in the *Doopsgezinde Jaarboekje* of 1923 (also a portrait there). vdZ.

Bintgens (or Bijntgens), **Thomas,** an elder of the Mennonite Flemish congregation at Franeker in the Dutch province of Friesland, purchased a house in 1588, and accepted a receipt for 800 florins, whereas he had actually paid only 700 florins. He did this with the consent of the seller, to prevent later bids. His fellow ministers, Jacob Keest, Joos Jans, and Jakob Berends most severely condemned this procedure, as a violation of justice and truth. They also considered it wrong of Bintgens to buy the house from a spendthrift and drunkard who was in debt; he should instead have paid off the creditors before he bought the house. An unexpressed point of opposition to Bintgens was also the feeling on the part of Jacob Keest and his followers that Bintgens was too severe in his application of the ban. When Bintgens was asked to justify his act to the church council he declared that he was sorry and would rather pay for the house twice than injure anyone; he had acted in ignorance. But the matter did not stop there. Bintgens' opponents demanded his deposition from the ministry. Three meetings of delegates from various congregations did not succeed in bringing about lasting unity. The quarrel grew sharper and involved gradually widening circles. The outcome was the rise of two parties, the *Huiskoopers* or Thomas-Bintgens group, and the *Contra-Huiskoopers* or the Jacob-Keest group; these epithets were gradually replaced by the generally used terms, viz., Old Flemish for the Huiskoopers, and Flemish (or *Jonge* and *Zachte* Flemish) for the Contra-Huiskoopers. (See also **Flemish;** *DB* 1912, 49-60;

Inv. Arch. Amst. I, Nos. 477, 479, 558; Kühler *Geschiedenis* I, 430 f.; *ML* I, 223.) NEFF.

Birch Bay United Missionary Church, Blaine, Wash., was organized in 1909. In 1952 D. S. Johnson was in charge of the congregation. A.L.H.

Birdaard, a town in the Dutch province of Friesland, where Leenaert Bouwens (*q.v.*) baptized 10 persons in 1563-65, and another 15 in 1568-82. Nothing is known of a congregation of Birdaard. The Mennonites of this town may have joined a congregation in the neighborhood. vdZ.

Birkenhof (see **Altkirch** and **Baumerthof**), an estate near Altkirch in Upper Alsace, on which it is known that Mennonite services were held as early as 1788. About two years later Peter Rich of Birkenhof was made elder of the congregation; he began a church record. He served more than 30 years as elder. His influence was felt far beyond his own congregation. He had great prestige everywhere among the Mennonites. A cemetery was laid out on the Birkenhof, and opened on Oct. 15, 1807. A quarrel grew out of the question of expenses of the cemetery and inadequate keeping of funeral records, which was settled only by the intervention of outside elders and preachers (Nov. 26, 1808). In 1825 a church was built here by the Mennonites. The congregation is in effect merged with Altkirch, but services are held at both places alternately. When communion is held at Birkenhof, the ordinance of footwashing is observed, one of two surviving cases of this practice among the Mennonites of Europe. (*ML* I, 224.) The membership in 1951 was 51 (*Almanach Mennonite,* 1952, p. 2; *ML* I, 224). NEFF.

Birney Mennonite Mission (GCM) among the North Cheyenne Indians is located eight miles south of the town of Birney, Mont., Rosebud Co., on the Tongue River Indian Reservation. This work was begun by P. A. Kliewer who was in charge until 1920. Habegger from Busby substituted in 1919-20, while the Kliewers had a year's furlough. Other workers were Mr. and Mrs. Alfred Wiebe, 1921-22; Otto B. Pankratz, 1923-26; native pastor Frank Littlewolf, 1926-42; and native pastor Milton Whiteman, 1942-47. A. Habegger has been in charge, coming from Busby and then from Lame Deer during the week to minister to the people here. Up to 1949, the total baptisms were 58, with a membership of 40 that year.

A.H.

Birth Rate, Mennonite. Birth rates are discussed as crude and refined. The crude rate refers to the number of births per thousand of the total population without regard to any other factors. The refined, corrected, or standard birth rate refers to the number of births per thousand according to selected factors such as sex, age, occupation, income, or marital status. An illustration of refined birth rate would be the number of births per 1,000 women between the ages of 15 and 45, which is generally considered the child-bearing period.

The birth rate in America and in Europe among the general population has been declining steadily since 1870. Although slight upturns have been noted since the late thirties and the early forties, the long-time decline is expected to continue. In 1940 the average American family size was about 3.75, reflecting a decline in the birth rate of about 30 per cent since 1850.

Among Mennonites the birth rate seems to vary according to physical and cultural environment. It is not possible to generalize about a Mennonite birth rate in all countries and in different branches of Mennonites. While no comprehensive study has ever been made of birth rate among Mennonites throughout the world, there is some evidence in America that Mennonite families in most groups are getting smaller, which of course means a declining birth rate. Local studies on Mennonite family size made among Mennonites in Elkhart Co., Ind., and in Marion and McPherson counties in Kansas in 1947 support the above generalization. The Indiana study clearly revealed that the birth rate had significantly declined in the last three generations in three of the four Mennonite groups studied. The rate of decline seemed to be in direct proportion to the degree of urbanization and accommodation to society. It was not due to a higher infant mortality rate or a later marriage age.

The Elkhart County Amish families averaged 8.8 children in the first generation (two generations ago), 9.4 in the second (one generation ago), and 8.7 in the third (the present generation). The Amish showed practically no decline in birth rate. In the same locality the figures for the (old) Mennonites were 7.0 children in the first generation, 5.9 in the second, and 4.8 in the third, for a decline of 2.2 children per family in three generations. A third group, namely, the Mennonite Brethren in Christ, revealed that the family size in the first generation was 7.7, 7.0 in the second, and 5.0 in the third, for a decline of 2.7 children per family in three generations. The fourth group, the General Conference Mennonites, had an average family size of 6.8 in the first generation, 5.8 in the second, and 3.9 children in the third, for a decline of 2.9 children per family in three generations. These figures are probably not a scientifically valid sample of Mennonite birth rate throughout America, but they reflect a general downward trend in a typical American Mennonite community. These figures also reflect the trend in America generally. A similar study done in a Kansas Mennonite Brethren congregation revealed that the average family sizes for the past three generations were: 7.0, 8.36, and 3.58. This decline reflects the same downward trend in the birth rate as found in the Indiana study.

According to statistics available on the number of children per family in the Chortitza Colony in Russia from 1890 to 1920, the average was seven. From 1920 to 1943 the family size sharply declined due to the violent interruption of the Soviet Revolution. Among the Old Colony Mennonites in Paraguay, a twenty-year record from 1931 to 1950 indicates an average family size of 5.6. The Fernheim Colony, which consists of Mennonites who came from Russia in 1930, has an average family size of 5.2 for the same period. In Durango, Mexico, the average family size in 1943 was 5.3. These figures all point to a relatively high birth rate among Mennonites in Russia prior to 1920 and in Mexico and Paraguay within the present generation. In the latter two countries, Mennonites have about two more children per family on the average than does the average American family.

The crude birth rate for a twenty-year period from 1931 to 1950 in the Menno and Fernheim colonies, Paraguay, was 54.1 and 44.4 respectively. This is higher than the national birth rate for any country in the world. Chile, the country with the highest birth rate in the world, stood at 34.6 per thousand, Japan at 29.9, the United States at 16.7, England and Wales, 14.8. The death rate for the same period in the two colonies referred to above was 11.8 for Menno and 7.6 for Fernheim. When compared with the four countries mentioned above, we see an even more phenomenal situation, namely, the low death rate in the colonies as compared with Chile, whose crude death rate in 1936 was 25.3; Japan 17.5; the United States 11.5; and England and Wales 12.1. It can be readily seen that the birth rate among these two oldest Paraguayan Mennonite colonies is still high. The twenty-year average annual net increase rate for Menno was 43.0 and 36.0 for Fernheim.

The chief reason for a declining birth rate in the United States among Mennonites seems to be the general process of urbanization. More and more Mennonites in North America have preferred fewer children and better opportunities and material advantages. Planned parenthood is another factor accounting in part for a declining birth rate. Modern urban conditions are not conducive to large families. The high cost of housing, the crowded living conditions, and, perhaps more important, the fact that children may be an economic liability rather than an asset are other reasons for declining birth rate.

The decline in birth rate may either be a short- or a long-term trend, depending upon the general economic, social, and political conditions at any period of time. It is conceivable that if social and economic conditions would significantly change, either due to natural or artificial causes, larger families would again become an asset and thus the birth rate increase. It is safe to conclude on the basis of evidence at hand that as Mennonite educational and economic levels rise, the family size tends to decline. The material comforts and cultural satisfactions seem to be preferred to increasing numbers of children. The desire for good education and high economic status seems to reflect a preference for material and social quality rather than biological quantity. In this respect many of the Mennonites seem to follow the general trends and reflect many of the general secular values, although more slowly and less conspicuously.

J.W.F.

A. Ehrt, *Das Mennonitentum in Russland von seiner Einwanderung bis zur Gegenwart* (Berlin-Leipzig, 1932); J. Fretz, *Pilgrims in Paraguay* (Scottdale, 1953); Howard Good, "A Study in Mennonite Family Trends in Elkhart County, Indiana," *Proceedings of the Sixth Annual Conference on Mennonite Cultural Problems* (North

Newton, 1947); I. G. Neufeld, "The Life Cycle of Mennonite Families in Marion County, Kansas," *Proceedings of the Sixth Annual Conference on Mennonite Cultural Problems* (North Newton, 1947); K. Stumpp, *Bericht über das Gebiet Chortitza* (Berlin, 1943).

Bisch, Rauff, of Odernheim (Palatinate), Germany, an Anabaptist preacher who represented the Anabaptists of the Palatinate at the disputation of Frankenthal (May 28-June 19, 1571). He was their spokesman, and on June 6 was asked to present the addresses of the other speakers, which had heretofore been the task of Hans Büchel (*q.v.*) of Mure in Lungau (Austria). Bisch was no match for the dialectics of the Palatine theologians; nevertheless his answers to the diffuse rejoinders and subtle questions of his opponents, especially of their spokesman, Peter Dathenus (*q.v.*), were sometimes very fitting; this was particularly true of his summarizing comments at the conclusion of the discussion of the assigned questions on confessional matters. Although he had been promised freedom of speech and personal security in the electoral invitation, Rauff Bisch nevertheless had to reckon with having his statements used against him in the future. He felt this and said it openly, when Dathenus tried to convince him in verbose dogmatic arguments. "We are surprised that you want to drive us into a net and trap with such questions." He finally declined to enter upon questions that were unfathomable to the human mind, and at the close of the disputation said, "We cannot burden our conscience with certain articles that we cannot with a clear conscience believe, but only want to cling to what we can answer for to God, for we know nothing better." Nothing is known of Bisch's subsequent life. He was probably not able to accomplish much in the Palatinate, for Elector Fredrick III forbade the Anabaptists to preach after the unsuccessful disputation, even though the officials did not very strictly apply these repressive measures.

HEGE.

Protocoll, Das ist alle handlung des gesprechs zu Franckenthal etc. (Heidelberg, 1571); Chr. Hege, *Die Täufer in der Kurpfalz* (Frankfurt, 1908) 117 ff.; *ML* I, 224.

Bischweiler, a town in Alsace, which was a part of the possessions of the barons of Eschenau when about 1535 an Anabaptist movement became evident here. At the wish of Ludwig von Eschenau, who was the bailiff of the Duke of Zweibrücken, the parson of Zweibrücken, Johann Schwebel, sent to Bischweiler "a friendly admonition and instruction to some who are suspected of rebaptism." The Anabaptists of Bischweiler wrote an anonymous reply to this letter, and presented it to the baron through a Hans Hoffner. Thereupon Schwebel directed a second, still longer warning to Hans Hoffner in Bischweiler. The author of the Anabaptist reply was perhaps Georg Pistor, who was the Protestant pastor at Ernstweiler near Zweibrücken and had to resign because of his Anabaptist inclination. (Fr. Jung, *Joh. Schwebel, der Reformator von Zweibrücken,* Kaiserslautern, 1910, 119 f. and 205; *ML* I, 225.)

NEFF.

Bisentz, a city in Moravia, location of a Hutterite Bruderhof established in 1545 (Beck, *Geschichts-Bücher,* 164). (*ML* I, 225.)

Bishop, the title used by several groups of Mennonites in America for the highest ministerial office. The corresponding term in Dutch was *oudste* (although *bisschop* was also occasionally used) and in German *Aeltester,* English translation "elder" (*q.v.*). In the United States those groups which descended from European immigrants who arrived after 1800 from Switzerland, Germany, or Russia, and did not affiliate with the Mennonite Church (MC) whose foundation and organization was laid by immigrants from Germany and Switzerland in the 18th century, used almost exclusively the German term "Aeltester" and later its English form "elder," but those who affiliated with the Mennonite Church adopted the term "bishop." However, in Canada, the older General Conference congregations, the Bergthal, the Kleine Gemeinde, and similar conservative groups use "bishop" freely in their English usage. The Eastern District Conference of the General Conference Mennonite Church, having originated in 1847-48 in a schism from the Mennonite Church (MC) in Eastern Pennsylvania, wavered, first using "bishop," but later after affiliation with the newer immigrant groups of the General Conference Church, adopted "elder." The following United States groups (and their Canadian congregations) use "bishop" exclusively: Mennonites (MC), Old Order Mennonites, Old Order Amish, Conservative Amish, Church of God in Christ, Mennonite, and smaller related groups. Vos claims "bisschop" was the term first used by Obbe Philips and Menno in the beginning in Holland, later supplanted by "oudste."

The history of the usage of the term "bishop" has not been fully traced. Without doubt the Mennonite Church (MC) in the United States is responsible for its introduction into the English ecclesiastical terminology of Mennonites, but exactly when this occurred is not certain. Christian Herr, a leader of the Lancaster Mennonite Conference, wrote a brief article on the Mennonites for I. D. Rupp's *History of all the Religious Denominations in the United States* (Harrisburg, 1848), in which he speaks of the threefold ministry of the Mennonites as "bishops, elders or ministers, and deacons." An 1849 remonstrance by the officials of the Deep Run Mennonite (MC) congregation of the Franconia Conference against the organization of an Oberholtzer congregation at that place, addressed to the Bucks County Court, is signed by two "bishops," two "ministers," and two "elders," where the title "elder" means "deacon" (J. C. Wenger, *History of the Mennonites of the Franconia Conference,* Telford, 1938, 363). The *Ordnung der Mennonitischen Gemeinschaft,* adopted and printed by the Oberholtzer group in 1848, says in the section *Von den Aemtern,* "Die Aemter unserer Gemeinschaft sind dreierlei: Erstens, Das Amt der Bestätigten oder Bischöfe; Zweitens, Das Amt der gemeinen Lehrer oder Prediger; Drittens,

Das Amt der Vorsteher oder Diaconen. Niemand kann zum Bestätigten oder Bischof gewählt werden . . . ." John H. Oberholtzer himself, though ordained to the office after he left the old church, assumed the title of "bishop," as is clearly indicated by the title of his 1860 book, *Der Wahre Charakter von J. H. Oberholtzer, Prediger und Bischof . . .*, and the obituary article about him which appeared in the 1896 *Mennonite Year Book and Almanac* calls him bishop and tells of his "ordination to the office of bishop" in 1847. A list of ordained men of the Ontario Mennonite Conference (MC) printed about 1853 lists "bishops, ministers, and deacons," and the printed 1864 German minutes of that conference use the German term "Bischöfe." (This conference had strong connections with the Franconia Conference, many of its families having emigrated from that area to Ontario 1780-1820.)

It is possible that the use of "bishop" was unintentionally promoted by the Dordrecht Confession of 1632 (first German edition 1664, first English edition 1712 in Amsterdam and 1727 in Philadelphia), which uses the term "bisschop" (Dutch), "Bischof" (German), as well as "oudste," "Aeltester," and "elder," and which was adopted as the official confession of the Pennsylvania Mennonites in 1725. At any rate, it seems clear that the Pennsylvania Mennonites as early as 1845 were using "bishop" in both English and German, and reserved "Aeltester" as the German word for "deacon." In view of the traditionalism of this group, it is most probable that this usage goes back into the 18th century at least. The Pennsylvania Amish and their descendants must have used "Bischof" (and more recently "Bishop") in the German for almost as long.

There is no evidence that "Aeltester" was regularly used for "bishop" by either the Amish or Mennonite groups of Pennsylvania (and their European Swiss, Alsatian, and South German ancestors). The corresponding German terms which they used were *Bestätigter Diener* (confirmed minister), *Völliger Diener,* or *Voller Diener* (full minister). It is probable that "oudste" or "Aeltester" (elder) was a more characteristic Dutch-North German-Prussian-Russian term and only in the 19th century came to be used in South Germany, France, and Switzerland, where it has apparently been the standard term for over a century. However, the *Concept of Cologne* (1591), printed in Holland in 1660, the oldest of the Dutch-Northwest German confessions, uses the term bishop in the following sentence (p. 110), *Een Bisschop of Leeraer sal onstraffelijck sijn.*

The official *Minister's Manual* of the Mennonite Church (MC), first published by John F. Funk at Elkhart in 1890, defines the office of bishop in the following paragraph:

> The bishop or elder in the Mennonite church is simply the minister who has been ordained to the special charge of caring for, and officiating in the church of a certain prescribed district. This district may contain but one place of worship, or a number of places, which are at considerable distances from each other. He may

have a number of fellow-ministers in his charge, to preach at the various places, and aid him in his work generally.

Earlier each congregation (the Amish still have this practice) had a bishop, several preachers, and one or two deacons, the number of preachers and deacons depending somewhat upon the size of the congregation. As the Mennonite settlements in Eastern Pennsylvania and Ontario and elsewhere expanded, the new congregations were considered as daughters of the older, and usually the bishop simply continued to exercise oversight over the daughter congregations as well. In fact the entire settlement was usually thought of as one "congregation." This accounts for the rise of the 'bishop district" (or diocese, although this latter term was almost never used), which in its largest extent seldom had more than 5-8 congregations and 1,500-2,000 members, often much less. The daughter Mennonite conferences followed the Lancaster-Franconia pattern of bishop districts. The Amish never permitted this evolution, however, and both the original Pennsylvania communities and the daughter Amish settlements have continued to adhere to this practice of each congregation having its own bishop. Among the Old Order Amish a new congregation or "district" is not considered fully organized and independent until it has its own independent bishop chosen from its own membership. The history of the Canadian General Conference Mennonite Church and related groups reveals the same pattern and development as that of the Eastern Pennsylvania Mennonites, only more sharply defined, with one bishop having oversight of as many as 15-30 groups, all viewed as one congregation or *Gemeinde*. For example, the Bergthal Church in Manitoba with almost 3,500 members and over 20 groups, until recently had only one bishop (now two), and the Rosenort Church in Saskatchewan with one bishop has almost as many groups and members. The Manitoba, Mexico, and Paraguay Old Colony and Sommerfelder groups (all of Manitoba origin) likewise have only one bishop, no matter how numerous the subgroups or congregations or how large the membership.

A bishop can normally be chosen only from among the already ordained ministers, although some Amish groups admit deacons to candidacy; thus a bishop ordination is always a second ordination. Usually the administration of ordination, baptism, marriage, the Lord's Supper, and discipline are exclusive functions of the bishop, along with presiding over the congregation in all its worship and business meetings, and pastoral responsibility.

Much prestige has usually been attached to the office of bishop in America. This was also the case in Russia and Prussia, and in earlier times in Holland and Germany as well, when the term "elder" meant the same thing as "bishop." However, the multiplication of "elders" in one congregation (Switzerland and South Germany-Badischer Verband) or the practice of ordaining almost all pastors to be elders and doing so almost at the beginning of their ministry, has greatly reduced the prestige and significance of the office in those groups where this is done; when all pastors become bishops, then there is no longer a bishop in the older sense.

Usually the differentiation between bishop and minister has not been one of rank so much as of function; accordingly in conference work and organization ministers usually have equal rights and privileges with bishops. An exception to this rule is the practice which has evolved through the years in the Lancaster Conference and to a lesser degree in the Franconia Conference, of treating the group of bishops as a sort of upper house in the conference, like the House of Bishops in the Episcopal Church of the United States. The group is called the Bishop Board, and has the sole right to initiate legislation in the conference sessions. Ministers are allowed to vote but not to "gainsay" the bishops. The Bishop Board meets in advance of the full session of conference to prepare the business and recommendations for the full conference.

There are in the Mennonite Church (MC) about 570 congregations and 71,500 members, with roughly 180 bishops, 860 ministers, and 380 deacons. The Old Order Amish with 15,000 members in 160 congregations have 161 bishops, 381 ministers, 155 deacons. The Conservative Amish with almost 6,000 members in 42 congregations have 42 bishops, 76 ministers, 18 deacons. The Old Order Mennonites with 5,500 members in 45 congregations have 14 bishops, 50 ministers, and 34 deacons. The Kleine Gemeinde of Manitoba with 2,000 members has 2 bishops, 17 ministers, 6 deacons. The Bergthal Church in Manitoba with 3,500 members has 2 bishops and 21 ministers. The General Conference of Mennonites of Canada with 15,500 members in 63 congregations has 32 bishops or elders (only 18 have died in the entire history of the conference) and 240 ministers.

For a treatment of the office of elder as practiced among the Mennonites of Europe and certain groups in America, see **Elder.** (K. Vos, "De keuze tot Doopsgezind Bisschop," in *Nederl. Archief v. Kerkgesch.* XVI, 1921; *ML* I, 224.)   H.S.B.

Bisschop, Jan and **Pieter,** born in Rotterdam, Jan in 1680, Pieter date unknown, sons of Esau Jansz Bisschop and Annetje Jans Cras. The father was a spinner of yarn; after his death in 1729 the sons Jan and Pieter carried on the business. Pieter died June 1, 1758. Under the management of the sons the business was greatly increased. They were also serious art collectors. Their collection later came into the possession of the art-lover Hope of Amsterdam. They were most interested in collecting books, shells, coins, and china. Their collection was so famous that Prince William of Orange and his wife visited it in 1768 and it attracted many foreigners. Both brothers were faithful members of the Mennonite church at Rotterdam and made generous gifts as long as they lived. Pieter had already bequeathed it a legacy; but at Jan's death on March 5, 1771, it was discovered that the congregation was the sole heir, inheriting 214,000 guilders. The congregation used this money at once to build the beautiful church that was dedicated in 1775, and was probably the most beautiful Mennonite church in the Netherlands. On May 14, 1940,

it was completely burned in the bombing raid. The catalog of the collection at Jan's death, containing 223 items, is printed in *Oud-Holland* XXVIII (1910) 161. (*N.N.B.Wb.* II, 169; *ML* I, 225.)   K.V.

Bisschop, Pieter de (dates of birth and death unknown), was chosen deacon in the Dutch Reformed refugee congregation of Frankfurt on Nov. 17, 1570. According to Vos he later also lived in Antwerp. After 1580 (at least until 1597) he lived in Rotterdam, where he was an elder of the Reformed Church. He was a grim opponent of the Mennonites. To that end he wrote among other things: *Antwoort-liedt op eens Wederdoopers Lasterliedt* . . . (5th ed., Rotterdam, 1600; the first edition was probably printed in 1593), and *Spieghel der Waterlantscher Wederdooperen Leughenkonst,* . . . (Rotterdam, 1597). Hans de Ries (*q.v.*) wrote against de Bisschop: *Verthoon van verscheyden onwaerheden ende loogen* . . . , of which no printed copy is known, but the manuscript is found in the Amsterdam Library (26 pages). (Vos, *Antwerpen,* 333, 378, 379; *N.N.B.Wb.* III, 117; *Catalogus Amst.,* 192, 354; *Inv. Arch. Amst.* I, 655, 656; *ML* I, 225.)   K.V., vɒZ.

Bitscherland, an Amish Mennonite congregation in the bailiwick of Bitsche, Alsace, probably formed by members of the congregations of Zweibrücken, Froensburg, and Struth. Its date of formation is unknown, but must be anterior to 1780, since in 1782 its elders are known to have written to Elder Jacob Kupferschmitt of the Salm congregation to request advice as to whether to rebaptize a family which had come from Holland. In this same period a list of the Anabaptists in the district was drawn up in order to prove to the prefect of Metz that only a few young men could be sent to work on the fortifications, which work was required of them instead of military service. The list names 22 families with 145 members. In 1808 the congregation was represented at the Saareck conference concerning military service, and was listed, together with the Struth congregation, as having given a total of 20 doubloons for the delegation to the government.

The following are known to have served as elders: Joseph Schertz, Christian Schantz (serving in 1808), Jacques Thomas (left for inner France around 1850), Nicolas Roggy (left for America at about the same time), Christian Schantz (d. 1886), Joseph Wolmer (d. 1892), Joseph Brunner (d. 1899), Christian Schantz (d. 1902), Jean Jordy (d. 1919). After Schantz' death in 1902 the remaining elements of the congregation, by then gravely weakened by emigration, attached themselves to the Saargemünd or Ixheim congregations across the border in the Palatinate. (P. Sommer, "Assemblée du Pays de Bitsche," *Christ Seul,* August 1931, 7-10.)   J.H.Y.

Bixel (Bixler, Bichsel), a Mennonite family name originating at Eggiwil in the Emmental, canton of Bern, Switzerland. The word "bichsel" is used for a rounded adze which was used to hollow out wooden troughs and spouts. It is likely that persons who made or used this tool were given this name during the 15th century.

The first mention of the name in connection with the Anabaptist faith is in 1537. Ulrich Bichsel was executed at Bern with six of his brethren during the latter part of 1537 or early part of 1538. He was the 15th Bernese Anabaptist to suffer this fate. Simon Bichsel was called before the authorities in 1621 and questioned concerning his Anabaptist faith. Various officials pointed out his errors and pleaded with him to recant. He answered them by saying that all their teaching, threats, and punishment will avail nothing as it is written in the Scriptures, "Go out from them."

Andres Bichsel appears to be the first of the family to have moved from the Emmental to the Jura. He arrived near Corgémont in 1717. During the following decade several other Bichsel families followed, most of them settling near Court on the Graitery Mountain and in the Chaluet Valley.

Probably the first of the families to migrate to America were John and Christian Bixler who settled near York and Hanover, Pa., about 1725; a third brother is said to have moved later to Virginia. In the early 19th century a branch of the family settled in western Pennsylvania near Butler (Bishop Joseph Bixler, 1778-1862), and in eastern Ohio near Columbiana (Bishop Joseph Bixler, 1813-95). Bishop Jacob Bixler (1877-1939) of Elkhart, Ind., was of this line. Descendants of the original immigrants now live in Pennsylvania, Virginia, Ohio, Indiana, and Illinois.

Jacob Bichsel and his wife were the first of the family in the new Swiss emigration to America in the 19th century. After arriving in 1821 they settled in the newly established Sonnenberg settlement in Wayne Co., Ohio, where most of their descendants live today. They use the name Bixler. Jacob's brother and sister, Peter and Verena, followed in 1824, settling in Holmes Co., Ohio. In 1845 Peter and his family moved to the Putnam Co., Ohio, settlement where most of his descendants now reside. They use the form of the name Bixel. Some members of these families are also found in the Berne, Ind., settlement.   D.L.G.

Müller, *Berner Täufer*, 78, 120, 248; P. B. Amstutz, *Geschichtliche Ereignisse der Mennoniten-Ansiedlung in Allen und Putnam County, Ohio* (Bluffton, 1925) 44-51. ML I, 219.

Bixler, Jacob K. (1877-1939), son of John and Barbara (Huber) Bixler, was born at Winesburg, Ohio, died at Elkhart, Ind. At the age of five he moved with his family to near Wakarusa, Ind., where he graduated from high school as one of the first Mennonite (MC) graduates in the midwest, then taught school for two years. In 1904 he was married to Susan Bailey, and ordained to the ministry of the Mennonite Church (MC), and in 1907 ordained a bishop. He became an influential leader in the Indiana-Michigan Mennonite Conference (*q.v.*) and Mission Board, and was the leader in establishing numerous mission congregations in the state of Michigan, while serving as secretary of the district mission board.   H.S.B.

Blaauw, a Dutch family, of which at least several generations were Mennonites. By 1450 this family was living at Westzaan near Amsterdam. Most of the members of this Blaauw family in the 17th and 18th centuries were Mennonites and well-to-do lumber dealers; e.g., Dirck Dircks (Blaauwe Dirk) at Westzaan, who died in 1680. Claas Gerritsz Blaauw, who was married to Guurtje Michiels Bruynvis, was a member of the Mennonite church of Zaandam. His son Gerrit, b. 1727 at Westzaan, baptized in the Zonist congregation at Amsterdam, d. there 1798, was first textile merchant in Amsterdam; in 1759-79 he lived at Ceylon as an agent of the Dutch East India Company. He was married to Cornelia Smidt, a daughter of Petrus Smidt, the well-known pastor of the Amsterdam Zonist congregation. Another descendant of this family, also called Gerrit Blaauw (1750-1825), was a member of the Amsterdam city council, then sheriff and burgomaster of Amsterdam, and also a Mennonite. His children did not belong to the Mennonite Church. Some Mennonite descendants of this family are still found at Amsterdam and other places.   vDZ.

Ned. Patriciaat VII (1916) 48; X (1919) 21-22; J. M. van Gelder, *Stamboek van Gelder* (Amsterdam, 1899) 180.

Blaauw, Gerrit, preacher of the Frisian Mennonite congregation at Wormerveer, 1727-80, an "experienced and intelligent research scholar in the privileges and customs of the Dutch Mennonites" (Samuel Muller), in 1765 published *Brief an den Heer . . . behelzende een antwoord op drie vragen, . . .* in which he urges the Mennonites, as loyal citizens to fulfill their duty to their country, and defends the rights of the Mennonites. In 1772 he wrote *Ontwerp tot meerdere aanweeking van leeraren,* which booklet he sent to the congregations. He was led to write this book by the great recession of the Dutch Mennonite congregations, which he attributed to the inadequate education of their ministers. He also published some sermons. (*Inv. Arch. Amst.* I, 684, 761; *DB* 1890, 82; *DJ* 1837, 67 ff. and 96; *Catalogus Amst.,* 188, 220, 249; *ML* I, 225.)   NEFF, vDZ.

Black Creek, in Willoughby Township, south of Niagara Falls, Ont., was a Mennonite settlement of over 200 according to the assessment records of Ontario in 1837. The meetinghouse of the congregation (MC) was known as the Riverside Church. It was located a few miles north of Black Creek on the River Road. The only evidence of its existence until the assessment records were found was a letter by Bishop Jacob Moyer of Vineland in 1831 to the ministers Christian Hershi and George Zavitz at Black Creek. George Zavitz was minister in Bertie Township, South. He and his brother John (1798-1872) served this church for the greater part of its active existence. Jacob Miller (1772-1841), whose wife was Barbara Hershey and who came from Maryland, located in this area in 1801. This probably gave rise to the name Miller Church, which was the earlier name of the Riverside Church. Miller is reputed by his descendants to have been a Mennonite minister active as far as Waterloo County. Jacob Miller, Jr. (1805-65), was a son of Jacob, Sr., reported as a Mennonite minister but inactive. Martin Weaver (1814-87) was ordained for this place late in life but did not preach. Joseph Wellick (1818-72), who after turning from the Catholic faith, married Esther Boyer, lived on the Sodom road in this township and became deacon. He with David Habecker, a Mennonite minister from east of Niagara Falls, conducted services also in a schoolhouse near the Wellick farm. The Willoughby Church (Riverside) was erected by public subscription in the community in 1827. It served both as a church and a school for many years. The Mennonites being in the majority used it most. The original log church gave place to a frame church about 1850, which stood unused for a quarter century before being removed at the time of the recent improving of the Niagara Boulevard along the west bank of the river. As the Mennonites lost out, preaching services were provided alternately by other active groups in the community. For many years before the Mennonites discontinued services, their services were held at eight-week intervals. Sunday school was conducted as early as 1827. (L. J. Burkholder, *Brief Hist. of the Mennonites in Ontario,* Toronto, 1935.)   J.C.F.

Black Creek Mennonite Brethren Church, 11 miles north of Courtenay, Vancouver Island, B.C., Canada, is a member of the Canadian Conference of the Mennonite Brethren Church of North America. The church was organized on Jan. 6, 1935, with 34 members under the leadership of Franz Friesen, who served as the first pastor. The 1953 membership was 67, all of whom were rural people. The first meetinghouse, with 150 seating capacity, in use in 1950, was built in December 1936. Ministers who have served the congregation are Franz Friesen, Isaak Goertzen, and John Z. Goertz.
                                                   J.A.G.

Black Creek United Mennonite Church (GCM), located in the vicinity of Black Creek, a village on Vancouver Island, B.C. The church has 186 members. The first settler, H. Schulz, came in October 1932, and two years later others came from the prairie provinces. For regular services they have met with the Mennonite Brethren from 1934 on, at first in private homes, and then in the district school. They built their first church, with 150 seats, in 1937. Services are conducted in German. N.F.

Black River Mennonite Church: see **Lewis County** (N.Y.).

Blacksmith, an Anabaptist martyr whose name is unknown, was put to death by beheading at Komen (Commines) in Flanders, Belgium, in 1551. He was executed in prison rather than in public because the authorities feared a popular demonstration. (*Mart. Mir.* D 105, E 502.)   vDZ.

Blagoveshchensk is a city on the Amur River of Siberian Russia in the vicinity of which Mennonites established a settlement after World War I. See **Amur Mennonite Settlement** and **Asiatic Russia.**
                                                   C.K.

Blaichner, Martin, a South German preacher of the Anabaptists, co-worker with Pilgram Marpeck in the preparation of the latter's writings.

Blaine County, Okla., about 45 miles northwest of Oklahoma City. Two groups of Mennonites set-

tled here. The Pleasant View Mennonite Church (MC) of the South Central Conference in the southwestern part of the county was organized in 1898. In 1950 there were 15 families living here and 20 families in Custer County adjoining Blaine on the west.

In the southeastern part of Blaine County a group of General Conference Mennonites settled at Geary in 1892. Several years later they organized the Geary Mennonite Church, which now has 40 members living in Blaine County and 76 living in Canadian and Kingfisher counties east of Blaine.
                                                   W.W.K.

Blaine Mennonite Brethren Church, of Blaine, Whatcom Co., Wash., is located within eight miles of the Canadian border, a mile from the Pacific. It is a member of the Pacific District Conference. It was organized in 1937 with 23 members and has grown to 182 (1953). A new building completed in 1949 has replaced the original assembly hall. Its leaders have been N. N. Hiebert, P. H. Karber, J. W. Fast, and D. P. Schultz. J.W.Fa.

Blainsport Mennonite Mission (MC) (before 1947 known as Cocalico) is a mission station of the Lancaster Mennonite Conference in northeastern Lancaster Co., Pa., in old Swamp Union Meetinghouse, built in 1865. The Indiantown-Bowmansville ministers held meetings in the vicinity in the last century, but not in this building. The Ephrata congregation reopened this house as a mission station in 1926 with Christian Mosemann and Daniel Stauffer as superintendents. The field workers of the Lancaster Mennonite Mission Board and the ministers of the Ephrata-Indiantown congregation preached here until Wilmer M. Eby was ordained for the work in 1938. Levi G. High in 1946 was ordained as deacon. In 1947 a brick church was built near Blainsport, two miles east of the Union House. In 1953 the membership was 63, with a Sunday-school enrollment of 136 and a summer Bible school with an average attendance of 155.
                                                   I.D.L.

Blair, Ont., a town near which land was sold to the New Mennonist Society for church purposes in 1872. Although there never was a Mennonite congregation in this community, there were some families sympathetic to the cause of the General Conference Mennonites in this area.   J.C.F.

Blair County in west-central Pennsylvania was first settled by Mennonites between 1790 and 1810 in Morrison's Cove, a valley at the southern extreme of Blair County extending into Bedford County. The first meetinghouse was near Martinsburg; one was later built at Roaring Spring for members in that vicinity. Of the 235 Mennonites now in the county, 85 who have allied themselves with the General Conference Mennonite Church now meet at Roaring Spring (*q.v.*) and Smith Corner (*q.v.*). A congregation of 80 members at Martinsburg (*q.v.*) and another of 70 at Altoona (*q.v.*), originally a mission endeavor of the Martinsburg congregation, belong to the Southwestern Pennsylvania Conference (MC).   B.W.B.

Blanc-Rupt, France, where an Amish Mennonite congregation was formed in the middle of the 19th century by Joseph Sommer (d. 1875), Pierre Sommer (d. 1878), and Jacob Sommer (d. 1877), who broke off from the Salm congregation, then under the leadership of Elder Augsburger. The Blanc-Rupt is the upper valley of the White Saar in a remote part of the Vosges Mountains, and the congregation centered in the farms around the chateau Turquestein.

The group was weakened by the death of its first leaders, by the reconciliation of some of its members with the Salm congregation, and by emigration to America or to less mountainous parts of Lorraine. The remainder finally became a part of the Repaix congregation around 1895 under the eldership of Christian Lehmann (d. 1909). J.H.Y.

Blanchard River Mennonite Church: see **Mount Pleasant** Church.

Blandford Mennonite Church (MC) in Blandford Township, Oxford Co., Ont., has among its early family names Basinger, Newschwander, Strickler, Miller, Baer, Stauffer, and Bingeman. A frame church was erected about 10 miles southwest of the Blenheim church and one and a half miles from Bright. As early as 1851 Blandford appointments are listed in the Meeting Calendar every fourth Sunday. These meetings were served by ministers from Waterloo County. Jacob Bretz, who became minister in 1839 at Wanner's, moved to Plattsville and probably held responsibility at Blandford, although the preaching was still done by several ministers as above. He died in 1879. John Basinger was ordained deacon Oct. 22, 1865, and resided near this place of worship. He died in December 1882.

The Waterloo conference in September 1892 provided that the meetings in Blandford be held only during the six months in the summer. In 1904 the interest in this field had so far dwindled that the April Conference authorized Moses Cressman to make sale of the building. The burial place is maintained by the community. In 1917 the Conference appointed M. Cressman trustee for the Blandford church property.

Since 1938 Mennonite services in Blandford Township have revived in a church on the 9th Concession, one mile east and south of the village of Bright where there is a community cemetery. This church formerly owned by the Evangelical organization has since come under the ownership of the cemetery board to serve as a community church. Brethren from the St. Jacobs congregation, Waterloo Co., Ont., for a number of years gave regular attention to Sunday school, preaching, and visitation until a few Mennonite families moved into the community and the care of it has come under the Mennonite Mission Board of Ontario. A few converts have been won so that there is a membership of seven. This new location is three miles east of the former site and cemetery.

J.C.F.

Blankenburger Allianzkonferenz (see **Alliance**) is in part a continuation of the meetings which Robert Pearsal Smith called into being on his evangelistic tour of Germany in 1875. It was founded in 1885 for the purpose of uniting and building up all true and active Christians into one body of Christ (*unum corpus Christi*). After 1918 it held meetings in Blankenburg in Thuringia, which were attended by some German and many Russian Mennonites. Among the latter it found many zealous supporters who have made large contributions to the work. The conferences were held annually until the fifty-second session in 1938. Jakob Kroeker (*q.v.*) was an outstanding worker in the conferences; he died on Dec. 12, 1948, after a long illness. The conferences could not be resumed until 1947, and the fifty-sixth was held in 1950. The separation of the East of Germany from the West, making it impossible for visitors or speakers from the West to come to Blankenburg, made it necessary to organize special conferences for the West; 1947 Marburg, 1948 Bielefeld, 1949 Libenzell, 1950 Wiesbaden. Contacts are maintained with the National Association of Evangelicals in the United States. The annual subjects for consideration have been: in 1947, "Christ, All and in All"; 1948, "The Work of the Holy Spirit according to Ephesians"; 1949, "The Glorious Hope of the Christians, according to I Pet. 1:3—2:10"; 1950, "The Returning Lord and the Waiting Church." The executive committee in 1950 consisted of Otto Kaiser, Kassel; Friedrich Heitmüller, Hamburg; Willy Diezel, Nürnberg. The conference is sponsored by the Blankenburger Allianz, a union of a number of *Gemeinschaften,* which has always been strongly evangelical and conservative in theology as well as pietistic in spirit. (*ML* I, 226.)   E.C.

Blaser, Peter, a Swiss Mennonite from Lauperswyl in the canton of Bern, who was imprisoned at Bern on Sept 20, 1710, with 52 fellow believers. There, in January 1711, in the name of his companions, he wrote a reply to the letter of consolation from the Mennonites in Amsterdam dated Dec. 9, 1710. The Dutch Mennonites also aided the prisoners with financial support. Through their intervention nearly 500 of the persecuted Mennonites were put on five boats and taken to Holland. Peter Blaser ran away from the transport in Basel, apparently seized by homesickness. In 1734 a Mennonite named Peter Blaser again appears in the Bern court records, having escaped "from the spinning-room" after his sons had repeatedly requested his temporary release. In 1742 he reappears in the country (Müller, *Berner Täufer*). (*ML* I, 226.)   NEFF.

Blasius of Grossen, an Anabaptist martyr, "a real leader (*Vorsteher*) of the sect," was burned at the stake in Tirol in 1531. (J. Loserth, *Der Anabaptismus in Tirol,* Vienna, 1892, 500.)

Blauch, Henry H., minister of the Mennonite Church (MC) was born near Johnstown, Pa., April 14, 1828, and died at Springs, Somerset Co., Pa., on June 8, 1904. He was the son of Jacob and Sarah Blauch and a grandson of Jacob Blauch, the first Mennonite bishop of the Johnstown district. He was married to Catherine Keim on May 25, 1851, and to this union were born eight children.

He united with the Mennonite Church in early

life and took up his abode in Elk Lick Twp., Somerset Co., Pa., then known as the Casselman River district. Here he was called to the ministry by a unanimous voice of the church on Sept. 6, 1853. He served the church at this place for more than 50 years (now the Springs congregation).

Henry H. Blauch's education was mostly in the German language, but he preached in both German and English. When he was ordained to the ministry, his church numbered 22 members, but in his lifetime it increased to 250 members. For several years Blauch was the only Mennonite minister in the southern part of Somerset County.

As the congregation had no house of worship, Blauch preached in schoolhouses at various points in both his native county and the adjoining county, Garrett Co., Md. However, during his lifetime the congregation built four meetinghouses.   E.E.B.

Blaupot, a Dutch family, first residing in Appingedam (q.v.), province of Groningen, later also in Norden, East Friesland, Germany, and other places. As early as 1660 Harmen Gerritsz Blaupot is found in Amsterdam, a member and deacon of the Lamist congregation as many of his descendants were also. Uko Blaupot, of Norden, was appointed ministerial candidate at the Amsterdam Mennonite Seminary in 1733, but it is not known if he ever served a congregation. Of the Appingedam branch mention should be made of Grietje Jans Blaupot, who in 1694 gave her house to the congregation to serve as a meetinghouse, and Jan Symons Blaupot, d. 1756, a well-to-do merchant, who from 1707 for more than 50 years was a minister of the congregation. His granddaughter Hester Blaupot was married to Izaak ten Cate, the Mennonite preacher of Noordbroek, and became the mother of the well-known Dutch Mennonite historian Steven Blaupot ten Cate (see **Cate, Steven Blaupot ten**).   vDZ.

Blaurer, Ambrosius (also Blarer or Blaarer), Swabian reformer, b. April 12, 1492, in Constance, d. Dec. 6, 1564, in Winterthur. In 1510 he entered the Benedictine monastery at Alpirsbach near Oberndorf. When Ambrosius Blaurer became acquainted with Luther's writings through his brother Thomas, a law student in Wittenberg, he accepted the Protestant doctrine, resigned his office as prior of the monastery, and retired to his parental home in Constance, remaining in seclusion until the council of Constance called him to the Protestant ministry on Feb. 25, 1525. In the following year the Catholic bishop and clergy withdrew from the city.

From Constance as a center Blaurer aided in bringing about the Reformation in various Swabian cities, giving his special attention to the suppression of the Anabaptists. He sought with all his strength to secure the unity of the church and to fetter every deviation. In contrast to the Saxon and Swiss reformers he opposed the use of capital punishment in religious matters. He emphasized indoctrination; where this failed he advocated compulsion. Capito (q.v.) wrote him on Sept. 13, 1528, that there were among the Anabaptists some pious souls, whom Blaurer could, with his gentleness, convert. But most of them, Blaurer says, were maliciously intent upon re-establishing the Mosaic law. In the city of Memmingen, which had often called upon him for advice, he secured the passage of a resolution on Dec. 9, 1529, demanding the expulsion of Anabaptists who refused to accept the teaching of the preachers (Schiess I, 18).

In the other cities he apparently met some opposition to this policy; for the Memmingen (q.v.) Resolutions of March 1, 1531, passed by the Upper German cities (Biberach, Isny, Constance, Lindau, Memmingen, and Ulm) which had joined the Smalkaldian League, rejected violent proceedings against the Anabaptists; Blaurer presided at this meeting and was also given the assignment of drawing up the resolutions. Regarding the Anabaptists the resolutions state that faith shall not be spread abroad in the world by the use of the sword or force but by the sword of the mighty Word of God; force had only brought a larger following and greater respect to the Anabaptists. Only those persons should be expelled who spread error, instigated mob action, and refused the oath and military service (Pressel, 169, 182).

Blaurer seems to have come into personal contact with the Anabaptists for the first time when he was called to Esslingen at the end of September 1531. In this city there had been a group of Anabaptists since about 1527, which had been ruthlessly persecuted by the city council before the introduction of the Reformation; many of its members had been martyred. Blaurer did not recognize the right of this evangelical group to do pastoral work. The Anabaptists had to adhere and be subject to him. In a letter to Martin Bucer in Strasbourg, written soon after his arrival, he complains "that the evil of the Anabaptists, which has firmly imbedded itself here, will not easily be uprooted" (Pressel, 204). But he soon had to admit that the Anabaptists were not criminals, but had a genuine longing for God's Word. His simple manner of preaching directly to the heart won him their confidence. They were attracted to him by the determination with which he, like them, insisted upon religious earnestness and moral purity of life. This he soon discovered. Two months later, Nov. 27, 1531, he wrote to Bucer, "I treat the Anabaptists in such a way that they love me and attend my sermons regularly and attentively; most of them have desisted from their error; the rest, of whom there are very few, will presumably do the same" (Schiess I, 292). He expressed himself similarly on Dec. 23, 1531 (Schiess I, 304), and on Feb. 2, 1532 (Schiess I, 321).

Early in June 1532, after Blaurer's return to Constance, a bitter quarrel arose in Esslingen among the clergy, which alienated the Anabaptists. Church discipline as introduced by Blaurer was no longer exercised; the life of many members was offensive. These unedifying conditions caused the Anabaptists to leave the church and again hold their own religious services. Blaurer was unable to pardon this step. The unity of the church seemed threatened by their separation. "More and more I hate," he wrote to his brother Thomas, Jan. 11, 1533, "this harmful sect, which is ruinous to the unity of the church, although or precisely because they are apparently so pious and innocent. Nevertheless we are also very guilty, because we do not insist on true repentance. The unlovely conduct of so many Protestant cities takes all the pleasure out of my work and life, and I fear serious punishment" (Schiess I, 379).

After his call to the university of Tübingen (1534) we hear little more about Blaurer's steps in opposing the Anabaptists. In Tübingen he drew up an official opinion concerning the punishment of the Anabaptists, at the request of Duke Ulrich, which was presented to Philip of Hesse on June 7, 1536, in the name of the theological faculty. Referring to the Old Testament and Augustine he granted the government the right to punish them even with death. But he warned against acting rashly, for some were merely followers. Those who refused to recant could be suitably punished by a prison sentence on bread and water. The preachers of the state church should frequently visit them in the hope of converting them (Hochhut).

The hymnbook published by Blaurer between 1545 and 1548, *Ein gmein Gsangbüchle,* contains songs written by Anabaptists—Dachser, Grünewald, Haetzer, and Hut (Spitta). In 1538 he had to leave Württemberg and in 1548 he had to flee from Constance; the rest of his life was spent as preacher in Winterthur and Biel (Switzerland).   HEGE.

K. Th. Keim, *Ambrosius Blarer, der schwäbische Reformator* (Stuttgart, 1860); Th. Pressel, *Ambrosius Blaurer* (Stuttgart and Elberfeld, 1861), in *Leben und ausgewählte Schriften der Väter und Begründer der reformierten Kirche* IX; T. Schiess, *Briefwechsel der Brüder Ambrosius und Thomas Blaurer* (Freiburg, 1908) I; J. J. Hottinger, *Helvet. Kirchengesch.* III (1708) 439; Hochhut, in *Ztschr f. hist. Theol.* XXVIII (1858) 566, 586-90, 591; Fr. Spitta, article on Blaurer's hymnal, in *Ztscht f. Kirchengesch.* XXXVIII (1920) 243 ff.; *ML* I, 226.

Blaurer, Thomas, a jurist, brother of the above, wrote a defense of the execution of Ludwig Haetzer (*q.v.*), whose martyrdom had created a great stir, with the title, *Wie Ludwig Hetzer zu Costanz mit dem Schwert gericht abgeschiyden ist* (Strasbourg, 1529). (*ML* I, 227.)   HEGE.

Blaurock (Cajacob), **Georg,** one of the founders of the first Swiss Brethren congregation in Zürich, was born *ca.* 1492 in Bonaduz, a village in Grisons, Switzerland. Nothing is known about his youth, except that he was matriculated as a student in the University of Leipzig for the summer semester of 1513. From 1516 to 1518 he was vicar in Trins in the diocese of Chur; so he must have received the usual education for the priesthood. Contrary to the oft-repeated assertion, there is no proof at all that he was a monk in the Premonstratensian monastery of St. Luke in Chur. In fact, the evidence is against his ever having been a monk at all.

When we next hear of Blaurock, he stands in the very midst of the young Anabaptist movement in Zürich in January 1525. He was actually the first person to receive adult baptism soon after the disputation of Jan. 17, 1525. The Hutterite chronicle tells how he first came to Zürich to consult with Zwingli concerning the Gospel, but being disappointed in him turned to Conrad Grebel and Felix Manz to find the truth which he was seeking.

When Blaurock came to Zürich he was already married. He was apparently in his prime, with a tall, powerful physique, a fiery eye, black hair, and a small bald spot. He was known by various names. His name was actually Jörg vom Hause Jakob. Some historians call him Georg Jakobi, others Bleurond; H. Bullinger calls him Weissmantel; Johannes Kessler speaks of a Georg von Huss and a Jakobs zu Bonaduz, considering two separate persons besides Blaurock. He was popularly called "der starke Jörg" because of his faith. He became best known by the name of Blaurock. The manner of his coming to this name is related in an Anabaptist chronicle thus: "It came about that one came to them from Chur, namely a priest by the name of Georg vom Hause Jakob, who was generally called Blaurock. As they were once discussing matters of faith in a meeting, this Georg vom Hause Jakob also added his ideas. Someone asked who had just spoken; then one said, that one in the blue coat had just spoken. Thus he received the name, because he was wearing a blue coat."

Blaurock immediately joined the Zürich Swiss Brethren. The Hutterite chronicle records, "He came to them, namely to Conrad Grebel (*q.v.*) and Felix Manz (*q.v.*), and talked to them about matters of faith, and in the pure fear of God had recognized and found that it was necessary to learn a true faith, active in love, through preaching from the Word of God, . . . and to remain steadfast in tribulation until the end."

That he took a prominent part in the first Anabaptist disputation (as stated by Cornelius) is doubtful, since he would then certainly have been banished from the city with the other non-resident Anabaptist leaders, Reublin (*q.v.*), Brötli (*q.v.*), Haetzer (*q.v.*), and Castelberger (*q.v.*). Very likely he came to Zürich after the disputation. It is certain that he was most influential in the young movement, and in its entire development. It was he who by his impetuous request introduced adult baptism and thereby gave the church just coming into existence the form in which it entered the conflict with the world. The Anabaptist chronicle mentioned above reports, "And it happened that they were together until fear struck them and came upon them, and they felt compelled in their hearts. Then they began to bend their knees before the highest God in Heaven and called upon Him as one who knows the heart and prayed Him to show them mercy. For flesh and blood and human wisdom did not lead them to this act, because they knew what they would have to endure and pay for it.

"After the prayer Georg vom Hause Jakob arose and entreated Grebel for God's sake to baptize him with the true Christian baptism upon his faith and understanding and when he had knelt with such request and desire, Conrad baptized him, because there was then no ordained minister for such work. When this had happened, the others likewise turned to Georg with the request that he baptize them, which he also did upon their request, and thus in the fear of God they committed themselves together to the name of the Lord, each confirmed the other to the service of the Gospel and began to teach and to keep the faith."

With ardent zeal the newly baptized entered the battlefield and proclaimed their doctrine. "Suddenly one saw a great many people, as though ready for a journey, girded with ropes, passing through Zürich. In the market places and squares they stood and preached of the improvement of life of conversion to guiltlessness and brotherly love." More than any others, Blaurock, "The second Paul," was thus engaged. Of undaunted courage and gifted with popular eloquence, he seemed created for the purpose of carrying the new doctrine out into the widest circles of the population. To a young man whom he was trying to convert, he said, "Marx, hitherto you have been a happy young man and must now become a different man; you must lay aside the old Adam and put on the new one and reform your life." To Thomann, an old man, he said the reverse; viz., that since he was an old man, near death, he should reform. Even more than through their words, Blaurock and his friends found adherents among the people through their manner of life.

With Grebel and Manz, Blaurock went from house to house as an "apostle of the Swiss Brethren," according to Acts 2:38-41, and from congregation to congregation to baptize, to administer communion and unify the Brethren. Their following grew visibly and with it their strength and boldness. On Sunday, January 29, 1525, Georg Blaurock appeared with a group of his followers in the church in Zollikon (*q.v.*) and stopped the Zwinglian assistant on his way to the pulpit with the question what he was going to do there. When the preacher answered, "Preach the Word of God," Blaurock said, "Not you, but I am sent to preach." Soon afterward (January 30, 1525) Felix Manz, Georg Blaurock, together with 25 natives of Zollikon were arrested and imprisoned in a room of the Augustinian monastery in Zürich. Upon a vow of peace, repayment of costs, security of 1,000 florins, and with the reprimand that they had done wrong and had dealt unreasonably offensively against God and their neighbor, they were released. Only Blaurock and Manz were detained in order to answer further before the commission.

Blaurock defended himself in a letter to the council, in which he says among other things, that Christ the Lord sent His disciples out to teach all peoples and gave them power to grant remission of sins, and as an outward sign of forgiveness to baptize them. When he too taught this, some had turned to him in tears and asked him to baptize them. This he could not refuse them, but had administered baptism to them according to their wish and called upon the name of Christ for them, and then further taught them love and unity and community of all things, as the apostles (Acts 2) demand, and that they should always be mindful of the death of Christ and not forget His shed blood, had showed the practice of Christ in the Last Supper, and had then broken bread together and drunk wine, so that they might remember

that they are all redeemed by one body of Christ and cleansed by one blood, and they were thus each the brother or sister of the other in Christ the Lord.

When he was cross-examined, Blaurock declared that he did not know anything to the contrary, but that he was the first to have himself baptized and eat of the Lord's Table, as God had given it to the disciples at the Last Supper, and had always in both respects met the wishes of those who desired them. Of Zwingli he said that he did violence to Scripture, and falsified it more than the "old pope." He offered to answer for this statement before the council or wherever they wished. On Feb. 18, 1525, the council decided that Georg von Husen of Chur be dismissed upon promise of peaceful conduct and then be appropriately dealt with later on. Blaurock, released Feb. 24, returned to Zollikon, where he held two meetings on Sunday, Feb. 26, for 200 persons. He baptized Heinrich Aberli (*q.v.*) in Jakob Hottinger's (*q.v.*) house, greeting him, according to Aberli's report, with the words, "God be praised that we all believe on Jesus and want to remain steadfast in this faith! Brother Heinrich, do you testify that the Lord Jesus Christ suffered for us and that what is written concerning Him is true?" When he answered affirmatively Blaurock baptized him "with a handful of water." The other meeting was held in Hans Maurer's house, in Zollikon, where he baptized those who desired it, including some women who received the rite with tears in their eyes.

Upon being informed of this meeting the council had the brethren seized individually and on March 11, 1525, determined that "anyone who had let himself be baptized since the affair in the Augustine monastery was to be fined a silver mark, and anyone who would in the future be baptized was to be expelled immediately with his wife and children." On March 16, nineteen Zollikoners were arrested. The trial, which lasted till March 25, revealed that Brotli, formerly of Zollikon, now living in exile, had sent to the Brethren there two letters to strengthen them in their faith. These letters asserted that Grebel and Manz were by no means defeated; no one knew with certainty that he had been baptized in infancy; the pope had instituted infant baptism; those who fall into sin should be banned; paying interest and tithes was right, etc. At the same time the Brethren of Zollikon sent a letter to the Zürich council, asking them to let the Word of God reign freely, to turn their attention to those who were willing to hear the Word, so that those who wished to obey the Word could be released from tribulation, and the council could have their wishes satisfied. They also requested that a public disputation be arranged, so that it might be disclosed who was in error.

Thereupon the council appointed a second Anabaptist disputation to be held March 20, as part of the hearings. The Brethren, especially Manz and Blaurock, who were still in prison, were to debate particularly the question of baptism with three secular priests and six members of the council. The principal speaker on the side of the Brethren, Conrad Grebel, was not present; from January to late April he was in Schaffhausen, St. Gall. Zwingli dealt extremely bluntly with Georg Blaurock, calling him a "great, foolish dreamer," so foolish that he was unable to read the German Testament before the council, although he had been a monk for several years; a fool, who in his presumption counted no one a child of God unless he was a "madman" like himself.

The disputation was without decisive results. The council proceeded more severely; it ordered that the Brethren be "very seriously spoken to"; they were to desist from "their harmful separations." Some fell away; Manz and Blaurock declared to the emissary of the council without circumlocution that they intended to stand by their interpretation and if the heavenly Father required them to baptize in the future they would baptize. Blaurock persistently refused to obey the demand to leave the country. Thereupon the council decided on March 25, 1525, that Blaurock and his wife should be shipped by boat to Chur, and a written promise be secured from the Chur authorities to keep him there. In case he would again come back, he should be rewarded in such a way that he would in the future be quiet.

The decision to expel Blaurock was apparently carried out, for Manz met him in Chur and went with him to the Zürich highlands, where to the great annoyance of Zwingli and the council, he won many adherents by his "eloquence that moved heart and senses, and which made him the favorite of the populace." His letter to Oswald Myconius belongs to this period; but this letter is lost. Zwingli calls it "so" dishonorable, shameful, prevaricating an epistle and also against the honorable council as he had never heard even a buffoon cry out against anyone." This leads to the surmise that the letter was suppressed by Zwingli and his friends.

These two leaders of the Brethren did not remain long in the Zürich highlands. In the middle of May they appeared in Chur (q.v.), Blaurock's home, where they worked to expand the Anabaptist movement begun by Andreas Castelberger, in the city as well as the canton, with considerable success, especially among the aged. Comander, the reformer of the Grisons, complains, "We must now exert all our energy against the Anabaptists; they have gathered here, and among the citizens there are many who secretly or openly adhere to them." To suppress the movement a mandate forbade rebaptism on penalty of life, honor, and goods. Consequently Blaurock and Manz were captured a few weeks after their arrival in Chur. Manz was compelled to return to Zürich with a letter dated July 18, 1525, and there he was imprisoned in the Wellenberg until Oct. 7. Blaurock was released by his numerous friends and escaped to Appenzell (q.v.), where he related to the Brethren how God had freed him from prison. This was interpreted as a fantasy and as a boast that, like Peter, he had escaped through closed doors. He apparently also spent time in the Chur prison.

After he had "restored the backslidden Brethren here, nursed the sick, and buried the dead," Blau-

rock went back to the Zürich highlands. Here he supported the work of Conrad Grebel with power and success. Beck's surmise (*Comeniushefte* 1898, 307) that he went to Basel disguised as a merchant and there participated in the disputation in Oecolampadius' house in August 1525 is not adequately supported by known facts.

Oct. 8 found Blaurock again in the Zürich highlands, apparently with Grebel. Before an audience of more than 200 he began to preach from the pulpit of the church in Hinwyl. "Whose is this place? If this place is God's, where the Word is to be proclaimed, then I am a messenger from the Father to proclaim the Word of God." When Parson Brennwald arrived he listened patiently until Blaurock began to speak on baptism. Then confusion ensued in the church. Brennwald hastened to Grüningen to report to Berger, the magistrate, and secure his assistance. When the latter arrived with his soldiers Blaurock was still in the pulpit, and was taken. Berger ordered the audience on the strength of their oath of duty to him, to take the captive to Grüningen. They refused and told him to look after it himself with his soldiers. Then Blaurock was put on a horse and led away by the magistrate and his soldiers. The populace, old and young, followed curiously. But he sang and was quite cheerful on his horse. The procession came upon a second Anabaptist meeting in Bezholz, attended by Grebel and Manz, the latter having been released from the Wellenberg the day before. Grebel was seized, but Manz managed to escape and was captured three weeks later, Oct. 31. All three, together with other Anabaptists, remained in prison, first in the castle in Grüningen, then in the Hexenturm prison in Zürich, until their escape on March 21, 1526.

The council was determined to put an end to the "corner-preaching and the rabble-rousing" that had spread through the county of Grüningen. Repeatedly the prisoners were cross-examined. A succession of incriminating witnesses arose against them, Zwingli first, then Leo Jud, Dr. Sebastian Hofmeister (q.v.), Provost Brennwald, and others, who accused them of "stirring up and seducing the populace, of mocking the regulations of the state and of the new church, its protegee, and trying to erect a separate church, whose task it was to overthrow the existing divine and human order."

Zwingli (as Beck reports), who boasted of having frequently asked the council not to make the Anabaptists suffer for their reviling and their wanton speech, and not to penalize them in body or in possessions, was on this occasion unable to avoid expressing his surmise, on the strength of all sorts of information at third hand, in which he apparently had complete confidence, that he believed it to be the serious intention of the Anabaptists to increase their numbers in order to overthrow the government. He said it was and always had been their idea, as he knew, to create a separate church of their own, to which only those who knew themselves to be without sin, should belong. He learned (he said) from a trustworthy man that Blaurock had boasted in Wyl of peculiar visions in which God revealed to him the great persecutions the children of God would have to endure and that he was to contend valiantly against the enemy of God; those who would not be baptized he called heathen.

Provost Brennwald reported that Blaurock had said in the church at Zollikon, that when there were a sufficient number of them so they could resist the council, let them see whether they could conquer them with a little squad. How little sedition there was in this statement is shown by the evidence of another witness, the canon Antoni Walder, who reported that he heard and understood them to say that in case the council of Zürich should proceed forcibly against the Brethren of Zollikon, they should not fear, nor care about force, but remain valiant and steadfast.

Blaurock defended himself most effectively against these charges: (saying) the statements attributed to him about inciting the populace to revolt were untrue; it was not true that he had boasted of miracles and visions at Wyl and of escaping through closed prison doors; he had not sworn to remain out of Zürich territory, for he would rather die than forswear God's earth, for the earth is the Lord's. Concerning the government, he thought that we should examine ourselves, as Paul says; we should work at the reform of our hearts and the perfection of our lives; then we will not need a government. In respect to the church, it had always been his opinion that all corrupt persons, all who lived in open sin and vice, were to be excluded and were not to consort with Christians. He did not favor community of goods, but a Christian will share his possessions, or he is not a Christian. (Manz asserted that this was also his view of community of goods: a good Christian would share with his neighbor if he was in need.) Since his last imprisonment he had not baptized in the canton of Zürich, but would do it at any time upon request. He admitted having openly accused the Zürich theologians of misleading the people and doing violence to Scripture, and in this sense being thieves and murderers according to John 10:1, where Jesus says, "He that entereth not by the door into the sheepfold [i.e., the church of Christ], the same is a thief and a robber."

In this state of affairs the council thought it best to institute a new disputation, which the Grüningen officials had also requested. This third Anabaptist disputation took place Nov. 6-8, 1525, in Zürich. Dr. Balthasar Hubmaier (*q.v.*) was to be the spokesman of the Brethren. But he was prevented from coming, since he was seized on his journey from Waldshut by Austrian soldiers and compelled to return to Waldshut. Thus as before, Grebel, Manz, and Blaurock were again responsible for defending their position against Zwingli, Leo Jud, and Grossmann. On the day's program were the three resolutions of Zwingli: (1) As children of God, the children of Christians shall not be refused baptism; (2) As in the Old Testament circumcision, so in the New Testament baptism shall be given to children; (3) Rebaptism has no basis, no example, no verification in God's Word.

For the course of the debate we must depend alone on the report of their opponents. According to their opinion and the verdict of the council it ended in the absolute defeat of the Brethren. But they did not feel by any means defeated, and complained loudly and bitterly about lack of freedom of speech and the mockery. The preachers had to hear many a word that aroused their displeasure. Thus Zwingli was addressed with, "You, Zwingli, have always resisted the papists with the statement that what is not founded on God's Word is not valid; now you say that there is much which is not in the Bible but is nevertheless of God. Where is now the positive word with which you opposed the suffragan Faber and all the monks?"

The council was entirely on the side of Zwingli and the Reformed preachers. It warned the Brethren seriously "to desist from their undertaking which had been openly proved fallacious." When this warning was not accepted, they were again imprisoned in the new tower. On Nov. 18, 1525, they were sentenced to be held in the new tower on mush, bread, and water as long as was pleasing to God and considered wise by "my lords." No one but the regular servants was to be admitted to them.

Grebel, Manz, and Blaurock were imprisoned in the tower in Zürich in accordance with the mandate of Nov. 18, 1525. Throughout the winter, additional Brethren were captured and added to the number in the tower. Hubmaier does not seem to have been placed in the same prison when he was imprisoned later in the winter. Grebel, according to reports, took advantage of the opportunity to strengthen the Brethren in prison by reading the Scripture and admonishing.

On March 5 and 6, 1526, the whole company of prisoners was given a second trial. The record of the trial reports very little about Grebel and Manz, and only a brief "confession" or letter from Blaurock. It is worthy of note, however, that Grebel requested permission to have a "writing" printed. On March 7 all the prisoners were again sentenced, this time to life imprisonment. Apparently the second trial was held for the purpose of preparing for the new and severe mandate which was issued against the Anabaptists on March 7, 1526. In this new mandate rebaptizing was sternly forbidden, and death by drowning was set as the punishment for all those who performed it.

But the lifelong imprisonment lasted only 14 days, for on March 21, 1526, all the prisoners escaped by means of a rope through an unlocked window. Grebel, Manz, and Blaurock at first were unwilling to take advantage of the opportunity but finally let themselves be persuaded. The drawbridge happened to be down; so they all got over the moat without any trouble. Two of the prisoners, William Exel of Wallis and Fridli Abyberg of Schwyz, elected to remain in the city and were caught again; through them the whole story of the escape became known and was entered upon the records. It is interesting to note their report that when the fleeing prisoners discussed whither they might go, some of them humorously suggested, "Let us go to the red Indians across the sea."

Whither the prisoners actually fled is not known in detail. Fourteen days after the escape Manz baptized a woman at Embrach, which lies north of Zürich in the county of Kyburg. In June 1526, Blaurock and Manz appeared in Grüningen according to an official report from that district. Grebel, however, was not with them. On Oct. 12, 1526, Felix Manz, together with Jakob Schupfelberg of Grüningen, was captured in St. Gall, but apparently released again, for on Dec. 3, 1526, Manz and Blaurock were arrested together in Grüningen. After a month's imprisonment in Zürich, Manz was executed by drowning on January 25, 1527, as the first martyr of the Anabaptists in Zürich.

Blaurock was treated as a non-resident, and as it could not be proved that he had violated the law of March 6 in the canton of Zürich he fared better. His sentence read, "Georg vom Hause Jakob, called Blaurock, who as a true instigator and chief agent of Anabaptism has previously been held in the dungeon of my lords and in hope of future improvement and that he would cease his erroneous plan of Anabaptism was graciously released, since his mere word was accepted without an oath as he wished it, yet he disregarded this; and although it was told him in clear words that if he ever returned into the realm and territory of our lords he would receive the penalty he deserved, he has nevertheless come back, and, even though he says he has not baptized since then, he has accused the preachers of doing violence to and falsifying Scripture in spite of the disputations, whereas rebaptism is altogether in opposition to and prejudicial to the Scripture as well as to common good usage, which has been preserved unanimously throughout all Christendom, and (rebaptism) has thus far created only offense and insurrection, he should for this seditious character, meeting in mobs and misconduct against Christian government and Christian authority be mercifully sentenced thus; the executioner shall be ordered to remove his clothing to the waist, tie his hands, and then beat him with rods from the Fish Market down the street to the gate in Niederdorf, . . . he is then to be banished under oath, the penalty for return being death by drowning."

On the day of Manz's execution this sentence was carried out. When Blaurock reached the gate at Niederdorf he refused to give the oath, saying that God had forbidden it. Then he was threatened with further imprisonment in Wellenberg to await further action by the council. "When Blaurock saw this he took the requested vow, and shook the dust off his clothing and shoes over the city."

Blaurock never returned to the canton of Zürich. But he nevertheless continued to aid the Brethren with word and deed. The petition of the Grüningen Brethren to the Diet of June 4, 1527, that "They be permitted to stay by the truth," is erroneously thought by Beck to betray Blaurock's views and phrasing, indicating his co-operation. It is, however, not certain that he took part in the compilation of the seven articles of Schleitheim (q.v.), as Beck assumes.

In January 1528 Blaurock went to Bern (q.v.)

with seven other Brethren to take part in the disputation that took place there Jan. 4-27; they were, however, not admitted, but were put in custody in the Dominican monastery. At the close of the disputation a trial was set for Jan. 17. Five preachers, including Zwingli, and the commander Schmidt tried to convince them of their error. They succeeded with Vinzenz Späting, but the others stuck to their opinion and were expelled.

The expelled Brethren went to Biel in the canton of Bern. There had been a large congregation here for some time, which owed its origin chiefly to Blaurock. They met secretly and quietly for their services, at first in the oak forest near "the big stone"; then when they were banished from this place, at Bittenberg near St. Bartholomew. But neither darkness nor mountains could shelter the poor Brethren when the government of Biel, pressed by Bern, decided to suppress them. March 9, 1528, it issued the edict which banished them; upon the streets and in the pulpits it was announced, threatening severe penalty upon anyone who offered them assistance or shelter.

Perhaps Blaurock now returned to the Grisons and was able to unfold a successful career in concealment. He seems also to have extended his influence to the canton of Appenzell. There he stepped once more into the open. On April 16, 1529, the high bailiff and the council of the canton of Appenzell wrote to Zürich requesting information concerning the recently imprisoned Georg Blaurock, as they were planning to sentence him on April 21 for baptizing and reappearing contrary to orders. Apparently the sentence was banishment and the threat of death upon returning.

Blaurock did not again enter Switzerland. In May 1529 he was in Tirol. The Anabaptist group which had formed at the Adige Valley and the Eisack had lost their preacher, Michael Kürschner, through death at the stake on June 2, 1529, in Innsbruck after long suffering. When Blaurock heard that the Brethren longed for God's Word he spared himself no trouble or danger to go at once to the orphaned congregation. With Hans Langegger of Ritten, a Tyrolese weaver, he traveled through Vintschgau, strengthening the Brethren everywhere and founding new congregations, as at Glurns, Schlanders, Meran, and Bozen as far as the solitudes of Ritten and to Clausen.

Blaurock's field of work was extensive—extending from Clausen to Neumarkt. His chief centers were Clausen, Guffidaun, Ritten, Vels, and Breitenberg near Leifers, below Bozen. In one of these places after the other where believers assembled from round about he held meetings, preaching and baptizing. At Clausen the Brethren from the Achtel, the Velturn, the mines of Mt. Pfunderer and Clausen met. As a rule meetings were held on holidays and at night across the bridge in the principality of Guffidaun. They could not keep such great numbers concealed long.

To escape pursuit Blaurock frequently changed the places of meeting, never avoiding the most strenuous journeys. Thus in June 1529 we find him in Vels, Tiers, in the ravines of the Kunder road and on Breitenberg. In July he held meetings at Ab-Penon, in the district of Kurtatsch, then at Vils near Neumarkt, and finally at Tramin on the Moos, where many believers received baptism. He was apparently most successful in Clausen; it was his favorite stopping-place, to which he returned after each trip, until the middle of August 1529.

Meanwhile the Innsbruck authorities had done their best to seize Blaurock and to suppress the Anabaptist movement entirely. They threatened to depose the manager (*Pfleger*) of Guffidaun unless he immediately put an end to the "mischief." He therefore redoubled his efforts to capture the leaders. On Aug. 14, 1529, he was able to report to the authorities that he had succeeded in capturing "two real leaders and Anabaptists, Georg von Chur and Hans Langegger," and imprisoning them in the Guffidaun castle. There he had questioned them and was now sending the report of the "indicated damnable and other heretical opinion and sects" they had confessed to, and requested the government to send such persons elsewhere to be tried on the rack and sentenced. The decision of the government, Aug. 19, stated that he should have proceeded according to the mandates against the two prisoners, since it was found that they were the actual leaders; but as this had not happened, he now received orders to question the Anabaptists and report who had baptized them, how many Brethren there were and who they were, and whether they had baptized, and not to spare them. But in order that this might take place with greater dignity, they had ordered Augustin Heyerling, the manager of Ritten, to be present at the trial, and had sent him secret instructions accordingly.

The poor prisoners were then cruelly tortured on Aug. 24, 1529, and the statements extorted from them were reported to Innsbruck. Thereupon Preu received the command on Aug. 26 to sentence the two captives, since they held to their faith, on the following Monday, Aug. 30. But when Preu answered that it was not his duty to take life, Sigmund Hagenauer, the judge at Rodeneck, was directed to sentence them according to the content of the mandates.

On Sept. 6, 1529, Blaurock and Langegger were burned at the stake in Clausen. "On this day," the brief report of Preu states, "Jörg Chur and Hans Weber were sentenced and executed because of their heretical faith."

The *Martyrs' Mirror* (D 21, E 430) gives a more detailed report: "About this time in 1529, Georg von dem Hause Jakob, named Blaurock (after he had spread and proclaimed the doctrine of the truth for two or three years in Switzerland and especially in Tirol, whither he himself had traveled, so that he could put his talent to interest and with his zeal for the house of God might be a tool for salvation) together with his companions was captured at Guffidaun and not far from Clausen was burned alive with fire, and indeed for the sake of the following articles: because he left his priesthood and the position he served in the papacy, because he considered infant baptism nothing and

preached a new baptism to the people, because he repudiated the Mass, as also the confessional as it was ordained by the clergy, and also that one must not call upon and worship the mother of Christ. For this reason he was executed, and as is fitting for a knight and hero of faith sacrificed body and life for it. When he was on the place of execution he spoke earnestly to the people and pointed them to the Scriptures."

The reasons cited here for the condemnation of Blaurock were quite different from those given in Zürich. Whereas sedition was chiefly emphasized in the charges there, here it was his falling away from the Catholic priesthood, from the Catholic Church, his repudiation of the Mass, the confessional, and the adoration of Mary that marked him as a criminal worthy of death. His pure, warm religious zeal, his deep moral earnestness were unassailable even by his most ruthless enemies.

Georg Blaurock was one of the noblest martyrs of the Christian Church. For the brotherhood he helped to found he cheerfully sacrificed everything, honor and respect, freedom and comfort, property and goods, wife and child, body and life for the sake of his Lord and Saviour. Under the sign of adult baptism he gave the brotherhood its actual reason for existence in the world.

"Manz and Blaurock," says a historian of the Grisons, "did not disappear without a trace. Their glorious goals—freedom of religion, liberty of conscience, the equality of all citizens before the law have become for our fatherland the most precious legacy of our fathers." Georg Blaurock is also known as the author of church hymns. Two of his songs are in the *Ausbund* (q.v.). Wackernagel has included them in his important work, *Das deutsche Kirchenlied*, perpetuating his name in the history of German hymnology. They are beautiful hymns, distinguished in form and content. The first, No. 5 in the *Ausbund*, begins with the words, "Gott führt ein recht Gericht und niemand mags ihm brechen." It consists of 33 stanzas and is an excellent hymn of faith. The second, No. 30 in the *Ausbund*, is his "swan song." It has 13 stanzas and is a moving testimony to the courage of his faith and his joy in the face of death.   NEFF.

Beck, *Geschichts-Bücher; idem,* "Georg Blaurock und die Anfänge des Anabaptismus in Graubünden und Tirol," published by J. Loserth in *Comeniushefte,* 1898, 295 ff.; *Gem.-Kal.* 1901; C. A. Cornelius, *Geschichte des münsterischen Aufruhrs* II (Leipzig, 1860); E. Egli, *Aktensammlung zur Gesch. der Züricher Ref.;* E. Egli, *Die Züricher Wiedertäufer zur Reformationszeit* (Zürich, 1878); J. C. Füsslin, *Beiträge zur Erläuterung der Kirchen-Ref.-Gesch.* (Zürich, 1741-53); J. Kessler, *Sabbata (Mitteilungen zur vaterländischen Gesch.* V, VI); R. Nitsche, *Gesch. der Wiedertäufer in der Schweiz* (Einsiedeln, 1885); Rob. de Porta, *Historia reformationis ecclesiarum Rhaeticarum* (Lindau and Chur, 1771 and 1774); Wackernagel, *Kirchenlied;* F. Jecklin, "Jörg Blaurock vom Hause Jakob," in *Jahresbericht der hist. antiq. Gesell. von Graubünden* XXI; Th. de Quervain, *Kirchliche und sociale Zustände in Bern unmittelbar nach Einführung der Ref.* (Bern, 1906) 120; O. Vasella, Von den Anfängen der Bündernerischen Täuferbewegung," in *Ztschr. f. schweiz. Gesch.* 1939; *BRN* VII; *ML* I, 227-34.

Blauwaert, Jan Matthijs: see Jan Matthijs van Middelburg.

Bleikers, Johann, of Crefeld, one of the earliest German immigrants to America, who arrived in America Oct. 6, 1683, with his family on the *Concord* (*ML* I, 234). He was a Quaker, but had previously been a Mennonite.   HEGE.

Blenckvliet, van, a former Mennonite family in the Netherlands, originally from Flanders. The members of this family were found in Haarlem, Rotterdam, and Dordrecht. In Haarlem Elisabeth van Blenckvliet and her husband Jaques van Damme in 1640 founded the old people's home called the Zuiderhofje, and in 1643 Elisabeth, then a widow, liberally endowed the orphanage of the Flemish congregation of Den Blok, founded 1634, and gave it an order. Jacob Arents van Blenckvliet was a preacher of the Old Flemish congregation of Rotterdam about 1635, while Adriaen Leendertsz van Blenckvliet was at the same time a deacon of this church. Fictoor Jans van Blenckvliet was a representative of the church of Dordrecht at the Flemish conference held at Haarlem in 1649.   vDZ.

Blenheim Mennonite Church (MC), on a county line road between Waterloo and Oxford counties in Ontario, serves the Mennonite families of the Ontario Mennonite Conference in the most southwesterly portion of Waterloo County. The congregation was organized in the year 1839 and until 1850 when the church was built, services were held in a schoolhouse near by. The land for church and cemetery was bought from Peter Erb. An addition to the church was built in 1859. In 1887 the building was moved slightly eastward and veneered with brick. During the summer of 1901 it was torn down and a new brick building erected. New Hamburg is the nearest town, four miles north. The ministers who served this congregation were Jacob Hallman, 1836-78; Joseph Nahrgang, 1878-1903; Isaiah Rosenberger, 1897-1907; Moses H. Shantz, 1907-38; Moses N. Baer, 1939-47. In 1953 the bishop in charge was Curtis C. Cressman. The deacons who served here were Jacob Bock, John Cressman, David Bergey, Gilbert Bergey, Omar Cressman. Arnold Cressman has been the minister since 1951.

The first evangelistic meetings were held by John S. Coffman, in 1891. The first Sunday school was organized in 1885. By 1953 the membership had grown to 93. (L. J. Burkholder, *Brief History of Mennonites in Ontario,* Toronto, 1935.)   J.C.F.

Blesczevoda, a village in Galicia, where there was a Mennonite congregation in the 19th century, which was later merged with the Lemberg congregation. (Mannhardt, *Jahrbuch* 1888, 78; *ML* I, 234.)

Blesdijk, Nikolaas Meyndertsz van, b. early in the 16th century in Blesdijk, Dutch province of Overijssel, attached himself early (1536) to Menno Simons and adhered zealously to his Christian doctrine. Ten years later he joined David Joris (*q.v.*). He was an educated man and thus became not only a warm partisan and admirer, but also the best qualified and effective defender of this remarkable Anabaptist leader; he clung for a long time to the conviction that Joris "was wakened by God, and that his writings came from the divine Spirit, that, indeed, no person could be compared to him"

(Nippold, 537). Nippold's idea that he is identical with Meynert von Emden (*q.v.*) is incorrect, for he was much younger than the latter (Vos, 66).

In 1544 Blesdijk already had to defend his master's cause. He attempted to save the Jorisite martyr Jurjen Ketel (*q.v.*) by writing a summary of Davidian doctrine to the Deventer council and offering to defend it in every city beyond imperial jurisdiction. His step was ignored. In 1544 he wrote *Billijcke Verantwoordinge ende Eenvoldige wederlegginghe op eenen Scheltlasterighen Brief door Dr Hier. Wilhelmi . . . teghens die heylsame leere D. J. aen weylandt Joncker Karel van Gelder geschreven.* It was printed in 1640 without naming the place of printing. Of greater significance was his appearance at the Lübeck disputation held in 1546, which was to be a debate between the Mennonites and the Jorisites. Besides Menno Simons and Blesdijk there were present Dirk Philips (*q.v.*), Leenaert Bouwens (*q.v.*), Gillis van Aken (*q.v.*), and Adam Pastor, in addition to several adherents of David Joris. Blesdijk debated with Gillis four hours. They argued principally about infant baptism; but instead of union, greater tension and hostility was the result.

In answer to Menno Simons' letter "to some persons who formerly agreed with me, but now think otherwise," Blesdijk wrote in 1546 *Christelijcke Verantwoordinghe, Ende billijcke nederlegginge des valschen onghegrondeden Oordeels, Lasterens ende Scheldens by Menno Symonsz, in eenen Sendtbrief wtgegeven . . . ,* printed in 1607 without naming place. This book includes three articles (Nippold, 534-44) and gives an unusually interesting view into the controversy and the points of opposition between the Mennonites and Jorisites.

In the same year (1546) Blesdijk published another book, *Weder-antwoort op zekeren Brief by Gellium onderteeckent, waer in hy sijne meyninge unde oordeel stelt op eenich Trachtaet geintituleert Een Christelijcke verantwoordinghe unde billijcke wederlegginghe* (published without place in 1607). In this book Blesdijk defends the action of the Jorisites in having their children baptized in the Reformed Church in order to be as inconspicuous as possible.

In the following year (1547) Blesdijk published a new book, *Eenvuldighe unde Christelijcke Berichtinghe op vijf Vraghen by eenighe van Men. Sym. gesintheyt voorgestelt* (without place in 1607), in which he answers these five questions in succession. The most important of these are, "Why does one not observe communion in the brotherhood?" and "Why is baptism, which is a command of the Lord, now neglected?" Blesdijk explains these signs of the covenant as outward ceremonies which have lost their meaning in the age of perfection which David Joris was called of God to proclaim.

Of particular importance is his book published in the same year (1547) with the title, *Hooft-Somma unde Gront van't gene wy wt die Leere D. J. hebben connen verstaen* (published without place in 1607). Here he gives a systematic presentation of the doctrine of David Joris (Nippold, 553-56).

Not long after the publication of these books

Blesdijk went to Basel, where David Joris was living in concealment under the name of Jan van Brugge. He married Joris' eldest daughter, Susanna, in 1550 or 1551. For some years he remained closely connected with his father-in-law. But gradually increasing doubts concerning the genuineness and significance of the revelations of the fanatical Anabaptist leader and the purity of his moral conduct began to alienate him. This is shown in the letters of Joris to his son-in-law, especially the one dated 1556 (Nippold, 591).

As yet there was no open dissension between them; but the defection of his most important adherent must have been a deep shock to Joris. His failing health could not withstand this blow. He died Aug. 25, 1556. Now Blesdijk expressed his opposition toward his father-in-law. In four tracts which he published in January, February, April, and May 1557, he attacked his teaching and especially his claim that his revelations were above those of the Bible. This is indicated by the verbose titles of these tracts, which have themselves been lost. (The titles are found in Nippold, 606.) Two of the four tracts were addressed to individual followers of Joris.

But even these polemics did not cause a complete split between Blesdijk and the Jorisites; this did not occur until two years later. Betrayal by a servant led to the discovery of the Jorisites. This created a great stir in Basel. Nobody thought or suspected that the highly respected family of Jan van Brugge belonged to the accursed sect of Anabaptists. Joris' corpse was exhumed and burned at the stake for heresy. His family and his adherents were imprisoned and subjected to a severe cross-examination, then dismissed upon the promise to make a confession of the true faith in the church and condemn the doctrine of the sect of the Anabaptists and have no more fellowship with them or their adherents. On June 6, 1559, they performed this penance.

Blesdijk escaped with a trifling loss. His books were confiscated while he was traveling to Holland to enlighten his fellow believers there and in North Germany. When he returned he immediately went to the preachers of the city and confessed to them his former error and his present belief. He was then placed in custody, but was on the whole leniently treated. He had presented the principal tenets of the Jorisites in 13 points, which were handed to the government and furnished it with a highly welcome foundation for both legal action and especially for the formulation of the refutation of Jorisite doctrine, which was drawn up in 11 points (Nippold, 615).

Soon afterwards Blesdijk moved to Freinsheim in the Palatinate as a Reformed preacher; he died there in 1584. Before his departure from Basel he composed his famous biography of David Joris (1559 and 1560), which he calls a part of a larger work on Anabaptism, which has unfortunately been lost. But this biography of Joris is our most important source for his teaching and life; it is written in Latin and has the title, *Davidii Georgii Holandi haeresiarchae vita et Doctrina* (Basel, 1559).

There are translations of this book in German (Basel, 1559) and French (Basel, 1560), and a new edition was printed in Latin in 1642 with the title, *Historia vitae, doctrinae ac rerum gestarum Davidis Georgii Haeresiarchae. Conscripta ab ipsius genero Nicolae Blesdikio. Nunc primum prodit in lucem ex musaeo Jacobi Revii, Daventriae 1642.*

In Freinsheim Blesdijk maintained friendly connections with his wife's relatives living in Basel. But his hostility to David Joris increased, as is eloquently shown in the refutation of the fallacious teachings of his father-in-law written in 1576 in behalf of the Palatine Church Council. The book itself is lost; we know of it only by Ubbo Emmius' mention of it. According to him this was the sharpest accusation published against Joris. It is possible that the pamphlet printed in Stade 1582 in Dutch translation, *Die gantsche Leeringhe van David Joriszoen int corte begrepen, tot nut van de onpartevdighen,* is a translation of this Palatine booklet.

NEFF.

Fr. Nippold, "David Joris von Delft, Sein Leben, seine Lehre und seine Sekte," in *Ztscht f. d. hist. Theol.,* 1863 and 1864; K. Vos, *Menno Simons* (Leiden, 1914); *DB* 1864, 130, 136; 1906, 3, 48; R. H. Bainton, *David Joris, Wiedertäufer und Kämpfer für Toleranz im 16. Jahrh.* (Leipzig, 1937); *ML* I, 235 f.

Blessum, a village in the Dutch province of Friesland. Here there was formerly a Mennonite church which probably came into existence between 1600 and 1620 or earlier. It was never large; about 1700 it had 32 members. It apparently also had little money, for throughout the 18th century it had to be supported by the Frisian Societeit. On May 24, 1764, it asked the Amsterdam church for help in building a church, for which it needed 1,000 additional florins. But in 1821—it had then only 30 members—it united with the Baard (*q.v.*) congregation. But only 23 of the 30 members transferred to Baard; the rest joined the Reformed Church.

J.L.

DB 1905, 29; 1909, 52; *Blaupot t. C., Friesland,* 188, 245, 306; *Inv. Arch. Amst.* II, No. 1545; H. J. Buse, "De verdwenen Doopsgez. gem. in Friesland," in *Vrije Fries* XXII (1915) reprint pp. 7-9; *ML* I, 236.

Bleyker, de, a family name. This Dutch family, which presumably stems from Flanders, has provided a large number of Dutch Mennonite preachers. A Jacob de Bleyker (or Bleeker) was a preacher in Sommelsdijk in 1693.

Jan Cornelisz de Bleyker, b. Nov. 1707, at Zierikzee, d. May 10, 1783, at Alkmaar, was called as a preacher to the Mennonite congregation of Aalsmeer in 1738, having probably served the Sommelsdijk congregation previously. He served in Aalsmeer, 1738-47, and in Alkmaar, 1747-83. His three sons were also Mennonite ministers: Michiel (1734-88) at Amsterdam (*q.v.*); Cornelis (1736-1816), preacher at Kolhorn and Barsingerhorn, 1758-70, and Twisk, 1770-96; Jacob (1754-90), preacher at Langendijk and Koedijk, 1780-81, at Oudesluis, 1781-90.

Michiel's son Jan de Bleyker (*ca.* 1765-1832) was also a preacher. He served the Emden congregation, 1792-93, Helder and Huisduinen, 1793-98, Ouddorp, 1798-1808, Aalsmeer, 1808-10, Huizinge and Westeremden, 1810-14, and again **Ouddorp,**

1814-24. With his son Michiel (1793-1875), who was a book dealer in Rotterdam and a deacon of the Mennonite church there, the male line of the family died out. (*DB* 1889, 84-89; 1907, 152-69; 1908, 106-15; *N.N.B.Wb.* I, 371 f.)   vdZ.

Bleyker, Michiel de, b. 1734, baptized Nov. 20, 1755, at Alkmaar, died Aug. 29, 1788, in Amsterdam. He studied at the Zonist seminary under Prof. Petrus A. Smidt and in December 1756 he became the preacher at Twisk. From October 1763 to May 1781 he was preacher at West Zaandam Nieuwe Huys, and from that date until his death he served the Zonist congregation at Amsterdam. He is the author of the following books: *Verhandeling wegens den aanleg, aart en't regt der waterlantsche . . . Sociëteit in Noord-Holland* (Amsterdam, 1766); *Aanmerkingen op de aanteekeningen van C. Vethman* (Amsterdam, 1766); *Immanueel beschouwd in vier kerkleerredenen* (Amsterdam, 1788); *Drietal van kerkleerredenen* (Purmerend, 1781); *Na-reeden bij wyze van Aanmerkingen over de verhandeling wegens de Natuur van onsen Middelaar* (Amsterdam, 1781); *Achttal leerredenen* (Utrecht, 1791). (*N.N.B.Wb.* I, 372; *Catalogus Amst.,* 145, 220, 247, 249; *ML* I, 236.)   K.V., vdZ.

Blickensdörfer, the name of a Mennonite family of Swiss origin, now found in South Germany and the United States. Its name derives from the hamlet of Blickenstorf in the parish of Baar, Switzerland. Its earliest proved appearance is in 1412 in Hedingen in the canton of Zürich.

The progenitor of most of the present-day bearers of the name is Hans Jakob Blickensdörfer, who settled on the Kohlhof (*q.v.*) in the district of Ludwigshafen (Palatinate) as hereditary lessee. Several direct descendants are still living on the Kohlhof or are members of that congregation even though they may live at some distance. Others moved at an earlier or later date into the regions of the Sembach and Friedelsheim congregations. In 1748 and 1753 four sons of Hans Jakob Blickensdörfer (Johannes, Ulrich, Christian, and Jost) emigrated to the United States. None of these continued in the Mennonite Church; so the family is not found among the Mennonites in America. One joined the Moravian Church at Lititz, Pa., and one the Dunkard (Brethren) Church, changing his name to Blickenstaff.

Georg Blickensdörfer (1754-1833), a grandson of the progenitor, was chosen elder in 1790. He was married to Magdalene Neff, a daughter of Peter Neff, elder of Assenheim. Also later on there were numerous interrelationships between the two families. He is considered the founder of the Kohlhof congregation, which met for the first time as an independent congregation in 1791 under his leadership. With the Herrnhuters (especially their settlement in Neuwied) he maintained active contacts which are to some extent still functioning.

Samuel Blickensdörfer, a great-grandson of the above, b. Jan. 3, 1848, at the Kohlhof, d. June 25, 1926, in Auerbach a.d. Bergstrasse, married to Katherine Krehbiel of the Weierhof, educated at the Basler Missionshaus and the university of Basel,

became a teacher at the school at Weierhof in the Palatinate, serving from 1874 to 1876. For the next three years he served the Kaiserslautern congregation as their first theologically trained minister. In 1879 he accepted a call to the Sembach Mennonite Church and in 1899 to the Friedrichstadt (Holstein) Church, remaining there until his retirement in 1920.

There are at present about 50 Mennonites with the name Blickensdörfer living in South Germany.
          P.S.
R. Wihr, *Die Rehhütter Chronik* (Ludwigshafen, 1937); *Gem.-Kal.* 1928, 34 ff. (biographical sketch with picture); *Menn. Adressbuch* (Karlsruhe, 1936); Jacob Blickensderfer, *Hist. of the Blickensderfer Family in America* (1899).

Bliem, Matthäus, weaver and preacher of the Mennonite congregation at Friesenheim in the Palatinate, died about 1740, published an extract from Gerrit Roosen's (*q.v.*) book, *Christliches Gemütsgespräch von dem geistlichen und seligmachenden Glauben und Erkenntnis der Wahrheit, so zu der Gottseligkeit führt in der Hoffnung des ewigen Lebens,* 1702, under the title, *Auszug aus Gerhardts Roosen, gewesenen Lehrer der Mennonitengemeinde Altona bei Hamburg, bestehend aus 35 Fragen und Antworten bei Information zur christlichen Wassertaufe.* It was used for a long time as a catechism in the South German churches (*ML* I, 236).   NEFF.

Blija, a town (pop. about 1,200) in the Dutch province of Friesland, where a Mennonite congregation was founded between 1600 and 1610, or even earlier. After a visit by the traveling elder, Jan Jacobsz, in Blija, a second church was formed here adhering to the Jan-Jacobsgezinden, which existed until 1767 and then merged with the other congregation. Later on Blija united with Holwerd (*q.v.*), retaining its own management for a time. The Blija congregation had about eight (1950) members in the town and vicinity. The church, built in 1806, was thoroughly renovated in 1853-54, but it was sold in 1935, the last service being held in it on Feb. 15, 1935. Every second Sunday the Mennonites of Blija attend services in Holwerd.
          J.L., vdZ.
Blaupot t.C., *Friesland,* 160, 164, 223, 306; *Ned. Arch. voor Kerkgesch.* XI, 227; *ML* I, 237.

Blijdenstein, an old Mennonite family which came to the Netherlands from Westphalia, Germany. Berndt and Adam van Blijdenstein were hatters in Burgsteinfurt (*q.v.*) in Westphalia. Berndt's house was destroyed by imperial troops in 1635. His widow obtained citizenship for herself and her children in the Overijssel town of Ootmarsum. His grandson Berent Berentsen van Blijdensteijn (1664-1705) settled in Enschede, Dutch province of Overijssel, in 1690 and married Maria Paschen, the daughter of a noted Mennonite family. Their sons Berent (1695-1755) and Benjamin (1701-74) founded a mercantile business (linseed, clothing). A son of Benjamin, Jan Bernard Blijdenstein, b. Feb. 18, 1756, at Enschede, d. there Dec. 10, 1826, founded the firm of Blijdenstein and Co., still existing (manufacture of textiles, later also banking). He was a well-educated man and had a good library which included the works of Menno Simons. The change in the Mennonite attitude toward government and the state is seen in the fact that in 1786 Jan Bernard accepted office in the Citizens' Council (*Burgercomitee*); in 1798 he was a representative in the legislature of the Batavian Republic (as the Netherlands were then called); and he was burgomaster of Enschede until 1819. He married Geertruida Schimmelpenninck, a Mennonite of Almelo.

Another noted member of this large family was Albert Jan Blijdenstein (March 15, 1829-Feb. 28, 1896) of Enschede, a grandson of the above Jan Bernard Blijdenstein. In addition to being a pillar in the Mennonite congregation, a codirector of the family weaving mills and director of the banking firm Blijdenstein and Co., established in 1801, he also served the community as a member of the provincial States of Overijssel (1866-78) and as a member of the upper chamber (1878-95). Furthermore, he was for many years chairman of the chamber of commerce in Enschede. He was deeply interested in sylviculture and was famous for his expert knowledge of trees; he took the initiative in the large-scale reclamation of waste heaths and was the founder and first chairman of the well-known Dutch Heath Society (*Nederlandse Heidemaatschappij*).

Abraham Blijdenstein was a Mennonite preacher; he served the congregations of Zwolle 1700-11, Enschede 1711-23, and Kampen 1723-27; he died in 1727.

Izaak de Stoppelaar Blijdensteyn, a Mennonite minister, was also a member of this family. From 1838 to 1857 he served successively the congregations at Mensingeweer, Enschede, and Sneek, and died at Sneek in 1857. (*Uit het verleden der Doopsgez. in Twenthe,* Borne, 61, 93-114; *Ned. Patriciaat* XXXIII, 1947, 7-54; *N.N.B.Wb.* I, 375.)

vDZ.

Block, Theodor Heinrich, an outstanding educator among the Mennonites of Russia, b. Nov. 9, 1885, at Rückenau in the Molotschna, a son of the teacher Heinrich Block, received his training at the Gnadenfeld Zentralschule and in the normal classes at Halbstadt, and spent four years (1907-11) at the Russian teachers' seminary in St. Petersburg. He taught as follows: 1904-7 elementary school; 1911-14 Gnadenfeld Zentralschule; 1915-20 Halbstadt Zentralschule, also Halbstadt girls' Gymnasium and Halbstadt Teachers' Seminary. With Peter J. Braun and K. A. Wiens(?) he served as official reporter on schools at the 1917 All-Mennonite Congress.

In 1920 Block fled from Russia, reaching Germany in December 1921 after a most difficult route through Turkey, Bulgaria, Rumania, and Czechoslovakia. From March 1922 to August 1923 he taught at the Ziegler boys' school at Wilhelmsdorf in Württemberg. In 1923 he married Else Belz of Stuttgart and was the father of six children. At that time he settled in Oberursel, where he served under the Deutsche Mennoniten-Hilfe (DMH) 1923-26 as administrator of the Lechfeld transient Mennonite refugee camp. In 1925-32 he worked for a life insurance company, then returned to teaching at Jüch-

sen near Meiningen, where he joined the NSDAP and became *Ortsgruppenleiter*. After 1936, when he appeared on the membership list of the Hamburg Mennonite Church, all trace of him has been lost. He published a number of volumes of poems: *Hungerlieder* (Bad Homburg, 1922); *Auf dem Pegasus durch die Assekuranz* (Berlin-Charlottenburg, 1930); also in May 1925 a poem celebrating the fourth centennial of the Mennonites (*Menn. Bl.*). For the *Mennonitisches Lexikon* he wrote numerous articles on the Mennonites of Russia. E.C.

Bliss United Missionary Church, Levering, Mich., was organized in approximately 1872. In 1948 Mrs. C. A. Neil was in charge of the congregation, which had a membership of 12. C.A.N.

Blok, Den (Vlaemschen), name of a well-known former meetinghouse of the Mennonites at Haarlem, Holland, in which the Flemish (later united Flemish, Frisian, and High German) congregation held its meetings for more than two centuries. In 1671, when a quarrel arose in this congregation, the meetinghouse was divided into two parts by erecting a stone wall in the middle of the building, in order that each group could use one part of the meetinghouse. (*DB* 1863, 143-44; the year 1670, mentioned here, is wrong, must be 1671.) vDZ.

Blokzijl, a town on the shore of the former Zuiderzee in the Dutch province of Overijssel (pop. 1,400 in 1947). Blokzijl was an insignificant village until it was made a fortress in 1580. By 1580 there was already a congregation here, which grew rapidly from this time on. In 1585 those who belonged to the shippers' guild were exempted from the oath; many Mennonites were at that time in the guild. Here the Dutch Mennonites found a place of safety at a time when a large part of the province was still in the hands of the Spaniards.

In the first half of the 17th century most of the population of Blokzijl was Mennonite. In 1656 the Mennonites furnished a loan to deepen the harbor; and three Mennonites accepted positions on the *Raad van Negen* (council of nine), which looked after the affairs of the harbor. In 1675 the Mennonites had acquired the right to appoint one of their number as *directeur van de Diepenningen* (director of the Diep pennies, the Diep being the approach to the harbor). All of this indicates the size and the influence of the congregations.

About 1700 there were three Mennonite congregations in Blokzijl. One of these was Flemish, sometimes called the *Huiskoopers* (*q.v.*). Claes Claesz (*q.v.*), a well-known elder and author, was a preacher here in the first half of the 17th century. On the old church formerly used by this congregation are still the words, *Pax huic domini, 1629.* About 1645 this congregation received a new church on the Noorderkaai. Its representatives were among the signatories of the Dordrecht Confession (*q.v.*) in 1632. In this congregation, which later also maintained an orphanage (now the sexton's home), the old strictness in the use of the ban and avoidance gave way to more moderate concepts in the course of the first half of the 17th century; consequently the congregation sided with the Lamists (*q.v.*) in 1665. The congregation was then called the "United Flemish, Frisian, and High German Mennonite congregation at Blokzijl." It is sometimes also known as the United Flemish and Waterlander congregation; but we must not draw too many inferences from this name, for there was no Waterlander congregation in Blokzijl, even less than a Frisian or Flemish. Toward the end of the 17th century very liberal ideas were proclaimed in the Noorderkaai congregation; in 1685-86 its preachers were accused of Socinianism (*q.v.*), but were acquitted. The preacher, Jacob Hendriks (Brouwer), who had written a book in 1698, *Onderwijs naer den Wegh ten Hemel*, was held in prison for nearly a year and was charged a severe fine. About 1700 a split occurred in the congregation, in which most of the members withdrew (see below), leaving scarcely 60, one third of whom had to receive financial support; they received financial assistance from Amsterdam and Haarlem in 1706. Little is known about the affairs of this congregation during the 18th century. In 1771 the church was burned down and was replaced by a new one in 1772, Amsterdam again lending its aid.

During the decade in the middle of the 19th century a new split took place, when the preacher, Volkert de Graaf, with a few members of the congregation, including the deacon, Adriaen Stuurman, joined the Moravian Brethren (Herrnhuter) in 1742, and began to hold Moravian services; in 1755 he broke his connections with the Moravians, though Adriaen Stuurman (d. 1763) and other Mennonites continued to support them. In 1786 this congregation called its first trained minister, namely, Jacob Ruertsz Veenstra.

The second congregation, which arose between 1650 and 1679, perhaps by dividing from the first, belonged to the Danzig Old Flemish (*q.v.*). This congregation, which had always been small, and of which no particulars are known, died out in 1782.

The third congregation was formed by a large number of members of the first congregation, who left out of dissatisfaction with its liberal preaching. They joined the Zonists and in 1700 built a church on Breestraat. In 1702 it had a membership of 260; because of the decline of the shipping industry in Blokzijl the number decreased to 123 in 1754.

In 1802 the Noorderkaai congregation united with the Breestraat congregation, so that there was now only one Mennonite congregation in Blokzijl, with about 165 members in 1810. The church on the Noorderkaai was no longer used; the church on Breestraat is still in use by the congregation. The congregation possesses a rich collection of silver communion utensils dating from about 1800-20 (5 cups and a bread plate) and also a silver vessel for baptism. It acquired an organ in 1858. The town is steadily declining, and with it the congregation. In 1840 there were still 140 members; in 1898, 162; in 1915, 90; and in 1950, 69. The congregation kept its Zonist character; it did not at first join the Algemeene Doopsgezinde Sociëteit, and did not care to use the Mennonite hymnal, but adopted the Reformed hymnal instead.

Besides the church at Blokzijl the congregation

has a subsidiary church on the Wetering, about an hour's walk from Blokzijl, where preaching services are held every two weeks. A Sunday school for the children, a women's circle, a youth's circle, and a girls' club are active in the congregation. The congregation belongs to Ring Zwolle. In the last half century the ministers have been J. W. van Stuyvenberg, 1897-1903; G. Hofstede Gzn., 1903-35; S. J. Verveld, 1935-40; H. J. Franken, 1942-45; Jacob Thiessen since 1946. vDZ.

Blaupot t.C., *Groningen* I and II, *passim; Inv. Arch. Amst.* I, 595; II, 1265, 1546-67; II, 2, Nos. 27-35; F. J. Stuurman, "De vroegere Mennisten-gemeenten in Blokzijl," in *Zondagsbode*, Nov. 13 and 20, 1939; *ML* I, 237.

Bloody Theater, or Martyrs' Mirror, . . . The (Dutch, *Het Bloedigh Tooneel, of Martelaers Spiegel . . .* ; German, *Der Blutige Schauplatz, oder Märtyrer-Spiegel. . . .* The first part of the title is seldom used): see **Martyrs' Mirror.**

Bloomfield, a village, population 30, of Dawson Co., Mont., located about half way between Glendive and Richey, is situated about 50 miles from the east border of the state and about 110 miles south of the Canadian border. It is the center of two Mennonite congregations—the Red Top Mennonite Church (MC), four miles east of Bloomfield, and the Bethlehem Mennonite Church (GCM), ten miles northeast of Bloomfield. Mennonites (MC) have recently been moving to Glendive while General Conference Mennonites have been moving to Richey and Glendive. Both conferences have mission stations in Glendive. G.G.D.

Blooming Glen Mennonite Church (MC), located in a village by the same name in Bucks Co., Pa., is affiliated with the Franconia Mennonite Conference. The original name was Perkasie, derived from Perkasie Manor, on which the first meetinghouse was built in 1753. When William Penn opened Perkasie Manor for settlement in 1735, among the earliest Mennonite settlers were Henry Funk, Christian Lederach, John Funk, Andrew Godshall, Valentine Kratz, and Hoopert Cassel. Familiar names such as Moyer, High, Hunsberger, Kulp, Rickert, Hunsicker, Yoder, Alderfer, Landis, Rosenberger, and Bishop came later. The name Perkasie was retained until about 1885, when the village name was changed to Blooming Glen.

As the congregation grew in number, larger meetinghouses were built in 1823, 1882, 1925 (addition), and 1938. The present church is a brick building with a seating capacity of 1,000 in the main auditorium.

The first minister who served at Blooming Glen was probably Abraham Swartz of Deep Run. The first preachers ordained for the congregation were probably Jacob Meyer (1758) and Samuel Meyer (1769). Later outstanding leaders were Isaac Oberholtzer, who was senior bishop in the Franconia conference at the time of the Oberholtzer schism in 1847, and Henry Rosenberger, who served the congregation as minister, 1885-95, and as bishop, 1895-1921. It was the support and leadership of Henry Rosenberger that brought about such significant innovations as the Sunday school (1887), evangelistic meetings by John S. Coffman (1896),

English preaching by Henry Anglemoyer (1900), support of foreign missions in India (1899), sewing circle (1915), Sunday evening services (1911), support of a foreign missionary (1918).

During the ministry of Wilson R. Moyer (1921-51) and Melvin A. Bishop (1930-53) the following new activities were introduced: (1) singing classes taught by J. W. Yoder and L. D. Hunsicker; (2) teachers' meetings (1921); (3) winter Bible school (1935); (4) summer Bible school (1946); young people's meetings (1948); (5) junior sewing circle (1945). Some changes in the form and order of worship services were made in 1949. The traditional introductory sermon (*Vorrede*) and the testimony following the sermon (*Zeugnis*) were discontinued and weekly Sunday morning services were introduced.

During an interim Paul Lederach served as pastor (Jan. 1951-Oct. 1952) and as bishop, serving conjointly with Joseph Gross (Jan. 1951-May 1953). David F. Derstine, Jr., was ordained as pastor in October 1951. Two deacons, Norman Moyer, ordained in 1921, and Franklin Alderfer, ordained in 1938, also serve the congregation.

Several changes in administration and organization took place during this more recent period (1951-53). Among them were (1) a quarterly workers' meeting; (2) the election of a board of five trustees; (3) the organization of a Christian Workers' Band with its various activities and projects for young people; (4) schedule of Sunday evening services to include a monthly song service, a C.W.B. meeting, a young people's meeting, and a church service; (5) by agreement with the Franconia Board of Missions and Charities responsibility was assumed for a mission outpost at Bridgewater Corners, Vermont. Several families moved into the area to assist with the activities, and the congregation agreed to supply the workers and regular support for Abram Landis, the pastor.

The congregation with the Sunday school and the young people's meeting support five adults and four children of missionary families, and the pastor and his wife of the Bethany Mennonite Church at Bridgewater Corners. Pastoral support of the home pastor was adopted by the congregation in 1951, and a home for the pastor was built in 1953. A very active Sunday school supports a number of mission projects and activities.

The Blooming Glen congregation, numbering 450 members, is the largest in the Bucks County district of the Franconia Mennonite Conference. Situated in a thriving farming community, it is largely rural in character. It includes also a number of businessmen, merchants, factory workers, and several doctors, nurses, and teachers. A large percentage of the young people attend high school and an increasing number of them enroll in church schools and colleges. A number of the young people of the congregation are now serving in various missions, church institutions, and relief projects both in the United States and in foreign countries. Q.L.

Bloomington, Ill., is a city of over 33,000 population located in McClean County in the heart of the Illinois corn belt. Most of the Mennonites living in the area are farmers and members of the Central Conference and the Evangelical Mennonite Conference, with churches in Normal, Meadows, Flanagan, Danvers, and Carlock. Mennonite institutions of the area include the Mennonite Hospital at Bloomington, the Old People's Home at Meadows, and the Salem Children's Orphanage at Flanagan. (W. B. Weaver, *History of the Central Conference Mennonite Church,* Danvers, Ill., 1926.) L.E.T.

Bloomington (Neb.) United Missionary Church had a membership of 40 in 1949. M.G.

Blösch, Emil, Dr., b. Jan. 11, 1838, at Burgdorf in the canton of Bern, d. Nov. 3, 1900, as professor of theology at the university in Bern. Under the title, *Zur Geschichte der Wiedertäufer,* he published in the *Archiv des historischen Vereins des Kantons Bern* XII (1889, 282-307) the sketches of the debate of Pastor Joh. Rud. Phil Forrer at Langnau with the Anabaptists there in 1621, mentioned by Müller (*Berner Täufer,* 118). In his work of two volumes, *Geschichte der Schweizerischen Reformierten Kirchen* (Bern, 1898), Blösch gives a rather detailed description of the Anabaptists, with an attempt to do them justice. (*ML* I, 237.) NEFF.

Blosser (Blaser, Bläser, Blasser), a Mennonite family name found in Switzerland as early as 1710. At that time Peter Blaser was a Mennonite prisoner in Bern. Later, on Aug. 27, 1739, Peter Blaser arrived in Philadelphia. Christian Blaser was in a group arriving in Philadelphia on Aug. 31, 1750. The family first settled in Pennsylvania and descendants moved to Virginia, Ohio, Indiana, Iowa, and other states, but are now found chiefly in Virginia and Ohio.

Prominent in this family was Preacher (MC) Noah O. Blosser (1859-1936) of New Stark, Ohio. John Blosser (1855-1921) (*q.v.*) of Rawson, Ohio, a bishop and evangelist, was an influential member of the Ohio conference (MC). Perry J. Blosser (1876-   ) of South English, Iowa, was ordained a bishop at the Liberty Church (MC) in 1929. Eugene Blosser (1916-   ), son of Perry J. Blosser, is a Mennonite missionary to Japan.

A Genealogical History of the Blosser Family as Known in America (Dayton, Va., 1903) was written by S. H. Blosser. More recently Mrs. Eli Blosser published *Blosser Family History* (North Lima, Ohio, *ca.* 1934), which contains 51 families and traces the descendants of Peter Blaser, the immigrant of 1739. H.H.HAR.

Blosser, John, b. Aug. 5, 1855, in Putnam Co., Ohio, d. July 28, 1921, in Hancock Co., Ohio. In 1869, with his widowed mother, the daughter of Bishop John Thut, and with his brothers and a sister, he moved to Hancock County where in 1876 the family helped to found the New Stark Mennonite Church (MC). On Dec. 26, 1876, he was married to Magdalena Brenneman, daughter of Bishop John M. Brenneman. They were the parents of three sons and four daughters. Declining to pass through the lot after an earlier ordination in the congregation had proved unsatisfactory, he was ordained to the ministry as the unanimous choice of the congregation in 1891 and to the office of bishop in 1905 (MC). In his early ministry, usually at great personal sacrifice, he devoted much time to evangelistic work. His efforts were singularly successful. In 1906, for example, following his series of meetings at West Liberty, Ohio, 17 young people chiefly from Amish Mennonite families united with the Bethel Mennonite Church. He was president of the Mennonite Book and Tract Society for a number of years and took a leading part in the Ohio Mennonite Conference and in the Ohio Sunday School Conference and various phases of church and young people's activities. He was much interested in the Christian education program of the church and in every effort for the welfare of her young people. His strong conviction of the potential value of the Elkhart Institute and especially of Goshen College as a means of stimulating missionary interest and of preparing young people for Christian vocations led to his election to the Mennonite Board of Education in 1901 and president of the Board in 1902. He served on the Board for 19 years and as president for 15. All of his children attended Goshen College; four graduated. His eldest son, C. B. Blosser, was a science instructor at Goshen College for 15 years and also served as dean.   J.S.U.

Blossers (MC), Nappanee, Ind. At an unknown date, possibly in the 1870's, a log meetinghouse was erected for the convenience of the Mennonites of the community in Harrison Twp., Elkhart Co., Ind., about 10 miles southwest of Goshen. So far as is known, the group which worshiped there was never organized as a separate congregation, nor did they have resident ministers; in 1887 it was reported that the Blosser church was "supplied by ministers from the surrounding districts" (Cassel). After the Wisler (*q.v.*) schism of 1871 in the Yellow Creek congregation (*q.v.*), the Wisler (Old Order) Mennonites used the Blosser meetinghouse as well as the Yellow Creek church building. The original log structure was replaced by a frame building about 1892. In 1949 the Old Order Mennonites enlarged and remodeled this frame building, and added a basement. The group who worship at Blossers are not organized as a separate congregation, but are a part of the Yellow Creek Old Order congregation.   J.C.W.

Blosser's Printing Press was founded by Abraham Blosser (1827-91), a lay member of the Mennonite church (MC), at his farm home located one mile southeast of Dale Enterprise, Va. A building approximately 15x30 ft., which was used as a printery, is still standing. His main publication was the *Watchful Pilgrim*, an eight-page semimonthly independent paper. The first issue was printed on Aug. 1, 1880, and was likely continued until 1888. David A. Taylor served as typesetter.

Blosser also printed his own tracts as well as his own English translation of Peter Burkholder's booklet entitled *Eine Verhandlung von den äusserlichen Wasser-Taufe* . . . (Harrisonburg, Va., 1816). He also did custom work.   H.A.B.

Blough Mennonite Church (MC) was the first Mennonite church established in Conemaugh Twp., Somerset Co., Pa. Located near Davidsville, it had its origin after Jacob Blough was ordained to the ministry in 1804. He was ordained bishop in 1814. The congregation is using its fourth building, three of them having been on the present grounds. The congregation belongs to the Southwestern Pennsylvania Conference and was the first to entertain the conference after its organization in 1876. Harry C. Blough, bishop, and John A. Lehman, minister, are now (1953) serving this congregation of 221 members.   A.K.

Blount, Richard, a preacher of the Brownist-Anabaptist group of Edward Barber (*q.v.*) in Amsterdam, was baptized by immersion in 1643 by the Collegiant Jan Batten, at Amsterdam. This was the beginning of baptism by immersion as the only acceptable method among the group now called Baptists.   vDZ.

J. G. de Hoop Scheffer and W. E. Griffis, *History of the Free Churchmen* (Ithaca, 1922).

Blue Ball, Pa., is a village located on the original Jacob Weaver 1723 tract in the Weaverland (Weberthal) district. In 1766 Robert Wallace bought of Jacob Weaver II a 12-acre tract and built the store and tavern "at the sign of the Blue Ball." It has been a town of retired Mennonites, and a Mennonite center for machine shop products, agricultural implements, and more recently banking. Weaver's Book Store and the Weaverland churches are near by. It is the center of a dense Mennonite settlement. The population is about 500.   I.D.L.

Blüetl, Hans, a Hutterite martyr, was captured on a missionary journey at Ried in the Innviertel (at that time Bavarian, now Austrian) in the house of a pretended brother who wished to receive the reward for his capture, was burned at the stake June 24, 1545, after futile attempts had been made by cunning and torture to make him abandon his faith. Even on the faggots he proclaimed the Gospel to the spectators. With great courage he endured the fiery death, singing hymns of praise until he collapsed. The traitor, tormented by remorse, committed suicide. An unknown author wrote Blüetl's story of suffering in a poem of 44 stanzas, "Aus Eifer der göttlichen Ehr," which appeared in the *Jahrbuch der Gesellschaft für die Geschichte der Protestanten in Oesterreich* XIII (1892) 82-91, as well as in *Die Lieder der Hutterischen Brüder* (Scottdale, 1914) 123-28. HEGE.

Beck, *Geschichts-Bücher*, 161-63; Wiswedel, *Bilder* II, 148; Wolkan, *Lieder*, 209; *Mart. Mir.* D 72, E 473; ML I, 237.

Bluffton (Ind.) Mennonite Civilian Public Service Camp No. 13 was opened east of Bluffton in June 1941. The work was under the direction of the United States Forest Service. In April 1942 the camp was moved to Medaryville, Ind., where there was the possibility of a larger work project. (M. Gingerich, *Service for Peace,* Akron, 1949.) M.G.

Bluffton, Ohio, is a village of 2,000 inhabitants, located in the northeastern corner of Allen County. It was surveyed in 1837 under the original name of Shannon, but in 1872 the name was changed to Bluffton. It is the home of Bluffton College (*q.v.*), the First Mennonite Church (*q.v.*), the Evangelical Mennonite Church (*q.v.*), and the Bluffton Community Hospital. The hospital was originally organized by the Mennonite churches of this community, but now turned over to the town and general public.

Between Bluffton on the eastern edge, and Pandora (*q.v.*), in Putnam County, seven miles northwest of Bluffton, is located the solid Mennonite Swiss community of some 2,000 members of four congregations of the General Conference Mennonite Church, one Reformed Mennonite, and one Evangelical Mennonite, the latter formerly called Defenceless Mennonite—all of Swiss extraction.

The pioneer Swiss settlers in this community were Michael Neuenschwander and family, who came here from near Belfort, France, just across from the Swiss border, by way of Wayne Co., Ohio; and in 1833 located on an unimproved timber farm, several miles northwest of the present village of Bluffton. Neuenschwander was followed the next two years by other Swiss, some by way of Wayne and Holmes counties, and others directly from Switzerland and from France just across the Swiss border. These were Christian Bucher, Christian Suter, John Moser, Ursus Amstutz, John, Christ, and Ulrich Boesiger, John Luginbuhl, and Christian Steiner. During the next 20 years, from the same Swiss and French regions, and from the Swiss settlement in Wayne County, new arrivals continued to augment this pioneer settlement with such names (in their modern anglicized spelling) as Amstutz, Althaus, Burkholder, Bixel, Basinger, Diller, Gerber, Gratz, Geiger, Hilty, Hofstettler, Lugibill, Lehman, Locher, Moser, Niswander, Schumaker, Schneck, Sommer, Suter, Steiner, Welty, Zuercher, etc.

The first minister in the new settlement was Christian Steiner, an ordained minister from near Belfort, France, who, arriving here in 1835, was invited to serve as minister, and began to hold services in the homes of the settlers. Complete congregational organization, however, was apparently not effected until two years later, when Christian Suter was selected as an additional minister and Christian Basinger as deacon. As the congregation grew, and as the older ministers died, new ministers and elders were selected from the home congregation by lot, to replace the old and serve the spiritual needs of the growing community. An outstanding elder, who served the congregation during the whole of the latter half of the century, was John Moser (*q.v.*), who was born in Wayne County, but arriving here in 1852, was elected minister the next year, 1853, a year long remembered as the year of the typhoid epidemic, when 30 members died of that disease. Moser was elected elder in 1864, and served faithfully in that capacity until his death in 1908. He was the last of the old guard, a prosperous farmer, with no special preparation for his ministerial calling, selected by lot, and unsalaried. During this long period of service he saw many of the old traditions and practices

changed to the newer methods more suited to the spirit of modern times—the introduction of Sunday schools, evangelistic meetings, an educated and salaried ministry, the passing of the German language as the sole language of worship, and the sponsoring of a college. (He laid the cornerstone of Central Mennonite College in 1901.) To his credit be it said that during all these changes he guided the course of the church, amid many differences among the members, without a serious break in the solidarity of the congregation. Moser was assisted in his later years, and followed as elder, by J. B. Baer (*q.v.*), 1903-9, the well-known traveling evangelist for a time for the General Conference Mennonites; and by William Gottschall (*q.v.*), 1909-23, the last pastor of the united congregation, before the separation into the four congregations now existing.

For the first few years worship was held in the homes of the members, but by 1840 there was a demand for a meetinghouse, which was built of logs, in the midst of the settlement, several miles northwest of Bluffton, in what is now Putnam County. This building was enlarged several times later, the last time in 1876, when it was known, because it was painted white, as the "Old White Church." In the meantime as the settlement moved toward the south, the members in that region desired a second meetinghouse for that area, which was built near the present Ebenezer Church, in 1846. This building, too, was rebuilt several times, and is now known as the Ebenezer Church. In 1888 a large brick building was erected several miles north of the Old White Church, now called the St. Johns Church, replacing the former.

By 1900 a number of the members from the country had moved into the two villages of Bluffton and Pandora, and demanding first, separate Sunday-school services, and, later, special worship service, finally built separate church buildings, Pandora in 1905, and Bluffton in 1906. The Pandora church, known as the Grace Church, formed an independent organization at this time, but the Bluffton church, known as the First Mennonite Church, remained a part of the main congregation until 1918, when it, too, became independent. When the St. Johns congregation also formed a separate organization in 1923, what had once been a single compact congregation now had separated into four, each with its own pastor and constitution—Grace, First Mennonite, St. Johns, Ebenezer.

This large Swiss church was not without its internal difficulties during the early years. Numerous outside influences frequently attempted to break the solidarity of the church with special religious practices and controversial ideas. In 1844 the followers of John Herr of Pennsylvania, the Reformed Mennonites, gained a few followers, who formed a new organization some years later and finally built a meetinghouse in 1876 near the Old White Church. In 1846 John Thut, who had arrived as a minister from the (old) Mennonites in Holmes County, after unsuccessfully attempting to introduce footwashing in connection with the communion services against the wishes of the other ministers, withdrew, and with a few followers organized a separate congregation, affiliating with the (old) Mennonites, under the name of the Zion congregation. The church usually went by the name of the American Mennonites locally, no doubt, to distinguish them from the large Swiss group, though the Zion group was composed largely of the same Swiss ancestry as the others. They erected a church building five miles west of Bluffton in 1857. The congregation was dissolved in 1925, and most of the remaining members joined the First Mennonite Church in Bluffton.

A little later, in 1884, Abraham Steiner, a minister in the Zion Church, because of some differences with other members, invited Henry Egli, the founder in Indiana some years before of what was known for a time as the Egli Church, to hold a series of meetings in near-by schoolhouses. Egli, who stressed especially a more emotional and evangelistic type of religious life than that practiced by either the Zion or Swiss congregations at the time, secured a number of followers from both groups, and organized what was known as the Defenceless Church, with a meetinghouse built in 1886 between the St. Johns and the Reformed Mennonite churches. This meetinghouse has recently been removed to Bluffton where the congregation now worships. The name has, however, been changed from Defenceless Mennonite to Evangelical Mennonite.

Some time later the Missionary Church Association found entrance into the membership of the Defenceless Church, and have occasionally gained a few scattered members from the other churches. They have congregations now both in Pandora and Bluffton. These defections have not grown large numerically and have not greatly influenced the course of church activities of the main Swiss body.

These Swiss Mennonites, coming as they did largely from the small farms in the foothills or the plateau of the Jura Mountains in Switzerland and the near-by Alsatian region just across the border, brought with them and retained here for the larger part of the century all the traditional religious practices and social customs of the Mennonite small farmer in the homeland. Life here at first was not easy. The timber on their small farms had to be cleared, markets were far away, and conveniences were few. Their religious life was equally simple. Their ministers were chosen by lot from the laity, without special preparation or education except that received by a few months' attendance in the winter in the little log schoolhouse in the neighborhood, and they served without salary. Religious worship was inclined to be formal and lengthy. The long prayers, the lengthy hymns from the old hymnal led by a *Vorsänger* in a slow tempo, the sermon, and the testimony of all the ministers and deacons present as to the soundness of the truth as delivered by the preacher of the day, all this took several hours of time. Discipline was strict. Excommunication for the breaking of the moral law or church regulations was not uncommon. Among the violations thus punishable were moral lapses, outside marriage, membership in a secret society, and others. Avoidance and footwashing, however, two controversial practices which were the source of a great deal of trouble all through Mennonite history, were not practiced by the church. Throughout the Civil War and up to World War I in 1917, they remained consistently nonresistant, both in theory and practice. The language of the pulpit remained German well into the beginning of the present century, though English is now used exclusively. But the Swiss dialect is still commonly heard on the streets of Pandora and Bluffton in everyday conversation by the middle-aged and older men and women.

With the exception of the social contacts and interchange of ministerial visits with their fellow Swiss communities in Wayne County, and Berne, Ind., the local Swiss church remained independent of any other church affiliations until well toward the close of the century. Changes were gradually taking place, however. Sunday schools were introduced in the late seventies. In 1893 the congregation entertained the session of the General Conference Mennonite Church, at which time it joined that conference. Members were moving to town. Both J. B. Baer and Gotschall were men of special training. Young people's meetings were introduced and mission interest stimulated. Young men were beginning to go to college and enter various professions, though few of these ever returned either to the church or home community. In 1900 this congregation together with the other congregations of the Middle District joined in the founding of Central Mennonite College. Today the four congregations which grew out of this original settlement are among the more progressive members of the General Conference. From this community have gone out within this recent period more than two score of missionaries, over a score of ministers serving in other fields of service, a number of doctors and lawyers, businessmen, high school teachers, college professors, and a number of leaders in political life, including several judges, one congressman, and one United States senator, the latter of whom lies buried in the Ebenezer cemetery. Not all of these were, of course, members of the Mennonite church. The following Mennonite congregations are now (1953) found in this community: General Conference—Ebenezer, 507; St. Johns, 230; Grace, 442; First Mennonite, 523; Reformed Mennonite, 50; and Evangelical Mennonite (Defenceless), 54.   C.H.S.

E. J. Hirschler, *Centenary Hist. of the Swiss-Menn. Churches of Putnam and Allen Counties, Ohio* (1937); D. Gratz, *Bernese Anabaptists* (Scottdale, 1953).

Bluffton College is an outgrowth of what was originally known as Central Mennonite College, founded in 1898 by the Middle District of the General Conference Mennonite Church, and located at Bluffton, Ohio. As early as 1896, the Middle District, at its conference session at Noble, Iowa, appointed a committee of three men—N. C. Hirschy of Wadsworth, Ohio, J. F. Lehman of Berne, Ind., and J. B. Baer of Bluffton, Ohio—to investigate the possibility of establishing a school of higher learning under Christian influences for the educating of the young people of the church. The committee, later increased to 7, believing that a conference with only 3,000 members was not large enough to finance a satisfactory school of this nature, first investigated the possibility of uniting in an educational project with the (old) Mennonites, who had just inaugurated a school at Elkhart, Ind., called the Elkhart Institute. The effort was unsuccessful, however.

At the conference session of 1898, held at Danvers, Ill., it was decided to found the institution, and Bluffton, Ohio, was selected as the location. The first building was erected in 1900, and the school was opened Nov. 5 of the same year, under the name of the Central Mennonite College. N. C. Hirschy was elected president, and D. F. Janzen of Elkhart and I. B. Beechy of Bluffton were added to the faculty. Others were added later for part-time work. Although called a college, the school offered only academy subjects, with additional courses in commercial subjects and music. There were 29 students on the opening day, nearly all from the local community, increased to 48 by the end of the year, 30 of whom had registered in the academy and the remainder divided between the commercial and music departments.

The growth of the school was slow, due to several factors. The development during the period of the growth of high schools everywhere was making the work of the academies increasingly unnecessary; the small membership of the Middle District Conference was not able to support a college efficiently; and unfortunately there was not sufficient harmony between the leaders of the school and local church community. There was continual expansion, though slight. In 1902 the junior college was added, giving two years of college instruction, with four students the first year. In 1904, the Herschler estate, valued at $40,000, was added to the endowment fund. In 1907 Edmund Hirschler joined the faculty, and a little later S. K. Mosiman, a former missionary to the American Indians, and but recently returned from Germany where he had been granted a Ph.D. degree from Jena.

Because of the handicaps above mentioned, the year 1908 was a critical year for the college, and a turning point in its history. President Hirschy had resigned his office, to be succeeded a little later by S. K. Mosiman; and William Gottschall from Pennsylvania became the pastor of the local congregation, thus bringing in new leadership to both the college and the church. The special independent college church congregation was liquidated, and a special endowment fund of $60,000 was planned, and later raised.

In spite of this new lease on life, however, it was doubtful whether the slender resources of the small Middle Conference were sufficient to promise any hope of developing the school into a full-fledged college. By 1913, the last year of the independent existence of Central Mennonite College, the total number of students registered for the year was 198, of whom 40 were registered in the junior college, and the remainder scattered through the other departments—commercial, music, Bible, and art, most of these for part time only. It is extremely doubtful whether Central Mennonite College could have survived many years longer with its slender financial and student backing had it not been that just at this time it fell heir to a new movement that greatly enlarged its constituency and financial backing.

The enlarged Bluffton College is the result of the vision of several of the educational leaders from different Mennonite groups for a united establishment of a standard college and theological seminary for all the Mennonite groups. Chief among these leaders were N. E. Byers, president of Goshen College, and S. K. Mosiman, president of Central Mennonite College. Two of the Mennonite colleges were granting college degrees at this time, Goshen and Bethel; but even these were not recognized by any accrediting agency as meeting the requirements of a standard college. There were a number of academies and Bible schools and two junior colleges—Central Mennonite and Freeman. Most of the smaller Mennonite groups had no college or school connections whatever. The movement above described had a threefold objective: (1) To provide a fully recognized standard college in connection with one of the colleges already established. (2) To unite in this common effort all the branches of the church including those smaller groups not yet supplied with educational institutions. (3) To supply the whole denomination with a theological seminary for the training of the ministers and church workers.

At a meeting held at Warsaw, Ind., on May 29, 1913, 24 of the educational leaders representing several of the larger branches of the church, decided unofficially to launch this experiment, and the following resolutions were adopted:

Resolved: That it is the sense of this meeting that an institution be established, representing the various branches of the Mennonite church, giving the undergraduate work of a standard college (courses leading to the A.B. and A.M. degrees), the theological and Biblical work of a standard seminary, and courses in music aiming at the thorough development of the musical ability of our people, and meeting the needs of our churches; and further, that the institution should be established in connection with one of the schools already controlled by the Mennonite people.

Accordingly a board of 15 directors was selected from the different branches of the church represented, and the location of the institution decided. Although Goshen and Bethel were the only Mennonite colleges at this time giving a full four-year college course, and thus the logical candidates for the new affiliation, yet neither found it expedient for various reasons to accept this responsibility; and so Central Mennonite, though but a small junior college, with an uncertain future, was chosen as the beneficiary of the new experiment, under the name of Bluffton College and Mennonite Seminary. S. K. Mosiman was retained as president of the new college, and N. E. Byers, who had resigned as president of Goshen, was elected as dean. C. Henry Smith, formerly dean of Goshen, was also added to the faculty. On Jan. 27, 1914, the board of trustees of the old Central Mennonite College, who eagerly welcomed this new turn in the affairs of the college, turned over the direction of the institution to the new board. At the same time under the direction of Dr. Mosiman, an extensive building program was inaugurated, which added to the campus within the year a central heating plant, a science hall, and a women's dormitory, the latter a gift of Mr. and Mrs. John Ropp of Bloomington, Ill., warm friends of the new movement.

As rapidly as possible the whole program inaugurated at Warsaw was put into operation, and the former junior college was transformed into a full-fledged four-year institution. During the first winter, J. A. Huffman, of the Mennonite Brethren in Christ Church, gave a course in Bible. The next year J. H. Langenwalter was selected as dean of the Mennonite Seminary, and additional members were added to the faculty as the student body grew in numbers. Under the able guidance of Dean Byers the necessary changes were soon made. Two years were added to the course of study and the first class of eight were granted the A.B. degree in 1915. In the years immediately following, G. A. Lehman was made head of the music department; the academy, up to this time the largest department of the school, was dropped, as was also the commercial department. Student organization also kept pace with the progress of the educational policies. Active young men's and young women's Christian associations were organized as was also a strong student volunteer mission band.

In 1921 the Mennonite Seminary became a separate institution, though it remained on the same campus, in close affiliation with the college. J. E. Hartzler became the first president, and P. E. Whitmer the first dean. The name was changed to Witmarsum Seminary.

In 1925, on the occasion of the twenty-fifth anniversary of the founding of the original Central Mennonite College, President Mosiman summarized the achievements of Bluffton up to that time. "The total enrollment in all departments at present (January 1925) is 395. Of these, 238 are in the college of liberal arts. Seventy per cent of the students are from Mennonite homes, and six branches of the denomination are represented; but twelve other denominations are also represented in the student body. They come from eleven different states with Ohio, Indiana, Illinois, and Pennsylvania leading in the order named. Two hundred forty-one A.B. degrees have been granted since 1914, besides a number of Master's degrees. Within the past ten years $500,000 has been collected, ninety per cent of which has come from Mennonite contributors. The eight buildings on the campus are valued at $260,000, while the permanent investments equal $367,000."

During the depression years of the middle thirties, and the war years of the early forties, student attendance was greatly reduced, and financial difficulties became severe, but the postwar years brought attendance back again to the highest point in the history of the school, approximately 400 in 1948, from 21 states and foreign countries, and the majority of them of the Mennonite faith. Since then attendance has again declined.

Students are given a large share in the government of student affairs. A student council, elected by the students themselves, assists the faculty in all matters of student discipline. The honor system applies to all student tests and examinations. The *Witmarsum* is the student college paper, and the *Ista,* the student annual. The official administration publication is the monthly *Bluffton College Bulletin.*

The curriculum is that of the usual liberal arts college, with special additional attention to religion, music, and fine arts. Twenty-one departments of study are grouped under four divisions— Christian fundamentals, arts and literature, material sciences, and social sciences.

While the college aims to be strictly broadly Christian and nonsectarian, yet in the Bible Department and among the Mennonite students, special emphasis is placed upon the traditional Mennonite faith, especially the peace teaching of the church. Among the active student organizations are two Gospel teams, one of men and the other of women; YMCA and YWCA organizations; an active peace action club; and an international relations club. A number of the faculty are members of the various boards and committees of the General Conference.

The faculty (1948) consists of 21 regular members, graduates of the leading universities and colleges of this country and abroad; and a number of part-time assistants. S. K. Mosiman, the first president of Bluffton College, retired in 1935, to be succeeded for a few years by A. S. Rosenberger. The present incumbent is Lloyd L. Ramseyer (1938-). N. E. Byers, the first dean of the college, retired in 1937 to be succeeded by J. S. Schultz (1937-54) and Robert Kreider (1954-).

The board of directors of the college consists of 16 members, 9 of whom are officially elected by three district conferences of the General Conference —the Eastern District, the Middle District, and the Central Conference. Four members are selected from the Mennonite church at large by the board itself; while two represent the alumni. There are also two advisory councils, one of men and the other of women. Dr. J. S. Slabaugh of Nappanee, Ind., has served for some years as the president of the board.†   C.H.S.

C. H. Smith and E. J. Hirschler, *The Story of Bluffton College* (Bluffton, 1925); *Bluffton College an Adventure in Faith 1900-1950* (Bluffton, 1950).

Bluffton College Bulletin, the official publication of Bluffton College, Bluffton, Ohio, was published monthly 1914-31, bimonthly 1931-42, and monthly since that date, distributed free to alumni and friends of the college.   L.L.R.

Bluffton (Ohio) Evangelical Mennonite Church was originally located about 2½ miles northwest of Bluffton but in 1940 the church was moved to its present location on South Jackson Street. In 1952 it had a membership of 60.   C.D.D.

Bluffton First Mennonite Church (GCM), Bluffton, Ohio, is one of the four congregations comprising the Swiss Mennonite community about Bluffton (*q.v.*), a member of the Middle District Conference. By 1900 a number of families of the settlement had moved into the village to enter different lines of business. They soon organized a special Sunday school for the town members, and later held occasional preaching services, first in the afternoons in the Lutheran church, and later in a rented up-town business building. By 1906 the congregation had grown large enough to justify a special building, and the present building was erected. It remained a part of the large Swiss congregation, however, and was served by the same ministers. By 1918 it asked for a separate organization, and a separate full-time minister was secured. Elmer Basinger was the first to serve in this capacity, to be succeeded in the years to follow by S. M. Musselman, A. S. Shelley, A. E. Kreider, H. T. Unruh, J. N. Smucker, and Alvin Beachy, the present pastor. The 1952 membership was 527.   C.H.S.

Bluffton Mennonite Deaconess Home and Hospital. The former Mennonite hospital in Bluffton, Ohio, had its origin in the Bluffton Sanatorium, a private stock company hospital founded by Dr. J. J. Suter, a local physician. The original institution consisted of a large brick private house remodeled into a 12-bed hospital, and an adjoining home used as a nurses' home located at Main Street and College Avenue. After several preliminary meetings of representatives of the various Mennonite churches of the Bluffton and Pandora communities, the first of which was held on April 6, 1919, it was decided to purchase the sanatorium for a hospital. The institution was formally taken over by the trustees of a newly formed nonprofit corporation on March 1, 1920, and renamed Mennonite Deaconess Home and Hospital. Special concern was expressed by the leaders of the movement that "the deaconess requirement and training shall be the prime feature of the institution." This high ideal was not realized.

From the beginning this new organization found it extremely difficult to meet the payments on its capital indebtedness and the deficits in its annual budget. Although considerable effort was put forth in financial drives and in personal solicitations, the Mennonite interests had to seek more and more aid from the local community. In recognition of this fact the name of the institution was changed to Bluffton Community Hospital in 1924. In the same year a Ladies' Auxiliary composed of a representative of each of the various churches of the city and community was formed which has given the institution active support throughout the years. In 1936 the real estate of the hospital was deeded to the city of Bluffton, and with the aid of a liberal federal grant a new hospital was built on Garau Street. This building is now owned by the city, but the hospital is equipped and administered by the trustees of the original Bluffton Community Hospital corporation and such general support as is needed is given by the Ladies' Auxiliary, the churches, the clubs, and other interests of the community.
                                                    I.W.B.

Bluffton (Ohio) Reformed Mennonite Church, called locally *Neu-Menist* and *Neu-Menite,* is located 2 miles north and 2½ miles west of Bluffton. The first meetings of the group were held in 1847, the first meetinghouse built in 1876, and the first ordained minister of the congregation took charge in 1882. In 1948 the membership was 47. John Steiner, Lima, Ohio, is the minister. The predominant family names in the congregation are Basinger, Steiner, Neuenschwander, and Nussbaum. J.L.K.

Blumenfeld, Blumengart, Blumenheim, Blumenhof, Blumenort, and Blumental are very common village names of Mennonite settlements of Russia, most of which have been transplanted to Canada, Mexico, and Paraguay. Some of them had their origin in Prussia. Many of them recurred in many of the Mennonite settlements of Russia. (See **Mennonite Village Names.**)   C.K.

Blumenfeld (often called Sagornoye), a village and Mennonite church in the Brazol (*q.v.*) colony in the Russian province of Ekaterinoslav, district of Alexandrovsk. The village was founded in 1864, contained 6,611 dessiatines (*ca.* 18,000 acres), numbered (1911) 337 inhabitants and had a school attended by 20 pupils. The Mennonite congregation of the same name was organized in 1872, members of which also lived in the neighboring villages, Silberfeld and Blumenheim, and which formed a subsidiary of the Lichtenau-Petershagen church. Ministers who served the congregation were D. Janzen, G. Wiens, and P. Janzen. (*ML* I, 238.)
                                                    HEGE.

Blumengard, a Hutterite Bruderhof, six miles southwest of Plum Coulee, Man., owns a little over 4,000 acres of land, which had formerly belonged to Mennonites who migrated to Mexico. It was settled by the Hutterites in 1922, when Johann Hofer moved to the site with 15 families. In 1933 Samuel Kleinsasser was chosen preacher. In 1938 he with 11 families founded the Sturgeon Creek Bruderhof four miles north of Headingly, Man. In 1942 Jakob Hofer was chosen preacher. In 1947 Blumengard numbered 118 souls, of whom 47 were baptized members.   D.D.

Blumengart was one of the last three villages of the Chortitza settlement (*q.v.*), established in 1824 by 14 families. In 1918 the village complex consisted of about 2,700 acres of land with a population of 213. Of these, 44, mostly men, were exiled and evacuated by 1941 when the Germans occupied the Ukraine during World War II. The remaining population was evacuated to Germany in 1943. About two thirds of these were repatriated by the Russians and one third found new homes in Canada and South America. Its church record covers the period 1796-1901. In 1942 the village had a church building, a school with 45 pupils and two teachers, and a kindergarten.   C.K.

Blumenheim (also called Verbovskoye), a village in the Mennonite Brazol (*q.v.*) settlement in the Russian province of Ekaterinoslav, district of Alexandrovsk, was founded in 1869, contained 3,360 dessiatines (about 9,000 acres), numbered (1911) 80 inhabitants and had a school attended (1911) by

20 children. In Blumenheim there had also been a Mennonite congregation with the same name since 1869, a subsidiary of the Lichtenau church. (*ML* I, 238.)   HEGE.

Blumenhof, a daughter colony established by the Chortitza Mennonites for the excess population, in the district of Pavlograd (*q.v.*) in the Russian province of Ekaterinoslav (*ML* I, 238).

Blumenort, a popular village name among the Mennonites of Prussian background. The name occurred in the Molotschna, Zagradovka, Siberia, Manitoba, and Mexico settlements and the Fernheim and Menno settlements in Paraguay. C.K.

Blumenort, a village in the Russian province of Taurida, district of Halbstadt, post office Orlovo. It was one of the Mennonite villages founded in 1804 on the Molotschna. With the exception of the village shepherd, the 566 (1911) souls in 76 families were German-speaking; there were among them two Jewish families who were tailors, and four Lutheran families from the Volga region. The rest were Mennonites, whose ancestors had come from Marienburg, Elbing, and Marienwerder in Prussia. Half of them belonged to the Ohrloff Mennonite Church and half to the Rückenau Mennonite Brethren Church; a few belonged to the Lichtenau congregation. They were all farmers and owned 1,616 dessiatines (*ca.* 4,300 acres) of land. The village had a school, attended by 40 children (*Neuer Haus- und Landwirtschafts-Kalender,* Odessa, 1910, 122). At Blumenort the initial steps were taken for the institution of the Mennonite school for the deaf. (Mannhardt, *Jahrbuch* 1888, 143-47; *ML* I, 239.)   M.W.

Blumenort Kleine Gemeinde Mennonite Church is located four miles north of Steinbach, Man. It is one of the largest in membership of the five Kleine Gemeinde districts in Manitoba. The 1948 baptized membership was 430; most of the members are rural people. From 1874 to 1918 church meetings were held in the village schoolhouses. A new church was built between the two larger school districts, Blumenort and Blumenhof, in 1918. David P. Reimer was ordained as bishop in 1948 to succeed his brother, Bishop P. P. Reimer, who emigrated to Mexico. Preachers serving at present are Cornelius R. Penner, John G. Barkman, Bernhard P. Doerksen, and Peter P. Friesen. The deacons are Aaron R. Reimer, Peter K. Dueck, and Cornelius R. Plett. Sunday school is held every Sunday and *Jugendverein* every four weeks. D.P.R.

Blumenort Mennonite Brethren Church near Blumenhof, Sask., was organized in 1926 under the leadership of Franz Martens and C. C. Penner with an initial membership of approximately 30. The church in which the services took place was purchased from the Old Colony Mennonites. The work was continued by Johann Funk, Heinrich Penner, and Johann Klaassen until the membership decreased and the group was merged with the Reinfeld M.B. congregation.   J.I.R.

Blumenort Mennonite Church (GCM) was founded in Blumenort, Man., in 1925. Jacob Klassen was chiefly responsible for bringing Mennonite refugees who had come from Russia since 1923 to settle here on the land between Gretna and Winkler, a distance of 30 miles, left by the Old Colony Mennonites when they migrated to Mexico. The villages where this group settled are Blumenort, four miles west of Gretna; Neuhorst, five miles farther west; Rosenort, two miles north; Schoenwiese, three miles farther north; Gnadental, between Rosenort and Schoenwiese, but four miles north; Reinland, two miles farther west; Hochfeld, five miles farther northwest; Osterwick, three miles farther west, and Chortitz, three miles north of Osterwick.

In 1925 the young congregation bought the church in Rosenort of the Old Colony for $800.00. It was evidently built in the early 1880's. In 1926 the settlers bought a second church at Reinland, also of the Old Colony Mennonites, for $500.00.

The group in Blumenort, together with some of the Sommerfeld church, bought a residence and arranged a church in it which has been used ever since. In 1942 Gnadental built a 28 x 50 ft. church with a good basement for $2,000. The settlement now has four churches for its regular Sunday services. About once a month a general meeting is held alternately in one of the first mentioned churches. In the first years there were a few other stations to be served, but since the members at Hochfeld have nearly all moved to Elm Creek, 65 miles to the north, and only two families are left in Schoenwiese, services are held at only four places.

At first there were only two preachers, Jacob Klassen, a farmer, and Peter Rempel, a teacher, who had come from Russia. In 1925 Johann P. Bueckert came from Russia, and was chosen and ordained as elder in 1928, and Cornelius Krahn, who had been chosen as preacher in Russia, was ordained in October 1925. In 1928 Heinrich Warkentin and Heinrich Albrecht were chosen as preachers. The former moved to Morris, and the latter died in 1933. Other preachers ordained here were: Heinrich Enns and Abram Bueckert, who are still serving; in 1935 Franz Sawatzky (farmer), Jacob Klassen (farmer), and Abram Teichroeb (now a Bible school teacher); and in 1942 Paul Schaefer (teacher) and Jacob K. Klassen (teacher), a son of the above Jacob Klassen, and a grandson of the founder. In addition to these, Johann Adrian (now a Bible school teacher in Winnipeg), who was chosen but not ordained to the ministry in Russia, has conducted greatly appreciated courses for Sunday-school teachers.

In Blumenort and Gnadental there are catechetical classes. Several weeks before Easter the young people to be baptized are given instruction; two weeks before Pentecost the candidates relate to the assembled congregation how they found Christ and accepted Him as their personal Saviour. On Monday after Pentecost they are baptized. On the following Sunday a meeting preparatory to communion is held, and communion is observed a week later. At this service the tradition is followed that the elder breaks the bread and distributes it to the members, who remain seated and then eat together. The cup is handed by the elder to the deacons, or preachers, who take it to the lay members, who then pass it around until it is empty. After the ceremony, Psalm 103 is read as a hymn of praise. Footwashing is not practiced. The church has three young people's organizations, which give a religious program every month. The total membership in 1953 was 364.   J.P.Bu.

Blumenthal Mennonite Church (GCM) in Alberta, composed of Mennonite immigrants from Russia since World War I, is a member of the Conference of Mennonites in Canada. Its church, 15 miles east and 2 miles south of Pincher Creek, was dedicated July 21, 1935. Since its first services in 1927, David P. Janzen has been the minister and leader of the congregation. The 1950 membership was 56.   F.J.

Blumstein, a village in the Russian province of Taurida, volost and post office Halbstadt, belonged to the Molotschna Colony, was founded in 1804. Most of the village was destroyed by fire on Sept. 4, 1817, but was soon rebuilt. Blumstein had 2,026 dessiatines (*ca.* 5,000 acres) of land and (1911) 606 inhabitants, who were all Mennonites with the exception of one Jewish family and four Lutheran families, and were almost all farmers; dyeing and small industries were also engaged in. The village supported a school with two teachers and about 60 pupils. Most of the Mennonites belonged to the Lichtenau Mennonite Church, some joined the Ohrloff congregation, and a few families belonged to the Rückenau Mennonite Brethren. (*Neuer Haus- und Landwirtschafts-Kalender,* Odessa, 1910, 114; *ML* I, 239.)   HEGE.

Board of Christian Service (GCM) was created when the new constitution of the General Conference Mennonite Church was adopted at its thirty-second session at Freeman, S.D., in August 1950.

This board is charged with all responsibilities of the conference in the broad areas of relief, peace, and mutual aid. It consists of 12 members, four of whom are elected at each regular session of the conference. The board has organized its work under various divisions which are responsible to the board. The Committee on Hospitals and Relief carries the administrative responsibilities for the interests of the conference in the field of relief, the work of hospitals, the homes for the aged and care of the orphans (see **Emergency Relief Board of GCM**). The Committee on Mutual Aid provides a service of counseling and guidance, promotes colonization efforts, and is authorized to receive and solicit funds for loans to persons needing help (for more information see **Mutual Aid Board of GCM**). The Committee on Peace Service carries responsibilities for the conference in regard to a program of Christian peace education and witnessing in the congregations of the conference and beyond (for more information see **Peace Committee of GCM**).

The Board of Christian Service has a full-time secretary with an office in the General Conference Headquarters, 722 Main St., Newton, Kan. C.K.

Board of Education of the General Conference Mennonite Church. One of the main reasons for organizing the General Conference in 1860 was to establish a school for the training of missionaries and ministers. This school was in operation as the Wadsworth (Ohio) school 1866-78. The Kansas (now Western District) Conference promoted a western school from 1879 on, which came into existence as the Halstead school (1882-92) and later Bethel College was founded (1893). However, the General Conference as such never actually established a policy of conference-owned and operated schools, and hence did not have a board of education to operate either Bethel, Bluffton (founded 1900), or Freeman (founded 1903) colleges. These schools were founded by district conferences, interested individuals and groups, or operated by self-perpetuating boards of trustees.

From the above, however, it is evident that the early educational efforts of the General and district conferences included the establishment of higher schools. In addition to these schools elementary parochial schools were operating in the various communities. At the 1905 General Conference session held at Mountain Lake, Minn., the question was raised as to the advisability of having an official conference committee charged with promoting and guiding the educational interest in the conference. In 1908 a Committee on Education was created, composed of five members, to prepare an outline of work in the field of education and present it to the next conference session. At the 1911 session at Bluffton, Ohio, this committee reported after it had made a rather extensive study by questionnaire as to what was expected along educational lines by church leaders. The chief concern of the committee all along was still with educational institutions and their problems.

Upon recommendation of the committee, at the 1914 conference at Meno, Okla., by amendment to the conference constitution, a Board of Education of six members was created to promote Sunday-school work, religious training in public schools, vacation Bible schools, assist academies and colleges, to help needy students, etc. To each of the six members of the newly created board was assigned a special area of work: J. K. Penner, the family; H. H. Ewert, elementary schools; D. H. Richert, the middle schools; J. H. Langenwalter, the Sunday schools and young people's societies; S. K. Mosiman, teaching of religion in public schools; S. M. Grubb, the preparation of a suitable list of books for young people. Much was done, especially in some areas. Soon a Sunday-school standard was adopted and a Sunday-school teacher-training program promoted. At the 1923 conference session at Freeman, S.D., great emphasis was again placed upon the importance of our colleges and a united financial campaign was authorized for endowment and buildings for our three colleges— Bethel, Bluffton, and Freeman. By resolutions Bethel and Bluffton were recognized as senior colleges and Freeman as a junior college. No new higher schools were to be established except by conference sanction. This procedure was followed later in connection with the Mennonite Biblical Seminary and Bible School in Chicago, the Rosthern

Junior College in Saskatchewan, and the Canadian Mennonite Bible College in Winnipeg. These conference schools report directly to the General Conference through the Board of Education.

In recent years the work of the Board of Education was expanded. The General Conference, in session at Upland, Cal., in 1935, instructed the Board of Education to try to revive the then dormant Witmarsum Theological Seminary so that graduate theological training in a conference institution would again be available. The Board of Education served as a link between the Witmarsum Board then still in existence and the executive committee of the conference in the reorganization of the seminary and its relocation at Chicago, Ill., in 1945 as the Mennonite Biblical Seminary and Bible School, operating in affiliation with the Bethany Biblical Seminary and Bible Training School of the Church of the Brethren.

Since 1944 the Board of Education employed a full-time executive secretary and gradually created a number of subcommittees, an organizational set-up that greatly increased the service and effectiveness of the board. (1) The Curriculum Committee created in 1945 was charged with providing a complete course of study for Sunday schools and teacher training, including catechism material. (2) The Young People's Advisory Committee worked with the executive committee of the Young People's Union and helped them plan and integrate their work. (3) The Inter-School Committee, composed of two board members and the heads of all seven conference schools of collegiate rank, dealt with common problems relating to Bethel College, Bluffton College, Freeman Junior College, Rosthern Junior College, Gretna Collegiate Institute, Canadian Mennonite Bible College, and the Mennonite Biblical Seminary. (4) The Committee on Academies and Bible Schools occupied itself with the welfare of academies and Bible schools. (5) The Ministers' Retreat Committee arranged for an annual retreat for ministers and their wives. (6) The Committee on Visual Aids promoted helpful material of that nature. (7) The Committee on Nursing Schools and Education dealt with the area indicated by its title. (8) The Committee on Ministerial Correspondence Courses worked with material in that area.

All committees were appointed by and responsible to the Board of Education. One or more board members, besides the executive secretary of the board, with other members appointed by the board, served on the various committees. Each committee met about twice a year and reported to the board at its annual meeting. The board in turn reported to the conference at its triennial session. The chairman of the Board of Education was a regular member of the executive committee of the General Conference.

Among other items of far-reaching importance that the Board of Education dealt with or initiated and referred to the conference executive committee for review and recommendation to the conference are: Civilian Public Service educational rehabilita-

tion; providing financial educational assistance for CPS young men; promoting the Foreign Student Exchange program by providing financial assistance for foreign students attending the colleges; presenting the need for co-ordinating conference activities which resulted in the creation of a Co-ordinating Committee working toward simplification of conference organization and revision of the constitution; a Suggested Standard for Ordination of Conference Ministers, which was reviewed by the executive committee of the conference and adopted by the conference; a Suggested Procedure for General Conference Recognition of Organizations and Institutions, which was reviewed by the executive committee and adopted by the conference.

The Board of Education did not own or operate any school or educational institution, each of which is under its own board. It has, however, been given general supervision of the recognized conference schools and co-operates with them. An official representative of the board is to attend the main annual business meeting of each conference school board. The trend in recent years has been in the direction of more conference control of these institutions. In 1950 the Board of Education was merged with the Board of Publication by action of the General Conference session of that year. See **Board of Education and Publication** for further history. E.G.K.

H. P. Krehbiel, *History of the Mennonite General Conference* I (Newton, 1898); II (Newton, 1938); *Minutes and Reports of the General Conference of the Mennonite Church of North America* (1860-1951); J. E. Hartzler, *Education Among the Mennonites of America* (Danvers, 1925).

Board of Education and Publication (GCM), formed by combining the former Board of Education and Board of Publication, was created when the new constitution of the General Conference Mennonite Church was adopted at its thirty-second session at Freeman, S.D., in August 1950.

This board is charged with all of the responsibilities of the conference in the areas of education and publication and consists of 12 members, four of which are elected at each regular session of the conference. The board has organized its work under the following divisions: Committee on Education in Church, Home, and Community (children's work, young people's work, leadership training, retreats, etc.); Committee on Educational Institutions (schools, student aid, etc.); Mennonite Biblical Seminary; Editorial Committee (which is responsible for all editorial work and visual aids); Publishing Committee (see **Board of Publication**); and Historical Committee (*q.v.*).

For a comprehensive treatment of activities of this board in the past, see the following articles: **Board of Education** and **Board of Publication**. The Board of Education and Publication has a full-time secretary with an office in the General Conference Headquarters, 722 Main St., Newton, Kan.   C.K.

Board of Emergency Relief (GCM): see **Emergency Relief Board**.

Board of Foreign Missions of the Mennonite Brethren Church of North America had its beginning in

1885 when that conference elected a "missions committee" to take over the responsibility for, and centralize the gathering of moneys for foreign missions and disburse them according to annual conference resolutions. Prior to this the treasurers of the various congregations reported such funds to the conference. The missions committee consisting of eight or more members had an executive section, made up of the chairman, secretary, and treasurer, which carried on the work. In 1896 the conference sought to facilitate the foreign missions endeavor by electing a "Committee on Foreign Missions," consisting of only five members. In addition to handling funds for foreign missions, this committee was given the responsibility of receiving and examining the candidates applying to the conference for foreign missions service.

When the Mennonite Brethren Conference which had been incorporated in 1900 under the name "The American Brethren Mission Union" had its charter amended in 1909, changing the name to "The Conference of the Mennonite Brethren Church of North America," and extending the scope of its activities, it also provided a more complete constitution which defined and enumerated the duties and powers of the "Board" of Foreign Missions.

The five members of the Board of Foreign Missions are elected for a three-year term by the regular triennial session of the General Mennonite Brethren Conference. After election the new board meets for organization, electing a chairman, two assistant chairmen, a recording secretary, and the executive secretary and treasurer. The duties of each member are defined in the constitution.

Since the Board of Foreign Missions is an elected committee of the General Mennonite Brethren Conference vested with the responsibility of looking after its foreign missions enterprise, it is directly responsible to the conference itself. At the triennial meeting, the board presents a complete report of the foreign missions activities, policies and principles pursued, standing of the treasury, extent of the fields, number and status of the missionaries, budgets and recommendations to the conference for consideration and action. Each of the district conferences receives an annual report from the Board of Foreign Missions. Although the district conference delegates have the right to inquire for information as well as to offer suggestions, they are not vested with the right to pass resolutions directly to the board. These must come by way of resolutions to the general conference.

Historically and in view of the importance placed upon the evangelization of the heathen, the conference has rather consistently chosen members for the Board of Foreign Missions from among the most outstanding leaders of the constituency, as for example Cornelius Wedel, Abraham Schellenberg, Heinrich Voth, N. N. Hiebert, H. S. Voth, J. H. Pankratz, H. W. Lohrenz, and others.

The areas of the board's work are three as given below.

(a) Geographic. Geographically the Gospel work entrusted by the Saviour, Jesus Christ, to the Mennonite Brethren Conference has through the direction of its Board of Foreign Missions, and through the services of its missionaries and its national workers been carried to the Comanche Indians and Mexicans of Oklahoma, to Hyderabad State of India, to Fukien, Kansu and Shensi provinces of China, to the Belgian Congo of Africa, to the Chaco Indians of Paraguay, to the Valle and Choco departments of Colombia, and to the Parana State of Brazil.

(b) Divisional. Divisionally the work has been done in four areas: (1) evangelization in the villages and the establishment and nurture of indigenous churches; (2) education, in operating elementary, middle, secondary, and Bible schools for the nationals; (3) medical service, by operating hospitals, clinics, and dispensaries; (4) publication, by supplying Christian literature, school books, Sunday-school materials, music, and periodicals in the native languages.

(c) Functional. Functionally the board has labored in the following areas: promoting the spiritual importance and interest in foreign missions within the conference; fostering sacrificial giving for missions; appealing for, selecting, accepting, processing, and sending out of missionaries; keeping in constant contact, encouraging, and maintaining from mission funds the missionary enterprises and the missionaries whether in active service or retired; providing principles, policies, and methods for the missions endeavor; and providing printed material on its foreign missions for church papers, and in the form of reports, maps, pamphlets, and books.   A.E.J.

Board of Missions (GCM) was formed by combining and reorganizing the former Foreign Missions Board (q.v.) and Home Missions Board (q.v.) when the new constitution of the General Conference Mennonite Church was adopted at its thirty-second session at Freeman, S.D., in August 1950. The board is "charged with all responsibility of the conference in the areas of missions and evangelism at home and abroad according to the instructions, decisions, and regulations of the conference." It consists of 12 members, four of whom are elected at each regular session of the conference, and is divided into the Section on Foreign Missions and Section on Home Missions. In addition to this the Board of Missions consists of a Church Unity Committee, Evangelism Committee, Mission Personnel Committee, and Ministry Committee.

The Board of Missions has a full-time secretary with an office in the General Conference Headquarters, 722 Main St., Newton, Kan.   C.K.

Board of Publication (GCM). The work of publication in the General Conference dates back to the early beginnings of the General Conference movement. On June 7, 1852, the first paper printed by John H. Oberholtzer appeared under the name of *Religiöser Botschafter* (q.v.) in Milford, Bucks Co., Pa. It was not long until a stock company was formed under the name "Mennonite Printing Union" (q.v.), with offices at Milford Square, Pa. The paper was now called *Das Christliche Volksblatt* (q.v.), the first number appearing July 30,

1856. In 1867 the name was changed to *Der Mennonitische Friedensbote* (*q.v.*) and in 1881 it was merged with a paper called *Zur Heimath* (*q.v.*) under the title *Christlicher Bundesbote* (*q.v.*). In the discussion on the points upon which the General Conference was to be organized (1860) the work of publications was considered, one of the resolutions stating, "That the Publishing House already in existence in our denomination is appreciated as a helpful institution and that it is hereby fraternally recommended to general support" (H. P. Krehbiel, *History of General Conference* I, 60).

At the eighth General Conference held at Wadsworth, Ohio, Nov. 25, 1878, the question of placing the work of publication under conference control was raised. In 1881 the Publication Board was created with A. B. Shelly, A. E. Funk, S. F. Sprunger, Christian Krehbiel, and Christian Schowalter as first members. The board was responsible to the conference and reported its work at every conference session.

In 1884, the board established the Mennonite Book Concern (*q.v.*) at Berne, Ind., as publishing agency and bookstore. The next year the board undertook the publication of a German Sunday-school paper, *Der Kinderbote* (*q.v.*). By 1887 the Mennonite Book Concern had sold over 11,000 volumes. J. F. Lehman, a member of the Publication Board, was made the business manager and served in this capacity for 34 years. The Publication Board now consisted of six members elected by the conference. In 1896 the following were members: N. B. Grubb, W. J. Ewert, H. J. Krehbiel, J. F. Lehman, J. Janzen, and J. van Steen.

In 1902 the need for an English periodical was expressed in conference session. The Eastern District Conference had been publishing *The Mennonite* (*q.v.*) which was now adopted as the General Conference weekly publication for which the Board of Publication became responsible. In addition to this the board also published the Sunday-school quarterly in 14,800 copies and in 1914 had also published by that time the following books: *Gesangbuch mit Noten; Mennonite Hymnal; Festklänge;* Cornelis Ris, *The Confession of Faith of the Mennonites* (German and English); *Handbook for Ministers* (German and English); *Catechism* (German and English); *Bundesbote-Kalender;* etc.

The reports of the Publication Board covering the years 1917-33 list among others the following additional books: *The Mennonites* by C. H. Smith; *Words to Young Christians* by C. H. Wedel; *A Plea for the Abolition of War* by H. J. Krehbiel; *Mennonite Hymn Book; The Coming of the Russian Mennonites* by C. H. Smith; *Mission Study Courses; Twenty-five Years with God in India; Mennonite Yearbook and Almanac; The Development of the Missionary and Philanthropic Interest Among the Mennonites of North America* by E. G. Kaufman and others.

In 1947 the Board of Publication opened, in addition to the Conference Book Store at Berne, Ind., one at Newton, Kan., and another one at Rosthern, Sask. The board also has interests in the Central Conference Book Store at Bloomington, Ill.

Since its beginning the General Conference investigated possibilities of establishing a conference publishing house. This was achieved when in 1949 the Mennonite Press (*q.v.*) was established, which is a joint enterprise of the Board of Publication and Bethel College and is located in the Grattan Building at North Newton, Kan. Most of the conference publications are now being printed here.

In 1950 the General Conference in session at Freeman, S.D., adopted a new constitution through which the Board of Publication and the Board of Education were merged under the new name, The Board of Education and Publication (*q.v.*). Under this board the Editorial Committee, the Publishing Committee, and the Historical Committee are aiding the Publication section in its work. In 1949 the Historical Committee started a Mennonite Historical Series published under the Board of Education and Publication. The publication efforts of the conference have been centralized and unified more than before.

Some of the outstanding publications of the board during the last years were *The Mennonite Hymnary* by Walter H. Hohmann and Lester Hostetler; *Handbook to the Mennonite Hymnary* by Lester Hostetler; *The Story of the Mennonites* (third edition) by C. Henry Smith; *The Fellowship of the Gospel,* Ruth Ratzlaff, ed.   D.C.W.

H. P. Krehbiel, *History of the Mennonite General Conference* I (Newton, 1898), II (Newton, 1938); *Minutes and Reports of the General Conference Mennonite Church,* 1860-1950.

Board of Trustees and Finance (GCM) was created when the new constitution of the General Conference Mennonite Church was adopted at its thirty-second session at Freeman, S.D., in August 1950. This board is responsible for the business administration of the conference, its properties, funds, and the budget. It consists of 12 members, four of which are elected at each regular session of the conference. The board has organized its work under the Trustees, the Finance Committee, and the Committee on Pensions.   C.K.

Bocher, Johanna: see Boucher, Jane.

Bocholt, a town in Westphalia (about four miles from Wesel and Emmerich), where in August 1536 a meeting of several extremist Anabaptist groups was held for the purpose of unification. It was attended by Melchiorites and Batenburgers; the Münsterite remnant was also represented. The expenses of the conference were defrayed by an Englishman named Henry, who is incidentally not identical with Heinrich Niclaes, as Krohn supposes. Among the leaders there were from Friesland Matthias of Balk, Tiardus of Sneek, and Siewerdus Klerik, a former teacher; from Gelderland Jan van Gulik, Christoffel and Heinrick of Zutphen; from England, Jan Matthysz of Middelburg and Johan of Utrecht; and from Holland (province) Johann of Maastricht and Johan of Schoonhoven. Several later fell into the hands of persecutors and were executed: Tiardus was beheaded in Leeuwarden, Jan Matthysz was burned at the stake in London, and Johan of Utrecht in Holland. Batenburg remained absent, probably to escape a condemnation of his doctrine (Nippold, *David Joris* I, 53). Strasbourg was not represented. David Joris managed at least apparently to bring about a temporary agreement on the disputed points, but on two main points the differences remained.

The resulting compromise was in substance as follows: Since the assembled parties were unified in most and the most important of the doctrines, and the dispute concerned only two chief points of issue, violent and bitter strife should be avoided. They should beseech God to grant light and show the way to unity. It was agreed that they should refrain from retaliation for insults, from legal force, from arbitrary physical and corporal punishment, and from plundering churches; they condemned all acts of this kind. And finally, adult baptism, which had been done away with by the Batenburgers, should again be administered to those whose piety was proved. After the meeting of elders at Bocholt in 1536 some Anabaptists are found here; some Anabaptists were arrested here in 1548. From their trials it is clear that they rejected the Münsterite teachings and principles; their preachers and elders were Leenhart Munsels, Adam Pastor (*q.v.*), and Hinrich Ebbinck (*q.v.*). Later on there must have been a Mennonite congregation at Bocholt, to which refugees both from England and the Netherlands had fled. Many Protestants too found shelter in Bocholt, for this town, in contrast with most Westphalian towns, which were entirely or at least predominantly Roman Catholic, was a Protestant town and the Mennonites were tolerated by the city government. In 1598 there were 26 Anabaptists in the town. But about 1608 by order of the ruler, the Bishop of Münster, all Mennonites (18 families) had to leave the town. A number of these families settled at Winterswijk in the Netherlands, where they founded a Mennonite congregation. HEGE, vDZ.

F. Nippold, "David Joris von Delft," in *Ztscht f. die hist. Theol.*, 1863-64; B. Krohn, *Gesch. der fanatischen . . . Wiedertäufer vornehmlich in Niederdeutschland* (Leipzig, 1758); L. Keller, *Gegenreformation am Niederrhein* (Leipzig, 1887); DB 1909, 105-6; F. C. Fleischer, *De doopsgez. gemeente te Winterswijk* (Winterswijk, 1911) 7-9; ML I, 239.

Bock, Friedrich Samuel (1716-86), professor of theology at Königsberg. In his two-volume work, *Historia Antitrinitariorum maxime Socinianorum ex fontibus magnamque partem monumentis et documentis manuscriptis* (Regensburg and Leipzig, 1784), he names men like Denk, Haetzer, David Joris, Adam Pastor, and various Dutch Mennonites as opponents of the doctrine of the Trinity. This book apparently became the foundation for later traditional church history. It is mentioned as a source in all important textbooks and is extensively used. Nevertheless Bock's assertions should be checked with special care (*ML* I, 239). NEFF.

Bockelson, Johan: see Jan van Leyden.

Böcker, Jakob, one of the founders of the Mennonite Brethren in Russia, signed the charter of Jan. 6, 1860, as well as the Ohrloff declaration of March 19, 1860, and the petition to the Ministry of the Interior of Dec. 30, 1863. He was a member of the Rudnerweide M.B. Church and on May 30, 1860, was chosen with Heinrich Hübert as elder of the newly founded Mennonite Brethren, and was ordained June 5. He was one of the first to be baptized by immersion; on Sept. 23 he and Heinrich Bartel baptized each other in the Molotschna. Böcker did not oppose the rising overemotional and libertinistic wing with adequate firmness and is thus partly responsible for its rapid increase and the consequent aberrations. In August 1863 he resigned as elder and was chosen "ruler" (*Regierer*), no doubt to lead the migration to the Kuban, which was just beginning. In 1875 he emigrated to America. After moving several times, he died in Fairview, Oklahoma. (Friesen, *Brüderschaft;* ML I, 240.) NEFF.

Bockschaft and **Streichenberg,** in Baden, Germany, where formerly a Mennonite congregation existed, founded about 1655. The members of this congregation in 1841 united with Ittlingen (*q.v.*) and since 1913 belong to the congregation of Sinsheim (*q.v.*).

Bocskay, Stephen, a Transylvanian prince (1556-1606), leader of the Hungarian revolt of 1604-5. Bocskay, with Bethlen Gabor (*q.v.*) and other Hungarian and Transylvanian partisans, led the revolt against Emperor Rudolf II, because Rudolf had threatened the religious freedom of the Hungarian Protestants. The entry of the Hungarian rebels and the Turkish troops into Moravia in May 1605 caused the Hutterian Brethren there untold suffering. Sixteen Bruderhofs (including 11 schools) were burned down, 87 inmates were murdered, 238 Hutterites were abducted, some to Turkey, of whom only 70 returned (Beck, *Geschichts-Bücher,* 347). It is not likely that Bocskay, who was fighting for freedom of religion, knew of the atrocities committed by the soldiers; Bethlen Gabor was a patron of the Anabaptists and had given them shelter on his estates in Transylvania. The event is described in a special chapter in the Hutterite chronicle.

The suffering of the Hutterian Brethren during this period of war is described in several songs known as the *Botschkay-Lieder* (Beck, 349). Three of them, by unknown authors, have been preserved: "Gott gib mir zu betrachten," 66 stanzas; "Herr Gott Vater im Himmelreich," 40 stanzas; and "Nun hören zu all in Gemein," 158 stanzas. (The last is reprinted in *Die Lieder der Hutterischen Brüder,* Scottdale, 1914, 804-12; see Wolkan, *Lieder,* 239; ML I, 240.) HEGE.

Bodensee, a congregation which originated in 1812 by the migration of Mennonites from the Heidelberg region, who settled north of the Bodensee (Lake Constance), now called Ueberlingen (*q.v.*). (*ML* I, 240.)

Bödigheim, a village in Baden near Adelsheim, meeting place (1874-84) of the Faussenhof congregation, later called Seligental, and now called Adelsheim. Bödigheim was the home of Simon Stumpf (*q.v.*), an early Zürich Anabaptist.

Bodmann, Ferdinand (1787-1822), who as chef of the second division of the prefecture in Mainz,

1810, issued a statistical yearbook of the Donnersberg Department (*Annuaire statistique du Departement du Mont Tonnere*), which gives a detailed favorable description of the Mennonites in the Palatinate during the French occupation. (*Gem.-Kal.* 1916, 122-26; *Menn. Bl.* 1914, No. 1; *ML* I, 240.)   NEFF.

Bodockh (also Bodock, Bodtock, Slavic: Potok Sarissky), a Hutterian Brethren Bruderhof in Transylvania, where there had previously been a Bruderhof at Alwinz (*q.v.*). The Brethren settled here upon a demand by Prince George Rákóczy I of Transylvania, who, like his son George II, was Calvinist. At first the Brethren were unwilling to obey the order; but when the prince proceeded with intimidation they decided in August 1645 to transfer the household at Tschäkowitz in Hungary to Bodockh on the estates of the Rákóczy family. The group prospered at first, but later they suffered from heavy taxation, and after a brief existence it died out, when the successor of George II (d. 1660), Franz Rákóczy, became Catholic. (Beck, *Geschichts-Bücher,* 472; *ML* I, 240.)   HEGE.

Boeckaert, Cornelis, Reformed visitor of the sick at Amsterdam, who disputed with Hans de Ries (*q.v.*), May 1596 at Amsterdam, at the end of de Ries' testimony. The next year de Ries wrote a tract to Boeckaert, which was published without de Ries' knowledge, titled, *Cort ende Claer Bewijs* . . . (n.p., 1597). Boeckaert wrote in reply: *Wederlegginge eens Tractaats* . . . (Amsterdam, 1597). (*Inv. Arch. Amst.* I, 495; *DB* 1864, 34-37; *Catalogus Amst.,* 212.)   vDZ.

Boehm, Martin (1725-1812), with Philip William Otterbein (1726-1813) the cofounder of the Church of the United Brethren in Christ, was born of Swiss-Palatine Mennonite parentage in what is now Lancaster Co., Pa., Nov. 30, 1725. After his marriage to Eve Steiner (1734-1822) in 1753, he was chosen by lot as preacher of the Pequea Mennonite congregation. His worries over his unworthiness as a minister were dispelled by a powerful conversion experience about 1758, when he began to preach "in power" the evangelical message of repentance and salvation by faith. Advanced to the office of bishop in 1759, he continued his preaching, making his famous visit to Virginia in 1761, where he came in contact with the "Great Awakening" evangelism of Whitefield and others. In 1767 he participated in the "great meeting" in Isaac Long's barn in the Conestoga Valley north of Landis Valley, where he met Otterbein, and the seed for the United Brethren in Christ Church (*q.v.*) took root. Ten years later, due to his association with non-Mennonites in the work of his widening ministry, and his revivalistic practices and beliefs, Martin Boehm was excommunicated by the Mennonite conference of Lancaster County, Pa. Into the United Brethren movement Boehm brought a considerable group of Mennonite converts and circuit-riders, while his colleague Otterbein brought groups of "awakened" members of the Reformed Church in Pennsylvania and Maryland. In addition to his importance for United Brethren history,

Martin Boehm's shadow falls across the early history of the Brethren in Christ (River Brethren). Also, he was the greatest single force in spreading Methodism through Lancaster County. His son Henry Boehm (1775-1875) became a prominent Methodist minister and left an invaluable volume of *Reminiscences,* which sheds light on his father's career. Martin Boehm died March 23, 1812, and his funeral sermon was preached by his friend, Bishop Francis Asbury of the Methodist Episcopal Church, at "Boehm's Chapel" near Willow Street in Lancaster Co., Pa., where he was buried.   D.Y.

Boeke, Isaac Herman, a son of the following Jan Boeke and Jenny de Stoppelaar Blijdenstein, was born in Amsterdam, Dec. 28, 1846, died at The Hague July 27, 1913. After his study at the University and the Mennonite Theological Seminary at Amsterdam, receiving the degree of ministerial candidate in 1870, he served the congregations of Zijldijk 1870-72, Hengelo 1872-75, Wormerveer-Zuid 1875-85, Hilversum 1885-93, and Amsterdam 1893 until he retired on Nov. 2, 1911.

In 1872 he married Sara Maria van Gelder of Wormerveer; their son Jan Boeke, b. Oct. 23, 1874, at Hengelo, who has been a professor in the school of medicine at the University of Utrecht and for a long period member and president of the board of the Utrecht Mennonite Church, is a well-known scholar, who published a number of outstanding medical books. Another son is Julius Herman Boeke, b. 1884 at Wormerveer, professor of economics at the University of Leiden and also a loyal member of the Mennonite congregation.   vDZ.

Boeke, Jan, b. April 14, 1805, at Zaandijk, d. July 9, 1854, at his country home at Breukelen, had originally business training but afterwards chose the ministry as a profession. In 1829 he was accepted by the A.D.S. as a candidate for the ministry after having studied at the Mennonite Seminary at Amsterdam. He served the congregations of Nijmegen (barely one-half year) and Amsterdam (1830-53). In 1853 he had to discontinue his charge and retire because of ill health. He was married to Jenny de Stoppelaar Blijdenstein. He performed his charge faithfully and was an example to his congregation of a true Biblical character. At the time of his death, Prof. S. Muller wrote a warm obituary, *Woord tot gedachtenis van Jan Boeke* (A Tribute to the Memory of Jan Boeke). In addition to being a Mennonite minister, Boeke gave his attention to spiritual concerns in other ways. For many years he was a member and the secretary of the executive committee of the Netherlands Bible Society (*Nederlandsch Bijbelgenootschap*) as well as a member and chairman of the executive committee of the Society for the General Welfare (*Maatschappij tot Nut van 't Algemeen*). In Amsterdam he was founder of the Louise-Bewaarschool (Kindergarten). Boeke wrote a great deal. Some of his didactic dissertations are (among others): *Schuitepraatje over de beleefdheid* (Conversation in a boat concerning politeness); *Over het dierenplagen* (About the teasing of animals); *Iets over onze wijze van begraven* (A bit about our manner of burial); *De ware liberaal als burger*

(The true liberal as a citizen). Besides these he wrote a number of popular religious pamphlets; e.g., *Paulus als voorbeeld van christelijke levenswijsheid* (Paul as an example of prudent Christian living); *Petrus, een gesprek aan de ontbijttafel* (Peter, a conversation for breakfast time); *Het Klaaghuis beter dan het huis der maaltijden* (The house of mourning better than the house of feasting); *Hoe onze rampen en ons leed zamenhangen met onze zonde* (How our catastrophes and our distress are related to our sin); *'s Heeren Geboortefeest* (The birthday celebration of the Lord); etc. The sermons preached by Boeke and his colleague, A. Doyer, on the occasion of the centenary of the Seminary and the third centennial of Menno Simons' renunciation of Catholicism, were published at Amsterdam in 1836. The speech he made upon the dedication of the church at Arnhem in 1852 appeared in print with the title: *Het betrachten der waarheid in liefde* (Ef. 4:15) (The practice of truth in love, Eph. 4:15). In collaboration with A. M. Cramer (*q.v.*) he published, *Twee brieven ter toelichting en toetsing der schets van J. H. Halbertsma, over de herkomst van de Doopsgezinden* (Two letters by way of elucidation and examination of the sketch written by J. H. Halbertsma concerning the origin of the Mennonites) (Amsterdam, 1844).

In behalf of religious education, he published *Handleiding bij het onderwijs in de Christelijke geloof- en pligtenleer* (Guide for education in Christian doctrines and ethics) (Amsterdam, 1837; 2nd ed., 1851); *Schriftuurlijke katechismus* (Scriptural Catechism) (Amsterdam, 1837; 2nd ed., 1847); and *Eenvoudige en beknopte Handleiding bij de voorbereiding tot den doop* (A simple and brief guide in connection with preparation for baptism) (Amsterdam, 1841). J.L., vDZ.

DB 1861, 156; 1885, 56; 1909, 9, 21, 149 ff.; Knuttel, *Nederlandsche Bibliotheek van Kerkgesch.*, 124; Chr. Sepp, *Bibliotheek van Nederlandsche Kerkgeschiedschrijvers*, 390; *Boekzaal der Geleerde Wereld*, 1854, II, 112 f.; Gorter, *Doopsgezinde Lectuur* I, 1854, *Kerknieuws*, 10 ff.; *Catalogus Amst.*, 11, 289, 308, 326; *N.N.B.Wb.* IV, 182; *ML* I, 241.

Boekenoogen, a family which originally lived in West Flanders in Belgium; Joos Bouckenoghe (Boekenoogen), head chaplain at Brugge and priest of the Roman Catholic Church at Ledeghem, was converted to the Mennonites and settled at Haarlem in the Netherlands as a weaver about 1580. His son Willem was also a Mennonite, but most of Willem's children became Quakers; one of them, Jan, emigrated to Pennsylvania in 1684 and was one of the first settlers of Philadelphia. Five of the children of Tanneken Symons B. (d. 1670 at Haarlem) were Quakers though she herself was apparently a Mennonite. The children of Jan B., a son of Willem and a velvet weaver, were, however, Mennonites about 1731, in Amsterdam and later in Haarlem.

A grandson of this Jan Boekenoogen, called Jan Gerrit Boekenoogen, b. at Haarlem 1802 and d. at Beverwijk 1877, married to Johanna Overbeek, studied at the Mennonite Theological Seminary at Amsterdam and became a ministerial candidate in 1826; he served the Mennonite congregations of

Ouddorp 1826-27 and Wormerveer-Zuid 1827-63. His son Lucas Fredrik Boekenoogen (1830-1909) was a manufacturer of vegetable oils at Wormerveer and became very well-to-do. He was married to Agatha Maria van Gelder. Jan Gerrit Boekenoogen (*q.v.*) and Gerrit Jacob Boekenoogen (*q.v.*) were their sons. vDZ.

Boekenoogen, Gerrit Jacob, son of Lucas Frederik B., was born at Wormerveer April 18, 1868, died at Leiden, Aug. 26, 1930, took his doctor's degree in Dutch literature at Leiden in 1896 with a thesis ("De Zaansche Volkstaal") on the folk language in the Zaan region. Afterwards he became editor of the *Woordenboek der Nederlandsche Taal* (Dictionary of the Dutch Language). In addition to this extensive labor, he found time to publish a number of the Old-Dutch folk books. Folklore, and especially engravings of child life (*kinderprenten*), of which he possessed a unique collection, received his devoted attention. He lived in Leiden and remained unmarried throughout life. He gave much time and concern to the Mennonite congregation at Leiden, which he served as deacon after 1896. He was also a member of the executive committee of the A.D.S. and of the board (Curatorium) of the Mennonite Seminary. He was a staunch and loyal friend of the noted historian, W. J. Kühler, who was minister of the congregation at Leiden from 1905 to 1912, as both had a great love for and knowledge of Dutch literature, art, and especially the history of the late Middle Ages, as well as the history of the Mennonites. Boekenoogen wrote a number of short themes on the subject of Mennonite history, which appeared in the *Zondagsbode* and the *Doopsgezinde Bijdragen*. Of special significance is his definitive study of the portraits of Menno Simons (*DB* 1916).vDZ.

J. W. Muller, *Levensbericht van Dr. G. J. Boekenoogen* (Leiden, 1921), which contains a complete list of his published writings.

Boekenoogen, Jan Gerrit, a Dutch Mennonite minister, son of Lucas Fredrik B., b. July 17, 1856, at Wormerveer, d. Jan. 7, 1933, at Bussum, studied at the university and the Mennonite seminary in Amsterdam, became a ministerial candidate in 1880, and served at Wormer and Jisp (1881-84), Hindeloopen (1884-85), and Krommenie (1885-1922). He received the Th.D. degree at Amsterdam in 1884. Except for his doctoral dissertation, he published only a few sermons. He compiled a new catalog of the Mennonite literature in the Amsterdam Library, which was published in 1919. (*Catalogus Amst.*, 317.) He was a member of the Teyler Theological Association at Haarlem and coeditor of *Teyler's Theologisch Tijdschrift. (Zondagsbode,* Jan. 15, 1933.) vDZ.

Boelaart, Jan, d. June 1762 at Harlingen, Dutch province of Friesland, author of the book, *De voorzigtige leidsman om de H. Schriften met nut te lezen* (Hoorn, 1770), was educated in Leiden and Amsterdam, where he studied at the Mennonite Seminary, and in 1744 became a ministerial candidate (*proponent*), and accepted the pulpit of the Mennonite church in Harlingen. Here he was very active when his colleague Johannes Stinstra (*q.v.*)

was suspended by the Frisian government. In December 1760 he retired for reasons of health. He translated two of Samuel Clarke's (*q.v.*) books into Dutch, and also wrote: *IV Godgeleerte Brieven over 't onderzoek der H. Schriften* (Haarlingen, 1763). J.L., vDZ.

DB 1868, 106; Chr. Sepp, *Johannes Stinstra en zijn tijd* (Amsterdam, 1865) II, *passim; Catalogus Amst.,* 220; *Inv. Arch. Amst.* II, No. 1899; *ML* I, 241.

Boelens, Allard, burgomaster of Amsterdam, was a friend of the Anabaptists; he entertained Jan van Leyden (*q.v.*) as his guest, and walked through the city streets (1534) with Jacob van Campen (*q.v.*), an Aanbaptist elder. (*DB* 1917, 195.) vDZ.

Boenes, Jean (Jan, Johan), was an influential preacher and elder of the Flemish congregation at Rotterdam in Holland after 1659. He and Bastiaan van Weenigem, his colleague, and Tieleman Jansz van Braght (*q.v.*) were among the *buitenmannen* (*q.v.*) who were called to Utrecht to restore order and peace in the congregation there. Here, according to a poem, *De Kristelikke Kruispoort* (The Christian Gateway of the Cross), written in 1661 by J. Six, Boenes' manner was one of implacability (see **Willem van Maurik**). A letter from Boenes regarding this matter was printed at Amsterdam (*q.v.*): "Copye eens Briefs, gesonden door Jean Boenes uyt Rotterdam, aen N.N. tot Amsterdam over het wederhouden eeniger Doopsgesinde leeraren van de Predickstoel en Kerckelycke Regeeringe binnen Uytrecht" (Copy of a letter sent by Jean Boenes at Rotterdam to N.N. at Amsterdam, regarding the restraint of several Mennonite ministers from the pulpit and ecclesiastical government in Utrecht) (*Catalogus Amst.,* 128). Boenes, who was married to Anna van Melsen, died Dec. 5, 1668, at Cadiz in Spain, where he was staying temporarily in connection with his business as a merchant. vDZ.

K. Vos, *Gesch. der Doopsgezinde Gemeente te Rotterdam* (1907, reprint) 18, 19, 42; *DB* 1916, 169-85.

Boer (De Boer), a Dutch Mennonite family, descending from Hans Baur (Bauer) and Anna Willener, Swiss Mennonites, who migrated in 1711 from Oberhofen, Swiss canton of Bern, to Sappemeer, Dutch province of Groningen. Here this family engaged in farming as they had in Switzerland. Their daughter Barbara married Peter Gerber, and their son Abraham married Trinette (Trijntje), daughter of the preacher Jacob Stähly. Abraham (1708-99), the father of Abraham Hansen Boer (1772-1859), later called himself de Boer. Abraham Hansen was married to Eke Coolman, a member of the Groningen Mennonite Coolman family (*q.v.*) and was the great-grandfather of M. G. de Boer (b. 1867), professor of Dutch history at the university of Amsterdam and author of a large number of historical books and papers, including a paper on his family, entitled *Vom Thunersee zum Sappemeer,* published in *Berner Ztscht für Gesch. und Heimatkunde,* 1947-I (also reprint). vDZ.

Boer, Francijntje, a Dutch Mennonite poet, b. Oct. 18, 1784, at Harlingen, d. March 7, 1852, at Heerenveen. She published *Dichtproeven* (1815); *Nieuwe Dichtproeven* (1821); *Gedichtjes voor kinderen* (1812); *Gedichtjes voor behoeftige kinderen* (1823); and *Laat ons leven tot elkanders nut en genoegen* (1850). She was not well-to-do; she earned the family's subsistence as a needle-woman and a cook-housekeeper. (*N.N.B.Wb.* I, 380; *ML* I, 241.)

NEFF, vDZ.

Boerma, Nicolaas Westendorp, b. 1872, d. Nov. 26, 1951, pastor of the Dutch Reformed Church at Blija 1898-1931, and at Budel 1931-37, was professor of ethics at the Amsterdam Mennonite Seminary 1935 (Oct. 23)-1945, and professor at the University of Amsterdam 1939-45. Among his publications should be mentioned *Realistische Ethiek* (Amsterdam, 1939), *Neen en Ja,* a collection of ethical-religious studies (Amsterdam, 1939), and in co-operation with J. Maarse, *De Wetenschap der Moraal* (Amsterdam, 1939), which was a collection of the manuscripts of I. J. de Bussy (*q.v.*), of whom Boerma was an attached disciple. vDZ.

Boetje, Gerrit Jochems, was appointed ministerial candidate by the Frisian Sociëteit (Mennonite Conference) in 1831; he served the congregation of Woudsend 1831-37 and Knollendam 1837-54, in which year he died. His sons Jochem (*q.v.*) and Herman (*q.v.*) were also Mennonite ministers.

vDZ.

Boetje, Herman, son of G. J. Boetje, b. 1846 at Knollendam, studied at the university and Mennonite seminary at Amsterdam; became a minister in 1870; served at the Mennonite congregations at Appelscha, 1871-73; Franeker, 1873-79; and Hengelo, 1879-1911; and after this lived at Arnhem, where he died Aug. 13, 1937. He wrote *Tafereelen uit het leven van Jezus* (Scenes from the Life of Jesus), 1875. In collaboration with J. Sepp he produced a new hymnal with the title, *Gezangen ten gebruike in Doopsgezinde gemeenten,* the so-called *Leidse Bundel* (Leiden Collection) (1st ed., Leiden, 1897; 5th ed., Leiden, 1918). To this collection Sepp and Boetje added a *Bloemlezing uit de Psalmen* (Anthology from the Psalms) (1st ed., Leiden, 1900; 3rd ed., Leiden, 1911). This collection, especially the songs, was in use in many Mennonite congregations until a new Mennonite collection appeared in 1943, sponsored by the Algemeene Doopsgezinde Sociëteit. vDZ.

Boetje, Jochem, b. Feb. 14, 1841, at Knollendam in the Netherlands, the son of the preacher G. J. Boetje, was ordained Oct. 23, 1864, as preacher of the Mennonite church at Burg on the island of Texel; July 5, 1868, became pastor at Koog a.d. Zaan; on Dec. 8, 1872, at Harlingen; and on May 4, 1884, at Amsterdam. He died July 29, 1890. He published *Rapport v.d. Commissie ter zake van het Emeritaatsfonds vor Doopsgezinde Leeraars in Friesland* Harlingen, 1876); *Tweede Rapport . . .* (Harlingen, 1876); "Over het opnemen van leden van Prot. Kerkgenootschappen in Doopsgezinde Gemeenten" (*DB* 1879); and "De Algemeene Doopsgezinde Sociëteit" (*Nieuw kerkelijke Weekblad,* 1870). J.L.

DB 1865, 168; 1868, 170; 1873, 190; 1885, 130; 1891, 113; *Catalogus Amst.,* 282, 286; *Dagblad voor Friesland,* April 4, 1884; *ML* I, 241.

Bogaert (Boomgaret), **Pieter Willemsz,** was a Mennonite preacher at Monnikendam (Holland), and in 1567 took an active part in the dispute between the Frisians and Flemish, siding with the former, and was banned by Dirk Philips. When Duke Alba (*q.v.*) came to Holland, Bogaert fled to Emden. Prince William of Orange wrote him here May 5, 1572, asking him to help in raising money among the Mennonites to continue his war against Spain. Bogaert complied and on July 19, accompanied by Dirck Jansz Cortenbosch (*q.v.*), was able to place 1,060 guilders at the disposal of the prince at Roermond, who gratefully accepted the sum. In the same year Monnikendam declared itself on the side of the prince, and Bogaert presumably returned home. The aid given by the Mennonites through his agency surely contributed to the tolerant attitude of the prince toward the Mennonites, for the prince repeatedly urged the strict Calvinists around him to a similar tolerance.

Bogaert was of a gentle disposition. He voiced his opposition to a repetition of baptism in the case of a transfer of membership. In 1588 he was made elder and in 1590 was banned by the stricter party together with the more moderate *Jonge* Frisians, Lubbert Gerritsz (*q.v.*) and Hoyte Renix (*q.v.*). In 1606 he was still living; in that year he wrote a letter from Monnikendam to C. P. Hooft, mayor of Amsterdam, a copy of which is in the archives of the Amsterdam church. The archives contain other documents from his hand, e.g., a pamphlet against Menno's book on the ban, and a letter of encouragement to Hans de Ries. A treatise titled *Een Munster end Wttocht also genaempt over Robert Roberts boeksken 1592* (see **Robert Roberts le Canu**) with the motto *Proeve wilt Behouwen* (P. W. Bogaert) is probably from his pen. But he is not to be confused with Pieter Willemsz, who wrote several religious poems and belonged to the strict opposing party. The correspondence with the Prince of Orange and the letter to Hooft are found in Blaupot t.C., *Holland* I, 381-84.   J.L.

Inv. Arch. Amst. I, Nos. 421 f., 478, 480 f., 488 f., 517, 630-34, 637, 639, 641; *DB* 1873, 8; 1898, 147; 1893, 62, 67, 70; *Archief Ned. Kerkgesch.* XI, 345; Blaupot t. C., *Holland* I, 84, 151, 259, 381; A. Brons, *Ursprung, Entwicklung und Schicksale der* . . . *Mennoniten* (Emden, 1912) 115; *ML* I, 241 f.

Bogatzky, Carl Heinrich von (1690-1774), one of the most popular and influential devotional writers of the Lutheran Church in Germany, a leader in the Pietist movement. After a study of law at the University of Jena (1713-15) he transferred to the University of Halle where he studied theology (1715-18) and came fully under the influence of A. H. Francke, the great Pietist leader. Unable to undertake a pastorate because of poor health, he spent his long life in a private pastoral ministry to many noble families, and also in institutions, first largely in his native Silesia, then after 1746 in Halle, where he ministered widely to students and young people.

Bogatzky's chief contribution was made, however, through his devotional writings, which, though not intellectually on a high plane, nevertheless had great influence because of their warm piety, deep sincerity, and simplicity of expression; they are among the best and most influential products of "Halle Pietism." *Güldenes Schatzkästlein der Kinder Gottes,* Bogatzky's first book (1718), became tremendously popular and has enjoyed countless editions. *Tägliches Hausbuch der Kinder Gottes* was another widely read volume. The *Schatzkästlein* appeared in a Philadelphia (Pa.) edition of 1811, a copy of which was possessed by the grandmother of John F. Funk in Eastern Pennsylvania. In far-off Waterloo Co., Ont., in the early years of the pioneer Mennonite settlement there, Heinrich Eby published in 1845 a 31-page extract from Bogatzky's *Das Leben Christi im Himmel,* under the title, *Eine Betrachtung über die Sünde wider den Heiligen Geist.* His writings were found in Mennonite homes.   H.S.B.

Böger, Salomon, a Hutterite miller of Moravia (d. 1610), who distinguished himself by his unusual activities to redeem Hutterite women dragged away by the Turks during a very bloody war raid in 1605. His story is to be found in a special Hutterite codex (yet unpublished) which contains 24 letters of Böger from his wanderings through Turkish Hungary and Turkey proper (1607-10) sent home to his congregation in Moravia. It is an unusual story of great struggle and tragedy, the earliest record of Anabaptist relief work as far as is known. For 13 years (1593-1606) a savage war raged between Turkey and the Holy Roman Empire along a frontier roughly identical with that between Czechoslovakia and Austria. The Hutterite colonies in Southern Moravia suffered severely, particularly because of their practiced nonresistance (*Geschicht-Buch,* 482-93). Böger felt urged to undertake whatever was possible to rescue not only his own wife and child but any prisoner who might have survived the assault. The community as such gave him little help, being in great distress itself. Böger spent a total of 32 months in Turkish territory (i.e., Hungary, Serbia, and Turkey proper), during which time he was able to redeem not more than six sisters and two brothers. He found no trace of his wife, although he went as far as Constantinople and even beyond (Nicea). A Hutterite physician of Nikolsburg, Balthasar Goller (*q.v.*), who accompanied the special imperial ambassador to the Sublime Porte (1608-9), had taken Böger along on this long and difficult trip, but lack of money and influence prevented any major success. The letters reveal all the hardship and anxiety of the man on his many trips up and down along the Danube. Finally in 1610 Colonel Kollonitsch, an outstanding (Calvinistic) nobleman and marshal, on whose estate in Slovakia Hutterite colonies were permitted to flourish, gave Böger a Turkish prisoner of war to be taken along as an exchange for any Hutterite to be discovered. From this last trip in 1610 Böger never returned; people at home surmised that he was slain by the Turk, who thus ransomed himself. The codex closes with the melancholy remark, "Now also he will have found his rest on behalf of his wife." The codex contains much valuable information concerning conditions inside Turkey, as well as a vivid picture of the plight of the colonies in Moravia and their spirit. (See **Bocskay**.)   R.F.

R. Friedmann, "Adventures of an Anabaptist in Turkey, 1607-1610," *MQR* XVII (1943) 73-86, with further bibliographical references. A transcript of the codex is to be found in the Mennonite Historical Library at Goshen College.

Bogerman, Johannes, b. about 1576 at Uplewert in East Friesland, d. Sept. 11, 1637, at Franeker (Dutch province of Friesland), well-known Reformed theologian, minister at Sneek (1599), Enkhuizen (1602), Leeuwarden (1603), and at the wish of Prince Maurice of Orange, temporary minister in The Hague (1618); in 1633 appointed professor of theology at the university of Franeker. Bogerman, who was an extremely ardent Calvinist, became best known as chairman of the great national synod of the Reformed Church held at Dordrecht in 1618-19, which proscribed the Remonstrants (*q.v.*) and gave the commission for a new Dutch translation of the Bible, the so-called *Statenvertaling*. The Remonstrants were, however, not the only object of his intolerance, but also the Mennonites. He insisted repeatedly that the provincial synods make regulations against the Mennonites. Together with his colleague Geldorpius, he translated Theodorus Beza's (*q.v.*) pamphlet concerning the execution of heretics (*De hæreticis*), which appeared in print in Sneek in 1601, and was dedicated to the town government of Sneek. In the foreword Bogerman and Geldorp urged the government to maintain true doctrine and to persecute the Mennonites. (*Biog. Wb.* I, 466-76 and the literature mentioned there.)   vDZ.

Bogomazov, a village in the Mennonite colony of New Samara, in the Russian province and district of Samara, founded in 1890 by emigrants from the Molotschna (*q.v.*) settlement. It was in 1915 composed of 40 families with 200 inhabitants, and had its own school (*ML* I, 242).   C.B.

Bohemia. From a manuscript of the Benedictine monastery at Raigern in Moravia we learn why Anabaptism did not achieve the same significance in Bohemia as in the adjacent Moravia, and why Anabaptist emissaries were able to go only to the German inhabitants. They were strenuously opposed not only by Catholicism, but also by the Czech Utraquists and the Bohemian Brethren. There was probably no lack of attempts on the part of the Anabaptists to gain a footing in Bohemia.

The appearance of Thomas Müntzer at Prague in 1521, where he preached in the churches of Bethlehem and Corpus Christi in Latin and German, and excited the populace, has, to be sure, nothing to do with the Anabaptist movement; but from the documents concerning court trials of 1527 in Ansbach and in Passau of 1528 it is known that the Anabaptist movement had gained some ground in southern Bohemia. The former records report that an Anabaptist lay in prison a year and seven weeks in Bohemia, and was released as if by a miracle; the latter report that in addition to Hans Reichenberger another Anabaptist, Hans, called the *kleine Männdel*, was engaged in southern Bohemia as an Anabaptist missionary.

In the town of Krumau in Bohemia Anabaptists gathered from the congregation of Hans Hut (*q.v.*) in neighboring Austria. When they learned of Jakob Hutter's activity in Moravia, 80 of them went from Krumau to the brotherhood in Austerlitz in 1529. Of these 80, only a small number came originally from Krumau. Even Hans Amon (*q.v.*), their leader, who was very influential in Tirol both before and after the migration, was a native of Bavaria. After 1529 there was also an Anabaptist congregation in Krumau.

When the situation of the Anabaptists in Moravia deteriorated in consequence of the Münster affair, one after another moved to Bohemia, until finally the Diet of 1534 passed severe mandates to prevent further immigration. One of the Anabaptists seized in Passau in the following year on their way out of Moravia and tried was Hans Betz (*q.v.*) of Eger, a weaver and poet who confessed his intention of going home. He remained imprisoned in Passau "for the sake of divine truth, and fell asleep in the Lord" there.

It was doubtless as a stroke against Anabaptist propaganda in Bohemia, that the Moravian Brethren (*q.v.*), for fear of being considered Anabaptist, formally abandoned the doctrine of rebaptism upon transfer of membership, at the Bunzlau Synod in 1534. From this time on one rarely meets an Anabaptist in Bohemia, except in Krumau. A remarkable personality among them was Klain Michel, or as he was called by his companions because of his trade, Michael Säfensieder or Seifensieder (*q.v.*), of Wallern in Bohemia. The story of his sufferings is told in letters written by him and by his fellow sufferers. Having been sent to the brotherhood in Tirol by Hans Amon in Moravia, he was imprisoned with two companions "in the sodomitic city of Vienna" and courageously confessed his faith. He knew the Czech language, for he wrote his wife a "Bohemian letter" from prison; his wife was Czech, and his children did not know German. He asks her, in case Brethren appear looking for work, to receive them and learn from them how to rear children. The letter indicates that the Anabaptists maintained connections with Bohemia. Michel Säfensieder and his two companions "endured death like mighty knights and lovers of God. They were burned to powder on Friday, March 31, 1536, in Vienna."

In the following year Hans Amon sent two epistles to the church in Krumau. In the first he demands complete union with the Moravian church; in the second he sends hearty greetings to persons mentioned by name and requests the prayers of the congregation. The bearer of this letter was Peter Walpot (*q.v.*), who was chosen as head of the entire Hutterite brotherhood in 1565. "It is our greatest joy," writes Amon, "to hear of your prosperity, that you are of one mind and are contending for the divine truth."

In the following decades the Bohemian Anabaptists are rarely mentioned. In the brotherhood in Moravia there are occasionally persons like "Bohemian David," or "Kasper Seidelmann, named Böhm," or "Gregory the Wicked," mentioned in

1550 and 1551 in the histories of the Hutterites, who came from the German parts of Bohemia. A detailed report of Aug. 23, 1556, about Jörg Körber from Bohemian-Aicha, has been preserved.

Among the Moravian Anabaptists there were skilled physicians. One of these, George Zobel, was called to the bedside of Emperor Rudolf II in Prague in 1581. "By the blessing of God the Emperor was raised to health through him." Eighteen years later Zobel's knowledge and help were again required by the imperial court.

When the well-known Moravian statesman, Karl von Zierotin, journeyed through Bohemia in September 1590, he found some Anabaptists near Elbogen, who were just returning to Moravia from an unsuccessful attempt at migration to Germany. We do not know whether or not they engaged in missionary work at Elbogen, as was their custom. The number of Anabaptists in Bohemia was certainly insignificant. The catastrophe which befell Protestantism after White Mountain ended their existence in Moravia and Bohemia.   LOSERTH.

Beck, *Geschichts-Bücher;* J. Loserth, "Deutsch-böhmische Wiedertäufer," in *Mitt. d. Vereins für Gesch. der Deutschen in Böhmen* XXX; *ML* I, 242.

Bohemian Brethren, a name frequently given to a remnant of the Hussites, who in 1467 organized a separate brotherhood in Bohemia (*q.v.*) and who have continued to the present day under the name Moravian (*q.v.*) Brethren (officially Unitas Fratrum). At the beginning of their history they held so many principles similar to the later Anabaptists (rejection of war, violence, and the oath, discipleship of Christ, strict discipline, the Bible as sole authority) that Ludwig Keller (*q.v.*) thought there was a historical connection, which however has never been proved and is most doubtful. The Hutterites are not to be confused with them. Peter Chelcicki (*q.v.*) (d. 1560), a forerunner of the group, an exceptionally fine leader, was very close in his views to the later Anabaptists. (See **Moravian Brethren.**)   H.S.B.

Böhmerle, Stephan, an Anabaptist martyr, beheaded in Esslingen Oct. 5, 1528, the first Anabaptist martyr there. (J. Rauscher, *Württemb. Kirchengesch.* III, 1934, 85; *ML* I, 610.)

Boissevain (Man.) Mennonite Brethren Church was organized Sept. 2, 1928, with a membership of 30 and was at first known as the Whitewater Mennonite Brethren Church. D. D. Derksen was its first leader and pastor and still serves the church in this capacity. The first meetings were held in the home of D. D. Derksen and later in a schoolhouse. In 1944 a church was erected in Boissevain with a seating capacity of 200 and the name was changed to Boissevain M.B. Church. The membership in 1951 was 85, all of whom were rural people. F. K. Dyck, H. B. Dueck, and A. J. Froese have also served the church as ministers.   F.K.D.

Bokhara was originally a large independent country in Central Asia. In 1868 General Konstantin von Kaufmann made the country subject to Russia. The chiliastic Mennonites of Samara made arrangements with him to settle in his province. When they arrived in Kaplanbek (*q.v.*) in 1880, they encountered difficulties in finding the place they had looked for, namely, where they would escape the "tribulations of the last days" and find complete exemption from military service. Therefore a group moved from Kaplanbek to Bokhara convinced that this was the country which God had prepared for them. They soon found out, however, that they were not welcome and were forced to return to the place from which they had come. After they had repeatedly attempted to force their way into Bokhara and settle there and had each time been forcibly sent back, they finally joined the group of Claasz Epp (*q.v.*) at Ak-Mechet (*q.v.*) in Khiva. The well-known educator and writer Martin Klaassen (*q.v.*) died and was buried in Bokhara during one of the attempts to settle in this country. Franz Bartsch (*q.v.*), the author of *Unser Auszug nach Mittelasien,* was also in this group.   C.K.

"Konstantin von Kaufmann" in *Meyers Grosses Konversations-Lexikon.* See also bibliography under other articles referred to.

Bolchen, a town in Lorraine (pop. 4,173 in 1910), 15 miles northeast of Metz. Amish Mennonites of Swiss descent settled around the town in the early 18th century, organizing themselves into a congregation known as Deutsch-Lothringen, which later, as the group increased and scattered, formed four congregations—Bolchen, Mörchingen, Luxembourg (*q.v.*), and Saar (*q.v.*). The group around Bolchen at first held its religious services in private homes, but about the middle of the 19th century two congregations were formed, the one meeting in Mörchingen (Morhange, *q.v.*), the other near Bolchen. Since the latter met in Diesen near Porzelat (district of Forbach), it became known for a time as Bolchen-Diesen. In 1916 it numbered 134 souls, including 58 children, its members mostly farmers, some miners. From the middle of the 19th century the congregation has had two cemeteries, in Dalem and Diesen. The Diesen (*q.v.*) congregation was organized in 1875, but was always closely related to Bolchen, and in recent years has absorbed Bolchen altogether, so that the latter has been dissolved. (*ML* I, 243.)   HEGE, H.S.B.

Boldt (Bolt, Baldt, Boltz), a Mennonite family name in West Prussia in the Frisian and Flemish congregations, which was first mentioned in 1655 at Danzig (*q.v.*), and in 1705 at Schönsee (*q.v.*) (Sosnovka). In 1776, 6 families of this name were listed in West Prussia (without Danzig), and in 1935, 13 persons. Members of the family emigrated to Russia and subsequently to Canada and South America.   G.R.

Boller, Heinrich, of Wadischwyl (Wädenswil) in Switzerland, one of the last victims of the Zürich persecution of the Swiss Brethren. He was imprisoned in 1644 in Zürich for his faith, as an aged man, and died of the privations imposed upon him (*Mart. Mir.* D 823, E 1121; *ML* I, 243).   O.H.

Bololo Mennonite Brethren Mission in Africa derived its name from the village in the Kasai District of the Belgian Congo (*q.v.*) near which the first station was built. In 1933 Henry G. Bartsch, who had been assisting at the Kafumba station of the Kwango District mission, set out in search of a location for a mission to the Dengese tribe. The field is roughly 50 miles north and south and 100 miles east and west, bounded on the north by the Lukenie and on the south by the Sankuru rivers. Dekese is the capital of the area. Between 1933 and 1942 other workers labored on this field at short intervals as follows: Eva Jantz, 1933-34; Lydia Jantz, 1933-35; Kathryn Harder, 1933-37; William Jantz, 3 months in 1933; Margaret Siemens, 1936-39; Herman Lentzmann, 1937-39, and Karl Kramer, 1938-42.

In 1943 the M.B. Conference officially accepted full responsibility for the Bololo Mission. When in 1946 the Wm. G. Baergs were sent out by the M.B. Board of Foreign Missions, the center of activity was shifted to Djongo Sanga, where a new station was built a half mile south of the village. Djongo Sanga, the only main station, has an elementary school, a church with regular worship services, a dispensary and several huts for hospital wards, three residences for missionaries, a boys' dormitory, and some small storage sheds. Besides the worship services, school, and medical work maintained on the station, the missionaries go out to the villages for itinerant preaching and to organize and supervise village schools. Other staff members are Mr. and Mrs. John C. Ratzlaff, Susie Brucks, and Elsie Guenther. The total church membership is 35. No ordination of national workers has yet taken place, although several nationals serve as evangelists. A.E.J.

Bolshevism is the name of a particular development and school of thought within the Marxist movement in Russia. In opposition to the more democratic Menshevik (minority) party the Bolshevik (majority) party favored the overthrowing of existing governments by force and the establishment of the "dictatorship of the proletariat." The Bolshevik party suppressed the Menshevik party as soon as it came to power in Russia in 1917.

Under Bolshevism the Mennonite communities and way of life were gradually disintegrated. This process was completed during World War II when most of the Mennonites of the Ukraine were evacuated to Siberia or Germany. Some of the latter found their way to Paraguay and Canada but most of them were "repatriated" by the Red army at the end of the war and sent to Siberia. See also **Russia, Concentration Camps,** and **Forced Labor.**
C.K.

Bolsward, a town in the Dutch province of Friesland (pop. 7,400 in 1947), which has a Mennonite congregation, which presumably originated between 1537 and 1550. Perhaps its proximity to Witmarsum and Menno's preaching there led to its rise. Bolsward was the home of the martyr Frans Dammasz (q.v.), who was burned at Leeuwarden on March 28, 1545. Between 1551 and 1565 Leenaert Bouwens baptized 68 persons in or near Bolsward. At the time of the dissension between the Flemish and the Frisians (1566-67), he sided with Hoyte Renix (q.v.), the noted elder who was banned by the Flemish and later united with the Young Frisians. Little is known of the history of the Mennonites of Bolsward. We know that in 1657 there were four Mennonite congregations in Bolsward, which had their own churches or meeting places. One of the congregations met in 1594 in a building on the Schilwijk (now Schildwijk), where the church is still standing. The other congregations worshiped on De Kampen, the Hoogstraat and Kerkstraat. One of these was probably a Janjacobsgezinden (q.v.) congregation. By 1710 all these congregations had merged into one. At this time the number of members not receiving charity (niet-gealimenteerde) was 130. The total membership in 1838 was 157; in 1898, 234; in 1952, 118. These members live in part in Bolsward, where they are engaged in business, and in part in the villages around Bolsward, where they are engaged in farming.

Miss D. Mesdag, a former member, gave this congregation a bequest in the form of an endowment known as the Instelling van Weldadigheid der Doopsgezinde Gemeente van Bolsward, for the benefit chiefly of needy widows and older women.

In 1914 the first woman became a member of the church council. The congregation, a member of Ring Bolsward, has an organization of women and one of young people. The church was enlarged in 1850; in 1938 the congregation bought a new parsonage. In 1951 an old people's home was built. Preachers since 1788 were Siemon Menalda, 1788-1813; Joost Halbertsma, 1814-21; G. Koopmans, 1821-31; W. van Hulst, 1831-58; H. A. van Gelder, 1858-63; A. W. Huidekoper, 1864-73; S. Kutsch Loyenga, 1871-87; W. J. van Douwen, 1887-92; J. Pottinga Hzn, 1893-1912; D. Kossen, 1913-32; M. J. Kosters Gzn, 1933-40; E. H. Boer, 1941-46; M. A. Hylkema, 1947-51; and since 1952 H. van Bilderbeek. vDZ.

Blaupot t. C., Friesland; Inv. Arch. Amst. I, Nos. 182, 607; II, Nos. 1568-93; DB 1901, 211; Ned. Archief v. Kerkgesch. XI (1914) 227 f.; ML I, 243.

Bolsward Ring. After the organization of Ring Akkrum (q.v.) in 1837, Ring Bolsward was established in 1840, with the name, Vereeniging van eenige doopsgezinde gemeenten en leeraren ter bevordering der predikdienst in Zuidwest-Friesland. It was organized by the following six congregations: Bolsward, Hindeloopen, Warns, Witmarsum, Workum, and Woudsend. Later other congregations joined it. The latest congregation admitted was Terschelling in 1896. The union, which holds an annual meeting of delegates from member congregations, has the name, Doopsgezinde Vereniging tot bevordering van de predikdienst en het godsdienstonderwijs in Zuidwestelijk Friesland. But it is usually known simply as "Ring Bolsward." Its purpose is to fill vacant pulpits with preachers of other congregations in the organization.

Ring Bolsward is at present made up of Baard, Balk, Bolsward, Franeker, Harlingen, Hindeloopen, Koudum, Makkum, Sneek, Staveren, Terschelling, Warns, Workum, Woudsend, IJlst, and IJtens. (H. J. Buse, "Beknopte gesch. van de Ring Bolsward van 1840-1913," ms.; ML I, 243.) vDZ.

Bolsweert, Frans van: see **Frans Dammasz.**

Bolt Eberli (Hippolyt Eberle), of Lachen, canton of Schwyz (Switzerland), an Anabaptist martyr, burned at the stake, May 29, 1525, in his home town (Egli, *Zwingliana* I, 141). Johannes Kessler relates in his *Sabbata* that he was a pious, kindhearted man. Several of the Swiss Brethren who had escaped from prison in Zürich in April 1525 came to him and notified him that they had other kindhearted brethren in St. Gall; they wished to go to them. Then he said, "I want to go to see the Brethren at St. Gall; for I have heard much concerning their faith." "But he was not rebaptized, but an opponent. But they persisted until he permitted himself to be baptized here in St. Gall, and since he knew the Scripture and was an eloquent speaker, they entreated him to be a preacher, and he declared himself ready to preach wherever they wished. . . . Then almost the entire city assembled at the Berlisberg to hear the peasant. . . . He preached in the city during the Easter holidays and every day in the following week . . . praised Anabaptism with beautiful words, announced special powers their followers were to receive, whereby all desire and pleasure in sin would be eradicated, and offered to baptize all who desired it. Then many citizens and peasants came. . . . After a week Bolt departed. But as soon as he returned to the region of Schwyz he was seized and sentenced to death by fire together with the priest who had been with him here; both approached the fire cheerfully and died willingly and undismayed." He was the first martyr of the Swiss Brethren in a Catholic canton. After Grebel's departure he worked in St. Gall. (Wackernagel, *Lieder; idem, Kirchenlied* V, 707; *MQR*, 1933, 208 f.; *ML* I, 245.)   NEFF.

Boltzinger (Poltzinger), **Leonhard,** an Anabaptist martyr, was seized in 1590 near Julbach in Bavaria. He was taken to Braunau, where he languished in the dungeon for 23 weeks. All attempts to make him recant failed; the most brutal torture was of no avail. On March 18, 1591, he was therefore beheaded at Julbach near Braunau. A hymn was written to commemorate his death, with his name in acrostic, beginning "Lasset uns von ganzer Seel lobsingen dem Gott Israel."
Wolkan, *Geschicht-Buch*, 432; *Lieder der Hutterischen Brüder* (Scottdale, 1914) 788; Wolkan, *Lieder*, 235; *Mart. Mir.* D 777, E 1080.

Bom, Cornelis, a Mennonite baker of Holland, place unknown, emigrated to Germantown, Pa., in 1683, and died there before 1689. (*MQR* VIII, October 1933, 234.) Cornelis Bom van Cranenburch, who in 1632 was a preacher of the Flemish Mennonite congregation at Schiedam, Dutch province of South Holland, and concerning whom some documents are found in the Amsterdam Archives (*Inv. Arch. Amst.* I, No. 593, II, 2, Nos. 329, 340, 348), is presumably not the same person as the emigrant of 1683. He may have been a relative. (*DB* 1884, 74.)   VDZ.

Bommel and **Ooltgensplaat,** two villages on the island of Over-Flakkee, in the Dutch province of South Holland, where there was once a Mennonite congregation. On Aug. 25, 1622, the Mennonites of Ooltgensplaat presented a petition to the council of Holland, asking that they might perform their marriages in their own meetinghouse, as they had

formerly done. This petition was refused. In 1626 Willem Jansz Exsel(t), as an elder of the Bommel congregation, signed the confession of J. Outerman (*q.v.*), and in 1632 he and Gijsbert Spiering signed the Dordrecht Confession. The Bommel congregation belonged to the Flemish branch. In 1664 the congregation joined the *Verbondt van Eenigheijdt,* a union of conservative churches in the Netherlands. It was signed by Nicolaes Gerritsz and Cornelis Jansz Munster of Bommel. The congregation then had only a few members. Cornelisz Jansz Munster in 1676 moved to Rotterdam, was accepted there without *attestatie* (certification), for there was no longer a congregation at Bommel, neither preacher nor laymen. (*DB* 1899, 183; 1908, 114, 115; Blaupot t.C., *Holland* I, 220, 330; *ML* I, 245.)   VDZ.

Bommel, Herman van (Hermann von Bommeln), formerly court chaplain of the Duke Karel van Gelre, in the Netherlands, joined the Anabaptists, and moved to Polish West Prussia, where he, March 28, 1547, obtained a large territory in the Danzig Werder (lowlands) for colonization of Dutch Anabaptists. He and Hugo Mathiszoon, a weaver from The Hague, were the preachers of the Danzig congregation about 1550.   VDZ.
DB 1917, 137; Horst Penner, *Ansiedlung Mennonitischer Niederländer im Weichselmündungsgebiet . . . (Schriftenreihe des Menn. Geschichtsvereins,* No. 3, 1940) 12-13; *MQR* XXXIII (October 1949) 235.

Bon Homme, a Hutterite Bruderhof 5 miles southwest of Benard, Man., founded in 1918 by Preacher Joseph Waldner and 14 families from the Bon Homme Bruderhof near Tabor, S.D. The move to Canada was made because Canada promised freedom from military service to conscientious objectors. Joseph Waldner died in 1934. In 1929 Michael Waldner and in 1934 Joseph Wollmann were chosen to the ministry. In 1947 this colony had a total of 180 souls, 72 being baptized members.   D.D.

Bon Homme, a Hutterite Bruderhof 20 miles west of Yankton, Bon Homme Co., S.D. It was founded in 1874. Preacher Michael Waldner reinstated communal living in Russia in 1859, supported by Jakob Hofer, who was later chosen preacher. But when Russia introduced universal military service these two preachers with several families emigrated to America and founded the first Hutterite Bruderhof in America. During a period of 74 years (1874-1948) this Bruderhof became the parent colony of 30 colonies in South Dakota and Manitoba, with a population of 2,767 souls, all born in the Bruderhofs. Michael Waldner died in 1889 and is buried here. Jakob Hofer moved out of this Bruderhof and founded the Milltown Bruderhof, where he died. Jakob Waldner, chosen as preacher at Bon Homme in 1875, died in the Milltown Bruderhof. Joseph Waldner, chosen as minister in 1880, died here in 1915. Michael Waldner, chosen as minister in 1907, died 1947, is also buried here. Joseph Wirz was chosen in 1945. There were 43 baptized members in a population of 108 in 1947.   D.D.

Bondgenoten (*Bundgenossen*), a term used by the first Anabaptists of Strasbourg and the Netherlands to designate their brotherhood. Karel Vos devoted a study to this subject (*DB* 1917, 82-90), and came to the conclusion that the term then signified covenanters in a league, i.e., persons bound together in the expectation of the imminent millennium. In this fashion the transition to revolutionary Anabaptism was easily made, so that "Bondgenoten" became synonymous with "Münsterites" and later, about 1544, with "Batenburgers," after which time the term died out.

This explanation has been found to be a very one-sided interpretation of the word. There were, to be sure, Münsterites and revolutionary Anabaptists who called themselves Bondgenoten, and the Batenburgers were referred to as "the Bondgenoten of the sword." But a statement made by Jan Paauw (beheaded at Amsterdam, March 6, 1535) at the time of his trial, "that the covenant is nothing other than that they (the Anabaptists) promise (i.e., to God) to walk in the ways of God, and without departing therefrom," indicates an entirely different viewpoint and does not have anything to do with a revolutionary persuasion. The term "Verbondt" as used by Melchior Hofmann (which is to be found in his book, *Van de Ordinantie Gods,* BRN V, 155-56) may have opened the door for the declaration that "Bondgenoten are persons who have a yearning outlook for a complete change in the social order" (Vos); but when Menno Simons in his tract against Jan van Leyden also calls himself a Bondgenoot, and contrasts the false Bondgenoten (those who employ violence) with the true, and says that many peaceful Mennonites after him were likewise called Bondgenoten, then we can see that the term cannot be used exclusively to designate the revolutionary Anabaptists.

The expression rather has its origin in I Peter 3:21 where baptism is viewed as a matter of good conscience (the Dutch Bible has a word meaning "covenant") toward God. In this sense the peaceful leader of the congregation at Strasbourg, Jacob Grosz, as early as 1527 refers to baptism as the covenant of a good conscience toward God, i.e., in the same sense in which Menno Simons and Dirk Philips later use the term. The term then means those who have accepted the sign of the covenant (*q.v.*), namely, the baptism of conversion. The emphasis was not placed so much on being bound together with each other in expectation of a new social order, but rather being bound with God, of which baptism is the sign. This is shown by the fact that many martyrs confessed that they were members of *'t verbondt,* i.e., the brotherhood.vDZ.

W. I. Leendertz, *Melchior Hofmann* (Haarlem, 1883); A. Hulshof, *Geschiedenis van de Doopsgezinden te Straatsburg* (Amsterdam, 1905); C. Krahn, *Menno Simons* (Karlsruhe, 1936) 22-31.

Bondo, seat of a Mennonite congregation on the Indonesian island of Java, on the former territory of the Dutch Mennonite Mission Association, organized as an independent church in 1940. This congregation of Javanese Christians has 106 baptized members; children of members number 179, catechumens 15. Since 1943 Barnawi has been the unordained minister. (*Verslag Doopsgez. Zending* 1949, 15-16.)   vDZ.

Bonnet. The headdress of Christian women has at times been prescribed in a particular form for re-

ligious purposes, especially by Catholic religious orders, but also by Protestant groups, such as the Salvation Army (founded 1865), which prescribes a characteristic bonnet for its women workers, and the deaconess societies in Europe and America.

However, the bonnet prescribed for most of the 19th century and the 20th century by certain American Mennonite groups of Swiss-South German extraction for all women members is something quite different, more related to the insistence of certain Russian Mennonite groups that their women continue to wear the simple peasant cloth kerchief instead of a hat than to a special garb for nuns or religious workers. In both cases without doubt the desire to maintain simplicity and nonconformity to the world with its changing styles of headdress has been a major motivating factor. However, the traditionalism of conservative rural culture in maintaining older forms of costume as over against the inroads of urban culture influences may also have played a part.

Another source of influence must be reckoned with, however, namely the Quaker bonnet. Since European Mennonites never had the bonnet practice for women, and since there is evidence that the oldest form of Mennonite and Amish headdress was not the bonnet (the conservative "Nebraska" Amish women of Belleville, Pa., still wear a broad-brimmed flat hat, and no bonnet, and some broad-brimmed beaver hats of early and mid-19th century use have been preserved among descendants of both Ontario [Vineland] Mennonite and Pennsylvania-Ohio Amish families) it is possible that it was Quaker influence which brought the bonnet into Eastern Pennsylvania Mennonite and Amish practice. In the Franconia conference area the contact between the Quakers and Mennonites was particularly close, and in colonial and later Pennsylvania the common position of the two groups on nonresistance, simplicity, and the nonswearing of oaths, created a strong bond of sympathy. The almost identical appearance of the Mennonite and Quaker bonnets adds weight to this supposition. Fortunately A. M. Gummère's careful study, *The Quaker, A Study in Costume* (Phila., 1901), contains an excellent chapter on "The Evolution of the Quaker Bonnet" (187-228), with illustrations. Photographs of two black Quaker bonnets of 1856 in this chapter could almost be taken for typical conservative Mennonite bonnets of 1950. It is true that during the 19th century the common headdress of American women also at times took on a form similar to the Quaker and Mennonite bonnet, and it is possible that the Mennonite bonnet was simply a retention of a type of headdress prevalent at a certain period, first retained by custom in resistance to style changes, and later required by religious and church sanctions.

Whatever the origin, the black bonnet, as distinct from the common woman's hat in various colors, became by the mid-19th century a prescribed part of the woman's costume in the United States sections of the Mennonite Church (MC), the Amish Mennonite Church, and all groups related to them. The more conservative the group, conference, or congregation, the more the older form of the bonnet (large size, front projection, and rear curtain down to the base of the neck) has been maintained. By the mid-20th century, however, in the Mennonite Church the bonnet had changed greatly in size and shape, becoming much smaller and more compact, and approaching in appearance the small close-fitting hat that often worn by American women today. In some sections the bonnet has almost disappeared among younger women, and in some congregations practically vanished altogether. The small size and simple character of much of the contemporary American woman's headdress has made this transition easier than in earlier times. Usually a simple dark-colored soft hat is adopted as a successor to the bonnet.

In form and material the bonnet has gone through several changes which need not be detailed here. The Old Order Amish women still wear the slat-bonnet which was formerly quite common, in which strips (slats) of cardboard or some stiff material are inserted into the cloth of that part of the bonnet which projects over the face to hold its shape. The cloth of the rear part of these bonnets usually extends down to the shoulders, and the projection over the face is so long as to make it impossible to see the face except from directly in front. Amish little girls also wear the same bonnet from babyhood. The women of the Reformed Mennonites in Eastern Pennsylvania and Maryland wear an older style gray bonnet.

The Mennonite women of Ontario did not adopt the "American" bonnet until well into the twenties of the 20th century. Before that they wore a variant type known as the "English" or "Queen Victoria" bonnet, which can be readily identified from the familiar pictures of Queen Victoria's later life. This bonnet was, however, not a uniquely Mennonite style, and was much worn by older women of all denominations in England and Canada in the late 19th century, particularly by conservative Methodist and Baptist women. (See Costume.) H.S.B.

A. M. Gummère, *The Quaker, A Study in Costume* (Phila., 1901); printed minutes and disciplines of various district conferences of the Mennonite Church (MC).

Bontemps, Pierre (Petrus), b. 1609, pastor of the French Reformed Church in Haarlem (Holland), strenuously opposed the Mennonites in a book he wrote in 1641 with the title, *Kort Bewijs van de menighvuldige doolingen der Wederdoopers ofte Mennisten;* it was issued in three editions, 1641, 1653, and 1661. Joost Hendriksz (*q.v.*) published a reply (1643), picturing the Anabaptist persecutions in Zürich in dark colors. Bontemps wrote a refutation, presenting the matter as if nothing of importance had happened in Zürich. A lengthy paper-war ensued. Three pamphlets against Bontemps appeared in Amsterdam, Haarlem, and Rotterdam; the last was written by Geeraerd van Vrijburgh. Bontemps replied in three pamphlets, which were in turn answered by van Vrijburgh. This was the conclusion of the affair. NEFF.

Catalogus Amst., 200-02; *DB* 1863, 133 f.; 1897, 117; Müller, *Berner Täufer,* 166; J. H. Ottius, *Annales Ana-*

baptistici (Basel, 1672) 295-301; *Biogr. Wb.* I, 489-90; *ML* I, 245.

Bontrager (Bontreger, Borntrager, Bornträger, Borntreger, Borntraeger), a Mennonite family name of Swiss origin. Martin Bornträger, an Amish Mennonite, was born in Switzerland and on Oct. 5, 1767, arrived in Philadelphia with three sons—John, Christian, and Andrew. The family located at Meyersdale in Somerset Co., Pa. It is said that Andrew later moved to Virginia and Christian to Indiana Co., Pa. The descendants of John are widely scattered in Amish and Mennonite communities in Ohio, Indiana, Illinois, Iowa, Kansas, and other states. Among the well-known Amish descendants was Joseph Bontreger (1811-1908), who was a deacon in Elkhart Co., Ind. Of his sons, two were chosen bishops, one a minister, and two deacons. A grandson, Bishop Eli J. Bontrager, of Shipshewana, Ind., is widely known both in Amish and in Mennonite circles.

In the 1951 *Mennonite Yearbook* three Old Order Amish Mennonite ordained Bontragers are listed for Illinois, fifteen for Indiana, five for Iowa, one for Kansas, three for Michigan, two for Ohio, one for Tennessee, and two for Wisconsin. In addition nine are listed for the Mennonite Church and one for the Conservative Amish Mennonite Church. M.G.

Sam R. Bontrager, *Family Record of Daniel J. Borntrager and His Descendants* (Haven, Kan., 1942); John E. Borntreger, *Descendants of Martin Borntraeger the Emigrant of 1767* (Scottdale, 1923).

Book and Tract Messenger, a four-page publication, appearing in September 1899 at Spring Grove, Pa., containing the history and constitution of the Mennonite Book and Tract Society (MC), a list of tracts published, and other items of interest relating to the Society's work. No further issues were published. N.P.S.

Bookstores, Mennonite. The first Mennonite bookstore in America was probably the one operated by the Mennonite Publishing Company at Elkhart, Ind., possibly established as early as 1867 by John F. Funk when he moved his printing business from Chicago to Elkhart. It was sold to James A. Bell in 1908, but has continued as a book and stationery store at the same location uninterruptedly to date.

The Western Publishing Co., Halstead, Kan., with David Goerz as manager, started a bookstore in Halstead in 1876; in 1880 it was taken over by Goerz, who also established a branch in Newton, Kan.

In 1882 Joel and B. F. Welty, two members of the First Mennonite Church at Berne, Ind., established a bookstore in the town of Berne. Two years later when the General Conference of the Mennonite Church of North America met at Berne, its Publication Board took over the Welty store, thus making it the first official Mennonite bookstore in America. By 1887 the establishment had sold over 11,000 volumes. In time it came to be known as the Mennonite Book Concern, and later the Mennonite Book Store. Two additional official bookstores serve the General Conference Mennonite Church. In 1946 the Mennonite Book Store was established in Newton, Kan. In 1947 the Mennonite

Book Store was opened in Rosthern, Sask. For several years previously a bookstore in Rosthern had operated under the auspices of the Canadian Mennonite Board of Colonization. The total investment in the three stores amounted to $30,000 in 1950.

John W. Weaver began a bookselling business in 1895 at Spring Grove, Pa. This may be considered the beginning of a service around which the present official bookstores of the Mennonite (MC) Church have been built. About this time John W. Weaver was appointed secretary-treasurer of the Mennonite Book and Tract Society, which in 1908 was absorbed by the Mennonite Publishing House, locating its headquarters in Scottdale, Pa. Weaver continued his growing book business personally until 1927, when the store, which then included a branch in Lancaster, Pa., was purchased by the Mennonite Publishing House. In 1937 the Golden Rule Book Store in Kitchener, Ont., was purchased by the House, and in 1939 the Graybill Book Store in Souderton, Pa., likewise. In 1942 the Gospel Book Store was established by the House in Goshen, Ind. At Scottdale, a bookstore has been a part of the House activities since the early days of the establishment. In each instance these stores have been profitable and have rendered an important service in their respective communities. The largest of these stores is the one in Lancaster, which has an inventory of approximately $55,000. The Golden Rule Book Store had an inventory of $31,000 and the Gospel Book Store had a stock of $27,000 in 1950.

The Mennonite Brethren Publishing House, Hillsboro, Kan., has operated a book business ever since it acquired the D. E. Harder bookstore in 1920, and the Christian Press Book Store, Winnipeg, Man., serves the Mennonite Brethren in Canada. The Mennonite Brethren in Christ (UMC) established the Bethel Publishing Co. Book Store, Elkhart, Ind., in 1927 and continue to operate it. No other branches of the church have official bookstores.

There are, however, a number of private bookstores serving the major Mennonite and Amish communities. The major private enterprise serving the United Missionary Church is the Leonard Book Store, Owen Sound, Ont. The Old Order Amish constituency is served by the Benjamin Esh Book Store, Ronks, Pa.; the L. A. Miller store, Arthur, Ill.; and the J. A. Raber store, Baltic, Ohio. Mennonite Brethren private bookstores include the Kroeker Book Store, now the Eitzen Book and Gift Shop, Mountain Lake, Minn.; and the Suderman bookstore in Reedley, Cal. D. W. Friesen and Son of Altona, Man., have for many decades served a large Canadian constituency. The Evangel Book Shop, Steinbach, Man., also serves Manitoba Mennonites. In western Canada the Christian Book Store was opened near Abbotsford, B.C., in 1946. The Klassen Book and Variety Store, Yarrow, B.C., was discontinued in 1951 because of the floods that swept through the Mennonite settlements of the area. The Herald Book Store, Newton, Kan., an outgrowth of the Beehive Book Store which was operated by the Krehbiel brothers, has served a large Mennonite constituency for many years. The Mennonite colleges all operate bookstores for the student-faculty community. Other smaller book concerns operated by Mennonites are scattered throughout various Mennonite communities in the United States, such as in Orrville, Ohio; Gretna, Steinbach, and Winkler, Man.; Peoria, Ill.; Henderson, Neb., and Freeman, S.D.

Most of the American Mennonite bookstores operate primarily as religious bookstores, Bible houses, and stationery stores. A few emphasize Mennonite publications, but the paucity of Mennonite books usually results in the display and promotion of a large amount of non-Mennonite literature. Thus the bookstores often become significant channels for the promotion of types of theology and piety which are not always congenial to the traditional historic Mennonite type.

In Holland there have never been special Mennonite bookstores or publishing houses, such as in America. From the oldest times Mennonite authors have had their books printed and published by non-Mennonites or Mennonites alike. Exceptions are the set of booklets for the Mennonites in the diaspora, the *Geschriftjes voor de Doopsgezinden in de Verstrooiing* (q.v.), which were published by a special committee and more recently certain booklets published by the A.D.S. That the Mennonites in the Netherlands have not had a publishing house of their own is due to the fact that they live in closer relationship with non-Mennonites and the culture of their country in general, than most of the Mennonites in other countries. There have, however, in the past been some well-known Dutch Mennonite printers and publishers, although they always dealt in non-Mennonite publications also. In the 16th century we find first at Emden, later on in Amsterdam, Nicolaes Biestkens (q.v.), who printed, in addition to the *Biestkens-Bible* (q.v.), at least one edition of the first martyr-book, the *Offer des Heeren* (q.v.), and also some old hymnbooks. Mennonite printers and publishers were numerous in the Netherlands during the 17th century. For example, in Amsterdam: J. A. Calom (q.v.), Jan Theunisz (q.v.), and particularly Jan Rieuwertsz (q.v.), who published many books written by Mennonites and Collegiants (q.v.), and whose bookshop was a meeting place of those Mennonites who were interested in books. In Haarlem were found H. P. van Wesbusch (q.v.) and Th. Fonteyn; in Hoorn, Zacharias Cornelisz (q.v.) and Iz. Willemsz; at de Rijp, Claes Jacobsz, etc. Today the widely known Dutch publishing houses of Tjeenk Willink at Haarlem, and de Bussy at Amsterdam, are of Mennonite background.

Among the Mennonites of Russia the following bookstores served their constituencies during the 19th and the beginning of the 20th centuries: *Chortitza Colony*, the three firms of Heese and Epp, David Epp, and Born at Chortitza, and the firm of D. P. Isaac at Schönwiese; *Molotschna Colony*, the firm of "Raduga" at Halbstadt, the firms Töws, Penner, and Isaak Fast at Gnadenfeld, Helen A. Janzen at Tiege, and Jacob Martens at Tiegenhagen; elsewhere, D. J. Warkentin at Memrik, A. P. Friesen at Davlekanovo, and others.

vDZ., M.G.

Boomkamp, Cornelis Jansz, was chosen preacher of the Frisian Mennonite congregation at Alkmaar, Dutch province of North Holland, April 19, 1699, and died there Jan. 14, 1739. By trade he was a house painter. He published *Christus de Messias* (Alkmaar, 1741). (*DB* 1891, 10; *Catalogus Amst.,* 244; *ML* I, 245.) J.L.

Boomkamp, Gijsbert (d. July 11, 1755, at Alkmaar), son of the above, rendered valuable service to the historiography of Holland, both local and national. He wrote many books, most of which are found in the library at Amsterdam. Of these works we mention especially *Stefanus de Diakon en Eerste Martelaar, ten voorbeelde in Rijm gebracht* (Alkmaar, 1743), in which he defends the view that alms collected from believers in church should be used exclusively for the poor. (*N.N.B. Wb.* I, 405-7; *ML* I, 245.) Neff, vdZ.

Boon, Gerrit, an Anabaptist martyr: see **Gerrit Cornelisz.**

Boone County Mennonite Brethren Church, one mile from Raeville, Neb., was founded in 1879 by 15 families who had come that year from Russia. Later, when the town of Petersburg was founded within an eighth of a mile of the church, the postal address became Petersburg. The lea'. r during the first three years was J. J. Regier. Th. membership rose to 50, but fear of intermarriage with Roman Catholics who settled among the Mennonites broke up the church. The church building was sold in 1897 and two years later most of the families had moved to Henderson or Jansen, Neb. I.G.N.

Boonsboro, Md., was the location of Unit 3 of Mennonite Civilian Public Service Camp No. 24, known as the Hagerstown camp. The unit was located on a farm purchased by the Old Order Amish Mennonites in the fall of 1941, and was operated under the Soil Conservation Service (U.S.-D.A.) until 1946. A certain amount of money per man was given the unit by the Mennonite Central Committee but the camp was then operated financially by the Amish entirely independent of MCC control. All but a very few of the campers were Amish. Their camp paper, *The Sun-Beam,* had the largest circulation of all Mennonite camp papers. (See **Civilian Public Service.**) M.G.

Boots. The population in the areas in Prussia, Poland, and Russia in which Mennonites lived wore leather boots reaching to the knees, and when the Mennonites from these areas migrated to North America 1873-80, in the prairie states and provinces, they naturally brought this practice with them. Here all but the most conservative adjusted themselves to their new environment in the matter of footwear, supplanting boots with shoes. The most conservative were the Old Colony Mennonites (*q.v.*) of Manitoba, and even among them all made the adjustment except the ministers, the guardians of tradition. Thus the Old Colony Mennonite ministers of Manitoba, Mexico, and Paraguay still wear the traditional boots (*Stiefel*) for which they believe to find sanction in Eph. 6:15, "An Beinen gestiefelt, als fertig zu treiben das Evangelium des Friedens" (Luther translation).

The older generations of all North American rural Mennonites, particularly the most conservative groups, also held fast to the older customs in footwear, wearing short boots, or old-style shoes with elastic instead of shoelaces. Still earlier the most conservative rural Mennonites in Europe continued to wear buckle-shoes or slippers (with knee-breeches) after this item of costume had generally been abandoned by the population. Elder Jacob Horsch of Würzburg-Giebelstadt, Germany, grandfather of John Horsch, was one of those who held longest to the buckle-shoes. H.S.B.

Boragan, a Mennonite village in the Russian province of Taurida (Crimea), founded in the early 1860's by emigrants from the Molotschna settlement, on land which they themselves purchased; the fields were acquired from the Tatars who were migrating to Turkey in consequence of financial failure. The village consisted in 1916 of about 15 families with 75 inhabitants. It had a school, which was under the Crimean school board, and which was used for religious services until the church in Karassan was built. The population belonged to the Karassan (*q.v.*) congregation; Karassan was about seven miles away (*ML* I, 246). C.B.

Borculo, Hans van, an Anabaptist martyr: see **Hans Collen.**

Borden Mennonite Brethren Church, formerly known as the Hoffnungsfeld Church, located 15 miles northeast of the town of Borden, northern Saskatchewan, is a member of the Canadian Conference of the M.B. Church. It was organized in 1906 under the leadership of David K. Klassen who served the church in this capacity for 13 years. In 1951 its membership was 86. Ministers who have served the congregation in the past are David K. Klassen, Elder David Dyck, John A. Harder, who served as leader 1919-35, Jacob J. Wiens, Jacob A. Nickel, and A. K. Rempel. J.H.E.

Boreel, Adam, Heer van Duynbeke, b. Nov. 2, 1603, at Middelburg in the Dutch province of Zeeland, d. 1667. He was learned and skilled in Hebrew. His idea of the nature of the Christian church, viz., that it should be an invisible church without organization or sacraments, was refuted by the Calvinist professors Maresius and Hoornbeek. His tract, *Onderhandeling noopende den broederlijcken Godtsdienst aangevangen in presentie der vrienden in Amsterdam,* and several manuscripts were preserved by Galenus Abrahamsz de Haan. Bock, in his book, *Historia Antitrinitariorum,* considers him a Socinian, following Sand's verdict.

In Amsterdam Boreel, together with Daniel van Breen and Michiel Coomans, led the Collegiant movement (*q.v.*). There he also met Galenus Abrahamsz de Haan, whom he influenced; to that extent Boreel is significant in our history. Galenus' idea that the true church could be found nowhere on earth was certainly nurtured by the anti-church views of Boreel. Neff.

H. L. Benthem, *Holl. Kirch- und Schulenstaat* (Frankfurt, 1688); C. B. Hylkema, *Reformateurs* I (Haarlem, 1900); II (Haarlem, 1902); Kühler, *Het Socinianisme in Nederland* (Leiden, 1912); *N.N.B. WB.* VI, 163-65; *ML* I, 246.

Borg, Jan ter, a Mennonite preacher at Amsterdam, in every respect a remarkable man. He was born Dec. 22, 1782, at Borne in the province of Overijssel, the son of the baker Koenrad Hendriks ter Borg and his wife Geesken Jans Hulshoff; at the age of ten he lost his father. Through the aid of friends at Borne and Amsterdam he was able to prepare himself for university study. Then he studied in Franeker and after October 1806 at the seminary and the Athenæum in Amsterdam, especially with the professors Hesselink and van Lennep.

June 20, 1810, having become a ministerial candidate, he received a call to Oldeboorn in the province of Friesland, which he accepted at the end of the year after marrying Fenneken Pol. In 1812-20 he served the congregation of Dantumawoude. On Feb. 13, 1820, after the death of Pastor A. H. van Gelder, he became a minister of the Mennonite Church of Amsterdam. He was honorable, gentle and kind in disposition; Dr. Sepp calls him "an unusual man, in whom clearness of intellect and soundness of judgment combined with a depth and sincerity of feeling, and so rich a gift of presentation combined with so original a gift of comprehension and reflection, that he produced a profound effect on Muller with his sermons." The fact that Prof. S. Muller, who for years was the guiding spirit of the brotherhood in Holland and who was himself noted for his extraordinary gift of preaching, was so moved by ter Borg is a particularly honorable testimonial for his talents. Others praised him for his genuine Johannine nature.

But gradually ter Borg came under the influence of the religious awakening that seized Holland at that time, known as the Réveil (q.v.), represented by men like Bilderdijck, da Costa, and Willem de Clercq. Especially when Thelwall, the English minister in Amsterdam, arose as a preacher of repentance (1825), ter Borg was deeply moved. He had undergone a great deal of sadness at home in the hypochondria of his wife and the death of three children. In 1826-28 he took a more and more Calvinistic view of redemption, predestination, the Trinity, etc., with the result that unity with his fellow ministers was destroyed and church services were attended by members of other denominations more than by Mennonites, and some parents hesitated to send their children to him for religious instruction. Consequently a committee of the church council drew up a report concerning ter Borg's relation to the congregation, with a statement by Muller, both of which have been preserved in the church archives. Although ter Borg was modestly but definitely defended by the poet J. van Oosterwijk Brun, a deacon, it was decided that it would be best to have ter Borg resign or to employ a fourth preacher besides him. At the same time Muller was appointed to the seminary and he and his colleague were each assigned half duty in the ministry, so that the situation was temporarily unchanged. In November 1828 ter Borg informed the church council that he had also gradually changed his views on baptism and now preferred infant baptism. On Dec. 18, 1828, he asked for release; this was granted in a dignified

manner with the title of pastor emeritus and a pension of 1,000 guilders. He remained in Amsterdam until 1831 and then moved to the village of Nigtevecht, where he died May 11, 1847. Although his sympathies were on the side of the Reformed, he apparently remained a Mennonite the rest of his life. Thus his personal friendship with Prof. S. Muller, in spite of all their differences of opinion in religious matters, remained intact until his death.

From his pen appeared: *Leerredenen* (Amsterdam, 1831); *Vier bijzondere leerredenen* (Amsterdam, 1833); in *Vaderlandsche Letteroefeningen* (1819) appeared the ter Borg address delivered at the meeting of the Frisian Societeit: "Heeft Menno Simons eene volstrekt algemeene weerloosheid gepredikt?" which he answered in the negative. (U. J. Reinders in *DB* 1897, 1-76; *DB* 1895, 122; 1898, 51; *ML* I, 246.)   J.L.

Borissopol, village No. 2 in the Arkadak Mennonite settlement, Russian province of Saratov, known after the Revolution as Krestyanskoye.

Borissovo, a Mennonite settlement in the Russian province of Ekaterinoslav, district of Bachmut (q.v.), founded in 1892 by members of the Chortitza colony on land purchased by them. It consisted of two villages, Kondratyevka and Nikolaipol, and owned a total of 5,100 hectares (13,000 acres). A farm unit contained 80 dessiatines (210 acres). In 1915 the colony numbered 80 families with 400 inhabitants. Each village had a school (*ML* I, 247).   C.B.

Born, a village in the Dutch province of Limburg, in the 16th century belonging to the dukedom of Jülich (q.v.), was shortly after 1530 a center of Anabaptist activity as were other villages in the neighborhood, such as Wassenberg (q.v.), Dieteren, Susteren, and Millen. The rise of Anabaptism was furthered by the fact that the Roman Catholic clergy in this area had shamefully neglected their task, as well as by the inclination toward the Reformation on the part of the bailiff, Wilhelm von Rennenberg. Lenart van Ysenbroek (q.v.) baptized here frequently. During and before September 1534, 30 Anabaptists, mostly men, were put to death, and in 1535 six more. This is stated by Rembert (*Wiedertäufer,* 419), without mentioning the source from which he drew, or giving the names of the victims. Peter Vrancken (q.v.) was beheaded in Born as a martyr; the year of his death is not known. It is mentioned that in 1557 there were still 14 living here who belonged to the Anabaptists; it appears that a congregation existed here. The well-known elder Lemke (q.v.) baptized a number of persons here in 1558. In spite of persecution the congregation maintained itself; in 1575 there were 18 Mennonite families in Born. In 1619 Anabaptists presented a petition to the government for religious freedom, which actually resulted in a lightening of their oppression. On Sept. 1, 1622, the Count Palatine, who was also the lord of Jülich decided to root out entirely the "souls of the Anabaptists, the rebaptized, or the Mennonites"; their gatherings were to be prevented; they were to be driven out of the country with confiscation of their goods if they refused to be converted to Roman Catholicism. Nevertheless, in 1670 there were Mennonites in Born and vicinity, for in this year their property was confiscated. Shortly afterwards the Mennonites disappeared from this area. vdZ.

W. Bax, *Het Protest. in het Bisdom Luik*, 2 vv. (The Hague, 1937, 1941) *passim;* Rembert, *Wiedertäufer*, 419 *et passim.*

Born, Feike, was appointed to the ministry May 20, 1850, in the Mennonite congregation at Drachten and Ureterp in the Dutch province of Friesland, moved to Joure on Dec. 3, 1854, and died there on April 14, 1886. On Oct. 27, 1861, he delivered an address for the newly founded congregation at Wolvega, which was published under the title, *De Gemeente van Christus Gods gebouw* (Leeuwarden, 1862). In addition he published *Krijgsroep tegen den Krijg* (Joure, 1870); *Leiddraad bij de opleiding der kinderen tot godsdienst en zedelijkheid* (Joure, 1878; second edition 1880 in Assen); *Vragen tot voorbereiding voor de Belijdenis in eene Doopsgezinde Gemeente* (Assen, undated; a second edition followed). (*DB* 1861, 132, 133; 1887, 146, 147; *Catalogus Amst.,* 296, 327; *ML* I, 247.) J.L.

Bornaige, Synken (Josyne), an Anabaptist martyr: see **Sijntgen, Kreupel.**

Borne, a town in the Dutch province of Overijssel (pop. *ca.* 12,000), the seat of a thriving textile industry and since about 1560, of a Mennonite congregation, the first members of which are said to have been weavers, refugees from Flanders; but judging by their names, they were more likely from Westphalia. They probably owed their safety to the magistrate of Twenthe, Count Bentinck, to whom they gave an annual gift of a piece of linen in gratitude for their protection. In the archives of the congregation there are still some letters from 1749 and 1769, in which the Mennonites of Borne and Hengelo offer such a gift to the magistrate. Borne, Hengelo, and Goor together formed a single congregation belonging to the Groninger Old Flemish. Well toward the close of the 18th century they were still observing footwashing with communion services, as was long the practice of the Groninger Old Flemish in the Netherlands.

In 1727 Borne separated peaceably from Hengelo and Goor. In the first half of the 18th century the well-known elder Hendrik Berents Hulshoff (*q.v.*) lived near Borne. Other noted preachers were Wolter ten Cate, 1736-96, and Jan Pol, 1766-1807. After Pol's death the congregation called as its first trained minister Laurens van Cleeff (1809). Originally the congregation held its meetings on the Oude Paschen, a farm near Zenderen, later in the church in the village. In 1824 the present church was built; a small organ was added in 1866, which was replaced by a larger one in 1871.

The congregation has always been very small; in 1733 it still had 94 members; in 1767 this number had decreased to 71; in 1834 it was only 30; in 1898, 57; in 1950, 80. The congregation belongs to Ring Twente; it has a Sunday school for the children, a women's circle, and a Bible circle.

During the last half century the congregation has been served by the following ministers: G. E.

Frerichs, 1890-1903; J. B. du Buy, 1903-12; F. J. de Holl, 1913-26; C. Nijdam, 1926-30; B. van der Goot, 1930-39; Miss H. C. Leignes Bakhoven, 1940-47; and J. Wieringa, 1947-52. F.J.dH., vdZ.

Inv. Arch. Amst. II, Nos. 1594-97; Blaupot t.C., *Groningen* I and II, *passim;* G. Heeringa, *Uit het verleden der Doopsgez. in Twenthe* (Borne) 70-78, 126-34; *ML* I, 247.

Borozenko, a Mennonite settlement founded in 1865-66 by Mennonites from the Chortitza colony on land purchased by themselves; the post office was Nikopol; the area 6,137 dessiatines (*ca.* 18,000 acres). It contained six villages: Nikolaital, Schöndorf, Felsenbach, Steinbach, Ebenfeld, and Blumenhof; population in 1910 was 600 with 120 families (Friesen, *Brüderschaft,* 677).

The settlement made satisfactory economic progress. As a congregation they were served in their baptismal and communion services by the elder of the old Chortitza settlement; but they later joined the Neu-Chortitza congregation, for they were located nearer to the latter.

The school system of Borozenko was very similar to that of Baratov (*q.v.*). Since the parents wished to keep their children on the farm, very few were sent to the Zentralschule.

World War I and its aftermath devastated these villages. Steinbach (and presumably Ebenfeld) was slaughtered off almost completely in a single night. The bandits caused much depredation in the other villages. The settlement was, however, somewhat negligent in the matter of emigration; they finally left the locality; particulars are not known. It is to be assumed that this settlement was completely destroyed in World War II. (*ML* I, 247.) P.A.R.

Borrekiek, an Anabaptist martyr: see **Pieter Pietersen.**

Borstentasters, the name of a small group of Mennonites in Holland banned by the Old Flemish Mennonites in 1620, who speedily united with other Mennonites. (*DB* 1863, 135; Kühler, *Geschiedenis* I, 433.) vdZ.

Bos, Ragger, a Dutch (untrained) Mennonite preacher, serving the congregations of Zwartsluis 1754-87, and Noordeind van Graft and Rijp 1787-96. Bos was one of the first Dutch Mennonite ministers to be interested in politics; he was an ardent adherent of the Patriots (*q.v.*), and in 1787 he had to flee because of his radical democratic views. Upon his return to Zwartsluis after a few months some trouble on this question arose in the congregation (*Inv. Arch. Amst.* I, No. 2445). Bos then moved to Graft. It was Bos who in 1789 in a conference of the Rijper Sociëteit (*q.v.*) advanced the idea of establishing a fund to aid the widows and orphans of Mennonite ministers. This fund (see **Fonds tot ondersteuning**) was actually founded in 1794. vdZ.

Bosch, de, a Mennonite family of Amsterdam. The progenitor of this family was Jeronimo de Bosch (I), who died in Spain in 1666, where he was poisoned because of the frank confession of his faith. All the members of the de Bosch family were interested in art, and many of them were skilled in drawing, painting, and writing poetry.

Some of the outstanding members were Jeronimo de Bosch II (1677-1767), apothecary and owner of a beautiful collection of drawings; Bernardus de Bosch I (*q.v.*); Johannes de Bosch (1713-85), who made drawings and copied paintings; Hendrik de Bosch (1720-72), Amsterdam city physician and Latin poet; Jeronimo de Bosch III (*q.v.*); Bernardus de Bosch II (1742-1816), owner of a fine collection of art, and poet; Goris de Bosch (1751-1804), also greatly interested in literature and painting. Jeronimo de Vries (*q.v.*), a Mennonite minister, was a descendant of the de Bosch family. (*N.N.B. Wb.* II, 218, 233-39.)   vdZ.

Bosch van Berg(h)e, Jan: see **Jan Durps,** an Anabaptist martyr.

Bosch, Bernardus (1746-1803), Reformed pastor in a number of Dutch churches 1770-78, after that active in politics—he was a Patriot (*q.v.*). He was also a poet, the author of some hymns in the *Groote Bundel* (*q.v.*), the songbook of the Amsterdam Zonist congregation of 1791. (*DB* 1867, 142-43; *Biogr. Wb.* I, 521-23.)   vdZ.

Bosch, Bernardus de, b. March 28, 1709, at Amsterdam, d. Oct. 27, 1786, a Dutch Mennonite poet. Critics said of him that he considered "delicate, pure, and gently flowing language the chief requirement of a poem." He wrote four small volumes entitled *Dichtlievende Verlustigingen* (Amsterdam, 1741-88), and *Taal- en Dichtkundige Aanmerkingen* in connection with these poems. Several translations of psalms published in the hymnbook of the *Laus Deo salus populo* society, which was used by the congregation in Amsterdam, were from his pen, as well as some songs that were found in Mennonite hymnals. He is not to be confused with the Reformed B. Bosch, several of whose songs were also found in Mennonite hymnals.   J.L.

DB 1867, 143; 1900, 78, 94; Kalff, *Gesch. der Nederl. Letterkunde* V (Groningen, 1910) 477-79, 573, 575; *N.N. B.Wb.* IV, 234; *ML* I, 247.

Bosch, Jeronimo de, b. March 23, 1740, at Amsterdam, d. there June 1, 1811, was an apothecary until 1773 and then became highest official in the Amsterdam secretariat. He was a Latin poet and highly regarded for his scholarship as well as his gentle and noble character. A poem of his on Napoleon Bonaparte was translated into Dutch, French, and German. The following works were published by him: *Over den staat der Zielen na den dood des lichaams* (1784); *De inhoud van den Ilias van Homerus* (1804, translated into German); *Lofrede op H. G. Oosterdijk* (Amsterdam, 1795); and *Lofrede op J. R. Deiman.*   J.L.

Kalff, *Gesch. der Ned. Letterkunde* VI (Groningen, 1910) 4, 156 ff., 319, 320, 321, 585-87; *N.N.B.Wb.* IV, 235-39; *ML* I, 248.

Bosch, Siegmund von, an Anabaptist hymn writer, three of whose hymns are in the *Ausbund* (*q.v.*). Two of them are found in Wackernagel, *Kirchenlied* V: "Gott Vater, Sohn, Heiliger Geist in Deinem höchsten Throne" (No. 783), and "So will ichs aber heben an singen in Gottes Ehre." The third, "Fröhlich so will ich singen," was formerly ascribed to an unknown Theodor Bosch (*Ausbund* No. 70). (See Rochus v. Liliencron, "Zur Liederdichtung

der Wiedertäufer," in *Mitteilungen aus dem Gebiet der öffentlichen Meinung während der zweiten Hälfte des 16. Jahrhunderts,* 1875, 12.) Siegmund Bosch was also an elder of the Swiss and South German Anabaptists and a collaborator with Pilgram Marpeck. The Basel (1822) edition of the Dordrecht confession of faith contains an appendix of hymns which were usually sung at worship services; it contains the second and third songs mentioned above. Bosch's hymns are also found in Wolkan, *Lieder* (*ML* I, 248).   NEFF.

Bosch, Theodor, to whom the *Ausbund* erroneously ascribes No. 70, "Fröhlich so will ich singen mit Lust ein Tageweis," is otherwise unknown. (*ML* I, 248.)   NEFF.

Bosch, Willem, a native of Alkmaar, Dutch province of North Holland, acquired his M.D. degree at the university of Groningen in 1717, and was later a physician at Haarlem, and at the same time (1716-37) the minister of the Lamist Mennonite congregation on the Klein Heiligland. He died in 1763. (*DB* 1868, 93; *Naamlijst,* 1743.)   vdZ.

Boschmann, Daniel, was elder of the Pleshanovo Mennonite Church (*q.v.*) in the province of Samara, Russia. Boschmann was ordained as minister in 1893 and as elder in 1904. Nothing else is known about his activities.   C.K.

Boshart (Bosser, Bossert, Buschert, Buzzard), a family name of Swiss origin found among the (old) Mennonites, and primarily among the Amish Mennonites of the United States and Canada. The Bosharts are located, or have lived, in Ontario, Michigan, Indiana, Iowa, Nebraska, and other states. The Buscherts are found principally in Ontario, while the Buzzards live in Pennsylvania but chiefly in Indiana. Daniel Kauffman in his *Mennonite Cyclopedic Dictionary* states that these are the descendants of George and Rachel Buzzard who lived in Northampton Co., Pa., in the latter part of the 18th century. A Palatine Mennonite census list of 1706 names a Bossert family living in Mannheim.   M.G.

Boskoop, a village in the Dutch province of South Holland, where there was once a Mennonite congregation. In the 17th century it belonged to the Flemish branch and was represented at the great Flemish conference at Haarlem in 1649. In 1680 there was no minister at this place; sometime before this date it had combined with the near-by Zevenhuizen (*q.v.*) congregation, but in 1680 this union was dissolved. The Boskoop congregation apparently became extinct soon after this date. vdZ.

Bossert, Gustav (1841-1925), outstanding research scholar in the field of the history of the Reformation in Württemberg, b. Oct. 21, 1841, at Täbingen near Rottweil, was Lutheran parson at Bächlingen near Langenburg, 1869-88, and in Nabern near Kirchheim, 1888-1907. His contribution to the history of Anabaptism was unique; he was one of the first modern scholars to sweep aside completely the sectarian prejudice which had for centuries severely handicapped the study of this movement, and to report the facts objectively and sympathetically. While he wrote no comprehensive work on the

Anabaptists, he did write a large number of detailed research articles and was the compiler and editor of the large volume of Anabaptist source documents of Württemberg with which the *Verein für Reformationsgeschichte* opened the great series of source volumes, *Quellen zur Geschichte der Wiedertäufer.*

Of Bossert's numerous studies in Anabaptist history the most striking are his account of the life and end of Michael Sattler (*q.v.*) and his extensive study of Augustin Bader (*q.v.*), the so-called king and prophet of the Anabaptists. In them Bossert presents the antipodes of the original movement. Michael Sattler, the ex-monk, the finest personality among the Swiss-South German Brethren, the probable author of the significant Seven Articles of Schleitheim, appears as the archetype of the peaceful group. This story, it seems, was Bossert's starting point in Anabaptist history. It was a remarkable deed for a Lutheran country pastor in the 1880's to publish for the first time the records of Sattler's trial and death (in the well-known periodical, *Die Christliche Welt*). In 1892 even the strong state church Protestant *Gustav Adolf Verein* had Bossert edit the story again. This was the estimate that this Lutheran pastor gave of Sattler: "Men of the spiritual breadth, of the courage and readiness for martyrdom of Michael Sattler, such men are the heroes who will preserve the kingdom. Perhaps sometime there will be a monument erected in Rottenburg for Sattler like those erected for Giordano Bruno in Rome and John Hus in Constance." Yet Michael Sattler was classed with such fantastic persons as Augustin Bader who were wrongly taken as representative Anabaptists. In fact the whole of Anabaptist history was treated by the scholars in such a misleading manner as to justify the state churches. Here again Bossert's painstaking researches revealed clearly the truth in the mystifying case of Augustin Bader. He very plainly proved that Augustin Bader had left the peaceful Anabaptists, who had also excommunicated him, when he started his fantastic program. The official historians, however, preferred mysteries to historical truth; the bloody action of the authorities needed justification. Just so the judges of 1527 who condemned Sattler had needed lies and deceit.

Why was it that the Anabaptists were not met in the spirit of the Gospel, and that recourse to bloody measures seems to have become "inevitable"? There is no doubt that everywhere the Anabaptists themselves proved to be much better provided with ammunition from the Gospel than the learned theologians were. Again and again Bossert shows that the public law was applied against the Anabaptists not because of creeds and forms of baptism but because of the Anabaptist ethic, which was considered a danger to the existing social order. In the case of Augustin Bader, Bossert points out clearly what a large part political considerations played in the persecution of the Anabaptists. The Württemberg Anabaptists were believed to be connected with the agitation by which the Duke of Württemberg was trying to regain his country from which he had been exiled in 1519 by the Swabian League. The actions of Augustin Bader, falsely assumed to be a leader of the Anabaptists, frightened the Austrian rulers of Württemberg and also other German princes. The Peasants' Revolt, suppressed only a few years before, was another cause for the suspicion of the authorities. Furthermore, just at this time the Turks were a serious threat to the Holy Roman Empire and it was again Ferdinand who was ordained to be Chief Defender. Eschatological utterances of some of the Anabaptists, referring to the Turks as divine agents in bringing in the millennium, were interpreted by the authorities to mean that the Anabaptists were allies of the Turks! It is again Bossert who shows that all these political charges were an absurdity.

Bossert's work in general is one of the few contributions by modern writers which throw light on the early period of persecution. His (and the other) researches are at the same time a remarkable support of the authenticity and high degree of accuracy of the oldest Mennonite historical work, the Dutch *Martyrs' Mirror* of 1660. Bossert goes farther than the *Martyrs' Mirror* by adding a great deal of information regarding the methods of persecution. For instance, he discovered a significant change in the methods of the Austrian government in Württemberg, which is recorded in Ferdinand's decree of Oct. 1, 1528, issued in Stuttgart, which ordered that the more bloody methods be dropped. Only a few months previously, Ferdinand had urged that Anabaptist leaders should be beheaded without trial, the Swabian League had sent out special squads of cavalry, and the dukes of Bavaria protected their boundaries with regular troops against the Anabaptists, inquisitorial methods having extinguished the movement within their duchies up to that time. Bossert suggests that the change in Württemberg came apparently from the effect of the cruel punishment of Michael Sattler, which had been a stimulus rather than a deterrent to the spread of Anabaptist ideas. One of Ferdinand's decrees (reprinted by Bossert as the first of his sources in his studies on Bader, IV, in the *Archiv für Reformationsgeschichte* XI, 1914, 18 f.) ordered the (Catholic) theologians of the University of Tübingen to instruct the Anabaptists *zur Ehre Gottes, zur Erhaltung des christlichen Glaubens und zum Besten des gemeinen christlichen Volkes.* In other words, the professors of Tübingen were to engage in disputations with the Anabaptists. Thus in effect the Catholics adopted Zwinglian methods in dealing with them. However, neither the milder policy which the Catholic authorities here introduced nor the semi-toleration urged by the Lutheran John Brenz, was successful. Fiercer methods were again introduced, with the result that finally all the important groups of Anabaptists in South Germany were exterminated.

The aim of this brief review of Bossert's work has been to demonstrate his successful and thorough contribution toward revealing the true character of the Anabaptist movement, which had been perverted in traditional literature as truly as the movement itself had been destroyed by the iron hand of the political authorities.

No complete list of Bossert's publications has been published. In the following catalog an attempt is made to collect all of Bossert's contributions which are of immediate value for Anabaptist history. Some are mentioned by Hege in his brief article on Bossert (*ML* I). The last great work Bossert undertook was the collection of all the archival material concerning the Anabaptists in Württemberg and Hohenlohe. Apparently he died just before the manuscript went to press.

Christian Hege rendered a great service in securing Bossert to write numerous articles for the *Mennonitisches Lexikon*. In these articles, the most important ones of which are named below, Bossert carefully boiled down his findings to give their essence in a most informing way. Unfortunately a chronic lack of finances made it impossible to carry out Hege's complete plan. No attempt is here made to collect the various reviews Bossert wrote on books on Anabaptist history and the like. The main part of his very constructive reviews was published in Harnack and Schürer's *Theologische Literaturzeitung* from 1885 on. They refer not only to his particular field, but also to the Reformation history of Switzerland, Austria, Poland, etc.

A. Books and Pamphlets

Das Blutgericht in Rottenburg am Neckar (the trial and death of Michael Sattler), enlarged reprint from the *Christliche Welt*, 1891, 22 ff., as No. 162 of the series (Bremen, 1892); Hartmann and Bossert, *Württembergische Kirchengesch.* (Calw, 1893); *Württembergische Geschichtsquellen* II (Stuttgart, 1895); *Beschreibung des Oberamts Rottenburg* I 1899 (Bossert wrote the historical section); *Quellen zur Gesch. der Wiedertäufer* I, *Herzogtum Württemberg* (Leipzig, 1930).

B. Articles in Encyclopedias

1. *HRE* (3d ed., Leipzig, 1896-1913). **Blarer, Ambrosius** (Hartmann revised), a Swabian reformer (1492-1564) of a rather fair-minded attitude toward Anabaptists; **Christoph, Herzog von Württemberg**; **Wilhelm Reublin**, **Michael Sattler**; **Jakob Strauss**.

2. *Mennonitisches Lexikon:* **Joachim Fleiner**, an Anabaptist martyr of 1530, son of a patrician of Ulm; **Friedrich, Herzog von Württemberg** (ruled 1593-1608, and was financially interested in the confiscated fortunes of the few Anabaptists still struggling for their life in Württemberg or leaving for Moravia to join the Hutterites); **Alfred Hegler**, a Tübingen theologian whose important work on *Geist und Schrift bei Sebastian Franck* (Freiburg, 1892) shed a very helpful light on the early Anabaptists; **Michael Sattler**; **Ulrich, Herzog von Württemberg**. The following articles on various cities and smaller places where the Anabaptist movement was of importance: **Gmünd**; **Hall**; **Heilbronn**; **Hohenwittlingen**; **Horb**; **Mantelhof**; **Reutlingen**; **Rottenburg**; **Schorndorf**; **Ulm**; **Weinsberg**. Comprehensive articles on larger territories like the dominion of **Hohenberg**, the principality of **Hohenlohe**, the Duchy of **Württemberg**. In an article on the **Schwäbischer Bund,** Bossert describes the measures of that mighty political group against the Anabaptist movement.

C. Articles in Periodicals and the Like

1. *Blätter fur württembergische Kirchengeschichte (Beiblatt zum württembergischen Kirchen- und Schulblatt):* "Rottenburg und die Herrschaft Hohenberg im Reformationszeitalter," 1886-95; "Wiedertäufer in Oberschwaben," 1888, 36 ff.; "Die Täufer in Rottenburg und Horb nach Sattlers Tod," 1892, 75 ff., 81 ff., 89 ff.; "Der Anabaptismus in Kirchheim," 1897, 112 ff.; "Berthold Aichele, der Bundesprofoss," 1897, 25 ff., 35 ff. (Aichele was the executive of the Swabian League and as such responsible for the death of many Anabaptists 1528-31); "Die Herrschaft Heidenheim in der Reformationszeit," 1898; "Beiträge zur Geschichte des Reformationsgesprächs in Worms, 1557," 1901; "Die Reformation in Blaufelden," 1901; "Die Reformation in Creglingen," 1903; "Beiträge zur Geschichte der Reformation in Württemberg," 1905; "Johann Brenz, der 'Reformator Württembergs' und seine Toleranzidee," 1911, 150 ff.

2. *Besondere Beilage des Staatsanzeigers für Württemberg:* "Der ritterschaftliche Adel und die Wiedertäufer, 1560-1600," 1895, 269 ff. (It is worthy of note in the history of Anabaptism that the lesser nobility often exercised toleration; economic as well as religious considerations played a role); "Eine amerikanische Quelle für Württembergische Geschichte und Literatur des sechzenten und siebzehnten Jahrhunderts," June 1, 1916 (referring to the Hutterites).

3. *Zeitschrift für die Geschichte des Oberrheins, Neue Folge;* "Die Reformation in Kürnbach," 1903; "Beiträge zur badisch-pfälzischen Reformationsgeschichte," 1902, 578 ff.; "Die Täufer in der Kurpfalz und dem Bistum Speyer," 1903, 71 ff.; "Wolf Kürschner, der Täufer von Bretten," 1908, 431 ff.

4. *Württembergische Jahrbücher für Statistik und Landeskunde:* "Recht und Brauch in Langenburg im 16. und 17. Jahrhundert," 1910; "Aus der Zeit der Fremdherrschaft 1519-1534," 1911, 73 ff.; "Zur Geschichte Stuttgarts in der ersten Hälfte des 16. Jahrhunderts," 1914, 62 ff., 135 ff.

5. *Archiv für Reformationsgeschichte, Texte und Untersuchungen:* "Augustin Bader von Augsburg, der Prophet und König, und seine Genossen nach den Prozessakten von 1530," X, 1913 and XI, 1914, a work of more than 230 pages, where all the available sources are reprinted. Hege, article **Bader**, gives an intelligent summary based on Bossert's research. A sensational story of Bader drawn from Bossert's articles by K. Loeffler is "Ein Vorläufer und ein Nachahmer des Münsterer Wiedertäuferkönigs . . . ," in *Deutsche Rundschau,* September 1923.

6. *Jahrbuch zur Geschichte des Protestantismus in Oesterreich:* "Hans Bünderlin," 1890, 61 ff. (after Pilgram Marpeck for a time a very influential leader of the South German Anabaptists. (See article **Bünderlin**); "Jacob Kautz, Schulmeister in Iglau," 1892, 54 ff.; "Zwei Linzer Reformationsschriftsteller," 1900, 131 ff., 1908, 1 ff. (concerns two Anabaptists both known as theological writers, Christoph and Leopold Freisleben alias Eleutherobion. (See **Eleutherobion.**)

Bossert had also a special liking for the Hutterites. Some of his writings about them concerned the

Scottdale edition of *Die Lieder der Hutterischen Brüder* in *Theologisches Literatur-Blatt* and in the Stuttgart newspaper *Schwäbischer Merkur*, 1915, here under the title, "Schwäbische Liederdichter in America." Bossert made no original study on the Hutterite Anabaptists; he was interested only in tracing Hutterite groups to Swabia. His last work on this topic was published in the Stuttgart newspaper supplement *Schwäbische Chronik:* "Wiedertäuferbischöfe aus Württemberg" (19. Juni 1920), and "Schwaben ausserhalb Schwabens" (February 1923). (E. Correll, "Gustav Bossert's Contribution to Mennonite History," *G. C. Record Rev. Suppl.,* May 1926, 28-34; *ML* I, 248.)   H.S.B.

Bosshard, Marx, of Zollikon in the canton of Zürich, a faithful follower of Conrad Grebel, with whom he traveled about in the highlands of Zürich Oberland in the Anabaptist cause in July 1525. When the two men were summoned to Zürich for trial on the charge of slander against Zwingli's *Taufbüchlein,* they addressed a petition to the city council on July 6, requesting a letter of safe conduct to attend the trial, which the council refused. When Bosshard nevertheless went to Zürich for the trial, he was thrown into prison, and was not released until Aug. 2. To secure his release he was forced to pay a fine of one mark in silver, post a bond of 100 pounds, and promise to desist from preaching and baptizing; he was given a warning, which was also meant for his companions, that "if they returned they would be left in the new tower until they thought they must suffocate." March 5 he was included in the court hearing regarding the meeting of the Zollikon Swiss Brethren in the inn "Zum Salmon." He complained that "my lords winked at Zwingli's faults and Zwingli at my lords." No details are known about his life. (Muralt-Schmid, *Quellen: Zürich,* 39 f., 42 f., 47, 59, 83, 85 ff., 89, 91, 96, 98, 100 f., 183 f., 381; *ML* I, 249.)   NEFF.

Bossler Mennonite Church (MC), located in Lancaster County between Elizabethtown and Maytown, is a member of the Lancaster Mennonite Conference. The first meetinghouse was built perhaps in 1811. In 1881 and 1902 new churches were built and the latter was remodeled in 1915 and 1948. This was the home congregation of Bishop Martin Rutt. In 1950 the congregation was served by Simon Garber and his son-in-law, Martin R. Kraybill, as ministers, John R. Kraybill as deacon. The membership was 105.   I.D.L.

Bote, Der, until 1926 *Der Mennonitische Immigrantenbote,* is a weekly publication founded, edited, and originally published by D. H. Epp at Rosthern, Sask. The first issue appeared on Jan. 16, 1924. From its beginning it served the immigrants coming to Canada from Russia after World War I, giving them a medium of contact, informing them about their new country, and providing them with spiritual and cultural nourishment in their mother tongue, the German language. The cultural level and content of the paper have always been commendable. In 1947 it and the *Christlicher Bundesbote* (*q.v.*) were merged and it thus became an organ of the General Conference Mennonite Church. D. H. Epp remained the editor and Cornelius Krahn became the assistant editor. Although the merged paper is published by the General Conference Publication Board, the place of publication has remained the same. The size was originally 9½ x 12½ inches but was enlarged after three years to 25 x 19 inches. In 1950 the number of pages was increased to 12 and the circulation was 4,500, of which 1,000 went to Europe and South America, whither many free copies were sent by the publishers to serve the refugees and new immigrants.   C.K.

Bote Press, The, at Rosthern, Sask., was started in 1931 by D. H. Epp, who purchased it from the Saskatchewan Valley News. Among the items printed regularly are: *Der Bote-Christlicher Bundesbote, Saskatchewan Valley News, Der Kinderbote,* various conference reports, catalogs, and annuals. At present (1953) the press has eight regular employees.   D.H.E.

Both, Hans, an Anabaptist preacher in Hesse, who was outstandingly zealous for Anabaptism in the border regions of Hesse and Thuringia in 1526. At first his sermons seemed to be full of apocalyptic ideas. A favorite theme was "the punishment of the world by a large army from the north." But he soon abandoned this topic, and worked in the sober spirit of the quiet Anabaptists, urged a serious sanctification of oneself, and emphasized an active expression of brotherly love. About 1530 he preached and baptized at Stadtlengstfeld on the Fulda in the bishopric of Fulda. Expelled from here he became the leader of the congregation at Sorge, not far from Hersfeld. Here he was able to further the Anabaptist cause extensively in the place of Melchior Rinck, who was seized Nov. 11, 1531, at Vacha.

Exiled in September 1533, Both emigrated at the head of his congregation to Moravia. But he could not adjust himself to the difference in the situation of the Anabaptists there. He was also unwilling to give to the brotherhood all the possessions the group had brought. But finally he yielded. Soon afterward there was doctrinal division. Hans Both, according to the writings of the Moravian Anabaptists, taught that there were neither angels nor devils. When the elders restrained him and called him heretical, he replied in vexation that they were attempting to block his stream of living water, and that Melchior Rinck preached the same doctrine. The dispute ended in the expulsion from the brotherhood of all who sided with Both. They now adhered to Philip Plener (*q.v.*) and Gabriel Ascherham (*q.v.*).

Not long afterward Hans Both, deprived of all his possessions by having given them to the church, returned to his home. A small remnant of the Anabaptists who had emigrated from Hesse and Thuringia to Moravia persevered there under suffering and persecution. At the end of October 1533 they wrote to Hans Both, urging him to remain steadfast and support the Brethren in the faith.

About four years later in August 1537 the Hutterian Brethren wrote an epistle to the congregation in Hesse, justifying their attitude toward Hans Both. Both apparently continued to work in Hesse. Nothing more is known of him. NEFF.

K. W. Hochhut, "Mitteilungen aus der protestant. Sektengesch. in der hessischen Kirche," in *Ztscht für die hist. Theol.*, 1859, 204-8; Beck, *Geschichts-Bücher*, 114; P. Wappler, *Die Stellung Kursachsens und des Landgrafen Philipp von Hessen zur Täuferbewegung* (Münster, 1910) 9, 46, 140, 185; *idem, Die Täuferbewegung in Thüringen* . . . (Jena, 1913) 50, 86, 100, 103 f.; *ML* I, 249.

Bothwell: see **Bethel** Mennonite Church, near Bothwell, Kent Co., Ont.

Botschafter, Der, periodical of the Mennonites of Russia, published twice a week. (Publisher, Joh. Thiessen, Ekaterinoslav; editors, David H. Epp and H. A. Ediger, Berdyansk.) It appeared usually in six pages, sometimes eight, with 2-4 pages of advertising. *Der Botschafter* was born of the need of another bond to preserve unity among the numerous Mennonite congregations scattered throughout Russia. In its columns it presented religious and devotional matter, and also followed all events in the field of politics, education, and science. The first issue appeared on Aug. 13, 1905, at Ekaterinoslav in the period of internal unrest and revolution. This fact was not without influence on the development of the paper. The frequent strikes in the printeries of the great manufacturing city caused many a delay. Other circumstances arose which finally made it necessary to transfer publication to Berdyansk. After that the *Botschafter* developed steadily. Its influence on the churches should not be underestimated. In questions of church organization and regulation it represented the traditional Mennonite position on a positive Christian foundation. The journal ceased publication in 1914 at the beginning of World War I. No further Mennonite periodical was published in Russia until *Unser Blatt* (*q.v.*) appeared in October 1925 as the official organ of the *Bundeskonferenz.* (*ML* I, 249.) D.H.E., C.K.

Botschafter des Heils in Christo, a 16-page bimonthly published and edited by John G. Stauffer, Quakertown, Pa. The first issue was dated January 1889. It was a continuation of *Die Gemeinde unterm Kreuz,* the last issue of which had appeared in November 1888, and which in turn was a continuation of *Die Kirche unterm Kreuz,* the first issue of which appeared in April 1885, edited by Stauffer at Quakertown. The periodical was discontinued, perhaps in 1891. (R. Friedmann, *Menn. Piety Through the Centuries,* Goshen, 1949, 256-60.) M.G.

Botschafter der Wahrheit, the official German organ of the Church of God in Christ, Mennonite, was founded in June 1897 by John Holdeman, who was also its editor until his death in 1900. It is now an 8-page semimonthly, 6½ x 9½ in., published in Manitoba. Other editors were in succession, John Dueck, Wilhelm Giesbrecht, Jacob T. Wiebe, A. G. Ensz, and again Jacob T. Wiebe, the present editor (1949). In 1949 its circulation was about 750. (*ML* I, 250.) J.T.W.

Botschert: see **Burtscheid.**

Botterman, Eppo, a preacher of the Waterlanders in Groningen, studied under Galenus Abrahamsz de Haan and was ordained May 12, 1700, at Groningen (Holland). He was also a respected member of the Collegiants (*q.v.*) and became their leader. Since this step caused offense in his congregation he resigned in 1714, but upon request resumed his office in 1725. Three years later the conservative Jacobus Rijsdijk was appointed as his colleague. Tension developed between them and Botterman was accused of favoring Socinian views (1739). He was acquitted of this suspicion by the directorate of the Reformed Church, but now Rijsdijk accused him of being actually Reformed. Rijsdijk went to Almelo in 1742, and relations improved. Botterman was a member of the directorate of the Frisian Doopsgezinde Sociëteit, which he had helped to found in 1695 and to which most of the congregations in the province of Friesland belonged, as did also the Groningen and Sappemeer congregations in the province of Groningen. He was still preaching in 1752. The date of his death is not known. He is the author of *Het ware Afbeeldsel van een Collegiant* (Leeuwarden, 1735), and *Vriendelijke en ernstige aanmerkingen op de verhandelinge van Ds. Jacobus Rijsdijk* (Groningen, 1742). K.V., vdZ.

Blaupot t.C., *Groningen* I, 166-71; *idem, Friesland,* 152, 187; *ML* I, 250; *Biogr. Wb.* I, 536-37; *Catalogus Amst.,* 136, 137.

Boucher (Bocher), **Jane** (also called Johanna of Kent), was sentenced to die at the stake in London as a follower of Melchior Hofmann (*q.v.*). The 12-year-old King Edward at first refused to sign the death warrant, but Archbishop Cranmer pressed him so long with the suggestion that she should be punished with death for her heresy according to the law of Moses that he finally yielded. He is said to have told Cranmer with tears, "Cranmer, I will sign the verdict at your risk and responsibility before God's judgment throne." Cranmer was deeply impressed, and he tried once more to induce her to recant; but she persisted and suffered death by fire on May 2, 1550 (*ML* erroneously 1549). Seven years later Cranmer suffered the same death. NEFF.

B. Krohn, *Gesch. der fanatischen und enthusiastischen Wiedertäufer vornehmlich Niederdeutschlands* (Leipzig, 1758) 392 f.; *Menn. Bl.,* 1856, 76; G. Weber, *Gesch. der akathol. Kirchen und Sekten von Grossbrittannien* (Leipzig, 1854) 97-106; R. Barclay, *The Inner Life of the Religious Societies of the Commonwealth* (2d ed., London, 1877) 38; *ML* I, 239, 585.

Boudewijne Boccaert, an Anabaptist martyr of Gent, was burned at the stake on the market place at Antwerp on May 20, 1573, because she had frequently visited the forbidden meetings of the Mennonites in Antwerp. (Génard, *Antw. Arch.-Blad* XIII, 112, 176; XIV, 90-91, No. 1021.) vdZ.

Boudewijns, Pieter, was the elder of the Danzig Old Flemish Mennonite congregation at Haarlem 1730-53, and at Amsterdam 1756-61. Through his catechism, *Onderwijzinge des Christelijken geloofs, volgens de belijdenis der Christenen die men de Oude Vlaamsche Mennoniten noemt* (Haarlem, 1743), he attained great influence; it found wide acceptance and was used by the conservative Mennonites long enough to necessitate another printing in 1825 at Sneek. In conservative congregations, e.g., Balk (*q.v.*), it was used as late as 1853. He also published *Korte schets van de onderwijzinge* (Haarlem, 1744). J.L., vDZ.

DB 1878, 22, 27; 1887, 92; 1892, 70, 78; *Catalogus Amst.*, 294; *Biogr. Wb.* I, 540; *ML* I, 250.

Boudewijnsvolk, a name of the former Danzig Old Flemish congregation at Haarlem, Holland, named for their elder Pieter Boudewijns; they held their meetings in a house called Het Goud Grendeltje (the little gold lock) on the Smalle Graft. vDZ.

Bouff, Wilhelm, an Anabaptist of Jülich. His confession (in the Düsseldorf state archives) throws much light on the doctrine, organization, and worship of the Anabaptist congregations in the 16th century. (Rembert, *Wiedertäufer,* 509 and 511; *ML* I, 250.) NEFF.

Boulay-Saint Victor, formerly the seat of a Mennonite congregation in France, now called Diesen (*q.v.*). (*Almanach Menn. du Cinquantenaire* 1901-51, 7.)

Bouma, Gellius Faber de: see Faber, Gellius.

Bouqueirao, four miles from Curitiba (*q.v.*), is the largest Mennonite settlement in Brazil, begun in 1938 by settlers from the Krauel (*q.v.*) colony in Santa Catharina State.

There are (1950) about 160 families living here, engaged almost exclusively in dairying. Most of them live in three villages, two of which are, however, now closed; i.e., there are a few non-Mennonites living in their area. The Mennonites are all well enough situated to make a good living. In addition, there are about 130 Mennonite families living at the fringes of Curitiba proper and within the city, half of whom are in the milk business, the other half engaged in skilled trades, factories, and independent business. Two churches, Mennonite Brethren and General Conference, are located in the area. P.K.

Bout, Josse, wrote under the initials J. B., *'t Merg van de Historien der Martelaren . . . alles in 't korte by een getrokken uyt de Groote Martelaars Spiegel der Doopsgesinde van Tileman Jansz van Bragt* (The Gist of the History of the Martyrs . . . Everything Condensed from the Large Martyrs' Mirror of the Mennonites by T. J. van Bragt) (Haarlem, 1699). According to Glasius, this book follows the first edition of van Braght, that of 1660, and Bout's condensation appeared first in an edition of 1671. This is incorrect. The source is van Braght's edition of 1685, and nothing is known concerning a 1671 edition of *'t Merg.*

A second edition of Bout's compilation appeared at Amsterdam in 1722; and another came out in 1736 "enlarged with engraved pictures," in which only the title-page was changed, the text being exactly the same as that of the 1722 edition. There was still another edition in 1769. The pictures are reproductions of the Jan Luikens engravings from the *Martyrs' Mirror* of 1685, but reduced in size, and reversed. (*Catalogus Amst.,* 16.) Of this work there has appeared an abbreviated German transla-

tion, *Das Andenken einiger heiligen Märtyrer,* published in Pennsylvania in 1745, 120 pp. (Bender, *Two Centuries; MQR* XXII, July 1948, 173.) About Josse Bout nothing further is known. He may be identical with Jacob Bout, who first belonged to the Remonstrants (*q.v.*), and later became a Mennonite. This Jacob Bout, who was married to Catharina Kool, at first lived at Zaandam and later at Amsterdam, becoming a member of the Lamist congregation in 1671. vDZ.

Bouterwek, Karl Wilhelm, b. Aug. 30, 1809, at Tarnowitz in Silesia, d. Dec. 22, 1868, in Elberfeld, a prominent educator, who spent the last years of his life in a thorough study of church history in Rhenish Prussia and Westphalia. In 1863 he founded the *Bergische Geschichtsverein* and became its president. In 1864 he discovered Bernhard Rothmann's book on vengeance, entitled *Ein ganz köstlicher Bericht von der Rache und Strafe des Babylonischen Greuels an alle wahre Israeliten und Bundesgenossen Christi hie und da zerstreuet, durch die Gemeinde Christi zu Münster* (December 1533). In 1864 Bouterwek also published *Zur Literatur und Geschichte der Wiedertäufer* (Bonn, 1864). This book contains the three pamphlets of the Münster Anabaptists, (1) *Bekenntnisse von beiden Sakramenten; unterzeichnet am 22. Okt. 1533 von Bernhard Rothmann, Joh. Kloprijs, Hermann Staprade, Henrik Roll, Dionysius Vynnen und Gotfriedus Stralen;* (2) *Restitution,* which like the above is presented with the full text and provided in part with important historical annotations; (3) the booklet, *Von der Rache des babylonischen Greuels.* In addition Bouterwek's book contains a *Bekenntnis einiger Personen, so der Wiedertaufe und des Münsterischen Unwesens halber allhie zu Wesel im Jahre 1535 eingezogen wurden,* and *Bericht des Henricus Greiss über die Wiedertäufer zu Wesel* (*ML* I, 250). NEFF.

Bouwen Lubberts, a preacher of the Mennonite congregation at Haarlem, Holland, who on April 25, 1557, on the evening before Joriaen Simonsz (*q.v.*) and Clement Dirksz (*q.v.*) were executed in that town, preached a sermon openly in the Schoutenstraat. Bouwen wrote a song on these two martyrs, "Hoort vrienden al hier in dit aertsche dal" (Hear, ye friends in this earthly vale), which is found in the *Liedtboecxken van den Offer des Heeren* (No. 20), and was also included in later Dutch songbooks. (*Offer,* 258, 586 ff.; *Mart. Mir.* D 179, E 563; Wolkan, *Lieder,* 63, 78.) vDZ.

Bouwens, Leenaert: see Leenaert Bouwens.

Bovenkarspel, Dutch province of North Holland, once the seat of a Mennonite congregation. As appears from the *Naamlijst* of 1731, the congregation was still in existence at that date, but by 1743 it had died out. At this place Leenaert Bouwens (*q.v.*) baptized six persons between 1551 and 1554. Nothing more is known about this congregation. vDZ.

Bovenknijpe, a village in the Dutch province of Friesland, not far from Heerenveen, where there were at least four, perhaps five Mennonite congregations, probably one each of Waterlanders, Frisians, Old Flemish, the Twisck group, and Jan Jacobsz group. These congregations also included some of the Mennonites living in Heerenveen and Mildam. One of them was founded in 1620 or between 1620 and 1640; the Old Flemish about 1650. The Jan Jacobsz branch had disappeared by 1727; nothing is heard of the Twisck group after this year either; the Frisians and Waterlanders united in 1741. In 1754 there was still an Old Flemish congregation at Bovenknijpe; it united with the neighboring Mildam congregation in 1767. The records of the old times are not always clear. Further written notations are defective and cannot always be harmonized, especially because several names are sometimes used for a single branch. In 1719 the preacher Jan Thomas was suspended by the government on a charge of Socinianism. In 1738 three Mennonite preachers at Knijpe, Wybe Pieters, Wytze Jeens, and Pieke Tjommes, were likewise charged with Socinianism. They refused to sign the declaration drawn up by the Frisian States in 1722. Wytze and Pieke were silenced on June 5, 1739.

Heerenveen and Bovenknijpe separated in 1780. Since then Bovenknijpe has been a separate congregation; it numbered 92 members at that time. One of their best-known preachers was A. S. Cuperus (q.v.), who served the congregation from 1790 to 1803 and was the people's deputy in the Diet of Friesland 1796-98. P. H. Veen, who wrote the history of these congregations, was its minister for 45 years. The membership in 1838 was 123; in 1861, 214; in 1898, 175; in 1915, 160; in 1950, 103. The Bovenknijpe congregation was the first Dutch congregation to appoint a woman as minister; she was Anna Zernike, and she served from November 1911 to her marriage in October 1915. Since then it has been served by the following ministers: P. G. van Slogteren, 1916-22; R. D. Boersma, 1922-24; J. Wuite, 1925-31; G. J. W. den Herder, 1931-33; M. J. Nolthenius, 1934-41; G. van Veen 1945-51, and since then Miss T. G. Siccama. The church was substantially remodeled in 1856. The congregation has a Sunday school, a women's circle, and a youth group. It belongs to Ring Akkrum. This congregation was one of the last ones to acquire an organ. This happened in 1901.   J.L.

P. H. Veen, *De Doopsgezinden in Schoterland;* Blaupot t.C., *Friesland;* Gorter, *Doopsgezinde Lectuur* III, 18, supplement; *Inv. Arch. Amst.* II, No. 1598; II, 2, No. 36; *DB* 1896, 149 ff.; *ML* I, 251.

Bower's Mennonite Church (MC): see **Clay County, Ind.**

Bowie Fish and Wild Life Camp No. 34, located 5½ miles east of Laurel, Md., was a Civilian Public Service camp established by an order of Selective Service in May 1942 under the National Park Service. It was at first jointly administered by the Brethren, Friends, and Mennonites, but was taken over by the Brethren in January 1945, and then later by the government. In April 1943 there were 19 Mennonites among the 60 campers. Drafted men working at the Akron, Pa., Mennonite Central Committee headquarters were listed on 34-D.S. (Detached Service). (See **Civilian Public Service.**)
                                              M.G.

Bowlings Creek (Beech, Ky.) Mennonite Gospel Mission (CAM). The first Bible school on Bowlings Creek was held in the summer of 1947. As the interest was good, Frank Dutcher and his wife were asked to move into the area and establish work there. Sunday school was started December 1947 with an attendance of 65. An acre of land with a small house was purchased for the mission home. Services were held in the schoolhouse. In the summer of 1949 a new house was built and now (1951) services are held in the basement of the new house. Most of the road to the mission is in the rocky creek bed and the means of transportation are walking, horseback, or wagon. The present membership is nine. Workers there are Frank and Gertrude Dutcher and Fannie Yoder. F.D.

Bowman, Moses S., the outstanding leader of the Mennonite church in Ontario in the second half of the 19th century, was born two miles east of Berlin, Waterloo Co., Ont., Nov. 9, 1819, as the eldest of eight children of Benjamin Baumann (1787-1874) and Susannah Bechtel (1797-1870), who in 1818 came to Canada from Lancaster Co., Pa. (Ezra Eby, *History of Waterloo Township*). Benjamin was the eldest son of Wendel Baumann (1758-1842) of Berks Co., Pa., who was third son of Preacher Christian Baumann (1724-90) of Berks County, Allegany Valley, who was the eldest son of pioneer Wendel Baumann, born in Switzerland about 1671, who at 17 years of age moved with his parents to Holland, then sailed for America after 1700.

On Oct. 8, 1844, Moses S. Bowman was married to Anna, daughter of Joseph and Barbara (Biehn) Cressman, born near Freeport, Aug. 7, 1838. In his family were six sons and six daughters. Two of his brothers, Tobias and Samuel, were ministers of the Mennonite Church; two of his sons, Moses C. and Ezra, were also ministers of the Mennonite Church; two of his daughters, Mrs. David Bergey and Mrs. Henry Baer, were the wives of deacons of the Mennonite Church. One grandchild, Moses S., is now minister of the Roseville Mennonite Church. One grandchild, Dr. Isaiah Bowman, was a former president of Johns Hopkins University and one of America's outstanding geographers.

Moses S. Bowman was educated in the elementary schools of Waterloo Township and thereafter did much by reading and study of the Bible to continue his self-education. One year after his marriage he moved to a farm near Mannheim, Waterloo County, where he resided for the remainder of his life. On May 1, 1853, he was ordained to the office of deacon of the Mennonite church in his home community. He was the first deacon of the Latschar church. In January 1859 he was ordained minister of the same church where he continued to serve until his death in 1898. When the Mennonite churches of Ontario organized their annual conference in 1873, he served as first moderator. In this capacity he served for many years. He was an enthusiastic Sunday-school promoter and became the first superintendent in his home church in 1874. He was one of the first to open the door to the evangelism of J. S. Coffman in Ontario. He was asked to preach many non-Mennonite funeral sermons.

Bowman's preaching was usually in German, largely extemporaneous and deliberate, and his messages gripping and convicting. His subject material was textual and expository. Favorite themes were heaven, the love of God, and assurance of salvation. He preached strongly against the use of tobacco and intoxicants. He sought the acquaintance of strangers and welcomed them, and especially sought the friendship and good will of children and young people with his kindly good humor. He is buried in the Latschar Mennonite cemetery near Mannheim, five miles west of Kitchener, Ont.
                                                            J.C.F.

Bowmansville Mennonite Church (MC) in Brecknock Twp., Lancaster Co., Pa., near Bowmansville, belongs to the Lancaster Mennonite Conference. The first Mennonite settlers were Jacob and Christian Good in 1738. The first preacher was Christian Bauman (1724-90). The congregation was organized probably in 1752, first worshiping in the home of Christian Good. The first meetinghouse was built in 1794 in the village of Bowmansville, and the second in 1875 a mile south of Bowmansville. In 1921 the third was built on the same spot. In 1851 in this congregation a division occurred over the free school system which left it in a weakened condition. In 1852 Bishop Jacob Mosemann (1795-1876) came from Trappstadt, Bavaria, Germany, to Lancaster County, Pennsylvania, and served in this congregation. His sermons were short, earnest, and convincing. The congregation took on new life near the close of his life. He ordained Benjamin Horning (1827-1903) as his successor in the ministry. Horning was one of the most eloquent pulpit orators of his day, the congregation growing in membership during his ministry. The 1953 membership was 427.   A.M.W.

Bowmansville Old Order Mennonite Church of Lancaster Co., Pa., worships in a meetinghouse one mile southeast of Bowmansville. It is a member of the Groffdale Conference under Bishop Aaron J. Sensenig.   E.M.S.

Bowne Mennonite Church (MC), located in Bowne Twp., Kent Co., near Clarksville, Mich., is a member of the Indiana-Michigan Mennonite Conference. The earliest settlers arrived here from Somerset Co., Pa., and Waterloo Co., Ont., in 1865. Public services were begun in the spring of 1866. During the year Peter Keim was ordained minister, and Herman Bentler deacon, by J. M. Brenneman from Allen Co., Ohio. In 1870 with the help of the Dunkards a log church house was built, which was used conjointly by both groups on alternate Sundays till 1879. In 1901 a frame structure seating 200 was built. The widely known J. S. Coffman held his first series of meetings at this place about 1880. The 1953 membership was 114, with T. E. Schrock serving as bishop; Daniel Zook, minister; and Harold Christophel, deacon. Resident bishops serving here in the past include John Speicher, 1867-?; and J. P. Miller, 1912-17. The ministers were Peter Keim, 1866-1904; Isaac Weaver, 1891-1917; and Aldus Brackbill, 1908-28. The deacons were Herman Bentler, 1866-1905; Joseph Mishler,

1900-28; Eli Zook, 1912-23; and George Stahl, 1925-48.   T.E.S.

Boxum, a town near Leeuwarden, Dutch province of Friesland, where Leenaert Bouwens (q.v.) baptized at least 52 persons in 1568-82. But nothing is known of a congregation in this town. The Mennonites may have joined the near-by congregation of Blessum (q.v.).   vDZ.

Boyertown Mennonite Church (MC) was formerly known as Colebrookdale, being located in that township in Berks Co., Pa. The first church was built between 1772 and 1780, as a convenience to save the members a six-mile trip to their home church at Hereford. Until 1953 Boyertown was a branch of the Hereford congregation. A new building replaced the old in 1819 and finally in 1879 the present one-story brick structure located on Reading Avenue in the center of the Boyertown business district was built.

The Oberholtzer schism of 1847 divided the congregation and both groups continued to worship in the building on alternate Sundays. In 1877, the new group sued the old group for equal rights in a proposed new building. When a decision was brought against the old group, they appealed to the Supreme Court of Pennsylvania in 1883. This resulted in a decision which declared the original group of the Franconia Conference to be the rightful owner of the property.

Sunday school was begun in 1899, was later discontinued, and revived in 1913. The group in 1953 had a membership of 33, served by Alfred Detweiler, a minister of the Rockhill congregation.
                                                            Q.L.

Boynton Mennonite Church (GCM), two miles south of Hopedale on the north edge of Boynton Twp., Tazewell Co., Ill., belongs to the Central Conference of Mennonites. Due to the desire of several Hessian Mennonite families, who differed from their Amish (now Mennonite) neighbors culturally, the congregation was organized on Sept. 15, 1901, under the guidance of Peter Schantz of Danvers, Ill. The original meetinghouse, dedicated Sept. 14, 1902, still serves the congregation, which (1953) numbers 104. Since 1942 the church has owned a parsonage in Hopedale.   M.F.F.

Bozen, a town in Tirol (Austria) at the confluence of the Talfer into the Eisack, where there are known to have been at least eleven Anabaptist executions, including those of Konrad Maier of Sterzingen and Madlem Steinerin of St. Jörgen (see **Blaurock, Georg**).

Brabant. In the 16th century the territory of Brabant comprised the present Belgian provinces of Brabant and Antwerp and the Dutch province of North Brabant (q.v.). Accordingly, a martyr song refers to the city of Lier, which at present is located in the province of Antwerp, as Lier in Brabant. In the former territory of Brabant not many Mennonites were to be found outside the city of Antwerp, nor were the martyrs as numerous here as in Flanders and Holland. In the present provinces of Antwerp and Brabant there are no longer any Mennonite congregations. (ML I, 252.)   vDZ.

Brabant, North, a Dutch province: see **North Brabant.**

Bracht, Tieleman van, author of a number of Dutch poems, is probably identical with Tieleman Jansz van Braght (*q.v.*).

Brackbill (Braechtbuehl, Brechbill, Brechbiel, Brechbuehl), a prominent family name in the Lancaster Mennonite Conference of Swiss origin. An outstanding figure in the family was Bishop Benedikt Brechbill (*q.v.*) of Trachselwald in the Emmental, canton of Bern, Switzerland. He was arrested in 1709, imprisoned, and the next year banished from Bern. He was active in enlisting the aid of the Dutch Mennonites in behalf of his fellow Swiss exiles in the Palatinate. Married to Maria Herr, daughter of Bishop Hans Herr (*q.v.*), he had four children, one of whom, Ulrich, succeeded him as a minister. In 1717 Bishop Benedict Brackbill, as the name has been anglicized, migrated to Lancaster County, Pa., and founded the Strasburg Mennonite congregation. He is said to have been an excellent singer and an able preacher. His death in 1720 marked the loss of the first Mennonite leader in the Pequea district. His son Ulrich was killed on the road to Philadelphia to which he was hauling farm produce in 1739. Sixth in line of descent from Benedict was Bishop C. M. Brackbill (1853-1936), also of the Pequea district of the Lancaster Conference. Other descendants include Minister Aldus Brackbill (1863-1941), his son M. T. Brackbill of the faculty of Eastern Mennonite College, and Minister Milton Brackbill of the Lancaster Mennonite Conference. An Amish couple, V. Brechbiel and wife of France, settled in Henry Co., Iowa, in 1855.   J.C.W.

Brackbill, Christian M. (1853-1936), was born in Salisbury Twp., Lancaster Co., Pa., Dec. 5, 1853, in the home of Joseph and Elizabeth Metzler Brackbill. He taught school for two years, attended a term of normal school, and then returned to the farm of his father. He married Elizabeth K. Denlinger Nov. 20, 1879, a daughter of Benjamin L. and Anna Kreider Denlinger, born Oct. 18, 1855. They had seven children. They were members of the Hershey church, probably before marriage, which was then rare. He was the first superintendent of the Hershey Sunday school and early a devotee of the mission cause. When it crystallized in the Sunday School Advocates in the middle nineties, he headed the organization for a short time.

On Sept. 17, 1896, Brackbill was ordained by Isaac Eby as a preacher in the Hershey-Paradise district. Though ordained when missions were not generally accepted, he continued his interest in missions and the Sunday school. He was a commanding figure in the pulpit and was very influential with the young people, being more progressive in spirit than many.

Upon the death of Isaac Eby in 1910, he was ordained bishop in the large Pequea-Mellinger-Strasburg district, serving ably until his death on March 8, 1936, leaving his imprint on the Lancaster Mennonite Conference.   I.D.L.

Braeside Home is a home for the aged to serve the Mennonite Conference (MC) of Ontario and the local community, with a capacity of 25 guests. It was established May 1, 1943, in the town of Preston, Ont., and placed in charge of a superintendent and matron, John A. and Dora Cressman. The formal opening and dedication was held on June 1, 1943. The deed for the property is held by the Mennonite Conference of Ontario. A management board, consisting of five brethren appointed yearly, with the superintendent as a nonvoting member, is responsible for its operation.† J.A.C.

Bragado, FCO, Argentina, 120 miles southwest of Buenos Aires, is the location of a Mennonite church under the Argentine Mennonite Conference (MC), a mission field under the Mennonite Board of Missions and Charities (Elkhart).

The Bible Institute for the Argentine Mennonite Church has also been located in Bragado since 1935. The boys' orphanage on a 20-acre farm and the girls' home are also located here.

One hears of the visits of Bible colporteurs to this place years ago, and it is also known that the Methodists had a Gospel hall for some time at the beginning of the present century at the very site of the present Mennonite church. When the first Mennonite missionaries, D. P. and Lillie Lantz, came to Bragado in 1926 they found no traces of any former Gospel work, but a city of 15,000 people without evangelical witness.

The first Gospel messages were given in a rented hall, and the first seven converts were baptized on Jan. 5, 1927. The following missionaries have served the church here: D. P. and Lillie Lantz, J. W. Shank, Amos and Edna Swartzentruber, Nelson and Ada Litwiller, L. S. and Edna Weber, and B. Frank and Anna H. Byler. To January 1949 a total of 124 persons were baptized in this church. Bragado is the county seat and there are several towns and villages scattered throughout the county. Gospel work is also being done in near-by towns and there are baptized believers in Mechita, General O'Brien, Comodoro Py, and Quiroga. The total Bragado membership in these towns is 120.

The missionaries who have had charge of the work in Bragado and its circuit have at the same time carried so many other responsibilities that it was not possible to realize what might have been done, had there been more workers and pastors on the field.†   N.L.

Braght, Tieleman Jansz van, a Dutch Mennonite elder, b. Jan. 29, 1625, in Dordrecht, d. Oct. 7, 1664. His father, like Tieleman van Braght himself, was a cloth merchant. The boy showed great talent. He applied himself at first to a study of languages and learned Latin, Greek, Hebrew, French, and German. In 1648 he was made preacher in his home town, and served in that office for 16 years, until his death. He was a warm defender of Mennonite principles, engaged in disputes on the streets, on ships, or wherever the occasion offered itself. One of his best-known disputes was that with Gerardus Aemilius (*q.v.*), the Reformed pastor of

Oud-Beyerland (see **Beyerland**), chiefly on the subject of infant baptism. Van Braght's knowledge, learning, skill in the Scriptures were clearly shown on this occasion.

Van Braght played an important role in the difficulties that developed in Holland about 1660 between the more progressive and the conservative Mennonites. He was completely on the side of the conservatives. The conservatives offered him the eldership of their Rotterdam congregation, but he declined it. In Utrecht he helped to depose the more progressive preachers, among them Willem van Maurik. Van Braght was the chairman of the Synod of Leiden (*q.v.*) of June 1660, where the conservative Mennonites united against Collegiantism.

In 1657 van Braght published his *School der zedelijke deugd* (School of Moral Virtue) to deter the young people from unvirtuous living and lead them to the true fear of God. This little work went through 18 editions. The original title was *De Schole der zedelijcke Deught, geopent voor de kinderen der Christenen*. With the eighth edition the word "zedelijcke" was omitted. The 18th edition appeared in 1824. But he became more famous for his publication of the *Martyrs' Mirror* (*q.v.*), which appeared under the following (1685) title: *Het Bloedig Tooneel of Martelaersspiegel der Doops-gesinde of Weerelose Christenen, Die om't getuygenis van Jesus haren Salighmaker geleden hebben ende gedood zijn, van Christi tijd af tot desen tijd toe. Versamelt uyt verscheyde geloofweerdige Chronijken, Memorien en Getuygenissen. Door T. J. V. Braght, Den Tweeden Druk. Bysonder vermeerdert met veele Autentijcke Stucken en over de hondert curieuse Konstplaten*. The first edition appeared in 1660, the second in 1685 with copper engravings by Jan Luyken (*q.v.*). The foreword of his first edition indicates his original plan to print the martyr book of 1631 without change, merely adding martyrs who had been discovered since that date; but he went much further. He gathered much information from city archives and made successful use of it. He also visited the congregations in South Germany; in March 1662 he was in Obersülzheim near Worms in the Palatinate. He was thus able to replace erroneous reports with correct ones, and did not hesitate to publish what had been hitherto uncertain or unknown.

According to modern standards his method of work was not scholarly; he accepted and published whole articles without checking their accuracy, and was historically inexact. His preferences and aversions also played a part. It must not be forgotten that he wrote for the purpose of edifying. But on the whole he can be considered reliable; nowhere is there intentional falsification. His reliability was thoroughly established by the late Samuel Cramer (*DB* 1899 and 1900). His work soon superseded the older martyr books. The *Offer des Heeren*, first published in 1562, as well as the other martyr books, was no longer widely known in the 18th century. A glance at the new edition of the *Offer des Heeren* (1904) shows how much of it van

Bragt used, but also that he altered it independently. His treatment of baptism, for instance, which he added for each century, is quite extensive and independent. Anyone wishing information concerning our oldest martyrs cannot afford to overlook van Braght, and will be amazed at the breadth of his reading and the fluency of his style. His fluency likely brought him fewer happy hours, for in 1660 he was summoned before the Reformed Church to answer for the boldness of his tone; but he managed to defend himself so well that his good name was merely enhanced thereby.

As a preacher van Braght was widely celebrated. The sermons which his brother published (*51 Predicatien, over verscheyde Schriftuerplaetsen*, Amsterdam, 1670, with portrait) are, to be sure, not the best that he produced. The Reformed Chr. Schotanus in *Van de Gronden der Mennistery ofte Waerschouwinghe over 't Bloed-tooneel van de Doopsgezinde van T. J. v. Bracht* (Leeuwarden, 1671) warns against the *Martyrs' Mirror*.

Tieleman van Braght also wrote some hymns; a few of them are inserted in the songbook of Klaas Stapel, *Lusthof des Gemoeds* (*q.v.*, 1681). T. van Bracht (or Braght), who is likely identical with the Dordrecht elder Tieleman van Braght, is the author of the following poems: *Anghstigh Swanengezangh, of Troosteloozê Vreede* (Dordrecht, 1647); *Kristus in't Vleesch, Kersgesang* (Dordrecht, 1716); *De gewiekte Kruiwagen* (Dordrecht, 1717); *Uitbreiding over Konings Salomons Lied der Liederen en Psalm XLV* (Delft, 1719). Besides Tieleman Jansz van Braght there were other van Braghts at Dordrecht, among them Cornelis van Braght, elder of the Dordrecht congregation from 1689 on and also a poet. Pieter van Braght, who was a brother of Tieleman, also wrote poems. (*DB* 1862, 104, 106.)

H.W., vDZ.

Schijn-Maatschoen, *Uitvoeriger Verh. van de Gesch. der Mennoniten* II (Amsterdam, 1744), 534-40, with portrait; Blaupot t. C., *Holland* I, 197-99, 285-87; *Inv. Arch. Amst.* I, Nos. 612, 613; *DJ* 1837, 96; *DB* 1862, 103 ff.; 1864, 125; 1869, 21 ff.; 1881, 35; 1882, 41; 1884, 39; 1887, 92; 1892, 72, 84; 1899, 65-164; 1900, 184-210; 1902, 170; *Bibliographie des Martyrologes Protestants Neerlandais* I (La Haye, 1890) 21-77; *Biogr. Wb.* I, 554-55; G. Franz, *Urk. Quellen z. hess. Ref.-Gesch.* IV: *Wiedertäuferakten 1527-1626* (Marburg, 1951) 21-26, 180-83, 266, 277; *ML* I, 252.

Braidl, Klaus (also called Klaus Schuster), the leader of the Hutterian Brethren in Moravia, 1583-1611. He united with them in 1550 and was chosen preacher in 1564. In that year he was sent as a missionary to the Palatinate, where he persuaded Farwendel, the elder of the Anabaptist congregation at Neustadt a.d.H., to join the Hutterites and emigrate to Moravia.

After the death of Hans Kräls (*q.v.*) Braidl was chosen as head of the entire brotherhood, and led it prudently for 28 years. He applied great care to the development of trades and handicraft in the communities, and set up various regulations, such as the "bath rule" in 1592, the "clothing rule" in 1603, and additions to the regulations of cobblers, dyers, and millers. He stepped into public view when Parson Christoph Andreas Fischer (*q.v.*)

slandered his brotherhood in his polemic (1603), *Von der Wiedertäufer verfluchtem Ursprung.* Braidl countered with a pamphlet, *Eine Widerlegung und warhaffte Verantwortung der alten grausamsten abscheulichen und unverschamisten, schmach und unwarhafftigen Beschuldigungen, so Christof Andreas Fischer, Pfarrherr zu Feldsberg, über uns Brüder erdacht,* 1604, which energetically repudiates the false accusations (Loserth, 61, 63, and 113). With the exception of Peter Riedemann's *Rechenschaft unserer Religion* this reply was the only publication of the Hutterian Brethren in the 16th century (Horsch, 110). A letter written by Braidl to Salomon Böger (1607), as well as letters written to him by Salomon Böger (*q.v.*) and B. Goller (1607-10) are in the possession of the Hutterian Brethren in North America. Braidl died Jan. 21, 1611, at the age of 82 at Neumühl near Polau, Moravia. Beck describes him as "steadfast, just, moderate in fortune, unyielding in misfortune." His successor was Sebastian Dietrich (*q.v.*).

HEGE.

Beck, *Geschichts-Bücher,* 195, 214, 216, 237, 287, and 360; J. Loserth, *Der Communismus der mährischen Wiedert. im 16. u. 17. Jahrh.* (Vienna, 1894); J. Horsch, *The Hutterian Brethren, 1528-1931* (Goshen, 1931); ML I, 253.

Brail (Brael), **Hans,** an Anabaptist martyr, who was arrested a few days before Ascension Day, 1557, in the Puster Valley (Austria). He was tortured severely several times, and the dungeon was so damp that his clothing rotted. He was held for two years, and then sentenced to the galleys (1559). However, on the way he managed to escape and rejoin the congregation of believers (*Mart. Mir.* D 175, E 560).

VDZ.

Braitenstainer, Burckhart, a Hutterite preacher in Moravia, ordained March 24, 1608. He wrote the song, "Billich heb ich zu singen an, dan ich herzlich verlangen han." Nothing further is known about him. (Beck, *Geschichts-Bücher,* 355; Wolkan, *Lieder,* 241; ML I, 253.)

NEFF.

Braitmichel, Kaspar (d. 1573), sometimes also called Kaspar Schneider because he was a tailor, the first chronicler of the Hutterite Brethren in Moravia. Born in Silesia like his fellow brother Peter Riedemann (*q.v.*), he joined the Hutterite brotherhood during its hardest time in the 1530's, perhaps as early as 1533. In 1538 he was chosen *Diener der Notdurft* (deacon). In the following year he was captured during a religious service at Steinabrunn (*q.v.*) together with 150 others and taken to nearby castle Falkenstein (Lower Austria), whence all the brethren were sent to Trieste for work on Venetian galleys. He managed somehow to escape, and then returned to Moravia or rather to adjoining Slovakia where new Bruderhofs had just been established. In 1548 he was chosen by the lot to be *Diener des Wortes* (preacher) of the Holitsch Bruderhof. Later on he seems to have moved back to Austerlitz in Moravia, which then was the center of the entire brotherhood. This move was perhaps due to his alert interest in the history of the group and his fine gift for writing. Perhaps he became the clerk of the *Vorsteher* or the archivist

of the brotherhood. In Austerlitz he died in peace in 1573.

Braitmichel was the beginner of the official church chronicle (*q.v.*) of the Hutterites called the *Geschichts-Buch,* which work he must have started toward the end of his life, during the period of the outstanding *Vorsteher* Peter Walpot (*q.v.*). He begins this work with an elaborate summary of church history "from the beginning of the world" to the year 1520, taken chiefly from Sebastian Franck's *Chronica* (*q.v.*). Then he continues his story up to the year 1542. In his signed preface he apologizes that he could not carry his work further due to his poor eyesight and other physical frailty. Yet we have also another chronicle from his hand, now in the library of the Hungarian Primate at Esztergom, Hungary (described as Codex I by Beck, *Geschichts-Bücher*), which runs again "from the beginning of the world" up to 1534 (the first 70 leaves). This chronicle served perhaps as a preliminary experiment in such annalistic activities, and may later have inspired the larger enterprise of the official Chronicle. In two other Hutterite codices one finds a short report of historical nature, *Wie die Brüder von dem Gabriel* (i.e., Ascherham) *sich mit uns vereinigt haben . . .* (in 1545), also drawn up by Braitmichel who most likely had been present at these negotiations and may even have taken the minutes of this event. This brief account was later incorporated into the larger Chronicle (Zieglschmid, *Chronik,* 250-57) by the continuer of Braitmichel's work, the brother Zapff (*q.v.*). Also two epistles from Braitmichel's hand have been preserved, one sent in 1568 to the brother Leonhard Dax (*q.v.*) and his fellow sufferers in prison at Alzey (*q.v.*), Palatinate, the other containing an admonition to repentance, sent to Silesia, his home country where the Gabrielite brethren lived. All this indicates that he filled an important position in the leadership of the brotherhood. Four hymns written by him are found in the *Lieder der Hutterischen Brüder* (1914, pp. 98-101, 175-78, 647-703): "Merkt auf, herzliebe Brüder mein" (12 stanzas); "O Herre Gott vom Himmelreich" (53 stanzas); "Christliche Art, Eifer und Trieb" (30 stanzas); "Ich schrei zu dir, O Herre Gott" (8 stanzas). (Wolkan, *Lieder,* 231; Loserth, *Communismus;* ML I, 253; see also **Chronicle, Hutterite.**)

R.F.

Brakel, Johan Engelbert van, b. Aug. 31, 1882, at Amsterdam, d. Aug. 14, 1950, at Baarn, was a prominent Dutch Mennonite minister. He studied theology at the University of Amsterdam and the Mennonite Seminary and finished his studies in 1907, being then a ministerial candidate. Successively he served the congregations of Witmarsum-Pingjum 1908-14, Hollum on the island of Ameland 1914-28, Koog-Zaandijk 1928-46, and Baarn 1946-47.

Van Brakel was warmly interested in missions. For many years he was a member of the board of the Dutch Mennonite Mission Society. In 1925, when a large number of Tobanese immigrants settled on the territory of Groot-Mandailing on the island of Sumatra (then Dutch East Indies), van Brakel actively advocated the preaching of the Gospel to this Tobanese people. This project was financially especially supported by the congregation of Heubuden in West Prussia.

After a visit to the Quakers at Woodbrooke, England, deeply impressed by their activities, van Brakel together with his colleagues T. O. Hylkema and C. Nijdam in 1917 founded the *Vereeniging voor Gemeentedagen van Doopsgezinden in Nederland* (see **Broederschapswerk**). From October 1922 to November 1928 he was the editor of the periodical of this association, called *Brieven* (*q.v.*), in which van Brakel wrote valuable essays, for example those on the Old Testament prophets and on Islam. He published some booklets for catechetical classes: *Christelijk Geloof* (1934); *De verkondiging van de Evangeliën* (1940). Further publications: *De Gerechtigheid, Kerngedachten uit de Brief aan de Romeinen* (Lochem n.d. 1948); *De Knecht des Heren* (an introduction to II Corinthians) (Lochem n.d. 1950) and a paper on "Justificatio en Sanctificatio bij Paulus," in *Nederl. Theol. Tijdschrift* (1942) II, 98-123. F. Kuiper wrote on van Brakel in *Menn. Life* VI, 4 (Oct. 1951) 4-5.   vdZ.

Branch Mountain, a mission station (MC) at Mathias, W. Va., under the Virginia Conference, listed in the *Mennonite Yearbook* 1913-25, last with a membership of 10 persons.   M.G.

Branchweilerhof, an old Mennonite settlement, surrounded by beautiful orchards, vineyards, meadows, and fields, near Neustadt a.d.Hardt, in the Palatinate, Germany, where there has been a Mennonite congregation since 1683. Here where two Roman roads crossed there was once an important citadel. Since the 16th century, when a hospital was built there on Roman foundations, it has also been called the Spitalhof. In 1705 the Jesuit monastery in Neustadt acquired possession of it. In the same year the Jesuits established a Latin school here, to the support of which also taxes on the income of the former hospital of Branchweiler had to be paid by the Mennonites living there.

The Palatine Elector Karl, in a document of Sept. 28, 1682, assigned the Branchweiler hospital with all the cultivated and waste land belonging to it at an annual fee with all its traditional "liberties, rights, and justice" to the following Mennonites: Fritz Dester and his wife Elisabeth, Jakob Weber and his wife Barbara, and Daniel Stauffer and his wife Anna "and all their physical heirs and descendants" in hereditary tenure. In matters of faith, they were forbidden to invite Mennonites from other places or any other Palatines to attend their meetings; they were also to refrain from rebaptism, but were not to be burdened with any other obligations than those in the contract. They were to cultivate the land properly, and "completely eradicate thorns, thickets, and brush, and clean up the land and make it arable."

In the difficult period following the Thirty Years' War skilled farmers were especially highly valued on the idle land in the depopulated country. When the Mennonites on the Branchweilerhof

were later on charged with "holding some scandalous, seditious, secret meetings," the Jesuits in Neustadt gave them the testimonial that they paid their required rentals and fees regularly, so that there was not the least cause for complaint; that they held no secret night meetings they (the Jesuits) would vouch for. It is signed on Feb. 27, 1740, by "Christophory Butzfeld p.d. Superior."

According to the records preserved in the State Archives in Karlsruhe, the families of Abraham Egly, Johann Gut, Daniel Hege, Wilhelm Meyer, Johann Ellenberger, and Jakob Dester were living on the estate in 1716. In 1724 the Christian Lichti family is mentioned for the first time. The financial circumstances of the inhabitants of the Spitalhof were described as moderate or poor. In 1741 the name Johann Janson occurs and a mixed marriage is indicated in that Philipp Griesing is required to pay his Mennonite wife's protection fee.

Ernst Müller (*Berner Täufer*, 211) reports of 1732: "The congregation on the Spitalhof, half an hour from Neustadt a.d.H., and the subordinate villages like Essingen, Duttweiler, and Mussbach (not Mossbach), 25 families. Preacher; Hans Dester; deacon, Jakob Gut." It should be noted that there was a small Amish congregation in near-by Essingen. In the Karlsruhe Mennonite list of 1717 the family of Christian Wenger is listed as living in Mussbach. About 1738 three Mennonite families lived there, Johannes Joder (Jotter), a linenweaver, Nikolaus Ellenberger, and Nikolaus Wittner who farmed "for half" of the produce. In Duttweiler the same list of 1717 names Johannes Janson, Friedrich Bergthold, and Abraham Egli as Mennonites. Egli was hereditary tenant of the estate of the monastery of St. Lambrecht. The other two failed financially. The property of Bergthold was sold at auction, March 20, 1723, to Ulrich Burkhardt for 750 florins. He did not stay long. In 1740 Johannes Lichti became tenant for the University of Heidelberg. In 1773 he appears on the Karlsruhe lists as the father of seven children; Isaak Bergthold is also listed. The Resolutions of Ibersheim of 1803 were signed for the Spitalhof congregation by Johann Bergthold.

On July 13, 1824, the first conference of the Mennonites of the Palatinate and Hesse met on the Spitalhof. It was attended by preachers and elders representing the congregations at Johanniskirchen (near Annweiler), Sembach, Weierhof, Altleiningen, Heppenheim a.d. Wiese, Friedelsheim, and Spitalhof. This conference was the result of the influence of the Baptist preacher Angas (*q.v.*). The preachers at Spitalhof were at that time Johannes Hirschler and Abraham Hege, both chosen in 1824. Heinrich Becker was the elder. The main decision of the conference was to support the foreign mission work of the English Baptists and to regulate the matter of alms. The second conference occurred in 1825, again on the Spitalhof, as well as the conferences of May 18, 1876, and May 15, 1895.

In 1855 Branchweilerhof had a membership of 35; in 1916 there were about 45 souls, most of them resident in Spitalhof; in 1952 there were 54 baptized members. For a long time the Friedelsheim preacher, Jakob Ellenberger, administered baptism and communion until 1879. Since 1880 the congregation has belonged to the *Badischer Verband* (*q.v.*). At the present time it has two preachers and a deacon. Services are held every Sunday in the old Gothic hospital chapel. (*ML* I, 254.) H.E.

Brand, Henrik Willemsz, b. about 1555 at Delft, d. 1627 at Zierikzee, one of the first Reformed preachers in the Dutch province of Zeeland. He conducted a disputation in November 1608 at Colijnsplaat on Noord-Beveland with the Mennonite preacher Frans de Knuyt. This disputation was published by the Reformed congregation in 1609 and then reprinted in 1620 in Middelburg and in 1646 in Dordrecht. (Blaupot t. C., *Holland* I, 194; II, 210; *N.N. B.Wb.* I; *ML* I, 255.)   HEGE.

Brandenberg, Friedrich, of Cologne, an Anabaptist martyr, the traveling companion of Jakob Hutter (*q.v.*), was executed in Tirol in 1532.

J. Loserth, *Der Anabaptismus in Tirol* II (1892) 507; H. Ammann, *Die Wiedertäufer in Michelsburg im Pustertal* (Brixen, 1896) 21.

Brandenburg, province of Prussia, which included Berlin until April 1, 1881. In the eastern part of the province, in Netzebruch, there was at Brenkenhoffswalde (*q.v.*) near Driesen a Mennonite congregation founded in 1765 by 35 families from the Culm lowlands (West Prussia), but extinct in 1834, since most of its members had emigrated to South Russia. A second Mennonite immigration into Brandenburg principally from West Prussia occurred after 1870 and led to the settlements near Berlin, especially in Schöneberg (1910, 63), Charlottenburg (1910, 50), Rixdorf-Neukölln (1910, 28), and Deutsch-Wilmersdorf (1910, 29), all now parts of Berlin. The membership has grown steadily, as is shown in the census statistics (the official source, *Preussische Statistik*).

District	1880	1885	1890	1895	1900	1905	1910
Potsdam	14	21	58	108	159	182	302
Frankfurt	4	9	18	18	8	12	26
Brandenburg	18	30	76	126	167	194	328

The great preponderance of men is conspicuous (1910, 189 men, 139 women), and is explained by the immigration of young men working and studying in the city. The Brandenburg Mennonites belong to the Berlin congregation (*q.v.*). (*ML* I, 255.)   HEGE.

Brandenburg-Ansbach, a Hohenzollern principality, ceded to Bavaria in 1806. At the time of the Reformation the Anabaptists here had attained a considerable following; the foundation was apparently laid about 1527 when Hans Hut (*q.v.*) and Eucharius Binder (*q.v.*) traveled from Lower Franconia to Austria (Falkenstein, *Schwäbische Chronik,* 194). Several years later Julius Lober, a refugee from Bruchsal and a leader of the congregation there, settled here; Bernhard Witgenannt, who accompanied him, was arrested, but was released when he recanted (*Ztscht für die Gesch. des Oberrheins* LIV, 1905, 84). The Anabaptist movement did not reach any great importance in the margravure (Schulin, *Ansbachische Ref.-Gesch.,* 41). Neverthe-

less the government issued several edicts against them. The moving force behind their suppression seems to have been Andreas Althamer (*q.v.*). In 1528 he wrote the polemic, *Ein Kurtze Unterricht den Pfarhern und Predigern,* against them. The influence of the Anabaptists, however, remained, as is shown by the church regulation of the margravure and Nürnberg published in 1533, which stipulates "(1) that godfathers should be present, especially because of the Anabaptists, who now pretend that they do not know whether they have been baptized or not, so that the godfathers can be the chief witnesses besides other persons; (2) that persons baptized privately should not be baptized again, which has heretofore been an unnecessary and false act, especially in order that the Anabaptists may not have a good reason for their error" (G. A. Will, *Beyträge zur Geschichte des Antibaptismus in Deutschland,* Nürnberg, 1733, 115).   HEGE.

H. Westermayer, *Die brandenburgisch-nürnbergische Kirchenvisitation und Kirchenordnung 1528-1533* (Erlangen, 1894); K. Schornbaum, *Quellen zur Geschichte der Wiedertäufer* II: *Markgraftum Brandenburg (Bayern,* I Abt.) (Leipzig 1934); *ibid. (Bayern,* II Abt.) (1951). The second volume contains supplementary Ansbach court records and also Anabaptist records of the Bavarian imperial cities of Kaufbeuren, Nördlingen, Regensburg, Rothenburg ob der Tauber, Weissenburg, and Schweinfurt. (*ML* I, 255.)

Brandhuber, Wolfgang, an Anabaptist martyr, a successful leader of the Anabaptists in Upper Austria. Little is known about the first years of his adherence to the group. He was born in Passau, where he preached and baptized in 1527. After the destruction of the congregation at Styria he moved to Linz and became the elder of the congregation there. Here a broad field of labor opened to him. From the capital as a center his influence was felt with blessing throughout the Austrian hereditary lands and in the bishopric of Passau. Everywhere he preached the Word of God, comforted and strengthened his hard-pressed brethren. In many adjacent villages congregations were formed: in Wels, Enns, Ried, Grein, Gallneukirchen, Gmunden, Lambach, Mauthausen, Schärding, Vöcklabruck, Püchl, and the Attersee many joined the new doctrine and were served by Brandhuber and other Linz preachers. "The moral simplicity and unostentatious greatness of the Gospel they proclaimed," writes Nicoladoni, the historian of Linz, "was of equal power with the character of the preachers—men whose moral conduct, frugality, and submission, and especially their loyalty to conviction, enthusiasm, and self-sacrifice even their enemies had to admit—upon the hearts of the people" (*Bünderlin,* 32).

Brandhuber's pastoral influence extended all the way to Tirol. This is known from a letter to the church in Rattenberg on the Inn, which throws much light on his attitudes and doctrine. Like all the Anabaptist leaders of that time he placed the greatest stress on a Scriptural faith, which is expressed in a spiritual life rejecting worldly grandeur, in patient endurance of suffering, and in mutual aid. His views on organization for the care of the poor and distribution of gifts of charity are worthy of note. "In the congregation each member is not to be his own steward or treasurer, but the resources of rich and poor shall be distributed by the one who is ordained by the church for that purpose; thus all things that serve to honor God should be held in common, as God gives, grants, and permits" (Beck, 88). A "command of community of goods" is not indicated here, as Nicoladoni (51) and following him the *Doopsgezinde Bijdragen* (1899, 115 and 153) assume. But his *Sendbrief an die Gemeinde Gottes* laid the foundation for the practice of community of goods, which was instituted among the Hutterian Brethren in 1528. He advises his members not to engage in business because of the risk of taking advantage of one's neighbor. He finds it irreconcilable with a true Christian life to take vengeance or go to war, but the government should be obeyed in all things that are not contrary to God's Word. He seems to have had connections with the Anabaptists in Thuringia; Paul Wappler mentions (*Thüringen*, 159 and 425) that the head of the Thuringian Anabaptists, Jakob Storger of Coburg, had been baptized at Wels in Upper Austria by Brandhuber.

Brandhuber's period of work was short. In 1529 he was seized at Linz with 70 members and was martyred with his fellow preacher, Hans Niedermayer. Hans Schlaffer, who had become acquainted with Brandhuber in Regensburg in 1527 and was beheaded in 1528 at Schwatz in Tirol, said that he had "found nothing in him but an ardent zeal for a devout Christian life." His successor was Peter Riedemann (*q.v.*), who later became the leader of the Hutterian Brethren in Moravia.

HEGE.

Beck, *Geschichts-Bücher*; Alex. Nicoladoni, *Johannes Bünderlin von Linz* (Berlin, 1893); *Mart. Mir.* D 24, E 433; Lydia Müller, *Glaubenszeugnisse oberdeutscher Taufgesinnter* I (Leipzig, 1938) 136-43; P. Wappler, *Die Täuferbewegung in Thüringen* (Jena, 1913); *ML* I, 255.

Brandon, Col., a preaching point (MC) under the Kansas-Nebraska Conference, listed in the *Mennonite Yearbook* 1913-18 with 18 members. M.G.

Brandschadenversicherung (see also *Mutual Aid*). Early Mennonite records show that a form of mutual fire insurance was practiced at least as early as the beginning of the 17th century by the Mennonites of Germany. In 1623 Mennonites living in the province of West Prussia organized the *Tiegenhöfer Privat-Brandordnung,* which was in operation until the end of the Mennonite settlements in Prussia. (This article deals only with the fire insurance practices among the descendants of this group.)

When in the late 18th century Mennonites from Germany migrated to Russia they took their system of mutual insurance along with them and, if anything, expanded and systematized its use. In Russia the Mennonites were all organized by districts. Insurance of buildings was compulsory except for a few types of buildings such as churches which were optional. Negligence in observing regulations could result in penalties. Each village had its representative in the district organization and each district or volost had its officers and appraisers.

All disputes were resolved by an established system of arbitration. Buildings had to be erected so as to meet the approval of the fire insurance regulations. So effectively did the Mennonite insurance plan work that it was introduced into the other German-speaking colonies in the area in 1868 by the Ministry of State Domain.

In the late 19th century when the large Mennonite migrations from Russia to North America occurred, the mutual insurance organizations were again taken with them and put into operation in the new lands. There are more than 20 such mutual aid insurance societies in existence in the United States and Canada today, about half of them having been started by the Swiss Mennonites and their descendants who settled in the eastern part of the United States.

The Old Colony Mennonites in Mexico and in Paraguay are organized to provide systematic protection for losses from fire exactly as their forefathers in Europe were a century or more ago. The name is the same. It is called the *Brandschadenversicherung.* In each village there is a *Brandschulze* or local village representative. The individual elected to serve as general director of the entire colony fire insurance organization is called the *Brandvorsteher.* Losses from fire are comparatively low but such losses as occur are shared by all the colonists according to their property valuation.

The newer colonists who settled in Paraguay as refugees from Europe after World Wars I and II are likewise organizing their colonies to secure mutual protection from fire losses. In the United States and Canada many Mennonites are now insuring in non-Mennonite companies. Several insurance societies that were once exclusively Mennonite have now enlarged and taken in anyone who wished to be insured, thus operating as a straight mutual insurance company without regard for religious affiliation. The former Mennonite Mutual Fire Insurance Co., Newton, Kan., now Midland Fire Insurance Co., is an example of this development. In West Prussia and in Russia all traces of such Mennonite organizations are now completely extinct. In North and South America, however, the mutual fire insurance plan is still strong. For a treatment of mutual fire insurance in other North American groups of Mennonites, see **Fire Insurance.**   J.W.F.

Brandt, Geeraerdt (or Gerardt), b. July 25, 1626, at Amsterdam, d. Oct. 12, 1685, at Amsterdam, was first a clockmaker, then studied theology and was a Remonstrant preacher in the Netherlands (Nieuwkoop 1652-60; Hoorn 1660-67; Amsterdam 1667-87); he wrote the anonymously published *Kort verhaal der Reformatie* (1657) and the later *Historie der Reformatie en andere kerkelijke geschiedenissen in en omtrent de Nederlanden* (Vol. I, Amsterdam, 1671, 2nd ed., 1677; Vol. II, Amsterdam, 1674). On the part of the Reformed Church in the Netherlands there was so much opposition to this work that Brandt did not continue it. His son Johannes published the third and fourth parts in 1704. It is written with excellent impartiality. This fact and the manner in which he relates all sorts of particulars give his work value even for the present as a source of our history. Mennonite history written before Schijn-Maatschoen, *Geschiedenis der Mennoniten* (1743-45), was largely based on Brandt.

A French translation of the first three parts was published in The Hague in 1704; an English translation in four parts was produced in London in 1720-23. vdZ.

G. M. C. Loeff, *De Nederlandsche Kerkgeschiedschrijver G. Brandt* (Utrecht, 1864); C. Sepp, *Bibl. der Nederl. Kerkgeschiedschrijvers*, 211-12; *Biogr. Wb.* I, 576-81; *ML* I, 256.

Brant Township Mennonite Church: see **Bruce County, Ont.**

Bratislava (German: Pressburg), capital of Slovakia (pop. 130,000), from 1541 to 1784 the capital of Hungary, because the greater part of Hungary, including Budapest, was then in the hands of the Turks. As the capital it was also the coronation city of the kings of Hungary (the Habsburgs), and the seat of the Palatine, the representative or viceroy of the king (who actually resided in Vienna), and the head of the Hungarian nobility. Bratislava was also the seat of the Hungarian Royal Diet until 1848, when it moved to Budapest and thereafter was called Parliament. The population of Bratislava was in 1930 roughly 40 per cent Slovakian, 30 per cent German, and 30 per cent Hungarian (or Magyar).

Since Anabaptists (Hutterites) lived in Slovakia since the middle of the 16th century (coming from adjoining Moravia), the name of Pressburg appears often in the Hutterite *Chronicle*. The nobles of Slovakia, needing these thrifty workers, opposed any persecution there, until the all-powerful state of the 18th century no longer depended upon these nobles. Then the government in Vienna undertook the systematic conversion to Catholicism or, if impossible, the expulsion of all nonconforming elements; this was done primarily by Jesuit or (after 1773) ex-Jesuit missionaries (see **Counter Reformation**). At that time all the numerous Hutterite manuscript books were confiscated, partly destroyed and partly stored away in various Catholic libraries. In Pressburg they were deposited in the library of the Jesuit College which was changed after 1773 into the "library of the Cathedral chapter" (*Dom Kapitel*). From its printed catalogue 34 such entries are known, all highly valuable 16th/17th century Anabaptist codices. In 1919, 30 of them were sold into private hands, while four codices are supposed to be still there.

In the 19th century Bratislava had a good Lutheran high school, called lyceum, and one of its principals collected seven 16th/17th-century Hutterite codices from near-by *Habaner* (*q.v.*) settlements. The library was later taken over by the *Evangelische Kirchengemeinde*. After 1939, the library is said to have been transferred to the Slovakian State Archives and Library, yet details are lacking. One or two of the "lost" 30 codices were bought back by this state archives. Also the city library has some Anabaptist material, primarily pictures; a good deal of original source material is

still on the private book market, of which Bratislava had been a center for a long time. R.F.

N. Knauz, *A Poszonyi Kaptalannak Keziratai* (Esztergom, Hungary, 1870) 324 pp. (the catalogue of the library of the Bratislava Cathedral Chapter, very detailed, with German titles); Fr. Kraus, *Nove prispevky k dejinam Habanov na Slovensku* (Bratislava, 1937) ("Recent Research about the Habaners in Slovakia"); this work reprints excerpts of the one recently purchased Hutterite Chronicle of 1648, together with other material and with some fine illustrations. See also *Menn. Gesch.-Bl.*, 1938, 61 f., where an account is given about the Hutterite Chronicle.

Bräul, Johann J., son of Johann Bräul, an early teacher of the village school in Orloff, South Russia. The father was an advocate of progressive methods in a period of transition in Mennonite education in Russia and the son absorbed these ideas. He attended the Halbstadt Zentralschule with Kornelius Unruh, and continued his education in Moscow and Odessa (1873-75) with him and with P. M. Friesen. He was the first Mennonite of the Molotschna to acquire a state license for teaching elementary schools in the city. In 1874-75 he was the zemstvo teacher in the two-class Orloff elementary school. In August 1875 he was engaged to teach the Russian language and Russian history and physics at the noted Ohrloff Zentralschule. To him a whole generation of Mennonite leaders owed the foundation of their intellectual and religious stamp. J. J. Bräul impressed upon all his students, Mennonite or non-Mennonite, a deep understanding of Russia's people, history, and culture. In 1884 while he was teaching at the Zentralschule, he passed with distinction the teacher's examination in Russian language, history, and geography. During the period of extreme tensions between the Russian school boards and the national minorities, which were to be degraded to an inferior position, Bräul rendered the Mennonite colonies a real service by his conciliatory mediation. He was accused of pro-Russian sympathies; but his deathbed declarations made it clear that he had at heart remained true to the brotherhood and its Christian confession of faith. His oldest son was J. J. Bräul, a graduate engineer, who settled in the Warthegau (western Poland near Posen) with the Mennonite settlers who were removed from Russia by the German army in the latter part of World War II. B.H.U.

Braun (Brown, Bruhn, Brun, Brunss, Bruens, Bruyn), a Mennonite family name in West Prussia, appearing in the rural Flemish congregations and at Danzig, first mentioned at Danzig in 1619. Twenty-two families of this name lived in West Prussia (without Danzig) in 1776, and 34 persons (including Elbing) in 1935. Members of this family migrated to Russia and subsequently to America. The name is represented among Mennonite ministers in British Columbia, Saskatchewan, Manitoba, and California. A. Braun has served many years as pastor at Ibersheim, Germany. H. J. Brown (GCM) of Freeman, S.D., was for many years a missionary in China. B. J. Braun of Dinuba, Cal., was president of the M.B. General Conference. Peter J. Braun was an outstanding teacher in the Mennonite schools of South Russia, and Heinrich

Braun was a publisher in South Russia. Also in the Netherlands, especially in the province of North Holland, the family of Bruyn or Bruin is often found among the Mennonites.   G.R.

Braun, Abraham A., son of Abraham Braun, Grossweide, a respected member of the Gnadenfeld Mennonite congregation, South Russia, was one of a group of Wüst (*q.v.*) brethren which included August Lehman, the elder of this congregation in Gnadenfeld, Andreas Flaming of Schardau, and Heinrich Schmidt of Pastwa, preachers of the congregation; in his later years Braun was a *Felsentaler Freund* (Friesen, *Brüderschaft,* 85 f.). Braun's father had the courage to admit Abr. Cornelsen into his home, who had been expelled in midwinter from the Elisabeththal school and who was living in the Nogai steppes in a freshly built, damp sod hut. Abraham Braun completed his courses for elementary teaching under Heinrich Franz I (1812-89) and the Lange brothers in the Gnadenfeld Vereinsschule. He taught in the village school in Neu-Halbstadt, then for 30 years in the Gnadenfeld school. He was also engaged as a teacher of Russian in the Gnadenfeld Zentralschule (Friesen, *Brüderschaft,* 622).   B.H.U.

Braun, Burkhard, an evangelist, one of the first preachers of the South German Anabaptists at the beginning of the Reformation. He was born in Ofen, was a goldbeater by vocation, and is known in the court records mostly as Burkhard von Ofen. Only a few facts have been handed down about his work. We hear of him first soon after the Martyrs' Synod, which met in Augsburg, Aug. 20, 1527. He apparently joined the Anabaptists at that time; in the following month he was arrested at Augsburg because he had been baptized, and on Oct. 1, 1527, was expelled from the city with his wife and children as a nonresident. He became a zealous worker in the vicinity of Augsburg as elder of the church; in Gögginen he baptized both Margarethe Anwald and Bernhard Zirgkendorffer (*q.v.*), who were therefore executed with Eitelhans Langenmantel (*q.v.*) May 11, 1528, at Weissenhorn. At Christmas 1527 he conducted a meeting in the big house near Wellenburg. Then he went to Passau, where he also preached and baptized in January 1528 and ordained the schoolmaster of Burghausen, Wolfgang Welser, as elder; this was related by the captured members of the congregation at Passau. Later he went to Moravia and joined the congregation in Austerlitz (*q.v.*). When this congregation divided in 1530 he sided with Georg Zaunring (*q.v.*) and Wilhelm Reublin (*q.v.*). When this group went to Auspitz (*q.v.*) he was given charge of the care and comfort of the sick and the children who were left behind and could not follow until homes were prepared for them in Austerlitz. In the same year he was banned because he criticized the church, but, as the chronicle states, the authorities could produce no evidence. Nothing is known of his later life. Hege.

Beck, *Geschichts-Bücher;* A. Nicoladoni, *Johannes Bünderlin von Linz* (Berlin, 1893); F. Roth, *Ztscht des hist. Vereins für Schwaben und Neuburg,* 1900, 1901; ML I, 256.

Braun, Georg, a South German Anabaptist martyr, who was beheaded at the end of February 1529 on the market square in Schweinfurt on the command of Count Wilhelm von Henneberg. He had been baptized in 1528 at an Anabaptist meeting at Sennfeld. On Dec. 19, 1528, a number of Anabaptists were seized in their homes. At their trial the information was given that several weavers of Schweinfurt had taken part in their meetings, who took to flight when they were summoned by the council. One of these, Georg Braun, returned voluntarily and presented himself to the authorities. He was imprisoned and cross-examined on Jan. 20, 1529, by the Schweinfurt parson, Johannes Ort. He confessed that he had erred and that he would change his Anabaptist views. But he soon repented of his recantation, made under the pressure of fear, and declared to a delegation of the council on Feb. 10, 1529, that he would persevere in his Anabaptist faith.

From the confession he made at this time we cite the following points: "The Anabaptists baptized none who did not wish it." "They did not meet to foment insurrection, but to instruct one another in God's Word." "If anyone consented to their cause and conduct, he had to promise them that he would refrain from blasphemy, the oath, excessive drinking and other debauchery and would serve God alone, and if anyone lacked food he would aid the destitute, but not those who would waste their food, but in everything be honest and kind." "Concerning the holy sacrament, he wanted to keep it as the Almighty God has instituted it. But no one could show him in the Scriptures that God meant the bread that He handed the disciples, but he did not think otherwise than that He meant the body which was there in person." "It was not true, as was reported, that women and girls were held in common among them, for that would not be godly, but devilish." "They do not forbid going to church." "Concerning government, he says that all government is instituted by God." (P. Wappler, *Die Täuferbewegung in Thüringen von 1526 bis 1584,* Jena, 1913; ML I, 257.) Neff.

Braun, Heinrich Jakob, b. April 30, 1873, at Alexanderwohl, South Russia, was a leading representative of the Mennonite Brethren of the Molotschna settlement. Braun was graduated from the Hamburg Baptist Seminary, was a minister, a director of the *Raduga* Publishing House (*q.v.*), and owner of two large estates. After the Revolution (1922) he left Russia to make his home in Germany, where he practiced healing. In 1924 he made a trip to South America to investigate settlement possibilities for Mennonites in Paraguay. He undertook this project entirely at his own initiative and on his own expense but submitted a comprehensive report to the Mennonitische Studienkommision delegated by the Mennonites of Russia to investigate settlement possibilities. He died June 24, 1946. His major achievements lie in the realm of promoting the publication and distribution of Christian literature among the Mennonites and others in Russia.   C.K.

Braun, Jacob, was the first elder of the Bergthal Mennonite settlement (*q.v.*) in South Russia. He was ordained in 1840 and was succeeded by Gerhard Wiebe (*q.v.*) who led the total Bergthal Mennonite group to America. Nothing else is known about Elder Jacob Braun.   C.K.

Braun, Johann Jakob, b. 1851 at Halbstadt in the Molotschna settlement in South Russia, son of Jacob Braun and Justina Giesbrecht, the third child, had two sisters and one brother. In 1875 he married Katharina Letkeman; to them were born three children. He attended a secondary school at Halbstadt, and became a schoolteacher at Blumstein (Molotschna settlement). He was a member of the Lichtenau Mennonite Church and became a minister there in 1876. Later he moved to Samoylovka, a new Mennonite settlement in the Ekaterinoslav province, serving as a leader of this young pioneer group. From 1906 to 1908 he was a minister at the Anadol forestry camp (*q.v.*) among young Mennonite men drafted for state service. After 1924, he was elder of the Samoylovka congregation. He died in 1928 of a heart attack.

The Samoylovka Mennonite Church which he served was founded in 1889. It had three ministers for a long time: Johann Braun, Johann Driedger, and Hermann Enns. It was served by elders of older churches until 1924, when Johann Braun was ordained an elder. After his death the church disintegrated.   J.H.E.

Braun, Peter Jacob, brother of A. Braun of Ibersheim, Germany, b. Feb. 9, 1880, Alexanderwohl, Russia, d. Sept. 24, 1933, Oberursel, Taunus, Germany. He was married to Maria Friesen. He was graduated from the Zentralschule and the Teacher's Training School, both at Halbstadt. After having taught school he enrolled at the St. Petersburg Teacher's Institute for further training. Following his graduation he taught at the schools at Halbstadt from which he had been graduated, and from 1909 to 1914 at the girls' Gymnasium at the same place. After the war he served as principal of the Teacher's Training School at Halbstadt. In 1924 he left Russia for Germany where he died a premature death of tuberculosis. Peter J. Braun was an outstanding educator among the Mennonites of Russia. His article, "The Educational System of the Mennonite Colonies in South Russia," appeared in the *MQR,* July 1929, 169-82.   C.K.

Brauns, Johann F. A., (d. 1851), pastor at Oesselse, Germany, author of the book, *Zur Verständigung über den Anabaptismus oder gemeinfassliche Widerlegung der Wiedertäufer zum ernsten Bedenken ihrer selbst und zur Warnung der protestantischen Gemeinde des Vaterlandes vorgelegt von I. F. Brauns mit einem Vorwort des Herrn Konsistorialrats und General-Superintendenten Dr. theol. Bauer in Elze zur Unterstützung eines angehenden "vaterlosen, gänzlich unbemittelten Missionszöglings"* (Hildesheim, 1844). This book is a warning in a warm, friendly tone, in the form of letters to a young friend Eduard, who wants to join the Anabaptists, to all Protestants against this transfer. The author apparently does not have reference to the Mennonites, for he never mentions them, but to the Baptists, whose origin he erroneously places in the Reformation period. When he relates that "the

daughter of an Anabaptist who had received communion from an orthodox preacher, was given nothing to eat because she had not gone to a Christian church, but had drunk the devil's brew in a cave of darkness," this would scarcely fit a Mennonite family in Hannover Province. Beyond this, the book is chiefly a long-winded justification and glorification of infant baptism. (*ML* I, 257.)   NEFF.

Bray, Guido de: see **Brez, Guy de.**

Brazil. The thousands of Mennonites who streamed into Moscow in the autumn of 1929 from all the settlements on Russian territory had only one goal in mind, namely, Canada. But only a small fraction of them reached this country. Escaping to Germany in November and December the refugees were temporarily sheltered in three camps, Mölln, Prenzlau, and Hammerstein, where over 5,000 were cared for. Previously efforts had been made, especially by B. H. Unruh in connection with the MCC, to open the road from Moscow to Canada. When this plan failed, and the situation at Moscow demanded quick action, B. H. Unruh sent a passionately inspired appeal to the Mennonite world as well as to the German government. The German Reichstag provided a large sum of money for the care of the refugees in Germany for the time being, and a national collection was carried through for *Brüder in Not.* But it was impossible to settle them in Germany. In this need two South American nations opened their doors to them: Brazil through the negotiations of the German government, and Paraguay through the offices of the MCC.

With the aid of the German government the emigration to Brazil was undertaken in early 1930. At that time the *Hollandsch Doopsgezind Emigranten Bureau* (H.D.E.B.: Dutch Mennonite Emigration Bureau) also assisted, acting on the motto: "It is our task to aid our brethren." On the memorable date of Jan. 16, 1930, the steamer *Monte Olivia* sailed from Hamburg with the first group of 33 families under the leadership of Heinrich Martins, and on Feb. 10 they arrived on the land of the Hanseatic Colonization Company in the state of Santa Catarina (*q.v.*) near Blumenau. They were assigned to the valley of the upper Krauel River, beyond Hammonia, which is today generally known as Witmarsum (*q.v.*). After three groups with a total of 150 families had settled here it was clear that the area was too small. The later groups, a total of 90 families, were then located on the Stoltz Plateau. In 1931 and 1932 a few additional families arrived. In June 1934 a group of 34 families from Harbin, China, was also brought to Brazil. These families formed the core of the Mennonite colonization in Brazil. There were about 280 in number.

In 1934 an emigration set in, at first from the Stoltz Plateau and then from Witmarsum. Most of those who moved went to Curitiba, the capital of Parana, the state adjoining Santa Catarina to the north and west. By 1951 the last of the Mennonite families had left the Stoltz Plateau. Several families and some unmarried persons went to Sao Paulo and other cities.

MENNONITE SETTLEMENTS IN
Brazil
AND NEAR-BY AREAS

▦ Mennonite Settlements

Scale of Miles
0   50   100   150

In 1949 the Mennonites in Brazil were distributed as follows: Witmarsum about 120 families, in Curitiba 258, in Sao Paulo (*q.v.*), Blumenau, Ponta Grossa, and elsewhere about 44 families, making a total of about 422 families, with about 2,300 souls. In 1949-52 the Witmarsum settlement also broke up, due to economic difficulties, about 70 families going to southern Rio Grande de Sul near Bage (*q.v.*), and the remainder to a new settlement, Neuwitmarsum, northwest of Curitiba, individuals scattered in other places being lost to the Mennonite brotherhood.

The two original settlements, Krauel (*q.v.*) and Stoltz Plateau, tried to organize their communities along the traditional lines to which the Mennonites were accustomed in Russia. In Witmarsum this order was followed to the end, with an *Oberschulze* (leader of the colony), the *Schulzen* of the various villages, and the village or settlement meetings, which discussed and settled all matters of common interest. In Curitiba, on the other hand, the civil life is not so cohesive, since there is no closed settlement there, and no colony or village organization has been formed.

The economic life of both settlements centers around the co-operative. This co-operative was originally merely the point of distribution of food and equipment which the German government furnished the settlers the first year. Then it became firmly established with the aid of the H.D.E.B. to help the settlers make the transition to independence and to form a basis for a sound development. The Dutch Mennonites furnished a cow for each family, gave the money for two feed mills, and funds to help weak families to become established. The co-operative in Witmarsum did a considerable volume of business, not only providing the Mennonites with the necessities, but also serving as a trading post for a wider area. It supported many charitable, cultural, and civil undertakings. In Curitiba the chief function of the co-operative is to furnish feed for the dairy herds of the Mennonites without the service of the middleman.

The most important product of Witmarsum was corn, which furnished both bread and cattle feed. Then there were the tubers, especially *aipim* (manioc) rich in starch, which was processed in a factory financed by the H.D.E.B. The most profitable products produced in Witmarsum were milk, *aipim,* wood from the forests, and pork. In Curitiba agriculture fills a less important place, and more stress is laid on dairying. The suburban Mennonites supply about three fourths of the milk consumed by the metropolis (pop. 160,000). Some Curitiba Mennonites are engaged in other industries, such as sawmills and plywood factories, and still others are employed in factories. Thus the Mennonites in Curitiba no longer form a compact social unit.

From the beginning the settlers tried to pattern their educational system on the traditions they had brought with them from Russia. They had among them an adequate number of teachers. From 1930 to 1938 they conducted their grade schools in this way and even established a secondary school (Zentralschule). Then the laws nationalizing all the schools of Brazil were passed; foreign teachers were abolished and Portuguese became the language of instruction in the elementary schools. Not until the close of the war (in Witmarsum to some extent before its close) could the children receive instruction in their specifically Mennonite heritage; school children were given religious instruction in the churches, and in both Curitiba and Witmarsum elementary Bible schools were opened for the older youth. The colony paper *Die Brücke* (*q.v.*), which was issued 1932-38, was suppressed by the laws of nationalization of 1938. In 1954 the Mennonites of Brazil had an organ, *Bibel und Pflug*.

The lack of physicians was a serious deficiency in the colonies. To be sure, the German Red Cross had equipped the settlers with medications for the beginning, and there were some who had experience in nursing. In response to the request of the colonies Dr. Peter Dyck, formerly of Russia, arrived in Witmarsum in 1935. A temporary hospital was built, which also housed the doctor's family. The doctor's wife, who had been a deaconess in the hospital in Muntau in South Russia, took upon herself this function in Brazil. Dr. Dyck also brought with him a gift of the Dutch Mennonites, amounting to 20,000 milreis, for a new hospital, which was built in 1937 with many a contribution by the local Mennonites. Its 12 beds were of great benefit not only to the colony, but also to non-Mennonites, caring for 250 patients annually, besides those who came merely for treatment. All those who brought trachoma with them from Russia were healed here. Infant mortality was sharply reduced. The expenses for the care of the sick were borne by the colony as a whole rather than by the patients.

During the first 16 years all religious services were held in the schools. The Mennonites and the Mennonite Brethren worshiped together. And when the first two Mennonite churches in Brazil were built in Curitiba in 1946 the work was done in unity and services are still conducted as a unit. In Witmarsum, on the other hand, the Mennonite Brethren built a separate church in 1948, and the General Conference Mennonites built two churches in 1949. The membership of the two Mennonite Brethren churches is 418, that of the three General Conference churches is 284. A serious question facing the congregations is the preservation of the principle of nonresistance. In 1949 the first Mennonite boys were called up for military service. For the two Witmarsum boys the colony leaders presented an appeal to the military authorities requesting release, which was granted. A similar step has not yet been taken by Curitiba, but the two colonies plan to work together as a unit in this matter. A more intensive indoctrination is also planned. Action is made difficult by the fact that the Mennonite group in Brazil is so small. While the original colonies in Santa Catarina were economically a failure, the newer settlements promise to be permanently successful. Culturally the colonies are of necessity becoming Portuguese, both

because of the national pressure and also the internal weakness (no schools, no literature, ecclesiastical strife). The most serious handicap, however, has been the weakness of the church life. There has been at times a serious lack of cohesion and of a sense of group responsibility, with resulting evidences of disintegration. The future is by no means hopeless and there are signs of real strengthening. Plans are being made for a church high school and Bible school.

To assist in ministering to the religious needs of the unorganized Mennonites in the metropolitan center of Sao Paulo, the Mennonite Central Committee established a religious and social center in 1947, which continued to render a valuable service. At various times the MCC has also sent representatives to aid the colonies in various ways, sometimes special commissioners for briefer visits, and also ministers for a two-year period. However, neither the MCC nor the H.D.E.B., nor any other organization except the German government ever had any administrative, financial, or moral responsibility for the Brazil colonies. In recent years both church groups in Brazil (MB and GCM) have joined the corresponding conferences in North America, which conferences have in turn rendered financial and other assistance to their affiliated groups in Brazil.

During the Hitler period in Germany, the Nazi influence became very strong among many Germans in Brazil and also affected seriously the Mennonite colonies. A movement to return to Germany led to the emigration of over 100 persons, mostly young people, but also some families. A few of these were settled in the Warthegau (western Poland). A few returned to Brazil after the war.   H.S.B.

Z. Kamerling, *De Doopsgezinden in Brazilie* (Amsterdam, n.d., 19 pp.); F. W. Brepohl, *Brasilien und die Einwanderung russlanddeutscher Mennoniten-Flüchtlinge* (Ponta Grossa, Parana, Brazil, 1930?); idem, *Flüchtlinge in Brasilien* (Ponta Grossa, Parana, Brazil, 1932, 20 pp.); P. Klassen, "Mennonites of Brazil," MQR XI (1937) 107-18; H. S. Bender, "With the Mennonite Colonies in Brazil and Paraguay, a Personal Narrative," MQR XIII (1939) 59-70; P. C. Hiebert, *Mitteilungen von der Reise nach Süd-Amerika* (Hillsboro, 1937) 18-31; A. E. Janzen, *Glimpses of South America* (Hillsboro, 1944) 117-23; W. and V. Smith, *Paraguayan Interlude* (Scottdale, 1950) 109-23; *Foreign Missions, Mennonite Brethren Mission, Brazil* (Hillsboro, Kan., 1948?, 21 pp.); J. W. Fretz, *Pilgrims in Paraguay* (Scottdale, 1953); see also the Brazilian Mennonite news journal, *Die Brücke*, 1932-37, and *Die neue Brücke*, 1938, both published at Witmarsum-Hammonia, Santa Catarina.

Brazil, Mennonite Brethren Mission in: see **Curitiba** (Brazil) M.B. Mission.

Brazol, D. N., was the name of the owner of a large estate from whom the Mennonites purchased 5,324 dessiatines (about 14,000 acres) of land in the Alexandrovka (*q.v.*) area in the province of Ekaterinoslav, Russia, on July 20, 1868. This land was located north of the Molotschna settlement and became the nucleus of the Schönfeld Mennonite settlement (*q.v.*), composed of villages and smaller and larger estates. Schönfeld was the center and volost of the growing and prosperous settlement. Blumenfeld (*q.v.*), which had been started in this district in 1848, was added to the Schönfeld volost in 1876. Between 1855 and 1875 a number of estates in this area were settled by Mennonites centering around Rosenhof (*q.v.*), and after 1875 Blumenheim (*q.v.*) was established.

At the time of World War I some 2,000 Mennonites lived in this area on 202 farms consisting of some 150,000 acres of land. The settlement had three places of worship, Schönfeld (*q.v.*), Blumenfeld (q.v.), and Rosenhof (*q.v.*). For a more detailed description see **Schönfeld Mennonite Settlement**. (*ML* I, 256.) C.K.

Breberen, a village near Aachen in Rhenish Prussia, where the Anabaptists were rather numerous in the 16th century. About 1534 the Wassenberger (*q.v.*) preachers, especially Johannes Campanus (*q.v.*), Johannes Kloprijs, Dionysius Vinne, Slachtscaep, and Roll (*q.v.*), were zealously active and won a large following (Rembert, *Wiedertäufer,* 150). There were Anabaptists here until the middle of the 16th century, but then they had to yield to the pressure of increasing persecution (Rembert, 431, 436, and 525). Much interesting light might have been thrown on this congregation at Jülich in the "Akten über Wiedertäufer in Breberen um 1554-10 bll. fol. Pap.," mentioned in *Uebersicht über den Inhalt der Kleineren Archive der Rheinprovinz* II (Bonn, 1904) 203, which were at that time in the possession of Pastor W. Lückerath in Waldfeucht (Heinsberg district, Rhenish Prussia), but could not be found in his literary estate. (*ML* I, 257.) HEGE.

Brechbill (Brechbühl, Brechbiehl, Brackbill), **Benedikt** (1665-ca. 1720), outstanding Swiss leader and pioneer Lancaster Co., Pa. (MC) leader, of Trachselwald in the canton of Bern, received into the Mennonite Church there at the age of 20, was made their preacher about 1699. In 1701 he married Marie Herr, a sister of Hans Herr (*q.v.*). Exiled twice for his faith, he returned each time. He tried to persuade his wife and children to leave with him and settle in Mannheim. But he was suddenly seized at his home early in the morning, bound, and taken to Bern, thrown into the tower, fastened to a chain, and left in the dungeon 18 weeks. Then he was taken to the "hospital" with other prisoners, where for 35 weeks he had to work "at the wool" from four in the morning until eight at night. On March 18, 1710, he was put on a ship with 56 other Mennonites for forcible deportation to America. He was released in Nijmegen and at once made his way via Cleve and Crefeld back to Mannheim. Here he was chosen elder of the congregation.

As the representative of the Dutch Mennonites he rendered a very useful service. He repeatedly wrote to Holland, reporting the unhappy state of the Mennonites in the Palatinate and in the canton of Bern. With Hans Bürcky and Melchior Zahler he traveled to Amsterdam at the invitation of the Dutch, and there answered 24 questions on conditions in Switzerland. To the Dutch government or to the city council of Amsterdam they presented a written self-defense, giving a clear, but brief confession of their faith (Brons, 198 f.). After numerous conferences and visits they left Amsterdam on

June 6, 1710, with a brotherly farewell and a gift of 50 guilders for travel expenses and returned to Mannheim. Bürcky and Zahler went on to Switzerland, where they were again imprisoned. Brechbill felt himself bound by his promise to the Dutch Mennonites at The Hague not to return to Switzerland without their consent. In a letter of May 7, 1711, he stated that his three children had arrived safely from Switzerland, but requested to be released from his promise because the Brethren in Switzerland desired his presence. He apparently did not enter upon this journey.

When the plan was announced to settle the Bernese Mennonites on a moor to cultivate it, Brechbill declared the project unacceptable. On the other hand, the idea of settling in Prussian Lithuania on a very favorable offer of the King of Prussia appealed to him. With Hans Ramseier and Uli Bauer he journeyed to Berlin and had a personal conference with King Frederick I of Prussia. Then they went to Lithuania to view the proffered land. Their impression was favorable, but they were unable to induce the Swiss to settle in Prussia.

Brechbill did not stay in Mannheim long. On Feb. 6, 1714, he wrote to Holland that conditions in the Palatinate were wretched in consequence of the war. This may have suggested the idea of emigrating to America. In the spring of 1717 we see him at the head of a large train of emigrating Palatine-Swiss Mennonites, who left for America from Rotterdam, arriving in Philadelphia, Aug. 24. He received from the Dutch Committee for Foreign Needs the sum of 4,000 guilders for distribution among the emigrants. The Mennonite Archives at Amsterdam contain a number of letters written by Brechbill, giving interesting information concerning the persecution of the Swiss and the Dutch aid.

Brechbill went at once to Strasburg, Lancaster Co., Pa., and claimed 150 acres of the John Funk tract and 100 more for his son Ulrich (later confirmed to his grandson John). The Brechbills had three children. Barbara married Jacob, son of Hans Groff, the ancestor of the Strasburg Groffs. Maudlin (Magdalena) married Emanuel, son of Hans Herr who was the paternal ancestor of John Herr (*q.v.*) and through the maternal side of Bishop Abraham Herr. Ulrich, the only son, also a preacher, was the ancestor of the Lancaster County Brackbills. Ulrich died in 1739 by an accident on the road to Philadelphia. The exact date of Benedikt Brechbill's death is not known.

It is quite possible that Benedikt Brechbill's home served also as a meetinghouse for worship in the Strasbourg section. A second "Brackbill home," serving in the same capacity, was built after Benedikt's death, in 1740. Brechbill not only took up land upon which he lived permanently but also assisted his fellow believers spiritually and even financially to start aright in the wilderness of Pennsylvania, not very far from the Hans Herr colony. He was noted for his fine singing in church services. He was a helpful minister on both sides of the Atlantic, and an outstanding relief worker during a time of testing and difficult migration.

While in Holland, he learned the Dutch language, which enabled him to translate J. P. Schabalie's popular work, *Wandering Soul* (*q.v.*), into High German (between 1710 and 1714). This is at least the present-day interpretation of the three initials B.B.B. on all German editions of this book. This translation provided his people with a fine devotional book in days of much distress.

NEFF, I.D.L.

Müller, *Berner Täufer;* J. C. Burkholder, "Benedikt Brechbühl, Hans Burkholder, and the Swiss Migration to Lancaster County," in *Papers read before the Lancaster County Historical Society* May 6, 1927 (*Proceedings* XXXI, 57 f.); M. Weaver, *Mennonites of Lancaster Conference* (Scottdale, 1931); R. Friedmann, *Mennonite Piety Through the Centuries* (Goshen, 1949) 114 ff.; A Brons, *Ursprung . . . der Mennoniten* (Norden, 1912); *Inv. Arch. Amst.* I, Nos. 1262-1371, *passim; ML* I, 258.

Brecht Alberts, an Anabaptist martyr. She was executed with nine others on May 15, 1535, at Amsterdam. (Grosheide, *Verhooren,* 58 f.)   vᴅZ.

Breda, a town in the predominantly Catholic Dutch province of North Brabant (pop. 85,294 in 1947; 86 per cent Catholic), the seat of a Mennonite congregation. At the time of the Reformation there were many Anabaptists in Breda. No fewer than seven martyrs suffered death here in 1572 for their faith. One of their members was Cornelis de Gyselaar, who married the widow of the martyred Valerius, called the Schoolmaster. The *Martyrs' Mirror* (D 603, E 930) describes at length the cruel tortures Cornelis Geleyn, another of the members, endured. In August 1572 several members were seized in the neighboring village of Nieuwvaart or Klundert at a well-attended religious service, which was betrayed to the magistrate. About 100 persons had assembled in the house of the martyrs Peter de Guliker and Jan Pieters, when they were surprised and seven of them taken. They had imagined themselves so secure here that Menno's friend, the elder Hans Busschaert (*q.v.*), had sent his son there. (*DB* 1912, 30-48, gives a letter written by the martyr Adriaen Jacob).

In the 17th century there was a congregation in Breda, which had several members living in Gertruidenberg and in Oosterhout. In 1664 they joined the Zonists and had as their preachers Jan Jans van de Langerijt and Augustijn Gerrits Hulstmann. The congregation presumably died out soon afterward. At any rate it no longer existed in 1731.

The Breda congregation was re-established on Nov. 22, 1896, by a number of Mennonite families living in the town. At the beginning B. Haga, the preacher of the Nijmegen congregation, came over to serve them once a month with preaching and catechetical instruction. In 1899 (the membership at that time was 72) the Breda congregation united with that at Dordrecht (*q.v.*) for ministerial service and instruction. This union lasted until 1945. In 1947 a similar combination was made with Eindhoven (*q.v.*). The membership at present (1953) stands at 96. The congregation does not own a meetinghouse. Since 1896 religious services have been held in the Lutheran church.

The Breda congregation has a woman's organization and Bible courses are held regularly. It belongs to the Zuidholland-Zeeuwsche Ring.

K.V., vᴅZ.

Blaupot t. C., *Holland* I, 341; II, 235; DB 1897, 256, 1899, 210; 1900, 224; 1912, 30-48; *ML* I, 258.

Breen, Daniel de (van Breen), b. 1594 at Haarlem, d. 1664 at Amsterdam, was secretary of the group of Remonstrant (*q.v.*) ministers at the Reformed Synod of Dordrecht in the Netherlands in 1618, but he soon withdrew from the Remonstrants and joined the Collegiants (*q.v.*). He founded the *college* of Amsterdam, of which he was an influential leader together with Adam Boreel (*q.v.*), the Mennonite minister Galenus Abrahamsz (*q.v.*), and Michiel Coomans. Daniel De Breen, who is said to have had much influence on Galenus, ardently defended the principle of nonresistance and the doctrines of millennialism. He wrote numerous theological books, including a compendium of the works of Erasmus. His *Opera Theologica* were edited at Amsterdam in 1664 by his nephew Frans de Kuiper. (*Biogr. Wb.* I, 604-6; Hylkema, *Reformateurs* II, Haarlem, 1902, 195.)   vᴅZ.

Bregenzer Wald (Bregenz Forest), the northern region in the Vorarlberg in Austria, which lies between the valleys of the Rhine, Walser, and Mittelberg, was very early a seat of the Anabaptists. In consequence of the severe regulations passed by the Swiss cantons against the Anabaptists after 1525 and 1526 the movement was nearly eradicated in eastern Switzerland. Only in the canton of Appenzell (*q.v.*) did they maintain a precarious existence. A craftsman from Au in the Bregenzer Wald, who had for some time lived in Switzerland and become acquainted with the doctrine of the Swiss Brethren, spread their doctrine at home upon his return in the region of the upper Bregenzer Wald (about 1570).

The authorities made futile attempts to eradicate them again and finally issued a mandate that the Anabaptists would either have to return to the Catholic Church or leave the country. Most of them preferred the latter course. Those remaining, if caught, were penalized with heavy fines and prison sentences. A stir was created by the trial of the three Anabaptists, Hans Berwig, Jakob Seiffrit, and Hans Sailer. Archduke Ferdinand sent a severe reprimand to the officials in Feldkirch, June 25, 1579, because of their negligence in this matter, and ordered, as an edict of Oct. 16, 1577, had already done, that those who refused to drop their faith were to be exiled and their property confiscated.

Hence in the years 1581-83 large numbers of Anabaptists migrated to Moravia, "the land of the saints." Only scattered individuals returned, while others were preparing to emigrate. The soul of the movement was Melchior Platzer, who had once been an apothecary, and later a preacher in Moravia. In June 1583 he was arrested at Feldkirch and taken to Rankweil castle, and dragged back to Feldkirch for trial; but all attempts to make him renounce his faith were in vain. He was therefore condemned to death. He approached the place of execution (Nov. 6, 1583) singing and admonishing the spectators to repentance. Now the Anabaptists left for Moravia in large groups; in 1585 alone 37 families went, leaving property worth 1,415 guilders behind.

But even in the following decades there were considerable numbers of Anabaptists in the Vorarlberg (*q.v.*). The success of Jakob Müller, who had been sent to the city and the diocese of Constance as church inspector by the bishop of Constance, Cardinal Marx Sitticus, induced Archduke Ferdinand to send this inspector to Bregenz; he succeeded in leading many Anabaptists back into the Catholic fold. The Jesuits who were sent to Bregenz in 1598 were even more successful.

But two decades later Anabaptism was still not extinct in the Bregenzer Wald; on May 24, 1618, one of them, Jost Wilhelm, was "executed with the sword in a village on the Eck," two miles from Bregenz; he was soon followed by Christine Brünner, who had "just set out to go to Moravia, like the patriarch Abraham, to escape from the idolatrous Chaldeans." She died at the same place on Aug. 8. The traces of Anabaptism were not extinguished in Au until about 1630.   LOSERTH.

Beck, *Geschichts-Bücher*, 283; J. Bergmann, *Die Wiedertäufer zu Au im inneren Bregenzer Walde u. ihre Auswanderung nach Mähren im Jahre 1585* (*Sitzungsberichte der kaiserl. Akademie der Wissenschaft* I, 248-57); J. Loserth, *Der Anabaptismus in Tirol* (1892) II, 220-28; *ML* I, 259.

Bregte Adams, wife of Frans Dirksz Quintijn (*q.v.*) or Frans Dirksz van Wormer, an Anabaptist martyr, was executed by drowning at Alkmaar, Dutch province of North Holland, on Feb. 1, 1536, because she had been rebaptized. Her husband had been burned at the stake at Alkmaar on the previous day. (G. Boomkamp, *Alkmaar en deszelfs Geschiedenissen,* 1747, 90; *DB* 1909, 18-20.) vdZ.

Breitinger, Johann Jakob (1575-1645), was the antistes (chief prelate or head) of the Zürich church from 1613 until his death. From 1593 to 1596 he studied in Germany and Holland at the Reformed universities, where he became closely associated with the scholars of the rigidly orthodox wing, whom he supported later as the delegate of the Swiss church at the Dordrecht Synod in its struggle with the Remonstrants. In 1611 Breitinger was called as preacher to Zürich. He fulfilled his duties as pastor and parson with a self-sacrificing spirit during the plague which was rampant in Zürich and thus won the sympathy of all classes, so that after the death of the old antistes Lehmann in 1613 he was called to fill his position at the Great Minster. His influence upon the Zürich church as well as the Swiss Reformed Church extended far beyond his lifetime; it is observable in his organization of the church into a substantial and decisive integral factor in the state. His life was centered in the church, the Zürich church in particular, as a religio-political concept.

Political life about 1600 had become more and more centralized and degenerated into a "family management." The church had no appreciable influence upon it; life in the canton was subjected to demoralizing influences, permitting the tendencies of the Counter Reformation, most evident in the field of education, to gain more and more ground, while the more earnest elements tended toward the loosely organized Swiss Brethren (Anabaptist) churches and in spirit joined them. This drift spread so much the more because the Swiss Brethren developed an extensive activity in charitable and welfare work and in the exercise of church principles, especially the ban, which had won the approval of even the former antistes Lehmann, and because the corrupt government was no longer guided by ethical motives. Breitinger found this state of affairs on his taking office, and since his was a practical temperament, he tried to take up the fight for the church at the weakest link in this chain of opposing factors.

His first significant step against the Swiss Brethren was a justification of the execution of Hans Landis (*q.v.*), one of the leaders and an elder of Swiss Brethren in the canton, who had paid the death penalty in 1614 because the state had counted his determination to remain with his church and not to emigrate as civil disobedience. The trial and the preliminary procedure give a fair picture of the progress the Swiss Brethren had made. The disputed points were still the same as was also the demand made by the Swiss Brethren that the church prove its sincerity by the Scriptural life of its members; but the relative strength of the Brethren had greatly increased. The council of the city of Zürich saw itself obliged to hold disputations in the country, into which Breitinger was also drawn, to induce the Brethren either to attend church or emigrate; the Brethren, however, did not consent, but let it come to a test to see which of the two parties had the greater following.

When this procedure proved futile, a persecution set in, accompanied by a serious reformation of the clergy. In 1613 a regulation was passed on the instruction of children; in 1615 a new hymnal replaced the one introduced in 1598; in 1616 a regulation of clothing, which included conduct in general. The synods became a stern tribunal for the irresponsible clergy who were largely responsible for the degeneracy of the canton; schools and instruction of children were pushed with all seriousness; Breitinger had attacked the essential points with reformatory results which extended far beyond his original purpose.

Breitinger's good intentions created for him an indisputable, superior position which his practical motives made the more secure, and which became disastrous to the progress of the Swiss Brethren. For it was first of all the Swiss Brethren who hindered Breitinger in the execution of the reforms for the unification of the canton by keeping the more earnest personalities from actual or even passive co-operation. But to save the church from the reproach of intolerance and to present it inviolable and unique above all others, he had to find a solution which would enable him to do justice to both sides, his own people and outward appearance, without losing sight of his goal. This solution he proposed in 1615 in the memorial against the Swiss Brethren. He says in it among other things: Sending them to the galleys should be avoided; it is better to convince them of the groundlessness of their views through the preachers. Those who nevertheless refused to attend church and were baptized should be heavily fined, their children declared illegitimate, because the marriages were not concluded according to church rules. But because the Anabaptists insisted so urgently on better church discipline and order, a committee should be formed to provide for improvement in church discipline and order.

These suggestions of Breitinger's were confirmed on Jan. 18, 1616, after two discussions in November and December and sent to other Protestant towns for opinion so that on the basis of these opinions it would be possible to reach some decision on a unified course of action against the Swiss Brethren at the meeting in Aarau set for February. The Aarau decision asserts unanimously that galley punishment should be abolished on the basis of scholarly opinion. The death penalty should be applied only to agitators. But all stressed the necessity of reform among the clergy, who would be able to do most to remove this evil.

These views remained basic for subsequent action and were modified only in the severity of their application.

The Thirty Years' War halted the movement, for Breitinger was deeply concerned with supporting the Protestant side, and Switzerland managed to avoid entanglement contrary to Breitinger's wishes. About 1630 he turned his attention again to questions of internal church politics, in order to bring his twenty years' struggle with the Swiss Brethren to a successful conclusion in their complete suppression and eradication in the canton of Zürich.

By Breitinger's orders a committee was appointed of members of state authorities, which should serve to assist, with the exercise of force, the clergy, who under Breitinger's direction were to lead in the struggle in order at the same time to meet the reproaches of the canton against the clergy for their harsh application of government regulations. In 1630 Breitinger composed a memorandum for the committee, discussing in detail the reasons for the necessity of resisting the Brethren. He speaks of the Anabaptist articles of faith in a very moderate tone, finds the sympathy for them comprehensible because of their way of life, and promises himself success against them only if the Reformed congregations recognize that the Anabaptists are wrong and deserving of punishment. Therefore it is necessary to explain the Bible and truth in their sermons, to exercise great patience toward the erring, and to attack no one or limit their freedom of conscience if they only lived quietly and honestly and attended (Reformed) church. Only in case of the exercise of rites and ceremonies and intentional separation, must the state exercise punitive authority. "If we do not apply these measures, we will have correct doctrine, but bad consciences on our side, and the sectarians will only become more hardened. . . ."

In 1633 Breitinger ordered a census to be taken by the clergy, which in addition to other questions of ecclesiastical and religious education in the canton was to count the Anabaptists. The result showed a total of 182 Anabaptists in all the villages of the canton, an insignificant number, which hardly corresponded with the measures undertaken against them. Aside from the fact that some parsons counted entire households as single individuals, and did not include children, so that the figure indicates the number of families rather than individuals, the parsons obviously considered it important to register the lowest possible number for their own districts, but had to admit a large number of suspected persons.

Contrary to Breitinger's wishes the government committee at this time took over the leadership, eliminating all secondary authority, and made use of the clergy only as a means in their struggle to establish order in the canton. The Anabaptists were required to formulate and present their religious views in writing; five congregations with 68 signatories complied. In general the individual statements agreed with the confession of faith presented shortly before, stating that (1) The foundation of their faith is Christ Jesus. (2) They believe and teach that Jesus is entirely the Son of God and of the Virgin Mary (referring to the divine-human nature of Christ). (3) Jesus Christ has completed redemption and eternal life can be acquired only through His "merit, justice, intercession and blood." (4) They made attendance at the Reformed church services dependent upon the introduction of the ban and excommunication. (5) In their conception of marriage "that it shall be one man and one woman, obligated in holy matrimony" they found no divisive influence. Those who attribute disorderliness to them were in error. (6) Baptism shall be administered only to those "who have been taught repentance and a change of life and believe in truth," that have been saved from sin by Jesus Christ. (7) In the matter of government they desired "no other government on the whole earth than you."

The point most opposed to Breitinger's intentions was doubtless their refusal to attend church as long as the ban was not introduced. Yet there is little evidence that the Brethren connected the use of the ban with the conception of a "church of holiness" to be evidenced at communion; it is rather the manner of life of many members of the Reformed Church that led to this demand. This admission was the point at issue according to the statements of imprisoned Swiss Brethren preachers, one of whom said they should not be made to suffer so merely for the sake of church attendance. To Breitinger it was important to attain at least external unity in the Swiss Reformed Church, since he must long since have been convinced of the impossibility of internal concessions. For until he achieved this outward unity he could hardly speak of success in his endeavors. Negotiations continued for several years, causing the Brethren continual excitement to be sure, but no immoderate pressure was applied. Breitinger even entered into discussions with them, but with no positive results. The

Brethren declined a public disputation for various reasons. They would not have been a match for Breitinger's dialectics. After all attempts had failed, Breitinger compiled a report to the government (1635), giving the outcome of the negotiations and suggesting measures for future procedure. This report became the basis of all later presentations, and parts of it were used in the letters of justification to the Dutch government and Reformed churches that had since 1641 shown sympathy for the persecuted Anabaptists.

In this report their refusal to bear arms or serve in possible war was stated as the occasion for proceedings against the Brethren; this was, to be sure, the immediate occasion, but it was by no means the basic cause. For the refusal to render armed service through an ensign to whom reference is made here, which led to the arrest of several Swiss Brethren, only started the fear that the Anabaptist movement might win the wealthier and socially influential circles. When Breitinger in this report expresses himself willing to make concessions excusing the Anabaptists from bearing arms, he thereby gives the impression of having proved clearly that he was willing and ready to make any concession to attain unity. But the reply of the Brethren, that Breitinger had granted the promise of freedom from military service only until they should be convinced by the Reformed preachers (or have convinced them), places Breitinger's intentions into a clear light and makes the distrust on the part of the Anabaptists very understandable. The treatment of individual articles of faith Breitinger touches only briefly, for the divergent points of doctrine were sufficiently well known. The important point to him is church attendance, for he would have expected no more of them than "merely to offer the outer ear of the body to the preaching of God's Word, but to keep their heart, faith, and conscience completely free and inviolate to agree or to disagree with what they hear." In the first draft made by Suter these words are added, "this is cheerfully and with kind words expected of them . . . this alone and nothing more." But these words were crossed out by Breitinger, since they would have made the contradiction and purpose too evident. Isolated cases of serious transgression (drunkenness, usury, immorality), for which the Brethren excommunicated the offender, are represented as general occurrences.

The most serious reproof is made by Breitinger himself in a long personal discussion concerning the inadequate instruction of children (by the Brethren) in the doctrines of faith and salvation, and he adds that this was one of the gravest reasons for compelling them to attend church. As for the rest, Breitinger does "not in the least wish to apply force to any persons in religious or doctrinal matters, . . . our intention is only that we and all our loyal subjects honor the one true God and Him whom He has sent, . . . to live in proper Christian unity, to bear with the weak in faith. . . ."

This report was obviously drawn up for the purpose of permitting the government to adopt certain measures and of outwardly creating the impression, above all among the populace, that these "proud" people, as Breitinger calls them instead of "obstinate," deserved their fate by their own attitude and that no one else could be blamed.

However unjustified, above all, the charge of inadequate instruction of the children was, actually contrary to facts and reports, this reproach contributed much to the irrevocable demands and punitive measures adopted by the government. The civil authorities carried on the contest most ruthlessly and cruelly, property was confiscated, the Swiss Brethren expelled from the country or held in prison. Breitinger's report served as a vindication to the people and later also to the Dutch authorities. The Brethren did not reply until several years later; their counterstatement, drawn up in 1645, is printed as an appendix in the 1655 edition of the *Ausbund* and in all American editions beginning in 1742.

When Breitinger died in 1645, there was no longer a Swiss Brethren church in the canton of Zürich; unity had thus been attained; but 20 years later Swiss students in Amsterdam reported that in the opinion of the important scholars the once uniquely exemplary Swiss Reformed Church had forfeited its position.   C.B.

Bergmann, *Die Täuferbewegung im Kanton Zürich bis 1660* (Leipzig, 1916); J. C. Mörikofer, *J. J. Breitinger und Zürich* (Leipzig, 1874); *Bilder aus dem kirchlichen Leben der Schweiz* (Leipzig, 1864); *ML* I, 259-62.

Bremen, Germany, a city of the Hanseatic League, where a second congregation of refugees was organized on Nov. 21, 1947, after the German collapse. It includes Bremen, Bremerhaven, Delmenhorst, and the districts of Wesermunde in the north, Rotenburg (Hanover) in the east, Hoya and Diepholz in the south. The membership numbers about 400 baptized and 150 unbaptized persons. Services are held in Bremen and eight subsidiary stations. Ernst Regehr (b. July 15, 1903, at Tiegenhof, minister since 1930 and elder since 1934 of the Rosenort congregation in West Prussia) was the elder until he went to Uruguay in 1948; since 1949 it is Albert Bartel (b. July 12, 1902, at Dragass, Schwetz district, minister since 1939 and elder since 1940 of the Tragheimerweide congregation). He is supported by the ministers of the West Prussian congregations, a deacon, and six elders. The congregation belongs to the *Vereinigung der Deutschen Mennoniten-Gemeinden.* (*Gem.-Kal.* 1951, 70.)
                                                   E.C.

Bremen (Ind.) United Missionary Church was organized March 1, 1934. In 1952 the congregation had 51 members, with R. McBrier serving as pastor.
                                                   G.B.

Bremer, Johannes, a Dutch Mennonite preacher, the son of the Remonstrant preacher of the same name and Remberta Zittart, daughter of the Leiden Mennonite preacher Gijsbert Zittart, was born April 8, 1694, at Hoorn. He studied in Amsterdam and in 1715 became a ministerial candidate in the Remonstrant brotherhood. But he received no regular position, and since his views coincided with those of the Mennonites he accepted a call to the Mennonite congregation at Leiden, and preached his inaugural sermon there June 2, 1720. At that time he very probably was himself rebaptized. In 1728 he received simultaneous calls to Haarlem and to the Lamist congregation in Amsterdam. He accepted the latter and worked there until his death, Feb. 20, 1757. His fellow preacher Joannes Deknatel, though in many respects opposed to his views, delivered a laudatory funeral sermon. In 1735 Bremer was one of the founders of the Amsterdam seminary for the education of ministers. He was married first to Catharina van der Hoeff and after her death in 1738 to Geertruyd van Eeghen (1698-1762).

The following books by Bremer have been published: *Rijmgedachten over het wenschelijkste op aarde* (Delft, 1718); *Lijkrede op den Remonstrantschen leeraar Joannes de Goede* (Amsterdam, 1738); *Grondbeginsels van de leere der waerheid, die naer de godzaligheid is, bij wijze van vragen en antwoorden opgesteld voor de Doopsgezinden* (Amsterdam, 1743 and frequently reprinted); *Handleiding tot waerheid en Deugd, inzonderheid gericht tot onderwijs van kleine kinderen* (Amsterdam, 1744); *Kort begrip van godgeleerde verhandelingen* (Amsterdam, 1747); *Ninive met den ondergang gedreigt; maar om zyn bekeering en boetvaardigheid gespaard en behouden* (Amsterdam, 1748); *Het verloste Nederland opgewekt tot een betaemelijke lof- en dankbetuiging aen den allerhoogsten God voor den geschonken Vreede* (Amsterdam, 1749, a sermon on Psalm 147:12-14); *Twee en dertig predikatien* (Amsterdam, 1757). J.L.

Biogr. Wb. I, 608-10; DB 1897, 167; C. Sepp, Gesch. der Predikkunde 234-37; idem, Joh. Stinstra en zijn tijd (1865) I, 193 v.v. 306; II, 188, 267; Catalogus Amst., 236, 245, 262 f.; ML I, 262.

Bremer, Koenraad, a Remonstrant minister at Amsterdam, who in 1740 published anonymously a treatise concerning Christian baptism, written by a deceased fellow minister, to which Bremer added five propositions concerning infant baptism (which he defended). Jan Wagenaar, the well-known Collegiant historian, answered Bremer, also anonymously, in *Onderzoek over de oudheid en schriftmatigheid van de Kinderdoop* (Investigation Concerning the Antiquity and Scripturalness of Infant Baptism) (Leiden, 1740; 2nd ed., Amsterdam, 1776); Herman Schijn and Abr. Verduin also answered Bremer, who replied with *Verdediging van de Verhandelingen, . . .* (Defense of the Propositions). (Blaupot t.C., *Holland* II, 30-31.) vDZ.

Brenkenhoffswalde and **Franztal,** villages in the Netzebruch near Driesen in Neumark, province of Brandenburg, Germany. In 1765 Frederick the Great, who had given Councilor Brenkenhoff charge of settling the marshy Netzebruch, permitted 35 Mennonite families expelled by Polish noblemen from the Culm lowlands to settle here; of these, 16 families with 95 persons were allocated in Brenkenhoffswalde and 19 families with 97 persons in the adjacent Franztal. They at once formed the Brenkenhoffswalde Mennonite congregation, which existed until 1834. The king gave them land and furnished lumber; until 1771 they were not taxed, and by a charter drawn up by the king himself

they were "completely free from military service and conscription." They belonged to the "Groninger Mennonites," or Groninger Old Flemish. This explains why they had not joined the larger Frisian congregation in the Culm lowlands at Schönsee, but had formed a congregation of their own with some scattered members at Thorn and Schwetz. They maintained contact and communion with these after they had come to Brenkenhoffswalde. According to the Dutch *Naamlijsten,* preachers of this congregation were Andreas Voet (Foth), Ernst Voet (Foth), Peter Jansz, Jacob Schmidt, and Peter Isaack.

The history of the church offers much that is of interest. A letter written by the church board to Harm Scholtens at Groningen (*Inv. Arch. Amst.* II, 2, No. 853), dated July 22, 1766, contains interesting particulars concerning the young congregation, which had already begun to build a meetinghouse. In 1788 the Lutheran teacher Wilhelm Lange of Brenkenhoffswalde, who had been appointed to the position by the government, asked permission of the authorities to transfer to the Mennonite faith, since he had grown up and been educated among Mennonites and was inwardly bound to them. On Oct. 24, 1788, he received permission to do so, on condition that his obligations to the state and his duties as a citizen would not suffer. Wilhelm Lange became a respected and influential member; in 1802 he was chosen preacher, and in 1810 elder, which office he still held when the congregation emigrated to Russia in 1834. In 1833 Lange had sent a petition to the Czar of Russia in the name of 40 families of Brenkenhoffswalde and Franztal to permit their immigration into Russia after permission to emigrate had been granted in 1828 to a certain Bengs of Brenkenhoffswalde by the government in Frankfurt a.O. It is probably to be assumed that the Mennonites in the Netzebruch did not see any possibility of acquiring more land, and therefore turned their attention to Russia, where most of the Groninger Mennonites from Culm and Schwetz had already gone. In 1823 there had been a small remnant of these families in Przechowo and Konopath near Schwetz, under the preacher Jakob Ratzlaff; but these also emigrated in 1824 to Alexanderwohl and other locations in South Russia.

Lange and his group received information on Jan. 10, 1834, through the Russian consulate in Danzig, that the czar would permit immigration on the following conditions: (1) presentation of a permit from the Prussian government to emigrate; (2) only families having at least five members would be admitted; (3) a sum of 800 rubles was to be deposited, which would be returned when they arrived. In that year the 40 families emigrated and found a hospitable reception in Alexanderwohl, but then founded the colony and church of Gnadenfeld (*q.v.*). The Mennonite church at Brenkenhoffswalde was thereby dissolved. The few remaining joined the state church, including their teacher Peter Janz, who later became a Protestant preacher.

According to information sent by Richard Schild, the teacher in Brenkenhoffswalde, to Stobbe, the teacher in Montau a generation ago, there were still various reminders of the former Mennonite colony. The church, which was housed in the same building as the school, was razed after serving for a time as a Protestant chapel. The Protestant church was located in the old Mennonite churchyard, which adjoined the present school. It was marked with a wooden sign, bearing the half-legible request to walk silently in order not to disturb the rest of the dead. Old Mennonite names, naturally mutilated, continued in Brenkenhoffswalde until 1945, such as Voth, Rettslag (Retzlaff), Nackert (Rickert), etc. (*ML* I, 263.)   H.G.M.

Brenneman (Branaman, Brannaman, Brenaman, Breneman, Breniman, Brenman, Brennaman, Brennemann, Brinneman), a Mennonite family name common in America. The ancestor of most of the American Brennemans was Melchior, who fled to Germany from his home in the canton of Bern (Switzerland) in 1671 because of the persecution of the Mennonites. The first of the family to come to America seems to have been the son of Melchior, also named Melchior, who settled in what is now Lancaster Co., Pa., probably in 1717. Among other Brennemans whose descendants are numerous in America was Nicolaus, who may have been a grandson of the above-named first Melchior. Nicolaus was born in 1736 and lived on an estate near Darmstadt in Germany. His descendants were mostly Amish Mennonites. In the late 18th and 19th centuries Amish Brennemans lived in Mengeringhausen, Waldeck, and other near-by villages; also near Marburg, Hessen.

A family history published in 1938 listed more than 3,200 persons under the name of Brenneman and its variants together with many thousands of others who are direct descendants of the several Brenneman ancestors treated in the book.

Among the Mennonite church leaders bearing this family name were Daniel Brenneman (*q.v.*) of Indiana, a leader in the founding of the Mennonite Brethren in Christ; John M. Brenneman (*q.v.*) of Ohio, bishop, author, and champion of Sunday schools, church literature, and evangelistic meetings; Christian K. Brenneman (1880-1919), city mission worker at Nampa, Idaho and Canton, Ohio, and George Brenneman (1821-89), a bishop of the Pike and Salem congregations in Ohio. Among the well-known Mennonite Brennemans today are Timothy Brenneman, formerly a missionary in Argentina and now the pastor of the Sarasota, Fla., church; Fred Brenneman, formerly a missionary to India and now a physician in Hesston, Kan., and Aldine Brenneman, a minister in the Virginia Mennonite Conference.   M.G.

C. D. Breneman, *A History of the Descendants of Abraham Breneman* (Elida, Ohio, 1939); A. H. Gerberich, *The Brenneman History* (Scottdale, 1938).

Brenneman, Daniel (1834-1919), son of Henry Brenneman, and great-grandson of Melchior Brenneman, a Mennonite exile from Switzerland who was one of the first settlers of Lancaster Co., Pa. (1717), was born June 8, 1834, near Bremen, Fairfield Co., Ohio. In 1838 his mother, a brother, and a sister died of smallpox, and he himself narrowly escaped. He was raised on the farm and attended the local school. He was converted in 1856 and soon after joined the Mennonite Church (MC). On March 22, 1857, he was married to Susannah Keagy of Augusta Co., Va. To this union 10 children, 5 sons and 5 daughters, were born. The youngest daughter, Phoebe (Mrs. C. F. Snyder), was a missionary to China, 1904-41. The oldest son, Timothy, was editor of the *Gospel Banner* (MBC), 1882-85. In 1864 he moved to Elkhart Co., Ind., where he lived until his death in 1919. In March 1908 he lost his wife after 51 years of married life. In April 1910 he was married to Della Troyer, who survived him.

From his youth Daniel Brenneman expected to be a minister. His father was a godly man who exerted a great and good influence over him. In 1857 Daniel was chosen by lot and ordained to the ministry in the Mennonite Church in Fairfield Co., Ohio. As time went on, he became a vigorous speaker and was considered one of the ablest among Mennonite preachers. He traveled extensively and was eagerly listened to wherever he went. He was noted for his progressive views and early in his ministry began to preach in English. In 1872 he with J. F. Funk conducted the first continued or revival meetings ever held in the Mennonite Church in the United States, at Masontown, Pa.

Gradually Brenneman became involved in the controversy between the progressive and conservative elements of the church, and in 1874, about 10 years after he located in Elkhart County, he found himself unable to remain with his denomination, having been excommunicated for disagreement with the church over methods of work. Together with Solomon Eby of Ontario he organized the Reformed Mennonites, a group that later became part of the Mennonite Brethren in Christ Church (now the United Missionary Church).

In 1876 Brenneman compiled and published a hymnbook, *The Balm of Gilead*. In July 1878 he began publishing the *Gospel Banner,* which has ever since been the official organ of the church. He served as editor and publisher until October 1882. For two years (1883-84) he edited and published the *Youth's Monitor,* a religious monthly paper for young people and children.

For 63 years he was a faithful herald of the Gospel. During his lifetime the Indiana and Ohio Conference, which he organized, grew to include some 1,700 members. He served for many years as a pastor, and for 12 years as Presiding Elder, in the latter capacity doing the work that later required two men. He was a member of the first seven General Conferences of the Mennonite Brethren in Christ Church, and during his entire career he never missed an annual conference.

He retained his mental alertness to the end. His travels extended from Virginia to California and through Canada, and his ministry was abundant both in sowing and the reaping. He reached the ripe old age of 85, dying on Sept. 10, 1919. His body lies interred in the Oak Ridge (City) cemetery, Goshen, Indiana. The Brenneman Memorial Church (UMC) in Goshen is named after him.†

E.R.S.

Gospel Banner, Sept. 24, 1919, 13; *Journal of the Indiana-Ohio Conf.* (MBC) 1920, 23-24; J. A. Huffman, *Hist. of the Menn. Brethren in Christ Church* (New Carlisle, 1920) Ch. V; Daniel Kauffman, *Menn. Cyclopedic Dictionary* (Scottdale, 1937) 39; J. C. Wenger, *Menn. Hist. Bulletin*, July 1948, 1.

Brenneman, John M. (May 28, 1816-Oct. 3, 1895), married Sophia Good in June 1837. Soon after their marriage they united with the Mennonite Church (MC) in Fairfield Co., Ohio. In April 1844 he was called to the ministry and served the Fairfield County congregation near Bremen until the fall of 1848, when he moved to Franklin Co., Ohio, where he was ordained bishop in 1849. In the spring of 1855 he moved to Allen Co., Ohio, where he lived for the remainder of his life. He was an earnest, zealous worker in the church and was so much absorbed in carrying out his task as overseer in the church that he gave little consideration to his temporal affairs. He made long, arduous trips to the West visiting brethren who had moved into isolated communities. On one occasion he took the train to Iowa to the end of the railroad, then drove 80 miles south in a two-horse wagon, and returned east on another railroad. He was away from home almost constantly preaching, holding baptism and communion services, and seeking to bring people of both Mennonite and non-Mennonite background into the church.

Although he was deeply concerned with the spiritual advancement of the church and with the Scriptural doctrines and teachings taught by the Mennonite Church he always was ready to adopt new methods. He was a pioneer in the organization of Sunday-school work in his own and other congregations even at the expense of losing friends or offending certain members of his congregation. He was inclined to look on the darker side of life. A section in one of his books is entitled "Why a Christian Should Not Laugh." He himself was said never to have laughed aloud. During his later years shaking palsy made him inactive in the ministry.

Brenneman had little formal education but attended elementary school with his own children after some of them were ten or twelve years old. He was a prolific writer for the *Herald of Truth*, but J. F. Funk once said that all of Brenneman's material needed complete editing. Even with this handicap he was a vigorous thinker and powerful preacher and evangelist. His first pamphlet, *Christianity and War*, edited and printed in 1863 by John F. Funk, probably the first American Mennonite publication on war, ran through several editions. He was the author of the following pamphlets, which appeared in both German and English editions: *Pride and Humility* (1867), *Plain Teaching* (1876); also *Aufmunterung der bussfertigen Sünder* (1877), and *Hope, Sanctification and a Noble Determination* (1893).

J.S.U.

Brenneman Memorial United Missionary Church, Goshen, Ind., was organized in January 1879, under the leadership of Daniel Brenneman, the founder of the Mennonite Brethren in Christ Church, and in whose memory the Goshen church is named. The church moved to the corner of Eighth and Jefferson streets in 1925, where a new meetinghouse had been constructed the previous year. The building was enlarged in 1944 to make possible the seating of 400. Its 1952 membership was 339. Ray P. Pannabecker was serving as its pastor. From 1943 to 1947 the congregation sent out five of its young people as foreign missionaries, all of whom were being supported by the Brenneman Memorial Church.

K.G.

Brenneman Memorial United Missionary Church, Lewellen, Garden Co., Neb., was organized as a congregation in 1928. Sunday school was started by the first settlers who arrived in 1908. In 1948 the membership was 33, with John P. Tschetter serving as pastor.

J.P.T.

Brennemans Mennonite Church (MC), now extinct, was located two miles west of Edom, Rockingham Co., Va., under the Virginia Mennonite Conference. The original church was built in 1826 on the farm of Melchior Brenneman (1775-1828), and was used for both school and church services. At some unknown date a larger church, 40 x 50 ft., was built, which was in continuous use until 1919, when the building was sold. What remained of the membership then worshiped at the Lindale (*q.v.*) Church one mile north of Edom. A Sunday school was conducted at Brennemans for some years beginning about the year 1870. Joseph Geil (1858-1945) attended this Sunday school as a barefoot boy. This was probably the first Sunday school held in the Northern District of the Virginia Conference.

T.S.

Brennwald, Karl, a Zürich Anabaptist in the earliest days of the movement, who was put into the dungeon of the Hexenturm with Grebel, Manz, and Blaurock soon after the third Anabaptist disputation. It was he who called attention to the unlocked shutter and thus led to the memorable flight from prison, March 21, 1526. Egli mentions two brief cross-examinations and his conversion through Roggenacher (*Wiedertäufer*, 54), and that captured Anabaptists said he was one of their preachers (74). Apparently he is identical with the Karlin mentioned in the article **Basel** (*q.v.*). (E. Egli, *Die Züricher Wiedertäufer zur Reformationszeit*, Zürich, 1878; *ML* I, 263.)

NEFF.

Brenz, Johannes, reformer of Swabia, b. 1499 at Weil (Neckar region in Württemberg), studied at Heidelberg, 1514-22, Lutheran preacher at Schwäbisch-Hall 1522-46, severely persecuted after the Interim of 1548, provost in Stuttgart, 1544, instigated the passing of a severe edict in 1558 against the Anabaptists and Schwenkfeld, who had influential friends at the court during Ulrich's (d. 1550) life. In 1527 he wrote the first Protestant catechism and co-operated in introducing the church order of Brandenburg-Ansbach, Nürnberg, and Württemberg. He died in 1570.

Like the other reformers, Brenz became a zealous opponent of the Anabaptists. At first he took a position against punitive procedure on the part of the state in religious matters and repeatedly defended the freedom of individual religious conviction. He frequently found occasion to express his opinion on prospective penalties against the Anabaptists. Though he did not favor complete toleration, he was nevertheless one of the few leaders of Protestantism in the period of the Reformation who openly opposed the death penalty for the Anabaptists. But in his later years he did not maintain this view consistently. In fact, as he grew older he grew visibly more intolerant, as was also the case with Luther. In his earlier writings he is not so much preaching love of one's neighbor as defending his own religious views over against the Catholic Church, with which the Protestant state church still had to reckon. But where the Protestant Church reigned he was of course unwilling to see the rise of another doctrinal point of view. He grants toleration only as long as the existence of his own church is not jeopardized thereby. He permits everybody to believe whatever he wishes, but not to express those beliefs unless they coincide with the views of the established church. Meetings for edification from God's Word, if held without the knowledge of the clergy, can according to his opinion only lead to division; it follows that the government therefore must interfere, "not as judge of the doctrine, but as judge of dissension, since it devolves upon their office to preserve a quiet and peaceful life among the subjects" (Hartmann, I, 296). Brenz even calls it sinful blasphemy when citizens separate from the church and arrange for their own assemblies without official permission. He requires the government not to permit any groupings in religious matters to arise in its territory. "The case is different when a government accepted by subjects of two or three different faiths permits each one to retain his old faith" (Hartmann, I, 297). Toward the Anabaptists he did not think this consideration applicable. For their suppression he recommended the forbidding of "civil manipulation" and expulsion from the country. It was merely clever calculating caution when he recommended a milder punishment in religious matters than the death penalty customarily used against Anabaptists. For, he writes, "Although governments at times persecute erroneous faith, their descendants may become so inured to persecuting that they persecute the true faith. . . . It is better to tolerate unorthodox faith four or ten times than to persecute the true faith only once."

Brenz actually resisted the death penalty in matters of faith by his deeds. He knew what dangers threatened his church if the old heresy laws of the Roman Catholic Church, which had been pushed into the background by the power of the popular movement, should be revived. A beginning had indeed been made by the mandate of Emperor Charles V of Jan. 4, 1528, which punished the repetition of baptism with death. What was true of the Anabaptists here might later threaten any other non-Catholic branch in case of political or religious realignment. He stated his doubts on the application of the death penalty in matters of faith in a book published in 1528, which bears the title,

Underricht Philips Melanchthon widder die leere der Widderteuffer. Ob ein weltliche öberkeit mit Götlichem und billichem Rechten mög die Widderteuffer durch jewer odder schwerd vom leben zu tode richten. Here Brenz denies the government the authority to decide religious questions with violence. If heresy is to be abolished by force, he writes, "why should one study the Holy Scriptures, since the hangman would then be found the most learned doctor." He threatens the governments with divine retribution if they hold judicial power over life and death in religious matters. "Anabaptism," he continues, "has not been more powerfully strengthened and furthered by anyone than by the authorities who in the very hour, without study of God's Word, have tyrannically proceeded against them with the sword. For in trying to meet spiritual wickedness with unjust means and using the temporal sword more and further than is commanded, they have angered the Lord our God with the misuse and tyranny of the temporal sword and He has in punishment upon men required the devil to rage ever more vehemently, and ever more powerfully to inflame man's error, so that afterward physical punishment brought no reform to the common people, but rather furthered their error."

Brenz requires that "only the Gospel and the Holy Scriptures be permitted to fight against heretics." In his book, after an attempt to justify infant baptism, he selects the points in the Anabaptist ideas that find analogies in the Catholic Church, in order to conclude that the death penalty should be applied to Catholics with the same right as to Anabaptists. In this way the Anabaptist views on their attitude toward government office, on the community of goods, and on rebaptism serve him as means to castigate doctrines of the Catholic Church, thereby creating the semblance of being a convinced defender of the Anabaptists. The doctrine of community of goods had in simple ignorance been taken from the Bible by the Anabaptists, "Should one always murder such a one at once, when he misunderstands a saying or two from the Bible? Who would then be safe from the sword? One finds in almost all holy teachers misunderstanding of several passages; should one kill them at once for that, and what kind of reasonableness would that be?" Monks and nuns also practice community of goods; if one is going to introduce the death penalty in this matter, it should be applied to the spiritual bishop and monks rather than the "poor Anabaptists who do not sell heaven and eternal life with deception." He also opposed the intention of imposing the death sentence upon the Anabaptists for refusing the oath and not finding it compatible with their conscience to take a government office. If they are to be killed for such reasons, "it should have been begun long ago with the clergy, priests and monks"; for they taught, "No clergyman shall exercise power over life and death. Without special dispensation they have not accepted any of this kind into their consecration and order. What is this but forbidding all true Christians to hold the office of temporal government? For all true Christians should be truly spiritual and the office of temporal government cannot be conducted without shedding blood. They are also the ones who have given the government neither oath nor vow nor other civil obligation, and this not out of the favor or permission of the government, but out of their own assumed right. Yea, where they have been pushed in these matters they have excommunicated the temporal authorities." In the matter of baptism Brenz also uses the Catholic clergy as an analogous case. "And if one," he writes, "wanted to martyr these people for the sake of their rebaptism, one would have to do the same to the pope and all his priests. For these have also rebaptized and do it yet; namely, if a child is baptized in haste at home by the women, they baptize it again in church. Is this not rebaptizing, exactly as the other Anabaptists do? They say, of course, if you are baptized, I baptize you in the name of the Father, etc. But why should the priests need this addition? They know from the statements of the women that the children have been baptized, why do they not leave it at that? The Anabaptists do not say either that they rebaptize but that they perform the first proper baptism. For they consider infant baptism no baptism at all, as the papists consider baptism by the women almost no baptism, although they do not show this outwardly."

Applying the death penalty for rebaptism Brenz considers absolutely inappropriate. Emperor Theodosius (says Brenz) to whom the mandate of Charles V of Jan. 4, 1528, refers, did not of his own will threaten Anabaptists with death; he merely wished to meet the wishes of the bloodthirsty bishop Nestorius of Constantinople, who in return had promised him armed aid against the Persians. It was not suitable for a Christian government to chastise with the executioner's sword persons who had only for lack of understanding fallen into error. Insurrection would not need to be feared from them, if the worldly sword were properly used; the chief cause of insurrection was the wicked life of the authorities. "Therefore," he concludes, "the government should avert its punitive hand from the Anabaptists and leave them to the Gospel for punishment; but otherwise provide for peaceful and honorable unity; for whoever acts against this, be he Anabaptist or not, he shall receive suitable punishment from it." "But if it is a duty to take life because of error, who would be allowed to live? There would be no end of killing."

The book was widely distributed and was published in many editions, five in German, four in Latin, two in Dutch, and one in French (W. Köhler, *Bibliographia Brentiana,* Berlin, 1904). But it did not influence the course of events. In the next year at the famous Diet of Speyer of 1529, the imperial law was passed against the Anabaptists, sanctioning the death penalty for rebaptism. The Evangelical representatives voted for it.

Brenz does not grant postponement of baptism on the basis of Christian liberty. A postponement of the baptism might arouse the suspicion of "Anabaptism" in one's neighbor; he should not be subjected to this offense. The government should compel the obstinate to hasten the baptism. It has the

authority to do this, for baptism is the foundation of Christian society. Whoever is born within the Christian social order of Christian parents, is born into the social order of the Church. "The principle of a single Church within the social structure can probably not be more clearly expressed; society, Christian society, and the Church coincide. Consequently the Church has the right to baptize the children belonging to it by birth. The withdrawal of their children from baptism on the part of the Anabaptists is an offense against the social order, and this has long since become deeply rooted" (W. Köhler, *Archiv für Ref.-Gesch.* IX, 1911-12, 96).

The presence of Anabaptists seems to have occupied Brenz later on as well; in 1544 he wrote to Bullinger of frequent journeys of their adherents through the region on their way from the Rhine to Moravia (Köhler, *Bibliographia Brentiana,* 362). He apparently came into personal contact with them; thus it is known that in April 1557 at Stuttgart he examined two Anabaptists, both named George Rapp from Pforzheim in Au, who had been arrested at Vaihingen; they were released because they were merely traveling through and had held no meetings (G. Bossert, *Ztscht für die Gesch. des Oberrheins* LIX, 1905, 76). On Aug. 24, 1557, at the request of Elector Otto Henry of the Palatinate, he with Jakob Andreae conducted the disputation with the Anabaptists at Pfeddersheim (*q.v.*), one of whose representatives, Diebold Winter, later complained to the Palatine Elector Frederick III, that things had been published about them which they had never thought of, to say nothing of talking about them (*Protocoll . . . des Gesprechs zu Frankenthal,* Heidelberg, 1571, 8).

Indicative of Brenz's later attitude on toleration is the publication issued soon after the Pfeddersheim disputation by the Protestant theologians' conference at Worms, *Prozess, wie es soll gehalten werden mit den Wiedertäufern,* which Brenz signed as a participant, and in which the theologians recommended the death penalty against the Anabaptists. In support of this harsh procedure, referring to Lev. 24 and Rom. 13, the very points are cited which Brenz had defended as pardonable errors in his book of 1528: the scruples of the Anabaptists against a conscientious Christian's holding government office, the refusal of the oath, and their views on community of goods; as a further point of accusation was cited their avoidance of lawsuits (Chr. Hege, *Die Täufer in der Kurpfalz,* Frankfurt, 1908, 93-99). HEGE.

Brentii opera, 8 vv. (Tübingen, 1576-90); Hartmann and Jäger, *Johannes Brenz,* 2 vv. (Hamburg, 1840); W. Köhler, *Bibliographia Brentiana* (Berlin, 1904); "Brenz," in *HRE* III, 386; *ML* I, 264-66.

Breslau, capital of the former province of Silesia, where a congregation of Anabaptists developed in the Reformation period. It was apparently founded in 1527 and maintained contact with the South German Anabaptist leaders; this is concluded from information given by Hans Hut (*q.v.*) at his trial in Augsburg, Oct. 5, 1527. He stated that Oswald (perhaps Oswald Glait?) and Hess were staying there (Meyer, 230). The founder of the congregation was probably Gabriel Ascherham (*q.v.*), who in 1528 led the Silesian Anabaptists to Moravia, especially Rossitz (*q.v.*) when they were severely persecuted in Silesia (Jäkel, 54). When they were no longer tolerated in Moravia some of them returned to Silesia in 1535. But they found an embittered enemy in the Silesian parson Dr. Ambrosius Moibanus (*q.v.*), who in a book published in 1537 with a preface by Luther, *Das herrliche Mandat Jesu Christi*, attacked them and the Schwenkfeldians; he brought about their expulsion from various Silesian towns.   HEGE.

P. Konrad, *Dr. Ambrosius Moibanus (Schriften des Vereins für Ref.-Gesch.* No. 34, 1891, 68-71); Meyer, in *Ztscht des Hist. Vereins für Schwaben und Neuburg* I (1874); J. Jäkel, *Gesch. der Wiedertäufer in Ober-Oesterreich* (1889); *ML* I, 266.

Breslau, a small town in Ontario, approximately five miles northeast of Kitchener, is the home of the Breslau United Missionary Church and the Cressman Mennonite Church.   M.G.

Breslau Codex, a manuscript from the middle of the 17th century in octavo, 236 pages, with the date "(16..)" on the cover, obviously attributable to a Moravian Anabaptist, in the Breslau university library, found under Sig. IV. duod. 8. The title reads, *Chronica und kurze Historia, gezogen aus den alten Geschichten und glaubwürdigen Chroniken—wie Gott von Anfang der Welt mit seinen Gläubigen ihm selbst zum Ruhm gehandelt durch alle Geschlechter von Adam bis auf Christum sich so wunderbarlich erzeigt und von Christo bis auf gegenwärtige letzte zeit mit seinen Auserwählten gehandelt hat.* The data of the "most recent times" are related in this chronicle of 1524 to 1648. The fate of this ms, in view of the severe destruction in Breslau at end of World War II and occupation by the Poles, is uncertain. (*ML* I, 266.)   NEFF.

Breslau United Missionary Church, Waterloo Co., Ont., was organized April 26, 1884. At that time a meetinghouse was built with seating capacity of 200 and is still in use. The 1948 membership was 82 and John W. Colley was serving as pastor. J.W.C.

Brethren is the only title used by the Anabaptists among themselves from the very beginning. In all the records (confessions, trials, wills, etc.) the name "Brethren" is applied to fellow believers again and again. Now and then in a special designation is added: thus there were Swiss Brethren, Moravian Brethren, etc.

The term "brethren" has actually become an earmark of the Anabaptists and like-minded Christians. Luther says in his *Auslegung des Johannes-Evangeliums* (1528-29, Erlangen ed., I, 437), "They (the fanatics) carry this beautiful, lovely word brethren in such misuse, that we can hardly use it any longer." Ludwig Keller shows that the name was used from the beginning among members of what he called the Old Evangelical brotherhood (dissident groups). It was adopted particularly by the Waldenses, Friends of God, and mystics of the Middle Ages (Keller, *Reformation*).

It is still in common use among the Mennonites in all countries as a term of address within the brotherhood, more particularly among those who have retained the simpler and warmer type of piety.

The term "brotherhood" (Dutch, *broederschap;* German, *Bruderschaft*) has been used from the earliest times, as is logical, as a designation for the Anabaptist-Mennonite group by its own members, along with "Gemeente," "Gemeinde," and in English "church." Hendrik van Maastricht, who was put to death in 1534, said that Pieter Govertsz was considered to be a member of the "broederschap" (Grosheide, *Verhooren,* 175), and concerning Hückelhofen in Jülich it is said that a "Bruderschaft" has been started, but it soon disappeared, viz., as a result of the severe edicts (Rembert, *Wiedertäufer,* 73). The term is quite commonly used in Holland today, much less in other Mennonite areas. Among the Mennonites in Holland the word "Broederschap" in the 17th and 18th century was also used for meetings of the male members of a congregation for the purpose of voting, etc., as in Russia "Bruderschaft" (*q.v.*) came to mean the meeting of the voting male members of the congregation. (*ML* I, 278.)   NEFF, H.S.B.

Brethren Church, a branch of the Dunkard denomination often called "Progressive Brethren," which separated from the main body of the church in 1881-83. (See **Brethren, Church of the.**)

Brethren, Church of the. This body of Christians originated at Schwarzenau, county of Wittgenstein, Germany, in 1708. A group of eight Pietists, of whom Alexander Mack was the leading spirit, formed a covenant to live in all things according to the New Testament and to be governed by it. They adopted no name and did not think of themselves at first as a denomination. They referred to one another simply as "the brethren," whence the name which is now a legal corporate title. The name was long vague. Their leading teaching concerning baptism by immersion gave them the name "Tunkers." The forms of this name are legion, although recently writers have been concentrating on the spelling "Dunker." Since this would be a German equivalent of "baptist," the name German Baptist was often used for them in pre-Revolutionary Pennsylvania and later. However, the origin of this group is definitely continental Anabaptist and Pietist, and is not to be connected in any way with the English Baptist movement. The Brethren are most accurately represented at the point at which Pietism and the Anabaptist movement intersect.

Pietism is the great German revival movement associated with the names of Philip Jakob Spener (1635-1705) and his disciple and junior colleague August Hermann Francke (1663-1727). The message of Pietism was the emphasis upon goodness of heart, disposition, and conduct as the only valid evidence that a man was a true Christian. Hence Pietists spoke much of conversion, but they always meant a conversion to practical goodness.

The pietistic emphasis created fierce controversy. To many they seemed to be preaching salvation through works. To themselves they seemed to be teaching a true spirituality. To an impartial student the reconciliation seems to be that Pietism is a species of subjective ethical mysticism. It is properly designated Christian on account of its devout (and it was devout rather than creedal or critical or academic) acceptance of the canonical Scriptures as God's Word and the norm of spiritual life.

When the pietistic emphasis was carried too far it resulted in disregard of and contempt for and finally separation from the state church. Spener and Francke condemned separatism; nevertheless soon many Pietists outran their guides and separated from the organized Church. They are known as "Separatists," and the reader must distinguish this term in German church history from its usage in English church history.

Alexander Mack and all his associates had been Separatists, who came to Schwarzenau for various reasons. There Count Henry permitted them to live quietly and the imperial laws against dissenters were unenforced. At Schwarzenau, Mack and others found the regime of "no organized Church," i.e., complete unregulated religious individualism, to be unsatisfactory.

In the meantime they had come under the influence of the writings of Gottfried Arnold (1666-1714), the brilliant and somewhat original and erratic pietistic scholar. Arnold has been called with truth the "father of modern church history." His researches into primitive Christian life and institutions were outstanding. Arnold's description of primitive church life impressed Mack and his friends. In Arnold they read that the early form of baptism had been trine immersion, and that the *agape* or fellowship meal had been long cherished in the early church and held in connection with the communion. Arnold wrote of the practice of footwashing as a rite, the kiss of peace, and the anointing of the sick with oil as rites of the early Christians. He portrayed the nonresistance, nonswearing, and the non-worldly emphasis of early Christianity.

The likeness of these ideas to the principles and practices of the existing Anabaptist-Mennonite congregations is patent. But Arnold's studies gave a new basis in history and a newer, greater authority for these ideas. In 1708 after some months of Bible study and prayer, and meeting in homes, a church organization was formed. The literature of the times refers to the Brethren as the "new Baptists."

In 1715 a group moved to Crefeld, where they were called *Dompelaars* (*q.v.*), and where they had close contact with the Mennonites.

Petty persecution induced emigration, especially when joined with the financial promises of Penn's agents. The Brethren came to Pennsylvania in two main parties. Peter Becker led a party from Crefeld in 1719. Alexander Mack led the larger party in 1729 from Holland (to which they had fled from Schwarzenau in 1720 after the death of Count Henry). Both groups settled at Germantown, but quickly spread to the area of available land in what is now Lancaster Co., Pa. The first organization was made in the Mennonite church in Germantown. The immigrants totaled only 219.

From this German area of eastern Pennsylvania, the spread of the church has paralleled the pattern of American western expansion. By 1851, the church was on practically the same territory it now occupies, although the number of congregations and the membership have greatly multiplied.

In Pennsylvania, the erratic Johann Konrad Beissel (*q.v.*) led a schism (1728) which resulted in the now extinct Ephrata monastic community. There were no further significant divisions in Brethren ranks until 1881-83. At that time the increasing urbanization and industrialization of American life so disturbed the Brethren that it resulted in a double schism. A minority party felt that the annual meeting was sanctioning innovations and that the old simplicity and fraternity was disappearing; so they withdrew and continued as the Old Order German Baptist Brethren. But the other extreme felt the annual meeting was hopelessly reactionary and that it had grown autocratic, and so calling themselves "progressives" (official name, "The Brethren Church") they too seceded. The main body continued and was popularly called "the conservatives." In 1908 (bicentennial year) the annual meeting or annual conference as it has come to be called, adopted the legal name "Church of the Brethren." Of recent years, especially in summer camps and student age groups, the name "Dunker" has come again into wide and this time in an affectionate and proud usage. In 1926 a small schism arose at Goshen, Ind., which called itself "Dunkard Brethren." It was a second "Old Order" movement and has remained small.

Foreign missions first found expression in 1876, when Christian Hope, a Danish convert in this country, returned to his homeland to share his new-found faith with old friends and relatives. Today organized missions are at work in India (since 1894), in China (1908), Nigeria (1922), and Ecuador (1946).

The Brethren Service Committee (now Brethren Service Commission) emerged from the troubled years of World War II. It was established by the conference in 1940. Its first task was to look after the conscientious objectors, of whom the church furnished 992 for Civilian Public Service. Although the church took a strong official position against all military service, in practice it left it to the conscience of the members to take noncombatant service or even full military service. In the confusion of the war more took military service than was expected. While the Service Commission is a frank imitation of the well-known Friends' Service Committee, it may be regarded as an indigenous expression of the Pietism inherent in the Brethren heritage with a desire to give a peace witness. Its work has been literally world-wide but has been rapidly adapted to the shifting panorama of the world's suffering. It has carried on much relief work for war sufferers in Europe and China.

The Church maintains six colleges, Juniata, Bridgewater, Manchester, McPherson, La Verne, and Elizabethtown, and Bethany Biblical Seminary of Chicago, which is a standard theological seminary with a training school affiliated. Mennonite Biblical Seminary (*q.v.*) is affiliated with Bethany Biblical Seminary (since 1945).

At the Annual Conference held at Orlando, Fla., in 1947 a comprehensive reorganization of the overhead denominational machinery was adopted. The congregation presided over by an elder remains the primary unit of organization. The congregations are grouped into districts. There are 49 districts in the United States and Canada. The districts are represented by delegates (who must be elders) and these form the Standing Committee of Annual Conference which receives all reports and prepares business for the conference. Each congregation may have at least one conference delegate elected by the local council. Large congregations may have delegates in proportion to membership.

For 60 years the conference has had a miscellaneous and changing assortment of committees and boards to make its work effective. In 1947 these were all summarily replaced by a General Brotherhood Board of 25 members chosen by the annual conference. The board divides itself into "commissions" for convenience to oversee the work and also acts as a unit. At present there are five "commissions." A publishing house called The Brethren House is located at Elgin, Illinois. The official journal of the brotherhood is *The Gospel Messenger.*

The Brethren Yearbook for 1949 listed for the United States and Canada 1,023 congregations with 185,799 members. The mission fields reported 13,597 members. Of the churches, 392 reported full-time pastors and 394 reported part-time pastoral service. The free or voluntary ministerial service is not extinct, although the trend seems to be in the direction of the professional ministry.

The church uniformly maintains that its only creed is the New Testament. In a nonliturgical church such as the Brethren, cultural inheritance and geography will inevitably, with the passage of time, cause some differences in local customs. Yet the Brethren have preserved a remarkable homogeneity, the great annual meeting, which is an annual reunion as well, being a definite element in preserving unity of outlook.

There is no binding creed other than the New Testament itself, yet the following widely circulated statement may be regarded as a fair presentation of Brethren doctrine.

1. This body of Christians originated in the 18th century, the church being a natural outgrowth of the Pietistic movement following the Reformation.

2. Firmly accepts and teaches the fundamental evangelical doctrines of the inspiration of the Bible, the personality of the Holy Spirit, the virgin birth, the deity of Christ, the sin-pardoning value of his atonement, his resurrection from the tomb, ascension and personal and visible return, and resurrection both of the just and unjust (John 5:28, 29; I Thess. 4:13-18).

3. Observes the following New Testament rites: Baptism of penitent believers by trine immersion for the remission of sins (Matt. 28:19; Acts 2:38); feet-washing (John 13:1-20; I Tim. 5:10); love feast (Luke 22:20; John 13:4; I Cor. 11:17-34; Jude 12); communion (Matt. 26:26-30); the Christian salutation (Rom. 16:16; Acts 20:37); proper appearance in worship (I Cor. 11:2-16); the anointing for healing in the name of the Lord (James 5:13-18;

Mark 6:13); laying on of hands (Acts 8:17; 19:6; I Tim. 4:14). These rites are representative of spiritual facts which obtain in the lives of true believers and as such are essential factors in the development of the Christian life.

4. Emphasizes daily devotion for the individual and family worship for the home (Eph. 6:18-20; Philip. 4:8, 9); stewardship of time, talents and money (Matt. 25:14-30); taking care of the fatherless, widows, poor, sick and aged (Acts 6:1-7).

5. Opposes on Scriptural grounds: War and the taking of human life (Matt. 5:21-26, 43, 44; Rom. 12:19-21; Isa. 53:7-12); violence in personal and industrial controversy (Matt. 7:12; Rom. 13:8-10); intemperance in all things (Titus 2:2; Gal. 5:19-26; Eph. 5:18); going to law, especially against our Christian brethren (I Cor. 6:1-9); divorce and remarriage except for the one Scriptural reason (Matt. 19:9); every form of oath (Matt. 5:33-37; James 5:12); membership in secret, oath-bound societies (II Cor. 6:14-18); games of chance and sinful amusements (I Thess. 5:22; I Peter 2:11; Rom. 12:17); extravagant and immodest dress (I Tim. 2:8-10; I Peter 3:1-6).

6. Labors earnestly in harmony with the Great Commission, for the evangelization of the world, for the conversion of men to Jesus Christ, and for the realization of the life of Jesus Christ in every believer (Matt. 28:18-20; Mark 16:15, 16; II Cor. 3:18).

7. Maintains the New Testament as its only creed, in harmony with which the above brief statement is made.

Except for the mode of baptism by immersion and the requirement of wearing the beard by ministers, which was long maintained, Mennonites and Brethren as denominations had so much in common in their earlier history that they were often confused by outsiders. In dress the Brethren dressed as "plain" as the Mennonites until recent times, and in Eastern Pennsylvania many Brethren still dress "plain." In recent times the tendency of the Brethren to revise or abandon certain earlier distinctive Brethren practices has created a wider gap between the two groups.

The Brethren were in their earlier history much more aggressive than the Mennonites, hence have grown much more rapidly and secured a larger proportion of members from the "outside." Numerous Mennonites were won by early Brethren evangelistic efforts and many names in the Brethren Church of today are Mennonite in origin; e.g., Bowman, Moyer, Ziegler. The original number of Brethren immigrants was about 200, compared to the Mennonite immigrants numbering 3-4,000 during the colonial period.

In numerous cases the Brethren and Mennonites have settled in the same general areas; e.g., Lancaster Co., Pa., the Shenandoah Valley of Virginia, and Elkhart Co., Ind. However, little fraternization has taken place on the local level, largely because of the earlier sharp Brethren emphasis on immersion. In recent times in World War II and later, Mennonites and Brethren have had considerable contact and co-operation through their national organizations for conscientious objectors and alternative service, they being two of the Historic Peace Churches. The National Service Board for Religious Objectors, after the withdrawal of the Friends in 1945, has been constituted by the Brethren Service Committee and the Mennonite Central Committee.

F.E.M.

M. G. Brumbaugh, *A History of the German Baptist Brethren in Europe and America* (Mt. Morris, 1899); Otho Winger, *History and Doctrines of the Church of the Brethren* (Elgin, 1919); J. E. Miller, *The Story of Our Church* (Elgin, 1941); *Brethren Builders in Our Century* (Elgin, 1952); S. Z. Sharp, *Educational History of the Church of the Brethren* (Elgin, 1923); E. S. Moyer, *Missions in the Church of the Brethren* (Elgin, 1931); F. D. Dove, *Cultural Changes in the Church of the Brethren* (Phila., 1932); J. H. Ziegler, *The Broken Cup, Three Generations of Dunkers* (Elgin, 1942); H. R. Holsinger, *A History of the Tunkers and the Brethren Church* (1901); F. Nieper, *Die ersten deutschen Auswanderer von Krefeld nach Pennsylvanien* (Neukirchen, 1940), treats in detail the pietistic background of the Brethren and their early relation to the Mennonites.

Brethren in Christ. In the latter part of 1750, about 30 Mennonite families in the canton of Basel, Switzerland, after a long period of persecution, during which they suffered both imprisonment and loss of property, decided to emigrate westward. They went first to England, and in the fall of 1751 set sail for America. The voyage across the Atlantic was disastrous; one of the ships with all their goods was lost, and they landed destitute. One company, including John and Jacob Engle and others whose names are uncertain, settled near the Susquehanna, in western Lancaster Co., Pa., in early 1752.

In 1770, as a result of the labors of some members of the Lutheran, Mennonite, and Baptist churches, who were grieved at what they considered the formalism which then characterized the churches, there was, in that region, a notable revival, which was attended by many conversions. It was conducted principally by Otterbein, Boehm, Bochran, and the Engles, representing the different bodies. Subsequently difference of views arose in regard to the form of baptism, some holding that the applicant should make choice of the method, while others claimed that trine immersion was the only proper form. The result was that they mutually agreed to work independently, in accordance with their various interpretations of the Scriptures.

The believers in trine immersion associated with the Engles, many of them former Mennonites, had no regular organization, but were in the habit of designating the various communities as brotherhoods. There was thus the Brotherhood down by the River, meaning in the southern part of Lancaster County; also the Brotherhood in the North, the Brotherhood in Dauphin, the Brotherhood in Lebanon, the Brotherhood in Bucks and Montgomery, etc. The outlying brotherhoods looked to the brotherhood in the southern part of Lancaster County as the home of the organization, and it was probably due to this fact that the general term "River Brethren" was given to the entire body. Another explanation has been given by some, namely, that they were in the habit of baptizing in the river. With the development of these brotherhoods, it seemed advisable to select someone to perform the duties of the ministerial office, and the choice fell upon Jacob Engle, who thus became their first minister.

A small faction of the Brethren in Christ broke off in 1838 in Ohio under the leadership of John Wenger, who were joined shortly thereafter by John Swank, formerly of the United Brethren Church. In 1860 Swank broke off with a small faction from this Wenger group, which in 1883 united with the Evangelical United Mennonites led by Daniel Brenneman, to become the Mennonite Brethren in Christ. Later, portions of the Wenger group joined the M.B.C., one congregation doing so as late as 1920. The small remnant of the Wenger group has since adopted the name Pentecostal Brethren in Christ.

In course of time dissensions arose concerning what would now be called minor points, which ultimately caused divisions. In 1843 the body known as "Yorkers" or, as some call them, "Old Order" Brethren, withdrew, and in 1853 the body known as "Brinser," but later as "United Zion's Children," also withdrew, both in eastern Pennsylvania.

At first the organization of the River Brethren was simple, but as their numbers increased a more permanent form became necessary, and about 1820 the present ecclesiastical organization was adopted. During the Civil War some of the members, although proclaiming the doctrine of nonresistance, were drafted for military service, and it became evident that the denomination must secure legal recognition as a religious organization holding that doctrine. Steps to secure such recognition were taken at a private council held in Lancaster, Pa., as early as 1862, at which time those who remained after the separation of the other two branches, and who constituted the great majority of the Brethren, decided to adopt the name "Brethren in Christ" instead of "River Brethren," which was done the following year. In 1904 the organization was incorporated according to the laws of the State of Pennsylvania as "a religious body for the worship of Almighty God," with headquarters at Harrisburg.

The Brethren in Christ have not accepted any historical creed or confession, but generally regard the authority of the Holy Scriptures and recognize the importance of the teachings of Christ and doctrines of the New Testament. They believe that the church is "built on faith in an almighty, triune, eternal, self-existent God—Father, Son, and Holy Spirit." They accept the doctrines of the immortality of the soul; redemption through Jesus Christ as the Son of God, who makes atonement for the sins of the world; and regeneration through the influence of the Holy Spirit, developing into holy living. They hold that trine immersion is the only proper form of baptism, practice confession of sins to God and man, and observe the Lord's Supper and communion, accompanying it by the ceremony of footwashing. The recognition of Christ, not only as Saviour, but as Lord and Master and King, involves in their view the acceptance of the tenets and principles of His government. Accordingly, they believe that, inasmuch as He is Prince of

Peace, His kingdom is of peace, and as His subjects, they should abstain from the employment of carnal forces which involve the taking of human life. For this reason the doctrine of nonresistance, in a qualified sense, is a feature of their belief. They consider Freemasonry and all other secret societies to be anti-Christian; they believe in prayer veiling for women, and they advocate the wearing of modest apparel, with nonconformity to the fashions of the world.

The ecclesiastical organization of the denomination includes the local church, a system of district councils, state councils, and a general conference. The officers of the church are bishops, ministers, and deacons. The bishops preside at all council meetings, officiate at marriages and in the observance of the ordinances, and exercise all functions of the ministry. The ministers are specifically the teaching body, but also do parish visiting, and by request of the bishop, in his absence administer the ordinances. The denomination in a slow transition is changing from a self-supported ministry to support by contributions, and salary for full-time pastors. The deacons have charge of the business affairs of the churches, serve at the communion table, look after the poor, and also do some visiting in the parish. The membership of the general conference, which meets annually, includes laymen as delegates as well as ministers.

The general activities of the church in education, publication, charitable and missionary interests are directed by general church boards, responsible to the general conference. Eight boards function in their respective areas of endeavor—General, Executive, Benevolence, Foreign Mission, Home Mission, Christian Education, Publication, and Board for Schools and Colleges.

In 1951 the Brethren in Christ Church had in the United States and Canada 138 churches, with a membership of 6,807 residing in 13 different states and 2 provinces. Of these congregations, 54 were in Pennsylvania, 14 in Ontario, 10 in Ohio, 8 in Michigan, 7 in Kentucky, and 5 each in California and Kansas. The church contributed $613,223.05 during 1950 to all phases of the church program, an average of $90.08 per member. The Sunday-school enrollment stands at 14,760.

The church is aggressively missionary in interest and program. Sixty-eight workers are active in the foreign mission fields of India and Rhodesia, South Africa. In southern Rhodesia there are 72 out-schools and in northern Rhodesia there are 38. There are 3,372 baptized members on these foreign mission fields, with 3,694 additional persons enrolled in membership inquirers' classes. 11,893 students are enrolled in mission elementary, boarding and teacher-training schools.

The educational interests of the denomination are served by two colleges and two academies—Messiah College, Grantham, Pa., and Upland College, Upland, Cal., a high school in Ontario, and another in Oklahoma. In 1950 the number of students enrolled in these institutions was 512. Contributions to the support of these schools during 1950 were listed at $33,823.98.

For a number of years the Brethren in Christ have worked with the Mennonites in the area of peace witnessing. When the first conference for administrators of Mennonite colleges was held at Winona Lake, Aug. 7-8, 1942, Messiah College was represented and participated in the discussion of immediate problems confronting the Mennonite colleges as a result of the war. Meeting regularly two or three times annually since that year, the organization came to be known as the Council of Mennonite and Affiliated Colleges, including Upland (formerly Beulah) College as well as Messiah College.

In 1940 the Brethren in Christ Church appointed a member on the Mennonite Central Committee and co-operated wholeheartedly in the program of Civilian Public Service and Relief. During the years 1940-50 the Brethren in Christ Church contributed to the Mennonite Central Committee $142,183.22 in support of Civilian Public Service and $109,462.12 to War Sufferers' Relief and other phases of work supported by the Mennonite Central Committee. Of the more than 600 Mennonite Central Committee relief workers in the period beginning with World War II, 19 were members of the Brethren in Christ Church. (Five paragraphs of this article are quoted from the report of Department of Commerce, *Census of the Religious Bodies* of 1916. Research now under way indicates the article is not correct in all historical details. Statistical information in the article is supplied from the records of the General Conference.)   C.N.H.

A. W. Climenhaga, *History of the Brethren in Christ Church* (Nappanee, Ind., 1942); *Origin and History of the Tunker Church in Canada* (Ridgeway, Ont., 1918); *Brief History of United Zion's Children Church* (1917); J. A. Huffman, *History of the Mennonite Brethren in Christ Church* (New Carlisle, Ohio, 1920) 81-95.

Brethren of the Common Life (Dutch name, *Broeders des gemeenen levens*), a religious brotherhood founded in Holland about the middle of the 14th century by Gerrit Groote and Florens Radewynsz. Their purpose was to counteract the secularized life of the church by creating and promoting a truly pious Christian life shut away from worldly life, but actively engaged in earnest work for their fellow men, especially in education. They lived in community houses, men and women in separate buildings. They were not bound by a vow; anyone could leave the community life at will. Obedience, celibacy, and poverty, the three fundamental monastic rules, were also practiced by them, but without a vow. Voluntary renunciation of private possessions and community of goods were based on the example of the early Christian church, and the pledge to work was based on Bible passages like I Thess. 4:11, "Study to be quiet, and to do your own business, and to work with your own hands."

What distinguished them from the monastic orders, which had at that time degenerated, was their genuine piety, their repudiation of the monastic vow, and their opposition to begging. In other respects life in their houses was regulated with monastic strictness. The spirit of love, shown in humility, obedience, community life, and chastity, was to permeate and govern all the inmates. The day from three in the morning until nine at night was divided between work and spiritual exercise.

The tasks of the Brethren varied. All kinds of handicraft, gardening, agriculture, and fishing were carried on. The educated clergy occupied themselves chiefly with copying books, making a great contribution of lasting value along this line. Even today there are in public and private libraries, especially in Holland, an uncommonly large number of manuscripts which originated in these communities.

In the center of mutual edification were the collations. These were devotional addresses which were occasionally interrupted by questions and answers or alternated with longer conversations. The collations were of two kinds. One was intended for the common people, and took place on Sundays and holidays, when the doors of their houses were opened to the public; the other was meant only for inmates and was held daily in connection with the common noon and evening meals.

Such communal houses were located in Holland in Deventer, Zwolle, Amersfoort, Hulsberger near Hattem, Hoorn, Delft, Gouda, 's Hertogenbosch, Doesburg, Groningen, Harderwijk, Utrecht, Nijmegen, Albergen; in Belgium at Liége, Louvain, Gent, Brussels, Grammont near Oudenaerde, Mechelen; Cambray in France; in Germany at Münster, Cologne, Wesel, Osnabrück, Emmerich, Trier, Herford, Hildesheim, Kassel, Butzbach, Marburg, Königsstein (Nassau), Urach in Württemberg (see *HRE* III, 439), Magdeburg, Merseburg, Rostock, and Culm (West Prussia).

The significance of the Brotherhood of the Common Life in pre-Reformation times was profound. Their genuinely pious, serious way of life as well as in their instruction and their preaching were exceedingly fraught with blessing. Their collations attracted many. Although their influence in the transformation of the educational system was less inclusive and sweeping than has sometimes been assumed, it was nevertheless of lasting effect; on the whole it may be asserted that in many respects it prepared the way for the Reformation. When the Reformation came into the country the task of the brotherhood was fulfilled; its houses were gradually dissolved; it ceased to exist.

There is no evidence of any connection with the Anabaptist brotherhood; the Brethren of the Common Life adhered to Catholic doctrine and always remained loyal to it. There is no trace of separation from the Catholic Church. W. J. Kühler, the Dutch Mennonite historian, held that the soil for the Anabaptist movement in Holland was prepared in part by the Brethren.   NEFF.

W. Moll, *Kerkgesch. v. Nederland voor de Hervorming* II (Arnhem, 1867) 2, pp. 164-78; R. R. Post, *De moderne Devotie* (Amsterdam, 1940); Kühler, *Geschiedenis* I, 24-32; *ML* I, 279; A. Hyma, *The Brethren of the Common Life* (New York, 1951).

Brethren of the Free Spirit, the name of a peculiar, quietistic-pantheistic group in the Christian Church in the Middle Ages whose history is still largely unknown. It was influenced by the mystics and leaned toward Libertinism. The fundamental ideas in their doctrine, traced back to Amalarich of Bena

(d. 1204 as professor of theology in Paris) are as follows: In the human soul and all earthly things the divine substance is present. The merging of the soul in God is the final goal of all religion. Whoever attains this, the "perfect one," is sinless; his will is God's will. The commandments and means of grace are meaningless to him. Since all human conduct has been determined from eternity, all freedom of the human will is eliminated and moral striving without value. One must permit the Spirit to rule in him freely and allow himself to develop. This doctrine of unrestrained freedom of spirit was attributed to the Waldenses by their Catholic opponents (Keller, *Reformation*, 156; *HRE*, 485). It is also charged against the Beguines and Beghards without warrant. It is apparently incorrect to try to define the development and organization of the Brethren as a unified brotherhood, a "sect of the free spirit." They were rather isolated groups that arose within and in opposition to the church. Perhaps some widely circulated writings hostile to the church, like *Die neun Felsen* in their original formulation and *Schwester Kathrei* were an important factor in their rise. Among the advocates of the doctrine were Margarete Porete (burned in Paris in 1310), Marie of Valenciennes, Hadewig Bloemmard of Brussels, who opposed Ruysbroek about 1330, Berthold of Rohrbach (burned at Speyer in 1356), and Hermann Küchener of Nürnberg. Whether Walter of the Netherlands (executed at Cologne in 1322), whom Keller calls an apostle of the Waldenses, belonged to them is very doubtful (*HRE*, 471). Still less should the "Friend of God," Nikolaus of Basel (*q.v.*) be mentioned in connection with them.

The accusation made again and again against the Anabaptists that they belonged to the "sect of the free spirit" was probably based on the unfounded assumption that they advocated the doctrine of sinlessness. (*HRE* III, 467-472; Keller, 124, 153 ff.; *ML* I, 278.)   NEFF.

Bretten, a district in the *Kreis* of Karlsruhe in Baden. In the vicinity of the town of Bretten, the place of Philip Melanchthon's birth, the Anabaptists were already numerous by 1528 among the populace, whose desire for reform in religious conditions remained unsatisfied. Information concerning the spread of the new doctrine is still quite fragmentary. The Anabaptists held their meetings in lonely regions and in forests which afforded them some protection from persecution. About 1531 their services were often attended by 200 to 300 persons. As meeting places they used isolated homes in Neibsheim, Hagenmühle near Bauerbach, as well as Mühlen near Gondelsheim and Flehingen, and also the woods between Flehingen and Bretten. Many participants suffered martyrdom for separating from the old church (see **Wolf Kürschner**). From figures compiled by the Hutterian Brethren it is known that in the city of Bretten alone nine Anabaptists were executed, including Friedrich Schuster of Bretten and Wendel Maurer (Beck, 279) who are mentioned by name; another source names Wolf of Gritznis (Wolkan, 30), who baptized, and was therefore a preacher.

The oldest court records giving information about the spread of Anabaptist doctrine are found in Bauerbach (*q.v.*), a village (1910, 786 inhabitants) which at that time belonged to the bishopric of Speyer, and which is today still almost entirely Catholic, where there had long been dissatisfaction with clerical rule. The clergy were aware of this spirit of dissatisfaction; they no longer trusted the populace and behind the most innocent movements suspected antiecclesiastical trends. Thus the bailiff of the local chapter, Peter Ochs, saw in a rifle-match planned in the summer of 1530 by the people of Bauernbach merely a pretext for an Anabaptist meeting. The Anabaptists openly resisted the church by refusing the last sacraments, which happened for the first time in the fall of 1530, and which was punished by refusal of a church burial as well as close observation of several families, who were suspected of giving lodging to strangers passing through. Several fled for fear of punishment; on their return they were imprisoned. Their preacher was Konrad Scheid, a citizen of Bauerbach, who had also fled, but who returned in February 1531 and conducted services in the various homes (Bossert, 73; Wolkan, 31). He seems to have avoided imprisonment by a second flight. The measures against the Anabaptists were not strictly carried out, for the mayor himself was considered one of them. Andreas von Neiss, who died as a martyr at Neuburg a.D. before 1535, preached and baptized in Bauerbach (Wolkan, 29). Most of the adherents of the persecuted congregation probably emigrated to Moravia; emigrations from Bauerbach are mentioned in the records as late as 1544 (Bossert, 74).

The Anabaptists also attained a considerable following in Kürnbach, a village located east of Bauerbach, today almost exclusively Protestant (1910, 1,372 inhabitants). Here Blasius Kuhn of Bruchsal preached their doctrine from about 1530 to 1532. At Zaberfeld Michael Jungmann from Kürnbach was baptized with four companions. He was soon discovered and arrested, but gained his freedom by recanting, fled to Moravia, and later settled in Durlach, where he renewed contact with his home town. Meanwhile Anabaptist doctrine won new adherents in Kürnbach because of the inadequacy of the parson; they can be traced to the end of the 16th century (Becker, 113 ff.). Also in Büchig, Flehingen, Gondelsheim, and Neibsheim Anabaptist doctrine had found entry between 1531 and 1538 (Bossert, 75). But their further expansion was violently suppressed, at that time by the Catholic Church, and later by the Reformed and Lutheran clergy.

In 1589 the Reformed church council of the Palatinate had ceremonious attempts made to convert four Anabaptists at Bretten. Summoning all his scholarship, the Reformed pastor George Henfell tried to make it clear to them that they were following false doctrines. On March 17, 1589, he wrote to the council that he had done this very difficult task almost unaided, and had become "hoarse and almost sick" in consequence. In the presence of the officials he had explained to "the Anabaptist priests" the Christian faith, the holy sacraments, as

well as the Ten Commandments and refuted their errors according to the "Frankenthal colloquium and other learned books." He was successful with only one of them, Wendel Oberholtzer; the others declared that they stood by their faith and would leave the country (Hege, 147). The Anabaptists not tolerated in the Palatinate for the most part still went to Moravia.

After the Thirty Years' War adherents of the sects outside the established churches were welcomed to rebuild the devastated country. A number of Mennonite families expelled from Switzerland settled near Bretten and formed the Wössingen (*q.v.*) congregation; in the second half of the 19th century a second congregation was formed on the Heimbronnerhof by the Michael Hahn group. The census of 1910 showed 80 Mennonites living in the district of Bretten (see **Baden**); they lived at the following places: Bretten 1, Bonartshäuserhof near Gondelsheim 17, Erdbeerhof near Gondelsheim 7, Heimbronnerhof near Stein 5, Menzingen 7, Talmühle near Ruit 8, and Wössingen 27. In 1952 the congregation had a membership of 30 souls (27 baptized members), with an elder and two preachers.   HEGE.

Beck, *Geschichts-Bücher;* Becker, "Die Wiedertäufer in Kürnbach," in *Archiv f. hessische Gesch. u. Altertumskunde* (1903, supplement I) 113, 139; *Beiträge zur Statistik des Grosherzogtums Baden* (Karlsruhe, 1911) No. 63, p. 147; G. Bossert, "Beiträge zur badisch-pfälz. Ref.-Gesch.," in *Ztschr. f.d. Gesch. d. Oberrheins* (1904) LIX, 71-88; Chr. Hege, *Die Täufer in der Kurpfalz* (Frankfurt, 1908); Wolkan, *Lieder; ML* I, 267.

Breuning, Franz, a prominent member of the Augsburg Anabaptists, was beaten Jan. 20, 1528, and expelled from the city. He was the son of the mastersinger George Breuning, a master weaver of Augsburg, born about 1440. George Breuning's two epistles, "Von der Liebe Gottes" and especially his three hymns "Von Gott und von Christo," printed in 1503, were widely used by the brotherhood. The former was evidently published in a new edition in 1525 by Jakob Dachser and Siegmund Salminger, the leaders of the Augsburg congregation. Salminger included the hymns in his hymnal, *Der ganze Psalter,* published in 1537. It was reprinted from this hymnal by Wackernagel, *Kirchenlied* II, 823. One of them, "Gott ist ewig," became known through the adaptation by Johannes Böschenstein. George Breuning's works show the influence of German Mysticism. The fact that his son was an Anabaptist, and that his writings were highly regarded by them is significant evidence of a relationship between the two intellectual movements of the Reformation period. (*Monatshefte der Comenius-Gesellschaft,* 1903, 280; 1904, 74 f. *ML* I, 268.)   NEFF.

Breuning, Hans, an Anabaptist from Dachrieden near Mühlhausen in Thuringia, was arrested early in May 1533 with six fellow believers and imprisoned in Mühlhausen. They refused to name their leaders or brethren and desired to die in their faith, "thinking that their suffering was Christ's suffering." They were sentenced to death; but Philipp of Hesse, who held a protectorate over Mühlhausen conjointly with Saxony after 1525, did not give his consent. He commissioned the parson of Hersfeld, Balthasar Raidt, to persuade the prisoners of their error. By his skill and gentleness he brought about their public confession and recantation after an imprisonment of 21 weeks. Soon afterward Hans Breuning apparently again joined the Anabaptists. In the court records of 1534 his name occurs frequently as the co-worker and companion of Ludwig Spon (*q.v.*); he was supposedly baptized by Claus Scharf (*q.v.*), but he definitely denied this in his confession. He seems to have bought his freedom by recanting all of this. Nothing more is known of him. Perhaps he went to Moravia, for he longed for a peaceful residence.　　　　　　　NEFF.

P. Wappler, *Die Stellung Kursachsens und des Landgrafen Philipp von Hessen zur Täuferbewegung* (Münster, 1910); idem, *Die Täuferbewegung in Thüringen* (Jena, 1913); Fr. Roth, "Der Meistersinger Georg Breuning und die religiöse Bewegung der Waldenser und Täufer im 15. u. 16. Jahrh.," in *Beiträge zur bayr. Kirchengesch.*, 1904, 226; *ML* I, 268.

Brez, Guy de (Guido de Bray, or de Brès), one of the most important Reformed leaders in the Reformation in Belgium, was born in 1522 at Bergen in Henegau. His pious mother, a Catholic, instilled love and honor for the church into his mind, and he was always a deeply religious man even after he changed his attitude toward the church. During his apprenticeship with a glass painter he came in contact with Protestants, and through constant study of the Bible he was led to leave the Catholic Church between the ages of 18 and 25, and joined the Reformed Church.

When persecution reached Bergen in 1548, he fled to England, returned in 1552 and settled in Rijssel (Lille) in France, where he preached zealously for four years. In 1556 he fled to Gent, then to Frankfurt, and finally to Switzerland to continue his theological studies in Geneva and Lausanne. In 1559 he returned to Belgium, and stayed in relative concealment at Doornik and from there visited Rijssel, Valenciennes, Bergen, and Antwerp. Then persecution reached Doornik in 1561, and de Brez fled to Sedan, where he entered the service of Henri Robert de la Marck, lord of Bouillon, where he stayed until 1566. In that year the consistory of Antwerp called him to preach; he had scarcely arrived there when Valenciennes requested his service as preacher; he accepted the latter. After the iconoclasm of Aug. 24, 1566, he preached in the Groote Kerk to a large audience. But in December General Noircarmes began a siege of the city, and took it March 23, 1567. For a while de Brez managed to remain hidden with the other preachers and eventually to escape; but he was overtaken and after repeated trials condemned to death by hanging. He was executed May 31, 1567.

De Brez was very close to Calvin in his views, and in addition to his other writings, his formulation of the Dutch Reformed creed (1561) was of lasting influence on his countrymen. Nevertheless he was broad-minded enough to co-operate in achieving Prince William's pet project, namely, the unification of Lutherans and Reformed. So much the more remarkable is his aversion to the Anabaptists, with whom he disputed several times, for instance at Frankfurt, and whom he violently attacked in his book, *La Racine, Source et fondement des Anabaptistes* . . . , published in 1565. It was published in Dutch translation in 1570 with the title, *De Wortel, den oorspronck ende het fundament der Weederdooperen oft Herdooperen van onsen tijde. Met overvloedige wederlegginghe der sonderlincste argumenten, door de welcke sij ghewoon zijn de gemeijnte onses Heeren J. C. te beroeren ende den eenvuldige te verleyden.* Besides the edition of 1570, there are editions of the Dutch translation in 1585 (GCL) and 1608 and a copy of the original French edition extant, evidence that de Brez was widely read. Bakhuizen van den Brink, a competent historian, makes this comment: "It is true he zealously promoted the eradication of the Mennonites; but he was born and reared in a community where they were regarded with aversion and where public opinion considered them the descendants of those publicans and bogeys who have traditionally been branded as archheretics." An English edition was published in 1668 at Cambridge, Mass., under the title, *Rise, Spring, and Foundation of the Anabaptists.*　　　J.L.

Biogr. Wb., 594-603; L. A. van Langeraad, *Guido de Bray, zijn leven en werken* (Zierikzee, 1884); W. F. Dankbaar, *Hoogtepunten uit het nederl. Calvinisme in de 16e eeuw* (Haarlem, 1946) Chap. I, 5-40; "De gemeenten onder het kruis en het levenswerk van Guido de Bres"; *ML* I, 268.

Brick (or **Willow Street**) Mennonite Church (MC) is located a mile southeast of Willow Street in the center of Hans Herr's original settlement in Lancaster Co., Pa. Christian Herr I, his son and successor, built a large sandstone house on the Conestoga Road in 1719, the oldest church and dwelling house still standing anywhere in Lancaster County. In 1849 near the present site of the church and adjoining the cemetery, the first brick church was built. The next year Amos Herr, the first preacher in the Lancaster Conference to preach in English, was ordained here. He was also a consistent advocate of Sunday schools and when by the action of the Lancaster (Spring) Conference in 1871 Sunday schools were recognized as part of the church program, the Brick was the first school organized. The average attendance is now 257. The present building was erected in 1889 and enlarged and remodeled in 1937. The present (1953) membership is 250. It is the home congregation of the present bishop, Jacob T. Harnish. It is on the ministerial circuit with Strasburg and Sunnyside, and together with the New Providence-Mechanic Grove circuit, Mt. Vernon and Sunnyside, constitutes the bishop district.　　　I.D.L.

Bridgeport, a village near Kitchener, Ont., a short distance from which was located the Union church, built in 1848, in which Mennonites, United Brethren, and Lutherans at various times held services. Perhaps as early as 1890, Mennonites conducted Sunday school in the church and a few years later had preaching services there every four weeks, although they never organized a congregation. Around 1918 Mennonite meetings were discontinued and the work closed.　　　L.J.B.

Bridgeport Mennonite Mission (MC). Bridgeport is a small borough, largely Roman Catholic in population, on the west side of the Schuylkill River opposite Norristown, Pa. Efforts toward establishment of a Mennonite mission were begun in 1945; the resulting mission station was an outgrowth of the Norristown Mission under the direction of Markley Clemmer. Located at 318 DeKalb St., the mission is controlled by the Franconia Mennonite Board of Missions and Charities. The mission congregation in 1953 had a membership of 25. Q.L.

Brielle (or den Briel), a town in the Dutch province of South Holland. Anabaptists were found here very early. Cornelis wt den Briel (*q.v.*) baptized Janneke Melchior Symonsz here in 1533. About New Year 1534 Jan Beuckelsz and Gert thom Closter, two apostles of Jan Matthys, visited Brielle; Gert baptized 15 or 16 persons here. In 1534 Anneke Jans (*q.v.*) was also baptized here by Meyndert of Emden (or of Delft), who soon thereafter fled to England with her husband Arent Jansz, where Arent died; Anneke was seized upon her return to Netherlands and was drowned. Two other Mennonites of Briel died as martyrs, viz., Hendrik Arents (*q.v.*) and Job Janze (*q.v.*), both in 1568. There is no information concerning a congregation during this time. In 1568 Jan Willems performed a marriage here "after the teachings of Menno."

When Brielle was taken by the *Geuzen* (followers of the Prince of Orange) on April 1, 1572, and Catholicism was compelled to yield to the Reformed faith, there was apparently a considerable number of Anabaptists, who had some difficulties with the Reformed concerning marriages and military service; they were relieved of such service by the payment of a set fee. This money was used to support the poor of the Reformed Church, and later (1656) for the general poor fund. There were also some complaints made by the Reformed council concerning the transfer of members to the Mennonites. Nevertheless the conditions were better here than in many other Dutch towns. On Sept. 9, 1589, the Mennonites were even by law admitted to the city council. It is, however, not known that any Mennonites ever actually had a seat on the council.

Brielle also had its Mennonite divisions, with the result that we find three congregations in the town. The Flemish and the Waterlander congregations had their own churches. Whether the *Huiskoopers* (Old Flemish) also had a meetinghouse of their own is not known. This congregation was in existence until about 1720. Though all records of the membership of these congregations are missing, the number must have been large about 1650.

In the second half of the 17th century the Flemish congregation, which seems to have united with the Waterlanders in 1700, belonged to the Lamists (*q.v.*). In 1642 the ministers were Daniel Danielse Breys (Buys?) and Leenaert Jacobse (Coornkooper). Until about 1687 Jan Abrahamsz was a minister. He was followed in 1688 by Evert Buys.

The united congregation did not thrive either, in spite of the financial and moral support of the Rotterdam congregation; its membership declined rapidly. The members made contacts with the Remonstrants; thus in 1715 their deacon Pieter Zonnevijl united with the Remonstrants with the announcement that he (and other Mennonites) were joining "with the stipulation that they might remain true to their feelings about their views on the bearing of arms."

Although the Brielle congregation does not occur in the *Naamlijsten* issued after 1731, it was still in existence, though in a weak state, judging by the *Resolutieboek,* with entries until 1801. In 1754 there were, however, no male members left in the membership. vDZ.

H. de Jager, in *Navorscher,* 1882, 1894, especially the latter, pp. 101-23, "Bizonderheden betr. de Mennoniten te Brielle"; C. Veltenaar, *Het Kerkelijk-leven der Gereformeerden in den Briel tot 1816* (Amsterdam, 1915) 20-28, 91-98, 125-203, 333-39; *DB* 1917, 99; C. H. Hulshoff, "Bezoekreis van Hendrik Berents Hulshoff . . . in 1719," in *Bijdr. en Mededeelingen v.h. Hist. Genootschap* LIX (Utrecht, 1938) 33; Nos. 143, 243, 417, 821, 840, 896, 907, 1128; II, Nos. 1599-1606, 1610, 1874; *DB* 1872, 67; 1892, 115, 124-26; 1899, 99.

Brielsche Landt, Het. In the *Handelinge van de Vereenigde Vlaemsche en Duytsche Gemeentens* (Transactions of the United Flemish and German Congregations) of 1649, a meeting of these groups having been held at Haarlem, Dutch province of North Holland in that year, a congregation by this name occurs. The congregation was not represented and during this period of time had no minister. It is not quite clear which congregation is meant. It could be Brielle (*q.v.*), but also a combination of small congregations in the neighborhood of Brielle, the members of which lived in the villages of Geervliet, Heenvliet, Spijkenisse, and Zuidland, all on the island of Voorne-Putten which is located in the Dutch province of South Holland, and all indicated under these separate names at a meeting of the Flemish at Leiden in 1660. vDZ.

Brieven, a Dutch periodical published by the *Vereniging voor Doopsgezind Broederschapswerk* (*q.v.*), formerly called the *Vereniging voor Gemeentedagen* (*q.v.*). This periodical is distinctive, especially so in the early years, in that it is composed mostly of letters from readers. The first issue appeared May 1918. Initially the issues appeared irregularly, and from January 1925 to April 1942 the *Brieven* appeared monthly; after this date they were discontinued by order of the German military authorities. Beginning in 1946 this periodical was again published, at first irregularly, but at present three or four times a year. Originally the *Brieven* was edited by a committee; from 1920 to April 1922, P. G. Slogteren was in charge of the editing, followed by J. E. van Brakel, October 1922 (*Brieven* No. 14) to November 1928; thereafter W. H. toe Water, January 1929 to November 1936; and A. H. A. Bakker from December 1936 to April 1942. It was usually 24 pages in size, but occasionally much larger for special issues.

The *Brieven* provide a good insight into what has transpired in the Mennonite brotherhood in the Netherlands those years and witness to the spiritual renewal which has taken place through the efforts of the *Vereniging voor Gemeentedagen.* vDZ.

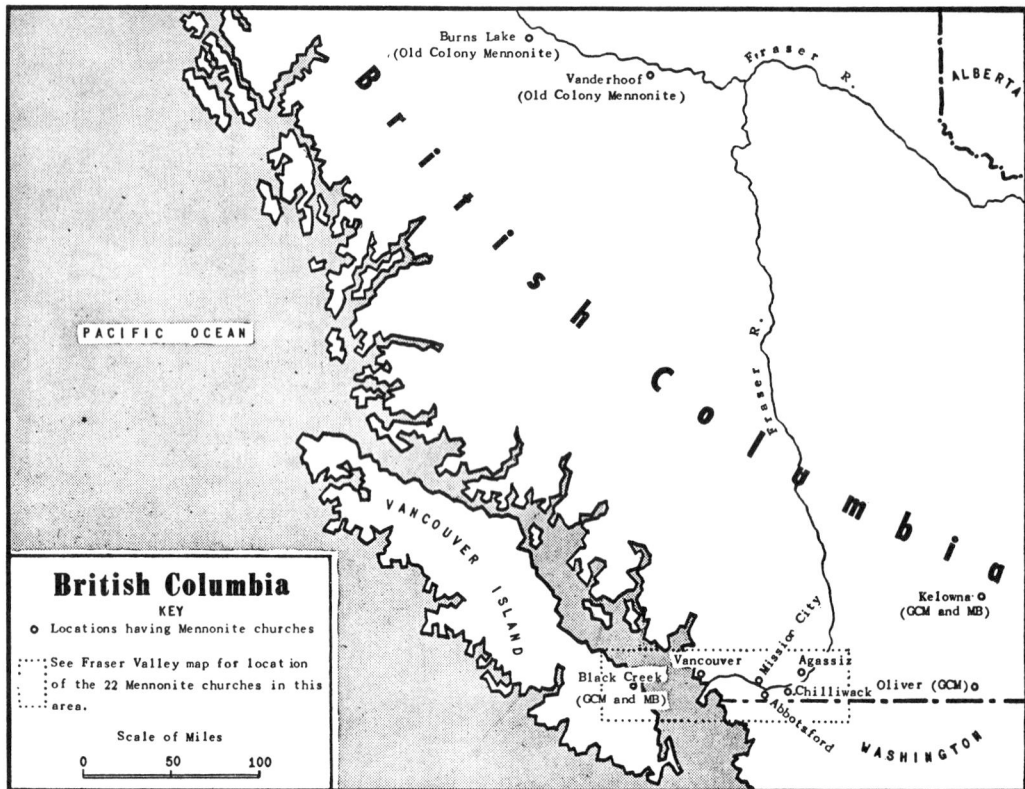

Bright Mennonite Mission: see **Blandford Town-ship, Ont.**

Bright United Missionary Church (now closed), located in the Kitchener district, was one of the earliest appointments of the Ontario (UMC) Conference. A church was built around 1877, the first preacher being Menno Bowman. The work was closed in 1945 and the members transferred to the church at New Dundee.   E.R.S.

Brighton Mennonite Church (EM), of Chicago, Ill., was previously named Hoyne Avenue Mission (1907), Mennonite Rescue Mission (1908-16), and Brighton Mission Chapel (1916-40). In January 1940 the name was changed to Brighton Mennonite Church of Chicago. In 1919 an almost new church was bought one-half mile east of the mission hall at 34th Place and Wolcott St. In November 1919 the congregation moved into the present quarters. It has a present membership of 80. In 1916 this work was placed in charge of G. P. Schultz. Two hundred and thirty-four persons have been baptized since 1916. At its peak the highest average Sunday-school attendance was never over 250. The shifting of population and changes in religious trends of the newcomers caused a 50 per cent decrease in the Sunday-school attendance and church membership.   G.P.S.

Britainville, 15 miles south of Gore Bay in Campbell Twp., Manitoulin Island, Ontario, the location of a community church built around 1888. Here the Mennonite Brethren in Christ (now United Missionary Church) have had charge of the Sunday school for the past 25 years.   M.G.

British Columbia is the "California" of Canada. Thousands have been attracted to Canada's Pacific shores by the mild climate and the pleasant, fertile valleys. In the period 1941-44 alone, over 90,000 Canadians migrated to the West Coast province. The province is Canada's third largest, with an area of 366,255 square miles, largely mountainous. The coast line is very irregular, indented with many fiord-like inlets, and measures 7,000 miles in length. The province extends from the Pacific to the height of land in the Rocky Mountains, a maximum of 600 miles, and from Alaska to the State of Washington.

In 1846 the Oregon Treaty cut the Northwest in two, drawing the present international boundary line between the United States and Canada at the 49th parallel of latitude. Vancouver Island was created a Crown colony of Great Britain in 1849. In 1858 the mainland was also made a Crown colony, thus ending the rule of the fur-trading companies. The island and the mainland united to form British Columbia in 1866, and in 1871 British Columbia became a province of the newly formed Dominion of Canada. At that time the province contained 36,000 whites. At present, well over one million people inhabit the cities and the valleys of the province. Lumbering, mining, fishing, agriculture, and manufacturing are the major pursuits of the people.

Mennonites have come to British Columbia in large numbers. The first came in 1928, mainly from the prairies, and built homes in what is now the town of Yarrow, about 40 miles inland from Vancouver. The settlers were poor and worked at any jobs that offered themselves, in the forests, on the farms, in the hop fields, and thus managed to eke out a bare living for themselves and their families. The settlement grew very rapidly, its present population being over 2,000. It is British Columbia's largest single Mennonite community, and is unique in that it is a completely Mennonite town. Most of the settlers came, here as elsewhere, from the drought-stricken areas of the prairie provinces after 1940, or from the new immigration from Russia after 1947.

The area around the town of Abbotsford, a few miles west of Yarrow, was the next site chosen by the Mennonites for settlement. The land was covered with light timber, and heavily dotted with the giant stumps of large, old trees. Several families began the difficult task of hewing homes out of the forest in 1930. They were very poor, the depression was at its height, and the only equipment available for land clearing was the ax and the saw. The group's only income was derived from what little could be earned in working for others. It was not until 1939 that economic independence was beginning to be attained. But thereafter great forward strides were made. Bulldozer, dynamite, and fire soon conquered the stumps, and the land was made ready for farming. Today comfortable farms cover the area.

In looking for a means of livelihood many Mennonites went to the near-by city of Vancouver. A permanent group developed there, and the city now has two sizable congregations, General Conference Mennonite and Mennonite Brethren.

As their numbers increased, the Mennonites diffused throughout the whole of the lower Fraser River Valley. Congregations are now to be found at Vancouver, Strawberry Hill, Aldergrove, Abbotsford, Matsqui, Mission, Arnold, Yarrow, Greendale, Chilliwack, East Chilliwack, Black Creek on Vancouver Island, and Kalowna in the interior, a total of 22. The most numerous group is the Mennonite Brethren, followed by the General Conference Mennonites. There are also small groups of Evangelical Mennonite Brethren, and a number of Holdeman Mennonites (Church of God in Christ, Mennonite). Four Bible schools are maintained. At one time there were three private Mennonite high schools, but at present only one remains, that at Abbotsford.

The Mennonite community of British Columbia has grown from a few persons in 1928 to over 15,000 in 1951 (2,000 D.P.'s from Europe have settled in B.C. since 1947), living in an area about 70 miles long by 15 miles wide. With the exception of those in the city congregations, almost all are engaged in dairying, small fruit growing, or poultry raising.   C.F.K.

British Columbia Provincial Mennonite Brethren Conference was organized on Oct. 31, 1931, with three local churches, Agassiz, Sardis, and Yarrow, having an approximate total membership of 170.

Attracted by the mild climate and large farm incomes, the M.B. membership of this area increased until 1948, after which a recession occurred, due to economic difficulties and floods. In 1949 there were 13 churches in the conference with a total membership of 3,077. The churches are located in the southwest part of British Columbia, with eleven in the Fraser Valley, one in the Okanagan Valley, and one on Vancouver Island, in an area stretching about 200 miles eastward from the Pacific coast along the United States border.

Activities in the conference include Bible conferences, youth conferences, tract mission work, radio broadcasts, a city mission in Vancouver, and widespread daily vacation Bible school work. The institutions of the conference include a girls' home in Vancouver, the West Coast Children's Mission, three Bible schools in Yarrow, South Abbotsford, and East Chilliwack, and a high school in North Abbotsford. The conference has been active in the resettling of European refugees and in the support of the relief program of the Mennonite Central Committee. C. C. Peters, secretary of the conference until 1948, contributed much to the establishment of the conference.   G.H.S.

Britton Run Mennonite Church (MC), located in Crawford County in northwestern Pennsylvania. In 1931 Amish Mennonite settlers arrived in the vicinity of Britton Run. After J. C. Provins of Scottdale, Pa., and Will Howitt of Portage Co., Ohio, canvassed the community for funds to purchase a deserted church building in the village, the Ohio State Mission Board helped to organize the congregation and furnished workers. Several Mennonite families from Nebraska joined the settlement. The family of Eli Kramer and others from Madison Co., Ohio, came within the next few years. Lewis Kletzly, the first licensed minister, later moved to Beaver Dam, 15 miles north. Early workers included Nelson King from Logan Co., Ohio, and I. B. Witmer, a nonresident minister from Leetonia, Ohio. The 1953 membership is 60 and the pastor J. W. Birky.   J.S.U.

Brixen, a city and district in Tirol, was formerly (after 992) an independent prince-bishopric, in which there were large numbers of Anabaptists by 1527. On Dec. 23, 1527, the prince-bishop had sent out the order to watch roaming agitators, "among whom there are said to be some who preach in corners about the new sect and rebaptism." These should be immediately imprisoned. The Innsbruck government sent the bishop the printed mandates on the eradication of the Anabaptists with the request that he publicize them in Brixen.

In the following years Anabaptists are found both north and south of the Brenner in constantly increasing numbers, and sharp edicts are repeatedly issued against them. Nor did the bishop escape criticism for proceeding "with too slight and lax sentences" against the Brixen Anabaptists. He should henceforth follow the mandates. For it was in the Brixen fief of Michelsburg that Anabaptism had taken root. Numbers of Anabaptists were taken from here to Brixen and sentenced to death, with the exception of those of whom it was said "that they were in general quite simple and of slight intelligence." Among those released was Agnes, the sister of Jakob Hutter (*q.v.*) of Moos, the founder of the Hutterian Brethren; among those executed was Gregor Weber of Pflaurenz, who was frequently mentioned in the Puster Valley, Hutter's most intimate friend and a preacher.

In spite of the severity emphatically demanded by the government and exercised by the authorities against the Anabaptists their numbers continued to grow; it was difficult to seize them, for they moved with great caution, assembled in remote places, placed guards, and were sometimes warned of imminent danger by friends. In order to capture the objects of their persecution in the woods and quarries, it was often necessary to combine the police force of two or three counties. We still have the oldest confessions of the Anabaptists in Michelsburg.

Here persecution raged most violently and here Jakob Hutter engaged in his frequently described work (Loserth, *Der Anabaptismus in Tirol* I, 56 ff.). "Like monks" the Tyrolese from this district streamed into Moravia. There was strife between the bishop of Brixen and the Innsbruck government on the exercise of regional jurisdiction, but in the matter of persecuting the Anabaptists they were of one mind; hence there were many victims in Brixen. Mandate upon mandate was issued against them, and repeatedly there is censure for the negligence, carelessness, and laxity of the officials, without which the movement could not have become so deeply rooted. Henceforth captured Anabaptists should be tried with "severe questioning" (i.e., on the rack) and punished according to the mandates. Whoever would shelter them or intentionally conceal them should be imprisoned and likewise severely questioned. Instructions were given in minutest detail on methods of procedure, the questions to be asked, how the expenses of the persecution are to be met, and what to do with the possessions of those punished; and lax officials were called to account.

Nevertheless the Anabaptist movement was not stamped out of Michelsburg in the following years, and the revolution in Münster gave all the powers hostile to the Anabaptists a most powerful weapon; for now even those who had heretofore been less severe lost their sympathy. While the news was being spread in Moravia "that there are not many Brethren left in the higher lands," persecution also flared up in Moravia, and many of the Anabaptists, including Jakob Hutter, returned to their old home, where of course no better lot awaited them. Even though the execution of Hutter (1536), "who had given a good lesson in his death," weakened the movement in the bishopric of Brixen, others soon followed in his steps and in the same year Anabaptists were again reported in Michelsburg. All efforts to master the situation seemed futile, for a large part of the populace openly sided with them or at least aided them. Hence the laments of the episcopal and civil officials that they could hardly depend on anyone. The defection from the Catholic Church was so marked that the number of those who had neglected the Easter confessional was announced as 600. After Hutter's death the movement centered about Offrus (Onufrius) Griesinger (*q.v.*), and so the persecution continued in the following years.

In 1538 the Brixen government made the first serious attempt not to combat Anabaptism with violence alone, but also with open indoctrination by the priest Dr. Gallus Müller; but the capture and execution of Griesinger had a greater effect, without, however, wiping out the movement; for now it received a new leader in Hans Amon (*q.v.*), called Tuchmacher, who came in haste from Moravia, and the mandates which were issued from time to time had so little effect that even members of the nobility joined the Anabaptists. A consultation between the Tyrolean government and that of Brixen in October 1539 on methods of stopping the spread of the movement, resulted in a tightening of the old orders; but now it was noted that no fewer than 600 persons had been executed in Tirol and in spite of this or perhaps because of it the numbers had increased.

After 1540 the movement took a smoother course. Adherents attempted to remain loyal to the faith in secret and escape to Moravia where there was complete toleration. Anabaptist trials became less numerous, the procedure of the authorities grew more lenient, and the death penalty was imposed only on the preachers. The recognition that capital punishment alone would not suffice found general acceptance, and finally even Ferdinand I declared that he had "a horror" of these never-ending executions and that he considered it an error to exercise the extreme severity of the mandates against these poor misled people. More and more the principle was accepted that more was to be gained by indoctrination than by severity.

Sometimes the governments supported the flight to Moravia. At that time Ulrich Stadler, a native of Brixen, died there; he had been an influential preacher in Moravia, and had produced some important writings. The migration to Moravia did not end during the next two decades, and Brethren from Moravia found their way into Tirol. We know of a letter sent by the congregation at Auspitz in Moravia on Aug. 13, 1557, to a citizen of Brixen, and ten years later we learn that there are Anabaptists there; when the more liberal practices were adopted in Moravia in the days of Maximilian II, which they themselves called "the golden time," the immigration increased until the end of the century when their situation in Moravia deteriorated. When Anabaptism became extinct in southern Tirol cannot be ascertained from court records, but there are still traces of its presence in the first decades of the 17th century. LOSERTH.

Beck, *Geschichts-Bücher*; J. v. Kripp, *Ein Beitrag zur Geschichte der Wiedertäufer in Tirol* (Progr. d. K. K. Staatsgymnasiums in Innsbruck 1857); J. Loserth, *Der Anabaptismus in Tirol* (Vienna, 1892); H. Amman, *Die Wiedertäufer in Michelsburg im Pustertal und deren Urgichten* (Progr. des K. K. Staatsgymnasiums in Brixen 1896 and 1899); ML I, 269.

Brno (German, Brünn), capital of Moravia, Czechoslovakia (pop. 270,000), formerly the seat of the Moravian Provincial Diet or Estates (Landtag).

Moravia once belonged to the kingdom of Bohemia and with it fell to the Habsburgs (*q.v.*) in 1526. Since 1918, it has been part of the Czechoslovakian Republic. Since the 18th century Brno is also the seat of a Catholic bishop, while formerly it belonged to the diocese of Olomuce (Olmütz). The Hutterite *Chronicle* reports that in the 16th century four Anabaptist brethren were martyred in this city, among them Thoman and Balthasar Waldhausen (*q.v.*) in 1528, and Wilhelm Griesbacher of Tirol in 1535. As seat of the Provincial Diet, the city is often mentioned in the Chronicle, particularly at the time of the imminent outbreak of the Thirty Years' War. Brno has a Provincial State Archive (*Landesarchiv*) which contains most valuable Anabaptist source material, namely, 15 Hutterite manuscript books (about half of them of the 16th and 17th centuries) and the famous *Beck Collection,* comprising 104 files with transcripts and some originals of practically everything Hutterite, or of some relationship to this brotherhood. (See Beck, Joseph.) The material was widely used by scholars up to the great political changes around 1940. (See **Moravia.**)   R.F.

H. S. Bender, "Anabaptist Manuscripts in the Archives at Brno, Czechoslovakia," *MQR*, 1949, 105-7 (lists, however, only 12 codices instead of 15).

Broad Street Mennonite Church (MC), Harrisonburg, Va. Work was begun among the colored people of Harrisonburg by the Young People's Christian Association of Eastern Mennonite College in 1937. A rented building on East Gay Street served as a center for this work until 1945 when a church was built on Broad Street. The first superintendent was Ernest Swartzentruber. He was followed by Ralph M. Shank, the present pastor of the congregation. There are 17 members with an average Sunday-school attendance of 70. H.A.B.

Broadcasting: see **Radio Programs, Mennonite.**

Broadway, Va., a town of 600 inhabitants in the northern part of Rockingham County. It is the general center of a Mennonite (MC) community comprising the Zion and Trissels congregations, the latter being the oldest active congregation within the Virginia Conference. From this center mission extension activity has been carried on in the adjacent counties of Virginia and West Virginia for three generations. A number of smaller congregations have resulted as an outgrowth of this work. Mennonites of this community have for the most part been engaged in farming, with specialization in poultry, dairying, and horticulture. They were pioneers in the system of contract feeding of broilers which has so largely affected the economic life of the northern counties of Virginia and the eastern counties of West Virginia.   J.Wa.S.

Brockes, Berthold Heinrich (1680-1747), a city senator of Hamburg, author of the famous *Irdisches Vergnügen in Gott,* a collection of religious observations on nature. He was a friend of Jakob Denner (*q.v.*), the noted Mennonite preacher, and wrote a poem on his death. (*ML* I, 271.)   Neff.

Brödli, Hans: see **Brötli, Johannes.**

Broederschap, a Dutch word which in the 16th-18th centuries meant the meeting of the *Broeders* (male

members of the church), who, usually after the service had finished, were asked to stay in the meetinghouse to decide on special questions as, for example, to choose preachers, elders, and deacons, to pronounce or lift the ban; nowadays this word, an equivalent of the English "brotherhood," is often used to indicate the Mennonite Church in Holland as a whole (*Doopsgezinde Broederschap*). See also **Brethren** and **Bruderschaft.**   vDZ.

Broederschapshuis, the name given in Holland to the Mennonite campgrounds and houses which are available to Mennonites, as well as others, as quarters for conferences and vacation periods. In 1950 the following broederschapshuizen were in existence: Elspeet (*q.v.*) founded 1925; Fredeshiem (*q.v.*) near Steenwijk, founded 1929; Schoorl (*q.v.*) founded 1932; Bilthoven (*q.v.*) founded 1936; Kraggehuis (*q.v.*) founded 1921, and Samen Een (*q.v.*) founded 1932, both near Giethoorn.   vDZ.

Broederschapswerk, Commissie voor Doopsgezind (Committee for Mennonite Brotherhood Work), the present sponsor of what was formerly called the *Gemeentedagbeweging* (*q.v.*), which came into being to a considerable extent under Quaker influence. In 1903 a Quaker organization for religious and church instruction was established at Woodbrooke, near Birmingham, England, which was attended by many people of Holland. Upon their return to Holland, these Woodbrooke people held conferences at Barchem. On April 12, 1917, T. O. Hylkema, the Mennonite minister of Giethoorn, called a meeting of those present to discuss with him the organization of a conference, which came into being and was later known as the *Gemeentedag van Doopsgezinden* (Church-Day Conference of Mennonites), for the promotion of faith in the individual and in the brotherhood. On Aug. 2, 1917, the first *Gemeentedag* of the Mennonites met in the church at Utrecht, followed by annual meetings since that time. (A preliminary step in this movement may be seen in a meeting called at Amsterdam in 1915 by J. Lagas.) Participants had come from various congregations. The focal center of the discussions was the questions of nonresistance and baptism.

The gemeentedag movement cannot be said to have had a precise goal. It was the intense desire of the leaders to kindle a fire among the Dutch Mennonites, which would continue to burn. Among the Quakers, who had in the 19th century fallen into a decline, a powerful revival had taken place in 1880. Why could not this spirit communicate itself to the Mennonites of the Netherlands, who were so closely related to the Quakers and who had likewise suffered a decline in the 19th century? Careful ministers at first urged caution toward the movement, which to them seemed without purpose and a reaction against existing views. The leaders of the movement sought to re-establish the ancient Mennonite customs, doctrines, and institutions. The great achievement of the 19th century, the Algemene Doopsgezinde Sociëteit (*q.v.*), had been to give the Dutch Mennonites an educated ministry. But in the new movement the watchword was: not only the ministers, but all believers are priests. The sociëteit, the seminary, the liberal theology were to be eliminated. The movement was considered to be in opposition to the established order. At times the leaders had visions of a return to the faith of the fathers on the foundation of Jesus Christ (I Cor. 3:11) in contrast to the liberal views of the 18th and 19th centuries. Derisive allusions were made by their opponents to an analogy between the Neo-Calvinists and the Neo-Mennonites. But the majority of the leaders did not agree with this attitude. T. O. Hylkema, who set the tone from the beginning, was untiring in proclaiming a positive goal, impelled by his faith in the task of the church in the present age. The movement was to be a ferment in renewing the entire brotherhood. The sleeping brotherhood should be aroused and put the talents entrusted to it into the service of Christ for the salvation of the world. Accordingly the *Gemeentedagbeweging* brought new inspiration to the Dutch Mennonites, but not a new theological direction; while many of its leaders have been strongly evangelical, the movement itself is neutral, and offers a place to all and wishes to unite all with itself, though the Christocentric idea has predominated in the leadership from the first.

A general gemeentedag was held annually, from 1917 to 1919 in Utrecht, later in Lunteren in cabins on the heath. The number of participants has been usually about 100. In addition, there are regional gemeentedag meetings in North Holland, Friesland, etc., attended sometimes by 300 persons. In connection with these meetings there is also a Youth Day (the first day in May 1922) at Lunteren and later also in the provinces. Youth organizations have been formed in various cities, more than 40 of which are united in the Mennonite Youth Secretariat. Mennonites between the ages of 18 and 36 may join. Camps for boys and girls are held in the summer, for the first time in 1920 in Oud-Reemst on the Veluwe for boys. Anyone interested in the aims of the gemeentedag movement may join as a "co-worker." It holds its meetings in conjunction with the gemeentedag conferences, the first in 1921. The group discusses practical work in the service of the Gospel and organizes itself into various interest groups to promote missions, Bible study, nonresistance, abstinence, etc. There are about 1,000 of these "co-workers."

At Pentecost 1925 the gemeentedag organization opened the *Doopsgezind Broederschapshuis* (Mennonite Brotherhood House) in Elspeet (*q.v.*). Several barracks were built, offering lodgings for 50 guests as well as dining-rooms and kitchens. During the first summer about 500 vacation guests came to the camp for short periods. In 1926 the "Clubhouse" was built with social rooms and sleeping quarters for 50 quests. Several conferences were also held here during the summer. A building for meetings was also planned, as well as additional dormitories sufficient so that 150 persons could be lodged at a single time. (*ML* II, 59.)

C.N.

The broederschapshuis at Elspeet grew in a short time to be indeed an ideal and frequently visited center of Mennonite life. After the main building and five barrack-dormitories were erected, a simple but artistic chapel of wood was added to complete the whole.

The first broederschapshuis was used as a conference center. A Brotherhood Week (*Broederschapshuisweek*) and a General Work Conference (*Algemeene Arbeids-samenkomst*) were held each year. Elspeet offered a hospitable place not only for these two central conferences, but also for the social-religious work in behalf of those who were affected by mass unemployment in the years of economic depression (called *crisiswerk*).

Between the conference periods the broederschapshuis was set aside for vacation use (called *vacantieverblijf*). Many families spent their vacation at Elspeet, especially during the summer months. During these periods a minister and his wife were always present to provide the leadership. Many vacationers look back with deep gratitude to the time they spent at Elspeet. The spiritual isolation in which a person frequently lives in modern times was broken through at Elspeet, and persons present found themselves accepted in a great spiritual fellowship.

Before long there came the founding of a second broederschapshuis. The financial risk of the Elspeet broederschapshuis was borne by the association named Broederschapshuis Committee-Elspeet (*Broederschapshuis Commissie-Elspeet*). When a second broederschapshuis was started, the *Gemeentedagbeweging* took upon itself the risk for building and development. This new project took place in the dunes region of North Holland slightly south of Schoorl. This broederschapshuis also developed rapidly despite the unfavorable times. Between the years 1928 and 1940 the third and the fourth broederschapshuis were erected in the neighborhood of Steenwijk (named "Fredeshiem") and at Bilthoven, respectively.

Through the efforts of the *Gemeentedagbeweging*, the spiritual life of the Mennonite brotherhood between World Wars I and II was enriched and deepened. Of great significance, moreover, is the fact that the Mennonite Youth Union (*Doopsgezinde Jongerenbond*, D.J.B.) was founded. This took place in 1926, although already before this date youth conferences had been held in connection with the gemeentedag. In 1928 the youth organization became independent.

Of the subcommittees and work groups, the most important are as follows:

(1) The General Camp Committee (*De Algemene Kamp Commissie*, A.K.C.), which organized a large number of summer camps for catechumens (among other places, at Elspeet and Giethoorn).

(2) The Committee for Bible Study (*De Commissie voor Bijbelstudie*).

(3) The Work Group against Military Service (*De Arbeidsgroep tegen de Krijgsdienst*).

The place which the broederschapshuis at Elspeet occupied in the *Gemeentedagbeweging* was so central that shortly before the outbreak of World War II it was decided to change the name to The Elspeet Association (*Elspeetse Vereniging*).

The responsibility for the work of the Elspeet

Association is vested in the yearly meeting, called the General Work Conference (*Algemene Arbeidssamenkomst*), while leadership in the customary work is carried on by the General Gemeentedag Committee (*Algemene Gemeentedag Commissie*) in which members of all the committees, work groups, and regional organizations sit. In this group there is also an executive committee which transacts current matters. In this manner the co-ordination of so variegated a work is preserved.

During the war years, 1940-45, the Elspeet program underwent radical changes. In the first place, it was compelled to change its form of organization in order to evade a prohibition made by the occupying National-Socialist government. Consequently, the Elspeet Association underwent a metamorphosis and in the summer of 1940 became a committee of the Algemene Doopsgezinde Sociëteit. The new name was *A.D.S. Commissie voor Broederschapswerk*. It turned out that in practice the same service was continued by the same persons. However, in the last years of this period a paralysis of the work could not be prevented and it came to a partial standstill. There were various causes for this situation. Already in the first months of the war, the broederschapshuis at Schoorl was requisitioned for military purposes. Here building after building was demolished, so that in May 1945 only the main building remained, also in a dilapidated condition.

Somewhat similar circumstances transpired at Elspeet, the oldest and largest broederschapshuis, although on a somewhat less devastating scale. The buildings and grounds were subjected to great destruction; one of the dormitories, at the time of the allied occupation in the summer of 1945, was entirely destroyed by fire.

Besides this damage in a material sense the dark period of World War II produced little gain in a spiritual sense although internally the relations of the brotherhood were improved. By means of the co-operation of the A.D.S., an appreciation for the Elspeet work grew to an extent not existing during the first period. However, after the termination of World War II, the Elspeet Association resumed its work independently, and the relationship to the A.D.S. remained only one of personnel. During and after World War II, W. I. Fleischer was chairman. The first year (beginning January 1947) was devoted to a restoration of contact with members, of which many had changed addresses during the war as a result of evacuation and other reasons. Also, a number of emergency repairs were performed on the buildings at Elspeet, so that at least small groups of people could again be accommodated. A reorganization of the Association was prepared. A new name and a new form of organization were sought. The new name decided upon was Fellowship for Mennonite Church Work (*Gemeenschap voor Doopsgezind Broederschapswerk*, G.D.B.). The G.D.B. set itself to the aim of "building on the foundation laid in Christ Jesus, to strengthen the personal religious life and the church life of the Mennonites in the Netherlands, and to engage in services of love." The G.D.B. now recognizes three

kinds of members: (*a*) individual members, (*b*) congregations, (*c*) other associations or organizations in a federal relationship whereby such groups retain their autonomy.

The Elspeet work prospered again. The prewar level was again reached and passed. The principal branches of service are summarized below:

1. The Committee for Bible Study (*De Commissie voor Bijbelstudie*) has published a guide for the study of the Gospel of Luke, and in addition is responsible for the regular Bible column in the *Algemeen Doopsgezind Weekblad*.

2. The Mennonite Peace Group (*De Doopsgezinde Vredesgroep*) after World War II attained a greater prosperity than that of the Work Group against Military Service before World War II. The Peace Group developed from a committee to an independent organization with its own membership, executive committee, and conference program.

3. The General Camp Committee (*De Algemene Kamp Commissie*) extended its work, so that each summer there are a total of 15 camps organized for catechumens with a total of approximately 500 participants.

4. To help persons affected by current crises, the Committee for Fellowship Weeks (*Commissie voor Gemeenschapsweken*) provides yearly four retreats where fatigued women are given an opportunity to renew their bodily and especially spiritual strength.

5. The Committee for Student Conferences (*De Commissie voor Studenten Conferenties*) sponsors an annual conference for theological students and for ministers.

6. The Committee for Conferences for Church Board Members (*De Commissie voor Kerkeraadsledenconferenties*) organizes yearly a conference for church board members, which is usually very well attended. Among other things, attention is given to the spiritual background necessary for the work of such members.

7. The Committee for the Study of Faith (*De Commissie voor Geloofsbezinning*) devotes its monthly meetings to a study of actual theological problems, while at the same time considering what is distinctively Mennonite.

8. The Committee for Catechism (*De Commissie voor Catechetiek*) gives attention to the possibilities of arriving at more similarity in methods of catechizing, and occupied itself, among other things, with the compilation of a book on faith for catechumens.

The seventh and eighth committees are committees which came into existence through the G.D.B. in co-operation with the A.D.S.

In addition to the conferences and meetings which were started before 1940, and which are continuing, other gatherings were organized after the war. In the current program the following conferences appear: Brotherhood Conference (*Broederschapsweek*), General Work Meeting (*Arbeidssamenkomst*), Family Conferences (*Gezinsweken*), Ministers' Conference (*Predikantenweek*), Conference for Scholars (*Gestudeerdenconferentie*), Retreat Conferences (*Retraitesamenkomsten*). Besides this there are special conferences for committees and organizations federally united with the Association.

The group-members federally united with the Elspeet Association are: (a) "Foundation for Meeting Special Needs Within and Without the Mennonite Brotherhood" (*Stichting voor Bijzondere Noden in de Doopsgezinde Broederschap en daarbuiten*), (b) "The Mennonite Society for Propagation of the Gospel" (*Doopsgezinde Vereniging voor Evangelieverbreiding*, or *Zendings Vereniging*), (c) "The Mennonite Youth Union" (*De Doopsgezinde Jongerenbond*, D.J.B.), (d) "The Frisian Mennonite Youth Union" (*De Friese Doopsgezinde Jongerenbond*, F.D.J.B.).

The Fellowship for Mennonite Church Work has a present (1953) total of 1,200 individual members, and in addition congregations which have joined the organization. The organ of the movement is called *Brieven* (q.v.) and appears four or five times in a year. The executive committee of the G.D.B. is now composed of D. Richards, chairman; Miss M. Kuitse, secretary; and G. H. Blaauw, Jr., treasurer.

After the restoration of war damages, the broederschapshuis at Elspeet is again able to accommodate some 200 guests, while the broederschapshuis at Schoorl is able to provide sleeping accommodations for about 100 persons.

To sum up, we can thankfully state that manifold blessings have gone out to the congregations and the brotherhood from the *Gemeentedagbeweging*, both in the past and the continuation. This movement had an influence of renewing, strengthening, and a furthering of fellowship in the development of Mennonite life in the Netherlands during the first half of the 20th century.　　　　R. DZ.

Several issues of *Brieven*; *Onze eerste tien jaren*, Wolvega, 1927; C. Nijdam, "Remembrance: The First Ten Years of the Gemeentedag Movement in Holland," *MQR* II, 1928, 54-65.

Broek, a hamlet in the Dutch province of Friesland, where Leenaert Bouwens (q.v.) baptized 6 persons in 1554-56 and 22 in 1563-65. Since there are two villages of this name in Friesland, it is not clear whether Broek near Joure (q.v.) or Broek near Dantumawoude (q.v.) is meant. The newly baptized may have joined the near-by Mennonite congregation, of which there was one in both Joure and Dantumawoude.　　　　vDZ.

Broek op Langendijk, a Mennonite congregation in the Dutch province of North Holland. It formerly was called Lange- and Koedijk and belonged to the Frisian wing. Of its history little is known, but it must be very old, for as early as 1567 mention is made of Mennonites living there. In 1727 the preachers of the congregation were Willem Cornelis Keyser and Dirk de Vries; in 1751 Jan Hand; in 1783 Jan Hellingman, and in 1806 Jan Eenigenburg. Among the most important of the preachers who ministered to this congregation in the 19th century were A. W. Wybrands, the noted church historian, and F. C. Fleischer (q.v.), the founder of the Green Cross, 1897-1902. After him the congregation was served by the ministers F. ten Cate 1903-7; W. Banga, 1907-14; A. de Jong, 1914-38;

J. Oosterbaan, 1938-40; Miss M. C. Schepman, 1942-50, and M. J. Nolthenius since 1951. In 1860 the membership was 36; in 1900, 90; in 1950, 120. The congregation acquired a new church in 1858 (dedicated Nov. 7). In the congregation there is an active Sunday school for children and a women's organization.　　　　K.V.

Blaupot t. C., *Holland* I, 251; II, 204, 233; *ML* I, 271; *Inv. Arch. Amst.* I, No. 411; II, Nos. 1607-8; II 2, No. 37.

Broeks, Jacob, was a shoemaker and preacher of the Mennonite congregation at Terhorne, in the Dutch province of Friesland. When the Moravian Brethren (q.v.) settled in the Netherlands they found some adherents among the Mennonites. Jacob Broeks, who joined the Moravians in 1756 together with Sybern Claases, one of the members of his congregation, caused some difficulty in his congregation. (W. Lütjeharms, *Het Philadelphisch-Oecumenisch streven der Hernhutters in de Nederlanden in de 18e eeuw,* Zeist, 1935, 65.)　　　　vDZ.

Broer Cornelis: see Cornelis Adriaensz.

Broese van Groenou, Herman, b. Feb. 19, 1822, at Kampen, a son of Jacobus Adolf Broese and Geertruide van Groenou. He studied at the University of Utrecht and the Amsterdam Mennonite Seminary and in 1847 became preacher at Medemblik; in 1852 he went to Aardenburg. On Aug. 19, 1883, he preached his farewell sermon in Aardenburg and retired to Leiden, where he died July 12, 1894. The *Doopsgezinde Bijdragen* published his historical study on the Aardenburg (q.v.) congregation under the title, "Uit het verleden der Doopsgezinde gemeente te Aardenburg" (*DB* 1876, 80-115; 1877, 1-42; 1879, 14-53; 1881, 1-33; 1883, 1-29; 1884, 32-63), and "Verklaring van een ouden scheldnaam der Doopsgezinden" (*DB* 1882, 34-40). Under the pen name Herman he wrote articles for the periodicals *Nederland* (1851), *Album van schoone Kunsten, Kunstkroniek, Drenthina, Evangeliespiegel, Evang. Penningmagazijn,* and also wrote about den Reynaert and about a painting by Ary Scheffer, "Christus als Vergelder" (1851). (*Biogr. Wb.* I, 644 and 645; *ML* I, 271.)　　　　J.L.

Broken View Mennonite Church (MC) is located four miles north and two miles northeast of Broken Bow, Neb. It was organized in June 1923 by Daniel Lapp and now (1953) has 46 members, with Royden Schweitzer as minister. Its meetinghouse was built in 1938.　　　　M.G.

Brons, Anna (nee Cremer ten Doornkaat), wife of Councillor Isaak Brons (q.v.) in Emden, b. Nov. 23, 1810, in Norden, East Friesland. She is widely known in German Mennonite circles as the author of a very meritorious book, *Ursprung, Entwicklung und Schicksale der Taufgesinnten oder Mennoniten, in kurzen Zügen übersichtlich dargestellt von Frauenhand* (Norden, 1884). This work was published in a third edition in 1912, revised by E. M. ten Cate.

She spent her youth in the home of her uncle S. D. Cremer in Norden, for her mother, his sister, had died at her birth. Her youth passed happily and harmoniously under the careful supervision of her uncle. Very active intellectually, she most advantageously assimilated the manifold good impressions which she had absorbed from the family traditions and the wholesome church life, borne by a Mennonite consciousness. On Nov. 12, 1830, she was married to Isaak Brons at Emden, a deeply religious man, also borne by a definitely Mennonite consciousness. In their thoroughly happy marriage of 55 years' duration she stood faithfully at his side as a companion of equal rank and reared her large family in complete harmony with her husband. She took a lively interest in all of her husband's work and was his perfect complement. When in 1856 following an illness he was compelled to drop his customary occupations and use his eyes only a few hours daily, she regularly devoted several hours a day to reading to him all that had formerly interested him. Thus she won a deeper than customary insight into scientific, religious, and social fields.

She was especially interested in the history of the Mennonites. The competent preachers who served the Emden church during her lifetime, van Hülst, S. Cramer, who later became professor at Amsterdam, and J. P. Müller, stimulated her to extend and deepen the knowledge she had gained by private study of Menno's writings and other works. Thus various larger and smaller articles came from her pen, extracts from the works of greater Mennonite significance. Finally she worked these articles over into a whole with a view to the generation growing up about her. Thus the book mentioned above gradually took form. At that time the German Mennonites lacked a survey of the total Mennonite picture. Aside from several monographs like those of B. C. Roosen and C. Harder on Menno Simons and D. Philips, only the *Mennonitische Blätter,* founded in 1854 by J. Mannhardt in Danzig, offered the German Mennonites an opportunity to become acquainted with Mennonite interests, history, and present conditions. Mrs. Brons was an unusually zealous and active worker on the *Mennonitische Blätter* even in her advanced years. The 1880's were particularly eventful for the development of the German Mennonites. In 1880 Dr. Ludwig Keller's *Geschichte der Wiedertäufer und ihres Reichs zu Münster* appeared, the first of the series of books which this scholar published in rapid succession on the beginnings of the Anabaptist movement, and which rendered the Mennonites a most distinguished service.

In 1884, when the first edition of her book was published, representatives of the Mennonite churches of Germany met in Berlin in November at the instigation of Dr. S. Cramer and discussed the formation of a union of these churches, which later came into being as the *Vereinigung* (*q.v.*). Among the most ardent promoters of this union were Anna Brons and her oldest son, consul Bernhard Brons, Jr. (*q.v.*), of Emden. Until her death she took an active part in building up the inner structure of the *Vereinigung.* She kept up a correspondence with all the promoters of the new organization and supported it in various other ways. Her ideal was a union of all German Mennonite congregations, similar to the Dutch Algemene Doopsgezinde

Sociëteit, which would permit the congregations to remain independent and yet support each other in preserving the Mennonite way of life. Several other articles appeared from her pen in her old age, warmly sponsoring the Mennonite ideal of a Christian community. This kind of work gave her the deepest satisfaction and earned the respect of wide circles of Mennonites for her unflagging energy. She died in Emden April 2, 1902, at the age of 91 years. (*Gem.-Kal.* 1904, 43-73; S. Cramer, "Mevrouw Brons," in *DB* 1902, 103-14; *ML* I, 272.)   H.vdS.

Brons, Bernhard, Jr., b. Oct. 15, 1831, in Emden, d. June 8, 1911, at Gronau at the home of his son-in-law J. van Delden. Bernhard Brons was the oldest son of Isaak (*q.v.*) and Anna (*q.v.*) Brons and was one of the most capable leaders of the German Mennonites of his day. In his parental home he developed an inexhaustible pleasure in work and a successful career in the field of business as well as congregational affairs. He was deacon of the Emden church from 1872 until the end of his life. He played a prominent part in the founding of the *Vereinigung der Mennoniten-Gemeinden im Deutschen Reich,* and devoted his best gifts to its promotion. With wise counsel and generous hand in complete agreement with his mother he worked for the strengthening of Mennonite consciousness. He was a pillar not only of his home church in Emden, but of the entire German Mennonite brotherhood. With poetic turns in word and deed he most emphatically advocated his conception of Mennonitism, which resembled the Dutch idea. He served in various organizations for the general welfare of the city, the Kant Society, as well as in politics. For 14 years he served Emden well as a member of the city council. He lost his two sons through death, one of them early, the second at the age of 22 years of heart trouble. Only a daughter survived, who faithfully nurtured her spiritual inheritance with her like-minded husband.   H.vdS.

L. Keller, "Bernhard Brons," in *Monatshefte der Comenius-Gesellschaft,* 1911, 185-89, and 1910, 95 ff.; *DJ* 1913, 21-36 with portrait; *ML* I, 273.

Brons, Isaak, b. April 3, 1802, at Emden, d. March 12, 1886, at Emden, deacon of the Mennonite church there until 1872. At the age of 17 he lost his father and faithfully supported his mother. The Mennonite virtues of perseverance and patience in addition to a deeply religious earnestness characterized him throughout his life. The writings of the Romantics exerted a pronounced effect on his development in his youth, and he was an enthusiastic admirer of Schiller. In 1826 he settled in Emden and established his prosperous mercantile business. On Nov. 12, 1830, he married Anna Cremer ten Doornkaat and found in her a sympathetic and loyal companion. (See **Brons, Anna.**)

In the city council his opinions were gladly heard, although his zealous political activity in the interests of a strong and unified Germany was not favorably regarded by the Hannoverian government of the time. In 1849 he represented East Friesland with other delegates in the German parliament at Frankfurt and agitated for the *National-*

Verein founded in 1861 by R. von Bennigsen. With some like-minded friends he also founded a Navy Society for East Friesland in 1861, and was chosen its permanent chairman. Though the Hannoverian government did not view the efforts to establish a Prussian fleet with favor, Isaak Brons was not deterred from working with all his might for the National Union and the Naval Society. In 1863 he represented East Friesland at a Diet of cities when the fiftieth anniversary of the Battle of Leipzig was celebrated. When the Reichstag of the North German *Bund* was called in 1867 to draft a constitution, he represented his electoral district and took an active part in its work. But then he withdrew from politics, on the ground that younger men could more adequately represent the district with honor. Until 1872 he retained his membership in the civic association (*Bürgerschaft*). Then he resigned this position and also his office of deacon in the church.

Isaak Brons accomplished much for his native city, his country, and his church and earned the respect of all. In addition, in complete understanding with his wife, he devoted much energy to rearing his children as useful citizens and wholesome, convinced Mennonites. It was a well-earned testimony to the community of spirit with his wife that she dedicated her book, *Ursprung, Entwicklung und Schicksale der Taufgesinnten oder Mennoniten, in kurzen Zügen übersichtlich dargestellt von Frauenhand*, to him for his eighty-third birthday. His wife describes his character with these words: "A man equipped with enormous energy, strength of will and determination, with significant talents and a many-sided intelligence. As a faithful steward he honorably and honestly invested the pound entrusted to him, so that a corresponding success was not lacking. But he never exalted himself, and never sought positions of honor. He accepted them only when it was demanded of him. The thrift practiced in his parental home remained characteristic of him; unnecessary extravagance roused his anger. But on the proper occasions he avoided no expenditures. He reared his children in the same spirit, and was able to see the blessing derived from it in his children and children's children, and beyond." (*Gem.-Kal.* 1900, 43-57; *ML* I, 273.)   H.vdS.

Bronson, a town in southern Michigan, was the location of the now extinct Pleasant Hill Mennonite Church (MC) of the Indiana-Michigan Mennonite Conference. The United Missionary Church has a congregation known as Pleasant Hill five miles southwest of the town.   M.G.

Brook Lane Farm, a hospital near Hagerstown, Md., owned and operated by the Mennonite Central Committee for the benefit of patients requiring immediate relief from acute emotional or mental disturbance. The idea of Brook Lane Farm grew out of the experiences of Mennonite young people who worked in mental hospitals during the World War II period, and so on a farm used by a Civilian Public Service unit during the war, the MCC opened this hospital in 1948, which it owns and

operates. With semiprivate rooms for 29 active treatment and observation patients, the average number of patients for 1953 was 25.†   M.G.

Bröskerfelde, a part of the village of Bröske, district of Marienburg, West Prussia, became important in Mennonite history by the establishment of a patrons' school (*Vereinsschule*) founded on Christian principles in 1836 and its successful conduct for 30 years. A missionary society was formed in the 1830's among the members of the Mennonite churches in Ladekopp and the vicinity, which was a branch of the Danzig Missionary Society, whose center was located in the old city of Danzig, where the society held its annual missionary festival in the Marienkirche, which was also attended by representatives of the Bröskerfelde Hilfsverein (branch society).

On the governing board of the Danzig Missionary Society, in addition to the pastors Karmann, Blech, Kniewel, and others was also Jakob Mannhardt, pastor of the Danzig Mennonite Church from 1836 to 1885, and founder of the *Mennonitische Blätter*. In addition to the newly awakened missionary spirit, the local society also recognized the necessity for offering Mennonite youth a Christian education; this led to the establishment of the school mentioned above. Of these endeavors Johann Töws, the widely known and respected preacher and elder of the Ladekopp congregation, is properly considered the soul and inspiration; he donated the site for the school as well as for the grounds. The first teacher was Friedrich Wilhelm Lange of the Brenkenhoffswalde (*q.v.*) Mennonite congregation, who later became very well known in Mennonite circles. Under his intelligent direction the school quickly became a center for implanting genuine Christianity. Students from far and near in the churches of West Prussia attended his sterling instruction. Unfortunately after two years Lange went to the Molotschna in South Russia. He was succeeded in 1838 or 1839 by Karl Gottlieb Roller, a teacher in Bütow, Pomerania, who faithfully devoted himself to his task for nearly 20 years. The seed scattered here bore much fruit; for a considerable number of his pupils later became consecrated preachers. The curriculum, with the exception of the daily classes in religion and Bible study, resembled that of a German higher elementary school. When Roller resigned for reasons of health, a young Reich of Danzig was appointed to succeed him; but he instead went to the teachers' seminary in Marienburg in 1862. In the same year Johannes Claassen (*q.v.*), who had studied at the university of Berlin for several years, was employed as teacher. He served until the spring of 1866. During his term the school enjoyed another period of prosperity, with an enrollment of 60. As long as Claassen was teacher the monthly missionary meetings were held in the school. After the older generation, who had been deeply concerned in matters pertaining to the kingdom of God, had emigrated to Russia or America, the school gradually died out, presumably for lack of interest. The building was temporarily rented out and about 1880 sold and torn down. (*ML* I, 274.)   J.E.

Brotherhood (Dutch, *broederschap*). The concept of the church as a brotherhood, a central idea in Anabaptism, is discussed under **Church.** See also **Mutual Aid.** Recently many American Mennonite congregations have organized men's brotherhoods (*q.v.*). (See also **Bruderschaft.**)   H.S.B.

Brotherhood Mutual Insurance Company was organized in 1917 under the name, the Brotherhood Aid Association of the Defenseless Mennonite Conference. Nine directors chosen from the various churches of the conference formed the board of directors of the association which was formed to give protection in case of fire or storm losses to its members. Coverage was later extended to members of other church bodies. By 1935 the organization was changed to a legal mutual insurance company and formed independent of conference direction in order to comply with state and federal regulations. Until 1939 the central office was located at Grabill, Ind.; in that year it was moved to Fort Wayne, Ind. Insurance in force in 1950 is over $66,000,000, extended principally to policy holders in the states of Indiana, Illinois, Michigan, and Ohio. In addition to fire and storm coverage, the company now offers health, accident, and life insurance. J.H.S.

Brötli, Johannes (also called Panicellus), originally from Grisons, once a pastor at Quarten, moved to the vicinity of Zürich as an assistant preacher in Zollikon, and instructed the peasants in the Gospel, "following Paul's example, not living on tithes and offerings, but by the work of his hands" (Cornelius II, 17); preacher in Zollikon (canton of Zürich), who joined the Anabaptist movement immediately after its inception. He was one of the signatories of the second letter of the Swiss Brethren to Thomas Müntzer of Sept. 5, 1524. On account of a quarrel with the assistant at the Grossmünster he was questioned by the city council, Dec. 21, 1524. On the day after the first Anabaptist disputation (Jan. 17, 1525) he was expelled from the city and canton of Zürich, and went to Hallau in the canton of Schaffhausen. On April 4, 1525, the city council sent a letter to Schaffhausen, warning the authorities against Brötli, stating that he had by his rejection of infant baptism and introduction of rebaptism misled the poor, simple populace and created a noticeable restlessness in the city and canton, which, if it had not been suppressed, might have led to the abolition of all government; they had therefore banished Brötli from the city's jurisdiction with Wilhelm Reublin, Ludwig Haetzer, and Andreas Castelberger on Jan. 21, 1525, and did not want to conceal this from the Schaffhausen authorities, for they had heard that three persons had gone to Hallau behind their backs to testify that Brötli had conducted himself honorably in Zürich (Stähelin, *Briefe* I, 344). From Hallau Brötli sent two epistles to his former congregation in Zollikon in February and March of 1525 (published in Füsslin I, 201-27).

With Reublin, Brötli worked in Hallau with great success for the Anabaptist movement. Nearly the entire community was baptized and protected its preacher from the council in Schaffhausen. They were supported by Waldshut. But when the latter city passed into Austrian hands the Swiss Brethren were also suppressed in Hallau. Most of them fled. Of Brötli it is asserted (*Mart. Mir.* D 17, E 427) that he was burned at the stake in 1528 (he is called Hans Pretle here; see Füsslin I, 201, note). Details of his death are unfortunately not given.   NEFF.

C. A. Cornelius, *Gesch. des Münsterischen Aufruhrs* II (Leipzig, 1860) 17; E. Egli, *Die Züricher Wiedertäufer zur Reformationszeit* (Zürich, 1878); J. Füsslin, *Beyträge zur Erläuterung der Kirchenreformationsgeschichten des Schweitzerlandes,* 5 vv. (Zürich, 1741-53); E. Stähelin, *Briefe und Akten zum Leben Oekolampads* I (Leipzig, 1927); idem, *Zwingli* I, 473 ff.; J. Zimmermann, *Thomas Münzer* (Berlin, 1925) 150; *ML* I, 275.

Brouwer, Jacob Hendriks, was a preacher in the Noorderkaai congregation at Blokzijl (*q.v.*). He sought financial support in the Amsterdam congregation for himself and two of his members when he was arrested and had further difficulties on account of his booklet, *Onderwijs naer den wegh ten Hemel* (1698), being charged with Socinianism (letter of March 26, 1707; *Inv. Arch. Amst.* II, No. 1548).   VDZ.

Brouwer, Jan, a Dutch Mennonite preacher, b. April 20, 1760, at Franeker, studied at the Mennonite seminary in Amsterdam, was called as ministerial candidate to Leeuwarden in 1785, where he remained in active service until 1822 (d. April 11, 1838), and earned general respect. He was an early member of the council of the Algemeene Doopsgezinde Sociëteit (1811), and did outstanding work in the field of philosophy. Three times he received the gold medal of the Teyler's *Godgeleerd Genootschap* and twice the silver medal. The following are some of his works: *Redevoering bij gelegenheid van het Nationaal Feest,* 19 Dec. 1799 (Leeuwarden, 1800); *25-jarige leerrede over de onveranderlijkheid der leere van en aangaande Jezus Christus* (Leeuwarden, 1810); *Dankrede wegens den vrede, uitgesproken 20. Juli 1814; Leerrede op het derde eeuwfeest der Kerkhervorming* (Leeuwarden, 1818). In 1797 he was engaged in a pen battle with the Reformed preacher E. Kist on the statement in the Heidelberg catechism, "We are inclined by nature to hate God and our neighbor." He was known as a man of great achievement, capable and well educated, a good theologian, in short, a man of importance. (*Biogr. Wb.* I, 648-50; *Catalogus Amst.,* 44, 253, 293, 311, 319; *DJ* 1837, 120 f.; III, 1850, 143; *ML* I, 275.) J.L.

Brouwer, Jelle, b. at Franeker about 1725; in 1749 ministerial candidate, then preacher in Cleve, Germany, chosen with the approval of the church council of the Mennonite congregation in Amsterdam, from Jan. 1, 1750, to his death, Jan. 9, 1782. He delivered the funeral address for Abraham Alders, preacher at Goch, which was published in 1774. He was succeeded by his son Pieter Brouwer (*q.v.*). (*Catalogus Amst.,* 253.)   VDZ.

Brouwer, Pieter, b. April 26, 1758, at Cleve, d. Sept. 22, 1832, at Utrecht. He was the son of Jelle Brouwer (*q.v.*), was educated at the Mennonite Seminary at Amsterdam and served as pastor in the congregations of Enschede, 1781-82, Cleve, 1782-86, and Utrecht, 1786-1828.   VDZ.

Brouwer, Pieter, b. Oct. 20, 1820, at Utrecht, d. Jan. 15, 1894, son of the above Pieter Brouwer, studied at the Mennonite Seminary, was a pastor of the Dutch Mennonite churches of Gorredijk and Lippenhuizen 1844-57, Warns 1857-63, and Aalsmeer 1863-68. He published *Korte Belijdenis des Geloofs* (1st ed. 1850, 5th ed., n.d., 1889); *Leerredenen (gehouden te Aalsmeer 1870-74)* (Amsterdam, 1898), and two papers on catechetical instruction in *Geloof en Vrijheid* (1891 and 1893). (*DB* 1894, 169; *De Zondagsbode,* Jan. 21 and 28, 1894; *Catalogus Amst.,* 317, 327, 328.) vDZ.

Brouwer, Wytze Jeens, a Mennonite preacher, who served the congregation of Heerenveen-Knijpe (Dutch province of Friesland) in 1736-38 and 1743-72, when he retired. Brouwer was a Collegiant (*q.v.*) as well as his colleagues in the congregation, Wybe Pieters Zeeman and Pieke Tjommes (*q.v.*). At the Frisian Reformed Synod of Zevenwolden in 1738 these three preachers were accused of teaching Socinian (*q.v.*) doctrines. On Sept. 3, 1738, the governor of Schoterland forbade them to preach and to give religious instruction, and on June 5, 1739, Brouwer and Pieke Tjommes were suspended from their ministry by the States of Friesland, Zeeman being permitted to preach again. On April 25, 1743, Brouwer and Pieke Tjommes were allowed to resume their services. vDZ.

P. H. Veen, *De Doopsgezinden in Schoterland* (Leeuwarden, 1869) 34-35, 42, 65-75, 165, 167-72.

Brouwershaven, a village in the Dutch province of Zeeland, where there was once a Mennonite congregation. The martyr Valerius de Schoolmeester came from this town. The congregation belonged to the Flemish branch. Delegates from this congregation were present at the Flemish conference at Haarlem in 1649. The congregation had no minister at the time. Later the congregation chose to join the Lamist side. In September 1694 the congregation collected 66 guilders for the brethren in the Palatinate. About 1750 the few remaining members united with the congregation at Zierikzee (*q.v.*), (Blaupot t.C., *Holland* I, 330, 342; II, 42; *Inv. Arch. Amst.* II, Nos. 1267 f., 1609; *DB* 1907, 169; 1908, 14.) vDZ.

Brown City United Missionary Church was the first church to be built in the Michigan Conference. It was dedicated Nov. 22, 1885, Bernhard Kreutziger being the first pastor. Destroyed by fire in 1894, a new site was procured and the present brick church was built the following year under Ebenezer Anthony. The first Michigan annual conference met here in April 1897. Altogether 20 annual conferences have been held in this church and two General Conferences (1908 and 1924). In 1952 there were 138 members, the pastor since 1946 being H. L. Matteson. E.R.S.

Browne, Robert (1550-1636), of Tolethorpe in Rutland County, England. He is the father of the idea of Independentism, i.e., a religion independent of the state, which became reality in England in Congregationalism. He possessed a passionate, impulsive nature of rare gifts, and was descended from a respected family. At first he was a clergyman in the state church, and then joined the Puritans. Under his leading the first Separatist church arose in Norwich in 1580.

The ideas defended by Browne, such as the independence of the church from the state and the selection of preachers from the congregation, are related to Anabaptist principles. He himself declared that he and his followers were called Anabaptists. Perhaps he had connections with the Dutch who were then staying in Norwich and were later condemned as Anabaptists. Complete independence from them is impossible. Without doubt the Dutch colony in Norwich had great influence upon the establishing of the first Congregationalist church, and Browne must have borrowed his ideas from Anabaptism. His motto was no longer a purification of the church but a separation from it; i.e., the separation of religious matters from state control. With clearness of principle and fiery progagandistic zeal he presented these modern ideas in his preaching and writing. In the fall of 1581 he emigrated to Middelburg, Dutch province of Zeeland, with his little congregation, but returned in 1583 after much strife.

This was the end of his historic career. He was reconciled with the state church. In the village Achurch (bishopric of Peterborough) he lived 40 years longer. His apparently characterless submission to the state church, although he held the same ideas as before, is explained by the fact that after his imprisonment in 1585 he was mentally abnormal. E.M.TC.

C. Burrage, *The True Story of Robert Browne* (London, 1906); Powicke, *Robert Browne* (London, 1910); C. Burrage, "Robert Browne and the First English Congregational Church," in *The Early English Dissenters* I (London, 1912) 94-117; J. G. de Hoop Scheffer and W. E. Griffis, *Hist. of the Free Churchmen* (Ithaca, 1922); W. B. Selbie, "Robert Browne and the Brownists," Chap. II in *Congregationalism* (London, 1927); *ML* I, 275.

Brownists. This group, named after Robert Browne (*q.v.*), which had many contacts with the English Anabaptists and Dutch Mennonites, formed a number of independent churches in England and Holland, after Browne himself had returned to the English state church in 1586. For this reason they usually avoided the name of Brownists. They increased rapidly: in 1592 they are said to have numbered 20,000 members in England. From 1592 to 1597 they were subjected to severe persecution. On April 6, 1593, Barrowe and John Greenwood were put to death, and on May 29, 1593, John Penry, all charged with high treason. Penry penned a farewell letter to his congregation, in which among other things he wrote: "And my good brethren, seeing banishment with loss of goods is likely to betide you all, prepare yourselves for this hard entreaty, and rejoice that you are made worthy for Christ's cause to suffer and bear all these things. And I beseech you, in the bowels of Jesus Christ, that none of you in this case look upon his particular estate, but regard the general state of the church of God, that the same may go and be kept together, whithersoever it shall please God to send you." In this letter we have the first intimation of emigration. Many brethren fled to Holland, of whom a number eventually returned. In 1611 two other members of this church suffered martyrdom, when Bartholomew Legate and Edward Wightman were arrested and after a long imprisonment burned at the stake in London, on March 18 and April 11, 1612, respectively. The Brownists were not Mennonites; their church leaders both in England and Holland, such as Francis Johnson, Henry Ainsworth, Thomas Helwys, Leonard Busher, John Murton, emphatically refused to join the Mennonite Church. But they were usually on good terms with the Mennonites, and many of the Brownist churches in England and Holland, which were sometimes called Anabaptists or even Mennonites, rejected infant baptism and adopted the practice of baptizing adults. On Nov. 12, 1626, five "Anabaptist" churches of England, viz., London, Lincoln, Sarum, Coventry, and Tyverton, wrote a letter to Hans de Ries (*q.v.*) and other leaders of the Waterlander Mennonites in Amsterdam with the object of forming a union with them. This letter, written in the name of 150 Anabaptists, was delivered in Amsterdam personally by two deputies of "high rank." But the union between the English Brownists and the Dutch Mennonites was not established. The fact that the Brownists had sworn an oath of allegiance to the king seems to have been a drawback to de Ries and other leaders. As early as 1624 and 1625 there had been some correspondence between Hans de Ries and Elias Tookey, an Anabaptist (Brownist) from London, on the subject of the use of the oath under certain circumstances. In any case the matter of union was dropped because there were "too large differences in the doctrines," as de Ries states (J. Dyserinck, 14-17).

In England most of the Brownist churches, each independent of the other, were absorbed in the general movement of Independentism during the early 17th century, while also many Brownists joined the Baptist churches or the Quakers.

In Amsterdam, where many Brownist refugees sought safety (in 1608 alone three or four hundred souls from Scrooby fled to Amsterdam), they had in the late 16th and the early 17th centuries four or five Brownist congregations, which were all independent of each other; that of Johnson and Ainsworth (*q.v.*) since 1593; that of John Smyth (*q.v.*), which united in 1615 with the Mennonites (Waterlanders), since 1606; that of John Robinson since 1608; that of Thomas Helwys since 1609, and maybe still another one, of which Leonard Busher (*q.v.*) was the leader. All of these groups disappeared soon, because their members returned to England, but the oldest group, though steadily decreasing, existed in Amsterdam until 1701. At that time the congregation had five members, four of whom joined the English Reformed Church in Amsterdam. vnZ.

J. G. de Hoop Scheffer and W. E. Griffis, *Hist. of the Free Churchmen* (Ithaca, 1922); W. B. Selbie, *Congregationalism* (London, 1927) Chap. II, "Robert Browne and the Brownists"; J. Dyserinck, *De Vrijstelling van den Eed voor Doopsgezinden* (Haarlem, 1883).

Brubacher (Brubacker, Brubaker, Brubaher, Brupacher), a Swiss Mennonite family name from the canton of Zürich. One of the converts of Blaurock (*q.v.*) was a certain Hans Brubacher of Zumikon,

canton of Zürich. Another Hans Brubacher emigrated to Lancaster Co., Pa., about the year 1710. The family genealogist, Jacob N. Brubacher, says that Hans came from Switzerland. It is indeed certain that the family is Swiss, but the writer gives no proof of his assertion that the immigrant himself came immediately from Switzerland. Immigrant Hans settled on 500 acres of land along the Little Conestoga in West Hempfield Township, Lancaster County, and there built a grist- and sawmill. Of the nine sons and one daughter, all remained in Lancaster County except Abraham who settled in Virginia. The family has provided much leadership for the Lancaster Mennonite Conference; the following served as bishops: Abraham Brubaker (1731-1811), his son Abraham (1774-1850), Jacob (1751-1831), John (1795-1870), Jacob N. Brubacher (1838-1913), and Isaac H. Brubaker (1858-1933). Of these leaders, by far the most influential was Jacob N. Brubacher (*q.v.*), author of the genealogy, bishop for 46 years, and moderator of the Lancaster Conference for over 25 years. Brubacher was perhaps the strongest leader in the Lancaster Conference during the last hundred years or more.

The Brubaker family is now found mainly in Pennsylvania, Virginia, Ontario, Ohio, Indiana, Illinois, and Missouri. J.C.W.

J. N. Brubacher, *The Brubacher Genealogy in America* (Elkhart, 1884); Daniel Kauffman, *Mennonite Cyclopedic Dictionary* (Scottdale, 1937).

Brubacher, Daniel M. (1840-1921), was ordained preacher in 1876 for the New Conestoga Meetinghouse (OOM), Woolwich Twp., Waterloo Co., Ont. In 1909 he withdrew from the Wisler (Martinite) group and worshiped with the dissident group in private houses. At one time he lived with a group at Brutus, Mich., but when these were scattered, he returned to Ontario. There he joined forces with the two David Martins in 1917. He ordained his son Menno as minister, broke with the David Martin group later, and died in 1921 with but a few adherents. I.D.L.

Brubacher, Hans, an Anabaptist from Zumikon in the canton of Zürich, who was seized early in 1530 in the Zürich Unterland and cross-examined with others. His statements offer an interesting insight into the faith of the Swiss Brethren of that period. Among other things he confessed: "Since Christ has forbidden the killing of anyone, both in the old law, the Ten Commandments, and in the Gospel, a government with a Christian mind cannot kill either thieves or murderers; but according to the words of Paul, it should put these into prison until they have been taught. Furthermore, Christ said yea should be yea, and nay, nay; since we can do or have nothing of ourselves but are dearly bought, we should live thus toward each other: what one has consented to in loyalty or faith, that he should do in deeds, and not swear an oath. He has heard, been taught, and believes that the preachers of the day have never explained the Holy Scriptures and Divine Word correctly, nor correctly presented to the Christians the cup of Christ with the blood even to this day . . . and have not properly declared to the simple populace the Holy Spirit and His work, and where life comes from and much more that Christians must know." (E. Egli, *Die Züricher Wiedertäufer zur Reformationszeit,* Zürich, 1878, 88 f.) Nothing more is known of him. (*ML* I, 276.)   NEFF.

Brubacher, Heinrich, was born in Einsiedel (Lemberg) in Galicia, then Austria, now USSR, in 1806. The village was founded by Mennonites of the Palatinate who had been invited to settle in Galicia by Joseph II in 1784. At that time Heinrich's grandfather, Tobias Brubacher, born in Albersheim in the Nassau-Weilburg district, took over farm number two in the village. In 1795 his son Philipp married Susanna Rubin; Heinrich was the third child and only son of this union. He attended the village school and then took over his father's farm. His marriage to Elisabeth Klein in 1826 was blessed with four daughters. Upon the death of his wife in 1843, he married Elisabeth Schmalenberg. In 1837 Heinrich Brubacher was ordained to the ministry and in 1845 to the eldership in Einsiedel. In 1858 he gave farm number two to his youngest son-in-law and took over farm number four. In 1871 he emigrated to the daughter colony at Dobrovlany near Strij, which his son-in-law Peter Müller had established the year before. Heinrich settled on the farm called Stary Dvor. He continued to serve as elder in the new settlement and died in 1893 at the age of 87.   Wa.K.

P. Bachman, *1784-1934 Mennoniten in Kleinpolen, Gedenkbuch zur Erinnerung an die Einwanderung der Mennoniten nach Kleinpolen (Galizien) vor 150 Jahren* (Lemberg, 1934). This book contains the genealogies of the Mennonite families in Galicia.

Brubacher, Jacob N. (1838-1913), leading Lancaster Conference bishop in the last half of the 19th century, whose name became a household word in Mennonite (MC) homes in Lancaster Co., Pa. His 46 years as bishop in his district and 25 years as moderator of Lancaster Mennonite Conference gave him a large place in the counsels of the church and the affections of his people. He was born on a farm near Mount Joy, Pa., July 25, 1838, the son of Sem and Magdalena (Nissley) Brubacher, and died near the place of his birth, Oct. 9, 1913. On Nov. 1, 1857, he was married to Barbara Stauffer. They began farming on the farm where he was born.

Brubacher lived through the years when Sunday schools were first accepted in his conference, and in this he was a pioneer. In 1862 he took a carload of fat cattle to the Philadelphia market. Arriving too late to sell them, he remained over Sunday, and while there he attended an Episcopal Sunday school. He was so impressed with the import of this kind of instruction that he returned home and sought to enlist others to undertake this new type of work. A year later he opened the first Sunday school in the Lancaster Conference in the Pike schoolhouse near his home in June 1863. This did not have official church approval and so met considerable criticism. When he was ordained to the ministry in 1865 in his home congregation at Landisville he closed the school because of this criticism. But his efforts during these few years certainly helped to pave the way for the approval of Sunday schools by the conference in 1872. In

1876 Brubacher organized the first official Sunday school in the conference in his home congregation at Landisville and became its first superintendent.

On Dec. 25, 1867, Brubacher was ordained bishop and during the 46 years he served as bishop he stamped his personality on his churches. He was a good executive. He never had more than a grade school education but he was well read and a good expositor of the Bible. He is well remembered by his practice of reading his text, then closing his Bible and proceeding with his message without opening his Bible again or using notes.

He was a lover of good singing. His comments on hymns and their singing were a worth-while contribution to the singing of the congregation. He devoted much time to visitation work; his visits were usually short. From this practice it became a common saying when someone made a short visit to call it a "Jacob's visit." He is known as the strong man of the conference. His keen intellect and good knowledge of the Word and his forceful personality made room for him. He was a strict disciplinarian. He is still quoted more often than any other man of the conference, and to this day his influence is still felt in his bishop district and in his conference.

Brubacher was well known beyond the Lancaster Conference borders. God gave him a robust body and he used it to serve his Lord and his church far and wide. He assisted in the organization of Southwestern Pennsylvania Conference and also in the work of the Franklin Co., Pa.-Washington Co., Md. Conference. (I. D. Landis, "The Life and Work of Jacob N. Brubacher," *Menn. Hist. Bulletin* II, 1, April, 1941.)   H.F.G.

Brubacher Mennonite Church (MC), now extinct, once located between Five Points and Paradise Hill in Richland Co., Ohio (after 1840, Ashland Co.), founded about 1820 by families from Lancaster Co., Pa., soon joined by Swiss immigrants (Nussbaum and Imhoff) and after 1830 by the Palatines, Risser, Beutler, and Hartman. Early ministers seem to have been John Kauffman and Christian Kauffman, the latter a deacon; John Nussbaum and Joseph Freed (according to tradition ordained on the same day) before 1830; Isaac Kilmer who moved from Juniata Co., Pa.; the Palatines, John Risser and Jacob Beutler, and apparently somewhat later John Hartman. The group was served by Bishop Jacob Nold, of Columbiana Co., Ohio, who seems to have ordained Kilmer bishop after 1830.

The congregation built a meetinghouse near Five Points and somewhat later another at Pleasant Ridge five miles east and southeast. The congregation lost a minister and a number of members to the River Brethren who founded Chestnut Grove and Forest Grove near Five Points about 1840. Beutler moved to Mahaska Co., Iowa; Nussbaum to Elkhart Co., Ind.; Freed and Kilmer to western Richland and eastern Crawford counties, Ohio. Risser helped found the General Conference congregation south of Ashland after most of his family united with the Presbyterian Church.

Members of the congregation scattered, some moving to Ohio counties farther west, some to

Indiana, Illinois, Iowa, Kansas, and Oklahoma. When the Wisler (OOM) schism developed about 1870 the few remaining members divided, a few following Imhoff who finally joined the Wisler congregation in Chester Township, Wayne County. After 1880 the Pleasant Ridge and the General Conference congregations dissolved and the remaining members united with some Methodists, Presbyterians, and Reformed to organize the Stone Lutheran Church south of Ashland. This church and the Chestnut Grove Brethren in Christ Church near Five Points are in a flourishing condition. All the others are extinct.

Burial grounds are located on the old Brubacher farm near Five Points, on the Pleasant Ridge and Forest Grove sites, on the grounds of the former General Conference Church, the cemetery near Olivesburg, and the Ohl cemetery southwest of Ashland. J.S.U.

Brubaker, John K., b. March 8, 1844, near Rohrerstown, Lancaster Co., Pa., the son of Jacob Brubaker (1816-68), of the sixth generation of pioneer John (d. 1748), who settled west of Lancaster. His profession was veterinary medicine. He was called to the ministry at Millersville, Pa., on Nov. 8, 1879. Brubaker preached English, when only two others in the conference, Amos Herr and Isaac Eby, used that language. For this reason he was called for funerals both within and without the Mennonite Church, near and afar. He saw Sunday school opened at his meetinghouses in '87 and '96, and a new church built at Rohrerstown in '95. He was interested in evangelistic meetings long before his brethren. From March 14 to July 22, 1896, he and J. S. Lehman made an evangelistic trip to Alaska, visiting many small congregations of the West. He held meetings for two or three weeks in Lagrange Co., Ind., and in Wayne Co., Ohio. After a five weeks' illness he died in 1898 at the age of 54 and was buried at Brubaker's cemetery near Rohrerstown. I.D.L.

Brubaker Schoolhouse in eastern Snyder Co., Pa., was the second meeting place for the Graybill (present Cross Roads) congregation (Lancaster Mennonite Conference) during the early 1880's. Samuel Winey was the bishop, Thomas and Solomon Graybill the ministers, and Abel Shirk and John Overholtzer the deacons. Services were held here every four weeks. This congregation in 1890 built the Susquehanna meetinghouse in 1890, where they still worship. I.D.L.

Brubaker's Mennonite Meetinghouse (MC) was located a mile north of Rohrerstown, Lancaster Co., Pa. The Abbeyville congregation moved its worship to this location in 1792, where a beautiful cemetery still marks the site. Here Bishop Jacob Brubaker, a moderator of Lancaster Conference, preached. This meetinghouse was replaced by a larger church in 1854, which served until 1895, when the congregation built a new church in Rohrerstown. I.D.L.

Bruce County, Ont., extinct Mennonite congregations include the Port Elgin Church located near Port Elgin in Saugeen Township. Several Men-

nonite (MC) families left Waterloo County in 1854 and located in this area. Within four years a congregation was organized and Solomon Eby was ordained as minister and his father, Martin Eby, as deacon. The first meetinghouse was built at Port Elgin in 1861 on a farm near the lake. The congregation was a part of the Mennonite Conference of Ontario until 1868, when Eby, with most of the members, left the conference and began a movement which resulted in the Ontario wing of the Mennonite Brethren in Christ Church (now UMC). After this, services were held in the homes with ministers supplied from Waterloo County. From 1876 communion services were provided twice a year at one or another of the homes which were located in the two townships of Culross and Brant, which were accordingly listed in the Meeting Calendar of the Ontario Conference as preaching places. In 1876 communion was held on three successive days beginning with Sunday at Port Elgin, Hanover, and Culross, and this arrangement was followed twice a year for three years; then continued for Hanover (*q.v.*) and Port Elgin in this regular order until 1901. At the beginning of the new century services were discontinued because some families returned to Waterloo County and others were absorbed in the M.B.C. and German Lutheran churches in that neighborhood. Among families in these upper townships were the names of Schwartz, Reier, Bergey, Dirstien, and Haase. (See **Elmwood.**) J.C.F.

Bruce Peninsula United Missionary Church, located 45 miles north of Owen Sound in Ontario, was established in 1885. The first meetinghouse was built in 1904. In 1950 the membership was 37. M.G.

Bruch, Klaus, a citizen of Strasbourg (Alsace) in whose house an Anabaptist meeting was broken up early in 1529. The worshipers were arrested and were subjected to several cross-examinations using torture. (T. Röhrich, *Ztscht für die hist. Theol.*, 1860, 48; *ML* I, 276.) HEGE.

Bruchhausen, a hamlet in the district of Heidelberg (Baden), belonged to the monastery Schönau from 1152 to the 16th century, when it was transferred to the domain of the Palatinate, and with its 800 acres of cultivated land and 500 acres of meadow, was one of the five largest estates in the Palatinate (*Ztscht für die Gesch. des Oberrheins,* 1854, 45). After the Thirty Years' War some Mennonite families expelled from Switzerland were accepted here. The oldest list, found in the State Archives at Karlsruhe, enumerates in 1716 the following heads of families: Melchior Fellmann, H. Jakob Schneider, and H. Jakob Hackmann (Bachmann?); a list of July 13, 1743, names Joh. Bühlher, Melchior Haury, Melchior Fellmann's widow, Jakob Fellmann's widow, and Hans Bachmann's widow; a list of 1759 names Wilhelm Eschelmann, Jos. Graf, Isaak Berky, Jos. Bühler, J. Bachmann, and Michael Neukommer. They belonged to the Mennonite congregation of Rohrhof (Schwetzingen district), which according to a church record of 1731 was served by Jakob Fellmann and Melchior Fellmann of Bruchhausen (Müller, *Berner Täufer,*

211). At the beginning of the 19th century meetings were also held in Bruchhausen, where there were more Mennonites than at Rohrhof; in 1829 35 Mennonites lived in Bruchhausen, and only 22 in Rohrhof. After 1840 only Bruchhausen is listed as a congregation. Because of emigration it declined rapidly and was dissolved in 1888. Its last preacher and elder was Johannes Neff, who died Sept. 8, 1891. (*ML* I, 276.) HEGE.

Bruchhäuserhof, once the seat of a Mennonite congregation numbering 130 souls. (See **Bruchhausen**; *DJ* 1840, 77.)

Bruchsal, a district in Baden, Karlsruhe area. In this territory, most of which belonged to the bishopric of Speyer in the Reformation period, Anabaptism had gained a footing early in the second quarter of the 16th century. The town of Bruchsal was the center of the South German Anabaptists. Here a large congregation quietly developed, from which the doctrine spread into the neighboring parts of the Palatinate.

The first preacher seems to have been Philip Plener (also called Weber), who came originally either from Strasbourg or Bruchsal, and who preached the Gospel with great success in this region in 1527. He apparently did not stay here long; for we meet him soon afterward near Heidelberg, where he was also very successful. In Bruchsal he had won a zealous companion in Blasius Kuhn, who traveled from place to place, preaching and baptizing. Leadership of the Bruchsal congregation, which in 1530 numbered 500, was assumed by Julius Lober from Zürich. The rapid increase in membership could not remain concealed from the clergy. In 1529 the bishopric of Bruchsal complained about it to the bishop of Speyer. With very severe measures the episcopal officials attacked the brotherhood. No details have been handed down about the persecution they introduced; but the brief notices of the court records indicate that the congregation was harshly suppressed. In 1531 five Anabaptists suffered a martyr's death (Beck, 311). Many members fled, most of them under the leadership of Blasius Kuhn to Auspitz in Moravia into the church of their former preacher Philip Plener (Beck, 71). A part of the Bruchsal congregation wished to return to their old home when persecution set in in Moravia, but were seized at Passau, Sept. 14, 1535. The records of the trials list from Bruchsal Michael Khumbauf, widow Barbara, Apollonia and Hans Fuchs, all baptized by Philip Plener; Gertraut Treytl (Michael Schneider's wife), baptized by Julius Lober; Anna (wife of Michel of Bruchsal), baptized by Konrad Scheid; and Anna of Durlach (Hans Steuber's wife), baptized by Hans Kellner (Wolkan, 30). They were fellow prisoners in the castle dungeon at Passau with the Anabaptists who laid the foundation of the *Ausbund* (*q.v.*) with the hymns they wrote here.

In the town of Bruchsal there were traces of Anabaptists until 1545 in spite of sharp watchfulness. In the adjacent villages the movement was also felt early. In Oberöwisheim they had a large following; the manager reported in 1531 that they held meetings there and asked for regulations to deal

with them. In February 1532 some Anabaptists were thereupon arrested, and their devotional literature taken away. They were thrown into prison and placed into the stocks, freezing their feet in the cold. Their property was confiscated and their children were forcibly baptized (Bossert, 84).

In the neighboring Zeutern 12 men and women were captured in April 1531 and taken to Kislau (now a police house of correction) with their spokesman Michael N. They were so thoroughly convinced of the truth of their faith, that all attempts of the clergy to convert them failed and threats of punishment did not move them. The expectation of the imminent return of Christ had filled them with such hope, that Michael N. declared to the cathedral preacher Dr. Gro of Speyer, "though he or more of them were to be killed, the Anabaptist cause would not be eradicated; for it was so widespread and so numerous that it would be impossible to wipe it out" (Bossert, 79). Another prisoner at Kislau declined to recant, but offered to emigrate. If they refused to permit this he would suffer death (Bossert, 84). There were also some Anabaptists in Mingolsheim and Heidelsheim at this time; the latter village was the home of Wendel Metzger, who was a very active preacher in the vicinity of Bruchsal about 1539.

About the middle of the 16th century the Anabaptist movement in the region of the present Bruchsal district was totally suppressed; it was not revived even in the time of toleration. Recently some isolated Mennonite families settled there (see **Baden**). According to the census of Dec. 1, 1910, there were 16 Mennonites in the district, six of them in Waghäusel and two in Bruchsal. HEGE.

Beck, *Geschichts-Bücher*; *Beiträge zur Statistik des Grossherzogtums Baden*, No. 63, p. 148; G. Bossert, "Beiträge z. badisch-pfälz. Ref.-Gesch.," in *Ztschr. f.d. Gesch. d. Oberrheins* LIX (1904) 71-88; Wolkan, *Lieder*; *ML* I, 277.

Bruck, seat of the district government in Styria (Austria), where the Anabaptist movement became widespread in the 16th century. Here nine men and three women were martyred in 1528. It was a moving tragedy that was played here. While the Brethren were bound and led to the place of execution, they were undismayed and said, "Today we will suffer at this place for the sake of God's Word and offer Him our sacrifice." They appealed earnestly to the conscience of the councilors of Bruck, warning them against shedding innocent blood. The youngest wished to be the first to receive the death blow. The chronicle says, "They were undismayed and it was wonderful to see how cheerfully they shed their blood." The three sisters likewise went to their death by drowning with joyful hearts. Some considered their steadfastness as the work of the devil, but others were moved to exclaim, "God must be doing this; otherwise it would not be possible." The song, "Nun wollen wir aber singen jetzt und zu dieser Frist" (16 stanzas), deals with this execution. It is found in Wackernagel, *Kirchenlied* III, 467, and in the *Lieder der Hutterischen Brüder* (Scottdale, 1914) 25. HEGE.

J. Loserth, "Wiedertäufer in Steiermark," in *Mittei-

lungen des hist. Vereins zu Steiermark LXII (Graz, 1894) 125; Beck, *Geschichts-Bücher,* 68; ML I, 277.

Bruck, Johann von (or Jan van Bruggen), pseudonym adopted by David Joris (*q.v.*), under which he lived in Basel from 1544 until his death in 1556. The von Bruck family, descendants of David Joris' oldest son Georg (Jörg), lived in Basel until 1750, when the last male descendant, the saddler Johann Jakob von Bruck, died there May 30. (P. Burckhardt, *David Joris und seine Gemeinde in Basel,* 1949, reprint, 105-96.) vDZ.

Brücke, Die, Mennonite news periodical of Brazil, published privately May 1932 to June 1937, first by Peter J. Klassen and Heinrich Martins, then after June 1933 by Klassen alone, as an 8-page bimonthly; then beginning January 1935, as a monthly, 8 x 12 in., in 1937 changed to a 4-page 12 x 15 in. paper. Although published at Witmarsum-Hammonia, state of Santa Catarina, and therefore really the organ of the Krauel Colony, it attempted to serve all the Mennonites in Brazil. After a six-month suspension, the Krauel Colony officially took over the publication with a subsidy from Germany, with Heinrich Martins as editor, making it an 8-page 8 x 12 in. monthly again, beginning in January 1938 under the name *Die neue Brücke.* Publication ceased with the September-October 1938 16-page double number. Until 1954 the Mennonites of Brazil have had no periodical of their own. H.S.B.

Brücke, Die neue, successor to *Die Brücke* (*q.v.*), an 8-page monthly, appeared only January-October 1938 as the organ of the Krauel Mennonite Colony, Witmarsum-Hammonia, Santa Catarina, Brazil. (See **Bibel und Pflug.**) H.S.B.

Bruckmaier, Georg (also Pruckmaier), a Hutterite martyr, was seized with two companions, Hans Aichner and Wolff Rauffer, on Wednesday after Easter in 1585 in an inn on the Geyersberg in the upper Tavern near Ried in Upper Austria (at that time Bavarian), while traveling through. The host suspected that they were Anabaptists, for they prayed before and after eating, and reported to the authorities that "there were some people like Anabaptists in his inn." They were taken to Burghausen, where another Brother, Leonhard Sumerauer (*q.v.*), had been imprisoned since the previous summer. The city parson of Burghausen and other theologians tried to make them renounce their faith, but in vain. On July 5, 1585, Sumerauer was executed. The parson's warning that their fate would be the same unless they recanted made no impression. After 14 weeks in the dungeon they joyfully met their death. On the site of execution Bruckmaier said, "Now that we must die, we die only for the sake of divine truth; for we have done evil to no man." They said farewell and were permitted to pray together. Bruckmaier was executed first, then Aichner, and finally Rauffer. The executioner was so moved by their innocence that he exclaimed, "These people have a stronger faith than I or anyone here. I would rather have killed 30 robbers than these men. God have mercy!" (Beck, 293.)

Bruckmaier is the author of several hymns: the *Jonaslied,* "Mein fröhlich Herz und auch Gemüt verursacht mich von Gottes Güt (22 stanzas), and the *Väterlied,* "Gott, du gewaltiger Herre, in deiner Majestät" (105 stanzas), which devotes several stanzas to each of the leaders of the Hutterian brotherhood and after Bruckmaier's death was continued until 1734 by unknown authors; and "Dieweil uns musst verlassen" (22 stanzas). All three were published in *Die Lieder der Hutterischen Brüder* (Scottdale, 1914) 768-85. Two additional hymns are still in the Austrian archives. His death is commemorated in a song of 44 stanzas, "Von den 5 Brüdern, die man zu Baierland gericht" (published by Th. Unger in *Jahrb. der Gesellschaft f. die Gesch. des Protestantismus in Oesterreich,* 1925, 144-54). HEGE.

Beck, *Geschichts-Bücher;* P. Dedic, *Der Protestantismus in Steiermark* (Leipzig, 1930) 14; R. Wolkan, *Lieder,* 238; Wiswedel, *Bilder* II, 159; *Mart. Mir.* D 754, E 1060; ML I, 278.

Brüder in Not, a German relief organization composed of representatives of the Red Cross, the Catholic Caritas, the Evangelical Church charity, the Labor charity, and the Mennonites, to raise funds to aid the refugees who came out of Russia in November and December 1929, most of whom were Mennonites. Prof. B. H. Unruh was the Mennonite representative. Large sums of money were raised by a united appeal, led by President Hindenburg, who contributed 50,000 marks, which were used to pay expenses for the maintenance of the refugees in the three camps at Mölln, Prenzlau, and Hammerstein, until the emigration overseas to Brazil and Paraguay was relatively completed (by August 1930). H.S.B.

Bruderfeld Mennonite Brethren Church, located six miles west of Waldheim, Sask., is a member of the Canadian Conference of the M.B. Church, and one of the very first congregations of this group in Canada. During the years 1897-99 a number of families came from Minnesota and South Dakota to pioneer in this new country. They met for worship in the various homes until 1901, when they organized a church with Isaac Neufeld as deacon and provisional leader. They also built a church, which was replaced by a 32 ft. x 66 ft. structure in 1911. The 1951 membership was 91. The church has been under the leadership of the following brethren: Peter Dyck, 1904-7; Heinrich Zimmerman, 1907-10; Elder David Dyck, 1910-22; H. A. Willems, 1922-52; H. M. Willems, 1952- . J.H.E.

Bruderhof (also called Haushaben), name for the community settlements of the Hutterites in Moravia and Slovakia, found today in similar fashion also in South Dakota and Canada. Since community of goods (*q.v.*) is one of the main principles of the Hutterian Brethren, it was quite natural that from the very beginning of their settlement in Moravia they established such "collective farms" (if it is permissible to use this modern term, forgetting for a moment the great difference in the ideology of Anabaptist communism and Soviet communism). The Bruderhofs were a unique undertaking without any model before them, yet highly successful and for that reason still today practiced among the Hutterian Brethren. These Bruderhofs were quite elaborate establishments consisting as a rule of several larger and smaller houses (one such farm in Slovakia had no fewer than 47 buildings), usually around a village common or square. The ground floor of the buildings was used for community living: dining hall, kitchen, and rooms for nursery, school, laundry, spinning, weaving, and sewing, and also for maternity rooms. The roofs (thatch mixed with clay to make them fireproof, a much-discussed invention of the Brethren) were high and steep so that the attics contained two stories of small chambers (*Stuben, Oertel*) where the married couples lived with their small children. These houses must once have distinguished themselves from the poor shacks of most of the peasants of the 16th and 17th centuries. "They have the most beautiful houses," exclaimed even the archfoe of the Brethren, the Catholic priest Christoph Andreas Fischer (*q.v.*), in 1605. A few of these houses still stand today in Slovakia. Some of the Bruderhofs in America are not unlike those of the far-off origins. A very graphic picture of these 16th-century houses may be found in a contemporary woodcut on the title page of the polemical book by Christoffer Erhard (*q.v.*), *Gründliche kurtz verfasste Historia* . . . (Munich, 1589). It shows a house with the thatched roof and two stories of windows in it, and in front of the house a man, woman, and child in the typical Hutterite garb. (This is perhaps the only original picture of the old Hutterites in existence.)

Each Bruderhof tried to be as self-sufficient as possible. It had not only its own fields, woods, ponds, mills, on the estates of the nobles, but also a great number of workshops, some of them of great renown. There were the shops of the black- and locksmiths, of the saddlers and shoemakers, of the carpenters, potters (see **Ceramics**), cutlers (*Messerschmiede,* see **Crafts**), wagonmakers, and furriers. They had also well-known breweries (the Hutterites still drink beer), and occasionally wineries. Their *Kellermeister* (both stewards of the vineyards, and of the revenues of the wineries, also keeper of the feudal wine cellars) were most in demand as masters in their field. Each household was managed by one responsible brother elected for this office, the *Diener der Notdurft,* the steward or keeper of the house. He had to purchase all that was needed—wool, cotton, and hemp, iron and other metals, wine and salt. His purchases were made with the proceeds of all the trades and crafts, and the material distributed as needed (see **Community of Goods**). He also organized the work on farm and shop, and directed everyone to his job according to the needs of the entire group. In North America the unlovely title of "boss" became the English designation for this office.

The afore-mentioned Fischer gives not only a very lively description of these community houses, but on the title pages of one of his pamphlets, entitled *Der Hutterische Taubenkobel* (1607), he has also a woodcut to illustrate his contention that the Brethren lived in these houses like doves in a dovecote. In another of his angry pamphlets, entitled *54 erhebliche Ursachen* . . . (1605), he mentions over 70 such households in southern Moravia, in each of which from 500 to 600 persons (including children) were said to be living, and in a few even as many as a thousand or more. (These statements are probably exaggerated.) He warns the authorities about the increase in number of these places, and pleads that the Brethren should not be tolerated any longer in Moravia. It was the climax of the Austrian Counter Reformation (*q.v.*); one should also keep in mind that these Bruderhofs were truly thriving, and that they were the object of much envy among the surrounding peasant-farmers. The landed nobles, however, gladly availed themselves of the unusual skill and industriousness of these "heretics."

The number of these Bruderhofs is a much-discussed theme. Loserth (*ML II,* 267) counts around 90 such settlements in Moravia, while Fischer claims but 70. F. Hruby, *Die Wiedertäufer in Mähren* (1935), is much more conservative in his well-documented estimates. He reports (for Moravia only) 21 such Bruderhofs in 1545, which number almost trebles to 57 in the "Golden Era" around 1589. Then came bad times, a Turkish War (1605) with its devastations, and the preliminaries of the Thirty Years' War, the high point of the Catholic Counter Reformation. By 1619 only 45 such collective farms are reported, and by 1622, not more than 24. The number of Bruderhofs in Slovakia is nowhere reported, but one may assume that there were hardly more than 20 altogether. Some of the buildings still stand today. (Pictures in L. Müller and in R. Friedmann; see bibliography.)

Each household had between 200 and 400 persons, one third roughly of this number not yet baptized children. The number of 1,000 inhabitants or more seems to be exaggerated—except for times of great disaster. Taking an average of 300 per unit, we arrive at the following approximate figures of Anabaptist population in Moravia:

1545	6,300
1589	17,100
1619	13,500
1622	7,200 (according to Hruby)

(In 1622, all these more than 7,000 Brethren were expelled from Moravia, and no Bruderhof was spared. It was the final end of the communal life in that country.) Sixteenth-century authors give quite different figures, varying between 20,000 and 70,000, and Johann Amos Comenius even claims that each Bruderhof held a population of between two and three thousand. This information has to be taken with caution; Hruby's calculations sound much more likely.

Today the Hutterite census, according to Joseph W. Eaton (*MQR,* January 1951), shows 96 Bruderhofs with a population of 9,211.

As to the economic value of the Bruderhofs in the Golden Age of Hutterite history (late 16th century), the estimates are likewise somewhat vague. Loserth draws conclusions from a remark in the Chronicle that one single household was taxed 100 florins (gold pieces) and even more. Hruby (p. 91) found in one letter of Emperor Ferdinand II that up to 1620, at least 30,000 florins were confiscated from the Hutterites in southern Moravia. (He had very little power in Slovakia.) This is a tremendously large sum considering the devaluation of the currency at the time of the outbreak of the Thirty Years' War. Since the Brethren could still salvage some means when fleeing into Slovakia, their total fortune is estimated by Hruby as possibly more than 60,000 florins. Hence the ever-repeated urge of the emperor (himself in never-ending need of money) to press the Brethren for all their hidden savings. Hruby's account of this topic is highly informative and well documented.

Varying are also the reports concerning the hygiene in these collective housings. Some reports stress their great cleanliness, unusual for the standards of 16th-century peasantry (Loserth, *Communismus*, 281 f.). Particularly the concern for the healthy upbringing of the children in nurseries and schools is emphasized time and again. Yet, a foreign visitor in 1612 (Hruby, 127 f.) has this to report (translated from the Latin): "For their education they crowd together 200 to 300 children in great filth and stench. Hence a great number of them die early." Of course this is a report of the declining years, but it could be stated fairly generally that, in spite of their excellent physicians, the knowledge of fighting epidemics was yet too poor to prevent a high infant mortality, particularly in the houses that were overcrowded with children (Loserth, 248; Hruby, 75). It is doubtful, however, whether it was worse than at any other place of the 16th century. Today, the Bruderhofs in America have both cleanliness and good health.

The Bruderhof was also the place of worship since there was no separate chapel. It was in the common dining room that they celebrated and still celebrate the Lord's Supper at certain intervals, coming together from the entire Bruderhof or even from several in the vicinity. It is understandable that this type of living together, working, caring and suffering together, produced a very closely knit fellowship. Mutual aid existed as a matter of fact, as well as a spirit of togetherness unknown anywhere else. (See also **Habaner** and **Community of Goods**; *ML* II, 266 f., **Haushaben**.)   R.F.

Loserth, *Communismus;* L. Müller, *Der Kommunismus der mährischen Wiedertäufer* (Leipzig, 1928); J. Horsch, *The Hutterian Brethren* (Goshen, 1931); F. Hruby, *Die Wiedertäufer in Mähren* (Leipzig, 1935); and R. Friedmann, "Die Habaner in der Slovakei," in *Wiener Ztscht f. Volkskunde,* 1927. Also the old polemical writings by C. Erhard (1588) and C. A. Fischer (1605 and 1607).

Brüderlich Vereinigung. The first known Swiss Brethren or Anabaptist confession of faith was entitled *Brüderlich Vereinigung etzlicher Kinder Gottes sieben Artikel betreffend . . .* ("Brotherly Union of a Number of Children of God Concerning Seven Articles"). It was drawn up at Schlatten (dialect for Schleitheim), canton of Schaffhausen, Switzerland, on St. Matthias Day, Feb. 24, 1527. The author was almost certainly Michael Sattler; this is evident from the reference to "our assembly, and . . . that which was resolved on therein" in a pastoral letter of Sattler, as well as from a reference in a letter from 50 Swiss Brethren elders to Menno Simons which mentions a brother in whose house the *"verdragh* (agreement) of Michael Sattler" had been made.

The confession treats of seven topics: baptism, excommunication, the Lord's Supper, separation from the world, shepherds, nonresistance, and the oath. Each of these subjects is discussed briefly and clearly, and is based on the Word of God. Baptism is made a symbol of Christian faith and of one's intention to live a life united with Christ in His death and resurrection. Those who twice refuse private admonition shall on the third occasion be excommunicated from the brotherhood because of their life of sin. Only those can be admitted to the Lord's table who have been united beforehand by Christian baptism and by a common separation from sin. The child of God is called upon by Christ to withdraw from every institution and person which is not truly Christian. Only one church officer is mentioned, the *Hirt* (shepherd, pastor) whose duties are to read, admonish, teach, warn, discipline, excommunicate, to lead in prayer, to administer the Lord's Supper, and to undertake the general oversight of the congregation. The child of God is to follow absolutely the law of love as taught by the New Testament, and leave the worldly sword to the officers of the state as ordained by God. Oaths are held to be inconsistent for finite creatures, and forbidden for the Christian by the express commands of Scripture. The Schleitheim confession does not give a complete summary of Christian faith, but treats only of the unique emphases of the evangelical Anabaptists of that era or perhaps of the points which were particularly challenged, either by the opponents or by erring brethren within.

The following four editions are known: 1533 (reprinted by Walther Köhler in 1908 as Heft 3 of Band 2, *Flugschriften aus den ersten Jahren der Reformation* together with valuable introduction); a contemporary but undated edition (reprinted by Heinrich Böhmer in *Urkunden zur Geschichte des Bauernkrieges und der Wiedertäufer*, Bonn, 1910, 2d and 3d ed. in 1921 and 1933); a later undated edition of the mid-16th century, unique copy in Goshen College Library; and an edition of 1686 bound with *Christliches Glaubensbekantnus*. An English translation of the 1533 edition by J. C. Wenger in *MQR*, 1945, 247-53. Each of the German prints appears together with other items in a single booklet. John Horsch published an English translation in *Gospel Herald* (1938) and the German text in the *Menn. Rundschau* (1912). The English text given by W. J. McGlothlin in *Baptist Confessions of Faith* (Philadelphia, 1911) 3-9 is a translation of the inadequate Latin form of the articles as given by Zwingli in the *Elenchus* of 1527, which is a translation from a German manuscript copy. Contemporary manuscript copies are in the Heidelberg University Library, Bern Staatsarchiv, and three formerly in Bratislava, Czechoslovakia. Dutch editions appeared in 1560 and 1565 (reprinted by S. Cramer in *BRN V* (1909) 585-613. Beck had published one of the Bratislava copies in his *Geschichts-Bücher* (1883). Ernst Müller published the Bern copy in his *Berner Täufer* (1895), and Beatrice Jenny published it (1951) in full in a critical edition. A lost French translation was used by Calvin in his attack against the Anabaptists of 1544 (*Brieve Instruction*), in which he specifically refutes the confession point by point.   J.C.W.

J. C. Wenger, "The Schleitheim Confession of Faith," *MQR* XIX (Oct. 1945) 243-53, and the literature cited there, particularly R. Friedmann, "The Schleitheim Confession (1927) and Other Doctrinal Writings of the Swiss Brethren in a Hitherto Unknown Edition," *MQR* XVI (Jan. 1942) 82-98, and Fritz Blanke, "Beobachtungen zum ältesten Täuferbekenntnis," *Archiv für Ref.-Gesch.* XXXVII (1940) 240-49; Beatrice Jenny, *Das Schleitheimer Täuferbekenntnis 1527* (Thayngen, 1951).

Brüderliche Vereinigung zwischen uns und etlichen Brüdern am Rheinstrom, a Hutterite tract of 1556-57, written by the Hutterite missionary brother Hänsel Schmidt or Raiffer (*q.v.*) who was then working in the area of Kreuznach (Palatinate) and Aachen (Lower Rhine province). It exists in two handwritten books, now in the Primatial library of Esztergom, Hungary, in form of an appendix to the otherwise well-known *Sendbrief* by Andreas Ehrenpreis (*q.v.*) of 1652. Its significance lies in its statement of the fundamental doctrinal and practical points in which the Hutterites distinguish themselves from the Swiss Brethren who lived in that area. The tract consists of two parts, (1) the negotiations in Kreuznach with a brother Lorenz Huef and his fellow Swiss brethren, in 1556, with whom seven points were discussed, and (2) similar negotiations in Aachen in 1557 with the Swiss brother Hans Arbeiter (*q.v.*), discussing not less than 17 points of doctrine and practical distinctions. Hänsel Schmidt, always an effective missionary worker of the Hutterites, could win both groups for his brotherhood, only to be caught himself finally by the authorities of Aachen and to suffer martyrdom for his faith's sake in 1558. The tract says expressly that the brethren in Kreuznach demanded a written statement concerning the seven points with all Scriptural references, which was also done, whereupon the statement was read before the entire congregation of the Swiss Brethren. This is apparently the document which forms the major part of the pamphlet at hand. Schmidt drew it up himself out of his intimate knowledge of Hutterite teaching. The seven points discussed concern: marriage, taxes for war (*Blutgeld*), separation from other groups who claim to be brethren, support of ministers and deacons for their secular needs, "idol worship" (meaning the Catholic Mass), the buying of houses in Moravia, and finally, who should move to Moravia. The 17 points of the *Aachen Gespräch* (for which no Scriptural references are presented—perhaps because no written statement was asked for) deal with much more central issues, such as original sin, incarnation of Christ, community of goods, ban, etc.

The text is preserved in full in the two codices IX and XI of Beck's description (*Geschichts-Bücher*) from which Beck prints only the main parts without the doctrinal details (225-29). The larger chronicle (ed. Zieglschmid) contains the full text (359-67, and 384) including the Scriptural references. It represents a complete copy of the original tract. The Ehrenpreis epistle, finally, our prime source, was published by the Hutterian Brethren in 1920 (Scottdale, Pa.) from a manuscript preserved by the Hutterites in South Dakota, and here again one finds the complete text of the tract on pages 155-183. In this *Sendbrief,* to which Ehrenpreis himself had apparently appended this doctrinal statement from a now lost original, this otherwise unnamed tract is given the heading (in Beck, 225) *Brüderliche Vereinigung etc.,* reminiscent of the similar title of the oldest doctrinal statement of the Anabaptists, the *Brüderlich Vereinigung etlicher Kinder Gottes* (*q.v.*) of Schleitheim, 1527.

The document is very significant for its discussion of relations between the various Anabaptist groups.   R.F.

Bruderordnung der Krimmer Mennoniten Brüdergemeinde, a mutual aid organization of the Krimmer Mennonite Brethren, had its origin in 1881 in Gnadenau, near Hillsboro, Kan., and continued to operate within the Krimmer Mennonite Brethren Church until Dec. 1, 1927. The two men largely responsible for its origin were Abraham Harms and Cornelius Duerksen, both teachers who had come from Russia. On the first committee were Johann A. Flaming, Johann Regehr, and P. A. Wiebe, all of Gnadenau. Later each district had its committee to evaluate property and to appraise losses, which were paid by the main secretary-treasurer, who was elected by the whole conference. Originally the organization served a twofold purpose, namely, to assist in case of loss by fire, and to make assessments according to household evaluation for special financial obligations of the church. The latter was soon discontinued, however, and it became an organization solely for aid in case of loss in storm, fire, tornado, and other causes. Property enlistment reached $1,500,000 at its high point. Participation was limited to church members.   C.F.P.

K.M.B. Yearbooks up to 1927, especially 1921 and 1927; *Regeln der Bruderordnung der Krimmer Mennoniten Brüdergemeinde* (1909); *Konferenzbeschlüsse der Krimmer Mennoniten Brüdergemeinde von Nordamerika zwischen den Jahren 1882 bis 1940.*

Bruderschaft was the name for congregational meetings (attended by men only) among the Mennonites of Prussia and Russia. The elder of a congregation called the *Bruderschaft* and was in charge of the meeting at which any matter pertaining to the congregational life would be taken up and acted upon. In America, particularly where the English was introduced, the term *Bruderschaft* among the Mennonites from Russia gradually disappeared although it is still used among the more conservative groups such as the Old Colony Mennonites. The Mennonite Brethren substituted the name *Gemeindestunde* for *Bruderschaft.*   C.K.

Brudertal Mennonite Church (GCM), located approximately six miles northeast of Hillsboro, Marion Co., Kan., was organized on Dec. 26, 1874. The congregation joined the Western District Mennonite Conference and the General Conference Mennonites in 1878 and was incorporated under the laws of the state of Kansas in 1887.

The first membership of the congregation was composed entirely of Mennonite immigrants from South Russia and West Prussia in 1873 and subsequent years, largely because of the threat of compulsory military training. The majority of the membership today still are descendants of that original stock. The able Wilhelm Ewert, former elder of the church at Ober-Nessau, Poland, was the first elder of the congregation, serving until his death in 1887.

To meet the problems arising out of such a varied background a written constitution to serve as a guide for the congregation was drawn up soon after its organization. This was revised in 1895 and again in 1939, when it was also translated into the English language.

In the beginning the German language was used exclusively in the worship and church life. For many years what is now known as the daily vacation Bible school was conducted in that language. Among the practices observed were close communion, footwashing, worship services every Sunday and on holidays with two being observed on Christmas, Easter, and Pentecost, marriage between Mennonites only, and refusal of military service, swearing of oaths, secret societies, and litigation. However, participation in voting and the holding of public office was never frowned upon.

For the last 20 years there has been a gradual transition to the exclusive use of the English language both in the homes of the members and in the church. The practices also have changed so that today communion is open, footwashing has been discontinued, there is no barrier to marriage with members of other Protestant faiths, and there are no second holidays with the exception of Christmas. However, the other practices mentioned above are still largely held.

While regular midweek prayer meetings and Sunday evening preaching services have never been held, the universal week of prayer and a week of meetings for the deepening of the spiritual life have long been observed annually. The practice of catechetical instruction for prospective church members and baptism upon confession of faith have always been adhered to. Among the several organizations of the church are the Sunday school, two Christian Endeavor societies, two ladies' missionary societies, a men's brotherhood, a choir, and a Bethel College Fellowship. Finances for local needs are raised by dues on membership and a percentage levy on property and income. Conference and other causes are supported by offerings.

The early growth of the church was rapid, due to the arrival of numerous immigrant families. But with the settling of the land and the formation of neighboring congregations of Mennonites and other Protestant faiths the membership of the church has been unusually stationary. At present (1952) there are 200 members. The membership has been predominantly rural although at present the number who are following nonagricultural pursuits is increasing.

Elders who have served the church are Wilhelm Ewert, Benjamin Unruh, Wilhelm J. Ewert, and Arnold E. Funk. In addition the following have served as ministers and evangelists: Jacob Funk, Jacob W. Penner, Abraham Balzer, David Goertz, Paul Mouttet, and John P. Suderman. All of the above-named with the exception of Benjamin Unruh were selected from the membership of the congregation. Mission workers who have gone out from the church are Mr. and Mrs. P. W. Penner, Elizabeth Goertz, Otto B. Pankratz, and Mr. and Mrs. John P. Suderman. (Ray Funk, "Bruderthal—Seventy-five Years Ago," *Mennonite Life,* July 1949, 4-6.) A.E.F.

Bruderthaler, a name once used by a number of congregations in the present Evangelical Mennonite Brethren Conference, viz., at Mountain Lake, Minn.; Marion, S.D.; Aberdeen, Idaho; Chinook, Mont.; Steinbach, Man.; Dallas, Ore.; and Langham, Sask. The Bruderthaler Church in Minnesota was one of the two groups which formed the conference later called the E.M.B. For a time the conference was popularly known as the Bruderthaler Gemeinde. The name has now been dropped and the congregations commonly call themselves the E.M.B. Church with the name of the location. Articles on these congregations will therefore be found in this *Encyclopedia* under the name of the town where found, followed by "E.M.B. Church." M.G.

Bruderthaler Evangelical Mennonite Brethren Church, now extinct, was organized with 25 members in July 1935, under the leadership of J. H. Klassen, at Fairholme, Sask. In 1936 a church was built four miles from Fairholme. The membership of fifty decreased to eight because of crop failures. Since 1947 the conference has operated a Scripture Mission in Fairholme with Ed. Dirks as minister. J.H.K.

Brugge (*Bruges*), capital of West Flanders, Belgium (pop. about 54,000). There were Anabaptists here probably as early as 1530, who fled to this place after the passing of the Edict of Speyer in 1529. At any rate there was a very active congregation here in 1534, which was untouched by the fanaticism of Münster. During the 16th century there was a large congregation in this city. The notorious heretic hunter, Brother Cornelis Adriaensz (*q.v.*), speaks of no less than 700 Anabaptists living there. Leenaert Bouwens was, however, not active here. A very large number of martyrs came from this city. Van Braght names at least 24. The actual figure was 47, two of whom died in prison, two were buried alive, and 43 died at the stake. For eleven who gave their lives on Dec. 10, 1561, a hymn was written, beginning "Genade ende vrede moet god vreezende zijn" (Wackernagel, *Lieder,* 130).

Seven martyrs were executed in 1538; one in 1552, seven in 1558, twelve in 1561, eleven in 1568, two in 1569, five in 1570, and two in 1573. The fact that on one occasion twelve and on another eleven were burned at one time suggests that the church was a large one; for otherwise it would not have been possible to capture so many at once. Special mention should be made of Jacob de Swarte (executed at Brugge Aug. 15, 1558), because his entire family was arrested in 1563 in Lille, where his father Jan was deacon; he died at the stake with his wife and four sons. The most important of the martyrs of Brugge were the two preachers and elders, Jacob de Roore or Keersgieter (*q.v.*) (chandler) and Herman van Vlekwijk (*q.v.*), who were burned to death on July 18, 1569. Their cross-examination by Cornelis Adriaensz, and their letters, are given at length in the *Martyrs' Mirror*.

Nothing further is known concerning the Brugge congregation. With the death of the last martyrs, Mattheus Kuese and Adriaen van der Zwalme (Aug. 7, 1573), it was apparently extinct, though in 1636 there were still some Mennonites in or near Brugge. In this year Pieter Hoop and Maerten Languut, Mennonites from the Dutch province of Zeeland visiting the brethren in Brugge, were put in prison here for more than half a year. About the same time other Mennonites living here, as Cornelis Dyserinck (*q.v.*), left the city and moved to the Netherlands. Since that time there have been no Mennonites here.　　　　　K.V., vdZ.

H. Q. Janssen, *Kerkhervorming in Brugge*, 2 vv. (Arnhem, 1868); A. L. E. Verheyden, *Het Brugsche Martyrologium* (Brussels, n.d., 1944); *DB* 1876, 84; 1877, 7; *ML* I, 285.

Bruggencate, ten, a Dutch family, originally from the district of Twenthe, province of Overijssel, one branch of which belonged to the Mennonites. Jan Bernards ten Bruggencate, b. 1833 at Almelo, d. 1871 at Noordbroek, was the minister of the Noordbroek congregation 1859-71. Bernard ten Bruggencate, b. 1839 at Almelo, d. 1903 at Groningen, served Baard in 1863-74 and Noordbroek in 1874-1900. Henriette C. ten Bruggencate, b. 1893, married A. Voorhoeve, who served first the Protestant church of Batavia, Dutch East Indies, and later the Mennonite church of Rotterdam in 1936-48.　　vdZ.

Brügger, Christian, one of the "leading Anabaptists and rabble-rousers" from Rohrbach in the canton of Bern, participated in the disputation at Zofingen (July 1-9, 1532), and was afterwards arrested. For identification and probably to sign the records of the disputation he was taken to Aarau. Here he was told that if he "renounced his sect" he would be released; if not he would be banished and if he returned, drowned. When he returned he was again imprisoned. Nothing more is known of him. (Müller, *Berner Täufer*, 35 f.; *ML* I, 286.)　　Neff.

Bruin, sometimes also spelled Bruyn, common Dutch family name, especially in the province of North Holland. Some members of a Mennonite branch were ministers: Claas Bruin (*q.v.*); Pieter Bruin, who served de Rijp from 1717 to about 1771; Gijsbert Bruin, preacher of Noordeind van Graft en Rijp from 1730 to about 1778; Willem Bruin (*q.v.*), two of whose sons also went into the ministry: Jan Bruin, serving IJlst in 1818-27 and Koog-Zaandijk in 1827-58, and Pieter Bruin, serving Noordeind van Graft in 1824-61, and others.　　vdZ.

Bruin, Claas, b. Feb. 20, 1671, often preached in the Amsterdam Bloemstraat Old Frisian church where his father was minister. He was himself never ordained, although he had great gifts in that

field. Until his death (1732) he was a bookkeeper in a commercial firm.

In his youth his manifold talents were evident. He devoted himself especially to writing poetry. His first attempt was the "De Aardbeving" in 1692. He was also fond of using Bible stories. In 1724 he published *Bijbelsche Tooneelpoëzy,* containing "Abrahams Offerhande," "Sauls dood," "Davids gestrafte hoogmoed." *Het leven van den Apostel Paulus, in dichtmaat afgebeelt,* appeared in 1734 in Amsterdam. The best known of his numerous works are two travel books in poetry, *Kleefsche en Zuid-Hollandsche Arkadia* (Amsterdam, 1716) and *Noordhollandsche Arkadia* (Amsterdam, 1732). He may also be the Claas Bruin who wrote a poem under each of the pictures of Haemstede's *Historie der Martelaren* (Leiden, 1747). His poems were not particularly original or inspired, on the whole somewhat tedious, and their cumbersomeness will repel many a reader. But he was a skilled linguist, and as such is highly regarded by prominent men.　　H.W., vdZ.

Wagenaar, Beschrijving van Amsterdam; Schotel, Bijdragen tot Boeken en Menschenkennis II and III; *N.N. B.Wb.* VI, 223; G. Kalff, *Gesch. der Ned. Letterkunde* V (The Hague, 1910) 446-48, 512; *Catalogus Amst.,* 235; *ML* I, 286.

Bruin, Willem (b. 1759 at de Rijp, d. Oct. 22, 1826, at Westzaan), pastor of the Mennonite church at Kolhorn, Wieringen, and Westzaan (op het Noord), all in the Dutch province of North Holland. He was one of the lay preachers who distinguished themselves by unusual capability in the ministry and in writing. Deprived of his parents in early childhood, and entirely without means, he grew up in the orphanage of his home town de Rijp in North Holland. In spite of his extraordinary talents, evident in his schoolwork, he was taught the carpenter's and mill-builder's trade, in which he did competent work. In his youth he applied himself to religious studies, stimulated by de Groot's book, *Over de Waarheid van den christlijken Godsdienst* (On the Truth of the Christian Religion). At the age of 22 he was baptized.

His pastor P. Hartman recognized his great gifts and his interest in religious questions, and suggested that he become a preacher. But there was no fund to finance his training; so Bruin devoted all his spare time to studying alone and with his pastor. After six months he preached his first sermon in the vacant pulpit of the church at Kolhorn and Barsingerhorn (1783) and was called to serve there as preacher after passing an examination conducted by the preachers Jan ten Kate and Sybrand Martens and being declared capable of the service. In 1784 he became a minister on the island of Wieringen and in 1786 in Westzaan, where he served with great blessing over 40 years (1786-1826).

The following titles are evidence of his literary work: *Het lot der menschen na hunnen dood* (Haarlem, 1793); *De levensgeschiedenis van Jezus* . . . (1794); *Gemeenzame Beschouwingen over den Godsdienst* (Amsterdam, 1795); *Godsdienstige en wijsgeerige beschouwingen van de jongste Staatsomwentelingen in Europa* (Amsterdam, 1799); *Proeve over de wijsheid van God, in het ontwerp der*

Evangelische Bedeeling (Amsterdam, 1810). For his paper, "Kan men met grond beweren, dat de menschen immer alleen door middel van hunne menschelijke rede of redekavelingen . . . tot de regte denkbeelden van Godlijke zaken zouden hebben kunnen komen?" (1796), he received the silver medal of the Teyler Theological Society at Haarlem. Besides all this he published a novel and some historical studies. (*DJ* 1837, 114-25; *ML* I, 286.)

NEFF, VDZ.

Bruinvis (sometimes written Bruynvis or Bruinvisch), a Mennonite family of Alkmaar (Dutch province of North Holland), many of whom served the Mennonite congregation at Alkmaar (*q.v.*) as deacons. A Pieter Bruynvis was deacon of the Flemish and Waterlander congregation in 1720 and treasurer 1721-23 and 1727. Most members of this family, however, belonged to the Frisian congregation at Alkmaar. The first Bruynvis listed in the records of this church is Jan Bruynvis, baptized March 18, 1731. He was a deacon in 1756 and died June 20, 1766. His son Cornelis Bruinvis (May 30, 1736, to March 6, 1810, *q.v.*) served after April 1, 1778, as a deacon and for many years as president of the church board. He prepared the union of the two Alkmaar congregations in 1810. He was the author of a paper (in *DB* 1880, 48 pp.) on the Mennonites at Alkmaar. Pieter Bruynvis (March 6, 1744, to Oct. 14, 1814), a brother of this Cornelis, was also a deacon at about the same time and 1778-1810 served the Frisian congregation and 1810-14 the United congregation. Further we find the following members of this family, all deacons and almost all for a long period of years: Pieter Bruynvis, Czn. (1764-1842), was deacon 1810-42; Jan Bruynvis, 1813-16; Cornelis Voorhout Bruynvis, 1816-42; Cornelis Bruynvis, 1820-37; Cornelis Pieter Bruynvis (1827-73) a deacon; Jacobus Bruynvis, 1842-71; Hendrik Jacobus Bruynvis, 1859-94; Cornelis Willem Bruynvis (*q.v.*) 1881-96 (d. 1922). The regency of the Gerrit Wildeman old people's home was for almost two centuries from generation to generation in the Bruynvis family. VDZ.

J. de Lange Czn., *Beknopte Geschiedenis der Doopsgezinde Gemeente te Alkmaar* (1927) *passim; DB* 1880 48-65; 1882, 83-101; 1891, 8, 16.

Bruinvis, Cornelis, b. May 30, 1736, d. March 6, 1810, a deacon in the Frisian church at Alkmaar (*q.v.*), wrote historical sketches, which were published in the *Doopsgezinde Bijdragen* 1880, p. 48 ff.; 1882, 83 ff.; 1883, 30 ff., and offer valuable insight into the church life of this Dutch Mennonite congregation. (*ML* I, 287.)   NEFF.

Bruinvis, Cornelis Willem, a member of the Mennonite Bruinvis family of Alkmaar, Dutch province of North Holland, b. June 26, 1829, d. April 1922, son of Cornelis Pieter Bruinvis, an apothecary, and Alida de Lange. In 1859 he married Miss Schreuder (d. 1916). This marriage remained childless. He was a man of great energy and of admirable versatility. First, at the age of 14, he was placed in a notary's office. Soon he turned to architecture and became an architectural draftsman; in 1856 he was architect of the Mennonite church of Broek op Langendijk (*q.v.*). About the same time he studied chemistry and assisted his father in the apothecary shop. From 1854 to 1882 he was editor of the *Alkmaarsche Courant* and during his whole life he remained a newspaperman. From 1859 to 1870 he was, like his father, an apothecary. From 1874 to 1898 he was engaged in politics, serving his native town 1874-88 as a member of the town council and 1888-99 as sheriff. He was always interested in history; especially that of Alkmaar received his warm attention and on it he published many papers. At the age of 20 he was appointed recorder of the city of Alkmaar and *Stadsarchivaris* and thoroughly reorganized the city archives. He worked here until 1920, when he was 90 years old! Of his numerous publications should be mentioned some papers on the Mennonites in *Doopsgezinde Bijdragen;* for the *Nieuw Nederl. Biographisch Woordenboek* he wrote nearly 300 articles. He was a loyal member of the Mennonite church of Alkmaar, which he served as deacon 1881-96.   VDZ.

H. E. van Gelder, "Levensbericht van C. W. Bruinvis," in *Levensberichten van de Maatschappij v. Ned. Letterkunde* (Leiden) 1922, 110-34, contains a complete list of his publications.

Bruinvis(ch), Jan, a member of the Alkmaar Mennonite Bruinvis family (*q.v.*), lived in Königsberg, Prussia, where he had established the largest warehouse in that city. He assisted with word and deed the Lithuanian Mennonites, who by an edict of Frederick William of Prussia (Feb. 22, 1732) had been expelled from Königsberg (*q.v.*), but were later allowed to return and stay in the territory, the decree having been revoked. He acted as a mediator between these Mennonites and the Dutch *Fonds voor Buitenlandsche Nooden* (*q.v.*) and wrote a number of letters to Amsterdam, the first of which is dated Aug. 12, 1711, and the latest June 23, 1744. A number of Lithuanian Mennonite families took ship at Königsberg for Holland; of these Bruinvis sent a list to the Amsterdam *Commissie.* Most of them returned in course of time. Bruinvis had assisted them in procuring passage to Holland, and when they returned, he helped them find land and houses, authorized financially to do so by the Dutch *Commissie.* He also acted in behalf of the congregation of the Elbing Werder at Markushof. Bruinvis was a wealthy man, who liberally gave large amounts of money of his own for the sake of the oppressed Mennonites. Bruinvis was a member—and presumably a deacon—of the Königsberg Mennonite congregation. In a letter written by Jan Pieter Spronck, the minister of the church, dated May 16, 1735, to the Dutch committee (*Inv. Arch. Amst.* II, 2, No. 796) Bruinvis is accused of marrying outside the church, and of consenting to have his children baptized as infants. Nothing is known about his life; even the years of birth and death are unknown and it is not clear whether he himself after returning from Prussia to Holland, or his son, founded (about 1750) the Handelshuis (trading company) Bruinvis en Barreveld at Amsterdam.   VDZ.

Inv. Arch. Amst. I, Nos. 1236, 1593, 1653, 1665, 1672, 1686, 1692, 1696, 1933, 2119; II, 2, Nos. 699, 746, 749, 753, 755, 758, 760 f., 765 f., 770, 772, 779, 784 f., 796, 806 f.; E. Randt, *Die Menn. in Ost-Preussen und Lithauen* (1912) 57.

Brundage, Daniel (1812-95), pioneer bishop of the Mennonite church (MC) in Kansas, was born in Ontario. While living in Canada he was ordained to the ministry. Later he moved to Elkhart Co., Ind. In 1869 he moved to Missouri, where he was ordained bishop of the Bethel congregation, near Tipton, Moniteau Co., on May 28, 1870. After a tornado destroyed his buildings and personal property in 1872, he moved to Kansas the next year and settled in McPherson County, where he organized the Spring Valley congregation. During the years 1873-81 (?) and 1887-89, he served the Kansas congregations as bishop, traveling in his two-wheeled springless cart to one of the four churches in his circuit each Sunday. He was known as "Old Faithful Bishop Brundage." In 1889 he discontinued his services and moved to Elkhart Co., Ind., where he retired.   M.G.

Brunfels, Otto (*ca.* 1488-1534), a native of Mainz, Germany, city physician in Bern, Switzerland. In his youth he entered the Carthusian monastery at Mainz, left it at the beginning of the Reformation to follow Luther. He found a reception at the Ebernburg by Franz von Sickingen. Ulrich von Hutten secured for him the position of parson at Steinheim (December 1521). Expelled from this place he found temporary refuge in Frankfurt a.M. On his way to Zwingli in Switzerland he was detained in Neuenburg in Breisgau, and took over the office of preacher there. Here he seems to have become acquainted with Anabaptist endeavors in nearby Zürich. This is suggested by his book, *Von dem Pfaffen Zehnden hundert und zwen und fiertzig Schlussreden,* in which he denounces the tithe and demands that it be used for the poor. In March 1524 he located in Strasbourg, where he made a living by teaching and studied medicine. Here he published the book, *Pandectarum veteris et novi testamenti Libri XII,* in which he championed the priesthood of all believers, attacked the tithe, and repudiated the oath. He associated with the Anabaptists of Strasbourg, L. Hackfurt, Friedolin Meyer, and others (Keller, 274). In September 1528 he published *Precationes biblicae sanctorum patrum* which he translated into German as *Biblisches Gebetbüchlein.* Menno Simons makes a reference to Brunfels (*Opera omnia,* 275). Brunfels vigorously opposed the punishment of Anabaptists (see the book, *Von Ketzeren. Ob man auch die verfolgen oder wie man mit jnen handlen solle,* compiled by Martinus Bellius, 1554, p. 68, a copy in the national library at Cassel). At the Strasbourg Synod, 1533, he opposed the articles concerning the rights of the government in matters of faith. In the fall of 1533 he settled in Basel as a physician. In natural science and the healing art he attained epoch-making significance. Karl Linné calls him the "father of modern botany."   NEFF.

C. Gerbert, *Gesch. der Strassburger Sektenbewegung* (1889) 164; F. W. E. Roth, "Otto Brunfels," in *Ztscht f. d. Gesch. d. Oberrheins* (1894) 284-320; *idem,* "Die Schriften des Otto Brunfels 1519-1536," in *Jahrbuch f. Geschichte, Sprache u. Literatur Elsass-Lothringens* (1900) 257-88; Erich Sanwald, *Otto Brunfels 1488-1534. Ein Beitrag zur Gesch. des Humanismus und der Reformation.* 1. Hälfte 1488-1524 (Teildruck) Diss. Munich (Bottrop i.W., 1932); ML I, 287.

Brunk (Bronk, Bronck), a Swiss family name found among the Mennonites in the Palatinate about 1700 and among the American Mennonites since the last quarter of the 18th century. About 1773 Jacob Brunk came to America from Europe, settled first in Pennsylvania, and in 1795 in Frederick Co., Va. His sons Christian, Joseph, and George located in Maryland. Christian's son Christian (1832-1906) was a Mennonite preacher near Winchester, Va., and his son George (1831-?) served as a preacher first at Broadway, Va., and later at Elida, Ohio. A number of the descendants of George Brunk (born 1831) were ministers and deacons in the Mennonite Church (MC). The most influential members of the Brunk family in the Mennonite Church have been Bishop George R. Brunk (*q.v.,* 1871-1938) first of Kansas, later Virginia, founder and first editor of *The Sword and Trumpet,* and author of *Ready Scriptural Reasons* (Scottdale, 1926); and his sons, Bishop Truman Brunk, who had often served as moderator of the Virginia Conference, and George R. Brunk, Jr., a Mennonite evangelist.

The Brunks have also been prominent in musical circles in the Mennonite Church. Christian H. Brunk (1845-1921) was an active layman and music composer of Rockingham Co., Va.; he served on the committee which compiled the *Church and Sunday School Hymnal* (1902). He also compiled a Sunday-school hymnbook entitled, *Bible School Hymns and Sacred Songs* (Elkhart, 1883). John D. Brunk (1872-1926) (*q.v.*) came from Rockingham Co., Va., was a composer of music, and served as professor of music in Goshen College. He was the music editor of the *Church Hymnal, Mennonite* (Scottdale, 1927), the best hymnbook of his body of Mennonites.   J.C.W.

Brunk, George R., prominent leader of the Mennonite Church (MC) in Virginia, the son of Henry G. and Susan Heatwole Brunk, was born at Geneseo, Ill., on Dec. 31, 1871. When he was two years old the family took a prairie schooner for the Kansas plains. George's father died eight days after their arrival and as a consequence the first years here were difficult ones. He married Katie Wenger of Harrisonburg, Va., in 1900. After ten years of service in Kansas the Brunk family moved to Denbigh, Va., in 1910, where he became bishop of the Mennonite churches in southeastern Virginia.

Brunk early acquired a library of his own which he made constant use of in his intellectual development. He was saved for work in the Mennonite Church by the appeal and prayers of his mother, the counsel of his uncle R. J. Heatwole, and the tactful solicitation of John S. Coffman. He was ordained to the ministry on Oct. 1, 1893, and to the office of bishop on Oct. 23, 1898. He served the church at large as an evangelist and a Bible conference speaker. He served as a member of the Mennonite Board of Education for many years, and took an active interest in the Eastern Mennonite College as vice-president of its board of trustees until 1924, and as a member of its Religious Welfare Committee. His literary contributions are found in a book entitled *Ready Scriptural Reasons*

(Scottdale, 1926) and articles in *The Sword and Trumpet* (q.v.), a quarterly journal which he established in 1927 and edited until his death in 1938.

His leadership in the Mennonite Church included both progressive and conservative elements. He was an advocate of new methods of work, but he vigorously fought the introduction of modernism and Calvinism in Mennonite churches.

He was the father of nine children, among them Bishop Truman Brunk of Denbigh, Va., and George R., Jr., and Lawrence, sponsors of the Brunk Brothers' Revival Campaign. **H.A.B.**

Brunk, John David (1872-1926), music composer and teacher, son of Samuel and Susanna Brunk, was born March 13, 1872, near Harrisonburg, Va. He was married to Mary Kathryn Martin of Hagerstown, Md., Sept. 2, 1897. They had seven children.

After finishing his elementary schooling in the local school near the homestead, he went to Bridgewater College for his academy and early music training. He spent two years at New England Conservatory, Boston, Mass., where he studied harmony and composition with George W. Chadwick. Later he attended American Conservatory, Chicago, Ill. His advanced studies here were under Adolph Weidig. Besides having a thorough training in theory and composition, he was a gifted pianist as well as vocalist. He taught three years at West Central Academy, Mt. Clinton, Va., and five years at Bridgewater College, Bridgewater, Va., before coming to Goshen College, Goshen, Ind., in 1906. Here he organized and started the music department, serving as director of the school of music and professor of voice and theory, 1906-13.

Brunk was a member of the Mennonite Church (MC) and a leader in church music. As editor, he headed a music committee appointed by the Ohio and Virginia conferences to compile a hymnbook for use in Sunday school and the church, the *Church and Sunday School Hymnal*, published in 1902, and in 1911 he edited a supplement to enrich the hymn materials in the book. His next published work was a book to be used for singing classes in the churches, *Educational Vocal Studies*, in 1912. In 1913 the Mennonite General Conference (MC) appointed a music committee to compile and publish a book of Gospel songs, known as *Life Songs*. He was appointed secretary and music editor of the committee, a position he held until his death. *Life Songs* was published in 1916. During the years 1913 and 1914 he, in co-operation with John W. Wayland as hymn writer, composed a cantata containing songs and hymns of the life of Christ called *Salvation Story*, which was never published, although some numbers from this manuscript appear in *Life Songs* and in the *Hymnal*. His last work as editor was as music editor of the *Church Hymnal*. His fine work in selecting, arranging, and composing of tunes has made this book a monument to his memory. It was published in 1927.

John D. Brunk was not only a compiler of hymns and tunes but also an able composer, writing many hymn tunes and Gospel song tunes in the spirit of the church and for her use. He was also greatly loved and respected by his many pupils. He was untiring in his efforts to raise the standard of church music in the Mennonite Church. He died Feb. 5, 1926, in his home near Elkhart, Ind. Interment was in the Prairie Street cemetery, Elkhart. **W.E.Y.**

Brunk Brothers Revival Campaign, an influential revival work among the Mennonites (MC) of North America, begun in 1951, carried on by Preacher George R. Brunk (1911-   ) of Denbigh, Va., the evangelist, and his layman brother Lawrence (1917-   ), who served as business manager and song leader. This team of Christian workers, using a large tent seating 6,000 persons, moved from one large Mennonite center to another during the open season from April to October, holding nightly meetings in a community for 3-4 weeks, to revive the church and evangelize non-Christians. The following communities have been served to date: 1951, Lancaster, Pa., Souderton, Pa., Orrville, Ohio, Manheim, Pa.; 1952, Johnstown, Pa., Waterloo-Kitchener, Ont., Goshen, Ind., Harrisonburg, Va., Morgantown, Pa., as well as two campaigns in Florida in the winter of 1952. In each series of meetings from 1,000 to 2,000 persons accepted Christ for the first time, renewed their covenant as members, or made a deeper consecration as Christians. The work was financed solely by offerings. Although modern methods of organization were used, the methods of preaching and the sermon content, etc., were simple and in conformity with good evangelical Christian and historic Mennonite faith. George R. Brunk is a graduate (B.D.) of Union Theological Seminary at Richmond, Va., and a former teacher of Bible at Eastern Mennonite College at Harrisonburg, Va. **H.S.B.**

Brunner, Charles H., an outstanding leader of the Mennonite Brethren in Christ Church in eastern Pennsylvania. He was the son of Joel S. and Rebecca (Gehman) Brunner, born Jan. 2, 1864, at Zionsville, Lehigh Co., Pa. He married Sarah C. Musselman Sept. 29, 1888, to whom were born one son (deceased) and one daughter. He had a public school education.

He was converted in 1878 and the same year joined the Evangelical Mennonites (in 1883 this group helped to form the Mennonite Brethren in Christ Church). He entered the ministry in 1893 and was ordained in 1896. He served as pastor in the Pennsylvania Conference for 40 years, 1893-98 and 1907-42, as follows: Lehighton, 1893-94; Royersford, 1894-96; Reading, 1896-98, 1907-10; Bethlehem, 1910-14; Allentown (Bethel), 1914-20; Bethlehem, 1920-23; Philadelphia (Salem), 1923-33; and Emmaus, 1933-42. He was Presiding Elder for six years, 1898-1902 and 1905-7.

In 1899 he organized the Gospel Herald Society, which is still the Home Missionary Society of the Conference, and was its first president, serving from 1899 to 1905.

Brunner also served as editor of the *Gospel Banner*, official organ of the Mennonite Brethren in Christ, 1908-12. He was the first editor of the Pennsylvania Conference Yearbook. He was conference secretary for 44 years, 1891-99 and 1906-42.

He was a member of 10 general conferences, 1896 to 1936 inclusive, and chairman of the general conference at Kitchener, Ont., in 1900.

Brunner retired from the active ministry in 1943 although he continued as an associate editor of the *Gospel Banner*. He died Nov. 20, 1948. E.R.S.

Brünnerin, Christine, a Hutterite martyr, who was executed in 1618 together with Jost Wilhelm, in Bregenz, Austria. The song, "Von Gott und seines Geistes Stärk, wie er im Glauben führt sein Werk," was written on their martyrdom (Wolkan, *Lieder*, 236; see **Bregenzer Wald**). Christine Brünnerin had not yet been baptized, but was in the act of emigrating to join the Hutterian Brethren in Moravia when she was arrested. (*ML* I, 287.)
                                                    NEFF.

Brunt, Reinier, attorney-general of the Court of Holland, which was seated in The Hague, afterwards chief justice of this court, in the first half of the 16th century. As a result of his intensive efforts and his fierce hatred for the Anabaptists, many were apprehended and executed. The archives of the Mennonite congregation at Amsterdam contain a large number of his letters and reports. He especially hunted down the Anabaptists in the Dutch province of North Holland 1534-38. (*Inv. Arch. Amst.* I.)
                                                    vDZ.

Brushy Run Mennonite Church (MC) is located on the east side of the Allegheny Mountains, three miles south of Onego, in Pendleton Co., W. Va. This was likely an early preaching point. The church was built here in 1933. It was once a strong Mennonite mission congregation of the Middle District of the Virginia Conference (MC), but now (1949) there are only three members. H.A.B.

Brussel, Bernhard, an Anabaptist of Niederdorla, a village near Mühlhausen in Thuringia, Germany, a linen weaver by trade, was subjected to a cross-examination there in September 1564 with some fellow believers, in which he confesses that the Evangelical preachers cannot teach properly because they are not called by lot and are themselves "weak, sinful persons," whose teachings are disregarded by their hearers; infant baptism he considers wrong and unnecessary for salvation, because infants cannot be taught. He denies that the true body and blood of Christ are in the holy communion; he cannot believe that Christ is at the right hand of God and yet be received in the sacrament. He grants a Christian the right of private possessions; he confesses that the government is ordained of God and does well in punishing evil; it is obligatory to pay it its dues. But he considers the oath wrong because the truth should be spoken without any oath, and one should simply say yea and nay.

After this examination the Anabaptists were told to leave the country within a week. If they refused, their confession would be sent to the judge, and his verdict, whether the death penalty or not, would immediately be carried out. They were given until Christmas to reform. When they refused to leave the country, they were tried again on Nov. 26, 1564; if they still persevered in their opinion, they would be given the customary penalty of death

by fire. At the third trial, Jan. 17, 1565, Bernhard Brussel again courageously confessed his faith. It is interesting to note that he now gives Biblical reasons. On the communion he refers to John 6:63 ("The flesh profiteth nothing: the words that I speak unto you, they are spirit, and they are life") and I Cor. 10:16, with the comment that the bread is the communion of the body of Christ and the body of Christ Himself; this must in truth be eaten in the spirit and in faith, and cannot be taken in the sacrament. On the oath he points to Matt. 6:34 ff., on the rejection of lawsuits to Luke 6:29 and 37. In conclusion he says that the government has no authority to judge him in matters of faith, and is therefore dealing with him in an unchristian way in separating him from his wife and children; what God hath joined together, let no man put asunder. Since it is written in Matt. 13:29 that the tares should not be separated from the wheat, the government has no right to remove or punish religious error.

Five days later, Jan. 22, 1565, Bernhard Brussel was imprisoned in Mühlhausen. Here he promised to reform and was permitted some liberty. On May 17, 1565, the fourth trial took place. The prisoners now confessed that they had done wrong and been in error; they would gladly recant publicly and accept any penalty. But they had hardly been released when they broke their promise. We do not know what happened to Bernhard Brussel; two of his companions were burned at the stake. (P. Wappler, *Die Täuferbewegung in Thüringen von 1526-1684*, Jena, 1913; *ML* I, 288.) NEFF.

Brussel (Bruyssel), **Michiel van,** an Anabaptist martyr: see **Michiel Willems.**

Brussels (Flemish, *Brussel;* French, *Bruxelles*), since 1830 the capital of Belgium, pop. (1947) 187,000, and Greater Brussels 952,500, where Anabaptist doctrine was spread in the 16th century. Since the city was then the residence of the chief magistrate, the Inquisition tracked down heretics more ruthlessly than in other places. There were probably fewer Anabaptists here than in Brugge, Gent, and Antwerp; nevertheless Leenaert Bouwens baptized at least 23 persons there between 1554 and 1557. The last Anabaptist to suffer death in Belgium was Anneken van den Hove (*q.v.*), who was buried alive July 19, 1597, according to van Braght, who also records the execution of Govert Jaspers van Goes in 1558 and Hans van der Straeten of Kortrijk at the stake in 1571. In his study of martyrs at Brussels, Verheyden lists eight Mennonite martyrs in this city, the first of whom was Wouter van Stoelwijk (*q.v.*), arrested Feb. 11, 1538, and executed in 1541, exact date unknown; but according to a document of September 1539 (*Inv. Arch. Amst.* I, No. 215) some Anabaptists were put to death at Brussels as early as 1539. A letter written by Regent Mary of Hungary to the Court of Holland, dated April 25, 1542 (*Inv. Arch. Amst.* I, No. 245), states that an Anabaptist had indicated a number of persons at Brussels who were infected with the heresy of Anabaptism; but in this period, as far as we know from the official records, no martyrs died at Brussels. There must have been a Mennonite congregation in Brussels, at least as early as 1541. The martyr Wouter van Stoelwijk gives some particulars about the congregation, which seems to have been only a small group of rather well-to-do people. The congregation still existed in 1594, but nothing is known of its history nor the time it dissolved. The relief work carried on in Belgium by the North American Mennonites, 1946-50, had its headquarters in Brussels. Two Mennonite missionary couples have been stationed there since that time. The missionaries sent to the Belgian Congo by the Congo Inland Mission, a North American Mennonite mission board, who must learn the French language by residence in Belgium, all normally spend a year of study in Belgium before proceeding to the field. (Verheyden, *Courtrai-Bruxelles,* 46, 48, 49, 57, 58; *ML* I, 288.) K.V., vDZ.

Brutus (Mich.) Old Order Mennonite Church had its origin about 1886, when the Wisler (OOM) faction withdrew from the parent Maple River (MC) congregation. In 1935 the group still had 60 members, but it gradually declined, so that at its last listing in the 1943 *Mennonite Yearbook* it had only ten members. M.G.

Bruyn, a Mennonite family of Amsterdam, related by marriage to many well-known Mennonite families, such as Centen, Cramer, Heiliger, Hulshoff, Kops, van Oosterwijk, Schellinger, van Vollenhoven. They were members of the Lamist congregation of Amsterdam. Some of the family served as deacons: Willem B., 1669-74; Ysbrand B., 1702-7 and 1716-21; Abraham B., 1779-84. Three ministers of the Bruyn family were C. C. Bruyn, who published *Vijf en twintig predicatiën* (Leeuwarden, 1692) (the congregation which he served is unknown), Kornelis Bruyn, who served Sneek in 1746-72 and Nijmegen in 1772-83, and Pieter Bruyn (1830-97), who was pastor of the congregation of Rottevalle-Witveen 1854-55, and Alkmaar 1855-62. In 1862 he resigned, because his extreme modernistic theological views were not accepted by his congregation. vDZ.

J. G. de Groot Jamin, Jr., *Geslachtslijst van de familie Bruyn* (Amsterdam, 1886); *Catalogus Amst.,* 241; J. de Lange C. Jzn., *Beknopte Gesch. der Doopsgez. Gemeente te Alkmaar* (1927) 110, 112, 123, 157; *Zondagsbode,* Feb. 27, 1908.

Bruyn de Wever, an Anabaptist martyr, who was seized with eleven companions (see **Anthonis de Wever**), March 11, 1571, by the Spaniards and beheaded May 25, at Deventer. (*Mart. Mir.* D 550, E 885; *DB* 1919, 29 ff.; *ML* I, 288.) NEFF.

Bucer (Butzer), **Martin,** the noted Strasbourg (*q.v.*) reformer, b. Nov. 10, 1491, at Schlettstadt in Alsace, d. Feb. 28, 1551, at Cambridge in England. At the age of 15 he entered the Dominican monastery as a student; in 1517 he matriculated at the university of Heidelberg, where he became acquainted with Luther and opened a correspondence with him. In 1520 he left the monastery cell and after a temporary stay in Speyer he found shelter on the Ebernburg of Franz von Sickingen. In 1521 he became chaplain at the court of the Elector Palatine Frederick, whom he followed to Worms and Nürn-

berg; in 1522, on the advice of his friend Ulrich von Hutten, he accepted the pastorate of Landstuhl in the Palatinate, the residence of Franz von Sickingen. Here he married a former nun. But in the same year because of the disturbances of war brought upon the town by the siege of the fortress of Sickingen by the Elector of Treves he was compelled to flee. He went to Weissenburg in Alsace and there founded a Lutheran congregation. In April 1523 he went to Strasbourg, where he worked with Wolfgang Capito (*q.v.*), Caspar Hedio, and Matthias Zell (*q.v.*). Bucer surpassed them all, an extraordinarily successful reformer. When the city council introduced the Interim in 1549 he emigrated to England, where he was received with great honor. After a brief but outstanding service on the faculty of Cambridge University he died.

Bucer's reformatory work was of wide significance. His influence extended throughout South Germany. Everywhere he strove zealously to bring about the unification of Protestants and to arbitrate between disputing parties. His warm love for the Protestant Church, his clear view, and his conciliatory attitude facilitated his role as intermediator.

He was particularly successful in dealing with the Anabaptists. He rejected the principle of the use of force and compulsion and tried to win them by means of private conversations and public persuasion at cross-examinations and disputations. His learning, his deep knowledge of the Scriptures, his judgment, his cleverness and ready wit stood him in good stead. Very wisely he always stressed the common, unifying points and toned down the divisive points. He was also very quick to detect his opponent's weakness and use it to his own end. Thus he succeeded in persuading many Anabaptists to return to the Reformed Church. When he could not accomplish it with words he called on the government to imprison or expel the Anabaptist; this happened in Strasbourg with increasing frequency; but he never sanctioned the death penalty. On Oct. 16, 1532, Bucer and some of the preachers requested that the council order a disputation with the Anabaptists, of course only for the purpose of being able the better to suppress them after the hearing on pretended grounds. In 1533 Bucer published a Latin broadside in justification of infant baptism *(What Is to Be Held of Infant Baptism According to the Holy Scriptures),* but accomplished little thereby. The council was probably influenced by Capito's opposition to persecution. Capito's views were definitely expressed in a letter he wrote April 17, 1533, to the Zwinglian preacher Mäuschen (Musculus) in Augsburg, where he says: "Bucer is working for a government order to retain infant baptism. I do not want to stand in his way, but he must leave me out of the game, for I know well that the supports of infant baptism cannot be proved" (Thudichum). [Contrary to Neff's idea, Hege held the view that Bucer was of the opinion that the Anabaptists were deserving of death.] On Dec. 17, 1546, he wrote to Philip IV of Hanau-Lichtenberg, that although on the basis of divine law the Anabaptists were deserving of death, this punishment should not be inflicted at the present time, because it was not being used against the vices of the Papists and the disregard of the Epicureans for religion (Hoffmann). Led by his experiences in combating the Anabaptists Bucer became the founder of confirmation.

Like Zwingli, Bucer also was at first very near the Anabaptist position in the matter of baptism. In December 1524 he wrote to Luther in the name of his co-preachers, "Baptism is an external matter. Baptizing those who have been taught to confess Christ would probably be more Scriptural and would destroy the error of the danger to salvation of the unbaptized. But they wanted to conform to the general custom: if only a time could be set for the instruction of those whom we, as far as we can remember, have baptized." In his book on the reason for the innovations in the congregation in Strasbourg on Dec. 26, 1524, he wrote, "Mere water baptism does not save. Where anyone wishes to postpone baptism and is able to do this without destroying love and harmony among those with whom he lives, we will not quarrel with him or condemn him. Let each be sure of his opinion." On Sept. 26, 1527, he said in a letter to Zwingli, that infant baptism is indeed Scriptural, but he was willing, where it was custom to baptize adults, to tolerate it for the present. But when the Anabaptists continued to increase in numbers he considered it necessary for the sake of the church that the government order the baptism of infants. In 1534 he finally brought it about that the magistrate of Strasbourg issued this order.

Another aid to Bucer in his winning of Anabaptists was his attitude to church discipline. With great determination he insisted on having stricter discipline introduced. "We absolutely need," he wrote Feb. 20, 1531, "a certain church discipline because of the imperfect; as it is we are without any order. Through this very fact the Anabaptists, these arch-heretics, win their way to the simpler hearts with their blasphemies. For we have scarcely a sign of the old church to show wherein we have the discipline and service of the brotherhood in view" (Gerbert, 157). But the council would not listen to him.

At the beginning of the Reformation Strasbourg was an asylum for those persecuted and suppressed for their faith. Almost all the leading South German Anabaptist preachers came here. Thus a thriving congregation arose here. The first of these leaders who came to Strasbourg was Balthasar Hubmaier (q.v.). In the summer of 1525 he came to Strasbourg from Waldshut to publish his book, *Von der christlichen Taufe der Gläubigen.* In March 1526 Wilhelm Reublin (q.v.) appeared. The congregation grew. Among its adherents were Jörg Ziegler and Hans Wolf of Benfeld. Of the latter Bucer gave the testimony "that he always conducted himself as a good man" (Bucer to Zwingli, May 17, 1526). Later, to be sure, he had some most unpleasant experiences with him when he without moderation attacked the Strasbourg clergy. Bucer apparently did not meet the first-named leaders. Soon afterward he began his task of converting the Anabaptists.

Bucer was asked to assist at the cross-examination of Jakob Gross (q.v.) from Waldshut and four other Anabaptists arrested in Strasbourg on Aug. 9, 1526. The questions of infant baptism, government, and other points were to be discussed. Bucer did not consent to the first point, probably at that time not feeling able to prove it from Scripture. When Jakob Gross confessed that he had been expelled from Waldshut because he had not obeyed the order of the government to take up arms against the peasants in Zell, Bucer asked whether it is permissible to refuse to obey the government. Gross replied, that as far as he was concerned he would render obedience to the government, but that he would refuse to kill anyone, because it was not commanded by God. Then Bucer asked the catchy question whether he would call the government, which of course bears the sword, Christian. When Gross noticed that Bucer was about to entangle him in his own words he replied cautiously and evasively that he would leave the judgment to God; he acknowledged that the sword was given and commanded to temporal government to punish the wicked and edify the good. In general Gross did not seem favorably impressed by Bucer when he complained that "Bucer had commended him to the devil" (Cornelius, II, 268).

In the fall of 1526 Ludwig Haetzer (q.v.) came to Strasbourg and was hospitably received in Capito's home. Possibly early in November Hans Denk (q.v.) arrived. Michael Sattler (q.v.) was also in the city at that time. It is very interesting to note the difference in the attitude of the reformers toward them. Sattler was most graciously and even fraternally received. But Haetzer and especially Denk were most violently opposed. In their booklet, *Getreue Warnung der Prediger des Evangelii zu Strassburg über die Artikel, so Jakob Kautz, Prediger zu Worms kürzlich hat ausgehen lassen, die Frucht der Schrift und Gottes Worts, die Kindertaufe und Erlösung unseres Herrn samt anderem, darin Hans Denk und andere Wiedertäufer schweren Irrtum erregen, betreffend, I. Joh. 4, 1,* of July 2, 1527, prepared chiefly by Bucer, Michael Sattler is called "a dear friend of God," "a martyr of Christ," although he is a "leader of the Anabaptists." And in the touchingly beautiful letter of farewell written by Sattler to "his beloved brethren in God, Capito and Bucer" (spring of 1527), he says that he had conversed with them "in brotherly propriety and friendliness," and closes with the words, "The Lord be with all of you dear brethren in God" (Röhrich, 31).

Toward Hans Denk their attitude was different. When he had been there only a few weeks Bucer and Capito complained in letters to Zwingli and Blaurer that he had brought confusion to their churches. On Dec. 22, 1526, a disputation was held between Bucer and Denk in the presence of 400 citizens. The council, not knowing of public participation in the disputation, had sent two delegates. Capito was also there, but did not take part. The discussion was based on Denk's book, *Vom Gesetz Gottes;* hence it must have dealt principally with the doctrines of reconciliation and salvation, though no details are known about the course of the debate. Evidently Bucer succeeded in convincing the councilors that it would be good for the city if Denk left. Two days later he was expelled from the city.

Bucer was probably aware of the superiority of the great Anabaptist leader, and feared that his influence would cause his congregation to crumble, hence his violent opposition. His verdict in the *Getreuen Warnung* on Denk was utterly unjust. He twisted Denk's statements, and gave them a false meaning. He called Denk's language so dark and confused that none of his adherents could understand *Vom Gesetz Gottes;* Denk used ambiguous phrases so that his statements could be twisted and turned to suit the required answer. This is of course a great exaggeration, even though it must be admitted that Denk's language is hard to understand. But Bucer also made the accusation that Denk "was unwilling to bind his spirit to the Scriptures" and "wanted to overthrow the Scriptures as of no avail." That this is not the case can be seen if one examines Denk's writings carefully and without prejudice.

Beyond this, Bucer declared, "Denk wished to make sin a vain delusion, i.e., nothing." Thus he misinterprets expressions in Denk's books as "Sin, as committed by man, is nothing against God," or "For sin is to be reckoned against God, and be it ever so great, God can and will and has overcome it." Bucer also went too far when in the detailed discussion of the last two statements of the seven theses of Kautz he called Denk's doctrine of the freedom of the will an obvious denial of salvation through Christ and asserted that he declared human nature, which is of course entirely corrupt, to be righteous. But he was altogether unreasonable in asserting, "Denk was unwilling to disapprove the deed committed in St. Gall, when one beheaded his brother." He evidently relied here on rumor. The fact that he credulously received it and made use of it shows clearly enough how incapable he was of judging the noble-minded Anabaptist leader.

Bucer's attitude to Martin Cellarius (*q.v.*) was similar. Cellarius had also come to Strasbourg in November 1526, and been received by Capito. Bucer celebrated him as a man of unusual greatness of spirit (Bucer's letter to Farel, Dec. 13, 1526). But when Capito became more and more deeply influenced by Cellarius and in warm words of recommendation wrote the foreword to his book, *De operibus Dei,* and finally in his commentary on Hosea openly advocated Anabaptist views, the friendship between the two reformers nearly came to a break. Bucer turned to Zwingli and Oecolampadius for help and urgently requested them to exert all their influence on changing Capito's mind. This was done. A complete break between Capito and Bucer was averted; the estrangement lasted until 1533. Bucer placed the blame on Cellarius and heaped the bitterest reproaches upon him, calling him a man "completely ruined by Anabaptism," and warning his friends of him. He was obviously very unjust.

In his attitude toward the Anabaptists Bucer became increasingly severe. When he noticed that he accomplished little by persuasion and that the Anabaptist movement in the city continued to grow, he appealed to the council with his fellow preachers with the request that they undertake more energetic measures against the Anabaptists. As a result a severe mandate was issued on July 27, 1527, against the Anabaptists, commanding all the citizens, inhabitants, clergy, and laymen in city and country to guard against such erroneous, unscriptural misleading, to get rid of the Anabaptists or their adherents, and offer none of them shelter, food, drink, or concealment. The mandate was immediately put into effect. The Anabaptists wherever found were seized, tried, and in part expelled from the city. Many of the remaining took the oath of citizenship. On Feb. 8, 1528, Bucer wrote to Ambrosius Blaurer (*q.v.*) that all the Anabaptists had sworn the oath, but he feared that they had done so merely to continue to live in the city and could do more harm than before.

Early in August 1528 the council managed to break up an Anabaptist meeting at "the Plow." On Aug. 15 the prisoners were tried in the presence of Bucer and Capito. In his commentary on Zephaniah, Bucer stated that one of the Anabaptists asserted on the basis of I John 3:8 and 9, that no one who sinned could be a Christian and denied that he sinned. He of course felt temptations to sin, but the Holy Spirit suppressed them. When Bucer called his attention to the petition in the Lord's Prayer, "forgive us our debts," the other was embarrassed; he observed that the prayer had been given to the apostles before they received the Holy Spirit; after Pentecost they no longer prayed thus. He could not do so either, for he was not aware of any sin. Judging from this, these Anabaptists belonged to the fanatical wing. Several days later they were tried again. The reformers had hopes of being able to lead them to better understanding. They succeeded in only one case. The others persevered in their conviction.

In the middle of August 1528 another meeting of Anabaptists, held in the house "aan de Kade," was surprised. This time the Anabaptist leaders Kautz (*q.v.*), Reublin, and Pilgram Marpeck were among them, as well as prominent citizens like Friedolin Meyer and Lux Hackfurt. Bucer, who had already talked to Kautz in June 1528 (Bucer to Zwingli, June 24, 1528), wanted a public disputation with them; he said from the pulpit that he "was not afraid of the pride and fluency"; but the council decided that Kautz and Reublin should be privately instructed from the Scriptures, but agreed that it might be done in writing. Bucer and the other city preachers turned in a refutation of Anabaptist views; and Kautz and Reublin sent in a frank statement of their faith, especially on baptism (Röhrich, 44). Then the preachers were ordered to deal with them orally, but without result; for the Anabaptists wished to defend their faith before the congregation or at least before the magistracy. Thereupon the preachers again requested the council to permit a public disputation, "because these two are among the most important of those called Anabaptists, and have respect not alone here but also as far as the sect is scattered, and many adhere to them." But the council continued to refuse it. Then Kautz and Reublin compiled a detailed statement of their faith, which is unfortunately lost; only its rebuttal by the city preachers is preserved (City Archives at Strasbourg, AA Ladula, No. 399 (9); Hulshof, note, p. 89).

In this document (Hulshof, 93 ff.) Bucer sets forth: the fact that "many pious persons are unfortunately laden with the Anabaptist error, but otherwise conduct themselves well and do not seek division" is not so serious "if one baptizes only the aged; unity should be preserved with these in all charity; for no one on earth is without error and mistakes; but there is the poison, where separation, division, and contempt for true Christians is found, with which unfortunately a large part of the Anabaptists is laden."

Bucer's first concern was the preservation of the unity of the church. For this he struggled and labored. All his wrath was aroused by the separation of the Anabaptists from the church protected by the authority of the state, and their establishing their own brotherhood; this angered him to the point of boundless resistance, even to spreading false accusations. About two weeks before Easter in 1529 he together with Hedio and Zell sent a report to the council (Cornelius II, 274), expressing the suspicion that "some intend to make all things common property and compel everyone to accept their faith by means of the sword; besides they act contrary to Scripture with regard to marriage." In consequence the council had some of the outstanding prisoners tortured; but "none would confess that they had the women in common or were planning any revolt or anything of the sort."

Bucer had a "grim pleasure" in these tortures and other severe measures. In July 1529 he wrote to Zwingli, "The ruthlessness of the Anabaptists has compelled the council to proceed more severely against them. Then Satan fell miserably. They, the unyielding, were quite softened, partly by banishment and partly by confinement in a dungeon. Those who were made quite wild by the most friendly Scriptural opinions soon changed their conduct; the bailiff had only to say 'he is expelled, or throw him into a deeper dungeon.'"

The growth of the Anabaptists in the city caused Bucer great concern. In a letter of Dec. 11, 1531, he inquired of Blaurer how he managed to win so many Anabaptists over. The failure of his efforts made his attitude toward them more and more rude and biased. This attitude is reflected in his treatment of Pilgram Marpeck. He described the character of this highly gifted and estimable Anabaptist leader at great length in his letters to Blaurer and Blaurer's sister Margarethe, who was deeply interested in Marpeck's personality. He could not close his mind to the excellencies and virtues of this man. "He is of fine and irreproachable conduct;—but he has cleverly laid aside the coarser vices; the spiritual ones affect him so much the more grossly." He resented most of all Mar-

peck's refusal to yield his separation from the church. "Pilgram will not desist from his baptism and from persuading the people that swearing and bearing arms are wrong; therefore I fear that he will be expelled from the city. For this reason be on your guard if he comes to you, not to be deceived by appearances" (Bucer to Margarethe Blaurer, Oct. 23, 1531).

Bucer had three discussions with Pilgram Marpeck, twice before the entire magistracy, and once before a committee appointed by them, chiefly on the attitude to government and infant baptism, but without result. In the course of the last conversation, Jan. 18, 1532, Bucer violently attacked his opponent with the words, "The fact that you Anabaptists, who make us out to be the enemies (Christ, thieves, and murderers of souls, do not expel and slay us, is only due to your lack of power. If you had it, I do not doubt that the spirit which keeps producing new ideas in you would soon teach you to kill all of us." Finally Bucer summarized all his accusations against Marpeck in a document which he presented to the council, in consequence of which Marpeck was expelled from Strasbourg. Before leaving the city the latter wrote a detailed defense of his faith, refuting Bucer's statement (published in *MQR* XII, 1938, 167-202), and wrote a letter of farewell to the magistracy, which "by its simple sincere tone says not a little for the character of the man" (Gerbert, 105; Röhrich, 57; *Monatshefte der Comenius-Gesellschaft*, 1896, 311).

We shall omit an account of Bucer's relations with Sebastian Franck (*q.v.*) and Kaspar Schwenckfeld (*q.v.*), who were close to the Anabaptist brotherhood, and mention his attitude toward Melchior Hofmann (*q.v.*). He came to Strasbourg in June 1529 and at once joined the Anabaptists. On June 30, 1529, Bucer announced his arrival to Zwingli. Although Hofmann's two visits to Strasbourg were brief, his influence must have been extraordinary. There were fanatical aberrations. Wonderful "visions" and "revelations" were reported. Bucer was alarmed by "revolting and impious idolatries" he saw in the city, causing him sometimes to despair of the future of his church (letter to Blaurer, March or April 18, 1532, Hulshof, 121, 249). He lamented it in a letter to the council in October 1532. In the spring of 1533 Hofmann made his third appearance in Strasbourg, and was captured a few weeks later, in May. According to a letter written by Bucer to Bishop Christian in Augsburg (Cornelius II, 355), Hofmann offered himself to the magistracy for arrest in order to fulfill a prophecy of a glorious conclusion of the mission entrusted to him by God.

On June 3-14, 1533, the great synod of the Strasbourg church was held. Sixteen articles of faith drawn up by Bucer were discussed and accepted. Only a small "Epicurean" party, including Otto Brunfels, made some objection (Bucer's letter to Blaurer of Feb. 3, 1534). Nearly all of the 16 articles referred to the Anabaptists. Their doctrines are often explicitly attacked in footnotes.

Without mentioning the Anabaptists, they refuted their position on the incarnation, baptism, communion, and the relation to government. This is evidence of the profound influence of the Anabaptists on the Protestant church in Strasbourg (Hulshof, 139 ff.).

The second part of the synod was devoted to the public disputation with the "sect leaders." The disputation with Melchior Hofmann was held on June 11-13. Bucer's *Handlung inn dem öffentlichen gesprech zu Strassburg jüngst in der öffentlichen Synode gehalten gegen M. Hofmann durch die Prediger daselbst 1533* (copy in Goshen College Library), gives an exact account. Hofmann also published an open letter entitled *Ein Sendbrief an alle gottesfürchtigen Liebhaber der ewigen Wahrheit, in welchem angezeigt sind die Artikel des Melchior Hofmann, derhalber ihn die Lehrer zu Strassburg als einen Ketzer verdammt und im Gefängnis mit Trübsal, Qual, Spott und Schande gekrönt und besoldet haben.* It is not as exhaustive as Bucer's pamphlet, which seeks to refute Hofmann's teachings in detail (zur Linden, 329-36; Hulshof, 145-48).

Bucer was intellectually greatly superior to Hofmann. Mockingly he advised the Anabaptist to stop preaching and stick to his trade. His superior bearing in this disputation enhanced his prestige and strengthened his position in the city, and he was celebrated far and wide as the successful combatant of the heretics. This reputation induced Philip of Hesse to summon him to convert the Anabaptists imprisoned in Marburg.

But before this Bucer still had to undergo a difficult struggle with the Anabaptists in Strasbourg, who were holding frequent, well-attended meetings, in which visiting Anabaptists participated. They had connections all the way to Moravia. Kilian Aurbacher, a preacher in the Austerlitz (*q.v.*) congregation, wrote a letter to Bucer in 1534, violently accusing him of causing the lords of Strasbourg, who had formerly received and shown pity for the believing brethren of the Lord Christ, who were in all the German lands exiled, expelled, martyred, and killed, now to take such a hard attitude. "Who gave you, I ask, power and authority to forbid the teaching of Christ to those who fear the Lord, serve Him, and sincerely desire to follow Him, and want to obey the government as far as is reasonable and proper, and live in all deference, meekness, patience, and charity toward all men. . . . You poor, wretched, blind preachers, where you preach you see to it that you are girt on one side with the sword of the Lord and on the other with the sword of the government; while you have this at your side you are happy and can well speak of faith; but when you lose it, all is over and you run away as has often happened. . . . You have driven the poor lambs of Christ out of their poor huts into the cold winter. Can you not understand and see how Christian your conduct is and what evangelical fruit it bears? Is this sheltering or showing mercy to the poor, wretched exiles? Is this being conformed to the Gospel of Christ

and His apostles?" (Hulshof, 165 f.) Bucer dealt repeatedly with imprisoned Anabaptists in the period following; one of these was Cornelius Polderman, who thought that Bucer had the right name, "for he snuffed the lights of the people of Strasbourg and their eternal welfare and salvation, so that they now grope along a wall like the blind at noon" (Cornelius II, 74-85). Bucer apparently induced only a few to repudiate their convictions, but in Hesse he was so much the more successful.

In August 1538 Philip of Hesse invited Bucer to Hesse. Bucer accepted in a letter dated Sept. 20. On Oct. 29 he arrived in Marburg from Cassel, where he first consulted the Landgrave. The disputation with the imprisoned Anabaptists took place on the next two days. He was completely successful (Hochhut, 627-44). He conducted the discussions with admirable skill. He stressed the need for the ban according to Matt. 18, I Cor. 5, and II Thess. 3. "Where there is no discipline and ban there can be no church." In sharp words he lashed at their usury which offended the Anabaptists. Earnestly he impressed upon them their error in condemning infant baptism; just as one does not refuse communion to women because they are not mentioned at its institution, children should not be denied baptism. The church is right in baptizing infants; it follows the baptismal command in Matt. 28, "baptizing them and teaching them." Obedience should be given the government in all things not opposed to God's Word; where this is not obviously the case, the subject should be obedient to the advice of the government and not set himself up as a judge of the government and its command. But if a subject knows that the government commands him to do an open wrong, he shall not, like Saul's guards, seek to kill the priests.

In this manner he won the Anabaptists over. On Dec. 9, 1538, nine Anabaptist prisoners drew up a confession of faith which almost entirely abandoned their former position (Hochhut, 612-22). Bucer and the Protestant clergy expressed their pleasure in a verbose document (Hochhut, 622-26): "Even though they do not completely confess their wrong and do not seem to understand that they have committed serious sin in rebaptizing, they [the clergy] after all praise God for aiding them to return to the church, in which may He preserve and strengthen them and us."

The most important of these converts was Peter Tasch (*q.v.*), "the acknowledged head of the Anabaptists in all Hesse, whose widely ramified connections extended to England" (Wappler, 78). The Landgrave and the preachers were elated by the success of the Alsatian reformer. On his suggestion Tasch was used to convert the Hessian Anabaptists. According to Bucer, Tasch led about 200 persons from their Anabaptist views. Tasch and Eysenburg, also a former Anabaptist, were called to Strasbourg, probably in the hope that they might induce Melchior Hofmann to renounce his faith. Their conversation on May 5, 1539, with the Anabaptist leader, who was greatly weakened by his chains, lasted six hours; this was repeated five hours on four successive days. But they did not succeed, nor did the other Strasbourg reformers, in moving him.

After this nothing more is heard of Bucer's efforts to convert the Anabaptists. A mightier took his place—Calvin (*q.v.*). Bucer was in Switzerland during the synod of the Strasbourg church in 1539, which was first of all concerned with opposing the Anabaptists. Calvin was the spokesman. Was Bucer perhaps in a gentler mood toward the Anabaptists because of his success? On March 17, 1540, he appealed briefly to Philip for Melchior Rinck (*q.v.*), who had been condemned to perpetual prison, with the result that Rinck was transferred "to mild arrest in a room built especially for the purpose."

Bucer introduced confirmation into the Protestant church. He had already expressed this idea in 1534 in his book *Ad monasteriensis*. It was first recommended for adoption in the *Ziegenhainer Zuchtordnung*, 1538, which was principally his work. Consideration for the Anabaptists induced him to introduce confirmation as a sort of substitute for baptism on confession of faith. Thus confirmation seems to be a concession to the Anabaptists (*Menn. Bl.*, 1912, 91; 34 ff.).

Bucer's attack on the Anabaptists in his commentary on the Gospels, which is reflected in its various editions, is a chapter in itself. It is fully presented by A. Lang in *Der Evangelienkommentar Martin Butzers und die Grundzüge seiner Theologie*. He says (45), "Bucer is most considerate to the powerful opposing party of Anabaptists, who are in the consciousness of the people often considered holier than the reformers themselves. He relates personal contacts and conversations with the Anabaptists.—Doubtless Bucer's commentaries offer the historian many a line to illustrate the Anabaptist movement."

On the whole Bucer was a severe, but moderate opponent of the Anabaptists. Although he finally also believed that he could not get along without government measures of force in combating them, he nevertheless protected them from the bloodiest persecution. He never spoke in favor of the death penalty. As far as is known, it was never applied in Strasbourg against the Anabaptists.   NEFF.

J. W. Baum, *Capito und Butzer* (Elberfeld, 1860); *HRE* III, 603 ff.; C. Cornelius, *Gesch. des Münst. Aufruhrs* II (Leipzig, 1860); C. Gerbert, *Gesch. der Strassburger Sektenbewegung zur Zeit der Ref. 1524-1534* (Strassburg, 1889); K. Hochhut, "Mitteilungen aus der protestantischen Sektengesch. in der hessischen Kirche," in *Ztscht für die hist. Theol.* 1858, 538-644; A. Hulshof, *Geschiedenis van de Doopsgez. te Straatsburg van 1525 tot 1557* (Amsterdam, 1905); B. Krohn, *Gesch. der fan. und enth. Wiedertäufer vornehmlich in Niederdeutschland* (1758); T. Röhrich, "Zur Gesch. der Strassburger Wiedertäufer in den Jahren 1527-1543," in *Ztscht f.d. hist. Theol.*, 1860, 1-120; P. Wappler, *Die Stellung Kursachsens und des Landgrafen Philipp von Hessen zur Täuferbewegung* (Münster, 1910); F. zur Linden, *Melchior Hofmann* (Haarlem, 1885); *Ztscht f. Kirchengesch.*, 1885, 473; H. Hoffmann, *Reformation und Gewissensfreiheit*, 23, 37; W. Diehl, "M. Butzers Bedeutung für das kirchliche Leben in Hessen," in *Schriften des Vereins für Ref.-Gesch.*, No. 83 (Leipzig, 1904); G. Anrich, *Martin Butzer* (Strassburg, 1914); G. Wolf, *Quellenkunde zur deutschen Ref.-Gesch.* II, Part 2 (Gotha, 1922); W. Bellardi, *Die Gesch. der "christlichen Gemeinschaft" in Strassburg (1546-1550)* (Leipzig, 1934); A. Lang, "Butzer in England," in *Archiv f. Ref.-Gesch.*, 1941, 230 f.;

idem., M. Butzer's last letter, *loc. cit.*; Rudolf **Schultz,** *Martin Butzers Anschauung von der christlichen Oberkeit dargestellt im Rahmen der reformatorischen Staats- und Kirchentheorien* doct. diss. Freiburg, 1932; N. Paulus, *Die Strassburger Reformatoren und die Gewissensfreiheit* (Freiburg, 1895, Catholic); H. Eells, *Martin Bucer* (New Haven-London, 1931); *ML* I, 307-13. H. Bornkamm, *Martin Bucers Bedeutung für die europäische Reformationsgeschichte (Schriften d. Ver. f. Ref.-gesch.* No. 169, Gütersloh, 1952) contains a complete list of works by and about Bucer; W. Pauck, *The Heritage of the Reformation* (Boston, 1950).

Buchanan County (Iowa) Amish settlement had its beginning in the fall of 1914. In that fall and winter seven families from Johnson Co., Iowa, migrated to Buchanan County to make their home. They chose this location because it was a level country, land values were not too high, and it was not too long or too difficult a move. A number of other families came later from Johnson County but the larger number of later settlers were from Kansas. There were also families from Wisconsin and Indiana as well as some others. The people live mostly in Buchanan County, but there are some in Blackhawk County and adjoining counties in northeastern Iowa. The addresses most common are Oelwein, Fairbank, Hazleton, and Independence.

The primary motive for a new settlement was dissatisfaction with the Amish churches in Johnson and Washington counties, Iowa. The churches in Buchanan County are somewhat more conservative in attire, as well as in some other things. The first ministers were William Miller and Jerry Stutzman. The settlement grew slowly at first, then more rapidly, and at present there are six congregations, each with its bishop and other ministers. T.H.M.

Büchel, Hans, an Anabaptist preacher and hymn writer, born in Murau in the Murtal (Salzburg), was one of the spokesmen of the Anabaptists in the Frankenthal disputation instituted by the Elector Frederick III of the Palatinate (May 28 to June 19, 1571). He was a nonresident representative, but did not attend all the sessions. He seems to have been an important leader of the South German Anabaptists; this is indicated by his being chosen as the speaker of the Anabaptists at the opening of the disputation. However, on June 6 a preacher from the Palatinate, Rauff Bisch (*q.v.*) of Obernheim, took his place. Büchel had appeared in public before this; when soon after the disputation at Pfeddersheim (*q.v.*) the theologians assembled at Worms in 1557 recommended the death penalty against the Anabaptists in their pamphlet, *Prozess, wie es soll gehalten werden mit den Wiedertäufern*, he wrote a long poem of consolation which begins, "Ein gfare zeit vor nie erhört, seit Gott erschuf Himmel und Erd" (20 stanzas). It is found in the *Ausbund*, No. 46, and also in Wackernagel, *Kirchenlied* V, 740. In addition the following of his hymns are still extant: (1) "Als man zählt tausend fünfhundert Jahr, sieben und fünfzig eben" (20 stanzas, *Ausbund* No. 29 and Wackernagel V, 738); (2) "Ambrosius klärlich beschrieb ein geschicht von christenlicher Lieb" (17 stanzas, *Ausbund* No. 9 and Wackernagel V, 737); (3) "Es begab sich auf ein zeite, als ich vertrieben war" (32 stanzas, *Ausbund* No. 45 and Wackernagel V, 749; (4) "Herr, starker Gott ins Himmels Thron, ich bitt durch deinen lieben Sohn" (21 stanzas, *Ausbund* No. 71 and Wackernagel V, 743). The first two of these are martyr hymns; the first is dedicated to Algerius (*q.v.*) who was burned at the stake in Rome in 1557, the second to a maiden and a youth whom Valerius executed. In the other Büchel laments the troubles and persecutions of the Anabaptists. Wackernagel's assumption that Büchel is also the author of the songs in the *Ausbund* signed "H. B." is incorrect; these songs were written by Hans Betz (*q.v.*). Very little is known of Büchel's life and work. Of his later period we know only that in 1584 he lived in Wildeck (near Heilbronn) under the protection of Albrecht of Löwenstein.   HEGE.

Chr. Hege, *Die Täufer in der Kurpfalz* (Frankfurt, 1908); *Protokoll, Das ist alle handlung des gesprechs zu Frankenthal* (Heidelberg, 1571); Wolkan, *Lieder; ML* I, 289.

Büchelhof, the name given in a list of 1731 to a Mennonite congregation in Baden (district of Sinsheim), "two and one-half hours from Wimpfen a.N. toward the northwest" (Müller, *Berner Täufer,* 209). It was founded by Mennonite immigrants expelled from Switzerland at the end of the 17th century and the beginning of the 18th, who settled on the two estates, Oberbiegelhof, owned since 1329 by the von Helmstatt family (*Ztscht f. d. Gesch. des Oberrheins,* 1863, 188), and Unterbiegelhof, property of the von Degenfeld family, or in their neighborhood; the latter is still tenanted by Mennonites, and the former was until 1910 (three generations of the Hege family occupied it 1822-1910). In the 18th century the congregation merged with Hasselbach (*q.v.*). (*ML* I, 289.)   HEGE.

Bucher (Bücher, Bougher, Bogar), a Swiss Mennonite family, found today among both the German and American Mennonites. In the early 18th century a Martin Boger was married to the daughter of immigrant Christian Bomberger of Lancaster Co., Pa. Among the Buchers who have served as ministers in the Lancaster Conference are Jonas W. Bucher (1828-1904), minister of the Mummasburg congregation from 1897; and John B. Bucher, ordained in the Hammer Creek congregation in 1892; also Simon Bucher, bishop 1940- .   J.C.W.

Buchner, Andreas, an Anabaptist martyr, was beheaded in the Vintschgau, Austria. He was leading a party of Anabaptists from Tirol to Moravia (V. A. Winter, *Gesch. der bayr. Wiedertäufer,* Munich, 1809, 138).

Bückert (Bueckert, Bieckert, Bickert), a Mennonite family name in the rural Flemish congregations of West Prussia. In 1776 five families of this name were listed in West Prussia (without Danzig), and in 1935 nineteen persons. The name is also found among the Mennonites of South Russia and Manitoba. J. P. Bueckert, Gretna, Man., is elder of the Blumenort congregation.   G.R.

Bucks County, located in southeastern Pennsylvania along the Delaware River, was one of the three original counties in the province. William Penn named it after Buckinghamshire of England. His residence, Pennsbury Manor, now restored, is located in southern Bucks County. Chief cities in the Mennonite northern half of the county are Doylestown and Quakertown. The first settlers were English Quakers. German settlers came into Bucks County from the expanding settlements of Montgomery County in the west. The earliest Mennonite settlement in Bucks County was probably in Bedminster Township which was created in 1742. Its first meetinghouse was built about 1746.

The Mennonite congregations in Bucks County totaled about 2,700 baptized members in 1950, about two thirds of whom belong to the Franconia Conference (MC), with 10 organized congregations, and one third to the Eastern District Conference (GCM), with 7 congregations.

It was at the Swamp Church near Quakertown, Pa., where the historic 1847 division occurred in the Franconia Conference. The more progressive group, led by John H. Oberholtzer (*q.v.*), later became the Eastern District Conference of the General Conference Mennonite Church. There is also one congregation of the Mennonite Brethren in Christ in Bucks County, at Quakertown.

The Mennonite settlement extends from central Bucks County north into Lehigh and Berks counties and west into Montgomery County. (See map of Bucks County, p. 462.)   Q.L.

Buckwalter (Buckwalder, Bookwalter, Buchwalder, Buchwalter, Boughwalder), a Swiss Mennonite family name represented in America chiefly in the Franconia and Lancaster conferences (MC). Johannes Buckwalter of Berks Co., Pa., was naturalized in 1730. Tax records of 1734 in the same county include a Jacob Buckwalter. In 1751 one of the trustees of the Coventry Mennonite Church in Chester Co., Pa., was Johannes Buckwalter; he may or may not have been identical with the Berks County settler of 1730. John Buckwalter (1749-1835) was a Mennonite minister in the Phoenixville and Charlestown Mennonite congregations of Chester Co., Pa. David Buckwalter (1809-91) was minister at near-by Coventry and Vincent 1854-91.

Louis and Joseph Boughwalder settled in Lancaster County in 1723 and 1747 respectively. In the ministry the following served: Henry Buckwalter (*ca.* 1740-1805) who was a minister in the Mellinger congregation, as was David Buckwalter (*ca.* 1821-1906); Michael Buckwalter (*ca.* 1809-76), a deacon in the same congregation, one of the largest in the conference; Ira J. Buckwalter (1870-1950), a minister in the Martins and Pleasant View Mennonite congregations in eastern Ohio from 1893, and bishop from 1895, and who at the time of his death in 1950 had been a bishop longer than any living leader in the Mennonite Church (MC). Among the living Mennonite leaders by the name of Buckwalter should be mentioned Bishop Earl Buckwalter of Hesston, Kans., and his two missionary sons, Albert in Argentina and Ralph in Japan, and Ira J. Buckwalter, who has been serving as treasurer of the Eastern Mennonite Board of Missions and Charities.   J.C.W.

Bucovic, a village east of Austerlitz in Moravia, where the Hutterian Brethren established a Bruderhof in 1536. It was at that time the property of Anna von Ojnic. The head of the congregation

Bucks-Montgomery

Counties, Pennsylvania.

KEY

o - Towns
• - Mennonite Churches
⊙ - Towns having Mennonite Churches.
b - Convalescent Home
d - Home for the aged

was Ulrich Stadler (d. 1540). From here the Brethren found entry in the following years into Bohnslavic, Urschitz, and Milonic. At about this time a congregation of Picards also arose in Bucovic (Beck, *Geschichts-Bücher,* 129; *ML* I, 289). HEGE.

Buddeus (Budde), **Johann Franz** (1667-1729), professor of theology at the University of Jena. In his book, *Historische und theologische Einleitung in die vornehmsten Religions-streitigkeiten* (1724 and 1728), he also discusses the Mennonites, calling them fanatics because they "place the chief emphasis on spiritual means, and reject all outward means, which God has also ordained." The presentation of the rise and development of Anabaptism, which is a pleasant deviation from traditional historical research, is based principally on Joachim Christian Jehring's (*q.v.*) book, *Historie von den Begebenheiten, Streitigkeiten und Trennungen, so unter den Taufgesinnten oder Mennisten von ihrem Ursprung an bis auf das Jahr 1615 entstanden* (see **Beginsel . . .**), for which Buddeus wrote the foreword. Like Hoornbeek, in his *Summa controversiarum* V, 366, Buddeus distinguishes three classes of Mennonite preachers: (1) *dogmata communia,* found among all Anabaptists; (2) *dogmata specialia,* found among some of their sects; (3) *dogmata specialissima,* who have been taught by one person or another. He adds, "Very few of these people, to be sure, are interested in study; nevertheless there have been some among them who were prominent in writing and public preaching." (*ML* I, 289.)   NEFF.

Budget, The, has been published weekly in Sugarcreek, Tuscarawas Co., Ohio, since its first issue, May 15, 1890. For over 30 years the paper was published and edited by Amish Mennonites and was widely circulated among them from coast to coast. The correspondence from their communities gives it considerable historical value. Two of the leading proprietors and editors were J. C. Miller and S. H. Miller, the latter an Amish Mennonite minister. Since 1920, the *Budget* has been out of

Mennonite control, but it continues to carry much Old Order Amish local news and is widely read in their communities. The paper was known as *The Weekly Budget* up to the time the Royal Printing Company began publishing it in 1920.   M.G.

Budkaw (Budkau), a Moravian village situated between Jamnitz and Budwitz, where the Hutterian Brethren established a Bruderhof in 1597, from which they were, however, driven by the oppressions of war in 1602. (Beck, *Geschichts-Bücher*, 335; *ML* I, 289.)   HEGE.

Buenos Aires, the capital of the Argentine Republic and a seaport city of over four million population. The first missionaries to work in Argentina under the Mennonite Board of Missions and Charities (Elkhart, Ind.) arrived in Buenos Aires in 1917. Because most of the missionaries of other boards working in Argentina had located in Buenos Aires, the first workers, the Shanks and Hersheys, moved to the rural districts of the southwest where there were a dozen or more towns and cities of five to fifteen thousand. In these centers, along the Western Railway, the foundations were laid, beginning in Pehuajo in 1919. As more missionaries were sent, more work was opened, churches were built, orphanages were established, the Bible School and the printery filled a needy place in the mission. In the first 20 years the membership had grown to over 500 baptized believers.

However, by 1939, the rural churches were steadily losing members who had moved to Buenos Aires because of economic inducements. The managing committee of the mission resolved that missionaries Shank and Litwiller make themselves responsible for the scattered members in Buenos Aires and its suburbs. By means of a circular letter a group of 43 were gathered for the first meeting, a preaching service held in the YMCA. Plans were made for regular meetings, which were held in halls either loaned or rented for that purpose.

By 1941 the L. S. Webers were sent to Buenos Aires to shepherd the flock. Because of a lack of workers, the Webers were moved to Bragado by December 1944. In the meantime, the Albano Luayza family had moved to Ramos Mejia, a suburb of Buenos Aires, and in December 1944 Luayza also took charge of the Buenos Aires congregation. The mission bought its first property in Buenos Aires in June 1946.

Because of governmental regulations which required the mission to have a central office in Buenos Aires, and because of the continued movement of members from the country to the capital, and for the sake of a remnant of Russian Mennonite refugees who stayed in Buenos Aires in the migration of 1947 from Germany to Paraguay, it was decided that the Litwillers should go to Buenos Aires to take charge of the work. Accordingly, in July 1949 a large property was purchased and by November 1949 work was inaugurated. The present chapel was used not only for worship services for the Argentine Mennonite Church but also for the Russian Mennonites. Sponsored by the Mennonite Central Committee, the Russian Mennonites, under the pastoral care of Martin Duerksen and the advisory supervision of Nelson Litwiller, have been meeting since October 1950 in a rented hall in Villa Ballester, a suburb of Buenos Aires. There are approximately 400 Russian Mennonites in Argentina today (a few German Mennonites among them), most of whom live in Buenos Aires and its suburbs. The membership of the Mennonite Church (MC) in Ramos Mejia under Pastor Luayza numbers approximately 40 (1951) while the membership in Buenos Aires proper is 30.   N.L.

Buens (Biens), **Claesken,** an Anabaptist martyr: see **Claesken,** the wife of Jan de Swarte.

Bugenhagen, Johann (Doctor Pomeranus), the reformer of Pomerania, b. June 24, 1485, at Wollin, educated at the University of Greifswald, was made rector of the city school at Treptow a.R.; on April 29, 1521, he matriculated at the University of Wittenberg, and soon became an enthusiastic follower and effective co-worker of Luther. Having become city pastor in Wittenberg and a professor at the university, he performed Luther's wedding ceremony. He died April 20, 1558. His historical importance lies in the organization of churches and schools in various states of North Germany, especially in Hamburg (where his work was interrupted by an invitation to the Flensburg disputation), in Lübeck, and in Pomerania.

In his attitude toward the Anabaptists Bugenhagen closely followed Luther. He was a signatory of the opinion of the Wittenberg theologians of June 5, 1536. Among his books were found two documents (*Theol. Stud. und Krit.,* 1886, 164), in which he refuted point by point the so-called Augsburg Articles (Anabaptist) ("the following articles some in Augsburg presented to the council and willingly confessed that they consider them true, for which they are lying in prison") and the Nikolsburg Articles (see **Confessions of Faith**), which he uncritically ascribed (in line with the common assumption) to Balthasar Hubmaier (Cornelius, *Geschichte des Münst. Aufruhrs* II, 279-82). In his conflict with the Anti-Trinitarian Joh. Campanus, Bugenhagen published a new edition of Athanasius, *Contra idolatrium et de fide sancta.* He also wrote a foreword to the book by Dorpius on the fall of Münster, and *Bekenntnis von seinem Glauben und Lehre, geschrieben an einen Wiedertäuffer zu Wittenberg* (Nürnberg, 1536), the first edition of which had appeared in the preceding year under the title, *Bekenntnis Bugenhagens von seinem Glauben und Lehre, geschrieben an einen Wiedertäufer.* The Anabaptist cited in the foreword is Hans Sturm of Styria, Upper Austria, in whose conversion Bugenhagen took a special interest.

Of unusual interest is Bugenhagen's part in the Flensburg disputation of April 8, 1529, held against Melchior Hofmann and some of his followers. Bugenhagen presided with Duke Christian. Chief spokesman was Hermann Fast, the reformer of Husum. In conclusion Bugenhagen summarized all of Hofmann's articles in a lengthy refutation. When Hofmann published his *Dialogus* describing the course of the debate, Bugenhagen published the official record of the disputation, which Krohn put into his *Geschichte der fanatischen und enthusias-tischen Wiedertäufer* . . . (Leipzig, 1758) 153-200.

In the first part of the book, *Von den vngeborn Kindern/ und von den Kindern/ die wir nicht teuffen können/ Vnd wolten doch gern/ nach Christus befehl/ Vnd sonst von der Tauffe* . . . (1557), Bugenhagen speaks about baptism in general and attempts to refute the views of the Anabaptists along these lines. His arguments are the usual ones, namely, that baptism and circumcision are the same and that baptism therefore should be administered to children, etc. At the end of the major part of the book he relates that Luther had instructed him to write the book, had read it and was pleased by it. However, Luther had asked him to add something to comfort the mothers whose children had died before they were baptized. After Luther himself has added some seven pages on this subject Bugenhagen takes up the subject. Again some references and attempts at refutation of Anabaptist views are made. The book is also significant as a source of information regarding baptismal practices and modes in the days of the Reformation. Krohn asserts also that in the *Martyrs' Mirror* of 1660, v. II, p. 77, van Braght stated that Bugenhagen had opposed infant baptism in his book, *Von den ungeborenen;* this error was corrected in the 1685 edition of the *Martyrs' Mirror.* NEFF, C.K.

H. Dorpius, *Wahrhaftige Historie, wie das Evangelium zu Münster angefangen und durch die Wiedertäufer zerstöret wieder aufgehört hat 1536,* Salig III, 402; *Ztscht f. Kirchengesch.,* 1911, 297; *Archiv f. Ref.-Gesch.,* 1933; W. Ruccius, *John Bugenhagen Pomeranus, a Biographical Sketch* (Philadelphia, 1925); ML I, 290.

Buggy. The Old Order Amish go to market, to town, and to church in a buggy, the "Wägeli." Like many current Amish practices the use of the buggy is a survival of an earlier general transportation pattern simplified to suit the Amish order of unworldly living and preserved in a rigidly prescribed form. The general type is a rectangular vehicle with a square top and sides, void of dashboard or whip socket, and without adornment. The occupant enters and leaves the vehicle in front by means of a step attached to the shafts. Certain Old Order Mennonites in Lancaster Co., Pa., Wayne Co., Ohio, Elkhart Co., Ind., and Waterloo Co., Ont., use similar vehicles. Both O.O. Amish and O.O. Mennonites forbid the ownership of automobiles by their members.

It has been a custom in most sections for the unmarried young Amish man to drive an open buggy without a top because it appeared less like the required Amish pattern. A few years ago in northern Indiana several young Amish men laid aside their pride in favor of the greater comfort and protection from the weather afforded by the top buggy. In spite of jeers, the top buggy is gaining favor among the young men.

The buggy may take slightly different forms and colors in different Amish communities. In some sections, in the Kishacoquillas Valley in Mifflin Co., Pa., for instance, after the Old Order Amish congregations had suffered several divisions, the color of the buggy was one of the distinguishing features of the various congregations, some pre-scribing yellow, some black, and some white. In Union Co., Pa., the color was yellow; the oilcloth for the curtains was made by painting several thicknesses of cheesecloth with yellow paint.

In Union County and in some other sections glass windows were proscribed as too worldly. On one occasion while one of the members, a cabinetmaker, who served as casket maker for the congregation, was using his buggy to convey a casket to the cemetery, the first buggy following broke a singletree; and, not knowing that the relatives were not following, he drove on nearly half a mile ahead of the procession. In order to avoid such embarrassment in the future the congregation voted to permit him to have a very small piece of glass in the rear curtain of his buggy.

As the Amish moved westward, some communities gradually departed from the stricter old style. In adjoining Logan and Champaign counties in Ohio, the permitted differences were a cause of friction. At least one young man left the Logan County congregation to unite with the congregation in Champaign because the latter permitted certain "fancy" modifications of the older pattern.

In Old Order Amish congregations failure to observe the prescribed pattern places the member under censure of the church, and persistence in disobedience leads to excommunication. On one occasion in Logan Co., Ohio, a minister who was in greatly straitened circumstances had an opportunity to purchase an old phaeton at a farm sale. His refusal to meet the demand of a fellow minister to dispose of this worldly vehicle became one of the causes for his severing his connection with the Amish Church and uniting with the Old Order German Baptist Brethren (Dunkards).

Among the Russo-German Mennonites the Old Colony Mennonites (*q.v.*) are opposed to the use of automobiles. Originally they used in Manitoba homemade wagons only and were opposed to the use of Canadian made wagons and buggies. Gradually the Canadian manufactured wagons and later the buggies found acceptance. Among the Old Colony Mennonites of Mexico it is permissible to use homemade vehicles with rubber tires drawn by horses, buggies to go to church and tractors to plow the fields; but automobiles are strictly prohibited. The buggies are the kind commonly in use in America before the coming of the automobile. The Sommerfeld Mennonites in Mexico and Paraguay are not quite as strict along these lines.

J.S.U.

Bühel (also called Beyhel), **Konrad van,** an Anabaptist in Strasbourg (Alsace), who was arrested because he visited Melchior Hofmann in prison. On May 29, 1539, he was tried and banished from the city on penalty of death by drowning if he returned. At his trial he said that he had visited Hofmann twice, "because we ought to comfort prisoners." Evidently he was induced to do this by the rumor current among the Strasbourg Anabaptists that Hofmann had recanted under the influence of the former Anabaptists Tasch and Eysenburg. Hofmann assured him that he adhered as firmly as ever to the truth. When Bühel asked how long it would be before the Judgment, Hofmann replied, that he knew of no Judgment Day; there would be times on earth when peace, joy, and righteousness reigned. Furthermore, Melchior admonished him that "he should just be pious and live quietly, keep his marriage intact and create no mobs; for he had no calling for this; he should also inform the brethren not to hold forbidden meetings in the forests, but should rather think of the Peasants' War, of Zwingli in Switzerland, and the Münster rebellion. They should keep the government in mind, especially that of Strasbourg, for it was a pious government." NEFF.

T. W. Röhrich, "Zur Gesch. der strassburgischen Wiedertäufer," in *Ztscht f. die hist. Theol.*, 1860, 114; F. O. zur Linden, *Melchior Hofmann* (Haarlem, 1885) 400; W. Leendertz, *Melchior Hofmann* (Haarlem, 1883) 325; *ML* I, 290.

Buhler, a Mennonite town in Reno Co., Kan., located on the Little Arkansas River 12 miles northeast of Hutchinson, has a population of about 650, almost 100 per cent Mennonite. Approximately 2,000 Mennonites live within shopping distance of the town. There are a General Conference Mennonite church and a Mennonite Brethren church in Buhler and a number of other Mennonite churches in the vicinity.

Buhler was first called Hamburg. In 1877 Bernhard Buhler settled in Reno County, becoming the cofounder and elder of the Hebron Mennonite Church (*q.v.*). Hamburg was incorporated under the name of Buhler in honor of A. B. Buhler, son of Bernhard Buhler, who had established a bank there. The town has a number of business enterprises and an old people's home. It has no theater and no intoxicating drinks are sold there. Most of the inhabitants and the rural population are descendants of Mennonites who came from the various places in the Molotschna settlement in Russia. Although Low German is still used, English has become the chief means of communication. C.K.

Buhler (Buler, Boular, von Bulaer, Bullaert, Buhlert, Buylaert, von Bulart, von Bular, Bulaert), a Mennonite family name in Danzig and Tiegenhof, West Prussia, originally urban and of Flemish affiliation, first mentioned in 1586. It is now extinct in West Prussia, but was transplanted to Russia and subsequently to the United States. Among the better known members of the family were Abraham Buhler, elder of the Grosswerder congregation 1726-29; Hans Buhler, elder of the same congregation 1741-54; Abraham Buhler, son of Hans, distinguished minister at Rosenort 1753-91; Jakob Buhler (d. 1855), minister at Berdyansk, South Russia, friend and early adherent of Pastor Edward Wüst, and Bernhard Buhler, minister at Berdyansk, and after migrating to America, elder of a church at Buhler (*q.v.*), Kan., which carries the family name. Buler also seems to be a Swiss Mennonite name. Hans Buler, a tailor, emigrated from Bern in 1711. G.R.

Bühler, Heinrich, a Mennonite from Brütisell in the Kyburg district of the canton of Zürich (Switzerland), had emigrated to Moravia in 1602 with his wife and children. He returned four times as an emissary of the Hutterian Brethren to promote emigration to Moravia. On the fourth trip he carried with him many letters from the Swiss in Moravia for their loved ones at home. He was imprisoned with his companion Joachim Arter in the Wellenberg in Zürich. At his trial he stated that he had come from Weselen (a Hutterite Bruderhof) and had received a commission from them to visit his friends in Switzerland, to persuade them to emigrate to Moravia. He had been in Switzerland six weeks. On July 6, 1614, the two men were released, after promising not to return; a return would be construed as perjury and would be punished accordingly. Their return to Moravia was delayed until fall. Nothing more is known about them. (Loserth, *Communismus; ML* I, 290.) NEFF.

Buhler Mennonite Brethren Church in Buhler (*q.v.*), Reno Co., Kan., started as a Sunday school in about 1901 and began to conduct church services in a grade school building in 1904. In 1908 the first frame church was erected. Under the services of Elder Henry Adrian this church became an independent body, working, however, in close relationship with its mother church, the near-by Ebenezer Mennonite Brethren Church (*q.v.*). In 1921 the Ebenezer Mennonite Brethren Church transferred to Buhler as a body, and built the present frame structure, 60 x 56 ft., in 1923. In 1926 the Mennonite Brethren Church of Inman, Kan., joined the Buhler congregation. The 1951 membership of 512 has Sunday school, Sunday morning and evening worship, a midweek service, as well as a young people's organization, sewing circles, men's organization, and three choirs. Other ministers who have served this church are P. R. Lange, J. B. Toews, C. E. Fast, H. P. Wiebe, J. E. Hildebrandt, Ervin Adrian, and Jacob J. Toews, the present pastor. J.J.T.

Buhler Mennonite Church (GCM) located in Buhler, Reno Co., Kan., is a member of the Western District Conference. This congregation was organized on Dec. 27, 1920. The first meetinghouse, however, was built in 1913, while the members still belonged to the near-by Hoffnungsau Church, of which the Buhler Mennonite Church is an offspring. The present church was built in 1927. The 1953 membership was 367. H.F.

Buitenlandsche Nooden (Foreign Needs): see **Fonds voor Buitenlandsche Nooden.**

Buitenmannen (or Buitenleraars), the name given in the Netherlands to the Mennonite elders and ministers, who were called in from another congregation, for example, to settle a difference and reconcile the parties concerned. In connection with the schism between the Flemish and Frisians in the congregation at Franeker in 1567, the *buitenmannen* mediated in vain. They also acted in connection with the *Lammerenkrijg* (1660-64). vDZ.

Buitenpost, a village in the northeast of the Dutch province of Friesland, where Leenaert Bouwens baptized about 14 persons 1568-82. It is not certain that a congregation arose at that time, but soon after 1620 there was a congregation here. In 1742 a church was built here and dedicated by A. Wynada, preacher at Haarlem, in a sermon entitled *David's liefde tot Gods huis, Leerrede over Ps. 26:8* (Amsterdam, 1743). In 1745 it united with the neighboring congregation at Kollum (*q.v.*), and in 1835 it was dissolved; the remaining members (there were only six left) joined the church at Surhuisterveen. The congregation owned a church at that time, which was remodeled into a double house and rented out, as well as a capital of 2,800 guilders. There is now a Mennonite group living in Buitenpost, consisting of about 20 members; they belong to the Veenwouden (*q.v.*) congregation.

J.L., vᴅZ.

Blaupot t.C., *Friesland*, 88, 192, 193, 245, 306; *Catalogus Amst.*, 147; H. J. Buse, "De verdwenen Dg. Gem. in Friesland," in *Vrije Fries* XXII (1915) reprint, 9; *ML* I, 291.

Buitenpost, Rogerus, was like many other Mennonite preachers, a physician, for he wrote a medical dissertation. From his book, *Kort Begrip van den Christelijken godsdienst voor de Doopsgezinde gemeente te Krommenie* (Amsterdam, 1742), we gather that he must have been the preacher there, although Blaupot ten Cate does not include him in his list of preachers at the end of his book, *Rede ter gedachtenis van het 300 jarig bestaan van een Doopsgezinde gemeente te Zaandam*. He names him rather as the preacher of the neighboring congregation Koog and Zaandijk. Buitenpost studied at the seminary in Amsterdam; he matriculated on July 14, 1729. Besides the above booklet he also published *Eerste beginselen van de leere des Geloofs* (Amsterdam, 1740) and *Onderwijzinge in den Christelijken godsdienst* (Amsterdam, 1744).

J.L.

Blaupot t.C., *Rede* (as above) p. 52; *Album Academicum van het Athenaeum en de Universiteit van Amsterdam*, 512; *Catalogus Amst.*, 293, 299; *ML* I, 291.

Buitentrouw ("outside marriage"), the term once used by the Dutch Mennonites when a member of the church married a non-Mennonite or a member of another branch of Mennonites, as, for example, when a member of the Flemish branch married into the Waterlanders. The stricter branches maintained the position against such marriages until the beginning of the 18th century and banned those who made such marriages. The Waterlanders soon relinquished the *buitentrouw*. Their church regulations of 1581 still ruled against it, but in practice those members who married outside the brotherhood were no longer banned. Before long many mixed marriages took place among the Waterlanders and gradually also among the other Mennonite branches. At present the Dutch Mennonites have no ruling whatever in regard to marriage with non-Mennonites. "Outside marriage" was also forbidden originally by the Swiss and German Mennonites as well as by their descendants in other countries, including Russia and North America. In the most conservative groups it is still forbidden on pain of excommunication. (See **Marriage**.) vᴅZ.

Bukiroba Mennonite Church (MC), located six miles east of Musoma, Tanganyika, is the central station of the Mennonite Mission, serving several small tribes. Work was begun there on Dec. 4, 1935, by the Clinton Fersters and the Elam Stauffers. The 1953 membership stood at 62 members. John Leatherman had the pastoral oversight of this church during its early years. The work is under the Eastern (Lancaster) Mennonite Board of Missions and Charities. E.W.S.

Buller (Büller), a Mennonite family name in the Old Flemish congregations in West Prussia, first mentioned at Schönsee (*q.v.*) (Sosnovka) in 1695. All members of this family emigrated to Russia (Molotschna settlement) in the first third of the 19th century, and subsequently to Kansas and Nebraska, from where they have spread into other states. Jacob Buller (*q.v.*), elder of the Alexanderwohl congregation in South Russia and later at Goessel, Kan., was one of the 12 delegates sent to America in 1873 to prepare for the migration. J. W. Buller was the founder of the Buller Manufacturing Co., Hillsboro, Kan. Peter P. Buller (b. 1874) served for many years as minister of the Alexanderwohl Church and later of the Goessel Mennonite Church in Kansas. Harold Buller, Mountain Lake, Minn., served as director of the Mennonite Central Committee relief program in Europe, 1949-51, and is now pastor of the Bethel College Mennonite Church. G.R.

Buller, Jacob, Elder of the Alexanderwohl Mennonite Church (*q.v.*) of the Goessel, Kan., community, was born June 10, 1827, in the village of Alexanderwohl, South Russia. In 1859 he was elected minister of the Alexanderwohl Mennonite Church and in 1869 its elder. When in the early seventies it became evident that Mennonites in Russia would have to look for a new home if Mennonite principles were not to suffer, he with eleven other Mennonite delegates was sent to North America to investigate places for prospective settlements. This inspection tour took about five months. Before the 1874 exodus he had been sent to Hamburg, Germany, with 15,000 Russian rubles to be exchanged for foreign currency. On Oct. 8, 1874, he with the majority of the members of the Alexanderwohl Church arrived at the place of destination and settled on the prairies north of Newton, Kan., where he continued as elder of the new Alexanderwohl congregation. During the pioneer years he and his associate ministers proved themselves able leaders of their flock. As to his ministry, his messages were simple and fundamental. A naturally strong voice helped to make his sermons emphatic. He believed in and practiced a strong church discipline. His bearing and speech bore testimony of the seriousness of life; however, a natural sense of humor made conversation with him a delight. He served his church without remuneration as was customary in those days. Contributions by the railroad company given as compensation for leadership he turned into the channels of the church treasury. During his last years ill health prevented him from rendering any public service. He died April 6, 1901.

P.P.B.

Buller, Peter, was elder of the Deutsch-Wymysle Mennonite church (*q.v.*) near Warsaw from 1838 on. He was ordained as minister in 1836. Nothing else is known about his life and activities. C.K.

Bulles, Les, a Mennonite congregation in the Jura district of the cantons of Bern and Neuchatel, with a meetinghouse (built in 1894) located in the hamlet of Bulles near La Chaux de Fonds at the far western end of the Jura Mountain plateau. Until 1923 it was a part of the larger congregation called Chaux d'Abel - Chaux de Fonds, which had two meetinghouses, the second being Chaux d'Abel built in 1905. The original congregation was formed by a late 19th-century merger of the Amish and Mennonite groups living in this area, the Amish La Ferriére, the Mennonite Chaux d'Abel. The earliest settlers in this vicinity probably came from the Emmenthal and Thun districts of the canton of Bern in the first decades of the 18th century. In 1882 the first Bible Conference (*Bibelkurs*) among the Mennonites of Switzerland was held in the Chaux de Fonds area followed by regular annual sessions attended by many from the other congregations. A number of outside evangelists contributed to the spiritual awakening in the Swiss congregations at the beginning of the 20th century and served in this annual Bible conference. Among them was Georg Steinberger of Rämismühle (canton of Zürich), and after 1904 Jakob Vetter, founder of the German Tent Mission. A prominent leader of the congregation was Elder David Ummel of Chaux d'Abel (elder 1837-96) who reached the age of 95 years. Other elders have been A. Geiser, ?-1902; Michael Nussbaumer, 1878-1917; David Ummel, 1887-1918; Heinrich Ummel, 1902-30; and Louis Geiser, since 1935, the present elder of the congregation. The 1950 membership was *ca.* 130 baptized, with 50 families. The congregation has a Sunday school and a chorus. Located as it is in the midst of a completely French-speaking environment and having no German school, the congregation is gradually changing its language from German to French.   H.S.B.

Bullinger, Heinrich (1504-75), chief pastor of the Reformed Church in Zürich, Switzerland, was born July 18, 1504, at Bremgarten in Aargau. He was educated under humanistic influence in Cologne. After serving his home church as pastor for two years, he withdrew from papal activities on the urging of his friends, and fled to Zürich, where he was offered Zwingli's position after his death in 1531. In his position of chief pastor of Zürich, which he held until his death in 1575, he developed the plans laid by Zwingli for the newly established Reformed Church into a firm structure. His influence extended far beyond Switzerland, over Italy, Holland, France, England, Bohemia, Transylvania, Hungary, and Poland.

Bullinger's first contact with the Swiss Brethren, according to his diary, occurred at the disputation in Zürich on Jan. 17, 1525. He says briefly, "Amazing is the impertinence of the Anabaptists," but wrote a few tracts dealing with the topics under discussion. It was his especial mission to insure the existence of his church and secure it everywhere by a definite, systematic, and foresighted attack on the Swiss Brethren. His public attitude toward them is shown in the following writings:

(1) *Von dem unverschampten fräfel, ergerlichem verwyrren unnd unwarhafftem leeren der selbsgesandten Widertöufflern, vier gespräch Bücher, zu verwarnenn den einfalten, Durch Heinrychen Bullinger geschriebenn. Een guter bericht vonn Zinsen. Ouch ein schöne underwysung von Zähenden* (Zürich, 1531, 178 leaves).

(2) *Bedenken der Herren Gelehrten zu Zürich, welches dieselbigen A. 1535, dem Rate daselbst der Wiedertäufer halben übergeben* (1535, reprinted in Füsslin III, 190-201).

(3) *Der Widertöufferen Vrsprung, fürgang, secten, wäsen fürnemme vnd gemeine jrer leer artickel, ouch jre gründ vnd warumb sy sich absünderind ... mit widerlegung vnd antwort vff alle vnd yede jre gründ und artickel, sampt ... vermanen, dass sy jres irrthumbs vnd absünderens abstandind vnd sich mit der kirchen Christi vereinigind, abgeteilt in VI Bücher und beschriben durch Heinrychen Bullingern ...* (Zürich, 1560, 2d ed. in 1561, title above).

(4) A long letter to Egli in Chur, of Oct. 13, 1570. (State archives of Zürich, E. II, 342, 606; reprinted in *Korrespondenz Bullingers mit den Graubündnern* III, 221 ff.)

Von dem unverschampten frävel (q.v.) is an earnest effort to refute in a book intended for popular consumption the basic tenets of the Anabaptists. It was much in demand by those who had to deal with the "hazard" of Anabaptism. It provides us with a summary of what Bullinger considered to be the main doctrines and emphases of the Swiss Brethren, together with his attempted refutation. It appeared in a Dutch edition in 1569.

In the early 1530's the Anabaptist movement definitely receded, the government grew more lenient, and the Diet of the four cities in 1533 advised milder measures. But the Münster affair became the occasion for sharper procedure. In Bern a persecution broke out, so that many Anabaptists fled to Zürich territory and forced the council of Zürich to take a position. In this connection the "opinion of the scholars" of 1535 was drawn up under the influence of Bullinger (printed in full in J. C. Füssli, *Beiträge* III, 190-201). This document is a justification and a statement of reasons for the procedure of the authorities against the Anabaptists as a sect, and their Scriptural punishment. It is significant that this statement deals in detail with the question of faith as a gift of God, for as long as this question was not decided a remnant of doubt remained in the minds of not only the lower classes against the church, which might be of advantage to the Anabaptists. Their attitude toward Anabaptist doctrine was more or less determined by the nature of their conception of faith. Furthermore, it was important to protect the young church from the charge that in the persecution of dissenters they were no better than the Catholic Church, and the seriousness of the question may have caused many to be concerned with the content of faith—as is clearly seen in a letter from Haller to Bucer—rather than to harmonize it with the demands of the time through a historical or dogmatic interpretation. In the *Bedenken* the authors (namely, the Zürich clergy) limit themselves to refuting the Anabaptist concept by citing the Old Testament and delimiting the idea of faith as a "free" gift as they understood it. By demonstrating that Anabaptists were a sect, they also justified their punishment, without having been guilty of wrongdoing. A classification of the sects according to the enormity of their error, the distinctions between the various degrees, is for the most part written with the Anabaptists in mind, even though it speaks of sectarians in general and only at the end mentions the Anabaptists and condemns them on the basis of the well-known consequences of "common Anabaptist doctrine" (contempt for the sacraments, disturbance of the peace, refusal of obedience to the government, etc.). The only new point presented is the form of Anabaptist trials, since the question of infant baptism merely led to evasions and only an examination in all the Articles would lead to more definite results. Nevertheless the attitude toward the Anabaptists had changed in that each deviating opinion was no longer punished with death, but that "individuals should be punished according to the degree of deviation and the receptivity for the church concept, according to the state of the affair and divine, temporal, and imperial law," i.e., to the death penalty.

The *Bedenken* specified the directions for dealing with the Anabaptists and was strictly observed. The Anabaptists replied by mass emigrations to Moravia.

The 1540's and 1550's gave Bullinger little opportunity to express himself against the Anabaptists. Their activities only rarely extended beyond their own brotherhood. The development of church discipline and conformation of their manner of life to the requirements of the Sermon on the Mount remained their principal objective and were in the 1560's the nucleus to which the populace attached itself and called a new movement into being.

It would be possible to connect this new movement with Bullinger's history, *Der Wiedertöufferen Ursprung,* published in 1560, and thus explain it as the second refutation of the Anabaptists in his own country. But this is not actually the case, as is indicated in a letter to Fabricius. Bullinger writes on Dec. 8, 1559, that he is fully occupied by a German book *contra anabaptistarum sectas omnes,* long requested by many North Germans, for the "Anabaptist pest" was particularly strong in those regions. He had to make a thorough revision of the four books he wrote 29 years before, and finished the first in two weeks, so that it could be publicized at the next market (Frankfurt *Frühjahrsmesse*). That the *Wiedertöufferen Ursprung* was in part based on his earlier polemic, *Von dem unverschampten frävel* (1531), and that it was a hasty revision, is of significance. It reveals once again Bullinger's impression of the Anabaptists over a three-decade span of time. In the eyes of Bullinger there were but two churches, Reformed and Catholic; the Anabaptists were not a church but a sect.

This point of view recognizing only two churches is even more obvious in Bullinger's practical work, as his letters to the Poles show, in which he recommends the suppression of the least expression of opinion contrary to the dogmas of the church.

The principle peculiar to the Anabaptists, viz., that the church does not have the authority to proceed with force against matters of conscience, found supporters even in the ranks of leading clergymen (Gantner in Chur; see letters of Bullinger to Egli in *Korrespondenz mit den Graubündnern,* pp. 1565-70 ff.). With all the means at his disposal Bullinger, through Egli, the parson in Chur, seeks to keep the Reformed Church pure and free of subjective expressions of opinion.

In a letter of Oct. 13, 1570, to Egli, Bullinger for the last time carries on a theoretical argument with the Anabaptists; nothing essential is added to his previous views. He proceeds from the consequences of Anabaptist doctrine and even in questions of minor importance he looks for Anabaptist suggestions which he stamps as "really seditious . . . articles"; even the mere charge that Gantner wants to treat the Anabaptists more leniently elicits the statement, "this article stinks of sedition."

Tolerance toward the Anabaptists can be spoken of only in a very limited sense, since Bullinger thinks that they as sectarians cannot demand it. His words to Faber, "We do not exercise force against those who do not adhere to our faith; for faith is a free gift of God, which cannot be forced; therefore faith can be neither bidden nor forbidden" (see *HRE,* article "Bullinger"), obviously have reference only to divergencies within the evangelical church (and to the Catholic creed). He was able to avoid the attempt, resulting from the decline of the church at the end of the 16th century, to accept the Anabaptist principles of church order, for at this time church and state were still more closely connected, so that no further forms were required within the church to preserve order. Until the end he was a determined opponent of the Anabaptist movement.

He is largely responsible for the theory that the Zürich Anabaptists got their views from Thomas Müntzer, a view which H. S. Bender completely refuted in his *Conrad Grebel,* 110-19, where he traces the development of Bullinger's theory on this point. C.B.

H. S. Bender, *Conrad Grebel* (Goshen, 1950); C. Bergmann, *Die Täuferbewegung im Kanton Zürich bis 1660* (Leipzig, 1916); H. Bullinger: *Diarium der Jahre 1504-1574* (ed. E. Egli, Basel, 1904); H. Bullinger, *Ref. Gesch.* (Frauenfeld, 1838, 1840); H. Bullinger, *Von dem unverschampten fräfel* (Zürich, 1531); idem, *Der Wiedertöufferen Ursprung* (Zürich, 1560); E. Egli, *Die Züricher Wiedertäufer zur Ref.-Zeit* (Zürich, 1878); idem, *Die St. Galler Täufer* (Zürich, 1887); E. Egli and R. Schoch, *Johannes Kesslers Sabbata* (St. Gall, 1902); N. Paulus, "Heinrich Bullinger und seine Toleranzideen," in *Hist. Jahrbuch* XXVI (1905) 576-87; T. Schiess, *Bullingers Korrespondenz mit den Graubündnern 1533-1575* (Basel, 1904 ff.); G. von Schulthess-Rechberg, *Heinrich Bullinger, der Nachfolger Zwinglis* (Halle, 1904); T. Wotschke, *Der Briefwechsel der Schweizer mit den Polen* (Leipzig, 1908); W. Wuhrmann: *Register zu Heinrich Bullingers Ref.-Gesch.* (Zürich, 1913); *ML* I, 291-98.

Bumangi Mennonite Church (MC) is located 25 miles east of Musoma, Tanganyika, in the Zanaki tribe. The work in this tribe was begun May 18, 1937, by J. Clyde Shenks and the Clinton Fersters. The beginning of the church was on July 30, 1940, when three men were baptized and received into church fellowship. J. Clyde Shenk has had pastoral oversight of the Bumangi church from its beginning. The 1953 membership stood at 75 members.

E.W.S.

Bundel, Groote (Large Collection), the popular designation for the Dutch Mennonite hymnbook adopted by the Amsterdam congregation de Zon in 1796 and soon also used by many other congregations. The official title was: *Christelijke Gezangen voor de openbaare godsdienstoefeningen.* It was first published by J. C. Sepp en Zoon at Amsterdam and contained 165 songs. The hymnbook issued by the Mennonite congregation at Altona, Germany (1802), under exactly the same title, took some hymns from the *Groote Bundel.* When de Zon united with Lam in 1801, the *Groote Bundel* remained in use. In Amsterdam it was discontinued in 1870, but in 1900 it was still used in 35 congregations, in 1940 only by the congregation of Holwerd, which used it until 1946. (*DB* 1865, 74, 84 ff.; 1900, 102 ff.)

vD**Z.**

Bundel, Kleine (Small Collection), the popular designation for a Dutch Mennonite hymnbook of the church bij 't Lam en van den Toren at Amsterdam (*q.v.*), adopted in 1792. It was first printed by Uylenbroek, van Hulst, and van Aken at Amsterdam in 1792, with the title *Christelijke Gezangen ten gebruike der Doopsgezinde Gemeente vergaderende by het Lam en den Toren, te Amsterdam.* It contains 68 hymns. When the Lam and Toren congregation united with the Zon congregation (1801), this hymnal was continued in use together with the *Groote Bundel.* It was discontinued in 1870. It was also used in many other places besides Amsterdam, but during the second half of the 19th century it was replaced in a number of congregations by new hymnals. In 1900 it was still used in seven congregations, and in 1940 only in Holwerd (until 1946). (*DB* 1865, 73 ff.; 83-4; 1900, 103 ff.)

vD**Z.**

Bünderlin, Hans (Johannes Wunderl, 1499-1533), a teacher and friend of Sebastian Franck (*q.v.*), and like him a spiritual reformer, at first joined the Anabaptists, but later left them and attacked them in speech and in writing. He was born in Linz in Upper Austria. On Sept. 19, 1515, he matriculated as an auditor at the University of Vienna. In 1519 he left the city. He may then, as Nicoladoni assumes, have wandered about as a traveling scholar. Gustav Bossert (*Jahrbücher für Protestantismus in Oesterreich* XV, 36) established his identity with Hans Fischer, the former secretary of Baron Bartholomäus von Stahremberg. He acquired this name from his father's occupation. Nicoladoni still treats the two as separate individuals.

Very likely Bünderlin went to Augsburg in the spring of 1526. Here he became acquainted with Hans Denk, who exerted the greatest influence on his religious views, and perhaps induced him to join the Anabaptists. In Augsburg he was baptized, as he states in his trial at Strasbourg March 16, 1529. From here he was probably sent to his home town of Linz as an "apostle of the Anabaptists," where he appeared in 1526. He accepted the secre-

tarial position of von Stahremberg and was very active as the leader of the Anabaptists in Linz and Wels. But he had to flee and went to Nikolsburg (*q.v.*) in Moravia, where the lords of Liechtenstein offered the Anabaptists a haven. Perhaps he participated in the disputation between Hubmaier and Hut, which was attended by a throng of Anabaptist preachers. As persecution by the Austrians became increasingly violent he had to flee from here too. At the beginning of 1528 he was in Strasbourg. He was imprisoned twice (Nicoladoni, 118). His second arrest took place in the house of the boatman Klaus Bruch (*q.v.*), at a meeting which he had called and where a portion of a booklet he had written was read aloud. From this it is known that he was actually an "apostle" of the Anabaptists; for meetings of this kind were usually held only upon their arrival at places where there were Anabaptists.

In 1529 he left Strasbourg for Constance, where Johannes Zwick, the reformer of the city, received him in his house as an opponent of the Anabaptists. Zwick's colleagues warned him of his "dangerous" guest. He therefore inquired of Oecolampadius for information about the visitor. Oecolampadius sharply condemned Bünderlin and his writings as "dark and accursed." This caused Zwick to insist on Bünderlin's departure from the city. He apparently next went from Constance to Prussia, perhaps under the direction of Caspar Schwenckfeld. Bossert (*Jahrbücher* XIII, 54) proves that Bünderlin was expelled from Prussia in August 1532. At this point all trace of him is lost. Nicoladoni surmises that he was captured in May 1533 in Litium (?) and there executed as a heretic.

Nor is there more information on Bünderlin's connection with Schwenkfeld. But Sebastian Franck speaks enthusiastically about Bünderlin in a letter to Joh. Campanus (*q.v.*) in 1531. He calls him "a learned, amazingly pious man, quite dead to the world." "I also wish to be baptized with the same baptism as he received." "He was indeed a man firm and strong in the Scriptures and gifted with a serene and especial understanding, mightily to entangle and overcome his enemies. But for the sake of the faith he did not wish to be involved in strife or dissension; for it was his view that a Christian is not a sower of discord, but should have his example only in Christ and His first church. He knew all the reasons in the Scriptures, and knew why a thing was said, and explained it according to the spirit, and not according to the letter like the scribes, especially Luther. He did not know whether Bünderlin was his brother in the faith, but he was a pleasant and desirable guest, frank and—speaking honestly—much more learned and pious than he himself, miserable man. He could therefore do much more in many matters than he; he could also be more open and free; for he had neither wife nor child" (Nicoladoni, 125 f.).

Nicoladoni gives the principal contents of four books by Bünderlin (132-55):

(1) *Ein gemayne Berechnung über der Heiligen Schrift Inhalt, aus derselben natürlichen Verstand (mit Anzeigung ihres Missverstands, Grund und*

Ursprung) einzuleiten, durch etlichen Punkten Gegensatz Erklärung, dabei man die andern, so vielfältig in der Schrift verfasst sind, auch abnehmen mag. In vier Teyl durch Joanem Bünderlin von Lyntz gestellet.—Prüfet alles und behaltet das gut. I. Thess. 5. Urteilet nit vor der Zeit (Strasbourg, 1529).

(2) The second book of Bünderlin appeared under the title, *Aus was Ursach sich Gott in die Nyder gelassen und in Christo vermenschet ist, durch welchen und wie er des menschen Fall in ihm selbs durch den gesandten Messiah versunnt und widerpracht hat. Röm. 11: Denn aus in und durch in und in in sein alle Dinge.* At the end, "*Durch Joh. Bünderlin von Lyntz*" (Strasbourg, 1529).

(3) In 1530, without stating the place of publication, a new work by Bünderlin appeared, titled *Erklärung durch Vergleichung der biblischen geschrifft, dass der Wassertauf sampt anderen äusserlichen Gebräuchen in der Apostolischen Kirchen geübet, on Gottes befelch und zeugniss der Geschrifft von etlichen dieser Zeit wider eefert wird. Sintemalen der Antichrist die-selben allzehand nach der Apostel abgang verwüst hat. Welche Verwüstung dann bis an das ende bleibt. Dan. 11. Joh. 4—Gott ist ein Geist und die in anbettend, die müssen in geist und in der warheit eeren und anbeten.*

(4) *Ein gemyne einlayttung in den aygentlichen Verstand Mosi und der Profeten, wie man sie lesen und in Allegorien mit dem neuen Testament vergleichen und auslegen soll. Ann vilen und den notwendigen Punkten gemehret, gebessert und von newem corrigirt. Mit Dannenthuung der letzten Clausulen, so aus unverstand vorhin dran gehenkt ist. I. Thess. V. Den Geist lescht nit auss. Weissagung verachtet nit. Prüfet alles und das gut behaltet. MDXXIX.*

The royal library of Dresden contains a copy of the first three Bünderlin writings, including the tract on baptism which has hitherto been used only in a single copy found in the library of the university of Utrecht.

In these writings we become acquainted with a pantheistic-mystical, speculative-theosophist and subjectivistic-rationalistic viewpoint of the author, who ranks among the most liberal theologians of his day. The first book reveals a dependence on Hans Denk. With warm words he champions tolerance in matters of faith, emphasizes the inner Word, which he places above the outer, and demands a purely spiritual worship with the absence of all outward ceremony. Christ's work of redemption consists in our acknowledging God's love in His mission and in becoming His disciples. The third book is the most important; it shows clearly that his ideas are not based on Anabaptist principles. Only those are the blessed who adhere to no outer party or sect. Only the inward devotion of the heart is true worship, which makes the outward unnecessary. Baptism should not be made a burden on the conscience of sinful man. Christians do not need baptism, for as Christians they do not assemble for battle, but each clings to God in spirit

and serves God, without the attention or motivation of others, and nobody needs to be concerned as in the external Israel as to who is or remains a Christian.

We can understand that the Biblicistic Anabaptists rejected and opposed his teaching. Pilgram Marpeck wrote a refutation against Bünderlin under the title, *Ain Clarer vast nützlicher unterricht, wider etliche trück und schleichendt geister, so jetzt in verborgener weis ausgeen dadurch vil frommer hertzen verirrt und verführt werden, kürzlich, getreuer warnung wegn herfürgebracht 1. betreffend das apostel ampt, 2. das bischoffampt, 3. die Ceremonien Christi, 4. Unterschiedt der Gottheit und menschheit Christi, 5. die Sendung und Wort eenes newen propheten, 6. gebet ein gut werk Corneli. Prov. XXI. Es ist dem gerechten ein freud zu tun was recht is, aber ein forcht der übelthäter. Nit was, sonder das. MDXXXI.* (Hulshof, 99.) This book was unfortunately lost in the fire of 1870 in Strasbourg; it might have given interesting information on Bünderlin's relation to the Anabaptists.

NEFF.

Monatshefte der Comenius-Gesellschaft, 1893, 199; 1894, 96, 103; 1895, 59; A. Nicoladoni, *Johannes Bünderlin von Linz und die oberösterreichischen Täufergemeinden in den Jahren 1525-1531* (Berlin, 1893); Hulshof, *Gesch. van de Doopsgez. te Straatsburg van 1525 tot 1557* (Amsterdam, 1905); Rembert, *Wiedertäufer*; G. Bossert, "Hans Bünderlins Vorgeschichte," in *Jahrbuch der Gesellschaft f. d. Gesch. des Prot. in Oesterreich*, 1890, 161; Rufus Jones, *Spiritual Reformers of the Sixteenth Century* (London 1914) Chapter III; R. Stadelmann, *Vom Geist des ausgehenden Mittelalters* (Halle, 1929); W. Köhler, "Hans Bünderlin," in *RGG I* (2d ed.) col. 1345; *ML I*, 298.

Bundesbote-Kalender was published by the General Conference Mennonite Church annually 1886-1947. In content and appearance it was very similar to other German almanacs published in America. It usually carried a calendar page for each month, some religious stories, biographies of Mennonite leaders, and events and chapters from Mennonite history everywhere. Much valuable biographical and historical information has been accumulated on the pages of the *Bundesbote-Kalender*. S. F. Sprunger and C. E. Krehbiel were among its editors.

In 1947 when the conference paper, *Christlicher Bundesbote* (q.v.), was merged with *Der Bote* (q.v.), the title of the *Bundesbote-Kalender* was changed to *Mennonitisches Jahrbuch* (q.v.) which appeared for the first time under the new name in 1948.   C.K.

Bundling is usually associated with the Amish as a form of courtship in which the young people, fully clothed except for their shoes, occupy the same bed. The custom seems to have been quite general among them until the beginning of the 19th century. Somerset County (Pa.) Amish ministers condemned the practice in a conference in 1830. Later several families left Somerset County to found a colony in Iowa hoping to leave the custom behind, but their efforts were not entirely successful. In Lancaster Co., Pa., the custom died out in some sections before 1880. Although disapproved by the Amish ministers and many family heads, the custom lingers on in parts of northern Indiana and elsewhere. One reason for the persistence of bundling among the Amish probably is their extreme reluctance to relinquish the customs practiced by the forefathers. Such long-established customs have acquired an almost religious significance. Either the custom is not so generally practiced as is commonly believed, however, or Amish young people observe it in a spirit of self-restraint. At any rate cases of illegitimacy are rare among the Amish. Bundling was not a custom confined to Amish families, but according to a research article in *The Mentor* (October 1929) it was imported to America in the 17th and 18th centuries with the Welsh, the English, the Dutch, the Germans, and even the Calvinistic Scotch. Jonathan Edwards preached against bundling, and Boston, Salem, and New York proscribed it by law. It is still to be found in a few townships in New England, survives in vestige form in Wisconsin and Minnesota, and is practiced in the mountains of Kentucky, West Virginia, Tennessee, and North Carolina. J.S.U.

Bunker Hill unaffiliated Amish Mennonite Church, Fredericksburg, Ohio, was first listed in the 1949 *Mennonite Yearbook and Directory*. In 1953 the 28 members were being served by preachers Jeremiah Schlabach and Noah Miller. M.G.

Bunschoten, a village in the Dutch province of Utrecht on the shore of the Zuiderzee, in which there was once a Mennonite congregation with its church building; it was sometimes called Spakenburg (*q.v.*), the name of the near-by village. It must have been in existence in 1581; about this time Leenaert Bouwens baptized 13 persons here, and in 1606 the Reformed preacher complained about their "audacious" conduct, for they already possessed a meetinghouse where they could meet undisturbed. In September 1647 delegates from Bunschoten took part in the conference of Waterlanders in Amsterdam. In 1733 the church contributed 112 florins to the Fund for Foreign Relief. In the middle of the 17th century, when the shortage of preachers in the Dutch churches was very acute, the church at Bunschoten had its own minister. After the death of Jan Barents (1685), the congregation was served by Teunis Adriaansz, preacher at Huizen (*q.v.*). After his death in December 1688 the church at Utrecht came to its aid. In 1699 Bunschoten was called a subsidiary of the Amersfoort (*q.v.*) congregation. In 1702 Bunschoten suffered a flood and the congregation suffered severe losses. From Dutch Mennonites they received contributions of 4,000 florins. In 1704 they had again received a preacher in Klaas Jelisz Huisman; but they were unable to raise funds for his salary. The other congregations could no longer make adequate contributions, and the church died out shortly after 1731, the children being received into the Reformed Church. The church building passed into the possession of the civic community, which sold it at the end of the 18th century. (*DB* 1863, 79-80, 95-98; 1872, 67; 1892, 108, 115, 125 f.; 1907, 78; 1910 f.; 1918, 127-29, 133-37; *Inv. Arch. Amst.* 95-98; 1918, 127-29, 133-37; *Inv. Arch. Amst.* II,

II, Nos. 833, 1522, 1610; II, 2, No. 38; *ML* I, 300.) NEFF.

Burchett Flat is a schoolhouse located three miles south of Relief, in Morgan Co., Ky. The nearest large town is Paintsville. Mennonites (MC), working under the Virginia Mennonite Board of Missions and Charities, have conducted regular Sunday services in the schoolhouse since the summer of 1943. One baptized member and two resident workers are located near Relief. L.C.S.

Burckhardt, Paul, b. Jan. 9, 1873, principal of a Töchterschule at Basel, author of the excellent book, *Die Basler Täufer. Ein Beitrag zur Schweizerischen Reformationsgeschichte* (Basel, 1898), which presents an account of the Anabaptist movement in the canton of Basel (*q.v.*) until the 19th century, based on thorough research. In 1949 he published *David Joris und seine Gemeinde in Basel,* 106 pp., a reprint from *Basler Ztscht für Gesch. und Altertumskunde. (Basler Biographien* I, 1900; *ML* I, 300.) NEFF.

Burcky's Schoolhouse, a former unorganized congregation (MC) near Tiskilwa, Ill., also called Ohio Station.

Bure, Idelette de, wife of John Calvin (*q.v.*), whom she married in August 1540, at Strasbourg in Alsace. She was for a time an Anabaptist, and had previously been married to an Anabaptist of Liège, Jean Stordeur (also called Storder and Stordene), who died of the plague. After the birth of a son Jacque in 1542, who lived only a few days, Idelette slowly succumbed, and died on March 29, 1549. Little is known about her life; but Calvin's loss is seen in a letter of April 2, 1549, to his friend Farel in Neuchâtel. (R. Schwarz, *Joh. Calvins Lebenswerk in seinen Briefen,* Tübingen, 1909, 338 f.)

Whether Idelette contributed to the Anabaptist influence on Calvin, which some believe is evident in Calvin's strict church discipline, is uncertain. It is true that soon after his arrival in Strasbourg in 1538 Calvin made contacts with the Anabaptists, and that some of the French Anabaptist refugees, finding it difficult to understand their German-speaking brethren, joined the French church which Calvin organized here, a step which was perhaps made easier because Calvin introduced into his church one of the principal Anabaptist demands, i.e., strict church discipline. But there is no concrete evidence of Idelette's part in this.

N. Weiss, professor and librarian at the university of Strasbourg, reports that a portrait of Idelette was extant at Fontenay, rue Roses 1907. The picture is a photographic copy of a painting on wood; it shows her unusually sharp features and long nose. (*Menn. Bl.,* 1909, 36; *ML* I, 300.) H.S.B.

Bureau County, Ill., is located in north central Illinois, about 120 miles southwest of Chicago and 50 miles north of Peoria. The Mennonites are located mostly in the southern part of the county. There are three Mennonite churches in the county, Willow Springs Mennonite Church (MC), four miles southwest of Tiskilwa; Tiskilwa Mennonite Church (GCM), in Tiskilwa; Rockwell Mennonite

Church (MC), in Sheffield. These three churches have a combined membership of about 220. This makes a Mennonite population of about 350 including the children.   E.I.C.

Buren, a small town in the Dutch province of Gelderland where there were Mennonites as early as 1563, Leenaert Bouwens baptizing eight persons here between 1563 and 1565, and where in 1649 a congregation belonging to the Flemish branch existed, which, however, disappeared soon afterwards. (*Inv. Arch. Amst.* I, No. 408; Blaupot t. C., *Holland* I, 222, 330; II, 45.)   vDZ.

Burg, Den, pop. 5,000, principal town on the Dutch island of Texel (*q.v.*), where soon after 1530 Anabaptism gained a foothold. On Sept. 15, 1534, an Anabaptist of Texel, Thijs Olbrants, received the death sentence; Sept. 15, 1534, 12 Anabaptists were banned for life; on Dec. 16, 1564, Jan Gerrits of Texel was burned at the stake in The Hague. During these years a congregation existed of which Simon Fijts was the minister in 1569. Between 1563 and 1582 Leenaert Bouwens (*q.v.*) visited the island twice and baptized 13 persons there.

Shortly after this we also find division here among the Mennonites. In Den Burg there were two congregations, one Frisian and the other Flemish. The former had its church on the site where the present church now stands; the Flemish church still exists as a warehouse at Achter de Wal. About 1660 the parties were no longer strictly separated from each other. Shortly after this date the Flemish formed one congregation with members of the near-by villages of Oosterend (*q.v.*), de Waal (*q.v.*), and Den Hoorn (*q.v.*), in which union the Waterlander congregations from Oosterend and de Waal were also included. From this federation Den Hoorn separated in 1707. In 1772 (July 19) the Frisians joined the United Flemish and Waterlanders and the church building was enlarged in 1774. It was intended that henceforth there should be one congregation on the island with a single church board and administration of all property. The congregation of Den Hoorn, however, did not go along with this union. There is a letter (*Inv. Arch. Amst.* II, No. 1636) written about 1775 by members of Den Burg, "who on account of the orthodoxy and the intolerance of Ds. Jan Stuurman have separated themselves and established their own church," to the church board of the Lamist congregation at Amsterdam, requesting subsidy for the support of their minister Gerbrands, which they received. Concerning this separated congregation nothing more is known. It presumably maintained its position for only a short time. Concerning the further history there is not much to relate. About 1780 the congregation held steadfastly to the principle of nonresistance and in 1807 still obtained freedom of military service from Louis Napoleon, who was then king of Holland. In 1857 the size of the congregation made an enlargement of the church necessary, and in 1869 an organ was acquired. The membership totaled approximately 200 in the Flemish congregation in 1731. At the time of the union in 1772 there were 359 members; in

1814, 307; in 1861, 498; in 1898, 680 in addition to 40 in Den Hoorn; in 1950, 650.

The congregation at Den Hoorn joined with this church in 1949, so that at present there is only cne congregation at Den Burg, Waal, Oosterend, and Den Hoorn, now called the Mennonite congregation of Texel. The ministers during the past century were: J. Huizinga, 1844-79; A. W. Huidekoper, 1861-63; J. Boetje, 1864-68; C. J. Bakker, 1868-71; H. Koekebakker, 1871-75; P. S. Bakels, 1876-79; S. F. van der Ploeg, 1880-84; R. Kuperus, 1889-1919; C. C. de Maar, 1919-25; Dr. A. Vis, 1925-39; K. T. Gorter, 1939-41; J. Knot, 1941-46; Th. van der Veer, 1942-46; Th. van Veen 1947-53.

The congregation has an active family help organization; there are also youth organizations and work is done in behalf of young people. An old people's home is in the process of being started in co-operation with the other Protestant denominations.   vDZ.

Inv. Arch. Amst. II, Nos. 1611-38; *DB* 1861, 168 f.; 1873, 140-74; Blaupot t. C., *Holland* I, II, *passim*; *ML* I, 301.

Burger, Martin, a Swiss Mennonite, born "auf der Burg," in 1643 joined the Mennonite congregation in Rynach, canton of Bern, and was consequently seized on March 2, 1646, and cross-examined on Jan. 6, 1648, in which he made detailed statements about his confession of faith. He says that he left the state church because its doctrine and life did not agree; therefore he united with the Anabaptists because he heard that they were a peaceful and upright people; he had also found that they gave alms, loved one another, did not swear, and were not unchaste. Therefore he wanted to stay with them. Concerning infant baptism he says he does not believe that it harms the children, but whether it is beneficial he will leave to God. The Bible says, "He who believes and is baptized"; faith must precede baptism. But a child knowing nothing about faith can neither consent nor refuse. The government is instituted by God to punish the evil and protect the good, and a Christian can be a member of the government if he conducts himself according to God's will. Of warfare he replies that Christ has proclaimed peace and commanded prayer for the enemy.

Concerning the oath he states that it is said at a certain place that the oath settles a thing. But he remains with yea, yea and nay, nay. Again on Jan. 13, 1648, he and Hans Stentz were asked whether they will change their minds. Then Martin Burger declared that he would stick to that which God has given him to understand, let it cost what it would. Thereupon both were placed in the penitentiary at Zürich, but soon escaped. Nothing more is known of Martin Burger. (Müller, *Berner Täufer,* 107-15; *ML* I, 302.)   Neff.

Burghart, Jacobus, a German engraver, who is supposed to have lived during the second half of the 18th century in East Friesland and of whom nothing more is known, engraved a portrait of Menno Simons in 1683 (known as the Hamburg-Altona portrait). This picture, first edited by Petrus Grooten, was widely accepted among the Mennonites.

In 1889 the congregation of Hamburg-Altona procured a new edition (Kunstverlag, Hermann Braams, Norden-Norderney). vdZ.

N.N.B.Wb. II, 281; Thieme-Becker V (Leipzig, 1911) 251; *DB* 1916, 77-80; *Menn. Bl.,* 1889, 113.

Burghausen, a town in Upper Austria, the seat of an early Anabaptist congregation and later the scene of the imprisonment of several Anabaptist leaders, among them Hans Aichner, Wolff Rauffer, and Leonard Sumerauer. (See **Bavaria** and **Bruckmaier**; Wolkan, *Geschichts-Buch,* 237; Beck, *Geschichts-Bücher,* 277.)

Burgmann, Johannes Christianus (1697-1775), professor at the University of Rostock (from 1754), Germany, in 1733 wrote a thesis on Obbe Philips and the Obbenites (full title: "Commentatio Historico-ecclesiastica. De Ubbone Philippi et Ubbonistis, subjecta brevi disquisitione de habitu doctrinae Mennonitarum"). A copy of this thesis is now in the Amsterdam Mennonite Library. By the same author is the book *De historiae mennoniticae fontibus et subsidiis* (Rostock, 1732) (Sources and Resources of Mennonite History), which is also to be found in the Amsterdam Library. In these two writings Burgmann proves himself to be an excellent authority on Mennonite history. (*BRN* V, 94; *ML* I, 302; Meussel, *Teutsche Schriftsteller* I, 1802, 743.) Neff.

Burgsteinfurt, a small town in Westphalia (Germany), between Münster and the Dutch border, where there was once a Mennonite congregation, probably consisting chiefly of Mennonite refugees from Twente, Holland, who had a very difficult time about 1600 and emigrated to Burgsteinfurt. After the attack upon Burgsteinfurt by imperial troops in 1635 many Mennonites returned to Holland, to Twente, Deventer, Zwolle, and Alkmaar. The Blijdenstein family (*q.v.*) came from Burgsteinfurt; also Hendrik Paschen Gerritszoon, a merchant, the father of Isaac Paschen, who became a preacher of Enschede; also Berent Paschen and Jan Franken, the pastor of the Enschede congregation, who died in 1764 at the age of nearly 105. In 1786 the Burgsteinfurt congregation was still in existence; Jan ten Cate Szn. of Enschede was the preacher. The time of its extinction is not known. In *DB* 1885 (p. 14) there is a note that the remaining funds of the congregation and also some communion silver passed into the possession of the Prince of Bentheim, on whose territory Burgsteinfurt was situated. (G. Heeringa, *Uit het verleden der Doopsgezinden in Twenthe,* Borne, n.d.) vdZ.

Burgweinting (near Regensburg, Bavaria) *Home for the Aged,* founded (April 1929) and operated by *Christenpflicht* (*q.v.*), Bavarian Mennonite relief agency, has a capacity of 25. H.S.B.

Burial. To bury the dead is a Christian custom, adopted from the Jews. The heathen usually cremated their dead. In the New Testament two burials are recorded. Ananias and Sapphira were carried to their grave by young members of the church (Acts 5:10), and Stephen (Acts 8:2) by "devout men."

In the earliest Christian church burial was already a congregational affair. Tertullian and other church fathers relate that the churches took care of the burial of their poor, and that they had common burying grounds. The entire congregation participated in the religious rite. This participation was based on a regard for the body as the "organ of the spirit," and on the belief in the resurrection. Funeral sermons in the modern sense were unknown. The funeral procession, which took place by day, was to express the joy in overcoming death. The custom of throwing three shovelfuls of earth originated in the Middle Ages. The dedication of the corpse came at a much later period.

In modern times cremation has been widely accepted. The Catholic Church does not accept it; its priests are forbidden any participation in the procedure. In most Protestant churches it is optional; ministers may take partial or complete charge of cremation. Among European Mennonites it is also occasionally practiced, especially in the city churches; many country churches oppose it.

Practices in Europe. From the beginning the Mennonites have buried their dead in accordance with local custom, and in common cemeteries. Several exceptions to this custom have been noted. Emil Egli (*Die Züricher Täufer, 37*) related that a Michel Meier helped his brother bury his wife in a meadow. Ernst Müller (*Berner Täufer,* 62) states that he heard a Mennonite in the Jura say they should not be compelled to bury their dead in the churchyard, but that each should be permitted to bury his dead on his own land. P. Burckhardt (*Die Basler Täufer,* 64) reports that the Mennonites preferred to bury their dead in a place of their own choosing. All of these are no doubt isolated cases. Where European Mennonites decided to lay out their own cemetery it was as a rule because the use of the common community burying ground was denied them or made very difficult. This is probably the reason for Preacher Risser's note in the church book of the Mennonites of Sembach: "Wherever several Mennonite families lived in a community, they had their own burial grounds." When the Mennonites buried their dead in common burying grounds, whether for Protestants or for all Christian creeds, their preachers delivered a sermon and at the conclusion thanked the authorities for the privilege of using the cemetery. (See "Friedhof" in *Gem.-Kal.* 1892, 93.)

In 1541 the preachers Cantzenius and Erasmus submitted to the city council of Bern their opinion that it seemed doubtful to them, whether the Anabaptists who die in their error are saved, and whether they should not be separated in burial from other, ordinary Christians, as they (the Anabaptists) have separated themselves in life"; whereupon the council replied that "they, the councillors, did not wish to interfere with God's judgment regarding the salvation of Anabaptists. Error is not always damned; we do not wish to separate their corpses from other believers, since other evil persons who are executed for their crimes, are buried at the upper almshouse" (Müller, *Berner Täufer,* 82 f.).

On June 5, 1694, the council of Bern was again

occupied with the question whether Mennonites should be buried in the churchyards with other Christians. "Honorable persons" had taken offense. The council answered that the right of burial could not be refused them, but that in the future their burials should be conducted without a funeral procession. But in the next year (Feb. 27, 1695) instructions were issued to officials that "Mennonites as excommunicated persons shall not be buried in a churchyard or other customary burying ground." In 1729 the *Täuferkammer* was asked for an opinion; it was divided. Some favored retaining the regulation of 1695, "because the plain man considers burial in a churchyard very important, and many might be frightened away from joining a sect which, as they can see, is segregated from the rest even after death." The others did not consider them less Christian than the Christian-minded, who were not denied the churchyard. Presumably the regulation of 1695 remained in force. In 1729 the cabinetmaker Lerch was compelled by the magistrate to bury his Mennonite sister in a remote spot on his little farm.

Concerning Holland there is not much to report. When the period of persecution was over in Holland, the Mennonites were buried in the customary manner; i.e., the more important ones in the Reformed churches, e.g., Hans de Ries in the Grootekerk at Alkmaar in 1638, and the plain people in the cemeteries. It was done in this way until burial in the churches was forbidden. The Mennonites of Holland have never had their own cemeteries. During the 16th, 17th, and part of the 18th centuries no mourning service was held. The preachers were usually not present at the burial: the poor of the congregation (the so-called *gealimenteerden*) and those who had few or no relatives were conducted to the grave by the deacons. Only in the 19th century did the Mennonites adopt the practice of the Reformed Church, of having the pastor conduct the entire funeral service and give a talk at the home of the deceased or at the graveside. In the last half century it has become more and more customary in the rural congregations to hold a funeral service in the church before interment.

In the Palatinate the Mennonites followed the same burial customs as the Lutherans and Reformed. They buried their dead unhesitatingly in the churchyard. The bells were rung, the school children accompanied the funeral train with singing, the Lutheran or Reformed parson gave the funeral address, or in his absence, the teacher read it. It continued so for 50 years after their settling there in 1664. On July 6, 1714, the Catholic priest of Spiesheim near Alzey complained that an "Anabaptist by the name of Hahn delivered a public funeral sermon in the churchyard," and requested a suppression of this "offense." Hahn was fined 10 Reichstalers, and the Mennonites were no longer permitted to bury their dead in the cemeteries of the three tolerated creeds (Catholic, Lutheran, Reformed), nor to hold public burial speeches. A petition of the Mennonites of October 1714 brought about the regulation that the Mennonites could be buried in the cemeteries of the three tolerated religions, but only in special parts reserved for them, isolated from the others. On May 31, 1743, an electoral decree went to all the *Oberämter* that Mennonites could now be buried quietly, without public singing or other show. A Mennonite request of Feb. 27, 1746, was refused; it was decided that they could in no case be buried in a cemetery used by the Catholics. In Kaiserslautern a revolting incident occurred in 1780; a Mennonite woman who had been buried in a Catholic cemetery with church honors, was exhumed and at night buried outside the cemetery walls. In 1785 the Protestant and Catholic parsons in Winnweiler quarreled about Mennonite burial fees, which the Catholic priest claimed for himself. It was settled by giving each a part (*Kirchenbuch der Mennoniten-Gemeinde Sembach*).

The 19th century brought toleration on this point to the Mennonites in Bavaria. A government rescript of Nov. 1, 1807, stated "in answer to the petition of N., the tenant of the N-hof near N, and the other Mennonites living there, asking that burial of their members be permitted according to their custom, without calling in a Catholic priest for a fee, considering that Catholic ceremonies at the burial of a non-Catholic constitute a presumption contrary to freedom of religion and conscience, and considering that the Anabaptists also are entitled to the privileges of our religious edict, we determine that the above custom be observed, and the pastors be instructed to regard it in similar cases hereafter." The government decision of Oct. 12, 1847, again assured to the Mennonites the right of burial in the common burial grounds.

In West Prussia, where in several towns the Mennonites paid burial fees to the Protestant or Catholic parsons, some difficulties arose in the 1890's in connection with the burial of their dead. A Mennonite preacher was sued for delivering a funeral sermon in the Catholic cemetery at Marienau against the priest's express order. This was forbidden by the decree of Feb. 13, 1852, which states that it is permitted only to the clergy to give addresses at the grave, and forbids lay addresses. He was declared innocent by the jury and in the court of appeals at Elbing on Oct. 9, 1898, on the ground that "the church at Rosenort had corporation rights and was an accepted religious organization, so that its preachers are clergymen in the sense of the regulation referred to, and the funeral sermon delivered by him is not to be considered a lay address."

In Baden it was long customary to have the Protestant pastors bury the Mennonite dead without the participation of their own preachers and elders. Ulrich Hege, the editor of the *Gemeindeblatt,* energetically and successfully protested against this practice (1896, 11). It occurs very rarely now.

Practices in America. In America no difficulties in obtaining burial privileges have been experienced. The Amish who had no church buildings often had family cemeteries on their farms. In Holmes Co., Ohio, the Old Order Amish follow this practice to this day. In later years it has become customary, however, to have congregational burial sites.

In one of the Amish cemeteries near Arthur, Ill.,

the dead are buried in rows in the order of their death, without regard for family connections. The Moravians also have this practice.

In the early Mennonite settlements in America, generally as soon as church sites were obtained, burial plots were procured also. Most Mennonite congregations in the United States and Canada now have their own cemeteries, generally near the church and often on adjacent grounds. Those Mennonites, however, who came to the Americas from Russia in the 1870's and later and settled in villages did not always establish congregational but sometimes community cemeteries. This practice is followed in Mexico and Paraguay.

In the congregational cemeteries, burial rights were generally open to any family in the community, with no charge made for burial privileges. At the time of the first death in a family a plot in the church cemetery was selected by the family and the sexton, which area was then reserved for that family. This plan was not always followed, however, as is illustrated by the Mennonite cemetery near Donnellson, Iowa, where for many years the dead were buried in rows in the order of their death. Not all American Mennonite congregations have their own cemeteries, for in certain communities several churches may use a common burial ground, while in other communities, Mennonites patronize city or public cemeteries. (See **Cemeteries** and **Funeral Practices**; C. H. Smith, *The Menn. Immigration to Pennsylvania in the Eighteenth Century,* Norristown, 1929, 49-54; *ML* I, 154-57.)
NEFF, M.G.

Burieu, Cathalijne, an Anabaptist martyr: see **Cathalijne Loury.**

Burkhard, Martin, an Anabaptist martyr, was one of the leaders (*Vorsteher*) of the congregation at Kaufbeuren who were chosen during the week of Augustin Bader's (*q.v.*) visit early in 1528. He was a victim of the cruel persecution, which broke with annihilating violence over the young church, making a permanent settlement of Anabaptists there impossible. On the morning of June 13, 1528, he was beheaded with three other leaders. (*Archiv für Ref.-Gesch.* X, 1913, 128; *ML* I, 302.)   O.H.

Burkhart (Burghart, Burckhard, Burkhardt), a Swiss Mennonite family name found today in Germany as well as in North America. Neff's *Adressbuch* (1936) lists the name in the Frankfurt congregation. The name also occurs among the Mennonites of East Germany and North Germany (F. Crous). The Palatine Census Lists of 1685 mention an Ulrich Burckhard at Heyerhof, and in 1724 an Ulrich Burkhart was living at Duttweiler. Among the Hutterian Brethren, mention is made of Burckhart of Ofen (now in Hungary), a preacher in the first years of that brotherhood.

One of the earliest Burkhart immigrants to North America was Joseph Burkhart, who migrated from Switzerland to Lancaster Co., Pa., in 1751. The Burkhart family has been well represented in Lancaster County, Pennsylvania, since that time. The immigrant's son Peter located in Ontario in 1820 where many of his descendants adhere to the Old Order Mennonite Church. At least five Burkharts have been ministers or deacons in the Lancaster Conference. In 1751 a Michael Burghart and a Frantz Burghart arrived in Pennsylvania, but it is not known where they and their descendants settled. Abram Burkhart served for many decades as a deacon at Sterling, Ill., having been ordained in 1895.   J.C.W.

Burkholder (Borcholder, Borcholter, Borckholder, Borgholder, Borkholder, Burckhalter, Burckholder, Burgholder, Burgholdter, Burkhalter, Burkalter), a Bernese Swiss Mennonite family having many descendants in Europe and North America, including a large number of leaders in the Mennonite Church. The name is said to spring from a place in Switzerland called Burghalde. One of the earliest Mennonite leaders of this name was Hans Burkholder of Bern, born about 1617, a minister of the church. He escaped from prison in 1658 and averted a forced deportation to Holland. In 1669 he was again in prison in Bern, and once more escaped. Two years later he with his wife and seven children were living in Kriegsheim in the Palatinate. Later the family located at Gerolsheim. His son Hans became a Mennonite minister at Gerolsheim in 1702, and was later ordained as an elder. He served faithfully for many decades, dying in 1752. He was very active in corresponding with the Dutch Mennonites about the plight of his fellow Bernese exiles in the Palatinate. His son, Christian Burkholder, was also a minister, and like his father carried on correspondence with Johannes Deknatel and others in Holland. (*Inv. Arch. Amst.* I, Nos. 1521-36). The name Burkholder is still found among the Mennonites of Europe, Anna Borkholder being listed in the *Adressbuch* of Neff as a member of the Durlach congregation in Baden in South Germany.

The Burkholders of North America are descendants of various immigrants. One of the earliest was a Hans Burkholder who had been ordained as an elder in Switzerland, and who settled in Lancaster Co., Pa., in 1717. He is credited with having organized the Stone congregation near New Danville. His relation to the Burkholders listed above is not known. He died about 1745.

An Abraham Burkholder came to America in 1717 and settled in York Co., Pa., but the area is now in Dauphin County. In 1732 an Ulrich Burkholder came to Lancaster County. A year later another Ulrich arrived, settling in Northampton County, and his descendants are now scattered through the West, many of them being members of the Reformed Church.

In 1755 a Christian Burkholder made arrangements to migrate from Switzerland to America, but died before leaving. His widow and six children came and settled in Lancaster Co., Pa. His son Christian Burkholder (1746-1809) (*q.v.*) became a minister in 1770 and a bishop in 1780, serving in the Groffdale congregation. He is the author of the *Anrede an die Jugend* (Ephrata, 1804) (Address to Youth), printed as Part IV of all American editions (German and English) of Roosen's *Conversation on Christian Faith* after 1837. Christian's brother Peter moved to the Shenandoah Valley, Virginia, where his son, also named Peter Burkholder (1783-1846) (*q.v.*), too became a minister (1805), bishop (1837), and an author of note; he edited the Twisck Confession of 33 Articles from the *Martyrs' Mirror,* wrote a book on baptism in 1816, another on predestination, and a third entitled, *Nine Reflections on the Holy Scriptures.* His son Martin Burkholder (1817-60) was ordained a minister in 1839 and succeeded his father as bishop following the latter's death in 1846. Another grandson of Peter who located in Virginia was John Burkholder (1838-1909) of Mahoning Co., Ohio, ordained as minister in 1879 and as bishop in 1886. David Burkholder (1835-1923) of Nappanee, Ind., ordained minister in 1880, and bishop in 1904, was another scion of this same Peter Burkholder. Another descendant was Christian of Ontario, whose son Benjamin located in Marion Co., Kan. Benjamin's grandson, Ezra Burkholder, was a millionaire banker, merchant, and landowner. There are still several Burkholder ministers among the Mennonites of Virginia.

One of the recent church leaders, descendant of the immigrant Ulrich of 1732, was Joseph Burkholder (1803-75), of the Manor-Conestoga district of the Lancaster Conference, ordained to the ministry in 1846, and as bishop, 1864. His grandson, Christian C. Burkholder (1865-1931), was a Brethren in Christ bishop, and president of Beulah College, Upland, Cal.

Among the more recent leaders should be mentioned Lewis J. Burkholder (*q.v.*) (1875-1949), Markham, Ont., minister of the Cedar Grove congregation, 1896-1949, and author of *History of the Mennonites in Ontario* (1935); and Oscar Burkholder (1886-   ), minister at Breslau, Ont., since 1912, teacher in the Ontario Mennonite Bible School since 1917, and principal of the school since 1949. Among the 19th-century Bernese Swiss who settled in the Berne, Ind., and Bluffton, Ohio, communities (GCM), there were several Burkhalter families. Edward Burkhalter and Martha Burkhalter, missionaries in India, come from the Berne community, and Harold D. Burkholder, president of Grace Bible Institute, comes from the Bluffton region. There are also some Burkholders among the Old Order Amish, chiefly in northern Indiana, where there are several ministers by this name and a bishop, David O. Burkholder, of Nappanee, Ind. (*Burkholder Family Reunion reports, 1926-   .*)

J.C.W.

Burkholder, Christian (1746-1809), outstanding Mennonite (MC) bishop of Lancaster Co., Pa., was the son of Christian Burkholder, Sr., of Gerolsheim in the Palatinate, a prominent leader who did much to aid his afflicted brethren in the Upper Rhine area. While preparing for the emigration to Pennsylvania the elder Burkholder died (March 1755), leaving a widow with six small children, the oldest being Christian, Jr., then aged nine. The brave woman managed the voyage (then a difficult enterprise), and settled (1755) in Earl Twp., Lancaster Co., Pa. Christian grew up during the French and Indian War in this new Mennonite community which his father had partly planned and visualized. Before the Revolutionary War Christian married Anna Groff, a granddaughter of the pioneer Hans Groff. They made their farmstead home north of Farmersville. He was a brother of Peter Burkholder (the father of the later bishop, Peter Burkholder, of Virginia) and of Ulrich Burkholder, preacher at Bowmansville. He himself was a successful preacher and the father of eight children.

In 1770 Christian was ordained at Groffdale, and was chosen bishop in 1780 for Earl and Brecknock townships. As such he was very active, traveling much and establishing new churches. He preached in the schoolhouse meetinghouse which had been built in 1755 on the land of Henry Landis (son-in-law of Hans Groff). The Weaverland Church (1766) was then the only other meetinghouse in his district.

About 1790 a German Methodist movement sprang up in Pennsylvania. In 1792 Jacob Albright began organizing the Evangelical Association (*q.v.*), which had a center also at Hahnstown of Burkholder's district. This movement proved to be a great temptation mainly to the younger generation to whom the revivalistic type of church movement strongly appealed. This most likely led Burkholder to counteract it in order to keep the youth in the Mennonite fold. The result is his renowned "Address to Youth Regarding True Repentance" (*Nützliche und erbauliche Anrede an die Jugend von der wahren Busse*), of 1792. We do not know whether these speeches were actually given (as might be assumed) or just written down for private circulation. In any case they were not printed until 1804. The address is a very strong and forceful appeal to loyalty to the time-honored and tested Christian way of the Mennonites, a teaching of the fundamentals of Christian living, and an exhortation to those of "faithful heart," showing them the true values of the faith of their fathers. It was an outstanding contribution to religious education, somewhat reminiscent of van Braght's *School of Moral Virtue* (*School der Deugd*). Eight German editions and five English during the 19th century prove the vitality of this small book. The first edition of 1804 was published without naming the author. A second, enlarged and somewhat changed edition, now signed by 27 ministers (all of the Lancaster Conference), was brought out later in the same year. It was probably adopted as an official church edition. Since 1839 the *Anrede* was printed as an appendix to G. Roosen's *Christliches Gemütsgespräch* (*q.v.*), with which it has much in common; and in 1857, when the latter was translated into English, Burkholder's *Address* was also translated and again appended as Part IV to the *Conversation on Saving Faith.*

The book consists of three parts: (1) Concerning true repentance (this is the central theme of the entire book); (2) Concerning saving faith, and pure love of God and one's neighbor (later this part was divided, and the section on love made an independent item exhorting people to yearn after true discipleship in brotherly love); (3) Concerning obedience to the Word of God and the full surrender of the soul into God's hand. A smaller tract "Warning against Backsliding" followed. The second edition has a few new items of a more emotional, pietistic nature.

The book would still be profitable and attractive reading, formulating the Mennonite position over against that of the newer (revivalistic) churches. It is the last literary product of the "colonial period" of the Mennonites. I. D. Landis presents in his article on Burkholder (see Bibliography) a thorough analysis of its contents. **I.D.L., R.F.**

I. D. Landis, "Bishop Christian Burkholder of Groffdale (1746-1809)," *MQR*, 1944, 145 f.; M. Weaver, *Menn. of Lancaster Conf.* (1931) 125 ff.; H. S. Bender, "Literature and Hymnology of the Menn. of Lancaster County," *MQR*, 1932, 160 ff.; R. Friedmann, *Menn. Piety Through the Centuries* (Goshen, 1949) 238-44.

Burkholder (sometimes spelled Borckholder and is the same name as Burghalter), **Hans**, the name of three different Swiss Mennonite preachers of the 17th and 18th centuries.

(1) The oldest known member of the entire Burkholder family was a Hans Burkholder "aus den Schniggenen" in the canton of Bern, born around 1617. Of him is only known that he was to be deported to Holland with 12 companions, but escaped from prison Nov. 26, 1658. A few years later he was seized again, but again managed to escape in 1669. Eventually, in 1671, he emigrated into the Palatinate together with his wife and seven children. Most likely he settled in Kriegsheim (Müller, *Berner Täufer*, 191; *ML* I, 302).

(2) Possibly the son of the above. This Hans Burkholder was made preacher of the Mennonite congregation at Gerolsheim, Palatinate, in 1702. Repeatedly he sent requests to the brethren in Holland for support of his hard-pressed and impoverished congregation. After having experienced much hardship through the relentless Palatinate government, he died in 1752. Though an emigration to America was visualized, the plan was never carried out (Müller, *loc. cit.,* 208; J. C. Burkholder in *Report of the First Burkholder Family Reunion,* 1926, where five letters of H.B. to the Dutch brethren are reprinted). The Amsterdam Mennonite Archives contain a number of letters by him, the first dated Oct. 1, 1730, the last one Aug. 4, 1751 (*Inv. Arch. Amst.* I, Nos. 1454-67; 1474-75; 1484-92; 1499-1520).

(3) Hans B., the first of his name to come to America. He was a deacon, teacher, and preacher of the Langnau Mennonite congregation in the Emmental in Switzerland (canton of Bern). He, too, had to pass through severe imprisonment 1708-10, of which a report from his hand is still extant. The Bern authorities wanted to get rid of the entire Anabaptist-Mennonite group, and simply loaded 57 of them on a boat (on the Rhine) to have them deported straight to America (1710). At Mannheim one group left this vessel (the weaker and sick ones) while the rest went on to Nijmegen, Holland, where they were kindly received by brethren and promised support. But it took seven more

years until the entire group under the strong leadership of Benedikt Brechbill (*q.v.*) and Hans Burkholder could undertake the great voyage to Pennsylvania. In 1717, Hans Burkholder settled on the Conestoga Creek (Lancaster County) on land which John Funck had purchased from William Penn.
R.F.

J. C. Burkholder in *Papers read before the Lancaster County Historical Society,* May 6, 1927, 57-62, and in the *Report of the First Burkholder Family Reunion,* Sept. 3, 1926; M. G. Weaver, *Mennonites of Lancaster Conference* (Scottdale, 1931) 125-28.

Burkholder, Lewis Josephus (1875-1949), b. June 15, 1875, near Markham, Ont., of an old Mennonite family, d. Sept. 28, 1949, on the farm where he was born and lived all his life, married twice, father of two children. He was ordained to the ministry of the Mennonite Church (MC) in 1896 for the Cedar Grove congregation, which he served for 53 years uninterruptedly. He was an active leader in the Ontario Mennonite Conference (MC) serving as conference moderator for many years, as chairman of the mission board, assistant moderator of the Mennonite General Conference, officer of the Nonresistant Relief Organization of Ontario, and teacher in the Ontario Mennonite Bible School. He was for years the historian of the Ontario Mennonite Conference and the author of *A Brief History of the Mennonites in Ontario* (Toronto, 1935), a substantial and valuable historical volume.
H.S.B.

Burkholder, Peter (1783-1846), a prominent Mennonite bishop in Virginia in the first half of the 19th century, the son of Peter and Margaret Huber Burkholder of the first generation of Burkholders in this country, was born in Lancaster Co., Pa., Aug. 27, 1783, and died Dec. 24, 1846; he was buried in the Weaver's cemetery. In 1790 the family migrated to the Shenandoah Valley and located in Dale Enterprise in Rockingham Co., Va. Peter was married to Elisabeth Coffman in 1803, to which union nine children were born.

Peter Burkholder was ordained to the ministry in the Mennonite Church (MC) in 1805 at the age of 21. About 32 years later he was ordained to the office of bishop. He was an outstanding and progressive leader among the Mennonites of Virginia. He defended pouring against immersion as being the Scriptural mode of baptism in a booklet entitled *Eine Verhandlung von der äusserlichen Wasser-Taufe* (Harrisonburg, 1816, English edition in 1882 at Dale Enterprise, Va.). He took his stand with the church in 1825 when a division was imminent. He encouraged the expansion of the church by preaching at outposts, such as Mount Clinton and Chimney Rocks. His delivery was marked with pathos. Joseph Funk wrote of him as "our beloved pastor." **H.A.B.**

In 1837 a book appeared at Winchester, Va., with the following lengthy title: *The Confession of Faith of the Christians known by the name of Mennonites, in Thirty-Three Articles; with a short Extract from their Catechism.* Translated from the German and accompanied with notes. To which is added an Introduction. Also, Nine Reflections, from different Passages of the Scriptures, Illustrative of the

Confession, Faith and Practice; By Peter Burkholder, Pastor of the Church of the Mennonites; Written by him in the German Language, and from his manuscript translated, together with the foregoing Articles, by Joseph Funk. The Confession is the P. J. Twisck 33 Articles found in the *Martyrs' Mirror*. The Introduction of 27 pages is an independent writing, designed "to adduce some testimony to prove the antiquity of our religious confession of faith and from Dr. Mosheim's *Ecclesiastical History*." It has been claimed that Peter Burkholder "compiled the confession," i.e., arranged for its publication in English. However, since everything which he wrote was translated from the German by Joseph Funk, as is clearly stated on the title page of the *Nine Reflections,* and as is stated of the additional material at the end of the book, including "Of the Administration of Baptism" (pp. 405-14), "Of the Mode and Practice of the Administration of Baptism" (414-17), and "On Predestination" (435-61), and since it is not indicated that the Introduction was translated, it is most likely that Joseph Funk, and not Peter Burkholder, was the author of the Introduction, the translator of all the material in the book, and the compiler of the volume. The *Treatise on Predestination* was reprinted as an appendage to *Christian Conversation on Saving Faith* (Lancaster, 1857) and in all succeeding reprints of the same. The "Extract from the Catechism" which appears on pp. 424-34 is not by Burkholder, but a translation of *Kurze Unterweisung aus der Schrift,* first published in 1690 in Danzig, and added to the *Christliches Gemütsgespräch* in its first (1769) American edition and all later German and English editions.

H.S.B.

A. Blosser, "Additional Statistics of the Ancestry and Family of the Aforenamed Peter Burkholder," pp. 59-61 in *A Treatise on Baptism and the Lord's Supper; Written by Bish. Peter Burkholder in the Year 1815 in the German Language and Translated into the English Language and Printed by Abraham Blosser* (Dale Enterprise, Va., 1882); *ML* I, 303.

Burkholder Conservative Amish Mennonite Church (not under the Conservative Amish Mennonite Conference), located two miles northwest of Nappanee, Elkhart Co., Ind., was organized on April 28, 1940, with 24 members, under the leadership of David O. Burkholder, who served as the first pastor. The meetinghouse, seating 400, was dedicated on Sept. 26, 1943. The ministers serving the church in 1953 were Bishop David O. Burkholder, Jacob L. Mast, Irvin D. Miller, and Steve Yoder, with a membership of 76. The group comes entirely from the Old Order Amish of the community.

D.O.B.

Bürky, Hans, from Giebel near Langnau in the canton of Bern, Switzerland, a preacher of the Mennonite church there. After long evading capture by the government, he was seized in July 1708 by treachery, and taken from his wife and 12 children to the castle of Trachselwald. Here he fell ill, and a few days later was placed in solitary confinement in a dungeon of the tower in Bern for 17 weeks. Then he was transferred to another prison known as the "Insel," and from there was taken to the poorhouse, where he had to work "at the wool" for 35 weeks from 6:00 in the morning until 8:00 at night. On March 18, 1710, he was put on a ship with 56 other Mennonites for deportation to America, but they were released in Nijmegen, Holland. With most of the group he went to Cleve, where they were kindly received and lodged by the Mennonites. They remained here over Sunday; perhaps Bürky conducted the church service (Müller, 272). With Benedikt Brechbill (*q.v.*) and Melchior Zahler he was invited to Amsterdam by the Mennonites there; here they reported conditions in their Swiss home before the city council and in many conferences. But homesickness soon drew him back to Switzerland to his family in disregard of all requests and warnings. Here he was again captured. His children and the servant Uli Gerber violently resisted his arrest and were consequently sharply punished. After a short imprisonment Hans Bürky was again placed on the *Emmentaler,* an emigrant boat, for deportation to Holland on July 13, 1711. He was made one of three supervisors on the boat. In Basel he refused to proceed; only the threat of Runkel, the man in charge, to take him in chains induced him to stay; but he escaped at Breisach. It is not known whether he returned to his family. In the Amish division he seems to have played an important role, but no details are known. The name Bürky is common among the Mennonites of the Palatinate and America (*Inv. Arch. Amst.* I, Nos. 1262 f., 1302, 1341; Müller, *Berner Täufer; ML* I, 303). Neff.

Burlington Railroad. The Burlington-Missouri Railroad Company, a division of the present Chicago, Burlington and Quincy road, induced a number of the Russian Mennonite immigrants of 1874, through their railroad representative, A. E. Touzalin, to locate on the railroad lands near Beatrice, Neb. The leader among the Russian immigrants was Cornelius Jansen, after whose son the town of Jansen later was named. The railroad company vied with the Santa Fe in Kansas, in offering the Mennonites cheap railroad lands, reduced freight rates, immigrant houses, gifts, and passes. Nebraska received only a minor portion of the immigrant settlers, however.

C.H.S.

Richard Overton, *Burlington West, A Colonization History of the Burlington Railroad* (Cambridge, 1941); C. Henry Smith, *The Coming of the Russian Mennonites* (Berne, 1927) 66, 120 f., 171-75.

Burns, with a population of about 330, is located in southeast Marion Co., Kan. Mennonites have settled in this community only within the last ten or twelve years. The General Conference Mennonite Church, with their church building located about two miles northwest of town, and the Church of God in Christ Mennonite, with their building in town, are represented with about 35 families each. Most families live south and west of town. Practically all are farmers.

H.W.G.

Burns Church of God in Christ Mennonite Church is located in Burns, Marion Co., Kan., and was organized in 1938. Worship services were conducted in several places in the community until the present church building was purchased. Ernest F. Wiggers is the preacher in charge. Allan Schmidt was ordained as deacon in 1945. The church membership is 161, and the Sunday-school enrollment 204 (1953). The sewing circle is active in supporting missions, hospitals, and relief work.　E.F.W.

Burns First Mennonite Church (GCM), Burns, Marion Co., Kan., is a member of the Western District Conference. The present congregation, composed of 98 members, all of whom are farm folk, had its beginning when it was organized on June 16, 1944, with 30 charter members. The meetinghouse was dedicated Nov. 25, 1947.

H.W.G.

Burr Oak Mennonite Church (MC), Rensselaer, Ind. In May 1918 J. K. Bixler of the Indiana-Michigan Mennonite Mission Board first visited this field and met with the six members that were here at that time. For the first five years, ministers were sent down about once a month. During this time the services were held in a schoolhouse, a vacant dwelling, and in a Baptist church. In 1925 with the help of the mission board a church, 24 x 38, was built. It was dedicated on Oct. 4 of the same year, at which time Floyd Weaver of the Yellow Creek congregation (Ind.) was ordained. At this time there were 16 members. In 1945 Weaver resigned as pastor on account of his health; Henry J. Stoll was asked to take charge of the work, and was ordained in 1951. The membership in 1953 was 57, and the congregation is now fully organized under the Indiana-Michigan Mennonite Conference. It is largely Amish in background. H.J.S.

Burrage, Henry Sweetser (1837-1926), American (New England) Baptist clergyman, editor, and historian, editor of *Zion's Advocate* 1873-1905, author of *A History of the Anabaptists in Switzerland* (Phila., 1882, 231 pp.), *Baptist Hymn Writers and their Hymns* (Portland, 1888, 682 pp.), containing a section on "Anabaptist Hymn Writers and their Hymns," pp. 1-26, and an Anabaptist novel, *True to the End* (Phila., 1895, 192 pp., German edition at Cassel, 1920, *Getreu bis ans Ende, Eine Täufererzählung zur Zeit Zwinglis*). His son Champlin (1874-), domiciled in England, also wrote historical works bearing on Anabaptist history: *The Church Covenant Idea, Its Origin and Development* (Phila., 1904, 230 pp.) and *The Early English Dissenters in the Light of Recent Research (1550-1641)* 2 vv. (Cambridge, 1912). (*ML* I, 303.)

H.S.B.

Burrton Mennonite Church (GCM) located in Burrton, Harvey Co., Kan., is a member of the Western District Conference. The church was organized on June 2, 1907, with 25 charter members, under the leadership of H. P. Krehbiel, who served as the first pastor. In 1952 the membership was 107, mostly rural. The first meetinghouse, a frame structure with a seating capacity of 130, which is still in use, was built in 1910. Other ministers who have served the congregation are Walter H. Dyck, Jacob J. Regier, Jr., Arnold A. Epp, Roy Henry, and Abe Peters. (*ML* I, 303.)　A.A.E.

Burtscheid (also spelled Botschert or Borchet), a town in the Rhine Province of Prussia, southeast of Aachen, seat of a Mennonite congregation with a church here and in the neighboring Dutch village of Vaals. This congregation was united with the one at Maastricht in the 18th century. Until 1768 the ministers lived in Burtscheid. About 1730 A. van Leuvenig was a member of the church board; Barthelomeus van Leuvenig (*q.v.*), a relative of his, who was a native of Burtscheid, was a preacher of the Lamist congregation in Amsterdam. Burtscheid and Vaals separated from Maastricht in 1768, but never had a preacher of their own, and the congregation vanished about 1793. About 1610 members of the Burtscheid Mennonite congregation were administrators of the property of the Catholic church of St. Michael. Though the congregation received an annual subsidy from Amsterdam from 1732, it made two large contributions (considering its small membership) to the Fund for Foreign Needs—525 guilders in 1733, and 550 in 1736. (See Bibliography in **Aachen, Maastricht,** and **Vaals.**

NEFF.

DB 1863, 6 f., 84; Hansen, "Die Wiedertäufer in Aachen," in *Ztscht des Aachener Geschichtsvereins* VI, 316; *ML* I, 304.

Burwalde (Russian, *Baburka*), a village of the Mennonite Chortitza settlement, province of Ekaterinoslav, South Russia, was founded in 1903 and located eight miles from the village of Chortitza. In 1913 the population was 400 and the village had 35 farms and 7,500 acres of land. In 1918 there were 51 farms and a Mennonite population of 536. In 1941 the Mennonite population had decreased to 320 while the total was 683. Seven persons had been killed as a result of the Revolution, 4 starved to death, 72 were exiled between 1929 and 1941, and 12 were evacuated by the Russians during World War II. Most of the remaining Mennonites were evacuated westward by the Germans in 1943. It is not known how many of them were sent back by the Soviets or how many reached Paraguay or Canada.

Burwalde had its own school and a church building erected in 1864. The congregation belonged to the Chortitza Mennonite Church (*q.v.*). (*ML* I, 304.)　C.K.

Burwalde Mennonite Brethren Church. At Burwalde (Baburka), eight miles southeast of Chortitza, a branch of the Einlage (*q.v.*) M.B. Church was organized in 1876 when Johann Hildebrandt, his wife, and his mother were converted and joined the M.B. Church over very stiff protests and opposition on the part of their relatives and neighbors. Little spiritual life was present at that time in most of the Mennonite villages. So Hildebrandt arranged for spiritual Sunday meetings in his home (*grosse Stube*). It was some years later that several people of Rosengart (Novoslobodka), a few miles west of Burwalde, joined the M.B. Church, and met with the small group at Burwalde. Among the later converts at Burwalde was Abr. Klassen, a very energetic personal worker and contender for the faith, though he had much opposition from his own family. Hildebrandt suddenly passed to his reward early in the 20th century. Because of this loss to the Burwalde group and the growing of the number of members in Rosengart and Kronstal, west of Rosengart, a church was built and the services of these groups held at Kronstal (Dolinsk).

P.H.B.

Busau Mennonite Church, located in the village of Busau, Yevpatoriya, Crimea, was founded in 1884 under the name Ettingerbrun Mennonite Church as a result of a Mennonite migration from the mother settlements in the Ukraine to the Crimea (*q.v.*). The members of the congregation lived in the following villages: Sarybash, Tokulchak, Muni, Temirbulat, Yapuntchi, Safronovka, Yalantush, Kutyuki, Busau, Aktatchi, and Montonai. Most of the members were engaged in farming.

The first elder of the congregation was Friedrich Raabe (1884-90). The congregation was without an elder from 1890 to 1901. During this time Elder Abr. Friesen of the Karassan Mennonite Church conducted baptismal services and the Lord's Supper. During this period a number of members joined the Mennonite Brethren. In 1901 Heinrich Martins, who had been ordained as minister in 1892, was installed as elder of the congregation. It was at this time that the name of the congregation was changed from Ettingerbrun to Busau Mennonite Church. Martins died in 1905 after a short but active period of service. He was succeeded in 1906 by Peter Friedrichsen, who served the congregation until 1926, when H. Dück became the leader of the congregation.

Bible studies and conferences as well as song festivals did much to enrich and strengthen the spiritual and cultural life of the congregation. Under the Soviets the large congregation was divided into groups consisting of 20 members each. In 1905 the total population of the congregation was 632, of whom 272 were members. The enrollment in the Sunday school at that time consisted of 55 pupils.

In addition to the elders mentioned, the following ministers served the Busau Mennonite Church: Peter Stobbe, Abr. Rempel, Abr. Bärg, Abr. Unruh, Jakob Harder, Peter Wohlgemut, Franz Wiens, Karl Friedrichsen, P. Martens, Wilhelm Voth, Abr. Dick, Joh. Heinrichs, Joh. Martens, H. P. Friedrichsen, and J. Driediger. Little is known about the experiences and the disintegration of the congregation under the Soviets. C.K.

H. H. Friedrichsen, "Die Geschichte der Busauer Menn.-Gemeinde," *Unser Blatt* II, No. 8 (May 1927) 236-38; P. M. Friesen, *Brüderschaft,* 709.

Busau-Aktatchi (also called Aktatchi), a small Mennonite village in the Russian province of Taurida, 13 miles from the sea-coast city of Yevpatoriya, 16 miles from the nearest railway station, Kurman-Kemeltchi, 10 miles from the post office Aibar. The village was founded in 1886, consisted of 5 farms and a school lot, and covered 1,350 dessiatines (about 3,000 acres) of plain. In 1913 there were 42 inhabitants, engaged in agriculture, all members of the Busau Mennonite Church. Originally the group had been a part of the Karassan (*q.v.*) congregation. The first elder was Friedrich Raabe (1884-90) followed by H. H. Martins (1902). (*ML* I, 304.) H.R.

Busby Mennonite Mission Church (GCM) is located at Busby, on the Tongue River Indian Reservation

in southeastern Montana, home of the Northern Cheyenne Indians. The work was begun in 1904, by Mr. and Mrs. G. A. Linscheid, who remained in the work until 1920. Other workers were Agnes Williams, 1905-6; Mr. and Mrs. P. A. Kliewer, 1908-10; Mr. and Mrs. H. T. Neufeld, 1911-15; Mr. and Mrs. Alfred Habegger, 1918-49; Mr. and Mrs. Malcolm Wenger, 1944-53; and Mr. and Mrs. David L. Habegger, 1949-50; Mr. and Mrs. John W. Boehr, 1953- . Over 200 have been baptized since the work began, with a 1949 membership of about 100. Both the Cheyenne and English languages are used in this mission work. (*ML* I, 304.) A.H.

Busch, Dirk Gerrits van den: see **Dirk Gerritsz.**

Busch, Philipp, an Anabaptist from Königsberg in Franconia, Germany, who according to his confession, was baptized by Hans Hut (*q.v.*). Since he remained true to his faith at his trial at Frankenhausen, Jan. 17, 1530, he presumably suffered a martyr's death with his companions. He may have been one of the four Anabaptists who were drowned in Frankenhausen in 1530. (P. Wappler, *Die Täuferbewegung in Thüringen, Jena,* 1913, 93, 313; *ML* I, 304.) NEFF.

Busenitz (Bussnitz, Buzenes), a West Prussian Mennonite family of the Flemish group, originally urban. The last family bearing this name moved to Kansas in 1894, where it is spreading again. Johann Busenitz together with Heinrich Donner represented the West Prussian Mennonites, 1777-80, in negotiations with the government, which led successfully to the special *Privilegium* of Frederick II in 1780. G.R.

Busher, Leonard, a refugee from London, living in Amsterdam about 1610. He was the head of a party of Teleiobaptists (i.e., of people who practiced adult baptism). He was a friend of Thomas Helwys (*q.v.*), a Brownist leader. Busher is also the author of a treatise, *Religious Peace or a Plea for Liberty of Conscience,* which was printed anonymously in England several times, and also of *Persecution for Religion Judg'd and Condemn'd . . . Proving That no Man Ought to be Persecuted for His Religion* (n.p., 1662, reprint), likewise anonymous. The group mentioned above was not Mennonite, as is stated in *Prophane Schism* (p. 65) by Christian Lawne, but a separated group of Brownists (*q.v.*), who later probably joined the Baptists in England; Busher himself also returned to England about 1614. vDZ.

J. G. de Hoop Scheffer and W. E. Griffis, *History of the Free Churchmen* (Ithaca, 1922) 171, 176, 177; *Catalogus Amst.,* 158.

Business is the general term applied to the activity of making a living, but it is usually used specifically to refer to the activity of buying and selling or rendering service for profit. It may also be used to describe the manufacturing of commodities for sale at a profit. The term "business" is distinguished from the term "profession," which is a form of service in exchange for a fee or a salary, and business is activity distinguished from manual labor for a wage. It is also usually distinguished from farming.

It is well known that business as a buying and

selling activity for profit was long frowned upon by Christians as an unethical way of making a living and not worthy of a Christian calling. Charging of interest for the use of money, and buying and selling for a profit was considered contrary to the high standards of Christian ethics. Before the Reformation, no respectable Christians engaged in "business." John Calvin is generally credited with having been among the earliest Christians to justify business as a calling through which pious individuals could glorify God as well as through any other enterprise.

However, long after the Reformation various religious groups still hesitated to approve business as an acceptable Christian enterprise. Mennonites, longer than any other religious group, forbade their members to engage in profit-making businesses. In the early history of the Mennonite Church, the vocations represented were chiefly those of farming, skilled crafts, such as weaving, and unskilled or common labor. One does not find Mennonites engaged in business enterprises for profit. Among the Old Order Amish in the United States, and the Old Colony Mennonites in Canada, Mexico, and Paraguay this ancient antipathy to business as a way of making a living is still maintained. Members of these groups are forbidden to engage in business enterprises. Only agriculture, or activity very closely related to it, is tolerated. There is corresponding opposition to living in cities and towns.

In Europe, especially in Holland and North Germany, already in the 17th century Mennonites engaged in profit-making enterprises. They had found refuge in the more tolerant cities and industrial centers, such as Rotterdam, Amsterdam, Emden, Hamburg, Danzig, and Königsberg, and with thrift and industriousness, soon began to accumulate fortunes from such commercial ventures as shipping, banking, and merchandising. Very few of those so engaged, however, emigrated to America. Mennonites coming to North and South America have been farmers almost exclusively. Even those whose forefathers have been in America for two centuries have only in the last 50 years begun to forsake the rural for the urban areas and the agricultural pursuits for the industrial and commercial occupations.

Where Mennonites have entered business, it has usually begun in areas closely allied to agriculture, such as buying and selling feed and grain, milling, hatcheries, small factories and repair shops, garages, and general merchandising stores. In more recent years there has been an increase in the number of Mennonites establishing manufacturing plants. On the whole, however, there are few large and well-established American Mennonite manufacturing plants or merchandising establishments in comparison to those of the Mennonites in the industrial sections of North Germany and Holland. The number of Mennonites gainfully employed in business, either in their own or as employees of business establishments operated by others, is probably between 15 and 25 per cent of all gainfully employed Mennonites, but the percentage of Mennonites so

engaged seems to be gradually increasing. The excess of migration from rural to urban areas since 1920 for the United States as a whole has made itself felt among Mennonites as well. Mennonites who move to cities often give up their affiliation with the Mennonite Church, and thus when they become established in business they are no longer considered Mennonites.

In the South American colonies the same pattern of development seems to be common. In the beginning everybody was engaged in agriculture. Gradually small service centers, stores, and the like were developed to provide for the needs of the agriculturalists. As these grow, a larger percentage of individuals become engaged in nonagricultural enterprises. In one significant area the development in South America differs from that in North America, *viz.*, in their attitude toward co-operatives.

Among the South American Mennonites business is conducted on a co-operative basis, whereas in North America the tradition is highly individualistic, and Mennonites have not organized or promoted many co-operative business enterprises. In South America co-operative businesses have frequently been a necessity for survival, whereas in North America co-operatives are now looked upon as a desirable way of doing business and are most popular among Mennonite farmers, though some Mennonites are opposed to accepting membership in co-operative associations for fear of becoming "unequally yoked." In North America co-operatives and mutual aid seem to be growing, while in South America individual business enterprises are increasing in number. Today the Mennonites in North America have fully and uncritically accepted the theory of capitalism and the profit motive in business.   J.W.F.

Business among the Mennonites in France and Switzerland

The Swiss and French Mennonites until recently have been exclusively agricultural in occupation, and they are still largely so. In a few cases, in Alsace in particular, the farms are really operated as large businesses, but commercial and manufacturing enterprises are few and usually small. The largest of these in this two-country area are probably the enterprises of Joseph and Jean Kennel. brothers at Chassey (Haute-Marne), France. The Joseph Kennel operations include a sawmill and lumber-export business, a furniture factory, and a co-operative cheese factory. Jean Kennel has organized a chain of rural co-operatives which operates elevators, sells farm machinery, seed, and fertilizer, and does custom farming. Emile Winter at Schirmeck operates a small textile factory. A few French Mennonites are retail merchants. In Switzerland there is no large business among the Mennonites except the wholesale flower-growing businesses of the Doblers at Muttenz near Basel and Samuel Nussbaumer in Zürich. Fritz Wüthrich operates a small hand weaving establishment near Langnau. The total number of Mennonite businessmen in these two countries is so small as to have no effect upon the basically agricultural character of the churches.   J.H.Y.

Business Among the Mennonites in Germany

In Germany there have always been basically two types of Mennonites, the urban congregations of Northwest Germany (Emden area, Crefeld, and later Gronau) and Schleswig-Holstein, including Hamburg-Altona and Friedrichstadt, to which should be added Danzig, Elbing, and Königsberg in the east, and then the rural congregations of the Vistula Delta and South Germany. The former not only included many businessmen from the very beginning but have furnished outstanding business leaders for Germany. A number of Danzig Mennonites, for instance, were presidents of the Chamber of Commerce there. Mennonites were traders, shippers, millers, and oil pressers, distillers, and brewers, millwrights and shipbuilders, and great textile manufacturers. The city of Altona owes its development in the 17th and 18th centuries largely to the Mennonites. Whaling became a Mennonite specialty, and Mennonite shippers handled much of the business of the port. Hinrich van der Smissen I (1632-1737), the chief of the most important trading firm of Altona at the beginning of the 18th century, was known as a city builder. He owned and operated a variety of business enterprises. Later at Hamburg, Berend Roosen was the leading shipowner of the leading commercial city of Germany, a princely merchant. The first Mennonite church in this city was built from 5 per cent of the net profits of one whaling trip in 1674-75. Although Mennonites ultimately discontinued their interests in whaling and shipping they continued to be wholesale merchants in Hamburg as before, some of them outstanding to the present day.

Likewise in East Friesland the Mennonites played a prominent role in the wholesale and sea trade. In the 18th century the Bouman family at Emden controlled oil mills, a distillery, the grain trade, the shipping trade and whaling, while the van Horn, Rahusen, Bavink, and Vissering families at Leer were wholesale merchants. For the 19th and beginning 20th centuries at Norden the Ten Doornkaat-Koolman family, at Emden the Brons family, at Leer the Brouer family are to be mentioned; that they were people of consequence is frequently evident by their being appointed to consulships or having the title of *Kommerzienrat* (Councilor of Commerce) or even *Geheimer Kommerzienrat* (Privy Councilor of Commerce). Jan ten Doornkaat Koolman was one of the greatest distillers of 19th-century Germany with his great plant at Norden. The distillery is still flourishing. In the 17th and into the 19th century there was a noted Mennonite distillery in Danzig whose products were known far beyond the borders of Germany, especially the Danziger Goldwasser brandy.

Still more outstanding have been the great Mennonite textile firms of Westphalia and the Rhineland, namely, those founded and operated by the van Delden, Stroink, and related families at Gronau (cotton) and at Ahaus (jute). In 1854 Matthieu van Delden founded a weaving and spinning mill at Gronau. The firm of Gerrit van Delden (founded in 1876) operated the largest cotton spinning mills on the European continent (it is still one of the largest). Hendrik van Delden (d. 1950), the son of Gerrit, was president, first of the German, and then of the International Union of Spinning Mills. These textile firms were founded by Dutch Mennonites who came to Germany in the early 1800's.

The Lower Rhine congregations of Emmerich, Rees, Cleve, and Goch, and especially Crefeld, had from the beginning (16th century) many linen weavers among them. But the great silk industry of Crefeld was established there by the von der Leyen family in the 17th century. In a short time it became a world-renowned firm, the economic mainstay of Crefeld. In 1768 it employed 724 machines and more than 3,000 workers in Crefeld and its neighborhood, whereas the whole town had only 6,000 inhabitants. In 1789, among the 1,485 artisans of Crefeld 625 were Mennonites "of considerable means and splendid knowledge and ability," according to a report of the Prussian government of Cleve. Fredrick Wilhelm II granted patents of nobility to the von der Leyens in reward for their great contribution to the welfare of the Prussian state. In the 19th century the big firm of the von der Leyens disappeared, but new Mennonite enterprises sprang up, and throughout the century the leading businessmen of the city were members of the large Mennonite church there, among them Hermann von Beckerath (d. 1870), a banker; Karl Wilhelm Crous (d. 1904), a big dealer in raw silk; and Heinrich Müller-Brüderlin (d. 1917), the biggest taxpayer of the city at the turn of the century. The Mennonite firms of Crefeld are still prominent though no longer so dominant as once.

Among the South German Mennonites very few of the farming families have entered business. Peter Kinzing of Neuwied, the gifted mechanic and clockmaker of the later 18th century, should be mentioned. There have been occasional millers, merchants, and small manufacturers in the Palatinate and Southwest Germany, but most of the Mennonites of these areas have remained rural.

The change in business occupations and trades open to and entered by Mennonites in Germany is worthy of note. At first in most cities only a few trades were open to Mennonites, others being forbidden. Thus in the 17th and 18th centuries Mennonites frequently became distillers because this was one of the few businesses with a product of general use, which was open to them. (See **Alcohol among the Mennonites of N.W. Germany**, also **Alcohol . . . West Prussia.**) Some Mennonites were makers of gold lace for the same reason. Friedrichstadt (Schleswig), a newly founded city of special character, was a unique exception, where the Mennonites early controlled most of the trade of the town. There, in the 17th and 18th centuries, they were to be found in all trades; "they were bakers and butchers, millers and oil pressers, distillers and brewers, tailors and shoemakers, weavers and dyers, wool carders, hatters, and soap boilers, masons and carpenters, smiths and glaziers, millwrights and shipbuilders, shopkeepers and wholesale dealers, in possession of a sugar factory and a starch factory." But by 1800 more and more trades were opened to Mennonites and entered by them, until soon all barriers were dropped. The *Mennonitisches Adress-buch* of 1936 lists Mennonites in the following trades and businesses: baker, butcher, distiller, pastry-cook, manufacturer, shoemaker, tailor, weaver, carpenter, glazier, mason, painter, upholsterer, engineer, machinist, mechanic, plumber, blacksmith, auctioneer, banker, bookkeeper, chemist, innkeeper, shopkeeper, merchant, pilot, seaman, shipbuilder, shipowner, carrier, ferryman, taximan, bookbinder, bookseller, printer, dentist, optician.   H.S.B.

Heinz Münte, *Das Altonaer Handlungshaus van der Smissen 1682-1824* (Altona, 1932); B. K. Roosen, *Geschichte unseres Hauses* (Hamburg, 1905); A. Fast, *Die Kulturleistungen der Mennoniten in Ostfriesland und Münsterland* (Emden, 1947); G. van Beckerath, "Die wirtschaftliche Bedeutung der Krefelder Mennoniten im 17. und 18. Jahrhundert" (Crefeld, 1952, unpublished dissertation at Bonn University); Ernst Crous, "The Mennonites in Germany Since the Thirty Years' War," *MQR* XXV (1951) 235-62; W. Kurschat, *Das Haus Friedrich und Heinrich von der Leyen in Krefeld* (Frankfurt, 1933).

Business Among the Mennonites in Holland

In the Netherlands Mennonites (before 1795 excluded from the governmental positions) were much engaged in business, besides being in agriculture and cattle-breeding. Particularly in the second half of the 17th century and in the 18th they held leading positions in the lumber trade (Zaandam, Workum, Harlingen, Groningen), in shipbuilding (Zaandistrict, Sneek), while ship-chandleries in many seaports were owned by Mennonites. The herring-fishery was for a large part operated by Mennonites (de Rijp), and whale-fishing was a Mennonite business (de Rijp, Warns, Ameland). Though there were some exceptions (H. H. van Warendorp, *q.v.*), Mennonites did not take much part in the Dutch East Indies Company, because the ships sailing to the Far East had to be provided with cannon or convoyed by warships for protection against the pirates. Instead of the excellent revenues of this trade they usually preferred the somewhat smaller, but still important profits of the Baltic Sea trade, in which many Mennonites were engaged. Mennonite ships from Holland sailed to many Baltic ports, such as Copenhagen, Danzig, Königsberg, Riga, and St. Petersburg. Seventy *fluiten* (large sailing-vessels) from the little town of Molkwerum in Friesland are said to have cast anchor at one time in the harbor of Riga in Russia (*DB* 1874, 86). And although not many Mennonite boats visited the Levant, the ships of van Eeghen (*q.v.*) and van Lennep (*q.v.*) did regularly carry Dutch and German products to Smyrna and other Levantine ports. The shipping trade to Iceland and Greenland generally was handled by Mennonites. As was the case in Norden, Danzig, and Königsberg, Mennonites in Holland were gin and brandy distillers, for instance, Doyer at Zwolle and van Calcar at Hoogezand.

Besides shipping and trade, a considerable number of Mennonites have been and still are engaged in banking, and also in insurance. Many of the old sawmills and oil presses operated by wind on the Zaan River, which have mostly disappeared now and been replaced by modern mills driven by steam or electricity, were Mennonite. There are still a number of big businesses and industries in Holland which were owned by Mennonites, for example the Honig factories (flour and related products, also vegetable oil products) at Koog aan de Zaan, the W. Middelhoven lumber business and P. Schoen's world-famous dye-factories, both at Zaandam, the Ten Cate factories (world-known textile industry) at Almelo in the province of Overijssel, etc. The flower-export of Aalsmeer (*q.v.*), mostly in Mennonite hands, should also be mentioned here. There are not many Mennonites among the bulb-growers, however. Two outstanding grocery chains, each with more than 300 shops throughout the country, those of Albert Heyn and Simon de Wit, both had their beginning in a grocery store at Zaandam about 1890, with Mennonites as founders. Many Mennonites still hold leading positions in the wholesale trade of different branches, which are not seldom also financed by Mennonites.   vDZ.

Business Among the Mennonites in North America

In the United States Mennonites entered business first, of course, in the oldest settlements in eastern Pennsylvania. Soon after the Civil War (1865 ff.) Mennonites of the Franconia Conference District entered the business of supplying butter, eggs, and fresh meats and fowl to the residents of Philadelphia as commission merchants, and many Mennonites have continued in this business very successfully down to the present time. Around the turn of the 19th century Miller, Hess and Co. (majority ownership Mennonite) was established at Akron, Pa., as a substantial shoe manufacturing business with several (now five) subsidiary companies, in which Orie O. Miller has been a leading figure. In the region of Biglerville and Orrtanna, near Gettysburg, several Musselman families entered the apple (and cherry) canning business, and the C. H. Musselman Company has become one of the leaders in processing apple products and other fruit. The J. M. Smucker Company at Orrville, Ohio, about the same time became a leading apple butter factory, making also jellies and jams of other fruits. The Yoder Greenhouses of Wooster, Ohio, have become very large producers of cut flowers. Archbold, Ohio, has become a center of Mennonite woodworking industries. Berne, Ind., has a Mennonite overall and shirt company and a furniture manufacturing company. Several Mennonite farm implement specialty factories have developed, among them the Ulrich Products Corporation at Roanoke, Ill., and the Hesston Manufacturing Co. at Hesston, Kan. At Altona, Man., several large processing mills have developed, especially one for sunflower-seed oil. The large Newton (Kan.) flour mills were established by B. Warkentin (branches in Kansas City and Halstead) and R. Goerz, thus continuing the tradition established in Russia. At Manson, Iowa, the Wieston Grain Co. has three large grain elevators. This list of Mennonite manufacturers by no means exhausts the list either in type or in location, for a vast number of Mennonites have entered into business throughout the length and breadth of the United States and Canada, although west of Pennsylvania agricultural pursuits still predominate.

A large number of Mennonite farmers now operate chicken or turkey farms with capacities up to

100,000 broilers per year, and several large processing plants have been established, particularly the Maplecrest firm (A. C. Gingerich) at Wellman, Iowa, and Denver, Col., and Pine Manor Farm (Milo and Annas Miller) at Goshen, Ind. Elkhart Co., Ind., and the region of Harrisonburg, Va., have become great centers for the production of broilers, and Johnson-Washington counties in Iowa a major producer of turkeys. There are also many Mennonite hatcheries, one of the largest being the Shenk Hatchery at Harrisonburg, Va. Numerous Mennonite feed mills have been established, some very large, which produce and distribute stock and poultry feeds. In Ohio and Indiana several large stock auctions are operated by Mennonites, e.g., the Lugbill Bros. at Archbold, Ohio. A large potato chip industry has been built up by Edward Snyder at Preston, Ont. Occasionally Mennonites become commission merchants on a large scale, selling eggs, chickens, and produce to the big metropolitan markets ("butter and egg men"). Abraham Schellenberg of Saskatoon, Sask., has developed a chain of grocery stores which are located in all major cities of the province. An outstanding business was developed by David Redekop and his sons in Cuauhtemoc, Mexico, which serves some 10,000 Old Colony Mennonites of that area. Among the larger privately owned printing establishments is the Herald Publishing Co. of Newton, Kan., and D. W. Friesen and Sons of Altona, Man.

The list of other businesses in which Mennonites have entered is very extensive: contractors and builders, banks and finance companies, creameries and dairies, grain companies and elevators, flour mills and feed mills, milk condenseries, produce houses, and large numbers of mercantile companies, lumber companies, oil companies and service stations, plumbing shops, radio shops, drugstores, bookstores, blacksmith shops, implement companies, and many others are to be found, one or more in every Mennonite community. Fire and burial insurance have been handled largely by mutual aid organizations, but one Mennonite firm has become a rather large commercial company—the Brotherhood Mutual Fire Insurance Co. (and its subsidiary, the B. M. Life Insurance Co.) of Fort Wayne, Ind. *Who's Who Among the Mennonites* offers a classified directory of Mennonite business firms in the United States and Canada (pp. 299-314), which, though professedly not exhaustive, lists almost a thousand Mennonite business firms. Some of the towns and cities in which Mennonite enterprises are found in greater numbers or are predominant are as follows: Newton, Moundridge, Hillsboro, Kan.; Beatrice, Neb.; Freeman and Marion, S.D.; Altona, Steinbach, and Winkler, Man. A number of Mennonite-controlled banks can be found in towns like Newton, Moundridge, and Hillsboro, Kan., as well as other places, and in some communities Mennonites hold large amounts of local bank stock and serve as bank presidents and other bank officers. A unique feature are the Credit Union Banks (*q.v.*).

The co-operative (*q.v.*) movement has not made much progress in Mennonite communities, partly because of the strong Mennonite emphasis upon in-dividual enterprise in business and a certain fear of socialism in some quarters. In a few places, however, chiefly in Manitoba, co-operative enterprises have taken the place of individual business. An outstanding illustration of a (largely) Mennonite co-operative business is Co-operative Vegetable Oils, Limited, at Altona, Man.   H.S.B.

Numerous short descriptive articles on the business and economic aspects of North American Mennonite communities, as well as on individual business and businessmen, have appeared in *Mennonite Life* and *Mennonite Community*. The following lists of articles are chronologically arranged without author names.

Mennonite Life 1947-53. The Economic Life of the Berne Community, July 1947, 19; The Citrus Fruit Industry of Southern California, Oct. 1947, 4-7; Mennonite Citrus Fruit Growers, Oct. 1947, 8; Sixty Years in the Banking Business, Jan. 1948, 38-41; Sunflower Rebuilds Community, July 1949, 28-32; The Crosstown Credit Union, July 1949, 32; D. G. Rempel's Adventure in Toy Manufacturing, Jan. 1950, 41-43; Wiebe's Diary—A Story of Ambition and Work, April 1950, 24-26; Mennonites in South Dakota, July 1950, p. I-V; The Grape and Raisin Industry, Oct. 1950, 4-9; The Fruit and Vegetable Industry in Ontario, Oct. 1950, 24-26; Turkey Growing in Mt. Lake, Oct. 1950, 35-38; The Mennonites in Winnipeg (Industry and Business), Jan. 1951, 16, 20-23; Mennonite Community at Meade, July 1951, 8-13; A Printery on the Prairie, Jan. 1952, 16 f.; The Shafter-Wasco Community, Oct. 1952, 158-64; Mennonites of Wichita (How They Live and Work), Jan. 1953, 9-11; From Farmer to Officer Craftsman, Jan. 1953, 36-38; The Buhler Mill and Elevator Co., April 1953, 82-86; The J. J. Wiebe Lumber Co., July 1953, 127 f.

Mennonite Community 1947-53. Occupations Among the Mennonites of Bucks and Montgomery Counties, July 1947, 6 f.; A Community Builds for 50 Years, Sept. 1947, 19-23; Dairy Industry of Elkhart County, Incorporated, May 1948, 17-23; The Turkey Industry at Wellman, Nov. 1948, 18-23; The Howard-Miami Community, Dec. 1948, 18-21; Community at Gulfport, Mississippi, Jan. 1949, 18-23; Community at Hubbard, Oregon, Feb. 1949, 18-23; The Brick and Tile Industry, Hubbard, Oregon, Feb. 1949, 24 f.; A Community Develops Its Own Woodcraft Industry, July 1949, 18 f.; A Chair Shop of My Own (Horning's Chair Shop), Oct. 1949, 24 f.; The Poultry Industry of Elkhart County, Nov. 1941, 6-10; The Goodville Mutual Casualty Company, Feb. 1950, 12 f.; The Archbold Community, May 1950, 6-11; Church, Community Flourish at Pigeon, Michigan, July 1950, 32; Lumbering in the Northwest, Aug. 1950, 6-10; Mennonite Contributions to Poultry Industry in Shenandoah Valley, Nov. 1950, 6-11; The Mennonites in Woodford County, Illinois, Dec. 1950, 6-11, 33; The Story of the Community at Kidron, Ohio, March 1951, 6-11, 15; The Mennonite Community of Washington County, Maryland, May 1951, 6-11, 32 f.; New Communities in York and Adams Counties, Pennsylvania, July 1951, 10-12; Growth of Industries at Hesston, Kansas, Aug. 1951, 6-11; The Mennonite Mutual Insurance Company, Sept. 1951, 12 f.; Church Community in Wayne County, Ohio, Oct. 1951, 6-11; Your Visit to the Grantsville and Springs Communities, Maryland, Dec. 1951, 6-11; A Farm Community Builds Its Own Industry, Oct. 1952, 17-19.

Business Among the Mennonites in Russia

Among the Mennonites in Russia business started when they found themselves producing cattle, horses, eggs, butter, ham, grain, etc., without the benefit of convenient markets. Some of the Mennonites, such as the young Johann Cornies, began to take produce to the markets of Sevastopol, Kertch, Taganrog, Berdyansk, Kharkov, and Ekaterinoslav. Returning, these small merchants took with them cloth, groceries, tools, machinery, etc. With the growing wheat production, Mennonite wheat dealers could be found in all settlements. Berdyansk (*q.v.*) was outstanding in this respect.

Lumber yards operated by Mennonites were found in Einlage near Chortitza. Popularity of the dairy cows produced by the Mennonites caused many to go into export business. The same must be said about the farm machinery (*q.v.*) produced in Mennonite factories. A number of business schools prepared young men for business.

This growing interest in business caused many Mennonites to establish businesses in non-Mennonite communities and cities. This trend became very strongly noticeable just before World War I. In 1908 there were 576 Mennonite business enterprises and industries valued at 5,494,878 rubles. Some of the major centers of Mennonite industry and business enterprise were Chortitza (*q.v.*), Zaporozhe (*q.v.*), Halbstadt (*q.v.*), Berdyansk (*q.v.*), and Ekaterinoslav (*q.v.*).   C.K.

Busschaert, Hans Bouwens (also called Hans de Weber), born in Flanders or Brabant, and worked chiefly in Belgium. In 1555 Menno ordained him as a Mennonite elder. Menno later related this incident about him: One day a mayor in Flanders halted the coach in which he was traveling and asked for Busschaert. Busschaert then asked his fellow travelers whether Busschaert was in the coach, and they, not knowing him, answered negatively. Then he said to the mayor, "They say he is not here."

In the disputes between the Frisians and Flemish 1566-68 Busschaert played a leading part. He joined the Flemish, and he and Jacob Pieters van der Meulen (*q.v.*) were their leaders. First he banned the *bekommerde Mennisten* (*q.v.*), the followers of Paulus Bussemaker. In the dispute which arose in 1586 among the Flemish over the sale of a house and resulted in a division into Flemish and Young Flemish or *Huiskoopers* (*q.v.*) and *Contrahuiskoopers* (*q.v.*), he was one of the leaders in the former group. Finally in 1598 he became involved in a dispute with J. P. van der Meulen (*q.v.*) concerning a case of bankruptcy, in which each banned the other.

He enjoyed taking part in disputations with the Reformed. A disputation with Adriaen Jeroens in 1566 at Westersouburg (Zeeland) was broken up by the government, and the attendants were dispersed. He also played a part, though minor, in the great disputation at Emden in 1578, where Pieter van Keulen brilliantly saved the honor of the Mennonites. In 1570-71 he baptized in the Antwerp congregation. In 1571 he was living in Cologne. He traveled much, proclaiming the Gospel and administering communion and baptism. Herman de Timmerman (*q.v.*), a martyr, stated in his trial that Busschaert had a red beard. (K. Vos, *Menno Simons*, Leiden, 1914, 145-47; *DB* 1868, 26; 1893, 12-79; 1908, 12, 14, 63; *ML* I, 304.)   K.V.

Bussemaker, Paulus, is named the leader of an otherwise unknown Mennonite Flemish group who were called the *heilsamen* (holy ones). About 1580 he was excommunicated from his own group by Hans Busschaert and Jacob Pieters van den Meulen. (Vos, *Antwerpen*, 355; *BRN* VII, 70.)   vDZ.

Bussiere, M. Th. de (d. 1865), author of *Les Anabaptistes (Histoire de la Luthéranisme, de l' Anabaptisme et du régne de Jean Bockelsohn á Munster)* (Paris, 1853, 475 pp.). This book by a Roman Catholic author is of no value for students of Anabaptism. (*Catalogus Amst.*, 55; *ML* I, 305.) vDZ

Bussum, a town in the Dutch province of North Holland, about 15 miles to the east of Amsterdam, pop. about 34,000, seat of the Naarden-Bussum congregation, with a church in Bussum. At the beginning of the 20th century many Mennonites, chiefly from Amsterdam, located here. The church board from near-by Hilversum, to which the members in Bussum belonged at that time, formed the Bussum fellowship in 1908, administered by a committee of five members, of which the chairman was a member of the church board at Hilversum. Originally one preaching service was held each month in the building of the *Nederlandse Protestantenbond* (first service on Jan. 24, 1909). In the year 1915 the fellowship became a congregation entirely independent of Hilversum and chose its own church board. Initially, it was hardly possible to have a service each month, although at the time there was a program of religious education, conducted first by the emeritus ministers, among whom was Tj. Kielstra (*q.v.*), and later on by several other ministers, among whom were W. Luikinga, M. L. Onnes, and J. L. de Wagenmaker. Of great importance was the erection of their own church, which was dedicated July 8, 1923. In 1939 the congregation received their first permanent minister in O. T. Hylkema, who served the congregation until 1944, and was followed by the present minister, D. Richards. While the number of members varied very little at first (150 in 1917; 160 in 1926), it has grown rapidly since about 1930. At present (1951) there are 435 members. The congregation also has a Sunday school for children, and fellowships for women, men, and youth (*DB* 1908, 206; 1909, 187; 1918, 155; *ML* I, 305).   vDZ

Bussy, Izaak Jan le Cosquino de, b. Sept. 13, 1846, at Utrecht; d. Oct. 5, 1920, at Hilversum, Holland, a student at the Amsterdam Mennonite Seminary (1865-70); minister of the Mennonite churches at Edam (1870-72), Wormerveer (1872-78), and Amsterdam (1878-84); archivist at Deventer (1889-92); teacher of philosophy of religion and ethics at the Amsterdam University and the Mennonite Seminary 1892-1916.

Religious ideas, as de Bussy teaches, are interpretations of a religious mind; they give a visible form to what a person feels of his relation to a Power which he does not observe in the world around him. They do, however, not reveal the reality around us, but the reality in us. Scientific ideas and religious ideas come from different functions of the mind; between these there is no direct relation. Religion has nothing to do, directly, with a (scientific) conception of the world; it is a way of looking at the world in the light of emotions. In the disposition of our mind a higher reality reveals itself than that which we may observe in the world of phenomena; the conceptions in which this interprets itself are always in the domain of transcendence. The truth of our religious conceptions can not be proved by contemplating the world, but only by the eye that beholds and by nothing else but a call on being normal, on the health of mind of the beholder; truth is nothing else but a state of mind. In metaphysics (i.e., concerning the question as to whether the contents of religious ideas are adequate metaphysically), de Bussy is an abstentionist, abstaining from a conclusion; but he does so as a scholar, from the intellectual function of his mind; as a human being with a religious heart he is sure of the truth of his religious ideas. Religious ideas are brought to us by culture. In the spiritual world, in which we live, we find the conception of a transcendental Power and its character.

As truth of faith does not come to us from a perceptible world, so too, according to de Bussy, our specifically ethical thoughts, our ideas about ethical right and wrong, do not flow from an outside world. Right and wrong do not exist in a world of phenomena; they only exist in the human mind; virtues and vices are not visible in the outside world. Traits of character, dispositions, inclinations are neither good nor bad in themselves, but we "think" they are good or bad. The object of our moral judgment is the character of man, more exactly, the idea of the character of a man, we have formed in our mind. Everything we think (ethically) to be right or wrong can be reduced in the last instance to human character; we do not call acts as such good or bad; if we (metaphorically) call an act good or bad, we properly mean that the acting person is good or bad according to our view, in so far as we get to know him from this act, the aim of his act, or the choice of means to realize the act.

We measure the character of a person after a standard which we have in our mind; this standard consists of ideas of virtues and vices. The question as to how we can come to judge ethically, and the question as to the origin of our standard of moral judgment, is answered by de Bussy in this way, that neither function nor standard are inborn, but are brought to us by culture. We only can say that we are capable of ideas of virtues and vices. It is evident that de Bussy represents the extreme modernist point of view.

Izaäk Jan le Cosquino de Bussy was a grandson of Félicité Sophie and Louis le Cosquino de Bussy, who about 1793 immigrated from France to Holland and lived in Utrecht as a teacher. A son of Izaak de Bussy was Arthur le Cosquino de Bussy, b. 1884 at Amsterdam, d. there July 24, 1953. He studied law and was archivist of the city of Amsterdam. He served the churches at Utrecht and Amsterdam as a deacon, was for a number of years a member of the board of the Amsterdam Mennonite Seminary and treasurer of the *Zwolsche Kas* (*q.v.*).

J.Marse.

Writings of de Bussy: *Ethisch Idealisme,* 1875; *Over de waarde en den inhoud van godsdienstige voorstellingen,* 1880; *Een tiental preeken,* 1883; *De maatstaf van het zedelijk oordeel en het voorwerp van het godsdienstig geloof,* 1889; *Wijsgerige*

wetenschap en persoonlijke overtuiging, 1892; *Inleiding tot de zedekunde,* 1898; *De koopman uit een zedekundig oogpunt,* 1905; *Het zedelijk beoordeelen* I, 1915, II, 1920; articles in *Theol. Tijdschrift* 1878, 1882, 1888, 1891, 1895; in *Teyler's Theol. Tijdschrift* 1903, 1907, 1908, 1909, 1910. After his death appeared: *Opstellen van I. J. de Bussy,* bewerkt door Dr. J. Maarse en Dr. N. Westendorp Boerma, 1926; *De wetenschap der moraal,* bewerkt door Dr. J. Maarse en Dr. N. Westendorp Boerma, 1939; *Over den oorsprong van het zedelijk beoordeelen,* bewerkt door Dr. J. Maarse, 1947. (*DJ* 1922, 46-63; *ML* I, 305.)

Butler County, Kan., in the east-central part of the state, has a Mennonite settlement in its northwest corner, which includes the following congregations, the first three of which are members of the General Conference Mennonite Church and the fourth a member of the Church of God in Christ, Mennonite: the Emmaus Mennonite Church (*q.v.*) near Whitewater, organized in 1877; the Zion Mennonite Church (*q.v.*) in Elbing, organized in 1883; the Swiss Mennonite Church near Whitewater, organized in 1885; and the Church of God in Christ Mennonite congregation (*q.v.*) at Burns, organized in 1939. In the city of Elbing the Berean Christian Laymen's Association, a Mennonite corporation, owns and operates the Berean Academy (*q.v.*), a four-year high school. L.A.J.

Butler County, Mo., was the home of a small group of Old Order Amish Mennonites from about 1920 to 1924. About 15 families, consisting of settlers mostly from Reno Co., Kan., including families of Miller, Bontrager, Glick, Amstutz, Troyer, Hostetler, Chupp, and Mast, lived in the area between Poplar Bluff and Harviell. The one and only minister of the group was Chriss Bontrager. The settlement was never very substantial, and in 1924 most of the Amish moved 50 miles east to Scott County and to other states. The Amish buried a few of their people in the county, but later took up their remains and shipped them to Kansas.

J.A.H.

Butler County, Ohio, a county in the extreme southwestern corner of the state, with Hamilton as the county seat. In this county was founded in 1819 the first of the Alsatian and South German Amish settlements in North America, of the Amish migration to America following the European Napoleonic wars. Butler County became a brief stopping place for many of the Amish immigrants later moving on to Illinois and Iowa. Among later Amish leaders who tarried here for a while were Christian Ropp, Peter Naffziger, Joseph Stuckey, all later of Illinois; and Joseph Goldschmidt of Iowa. The present congregation, with a meetinghouse in the village of Trenton, is now called the Apostolic Mennonite Church (*q.v.*) and is a member of the General Conference branch. C.H.S.

Butler County Mennonite Brethren Church, located near Cassidy, Kan., was organized in the later 1880's by Abraham Cornelsen, Sr., who had been elected to the ministry in Russia, when four families belonging to the Mennonite Brethren Church moved there. By 1893 approximately 20 families belonged to the group, but soon after that began to disperse because of poverty and the offer of free homesteads in Oklahoma. Some families moved to Canada, and at the turn of the century the group had dissolved. A. Cornelsen, after trying his fortune in Marion Co., Kan., became the leader of the church at Hooker, Okla., in 1906. **I.G.N.**

Butterfield, Minn., is located in the south central part of the state and is in the western end of Watonwan County. It has a population of approximately 600 inhabitants. There are at least 500 Mennonites living within the town and in the surrounding community. A much larger group is within shopping distance of the town. A considerable number come from the St. James and Mountain Lake Mennonite communities to shop at Miller's store. Most of the Mennonites of these areas are farmers.

The Mennonites living in this area are mostly General Conference Mennonites with a sprinkling of E.M.B.'s. Most of these people live north and east of the town. A goodly number reside west and south, connecting with the Mountain Lake area. Some of these people have lived here since 1874. The settlement took shape largely after 1876. In the late eighties and early nineties the Galician Mennonites also came into the area. There are two Mennonite churches in the vicinity, one in town and the other five miles northeast of Butterfield. At present there are no other Mennonite institutions although a number of years ago there was a German Mennonite Bible school on the premises of the First Mennonite Church property northeast of Butterfield. The building was torn down in 1952, and the lumber used for a parsonage. **M.M.L.**

Butterfield First Mennonite Church: see **First** Mennonite Church of Butterfield, Minnesota.

Butterfield Mennonite Church (GCM) in Butterfield, Minn., had its origin in the Menno Simons Mennonite Church (*q.v.*), which united with the Salem Mennonite Church (*q.v.*) in 1915, withdrew in 1921, reorganized, and built a church in 1922, known as the Mennonite Church of Butterfield. **J.J.F.**

Butsch, a baronetcy (*Herrschaft*) in Moravia, where the Hutterian Brethren had a Bruderhof (*Arch. f. Ref.-Gesch.,* 1933, 97).

Buyck, Joost Sijbrandsz, b. 1505 at Amsterdam, d. Feb. 10, 1588, at Leiden, promoted to the rank of a noble by King Christian of Denmark in 1521, became sheriff at Amsterdam in 1532, and burgomaster of this city for the first time in 1549 and was thereafter re-elected 17 times. He defended the town against the Reformation, and when Amsterdam fell, i.e., the Catholics lost, in 1578, Buyck was banned. Holding the office of sheriff, he was present in connection with many court procedures against the Anabaptists and Mennonites. In these instances he showed himself a decided opponent but moderate in his judgment. Of significance is his writing concerning the rise of the Anabaptists: *Nieuwe maaren of verhaal van tegen voorgevallen is binnen Amsterdam en op andere plaatsen in de jaren 1534 tot 1536* (The latest tidings or the story

of those happenings in Amsterdam and other places during the years 1534 to 1536). This work, which has the faults of all the historical writing of that period—prejudice and partisanship—contains many valuable particulars concerning this period. It was reprinted by P. Scheltema in *Amstel's Oudheid* (1856) II. (*N.N.B.Wb.,* VI, 244.) vDZ.

Buys (also Buis), a common Dutch family name, which is also found among the Mennonites. Evert Buys is mentioned in 1688 as preacher of the Mennonite congregation at Brielle (*Inv. Arch. Amst.* I, No. 840). Cornelis Buys was preacher of the Flemish congregation at Aalsmeer in the first quarter of the 18th century (*Naamlijst* of 1731). In the congregation of *de oude vermaning* at Aalsmeer, which was served until 1866 by untrained preachers, four members of this family were serving during the 19th century. Willem Willems Buys, elder 1822-50; Gerrit Buys, preacher, later elder, 1849-66; Jan Buys, preacher 1855-66, and Willem Gerritsz Buys, preacher until 1866. (*DB* 1902, 241.) The name of Buys is still very common among the Mennonites of Aalsmeer. In Zaandam, where Jan Jacobsz Buys was a preacher in the *Oude Huys* from 1746 until his death in 1753, a large number of the Buys family served as deacons. vDZ.

S. Lootsma, *Het Nieuwe Huys* (Zaandam, 1937) 190, 195 f., 201.

Buys, Willem Jansz, is the printer of the eighth edition of *Het Offer des Heeren* (*q.v.*), which with the *Liedtboecxken* (hymnbook) appeared in 1590 ("T'Amstelredam. Bij Willem Jansz. Buys, Woonende in de Waermoestrate, in den Liesveltschen Bybel"). Buys also published in 1595 the tenth edition of the *Offer* and the *Liedtboecxken* and some other songbooks of the Mennonites (*BRN* II, 14, 16). vDZ.

Buyser, Jan de, a native of the Netherlands, probably from Amsterdam, was a minister of the Flemish congregation of the *Huiskoopers* (*q.v.*) at Hamburg-Altona shortly after 1640, which congregation he served until 1670. He wrote *Christelijck Huys-boeck ende het eendrachligh gheluyt in de Geestelijcken Tempel Salomons, oft Gemeeynte Jesu Christi* (Christian House-Book, and the Harmonious Peal in the Spiritual Temple of Solomon, or the Church of Jesus Christ), printed at Hoorn in 1643. It consists of a collection of writings by various Mennonite authors and is intended for family reading. The *Huys-boeck* is a large volume of 980 pages. The first part (pp. 1-625) contains 12 articles of faith on which the author comments with quotations from the works of Menno Simons, Dirk Philips, Vincent de Hondt, and other influential Mennonite authors. The second part (pp. 627-821) is taken up with a "Further Explanation" (*Naerder Verklaringhe*) of the above articles, while in the third part of this book (pp. 823-980), called "Necessary Instruction" (*Hoogh-noodige Vertooninge*), the author provides still another commentary on some of the articles of faith.

Besides the *Huys-boeck* de Buyser also published *Christi Hemelvaert* (The Ascension of Christ), which seems to have been lost, and *Naerder verklaringe over mijn klein Boeckjen ghetytuleert*

"Christi Hemelvaert" (Altona, 1664). His *Christe-lijck Huys-boeck* was written as a devotional and doctrinal reader for his own group, the Dutch-speaking *Huiskoopers.* vDZ., R.F.

R. Friedmann, *Menn. Piety Through the Centuries* (Goshen, 1949) 152 f.; *Menn. Bl.,* 1854, *Catalogus Amst.,* 173; *ML* I, 313.

Buyser, Jan Gerrits, a preacher of the Dutch Mennonite congregation at Uithoorn from Feb. 8, 1660, to Sept. 24, 1695, when he died. After his death 32 of his sermons were published (Amsterdam, 1697) by Klaasz Jansz Man, his colleague (who also delivered his funeral sermon), with an appendix on the administration of baptism and communion (by going to the table, according to the Waterlander custom), and instruction to establish preachers in the Word. (Schijn-Maatschoen, *Gesch. der Mennoniten* II, Amsterdam, 1744, 656-58: *Catalogus Amst.,* 250; *ML* I, 313.) NEFF.

Buyser, Lieven de, a member of the Flemish Mennonite congregation at Amsterdam, author of *Verklaringe van den Droevigen Handel der Ghemeynte Gods tot Amsterdam . . .* (Amsterdam, 1616). (*DB* 1896, 100 ff.; *Catalogus Amst.,* 111; *ML* I. 313.) NEFF.

Byerland Mennonite Meetinghouse in Lancaster Co., Pa., is the meeting place of a congregation of the Lancaster Mennonite Conference (MC). Samuel and Mary Boyer sold one acre of their farm Dec. 10, 1755, along a road, now abandoned north of the James H. Hess farm home, Pequea Twp., Lancaster Co., Pa., to Charles Christopher and Jacob Boehm, deacons, whereon was built a small log meetinghouse, still standing (1950), although moved from its first location a few miles. The next church, one-half mile away on an elevated site along the Pequea Valley Road, was built in 1848 when Jacob Brenneman and Henry Charles were deacons. A large cemetery adjoins the church grounds. The present well-preserved brick church built in 1879 was extensively remodeled in 1953. It became part of the New Danville-River Corner circuit. Rawlinsville is a mission outgrowth of the congregation. The 1953 membership was 199. Ministers now serving (1953) are Maris Hess and James H. Hess; Howard Eshleman is deacon.

I.D.L.

Bylandt, von, a family of earls having its seat in Rheydt (*q.v.*) in Rhenish Prussia, which for more than 100 years offered toleration and protection from the repressions of the government to Anabaptists living on their estates. At first Otto von Bylandt, who played an influential role of power in the court of Duke William in Düsseldorf, protected them against all persecution by the imperial government. "In 1594 the first Anabaptist, Peter auf der Heuren, is mentioned. Ten years later their number had increased; they conducted their services in night meetings with singing and preaching. In 1646 they seem to have been organized in a congregation with their own deacons. At the end of the 17th century the von Bylandt family offered them residence within the castle walls until they were forcibly expelled on July 16 on command of the Palatine elector." (Rembert, *Wiedertäufer,* 158, 426, 530; *ML* I, 314.) NEFF.

Byler (Beiler, Beyler), an Amish family name of Swiss origin. The ancestor of most of the family in America was Jacob Beiler, born in Switzerland, who came to America on the *Charming Polly* in 1737. He with his family settled in the Oley Valley in Berks Co., Pa., but later moved to Lebanon Valley, and finally settled in Lancaster County, where he died. A grandson, Hans Beiler, was the pioneer Amish bishop in the Kishacoquillas Valley, Pennsylvania. The family historian, C. Z. Mast, estimated in 1923 that there were 6,000 living descendants of Jacob Beiler in America. In 1951 these descendants lived principally in Ohio and Pennsylvania. In Ohio there were seven Byler Old Order Amish Mennonite ministers and in Pennsylvania eleven Beiler and ten Byler Old Order Amish Mennonite ordained men.

Among the better-known descendants of Jacob Beiler was his great-grandson Bishop David Beiler (1786-1871), Lancaster Co., Pa., author of *Das wahre Christentum* (Lancaster, 1888). Another well-known Amish bishop was Solomon Beiler (1799-1888) of Mifflin Co., Pa., whose advocacy of baptism in the water led to the separation of his congregation from the Old Order Amish Church. B. Frank Byler of West Liberty, Ohio, is now a missionary (MC) in Argentina. Clayton Beyler is a minister and Bible teacher at Hesston College.

M.G.

C. Z. Mast, "The Beiler Family," *Christian Monitor,* March, 1923; John Umble, "Memoirs of an Amish Bishop" (David Beiler), *MQR* XXII, 2, 94.

C

Cachipay Mennonite Mission (GCM), a school and evangelistic center located on a small farm near Cachipay, Cund., Colombia, about 40 miles southwest of Bogotá, the capital. The work began in the fall of 1945, with the arrival of Mr. and Mrs. Gerald Stucky, Janet Soldner, and Mary Becker. They studied the Spanish language for one year in Medellin, and then began active work on Feb. 1, 1946, opening a boarding school for underprivileged children, most of whom are the children of lepers. The school operates with the co-operation of the American Leprosy Missions, who have heavily subscribed to the financial obligations of this work. In 1947 the school was organized as the Colegio Evangelico Colombiano with 24 children, and the mission was incorporated under the laws of Colombia as the Misión Menonita Colombiana. The school now has a capacity of about 100 children. The mission staff has been increased to include Miss Alice Bachert (1948), Mr. and Mrs. LaVerne A. Rutschman (1948), and Mr. and Mrs. Arthur Keiser (1949). The school serves as the hub for the evangelistic activities of the mission. In Cachipay there is an active and growing congregation of believers with a membership of approximately 60 (1953).

G.S.

Caddo Mennonite Brethren Church, now extinct, a member of the Southern District Conference, was founded in 1905 when Mennonite families filed claims for homesteads on the newly opened Caddo Indian Reservation in Oklahoma, and dissolved in 1919. Henry Bergthold was the leader from the beginning until about 1917. In 1913 the membership was 49, but because of the sandy soil and poor crops most of the members moved to Corn, Okla. The last minister was A. B. Schmidt. (*ML* I, 314.)

I.G.N.

Cadzand, a village in the Dutch province of Zeeland near the Belgian border, once the seat of a Mennonite congregation. About 1580 Mennonites were already reported in the district of Cadzand, which at that time was an island (until by reclamation of land it became a part of Dutch Flanders in 1623). In 1629 the minister of the congregation was Bartholomeus van den Daele (also known as B. den Mulier). By 1657 the congregation had already acquired a simple meetinghouse near the village of Nieuwvliet, and after 1660 was generally known as Nieuwvliet (*q.v.*), but sometimes also as Groede (*q.v.*). Not much is known concerning the history of this congregation. In 1657 it was granted a charter by the States-General to perform the marriages of its members. The congregation became smaller and smaller; about 1670 there were 90 members; in 1730 barely 40. In the 17th century the congregation belonged to the Flemish (*q.v.*) branch; representatives from the congregation of Cadzand were present at the Flemish conference at Haarlem in 1649; and presumably the ministers of this congregation signed for "Zeelandt" the Flemish Confession of Faith at Dordrecht in 1632. During the time of the wars with France the con-

gregation became impoverished. In 1712, and repeatedly later, it asked financial support from other congregations. In 1721 it was stated that the congregation consisted entirely of poverty-stricken members. To support a minister was for the congregation frequently difficult. From 1713 to about 1726 Roelof Agges Jonker (d. 1730) was minister here, but he was suspended because of misconduct. In 1733 it is known that both the congregation and the church building were in a deplorable condition. From 1735 to 1753 Joannes (Jan) Francken was the elder at this place, but was not an asset to the congregation. It is not surprising, therefore, that in 1754 the congregation began a serious deterioration. In 1758 the ministerial candidate N. Klopper served here several months, and after this the pulpit was vacant. Jan Nieuwenhuizen (*q.v.*), minister at near-by Aardenburg, preached regularly at Nieuwvliet, 1765-71. After his departure the services were suspended.

On June 10, 1779, the congregation at Aardenburg took over the debts and possessions of the Cadzand congregation, and the few remaining members joined the church at Aardenburg. The church building was razed in 1788. (*Inv. Arch. Amst.* II, 1639-76; *DB* 1879, 20; 1884, 108; 1889, 90-116.)

vDZ.

Cajacob, identical with Blaurock, Georg (Jörg) (*q.v.*).

Calcar, van (Calker, Calcker, Kalkar, Kalker, Kalcker), a Dutch Mennonite family of Deventer during the 17th century. The archives of the Mennonite congregation of Deventer contain a genealogy of this family. Matheus van Calcar, married to Hendrikje van Delden, born at Burgsteinfurt in Westphalia in 1616, lived in Deventer. So he or his father may have migrated from Burgsteinfurt to Deventer. In Deventer the family belonged to the Old Flemish congregation. In 1711 Berend (?) van Calcar, a merchant and member of this church at Deventer, took care of seven Swiss Mennonite immigrants and sheltered them in his house. His son Jan van Calcar (*q.v.*) left the Old Flemish church and joined the Old Swiss Brethren congregation at Hoogezand. About 1720 a group of Old Flemish Mennonites left Deventer and migrated to Hoogezand, because they were dissatisfied with the worldliness and low doctrinal standards of the Deventer congregation, and joined the Swiss congregation in Hoogezand. Among this group were many members of the van Calcar family (*DB* 1919, 74-75). But other van Calcars remained at Deventer. Here most of the van Calcars were engaged in business. One of their descendants founded a distillery still existing at Hoogezand. Some of the van Calcar family lived in Groningen and were merchants and later on lumber dealers. They belonged here as in Deventer to the Old Flemish congregations. In 1695 Abraham Albertz van Calcker and Jan van Kalckar are named as contributors to this church.

A few members of this family have served Mennonite congregations as ministers. Isaac van Calker served the Old Flemish congregation of Zaandam 1711-ca. 56. Jan van Kalker (Calkar), not the man named above, was a preacher of the Swiss Brethren (*Nieuwe Zwitzers*) at Groningen and Sappemeer 1755-72. Isaäk van Kalker (Calcar) served this congregation 1770-96. Jan van Kalker was minister at Noordbroek 1776-82, Neustadt-Gödens 1782-88, and Knijpe (later called Heerenveen) 1788-1821; Pieter van Kalker at Sappemeer 1786-1807. Hendrik van Calcar served the congregation of Hindeloopen and Molkwerum 1863-65, Veenwouden 1865-80, Noordhorn 1880-86, and Zijpe 1886-1906; his son J. D. van Calcar was pastor of Warns 1901-3, and Beverwijk 1906-37. J. D. van Calcar was also for many years a teacher of Bible and church history at the state training college for teachers at Haarlem. He wrote a manual on religion called *De Groote Lijnen* (Groningen, 1927) and some Biblical plays: *Job* (1924), *Verlaten ?* (1926), and *Michal* (1927). (See also **Kalker, van.**)   vDZ.

Calcar (Calker), **Jan van** (1696-1773), b. at Deventer, Dutch province of Overijssel. He left his home church (Old Flemish) and joined the congregation of the Swiss Brethren at Hoogezand, Dutch province of Groningen, being baptized here in 1716 by Hans Ancken, Elder of the United Palatine and Swiss Brethren, who had immigrated from Switzerland in 1711. Jan van Calcar was a very pious and ascetic man, who left his business in order to live in the country and to do farm work, which seemed to him more according to the Gospel than business. In 1736 he met Zinzendorf (*q.v.*), the leader of the Moravian Brethren, and became an ardent follower of this movement, without leaving his Swiss Mennonite Church. Van Calcar also urged his father-in-law W. Ebbing, who was at this time a sheriff and a member of the Reformed Church, to be converted and to leave his office; Ebbing migrated with his family to Hoogezand and also joined the Swiss Mennonite Church. Ebbing's daughters do not seem to have joined the Mennonite Church, but held important offices in the Moravian brotherhood. Hendrika Ebbing became in 1760 "Generalältestin der ledigen Schwestern" (Head of the Unmarried Sisters) at Herrnhut. A *Levensbericht* (Autobiography), written by Jan van Calcar himself, is found in the archives of the Mennonite congregation of Amsterdam. (W. Lütjeharms, *Het philadelfisch-oecumenisch streven der Hernhutters in de Nederlanden in de achttiende eeuw*, Zeist, 1935, 137.)   vDZ.

Caldwell (Idaho) **First** Mennonite Church (GCM), a member of the Pacific District Conference, was organized on May 25, 1947, with a membership of 24, by pioneers who had settled at Caldwell around 1902. Others came from Oregon and Nebraska, 1941-46. The church was dedicated on April 18, 1948. Prominent names are Ulrich, Dick, Huebert, and Schmidt. Its 1952 membership was 34.
          M.H.K.

Caledonia (Mich.) Mennonite (MC) Church, now extinct, in Kent County, where Mennonite (MC)

settlers built a church in 1865. Many of the first settlers in 1864-65 came from Ontario; others were from Indiana, Ohio, and Pennsylvania. Resident ministers included Abram Detweiler, Henry Wismer, Peter Steiner, Jacob Hahn, Christian C. Beery, and Christian G. Wenger. By 1867 there were 40 members, but the congregation never prospered. In 1881 a new church was built. Ten years later disagreements on doctrine and other matters arose and helped bring about the dissolution of the congregation by 1910. The building burned in 1923. The present Bowne Church (*q.v.*) is located about twelve miles from the site of the Caledonia Church but the two congregations were always distinct and independent.   J.C.W.

Calendar of Appointments, a small pamphlet giving a complete list of the church appointments for the coming year, i.e., the "appointed" dates of meeting of the regular Sunday services and the special services such as "inquiry" or "preparatory" service and communion service of the several Mennonite congregations in a conference district or regional area, and also the annual and semiannual conferences and ministers' meetings. Used only in the Mennonite Church (MC), it was designed to help ministers and lay-members desiring to attend the services of sister congregations on the "off Sundays," i.e., on the Sundays when no services were held at home (the almost universal practice was to hold the regular services biweekly only, for outlying places only monthly, and only in the mornings). Ministers were sometimes sent to "fill appointments" in the absence or illness of the home ministers.

Two of these "Meeting Calendars" are known, one for eastern Pennsylvania, one for Ontario. Which is first is not known. Although it seems probable that the one for eastern Pennsylvania preceded, the oldest extant copy is for 1854, while the first edition of the one for Ontario was for 1836 in German. The latter was published in German only, 1836-89, then in both a German and English edition from 1890 for some years until the German was discontinued. As a result of the Old Order Mennonite schism of 1890, the seceding group continued the publication of the Calendar in German, later displaced by English. Both groups have continued the series numbering as 1836, counting number 1 as 1836. The German edition title was *Calender für die Versammlungen der Mennoniten-Gemeinde in —— (provincial name changed from "Ober Canada" to "Canada West" and then to "Ontario"). From the beginning the Calendar contained a separate list of all ordained men. In 1917 the minutes and reports of the annual meetings of the conference and mission board were added, and later of other organizations.

Of the 1854 eastern Pennsylvania Calendar, the oldest extant was in English (no German edition at any time apparently) bearing the title, *Calendar of Mennonite Meetings in Lancaster County, Pa.* By 1880, the next extant copy, it was called *Meeting Calendar of all the Mennonite Churches in Eastern Pennsylvania* (excluding of course other branches but including the Franconia Conference and the Franklin County churches) and carried a complete directory of ordained men with addresses and congregational connections. By 1885 the Washington Co., Md., district was added. In recent years it has carried a full calendar of special meetings, ministerial statistics, mission board members' lists, etc., and is edited by Ira D. Landis.

In 1872 a *Meeting Calendar, of a Part of the Mennonite Churches in the United States with a List of Ministers' Names and Addresses* was published in similar form by J. F. Funk and Bro. at Elkhart, Ind., called a *Supplement to the Herald of Truth* and distributed free to all *Herald* subscribers. Whether further issues appeared is unknown but unlikely. The real continuance of this publication came in the *Mennonite Yearbook and Directory,* 1905- , now published by the Mennonite Publishing House (Scottdale, Pa.), which from the beginning published along with a ministerial directory with addresses lists of all (old) Mennonite congregations by conferences together with the ministers attached to each and the "appointments" for Sunday services. This directory of services and ministers, still continued in the current annual volume without change even though now most congregations meet regularly every Sunday, is unique in Mennonite literature. (*ML* II, 452.)   H.S.B.

Caley (Alberta) Hutterite Bruderhof was founded in 1936 by members of the Raley Bruderhof. Their preacher was Paul Walter, who was chosen in 1938 and confirmed later. In 1947 the Caley Bruderhof number 85 souls, with 30 baptized members.

D.D.

Calhoun County (Mich.) Old Order Amish settlement is a small group located in the southeastern part of the county near Homer. The original settlers came from Lagrange Co., Ind.; others came later from Daviess Co., Ind., and St. Joseph Co., Mich. Church services have been held since Dec. 1, 1941. In 1949 Alvin J. Yoder was serving as resident minister, and Henry N. Miller of Middlebury, Ind., had bishop oversight.   J.A.H.

California. Mennonite history in California was begun in the late 19th century by pioneers of the General Conference Mennonites. Perhaps the first Mennonite to reach California was Henry Rees of Ashland, Ohio, who settled in Pomona in 1887. The first Mennonite church to be organized in California was established in 1897, 15 miles west of Paso Robles, and named the San Marcos Mennonite Church (GCM). Mennonites arrived in California in increasing numbers, so that by 1903 churches were established in Paso Robles and Upland, members of the latter congregation having arrived as early as 1887. The year 1903 also saw Mennonites arriving in Reedley, where a church was formed in 1906, which grew to be the largest General Conference congregation in California, having a present baptized membership of around 600. As early as 1906 General Conference Mennonites began to meet in homes for worship in the Los Angeles area but it was not until 1918 that a church was organized. Later, in 1921, another congregation

was formed in Winton and in 1935 a new General Conference group came into existence in Shafter. Approximately 1,600 General Conference Mennonites now make their home in California. A congregation at Woodlake has ceased to exist, its members having moved to other Mennonite settlements.

The second group, chronologically, to settle in California were the Mennonite Brethren, now the largest Mennonite branch in California both in total membership (over 3,500) and in number of active congregations (12). The first church to be organized was the Reedley congregation in 1905, the first settlers having arrived one year earlier. The Reedley M.B. Church has grown to be not only the largest Mennonite congregation in California, but it also has become the largest church in the North American Mennonite Brethren conference. The total baptized membership is approximately 1,350. A new church has just been built with a seating capacity of 2,200. Also in 1904 Mennonite Brethren families arrived in Escondido, near San Diego, and formed a congregation in 1905. This group, however, was of short duration due to lack of leadership. The Rosedale M.B. Church was organized in 1909, Bakersfield in 1910, Lodi approximately 1915, Shafter in 1918, Fairmead (now Madera) in 1919, Winton in 1922, Orland in 1923, Los Angeles in 1924, Dinuba in 1925, San Jose in 1940, and Fresno in 1942.

The Krimmer Mennonite Brethren have established a single church in California, organized on March 17, 1911, near Dinuba as the Zion Krimmer M.B. Church, which now has a membership of 250. Its building was remodeled and enlarged in 1941. Most of the early members of this congregation came from South Dakota and Kansas.

The (old) Mennonites were the fourth group to settle in California. Although members of this group arrived in the Dinuba area as early as 1905, a congregation was never organized in this locality. Others settled near Corning, north of Sacramento, in 1907 and later. Another group located in the area near Terra Bella in 1909 and during the following years. A Sunday school was organized in Pasadena in 1915. Early (old) Mennonite settlers established their homes in the Upland, Orange, and Los Angeles area. Their first organized congregation was the one in Los Angeles organized in 1921, where Sunday school had been conducted since 1917. The second church to be established in California by this conference was in Winton in 1931. The Upland congregation was organized in 1943 and has grown to be the largest, having 83 members. The California (old) Mennonites now number about 220.

In 1911 the first members of the Church of God in Christ Mennonite Church came to California. The Benjamin T. Koehn and Jacob B. Ratzlaff families from Canada and the Jacob Hoeppner family from Hillsboro, Kan., settled in the vicinity of what is now Winton, a congregation being organized there in 1912 having 12 members. Later, in 1944, the second church of this conference was established in Livingston, members of this group having lived in this area since 1912. The Winton

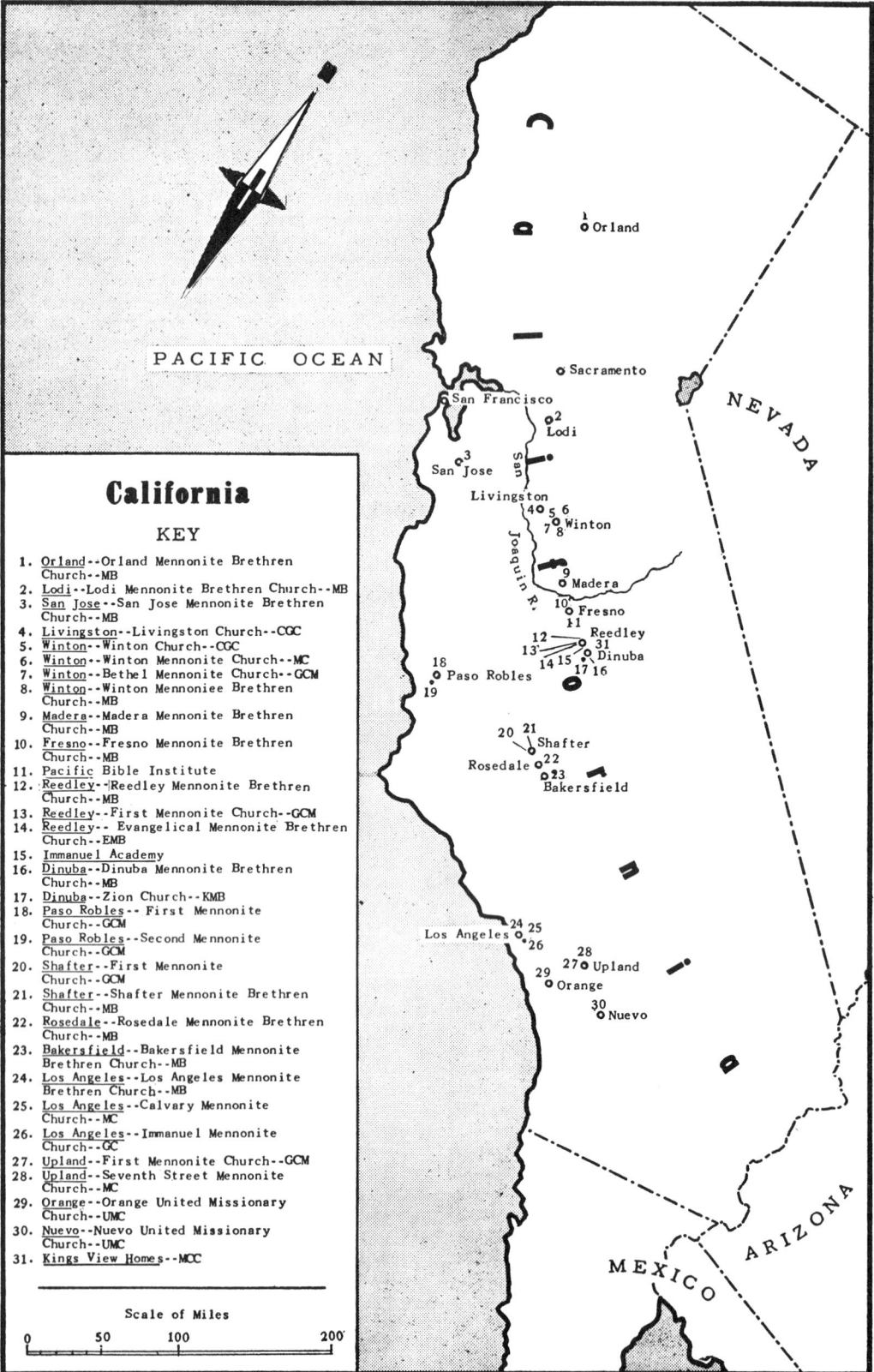

PACIFIC OCEAN

Orland

NEVADA

Sacramento

San Francisco

2 Lodi

3 San Jose

San Joaquin R.

Livingston
4 5 6
7 8 Winton

9 Madera

10 Fresno
11

12 Reedley
13 31
14 15 Dinuba
17 16

18 Paso Robles
19

20 21 Shafter
Rosedale 22
23
Bakersfield

24 25
Los Angeles 26
28
27 Upland
29
Orange
30 Nuevo

ARIZONA

MEXICO

California

KEY

1. <u>Orland</u>--Orland Mennonite Brethren Church--MB
2. <u>Lodi</u>--Lodi Mennonite Brethren Church--MB
3. <u>San Jose</u>--San Jose Mennonite Brethren Church--MB
4. <u>Livingston</u>--Livingston Church--CGC
5. <u>Winton</u>--Winton Church--CGC
6. <u>Winton</u>--Winton Mennonite Church--MC
7. <u>Winton</u>--Bethel Mennonite Church--GCM
8. <u>Winton</u>--Winton Mennoniee Brethren Church--MB
9. <u>Madera</u>--Madera Mennonite Brethren Church--MB
10. <u>Fresno</u>--Fresno Mennonite Brethren Church--MB
11. <u>Pacific</u> Bible Institute
12. <u>Reedley</u>--Reedley Mennonite Brethren Church--MB
13. <u>Reedley</u>--First Mennonite Church--GCM
14. <u>Reedley</u>-- Evangelical Mennonite Brethren Church--EMB
15. <u>Immanuel</u> Academy
16. <u>Dinuba</u>--Dinuba Mennonite Brethren Church--MB
17. <u>Dinuba</u>--Zion Church--KMB
18. <u>Paso Robles</u>-- First Mennonite Church--GCM
19. <u>Paso Robles</u>--Second Mennonite Church--GCM
20. <u>Shafter</u>--First Mennonite Church--GCM
21. <u>Shafter</u>--Shafter Mennonite Brethren Church--MB
22. <u>Rosedale</u>--Rosedale Mennonite Brethren Church--MB
23. <u>Bakersfield</u>--Bakersfield Mennonite Brethren Church--MB
24. <u>Los Angeles</u>--Los Angeles Mennonite Brethren Church--MB
25. <u>Los Angeles</u>--Calvary Mennonite Church--MC
26. <u>Los Angeles</u>--Immanuel Mennonite Church--GC
27. <u>Upland</u>--First Mennonite Church--GCM
28. <u>Upland</u>--Seventh Street Mennonite Church--MC
29. <u>Orange</u>--Orange United Missionary Church--UMC
30. <u>Nuevo</u>--Nuevo United Missionary Church--UMC
31. <u>Kings View Homes</u>--MCC

Scale of Miles

0   50   100   200

group grew to be the largest, numbering approximately 350 members. The Livingston group numbers about 100.

Factors that have operated in determining the location and growth of the various Mennonite communities were principally economic and climatic. The Mennonites have contributed much toward improvement of their respective communities located in the fertile San Joaquin Valley. Essentially the 6,000 Mennonites of California are farmers and still remain largely a people whose life is closely linked with the soil. Nearly one half of all California Mennonites live in the Reedley-Dinuba area, the center of the world's largest fruit-growing district.

A notable exception to this rule, however, is the recently established (1940) Mennonite Brethren Church of San Jose with its approximately 250 members, reported to be 95 per cent urban, whose chief occupation is day labor in the San Jose industries. In general, the slow but perceptible movement from farm to city is the result of young people seeking employment and business opportunities, and older people retiring from farm life. Along with this movement to the city there is a corresponding tendency to adopt urban ways of life, thus hastening the social process of assimilation into the American culture pattern. In some areas there is little to distinguish the Mennonite from his non-Mennonite neighbor and the distinctive Mennonite way of life has all but disappeared.

When asked whether Mennonitism, i.e., the Mennonite heritage, way of life, doctrines, separation from the world, etc., is as strongly emphasized today as during the early days of settlement in California, some stated that "there seem to be some weaknesses appearing," "by the conference, yes, but not by individual members," and, "in more liberal terms, the termination of the isolation due to language barriers having brought about a community responsibility." These comments indicate a movement toward the more complete acceptance of social responsibilities simultaneous with the loosening of ethnic and group ties. California Mennonites are actively engaged in home mission activities within the state, an evidence that they are concerned about the spiritual welfare of their neighbors.

California Mennonites have established a number of institutions. Outstanding is the Immanuel Academy in Reedley, founded in 1912. Although the Reedley and Dinuba M.B. churches together with the Zion K.M.B. Church carry most of the economic and administrative responsibility for this school, students and contributions are gladly received from any Mennonite group. The Pacific Bible Institute of Fresno, founded in 1944 and supported by the Pacific Coast Conference of the Mennonite Brethren, offers college level instruction to all Mennonite students interested. The Mennonite Aid Plan established in 1922 and the Mennonite Aid Society established in 1941, whose offices are located in Reedley, enjoy wide support from various Mennonite groups. Thus fire and life insurance is offered to Mennonites by a growing Mennonite

financial organization. The Mennonite Old People's Home established in Reedley in 1943 by the Mennonite Brethren offers a haven for aged Mennonites of all groups. Kings View Homes, the newly established (1951) Mennonite mental hospital, an MCC project, is located near Reedley. Unitedly the Mennonites of California support the work of the MCC and it is here that they co-operate most wholeheartedly. Just as some Mennonite localities became noted for having their names on sacks of flour sent to Europe by the MCC, so California Mennonite congregations became known by their names which appeared on countless boxes of fruit and raisins, shipped by the ton to Europe and Paraguay.

Most California Mennonite churches report that their congregations are growing. Few non-Mennonites are being added and but a small proportion of this increase is due to a local increase in population. The unprecedented migration of Americans to the west coast in recent years perhaps accounts for most of the Mennonite population increase in California.

California Mennonites constitute an active, prosperous, and progressive part of the American Mennonitism. They too are experiencing the uncertainties as well as the opportunities which come with all social change. A valiant effort is being made to preserve that which is good in the old, sift out the unwholesome in the new, direct the energies of their youth into channels consistent with their faith, and meet the demands of newly discovered social responsibilities.   L.R.J.

H. D. Burkholder, *The Story of Our Conference and Churches* (N. Newton, 1951); A. C. Ewy, "The Grape and Raisin Industry," *Menn. Life,* October 1950; Vernon Neufeld, "The Shafter-Wasco Community," *Menn. Life,* October 1952; J. H. Lohrenz, *The Menn. Brethren Church* (Hillsboro, 1950) 159-76; ML II, 453.

California Mennonite Brethren Youth Bible Camp. The Pacific District M.B. Youth Fellowship committee directs the program for an annual high-school and young adult Bible camp. The high-school age camp is conducted during the second whole week of July and the young adult camp during the three-day Labor Day week end. Both camps are scheduled for the Hartland Bible Conference Grounds near Badger, Cal. The committee was first organized in October 1948. Each year on the evening preceding the regular District Conference, the Youth Fellowship has its report and election meeting. Youth delegates from all of the churches (each delegate representing fifteen young people—high school through thirty years) select the officers for the coming year. The term of office is three years. The committee includes five young people and three adult advisers. The Youth Fellowship elects the five young people and one adult adviser. The other adult advisers are elected by the District Conference.   W.L.P.

Calkins (Mont.) Mennonite Church (MC), now extinct. The first Mennonite families moved into this community in the fall of 1915 and were organized into a congregation Dec. 9, 1917, at which time Frank Roth was ordained their minister by his father Jake Roth. John Hochstetler was ordained by I. S. Mast on Nov. 11, 1921, to fill the vacancy left by Roth, who moved away. The congregation was under the Dakota-Montana Conference (now North Central), I. S. Mast having bishop oversight. Services ceased in the fall of 1928, when nearly all of the families had moved away because of hard times.   F.E.K.

Calleken Claes: see **Cathalijne** and **Suzanna Claes.**

Calleken (Catherine) **Meere,** an Anabaptist martyr, born at Wyncle, Flanders, daughter of Pieter, unmarried, was burned at the stake on the Vrijdagsmarkt at Gent, Belgium, July 28, 1573, at 11 A.M., together with Jacob van den Weghe, Francois (Fransoys) van Leuvene, and Hendrick (*q.v.*) Bauwens. These martyrs could not speak to the people because of a gag put in their mouths. The people present at their execution, being in sympathy with the martyrs, vainly tried to prevent the execution. (Verheyden, *Gent,* 64, No. 227.)   vDZ.

Calleken (Lijnken, Lijntgen, Lijsken) **Meevels,** an Anabaptist martyr, was burned at the stake at Antwerp, on Feb. 26, 1571, together with Maerten van Wijk and her husband Jan van de Walle (*q.v.*). She was a native of Kortrijk (Courtrai), Belgium, and was 40 years of age. Two years before the execution she was married at Antwerp by Michiel de Leertouwer (*q.v.*), the preacher of the Antwerp Mennonite congregation. About 11 or 12 years before she was put to death, she had been rebaptized at Doornik (Tournai), Belgium, by Joachim Vermeeren (*q.v.*). She signed the trial herself: Ic Kalleken Meeuwels. She remained steadfast and died as a true lamb of the Saviour. (*Antw. Arch.-Bl.* XIII, 15, 28, 34, 38, 43, 63; XIV, 76-77, No. 869.)   vDZ.

Calleken Steens (also called Calleken Swef or Catignies Swelz), an Anabaptist martyr, the daughter of Andries and wife of Augustijn, a native of Sweghem, Flanders, was put to death for her faith by being burned at Rijssel (Lille, France) in 1564, probably Feb. 22, with Janneken Cabiljaus (*q.v.*). (*Mart. Mir.* D 300, E 664; *Bibliographie,* No. 737.)   vDZ.

Calom (or Colom), **Jacob Aertz,** b. Oct. 10, 1599, at Dordrecht, d. May 10, 1678, at Amsterdam, was baptized in the Amsterdam Waterlander congregation, Sept. 25, 1622, and remained a member of this congregation until his death. He was a bookseller and published among others a large number of Mennonite books. In the dispute in the Waterlander congregation about the charge of Socinianism made against Nittert Obbes (*q.v.*), Calom published a pamphlet in Obbes' defense, titled *Antwoord op seeckere drie vragen,* of which he was probably the author. At least one of his daughters was a member of the Waterlander congregation, but all of his sons joined the Reformed Church.

Calom was very expert in matters of mathematics and navigation; he wrote various cartographic books, and besides these technical works: *Troost der Zeevaart* (Comfort of Navigation) (Amsterdam, 1651) and *Onderrigting in de Konst der Zeevaart* (Instruction in the Art of Navigation). vDZ.

Van der Aa, *Biogr. Wb.* III, 193; *Catalogus Amst.,* 105; *Jaarboek Amstelodamum* XXV (1928) 85-88.

Calvaart, a Mennonite family name found in Flanders and Holland. Daniel Calvaerd(t) (*q.v.*) was an Anabaptist martyr. In the 17th century members of this family (also spelled Kalvaart) are found in the Mennonite congregations of Leiden and Haarlem. Both Crijn Pietersz Calvaart and Joost Calvaart were deacons of the church at Leiden about 1675. (See Supplement for addition.)   vDZ.

Calvary Gospel Chapel (EMC), Poplar, Mont., a mission station among the Indians, in charge of Mr. and Mrs. Abe Teichroew.   M.G.

Calvary Hour: see **Radio Programs, Mennonite.**

Calvary Memorial Church (EMC), Chicago, Ill. The Salem Gospel Mission at 248 Root St., Chicago, was opened on June 24, 1908, with Mr. and Mrs. J. K. Gerig as superintendent and matron. The outgrowth of this work was the Southwest Gospel Tabernacle located at 1217 West 72nd St., which was erected in 1930. The Calvary Memorial Church was organized as an outgrowth of the Tabernacle in 1944. The congregation is operating as a self-sustaining church. It has a two-story brick church and a six-room brick veneer parsonage at 221 West 72nd St. The membership in 1947 was 61. I.R.C.

Calvary Mennonite Brethren in Christ Church, Coopersburg, Pa., was organized in 1869. In 1953 the congregation had 137 members and Herbert W. Hartman was the pastor.   H.W.H.

Calvary Mennonite Brethren in Christ Church, Shamokin, Pa., was organized in 1915 with H. A. Kauffman as pastor. The present (1950) meetinghouse was built in 1938. The congregation is a member of the M.B.C. Conference of Pennsylvania and in 1950 had 164 members, with F. M. Hottel serving as pastor.   F.M.H.

Calvary Mennonite Church (MC), Los Angeles, Cal. Although a few Mennonites were living in the Los Angeles area as early as 1912, no definite meeting place was established until 1916, when a Sunday school was organized at Pasadena. The Sunday school was moved to Los Angeles in 1917, the location changing four times, 1917-20. On Nov. 7, 1920 (or 1921), the congregation was organized as the Los Angeles Mennonite Church at the present location, 151 West 73rd St., with about 60 members. In May 1942 the name was changed to Calvary Mennonite Church. The 1952 membership was 74. Until September 1948 the congregation was an affiliate of the Mennonite Conference of the Pacific Coast District, and then became a member of the newly organized South Pacific Mennonite Conference. The present pastor is John Zehr.

P.Bu.

Calvary Mennonite Church (GCM), Washington, Ill., formerly known as the East Washington Church, held its first meeting in May 1866, when Jonathan Yoder began to preach for those Amish families of Woodford and Tazewell counties who did not have church privileges in their community. The people worshiped in private homes until 1869.

A 30 x 40 ft. church was built a few miles east of Washington in 1869. This was replaced in 1906 by a new frame building, and in 1925 by a brick building in the town of Washington. At that time (1925) the name of the church was changed from East Washington Church to Calvary Mennonite Church. In 1952 there were 540 members. In 1892 a language difference caused a division of the congregation; the pastor, Michael Kinsinger, and a group of people sympathetic to his views organized the South Washington Church (*q.v.*). (W. B. Weaver, *Hist. of the Central Conf. Menn. Church,* Danvers, 1926.) G.Mi.

Calvary Mennonite Church (MC), located in Greensburg, Kiowa Co., Kan., a member of the South Central Conference District, was organized in October 1932, with E. M. Yost as pastor and H. A. Diener of Hutchinson, Kan., as bishop. The congregation in 1952 had 76 baptized members, only a few of whom had been members of the Mennonite Church (MC), the majority having come from the Church of God in Christ Mennonites, and some from the General Conference and Krimmer Mennonite Brethren. P. A. Friesen, returned missionary from India, was bishop and pastor of the congregation 1945-50. Others who have served in the ministry of the congregation include Samuel Janzen and Deacon A. F. Willems, with Earl Buckwalter as bishop since 1950. S.J.

Calvary Mennonite Church (GCM), located in Barlow, Clackamas Co., Ore., a member of the Pacific District Conference, was organized on Aug. 6, 1944, with 51 members under the leadership of Paul N. Roth, who still serves as pastor. The charter members had earlier left the Zion Mennonite (MC) Church near Hubbard. The present membership of 131 (1953) is nearly 30 per cent non-Mennonite in background. The present building, which has served three denominations in the past, has been enlarged and remodeled, and easily seats 225. P.N.R.

Calvary Mennonite Church (GCM) Quarryville, Pa., is located in a village about 18 miles southeast of Lancaster. The church was established by the Board of Home Missions of the General Conference, under whose jurisdiction it is at the present time. S. S. Amstutz was sent to this field in 1919 and the congregation was organized about 1923. The present frame church was erected in 1921 and dedicated in 1922. At one time the membership had reached 70 but in 1952 it was only 49. A.J.N.

Calvary Mennonite Church, Souderton, Pa., an unaffiliated congregation, was organized in 1950 by dissidents who had withdrawn from several congregations of the Franconia (MC) Conference because of dissatisfaction with some of the aspects of the conference discipline. William Anders, a minister of the Towamencin congregation, became their leader. A new meetinghouse has been built (1952). The present membership (1952) is 160. H.S.B.

Calvary United Missionary Church, Detroit, Mich., was organized in 1926 with eleven charter members, work having been carried on in the city since 1914. In 1948 the membership was 97, with Lester L. Rassi serving as pastor. L.L.Ras.

Calvin, John, the great reformer, was born at Noyon, Picardy, France, on July 10, 1509, and died May 27, 1564, at Geneva. His father, a lawyer, was a respected man, and his mother, the daughter of a well-to-do councilor in Noyon, was a pious woman, who implanted in the talented boy's receptive mind his earnest religious sense. At the age of twelve he received a church benefice, the income of which enabled him to study law in Paris. His residence in the universities of Bourges and Orleans made a permanent impression on him, for he met there men like Melchior Wolmar and Robert Olivetan, who sympathized with Luther's teaching.

By 1534 he had broken completely with his past, left the Catholic Church, and devoted himself to the study of theology. He could, of course, not remain in Paris, where his life was no longer certain; he stayed briefly in Angoulême, Nerac, and Noyon, and then went to Strasbourg and Basel, and in 1536 published his famous *Institutio religionis christianae,* which "secured for him the leadership of the Reformed Church for centuries." Then he went to Italy, where he spent some time at the court of the Duchess of Ferrara. On his return to Strasbourg by way of Geneva, William Farel detained him at Geneva and won his co-operation in the work of the Reformation. Calvin was soon in the foreground of the Protestant movement in the city. With energy and severity he introduced ecclesiastic reforms, which roused his opponents to stubborn resistance. On Feb. 3, 1538, they obtained control of the city in the election of councilors, and Calvin and Farel had to leave, betaking themselves to Basel. In September 1538 Calvin went on to Strasbourg, where he spent three years of great significance for his religious outlook. Then he returned to Geneva and there created a religious organization that for centuries was a model of Christian order and morals for the entire Protestant Church, and through his extensive correspondence he extended his activity throughout Protestant Christendom. Toward antagonists he was ruthlessly intolerant. Michael Servetus, the noted physician and scientist, had to atone at the stake for his denial of the Trinity. Calvin was also unyielding in his dealings with the Anabaptists, though he never recommended the death penalty. With an understanding rare at the time he distinguished between the seditious-fanatical Anabaptists and the quiet, simple, pious group, winning many of the latter over to the Reformed Church by his powers of persuasion.

Calvin had already made contacts with the Anabaptists during his first stay in Geneva. Early in 1537 some Dutch Anabaptists had come to Geneva and, to the dismay of Calvin and Farel, found acceptance for their preaching. Two of them, Hermann of Gerbihan or Gerbehaye (Hulshof, 187, note) and Andry Bendit of Engelen in Brabant, were taken before the council on March 9, 1537. These men wanted to defend their faith in a public disputation with the Geneva reformers, and after some hesitation the council consented. The disputation was held on March 16 in the Franciscan monastery of Riva; it lasted two days, and dealt with baptism, ban, the nature of the soul. According to the official report of the council Calvin did not participate directly; hence Gaberel, Beza, and others cannot be right in saying that Calvin brilliantly defeated the Anabaptists (Hulshof, 186 ff.). It seems instead that the Anabaptists withstood Farel with some success, even though they expressed themselves awkwardly. The council, of course, declared them defeated and expelled them from the city. Soon after, on March 29, there was a second disputation in Geneva, in which Calvin took part, with two Anabaptists of Liége, Jean Bomeromenus, a printer, and Jean Stordeur, uneducated men, by no means a match for the reformers; but they defended their faith with courage. On March 30 both were banished but their influence was felt in the city for a long time. On Sept. 7, 1537, the clergy reported to the council that there were several Anabaptists among the inhabitants of the city.

When Calvin came to Strasbourg he made contacts with the Anabaptists there. His attitude toward them is shown in a letter he wrote on Sept. 11, 1538, soon after his arrival, to Farel in Neuchâtel, saying, "In Metz, where everything is already hostile to the true religion and the council has sworn to annihilate it with the assistance of the priest, the leaven of the Anabaptists has slipped in to create new offense. Two were thrown into the Moselle, one was disgracefully branded and expelled. As far as I could ascertain, one of them was the barber who accompanied Hermann (von Gerbihan). I fear that this pestilence is widespread among the common people in Metz" (Schwarz I, 45; see Hulshof, 193).

At the synod of the Strasbourg Evangelical Church in 1539, which was held chiefly to deal with the Anabaptists, Calvin was the spokesman. He persuaded two Anabaptists whom he had already met in Geneva to renounce their faith in favor of the Reformed confession. These were Jean Stordeur, whose widow, Idelette de Bure (q.v.) Calvin married on Bucer's suggestion in August 1540, and Hermann of Gerbihan. He gave details in his letters to Farel. On Feb. 6, 1540, he wrote, "The Anabaptist Hermann, who had a disputation with us in Geneva, asked me for a conference. He grants that he was in serious error on infant baptism, Christ's humanity, and many other points. On some other questions he still has some doubts, but he is hopeful because he has already overcome so much. His companion Jean (Stordeur) has finally brought his son, who is already quite large, for baptism. I hesitated a while because of the child's weakness, since he said that was his principal reason for postponing the baptism. Finally he said he would not stop the people whose obstinate insistence on baptism he could by no means withstand" (Schwarz I, 87 f.).

Three weeks later, on Feb. 26, Calvin wrote to Farel, "Hermann has, if I am not mistaken, in good faith returned to the church. He has confessed that outside the church there is no salvation, and that the true church is with us; therefore, it was apostasy when he belonged to a sect separated

from it; for this misstep he asked forgiveness. He accepted instruction on the freedom of the will, the deity and humanity of Christ, rebirth, infant baptism, and other things. Only on the question of predestination he hesitated somewhat; yet he almost subscribed to this too, except that he could not understand the difference between the foreknowledge of God and foreordination. But he asked that this might not prevent his being received into the fellowship of the church with his children. I received him with fitting readiness, and when he asked forgiveness I gave him my hand in the name of the church; then I baptized his little daughter, who is over two years old. If my faith does not deceive me, he is a pious man. When I admonished him to lead others back to the right way, he said: 'That is the least that I can do, to exert myself no less in building up than I did before in tearing down.' Jean too, who lives in Ulm, is said to have come to his senses. But in order that we may not boast of these things, the Lord humbles us in a thousand ways" (Schwarz I, 90).

This Jean was probably Johannes Bomeromenus (Hulshof, 106), who was banished from Strasbourg in 1537 and had probably gone to Metz, and not Jean Stordeur, as is often assumed. The greatest achievement in Calvin's conversion labors in Strasbourg was the return of the former preacher of the St. Nikolai Church, Paul Volz, to the Reformed Church. But he had not gone to the Anabaptists, as Krohn and others including zur Linden suppose, but to the Schwenkfeldians (Hulshof, 197; Röhrich, *Mitteilungen* III, 215). Beza reports that Calvin converted many Anabaptists in Strasbourg; but this is at least exaggerated. No names are known of any others whom he won; but the number of children Calvin received into the church is said to have been large.

On Jan. 21, 1546, Calvin wrote to Farel in Neuchâtel that he had just met an Anabaptist Belot (*q.v.*) in Geneva. The letter also throws light on Calvin's attitude to the Anabaptists at that time. He says, "In these days an Anabaptist, when he was laying out foolish writings publicly for sale, was at my instigation arrested. You of course know the nature of these people from experience. But I have never been aware of such wild defiance before. Although I first addressed him politely, as is my custom, it did not suit him for a moment to talk otherwise with me than if he were dealing with a dog. When they led him to the city hall, he at once wanted to sit beside the first syndic; when he was turned away from there, he gave himself with raised head and rolling eyes the majestic aspect of a prophet and answered if it suited him with a few words the questions directed to him; frequently he was altogether silent. A dispute then arose between us on swearing. When I asked him if the law of the Lord did not give us directions for living, he uttered the horrible dogma of the Anabaptists: The Old Testament is done away! I quoted the words of Paul. All Scripture is profitable, that the man of God may be perfect, throughly furnished unto all good works (II Tim. 3:16, 17). I insisted that he answer; but not a word could I get out of him.

Therefore I now explained this entire question, so that everyone might recognize the invincible ignorance of this man together with his equally great impudence. When he saw himself thus pushed, he uttered the usual frivolous phrase of the sectarians, that no man has a more comfortable life than the parsons. I answered with a few words, not so much to defend our class as to ward off the boldness of this beast. Then he called me covetous. This produced general laughter; for all knew that I had just this year refused a large personal salary and indeed so seriously that I assured them under oath that I would not preach another sermon if they did not leave off. They knew too that I had not only refused such extraordinary generosity, but had even returned some of my regular salary, not less than 20 crowns. And so he was attacked by all with abusive terms. I answered modestly, he would probably be rich in my position; it was no sign of avarice if I am poor with all the opportunity of becoming rich; but he could be accused by me on a matter of life and death, namely of theft; if he denied it I would offer my head for punishment for slander if it were not true. For it was certain that he was selling broadsheets for two and a half sous which had cost him four deniers. And it was not due to a fixed tax that he sold them so dearly. When he was silent as usual I began to talk about the sinlessness of the Anabaptists. When he had sufficiently shown his defiance, he was expelled from the city. Two days later, when he was again seized in the city, he was beaten, his books publicly burned, and he himself was told not to come again, on penalty of the gallows. This is a man or rather a beast of desperate wickedness."

It is a pity that nothing more is known about this Belot.

Calvin deals with the Anabaptists in three books. The first, *Psychopannychia,* which contains the name Anabaptist for the first time, attacks the doctrine of the "sleep of the soul." The position of the German Anabaptists on the question is not known, but in France the doctrine was so widespread among the Anabaptists in the 1530's that Calvin found it necessary to write a tract against the sleep of the soul, which was published in 1542 in Strasbourg and had the title, *Vivere apud Christum, non dormire animas sanctas, qui in fide Christi decedunt* (*Corpus Reformatorum* XXIII, 170 ff.; a new edition by W. Zimmerli in 1932). In 1545 appeared an almost unaltered second edition with the new title, *Psychopannychia, qua repellitur quorundam imperitorum error, qui animas post mortem usque ad ultimum judicium dormire putant.* The word "Psychopannychia," which really means "wakefulness of the soul," quite the reverse of "sleep of the soul," was later misunderstood to mean sleep (Zimmerli, 10). The original draft of this booklet was written in 1534, while Calvin was living in France. The *Brieve Instruction* (see below) also attacks the doctrine of the sleep of the soul. (Concerning the further course of the teaching of the sleep of the soul in Socinianism and in the religious movements of the revolution in England, see Karl Müller, *Kirchengeschichte* II, 2, 136, 470, note 4.) The sec-

ond book, entitled *Brieve Instruction pour armer tous bons fideles contre les Erreurs de la secte des anabaptistes, Geneve 1544,* is a refutation of the Seven Articles of Schleitheim, *Brüderliche Vereinigung . . . ,* which was sent to him for refutation (Hulshof, 189). In the introduction he says that the Anabaptists in contrast to the Libertines recognized the Holy Scriptures and like the church accepted it as a guide for living, and that there was thus a common foundation from which an effort could be made to reach an understanding. This book deals with the following: (1) infant baptism; (2) the ban; (3) admitting to communion, "on which they say nothing with which we do not agree"; (4) the right to bear arms; (5) the shepherds (preachers); (6) the power of princes; (7) the oath. In addition two points are treated which were not held by all Anabaptists: the Incarnation, and the life of the soul between death and the resurrection (zur Linden, 416).

In the third book, *Contre la secte phantastique et furieuse des Libertins, qui se nomment spirituels* (*Geneve, 1545*), Calvin expressly acquits the Anabaptists of the unrestrained doctrines and deeds of the Libertines. He says that there were at first some Anabaptists who thought and taught as they did, but it was generally recognized that such absurdity is contrary to reason, and their best authors are ashamed of such doctrines.

Calvin's judgment of Menno Simons is incomprehensible; he knew him only through a letter from Martin Micronius (*q.v.*). In an opinion he sent to Micronius he said, "Nothing can be prouder, nothing more impudent than this donkey" (Calv. IV, 176; *HRE* XII, 592).

Calvin's close acquaintance with the Anabaptists was bound to be of influence upon him. Even if it is not true, as has been asserted, that he took his doctrine of the communion from them, it is certain that their doctrine and practice of church discipline was of significance as a pattern. He himself indignantly denied this idea and said that the Anabaptists had taken their idea of church discipline over from him. "That the ban is a good and sacred institution we do not deny; and we confess that it is not only useful but even essential to the church. Yea, what these unfortunate and thankless people teach about it they learned from us, only they in their ignorance and presumption have ruined the doctrine which we keep pure" (zur Linden, 417). The falsity of this position is obvious; the Anabaptists held this doctrine of church discipline (the Seven Articles of Schleitheim were adopted in 1527) at a time when Calvin was still a Catholic and scarcely 18 years old. Concerning Anabaptism in Calvin's *Institutes,* see W. Köhler in *Menn. Gesch.-Bl.,* 1937, 1-4; Calvin's *Opuscula* (Geneva, 1563) also contains *Contra Anabaptistas.* See also A. Erichson, *Bibliographia Calviniana* (Berlin, 1900) 26.

NEFF.

HRE III and XII; Abr. Hulshof, *Geschiedenis van de doopsgezinden te Straatsburg van 1525 tot 1537* (Amsterdam, 1905); R. Schwarz, *Joh. Calvins Lebenswerk in seinen Briefen,* 2 VV. (Tübingen, 1909); F. O. zur Linden, *Melchior Hofmann, ein Prophet der Wiedertäufer* (Haarlem, 1885); S. H. Guistorp, *Calvin's Eschatologie*

(1941); J. G. de Hoop Scheffer, "Calvijn tegen Menno Simons," in *DB* 1873, 80-103; W. Walker, *John Calvin* (N.Y., 1906); G. Harkness, *John Calvin, the Man and His Ethics* (N.Y., 1931); J. Calvin, *Institutes of the Christian Religion* (7th Amer. ed., Phila., 2 vv., n.d.); *ML* I, 314-17.

Calvinism and Mennonitism, although agreed in rejecting the Roman Catholic doctrines of the church, the hierarchy, and the sacraments, and in accepting the Bible as the only source of doctrine, differ significantly both in doctrines and in polity. In the past there have been many conflicts between Calvinists and Mennonites. Calvinists, formerly very staunch in their opinion that Calvinism is the only true form of Christianity, often despised and even persecuted non-Calvinists, although with the exception of Michael Servetus (*q.v.*) they did not put their antagonists to death.

In the Palatinate and in the duchy of Jülich, Germany, Mennonites sometimes were forced by Calvinistic rulers to leave the country, but it was especially in the Netherlands that Calvinism and Mennonitism collided and struggled for centuries.

The main controversial issues from the side of Calvinism (see also **Calvin**) were: rejection of infant baptism, non-swearing of oaths, refusal to bear arms, refusal to serve in governmental offices, and the practice of avoidance (*q.v.*). Occasionally the Mennonites were also charged with false doctrines such as unorthodoxy in regard to the Trinity, and denial of the deity of Christ and the atonement.

Calvinism attacked Mennonitism particularly in four ways:

1. Recommending that Reformed ministers enter the Mennonite meetinghouses to refute the preachers and "to convince them of their false teachings." This advice was already given by one of the first Reformed synods, held in 1574 at Dordrecht. It was followed, among others, by Ruardus Acronius, who in 1594 broke into a Mennonite meeting near Leeuwarden, interrupted the preacher, and violently attacked the Mennonite principles. But this method of fighting the Mennonites proved to be very unsuccessful and was soon abandoned.

2. Organizing public disputations (*q.v.*). The most important of these debates were those of Frankenthal (*q.v.*) in 1571 and Emden (*q.v.*) in 1578, and that at Leeuwarden (*q.v.*) in 1596 between the afore-mentioned Reformed minister Ruardus Acronius and the Mennonite preacher Pieter van Ceulen (*q.v.*).

3. Combating the Mennonites in writing. Numerous polemic books were published by Calvinistic theologians against Anabaptists and Mennonites. We mention only a few: Guy de Brèz (*q.v.*), *La racine, source et fondement des Anabaptistes* (1565), with Dutch translation: *Den Wortel, oorspronck ende het fundament der Wederdoperen* (1570, reprint 1589, 1608); Jean Taffin (translated from the French), *Onderwijsinghe teghen de dwalinghen der Wederdoopers,* 1590; Marnix van St-Aldegonde (*q.v.*), *Ondersoeckinge ende grondelycke wederlegginghe der geestdrijversche Leere* (1595), in which the author insists on capital punishment of the Mennonites; H. Faukelius, *Babel, dat is de Verwerringhe der Wederdooperen onder malkanderen*

(1621 and reprint, n.d.); A. Dooreslaer and P. Austro-Sylvius, *Grondige ende klare vertooninghe van het onderscheydt in de voornaemste hooftstucken der christelijcken religie tusschen de Gereformeerden ende de Wederdooperen* (1637, repr. 1649); P. Bontemps, *Bewijs van de menighvuldighe doolingen van de Wederdoopers often Mennisten* (1641, repr. 1653, 1661); F. Spanhemius Sr., *Variae Disputationes Anti-Anabaptisticae* (1643); idem, *Controversiarum de Religione Elenchus* (1694); Joh. Hoornbeek, *Summa Controversiarum Religionis* (1653); Chr. Schotanus, *Van de gronden der Mennisterij* (1671); F. Spanhemius Jr., *Controversiarum de Religione* (1757).

Mennonites defended themselves against these attacks. The most notable Mennonite replies are: Claes Claesz, *Bekentenisse van de voornaemste Stucken des Christelijcken Gheloofs* (1624, repr. 1650); Anthoni Jacobsz Roscius, *Babel, d.i. Verwerringe der Kinderdooperen onder malcanderen* (1626); E. A. van Dooregeest, *Brief aan den Heer F. Spanhemius* (1693, repr. 1693, 1700); Galenus Abrahamsz, *Verdediging der Christenen die Doopsgezinde genaamd worden* (1699).

4. Pressing both state and city authorities to take measures against the Mennonites. As late as 1795 in the Netherlands the Reformed Church was a state church, and Mennonites and other nonconformists were accordingly only tolerated. Often —but usually without success—Calvinist ministers and church councils tried to persuade the government to close or even to tear down Mennonite meetinghouses, forbid their services, deny them legacies from estates. They also insisted on the issuance of orders—which often occurred—that Mennonites must have their marriages performed in Reformed churches, and that they should be compelled to swear oaths and to render military service, etc. In these oral or written petitions the Calvinists mostly tried to persuade the authorities by pointing out the danger of the Mennonites to the state and public order, insinuating their reputed descent from the revolutionary Münsterites.

In the 18th century disputations were no longer held, and Calvinistic polemical books and complaints to the government rapidly decreased. Occasionally an action was still brought against the Mennonites, as for instance in the cases of Jan Thomas (*q.v.*) in 1719 and Johannes Stinstra (*q.v.*) in 1742. The agitation of the Calvinists then was usually based upon a charge of unorthodoxy, i.e., Socinianism (*q.v.*).

After 1770 Calvinism no longer troubled Mennonitism.   vDZ.

N. van der Zijpp, "Gereformeerden contra Doopsgezinden in vroegere eeuwen," in *Algemeen Doopsgez. Weekblad*, Feb. 25-Dec. 2, 1950; idem, *Gesch. der Doopsgezinden in Nederland* (Arnhem, 1952) 135-42, 159-62.

Cambria County, Pa., a coal and industrial area in the southwestern part of the state, county seat Johnstown, lies north of Somerset County, which has long been the seat of considerable Amish and Mennonite settlements. A small corner of this settlement reaches over into Cambria County, where the Weaver Church (*q.v.*) is located. In recent years three new congregations have been established in the southern part of the county as the result of mission extension work, Elton (*q.v.*), Walsall (*q.v.*), and one in Johnstown (*q.v.*). The latter city was founded by an Amish Mennonite, J. Johns (Tschantz) soon after 1800, after whom the city is named. (*ML* I, 317.)   H.S.B.

Camillo Renato: see Italy.

Camino Mennonite Civilian Public Service Camp No. 31, often known as Camp Snowline, was located approximately 60 miles east of Sacramento, and 3 miles west of Camino, Cal. The camp was operated under the U.S. Forestry Service from April 1942 to December 1946. In the early autumn of 1945 more than 180 men were located here, engaged principally in forest fire prevention and fighting and related tasks. (M. Gingerich, *Service for Peace*, Akron, Pa., 1949.)   M.G.

Camp, Guillaume de, an Anabaptist martyr: see **Willem van Ackere.**

Camp Meetings, a type of open-air revival meeting that became popular in America in the first years of the 19th century. The origin cannot be stated exactly but evangelistic meetings in Virginia and North Carolina, well before 1800, attracted such large crowds that they had to be held outdoors. In Kentucky and Tennessee these became occasions for protracted outdoor services. Perhaps the best-known early camp meeting was that at Cane Ridge, Ky., in 1801, where over 20,000 people gathered. Visitors brought their own provisions and slept in covered wagons or put up tents. Stands were erected for four or five preachers to speak at once. At night the grounds were lighted by camp fires and the exhortation, weeping, praying, and singing continued. Physical manifestations as falling, laughing, and the "jerks" were common. Camp meetings were used by all the larger churches on the frontier —Methodists, Presbyterians, Baptists, but they were much criticized and largely dropped by the latter two. Among the Methodists the camp meeting became an institution and enabled them to reach large numbers of unchurched people. The more spectacular features disappeared as frontier conditions changed, and by the latter half of the century regular grounds were maintained with assembly halls, cottages, and educational features in the program. The Methodist campground at Chautauqua, N.Y., became, in fact, an educational institution after 1874 and gave rise to the Chautauqua movement. The campgrounds were located in groves of trees or on lakesides.

Most Mennonites reacted against emotional revivals including camp meetings; but they were accepted by the Mennonite Brethren in Christ (United Missionary Church) 1875 ff., and continue to be held annually in every conference district of that group. Youth camps, summer conferences, and the summer retreats common among many Mennonite groups are modified forms of the old camp meeting.
                                        S.F.P.

W. W. Sweet, *Revivalism in America* (N.Y., 1944); Elmer Clark, *The Small Sects in America* (rev. ed. 1949, Nashville); C. A. Johnson, "The Frontier Camp Meeting" (Ph.D. thesis, Northwestern University, 1950).

Campanus, Johannes (*ca.* 1500-75), one of the leading minds of the "left wing" of the Reformation in the Lower Rhine area (duchy of Jülich), leaning toward a spiritualistic interpretation of Christian thought, thus belonging to the group of "spiritual reformers" (like Sebastian Franck or Bünderlin). Rembert evaluates Campanus thus: "Campanus impressed upon the entire movement in Jülich the stamp of his spirit. He was the driving force and spiritual leader until displaced by Menno Simons and his followers, who turned the movement into a different direction" (Rembert, *Wiedertäufer,* 265). His influence upon Bernt Rothmann, the theological leader of the Münsterites (1533-35), is strongly suggested by Karl Rembert but there is no proof of any direct connection. He was not an Anabaptist, though some of his thoughts are suggestive of Anabaptist tenets. Rembert is inclined to interpret Campanus as a sort of free-lance Anabaptist, while Dunin-Borkowski claims that his thoughts on baptism are definitely not Anabaptist. Campanus belongs to the group of humanistically trained theologians (upon whom Erasmus had some influence) who between 1520 and 1535 shifted so much in their position from Catholicism to Lutheranism, then into the direction of Anabaptism (untheological, Biblical Christianity), and finally to a free and near gnostic Christianity. Campanus was never an aggressive promoter of his ideas; he was more the "idealistic" (i.e., unrealistic) scholar and dreamer, and as such less offensive to the nobles of the Rhineland than the consistent and practical Anabaptists. He was never the leader of an organized group. His significance for Mennonite history rests chiefly upon ideas expressed in his one major book, the *Göttlicher und Heiliger Schrift/vor vielen Jahren verdunkelt und durch unheilsame Lehr und Lehrer (aus göttlicher Zulassung) verfinstert/Restitution und Besserung. Anno 1532* (8°, 170 pages; extant in two copies). This book is extensively discussed and described by Karl Rembert (*Wiedertäufer,* 242-64), and Dunin-Borkowski (see Bibliography) also gives large excerpts (113-15).

Between 1520 and 1530 Campanus was unhesitatingly an admirer of Luther. But neither the latter nor Melanchthon was willing to go along with Campanus' unorthodox Bible expositions and his interpretation of doctrines and ordinances. In fact, it is most probable, as Rembert has shown, that the condemnation of the "new Samosatenes" (i.e., Anti-Trinitarians) in the Lutheran *Augsburg Confession* of 1530 is directed specifically against the teachings of Campanus. In 1531, Sebastian Franck sent a lengthy epistle to Campanus welcoming the spiritual kinship between himself and Campanus (Hegler, 264-67). In the duchy of Jülich the Lutheran Reformation was not fully carried out until the 1540's. For that reason Campanus could continue his literary activities and correspondence unmolested, in spite of Melanchthon's repeated request to have him arrested (letters to the court chaplain K. Heresbach). But when (1553) the Servetus case exploded (the publication of his book against the Trinity, and the subsequent burning at the stake in Geneva), the excitement of the new

Protestant orthodoxy regarding all "liberal" theology was felt even as far as Jülich. Campanus, always suspect of some confused interpretation of the doctrine of Trinity, was put under arrest (though apparently an easy one) for the next 20 years, to be released only shortly before his death. Many a theologian, Lutheran and Catholic, tried to bring him back to orthodox teachings, but it was in vain. He remained the old "idealist" all the while, leaning in his last days even strongly to some sort of chiliasm as Melchior Hofmann had done (namely, believing in the imminence of the end of the world).

Campanus' major book, *Contra Totum Post Apostolos Mundum* (about 1530), seems to have been lost. We know but the shortened German version of 1531 (see above). Regarding baptism, which is said to stand in the very center of his teaching (Rembert, 353 ff.), he claims rightly that knowledge and understanding have to precede baptism. He then explains baptism as a covenant comparable to that between bride and bridegroom. But since he neglects to argue in Anabaptist fashion against infant baptism, or to establish a special ordinance for adult baptism, his presentation remains theoretical, unrealistic, and visionary. He believes in the freedom of the will; hence justification comes through faith *and* works. He teaches that a true Christian should not seek litigation and should never go to court. Government is permitted by God for the sake of the ungodly. Obviously, some of these thoughts approach Anabaptist positions. And yet, on the whole, Campanus does not belong at all to the camp of the Anabaptists proper because of his utterly unrealistic or unconcrete type of Christianity.

Regarding the idea of *Restitution* Rembert claims that Campanus was the very originator of this term, central indeed for the entire "Left Wing" of the Reformation. "For 1400 years," he wrote in 1531, "the true church has not existed. But now the time of restitution has come" (Rembert, 244). We know three renowned books bearing in their title this term "restitution": Campanus' work of 1531 (approvingly mentioned by Sebastian Franck in his *Chronica* of 1536), Bernt Rothmann's pamphlet of 1534, the programmatical book of the Münsterite experiment, and finally Michel Servetus' *Restitutio Christianismi* of 1553, with its strictly Anti-Trinitarian purpose or bias.

The contact between Campanus and the Münsterites is rather obscure. According to Rembert, Campanus had much influence upon the so-called Wassenberg preachers who later turned Münsterite. From them Rothmann may have learned the ideas of Campanus. Rembert claims that the latter is the very father of the Münsterite idea of "restitution," and that "no doubt Campanus was known to Rothmann." However, from Campanus we never hear any reaction to the Münsterite events, and he seemed to have been quite unconcerned with this experiment of restitution and its failure. According to Rembert, the two booklets by Campanus and Rothmann are in many regards very similar and of like organization.   R.F.

The only genuine and thorough work of research regarding Campanus was done by Karl Rembert in his *Die "Wiedertäufer" im Herzogtum Jülich* (Berlin, 1899), of which his lengthy article, *ML* I, 317-24 (1913), is but an elaborate excerpt. St. von Dunin-Borkowski, "Quellen zur Vorgeschichte der Unitarier des 16. Jahrhunderts," in *75 Jahre Stella Matutina* (Feldkirch, Austria, 1931), on 113-15 discusses Campanus' main book, chiefly from the angle of his "ditheism." A. Hegler, *Geist und Schrift bei Sebastian Franck* (1892), deals on 50-53 and 264-67 with Franck's epistle to Campanus of 1531. See also W. Bax, *Het Protestantisme in het Bisdom Luik* I (The Hague, 1937) 43-45; *ML* I, 317-25.

Campen, Jacob van, a bishop and leader of the Anabaptists at Amsterdam: see **Jacob van Campen.**

Camphuysen, Dirk Rafaelsz, though not a Mennonite, deserves mention here because of his influence as a poet on Dutch Mennonite religious verse. He was born about 1586 in Gorinchem and studied at the university of Leiden. Then he was a teacher, first in his native city, and later in Utrecht, and preached several times for the Mennonites in Waterland. In 1617 he became a Reformed preacher in Vleuten in the Dutch province of Utrecht, but in 1619 was removed from office and in 1620 banished because he favored Remonstrant ideas. He hid in Amsterdam for a time, then went to Norden in East Friesland, and later to Harlingen and Ameland, until in 1623 he was finally permitted to settle in Dokkum and open a store. In 1625 he refused a call as professor in Rakow and died on July 19, 1626. Camphuysen wrote a translation of the Psalms in verse, a large part of which was taken into the new collection of Psalms adopted by many Lamist Mennonite churches. They are also in the hymnal of the Mennonite church at Haarlem (republished in 1713 and 1756). Among his writings were *Stichtelyke Rymen om te lezen of te zingen; onderscheiden in IV Deelen,* which was reprinted at least 12 times, and *Uytbreyding over de Psalmen des Propheten Davids,* which also went through many editions. Camphuysen's devotional poems were also known and loved in Mennonite circles. At the beginning of the 19th century one of Camphuysen's books, probably his *Stichtelyke Rymen,* was still the songbook of the Mennonite congregations at Leeuwarden and Grouw (*DB* 1900, 90). (L. A. Rademaker, *D. Camphuysen,* Gouda, 1898; *Catalogus Amst.,* 275 f., 279; *ML* I, 325.)
                                                                    J.L.

Campius, Johannes (also called Johann von Campen), is not to be confused with Johannes Campanus (*q.v.*). Campius, whose proper name was Wulff, was first a monk, shortly after 1526 a Lutheran preacher at Itzehoe, North Germany, and in 1529 a colloquent at the dispute at Flensburg on the side of Melchior Hofmann. After much wandering he moved to Soest in Westphalia, where he lived and preached 1531-33. Luther warned against him. Whether he was an Anabaptist at this time is not clear. Nothing of his life is known after his departure from Soest, July 1533. It is very likely, however, that he was active in Münster in 1534. (Rembert, *Wiedertäufer,* 287-94.)   vDZ

Campo 45 Bethel Mission: see **Bethel Mission.**

Camps: see **Summer Camps.**

Camrose, a Hutterian Bruderhof, established in 1949 near Camrose, Alberta. It had a population of 83 in 1950.   M.G.

Canaan Amish Mennonite, Church, located five miles southwest of Plain City, in Canaan Twp., Madison Co., Ohio, unaffiliated, was organized June 12, 1938, with 23 members under the leadership of M. M. Beachy of Salisbury, Pa. Until the meetinghouse was built in 1940, meetings were held in a vacant farmhouse. The 1952 membership was 52. Ministers who have served the congregation were Eldon Troyer, Robert Kaufman, and Emery Yutzy. The congregation suffered a division in 1953, when the more conservative half withdrew.   E.Y.

Canada. This country covers the whole of the North American continent north of the United States, excepting Alaska. Her area of 3,847,597 square miles is greater than the whole of Europe. The physical characteristics and the extreme cold of the northern part make that section uninhabitable. More than 90 per cent of the nation's estimated more than 14,000,000 people live in the narrow belt bordering on the United States.

On the Atlantic seaboard are the four Maritime Provinces of Nova Scotia, New Brunswick, Prince Edward Island, and Newfoundland. The latter was Britain's first colonial possession, taken in 1583. The land is heavily forested with the exception of Prince Edward Island, and the cleared portions form excellent farming districts, except for northern Newfoundland, which is rocky, barren, and bleak. The region's 1,454,410 people gain their livelihood mainly from the products of the farm, the forest, and the sea. There are no Mennonites living in this area.

Next, the Laurentian Shield, as it is commonly known, is an area of low-lying, evergreen-clad hills, forming a huge basin centering on Hudson Bay in the north. The trapper, the miner, and the logger are its only inhabitants. There is a wealth of minerals in this remote territory. Canada leads the world in the production of nickel and asbestos. Gold, silver, copper, lead, and iron are among other minerals found here. The pulp and paper industry has gained tremendous proportions. The centers of population of this region lie just to the south of the Shield, in the valley of the St. Lawrence River and on the shores of the lower Great Lakes. The St. Lawrence Valley is the center of the French Canadian population, and contains Montreal, Canada's largest city, as well as Quebec, the oldest city. In the vicinity of the lower Great Lakes is found the center of the English-speaking community of Canada. These two areas combined contain the largest proportion of Canadian industrial establishments. Mennonites are to be found only in southern Ontario, having established the first Mennonite settlements in Canada here 1786 ff.

West of the Great Lakes lie the prairies, an ocean of wheat waving in the west winds, and stretching from the Red River to the Rockies, the "bread basket" of the world. Approximately one billion bushels of the several grains, wheat, oats, barley, are produced annually. On this land also are raised 10 million cattle, 8 million hogs, and 3.5 million sheep. Almost everywhere mixed farming is the rule. Nearly 2.5 million people live on the prairies. The three prairie provinces are Manitoba, Saskatchewan, and Alberta. Large numbers of Mennonites are to be found here, the first having come from Russia to Manitoba in 1874.

Between the prairies and the Pacific Ocean lie the mountains. There are several parallel ranges, of which the Rockies are the best known, and the highest and most rugged. In this whole mountainous region there are only a very few valleys that are inhabited. The coast range of mountains everywhere drops abruptly to the sea. Only the few long-lying coastal valleys are habitable. The most important of these is the valley of the lower Fraser River. At the head of this valley is Canada's great Pacific seaport, Vancouver. In the valley, dairying, poultry farming, and berry and fruit growing are the important occupations. Large and growing Mennonite settlements were established here 1928 ff.

Canada's northland is inhabited only by a few trappers, traders, and Eskimos. The airplane has made this arctic north increasingly accessible. There are many mines in the far north whose only contact with civilization is by airplane.

Almost all the people of Canada are of European origin. The two basic stocks are French and British. The British total 5,716,000 and the French Canadians, living largely in the province of Quebec, number upwards of 3,483,000. There are large numbers of Germans, Scandinavians, Ukrainians, Jews, Dutch, Poles, Italians, and others representing almost every nation on the globe. Indians and Eskimos have dwindled to 125,000. Mennonites of all descriptions number about 120,000 souls. The Roman Catholic Church claims about 42 per cent of the population, and enjoys special privileges in the province of Quebec. The Protestants constitute 55 per cent of the population. The Anglican and Presbyterian churches are prominent. The urban dwellers have outnumbered the rural in Canada since 1921. At present, 54 per cent of Canada's population lives in cities and towns. Canada is no longer merely a producer of primary raw materials. Heavy industry today accounts for 45 per cent of gross production, agriculture 20 per cent.

Newfoundland was discovered in 1497 by John Cabot, who was sponsored by a group of Bristol merchants. Jacques Cartier took possession of the land around the Gulf of St. Lawrence for the King of France in 1534. In 1583 Newfoundland was claimed by the English. Britain defeated France in the Seven Years' War and, as a result, Canada came under British control in 1763. In the hundred years following 1763, the colony grew rapidly and kept up a continuous struggle for self-government, which was granted in 1867 when the provinces of Quebec, Ontario, Nova Scotia, and New Brunswick entered into a confederation with Dominion status within the British Empire. The Canadian Pacific Railway linked British Columbia to the rest of the Dominion in 1885, and the other provinces joined soon. The Dominion of Canada is a democracy. It is ruled by a Parliament consisting of the King, represented by the Governor-General, the Senate, and the House of Commons. The Senate is appointed and the members of the Commons are elected by the people. The Prime

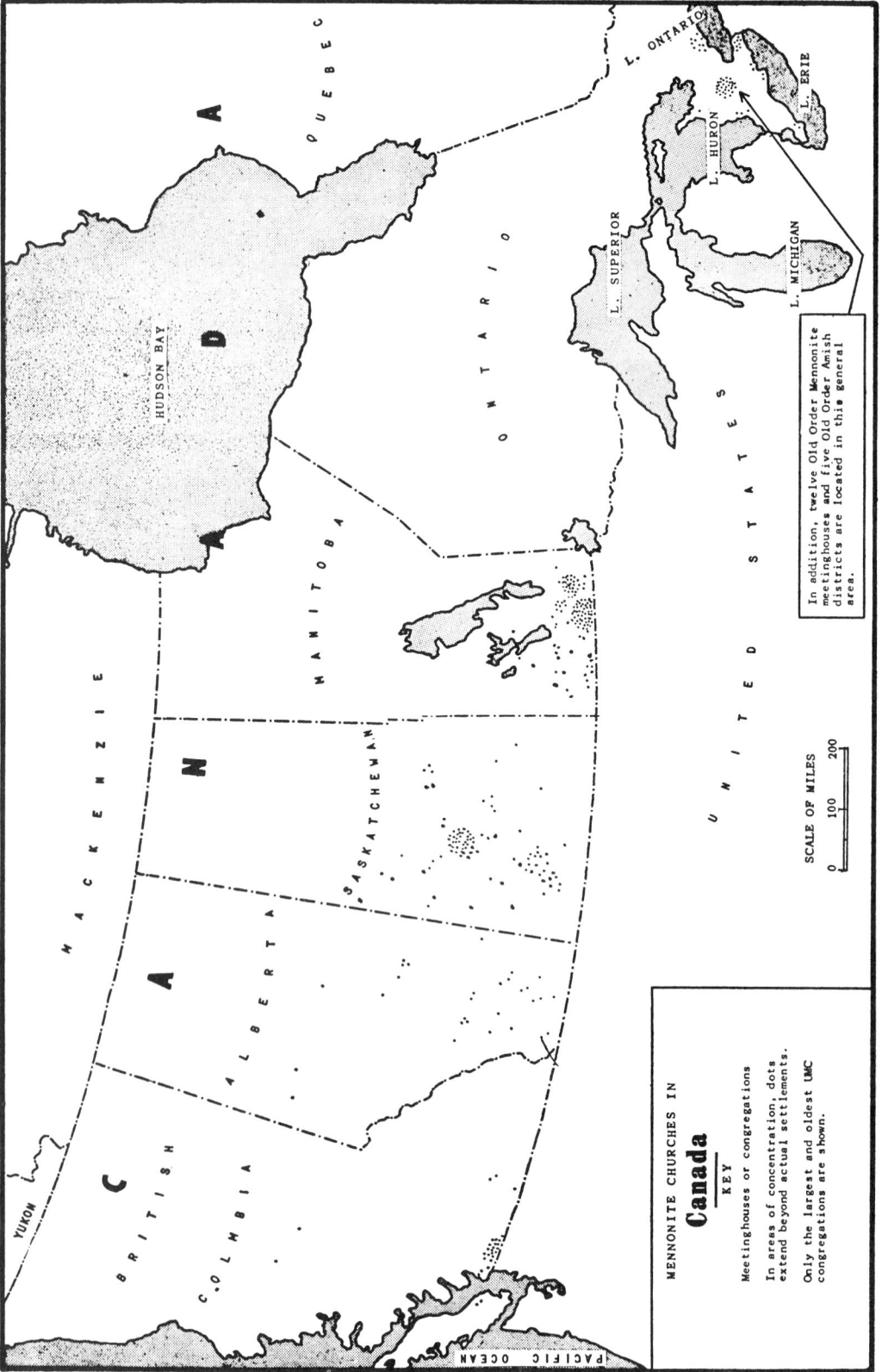

MENNONITE CHURCHES IN

Canada

KEY

Meetinghouses or congregations

In areas of concentration, dots extend beyond actual settlements.

Only the largest and oldest UMC congregations are shown.

In addition, twelve Old Order Mennonite meetinghouses and five Old Order Amish districts are located in this general area.

SCALE OF MILES

0   100   200

Minister and his ministers are members of the Commons or the Senate. The Cabinet holds office only while it enjoys the confidence of the representatives of the people.

This democratic country has become a home for many Mennonites in their search for a land of religious freedom. The first group came from eastern Pennsylvania to the Niagara peninsula in 1786 to settle in Welland and Lincoln counties of what later became the province of Ontario (*q.v.*). In the years immediately following, others came, locating principally in three centers: Waterloo County (*q.v.*), the Markham (*q.v.*) district, and the Niagara (*q.v.*) district. They were among the pioneers of Canada. The little Mennonite village of Ebytown in Waterloo County, named Berlin in 1827, has become the present large city of Kitchener (*q.v.*), the center of the largest compact Mennonite settlement in Canada. Between 1786 and 1825 about 2,000 Mennonites migrated from Pennsylvania to Ontario. The first congregation of Amish Mennonites was organized in Waterloo County in 1824, coming from Bavaria and Alsace-Lorraine.

A second influx of Mennonites began in 1874, this time from the steppes of faraway southern Russia. They settled on the virgin prairie of Manitoba (*q.v.*). The government reserved two blocks of land for them, one on each side of the Red River —the East Reserve (*q.v.*) and West Reserve (*q.v.*). They were among the first to attempt to live on the plains away from the rivers. After overcoming severe and prolonged hardships, this group succeeded in making of the two "reserves" one of the most substantial and desirable farming areas in the West. Jacob Y. Shantz (*q.v.*), a layman of Waterloo County, played a great role in establishing these settlements.

The third and largest wave of Mennonite immigrants to Canada from Russia began in 1922, and continued through to 1930. This movement brought well over 20,000 Mennonites into Canada, the majority of whom settled on farms in the West. This settlement differed from the previous ones in that it was, in most cases, impossible to obtain large blocks of land, and the settlers had to be interspersed with the rest of the population. Frequently the new settlers went to the cities temporarily where money could be earned more directly and more easily. Some stayed in the cities, and thus the urbanization of the Mennonite population of western Canada began. At present both Kitchener-Waterloo and Winnipeg have five or more Mennonite congregations. Saskatoon and Vancouver are other larger Canadian cities containing relatively large Mennonite populations. The emigration of several thousand Manitoba and Saskatchewan Mennonites to Mexico and Paraguay (1921-27) during this time should not be forgotten.

The fourth wave of immigration, 1947-52, from Russia (via Germany) brought another group of more than 7,000, largely to the west. This time over 200 German Mennonites from the former Danzig area joined the migrants.

Internal westward migration movements should be noted. The first of these (1890 ff.) took Manitoba General Conference Mennonites to Saskatchewan, particularly around Rosthern and Herbert. From 1891 to 1903 several small groups of Ontario Mennonites, representing both the Mennonite Brethren in Christ and the Mennonites (MC), settled in Central Alberta, a small group of the latter also in Saskatchewan. The greatest movement of all, however, beginning in 1925 and still continuing, was from the prairie provinces to the Fraser Valley of British Columbia. According to the 1951 census the total Mennonite population of 125,938 was distributed over the Canadian provinces as follows: Manitoba, 44,667; Saskatchewan, 26,270; Ontario, 25,796; British Columbia, 15,387; Alberta, 13,529; Quebec, 220; Nova Scotia, 23; New Brunswick, 30; Prince Edward Island, 6; Newfoundland, 3. The largest city populations (in cities over 5,000) are as follows: Winnipeg, 3,460; Saskatoon, 1,663; Kitchener, 1,646; Vancouver, 1,624; Swift Current, 621; Waterloo, 527; St. Catherines, 510.

The education of their children has been of great concern to the Mennonites of Canada, the first Mennonite school, the Mennonite Collegiate Institute at Gretna, Man., having been established as early as 1891. Here the religious aspect has come first, as the many small Bible schools dotting the Mennonite settlements testify. The Mennonite Brethren, the General Conference Mennonites, the United Missionary Church, and the Mennonites (MC) each have a Bible college. The colleges or Bible institutes of the first two conferences are located in Winnipeg, Man., and the other two in Kitchener, Ont. Every province in which Mennonites reside now has a Mennonite high school: Saskatchewan, Alberta, and British Columbia have one each, and Manitoba and Ontario have two each. In these institutions the regular courses are taught, in addition to some religious instruction, some Mennonite history, and the German language. However, the majority of the Mennonite young people attend the public schools.

Organizationally the various Mennonite district or provincial conferences in Canada belong to the general conferences of their bodies, which represent both the United States and Canada, although the relation of the Canadian Conference of the G.C. Mennonite Church is somewhat different from the relationship in the case of the M.B. and the Mennonite (MC) conferences. The first conference organized in Canada was the Ontario Mennonite (MC), organized about 1825. The Canadian Mennonite Conference (GCM) was organized in 1903. The Canadian Mennonites generally support the church-wide boards and institutions of their denominational connections instead of organizing separately for the Canadian constituents. However, several intergroup Canadian Mennonite organizations have developed to serve exclusively Canadian Mennonite interests and needs, such as the Canadian Mennonite Board of Colonization (*q.v.*), the Non-Resistant Relief Organization (Ontario) (*q.v.*), the Conference of Historic Peace Churches (Ontario) (*q.v.*), the Western Canada Mennonite Central Relief Committee. And in Ontario the Brethren in Christ co-operate closely with the Mennonites in relief and peace work. All Canadian Mennonites co-operate with the Mennonite Central Committee, which has a Canadian headquarters in Waterloo, Ont. In a real sense the Canadian Mennonites and the Mennonites of the United States constitute a unified North American group, in which the political boundary between the two nations has little significance. The complete absence of any significant hindrance to a free crossing of the border, as well as the common Anglo-Saxon culture and English language, together with great similarity in political, social, and religious institutions, has made this genuine Mennonite unity possible. There is actually no distinctive Canadian Mennonitism, as contrasted to that of the United States, except that most of the Canadian Mennonites of Russian background still use the German language in their worship services, and have not come as much under the influence of North American Protestantism as their counterpart bodies in the United States.

The relation of the Canadian Mennonites to the state with reference to military service is discussed in detail elsewhere (see **Military Service**). Suffice it to say here that the Canadian government has always been generous in dealing with conscientious objectors. There has never been compulsory military training or service in Canada except during wartime. In the war of 1812-15 between England and the United States, some of the Mennonite settlers of the Waterloo County area were impressed with their horses and wagons to aid in military transport. Mennonites (and Quakers and Tunkers) were always excused from militia duty on payment of a nominal exemption fee. The immigrants from Russia 1874-80 received special written assurances that they would be free from military service. In World War I Mennonites were exempt from all service although occasional difficulties arose. In World War II alternative civilian service was required (see **Alternative Service Camps**), and a generally satisfactory solution of the problems related to this question was found.

The Mennonites of Manitoba of the 1874-80 immigration remained culturally and linguistically (as well as religiously) distinct from their Canadian Anglo-Saxon neighbors, maintaining the German language and even German schools. This cultural autonomy, expressly tolerated by the government at the beginning (the cultural autonomy of the French Canadians made this easy and natural), caused no difficulties until rising Canadian nationalism with its insistence on cultural uniformity brought pressure on the Mennonites for cultural assimilation. This came to a climax in World War I when the situation was complicated by the bitter Canadian anti-German feeling. When the Manitoba government prohibited German schools in 1914, the more conservative Mennonite groups felt their security threatened, and most of them sought and found homes elsewhere (1922-27) in Mexico and Paraguay (see **Old Colony Mennonites**).

The conservative Manitoba Mennonites, often called Old Colony, but actually properly called Chortitza or Sommerfeld groups, present a strikingly different phenomenon in North American Mennonite

history, similar in some ways, however, to the Old Order Amish (*q.v.*) and the Hutterian Brethren. Their attempt to maintain complete cultural autonomy on religious grounds failed, in contrast to the successful maintenance of such autonomy by the Mennonites in Russia from whence they came. Not only did they fail in their attempt—they suffered a tragic degree of cultural and religious deterioration, partly because they were too small a group, but partly also because they were completely cut off from all outside sources of cultural renewal. The removal to Mexico and Paraguay has only intensified their isolation and cultural introversion.

The older Mennonite group in Ontario, of Pennsylvania origin, early made a successful transition to Canadianization as an English-speaking, culturally progressive, but sturdily Mennonite body, although a fraction, the Old Order Mennonites, has continued a certain degree of cultural retardation. The large newer immigrant group from Russia (1922-30), coming with a higher cultural and religious level to begin with, has not followed the pattern of the Old Colony Manitoba group but rather that of the Ontario group, although the first generation has strongly maintained the German language.

The Canadian government for its part has consistently evidenced a high regard for the Mennonites, no doubt largely because of their solid contribution to the national welfare through their community building and their agricultural achievements in both Ontario and the prairie provinces. The late and long-time Prime Minister W. L. Mackenzie King was a native of Waterloo Co., Ont., and knew the Mennonites well. His influence was frequently brought to bear on their behalf in times of difficulty with the state and in connection with immigration policies.

Mennonite membership in Canada by Conference groups in 1951 was (baptized):

General Conference Mennonites	15,500
Mennonite Brethren	9,579
Mennonite Church (MC)	6,335
Sommerfelder Mennonites	3,785
United Missionary	2,866
Old Colony Mennonites	2,049
Evangelical Mennonites (Kl. Gem.)	1,895
Old Order (Wisler) Mennonites	1,840
Rudnerweide Mennonites	1,800
Chortitz Mennonites	1,408
Church of God in Christ, Mennonites	1,292
Evangelical Mennonite (former E.M.B.)	630
Old Order Amish Mennonites	610
Krimmer Mennonite Brethren	310
Reformed Mennonites	221
Total	40,120

C.F.K.

There is little literature in English on the general history of the Mennonites in Canada. In the German language there is: P. J. Schaefer, *Die Mennoniten in Canada*, which is Part 3 of *Woher? Wohin? Mennoniten!* (Altona, Man., 1945); H. Lehmann, *Das Deutschtum in Westkanada* (Berlin, 1939); E. K. Francis, "The Mennonite School Problem in Manitoba," *MQR XXVII* (1953) 204-36; *idem*, "A Bibliography of the Menn. in Manitoba," *loc. cit.*, 237-47; C. Henry Smith, *The Coming of the Russian Menn. . . . 1874-1884* (Berne, 1927); S. C. Yoder, *For Conscience Sake* (Goshen, 1940); B.

Ewert, ed., *Wichtige Dokumente betreffs der Wehrfreiheit der Mennoniten in Canada* (Gretna, 1917); *ML* II, 456-58; *Erfahrungen der Menn. in Canada während des zweiten Weltkrieges* (Steinbach, n.d.).

Canada Colonization Association was a subsidiary of the Department of Immigration and Colonization of the Canadian Pacific Railway Company which gave valuable assistance to Mennonite land settlement in Western Canada after World War I. It was organized by Col. Dennis in 1919 as a private organization, but was soon taken over by the Canadian Pacific Railway. T. O. F. Herzer was its long-time director. See **Mennonite Land Settlement Board.** (J. B. Hedges, *Building the Canadian West*. N.Y., 1939.)   J.G.

Canada and States Mennonite Insurance Association. This organization originated in the Molotschna and Chortitza colonies of Russia, and was brought to Manitoba in 1874. It was joined by Mennonites in the Dakotas, Minnesota, Montana, and Nebraska as they settled there. The Middle West is at present the area of responsibility although it is expanding rapidly into other states and joining with other Mennonite organizations. It offers insurance against fire, storm, hail, and the natural catastrophes. Movable and immovable property are insured. Premiums are gauged according to losses. At present, an insured risk of $29 million is carried. Operated on Christian principles, it adheres to the traditional practice of assisting a "brother in need." J.K.R.

Canadian Conference of the Mennonite Brethren Church of North America.

I. The Beginning and Early History of the Conference (1910-24). The Canadian Conference of the Mennonite Brethren Church of North America, in earlier years known as the Northern District Conference of the Mennonite Brethren Church, had its beginning in 1910. Until then, the entire M.B. Church in the United States and Canada functioned as one general conference. There were no Mennonite Brethren among the original Mennonite settlers in Manitoba.

The conference convened for its first annual session at Herbert, Sask., June 27 and 28, 1910. At this meeting the thirteen M.B. churches in Saskatchewan, with a total membership of nearly 1,000, were represented by 64 delegates. The conference organized with David Dyck as chairman, Benjamin Janz, assistant chairman, and J. F. Harms, secretary. The two M.B. churches in Manitoba, Winkler and Winnipeg, joined this conference in 1913. Since the Saskatchewan churches constituted two groups, northern and southern, the conference was often subdivided into three circuits (*Kreise*), the northern Saskatchewan circuit known as the Rosthern Kreis, the southern Saskatchewan circuit as Herbert Kreis, and the Manitoba Kreis. In 1914 the total membership of the conference was 1,317.

Home mission work has been the most important activity of the conference in its earlier years as well as later. At its first session, the conference elected a home mission committee composed of three members: David Harms, chairman, Jacob W. Thiessen, secretary, and Heinrich Aaron Thiessen, treasurer. These three continued in this committee many years and rendered valuable service to the conference. The home mission work arranged for by the conference consisted of conducting evangelistic services in the churches, caring for the small groups in new settlements, doing extension work in localities where no evangelistic work was done, and colporteur work by which Bibles and Christian literature were sold.

Among the conference workers engaged as evangelists for a greater length of time who rendered valuable service should be mentioned the following: C. N. Hiebert, J. H. Ewert, H. A. Neufeld, Jacob Wiens, John J. Kroeker, H. S. Voth, H. P. Janz, C. J. Kliewer, H. S. Rempel, H. H. Nikkel, and J. F. Redekop. The conference also took a keen interest in the Russian settlements of Saskatchewan, among whom two M.B. congregations were established, one at Eagle Creek and the other at Petrofka. Hermann Fast (*q.v.*) especially rendered valuable service here.

Among the leaders of the early years should be mentioned Elder David Dyck, Elder Benjamin Janz, Heinrich A. Neufeld, J. F. Harms, Jacob Lepp, David K. Klassen, John Warkentin, John P. Wiebe, H. S. Voth, and S. L. Hodel. Most of these have been very active in the conference sessions, in holding Bible conferences in the churches, and in furthering the various conference projects.

The conference early began a city mission in Winnipeg, which ultimately led to the organization of a local church. Wm. J. Bestvater was the first city missionary, followed by E. H. Nikkel, and after that by C. N. Hiebert, who served for many years. Anna J. Thiessen entered this work almost at its beginning and was still active in 1949.

Among the other early conference activities should be mentioned the Bible School at Herbert, and the Home for the Aged at Winkler. Courses intended for the training of choir directors and choir singers were also arranged for by the conference.

II. Expansion of the Conference and Its Activities, 1924-36. These twelve years mark a period of rapid growth and expansion of the conference, largely due to the new immigrants from Russia 1923 ff. At the beginning of 1924 the conference consisted of 22 congregations with a membership of 1,771. At the close of 1936 there were 63 churches and groups having a total membership of 5,562. These spread over Manitoba, Saskatchewan, and Alberta, and there were small beginnings of congregations in British Columbia.

The effective home mission activities partly accounted for this rapid growth, but the main contributing factor was the immigration of many Mennonites from Russia, 1923-30, a fairly large percentage of whom had been members of M.B. churches in Russia. Wherever they settled, they either joined M.B. churches or formed new churches and affiliated themselves with the conference.

The coming in of so many new members and the rapid growth of the churches raised some new and difficult problems which the conference solved in an effective way. Economically most of the newly arrived members were without means; so the churches assisted with clothing, food, living quarters, provided work, and helped them to procure farm land and homes. It required some time as well as Christian forbearance for these elements, the early Canadian members and the newly arrived brethren, to become fully amalgamated into one functioning conference.

The conference has profited greatly in cultural as well as in spiritual respects through the coming of the brethren from Russia. A number of effective and experienced leaders, ministers, educators, and other workers became an asset to the conference. Among these should be mentioned in a special way Herman A. Neufeld, Wm. Dyck, Jacob W. Reimer, John G. Wiens, Abr. H. Unruh, Gerhard Unruh, F. F. Isaac, C. F. Klassen, C. A. DeFehr, D. D. Duerksen, and H. Goossen, whose services were in Manitoba; Isaac Regehr, H. A. Regier, Jacob G. Thiessen in Saskatchewan; B. B. Janz, J. A. Toews, A. A. Toews in Alberta; J. A. Harder, C. C. Peters, Abr. Nachtigal, J. P. Braun, F. C. Thiessen in British Columbia.

The conference continued its home mission work with vigor and expanded it. The many new and small settlements made this work very necessary. The city mission in Winnipeg continued and since many of the new immigrants settled in this city, three large M.B. churches developed. The Mary-Martha Home for Mennonite working girls in the city was established in 1927 under the supervision of Anna J. Thiessen and afforded a spiritual home for hundreds of girls lacking parental care. City missions, which also included homes for working girls, were begun in Saskatoon, Sask., and in Vancouver, B.C. Mr. and Mrs. H. S. Rempel have served as missionaries of the former for many years and built up a church congregation.

The congregations realized the need and importance of Bible instruction for its young people and encouraged the establishing of Bible schools. The one at Herbert continued, and other schools were established at Hepburn, Sask., at Winkler, Man., and at Coaldale and Gem, Alta. Though these schools were not directly supervised or financed by the conference, the conference continued to encourage them, received reports of their work, and from them received many of its best young workers.

III. The Growth of the Conference and Its Activities, 1936-49. This period marks a time of further growth and increase of the conference activities. New problems, economical and ecclesiastical, arose and were solved with remarkable success. During this time the conference expanded westward and eastward. While the churches in Alberta continued to increase for some time, a great rush to the Fraser Valley took place and in a short time large congregations grew up, so that in 1949 nearly one third of the conference membership was found in this province. The main reason for this westward emigration was the continuous failure of crops in the prairie belt of Saskatchewan. The effect on the churches of this area was a marked decline of membership and in some cases the discontinuation of churches.

The M.B. churches in Ontario, which grew out of the immigration of 1923-30 from Russia, had organized as a separate M.B. conference, but in 1944 joined the Canadian Conference as well as the General M.B. Conference of North America. With this addition the Canadian Conference increased in numbers, and received several strong leaders, among whom were H. H. Janzen and Isaac Thiessen.

The conference has reorganized its home mission effort in that it has delegated this work to the five provincial conferences, which report on their work at the annual conference. The spiritual welfare of the church is under the supervision of the Committee of Reference and Counsel (*Fürsorge-Komitee*). In 1916 the conference framed and adopted a constitution and was incorporated as a religious body in Canada, after which it regulated its procedures and conducted its work through the several elected boards and committees.

There had been a steady advance in educational effort. Nine Bible schools and five church high schools were in operation in 1949 and many young people were availing themselves of educational opportunities. In 1944 the conference established the Mennonite Brethren Bible College in Winnipeg for training ministers, evangelists, Bible teachers, and other workers. The college is under the direction of a committee of nine members elected by the conference. A. H. Unruh, H. H. Janzen, and J. B. Toews have had a leading place in establishing the school and on the faculty staff. In 1947 the conference accepted full responsibility for the operation of the Bethesda Mental Hospital at Vineland, Ont., of which Heinrich Wiebe was superintendent.

Since World War II the conference has taken an active part in relief work, principally through the MCC. The conference has done its share in caring and providing for the large number of displaced Mennonites who have come from Europe into Canada, some of whom have joined M.B. churches. Recently several M.B. emigrant families from Brazil and Paraguay have come to Canada and joined M.B. churches.

The churches constituting the conference have experienced a gradual and continuous growth during this period. In 1951 there were 75 congregations with a total membership of 10,783. The conference has convened annually since 1910 except in 1940. The German language is used in its deliberations.

The Canadian M.B. Conference bears the same relationship to the General Conference of the M.B. Church of North America as the several district conferences in the United States. (*Yearbooks* of the conference, 1910-52; J. H. Lohrenz, *The Mennonite Brethren Church*, Hillsboro, 1950.) J.H.Lo.

Canadian Mennonite Bible College, 515 Wellington Crescent, Winnipeg, Man., offers a Bible education to young people seeking to prepare themselves for Christian service, operating under the General Conference Mennonite Church of Canada.

Consideration of the establishment of such a school was begun by the Conference in 1941. Twice (1942, 1945) the conference decided that a course in theology should be added to the four-year Bible program of the Rosthern (Sask.) Academy, but lack of staff prevented this. Finally a separate school was established in Winnipeg in the basement rooms of the Bethel Mission Church with a three-year curriculum patterned after the Bible Department of Bethel College at Newton, Kan.

On Oct. 5, 1947, the Bible College was opened and dedicated. A. J. Regier, president, I. I. Friesen, P. A. Rempel, Henry Wall, and John Konrad comprised the teaching staff, while the enrollment numbered 33 students. In the following year the staff increased to 7, and the student body to 49.

The present building, the former Smith mansion, located in a desirable residential district on the banks of the Assiniboine River, was purchased in 1949, and the College began the 1949-50 season in the present quarters, with a staff of 9 instructors and a student enrollment of 74. The present president (since 1951) is I. I. Friesen.   H.H.F.

Canadian Mennonite Board of Colonization. When after World War I the Mennonites of Russia were famine-stricken and suffered many other hardships, the Mennonites of Western Canada were among those who wished to extend every possible help. On Oct. 18, 1920, therefore 14 representatives of the various Mennonite churches in Manitoba, Saskatchewan, and Alberta met in Regina, Sask., to organize a Canadian Central Committee similar to the Mennonite Central Committee just organized in the United States, which should be in charge of a united Canadian relief program for our suffering brethren in Russia. A committee of five was elected: P. P. Epp, Morden, Man.; Abram Loewen, Acme, Alta.; C. K. Unruh, Hepburn, Sask.; P. M. Schmidt, Drake, Sask.; and John Thiessen, Greenfarm, Sask. This committee elected its executive as follows: P. P. Epp, chairman; John Thiessen, secretary; and C. K. Unruh, treasurer. Twenty-five conveners were appointed to organize local relief committees and direct the relief work in the Mennonite churches. It was also decided that if at all possible the relief work should be done jointly and in co-operation with the Mennonites in the United States. (See **Central Mennonite** *Immigration Committee.*)

A little later the Russian Mennonites sent a delegation to investigate immigration and settlement possibilities in Mexico, the United States, and Canada. Of these countries Canada alone finally consented to open its doors to the prospective immigrants. In order to assist in the prospective Mennonite immigration movement to Canada, an organization was effected at a meeting of representatives of the Canadian Central Committee in the home of H. H. Ewert, Gretna, Man., on May 17, 1922, under the name of "Canadian Mennonite Board of Colonization," with headquarters at Rosthern, Sask. A. A. Friesen, who had been one of the four delegates from Russia, was appointed corresponding secretary and later secretary-treasurer of the Board, and David Toews of Rosthern, chairman. Various representations had already been made to the federal and the western Canada provincial governments in connection with this Mennonite immigrant movement. The Canadian Pacific Railway Company was also interviewed with reference to the transportation of the Mennonites from Russia to Canada. Gerhard Ens of Rosthern, who had been a member of the Saskatchewan Legislature, rendered a very valuable service as intermediary between the Mennonite Board and government officials. At his suggestion a joint stock company to finance the immigration and more effectively settle the prospective Mennonite immigrants was planned. This, however, did not materialize due to lack of financial support.

On June 20, 1922, Col. J. S. Dennis, Chief Commissioner of the Department of Colonization and Development of the C.P.R., advised the Canadian Mennonite Board of Colonization that the C.P.R. was prepared to enter into a contract with the Board to transport 3,000 Mennonites from Russia to Canada on a credit basis. At a meeting of the Board on June 26, 1922, this generous offer was accepted and the chairman, David Toews, was authorized to sign the contract on behalf of the Board. The co-operating Mennonite groups in this movement were the General Conference, the Mennonite Brethren, the Mennonite Church (MC), the Church of God in Christ Mennonites, and the Evangelical Mennonite Brethren.

David Toews consistently stressed the fact that this undertaking was a missionary project based on faith. There was, however, strong opposition by some of the Mennonite communities to the above credit contract and its implications.

The first group of the new Mennonite immigrants arrived in Canada in July 1923. Similar contracts were entered into every year up to 1930. Over 21,000 Mennonites were brought to Canada under these contracts. The total credit for transportation extended by the C.P.R. amounted to $1,767,398.68. The last of this principal sum was paid back in 1946. In addition a total sum of $180,000 was paid as interest. The balance of the accrued interest due, amounting to about 1½ million dollars, was canceled by the C.P.R., and the interest payment of $180,000 was placed in a suspended account by the C.P.R. to serve as a collateral for a future possible credit movement.

Accommodation and maintenance was provided for the newcomers by the Canadian Mennonites who opened their homes to them on their arrival or assisted them in finding necessary accommodation. The Mennonites of the United States also greatly assisted them by sending thousands of pounds of clothing and large sums of money to the Canadian Board for the needy and sick. Many hospital bills and other needs could thus be met and in quite a few cases deportations prevented. They also advanced approximately $250,000 in loans to be applied on the transportation debt, all of which has since been repaid.

In order to aid the settling of the newly arrived Mennonites, Col. Dennis suggested that a Mennonite Land Settlement Board (*q.v.*) be organized to separate the land settlement work from the work of the Colonization Board. The Land Settlement Board was organized in July 1924. It consisted of nine members, on which the Canadian Mennonite Board of Colonization, the Mennonite immigrants who now had their own organization known as the Central Mennonite Immigration Committee (*q.v.*), and the C.P.R. each had three representatives. The underlying principle in this settlement work was "to settle the largest number of Mennonite immigrants in the best possible way for the least possible expense." This work was financed by the Canada Colonization Association, a subsidiary of the Colonization Department of the C.P.R. All commission contracts were made in the name of the Canada Colonization Association as security for the advances made. The commissions received, however, were not sufficient to cover expenses and the Mennonite Land Settlement Board was later absorbed by the Canada Colonization Association.

The Canadian Mennonite Board of Colonization appointed collectors to collect transportation accounts from the immigrants. H. B. Janz served in this capacity for a number of years and was succeeded by C. F. Klassen in the spring of 1930. Klassen continued this work until he went to Europe immediately following World War II in 1945 under the auspices of the Mennonite Central Committee to direct the emigration of Mennonite refugees from Europe. The expenses in connection with this collection work were also financed by the Canada Colonization Association.

David Toews very capably served as chairman of the Canadian Mennonite Board of Colonization from its inception until failing health forced him to resign on April 4, 1946. J. J. Thiessen of Saskatoon, Sask., was then elected as his successor, and has served continuously since. Just two months later D. P. Enns, who had faithfully and efficiently served as secretary-treasurer of the Board for twenty years, suddenly died. He was succeeded by J. Gerbrandt, a member of the Board since before the arrival of the first Mennonite immigrants in 1923.

In the period 1930-35, when the Liberal Government under the leadership of the Hon. W. L. Mackenzie King was replaced by the Conservative party led by the Hon. R. B. Bennett and very adverse economic conditions prevailed throughout the world, further Mennonite immigration to Canada under the above scheme was prohibited. The Mennonites remaining in Russia were in great distress. During the years 1929 to 1938 the amount of $211,218.36 was received by the Canadian Mennonite Board of Colonization for transmission to Russia. Of this a large proportion was contributed by the relatives who were fortunate enough to have come to Canada in the previous decade. By the end of 1950 the above sum for foreign relief purposes had increased to $230,773.43. Since the beginning of World War II remittances were mostly sent to Mennonites in South America and western Europe.

In July 1947 the office of the Board was moved from Rosthern to Saskatoon, Sask. In the same year a new movement of Mennonite refugees to Canada started. The applications of prospective Mennonite immigrants for admission to Canada were largely prepared and then submitted to the Canadian immigration authorities by the Board or its provincial committees. The processing overseas was handled by the MCC representatives. Up to August 1953 over 8,500 Mennonites had come to Canada in this latest movement, the majority coming to close relatives. Others were placed on farms as sugar beet workers or general farm workers. A considerable number of domestics have also found new homes in Canada. Quite a few widows with their children were permitted to come as domestics. The above immigration involved an outlay of over one million dollars for transportation charges, most of which was advanced by the close relatives, but the Mennonite Board and the provincial committees also gave considerable assistance.

On May 24, 1951, the Canadian Mennonite Board of Colonization signed a contract with the C.P.R. for a new credit movement for the amount of the above-mentioned suspended interest of $180,000. The first group of 48 credit passengers arrived in Canada on July 25, 1951. Most of these were Mennonites from the former Danzig area of Germany, who with but few exceptions have no relatives in Canada. Repeated representations by the chairman of the Board, J. J. Thiessen, to the Canadian Government were necessary before the Danzig Mennonites were finally more freely admitted to Canada.

The chief participants in the work of the Canadian Mennonite Board of Colonization at present are the General Conference and the Mennonite Brethren churches in Canada, although a representative of the Mennonite Church (MC) has always served on the executive committee.   J.G.

Canadian Mennonite Relief Committee was organized on Dec. 30, 1940, by a group of Mennonite churches, chiefly in Manitoba, the membership of which is composed almost exclusively of descendants of the Russian Mennonite immigration of 1874. A common background, common experiences in matters pertaining to peace problems in World War I, and a common position relative to alternative service in World War II were the bonds which united these churches for the purpose of giving a positive peace witness. The otherwise completely independent churches represented in this relief organization are the Bergthal, Sommerfeld, Rudnerweide, Kleine Gemeinde, Church of God in Christ Mennonite, Chortitz, Evangelical Mennonite Brethren, and the Old Colony groups. Their total membership approximates 10,000.

The leading persons responsible for the creation of this relief organization were David Schulz, J. F. Barkman, H. R. Reimer, Jacob S. Rempel, and J. G. Toews. J. S. Rempel was chairman until his death in 1947, when G. S. Rempel succeeded him to that office. J. G. Toews served as secretary-treasurer of the organization until 1950, when J. F. Unrau of Rosenfeld, Man., assumed this office.

All the above-named churches have representation on the committee and members hold office during the pleasure of their respective churches. The object of the organization is to collect funds and material aid for relief purposes, all of which is channeled to the relief fields through the Mennonite Central Committee.

The financial reports of the organization show that 1947 was the peak year for its activities. Contributions for the year were: cash, $76,328.81; clothing, $88,325.57; food, $86,936.78; total, $242,591.16.

The financial reports for subsequent years show a marked decline in total contributions; furthermore the major portion of the cash contributions was directed toward refugee migration, this item for 1949 being $21,000.

In 1948 the Sommerfelder and the Chortitz churches withdrew from the organization because they felt that the emergency stage of the relief program was over. They, however, continued to contribute material aid as well as cash in aid of their brethren in Paraguay and Mexico, availing themselves of MCC channels in forwarding their contributions to the relief fields. J.G.T.

Canadian Northwest Conference (UMC), one of the eight district conferences of this body, formerly the Mennonite Brethren in Christ. Settlers of this group from Ontario first located at Didsbury, Alta., in 1894, then at Carstairs in 1900, and at Castor in 1906. Sons of the early pioneers moved to Alsask, Sask., in 1910. The first pastor in the Didsbury area was Elder J. B. Detwiler, 1894-1911. In 1906 Elder H. Goudie from Ontario organized the churches into a mission conference under the Ontario Conference. This was reorganized as an independent conference the following year and recognized by the General Conference of the church in 1909 under the name of the Canadian Northwest Conference.

The conference has maintained a strong emphasis on evangelistic efforts through revival, tabernacle, and camp meetings. Beulah Mission in Edmonton (1907) and Beulah Home for Girls (1910) were supported. The first missionary couple of the conference sailed for Nigeria, West Africa, in 1918, though the conference had assumed support of an Ontario couple since 1909. The Mountain View Bible College, founded as a Bible school at Didsbury in 1926, serves as the official school of the Conference.

Conference statistics for the year 1949 show 498 communicant members, 24 ordained ministers, and 12 probationers. S.F.P.

J. A. Huffman, *Hist. of the Menn. Brethren in Christ Church* (New Carlisle, 1920); E. R. Storms, *United Missionary Church Year Book, 1950* (Kitchener).

Canadian Pacific Railway Company (C.P.R.) was formed to give British Columbia rail connections with the eastern provinces. Building the C.P.R. was one of the most formidable tasks in the history of railroad construction, especially building the line north of Lake Superior, and driving the railroad through the Rocky Mountains and the ranges beyond them. Both tasks were accomplished, and the railroad was completed five years earlier than the contract required, on Nov. 7, 1885. The Confederation of Canada was consolidated, and the C.P.R. was ready to begin its world transportation service.

The C.P.R. has played a very important role in the history of the Canadian Mennonites of the last three decades. When the Bolsheviks came to power in Russia in October 1917, their political and economic dictatorship brought starvation to millions of Russians, and also persecution to the church. The Mennonites of Russia turned to their coreli-

gionists in North America for help. In America the Mennonite Central Committee and in Canada the Canadian Mennonite Board of Colonization (*q.v.*) were organized. The MCC has not only saved thousands from death by starvation (see *Feeding the Hungry*), but indirectly also helped the Mennonites in Russia to get official permission from the Soviets to start their migration to Canada.

In the early 1920's the Canadian Mennonite Board of Colonization approached the C.P.R. with a proposal to move Mennonites from Russia to Canada on credit. This request was granted by the C.P.R., and from 1923 to 1930 over 21,000 Mennonites came, most of them on credit. This was a unique undertaking in the 400-year history of the Mennonites. A private business concern extended a credit of nearly two million dollars to poor homeless people for their transportation from Soviet Russia, without any security. With God's help, this debt was fully paid off to the C.P.R. C.F.K.

J. B. Hedges, *Building the Canadian West* (N.Y., 1939); H. A. Innis, *A History of the Canadian Pacific Railway* (London, 1923).

Canan Station, a suburb of Altoona, Pa., pop. (1952) 430, mostly of the laboring class, where workers at the Altoona Mennonite (MC) Mission (*q.v.*) conducted Sunday-school services on Saturday afternoon in a public school for 23 years, until 1951, when the time was changed to Sunday afternoon. Twelve members of the Mennonite Church live in the area. Plans are to build a chapel as soon as funds are available. F.B.

Canelones, Uruguay, a town 34 miles north of Montevideo in an area that is the most highly developed in fruit growing and dairying in all Uruguay. Near Canelones 6 Mennonite families were living in 1950, on a plot originally intended for 42 families; but because of differences in opinion on such matters as the terms for repayment of the purchase price of the land and the internal government of the future colony, most of the original group looked elsewhere for opportunity. The main undertaking at Canelones is dairying, with hog raising and truck gardening as side lines. W.T.S.

Canton, Kan., a town of 775 inhabitants, midway between McPherson and Hillsboro, in the eastern part of McPherson County. Between 30 and 40 per cent of the people living in its trade territory are Mennonites, most of whom came originally from Karolswalde, Poland, and are now affiliated with the Church of God in Christ, Mennonite (see **Lone Tree Church**). The members of the Emmanuel (*q.v.*) Mennonite Church (GCM) are of the same background. Here is also located the Spring Valley (*q.v.*) Mennonite Church (MC). C.D.

Canton, Ohio, is the county seat of Stark County in northeast section of the state, with a (1948) population of 137,000. It is a city of diversified industry in a large agricultural area. The steel industry is prominent because of the soft coal fields near by and the availability of iron ore, via Great Lakes transportation to Cleveland.

Mennonites first came to this area in 1806 from Washington Co., Md., and later from Pennsylvania.

There are many present non-Mennonites in Canton who are direct descendants of these early Mennonite immigrants. Approximately 1,500 Mennonites of all branches now live in the county, with only 65 members within the city itself. Many are employed in the city, daily commuting to their work from their homes in the country. The Mennonite branches represented are Mennonite (MC), Conservative Amish Mennonite, Old Order Amish. These settlements lie mostly northeast of the city with some in the extreme western part of the county.

The first Mennonite church in the county was built about 1823 of logs on land donated by Jacob Rowland, Sr. This church, known as the Rowland Mennonite congregation, was located approximately one mile east of the town of Canton. These early Mennonites owned farms in the community surrounding the town, practically all of which have now been absorbed by the growing city. About 1874 the log church was replaced with a brick building. Gradually, as the city grew out beyond the church, the community changed, and the church became a city congregation. With the passing of the rural community and the absorption of the members in the city life, the congregation dwindled in membership. Many of the farm owners, upon selling their land, moved out of the community to other rural sections, while still others united with larger city churches. In November 1904 the congregation was re-established as a mission (see **Canton First** Mennonite Church) under the Ohio Mennonite and the Eastern A.M. conferences.

A General Conference Mennonite congregation was briefly in existence, *ca.* 1893-98 (see **Canton Mennonite Church**). J.J.H.

Canton (Ohio) **First** Mennonite (MC) Church, formerly known as Canton Mennonite Mission, is located at 1935-39 Third Street S.E., in the eastern part of the city of Canton, Stark Co., Ohio, where a parsonage was erected in 1912 and a church building in 1915.

The mission was founded in 1904 by a joint committee representing the Ohio Mennonite (MC) and the Eastern Amish Mennonite conferences. This action grew out of a request for reopening the Mennonite church located at this place approximately 1823-99, whose services had been discontinued for about five years. John A. Liechty was appointed as first superintendent and pastor. In 1907 the property and administration of the mission was given to the Mennonite Board of Missions and Charities, at Elkhart, Ind. A branch was opened by P. R. Lantz in an industrial area on Sept. 21, 1909, known as "The Happy Hour Mission," which was discontinued about five years later. A six weeks' Bible school was organized in 1912 by P. R. Lantz and I. W. Royer. The first sessions were held in January and February of 1913. This school, called the Canton Bible School, has continued intermittently since, with the students sharing in the program and work of the mission.

Following is a list of the superintendent-pastors with their period of service: J. A. Liechty, 1904-6; P. R. Lantz, 1906-12; George M. Hostetler, 1912-14;

C. K. Brenneman, 1914-19; N. E. Troyer, 1919-23; O. N. Johns, 1923-26; C. C. King, 1926-27; E. A. Shank, 1927-31; M. C. Lehman, June-August 1931; William G. Detweiler, 1931-38; J. J. Hostetler, 1938-52; Allen Ebersole, 1952- . Eight ordinations have been held at the Canton church: Michael Rohrer, 1868, bishop; P. R. Lantz, 1907, minister; E. F. Hartzler, 1910, minister; O. N. Johns, 1923, minister; William G. Detweiler, 1933, minister; J. J. Hostetler, 1939, minister; D. Walter Miller, 1941, deacon; Allen Ebersole, 1953, bishop.

During the years 1938-44 the mission carried on a branch work in the Hartville community, about twelve miles north of Canton, which developed into an organized congregation known as the Hartville (*q.v.*) Mennonite Church, now having a membership of over 200. Another branch was begun in 1945 in a suburban area known as the Moreland Allotment, southeast of the city, with summer Bible school, evangelistic meetings, and Sunday school in a renovated barn. In 1948 this field was taken over by another denomination.

The mission at Canton was first organized in 1904 with three members and five imported workers. Thousands have been ministered unto, hundreds have been converted, and the membership has grown from year to year. Many members, however, transferred their membership to other places, including the new Hartville congregation, while still others withdrew. In 1952 the membership stood at 82.

The background of this mission congregation involves the history of the Rowland Mennonite Church, in existence in Canton 1823 to 1899. Jacob Rowland, Sr., a Mennonite who came in 1810 from Maryland to a farm one mile east of the village of Canton, about 1823 gave a parcel of ground for a cemetery and church, and built a log meetinghouse. About 1830 Joseph Rohrer was in charge of the congregation as pastor, continuing until about 1852 when he moved to Indiana. From 1852 to 1863 the congregation was served by visiting ministers, Smith and Newcomer, from Columbiana Co., Ohio. About 1874 this log building was replaced with a brick structure. Gradually, as the village became a city, it enveloped the small church and absorbed the rural community. Many of the members moved out, while others united with various city churches. In 1893 the bishop and pastor, Michael Rohrer, died, leaving the small congregation without leadership. Services continued with less frequency, the congregation being served only by visiting ministers. Several attempts were made at reviving the work during those years. Menno S. Steiner moved into the community during this time for about a year. The work, however, dwindled and services were discontinued about 1899 by the Mennonites (MC) until the opening of the mission in 1904, which took over the Rowland church property for its use. (*ML* I, 325.)
J.J.H.

Canton (Ohio) **Mennonite Church** (GCM), now extinct. About 1856 Michael J. Kreibuill came to this community from Alsace with other settlers, who began services among themselves. The first meeting was at the John Sommers' home, north of the city. Later services were held in the Jacob Kreibuill barn, near Maximo, about twelve miles northeast of the city. These services were held about two or three times per year, lasting two or three days at a time, on occasions when General Conference ministers came into the community.

The group was organized into a congregation about 1893, with an Oberlin student as part-time pastor. H. P. Krehbiel, also an Oberlin student from Kansas, was then called to serve as pastor until 1898. Services were conducted during this time in the Rowland Mennonite Church every two weeks, alternating with the (old) Mennonites. An attempt was made about this time to purchase an abandoned church building and to move it to the eastern part of the city. Some difficulties arose concerning this project which resulted in differences of opinion which caused some of the group to withdraw. After 1898 special services were held only occasionally, when visiting ministers came into the community. The remaining members transferred their membership to the church at Wadsworth, Ohio, and to the newly organized Canton Mennonite Mission (*q.v.*) of the Mennonite Church (MC). A few of these people still live in the community and attend the Wadsworth Church for special services and communion. (See J. S. Umble, *Ohio Mennonite Sunday Schools,* Goshen, 1941.) J.J.H.

Canton Mennonite Mission: see **Canton** (Ohio) **First** Mennonite Church.

Cantonment, a Mennonite mission (GCM) among the Cheyenne Indians, located on the North Canada River, a few miles north of Canton, Okla. The "Cantonment" once housed a division of cavalry, stationed here to guard the Cheyennes. On Oct. 2, 1882, the empty buildings of the cantonment were turned over to the mission to be used as a school. Today it consists only of a few government buildings, residences of officials, and two small mission buildings.

The mission school was opened in 1883 by S. S. Haury (*q.v.*) and continued until 1901 under the leadership of a number of missionary teachers. When it was abandoned because a new large government school was established near by it was decided to station a missionary in Cantonment. Rodolphe Petter (*q.v.*) and his wife, both natives of Switzerland, accepted this task, reduced the language to writing, and translated parts of the Bible. A chapel was built for regular worship services.

Since Cantonment was for a while also an Arapahoe center, in 1897 A. Funk was appointed to this place to work among them. But the Arapahoes (*q.v.*) were moving south; so it was decided to move their missionary with them, and Cantonment once more became a center only for Cheyenne mission work. At the request of Chief Oechowo, a subsidiary station was opened about ten miles from Cantonment to better serve the field, which extended 30 miles to the west. This station, named Fonda (*q.v.*), consisted of a chapel, a small frame house for the use of the missionary when he was there, and a small dwelling for the Indian assistant.

The Cantonment station had about 600 Indians, who, however, lived widely scattered. Of these, 114 had been received into the church by baptism by about 1915.

Government officials often came to Cantonment to look after the economic and physical welfare of the Indians, but because they had short terms they did not become personally acquainted with the Indians and did not understand their language. Therefore Indians came to the mission every day with all sorts of matters for advice and help. This practical help was always combined with spiritual aid.

After the Petters were transferred to work among the Cheyennes in Montana, the Albert Claassens, Bertha Kinsinger (later Mrs. Petter), and Agnes W. Williams worked here from 1914 to 1917. The G. A. Linscheids served at Cantonment from 1920 until the fall of 1938, when they were succeeded by the Benno Toews. They continued until the spring of 1940, when the Arthur Friesens became their successors. On April 19, 1947, they transferred to Clinton. The Alfred Wiebes then came to take over the responsibility for Canton, Longdale, and Fonda, and are still serving there.

Since the Indian population drifted away from Cantonment the old church there was razed and its material used in 1926 to build a new church at Longdale (*q.v.*), across the river. Work at Fonda continued with a meeting in Cheyenne each Sunday. The government school at Fonda was closed in 1927 (?); the work has continued there, as well as at Longdale and Canton to the present.

In Theodor Fontane's novel *Quitt* (Berlin, 1891) the scene of the second part is the Cantonment Mennonite Mission. R.P., Wi.K.

H. P. Krehbiel, *The Hist. of the Gen. Conference of the Menn. of N. A.* (Canton, 1898) 282-343; E. G. Kaufman, *The Development of the Missionary and Philanthropic Interest Among the Menn. of N. A.* (Berne, 1931) 103-10 and 135-51; A. Zieglschmid, "Truth and Fiction and Mennonites in . . . *Quitt,*" *MQR* XVI (1942) 223-46; E. Correll in *ML* I, 661, 325.

Canu, Robbert Robbertsz: see **Robbertsz, Robbert.**

Capasin, Sask., located about 150 miles northwest of Rosthern, is a small district of the Rosenort Mennonite Church with its seat in Rosthern, Sask., between the North and South Saskatchewan rivers. The Rosenort Church has about a dozen districts and about 1,500 members. Capasin is the district farthest from Rosthern and is the only district on the left side of the North Saskatchewan River. In 1952 this district had 37 church members and 37 children. J.G.R.

Cape Chin (Ont.) United Missionary Church, Ontario Conference, is located on the Bruce Peninsula. The church was dedicated on May 23, 1937, services having previously been held in the Hays' schoolhouse. In 1951 there were 30 members, the pastor being Clinton Bell. E.R.S.

Capeland Mennonite Church (GCM) is a small country congregation with its meeting place two miles west of Main Centre, Sask. It was originally a part of the Herbert General Conference Mennonite Church, but because it wished to practice both forms of baptism, i.e., pouring and also immersing, it was organized separately under the leadership of John J. Nickel on Oct. 2, 1940. In 1941 the congregation was received into the membership of the General Conference of Mennonites of North America, and in 1943 into the Canadian District Conference. The membership at present (1952) is 29, and is under the lay leadership of Anton E. Nickel.

J.W.N.

Capilla del Monte (Argentina) Mennonite Church (MC) is located in Capilla del Monte, a town of approximately 5,000 inhabitants, situated in the heart of the Cordoba hills in the province of Cordoba. In 1935 D. P. Lantz and wife visited the town, distributed tracts and Gospel literature, and made some personal contacts. By 1941 the Argentine Mission decided to rent a room, where weekly meetings were then held. The Calvin Holdermans also co-operated in 1941. In 1942 the Argentine pastor Pablo Cavadore with his wife moved to this town. In due time a chapel and pastoral residence were constructed. Although there have been times of spiritual quickening, the 1952 membership was only 10.

N.L.

Capito, Wolfgang, reformer of Strasbourg, b. 1478 at Hagenau, son of the respected councilor Johann Köpfel, studied at the universities of Ingolstadt, Freiburg, and Basel, first medicine, then jurisprudence, and later theology, and in 1512 was made cathedral preacher at Bruchsal on the recommendation of Philip von Rosenberg, Bishop of Speyer. Here he became a friend of Melanchthon. In 1515 he was made cathedral preacher at Basel, in 1519 chaplain to the Archbishop of Mainz, and in 1523 provost at the church of St. Thomas in Strasbourg, where he turned his energy to the Reformation. With Caspar Hedio and Matthias Zell (*q.v.*), and especially Martin Bucer (*q.v.*) he worked with unflagging zeal for the Protestant cause until his death by the plague in 1541.

Of all the reformers Capito was nearest the Anabaptists. He was the close friend of several of them. In general he judged them favorably, and "asserts that he regarded most of them as God's elect, gifted with the fear of the Lord, and some also as steadfast confessors of the glory of God, yea, loved them as dear brethren." For a time it seemed that he might step completely over to their side and become their mighty leader; but this did not happen. We shall present first his theological position as revealed principally in his commentary on Hosea, and then his relation to the Anabaptists separately.

Capito opposed infant baptism. To him (as to Denk) the sacraments are only outward ceremonies, symbolic acts; as such they do not belong to Christ's kingdom; for this is within us and is nothing but righteousness, peace, and joy in the Holy Ghost. Just as little may the sacraments be thought of as a means of gathering and preserving the church. The generating, ruling, and preserving power of the church is rather the Spirit, who as a gift of God simply comes down from above; the sacraments are merely symbols of the life of the Spirit already present in the believer. Baptism is actually a confession of the faith dawning upon us and a declaration of the determination to kill the flesh and follow the leading of the Spirit. From this the inadmissibility of infant baptism follows. In this conception of baptism and the ordinances Capito touched the Anabaptist position most closely. To be sure, he repudiated rebaptism. The wish of the Anabaptists in this respect he called a clinging to the vain elements of the world. "Those are farthest from the kingdom of God, who today are working with all their might to have baptism repeated after hearing the Word" (*Hosea,* 33 B and 34 A). He favored accepting infant baptism as a practical measure (Capito, *Kinderbericht,* 1529, 30 A; Hulshof, 71, and Usteri, 463 ff.).

The Scriptures are to Capito the Word of God as the work of the Holy Spirit who has spoken through men; but the outer Word is only a dead letter, which one must guard against idolizing. It is only a witness of the truth, not the actual and highest source of the understanding of the things of God. This source is God Himself and His Spirit. We have the true teacher within us, the Spirit of truth, who instructs in the stillness of the heart. Through Him we have the law of God written in our hearts, which is the only way to know Him. True faith then is not based on the word of Scripture, but on the inner, living word of God, that light of the soul which illuminates us.—The object of the outer Word in Scripture and preaching is to remind us of God's works and thereby awaken our spirit and implant faith in us. In addition we have in the Scriptures a touchstone for all that seeks to be regarded as Christian truth and divine revelation, not only for every false doctrine, but also for the inspirations we receive within ourselves; for great caution is needed lest we accept human inventions instead of the divine, or consider that to be the will of the Lord which only our ungodly flesh substitutes for it. It is therefore necessary to compare with the Scriptures all that particularly moves and pleases us; they are the most dependable guide, by which we put in order our wrong emotions; i.e., by which we are to prove their solution only in the spirit.

It is clear that Capito expressed ideas that recurred in the writings of Denk (*q.v.*) and other Anabaptists in his position on the Scriptures, when he contrasted the dead letter with the Spirit and subordinated the former to the latter, distinguishing between the outer word and a living, inner word, when he did not rank the Bible as the supreme source of revelation but as a witness, since the knowledge of God has its basis in the spirit and makes itself known in all the works of God, when he often speaks of the anointing perceived within the heart. Note also his statements about the apparent contradictions in the Bible, which find their solution only in the spirit.

Capito's chiliasm is also closely allied to the Anabaptist concept. He distinguished three periods in the era of the exalted Christ: (1) the apostolic age, (2) the reign of Antichrist, and (3) the age of Christ's absolute reign on earth after the fall of the man of sin. The third period is divided into beginning, progress, and fulfillment. The beginning is the Reformation period; the impending severe persecutions of its adherents Capito takes for sure proof that salvation has come near. Pure and simple preaching of the Gospel will bring about the victory of Christ, who will immediately, as King of Glory, take upon Himself the power over all things. In addition the heathen throngs will be converted and all Israel will be saved. This perfect reign of Christ will be followed by eternal glory and the resurrection of all the saints. At first Capito interprets the millennium as a spiritual reign of the perfect knowledge of God and brotherly love. All outward things, including baptism and communion, will be done away; Christ will be all in all through His spirit. But this spiritual glory of the perfected kingdom of God will be clearly reflected in human relationships as well; it will be a universal reign of peace. No race will lift the sword again against another. There will be no need of temporal kings. The Jews will occupy a favored position; the prophets have foretold this. Denk made similar assertions. Yet in all these points Capito was materially influenced by Cellarius; this is especially the case in his position on the doctrine of election.

Capito held that there are two classes of men, elect and rejected, or vessels of mercy whom God has determined from eternity to eternity for blessedness, and vessels of wrath whom He has prepared for destruction. The only basis for this contrast is the free, eternal, and unchangeable decree of God. The former have implanted within them from birth a seed of piety, a religious and moral inclination to the good, whereas the others carry within them the seed of vice (Heberle, 297-306). He denied all freedom of the will: "Freedom of the will is the worst plague of true religion."

Even more definitely Capito attacks the Anabaptists when he speaks of the separation of believers from unbelievers; he will grant only spiritual separation. The individual must not fraternize with their teachings or with obvious sinners; but this avoidance shall never become a public matter or lead to excommunication. Furthermore he attacks the Anabaptist rejection of warfare and demands obedience to the government when it calls its subjects to defend the nation. Christ's teaching that we shall resist evil is meant only for the individual Christian. It is the duty of the government to defend the helpless, and the duty of the individual to support the government. He vigorously attacks the repudiation of the oath, calling the oath an act of worship. Christ did not repeal the law or make a law, but re-established divine law in its original purity; by their refusal to render the oath the Anabaptists are trying to overthrow the basis of morality under the pretext of piety. To refuse the oath offends the public peace, the legal order instituted by the Lord, and, most important of all, brotherly love. Finally Capito condemns the Anabaptist position on rejection of the preaching office and the practice of lay preaching. All this makes it quite clear that, after all, Capito was far removed from Anabaptism.

When Capito had been in Strasbourg scarcely a year he came in contact with the beginnings of the

34

Anabaptist movement. Late in 1524 Carlstadt (*q.v.*) had come to Strasbourg for a short time, and his writings advocating the rejection of infant baptism had been distributed in the city. Thus the attention of the Strasbourg clergy was directed to this important question. Capito wrote to Zwingli on Dec. 31, 1524, that he would give the question of infant baptism more thought; he feared that many would be misled by ruinous doctrines in writings he had not yet seen. He made a similar statement in a letter to Bugenhagen on Oct. 8, 1525, reporting also, "A preacher from Waldshut appeared here, who proclaimed the need of rebaptism. Persons who were not baptized anew were condemned, as though salvation were bound to the element of water." He apparently did not come in personal contact with Balthasar Hubmaier (*q.v.*), the preacher referred to, who spent a short time in Strasbourg in 1525, but he felt the influence of this energetic Anabaptist leader. On Feb. 6, 1526, he lamented in a letter to Zwingli that many in the city were no longer having their children baptized.

Soon after this, Capito made his first personal acquaintance with an Anabaptist. It was Wilhelm Reublin (*q.v.*), who came to Strasbourg in March 1526, and with whom he disputed in his home on the matter of baptism. When Reublin then circulated the report (letter of Capito to Zwingli, April 6, 1526) that the clergy had espoused Anabaptism, and did not venture to advocate it only out of fear of temporal force, he was three times challenged to a disputation on baptism. He declined because he did not think it necessary; nor did he consent to a public disputation, but left the city, perhaps on the advice of Matthäus Zell, who knew nothing about the plan for a public disputation. On the whole Reublin seems to have made a favorable impression on Capito. Capito called him "a pious man of upright appearance" (Hulshof, 10).

Capito had unpleasant experiences with the Anabaptist Hans Wolf (*q.v.*) of Benfeld, who was obviously a fanatic, and preached that the world would be destroyed in seven years at the stroke of twelve on Ascension Day. Capito took him into his house several days to change his views, but Wolf became all the bolder in attacking the clergy and was therefore sent back to Benfeld on July 30, 1526, on a threat of death if he again annoyed the clergy of Strasbourg (letters to Zwingli May 16 and June 11, 1526; see also Hulshof's correction of Gerbert's account 14-18). Now Capito hoped that Anabaptism had disappeared from the city (letter to Zwingli Sept. 30, 1526), but it was a false hope.

A few weeks later the three Anabaptist leaders, Haetzer (*q.v.*), Denk, and Sattler (*q.v.*), came to Strasbourg. Haetzer apparently came first. Capito received him in his home. They had perhaps been friends as students at Freiburg; and Capito respected Haetzer's learning. Haetzer at first avoided all contact with the Anabaptists, working in seclusion on his translation of Isaiah, perhaps aided by Capito, until he received better help from Hans Denk. Haetzer was, however, soon expelled from the city (the elaboration of the affair by Gerbert, 45 ff., is based on a false evaluation of Haetzer), and it was his opinion that Capito had shown him the door to avoid embarrassment.

Nor was Capito able to be friends with Hans Denk. Before Denk's appearance he had considered the Anabaptists "perverted, eccentric persons, puffed up with vanities, but otherwise quite harmless" (letter of June 11, 1526, to Zwingli), but after Denk's brief influence he saw in them a perilous threat to the evangelical cause in the city (letter to Zwingli, Dec. 26, 1526). Before he had become personally acquainted with him he agreed with the general unfavorable opinion of him (letter to Zwingli, Dec. 10, 1526), calling him a sly and variable man, who brashly and insolently slanders all the preachers everywhere (which Keller repeats erroneously on p. 156); but after listening to Denk's disputation with Bucer, Capito praised Denk's morally clean life, the dexterity of his mind, and his attractive personality (letter of Dec. 26, 1526; Hulshof, 26). But Capito was particularly offended by Denk's doctrine of the atonement. In the letter of Dec. 26 he said, "Denk has most artfully presented the contents of his book (*Vom Gesetz Gottes*); once he affirmed, and then he denied; then he again yielded and with remarkable skill he sought all sorts of loopholes. Meanwhile we were satisfied to hear his admission that he agreed with us on the main points, whereas he is actually far removed from us." In the letter of Dec. 10 he said, "I do not understand the spirit of such people. I only know that they are not of God, they, who take away from us the center of Christianity, and do not even leave us our trust in Christ's suffering." In Denk he saw a "complete repudiation of the doctrine of faith" and expressed his satisfaction in seeing him banished from the city.

But toward Michael Sattler Capito developed a warm friendliness, and also received him into his home. Sattler's genuine piety and Biblicism won his complete sympathy. When the Anabaptists were imprisoned after Denk's expulsion, Sattler was permitted to remain free at the instance of Bucer and Capito. But he was too honest to endure freedom while his brethren suffered imprisonment. "He could not stay without great blasphemy," he said in his beautiful letter of farewell to the reformers (see **Bucer**) and left the city. He requested a disputation with Bucer and Capito before leaving, in order to prove his faith from the Scriptures. His request was granted and the disputation was conducted in a friendly spirit with a brotherly exchange of ideas. Then he parted from them. Several months later he suffered a most terrible martyr's death in Rottenburg a.N.

Capito was shocked by the news of Sattler's execution. He wrote a long letter to the council of Horb, where several of Sattler's fellow believers still lay in prison, warmly commending them. "Blasphemers may of course be punished; but Michael Sattler and his adherents could not be suspected of this; for they are not blasphemers, as far as we know, unless one regards as blasphemy the fact that these poor people have resolved to avoid the luxury of playing, drinking, gluttony, adultery, warfare, killing, slander, and carnal lusts

and to flee what is worldly and carnal" (Hulshof, 66). Also a letter of consolation, "To my dear brethren and sisters, who are now witnessing for Christ the Crucified in their bodies by imprisonment and suffering in Horb," is said by Heberle to have been written by Capito (Heberle, 309). The original is in the Basel church archives (Baum, 375, and Hulshof, 67). It is signed, "A faithful brother and partaker of your hope in the Lord, whose name is known to God."

Of special interest is Hulshof's assertion (p. 62) that on the same day Capito composed his statement entitled "Whether the Anabaptists Endure Death Because of Piety or Fanaticism" (ms. in Basel Church Archives; Röhrich, 39). There is a document identical with it in Simmler's collection of letters in the Zürich state archives, entitled "Capitos Fürsprache für die Wiedertäufer, 31. Mai 1527." Hence Röhrich and others are in error in dating Capito's statement 1528. Together with the letter to Horb already mentioned, it is an extraordinarily beautiful proof of Capito's genuinely evangelical, tolerant mind, not found in the other reformers.

After Denk's expulsion and Sattler's departure Capito hoped that his struggle with the Anabaptists was over (letter to Zwingli, Jan. 22, 1527), but he was mistaken. He was to become much more intimately connected with them. Their resistance was, of course, broken. "The Anabaptists have not entirely ceased, but neither are they a threat," he wrote to Zwingli on Feb. 28, 1527. "We must just pay more attention to the simple in the future." There was no trace (said he) of a revolt, for a rumor had spread that the exiling of Denk threatened to bring about a revolt in the city (Keller, 165). But Capito became more and more worried about the activity of the Anabaptists in Strasbourg. "They are increasing in great numbers," he writes to Zwingli on April 8, 1527, "instructed in very poor articles of faith. One of our chief worries about them is that they will destroy respect for the Word. I would never have surmised what we are now experiencing. It is the severest trial of the Lord." On July 7, 1527, he reports to Zwingli, "The Anabaptists cause us great distress." In a letter to Zwingli of Nov. 7, 1527, he complains still more bitterly about the growth of the Anabaptists: "Daily their number increases, and they keep introducing new ideas which have not the least connection with the glory of God. I regret that so many good people are enmeshed in the affair."

In the meantime Capito's religious views had been approaching those of the Anabaptists, chiefly under the influence of Cellarius (*q.v.*). On Aug. 18, 1527, Capito reports to Zwingli the debate held between Cellarius and Denk in the presence of Haetzer in December 1526: "By his modest dignity Cellarius won Denk so completely to his side that he agreed in all points; he also threw light on Denk's book on the freedom of the will by way of apostolic ideas, so that Denk solemnly assured him that everything was now completely arranged" (Gerbert, 34; Hulshof, 39; Keller, 159, who takes a different view of this passage in the letter). These statements show Capito's pronounced bias in favor of Cellarius, whose influence on Capito continued to increase. In July 1527 he wrote the foreword to Cellarius' book, *De operibus dei,* warmly recommending it. Bucer and Zwingli were astonished. Scarcely a year later (April 1528) Capito's commentary on Hosea was published, in which he presented the views already mentioned, which are in part very close to those of the Anabaptists. Alarmed, Bucer asked Zwingli and Oecolampadius for help in releasing Capito from this influence. This plan succeeded. Very cleverly Zwingli addressed a letter to both Capito and Bucer on June 16, 1528, which produced the effect desired; i.e., Capito took a more reserved attitude toward Cellarius and the Anabaptists. O. E. Strasser writes in *Capitos Beziehungen zu Bern* (Leipzig, 1928), 31 f.: "As a silent observer Capito must have attended the entire colloquy at Bern on Jan. 6, 1528. The thing that filled him most in this entire period he probably shows us himself in his commentary on Hosea, at the place where he recalls the Bern disputation (in *Hoseam* 270b), by his mention of only the act of amnesty toward some Anabaptists. This incident seems to have moved him most, an incident that is not even mentioned in the official records. In this matter Capito grows warm. Forgetting restraint, he betrays, as he had already done by his characteristic participation in the debate when it concerned the Spirit, what occupied Capito during the Bern disputation which was to be of such great significance to the Swiss and South German Reformation; i.e., it was the Anabaptist concept. Capito lived in Anabaptism at that time. . . ."

Of great significance to us is this passage from the letter of justification he wrote to Zwingli on July 31, 1528: "I make a clear distinction among the Anabaptists. There are among them principals and leaders, whom they themselves call 'Vorsteher'; all of these avoid me as the mouse does the cat; I cannot bear them; for all of them, as many as I have seen, are full of secret intrigues and craftiness. There are others who are distinguished by an admirable simplicity of spirit, who are injured by the error they cling to. If one deals gently with these and gives them time, they come toward our side. I do not reject these unless after long treatment I have found them obstinate. . . ."

In two other letters Capito wrote in a similar vein. He wrote one on Sept. 13, 1528, to Ambrosius Blaurer: "Among the Anabaptists I have found excellent souls, receptive to true piety, who can by your kindness be led back to the fold of Christ from which they have thoughtlessly strayed through ignorance and lack of understanding of Christ and His kingdom. In addition there are also many among them who are filled not only with errors but also with malevolent intentions, and plan agitation and revolt, and that by means of a reestablishment of the Mosaic law. . . ."

Of interest is Capito's correctly recognized and consistently maintained distinction between the quiet and the revolutionary Anabaptists.

In the second letter, written to Musculus on April 17, 1530 (Hulshof, 72, 127; Baum dates it 1533,

Gerbert probably correctly 1528), Capito objected to Bucer's violent procedure in dealing with the Anabaptists. He says: "I am in absolute agreement with your treating these poor people with pity and kindness herein; you have my complete and entire consent; for the harm they do is not serious. I am constantly shocked by the ruthless procedure of my brethren against them. . . .

"Bucer is urging a government command on infant baptism, which I at present do not wish to abolish. But I do not want to block him, only he must count me out; for I know very well that the supports produced for infant baptism have no convincing power." Here Capito once more urged the exercise of gentleness and consideration toward the Anabaptists and leaving the judgment to God.

Capito's lenient attitude was carried out in his deeds. In the numerous examinations of Anabaptists during 1528 Capito took pains to change their opinions by kind encouragement. He made an especial attempt to gain their consent to giving the customary constitutional oath which was required every January. He reports his success in a letter to the bailiff Nikolaus Kniebiss (Röhrich, 42): "He presented their error to them; if they referred to Matt. 5 he pointed out that this passage was directed against the Pharisees who swore falsely. . . ."

He also treated Pilgram Marpeck (*q.v.*) benevolently. He had a conversation with him before he was imprisoned. "But it did not take effect." During his confinement Capito visited him and encouraged him. Not until Capito left the city for an extended journey was Marpeck expelled from the city. It can be assumed that Capito protected him. It must also be mentioned that Capito gave Caspar Schwenckfeld (*q.v.*) board and lodging in his home for two years, and that in the summer of 1531 he received Bernhard Rothmann (*q.v.*) and Michael Servetus as guests. Nothing shows more clearly than this his liberal attitude, even though these men were not yet so notorious as heretics as they were later.

About 1533 Capito's attitude toward the Anabaptists underwent a definite change, and now he sided completely with Bucer. This came about as the result of an extended journey through Switzerland and South Germany from December 1531 to April 1532, made on the insistent urging of Bucer. One object was to relieve Capito of the melancholia that overtook him after a serious illness in 1529 and especially after the death of his wife (1531) and Zwingli; he also wished to divert Capito from his intention to marry the widow of Augustin Bader (*q.v.*) (see Capito's letters to Vadian, Sept. 18 and Oct. 10, 1531) in order to have him marry the widow of Oecolampadius, who had died on Nov. 21, 1531. Both aims were accomplished. Capito returned a different man. The friendly reception he enjoyed everywhere, the success of his endeavors for unification, had won him completely for his church. In April 1532 he married the widow of Oecolampadius.

From this time on his attitude toward the Anabaptists and all who stood aloof from his church is changed. With great satisfaction Bucer wrote to

Ambrosius Blaurer (Oct. 11 and Nov. 16, 1532), "Capito is entirely one of us, had it only been always thus." In his letter to Musculus (Nov. 23, 1532) Bucer wrote, "At first Capito was too lenient, now he is determined and severe enough." Whereas he had formerly called Schwenckfeld his dear brother, he cannot now do enough to warn others of this sectarian (Gerbert, 189). He favored the application of sterner measures against Melchior Hofmann (*q.v.*) and his adherents.

Capito's altered frame of mind is clearly set forth in a popular pamphlet, *Eine wunderbare Geschichte und ernstliche Warnung Gottes, so auch an ein Wiedertäufer, genannt Claus Frey, zugetragen hat, . . .* (1534) (see Röhrich, 80-99). He knows nothing good to say about the Anabaptists any more. Their piety and virtue are only outward show, of which he warns his people. He sees all mischief in separation from the church; he uses the unfortunate aberrations of a man who was living in common law marriage to paint in the darkest colors how far astray separation leads. Whereas he had previously praised the courage of martyred Anabaptists (especially in his *Apologie,* 1527), he now designates it as the work of the devil. "It is the manner of heretics, especially because they have no Scriptural foundation, to prove their deception with a defiant death (Röhrich, 94). The devil can also strengthen the heart out of desperation!" (Röhrich, 92). In conclusion he enumerates all the shameful deeds of the Anabaptists, how they are intent upon "slaying all priests, monks, princes, noblemen, citizens, and peasants, be they Catholic, Lutheran, or Zwinglian. Innumerable terrible plans of this kind are concealed under the sourfaced looks and highly spiritual conversation.— May God preserve all the goodhearted from going astray and from self-directed planning, especially in matters of faith, so that they may continue to come to the true knowledge in and through the church of Christ."

And yet this very man had once given the excellent and true testimony to the Anabaptist movement: "Meanwhile a great benefit flows from their rise to all the churches—the people are more careful, the leaders are more alert, and all offices are better provided for. Where Christ has not yet been preached, there one is of course safe from such a plague; but the people suffer from a much more serious evil, namely, a lack of God's Word."

However near Capito was in many respects to the Anabaptist position, he was still far from being one. For a time, it is certain, he surpassed all his contemporaries in correct and clear understanding, generous tolerance, and benevolent judgment of the Anabaptists.

(Concerning Capito's relation to Anabaptism see also his letter to Michael Keller of May 17, 1528, in *Archiv für Ref.-Gesch.,* 1937, 157-59. Capito's inner and outer turning away from the Anabaptists toward the Strasburg church system is described by Fr. Thudichun in *Die Deutsche Reformation 1517-1537* II, Leipzig, 1909, 619-20.)   Neff.

J. Baum, *Capito und Butzer* (Eberfeld, 1860); C. Gerbert, *Gesch. der Strassburger Sektenbewegung* (Stras-

bourg, 1889); J. Heberle, "Capitos Verhältnis zum Anabaptismus," in *Ztscht f. d. hist. Theol.,* 1857, 285 ff.; A. Hulshof, *Gesch. van de Doopsgezinden te Straatsburg van 1525 tot 1557* (Amsterdam, 1905); L. Keller, *Ein Apostel der Wiedertäufer* (Leipzig, 1882) 148 ff.; T. W. Röhrich, "Zur Gesch. der Strassburger Wiedertäufer 1527-1543," in *Ztscht f. d. hist. Theol.* (1860); J. Usteri, *Die Stellung der Strassburger Reformatoren Butzer und Capito zur Tauffrage* (1884) 456 ff.; *HRE* III, 715 ff.; *ML* I, 326-33.

Cardinaal, a Dutch Mennonite family descending from Nen Jansz, who lived at Zaandam or Westzaan about 1500. Hendrick Hendricksz Cardinaal (1644-1702), shipbuilder and lumber dealer at Zaandam, was a friend of Czar Peter of Russia, who lived for some time at Zaandam. His son Jacob Hendriksz Cardinaal (1682-1735), a wealthy shipbuilder and lumber merchant, owner of an oil-mill and whaling boats which hunted near Greenland, served the Zaandam Mennonite congregation of the *Nieuwe Huys* as deacon from 1726 until his death in 1735, as did his grandson Cornelis Cardinaal from 1778 until his death in 1804.

Only one member of this Cornelis Cardinaal (see below) went into the ministry. The two sons of this Cornelis Cardinaal, Cornelis (1833-97) and Pieter (1834-89), living at Almelo, started a linen business; about 1855 they founded a steam-powered weaving mill, in 1870 also a spinning mill (*Almelosche Stoomspinnerij*). (*Ned. Partriciaat* VIII, 95-102; X, 168-69.)   vDZ.

Cardinaal Jr., Cornelis, a Dutch Mennonite minister, son of Cornelis Cardinaal and Anna Ris, b. Jan. 8, 1808, at West-Zaandam, d. Jan. 8, 1890, at Almelo, married to Sara Alida van Gelder (1807-54) of Wormerveer. Cardinaal studied at the University and the Mennonite Theological Seminary of Amsterdam, became a ministerial candidate in 1831, and served the congregations of Wormer and Jisp 1832-34, Warga 1834-38, and Almelo 1838-73. He published *Leerrede over Jacobus 4. 14 a* (Almelo, 1868); *En vijftal schetsen uit de oude doos* (Almelo, 1881); *Eene vertelling van grootvader voor zijn kleinzoon* (Almelo, 1884). (Van Alphen, *Nieuwkerk. Handb.,* 1889, Supplement, p. 23; 1891, Supplement CXLI; *ML* I, 333.)   J.L.

CARE. The Co-operative for American Remittances to Europe, universally known as CARE, was conceived for the purpose of making available to American individuals and organizations for foreign relief the vast stores of surplus army rations following World War II. It was organized by the leading American relief groups to render a nonprofit, safe, personalized, packaged relief service with delivery to specific recipients guaranteed. This plan found such wide acceptance that upon the exhaustion of army rations, CARE developed its own food and textile packages. Its area of service later included books and enveloped Asia, making CARE the leading relief organization arising out of the postwar period.

The Mennonite Central Committee was a charter member of CARE and was represented on its Board of Directors until July 1954. The Mennonite constituency purchased over $360,000 worth of CARE packages in the first four years. During the same period the MCC benefited by $80,000 through CARE's surplus and general relief distribution.

J.N.W.

Carel van Mander (Vermander): see **Mander, Carel van.**

Carel (Caerle) **Thys,** an Anabaptist martyr, was burned at the stake at Antwerp on March 14, 1570, together with Hans Kuene (*q.v.*), because he had been rebaptized. (*Antw. Arch.-Bl.* XII, 445, 453; XIV, 72-73, No. 802.)

vDZ.

Carel van Tiegem (Thiegem), an Anabaptist martyr, b. at Kortrijk (Courtrai) in Flanders, and died at the stake there, Dec. 20, 1550 (*Mart. Mir.* incorrectly, 1559). He had formerly been a shoemaker, but at the time of his arrest he was a weaver. His goods were confiscated. During the execution a special guard was set up, because the magistrates feared a popular uprising. (*Mart. Mir.* D 242, E 617; Verheyden, *Courtrai-Bruxelles* 35, No. 11.)

vDZ.

Carinthia (Kärnten), a province of Austria (area 4,460 sq. mi.; pop. 474,000). Long after the Anabaptist movement had reached the other parts of Austria, it came also to Carinthia; but its spread here was less extensive than in Tirol (*q.v.*) or elsewhere. There is only sparse information regarding the Carinthian Anabaptists of the early 1520's. Any strong propaganda for the movement was made as difficult here as in Styria (*q.v.*), mainly because the Protestant estates zealously prevented its penetration into this duchy, and thus aided the (Catholic) Habsburg government. But it seems very probable that there were a large number of Anabaptists there, for the general mandates and other orders against Anabaptists, issued in Lower and Upper Austria, were also published in Carinthia.

It may be assumed that the Anabaptist movement entered Carinthia from the Pustertal (*q.v.*) of the Tirol in the late 1520's. The chronicles of 1531 state that Brother Balthasar Mayer, a cooper and preacher at Wolfsberg in Carinthia, was one of three seized and beheaded there. "All of them testified to the truth with their blood." Unfortunately there is no indication as to whether Mayer had been preaching at Wolfsberg for some time, or had been merely passing through when seized.

Special regulations to stop the spread of the movement in Carinthia were issued in the 1530's. A mandate of King Ferdinand I issued to the governor Veit Weltzer on May 7, 1532, and the orders sent out by Weltzer to all the authorities of Carinthia to track down the Anabaptists, to take them prisoner, and to punish them in accord with the orders issued for all five countries of Inner Austria (the two Austrias, Styria, Carinthia, and Carniola), show that the Anabaptist movement had taken firm roots in Carinthia, too. Three years later the government had the mandate of Ferdinand I against the spread of "the new deceptive sects" of Feb. 15, 1535, also published in Carinthia. It is very probable that here as in Styria the older general mandates were frequently repeated, in order to ferret out the Anabaptists. Since the situation in Carinthia was not different from that in Styria,

we refer to an opinion that the Styrian vicegerent Michael Meixner delivered in 1537: "For forty years church and government have been failing, to the advantage of the Anabaptists and other sects."

But even though there were Anabaptists in Carinthia, their teaching had not taken such deep roots as in Tirol. In the next few years only isolated references to Anabaptists are found. On April 16, 1538, two brothers, Matthäus Peckh and Jakob Tanferer, recanted before Vice-regent Francis of Tannhausen and were pardoned. On Wednesday before Christmas 1538 Hans Seidl (*q.v.*) of Murau and Hans Donner (*q.v.*) of Wels were seized and soon afterwards put to death.

In St. Veit, the former capital, a strong movement for ecclesiastical reform was apparently in progress. Book dealers who sold "heretical" books in this line were given prison sentences. The county clerk Hans Knysler sent a report to the king, inquiring what should be done with the Anabaptists and their books. Friends of the new movement were found even among the city councilors. In Villach Anabaptist activities are also reported.

The most outstanding of the Carinthian Anabaptists was Antoni Erfordter (*q.v.*), whose farewell letter, the *Urlaubsbrief* of 1538, deserves particular attention. It is a sermon calling to repentance from the immorality and spiritual poverty of his contemporaries. In lurid colors he portrays the soil in which Anabaptism tries to take root. "Don't be surprised that scarcely two God-fearing men can be found here in Klagenfurt, St. Veit, and Völkermarkt, indeed perhaps in the entire country." That is why he cannot bear any longer to remain in Carinthia. He went to Moravia where he was made *Diener des Wortes*. In 1541 he died; it is uncertain whether at Schäkwitz or at Pausram near Auspitz, where the largest brotherhoods were located.

It is known that in 1540 Anabaptism was still active in Carinthia. From a letter of that year by Hans Amon (*q.v.*), who succeeded Jakob Hutter (*q.v.*) as head of the entire brotherhood, we learn that Lamprecht Kreutztaler and Kaspar Schmidt were working for the Lord in Carinthia, and that also Michel Schneider and Hänsel Coll were in their home town in that country.

The Anabaptists had a strong brotherhood in Ortenburg led by Michael Madschidl or Kleinmichel (*q.v.*). The chronicles relate that he was seized in Ortenburg with his wife and a cobbler named Hans Gurtzham (*q.v.*). A deacon and the parson of Villach put forth much effort to convert them, but were worsted by the superior Biblical knowledge of the defendants. The prisoners were then taken in chains to Oberdrauburg via Spittal, and on across Styria to Vienna. In prison they met Hans Staudach (*q.v.*) and three other brethren, "who were led to the slaughter after St. Matthew's day. . . . They were firm as a stone wall." Gurtzham commemorated their death in a song. Madschidl, in prison, remained true to his faith. He wrote to the brotherhood in Moravia that they would continue to be true to the Lord until death.

But he was destined to have a peaceful end. Three years after his imprisonment a fire broke out in Vienna. During the tumult he escaped with his Liesel through "the providence of God" and the aid of a citizen, and reached the church in Moravia. After another year in prison Gurtzham was drowned in the Danube on June 27, 1550. Madschidl died as an "elder of the church and an apostle of Jesus Christ and of the church after suffering much tribulation and imprisonment" in 1553 at Altenmarkt in Moravia. A summary list of martyrs of later origin lists ten Anabaptists executed in Carinthia: seven at St. Veit and three at Wolfberg.

After the 1550's little is heard of Anabaptists in Carinthia or in the other two cantons of inner Austria. The religious peace of Augsburg of 1555 had recognized the right of only one Protestant church in the Holy Roman Empire, namely, the Lutheran, which then dominated political and military affairs. Though they were themselves merely tolerated in Austria, yet they considered it their duty to keep all other Protestant branches out of the country. In this they co-operated with the Catholics. Hence no Calvinist, and no member of the numerous Protestant sects was tolerated any longer.   LOSERTH, R.F.

J. Beck, "Ein Beitrag zur Geschichte der Wiedertäufer in Kärnten," in *Archiv des histor. Vereins für Kärnten;* J. Loserth, "The Anabaptists in Carinthia," *MQR* XXI (1947) 235-47; concerning Erfordter's *Urlaubsbrief* see bibliography on *"Erfordter";* *ML* II, 465-68.

Carinthian Exiles. Nearly two full centuries after the Counter Reformation had begun its work in Austria, catholicizing by compulsion a country which by 1550 had been predominantly Protestant, a reaction broke out in Carinthia. It led to renewed emigration by citizens and peasants, who were not willing to give up their Protestant faith, and were ready to suffer much hardship for the sake of this faith. The information on this emigration is found in the writings of a recently discovered Anabaptist historian, Johannes Waldner (*q.v.*, d. 1824), who as a child participated in this trek with his parents, and was familiar with these events from the conversation of his parents and their associates. He relates that the peasants in Carinthia began to avoid going to church, and studied the Bible and other religious books at home, and held secret meetings at night in all sorts of weather. The movement spread over the country, principally through the Gail Valley, and in the district of Himmelsberg and Spittal. In the early 1750's sharp governmental investigations took place.

All who confessed the Protestant (Lutheran) faith and were not willing to desist, had to sell their property, but were not expelled into the foreign lands to increase their forces, but were sent to Transylvania (the easternmost part of former Hungary), where Empress Maria Theresa had ordered that they be assigned to land specially designated for them.

Many young persons now left their parents, friends, and acquaintances, among them the parents of the author of the account. Waldner lists them by name, and we must give some of these names, for they are still found among the Hutterian Brethren. Johannes Kleinsasser, who was for many years the head of the brotherhood, led them in the toilsome journey over the Transylvanian Alps into Wallachia, from there, aided by the Russian field marshal, Count Rumyantsev, to Little Russia, where this company became the parent of thriving colonies. George Waldner, the father of the narrator, emigrated with his wife and three children. Christoph Glanzer emigrated with his wife, two children, and three brothers; the oldest of these left his wife, the other two were youths of eighteen and twenty. Other families were: Hofer of St. Peter, Nägeler of the Paternion, Gual of Himmelsberg, Müller of Lentsach, Egarter of St. Peter, Platner, Amlacher, Resch, Winkler, and Bichler. These names do not include all the emigrants, but only those who later joined the Hutterian Brotherhood (*Klein-Gesch.-Buch*, 268-70).

In Carinthia all of these emigrants had been Lutheran. The government placed wagons at their disposal for their departure. Several days after they had arrived in the village of Romos in Transylvania in October 1755, a Lutheran councilor and a clergyman came to announce the imperial will to them: since they could not remain in Carinthia, where only the Catholic faith was tolerated, the Empress had sent them here. "Here you can have the Gospel as you desire it. To be assured of your loyalty, however, she demands an oath of loyalty of you." They protested that the oath was contrary to the Gospel, for which they had left home. "How can you," cries out the zealous Matthias Hofer, "demand of us what Christ (Matt. 5 and John 17) has forbidden?" The councilor replied, "You can read well, but you do not understand. Read Romans 13 about him who resists authority."

Probably the majority yielded, and they were given sites for settlement as promised. Those who refused to yield were excluded from this privilege, and had to work as laborers or artisans in the villages and towns. Two of them, Andreas Wurz and George Waldner, went to Alwinz (*q.v.*), a half-day's journey from Romos, where the Transylvanian prince, Bethlen Gabor, had once given a homestead to the Hutterites when they were refugees from Moravia. Here they met a brotherhood with whom they were in complete agreement on all essentials, such as baptism, communion, government, war, and divorce, whose services of worship appealed to them, and whose books and writings pleased them. Although these Alwinz Hutterites were no longer on their highest standard, having abandoned the principle of communal living, the new transmigrants now joined them, ready to accept persecutions coming upon them from two directions, Catholic and Lutheran.

However, the Carinthian group worshiped apart from the others; every Sunday they met in the home of Andreas Wurz, prayed, sang, and read their Bibles together. At the end of April 1762 Hans Kleinsasser and Josef Müller were baptized. Kleinsasser was chosen leader of the brotherhood on trial, and confirmed in January 1763, after receiving instruction in the essentials of his pastoral charge.

But previously the group had put in order its spiritual and temporal affairs at Kreuz (*q.v.*), where most of them were united. They had asked their Alwinz friends for counsel and aid. These advised them that two or three of the most gifted brethren be chosen, and the one receiving most votes should be their leader. On July 26 thirteen were baptized. Now the school regulations were set up and the training of children begun. They were taught reading and writing and Christian doctrine, and two sisters, Christina and Elisabeth Winkler, were appointed to look after their physical needs. Joseph Müller was made deacon and Joseph Kleinsasser his assistant. The others worked for the common good, each according to his ability. They met daily for prayer. But increasing pressure from the outside soon compelled them to look about for a quieter place for settlement.

The brethren Joseph Kuhr (*q.v.*) and Johannes Stahl, who had both previously suffered severe torture in prison, were appointed to look for suitable places in Poland, Wallachia, and Moldavia. They returned with favorable information. In Kreuz they learned of the evil intentions of the Jesuit Delphini, upon whose advice it had been decided to take their children from them and educate them at the Catholic orphanage in Hermannstadt. The older generation were to be put in prison, and then if they did not recant, be banished from the country, as had already been done with Kuhr and Stahl. A great fear fell upon the small company. Then Brother Joseph Kuhr related that in Moldavia and Wallachia nobody was molested on account of his faith. This news gave the Brethren courage to migrate. On Oct. 3, 1767, a group of 67 souls left. The brotherhood had existed just six years at Kreuz, the starting point of the new migration.　LOSERTH, R.F.

J. Loserth, "The Decline and Revival of the Hutterites," *MQR* IV (1930) 93-112; Zieglschmid, *Klein-Geschichtsbuch,* contains Johannes Waldner's *Denkwürdigkeiten* 1752-1802 (259-402); E. Nowotny, *Die Transmigration . . . österreichischer Protestanten nach Siebenbürgen im 18. Jh.* (Jena, 1931).

Carlin, an Anabaptist of Zürich, probably identical with Carl Brennwald (*q.v.*), who put the articles of his faith in writing, and read them to the city council of Basel (*q.v.*) on June 30, 1527. Oecolampadius (*q.v.*), on the order of the council, composed a written reply, which was printed under the title: *Underrichtung von dem Widertauff, von der Oberkeit, und von dem Eyd, auf Carlins N. Widertauffers Artickel. Antwort auff Balthasar Huobmeiers Büchlein wider der Predicanten gespräch zuo Basel, von dem Kindertauff* (Basel, 1527). (P. Burckhardt, *Die Basler Täufer,* Basel, 1898, 21; *ML* II, 463.)
　NEFF.

Carlock (Ill.) Mennonite Church (GCM) was established because a number of families belonging to the North Danvers Mennonite Church (*q.v.*) had moved to town and found it inconvenient to attend services in the country. The Ladies' Aid was organized as a branch of the North Danvers Ladies' Aid in April 1912. The organization of a prayer-meeting circle and a Christian Endeavor Society held conjointly with meetings of the United Presbyterian Church finally resulted in the organization of a

Mennonite congregation on April 14, 1914. For a while services were held in the town hall, but in January 1916 a new church was dedicated. In 1952 the church had 159 members.　G.Mi.

Carlos Casares Mennonite Church (MC) is a congregation in the city of Carlos Casares, on the Buenos Aires-Santa Rosa branch of the Ferro Carril Oeste (Western Railroad), county seat of Carlos Casares County in the province of Buenos Aires, Argentina. The work here was begun in October 1922 by W. G. Lauver and wife under the Mennonite Board of Missions and Charities and formally organized in March 1923. The 1952 membership was 55, most of Spanish, Italian, and Indo-Argentine descent. The following pastors have served the congregation: W. G. Lauver, 1922-27, 1929-37; J. W. Shank, 1928; Elvin V. Snyder, 1937-47; B. Frank Byler, 1947-49; and John Koppenhaver, 1949- .

The city of Carlos Casares, population 12,000, has a proportion of about 50 per cent Jews, who were brought from Russia and Poland thirty or forty years ago by Baron Mauricio Hirsch, and settled on farms of 50-200 acres in Casares County, where a few are still on their land, although the majority of them have set up some business in the city. There are, therefore, three synagogues in this city, besides a new Roman Catholic church built in 1945 and the Mennonite church built in 1937. Very few of the Jews have accepted Christianity. Most of the evangelical Christians are of Spanish descent, and a few are Italian.

A rural colportage experiment was begun in 1941, which has resulted in a remarkable witness for the Gospel. Federico Prottor, a Polish Christian and a member of the Carlos Casares Mennonite Church, hired for this work, distributed over 600 Bibles, 4,000 Testaments, and thousands of Scripture portions and tracts during his six years of work. (J. W. Shank *et al., The Gospel Under the Southern Cross,* Scottdale, 1943.)　E.V.S.

Carlstadt (Andreas Rudolf Bodenstein, b. at Karlstadt a.M.) (1480?-1541) studied scholastic philosophy and theology at the universities of Erfurt (1499) and Cologne (1503), became an influential professor of theology at the University of Wittenberg (1505-22), in a short time winning high honors and offices. In 1516 he acquired the juristic doctorate (in Siena) and the prospect of a higher ecclesiastical position.

Returning from Rome and Siena to Wittenberg early in 1517, he joined Luther in promoting the Reformation. Influenced by Augustine, the German mystics, and Luther, he attacked with tongue and pen the known errors and abuses of the Catholic Church. In this he was on Luther's side; but in his efforts at reform and his doctrinal ideas he went his own way, which often brought him close to the position of Anabaptism.

Carlstadt was a Biblical theologian. "Turn your eyes and ears toward the Scriptures!" The text and canon he regarded with remarkably scholarly independence and freedom; yet he insisted on the unconditional spiritual authority of the entire Bible, including the Epistle of James (*q.v.*), which he,

contrary to Luther and in accord with the Anabaptists, valued very highly for its ethical content.
In the summer semester of 1520 he declared before
a large audience: "I am grieved by the bold depre-
ciation of James" by Luther. Faith and works belong together organically. "Beware that you do not
take a paper and loveless faith for the greatest
work," he warned the Lutherans, who at once accused him of legalism and fanaticism.

As early as 1521 he took a genuinely Anabaptist
position on the oath: "It would be better if oaths
were discarded, because through oaths no one becomes better; many, however, become worse. He
who does not honor God will never honor an oath.
Therefore let it fall into disuse."

At the communion service held with a large congregation at Christmas 1521, which was the first to
be observed in both kinds, he emphatically stressed
the necessity for faith in receiving the emblems.
Outward formalism and images in the churches he
considered reprehensible. "Having images in our
churches is contrary to the first commandment:
Thou shalt have no other gods!" Nevertheless
Carlstadt cannot be held responsible for the iconoclasm of the masses early in 1522. He had scarcely
any contact with the Zwickau (*q.v.*) prophets and
Thomas Müntzer (*q.v*). "There is a deep chasm
between their views and Carlstadt's religious thinking" (Barge, 403). Carlstadt disliked disorder and
always defended orderly government. In his church
innovations and social improvements (abolition of
begging) he proceeded hand in hand with the Wittenberg council, and was the instigator of the famous "Ordnung der Stadt Wittenberg," which the
council passed on Jan. 24, 1522.

Elector Frederick III was, however, displeased
with Carlstadt's conspicuous reforms, especially in
his change of the cult. So the Mass was restored,
Luther having come from the Wartburg to Wittenberg on March 6 for that very purpose. Carlstadt
retreated to his pastorate in Orlamünde and here
continued his reformation. As an ardent exponent
of the priesthood of the believers—he himself
wished to be called a "new layman" and took off
his priestly robes—he now sharply attacked the
Mass, without Luther's regard for "weaker brethren." He spiritualized the sacraments, denying the
necessity of baptism and communion. These reforms disturbed Wittenberg to the extent that Luther had him banished from electoral territory in
September 1524; he then fled to South Germany
and Switzerland.

The Swiss Brethren, who eagerly read his tracts,
sided with Carlstadt against Luther. Conrad Grebel
(*q.v.*), who was corresponding with Carlstadt,
wrote to Vadian, "A reasonable reader will judge
from the Carlstadt books that Luther is retrogress-
ing, and that he is an excellent procrastinator and a
competent defender of his scandal." In the letter
Grebel and his associates wrote to Müntzer on Sept.
5, 1524 (the letter written to Carlstadt by Andrew
Castelberger, *q.v.,* in the name of the group was
unfortunately lost), Carlstadt was frequently mentioned.

Against infant baptism Carlstadt, unlike the Ana-

baptists, spoke only incidentally, classing it as an
"outward thing" with circumcision. He said, to be
sure, that it was better to postpone baptism until
the candidate was sure of his faith, and that it was
superficial of Luther to baptize infants who do not
understand their lusts, to say nothing of the death
of their lusts through Christ. Carlstadt's wife refused to have her own son baptized (1525).

After a short meeting with the Swiss Brethren in
Zürich, in October 1524, there were apparently no
contacts between them and Carlstadt. They did not
enter into his dispute on the communion, though
they read and distributed his tract on the subject;
its printing in Basel was arranged for by Felix
Manz (*q.v.*) and Carlstadt's son-in-law, Dr. Gerhard Westerburg (*q.v.*).

Ludwig Haetzer (*q.v.*), however, was banished
from Augsburg for siding with Carlstadt against
Urban Rhegius (*q.v.*) in the dispute on communion.
—The strange view of Carlstadt that in the words,
"This is my body," Christ was referring to His
own body, was accepted in some Anabaptist circles,
as the testimony of Veit Frick of Württemberg
(Gutenberg) before the magistrates on July 29,
1563, shows: The words, This is my body, and this
is my blood, had reference to Christ's body and not
to the bread and wine; the meaning is, this body
sitting at table with the disciples must be given and
His blood shed, and bread and wine are a symbol
and memento of this suffering and death (Bossert,
228).

Caspar Schwenckfeld (*q.v.*) in his *Judicium*
(*q.v.*) also accuses the Anabaptists of having adopted Carlstadt's view of communion. Nor does Marpeck (*q.v.*) in his *Verantwortung* repudiate the
idea: "When Christ says, this is my body which is
given for you, we believe it naturally as referring
to His real body which sat at table, was betrayed,
and truly given for us. But of the bread and wine
we understand it figuratively, as the bread that we
break and the wine that we drink is a memorial of
the body and blood of Christ; thereby we shall remember that Christ gave His body and shed His
blood for us" (Loserth, 56).

Against Carlstadt's doctrine of the communion
Luther wrote his libelous pamphlet, *Wider die
himmlischen Propheten,* which at the same time
attacks the Zwinglians. In Rothenburg Carlstadt
replied with three pamphlets. The Rothenburg
schoolmaster, Valentine Ickelsamer, also defended
him against Luther in his *Klag etlicher Brüder an
alle Christen von der grossen Ungerechtigkeit und
Tyrannei, so Endressen Bodenstein von Carlstadt
jetzo von Luther zu Wittenberg geschieht.*

The sharp opposition between Carlstadt and
Luther must be considered not only a matter of
personalities, but also one of content. For when
Carlstadt had to flee Rothenburg and begged Luther to receive him, Luther consented to let him
return to Wittenberg on condition that Carlstadt
recant his heterodox views on the communion and
refrain from lecturing. But the old opposition could
not be suppressed, and he finally had to flee again.

Carlstadt now turned toward Holstein at Melchior
Hofmann's (*q.v.*) invitation, to take part in the

Flensburg disputation on the communion, but was not admitted. After Hofmann was expelled from the country the two met again briefly in East Friesland, where Carlstadt remained nearly a year under the protection of the Zwinglian Ulrich von Dornum, writing polemics against Luther and his doctrines. Compelled to leave the domains of the strictly Lutheran Count Enno (*q.v.*), he sought protection in Switzerland. With recommendations from Bucer in Strasbourg and Oecolampadius in Basel, he went to Zwingli in Zürich, who helped him to a position as proofreader in the Froschauer print shop and later as deacon at the Spital.

In Zürich and Altstätten, where he had a temporary pastorate, Carlstadt allied himself with the Zwinglians, who defended him against Luther's attacks. In 1534 he was called to Basel as preacher at St. Peter's and professor at the university. He died of the plague on Dec. 24, 1541.

The elusive relationship between Carlstadt and the Anabaptist movement deserves further study. In his Wittenberg period he was certainly a near-Anabaptist, yet his visit to the Zürich brethren did not result in a union. Why did he not become an Anabaptist?   G.H.

H. Barge, *Andreas Bodenstein von Karlstadt*, 2 vv. (Leipzig, 1905); idem, *Frühprotestantisches Gemeindechristentum in Wittenberg und Orlamünde* (Leipzig, 1909); K. Müller, *Luther und Karlstadt* (Tübingen, 1907); *RGG* III, Col. 632 ff.; *Gedenkschrift der Mennoniten*, 49 ff. und 65 ff.; H. Erbkam, *Gesch. der prot. Sekten*, 174 ff.; Hertzsch, *Karlstadt und seine Bedeutung für das Luthertum* (Gotha, 1932); C. Sachsse, *D. Balthasar Hubmaier als Theologe* (Berlin, 1915) 154-57; J. Loserth, *Quellen und Forschungen zur Gesch. der oberdeutschen Taufgesinnten* (Vienna, 1929); G. Bossert, *Quellen zur Gesch. der Wiedertäufer I; Herzogtum Württemberg* (Leipzig, 1930); H. S. Bender, *Conrad Grebel* (Goshen, 1950); *ML* II, 463-65.

Carmichael, Mahlon J. (1869-1948), presiding elder of the Pacific Conference (UMC), was ordained by the Nebraska Conference in 1900. He married Eva Taylor in 1900 and after her death Bertha Bartlett in 1907. Three children were born to him by the first marriage and two by the second. He held pastorates at Newton, Kan.; Stuttgart, Ark.; La Junta, Col.; Yakima, Wash.; Mt. View, Wash.; Filer, Idaho; and McMinnville, Ore. He served as presiding elder of the Pacific Conference during various terms following 1906.   M.G.

Carpenter Mennonite Church (MC) in Lancaster Co., Pa. Dr. Heinrich Zimmermann came from the canton of Zürich (Switzerland) to Germantown, Pa., in 1706. He first bought land in Lampeter and in 1733 in West Earl Twp., Lancaster County. His two sons, Henry and Gabriel, started a family cemetery here along the Brownstown to Mechanicsburg Road in 1750. The cemetery was enlarged in 1821 and a union stone church was built near by in 1824. On Nov. 26, 1939, a Mennonite Sunday school was opened here. In October 1942 the Lancaster Mennonite Conference accepted it as a congregation in the Mahlon Witmer district, using the newly renovated old stone church. The membership in 1953 was 73, average Sunday-school attendance 84, summer Bible school enrollment 200. Michael N. Wenger is minister and John W. Wentling deacon.   I.D.L.

Carpenter (Neb.) United Missionary Church is a member of the Nebraska Conference. The present church, located eight miles west of Carpenter, was dedicated May 25, 1941, under John P. Tschetter as pastor. In 1951 there were 40 members.   E.R.S.

Carpenter (S.D.) United Missionary Church is located eight miles west of Carpenter. Organized about 1928, it had a membership of 38 in 1952.
                                                       C.F.G.

Carr Mennonite Church (MC) is located on the North Fork of the South Branch of the Potomac River in Randolph Co., W. Va. Regular work was begun in the Carr schoolhouse in 1932. A meetinghouse was built in 1948. It is a Mennonite mission church of the Middle District of the Virginia Conference and a flourishing mountain congregation with 49 members. (*ML* I, 334.)   H.A.B.

Carr Schoolhouse is located near the North Fork of the South Branch of the Potomac River in Pendleton Co., W. Va. Regular church work (MC) was begun here in 1932. The work prospered until there were about 50 members in 1948. A church was built in that year on the North Fork River and is known as the North Fork Mennonite Church. No religious services have been held at the Carr Schoolhouse since.   H.A.B.

Carson Mennonite Brethren Church in Cottonwood Co., Minn., was organized by six families on June 11, 1877, under the leadership of Heinrich Voth (*q.v.*). In 1879 the church joined the Conference of the Mennonite Brethren Church of North America. The first meetinghouse was constructed in 1885 near a scenic creek about three miles north of Bingham Lake. Because members living in and south of Mountain Lake could not attend regularly, another meetinghouse was built about five miles south of Mountain Lake. Elder Voth served as pastor of both churches until 1918, when he moved to Canada. In 1893 the church at Bingham Lake, now known as the Carson Church, erected a new building. A. J. Wiebe, who was elected in 1899 and later ordained as a minister, served as pastor of the church from 1918 to 1941. He was succeeded by B. J. Braun, who served until 1945, when Wm. Neufeld, the present pastor, became his successor. Others who have assisted in the ministry are Johann Wiens, Peter H. Ewert, H. S. Voth, Henry E. Wiens, David Hooge, John H. Wiens, and J. D. Wiens. The work of foreign missions has been stressed throughout the history of the church. In 1896 Henry and Maria Ensz left for Africa. John H. and Maria Voth sailed for India in 1908. In 1927 John A. and Viola Wiebe proceeded to India. Edna Gerdes also went to India in 1946. Other workers are laboring among the Indian tribes of North America. In 1949 the church moved to its new location in Delft, where a building measuring 84 x 32 ft., with a seating capacity of 350, was dedicated on March 13. In 1953 the membership of the church was 164.   J.A.W.

Carthage (Jasper Co., Mo.) Church of God in Christ Mennonite Church, now extinct, had nine members in 1911. The church, located seven miles northeast of Carthage, had Henry Herr as its leader. (*ML* I, 334.)   M.G.

Casier (or Cesaer), **Joost,** was a deacon of the Waterlander Mennonite congregation at Leiden, Holland, at least until 1656. In a letter of 1614 he signed his name with the French addition, *diaque des Valon a Leiden.* The letter, also signed in French by Jean de Mortier as *Evesque* (bishop) and Jean des Mullier as *Serviteur* (preacher), seems to indicate the existence of a separate congregation called *Vallons,* i.e., French-speaking Mennonites, originally from the Walloon district of Belgium (see also **Leiden**).   vDZ.

L. G. le Poole, *Bijdrage tot de kennis van . . . de Doopsgez. te Leiden* (Leiden, 1905) 33, 61, 62, 83.

Caspar, an Anabaptist martyr of Schöneck, was put to death by beheading at Ries in Fluchttal near Brixen, Tirol, about 1528. Caspar and Vilgard (*q.v.*), who was executed with him, left behind an admonition to the brethren, which is found in the *Martyrs' Mirror.* (*Mart. Mir.* D 19, E 429; *ML* II, 469.)

Caspar, a shoemaker, an Anabaptist martyr who was beheaded in 1538 at Michelsburg in Priestertal (Pustertal?), Austria, with Martin of Vilgraten. (*Mart. Mir.* D 43, E 449.)   vDZ.

Cass County, Mo., approximately 40 miles southeast of Kansas City, now (1951) contains a Mennonite congregation (MC) of 250 members. For many years it had two congregations, numbering in 1908 a total of 480 members. Amish Mennonite settlers moved into the area as early as 1860, but regular church services were not held until 1866. Two years later they organized the Clearfork congregation (*q.v.*). Out of this church developed the Sycamore Grove (*q.v.*) and the Bethel (*q.v.*) congregations, both in the Garden City area in the southeastern part of the county.   M.G.

Cassander, Georg, an outstanding Catholic scholar, born at Pittham near Brugge, died in Cologne, Feb. 3, 1566, noted for his exceedingly rare tolerance toward persons of other faiths. He was frequently used to convert Anabaptists, as in the case of Johannes Campanus (*q.v.*), and especially of Matthias Servaes (*q.v.*). The latter pictures him in his letters (*Mart. Mir.* E 690) as a man little and feeble of body, who . . . laid many little snares, to take captive my mind." In his *Opera,* published in Paris in 1616, Cassander presents two extremely interesting conversations with Servaes (Rembert, 476, note 4). He was obviously deeply impressed by Servaes' faith, firmly rooted in the Bible, and by his constancy in the face of death. He deeply regretted that the imperial laws inexorably demanded the death penalty for the young Anabaptist, and believed that the Anabaptists should be converted by teaching and instruction rather than punished with the sword. Summoned by the Duke of Cleve, Cassander went to Duisburg to convert the Anabaptists (Ottius, *Annales Anabaptistici,* 122). To this end he wrote a pamphlet on infant baptism, which he read to Servaes. He mentioned another booklet he wrote to combat the Anabaptists with the title, *Libellus Adversus Anabaptistas* (Rembert, 546, note 6). Because of his pacific attitude Ferdinand I called him to his court to assist in the task of reconciling the creeds, but it did not take place.

Cassander's influence was not of long duration because his position lacked definiteness.   NEFF.

Rembert, *Wiedertäufer;* K. Vos, *Menno Simons* (Leiden, 1914) 315 f.; Schyn-Maatschoen, *Gesch. der . . . Menn.* (Amsterdam, 1743) I, 287; *Ztscht des Bergischen Geschichtsvereins* (Elberfeld, 1899) 2 ff.; *HRE* III, 742 f.; M. Nolte, *Georgius Cassander en zijn oecumenisch streven* (Nijmegen, 1951); *ML* I, 334.

Cassel (also Kassel), a Mennonite family name prominent in early eastern Pennsylvania Mennonite history, particularly in the Franconia Conference area. J. C. Wenger in his *History of the Mennonites of the Franconia Conference* lists 26 Cassels and 7 Kassels. The name appears in the Palatine Mennonite census lists of 1664 under Kriegsheim and Gerolsheim. D. K. Cassel in his *Genealogical History of the Cassel Family in America* (Norristown, 1896) states that Johannes Cassel and family arrived in Philadelphia from Kriegsheim in 1686 and settled in Germantown. A Hendrick (Heinrich) Kassel is mentioned among the 52 members of the Germantown Mennonite Church in 1708. The Cassel immigrant, however, whose family became most prominent in eastern Mennonite areas was Hupert, who came to Philadelphia from Kriegsheim between 1715 and 1720. By 1725 he was living in the Skippack (*q.v.*) community where he was among the signers of a petition to have a township surveyed. His brother Julius Cassel (Yilles Kassel) came to America in 1727 and farmed at Skippack, where he also preached. Wenger gives brief biographies of five other Cassels who served in the Mennonite ministry of eastern Pennsylvania between 1708 and 1922. Among the prominent members of the Cassel family were the noted antiquary Abraham H. Cassel and the historian Daniel Kolb Cassel of Germantown, who was the author of three volumes of family history —the *Kulp Family,* the *Cassel Family,* and the *Rittenhouse Family.* His *History of the Mennonites* (Philadelphia, 1888) was the first book on the subject to be published in America.

Obituaries of Cassels appearing in Mennonite periodicals indicate a spread to Lancaster and Montgomery counties, Pa., and to Ontario.   M.G.

Cassel, Daniel K., was born on April 22, 1820, in Upper Salford Twp., Montgomery Co., Pa., the son of farmer-weaver Jacob and Wilhelmina Kulp Cassel, and the sixth generation from Hupert Cassel, the Mennonite immigrant weaver who settled in Germantown, Pa., about 1720. Daniel, the oldest of four children, was early taught the art of weaving by his father.

In his youth he manifested studious habits, supplementing his limited grammar school experience with intensive private reading, often late into the night. At the age of nineteen he began to teach in local schools and for twenty years continued to do so, introducing such new subjects as geography and higher mathematics into the simple curriculum of the day. During these years he published two German booklets: a book of prayers and songs, and a catechism for religious instruction of his pupils. In all probability Daniel attended the Salford Mennonite Church in these early days. He organized a Sunday school at Alderfer's, below Harleysville, in 1855, the first one in the community. On Feb. 16, 1845, he married Elizabeth Kolb, daughter of Jacob Kolb, preacher at Salford. Three sons were born to them: Simeon in 1846, Jonas in 1849, and Abel in 1852.

In later years Daniel and Elizabeth Cassel lived in Philadelphia at 4333 Germantown Avenue. The leisure of later years and his return to romantic Germantown stimulated the religious and historical activities which he had anticipated all his life. He joined the historic Germantown Mennonite Church (GCM), serving as deacon from about 1886 until his death. In 1888 he published his well-known *History of the Mennonites,* the first extensive history of American Mennonites. In spite of its errors, disunity, and sketchiness, it was a noble pioneering achievement in the days when there was little interest in Mennonite history. It is especially valuable for its congregational histories and various documents preserved and printed in full. Two years later it was expanded and reprinted in German under the title, *Geschichte der Mennoniten.* During these years he also compiled genealogies of the Rittenhouse, Kulp, and Cassel families.

The titles of his known works are: *Eine schoene Sammlung auserlesener Gebete und Lieder zum Gebrauch der Jugend* (Sumneytown, 1844); *Katechismus oder kurze und einfältige Unterweisung nebst den Zehn Geboten* (Skippachville, 1851); *History of the Mennonites* (Philadelphia, 1888); *Geschichte der Mennoniten* (Philadelphia, 1890); *A Genea-Biographical History of the Rittenhouse Family* (Philadelphia, 1893); *A Genealogical History of the Kolb, Kulp or Culp Family* (Norristown, 1895); *A Genealogical History of the Cassel Family* (Norristown, 1896); *The Family Record of David Rittenhouse* (Norristown, 1897).

He was an early stockholder and member of the Bethel College Corporation controlling Bethel College, North Newton, Kan. Two of his belongings, a large volume of the four Gospels in twelve languages and a manuscript copy of his will, are now in the possession of Jacob R. Fretz and the writer respectively. He died on Feb. 19, 1898, and was laid to rest in the historic Germantown burial ground beside his ancestors.   J.H.F.

A Genealogical History of the Kolb, Kulp or Culp Family (Norristown, 1895) 61 ff.; *A Genealogical History of the Cassel Family* (Norristown, 1896) 98 ff.; see also "One by One." *The Mennonite,* March 1898, p. 44; *ML* I, 334.

Cassel, Heinrich, a Mennonite preacher at Gerolsheim in the Palatinate, wrote a booklet against the Quakers, *Eine Entdeckung der Quäker oder Beber,* and sent it to his relatives and friends who had joined the Quakers. (*Menn. Bl.* 1854, 43; 1912, 11 ff.; *ML* I, 334.)   NEFF.

Casselman Mennonite Church (MC) is located several miles south of Grantsville, Garrett Co., western Maryland, in the beautiful valley of the Casselman River. The community had its first services in 1874, probably in the homes, and later in the Ridgeley schoolhouse. The Casselman church was built in 1889. In 1952 it had a membership of 55, with Milton B. Miller serving as bishop. It is a member of the Southwestern Pennsylvania Conference. (*ML* I, 335.)   A.Ka.

Casselman River Conservative Amish Mennonite congregation, located in Somerset Co., Pa., and Garrett Co., Md., is a member of the C.A.M. Conference, and worships in three meetinghouses: Maple Glen, near Grantsville, Md.; Oak Dale, near Salisbury, Pa.; and Cherry Glade, near Bittinger, Md.

The congregation dates back to about 1770-75, when the first Amish pioneers settled along the Casselman River, the settlement extending within a few decades on both sides of the Pennsylvania-Maryland state line. (See **Somerset Co., Pa., and Garrett Co., Md.**)

Differences in the Amish Church in these counties resulted in a division in 1895. Of the two groups, the more liberal became the C.A.M. congregation with a membership of 118, under the leadership of Bishop Joel J. Miller, Minister Jacob S. Miller, and deacons Elias D. Hershberger and John Brenneman. These men had been ordained in the Amish Church and served the charge on the Maryland side of the line before the division, with the exception of Elias D. Hershberger, who served as deacon in the charge on the Pennsylvania side of the state line.

Of the four Amish meetinghouses in the two counties, the two in Garrett Co., Md., became the property of this congregation at the time of the division. Maple Glen, built in 1881, was used until 1946, when it was replaced by a new frame structure, with initial services held on Pentecost, May 16, 1948. Cherry Glade, a frame structure, also built in 1881, continues in use. Oak Dale, a frame structure, was built in 1896 to serve the northern end of the congregation. All ministers in the district serve in turn at the three meetinghouses.

The first English sermon was preached at a funeral in July 1898 by Jonas B. Miller. Currently the German and English languages are both used in the services. Sunday schools had been organized in the Amish Church before the division, as early as 1893, and continued from the beginning of this congregation. The membership in the district in 1952 was 242; it is entirely rural.

Ministers and bishops who have served the congregation are: Joel J. Miller, ordained preacher in 1880, bishop 1887-1915; Jacob S. Miller, 1886-1915; Jonas B. Miller, 1897-1952; Noah J. Brenneman, 1913-48; Christian W. Bender, minister in 1915, bishop 1916- ; Shem Peachey, 1930- ; Ivan J. Miller, 1938- ; Mark Peachey, 1946- ; Simon D. Beachy, 1946- ; Paul E. Yoder, 1952- .   I.J.M.

Castelberger, Andreas (Andres auf der Stültzen), a follower of Conrad Grebel in the first Swiss Brethren group at Zürich, also called *Andres auf der Krucken* (crutches), or simply the *Stültzer;* in Chur he was called *hinkender* (limping) *Andres,* because he was a cripple. He was from the canton of Grisons and a bookseller by trade. As early as 1522, before he joined the Anabaptists, he had shown himself a successful "innovator." He was expressly forbidden to continue his meetings with the "confused people," which were attended by large numbers. At these meetings—so the witnesses said at the trial—he had given an exegesis of Romans and preached particularly against pride and usury, church benefices, and war. He joined the new Anabaptist movement with enthusiasm, but he could not stay in Zürich more than a short time, for the non-Zürich followers of the group, including Andreas, were expelled by the mandate of Jan. 18, 1525. In consideration of his illness the Zürich council granted his request to postpone his expulsion by permitting him to stay a month longer, but he was forbidden to preach (letter to the council published in *Anzeiger für Schweizerische Geschichte*, 1900, No. 3, 329-31). He later returned to his homeland in Chur, and was also very successful in the Anabaptist cause there. A letter written by Conrad Grebel to Castelberger in May 1525 was published with annotations in *MQR* I (July 1927) 41-52. (H. S. Bender, *Conrad Grebel*, Goshen, 1950; *ML* I, 71.)   NEFF.

Castellio, Sebastien, b. 1515 at St. Martin du Fresne in the French Savoy, d. Dec. 29, 1563, at Basel, was influenced to join the Reformation as a result of Calvin's *Institutio Religionis Christianae*. For some time he worked with Calvin at Strasbourg and Geneva, but as a result of Castellio's translation of the Bible, and particularly his humanistic opinions as opposed to Calvin's dogmatism and intolerance, their ways separated. Castellio, who in the meantime had acquired a professorship in Greek at the University of Basel, became a great champion of freedom of conscience and belief in the 16th century. As such he condemned the concepts of Calvin and Beza and their Reformation party, especially the claim that the state had the right to persecute with the sword those who would not conform their thinking. According to Castellio, the execution of heretics was entirely unlawful. Castellio wrote *De haereticis an sint persequendi* (Whether Heretics Should Be Persecuted). It was translated into French with the title, *Traité des hérétiques a savoir si on les doit persécuter* (new edition, Geneva, 1913). In this book Castellio also considers the Anabaptists, although he does not share their principles and beliefs. For his toleration as well as for his objective judgment of the Anabaptists, Castellio occupies a unique position in the history of the 16th century.   vDZ.

F. Buisson, *S. Castellio, Sa vie et son oeuvre* (Paris, 1892) 2 vv.; R. H. Bainton, *The Travail of Religious Liberty* (Philadelphia, 1951) 97-124; P. Burckhardt, *David Joris und seine Familie in Basel* (1949), reprint 37-44 *et passim; DB* 1916, 110-12; *Castellioniana*, four studies by Bainton, Becker, Valkhoff, and van der Woude (Leiden, 1951); *Autour de M. Servet et de S. Castellion* (Haarlem, 1953); N. van der Zijpp, *Castellio*, in *Stemmen uit de Doopsgez. Broederschap* II (Assen, 1953) 58-63.

Castor (Alberta) United Missionary Church began having services in October 1942. A stucco building, with seating capacity of 100, was dedicated Aug. 17, 1947. In 1948 Ray Shantz served as pastor and the membership (including Markham) was 31.   R.S.

Castricum, in the Dutch province of North Holland, where a number of resident Mennonites (21 in 1952) meet regularly. The circle (*kring*), belonging to the congregation of Beverwijk (*q.v.*),

started in 1946, and now (1953) has 21 members.
        vDZ.

Catabaptist, a name used for a time (1525 ff.) for the Swiss Anabaptists by Zwingli and Oecolampadius in their Latin writings. It did not, however, succeed in displacing "Anabaptist," which became the standard term. It is an original Greek word translated into Latin, not found in German or English.

The exhaustive discussion of the meaning of the word by Fritz Blanke in the commentary to Zwingli's *In Catabaptistarum strophas elenchus* (*Huldreich Zwinglis sämtliche Werke* VI, 21-22, Leipzig, 1935?) points out that Oecolampadius first proposed it in a letter of Oct. 12, 1525, to Zwingli, taking it consciously from a fourth-century writing of Gregory of Nazianzus, recommending that it be used in place of "Anabaptist," which had already come into use. The most prominent use of the word is in Zwingli's 1527 *Elenchus*. The word is actually used in essentially the same meaning as "Anabaptist," i.e., rebaptizer, but carries the additional connotation of "anti-baptist," i.e., attempting to destroy the true baptism. Schijn (*q.v.*) considered "Catabaptists" the best designation for the Anabaptists, explaining that "kata" means to act in accord with true baptism; he approved it because the Anabaptists act according to Biblical doctrine, i.e., they practice baptism Scripturally.
        H.S.B.

G. Maatschoen, *Geschiedenis der Menn.* (Amsterdam, 1743) pp. XCVII-CI, where Fred. Spanheim in *Elenchus Controversiarium* (1694) p. 86, is also cited; *ML* II, 469.

Catalogus van de Bibliotheek *der Vereenigde Doopsgezinde Gemeente te Amsterdam.* The Amsterdam Mennonite library possesses an old catalog in manuscript, dating from the 17th century: *Catalogus der boeken op de kerkekamer bewaard, meerendeels Mennonitica.* In 1796 Prof. Hesselink made a systematic catalog, which he provided with a Latin preface. This manuscript was not printed, however, as seems to have been the intention (*Inv. Arch. Amst.* II, 618). There was no printed catalog before 1854. In this year Prof. Samuel Muller edited a catalog of the rich and valuable collection of the Amsterdam Mennonite Library, as far as it deals with Mennonite history: *Catalogus van Doopsgezinde Geschriften behoorende tot de bibliotheek der Ver. Doopsgez. Gemeente te Amsterdam* (Amsterdam, 1854, 72 pp.). In 1885-88 J. G. de Hoop Scheffer, also of the Seminary faculty, prepared a *Catalogus van de Bibliotheek der Ver. Deepsgez. Gemeente te Amsterdam,* in two volumes, containing the titles of all the books of the library: Vol. I, theology in general and philosophy (1885, 430 pp.); Vol. II, (*a*) *Teleiobaptistica* (books dealing with Mennonite history, as well as books written by Mennonites); (*b*) *Oude en nieuwe letteren* (1888, 481 pp.). In 1919 J. G. Boekenoogen published a *Catalogus der werken over de Doopsgezinden en hunne Geschiedenis aanwezig in de Bibliotheek der Ver. Doopsgez. Gemeente te Amsterdam* (Amsterdam, 1919, 375 pp.). Of this catalog the Mennonite Historical Society of Goshen College published an *Index* in mimeographed form (Goshen, 1950, 64 pp.). vDZ.

Cate, ten (ten Cathe, or ten Kate), an extensive family in the Netherlands, originally residing in the district of Twenthe, province of Overijssel, many of whose members belonged and still belong to the Mennonite Church. The genealogy of this family has been only partly written. H. A. Vorsterman van Oyen assembled a number of data about the ten Cate family in *Stam- en Wapenboek van aanzienlijke Nederlandsche Familiën* II, 144, 145. The genealogy of the descendants of Teunis Lammerts ten Cate of Borne, Twenthe, then migrating to Friesland, has been written and published by G. ten Cate in *Geslachtslijst van den Frieschen tak der familie ten Cate* (n.p., n.d.—1896). It seems that there are four or five branches of this family, but it is not clear if and how these branches are connected and go back to one ancestor. It is said that in the 16th century the original residence of this family was a farm at Zenderen near Borne, but they may have lived also at other places in Twenthe.

Rather well known is the genealogy of a branch living at Almelo, Twenthe, from about 1600. This branch is entirely Mennonite; the first known member of this branch is Jan Hermansz ten Cate, b. about 1575. A descendant of this Jan ten Cate is Hendrik ten Cate, b. 1743, who was the founder of the now world-famous textile factories at Almelo, *Fa H. ten Cate Hz en Co.* In his old notebook this Hendrik ten Cate, who was a cloth merchant, tells how he bought pieces of linen from the farmers in Twenthe, who were weavers during the winter. In 1760 he began to send bales of cloth to the Caribbean Islands, which the captains of the sailing vessels traded for gold and coffee; in the next century they sold the linen here and elsewhere for cash. This kind of trade, selling the linen which was bought from Twenthian home-weavers, lasted until 1860. In this year Egbert ten Cate, a great-grandson of Hendrik, founded a weaving factory at Almelo; the products, now chiefly cotton, were sent to many countries and especially to the Dutch East Indies. The business continued to expand, and in 1898 a second steam-powered weaving mill was founded in Almelo, in 1912 a third one, and in 1929 a fourth one. In 1924 a thread manufactory was founded, the yarns having previously been imported from England. A second spinning mill was put into use in 1929. After 1945 important modernizations, improvements, and enlargements were made, and in 1952 a merger of the Royal Steam Powered Weaveries at Nijverdal with the Almelo factories took place. The large and modern factories conducted by the descendants of the ten Cate family now have more than 4,000 looms and 157,000 spinning spindles. The annual consumption of cotton amounts to some 6 million kilograms; every week more than three quarters of a million yards of cloth are produced and find their destination both on the home market and in some 30 countries all over the world. The number of employees is more than 5,000.

From olden times weaving has been the occupation of the ten Cate family, and not only of the Almelo branch. The first known members of this family were home-weavers, who at the same time were engaged in agriculture. According to a family tradition they had some contacts with Waldensian weavers in Flanders as early as the 15th century. But this tradition is not very probable. Another tradition states that they had some contacts with Westphalian Anabaptists. This may be possible, though it has not been proved.

Many members of this family since about 1600 have been members of the Mennonite Church. A petition of Oct. 10, 1612, which was sent in the name of "the congregation, who are called Mennonites in Twenthe" to the magistrate of Deventer (Blaupot ten Cate, *Groningen* II, 59), was signed among others by Arent ten Cate of Goor, Wolter Lammerts (ten Cate) of Enschede, Gerrit Tonnis (ten Cate) en Tonnis Gerrits (ten Cate) of Borne, while Berent Lammerts and Willen Berends of Almelo, who also signed the petition, are supposed to have been members of the ten Cate family too. All these men must have been preachers or deacons of the Mennonite Church. In the baptismal books of all four congregations which now exist in Twenthe (Almelo, Borne, Hengelo, Enschede) the ten Cates are numerous; in the records of other congregations such as Amsterdam *bij't Lam,* Deventer, Sneek, IJlst, and many others, their names are also found in large numbers.

Many members of this family have served as ministers in Mennonite congregations: Jan Lammerts ten Cate (1638-78), married to Geertje Kops, was a minister of the Old Flemish congregation of Deventer from 1669 to his death (*DB* 1919, 49, 60-61); about the same time Jan Jansz ten Cate, b. about 1625 and married to Maria Willink, was preacher at Almelo. Hendrik ten Cate was preacher of the Amsterdam Lamist congregation 1677-94, and Jan ten Cate at the same church 1677-79. Wolter ten Cate (*q.v.*), minister and elder; Jan Teunis ten Cate (d. 1798) served at Middelie 1781-83 and Alkmaar 1783-98; Gerardus ten Cate Thzn, minister at Almelo 1753-55, Westzaandam 1755-72, and again Almelo 1772-1810(?), author of *Antwoord op een brief* (n.p., n.d.); *De wederdoop gewraakt* (n.p., n.d.); *Antwoord op de aanspraak van Justus Benevolens* (Zaandam, 1758); *Kort berigt wegens den Heer Anth. van der Os . . .* (n.p. 1765); *Historisch Verhaal id, . . .* (Zaandam, 1766). In 1777 this Gerardus ten Cate made a proposal in the meeting of the Zonist Sociëteit (*q.v.*) to unite all the Dutch Mennonites in one conference (*Inv. Arch. Amst.* I, No. 940); Isaac ten Cate, b. at Goor, d. 1839 at Noordbroek, was minister there from 1796 to 1839; Egbert David ten Cate, minister at Almelo 1811-38; Herman I. ten Cate, d. 1858, minister at Pieterzijl 1828-58; Herman ten Cate, Herm. zn. (1804-64), married to Judith Paschen, minister at Hengelo 1829-64; Lambertus ten Cate Coster, d. 1877, minister at Zwolle 1833-58; Steven Blaupot ten Cate (*q.v.*); Isaac ten Cate Fennema (1810-86), married to Evadina ten Cate, served at Nijmegen 1834-60; Herman ten Cate Hoedemaker (1823-1902), married to Geertruid ten Cate, served the following congregations: Mensingeweer 1849-50, Noordbroek

1850-52, Grouw 1852-56, and Deventer 1856-89; Gerrit ten Cate (*q.v.*); A. Hermansz ten Cate (d. 1920) served the following congregations: Zijldijk 1857-66, Gorredijk 1866-70, Dantumawoude 1870-77, Midwolda 1877-83, Warns 1883-93, and Oudebildtzijl 1893-99, in which year he retired. He published *De Roeping der kerk* (Oosterwolde, 1867), which was a sermon he preached on Nov. 7, 1867, when he dedicated the church of the newly-founded congregation of Appelsga (*q.v.*). E. M. ten Cate (*q.v.*); Frederik ten Cate (1878-1944), served at Broek op Langendijk 1903-7, Leermens-Loppersum 1907-12, Purmerend 1912-16, Sappemeer 1916-35, and Leiden 1935-43. (See also **Kate, ten**.)   vɒZ.

Cate, Egbertus Marius ten, b. Dec. 6, 1868, d. Dec. 21, 1926, Dutch Mennonite minister. After having finished his theological studies at the Amsterdam University and the Mennonite Seminary, became a ministerial candidate in 1893. He served the congregations of Noordhorn 1894-96, Monnikendam 1896-1904, and Apeldoorn 1904-24. On Sept. 24, 1924, he collapsed in the pulpit. As the pastor of Monnikendam and later of Apeldoorn, he also took care (from 1903) of a group of Mennonites at Amersfoort (*q.v.*). When this group became an independent congregation (1919) ten Cate served also this congregation until he retired. Ten Cate was much interested in Mennonite history and wrote many articles in the Dutch weekly, *De Zondagsbode* and Dutch non-Mennonite periodicals. He contributed important articles to the *Doopsgezinde Bijdragen* (issues of 1899, 1903, 1904, 1906, 1911, 1918). Ten Cate also revised and edited in 1912 the third edition of A. Brons *Ursprung, Entwicklung und Schicksale der altevangelischen Taufgesinnten oder Mennoniten. (De Zondagsbode.* Jan. 2, 1927.)   vɒZ.

Cate, Gerrit ten, a Dutch Mennonite preacher, b. Oct. 14, 1825, at Sneek, the son of the mayor Steven ten Cate and his wife Johanna van Delden. In 1851 he became minister at Wormerveer-Noord, in 1852 married Maria Anna Craandijk, who died in 1896. In 1858 he took over the congregation at Drachten, and in 1883, when he began to age, the much smaller one at Wolvega where he served until his retirement in 1891. After that he resided in The Hague, in Apeldoorn, and in Doorn, where he died on July 13, 1910. He was an adherent of the modernist movement and in 1868 agitated for the formation of a general union of all liberals of Holland. He did not succeed, but his work was the first step toward the *Protestantenbond* formed in 1870. Ten Cate was an editor of the Dutch Mennonite weekly, *De Zondagsbode,* from October 1890 to November 1894. His article in *DB* 1894, 71-115, "Wat kan voor onze Broeders en Zusters in de Verstrooiing gedaan worden" (What Can Be Done for Our Brethren and Sisters in the Diaspora), gave rise to the *Commissie tot de Verstrooiden* (a committee which looked after Mennonites living where there are no congregations and provided for regular visits to them). An especial service of ten Cate was his research in the archives on old Mennonite families. Some of the fruits of his work

were published in the *Zondagsbode,* and he bequeathed much of the data he collected to the Amsterdam Mennonite library.

Some of his publications were *De Hernhutters in Akkrum* (*DB* 1885, 68-90); *Geschiedkundig overzicht van de Doopsgezinde Gemeente van Drachten en Ureterp* (1890); *Korte schets van de Doopsgezinde gemeente der Oude Vlamingen te Sneek* (*DB* 1890, 87-123); *Geschiedenis der Doopsgezinde gemeente te 's Gravenhage,* a history of the decline and revival of the congregation at The Hague (1896, 2nd ed. Leiden, 1908, 3d ed. The Hague, 1914); *Geslachtlijst van de Familie Halbertsma* (1897); *Geslachtlijst der Familie Vissering* (1903); *Geslachtlijst van den Friesschen tak der familie ten Cate* (1896). (*DB* 1910, 210-17; *DJ* 1911, 21-32, with portrait; *Catalogus Amst.,* 42, 44, 47, 15; *ML* I, 335.)   J.L., vɒZ.

Cate, Steven Blaupot ten, a Dutch Mennonite minister and historiographer, a son of Isaak ten Cate, the Mennonite minister in Noordbroek (province of Groningen), and his wife Hester Blaupot, was born there on Jan. 29, 1807. In Zaandam he had the privilege of instruction by Pastor S. E. Wieling, and then entered the seminary at Amsterdam. In 1830 he became a candidate and was called to Akkrum, where he served as pastor until 1839, when he took charge of Zaandam-Oost. He also served this church nine years, resigning on Aug. 6, 1848. On Jan. 1, 1851, he was made a member of the provincial council and in the fall of 1851 he entered the second chamber of the States-General. His political activity, however, ended in 1859, when on July 28 he was appointed inspector of the public schools in the province of Groningen. He devoted himself to this task until 1880, when the decline of his vision gradually made work impossible. After retirement he lived four years at Hoogezand, where he died on Sept. 9, 1884. In an obituary the statement was made, "In his death an active and capable man has passed away, who zealously used the talents God granted him and who rendered meritorious service to human society in many fields." The *Maatschappij der Nederl. Letterkunde* made him a member in 1842, the *Genootschap voor Kunsten en Wetenschappen* of the province of Utrecht in 1844, and the *Genootschap voor Wetenschappen* of the province of Zeeland in 1845; the government honored his services with the Knight's Cross of the Dutch Lion.

Ten Cate began his literary work very early. In 1825 the *Maatschappij tot Nut van't Algemeen* awarded him the silver medal for his competitive essay, "Biographies of Native Men and Women from the Southern Provinces." Twice, in 1827 and 1828, he received the *accessit* in competitions of the Academy at Liege, in the second instance with a *magna cum laude.* In 1834 he won another prize from the *Maatschappij tot Nut van't Algemeen* for a "History of the Trade and Navigation of Holland," and in 1841 from the Zaandam branch of the same society for his "Treatise on the Stimulation and Spread of Charity in Zaandam." This essay reveals his knowledge of and service in the field of social welfare, which are best presented in his prize-winning essay, *Eene duidelijke en bepaalde aanwijzing van de grondslagen, op welk een doelmatig ingericht armwezen in ons vaderland zou moeten rusten,* which was crowned in 1850 with a gold medal. He had already published a preparatory study, "De Staatszoorg voor de armen." In 1851 he published the *Tijdschrift voor het armwezen* and as a member of the Chamber he worked for the passage of the law of 1854 for the care of the poor.

Meanwhile he had already established his reputation as a historiographer, especially in Mennonite history. In 1832 he published *Oud-Nederland uit den grootsten nood gered,* a reminder of the eighty years' warfare for the liberation of Holland and the year of misfortune, 1672. In 1834 appeared *Over Doop en Doopsgezinden. Handboekje;* in 1839 his volume on Friesland, in 1842 two volumes on Groningen, Overijssel, and East Friesland; and finally in 1847 two volumes on Holland, Zeeland, Utrecht, and Gelderland. These works are of the greatest importance for the understanding of Dutch Mennonite history, especially since ten Cate's work is very scholarly; he took pains to gather and incorporate materials from many sources. These books are said to have been "much plundered and little praised" (*DB* 1904, 142). In between he published in 1844 his research on the Waldensian origin of the Dutch Anabaptists, *Geschiedkundig onderzoek naar den Waldenzischen oorsprong der Nederlandsche Doopsgezinden* (Amsterdam, 1844), and had become involved in a friendly dispute with Pastor B. ter Haar, of the Reformed Church in Amsterdam and author of a history of the Reformation, in the defense of his position, viz., that a Waldensian origin can be proved. Both defended their views, and ten Cate did this again in his history of the Dutch Mennonites (see above) as well as in an open letter which Prof. Samuel Müller put into the *Doopsgezind Jaarboekje* in 1850, "Brief van S. Blaupot ten Cate aan N.N. over de oorsprong van de Doopsgezinden en hunne betrekking tot de Wederdoopers." In 1844, too, after J. H. Halbertsma (*q.v.*) had published his book on the *Doopsgezinden,* ten Cate wrote *Gedachten over de Getals-vermindering bij de Doopsgez. in Nederland . . .* (Amsterdam, 1844).

Besides these, the following writings were published by him: *Onderzoek naar den invloed van den Franschen volksaard op den tydgeest van Europa* (1833); *Grondslagen voor de Vereeniging tot plaatselijk nut te Zaandam* (Zaandam, 1841); *Rede ter gedachtenis van het 300-jarig bestaan van eene Doopsgezinde gemeente te Zaandam* (Zaandam, 1843) and a booklet for catechetical instruction, *Over Doop en Doopsgezinden* (Leeuwarden, 1834, 2d ed. 1835). (*Levensberichten van d. Maatsch. der Ned. Letterkunde,* Leiden, 1885, 23-46; *Biogr. Wb.* II, 26-29; *ML* I, 335 f.)   J.L., vDZ.

Cate, Wolter ten, b. Aug. 28, 1701, at Hengelo in Twente, a district in the Dutch province of Overijssel, d. at the same place, Aug. 8, 1796. In 1720 he took over his father's textile factory, developed it into a flourishing industry, and consequently became wealthy. He was one of the founders of big industry in Twente. According to a tradition, he was taught the skill of damask manufacturing by weavers from Danzig. Wolter ten Cate, himself descended from a very old Mennonite family, was married in 1725 to Tjilke Jans Dijk, of a well-known Mennonite family in Groningen. The marriage was childless. Ten Cate gave much of his time, devotion, and money to the church. In 1736 he was chosen minister of the Groninger Old Flemish congregation at Borne, although he lived in Hengelo. This congregation he served until 1757, when he became minister of the congregation at Hengelo. In 1755 he was chosen overseer (*opziener*) of the Groninger Old Flemish congregation, a position which was similar to that of elder (*oudste*). Henceforth it was his task to visit the various congregations in the Netherlands, a charge he performed with great zeal. In the congregation he was a person of great influence. Wolter-Oom (Uncle Wolter), as he was called, was a veritable patriarch among his own people. He exerted a marked influence on the confession of faith drawn up by the Groninger Old Flemish in 1755. His material bounty he shared liberally with his congregation; in 1791, toward the end of his life, he made it possible for his congregation at Hengelo to have a new church, but with the emphatic stipulation that above all it should be sober and simple in appearance.   vDZ.

Uit het Verleden der Dg. in Twenthe (Borne, n.d. 117-18; 135-41; B. Rusburg, *Iets over W. en J. ten Cate als oprigters der fabrijken . . . te Hengelo* (n.p., n.d.).

Catechetical Instruction. *North America.* American Mennonite groups vary considerably in their attitudes toward and in their use of catechetical instruction. Among the major groups who do not officially provide such instruction are the Mennonite Brethren Church, the Evangelical Mennonite Brethren, the Church of God in Christ Mennonite (Holdeman), and the United Missionary Church (formerly Mennonite Brethren in Christ). These groups strongly emphasize a crisis conversion experience as a prerequisite to church membership and tend to minimize the benefits of an instructional period, although some leaders in these groups indicate a personal appreciation of such instruction and report that in some local churches of their groups efforts are being made to provide it. In the Mennonite Brethren Church, for example, a booklet called *Fundamentals of Faith in Question and Answer* was published in 1943 under the direction of The Board of Home Missions of the Southern District Conference of the Mennonite Brethren Church of North America. This was designed for use "in church Bible classes, in our Bible schools, and vacation Bible schools." The preface, however, expressed the concern that "the learning of its contents may never be substituted for regeneration or a personal experience of religion."

Two conferences of the Mennonite Brethren in Christ petitioned their General Conference in 1924 for a "Book of Instruction" for the youth of the church. As a result a committee was appointed and in 1930 a "Book of Religious Instruction" was published by the executive committee. Containing 110 pages, the book was compiled and edited by Elder Samuel Goudie, a district superintendent of the Ontario Conference. This catechism has been used in several churches in various conferences but has never been employed by the church as a whole.

The Old Order Amish, who generally oppose Sunday schools, do provide catechetical instruction for those who desire to unite with the church. This usually occurs between the ages of 14-18. Instead of following a catechism book, however, the instruction usually consists of direct teaching of the Bible and of the orders and rules of the church, arranged and presented by the minister.

The Old Colony Mennonites also give instruction before baptism, which usually occurs at about the age of 19. They use their own edition of the *Katechismus oder Kurze und Einfache Unterweisung aus der Heiligen Schrift*. The memorization method of instruction is generally used.

Catechetical instruction patterns among the (old) Mennonites are apparently not standardized. Usually candidates for baptism, between the ages of 11-17, are instructed in from four to twelve sessions, sometimes longer. Some congregations still use the Dordrecht Confession of Faith with the traditional catechism as the basis for instruction. Daniel Kauffman's *One Thousand Questions and Answers* (1908) was long in use in the East and is still used in some quarters. More recently Chester Lehman's *Junior Catechism* and *Instruction to Beginners in the Christian Life,* edited by John L. Horst, has come into use. Other materials are still in the process of preparation.

In the General Conference Mennonite Church catechetical instruction is almost universally employed but the patterns are not uniform. In German-speaking churches the General Conference edition of the *Katechismus* is employed, while in the others the English catechism (revised 1937) is in most common use. Some churches, however, use *A Guide to Christian Teaching* by Arthur Rosenberger, while some local churches have worked out their own courses of instruction. A recent innovation is the publication of a pupil's catechism workbook, edited by Walter Gering, to supplement the use of the catechism and to introduce better pedagogical procedure.   E.W.

Holland. From the beginning of Anabaptism in Holland until 1670 religious education was the task of the parents. The oldest catechism, that of Pieter Jansz Twisck, *Catechismus,* 1633, was intentionally composed for the purpose of instructing parents how to teach the Mennonite principles and doctrines to their children, but about 1670, as the interest of the parents in instructing their children decreased, the churches took over the task of religious education. At this time the church boards of many congregations ordered their ministers to instruct the children, but many ministers thought it wrong. In 1692 E. A. van Dooregeest (*q.v.*), the Mennonite preacher of de Rijp, wrote that this was not the task of the preacher, but that parents should educate their children in the teachings and admonition of the Lord; and as late as 1760, K. de Vries,

a Lamist minister of Amsterdam, warned from the pulpit against religious teaching by the ministers.

But gradually it became the practice for the ministers to give the instruction. Only in the Old Flemish branch did the parents continue to give religious instruction until the middle of the 18th century. In both the Lamist and Zonist congregations the teaching by the ministers at first took place on Sunday morning after the regular church service, all the children being at first assembled in the church at the same time. But soon the boys were separated from the girls, and also the younger ones from older. Later the catechism classes were held on a week day, usually Wednesday. At present the young people, divided into groups according to age (from about the 12th until at least their 18th year), have an annual course of instruction. During the last year of this course they are prepared for baptism. In former times the teachers generally used a catechism book, of which there have been from 1633 until now more than 140 different compilations. Now ministers often compose their own catechism.   vDZ.

N. van der Zijpp, *Gesch. der Doopsgez. in Nederland* (Arnhem, 1952) 127 f.; Kühler, *Geschiedenis* III, 4-7; *DJ* 1850, 107-10; *DB* 1868, 107-10; 1869, 94, 102, 104.

Remainder of Europe. In Germany the Dutch-speaking congregations in the North (Danzig and surrounding area, Hamburg-Altona, Emden and region, and Crefeld) followed the example of the Dutch churches and used Dutch materials. Gradually German catechisms were published, such as Georg Hansen's *Glaubensbericht* at Danzig 1671, G. Roosen's justly popular *Christliches Gemüthsgespräch* of 1702 at Hamburg, and the widely used Elbing-Waldeck *Kurze und einfältige Unterweisung aus der Heiligen Schrift* (1778 in Elbing, 1797 in Waldeck). The very first German catechism was the 1690 *Kurze Unterweisung aus der Schrift,* published most likely at Danzig. This booklet was used in Russia where it was reprinted first in 1853. The South German Mennonites produced their own catechisms in the 19th century; for the Palatinate Molenaar's *Katechismus der Christlichen Lehre* of 1841, and for the Badischer Verband the *Christliches Lehrbüchlein* of 1865.

Apparently the South German Mennonites, being of Swiss origin, were much slower to introduce catechetical instruction, as is evidenced by the late appearance of their books. The Amish Mennonites never produced a catechism of their own, but used the Prussian Elbing catechism widely (editions Waldeck, 1797; Strasbourg, 1801; Giessen, 1834; Zweibrücken, 1855; French translation, Montbéliard, 1822). The Swiss Mennonites were very slow in adopting the catechetical method, introducing the *Lehrbüchlein* of the Baden Conference toward the end of the 19th century. The Alsatian congregations had done the same thing somewhat earlier. Today the catechetical method is almost universal among the German- and French-speaking churches of Europe. The only exception was the Mennonite Brethren churches of Russia.

South America. The newly established colonies

in Paraguay, Brazil, and Uruguay have followed the model of their European or Canadian mother churches.

For a detailed bibliography see the article **Catechism.** (*ML* II, 469-71.)   H.S.B.

Catechism, designation for the booklets in which the main outline of Christian doctrine is presented (usually with Scripture references) in the form of questions and answers, for the instruction of youth. The term originated in the Reformation period, apparently having been used first by Johannes Brenz (*q.v.*) in 1528, although the practice of catechetical instruction (*q.v.*) goes back to early Christian times. The oldest Protestant catechism was probably Luther's *Kurze Form der 10 Gebote, des Glaubens, des Vaterunsers* of 1520. Well known are Luther's large and small catechisms, both of 1529. With these and the Brenz catechism must be ranked the Reformed *Heidelberg Catechismus* of 1563. The first Roman Catholic catechism appeared in 1535. The standard Anglican catechism is dated 1604, and the Presbyterian (Westminster) 1646 and 1647.

Among Anabaptist publications, Balthasar Hubmaier's may be considered the oldest catechism, bearing the title, *Ein Christennliche Leertafel, die ein yedlicher mensch, ee vnd er im Wasser getaufft wirdt, vor wissen solle* (Nikolsburg 1526). In it Hubmaier treats the various points of doctrine in the form of a conversation between Hans and Leonhard von Liechtenstein.

It is not probable that Hubmaier's catechism was actually used as such. For a long time there is no indication that a catechism was used by the Anabaptists (except among the Hutterian Brethren, Walpot's, *q.v..*, catechism) in addition to the Bible in youth instruction. The Dutch Mennonites were the first known to use them, and produced over 140 different forms 1633-1950, none of which became universally accepted or dominant.

The Swiss and South German Anabaptists, and their later descendants as Mennonites, never produced a catechism of their own (except a Swiss *Katechismus der christlichen Lehre,* Basel 1830 and Langnau 1879), and did not use a catechism booklet of any sort, even a borrowed one, until the later 18th century. It was the North Germans, under Dutch influence, who introduced the catechism among the German-speaking Mennonites, and two of their productions became very popular among the South Germans and the Pennsylvania Mennonites as well as among the Russian Mennonites.

The first German catechism, very brief, called *Kurze Unterweisung aus der Schrift,* with 36 questions and answers, which appeared in Danzig in 1690, has been very popular. It has appeared attached to all American editions, both German and English, of the *Christliches Gemüthsgespräch* (first edition, Ephrata 1769; first English edition, Lancaster 1857) and in condensed form in Christian Burkholder's *Anrede an die Jugend* (Lancaster 1804, first English edition, Lancaster 1857). It appeared in Spanish in 1927 (*Breve Catecismo*) along with the Dordrecht *Confesion de Fe* at Pehuajo, Argentina.

However, the first comprehensive German catechism was this same *Christliches Gemüthsgespräch* of Gerrit Roosen, minister of the Hamburg church, first published at Ratzeburg in 1702, containing 148 questions and answers. It was reprinted five times in Germany 1727, 1766, 1783, 1816, and 1838 (all without indication of place), after which it went out of use there, being supplanted by Molenaar's *Katechismus der christlichen Lehre* of 1841 for the Palatinate and by the *Christliches Lehrbüchlein* of 1865 in Baden. In America there were 14 German editions of it (1769, 1770, 1790, 1811, 1836, 1839, 1846, 1848, 1868, 1871, 1873, 1891, 1902, 1930), and six English (1857, 1870, 1878, 1892, 1921, 1941). Strangely the book also contains the Prussian catechism of 1690, and for several editions a third short catechism by A. Z. It was not used by the Amish. It was reprinted in Biel, Switzerland, in 1877.

A third popular catechism, *Kurze und einfältige Unterweisung aus der Heiligen Schrift,* though first published in Elbing in 1778, became *the* catechism of the Amish congregations in both Europe and America, with German editions in Waldeck 1797, Strasbourg 1801, Giessen 1834, Zweibrücken 1856, 1880, Regensburg 1877, Montbéliard (Mümpelgart) 1855, 1860, and 1891. French language editions appeared at Nancy 1862, Neufchateau 1869, Baccarat 1898, and Montbéliard 1922, under the title *Catechisme ou Instruction tirée de l' Ecriture Sainte.* Meanwhile the West Prussians themselves were constantly reprinting it: Elbing 1794, Marienwerder 1802, 1862, Marienburg (n.d.), Elbing 1806, ——, 1833, 1837, 1890, Marienburg 1935 (tenth edition). The West Prussian immigrants published it at Odessa 1851, 1865, St. Petersburg 1870, Berdyansk 1874, 1879, Odessa again in 1890, Halbstadt 1898 and 1912, and at Stuttgart, Germany, in 1860. There was an edition of 1845 published by Philip Machold, but no place given.

In America the Elbing catechism was first printed at Ephrata (Pa.) in 1824 (for the Mennonites of Waterloo Co., Ont.), with reprints Doylestown 1844, Berlin 1845, Schippach 1848, Milford Square 1863, 1879 (2), Elkhart 1869, 1872, 1878, 1881, 1888, 1892, 1898 (EMB), 1900, 1907 (EMB), 1914, 1918, Scottdale 1929 (11th edition), Berne (revised) 1897, 1898, 1901, 1924, and 1926, 1935 (revised edition for Canada). There was an Amish edition at Berne, 1925, "Im Auftrage der Amisch Christlichen Gemeinde von Berne." The Old Colony Mennonites of Mexico published it in 1943 and 1950 (Cuauhtemoc). The *Rundschau* (MB) Publishing House of Winnipeg, now the Christian Press, began to publish the catechism in German about 1924; the 1927 edition is labeled the 13th, with the 1940 edition, issued for the Kleine Gemeinde, labeled the 19th. The Old Order Amish publisher, L. A. Miller, Arthur, Ill., issued editions in 1928 and 1940. English editions appeared as follows: (Rupp Translation) Lancaster 1849, Milford Square 1878, Quakertown 1889, and (revised Elkhart translation) at Elkhart 1874, 1881, 1883, 1889, 1898, 1905; at Berne (new tr. from revised German) 1897, 1904, 1917, 1922, 1925, 1928, 1931; (again revised) 1934, 1937. It is worth noting that this catechism thus became not only the catechism of the Amish in America, but also of the Mennonites (MC), the General Conference Mennonites, the Evangelical Mennonite Brethren, and the Kleine Gemeinde (now called Evangelical Mennonites). It is nothing short of astounding to discover that the Elbing-Waldeck catechism became the standard source of doctrinal, prebaptismal instruction for such widespread groups as the American groups just listed, the Mennonites of Russia (except the M.B. group 1860 ff.), those of West Prussia, and those of France; further that it is still in widespread use in North America wherever catechisms are used, in both English and German; and finally, that no other catechism, except the much larger and somewhat different *Gemüthsgespräch*—and that only among the Mennonites (MC) of Eastern Pennsylvania—has ever successfully competed with it in any language in these countries. Does this not explain, in part at least, the widespread doctrinal agreement among these groups? Since it contains a strong article on nonresistance one may assume that it also contributed to the steadfast maintenance of this doctrine.

Numerous other catechisms of lesser popularity were produced and used in Germany. Among them are Johannes Molenaar's *Katechismus der christlichen Lehre,* Leipzig 1841, 1854; revised and condensed as *Katechismus der christlichen Lehre,* Worms 1861 and Karlsruhe 1922; *Christliches Lehrbüchlein,* Heilbronn 1865, 1868, Sinsheim 1893 (condensed), 1913, Stuttgart 1922, Langnau (edition for the Swiss churches) 1943. At Crefeld in 1836 and 1852 appeared *Christliche Lehre,* revised by E. Weydmann in 1888, the same further revised in 1898. The Dutch Mennonite preacher Joannes Deknatel's *Anleitung zum Christlichen Glauben* (Dutch editions 1746, 1747, and 1764) appeared in German editions in 1756 (Amsterdam), Neuwied 1790, Worms 1829, Alzey 1839. A number of catechisms were issued in West Prussia: Georg Hansen, *Ein Glaubensbericht vor die Jugend,* Danzig 1671; Joh. Peter Sprunk, *Katechismus* (1723-43); *Konfession oder kurzer, einfältiger Glaubensunterricht der altflamischem Taufgesinnten Gemeinde in Preussen im Jahre 1730 in Fragen und Antworten,* 1768; Hermann Jantzen, *Confession oder kurzer Glaubensunterricht derer bekannten Taufgesinnten Gemeinden in Preussen, Zur Erbauung der Jugend . . . in 92 Fragen und Antworten,* 1741; Jakob de Veer, *Catechismus oder biblischer Religionsunterricht in Frage und Antwort,* Danzig 1791. The Conference of East and West Prussian churches in 1935 authorized the preparation of a new catechism based on the Palatine - Hessian and the Flemish - Frisian - West Prussian booklets and appointed a commission for this purpose. In 1936 the attempt was given up and the congregations were advised to use whatever catechisms they pleased.

Two regular new catechisms were attempted in America. The first was *Katechismus der Christlichen Lehre* prepared by a committee appointed for that purpose by the General Conference of the Mennonites of North America in 1868 and published in 1882 by Christian Schowalter at Primrose, Iowa. If it was designed to displace the older Elbing catechism already in time-honored use in the congregations of the conference, it failed, for no further editions appeared, while the Elbing catechism has continued in use to the present day. The Old Order Amish *Katechismus für kleine Kinder,* prepared by S. D. Guengerich of Johnson Co., Iowa, and first published at Elkhart in 1888, was more successful. It has gone through five editions (Elkhart 1888, 1903, 1916, and Arthur, Ill., 1928 and 1940) and is still in use. The full title is *Katechismus für kleine Kinder. Zum Gebrauch für Schulen, Sonntagsschulen und Familien. Besonders bearbeitet für die Kleinkinder-Klassen zur Grundlage eines evangelischen Religions-Unterrichts.* In spite of the group's rejection of the catechetical method, a book of doctrinal instruction very similar to a catechism has been published in recent years by the Mennonite Brethren Church (Hillsboro, Kan., 1943 and 1946) bearing the title *Fundamentals of Faith in Questions and Answer Form* (prepared under the direction of the Board of Home Missions of the Southern District Conference), 66 pages.

David H. Epp, minister in the Chortitza Mennonite congregation in South Russia, published in 1896 (new edition at Odessa-Ekaterinoslav in 1899, Canadian edition at Rosthern 1941) an extensive commentary on the Elbing catechism entitled *Kurze Erklärungen u. Erläuterungen zum "Katechismus der christlichen, taufgesinnten Gemeinden so Mennoniten genannt werden"* (258 pp.) to which is attached a brief survey of Mennonite history (36 pp.) and a list of Mennonite periodicals. C. H. Wedel, professor at Bethel College, Newton, Kan., did much the same thing in 1910 in his *Meditationen zu den Fragen und Antworten unseres Katechismus* (322 pp.). In 1951 Walter Gering wrote a Catechism *Workbook* (Newton, Kan.) to be used as an aid for ministers in teaching the catechism.

A number of short pamphlets similar to catechisms have been published in America. H. D. Penner's *Kurzer Leitfaden für den Religionsunterricht in der Kinderlehre* (Hillsboro 1912), the Hutterite *Einige Fragen und ihre Beantwortung für die reifere Jugend* (before 1928), and Chester K. Lehman's *Junior Catechism* (Scottdale 1933, reprinted as late as 1944) should be mentioned here.

As has been noted, many of the catechism editions did not appear as separate publications, but in combination, usually with a confession of faith, sometimes with a collection of prayers and hymns added.

Theologically the various catechisms reflect the current climate in the Mennonite churches where they were composed. Mostly they reveal some departure from the earlier strict Anabaptist doctrinal and ethical position in the direction of Pietism (Deknatel's *Anleitung* for instance) or standard Lutheranism (Roosen's *Gemüthsgespräch*). The Elbing-Waldeck catechism remained closer to original Anabaptism than any other.

It has been the policy of the Mennonite Brethren

Church to reject all catechisms and catechetical instruction from its beginning in Russia, in favor of an emphasis on evangelistic preaching and conversion. This and the obvious nonuse of the catechetical method and nonpublication of a catechism by Anabaptist-Mennonites in any country for the first century and a quarter of their history poses the question as to whether catechisms are an importation, foreign to the genius of Anabaptism, whose use indicates a spiritual decline of the brotherhood and departure from its original character and type of piety, or whether it was actually a fruitful adaptation from the outside, useful and beneficial throughout the long history of its use in the Amish and Mennonite churches of Germany, France, Prussia, Russia, Holland, and North America. (*ML* II, 469 f.)† NEFF, H.S.B.

Cathalijne (Calleken) and **Suzanneken Claes,** Anabaptist martyrs, the daughters of Lieven (*q.v.*), who was put to death at Gent, Belgium, on Sept. 27, 1549. They had been baptized at Gent in the spring of 1572 by the bishop Paulus van Meenen (*q.v.*). Both were unmarried; Suzanne was 25, Calleken 24 years old; they were living in Gent. First they were imprisoned in the city prison, and after the inquisitors had vainly tried to make them renounce their faith, they were burned at the stake on the Vrijdagsmarkt on Dec. 3 (*Mart. Mir.,* Dec. 4), 1573. Before the execution took place a ball was put in their mouths, preventing them from speaking to the people who had assembled to watch the execution. Calleken is called Calleken Draeyarts by van Braght in the *Martyrs' Mirror;* this name was not found, however, by Dr. Verheyden, who studied the official documents. (*Mart. Mir.* D 674, E 991; Verheyden, *Gent* 65, Nos. 232-33; *ML* I, 358.) VDZ.

Cathalijne Loury (or Burieu), an Anabaptist martyr, wife of Pieter Michiels, a native of Zwevegem, Flanders, was burned for her faith at Brugge, Belgium, in 1568. She belonged to the congregation which was led by Jacob de Rore (*q.v.*), and of which 14 members were seized in February 1568 by the henchmen of the Inquisition. Nine of them forsook their faith, but Cathalijne and four others remained faithful to the cruel death. The exact date of her execution is not known; it must have taken place between April 13 and July 28, of 1568 (Verheyden, *Brugge,* 54, No. 53). VDZ.

Catharina (Katherijn), an Anabaptist martyr, executed April 19, 1551. She came from Lier (Belgian Brabant), was apprehended at Gent by treachery, and condemned to be burned to death. On the scaffold she requested that the thongs be removed from her hands that she might pray. When this was refused she knelt with her hands bound. When she was tied to the stake, a "seducer" tried to dissuade her from the faith, but she asked him to leave her in peace. After this she suffered cruel death by fire together with Joris (Goris Cooman, *q.v.*), *Wouter* (Wouter van der Weyden), Grietgen (Margriete vanden Berghe, *q.v.*), and Naentken (N. Bornaige, *q.v.*). A song concerning these five martyrs is found in the *Liedtboecxken vanden Offer*

des Heeren (No. 4): "Doemen vijftienhondert schreve, Daertoe een en vijftig jaer." VDZ.
   Offer, 516-21; *Mart. Mir.* D 106, E 503; Verheyden, *Gent,* 14, No. 25; Wolkan, *Lieder,* 61; *ML* II, 472.

Catharina Müllerin (the wife of Müller, or the wife of a miller), an old woman, was arrested at Zürich, Switzerland, in 1639; she had, while in prison, to endure much for the sake of the truth, but finally she was released. (*Mart. Mir.* D 813, E 1,111.) VDZ.

Catharina and **Lijsbeth Somerhuys,** Anabaptist martyrs, seized by the Spaniards in the Dutch town of Deventer, March 11, 1571, with ten other Mennonites. These two women, both unmarried, were the daughters of Albert Somerhuys, the registrar of Deventer. They were put in prison in the Noordenbergertoren together with the others and had a very severe and cruel imprisonment. Some of the 12 Mennonites recanted, but only for a short time, and all died for their faith. But Catharina and Lijsbeth never recanted. When the Catholic priest visited them in prison, Catharina disputed frankly with him; the priest tried to demonstrate the truth of the Roman Catholic faith from the Old Testament, but Catharina answered that she preferred the New Testament and showed him from the New Testament that his assertions were dull and unscriptural. Both women were sentenced to death. Leaving the prison they sang the song, "Mijn Godt, waer sal ick henen gaen" (My God, whither shall I go). They were taken to the stakes, but after a short time they were returned to the prison. Ydse Gaukes (*q.v.*), who was one of their group, mentions in his first letter (*Mart. Mir.*) that Catharina was cruelly tortured together with two other women and two men. She had to wait some weeks before the hour of their execution struck. On June 16. 1571, both were burned at the stake at the Brink (a market place). Van Braght relates that at the moment of the execution of these six martyrs a miracle occurred: a crashing noise was heard, like thunder, and the spectators were thrown to the earth. Albert Somerhuys, the father of Catharina and Lijsbeth, was arrested soon after the execution and condemned to life imprisonment, but soon he died in prison, obviously by poison administered to him by a Catholic priest. (*Mart. Mir.* D 552-54, E 885-88; *DB* 1919, 29-37.) VDZ.

Cathars (Cathari or Catharists), a religious sect of the 11th century of remote Balkan origin, representing a renewal of Manichaeism, which spread through northern Italy and southern France. Their belief was based on a dualistic conception of the world. The visible world is subject to evil, the devil; the invisible world is subject to God. Satan, with Moses as his tool, delayed the redemptive work of God (hence they rejected the legal books of the Old Testament) until it was carried through by Christ, who had only apparently assumed human nature. Since the soul is the divine part of man, it must be freed from matter to enter the kingdom of light. On this basis they rejected marriage, forbade the eating of meat, demanded complete chastity, and denied the resurrection. They were hostile to the external church. Baptism and communion had no meaning for them, and they rejected the adoration of images. In the place of the two sacraments they believed in the baptism of the spirit (*consolamentum*) through the laying on of hands, and strict moral demands (poverty, chastity, asceticism), which were certain to lead to blessedness unless some sin was committed afterward.

The *perfecti,* with their severely moral conduct, exerted great influence on the people and through their itinerant preaching won many believers (*credentes*), who did not, however, leave the Catholic Church.

In southern France, where the moral and cultural level of the Catholic clergy was particularly low, the movement became very powerful. About 1200 most of the princes and barons were *credentes.* In the cities and castles *perfecti* preached openly and built chapels and schools for boys and girls. The Catholic Church here led a merely tolerated existence. Since the church was unable to subdue these Cathars, here known as Albigenses (after Albi, a city in southern France where they were very numerous), with spiritual weapons, she organized a crusade against them and in a bloody war lasting 20 years finally succeeded in crushing the movement.

The Cathars in Spain, Italy, and Germany were wiped out by the Inquisition (*q.v.*). Yet they did not disappear without leaving their traces behind. In 1215 the Catholic doctrine of transubstantiation was made a dogma in order to oppose the dualism of the Cathars. The *consolamentum* led to the development of the sacrament of the extreme unction; and the moral rigor of the Cathars led to the begging monastic orders.

The Cathars cannot be considered forerunners of the Anabaptists. Though both groups rejected infant baptism, their motives were far apart. The Anabaptists based their doctrine on the Bible, the Cathars on the (essentially Persian and pagan) opposition between light and matter, which completely devaluates everything earthly. Spiritual baptism brought redemption from the world, but if even a single sin was committed afterward, salvation was forfeited. In order to avoid committing any possible sin after receiving this baptism, many chose to die (by hunger). In the matter of the rejection of war and of killing likewise, the Anabaptists based their belief on the Biblical prohibition, whereas the Cathars' belief was founded on their un-Biblical (though deep) conception of sin as the inclination toward matter; hence the eating of meat, killing of animals and human beings, sexual relations, and the owning of property were equally serious sins. He who rids himself of these things is saved; the ascetic life is therefore the guarantee of eternal life. The Anabaptists also were distinguished for their purity of conduct, as their preference for the Sermon on the Mount indicates, but they conceived moral living as a natural conduct of the regenerated man who follows in the steps of Christ. There was an equally serious difference between the two groups in the idea of the church. In spite of the great attraction of the Cathar doctrines for the masses, they made

a sharp distinction between the *credentes* and the *perfecti,* and in spite of their opposition to clerical domination, they developed a sort of hierarchy in the course of time. We even hear of a Cathar pope!

In summary, it may be said that precisely the points of doctrine that are apparently common to both Cathars and Anabaptists show most clearly the fundamental difference between them, the difference between Persian religiosity and Christianity. Nor are there any external connecting lines between them. Catharism of all branches was literally wiped out by fire and sword.   H.Q.

"Katharer," in *HRE* and *RGG; Ztscht f. hist. Theol.* (1847) IV; L. Keller, *Johann von Staupitz . . .* (Leipzig, 1888) 92 and 247; Edm. Broecx, *Le Catharisme* (Hoogstraten, 1916); J. Lindeboom, *Stiefkinderen von het Christendom* (The Hague, 1929) 43-66; E. Holmes, *The Albigensian or Catharist Heresy. A Story and a Study* (London, 1925); H. C. Lea, *A History of the Inquisition of the Middle Ages* (N.Y., 3 vv. 1888). *ML* II, 471.

Catherine II, empress of Russia 1762-96, called the Mennonites as competent colonists (see **Chortitza**) into her recently acquired lands in the Ukraine. On July 22, 1763, she issued a manifesto guaranteeing to all German immigrants, regardless of creed, freedom of speech, schools, and religion; autonomous government of villages, communities, and colonist areas; and, above all, freedom from military service. By means of a special document signed by George von Trappe she invited the Mennonites in West Prussia to immigrate to Russia, promising them complete freedom "for all time," and 65 dessiatines (*ca.* 165 acres) of land for each family. On Aug. 7, 1786, the document was read aloud at a public meeting at Danzig. In autumn of the same year Höppner (*q.v.*) and Bartsch (*q.v.*) went to Russia as deputies of the Prussian Mennonites. They were ceremoniously received by the empress, who was on her journey to Taurida, and "out of special grace and favor" they had to accompany her to the Crimea. The empress remained friendly to the Mennonites throughout her life.

NEFF.

G. Thomson, *Catherine the Great and the Expansion of Russia* (N.Y., 1950); *ML* II, 472.

Catholicism and Anabaptism. This is a theme which has not yet been thoroughly studied. Of course the Catholic encyclopedias contain articles on the Anabaptists (F. X. Funk in the *Kirchenlexikon* by Wetzer and Welte, and N. A. Weber in the *Catholic Encyclopedia*), but the very use of the designation *Wiedertäufer* in German denotes not merely a popular wrong usage of the word, but rather a dogmatic judgment that ranks the Anabaptism of the Reformation period into the traditional chain of *rebaptizantes* in order to be able to strike at them with the traditional edicts issued against these.

The teaching office of the Catholic Church has never, to our knowledge, had any particular interest in the Anabaptists of the 16th century—not so much because they did not seem important enough, or because punishment by the temporal arm, be it that of the emperor or that of temporal or spiritual regional rulers, was effective, but because they saw no problem here; the matter had long since been settled—negatively—ever since the conflicts with heretics in baptism in the third century and in rejection of the Donatists and medieval heretics, in the establishment of a single baptism. "We believe that in the one, true, catholic, and apostolic church one (i.e., a single) baptism is given," was a statement passed at the Council of Lyons in 1274; and Augustine said in his commentary on Psalm 54: "Nor had baptism received full treatment before the outside rebaptizers (he means the Novatians) raised their objections." (See also the ruling of the *Codex Theodosianus* of A.D. 373: baptism must not be repeated, in C. Kirch, *Enchiridion,* 1910, 468, and other places in the table of contents.)

Nevertheless the Anabaptists played a part in the great general agreement Catholicism made with the Reformation in the Council of Trent. Zwingli's old opponent, Johann Faber, mentions them as early as July 6, 1536, in a preliminary opinion to Pope Paul III, as "The most ruinous sect, not unlike the errors of the Donatists," and states that it was urgently necessary to "have their books." It must not be overlooked that these words were written soon after the catastrophe of Münster, which continued to have its effect in the later councils as a horrible example. To find the Anabaptists lumped together with the Sacramentalists is not surprising. The Lutherans did the same.

In the numerous tracts connected with the Tridentine Council, the Anabaptists are opposed by Johann Haner, Johann Cochlaeus, Hieronymus Alexander, and Francis Reghini, usually in connection with the ordinance of baptism, concerning which "the Anabaptists assert that it must be repeated." Nicolas de Ponte, the orator of Duke Albrecht of Bavaria, in his speech of June 27, 1562, at the council, mentions the Anabaptists with the Zwinglians, Lutherans, Flaccians, and Manichaeists. On July 1, 1562, there was discussion in the general assembly of the council as to whether the article on the communion should be formulated against the Zwinglians and Anabaptists, or against the Protestants, with whom the two above groups are apparently not included. The Augustinian General Seripandus in the session of Feb. 17, 1547, condemned the "Anabaptists with the Donatists." When the *Concilium Tridentinum,* the great work of the *Görresgesellschaft,* to which we owe these notes, is published, the significance of Anabaptism to the council can be exactly determined.

At any rate, the following canons of Session VII of the council are aimed at Anabaptists: Canon 11, "If anyone says that a true and properly administered baptism must be repeated with one who has denied the Christian faith among unbelievers, when he repents, he shall be banned"; Canon 12, "If anyone says that none shall be baptized except at the age at which Christ was baptized or immediately facing death, he shall be banned"; Canon 13, "If anyone says that children are not to be reckoned among the believers after baptism because they do not have the act of faith, and must therefore be baptized again when they come to years of accountability, or that it would be better to postpone their baptism than to baptize only in the faith of the

church those who do not believe by an independent act of faith, he shall be banned."

The new law book of the Catholic Church, the *Codex iuris canonici,* takes for granted as self-evident that infant baptism is necessary to salvation (canon 737), rules (canon 770) that children should be baptized as soon as possible, stresses (canon 732) that the rite of baptism cannot be repeated, and has the *Professio catholicae fidei* placed at the head. It expressly acknowledges the decisions of Trent as binding.

Catholic publication of the 16th century against the Anabaptists was not so lively as that of the Protestants; nevertheless in their polemic against the Reformation, particularly against the Sacramentalists, many a word was directed against the Anabaptists. The fact that Anabaptism emanated from the Protestant movement and set up its tenets against it, was bound to evoke a very different opposition on the part of the Protestants than that of the Catholics, who opposed Anabaptism essentially as a part of Protestantism. The Dominican Ambrosius Pelargus wrote at Freiburg i.Br. in 1530, *In Anabaptistarum errores aliquot;* in 1531, *In Eleutherobaptistas* (Against Those Who Will Not Acknowledge the Necessity of Baptism); in 1531, *An fas sit in Anabaptistas adeoque in Haereticos poena capitis animadvertere.* Also the booklet of Pelargus against Oecolampadius, *Refutatio consilii Oecolampadii de differendo parvulorum baptismo in trimulam aut quadrimulam usque aetatem 1530* belongs in this list. (N. Paulus, *Die deutschen Dominikaner im Kampfe gegen Luther,* 1903, 199 ff.) The most important—because it is the only complete presentation by an eyewitness-source for the history of the Anabaptist kingdom in Münster, Hermann von Kerssenbroich's *Anabaptistici furoris Monasterium inclitam Westphaliae metropolim evertentis historica narratio,* comes from a Catholic, who judges from the point of view of his church.

Since one of the most important measures of the Counter Reformation was the sending out of papal nuncios into the endangered regions, the reports of these emissaries naturally contain material on the Anabaptists (but probably not too abundant) in places where there were some living in territory to be recatholicized at the end of the 16th century. It must suffice here to point out this source (L. Just, "Die Erforschung der päpstlichen Nuntiaturen, Stand und Aufgaben, besonders in Deutschland," in *Quellen und Forschungen aus italienischen Archiven* XXIV, 1932). Details belong to the history of the Catholic territories. No less valuable are the episcopal diocesan reports to Rome, the importance of which is indicated by the work of J. Schmidlin (3 vv.), *Die kirchlichen Zustände in Deutschland vor dem 30jährigen Kriege nach den bischöflichen Diözesanberichten an den Hl. Stuhl* (1908-10).

Though there can be no doubt that the struggle of the Anabaptists against the ethical sterility of infant baptism released a strong reaction in favor of an ethical renewal of the covenant of baptism (see **Confirmation**), it must also be mentioned that in the contemporary Catholic Church in connection with the revival and invigorating of the entire liturgy, the "Belebung des Taufbewusstseins" (title of a treatise by P. Parsch in *Bibel und Liturgie,* No. 6, 1932) or "Tauf und Tauferneuerung" (*Volksliturgische Andachten,* No. 18, 1929) was vigorously discussed. The Catholic periodical for the St. Bernard pastorate in Frankfurt (Vol. VI, 1932, No. 3) stated:

"However we exert ourselves, we have no baptismal experience that goes with us. The day of our first holy communion is unforgettable, the day of our sacramental marriage stands large and ineradicable in our souls. But our baptism occurred while our soul was still in slumber, and was not yet capable of an experience. However, we live constantly from our baptism, as the tree from its roots, we constantly call ourselves by the name of Christian like a family name. Therefore the church wants to make up for the missing experience. So on Saturday before Easter she places us around the baptismal font, fills it with water, consecrates it as a sacred source of supernatural life, sprinkles us with it in memory of our first washing, gives us some to take home, that we may use it in the morning and evening. Do you think of this when the priest carries it through the church every Sunday before High Mass, when you bless yourself upon entering and leaving the church, upon leaving and returning to your home? Our annual belated baptismal experience shall be so great and powerful that we need a whole year to live it up."

Here it is not confirmation but the consecrated holy water that becomes the moment of the baptismal renewal, and it is a daily renewal.

At other places the pastor is strongly urged to speak of this first and most important sacrament from time to time in religious instruction, in preaching, and in school and explain it with translations of the ritual and prayer. Or, in contrast to the practice of administering the sacrament in a corner of the church, only before the nearest relatives, quickly and unceremoniously, "baptism should become an affair for the entire congregation with a short address. The individual Christian is expected to renew his baptism with special meditation on his baptismal day."

Historical teaching grants that in the primitive church the baptismal candidates were "mostly adults," and that the rite was preceded by the threefold question put to the candidate, whether he believed in the Father, Son, and Holy Ghost—questions which are to have meaning only in relation to original adult baptism, but are now answered by the baptized infant's godfather. Thus there are still some old Christian elements alive in the Catholic Church. But the points of contact between Anabaptism and Catholicism should not be overrated. The fundamental, radical difference remains.

The hierarchy, which Anabaptism, based on the concept of the priesthood of all believers, rejects, is everything in Catholicism; without the priest no salvation. Sociologically the Catholic Church is an institution with firmly established resources of salvation, which it gives to believers born into it, in

strictly canalized methods; the Anabaptist **group** is a brotherhood into which one enters by **the act** of personal confession, and which is for its **members** only the form of the common life, never a compulsory institution. The living organism of all **the** members, which among the Dutch Mennonites eliminated even sex distinctions (in Germany **the** question did not become acute, and elsewhere I Cor. 14:34 f. is binding), and which lets the Anabaptists act as a body, is in Catholicism split by the distinction between clergy and laity, which in spite of all revival of the "lay apostleship" grants the layman no independence of any kind, and keeps women from any contact with the altar (literally and symbolically).

Whereas Anabaptism strictly speaking has no sacraments, i.e., it knows no means of grace attached to outward symbols, but rather sees in communion and baptism acts of confession on the part of the believer or the believing community, the seven Catholic sacraments are interpreted as being strictly "sacramental"; independently of the state or quality of the recipient the means of grace is attached to the so-called material of the sacrament with partly spiritual and partly physical effect and becomes effective by the mere performance of the rite. The charge of sacrament magic cannot be denied (though it does not apply to all individual cases). This is particularly true of baptism.

The principle (canon 737 of *Codex jur. can.*) that baptism is necessary to salvation (also in the Lutheranism of the Confession of Augsburg of 1530) is carried out to its furthest implications. Salvation actually depends on the act of baptism, even though the damnation of children dying unbaptized is not expressly stated and a particular act of grace is possible in such a case. In an emergency —and only then—can a layman, or even a woman administer baptism, father or mother only if there is danger of death and no one else is at hand; very exact stipulations are made about a possible baptism of an unborn child or of limbs that have made their appearance in the world, or the baptism of monstrosities, or on conditional baptism (for instance, in case of doubt as to whether the child is living or dead) (canon 742-49).

There are unbridgeable differences between Catholicism and Anabaptism. **W.K.**

Catholic authors who wrote against Anabaptism and Mennonitism were: Johann Faber, *Adversus Doctorem Balthasarum Pacimontanum* (Leipzig, 1528); Bartholomeus Arnoldi de Usingen, *Anabaptismus contra Rebaptisantes* (Cologne, 1529); L. Dickius, *Adversus impios anabaptistarum errores* (Haganoae, 1530); Joh. Corbachius, *Contra Anabaptistos* (Cologne, 1535); Martin Duncanus, *Anabaptisticae haereseos confutatio* (Antwerp, 1549); Cunerus Peter, *Den Schilt teghen die Wederdoopers* (Lyons, 1568); Chr. Erhard, *Salus ex inimicis. Goliaths Schwerdt* (Ingolstadt); Chr. Erhard, *Gründliche kurtz verfaste Historia, von den Münsterischen Widertauffern . . .* (Munich, 1589); P. de Bisschop, *Spieghel der Waterlantscher Wederdooperen Leughenkonst . . .* (Rotterdam, 1597); Franc. Costerus, *Toetsteen van de versierde Apostolische Successie eens Wederdoopers . . .* (Antwerp, 1603); C. Gallus, *Malleus Anabaptistarum* (Arnhem, 1606); (S. Walraven), *Successio Anabaptistica . . .* (Cologne, 1603, 1612); C. A. Fischer, *Von der Widertauffer verfluchten Ursprung, Gottlosen Lehre . . .* (Bruck a.d. Teya, 1603); idem, *Antwort auff die Widerlegung so Clauss Breutel der Widertauffer König . . .*

Bruck, 1603); *idem, Vier und funfftzig Erhebliche Ur-chen—Warumb die Widertauffer nicht sein im Land zu yden* (Ingolstadt, 1607); *idem, Der Hutterischen Wider-uffer Taubenkobel* (Ingolstadt, 1607); Georg Eder, *vangelische Inquisition wahrer und falscher Religion* Dillingen, 1573, reprint Ingolstadt, 1580); *ML* II, 472-74.

Catlin Mennonite Church (MC) is located in Catlin Twp., Marion Co., Kan., 1 mile west, and 3½ miles north of Peabody. The first Mennonite family, the Henry Hornbergers, arrived from Pennsylvania in 1873. Among the later settlers who arrived by 1886 appear such names as Cockley, Evers, Doerr, Snyder, Dohner, Wismer, Newcomer, Shelly, Beck, and Gish. They came from Pennsylvania, Virginia, Missouri, and Ontario. The congregation was organized before 1880. A Sunday school was organized in 1888. In 1886, when the present church was built, the membership of the congregation was 65. The first minister was John Evers, who was ordained in Virginia in 1859. Its first bishop was Daniel Brundage (*q.v.*), the pioneer Mennonite bishop of Kansas. During the earlier period of the congregation, fellowship was enjoyed with two small Mennonite settlements in Marion County, the one near Canada, the other near Marion Center. Both of these small settlements are now extinct. It was at the Catlin Church in the 1899 session of the Kansas-Nebraska conference, after a heated discussion, that the possibility of the reception of the Holy Spirit subsequent to conversion was accepted. This action caused serious difficulty in Kansas Mennonite circles later. The 1953 membership was 21. Laurence Horst was serving as pastor.   G.G.Y.

Catonsville, Md., see **Spring Grove State Hospital.**

Catrou, Francois (1659-1737), a French Jesuit priest and historian, author of *Histoire des Anabaptistes* (added title page *Histoire du fanatisme dans les religions protestantes depuis son origine*) (Paris, 1706, Claude Cellier), copy in Amsterdam Mennonite Library and GCL. Later the work was enlarged and published under the modified title, *Histoire du fanatisme des religions protestantes, de l' Anabaptisme, du davidisme . . .* (Paris, 1733, best ed. at Paris, 1740, 2 vv., 12 mo.). The work has little historical value, apparently not based on original sources, but was influential for French Catholic opinion. Whether two other French books bearing the title *Histoire des Anabaptistes,* which were published anonymously, one in Paris and one in Amsterdam about the same time, were by Catrou is uncertain—probably not, and they were probably not by one and the same author. (1) *Histoire des Anabatistes* (sic!) *ou Relation curieuse de leur doctrine, Règne & Révolutions, tant en Allemagne Holland qu' Angleterre, ou il êt traité de plusieurs sectes de Mennonites, Kouakres, autres qui en sont provenus* (Paris, Charles Clouzier, 1695) (copy at GCL, Amsterdam, and Hamburg) and (2) *Histoire des Anabaptistes contenant leur doctrines, les diverses opinions qui les divisent en plusieurs Sectes* (Amsterdam, Jaques Desbordes, 1700; at Amsterdam) (1702 ed. at GCL). The antiquarian catalog, No. 585 (*Occultism*), of Theodor Ackermann in Munich attributes the former to Catrou, giving "Barbier II, 740" as his source. The first book is in

effect a translation of Lambertus Hortensius, *Tumultum anabaptistarum* (1548), which appeared in several Dutch editions in the 17th century including one in Amsterdam in 1699. The pictures in the 1699 Hortensius edition and the two anonymous volumes are almost identical, including the frontispiece. (*ML* I, 336.)   NEFF, H.S.B.

Cattenburgh, Adriaan van, b. Nov. 2, 1664, at Rotterdam, d. March 5, 1743, at Utrecht. After completing his study at the Athenaeum and the Remonstrant (*q.v.*) seminary at Amsterdam, became Remonstrant minister at Rotterdam and later professor (1712-37) at the Remonstrant seminary in Amsterdam. He is honored as the father of Remonstrant historiography. He sought to remove from his denomination once and for all the suspicion of Socinianism as entertained by the Reformed clergy.

Mennonite students preparing for the ministry also attended his lectures, for at this time there was not yet a Mennonite seminary. They attended his classes with many good results, as they had those of his predecessor, the renowned Philippus van Limborch. In 1726, however, Cattenburgh began to take an open and in many respects hostile attitude toward the Mennonites on the issue of nonswearing of oaths. In his book, *Specilegium theologiae christianae* (Amsterdam, 1726; Liber IV), Chap. 29, "De Juramento," and in the translation of this chapter, "Verhandelingen van den Eedt" (Discourses Concerning the Oath, 1729), he gave clear expression to his views. His antipathy to adult baptism also made difficulties because he became more and more partisan in the defense of infant baptism. On this matter he was opposed by Herman Schijn (*q.v.*), Gerardus Maatschoen (*q.v.*), and especially by Abraham Verduin (*q.v.*).

The attitude of Cattenburgh, which was said to be "hostile to the name and the distinctive doctrines of the Mennonites," contributed appreciably to the fact that in 1735 the Mennonite Lamist congregation in Amsterdam took action to found its own Mennonite seminary (*Biogr. Wb.* II, 30-32; *DB* 1868, 54; 1918, 73).   vDZ.

Caucasus, a part of Russia between the Black and Caspian seas, area 154,250 sq. mi., pop. (1950) 14,410,000, predominantly mountain people of Turkish and Tatar origin. Caucasus was incorporated into Russia in 1861.

North Caucasus became the site of several Mennonite colonies. The original settlements in Caucasus fell in the period of strong separatist movements and ensuing religious divisions within the Mennonite circles of the mother colonies in the Ukraine. In the early years "from the base in South Russia proceed only the religiously and morally motivated secessions into Caucasus" (A. Ehrt, *Das Mennonitentum in Russland,* 80): the Templars, a rationalistic wing, to the Tempelhof near Pyatigorsk, and the newly emerging Mennonite Brethren with pietistic tendencies to Kuban. In later years sociological reasons predominated, the settlement at the Terek arising because of the overpopulation of the mother colony of Molotschna.

The founders of the Mennonite settlements in

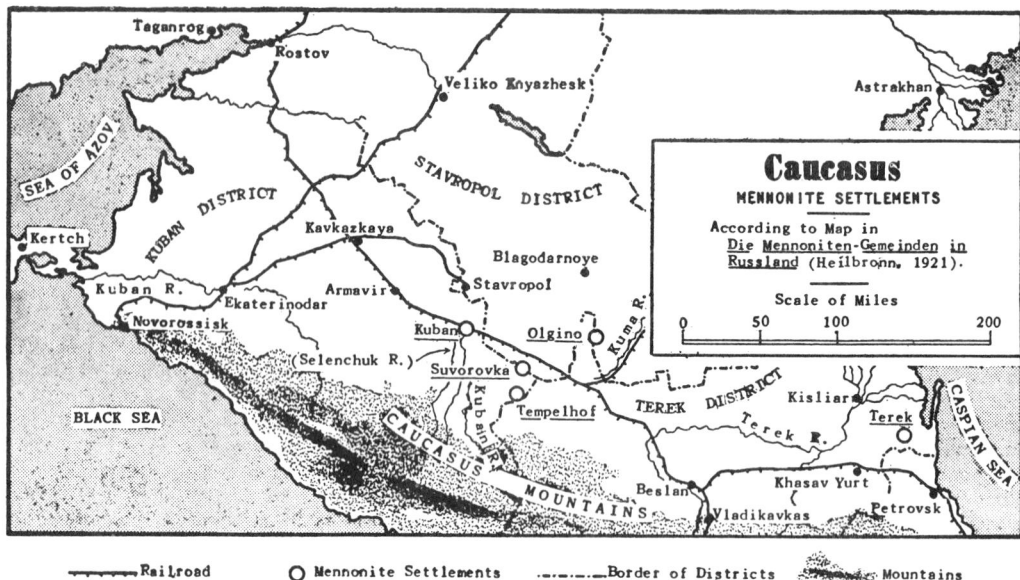

Caucasus came from the Molotschna and Chortitza settlements as well as from the daughter colonies like Zagradovka and Kuban. The Mennonite settlements here were only a minor part of a large Russian settlement movement after Caucasus had been incorporated into Russia, and the Mennonites were only a small group among the many settlers of German extraction who found a new haven of religious freedom and cheap land there.

The first Mennonite settlement established on the Kuban River (1863-66) in the district of Batalpashinsk became known as the Kuban settlement (*q.v.*). It comprised 17,500 acres of land in two villages. This settlement consisted mostly of members of the Mennonite Brethren Church. After World War I it had a population of 1,000. The Kuban (*q.v.*) Mennonite Brethren Church was established in 1864 and had a total population of 502 in 1905. The Wohldemfürst-Alexanderfeld Mennonite Church (*q.v.*) was organized in 1885 and had a total population of 270 in 1905.

The second settlement, consisting of two villages —Tempelhof (*q.v.*) and Orbelianovka—was established in 1866 on 27,000 acres of land in the province of Stavropol and had a population of 700 after World War I. The population of Tempelhof consisted of Friends of Jerusalem (*Jerusalemsfreunde, q.v.*), who had come from the Molotschna settlement; the inhabitants of Orbelianovka were non-Mennonites who had joined the settlement, and the Alexandrodar Mennonite Church of the Friends of Jerusalem (*q.v.;* see also **Johann Lange**).

The Suvorovka (*q.v.*) settlement was located in the province of Stavropol in the district of Alexandrovsk and was established by Mennonites from Zagradovka in 1894. It consisted of four villages on 10,000 acres of land with a population of 1,000 after World War I.

The Olgino (*q.v.*) settlement, located in the province of Stavropol, was established in 1895 and consisted of 4 villages with an area of 12,000 acres.

After World War I the population was 1,000, and belonged to the Olgino (*q.v.*) Mennonite Church of Friends of Jerusalem.

Terek (*q.v.*) was the largest, latest, and least successful settlement of the Mennonites in the Caucasus. Established in 1901 by settlers from the Molotschna, it consisted of 17 villages on 67,000 acres of land with a population of 3,400. The Terek Mennonite Church (*q.v.*), established in 1902, and the Terek Mennonite Brethren Church (*q.v.*) cared for the spiritual welfare of the settlement.

The available land in the various settlements was adequate. With the exception of Terek, all the colonies developed normally, and became in part model farms and colonies. The original difficulties were very real. The settlers had come into a region that was very different from their homeland in climate, in topography, and in ethnic characteristics. The neighboring Tatars, Circassians, etc., still held to primitive methods of agriculture; there was no one to give advice, and they had to learn by experiment. Various futile attempts consumed time and money, such as cheese making, silkworm culture, and vineyards, until they concentrated on cattle raising and fruit growing, which were eminently successful. In Olgino, where agriculture was the principal occupation, Mennonite methods were also successful and served as models to the surrounding Russian villages. Factories, mills, co-operatives, and ther industries soon did a thriving business as well.

The Mennonites of North Caucasus were peacemakers and pioneers all along the line; their work was repeatedly recognized and rewarded by the czarist government. Their mental alertness was expressed in the excellent development of churches, schools, and organizations, setting them apart not only from the native population, but also from other Mennonite groups. Only World War I and the Revolution disrupted their progress, and the communist way of life and World War II destroyed their settlements and achievements.

The Terek settlement, the farthest east of all, was the first to disappear as a result of the troubles following the war and the Revolution. Repeated robberies and even murders at the hands of their non-Russian neighbors led to an evacuation of the entire settlement in February 1918 to other parts of Caucasus. The return of a part of the colonists in the spring of 1921 was a mistake, for in 1923 conditions again became so bad that families began to leave, and in May 1925 the settlement was finally completely evacuated. Most of the Terek colonists reached Canada in the 1922-25 migration.

The remaining Mennonites of Caucasus were mostly exiled during the Soviet era and the last were evacuated to Asiatic Russia when the Germans invaded Russia in 1941. Very few reached Canada and South America after World War II. (See also **Russia, Ukraine.**)   TH.B., C.K.

Friesen, *Brüderschaft;* C. P. Toews, *Die Tereker Ansiedlung* (Steinbach, Man., 1945); H. Dirks, *Statistik der Menn.-Gemeinden* (1905); W. Quiring, *Die Mundart von Chortitza in Süd-Russland* (Munich, 1928); Fr. Isaak, *Die Molotschnaer Mennoniten* (Halbstadt, 1908); *Die Kubaner Ansiedlung* (Steinbach, 1953); *Die deutschen Siedlungen in der Sowjetunion* IV: *Dongebiet und Kaukasus* (Berlin, 1941); *ML* II, 475.

Cavalier County, N.D., home of approximately 540 Mennonites, is located in the northeastern part of the state. The Mennonites, though scattered, are located chiefly in the southwestern part of the county. Approximately 75 per cent are members of the General Conference Mennonite Church, 15 per cent are Mennonite Brethren, and 10 per cent are Church of God in Christ Mennonites. The first Mennonite settlers perhaps arrived in the county in the early 1880's. There are in the county five Mennonite churches and the Bethany Bible Academy, which is located in Munich.   H.O.

Cave (W. Va.) was the name of a schoolhouse 2 miles southwest of Whitmer, where a congregation (MC) of 10 Mennonites was worshiping in 1911.   M.G.

Cecilia Jheronimusd, an Anabaptist martyr, the wife of Jacob Claesz (*q.v.*) of Landsmeer, was burned at the stake at Amsterdam, Nov. 9, 1549, together with her husband. This Cecilia, who was a native of the village of Wormer, is the same person as the martyr Seli listed by van Braght, whose martyrdom he places in 1542 (*Mart. Mir.* D 85, E 485; *Inv. Arch. Amst.* I, No. 357; *DB* 1917, 173; Grosheide, *Bijdrage,* 158, 308).   vDZ.

Cedar County, Mo., once the location of an Amish Mennonite community, now extinct. Their church was organized in 1870. Two years later a plea for funds to be used for building a meetinghouse was signed by Bishop Samuel Yoder, preachers John Snyder and Joseph Kauffman, and Jonathan Krichbaum. Twenty-two families, mostly Amish Mennonite, were members of the congregation at that time. Around 1890, members of the congregation joined the "Egly Amish" (Defenseless Mennonites), but by the first decade of the 20th century the church had ceased to exist.   M.G.

Cedar Creek Mennonite Church (MC), located in Manson, Calhoun Co., Iowa, was organized in 1898 by settlers from Woodford and Bureau counties, Ill., and is a member of the Iowa-Nebraska Conference. In 1903 the first meetinghouse was built, called the Cedar Creek Mennonite Church. In 1913 a larger church was erected in northwest Manson. The name Cedar Creek has never been officially changed, but this congregation is more frequently known as the Manson Mennonite Church. Missionary emphasis has generally prevailed as is evidenced by the fact that through the years approximately 52 members have been received from non-Mennonite homes. Minnie Swartzendruber Graber, Don McCammon, Wilbur and Grace Nachtigall, and Marie Kauffman are missionaries sent out from this church. Several others are volunteers (1948). The 1953 membership was 264. Edward Birkey and Nicholas Stoltzfus are serving in the ministry of the congregation (1953). (*ML* I, 336.)   N.S.

Cedar Grove Mennonite Church (MC) in York Co., Ont. From about 1824 the grounds here were used for burial purposes. In 1861 Samuel Reesor, grandfather of L. J. Burkholder, owner of the property, built a frame meetinghouse, and gave it to the Mennonite Church. Regular services are recorded for this place since 1867. The preaching was in German until 1882. This church was neighbor to the Reesor Wisler Mennonite Church and served the members of the Mennonite conference in the southeastern part of Markham Twp., York County. About the year 1864 a Sunday school was opened by neighbors and conducted for several years, and again in 1887 a union Sunday school was organized at this place and carried on until 1895. In 1896 a Mennonite Sunday school was organized which, with a few interruptions between 1905 and 1932 when the Wideman Sunday school served both churches, has now again been regular at Cedar Grove. Ministers who served here were Samuel Hoover of Ontario County; Samuel R. Hoover of Markham; John G. Hoover; Lewis J. Burkholder, and A. Lorne Burkholder. At this place Oscar Burkholder was ordained to the ministry in 1912. Here Samuel G. Reesor, a deacon, expired in the pulpit while at prayer in August 1913. Other deacons who served at this place were Jacob G. Reesor, Isaiah Hoover, Amos Burkholder. The 1952 membership of this church was 39. (L. J. Burkholder, *Brief History of Mennonites in Ontario,* Markham, 1935.)   J.C.F.

Cedar Grove Mennonite Church (MC), located three miles south of Greencastle, Franklin Co., Pa., became an independent congregation in 1937, having until that time been a member of the Washington Co., Md., and Franklin Co., Pa., Conference. In 1951 it was received into the Ohio Mennonite and Eastern A.M. Conference. The meetinghouse was built and the congregation organized with about 50 members in 1905. Services were conducted by ministers of the Washington County churches 5-15 miles away. In 1911 A. Dorsey Martin of Scottdale, Pa., formerly of this community, became the first resident minister. Other ministers who have served the congregation are: Bishop Geo. S. Keener, John F. Grove, Glen Diller, and Abram M. Baer. In 1929 the brick building burned but was rebuilt with an addition, which makes a seating capacity of 500. The current membership (1952) is 189, mostly rural people. (*ML* I, 336.)   J.F.G.

Cedar Hill Mission Sunday School (MC) was opened in 1936 in a schoolhouse in West Donegal Township two miles north of the Good Church in Lancaster Co., Pa., under the Lancaster Mennonite Conference. The present attendance is 40. The summer Bible school attendance averages 108.
                                                                I.D.L.

Cedar Point Church of God in Christ Mennonite Church, now extinct, was organized in 1887, several miles south of Cedar Point, Chase Co., Kan., with John A. Holdeman as pastor, with a membership of 14. Meetings were held in schoolhouses. The congregation was dissolved in 1913.   F.H.W.

Cedar Road United Missionary Church, Mishawaka, Ind., whose new church seating 175 was dedicated Oct. 22, 1950. The rapid growth of the membership of the congregation resulted in plans being made in 1952 for the enlargement of the building. The present (1953) membership is 53.   M.G.

Cedar Vale Mennonite Church (MC), now extinct, was located near Birmingham, Jackson Co., Kan. The Mennonite settlement was started about 1880. Perhaps the first to arrive was the J. G. Longenecker family of Lancaster Co., Pa. The first settlers thought that a substantial Mennonite community would be formed. This was not the case, but among those who did join the settlement appear such names as Hamilton, Garber, Winey, and Mast. The only resident minister to serve the congregation was Jacob L. Winey. He was ordained in the Catlin Church near Peabody, Kan., in 1887, and moved to Jackson County in 1895, where he died in 1902.

At first the members worshiped in the Methodist church in Birmingham. On one occasion a class of five were baptized in this church by J. M. Shenk of Elida, Ohio. Later, under the leadership of Jacob Winey, the congregation worshiped in the Cedar Vale schoolhouse, and after his death in the New Harmony rural Methodist church.

The congregation was never large. In 1902 twelve members were reported. By 1906 it was apparent that the congregation would not survive and the majority of the remaining members relocated in better established Mennonite settlements. Some of the members remained and became active in other denominations.   G.G.Y.

Cedarville Hope Mission (UMC) is located five miles west of Oakville, Grays Harbor Co., Wash. In 1948 meetings were held in a rented building seating 60. F. M. Wolf served as pastor. F.M.W.

Cellarius (Borrhaus, Burress), **Martin,** b. 1499 at Stuttgart, Germany, studied at the University of Tübingen, where he became a friend of Melanchthon, then in Ingolstadt under Reuchlin, from whom he acquired a thorough knowledge of Greek and Hebrew. A dispute with Johann Eck, Luther's noted opponent, led him to Wittenberg. Having here become an ardent follower of Martin Luther, he came under the influence of Marcus Stübner (*q.v.*), one of the Zwickau prophets. Via Stuttgart he betook himself to Switzerland, where he met

Felix Manz. He apparently remained for some time; but he left Zürich before the first Anabaptist disputation on Jan. 17, 1525, and proceeded through Austria and Poland to Prussia. In Prussia he was placed in mild arrest and then released on the promise to go to Wittenberg and present himself to Martin Luther for a conversation, which dealt with the doctrine of predestination. Luther invited him to remain, but he settled in South Germany.

In late November 1525, he came to Strasbourg, where Capito received him in his home, though not without some hesitancy. "Before I saw him," he wrote to Zwingli on Sept. 21, 1527, "I hated him bitterly. For I had heard nothing from those who knew him but foolishness, pride, arrogance, and sedition." Gradually Capito came entirely under the influence of this important man. He wrote the introduction to *De operibus dei,* which Cellarius published in July 1527. He says, "Martin Cellarius came here on a journey, a man of God and gifted with an excellent spirit. When he heard of the condition of our church . . . he resolved to come to an understanding with us concerning the faith. We were very willing, met, debated with each other, and both sides discussed in detail how the glory of God must be still more gloriously revealed in our time. . . . The truth was much clearer to him. . . . Then . . . each assured the other of our mutual faith and the grace we had received."

Zwingli felt uneasy about this enthusiastic friendship between Capito and Cellarius. He recalled too vividly how a few years before, he had collided with Cellarius in Zürich and pressed him for his Anabaptist views. He warned his Strasbourg friend of Cellarius. Capito replied on Aug. 15, 1527, defending his friend, "Martin Cellarius is far better than his reputation. . . . I write this to you to clear our common brother of the suspicion of Anabaptism and present him as an elect servant. . . . When the Anabaptists charged you with cruelty in the execution of Manz, he stood bravely on our side and still does so, defending your innocence as that of a splendid child of God."

Probably at Capito's request Cellarius wrote to Zwingli on Aug. 31, 1527, defending himself against the reproach of Anabaptism. "If some reckon me among the Anabaptists, I do not doubt that my book (*De operibus dei*) will easily cure them of this suspicion. It acknowledges the justification of government, repudiates the doctrine of the free will, glorifies the power of election above all else . . . , allows a free use of the outward ceremonies according to the norm of love and the *regula fidei* and finally its aim is particularly the glory of God and the salvation of the church."

But Zwingli could not so easily give up his suspicion. Once more Capito defended Cellarius in a letter to Zwingli on Sept. 21, 1527, and used in his favor his aversion to the Anabaptists, his sanction of the Strasbourg government, the assistance he gave the preachers, and his excellent character.

Without question it is due to the influence of Cellarius that Capito's views were so closely related to those of the Anabaptists. This is expressed in his commentary on Hosea. Bucer was quite horrified by it. He too had at first a most favorable opinion of Cellarius. In a letter to Farel, Dec. 13, 1526, he praised his greatness of spirit (see **Bucer**). He too defended him in a letter to Zwingli on Sept. 26, 1527: "What you have written us warning us about Cellarius we have gratefully received; but because one would have to call the bright light dark if we did not confess that Cellarius is thoroughly pious, we will beware of admitting suspicions that are foreign to love. Yet I confess that I would give much to have him accept our view of baptism. While in everything else he confesses the same as we, while he lives blamelessly and sanctions nothing less than the raving of the Anabaptists, we cannot reject him." But when Bucer perceived the predominant influence of Cellarius on his friend Capito, he changed his mind. How different is his verdict in a letter to Zwingli on April 15, 1528: "What you feared has happened. Cellarius, who is motivated by a true Anabaptist spirit, has tricked our Capito by his association with him." A bitter hostility developed between Cellarius and Bucer, which nearly descended to acts of violence. "He, Cellarius, the dwarf, nearly attacked me, the giant, on the street," writes Bucer in this letter.

Bucer now asked Zwingli and Oecolampadius to exert all their influence to remove Capito from the dangerous influence of Cellarius. Thereupon Zwingli addressed a skillfully composed letter to both Bucer and Capito together, most sharply attacking Cellarius and calling attention to the great dangers threatening the Strasbourg church through him. This took effect. Capito broke with him. Cellarius left Strasbourg for a teaching career at Basel in 1536, first as professor of rhetoric, then as professor of theology. After an eventful life he died in Basel on Oct. 11, 1565.

Cellarius was not an Anabaptist. His connections with the Zürich Anabaptists were temporary. In Strasbourg he did not adhere to the Anabaptists. He opposed Denk from the very beginning. At the colloquium which he and Haetzer held with Denk at the wish of the Strasbourg preachers in December 1526, he attacked Denk's doctrine of the freedom of the will expressed in his pamphlet, *Was geredt sei.* Denk wisely yielded and stressed the points of agreement between them; so they parted in perfect peace and Cellarius thought he had converted Denk (Hulshof, 39). Cellarius apparently never gave up his view that infant baptism is not justified, but held baptism to be an external matter to be left to the individual. Bock, in his *Historia Antitrinitariorum,* counts him an Anti-Trinitarian, though unjustly, and lists his numerous writings. Menno Simons quotes *De operibus dei* in matters pertaining to baptism (Krahn, *Menno Simons,* 46).

NEFF.

C. Gerbert, *Gesch. der Strassburger Sektenbewegung z.Zt. der Ref. 1524 bis 1534* (Strasbourg, 1889); *HRE* III; L. Keller, *Ein Apostel der Wiedertäufer* (Leipzig, 1882); A. Hulshof, *Gesch. van de Doopsgezinden te Straatsburg van 1525-1557* (Amsterdam, 1905); *Basler Jahrbuch 1900,* 47-84, article by Bernhard Riggenbach; J. Heberle, "Die Anfänge des Anabaptismus in der Schweiz," in *Jahrbücher für deutsche Theol.* 1858, 262 f.; K. T. Keim, "Haetzer," in *Jahrbücher für deutsche Theol.,* 1856, 215 ff.; *ML* I, 336-38.

Cemeteries. European Mennonites in their earlier history experienced considerable difficulty in obtaining burial privileges in the public cemeteries. In time, however, these restrictions were removed. For example, a statement from the Department for Internal Affairs of the Kingdom of Bavaria declared on Oct. 12, 1847, "The general wording of this law leaves no doubt that the common use of the cemetery is also for private denominations such as the Mennonites."

In the Palatinate, West Prussia, and Russia the Mennonites according to the customs of those areas buried their dead in the churchyards or in near-by burial lots. The historic Danzig Mennonite Church, for example, had its cemetery in an adjacent plot. In Russia the cemeteries were generally located either adjacent to the public school or on the lot which was reserved by the village for the school or close to but outside the village. The cemeteries were often lined with large poplar trees.

The location of Mennonite cemeteries in America varies. The oldest Mennonite church in America, at Germantown in Philadelphia, has gravestones near the front door and along several sides of the building. Many of the older Mennonite cemeteries in Pennsylvania, Ontario, and Ohio are in the churchyards or in adjacent lots. In some of the younger western churches, however, the cemeteries are often located some distance from the churches. Amish congregations frequently use family cemeteries located on the farms of leading families in the community, and one congregation might use several such cemeteries. As cemeteries were often started before churches were built in Amish Mennonite communities, their cemeteries and churches were sometimes separated by a distance of a fraction of a mile or more. Each colony of the Hutterian Brethren owns its cemetery, which is always a short distance from the colony village. Members only are buried there and the graves are marked by homemade gravestones.

Various methods of Mennonite cemetery control are used. Usually the cemetery is owned by the church and is under the control of church or special cemetery trustees who appoint a caretaker. In other places, cemetery associations are formed to guarantee the proper care and financing of the grounds. Such, for example, is the Zion Mennonite Cemetery Association at Donnellson, Iowa. The Oak Grove congregation in Champaign Co., Ohio, has established an endowment fund to finance the care of its cemetery.

Although Mennonite church cemeteries are used primarily by members of the congregation, other groups are not barred; thus they often serve as community burial grounds. The bodies of deceased relatives who have moved away or have left the faith are sometimes interred in the home congregation burial ground. Some congregations, on the other hand, have no cemeteries but instead use municipal or public burial sites.

In general, Mennonite cemeteries, as is true of church premises, are well lawned and properly cared for. With their emphasis upon simplicity, Mennonites have seldom used large tombstones or monuments. The Amish regulate the maximum size that may be used in their cemeteries. The result is that the typical Mennonite burial site expresses the equality of the brethren and their opposition to costly display. Although family burial plots are almost uniformly customary in Mennonite cemeteries, several groups have the practice of burying the dead in rows according to the time of their death. Such is the custom in certain Church of God in Christ Mennonite communities, in some Old Order Amish communities, as at Arthur, Ill., among many of the Manitoba Mennonites, and among the Old Colony Mennonites of Mexico. The conservative Mennonites of Manitoba, Mexico, and Paraguay have no tombstones on the graves. (See **Burial** and **Funeral Customs**.)   M.G.

Centen, a Mennonite family of Amsterdam, whose members belonged to the High German congregation, and after the unification of this church with the Flemish group, to the United Frisian, Flemish, and High-German congregation (church *bij't Lam*). Jan Cents (also written Centen) (*q.v.*) signed the confession which is named for him. Job Sieuwertsz Centen I, b. 1639 at Amsterdam, who between 1679 and 1704 served his congregation four times as deacon, was painted in 1713 by Christoffel Lubienietski; he and his wife Maria van de Rijp founded an old people's home, called Rijpenhofje, which in 1747 was bequeathed to the church *bij't Lam*. Gosen Centen, painted by Govert Flinck, is supposed to be his brother. Gozewijn Centen, painted with his family by Lubienietzki, who was a regent (governor) of the Rijpenhofje, was likely a son of Job Sieuwertsz Centen I. Job Sieuwertsz Centen II, b. about 1690 and baptized in the church *bij't Lam* on Feb. 8, 1711, must be the grandson of J. S. Centen I. This J. S. Centen II was for many years secretary of the Dutch Mennonite Committee of Foreign Needs (*Commissie voor Buitenlandsche Nooden*).

Many members of this family, which died out in the beginning of the 19th century, have served the congregation *bij't Lam* as deacons.   vDZ.

Central Amish Mennonite Church (MC), Fulton Co., Ohio. The first settlers of this congregation came from Upper Alsace in 1834. Two related groups formed the congregation. Those in Fulton County were chiefly German-speaking and those across the line in Williams County in what is now the Lockport neighborhood spoke French. The congregation was organized in 1834-35, and the first ministers were Christian Beck and Christian Rupp. Like most Amish congregations, they met in the homes of members until 1869, when the Central Church was built north of Archbold. With the growth of the congregation additional meetinghouses became necessary. In 1908 the congregation built the West Clinton Church in West Clinton Township east of Pettisville and the Lockport Church in Williams County north of Stryker. During the latter part of the 19th century and the beginning of the 20th the families of Deacon (later ordained Bishop) Eli Frey and Deacon Jacob C. Frey occupied a leading role in the history of the congregation. Eli Frey was the first lay

Sunday-school superintendent. After its first organization about 1871, the leaders yielded to violent opposition and closed the school for a number of years. First superintendents were preachers Jeptha Wise and Jacob Nafziger, but it was encouraged by Bishop Christian Stuckey and several other ministers. Even after the Lockport and West Clinton churches had been built, the members worshiping at the three churches continued as one congregational organization. Beginning in 1908 each, however, had its own Sunday-school organization.

The Lockport and West Clinton churches were remodeled in 1930 and 1935 respectively to provide classrooms for the younger Sunday-school classes. The congregation built several additions to the Central Church which had been built in 1869 and dedicated in 1870. The old building was replaced by a large brick structure, completely modern, in 1936. Within recent years the congregation has become one of the most aggressive in mission and Sunday-school work of any congregation in the conference. Members of the congregation still prefer to be known as Amish Mennonites rather than Mennonites. The groups meeting at Central, Lockport, and West Clinton are now organized as individual congregations. Several other congregations have been organized—Bancroft near Toledo, Tedrow near Wauseon, and Pine Grove south of Stryker. The membership of Central in 1952 was 765.

The Central Church has suffered two schisms: (1) the Church of God in Christ (Holdeman) group in 1863, whose church is located in Pettisville, and (2) the Evangelical Mennonite (Egly-Defenseless) group in 1870, whose churches are in Archbold (1870) and Wauseon (1945). (See **Fulton County**.)   J.S.U.

Central Asia: see **Asiatic Russia**. For map see **Siberia**.

Central Conference Mennonite Church existed as a distinct organized Mennonite denominational body 1908-46, the name having been officially adopted in 1914 as a change from "Central Illinois Mennonite Conference." In 1945 the group joined the General Conference Mennonite Church in a body as a district conference, retaining the name "Central Conference," and its distinct organization. In 1957 it merged with the Middle District Conference to form the present Central District of the General Conference Mennonite Church. Before full official organization in 1908, the 12 congregations which formed the group, largely located in Central Illinois, had been loosely affiliated as a distinct denomination with an annual ministerial meeting beginning in 1899 (and earlier unorganized, since 1872, when the parent congregation ceased to affiliate with the Amish Mennonite General Conference). Since the leader in the 1872 withdrawal was Bishop Joseph Stuckey (*q.v.*), the group was long popularly known as "the Stuckey Mennonites." The word "Amish" was dropped from the official name in 1908.

The mother church of the Central Conference was the present North Danvers Church, organized in 1835 (first called Rock Creek), often called the Yoder Church because of its outstanding bishop

Jonathan Yoder (1795-1869). Joseph Stuckey (1825-1902), ordained bishop of this congregation in 1864, a man of unusual ability and leadership, occasioned the division in 1872 by refusing to excommunicate a member of the congregation who taught universalism, as was requested by the Amish conference. Although no other congregations joined Stuckey, except the two small congregations at Meadows and Washington, Ill., which were under his oversight, his following grew. Locally new congregations were organized. Two Stuckey congregations were established by colonization, at Aurora, Neb. (1885), and Goodland, Ind. (1897), and one congregation at Topeka, Ind. (1902), which left the old church there, joined the group. There were nine Illinois churches, the mother church, with South Danvers (1859), East White Oak (1892), Meadows (1891), Washington, later called Calvary (1866), Pekin (1905), Flanagan (1878), Congerville (1898), Anchor (1894).

Although Stuckey remained free from all conference affiliation he was in close touch through the years 1872-98 with the General Conference Mennonite Church and other Mennonite groups. A report of the North Danvers congregation is found in an 1890 report of the General Conference Mennonite Church. Stuckey's notebooks also reveal that through travel and correspondence and the church papers he was in continual touch with Mennonite leaders of other conferences. In this period he also took a great deal of interest in congregations which had similar experiences to his. He has been even blamed for causing divisions in churches. This does not seem to be the case, but it can truthfully be said that he was always willing to assist through his effective leadership where a group of people were without conference affiliation or the proper leadership to make progress. His records show that he traveled both east and west, visiting congregations and groups of people who needed help, encouraging the work, ordaining bishops and ministers, and helping congregations to succeed.

Through the years 1883-98 a number of young ministers were ordained by Stuckey in various congregations, such as Aaron Augspurger, J. H. King, Peter Schantz, and Emanuel Troyer. These men felt the need of greater unity and co-operation between the congregations. A meeting was held at the home of J. H. King, Aug. 5, 1899, and the second at North Danvers, Sept. 26, 1899. At the second meeting definite plans were made to have an annual conference. The conferences from 1899 to 1907 were largely in the nature of Bible study and a discussion of the doctrines of the church. The meetings were inspirational, not legislative. But after institutions were established and activities in the church increased it was found necessary to be more closely organized, and so a constitutionally organized conference was created with 12 congregations as charter members. The first conference held under the new organization was at the North Danvers Church, Sept. 10, 1908. There were in 1951, 20 congregations in the conference with a membership of 3,252.

The second period of organized conference history, 1908-51, shows further extension in the establishment of congregations but especially an interest in missions and the establishment of institutions. Elders Peter Schantz and Emanuel Troyer were outstanding in their leadership in these fields in the earlier years, with Troyer, W. B. Weaver, Allen Yoder, and Raymond Hartzler in the later years.

The first mission work to be established in the conference was home missions. A Home Mission Board was organized in 1908 and the first mission station established on June 20, 1909, which later became the Mennonite Gospel Mission of Chicago. In 1914, the second mission station was established in Peoria and called the Mennonite Gospel Mission. The third mission, the 26th Street Mission in Chicago, was taken over from the Mennonite Church (MC) under the leadership of A. M. Eash and admitted into the conference in 1923.

After several years of mission work under the Africa Inland Mission, the conference established its own foreign mission work in co-operation with the Defenseless Mennonites (now Evangelical) in the Belgian Congo, establishing a joint board, the new Congo Inland Mission (q.v.) Board, whose first workers were sent out in April 1911.

In this same period the Old People's Home was established at Meadows (1922), the Mennonite Hospital at Bloomington (1919), and a joint program in college and seminary work was undertaken, supporting Bluffton College and Witmarsum Seminary, and later the Mennonite Biblical Seminary in Chicago. W.B.W.

Central District Conference of the Mennonite Brethren Church of North America had its beginning as a result of a provision made by the M.B. General Conference in 1909. This conference arranged to divide its constituency into three distinct conferences—Northern, Central, and Southern.

According to this provision the M.B. congregations in the states of Nebraska, Minnesota, South Dakota, North Dakota, Michigan, Colorado, and Oregon and those of the province Manitoba, Canada, constituted the Central District Conference. This conference convened for its first annual meeting Oct. 17 and 18, 1910, in the M.B. Church at Bingham Lake, Minn., and organized itself. Sixteen local churches were represented by 48 delegates. These churches at that time had a total membership of 1,359.

In 1912 the churches of Manitoba withdrew and joined the Northern or Canadian District Conference, and those of Colorado joined the Southern District Conference, while those of Oregon joined the Pacific District Conference a year later. In 1915 M.B. churches began in Montana, and these joined the Central District Conference. Up to the present the conference has convened for its annual meetings regularly except in 1918. At these meetings a mission festival is held on a Sunday and other meetings of a devotional character are held. Two days are usually devoted to business sessions where its work is transacted. An annual yearbook containing the report of the conference is published. Until 1942 the conferences were conducted in the German language. Since then the change has been gradually made to the English.

The activity of the conference consists mainly in arranging and doing home mission work and in providing and caring for the churches. Its home mission effort is supervised and directed by a Home Mission Committee of three members—chairman, secretary, and treasurer. The care and supervision of the churches is in the hands of the Committee for Reference and Counsel. The various phases of the M.B. General Conference work, such as foreign missions, publication, city missions, education, and relief, are reported at the district conferences.

The conference has done some extension home mission work. In its early years, the two Russian M.B. congregations at Kief and Dogden, N.D., were affiliated with the conference, and mission work among Russians was done. Later the conference began mission work in the timber area of northern Minnesota where Rev. and Mrs. J. H. Wiens worked at Mildred as missionaries for many years.

Among the ministers who have been outstanding conference leaders and who have done extensive itinerating work in the church may be mentioned Elder Heinrich Voth, Elder J. J. Kliewer, Elder Gerhard P. Regier, N. N. Hiebert, H. S. Voth, Gerhard Wiens, Johann Abrams, Isaac Wall, Ludwig Seibel, Christian Reimche, J. F. Thiessen, A. A. Dick, H. E. Wiens, and G. H. Jantzen.

Traveling evangelists who have worked extensively and conducted many evangelistic meetings in the churches are J. S. Regier, H. S. Voth, C. N. Hiebert, Adam Ross, J. H. Ewert, D. F. Strauss, H. D. Wiebe, David Hooge, and John Siemens. (*Year Books* of the Central District Conference of the M.B. Church, 1910- ; J. H. Lohrenz, *The Mennonite Brethren Church,* Hillsboro, 1950.) J.H.Lo.

Central Illinois Conference: see Central Conference Mennonite Church.

Central Mennonite Board of Home and Foreign Missions was incorporated in Illinois on Oct. 26, 1909, four years after the Central Conference Mennonite Church (*q.v.*) first began to take an active interest in home and foreign mission work on an organized basis. The object for which it was formed as stated in the original articles of incorporation is as follows: "to systematize and extend the work of evangelization, to encourage, establish and support Home and Foreign Missions and Mission work, to receive and hold all donations and bequests, both personal and real estate, to be used only for missions purposes, and under the patronage and management of the Central Illinois Conference of Mennonites." The foreign mission work of the conference has been centered in the work in the Belgian Congo of Africa, and has been a joint work with the Evangelical Mennonite Conference (*q.v.*) working together under the Congo Inland Mission (*q.v.*) Board. City missions have been maintained in Chicago and Peoria, Ill., but in line with the peculiar genius of the Mennonite people for work in rural areas, the two Chicago missions have been closed and a conscious effort is being made to reach and to expand in the rural areas of home mission work. L.E.T.

Central Mennonite Church (MC), located in Elida, Allen Co., Ohio, was organized in December 1925 by a group excommunicated in 1924 from the Salem-Pike congregation and joined later by the Sunday-school superintendents, Ruda R. Brenneman and Menno L. Troyer, and one of the ministers, Andrew Brenneman. After the group requested and was granted by the Ohio Mennonite and Eastern A.M. Conference permission to organize a separate congregation, they purchased a vacant church building in Elida. Ordinations: M. L. Troyer, deacon 1927, minister 1940, bishop 1950; Timothy H. Brenneman, minister 1938, appointed missionary to Argentina. Present membership (1953) 99; ministers, Andrew Brenneman, Menno L. Troyer. J.S.U.

Central Mennonite College was established in 1900 by the Middle District Conference of the General Conference Mennonite Church at Bluffton, Ohio, and later (1913) called Bluffton College (*q.v.*). This district conference was composed of 12 churches with a total membership of about 3,000. The purpose of the college was to give to Mennonite young people the opportunity of securing an education under Christian auspices in harmony with the beliefs of the Mennonite Church. At the annual conference in 1898 a board of trustees was elected to establish a college at Bluffton. Those elected were J. H. Tschantz, J. F. Lehman, J. A. Amstutz, Gerhard Vogt, J. C. Mehl, H. J. Krehbiel, J. W. Leatherman, H. P. Krehbiel, and P. E. Stuckey. The first president was N. C. Hirschy (*q.v.*), pastor of the Wadsworth (Ohio) Mennonite Church.

The college opened Nov. 5, 1900. During the first year 47 students were enrolled in academy and commercial courses. Freshman college work was first offered in 1902 with four students, and later, a two-year junior college course was given. In 1908, upon the resignation of President Hirschy, S. K. Mosiman (*q.v.*) was elected president. In 1913 representatives of five branches of Mennonites organized Bluffton College (*q.v.*) and the Mennonite Seminary, taking over the plant and resources of Central Mennonite College and developing a four-year standard college and graduate seminary.

Because of its limited constituency Central Mennonite College was small and its offerings limited, but since both presidents were thoroughly trained and men of culture and genuine Christian character, a good foundation was laid for Bluffton College with a much larger constituency. (*The Story of Bluffton College,* Bluffton, 1925.) N.E.B.

Central Mennonite Immigration Committee (*Das zentrale Mennonitische Immigrantenkomitee*) was founded in 1923 among the newly arrived Mennonite immigrants in Canada to serve in an advisory capacity to the Canadian Mennonite Board of Colonization (*q.v.*). At a meeting in Eigenheim, Sask., 12 members were elected. In 1925 the immigrants of other provinces joined and the committee was reorganized consisting of five members.

In a meeting at Reinland, Man., in 1927 the organization was completed and a constitution adopted. The following year provincial committees were elected and all immigrants became members of the organization. Some of the duties of the CMIC (*ZMIK*) were to advise the Canadian Mennonite Board of Colonization in helping the immigrants establish new homes and to build Mennonite communities. The committee helped in distributing aid and loans coming from the Mennonites in the United States, presenting to the Soviet government lists of relatives requesting permission to leave Russia, finding large tracts of land for settlement for the ever-increasing number of immigrants, collecting the debt to the railroads which had financed the passage of the immigrants, obtaining German books for homes and schools, aiding orphans in getting refunds of the loans given by their parents to the German government during the occupation of the Ukraine.

In spite of all efforts, the committee was unable to purchase large tracts of land such as were made available by the Old Colony Mennonites of Manitoba, Swift Current and Hague, Sask., since this was during the depression. The greatest accomplishment of the committee lay without question in obtaining German and religious books for the immigrants and thus establishing a cultural basis for the future. During the years 1923-44 over 12,000 books were distributed. The sum of $6,531 was returned to the Mennonites who had loaned the money to the German government during the occupation of the Ukraine.

The provincial committees were gradually strengthened and the CMIC lost its significance, since it had accomplished as much as possible. At a meeting of the committee held at Rosthern on May 30 and 31, 1934, it was decided to merge it completely with the Canadian Mennonite Board of Colonization. This was approved by the board at a meeting in Saskatoon July 26, 1934. The work of the CMIC was continued in a number of subcommittees of the board. (D. H. Epp, "Das Zentrale Mennonitische Immigrantenkomitee," *Bote* XXV, July 21 and 28, 1948.)   C.K.

Central Mennonite Publication Board, the official publication agency of the Central Conference of Mennonites, was established by action of the conference in 1917. For some years previously the work of publication had been sponsored by a publication committee. The board consists of five members, four generally laymen, one being elected annually by the conference for a four-year term, and the editor and business manager as a fifth member.

Principal items of publication sponsored by the board are *The Christian Evangel* and *Central Conference Yearbook*. The board also operates a business office for the purchasing of Sunday-school materials, books, Bibles, and miscellaneous supplies desired by churches or their auxiliary organizations. The present editorial and business office is located at 809 North Evans St., Bloomington, Ill. R.L.H.

Centralia, Mo.: see **Audrain County, Mo.**

Centralia (Boone Co., Mo.) Defenseless Mennonite Church, now extinct, had 21 members in 1911. The church was located six miles southeast of Centralia and was served by two ministers, L. Zehr and J. C. Bertschi.   M.G.

Cents (Centsz, Centsen), **Jan,** a Dutch Mennonite of Amsterdam, probably a deacon of the church, who with 13 other members of the Frisian and High German congregation at Amsterdam signed the *Korte Confessie ofte Belijdenisse des Gheloofs,* of 1630 (see **Confessions**). Jan Cents signed first; for this reason the confession was named the *Jan Cents' Confessie.* He may have been the author or planner of this confession. Of Jan Cents nothing further is known. He must have belonged to the well-known Centen (*q.v.*) family at Amsterdam.

vDZ.

Ceramics. One of the crafts engaged in by the Hutterian Brethren in Moravia which attracted much attention was the art of ceramics or pottery. Their chronicles speak of it merely as the potter's trade (*Hafnergewerbe*), but the earthenware produced in their shops included more than is commonly understood by this term. There were all kinds of articles for domestic use, such as plates, bowls, vases, and pitchers, many of them having artistic value.

The importance of these products was not recognized until recent times. Items are found in several museums, but their source was unknown, and even today, though it has been definitely established that they are Hutterite products, they are incorrectly listed in the literature describing them. They are usually called *Habaner faience;* but they were produced before the Thirty Years' War, and the name Habaner (*q.v.*) is used only to designate those Hutterites in Hungary who under government pressure turned Catholic in the 18th century. The Habaner were still engaged in pottery, but the china which has aroused the interest of investigators is the Hutterite product of the earlier period. The Hutterite chinaware is worked out with delicate artistry, especially dinnerware, which was much used for gift purposes by the nobility. A letter written on Oct. 5, 1612, states that Johann Dionys von Zierotin at Seelowitz near Brno sent the wife of the Margrave of Brandenburg, Johann Georg, a large load, drawn by four horses, of "white earthen dishes of all sorts and several pairs of knives, such as the Anabaptists here regularly manufacture."

In the period preceding the outbreak of the Thirty Years' War it was common usage among the noble families in Moravia to have a large supply of chinaware from the Hutterite colonies. In the castles of Catholic noblemen, who were in many cases friendly toward the Hutterites, their products were used, usually expensive pieces. The inventories still in existence speak for the popularity of Hutterite faience. The inventory of 1615 of a room in the castle of Ladislaus Berka, the adviser of the Prag government under Rudolf II, lists besides valuable silver, also "41 white Anabaptist earthen dishes." The "confiscation commission" appointed in 1621 after the Bohemian revolt found in a series of drawers in the castle of Adam Schampach von Pottenstein in Weissenkirchen "eleven Anabaptist dishes," and in a green painted chest "much Anabaptist china and glass." Some of this confiscated ware was taken to Vienna in 1624 as a gift from

Emperor Ferdinand II to Empress Eleonora. There is probably not an inventory of a Moravian castle which does not list some Hutterite faience.

Hutterite art objects were also purchased by the Moravian barons for foreign noblemen. The correspondence of Johann Dionys (of the Zierotin family) shows that in 1611 he bought for the Margrave of Brandenburg a richly gilded carriage of their workmanship; in 1609 iron bedsteads were ordered for the Austrian nobleman, Wolf Sigmund von Losenstein, and in 1613 through the latter for the imperial vice chancellor. Hutterite knives and earthenware were delivered to friends in Silesia. An inventory of May 26, 1618, in the archives of the castle of Falkenberg in Upper Silesia, listing the estate left by Weighard von Promitz and Polyx, has as item 37, "a blue Anabaptist jug mounted in silver and gilded"; as item 194, "Anabaptist dishes, jugs, pitcher, basins, and bowls"; another lists "25 pairs of Anabaptist knives."

Hutterite products were likewise popular in middle-class circles. The description of the home of Anna Zedlarin in Zlin, Moravia, Sept. 22, 1622, lists in one room "not a little Anabaptist china and glass," in another room a cupboard containing "Anabaptist dishes," in a third, "a smaller painted cupboard full of various glass jugs and other Anabaptist dishes."

The production of chinaware was very profitable to the Hutterite brotherhood. Their shops were the only ones in Moravia. The secret of its china manufacture was strictly guarded in all countries, and was known only to a few. Where the Hutterites learned it is not known. It is not unlikely that some of the refugees from Italy were ceramic craftsmen, as for instance those who escaped from Ferrara (q.v.), which was at that time a pottery center, and which lies only 45 miles north of Faënza, then the center of majolica manufacture. They built their first faience potteries in Gostal (q.v.) in 1593, near Lundenburg, and in Neudorf near Hradisch.

The Hutterite faience differs from the products of other countries in the choice of motif used in decoration. Pictures and figures that might be offensive to religious sensibilities they avoided. By principle they never pictured the human figure. Even animal figures are absent. Plant forms were the favorite motifs. The shapes were also limited by regulation: the *Hafnerordnung* of Dec. 11, 1612, specified that jugs and cups must not be shaped like books, shoes, etc. (see **Dietrich, Sebastian**).

When the Hutterites were expelled from Moravia in 1622, they took the secret of china manufacture with them. They used not only special kinds of yellow and white clay, some of which they had to get from distant places, but also definite dyes and mixtures for the ornamentation of the glaze. "They observed a process of their own in the manufacture, with a constantly growing feeling for good form, for lively but harmoniously shaded colors, which we still admire. It was actually impossible to find an equivalent substitute for their work."

Specialized literature has given valuable clues in recent years. An interesting pictorial survey of Hutterite faience is given by Karl Layer, the director of the Hungarian museum for crafts in Budapest in *Oberungarische Habaner-Fayencen* (Berlin, 1927). Seven other treatises in the Czech language by Karl Cernohorsky of the Silesian museum in Troppau, with the following titles (translated into German): *Beiträge zur Geschichte der mährischen Fayence* (Troppau, 1928); *Die Erzeugung der Wischauer Fayence* (Wischau, 1928); *Die Anfänge der Habaner-Fayence-Produktion,* with 35 photographs illustrating the masterpieces of the Hutterian Brethren 1598-1634 (Troppau, 1931; an excerpt in the German language is added, and was reprinted in "Festschrift zum 60. Geburtstage von E. W. Braun," Augsburg, 1932); *Der heutige Stand der Erforschung der sog. Habaner Fayencen* (Prague, 1932), *Die Fayenceerzeugung in Wischau* (Prag, 1932); *Wiedertäuferische Schale aus dem Jahre 1605 aus den Sammlungen des Städtischen Museums in Böhm. Budweis* (1932); *Die Fayenceerzeugung in Bucowic* (Bucovic, 1933). There is a catalog of an exposition of Hutterite ceramics displayed in Troppau in 1925. Interesting information from Czech sources is given by Dr. Frantisek Hruby, director of Moravian archives in Brno, in *Die Wiedertäufer in Mähren* (Leipzig, 1935). Robert Friedmann published a few pictures of these museum pieces in *Mennonite Life,* July 1946, 42 f. (*M. Life,* Jan. 1953, 34 f; *ML* II, 482.)†   HEGE.

Cervaes, Matthias, an Anabaptist martyr: see **Matthijs Servaes.**

Ceulen (Coelen, Keulen), **Pieter** (Peter), Dutch Anabaptist leader: see **Peter van Coelen.**

C. E. Witness, the official organ of the Eastern District Young People's Union of the General Conference Mennonite Church, began in May 1941. It was a fourteen-page mimeographed paper until it appeared as a four-page printed periodical in July 1946. The last issue was dated November 1947, after which it was merged with the *Messenger,* the official quarterly paper of the Eastern District Conference.   G.Mo.

Chaco (or Gran Chaco), a large area in central South America divided among the countries of Argentina, Paraguay, Bolivia, and Brazil. It is in a sense a northern extension of the Argentine pampa, though, unlike the latter, the Chaco is broken up into alternating patches of open grassland and more or less scrubby woodland with the latter predominating. The area is a flat alluvial plain composed of unconsolidated sands and clays. Hills are almost nonexistent, and rarely is solid rock or even a solitary stone or pebble to be found. Geologists are of the opinion that this area was at one time the bed of a great inland sea which for ages since has been receiving the alluvial washings from the foothills of the Andes. Except for the Bermejo River and the Pilcomayo, which forms the boundary between the Argentine and Paraguayan Chaco, the region is drained imperfectly by small channels leading toward the Paraguay River. Some swampy areas and marshes appear during the rainy season, but the idea conveyed by some writers, that much of the region is a swampy area covered with water most of the time, is misleading.

Various explanations have been given of the origin of the word "Chaco." Perhaps the most plausible is that the word comes from the Quechua Indian word "chacu," which means an abundance of animal life (hence the term hunting ground as sometimes applied), the Spanish changing the word to "chaco."

The part of the Chaco south of the Bermejo River is known as the Chaco Austral; that between the Bermejo and the Pilcomayo as the Chaco Central; and that north of the Pilcomayo as the Chaco Boreal. Though the boundaries of such an area are somewhat indeterminate, the Gran Chaco, as the entire region is sometimes called, covers 200,000 square miles or more.

The Paraguayan Chaco, with which this article is primarily concerned, consists of that part of Paraguay lying west of the Paraguay River, approximately 100,000 square miles, or close to two thirds of the area of the entire country, the rest lying east of the river. These two parts are quite different and have had little contact with or influence upon each other until recently. Paraguayan population figures are only estimates at best, but the Chaco inhabitants, many of whom are Indians, probably number less than 100,000, as compared with the 1,000,000 or more in Paraguay proper. The chief Indian tribes include the Maccas, Lenguas, Chulupis, Tobas, Chiriguanos, Chamacocos, and the savage Moros who have attacked and killed several Mennonites in an outlying village. Probably coming from the Andes, many of the more remote Chaco Indians show marked Quechua features. These tribes, unlike the Guaranis in Paraguay proper, have entered little into the history of the country, and their chief influence has been to make the Chaco so inhospitable to the white man that its inhabitants have until recently remained "an unknown people in an unknown land." Thanks, among other factors, to the settlements made in the interior by the Mennonites, the land and the people are no longer mysterious or unknown.

As to resources, the Chaco is known for its hardwoods, including the *Quebracho* ("axebreaker") *Colorado,* from which tannin is made. A few important tannin factories are located on the Paraguay River. Another industry becoming increasingly important and shared by the Mennonites is that of cattle raising. The Mennonites have also demonstrated that farming can be carried on with profit in the Chaco, although there are some obstacles. Rainfall, adequate near the Paraguay River, becomes insufficient and uncertain farther west. Because of uneven distribution, the high temperatures in summer, and the sandy nature of some of the soil, the rainfall in the Mennonite colonies, which may vary from some twenty to some thirty inches annually, is at times inadequate for good agricultural production. Another serious obstacle is the grasshoppers. The Mennonites have shown that the following crops can be grown in the Chaco: manioc, cotton, kaffir corn, peanuts, beans, cane, citrus fruit, melons, sweet potatoes, and pumpkins.

36

A few additional garden vegetables and subtropical fruits can be produced in limited amounts. One resource which Paraguay hoped to find in the Chaco, as Bolivia had, was oil. But a very long and intensive search made by a United States oil company apparently was not successful.

The discovery of oil on the Bolivian side and the coming of the Mennonites into the disputed area were among the many complicated factors which led to the Chaco War between Bolivia and Paraguay, 1932-35. With the forming of the peace treaty the Chaco boundary between the two countries, for the first time in history, has been definitely determined.

Menno (*q.v.*), the first Mennonite colony established in the Chaco, was founded in 1927 by Canadian Mennonites and is located a little over 100 miles west and a few miles south of Puerto Casado, a Paraguayan river port. Menno now has a population of about 3,000. Fernheim (*q.v.*), founded in 1930 by Mennonites from Russia, is located just to the west and north of Menno and has a population of 2,500. Neuland (*q.v.*), with a similar population, was founded by Russian Mennonite refugees in 1947, and is located some twenty miles south of Fernheim. Isolated Mennonite families are distributed in the region surrounding the colonies, engaged in cattle grazing. A few Mennonite merchants are located at Fortin López de Filippis, the center of the Paraguayan government administration, located about 60 miles west of Filadelfia (*q.v.*), the capital of Fernheim Colony.

Since 1943 a mission has been carried on in the Argentine (Central) Chaco by the Mennonites (MC). (See **Chaco Indian Mennonite Mission;** see also map of Chaco, p. 546.)   W.H.S.

W. H. Smith, *Paraguayan Interlude—Observations and Impressions* (Scottdale, 1950); J. W. Fretz, *Pilgrims in Paraguay* (Scottdale, 1953); J. E. Bender, *Paraguay Calling,* Part 1 (mimeographed, Akron, Pa.); W. Quiring, *Deusche erschliessen den Chaco* (Karlsruhe, 1936); *idem, Russlanddeutsche suchen eine Heimat* (Karlsruhe, 1938).

Chaco (Argentina) **Indian Mennonite Mission** (MC). One thousand miles northeast of Pehuajo, the first station of the Argentine Mennonite Mission, lies central Chaco where a Mennonite Indian mission is located. The Indians of the Chaco in their wild state were nomadic collectors, fishermen, and hunters. While their way of life has been much modified by contact with the whites, yet they find it hard to cast aside their agelong superstitions and tribal customs, including witchcraft and quackery. A bit of haphazard farming, a lot of roving around, and the pursuance of occasional jobs on cotton plantations—this is the life of the remaining 10,000 or fewer Indians of the Argentine Chaco today.

In government-controlled reductions for the Indians, such as Napalpi, 40 miles from the Mennonite mission, efforts have been made to aid the Indians through cattle raising, farming, and elementary education, but nothing has been done for their moral and spiritual uplift. Even Catholic missions so vigorously developed in past centuries have all but disappeared. Protestant efforts of the past 60 years so nobly made in Paraguay and north-

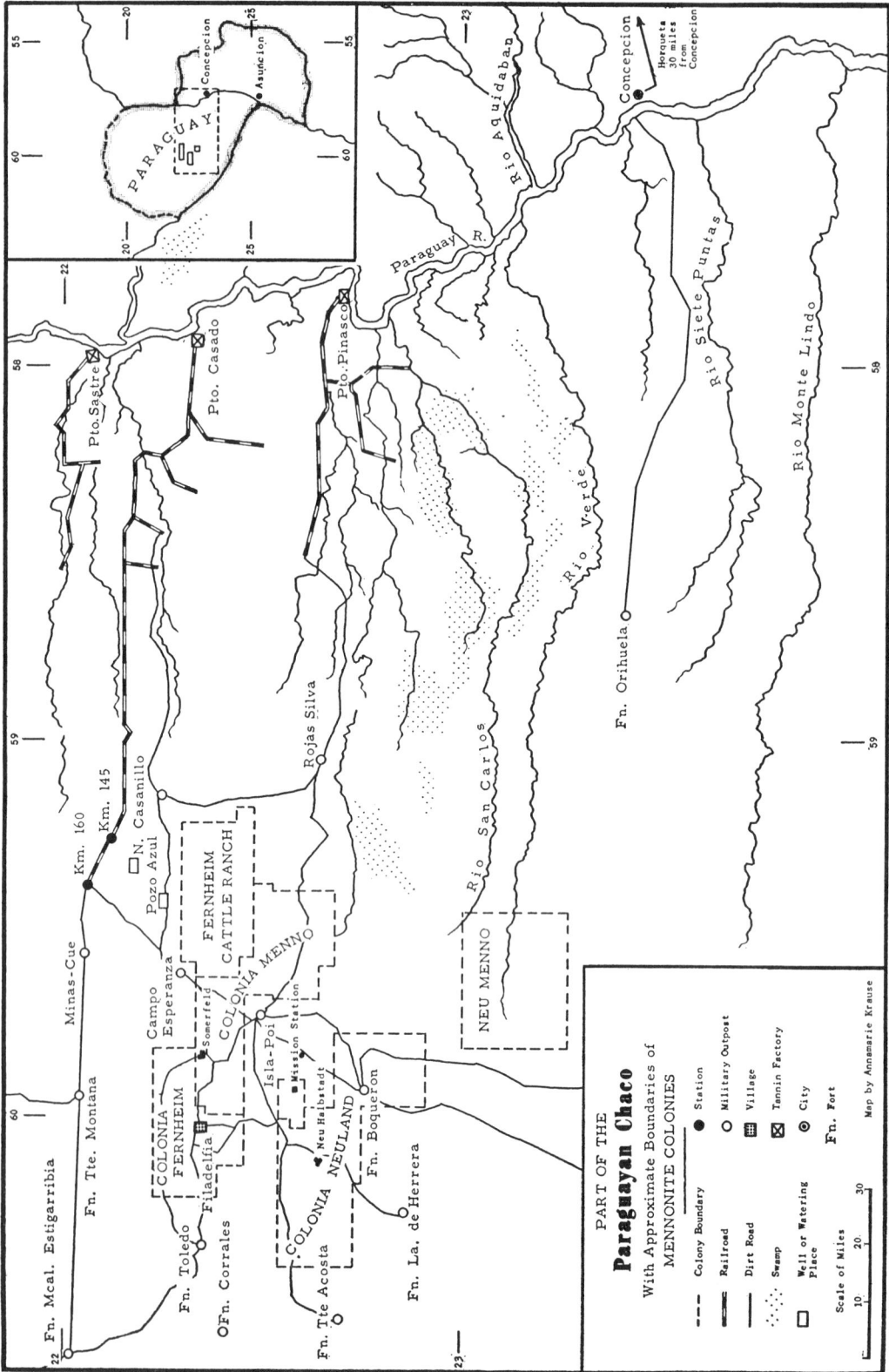

PART OF THE

Paraguayan Chaco

With Approximate Boundaries of
MENNONITE COLONIES

Map by Annamarie Krause

Colony Boundary	● Station	● City
Railroad	○ Military Outpost	⊠ Fort
Dirt Road	⊞ Village	
Swamp	⊠ Tannin Factory	
□ Well or Watering Place		

Scale of Miles

10 20 30

ern Argentina by the Anglicans and later by a few independent groups are still alive and growing but inadequate to meet the pressing needs of the Indians.

In March 1943 the Shanks and Holdermans, appointed by the Argentine Mennonite Mission, began their travels over the great northern region of Argentina in search of unevangelized groups of Indians. Finally by May central Chaco was chosen as the most strategic region for the new mission. Two months later work was begun in a Toba Indian colony of some 300 souls near Tres Isletas and within a month work on a church-school building was started. Some months later land was purchased some 18 miles farther south and nearer the thriving town of Saenz Pena. Here a new Indian colony was formed. This became the central station under the name "Nam Cum," where the Mennonites have aimed to emphasize preaching, Bible training, medical and nursing service, day school, better farming and industrial work. The third station 18 miles to the east was opened in 1944. In rustic buildings of their own construction the Indians gather for services and afterward bring their sick out under the trees for treatment.

The personnel of the mission during its first years was as follows: Calvin and Frances Holderman, 1943-46; J. W. and Selena Shank, 1943-50; John and Edith Tuck, 1947-49; Una Cressman, 1948-52; Samuel E. and Ella May Miller, 1949-52; Mabel Cressman, 1950-53; Albert and Lois Buckwalter, 1951- ; John and Maryann Litwiller, 1953- . The 1953 membership was 82. J.W.S.

Chalkley, Thomas (1675-1741), a Quaker missionary who worked among the Mennonites in Holland and the Rhineland. It was a time when a rapprochement between Quakers and Mennonites was much sought both in Germany (Crefeld) and Pennsylvania (Germantown), so that historians speak of Quaker-Mennonites or Mennonite-Quakers. Chalkley was born near London but emigrated to Pennsylvania before 1700. In 1709 he visited Northwest Germany and then jotted down in his journal, "There is a great people which they call Menonists who are very near the truth, and the fields are white unto harvest among divers of that people, spiritually speaking." Chalkley traveled as a missionary "minister" of the Monthly Meeting of the Friends in Philadelphia practically all his life, up and down the colonies of America, and also in England and the European continent. He kept a careful diary, which was published in *A Collection of the Works of Thomas Chalkley* (Philadelphia, 1790). It covers all his "life, labours, and travels" up to his death on the island of Tortola, W.I. R.F.

Chambersburg Mennonite Church (MC) is located one-tenth mile north of Chambersburg in Green Twp., Franklin Co., Pa. The congregation is under the Washington Co., Md., and Franklin Co., Pa., Conference. The total baptized membership (1953) is approximately 265.

This congregation was organized in the latter part of the 18th century under the leadership of Daniel Lehman (b. 1742), who was ordained bishop in Lancaster County so that he might have charge of the Mennonites who had settled in the Chambersburg community. The first church was built in 1804 of log construction on land given by Daniel Lehman from a farm he purchased when he moved to Chambersburg. Lehman preached the first sermon in the new church in September 1804, and died Sept. 22, 1804, before the next regular service.

In 1857 an addition of brick was built to the original log church. In 1872 this structure was replaced by a new house built entirely of brick, 40 x 60 ft. The third and present church was built in 1908, also of brick, 52 x 76 ft., on the same land, but on a slightly different location. R.F.L.

Chamococo Indians are located on the west side of the Paraguay River from Casado north as far as Bahia Negra. Most of them make a living as woodcutters or as laborers on ranches and harbors. Originally the Chamococos were a forest tribe. It is believed that they are only a small tribe. They speak their own language, but most of their chiefs and other prominent men, and also many of their young people know Spanish well enough to use it when dealing with their employers. The New Tribes Mission which at first had its headquarters in the Mennonite settlements of Filadelfia, Paraguay, is doing some mission work among these Indians at Bahia Negra. The Catholic priests are also trying to win as many as possible for the Catholic Church. J. H. Franz.

Champa Mission Station (GCM), Madhya Pradesh, India, can be described in three parts: (1) the Champa station or compound; (2) the Leprosy Home and Hospital; (3) the medical station.

The Champa compound comprises 8.8 acres of land registered Oct. 20, 1901. The station was opened by P. A. Penner (q.v.), who arrived in India on Dec. 9, 1900, and retired from the India service in April 1941. Others who worked at this station were: the P. J. Wienses, F. J. Isaacs, O. A. Waltners, P. W. Penners, and Miss C. L. Kuehny. Besides two missionary bungalows, there are also a primary school, a church, and a Christian suburb for Indian Christians and widows.

The Bethesda Leprosy Home and Hospital is situated on the east bank of the Hasdeo River. It comprises three walled compounds for women, men, and school respectively. There are over 40 wards for the patients. There are two hospital wards with an attached operating theater. A dispensary, church, quarters for the healthy staff, and observation ward are other buildings. The Home also owns some land outside of these compounds for cultivation. This land is in seven sections. The homes for the healthy children of leprous patients are connected with the Champa compound. Leprosy work began in April 1902. The following have acted as superintendents of the home: P. A. Penner, E. B. Steiner, H. R. Bauman, P. W. Penner, O. A. Waltner, A. E. Jantzen. Eva Pauls served here as a nurse for a number of years.

The medical station occupies a centrally located tract of 16 acres, registered Oct. 26, 1925. Dispensary work was started in July 1926 by Miss Loretta Lehman and Dr. Caroline Banwar. The medical station now has two missionary bungalows, an Indian nurses' bungalow, dispensary building, operating suite, six wards, kitchen and grain storeroom, barn, two garages (double), warehouse for missionary personal effects when on furlough, power house, and Indian staff quarters. The hospital has 50 beds. There is an X ray. The following missionaries have served here: Misses Loretta Lehman, Alida Schrag, Elenore Schmidt, Eva Pauls, Dr. and Mrs. H. R. Bauman, and Rev. and Mrs. H. C. Ratzlaff. Mrs. Menno Diener and Miss Leona Cressman did secretarial work.

Two churches serve the area. The Bethesda Church is on the grounds of the leprosy home and has a membership of over 300. The Champa Church also has a membership of more than 300. H.R.B.

Champaign County, Ill., one of the largest counties in the state, lies 130 miles directly south of Chicago in the fertile corn belt of the Midwest. With the exception of a few industries and the University of Illinois in Champaign-Urbana and a military base at Rantoul, the county is devoted largely to agricultural pursuits.

A settlement of over 500 Mennonites (MC) is located in and near the northwest corner of the county near Fisher. The first Mennonite settlers arrived in this county around 1883 from Tazewell Co., Ill. The greater part of the settlement is in the county, but about 100 members live in McLean County to the west and in Ford County to the north.

The East Bend Church (MC), the only Mennonite church in the county, is located in East Bend Township, two miles north and one mile east of Fisher. The East Bend Church together with its mission station at Dewey serves all of the Mennonites in this settlement. K.L.M.

Champaign County (pop. 25,000), Ohio, organized in 1805, lies in the fertile agricultural section in the west-central part of the state. The county seat is Urbana. An Amish Mennonite settlement founded on the northern border of the county about 1846 by settlers from Wayne and Fairfield counties, Ohio, and Mifflin Co., Pa., is now the Oak Grove congregation with a membership of 269 in Salem Township in the north central part of the county. An earlier Mennonite settlement, now extinct, left in Salem Township families bearing the names Herr, Weidman, Gehman, Funk, and Mast, whose ancestors founded the first Methodist church in the county. With Logan County (pop. 30,000) on the north, containing the South Union and Bethel congregations, Champaign has been an important Amish Mennonite center for more than a century. The combined membership of the three congregations (Ohio and Eastern A.M. Joint Conference), all near West Liberty, is 731 (1953). J.S.U.

Ch'ang-Yuan, a county (*hsien*) in the southern tip of the province of Hopei, China, area about 900 square miles with the Yellow River flowing through the middle. Besides the county seat, which is also called Ch'ang-yuan and is a walled city of 25,000 inhabitants, there are 700 small villages and 50 larger market towns with a total population of about 381,000.

Mission work was conducted in the county by the General Conference Mennonite Church since 1915 with buildings for church, primary schools, and workers' homes in the city of Ch'ang-yuan. In 1940 there were 5 congregations and several preaching places in the county with 12 Chinese workers and 200 baptized Christians. S.F.P.

Channing Bible Chapel (EMB) in Channing, Dickinson Co., Upper Mich., was dedicated in October 1944 as a result of home mission work. On May 3, 1943, Leander D. Fast of Mountain Lake, Minn., located in this railroad town of about 600 people and began services in a small rented store building in September 1943. In January 1944 an old building was bought and remodeled. Leander Fast served until May 30, 1948, and was followed by Arnold Wall of Dallas, Ore. The area served in this work includes a field of about 20 x 50 miles in which there is no other Gospel witness. L.D.F.

Chapel Hill United Missionary Church, located two miles northeast of Union, Mich., is a congregation of the Indiana Conference. The first meetings were held in 1911 with Elmer D. Mast as pastor. A church was dedicated June 6, 1920, under H. E. Miller. In 1952 there were 37 members with an average Sunday-school attendance of 76. The pastor was Dean Freed. E.R.S.

Chapel Mennonite Church, now extinct, located near New Stark, a village in Ohio, hence sometimes called the New Stark congregation, was founded by Mennonites from Stark County, Ohio, and several families who were the descendants of Bishop John Thut of Bluffton, Ohio. The settlement dates from 1839 but the congregation was not organized until 1876. The church was built two years later. In earlier years the members belonged to the Riley Creek Church (later Zion) near Bluffton. John Blosser was the first superintendent of the Sunday school organized in 1878. After his ordination to the ministry in 1891, he was succeeded by his brother Noah. John Blosser was ordained bishop in 1895 and served for many years as president of the Mennonite Board of Education. He also was active as an evangelist. After his death in 1921 his brother Noah served as pastor. When the congregation became involved in difficulties with the Ohio Mennonite Conference (MC) it withdrew from the conference in 1927 and transferred its membership to the General Conference Mennonite Church. Noah losser was then ordained elder and served until his death in 1936. The congregation declined in membership until it united with the few remaining members of the Presbyterian Church and others in New Stark to form the New Stark Community Church. J.S.U.

Chappell, Neb.: see **East Fairview.**

Charitable Institutions Board of the Church of God in Christ Mennonite (7 members) was created by the 1947 General Conference to advise the various local institutional boards. P.G.H.

Chariton County, Mo., the location of a Mennonite (MC) settlement north of Brunswick, now extinct, to which Mennonites first moved in 1869 (*Herald of Truth*, March 1870). When J. S. Coffman held meetings there in 1890 he reported a membership of five, which included the families of J. L. Kreider and Fred Brunk. Earlier Beachtels and Overholts had lived in the community. M.G.

Charkow: see **Kharkov.**

Charles (originally Karli or Karle), a Mennonite family of Swiss background located principally in Lancaster Co., Pa. The founder of this family was Henry Charles who came to America in 1737. After farming near Germantown for eight years, he moved to Manor Twp., Lancaster County. At least ten descendants carrying the family name have served or are now serving in the ministry of the Mennonite Church (MC). Among them was John D. Charles (*q.v.*), at one time dean of Hesston College. M.G.

Charles V (1500-58), Emperor of the Holy Roman Empire, 1519-56. The course of the Reformation was determined in no small degree by the circumstance that the heirs of Maximilian I, his grandsons Charles V and Ferdinand I, had grown up in circles that were only slightly touched by the movement toward a reformation of the Roman Church. Neither could be considered German, either by descent or education. The house of Hapsburg had grown from a German dynasty into a world power. By his connections with Burgundy, Charles was drawn into the wars with France, by those with Spain into the Moorish wars, and as a Holy Roman Emperor he was responsible to protect the church. From these viewpoints the historian must consider Charles's attitude toward the great religious movement of the 16th century.

Charles was born Feb. 20, 1500, at Gent (now Belgium), and spent his youth in the Netherlands, which he always regarded with affection. Since his father, Philip of Burgundy, died in 1506, and his mother Joanna (third child of Ferdinand of Aragon and Isabella of Castile) suffered from a clouded intellect, he succeeded to the Netherlands possessions and to the county of Burgundy, and after Ferdinand's death also to the Spanish lands. His teacher was Adriaen of Utrecht (Pope 1522 f.), a pious and learned theologian, under whose tutelage he acquired the strictly religious, gloomy view of the world which characterized him throughout his life. In addition to French, which may be considered his native tongue, he spoke some Latin and Spanish; of German he knew only a few words. In 1519 he was elected emperor at Frankfurt, in spite of all the efforts of his rival, Francis I of France, to defeat him. His arrival in Germany was welcomed in many circles, especially by the Imperial Knights and the Humanists. The former hoped that he would put an end to the oppressive might of the princely oligarchy, the latter, that he would promote the movement begun by Luther.

But Charles, who had come to Aachen (Germany) on Oct. 22, 1520, and there been crowned and anointed, remained solidly with the old Roman Church. In the Netherlands he had already affirmed the prohibition of Luther's works, and as far as his influence extended, they were destroyed. On Jan. 28, 1521, he opened the Diet at Worms, which put Luther under the ban of the empire in the Edict of Worms of May 26. But this edict did not have the desired results. Since it was published in only a part of the empire, and the Emperor was much absent, the authorities did not block the progress of the new doctrines. The Reformation took its course.

Meanwhile, from Switzerland the Anabaptist movement, founded in January 1525 in Zürich by Grebel, Manz, and Blaurock, spread over a large part of the empire, especially into the Austrian Alps, where Charles could not master the situation no matter how many mandates he issued against them, because he was so deeply involved in the French and Turkish wars, that he was kept away from Germany throughout a quarter of a century.

Under these circumstances the new doctrine continued to spread; neither Charles nor his regent, Duke Ferdinand of Austria, could prevent it. By 1524 the Diet of Nürnberg sided with the Lutheran Reformation, and even though the princes in the Regensburg Diet were inclined to support the Emperor in carrying out the Edict of Worms, nevertheless political conditions, especially the alliance of the Pope with Charles's enemies, compelled him to yield. He tried to win the Protestant princes to his side by lenience in religious matters, and so it was decided at the Diet of Speyer, in 1526, that every imperial estate should conduct his ecclesiastical affairs "as he could answer for it before God and the Emperor." Thus the Reformation was left to the individual governments. Not until the second war with France had come to an end in the so-called Ladies' Peace at Cambrai (1529), was Charles's energy directed to countering the further spread of the Reformation. In actual fact, Charles had made agreements to eradicate the new teaching, in his treaties of peace with the Pope and with France. In that year at a Diet held at Speyer a decree was issued to annul the concession of 1526, but a minority of princes and cities protested. Thus the empire really fell into two parts, one Protestant and the other Catholic.

Both parts turned with ruthless severity and violence against the Anabaptists. The same Diet that granted religious freedom to the Protestants passed the most horrifying law to eradicate the Anabaptists. The mandate of Charles, of Jan. 4, 1528, in which he, as "protector of the most holy Christian faith," ruled "that each and every Anabaptist and rebaptized person, man or woman of accountable age, shall be brought from natural life to death with fire and sword and the like," was elevated to an imperial law; on April 23, 1529, it was sanctioned by the consent of the assembled imperial estates. At the Diet of Augsburg (1530) it was reaffirmed; at the Diet of Frankfurt (1531) it was declared to have "been issued somewhat too hastily," but was retained; at the Diet of Speyer in 1544 it was extended by the additional clause, that those "who have been negligent in denouncing [heretics] shall be punished according to their deserts." The last Diet to occupy itself with it was the Diet of Augsburg in 1551, which decided that all judges and bailiffs who refused to pronounce the death sentence against Anabaptists should be deposed and punished by fine and imprisonment. In February 1540 Charles V returned from Spain to the Netherlands to discipline rebellious Gent. "From Brussels he issued sharpened proclamations against the heretics and Anabaptists. Flanders in particular suffered 'under the renewal of persecution" (Hans Rott, "Karl V.," in *Neues Archiv f. die Gesch. der Stadt Heidelberg* IX, 1911, 153). Rott refers to Hoofstede de Groot. (See de Groot, *100 Jahre aus der Gesch. der Ref. in den Niederlanden*, 1893, 126.) P. Kalkoff shows that Charles's first proclamation of Sept. 28, 1520, against the Protestants in the Netherlands (ARG I, 279) is identical with the mandate issued on March 22 or 30, 1521. (See *Theol. Lit.-Zeit.*, 1905, col. 342.)

In the Netherlands and Belgium the influence of Charles was very great; in the Southern Netherlands (now Belgium), all of which with the exception of the bishopric of Liége belonged to the crown lands, he had absolute power. Likewise he exercised full authority in the provinces of Holland and Zeeland, which he had also inherited. Gradually he acquired possession of the whole of the Netherlands. By war, purchase, or political manipulation he acquired Friesland in 1515, the Bishopric of Utrecht (provinces of Utrecht and Overijssel) in 1528, Groningen (Groningen, Ommelanden, and Drenthe) in 1536, and Gelderland in 1543. Since he was not thwarted here by princes and Diets as in Germany, he could enforce his measures to suppress heresy and prevent the Reformation. Besides the general mandates sanctioned by Diets and valid for the entire empire, several special mandates (*q.v.*) were issued for these territories, and particularly against Anabaptism. A special form of the Inquisition (*q.v.*) was introduced as early as 1522; both imperial regents in the Netherlands, Margaretha of Austria, 1507-30, and Maria of Hungary, 1531-55, were given strict instructions to prevent and suppress heresy.

The further attempts of Charles V to suppress Protestantism were fruitless. To be sure, he defeated the Protestant princes in the Schmalkaldian war (1547), and thereupon issued the Augsburg Interim (1548), which permitted to Protestants the lay communion in both forms, marriage of the clergy, as well as the continued use of church property; but it satisfied neither the Protestants nor the Catholics. Finally he was compelled to sign the treaty of Passau (1552), which gave the Protestants free exercise of their religion until a general Diet should be called, which met three years later in Augsburg. It granted to the Protestant estates of the Lutheran confession complete religious liberty and political equality with the Catholic estates. Excluded from this religious peace were the Reformed and the Anabaptists.

Charles V was not pleased with this solution of ecclesiastic confusion. Political failures, severe physical illness, and increasing melancholia induced him to pass his crowns to his successors. At a brilliant assembly in Brussels (October 1555) he ceded his Italian and Burgundian lands to his son Philip, and later (January 1556) also his Spanish domains and those in the New World; finally he also abdicated the imperial crown to his brother Ferdinand. He retired to the vicinity of the Jeromite monastery of St. Justus in Estremadura, Spain, where he died, Sept. 21, 1558.   LOSERTH, vDZ.

H. Baumgarten, *Gesch. Karls V.* (3 vv. 1885-92); W. Maurenbrecher, *Karl V. und die deutschen Protestanten 1545-1555* (1865); L. v. Ranke, *Deutsche Gesch. im Zeitalter der Ref.* (6 vv., 7th ed., 1894); K. Brandi, *Emperor Charles V* (N.Y., 1939); *ML* II, 460.

Charles XII, the well-known king of Sweden. For his encounter with Stephan Funk, a Mennonite preacher, see **Funk, Stephan.**

Charles (of Thiegem): see **Karel van Tiegem.**

Charles, John Denlinger (1878-1923), prominent Mennonite (MC) educator, was born in Lancaster Co., Pa., in Washington Boro, June 29, 1878, of Swiss background, to John Funk and Annie Denlinger Charles. He was the second in a family of two boys. His education began in the local grade school known as Harmony Hall, progressed through the state normal school at Millersville, Pa. (class of 1899), Franklin and Marshall College, Lancaster, Pa. (B.A., 1905), and Columbia University, New York (M.A., 1914).

On May 3, 1906, he married Amelia (née) Charles and moved to Kansas City, Kan., to become superintendent of the Mennonite mission there, serving 1906-9. He was called from this position in 1909 to be a member of the first faculty of Hesston Academy and Bible School, then being founded at Hesston, Kan. He served in that capacity and later also as dean and registrar, the remainder of his life. Five children were born into the family—Irvin, Anna, John, Stanley, and Harold.

Charles united with the church at the age of 18 (1896) and was ordained to the ministry May 4, 1908. He served as minister to the Hesston congregation during the fourteen years of his life there and in many other positions of trust in the church: as Sunday-school field secretary, as chairman of the General Conference Committee on Fundamentals, as secretary of the committee for revision of the Book of Doctrine, as a member of the General Music Committee, and at the time of his death he also was secretary of the district mission board (*Gospel Herald*, Sept. 7, 1923). His last illness interrupted an evangelistic tour of the Pacific coast states in July 1923. He died on Aug. 30, 1923.

Among his writings two books are recorded: *Fallacies of Evolution* (1917), and *Present Day Religions* (1921), both published by the Mennonite Publishing House, Scottdale, Pa.   P.V.S.

Charles Louis, Elector Palatine, 1648-80, gave much attention to the problem of rebuilding the lands of the Palatinate devastated by the Thirty Years' War. For this purpose he admitted Mennonites coming from the Netherlands or expelled from Switzerland. Utilitarian considerations outweighed religious scruples. For a long time the Mennonites in the Palatinate were not granted religious freedom "as a dangerous and refractory sect." Repeated heavy fines were levied upon them as a penalty for holding "secret meetings"; they must refrain from meeting secretly or be expelled. On Aug. 14, 1661, they begged permission to hold their meetings quietly, but were refused. They should understand that they had never been permitted free *exercitium religionis,* because it was contrary to the imperial "recesses," but every time they meet a fine should be imposed on each person (April 30, 1664). But on August 4, 1664, a significant general "Concession" was made, probably initiated by the Elector himself. A letter from the King of England and the intervention of influential Quakers may have led him to this decision (German text in *ML* II, 461 f.).

Charles Louis, who opposed the spirit of intolerance in his country and was interested in a union of the churches, continued his benevolence to the Mennonites and protected them from the attempts of his officials to suppress them. In Mannheim he permitted them to build a chapel at the Rheintor, likewise he allowed also the Hutterian Brethren to build a Bruderhof in this city with a large plot of land of their own.

Charles Louis has a place of grateful remembrance among the Mennonites. They liked to recall his paternalistic benevolence. The incident Anna Brons relates (*Ursprung,* 203), taken from folk stories, is characteristic: One day, riding through the countryside, the thriving farm of a Mennonite in the Pfrimm Valley caught his eye; he was told that on this farm things were not all aboveboard, for the farmer was a counterfeiter. The Elector requested that the farmer show him his counterfeiting mint, whereupon he showed the Elector his calloused hands, with which he had, with God's blessing, found the money in his fields. "If that is the way it is," said the Elector, "may your coin remain." He told the farmer to teach his children this method of minting, to their welfare and that of the entire country. NEFF.

K. Hauck, *Karl Ludwig, . . .* (Leipzig, 1903); Nüssle, *Bilder und Beiträge zur kirchl. Gesch. der Stadt Mannheim* (1901); J. Ellenberger, *Bilder aus dem Pilgerleben* vol. III 1883); A. Brons, *Ursprung, Entwicklung und Schicksale der . . . Mennoniten* (Emden, 1912); *ML* II, 461 f.

Charles Philip, Elector Palatine, 1716-42. The period of his rule was one of oppression for the Mennonites. Because of their religious separatism they were made to endure much hardship. Even the confirmation of their civic privileges, which the Mennonites asked for in 1717, was granted only after much trouble. Charles Philip finally ordered that they should be tolerated as before, without, however, being permitted to have public church buildings. For the confirmation of this concession the court council demanded payment of 1,500 florins, which Philip William had allegedly required in 1686 upon assuming the government. Although this assumption was proved an error, the government years later, in 1730, when the coffers were empty, insisted that the Mennonites pay the sum.

Great hardship came to the Mennonites by the application of the "right of redemption" against them. This law permitted a Catholic, Lutheran, or Calvinist to "redeem" any piece of land from an Anabaptist (as Mennonites then were contemptuously called) just by paying to him the purchase price without regard to the previous legal purchase of this property or any improvement in value since the original purchase. One particularly serious case happened in 1726 (with a certain Landes as victim). It was only after a long struggle that in 1737 this law was limited to three years, after which period no foreign "redemption" was any longer allowed.

Early in 1740 a new blow fell upon the Mennonites in the increase of the protection fee from 6 florins to 12 per person; the government took this step because of an alleged increase in the number of Mennonites. In spite of repeated petitions and the intervention of the noble owners of the land on their behalf, the Mennonites had to pay this amount until Charles Theodore became elector. A number of letters written to Amsterdam by Hans Burckholder and other Mennonite leaders in the Palatinate and now found in the Mennonite Archives of Amsterdam give detailed information about these difficulties. (*Inv. Arch. Amst.* I, Nos. 1447, 1458, 1470, 1473, 1476-83, 1486.) G.H.

E. Correll, *Das schweizerische Täufermennonitentum* (Tübingen, 1912) 88 ff.; *Christlicher Gem.-Kal.* 1912, 120-34; Chr. Hege, *Die Täufer in der Kurpfalz* (Frankfurt, 1908); *ML* II, 462.

Charlestown Mennonite Church (MC), now extinct, located in Chester Co., Pa., probably dates back to 1795 when a deed was conveyed to five trustees, one of whom was Bishop Mathias Pennypacker (1742-1808), the great-grandfather of Samuel W. Pennypacker, a former governor of Pennsylvania. Bishop Pennypacker, who had charge of the Phoenixville congregation, was no doubt the founder of the Charlestown congregation. No date is known for the erection of the meetinghouse. Tradition tells us that the building still standing in 1867 was not then being used for services. The old building finally collapsed and was removed so that no trace of church or cemetery remains. Q.L.

Charlesville Station was one of two stations to be established by the Congo Inland Mission (*q.v.*) with the beginning of active work on the field in 1912. It is located nearly 1,000 miles inland from the coast on the Kasai River, a leading tributary of the Congo River, in the territory of the Baluba-Lulua people. The site was chosen partly because of its transport possibilities and until recent years it served as the transport center for the four stations then in the field. The mission office and mission press are also located here.

Charlesville is the largest of seven stations, being one of the oldest, and having enjoyed generally more favorable conditions for expansion of its work. The report for 1948 lists the following: missionaries, 10; native pastors and deacons, 7; baptisms during the year, 187; church members, 5,238; professed Christians under instruction for baptism, 648; communities where the Word is given out regularly, 152; rural schools, 142; rural teacher-evangelists, 152; average attendance of all schools, 6,666; native medical helpers, 3; new cases treated, 2,413. R.L.H.

Charlo de Wael, an unmarried man, an Anabaptist martyr, was, according to van Braght (*Mart. Mir.*), burned at the stake at Hondschoote in Flanders in 1562, together with six other martyrs. But according to de Coussemaker he is identical with Charlo Vivier, born at Relly and burned at the stake as a Mennonite at Artois, France, on March 9, 1561.

vD Z.

Mart. Mir. D 298, E 663; *Bibliographie,* No. 826; E. de Coussemaker, *Troubles Religieux du XVIe Siècle dans la Flandre Maritime 1560-1570* I (Brugge, 1877).

Chartsch: see **Khartch.**

Chassaw-Jurt: see **Khasav Yurt.**

Chatenois (Kestenholz), a village in the Leber Valley in Alsace, 12 miles east of Sainte-Marie-aux-Mines (Markirch) and 3 miles west of Sele-stat (Schlettstadt), also formerly the name of a Mennonite church (*Gem.-Kal.,* 1911-22), which was later known as Markirch (*q.v.*), and then as Weilertal (Val-de-Villé). The variation in name is due to the fact that the congregation did not have a church building, but met in the homes of the various members. (*ML* II, 484.) P.S.

Chaux d'Abel, a Mennonite congregation on Mt. Sonvilier in the Jura district in the canton of Bern, Switzerland, listed as early as 1888 in Mannhardt's *Jahrbuch,* later merged with the Amish congregation La Ferriere, and called Chaux d'Abel-Chaux de Fonds until 1923 (after 1930 Chaux d'Abel-Berg and Chaux d'Abel-Kapelle). The ancestors of the present members settled here on the peaks of the Bernese Jura in the period of persecution as refugees, chiefly from the Emmental. They retained the German language in the midst of the French-speaking population. By emigration to America the church has suffered great losses since 1875. After a revival in 1892, the result of the work of Georg Steinberger, a preacher from the school at Rämismühle in the canton of Zürich, the congregation, assisted by the youth organization, erected a chapel in 1905. David Ummel (*q.v.*) of Chaux d'Abel, an elder 1837-96, an outstanding leader, founded a German school in Chaux d'Abel in 1862, and in 1903 donated the building to the congregation. On Feb. 5, 1917, it burned down; in its place a new school was built with accommodations for 40 or 50 children and put into service on Nov. 4, 1917. The German school is still in operation (1952). Later prominent elders were David Ummel, 1887-1918, and Heinrich Ummel, 1912-30. In 1923 the Chaux d'Abel group was organized as a congregation, with David Geiser and Abraham Geiser as elders. Chaux de Fonds was later renamed Bulles (*q.v.*). In 1930 the congregation was divided again into two parts: Chaux d'Abel-Berg with David Geiser as elder and 50 members in 1952, and Chaux d'Abel-Kapelle with Gottlieb Loosli as elder and 100 members in 1952. David Geiser died in 1950, and was succeeded by David Lerch as elder. (*ML* I, 340.) H.S.B.

Chaux de Fonds, La, Mennonite congregation in Switzerland: see **Bulles** and **Chaux d'Abel.**

Chelciki, Peter (active 1420-60), a remarkable Czech Christian leader (farmer, no priest), an apostle of complete nonresistance and advocate of a high type of Christian discipleship, a forerunner of the Bohemian Brethren (opponent of the Taborites), in many respects much like the early Anabaptists. He was the author of numerous books and pamphlets, the chief being *The Net of Faith.*

H.S.B.

Carl Vogl, *Peter Cheltschizki, Ein Prophet an der Wende der Zeiten* (Zürich, 1926). See discussion by H. S. Bender in *MQR,* 1930, 220-27.

Chengtu, Szechwan, West China Mission (GCM) was not in the original plan for the West China Mission, but when approaching hostilities made it seem wise to move from Paoki, the work was transferred to Chengtu. Here the P. J. Boehrs, Aganetha Fast, and the Wuthrichs, joined in the summer of 1948 by W. C. Voth and Elisabeth Goertz from the United States, found an unreached section with a population of about 150,000. Sunday services were first held in the missionary home, later in a little adapted chapel near by. Women's meetings, Bible classes, and children's activities were carried on, as well as home, hospital, and prison visitation. For part of every day, beginning in October 1948, a tea shop was rented in which a small clinic was set up and the Word was preached nightly. Wilhelmina Kuyf arrived in December.

In April 1949 a property was rented outside the city gate, facing on a busy main street, which provided space for a clinic, three beds for lying-in mothers (more than 200 babies were born there), workers' quarters, and a Gospel hall, where nightly services were also held.

Instruction classes at both places resulted in many candidates for baptism. A number of these are now in the group of 120 Christians who meet in these two places, and who compose the church there; others have returned to their home communities, or have gone to different areas to work or study.

When the missionaries withdrew in 1951 these Christians, together with two groups of inquirers, were carrying on the various activities of the church, directed by a committee of seven, who were elected at the annual church meeting. The pastor, an ordained man, is a trusted shepherd, and with the other workers is committed to the task of making Christ known and working out Christian principles in the "New Age" which has come to China.

Wi.K.

Cheraw, Col., the only town in the Holbrook Valley, lies ten miles north of La Junta in Otero County, and has a population of 184. The first Mennonite settlers moved into Holbrook Valley at the beginning of the present century. The East Holbrook Mennonite Church (MC), two miles east of Cheraw, had 130 members in 1949. From about 1900 to 1935 a Mennonite Brethren in Christ church also existed in the community. E.K.

Cherokee County, Kan. Preacher S. A. Mishler (MC) and a few other Mennonites were living at Columbus in this county in the 1890's. M.G.

Cherry Box: see **Mt. Pisgah.**

Cherry Glade Conservative Amish Mennonite Church, Bittinger, Md.: see **Casselman River Congregation.**

Cherson: see **Kherson.**

Chesley Lake Camp is located near Allenford, Ont. Purchased by members of the Ontario Mennonite Conference (MC) in 1947, the site comprises 40 acres and has a chapel and cabins. Since 1948 the camp has had a varied program of summer activities, including boys', girls', and young people's camps. M.G.

Chester County, located in southeastern Pennsylvania, pop. 136,000, was the site of a number of early Mennonite and Amish Mennonite settlements. The first settlers, Mennonites from Switzerland and the Palatinate, settled in the region of Pottstown, Coventry, Phoenixville, Royersford, and Spring City about 1718-20 and in the following years. The first Amish settled near Malvern and Frazer about 1750-60. The two oldest settlements of Mennonites in Chester County built the Vincent (*q.v.*) and Coventry (*q.v.*) meetinghouses about the middle of the 18th century (Coventry possibly as early as 1735); Coventry became extinct as a congregation about 1914 but Vincent now (1952) has 150 members. The Charlestown (*q.v.*) Mennonite meetinghouse was built about 1789 and was in use about fifty years when the congregation became extinct; its first bishop was Matthias Pannebecker (see **Pannebecker**), great-grandfather of Governor S. W. Pennypacker of Pennsylvania. The fourth location in Chester County where the Mennonites built a meetinghouse was Phoenixville (*q.v.*): the first building was started in 1772 and was later known as Buckwalters' and Morgans' School House; the second was built at Main and Church streets in 1794 and rebuilt in 1873, but the property was taken over by the Lutherans in 1875. Preacher Jacob Beidler was instrumental in erecting the Diamond Rock (*q.v.*) Mennonite meetinghouse in 1835, but it was not used much after his death (1864). All of these congregations belonged or still belong to the Franconia Conference (MC). The other Mennonite congregations in Chester County are of recent origin, since 1917: Frazer (*q.v.*), Coatesville (*q.v.*), Parkesburg (*q.v.*), and Homeville (*q.v.*), and belong to the Lancaster Conference (MC).

The oldest Amish Mennonite meetinghouse in America was erected near Malvern in Chester County in 1795, and was called Goshen or Chester Valley. The bishop oversight was in charge of Jacob Mast (1738-1808), who had become a bishop in 1788. The congregation became extinct some time after his death, and the building was accidentally burned in 1895; the walls, however, are still standing. The Amish had settled in Chester County in 1760, led by Jacob Mast, coming to Chester from Bern Township, Berks County (*q.v.*). Although the Goshen group died out, the Amish flourished in both the Conestoga and Pequea valleys; most of their members now reside in Lancaster County, however. From 1869 until 1877 there was some dissension among the Amish of the area which resulted in the formation of two separate groups: the Amish Mennonites who built the Conestoga A.M. Church in Berks County in 1882, and the Old Order Amish who clung more tenaciously to the discipline and piety of their elders. The Maple Grove A.M. Church in Chester County near Atglen was built in 1909, and was originally an outpost of the Millwood A.M. congregation of Lancaster County. The Conestoga and Maple Grove congregations belong to the Ohio and Eastern A.M. Conference, whereas Millwood, which formerly belonged to the same conference, a few years ago joined the Lancaster Conference. A considerable number of the members of all three congregations live in Chester County.

There are two Christian day schools in the county, West Fallowfield Mennonite School, and Parkesburg Mennonite School, with a total enrollment (1948-49) of 73 pupils. G.B.S., J.C.W.

J. C. Wenger, *History of the Mennonites of the Franconia Conference* (Telford, 1937); C. Z. Mast, *Annals of the Conestoga Valley in Lancaster, Berks and Chester Counties* (Scottdale, 1942).

Chester (Pa.) Mennonite Brethren in Christ Church was established in 1926 under the Gospel Herald Society, when a building was purchased. In 1936 it became part of the Pennsylvania Conference with E. B. Hartman as pastor until 1941. Other pastors have been J. B. Henry, 1941-45, and J. E. Golla since 1945. In 1950 there were 111 members and the Sunday school had an average attendance of 204. E.R.S.

Chester Mennonite Church (OOM), located near Wooster, Chester Twp., Wayne Co., Ohio, formerly called the Eight Square Mennonite Church, is a member of the Ohio and Indiana Conference of the Old Order (Wisler) Mennonite Church. The settlement, made in the late 1820's, was one group until 1858, when John Holdeman formed the Church of God in Christ, Mennonite, which group reportedly left the community in 1884. It is commonly accepted that the entire congregation sided with the Wisler movement in 1873 in rejecting English preaching and the Sunday school. In the spring of 1907, the larger part of the congregation sided with the Bishop Martin group of Indiana, which rejected some modern inventions (chiefly the telephone) and English preaching and withdrew. The withdrawing group now is called the Eight Square Mennonite Church (*q.v.*). The 10 remaining members, with no minister, were served once a month by ministers of sister groups of eastern Ohio for many years. With 42 members (1950) the group now worships on alternate Sundays in a frame building built in 1873 which replaced a log house reportedly built in the 1840's. Ministers who served the congregation are John Shaum, Peter Troxel, Peter Landis, Peter Imhoff, and Daniel Martin (the latter two left the group in 1907 but Martin rejoined in 1940), and since 1944, C. J. Good. H.B.

Chestnut Hill Mennonite Church (MC) in Lancaster Co., Pa., a member of Lancaster Conference, is located one mile west of Silver Spring on the Marietta Pike on land originally warranted to Joseph Sherrock in 1740. In 1790 Martin Greider and Michael Hoffman deeded a tract to Samuel Nissley, Michael Seichrist, and Joseph Sherck, ministers of the "Hempfield Mennonist Religious Society." The log meetinghouse erected on it was used until 1874, when the present brick church was built. This was enlarged and remodeled in 1909 and 1947. The burial ground is at the Salunga and Landisville meetinghouses, which were for many years a part of the ministerial circuit. The congregation numbered 133 members in 1953. The Sunday school, started in 1884, now averages 130. A circuit young people's meeting started in 1946 is well attended. Henry E. Lutz is the bishop, Jacob L. and H. Raymond Charles are the ministers, and Martin S. Newcomer the deacon.   I.D.L.

Chestnut Ridge Mennonite Church (OOM), located near Orrville, Wayne Co., Ohio, is a member of the Ohio and Indiana Conference of the Old Order (Wisler) Mennonite Church. It worships on alternate Sundays in the County Line Mennonite Church. The congregation began when it separated in 1873 from the Martin's Mennonite Church and the Pleasant View Mennonite Church (which were one congregation until 1930) in objection to English preaching and Sunday school. Sunday services were alternated with the Martin's congregation until 1908 when the present frame building (Chestnut Ridge) was built, which was remodeled in 1939. In 1907 a group led by Daniel Brubaker withdrew and joined the Bishop Martin group of Indiana which rejected modern inventions (chiefly the telephone) and English preaching. Ministers who have served the congregation, which now has a membership of 160 (1950), are Benjamin Good, David Wenger, Henry Hursh, Jacob Tyson, Daniel Brubaker, Elmer Good and Cleophas Steiner. In 1953 a group withdrew to affiliate with the Virginia (MC) Conference.   H.B.

Chestnut Spring Mennonite Church: see **Springs** Mennonite Church.

Cheyenne and Arapaho Messenger. The first number of this periodical was dated January 1930 and was published at Canton, Okla., as a four-page monthly by the Workers Conference of the General Conference Mennonite missionaries working among the Indians of Oklahoma. To December 1938 it was edited by G. A. Linscheid and after that by J. B. Ediger until its discontinuance in December 1939. In 1898 or 1899 a somewhat similar periodical under the title *The Cheyenne and Arapaho Sword* was launched by the Mennonite missionaries in Oklahoma.   M.G.

Cheyenne Indians today comprise two major groups—the southern (Oklahoma) and the northern (Montana). Originally one tribe, they were separated through the westward movement of the whites and were the last ones among the Indians to be subdued and placed on reservations.

The General Conference Mennonite Church started its first mission work among the Cheyenne Indians of Oklahoma in 1880 by building a school at Darlington (*q.v.*) for Arapaho children to which some Cheyenne children were admitted. Another school for Cheyennes was established in 1883 at Cantonment, which was soon attended by as many as 75 children. A second step was the establishment of mission stations at Cantonment (*q.v.*), 1882; Clinton (*q.v.*), 1894; Hammon (*q.v.*), 1898; and Fonda (*q.v.*), 1907. The Cantonment

Church was moved to Longdale, Oklahoma, in 1929.

Since there was no literature in Cheyenne, Rodolphe Petter (*q.v.*) reduced their language to writing, compiled a grammar and dictionary, and translated portions of the Bible, the *Pilgrims' Progress,* and songs which were used by the missionaries in their work. Gradually Sunday school, daily vacation Bible school, young people's retreats, and other activities became regular features of the work among the Cheyennes.

Today most of the Cheyenne children attend public schools with their white neighbors. Many intermarry with other tribes and whites. Some of the old tribal customs, organizations, and traditions remain. Over 900 Cheyennes have been baptized since the beginning of mission work in Oklahoma. The present membership is 400.

The General Conference mission work among the Cheyennes in Montana was started in 1904 at Busby (*q.v.*), and spread to Lame Deer (*q.v.*), Birney, and Ashland. The closed reservation land was allotted to the Cheyennes in 1926. The remaining land they were permitted to rent out. The Cheyennes live mostly in villages. There are government schools at the villages Busby and Birney. The work among the northern Cheyennes is similar to that among the southern. Over 500 Cheyennes have been baptized since the work began, and 250 are members of the church at present.

Cheyennes in general are learning the English language; intermarriage with whites and other tribes hastens the abandonment of their own language. Modern conveniences speed up the change of life among them. Mission work has had a great influence in curtailing the influence of the Indian medicine men and women who were the chief sponsors of the old way of life. Although the influence of disintegrating forces is evident, the power of the Gospel is becoming increasingly noticeable in the lives of many of the Cheyennes.   A.H.

H. P. Krehbiel, *Hist. of the General Conf. of Menn. of N.A.* (Canton, 1898); *ML* I, 341.

Cheyenne Mennonite Mission Church (GCM), more commonly known as the Deer Creek Mennonite Church (Indian), located six miles south of Thomas, Custer Co., Okla., was organized in 1928 with 11 members, under the leadership of J. B. Ediger. In 1924, to avoid confusion, the various denominations working in the area turned this field over to the General Conference Mennonite Church, since they were already working near by. Services were held once each month in private homes. In February 1930 the new church was dedicated and services have been held every Sunday since then. The membership in 1949 was 38. Missionaries who have served the congregation are the J. B. Edigers, H. J. Kliewers, Arthur Friesens, and now the Herbert M. Dalkes.   H.M.D.

Chicago, Ill., second largest city of the United States (pop. 1950: 3,606,436), is today the home of nine Mennonite congregations. Several score Mennonite students are always to be found in the many educational institutions of the city. The Mennonite Central Committee customarily holds its annual sessions, executive and section meetings in Chicago.

Chicago

Street Numbers
7200N
6400
5600
4800
4000
3200
2400
1600
800N
0
1200S
2200
3100
3900
4700
5500
6300
7100
7900
8700
9500
10300
11100
11900
12700
13500S

Map labels:
Lincoln Ave.
Gospel Mission (KMB)
Moody Bible Institute
Bethany Seminary
Chicago Loop
Mexican Mission (MC)
Bethel Menn. (MC)
Dearborn St. Mission (MC)
Menn. Home Mission (MC)
Brighton Menn. (EM)
Grace Menn. (GCM)
Woodlawn Menn. (GCM)
Menn. Seminary (GCM)
Brethren in Christ Mission
First Menn. (GCM)
Calvary Memorial (EM)

7200W 6400 5600 4800 4000 3200 2400 1600 800W 0 800E 1600 2400 3200 4000E

From April 1953
Mennonite Life

The first Mennonite church (MC) in Chicago was organized in 1866 by two businessmen, Peter Neff and John F. Funk. The congregation continued until 1871, when the small meetinghouse was destroyed in the great Chicago fire.

John F. Funk (q.v.), a co-worker for several years with D. L. Moody, laid the foundations for the publication work of the Mennonite Church (MC) when he started his publishing company in Chicago in 1864, which he then transferred in 1867 to Elkhart, Ind. Funk published the *Herald of Truth* and the *Herold der Wahrheit*, both founded in 1864 and "devoted to the interests of the denomination of Christians known as 'the Mennonites.' "

Chicago has been the scene of pioneer efforts of the Mennonites in city mission work. In many instances the work was begun spontaneously by interested individuals and groups with the conferences subsequently authorizing and supporting the already operating programs. The first Mennonite (MC) mission in Chicago was established at 145 West 18th Street in 1893 with M. S. Steiner as superintendent. This mission was suspended in 1895 but was re-established in 1896 under the auspices of the Mennonite Evangelizing and Benevolent Board (MC). Other conferences inaugurated mission work in Chicago during the next two decades: Evangelical Mennonite Brethren, 1907; Evangelical Mennonite Conference (Defenseless), 1908; Central Conference, 1909; General Conference, 1914; and Krimmer Mennonite Brethren, 1915.

M. B. Fast and later D. M. Hofer and J. W.

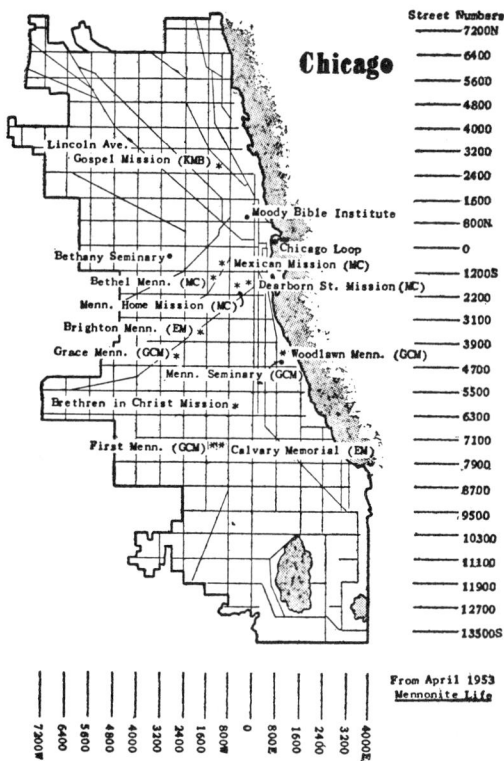

Tschetter edited and published in Chicago the *Wahrheitsfreund,* which came to be the official publication of the Krimmer Mennonite Brethren.

The General Conference Mennonites in 1945 established in Chicago the Mennonite Biblical Seminary (q.v.) in affiliation with Bethany Biblical Seminary (Church of the Brethren).

Following are the Mennonite congregations in Chicago, their addresses, conference affiliations, and dates of origin: Mennonite Home Mission, 1907 S. Union (MC), 1893; Bethel Mennonite Church, Loomis and 14th Place (MC), 1950; Mennonite Mexican Mission, 1014 Blue Island (MC), 1932; First Mennonite Church, 73rd and Lafflin (GCM), 1914; Grace Mennonite Church, 4221 S. Rockwell (GCM), 1916; Woodlawn Mennonite Church, 46th and Woodlawn (GCM), 1950; Brighton Mennonite Church, 34th Place and Wollcott (EMB), 1907; Calvary Memorial Church, 1217 W. 72nd St. (EM), 1908; and Lincoln Avenue Gospel Mission, 2812 Lincoln Avenue (KMB), 1915.   R.K.

Bender, *Two Centuries,* 28-32, 143; J. W. Fretz, "A Study of Mennonite Religious Institutions in Chicago," unpublished B.D. thesis, Chicago Theological Seminary, 1940; E. G. Kaufman, *The Development of the Missionary and Philanthropic Interest Among the Mennonites of North America* (Berne, 1931); Emma Oyer, *What God Hath Wrought in a Half Century at the Mennonite Home Mission* (Elkhart, 1949); W. B. Weaver, *Hist. of the Central Conference Mennonite Church* (Danvers, 1926) 134-37, 139-40; H. Weber, *The Centennial History of the Mennonites of Illinois, 1829-1929* (Scottdale, 1931); the Mennonites of Chicago were featured in the April 1953 issue of *Menn. Life.*

Chicago Avenue Mennonite Church (MC) is located in the northwest section of the city of Harrisonburg, Va. The work here, begun by the YPCA of the Eastern Mennonite College, was soon taken over by the Virginia Mennonite Board of Missions and Charities. A United Brethren church was rented in 1937 and then purchased in 1939. The church was known as the White Mission for a number of years. The congregation grew rapidly as it drew members and support from both the Middle and Northern districts of the Virginia Mennonite Conference. In 1947 it was organized as a separate congregation under the name of Chicago Avenue Mennonite Church. There were 114 members in 1952.   H.A.B.

Chicago (Ill.) First Mennonite Church (GCM) had its beginning in a surge of city mission interest in the General Conference Mennonite Church between 1902 and 1920, and was the second of about eight city missions established. It began in 1914 as a rescue mission in the commercial center of Englewood (63d St. near Halsted St.). Its leaders turned to work with people (primarily children) of more stability in the new community of West Englewood in 1915, and soon two store-front chapels (Ashland Ave. near 72d St.) became inadequate. A financial campaign among the churches of the Eastern, Middle, Western, and Northern districts between 1916 and 1918, conducted personally by the founder of the work, W. W. Miller, resulted in the construction of a church at 73rd and Lafflin, off the main avenue, in 1918, and the subsequent organization of a congregation. Since Miller's initial pastorate of eight years and A. H. Leaman's of nine years, the congregation has had six other pastors. Leland Harder became pastor in June 1952. Membership in 1953 was 70. (Leland Harder, *Seventy-Third and Lafflin,* Chicago, 1952.)   L.Ha.

Chicago Mennonite Gospel Mission, 6201 Carpenter St., Chicago, Ill., an extinct mission station, was founded in 1909 as the initial step in home mission work by the Central Conference of Mennonites. It was first located at 843 West 63d Street. The property at the Carpenter Street location was purchased in 1910 and rebuilt for mission purposes. For many years it was known as the Mennonite Home Chapel. The membership at one time was near 60, but successive population shifts removed the chief elements in the mission constituency, and the work was continued for some years with increasing difficulty. The Home Mission Committee discontinued its organized program at the close of 1947 and the property was sold soon after.   R.L.H.

Chihuahua (pop. 841,000), the largest of the twenty-eight states in the Republic of Mexico, lies along the United States border facing the states of New Mexico and Texas, an arid, sandy plain extending 300-350 miles inland from the Rio Grande River. Large stretches of the state have practically no rainfall. The elevated plateaus and valleys have a heavier rainfall but in most cases the total is less than twenty inches a year. Where irrigation is practiced the soil has been shown to be highly fertile. Mining is the most important industry of the state, although stock raising is a close second. The state of Chihuahua along with the state of Durango originally formed the province of Nueva Viscaya. The principal city is Chihuahua, the capital, with a population of 56,000, located 227 miles south of El Paso, Tex.

The city and the state of Chihuahua are of special interest to the Mennonites because of the 15,000 Mennonites (1950) located 75 miles west and north of the city of Chihuahua. The largest group is the Old Colony Mennonites settled in three distinct yet relatively adjacent areas. The separately organized settlements are known as the Manitoba, the Swift Current, and the Santa Clara settlements. The Old Colony population is something over 14,000. The second largest group is the Sommerfelder Mennonites who number about 800. These two groups migrated to Mexico in the 1922-27 period. The third largest group is the Kleine Gemeinde, which numbers about 700 and, along with the Sommerfelder and one settlement of Old Colonists, is located in the Santa Clara area. All three of the above-mentioned groups came originally from Manitoba. A fourth group, the Church of God in Christ Mennonites, have a mission station adjacent to the large Manitoba Old Colony. This group numbers less than a hundred. Its original members came from Oklahoma. The fifth group is the General Conference group located in the city of Cuauhtemoc. It is composed of the remnant of about 50 refugee families who escaped from Russia after World War I and temporarily settled in Mexico. Most of this group has since migrated to the United States and

Canada. It maintains a church and an evangelical witness in Cuauhtemoc.

The Mennonite Central Committee carries on a service program in Mexico. In co-operation with the General Conference Mennonites, two schools have been operated, one in Santa Clara and the other in Cuauhtemoc; a Mexican hospital is being administered, clinical work is done in the colonies, and agricultural information is supplied to Mennonite farmers. During the severe drought years of the early fifties relief in the form of flour, seed oats, and funds to dig central irrigation wells were supplied.

Of major significance for the state of Chihuahua is the large contribution that Mennonites have made to the development of agriculture. Dairy products, fresh and cured meats, and a number of cereal crops, chief of which is oats, have all been produced by Mennonites in large quantities. Before their settlement in the 1920's, there was practically no production of these commodities for commercial use, with the exception of the range cattle sent to northern markets. (J. W. Fretz, *Menn. Colonization in Mexico,* Akron, 1945; W. Schmiedehaus, *Ein feste Burg,* Cuauhtemoc, 1948.)   J.W.F.

Chihuahua (Mexico) Kleine Gemeinde Mennonite Church is located about 200 miles south of the American border in the "Quellen Kolonie." A tract of approximately 35,000 acres was bought in the region between Namaquipa and Santa Clara in 1948. The immigration from Manitoba began the same year, so that the membership by the close of the year was approximately 160 baptized members, and 262 not baptized. At first church services were held in a large building built on this land by the former owners as a granary. In 1949 a new church was built. Ministers who immigrated the first year with this group were Bishop P. P. Reimer and A. J. Thiessen from the Blumenort district of Manitoba; Cor. R. Reimer from Kleefeld, Man.; and B. R. Dueck and (deacon) P. J. Dueck of Morris, Man. Bishop Reimer died April 8, 1949. Evening schools are attended by the youth above the public-school age for the purpose of studying the Scripture and the German language.   D.P.R.

Chihuahua Mennonite Brethren Church for Latin Americans, located in Chihuahua, a village five miles west of Mission, Texas, was organized April 27, 1941, by Harry Neufeld of Los Ebanos, Texas, under the Southern District of the Mennonite Brethren Conference. In 1942 Henry F. Thomas took charge of the mission church. A larger church was dedicated April 28, 1946. The members of the church are Latin Americans of Texas and Mexico. Many are poor and migrant workers. Some of them have returned to their native land. Inosencio Garcia, ordained Dec. 28, 1952, is assistant. H.F.T.

Children's Companion is a four-page illustrated weekly, containing stories, activities, suggestions, and correspondence from readers, published by the Bethel Publishing Company (UMC), Elkhart, Ind., for children of junior and intermediate ages. Dr. J. A. Huffman, Winona Lake, Ind., has been editor since the periodical began in 1929.   N.P.S.

Chiliasm, the doctrine of a thousand-year reign of Christ on earth following His second coming for His saints. The term comes from the Greek word for "thousand" and the chief N.T. passage upon which the view is based is Rev. 20:1-10. Modern chiliasts base much of their teaching, however, upon a literal interpretation and application of Old Testament prophecies regarding the Jewish kingdom. The views of the Jewish apocalyptic books on the glory of the Messianic days also exerted some influence on the chiliasts of the second century Christian Church. Papias, for instance, quoted from Baruch 29 to show how fruitful the earth would be during the millennial reign of Christ.

In modern times the term "millennialism" or "premillennialism" is more commonly used instead of "chiliasm." The "pre" refers to the second coming of Christ as being "before" the establishment of the earthly kingdom. Postmillennialism holds that Christ will return after the kingdom of God had been realized spiritually. Amillennialism (also called nonmillennialism) holds that there will be no earthly kingdom at all and that there will be no golden age spiritually before the second coming of Christ.

Among the early (2nd-5th centuries) adherents of chiliasm may be mentioned: Papias, Justin Martyr, Irenaeus, Tertullian, Commodianus, Victorinus, and Lactantius. On the other hand, there is no trace of it in Clement of Rome, Ignatius, Polycarp, Tatian, Athenagoras, or Theophilus; and it is specifically opposed by Clement of Alexandria, Origen, Jerome, and Augustine. Typical of the chiliasm of A.D. 200 is Irenaeus: the world is to last six thousand years, comparable to the six creative days, and then shall come the millennial "day" of one thousand years, God's Sabbath. Near the end of the sixth day Antichrist will appear. At the end of the sixth day Christ will appear in glory and triumph over His enemies, and then reign on earth for one thousand years. During this time Jerusalem will be rebuilt and the earth will become very fruitful. Peace and righteousness will prevail. At the end of this millennium Christ will hold the judgment and effect the new creation. (For Irenaeus Christ's millennial reign did not have a Jewish character; it was not modern dispensationalism.)

Of the forty early Church Fathers (not counting schismatics) who left writings, about eight held to chiliasm. By the fourth century the view was almost dead and remained so for a thousand years. All the leading reformers rejected chiliasm, as did the historic creeds of Christendom. Except for Melchior Hofmann, only a few fringe figures of the Anabaptist movement were chiliastic; all the major leaders held to views which would now be called amillennial (nonmillennial). Menno Simons explicitly rejected chiliasm (summary of relevant quotations in Ira D. Landis, *The Faith of Our Fathers on Eschatology*, Chap. I). There is no trace of chiliasm in any of the older Mennonite confessions of faith: Schleitheim (1527), Twisck (*ca.* 1617), the Dutch Mennonite deposition of 1626, Olive Branch (1627), Jan Cents (1630), Dordrecht (1632), or Prussian (1660, 1678).

The four major sources of chiliasm in the modern Protestant Church are (1) Pietism, of which a good representative is the mild chiliast Johann A. Bengel (d. 1752); (2) the Plymouth Brethren, who originated in England under the leadership of J. N. Darby (1800-82) about 1830; (3) the Adventist bodies, whose chief founder was William Miller (1782-1849) about 1845; and (4) the *Reference Bible* of C. I. Scofield (1853-1921), first published in 1909. Both the Plymouth Brethren and Scofield hold to a modern form of chiliasm known as dispensationalism. According to this neo-chiliasm, redemptive history is to be divided into seven dispensations in each of which God deals with man on different terms, and each of which ends in human failure and divine judgment. The church, say dispensationalists, is not in O.T. prophecy, and Christians are not bound to keep "kingdom ethics" including the Sermon on the Mount; Jesus first offered the kingdom to the Jews but was rejected, upon which this Jewish kingdom was "postponed" to the millennial age; the Jews will be converted *en masse* at the sight of Christ at His "revelation" seven years after the "rapture" of the church; during the millennium the Jews will lead the nations, the Gentiles will keep the O.T. Jewish feasts, Jewish sacrifices and temple worship will be reinstituted, and the Jewish Sabbath will be observed. The church is thus a sort of parenthesis between the Jewish rejection of Christ as their King, and the Jewish kingdom of Christ which will obtain in the millennium. This dispensationalism has gained considerable acceptance in Bible schools and institutes, through prophecy journals and magazines, prophetic conferences, etc., in modern American Protestantism in the last fifty years, less in England and continental Europe.

The nondispensational type of chiliasm was also held by a number of German religious writers and theologians of the 19th century: Jung-Stilling, Auberlen, Hahn, Stier, Ross, Oetinger, Rothe, Lange, Hofmann, Delitzsch, and Meyer. Most of the writers on systematic theology rejected chiliasm, while a number of leading exegetes accepted classic chiliasm but not dispensationalism.

As was mentioned above there is no trace of chiliasm in the first generation of the main line of the Anabaptists, whether Swiss, Dutch, or German, represented by such men as Conrad Grebel, Michael Sattler, Hans Langenmantel, Pilgram Marpeck, Thomas von Imbroich, Obbe Philips, Menno Simons, Dirk Philips, Leenaert Bouwens, and the Hutterites Jakob Hutter and Peter Riedemann. From many of these leaders we have tracts, books, or letters, which more or less clearly delineate their doctrinal position, and none of these leaders exhibits chiliastic views. For that one must go to such persons as Melchior Hofmann (Strasbourg, Emden, Holland), Hans Hut (Augsburg, Bavaria), and the revolutionary Münsterite movement (a degenerate form of Melchiorism). Hut (d. 1527) expected Christ to return about 1530 and to set up a spiritual, though not a physical, kingdom. So far as is now known the chiliasm of Hut never was accepted by his fellow leaders and had no later influence. Melchior Hofmann (d. 1543), who became an Anabaptist of a unique type in 1530, was an ardent chiliast, and though he had no influence on the Swiss and was expressly repudiated by the Swiss Brethren who took part in the Bern disputation of 1538, he had considerable influence in Northwest Germany (Emden, 1530) and Holland (1530-33) and is responsible for the chiliasm which appeared there in the early years (up to 1540). His chiliasm finally found an outlet in the violent Münsterite movement (1534-35), though he himself never advocated violence.

The Philips brothers and Menno Simons succeeded in purging the Obbenite-Mennonite brotherhood (1533-44) of all Münsterism and chiliastic tendencies, and as a result of Münster the later Anabaptists and Mennonites became very careful in this matter. There seems to be no further trace of chiliasm among the Dutch, German, or Swiss Mennonites until at least two centuries later.

The question therefore arises as to time and circumstances of the entrance of chiliasm (premillennialism) into the modern Mennonite Church. This took place in the latter part of the 19th or early part of the 20th century, depending on which country is involved. Russia came first, South Germany, America, and Switzerland following in that order, but none interdependent. Modern Dutch Mennonites have manifested no interest in chiliasm at all. The writings of Johann Heinrich Jung (pen name: Stilling, 1740-1817) were of some influence in leading some of the Russian Mennonites to adopt millennial views. Plymouth Brethren influence came from England to Russia, mediated in part through Germany. Claasz Epp (q.v.) adopted chiliastic views and in 1880 led a group of his followers into central Asia to escape the Antichrist and to wait for the Lord. He set the date for the Lord's return at March 8, 1889, later postponed by two years. Epp (d. 1913) became increasingly unbalanced and fanatical and finally alienated most of his deluded followers.

Around the turn of the present century Mennonites in many lands, Switzerland, France, Germany, and America, began to experience their first contact with millennialism in their own ranks. Young men attended Bible schools where premillennialism was taught, and returned home with "keys" to the interpretation of Daniel and Revelation, both of which are books containing much figurative and symbolical material which had not been much studied or taught by Mennonites, even by the ministers, before that time. (There were exceptions of course: P. J. Twisck, 1565-1636, had written an exposition of Revelation 20, and Jakob Denner, 1659-1746, had included a sermon on this passage in his book of sermons entitled *Betrachtungen,* 1730. Heinrich Funck [d. 1760], a Mennonite bishop in the Franconia Conference, had also written an exposition of the law and its fulfillment in Christ, entitled *Eine Restitution oder Erklärung einiger Hauptpunkte des Gesetzes,* which was published in 1763 in Philadelphia.)

In the 1890's a number of American Mennonite (MC) young men studied at Moody Bible Institute in Chicago and became teachers of the premillennial view in their branch. Among them were A. D. Wenger (1867-1935), Aaron Loucks (1864-1945), E. J. Berkey (1874-1954), S. F. Coffman (1872-), and A. I. Yoder (1866-1932). A. D. Wenger was the first to teach premillennialism in his branch of the Mennonite brotherhood (MC), according to his own claim, apparently at a Bible conference held at Johnstown, Pa., Dec. 27, 1897-Jan. 7, 1898. Of Wenger's lectures the venerable John S. Coffman wrote (with restraint and charity): "A. D. Wenger, of Millersville, Pa., gave a connected lecture on Unfulfilled Prophecies. The prophecies more especially noticed are those by the Old Testament prophets, and of Christ as given in the New Testament, relative to the second coming of the Lord, the resurrection of the saints, the millennium, the loosing of Satan, and the last judgment. The manner in which this was treated was somewhat new, and is by no means the generally accepted view of the Mennonite people. The Scriptures do teach to a certainty that Christ is coming again; and it is certainly profitable to study that fact so as to be ready when He does come. There are, however, uncertainties concerning the literal application of the few passages relative to the millennium that make it unsafe to go into speculation concerning it as many speakers and writers have done." In addition to A. D. Wenger, the following influential premillenarians of the Mennonite Church (MC) should be mentioned: J. A. Ressler (1867-1936), J. B. Smith (1870-1951), George R. Brunk (1871-1938), John Thut (1879-1950), and John H. Mosemann (1877-1938). Among the leaders in the same period who held the amillennial view in the Mennonite Church were John F. Funk (1835-1930), John M. Brenneman (1816-95), John S. Coffman (1848-99), Daniel Kauffman (1865-1944), John Horsch (1867-1941), Andrew S. Mack (1836-1917), Abner G. Yoder (1879-1942), and E. L. Frey (1856-1942). The premillennial view made rapid progress in the (old) Mennonite group only after World War I. At the present time probably nearly half of the (old) Mennonites (MC) hold this view. In recent times premillennialism is receding somewhat. The church has never officially recognized or adopted premillennialism, except in two district conferences, whereas two district conferences prohibit this teaching directly. Dispensationalism has never secured a hold in the group.

The more conservative groups of Mennonites, who have had little contact with modern theological influences, such as the Old Order Mennonites, Old Order Amish, Conservative Amish, Church of God in Christ Mennonites, and the conservative Manitoba groups, have remained relatively untouched by modern chiliasm.

The General Conference Mennonite Church, because of the variety of groups of differing origin constituting its membership, is somewhat less uniform in its teaching. In the statement of faith adopted in 1941, it is stated, "We believe in . . . His personal triumphant return." There is no further elaboration on this statement as to the nature of Christ's rule. Premillennialism has never been officially recognized as the position of the church, but the teaching of premillennial Bible schools and periodicals has had considerable influence upon the preaching of some ministers, and there are numerous premillennialists, including some outspoken dispensationalists. The Grace Bible Institute, founded in 1945 at Omaha, Neb., largely G.C., though actually inter-Mennonite in control, espouses premillennialism. There is considerable tension over the issue in some quarters.

Only two American Mennonite bodies are officially committed to premillennialism in their adopted confessions of faith: the Evangelical Mennonite Church (formerly Defenseless Mennonites), and the United Missionary Church (formerly Mennonite Brethren in Christ). The Mennonite Brethren Church, the Evangelical Mennonite Church, and the Krimmer Mennonite Brethren are almost solidly premillennial, though not officially committed.

In Europe premillennialism never entered the North German or West Prussian churches, and very little in any other area. Some few ministers among the present leaders in the German *Badischer Verband,* and in the Swiss, Alsatian, and French churches have adopted it, but by no means the majority. Some chiliastic influence has been mediated through the Bible schools attended by Mennonites in Germany and Switzerland.

In Russia chiliasm found entrance only late in the 19th century and then almost exclusively in the Mennonite Brethren group. Isaak Peters (*q.v.*), an elder in Russia before he came to America in 1874, where he was cofounder of the present E.M.B. Church, and who is rated by P. M. Friesen (*Brüderschaft*) as an authority in the old Mennonite literature and traditions, particularly in Russia, is quoted as writing in 1910 (*Brüderschaft,* 264) as follows: "Menno Simons never believed in the millennium, and whoever believes in it is no Mennonite." Friesen, himself an *Allianz*-Mennonite, described the situation among the Mennonites in Russia regarding chiliasm as follows: "That chiliasm is contrary to old-Mennonite teaching is certain . . . . We pass over the question of the Biblical justification of this teaching; only we have asked ourselves hundreds of times, What benefit has the manner in which this teaching has been promoted among us in the last half century and particularly in the last eight years, brought us in connection with our sanctification (*Unsere Heiligung durch und durch*) and our greater effectiveness in being the salt of the earth and light of the world? . . . We ourselves have no positive answer to give." Heinrich Dirks (*q.v.,* 1842-1915), an influential elder of Gnadenfeld (1881-1915), first Russian Mennonite missionary (1869-81), not an M.B., apparently held to a mild form of chiliasm. For the history and present status of chiliasm in the Mennonite Brethren group see the account immediately below.

J.C.W.

Chiliasm as accepted and taught in the Mennonite Brethren Church. This doctrine entered the M.B. Church in Russia for the first time when a number of preachers from England, Switzerland, and other countries visited our churches and began to preach on that subject. Among them were Broadband and Baedecker from England, Stroeter from Germany, whose powerful preaching had great influence, and also a certain Widmer from Switzerland. This was the first time that this doctrine had been taught among the Mennonites of Russia, and quite a few of the leading brethren accepted it.

Jakob W. Reimer, preacher of Rückenau, Russia, became a leading advocate of chiliasm. As an evangelist and Bible expositor of great fame among the Mennonites in Russia, he engaged himself in a thorough study of Daniel and Revelation. His booklet *Der wundervolle Ratschluss Gottes mit der Menschheit* (The Wonderful Plan of Salvation of God with Men), already in its fifth edition, may be taken as typical of the Mennonite Brethren position. A few quotations from it follow:

"*A Beautiful Picture of the Future:* God will make a new covenant with His people. The citizens of the coming Messianic Kingdom will receive forgiveness of sins, a new heart, and the spirit of their God. God will make such people of them as will walk in His ways. They shall all know the Lord. As the water covers the sea, the land shall be full of the knowledge of the Lord. Jerusalem shall be again the place of the manifestation of God.

"The heathen will also partake of the blessings of the new City of God. This will extend over the whole earth. The nations will come to Jerusalem to worship the King, the ruler of the world, and to be instructed in His ways.

"The godless will be destroyed out of the land. For the righteous, death will be abolished forever. All nations will live in peace. Everyone will dwell under his own vine and fig tree, without fear. The whole creation will experience an amazing change.

"*The Millennium.* Christ will be the King on earth, and will reign with His saints over all the nations. 'The times of refreshing' have come. Peace reigns over all.

"But even though the reign of the King Jesus Christ will be glorious, not all the inhabitants of the earth will be truly loyal. . . . Also in the millennium there will be not a few who will love the darkness more than light. In their heart many will scorn the government of the incomparable King, Jesus Christ."

Another paragraph follows, in which Reimer speaks about the Last Judgment, the "Great White Throne." "The 1,000-year Sabbath will come to an end, and God will put the whole world to another test. Satan will be released from his prison for a short period of time and will go out to seduce the nations. Many will follow his tempting voice and join him in his mad attempt to overthrow Christ, the King of Kings. . . . Then will come the final fulfillment of the glorious Plan of God's Salvation."

This teaching has been unofficially accepted in the course of the years by the entire Mennonite Brethren Church. Today one would hardly find any congregation and very few individual members who would oppose the teaching on chiliasm as given above. The Conference of the Mennonite

Brethren Church has appointed a committee to revise its confession of faith. It is most probable that certain paragraphs will be added giving the chiliastic conception as to the coming of the Lord, the rapture of the church, the time of tribulation, the millennium, and the final events connected with the coming of the kingdom of God.　　H.H.J.

Floyd E. Hamilton, *The Basis of Millennial Faith* (Grand Rapids, 1942); J. S. Coffman, *Outlines and Notes Used at the Bible Conference* . . . (Elkhart, 1898) 4, 5; Jakob Denner, *Christliche und erbauliche Betrachtungen* (Philadelphia, 1860); E. Händiges, "*Chiliasmus,*" *ML* I, 342-47; Ira D. Landis, *The Faith of Our Fathers on Eschatology* (Lititz, Pa., 1946); C. K. Lehman, *The Fulfillment of Prophecy* (Scottdale, Pa., 1950); W. H. Rutgers, *Premillennialism in America* (Goes, Holland, 1930); P. J. Twisck, *The Peaceful Kingdom of Christ* (Elkhart, 1913); J. C. Wenger, *The Doctrines of the Mennonites* (Scottdale, 1950); *idem, Christ the Redeemer and Judge* (Scottdale, 1942); C. Henry Smith, *The Story of the Mennonites* (Newton, 1950) 456-62; *Prophecy Conference. Report of Conference Held at Elkhart, Ind., April 2-5, 1952* (Scottdale, 1953); J. W. Reimer, *Der wundervolle Ratschluss Gottes* . . . (Hillsboro, n.d.); *ML* I, 342-47.

Chilliwack (British Columbia) **First** Mennonite Church (GCM) was organized in September 1947 with a charter membership of thirty-eight. Services are conducted in German by Gerhard D. Loewen. The congregation is a member of the Canadian Mennonite Conference.　　P.J.D.

Chilliwack (British Columbia) **Mennonite Brethren Church,** located in the Fraser Valley, is a member of the Provincial, Canadian and General Conference of the M.B. Church of North America. With 98 members it was organized May 15, 1947. Six years later its membership was 243. The chapel, erected in 1947 and dedicated on December 7 of the same year, accommodates 475 persons and the basement provides room for ten Sunday-school classes. The leading minister since organization has been J. I. Bergen, and assisting ministers have been G. Penner, H. Fast, M. Hamm, H. Toews, N. A. Rempel, Paul Rogalsky, and P. Doerksen. J.I.B.

Chin (Rock Lake) Hutterite Bruderhof near Wrentham, Alta., was founded in 1934. Preachers are Andreas Gross, chosen to the ministry in the Old Elm Spring Bruderhof in South Dakota in 1911, and Samuel Dekker, chosen in the Chin Bruderhof in 1936. In 1947 the Bruderhof numbered 140 baptized members and 56 unbaptized persons.　　D.D.

China Mennonite Mission Society, an organization formed among the supporters of the mission work started by H. C. Bartel in North China. Bartel first went to China in 1901 and after four years of service with the South Chihli Mission started independent work at Ts'ao-hsien, Shantung. Adjacent areas were added to the field—Shan-hsien to the east in 1906, Ts'ao-chow to the west in 1909, and later the Honan counties of K'ao-ch'eng and Yüch'eng.

By 1911 sixteen additional workers had arrived. The staff then came from the Krimmer Mennonite Brethren, the Evangelical Mennonite Brethren, the Mennonite Brethren, and the Missionary Church Association. A home organization was effected in 1912 based on supporters in these four groups, the board being incorporated in 1913 as the China Mennonite Mission Society. At the peak of mission work in 1916 there were 30 missionaries. Types of endeavor included evangelistic work with a Bible school, an orphanage with agricultural and industrial training, and a home for old women. In 1942, during the Japanese occupation, the Bartels moved west and again opened new work in Kansu province. The total number of communicants was estimated at about 2,500.

Difficulties of administration impressed the need for reorganization of the board and at a meeting on May 7, 1946, various proposals were considered. As finally agreed upon the Evangelical Mennonite Brethren accepted responsibility for the original Shantung-Honan field, while the Mennonite Brethren and the Krimmer Mennonite Brethren accepted the new Kansu field. With this agreement the China Mennonite Mission Society was dissolved.　　S.F.P.

China Missions of the Mennonites. The first Mennonite missionaries to enter China were sent out from the United States in the 1890's but served under non-Mennonite boards. Mission work under Mennonite boards began after 1900 and may be summarized under six heads, viz., the China Mennonite Mission Society, the China Mission of the General Conference Mennonites, the South and West China Missions of the Mennonite Brethren, the Mongolia Mission of the Krimmer Mennonite Brethren, and the postwar attempts of the United Missionary Society and the Mennonites (MC) to establish new work.

The China Mennonite Mission Society (q.v.) operated from 1905 until 1946, when the Society was dissolved and its work taken over by the participating groups, the Mennonite Brethren and Krimmer Mennonite Brethren taking responsibility for the western field in Szechwan-Kansu and the Evangelical Mennonite Brethren in Shantung-Honan.

The General Conference Mennonite Mission. The China Mission of the General Conference Mennonites was begun as an independent venture by Mr. and Mrs. H. J. Brown in 1909, and in 1911 was located at Kaichow, Hopeh. In 1914 this work was taken over by the Foreign Mission Board of the General Conference and additional workers sent out. By 1920 there were 14 missionaries on the field, primary school work had been started, and a large church building completed at Kaichow. The field expanded to include all of the tip of Hopeh province south of Ta-ming, an area 100 miles long and 40 miles wide with a population of 2¼ million. In this field were seven major centers with buildings erected by foreign funds.

Evangelistic work was carried on from the beginning with Chinese evangelists assisting in outstations, traveling work, instruction classes, and as colporteurs and Bible women. Educational work included full primary work at the seven centers and lower primary at a number of other places. Boarding schools were opened at Kaichow and Ta-ming, the former developing eventually into a full senior

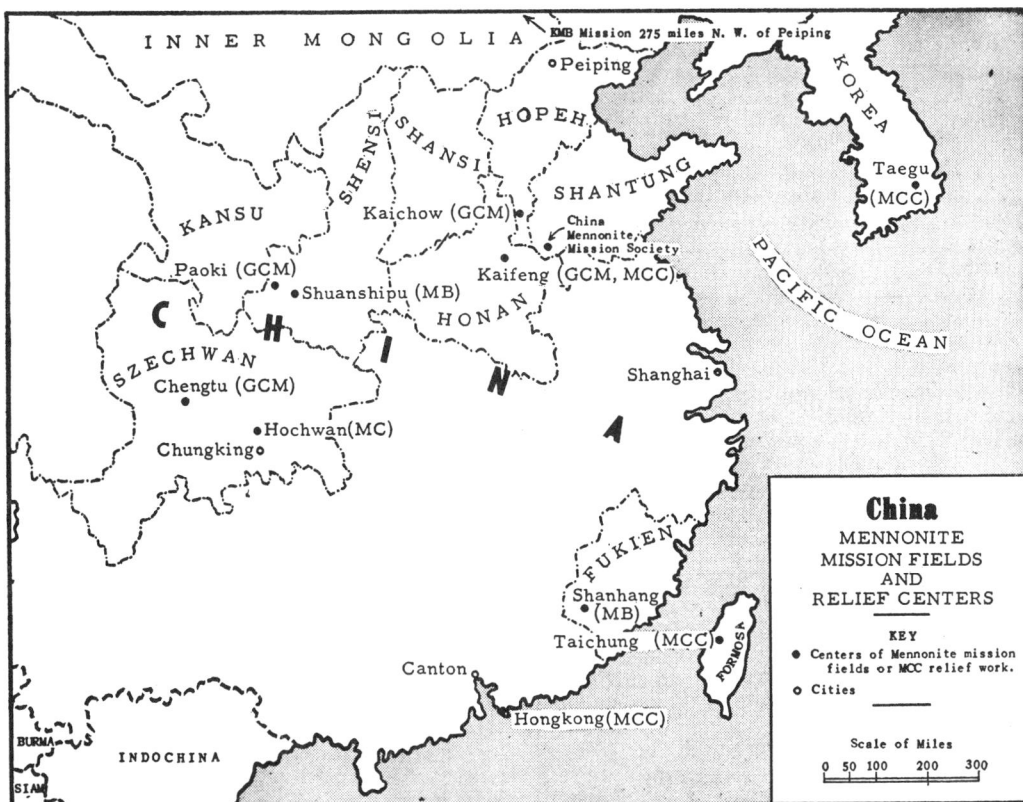

China
MENNONITE
MISSION FIELDS
AND
RELIEF CENTERS

KEY
● Centers of Mennonite mission
 fields or MCC relief work.
○ Cities

Scale of Miles
0 50 100 200 300

high school. Medical work began with a dispensary at Kaichow which grew to become an 80-bed institution with outstation clinic work and a well-developed school of nursing.

The mission had its last normal year in 1940. In the following two years all missionaries either evacuated or were interned. There were at that time 2,273 communicants in 24 organized churches and 40 preaching places. The churches and missionaries had organized in 1938 a Field Conference with a General Committee for administrative purposes. This organization took over the work during the war and since the Communist occupation. There has been little contact in the interval but reports show continued activity.

After the close of the war eleven missionaries returned to China. Due to ensuing civil war the work was interrupted and they were forced to move, working successively at Kaifeng, Honan; Paoki, Shensi; and Chengtu, Szechwan. As Communist control was established, it became increasingly difficult for foreign missionaries to work and many found it advisable to leave the country. By 1950 only four of the eleven remained. Two of these were granted exit permits and left in February 1951. The other two, P. J. Boehr and wife, were detained on account of accusations against him. He was arrested and subjected to house imprisonment, and was finally escorted from the country in May 1951. Mrs. Boehr followed shortly after.

The Mennonite Brethren of America participated

in the work of the China Mennonite Mission Society and provided perhaps a dozen workers through the years. The South China Mission, however, was the first that came to be formally sponsored by the church. It was started independently by Mr. and Mrs. F. J. Wiens in 1911 among the Hakkas at Shanhang in Fukien province. The home church was interested from the beginning and in 1919 accepted conference responsibility for the mission. Six new missionaries were sent out in the next two years and more later. Evangelistic work, schools for boys and women, and a Bible School for training evangelists were conducted. In 1921, 450 members were reported, also 11 outstations manned by Chinese evangelists and 17 schools with 30 teachers.

Recurrent political unrest caused the evacuation of the missionaries in 1927. Although return was attempted in 1929 it was unsuccessful. Again in 1933 work was attempted but with only limited success. In 1947 Roland Wiens, son of the founder, and his wife returned for a third attempt. In spite of lack of communications, difficulty of money exchange, and Communist occupation, the couple remained until May 1951, when they left the field for Hong Kong and were transferred to work in Japan.

The West China Mission of the Mennonite Brethren came about through the dissolution of the China Mennonite Mission Society in 1946, at which time the Mennonite Brethren accepted responsibility for work that the Society had started on the

Szechwan-Kansu border. Eight missionaries were sent out after the war for a short period of active work, but all found it necessary to return. The last to leave was H. C. Bartel, who was the founder of Mennonite work in China. He traveled to the coast and returned home in May 1952.

The Krimmer Mennonite Brethren. H. C. Bartel, the founder of the China Mennonite Mission, was from this group and went to China as early as 1901. Others from the K.M.B. also worked under the same Society; as many as 13 were serving in 1922. Though the K.M.B. Church was never officially connected with it, regular support was given through individual contributors. In 1922 F. V. Wiebe and family were sent to China with instructions, after learning the language at the China Mennonite Mission, to begin a work of their own. This was done in 1923 when a station was opened at Cho-tze-shan, a city of 4,000 in Suiyuan province, Mongolia. The field selected was about 150 miles long and 50 wide with a population of 60,000, largely Chinese but partly Mongolian. At Cho-tze-shan, the main center, the mission had a 4½-acre compound with homes, church, elementary school, and clinic. The major emphasis in work was on evangelism, with preaching, women's work, colportage, outstation meetings, and instruction classes. Churches were organized at four centers and encouraged to become indigenous and self-supporting. Under the Japanese-sponsored government missionaries were welcomed but their activities much restricted. A total of 16 missionaries served on the field between 1923 and World War II. After the war four missionaries went back to the field and in 1947 organized the Chinese Christian Church Conference. Due to disturbed conditions the missionaries had all returned home by 1949 and work continued as possible under the Chinese.

The United Missionary Society. This is the mission board of the Mennonite Brethren in Christ who, after 1948, were officially known as the United Missionary Church. Their first missionaries, William Shantz and C. F. Snyder, went out to China in 1895 and 1897 under the Christian and Missionary Alliance. In 1923 Bessie Cordell was sent to China under the National Holiness Association though supported largely by her own group. After World War II Miss Cordell was located at Tientsin and became interested in orphan children. She proposed that her church start missionary work with an orphanage. This was approved in 1948 and work begun. It was barely started before Communist occupation caused the evacuation of Miss Cordell and the work was left in Chinese hands.

The Mennonite Board of Missions and Charities. In 1942 the matter of opening work in China was discussed at the annual mission board meeting of the Mennonites (MC) but action delayed until after the war. The board secretary made an investigation of the field in 1946 with recommendations and the following year a party of five sailed for China. After a year of language study work was opened in the area centering about Hochwan, Szechwan. Communist movements, however, so restricted the

activities that missionaries were withdrawn to Chengtu in 1950 and their evacuation requested by the board. One of the group, Don McCammon, was arrested in December 1950 on a charge of disrespect to the new government and after a public trial deported. The rest also left by the middle of 1951.

The Tangshan (Kuhlman) Mission might be mentioned, for, although it was not a Mennonite mission, it was closely related to the Mennonites. Ernest Kuhlman from Germany went to China in 1907 and there married Maria Dyck from Elbing, Kan., who was serving under the China Mennonite Mission. The work at Tang-shan, Kiangsu, was begun in 1911 and served three counties in Kiangsu and Honan. Twelve foreign workers were engaged in this work, seven being from Europe and five from America. Financial support came about half from Germany and half from Mennonite churches and individuals in the United States and Canada. In 1923 there was some discussion of a closer connection with the General Conference but negotiations got no further than an agreement that the Foreign Mission Board of the General Conference would forward to the Kuhlman mission funds sent to them for that purpose. The Tangshan Mission carried on evangelistic work, schoolwork, and a Bible school after 1938. There were 900 baptized believers by 1941 with 15 congregations and 20 preaching places. From 1935 on, all responsibility for the maintenance of church property and pastors' salaries was in the hands of the Chinese church. With the war the missionaries evacuated to Tsingtao and later left China. The dispensary and school were closed but evangelistic work has been continued by the Chinese church.   S.F.P.

Ed. G. Kaufman, *The Development of the Missionary and Philanthropic Interest Among Mennonites* (Berne, 1931); E. R. Storms, *What God Hath Wrought* (Springfield, 1948); J. H. Lohrenz, *The Mennonite Brethren Church* (Hillsboro, 1950); G. W. Peters, *The Growth of Foreign Missions in the Mennonite Brethren Church* (Hillsboro, 1952); H. J. Brown, *Chips of Experiences* (n.p., n.d.), and *In Japanese Hands* (North Newton, 1943); Dorothy McCammon, *We Tried to Stay* (Scottdale, 1953); also mission board reports, conference minutes, and yearbooks of the different groups.

China-Home Bond, a periodical published by the China Mission of the General Conference Mennonite Church at Kaichow, Hopeh, China. Its appearance was irregular, there being in the year 1940 four single issues of four pages and two double issues of eight pages. S. F. Pannabecker served as its first editor from January 1939 to August 1941, when Marie J. Regier took over responsibility; but after two more issues the periodical suspended publication because of the growing political tension.
                    S.F.P.

Chinook Mennonite Brethren Church, now extinct, located north of Chinook, Mont., a congregation of the Central District Conference, was organized in 1916, with 40 members, by Heinrich Voth. A building 28 x 36 ft. was erected. J. M. Enns served as the first pastor until 1920, when he moved away. Then J. J. Buller was placed in charge. As other members moved away, the church was dissolved.
                    A.A.D.

Chippawa is a town in Welland Co., Ont., on the Niagara River a few miles south of the Canadian Niagara Falls. One main travel route of the Mennonite pioneers immigrating from Pennsylvania crossed high up on the Niagara River from Black Rock to the Canadian side, followed the river north through Black Creek and used the Boyer farm, some eight miles south of Chippawa, as a stopping place and Chippawa as the point to turn into the peninsula to the Short Hills south of Vineland, to the Twenty at Vineland, and westward. South of Chippawa on the Sodom Road lived Deacon Joseph Wellick, who served in the Willowby Township Church (MC) at Riverside near Boyer's and in whose home services were sometimes conducted.

J.C.F.

Chippewa, a former name of the Crown Hill Mennonite Church (MC), Orrville, Ohio, was founded in 1825 by Mennonites from Alsace. The names of the first settlers were Amstutz, Bösinger, Burkholder, Dähler, Lugibühl, Neuenschwander, Steiner, and Suter. (See **Crown Hill.**) HEGE.

D. K. Cassel, *History of the Mennonites* (Philadelphia, 1888) 199; Müller, *Berner Täufer*, 370; *ML* I, 347; D. L. Gratz, *Bernese Anabaptists* (Scottdale, 1953) 145-46.

Chiva: see **Khiva.**

Choirs, singing groups organized to render special numbers of music at regular church services and other meetings, are only recent in the Mennonite Church, beginning probably about the end of the 19th century. They have, however, become a regular part of the Sunday morning service, supporting the congregational singing and rendering anthems or special hymns, among certain groups in North America, such as the General Conference Mennonite Church, the Mennonite Brethren, the Evangelical Mennonite Brethren, the United Missionary Church, and the Evangelical Mennonites, although not among the more conservative groups such as the Mennonites (MC), the Amish groups, etc. Since choirs commonly require musical accompaniment, they have been introduced for regular Sunday services only in congregations using reed organs, pipe organs, or pianos in worship, except in Russia where choirs came in long before musical instruments. They have been unknown for this purpose in any Western European Mennonite groups, although in Switzerland, South Germany, and France, choirs have been in use for the past fifty years in a few places, particularly in Switzerland and near-by Alsace and France, to sing at special occasions, not in the regular Sunday services. In Holland and northwest Germany they are unknown, although organs are used. Among the Mennonites (MC) of North America, choruses (the word "choir" is distinctly avoided because it is thought to savor of professionalism, though this implication is not necessarily true) have been organized in various congregations since World War I, largely as the result of the influence of the church colleges, where a cappella chorus singing is strongly promoted, and whose choruses have for many years made annual tours, giving programs in various areas of the constituency. Quartets are

also quite common in this group, singing at special occasions. In the conservative Lancaster Conference of this group, however, special music of any kind, chorus or other, is still forbidden in the meetinghouses. The same policy is followed in all the more conservative Mennonite and Amish groups in North America.

The historic emphasis upon congregational singing and simplicity of worship has been a strong restraining influence against the introduction of special music, particularly by choirs, in Mennonite churches. The older pattern of a lay, untrained, and unsupported ministry is almost always accompanied by a nonliturgical form of worship without choirs. The strong sense of equality and brotherhood has often expressed itself in opposition to emphasizing the special service of a certain few in corporate worship, as well as against paid professional services. Paid choirs are unknown in Mennonite churches anywhere, although paid choir directors are to be found in some G.C.M. and M.B. congregations.

The attitude of the reformers toward the use of special music, choral and instrumental, in worship was determined by their concept of the church and the nature of the church service. The emphasis upon the preaching of the Word and the response of the congregation, coupled with the priesthood of all believers as over against the special functioning of the priests and clerical assistants, and the opposition to liturgy, particularly in Latin, resulted in a strong emphasis upon congregational singing and opposition to clerical or lay choirs in the regular worship, which has continued to the present day. During the first Protestant century choirs were practically unknown. The Reformed churches in particular insisted upon a simple nonliturgical congregational worship. Zwingli even rejected all music and singing at the outset, as did Conrad Grebel (letter to Müntzer, Sept. 4, 1524). However, this was a rejection of liturgy rather than of congregational singing. H.S.B.

Choirs in Prussia and Russia and Descendant Groups in America. The use of the *Choralbuch* with notes or ciphers among the Mennonites of Danzig, Prussia, and Russia followed the introduction of the organ and piano among the Mennonites of Prussia (see introduction to *Choralbuch,* 1898). This *Choralbuch* was originally used for congregational singing, but also for choirs as stated on the title page. Evidently these choirs originally did not participate in the regular Sunday morning worship service. This is a later development. The *Choralbuch* (anthology of tunes) of H. Franz, whose collection in manuscript form was begun in 1837, is evidence that there was a movement at the beginning of the 19th century to improve the traditional singing by means of special groups and training in schools using four-part and unison singing. This reform of singing started by Franz and others in schools gradually found its way into the homes. Choirs were organized and transformed the traditional somewhat corrupted singing, using melodies from the *Choralbuch* (*q.v.*). This process continued throughout the 19th century until choirs and their participation in the worship became generally accepted among the Mennonites in Russia at the beginning of the present century.

The time when this happened, the songs used, and also the gradual acceptance of the choir can be gathered from various sources. Originally the music and the songs for this purpose were copied by individuals. Numerous copies of these handwritten books, dating back as far as the middle of the past century, have been brought to this country by the immigrants of the 1870's and have found their way into the Bethel College Historical Library. Difficulties encountered during the introduction of the choir into Mennonite communities are vividly portrayed by J. H. Janzen, *Aus meinem Leben* (37-39). But most of the Mennonite congregations in Russia introduced the choir, not only to sing at special occasions, but also in regular worship services. Today the choir as an aid in worship is accepted by all Mennonites coming originally from Russia and Prussia and now residing in United States, Canada, and South America, with the exception of such conservative groups as the Old Colony Mennonites and the Church of God in Christ, Mennonite. In addition to the programs given during the Sunday worship annual song festivals have been popular for many decades, the best known being those of the Kansas and the Manitoba Mennonite communities, in which 20 to 30 choirs take part. All Mennonite colleges and schools have choirs. In 1952 the Bethel College choir made a trip to Europe, singing in many Mennonite congregations in Germany, Holland, and Switzerland, as well as at the Fifth Mennonite World Conference. Few congregations, however, have choirs which are permanently a part of the Sunday morning worship and sit regularly in choir seats facing the congregation, as is common in American Protestant churches. (See the various articles on singing and music in the April issue of *Menn. Life*, 1948.)   C.K.

Choir-singing among the Mennonite Brethren in Russia. Choir singing was introduced early among the Mennonite Brethren in Russia—about 1870-75. The M.B. groups who emigrated to the United States in the 1870's took the practice with them. Songs used were mostly out of Ernst Gebhardt's *Frohe Botschaft* (Germany), which was very popular. The use of these songs both in the congregational services and in homes, even at work in the fields, contributed much to the rapid spread of the M.B. movement as had Luther's songs in the Reformation period. Young people especially were attracted by the singing of these songs. Since the population of the villages was often mixed Mennonite and Mennonite Brethren, after some time village choirs were formed in which all took part, although the Mennonite Church did not introduce choir singing into the Sunday services as early as the Mennonite Brethren did. The songs for these village choirs were customarily hectographed locally. Ultimately the M.B. congregations came to use mostly Born's *Liederperlen* for their choirs. In the last years before the Revolution both the village choirs and the congregational choirs served as a

good bridge for better relations between the two groups, since the song festivals were often held jointly in the churches.

In Russia all groups, both in schools and choirs, used the number notation system (*Ziffern*), which was a great improvement over the congregational singing from hymnals without notes. Instruments were never used in Russia in the M.B. services, nor in the Mennonite churches. The one exception was the Mennonite church in Gnadenfeld. Even in the homes, it was only in the last years before the Revolution that a few reed organs appeared. When the Russian groups, both M.B. and G.C.M., came to North America in the early 1920's they soon adopted the American system of notation and the use of instruments as well.   B.B.J.

Choral-Books (*Choralbuch*). From the beginning the Anabaptists were averse to the cultivation of the type of music used in the worship of the Roman Catholic and Protestant state churches. The martyr hymns of the first Anabaptist hymnals were sung only to familiar folk tunes. Later, however (18th century), the hymnals of the state churches came into general use. Thus in the Palatinate the old Palatine hymnal was used in nearly all the congregations. Only in Holland was a distinctive Mennonite collection of songs produced. Choral-books (collections of chorals) did not come into general use in Holland until the first organs were put into the churches: Utrecht in 1765, Haarlem in 1771, Amsterdam in 1773, Rotterdam in 1776, Zaandam in 1782, etc.

The city congregation in Danzig had a manuscript choral-book of its own since the installation of its organ in 1805; it was revised and recopied in 1905. The original of 1805 is now in the custody of the Bethel College Historical Library.

When the Mennonite hymnal of 1832, *Christliches Gesangbuch, Zunächst für den Gebrauch der Taufgesinnten in der Pfalz,* was introduced in the Palatinate, the principal hymns of which were provided with melodies, J. Ellenberger I, preacher of Friedelsheim, made up a book of four-part harmonies for the hymnal, and had it lithographed. It found its way into most Mennonite homes. Ellenberger was also the first Mennonite minister of the Palatinate to cultivate successful singing in choruses, establishing a mixed chorus, and later a men's chorus; the former remained in existence until the beginning of the 20th century. Also in the Weierhof congregation choral music was successfully used and cultivated with artistic understanding. When the new hymnal of 1856, titled *Gesangbuch zum gottesdienstlichen und häuslichen Gebrauch in Evangelischen Mennoniten-Gemeinden,* came into use in the congregations of Hesse and the Palatinate, Ellenberger also furnished a lithographed book of four-part harmonies for it under the title, *Vierstimmige Melodien zu dem Gesangbuch zum gottesdienstlichen und häuslichen Gebrauche in Evangelischen Mennoniten-Gemeinden* (Dürkheim, 1856). In 1874 a new edition appeared in book form (3d revised ed., 1897), with the G clef for the soprano and alto in place of the C clef, which was no longer understood by many singers and organists.

The movement of the 19th century to promote the use of the original pure melodies in church services led to the appearance of a new edition of the above under the auspices of Thomas Löwenberg of Ibersheim and L. Wettschureck of the Weierhof school, in which some runs and elaborations were removed from the tunes, and the melody and rhythm largely restored to their primitive form. Wettschureck also worked out in co-operation with a committee a new choral-book for the hymnal issued in 1910 by the Conference of the Mennonites of South Germany, in which each song was provided with a four-part harmony.

In 1883, when Thiensdorf became the first rural church in West Prussia to install an organ, the Protestant choral-book of the churches' of East and West Prussia was adopted; however, some other tunes considered necessary were added by hand. As all the Mennonite churches of West Prussia gradually installed organs or at least parlor organs, a need was felt for a choral-book of their own; it was produced in 1898 (second edition 1935) by a committee, and was thereafter used in the Mennonite congregations of West Prussia, sometimes in addition to the Protestant hymnal. It bears the title *Choralbuch zu den Gesangbüchern für Mennoniten-Gemeinden, herausgegeben von der Konferenz der Ost- und Westpreussischen Mennoniten-Gemeinden.*

The North American Mennonites by about 1890 furnished each hymn of their hymnals with a four-part harmony, making the use of a separate choral-book superfluous; hence no choral-book has ever been published by the Mennonites here. The only exception to this is the reprinting of the Franz *Choralbuch* for the Manitoba Mennonites of Russian origin.

For an account of the Franz choral-book used by the Mennonites of South Russia, see the following article. A new choral-book was published in 1914 by the Mennonite General Conference at Halbstadt, with the following title: *Choralbuch zum Gebrauch für Kirche, Schule und Haus, mit Berücksichtigung des mennonitischen Gesangbuches, zusammengestellt im Auftrage der Allgemeinen Konferenz der Mennoniten-Gemeinden Russlands* (first ed., Halbstadt, Taurida, 1914). (V. Neufeld, "The Danzig Choral Buch," *Menn. Life,* April 1948, 35; *ML* I, 347.) NEFF.

Choralbuch zunächst zum Gebrauch in den mennonitischen Schulen Südrusslands, edited by Heinrich Franz (1812-89), a book of melodies for the hymns of the Mennonite church hymnal of South Russia, first edition at Leipzig, Germany, 1860, second European edition at Leipzig, 1880, American editions as follows: Elkhart, Ind., 1878, 1918, and two editions in Manitoba, the last or the fifth at Altona. The last edition bears the modified subtitle, *Zum Gebrauch in den mennonitischen Schulen und Kirchen in Canada.* The popular name of this songbook has been *Choralbuch mit Ziffern,* i.e., songbook with numbers, since the musical notes are indicated by numbers and not by the commonly used notation system. The book is in two parts, the first containing "all the melodies to the hymns in the *Mennonite Church Hymnal,*" 163 in number, the second containing "112 selected melodies for church, school, and home." All editions are identical except that the European editions give four-part notation, while the American editions give only one-part notation and are thus much smaller. In 1897, a greatly revised edition was published at Neu-Halbstadt, Taurida, under the title *Choralbuch, dem neuen mennonitischen Gesangbuche entsprechend, zum Gebrauch in Kirche, Schule und Haus,* edited by Wilhelm Neufeld, containing a total of only 133 melodies.

The original Franz *Choralbuch* was first prepared in manuscript form for use in the school which Franz taught, but gradually made its way through the Mennonite schools and churches of South Russia. P. M. Friesen (*Brüderschaft,* 587) said in 1910 that Franz's *Choralbuch* "transformed the singing of the Russian Mennonites and still substantially dominates it." D.H.E.

Chorister (*Vorsänger*), the song leader for the hymns sung in the worship of the Anabaptist-Mennonite congregations in all countries before the introduction of the (reed or pipe) organ. The origin of the office is lost in antiquity.

In the Swiss congregations and their descendant groups, the office was in essence a voluntary one, but once assumed, was retained for life. Usually there were several in a congregation, who took turns. In early days in Eastern Pennsylvania and daughter settlements, it became customary for the choristers, usually three to seven in number, to sit around a table in the front of the meetinghouse, a custom which is still followed by the Old Order Mennonites of eastern Pennsylvania. Later the choristers sat in the front benches. Not until the 1920's did choristers in the Mennonite (MC) congregations arise and face the congregation while leading, or use gestures to mark the time. After this transition the chorister, almost never the minister, selected and announced the hymns, although in the Lancaster Mennonite Conference, for instance, it is still customary for the minister to announce the hymn sung before the sermon. In the earlier days the chorister sometimes "lined" the hymns; i.e., he read each line of the hymn before the congregation sang it. This custom, not uniquely Mennonite, probably arose because of the lack of hymnbooks. In more recent times the Mennonite (MC) congregations elect their choristers, sometimes at the annual business meeting, for a one-year term. In earlier times the tuning fork was used to get the right pitch, now the pitch pipe. The Conservative Amish Mennonites, and the Church of God in Christ Mennonites, as well as the Mennonites (MC) and other conservative groups do not use musical instruments (*q.v.*) in their worship but have congregational singing led by the choristers, in contrast to other Mennonite groups who have accepted the organ or piano or both, even though some continued the use of choristers along with the instrument.

The Old Order Amish Mennonites have no

officially appointed choristers. Any brother of the church who has the ability and the informal training necessary to lead in the singing of the difficult tunes handed down orally from generation to generation, may at the proper time in the services announce the number of a hymn and lead it. He does not rise nor does he sit in a special place as he leads the hymn. He always begins the verse alone, the congregation not falling in until the second note.

In Holland most if not all the congregations formerly must have had a chorister, known as the *voorsinger* or *voorzanger*. Small congregations had one chorister, larger congregations two or more. Among the Groninger Old Flemish and the Old Frisians the chorister used to choose the hymns which were to be sung; in the other congregations he led the singing of the hymns, which were announced by the preacher. In some congregations the Psalms were sung regularly, beginning with Psalm 1 and finishing with Psalm 150, and then beginning again with Psalm 1. In 1620 the chorister of the Flemish congregation at Leiden was instructed that he should omit the Psalms of vengeance (Le Poole, 20). After the introduction of organs (about 1775) the chorister became superfluous, strictly speaking, but still held his office, and in a few congregations the chorister stood before the pulpit leading the singing until the beginning of this century. The chorister, who usually was chosen for life, customarily received a small salary, especially in city churches; in some cases he also read the opening Scripture.

The institution of choristers was taken along when the Mennonites moved from Holland to Prussia and from Prussia to Russia, 1789-1820. Since the choristers were chosen by secret ballot, just as were the ministers and the deacons, this position was held in high esteem. For this reason it was desired by many church members. In church, as well as at festivities in the homes, the choristers occupied a place of honor. They entered the church before the ministers. As a rule there were several choristers in one congregation, at times even four or five. The first chorister would call out the first line and the number of the first song. He would also start the song, whereupon the other choristers and then the whole congregation would join in. During the second song the ministers entered.

This custom was adhered to in most churches of Russia for more than a century. It was not until the last few decades before World War I that the first musical instruments were introduced into the churches. Although the choristers remained in their position, their service decreased in importance. Where well-trained choristers, usually using tuning forks, led the singing, the song was started on the right pitch, otherwise the pitch was not always satisfactory. On the whole, however, it was remarkable how the choristers, who received no special musical training, still made good progress in this art of leading the singing, mainly through devoted practice.

When the Mennonites, in the seventies of the last century, immigrated from Russia to the United States and Canada, they transplanted into their new homeland the practice of appointing choristers. Since the Mennonites who settled in the United States from Russia as a whole were more progressive than those settling in Canada, the musical instrument and the choir largely replaced the chorister in their churches. This trend beginning in the late 19th century was completed by the end of the first quarter of the 20th century.

In Canada, on the other hand, the use of choristers prevailed much longer. This was especially true of the group which is usually called the Old Colony Mennonites. Here the choristers still hold their position of importance, and choirs and instruments are unknown. The Mennonites who came to Canada from Russia in the 1920's continued the practice of choristers in so far as they organized independent churches, but here also the musical instruments is gradually displacing the chorister. In South America, where the Mennonite immigrants from Russia in 1930 and after lived in closed settlements, and in Mexico, the practice of having choristers has also continued.

The congregations of original Swiss-South German background in the G.C. Mennonite Church, no matter how remote the background, retained the chorister much longer than those of Prussian and Russian background. In the congregations of Swiss-Alsatian-Amish background, such as Eden (Moundridge), choristers were elected, usually three. The office was quite an honor and there was some friendly rivalry. They also served as choir directors. In the congregational singing, the choristers took turns in leading the hymns. They sat in front, announced the hymns, lined them, and led out, and were always a little ahead of the congregation. In the Eastern District Conference choristers still hold an important and honored position in most of the congregations, although a few churches now depend on the choir and the instrument to lead the singing.

The Hutterian Brethren, like the Old Order Amish, have no officially appointed choristers. The minister chooses the hymn, announces it, and then reads the first line. Any brother of the church who has the ability and informal training necessary to lead in the singing of the tunes handed down orally may then lead the hymn. After the first line is read and sung, the minister reads the second line, which is then sung. This routine is followed to the end of the hymn. The chorister does not stand or sit in a special place and no musical instruments are ever used. These practices have been followed without change for many generations.

J.G.R.

L. G. le Poole, *Bijdr. tot de kennis van. . . . de Doopsgez. te Leiden* (Leiden, 1905) 20; see also *Inv. Arch. Amst.* II, Nos. 800-6.

Chortitz Mennonite Church, East Reserve, Man. When in 1890 the conservative members of the Bergthal Mennonite Church (*q.v.*) separated from the more progressive members in the West Reserve because of the question of higher education, much debated among the Mennonites in Manitoba, they organized a new group, electing Abram Doerksen as their bishop and also a number of elders. This newly formed group was called the Sommerfeld Mennonite Church (*q.v.*) because Bishop Doerksen resided in the village of Sommerfeld. Bishop Gerhard Wiebe, on the East Reserve, and the elders and church members of his group threw in their lot, as being one, with the new Sommerfeld Mennonites on the West Reserve. Because Bishop Gerhard Wiebe lived in the village of Chortitz, their congregation was known from then on as the Chortitz Mennonite Church.

Then as now, Sunday schools, choirs, young people's societies, and similar organizations were outside the realm of their church activities. No spiritual fellowship with other Mennonite church groups or congregations is tolerated. Concerning civil and social activities, however, they take a more friendly and tolerant attitude toward their brethren. They also contribute to charity and public relief at home and abroad. Before the trek to Paraguay in June 1948, the Chortitz Mennonite Church had approximately 600 families with around 1,500 members, 12 preachers, 6 stations of worship, but only 4 church buildings, with one of them located in the village of Chortitz. A number of families from this district, some 1,700 souls all told, joined a Sommerfeld group from the West Reserve and emigrated to Paraguay in 1948.   H.H.H.

Chortitz Mennonite Church, Menno, Chaco, Paraguay, was founded by Mennonites coming from Manitoba and Saskatchewan after World War I. The Mennonites of the East Reserve, Man., had come from the Bergthal settlement in Russia. In Manitoba they became known as Chortitza Mennonites, because they had originally come from the Chortitza settlement in Russia. Some moved from the East Reserve to the West Reserve and became known as Bergthaler and Sommerfelder. From here some moved to Saskatchewan, calling their church the Bergthal Church. Of these Chortitza, Sommerfelder, and Bergthal (Saskatchewan) Mennonites, 1,743 souls left Canada in 1926-27 (see **Menno**) for the Paraguayan Chaco. Later 328 returned to Canada, leaving 1,415 who were registered as members of the new church called the Chortitz Church of Menno. Currently the membership is 1,105 (1949), served by 11 ministers and 4 deacons with Martin C. Friesen of Osterwick as elder. Church services are held regularly every Sunday morning at the church in Osterwick, built in 1932 of adobe bricks and metal roof with a seating capacity of 350, and in 18 surrounding village schools throughout the colony in rotation according to the number of ministers available. No musical instruments are used during the services and the Mennonite hymnary (*Gesangbuch*) is used exclusively. Sunday schools are not held but summer vacation Bible schools are frequently arranged. Footwashing is not practiced. Church discipline and the use of the ban are receiving increased attention in recent years.
      M.C.F.

Chortitza (Khortitsa, Chortitz), a tributary of the Dnieper River (Ukraine), on which the Mennonites settled in 1789 naming the first village after the stream. The village of Chortitza (*q.v.*) developed into a most significant center, so that the whole district became known as the Chortitza settlement (*q.v.*). The village name was transplanted by Mennonites from Chortitza to the West Reserve of Manitoba (1874) and from there to Paraguay. Chortitza settlers established a village by that name also in the Orenburg settlement (*q.v.*) in 1894.   C.K.

Chortitza, a village in the province of Ekaterinoslav, of the district of Chortitza, belonging to the first Mennonite settlement in Russia founded in 1789 near Alexandrovsk, situated on the Dnieper, with about 6,100 acres of land. In the village there were a Greek Orthodox and a Mennonite church, a secondary school established in 1842 (see **Chortitza Zentralschule**), a preparatory school with a two years' course established in 1890, a girls' school established in 1895, for the founding of which Abraham Neufeld, the well-known teacher at the Zentralschule and later director of the German Realschule in Berdyansk, rendered great service, 2 elementary schools, 131 business establishments, among them three important factories of agricultural machinery (Lepp and Wallmann, Koop, Hildebrandt). The railway station of Chortitza was near the village and had telegraph, telephone, and district government offices. The obelisk erected on the square in 1889 commemorated the centennial of Mennonite settlements in Russia. Chortitza was one of the chief intellectual centers of the Mennonite settlements in Russia.

During the Revolution (1917) and after, the village of Chortitza suffered much and underwent a great change. Through the nationalization and enlargement of the Mennonite industries and the exile of Mennonites a shift in population occurred. In 1941 the population consisted of 2,178 Mennonites and nearly 12,000 Russians and other nationalities. (For further information see **Chortitza Settlement, Chortitza Mennonite Church, Chortitza Zentralschule,** and **Agriculture.**) (*ML* I, 351.)
      C.B.

Chortitza Mädchenschule (secondary school for girls), Ukraine, Russia, was founded through private initiative in 1895. For some time the girls had been attending the Chortitza Zentralschule; but this practice was later forbidden by the *Fürsorgekomitee* at Odessa. For this reason it was felt that a special secondary school for girls should be established. Since the Chortitza *Gebietsamt* hesitated to sponsor the project some friends of education organized an association. Educators who particularly promoted the cause were David H. Epp, A. A. Neufeld, and Jacob A. Klassen. The financial sponsors were mostly Mennonite industrialists of Chortitza and the city of Ekaterinoslav. In 1900 the Department of Education approved the school with the following required curriculum: religion, Russian, German, mathematics, history, geography, science, art, penmanship, music, and crafts. The school started with a three-year course and added a fourth year in 1899. A new modern and well-equipped building was erected in 1904, made possible by a gift of 10,000 rubles ($5,000) from Mrs. K. Wallmann. J. J. Thiessen of Ekaterinoslav, the chairman of the school board, especially promoted the school. Most of the teachers were women.

The school was opened in 1895 with 17 girls and had an enrollment of 116 in 1913. Many of the graduates continued their studies, obtained teacher's certificates, and taught school. A certain number of needy girls and daughters of teachers and ministers could attend without paying tuition. The Chortitza *Mädchenschule* was highly influential in raising the standard of education and the cultural level of the settlement. Some 600 girls attended the school during its 25 years of existence. After the Revolution, when the Zentralschule became co-educational, the *Mädchenschule* was closed (1920) by the Soviets and it became a Ukrainian school. Teachers during the last year were: Agnes J. Klassen, Peter P. Neufeld, Lena Froese, Lise Epp, and Sophie Thiessen.   C.K.

H. Epp, "Die Chortitzer Mädchenschule," *Menn. Jahrbuch* (Berdyansk, 1913) 91-102; *Glückliche sonnige Schulzeit* (Niagara-on-the-Lake, Ont., n.d.).

Chortitza Mennonite Church was the first Mennonite congregation organized in Russia and was located in the village of Chortitza, Ukraine. The settlers were composed of members of the Flemish (q.v.) and Frisian (q.v.) congregations of the Danzig area who had been urged by the Russian government to unite and had been encouraged in the same direction by the Old Flemish Mennonite Church of Amsterdam. There were no elders and ministers among the first settlers who spent the winter in Dubrovna (q.v.). Upon request the Danzig mother congregations appointed 12 ministerial candidates by letter, among whom were Jacob Wiens, Gerhard Neufeld, and Behrendt Penner, representing both the Flemish and Frisians. No elder was elected. One of the main causes of the many pioneer difficulties which the new settlement endured and also a factor in the continued separation of the Flemish and Frisian Mennonites was the lack of spiritual leadership. The Frisians settled in separate villages and organized the Kronsweide Mennonite Church (q.v.).

By far the largest number of settlers belonged to the Flemish group, which was expecting an elder from Prussia to come to help them organize and appoint an elder (bishop). Elder Peter Epp of Danzig, who had been appointed for this task, died before he could leave. Then at a congregational meeting at Chortitza in 1790 the minister Behrendt Penner was elected as elder and installed by letter from Danzig. The first meetings took place in an abandoned mill. Soon a meetinghouse was erected. When Penner died in 1791 Johann Wiebe and David Epp were elected as coelders and ordained by C. Warkentin, who had come from Danzig with Elder Cornelius Regier for this purpose, the latter having died in Russia before he could fulfill his task.

Much disturbance was caused in the congregational life through the accusations launched against Johann Bartsch (q.v.) and Jacob Höppner (q.v.), the original delegates who had selected the land

for settlement. The securing of the promised imperial *Privilegium* (q.v.) took much time and effort, but it was finally obtained in St. Petersburg and signed by Paul I (q.v.) in 1800. Unrest was also caused later by a controversy between the Agricultural Association (q.v.), the *Gebietsamt* (q.v.), and the church leaders.

In the 1830's the old meetinghouse was replaced by a large two-story stone structure with a tile roof, which in its plain structural design was reminiscent of the Dutch and Prussian meetinghouses (e.g., Heubuden). This building was used until the Mennonites left Chortitza in 1943. Although the Chortitza church and village remained the center of the church, branch meetinghouses were also erected in Neuendorf, Burwalde (1862), Osterwick (1872), and Einlage. In other villages services were held in schoolhouses.

In addition to these churches, some daughter settlements also remained branches of the Chortitza mother church, viz., Fürstenland (q.v.) (after its elder left for America), Neu-Chortitza (q.v.), Borozenko (q.v.), Nikolaifeld (q.v.), and others. Some of them, for example the Bergthal Mennonite Church (q.v.), gradually became independent. As long as these branch congregations had no duly appointed and installed elder (bishop), the elder of the Chortitza Mennonite Church performed baptism, conducted the Lord's Supper, and was the leader. The ministerial body (*Lehrdienst* or *Kirchenkonvent*), composed of elder, ministers, and deacons, was the governing body of the large congregation. In the matters pertaining to baptism, Lord's Supper, and church discipline, the congregation followed the practice of the Flemish.

The spiritual and cultural life of the first decades was on a rather low level, as can be expected under the circumstances. Conditions improved with the overcoming of the period of strife and economic difficulties, and the raising of the educational and spiritual level through capable leadership. During the second part of the past century it became the practice to elect ministers from the ranks of teachers. Many of the outstanding elders and ministers had been teachers of the Chortitza Zentralschule or the preparatory school. This era introduced greater appreciation not only of the Christian-Mennonite heritage but also of the German and Russian culture. An adjustment to the new environment was gradually taking place, partly under pressure, partly voluntarily. In the 1870's this question became a matter of great concern and disturbance when the development was climaxed by the introduction of universal military conscription in Russia. The more conservative element, approximately one third of all Chortitza Mennonites, which was least willing to take any step in this direction or to accept an alternative state service, left for America. Although such leaders as Heinrich Epp, teacher and elder, were very active in preserving the principles and the rights of the *Privilegium* of the Mennonites, they did not advocate emigration. On the other hand, the elders of the daughter colonies of Bergthal (Gerhard Wiebe) and Fürstenland (Johann Wiebe) not only actively promoted this cause but also succeeded almost entirely in taking their flocks with them. They were joined by many from the Chortitza village. In contrast to the Molotschna Mennonites, who settled in the United States, they went to Manitoba, where they became known as Old Colony (*q.v.*), Bergthal (*q.v.*), Chortitza (*q.v.*), Sommerfeld (*q.v.*) Mennonites.

The leadership of the Chortitza congregation has also played an important role in promoting missions, publications, and other activities of the *Allgemeine Mennonitische Bundeskonferenz* (*q.v.*) in Russia.

In addition to the separation of the Frisian from the Flemish at the beginning of the settlement, another separation occurred during the 1860's, when the Mennonite Brethren Church (*q.v.*) was founded in 1860 ff. Pietistic and Baptist influences caused a religious revival in the village of Einlage. The rigid adherence of the leaders to established religious practices without much consideration for some justifiable innovations, and the zeal of those converted to new practices and principles brought the matter to a climax just as was the case at the Molotschna. (See **Einlage Mennonite Brethren Church** and **Mennonite Brethren**.) The *Allianzgemeinde,* founded by P. M. Friesen in 1905, which followed a middle road between the Mennonite Church and the Mennonite Brethren, found some followers in the Chortitza Mennonite Church.

Evangelistic meetings, Bible study groups, prayer meetings, Sunday schools, choirs, the use of musical instruments, and other more recent means and methods of promoting religious life and activities were gradually accepted. The congregation never practiced footwashing. In the use of alcoholic beverages and smoking, moderation was stressed.

With the outbreak of the Revolution in 1917 the congregation began to encounter great difficulties, although it also received substantial material aid through the relief program of the American Mennonites of 1919-21. Its aging elder, Isaak Dyck, died and was succeeded by Peter P. Neufeld in 1922. At that time new hope and life began to fill the hearts after years of hardships, murder, epidemics, and starvation; Bible studies, conferences, and music festivals became common. Nevertheless,

in 1922-25 many members left for America. When the NEP period ended and antireligious propaganda and the exile of kulaks set in, most religious work was gradually stopped. The work of the ministers was confined to preaching. Religious instruction and baptism of the young people were made illegal. Ministers had to pay fines. After the death of Elder Peter P. Neufeld (1927) his successor, David H. Epp, could do his work only under the greatest difficulties until he was forced to discontinue to function as elder in 1929, after which the office of elder remained unfilled. The ministers that had not yet been exiled or given up their vocation did their work quietly as long as they could. In 1934 the minister Aron P. Töws was exiled, never to return. Heinrich Winter was exiled in 1935, returned in 1940, and undertook the tasks of minister and elder when the Germans occupied the Ukraine. The churches had been closed for years or had been used for other purposes. The Chortitza church had been used as a cinema. In 1942 a number of ministers were elected and the first baptismal service was held, with around 300 baptized. The following year, during which the total congregation was evacuated to Germany in October, the number of baptisms was even greater. Today the surviving members of the Chortitza congregation are scattered in Canada, South America, and Siberia. Some of the Chortitza members became unfaithful in the hour of trial, but most remained steadfast, testifying for the Lord even unto death.

The Chortitza Mennonite Church was founded in 1790. In 1905 it had a membership of 1,504 at Chortitza proper, 732 at Neuenburg, 726 at Osterwick, and 601 at Burwalde, a total of 3,563. The total population, including children, was 7,860, not including the daughter settlements. In 1927 the total membership for the same group was 3,287 (6,968 including children). The decrease in membership is probably due to emigration to Canada and to increased antireligious propaganda and persecution. Of the members of the Chortitza Mennonite Church, 542 had secondary education and 6 had university training. The congregation had 17 ministers, 10 deacons, and one elder; of these 10 had a secondary education and one theological training (*Unser Blatt,* 1927, 176).

For literature see **Chortitza Mennonite Settlement.** C.K.

Chortitza (Khortitsa) **Mennonite Settlement** was located on the left bank of the Dnieper River between the cities of Ekaterinoslav (Dnepropetrovsk) and Alexandrovsk (Zaporozhe) in the Ukraine, Russia. This was the first Mennonite settlement in Russia, established in 1789. The settlers came from the Danzig area upon invitation by Catherine II. The object of the Russian government was to have the border regions settled by a stable agricultural population. It sent representatives into foreign countries (Germany and Bulgaria) to examine and secure suitable immigrants. The attention of the government was probably directed to the Mennonites by the Lutheran pastor of Nassenhuben near

Elders of the Chortitza Mennonite Church

	Elected Minister	Ordained Elder	Died
1. Behrendt Penner	1788/89	1790	1791
2. Johann Wiebe	1791	1794*	1823
3. David Epp	1791	1794*	1802
4. Peter Bergen	----	1806*	1809
5. Jakob Dyck I	----	1812*	1854
6. Jakob Dyck II	----	1851*	1855
7. Gerhard Dyck	1848	1855*	1887
8. Heinrich Epp	1864	1885	1896
9. Isaak Dyck	1876	1896	(?)
10. Peter P. Neufeld	1914	1922	1927
11. David H. Epp	1886	1927	1934

* Coelder.

Danzig, Joh. Reinh. Forster (d. 1769 at Dirschau, West Prussia), who at the request of Catherine traveled through Russia in the 1760's, especially visiting the (non-Mennonite) settlements in the province of Samara.

The Beginning. The general economic conditions in Germany, and particularly the position of the Mennonites in the regions of West Prussia after the annexation of Poland, had produced a feeling of anxiety among the Mennonites, so that the first invitation of the Russian commissioner Trappe (*q.v.*) to the elders of the Danzig churches in 1786 was received with great reserve in order not to antagonize the Danzig city council, though 60 families were found willing to emigrate. According to Mennonite tradition two deputies, Jakob Höppner of Nehrung and Johann Bartsch of Danzig, were appointed by the congregations and sent to Russia to inspect the land and draw up the necessary agreements. Supported by Trappe and the Russian consulate in Danzig the delegates undertook their journey in 1787. After a conference with Catherine II (May 13, 1787) and the proper authorities, and after defining their rights and duties along economic and especially religious lines (apportioning of land, support, tax-free years, self-government, free exercise of religion) to the satisfaction of all concerned, they returned in the same year. Meanwhile Trappe had secured information about the attitudes and manner of life of the Mennonites in Holland, and when the Danzig authorities expressed their displeasure with his plans, he went temporarily to Marienwerder. Since he was able to meet the peculiarities and wishes of the Mennonites with understanding, he soon won further confidence. The return of the deputies and the imminent edict of Frederick William II of 1789 caused the mood already present to mature to a quick decision, with the result that in spite of the continued aloofness of the elders a greatly increased number of families declared themselves willing to emigrate when negotiations were resumed in 1788, and with or without the consent of the Danzig authorities applied to the Russian consulate for passports.

In the fall of 1788 two groups of emigrants were organized, numbering 228 families, who spent the winter in Dubrovna in the province of Mogilev. In 1797 a second train of 118 families followed; several families had meanwhile decided to join the first party; thus about 400 emigrant families became the basis of the settlement. In 1819 the settlement consisted of 560 families with 2,888 souls, in 1910 about 2,000 families with about 12,000 souls. The increase in population was at first 5 per cent annually.

Economic Progress. At first the settlers were divided into 15 villages; by 1824 three others had been established to provide for the surplus of population. The government at first assigned 89,100 acres, but increase in population and prosperity caused the colony management early to acquire land for daughter colonies (about 190,000 acres). With the increasing prosperity several groups settled on land they had themselves acquired (about 108,000 acres), bringing the ultimate total of the land belonging to the Chortitza settlement to about 405,000 acres, not including rented land and privately owned estates.

Vocationally the first settlers were craftsmen and small manufacturers. In 1819, thirty years after the founding, 300 manual craftsmen could still make a living; their products were used not only in the agricultural growth of the colony, but also outside. They also farmed as a side line. Domestic industry was in general limited to wool spinning (1819, 557 spinning wheels) and weaving (49 looms), for many of the immigrants had been weavers in Danzig. The land apportioned to them could not all be cultivated yet, and was therefore used in profitable sheep grazing. Not until later did agriculture displace these side lines. By 1819 the nearly treeless tract had been planted with 30,000 fruit trees, 35,000 other trees, 1,000 grapevines, and about 25,000 mulberry trees, since the silk industry after 1810 had become a lucrative side line (according to Reisswitz and Wadzek). In the 1830's and 1840's these beginnings were greatly stimulated under the leadership of Johann Cornies (*q.v.*), the representative of the government in the colonies, who was himself a resident of the Molotschna settlement. Not until after the 1860's did agriculture move into the foreground and lead to the manufacturing of agricultural machinery, the importance of which extended far beyond the Mennonite settlements, and which continued to grow until World War I. The settlement passed through the regular steps of colonization, determined by the quality of the settlers and by the slow adaptation to new economic conditions: from the repetition of customary practices, to the proper exploitation of the soil by a more adventurous spirit, and finally to the integration in the total national economic pattern. These three steps are represented by (1) the years of settlement, (2) 1820-60, and (3) 1860-1917. The solicitude of the government is clearly discernible throughout the first two periods, in spite of many unfaithful and inexpert officials. It did not withdraw until after the liberation of the Russian peasants (1861), when the development had taken its sure and proper course and government aid was no longer needed.

The rapid industrialization of Europe toward the middle of the 19th century and the increasing demand for grain laid the foundation for the expansion of grain farming on the Russian steppes. The Mennonites of Chortitza were leaders in agricultural improvement, in the discovery of the most suitable variety of grain, and in the production of agricultural machinery. Peter Lepp founded the first factory in Chortitza in 1853. In 1888 there were eight such factories, and in 1907 there were sixteen. Plows, drills, wagons, mowers, threshing machines, fanning mills, and steam engines produced by Mennonites found ready acceptance also among the Russian population. Some of the outstanding Mennonite factories were Hildebrandt and Pries, Lepp and Wallmann, and A. Koop and Company. As a result of the increased grain production an expanding grain and milling industry developed.

One of the largest concerns was Niebuhr and Company. Starch factories, brickyards, and other industries followed. Chortitza and Alexandrovsk (*q.v.*) were the centers for these industries.

Leadership. Development in spiritual matters ran a far more complicated course and must be considered more dependent on the will of the leaders and their relation to those they were leading. The original immigrants had two characteristics—outward poverty and defective insight, to say nothing of the division into Frisian and Flemish congregations (Danzig, Neugarten, Marienwerder). The Russian government was interested in having a homogeneous church; therefore Trappe sought to form a single brotherhood with the support of the Dutch Mennonites. But the conference of elders on June 28, 1788, in Rosenort (Elbing) found among the emigrants no competent personality agreeable to both sides, so that the emigrants went to their new foreign home without a church organization. Undesirable consequences were already evident in their winter quarters; want of worship services interrupted their traditional life. The election of two readers for divine services was of no avail. The request to the mother church for the ordination of a minister was only tardily granted when they had already settled. The inadequacies of the early period, the death of the first elder they chose and ordained by letter, Behrendt Penner (d. 1791), and the strife concerning his successor, friction between the deputies who had charge of temporal government and the ministers, who by tradition were the "rulers," and finally calling on the government authorities in the dispute, created an unedifying situation and split the church into two camps, so that the quarrel could be settled only by strictly impartial judges. The groups appealed again to the mother church in Prussia, which sent the elders Cornelius Regier of Heubuden and Cornelius Warkentin of Rosenort (Elbing) to settle the dispute; this was accomplished with great effort and self-sacrifice. Church matters in the Flemish congregation (Chortitza) as well as the Frisian congregation (Kronsweide) were adjusted, elders and ministers were chosen and ordained, and a tolerable relationship established. Elder Cornelius Regier died in Chortitza on this journey (1794); his work was finished by his younger colleague Warkentin. But a union of the two congregations, as desired by the government, did not occur.

The division of jurisdiction as between the deputies (Höppner and Bartsch) and the ministers did not eliminate friction, and strife flared up periodically, which even led to the excommunication and imprisonment of Höppner. The fault cannot now be ascertained, but probably lay chiefly in jurisdictional disputes, for temporal and spiritual authority were in some instances hard to separate and were even later not entirely separated. Friction of this kind also arose in the period of Johann Cornies' work, who, as a member of the directorate of the Agricultural Association (*q.v.*) formed in 1832, planned larger organizations which he could carry out only by the support of the collective church. Since the representatives of the church were at the same time personally involved, they sometimes concealed their likes and dislikes behind the church or religious ideology and distorted the facts. In the conflict between the Chortitza churches and the Agricultural Association, the jurisdiction of the church was limited; but the church thereby merely lost a source of friction as also in the assignment of jurisdiction to temporal village authority.

Education. An additional source of friction arose from the assignment of school supervision to the Agricultural Association, thus forming the basis for the school council. After the colony was really established, much thought was given to the care of schools. Nevertheless, following the example of the home community in West Prussia, the schools were limited to a very narrow scope of instruction—reading, writing, arithmetic, and Bible and catechism. This was the extent and the content. Teachers were haphazardly assigned. These inadequate conditions, which the supervisory assembly could not change, remained until the founding of the Chortitza Zentralschule (*q.v.*) in 1842 in the village of Chortitza. The new school was to provide further education and also serve as a normal school for teachers. Idealistic and farsighted men as teachers and members of the board (H. Heese, G. H. Epp, J. Janzen, A. Neufeld) gave the school the character of a German educational institution and furnished the teachers for the village schools. Science, languages, mathematics, etc., were under the supervision of the school board, and religion under the representatives of the church. In 1871, when the Agricultural Association was dissolved, the school board also lost its authority to supervise, and in 1881 education among the Mennonites became subject to the Department of Education. The board barely remained in existence until it took over, in conjunction with the church, the supervision of the German language instruction and on its own initiative was able to revive its fruitful work. The district of Chortitza, both in its own settlement and in its daughter settlements, laid great stress on education and spared no expense to make a standard education possible. Chortitza had 40 teachers with 1,500 pupils; the total including the Mennonite subsidiaries of the Chortitza settlement in the province of Ekaterinoslav numbered about 150 teachers with nearly 5,000 pupils (1918). School matters were always a community concern, independent of church denominational relationships.

In matters of administration Chortitza had its county headquarters (*Gebietsamt* or district administration) in the village of Chortitza with a mayor (*Oberschulze, q.v.*) and secretary (*Gebietsschreiber*). This administration was originally responsible to the Russian supervisory office (*Fürsorge-Komitee, q.v.*) in Odessa, and later to the local Russian authorities. The Agricultural Association played an important role in Chortitza but never gained the influence it had under Cornies in the Molotschna. Health and hospital care developed rapidly at the turn of the last century when a hospital was erected and physicians employed. (See M. Hottmann, "Dr. Th. Hottmann," *Mennonitisches Jahrbuch,* 1953.)   C.B.

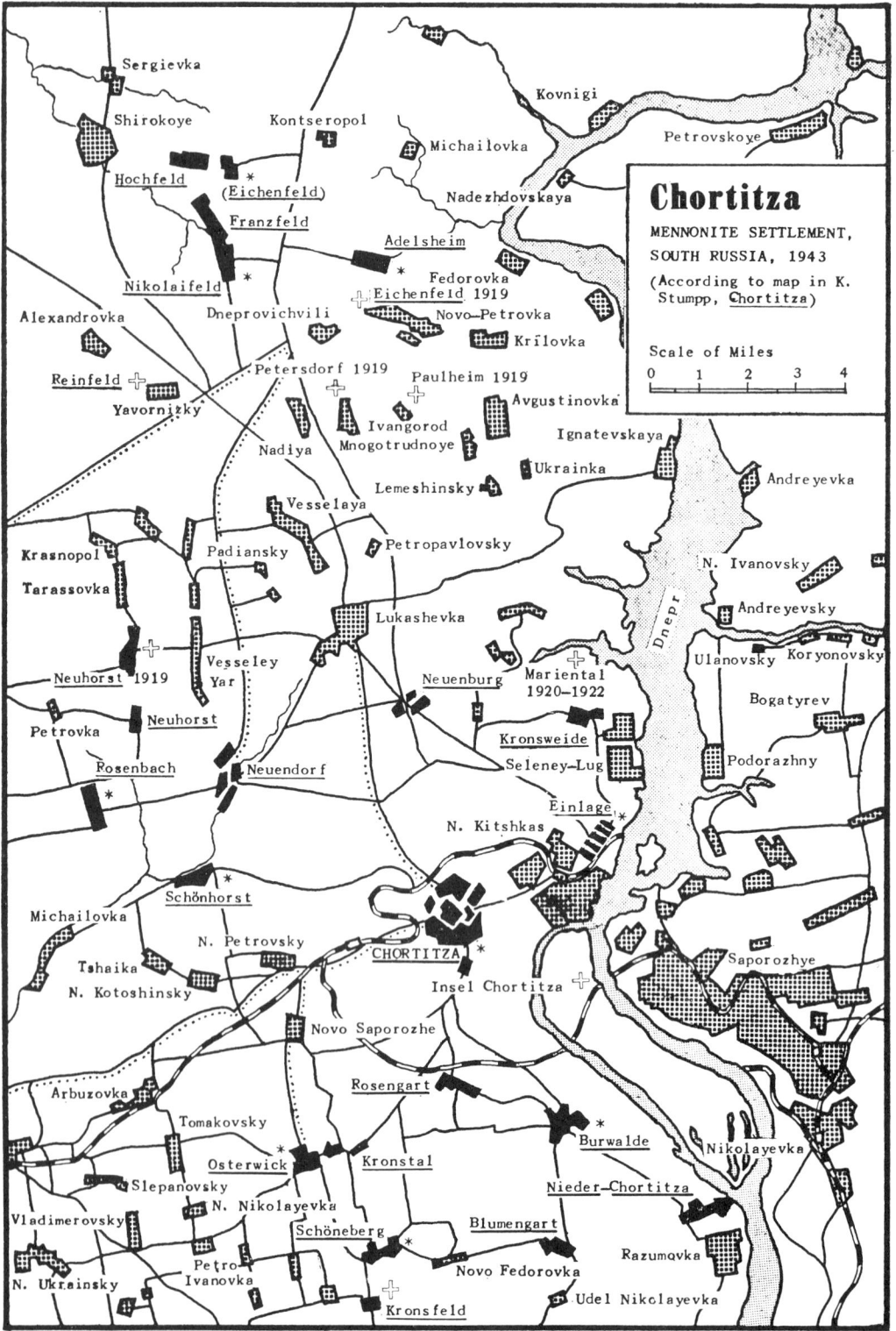

Sergievka

Shirokoye

Kontseropol

Kovnigi

Petrovskoye

Michailovka

Hochfeld

*

(Eichenfeld)

Nadezhdovskaya

Franzfeld

Adelsheim

Nikolaifeld

*

Fedorovka

Eichenfeld 1919

Novo-Petrovka

Alexandrovka

Dneprovichvili

Krïlovka

Reinfeld

Petersdorf 1919

Paulheim 1919

Yavornizky

Avgustinovka

Ivangorod

Nadiya

Mnogotrudnoye

Ignatevskaya

Andreyevka

Lemeshinsky

Ukrainka

Vesselaya

Krasnopol

Padiansky

Petropavlovsky

N. Ivanovsky

Tarassovka

Andreyevsky

Lukashevka

Dnepr

Ulanovsky

Koryonovsky

Neuhorst 1919

Vesseley
Yar

Neuenburg

Mariental
1920-1922

Bogatyrev

Neuhorst

Petrovka

Kronsweide

Podorazhny

Rosenbach

Neuendorf

Seleney-Lug

*

Einlage

N. Kitshkas

*

Michailovka

Schönhorst

*

N. Petrovsky

CHORTITZA

*

Saporozhye

Tshaika

N. Kotoshinsky

Insel Chortitza

Novo Saporozhe

Arbuzovka

Tomakovsky

Rosengart

Burwalde

*

Nikolayevka

Osterwick

Kronstal

Nieder-Chortitza

*

Slepanovsky

N. Nikolayevka

Vladimerovsky

Schöneberg

Blumengart

Razumovka

*

Petro-
Ivanovka

Novo Fedorovka

N. Ukrainsky

Kronsfeld

Udel Nikolayevka

Chortitza

MENNONITE SETTLEMENT,
SOUTH RUSSIA, 1943

(According to map in K.
Stumpp, Chortitza)

Scale of Miles

0   1   2   3   4

Mennonite
place

Mennonite
Churches

Destroyed
Mennonite place

Ukrainian
place

Road

Railroad

Telegraph

Mennonite
villages
underlined

Under Communism. With the outbreak of the Revolution in 1917 the agricultural and industrial development of the Chortitza settlement came to a standstill. From 1917 to 1922 the Chortitza settlement was the battleground of various armies, including the Reds, the Whites, and the Makhnov bands, and was plagued by starvation and epidemics. In 1919 alone, 245 persons were murdered. Through the New Economic Policy (NEP) some temporary economic improvement was brought about. The population of the Mennonite villages of the Chortitza settlement increased from 11,666 in 1918 to 13,965 in 1941.

For the first few years of this period the Mennonites were able to maintain their schools, organize their agricultural associations, and continue their religious services. With the erection of the Dneprostroy dam and the nationalization and enlargement of the Mennonite factories and milling industries, a tremendous influx of non-Mennonite population came into the Chortitza settlement. In addition to 2,178 Mennonites, the village of Chortitza had nearly 12,000 Ukrainians, Russians, and persons of other nationalities in 1941. As a result many mixed marriages took place.

Many Chortitza Mennonites, especially among the cultural leaders, left Russia in 1922-27 and went to Canada. The year 1927-28 marked the end of the NEP, the time of relative freedom, the possibility of emigrating to America; it was followed by five-year plans and speeded-up collectivization, industrialization, and the exile of ministers and kulaks to Siberia and the Far North. From 1929 to 1941 a total of 1,456 Mennonites were exiled from the Chortitza settlement (before the outbreak of the war). The size of the family decreased rapidly. The average number of children per family had originally been 6.2. When in 1929 Mennonites from all parts of Russia came to Moscow to secure passports in order to leave the country, the Chortitza Mennonites were strongly represented.

A new reduction of the population occurred after the outbreak of the war with Germany in 1941. It was the intention of the Soviet government to evacuate the total civilian population eastward, particularly the element of German background. In the settlements east of the Dnieper River they succeeded quite well. Because of the German Blitz war they were not so successful in the settlements west of the river. Yet they evacuated 831 from the Chortitza settlement. When the German army finally occupied the Ukraine, 2,287 of the 13,965 Mennonites of the Chortitza had been exiled or evacuated. Forty-three per cent of the families had been deprived of the breadwinner.

The End. During the German occupation of the Ukraine (1941-43) the Mennonite farmers gradually returned to private farming, and the educational system of former years was revived. The Chortitza Zentralschule even commemorated its centennial in 1942. However, this revival of cultural traditions was only of short duration. In the fall of 1943 Germany began to evacuate the Mennonite settlements of the Ukraine. From September 28 to October 20 the inhabitants were taken to Germany in trains consisting of some fifty freight cars, each carrying approximately 1,200 persons. Most of them reached their destination within ten days. They were to be settled in West Prussia and the Warthegau (formerly the province of Posen in western Poland).

When in January 1945 the Red army entered Germany most of the newly settled Mennonites fled westward, scattering all over the country. Not all were able to escape from the Russian zone and even those that found themselves in the Western zones were sometimes turned over to the Russian officers for repatriation. It is estimated that a total of 35,000 Mennonites from Russia had been evacuated to Germany, of whom about two thirds were forcibly repatriated by the Russians. Of those 35,000, approximately 11,678 were from the Chortitza settlement. If two thirds of them were also returned to Russia it would leave about 4,000 who have found new homes in Canada and South America. Those that were returned to Russia sent beyond the Ural Mountains. Individuals may have returned to their former homes but the Chortitza Mennonite settlement exists no more, except in the minds and hearts of those who once called it their home.　　　　　　　　　　**C.K.**

Chortitza Settlement
Mennonite Villages, Population, Exile, Evacuation: 1789-1941

Village	Year of Founding	Pop. 1914/18	Killed 1919	Exiled 1929-41	Evacuated 1941	Total Exiled and Evacuated
1. Chortitza	1789	2861	13	327	187	514
2. Adelsheim	1869	334	4	21	11	32
3. Einlage	1790	600	9	245	23	268
4. Franzfeld	1869	466	11	85	24	109
5. Hochfeld	1869	313	19	53	12	65
6. Kronsweide	1789	408	13	13	----	13
7. Nikolaifeld	1869	221	13	113	4	117
8. Neuendorf	1790	1050	13	123	39	162
9. Neuhorst	1790	315	2	3	1	4
10 Neuenburg	1789	280	7	17	11	28
11. Rosenbach	1928/29	new	..	5	3	8
12. Schönhorst	1790	689	4	51	15	66
13. Blumengart	1824	213	3	37	7	44
14. Burwalde	1803	536	7	72	8	80
15. Osterwick	1822	1550	3	81	136	217
16. Rosengart	1824	260	..	14	51	65
17. Nieder-Chortitza	1803	835	21	83	276	359
18. Schöneberg	1816	275	1	43	10	53
19. Kronstal	1809	460	1	70	13	83
Total		11666	144	1456	831	2287

(From K. Stumpp, *Bericht über das Gebiet Chortitza.*)

P. Hildebrandt, *Erste Auswanderung der Mennoniten aus dem Danziger Gebiet nach Südrussland* (Halbstadt, 1888); D. H. Epp, *Die Chortitzer Mennoniten* (Odessa, 1889); Friesen, *Brüderschaft;* A. Klaus, *Unsere Kolonien* (Odessa, 1887); C. E. Bondar, *Sekta Mennonitov v Rossii* (Petrograd, 1916); J. Quiring, *Die Mundart von Chortitza in Süd-Russland* (Munich, 1928); A. Ehrt, *Das Mennonitentum in Russland . . .* (Berlin, 1932); D. G. Rempel, "The Mennonite Colonies in New Russia . . ."

(Unpublished doctoral dissertation at Stanford University, 1933); H. Quiring, "Die Auswanderung der Mennoniten aus Preussen 1788-1870" (*Auslanddeutsche Volksforschung* II, 1, 66-71, Stuttgart, 1938); K. Stumpp, *Bericht über das Gebiet Chortitza . . .* (Berlin, 1943); Gerhard Fast, "The Mennonites under Stalin and Hitler," *Menn. Life*, April 1947, 18 ff.; W. Kuhn, "Cultural Achievements of the Chortitza Mennonites," *Menn. Life*, July 1948, 35-38; Dietrich Neufeld, *Tagebuch aus dem Reiche des Totentanzes* (Emden, 1921); *ML* I, 348-51.

Chortitza Zentralschule was the third secondary school established by the Mennonites of the Ukraine, South Russia, and the first in the Chortitza settlement. In order to enable the Mennonites to learn the Russian language the government through the *Fürsorgekomitee* (*q.v.*) encouraged the establishment of a secondary school in Chortitza, for which the *Kirchenkonvent* (*q.v.*) in co-operation with the Agricultural Association (*q.v.*) prepared a plan. It was approved by the *Fürsorgekomitee* on June 3, 1842, with the provision that six needy boys be admitted free of charge. Heinrich Heese (*q.v.*) was the first teacher, 1842-46, succeeded by Heinrich Franz (*q.v.*), 1846-58. Although both men had received a fairly good training in Germany the school remained on a rather low level during their period of administration, mostly because of opposition, misunderstanding, and disagreement among leaders and constituency. And yet it was through the devoted and untiring efforts of these pioneers that the foundation was laid for a good secondary school, which became the center of Chortitza's cultural life as envisioned by its first teachers.

Considerably more progress was made under Heinrich Epp (*q.v.*), who had received his training at Steinbach and the Chortitza Zentralschule, and had taught in a number of schools. He obtained the Russian teacher's certificate in Ekaterinoslav. The Zentralschule received an endowment of some 54,000 rubles and used during the first years only 600 rubles annually of the income from it. In 1870 a second building was erected and during the following year a teacher for Russian was engaged (Schalawski). Wilhelm Penner (see **Penner**), a graduate of the Ekaterinoslav Gymnasium, filled this position 1874-81.

Under P. M. Riediger, 1879-92, and J. A. Klassen, 1881-95, the objectives of the Zentralschule were enlarged. Formerly the Russian language had been taught as a foreign language, but now all subjects, with the exception of German and religion, were taught in the Russian language.

Under the leadership of A. A. Neufeld (*q.v.*), the first teacher with a university training (Odessa and Berlin), the school commemorated its 50th anniversary in 1892. During Neufeld's time (1890-1905) the Zentralschule was reorganized and the educational level of all elementary schools was raised. In 1890 a two-year teacher's training course and a *Musterschule* (an elementary school for practice teaching) were added to the Zentralschule which now offered a four-year course. Before World War I the two-year teacher's training course became a three-year *Lehrerseminar* (normal school). A new structure for it was erected in 1912. The plan to add a theological seminary was never realized.

The enrollment was 52 in 1872-73, 90 in 1876-77, and 183 in 1900-1. The budget in 1903-4 was 13,750 rubles. In 1914 the school had the following teachers: P. J. Penner, Dietrich H. Epp (*q.v.*), Heinrich H. Epp (*q.v.*), J. J. Klassen, H. J. Dyck, J. A. Froese, J. A. Rempel, A. A. Vogt, and A. J. Wiebe. From 1891 to 1903, 90 students obtained a teacher's certificate.

After the Revolution the Zentralschule was changed into a Seven-Class German Work School (1920-30) and the *Lehrerseminar* into an independent *Pädtechnikum*, later named *Pädshkola*. Gradually the spirit of the schools was changed. Some teachers emigrated to America; others were exiled. The growing Russian industrial population of Chortitza also had its influence on the schools. From 1938-41 the former Zentralschule became a Russian ten-class school, which was still attended by Mennonite pupils in addition to the many other nationalities. In spite of antireligious instruction and pressure there were no members of the communist youth organization among the Mennonite graduates.

During the German occupation (1941-43) the school was again converted into the Zentralschule and continued the Mennonite tradition, even commemorating its hundredth anniversary on June 28, 1942. With the evacuation of the Mennonites to Germany in 1943 came the end of the Chortitza Zentralschule. The memory of the school lives on in the minds of its many graduates now residing in Canada and South America. Teachers and graduates established the *Echo-Verlag*, a publishing enterprise, in memory of their alma mater in 1944. Numerous books pertaining to the Mennonites of Russia have already been published by this organization. How much the Chortitza Zentralschule contributed through the training of spiritual, cultural, and economic leadership during the hundred years of its existence is hard to overestimate. (For curriculum and additional information see also **Education Among the Mennonites in Russia** and **Zentralschule.**)   C.K.

A. Neufeld, *Die Chortitzer Centralschule 1842-1892* (Berdyansk, 1893); *Heinrich Epp, Kirchenältester der Mennonitengemeinde zu Chortitza* (Leipzig, 1897); Friesen, *Brüderschaft*, 612-21; D. H. Epp, *Die ehemaligen Schüler der Chortitzer Zentralschule in Kanada* (Echo-Verlag, 1944); L. Froese, "Das pädagogische Kultursystem der mennonitischen Siedlungsgruppe in Russland" (Göttingen Ph.D. dissertation, 1949, mimeographed and placed in all Mennonite higher school libraries). In connection with the hundredth anniversary of the Chortitza Zentralschule the *Bote* (Rosthern, Sask.) published numerous reminiscences by former teachers and students of the school. See *Bote* Dec. 10 and 23, 1942; and in 1943, Jan. 6, 20, and 27, Feb. 24, March 17 and 31, April 7 and 14, March 12, June 2 and 16, and July 21 and 28, Aug. 11, *et seq.*; also Nov. 7, 1951.

Chortitzaer Mennonitischer Kirchenkonvent. In the Mennonite Church in Russia, in accord with the autonomy of the individual congregation, each congregation organized its own board of directors (*Kirchenvorstand*), known as the *Konvent*. It was composed of the elder, preachers, and deacons. All of them together formed the committee known variously as the *Lehrdienst, Kirchenvorstand, Konferenz,* or *Kirchenkonvent*. The Mennonites settling in larger areas of Russia united in major church unions, which were also called *Kirchenkonferenz* or *Kirchenkonvent*. This was the origin of the *Chortitzaer Mennonitischer Kirchenkonvent*.

The 18 villages of the Chortitza formed the first Mennonite settlement in Russia. All of the elders of the church district automatically belonged to the *Chortitzaer Mennonitischer Kirchenkonvent;* probably not all the preachers were included, but at least those who were chosen by their individual congregations were members.

This *Kirchenkonvent* was not a board with executive authority. It had no power to pass regulations for the various congregations. Resolutions were of course passed at its sessions, but they were given binding force only by the congregations after they had been approved and adopted at the congregational meeting. In this way the autonomy of the individual congregation was fully preserved. A.B.

Friesen, *Brüderschaft;* A. Klaus, *Unsre Kolonien* (Odessa, 1887); P. M. Friesen, *Konfession oder Sekte* (printed as a manuscript).

Christ Seul, the organ of the Association of French-speaking Mennonite congregations of France, originated in connection with the conferences that have been held since 1901. At first a report was published after every conference beginning in 1902, to which several articles were soon added. Since 1907 the paper has appeared regularly, at first under the title, *Bulletin de la Conference des Eglises évangéliques-mennonites françaises,* and beginning in June 1907 *Christ Seul.* From August 1908 it was published in a monthly edition of 700 copies. Because of the war it ceased publication in 1914, to be resumed in October 1927. A second time because of war it discontinued in 1941, to be resumed in April 1945. From May 1943 to March 1945 a substitute *Bulletin Mennonite* was published, first in typed or mimeographed form and from January 1945 printed. The editor from the beginning to 1941 was Pierre Sommer, assisted by Pierre Kennel until 1914. Since 1945 the editor has been Pierre Widmer. The journal has carried much historical information, largely written by Pierre Sommer, including a series of historical sketches of all French Mennonite congregations in 49 installments 1930-33. P.S.

Pierre Widmer, "Les Debuts de Christ Seul," in *Almanach Mennonite du Cinquantenaire 1901-1951* (Grand Charmant, 1951); *ML* I, 351.

Christelijck Huys-boeck. This heavy quarto volume (Hoorn, Holland, 1643), written by Jan de Buyser (*q.v.*), a preacher of the Dutch-speaking Mennonite congregation of the Huiskoopers (*q.v.*) in Hamburg-Altona 1640-70, is a devotional and doctrinal reader, containing the major enunciations of the Mennonite Fathers and contemporary leaders on many topics. In this Mennonite anthology Vincent de Hondt (*q.v.*) is more frequently quoted than any other author; so it is clear that to the compiler de Hondt's authority was quite superior to that of any other Mennonite leader. The book has never been critically analyzed. It is a fact, however, that its "radicalism," which was striving toward a pure church without spot or wrinkle, had some appeal

to the stricter Mennonites of the Netherlands and North Germany. Later, when the group had completely died out, the book still continued to be cherished among the Mennonites as a devotional manual as long as the Dutch language was used in the Hamburg-Altona congregation, i.e., until about 1820. R.F.

B. K. Roosen, *Gesch. der Menn.-Gem. Hamburg-Altona* (Altona, 1886-87); A. Brons, *Ursprung . . . der Taufgesinnten* (Norden, 1884, 3rd ed., 1914).

Christelijke Gezangen. This is a general title of a number of Dutch Mennonite hymnbooks: (1) *Christelyke Gezangen ten gebruike der Doopsgez. Gemeente, vergaderende bij 't Lam en den Toren* (1791); this is known as the *Kleine Bundel* (*q.v.*); (2) *Christelijke Gezangen voor de openbaare godsdienstoefeningen* (1796), known as the *Groote Bundel* (*q.v.*); (3) *Christelijke Gezangen en Liederen ten dienste der Ver. Doopsgez. Gemeente Haarlem* (1804), known as the *Haarlemsche Gezangen;* (4) *Christelijke Gezangen* (Amsterdam, 1848, two volumes), known as *Oude Amsterdamsche Bundels;* (5) *Christelijke Kerkgezangen, Haarlem* (Amsterdam, 1851), known as the *Nieuwe Haarlemsche Bundel;* (6) *Christelijke Liederen* (two volumes, Amsterdam, 1870, known as the *Nieuwe Amsterdamsche Bundels;* (7) *119 Christelijke Kerkgezangen* (Groningen, 1893), see **Kerkgezangen;** (8) *Christelijke Liederen* (Amsterdam, 1916); a small volume, that was used in the Amsterdam congregation until 1945, in addition to the two hymnbooks of 1870 (no. VI). Concerning these hymnbooks see *DB* 1900, 102-24; *Catalogus Amst.,* 278, 329-30. vDZ.

Christen, Christen (van Braght, *Mart. Mir.,* calls him Christen Christiaens), who according to van Braght was imprisoned in 1659 at Bern, Switzerland, with six of his fellow preachers and deacons. They had to choose between joining the Reformed Church, expulsion, or death. An official report of Jan. 20, 1660, states that there were not six men, but eleven, and that Christen was a native of Langnau. A song found in the *Geistliches Liederbüchlein* of 1696 gives the information that in January 1659 a meeting of the Swiss Brethren at Dürsrütti near Langnau in the *Emmental* was surprised and a number of men were arrested at Trachselwald, then taken to Bern. Van Braght says nothing is known concerning their choice or their fate, but Müller, *Berner Täufer,* gives the information that after repeated attempts to convert them to the state church they were taken by boat to Holland on Sept. 10, 1660. Christen and at least one brother, Benedicht Baumgartner, succeeded in returning to Switzerland. Nothing further is known about these two men. The arrest and mistreatment of the eleven brethren in the Bernese prison was reported to Hans Vlamingh (*q.v.*) in Amsterdam, and led to the intercession of the Dutch government with the Bernese magistrates (1660) and to measures taken by the Dutch Mennonites in behalf of their Swiss brethren. vDZ.

Mart. Mir. D 826, E 124; Müller, *Berner Täufer,* 1895, 123 ff., 173 f., 179 f., 191.

Christenpflicht (*Mennonitisches Hilfswerk Christenpflicht,* tr., "The Christian's Duty"), a South German Mennonite relief organization, founded in 1920, incorporated. The great war which for 51 months shook the world to its foundations demanded a frightful toll of lives. In addition the Central Powers suffered from the blockade, and the disturbed economic and monetary systems threw a large part of the population into indescribable misery. The refugees from territories ceded to other powers burdened the economic system still further.

In this time of need all Germans, especially those with religious motivation, including the Mennonites, came to the aid of the most destitute. Lene Bühler (1858-1936) of Harlanden near Ingolstadt, who had lived for some time in America, now received from her friends in America gifts of money to be used for the needy. She set up a soup kitchen in Ingolstadt, using also food donated by the Mennonites of the vicinity. In the inflation of German currency the purchasing power of the dollar became so great that she could no longer manage the project alone.

Then the American Mennonites asked Michael Horsch, the elder of the Ingolstadt congregation, to form an organization for the relief of the most urgent distress in the neediest districts. Thus Christenpflicht was organized by the Mennonites of Bavaria. Generous gifts of money given by American Mennonites were cabled to a bank in Ingolstadt to be distributed by Christenpflicht. In cooperation with the local authorities, who carried out the distribution free of charge, under the direction of committees manned as much as possible by Mennonites, the apparatus functioned almost entirely without overhead expense; in 1921, for instance, the cost of distribution was only 1.3 per cent of the turnover. In addition to Ingolstadt relief was given to the needy of all creeds in Munich, Augsburg, Würzburg, and the Erzgebirge in Saxony. The supervisor of Christenpflicht in the Erzgebirge was Pastor Richter of Scheibenberg.

Twice a week food certificates were handed out which were exchanged for food in the local stores and which Christenpflicht then redeemed. The food contributed directly by the German Mennonites was handed out in special stations. During the inflation of 1920-23 an average of 12,000 persons were provided twice a week with essential food. The head of Christenpflicht, Michael Horsch (*q.v.*), of Hellmannsberg, reported at the Mennonite World Relief Conference at Danzig in 1930 that in this period the organization disposed of 259,600 marks, which had a purchasing power of 2,500,000 marks. During this time several transports of undernourished children of the Erzgebirge, selected by a Mennonite physician, Dr. Hermann Neff, were sent to Mennonite farms. The Mennonites themselves, being on the whole successful farmers, needed little aid.

Soon there was opportunity to aid the Mennonites emigrating from Russia. In 1924-25, 15,000 entered Canada alone, nearly all of whom had been in Germany before being admitted to America. Many of them had to stay in Germany for years because of their health and other reasons. For them Christenpflicht and *Deutsche Mennoniten-Hilfe* (*q.v.*) used the army grounds of Lechfeld (*q.v.*) as a camp until they were admitted to Canada.

In 1930 Christenpflicht received from Babette Ringenberg a former Hochstettler estate in Burgweinting near Regensburg with the stipulation that it be made a Mennonite deaconess home. Christenpflicht in a meeting in this house on Dec. 15, 1931, agreed that since the original purpose of its organization had been fulfilled, it would turn its attention to deaconess work. But because of a lack of volunteers among Mennonite girls this work never developed. In 1929 the house was in charge of sisters from the mother-house of Hensoltshöhe (Middle Franconia) under the direction of Elise Hochstettler, a Mennonite deaconess.

In 1929, in connection with the policy of agrarian collectivization in Russia a new wave of immigrants set in, who were also offered asylum in Germany. Again there were numerous Mennonites among them. Christenpflicht admitted a number of aged women, for whom camp life was too difficult, into its deaconess home in Burgweinting. Since their departure the home has been used chiefly as a home for the aged.

A new task for Christenpflicht arose in connection with the suffering occasioned by World War II, both in the relief of destitute war sufferers in their home regions, and in the aid to refugees from former German settlements in the East and Mennonite refugees from Russia and the Danzig area. This new work, which included also a spiritual ministry to scattered Mennonite refugees, began in early 1946. Food and funds were contributed by South German Mennonites, especially the farmers, but the major source of supply, both food and clothing, was the Mennonite Central Committee. Since the MCC was never granted permission to operate direct relief in the American zone, it was compelled to send its food and clothing to other agencies for distribution, chiefly the *Evangelisches Hilfswerk,* which was the relief agency of the Lutheran state church. As soon as Christenpflicht was licensed by the American military government to serve as a distribution agency (1947), it was given generous stocks of MCC food and clothing, although it also received some supplies through *Evangelisches Hilfswerk* in 1946. Under MCC general direction it set up distributions in the severely damaged cities of Heilbronn, Pforzheim, Munich, Regensburg, and Nürnberg. It also operated an extensive package distribution program in other needy areas in South and Middle Germany, and the Russian zone, particularly for Mennonite refugees. The package service to the Russian zone continued as late as 1952.

Organizationally Christenpflicht was composed of a group of ten representatives of the Mennonite congregations of Bavaria, a self-perpetuating body which was incorporated Jan. 29, 1922, at Ingolstadt, Bavaria, as an *Eingetragener Verein.* Its headquarters were always at the home of Michael Horsch at his farm at Hellmannsberg, near Ingolstadt until his death Oct. 1, 1949, when they were transferred to Ingolstadt. The warehouse was always in Ingolstadt. Michael Horsch, who was the elder of the Ingolstadt Mennonite congregation, was its chairman and executive officer from the beginning until his death. Since then Albert Schantz, a Mennonite layman of Wolfersdorf, Bavaria, who was the long-time treasurer, has served as chairman. Christenpflicht, though conceived and carried through as a work of the South German (*Verband*) Mennonite churches, was in a real sense the lengthened "shadow of one man, Michael Horsch, whose vision, devotion and personal labors made Christenpflicht what it was and continues to be, a uniquely effective Christian relief work, to serve 'the poorest of the poor' in the name of Christ." A.S.

Mennonitische Welt - Hilfskonferenz Danzig 1930 (Weierhof, 1930) 71-73 and 104-9; Albert Schantz, "Das Mennonitische Hilfswerk 'Christenpflicht,'" *Gbl.*, 1949 (Karlsruhe, Baden); *ML* III, 110.

Christiaen, the son of Jan de Swarte (*q.v.*), an Anabaptist martyr, born at Nijpkerke (Nieppe), Belgium, was burned at the stake at Rijssel (Lille) in France on March 27, 1563, together with his mother and his two brothers Hans and Mahieu. (*Mart. Mir.* D 299, E 664.) vDZ.

Christia(e)n, an Anabaptist martyr of Bavaria, beheaded in Wermes (Worms?) in 1555; though he had been a member of the brotherhood only a short time, he remained steadfast and died for openly confessing his faith. (*Mart. Mir.* D 162, E 550; *ML* I, 351.) vDZ.

Christiaen Arents (or Adriaensz) was present at the disputation with the Reformed, held in Emden, Feb. 27—May 17, 1578. He was an elder or minister of the Mennonite congregation at Delft. (K. Vos, *Menno Simons,* Leiden, 1914, 307.) vDZ.

Christiaen Janssens (called Langedul), an Anabaptist martyr, was seized on Aug. 10, 1567, on his way to a village where he was to settle a dispute, and on Sept. 13, 1567, he was put to death with three brethren at Antwerp, Belgium. Van Braght (*Mart. Mir.*) prints four letters written by him; three to his wife Maeyken Raeds, and one to his brother and sister. They are eloquent testimonies to his firm faith, which he confessed with joy, to his warm love for wife and family, of whom he thinks with anxiety, and of his patient endurance, which he describes without rancor. He comforts and strengthens them and wishes for them true faith "as I have often done; we must give such to the Lord, but one must also ask Him for it and desire it sincerely. Oh, if I could die for my friends, that they might acquire salvation. How gladly would I do it!" (*Mart. Mir.* D 345, E 704; *Antw. Arch.-Bl.* IX, 460, 461; X, 65; XIV, 46 f., No. 522; *ML* II, 617.) NEFF, vDZ.

Christiaen Kemels, a Dutch Mennonite who fled from the Netherlands to England and was arrested in London in 1575 and put in prison with Hendrik Terwoort, Jan Pietersz, Gerrit van Byler, and others. The petition to Queen Elizabeth, the Confession of Faith, and a letter to John Fox, all found in the *Martyrs' Mirror* (D 710-12, E 1009, 1022-24), were signed by Christiaen Kemels. Whereas Hendrik

Terwoort and Jan Pietersz were executed and Gerrit van Byler and others set free, Christiaen died in the Newgate prison before the sentence was passed. This is related in a song, *Een nieu Liedeken,* . . . found in the 1579 edition of a very rare booklet (in the Amsterdam Mennonite Library): *Confession of Thomas van Imbroeck* (*Catalogus Amst.,* 59).
vDZ.

Christiaen de Rijcke (or Christiaen Rijken, or Rijcen), an Anabaptist martyr, executed at Hondschoote, Flanders, Belgium, on April 7, 1588. He was likely a relative of the martyr Willem de Rijke (*q.v.*). He was taken prisoner in December 1587, remained steadfast through severe and cruel tortures, and was burned at the stake.

Soon after his death a book appeared, *'T getuygenisse ende naeghelaten schriften van Christiaen Rijcen en Adriaen Jansz* (Haarlem, 1588). This rare volume, a copy of which is found in the Amsterdam Mennonite Library, contains besides the letters of Adriaen Jansz sixteen letters by Christiaen Rijcen and seven songs. At the end of the book there is a song by K.V.M. (Carel van Mander, *q.v.*) celebrating the suffering and death of Christiaen; this song, beginning "Eylaes hoe mach gheschieden, dat eenen Christen goed," is also inserted in *De gulden Harpe,* a hymnbook by van Mander (Haarlem, 1627). From *'T getuygenisse* eight letters by Christiaen were copied by van Braght in the *Martyrs' Mirror* (Nos. 1, 3, 8, 9, 11, 14-16). They are an account of his trial, which he wrote to his wife, Jan. 2, 1588, a letter to a brother, of Jan. 17, 1588, and five other letters to his wife (dated Feb. 27, March 12, March 19, March 27, and a note shortly before his sentence, undated). These letters show clearly how the Roman Catholic priest tried to make him recant, but also how he believed loyally in his Saviour. Hans Alenson (*q.v.*) tells in his *Tegenbericht* (*BRN* VII, 249) that he often spoke with Christiaen de Rijcke while he (Christiaen) lived at Leiden where he was a preacher. Alenson visited the place where his friend had been executed two years after his death. He states that Christiaen did not agree with the practice of shunning and avoiding held by some Mennonite leaders, and mentions that Christiaen was suspended from his ministry (he must therefore have been a preacher) because of his mildness in the matter of discipline. vDZ.

Mart. Mir. D 757-63, E 1063-69; *Bibliographie* I, 319-31, 668; II, List of Martyrs, No. 661; *Catalogus Amst.,* 101.

Christiaen van Wettere(n), born at Gent, Belgium, an Anabaptist martyr, by trade a *dobbelweerckere,* was burned at the stake on the Vrijdagsmarkt at Gent, on Nov. 9, 1563, together with Antheunis Behaghe (*q.v.*). His name is listed as No. 12 in the song, "Liedeken van 41 Vrienden," in the *Liedtboecxken vanden Offer des Heeren.* (*Offer,* 651; *Mart. Mir.* D 300, E 666; Verheyden, *Gent,* 30, No. 96; *ML* I, 351.) vDZ.

Christian (called Christiaen uyt den Eukeraet in *Mart. Mir.*), an Anabaptist martyr, beheaded with three fellow believers at Blankenburg, Holland(?), in 1552. (*Mart. Mir.* D 132, E 526.) vDZ.

Christian, an extinct village of a Mennonite settlement located in Garden and Alta Twps., Harvey Co., extending into Mound and Turkey Creek Twps., McPherson Co., Kan. Christian and Daniel Krehbiel, Christian Hirschler, and Christian Voran purchased land, the corners of which joined one mile south of the present town of Moundridge. They jointly laid out a town site in 1874 and named it Christian, the name of three of the landowners.

Soon Daniel Krehbiel built a store on his land as the first business place of the town. Christian Ellenberger built a blacksmith shop near by. A church building dedicated March 4, 1877, was constructed across the corner on Christian Krehbiel's land. About 1884 or 1885 William Galle and Peter J. Galle established a store near the church.

The first post office of the town was located in the home of Christian Hirschler, who was appointed postmaster July 13, 1876. On April 3, 1877, Daniel Krehbiel was appointed postmaster and the post office was moved into his store. Upon the appointment of William Galle as postmaster Feb. 10, 1886, the post office was moved into the Galle store.

In 1886 the El Dorado-McPherson branch of the Missouri Pacific established a station just one mile north of Christian and named it Moundridge. Christian was then dissolved, and all the business buildings were moved to Moundridge. Christian had only five homes, and the five families living in them comprised the whole population. The First Mennonite Church of Christian (*q.v.*) in Moundridge has its name from this town. When the church building dedicated in 1877 became too small a larger building was constructed at Christian and dedicated Feb. 10, 1884. The original building was moved to Moundridge in 1888 to house the West Zion Mennonite Church (*q.v.*), and the building erected in 1884 was also moved to Moundridge in 1908 and continued in use of the First Mennonite Church of Christian until 1950. On Nov. 5, 1950, this congregation dedicated a new building erected on the same grounds.   P.P.W.

Christian Education. Christian education as used here includes all the methods Mennonites have used to impart Biblical knowledge and faith to their children with special reference to the noninstitutional means. These methods include home instruction, catechetical instruction, Sunday schools, young people's work, daily vacation Bible schools, weekday church schools, Bible conferences, winter Bible schools, and study classes. As some of these methods will be treated in detail elsewhere in these volumes, the purpose here is to show the historical sequence and something of their interrelation.

Home Instruction. The Anabaptist movement, though inaugurated partly by theologically trained men, was primarily a movement of the common people. Especially was this so as persecution removed the trained leaders and forced the movement underground. Education in its secular aspect as well as theological education held no appeal for them, for it was precisely with the educated men that they disagreed. Yet the Anabaptists and early

Mennonites were forced to a Christian education of their own type for two very cogent reasons. First, their reliance on the Scriptures as the final authority demanded that every man be able to read and interpret them for himself. Secondly, the responsibility for bringing up children so that they would voluntarily choose the right enforced a kind of child training that was real Christian education. Menno himself wrote specifically on the education of children, pointing out the special responsibility which Christian parents have for their own children. "For why," he asks, "teach those not of our own household when we take no pains to preserve our own families in the love and fear of God?" As to content, Menno emphasized first the need of moral instruction—that children fear and love God, walk in modesty, honor and obey parents, use good language and be truthful, not stubborn and self-willed nor seeking worldly honor, fame, or wealth. He urged also that children be instructed in reading and writing and further that they be taught habits of industry and be given an opportunity to learn a trade. As to method it is primarily home training that he relied upon. Parents are first to show themselves as patterns and examples; they are to start early and train children from youth up, teaching them in proportion to their degree of understanding; they are to admonish children with strictness, yet without bitterness or anger. It was this type of parental training that was the basis of early Mennonite Christian education. In fact some such type of home training has been recognized as desirable by Mennonites through the centuries.

Among the Hutterian Brethren with their communal type of living child training early developed into schools of the more formal pattern which were operated by the Bruderhof. They were apparently limited to primary schools with women as teachers for the kindergarten and men for the older children. Both Peter Riedemann's *Rechenschaft* (*q.v.*), written in 1545, and a Hutterite *Schulordnung* of 1578 reveal a deep sense of responsibility for child training and outline relatively advanced methods whereby children were trained according to their abilities with kindness though also with strictness. Beginning with Scripture and prayer, which children early learned to repeat, they were taught about God and His purposes, then obedience to parents and from that obedience to God. The last stage of education was the teaching of some kind of work or trade to which their talents were bent. Thus equipped young people were expected to "seek eternal things" and were ready for baptism on confession of faith and to take their place in the Christian community.

Catechetical Instruction (*q.v.*). With the emphasis on Christian training in the home, catechisms came into common use. Originally written as statements or explanations of faith, they came to be enlarged into home devotional booklets. Friedmann, in his *Mennonite Piety Through the Centuries,* discusses in detail the composition and purpose of some of these which became popular. The earliest were published by Dutch authors: P. J.

Twisck (*q.v.*) in 1633, Reynier Wijbrants (*q.v.*) in 1640, and T. J. van Braght (*q.v.*), the author of the *Martyrs' Mirror*, in 1657. Very popular among the North-German Mennonites were van Sittert's *Christliches Glaubensbekentnus* of 1664, published in Amsterdam, and the anonymous Prussian *Confession oder kurzes und einfältiges Glaubensbekenntnis* of 1660. They were originally similar in content and purpose and became more so in later editions through borrowing. Both were prepared as guides for devotional practice or private worship and as such became popular in family worship and home training of children in religion and morals. The family use of the latter book is indicated by the fact that it was printed in the German language one hundred years before Prussian Mennonites permitted the change from Dutch to German in the pulpit. The host of successive editions of these books indicates their popularity and wide circulation among Mennonites in Germany, Russia, and America. A third booklet equally popular but more specifically a prayer book was the *Ernsthafte Christenpflicht* of 1739, which drew from Swiss sources. Through these books and many others less popular but of the same type, children and youth were taught the essentials of Christian truth. The Russian manual particularly was apparently designed for the examination of young candidates. American adaptations of these materials and English translations, along with the Bible, have until recent years been the instructional materials in catechism classes in America. Such classes, usually taught by the pastor and supplemented by home teaching, have been characteristic of most Mennonite branches in America as the preparation for church membership.

Sunday schools (*q.v.*). As the catechism method became more formalized, efforts were made to adapt it to new conditions. This was particularly true in America as the Great Awakening of the early 19th century revitalized spiritual life and fostered new organizations. The Sunday school was one of these new developments, coming into American life after 1810. Being originally an institution of the English language churches, it was slow in making itself acceptable to the German-speaking Mennonites, coming in largely after 1860. Some preparation was found in adaptations of the catechism method, such as the *Kinderlehre* of J. H. Oberholtzer, as early as 1847. Here the children were gathered together on Sundays to practice singing and memorize Scripture and catechism. The pastor was prominent in the work but others assisted. Though strictly speaking not a Sunday school, this method had some of the features of the Sunday school and was one of the earliest attempts in that direction. A few Sunday schools are known to have had brief existence in connection with Mennonite churches about this time but real Sunday schools on a permanent basis were not organized for at least another ten years. By the 70's there were a considerable number and the first Sunday-school convention among Mennonite churches (GCM) was held in Philadelphia in 1876. In the 90's such conventions became popular gatherings in most conferences, and Sunday schools were current in all congregations except those few more conservative branches which have resisted in principle all innovations. For many it was regarded as the main agency for religious instruction of the young and was attended by all children. The International Uniform Lessons have been mainly used but graded lessons are provided in many churches, and publishing houses of the different branches provide a variety of helps both for the International Uniform and for the graded lessons.

In the Netherlands Sunday schools, now found in nearly all congregations for children from about 6 to 12 years, started shortly after 1900. In Germany, Switzerland, and France it started much later, largely after World War II. Educational materials for Sunday schools and summer Bible schools in these latter countries are being published under the sponsorship of a joint committee representing the Mennonite Publishing House of Scottdale, Pa., and the interested groups in the European countries.

In Holland most Mennonite churches now have Sunday schools (for children only). The West Hill type for children and adolescent youth was largely introduced only since 1920. Sunday schools are just now being introduced into the Mennonite churches of Switzerland, Alsace, and South Germany.

Young People's Work. Another form of activity closely related to Christian education is the work of young people's societies. The experience in expression and administration and self-directed study and service has made the various forms of young people's work recognized as efficient aids in the training of young people for the church. In as far as such work was introduced as an innovation it, like Sunday schools, was accepted only slowly. Especially was this true where interdenominational contacts were involved. There is record of a young people's society organized in the Halstead, Kan., church (GCM) as early as 1885 and one in the Hereford (GCM) church in Pennsylvania in 1886. The latter was associated with the Christian Endeavor movement. Before 1900 there were young people's conventions in some areas and in general young people's meetings were sanctioned. One of the most profitable developments of young people's work has been the retreats which have become common in the last twenty-five years. Here a strong evangelistic emphasis has been combined with serious study of Mennonite heritage and a voluntary service program. (See **Christian Endeavor.**)

Among the Mennonites (MC), young people's activities have appeared in the form of young people's Bible meetings (*q.v.*) with active Sunday evening services. As early as 1877 the Ontario Mennonite Conference (MC) had taken official action to approve youth gatherings. The young people's Bible meeting, however, very likely developed out of the earlier children's meetings. The Prairie Street Church, of Elkhart, Ind., in 1887 changed its children's meetings into a young people's meeting. A serious and systematic Bible study has been developed in these meetings based on a conference publication called *The Program Builder* and edited for this purpose.

In Holland youth activities started about 1920 (see **Doopsgezinde** *Jeugdraad*, **Doopsgezinde** *Jongeren Bond;* **Friese** *Doopsgezinde Jongeren Bond*). Much the same time young people's work was started in South Germany (see **Jugendkommission**), and somewhat later in Switzerland. In France it began only recently, largely since World War II; whereas in Holland youth activities consisted largely of what the young people did for themselves, in the other countries they consisted largely of what the conferences and congregations did for their youth.

Summer Bible Schools (q.v.). The Daily Vacation Bible School movement found a response among Mennonite churches in the 20's of this century but it was only within the last twenty years that serious attention has been paid to this form of Christian education. In 1948 the Mennonite Publishing House of Scottdale, Pa., issued the Herald Press Summer Bible School Series designed to provide pupils' material in workbook form and a teacher's guide for thirteen age levels from nursery to the second year of high school. This was the culmination of several years of activity and growth in summer Bible schools in which the demand was realized for material which should be consistent with the basic Anabaptist-Mennonite philosophy that "faith and doctrine are to be expressed in dynamic Christian living." The course proved very popular and the first printing, expected to last for several years, was sold out the first summer. The Mennonite Church (MC), which sponsored the printing of the series reported 609 summer Bible schools with a total enrollment of 64,307 pupils for the year 1951. The General Conference Mennonite Church, next largest in membership, has adopted the same series with modifications to suit and reported 127 Bible schools with 5,845 pupils enrolled for 1950. The series is used widely by Protestant groups other than Mennonite as well as by various Mennonite branches.

Weekday Bible Schools (q.v.). Mennonites have also participated in weekday church schools in which public-school pupils are gathered for religious instruction. In some cases such classes have met in the school building and were taught by a minister or a church worker at designated periods; in other cases they have met in the church with the children released from school for the period. Afternoon or evening classes held outside of school time and meeting at the church are modifications of the same plan but not on released time.

Although it is not the purpose of this article to go into the part played by educational institutions in Christian education, yet it must be pointed out that such institutions have been an essential part of the whole program. Before the middle of the 19th century there was among the Mennonites no conception of education apart from Christian education. Such secular education as there was, was given in parochial schools or private schools. The former invariably regarded moral and spiritual training as its basic responsibility. Parochial schools

only gradually blended into the American public school system and in some communities still persist. In others again attempts have been made in recent years to revive this type of school. Church-sponsored Bible schools (*q.v.*) and high schools have grown out of the parochial school while colleges and seminaries have also found their primary purpose in relating modern education to Christian faith and living as taught by the church.

Winter Bible Schools (q.v.). In the Mennonite Church (MC), short term Bible schools for older young people, held for two to six weeks during the winter, came into being about 1900 starting at Goshen College. The movement has spread, until at the present time some twenty such schools serve over a thousand students in an effective adult education program.

Bible Conferences (q.v.), popular chiefly in North America but also in Europe to a lesser degree (South Germany, Switzerland, France, and Russia) since about 1900 have also served well in adult education.

Study Classes. Many congregations in North America, particularly among the Mennonites (MC), have used weekday evening study classes in Bible study, missions, doctrine, teacher training, etc., as an effective adult education method. In the Mennonite Church (MC) a systematic and comprehensive program of promotion of these study classes has been developed.

Co-ordination of the Program of Christian Education. In the highly organized North American churches, centralized direction, or at least promotion, co-ordination, and assistance of the church-wide program of Christian education has developed, particularly in the Mennonite Church (MC). In this group the Commission for Christian Education (*q.v.*) since 1937 and its predecessor, the General Sunday School Committee founded in 1913, have served this function.

Europe. In Europe outside of Russia the program of Christian education has been far less comprehensive than in America and largely limited to catechetical instruction, except for the Bible schools and Bible conferences. In Russia, however, the Mennonite school program, with its village schools and higher schools, incorporated regular religious instruction and was the chief agency for the Christian education of children and youth.   S.F.P.

Menno Simons, *Complete Works* (Elkhart, 1871) I, 273-76; John Horsch, *The Hutterian Brethren, 1528-1931* . . . (Goshen, 1931) 33-36; Hasenberg, trans., *Account of our Religion, Doctrine, and Faith given by Peter Rideman* (1950) 130-31; R. Friedmann, *Mennonite Piety Through the Centuries* (Goshen, 1949) 117-30; J. E. Hartzler, *Education Among the Mennonites of America* (Danvers, Ill., 1925); H. S. Bender, *Mennonite Sunday School Centennial* (Scottdale, 1940); J. H. Lohrentz, *The Mennonite Brethren Church* (Hillsboro, Kan., 1950); P. Lederach, "The History of the Young People's Bible Meetings," *MQR* XXVI (1952) 216-31; also yearbooks, conference reports, and church periodicals; C. Fretz, "History of Winter Bible Schools in the Mennonite Church," *MQR* XVI (1942) 178-95; Q. Leatherman, "Christopher Dock, Mennonite Schoolmaster," *MQR* XVI (1942) 32-44; P. R. Shelly, *Religious Education and Mennonite Piety Among the Mennonites of Southeastern Pennsylvania: 1870-1943* (Newton, Kan., 1950); J. F. Moyer, *Religious Education in the Mennonite*

Churches Comprising the Middle District Conference (Pandora, Ohio, 1920); M. S. Harder, "The Origin, Philosophy, and Development of Education Among the Mennonites" (U. of So. Cal., Los Angeles, Ph.D. Thesis, 1949, unpublished); P. Lederach, "History of Religious Education in the Mennonite Church" (Southwestern Baptist Theol. Seminary, Ft. Worth, Tex., Th.D. Thesis, 1949, unpublished)

Christian Endeavor. The first young people's society in General Conference Mennonite churches was organized in 1886 in the First Mennonite Church, Philadelphia, Pa., aiming to give more opportunity and better training for more effective service in Christ's kingdom. The young people's movement in the General Conference was stimulated by the Young People's Society of Christian Endeavor, founded as an interdenominational organization in 1881, and took over the name Christian Endeavor Society from it. Later the general organization took the name Young People's Union, although local congregational meetings are still called "Christian Endeavor." By 1898 there were at least 26 such organizations in the General Conference Church, by 1923 some 100, and at present it is taken for granted that every conference congregation has a young people's society. As early as 1898 many societies, besides their regular weekly or semimonthly meeting of a devotional nature, took an interest in missions and made contributions of clothing, Bibles, or money to that cause.

As the number of societies increased, young people's conventions were organized. Since 1917 the young people have had one evening for their program during the regular triennial sessions of the conference. Since 1926, the young people have had their own executive committee and in 1938 at the Saskatoon Conference, the Young People's Union (*q.v.*) was organized to stimulate and integrate various activities. Each district conference is represented on the executive committee which operates under the Board of Education and Publication of the conference. This committee, with its own editor, has a section in the weekly issue of the *Mennonite*, which is devoted to their interests. Since 1926 annual young people's retreats have been held. More recently, retreat grounds have been acquired and developed in various districts. Besides raising many thousands of dollars each year for missions, education, relief, etc., the Young People's Union has promoted voluntary service for a summer or a year at home or abroad in recent years and increasing numbers of young people are participating. All work is done under and in cooperation with the General Conference.

The first Christian Endeavor Society of the Central Conference Mennonite Church, now a district conference of the General Conference Mennonite Church, the only other Mennonite conference to use this name for its young people's societies, was organized in the North Danvers, Ill., congregation in 1892. The 1911 conference appointed a field committee to visit all of the societies in the conference. This visit to nine societies led to the appointment of a field secretary, who was instrumental in organizing the first Christian Endeavor Rally to be held in the conference, in 1913. In the 1914 conference a Christian Endeavor Union was formed.

Beginning in 1917 the union has used the topics of the United Society of Christian Endeavor but has adapted the materials for its own purposes. Since the merging of the above two conferences, their young people's work is under the Young People's Union.   E.G.K.

Ed. G. Kaufman, *Our Mission as a Church of Christ, Mennonites and Their Heritage*, No. IV; *Official Minutes and Reports of the General Conference of the Mennonite Church of North America, 1860-1947*; W. B. Weaver, *History of the Central Conference Mennonite Church* (Danvers, 1926).

Christian Evangel, the official monthly organ of the Central Conference of Mennonites, appeared in July 1910. Its initiation marked the culmination of a growing conviction on the part of a number of conference leaders regarding the need of such organ. During most of this period it has been a 24-page monthly. Cost of publication is now underwritten by the conference and the *Evangel* is sent without charge to all members of Central Conference churches, such cost being allocated to the churches on a per capita basis. Roster of editors is: A. B. Rutt, 1910-13; Lee Lantz, 1913-16; Ben Esch, 1916-19; A. S. Bechtel, 1919-20; L. B. Haigh, 1920-23; W. B. Weaver, 1923-25; H. E. Nunemaker, 1925-26; W. B. Weaver, 1926-38; and R. L. Hartzler, 1938-   .   R.L.H.

Christian Exponent, a 16-page biweekly Mennonite journal published Jan. 4, 1924, to Sept. 25, 1928, the organ of a movement in the Mennonite Church (MC) which attempted to establish a counterweight against the more conservative main body of the church which had caused the temporary closing of Goshen College 1923-24. It was promoted largely by sympathizers with the "old" Goshen, and though conducted on a high level, ultimately the group behind it disintegrated, some joining the General Conference Mennonite Church, the others adapting themselves to the new regime at Goshen and to the general constructive conservative trend in the old church. Editors were Vernon Smucker, 1924-26, and Lester Hostetler, 1927-28. In its fourth and last year the journal became openly "all-Mennonite," when it became clear that its cause in the old church was lost.   H.S.B.

Christian Fellowship is a Mennonite Brethren organization of and for the young people of the denomination. The organization is local but also denominational in scope. It is under the supervision and guidance of district conference youth committees and they in turn work in co-operation with the General Conference Christian Fellowship Committee. The organization was initiated in 1940 for the purpose of providing a time and place for separate Bible instruction and church and conference training for young people. Its objectives are fourfold and each local organization is divided into four study and service departments, viz., the missionary, the educational, the recreational or Christian service, and the devotional departments. Each department is headed by a chairman and assistants. The department then provides study material for their programs and seeks work projects for the entire group. The whole organization is headed by an executive committee with a president at the head. Services are held Sunday evenings before the evening service. Some churches also include children's fellowship in separate meetings. In most of the conference districts the Christian Fellowship also sponsors a summer youth camp under the supervision of the district youth committee.

J.W.V.

Christian Fellowship Chapel (EMB), Winnipeg, Man., was informally organized on Sept. 1, 1944, and formally organized in 1947 with Arno Wiebe as its first pastor. It was formally recognized as an EMB church at the annual EMB conference in Dallas, Ore., in 1950. The church consists of 36 members (1950). It has a board of five trustees and a secretary-treasurer. The church has an active Sunday school, young people's group, midweek prayer group and sponsors a mission program.

W.R.G.

Christian (Kan.) **First** Mennonite Church (GCM) of Christian derived its name from the country village and post office called Christian (*q.v.*), near which its church was built, one mile south of what is now Moundridge, Kan. It was organized on March 26, 1878, before the advent of the railroad and the founding of Moundridge.

The first church was dedicated on March 4, 1877. Though enlarged in 1880, it was replaced by a new church, which was dedicated on Feb. 10, 1884. In 1908 it was moved a half-mile north into the city limits of Moundridge. A new building of brick was constructed in 1948. The congregation has a membership of over 280.

The original settlers were of South German stock who came to this country in 1852 to 1855 and settled in Lee Co., Iowa, and at Summerfield, Ill. In 1874 and the following years many of them moved to Harvey and McPherson counties, Kan. Later many families of the Swiss Mennonite group that immigrated into Kansas from the province of Volhynia, Polish Russia, in 1874 united with this church.

Valentine Krehbiel served as elder from 1878 to 1901. From 1902 to 1908 John C. Goering served as minister and from 1908 to 1917 as elder. P. P. Wedel served the Christian Church from 1917 to 1951. He was elder for over 33 years. After his resignation, Edmond J. Miller accepted the call in 1951. In 1950 the congregation dedicated a new church, the sanctuary 37 x 94 ft. and educational wing 30 x 36 ft. In 1953 the congregation had a membership of 275.

P.P.W.

Christian Leader, the official youth paper of the Mennonite Brethren Conference of North America, was begun March 1, 1937, as a monthly 32-page paper, 9 x 6 in. The size was changed to a 16-page paper, 8 x 11 in., in March 1943, and it became a semimonthly in April 1946. It serves the conference young people as well as English-speaking adults as an official conference publication. It contains devotional articles, missionary reports, field notes from various churches, peace and voluntary service notes, educational articles, and other news and features that might inform and edify a conference constituency. The paper is printed and published by the Mennonite Brethren Publishing House, Hillsboro, Kan., and edited by J. W. Vogt of Corn, Okla. The circulation in 1949 was approximately 2,300, mostly in the Mennonite Brethren churches of the United States.

J.W.V.

Christian Life Conference, a name for an inspirational conference held in recent years in Mennonite (MC) congregations. Hesston (Kansas) College students and instructors attended a "Christian Life Conference" at the Pleasant Valley Mennonite Church near Harper, Kan., during the Easter vacation in 1926. A similar conference was held at the Home Mission in Chicago in March 1926. Such a conference was held also at the Mennonite Church near Metamora, Ill., during the Christmas vacation in 1928.

The Christian Life Conference had its inception in a Young Men's Conference held at the Pennsylvania Church near Hesston on Dec. 31, 1917, and Jan. 1, 1918. The conference was called to enable the young men to discuss problems relating to the Mennonite testimony during the war. The success of this meeting led to its continuance the next year as a Young People's Conference with both young men and young women participating. This conference was held annually until 1926 when its name was changed to Christian Life Conference.

Noah Oyer, Dean of Goshen College, who was a member of and deeply interested in the General Sunday School Committee, the Young People's Problems Committee, and Young People's Bible Meeting Topics Committee, is credited with arranging for the first Christian Life Conference held at Goshen College in 1927 at the conclusion of the annual Winter Bible Term. It had been advertised as a "conference for old and young, but especially for the young people of the Mennonite Church."

Interest in this annual conference at Goshen College was very good from the beginning. On several occasions many were unable to find room in Assembly Hall and the adjoining classrooms. It continues to be one of the most inspiring and helpful meetings of the college year. Hesston College seems to have held no Christian Life Conference as such in 1927, but in connection with Young People's Week during the Special Bible Term Daniel Kauffman gave talks on the Christian life and also "Life Work Talks." Hesston College held a Christian Life Conference in 1928 and Eastern Mennonite School in 1929. At the latter institution the two-day conference concluded a ministers' week. Such meetings are still quite general throughout the Mennonite Church (MC) east and west. They are held in connection with the Winter Bible Schools and by individual congregations. The Canton Bible School held one in 1947, the Spring Mount Mission in the same year, and the Blainsport Church at Reinholds, Pa., in 1948.

J.S.U.

Christian Living, a 48-page monthly magazine for home and community, a merger of the *Christian Monitor* (1909-53) and the *Mennonite Community* (1947-53), first issue January, 1954, published by the Mennonite Publishing House, Scottdale, Pa. The initial editorial staff consisted of Millard Lind, editor, Daniel Hertzler, John A. Hostetler, and Alta Mae Erb. Circulation was 14,000.

H.S.B.

Christian Ministry, a 64-page (6" x 9") quarterly published by Mennonite Publishing House, Scottdale, Pa., since 1948, John R. Mumaw, editor. It has a (1952) circulation of 1,800. It is a channel of promotion to guide the minister and lay leader in the work of the church. It provides inspiration, information, guidance, interpretation, and exposition. It covers matters pertaining to preaching, pastoral work, church administration, ecclesiastical issues, source materials, and doctrine.   J.R.M.

Christian Monitor, a 32-page monthly magazine (MC) for the home and Christian worker, containing departments on the Christian life, home, education, missions, Sunday school, young people's Bible meeting, and world news, was published by the Mennonite Publishing House, Scottdale, Pa., from January 1909 to December 1953. Editors have been H. F. Reist 1909-19, Vernon Smucker 1920-23, C. F. Derstine 1923-29, and John L. Horst 1930-53. It had a monthly circulation of approximately 11,306 (1951). In January 1954 it was merged with the *Mennonite Community* to form a new magazine entitled *Christian Living.*   J.L.H.

Christian Nurse, a bimonthly 8-page journal published by the Mennonite (MC) Nurses Association, first issue April 1947, successor to *Mennonursing* (March 1945).

Christian Press, Ltd. In 1923 the publication of the two German-language weeklies of the Mennonite Publishing House in Scottdale, Pa., *Mennonitische Rundschau* and *Christlicher Jugendfreund,* was transferred to Winnipeg, Man., by Hermann Neufeld, who at that time established the Rundschau Publishing House. In 1940 this house was reorganized into the present Christian Press, Ltd., a firm which is owned jointly by the Mennonite Brethren Conference of Canada (⅛ of the stock) and private shareholders (⅞), who are all Mennonites. The main objective is to publish Christian periodicals for German-reading Mennonites the world over. Mennonite church literature and other Christian literature in eight different languages is being published.

The company owns the house and printing shop at 159 Kelvin St., Winnipeg. C. A. DeFehr is the president of the company. Henry F. Klassen is the managing director and editor of its two major publications, which are the *Mennonitische Rundschau* (1877-), widely known as one of the oldest Mennonite publications in North America now in circulation, and the *Konferenz-Jugendblatt,* published every two months since 1944, an illustrated magazine in both English and German for the young people of the Mennonite Brethren Conference of Canada.   H.F.K.

Christian Review, a periodical first published April 10, 1926, by the Rundschau Publishing House, Winnipeg, Man., to fill the need for a religious English paper for the German-speaking Mennonites who immigrated from Russia. Published weekly for the first three months, and monthly thereafter, it was discontinued in November 1928. E. S. Hallman served as editor.   E.S.H.

Christian School, a monthly (August to May) 8-page journal published by the Mennonite Publishing House, Scottdale, Pa., in co-operation with the General Educational Council of the Mennonite Church (MC), first issue January 1949.

Christian Witness, a 16-page biweekly publication of the Krimmer Mennonite Brethren Conference, has been published since January 1941 for the purpose of informing its members of the work of the churches and the activities of the conference and its missionary endeavors. Devotional meditations and sermonettes are printed to provide food for spiritual growth. William J. Johnson, Hillsboro, Kan., has been the editor since October 1948. Before this J. H. Klassen, Rachel Wiebe Hiebert, and A. L. Friesen served as editors. It is printed by the Salem Publishing House, Inman, Kan.   W.J.J.

Christian Workers' Conference. This is the name applied to the Mennonite (MC) district conference formerly known as the Sunday School Conference and in Ohio for a number of years as the Sunday School and Young People's Meeting Conference. In both the Ohio and the Indiana-Michigan conference districts the "Sunday School Conference" became the Christian Workers' Conference in 1943.

Before 1921 a number of Mennonite (MC) congregations in Central Kansas held an annual Christian Workers' Conference over the Easter week end. In 1921 this conference was held at Larned, Kan., with good attendance and interest. In 1922 the Missouri-Kansas Conference, where lay delegates had equal voice in conference with ministers, voted to encourage Christian Workers' conferences under certain conditions. In that year at the same place a Sunday School Conference, a Young People's Conference, and a Missions Conference, each with separate sessions, followed successively at the close of the church conference. In 1923 "Christian Workers' Conference" was used as a covering name and organization for these three conferences but each retained its separate name and sessions. In subsequent years these subsidiary conferences were held, sometimes before the church conference, under the title "Christian Workers' Conference" or sometimes merely "Workers' Conference" but the various interests retained their special designation. In more recent years other special interests were included under the Christian Workers' Conference—Teachers' Conference (1941), Sewing Circle Conference (1941), The Christian Home Conference (1941), Christian Life Conference (1942), and also a Civilian Public Service Program (1942), Marriage and Home Conference (1943), and Christian Education Conference (1943).

Since the organization of the Commission for Christian Education and Young People's Work, the South Central Conference elects a Christian Education Cabinet to plan the activities formerly included under the Christian Workers' Conference. In most districts this conference has replaced the Sunday School Conference.

The term "Christian Worker" was used much earlier, however, in the title, *The Christian Worker's Manual,* the general title of a projected series of three booklets "The Ministry," "The Sunday School," and "Missions." The publication was authorized by General Conference (MC) in 1911 and "The Sunday School" was published in 1913. *The Christian Worker* also is the title of a book by Daniel Kauffman published in 1922 under the auspices of the Mennonite Board of Missions and Charities. A "Workers' Meeting," a combination of Sunday-school meeting, harvest meeting, and evangelism, was held in the Ephrata Mennonite Church over the Labor Day week end, Sept. 3-5, 1927.

Until within recent years the Central Illinois Conference has made the most extensive use of the term "Christian Workers." In the December 1910 issue of *The Christian Evangel,* the editor begins a new feature, "Christian Workers' Section." This is continued and amplified in succeeding issues to include personal work, C.E. topics, and the Sunday-school lessons. In 1912 the editor of the *Evangel,* A. B. Rutt, was one of the speakers at the first annual "Soul-Winning Conference for Christian Workers," an interdenominational venture held at the Euclid Avenue Baptist Church in St. Louis, Mo. He also gave an address in the closing session of the second conference held at the same place in January 1913. Beginning in January 1917 the Central Illinois Conference of Mennonites annually held a Christian Workers' Conference. This was in addition to and separate from the annual church conference held in August each year. In January 1919, this conference devoted one day each to missions, Sunday school and young people, education, pastoral work, and denominational interests. The conferences consisted chiefly of inspirational addresses. By 1925 when the young people requested course instruction in various subjects the Christian Workers' Conference was replaced by the Christian Workers' Institute. In 1926 a committee was appointed to outline courses. J.S.U.

Christijntgen, an Anabaptist martyr, wife of the martyr Willem Vernon (*q.v.*). Willem had been arrested on Ascension Day, May 4, 1570, when a meeting of the congregation was held in the environs of Brugge, Belgium. Christijntgen, who had been able to escape, was seized in Brugge that same night by the burgomaster. Together with Grietgen (*q.v.*), the wife of Kaerle de Raedt, because she remained steadfast in the truth, she was burned at the stake in the castle of Brugge. Van Braght (*Mart. Mir.*) states that this execution took place in 1568. This is wrong. Christijntgen and Grietgen were put to death in 1570, the exact date being uncertain (probably May 20). (*Mart. Mir.* I) 369, E 725; Verheyden, *Brugge,* 62, No. 68.) vDZ.

Christina Michiels Barents, an Anabaptist martyr, who was drowned at Rotterdam on Jan. 24, 1539, with Anneken Jans (*q.v.*). She was born at Leuven (Louvain) in Belgium, was about fifty years old, was baptized in her house in Steenstrate at Leuven by Johannes, "who was from Maastricht or thereabouts" (she probably means Jan Smeitgen, *q.v.,* of Maastricht), together with her husband Mathijs van der Donck, "a surgeon and physician." (*Mart. Mir.* D 143, strangely not in the 1950 English edition, but in the German edition of Pirmasens, 1780, p. 62 f.) vDZ.

Christina Stichting, a foundation which has its seat at Amsterdam and owes its existence to a bequest made by Christina de Bosch Kemper (*q.v.*), an outstanding Dutch Mennonite, who died in 1924. The funds, which are administered by a board of Mennonite regents, have been assigned to the purpose of improving the lot of unmarried women or widows by financial support. First and foremost the founder intended to help Mennonites, but other women are also considered. vDZ.

Christliche (Adams Co., Ind.), the name of an independent Amish congregation which in 1911 had 69 members and worshiped 4 miles northwest of Berne. Among the preachers were David Schwartz and Jacob J. Schwartz. It is now extinct. M.G.

Christliche Volksblatt, Das, a 4-page, biweekly 15 x 22 in. German religious journal, edited by John H. Oberholtzer, first issue July 30, 1856. It followed the *Religiöser Botschafter* (*q.v.*), which had been started by Oberholtzer in the same town in 1852. The first paper had been a private venture, while *Das Christliche Volksblatt* was published by a stock company, the *Mennonitischer Druck-Verein,* Milford Square, Pa. In January 1867 the name was changed to *Der Mennonitische Friedensbote* (*q.v.*), and under this name continued until 1882, when it was merged with *Zur Heimath* (*q.v.*) to become the *Christlicher Bundesbote.* These papers were forerunners of the later official periodicals of the General Conference Mennonite Church. P.R.S.

Christlicher Bundesbote, founded in 1882, the official German weekly of the General Conference Mennonite Church, had its forerunners in the *Religiöser Botschafter* (*q.v.*) (1852-56), *Das Christliche Volksblatt* (*q.v.*) (1867-81), *Zur Heimath* (*q.v.*) (1875-81), and *Nachrichten aus der Heidenwelt* (*q.v.*) (1877-82). It came into being by merging the latter three, which represented respectively the Mennonites of the eastern United States, recent immigrants from Russia, and missionary interests. Thus the *Bundesbote* became the first G.C.M. paper, appearing first semimonthly and later weekly. Editors were David Goerz, 1882-85; J. A. Sommer, 1886-1911; C. van der Smissen, 1912-30; and C. E Krehbiel, 1930-47. The original larger size was reduced in 1930 to 8 x 11 in., with 16 pages.

In 1947 the *Bundesbote* was merged with the Canadian Mennonite weekly *Der Bote* (*q.v.*), retaining its name *Christlicher Bundesbote* in the subtitle. The editor of *Der Bote,* D. H. Epp, was given an assistant editor in Cornelius Krahn. The circulation of the merged paper was 4,500 in 1950. With the change of the reading constituency and editors the content has changed somewhat from that of the preceding period. Originally the paper served a Pennsylvania-Swiss-South German and Russian Mennonite constituency of the United States. Now it is read mostly in Canada and South America. It contains devotional messages, biographical and historical material, and information about congregations, mission fields, institutions, and Mennonites in other countries.

The great contribution which the *Christlicher Bundesbote* has made lies in the following areas: uniting Mennonites of entirely different cultural and religious backgrounds and promoting endeavors such as Sunday school, missions, evangelism, education, philanthropic institutions, literature, the Mennonite heritage and principles, and a conference consciousness. **C.K.**

A. B. Schelly, "Mennonitische Kirchenblätter," in *Bundesbote-Kalender*, 1898, 26; B. Bargen, "General Conference Mennonite Press," in *Mennonite Life*, January, 1951, 35; *ML* I, 351 f.

Christlicher Familienfreund, the organ of the Kleine Gemeinde (since 1952 called Evangelical Mennonite Church), began as a monthly periodical in January 1935. After twelve years, it became a biweekly. Printed by the Christian Press of Winnipeg four years, it has since been produced by Derksen Printers, Steinbach, Man. The paper is 6 x 9 in., averages 16-18 pages, and has a circulation of approximately 1100. Its editor has from the beginning been David P. Reimer. **D.P.R.**

Christlicher Familienkalender, a Russian Mennonite almanac edited by A. Kröker, was founded in 1897. During its first two years it was printed by Peter Neufeld in Halbstadt; from 1899 to 1904 by A. Schulze in Odessa; and after 1905 in the printing establishment of J. J. Braun, which was later merged with "Raduga." Although its object was to disseminate general information on Mennonite life, it also provided general Christian reading material and was therefore purchased by many non-Mennonites. As it was the only almanac published by the Mennonites in Russia, it was read by nearly every Mennonite family and reached a circulation of 15,000 copies yearly. Because of World War I, publication was suspended in 1916 and 1917, but was resumed for 1918 and 1919.

In contrast to the German *Christlicher Gemeinde-Kalender* (*q.v.*), the Russian almanac practically never published Mennonite historical material and never published a Mennonite directory or statistics of any sort. (See the editorial of 1903 vigorously rejecting proposals to include them.) Kröker did publish quite regularly a directory of German colonies (villages) in Russia. The chief reason given for leaving out a Mennonite directory was lack of space which the editor wished to reserve for the literary section. However, there was an extraordinarily large advertising section. In 1912, for instance, 106 pages of 248 were devoted to advertisements. Space was available for articles such as "Memories of the Russo-Japanese War" and detailed lists of all the members of the Czar's family and close relatives. However, the advertisements themselves have considerable historical value today since they reflect much of the economic activity of the Mennonites of Russia. It is evident, however, that the editor's policy called for a general Christian publication with no particular Mennonite character. (*ML* I, 352.) **H.S.B.**

Christlicher Familien-Kalender was published by David Goerz, Halstead, Kan., for the years 1884 and 85. The former was not an original publication and contained no material on Mennonites, and the second contained little such material. A copy of both issues is found in the Bethel College Historical Library, and a copy of the 1885 issue in the Goshen College Historical Library. (Bender, *Two Centuries,* 98.) **C.K.**

Christlicher Gemeinde-Kalender, an annual published by the South German Mennonite Conference beginning in 1892 usually in editions of 2,000. At the conference of the Mennonites of the Palatinate and Baden (*Konferenz der Süddeutschen Mennoniten*) on Nov. 11, 1890, Preacher Jakob Ellenberger of Friedelsheim promoted the idea of publishing an almanac, and found almost unanimous approval. A committee was chosen (Jakob Ellenberger of Friedelsheim, Ph. Kieferndorf of Monsheim, Christian Neff of Weierhof, Christian Hege of Breitenau, Philipp Hege of Oberbiegelhof, and Jakob Hege of Reihen) to plan the almanac. Besides the calendar, the almanac contains a section of information and entertainment, with usually a story or two and various articles on the history and present state of the Mennonite brotherhood. Its contents make it a very important source for the study of Mennonite history. An important feature has been the directory of all Mennonite congregations in Europe outside of Holland and Russia. The 1898 issue had only West Prussia, 1899 all Germany; 1902 first included France, Switzerland, and Luxembourg. It was suspended 1942-50 inclusive because of the war and postwar difficulties. Editors were: J. Ellenberger, 1892-1901; J. Hege, 1892-1912; A. Hirschler, 1902-32; A. Braun, 1933-41; P. Schowalter, 1951- . The West Prussian Mennonite Conference became joint publisher in 1934. **NEFF.**

Christlicher Jugendfreund (1878-1951), the first youth periodical published anywhere in the Mennonite world, established in January 1878 by S. D. Guengerich, an Old Order Amish layman of Amish, Iowa, as a private venture, taken over in 1881 by the Mennonite Publishing Company of Elkhart, Ind., and published by them until its sale to the Mennonite Publishing House of Scottdale, Pa., in 1908 and by them to the Rundschau Publishing House of Winnipeg, Man. (MB, later called Christian Press), in 1923. The last issue appeared May 30, 1951, after which a department was introduced in the *Mennonitische Rundschau* with the title *Christlicher Jugendfreund.* **H.S.B.**

Christliches Gemütsgespräch, one of the most popular catechisms among the Mennonites of Europe and America. It was drawn up by Gerhard Roosen (*q.v.*) of Hamburg-Altona, and first published in 1702 when its author was 90 years of age. (Whether he wrote it then or earlier is not known.) Twenty-two editions are known but most likely more editions were printed. In Europe six editions came out between 1702 and 1838, while America has seen eleven German editions since 1769, and five English editions since 1857. The full title of the book runs as follows in English: *Christian Spiritual Conversation on Saving Faith and the Acknowledging of the Truth Which Is After Godliness in Hope of Eternal Life* (Tit. 1:1, 2), *in Questions and*

Answers for the Rising Youth, by Which They May Be Incited and Encouraged to a Wholesome Practice of Life.

This book is the first complete German Mennonite catechism in existence. It represents the work of a well-settled denomination of respectable city dwellers who wanted to prove their complete harmlessness and orthodoxy to their non-Mennonite neighbors. Altogether there are 148 questions and answers in 24 sections. One whole third of the text is devoted to the first article of faith, the doctrine of God, demonstrating the creedal strictness of the Mennonites regarding the Trinity and related points. Doctrinal items also prevail elsewhere though softened down wherever possible. No total depravity is taught as in the Prussian catechism. The practical teachings of the Mennonites are but lightly touched; nonresistance is taught on less than one page, and nonconformity is not taught at all. There is no talk of a suffering church. The entire tone is mild, nonprovocative, and assimilatory.

Roosen had of course certain models to draw from: Dutch catechisms which likewise stressed the doctrinal angle and tried to be nonprovocative, and also G. Hansen's *Glaubensbericht an die Jugend* (1671), which book, however, is much stronger and more uncompromising than the *Gemütsgespräch,* and for that reason never became as popular as the latter (see **Catechisms**). Yet all these models were just suggestive to Roosen and not actual sources. Hence the *Gemütsgespräch* must be considered as his original work. Due to its moderation it became more widely used than any other catechism of its size. R.F.

R. Friedmann, *Menn. Piety Through the Centuries* (1949) 144-47; B. K. Roosen, *Gerhard Roosen* (1854); American editions are listed in Bender, *Two Centuries.*

Christliches Jahrbuch zur Belehrung und Unterhaltung, published 1902-5 (the last year under the changed title, *Fürs Christliche Haus. Belehrendes und Unterhaltendes für Jung und Alt*), edited and published by J. and A. Kroeker of Spat, Crimea, Russia, printed (except for the last year) in Cassel, Germany, a small annual handbook of 145-68 pages, containing general religious and literary articles, with a small amount of Mennonite historical material. It is not a yearbook in the common meaning of the term as a directory and statistical handbook. H.S.B.

Christoffel, an Anabaptist martyr of Geistens, beheaded in 1552 with three companions at Blankenburg (*Mart. Mir.* D 132, E 526; *ML* I, 352). The name Christoffel was common among the Mennonites in Switzerland and the Palatinate, and is still found in America. NEFF.

Christoffel Buyse (Buyze), an Anabaptist martyr, was according to the song, "Een Liedeken van XLI Vrienden" (*Offer des Heeren*), executed at Gent, Belgium, in 1569, with four other martyrs. Verheyden, who studied the sources in Gent, did not find any mention of him. (*Offer,* 649-54; *Mart. Mir.* D 407, E 759; Verheyden, *Gent,* 56; *ML* I, 313.) vDZ.

Christoffel Fierens, an Anabaptist martyr, who was executed Dec. 5, 1572, at Meenen (Menin) in Flanders with Willem de Rijke (le Riche) by burning at the stake. Rembry-Barth, *Historie de Menin,* mentions only the latter; but on the basis of the details offered by van Braght (*Mart. Mir.*) his account must be considered the correct one. The mayor Cornelis of Eeckhoute attempted to have Willem, who was evidently a respected citizen (perhaps from the family of the preacher Christiaen Rijcken), released on the ground that he was ignorant. The inquisitor therefore tested Willem's understanding of purgatory and discovered the contrary. Later, in consequence of the war, the mayor fled to Brugge and lost his property. At the execution a brother called out to Willem, "Dear brother, fight bravely for the truth." Christoffel answered, "O people, consider your salvation; for this is the way to life. . . . Sell your clothing and buy Testaments and note the words of God therein: for therein you will find life, and do not fear them who slay the body, but fear him who has the power to cast body and soul into hell." The hangman cut off this effective testimony by means of gags. (*Mart. Mir.* D 640, E 961; *ML* I, 643.) K.V.

Christoffel (or Christoph) **van Zutphen** (also called Guldemont), a Dutch Anabaptist leader, was present in August 1535 at a meeting of Anabaptist leaders at Bocholt (*q.v.*) in Germany. Of his activities nothing is known but the fact that he administered baptism. Likely he belonged to the Münsterite wing of Anabaptism. (*DB* 1917, 117, No. 73; 1919, 193.) vDZ.

Christoph, a native of Meissen or Mühlhausen, a cobbler by trade, an apostle of the Anabaptists in Thuringia, who together with Hans Römer (*q.v.*), Christoph Peisker (*q.v.*), and Volkmar Fischer (*q.v.*) was very successful in the Anabaptist cause in the region of Erfurt and Mühlhausen after 1525. Wappler (*Die Stellung,* 46, and *Täuferbewegung,* 41-44) counts them among the "wild, fanatical Anabaptists," who had even planned an attack on the city of Erfurt on New Year's Day 1528. The tailor Niklaus admitted the intended coup. Thereupon many Anabaptists were arrested, and Niklaus and twelve others were executed. On Dec. 2, 1527, the council of Erfurt sent to the neighboring governments a proclamation of warning against the four apostles named above, stating that "among other things, they preached that God has sent them to restore fallen Jerusalem; for the world will not stand longer than twenty-one months; and at Alich they baptized more than 20 persons; likewise at other places, as in Hesse at Ballhausen, Schwertstedt, and Sondershausen; the preachers told those whom they baptized to watch on the mountain and remain together; for it will rain locusts; that there are 500 preachers who roam through the country and have many adherents to their cause at Magdeburg." This letter apparently caused consternation and unleashed a cruel persecution of the Anabaptists. In the records of later trials the name of Christoph of Meissen appears as one who administered baptism. Volkmar Fischer stated on March 9, 1535 (Wappler, *Täuferbewegung,* 373), that he had made an agreement with Christoph the carpenter "to kill those who were not of their faith."

Whether this confession is not solely the product of the tortures of the rack remains to be determined by future investigation.

According to Wappler (*Täuferbewegung*, 41), Christoph of Meissen is perhaps identical with Christoph Rudolf of Oberdorla, who was later also called Christoph of Eichen (see **Rudolph, Christoph**).   Neff.

P. Wappler, *Die Stellung Kursachsens und des Landgrafen Philipp von Hessen* (Münster, 1910); idem, *Die Täuferbewegung in Thüringen* (Münster, 1913); Franz, *Quellen: Hessen*, 55, 58, 196, 317-19; *ML* 352.

Chronica, Zeytbuch vnd geschychtbibel *von anbegyn bisz inn disz gegenwertig M.D. xxxj. jar. Darinn beide Gottes vnd der welt lauff/ hendel/art/ wort/werck/thun lassen/kriegen/wesen/vnd leben ersehen vnd begriffen wirt. Mit vil wunderbarlichen gedechtniszwürdigen worten vnd thatten/ guten vnd bösen Regimenten/Decreten, etc. Von allen Römischen Keisern/Bäpsten/Concilien/Ketzern/Orden vnd Secten/beide Juden/vnd Christen. Von dem vrsprung vnd vrhab aller breüch vnd miszbreüch der Römischen kirchen/als der Bilder/ H.err/ Messz/Ceremonien. etc. so yetz im Bapstumb im schwanck geen/wie eins nach dem anderen sey einbrochen/was/wa/wann/ durch wen/vnd warumb. Ankunfft viler Reich/breüch/neüwer fünd. etc. Summa hierinn findestu gleich ein begriff/ summari/innhalt vnd schatzkammer/nit aller/sunder der Chronick wirdigsten/ausserlessnen Historien, eingeleibt/vnnd ausz vilen von weittem doch angenummenen glaubwirdigen Büchern/gleich als mein ymmen korb müselig zusamen tragen/in seer gutter ordnung für die augen gestelt/vnd in iij Chronick oder hauptbücher/verfasst. Durch Sebastianum Francken von Wörd/vormals in teütscher zungen/nie gehört noch gelesen. Innhalt begriff vnd gleichsam ein Inuentarium vnd Register diser gantzen Chronicken/findestu zuruck disz plats. Kumpt her vnd schauwet die werck des Herren. Psalm. xlvj. lxiiy[=66] Anno. M.C.XXXI. Colophon: Getruckt zu Straszburg. Durch Balthassar Beck. Vnd vollendet am Fünfften tag des Herbstmonats. Im Jar. M.D. XXXj.* Strasbourg, 1531). This is a big folio volume of more than 1,000 pages, most important for the history of ideas of early Anabaptism. It might be called the main source of the Anabaptist Brethren for their knowledge of church history and the history of Christian doctrines. Since Sebastian Franck (*q.v.*), in spite of his outspoken Christian-spiritual interests, might yet be termed a Humanist scholar, the book became the very link between Anabaptism and Humanism. Here was a text at the same time reliable and thorough and yet acceptable to those radical Christians who just a few years earlier had started their challenging movement. Franck was in open sympathy with this trend toward a predominantly inward Christianity, away from all ecclesiastical institutionalism. But, as a typical spiritualistic individualist, he yet kept aloof from any closer engagement to a movement which stressed brotherhood and the discipline involved. He remained a spiritualist and was not willing to try the way of discipleship.

Franck had discovered, perhaps for the first time in history, a stream of nonconformist and non-ecclesiastical Christianity through the ages, something which in more recent times has been called "old-evangelical brotherhoods," and for which his age had but the derogatory term *Ketzer* (heretic). He now set out to ennoble this word and to prove that these heretics were actually the better Christians, nearer to truth, than those of the official churches. Thus he started a type of literature which later became known as *Ketzerhistorien*.

It was in the most brisk atmosphere of Strasbourg (where Franck lived in 1529 to 1531) that he conceived the plan to write a complete "world history" comprising both the secular and the spiritual viewpoints. This enterprise grew into a heavy volume, exceedingly well written, and likewise most carefully printed. It should soon have become a real *Volksbuch*, or as we today would say, a best-seller. But it was too radical in its philosophy, shocking nearly every party and making as many enemies as it made friends. On order of the magistrates Franck was expelled from Strasbourg with wife and child just because he had published this unusual book. Ernst Troeltsch calls it correctly "the outstanding defense brief (*Schutzschrift*) for the Protestant sects." The nonconformist groups responded accordingly as will be demonstrated later.

The book is made up of three parts: (1) the story of mankind from Adam to Christ; (2) the story of emperors and temporal events; (3) the story of popes and spiritual happenings (church history). It is in this third and most important part that the famous *Ketzerchronik* appeared, the story of the non-Catholics who dared to think in their own way. To us it is the most interesting section of the entire volume, primarily for its uniquely fair picture of the Anabaptists. Franck who had broken not only with the Roman Church but with the Lutherans as well, was convinced that truth (as he saw it) has ever been and is also now persecuted under the pretext of "heresy" (*Ketzerei*). "If wishing would help," he exclaims, "I for myself would rather bear the fate of an heretic condemned by the popes, than that of a saint figuring in the calendar of the popes." And thus he starts to picture sympathetically his "Ketzers," one after another down through the alphabet.

It is a strange mixture which he thus presents. For instance, under the letter "M" we find many pages dealing with Martin Luther, and then follow again several pages dealing with "Michael Sattler, Jörg Wagner, Lienhart Kaiser" (three renowned Anabaptist martyrs of the 1520's). Under the letter "W" we find a 17-page study of the *Wiedertäufer* (Anabaptists), most remarkable for the fine grasp of their main features. A. Hegler (*Geist und Schrift bei Sebastian Franck*, 1892, 271) was right in claiming that this part of the *Chronica* is perhaps the best section of the entire book, written with an inner participation and even compassion. One must keep in mind that the book was written in 1530-31, when Anabaptism had been just a few years in existence, and was slandered everywhere. But Franck had many personal contacts with representatives of this movement, in Nürnberg, Augsburg, and above all in Strasbourg, then a place of refuge for many (also Pilgram Marpeck was then in this city, and he is quoted by Franck in his *Weltbuch,* 1534, fol. 44b). He shares many of their viewpoints, though he disapproves at the same time of others, e.g., the ceremony of adult baptism which to him seems unnecessary and external.

His story of the Anabaptists begins about as follows: "In the year 1526, right after the Peasants' War, a new sect or separated church arose which wanted to follow the letter of the Scriptures, called Anabaptists; they began to separate themselves by means of baptizing their members, disclaiming anything common with other churches whom they considered unchristian. Their elders or bishops were first Dr. Balthasar Hubmaier, Melchior Rinck, Hans Hut, Johannes Denk, Ludwig Haetzer. They made such quick progress that their teaching soon spread over the entire country (Germany?). They baptized many thousands, among them a great number of good-hearted people who earnestly strove after God and were now attracted to these brethren who so rigidly stuck to the letter of the Scriptures and who made such a good impression. For as far as could be observed, they taught nothing but love, faith, and the cross. They showed themselves humble, and patient under much suffering; they broke bread with one another as an evidence of unity and love. They helped each other faithfully with mutual love, lending and giving, and taught that all things should be held in common [NB. This was taught in Moravia only]. They called each other brethren, but those who were not of their sect they scarcely greeted. They died as martyrs, patiently and humbly enduring all persecutions."

Franck is surprisingly well informed about the brotherhood in Moravia which had just begun setting up their community of goods. (Jakob Hutter had not yet arrived at that time.) "Like monks they have regulations concerning eating, drinking, dress, silence, speech. Some arrogate for themselves the apostolic life and the mode of the primitive church [at Jerusalem], and for that reason they keep strictly to the letter, wash each other's feet, go from place to place to preach and to speak of calling and mission." "They all teach to be obedient to the authorities unless it is against God's commandment. And they are ready to suffer violence for that. All those whom I have asked answered thus: they are here to suffer for Christ's sake with patience, and not to fight with impatience. No Christian should ever go to war. For the Gospel does not ask to be confirmed with the fist (as the peasants did) but with suffering and dying. . . . For that there is no need to worry about rebellion on their part, as the devil insinuates to the many who then tyrannize these poor people. God is strong enough to stop any heresy, if there is any. If I were pope, emperor, or Turk, I would be less concerned about rebellion by these people than by anybody else." "Christians have the ban not the sword among themselves."

With all his admiration, Sebastian Franck, the spiritualist and individualist, does not approve two very central points of Anabaptist teaching: their Scriptural literalism, and their principle of separation from the world. "The letter," he says, "makes heretics (meaning sectarians), for what matters is not the letter but its meaning which Christ had in mind (*der Sinn Christi*)." That was also the position of the later Hans Denk and of Bünderlin, and of all the other "spiritual reformers" of that age. It makes for individualism at the same time. "Therefore I pray that Anabaptists may walk in the truth, do repentance, live God-fearing and concernedly, but—that they may not separate from the world." To this Hegler (*Geist und Schrift,* 272) remarks interestingly: "It appears as if the fate of Hans Denk stood before his mind as a warning. Franck does not believe in a community of saints which can never exclude altogether some mean elements. Denk appears to him as proof that a separated church has no justification, considering the disappointment of this man after so many years with the brethren."

Through the next decades the book had great influence upon Anabaptist circles. Joseph Beck, the editor of the *Geschichts-Bücher der Wiedertäufer in Oesterreich* (Vienna, 1883), states very significantly that the entire historical introduction of the Hutterite chronicle is nothing but an elaborate excerpt from the *Chronica* by Franck. (Beck, p. 9, footnote, which tells us that this introduction deals with the story of the early church, the persecutions, and the church development from Arius to 1519.) The same holds true with Menno Simons, of whom Cornelius Krahn (*Menno Simons,* 1936, 40) claims that a great number of his quotations of a historical nature were taken from this book. Menno's knowledge of the old authors seems to go back to Franck. Dirk Philips, likewise, borrows many phrases and statements from Franck, referring to him time and again (*BRN* X, 83, 110, 483; V, 4, 11, 37; see also IV and VII). In a special tract, *Verantwoordinghe ende Refutation op twee Sendbrieven Sebastiani Franck* (*BRN* X, 481 ff.), Philips expressly takes issue with Franck's viewpoint concerning the interpretation of the Scriptures (Sepp, *Geschiedkundige Nasporingen,* 1872, 163). Also the well-known Rhenish Anabaptist Thomas von Imbroich quotes Franck's *Chronica* frequently (Rembert, *Wiedertäufer,* 468). We learn further that the Old Flemish martyrs' chronicle, *Historie der Martelaren* (Hoorn, 1617), contains a number of martyrs' stories taken from the *Chronica,* thus proving again the popularity of this book among all branches of Anabaptism (*DB* 1870, 75). The same must have been true with the Mennonites in Prussia, who, though belatedly, had also produced a volume of martyr stories. Isaac van Dühren (*q.v.*) in his *Geschichte der Märtyrer* (Königsberg, 1787) expressly quotes Sebastian Franck's *Chronik der römischen Ketzer* as one of his sources, and it seems that by using it he had gone beyond the material of the older martyr books. Also in South Germany the Anabaptists were well acquainted with the work. Pilgram Marpeck (who must once have known Franck) quotes the *Chronica* in his *Verantwortung* of 1542 when discussing the communism of the earliest church (Hege in

Gedenkschrift zum 400 jährigen Jubiläum der Mennoniten, 1925, 265). In fact Hans v. Schubert proved that those brethren who defended some sort of community of goods were at least partly influenced by a quotation found in Franck's *Chronica* (*Akademie d. Wiss. in Heidelberg* XI, 1919, 14 and *passim*). Friedmann proved the same for an outstanding dogmatic tract of the Hutterites of about 1547 (*Arch. f. Ref.-Gesch.* 1931, 235). Furthermore, the church historical arguments in this tract, quotations from councils and papal edicts concerning the rise of infant baptism in the Roman Church, were taken altogether from this great book which thus served for many generations as a source of learning and education among the brethren.—For its author, to be sure, the publication of the *Chronica* meant hardship and homelessness, because he had antagonized nearly everybody of status and influence. Since Franck, however, was not willing to commit himself to any group, it meant also at the same time isolation and the "noble loneliness" of a spiritual individualist. (See **Franck; Clemens, Epistle** No. IV.) **R.F.**

The best book is still A. Hegler, *Geist und Schrift bei Sebastian Franck* (1892). His *Beiträge zur Gesch. der Mystik in der Reformationszeit* were posthumously edited by W. Köhler (1905). More recent is R. Stadelmann, *Vom Geist des ausgehenden Mittelalters. Studien zur Gesch. der Weltanschauung von Nicolaus Cusa bis Sebastian Franck* (1929); R. M. Jones, *Spiritual Reformers of the Sixteenth Century* (London, 1914); **A. Reimann,** *Sebastian Franck als Geschichtsphilosoph* (1921); W. Köhler's article in *RGG* II (1928); L. Keller, *Reformation;* idem, *Johann Staupitz und die Anfänge der Reformation* (1888); Ernst Troeltsch, *Social Teachings of the Christian Churches* (German 1912, English 1930); Rembert, *Wiedertäufer;* C. Krahn, *Menno Simons* (Karlsruhe, 1936); C. Sepp, *Geschiedkundige Nasporingen* I (1872; very valuable); Hans v. Schubert, *Der Kommunismus der Wiedertäufer in Münster und seine Quellen* (*Sitzungsberichte der Heidelberger Akad. d. Wissenschaften,* 1919) XI (claims that the *Chronica* was most influential upon B. Rothmann); R. Friedmann, "Eine dogmatische Hauptschrift der Hutterischen Täufergemeinden in Mähren," in *Arch. f. Ref.-Gesch.* XXVIII (1931); W. E. Peuckert, *Sebastian Franck* (Munich, 1943).

Chronicles, Hutterite. Among the many groups of 16th century Anabaptists not one was as history-minded as the Hutterites in Moravia. At the headquarters of their *Vorsteher* (bishops) they seem to have kept orderly archives where all material of significance was collected, incoming and outgoing epistles, official writings, doctrinal statements, records about martyrs, records about the affairs of the brotherhood itself, notes on weather, on prices of farm products, regulations (*Ordnungen*), speeches of elders, and all the rest. It was the fountain from which inspiration and strength could be gained and the assurance that their way was the right one. Wherever brethren were examined by the authorities they knew how to answer because they knew their history and the previous testimonies of their brethren. Numerous copies of this material were made (see **Epistles**), and often collected in well-bound books or codices. At these headquarters the Brethren must also have kept a small library, containing such books as Eusebius' *Church History* (see **Eusebius**), Sebastian Franck's *Chronica* (*q.v.*), and other works in church history, then all the

printed books by Hubmaier (*q.v.*), Denk, (*q.v.*), Hans Hut (*q.v.*), and related men, and pamphlets like Michael Sattler's (*q.v.*) Epistles together with the story of his trial and end, the story of G. Wagner's or Leonhard Kaiser's martyrdom, and many more like them (see *MQR,* 1942, 83), then also various Bible concordances which were often carefully copied (see *Arch. f. Ref.-Gesch.,* 1931, 225 f.), and so on.

During the "golden era" of the brotherhood in Moravia, the time of the *Vorsteher* Peter Walpot (*q.v.*), 1565-78, the idea must have arisen to collect all this material in an official "chronicle" to keep the memory of the great happenings alive, particularly the "heroic beginnings" and also to offer an object lesson to later generations. Perhaps they meant also to vindicate their peculiar way of life; and, not the least, the martyrdom of the many witnesses to truth should find a permanent record for posterity. Thus the work was begun, perhaps on suggestion of Peter Walpot, by the *Diener des Wortes* Kaspar Braitmichel (*q.v.*). From the preface, where he apologizes that for reasons of poor eyesight and other frailties he could not carry on his work beyond the year 1542, we might assume that he wrote this book toward the end of his life. He died in 1573 in Austerlitz (Moravia), the seat of the *Vorsteher* and (probably) also of the archives. His original manuscript is no longer extant; it was copied, however, by Hauptrecht Zapff, the clerk of the next *Vorsteher* Kräl (1578-83) and the following *Vorsteher* Klaus Braidl (1583-1611). This Zapff manuscript is still extant, incidentally also a work of outstanding penmanship and artistic illumination. After Zapff, six more scribes or annalists continued this work in the given fashion, until the year 1665, when the manuscript abruptly ends with a letter of supplication to the brethren in Holland. Only one master copy of this chronicle exists, or as it was called the *Geschichts-Buch und kurzer Durchgang vom Anfang der Welt* . . . , also called *Unser Gemain Geschicht-Buch.* It is a bulky volume of 612 folio leaves, bound in leather and with the usual brass buckles. As their greatest treasure the Brethren kept it with utmost care, carrying it along on all their pilgrimages through the ages. Today it is with the Brethren in America. It is commonly called the *Great Chronicle.*

For about 130 years no continuation of the Zapff manuscript was ever considered. It was the time of the decline of the brotherhood. But then, the revived brotherhood, then living in Russia, had the good fortune of having in their midst a man of outspoken gift in historiography: Johannes Waldner (*q.v.*) (1749-1824), bishop of the brotherhood from 1794 to his death. Waldner, a Carinthian by birth, studied all the old records, including the *Great Chronicle,* and decided to write a sequel to the first chronicle. He worked on this important enterprise from 1793 to 1802; we do not know why he stopped at this year. In this book, called by himself *Denkwürdigkeiten* (*Memorabilia*), he first briefly repeated the entire story of the former book, to be sure, with new and significant additions, then he carried the story forward from the year 1665 to the moment when the Carinthian transmigrants (see **Carinthia**) joined the nearly extinct brotherhood in Transylvania around 1755 (getting his material from written and oral sources otherwise unknown). And finally he told in broad details all the vicissitudes of the brotherhood which he had shared himself or, at least, had witnessed. While the older book, from now on called the *Great Chronicle,* was fairly unartistic in its form, more annals than history, the new book, now called the *Small Chronicle, Das Klein-Geschichtsbuch der Hutterischen Brüder,* is a real masterwork of historiography, a pragmatic account of great unity and dynamic. The manuscript consists of 370 folio leaves.

After Waldner's death very little was done to carry on this kind of work, and later notes are scanty and poor. This manuscript also exists in only one master copy in one of the Bruderhofs in Canada.

These Chronicles then are the two major source books of our knowledge of the Hutterites whose story thus became better known and more easily accessible than that of any other Anabaptist group. However, they represent by no means the only historical material from this group. It is highly characteristic for the history-mindedness of the Hutterites that many a brother undertook similar literary enterprises though on a smaller scale. These books were usually called *Denkbüchlein* or memorandum booklets, sometimes also simply *Chronicle.* To a certain extent they are but excerpts from the "larger" chronicle, omitting much of the non-annalistic material, but partly they are original works with their own (unknown, mostly oral) sources. They partly overlap and have the same contents, but partly they bring new data otherwise not available, enriching thus our knowledge in many a detail. Of these smaller chronicles we know about 19 different specimens. Joseph v. Beck gives an account of them in the introduction of his remarkable edition of these chronicles, published under the title *Die Geschichts-Bücher* (note the plural) *der Wiedertäufer in Osterreich-Ungarn,* etc., *von 1526 bis 1785* (Vienna, 1883, in *Fontes Rerum Austriacarum* XLIII). He enumerates them as codices A to T. The best known of them is perhaps the codex "A," the "Resch-chronicle" (named after its writer who carried the work on until his death in 1592, while later brethren continued it until 1639), entitled *Ein klein gründliches Denkbüchlein darin wird begriffen und angezeigt was sich seit dem 1524 Jahr mit den rechten christgläubigen und frommen Menschen hat zugetragen, und wie die Gemein Gottes wiederum hat angefangen* (meaning the restitution of the primitive church after 1400 years of decline) *und vermehrt hat.* Another remarkable book is codex "I," *Beschreibung der Geschichten . . . wie und was Gott mit seinen Gläubigen . . . vom Anfang der Welt gehandelt und bis auf die jetzige Zeit sich kräftig in ihnen bewiesen . . . durch Kaspar Braitmichel oder Schneider gestellt, und jetzt* (i.e., 1591) *wieder angefangen zu schreiben . . . C.K.* Only part of the first hundred leaves seems to go back to Braitmichel, the rest (200 leaves) are a copy of the

Resch codex. Whether Braitmichel himself made excerpts from his own "larger" chronicle or, what is more likely, whether this book represents a preliminary experiment in chronicling (and also in church history—as the title indicates), must remain a moot question.

These codices are usually octavo size, comprising between 200 and 300 leaves, produced in beautiful handwriting. Seven of them begin with a brief summary of the history of the church from the time of Constantine (when it was considered that the true church began its decline) up to about 1520. This part is but an excerpt from Seb. Franck's popular *Chronica* (*q.v.*). In the *Great Chronicle* this introduction is more elaborate and takes up 32 (or 44) pages in print. Most of these chronicles continue their story almost to the end of the 17th century, several authors working successively on them similar to the way in which the *Great Chronicle* was composed. A complete comparison of both the *Great Chronicle* and these 19 smaller ones has never been undertaken. Much material is identical but quite a bit is also new and different. In completeness and spiritual intent the *Great Chronicle* is certainly superior to the others.

More than one fifth of this *Great Chronicle* is made up of inserts of doctrinal statements and epistles (*Sendbriefe*); among the latter we find some of the finest ever written by Hutterites, such as those by Jakob Hutter, Riedemann, Peter Walpot, Paul Glock, etc. (see *MQR,* 1945, 27 ff.). From Hutterite epistle books extant (see **Epistles, Hutterite**) it becomes apparent that also a great part of the remaining story was drawn from these unusual prime sources, a point to which particularly Wolkan called attention in his ed. of 1923. Likewise hymns, so numerous among Hutterites (see **Hymns, Hutterite**), have served as a welcome source mainly for the stories of martyred brethren. The *Great Chronicle* contains also most welcome doctrinal material taken from proceedings of religious debates or from other documents in the archive. For instance, only the *Great Chronicle* has the *Five Articles of the Greatest Disagreement between Us and the World* of 1547 (see **Article Book**), written most likely around 1570 by Peter Walpot, or the *Brüderliche Vereinigung zw. uns und etlichen Brüdern am Rheinstrom* of 1556, written by Hänsel Raiffer. At the year 1571, a lengthy insert describes in detail the organization and the work of the brotherhood (written perhaps by Peter Walpot), a major source for our knowledge of the life of the Hutterites.

For a long time the *Great Chronicle* was not known to European scholars, since it existed only in a faraway colony in Russia and was then taken to America. Only the chronicles which had been confiscated by Jesuits in the 18th century and kept in different libraries of Europe were known. Joseph v. Beck (*q.v.*) assiduously collected and copied most of them and then undertook the difficult task of combining all his material mosaic fashion. He added whatever pertinent material he could get hold of otherwise and thus produced an admirable and still very usable work, the *Geschichts-Bücher* (1883), of about 700 pages.

In 1908 Rudolf Wolkan of Vienna, Austria, learned through John Horsch (*q.v.*) for the first time of the existence of the original chronicle and from a transcription received from the brethren in America prepared an edition of this volume entitled *Geschicht-Buch* (note the singular over against Beck's plural) *der Hutterischen Brüder* (Vienna, 1923) in 750 pages. The language of this edition is adjusted to the present-day usage of High German. In footnotes much valuable material from epistles is added. It can be safely said that the Beck and Wolkan editions well supplement each other.

In 1943 another edition of the same book was published, this time in America, entitled *Die älteste Chronik der Hutterischen Brüder* (Carl Schurz Foundation, Philadelphia, 1943). It was prepared by A. J. F. Zieglschmid (then professor of German literature at Northwestern University, Evanston, Ill.) and was brought out in a letter-perfect edition of the original text (spelling, punctuation, etc.). It is a bulky volume of more than 1,100 pages and 20 plates (with samples of the handwriting). It contains many valuable helps—glossary, bibliography, and so on.

Four years later, in 1947, Prof. Zieglschmid published the sequel, the *Klein-Geschichtsbuch der Hutterischen Brüder* (again Carl Schurz Foundation). It is a first edition taken from the hitherto unknown *Denkwürdigkeiten* of Johannes Waldner, which was kept in custody on a Bruderhof in Canada. Though called *Small Chronicle,* the volume is almost as bulky as the *Great Chronicle,* having 856 quarto pages. This edition is done in modernized language like the Wolkan book, and contains again an extensive apparatus. Its bibliography of more than 300 items is by far the most exhaustive one on the Hutterites in existence. As was mentioned above, Waldner's text goes only as far as 1802. From 1802 to 1947 very few notes are found in the manuscript, and the editor was compelled to supply supplementary material from even the remotest sources attainable (pp. 410-500). In an Appendix (500-686) a nearly complete collection of *Gemeinde-Ordnungen* (regulations or ordinances for the brotherhood) from 1651 to 1873 is published, further the revealing travel diary of Paul Tschetter (1873) while on a search for a place of settlement in America, then Canadian documents (since 1872), list of colonies, preachers, etc.

Waldner's text of the *Small Chronicle* gives more than mere annals. Skillfully he emphasizes the dynamic evolution, condensing the earlier story to what is of true significance and adding material not known heretofore. Of great value are inserted selections of sermons which were to help revive the former spirit and strengthen the loyalty to the original institutions (204-14). They were taken from one of the remarkable sermon collections which up to this day have been preserved in the colonies and are still in use at their worship services. An ordinance of 1633 by Ehrenpreis concerning nonresistance is another welcome insert into the text (translated in *MQR,* 1951). Since Waldner's description of the sufferings in Transylvania and the exodus to Russia (1767 ff.) is based on his own

experiences, the last part of his "memorabilia" is particularly dramatic and well written, proving that these Carinthian newcomers had certainly grasped something of the spirit of the Hutterite forefathers. R.F.

The editions of the larger and smaller chronicles by Beck, Wolkan, and Zieglschmid are mentioned in the text. Zieglschmid described "The Hutterite Chronicle" in *American-German Review,* 1942, and his edition is fully discussed by J. A. Waltz in the *Journal of English and German Philology,* October, 1944. As for Waldner's Chronicle see J. Loserth, "The Decline and Revival of the Hutterites," *MQR,* IV (1930) 93-112. As for the sources see also R. Friedmann, "The Epistles of the Hutterian Brethren," *MQR* XX (1946) 147-77.

Chulupi Indian Mission (MB), located in the Mennonite Colony Fernheim in the Paraguayan Chaco, has its headquarters in the town of Filadelfia of the same colony. The Chulupi Indian, of medium height, tough and wiry, is usually a willing worker and generally considered more intelligent and temperamental than the neighboring Lengua Indian tribe. The Chulupi first came to Fernheim in 1934 from the Pilcomayo River area, southwest of the Mennonite settlement. As more Indians arrived the Fernheim churches felt the need for a mission to them and in 1946 the first missionaries, Jakob and Helene Franz of Coaldale, Alta., were sent to Fernheim by the Mennonite Brethren Board of Foreign Missions of North America, to assist the local churches in this undertaking. In 1949 two other missionaries, Kornelius Isaak and Gerhard Hein of Fernheim Colony, were added to the working staff. Especial difficulty is encountered by the staff in learning the unwritten Chulupi language, and in the nomadic unstable habits of the tribe. There has been no interference from the Catholic Church thus far. The mission is supported by the Mennonite Brethren Board of Foreign Missions in co-operation with the churches in the Chaco. J.H.F.

Chur, capital (pop. 19,256) of the Swiss canton of Grisons (Graubünden), which in the Reformation was made up of three independent democratic states, the Gotteshausbund (southern part, Engadin, after 1367), the Oberbund or Graubund (western part, 1395-1425, Disentis, Rhäzüns, Misox, Flumns, Rheinwald), and the Zehngerichtenbund (eastern part, 1436, Davos, Prätigau, Schanfigg, Churwalden). The legal influence of the bishop's supremacy was, however, not sharply defined; Austria also exercised jurisdiction and claimed territorial supremacy. Concerning the beginnings here of the Reformation and the Anabaptist movement connected with it, little is known, since a part of the archives as well as the protocols of the council were burned. Nevertheless, from the chronicles of the later years and the wealth of correspondence among the leaders of the Reformation in Chur and in Zürich as well as in St. Gall, it is clear that in principles and intensity the movement paralleled that in the other cantons, and that especially two factors were decisive for the Anabaptist movement: the common assumptions, found also in other territories, expressed by the thinking and attitude of the people toward the Catholic Church, and the initial influence of the oppositional leaders of the

Reformation, later on of particular Anabaptist preachers.

Salzmann (Salandronius), a teacher in the monastery at Chur, reports to Vadian in St. Gall in 1521, that the progress of the Reformation in Germany was being tensely watched, and that the pamphlets, as, for instance, the *Conclusions* of Carlstadt (*q.v.*) against Eck, were eagerly read, and adds, "You may soon be able to see the inhabitants of Rhaetia shake off the yoke of the Babylonian captivity." In 1522 the federal authorities especially designated particularly Sargans as speaking and acting improperly toward the faith. In 1523 chaplain Brötli, who later became known in the Anabaptist circles of Zürich (1524), opposes the Catholic Church with views that offer a preview of a part of Anabaptist doctrine, even though rebaptism did not yet appear, On April 13, 1523, the Oberbund and the Zehngerichtenbund, together with Chur, draw up the first articles, which were a year later recognized and confirmed, giving the populace a voice in the filling of pastoral vacancies and obligating the clergy to serve in person the congregations from whom they obtained their benefices. Consequently the Catholic dignitaries lost the churches in Chur and had to yield the church of St. Martin to Comander (Dorfmann), who had been called by the congregation. Comander worked in constant agreement with Zwingli for him and his views, so that by the end of 1525 forty clergymen requested the council to permit a disputation with the Catholics, which took place on Jan. 8 and 9, 1526, in Ilanz. Comander had drawn up 18 theses against the church, the first of which founded faith and the church on the pure Word of God. He had previously published his theses and distributed them among the populace. At the disputation, the report of which was written by Dr. Hofmeister (*q.v.*) of Schaffhausen (Füsslin, *Beiträge* I), no specifically Anabaptist views are presented beyond the common ideas from which arose the opposition to the Catholic Church (Bible, indications of the church ban, and mutual, though not communistic assistance).

The Anabaptists were not represented at the disputation, although they had previously attracted definite attention and had already appeared openly. For even if one is willing to overlook the first mention of Andreas Castelberger (in 1522 he is called a "villainous fellow"), George Blaurock (*q.v.*) was without doubt active before the close of 1524 or the beginning of 1525, when he made his influence felt in Zürich and Zollikon, though not as an Anabaptist before early 1525. These views may have caused less excitement in Chur because the democratic government had made some concessions to popular feeling, especially in economic matters. But the influence of the Anabaptist leaders had taken effect at least by the beginning of 1525. That Andreas Castelberger (*q.v.*) had connections in Chur and sent books there is seen from his letter to the council of Zürich (Jecklin). Blaurock too, after his expulsion from Zürich on March 25, 1525, turned to Chur. The chronicler Eichhorn reports that the Anabaptists in Grisons began to stir about

this time and Salzmann writes to Zwingli (May 15, 1525), that the spirit of Grebel (*q.v.*) and Manz (*q.v.*) also haunted the regions of Grisons. In July 1525 Manz was arrested there. The council of Chur reported to Zürich that he had created offense and dissension "with the rebaptism of old people and corner preaching." Manz was expelled.

It seems that in this period the Anabaptist movement was at its peak, since pathological psychic aberrations, as one finds them in periods of extreme excitement of the masses (such as the phenomena in St. Gall, *q.v.*), are reported. Comander also complains in his letters to Zwingli about the attitude of the Anabaptists and the increasing influence of Anabaptist preaching, which caused the populace to waver and seriously hampered the progress of the Reformation. He called them Pseudobaptists, in order to give the movement a label (Zwingli *W.W.N.* 374, of Aug. 8, 1525) and also mentions Castelberger as carrying on in Chur. It cannot be determined to what extent the Reformed clergy themselves contributed to this confusion by ambiguous interpretation of various statements of faith. It is certain that the question of the regulation of communion and the ban divided the leaders of Zwingli's party and created shades of opinion varying from the views of the Reformers to those of the extreme Anabaptists. The course of the chaplain Ulrich Bolt (*q.v.*) of Fläsch, a member of the Reformed party in 1524, and in June 1525 (Zwingli *W.W.N.* 372) requested Zwingli to explain the question, but later joined the Anabaptists, is only one illustration of the conditions of the time and the persons connected with it. These conditions required clarification, which was to result from the disputation at Ilanz in January 1526. For the Reformed, in spite of the unconcealed intention of the Bishop (Paulus Ziegler, 1503-41) to discredit it, this disputation created unity. The Anabaptists were soon to feel the effect of this unity. By order of the diet of the three confederations at Chur (February 1526) the Anabaptists imprisoned at Fläsch, 18 men and 60 *Hüter*(?) were placed on trial at Maienfeld. Salzmann reports to Vadian that all recanted, including the leaders; they were therefore fined 25 to 120 guilders and dismissed (de Porta). But this assertion contradicts the statement by Strickler that "they did not renounce their error but were found quite obstinate; but finally after adequate promise of the Fläsch community to grant them their rights at the next diet they were released" (Strickler, *Abschiede*). Nevertheless Salzmann reported to Zwingli (April 1, 1526) that the Anabaptists had established a nucleus (*Brutnest*), encouraged and strengthened by those who had just previously escaped from the tower in Zürich (Manz, Grebel, Blaurock were imprisoned in Zürich on Nov. 18, 1525, but escaped March 21). Grebel fled to Maienfeld in the summer of 1526, where he had a sister living and where he died of the plague.

This agitation led to a stern order on May 20, 1526, forbidding all sects in the Bunden territory on penalty of death; following this edict conditions seem quieter. For when Zürich invited the confederations and Chur to participate in a joint session to agree on proceedings against the Anabaptists, Chur replied on Aug. 5, 1527, that at present they had no trouble with the Anabaptists, and knew of no one connected with this sect (Strickler). It is not possible to ascertain whether this statement agrees with fact or to what degree. Nevertheless Comander had to report to Zwingli as early as March 17, 1528, that they needed all their strength against the Catabaptists (as Zwingli called them), who had again assembled among them. "There are many citizens who secretly or openly tolerated them and the cripple Andreas (Castelberger) was also active in the city and confused many." The Anabaptists also received support, or at least no particular persecution, from the abbot Theodore Schlegel, who had become an opponent of the Reformation after having been a friend, and may incorrectly have given rise to the assumption that the Anabaptists were supported by the Catholic party. This supposed favor has no factual proof. Schlegel was beheaded in 1529 on a charge of endangering the laws of the state.

For the 1530's no facts are known about the Anabaptist movement. A second disputation occasioned by Comander and authorized by the council of Chur was announced for the Monday after Easter in 1531 at Ilanz, but it is not known that it took place. Martial incidents in Italy may have prevented it. The 12 articles set up by Comander and Gallizius, which were to be defended by the Scriptures of the Old and New Testaments but not by the doctrinal statements of the church fathers, reveal the advantage the Reformers managed to secure for themselves. The meaning of the articles is the same as those of 1526, only in article 11 communion is added according to Zwingli's conception "as a memorial and thanksgiving after proper arrangement," which signified a retrenchment compared with the previous one and a move farther away from the Anabaptists, since in 1526 no objections could be made against the frequent repetition of communion, which was considered right by the Anabaptists, and which had at first been permitted by the Reformed. The communion and the Christian ban, which are not indicated in the first articles, were to replace the Mass. The twelfth point of 1531 is pointed directly at the Anabaptists and specifies that "rebaptism is an error and a corruption against God's Word and doctrine." It was not included in the 18 articles of 1526.

The letters of the reformers only rarely refer to the Anabaptist movement in this period filled with unrest. As in the other cantons the movement seems to have been halted. After the death of the bishop of Chur in 1541, the congregations of the Gotteshausbund and Chur ruled that in the future the bishops to be chosen had to swear to six articles which determined the rights and limitations of the bishop's power and assured equality of rights among the various religious views. Through this imperial capitulation the progress of the Reformed Church was greatly forwarded (Mayer, Campell). When in 1544 the federal diet at Chur granted residence in Grisons to all who had been exiled from their homes for their faith, on condition that they adhere to the true doctrine and not undertake anything against the state, Grisons opened its doors to the influx and influence of various religious views.

Of importance to Chur was a movement in the 1560's led by Gantner, the second parson in Chur, which possibly arose from the influence of the more liberal Italian ideas, but even more from the recognition of the close connection of the church with the state and with the closely related suppression of Anabaptist views. The part played by personal antipathy toward Egli, the disciple of Bullinger, who had been made first pastor in Chur at Bullinger's instigation, in sharpening the friction can have no bearing on the factual side of the affair. The dispute was centered on the question of the right of the authorities to proceed against the Anabaptists and whether one could compel them to believe contrary to their conscience. The quarrel was brought about by the book dealer Frell (*q.v.*) in Chur, who had already previously been called to account by Fabricius (then deceased) for the sale of Anabaptist books. He is described as a quiet, religiously thoughtful man, seems to have belonged to a religiously purified Anabaptist congregation, and was nonetheless to be expelled in 1570. Gantner interceded for him against Egli's demands and based his opinion on the equality of rights of dissenters on Matt. 13, that Christ had permitted tares to grow, that the apostles punished no one except by the ban, and that this ban was necessary to the church; he also rejected the binding character of the Old Testament on disciples of the New, also the oath, demanding recognition of yea and nay; faith is to be determined freely as a pure gift of God and not by force; his position on baptism is not expressed. Bullinger became greatly agitated by this dispute, and called the article on the oath, the valuation of the Old Testament and the ban "seditious Anabaptist" articles and supported Egli through numerous letters in refuting the debated points. The recognition of one of these articles sufficed for Bullinger to imagine "Anabaptist terrors," among whom he also reckoned Servetus, although he was never an Anabaptist. (Bullinger claimed Servetus to be an Anabaptist, and proved it several times.) On Bullinger's recommendation Gantner was expelled, but found refuge in Schanfigg. This congregation had obtained permission to call him as their pastor, evidence of the sympathy his views had found. Egli's officiousness and several tactical errors may also have contributed to Gantner's popularity.

It is not easy to determine whether the views of Frell and Gantner are directly Anabaptist or rather those of an enlightened Christian spirit. Other influences, especially Schwenckfeldian, seem to have made themselves felt; yet their disparagement of infant baptism and the teachings of the older Zwingli in this connection, as well as their opposition to military service definitely indicate Anabaptist origin and agreement of opinion. But these few known representatives are not conclusive evidence of the existence of quiet, settled Anabaptist congregations. Neither is Bullinger's supposition that every deviating opinion carried the germ of

Anabaptist heresy sound. There is no information on the further development of the Anabaptist movement in Chur. The Anabaptist congregation at Ilanz in Grisons maintained itself, unknown to the government, until the late 1560's under the leadership of Leupold Scharnschlager (*q.v.*, d. 1563). The strife and disturbances which broke out in the last quarter of the 16th century and occupied the church of Chur were Arian in nature and were more concerned with the Trinity and the dual nature of Christ. C.B.

H. Campell, "Historia Rhaetica," in *Quellen zur Schweiz. Gesch.* VIII, IX; Bullingers Korrespondenz mit den Graubündnern," *op. cit.*, XXIII, XXIV, XXV; Auhorn, *Heilige Wiedergeburt der evang. Kirch in den gemeinen dreien Pundten der freien hohen Rhaetia;* Rosius de Porta, *Historia Reformationis* (Chur, 1770); J. C. Füsslin, *Beiträge zur Erläuterung der Kirchen-Ref.-Gesch. des Schweizerlandes* (Zürich, 1741-53, 5 vv.); J. v. Beck. "Georg Blaurock und die Anfänge des Anabaptismus in Graubünden und Tirol," in *Vorträge der Comenius-Gesellschaft* (Berlin, 1899) VII, Nos. 1 and 2; F. Jecklin, "Beitrag zur Churer Ref.-Gesch.," in *Anzeig. für schw. Gesch.,* 1895, No. 3; *idem,* "Beiträge zur bündnerischen Ref.-Gesch.," *op. cit.,* 1899, No. 5; *idem,* "Zur Gesch. der Wiedertäufer," *op. cit.,* 1900, No. 3; Kind, *Die Ref. in den Bistümern Chur und Como* (Chur, 1858); J. G. Mayer, *Gesch. der Bistümer Chur* (2 vv., Stans, 1914) (Catholic viewpoint); O. Vasella, "Von den Anfängen der Bündnerischen Täuferbewegung," in *Ztscht f. schw. Gesch.* XIX (1939) 165-84; J. ten Doornkaat Koolman, "Leupold Scharnschlager und die verborgene Täufergemeinde in Graubünden," *Zwingliana* IV (Zurich, 1926) 329-37; Simon Rageth, "Die Autobiographie des Täufers Georg Frell von Chur," *Zwingliana* VII, (1942)) 444-69 (Frell was, however, probably not an Anabaptist, but a Schwenckfelder); J. Loserth, "Ueber die Beziehungen der Mährischen Wiedertäufer zu ihren Glaubensgenossen in Augsburg und in Graubünden," in *Ztscht d. deutschen Vereines f. d. Gesch. Mährens und Schlesiens* XXVII (1925) 48 ff.; *ibid.,* XXX (1928) 9-11; ML I, 353-55.

Church, in the English Bible the translation of the Greek New Testament word *ecclesia,* which is translated in the Luther Bible as *Gemeinde* (not *Kirche*). *Ecclesia* is in turn the translation in the Greek Old Testament (Septuagint) of the Hebrew word *Qahal* meaning "people of God" or the Jewish religious congregation, and accordingly means in the New Testament the new "people of God." In secular Greek *ecclesia* was used to mean "duly summoned assembly of the people," derived from the root meaning of "calling out the citizens from their homes." The popular etymology from the Greek word, making the church a body "called out from the world," has no basis in fact, although the doctrine of separation from the world is a New Testament teaching. "Church" in the New Testament may mean either the entire body of Christian believers as the general church, or a local congregation as a particular church. In either case the N.T. concept of the church is that of a body of disciples of Christ, united by faith to Him as Saviour and Lord, regenerated by the Holy Spirit, sharing a fellowship of mutual love and brotherhood with one another, witnessing individually and corporately for Christ in the world. The church is Christ's church, founded by Him, responsible to Him. After several centuries during which it at first maintained more or less its original character and later developed into a hierarchical institute of salvation, the church entered a new phase in which it compromised with the world and became a state church. Thereby it lost most of its original N.T. character and became a great and powerful socio-religious institution. Having at first based its faith, life, and organization on the Bible, it gradually came to base itself largely on its own tradition and the teachings of the Church Fathers, thus making the Church in effect the primary authority, the Scriptures secondary. The Reformation of the 16th century broke off a large segment of the Roman Church in the West, in which the Bible was restored as the sole authority for faith and practice, and the N.T. Gospel largely revived, but the medieval concept of the mass state church retained. The Anabaptist movement broke completely with this mass state church concept, and restored the N.T. concept of the church of believers.

One of the most characteristic features of Anabaptism is its church concept. The church (*Gemeinde*), according to the Anabaptists, is a voluntary and exclusive fellowship of truly converted believers in Christ, committed to follow Him in full obedience as Lord; it is a brotherhood, not an institution. It is completely separated from the state, which is to have no power over the church; and the members of the church in turn do not hold office in the magistracy. There is to be complete freedom of conscience, no use of force or compulsion by state or church; faith must be free. In these principles the Anabaptists were pioneers and forerunners of modern religious liberty and the free church. This church concept was held in sharp distinction from the prevailing inclusive concept of both Catholic and Protestant state-church-ism, namely, that of the mass church (*Volkskirche*) coterminous with the population of a state, into which all citizens are in effect born and are to be formally incorporated by universal and compulsory infant baptism and in which they remain until death.

This church concept was held by Anabaptists universally, beginning in Switzerland in 1525, when the Swiss Brethren separated from the Zwinglian Reformation, then also among the Dutch-North German group in 1530 ff., and by the various Tyrol-Austria-Moravia groups, including the Hutterites. There were some minor variations however. The Hutterian Brethren, beginning in 1528, modified this concept by establishing a communal brotherhood in which all private property is abolished, and in which the church includes and orders the total life of its members. The opposite tendency, the spiritualistic one, in which the place of the church is minimized and the chief weight is placed upon the individual and his autonomy within the brotherhood, also appeared in the early days of the Anabaptist movement, but found no permanent place in it, except in the later Dutch Mennonites. The representatives of this spirit either died early (e.g., Hans Denk, *q.v.,* who died in 1527, expressing regret that he had baptized anyone), or withdrew (e.g., Christian Entfelder, *q.v.,* of South Germany, who was in the movement only one year, 1529-30, and Obbe Philips, *q.v.,* of Friesland, who withdrew in 1540), or never actually joined any local congregation. In fact, modern scholarship now carefully distinguishes the Spiritualists from the Anabaptists as a distinct movement, a distinction which Alfred Hegler (d. 1902) first clearly stated. Later the spiritualistic tendency exerted more influence among the Dutch Mennonites, although Menno Simons (q.v.) and Dirk Philips (q.v.), the outstanding early leaders, were strongly of the opposite position. According to S. Hoekstra (*Beginselen en leer der oude Doopsgezinden*) the Dutch Anabaptists' theology is centered in the New Testament *ecclesia*. Some modern Dutch Mennonite scholarship does not agree with this interpretation, although according to Cornelius Krahn, it is in error in doing so. Krahn says: "Kühler constructs the theory that the genuine Anabaptism is that of individual piety, which throughout Mennonite history struggles with the strictly supervised and disciplined *ecclesia*. According to Kühler, therefore, the martyrs, the Waterlanders, and other liberal factions represent genuine Anabaptism, while the strict and conservative followers of Menno Simons have deviated from it. Thus the liberal Doopsgezinde religious beliefs of the 19th century are conjectured into the sixteenth century Anabaptism" (C. Krahn, "Historiography of the Mennonites in the Netherlands," *MQR* XVIII, 1944, 195-224). Krahn says further in the same place, "The Dutch Mennonites have been [were] most consistent in establishing a church without spot or wrinkle. They practiced the principle of nonconformity to the world more rigidly than any other Mennonite church." The only full-length Anabaptist treatise on the church, that by Dirk Philips, *Van die Ghemeynte Godts, hoe die van den beginne gheweest is, waer die beḳent, ende van alle Secten onderscheyden wert, Een corte Beḳentenisse* (published separately, then as a part of his *Enchiridion* in 1564, reprinted in *B.R.N.* X, 1914, pp. 377-414), fully supports Krahn's views. F. Pijper, the *B.R.N.* editor of Philips' works, says of the *Enchiridion,* "No second work exists, wherein the teachings of the oldest Doopsgezinden are expounded with so great clarity and many-sidedness."

Since the Anabaptist conception of the church is ultimately derivative from its concept of Christianity as discipleship, i.e., complete obedience by the individual to Christ and the living of a holy life patterned after His example and teachings, an essential idea in it is that the church must be holy, composed exclusively of practicing disciples, and kept pure. It is a church of order, in which the body determines the pattern of life for its members, and therefore has authority over the individual's behavior. It controls admission of new members, requiring evidence of repentance, the new birth, and a holy life, and maintains the purity of the church through discipline (q.v.) using the ban (q.v.) or excommunication. Adopting the program of Christ for the church (Eph. 5:27) as their aim, the Anabaptists sincerely sought to achieve a church "not having spot or wrinkle or any such thing; but that it should be holy and without blemish." They cannot however rightly be charged on this account

with perfectionism, for their position expressly provided for discipline for sinning church members. It must also be remembered that they took their position in opposition to the Lutheran and Zwinglian churches, who did not at first attempt any discipline except for heresy. Actually the introduction of a certain amount of discipline in the Swiss Zwinglian churches, as well as in Hessen, Strasbourg, and elsewhere, can be attributed at least in part to the direct challenge of the Anabaptist critique which was outspoken, vigorous, and continuous. Repeatedly, when Anabaptists were questioned by state church leaders either in free discussions or in court trials, as to the reason for their separation from the official church, they cited the lack of discipline. The state church could not be the true church of Christ because it tolerated in its midst all kinds of sin. Menno Simons sets forth this point clearly in a classic statement (in *A Brief and Clear Confession,* 1544) where he says: "Secondly, cleanse your church also. Exclude, according to the Word of God, all adulterers and fornicators, drunkards, slanderers, swearers, those who lead a shameful and inordinate life, the proud, avaricious, idolatrous, disobedient unto God, whoremongers and the like, that you may become the holy, Christian church which is without spot or blemish, which is as a city built upon a rock. In case these are truly observed and found with you, and besides, a free Christian doctrine, the true ministration of the sacraments of Christ, not according to the opinion of men or of the learned but according to the true doctrine of Christ and his apostles—again, the fear and love of God, and an unblamable life, according to God's Word, then you will ever have us as your brethren; for it is such we seek. But if you remain as you are, then I say publicly, better to die than to enter into your doctrine, sacraments, life, and church, as was said above" (*Complete Works,* Elkhart, 1871, II, 345).

Pilgram Marpeck (d. 1556, q.v.), the outstanding leader in the South, takes an identical position. His great work, the *Verantwortung* of 1544 (edited by Loserth in 1929), deals at several places with the concept of the church, particularly on the need for the organization and operation of a visible church, willing to stand openly for the Gospel in spite of persecution, this in opposition to Schwenkfeld's (q.v.) doctrine of suspending the actual organization of the church until a more favorable time. "The Church of Christ, inwardly as spiritual, and outwardly as a body before the world, consists of men born of God; they bear in their cleansed flesh and blood the sonship of God in the unity of the Holy Spirit with cleansed minds and dispositions" (*Verantwortung,* 294).

This stress upon the holy and pure character of the church is so strong throughout the Anabaptist movement that it may well be taken as their decisive mark of the true church. Menno Simons, however, lists six marks of the true church: (1) unadulterated pure doctrine; (2) Scriptural use of baptism and the Lord's Supper; (3) obedience to the Word of God; (4) unfeigned brotherly love; (5) candid confession of God and Christ; (6) persecution and tribulation for the sake of the Word of the Lord (I, 301; II, 83). Littell (*Anabaptist View of the Church*, 1952) holds that the controlling idea in the Anabaptist concept of the church was the restoration of the primitive (apostolic) N.T. church. Certainly this was an important element in their doctrine; however, it is seldom directly and systematically set forth. Max Göbel (*Geschichte des christlichen Lebens . . .* , 1848) focuses the Anabaptist doctrine of the church somewhat differently as follows: "The essential and distinguishing characteristic of this church is its great emphasis upon the actual personal conversion and regeneration of every Christian."

The Anabaptist concept of the church, whatever may be its precise definition, was one of the most powerful ideas in the whole range of Anabaptist doctrine, and in subsequent centuries in Mennonite doctrine. Cornelius Krahn even speaks of the theology of Menno Simons as "ecclesiocentric." For Anabaptists-Mennonites the preaching of the Gospel was to issue finally in a redeemed community. Hence, in contrast to the Lutheran emphasis on the preaching of the Word and the right administration of the sacraments, the Anabaptist-Mennonite emphasis always fell on the establishment of the true church through the adherence of true believer-disciples (the term believers—*Gläubige*—is seldom used in the earlier Anabaptist-Mennonite literature), through its separation from the world, and through its right discipline. Admission to this church was theoretically possible only on the basis of true personal faith and conversion.

The history of the practice of the Anabaptist-Mennonite church concept reveals that although the ideal has been continuously asserted down to the present in confessions, catechisms, sermons, and doctrinal writings, actually it was often obscured or even lost in practice. The problem became most acute in the closed Mennonite settlements or colonies in East and West Prussia (*q.v.*) and Russia (*q.v.*) (but only slightly less so in all the congregations in Europe and America), where the brotherhood constituted a distinct community of families sharply separated, even culturally, from the surrounding society, and strongly under the influence of tradition. Increasingly church membership was based on family connection and catechetical instruction, and became conventional, with much of the original idea of conversion and vital personal experience lost. It became customary for all children to be baptized at a traditional age, 15-18 (in Russia more commonly 20-22, as among the Amish also). In Russia, Mennonites were commonly thought of as a "people" as well as a church, and a cultural Mennonitism developed. The extreme form of this is probably found today in the Old Colony Mennonites (*q.v.*) of Manitoba, Mexico, and Paraguay, but it also existed (and still exists?) among some better educated elements who consider themselves to be Mennonites though not baptized or in any real way vitally connected with the church. In other areas in North America, particularly in the Mennonite Church (MC), the age of baptism has recently become so low (numerous cases of ten years and below) that, in spite of the outward form of voluntarism and even profession of conversion, the actual practice tends toward child baptism. In Holland in recent years the contrary tendency has operated to raise the age of baptism (many baptized at 20 years and upward) and to emphasize exclusively adult commitment. In those circles in Germany (*q.v.*) and Switzerland (*q.v.*) as well as in America where pietistic influences and religious awakenings have been strong, the dangers of traditionalism have been largely or in part overcome by the development of more vital personal experience and vigorous teaching and practice. The rise of the Mennonite Brethren (*q.v.*) group in Russia (1860 ff.) can be viewed as an attempt to restore the lost original ideal of the church of converted believers, which in turn had a wholesome effect on the total Mennonite brotherhood in that country.

Another aspect of the Anabaptist-Mennonite church view is the concept of the church as a brotherhood. On the one hand this carries an anti-hierarchical emphasis, minimizing the clerical character of the church offices (elder, preacher, deacon) and maintaining a lay ministry over against a professional and salaried ministry, or at least emphasizing lay responsibility and lay participation. On the other hand it emphasizes responsibility for mutual aid in economic life. Here again the brotherhood idea has often been obscured. In some cases hierarchical development has taken place, in which the office of elder-bishop secured great prestige and power and in effect produced a rule by bishops; in other cases a professionalism has come in, with little to distinguish the Mennonite minister from the parson of the established church and with a reduction of lay participation in the life of the church. The mutual aid idea has at times also almost vanished under the rise of wealthy classes with a typical "business" or capitalistic attitude toward their less privileged fellow members. Note, for instance, the plight of the landless (*q.v.*) in the Russian Mennonite settlements in the 19th century.

In church polity, the original Anabaptist movement was strongly congregational, although the synodal idea was not altogether absent (Schleitheim conference of 1527, meetings of elders under Menno Simons' leadership such as Wismar, *q.v.*, in 1552, the Strasbourg conferences of 1555, 1557, etc.). Later the synodal idea became much stronger with the rise of the "conferences" in the 19th century in almost all countries (see **Conference**). In some Mennonite groups—e.g., the Mennonite Brethren and the Mennonite Church (MC)—the synodal idea has conquered; authoritative government by conferences is now the rule. The General Conference Mennonite Church (*q.v.*) has retained the congregational polity. In Holland, after a period of variation in the 17th and 18th centuries, when the equivalents of conferences (*Sociëteit*) had much power in the various factional groups, the congregational polity was fully restored, and the autonomy of the local church is now universally practiced.

A study of the fifteen significant Mennonite confessions of faith (*q.v.*) produced before 1800 (1527,

1538, 1545, 1577, 1578, 1591, 1600, 1610, 1627, 1678, 1702, 1749, 1773, 1792), including two unprinted Hessian confessions of 1538 and 1578, and including all the historic confessions still in use in America (see **Confessions**), reveals the following material on the church. Eleven of the fifteen have an article on the church—all except 1527, 1538, 1591, 1627; thirteen have an article on church offices—all but 1538 and 1578 (the two Hessian confessions); and all fifteen have an article on church discipline (ban or shunning). All these confessions teach substantially the same doctrine on all three points. Emil Händiges, who has carefully studied the teaching of the confessions on the doctrine of the church (Chapter 5, "Die Lehre von der Gemeinde im besonderen nach den Bekenntnisschriften dargestellt," in his book, *Die Lehre der Mennoniten in Geschichte und Gegenwart* 1921), says, "All the confessions of the 17th century (he cites 1600, 1626, 1630, 1632) adhere closely to Menno Simons' and Dirk Philips' [views on the church]. The 1702 confession by Gerhard Roosen (*q.v.*) contains nothing unique. The first later confession to have something characteristic is the 1766 Cornelis Ris, which is more tolerant. . . . The later confessions and catechisms furnish no new points of view. The specifically Mennonite position (in addition to the general Christian description of the church) is always [to hold] as marks of the true church; the emphasis on repentance, conversion, and the new birth as prerequisites for membership; the Scriptural practice of baptism and communion; the requirement of the ban; the rejection of military service and the oath, and occasionally also the requirement of feet-washing. Also the priesthood of all believers and the autonomy of the local congregation are held as an indispensable heritage of faith from the fathers."

As to the "offices in the church," the confessions regularly, from 1577 on, call for a threefold ministry, namely, bishop-elder (*q.v.*), preacher (*q.v.*), and deacon (*q.v.*). Only the Dordrecht (1632) Confession (*q.v.*) also speaks of the office of deaconess. The Schleitheim (1527) Confession (*q.v.*) has a strong article on the office of shepherd (*Hirt*) only; apparently the threefold ministry had not yet developed. The same is true of the Peter Riedemann's *Rechenschaft* (*q.v.*) of 1545, although here reference is made to assistant ministers and other officials of the Hutterite Bruderhofs. The Schleitheim definition of the function of the shepherd (later bishop-elder) is characteristic: "This office shall be to read, to admonish and teach, to warn, to discipline, to ban in the church, to lead out in prayer for the advancement of all the brethren and sisters, to lift up the bread when it is broken, and in all things to see to the care of the body of Christ, in order that it may be built up and developed."

The confessions are unanimous in the requirement of discipline by the use of the ban or excommunication (shunning or avoidance, *q.v.*, *Meidung*, was added in the Dutch-North German confessions) to keep the church pure of transgressors. They uniformly base this on the teaching of Jesus in Matthew 18:15-17. Conrad Grebel (*q.v.*) called for the ban on the basis of Matthew 18 as early as 1524 in his letter to Thomas Müntzer. The practice of strict discipline on this basis was generally maintained by all Mennonite groups (except Holland) until into the 19th century, and is still maintained by most North American groups. In Holland and Northwest Germany it has been completely abandoned, but in Russia, Southeast Germany, Switzerland, and France discipline has been maintained until the present, with some variation in degree.

In spite of considerable variation in application, Mennonites round the world still unitedly hold to the concept of a believers' church and the brotherhood idea, and still emphasize the central importance of the church in Christian faith and life. The range of concrete practice is still wide, from the Hutterite communal brotherhood, to the strongly disciplined, more authoritarian standard synodal groups (M.C., M.B., C.G.C., *Badischer Verband*) and on to the loosely associated denominational type (General Conference Mennonite, South German Conference) and the highly individualistic Dutch Mennonites, with many degrees of variation in between these major types. In some quarters the church concept itself has been obscured, and no clear line of theology or practice is maintained. The increasing tendency, particularly in the less conservative groups, has been to move from the brotherhood type to the denominational, whereas the more conservative groups as a whole succeed in perpetuating more faithfully the original brotherhood concept.

The original Anabaptist movement rejected the idea of an invisible church, which was the invention of Luther, holding that the Christian community in any particular place is as visible as the Christian man, and that its Christian character must be "in evidence." The intrusion of the concept of an invisible church into Mennonite thought is an evidence of outside influence, usually pietistic. Nor did the Anabaptists ever move in the direction of a crypto-ecclesia. For them an essential aspect of the church is its readiness to take an open stand for its Lord and suffer for Him. In fact the idea of a suffering church is a very prominent one in Anabaptist testimonies and literature. It is correlative with the idea of martyrdom (*q.v.*) and victory through suffering. As Christ, the head of the church, conquered through the cross, so shall His church. In later (19th, 20th century) developments, after persecution was past, this courageous faith and devotion was often replaced by an all too quick compromise with the world and an easy yielding to the demands of the state, particularly in such matters as military service. H.S.B.

F. H. Littell, *The Anabaptist View of the Church* (N.Y., 1952); F. Heyer, *Der Kirchenbegriff der Schwärmer* (Leipzig, 1939); C. Krahn, *Menno Simons* (Karlsruhe, 1936), especially "Mennos Gemeindebegriff im Rahmen seiner Theologie," pp. 103-76; E. Händiges, *Die Lehre der Mennoniten in Geschichte und Gegenwart nach den Quellen dargestellt* (Ludwigshafen, 1921); C. Burrage, *The Church Covenant Idea* (Philadelphia, 1904); S. Hoekstra, *Beginselen en leer der oude Doopsgezinden* (Amsterdam, 1863); Dirk Philips, *Van die Ghemeynte Godts* (n.p., n.d., after 1559, reprinted in *Enchiridion*, n.p., 1564); F. W. Dillistone, *The Structure of the Divine Society* (Philadelphia, 1951);

K. L. Schmidt, *The Church* (*Bible Key Words II*) (London, 1950); J. Wach, *Church, Denomination and Sect* (Evanston, Ill., 1946); *The Nature of the Church, Papers Presented to the Theological Commission Appointed by The Continuation Committee of the World Conference on Faith and Order* (London, 1952; the papers in this last volume report the views of the nature of the church held by each of the leading Catholic and Protestant churches); A. Keller, *Church and State on the European Continent* (London, 1936); W. Pauck, "The Idea of the Church in Christian History," *Church History* XXI (1952) 191-214; N. van der Zijpp, "The Conception of Our Fathers Regarding the Church," *MQR* XXVII (1953) 91-99; H. W. Meihuizen, "Spiritualistic Tendencies and Movements Among the Dutch Mennonites of the 16th and 17th Centuries," *MQR* XXVII (1953) 259-304; E. Heimann, "The Hutterite Doctrines of the Church and Common Life," *MQR* XXVI (1952) 22-47, 142-60; E. Waltner, "The Anabaptist Conception of the Church," *MQR* XXV (1951) 5-16; R. Kreider, "The Anabaptist Conception of the Church in the Russian Mennonite Environment 1789-1870," *MQR* XXV (1951) 34-46; F. H. Littell, "The Anabaptist Doctrine of the Restitution of the True Church," *MQR* XXIV (1950) 12-24; H. S. Bender, "The Mennonite Conception of the Church and Its Relation to Community Building," *MQR* XIX (1945) 179-214; J. C. Wenger, "The Theology of Pilgram Marpeck," *MQR* XII (1938) 205-56, particularly "6. Ecclesiology," pp. 241-53. Daniel Kauffman, "The Doctrine of the Church," which is Part VI, pp. 311-439, of *Doctrines of the Bible* (Scottdale, 1929), contains besides a chapter on "The Christian Church," pp. 319-32, one on "The Ministry" by D. H. Bender, pp. 333-62, and one by the same author on "The Congregation," pp. 363-77, followed by a discussion of "The Christian Ordinances" by Daniel Kauffman, pp. 378-439. This book represents the standard position of the Mennonite Church (MC), and is the only extensive modern Mennonite publication in this field.

Church and Mission News, a monthly 4-page organ of the Mennonite (MC) Mission Board of Ontario, first issued as a bimonthly in January 1940 with 4 pages, changed to a monthly in January 1951. It is the successor to *Mission News Bulletin,* issued as a single-page bimonthly beginning in January 1936.

Church and Sunday School Hymnal was compiled by committees appointed by the Ohio and Virginia conferences (MC). The editorial work was done by J. D. Brunk. The book was published in octavo, with shaped notes, also in word edition, by J. S. Shoemaker, Freeport, Ill., in 1902. It was turned over to the Mennonite Publishing House, Scottdale, Pa., in 1908. It contained 412 numbers, with appendix of 50 German hymns in words only. In 1911 a supplement of 120 numbers was added. Twenty-five years after the publication of the official *Church Hymnal* in 1927, it is still used in many churches. P.E.

Church of God in Christ, Mennonite, is the result of a spiritual awakening through the instrumentality of John Holdeman in 1859. John Holdeman was born Jan. 31, 1832, near New Pittsburg, Wayne Co., Ohio. His parents, Amos and Nancy (Yoder) Holdeman, were members of the Mennonite Church (MC), in which faith John Holdeman was brought up. He was a thoughtful and impressionable youth, and at the age of twelve years he had a definite religious experience of the new birth and forgiveness of sins. He reconsecrated his life at the age of twenty-one and was at that time baptized and received into the Mennonite Church (MC) by Bishop Abraham Rohrer in October 1853. For several years he was connected with the above-named church and in consequence of being a member of this church, he was brought to perceive more fully and clearly the decay and the errors into which he believed the church had drifted, which wrought within him much prayerful concern and travail of soul. His understanding of the condition of the church was, he believed, revealed to him by the Lord. He stressed the absolute necessity of the new birth and being baptized with the Holy Ghost, as well as a return to the faith of the fathers in practicing a more spiritual child training, disciplining unfaithful members, Scriptural avoidance of apostates, avoiding of worldly minded churches, associations, etc.

Being of a zealous mind and of energetic convictions, though endeavoring to follow peace with all men, he nevertheless, as he says, soon discovered opposition on the part of those who were not willing to yield to his pleas for a return to the primitive Gospel way of life and doctrine. This was the primary and fundamental cause of the cleavage which, six years after his admission into the Mennonite Church, resulted in his separation from that brotherhood, after all efforts to work in fellowship on the old ground and foundation failed, which he had sought with much concern, prayer, supplication, and pleadings with the elders of the church.

In 1859 John Holdeman with a number of others began to hold separate meetings. Not long after, others joined with John Holdeman laboring and preaching as they believed in the old-time Gospel. He soon established a separate organization which was named "The Church of God in Christ, Mennonite." The newly organized church struggled with and weathered many difficult trials, and for a time progressed slowly until other brethren united in the labors with him so that the faith was carried to different states and Canada, where congregations were formed. The first brethren to be ordained into the ministry were Frank Seidner and Mark Seiler, both of Ohio, men of spiritual gifts and power. Soon others followed, including Peter Toews and Wilhelm Giesbrecht of Manitoba, Tobias A. Unruh of Kansas, F. C. Fricke of Michigan, and H. J. Mininger of Pennsylvania.

Key to Map of Church of God in Christ Mennonite Congregations

1. Glenn, Cal.; 2. Livingston, Cal.; 3. Winton, Cal.; 4. Pleasant Valley, Crowley, Col.; 5. Walnut Hill, Fla.; 6. Georgia, Stapleton, Ga.; 7. Mountain View, Bonners Ferry, Idaho; 8. Alexanderfeld, Hillsboro, Kan.; 9. Bethel, Greensburg, Kan.; 10. Eden, Burns, Kans.; 11. Cimarron, Kan.; 12. Emmanuel, Fredonia, Kan.; 13. Grace Mennonite, Halstead, Kan.; 14. Logan, Durham, Kan.; 15. Lone Tree, Galva, Kan.; 16. Meridian, Hesston, Kan.; 17. Montezuma, Kan.; 18. Salem, Copeland, Kan.; 19. Scott Mennonite, Scott City, Kan.; 20. Wallace, Kan.; 21. Zion, Inman, Kan.; 22. Highland, De Ridder, La.; 23. Newark, Ithaca, Mich.; 24. Harrison, Mich.; 25. Emmanuel, Rich Hill, Mo.; 26. Grafton, N.D.; 27. North Unity, Wales, N.D.; 28. Pettisville, Wauseon, Ohio; 29. Fairview, Okla.; 30. Plainview, Chickasha, Okla.; 31. Pleasant View, Goltry, Okla.; 32. Cloverdale, Creswell, Oreg.; 33. Abbotsford, Mt. Lehman, B.C.; 34. Linden, Swalwell, Alberta; 35. Oras, Alberta; 36. Rosedale, Crooked Creek, Alberta; 37. Greenland, St. Anne, Man.; 38. Kleefeld, Man.; 39. Rosenort, Man.; 40. Steinbach, Man.; 41. Whitemouth, Man.; 42. Bethel, Cuauhtemoc, Chih., Mex.; 43. La Junta, Chih., Mex.; 44. Spanish American Mission, Tucumcari, N.M.; 45. Sunchild Indian Mission, Rocky Mt. House, Alberta.

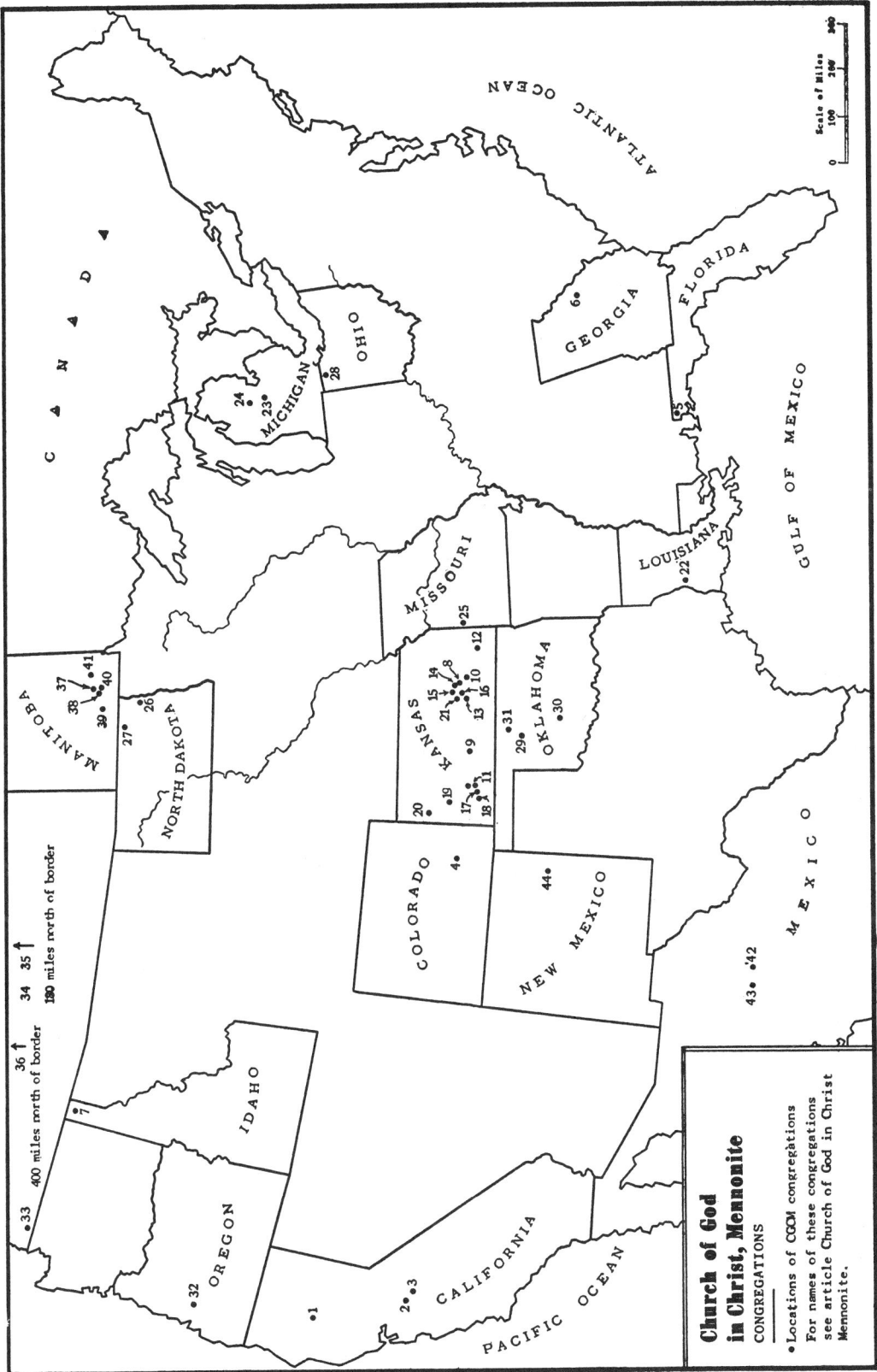

Church of God
in Christ, Mennonite
CONGREGATIONS

• Locations of COM congregations

For names of these congregations
see article Church of God in Christ
Mennonite.

When the immigration of Mennonites from Russia took place in 1874 and later, quite a few of their number joined the Church of God in Christ, Mennonite, both in Kansas and in Canada. Many of the Mennonites of the Kleine Gemeinde, under the leadership of Elder Peter Toews and Wilhelm Giesbrecht, were united to the faith. And in Kansas, Tobias A. Unruh (a former minister from the General Conference Church) and Benjamin Schmidt were active in bringing many into the church; also David Holdeman of Hesston, Kan., formerly of Indiana, did much in promoting the new congregations. The church began to increase and to spread to different states in the United States and to different provinces in Canada, until in 1949 there were 41 congregations in the United States and Canada, with a baptized membership of about 4,500, including 88 ministers and 62 deacons. The church has mission stations in Mexico and New Mexico with three ordained Spanish ministers, and an Indian mission station in Canada.

Elder John Holdeman believed in a true lineage of the church of God, and stressed that to claim this lineage the church must believe and practice the same confession of faith through the centuries from the time of the apostles to the end of the world. He taught that the church was established on the day of Pentecost and continued through the centuries until this present time, having like faith and practice, emphasizing that ". . . upon this rock [Christ] I will build my church; and the gates of hell shall not prevail against it" (Matt. 16:18). John Holdeman believed and taught and the church believes and teaches likewise that the Holy Scripture is the inspired Word of God and the infallible guide whereby all doctrine and teaching must be governed. It accepts the Eighteen Articles of Faith (*Dordrecht Confession*) as drawn up at a peace convention at Dordrecht, Holland, April 21, 1632, as a true evangelical confession. These articles are taught and practiced throughout all the churches. This denomination also accepts doctrines not so clearly set forth in the Eighteen Articles, such as nonconformity to the world in dress, bodily adornment, worldly sports and amusements.

The church holds to a twofold ministry, viz., elders or bishops (ministers), and deacons. While elders may differ in gifts and hence in responsibility, officially they are all equal. Baptism is administered by pouring to those that have been born again, having received remission of sins through the atoning blood of Christ, and are willing to conform their life to the faith and practice of the church. The church accepts as obligatory the great commission, "Go ye therefore, and teach all nations . . . ," in obedience to our Lord and Master as well as the constraint of the love of Christ and the responsibility toward our fellow men. It believes that the letter and the spirit of the Gospel are emphatically against strife, contention, and carnal warfare and that, therefore, no believer should have any part in carnal strife, whether between individuals, in lawsuits, or in conflicts between nations; that church and state, although both ordained of God, are separate institutions and serve different purposes; that believers should have no part in oath-bound secret organizations and that membership in such disqualifies them for church membership; and that Christian people should be temperate in all things lawful and abstain from the use of intoxicants, tobacco, and kindred carnal habits.

The nonmillennial or amillennial view of Christ's reign and kingdom on earth is accepted as Scriptural. The church teaches that the present dispensation is the last and only time in which salvation is offered, and that at the second advent Christ will receive the redeemed and judge the world in righteousness; and that Christians should "follow peace with all men, and holiness, without which no man shall see the Lord" (Heb. 12:14). The governing body of the church is the General Conference, whose decisions are binding upon all members of the church, and which convenes on the decision of a two-thirds affirmative vote of all ministers, deacons, and delegates.

The church has an active mission board, a publication board, and other committees deemed appropriate to the furtherance of its activities. It operates Mercy Hospital at Moundridge, Kan.; two homes for the aged, Bethel Home at Montezuma, Kan., and Linden Home at Linden, Alta.; and the Bethel Hospital at Cuauhtemoc, Chih., Campo 45, Mexico. Its periodicals are *Messenger of Truth,* Goltry, Okla., and *Botschafter der Wahrheit,* Steinbach, Man.

In 1953 the church had the following number of congregations: California, 3; Colorado, 1; Florida, 1; Idaho, 1; Kansas, 14; Louisiana, 1; Michigan, 2; Missouri, 1; North Dakota, 2; Ohio, 1; Oklahoma, 3; Oregon, 1; British Columbia, 1; Alberta, 3; Manitoba, 5; Georgia, 1; and Mexico, 2. One mission station in New Mexico and one in Alberta had a membership of 20. The total membership is 5,308, of whom 1,334 are in Canada.   P.G.H.

John Holdeman, *The Old Ground and Foundation* (Lancaster, 1863); idem, *A History of the Church of God* (Lancaster, 1876); John Penner, *A Concise History of the Church of God* (Hillsboro, 1951?); *Year Book of the Church of God in Christ, Mennonite,* 1944- ; *Conference Reports From 1896-1950, Church of God in Christ, Mennonite* (Cumulative); *The Confession of Faith and Minister's Manual of the Church of God in Christ, Mennonite* (2nd ed. 1952?).

Church of God in Christ, Mennonite, Mission Board, Inc., Moundridge, Kan., is the official central organization of the conference, empowered to receive and make use of monies, lands, wills, etc., for mission purposes. Through it the general mission program and activities of the church are carried out. The Mission Board is the outgrowth of the Western District Mission Board, of which A. L. Yost of Moundridge was the first chairman. Mission activities were carried on before its organization in 1921. In 1933 the Mission Board was formed. It is composed of nine members, five of whom are executive. It has a chairman, a secretary, a treasurer, and six other members. All districts in the United States and in Canada are represented. The terms of three members expire at each conference, with conference usually convening at intervals of from three to four years. The board is responsible to the general conference of the church. Its annual current budget in 1950 was approximately $15,000. The outstanding achievements of the board have been, first, to start mission work in Mexico, and second, the successful operation of a hospital and school program in Mexico.   P.G.H.

Church of the Brethren: see **Brethren, The Church of the.**

Church Papers: see **Periodicals.**

Church Record Books (congregational records), the the book in which a record is kept of church functions for individual members, as baptisms, marriages, funerals, etc. The Israelites of old kept similar books in their birth books and genealogies. Not in order to ascertain the fighting strength or to determine taxes were the names of the members entered, but as citizens of a kingdom of God which was expanding farther and farther. That has been the actual purpose of the church book down to the present.

The first beginnings of such a record are found in Zürich, where Pastor Johannes Brennwald introduced a list of baptized members as early as 1525 (Egli, *Die Züricher Wiedertäufer,* 42). On May 24, 1526 (Egli, 58), on Zwingli's advice the Zürich council decided to introduce church records on the ground that many were not having their children baptized, or said they had been baptized when that was not the case. Thus the Swiss Brethren were the cause of the first introduction of the use of church records. Later on marriage and burial lists were added to the Reformed baptismal lists. Later still came the confirmation registers. Records concerning church discipline and other proceedings in the church were called "family books"; in them an exact record was kept according to families.

Later the church records began to have significance as a source of the study of ethnology and—first in England—sociology. In other countries, as in Prussia, they had to serve the wishes and requirements of civil government; they were used for purposes of court proceedings, army musters, and taxes. This practice ended when the French Revolution completely separated the government records from the church records, restoring the latter to their legitimate function.

The Anabaptists in Switzerland, Germany, and Austria kept no church records so far as is known throughout the 16th century and later. The Swiss Mennonites did not introduce them until modern times.

Among the Dutch, Prussian, and Russian Mennonites there seems never to have been objection to keeping a record of church members. The oldest "church record" in the north seems to be the one by Leenaert Bouwens (*q.v.*), who baptized more than 10,000 individuals and kept a record from 1551 to 1582. Other elders during the 16th and 17th centuries continued this tradition (see K. Vos, "De copia der oudsten en dooplijsten van de Harde Vriezen uit de 16 en 17 eeuw," *Nederlandsch Archief voor Kerkgeschiedenis* XI, 4, 1914). The *Inventaris der Archiefstukken* (Vol. II) of the Mennonite Church of Amsterdam lists (pp. 1 ff.) church records of the various congregations starting with the year 1612. The archives of the Mennonite Church of Amsterdam have the largest collection of church records. Some of the Haarlem records date back to 1606.

The Amsterdam congregations kept a *Doopboeck,* in which the persons who had been baptized were enrolled, a *Trou-boeck* for the registering of the marriages performed in the church, a *Banboeck,* or book of the "gebreckleke lidmaten," in which the names of those who were disciplined were entered. *Kinderboeken,* or books in which the names of the children of the members were enrolled, and which are found for example in Amsterdam and Rotterdam, date from about 1715. By about 1660 all congregations maintained a *Lidmatenboeck* (book of members). During the Napoleonic regime (1810-14) most Dutch Mennonite congregations were obliged to hand over their church books, both *Doop-* and *Kinderboeken,* to the state officers, because a "list of all citizens, children included" (register) was to be compiled. Not always were the old books returned.

In South Germany, in some areas where Mennonites settled after the Thirty Years' War, particularly in the Palatinate and Hesse, records of Mennonite births, deaths, and marriages were included in the parish church books of the state church. When the German Mennonite congregations began to introduce church books of their own is not known, but probably not before the 19th century. The 18th century immigrants to Pennsylvania, and the 19th century Amish immigrants from Alsace and Bavaria as well as the Swiss immigrants did not establish church books in this country, and the groups descending from these immigrants to this day do not have church books in the usual European sense. In fact, the more conservative groups object to church books as being an evidence of pride. The only exceptions to the above are two alms books containing the deacon's annual report of the alms funds together with the signatures of all the ministers, of the Skippack, Pa. (MC), congregation (1738-) and the Franconia, Pa. (MC), congregation (1767-). However, many bishops kept their own private records of baptisms, marriages, ordinations, and funerals conducted by themselves.

Among European Mennonites, congregations which have long had a trained and salaried minister have usually kept church books. Congregations with a lay minister have not so often had them. However, there are notable exceptions. The congregation at Montbéliard has maintained a church book since about 1750. In West Prussia the church books were established in most congregations about 1772, by order of the new (Prussian) government, and were maintained up to the destruction of the congregations in 1945. For instance, the Heubuden congregation maintained a *Taufregister* (baptismal register) 1770-1944, and a *Geburts-, Heirats- und Sterberegister* (register of births, marriages, and deaths) 1772-1944. The *Taufregister* of the Grosse Werder church (including Rosenort, Tiegenhagen, Ladekopp, and Fürstenwerder, 1782-1840, with an appendix on the votes on minister and elder) was deposited with the Danzig State Archives. An official membership roll with residence and dates of birth, baptism, marriage, and death was maintained by the Heubuden congregation from 1888 on. Some of the West Prussian church books have been saved, either in original or copies. For instance, Gustav Reimer (now Montevideo, Uruguay) has copies of the 1770-1944 and 1771-1944 books mentioned above, as well as the original of the 1888-1944 membership register. A considerable number of the West Prussian church books are now in the Mennonite research center (*Forschungsstelle*) in Göttingen.

The first entry in the church record of the Danzig Mennonite church goes back to the year 1667 and was made by Elder Peter Classen in the Dutch language. This copy is now in the custody of the Bethel College Historical Library. Elder Johann Andreas brought the church records of the Elbing-Ellerwald Mennonite Church to America during the 1870's. Particularly the annotated entries of Elder Gerhard Wiebe were of significance. C. H. Wedel summarized the contents in *Monatsblätter aus Bethel College* starting in January 1904, in a number of issues. Later a volume of this church record was returned to Elbing and is now in the Göttingen center. Some of the volumes of the church record have been preserved in this country.

The Alexanderwohl Mennonite Church of Russia, which moved to Kansas as an entity in 1874, brought its church record along which was started in Prussia. The first entry, the birth of a member, dates back to 1640. This is the oldest church record of any Mennonite congregation in America.

The Mennonites in Galicia were compelled by the government to keep a church book, called *"Matrikel,"* which had legal force and significance.

When the Germans occupied the Ukraine in 1941-43 they found church records in most of the Mennonite congregations of Chortitza, and used them extensively for study purposes. Most of them were lost during the final stages of the war.

In America most of the General Conference Mennonite congregations have kept church records from the time of the founding of the congregations, particularly those that immigrated from Germany and Russia in the 19th century. The Historical Committee of the Conference is now launching a project to microfilm church records which are in danger of gradual deterioration or sudden destruction. The Bethel College Historical Library has quite a number of original church records of G.C. congregations, including some brought along from Europe. Most M.C. congregations now have membership books.   NEFF, C.K.

J. C. Wenger, "Almsbook of the Skippack Mennonite Church 1738-1926," *MQR* X (1926) 138-48; *idem*, "Alms Book of the Franconia Mennonite Church, 1767-1926," *MQR* X (1936) 161-72; M. Gingerich, "The Alexanderwohl Schnurbuch," *Menn. Life* I (January 1946) 45.

Church Seals were in use among the Mennonite congregations in Prussia, Poland, and Russia, from where this practice was transplanted to America. The best sources for the study of church seals are the church letters brought along by Mennonite immigrants of 1874. Some congregations, such as the Bethel Mennonite Church and Hoffnungsau Mennonite Church, Inman, Kan., and the Bruderthal Mennonite Church, Hillsboro, Kan., have preserved the church letters (*q.v.*) of the charter members brought along from various congregations in Russia, Poland, and Prussia, all of which are signed by the elders who affixed the seals of the congregation to them. The seal, usually round or oval, has the name of the congregation around a symbol or picture in the center. Two commonly used themes in the picture are John the Baptist baptizing Jesus in the Jordan (Margenau, Pordenau, Lichtenau, Petershagen, Berdyansk, etc.), and the open Bible (Rudnerweide, Obernessau, Gnadenfeld, Karassan, Alexanderwohl, etc.). Sometimes the cross, the cup, an anchor, or other symbols are added to the Bible. Some congregations used a wax seal.

Most of the Mennonite congregations of the prairie states and provinces of direct European origin, as well as those of Mexico and Paraguay, still have a church seal which is used to impress the official documents of the church. The seal usually bears the name of the church and possibly a Scripture passage and is used on baptismal certificates, church letters, and other statements or correspondence.

In the Netherlands only the church of Aardenburg possesses a seal. It shows a lamb on a pasture and is surrounded by the legend: *De Kerck het Lam tot Aerdenburgh.*   C.K.

Church Unity Committee: see **Committee on Church Unity.**

Church World Service, with its executive office in New York, is an interdenominational organization concerned particularly with the placing of refugees and displaced persons and with overseas relief. In 1952 the organization assumed control of CROP (*q.v.*), which it had been supporting from its beginning several years earlier. The MCC co-operated with Church World Service in China relief, in the Philippines where two workers were seconded to that organization, in Okinawa, and in placing over 600 non-Mennonite European refugees in the United States under Mennonite sponsors.   M.G.

Churchtown Mennonite Church (MC) in Cumberland Co., Pa., originated in 1835, when Preacher John Erb gave land for a meetinghouse three miles east of Carlisle. In 1885 another meetinghouse was built in Churchtown. The membership was low for some years, but now as a mission station the work has been revived. The Sunday-school attendance is 66 (average). Under the leadership of William M. Strong, bishop, Mervin J. Baer, minister, the membership (1954) is 23.

Churchtown Mennonite Church (MC) at Narvon, Lancaster Co., Pa., is a member of the Lancaster Conference. The Mennonites of this area first rode or walked the four to six miles to the Weaverland Church. When Christian Shirk was ordained at the Weaverland Church in 1837, the brethren obtained the use of a log schoolhouse near his home for a meetinghouse and later a larger one. In 1879 an acre along Route 23, one mile east of Churchtown, was purchased and a substantial frame house was built on it, which was again enlarged and re-modeled in 1947. Benjamin Weaver, later bishop, opened a Sunday school here in 1894. The 1953 membership of the church was 112. J. Paul Graybill is bishop and the Weaverland circuit ministers have charge of the congregation. I. B. Good especially built up this congregation.   I.D.L.

Churchtown Old Order Mennonite meetinghouse is located at the east end of Churchtown, Lancaster Co., Pa. The building was constructed in 1910. The congregation belongs to the Groffdale Conference, under Bishops Joseph O. Wenger and A. Z. Sensenig. Preachers serving the congregation are Samuel S. Horning and Isaac W. Zimmerman. E.M.S.

Cijnken van Geldere: see Sijntgen van Gelder.

Cillich (Killig), **Andreas,** a Hutterite who in 1725 wrote a hymn, "Ein neues trauriges Lied von der Verfolgung so sich zu Grossschitzen hat begeben." It has 80 stanzas and begins with the words, "Mein geist lasst mich nicht ruen gewisslich zu aller stundt." Printed in *Die Lieder der Hutterischen Brüder* (Scottdale, 1914) 879-85. (Wolkan, *Lieder,* 243; *ML* II, 487.)   NEFF.

Cimarron Church of God in Christ Mennonite Church is located 1¼ miles south of Cimarron, Gray Co., Kan. It was organized in 1914. The first meetings were held in homes and later in a schoolhouse, with Henry A. Koehn as pastor. Later Reuben J. Koehn and Ben T. Koehn were ordained to the ministry and Jake Wadel and Henry Redger as deacons. The three former brethren moved to other congregations and Sam L. Fricke moved in and served as pastor until his death in 1947, after which H. J. Mininger served for a while. It had a Sunday-school enrollment of 68 and a membership of 72 in 1953. The congregation is active in supporting missions, MCC, and relief. It has an active sewing circle.   A.U.

City Missions. City missions are a form of home mission work or church extension, practiced in one form or another by most Protestant and Catholic churches. In European countries, where because of the state church system the entire population is nominally Christian, city missions are an organized attempt to reach and reclaim for the church the large numbers of city people who have become alienated from the church and Christianity because of the peculiar conditions of life in the cities, in particular modern industrialization, or who, having left the home villages and small towns, have not established connections with the church in their new city homes. In England the free or nonconformist churches have also established city missions among the Christian population nominally belonging to the state church. The same is true of the work of the free churches on the European continent, where such denominations as Methodist, Baptist, and Brethren have established themselves largely through city mission work. In the United States and Canada where, except in Catholic Quebec, there have been no state churches since early times, city missions have been largely church extension work (the new congregation often being called a "mission" so long as it is not self-supporting), or have taken the form of "rescue" missions among the down-and-out. Another form consists in institutional social service work in slum and underprivileged areas, often called "institutional churches."

Europe. Apparently the first city mission was the one organized in Glasgow in 1826. The London City Mission was next organized in 1835 with the help of Lord Shaftesbury. Both of these missions were in effect united activities of already existing Christian action societies. In Germany J. H. Wichern, influenced by the London City Mission, began similar work in 1848 by organizing the "Hamburg Society for Inner Mission." The German "Inner Mission" work has grown largely since that time. By 1900, 70 other German cities had followed the example of Hamburg (and Berlin). The YMCA, organized in England in 1844, originally contributed much to city mission work. The Salvation Army, organized by William Booth in London in 1865 (1878), has been essentially a city mission organization.

United States. The New York City Mission and Tract Society, a nondenominational group, the oldest organization for city mission work in North America, was organized first as a band of volunteer workers to encourage nonchurch people to attend the city's churches, then (by 1833) began to employ paid workers, and finally (1867) began to build churches. Later it organized institutional churches. Its example was followed in many other cities of the United States and Canada. However, most denominations soon organized "home mission" work in the cities, sometimes under this name, sometimes as "city missions" or as "church extension." The enormous flood of foreign immigration in the 19th century led to much city mission work among immigrant groups.

Mennonites. City mission work has been unknown among Mennonites anywhere except in the United States and Canada. Apart from the original Germantown village church in 1683, the first truly city churches in America were established in Philadelphia (GCM) in 1865, in Elkhart, Ind. (MC), in 1871 and Lancaster, Pa. (MC), in 1876; the city of Kitchener (Berlin) grew up around the First Mennonite Church (MC, 1813) of that city. Apart from the late rise of such city churches, North American Mennonitism has been exclusively rural and is still largely so. This rural character combined with the late rise of the missionary and philanthropic interest among the Mennonites accounts for the complete lack of interest and work in city missions until the end of the 19th century.

The first North American Mennonite city missions were established by the Mennonite Church (MC): Chicago 1893, Lancaster 1896, Philadelphia 1899, Canton (Ohio) 1903, Fort Wayne (Ind.) 1905. This type of work in the denomination grew steadily and in almost all major sections of this group one or more city missions were established. After World War II a new burst of activity followed, especially in the East. In 1953 the yearbook of this group listed 256 home missions with a membership of 5,597, most of which were in cities or towns. The Mennonite Brethren in Christ group was the next to start city mission work, with South Bend, Ind., in 1895, Dayton, Ohio, in 1896, Grand Rapids, Mich., in 1897. In the early decades of the 20th century this small denomination was at one time operating over 100 city missions. Gradually almost all of these became established congregations, and in later times the church extension type of work has largely superseded the city mission type. The Central Conference Church started the first of its city missions in 1909 in Chicago with later a second in Chicago, and one in Peoria. The G.C.M. Church started its first city mission in 1901 in Los Angeles, followed by one in Chicago in 1914. The church extension emphasis has always dominated over the city mission interest and consequently few city missions were ever operated at one time. In the Mennonite Brethren Church each district conference operates at least one city mission, and the M.B. General Conference agency operates two city missions—at Minneapolis and Winnipeg. Some of the smaller groups (KMB, EMC) have established one or more city missions. At one time there were nine Mennonite city missions in Chicago operated by six different conferences.

Administratively the Mennonite city missions in North America have been either under home mission or city mission boards or societies, or directly under conference mission committees or district conference administration. Only in the Mennonite Church (MC) and (recently) the General Conference Mennonite Church have foreign missions and home (city) missions been combined under one board. In character many of the city missions have served the combined purpose of ministering to rural Mennonites moving to the city, and of evangelizing non-Christians and non-Mennonites. Except in the case of the Mennonite Brethren in Christ, the city mission efforts have not been successful in establishing strong "indigenous" city congregations composed of non-Mennonite converts. The rural mindset, frequent lack of trained workers, inability to adapt to new conditions, and similar facts have been handicaps.   H.S.B.

Ed. G. Kaufman, *The Development of the Missionary and Philanthropic Interest Among the Mennonites of North America* (Berne, 1931); A. M. Erb, *Our Home Missions* (Scottdale, 1920); idem, *Studies in Mennonite City Missions* (Scottdale, 1937); J. D. Mininger, *Exalting Christ in the City, or the Why, What, and How of City Missions* (Scottdale, 1937); Emma Oyer, *What Hath God Wrought in a Half Century at the Mennonite Home Mission* [Chicago] (Elkhart, 1949); A. M. Eash, *After Ten Years* [26th Street Mennonite Mission in Chicago 1906-16] (Chicago, 1916); J. A. Huffman, *History of the Mennonite Brethren in Christ Church*, Chap. XV, "City Missions," 202-13 (New Carlisle, 1929); *The Annual Report of the Mennonite Board of Missions and Charities* (1905-) regularly contains descriptive and statistical summaries of the city mission work of the Mennonite Church (MC). The printed reports of other conference mission boards, as well as certain conference yearbooks, also contain some information and statistical data.

City Missions Committee of the Mennonite Brethren Conference of North America. Among those participating in the organization of this committee in 1907 were J. J. Kliewer of Henderson, Neb., and N. N. Hiebert and J. C. Dick of Mountain Lake, Minn. The work of the committee consists of directing the city missions in Minneapolis, Minn., and Winnipeg, Man. Its annual budget in 1950 was $16,000. It submits annual reports to the general conference of the church. Since most of the city missions founded in the past 25 years have remained under the district conferences, the field of work of the City Missions Committee has remained limited. Each of the district conferences operates one or more city missions directly.   P.C.H.

City Terrace Mission Chapel (MB), 3806 Whiteside St., Los Angeles 33, Cal., was begun in 1926 by the A. W. Friesens, who are still in charge of the work (1949). The mission is located in East Los Angeles, a district populated largely by Jews and Catholics. As a result of this mission work a number have been baptized. The membership numbered 47 in 1949. In 1940 the Pacific District Conference of the Mennonite Brethren Church officially accepted the mission and in 1942 the present buildings were erected and dedicated.   P.F.W.

Civilian Public Service, a plan of service provided under the United States Selective Service and Training Act of 1940 for conscientious objectors who were unwilling to perform any kind of military service whatsoever. In the six and one-half years that men were drafted under this law, nearly 12,000 young men were assigned to Civilian Public Service camps to perform "work of national importance." Of these, 4,665 or 38 per cent were Mennonites. At least 86 other sects and denominations had three or more men each in CPS camps. Following the Mennonites in number of men in the camps were the Brethren, Friends, and the Methodists, who ranked second, third, and fourth respectively.

During World War I, American conscientious objectors were actually drafted into the army, where they were expected to perform noncombatant service. The refusal of large numbers of these men to wear the military uniform or to engage in work connected with the military produced difficult problems for the army as well as for the young men who were placed under pressure to do that which their consciences forbade, and led to a more liberalized program during World War II. When in 1940, legislation for a draft law was being considered in Congress, the historic peace churches as well as other denominations presented their desire for a more liberal program to the proper authorities, with the result that the law finally passed was superior to former ones in four respects. The basis for objection was broadened to include all of those who by reason of religious training and belief could not participate in war. When a local draft board refused the classification a registrant desired, he was given the right of appeal under the new law. Perhaps most important was the new provision for assignment, in lieu of induction into the army, to work of national importance under civilian direction. The fourth improvement was placing conscientious objectors under civilian control and making violations of the law subject to the Federal courts rather than military courts.

These gains were in part the result of interchurch co-operation of the Historic Peace Churches,

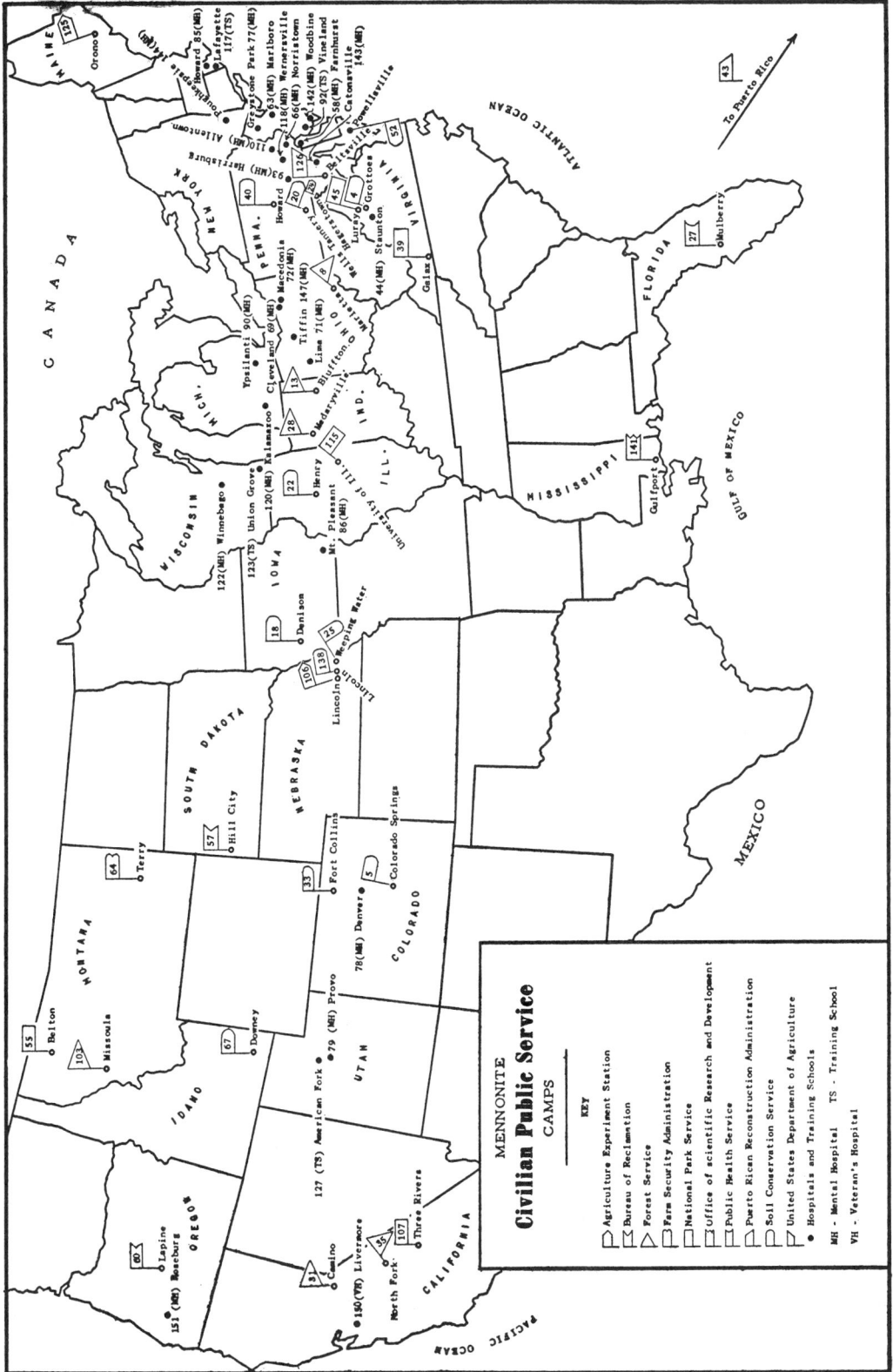

Brethren, Friends, and Mennonites, in the period between the two wars, when representatives of these groups met occasionally to consider their problems and to come to a common mind concerning the kind of program they would desire for conscientious objectors. Among the most important of these conferences was the one held at Newton, Kan., in 1935, when a "Plan of Unified Action in Case the United States Is Involved in War" was adopted. This called for a program of alternative civilian service in lieu of service in the armed forces.

Out of this co-operative effort came also the National Council for Religious Conscientious Objectors, later known as the National Service Board for Religious Objectors, which represented not only the Historic Peace Churches but also many other denominations to the government during World War II. This organization, however, was also the result of government initiative, for as is stated in its official report *Conscientious Objection,* "These groups (the three Historic Peace Churches) were now desirous also of the privilege of operating work units of conscientious objectors. It was evident that they had rather different ideas than the System for the administration of such units and it was anticipated that misunderstandings and confusion would be the outcome of separate agreements with the several groups. It was therefore suggested that one central representative body be formed through which all matters could be cleared by Selective Service."

The first registration under the new draft law occurred on Oct. 16, 1940, but it was not until April 11 of the following year that the President authorized the establishment and designation of work of national importance for conscientious objectors. In the meantime conscientious objectors who had registered with their local draft boards were placed into class I-A-O if they were willing to accept induction into the army, there to perform noncombatant service, usually in hospital or medical work. Those not willing to accept induction into the army were classified IV-E after they had filled out convincingly "Form 47," which asked questions designed to reveal the sincerity of their position.

In May 1941 the first Mennonite Civilian Public Service camp was opened, near Grottoes, Va. The camp consisted of four barrack dormitories, a large dining room, offices, staff quarters, and other buildings, all formerly used by the government for young men engaged in the work of the Civilian Conservation Corps. During the next several years many such CCC camps were used as the "base camps" for drafted conscientious objectors.

This first Mennonite camp was established to engage in soil conservation. Before the end of CPS, eleven soil conservation camps scattered from Maryland to Idaho had been or were being operated by the Mennonite Central Committee, acting for the Mennonites of the United States. Early in the CPS program, it was assumed that since farming was the leading profession among Mennonites, most of

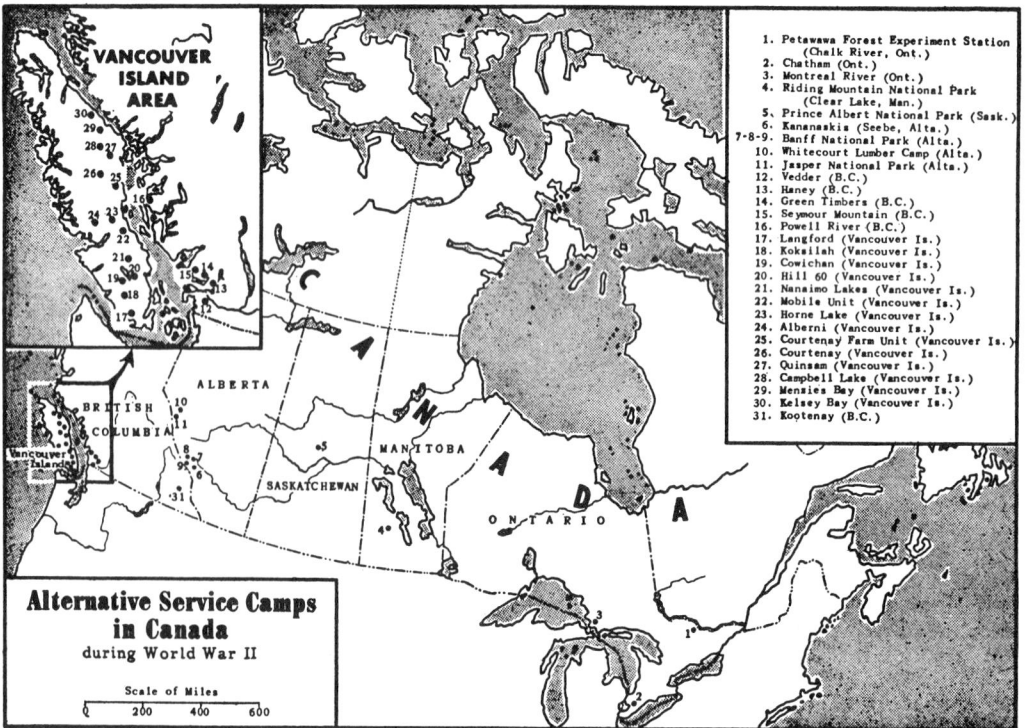

Alternative Service Camps in Canada during World War II

1. Petawawa Forest Experiment Station (Chalk River, Ont.)
2. Chatham (Ont.)
3. Montreal River (Ont.)
4. Riding Mountain National Park (Clear Lake, Man.)
5. Prince Albert National Park (Sask.)
6. Kananaskis (Seebe, Alta.)
7-8-9. Banff National Park (Alta.)
10. Whitecourt Lumber Camp (Alta.)
11. Jasper National Park (Alta.)
12. Vedder (B.C.)
13. Haney (B.C.)
14. Green Timbers (B.C.)
15. Seymour Mountain (B.C.)
16. Powell River (B.C.)
17. Langford (Vancouver Is.)
18. Koksilah (Vancouver Is.)
19. Cowichan (Vancouver Is.)
20. Hill 60 (Vancouver Is.)
21. Nanaimo Lakes (Vancouver Is.)
22. Mobile Unit (Vancouver Is.)
23. Horne Lake (Vancouver Is.)
24. Alberni (Vancouver Is.)
25. Courtenay Farm Unit (Vancouver Is.)
26. Courtenay (Vancouver Is.)
27. Quinsam (Vancouver Is.)
28. Campbell Lake (Vancouver Is.)
29. Menzies Bay (Vancouver Is.)
30. Kelsey Bay (Vancouver Is.)
31. Kootenay (B.C.)

the drafted men would prefer this kind of service. When an increasing number of men came from nonfarm backgrounds, other types of work were opened so that by September 1945 only 19 per cent of the Mennonite men were in soil conservation. An equal number, however, were engaged in other forms of agricultural service, including dairy units.

A second type of work was that done under the direction of the United States Forest Service. The first Forest Service camp operated by the MCC was the one at Marietta, Ohio, which opened in June 1941. Others were operated in Indiana, Montana, and California, a total of six. Although the major purpose of the western camps was to prevent or stop forest fires, much time was spent in building forest trails, caring for nursery stock, and engaging in pest control. One of the most spectacular services was that of the parachute jumpers who were trained to parachute to the scene of a forest fire there to engage in the usual fire-fighting techniques.

Four MCC camps, located in Virginia, Montana, and California, were under the National Park Service. In 1945 approximately 10 per cent of the men in Mennonite camps were in this work. Various types of maintenance work as well as fire fighting in national parks were performed by these men. The two camps under the Bureau of Reclamation worked on the construction of dams and a third camp divided its work between this Bureau and the Farm Security Administration, developing an irrigation project in the Yellowstone River Valley.

Other service in the field of agriculture was performed in small units such as the one at the Nebraska Agricultural Experiment Station. A CPS Reserve was made up of men who acted as livestock attendants on boats of cattle and horses sent to Europe. In May 1942 the first group of men from a Mennonite camp to serve in a dairy unit were placed in Wisconsin. By August 1945 the Mennonites had over 550 men in dairy work, among whom were a considerable number engaged in dairy herd testing.

Of an entirely different nature was work in the dangerously undermanned mental hospitals and training schools. In August 1942 the first men from a Mennonite camp to work in a state mental hospital arrived at Western State Hospital, in Staunton, Va. By December 1945 more than 1,500 men had served in mental hospital units under MCC administration. Other men served under the United States Public Health in Florida and Mississippi where the work centered around hookworm control. A unit in Puerto Rico spent part of its time working with the same problem. Receiving much publicity were the "guinea pig" units, in which men working under the Office of Scientific Research and Development subjected themselves to various experiments designed to gain information having to do with nutrition and disease.

The camps and units operated either individually by the MCC or jointly with another church agency are given below in order of establishment.

Camp No.	Camp Name	Location	Operating Group	Technical Agency	Capacity	Date Approved	Date Closed
4	Grottoes	Grottoes, Va.	MCC	SCS	150	Mar. 14, 1941	May 31, 1946
5	Colorado Springs	Colorado Springs, Col.	MCC	SCS	165	Mar. 14, 1941	Apr. 12, 1946
8	Marietta	Marietta, Ohio	BSC-MCC	FS	50	Apr. 19, 1941	Apr. 30, 1943
13	Bluffton	Bluffton, Ind.	MCC	FS	150	May 7, 1941	Apr. 8, 1942
18	Denison	Denison, Iowa	MCC	SCS	150	Aug. 2, 1941	Aug. 31, 1946
20	Sideling Hill	Wells Tannery, Pa.	MCC	SCS	120	Aug. 22, 1941	Oct. 15, 1944
22	Henry	Henry, Ill.	MCC	SCS	135	Nov. 17, 1941	Nov. 16, 1942
24	Washington Co.	Hagerstown, Md.	BSC-MCC	SCS	175	Dec. 31, 1941	Sept. 30, 1946
25	Weeping Water	Weeping Water, Neb.	MCC	SCS	175	Feb. 11, 1942	Apr. 30, 1943
27	Florida State Board of Health	Crestview, Fla.	BSC-MCC	PHS	100	Apr. 1, 1942	Dec. 10, 1946
28	Jasper-Pulaski	Medaryville, Ind.	MCC	FS	150	Apr. 1, 1942	Mar. 31, 1946
31	Placerville	Camino, Cal.	MCC	FS	200	Apr. 1, 1942	Dec. 10, 1946
33	Fort Collins	Fort Collins, Col.	MCC	SCS	200	May 6, 1942	Sept. 30, 1946
35	North Fork	North Fork, Cal.	MCC	FS	200	May 20, 1942	Feb. 28, 1946
39	Galax	Galax, Va.	MCC	NPS	150	May 23, 1942	May 17, 1943
40	Howard	Howard, Pa.	MCC	SCS	100	May 27, 1942	Apr. 30, 1943
43	Puerto Rico	San Juan, P.R.	BSC-MCC	PRRA	75	June 20, 1942	Mar. 31, 1947
44	Western State Hospital	Staunton, Va.	MCC	SMH	56	July 15, 1942	Sept. 1, 1946
45	Shenandoah National Park	Luray, Va.	MCC	NPS	150	July 27, 1942	June 30, 1946
52	Powellsville	Powellsville, Md.	MCC-FSC	SCS	175	Aug. 25, 1942	Mar. 31, 1947
55	Belton	Belton, Mont.	MCC	NPS	200	Sept. 7, 1942	Sept. 30, 1946
57	Hill City	Hill City, S.D.	MCC	BR	200	Sept. 23, 1942	Feb. 28, 1946
58	Delaware State Hospital	Farnhurst, Del.	MCC	SMH	40	Sept. 18, 1942	Nov. 15, 1946
60	Lapine	Lapine, Ore.	MCC	BR	300	Oct. 7, 1942	Dec. 31, 1943

Camp No.	Camp Name	Location	Group	Technical Agency	Capacity	Date Approved	Date Closed
63	New Jersey State Hospital	Marlboro, N.J.	MCC	SMH	65	Nov. 5, 1942	Dec. 10, 1946
64	Terry	Terry, Mont.	MCC	SCS-FSA	100	Nov. 10, 1942	June 30, 1946
66	Norristown Hospital	Norristown, Pa.	MCC	SMH	95	Nov. 5, 1942	Oct. 31, 1946
67	Downey	Downey, Idaho	MCC	SCS	150	Nov. 7, 1942	Dec. 31, 1945
69	Cleveland State Hospital	Cleveland, Ohio	MCC-FSC	SMH	30	Nov. 26, 1942	Sept. 30, 1946
71	Lima State Hospital	Lima, Ohio	MCC	SMH	12	Nov. 26, 1942	Sept. 30, 1946
72	Hawthornden State Hospital	Macedonia, Ohio	MCC	SMH	20	Nov. 26, 1942	Oct. 1, 1946
77	Greystone Park State Hospital	Greystone Park, N.J.	MCC	SMH	95	Jan. 6, 1943	Oct. 31, 1946
78	Colorado Psychopathic Hospital	Denver, Col.	MCC	SMH	15	Jan. 7, 1943	Mar. 25, 1946
79	Utah State Hospital	Provo, Utah	MCC	SMH	25	Jan. 16, 1943	Apr. 30, 1946
85	Rhode Island State Hospital	Howard, R.I.	MCC	SMH	60	Jan. 29, 1943	Nov. 19, 1946
86	Mount Pleasant State Hospital	Mount Pleasant, Iowa	MCC	SMH	33	Feb. 1, 1943	Oct. 1, 1946
90	Ypsilanti State Hospital	Ypsilanti, Mich.	MCC	SMH	75	Mar. 4, 1943	Oct. 5, 1946
92	Vineland	Vineland, N.J.	MCC	STS	16	Mar. 16, 1943	June 14, 1946
93	Harrisburg State Hospital	Harrisburg, Pa.	MCC	SMH	35	Mar. 20, 1943	Aug. 24, 1946
97	Dairy Farm Project		Coop	DA		Apr. 9, 1943	Oct. 31, 1946
.1	San Joaquin Co.	California	MCC		40	Apr. 1, 1943	Aug. 21, 1946
.2	El Paso County	Colorado	MCC		25	Apr. 1, 1943	Aug. 31, 1946
.5	Worcester Co.	Massachusetts	MCC		20	Feb. 28, 1945	Nov. 22, 1946
.9	Queen Annes County	Maryland	MCC		20	Feb. 1, 1945	Oct. 12, 1946
.10	Genesee County	Michigan	MCC		20	May 1, 1943	Oct. 30, 1946
.11	Lenawee County	Michigan	MCC		20	Apr. 1, 1943	Sept. 16, 1946
.12	Hillsborough Co.	New Hampshire	MCC		20	Feb. 28, 1945	Sept. 18, 1946
.19	Cuyahoga Co.	Ohio	MCC		13	Apr. 1, 1943	June 19, 1946
.20	Lorain County	Ohio	MCC		2	Apr. 1, 1943	Apr. 8, 1946
.21	Summit County	Ohio	MCC		20	Apr. 1, 1943	Aug. 23, 1946
.22	Wayne County	Ohio	MCC		25	Apr. 1, 1943	Mar. 1, 1946
.24	Tillamook Co.	Oregon	MCC		20	June 1, 1945	Sept. 18, 1946
.25	Allegheny Co.	Pennsylvania	FSC-MCC		10	Apr. 1, 1943	Oct. 23, 1946
.26	Lancaster Co.	Pennsylvania	MCC		20	May 1, 1943	Oct. 23, 1946
.28	York County	Pennsylvania	MCC		20	Apr. 1, 1943	June 22, 1946
.29	King County	Washington	BSC-MCC		15	Apr. 1, 1943	May 27, 1946
.30	Dane County	Wisconsin	MCC		20	Apr. 1, 1943	Aug. 30, 1946
.31	Dodge County	Wisconsin	MCC		20	May 1, 1942	Sept. 18, 1946
.32	Fond du Lac Co.	Wisconsin	MCC		20	Apr. 1, 1943	Sept. 12, 1946
.33	Green County	Wisconsin	MCC		20	Apr. 1, 1943	June 26, 1946
.34	Outagamie Co.	Wisconsin	MCC		20	Apr. 1, 1943	Aug. 28, 1946
100	Dairy Herd Testing		Coop	DA			
.5	Iowa	Iowa	MCC		13	Aug. 1, 1943	June 28, 1946
.6	Maine	Maine	MCC		17	Nov. 1, 1943	Sept. 28, 1946
.8	Michigan	Michigan	MCC		52	May 1, 1943	Aug. 21, 1946
.11	Pennsylvania	Pennsylvania	MCC		68	Mar. 1, 1943	Sept. 23, 1946
103	Missoula	Huson, Mont.	MCC	FS	250	Apr. 24, 1943	Dec. 31, 1945
106	Lincoln Experiment Station	Lincoln, Neb.	MCC	EXS	40	May 4, 1943	Oct. 16, 1946
107	Three Rivers	Three Rivers, Cal.	MCC	NPS	150	May 5, 1943	May 31, 1946

Camp No.	Camp Name	Location	Group	Technical Agency	Capacity	Date Approved	Date Closed
110	Allentown State Hospital	Allentown, Pa.	MCC	SMH	25	May 31, 1943	May 13, 1946
115	Office of Scientific Research and Development	Various places	Coop	OSRD		Aug. 31, 1943	Dec. 31, 1946
117	Exeter	Lafayette, R.I.	MCC	STS	15	Oct. 29, 1943	Sept. 1, 1946
118	Western State Hospital	Wernersville, Pa.	MCC	SMH	25	Nov. 3, 1943	June 27, 1946
120	Kalamazoo State Hospital	Kalamazoo, Mich.	MCC	SMH	30	Nov. 3, 1943	June 22, 1946
122	Winnebago State Hospital	Winnebago, Wis.	MCC	SMH	15	Nov. 8, 1943	Feb. 28, 1946
123	Union Grove	Union Grove, Wis.	MCC	STS	25	Nov. 8, 1943	Aug. 20, 1946
125	University of Maine Experiment Station	Orono, Maine	MCC	EXS	10	Nov. 22, 1943	May 15, 1946
126	Beltsville Research	Beltsville, Md.	MCC	EXS	35	Nov. 29, 1943	Dec. 31, 1946
127	American Fork	American Fork, Utah	MCC	STS	15	Nov. 30, 1943	Jan. 10, 1946
138	Lincoln	Lincoln, Neb.	MCC	SCS	85	Sept. 11, 1944	Oct. 15, 1946
140	Office of the Surgeon General	Various places	Coop	SGO		Dec. 18, 1944	Dec. 10, 1946
141	Mississippi State Board of Health	Gulfport, Miss.	MCC	PHS	40	Jan. 17, 1944	Dec. 10, 1946
142	Woodbine	Woodbine, N.J.	MCC	STS	20	Jan. 17, 1944	Sept. 30, 1946
143	Spring Grove State Hospital	Catonsville, Md.	MCC	SMH	35	Jan. 22, 1945	Aug. 15, 1946
144	Hudson Grove State Hospital	Poughkeepsie, N.Y.	MCC	SMH	30	Mar. 6, 1945	Mar. 30, 1946
146	New York State Experiment Sta.	Ithaca, N.Y.	MCC	EXS	6	Apr. 5, 1945	June 24, 1946
147	Tiffin	Tiffin, Ohio	MCC	STS	25	Apr. 25, 1945	Nov. 12, 1945
150	Livermore Veterans' Hospital	Livermore, Cal.	MCC	VAH	130	Nov. 13, 1945	Dec. 10, 1946
151	Roseburg Veterans' Hospital	Roseburg, Ore.	MCC	VAH	40	Dec. 18, 1945	Dec. 10, 1946

KEY

BSC	Brethren Service Committee	NPS	National Park Service
Coop	Co-operative, by all religious agencies	OSRD	Office of Scientific Research and Development
FSC	Friends Service Committee	PHS	Public Health Service
MCC	Mennonite Central Committee	PRRA	Puerto Rico Reconstruction Administration
BR	Bureau of Reclamation	SCS	Soil Conservation Service
DA	Department of Agriculture	SGO	Surgeon General's Office
EXS	Extension Service, U.S.D.A.	SMH	State Mental Hospital
FS	United States Forest Service	STS	State Training School
FSA	Farm Security Administration	VAH	Veterans' Administration Hospital

During the 1941-47 period of CPS, the men assigned to Mennonite camps performed a total of 2,296,175 man-days of service, exclusive of the work in CPS camps numbers 27, 43, 97, and 100, which were operated jointly by two or more agencies. At least 120 different types of work were done according to the Works Progress Reports in the Selective Service Records Offices. As the draftees were not paid for the work performed in the base camps, and only given maintenance wages of $15 per month in the special projects (using the basic army pay of $50 a month for estimation) men in Mennonite CPS contributed approximately $4 million worth of labor to the federal and state governments. The federal government spent approximately $1 1/3 million on CPS. Thus the United States benefited to the figure of $2 2/3 million from the contribution of men drafted to Mennonite CPS camps.

To operate the camps under Mennonite direction, the churches contributed to the Mennonite Central Committee in money and goods a total of over $3 million. Early in the planning for the CPS program, the MCC set up a quota system for raising funds to pay for the administration of the program, under which it was suggested that all members of Mennonite churches should contribute 50 cents per member up to Aug. 1, 1941. Other quotas were adopted from time to time so that by the end of CPS every Mennonite who had met the suggested quotas had given $21.45. Certain branches of the church contributed more than this amount, while others fell far short of this figure. As the quotas were not mandatory, the MCC made no attempt to compel the churches to give the suggested amounts. Gifts-in-kind contributed by the churches included large quantities of food, particularly canned goods. In addition to the moneys and gifts collected for CPS by the MCC, congregations and individuals gave individual gifts to men in camp. Certain conferences and congregations also gave money payments to their men at the time of their demobilization. The Lancaster Mennonite Conference, for instance, gave each man a gift of $10 per month for the time he had spent in CPS. As many of the drafted men who served without pay in CPS had dependents, the various Mennonite groups were urged to take care of these who were their own members in need. Those cases that were not handled in this manner were dealt with directly by the MCC.

The camps were operated under a system of divided responsibility. Selective Service agreed to "furnish general administrative and policy supervision and inspection, and will pay the men's transportation costs to the camps." The National Service Board for Religious Objectors representing the churches that had large numbers of conscientious objectors agreed for a temporary period "to undertake the task of financing and furnishing all other necessary parts of the program, including actual day-to-day supervision and control of the camps (under such rules and regulations and administrative supervision as is laid down by Selective Service), to supply subsistence, necessary buildings, hospital care, and generally all things necessary for the care and maintenance of the men." This temporary agreement was renewed from time to time, and by the end of the draft the Mennonites were still co-operating in this arrangement, although certain other groups had withdrawn, having come to feel that this contract made them a party with the government in the enforcement of the conscription system and disagreeing with certain regulations of S.S. which they regarded as being arbitrary.

This dual control of the camps although it may have operated better in Mennonite camps than in some others was the object of much criticism both by camp leaders who felt that the lines of authority were not clearly drawn and by S.S. officials who felt that the plan interfered with effective discipline. Selective Service, therefore, recommended that in any future program dual control be eliminated in favor of complete government control.

During the early days of Mennonite CPS camps, older men, who were usually ministers, were appointed by the MCC to be camp directors. As the program developed, younger men who were draftees were generally selected, with satisfactory results. To the surprise of many observers, CPS developed a comparatively large number of capable young leaders, who were called upon constantly to make decisions that were perhaps more difficult than those facing the pastor of an average Mennonite congregation. Since the close of the program, a large number of these young men have been assigned responsible positions in the ministry as well as in other church offices.

The Historic Peace Churches were willing to accept the responsibilities listed above in the agreement with Selective Service because this arrangement gave them the opportunity to follow their men to camp in order to minister to them. The churches not only provided regular religious services for their men but also set up educational programs that included Bible and devotional courses as well as crafts and regular high-school and college courses. In time each Mennonite camp was assigned an educational director who co-operated with the camp manager in organizing and administering a well-arranged program designed to give the camper meaningful and creative experiences during his off-work hours. Courses were taught by camp staff, campers, government staff men, and by church and school leaders who visited the camps regularly.

It was no easy task to provide an adequate spiritual ministry for the men. In the early months of the program, ministers were appointed to the camp directorships but in time it was learned that the administrative work and spiritual ministry in a camp did not belong to the same office. It also became difficult to obtain enough ministers to supply the rapidly increasing number of camps. As a result area pastors were appointed when obtainable and in other cases Mennonite ministers in the nearby states took turns in visiting the camps. This plan worked more satisfactorily in the east than in the west, where travel distances were greater. One of the chief failures of the entire MCC-CPS program was in not supplying enough camp pastors or in not having a large enough number of qualified ministers available for a regular program of services in the camps. In spite of this lack of a well-organized program of spiritual ministry and in spite of the fact that the campers were living under abnormal conditions, away from the sheltering influences of the home community and thrown in with many others whose views on various subjects were novel, the majority of men in a carefully sampled poll of opinion declared that as a result of their CPS experiences they held to the doctrines of their church more strongly than before while another 34 per cent declared that their loyalty had remained the same. Living in close proximity to men from many faiths and environments produced a re-examination of convictions and traditions that on the whole proved wholesome to the majority of men.

CPS created a new respect for the government which granted to CO's a greater amount of religious liberty than had formerly been enjoyed during wartimes in the United States. It gave thousands of young men the opportunity to witness to their religious convictions not only by the act of going into CPS but also by the way in which they lived together and in the quality of work which they did. It gave young men an opportunity to build the kind of camp community life that covered all areas of life—physical, social, educational, cultural, spiritual. As there were no traditions or patterns to follow, much experimentation was possible. It widened their knowledge of Mennonitism, it brought about a re-examination of their peace position, it taught them new skills and introduced them to new areas and environments, it taught them and their elders that young people could be trusted to carry responsibility, and it aroused their interest in new areas of service, particularly in mental hospitals and in public health work as well as in conservation.

Many CPS groups have organized reunions which have met yearly, or less often, since the close of the war. Here friendships are renewed and interests as broad, and broader, than Mennonitism are maintained. Yearly these groups are turning their attention away increasingly from their past experiences to the present and future challenges facing nonresistant Christians. Several groups are sponsoring programs of peace education and are engaging in service projects.

On the other hand, the CPS program revealed certain weaknesses. Less than half of all drafted Mennonite men chose to go into CPS, averaging the records of those conservative branches in which nearly all drafted men had gone to CPS with the more liberal groups which no longer exercised church discipline on participation in the military, revealing to what degree the historic position of the church on the participation in war had been surrendered. It also revealed that many CO's had a superficial understanding of their position and had little depth of spiritual experience. Intolerance and lack of love for each other led to tensions among campers. Working without pay and sometimes on jobs that appeared insignificant had a demoralizing effect on many men. It remains to be seen what the long-range effects of conscription on 8,000 young Mennonites will have been. Some who witnessed government red tape and inefficiency in certain areas reacted by developing cynicism and a lack of co-operation toward government.

The MCC on the basis of its experience made certain recommendations for any future program of civilian public service. It suggested that the government should have basic administrative responsibility for administering the draft but should then turn the drafted conscientious objectors over to the church service agencies. They also recommended that in the future the men be given pay and that the program be strictly under the control of civilian agencies of the government in a statement presented to the House Military Affairs Committee in 1945.

The Selective Service System also brought its recommendations in its two-volume report to the President (*Conscientious Objection*, 1950). Their twelve points are summarized below: (1) any future draft law should make provision "for civilian duty in work of national importance"; (2) the drafted CO should be given more rights and privileges in the next law, including pay and family allowance; (3) there should be more effective methods of determining the validity of claims for a CO classification, with more help available from the Justice Department; (4) there should be provisions for immediate and continuous detention of the troublemakers in the camps so that they can not damage the morale of the camp or the reputation of the program; (5) the camp system should be continued but the camp director should be an employee of the agency for which work is being done; (6) those assigned to CPS camps should be given the same rigid physical and mental examinations as are given to those assigned to the military; (7) objectors who violate Selective Service laws should be tried by the civil courts but these cases should be given priority; (8) the objector who feels that justice has not been done him should be given a prompt hearing; (9) the objector accused of violations should be allowed to comply with the law during court proceedings; (10) there should be established and applied early "comprehensive statistical and other records and reports on the activities of the System in the field"; (11) there should be a "wide variety of regular projects, manual in nature, and also of special ones, skilled and professional"; and (12) much study should be given by the government to camp organization and administration, the national significance of various projects as well as those overseas, and the most effective use of CO man power. (See **Alternative Service** Work Camps for the Canadian camps for conscientious objectors during World War II.)

M.G.

M. Gingerich, *Service for Peace, A History of Mennonite Civilian Public Service* (Akron, Pa., 1949); an annotated bibliography appears on pp. 425-28; *Conscientious Objection*. Special Monograph No. 11, Selective Service System (1950); L. Eisan, *Pathways of Peace—A History of the Civilian Public Service Program Administered by the Brethren Service Committee* (Elgin, Ill., 1948); M. Q. Sibley and P. E. Jacob, *Conscription and Conscience: The American State and the Conscientious Objector, 1940-1947* (Ithaca, N.Y., 1952); E. Yoder and D. Smucker, *The Christian and Conscription—An Inquiry Designed as a Preface to Action* (Akron, Pa., 1945).

Claassen (Claasen, Classen, Claesz, Claussen, Klaassen, Klassen, Klaeszen), a Mennonite family name which originated in the Netherlands. In Prussia it was first mentioned in 1552 at Schmerblock. In 1776, 107 families carried this name in West Prussia (without Danzig); in 1910, 409 persons; and in 1935 (without Elbing), 420 persons. In Prussia it was one of the most common Mennonite family names, occurring mostly in the Flemish congregations. An outstanding representative of the family was Peter Claassen, the second elder of the Grosse Werder congregation, 1645-79. Peter Claassen (1828-1901), a minister of the Heubuden congregation, emigrated to America in 1878 and was instrumental in founding the First Mennonite Church at Newton, Kan. (*Bundesbote Kalender* 1902, 33 f.).

The members of the Claassen family who went to Russia at the close of the 18th century and settled in Chortitza usually spelled their name "Klassen," while those who settled later at the Molotschna and in Samara used the forms "Claassen" and

"Klaassen." Some of the outstanding bearers of this name in Russia were Elder Peter Klassen (1825-1902), David I. Claassen (*q.v.*), all-Mennonite representative of the Forestry Service, J. J. Klassen (1856-1919), the managing secretary of the Chortitza district, Martin Klaassen (*q.v.*), writer of a Mennonite history, and Jakob A. Klassen (1847-1919) (*q.v.*), an educator in Chortitza.

In America the two predominant forms of the name are "Klassen" (usually from Russia) and "Claassen" (usually from Prussia). Cornelius F. Claassen (1859-1941) was president of the Kansas State Bank at Newton and treasurer of the G.C. Emergency Relief Board. Johannes Claassen (*q.v.*), writer of numerous books on philosophical, theological, and literary subjects, was a Prussian Mennonite. Among the many other prominent members of this widespread and well-known family may be mentioned: Johannes Claassen (*q.v.*), one of the founders of the Mennonite Brethren in Russia in 1860; Johannes Klaassen, long-time missionary to Java (1872-1950); C. F. Klassen (1894-1954), vice-chairman of the All-Mennonite Russian Agricultural Union in Russia, since 1927 in Canada, active in colonization and refugee migration work; J. P. Klassen (1872-1942), elder at Dundurn, Sask.; J. P. Klassen (1868-   ), elder of Schönwiese Church (Winnipeg); H. A. Claassen (1883-1954), missionary and elder (Beatrice, Neb.); J. P. Klassen (1888-   ), Professor of Art (Bluffton); P. J. Klassen, writer and minister (B.C.); and H. F. Klassen, Winnipeg, Man., editor of the *Mennonitische Rundschau*. (D. J. Classen, *History of the Classen Family,* Bakersfield.)

G.R.

Claassen, David Ivanovitch, b. May 9, 1855, in the village of Liebenau, Molotschna, Ukraine, as the sixth child of Johann and Catharina (Reimer) Claassen. He had five brothers and four sisters. In the 1860's he moved with his parents to Kuban, where his father succeeded in acquiring a tract of land from the government for the settlement of the members of the newly organized M.B. Church. Young David Claassen (who was generally known as David Ivanovitch) was richly talented. His sincere Christian faith and his kindness to the poor and the lower classes soon made him one of the outstanding leaders of the Kuban settlement.

On April 10, 1882, he married Anna Reimer. Little is known about his family. One son, Nikolai Claassen, a beloved physician, was shot to death by the Bolsheviks, together with his wife Helma (Meyer), in the city of Losowaya.

His positions and services were many. He was an ordained minister of the M.B. Church. For some years he served also as *Oberschulze* (chief magistrate) of the Kuban settlement. His first official meeting he opened with prayer. For 24 years, until 1902, he served as principal and instructor of a progressive high school, which also had been founded by him. For his outstanding achievements in the field of horticulture he was honored by the Russian government.

In the year 1906 he was called to the Molotschna colony, where he served as instructor of German in the Zentralschule as well as in the normal school at Halbstadt. Soon after his arrival he was elected to the position of president of the educational board of the Molotschna settlement. A great responsibility was entrusted to him when he was appointed the chief director of Alternative Service for all the Mennonites of Russia. For nine years, including the critical years of World War I, he served in this capacity. He was very likely the author of the printed annual reports. After the Revolution of 1917 he went back to Kuban, where he lost all his property. Later he was also arrested and kept in prison for a long time. After his release, he came home a sick man. He died at the age of 77 and was buried at Wohldemfürst on Nov. 1, 1932.

His biography is published in *Mennonitische Märtyrer* (1949) by A. A. Töws, Abbotsford, B.C. His life story is also found in a pamphlet written by his brother D. J. Classen, Bakersfield, Cal., under the title *History of the Classen Family.*   A.A.T.

Claassen, Johannes, one of the founders of the Mennonite Brethren in Russia, born in Orlofferfelde near Tiegenhof in West Prussia, emigrated as a child to Russia with his widowed mother and later established a home in Liebenau. As a member of the Gnadenfeld congregation he was one of the group of brethren who called the *Bruderschule* into being, which like the *Rauhe Haus* in Hamburg was to offer "better education, above all, strictly Christian training," with special attention to gifted orphans. In this cause Claassen twice traveled to St. Petersburg and Reval and secured through the *Fürsorgekomitee* in Odessa recognition of the school as a teacher-training institution for Mennonites.

Soon after this, the momentous break occurred which led to the founding of the Mennonite Brethren. In the fall of 1859 several members of the Gnadenfeld church began to hold communion services in their homes. They were called to account and threatened with exclusion from the church if they continued this practice, which violated church regulations. Division followed. About 25 members withdrew, led by Johannes Claassen and Jakob Reimer (*q.v.*), neither of whom had taken part in the communion service. On Jan. 6, 1860, they signed a charter in Elisabethtal, which was at the same time a statement of their faith (Friesen, *Brüderschaft,* 189-91).

Johannes Claassen, Abr. Cornelsen, and Jakob Kooper were chosen as deputies of the new brotherhood. In a letter to the Halbstadt *Gebietsamt* on Jan. 23, 1860, they declared that they intended to found a Mennonite congregation of their own. Meanwhile the elders of the Molotschna churches had applied to the *Gebietsamt* for assistance; this office on Jan. 28 forbade all religious meetings of the Brethren. It appears that the three deputies were intimidated and on Feb. 10 signed a document promising "to take no further steps in this matter without first securing the express permission of the higher authorities" (Friesen, 195).

On March 19 the Brethren declared in a new statement "that they did not wish to form a new church, but as Mennonites to live peaceably together in the faith of the fathers, and would even now be happy to return to the Mennonite brotherhood if the preachers would earnestly oppose the decline of the church according to the Word of God" (Friesen, 198 f.). A week later Johannes Claassen quietly went to St. Petersburg; but he accomplished "little enough" and realized that "the matter is very difficult." After his return he advised his brethren to choose their own preachers, and to exclude him and the two other signatories to the charter from consideration. The election, held on March 23, 1860, resulted in the choice of Heinrich Hübert (q.v.) and Jakob Böcker (q.v.).

The break was not complete. Their opponents did what they could to prevent state recognition of the group. At the end of November 1860 Johannes Claassen made a second journey to St. Petersburg for the new brotherhood and at its expense, to acquire civil and ecclesiastical recognition. He remained there until the end of June 1862. On May 15, 1862, he presented a petition to the Emperor (Friesen, 297-303). The result was the provision that "ecclesiastical separation shall in no case incur a loss of civil rights or persecution by police authorities."

Now the matter of a new site for colonization became paramount. On June 30, 1862, Johannes Claassen had returned from St. Petersburg, and on Aug. 18 he was already en route with five other brethren to seek suitable lands in Caucasus. He thereby became the founder of the thriving Mennonite colony on the Kuban; permission for its establishment was given on March 4, 1864 (Friesen, 341), by the Land Office (*Ministerium für Domänen*) upon the presentation of a written petition on Dec. 30, 1863. On May 30, 1866, Claassen also received from the government the confirmation of Mennonite religious privileges.

During his absence in St. Petersburg the "overjoyful," fanatical tendency appeared. At first Claassen sought to mediate and failed to oppose it energetically enough to prevent its rapid growth and the ensuing aberrations. He had to interrupt his stay in Kuban, where he was engaged in establishing the new colony with great self-sacrifice in the face of serious difficulties. May 4 he returned to his home and by his apt and decisive intervention in June 1865 (June protocol, pp. 234, 334-74), he succeeded in removing the excesses and establishing "order well-pleasing to God." July 20 he returned to Kuban and remained there until his death.

Claassen was again most unpleasantly troubled on account of his religious position. He was arraigned with two brethren before the authorities at Halbstadt, but after a brief conference with the colonial inspector in Prischib he was released. In 1869 he was elected *Oberschulze*. In this capacity it was his duty in 1871 to travel to the city of Vladikavkas to the reception of Alexander II, whereupon he received in 1872 the silver medal and in 1874 the gold, both on the ribbon (*Ordensband*). Besides these he received from the government a gold watch with an inscription recognizing his services in the colonization of Russia. In 1870 he was visited in his own home by the Grand Duke Michael Nikolayevitch. On Dec. 27, 1876, he died,

at the age of 56, in Wohldemfürst (q.v.) P. M. Friesen rated him with Johann Cornies (q.v.) and Bernhard Harder (q.v.) as one of the greatest contributors to the cause of Mennonitism in Russia. (*ML* I, 356.) NEFF.

Claassen, Johannes (1835-98), an eccentric scholar, of a strict Mennonite family in Königsberg, began the study of agriculture, and when he found this subject unsuited to him he turned to business. He remained in business for several years, devoting his spare time to literature and art. His employer in Danzig, recognizing and appreciating his pursuit of knowledge, made it possible for him to study at the University of Berlin, where he enthusiastically studied theology under Hengstenberg and Steinmeyer, as well as philosophy and other subjects of interest to him.

After one and one-half years at the university he concluded his studies by traveling through almost all of Germany, paying particular attention to church architecture. Then he was supposed to become a Mennonite preacher, and delivered several sermons in Ibersheim, where his cousin Neufeld had charge of the congregation. For five years he taught in the Mennonite school at Bröskerfelde (q.v.) near Marienburg, which was to have developed into a Mennonite theological seminary; this project however failed. In 1869 he accepted a teaching position in the noted Zahnsche Erziehungsanstalt near Mörs, and remained here too for five years. He now became connected with theosophists who called themselves "Friends of God," whose system seemed to satisfy his seeking spirit. He maintained this contact with the theosophists at Elberfeld for eight years. In 1882 he went to Münster, where he was kindly received by friends and relatives of the poet Annette von Droste-Hülshoff. Besides his literary activity he conducted Bible classes in the Evangelical hospital there. In 1890 he was called to Calw to prepare a revision of the *Calwer Bibelkonkordanz*. He remained in Calw the rest of his life, lecturing in Tübingen, Stuttgart, Frankfurt, and other places. He also visited Mennonite churches like Weierhof, conducting Bible classes. He refused to hold any office; nor did his accept a chair of theosophy, which friends had planned to create for him. He was a prolific writer on literary and philosophical subjects. (For a list of his publications see *ML* I, 347 f.) As a contributor to the *Mennonitische Blätter* he wrote the articles, "Unser Bekenntnis," 1863, p. 44; "Nehmet, leset," 1865, p. 63; "Unser Bekenntnis—mein Bekenntnis," 1866, pp. 5-7; "Zwei erste Worte—zum letzten," 1866, p. 30 (see also *Menn. Bl.*, 1898, 45, 83). NEFF.

Clachan was a small rural center near Aldboro (q.v.), Bothwell (q.v.), and Mosa (q.v.), meeting places in southwestern Ontario, under the Mennonite Conference of Ontario (MC). Mennonites had located in this area by 1870. Clachan Hall served for some of their services until 1940. More recently the Bethel Mennonite Church was built and used by the Mennonites of this area. J.C.F.

Claerken, an Anabaptist martyr, whose official name was Clairette Boucket, or Bocquette, wife of the martyr Maerten (*q.v.*) de Wael (Martin le Josne), was secretly executed on July 6, 1557, in the Steen prison in Antwerp, by being drowned in a sack, together with Margrite Venneau (see **Margriete, Jeroons huysvrou**) and Janneken op Dextelaer (*q.v.*). After they were put to death, their naked bodies were thrown into the Schelde River. In the song, "Liedeken van 72 Vrienden" (Claerken's name is listed as No. 22), it is said of these women:

Op den Steen verdroncken, siet openbaer,
Int Schelt geworpen daer naer,
Daer heeft men se sien drijven
Opt water, met schoone witte lijven.

This song is included in the *Liedtboecxken van den Offer des Heeren* (No. 16). (*Offer*, 565; *Mart. Mir.* D 185, E 569; Wolkan, *Lieder*, 63, 72; *Antw. Arch.-Blad* VIII, 434, 438; XIV, 22-23, No. 248.)   vDZ.

Claes of Armentières (in France), an Anabaptist martyr, whose official name was Nicolas de Stevele, was burned at the stake at Antwerp, Oct. 7, 1575, together with Lijntjen. By trade he was a maker of embroidery. (*Mart. Mir.* D 693, E 1008; *Antw. Arch.-Blad* XIII, 195; XIV, 96-97, No. 1092; *ML* I, 358.)   vDZ.

Claes (Nicolaes de Swarte), an Anabaptist martyr, the son of Jan de Swarte (*q.v.*), born at Nijpkercke (Nieppe), Belgium, was taken prisoner at Halewijn (Halluin) in the Belgian province of Flanders, and on March 17, 1563, together with his father, put to death by burning at the stake at Rijssel (Lille) in France. (*Mart. Mir.* D 299, E 664.)   vDZ.

Claes Adriaens Proper of Rotterdam, Holland, was sentenced to death by the Court of Holland on April 21, 1558, because he had created a disturbance during the execution of the Anabaptist martyr Jan Hendriksz (*q.v.*) in a vain attempt to liberate this victim and others who were to be executed. It is not clear whether Claes Adriaens was an Anabaptist himself; likely he was not.   vDZ.

Inv. Arch. Amst. I, No. 385; I. M. J. Hoog, *De Martelaren der Hervorming* (Schiedam, 1885) 237 ff.

Claes van Alkmaar, a Dutch Anabaptist, one of the twelve apostles sent out by Jan Matthys in late 1533. Claes went to Groningen, where soon afterward the Zandt rebellion of the Anabaptists took place. Later he was in Münster, and from there returned to Groningen. He may also have preached in Delft. In November 1535 he was imprisoned in Bergen op Zoom (Dutch province of Brabant), and was executed in December of that year. (*DB* 1906, 28; 1909, 12; 1917, 98, 105.)   vDZ.

Claes Arentsz, Elder of the Flemish Mennonite church of Nieuwe Zijpe (*q.v.*) in the Netherlands, had spoken slightingly of infant baptism while performing a baptismal service at de Waal on the island of Texel on March 3, 1649. For this he was imprisoned on a charge brought by the Reformed minister J. G. Moldanus, author of *Christen-Kinder-doopswaerheydt* (1650). Arentsz was soon released on bail, but was forced to dispute with Moldanus and the other Reformed ministers of the island. In this disputation he was assisted by Galenus Abra-

hamsz (*q.v.*) and two other preachers of Amsterdam. After the dispute Arentsz was ordered never to publicly oppose infant baptism. At a meeting of conservative Flemish elders, preachers, and deacons held at Leiden in June 1660, and presided over by van Braght, Arentsz was invited to give two addresses.   vDZ.

Blaupot t. C., *Holland* I, 195-97; H. W. Meihuizen, *Galenus Abrahamsz* (Haarlem, 1953).

Claes Claesz of Beverwijk, Dutch province of North Holland, an Anabaptist martyr, was burned at the stake July 1, 1535, probably at The Hague. (*Inv. Arch. Amst.* I, 745.)   vDZ.

Claes Claesz (Claes Claesz Joncker), an Anabaptist martyr of Krommeniërdijk, Dutch province of North Holland, was, with eight others, put to death for his faith, probably in 1534. (Van Braght's date of 1542 cannot be correct.) (*Mart. Mir.* D 62, E 465; *Bibliographie,* No. 142; *DB* 1917, 170; *ML* II, 432.)   vDZ.

Claes Claesz of Monnikendam, Dutch province of North Holland, an Anabaptist, was put to death at Amsterdam, March 6, 1535. On Jan. 10 of this year he had bought weapons at Amsterdam. Obviously he belonged to the revolutionary wing of Anabaptism. (Grosheide, *Verhooren,* 53-55.)   vDZ.

Claes Claesz of Westzaan, Dutch province of North Holland, an Anabaptist martyr, was burned at the stake at Amsterdam, April 25, 1534. (*DB* 1917, 121, No. 136.)   vDZ.

Claes Claesz of Wormer, Dutch province of North Holland, is identical with Claes Claesz Joncker (*q.v.*).

Claes Cornelisz of Amsterdam was executed by hanging, on June 1, 1535. Claes was the son of Hillegont Petersdochter, who lived in the house d'Engel, where Anabaptists sometimes stayed. It is not clear whether Claes was an Anabaptist himself; he may have been punished by death for merely sheltering Anabaptists. (Grosheide, *Bijdrage,* 60, 305.)   vDZ.

Claes Denysse (called in the *Mart. Mir.* D 603, "*De knecht van Peter de Gulicker,*" i.e., the servant of P. de G.). He was a weaver and 18 years old; he could not read nor write, and had not yet been baptized, because he was still too young and "at this time not well enough founded in the true Christian belief." He was taken prisoner on Aug. 5, 1571 (*Mart. Mir.* incorrectly 1572), at Klundert (*q.v.*), when a meeting held in the house of his master was surprised by the sheriff. He was examined before the court several times, the last time being Sept. 17, 1571. Shortly after this he must have been executed. Notwithstanding his lack of knowledge and culture, Claes remained steadfast and died as a true martyr, while his master recanted. (*Mart. Mir.* D 603-5, E 929; *DB* 1912, 36-37, 42.)   vDZ.

Claes Dircxsoon, an otherwise unknown Anabaptist martyr, was executed at Leeuwarden, Dutch province of Friesland, on April 10, 1535, because he had been rebaptized. (K. Vos, *Menno Simons,* Leiden, 1914, 228.)   vDZ.

Claes Dircxzn Mug, a revolutionary Anabaptist of Benschop, Dutch province of Utrecht, who together with some others came by ship from Antwerp, Belgium, to Amsterdam, where they were all arrested. Claes was executed by hanging at Amsterdam on Aug. 9, 1540. (Grosheide, *Bijdrage,* 145-46, 308.) vDZ.

Claes Dirksz, an Anabaptist martyr, taken prisoner at Krommeniërdijk, Dutch province of North Holland, was, according to van Braght (*Mart. Mir.*), put to death in 1542. This is certainly wrong. In all probability it was 1534 (see *DB* 1917, 170), on April 27. Claes, who had participated in the journey to Münster in March 1534 (see **Bergklooster**), was beheaded. vDZ.

> *Mart. Mir.* D 62, E 465; *Inv. Arch. Amst.* I, 745; *DB* 1917, 121, No. 140; *ML* I, 442, where this martyr is called Nicolaus Dietrich.

Claes Ganglofs, Dutch Mennonite elder: see **Ganglofs, Claes.**

Claes Gerbrandsz, an Anabaptist martyr, was burned at the stake on Aug. 6, 1552, at Amsterdam with five brethren, because he attended the meetings of the Mennonites. He came from Wormer, in the Dutch province of North Holland, and was a weaver by trade. At the time of his trial, he declared that he had heard Menno Simons preach more than ten years before. He had not yet been baptized on the confession of his faith, although he would gladly have done so if he had had the opportunity. This case is again an indication that those who desired to be baptized sometimes had to wait for years before the elder considered them worthy. Claes and the other brethren endured the grim ordeal with all steadfastness. (*Mart. Mir.* D 142 f., E 536; *ML* II, 76.) vDZ.

Claes Jan Nachtegaelsz, an Anabaptist martyr, b. at Dülmen, Westphalia, living in the Netherlands, admitted that he had been (re)baptized. He was beheaded at Utrecht, June 11, 1539. (*Berigten Hist. Genootschap, Utrecht* IV, 2, 1851, 139.) vDZ.

Claes Janssen, by trade a *glaismaicker* (glass blower, or painter on glass), was sentenced to death, May 14, 1535, at Amsterdam, because he had taken part in the Anabaptist revolt at Amsterdam, May 10-11. He was executed with 10 companions in a barbarous manner. (Grosheide, *Verhooren,* 63, 64.) vDZ.

Claes Jansz, a baker at Haarlem, Dutch province of North Holland, an Anabaptist martyr, confessed under torture that he had been rebaptized, and was beheaded at Haarlem in 1535, date unknown. (*Inv. Arch. Amst.* I, 750; *DB* 1917, 153; *Bijdragen en Meded. Hist. Genootschap, Utrecht* XLI, 1920, 202, 203.) vDZ.

Claes Jansz, a revolutionary Anabaptist and citizen of Hazerswoude, Dutch province of South Holland, who took part in the Anabaptist revolts at Hazerswoude (*q.v.*) on Dec. 31, 1535, and Poeldijk (*q.v.*) in February 1536, and was executed at The Hague on March 13, 1536, in a very cruel way, his heart being cut out of his body. vDZ.

> *Inv. Arch. Amst.* I, No. 744; E. van Bergen, "De wederdoopers in het Westland," in *Bijdr. voor de Gesch. van het Bisdom Haarlem* XXVIII (Leiden, 1903) 276-77.

Claes Jansz Brongers, an Anabaptist martyr, beheaded June 1, 1549, at Leeuwarden, Dutch province of Friesland, because he had received Menno Simons in his house about six weeks before his death and had invited him to stay. Furthermore, he possessed books written by Menno Simons, which he distributed. Above all, he had attended the meetings of the Mennonites for many years. (*Inv. Arch. Amst.* I, 356; *DB* 1865, 113-14; K. Vos, *Menno Simons* (Leiden, 1914) 69, 232-33.) vDZ.

Claes Jansz Leke, a native of Poeldijk (*q.v.*), Dutch province of South Holland, a revolutionary Anabaptist, was involved in the Anabaptist revolt at Poeldijk on March 8-9, 1536, and for this reason was beheaded at The Hague. vDZ.

> *Inv. Arch. Amst.* I, No. 745; E. van Bergen, "De Wederdoopers in het Westland," in *Bijdr. voor de Gesch. van het Bisdom Haarlem* XXVIII (Leiden, 1903) 279-80.

Claes Jansz van Oostsanen, a Dutch Anabaptist martyr, was sentenced by the Court of Holland on Aug. 27, 1534, to die by being beheaded, while his wife Truitje Gysberts was sentenced on the same day to be drowned. Both had participated in the journey to Münster and were arrested at Bergklooster (*q.v.*). (*Inv. Arch. Amst.* I, Nos. 744, 745.) vDZ.

Claes Leks, an Anabaptist martyr, born at Ostende, Belgium, was summoned to the courthouse in 1548 and subjected to a cross-examination, in which "he made a good confession of his faith." He was well spoken of for the alms he distributed among the poor. Because he refused to desist from his faith, he was condemned to death at the stake, "and offered up his sacrifice as a true child of God." (*Mart. Mir.* D 81, E 481; *ML* II, 635.) NEFF.

Claes van Le(eu)wen, husband of the Dutch Anabaptist martyr Cornelia (*q.v.*), was a director of the Latin school at Zutphen, Dutch province of Gelderland. When after his death it was learned in 1549 that he had belonged to the Anabaptist brotherhood, his corpse was exhumed and buried in unhallowed ground. (*DB* 1881, 42.) vDZ.

Claes Matthijszoon, an Anabaptist leader of Knolendam, Dutch province of North Holland, was burned at the stake on April 10, 1534, at The Hague, because "he had a bad opinion of the Holy Sacrament and was extremely obstinate." He was executed together with Jan Dircks of Alkmaar and another martyr also called Jan Dirkzoon. Of these three victims the Council of Holland wrote to the regent of the Emperor, Maria of Hungary at Brussels, that "they went to their death as sheep, which was wonderful and miserable to behold." (*Inv. Arch. Amst.* I, Nos. 31, 745; *DB* 1905, 173; 1917, 131, No. 129.) vDZ.

Claes Melisz, an Anabaptist martyr, who with other brethren and sisters was apprehended at "Krommenieërdijk in Waterlandt," in the Dutch province of North Holland, was likely put to death in 1534 (certainly not 1542, as van Braght, *Mart. Mir.,* indicates). (*Mart. Mir.* D 62, E 465; *DB* 1917, 170.) vDZ.

Claes Meselaer, a member of the Cleves (Germany) city council. When in 1551 the Anabaptist Willem de Kistenmaker (*q.v.*) was to be sentenced he was unwilling to sit on the council and remained at home reporting himself ill. Thereupon the mayor and the six councilors came to his bed to take his vote. Meselaer declared that he would not condemn such a pious man; the mayor replied, "Thereby you will fall into disfavor with our gracious prince and lord, Duke William." "I would rather be in disfavor with the prince than with the Highest," was his reply. He gave up his position as councilor and later became a member of the brotherhood. (*Mart. Mir.* D 131, E 525; *DB* 1899, 139; *ML* III, 117.)

Neff.

Claes Opreyder, an Anabaptist martyr, was taken prisoner by the Spaniards at Deventer, Dutch province of Overijssel, on March 11, 1571, together with 11 other Mennonites. He was burned at the stake at Deventer on June 16, 1571. After he had ascended the scaffold platform he knelt for prayer, but the executioner disturbed him because the Spaniards wanted to avoid the impression that he was a man of faith. (*Mart. Mir.* D 552 ff., E 885 ff., *DB* 1919, 29-37; *ML* III, 307.)   vDZ.

Claes, Pieter, an Anabaptist martyr: see **Pieter Claes Jansz van Wormer.**

Claes (de) **Praet,** an Anabaptist martyr, executed at Gent, Belgium, by burning at the stake, probably in the last half of 1556 or early months of 1557. Claes had been deeply impressed by witnessing the death of some steadfast Anabaptist martyrs. He had been baptized in 1552 at Antwerp. Shortly before his imprisonment he had visited the Mennonites in Emderland, both for trade and spiritual contacts. He was married and had children. Nothing further is known about his life. His imprisonment lasted about two months. *Het Offer des Heeren* and later martyr books contain a letter of Claes, written from his prison, in which he speaks at length of his trials. At the end of this letter Claes greets "the whole church, scattered in all countries." The hymn says that Claes willingly came to the stake, to which he was bound for burning. Concerning Claes the hymn was written: "De werlt op de Christen verstoort, vangen, dooden aen menich oort" (The world, annoyed by the Christians, seizes and kills them at many places), which is included in *Het Offer des Heeren*. (*Offer,* 239-56; *Mart. Mir.* D 167-73, E 554-60; Verheyden, *Gent,* 23, No. 45; Wolkan, *Lieder,* 66.)   vDZ.

Claes Roders, an Anabaptist martyr of Wormer, Dutch province of North Holland, was executed at Enkhuizen, North Holland. The year of execution is unknown. (*Mart. Mir.* D 61, E 464.)   vDZ.

Claes Sybrands van Wessanen, a Dutch Anabaptist martyr, who had joined the Anabaptists who sailed from Amsterdam to Hasselt, in order to go on to Münster. He was arrested at Bergklooster (*q.v.*) and sentenced to death by the Court of Holland on June 3, 1534, and then beheaded at The Hague. (*Inv. Arch. Amst.* I, Nos. 744, 745.)   vDZ.

Claes van Venlo, an Anabaptist and *Naaktlooper* (*q.v.*), was beheaded at Amsterdam on Feb. 25, 1535. (Grosheide, *Verhooren,* 57, 58.)   vDZ.

Claes (de) **Wever,** a Dutch Anabaptist martyr, was imprisoned at The Hague but managed to escape from prison. Later on he was active in Bergen op Zoom, Dutch province of North Brabant, and arrested here in November 1535. After being tortured he was executed before Dec. 12, 1535. He belonged to the revolutionary wing of Anabaptism. (*Inv. Arch. Amst.* I, Nos. 141, 143.)   vDZ.

Claes Willemsz, an Anabaptist martyr who had held Anabaptist meetings in his house at Sloten near Amsterdam, and was himself an Anabaptist preacher, was executed at Haarlem, Dutch province of North Holland, about 1539. (Grosheide, *Bijdrage,* 103.)   vDZ.

Claes-Wolters-Volk, followers of Claes Wolters Cops (see **Kops**), a Mennonite preacher in the Dutch town of Haarlem, United High German and Frisian congregation. Cops and his followers in 1611 separated from this congregation, whose leader was Leenaerdt Clock (*q.v.*). As late as 1635 the name of Claes-Wolters-Volk was still common for a group of High German Mennonites at Leiden, Holland.   vDZ.

L. G. le Poole, Bijdr. tot . . . het kerkelijk leven onder de Doopsgez. . . . te Leiden (Leiden, 1905) 25.

Claes Ysbrands of Monnikendam, Dutch province of North Holland, an Anabaptist preacher and leader who is said to have baptized many people, was beheaded at The Hague on April 28, 1535 (not in May 1535 at Monnikendam, as was formerly generally accepted). Of his activities we only know that he was very active in his home town of Monnikendam.   vDZ.

Inv. Arch. Amst. I, Nos. 117a, 745; DB 1917, 118 No. 87; Mellink, Wederdopers, 163.

Claesen (Clazen), **Teunis,** minister of the (Groninger) Old Flemish congregation at Rasquert, Dutch province of Groningen, and elder (*opziener*) of the (Groninger) Old Flemish after 1755, composed a *Verklaringe van de Geloofsbelijdenisse der Doopsgesinden bekent onder de Naam van oude Vlamingen* (Groningen, 1762). He died before 1766. (Blaupot t. C., *Groningen* I, 133 f.; *Catalogus Amst.,* 173.)   vDZ.

Claesen (Klaesken), wife of Frans (Francoys) de Swarte, b. at Meteren, Flanders, an Anabaptist martyr, was put to death on Oct. 3, 1562, at Hondschoote, Flanders, Belgium, with her sister Proentgen (*q.v.*), the wife of Karel van de Velde (*q.v.*). The two women were drowned secretly in a tub, remaining steadfast in the truth. (*Mart. Mir.* D 298, E 662.)   vDZ.

Claesken (Klaesken or Claesken Pertrijs), the wife of Jan de Swarte (*q.v.*), an Anabaptist martyr, taken prisoner at Halewijn (Halluin) in French Flanders, together with her husband, four sons, and a group of brethren and sisters of the church. She was burned at the stake at Rijssel (Lille) in France on March 27, 1563, together with three of her sons, Christiaen, Hans, and Mahieu, after her husband and her son Claes had given their lives by burning 10 days before.

The *Martyrol. Prot. Neerl.* states that Claesken, whose official name was Claisse Florissone, also called Buens or Bienes, was not executed at Rijssel but at Hondschoote in Flanders, the date being April 27, 1563, but this must be an error. (*Mart. Mir.* D 299, E 664; *Bibliographie* II, 421.)   vdZ.

Claesken Gaeledochter, an Anabaptist martyr. She was baptized by Gillis van Aken (*q.v.*) "near Workum in the open field" about 1549, was seized at the end of 1558 or the beginning of 1559 and subjected to cross-examination seven times. With admirable knowledge of Scripture and skill in answering she testified to her faith. She had three sons, whom she did not want to leave "for all the world" and for whose future she was deeply concerned. *Het Offer des Heeren* and also van Braght's *Martyrs' Mirror* contain two letters written by her, which are a remarkable monument to her pious faith and warm affection. On March 14, 1559, she was executed by drowning with her husband Hendrik Eeuwesz (*q.v.*) and Jacques d'Auchy (*q.v.*) at Leeuwarden, Dutch province of Friesland. An anonymous poet wrote a poem on her death, beginning "Een liedeken met vreuchden goet verhalen wij met sangen." (Wolkan, *Lieder,* 67; *Offer,* 324-41; *DB* 1899, 33-50; *Mart. Mir.* D 236-42, E 611; *ML* I, 358.)   Neff.

Claessens, Jan, of Grouw, Friesland: see **Klaasz, Jan.**

Claesz, Claes, an elder in the Flemish congregation at Blokzijl, Dutch province of Overijssel, in the first half of the 17th century, who enjoyed the regard of the moderate branch. He endeavored by lenience and a conciliatory attitude to unite the various branches of the Mennonites of Holland. Gifted with foresight he was always able to maintain an impartial and moderate attitude and to turn to account the good points of his opponents. Among his bitterest opponents were P. J. Twisck, Vincent de Hondt, and Jan Luies. These would have no part in unification, since in their opinion Claesz did not exercise the ban strictly enough. In a meeting at Middelstum on Sept. 18, 1628, Jan Luies and Claesz fell into arguing, and the result was the separation of the Groninger Old Flemish (*q.v.*). In reply to the violent polemic of Herman Faukelius, a Reformed preacher at Middelburg and well-known opponent of the Mennonites, entitled *Babel, dat is verwerringhe der Wederdooperen onder malcanderen over meest alle stucken des Christelijcken Geloofs en Leere,* he wrote *Bekenntenisse van de voornaemste Stucken des Christelijken gheloofs en der Leere* (Amsterdam, 1624, 2d ed. Utrecht, 1650). It contains 23 articles and forms a valuable confession of faith of the Mennonites. Others of his writings are the following: *Eenvuldige vertrouwinge, Waer inne naectelijck uyt de H. Schrifture aengewesen wort, dat Gods Gemeente, niet op eeniger menschen vroomheyt, oude gewoonten, traditien, ofte lange belevingen, Dan alleen op den hoecsteen Christum, Sijne heylsame leere, ende onberispelijck leven ghefondeert staet* (Amsterdam, 1610); *Copye eens Briefs of Voorlooper, om niet ligtvaardig te oordeelen* (Amsterdam, 1613). In reply P. J. Twisck published *Vreeds-Beletzel,* which Claesz answered with *Vreeds-Beletzel van P. J. Twisck beantwoordt en wederleyt* (Amsterdam, 1629); *Predikatie of verklaringhe over Luc. 10. 25-28* (Amsterdam, 1624), a sermon

of 104 pages, but according to Maatschoen doubly worth reading; *Onschult, ende bestraffinghe des onschriftmatighen oordeels, 'twelck by Jan Luyes . . .* (Amsterdam, 1627); *Schriftuerlijk tractaet over het wederaennemen der boetvaerdighe buytengetroude* (Haarlem, 1634); *Propositie of Voorstelling dat de eens geloofs gezinde Christenen niet behooren gescheiden te blyven* (Haarlem, 1634). A letter to Vincent de Hondt is added to this book. In addition Claesz was the author of a number of hymns, several of which are printed in Stapel's *Lusthof,* 1681.

Claesz was one of the signatories of the union of the Flemish, which came into being at Dordrecht in 1632.   J.L.

H. Schijn and G. Maatschoen, *Uitvoeriger Verhandeling van de Geschiedenisse der Mennonisten* (Amsterdam, 1744) 439-82; Blaupot t. C., *Groningen* I. 60-63; *DB* 1876, 38; 1897, 118; 1900, 90; 1883, 6, 8; *Catalogus Amst.,* 104, 185, 198; Kühler, *Geschiedenis* II, 76 ff., 82 ff., 192; *Inv. Arch. Amst.* I, Nos. 558, 573, 589; II, 1239; *ML* I, 358.

Clara Joostendochter, an unmarried woman, was taken prisoner May 24, 1539, in the house of Lambrecht Duppijn (*q.v.*) at Haarlem, Dutch province of North Holland, where a meeting was held. After a cross-examination on the rack she was drowned on June 3, 1539, at Haarlem. Likely she was a follower of David Joris (*q.v.*). (*Bijdr. en Mededeelingen van het Hist. Genootschap, Utrecht* XLI, 1920, 199-201, 208, 209, 211, 218.)   vdZ.

Clara Vrencken (or Vrancken), sister-in-law of Metken (*q.v.*), an Anabaptist martyr, was burned at the stake on Aug. 22, 1549, at Valkenburg, Dutch province of Limburg. She was baptized and lived at Visschersweert (*q.v.*). The imprisonment lasted 15 days. Further particulars are lacking. (W. Bax, *Het Protestantisme in het Bisdom Luik, . . .* The Hague, 1937, I, 327; *Inv. Arch. Amst.* I, No. 357.)   vdZ.

Clarenbach, Adolf, a widely celebrated Protestant martyr, who was burned at the stake in Cologne, Germany, on Sept. 28, 1529, with Peter Fliesteden (*q.v.*). He was born at the close of the 15th century on the farm "zum Busche," which belonged to the ecclesiastical district of Lüttringhausen near Lennep. Until 1514 he studied in Münster, probably in the school of the Brethren of the Common Life, in 1517 acquired the Master's degree at Cologne, and then became a humanist teacher in Münster, but never a cleric. In 1524 he became second master of the city school at Wesel, where he became a friend of Johann Klopreis (*q.v.*). Expelled from Wesel because of his Protestant convictions (Sept. 11, 1525), he betook himself to Osnabrück accompanied by a large number of students, took a position as a Latin teacher in the house of a pious widow, and also lectured on several books of the New Testament. Expelled again, he went to Lennep at Easter 1527. Here he wrote his most important book, in which he treated the evangelical faith as a matter of faith, hope, and charity in contrast to law, and sharply exposed the errors of the Catholic Church. But he could not stay here either. He turned to Büderich to his friend Klopreis, and when Klopreis was summoned to **Cologne**

the second time because of his heretical views, he accompanied him to defend and encourage him. Both were arrested on April 3, 1528. Whereas Klopreis escaped on New Year's night, Clarenbach remained in a prison cell with Peter Fliesteden. After unspeakable suffering, during which they comforted each other, both suffered a martyr's death. Clarenbach was heard to cry from the flames, "Lord, into Thy hands I commend my spirit." The third centennial of their death was publicly celebrated in 1829. On the elevation between Lennep and Lüttringhausen a stone with an appropriate inscription was erected to the memory of Clarenbach.

Was Clarenbach a follower of Luther, an Anabaptist, or perhaps a member of the old-evangelical churches which had their seat in the Rhine region until the Middle Ages? Keller, Rembert, and others thought the last was the case; C. Kraft and G. Bossert claim him positively for the Lutheran Church. Johannes Hillmann and Eduard Bratke (article in *HRE*) see in him an independent personality. It is nevertheless very probable that he was influenced by Anabaptist ideas and thoughts, which were strongly represented in the region of Cologne. His positive rejection of the oath, his relation to the "brethren," such as Klopreis, Westerburg, etc., his concept of communion and baptism, which he calls a dying of all carnal desires and a putting on of the new man, makes this clear. But with the scarcity of material on the subject his Anabaptism can hardly be conclusively proved.

NEFF.

G. Bossert in *Lit. Centralblatt* 1899, No. 39, Col. 1317: X, 508-13; Joh. Hillmann, *Die evang. Gemeinde Wesel* . . . (Düsseldorf, 1896); C. Kraft, *Die Geschichte der beiden Märtyrer der evang. Kirche Adolf Clarenbach und Peter Fliesteden* (Elberfeld, 1886); Keller, *Reformation; Rembert, Wiedertäufer; Menn. Bl.,* 1898, 66 ff.; Ludovicus Rabus, *Historien der Heyligen auserwelten Gottes Zeugen Bekenner und Märtyrer* (Strasbourg, 1557); C. A. Cornelius, *Gesch. des Münsterischen Aufruhrs* I, 272-78; *ML* I, 359.

Clarence, New York, is a village with a population of approximately 660, located in Erie County, 12 miles east of Buffalo. Approximately 20 Mennonite families, of which about 20 per cent live in town, representing two branches, the Mennonites (MC) and the Conservative Amish Mennonites, live in the vicinity in which the village is rather centrally located. Mennonites originally located in this community in the early part of the 19th century, but church life disintegrated after the death of Bishop John Lapp in 1878 and after Preacher Jacob Krehbiel, Jr., left the Mennonite Church (MC) in 1880 taking a considerable number of members with him into the General Conference Mennonite Church. Another settlement was made between 1920 and 1930. The present Mennonite Church (MC) is the result of this later settlement. E.D.

Clarence (N.Y.) Conservative Amish Mennonite Church, now extinct, was organized in December 1921 by Christian Nafziger of Lewis Co., N.Y., with Lewis Eichorn as the minister. The settlers came from different parts of the United States and Canada. During the first few years services were held at the Sandhill Church, later at the old Stone

Mennonite Church, and still later at the Lewis Eichorn home. In 1929 the church was reorganized by John A. Stoltzfus, Lancaster Co., Pa., but not under a conference. In November 1934 Joseph Roth was ordained to the ministry by John A. Stoltzfus. Some years later the Pine City schoolhouse, two miles from Clarence, was bought for a meetinghouse, and was generally known as the Eichorn Church. Many members moved away. Lewis Eichorn died on Feb. 17, 1945. Services were held until March 14, 1948; at that time nine members were left.   A.E.

Clarence Center, a village 30 miles east of Buffalo, N.Y., was the location of two Mennonite churches now extinct. The Good's Stone Church and cemetery was the first and belonged to the Mennonite Conference (MC) of Ontario. The Cox cemetery, a mile nearer Clarence Center, marks the location for the place of worship of a General Conference Mennonite group organized under Jacob Krehbiel, Jr. (1835-1917). He was a son of·Deacon Frederick Krehbiel (1806-63) and grandson of Bishop Jacob Krehbiel (*q.v.*) (1780-1860), who came to Erie Co., N.Y., from Germany. Jacob, Jr., was ordained to the ministry under the Mennonite Conference (MC) of Ontario in 1872. He married Leah Strickler in 1866, daughter of Preacher John Strickler. Several families bearing the names of Eberhart, Lehman, Lapp, Ritz, Rhoades, Frick, Leib, Martin, Hummel, Sherer, and Roth affiliated with the General Conference Mennonites about 1880. Sometime after organization their worship services were held every two weeks in Clarence Center in a church rented from the United Brethren. After Jacob Krehbiel became inactive, these services were discontinued and the organization ceased. Descendants of these families have become members of local non-Mennonite churches.   J.C.F.

Clarence Center Mennonite Church (MC), a member of the Mennonite Conference of Ontario, is located near Clarence Center, N.Y. In 1824 a colony of Mennonites from Lancaster Co., Pa., among them the Leibs, Lehmans, Sherers, and Martins, settled around Clarence Center. It is reported that Johannes Roth of Lancaster County settled in Erie County south of Clarence Center early in the latter half of the 18th century. Their first minister was Jacob Lapp, who, according to Hartzler-Kauffman records, came in 1828. John Martin was the first deacon (Cassel, 169). In 1831 Jacob Krehbiel, a Mennonite minister, moved in from Germany. He became bishop in 1839. His son Frederick and Abraham Leib were ordained deacons with the growth of the congregation. They soon built a stone church (no longer standing) a few miles west of Clarence Center, known as Good's Church. The congregation prospered both by immigration and by accessions. John Lapp (1798-1878) became minister in 1828 and bishop about ten years later. Peter Lehman and Abram Lapp were also ordained ministers. Jacob Krehbiel, Jr., became minister in 1872 but withdrew about 1875, and affiliated with the General Conference Mennonites. Jacob Hahn, father of Sarah Lapp, missionary to India, became minister in 1866. The *Herald of Truth* in 1872 reported German Sunday school and services held here every Sunday. John Strickler, of the Miller Church (*q.v.*) near Clarence, later identified himself with this flock (MC). When John Lapp became inactive the church dwindled and with the loss of the Krehbiel followers became very weak. The Ontario Conference supplied the ministers for a number of years until about 1920, when new families moving in from various states gave rise to a revived congregation in a more easterly location. The Good cemetery is still the burying ground for the Clarence Center congregation.

Services were held in a school east of Lockport and in a small church near Gasport until a larger church was found, known as Sandhill. This church was used for more than ten years, and then the present church was built a few miles north of Clarence. Membership in those years grew to more than 300. During the 1940's some families again moved to other settlements. The church membership in 1949 was given as 177. The ministers in this 25-year period have been Irvin E. Burkhart, Chris L. Ressler, Jacob W. Birky, D. D. Kauffman, D. Edward Diener, with bishops S. F. Coffman, Moses H. Roth, Moses H. Shantz, Burton B. Weber, and A. Lewis Fretz (serving in 1954). J.C.F.

L. J. Burkholder, *Brief History of Mennonites in Ontario* (Toronto, 1935); D. K. Cassel, *History of the Mennonites* (Philadelphia, 1888).

Clarichen (*Clerqen, Clerckschen, Klarken, Klaren*), the name used for the Old Flemish Mennonites in Prussia. In 1678 a confession appeared: *Konfession . . . der Mennonisten in Preussen so man nennet die Clarichen* (ML I, 160). This name was unknown in the Netherlands; here they were usually called *Dantziger Oude Vlamingen* or *Huiskoopers* (*q.v.*). The name *Clerckschen* is also found in some letters written by Jan van Hoek (*q.v.*) of Danzig to the Committee on Foreign Needs at Amsterdam (*Inv. Arch. Amst.* I, Nos. 1620, 1622, 1632, 1646, 1664 in 1735-37). H. G. Mannhardt (*Die Danziger Mennoniten-Gemeinde*, 1919, p. 46) supposes that the name is of Dutch origin and means *klaar*, i.e., unambiguous. According to this explanation they are clear, or unequivocal ones.

H. B. Hulshoff (*De Bezoekreis van Hendrik Berends Hulshoff*, 1938, reprint, p. 5 note 1) is of opinion that the word *Klerk* is related to the medieval Dutch word *clerq*, which was still in use in the 16th century and which meant a man who in the Catholic Church had received the lower ordinations and was therefore wearing black clothing. The plain Mennonites of the Old Flemish branch, he says, were also dressed in dark clothes, hence they were called *Klerken*, or in the Low German dialect *Clarichen*. But this explanation does not satisfy. vdZ.

Clarion (Iowa) Amish Mennonite settlement: see **Wright County, Iowa.**

Clarke, Samuel, b. at Norwich, England, 1675, d. 1729, studied first mathematics and philosophy, then the New Testament, became chaplain-in-ordinary to Queen Anne of England, is the author of many treatises on theological subjects, including a book on the *Scripture Doctrine of the Trinity*

(1712). Clarke can be said to be the founder of rationalistic supranaturalism. Against deism and pantheism, which were much accepted and widely spread in his time, Clarke defends the contents of the Biblical revelation, which, however, he tries to explain with reason. Two of his books, *A Discourse concerning the Being and Attributes of God* (1705) and *A Discourse concerning the unchangeable Obligations of Natural Religion and the Truth and Certainty of the Christian Revelation* (1705), were translated into Dutch by the Mennonite minister Jan Boelaart (*q.v.*) in 1753 and 1769. J. Stinstra (*q.v.*), a Mennonite minister, also translated the sermons of Clarke into Dutch (9 vv. 1739-49). By these translations Clarke had some influence on the Mennonites in the Netherlands, and made the rationalism of the Dutch Mennonites in the 18th century more Scriptural than it was elsewhere. vdZ.

HRE IV, 129-30; Chr. Sepp, *Johannes Stinstra en zijn tijd* (Amsterdam, 1865) I, 6; II, 146, 167, 256.

Clarksburg United Missionary Church, a congregation of the Ontario Conference, located at Clarksburg near Georgian Bay, had a membership in 1951 of about a dozen. The appointment was closed in 1952. E.R.S.

Clarksville (Pa.) United Missionary Church belongs to the Ohio Conference. It was organized in 1933, with Joseph Sabo, Sr., as pastor. E.R.S.

Clasen (Claasen), **Eje,** was, according to the title and foreword of one of his books, an unlearned preacher of the small Mennonite church at Humsterland (*q.v.*), west of Groningen in Holland. He served from about 1780 until his death in 1813. He seems to have studied nature extensively and makes use of it in his sermons, of which he published *Leerrede* (1797), *Tweetal leerredenen* (Groningen, 1799), *Drie verhandelingen of leerredenen met Nareden over de beweging der aarde* (Groningen, 1803). (*Catalogus Amst.*, 311; ML I, 360.) J.L.

Claudine le Vettre (called Claudine le Vetter in *DB*), an Anabaptist martyr, the wife of Piersom (Pierson) des Muliers (*q.v.*), a God-fearing man who lived in Brugge and later in Meenen (Menin), Belgium. Piersom managed to escape, having been warned by a friend of the coming of the catchpolls. But Claudine, with a child upon her arm, was unable to do so, and after a valiant confession of her faith in Ieper (Ypres), Belgium, was executed in 1568. Her husband praised her for her great knowledge of the Scriptures; she also had a beautiful voice and encouraged many in prison by singing hymns. (*Mart. Mir.* D 383, E 737; *DB* 1875, 29; 1899, 104, 106; ML II, 644; III, 175.) NEFF.

Claudius, Matthias (1740-1815), a major lyric poet of Germany. Much of his verse is moralizing or religious in character, even strongly pietistic in his later life, and is marked by simplicity and humor. He published many of his poems in the *Wandsbecker Bote* (Wandsbeck Messenger), of which he was the editor. One of these is a poem of seven lines, titled "Hinz und Menno," Hinz boasting in the first six lines of his extensive knowledge of morals, and Menno (Simons) replying in a single line in Dutch, "But do you act accordingly?" (Maar doet gy ook daarna?) The *Church Hymnal* (MC) and the *Mennonite Hymnary* (GCM) both contain a poem written by Claudius, which was later set to music, viz., "We Plow the Fields and Scatter."

E.H.B.

Aus dem Wandsbecker Boten des Matthias Claudius (Die Blauen Bücher) (Leipzig, 1921) 14.

Claudy Centurio, an Anabaptist martyr, b. at Noyelles near Cambrai in France, a citizen of Brussels, was beheaded at Utrecht in the Netherlands on June 11, 1539, because he had been (re)baptized. Together with him his son Aert (*q.v.*) was executed. (*Berigten Hist. Genootschap, Utrecht* IV, 2, 1851, 139.)

vDZ.

Clay County, Ind. (pop. 30,000), south of the west-central part of the state, was formed by statute in 1825. In the early days it was a coal-mining center, but when coal began to fail, ten clay plants were in operation. With Owen County (pop. 13,000) on the east, the location of McCormicks Creek State Park, it became the home of a small struggling ultraconservative Mennonite settlement about 1860, made up chiefly of settlers who had come originally from Rockingham Co., Va., to Fairfield Co., Ohio, then to Logan Co., Ohio, where a small Mennonite settlement died out about 1869. Deacon George Funk, son of Bishop Daniel Funk of the extinct Mennonite church in Logan County, was one of the last ordained men in the congregation. Descendants of the Mennonites who remained in the community united with other denominations. One became a Methodist minister. Matthias Cooprider, grandfather of Dr. Florence Cooprider Friesen, moved from Clay City in southern Clay County to Marion Co., Kan., in 1876 and married as his third wife the widow of Henry Brunk, father of George R. Brunk.

J.S.U.

Clearbrook (British Columbia) Mennonite Brethren Church is located west of Abbotsford. In 1953 it had a membership of 328, with A. A. Toews as its leader.

M.G.

Clearfield County (Pa.) Mennonite Church: see **Rockton** Mennonite Church.

Clearfork Amish Mennonite Church (MC), now extinct, organized in Cass Co., Mo., in 1868, by settlers who had come from Ohio, Illinois, Michigan, and Pennsylvania. After worshiping in their homes for several years, they built the Clearfork Church in 1870. In the winter of 1875-76, a church split divided the congregation into two factions, the more liberal, known as the "Eicher people," finally obtaining control of the church building. The conservative group then built the Sycamore Grove Church. The Eicher group (see **Benjamin Eicher**) finally disbanded, although from among their members, through the preaching of John S. Coffman, were recruited a nucleus who established the Bethel Mennonite Church.

M.G.

Clearspring (Md.) **Camp.** Unit 4 of Civilian Public Service Camp No. 24, often known as the Hagerstown Camp, was located about five miles north of Clearspring on a farm owned by the Mennonite Publishing House, Scottdale, Pa. Although there were five units in the camp, each was operated independently of the others. Unit 4 was under the direction of the Mennonite Church (MC) and the Soil Conservation Service. It was opened in the spring of 1942. Two schools were held here for the campers, a farm and community school early in 1944 and a Christian workers' school beginning in November 1944. (M. Gingerich, *Service for Peace,* Akron, Pa., 1949.)

M.G.

Clearspring Mennonite Church (MC), located one mile south of Clearspring, Md., near U.S. Route 40, is a member of the Washington Co., Md., and Franklin Co., Pa., Mennonite Conference. The earliest meetinghouse was built in 1857 and rebuilt in 1912. Ministers who served the congregation include John Summers, John Rowland, Daniel Roth, Abr. Ebersole, and Josiah Brewer. Samuel R. Eby is serving as present pastor (1948), and M. K. Horst as bishop. The congregation consists of a rural people. Sunday school is conducted with every morning service, which is biweekly. The 1949 membership was 71.

J.D.R.

Clearwater Mennonite Church (MC), now extinct, was located near Youngstown, in east-central Alberta. The first settlers came to the area in 1910. The church was organized in 1912 by Bishop N. B. Stauffer. Ordained brethren who served the church were Isaac Miller, M. H. Schmitt, and Abe Reist, the latter being ordained there in 1919. Year after year of drought with only an occasional good crop was the cause of the abandonment of this district. The last Mennonite family left in 1924, moving to Tofield, Alta.

E.S.

Cleeff, van, a Dutch Mennonite family, of which the following members went into the ministry: Laurens van Cleeff of Zwolle, serving at Borne 1809-59; his *Afscheids-rede* of Nov. 15, 1857, was published at Zwolle in 1858 (*Catalogus Amst.,* 320); three of his sons also went into the ministry: Anthony Doyer van Cleeff, at Makkum 1835-76; Hendrik Arnoldus van Cleeff, at Rottevalle 1846-51, and Beemster 1851-85; Laurens van Cleeff, at Huizinge 1848-54, Warns-Staveren 1854-57, and Uithuizen 1857-94, author of a paper on the significance of the congregation in *DB* 1893, and a sermon commemorating his 25th year of service in this congregation of Uithuizen (1882, *Catalogus Amst.,* 320); Laurens van Cleeff J. Jzn, a cousin of Laurens, at Hallum 1876-82, Tjalleberd 1882-87, and Aalsmeer 1887-1905; he published (1901) a sermon on Psalm 16:6, commemorating the 25th anniversary of his ministerial service (*Catalogus Amst.,* 322; *DB* 1907, 184.)

vDZ.

Cleerke Hiems (Claerken), the daughter of Bartholomeus Hiems, an Anabaptist martyr, a native of Borculo, Dutch province of Gelderland, was sentenced to death at Antwerp and drowned at the Steen prison in Antwerp on March 20, 1560. (*Antw. Arch.-Blad* IX, 19, 22; XIV, 30-31, No. 338.)

vDZ.

Clemens was the name of a preaching appointment (MC) in Grey Twp., Huron Co., Ont., during the 1870's. It appears that a family by the name of Clemens lived there and that the Mennonites conducted services in this home for several years, at first with eight-week intervals and later near 1880 at four-week intervals. Ministers were supplied. There was no organized work. This appointment was under the Mennonite Conference of Ontario.

J.C.F.

Clemens (Clemons, Clemmens, Cleman, Clementz), a Mennonite family name which appears in the Palatine Mennonite census list as early as 1664 in the person of Jan Clamens living at Niederflörsheim (some researchers trace the name back to Clement of Toft, England, of the 16th century). In 1672 this Johann Clemeintz as deacon signed a letter of appeal sent to the Amsterdam Mennonites. In 1685 he is listed as still living as an old man at the same place. The first member of the family to come to America, Gerhardt Clemens, probably born in 1680, left the Palatinate and arrived in Pennsylvania in 1709, settling in Skippack, Montgomery Co., Pa. Some of his descendants moved to adjacent Chester County. In 1809 another of his descendants, Abraham Clemens, migrated to Waterloo Twp., Ont., where there can still be found a number of his posterity. Several of these Canadian Clemenses moved to the Grand Rapids, Mich., area. Although some Clemens families still are to be found in Michigan and Missouri as well as a few isolated families in other states, by far the largest number are concentrated in Montgomery County.

Four deacons named Clemens served the Mennonite churches in the Waterloo Twp., Ont., district during the 19th century. They were Abram C. (1803-72), Abram L. (1781-1845), Abram S. (1790-1867), and Henry L. (1802-76). Probably the most active member of the Clemens family in Mennonite Church affairs has been Jacob Cassel Clemens (1874-), who served as the first secretary of the Franconia (MC) Conference 1909-50, a minister in the same conference since 1906, a member of the Mennonite Publication Board for many years, and author of the Clemens family history listed below.

J.R.C.

J. C. Clemens, *The Genealogical History of the Clemens Family and Descendants of the Pioneer, Gerhardt Clemens* (Lansdale, Pa., 1948); E. S. Hallman, *The Hallman-Clemens Genealogy with a Family's Reminiscence* (Tuleta, Tex., n.d.); Ezra E. Eby, *A Biographical History of Waterloo Township* (Kitchener, 1895).

Clemens VII, pope 1523-34, was too deeply involved in the political affairs of his time, especially in the wars between Charles V and Francis I of France, to be greatly concerned with the Reformation in Germany, of which he had not the least comprehension. He believed he could suppress it with measures of violence, fire, sword, and the Inquisition. But he was too late. In October 1528 he ordered Charles V to "put an end to the innovations, which have already progressed to a denial of baptism and communion" (Ney, *Geschichte des Reichstags zu Speyer*, 1529, p. 7). It may therefore be assumed that Pope Clemens VII caused Charles to suppress the Anabaptists most ruthlessly, and that he was thus an essential factor in the passing of the cruel Edict of Speyer of April 23, 1529, calling for the complete suppression of the Anabaptists by death. (*ML* I, 360.)   NEFF.

Clemens, Epistle No. IV., a forgery of the 9th century, allegedly one of the major sources of the Anabaptist idea of community of goods (*q.v.*). This thesis was proposed by the German church historian Hans von Schubert in a paper in 1919, in which this idea is followed up with great erudition. The epistle was believed to have been written by Clemens, the first bishop (pope) in Rome, said to have been invested in his office by the Apostle Peter himself. The core of this epistle (in German translation) is contained in Sebastian Franck's *Chronica* of 1531 (*q.v.*), and runs as follows, "Read the fourth epistle (*margin:* of Clemens, concerning the community of goods of the first Christians) addressed to the entire church in Jerusalem, describing how they practiced a common life and how everything was in common possession. Yet, evil arose and established in Christianity the 'mine' and the 'thine'; in fact private property came up." Clemens was emphatically opposed to this and even quotes pagan wise men (philosophers) of Greece who had already recognized that it is but fair that all things should be held in common. Nobody has a right to claim possession of a thing that comes from God, as little as anybody may claim the sun, the air, and the elements. For as these things cannot be divided up, he says, so the other things cannot be parceled out either. All things are given (by God) for common use. He (Clemens) then nicely alludes to Psalm 132:1 and to the practice of the first Christians, Acts 4 and 5. (Franck, *Chronica*, "Vom Ursprung und Ankunft allerlei Irrsal im Amt der Messe," ed. 1531, fol. 495; ed. 1536, fol. 244.)

What shall be said about von Schubert's thesis? It is true that the Anabaptists read this passage; the Hutterites quote it in a great doctrinal book of 1547 (see **Article Book, Hutterite**); and Pilgram Marpeck mentions it in his *Vermahnung* of 1542 (*Gedenkschrift z. 400-jähr. Jubiläum der Menn.*, 1925, 265). Von Schubert mentions Bernhard Rothmann's books, *Bekenntnis von den beiden Sakramenten* (1533) and *Restitution christlicher Lehre* (1534), which had strongly influenced the Münsterite experiment. Rothmann admits that he found the idea that the Lord's Supper means a brotherly community of all things in Franck's *Chronica*. (Franck and Rothmann knew each other in Strasbourg, 1530-31.) Rothmann's idea of a "restitution" of the apostolic church (including its communism) might also have been influenced by Johannes Campanus (*q.v.*), who with great enthusiasm took up the ideas of the *Chronica*, above all that of restitution.

Von Schubert now undertakes an inquiry into the background of this frequently quoted passage from the Clemens epistle. Step by step he proceeds from Franck to the Humanist Johann Sichem, who in 1526 had published the Latin text of this epistle, taking it from the so-called Pseudo-Isidorian Decretals (written *ca.* A.D. 850) where this letter appears for the first time. Here it stands as an admonition by the alleged first pope to the Christians not to deviate from the rules of the apostolic church in Jerusalem. He, Clemens, a disciple of St. Peter, knows the apostles personally, and therefore it is his duty to enjoin upon every Christian obedience to the example of the apostles. The authority of Acts 2 and 4 is thus strengthened and emphasized. The roots of this forgery (it was a case of ecclesiastical politics) were found in the Pseudo-Clementine writings of the third century A.D. (in Rome), in which the *communis usus omnium quæ sunt in mundo* is again defended. In fact, von Schubert proves that the idea is still older, and he finds Stoic and other philosophies of the ancients which to a certain extent may be taken as the very background of the theme (mainly Seneca is quoted).

The further details may be omitted here; it may suffice to recognize that through the activity of Humanists this strange source became known even to unsophisticated common people. But it would be erroneous to conclude with von Schubert that this one rather brief passage served as the main source of the idea of a Christian community of goods, whether in the form of the Münsterites (which von Schubert alone visualizes) or in that of the Hutterites. It may be correct that Rothmann discussed the subject with Franck and got some encouragement from him, but it is still a long way from an ideal to its bitter practice (as chiefly that of Münster). As for the Hutterites, even less contacts can be produced. In any case, Franck's *Chronica* was published long after the community of goods had been established by the Hutterites in Moravia (1528), based on a strict obedience to Scripture. The idea of sharing material possessions with the needy was indeed present among the Anabaptists in Switzerland and near-by South Germany, Tirol, Austria, and Moravia from the beginning in 1525, so much so indeed that their enemies and persecutors (e.g., Zwingli) accused them of communism several years before the publication of the *Chronica,* or even the publication by Sichem in 1526. It is impossible that the idea came from Sichem.   R.F.

H. von Schubert, *Der Kommunismus der Wiedertäufer in Mähren (Sitzungsberichte der Heidelberger Akademie der Wissenschaften* 1919, XI); R. Friedmann, "Eine dogmatische Hauptschrift . . . ," in *Arch. f. Ref.-Gesch.,* 1931, 234-36.

Clement Dirksz, an Anabaptist martyr, by trade a weaver in Haarlem, Dutch province of North Holland, was there burned at the stake on April 26, 1557, with Joriaen Simonsz (*q.v.*). Their martyrdom is sung in three hymns: (1) "Hoort vrienden al hier in dit aertsche dal" (Hear, all ye friends here in this earthly vale), No. 20 of the *Liedtboecxken vanden offer des Heeren;* this song is attributed to Bouwen Lubberts (*q.v.*); (2) "Hoort toe ghy Christen scharen" (Hearken, ye hosts of Christians), found in *Een nieu Liedenboeck* (1562) and included in Wackernagel, *Lieder;* (3) "Hoort vrienden al te samen" (Hear ye friends altogether), found in *Veelderhande Liedekens* (1559). There is also a hymn composed by Clement Dirksz and his fellow sufferer Mary Joris (*q.v.*), found in *Veelderhande Liedekens,* which begins "Hoort doch nu al te samen" (Now hear ye, altogether); its last stanza begins: "D'een heet Clement en een hiet Mary."   Neff, vDZ.

Offer, 257, note 1, 586-91; *Mart. Mir.* D 178, E 563;

Wackernagel, *Lieder,* 133; Wolkan, *Lieder,* 63, 71, 78, 80, 84; F. C. Wieder, *De Schriftuerlijke Liedekens* (The Hague, 1900) index, p. 191; *ML* I, 449.

Clement Henricksz, an Anabaptist martyr, burned at the stake at Amsterdam, of which city he was a citizen, on Dec. 17, 1569. By trade he was a sailmaker. Clement, like Cornelis Jansz (*q.v.*), Jan Quirijnsz (*q.v.*), and Willem Jansz (*q.v.*), was a victim of the Spanish-inspired reaction in Amsterdam, particularly after the coming of Alba (*q.v.*) in 1568. Clement, as well as the other three brethren, were condemned to death by burning because they had attended Mennonite meetings and were thought to hold "stubborn heresy" although he had not yet been baptized. Cornelis, Jan, and Willem were executed on March 12, 1569, but the execution of Clement was repeatedly postponed. Possibly it was expected that he would after all return to the Roman Catholic fold. At any rate, information was given on March 24 that he appeared to be not unwilling to be heard again, and on April 21 that he doubted. Still, Clement remained loyal until death. On Dec. 17, after the execution had again been stayed several times, he had to go to the stake. With the bell ringing in order to prevent the crowd from understanding the words which he was expected to speak to them, he "gave up joyfully." He was strangled at a stake, and then burned.

The *Offer des Heeren* contains a letter from Clement, written in prison. Later on four other letters from him were discovered, also written from prison. They were included with the first letter in the *Groot Offerboek* of 1615 and all five copied by van Braght in his *Martyrs' Mirror.* In one of these letters, he wrote about the severe torture he had to endure.

There is a song about Clement Henricksz which begins, "So wie op den Steen Christum bout, Diens timmering mach blijven" (He who builds on Christ the Rock, his building will remain). This song is included in the *Offer des Heeren.* (*Offer,* 478-83; *Mart. Mir.* D 439, E 833; Grosheide, *Bijdrage,* 181-83, 310; Wolkan, *Lieder,* 69; *ML* II, 282.) vDZ.

Clementia Heynen: see **Mente.**

Clemmer, Josiah C. (b. May 1, 1827, d. June 28, 1905), a prominent bishop of the Franconia Mennonite (MC) Conference, a fourth-generation descendant of immigrant Henry Clemmer of 1738, lived and died on the original Clemmer homestead farm in Franconia Twp., Montgomery Co., Pa., near the village of Franconia. He was ordained preacher of the Franconia congregation on Nov. 9, 1860, and bishop in December 1867. He was an able preacher and effective leader of the moderate conservative type. He married Sarah Kulp Nov. 9, 1851 (8 children), and Lydia Derstine, Dec. 24, 1884.   J.C.C.

Clerckschen: see **Clarichen.**

Clercq, de, a Dutch Mennonite family originally from Flanders, Belgium. Geraerdt de Clercq, b. about 1530, who is thought to have been a Mennonite, migrated from Brugge to Emden, Germany, because of persecution between 1609 and 1622 and died there. His son Jacques de Clercq, b. 1555 at Gent, Belgium, a linen merchant of Brugge, who married Passchijntje Gryspeert of Rumbeeke (of the well-known Mennonite Grispeer or Grijspeert—*q.v.*—family). While most members of the de Clercq family remained Catholic, and their descendants are still living in Brugge, Jacques joined the Mennonite Church and left Flanders with his wife and two children to settle in Haarlem, Holland, in 1607, where he joined the Flemish congregation and died in 1609. It is not clear whether other Mennonites of this family name who are found in Aardenburg and Middelburg in the Dutch province of Zeeland were relatives of Jacques de Clercq. In Haarlem Jacques de Clercq evidently became a deacon and a friend of the well-known Elder Jacques Outerman (*q.v.*).

The de Clercq family lived in Haarlem for three or four generations. Then most members went to Amsterdam, where they were engaged in business and banking. Here in the 18th and 19th centuries no fewer than 18 members of this family served the church *bij't Lam* as deacons. In Middelburg, Zeeland, there must also have been a branch of this family: Jacob de Clercq was a minister of the Flemish congregation of this town in 1665. Willem de Clercq (*q.v.*) was a member of this family. To this family also belonged Pieter de Clercq, b. Jan. 21, 1849, at Amsterdam, d. May 9, 1934, at Zeist, married Maria Catharina Müller of Crefeld. Pieter de Clercq, a banker at Amsterdam, who was a deacon of the Amsterdam congregation, and later, while living at his country house at Veenwouden, a president of the Friesche Doopsgezinde Sociëteit (Mennonite Conference of Friesland), was very active in stimulating the reading of the Bible and in promoting the translation of the Bible into the Frisian language.   vDZ.

P. van Eeghen, *Familieboek de Clercq* (The Hague, 1940); *Ned. Patriciaat* II (1911) 60-68; XI (1920) 43-53; XIII (1923) 29-30.

Clercq, Willem de, son of Gerrit de Clercq and Maria de Vos, b. Jan. 15, 1795, at Amsterdam, d. there Feb. 4, 1844. Though it was the original plan that he enter the Mennonite Seminary in Amsterdam to become a preacher, a combination of circumstances caused him to enter his father's business. Later he was made secretary and then director of the Netherlands Trading Company. In this capacity he established the important Dutch textile industry in Twente in 1833. With Bilderdijk, da Costa, Groen van Prinsterer, and others, he was one of the leaders of the well-known revival movement in Holland called the *Réveil*. Under their influence he no longer felt comfortable in the Mennonite Church, was dissatisfied with the sermons of Prof. Samuel Muller, also thought that infant baptism agreed with the Scriptures better than adult baptism, and in 1825 transferred to the Reformed Church. Of interest is his correspondence with Isaak Molenaar, the Mennonite preacher at Crefeld (*DB* 1911, 74-92; *Menn. Bl.,* 1917, 74; 1918, 4 ff.), who vainly tried to prevent the step. After about 1831 he was under the influence of the noted *Réveil*-preacher, H. F. Kohlbrügge. In his *Dagboek* (Diary), published by Prof. Pierson, we can follow his religious development and the changes in his ideas step by step. De Clercq is especially well known for his rare ability to improvise verse. The Dutch Royal Institute for Literature published his treatise, *Verhandeling over de vraag: welken invloed heeft de vreemde letterkunde, inzonderheid de Italiaansche, Spaansche, Fransche en Duitsche gehad op de Nederlandsche taal en letterkunde sints het begin der 15. Eeuw tot op onze dagen* (Amsterdam, 1824).   J.L.

A. Pierson, *Willem de Clercq naar zijn dagboek* (2 vv., Haarlem, 1888); J. Bosscha, *Willem de Clercq herdacht* (The Hague, 1874); C. E. te Lintum, *Willem de Clercq, de mensch en zijn strijd* (Utrecht, 1938); *DB* 1895, 112; 1897, 16 ff., 47, 58, 66 ff.; *ML* I, 361.

Clericus, Johannes (Jean le Clerc), b. 1657 at Geneva, Switzerland, d. at Amsterdam in 1736, first belonged to the Calvinists, but soon withdrew from them because of the doctrine of predestination. He studied at the universities of Geneva and Saumur in France and visited England and Holland. In 1684 he was appointed to teach in the Remonstrant (*q.v.*) seminary of Amsterdam. He taught here for nearly 50 years—until 1728. His field was Latin, Greek, and Hebrew, and afterwards also philosophy. He published a large number of learned books in Latin and French. By his contemporaries he was accused of Socinian (*q.v.*) views and an unorthodox position concerning the doctrines of Trinity and original sin; he laid much stress upon practical Christianity, which Clericus said is taught very clearly in the Scriptures. As a professor of the Remonstrant seminary he had some influence on Mennonite ministers, many of whom, when training for the ministry, attended his lectures, until a Mennonite seminary was established in 1735. (*Biogr. Wb.* II, 83-104.)   vDZ.

Cleve (Cleves, Kleve), a German duchy situated on the Lower Rhine, on the important route from Switzerland and Upper Germany to the Netherlands; the larger part lies to the right of the Rhine, with the cities of Duisburg, Wesel, Rees, and Emmerich; the more beautiful part on the left, with Xanten, Goch, and the capital, Cleve. The fertile little country had become known through history (Drusus) and legend (Lohengrin). Duke John III (d. 1539) was very influential during the Reformation as a leader of German Protestantism. By his marriage with the heiress of Jülich, Berg, and Ravensberg he extended his realm into a territory almost the size of modern Saxony, making it the largest sovereignty in northwest Germany. His attitude toward the Reformation was therefore of the greatest importance. The boundaries of the duchy of Cleve touched the Netherlands, the duchy of Gelderland, and the regions of the church princes of Cologne and Münster.

The current church policies of these regions also had considerable influence on the neighbors. Since the dukes of Cleve took a rather independent position in religious matters, having liberated themselves almost entirely from the ecclesiastical courts, and since the landed estates possessed great power and the officials ruled rather self-sufficiently under John III as well as under his successor William the Wealthy, 1539-92, reformatory and separatist movements were at times able to develop freely. Characteristic of this independence was the duke's church regulation (*Kirchenordnung* of 1532) in which the duke, though not separated from the old church, nevertheless on his own authority formulated a constitution governing the innermost affairs of the church and proclaimed it without the co-operation of the clergy as a law, introducing it with a Declaration (1533). Along the Lower Rhine the soil was in any case a particularly fruitful one for separatistic movements. On the one hand we see the unparalleled cleavage betweeen the secular and spiritual authorities and a citizenry striving for political and social freedom; on the other hand there were the mystics, the forerunners of the movement known as Anabaptism (zur Linden, *Melchior Hofmann,* 14). In near-by Cologne, the matrix of medieval heresies and the refuge of all sorts of religious parties during the Reformation, the great German mystic, Master Eckhart (*q.v.*), reached the peak of his fame. Closely related to him was the author of the *Theologia Deutsch* (*q.v.*). Although Luther published it as a work of Tauler, nevertheless the Anabaptists considered it a product of their circles; in their later writings and statements at their trials passages from this booklet are quoted verbatim. Not far from that part of Cleve which lies on the left side of the Rhine is the tower of Kempen, whose son Thomas à Kempis gave us the world-famous book, *The Imitation of Christ,* in the 15th century. Anabaptist literature reveals how much those in the region of the Lower Rhine drew from the genuinely evangelical world of ideas in this region (Bouterwek, *Literatur der Wiedertäufer*).

Other sources of strength from which the Reformation and the Anabaptist movement drew included the Brethren of the Common Life (*q.v.*) of the 15th century. The most noted of them were natives of Cleve—Johann Pupper of Goch (d. 1475) and Johann Ruchrath of Wesel (d. 1481). A friend of the former was Cornelius Grapheus, who had published one of Pupper's books and written a foreword for two others. In 1522 he was condemned to death by the Inquisition in Antwerp (O. Clemen, *Joh. Pupper*). Grapheus was one of the *Freigeister* or *Christen zu Antorff,* to whom Luther addressed his well-known letter of 1525 (Rembert, *Wiedertäufer,* 165 ff., 174). Harnack says in his book on the history of dogma (*Dogmengeschichte* III, 3rd ed., 685 f.): "The further one progresses in the history of the Reformation in the various provinces and cities, the clearer it becomes that these Anabaptists, frequently bound with Waldensian and Hussite elements or going back to former medieval movements, were the soil of the Reformation and in some regions remained entwined with it for decades."

Among the Reformed of the Lower Rhine the conviction still lived on in the 17th century that the light of the Gospel did not dawn through the work of Luther in 1517, but through the pre-Reformation religious groups (*Comeniushefte* V, 63; see *ML* I, 362), whose adherents such as the Waldensians and Bohemian Brethren had fled as refugees from Saxony and Pomerania to this region. This is also the point of view from which the

sufferings and confessions of Adolf Clarenbach (*q.v.*) must be judged. In essence he was evangelical; he rejected purgatory and the oath, insisting on discipleship even in suffering, and calling his followers Christian brethren; and he concluded his statement before his inquisitors with the words, "I do not want to make any new articles, but stay with the old ones, which my mother taught me." We can certainly say that in spite of Lutheran influence he belonged to the Waldenses, who were frequently condemned as Anabaptists. In the course of his cross-examination both he and his friends even in the humbler ranks revealed such an amazing knowledge of the Bible, not of a naive kind, but thoroughly systematic, furnishing the accused the framework for their oral apologetics and polemics for all dogmatic and ethical questions, that the explanation must be sought elsewhere than in the appearance of Luther and his Bible. The roots must lie deeper than this.

Of especial importance in the unfolding of ecclesiastical and theological development along the Lower Rhine and also in the Cleve district was Erasmus of Rotterdam, who was also the product of the Brethren of the Common Life (at Deventer and Hertogenbosch). For a time he was in the humanistic circles at the court of John of Cleve, which was dominated by Konrad of Heresbach. John's attitude toward religious innovations and new movements was one of more than neutrality, for he placed all his hopes for the settlement of the religious confusions of the day upon a general council which was to be called. The *Kirchenordnung* of 1532 was presented to Erasmus for his criticism. It is no wonder that the numerous works and teachings of the honored guest were diligently read and distributed. He was cited by leading Anabaptists, such as Thomas von Imbroich and Adam Pastor, stressing as he did that the Christian life was in essence a matter of discipleship. From him they drew their arguments against infant baptism. He even undermined the doctrine of Trinity and was finally suspected as the father of all heresy and even as an Anabaptist.

New ideological material then came down the Rhine from Upper Germany. In the matter of adult baptism, the more democratic Upper Germans preceded the more conservative Low Germans. Here the rejection of tradition was combined with a petrified adherence to the Word, with stress on the ancient teachings and apostolic institutions. In 1529 polemic writings were taken away from a bookseller at the fair and burned. The inspectors of 1533 looked carefully for writings of Andreas Carlstadt (*q.v.*) and Dr. Gerhard Westerburg (*q.v.*). The latter deserved the credit for the rapid growth of Anabaptist congregations also in Cleve (Rembert, 45 ff.).

The hospitable town of Wesel was also a very significant point of attraction for all reformatory trends. The first heresy trial after Clarenbach's showed the existence of a congregation of Covenanters (*Bundesgenossen*). A citizen had declared, "Christ is not going to live in temples made with human hands. Infant baptism is nonsense." Therefore the duke lamented that unbelief was again rearing its head. The imperial mandate of 1529 was published, ordering that "all Lutherans who dared to baptize anew should be killed at once." At the end of the 1520's Wesel was a center of Anabaptism and finally a suburb of Münster (1534-35) (Wolters, 456; O. Clemen, 281; Rembert, 114). Very active propaganda was carried on in Wesel by the Münsterites during the siege. The route of the emissaries usually crossed Wesel. Such a large congregation developed here that from here the establishment of a New Zion was promoted; Wesel was even to become a second New Jerusalem.

Naturally such movements could not remain unnoticed. Severe persecution set in. In the numerous inquisitions of Wesel citizens the fourteen articles were an important basis for the examinations. Otto Vinck and Schlebusch were named as leaders of the congregation (Bouterwek, *Bergische Gesch.* I, 362 ff.) (Of great value are the Dorth manuscripts of the Wesel trials in the Düsseldorf archives.) One of the emissaries sent to Wesel was Heinrich Roll (*q.v.*), who was burned at the stake at Maastricht in 1534 (*BRN* V). Anholt near Wesel was the birthplace of Fabritius (1501), who released Johannes Klopreis from prison in Cologne when he was arrested with Clarenbach (Rembert, 310).

Very gradually the Anabaptists became settled again after the horrors of Münster. Moderate trends began to carry the day. Since Lutheranism was tolerated in the archbishopric of Cologne under Hermann von Wied, Menno Simons also appeared in Cologne and tried to arrange a disputation with the Reformed clergy in Wesel (Cramer, *Menno Simons,* 83). Though in the records of the synods of the Lower Rhine in the following years the Anabaptists are often mentioned, they are not called Mennonites until the 17th century. In spite of extreme bitterness against them, the scattered congregations gradually began to hold conferences on matters of church regulations and discipline. After the first meeting of this kind at Spaarndam (1534) there were others at Bocholt (Westphalia) and Goch (1547) (*DB* 1877). At the Goch conference Adam Pastor was sent out by Menno Simons to proclaim the Word, but was banned later that year on account of his unitarianism. Pastor chose Cleve as his field. In Goch he had converted many members of the "Wüllenamt" (*Annalen* 6).

In spite of all the imperial edicts issued in rapid succession, the government of the duchy of Cleve did not carry them out consistently, for more and more the landowning nobles came to appreciate the value of these industrious workers on their estates. In 1564 the Davidjorists in Wesel were prosecuted (two large volumes of documents in the Deventer library; Dorth Mss. XIV, p. 288; Keller, *Gegenreformation* II, 114 ff.; Rembert, 513). Hunted like wild beasts, the Anabaptists moved from one side of the border to the other, according to prevailing church policies. Many a strong character was won to the movement in these regions in the time of intolerance. An example was the geographer Gerhardus Mercator, who published his immortal works in Duisburg in 1554-94. In Duisburg the irenic Georg Cassander (*q.v.*) was used by the duke in the conversion of Anabaptists.

Although Menno Simons had long succeeded in eliminating the radical element from the Anabaptist movement in these regions, concealed aftereffects of the Münster excesses occasionally came to light, defaming the entire movement. In the Cleve region a Wilhelm Wilhelmsen and his band of "Anabaptists" caused some disturbance. In his book published in Emmerich in 1574 polygamy was frankly preached, just as the most brutal polygamy was advocated by this robber band. Wilhelmsen was executed at Dinslaken in 1580, after he had been guilty of robbery and murder in Emmerich and Wesel.

Gradually the fanatical hatred against the Mennonites subsided, and they were able in remote places to do their work and cultivate their ideals. Little is known of their activities in the late years of the 16th century. The Concept of Cologne was signed for Cleve by only one person, Louys Bouderwijns, in the name of the congregation at Rees. In Goch the Protestant Church congregation reported (1607) that it did not have its own school, but its schoolteacher was an Anabaptist (Keller, *Gegenreformation* II, 256). Mennonites from Jülich and Cleve were received into the Nijmegen congregation 1642-50.   K.R.

According to the *Martyrs' Mirror* martyrs from the district of Cleve were executed: at Amsterdam in 1539 (Jan Janssen van dem Berg, who had been baptized in 1538 at Delft by Claes with the lame hand); at Gent 1568 (Pieter van Cleve) and at Deventer in 1571 (Dirk and Janneken van Wesel—see **Dirk Wessels**); in 1551 Willem de Kistemaker (the Cabinetmaker) from Weess (Weeze), a village near Cleve, and Windel Ravens were executed at Cleve. In 1591 a mixed Anabaptist-Reformed congregation at Calcar was dissolved. In 1654 by an order of Frederick William, Elector of Brandenburg (whose dynasty had gained the duchy in the 17th century), the Mennonites were exempted from the oath and public offices. In 1721 their exemption from recruiting was confirmed by Frederick William I of Prussia (see his privileges for Crefeld dated January 1, 1721, and also the different attitude toward the Mennonites in East Prussia) in return for the annual payment of 500 reichstaler. The Prussian congregations in the west, Crefeld (previously belonging to the principality of Mörs), Cleve, Duisburg, Emmerich, Goch, Rees (previously belonging to the duchy of Cleve), and Hamm (previously belonging to the county of Mark) shared in this payment according to their financial abilities as follows: Crefeld 50 per cent; Emmerich 15 1/3 per cent; Goch 12 1/3 per cent; Cleve 11 1/3 per cent; Rees 5 per cent; Duisburg 3 1/2 per cent; Hamm 2 1/2 per cent.   E.C.

F. O. zur Linden, *Melchior Hofmann, Ein Prophet der Wiedertäufer . . .* (Haarlem, 1885); K. W. Bouterwek, *Zur Literatur und Gesch. der Wiedertäufer, besonders in den Rheinlanden* (Bonn, 1864); O. Clemen, *Johann Pupper von Goch* (Leipzig, 1896); Rembert, *Wiedertäufer;* A. Harnack, *Lehrbuch der Dogmengesch.* (Freiburg, 1888); *Theologische Arbeiten aus dem rhein. wiss. Predigerverein* (Bonn, 1886) p. 91; Wolters, *Reformations-*

geschichte der Stadt Wesel; A. M. Cramer, Het leven . . . van Menno Simons (Amsterdam, 1837); Annalen des hist. Vereins f. d. Niederrhein VI, p. 6; L. Keller, Die Gegenref. in Westfalen und am Niederrhein (Leipzig, 1887); Teschenmacher, "Annales ecclesiastici" (ms. in the Berlin State Library); H 'leppe, Geschichte der evang. Kirche von Cleve-Mark; P. C. J. Guyot, Bijdragen tot de Gesch. der Doopsgezinden te Nijmegen (Nijmegen, 1835); DB 1877; Menn. Bl., November 1887; Ernst Crous, "Die rechtliche Lage der Krefelder Mennonitengemeinde im 17. u. 18. Jh.," and "Urkunden u. Zeugnisse zur rechtlichen Stellung der Mennoniten in Krefeld" in Beiträge zur Geschichte rheinischer Mennoniten (Schriftenreihe des Mennonitischen Geschichtsvereins 2) (Weierhof, Palatinate, 1939) 29-49, 50-57 (illustrated); ML I, 361-64.

Cleve (Cleves, Kleve), a town (1950 pop. 28,704) in Germany, in the province of Nordrhein-Westfalen (Rhine Province), not far from the left bank of the Rhine and the Dutch border capital of the former duchy of Cleve, was formerly the seat of a Mennonite church. Already in 1534 there were Anabaptists in Cleve (Inv. Arch. Amst. I, No. 23). In 1546 Elder Thönis von Hastenrath stayed in Cleve and baptized there (DB 1909, 123). In 1569 a congregation existed in Cleve, which experienced the Frisian and Flemish controversies (Inv. Arch. Amst. I, No. 466). After the invasion by the French army (1672) many members fled to Nijmegen in the Netherlands (Inv. Arch. Amst. II, No. 2572). In 1679 the Mennonite congregation carried on an active correspondence with the Dutch churches. Their church, actually a mere chapel, was on the large square, in a row of houses on the east side; it was built in 1682 with the use of space in a private residence which had been purchased. In the same year, the first church record (Kerke-Boek) was begun; it speaks of the congregation as "very old." Among the members in this period were the Leendertz, Paulus, Utzelmann, Welsing, and Moerbeek families. From 1708 to 1713 Isaak Francken was its Vorleser (leeraar). The congregation received support from Holland, and in 1726 contributed to the Amsterdam Fonds voor Buitenlandsche Nooden.

In 1743 the membership numbered 60. Willem Leendertz was their Vorleser (Inv. Arch. Amst. II, No. 2580). By 1749, when they were stronger, they acquired a pastor of their own, viz., Jelle Brouwer (q.v.), who served until 1782, and was succeeded by his son Pieter Brouwer (q.v.), who served until 1786. Following preachers were A. Doyer, 1787-88; H. W. van der Ploeg, 1789-93; J. van Hulst, 1804-18; H. W. van Ploeg had charge of the Cleve congregation from 1818 to 1850, when it received A. C. Leendertz as its last minister, 1850-95.

In 1794, when the French occupied Cleve and used the Lutheran and Reformed churches for the storage of hay and as stables, the Mennonites also experienced evil times. In 1801 Prussia ceded Cleve to France, which did not return it until Napoleon's final defeat. The congregation dwindled so rapidly during this time that in the 1820's the members made an arrangement with the Goch congregation, whereby the latter's preacher van der Ploeg would look after all spiritual affairs in the Cleve church as also in the united church of Emmerich-Rees. In 1842 there were only 24 members remaining. When van der Ploeg at an advanced age had to sever relations with Emmerich and Cleve, each congregation chose a preacher. Emmerich received as its preacher P. W. van Zutphen, who had been serving for 14 years, and Cleve received the candidate of the Sociëteit, Abraham Cornelis Leendertz, a descendant of the founders of the congregation. Leendertz preached only in Dutch; he found a pleasant field of labor here, not so much in the steadily declining congregation (1787, 69; 1861, 41; 1868, 35; and 1878, 7 members), as in Dutch families living there in summer who regularly attended his services. After the death of van der Ploeg in 1853 Leendertz also conducted monthly services in Goch. In 1895, at the age of 73, he resigned.

The church is now extinct. The slight capital remaining after dissolving the congregation was transferred to Crefeld. The church building was leased to the Dutch Reformed congregation. Up to World War II several services were conducted there each summer by Dutch Mennonite preachers for the sake of Dutch Rhinebargees.

On the Lower Rhine, in the congregations of Emmerich, Rees, Cleve, and Goch, and especially Crefeld, linen weaving was the predominant occupation. Abraham Welsing of Rees, who became a citizen of Cleve in 1671, as late as 1716 was working here with 8 looms, 10 bondmen, 24 boys, and 100 women. C.A.L.

Ernst Crous, "The Mennonites in Germany since the Thirty Years' War" in MQR XXV, No. 4 (Goshen, October 1951) p. 250 f.; Inv. Arch. Amst. I, Nos. 23, 466; II, Nos. 1164, 2571-2575, 2626; DJ 1850, 63 f.; ML I, 364.

Cleve, Pierken van, an Anabaptist martyr: see Pieter Aelbrechts.

Cleveland (pop. 914,000), the metropolis of Ohio, located on Lake Erie. In the early 1830's and in the following years, a number of Mennonite families from the Palatinate, with such names as Risser, Leisy, Baehr, Pletcher, and Krehbiel, located near and within the limits of the present city. These families seemingly never organized a separate congregation, never had a meetinghouse of their own, nor a resident minister; for many years services were held in rented buildings by visiting ministers, including for several years after 1875, C. H. A. van der Smissen, who had charge of a church in near-by Ashland County. In 1862 Daniel Krehbiel, one of the prominent founders of the General Conference Mennonite Church, whose wife was a member of the Leisy family, moved from Iowa to Cleveland. In the General Conference sessions of 1869 to 1876 he served as a delegate from the Cleveland group. Krehbiel died in 1888. The congregation has long since become extinct. Some of the families moved away, and others joined other churches. Some of the descendants of the early settlers later played a prominent role in the business and political life of the city. The Leisys became the founders of the present well-known Leisy Brewery interests. From 1910 to 1912 Herman C. Baehr served as mayor of the city. It was a matter of newspaper comment at the time of their inauguration into office that both the mayor and his district attorney, Cyrus Locher, a Mennonite from Bluffton, Ohio, true to their Mennonite heritage, substituted for the official oath the simple affirmation.

In 1948 the Gladstone Mennonite Mission (colored) was established in Cleveland. It was originally sponsored by the Plainview Mennonite Church (MC), Aurora, Ohio, but is now under the Mennonite Board of Missions and Charities (Elkhart, Ind.). The Mennonite Witness to Israel (MC) mission, located southeast of the city, 52 Louis Road, Bedford, was established in 1947 and is under the Ohio Mennonite (MC) Mission Board. During World War II Mennonite conscientious objectors served in the several state mental hospitals in and near the city. In 1954 more than 140 Mennonite CO's (I-W men) were serving in the Cleveland area, with the Cleveland State Hospital as the chief employer. **C.H.S.**

Cleveland (Ohio) State Hospital. Civilian Public Service Unit No. 69⁴ was opened here under the administration of the Friends in December 1942, but was discontinued a year later. The Mennonites reopened the unit in April 1945, and remained in charge until it was terminated in October 1946. During the time that the unit had its full quota of men, they were given complete charge of the male infirmary, housing approximately 365 infirm and untidy mental patients. During the period when the Mennonites had charge of the unit, a total of 45 men were assigned to it. Women's summer service units under the direction of the Mennonite Central Committee served at the hospital in 1945 and 1946. (M. Gingerich, *Service for Peace,* Akron, Pa., 1949.) **M.G.**

Cleyndert, a Mennonite family found in the Dutch Zaan district north of Amsterdam. Most of them originally belonged to the Groningen Old Flemish congregation of Oostzaandam. They usually were grain merchants, and some of them were deacons in the church. A descendant of this family, Claes Cleyndert (1799-1842), and his son Hendrik Cleyndert (1825-87), both grain merchants, promoted the building of a church (1843) at Nieuwendam, near Amsterdam, where at this time some members of the Cleyndert family resided. The Nieuwendam meetinghouse, a frame building, was a gift of the Cleyndert family. **vDZ.**

Clinton Amish Mennonite Church, located 5½ miles east of Goshen, Ind., on State Road 4, was organized by former members of the Old Order Amish Mennonite Church on Ascension Day 1947. The congregation is not affiliated with any conference, but fellowships with the group of former Old Order congregations known as "Beachy Amish." The first meetinghouse was dedicated on Dec. 7, 1947. David A. Bontrager is the bishop of the congregation which has a membership of 107 (1951). **D.A.B.**

Clinton Brick Mennonite Church (MC), located in Clinton Twp., Elkhart Co., near Goshen, Ind., is a member of the Indiana-Michigan District Conference. The church was organized in 1854 with approximately 40 members, under the leadership of John Nusbaum, who served as the first pastor. The present membership (1954) stands at 154, most of whom are rural people. The first meetinghouse was a log structure, built in 1854, with a seating capacity of 100. In 1880 a new solid brick building was erected, which served the congregation until 1944, when it was destroyed by fire. In 1946 a new solid brick church was built which has a seating capacity of 300. Ministers who served for a length of time are John Nusbaum, Henry Miller, Peter Lehman, John Garber, David Garber, Samuel Honderich, Amos Nusbaum, Samuel S. Miller, and Amsa H. Kauffman, who is the present bishop. (Maxine Kauffman, "History of the Clinton Brick Mennonite Church," *MHB,* March-June 1945.) **A.H.K.**

Clinton Cheyenne (American Indian) Mennonite Church (GCM), located one mile east of Clinton, Custer Co., Okla., was organized Feb. 19, 1899. The mission station was established in 1894 by M. M. Horsch. In April 1951 a new church building was dedicated, replacing the old frame building erected in 1898. A total of 185 members have been added. The 1954 membership stood at 62, a number having transferred to the Hammon and Thomas Mennonite churches. The fiftieth anniversary was commemorated in 1949. Missionaries who have served are G. A. Linscheid, J. H. Epp, J. B. Ediger (40 years), and Arthur Friesen, the present missionary. **A.F.**

Clinton Frame Mennonite Church (MC), located in Clinton Twp., Elkhart Co., Ind., five miles east of Goshen, is a congregation of the Indiana-Michigan Conference of the Mennonite Church. This was the first Amish Mennonite church organized in Indiana. The first services were held on Easter Day of 1842.

The first meetinghouse was built in 1848 at the location where the present church stands, which was built in 1888 and enlarged in 1913 and 1949. Two divisions have occurred in the congregation. The first (Old Order Amish, 1855-65) was the result of differences on the question of whether to baptize in the meetinghouse or in a stream. The second division at Clinton Frame came in 1892 when approximately 40 members left to organize the Silver Street Mennonite Church (*q.v.*). Among the issues at that time were questions relating to the regulation of attire and open communion.

In July 1944 a church in the village of Benton, also in Elkhart County, about five miles southwest of the Clinton Frame Church, was purchased by the congregation and regular services have been held there ever since. In 1948 this Benton (*q.v.*) mission church became an independent congregation in the Indiana-Michigan Conference. This action took about 40 members out of the Clinton Frame congregation. The 1954 membership was 200.

Bishops who have served this church were Jonas Troyer, Benjamin Schrock, D. J. Johns, D. D.

Troyer, and Edwin J. Yoder. Ministers who have served are Christian Plank, Eli Miller, D. D. Troyer, Silas Yoder, Ira S. Johns, Verle Hoffman, Galen Johns, and Vernon Bontreger. Present ministers (1954) are Vernon Bontreger, pastor, and Ira S. Johns, minister. Deacons who have served are Daniel Schrock, Ira S. Johns, David Yontz, Vernon Bontreger, and Norman Kauffman.

The first Sunday school was organized in 1876. The first Mennonite (MC) Sunday-school conference in the United States was held at the Clinton Frame Church in 1892.   I.S.J.

Ira S. Johns, "Early Amish Settlers in Indiana and Clinton Frame Church History," in *MHB* III, 3; D. Schrock, *A History of the Clinton Frame Church* (Scottdale, 1927).

Clock (Klock), **Leenaerdt,** a Mennonite preacher, a native of Germany who settled in Holland probably before 1590. He is one of the most prolific writers of Dutch Mennonite devotional hymns. He was also the most important drafter of the Concept of Cologne (*Concept van Keulen* 1591) (*q.v.*), on the basis of which a part of the South German churches and of the High German churches in Holland united with a group of Frisians and some Waterlanders as the *Bevredigde Broederschap* (*q.v.*) (i.e., they had achieved peace). This union had the endorsement of the elders Hans Busschaert de Wever (*q.v.*), Hans de Ries (*q.v.*), and Lubbert Gerritsz (*q.v.*). When Clock moved to Haarlem he gradually grew stricter in his views, especially on mixed marriages and the ban (*q.v.*).

In 1608 Clock became involved in a dispute with the Waterlanders under Denys van Hulle. After he had vainly demanded of van Hulle that he resign his ministry (1611), he parted from him two years later because of difference of opinion on mixed marriages. Hans Matthijs, Jan Schellingwou, Anne Annesz, and Jan Eriksz went with Clock. A new High German congregation was formed in Amsterdam, which was but short-lived. This quarrel was the more lamentable because in 1604 Clock had attempted a reconciliation with all the Flemish, an attempt blocked chiefly by the opposition of Claes Ganglofs (*q.v.*) and the Groningen congregation. He had better success in his attempt at reconciliation with the Waterlanders in De Rijp under Cornelis Michielsz, who in 1611 had separated from the *Bevredigde Broederschap* at the instigation of Claes Wolter Kops (*q.v.*); but this division was healed in September of the same year at a large conference in Amsterdam. After the division of 1613, both parties preached in the church at Haarlem for a time. After Clock had vainly tried to lock the doors against the opposing party, his party tried to gain possession of the building by illegal methods. The title deed to the church property was made out in the name of Thomas van Dalen. His son Jacob Thomas van Dalen and his son-in-law Guillaume Stoppelaar sold the building on April 25, 1615, to Leenaerdt Clock; but the opposition prevented the sealing of the transaction. This unedifying quarrel ended in 1617 with the erection of a new building by each party. In the meantime Clock had left Haarlem and was living in Schoonhoven (*q.v.*), a

Dutch province of South Holland, where he became a copreacher of Jan Lammersz. A futile attempt at reconciliation was made in 1621. Clock resisted it, though his daughter Anneken was on the opposing side. The followers of Leenaerdt Clock in Haarlem, Amsterdam, and elsewhere were called the *Afgedeelden* (*q.v.*). They united with the Flemish in 1639.

Clock's place in Mennonite history rests in the main on his writings, which had lasting influence. As a hymn writer he was very successful, even though Wolkan is right in saying that many of his hymns lack poetic inspiration. This was due chiefly to his favorite practice of composing acrostics, i.e., hymns in which the initial letters of each stanza when read together give the name of a person. In the 1625 collection of 435 hymns, no fewer than 398 are of this kind. (Concerning the names see Th. J. J. Arnold in *Bibliographische Adversaria* II.) But other hymns are of lasting value; and his most popular hymn (No. 131 in the *Ausbund*) is still sung today by the Amish as the second hymn in every church service (see J. W. Yoder, *Amische Lieder,* 1942, No. 1). Clock published the following five hymnbooks: (*a*) *Veelderhande schriftuerlijcke nieuwe Liedekens* (Utrecht, 1593, combined with the following); (*b*) *Het groote Liedeboeck* (Leeuwarden, 1625); (*c*) *Kleyn Liedtboeck* (Haarlem, 1625); (*d*) *Vyftien schriftuerlijcke Liedekens* (Amsterdam, 1690); (*e*) *Vier en twintig schriftuerlijcke Liedekens* (Amsterdam, 1589). All these books became rather popular and passed through several editions. Some hymns were also translated into German (possibly by the author himself) and were adopted in two leading devotional manuals: the *Confession oder kurzes und einfältiges Glaubensbekenntnis . . . der Gemeinden in Preussen* (1751 ed.; here we find the hymn, "Lebt friedsam, spricht Christus der Herr"), and *Christliches Glaubensbekenntnis, . . . T.T.V.S.* (Amsterdam, 1664; see van Sittert), a most popular handbook, which contains seven of Clock's hymns.

But Clock's influence goes still further. In 1625, he published a *Forma eenigher Christelijcker Ghebeden* (A Formulary of Several Christian Prayers), which until recently was hardly noticed though it proved to be the very standard book upon which all later Mennonite prayer literature is built (Friedmann, *Menn. Piety,* 181 ff.). A German translation of this book appeared in T. T. van Sittert's manual of 1664 with 18 prayers (while the 1751 Prussian manual contains only 13 prayers). The preface says, "To the unanimous brotherhood in Prussia and to the believers everywhere assembled in Christ, dedicated by L. C. . . . ." indicating that Clock either had drawn up this prayer formulary expressly for the brethren in Prussia or that he later translated it from the Dutch for their sake. In any case, a few of these prayers became exceedingly popular, particularly the "general" prayers II and III (in van Sittert's manual). It has been proved that prayer II was time and again used and reshaped until it found its final form in the Swiss-Mennonite prayer book, *Ernsthafte Christenpflicht* (*q.v.*) of 1739 (Friedmann, 181-92). This is the more surprising as this prayer in its original form is rather colorless. Yet nothing else was available of Mennonite origin, particularly in the German language, for those who wanted a Mennonite prayer book. Thus van Sittert's edition found wide circulation both in the north and in the south of Germany.

In the early controversy of the Dutch Mennonite Church concerning the practice of silent or audible prayers (see **Prayer**), Clock stood on the side of those who preferred the audible prayer in worship. Knipscheer reports in his fine study of this controversy (*DB* 1897, 109 f.), that Leenaerdt Clock, who had come from Germany, spoke his prayers always "overloyt," i.e., audibly, as Hans de Ries used to do. Clock had also visited the congregations in Prussia and Poland in 1606 (*Inv. Arch. Amst.* II, 2930). In the quarrel between Clock and Cops in Haarlem the Prussian churches remained neutral.

With regard to Clock's doctrinal stand, Alenson (*q.v.*) claims that Clock placed great stress on Menno's peculiar doctrine of the incarnation. (See **Hymns, Prayers,** and **Prayerbooks.**)   K.V., R.F.

Kühler, *Geschiedenis* II, 1, pp. 72 ff., 88, 91 ff., 193; Blaupot t. C., *Holland; idem, Groningen; BRN* VII; Wolkan, *Lieder*, 113-17, 155 f.; R. Friedmann, *Menn. Piety Through the Centuries* (Goshen, 1949; see Index); *DB* 1897, 109 f.; *Biogr. Wb.* V, 27-30; *N.N.B.Wb.* III, 307; *Inv. Arch. Amst.* I, Nos. 482, 483, 520, 535, 542, 545, 546, 554, 555; II, Nos. 1193-1203, 2626 f., 2925 f., 2930 f.; *ML* I, 364 f.

Clocks. Clockmakers were to be found among the Anabaptists and Mennonites through the centuries. We learn that Hutterites, especially in the large Bruderhof of Pribitz, manufactured clocks for church towers in 1572 and 1609 and clocks (even costing 170 talers) for the brother of Emperor Matthew and for the Cardinal Franz von Dietrichstein in 1613. The Moravian nobleman Albrecht von Boskowitz in 1571 instructed them to paint the necessary faces for a clock in his castle at Czernahora (F. Hruby, *Die Wiedertäufer in Mähren,* Leipzig, 1935, 24 and 32/33; see also **Pribitz**).

In the Palatinate a century later we meet a whole dynasty of Mennonite clockmakers: two brothers of the well-known Martin and David Möllinger, viz., the famous Jacob Möllinger (1695-1763) in Neustadt an der Haardt and Joseph Möllinger (1715-72) in Zweibrücken (ducal clockmaker and master of the mint), also Jacob's son and grandson—Johannes Möllinger at Fischbach, clockmaker to the Count of Wartenberg, and a second Jacob Möllinger at Kaiserslautern; likewise an Elias Möllinger, who died 1854, also at Kaiserslautern. (See **Möllinger.**)

Noteworthy is the famous Mennonite clockmaker, Peter Kinzing (1745-1816) of Neuwied on the Rhine, an unusually skillful and creative craftsman, whose artistic and special clocks were mechanical wonders, "most of which found their way into the French, Russian, Prussian, Saxon, Württemberg and other German courts." On the occasion of a trip to France he was made "clockmaker to the queen." The famous writing desks of David Röntgen owe a large share of their reputation to the clocks which Kinzing built into them.

A famous Dutch Mennonite clockmaker was Hendrik van Heylbronn (*q.v.*) at Almelo.

The "Russian" or "Mennonite" clocks (*Wanduhren*) can still be found in some Mennonite homes in Canada, Mexico, South America, and in some of the prairie states. The Prussian Mennonites living along the Vistula River probably brought this clock with them from the Netherlands. Some of the clocks now found in Mennonite homes date back to the time when the Mennonites lived in Prussia prior to 1800. In Russia one of the first manufacturers of these "Mennonite" clocks at the middle of the past century was Peter Lepp of Chortitza. Prominent manufacturers of these clocks in Russia in the beginning of this century were David Kröger in the village of Rosenthal in the Chortitza settlement and Gerhard Mandtler of Lindenau in the Molotschna settlement, each of whom had a factory evaluated at about $5,000. The manufacturer C. Hildebrandt worked for years on a very complicated clock which included the days of the month and the planetary movements. Among the Mennonites that came to America in the 1870's there were a few men who kept these clocks in repair and at least one who made them.

These clocks could be found in nearly every Mennonite home in Russia and after 1874 also in the prairie states and provinces in America in the *grosse Stube* (parlor) hanging on the wall next to the door leading into the *Eckstube*. The mechanism was usually simple, operated by one heavy and one light weight. A clock that struck the hour had two heavy and two light weights. The brass parts, weights, pendulum, and hands, were always kept shining. The face of the clock, made of tin or wood, was twelve inches square and usually bore a flower motif and the year of its construction. Most of the surviving clocks brought to Canada and the United States in the 1870's are still in running condition. For a time during the adjustment of the Mennonites to their American environment there was little appreciation for these heirlooms; today they are scarce and sought after by Mennonites of Canada, United States, Mexico, and South America.   C.K.

Cloppenburch, Johannes, a Dutch Reformed preacher, b. May 13, 1592, in Amsterdam, studied at the university of Leiden, where he formed a friendship with Voetius, and later attended various **French,** German, and Swiss universities, until he was made preacher at Aalburg in 1616. In 1618 he was called to Heusden. Three years later he accepted a preaching position in Amsterdam. After falling out with the city government he was engaged as preacher in Brielle, 1630-40, and then as a professor at the universities of Harderwijk (until 1643) and Franeker, where he died on July 30, 1652. Cloppenburch distinguished himself as a zealous opponent of the Mennonites. In 1625 he published in Amsterdam *Gangraena Theologicae Anabaptisticae, d.i., Cancker van de leere der Wederdooperen, ontdeckt uyt hare eygene Schriften.* This book was later published in a more detailed version in the form of disputations in Latin (Franeker, 1645 and 1656). It was printed again when after Cloppenburch's death most of his writings were published by Professor a Marck (Amsterdam, 1684). It was probably this anti-Mennonite book that drew attention to the author and led to his appointment at the university in Harderwijk. (*Biogr. Wb.* II, 106-22; *DB* 1897, 116; *Catalogus Amst.*, 198, 202; *ML* I, 365.)   J.L.

Cloverdale Church of God in Christ Mennonite Church, organized in 1945, is located north of Creswell, Lane Co., Ore. Sunday-school and worship services are held every Sunday morning. It had a membership of 13 in 1950. Jacob G. Loewen was in charge of the services.   J.G.L.

Clyde Park Mennonite Church (MC), now extinct, 70 miles south of Calkins, Mont., was organized into a congregation with eight members on Nov. 12, 1921, by Bishop I. S. Mast. John Hochstetler filled the pulpit twice a month until the spring of 1924 when he moved there, remaining until the group left in 1926. Thirty-five was the largest membership. Hard times due to uncertain crops and the depression were the reasons given for discontinuing the work. They worshiped in a rented Methodist church four miles east of Clyde Park, Park Co., Mont.   F.E.K.

Cnoop (Knoop), a Mennonite family, in the 17th to 19th centuries living in Bolsward, Friesland, where they were merchants and often deacons of the local church. Wopke Claes Knoop, b. Feb. 2, 1740, at Bolsward, d. Nov. 20, 1801, at Amsterdam, was an ardent Patriot (*q.v.*), organizing the voluntary citizen soldiery in his home town. From September 1786 to May 1789 he was imprisoned in Leeuwarden, capital of Friesland, because of his radical democratic ideas. His daughter Janke was married to Rinse Koopmans (*q.v.*), Mennonite pastor and professor at the Amsterdam Mennonite Seminary. Rinse's son Wopco Cnoop Koopmans, like his father a pastor and a professor at the Seminary, was named for his patriotic grandfather. Some of the descendants bearing the family name Cnoop Koopmans have left the Mennonite Church.   vDZ.

Chr. Kroes-Ligtenberg, "Wopke Knoop, een Fries Patriot," in *Vrije Fries* XLI (Leeuwarden, 1953) 112-44.

CNRRA (Chinese National Relief and Rehabilitation Administration) was a Chinese government agency established by order of the Executive Yuan, Jan. 21, 1945, for the purpose of administering postwar relief and rehabilitation in China. Supplies to the amount of $945,196,000 were requested from the United Nations Relief and Rehabilitation Administration (UNRRA). Plans covered direct emergency relief in liberated areas, work projects, and rehabilitation measures. Responsibility for administration of projects was with CNRRA, but experts and advisers from UNRRA participated. Through interference by civil war, the relief program was much restricted but continued active in areas under Nationalist control. Relief efforts by voluntary agencies, including the MCC, were integrated as far as possible with the CNRRA program.   S.F.P.

Coal Creek, What Cheer, Iowa, was listed as a preaching point of the Liberty (MC) congregation in the *Mennonite Year-Book and Directory,* from 1913 (not listed in previous directory of 1908) through 1922. Services were held there once a month for the seven members.   M.G.

Coaldale is a village situated in the middle of an irrigation district in southern Alberta. This is a mixed-farming district, including dairying, for which the Mennonites built and manage a cheese factory. Sugar beets are also grown in this district, for which there are three sugar factories near by.

Most of the Mennonites of this area came to Canada from Russia between 1923 and 1930. The larger percentage belong to the Mennonite Brethren Church, which has about 605 members in this locality. In addition there are 136 Mennonites who are not members of a congregation.

The M.B. church building is 60 x 104 ft. Next to the church is the M.B. Bible school, which in 1954 had four teachers and 95 students. There is also a Mennonite high school which had three teachers and 50 students in 1950. The Coaldale Mennonite Church (GCM) had in that year about 285 members.   J.W.

Coaldale Home for the Aged, an institution operated by the Conference of the Mennonite Churches of Alberta, was founded by the annual conference in 1952. In 1954 it was in process of building.   J.J.K.

Coaldale Hospital, a Mennonite institution in Coaldale, Alta., was established in 1934. Among the Mennonite settlers at Coaldale who had come from Russia, it was a tradition that care of the sick and the poor was the responsibility of the community or the congregation. On this basis two organizations were formed in Coaldale: (1) The Coaldale Mennonite Health Society (C.M.H.S.), with the aim of bringing medical service within the reach of the poor; and (2) The Coaldale Hospital Society (C.H.S.), to make hospitalization easily accessible to everyone.

The C.M.H.S. was formed in 1928 and entered a contract with a Lethbridge physician, Dr. W. S. Galbraith, to render all his professional services to members of the society and their families for a monthly fee of $1.00 per family. The society started out with 25 members, but soon grew to over 300, with increasing advantages to the members. In 1932 a similar contract was made with the Galt Hospital in Lethbridge (10 miles distant). This brought health services up to a fairly high standard. But there still was the difficulty of language. This was also remedied when in 1933 Dr. D. L. Epp, of their own kin and creed, took over the contract of the C.M.H.S. and moved to Coaldale.

George Kroeker and John Martens, at the suggestion of Helen Martens, a local graduate nurse, tackled the task of bringing hospitalization to Coaldale. They rented a room in the old Bank Building, furnished it with the necessary equipment for a 3-bed "Nursing Home," and persuaded some friends to join in the undertaking, organizing the C.H.S. At first only nine members enrolled with a fee of $10.00 each. The nursing home was officially opened on Feb. 12, 1934, under the name of "Coaldale Hospital."

The same year the C.H.S. acquired its own premises in a more suitable location, and on Feb. 3, 1935, the new Coaldale Hospital was opened with Dr. Epp as physician and Helen Martens as matron. In its early years the hospital had a hard financial struggle. It has never lacked patients, but it was difficult to meet the demands for expansion, new surgical equipment, etc. The hospital now is equipped with twelve beds.

The physician in charge has always been the local doctor of the C.M.H.S. The hospital staff has always been short of registered nurses and has had to employ practical nurses.

The record of the hospital in 15 years is 714 major and 1,134 minor operations, 1,568 medical patients, 1,036 maternity cases, with a total of 31,192 hospital days. At present the C.H.S. has 23 members, the membership fee now being $25.00, and the net assets are $15,000.00. Dr. Epp has served the district for thirteen years, Helen Martens served during the first two years, Anna Regehr served as head nurse from 1936 to 1944, and A. A. Toews headed the hospital board for fourteen years. B.B.J.

Coaldale Mennonite Brethren Church, a member of the Northern District Conference, is located ten miles east of Lethbridge, southern Alberta. Nearly all Mennonites of this community have come from Russia since 1923. The first five immigrant families settled on "Lathrop's farm" in 1926. On May 23, 1926, 21 members met and organized this church with Klaas Enns as their temporary leader. Enns has justly been called the pioneer of the Coaldale Settlement as well as of the church. Soon the ministers Dav. Klassen, Jakob Wieler, and Frank Friesen came to Coaldale, and on Dec. 4, 1926, F. Friesen took over the leadership of the church. The following decade was one of rapid growth, which is clearly seen from the history of the church building. In 1928 the first church was built (32 x 52 ft.), which proved too small from the beginning, so that additions had to be made in 1929 and 1932. By 1939 it became necessary to build a new and still larger church. The new structure (60 x 104 ft.) has a seating capacity of about 1,000. In the last decade the flow of immigrants has decreased and a number of families have moved either to British Columbia or Ontario. The present membership (1953) of the church is 602. Church services as well as Sunday-school classes are held in the German language. The Sunday school had an enrollment of 395 children.

Since 1929 a Bible school provides opportunities for the training of Sunday-school teachers and other church workers. At present it has an enrollment of 100 students who receive instruction under four teachers in three classes. Young people who desire a secular education under Christian teachers attend the Alberta Mennonite High School at Coaldale.

The church has had capable and devoted workers, among whom B. B. Janz deserves special mention. His sacrificial services have been a great blessing not only to the local church, but also to the whole Conference and to the Mennonite people in general. Others who have faithfully served the church in various capacities are F. Friesen, David Klassen, J. A. Toews, A. Dueck, A. Epp, A. P. Willms, H. Kornelsen, and J. J. Unger. At present (1953) 13 ministers and 5 deacons serve the church. The leader is J. J. Siemens and the assistant leader is D. J. Pankratz. J.B.J.

Coaldale Mennonite Church (GCM) was organized in 1929 in the village of Coaldale, in southwestern Alberta, as a member of the Alberta Provincial Conference and also the Conference of Mennonites in Canada. At first services were conducted in the United Church. In 1931 construction of a place of worship was begun, and at first the basement only was used but on Jan. 10, 1937, dedication services were held in the completed church, which has a seating capacity of 300.

Peter Schellenberg is the minister in charge of this congregation, which had in 1951 a total baptized membership of 251, but there are three other ministers actively engaged in the ministry, and two retired. All are unsalaried. The German language is generally used in the services. A number of Mennonite families from Russia, Poland, and Prussia have joined the congregation in recent years. J.P.V.

Coalridge Mennonite Church (MC) is located near Dagmar, Mont. In 1906 a work was started at Skermo, N.D., which was later transferred to Coalridge. In 1912 a Sunday school was organized there by I. S. Mast. Ministers from other congregations preached here until 1916, when L. A. Kauffman moved in with his family and served until 1930. In 1926 J. E. Harshberger was ordained deacon and also served the congregation as leader of the Sunday school. The 1954 membership of 13 met in a schoolhouse for services. F.E.K.

Coatesville Mennonite Mission (MC), located in a steel center in Chester Co., Pa., was opened in 1929 by the Maple Grove-Millwood congregation. John E. Kennel, the present superintendent, was also the first superintendent. A store building, the third floor of the Fire Hall, and in 1930 the new building at 625 Walnut St. have been used as meeting places, under the auspices of the Eastern Board of Missions and Charities of the Lancaster Mennonite Conference. Frank Stoltzfus in 1940 became resident pastor. George B. Stoltzfus is the present (1954) pastor. A summer Bible school among the colored developed into the Newlinville mission station. The Coatesville membership in 1953 was 60, and the Sunday-school enrollment 80. I.D.L.

Cober, Peter, son of Nicholas and Nancy (Holm) Cober, was born May 7, 1853, in Puslinch Twp., Wellington Co., Ont. On Sept. 28, 1875, he married Martha Steinacher, to whom were born eight children, two of whom died in infancy.

Converted at the age of 21, the following year he united with the Mennonite Brethren in Christ Church (now the United Missionary Church). A few years later Cober moved to Michigan, and began preaching in 1881 at Brown City, the first pastor of the church there. He also served for a few years in the Indiana-Ohio Conference (at Bethel), being ordained by that conference in 1884. Soon afterward he returned to Ontario, where he spent most of his 42 years in the active ministry, serving pastorates at Markham, Kitchener, Kilsyth, New Dundee, Shrigley, Breslau, Maryboro, and Hespeler.

Cober was presiding elder of the Ontario conference for 10 years, 1895-1901 and 1903-7, and chairman of six conferences, 1898, 1899, 1900, 1901, 1905, and 1906. He also served at various times as conference evangelist and as a member of the several boards of the Ontario conference. He was a delegate to general conferences and chairman of one (Coopersburg, Pa., 1896).

In a few respects Peter Cober's record was unique. He was the first subscriber to the *Gospel Banner,* opened the first city mission of the Ontario Conference (Collingwood, Sept. 17, 1897), and attended 60 consecutive annual conferences (1881 to 1940 inclusive).

In 1923 he retired from pastoral work, residing at Kitchener, Ont., from then until his death March 23, 1941. Interment was made in Woodlawn cemetery.   E.R.S.

Cocalico Mennonite Mission: see **Blainsport** Mennonite Mission.

Cochlaeus, Johannes (1479-1552), like Eck, Emser, and Faber, one of the most outspoken and active literary opponents of Luther and all other Reformation currents. His name was actually Dobneck (Dobeneck). He was born in Wendelstein in Franconia of peasant parents, attended the university in near-by Nürnberg, where he was closely associated with the Humanists Johann and Willibald Pirkheimer, whose influence on his career was profound. At the university of Cologne he was a fellow student with Karl von Miltitz, Count Hermann von Neuenar, Ulrich von Hutten, and Crotus Rubianus, all of whom were prominent fighters of the Reformation period. His Nürnberg connections secured for him an office, a living, and recognition as a school rector in the city on the Pegnitz. In Nürnberg he also became associated with Dr. Gerhard Westerburg (*q.v.*) (Rembert, *Wiedertäufer,* 43, 118, 188), known in Anabaptist history. He spoke with enthusiasm of Ulrich von Hutten, entirely in the manner of the enemies of Rome. But in Rome on a tour of Italy he was promptly won for Rome and consecrated to the priesthood (1518). After zealous study at Rome he finally received through the papal chamberlain von Miltitz a German benefice, the deanery at the Liebfrauenstift at Frankfurt.

The letters written by Cochlaeus to several papal delegates reveal that he was writing histories of earlier heresies, in order to attack the reformers. Thus in May 1521 he was editing a book against the Waldenses following an old codex, *Ubi errores eorum (quibus novus hic haereticus participat) solidis reprobantur scripturis.* The second of his numerous works is the *Historia Alberti Krantz von den alten hussen zu Behemen in Keisers Sigmunds zeiten* (Strasbourg, 1523). More than twenty years later (1549) appeared his *Historia Hussitarum libri XII* (Friedensburg, 253 ff.).

Cochlaeus is best known for his uncommonly coarse polemics against Luther. Against his old schoolmate Westerburg (also called Doktor Fegfeuer), who in 1523 had published *Vom fegefewer und standt der verscheydten selen,* he wrote a tract dedicated to Duke Karl of Gelderland and Jülich, *Von Christgläubigen Seelen im fegfewer, wie yhn hilff und trost vonn lebendigen in Christlichen Kirchen geschehen soll* (1526). Naturally Westerburg did not fail to reply (Rembert, 43).

In 1527 Cochlaeus heard of the seven articles of faith of the Anabaptist Jakob Kautz (*q.v.*) at Worms. The pamphlet of the "heathen" Kautz, signed by "Ulrich Preto and Johannes Fryher, preachers at Worms with their Brethren," with the Anabaptist doctrine of the distinction between the outer and the inner Word, infant baptism, transubstantiation, the emphasis on discipleship, etc., receives from Cochlaeus a more than superficial refutation in *Articuli aliquot, a Jacobo Kautio Oecolampadiano, ad populum nuper Wormaciae aediti, partim a Lutheranis, partim a Johanne Cochlaeo doctore praestantissimo, reprobati* (MDXXVII).

It would be surprising if this passionate opponent of the Reformation and all Protestant endeavors had not occupied himself with the tragedy of the Anabaptists at Münster who, besieged by their deposed bishop, sent flaming leaflets and challenges into the world. In 1534 Nikolaus Faber at Leipzig printed a small volume by Cochlaeus with the title, *XXI Articuli anabaptistarum Monasteriensium, per Doctorem Cochleum confutati, adjuncta ostensione originis, ex qua deflexerunt. Appendix elegans, Ex Epistola Petri Plateani, Marpurgi in Hassia data, quae de anabaptistis et de civitate Monasteriensi multa commemorat.* (The same booklet also appeared in German, without the letter of Plateanus.) Again Cochlaeus exploited the opportunity to prove the Münsterites to be genuine disciples of Luther, who merely drew the logical conclusions from Luther's heresy of 1520. Otherwise it contained nothing new.

In the same year besides the German edition of the twenty-one articles there appeared a booklet, *Von neuen Schwermereyen sechs Capitel, den Christen und Ketzern heyden nötig zu lesen und höchlich zu bedenken, der Seelen Seligkeit betreffende* (Spahn, 183) at the end of which he deals with the Anabaptists and their presumed predecessors, the Arians, Donatists. But anyone hoping to find an original idea on the 15 pages will be disappointed. For Cochlaeus Luther is always the founder of the dangerous sect; compared with it the Anabaptists are insignificant. Hence his writings (*Catalogus brevis eorum, quae contra novas sectas scripsit,* 1548) yield little for the study of Anabaptist history.   K.R.

Kolde in *HRE* IV, 194-200; K. Otto, *Joh. Cochlaeus, der Humanist* (Breslau, 1898); M. Spahn, *Cochlaeus* (Berlin, 1898); J. Schlecht, *Hist. Jahrb.* 1898, 938; Kawerau, *Deutsche Literaturzeitung* (1898) 1005; W. Friedensburg, *Fortschritte in Kenntnis und Verständnis der Ref.* (in the series *Schiften des Vereins f. Ref.-Gesch.,* No. 100, 1910) 40; J. Grisar, *Luther* (Freiburg, 1911-12) 3 vv., *passim; ML* I, 365.

Cockley's Union House, once the seat of a Mennonite (MC) congregation, now extinct, was built by Lancaster Conference Mennonites together with non-Mennonites in 1848 near Michael Cochlin's about six miles south of Churchtown, Cumberland Co., Pa., the place near where Preacher Christian Herr settled. The Cumberland County ministers of the Lancaster Mennonite Conference (MC) took care of the services at this place. The peak membership was about 50.   I.D.L.

Coenraad Koch, an Anabaptist martyr: see **Koch, Konrad.**

Coesfeld, a village located west of Münster, Germany, was during the time of the Reformation the scene of Anabaptist activities. In 1532, when the Reformation movement reached the city, Bishop Franz of Waldeck warned against the movement and banished Johann Hunse, the preacher leading the movement. The following year Jan von Leiden worked here. When Heinrich von Tongern (Slachtscaep) was on his way to Münster on the invitation of Rothmann, he stopped in Coesfeld and preached to the people on the open street. A considerable number of the Coesfeld citizens went to Münster, where the "New Jerusalem" was to be established. It is probable that the Anabaptist movement in Coesfeld did not die out with the collapse of the "New Jerusalem," but its history has not yet been investigated.   **C.K.**

Rembert, *Wiedertäufer,* 307 f; L. Keller, *Geschichte der Wiedertäufer und ihres Reiches zu Münster* (Münster, 1880) 167, 143; K. H. Kirchhoff, "Die Wiedertäufer in Coesfeld," in *Westfälische Ztscht.,* 106 (1956), pp. 113-14.

Coffee Creek, a schoolhouse near Silver Hill, Ken., was the scene of Mennonite preaching from the summer of 1946 to the summer of 1948 under the Virginia Mennonite (MC) Conference.   **L.C.S.**

Coffins. American Mennonites largely followed the general American practice of using custom-built coffins until the 20th century, when commercially manufactured ones were introduced. In each community, a carpenter or cabinetmaker specialized in the production of coffins, keeping various sizes of planed boards on hand so that when a coffin was ordered, it could be delivered the next day. They were generally shaped to the body, becoming wider between the head and the place for the shoulders and narrowing down to less than ten inches at the foot end. Various degrees of ornamentation were used, although generally severe simplicity was practiced in styling the coffin. In some instances bleached muslin was used for lining. Earlier no handles were attached; the coffin was carried with the aid of wooden bars of boards, as is still the case among the Paraguay Mennonites. At the beginning of the present century a homemade coffin of this type may have cost from ten to fifteen dollars, although in recent years the cost has advanced to perhaps forty or fifty dollars. Coffins of this type were generally placed inside vaults or "rough boxes" made of one-inch lumber. The Old Order Amish who use the custom-built coffin and casket exclusively pay less than $110 on an average for the entire expense of a funeral in contrast to perhaps $500 as the average expense of an American Mennonite funeral. The practice of using homemade coffins is still followed not only among the Old Order Amish, but also among other conservative Mennonite groups in Canada, Mexico, and Paraguay. European Mennonites earlier followed this practice. In Russia the Mennonites adhered to it throughout their history. (See **Cemeteries** and **Burial.**) **M.G.**

Coffman, John S., pioneer Mennonite (MC) evangelist, was born in Rockingham Co., Va., Oct. 16, 1848, and died in Elkhart, Ind., July 22, 1899.

John Samuel was the eldest of 12 children born to Samuel and Frances Weaver Coffman. His birth occurred on the J. R. Keagy farm, near Mount Crawford, and he grew to manhood on his father's farm near Dale Enterprise. At the age of 16, Coffman was converted and baptized in Muddy Creek, near the Bank Church. A short time later, to avoid being drafted into the Southern army, he escaped into Cumberland Co., Pa., where he remained until the end of the war.

Coffman's formal education was limited, consisting chiefly of a number of terms in a night school established for the boys of the community by David A. Heatwole. By dint of much reading and private study, he was later able to pass the required examination to secure a teacher's certificate. He spent one term at Bridgewater Normal School in 1875.

On Nov. 11, 1869, Coffman was united in marriage to Elizabeth J. Heatwole, daughter of John G. and Elizabeth Rhodes Heatwole. Seven children were born to them: William, Samuel F., Jacob, Ansel, Fannie, Daniel, and Anna Barbara. The first three years of their married life they were tenants on the Margaret Rhodes farm near Dale Enterprise, after which Coffman purchased a 30-acre farm on Gravelly Hill, at the foot of Mole Hill. In 1874 he began teaching the grade school at Montezuma, where he taught for two winter terms, followed by two terms at Paul Summit.

On July 18, 1875, J. S. Coffman was chosen by lot and ordained to the Mennonite ministry at the Bank Church, near Rushville, Va. During the next four years he filled many appointments in Rockingham and Augusta counties and in West Virginia. Being gifted in music, Coffman conducted a number of singing schools in the community, which did much to stimulate four-part singing and instill an appreciation of the better type of church music.

It was on the invitation of John F. Funk, head of the Mennonite Publishing Co., Elkhart, Ind., that J. S. Coffman moved with his family to Elkhart in June 1879. Here he became the assistant editor of the *Herald of Truth,* contributing many original articles and editorials during the next few years. In 1880 he began to work on material for Sunday schools, and produced a small volume for teachers entitled *Infant Lesson Book.* A second edition of the work was published in 1891. Later he edited weekly lesson sheets for the *Words of Cheer,* and from 1890 to 1899 served as editor of the lesson helps which appeared first in monthly editions and then in quarterly form. Other editorial work included collaboration with Funk on the *Minister's Manual* and *Confession of Faith,* 1891; and a small booklet, *Fundamental Bible References,* 1891. He was a member of the committee of five chosen to compile *Hymns and Tunes,* published in 1890, and following the organization of the Mennonite Book and Tract Society in 1889, Coffman served as tract editor for a number of years, as well as president of the organization.

But it was as evangelist that Coffman made his greatest contribution to the Mennonite Church. Since "protracted" or evangelistic services were generally in disfavor at this time, as savoring too much of aggression, Coffman proceeded with the utmost caution, his natural tact and winning personality being great assets in breaking down barriers and paving the way for the spirit of evangelism characterizing the church of the 20th century. Early in his ministry Coffman became burdened for the welfare of the many small, newly established congregations, frequently found in the western and midwestern states, struggling bravely to compete for the interest of the young people with other large denominations. .He was particularly distressed by the number of young people being lost to the church through lack of spiritual encouragement and guidance.

Coffman's first series of evangelistic meetings was held in Kent Co., Mich., in June 1881. By the end of a week nine confessions had been made and the church greatly encouraged. During the next few years many invitations were received from all parts of the church for similar services, and by the end of the century practically every district of the church in the United States and Canada had benefited from his efforts, hundreds of individuals having been brought into church fellowship.

Coffman was a forceful and able speaker, commanding respect and attention from all classes of people. His effort was constantly directed toward building up the church, and major emphasis was placed upon teaching the Word and expounding the peculiar doctrines of the church. He also showed great charity and tact in his fellowship with the Amish congregations found in many Mennonite communities, and assisted in bringing about an amalgamation of a number of Mennonite and Amish congregations.

J. S. Coffman was a strong promoter of Sunday schools and young people's meetings. He assisted in the organization of the first Sunday-school conference held in Indiana, October 1892, and encouraged Biblical instruction in the churches in the form of Bible conferences. He was also a prominent figure in promoting missionary activity in the church.

Coffman was one of the earliest church leaders to sense the need of providing a liberal education for young people under the auspices of the church. On the opening of a business and normal school at Elkhart in the fall of 1894 by Dr. H. A. Mumaw, Coffman braved the storm of opposition from church leaders and laity and bent his energies toward supporting the institution. He became the second chairman of the board of trustees of the private organization known as the Elkhart Institute Association, and during the few remaining years of his life gave much of his time to promoting the work of the school, which was the forerunner of Goshen College.

Coffman's death, which occurred at his home in Elkhart at the age of 50, was attributed to a malignant growth in his stomach from which he had suffered for a number of years. Funeral services were held simultaneously in Elkhart and Virginia, and interment was made in the Prairie St. Cemetery at Elkhart.† B.F.C.

Coffman, Samuel (1822-94), Dayton, Va., bishop in the Middle District of the Virginia Mennonite Conference (MC) from 1861 to 1894. The seventh child of Christian and Anna Wenger Coffman, he was born in Greenbrier Co., W. Va., and moved to Virginia in 1847, where he died Aug. 28, 1894.

He married Frances Weaver on Nov. 11, 1847. They lived first in Augusta County, then in Rockingham County on Beaver Creek, at Dale Enterprise during the Civil War, and then on Dry River near the Bank Mennonite Church.

Coffman united with the Mennonite Church in 1848. Four years later he was ordained to the ministry and in 1861 to the office of bishop. He took a firm stand for the principles of the church during the Civil War. He was inclined to permit the changes which later were associated with the great awakening in the Mennonite Church.

He was the father of twelve children. Two became preachers—John S. Coffman, the pioneer Mennonite evangelist, and Joseph W. Coffman. A daughter, Mary, married L. J. Heatwole, who served the Virginia church as minister and bishop.

H.A.B.

Coghlan United Mennonite Church (GCM) is located near Langley Prairie, a town in British Columbia. On Jan. 1, 1948, the church had 117 baptized members. The first settlers, immigrants of the 1923-25 group from Russia, Jakob J. Reimer, Heinrich H. Dueck, Aron J. Jantzen, Johann D. Jantzen, and Jakob J. Baerg, came in 1934, organized a church in 1935, and built a meetinghouse in 1936, to which they later added a basement. The years 1946 and 1947 saw a considerable influx of new members. Berry culture and dairying are the important industries. German is the language used in worship and in most of the homes. The elder is Johannes Regier. Other ministers are A. J. Jantzen, J. J. Baerg, H. H. Dueck, and J. D. Siemens. The church has a Sunday school, a youth organization, a women's organization, regular Sunday morning services, and a midweek prayer meeting. Footwashing is not practiced. Church discipline, including confession, exclusion from communion, and expulsion, is practiced. Outstanding in the history of the church are Johann D. Jantzen and Elder Nickolai Bahnmann. H.H.D.

Colberg, Ehre-Gott Daniel, professor of theology at the university of Greifswald, wrote a voluminous book with the title, *Das Platonisch-Hermetische Christentum begreifend die historische Erzählung vom Ursprung und vielerlei Sekten der heutigen fanatischen Theologie unterm Namen der Paracelsisten, Weigelianer, Rosencreutzer, Quäker, Wiedertäufer, Bourignisten, Labadisten und Quietisten* (Leipzig, 1710). Chapter IX, 330-86, of this book deals with the Anabaptists. What the learned author repeats here as supposedly the result of scholarly research in Mennonite history is completely without value. He reveals not the least familiarity with the matter nor any understanding of this great spiritual movement. We find the current conception of their origin, character, and development as a sect dangerous to the state and to the soul presented without critical examination. Some headings of the ten paragraphs will be evidence of this: (1) "Die Weigelianer und Rosencreutzer sind subtile Wiedertäufer—Warum die Weigelianer und heutigen Wiedertäufer nicht Aufruhr anrichten?"

He answers this question briefly to this effect: because they do not have the power. (2) "Ursprung der Wiedertäufer. Claus Storch, Thomas Müntzer, Henr. Pfeiffer." (5) "Die Wiedertäufer sind vielerlei Art: Münzerianer, Huttiten, Augustinianer, Hofmannisten, Mennonisten, und Gabrieliter." The Augustinians, he says, derive from a certain Bohemian name Augustin, who was concealed for a time under the name of the Hussites, but finally broke out. He defended above the common Anabaptist errors the doctrine that the souls of believers will not see God until the Judgment Day, and that until then heaven is closed. (8) "Andere wiedertäuferische Sekten der Apostolischen, Geistlichen, Schweigenden, Betenden, Adiaphoristen, Enthusiasten, Adamiten, Grubenheimer, Libertiner, Familisten, A-B-C-Schüler." The Apostolics, he explains, also called footwashers, had as their ancestor Matth. Servatus (Servaes?), claimed to be the true followers of Christ, forsook their wives, children, and business, went without shoes, purses, and money, preached from the housetops, and had all things in common. Modern Anabaptists are almost all footwashers, as Joh. Hoornbeek shows from their writings. (*ML* I, 367.)   **Neff.**

Coldwater (Texas) Mennonite Brethren Church, now extinct, was organized Sept. 29, 1929, under the direction of J. J. Wiebe and B. A. Richert of Corn, Okla., with a membership of 40. The highest membership of the church was 209. Ministers who served in this church are A. L. Schellenberg, J. M. Enns, P. E. Nikkel, and J. H. Voth. Since nearly all the members of this congregation moved away, the church was dissolved in 1943.   P.L.R.

Colebrookdale, an area in eastern Bucks County, Pa. When the first Mennonites settled in what is now Bucks County, prior to 1725, this area of approximately 150 square miles was known as Manatawny or the Manatant District (*q.v.*). Later the area was known as Colebrookdale, a name which finally restricted to the area in which Boyertown is located. The term is used for this region to this day. More than 200 years ago the whole area of the extreme western corner of Bucks County became officially known as Hereford, from which the Hereford Mennonite churches took their name. The Mennonites who worshiped at Boyertown were spoken of as worshiping at Colebrookdale, and the Colebrookdale Mennonites until very recently were a part of the Hereford Mennonite Church.   E.E.S.J.

Colfax County, N. Mex., once the home of a group of Old Order Amish Mennonites, 1921-25. Eleven families from Reno Co., Kan., consisting of Bontragers, Nissleys, and Mullets, lived in the southeastern part of the county near Chico. The only minister of the church was Abe Nissley. Land agents were successful in inducing Amish as well as others to move into that part of the country. In 1921 bountiful crops were raised, but after that there was a severe drouth for many years, and the settlement disappeared. Most of the Amish returned to Kansas, while some went to Custer Co., Okla. J.A.H.

Colfax First Mennonite Church (GCM): see **Onecho Mennonite Church.**

Colfax United Missionary Church, located in Huron Co., Mich., was organized in 1898 by Bernard Kreutziger, and is a member of the Michigan Conference of that body. In 1950 the membership was 36 and William C. Weihl was serving as pastor.
                                        W.C.W.

Collectivization in Soviet Russia. On the night of Nov. 8, 1917, the Second All-Russian Congress passed a decree to eliminate all private possession of land without compensation. Though private use of land was for the time still being permitted, the Bolsheviki soon began to favor communal use of land and to organize communes and land co-operatives. During the Civil War (1917-21) many communes were formed which burst like bubbles. The experiment failed and with the introduction of the New Economic Policy (1921) private use of the soil in individual farms was again permitted without restriction, which soon brought about an agricultural boom. But this lasted only a few years, and the Fifteenth Congress of the Communist Party of the Soviet Union (December 1927) declared that the "unification and reformation of small peasant farms into great collectives" must be accomplished as the basic objective of the party in the villages.

Most of the peasants did not accept this policy and offered passive resistance; so the Bolsheviki resorted to increasingly sharp measures to press them into collective farms. These measures culminated in the "year of the great reform" (1929) in the "offensive along the entire front," which led to the "liquidation of the kulaks as a class" (kulak: Russian for "fist"; the term meant the more prosperous peasants). Confiscation of property, arrests, exile, banishment to concentration camps—these were the common measures applied to the peasants to force them into collectives.

In 1929, 25 million peasant farms were counted in the Soviet Union; in 1937 there were only 20 million, 5 million having been liquidated, involving 20-25 million souls! Where were they? Some of them had succeeded in submerging themselves in the cities, but most were in exile, in concentration camps, or dead. This great operation dealt a terrific blow to the supply of cattle and other livestock. From 1929 to 1932 the number of horses decreased from 34 million to less than 20 million; cattle decreased from 68 million to about 40 million; sheep and goats fell from 147 million to 52 million, and hogs from 21 million to 12 million.

In 1932 and 1933 the Soviet Union, particularly the Ukraine, suffered a severe famine, which claimed several million human victims. Thus the Soviet Union was able to reach its goal: of the 20 million remaining peasant families, 18.5 million were "united" in collectives by 1937. During recent years the collective farms have been combined into larger units and the number of such farms reduced. On the basis of a compulsory co-operative (*artel*), which became a law on Feb. 17, 1935, all production is socialized, especially that of food. The management is nominally elected by the members, but is actually appointed (at least the chairman) by the Party. The liquidation of the kulaks and the collectivization of agriculture were, according to Stalin's words, "a very deep revolutionary change, . . . in its consequences akin to the Revolution of October 1917."

This process, which was also applied to the church life, was catastrophic to the Mennonite settlements. Mennonite organizations had to cease all activity, and the Mennonite farmers were helplessly subject to arbitrary government. In 1929 they attempted to escape—they came to Moscow by the thousands to apply for emigration permits. But only a small number were successful (not even 6,000); the rest were sent back in locked cattle cars and suffered the common fate of farmers in Russia: they were banished to the forests of North and Northeast Russia, to the steppes of Kazakhstan (*q.v.*). The leaders were thrown into prison; how many of them have survived is not known. This was a devastation that has caused inestimable and irreparable damage. In the collectives it was of course impossible for the Mennonites, even when in the majority, to carry on any organized religious life of their own. The Mennonite Church as a distinct entity accordingly ceased to exist in the measure that collectivization was pushed through. However, the rate of collectivization varied somewhat in different regions. It seems to have proceeded much more slowly in Siberia, where Mennonite villages with private ownership persisted as late as 1935 and after. In some areas also, the Mennonite population remained almost intact, with little admixture of non-Mennonites in the villages and collectives. In such areas Mennonitism could still maintain itself to some degree, even though without organization. The release and ultimate repatriation in 1943 to Germany of some 35,000 (about 23,000 were again captured and returned to Russia) Mennonites, chiefly from the Chortitza area, show that in spite of collectivization and dilution Mennonitism was not destroyed.

The latest stage in Russian agricultural policy, made possible by mechanization, seems to be the establishment of large state farms, in which the last stage of socialization is reached where the individual farmer becomes merely a state employee.

P.F.F.

College Record, a monthly journal, was the official publication of Central Mennonite College, located at Bluffton, Ohio. First published in April 1902, it was replaced by the *Bluffton College Bulletin* when Central Mennonite was reorganized as Bluffton College in 1913.   L.L.R.

Colleges, Mennonite. Mennonite colleges are a product of the North American environment and are found in no other Mennonite area. Mennonites in Europe have long patronized institutions of higher learning but have not established advanced schools except in Russia, where they built excellent secondary and normal schools but no colleges; in Holland where they established a theological seminary; and in Germany which had its *Realanstalt am Donnersberg* (Weierhof), a secondary school.

The conviction that a democratic society could not function successfully unless its citizenry was educated resulted in the establishment of a free public school system in America during the first half of the 19th century. The phenomenal growth of free public elementary schools after the middle of the 19th century produced a general demand for secondary and higher schools of learning. From approximately 300 high schools in the United States in 1860, the number increased to approximately 12,000 by 1915. Tuition academies which had reached their highest number of 6,000 by 1860 were largely replaced by the free public high schools by 1915. Of the 494 colleges in the United States in 1900, more than half were founded after 1860. In the 1880-89 period 74 were established and in the next decade 54 were begun.

Although American Mennonites in their earliest settlements of eastern Pennsylvania had provided community schools for the elementary education of their children, they accepted the free public schools when these became common. Influenced by their non-Mennonite neighbors, Mennonite young people gradually began to attend academies and high schools and some went on to college. At first, those who attended school beyond the grades did so because they wished to prepare themselves for teaching. For instance, John F. Funk (*q.v.*), an outstanding Mennonite leader during the last half of the 19th century, in the 1850's attended Freeland Seminary (*q.v.*), founded by a Mennonite, and later taught school. Samuel Guengerich (*q.v.*), a schoolteacher and an Amish leader, attended a Pennsylvania normal school in the 1860's. Although no records are available to show how widely Mennonites patronized schools of higher learning during the last half of that century, it is evident that the number was increasing rapidly enough to cause the church concern. During the 1890's, for example, a number of young Mennonites, several of whom later became leaders in the Mennonite Church (MC), attended Ohio Normal University at Ada, Ohio.

Sensing the need for advanced training of their young people under church auspices, the General Conference Mennonites were the first to provide an official church school for them. In their 1861 conference, they approved the establishment of a theological institution, which resulted in the founding of the Wadsworth School (*q.v.*) in 1868. It had as its two chief goals the unification of Mennonites and the spreading of the Gospel. Although the school had a theology department, in time its normal school became the most popular department. No work on a college level, however, was offered during the ten years of the school's existence.

Before the close of the Wadsworth School, several thousand Mennonite immigrants from Russia and Prussia had settled in the Great Plains states. Having brought with them a tradition of parochial schools and a considerable number of experienced teachers, they immediately established elementary schools, which were slowly replaced by public schools in later years. As early as 1877 leaders of this group called for the establishment of a denominational school in Kansas. In 1879, after the close of Wadsworth, the General Conference decided to establish such an institution in Kansas. As a result, one was opened at Goessel in 1882 and moved to Halstead the next year, where it continued until 1893, when it was replaced by Bethel College (*q.v.*). This institution, therefore, has the distinction of being the first Mennonite college in America, having opened its doors in 1893 to students privileged to enroll in three departments, namely, preparatory, academy, and college. The first catalogue declared that among the purposes of the school was the training of teachers, of home and foreign missionaries, and of those wishing to prepare for vocations and professions. Its first A.B. degrees were granted in 1912. When the college was admitted to the North Central Association of Colleges in 1938, it was the first Mennonite school to achieve this distinction. Although students from many states attend Bethel, it serves primarily those of the General Conference Mennonite churches west of the Mississippi River. In 1950-51 its total enrollment was 487 students, of whom 316 were Mennonites. Of the 487 students, 305 were full time in the regular school year. During its history more than 8,000 students have been enrolled in its courses. From a net worth of slightly less than a half million dollars twenty years ago, the figure rose to more than one and a half million in 1952.

The General Conference Mennonite constituency east of the Mississippi River is served by Bluffton College (q.v.), Bluffton, Ohio. The closing of the Wadsworth School had left this area without an institution of higher learning but interest in a school did not disappear. In 1894 the Middle District Conference (GCM) appointed a committee to investigate the possibility of establishing a new school. Four years later the conference approved the establishment of a school at Bluffton, Ohio, and the cornerstone for the first building was laid in 1900. That autumn the first students were enrolled in the "Central Mennonite College," as the institution was called from 1900 to 1913. At first the school offered three courses, Bible, academy, and normal. College work was first offered in the 1902-3 school year. Progressive leaders realized that with the increasing number of Mennonites attending non-Mennonite colleges, a four-year college was necessary. It became apparent, however, that the constituency supporting Central Mennonite College was not large enough to support a four-year liberal arts school. The result was the reorganization of the school into Bluffton College and Mennonite Seminary in 1914, with representation from a number of Mennonite branches. Under the new organization, the school granted its first bachelor's degrees in 1915. The seminary remained a corporate part of Bluffton College until 1921 when it was separately organized as Witmarsum Theological Seminary (q.v.). On Bluffton's 40 acres of wooded land have appeared since 1900 the six buildings of the campus, Founders Hall, the latest, having been dedicated in 1952. The 296 students in 1950-51 came from 8 countries and provinces outside the United States and from 13 states, largely east of the Mississippi. Nearly one half of these students were Mennonites. Of the 296 students, 225 were full time in the nine-month school year. In 1953 Bluffton College was admitted to the North Central Association.

The first Mennonite institution of higher learning to grant bachelor's degrees was Goshen College (q.v.), which had its origin in Elkhart Institute (q.v.). Elkhart, Ind., a private school conducted by Dr. H. A. Mumaw, a practicing physician. Established in 1894, Elkhart Institute had as its purpose the providing of educational opportunities for the young people of the Mennonite Church (MC). In 1895 the Elkhart Institute Association was organized to direct the new school. Under Noah Byers' leadership the school became an academy, granting its first diploma in 1898. In September 1903 the school was removed to near-by Goshen, renamed Goshen College, and a junior college course was added. In 1908 the complete college course was established and in 1910 the first bachelor's degree was granted. Goshen College was admitted to the North Central Association of Colleges in 1941. By 1952 more than 10,000 students had been enrolled in its courses. Its total enrollment in 1950-51 was 912, of whom 640 were Mennonites. Of the 912 students, 570 were full time in the nine-month year. Although the school serves primarily young people of the Mennonite (MC) churches of the central states, 28 states and provinces were represented in its 1950-51 Mennonite student body.

In point of time, the next Mennonite college to be established was Tabor (q.v.). Located in Hillsboro, Kan., it opened its doors to students in September 1908. From its beginning to 1934, the school was owned, controlled, and operated by the Tabor College Corporation, representing primarily the interests of the Mennonite Brethren Church and the Krimmer Mennonite Brethren Church. Since 1935 Tabor College has been under the control of the Conference of the Mennonite Brethren of North America. With a background in Russia somewhat similar to that of the patrons who established Bethel College, the group soon after its arrival in America in the 1870's had established its parochial schools and had manifested an interest in education. For seven years, 1898-1905, the Mennonite Brethren of the Kansas area unofficially supported McPherson College, a Church of the Brethren school. During those seven years more than 200 Mennonite students were registered in McPherson College. With the establishment of Tabor College, Mennonite Brethren support was shifted away from McPherson to their new church school located near by. The school now has a College of Liberal Arts and Sciences and a College of Theology and grants degrees in both colleges. In 1950-51 the total enrollment was 295, of whom 250 were Mennonite. Of the total enrollment, 237 students were carrying full-time work in the regular school year.

Freeman Junior College, Freeman, S.D., known first as South Dakota Mennonite College, was established by the Mennonites who came to that state from Russia in the 1870's. Its founders wished to preserve the German language, to impart Biblical instruction, and to give the kind of Christian training for teaching and other vocations which their young people were not getting in the non-Mennonite schools they were attending. Instruction was first offered in the fall of 1903. The school has expanded until it now has 7 buildings on a 9-acre campus. Although the institution is not under the direct management of any one branch of the Mennonite

Church, it does represent the interests of various Mennonites in South Dakota and surrounding states, particularly the General Conference Mennonites. It now offers an academy course, a teacher-training course, a junior college course, and a business course. In 1950-51 its total attendance was 150, of whom 42 were enrolled in the junior college course. Of the total enrollment, 142 were Mennonites.

Hesston College, Hesston, Kan., was established in September 1909 by the Board of Education of the Mennonite General Conference (MC). The desire on the part of members of the Mennonite Church (MC) for a school to serve their constituency in the western states and the wish for a more conservative school than Goshen College were among the forces that brought Hesston College into existence. At first known as the Western Mennonite School, it became successively Hesston Academy and Bible School, and Hesston College and Bible School. In 1915-16 for the first time two years of college work were offered, but by 1918-19 a four-year college course was given. Beginning with the school year 1927-28, the school again offered only junior college work. In 1950-51 the total enrollment was 404, of whom 163 were college students, 149 being Mennonites.

Eastern Mennonite School was incorporated under the laws of Virginia in 1917 and the school was formally opened in October of that year, near Harrisonburg, Va. Founded by members of the Virginia Mennonite (MC) Conference, its purpose was "to supply the needs of the Church with loyal and competent workers" (*Annual Catalog, 1919-1920*). In addition to the argument of the need for a Mennonite school in the eastern states, there was also a conviction that a more conservative school was needed than could be found in the Mennonite conferences at that time. College work has been offered since 1921, and in 1930 accreditment was received as a standard junior college. In 1947 the college received approval for conferring the A.B., B.S., B.S. in Education, B.R.E., and Th.B. degrees. At that time its name was changed to Eastern Mennonite College (*q.v.*) and it is now controlled by a Board of Trustees appointed by the Virginia Mennonite Conference (MC). In 1950-51 the total enrollment of the school was 680, of whom 275 were college students, all being Mennonites.

Rosthern Junior College (*q.v.*), Rosthern, Sask., is an outgrowth of the German-English Academy founded in 1903 by Mennonite immigrants from Russia and other areas. In 1946 its name was changed to Rosthern Junior College. The total enrollment in 1950-51 was 121, of whom 47 were carrying college grade work, all being Mennonites.

Grace Bible College (*q.v.*), Omaha, Neb., was founded in 1943 for the training of Christian workers in the Mennonite denomination. With a total enrollment of 301 students in 1950-51, 223 were Mennonites. Of these, 154 were from the General Conference Mennonite Church and 43 from the Evangelical Mennonite Brethren. In line with a trend in Bible institutes, Grace is moving in the direction of offering college work and has recently conferred bachelor of arts degrees in Bible.

The Pacific Bible Institute (*q.v.*), Fresno, Cal., has likewise, beginning with its 1950-51 *Annual Catalog*, offered Bible college as well as Bible institute instruction. In 1951 it granted 10 bachelor of arts degrees. Operated by the Mennonite Brethren Conference and the Zion K.M.B. Church, the institute was opened in 1944. Its total enrollment for 1950-51 was 155, of whom 100 were doing work on the college level, all Mennonite.

The Mennonite Brethren Bible College (*q.v.*), Winnipeg, Man., granted 11 bachelor of arts degrees in Christian education in 1951. The college was opened for instruction in October 1944. In 1950-51 it had 180 students, all Mennonite but one. Other Mennonite schools reporting students of college grade but not conferring bachelor of arts degrees in 1951 include Canadian Mennonite Bible College (*q.v.*), Winnipeg, Man., 47 students, all Mennonite, and Mennonite Collegiate Institute (*q.v.*), Gretna, Man., 40 students, all Mennonite. A few other Mennonite Bible institutes and secondary schools in Canada offer a little work corresponding to the first year of college. For other schools offering some work of college grade see **Seminaries** and **Nursing Schools.**

The impact of Mennonite colleges upon the Mennonite church and other Christian groups in the area of the schools can be assessed only in a small measure by the use of statistics. The following table, however, will give a partial view of the growth of education in American Mennonite circles during the last two decades.

Year	Mennonite students	Non-Menn. students	Total	College students	Below college
1930-31	1515	655	2170	1234	946
1940-41	2101	608	2709	1581	1128
1950-51	5575	1111	6686	3464	3222

A half century ago the Mennonites of America were largely rural and only a very small per cent had attended high schools. Only a very small number of Mennonite preachers had any formal training. In the mid 20th century, the majority of the ministers in certain Mennonite conferences had had college training and in only the most conservative groups were there no formally trained ministers. Most of the ministers who had received formal training had spent one or more years in a Mennonite school. These leaders were able to present a challenging program to a youth no longer satisfied with the older patterns of church life. Young people's institutes, summer camps, Christian life conferences, voluntary service, Gospel teams, peace teams, choruses, and Mennonite youth fellowships were but a few of the many activities provided during the last two decades preceding the mid-century for Mennonite young people under the leadership and stimulation of the church colleges and of the men who had been trained there.

Both home and foreign missionaries representing the Mennonite conferences of America have in the large majority of instances received part or all of their advanced training in Mennonite colleges. As an example a missionary conference program given in one of the Mennonite colleges in 1952 listed its former students who were at that date serving in mission stations or in voluntary service outside the United States. The list contained 182 names.

In spite of the prominent place in Mennonite church work occupied by former students of Mennonite colleges it is true that a considerable number from some of the colleges have gone into professions that have taken them away from Mennonite communities and into other denominations. It has been a matter of great concern that so large a number of graduates have been lost to their home communities and that so few have remained in agriculture. In recent years, courses and conferences in Mennonite colleges have emphasized the opportunities of Mennonite community building, but it remains to be seen whether the movement away from the Mennonite communities and into the large cities can be checked and if the goal of training young people for service in the Mennonite Church can be more successfully achieved than it had been earlier.

To what degree higher education has brought a cultural adaptation by Mennonites to American society and has thus broken down the barriers of cultural isolation that for several centuries served as a means of maintaining Mennonite nonconformity cannot be measured accurately at this time. Certainly the colleges have given their young people an appreciation of the world's cultures, have acquainted them with the conflicting world views, and have helped them see their own group in a proper historical perspective. The impact of this has often been a weakening of the religious sect aspect of Mennonitism and sometimes the moving of the group closer to the main stream of Protestantism.

On the other hand, many additional factors breaking down Mennonite isolation very likely would have produced somewhat similar results to those brought about by higher education even if Mennonite colleges had not been established. On the positive side it should be added that Mennonite faculties have given Mennonite youth a new appreciation of their spiritual heritage and have taught them how to evaluate American culture in the light of New Testament principles. Outstanding in this contribution have been the journals *The Mennonite Quarterly Review* (*q.v.*) and *Mennonite Life* (*q.v.*). Scholarly books in the areas of Mennonite history, life, and practice produced by faculty members in several Mennonite colleges have helped educated Mennonite youth establish their thinking on a firmer basis than traditionalism. Rural life conferences, Mennonite historical society programs, Anabaptist theology seminars, Mennonite cultural problems conferences, Christian life conferences, and other similar programs largely sponsored by the church colleges have given the future Mennonite leaders an appreciation of and a loyalty to the basic New Testament principles, which in the thinking of the patrons of the colleges are sufficient reasons for their continuation. M.G.

J. E. Hartzler, *Education Among the Menn. of America* (Danvers, Ill., 1925); H. P. Peters, *History and Development of Education Among Menn. in Kansas* (Hillsboro, Kan., 1925); C. H. Smith, "The Education of a Menn. Country Boy" (unpublished biography, Bluffton, 1943); M. S. Harder, "The Origin, Philosophy, and Development of Education Among the Menn." (unpublished doctoral dissertation, University of So. Cal., 1949); Ed. G. Kaufman, "The Liberal Arts College in the Life of the Mennonite Church of America," *Proceedings of the Fourth Mennonite World Conference* (Akron, 1950) 276-87; S. Hertzler, "Attendance at Mennonite Schools and Colleges," annually in *MQR* since 1928.

Collegiants, a Protestant association of the 17th century in Holland, which called its meetings for religious services *collegia*. Its members were also called Rijnsburgers, since their main center was in Rijnsburg near Leiden. In the religious life of the Netherlands during the 17th and 18th centuries they played an important part. Their influence on the Mennonites was also marked.

The rise of the Collegiants was caused by the national synod of the Reformed Church which met at Dordrecht in 1618-19 and removed from office the Remonstrant (*q.v.*) preachers—about 300 of them. This fate also struck Chr. Sopingius, a preacher at Warmond near Leiden. In his absence Gijsbert van der Kodde proposed that they meet occasionally without a preacher, to read several chapters from the Bible, to pray, and to have a devotional address if anyone felt called to speak. This was done. A small circle, which was joined by Gijsbert's brothers, Jan and Orie van der Kodde, who lived in the adjacent Rijnsburg, soon met regularly. Such *exercitia* or *colloquia prophetica*, says van Slee, were in the days of the Reformation a common occurrence; they took place in Zürich, in London, and also in the Netherlands.

The movement soon spread beyond the immediate community. Men like Dirk Raphaelsz Camphuysen, Jan Geesteranus, and Jan Montanus, former preachers, joined it. Later the movement could even count statesmen like Conrad van Beuningen and Adrian Paats, and the historiographer Jan Wagenaar among its adherents.

The most outstanding principles of this spiritual movement were the conviction that all churches had forsaken the principles and practices of the apostolic church, and that none of the existing churches could lay claim to be the true church of Jesus Christ. This negative opinion of the Christian churches makes it clear why they hoped for and aimed at an evangelical renewal both in religious practices and principles, without actually establishing a new church and without assuming ecclesiastical practices and traditions. The Collegiants did not want church buildings nor pastors; they formed an anti-ecclesiastical and purely lay movement, and though many pastors of the churches were active in the collegia, they did so as private persons and not as church leaders; some Collegiants were members of a church (Reformed, Remonstrant, Mennonite) and remained so; others were members of no church.

In Rijnsburg the meetings were held in the home of one of the members, which was later bought and remodeled. This Groote Huis was adequate to provide lodgings for the steadily growing number of participants, who met at first always at Rijnsburg for devotions after the manner of the founders.

After 1640, when the collegia had been established throughout the country, Rijnsburg became the great center where conferences were held twice a year, at

Pentecost and in the latter part of August, to observe communion together and to baptize by immersion those who wished it. Immersion of adults was performed usually on Saturday morning before the large assembly. The baptismal candidate chose the one who was to baptize him. The chosen one then, after a song and prayer, preached a short sermon. Then the candidate made a confession of his faith, which the baptizer then analyzed. The latter reminded the audience that he held no particular office in virtue of which he should perform the ceremony; that the baptism did not signify membership in any particular group and that one could be a good Rijnsburger without being baptized. After prayer the ceremony was performed outdoors and the service concluded with singing and prayer.

Besides the general meetings held twice a year at Rijnsburg, the Collegiants met regularly in their local collegia. Such collegia were found in Rotterdam, Leiden, Amsterdam, and other cities of Holland, in many towns in North Holland and Friesland, and in the city of Groningen. The most important were those of Amsterdam and Rotterdam, existing until 1791 and 1787 respectively. In these collegia a meeting was usually held on Sunday afternoon; the program was composed of prayer, singing of hymns, and reading of the Scriptures, which were explained, and sometimes too an address on a religious theme. Nowhere did they have a special preacher or minister though ministers were allowed to speak in the meetings; each of those who were present had the right to address the meeting; for this reason the collegia were mostly called "Vrij-spreeck colleges." Only with one exception (Groningen), baptism and communion services were never held in the local collegia. The Collegiants had an orphanage in Amsterdam, called *De Oranjeappel* (*q.v.*).

The Collegiants had very close connections with the Dutch Mennonites, the result of some mutually shared ideas. Both believed in the priesthood of all believers. They also agreed on adult baptism, rejection of military service, simplicity in life and dress which prevented their pursuit of high office, and in the practical application of the Gospel in benevolence and provision for widows and orphans.

The contacts between the Collegiants and the Mennonites led now and then to quarrels. In Rotterdam, soon after 1640, a collegium was held in the anteroom of the Flemish Mennonite church, which was attended by the preachers of this congregation. This caused trouble. Elders of other churches called in to aid (among them van Braght, the author of the *Martyrs' Mirror*), deposed the ministers, most of whom then joined the Waterlander Church (1654). Then the Collegiants tried to make contacts with the Waterlander group in Rotterdam. Their ideas permeated so deeply into the Waterlander congregation, that an attempt was made to form a union with the Remonstrants in Rotterdam (1658). But a strong resistance asserted itself. The outward occasion for the tension was apparently the general invitation to communion given by Elder Jacob Osten and the fact that he had baptized persons who later joined the Remonstrants. The direct connections between the Collegiants and the Mennonites seem now to have been severed. An outstanding Collegiant was the Mennonite Jan Dyonisus Verburg. In Amsterdam and other places relations were similar to those in Rotterdam.

In almost all the Waterlander groups, the Collegiants had great influence. But nowhere—if this was their intention at all—did they succeed in making the Mennonite church turn Rijnsburger. Under the influence of Collegiantism the Waterlander congregation of Leeuwarden (*q.v.*) in 1715 put in their church a stone tub for baptism by immersion, which was removed in 1720 because it had given rise to discord in the congregation. Not only in the Waterlander, but also in many Flemish Mennonite congregations both advocates and opponents of the free-speaking practice were found. The more conservative Mennonites, such as the later Zonists, rejected this; they had a stricter idea of their church as a closed communion, fenced with baptism and confession and discipline, and abhorred "unlimited toleration" (*onbepaelde verdraegsaemheyt*), which through the influence of Collegiantism penetrated into many congregations, where all who so desired could take part in the holy communion even if they were members of other Protestant churches, and even if they were not baptized at all (see **Communion Call**).

As more and more members spread Collegiant ideas in the congregations, the fires of division flared up with great violence. Evidence of this is the *Lammerenkrijgh* (see **Galenus Abrahamsz de Haan** and **Amsterdam**).

The more liberal Lamist churches maintained cordial relations with the Collegiants. They were perhaps rarely as fraternal as in Harlingen, where after the withdrawal of the more conservative part of the congregation the others agreed to arrange their worship on the Rijnsburg pattern (1718). From the middle of the 18th century on, many Collegiants were received into the Mennonite churches. Toward the end of the 18th century the *collegia* disappeared. Their last meeting was held in Amsterdam in 1791. But their ideas had borne fruit, not only among the Mennonites, but also among other church groups. vDZ.

J. C. van Slee, *De Rijnsburger Colleginaten* (Haarlem, 1895); K. Meinsma, *Spinoza en zijn Kring* (The Hague, 1896); C. B. Hylkema, *Reformateurs* (1901 and 1902); W. J. Kühler, *Het Socinianisme in Nederland* (Leiden, 1912); *DB* 1900, 1-17; H. W. Meihuizen, *Galenus Abrahamsz* (Haarlem, 1954); W. Goeters, *Die Vorbereitung des Pietismus in der reformierten Kirche der Niederlande* (Leipzig, 1911); Chr. Burrage, "The Collegiants or Reynsburgers of Holland," in *The Review and Expositor* (Louisville) VII (1910); *Inv. Arch. Amst.* II, 2943-55; *ML* II, 521 f.

Collingwood United Missionary Church, located at Collingwood, Ont., on Georgian Bay, a member of the Ontario Conference, began as a city mission on Sept. 17, 1897, with Sarah Madden (Mrs. John Bolwell) and Eliza Williams in charge. A church building acquired in 1919 was used until 1954, when construction was begun on a new church under the leadership of the pastor, H. R. Priddle. E.R.S.

Collinsville Mennonite Brethren Church, a member of the Southern District M.B. Conference, located two miles south of Collinsville, Tulsa Co., Okla., was organized in November 1913 with Benjamin Wedel as the first leader. The first Mennonite settlers of Polish, Russian, and German background, came to this community in 1910 from Kansas, Nebraska, and Western Oklahoma. Approximately 20 families met in private homes for worship until permission was secured to meet in the Ellingwood school, 3½ miles southwest of Collinsville. On Feb. 21, 1918, it was decided to build a church, but World War I brought persecution for the Mennonites in this community because of the use of the German language and some of the families moved back to their original communities. Building plans, however, went on and in May 1919 services were conducted in the new church for the first time. Membership in 1924 was 100, but had declined to 76 in 1950. Most of the members are farmers. All services are now conducted in the English language.

I.G.N.

Colmar, capital of Upper Alsace, pop. (1950) 43,512, is the center of a Mennonite community which originated in the Reformation period. In the Colmar archives are the following documents dealing with the Anabaptists:

(1) Edict of King Ferdinand against the Anabaptists, May 26, 1535; (2) Edict of Emperor Ferdinand against them, July 5, 1561; (3) Mandate of Egenolphe of Ribeaupierre in Rappoltstein, June 28, 1561; (4) A notice concerning the Anabaptists in Ingersheim, July 2, 1572; (5) Doubts, Suspicions and Regulations concerning the Anabaptists, 1584; (6) Letter of the pastor of Sainte-Marie-aux-Mines, Jean la Bachelle, to Paul Ferry, Protestant pastor of Metz, March 12, 1643; (7) *Baillage de Sainte-Marie. Affaires religieuses Anabaptistes 1696-1712;* (8) A letter of the superintendent of Alsace to the magistrate of Colmar, Sept. 9, 1572, regarding the expulsion of the Anabaptists; (9) A record of Mennonite families in the offices of the subdelegation of Belfort, January 1870.

From the meager contents of these documents it is evident that Anabaptism found its way into the region of Colmar in the 1520's. But the ruthless persecution that soon set in completely crushed it. Only small remnants maintained themselves, if any at all. During the Thirty Years' War (1641) Mennonites exiled from Switzerland, especially from the canton of Bern, settled around Colmar and established the present congregation there. The number was increased by a continued stream of Swiss refugees, who lived in the surrounding villages and estates. In Jebsheim and in the mill at Ohnenheim they held their services. In Ohnenheim a conference of the Alsatian Mennonites was held in 1660, where they accepted the Dordrecht Confession (*q.v.*). It was signed by the preachers Hans Müller of Magenheim, Hans Ringer of Heidolsheim, Rudolf Egli of Künheim, and the deacons Ulrich Husser and Jakob Gachnauer of Ohnenheim, and Heinrich Frick of Künheim. The priest of Ohnenheim and Heidolsheim denounced their "conventicle." At his instigation the Count Palatine of Birkenfeld as the

heir of the Rappoltstein was urged to expel the Mennonites from Ohnenheim and to exterminate the "sect" by the roots. They were thereupon apparently more severely dealt with. On Sept. 7, 1769, Jakob Frey, an "Anabaptist" of Dürrenenzen in Upper Alsace, was sentenced by the court at Colmar to eternal banishment from the country and a fine of ten livres for refusing an oath demanded of him. In 1750 there were in Heidolsheim four Mennonite families, in Ohnenheim two, in Magenheim two, in Elsenheim one, Grussenheim one, Jebsheim seven, Artzenheim one, and in Künheim four. The number decreased later, when many emigrated to America.

At the conference in Essingen (*q.v.,* now Palatinate) on Nov. 21, 1779, Hans Rub and Bäntz Stucky signed for the Colmar church. The *Mennonitische Blätter* reports a Mennonite wedding on an estate near Colmar in 1779, giving an interesting description of the religious ceremony. At a meeting held on June 19, 1808, on the Bildauerhof, at which the question of release from military duty was discussed, Colmar was represented by Peter Schreck(?). A short letter of 1822 from the Colmar congregation to Birkenhof is signed by Sebastian Peterschmitt.

Details of congregational development to the end of the 19th century are not known, with the exception of a conference held in Münzenheim near Colmar in 1896 (see Alsace). Since that time meetings have been held regularly in the homes of the congregation, which extended from Ensisheim to beyond Sélestat, and for a time also in homes in Colmar. About 1910 services were held every two weeks in the Protestant school of Wolfganzen, a village on the railroad. During World War I this space was used for military purposes, and the congregation met in the town hall. At that time the following ministers served the congregation: Benjamin Peterschmitt, Munzenheim, elder; John Gingerich, Geiswasser, elder; Jacob Peterschmitt, Nambsheim, Jean Peterschmitt, Rheinfelderhof, Emil Peterschmitt, Fohrenhof, Heinrich Grieser, Ostheim, Joseph Sommer, Rappoltsweiler, preachers; Christian Augsburger, Hueb near Markolsheim, deacon. At that time the congregation had about 130 members.

Since the distance to Wolfganzen was too great for many members, a hall was shared with the Salvation Army in Colmar in 1920. At the same time weekly prayer meetings were held in the homes of families living in Colmar. The Colmar hall was the scene of two conferences of ministers of Alsace-Lorraine, 1920 and 1921, presided over by Valentin Pelsy of Sarrebourg.

In the spring of 1922 the congregation acquired a building of its own at 22 rue d'Ingersheim which they remodeled into an assembly room and an apartment. It was dedicated on Aug. 27, 1922. The members of the former Wolfganzen congregation who lived near Neuf-Brisach (*q.v.*) also acquired a building and organized a separate congregation. The Colmar congregation became a member of the Alsatian conference and has kept regular records since 1922. The language is predominantly German, though French is also occasionally used in preaching. Sunday school is conducted in both languages.

42

In 1931 the meetinghouse was enlarged and a new room added for the Sunday school. Colmar became the seat of the conference of Alsace-Lorraine; meetings of the conference were held regularly here until World War II. Bible courses were also conducted by ministers from the outside. During the German occupation meetings were for a time prohibited.

Since World War II the membership is about 70. The ministers since the separation from Neuf-Brisach have been: Benjamin Peterschmitt, who served more than 50 years as preacher and elder; Henri Volkmar of Colmar, preacher 1913-53, elder from 1938; Emil Kremer of Colmar, preacher 1924, elder 1927; Heinrich Grieser of Ostheim, d. 1924; Hans Nussbaumer of Schopenwihr, preacher 1923, elder 1927, moved to Altkirch in 1942; J. J. Wack of Colmar, preacher 1923, d. 1947; Emil Kempf of Wintzenheim, preacher 1920; Willi Peterschmitt of Munzenheim, preacher 1953- . Colmar ministers also served the congregations of Chatenois, Hang, Sarreguemines, Sarrebourg, and Pulversheim.

Typical family names are Baecher, Baechler, Bee, Egly, Hirschy, Neuhauser, Peterschmitt, and Schowalter. Most members are farmers, millers, or merchants. In 1953 the membership was 81. *(ML I, 367 f.)*   NEFF, H.V.

Cologne (Köln), capital of the Prussian Rhine province, pop. 590,000, was already in Reformation times a great, powerful city, an archiepiscopal see, had a highly regarded, well-attended university, was the center of an extensive trade, the fortress of Catholicism and at the same time the place of refuge of all the non-Catholic movements of the time, among which the Anabaptists played a prominent part. Numerous traces of pre-Reformation parties are also to be found here. Cologne can be called a center of the Waldensian groups, who held their meetings in secret basements and weavers' rooms. Wherever they came into the open or were discovered, they became victims of the Inquisition.

In the protocol of the Cologne council, Aug. 24, 1531, an archbishop's letter is mentioned which states that there were Anabaptists in the city. For two years nothing more is heard of them. In 1533 the Anabaptists began a greater activity. Perhaps the first Anabaptists were burned at this time (Rembert, 381).

In the center of the movement was the native of Cologne, Gerhard Westerburg (*q.v.*). He had gone to Münster early in 1534 and been baptized in Knipperdolling's house by Henric Rol (*q.v.*). With his brother Arnold he baptized many in Cologne. The movement was violently suppressed.

Later a congregation of peaceful Anabaptists had also formed at Cologne. When and how it came into being is not known. Menno Simons may have found them there, and may have contributed much to strengthening and building them up in his two years in the city territory (1544-46). Elder Teunis van Hastenrath (*q.v.*) baptized here about 1550 (*DB* 1909, 122). In 1551 a notice was issued by the Duke of Jülich to the city council of Cologne, that Schröder Nellis on the Domhof and the cobbler Heinrich on the Krummbüchel were Anabaptists.

This unleashed a cruel persecution. By far most of those seized in the city were not natives, but had come from outside. To prevent further influx of strangers whose creed was not known, the council issued the order not to tolerate the "unchristian, damned sect of Anabaptists," who, expelled from other places, had come here to hold their conventicles. All outsiders must present an attest from their home town concerning their origin, creed, etc., before they may be lodged.

When Thomas von Imbroich (*q.v.*) came to Cologne in 1554, he was introduced to the preacher of the brotherhood there by Johann Schuhmacher, a citizen of Cologne. He found a large congregation, most of whom had probably not been baptized yet as adults. The council issued an edict in 1554 warning that the imperial laws would be strictly observed in all cases of adult baptism. On July 10, 1555, this announcement was repeated. Two years later Thomas von Imbroich was arrested and executed on March 5, 1558. In the foreword of his "confession" to the council he protests his innocence of any seditious intentions with warmth and dignity.

In 1560 the city council was informed that the Anabaptist congregation there numbered 40 members, and that their leader and preacher was the capmaker, Heinrich Krufft (*q.v.*), "a small squarely built man"; they met frequently in the Neuenahrer or Moersischen Hof. They had appointed a regular "caller" whose duty it was to notify members of the meetings (*Ztscht für hist. Theol.*, 1860, 165, where an invitation issued by the Strasbourg Anabaptists is given verbatim).

In 1561 three Anabaptists were executed by drowning at Cologne, one of them being George Friesen (*q.v.*), and in 1562 two others were arrested. The church had increased to over 100 members. Faithfully they continued to meet in secret until they were betrayed by one of their own members in 1564. Thirty-three women and 24 men were thereupon seized and imprisoned in the various towers and gates of the city. Most of them were artisans, winedressers, washerwomen, and maids from other towns. Only two women belonged to the higher classes, the wife of the magistrate of Born and the *Stiftsfräulein* Margarete Werninckhofen. Among those arrested was Matthias (or Matthijs) Servaes (*q.v.*) of Ottenheim, who was put to death on June 30, 1565.

In August, September, and October 1565 a group of Anabaptists who "persisted stiff-necked in all their known errors" were expelled from the city; any who returned would be punished with death within 24 hours without mercy. About 1570 the well-known elder from Flanders, Hans Busschaert (*q.v.*) de Wever, lived in Cologne whither many Mennonites fled from Belgium in the next few years. Among those who had come from Antwerp were the parents of Joost van den Vondel (*q.v.*), who was born at Cologne in 1587.

The numerous protocols of the cross-examinations shed some light on the nature and inner life of the congregation. At the head stood the "principal preacher," called elder; there were four of them;

they had the oversight and rule over the church. Preachers were ordained by them. They served without fixed salary; they received only freewill gifts for their support. In 1609 a remarkable case is mentioned, where a preacher in Cologne received a daily income of six "albus" (Rembert, 509, note 3). The care of the poor was in charge of the deacons. In receiving members by baptism they acted with great caution. Scarcely one third of those who regularly attended their meetings were received in full membership. Anyone who maintained friendship with the Papists or other churches was regarded as a "sawed-off limb," and had to make confession before all the congregation.

Concerning communion services the following is known: "When communion was distributed the preacher took the bread and broke a piece of it for each, and as soon as it was given out and each had a piece in his hand, the preacher also took a piece for himself, put it into his mouth and ate it; and immediately, seeing this, the congregation did the same. The preacher, however, used no words, no ceremony, no blessing. As soon as the bread was eaten, the preacher took a bottle of wine or a cup, drank, and gave each of the members of it. On this wise they observed the breaking of bread."

In baptism the candidate knelt, the one administering baptism took water into his hand from a jug, poured it on the candidate's head with the words, "I baptize you on the faith you have confessed and accepted, in the name of the Father...." "Baptism does not save, only obedience does," said their creed. They recognized each other by the greeting, "Peace be with you!" They rejected community of goods. "The more powerful and wealthy give according to their means to the preachers and the poor and needy, so that they do not starve."

The church in Cologne had connections with Anabaptists in Holland (*DB* 1898, 109), Switzerland, and South Germany. In 1576 Hendrik von Berg, a member of the Cologne congregation, corresponded with the Dutch Elder Hans de Ries (*q.v.*). In the older books such as those by Burgmann, Hoornbeek, etc., a letter written by the Swiss Brethren to their brethren in Cologne is mentioned. In 1591 a conference of German and Dutch Mennonites met in Cologne to reach an agreement on several important points of church life. This took place in the Concept of Cologne (*q.v.*) (reprinted in Hege, *Die Täufer in der Kurpfalz,* 150-52). On the part of the congregation of Cologne the concept was signed by Ameldonck Leeuw, who is already mentioned as a preacher in 1569.

A church inspection made in 1597 in the archbishopric yielded a sad picture of conditions in the Catholic Church, which explains why Protestant preachers won large followings. There were also many Anabaptists in the city. Against them the mayors issued a stern warning on April 30, 1601, that they must leave the city within a week on penalty of death. The houses in which they held their services or whatever conventicles the heretics had, should be confiscated, the owners subject to the death penalty, the auditors be fined 100 guilders.

Non-Catholic baptism should be fined with 50 instead of 25 guilders as hitherto. All Protestants who had come to Cologne after 1590 must give up their citizenship and the protection of the city. By the end of May 300 persons, probably most of them Mennonites, had left the city.

After this, little or nothing is heard of the Mennonite church in Cologne. In 1637 a member of the congregation of Cologne came to Amsterdam, bringing along an *attestatie* (*q.v.*).   NEFF.

Rembert, *Wiedertäufer,* 380 ff.; P. Weiler, *Die kirchliche Reform im Erzbistum Köln* (Münster, 1931); Chr. Hege, *Die Täufer in der Kurpfalz* (Frankfurt, 1908); W. Ernst, *Briefwechsel Herzog Christophs von Württemberg* III (1902) 335; *Inv. Arch. Amst.* I, 401, 404, 466, 468, 469; *ML* II, 522-24.

Colombia Mennonite mission work is carried on by two branches of the Mennonite Church, both of them beginning in 1945. The Mennonite Brethren mission occupies a territory in Choco and in Valle on the Pacific coast and has three main stations, La Cumbre in Valle, Istmina and Noanama in Choco. Evangelistic, medical, educational, and linguistic work is done. There are 50 believers and a missionary staff of 16 members to date (October 1949).

The General Conference Mennonite Church is doing mission work in central Colombia in the department of Cundinamarca. Its principal work is located near Cachipay (*q.v.*), where they operate a home and school for underprivileged children, a large percentage of whom come from a background of leprosy. Evangelistic work is also done in Cachipay, Anolaima, La Mesa, and La Esperanza. There is an evangelical community of about 150, of whom 81 have been baptized (February 1954). There are nine members on the missionary staff.   G.S.

Colombia Mennonite Brethren Mission in South America had its beginning when Mr. and Mrs. Daniel A. Wirsche, who were sent there by the Board of Foreign Missions, arrived at Palmira, Valle, for the study of the Spanish language in April 1945. The mission acquired its first property when the Board purchased an unoccupied, independent mission station at La Cumbre, Valle, in the hills. The chief field of the mission, however, lies in the Choco, which stretches along the Pacific Ocean from the mouth of the San Juan River north to Panama and the Caribbean Sea. The population of the field is variously estimated at several hundred thousand to four hundred fifty thousand.

The main stations now are at La Cumbre, Valle, and at Istmina and Noanama, Choco. Other places serve as preaching centers. Besides being the seat of the first indigenous church, La Cumbre operates an elementary school for nationals as well as a school for missionary children patterned after the American eight-grade curriculum. The dispensary service in charge of a nurse is in its beginning stages. Istmina in the Choco harbors the indigenous church group of the Chocoans. A dispensary is conducted by a missionary nurse. Preparation is in progress for a school for nationals. Evangelization at the stations consists largely in house visitation and preaching in neighboring villages. Noanama is the center for linguistic work among the Indians. After the language has been reduced to writing and some translation of Scripture undertaken, evangelization among the Indians will be made possible.

The total number of believers on these three fields in 1949 stands at fifty. No ordination has yet taken place, although nationals are being employed as evangelists and teachers. The missionary staff consists of Mr. and Mrs. Daniel A. Wirsche, Mr. and Mrs. David Wirsche, Mr. and Mrs. John A. Dyck, Lillian Schafer, Annie E. Dyck, Kathryn Lentzner, Mary I. Schroeder, Lydia Golbek, Mr. and Mrs. Jacob A. Loewen, Mr. and Mrs. Harry K. Bartel, and Ruth Loewen.   A.E.J.

Colonia, Uruguay (pop. 130,000), capital of the state bearing the same name, is approximately 110 miles west of Montevideo, on the bank of the Rio de la Plata, and almost within sight of Buenos Aires, Argentina. Three hundred and fifty of the first Mennonite immigrants were quartered in an army barracks belonging to the Uruguay Ministry of Defense. The quarters were located in Colonia proper and the immigrants gradually found employment in the farm area surrounding the city. Colonia was cleared of Mennonites as the El Ombu project began taking form, until by August 1950 there were but 10 families remaining in the Colonia barracks.

Six families, numbering 30 people, made Colonia their permanent home. They were employed in factories and care for gardens part time.   W.T.S.

Colonies, Colonists, Mennonite, terms used in referring to Mennonite settlements, particularly in Russia. A. Klaus, author of *Unsere Kolonien* (1887), uses this term for all foreign rural settlements in Russia as seen from the Russian government's point of view as an attempt to settle unoccupied lands with permanent foreign settlers to serve as models for the native population, a policy which was begun under the reign of Czarina Elizabeth (1741-62) around 1750. The borders were closed to immigrants in 1819 with the exception of some Mennonites. The Russian colonization policy was described by Ehrt, *Das Mennonitentum in Russland* (Langensalza, 1932) 25-26.

The modern usage of the term to mean a "group of people transplanted from a mother country to another country but remaining subject to the parent state and country" is not quite accurate in the case of the Mennonites in Russia. The so-called "daughter colonies" in Russia were a result of a natural expansion sponsored by the mother settlements (colonies), to some degree promoted by the government. The Mennonite settlements later established in America (Manitoba, Mexico, Paraguay) were actually "colonies" of the mother settlements in Russia in a somewhat similar sense though never so called.

The term "colony" was not only used to designate a large compact settlement, but also sometimes to refer to single villages. The Hutterite Bruderhofs in Russia were referred to as "colonies." All foreign settlers in Russia were referred to by the government as "colonists," while the Mennonites usually spoke of themselves as "Mennonites" or "Germans" (*Dietsche*) and of other foreign settlers as "colonists." In order to avoid confusion it is best to speak of the Mennonites in Russia as "settlers" and "settlements" rather than "colonies" and "colonists" (see **Colonization**).   C.K.

Colonization is essentially a collective process of transplanting human beings from one geographic area to another. The process occurs when a group of like-minded people separates from a "parent" body or a similar cultural group and transplants itself to a new locality with the express purpose of establishing a separate organization. The essential difference between settlement and colonization is that settlement may occur when individuals, families, and small groups, together or independently, transfer their permanent residence from one area to another, without deliberate effort to maintain the previous cultural patterns or group identity.

The settler adapts his life and customs to the environment around him, whereas the colonist resists adaptation to his surrounding culture and tries to establish the familiar cultural patterns which he has brought with him. This cannot be done individually but must be done collectively.

There is a family characteristic about colonization that is well illustrated in the use of such terms as "mother" and "daughter" colonies. The first inclination of daughter colonies is to reproduce in the new community the same institutions and patterns of life that are found in the parent colony. As a spider spins his web out of his body, so new colonies tend to spin out of their own experiences and traditions a social organization similar to that of the parent body. In Mennonite history this is well demonstrated in the village patterns which have been transplanted by the Old Colony Mennonites from Russia to Canada, to Mexico, and to Paraguay. The Old Colony Mennonites established themselves in small European-type agricultural villages. In each of these countries today when new colonies are established they become replicas of those established in Russia a century and a half ago. One can find today the identical village patterns, the same space arrangement of houses and barns, and location of orchards and gardens, as that earlier used in Manitoba and Russia. Even the names given to the new villages are the same as those found in the mother colonies.

We may then define a Mennonite colony as a group of like-minded people with common interests and common ideals, living in a well-defined geographic area, the central and integrating idea around which the colony is organized being religious.

Mennonites have traditionally been great colonizers. Movement in groups is, in fact, generally the only way in which they have agreed to migrate. There is a long and conspicuous list of examples of successful colonization. When Mennonites came to America directly from Germany and Switzerland in the early 18th century, they colonized in eastern Pennsylvania. Their subsequent periodic expansion to states farther west was almost always by groups. When in the 1870's the Mennonites from Russia came in large numbers to Canada and the United States, they sent investigating parties ahead to scout carefully for colonization possibilities. Invitations to colonize were accepted only where there was opportunity for all migrating members to be accommodated in compact settlements as well as for their children in the future. Likewise, the movements of Mennonites to the Latin-American countries of Mexico, Paraguay, Brazil, and Uruguay are all examples of contemporary Mennonite colonization. From Ontario to British Columbia, and from Pennsylvania to California, Mennonites are settled in rather solid and compact cultural groups.

Among Mennonites, colonization is almost exclusively a rural phenomenon. This is probably true because of their preference for agriculture as a vocation. Rural areas also provide fewer disintegrating threats to the compact nature of Mennonite communities. The penetrating forces of secularism do not seem to undermine and destroy a group's religious qualities as rapidly in the rural areas as they do in the cities. North Kildonan, a suburb of Winnipeg, Man., is one city where Mennonites have colonized, several hundred Mennonite families having settled in this area. It is, however, a rare exception in the history of Mennonite colonization. Schönwiese, near Alexandrovsk, Russia, was also a suburban settlement.

Colonization seems almost essential if Mennonite religious principles and culture traits are to survive. The very genius of the Mennonites is their living in closely knit religious-centered communities. Without the sense of solidarity and mutual edification that close settlement and frequent social contact affords, the ideals of Mennonites can scarcely be maintained. The failure of American Mennonitism to establish itself firmly in any major American city (except Winnipeg) today would substantiate this point. For this reason, in times past and even today, Mennonites have attributed a basic importance to colonization. It is, in fact, an integral aspect of Mennonite philosophy.

After World War II, when new homes were sought for the displaced Mennonites who escaped from Russia or for those who were uprooted in Germany, it was in areas where large groups could be colonized anew or absorbed in established Mennonite communities. Mennonite refugees were not scattered at random throughout the countries of the world. The movement of 1,200 uprooted Mennonites from the Danzig area to Uruguay in 1949 and 1951 is a most recent illustration. Here through the combined efforts of American Mennonites two large tracts of land were purchased and colonies established. In this way a church could be established and the values, customs, and meaningful ways of life preserved. Thus in Uruguay as in Paraguay, Mennonites are attempting to set up colonies that will enable them to preserve their religious faith in the face of sharply contrasting ethnic, cultural, and religious conditions.

An essential ingredient to successful Mennonite colonization has always been the practice of mutual aid. Members of the transplanted brotherhoods have looked after each other's welfare. Often the resources of the whole group have been pooled and made equally available to all. At other times the wealthier advanced funds to the poor, who after becoming economically established repaid their loans. Aid was not confined to material assistance, but counsel and mutual encouragement were provided through conscious and unconscious group efforts. Mennonites in one country have repeatedly come to the aid of their brethren in other countries in case of need.

The successful record of colonization in older areas has often been used to open the door for entrance (and special privileges) to new areas. Sometimes this has been solely a result of the obvious and well-known achievements and reputation by Mennonite scholars and leaders. Sometimes studies have been prepared by government officials for governmental agencies considering applications or subsidies. The first type is well illustrated by the Russian government in 1786 ff., seeking out the West Prussian Mennonites for colonization purposes, because their reputation as farmers, as also the United States and Canadian governments seeking Russian Mennonites as colonists in 1873. The second is illustrated by memoranda prepared by representatives of Russian and American Mennonites in the period after World War I and World War II for Mexico, Paraguay, I.R.O. (International Refugee Organization), and the United States State Department. The third is illustrated by the action of the Uruguayan government in securing a report by a Uruguayan social scientist in connection with the movement of West Prussian Mennonites to that country.

The following table of successful Mennonite colonization movements lists only the major ones, ignoring minor groups and daughter colonies:

1. Holland to the Vistula and Nogat deltas in West Prussia, 1540-1625 (see **West Prussia**).

2. Switzerland to the Palatinate, 1650-90 (see **Palatinate**).

3. Switzerland and Palatinate to Eastern Pennsylvania, 1710-50 (see **Pennsylvania**).

4. West Prussia to the Ukraine, 1784-1800 (see **Russia**).

5. Palatinate and Alsace to Galicia and Volhynia, 1789-1820 (see **Galicia** and **Volhynia**).

6. Alsace and Switzerland (separately) to Ohio, Indiana, and Illinois, at various places, 1815-60 (see **Ohio, Indiana, Illinois**).

7. Ukraine to Kansas, Nebraska, Minnesota, Dakota, and Manitoba, 1873-80 (see the articles on the relevant states or provinces).

8. West Prussia to Kansas and Nebraska, 1873-80 (see **Kansas** and **Nebraska**).

9. Ukraine to Caucasus and West Siberia (separately), 1905-14 (see **Caucasus** and **Siberia**).

10. Manitoba to Mexico, 1922-25 (see **Mexico**).

11. Russia and Siberia to Canada, 1922-25 (see **Canada**).

12. Manitoba to Paraguay, 1926-28 (see **Paraguay**).

13. Russia and Siberia via Germany to Brazil, 1930 (see **Brazil**), and to Paraguay, 1930 and 1947-50 (see **Paraguay**).

14. Ukraine to Canada via Germany, 1947-50 (see **Canada**).

15. Prairie Provinces of Canada to British Columbia, 1935-50 (see **British Columbia**).

16. West Prussia and Galicia to Uruguay via Germany, 1949-51 (see **Uruguay**).　　　　J.W.F.

J. W. Fretz, *Mennonite Colonization: Lessons from the Past for the Future* (Akron, 1944); *idem*, "Recent Mennonite Community Building in Canada," in *MQR* XVII (1944) 5-21; *idem*, "Factors Contributing to Success and Failure in Mennonite Colonization," in *MQR* XXIV (1950) 130-35; A. Ehrt, *Das Mennonitentum in Russland* (Langensalza, 1932); C. H. Smith, *Coming of the Russian Mennonites* (Berne, 1927); *idem*, *The Mennonite Immigration to Pennsylvania in the Eighteenth Century* (Norristown, 1929); W. Quiring, *Deutsche erschliessen den Chaco* (Karlsruhe, 1936); *idem*, *Russlanddeutsche suchen eine Heimat* (Karlsruhe, 1938); C. A. Dawson, *Group Settlements: Ethnic Communities in Western Canada* (Toronto, 1936); R. England, *The Colonization of Western Canada* (London, 1936); E. Correll, "Mennonite Immigration into Manitoba, Documents and Sources" (1872-74) in *MQR* XI (1937) 196-227, 267-83, and XXII (1948) 43-57; *idem*, "Congressional Debates on the Mennonite Immigration from Russia 1873-74," in *MQR* XX (1946) 178-221; *idem*, "Canadian Agricultural Records on Mennonite Settlements" (1875-77), in *MQR* XXI (1947) 34-46; *idem*, "Sources on the Mennonite Immigration from Russia in the 1870's," in *MQR* XXIV (1950) 329-52; J. W. Warkentin, "Carving a Home out of the Primeval Forest," in *MQR* XXIV (1950) 142-48; K. Schnell, "John Funk and the Mennonite Migration of 1873-75," in *MQR* XXIV (1950) 199-229; M. Gingerich, "Jacob Y. Schantz, Promoter of the Mennonite Settlements in Manitoba," in *MQR* XXIV (1950) 230-47; J. Umble, "Factors Explaining the Disintegration of Mennonite Communities," in *Proceedings of the Seventh Annual Conference on Mennonite Cultural Problems* (North Newton, 1949) 112-28; C. Krahn, ed., *From the Steppes to the Prairies* (1874-1949) (Newton, 1949); D. Gratz, *Bernese Anabaptists* (Scottdale, 1953); E. Francis, *In Search of Utopia* (Altona, Man., 1955); *ML* II, 524.

Colorado (area 104,247 sq. miles; pop. 1,123,296), a state known for its Pikes Peak among the 200 or more peaks over 13,000 feet high. The discovery of gold in the Pikes Peak region in 1858 led to the first important settlements of English-speaking people. Mining is an important industry in the state.

But the chief attraction for Mennonite colonization is its agricultural resources. There is a wide arid plain on the eastern slope of the mountains which is adapted for stock raising and the production of grain and feed crops. The Arkansas and Platte River valleys furnished large areas of potential irrigation projects which through the years have been developed. Besides this eastern slope, there are the smaller rich valleys between the mountain ranges on the western slope which are well adapted to a varied agricultural program.

These agricultural possibilities attracted Mennonite (MC) colonization to several areas of the state, where churches have been established. One of the earliest of these was established near the close of the 19th century at Thurman, about 80 miles east of Denver. A few years later the colony at Limon was established. About 1900 the Holbrook irrigation project was developed near La Junta. Mennonite settlers under the leadership of J. M. Nunemaker, R. J. Heatwole, and others established rural homes here and the East Holbrook and La Junta Mennonite churches.

Another factor that contributed largely in the making of the Colorado Mennonite churches was the attraction of climate for health seekers. Following the Trudeau experiment in tuberculosis treatment, many sanatoria were established in the arid climate of the Rocky Mountains. Some Mennonites were thus induced to move west. These health seekers centered around La Junta. From the need created by this movement there was born the idea of a sanatorium built by the Mennonite Church. From this grew the Mennonite Sanitarium west of La Junta, and later the Mennonite Hospital and Sanitarium, and the La Junta Mennonite School of Nursing in La Junta.

In Rocky Ford, Col., another hospital was in building in 1953, to be operated by the Mennonite Church (MC) as an integral part of the Mennonite Hospital and Sanitarium of La Junta. The Mennonite Board of Missions and Charities has also negotiated a contract to operate a hospital to be built by the Glenwood Springs community. These two additions will add much to the resources of the church in taking care of the sick in Colorado.

Through these activities the Colorado Mennonite program was publicized throughout the Mennonite Church as a whole. This work also served to strengthen the Mennonite church program throughout the state.

Another factor aiding the growth of the church was the missionary activity of the Kansas, Nebraska, Missouri, and Iowa Mennonite (MC) churches. Some Mennonites were settled in Colorado Springs. Others came out for the summer for employment in the rush tourist season. This led to the suggestion that the church should establish a mission in Manitou Springs, both to conserve Mennonites who were there and to reach the tourist group for Christ. There is now a well-established congregation in Manitou Springs.

The Denver Mennonite Church was the outgrowth of missionary suggestions prompted by the affiliated nurses in Denver, sent there by the home school of nursing in La Junta. From a small mission effort, this work has grown to an established congregation.

The Pueblo church was also begun as a missionary venture sponsored through the La Junta Mennonite congregation. This was organized as a congregation in 1949. The work is not large, but is active as a missionary center with some support from the South Central Mennonite Conference Mission Board.

Thus through agricultural colonization, hospital institutional work, and missionary endeavor has this quite virile Mennonite program developed in Colorado.

Likewise a missionary program was started by the East Holbrook Mennonite Church among the Spanish people. This grew into a Spanish mission church at La Junta under the auspices of the General Mission Board, Elkhart, Ind.

The General Conference Mennonites have one congregation in Colorado, located at Vona. Its membership in 1954 was 20. A Mennonite Brethren congregation reported 50 members in 1948. The total number of baptized Mennonites in Colorado is therefore approximately 550.　　　　A.H.E.

Colorado Springs, Col., was the location of the second Mennonite Civilian Public Service Camp, which was opened three miles northeast of the city in June 1941. Under the Soil Conservation Service the campers chiefly built irrigation ditches, dams, and reservoirs, leveled land for irrigation, built fences, surveyed land, and engaged in emergency farm labor. A survey of the 143 campers in October 1942 showed that they came from 12 states, from 10 branches of the Mennonite brotherhood, and from 13 other denominations, the General Conference Mennonites having the largest number. The camp enjoyed excellent public relations with various civic groups who used their influence to keep it when in 1943 there were rumors that it might be closed. It was closed in May 1946. (M. Gingerich, *Service for Peace,* Akron, Pa., 1949.) M.G.

Colportage: see Tract Distribution.

Columbia Mennonite (MC) Mission in Lancaster Co., Pa., founded in 1907, was the fruition of the vision of Charles Byer. Under the Eastern Board of Missions and Charities of the Lancaster Mennonite Conference, C. Z. Martin became superintendent in 1920 and pastor in 1923. The present church building was erected in 1922 at a cost of $24,000. Summer Bible school (white and colored), Sunday school, sewing schools, children's meetings, regular services, and quarterly Bible meetings featured the work here. The membership in 1954 was 71, average Sunday-school attendance 160, average summer Bible school attendance 68 colored and 360 white; C. Z. Martin was the pastor, and B. B. Zimmerman the deacon. I.D.L.

Columbiana County (pop. 83,000), Ohio, lying along the eastern border of the state, was organized in 1803 and early received a large German population, including Mennonites from Bucks Co., Pa. (in 1807). During the first fifty years it became one of the four or five leading wool-growing counties in the Union. At present the large increase of the urban population in Columbiana and (adjoining) Mahoning counties on account of the growing importance of ceramic and steel manufactures is directing the agricultural interests of the Mennonites from general farming to poultry raising, dairying, and gardening. With Mahoning County (pop. 87,000), formed from it in 1846, Columbiana has long been a progressive and influential center of Ohio Mennonitism. The three Mennonite (MC) churches in northern Columbiana and southern Mahoning counties have a combined membership of 471, and a Wisler (OOM) congregation north of Columbiana has 60. J.S.U.

Colyn, Pieter, a burgomaster of Amsterdam, who protected the Anabaptists about 1535 and is said to have belonged to them, which is, however, an error; he likely was a Sacramentist (*q.v.*). (*DB* 1917, 195; 1919, 172, 174; Kühler, *Geschiedenis* I, 135, 177, 129.) vDZ.

Comans, a Dutch Mennonite family living at Rotterdam in the 17th century whose members belonged to the Flemish church in this town. Michiel Michielsz Comans was a preacher of this congregation, already serving in 1632; in that year he signed the Dordrecht Confession for his congregation of Rotterdam. He disagreed with his fellow preachers because of their conservatism and their belief that only the Flemish church could be considered

the true Christian church. Comans had been influenced by Collegiant (*q.v.*) principles, and believed the true church could also be found among other Christians, Mennonite as well as non-Mennonite. In 1655 he left the Flemish congregation and joined the Waterlander congregation, which he served as a preacher until his death in 1664.

His son Michiel Michielsz Comans, a cloth-dyer and a member of the Flemish church, left Rotterdam about 1645 to live in Amsterdam. Here he founded a Rijnsburg (*q.v.*) *college* about 1648, together with Adam Boreel and Daniel de Breen, and became an ardent participant. At the meetings of this *college* he came in close contact with Galenus Abrahamsz (*q.v.*), the preacher of the Flemish Mennonite church *bij't Lam* at Amsterdam and a warm friend of Collegiantism. Comans did not join the Mennonite church in Amsterdam, for he could not obtain a certificate of membership (*aanwijs*) from his Rotterdam congregation, since he was under censure there because of his advocacy of open communion. Michiel Michielsz Comans died in 1687. vDZ.

K. Vos, *Geschiedenis der Doopsgez. Gemeente te Rotterdam* (Rotterdam, 1907) 15, 17, 42, 43; J. C. van Slee, *De Rijnsburger Collegianten* (Haarlem, 1895) 135, 140, 162; H. W. Meihuizen, *Galenus Abrahamsz* (Haarlem, 1954), see "*Index.*"

Comenius (Komensky), Johann Amos, great educator, the last bishop of the old church of the Moravian and Bohemian Brethren, was born March 28, 1592, at Niwnic in Moravia, went to Herborn in Nassau, Germany, in 1611 to study theology, attended the university at Heidelberg in 1613, and journeyed to Amsterdam in 1614, where he met the wealthy merchant de Geer, who became his protector and patron.

Too young to take over a church office he assumed the principalship of the Brethren school at Prerau. Here he wrote *Prescriptions for an Easier Grammar,* which demanded consideration of the folk-speech in the school. From 1618 to 1621 he was preacher and school inspector in Fulnek. In 1621 he lost all his possessions as well as wife and child in the Spanish invasion. As a refugee he wandered about, strengthening the Brethren, and visited the cities of Görlitz, Frankfurt a.O., and Berlin.

In 1628 he left his home with thousands of the Brethren. At the boundary he fell on his knees and with tears prayed "that God would not depart from Moravia and Bohemia, but would retain a seed there." On Feb. 8, 1628, he went to Lissa in Poland and taught Latin at the Brethren Gymnasium there; from 1626 to 1641 he was rector of the school. Here he wrote his world-famous books, *The Great Didactic* (1636-37, first published 1657-58), with the motto, "Omnia sponte fluant, absit violentia rebus"; *Teachings of the Mother School; The Gate of Language* (1631); and previously, *The Labyrinth of the World and the Paradise of the Heart* (1623). In 1632 he was made secretary of the Moravian brotherhood and was put in charge of its student youth. In 1641 he was called to England and in 1642 to Sweden to reform the school system. In 1648 he was chosen bishop of the brotherhood. Now he had to take up residence in Lissa again.

The hope of the Brethren in the Peace of Westphalia failed them, for they were excluded from its provision of toleration and their existence destroyed. Comenius wrote *The Bequest of the Dying Mother, the Unitas Fratrum*, a book which cannot be read without emotion even today. In 1650, at the invitation of the Duke Siegmund Rakoczy he went to Hungary and organized the Saros Patok school. The death of the ruler caused him to return. In 1656 Lissa was destroyed by Sweden, and Comenius again lost all his possessions. Impoverished and worn, he resumed his wandering. He found brief asylum in Silesia. Driven from Frankfurt a.O. by the plague, he went to Hamburg and then to Amsterdam (1656), where he remained active until his death on Nov. 15, 1670.

Of the total of 106 books which Comenius wrote, two others must be specifically mentioned here. His *Orbis pictus* (1658) was in Goethe's time still considered the best book of pictures. Here he added the use of the visual sense to education, which had hitherto employed only the auditory sense. The book *The One Thing Needful* (1668), written two years before his death, offers the best insight into his religious position.

Comenius, the "seer of pedagogy," the founder of our modern theory of education, the greatest promoter of the German elementary school besides Luther and of instruction in the native tongue, the energetic defender of the Christian faith against all false doctrine and free-thinking, the champion of unity in the Protestant churches, a messenger of peace in the midst of the noise and strife of his time, held a position very near to that of the Mennonites. Although he had few actual contacts with them, he repeatedly defended them against attack. In his *Questions about the Unitas* (1663) he says, "The Anabaptists are preserved by their inner constitution which is more perfect than in any other brotherhood." In 1661 he takes their part against the unitarian Zwicker who had questioned their trinitarian orthodoxy, with the remark that he had from boyhood been acquainted with the Anabaptists of Hungary, and that these "simple people" had always held a belief in the Triune God. It is clear that Comenius referred to the Hutterites. Although Comenius was in Amsterdam from 1656 on, there is no evidence that he was acquainted with any other Mennonites or Anabaptists.

The third centennial of the birth of Comenius (1892) was a well-attended memorial. Mennonites also took part in it. At the public celebration in Danzig, H. G. Mannhardt gave an impressive address. The Elbing Mennonites arranged a church memorial service, which was attended by non-Mennonites. A dignified service was held in Amsterdam. The preliminary celebration held in Holland in the house of the onetime patron of Comenius, Laurens de Geer, was conducted by P. van Eeghen. NEFF.

J. Kvaczala, *J. A. Comenius* (Berlin, 1914); *Monatshefte der Comeniusgesellschaft* I, 19 ff., 75 ff.; 295 ff.; II, 85 ff., X (1912) 91 ff.; XXV, 158 ff.; J. Needham and R. F. Young, *The Teacher of Nations* (Cambridge, 1942); M. Spinka, *John Amos Comenius* (Chicago, 1942); *The Labyrinth of the World*, tr. by M. Spinka (Chicago, 1942); *ML* I, 368.

Comeniusgesellschaft. In memory of Johann Amos Comenius, the great pedagogue and theologian, at the instigation of Prof. Kleinert and Dr. Ludwig Keller, the *Comeniusgesellschaft* was founded in 1892 with headquarters in Berlin, with the following aims: (1) the publication of Comenius' most important works and letters, as well as those of his predecessors, teachers, and other like-minded persons; (2) research in the history and doctrine of the "old-evangelical" churches, especially by publication of the source materials; and (3) collection of books, manuscripts, and documents of historical importance.

To accomplish this aim the *Monatshefte der Comeniusgesellschaft* were published from 1892 to 1934, in addition to the *Comeniusblätter für Volkserziehung, Mitteilungen der Comeniusgesellschaft*. Leading Mennonites of Germany, Holland, America, and Russia joined this society at its inception. It received an annual financial contribution through the *Vereinigung der Mennoniten-Gemeinden im Deutschen Reich*. On its directorate the German Mennonites were represented (1917) by E. Goebel of Weierhof (Palatinate), and J. van Delden of Gronau (Westphalia), and the Dutch Mennonites by Prof. J. G. Appeldoorn in Amsterdam. The Amsterdam branch had a Mennonite minister, W. J. Leendertz, as secretary, with Prof. S. Cramer a member. In the earlier issues the *Monatshefte* printed important and valuable material on Mennonite history. Later it stressed social and ethical problems and pedagogical questions that contributed to the general welfare and public education. The Goshen College Library has the first 15 volumes of the *Monatshefte* (1892-1906); the Amsterdam Mennonite Library has 30 volumes of the *Monatshefte* (1892-1921) and 25 volumes of the *Comeniusblätter* (1895-1919). (*ML* I, 369.) NEFF.

Comes, Teunis: see **Komes.**

Comins (Mich.) Mennonite Church (GCM) began as a union Sunday school, sponsored by F. F. Stutesman and a number of Mennonite families living in that vicinity. Revival meetings were held in the fall of 1924; and in the summer of 1925 a congregation was organized and a church built. There were 166 members in 1953. G.Mi.

Commemorative Medals (Dutch *gedenkpenningen*) are medals made of gold, silver, or other metal to commemorate certain historical events. There are a few memorial medals concerning Mennonite history:

(1) A medal in silver and also in pewter engraved in 1736 by Martinus Holtzhey, to celebrate Menno Simons' leaving the Roman Catholic Church in 1536. This medal shows on one side a portrait of Menno and on the other side a poem in the Dutch language.

(2) A medal in bronze, issued in 1845 to commemorate the 150th anniversary of the Mennonite conference in Friesland. This medal, engraved by T. A. Keikes, shows the conference represented as a woman with a cross on her breast. An old man on her right points at a ruin of an old church; at the left a young man and a new church; before her a

cornucopia and a vase filled with coins. Legend: *1695 Friesche Doopsgezinde Sociëteit 1845.* On the other side the inscription: *ter gedagtenis aan III Julij MDCCCXLV.*

(3) A medal, issued in 1898 for the congregation of Hamburg-Altona for presentation to members who celebrated their silver wedding. The medal contains on one side a portrait of Menno Simons; the other side was intended for an inscription.

(4) A medal commemorating the 350th anniversary of Menno Simons' death, engraved in 1909 by Johannes von Langa for the Hamburg-Altona congregation. This medal shows a portrait of Menno Simons and the symbols of the seal of the Hamburg-Altona congregation, i.e., two palm trees divided by a body of water, and the all-seeing eye of God (exists in silver and bronze).

(5) A medal engraved by Johannes von Langa in 1911 on the occasion of the 25th anniversary of the Conference of German Mennonite congregations. One side shows the portrait of medal 4 (above) and laurel branches, other side an inscription with the names of the board of the *Vereinigung der Mennoniten-Gemeinden im Deutschen Reich* (exists in silver and in bronze).

(6) A medal commemorating the 25th anniversary of the Mennonite congregation of Berlin, Germany, engraved by Johannes von Langa in 1912. One side shows the portrait of Menno (as 4 above, but without laurel), the other side the inscription: *Zur Erinnerung a. d. 25-jährige Bestehen der Berliner Mennoniten Gemeinde 1912* (silver and bronze). (For Nos. 1-6 see *DB* 1916, 75 f., 95-98.)

(7) A medal in bronze, engraved in 1935 by A. Mazotti, commemorating the fall of the Münsterite kingdom of Jan van Leyden, July 1535. The medal shows on one side the city of Münster according to an old picture, with the city coat of arms; the other side has portraits of Jan van Leyden, Knipperdolling, and Krechting.   vDZ.

Commes, Jan, a Dutch Mennonite preacher from about 1690 and elder of the congregation of Zwolle, province of Overijssel, from 1702, is the author of a book against Jacobus Rijsdijk (*q.v.*), who had also been a preacher at Zwolle. Against this ardent champion of Mennonite orthodoxy Commes wrote *Den Veynzaart ontmaskert* (Zwolle, 1729). vDZ.

Commissie voor Buitenlandsche Nooden: see Fonds voor Buitenlandsche Nooden.

Commissie voor de Doopsgezinden in de Verstrooiing (Committee for Scattered Mennonites): see **Verstrooiing, Doopsgezinden in de.**

Commission for Anabaptist Affairs (*Täuferkammer*). The great growth of the Mennonites had induced the council of Bern to set up a special committee for the management of Anabaptist affairs on Jan. 4, 1659. This newly organized committee was composed of Wilhelm von Diessbach and Christian Willading of the council, Captain Daniel Morlot, and Magistrate Johann Stürler, and two clergymen, Professor Christoph Lüthard and Pastor Abraham de Losea. From this special committee developed the permanent *Täuferkammer,* which was to relieve the council of its Anabaptist problems. It was the duty of the committee to supervise the Anabaptist funds, to check the growth of the sect, make suggestions as to its elimination, to control the apprehension and banishment or pardoning of the Mennonites, and to be responsible for the execution of the mandates. A part of the confiscated property fell to the Commission.

The Commission worked systematically. Most of the Mennonites seized were sent over the border penniless. In 1709 the council could boast that more than 500 persons had been conducted to the border. But many came back because they had left their families behind or could not abandon their congregation.

To end their troubles with the Mennonites once for all, the Commission planned to deport them to the East Indies, since the prisons were overflowing, and expulsion was not effective; but this plan failed. Their next idea was to send them to America. The committee reached an agreement with a certain Mr. Ritter to have about 100 imprisoned Mennonites taken to the Carolinas (see **Bern**). For each Mennonite he actually transported he was to receive 45 talers from the Anabaptist fund. But this plan was foiled by the intervention of the Dutch **Mennonites.**

The work of this institution is recorded in the manuals of the Commission in the state archives of Bern, which fill four volumes in the period 1721-43, and in the *Täuferurbar,* the official inventory of confiscated Anabaptist property (see **Confiscation of Property**), which was instituted by a mandate of Feb. 23, 1729. This list in the state archives of Bern gives us an insight into the persecution which not only threatened the economic existence of numerous Mennonite families, but ruined them. The *Täuferurbar,* especially set up for this purpose, was to give information on the spread and development of Anabaptism in order the better to suppress it, and also to give an account on the use of confiscated property taken from them. But these books are not a justification of the course of the Bernese government regarding the Mennonites, but are instead a spot of disgrace in the history of the patrician government of Bern.

Gradually as the zeal for the preservation of church uniformity declined and the old orthodoxy paled in the Age of Enlightenment, religious intolerance gave way to the idea of "Liberty, Fraternity, and Equality." On Dec. 4, 1743, the council of Bern came to the unanimous decision to dissolve the *Täuferkammer.*   NEFF, S.G.

Müller, *Berner Täufer* 337 ff.; S. Geiser, *Die Taufgesinnten-Gemeinden* (Karlsruhe, 1931).

Commission for Christian Education, an organization under the Mennonite General Conference (MC), which created it in 1937 to take over the work of three previously established General Conference committees, namely, the General Sunday School Committee (est. 1915), the Young People's Bible Meeting Topics Committee (est. 1909), and the Young People's Problems Committee (est. 1921). It is composed of twelve members, ten elected by the General Conference and two co-opted, and meets semiannually. Its function is to supervise and assist the organized teaching agencies of

the church as they operate in the local congregation, as well as young people's activities with the exception of the summer camp program. The work of the Commission is carried on through one standing committee, viz., the Curriculum Committee of five members, two of whom are appointed by the Mennonite Publishing House, and ten secretaries for the following areas of work: Sunday schools, young people's Bible meetings, Christian workers' training, summer Bible schools, weekday Bible schools, young people's activities, missionary education, junior activities, home interests, and church music. The Curriculum Committee plans all curriculum materials for use in the local church program of Christian education, which are then produced by the Mennonite Publishing House. The youth work of the church, the Mennonite Youth Fellowship, is under the supervision of the Commission, the secretary of Young People's Activities being the sponsor of the national MYF, and a member of its General Council. The name of the Commission 1937-53 was Mennonite Commission for Christian Education and Young People's Work.
H.S.B.

Committee for Church Affairs: see **Komitee für Kirchliche Angelegenheiten.**

Committee of General Welfare and Public Relations operates under the direction of the Conference of the Mennonite Brethren Church of North America and also reports to and co-operates with the four district Mennonite Brethren conferences, which meet annually.

Until 1920 the relief work of the conference was directed by the members of the Board of Foreign Missions; then three committees were organized as follows: the Relief Committee; the Committee for Peace and Nonresistance; and the Committee for Colonization. At the adoption of the new constitution at the Reedley (Cal.) sessions of the conference in 1936, these three committees were discontinued and their duties assigned to the Committee of General Welfare and Public Relations.

The constitution provides for five members who serve for a period of three years between the triennial sessions of the General Conference, but because of the extension of the field and the widespread location of the congregations, three associate members were appointed to represent certain areas and special purposes at the 1949 conference session.

The purpose and work of the committee is outlined in Article XVI, Section 2, of the Constitution of the Conference under three headings as follows:

(*a*) The committee serves as Relief Committee in the ministry of general welfare by receiving money which it uses to alleviate physical suffering in countries visited by tribulation, aiding first, them that are of the household of faith, and then sufferers in larger circles.

(*b*) Through its representative on the Committee of Colonization it takes part in undertaking to find new homes for those who because of persecution on account of their faith were forced to leave their former homeland.

(*c*) In public relations the committee seeks to render mediating service, when conflicts arise in questions of civil rights and faith. The committee does preparatory work in this respect by recommending and distributing literature that presents the Christian's relationship to the government on Biblical grounds in order to keep alive the consciousness that it is the duty of the children of God to preserve peace.

The annual budget ranged from $188,000 in 1946 to $125,000 in 1949.

Some of the outstanding persons in the committee during the time since its organization were the following: J. W. Wiens, D. C. Eitzen, J. F. Harms, C. F. Klassen, B. B. Janz, P. C. Hiebert, and M. A. Kroeker.

Among the publications of the committee are: *Mitteilungen von der Reise nach Südamerika* (1937); *Our Attitude Towards War; Handbook on Peace* (1939); and *Is War a Crime?* P.C.H.

Committee on Church Unity functions under the Board of Missions of the General Conference Mennonite Church. Its purpose is to promote "unity among member churches of the Conference and among branches of Mennonites around the world." Among the other duties of this committee is the examination and recommendation of applications from congregations and conferences for admission into conference membership.

The committee was created at the 1929 session of the General Conference under the name of Comity Committee. At the conference session in 1935 the name was changed to Church Unity Committee. The committee contacts congregations, mostly those affiliated with district conferences but not with the General Conference, and invites them to join. It is also the responsibility of the committee to remove difficulties that arise in matters pertaining to practices and doctrines.

One of the major tasks of the committee has been to work out the plan by which the General Conference Mennonite Church and the Central Conference of Mennonites united in one body. This union, as well as the joining of numerous congregations in the United States, Canada, and some in South America, was due to a large degree to the efforts of the Committee on Church Unity, which is the name adopted in the new conference constitution of 1950. Leading members of the committee have been M. Horsch, Benjamin Ewert, W. F. Unruh, and Arnold Funk. (See reports of the committee since 1929 in *Minutes and Reports of the General Conference Mennonite Church.*) C.K.

Committee on Economic and Social Relations. A committee of the Mennonite (MC) General Conference, first established in 1939 as an appointive committee, and known at that time as the Committee on Industrial Relations. In 1943 it became a standing committee and in 1951 it was renamed the Committee on Economic and Social Relations. One of the first, and continuing major, tasks of the committee has been to assist the workingmen of the church to maintain the stand of the church (on grounds of nonresistance) against joining labor unions.

In 1941 the General Conference authorized the

committee to concern itself with the entire economic and social ethic of the New Testament as it related to the Christian brotherhood. A meeting of church leaders sponsored by the committee in 1943 recognized that urbanization and industrialization were changing the old ways of the brotherhood, and that new economic and social patterns were being set. It was believed that many of the young men then in Civilian Public Service without personal income would require assistance to establish themselves following their discharge. This led the committee to place increasing emphasis on mutual assistance within the church as an expression of Christian brotherhood. One result of this was the formation in 1945 of a new organization known as Mennonite Mutual Aid (*q.v.*) to function as a financial aid and counseling service, especially for young people lacking capital and financial experience. In 1949 a subsidiary organization, Mennonite Aid, Inc. (*q.v.*), was formed for mutual assistance in meeting the cost of unusual sickness, hospitalization, death and burial.

In 1945 the committee sponsored a study conference on Mennonite community life at Goshen College whose papers were published in the *Mennonite Quarterly Review* XIX (1945), 74-176. This conference was followed by annual conferences of a more popular type, held in local Mennonite communities, and designed to challenge the brotherhood to find the way of Christian ethics in its economic and social relationships. Beginning with 1949 these conferences were sponsored jointly with the Mennonite Community Association. Among other things, the committee has encouraged the trend toward the formation of small industries within the Mennonite communities which provide employment locally and thus discourage the disintegration of the community through the removal of its youth to larger industrial centers. One of the indirect results of this effort was the founding of the *Mennonite Community* (*q.v.*), a periodical devoted to the study of the material problems of the brotherhood, and stressing the application of the Gospel and Christian ethics to every aspect of the Christian's life, especially in economic and social relationships. In 1954 this journal was merged into a larger monthly journal called *Christian Living* (*q.v.*).

In the summer of 1951 the committee sponsored a students-in-industry unit in the city of Detroit designed to help students make a firsthand study of modern industrial life, and also a study conference on Christian community relations which resulted in the formulation of *A Statement of Concerns* on the social implications of the Gospel, including nonresistance in daily life, Christian ethics in business and the professions, organized labor, race and minority group relations, and other related concerns. This statement was published and widely circulated both within and without the church.

In 1952 the committee inaugurated a series of conferences of Mennonite industrial employers for the exchange of ideas on ways and means for promoting Christian labor relations in industry and included in its plans the publication of a series of pamphlets on Christian economic and social relations.

In 1953 the membership of the committee consisted of two ministers and six laymen representing agriculture and industry as well as the general interests of the church. One of the members was a Negro, emphasizing the committee's interest in Christian interracial relations. Guy F. Hershberger has served as executive secretary of the committee from its beginning in 1939.　　　　G.F.H.

Commonitio ofte Waerschouwinge, *aen de Vlaemsche Doopsgesinde Gemeynte binnen Amsterdam* (Admonition to the Flemish Mennonite Congregation of Amsterdam, n.p., 1665) is a six-page pamphlet. The anonymous author calls himself a *Voorstander, je een Lidtmaet der selve Gemeynte* (a member of this church). Some of the ministers of this church, he says, do not teach the way, that is, Christ in the right way; e.g., Galenus Abrahamsz (*q.v.*), David Spruyt (*q.v.*), and Frans Beuns. They are looked upon as Socinians (*q.v.*), and the author thinks this is likely the truth; he explains why he thinks so, examining the sermons delivered by Galenus and Spruyt. At the end of his booklet the author demands that they answer without ambiguity seven questions which he puts.　　　　vdZ.

Communion (Lord's Supper, *Abendmahl, Nachtmahl*) has always had only a symbolic meaning for the Anabaptists and Mennonites and is observed as the ordinance of the Lord and not a sacrament which in itself conveys the grace of God to the participant. The early Christians probably observed the Lord's Supper at every meeting for worship in accordance with the Lord's ordinance given in Matt. 26:26-28; Mark 14:22-25, etc. It was a memorial to the death of Christ and a means of the closest fellowship of the believers in Christ. In later centuries the sacrificial aspect surrounded by elaborate liturgical accompaniments was strongly emphasized so that the sacramental character predominated and the Lord's Supper became the "Sacrament," "Mass," or "Eucharist," as it is today in the Catholic Church, the Greek Orthodox Church, even the Anglican Church, the Lutheran Church, and some others. Bread and wine were believed to become actual flesh and blood of Christ (transubstantiation or consubstantiation) and partaking of them became a necessary means for securing forgiveness of sin.

During the Reformation this practice and concept were changed in the direction of the early Christian Church. The Anabaptists belonged to the wing which most radically broke with this tradition and restored the Biblical practice. Luther insisted on a literal interpretation of the words of Christ, "This *is* my body," while Zwingli interpreted it as meaning "This *signifies* my body." The early Anabaptists, who had originally closely associated with Zwingli, largely shared his views along these lines. Zwingli had adopted his interpretation which did away with the sacramental character of the Lord's Supper from the Dutch lawyer C. Hoen (*q.v.*), who had written on this subject in 1521. In the Netherlands those denying the sacramental character of the

Lord's Supper became known as "Sacramentists." It was this movement which influenced the early Dutch Anabaptists including such leaders as Menno Simons. Luther and the Lutherans commonly called the Zwinglians "Sacramentarians."

The first source of information regarding the attitude and beliefs of the early Swiss Anabaptists is a letter which Conrad Grebel and some friends wrote to Thomas Müntzer, dated Sept. 5, 1524: "The Lord's Supper was ordained by the Lord as a means of fellowship. Nothing more nor less should be used than the words found in Matthew 26, Mark 14, Luke 22, and I Corinthians 11. The minister of the congregation should read them from one of the Gospels or from Paul's letter. One should eat and drink in the spirit and in love. Even if it is only bread, if faith and brotherly love precede, it should be partaken of joyfully; and as often as it is practiced within the congregation it is to signify that we are truly one body and bread and are and wish to remain true brethren together" (Geiser, *Die Taufgesinnten-Gemeinden*, 330).

The *Schleitheim Articles* speak of the Lord's Supper as the breaking of "one bread in the remembrance of the broken body of Christ" and the drinking of the cup "as a remembrance of the shed blood of Christ" (*MQR* XIX, 1945, 248). Hans Denk, Balthasar Hubmaier, Pilgram Marpeck, and the other early leaders emphasized the fact that the Lord's Supper was ordained by Christ so that His disciples would commemorate His atoning death and have true fellowship in Him. The basic idea of the Catholic Church, the transubstantiation and the sacramental character, disappeared and the Biblical meaning of the Lord's Supper was restored.

It was during the celebration of the Mass that the priest Menno Simons began to doubt the Catholic teaching regarding the Mass. These "whisperings of the devil" must have come to Menno via the Sacramentist movement. After a long struggle he realized that the spirit of God was leading him to the Bible as a source of information. He now believed that the "outward man" receives in the Lord's Supper bread and wine, but that the "spiritual man receives through the promises of Christ the invisible bread and drink" (*Fundament*, 1539 H.i.i.j.2). Menno accused the Catholic Church of having made an idol of the Lord's Supper, which made Christ Himself superfluous. He emphasized strongly the symbolic character of the Lord's Supper which points to the one in whom all salvation is found—Christ. The Lord's Supper was a memorial of the death of Christ for men and a special occasion for self-examination (C. Krahn, *Menno Simons*, 18-21, 139-42).

Already in 1533 a booklet *Bekentenisse . . . ,* coming from the circle of Anabaptists in Holland, stated: "Two things are continually held before us in Christ, namely, that He is our Savior and example. We should remind ourselves in the Lord's Supper of what He has done for us and what we should do for Him. Thus we should contemplate these two things when we partake of the Lord's Supper, but not only reflect about them, but realize them with the highest expression of gratitude in our life" (v. d. Zijpp, *Geschiedenis . . .* , 1952, 117). Similar concerns and beliefs were expressed by other writers of the Netherlands during the 16th century (see D. Philips in *BRN* X, 111-34). During the 17th century the beliefs of the Mennonites of the Netherlands were formulated in confessions of faith including the teaching about the Lord's Supper. Basically they have remained the same throughout the centuries. The changes which took place pertain to the form and circumstances of observing the Lord's Supper.

During the early days of persecution, little attention could be paid to the outward form of the Lord's Supper. There was a very definite feeling and conviction that as much as possible of the outward form of the Catholic tradition should be done away with because of the idolatrous implications. Little attention was paid to uniformity of practice in the various parts of Europe where Anabaptists were located.

Rembert (*Wiedertäufer*, 510) reports regarding the communion services among the Anabaptists of the Lower Rhine in the late 16th century: "When the Lord's Supper was distributed the minister took the bread and broke a piece of it for each, and as soon as it was given out and each had a piece in his hand, the minister also took a piece for himself, put it into his mouth and ate it; and immediately, seeing this, the congregation did the same. The minister, however, used no words, no ceremonies, and no blessing. As soon as the bread was eaten, the minister took a bottle of wine or a cup, drank, and gave each of the members of it. On this wise they observe the breaking of bread."

In the 16th century severe persecution made development along uniform lines difficult. One of the differences seems to have been whether the bread and wine were to be distributed by the officiating elder or minister while the members kept their seats, or whether the members were to come to the front of the meeting place to receive the bread and wine, seated around a table. Vos, Kühler, van der Zijpp, *et al.*, are of the opinion that in the Netherlands it was the original practice to distribute the bread and wine to the participants in their seats, and that Hans de Ries, an elder of the Waterlanders, introduced the practice of handing the bread and wine to the participants seated at a table in groups around 1580. Thus it became the practice of the Waterlanders to observe the Lord's Supper seated around a table, while the Flemish received it from the elder in their seats. Later, when Flemish and Waterlander congregations united, a compromise was usually made. At one time of the year the Lord's Supper would be served around the table and at another time in the seats. This is the practice of the Amsterdam Mennonite Church to this day.

The widespread practice in certain groups of Mennonites in South and North Germany to have the members of the congregation come to the table in the front of the room to receive the bread has very likely no connection with this practice of the Waterlanders, but is due to Lutheran influences.

The practice of putting the bread into a cloth or handkerchief until it is eaten, in unison must be old, going back to the Catholic days when the actual presence of Christ in the bread and wine was a basic belief. According to Vos (*De avondmaalsbediening . . .*) this practice was observed among the early Dutch Mennonites but has disappeared completely. Among some of the Mennonites of Prussian, Polish, and Russian background in America, it is still practiced to this day (Beatrice, Gnadenberg, Rosenort, and other congregations). When the cup is passed from member to member the one receiving it turns to his neighbor who has not yet been served, asking with a silent nod for permission to help himself, to which the neighbor responds with a nod. The origin and full meaning of this practice is not known to the writer. It may have been the intention by this practice to indicate brotherly love and recognition. The practice is still in use in Berlin as well as in Göttingen, probably coming from West Prussia.

The vessels—cup, pitcher, and plates or baskets in which wine and bread were served—were originally very plain. They became more ornamental during the "Golden Age" (17th century) in the Netherlands. The cup and pitcher were originally earthenware or pewter and later sometimes silver, the first silver cups having been used at Zwolle in 1661. Etchings were common. This was also the case among the Mennonites in Prussia and Russia. Some of the vessels for communion services in Prussia and Russia (including cups from Chortitza dated 1842) have been brought to this country.

Originally not only elders (bishops) performed the function of administering the Lord's Supper but also ministers, deacons, and possibly lay members. Gradually the practice developed that elders (bishops) only could be in charge of this function. In later centuries when in some countries and conferences the traditional function of an elder (bishop) was restricted to one congregation and his authority and function were reduced to that of a minister of one congregation, each local minister administered the Lord's Supper. This has been the case among the Mennonites of Holland for many generations and is the practice among most of the Mennonite Brethren and General Conference congregations as well as other groups that have come from Europe to America during the past century. Among the groups of Swiss background such as the Mennonites (MC) and the Amish, or the Old Colony Mennonites, where the bishop system is still the prevailing practice, only the bishop can be in charge of a communion service. The preachers and deacons assist in the act. In Germany it is still the rule that only elders are in charge of the communion service.

Moral integrity, and unity and peace among the members were prerequisites for the observance of the Lord's Supper. For this reason it was always strongly emphasized that all differences and offenses should be removed between members before the Lord's Supper. This resulted in the practice among the Mennonites of Switzerland, South Germany, and Holland, of setting aside the Sunday before the observance of the Lord's Supper to cleanse the congregation as far as necessary and possible from all misunderstandings, and to clear all cases of necessary church discipline of individual members. If this was impossible some congregations would not observe the Lord's Supper, or individuals not "at peace" with fellow men and God would stay away. In Holland this meeting was called *enigheid houden*. Mannhardt reports that the Danzig Mennonites up to the 19th century were invited by the *Ansager* or *Umbitter* (a sort of deacon) to come to the Lord's Supper and that the ministers inquired whether there was anything among the members of the congregation that needed to be cleared to have peace. In an Old Flemish congregation of the Netherlands in 1753 two brethren were asked to take off their wigs for the communion service.

The emphasis on self-examination has remained in all Mennonite congregations, and the traditional Sunday or other day set aside for this purpose is still observed in many European congregations. In America it is observed among the Amish, the Mennonites (MC) and others, where this day before the communion service is known as the "Counsel Meeting." According to J. C. Wenger (*Glimpses*, 112) such meetings can take place a few days or weeks before the communion service. This practice existed also in the Netherlands and was in some congregations maintained until the end of the 19th century. (See further **Counsel Meeting**.) On this occasion church discipline is discussed and members are given opportunity to straighten things out if they are not in harmony with the standards of the church. Members who are "out of order" or not at peace with God and man, are "set back" from the communion and not allowed to participate until all matters have been made right. It is still the custom in these groups to have the congregation vote at the close of the preparatory service whether it is ready to proceed with the communion service as planned. Any considerable negative vote or even abstention results in a delay of the communion service until matters are cleared. The *Schleitheim* article on the "ban" states this principle clearly in referring to the disciplining of erring members, saying "this shall be done according to the regulation of the Spirit before the breaking of bread, so that we may break and eat one bread, with one mind and in one love, and may drink one cup" (*MQR* XIX, 248).

The early Anabaptists must have used ordinary bread for the communion. In the 17th century in the Flemish congregation of Rotterdam, Holland, a kind of crackers in the form of a figure "8," called *krakelingen,* were used instead of white bread. (Vos, 15.) In 1716 Jehring found the Mennonites of Norden using white bread which the elder broke, giving each member a piece. After that he filled eight pewter cups from a bottle of wine. The elder drank first and then the cups were passed from person to person. Several times the congregation knelt in silent prayer (Vos, 10). When Rues visited the Old Flemish of Holland a little later he found them using small pieces of white bread, which the minister broke and distributed, followed by the deacon with the basket of bread. The bread was eaten in unison. In front on the table were the cups and the bottles of wine covered with white linen. The elder filled the cups, drank first, and passed them from person to person. When one person passed the cup to the other he nodded without saying anything (Vos, 10).

The bread used for the communion must have been mostly unleavened, which was broken or cut. In Russia a conservative group insisted on breaking the bread (not cutting) because the Lord "took the bread and broke it" (*Apostolische Brüdergemeinde, q.v.*). The present usage among the Mennonite groups of America seems to be that unleavened bread has given way to leavened bread, which is cut in slices and then broken as it is distributed. In some congregations the bread is still homemade (sometimes baked in small pieces) but the majority buy the bread. In some congregations the members walk to the Lord's Table and receive the bread from the ministers, eating it after returning to their seats. But in the majority of congregations the bread is distributed by ministers and/or deacons, and the members then partake of it in unison. In those congregations which have bishops or elders, these do the distributing, and each recipient partakes at once upon being served.

Throughout the centuries members drank from a common cup; i.e., the congregation had up to a half-dozen chalices, which were filled and passed from member to member. The use of individual cups was started in Holland in 1896 (Vos, 13). By 1917 over half of the Dutch Mennonite congregations were using individual cups. In America the change from the common cup to the individual cup came after World War I. Most of the General Conference Mennonite churches have made this change, but most of the other groups still use the common cup. The usual reason offered for the change is the sanitary one.

For centuries the Mennonites used regular fermented wine; this is still the case among the European Mennonites. In America the change from wine to unfermented grape juice came with the turn of the last century. Most of the Mennonite congregations of the United States, and the Mennonites (MC) in Canada, have made this change. Among the Mennonites of Russian background in Canada, Mexico, and South America, the common cup and fermented wine are still in use. The change in the United States has been due to the influence of the total abstinence movements, which have had a great influence on the Mennonites.

The singing and praying during the Lord's Supper differ. Originally there was much silent kneeling prayer. Rues (*Aufrichtige Nachrichten . . . ,* 56) reports that during the 18th century the Dutch Mennonite elder preached and admonished his congregation while he was distributing the bread among the members. The Amish still use special prayers from the *Ernsthafte Christenpflicht.* The South German Mennonites have used for over one hundred years the *Formularbuch* which includes special prayers for this occasion. The Prussian Men-

nonites published *Abendmahlsandachten* as early as 1823 for use on such occasions. These are practices in which adjustments were made to the usage of the country. The Dutch Mennonites have resisted the use of the ministers' manuals to this day. Among the American Mennonites some General Conference congregations have been using such aids since the turn of the century.

The Lord's Supper was accompanied by footwashing in most of the Mennonite churches in the early centuries. Although this was not a fixed practice of the early Anabaptists it was gradually adopted by the Dutch-North German groups. Footwashing (*q.v.*) was practiced during the meeting at which the congregations were preparing for the Lord's Supper, or just preceding the Lord's Supper or immediately thereafter. The conservative groups in Holland, Prussia, and Russia had this practice. About one hundred years ago it had completely disappeared in Holland. In Russia only the Gnadenfeld and Alexanderwohl congregations, the Kleine Gemeinde and the Mennonite Brethren practiced it. The Alexanderwohl congregation discontinued the practice in America. The South German and Swiss Mennonites (who were not Amish) never adhered to it, but the Amish groups in South Germany, France (where all were Amish), and Switzerland did. The Amish and all who descend from the Amish, the Mennonites (MC) and related groups, and Hutterian Brethren practice it to this day. Thus the practice of footwashing, which originated among the Mennonites of Holland, was taken over by the Amish going to America (via the *Dordrecht Confession of Faith*), while in the country of its origin it long has been discontinued.

Since the Mass was celebrated every Sunday it can be assumed and is easily understandable that the early Anabaptists observed the Lord's Supper quite frequently, possibly at every meeting. Gradually the frequency must have decreased to twice a year. At times in the past the Lord's Supper could not be observed because of lack of unity and peace. During the time of extreme liberalism in Holland some congregations temporarily discontinued this practice altogether. In the Netherlands most congregations observe it only once a year. In most of the congregations in other countries it is observed at least twice a year, in a few four times, and occasionally even ten times a year, rarely only once.

As stated earlier, throughout the 16th century and in most places down to the 19th century only members in good standing could participate in the Lord's Supper. This practice, called close communion, was also followed by other evangelical denominations and is today still practiced by some large and small groups in America, e.g., the large Southern Baptist group. During the 17th and 18th centuries the Mennonites of Holland were divided on this question as to who should be admitted. The Zonists and other conservatives favored the retention of close communion, while the Lamists and others wanted to have not only all Mennonites of various groups admitted but also other professing Christians (v. d. Ziipp, 119, 244). Most of the European Mennonites today practice open communion, stating in their invitation something to the effect that all Christians are welcome to participate. In America this practice is followed by the General Conference Mennonite Church and some others, while the Mennonites (MC), the Mennonite Brethren, Krimmer Mennonite Brethren, the Amish, and the Hutterites generally observe close communion, i.e., only members of their own group in good standing are admitted.   C.K.

Van der Zijpp, *Geschiedenis der Doopsgezinden in Nederland* (Arnhem, 1952); S. F. Rues, *Aufrichtige Nachrichten . . .* (Jena, 1743); K. Vos, *De Avondmaals-bediening* (The Hague, 1915); E. Crous, "Vom Abendmahl," *Zionspilger* (Langnau) 1954, Nos. 3 and 4; K. Vos, *Geschiedenis der Doopsgez. Gemeente te Rotterdam* (Rotterdam, 1907); *ML* I, 6-10.

Communion Call (*Benodiging tot het Avondmaal des Heeren,* Invitation to the Lord's Supper). In the Dutch congregations much stress was laid on this *benodiging,* for the formula of the *benodiging* stated who was to partake. Originally only close communion was known. Safety required it. In the early 17th century it was customary to invite members of other congregations or other Mennonite groups to take part in the communion. The conservative groups opposed this practice. In several Flemish congregations strife was engendered by this question. In 1678, for instance, at Alkmaar all those were invited "who were baptized upon confession"; in Leiden the formula invited "all those who were baptized in their maturity and are at peace with their congregation." This *benodiging* was customary with the Zonists (*q.v.*). The Lamists used to have open communion. When the Flemish and Waterlander congregations in Leiden merged in 1701 they agreed on this *benodiging:* This table is the Lord's table . . . for those who confess the Lord Jesus in the knowledge of the truth, which is according to godliness. . . . Therefore we judge (*ordeelen*) as belonging to this table all nonresistant Christians, who have been baptized upon their faith, are free of the works of the flesh and offensive living and who entreat God daily for forgiveness for their weaknesses. But whereas there are Christians who differ from us on some points, if these are of an edifying life and a holy walk, and are not excluded by Christ the Lord in His Holy Word, and may be inclined to share with us this holy ceremony: with such we testify that we wish to observe the Holy Communion of the Lord, . . . (L. G. le Poole, *Bijdr. tot Kennis v.h. Kerk.-Leven onder de Doopsgezinden . . . te Leiden,* 1905, 94 f.).

Still broader was the *benodiging* adopted by the congregation at Rotterdam at its unification in 1700. There "all Christians who wish to take Holy Communion with us are heartily invited," so that Remonstrants and even unbaptized Collegiants could participate in the communion. Gradually this became the current formula. In most congregations, however, it was customary that only the members of the congregation take part. In Friesland this was the case until very recently. Members who moved out of the region kept their membership with the congregation in which they had been baptized and came from far and near to take part in the communion service.   vDZ.

Communism and the Mennonites. Some modern writers have considered the early Anabaptists to be forerunners of Marxian Communism (K. Kautzky, *Die Vorläufer des neueren Sozialismus . . .* ; Erich Kuttner, *Het Hongerjaar 1563*). Even the Mennonite historian K. Vos was somewhat inclined toward this interpretation, while his Dutch colleague W. Kühler claimed to have evidence that a great number of the early Anabaptists belonged to the middle and upper classes. B. H. Unruh dealt with this problem in "Die Revolution und das Täufertum" (*Gedenkschrift . . . ,* 1925, 19-47), and Robert Kreider recently investigated the "Vocations of Swiss and South German Anabaptists" (*Mennonite Life,* Jan. 1953), coming to the conclusion that "landowner and peasant, patrician and servant, master and apprentice were baptized together."

Many writers did not distinguish between the peaceful Anabaptists who later became known as Mennonites and the radical wing which ended with the catastrophe of Münster and the Batenburgers. To what extent even the two latter could be considered forerunners of modern Communism is a matter of opinion. Nevertheless the theme of the Münsterites and other radicals of the Reformation has not only been a matter of investigation of scholars and a welcome label for contemporaries to be used for all who deviated from the Catholic and Protestant established religious systems, but it has also been a favorite subject for novelists and dramatists to the present day (*Menn. Life,* April 1952, 86-87).

One of the common charges leveled at the early Anabaptists in the contemporary polemical literature, which appears repeatedly from the very beginning in Zürich in 1525, both in the court trials and disputations, and in attacks in pamphlets and books (Zwingli, Bullinger, Melanchthon, *et al.*), is that they taught and practiced communism, i.e., community of goods. Grebel and Manz had to defend themselves against this charge in their first trial in 1525, and Melanchthon makes it a major point in his *Underricht wider die Lere der widertauffer* of 1528, before either the Hutterite or the Münsterite practices could have been the ground for the accusation. Actually the early Swiss and German Anabaptists taught and practiced the sharing of their goods to support the needy brethren, but they never taught nor practiced community of goods as an ethical principle or as a socio-economic order. Their principle of Christian mutual aid, misunderstood or misrepresented by their enemies, was probably the cause for the charge of communism.

Among the peaceful Anabaptists who have survived persecution, the Hutterites (*q.v.*) deserve mention. They are Christian "communists," practicing a community of goods (*q.v.*) which they base on strictly Biblical principles, having nothing in common with Marxian materialistic philosophy. They practice a voluntary group communism, in contrast to a state communism established and maintained by force as the only permissible way of life.

A large percentage of the Mennonites in Europe

have been forced to confront Communism in our day. The Mennonites of Russia have been under Communism for the longest period of time and have suffered most. After the NEP period, when Stalin introduced the present rigid totalitarian Marxist line, liquidating private ownership, forcing all farmers into collectives and the kulaks into slave-labor camps, and breaking up the social and religious life and educational system of the Mennonites, it became apparent to most of the Mennonites in Russia that there was no room for a Christian democratic form of life in a Stalinist-Marxian society. Their petition to the government of Moscow in 1924 to grant them certain basic freedoms which they considered a minimum for the maintenance of their way of life was ignored (Smith, *Story,* 505). Some were so fortunate as to escape Russia at this time, while those that remained lost not only all the rights once given to the Mennonites of Russia but also all basic freedoms of any modern society.

At a Russian Mennonite congress in 1917 the relationship between Socialism and Christianity was discussed. One speaker stated that Christianity was not tied directly to any economic system whether socialistic or capitalistic, while another maintained that socialism was more closely related to Christianity than capitalism, although Christianity and socialism were not identical. Whatever the attitude of the Mennonites was toward socialism, they soon found out that there was no bridge between Christianity and Russian Marxian Communism. After World War I some 35,000 Mennonites of Russia, one third of the total number, escaped and found new homes in the Americas, mostly in Canada. During World War II about 25,000 Mennonites were evacuated from Russia to the West, of whom nearly two thirds were forcibly repatriated by the Russians and sent to Siberia and one third ultimately found their way to Canada or South America, a few remaining in Germany.

As an outcome of World War II and the extension of the Iron Curtain westward, all Mennonites of Danzig (*q.v.*), Prussia (*q.v.*), Poland (*q.v.*), and Galicia (*q.v.*) were evacuated from their homes and countries. Some were taken to Russian slave-labor camps, some perished, and most of the others are still living in western Germany. Nearly 2,000 have found their way to North and South America, particularly Uruguay (*q.v.*).

About 120,000 Mennonites have been affected directly by Communism, most of whom have lost their homes and other property. This number constitutes about one third of the Mennonites of the world. The number that was affected indirectly was much greater. All Mennonites originally coming from countries now behind the Iron Curtain have lost relatives. Those who left Russia since World War I have lost all their property and many family members.

In the Far East it is China where Mennonite missions have been affected by Communism. All missionaries have left China and it is impossible at this time to determine how much of their work

has been destroyed. (See **Russia, Ukraine, Concentration Camps, Siberia, Asia.**)
C.K.

C. Henry Smith, *The Story of the Mennonites* (Newton, 1950; K. Stumpp, *Bericht über das Gebiet Chortitza* (Berlin, 1943).

Community. The term "community" is used with a variety of meanings. Commonly it is used to refer to a group of people settled in a particular small geographic area and having a relatively large number of interests, activities, attitudes, traditions, and cultural aspects in common. It may be a village, town, township, or even city or county. In a certain sense a state or even a nation is sometimes called a community, though in a strict sense this is not possible. When applied to Mennonites, the term "community" has all of these meanings plus the connotation of a homogeneous religious group with clearly marked beliefs, principles, and characteristic social practices. In common usage the terms "Mennonite community" and "Mennonite church" (congregation) are used interchangeably almost to the point of being synonymous. There is, however, a sense in which the term "community" has a wider application than the term "church" since it includes persons who are not actually church members. Originally, church and community were one because the church was composed of adult believers only, but this is no longer the case. There are today adult nonchurch members whose family and cultural backgrounds are Mennonite but who never joined the Mennonite Church. These individuals consider themselves Mennonites of a sort and are generally so considered by others. This was particularly true in Russia where the Mennonite settlements were German Protestant cultural islands in the Slavic Greek Orthodox cultural body, and where in the latest period up to one third of the adult population were not baptized members. In the new settlements in South America, the percentage of unbaptized members has been still higher. The problem of racial or cultural (unbaptized) Mennonite community members existed in Russia and in other places also, such as the Danzig area earlier, and western Canada since 1922. In other words, membership in a Mennonite community has a cultural inference which is not confined to those who subscribe to the doctrines of the church nor those who adhere to the religious discipline required of members in an organized religious body.

When applied to Mennonites, then, the term "community " is basically a religious concept with certain sociological implications. The economic, the social, and the political aspects of the Mennonite community are all subordinate to the religious. The religious aspects are primary and all-pervasive. The roots of the Mennonite community are clearly discernible in the 16th-century genesis of the Mennonite Church which emerged in the "left wing" segment of the Reformation. A central reason for establishing a new church in the Reformation era was that the true church was to be composed of adult baptized believers only. Children and religiously indifferent adults were not to be considered members of the church, hence not of the

Christian community. Menno Simons' ideal of the church was described in the words "without spot or wrinkle." The sincere efforts of its members to live scrupulously righteous lives in a sinful world often made Mennonite communities conspicuous. Their constant and conscious effort to live under the guidance of God and after the pattern of Christ won for them the descriptive phrase "communities of the spirit." While not politically conscious, the Mennonite communities were characterized by the concern they expressed for democratic values, such as religious freedom, tolerance, individual rights, and congregational church government.

American Mennonite communities are today still characterized by their ethnically homogeneous character. In all of the older communities, one can still clearly discern the ethnic background of the Mennonites. There are three main Mennonite ethnic groups; namely, the Swiss, the Dutch, and the German, although even the German Mennonites may ultimately be traced back to either Holland or Switzerland, but of these the Dutch never appeared in community form in North America. The distinguishable characteristics are observable not only to the genealogist and the historian, but to anyone who listens to the speech, the dialect, and the accent of American Mennonites. Many Mennonites are bilingual. The Pennsylvania-German dialect is still universal among all Old Order Amish and Conservative Amish and very common in some of the Mennonite (MC) groups and many of those who have descended directly from the Swiss group. The German is also common among most of the Mennonites who have come originally from West Prussia and Russia. The Swiss who came directly from Switzerland to Ohio and Indiana, and those who came to Kansas and South Dakota by way of Polish Russia, still speak the Swiss dialect to some extent.

Mennonite communities, while affected by the culture of the times, are still rather largely characterized by the compact nature of their settlements. This is especially true of agricultural areas where the pull of the church in a community tends to draw its members into the community and by degrees drive out by the processes of competition, invasion, and succession, the non-Mennonite populations. The predominant occupation is still agriculture, although a noticeable shift of Mennonite population from the farms to the towns and cities has everywhere been evident during the first half of the 20th century. Where Mennonites have gone to cities, the solidarity of the communities has been shattered. There are only a few cases of Mennonite communities in urban areas, and most city Mennonite churches have been unable to maintain their traditional characteristics of solidarity. In fact, Mennonites moving to the cities have in large numbers lost their identity as Mennonites. A major exception to this is the large Mennonite population of Winnipeg, chiefly of the 1922 ff. and the 1947 ff. immigrations from Russia, compactly settled in several suburban areas of Winnipeg.

While most American communities still reflect a sense of solidarity, and to the non-Mennonite may appear to be culturally compact and somewhat isolated from the rest of the world, this is at times only a surface appearance. Every Mennonite community, including the Old Order Amish, has felt the impact of the revolutionary changes of the times. No community has escaped the penetrating poisons of modern secularism. The processes of accommodation, adaptation, and assimilation have been subtly going on and gradual changes taking place even though the significance of these changes has often not been recognized until long after the community has taken on the new characteristic.

Among factors accounting for the sociological changes in the structure and the character of the American community are the public school, the radio, the printing press, the automobile, and a host of other technological inventions which have changed the fundamental nature of living and earning a living. The public-school system with its compulsory education, its standardized textbooks, and its inevitable throwing together of children from a variety of religious, ethnic, and cultural backgrounds, plus the conscious effort to teach all people to think alike, has resulted in something of a standardization of behavior and acceptance of cultural values by Mennonites along with their fellow American citizens. Listening to nationally broadcast radio programs, reading highly illustrated magazines and newspapers, and participating in technical American recreational activities, have all tended to water down many of the American Mennonite patterns of behavior to something of a standard American norm. Intermarriage has taken place at a somewhat accelerated rate in recent decades, especially in areas where Mennonite populations are small, and where mating along exogamous lines is therefore the natural and inevitable result. Despite the many changes that have taken place in Mennonite communities, a relatively stable character is still manifested. The best index to this is perhaps the low rate of social disorganization. Cases of serious crime are a rare exception in Mennonite communities. The divorce rate, which is an index to family stability, is low and divorce is still the very rare exception in the Mennonite community. Mennonite communities are still characterized by industry, piety, and respect for law.

The small rural communities generally have been underestimated in their contribution to the stabilizing forces of a society, yet it is in such areas that the basic values of neighborliness, honesty, self-reliance, and reverence for life and property are most persistently developed. It is in this respect that Mennonite communities may have contributed a larger share to the strength of a national society than they have been given credit for. Because of variety in industry, sobriety, and thrift, most Mennonite communities have been economically prosperous, thus building up the economic resources and the property values, which again are considered assets to any existing society.

In recent years the growing awareness of the value of the Mennonite rural community as a source of strength for the brotherhood, as well as an awareness of the danger threatening this community, has led Mennonite scholars and leaders to a careful study of Mennonite community life and the conscious promotion of ways and means of strengthening it. The Mennonite Community Association (*q.v.*), organized in 1946 to serve primarily the Mennonite Church (MC), is an instance of this. Among its chief projects has been the publication of a monthly illustrated journal called *The Mennonite Community* (*q.v.*), founded in 1946, since 1950 published by the Mennonite Publishing House, Scottdale, Pa. The Committee on Industrial and Social Relations of the Mennonite (MC) General Conference is devoting increasing attention to this area of concern and interest, and among other activities holds an annual "Conference on the Mennonite Community" which meets successively in major centers of the church. G. F. Hershberger of Goshen College has been a leader in this movement.

The typical ethnically, culturally, and religiously homogeneous Mennonite community is possible only in rural areas where land availability has made possible fairly compact continuous settlement. This has been the case in the Swiss Jura, at places in Alsace and the Palatinate, and in West Prussia, only in restricted areas in Holland such as Friesland and the Zaanstreek, and not at all in the generally scattered type of rented farm economy and settlement in South Germany. In Russia, however, and in South America and Mexico, where the settlement was practically always on virgin soil and in closed colonies, Mennonite communities par excellence could be and were established. These communities, completely isolated from their environment by language, culture, and religion, with even a measure of political autonomy in Russia and Paraguay, had to assume complete social, cultural, and economic functions. They deserve and call for a more complete and thorough study than has yet been attempted.   J.W.F.

J. W. Fretz, *Mennonite Colonization: Lessons from the Past for the Future* (Akron, 1944); *idem, Mennonite Colonization in Mexico. An Introduction* (Akron, 1945); *idem, Christian Mutual Aid, a Handbook of Brotherhood Economics* (Akron, 1947); *idem, Pilgrims in Paraguay* (Scottdale, 1953); G. F. Hershberger, *Christian Relationships to State and Community* (Akron, 1945); *The Mennonite Community* (Scottdale, 1947-53); *Mennonite Life* (Newton, 1946-); *MQR* (Special Mennonite Community life number, April 1945).

Community of Goods. (A) *General.* The usual sources given for the practice of community of goods (communism) among Christians are the chapters in the *Book of Acts* (second, fourth, and fifth), where the economic practices of the primitive church in Jerusalem are described. The "having all things in common" described here was not based, to be sure, on a special commandment of Christ but represented rather a necessary makeshift according to the needs of the actual situation which arose from the presence of thousands of newly baptized Christians far away from their homes in the Jewish diaspora. Private property was not condemned in the teachings of Jesus, though also not praised. The concern for the poor was a natural outgrowth of the new law of brotherly love. Sharing of worldly goods has, to a certain extent, always been a practice of the earlier church, to the greatest amazement of the surrounding pagan world. It was what Troeltsch had fittingly called a "communism of love," something distinctly different from the practice of radical "community of goods" (see B).

The history of this idea through the ages cannot be told here. Its practice occurred mainly on the fringe of the general church development. The Gnostics and Donatists may be named here as well as some so-called "old-evangelical brotherhoods" (according to Ludwig Keller) such as Bogomiles, Waldensians, and Beghards (who maintained some common workshops). These groups, so varied in character otherwise, all showed a natural distrust in worldly possessions and an ascetic leaning toward the plain life and sharing as far as necessary with the brethren in need. But actual communistic living was practiced only by the monastic orders whose requirement of apostolic poverty led quite naturally to such practices. Yet for the monks it was less the point of brotherly love for those in need than one of escaping the temptation of "mammon" which produced these monastic forms of living.

Anabaptists who followed the idea of discipleship and of restitution of the primitive church also developed some ideas regarding the economic side of life. Their principle of nonconformity lent itself very naturally to a nonmaterialistic, puritanical concept of life in which man is but a steward of his worldly possessions which he must be ready to share at any time with others. The emphasis upon discipleship likewise brought forth the idea of caring for others and of sharing wherever a brother is in need (*Liebeskommunismus*). Only with the Hutterites did it also lead to a complete and nearly monastic establishment of community of goods, unique indeed within the entire history of the Christian churches on that point (see Section B). The distinctly spiritual background of the entire Anabaptist attitude toward worldly economy excludes completely any characterization of Anabaptism as a "forerunner of modern socialism," as Karl Kautsky has suggested. Anabaptism can in no way be understood as a "social movement" of the poorer classes, though since the unfortunate Peasants' War of 1524-25 it was often looked upon in this way by its opponents in order to disparage the movement as a whole.

Reports of Anabaptist leaders concerning worldly goods and their use abound. In these references the emphasis will be found always to be laid upon stewardship and brotherly sharing, not upon community of goods proper. Conrad Grebel, the very beginner of the movement in Switzerland, protests distinctly against the charge that he taught "that no one should be interested in his possession" (H. S. Bender, *Conrad Grebel,* 159 and 205, also the extensive footnotes 254, No. 29 and p. 276, No. 70). Felix Manz declares that he understands community of goods to be merely a willingness to aid the needy. George Blaurock, to be sure, made a written petition to the council of Zürich in which he also demonstrated "community of all things" by the example of the apostles, yet in a cross-examination he declared expressly that he did not favor community of possession. "He who is a good Christian should share what he has, else he is none." This was the traditional attitude of Anabaptists everywhere toward worldly goods.

As for Balthasar Hubmaier, he discusses the idea only once in his *Gespräch auf Meister Zwinglis Taufbüchlein* (1526, actually written in 1525) in the following manner: "Concerning community of goods I always taught that a man should have a concern for the other man, that the hungry be fed, the thirsty receive drink, etc. For we are not the masters of our possessions but stewards and distributors only. No one would say, take away what a man has and make it common. Rather he would say, let the coat go together with the mantle. . . .'"

Menno Simons, in his book *A Humble and Christian Justification and Replication* (*Works* II, 309) replies in detail to his opponents who "imagine and say, we have our possessions in common." "This accusation," he says, "is false and without all truth. We do not teach and practice community of goods but we teach and testify the Word of the Lord, that all true believers in Christ are of one body (I Cor. 12:13), partakers of one bread (I Cor. 10:17), have one God and one Lord (Eph. 4). Seeing then that they are one, as said, it is Christian and reasonable that they also have divine love among them and that one member cares for another, for both the Scriptures and nature teach this. . . . They show mercy and love, as much as is in them. They do not suffer a beggar among them. They have pity on the wants of the saints. They receive the wretched. They take strangers into their houses. They comfort the sad. They lend to the needy. They clothe the naked. They share their bread with the hungry. They do not turn their face from the poor nor do they regard their decrepit limbs and flesh (Isa. 58). This is the kind of brotherhood we teach, and not that some should take over and possess the land, soil, and properties of others, as we are falsely maligned, accused, and lied about by many. . . . Furthermore, this love, mercy, and brotherhood they teach and practice, and have taught and practiced for seventeen years in such form and manner in perpetual thanks to the Lord that although we have been robbed of a great part of our possession and are still daily robbed and taken, and many a pious, God-fearing father and mother is killed with fire, water, and sword, and we may have no safe and free place of abode, as can be seen, and the times are hard; nevertheless none of the pious nor the children left behind by the pious, who are willing to adapt themselves among us, have had to beg. . . . See, my dear readers, this accusation is fundamentally false and unjust, as are the others also. For although we know that the apostolic church had this practice in the beginning, as can be seen in the Acts of the Apostles, nevertheless we note from their epistles that it disappeared in their time . . . and was no longer practiced. Since we do not find it a permanent practice with the apostles . . . we

have not taught or practiced community of goods, but we urge earnestly and zealously to practice liberal giving, love, and mercy, as the apostolic writings teach and testify abundantly. . . . And even if we had taught and practiced community of goods, as we are falsely accused of doing, we would still not be doing otherwise than the holy apostles, full of the Holy Ghost, themselves did in the former church at Jerusalem in the beginning of the holy Christian Church, although they stopped the practice as has been said."

This represents certainly the general Anabaptist position everywhere, except for the Hutterites (whose case will be discussed under section B). In the Frankenthal Disputation (*q.v.*) of 1572 the question of community of goods came up as a special point. The Anabaptist leaders declared unanimously that they were opposed to this tenet of ill repute. "A Christian may buy and sell goods whenever it suits him." Strangely enough, Peter Walpot, bishop of the Hutterites, who was also present, did not specifically react to this discussion, apparently in order not to become a party to a dispute in this matter (see Wolkan, *Lieder,* 52).

All these quotations and many more are ample proof that no communism but only brotherly sharing was in the minds of those Brethren who took the evangelical advice seriously and tried to practice discipleship. And yet the Anabaptist repute was badly soiled for centuries by one single event which, strictly speaking, does not belong at all into the story of the evangelical Anabaptism but rather in that of the fanatical fringe of the "Left Wing" of the Reformation (which only too often is erroneously identified with Anabaptism in general). It is the Münsterite experiment of 1534-35, so violently repudiated by all peaceful Anabaptists of North and South alike. Here in Münster, it is true, a sort of wild communism was established and, strangely enough, justified on the basis of the old authorities. No doubt it was a tragic confusion of mind. Bernt Rothmann taught actually a radical communistic sharing of all things. In his *Bekenntnis von beiden Sakramenten* (1533), signed by the six elders, he quotes as his major authority (besides the Book of Acts) the spurious *Fourth Epistle of Clemens* which deals, at least partly, with the community of goods among the first Christians. Rothmann learned of this source from the *Chronica* (*q.v.*) of Sebastian Franck, 1531. Franck on his part had taken this quotation from a 1526 Latin edition of the Clementine Epistles. H. von Schubert followed up the story of this strange crowning witness to primitive Christian communism (which was actually a forgery of the 8th century A.D.), and found its origin in Plato and the Stoics. Franck, however, who was deeply impressed by this document (which he took for genuine), claimed that community of goods is a prime divine law and for that reason also a Christian law (Schubert, 15). *Das Gemein is rein, das Dein und Mein is unrein,* Franck says again in his *Paradoxa* of 1534. (See **Clemens, Epistle IV.**)

Rothmann, whose motives were certainly religious and not economic, became step by step more radical as is evident from his later book *Restitution* of 1534. His teachings led eventually to a compulsory community of goods (later even of wives), thus making a caricature of Christian living and discipleship. (Of course this had nothing to do any more with Franck's idealistic statements.) How the ideas of Rothmann and his collaborators were carried out and practiced and how this tragic experiment ended is told in the article on Münster. The event brought much harm to later Anabaptism and gave an excuse to increased persecutions. It had no relationship with genuine discipleship and its corollary, sharing of worldly goods with the brother and concern for the needy ones, principles which remained leading in all evangelical Anabaptism.

It is important to clarify a popular error which is also mentioned in the corresponding article **Gütergemeinschaft** (*ML* II, 201), namely, that the so-called Nikolsburg Articles (*q.v.*) expressly declare that whosoever possesses private property cannot be admitted at the Lord's Table. Today it is well known that this document was a forgery and had nothing to do with Anabaptist teaching, as has been proved by Wiswedel.   NEFF, R.F.

H. v. Schubert, "Der Kommunismus der Wiedertäufer in Münster und seine Quellen," in *Sitzungsberichte der Heidelberger Akademie,* 1919; Ernst Troeltsch, *The Social Teachings of the Christian Churches* (German edition, 1912, English translation, N.Y., 1930); K. Kautsky, *Vorläufer des neueren Sozialismus* (1913, also English translation). Among Mennonites, no special study has ever been undertaken in this field. See H. S. Bender, *Conrad Grebel* (Goshen, 1950) index under "Community of Goods."

(B) *Hutterite.* Very different from the interpretation of Christian community of things temporal as expressed in the first section (A) of this article is the position of the Hutterite brotherhoods who have been practicing full community of goods most successfully for more than 400 years (established in 1528), with some decades of interruption in Russia in the mid-19th century. Except for the monastic way of community living with its totally different spirit this is the only example in church history (and secular history as well) where a group (once about 50,000, today 10,000) has successfully carried out such an organization of complete community of goods for so long a time. Whenever the Brethren gave up this form of living due to tremendous pressure from the outside they declined, whenever they organized again they thrived. Still today their Bruderhofs (*q.v.*) are shining examples proving that, on a right foundation, such a life is not only possible but very satisfying to its participants.

In the first section (A) it was said that the true Christian idea of fellowship works toward sharing and caring (*Liebeskommunismus*) but not necessarily for full community of goods. In fact the Swiss Brethren and the Dutch Mennonites expressly declined such a radical interpretation of the Christian message and did so on good ground. In contradistinction, the Hutterites are emphatic that their point of view is the only true Christian one, that community of goods is the direct outgrowth of Christian love and that all other forms lack the

character of true discipleship. "If Christian love to the neighbor cannot achieve as much as community in things temporal, in assistance and counsel, then the blood of Christ does not cleanse a man from his sins" (Ehrenpreis, *Sendbrief* of 1652, 49). And again "to give up the true Christian community means to give up God" (Riedemann, 1545). Or also, "private property is the greatest enemy of love."

It would be misleading to assume that the Hutterite way of community living started as a measure only of mere emergency and situational need, comparable to that of the first Christian Church in Jerusalem (Acts 2 and 4). Perhaps this was true in the earliest years (1528 ff.) prior to the coming of Jakob Hutter (1533), but when this truly charismatic leader took up the reins and established a *Gemeinschaft* on strictly Christian spiritual foundations it became much more than an emergency experiment. It was a holy beginning, a radical actualization of the Christian commandment of love as Hutter and his fellow workers understood it. Here was *Nachfolge,* the practice of brotherly love by overcoming selfishness (*Eigennutz*) and the entering into complete brotherhood and unity of the spirit. Without giving up private and personal possessions, the leaders claimed, such a unity could never be achieved. To the Hutterite this way of life was his religion proper and within the community there could be no distinction between sacred and secular. God has commanded this way of life in which the total of man's sanctioned activities are sacred rather than secular. For this way they were ready to suffer martyrdom. "God helping we are ready rather to die than to give up the community," says a brother in 1540. It is important to point out that the German term *Gemeinschaft* as used by the Hutterite has a double connotation: brotherhood or fellowship, and community of goods.

From all this it becomes clear that the Hutterite Bruderhofs cannot be compared with Catholic monasteries. Not retreat from secular temptation brought the Brethren together but the conviction that only thus does Christian love become a reality. It is true that today one may hear a Hutterite brother justifying this life by reference to the story in the Book of Acts (4:32-37; 5:1-11) and that obedience to the Scriptures cannot mean anything else but community. But that is a rather external interpretation. In the 16th century such Scriptural "literalism" was certainly not the chief motive and could have easily been defeated. There is very little if anything legalistic among the Hutterites (at least in the first 150 years) and the reference to Acts 4 is more a Scriptural corroboration than the true ground for the practice of community of goods.

Community of goods, as Hutter and all the other leaders understood it (and defended it against all odds), is the direct outcome of a deeper interpretation of Christ's teaching of brotherly love. Love is no sentimental affair but a total giving of oneself to the fellowship. A true disciple cannot do otherwise. In 1652, Andreas Ehrenpreis (*q.v.*) published a booklet (reprinted 1920) entitled *Ein Sendbrief,*

Gemeinschaft, das höchste Gebot der Liebe betreffend (An Epistle Concerning Community of Goods, the Highest Commandment of Love).

There is yet another point suggested by the brethren, that of true *Gelassenheit.* (The word is hard to translate, perhaps best by "surrender" or "yieldedness" or even by "conquest of self.") Human nature in general is imperfect and a far cry from anything Christian. Natural man is selfish, self-centered, self-willed, which explains our basic estrangement from the Divine above us and from our fellow men next to us. In the great *Article Book* of 1547 stands the following statement: *Gottes Wort wär nicht so schwer, Wenn nur der Eigennutz nicht wär.* (God's word would not be so difficult [to carry out] if there were no human selfishness.) In order to become a true disciple of Christ (after an inner rebirth) man needs most of all a way that will assist him in his "conquest of selfishness." This they call *Gelassenheit,* yieldedness, giving up self-will, and committing oneself to God's will, i.e., brotherly love and community. One must not hang one's heart upon earthly goods but rather become free from that propensity. This can be achieved best by the voluntary practice of community of goods where nothing is one's own private property any more, not even one's own garment or walking stick. Thus the way of discipleship begins.

Living co-operatively—that is the Hutterite alternative to the "holy poverty" of the Franciscan movement, which latter, to be sure, is foreign to Anabaptism although both principles derive from the same spirit of search for a practical and concrete expression of love and discipleship.

It is not the purpose of this article to tell the story of the Hutterite experiment in detail. This will be done in the article **Hutterites.** That Hutter's motives were exclusively spiritual has already been emphasized; that they were sound is proved by 400 years of experience. Many collaborators and followers shared his views. Apologies for the Hutterite way abound; all authors on this subject quote from the rich and high-level Hutterite literature ample arguments for such a form of living, beginning with Hutter's epistles (1533-36) and ending with Ehrenpreis' *Sendbrief* of 1652. In general these arguments are much the same as those presented above. The Hutterites have two great doctrinal books which serve them as a foundation and justification for this life: Riedemann's *Rechenschaft* (1545) (*q.v.*) and the great *Article Book* (*q.v.*) of about 1547, written most likely by Peter Walpot (*q.v.*). While Riedemann devotes but four pages to the exposition of his arguments, Walpot devotes one whole article (of five) to this subject in his great doctrinal work. In abbreviated form it appears also in the *Great Chronicle.* Here the third article concerning "community of goods" covers pp. 285-96 in the Zieglschmid edition. "Love is a tie of perfection. Where she dwelleth she does not work partial but complete and entire community. To such a *Gelassenheit* (yieldedness, resignation) you have to adapt yourself; you must give up your own and become free from it if you want to be-

come a disciple. Love does not seek her own profit, hence she seeks certainly communion (*Gemeinschaft*). Communion is nothing else but having everything in common out of sheer love to the neighbor."

It is interesting to note that among the church historical arguments which Walpot adds to prove his points we meet again the *Fourth Epistle of Clemens* (discussed in Section A). It is found in the great *Article Book,* Art. III, item 148 (quoted in full in *Arch. f. Ref.-Gesch.,* 1931, 235). Beyond doubt it was borrowed from S. Franck's *Chronica* (*q.v.*) (Ed. 1531, fol. CCCCXCV; ed. 1536, fol. CCXLIIII). Certainly this (forged) epistle did not prove anything but could to some extent at least undergird the Hutterite position.

Perhaps the strongest argument for full communion of goods was found in the early Christian document, *The Teaching of the Twelve Apostles,* or *Didache* (about A.D. 120), where a novel interpretation of the Lord's Supper is presented. Since this argument is used time and again by the Brethren, also by Ehrenpreis in his *Sendbrief* (ed. 1920, p. 42 f.) and is even today quoted in Amish sermons (though without drawing the consequences), it is presented here in full. "As the grain-kernels are altogether merged, and each must give its contents or strength into the one flour and bread, likewise also the wine, where the grapes are crushed under the press and each grape gives away all its juice and all its strength into one wine. Whichever kernel and whichever grape, however, is not crushed and retains its strength for itself alone, such an one is unworthy and is cast out. This is what Christ wanted to bring home to his companions and guests at the Last Supper as an example of how they should be together in such a fellowship."

The most interesting fact of the Hutterite way is the unique compromise between community and family living, thus overcoming the pitfalls of monastic asceticism. To be sure, such family life has little room for romanticism, but it is nevertheless solid and healthy. Outstanding were the schools in these colonies, also the hygienic and medical achievements. Their crafts stood in high repute during the 16th and 17th century (cutlery, ceramics, etc.). Trading was completely excluded as a sinful business, "As the wise man saith: it is almost impossible for a merchant and trader to keep himself from sin. As a nail sticketh fast between door and hinge so doth sin stick close between buying and selling" (Riedemann, 126 f., quoting Eccles. 26:29 and 27:1-2).

Of course, the temptation of selfishness is always present and we read many complaints about a decline of the original principles. That was the reason why the leaders enjoined the ideas ever and anon, and why ordinances and regulations were issued by the elders, with the consent of the entire brotherhood, to insure the basic standards. But by and large, after many slumps and deviations the brotherhood returned to its former status, and as far as can be observed today, it is certainly ready to continue its way in the old pattern, even though the spirit of mission (once so strong among them) has died out. The principle that no one should have anything in private, neither clothing nor bedding, neither books nor any niceties, has in recent times been somewhat relaxed though more by indulgence than by approval. In times of crisis the old spirit of perfect brotherhood has always stood the test.

With regard to the actual carrying out of such a principle we can refer here only to the pertinent articles of this Encyclopedia: **Hutterites, Bruderhofs, Education, Discipline,** and to the literature listed below. No visitor at such a Hutterite Bruderhof can help being deeply impressed by this object lesson. This is as true today as it was in the 16th century when the communities flourished in Moravia and Slovakia under the protection of the nobles. The fact that even today but few Hutterites leave this kind of life seems to prove that it has a high appeal to each member. Strict regulation and discipline are practiced but since everything is done voluntarily and after common counseling, it is done cheerfully, and in the right spirit. The fact that in the 1920's a new Bruderhof of this type sprang up in Germany (see **Arnold, Eberhard**) and soon joined the wider Hutterite family, may further illustrate the vitality and appeal of the idea.   R.F.

Loserth, *Communismus;* Lydia Müller, *Der Kommunismus der mährischen Wiedertäufer* (Leipzig, 1927); J. Horsch, *The Hutterian Brethren* (Goshen, 1931); R. Friedmann, "Eine dogmatische Hauptschrift der Hutterischen Täufergemeinschaften," *Archiv f. Ref.-Gesch.,* 1931-32; *Proceedings of the Fifth Annual Conference on Menn. Cultural Problems,* held at Freeman, S.D., 1946 (in particular an article by Marie Waldner); Hans G. Fischer, *Jakob Hutter* (Newton, 1955); P. Rideman, *Account of Our Religion* (1950); *ML* I, 201-10.

Compass Mennonite Brethren Church, formerly known as the Northern Evangelical Church, located northwest of Meadow Lake, Sask., or approximately 250 miles northwest of Saskatoon, is a member of the Canadian Conference of the M.B. Church. The church was organized in 1938 under the leadership of Frank Janzen, with 12 members. Its (1953) minister is David Nickel, and the church has a membership of 28.   J.H.E.

Compromis, an agreement reached in 1566 or 1567 by two Dutch Mennonite groups, viz., the Flemish (*q.v.*) and the Frisians (*q.v.*), among whom there had been some differences since 1565. Jan Willemsz (*q.v.*) and Lubbert Gerritsz (*q.v.*) intermediated, and after much discussion succeeded in reconciling the two groups. The leaders of both sides agreed to submit the question to Jan Willemsz and Lubbert Gerritsz as judges and henceforth to keep peace. But the *Compromis* did not last and soon the two factions separated and remained so for about 75 years. The text of *Compromis* is found in V. P., *Successio Anabaptistica* (*BRN* VII, 62-64) and also in *Protocol, Dat is alle Handelinge des Gesprecks tot Emden* (Emden, 1579, Fol. 371 b.). Concerning the *Compromis,* what preceded and what followed, see the study of J. G. de Hoop Scheffer: *Het verbond der vier steden* in *DB* 1893 1-90 (concerning the name *Compromis* see p. 43 note 2). See also Kühler, *Geschiedenis* I, 406-18.   vDZ.

Compton (Mrs.), **Otelia Augspurger** (1858-1944), was born near Trenton, Butler Co., Ohio. Her parents were Samuel and Elise Holly Augspurger, both of German Mennonite ancestry.

She received her education in the public schools of Butler County and Western College, Oxford, Ohio, from which she graduated in 1886 after an interim of teaching in the public schools near her home. She was perhaps one of the first Mennonite women in America to graduate from college.

Soon after she graduated in 1886 she was married to Elias Compton, also of Butler County. He was professor of philosophy and later also dean of Wooster College, Wooster, Ohio, where they made their home.

Her children are Karl Taylor Compton, who has been president of Massachusetts Institute of Technology, Cambridge, Mass., and a scientist of note: Arthur Holly Compton, chancellor of Washington University, St. Louis, Mo., who was awarded the Nobel Prize in physics in 1927; Wilson Martindale Compton, president of Washington State College, Pullman, Wash., and also one of the U.S. delegates to the United Nations Assembly; and Mary Compton Rice, who has been a missionary in India for many years, and whose husband, C. Herbert Rice, is now president of Forman Christian College at Lahore, Pakistan.

Mrs. Compton was brought up in the Apostolic Mennonite Church of Trenton and was a member of it until her marriage, when she united with the church to which her husband belonged. She, however, kept up her interest in her mother church and attributed much of her strength of character to its influence and teaching.   J.E.A.

Concentration Camps in Soviet Russia have existed as long as the Soviet Union itself. Without them Soviet Communism is unthinkable. They have played and are still playing an extraordinary role in internal politics as well as in the national economy. Concentration camps have been used as a means to secure Communism in power, to silence the entire country, burying all its liberties, and in part to attain to its present economic status.

The removal of opposing political elements from the middle classes and military circles and their concentration in complete isolation in remote regions of the gigantic nation began while the struggle of the Communists against the counterrevolutionaries under Yudenich, Kolchak, Denikin, and Wrangel was still in progress. During those early years (1917-25), opposing elements were often simply shot. But later, when it became apparent to many sympathizers that their aims were being betrayed, they turned hostile to the party; these former comrades could not be simply shot; hence the party in power reverted to the czarist practice of banishing them to remote places.

Solovetsk, an ancient monastery, with an extensive complex of land and buildings on various islands of the White Sea, had already in the 1920's become notorious as a place of exile and a symbol of the system. Though other concentration camps were reopened in Siberia, Solovetsk was the most used and acquired a certain tragic notoriety.

Since the original purpose of these camps was the isolation of dangerous elements, the work done by them was of minor importance. In those early years of political and economic instability the care of the prisoners was very primitive and brutal; there was practically no hope of release. After some years, especially after 1929, when the reign of terror and violence was established throughout the entire country, concentration camps were thoroughly reorganized and turned into slave labor camps. Ordinary criminals were also sent here. Now the work performed by the prisoners became as important to the camps as the concept of exile and punishment; the work is also an important factor in the economy of the nation.

No statistics have ever been assembled, but it is known that large numbers of Mennonites were sent to the concentration camps, particularly from 1928 on, and that thousands of them perished under the terrible conditions in the camps.

The notorious concentration camps of the German National Socialist government 1933-45 (Dachau, Belsen, Oswiezcim, etc.) were not forced labor camps but actual mass prisons for the mass slaughter of Jews and detention of political prisoners and enemies of the regime. So far as is known, no German Mennonites were detained in these camps, except Hermann Epp, a member of the Danzig church board. Two Dutch Mennonite ministers, however, died in German concentration camps; they were A. Keuter of The Hague (1943) and A. du Croix of Winschoten (1943). The prisoner of war camps, and refugee camps operated by all governments during the war and after, are not properly called concentration camps. J.N.

A. A. Töws, *Mennonitische Märtyrer* (Winnipeg, 1949); Hans Harder, *In Wologdas weissen Wäldern* (Altona, 1934); D. Dalin and B. Nicolaevsky, *Forced Labor in Soviet Russia* (New Haven, 1947).

Concept of Cologne (*Concept van Keulen*), an agreement between the High German and Dutch Mennonites, which was signed on May 1, 1591, at Cologne. Various previous attempts had already been made to bring about union, but they were usually geographically limited. Participating in this conference at Cologne were Mennonites of the Rhine region from the North Sea to the borders of Switzerland.

The churches were trying to reach a fraternal agreement to bridge over differences that had formed between them. The Dutch churches realized that they had been too severe in their attitude toward other brethren, as in the use of the ban, and joined with the High Germans in signing a common confession of faith and an agreement on church regulations and conduct which was called a *Concept,* commonly known as the "Concept of Cologne" since it was published under that title in 1665 in *De Algemeene Belijdenissen* (see **Confessions of Faith**). It was never printed separately.

In doctrine, the belief in the Trinity was affirmed. "In Jesus Christ we recognize the only Son of the Father from eternity, born of Mary in the fulness of time through the power of the Most High and through the co-working of the Holy Spirit, who

was made flesh through the eternal Word of the Father. We acknowledge also the Holy Spirit, that He is a power of God and proceeds from the Father through the Son, promised by Christ and sent to comfort the believer. He who believes in this Son of God as the Savior and Redeemer promised and sent from God, he is free from all sins. . . . We also confess the resurrection of the body from the dead, both the righteous and the unrighteous, and believe that at the Last Judgment each will receive according as he has walked."

Concerning baptism and communion the *Concept* says: "The man who acknowledges himself to be sinful and brings forth the fruits of repentance, and proves that he gladly accepts the Word of Christ and requests baptism out of desire, him shall an irreproachable ordained minister baptize with water in the name of the Father, the Son, and the Holy Spirit. He who is thus minded and has been baptized, shall not be baptized again. All those who are thus baptized by the Spirit into one body (I Cor. 12:12) shall observe communion together with ordinary bread and wine, and thereby remember His great love and His bitter death."

The practical church regulations of the *Concept* sought to ease the severity of discipline in the Dutch churches. It was lamented that in many cases it had been misused, especially in the use of the ban applied in marriage (*q.v.,* see also **Avoidance**). Church discipline should serve to keep the church pure, but love should be allowed to reign, and brotherly admonition should not be neglected, as is explained in Matt. 18:15-18.

The preachers are to be chosen from the church, according to the *Concept*. They must be blameless, and may not serve until they have been proved. They are to be ordained by the laying on of the elder's hands. To care for the poor, deacons should be chosen according to the example of the apostolic church; they must distribute the gifts voluntarily given for that purpose, and are to keep silence in accord with Matt. 6:3. Further regulations are as follows.

One should allow footwashing to be performed on oneself if requested by a brother, and also wash his feet in sincere humility.

Marriage shall be concluded only between believers; transgression of this requirement is punished by exclusion from the communion before the congregation. If the transgressor shows a change of mind, "if one feels in him fruits worthy of repentance," then he shall again be admitted to communion. Married persons shall in all cases be admonished to be true to their marriage vows; they shall not leave a spouse or marry another.

A Christianity shown in deeds is required of the members. In accord with the teaching of Jesus and James, the oath is forbidden; "all words and deeds shall be affirmed by a truthful yea or nay, and nothing be added, and this shall be truly kept like a sworn oath." Retaliation is not permitted, "not only with external weapons, but one should not repay abuse with abuse." Merchants shall be content with modest profit. How much they may take cannot be prescribed. No one should be like the discontented and insatiable. Usury is an abomination and is regarded as shameful by all men. Warning is given against elaborate clothing, which "resembles the world more than it shows Christian humility." It is not possible to prescribe to each individual what he shall wear; in simple clothing and in all his deeds he shall be a light to the world.

In conclusion it was agreed "that every watchman of God's house shall in all faithfulness and in the strength of the Holy Spirit warn the people, thereby to keep himself and them pure from the ruin of the disobedient. In this manner one brother shall admonish and warn another with a fatherly heart, that the admonition may be more acceptable."

The agreements were signed by 15 representatives of the churches. Of the Dutch Mennonites, especially the Frisians supported them, but also many Waterlanders as well. Of the High (South) German churches, those of Alsace, the Breisgau, and the Palatinate joined; the names of the signatory congregations are Strasbourg, Wittenberg (probably Wissembourg in Alsace), Landau, Neustadt, Worms, and Kreuznach. Of the Lower Rhine region, representatives of the Mennonite churches at Gladbach, Cologne, Odenkirchen, Rees, and all the churches of the duchy of Berg (Rembert, 618) signed.

In drawing up the agreements, Leenaerdt Clock (*q.v.;* see also **Amsterdam**), a Mennonite of South Germany who later moved to Haarlem, took a leading part, probably writing most of it himself. His relations with the Waterlanders were severed in 1611 when he withdrew from them because of his increasingly severe views on mixed marriages and the ban. But this unfortunate event hardly touched the relations between the Dutch Mennonites and the High Germans. The Alsatian and Palatine churches in 1660 adopted the Dordrecht Confession (*q.v.*) drawn up in 1632, thus following the pattern of the *Concept* of 1591.

This agreement of Cologne served as a basis for future attempts at unification; the conference held under the chairmanship of Tieleman van Braght (*q.v.*) in 1651 (1649) at Haarlem between the Frisians and High Germans with the Flemish, accepted the *Olive Branch Confession* (*Olijftacxken,* 1629), the Confession of Jan Cents (1630), the Dordrecht Confession (1632), and the Concept of Cologne.

The bond which was formed in Cologne between the Dutch and High German Mennonites led beyond these agreements to practical deeds of brotherly love. In the 17th century, when the Swiss Mennonites were hard pressed by their government, the Dutch Mennonites persuaded the States-General to relieve this oppression and helped them settle in lands where they were tolerated. Thus the agreements reached in the Concept of Cologne had their effect on Mennonite history for a long time afterward. HEGE.

Chr. Hege, *Die Täufer in der Kurpfalz* (Frankfurt, 1908) 149-52; Rembert, *Wiedertäufer; Catalogus Amst.,* 168, 169, 353; Wolkan, *Lieder,* 153; Keller, *Reformation,* 478; *De Algemeene Belydenissen* (Haarlem, 1665) 1-7; *ML* II, 545-47.

Concerning a True Soldier of Christ, an Anabaptist tract of about 1533-35. It deserves great attention for its profound thoughts and power and its unusually fine presentation, an outstanding product of early Anabaptism, hitherto completely overlooked. It exists in one copy only in a Hutterite manuscript codex of 1570 (now of unknown location), which explains why it escaped wider attention. It is remarkable also as the only dogmatic contribution (as far as is known) which comes from the Philipite Brethren in Moravia (*q.v.*), a group similar to the Hutterites but without their community life. They did not survive the severe persecutions in Moravia in the 1530's. On their flight from Moravia to South Germany in 1535, many Brethren were captured in Passau and put into a dungeon of the castle. It was there that the oldest part of the *Ausbund* originated (Wolkan, *Lieder,* 27 ff.). Among these men, languishing in prison for many years, was also the author of our tract, Hans Haffner, whose name appears also in stanza 11 of No. 100 in the *Ausbund*. He came from Riblingen (*Württemberg*), and joined the Brethren in 1533, lay in Passau from 1535 to 1540 or 1541, and was finally released upon recantation. The tract *Concerning a True Soldier of Christ* must have been written between 1533 and 1535, while Haffner was active as a Philipite in Moravia. It seems to represent very distinctly the general Christian outlook and mood of the Philipites, at least of their elder Michel Schneider (Wolkan, 36). The tract, surprisingly found in a Hutterite manuscript, has not yet been published. Only an incomplete transcription has been preserved (at Goshen College Mennonite Historical Library). The manuscript itself seems to be lost. The main contents are described by Friedmann in *MQR* V (1931) 90-99. The complete title runs as follows, *Von einem wahrhaften Ritter Christi, und womit er gewappnet muss sein, damit er überwinden möge die Welt, das Fleisch, und den Teufel* (Concern a True Soldier of Christ, and Wherewith he Must be Armed in Order to Conquer the World, the Flesh, and the Devil). The allusion to Eph. 6:10 f. is obvious. In the codex the tract covers 23 leaves, written with greatest care. In view of the deviation of certain ideas of the tract from those of the Hutterites, its preservation at this place is remarkable.

A true soldier of Christ then needs four weapons: faith, love, hope, and inner surrender or *Gelassenheit.* Haffner wanted to demonstrate to everyone "how the true disciple of Christ should be. Let us therefore hear what belongs to a genuine soldier of Christ and of what character he ought to be or wherewith he must fight." The major stress of the tract falls on the idea of *Gelassenheit* (yieldedness, inner surrender, conquest of self), which is the discipline and test of a true disciple. "The world accepts Christ quite readily as a gift but from the point of view of suffering does not know Him at all. Yet whosoever wants to follow Christ must follow Him on the way of suffering."—"When we truly realize the love of God we will be ready to give up for love's sake even what God has given us." Resignation is the central theme of the tract. By it "a Christian is recognized." It means mortification of the flesh, an inner surrender of everything that is dear to us.

This is not the Hutterite position, which stresses more the principle of obedience over against that of yieldedness, nor is it that of the Swiss and South German Brethren, who show a more positive approach in their understanding of discipleship. This may explain why these groups survived and the Philipites disappeared. (R. Friedmann, "Concerning the True Soldier of Christ, a Hitherto Unknown Tract of the Philipite Brethren in Moravia," *MQR* V, 1931, 87-99.) R.F.

Concession (*Konzession*), the document of toleration and admission given the Mennonites in the Palatinate. The first was granted on Aug. 4, 1664, by elector Karl Ludwig, 1648-80. It was confirmed by each of his successors upon the request of all the Mennonites living in the Palatinate; by Carl, 1680-85, on Dec. 5, 1682; by Philip William, 1685-90, on Jan. 15, 1686; by John William, 1690-1716, on Feb. 18, 1698; by Carl Philip, 1716-43, on July 15, 1717; and by Carl Theodore, 1743-99, on Feb. 27, 1743. In other countries the term *Privilegium* (*q.v.*) was commonly used for the same type of document. (*ML* II, 547.) G.H.

Concord Mennonite Church (MC) is located 14 miles west of Knoxville, in Knox Co., Tenn. The abundance of cheap well-watered land and a mild climate attracted Amish Mennonites and Mennonites to this area soon after the Civil War. In 1874 the Mennonite community numbered 54 souls, 21 of whom were members of the church.

It seems that the Ohio Mennonites assumed some responsibility for the church there at first, but now the church is under the Virginia Conference. The Concord Church did not continue to grow. A number of the original families moved elsewhere. Today the presence of a large frame church and numerous graves in the yard adjacent to the church are mute testimonies to the existence of a once flourishing congregation. There were 17 members in 1954, with William Jennings the long-time resident bishop. H.A.B.

Concord, the name of the ship that carried the first German immigrant group from Europe to America, composed of 13 Mennonite-Quaker families of Crefeld. The ship left the Thames harbor at Gravesend on July 24, 1683, and after a difficult journey of two and one-half months arrived safely at Philadelphia on Oct. 6, 1683. It carried a complement of 40 crewmen and 120 passengers. HEGE.

Concordance (in Latin, *Concordantia*-agreement), a reference book used as an aid in the study of the Scriptures. With the spread of printed Bibles in the vernacular these books became rather popular, allowing a more intensive checking of the Scriptural texts and making the use of the Bible easier and more meaningful. There are two types of Bible concordances, verbal and topical. The first type is organized as an alphabetical index of all the chief words used in the Bible together with

their locations (Bible register), while the second is organized according to key concepts with corresponding passages indicated. The wide use of concordances in the Reformation period reflects the Biblicistic interests of the masses, in contrast to the spiritualizing tendencies of certain intellectuals who tended to minimize Scriptural studies or arguments and rely on direct inspiration. Since the Anabaptists and Mennonites were (and are) Biblicists, they showed a particular interest in such books, which to them were not only Bible indexes but to some extent real guides through the Bible for understanding and for arguing in disputations. This is particularly true with regard to the topical concordances, which are almost Bible "anthologies," in which selections are made according to certain theological and devotional principles.

The very first concordance is that made by Cardinal Hugo of St. Cher, about A.D. 1230, in Latin, of course. The first printed concordance was the Latin one by Conrad, printed at Strasbourg in 1470. The oldest known German printed concordance was made by Jörg Birckmeier, *Ein Zeigerbüchlein der Heiligen Geschrift,* printed by Froschauer at Zürich in 1525 (24 leaves, 8°), a verbal concordance which later was added to all editions of the Froschauer Bible (*q.v.*). (A copy in the Goshen College Library.)

The next work of the same type is a book by Leonhard Brunner, *Konkordanz und Zeiger der Sprüch und Historien aller biblischen Bücher* (Worms, 1529, and Strasbourg, 1530), a folio volume of 268 leaves. It is said that the author's views were near those of Hans Denk (*q.v.*) and Ludwig Haetzer (*q.v.*), whose translation of the Prophets he used. The work does not reveal any originality but is very elaborate. For example, the heading *Zeit* contains three columns of quotations dealing with "time." It was a popular, dictionary-like verbal concordance and saw one more folio edition in 1546 (Strasbourg) and one further condensed edition (in 12°) in 1567 in Basel. The Hutterite brother Ambrosy Resch (d. 1592) copied and enlarged this work, adding texts from the Apocrypha, thus creating a folio codex of 1,046 handwritten leaves (now in Bratislava). Only three other German verbal concordances of the 16th century are known: J. Danreuter (1561); P. Gedultig (1571); and M. Vogel (1587), although 44 Latin verbal concordances appeared during the century.

A very early topical concordance, almost surely of Anabaptist origin, is the *Concordanz und Zeiger der namhafftigsten Sprüch aller Biblischen Bücher alts und news Testaments* (presumably of the 1530's or 1540's). In 1560, a Dutch translation appeared (*BRN* V, 585 ff.), while several more German editions subsequently came out; one around 1600 (with 368 pages small size) of which a copy is in the Goshen College Library, then in 1693 and again in 1709. In none of the editions is the place of printing named, but it was most likely Basel or the Palatinate. Since this concordance first appeared together with several Anabaptist tracts and later became popular with the Swiss Brethren its Anabaptist origin is strongly suggested. George Thormann in his polemical *Probierstein . . . des Täufertums* (Bern, 1693) expressly states that "the Brethren made so much ado with their concordance booklet" (he may have had the edition of 1693 in mind), which suggests the Swiss origin of this work. It has not more than 66 topics, yet the very selection of them reveals an alert and devoted brother at work. The article *Verfolgung* (persecution) covers 18 pages, the article on "False Prophets and anti-Christ" covers 24 pages of quotations. Old and New Testament are quoted without distinction. In general, however, the Anabaptists prefer the New Testament.

No concordance of official Protestant origin is known before the 17th century, but we know of several more such books of Anabaptist background. There once existed the *Ratsbüchlein* of Hans Hut (*q.v.*), written about 1525-27, which the authorities found in the knapsack of Eitelhans Langenmantel (*q.v.*) at his arrest; it contained a catechism, a prayer, and a concordance of 78 entries (*Ztscht des Hist. Ver. f. Schwaben*, 1900, 39; also 1874). Hans Hut at his trial acknowledged the authorship of the booklet.

Another outstanding concordance of Anabaptist origin is Pilgram Marpeck's great anonymously published *Testamentserläuterung* of 1544 (417 leaves, 4°). It is a topical concordance of 125 chapters, juxtaposing texts of the Old and the New Testament (called "yesterday" and "today"). We do not know too much about the spread of this work, of which only two copies are known (in Zürich and Berlin), but apparently it was much read among South German Anabaptists, as references to it prove. Wiswedel (*Blätter für württ. Kirchengesch.*, 1937, 64-76) conjectures that it was the work not of Marpeck alone but of an entire group of earnest Bible students.

The Hutterites, too, had quite a number of such concordances among their manuscript books; yet it is next to impossible to trace the origin of most of these books. We know that one brother copied and enlarged the Brunner concordance. One codex (now in the Hungarian National Museum in Budapest), a topical concordance, is certainly a copy of a non-Hutterite work of high originality. Another codex concordance is of 1567 and still another of 1578, perhaps a copy of the *Concordanzbüchlein* mentioned above. (All these codices are listed in *Arch. f. Ref.-Gesch.*, 1931, 226-27.)

The topical concordance presupposes a certain creative editor; sometimes he does not feel bound to the alphabetical arrangement, and some of these books are rather diversified and arbitrary in their organization. Pilgram Marpeck's *Testamentserläuterung*, for instance, is of this kind. Sebastian Franck, himself not an Anabaptist but much read among the Brethren, published two works of this kind: the *Güldin Arch*, 1538, and *Das Verbütschierte Buch*, 1539. Both works are rather Bible "anthologies," arranged according to certain selected principles, sometimes demonstrating existing apparent contradictions within the Scriptures (the so-called *Schriftkrieg*).

The most extensive concordance of the topical type is the outstanding Dutch production by Pieter Jansz Twisck (*q.v.*), the leader of the strict Dutch Mennonite group of the Old Frisians (*q.v.*), *Concordantie der Heylighen Schrifturen. . . .* This work appeared first in 1615 at Hoorn as a large folio volume of 1,056 pages, and was reprinted in 1648 (at Haarlem). It is the work of an outstanding student of the Bible, and can be called a real guide through the Scriptures. In 1632, Twisck published a sequel to it, the *Bybelsch Naem ende Chronijck boeck* (Schijn-Maatschoen II, 1744, 518). Twisck also published *Na Beter. Een corte gheestelijcke verclaringhe vanden hoge Priester Aaron zijn Persoon, doen, Kledinghe, Borst-lap officie, Amt ende offerhanden . . .* (Hoorn, 1608); and *Namen, ofte Benaminghen Christi . . . op't A.B.C. gherecht* (Hoorn, 1615). An old Dutch concordance, the author of which is unknown, is *Handtboecxken, ofte Concordantie, Dat is: de ghelijckluydende plaetsen der Heyligher Schrift by een vergadert* (n.p., 1576; 2d ed., Rotterdam, 1614). Other concordances by Mennonite authors are: J.P.V.M. (Jacob Pietersz van der Meulen), *Collatio: S.Scripture, Dat is, Vergelijckinge der H. Schrifturen in verscheyden geloofs-saken . . .* (Dordrecht, 1602, *idem*, with an appendix, Dordrecht, 1602); J. P. S. (Jan Philipsz Schabaelje), *Harmonia, Ofte Eendrachtghe Verstellinghe der vier Evangelisten . . .* (Amsterdam, 1624); the same, *Sommarium, Ofte Corten Inhoudt des Bybels . . .* (Amsterdam, 1629, reprint Haarlem, 1654); K. Toornburg, *Concordantie van gelijkluydende piaatsen der H.S. . . .* (Alkmaar, 1695). The Amsterdam Mennonite Library has some fragments of a *Concordantie ofte schriftuerlyke catechismus* by an unknown author and undated, but likely from the 17th century. (*Inv. Arch. Amst.* I, No. 668.)

One more concordance of the 16th century has become known, which originated neither in Anabaptist nor in official Protestant church circles: it is Otto Brunfels' (d. 1534) *Pandectbüchlein beiläufig aller Sprüch beider Testament* (460 pp., 8°). It was first published in Latin in 1527 in Strasbourg, but was soon translated into German (German edd., 1529, Strasbourg, and 1533 and 1544, Augsburg. Ten Latin editions appeared between 1527 and 1576, and one Dutch edition). Again it is a topical concordance, inasmuch as it collects Scriptural texts according to certain topics in separate chapters, one for each topic. As it was published first in Strasbourg (Brunfels was a friend of Capito, *q.v.*), contacts with Anabaptists are highly probable.

The 17th century produced a number of concordances by official Protestant churchmen: in 1609 Konrad Agricola (Bauer) published a verbal concordance which became very popular; in 1610, Johann Piscator, principal of the academy at Herborn, Nassau, published his voluminous *Herborn Bibelwerk*, composed of Scripture portions with elaborate commentaries, and the *Bibel Register*, a verbal concordance of not less than 1,607 pages.

It was printed at the well-known "academic press" of Herborn. It must have been popular also among the Anabaptists, for Andreas Ehrenpreis (*q.v.*) mentions the book in his great *Sendbrief* of 1652, and worn-out copies are occasionally found in Mennonite homes even today. Other Protestant Bible concordances are by Johannes Janus (1650), G. Büchner (1750), which latter became particularly popular (29th edition 1927), the *Calwer Bibel Konkordanz* (1892), the second edition of which (1905) was prepared by the Mennonite scholar Johannes Claassen (*q.v.*, 3rd ed. 1923), and that of Otto Schmoller (1869, 5th ed. 1923).

The first English concordance to the entire Bible, *A Concordance,* was produced by John Marbeck in 1550. The most famous is that of Alexander Cruden, *A Complete Concordance,* first published in London in 1737, since published in countless revisions. It purports to list each occurrence of the significant words of Scripture (though it is not complete) and appends a concordance to the Apocryphal books. More exhaustive concordances are Robert Young's *Analytical Concordance to the Bible* (Edinburgh 1879, rev. ed., 1902) and James Strong's absolutely complete *Exhaustive Concordance of the Bible* (N.Y., 1894). J. B. R. Walker's *Comprehensive Concordance of the Holy Scriptures* (Boston, 1894) is similar to Cruden's but more complete. **R.F.**

The older study by H. E. Bindseil, "Ueber Bibel Konkordanzen," in *Theol. Studien und Krit.* (1870) 673-720, contains hardly anything regarding Anabaptist or Mennonite material. The Anabaptist material was collected by Robert Friedmann in two articles, "Eine dogmatische Hauptschrift der hutterischen Täufergemeinschaften in Mähren," *Arch. f. Ref.-Gesch.* XXVIII (1931) 224-33, and "The Schleitheim Confession," *MQR* XVI (1942) 95-98. See also G. Baring, "Die Wormser Propheten . . . ," in *Arch. f. Ref.-Gesch.* (1933) 38 (connecting Leonhard Brunner with Denk and Haetzer); W. Wiswedel, "Die Testamentserläuterung, ein Beitrag zur Täufergeschichte," in *Arch. f. Ref.-Gesch.* (1937) 64-76; finally S. Cramer in the Introduction to his edition of the commentary of 1560; *BRN* V (1909) 588 ff.; *ML* II, 541.

Concordat of the cities of Zürich, Bern, and St. Gall against the Swiss Brethren. On Aug. 2, 1527, the city of Zürich issued an invitation to the cities of Bern, St. Gall, Basel, Schaffhausen, Chur, and Appenzell to come to Zürich for a conference, to adopt unified measures for gaining control of the dangerous Anabaptists. The conference, which was held Aug. 12-14, 1527, agreed upon a mandate, which was signed by Zürich, Bern, and St. Gall and published under the following title, *Abschid der Stette Zürich, Bern und Saint Gallen von wegen der widerteüffer auszgangen* (1527). Some of its specifications were as follows:

(1) Whoever is suspect of the vice of Anabaptism will be summoned before the authorities and faithfully and seriously warned to desist and the penalties will be explained to him. (2) In order that this suspicion may come to light, every citizen is bound by his oath of loyalty to inform the authorities of any one suspected of Anabaptism. (3) Whoever openly belongs to this sect and refuses to be corrected and to desist, is subject to punishment by the authorities. (4) Foreign Anabaptists are to be expelled. A foreigner is defined as one who is born outside the jurisdiction of the cities and cantons entering upon this agreement. (5) Whoever is expelled, and in violation of his oath returns, shall be drowned without mercy. (6) Citizens who backslide and are again stained with Anabaptism shall pay a double fine. (7) Whoever persists in his error, becomes a preacher or leader of the sect, or, having sworn to amend his ways and to desist from his error, backslides, shall also be drowned. (8) Anabaptists should not be absent from communion; they shall observe it with the other people of their local church. (9) Since many innocent persons are enticed by the hypocritical doctrine of the Anabaptists, we reserve the right to modify the penalty according to circumstances. (10) If an Anabaptist flees from one of the regions bound by the agreement to another, he shall not be spared, but shall either be expelled or extradited. (11) If neighboring cantons or cities wish to join us in this agreement, they may do so at any time. (12) The messengers shall immediately announce this mandate to their home governmental authorities, who shall then determine the amount of the fines to be imposed.

On Sept. 6 Bern reported to Zürich that it had accepted the suggestions; concerning fines it reserved a free hand. Zürich wanted to have the concordat printed, but Bern, in a letter of Sept. 14, considered it unnecessary.

The baneful effect of this concordat was soon in evidence. The death penalty for Anabaptists provided in it was now also applied in Bern. It was the first mandate issued by Bern against the Anabaptists, and initiated a systematic persecution that lasted for centuries. **S.G.**

Allgemeine Eidgenössische Abschiede A.A. 243, State archives of Bern; Steck and Tobler, *Aktensammlung zur Gesch. der Berner Ref.,* Nos. 1280, 1310, 1320; S. Geiser, *Die Taufgesinnten-Gemeinden* (Karlsruhe, 1931) 147, 169; *ML* II, 542. A copy of the original *Abschid* is in the Goshen College Library.

Concordia Hospital, Winnipeg, Can. The founding of the Concordia Hospital dates back to Jan. 1, 1928, when at a meeting of a number of refugee students from Russia, it was resolved to found a Mennonite hospital in Winnipeg. When the Mennonite groups of Manitoba proved responsive to this idea, an appeal was made to the youth organizations of Canada and the United States in March of the same year that they assist in the realization of this plan. The result was that in a short time a considerable sum of money came together but it did not suffice by far for the opening of a regular hospital. Therefore it was resolved to begin with a maternity home. For this purpose a private home was rented on 291 Machray Ave., and the necessary equipment was bought. In the end of June the home with five beds was officially opened and the first maternity cases were admitted on July 28, 1928. The home was founded with the purpose of turning it over to the Mennonites once its need had been realized.

The opportune moment seemed to have arrived in 1929, when at the meeting held on Nov. 21, six members of the Mennonite churches were elected to the enlarged council. The meeting instructed this enlarged council to found a regular hospital. As the required monies were provided by personal loans, the transference of the maternity home to a house on 720 Beverley St. was possible in 1930, at which time it began to function as a regular private hospital. Until the year 1932 the hospital flourished but then the world-wide depression also hit Concordia. The people became too poor to seek medical attention or avail themselves of hospital care. To ameliorate this, a system of mutual health insurance was inaugurated which included doctor's care as well as hospitalization. This system gave the hospital new life and made possible the purchase of the Winnipeg Sanatorium in Elmwood, to which the hospital was transferred on April 13, 1934.

The present hospital has been recognized as a Public General Hospital by the provincial government. It has 50 beds and 16 bassinets, a well-equipped operating room, 2 obstetrical rooms, an X-ray department, and an up-to-date laboratory. It is operated by the Mennonite Hospital Society Concordia.   H.J.W.

Conestoga Amish Mennonite Church (MC) is located one-half mile west of Morgantown, in Caernarvon Twp., Lancaster Co., Pa. Its members, most of whom are farmers, are located in the three adjoining counties of Lancaster (q.v.), Berks (q.v.), and Chester (q.v.).

The church was founded in 1760 and is therefore the first permanent Amish Mennonite congregation in America. Among the first settlers were those having the family names of Mast, Hoelley, Hertzler, and Lapp. Jacob Mast (q.v.) served as the first resident minister of the congregation and was elected its bishop in 1788. The following bishops have served this church during the years indicated: Jacob Hertzler, 1760-86; Jacob Mast, 1788-1808; Peter Plank, 1808-31; John Plank, 1831-35; John Stoltzfus, 1835-37; David Beiler, 1837-45; John K. Stoltzfus, 1845-54; Christian Umble, 1854-77; John P. Mast, 1877-88; Gideon Stoltzfus, 1888-1908; John S. Mast (q.v.), 1908-51; and Ira A. Kurtz, 1944-   .

About 1869 differences of opinion arose within the congregation concerning the adoption of more progressive forms of worship. The most conservative minority withdrew from the congregation in 1877, thus establishing an O. O. Amish group in the community. The larger group soon after this built its first church, dedicating it in June 1882. The present edifice was erected in 1923.

In 1850 the membership of the church was 30, by 1882 it had grown to 80, by 1923 the number had increased to 225, and by 1952 the total was 380. The Conestoga Church has in recent years planted three organized churches under its bishop jurisdiction. The Rock Amish Mennonite Church (q.v.) was organized in 1936, the Oley Church in 1942, and the Zions Church in 1951. The three are situated in Berks County, within a radius of 25 miles. (C. Z. Mast and Robert E. Simpson, *Annals of the Conestoga Valley in Lancaster, Berks, and Chester Counties, Pennsylvania*, Elverson, Pa., 1942.)
                                                C.Z.M.

Conestoga Wagon. The Conestoga wagon was named for the valley in Lancaster Co., Pa., where it developed. It is contended that this wagon was first produced in America in Lancaster Co., Pa., by the Pennsylvania-German inhabitants. It was one of the chief freight carriers of the East from about 1750 until the coming of the railroads. Built with a boat-shaped body so that the load would shift less easily on hills, it presented a distinct appearance, although no two were alike, as they were often custom-built. It generally had a vermilion running gear, a Prussian blue wagon body, and a white canvas cover. Broad wheels kept it from getting stuck in the mud. It was generally pulled by four or six horses.

Mennonites were associated with the development and use of the wagon. M. G. Weaver, Mennonite historian of Lancaster County, wrote that his father Gideon Weaver built these wagons in the Conestoga Valley from 1836. One of the early Conestoga wagon teamsters, who as a youth began hauling freight across the Alleghenies, was Moses Hartz, who later became an Amish minister.

The story of the migration of the Mennonite Bricker brothers to Ontario from eastern Pennsylvania in a Conestoga wagon in 1802 has been made immortal by Mabel Dunham in her *Trail of the Conestoga* (q.v.). A Conestoga wagon used by early Mennonite immigrants on their trip to Ontario is preserved in the Waterloo County Historical Museum, Kitchener, Ont. A feature of the Waterloo County Centennial of 1952 was the driving of this wagon from Pennsylvania to Kitchener by Amzie Martin, a man of Mennonite descent. A Conestoga wagon of similar design and use is preserved in Vaughan Township, York County, Ont., by Amos Baker, an Old Order Dunker. (J. William Frey and H. C. Frey, *The Conestoga Wagon, A Pennsylvania Dutch Product*, Lancaster, Pa., 1947.)   M.G.

Conestogo (MC) was the meetinghouse and name used by the St. Jacobs, Ont., Mennonite Church (q.v.) before it moved to St. Jacobs in 1915. The first Conestogo meetinghouse was one of logs erected in 1844, followed by a frame building *ca.* 1852, both located on the east bank of the Conestogo River, two and one-half miles northwest of the village of St. Jacobs.   J.C.F.

Conestogo Old Order Mennonite Church, near St. Jacobs, Ont., was built in 1893 about four years after a schism separating the group from the Mennonite (MC) congregation. For some time after the schism, the question of which faction should hold the building remained unsettled. The Old Order Mennonites worshiped in the building known as the Conestogo church up to the end of 1892, while the Mennonites worshiped in a home about three miles distant near Conestogo. When the Old Order produced a church calendar entitled "Old Mennonite," the position was taken that they had changed their name, hence had no right to the Conestogo Mennonite church. Accordingly the Mennonites took possession of the building on Jan. 1, 1893.

The Old Order Mennonites then put up a new building about one mile south of their former place of worship, where they have held services up to the present time (1950). The minister was Daniel M. Brubacher (1840-1921), who was ordained in 1876. The minister in 1950 was Irvin Shantz. The membership worshiping here is counted as part of the Martin's district, which has over 1,000 members.

A.G.

Conestogo (Ont.) United Missionary Church, now extinct, organized about 1885, was located in the village of Conestogo. It had 42 members in 1901, but after 1911 gradually dissolved. The church building was later bought by the Lutherans.

J.C.F.

Conference, the name most commonly used both by German-speaking (*Konferenz*) and English-speaking Mennonites for the official meetings or synods of the ministerial leadership of the congregations. The original intent of the word was apparently to indicate the purpose to "confer" or counsel about matters of common concern relating to the spiritual welfare of the brotherhood, particularly matters of faith and life. The conferences were earlier composed solely of ordained men—elders, preachers, and deacons taking part. However, there were also special meetings of elders or bishops only, and it is sometimes difficult to determine the exact character of the meetings. At first the conferences were not regularly recurring meetings held at stated intervals, but met only as occasion required, particularly when it was felt necessary to try to arrive at a common policy which all the ministerial leadership in the various congregations could follow, or to reconcile differences. Usually resolutions were adopted expressing the agreements reached, but these did not at first have the binding force of ecclesiastical law.

The first conference was probably the one which met at Schleitheim, Switzerland, on Feb. 24, 1527. Its outcome was the *Seven Articles,* known as the *Brüderlich Vereinigung* (*q.v.*). Also important was the noteworthy Martyrs' Synod (*q.v.*), meeting at Augsburg, Germany, on Aug. 20, 1527, which led to an agreement among the leaders on the most important questions of religious life as well as to the adoption of a plan for the sending out of missionaries. Conferences were held at Spaarndam (1535) and Bocholt (summer 1536) in Northwest Germany, by the radical Anabaptists connected with the Münsterite revolutionaries. Controversy on the doctrine of the Incarnation and the ban in marriage was to be settled at meetings in the North under Menno Simons' leadership at Emden (1547), Goch (1547), Lübeck (1552), and finally at Wismar (1554), when the Wismar Resolutions (*q.v.*) of agreement were reached. A similar meeting at Harlingen, Holland (1557), failed. The same (and some other) questions occupied the great conferences at Strasbourg in 1555, 1557, 1568, and 1607 (also of 1630 at Hoffingen), when the Swiss and South German leaders met, and where among other things certain questions concerning practical life were settled. Unity was achieved in 1591 at a conference at Cologne which produced the confession of faith known as the Concept of Cologne (*q.v.*). Most of the numerous Dutch confessions of faith

of the 17th century were drawn up at conferences specifically called for such purposes. The meeting of the brethren of Alsace-Lorraine at Ohnenheim, Feb. 4, 1660, ended with the adoption of the Dordrecht Confession. The elders of the congregations of West Prussia and Danzig met frequently in the 16th and 17th centuries, not of course in one overall group, since the Flemish and Frisian and other divisions kept the several groups apart. These meetings of elders were, however, certainly the forerunners of the later West Prussian ministerial conferences. The Amish elders and ministers met on several occasions at Essingen in the Palatinate in the 17th and 18th centuries, e.g., 1779. The first recorded conference of the Mennonite Church of the Palatinate was 1688 at Obersülzen-Offstein. Of no small importance were the Mennonite conferences held at Ibersheim (*q.v.*) in the Rheinhessen-Pfalz area in 1803 and 1805.

Organized conferences with regular annual or semiannual meetings first appear in the late 18th and early 19th centuries. Among these are: the Swiss conference, meeting at least since 1779; in Germany, the Conference of the Hessian and Palatine Churches since the year 1824, the meetings of the ministers (*Lehrdienst*) of the congregations of West and East Prussia at least since 1834, the meetings of the ministers of the Baden-Württemberg-Bavaria congregations (*Badischer Verband, q.v.*), at least since 1840 (the meetings are held quarterly), the Conference of the South German Mennonites since 1887, and the Union of German Mennonite Congregations (*Vereinigung der deutschen Mennonitengemeinden, q.v.*) since 1886. Regular conferences have also been held in France since 1901, where two conferences exist, one for the French-speaking congregations and the other for Alsace. In America the oldest conference is the Lancaster (MC), meeting since about 1740, and the Franconia (MC) beginning about the same time; the very first meeting was that of Germantown in 1725, where the Dordrecht Confession was adopted. In Russia the meetings of the elders, known as *Aeltestenkonvent* (later *Kirchenkonvent*), began about 1840, with the regular conferences coming later (MB 1872, GCM 1883). In Holland the corresponding conference is the *Algemene Doopsgezinde Sociëteit* (*q.v.*), or General Mennonite Society, of which all the Dutch Mennonite churches are members, founded in 1811. Earlier, conferences (*Sociëteit*) of the several groups had been meeting separately.

Earlier the conferences were meetings of representatives of autonomous or semiautonomous congregations and they have continued to be so in Europe, except the *Badischer Verband*. During the 19th century, however, in America in the Mennonite (MC) and related groups these developed into authoritative ecclesiastical bodies with power over the local congregations and ministers. The general conference of this body (MC) is, however, only advisory and not authoritative over the district conferences. The Mennonite Brethren conferences in Russia and America have been authoritative, whereas in the General Conference Mennonite Church the district and general conference are not authoritative bodies. The character of the conferences varies from authoritative to advisory in the smaller American bodies. The Old Order Amish have not had any conferences in modern times. However, special Amish conferences were held in America occasionally (1809, 1837, 1865), and 1862-78 annual Amish general conferences were held.

Modern American Mennonite conferences add to their dealing with questions of doctrine, practice, discipline, and administration, also the direction and supervision of many and varied activities. They usually adopt constitutions and by-laws to govern their organization and procedures, as well as official disciplines (*q.v.*), which contain the basic rules and regulations governing the members.

An interesting modern development regarding conferences, which is characteristic chiefly of the North American groups, is the opening of the sessions to the general public, and the generous attendance of the conference sessions by the general membership of the church. This is particularly true of the general conferences of the various groups, but also of the many annual district conferences. The biennial general conferences of the Mennonite Church (MC), called "Mennonite General Conference," have often been attended by 2,000-6,000 persons, fewer than 250 of whom have been official delegates, and district conferences of this group are often attended by 1,000-2,000. To accommodate such large crowds great tents are put up and extensive catering arrangements made. The triennial general conference sessions of the G.C. Mennonites and the Mennonite Brethren also are attended by large crowds, although, having lay delegates, their conference attendants are to a greater proportion delegates. Attendance averages 1,000-2,500 persons. There is some of this in Europe, particularly in the Alsatian, French, and South German conferences, but none in Holland or the German *Badischer Verband* or *Vereinigung*.

The attendance of large crowds naturally changes the character of the conferences, since it becomes necessary to supply informational and inspirational addresses, often accompanied by special musical numbers. Some of the conferences then have most of the business sessions of the delegates in closed sessions, while the larger crowd is served with more general programs.

Since customarily all the "leaders" of the denomination attend, the conferences become much more than official synods, partaking of the character of a family gathering on a large scale, where acquaintances are made and renewed, fellowship intensified, and sympathetic personal face-to-face relationships made possible and maintained. This type of group relationship has a vital bearing on the solidarity and effective working relationships of the body. Even in the largest North American Mennonite branches it can be said that all the leaders and most of the ministers know each other personally and meet regularly. (*ML* II, 526 f.) NEFF, H.S.B.

Conference Messenger, bimonthly 8-page organ of the South Central Conference (MC), first issue September 1945 with 4 pages, changed in 1949 to 8.

Conference of Evangelical Mennonites: see **Evangelical Mennonite Conference.**

Conference of French-Speaking Mennonites (Association of the Evangelical-Mennonite Churches of France, French-Language Group). Those Mennonite congregations formed in French-speaking France (*q.v.*) maintained close connections with the sister congregations of Alsace, German-speaking Lorraine, the Palatinate, and the Saar. However, the annexation of Alsace-Lorraine by Germany (1871) and the transition to the French language in the congregations remaining on French soil (1875-1900) made it impracticable for French-speaking congregations to participate in the conferences held 1876, 1896, and 1907 by the congregations in Alsace and German Lorraine (see **Conference of the Mennonites of Alsace**).

On the initiative of Pierre Sommer and Valentin Pelsy a conference was called in Epinal in 1901, and was held annually or biennially from 1901 to 1914. It was officially organized as an *Association* in 1907. Following World War I and the return of Alsace-Lorraine to France an effort was made to unite this French-language conference with the German-language conference of Alsace-Lorraine, which was considered as the parent body. This attempt was, however, unsuccessful for practical reasons, although a number of meetings were held which were attended by both groups, and a general French *Association* was organized and legally registered in 1925. The French-language group then resumed separate sessions in 1927 under the name *Association des Eglises Evangéliques-Mennonites de France, Groupe de Langue Francaise.* This conference meets semiannually: at Valdoie on Easter Monday, and at Toul in early November. The conference deals with all matters of common interest to the congregations, including the use of donated funds, but has no jurisdiction over the internal concerns of the individual congregations. Its affairs are directed by a committee of elders and ministers of whom for some years J. B. Muller (Toul) has been the president, and Pierre Sommer, Grand Charmont par Montbéliard, the secretary-treasurer. The official headquarters is Chapelle de la Prairie, Montbéliard (Doubs). (*ML* II, 530.) J.H.Y.

Conference of Historic Peace Churches, an association of Canadian peace churches, was organized July 22, 1940, at Waterloo, Ont. The meeting was called by the Peace Problems Committees of the Brethren in Christ (Tunker), Mennonite, and Mennonite Brethren in Christ churches in view of the imminent introduction of compulsory military service. Churches represented are the Brethren in Christ, Mennonite Brethren in Christ, Old Order Mennonite, Amish Mennonite, Friends, Brethren, Old Order Dunkard, and the Ontario sections of the Mennonite Brethren and General Conference Mennonites. Close contact is maintained with the General Conference and Mennonite Brethren churches of Western Canada.

During the war years, the Conference was largely responsible for the interpretation of the nonresistant faith to the government, especially as the convictions of peace church adherents related to problems of army service. With the establishment of Alternative Service for Canadians of peace church persuasions, the Conference of Historic Peace Churches provided spiritual oversight for men in service. Since the war, the Conference has attempted to keep before the membership the historic Scriptural principles of nonresistance. At the same time, the Conference has remained alert to developments and changes in government policy which have bearing on the peace stand.

The Conference of Historic Peace Churches has worked in close co-operation with the MCC. This relationship has developed more systematically from the time of the war years until the present. On April 1, 1946, plans were adopted to affiliate the Non-Resistant Relief Organization (*q.v.*) with the Conference of Historic Peace Churches. By virtue of the fact of this affiliation completed on Sept. 10, 1946, four member officers of N.R.R.O. and the Military Problems Committee were added to the executive committee of the Conference of Historic Peace Churches. The officers in 1953 were as follows: E. J. Swalm, chairman; P. G. Lehman, vice-chairman; C. J. Rempel, secretary; M. R. Good, treasurer; additional members: J. B. Martin, Elven Shantz, Oscar Burkholder, S. F. Coffman.   H.S.B.

Conference of Mennonite Churches in Uruguay, a subsidiary of the Vereinigung in Germany, organized Feb. 21, 1953, includes three congregations of Danzig-West Prussian immigrants who came to Uruguay (*q.v.*) 1948-52—El Ombu, Gartental, and Montevideo.   H.S.B.

Conference of Mennonites in Canada (GCM) first met in 1903 in Hochstadt, Man. At first it was called Conference of Mennonites in Middle Canada, because only three provinces—Manitoba, Saskatchewan, and Alberta—belonged to the Conference. According to Benjamin Ewert, who took part in this conference and is still active, 15 delegates and guests were present at the first conference; others estimate that there were 19 delegates and guests. At the last conference there were between two and three thousand delegates and guests. This was in 1952, at the fiftieth anniversary of the Conference of Mennonites in Canada at Gretna, Man.

The Conference was organized to promote "home missions," because the Mennonites as a rule had large families, were looking for new land, and it was a great work to keep them together. At the first conference in 1903 in Hochstadt, two churches met—the Bergthal Church of Manitoba and the Rosenort Church of Saskatchewan. These two groups had the first Mennonite high schools— Gretna in Manitoba and Rosthern in Saskatchewan. Soon the churches that joined the Conference of Mennonites in Middle Canada became greatly enlarged, especially when the immigration set in in 1923 and brought some 20,000 Mennonites mostly from Russia to Canada in roughly seven years. Most of these immigrants joined churches of this Conference. When the Mennonites spread in large numbers westward to British Columbia and eastward to Ontario, the name "Middle Canada" was left out. In a few years the substitute name "General Conference" was dropped, too, because it always suggested the General Conference of Mennonites, who not only had many churches in North America, but spread also to South America. And there remained the name: The Conference of Mennonites in Canada.

The constitution of the Conference was adopted at the second conference (Eigenheim, Sask., 1904). The main part of the constitution is as follows: "The Conference has no authority to interfere in the internal matters of a congregation unless called to do so. It is not a legislative, but an advisory body. The union it promotes does not consist in agreeable forms and customs, but in unity of love, faith, and hope, and in connection with this a common work in the kingdom of God."

The main promoter of the Conference was David Toews, who served as chairman for 26 years (1914-40 with exception of 1936, when he was at the World Conference in Holland). John G. Rempel was secretary of the Conference for 18 years (1930-47), when he became elder. Since 1941 J. J. Thiessen of Saskatoon, Sask., has been chairman.

In 1952 the chronicle of the conference shows: 15,357 members, 26,953 members and children, 250 ministers, 35 elders, 108 churches, and $451,422.92 contributed by the congregations. The Conference of Mennonites in Canada is affiliated with the General Conference Mennonite Church.   J.G.R.

Conference of the Mennonites of Alsace (*-Lorraine*) (Association of the Evangelical-Mennonite Churches of France, comprising the German-language congregations of Alsace and Lorraine). In the 18th century the Amish churches in Alsace were quite active in holding conferences. There are numerous traces of general meetings, usually occupied chiefly with the problem of church discipline. Toward the end of the century and early in the 19th the military question occupied the foreground. The combined efforts of the total membership brought it about that throughout the Napoleonic wars Mennonites were permitted to give their required services in the medical corps or in transportation.

Later the conference ceased to function, and each congregation remained to itself, causing grave injury to the church life. Not until the end of the 19th century did matters improve. In 1876 a conference of the Mennonites of Alsace-Lorraine was held at Basel on the subject of footwashing. In 1896 a conference met at Munzenheim near Colmar, and stressed the need for such meetings. In 1907 the conference met in Pulversheim near Mulhouse and has been meeting regularly twice a year ever since except in the periods of 1915-19 and 1940-45. It was legally organized and registered in 1925. The congregation in Luxembourg now also belongs to the conference.

Since the return of Alsace-Lorraine to France after World War I the Alsatian conference is officially called the *Association des Eglises Evangéliques-Mennonites de France,* although the German language continues to predominate in both congregations and conference activities (for relations of this group with the French-language conference, see **Conference of French-Speaking Mennonites**).

Since the year 1925 the conference has been meeting semiannually, generally at Pfastatt, also at Sarrebourg or Colmar. Conference programs are prepared and proposals formulated by a committee of ministers and elders of which for many years Elder Joseph Widmer of Mulhouse-Modenheim has been president, and Elder Hans Nussbaumer of Altkirch-Schweighof, secretary; at conference sessions all those attending may participate in deliberations. The conferences concern themselves with home and foreign missions, charities, education, and other matters of common interest. A part of the session is always devoted to Bible exposition or doctrine. The official office is at 22 Rue d' Ingersheim, Colmar (Haut-Rhin).	P.So.

Conference of the Mennonite Brethren Church of North America. When Mennonite Brethren from Russia settled in the prairie states of the United States, 1874-80, they immediately felt the need of fellowship with one another and of a closer relationship among the several congregations. A way to effect such a union was early sought. On Sept. 28-30, 1878, eleven representative brethren from three Nebraska congregations and one in Kansas met near Henderson, Neb., to discuss matters of common concern. This meeting was, however, not fully representative of the M.B. churches and was later not recognized as an M.B. conference.

On Oct. 18-20, 1879, 22 delegates from M.B. churches in Kansas, Nebraska, Minnesota, and Dakota convened in the Henderson M.B. Church, organized and conducted the first M.B. Conference. The purpose in effecting this conference was to promote spiritual fellowship among the churches, to define and establish a united position on points of doctrine and practice, and to unite themselves for more effective mission effort and other activities.

From 1879 to 1909 this General Conference of the M.B. Church convened every fall, holding its meetings in one of the larger churches of the constituency. The conference Sunday was devoted to a mission festival; the evenings were used for evangelistic sermons or Bible addresses. During the conference a communion service was observed. The conference organized with a chairman, an assistant, and secretaries, and the required committees. Besides the delegates many visitors attended and the conference became an occasion for large gatherings. Beginning with 1883 the minutes and reports were printed in the form of an annual yearbook.

Home missions occupied an important place on the conference program and in its deliberations. The home mission work, as arranged for by the conference and directed by its Home Mission Committee, consisted in evangelistic meetings in all the churches as well as in neglected communities.

Beginning with 1884 the conference has published the *Zionsbote* as its church organ; in 1907 it transferred its publishing house, originally established at Medford, Okla., to McPherson, Kan. The Publishing House had been started as a private enterprise by J .F. Harms at Hillsboro, Kan. Later it was transferred to Medford, Okla., after which it was taken over as a conference-operated program and

moved to McPherson, Kan., for several years and from there back to Hillsboro, the present headquarters of the Mennonite Brethren Publishing House.

The need for a school of its own was expressed as early as 1883 and repeatedly mentioned in the following years. In 1898 a Conference Educational Committee was elected and a German Department School was opened in conjunction with McPherson College, McPherson, under the direction and instruction of J. F. Duerksen.

The desire to do foreign mission work was keenly felt in the conference from its beginning and financial support of missions with which the church was acquainted began in 1884. In 1889 the conference appointed a Foreign Missions Committee which was instructed to find a field among the American Indians· and suitable mission workers. This came to fruition in 1894, when Heinrich Kohfeld opened the first M.B. mission among the Comanche Indians in southern Oklahoma.

The conference has had many devout and efficient leaders, devoted and successful evangelists, and many other useful workers. The most outstanding conference leaders in early years were Abraham Schellenberg, Johann J. Regier, Cornelius Wedel, Heinrich Voth, Johann Foth, John F. Harms, David Dyck.

To care for the mission work opened in India in 1899, the conference was incorporated under the state laws of Kansas in 1900. In order to include all conference activities and to do all the work more efficiently, the conference adopted a constitution in 1908.

The conference has adhered to the doctrinal position held by the Mennonite Brethren in Russia, and in 1902 formally adopted the *Glaubensbekenntnis der Vereinigten Christlichen Taufgesinnten Mennoniten Brüdergemeinden in Russland* of 1902.

By 1909 the constituency of the M.B. Conference had spread over a large area in the United States and extended into Canada. Since it now became too difficult and too expensive for the conference to convene annually and have a fair representation of delegates from all the churches, it was divided into district conferences, each of which would hold an annual conference, do its own home mission work, and regulate the affairs of its churches. The M.B. General Conference has since 1909 met only once every three years to provide for the activities that concern the entire church. The four district conferences are (1) the Canadian, formerly known as the northern, comprising all the M.B. churches in Canada; (2) the central, including those in Minnesota, Michigan, Nebraska, South Dakota, North Dakota, and Montana; (3) the southern, representing those in Kansas, Oklahoma, Colorado, and Texas; (4) the Pacific, comprising those in California, Oregon, and Washington. The M.B. General Conference through its respective boards submits reports of its activities to the district conferences. In 1948 the conference of M.B. churches in Paraguay and Brazil was received into the General Conference as a district conference.

Foreign missions have since 1909 had an important place in conference activities, have received the wholehearted support of the constituency, and have a record of continuous expansion and growth. In addition to the mission to the Comanche Indians and the one in southern India, the conference has taken over fields in South China, West China, the Belgian Congo, Paraguay, Brazil, Colombia, Japan, Mexico, Ecuador, and Europe with responsibility for some 6,000,000 souls. Since the beginning of its foreign missions enterprise the Conference has sent out 228 missionaries, of whom 152 are still in active service. In early years as well as in more recent times, the conference has done mission work among Russians in Canada and in North Dakota. This is now done by the district conference.

The conference has expanded its publication efforts and in 1913 erected in Hillsboro, Kan., its present publishing house. Two periodicals, the *Zionsbote* in German and the *Christian Leader* in English, are being published as well as much material for Sunday schools.

A city mission under the direction of the Conference City Mission Committee was begun in Minneapolis, Minn., 1910, and among the Jews in Winnipeg, Man., in 1948. All city mission work except the above-named stations is now being done through the boards of the several district conferences which operate under the General Conference. This city mission work is now quite extensive.

A realization of the need for higher education and of training workers for the churches and mission constantly increased in the conference and in 1933 it took over Tabor College, Hillsboro, as a conference school, and has since operated this institution by its educational board.

With the aftereffects of the two world wars the need for extensive relief arose, and the conference has through its General Welfare and Public Relations Committee endeavored to do its share in alleviating the suffering as well as in the rehabilitation of displaced Mennonites and other suffering people, working through the MCC.

Among the leaders who have rendered valuable service are Abraham Schellenberg, Sr., Heinrich Voth, J. F. Harms, M. M. Just, N. N. Hiebert, A. L. Schellenberg, H. W. Lohrenz, H. S. Voth, P. C. Hiebert, A. E. Janzen, P. H. Berg, P. R. Lange, H. D. Wiebe, B. B. Janz, A. H. Unruh, and B. J. Braun.

At the 1936 conference a thorough revision of the constitution was accepted. Its new provisions covered all phases of conference work. The Committee of Reference and Counsel has the general oversight of the church and takes care of its spiritual welfare; the Board of Trustees holds in custody and manages the property and funds; the boards for foreign mission, city missions, publication, education, general welfare and public relations, Sunday school, youth, execute the work entrusted to them. The conference continues to grow and to increase its activities. At recent sessions churches have been represented by over 360 delegates and by many more visitors. (Yearbooks of the General Conference of the M.B. Church of North America, 1879-1951.)   J.H.L.

Conference of Pacifist Churches. At the close of World War I the Friends initiated a movement that

44

came to be known as the Conference of Pacifist Churches. The first meeting was held in Bluffton, Ohio, in August 1922, and was attended by a total of 95 Brethren, Friends, Mennonites, and others from 16 states, Canada, and England.

The second conference was held at Juniata College (Pa.) in December 1923; the third at Carlock, Ill., in 1926; the fourth in North Manchester, Ind., in 1927; and the last one at Mt. Morris, Ill., in March 1931. At the last conference H. P. Krehbiel (*q.v.*) stressed the differences between social and political pacifism as contrasted with New Testament pacifism. Krehbiel was appointed a Committee of One to arrange for the next meeting which convened in Newton, Kan., in October 1935 under the new name of the Conference of Historic Peace Churches. At this meeting a Continuation Committee (*q.v.*) was appointed, which has called meetings of the Historic Peace Churches at irregular intervals since that date. (M. Gingerich, *Service for Peace*, Akron, Pa., 1949, 25-31.)   M.G.

Conference of the Mennonites of East and West Prussia (*Konferenz der ost- und westpreussischen Mennonitengemeinden*). Soon after the immigration of Dutch Mennonites into the Vistula and Nogat region and of High Germans into the Culm swamps, we hear of meetings of the churches. At first the two branches, the Frisian and Flemish, held their meetings separately. About 1586 a closer union was formed among the five Frisian churches, and several years later they invited the High Germans to join this association. In bringing this about, Lubbert Gerritsz (*q.v.*) of Holland deserves much credit. With Hans de Ries he composed the confession of faith of 1581, of the united Flemish, Frisian, and High German groups. It remained in use for over three hundred years, until in 1895 a committee of four elders worked out a new one which replaced it.

In their negotiations with secular and church authorities for their hard-won privileges, the Frisians and Flemish co-operated. One of the successful spokesmen in the negotiations of 1640 was Hans Siemens, who had in 1639 been ordained as elder of the Flemish church in the Grossen Werder. The documents of the "privileges" were preserved by the Frisian churches.

Meetings were held when necessary in the homes of members. About 1740 it was customary to have the "brethren in service" of each congregation meet every Thursday. The Flemish churches decided in 1737 and 1740 to give special instruction to the young people who would want to join the church in two or three years.

Other matters of conference concern were the "prevalence of showy dress," suing at law, and especially what to do about young men who were forcibly taken as soldiers by the "Brandenburgs." In 1767 the first German hymnals were published. Through visiting preachers active communication was established between the churches. In 1778 the catechism drawn up by the elders Heinrich Donner and Gerhard Wiebe was adopted by both branches and printed. In 1785 a conference passed a resolution to apply church discipline against members who were guilty of open sin.

When Frederick the Great, after the first division of Poland, took over West Prussia without Danzig and Thorn, the collective churches decided to present him with a gift at the ceremony of homage at Marienburg on Sept. 22, 1772, and present a petition for free exercise of religion and exemption from conscription. A state regulation was passed requiring the Mennonites to pay an annual sum of 5,000 talers for the support of the military school at Culm in return for these privileges. The amount of this fee to be paid by each congregation was decided at the beginning of each year, and later every six years. In 1775 the conference sent Elder Heinrich Donner and Peter Regier, a preacher, to Berlin with a petition for recognition of the privileges they had been receiving from the Polish government, and for exemption from the fees demanded at some places by the established churches. On April 18, 1780, the *Gnadenprivilegium* of March 29, 1780, was received in Marienwerder.

On Sept. 19, 1786, Heinrich Donner (elder at Orlofferfelde) and Cornelius Warkentin (minister in Rosenort) were sent as delegates to the celebration of homage (Frederick William II) in Königsberg, in order to share in the "king's protection." In 1787 these two men were sent as delegates to Berlin on account of secret machinations against the Mennonites by the "Lutherans." They received a confirmation of the Privilegium, but with further restrictions on the acquisition of land. In consequence the emigration to Russia began in 1788, and received further impetus by the severe restrictions of the edict of July 30, 1789. The great number of meetings held indicates the natural excitement. They presented a petition complaining, "In the country which our ancestors with great difficulty and expense wrested from the sea, we have become strangers and many of us have had to leave the country with tears." Four delegates sent to Berlin received the concession on Nov. 24, 1803, which at least guaranteed to them for the future the land they then possessed.

On Oct. 28, 1806, the conference decided to send the king a gift of 30,000 talers as a "voluntary patriotic contribution" for the support of widows and orphans of soldiers. In 1811, the 10,000 talers loaned to the state in the previous year were given as an outright gift to the king.

Early in March 1813 six delegates were sent to Königsberg to negotiate for exemption from military service. The sum of 187,439 florins required in return was allocated among the churches. A petition sent to the king on Aug. 11 released the Mennonites from participation in the reserve army by an order of cabinet dated Aug. 25, 1813.

On Sept. 22, 1814, an earnest attempt was made to have church discipline enforced. In this year it was also decided to leave to each congregation the matter of joining the Bible Society. This step resulted in religious movements which were expressed in mission work, temperance, etc.

In 1820 and the following years the Mennonites were threatened with the loss of their leased land if they refused military service. But when a petition to the king made it clear that the land in question had been in Mennonite possession for centuries and that the ancestors of the present residents had cleared it for cultivation, the contracts were renewed to 1845 and then to 1865. In the meantime a change in the laws converted this leased land into Mennonite property.

The conference held at Schönsee on Oct. 26, 1834, was occupied with mutual encouragement in the service of the church. The conference maintained active contact with the colonies in Russia, and in 1838 sent 2,000 hymnals to the Molotschna colony.

On July 29, 1859, an important resolution was passed by the conference, eliminating the distinction between Frisian and Flemish. In 1861 special services were held to commemorate the tercentennial of the death of Menno Simons. Jakob Mannhardt of Danzig wrote a booklet for the occasion.

After 1848 the conference was again compelled to take steps to preserve military exemption. On Feb. 12, 1849, a deputation was sent to Berlin. In April a petition was sent to the government for release from jury service; this was refused, and the Mennonites yielded. On Jan. 13, 1862, the conference sent a petition to both houses of the Landtag with 2,047 signatures. The three deputies who presented it in Berlin were received by the king and the cabinet. In 1866 the sum assessed for the cadet school was trebled and used for the wounded. On Oct. 23, 1867, a deputation of five elders was chosen, which was received by the cabinet, the king, and the crown prince. Thereupon the cabinet order of March 3, 1868, was passed, permitting the Mennonites to serve without bearing arms.

Since 1879 records have been kept of the meetings of church officers. A common treasury was opened, and a committee of six elders chosen as the executive organ. The annual meeting was held on the second Thursday after Pentecost, other meetings being called as needed. At these meetings the elders, preachers, deacons, and chairmen of the church boards took part as representatives of the churches. The churches entertained the conference in rotation, with the elder of the local church serving as moderator. Business considered covered all questions of doctrine, church life, communication with other churches, and contact with government authorities.

The conference often collected funds for needy Mennonites; in 1801 for the church at Neuwied which had suffered from war, in 1883 and 1885 for the victims of floods, in 1885 for the church at Neudorferhof, in 1889 for the church which had burned down at Obernessau, in 1892 for need in Saratov.

The conference also supported foreign missions. In 1883 it was decided to send Nikolai Wiebe of Russia to the Barmen mission school. When he returned from the mission field in 1901 he was appointed traveling preacher, serving until his death in 1924. The conference provided for the pastoral care of Obernessau after 1914. In 1884 the fund for foreign missions was established. In 1913 a sum of 9,878 marks was raised as a national gift for missions in the German colonies.

In 1898 the conference issued a book of chorales as a supplement to the hymnal of 1869; in 1935 it was revised. In 1900 the conference decided to publish a collection of sermons; it appeared in two parts, in 1906 and 1909 respectively. In 1927 the conference began to make a small annual contribution for the support of the *Mennonitische Blätter,* and granted funds to students of theology from the churches of East and West Prussia.

In 1892, on the occasion of the celebration of the fourth centennial of the birth of Menno Simons, a *Festschrift* by H. G. Mannhardt was published. On Jan. 25, 1925, the fourth centennial of the church was celebrated at a meeting held at Heubuden on June 4, 1925.

At the suggestion of Pastor E. Göttner of Danzig the first general West-Prussian Mennonite conference, including the public, was held on Aug. 25, 1929. At these annual sessions, the feeling of brotherhood was strengthened by talks, sermons, addresses, congregational singing and choral groups; all members participated. An outcome of this general conference was the initiation of young people's work by the conference. On Oct. 25, 1932, the first *Jugendtag* of the district was held in Steegen. This youth conference also became an annual institution of East German Mennonitism.

In 1901, after an address by Mannhardt, the conference decided to exclude members who swore an oath. In 1903 it was decided to refuse to marry a divorced person; but after careful investigation the innocent party might under certain circumstances remarry. In 1914 the consecration of infants was discussed, and the decision was reached that in each case the parents should decide whether the child was to be presented in the church, though without ceremony. After the change in the state constitution in 1920 it was decided to retain the affirmation formula in place of the oath.

In the matter of the payment of taxes for the support of the established (state) church, the conference in 1924 appointed a "committee for questions of church law." Later the conference assumed the expense of two legal decisions, which canceled the obligation of Mennonites to pay taxes for the support of the Protestant church. In 1920 Mannhardt described the dire need of the Mennonite refugees from Russia, whereupon measures were undertaken to aid them. To discuss this problem a Mennonite world conference was held in Danzig from Aug. 29 to Sept. 2, 1930, which was supported by the conference of West Prussia.

The last regular session of the conference was held June 6, 1939. Special sessions were held later as follows: Oct. 6, 1939; Jan. 17, 1940; Feb. 21, 1940. There no doubt were special sessions during the war that followed, but the official minutes which have been preserved, covering the annual and special sessions beginning July 7, 1879 (also Oct. 26, 1834), contain nothing after Feb. 21, 1940.

This conference, often called the Kalthof Conference, because in later years it frequently met at Kalthof near Heubuden-Marienburg, was actually a conference of ordained men, who are always referred to in German as a group by the term *Lehrdienst,* and the conference is frequently called *Lehrdienstversammlung.* Within the conference the executive committee was a group of five elders, called *Aeltestenausschuss.* The official sessions were limited to the *Lehrdienst,* whereas the "conferences" of 1929 and later were popular inspirational meetings with mass attendance.

The destruction of the entire East and West Prussian settlements in 1945 and the survival of 7,000-8,000 refugees from these settlements in Western Germany, led to the reorganization of the conference (*Lehrdienstversammlung*) as a West German body. The first meeting was held at Hamburg, March 6-8, 1948.

This organization, although autonomous, is closely related to the *Vereinigung der Mennoniten-Gemeinden im . . .* (*q.v.*). Except for the city congregations of Danzig and Elbing and a few in the country, the West Prussian congregations had not joined the *Vereinigung* until its reorganization in 1934. (*ML* II, 530-32.)   A.D., H.S.B.

Conference of the Mennonites of South Germany (*Konferenz der Süddeutschen Mennoniten*). At the meeting of the Palatine and Hessian Conference at Eppstein, May 27, 1886, at the suggestion of J. J. Krehbiel, the initial step was taken to hold a joint conference with the *Badischer Verband* brethren. The idea fell on fertile soil. At the first experimental meeting on Feb. 17, 1887, at Ludwigshafen, attendance was meager. J. Ellenberger II of Friedelsheim, and J. Hege of Reihen, gave the introductory addresses on the "Blessing of Unity." With S. Blickensdörfer of Sembach as moderator, the matter of publication and of entry into the Union (*Vereinigung*) of the Mennonite Churches in Germany was briefly discussed, but no action taken. On Nov. 16 of the same year a second meeting took place at Ludwigshafen, at which the latter question was thoroughly discussed. Although no conclusion was reached, the conference itself was now on a solid footing with the name, "Conference of the Baden and Palatine Mennonites" (*Konferenz badisch-pfälzischer Mennoniten*).

On Nov. 14, 1888, about 60 brethren attended the third conference held at Ludwigshafen, at which the plan was made to discuss the fundamentals and principles of the brotherhood in successive meetings with a fraternal exchange of opinion. The first of these topics was church discipline. Three addresses were heard on the subject. In principle there was unity, but in the method of application opinions differed.

It was therefore fortunate that the topic chosen for the next session was "Past and Present," which, discussed by Christian Hege of Breitenau, established a neutral ground. Gradually the character of the conference developed. A Biblical devotional address opens the meeting. Then the topics under consideration are discussed. At first they dealt with fundamental Mennonite doctrines: the oath, on Nov. 17, 1891, by Philipp Kieferndorf (published in expanded form in 1893); baptism at three conferences, 1893-95, by Christian Hege of

Breitenau and Christian Neff of Weierhof; nonresistance in 1901 and communion in 1902, both by Neff.

On Nov. 11, 1890, it was decided upon a suggestion made by J. Ellenberger II of Friedelsheim to publish a yearbook, which has appeared regularly since 1892 (except 1942-50) called *Christlicher Gemeindekalender*, since 1951 called *Mennonitischer Gemeinde-Kalender*. A *Kalenderkommission,* a committee of six, was appointed to assist the editor, three from each of the two groups (Palatinate and Baden), later with additional members from outside the conference.

In 1906 (Nov. 28) the publication of a new hymnal was discussed and assigned to a committee consisting of six members from each of the two groups. The hymnal was published in 1910. It met universal approval and came into use in all the churches of South Germany. In 1950 a new and slightly revised edition was published. Since World War II it is the only Mennonite hymnal available in Germany. It is being increasingly adopted and used outside the conference (Neuwied 1952, Hamburg-Altona 1953, refugee congregations 1952-53).

After an address by Jakob Latscha of Frankfurt on the instruction of youth (Nov. 23, 1899), the care of the soldiers (*Soldatenfürsorge*) was taken into the program of work and a committee was appointed which, headed by Christian Hege of Frankfurt, rendered a great service, especially during World War I. When universal military service was abolished after the war, the work of the Soldiers' Committee was ended. It was replaced by the Youth Committee (*Jugendkommission:* see **Youth Work**), which is now composed of 11 members (originally 9). From 1920 to 1939 the Y.C. published *Mennonitische Jugendwarte* (*q.v.*) and since 1948 *Junge Gemeinde* (*q.v.*).

On Nov. 26, 1902, Christian Neff proposed giving the conference a firmer form and a broader basis by naming it the Conference of the South German Mennonites (*Konferenz der Süddeutschen Mennoniten*). An invitation was sent to all the South German churches to join by the payment of a small annual fee. Eight churches at first refused, but later joined. From 1903 to 1920 annual reports were published as booklets containing the addresses and committee reports; thereafter the minutes appeared in the two German Mennonite papers. The report for 1911 lists the members—1,203 names—alphabetically. Also the publication of pamphlets was considered, of which three were published: *Was sind Mennoniten?; Mennoniten keine Wiedertäufer;* and *Mennoniten keine Baptisten und Methodisten.* In 1925 the conference published a book, *Gedenkschrift zum 400-jährigen Jubiläum,* and the pamphlet, *Seid Eurer Väter wert,* and in 1948 *Botschaft und Nachfolge.*

On Nov. 28, 1911, it was decided to incorporate. A committee of 24 members was appointed to work out a constitution, adopted on Feb. 19, 1912.

In 1911 an attempt was made to appoint a visiting minister (*Reiseprediger*), but failed. But on May 29, 1912, E. Händiges was appointed as first visiting minister and was ordained to the ministry at the conference at Ludwigshafen on Nov. 20,

1912. Later Christian Guth was called to this office.

A branch conference was called into being in Bavaria and held its first session on March 8, 1914, at Regensburg.

In 1914 religious services were also begun in Darmstadt under the sponsorship of the conference, which from 1932 to 1936 were held alternately at Frankfurt and Darmstadt, then alone in Frankfurt until an independent congregation was organized there in 1948.

The outbreak of World War I created unusually great tasks for the conference. The first obligation, besides the work of the Soldiers' Committee (to send letters and packages to the soldiers in service), was to provide for the needs of members in regions damaged by the war, in Alsace-Lorraine, East Prussia, and Galicia. A call for relief gifts was issued and brought a generous response. E. Händiges and G. van der Smissen were sent to visit the severely suffering brethren in Alsace-Lorraine. A second visit, planned for Christian Neff and E. Händiges, was not permitted by the authorities.

On the other hand, the authorities were very accommodating on the visit of E. Händiges made on Sept. 16 and Oct. 15, 1915, to the Russian Mennonite men held as prisoners of war at Bütow (Westphalia). On this trip Händiges also visited the churches in West Prussia. He visited Bütow again on Jan. 10 and 11, 1917.

Since Händiges took over the pastorate at Ibersheim in 1918, his place was taken by Abraham Warkentin (July 30, 1920), who was ordained on Nov. 21, 1920, at Ludwigshafen. One of the main tasks falling upon him was the care of Russian Mennonite refugees, whom he sought out in the various camps, gave pastoral care, and supported with donations. This work developed into the "Mennonite Refugee Succor" (*Mennonitische Flüchtlingsfürsorge*), which was organized on the occasion of one of the conferences at Ludwigshafen (1920) and soon, under the new name *Deutsche Mennonitenhilfe* (*q.v.*), did a great work in the Lechfeld (*q.v.*) camp. At the close of the war, when the blockade created an acute shortage of food in Germany, many parcels of food and gifts of money were sent from America, which were distributed in the German cities through the *DMH*.

After the collapse of Germany there was rebuilding to do. At the conference which met at Heilbronn (for the first time) on Nov. 28, 1919, because the Palatinate was occupied territory and insurmountable difficulties prevented a meeting at Ludwigshafen, a program was set up for the future. Christian Guth (d. 1952) served as itinerant pastor (*Reiseprediger*) of the conference 1923-48.

Many efforts were made by the conference to obtain a much closer contact with the brotherhood in West Prussia as well as in other countries of Europe and abroad. After years of mutual visits and exchange of letters the conference had the courage to make an appeal for a world-wide conference of the brotherhood to be called in commemoration of the 400th anniversary of the founding of the Mennonite Church (1925). This became the first Mennonite World Conference.

A painful loss resulted from the compulsory withdrawal of the brethren from Alsace-Lorraine. Before the war (1912) the conference committee had been enlarged by the addition of two delegates from Alsace-Lorraine.

Besides its interest in home missions the conference also has helped to support the Dutch Mennonite missions in Java and Sumatra. Visits of missionaries at the conference sessions roused and sustained this interest; some of these missionaries were Hübert (1908 and 1909), Wiebe (1905 and 1906), Johannes Fast (1911); others living in Germany were P. Löwen of Würzburg, and Johannes Klaassen of Heilbronn. The first missionary trained and sent out by the Mennonites of South Germany was Hermann Schmitt of Deutschhof. On Oct. 24, 1926, he and his wife Helene Klaassen were ordained as missionaries near Bergzabern. At the end of 1934 Otto Stauffer of Obersülzen (Palatinate) and his wife Martha Klaassen were sent out. Both men lost their lives in the torpedoing of a British vessel evacuating them as internees from Java to India in 1942. In 1951 Liesel Hege of Ibersheim was sent to Java as a missionary nurse.

The great and chief leader of the conference was undoubtedly Christian Neff (*q.v.*). He led it from small beginnings into much broader and more active areas, in which he himself was the most energetic worker in all good things. From 1903 to his death in 1946 he was the chairman of the conference, successfully reconciling differences and building confidence. At present the conference is led by an executive committee of nine, with Abraham Braun of Ibersheim as chairman.

NEFF, P.S.

Chr. Neff, "50 Jahre Konferenz der Süddeutschen Mennoniten," *Gem.-Kal.* 1940, 74-82; *ML* II, 528-30.

Conference of the Mennonites of Switzerland *(Konferenz der altevangelischen Taufgesinnten-Gemeinden [Mennoniten] der Schweiz)*.

Representatives of the Swiss churches meet semiannually, at the end of March at Sonnenberg (Jura) and at the end of September at Langnau (Emmental). The conferences are usually attended by elders, preachers, and deacons for consultation and deliberation on church matters, with lay representatives participating as may be elected by the several congregations. The idea of the conference is based on old tradition. A letter of May 24, 1779, reveals that the preachers, deacons, and elders met annually on March 25 for a conference to discuss church affairs. A letter from "Biderichgraben, 2 stund hinder Biel in der schweitz," dated March 2, 1785, states that the "old customary conference" will be held on March 25. Not much is said in these letters about the business under consideration.

The task and purpose of the conference consisted not only of discussion of church affairs, but also in mutual admonition to faithfulness and love, as well as reproof in cases of unauthorized interference in church life, as when two preachers and their following were put out of church in 1835 in connection with the Samuel Fröhlich (*q.v.*) affair (see **Bern**).

A subject under lively discussion in the 1850's and 1870's was the annulment of military freedom for Mennonites, which led to negotiations with the cantonal government at Bern.

Since 1889 the proceedings have been carefully recorded. In that year the conference was occupied with thoughts of missions. A general fund was established and presented to the brotherhood in order to awaken a sense of missions through suitable addresses in the churches. Home missions also received increasing attention, and a missions committee was appointed to hold evangelistic meetings. The brethren were also commissioned to visit churches, families, and individuals.

Concerning internal questions of individual congregations the decision was made in 1890 that at least once a year a meeting of the brethren (*Brüderversammlung*) should be held, in which these matters could be discussed for the good of the congregation and the growth of the kingdom of God. Deacons were to report on the "poor fund" at these meetings, and delegates chosen to represent the congregation at the next general conference.

Regarding youth instruction the conference decided in 1892 to adopt the *Christliches Lehrbüchlein* of the Baden Mennonites. A Youth Commission (*Jugendkommission*) was established in 1935.

In 1898 the conference adopted a constitution and the name which appears at the head of this article. The question of incorporation was discussed. Since several congregations had recently built churches the question arose whether the congregations or conference should have the right of ownership. Autonomy again decided the issue, and it was left to each congregation to decide whether it wished to be incorporated. Only the school at Chaux d'Abel became the property of the conference.

In the course of time many a doctrinal question, such as baptism, communion, and church discipline, has been discussed. The devotional part of the conference usually consists of an introductory discussion of some Bible passage by the moderator and an instructive talk on some question of the day, usually a Biblical topic.

In 1920 the conference of the Swiss Mennonites joined the Federation of Free Churches in Switzerland (*Aarauer Verband*). (*ML* II, 527.)   S.G.

Conference of the Palatine and Hessian Mennonite Churches *(Konferenz der pfälzisch-hessischen Mennoniten-Gemeinden)*.

The momentum to organize this conference was given by W. H. Angas (*q.v.*), a Baptist preacher, after the plan of Johann Risser of Friedelsheim to call a "meeting of preachers and elders" at Pentecost in 1820 had failed to materialize. At the first session held at the Branchweilerhof (*q.v.*) on July 13, 1824, a resolution was passed to give some consideration to foreign missions on the first Sunday of each month and to put up an offering box in each church to collect funds for the missions of the English Baptists.

Successive conferences met at the Spitalhof (May 1825), Friedelsheim (Sept. 12, 1826), Weierhof (May 9, 1830), Sembach (Oct. 8, 1843; see *Gem.-Kal.*, 1918, 99-109), and Monsheim (June 2, 1844).

This last-named conference was very significant. The next two meetings, held respectively at Kühbörncheshof (May 10, 1852) and Eppstein (June 7, 1854), were called to consider particular matters. At the former it was decided to introduce a new ministers' manual or formulary (see **Formularies**), at the latter a new hymnal. There was now a lull in conference activities, until it was revived by a call issued by Ibersheim on Aug. 5, 1871.

On Feb. 20, 1872, a meeting was held at Monsheim, and on Oct. 29, 1872, at Sembach. The question under consideration was a proposed union of the South German churches with those of Northwest Germany; it was negatively decided at the next session meeting at Friedelsheim (May 28, 1874). Eleven years later the Palatine and Hessian brethren, in conference at Ernstweiler (May 28, 1885), declared themselves ready to join the Union of Mennonite Churches in Germany (*Vereinigung*).

Another significant decision was that passed at Monsheim on May 27, 1880, to establish a central relief fund. After the organization of the *Vereinigung* this fund involved only the Palatinate and Rheinhessen. At the conference held at Eppstein on May 27, 1886, this fund was named the *Mennonitische Hilfskasse*. Here it was also decided to plan a conference with the brethren of Baden, which led to the formation of the Conference of the Mennonites of South Germany (*q.v.*).

From the beginning the conference has been a brotherly association of the Mennonite congregations in the Palatinate and Rheinhessen (except the Deutschhof and Branchweilerhof congregations which belong to the *Badischer Verband, q.v.*) for the purpose of fellowship and the ordering of problems of common concern as they may arise. It has no separate program of work, since these matters are handled by the Conference of South German Churches to which all belong. Its chief expression has been the spring conference, which met annually for more than a century in rotation in the various congregations, but since World War II meets in the central cities of the Palatinate on account of the increasingly large attendance. The program of these conferences consists of sermons and Bible expositions, inspirational, informational, and practical addresses, and necessary business and reports. The conference is managed by a committee composed of representatives of all the congregations.

Subsidiary to the P.-H. conference is a "conference of preachers and congregational lay leaders," which meets usually annually in January largely to consider general and business matters. The preachers meet every two to three months for fellowship and counsel in a "preachers' conference." NEFF.

Chr. Neff, "Aus der Geschichte der Pfälzisch-Hessischen Konferenz," *Gem.-Kal.*, 1935, 85-101; 1936, 103-17; 1937, 95-102; *ML* II, 528.

Conference on Mennonite Cultural Problems met annually 1942-47 (Winona Lake, Ind.; Goshen, Ind.; North Newton, Kan.; Bluffton, Ohio; Freeman, S.D.; Hillsboro, Kan.), and since then biennially (Hillsboro, 1949; Grantham, Pa., 1951; Hesston, Kan., 1953), changing its name in 1951 to "Conference on Mennonite Educational and Cultural Problems." After its first session, which had been sponsored by a Conference on Mennonite Sociology which met at Chicago, Ill., Dec. 31, 1941, it was taken under the wing of the Council of Mennonite and Affiliated Colleges (*q.v.*), which regularly appoints the program committee, composed of representatives of the Mennonite colleges, and underwrites the cost of printing the *Proceedings* of each conference in book form. The conference is unofficial and open to the general public; its range of interest includes Mennonite sociology, ethics, education, community interests, and other topics relating to the total life of the Mennonite brotherhood. The sessions have attracted primarily faculty members of the participating colleges, public school teachers, ministers, and a scattering of laymen. The proceedings of the conferences are available from J. W. Fretz, North Newton, Kan., who has served as the secretary continuously from the beginning of the organization. Perhaps its most important achievements have been the creative writing it has stimulated, the research it has encouraged, and the body of information on the cultural life of Mennonites it has produced. It is the only officially sponsored American inter-Mennonite group that meets regularly for intellectual fellowship and discussion. The Mennonite Research Fellowship (*q.v.*) usually meets in connection with the conference.   H.S.B.

Conferences in Russia. The Mennonites who emigrated to Russia from Prussia (1788-1840) took with them their church institutions and customs. Though fully preserving the autonomy of the individual congregation, the leaders of the churches occasionally met for consultation and discussion. These meetings were called the "Council of the Elders" or *Aeltestenkonvent*, and later "Church Convention" or *Kirchenkonvent*. Klaus writes on this subject: "A meeting of the church elders of the Molotschna Mennonites decided on April 7, 1851, by majority vote, in the future to call itself a *Kirchenkonvent* (*q.v.*) with the provision that all controversy arising in the district concerning church matters and regulations should be presented to it for final consideration and decision."

Corresponding to the two settlements, Molotschna and Chortitza, there were organized a *Chortitzaer Mennonitischer Kirchenkonvent*, and a *Molotschnaer Mennonitischer Kirchenkonvent*. For a long time apparently only the elders voted, while preachers and deacons were advisory members of the conferences. Thus we find that the petitions presented to the civil authorities in the 1850's and 1860's were signed only by the elders.

The conference had no binding authority over the congregations, but rather its resolutions were considered suggestions to the congregations, and became authoritative only after adoption by the brotherhood of the local congregation; they could of course also be rejected by the brotherhood.

The increase of the Mennonite population in Russia, which led to the establishment of daughter colonies, created a need for a more closely knit relationship, and so the Mennonite Church congregations in 1883 formed a Federal Conference

(*Bundeskonferenz,* see **Allgemeine Bundeskonfe- renz der Mennonitengemeinden in Russland**). This conference met annually, and consisted of the elders and preachers of the congregations. At each session a moderator (usually an elder), an assistant moderator, and several secretaries were elected. It was the duty of the moderator to attend to business affairs of the conference, report to the conference the resolutions of the congregations, represent the churches to the civil authorities, prepare the agenda for the next conference, issue the call, and open it.

The Mennonite Brethren (*q.v., Mennoniten- Brüdergemeinde*) congregations of the Molotschna, Chortitza, and Kuban, which were organized in the 1860's, united in 1872 to form a federated con- gregation (*Mennoniten - Brüder - Bundesgemeinde*). This conference also met annually, and was com- posed of delegates from the individual congrega- tions. The autonomy of the congregation was pre- served here too. The organization was similar to that of the *Bundeskonferenz*. Both conferences con- sidered it their primary task to elevate and promote Christian living in the churches.

On Oct. 26-28, 1910, the General Mennonite Fed- eral Conference (*Allgemeine Mennonitische Bun- deskonferenz*) included for the first time also the *Mennoniten-Brüder-Bundesgemeinde,* and the *Mo- lotschnaer Evangelische Mennoniten Brüderschaft,* the last-named in union with the *Altonauer Evan- gelische Mennonitengemeinde* at Zagradovka. The General Conference thus now represented all the Mennonites of Russia. It met every three years, and was attended by delegates of the component con- ferences or congregations. The chief objective of the Conference was to protect the privileges once granted to the Mennonites, to preserve religious liberty and the autonomy of the churches, and to promote and establish the churches spiritually.

In 1909 the church conventions of the Molotschna and Chortitza in joint session at Schönwiese had appointed a "Committee on Faith" (*Glaubens- kommission*), consisting of three members, to take care of church relations with the state. This com- mittee was reappointed in 1910, and was later called the "Committee for Church Matters" (*Kom- mission für kirchliche Angelegenheiten, KfK q.v.*) and a lawyer was added to it as an advisory member. (*ML* II, 533.)

The General Federal Conference met for the last time at Moscow in 1926.   A.B.

Confession de Foi Chrétienne *des Chrétiens sans défense connus surtout dans les Pais-bas sous le nom de Mennonites* (Confession of Christian Faith of the Nonresistant Christians, who Especially in the Netherlands Are Known as Mennonites) is a booklet of 142 pages, published 1771 (n.p.), con- taining Preface, Confession (Dordrecht Confession, translated from a German edition of 1711), certifi- cate of a number of Alsatian brethren, 18 prayers, 7 hymns, all by Leonhard (Leenaerdt) Clock (*q.v.*), and a sermon on I Cor. 15:55-57, preached on the Sunday after Easter 1753 in the Mennonite church of Altona (*q.v.*) by the youngest preacher of that congregation (presumably it was Jan de Jager). This is the French edition of the Dordrecht Con-

fession of 1632. It was reprinted at Nancy in 1862. An earlier reputed edition of 1660 could not be verified.   **vdZ.**

Confession de Foy, Brieve, *touchant les principaus points de la doctrine chrestienne, enseignée et pra- tiquée par les Chrestiens, qu' on nomme communé- ment les Frisons et Alemans associés,* is a French translation from the Dutch, published in 1684 (n.p.), of the Jan Cents Confession of 1630. vdZ.

Confessions of Faith. The Christian Church early felt the need of establishing clearly and definitely the content of its faith and exactly delimiting it; this led to the formulation of confessions of faith or creeds. The three oldest are the ecumenical symbols: the *Apostles' Creed* (*q.v.*), the *Niceno- Constantinopolitan Creed,* so called because it was the result of two great general councils at Nicea (325) and at Constantinople (381), and the *Chalce- donian Creed,* adopted at the Council of Chalcedon (451). They are called ecumenical because they were and are today accepted by the whole Christian Church, East and West, as the most significant product of the doctrinal teaching of the early church. However, these creeds do not cover the entire range of Christian doctrine but only the points under dispute at that time.

In the Roman Catholic Church the *Confession of Trent* or the *Tridentinum,* which contains the doc- trinal resolutions of the Council of Trent from Dec. 13, 1545, to Dec. 4, 1556, is considered the final and authoritative norm of the faith of the church. The chief creed of the Greek Orthodox Church is the *Confessio Orthodoxa,* compiled at the instigation of Petrus Mogilas, metropolite at Kiev, printed in Amsterdam in 1662, and adopted by Peter the Great into the liturgy of the church.

In the Lutheran Church the *Confessio Augustana* or *Augsburg Confession* of 1530 (*q.v.*) is the "really decisive and in any case the most important con- fession." In addition, mention must be made of the *Formula of Concord,* published in 1580, which was to put an end to all doctrinal disputes. The most important confessions of the Reformed church are the *Basel Confession* of Jan. 21, 1534; the *Con- fessio Gallicana* of 1559, of the French Reformed Church; the *Confessio Belgica* of 1561, of the Dutch Reformed Church; the *Confessio Helvetica* of 1566, compiled by Bullinger, and recognized in Switzer- land and in the Palatinate; the *Confessio Fidei* of 1647, of the Scotch church; the *Hungarian Con- fession* of 1558, still valid with the Reformed of Hungary, and the *Westminster Confession* of 1648, which is the English and American Presbyterian creed.

The Anabaptists never attached the weight to creeds or confessions given to them by the re- mainder of Christendom; they were Biblicists who produced a large number of confessions, not as instruments to which the laity or ministry sub- scribed *ex anima,* but as instructional tools for the indoctrination of their young people and as wit- nesses to their faith for distribution in society or as a means of better understanding between differ- ing groups. Hans de Ries (1553-1638), one of the outstanding early Dutch Mennonite leaders, wrote in 1626 (*Apologia*, quoted in van der Zijpp's *Geschiedenis*, 1952, 89): "The confession is simply a short statement of what we believe we find in God's Word in contradistinction from others who also claim to hold to the Scriptures. And shall we be bound by it? We say no, it is subject to improvement." Van der Zijpp adds: "The main concern in the confessions was to learn to know one another. One did not write what had to be believed, but what was believed in the particular group." We read constantly also that the confessions were emphatically "subject to the Word of God."

The oldest Anabaptist confession is the *Seven Articles* of Schleitheim (*Brüderlich Vereinigung*, *q.v.*) of Feb. 4, 1527, compiled by Michael Sattler (*q.v.*). This is, however, not a true creed but rather an agreement on the doctrines, usages, and regulations peculiar to the Anabaptists. That which they held in common with the rest of Christendom is taken for granted and not discussed at all. The seven articles treat of baptism, excommunication, Lord's Supper, separation from the world, the church, nonresistance, and the oath. (Text in English translation in Wenger, *The Doctrines of the Mennonites*, Scottdale, 1950.)

The seven articles of Jakob Kautz (*q.v.*), which he fastened on the door of the Predigerkirche at Worms, June 9, 1527 (Chr. Hege, *Die Täufer in der Kurpfalz*, 34-37), are merely a personal confession and have no further significance. The eight *Nikolsburg Articles* (*q.v.*), which were printed in various versions in 1527 and 1528 and also as *Artikel der Augsburger neuen Christen*, and were often attributed to the Anabaptists, have now been proved by Wilhelm Wiswedel to be a forgery prepared by their enemies and falsely attributed to them.

Many confessions of individual (sometimes of groups) Anabaptists are found in the records of their trials; they afford a very important insight into the faith of the Anabaptists. (See the records in the *Martyrs' Mirror*; Müller, *Berner Täufer*, 42 f.; C. A. Cornelius, *Gesch. des Münsterischen Aufruhrs*; F. Roth, *Augsburgs Ref.-Gesch.*, and the recent publications of the *Täuferakten*, *q.v.*) The confession of the Anabaptists imprisoned at Marburg, of Dec. 10, 1538, by Peter Tesch, *Glaubensbekenntnis der in Marburg gefangenen Wiedertäufer* (printed in *Urkundliche Quellen zur hessischen Ref.-Gesch.*, IV. Band, *Wiedertäuferakten 1527-1626*, Marburg, 1951, 247-56), is worthy of note, because it throws light on the peculiar religious position of the Hessian Anabaptists. See also *Verantwortung und Widerlegung der Artikel, so jetzund im Land zu Hessen über die armen Davider (die man Wiedertäufer nennt) ausgegangen sind* (*ibid.*, 165-80). More important is *Das Bekenntnis der Schweizer Brüder in Hessen* (*ibid.*, 404-40) of 1578, published in English in the *MQR* XXIII (1949) 22-34 under the title *Confession of the Swiss Brethren in Hesse*.

Thomas von Imbroich's (d. 1558 at Cologne) *Confessio, Ein schöne bekanntnus eines frommen*

und Gottliebenden Christen of 88 pages (first ed. *ca.* 1560, later published 1702, 1742, and 1745 in *Güldene Aepfel in silbern Schalen*, Dutch ed. 1579, reprinted in the *Martyrs' Mirror* in 1660 and following editions), though a very influential book is not actually a full-fledged confession of faith, nor cast in the form of a confession, but a theological treatise mostly on baptism.

Pilgram Marpeck's *Rechenschaft meines Glaubens*, submitted to the Strasbourg Council in 1532, first published in *MQR* XXII (1938) 167-202, though more comprehensive, is likewise not a true confession but a defense of his faith.

The religious disputations (*q.v.*), such as were held at Zofingen (*q.v.*) in 1532, at Bern (*q.v.*) in 1538, at Frankenthal (*q.v.*) in 1571, at Emden (*q.v.*) in 1578, and Leeuwarden (*q.v.*) in 1596, the records of which were published in book form (except Bern, 1538), offer valuable testimony on the confessional position of the Anabaptists, but the records are not in themselves formulated confessions.

The *Abred* (Agreement) of the South German and Swiss preachers and elders at the various conferences, as at Strasbourg in 1568 (Müller, *Berner Täufer*, 50, and printed in *MQR* I, 1927, 57-68), the Amish discipline of 1779 (*MQR* XI, 1937), and the resolutions of the other Anabaptist and later Amish assemblies in Strasbourg and elsewhere from 1555 on (including the discussions of the Incarnation and other doctrines) down until the Ibersheim (Germany) conferences of 1803 and 1805, throw much light on the doctrines of the Mennonites and their ethical views; but these records are not true confessions of faith. For the most part these ministers' meetings deal with life rather than doctrine; the concern is with Christian conduct and church regulations, not dogmatics. The outcome is typically precepts, not creeds.

The outstanding confession of the Hutterian Brethren is Peter Riedemann's (*q.v.*) *Rechenschaft* (Accounting), written in prison in Hesse about 1545 and printed in 1565 under the title, *Rechenschaft unserer Religion, Leer und Glaubens, von den Brüdern, so man die Hutterischen nennt ausgangen*. It was reprinted in *Calvarys Antiquariatskatalog* (Berlin, 1870, 254-417), published in a new edition by the Hutterian Brethren in America in 1902 and by the Hutterian Brethren in England in a revised edition in 1938, and finally by the latter in an English translation in 1950 under the title *Account of Our Religion, Doctrine and Faith*. Klaus Felbinger's (*q.v.*) *Rechenschaft* should not be overlooked in this connection (printed in L. Müller's *Glaubenszeugnisse Oberdeutscher Taufgesinnter* II, No. 9).

The confession of the Dutch Waterlanders, compiled on Sept. 22, 1577, by Jacob Jansz (Scheedemaker), Hans de Ries, Simon Michiels, Simon Jacobs, and Albert Verspeck, is the oldest extant Anabaptist-Mennonite confession of faith. This confession is reported by Blaupot ten Cate (*Holland* I, 118-19; see also 285-89) and was published by E. M. ten Cate (*DB* 1904, 145-56). It contains 25 articles and breathes the lenient spirit which characterized the Waterlanders. Kühler says of this confession (*Geschiedenis* I, 356), "The authors wished only to express their own conviction; it was least of all intended to impose any compulsion or give a binding rule of faith." The *Verdrag der Broederen* (Emden, 1579) must also be considered as a confession of faith; it was signed by a number of Waterlander preachers, among them de Ries. (It is found in Blaupot t. C., *Groningen* I, 264-70.)

The booklet, *Beiträge zur Kenntnis der Mennoniten-Gemeinden in Europa und Amerika,* by von Reisswitz and Wadzeck (Berlin, 1821) mentions an unprinted confession which had been used in the church at Hoorn, Holland, in the 16th century, but of which nothing further is known.

The Concept of Cologne (*q.v.*) was compiled at the synod in Cologne, May 1, 1591, by the Elder Leenaerdt Clock (*q.v.*), and signed by 15 preachers of Holland and of the Lower Rhine, Frisians, and High Germans. Many Waterlanders adhered to this confession (see **Bevredigde Broederschap**). In condensed brevity and in liberal terms borne by the spirit of Christian charity, tolerance, and mutual regard, it states the Mennonite concept of the Christian faith. But it also is not a true creed, being rather a set of conclusions on points over which differences had arisen especially concerning the ban. It was printed in *De Algemeene Belydenissen . . . (q.v.)* (Amsterdam, 1665), 1-7. There is a copy in the Dutch language in Rembert, *Wiedertäufer,* 615-18, and in German in Chr. Hege, *Die Täufer in der Kurpfalz,* 150-52.

The oldest fully developed confession of faith of the Mennonites is probably the *Belydenisse naer Godts heylig woort,* printed in the *Martyrs' Mirror* in 1660 (1950 ed., 373-410), in 1837 published in English at Winchester, Va., as *The Confession of Faith.* It contains 33 articles, and presents the content of the Christian faith in great detail with thorough, exhaustive Biblical argumentation. When and where it originally appeared, and by whom it was drawn up is not stated, but it was probably first printed about 1600. The author has been determined to be Pieter Jansz Twisck (1565-1636).

Hans de Ries and Lubbert Gerritsz formulated the *Brief Confession of Faith (Corte Belijdenisse des Gheloofs, ende der voornaemster stucken der Christelijcke leere)* in 40 articles, first published at Hoorn in 1618 (reprints: Amsterdam, 1624, 1716, 1741; Hoorn, 1643, 1658, 1681; Rotterdam, 1740, revised edition by Pieter Jansz at Crommenie, 1654, 1660, and at Amsterdam, 1686). According to Cramer (in *HRE* 3rd ed., XII, 609) it was compiled in 1615. W. Mannhardt gives 1610 as the date in *Die Wehrfreiheit* and calls it the "Frisian-Waterlander Confession of 1610." (See **Amsterdam;** at the end of the article the occasion for its being written is related.) Schijn in his *Geschiedenis* gives 1580 as the date of its origin, which is repeated in the title page of the 1741 Dutch and German editions. Plitt's *Symbolik* (Erlangen, 1875) follows Schijn. In *Mennonitische Blätter,* 1856, 78, the year 1581 is mentioned. The problem of the origin of this confession was finally solved by Kühler (*Ge-*

schiedenis II, 1, 95). In 1608, when there was some thought that a group of English Brownists (*q.v.*) would unite with the Waterlanders, this group asked Hans de Ries to draw up a confession of faith. In collaboration with Lubbert Gerritsz, de Ries did this and presented to them a confession of 38 articles. In 1610 it was printed with two additional articles. It is usually known as the *Belijdenis van Hans de Ries* or *Waterlandsche Belijdenis.* Although it was composed by only two persons, its influence was widespread. A French translation was printed in 1684, a Latin one in 1723, and a German one in 1741 at Amsterdam.

The period 1615-65 was one of unusual production and use of confessions by the Dutch Mennonites. It was a time when repeated attempts, many successful, were made to heal the many schisms among them and to unite the brotherhood on the basis of acceptable statements of faith. The *Concept of Cologne* (1591) was the first such statement in which Frisians, Flemish, and High Germans (Swiss Brethren) united, and which was accepted by many Waterlanders. It was signed by representatives of congregations from Holland, the Rhine Country, Alsace, and Württemberg. The *Olive Branch Confession (Olijftacxken)* of 1627 (printed in 1629) was designed to bring about a union between the Frisian and Flemish churches. The 1630 Jan Cents Confession served a group of United Frisian and High German congregations. The 1632 *Dordrecht Confession* was definitely offered as a basis for peace between Flemish and Old Flemish. J. P. Schabalie's *Union of the Principal Articles of Faith (Vereenigingh van de principale Artijckelen des Geloofs)* of 1640, is an extract and summary of previously issued confessions of the Waterlanders, Flemish, and High Germans.

The final development was the attempt to secure common acceptance of several similar confessions, which were then published in collections. The first of these was the collection approved at Haarlem in 1649 by a group of Flemish and High Germans, containing the Olive Branch, Jan Cents, and Dordrecht confessions as approved, plus the *Concept of Cologne* and the *Outerman Confession* of 1626, apparently not printed, however, until 1666 with the title *Handelinge der Vereenigde Vlaemse en Duytse Doopsgesinde Gemeynten Gehouden tot Haerlem Ao 1649 in Junio, met de Dry Confessien Aldaer geapprobeert of Angenommen* (Vlissingen, 1666). An almost identical collection which appeared at Amsterdam the previous year was published apparently by the private initiative of a group of conservative Zonist leaders (Cramer says van Braght and Schijn), who wanted to use the authority of the older confessions in their struggle with the Lamists, and in an accompanying statement, *Bond of Unity (Verbondt van Eenigheydt),* prepared in 1664, declared their hope that its publication would "strengthen the bond of faith and love and prevent further disintegration of the congregations." It bears the title *De Algemeene Belydenissen der Verenighde Vlaemsche, Vriesche, en Hooghduytsche Doopsgesinde Gemeynte Gods* (Amsterdam, 1665). It contains the Cologne, Outerman,

Olive Branch, Jan Cents, and Dordrecht confessions, plus the *Verbondt van Eenigheydt.* It was reprinted in 1700 at Haarlem, and again in 1739 at Rotterdam with the addition of the Schabalie *Union* of 1640. `Another motive for some confessional activity was the threat of the unitarian influence coming from the Socinians who came from Poland to Holland and were influential there from about 1600 on. The 1626 confession of 12 Waterlander preachers was an attempt to counteract this influence.

One might wonder at the frequency of the "union confessions" and whether they succeeded in their purpose. Since there was no general and authoritative synod or conference of any of the schismatic groups (Flemish, Frisian, Waterlander) the union attempts were only representative of those individual leaders or congregations who chose to respond to the invitations to the "peace conferences," and the resulting confessions had only as much weight as the prestige of those who formulated or adopted the statements, or as the convincing quality of the contents produced. In fact, since the union attempts represented the concession on the part of the conferring congregations that each group could no longer claim to be the sole true church, the more conservative element opposed them for that very reason. Also, since the confessions represented a certain degree of theological sophistication which went beyond the simple Biblicistic faith of the earlier period of Anabaptist history, the same conservative groups objected to confessions in principle, claiming that the Bible was enough for them. K. Vos, in *ML* II, 120, says, referring to the confessions in the 1665 collection, *De Algemeene Belijdenissen,* the 33-article confession in the *Martyrs' Mirror,* and the *Brief Confession* of the Waterlanders issued in 1618 by Hans de Ries and Lubbert Gerritsz, "These confessions may be regarded as the most representative expressions of the faith of the Dutch Mennonites in the 17th century."

After the period of "peace" confession making was past, no new confessions were produced in Holland for a century. Thereafter the confessions were either the expression of the hardened holding fast by single schismatic groups to their separatistic positions (which were nevertheless abandoned by the early 19th century) or of an attempt to stem the growing tide of liberalism, such as the irenic confession prepared by Cornelis Ris in 1762 (published in 1766), which was a Zonist confession. Though not much used in Holland, it came into general use in North Germany (a German edition with commentary was published as early as 1776 in Hamburg, and another edition in 1850 at the same place) and West Prussia, and later became the unofficial confession of the General Conference Mennonite Church (German editions 1895 ff., English 1902 ff.).

Following are the Dutch confessions from 1615 on in chronological order.

Bekentenisse des Gheloofs, Nae Godes Woort, which appeared first in the Hoorn Martyr Book (*Historie der warachtighe getuygen*) of 1617, then separately at Hoorn in 1620 and 1626, was, according to Hans Alenson's *Tegenbericht,* the product of two Old Frisian preachers, Sijwaert Pietersz and P. J. Twisck.

F. de Knuyt was the author of a work of this general type, though not a confession in the strict sense of the word, *Onder Verbeteringe, een Corte Bekentenisse onses Geloofs,* first edition 1618 or earlier, reprints Amsterdam, 1623, 1642; Haarlem, 1625, 1684.

At Haarlem in 1622 appeared also *Kort Verhael ende Belijdenisse der ware Religie ende des Alderheylichsten geloofs,* by J. P. (Jan Pietersz van der Molen, or Vermeulen).

The 1626 anti-Unitarian *Korte Belijdenis der Waterl. gemeenten,* prepared by 12 Waterlander preachers, was reprinted at Rotterdam in 1740.

The *Belydenisse van den Eenigen Godt, Vader, Soon ende Heyligen Geest* was the one which Jacques Outerman (*q.v.*) of Haarlem in Holland presented to the deputies of the Dutch government on Oct. 8, 1626, and which was signed by several preachers of the Flemish. This confession deals only with the doctrine of the Trinity and the Incarnation, without division into articles. It is found in Latin in Schijn, *Hist. Menn.* (1729) 79-85. This one was also put into *De Alg. Belijdenissen,* 816 ff., and the *Martyrs' Mirror* (1950) 1106-8.

The *Olive Branch* (see **Amsterdam**) was composed in Amsterdam on Sept. 27, 1627. Its title is *Olijf-tacxken, of Schriftuerlijcke aenwijsingh, over wat lieden den Vrede Godts staet* (Haarlem, 1636, reprints Amsterdam, 1647, 1661. It also appeared in *De Alg. Belijdenissen,* 67-84). The preachers of the Flemish Lamist congregation in Amsterdam planned this confession for the purpose of healing the breaches among the divided Dutch Mennonites. Though it did not achieve this, it was widely accepted. It was still in use in the 18th century by the Hamburg-Altona (Germany) congregation. It is found in the *Martyrs' Mirror* (1950) 27-33.

The confession of Jan Cents at Amsterdam, dated Oct. 7, 1630, bore the title: *Korte Confessie ofte Belijdenisse des Gheloofs (der) Vereenighde Vriesen ende Hoochduytschen.* It contains 21 articles. It was apparently never printed separately but is found in *De Alg. Belijdenissen,* 55-90. Without the division into articles it is found also in *Martyrs' Mirror,* 33-38. In Latin it is found in Schijn, *Historiae Mennonitarum* (Amsterdam, 1729) 87-114.

The *Dordrecht Confession of Faith,* compiled by Adriaen Cornelisz, elder of the Flemish congregation at Dordrecht, was signed April 21, 1632, by 51 delegates from 17 Dutch churches including two Lower Rhine congregations. This *Confessie des Christelicken Geloofs* contains 18 articles. It is found in *De Algemeene Belijdenissen,* 91-128, and in the *Martyrs' Mirror* (1950) 38-44. It has been more generally accepted among the Mennonites of Europe and America than any other. It is more conservative than most other Dutch confessions of this time, teaching the old strict view of shunning. Its real aim was to restore peace among the Flemish Mennonites, whose unity had been broken by the House-Buyer (see **Huiskooper**) controversy. It was printed at Haarlem in 1633 and in 1658 at Rotterdam. A German translation of the 1658 edition was sent to the brethren in Alsace, where it was signed by 13 preachers of various churches who had met at Ohnenheim, Feb. 4, 1660. In 1664 and 1691 it was printed in Amsterdam in German under the title *Christliche Glaubens bekentnus der Waffenlosen und fürnehmlich in den Niederländern (Unter dem Nahmen der Mennonisten) Wohlbekanten Christen;* further German editions without place 1686, 1711, 1742; Basel, 1822; Zweibrücken, 1854; Mümpelgart, 1855; Regensburg, 1876. The 1711 German edition was translated into French and published in 1771 (n.p.) as *Confession de Foi Chrétienne,* and reprinted at Nancy in 1862. An earlier reputed French edition of about 1660 could not be verified. It was translated into English and published at Amsterdam in 1712 for the Pennsylvania Mennonites, who published it themselves in 1727 at Philadelphia as the first Mennonite book printed in North America, after officially adopting it in 1725 as their confession. The English title is *The Christian Confession of the Faith of the harmless Christians, in Netherlands known by the Name of Mennonists.* English reprints: New Market, Va., 1810; Niagara, Ont., 1811; Doylestown, Pa., 1814; West Chester, Pa., 1835; Skippackville, Pa., 1836; and many other reprints in various combinations.

This *Dordrecht Confession* became the authoritative confession of the German and French Amish churches (based upon the 1660 Ohnenheim adoption) and all the Mennonite groups in North America except those of Prussian or Russian Mennonite background arriving after 1870, or those who joined the General Conference Mennonite Church.

In 1659 appeared at Utrecht *Een Belijdenisse Aengaende de voornaemste Leer-Stucken des Christelijcken Godts-Dienst Gestelt door G. V. Aldendorp, A. V. Heuven, J. Andries, W. V. Maurick.*

The Groningen Old Swiss group published its confession in 1744 at Groningen, written by J. van Koomen, *Belydenisse des Geloofs onder de Doopsgez. Christenen.*

The Groningen Old Flemish Confession written by T. Popkes appeared in 1749 at Groningen under the title, *Een beknopt ontwerp of schets v. de geloofsbelydenisse der Mennonyten, onder de benam. v. Oude Vlaamingen.* Another Old Flemish confession appeared at Groningen in 1755 as *Geloofsbelydenisse der Doopsgesinden, bekent onder den Naam v. Oude Vlamingen* (reprints 1774, 1805, and once without date).

Cornelis Ris published in 1766 at Hoorn, *De geloofsleere der waare Mennoniten of Doopsgezinden.* This confession was recognized in 1773 by the Sociëteit of Mennonite churches whose delegates had met in the Zonist church in Amsterdam. A considerable number of the Dutch and some German congregations belonged to this Sociëteit at that time. For this reason this confession attained a wide distribution and a high regard among the Mennonites. It was printed in Hamburg in German in 1776 with the title, *Die Glaubenslehre der wahren Mennoniten oder Taufgesinnten aus deren*

öffentlichen Glaubensbekenntnissen zusammengezogen durch C. Ris nebst erläuterndem Vorbericht und Anhang. It was again translated and published by C. J. van der Smissen, minister of the Friedrichstadt church, in 1850 (Horn bei Hamburg). It contains 36 detailed articles. This was the last new confession produced by the Dutch Mennonites. The increasing emphasis among the Dutch Mennonites in the 19th and 20th centuries upon an "undogmatic" faith, and upon the autonomy of the individual Christian as well as the individual congregation, has outmoded such confessions of faith completely among them.

It may be noted that some commentaries on the confessions, and formulation of the confessional contents in catechetical form, were produced by preachers and theologians. E. A. van Dooregeest of De Ryp published such a book with 813 pages in 1692 (Amsterdam) under the title (translated) *Instruction in the Christian Doctrine According to the Confessions of the Doopsgezinden Wherein the Main Points of Faith are Strengthened with Scripture References, Comments, Refutation of Opposition-Arguments, in Questions and Answers.* The House-Buyer group issued such a booklet in 1708 at Steenwyck, called *Mennoniste Vrageboeck.* The Old Flemish confession of 1755 was treated in a similar way in two editions, one of 1762 and one undated. K. van Huyzen published in 1705 at Amsterdam a brief summary of doctrine based on the 1665 collection, *De Algemeene Belijdenissen,* entitled *Korte Inhoud van de Leere des Geloofs.* A similar book, *Korte Schets der Doopsgesinde Belydenisse* was published by D.P.C.I.L. at Amsterdam in 1701. Mention should be made of Galenus Abrahamsz' *Korte Grondstellingen,* which is the last part of his *Verdeediging der Christenen* (Amsterdam, 1699).

The chief confession of the West Prussian churches was the *Confession Oder Kurtze und Einfältige Glaubens-Bekentnis derer/ so man nennet/ Die vereinigte Flämische/ Friesische und Hochdeutsche Tauffsgesinnete/ oder Mennonisten in Preussen. Aussgegeben von denen obigen Gemeinen daselbsten; Gedruckt im Jahr Christi, 1660.* Wilhelm Mannhardt held it to be a translation of an older Dutch confession, but no one has yet identified the supposed original. (See his *Wehrfreiheit,* Appendix, p. xxiii.) It was reprinted in 1751 and 1756 without place, in 1781 at Elbing, 1854 at Graudenz, and in Russia three times, at Odessa in 1854, at Berdyansk in 1873 and in 1912. It was until recent times used by the West Prussian churches. In all editions beginning in 1690 there is an appendix, *Kurze Unterweisung aus der Schrift, so wir erachten denen zu wissen nötig, die sich zu der Gemeinschaft, der Christlichen Gemeine, welche man Mennonisten nennt, begeben wollen, verfasst in Fragen und Antworten.* The text follows that of the preceding confession. A further addition is the *Formular etlicher Christlicher Gebete* (L. Clock's collection).

The *Flaminger Bekenntnis* (Flemish Confession) of Georg Hansen (d. 1703), a preacher and elder of the Flemish Mennonite congregation at Danzig, was presented in 1678 to Stanislaus Sarnowski, the Bishop of Leslau. It was printed in Dutch at Amsterdam in 1696. A Latin and German edition was published, probably by a member of the Bishop's Commission, under the title, *Confession oder kurze und einfältige Glaubensbekenntniss der Mennonisten in Preussen, so man nennet die Clarichen. Im Jahre Christi, unseres Erlösers* (1678). Attached to this edition is the record of a religious cross-examination of Georg Hansen on Jan. 20, 1678. A copy is to be found in the Danzig city library. This confession was the vehicle of a merger of the Danzig Old Flemish churches in Holland and the Old Flemish churches in West Prussia which was solemnized and confirmed at joint communion services in Amsterdam, July 6, 1730, and in Haarlem, July 16. It is signed by four elders in Prussia and four elders in Holland as well as 70 preachers. A German edition was published by the Danzig church in the same year. In 1768 a new edition was published with a catechism and numerous appendices under the title, *Confession oder kurzer und einfältiger Glaubensbericht der flämischen Taufgesinnten Gemeinden in Preussen. In Fragen und Antworten verfasst der erwachsenen Jugend zum nötigen Unterricht. Gedenke an deinen Schöpfer in deiner Jugend.* It consists of 19 sections having separate headings but not numbered. This confession was reprinted in 1878 (?) at Elkhart, Ind., for the church in Turner Co., S.D., with a title which states it to be a reprint of the edition published in 1853 by the church of Rudnerweide, South Russia. It was again reprinted at Elkhart in 1893, in *Ein Fundamentbuch der Christlichen Lehre*, edited by Elder Isaac Peters of the Evangelical Mennonite Brethren.

In 1792 G. Wiebe, elder of the Flemish congregation at Elbing and Ellerwald, published at Elbing a new confession of 20 articles, *Glaubensbekenntniss der Mennoniten in Preussen*, which was much used in West Prussia and Russia, reprints at Elbing, 1836 and 1837, and in Russia in 1870 and 1874.

Several additional confessions prepared by individual German Mennonite ministers, but of no great significance or use, should be mentioned as follows: *Evangelisches Glaubensbekenntnis der Taufgesinnten Christen oder also genannten Mennonisten, wie solches in Altona öffentlich gelehrt und gepredigt wird*, compiled by Gerhard Roosen, 1702. It is found in Roosen's booklet, *Unschuld und Gegenbericht der Evg. Taufgesinnten Christen, so Mennonisten genannt werden . . .* (Ratzeburg, 1702). This booklet was used somewhat in the Palatinate.

Die Gottesgelehrtheit der Taufgesinnten Christen durch Cornelius van Huyzen, Lehrer der Taufgesinnten zu Emden 1713.

Confession oder kurzer Glaubensbericht der bekannten taufgesinnten Gemeinden in Preussen zur Erbauung der Jugend ausgegeben . . . , by Hermann Jantzen, the elder of the Flemish church at Elbing, 1741. (A copy could not be located or verified.)

In 1895 the rural Mennonite churches of West Prussia published a new confession of faith, combining the confessions of the Old Flemish and the Frisians. It was adopted at the annual conference at Marienau near Tiegenhagen on June 6, 1895.

Its title is also *Glaubensbekenntnis der Mennoniten in Preussen* (Marienburg, 1895, reprint Gütersloh, 1903).

In Russia the Mennonite Church, after using the 1660 Confession (Odessa, 1853; Berdyansk, 1873) and the 1792 *Glaubensbekenntniss der Mennoniten in Preussen* (editions of 1870 at St. Petersburg and 1874 at Berdyansk added the phrase "und Russland"), adopted a newly edited confession of faith in 1896, which was printed in 1898 in Halbstadt by P. Neufeld, with the title, *Glaubensbekenntnis der Mennoniten in Russland.*

The newly organized Mennonite Brethren Church had its first confession of 1876 printed at Basel, *Glaubensbekenntnis und Verfassung der Gläubig Getauften und Vereinigten Mennoniten-Brüdergemeinde in Russland.* The second revised edition, *Glaubensbekenntniss d. Ver. Chr. Taufges. M. Br.-G. in Russland* was printed by P. Neufeld at Halbstadt in 1902. This was reprinted at Gronau in Westfalen, Germany, in 1947 for the M.B. refugees who had come out of Russia during and after World War II, and in 1916, —, and 1952, at Hillsboro, Kan., as the "amerikanische Ausgabe," having been adopted by the M.B. General Conference in 1902. It was translated and published in English about 1940 at Hillsboro as *Confession of Faith of the Mennonite Brethren Church of North America, American edition.*

A certain amount of new confession building among Mennonites has taken place in recent times. In Europe the Mennonites in Galicia (then Austria, now Russia) published in 1871 and then in 1904 at Lemberg a confession first prepared by their Elder Johann Müller and then revised and edited by his son Johann Müller: *Glaubensbekenntnis für Taufgesinnte der Galizischen Mennoniten-Gemeinden.*

The Crefeld Mennonite congregation adopted a statement of "General Principles" in 1912, which is actually a confession of faith, though not so labeled. (See **Crefeld**, where the statement is given in full.) The theological position of this statement is extremely liberal, in marked contrast to the Dordrecht Confession of 1632, which had been signed by a minister of this congregation.

Joh. Kipfer, elder of the Mennonite congregation in the Emmental, prepared a confession of faith which his congregation adopted and published at Langnau in 1937: *Kurzgefasstes Glaubensbekenntnis der Altevangelischen Taufgesinnten-Gemeinden im Emmental.* It shows some adaptation to the pietistic emphasis, and also to the Reformed position in baptism. The Conference of Swiss Mennonites refused to adopt this confession as requested by Kipfer.

In North America the first new confession was that of the present United Missionary Church (formerly Mennonite Brethren in Christ), although it has never been called a "Confession." The first form was *Glaubenslehre und Kirchenzucht-Ordnung* (Skippackville, Pa., 1866), English form, *Doctrine of Faith and Church Discipline (idem, 1867).* In 1880 a revised edition appeared at Goshen, Ind., in both English and German, and again in 1889 at Berlin (now Kitchener), Ont., in both languages.

Later editions were in English only, Berlin, Ont., 1897 and 1905; New Carlisle, Ohio, 1920 and 1924, and later editions. In 1951 it was displaced by a new *Doctrines and Discipline of the United Missionary Church.*

The second such confession was *Glaubensbekenntnis der Mennoniten in Manitoba, Nordamerika,* prepared by Johannes Wiebe, elder of the church at Reinland, Man., in 1881 and printed the same year at Elkhart, with several reprints, such as Elkhart, 1889 and 1900, and Winnipeg, Man., in 1927.

Third, the Church of God in Christ, Mennonite, adopted and printed in 1896 (latest reprint 1952) its confession, called *Confession of Faith of the Church of God in Christ, Mennonite.* It had earlier printed the 33 articles of P. J. Twisck as its own.

The fourth new confession was that of the Evangelical Mennonite Brethren (Isaac Peters-Aaron Wall conference), published at Elkhart in 1907 as *Glaubens-Bekenntnis der Mennoniten in Nebraska und Kansas, Nord-Amerika.*

The fifth new confession was that of the Evangelical Mennonite Church, then called the Defenseless Mennonite Church, which published its *Confession of Faith, Rules and Discipline,* adopted in revised form at Archbold, Ohio, Aug. 30, 1917 (Chicago, 1917), later editions 1937 and 1949. Its 12 Articles of Faith teach not only the usual Mennonite doctrines, but also "second work of grace" or baptism of the Holy Spirit, divine healing, open communion, and premillennialism.

The Conference of Mennonites in Canada (GCM) published in 1930 a condensed and revised form of the Cornelis Ris confession, with the following explanatory title: *Glaubensbekenntnis der Mennoniten in Canada. Im Auftrage der Predigerkonferenz zusammengestellt und revidiert auf Grund der Bekenntnisse der Mennoniten in Preussen und Russland und von der Allgemeinen Konferenz in Winkler 1930 gutgeheissen und angenommen.*

The Mennonite Church (MC) in 1921, and the General Conference Mennonite Church in 1941, both officially adopted doctrinal statements which do not profess to be confessions of faith but are such in effect nevertheless. Both reflect the influence of the Fundamentalist-Modernist controversy which continued in the United States and Canada during the first half of the 20th century. (The G.C.M. group attempted a brief "revised" *Articles of Faith* in 14 articles, which though authorized in 1933 to be printed never were adopted.) The statement of the Mennonite Church (MC), which was adopted by its General Conference at Garden City, Mo., Aug. 24-26, 1921, is called *Christian Fundamentals,* and contains 18 articles. The conference expressly declared that "this statement does not supersede the eighteen articles of the Dort Confession, which the Church still confesses and teaches." The General Conference Mennonites, at their conference session at Souderton, Pa., Aug. 17-22, 1941, adopted an official *Statement of Doctrine* containing nine brief articles. Both churches have also adopted comprehensive declarations of faith on nonresistance, the Mennonite Church (MC) at its

session at Turner, Ore., in 1937, and again at Goshen, Ind., in 1950, the General Conference Mennonite Church at its 1941 Souderton sessions.

The Beatrice (Neb.) Mennonite Church (GCM) in 1918 published a condensed edition of the old Prussian confession under the title *Unser altes Glaubensbekenntnis in abgekürzter Darstellung.*

The Apostolic Christian Church ("New Amish") had its confession published at Elkhart in 1880, *Glaubensbekenntnis der Neuen Deutschen Baptisten-Gemeinde in den Vereinigten Staaten.*

Eine Konfession oder Glaubensbekenntnis der Taufgesinnten in Griechenland welche die 3 Christen von Thessalonich die nach Deutschland gekommen sind und allda bekannt haben den grund ihres glaubens is a confession written about 1540 on behalf of a mysterious group whose identity has not been fully clarified. (See **Thessalonian Anabaptists.**) The confession has been preserved only in manuscript form, handed down among the Amish. A copy is in the Goshen College Library. It is probable that the Thessalonian group was not Anabaptist but anti-Trinitarian.

Among the Mennonites confessions of faith earlier had no binding power or legal significance; they were and claimed to be nothing more than an easily intelligible expression of the confession of the church and the form for a commonly held content of faith. Now and again an attempt was made to compel recognition by both preachers and laymen as a binding authority upon them. In Holland this led to the division of the Zonists and Lamists (see **Amsterdam**). The latter thought it necessary to require unconditional recognition of the confessions of faith in order to "preserve the bond of faith and love and to prevent further injury to the church." The Lamists most definitely opposed this attempt. In general the Mennonites have held to the Protestant principle that the highest and only norm of all religious understanding, of faith, and of doctrine, is the Bible, the Word of God, which means that the Mennonite Church has not been a creedal church in the customary sense of the term. However, in recent times some groups and conferences in North America give more weight and almost binding power to the confession officially adopted by the conference. Since the beginning of the 19th century confessions of faith are no longer used in the Dutch congregations.

The theology of the Mennonite confessions of faith from the beginning has been uniformly orthodox evangelical, avoiding the particularities of the classic Lutheran and Reformed formulations, and reflecting quite well the original Anabaptist insights and emphases. The later (18th century and after) confessions reveal slightly more assimilation to the current Protestant orthodoxy or pietism, but except for a few modern statements which teach such doctrines as the second work of grace, baptism by immersion, open communion, and chiliasm, the confessions agree remarkably in presenting simply, and with many Biblical allusions and citations, the same doctrines as taught originally by Grebel, Manz, Blaurock, Marpeck, Obbe and Dirk Philips, and Menno Simons; viz., separation of church and state, believers' baptism, nonresistance, liberty of conscience, church discipline, separation from the world, the avoidance of litigation, and the non-swearing of oaths, as well as the main orthodox Protestant doctrines. These confessions have undoubtedly done much to preserve the doctrinal and ethical homogeneity of the total Mennonite brotherhood in the absence of formal works of theology. This does not apply of course to those congregations in Holland and Germany which have dropped the use of confessions altogether and taken on liberal theology and accommodated themselves to current ethics.   NEFF, J.C.W., H.S.B.

S. Cramer, "Die Mennoniten" in *HRE* XII (1902); Friesen, *Brüderschaft;* A. Hunzinger, *Das Religions-, Kirchen- und Schulwesen der Mennoniten* (1830); W. Mannhardt, *Die Wehrfreiheit der Altpreussischen Mennoniten* (1863); *Menn. Bl.,* 1856, 1857, 1885, 1886; Müller, *Berner Täufer* (1895); G. Plitt, *Abriss der Symbolik* (Erlangen, 1875); Reisswitz and Wadzeck, *Beiträge zur Kenntnis der Mennoniten-Gemeinden in Europa und Amerika* (Berlin, 1821); H. Schijn, *Historiae Mennonitarum* (Amsterdam, 1729); Fritz Blanke, "Beobachtungen zum ältesten Täuferbekenntnis," in *Arch. f. Ref.-Gesch.* XXXVIII (1940) 242-49; R. Friedmann, *Menn. Piety Through the Centuries* (Goshen, 1949); Beatrice Jenny, *Das Schleitheimer Täuferbekenntnis 1527,* reprint from *Schaffhäuser Beiträge,* 1951 (see review by Arthur Rich in *Theol. Ztscht* VIII, 1952, 309-14); *ML* II, 119.

Confirmation is the ceremony in the Protestant Church by which the young person (baptized as an infant) at the age of 14 to 16 is received as a member of the church and admitted to communion with a ceremony of consecration by the minister, upon the confession of faith after instruction by the preacher and an examination passed before the assembled church.

The attempt has been made to trace confirmation back to apostolic times and to equate it to the laying on of hands by the apostles at baptism, by which act the gift of the Holy Spirit was given the candidate, based on passages like Acts 8:14-18; 19:5, 6; II Cor. 1:21 (*qui autem confirmat nos vobiscum in Christo, et qui unxit nos Deus*), and Heb. 6:1, 2. But the proof is not established in any of these passages. It must be pointed out that in Acts the laying on of hands is always mentioned as immediately following baptism; nowhere is the character of an apostolic symbol of the covenant ascribed to it. And finally, its separation from baptism or ordination is without Biblical precedent.

Confirmation in the Protestant Church corresponds more or less to that in the old Catholic Church. In the Greek Orthodox Church it is considered an adaptation of apostolic laying on of hands made by the successors of the apostles, and is administered in connection with baptism as the "seal of the Holy Spirit."

Confirmation can be traced far back in Roman Catholic history, where it was separated from baptism and made a sacrament. Tertullian (d. *ca.* 220) distinguishes between baptism and confirmation when he writes, "The body is washed, that the soul may be made spotless; the body is anointed, that the soul may be consecrated; the body is signed, that the soul may be consecrated; the body is shaded by the laying on of hands, that the soul may

be illumined by the Spirit" (*De resurrectione carnis,* p. 8).

In the 4th and 5th centuries confirmation became definitely an act reserved to the bishop, and as adult baptism became rarer, confirmation was applied to those who had been baptized as infants. For the Roman Catholic it is the second of the seven sacraments and was confirmed as such by the synods of Lyons (1274) and Florence (1439); the council of Trent (1545-63) emphatically declares confirmation to be a "true and real sacrament" (*Sess. 7, can. 1, de confirmatione*).

From the beginning of the Reformation the Protestant Church rejected the sacrament of confirmation, because it lacked the signs of a true sacrament, viz., institution by Jesus and a special promise, and because it was prejudicial to baptism. Luther called confirmation, consecration of the priests, and extreme unction "church customs."

In spite of this rejection the need soon arose out of the rejection of adult baptism and the baptismal vow as it was demanded by the Anabaptists, to create an equivalent and to invent a rite similar to Catholic confirmation, by which admission to church membership would become a solemn act. Adam Weiss, a reformer of Brandenburg-Ansbach, had already in 1527 suggested that in all the churches the children of accountable age should be annually instructed by the pastors on "baptism, faith, prayer" (G. Bossert, 185). But his suggestion was not followed (*Beiträge zur bayrischen Kirchengesch.* IV, 1898, 191).

The *Apologie* of the Augsburg Confession of 1530 again rejects confirmation; article XIII (VII) says, "Confirmation and extreme unction are ceremonies which come from the Fathers and have never been held necessary for salvation, for they have neither God's word nor command. Therefore it is well to distinguish them from [baptism and communion], which are instituted and commanded in God's Word and have a promise attached."

Not until they were involved in conflict with the Anabaptists, who insisted on a baptismal vow to live a Christian life, was confirmation introduced into the Protestant churches. The beginning was made by Martin Bucer, the reformer of Strasbourg. Calvin was also influenced during his sojourn in Strasbourg. Already at the great synod of Strasbourg in 1533, Caspar Schwenckfeld, under Anabaptist influence, raised the demand, "If they could not agree to abolish infant baptism, then at least a ceremony should be introduced, whereby baptized children, when they are grown, would be dedicated to Christendom." Bucer adopts this suggestion in his book (1534) *Ad Monasterienses,* and meets the Anabaptists half-way by recommending that all who had been baptized as infants and who had received catechetical instruction should be consecrated by the laying on of hands as independent members of the church.

But this plan was not adopted in Strasbourg. Later, when Bucer was called to Hesse (*q.v.*) to assist in a similar ecclesiastical situation, he proceeded with his plan, in order to counteract Anabaptist reproaches. Thereby Bucer became the founder of Protestant confirmation. This took place in the following manner:

In order to resist the rapid spread of Anabaptism in his land, Landgrave Philip called Bucer to Hesse in 1538. Not with violence, but with gentle persuasion the Anabaptists were to be won to the church. "We wanted to act graciously and leniently once more," says the landgrave in a letter to the Anabaptists, "and we have therefore appointed a God-fearing man to converse with you kindly about your error and to instruct you in the fundamentals" (Hochhuth, 612; Franz, No. 76).

Bucer complied with the wishes of the landgrave and held a disputation with the Anabaptist leaders (Peter Tasch, Hermann Bastian, Georg Schnabel, Leonhart Fälber, Peter Lose), some of whom had already been put in prison at Marburg. But he was countered with so many well-founded complaints against the church that he had to give in. When Georg Schnabel, whom he had appointed spokesman of the Anabaptists, said that in the church one took communion with "drunkards, usurers and fornicators," he replied that matters would be corrected (Hochhuth, 363), and to the charge that in baptism the apostolic order was not observed, children were baptized, but not taught repentance and Christian conduct, Bucer could only reply, "The children, when they are grown, should be faithfully catechized and taught all things that the Lord has commanded" (Hochhuth, 637). Hermann Bastian pointed out the lack of church discipline in the face of the increasing prevalence of vice among the people. It had indeed been said a year ago that the ban was to be instituted, but nothing had been done. "The church cannot exist without the ban and faith," with which Bucer agreed: "It is true; where there is no discipline and faith there is no church" (Hochhuth, 642).

Correctly realizing that here it was not a matter merely of defense, but of taking serious measures to remove the offenses that stirred up Anabaptist resistance, Bucer made the suggestion in Wittenberg, in a letter to the landgrave, Nov. 17, 1538, that all these complaints be brought before the proposed synod at Ziegenhain for action, "because they could in no other way make the Anabaptists more tractable or warn the common people better than by seriously practicing Christian discipline."

The synod met at the end of November 1538 at Ziegenhain (Kassel district). Following Bucer's suggestion, the *Ziegenhainer Zuchtordnung* of 1538 was set up. In its framework confirmation was introduced in the churches of the Reformation. The order stipulates that all children had to attend catechismal instruction, and on a holiday they were to be presented to the pastor in church, who would examine them on the principal doctrines of the Christian faith. After the children have "publicly yielded themselves to Christ the Lord and His church, they are to be confirmed by the laying on of hands and admonished to accept willingly at all times Christian discipline and punishment from every Christian, but principally from their pastor, and to obey" (Diehl, 5-13).

It was the landgrave's wish that the regulations for discipline should be first tried out in the individual communities, as Kassel and Marburg, and the details of enforcement worked out. This was done in a few days in Kassel in the Confirmation Formulary of Kassel of 1538, which states in its introduction: "Manner and usage is described in the Ziegenhain regulations for discipline, which we hope to put into effect here." Comparison of the Ziegenhain regulations and the Kassel Formulary reveals great similarity (Diehl, 19, 124 ff.). The confirmation ceremony prescribed in these orders was confirmed by the *Hessische Agende* of 1574.

From Hesse the ceremony of confirmation was introduced to other regions in the 16th century, in Strasbourg, e.g., soon after 1538, certainly before 1548. All the confirmation regulations of the 16th and 17th centuries, with the exception of the Pomeranian of 1565, were influenced by that of Hesse (*Menn. Bl.,* 1912, 43). Even the confirmation liturgy in the English *Book of Common Prayer* is obviously a result of Bucer's authoritative influence. In the Protestant liturgies published in Hesse before Bucer's disputation with the Anabaptists there are no directions for confirmation. Instructions on confirmation with public confession before the church are not found until 1543, in a liturgy which Ott Heinrich as regent of Pfalz-Sulzbach introduced after the Reformation there (Lamb, 97 ff.).

In many places the authorities hesitated to follow Hesse's example. Voices were heard for and against confirmation. In the *Wittenbergische Reformation* (liturgy) of 1545, which was signed by Luther, Bugenhagen, Cruciger, Maier, and Melanchthon, it is urged that "this would be very necessary in all the churches, to hold the catechism on certain definite days, to instruct youth in all the necessary articles of Christian doctrine. For this purpose confirmation might be established, namely when a child has reached an accountable age, to hear his confession publicly, and to ask whether he would remain in this one godly doctrine and church, and offer a prayer after the confession and consent with the laying on of hands. This would be a useful ceremony, not only for appearance, but rather for the preservation of true doctrine and pure understanding, and useful for good discipline" (Sehling I, 211).

More definite are the instructions in the liturgy of Henry IV of Reuss, of Aug. 30, 1552: "Instead of confirmation, the youth should be industriously trained in the catechism on fast days, and those who are capable of receiving the worthy sacrament of the communion of Christ should be given it on Maundy Thursday and then be regarded as confirmed Christians" (Sehling II, 156). Open confession before the church is required in the Palatine liturgy of 1563, the Pomeranian of 1573, that of Hohenlohe of 1577, and of Mecklenburg of 1602. In Mühlhausen, Thuringia, superintendent Sebastian Starcke raised the question with the clergy (about 1574) whether children should be given a public examination before admission to communion. It was negatively answered as "inopportune" at the moment (Sehling II, 336). The introduction of confirmation took longest in Hamburg; not until 1832 was it adopted there.

In the discussion on infant baptism between Hans Denk and Johann Bader (*q.v.*) in Landau, Bader agreed with Denk that the compulsory baptism of infants against the wishes of the parents would be of no avail. He considered infant baptism of value only if the children were made aware of the meaning of their baptism when they reach the age of understanding; it was of no value unless the parents "train and instruct their children at the right and proper time, of the meaning of their baptism and the teachings of Jesus and do this as faithfully and as earnestly as they have previously hastened with baptism. For if this does not occur, the parents sin against God and the children, and it would be much better to dispense with baptism if this is not done." Bader is here obviously showing that most people die without having learned "what Christian baptism is and to what end a man can use his baptism" (Chr. Hege, *Täufer*, 17).

Oswald Myconius, in his exposition of the Gospel of Mark, which he dedicated to the mayor of Basel in 1538, complains about the neglect of the young people (Hagenbach, 414-16).

"In Württemberg Hochstetter's demand for the institution of confirmation does not cease after 1692 until its introduction is recognized as being essential in the struggle with separatism in 1721" (G. Bossert in his discussion of Chr. Kolb's *Die Anfänge des Pietismus und Separatismus in Württemberg, Theol. L.Z.* 1902, col. 622).

It was the great service of Pietism and especially Philip Jakob Spener to deepen youth instruction and make it more meaningful and to urge a personal experience of grace for the one confirmed. The subjective element comes further into the foreground. The children were to enter consciously into the covenant which God made with them at their baptism. Likewise also the Moravians placed the emphasis on a renewal of heart, whereby the child, having reached understanding, could renew his baptismal covenant.

The influence of Anabaptism on the development of Protestant confirmation is today openly admitted. Besides Wilhelm Diehl, E. P. Hansen has also expressly pointed out these connections.

For us it is important to make it clear that confirmation, as H. van der Smissen says, "was originally to serve as a church institution created to meet Anabaptist demands—it was a step in the direction of the center of their concept of the church—and to make their demands invalid. These demands are today recognized as justified in ever-expanding circles, namely the need for the individual Christian's conscious determination and will to accept Christ as Lord and to follow Him, come what may. This determination made of our fathers the courageous witnesses and martyrs whom the world today recognizes and praises" (*Menn. Bl.,* 1912, 52).

During the period of Rationalism (18th century), confirmation lost much of its original meaning. Men like Stöcker and Mahling very earnestly pointed out the harm done, which gradually came to

light and which loudly called for a thorough revision of the practice. This has, however, not been done. Confirmation remains an imperfect substitute for adult baptism.   E.H., E.T.

G. Bossert, *Theol. Studien aus Württemberg* (1882); E. Burgck, *Die Konfirmation, ihre geschichtliche Entwicklung, Bedeutung, und praktische Ausgestaltung* (1900); W. Caspari, *Die evangelische Konfirmation* (1890); H. Claus, "Zur Geschichte der Konfirmation," in *Beiträge zur bayr. Kirchengesch.* XXIII (1917); W. Diehl, *Zur Gesch. der Konfirmation* (Giessen, 1897); O. Grätz, "Die Konfirmation nach ihrer biblischen Begründung, Geschichte und Zukunft," in *All. Ev. Luth. Kirchenzeitung* (Leipzig, 1901); K. Hagenbach, *Johann Oekolampad und Oswald Mykonius* (Elberfeld, 1859); E. P. Hansen, *Gesch. der Konfirmation in Schleswig-Holstein* . . . (Kiel, 1911; see also *Ztscht f. Kirchengesch.*, 1913, 463); Chr. Hege, "Hesse" in *ML* II; idem, *Die Täufer in der Kurpfalz* (Frankfurt, 1908); K. W. H. Hochhuth, "Landgraf Philipp und die Wiedertäufer," in *Ztscht f. d. hist. Theol.*, 1858; Fr. Loofs, *Symbolik* I (1902); idem, *Dogmengesch.* (1906); V. Schultze, "Ein unbekanntes Luther. Konf.- Bekenntnis von 1529," in *Neue kirchliche Ztscht,* 1900, 233-42; von Zezschwitz, "Der Zusammenhang der ersten Formen einer protestantischen Konfirmation mit der Wiedertaufe," in *Pastoralblätter* (Stuttgart, 1864); *Catalogus Amst.*, 140; S. R. Naumann, *Der ev. Rel.-Unterricht im Zeitalter der Ref.* (*Programm Berlin* XXVI, 1899, 4); Th. Zahn, "Zur Gesch. der Konfirmation im Unterfränkischen," in *Ztscht für bayr. Kirchengesch.*, 1929, 134; E. Sehling, *Die evangelischen Kirchenordnungen des 16. Jahrhunderts* I (1902), II (1904); K. Lamb, "Gesch. der Konf. in der Pfalz," *Beitr. z. bayr. Kirchengesch.* X (1904); Franz, *TA: Hessen; ML* II, 534-36.

Confiscation of Property. In the 16th century the Anabaptists not only forfeited their lives when they were baptized upon confession of their faith; their property was also seized by the authorities. In the Netherlands during the time of persecution the property of martyrs who were sentenced was usually confiscated, though this is not always expressly declared in the sentences. The proceeds of the property of a martyr who was executed or of a person banished from the city or the province accrued partly to the public treasury, and partly to the emperor; sometimes a part of the proceeds was given to the person who had denounced or betrayed the "heretic." The very earliest mandates issued against them contain threats of such punishment. The mandate of Louis V, Elector Palatine, March 5, 1528, determined that anyone "who had previously been baptized according to Christian order" would be punished with "loss of life by fire, and confiscation of possessions and property" if he allowed himself to be rebaptized (Hege, 59). Confiscation was retained for several centuries as a punishment for membership with the Anabaptists. A comprehensive study of confiscation of Anabaptist property has not yet been made.

Exceptional severity in confiscation characterized the Swiss cantons. In Bern, when the emigrating Swiss Brethren sold their properties these were to be confiscated from the buyer by a decree of April 23, 1610; the buyer was then supposed to be repaid by the seller. Thus sale became impossible. But finally this confiscation by the state became so offensive to public opinion that a Bern mandate of Aug. 19, 1678, specified that confiscated Anabaptist property should be managed by the local communities. The income from these properties flowed into the church and school funds of the community (Müller, 131).

In the Palatinate in the last third of the 16th century, the Anabaptists who refused "to return to the right church" were expelled and their property was confiscated by the state. It was returned as soon as the exile promised to return into the state church. If an exile died "in wretchedness," his property was given to the surviving relatives or friends (Hege, 137-41).

In the duchy of Württemberg, property confiscated from Anabaptists was occasionally arbitrarily disposed of, causing loud complaints in the Landtag in 1594. Formerly the property of emigrants to Moravia had been returned to the heirs, but now petitions for the release of Anabaptist hereditary property were as a rule denied. "A matter of faith becomes a matter of finance." At the demand of Duke Frederick, confiscated Anabaptist funds were applied to the church at Freudenstadt. In 1606 the funds collected from Anabaptists by the Austrian government during its occupation amounted to 40,000 fl.; in 1636 they decreased to 24,000 fl. (Bossert, 38).

Confiscation was practiced longest in Zürich. Here too the aim was to compel the Anabaptists either to recant or to emigrate by injuring them financially. This measure had already been extensively discussed about 1550 at a synod in Aarau, but was not applied until 1598. At first this confiscated Anabaptist property was used to aid the children or those who recanted; later it was used to support hospitals, schools, and churches. Anabaptist property was also frequently applied to the printing of Bibles, which the government took over in 1618. These funds were also used to cover the cost of tracing and seizing Anabaptists, as well as the support of imprisoned Anabaptists. Thus the fund was sharply reduced. Not until a number of well-to-do Anabaptists were seized did the fund appreciably increase. Thereby the community fund for the support of the poor also fell into the hands of the government. Frequently the confiscated properties later fell into the private possession of officials. In 1798 the Anabaptist fund had grown to 325,402 pounds. Appeals made by heirs for repayment were only rarely granted, and then only if there was proof that they had returned to the state church (Bergmann, 136-45).

The confiscation of Anabaptist property by the state was first assumed by the canton of Bern to be a self-evident right; later this measure was disapproved by the people. It was therefore decided that confiscated Anabaptist-Mennonite property should be kept in the local community as a separate fund. Täufergut (Anabaptist Property) was the name given the cash capital confiscated from the arrested Mennonites. The income from this fund was used for the churches and schools of the community.

The severe Bernese mandate of Sept. 8, 1670, stipulated that those Mennonites who would "yield to attend the sermons and the use of the holy sacraments" should be permitted to keep their property; but those who remained obstinately with their faith should have their property publicly sold at auction and the proceeds turned over to the manager of the church fund, who should make an annual report to the government on this fund. In case such "unconvertible Anabaptists die, their property shall remain in the church fund and be used for schools and the poor." Under certain circumstances the farms of these "stiff-necked and disobedient fellows" who were already behind bars, if the land was farmed by the prisoner's wife and children, should be placed in the hands of a guardian and if it seemed advisable sold, and the proceeds given the children only if they would submit to the orders of the established church. This mandate specified further that the property of those Mennonites who were in exile should be sold and this money also added to the fund in the care of the church. The government made an effort to banish the Mennonites as penniless as possible and keep the money in Switzerland.

Later, when the permanent Commission for Anabaptist Affairs (*q.v.*) was appointed, this commission assumed the care of the Anabaptist properties, which were put into the *Täufergutsfonds*. After the costs had been met, the remainder of the proceeds of the sale should be listed in the *Täufer-Urbar*, so that it would at all times be possible to see what had been done with the money. These Anabaptist property accounts are still to be found in the archives at Bern, as well as a *Zinss-Rodel* for Anabaptist funds (begun in 1614). Enormous sums were taken by the state from honest citizens. If a Mennonite was converted and joined the state church, abandoning Anabaptism for good, his property was restored to him; but this happened only rarely. The confiscated money remaining in the fund was used for church and school buildings. Thus the parish of Roggwil received 2,000 pounds of Anabaptist money for the renovation of the church. Huttwil used 500 guilders of Anabaptist money in building a new church. The parish of Schwarzenegg in Thun in 1692 drew a sum from the Anabaptist fund that would in modern currency be worth about $4,000.   HEGE, S.G.

C. Bergmann, *Die Täuferbewegung im Kanton Zürich* (Leipzig, 1916); G. Bossert, "Aus der nebenkirchlichen religiösen Bewegung der Reformationszeit in Württemberg," in *Blätter für württembergische Kirchengesch.* I and II (1926) 1-41; Chr. Hege, *Die Täufer in der Kurpfalz* (Frankfurt, 1908); Müller, *Berner Täufer*; Eberhard Teufel, "Die Beschlagnahme und Verwaltung des Täufergutes durch den Fiskus im Herzogtum Württemberg im 16. u. 17. Jahrhundert," in *Theol. Ztscht* VIII (July/August, 1952) 296-304; Delbert Gratz, *Bernese Anabaptists* (Scottdale, 1952); Grosheide, *Bijdrage*, 72-87, 228-30; I. M. J. Hoog, *De Martelaren der Hervorming in Nederland* (Schiedam, 1885) 195-96; *ML* II, 210.

Congerville (Ill.) Mennonite Church (GCM), located in Woodford County, was the first Amish church to be established in a village. A few Mennonite families moved into the community and opened a Sunday school in 1891. In January 1896 Peter Schantz organized the congregation at this place. In 1917 the remodeled church earlier purchased from the Christian Church and moved into Congerville was rededicated. When the Central Illinois Conference of Mennonites was formed in

1908 Congerville was a charter member. The congregation had 100 members in 1951.   G.Mi.

Congo Inland Mission was organized at Meadows, Ill., on March 22, 1911, by the Defenseless Mennonites and the Central Conference of Mennonites. The following members, consisting of four from each conference, served on the organizing committee: Valentine Strubhar, C. R. Egle, J. H. King, Peter Schantz, Benjamin Rupp, Aaron Augspurger, J. K. Gerig, and D. N. Claudon. The official name of this committee was "The United Mennonite Board of Missions," but on Jan. 23, 1912, the name was changed to "The Congo Inland Mission" and incorporated as such.

In 1911 L. B. Haigh and wife were sent to the Congo to investigate the field which had been recommended to them by the Presbyterian missionaries in the Congo, from whom they received much help. The following year the board decided to begin work in this field along the Kasai River. Alvin James Stephenson, a former Baptist missionary who had served two terms in the Congo, was sent to help the Haighs start the work. Before a year of service, he died on the field on Feb. 16, 1913.

After preliminary itinerating work, the village of Kalamba was made the center of missionary activities and Djoka Punda, later named Charlesville, the transport station. On Jan. 24, 1913, the mission force was strengthened with the arrival of Aaron Janzen and wife, Sarah Kroeker, and Walter Scott Herr. In January 1915 the first two converts of the

Congo Inland Mission were baptized at Djoka Punda and the first native church organized with a membership of 12, of whom 10 came from the near-by mission at Luebo. Medical work was carried on from the beginning, Oscar Anderson being the first physician on the field.

Outstations were continually being opened and in 1917 a training school was established at Djoka Punda to train natives for this work. In 1918 a girls' home was established both at Djoka Punda and Kalamba. A new mission station at Nyanga was opened in 1921. In May 1923 another station was opened at Mukedi. By the end of 1923 the church membership at the four stations was 200, by 1932 there were 1,200 members, and by 1936 the number of baptized Christians on the Congo Inland Mission field was 3,145. Between 1911 and 1936, 89 missionaries served in this work.

The mission carries on evangelistic, industrial, educational, and medical work. Each of the four stations has a boys' and a girls' school and natives trained to teach in the outstations. One of the most important activities has been the translation of the New Testament into the Kipenda language. This task was done at the Mukedi station and required nine years to complete.

At present (1954) the work of the mission is controlled by a board of 18 members, 6 from the Central Conference of Mennonites, 6 from the Evangelical Mennonite Conference, 3 from the Evangelical Mennonite Brethren Conference, and 3 from the General Conference Mennonite Church.

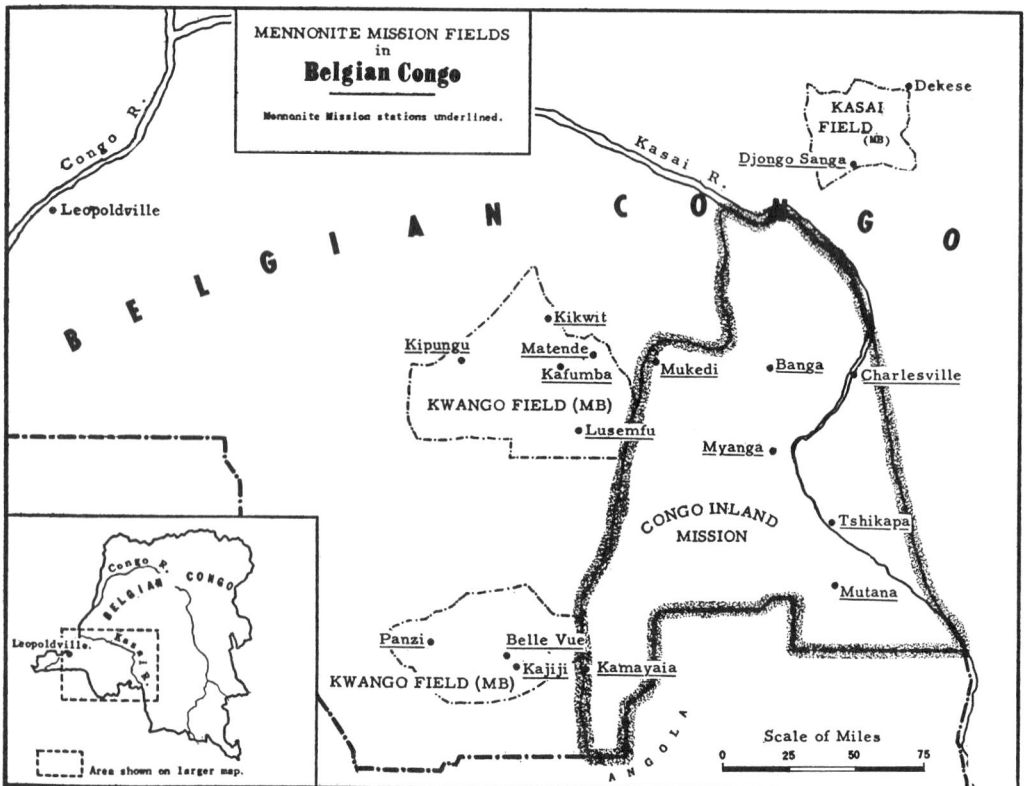

MENNONITE MISSION FIELDS in **Belgian Congo**

Mennonite Mission stations underlined.

The annual budget is $161,000. The official organ of the board is the *Congo Missionary Messenger*, published bimonthly. The total baptized membership on the field in 1954 was almost 15,000. A.N.

Congo Missionary Messenger, the organ of the Congo Inland Mission Board, is published at its home office, 4610 S. Woodlawn Ave., Chicago, Ill., and printed by the Economy Printing Company, Berne, Ind. Its first issue was dated August 1929. The purpose of this 24-page, bimonthly organ is to keep the constituency informed of the progress and needs of the work in the C.I.M. field in the Belgian Congo. The contents consists mainly of letters and articles by missionaries on the field, and in 1953 3,700 copies were sent without charge to all families of the supporting constituency.   R.L.H.

Congregational Church. The present-day Congregational Church had its roots in the Reformation period in England, where there were many who were ready for a more thorough reformation than that of slow-moving hierarchical Anglicanism. Since the days of John Wyclif the leaven of reformation had been at work. The influence of the Anabaptists and Luther was also felt in England. Contemporary documents repeatedly speak of the presence of Anabaptists in the eastern counties of England just across the English Channel from Holland where Anabaptists early developed strength. There was constant travel between the two countries, with exchange of ideas and influences. Dutch Anabaptists and Mennonites are credited by historians with contributing democratic ideas, religious and social, to the Reformation in these eastern counties in England. These ideas together with influences from the Zwinglian and Calvinistic continental Reformation, though not effective in the main line of the Anglican Church, came to expression in the Puritan and Independent movements.

The rift between the Puritan and the Anglican parties in the Church of England was too deep to bridge. The thoroughgoing Puritans were persecuted by church and state. Groups of uncompromising dissenters, who because they separated completely from the established church were called "Separatists" or "Independents," sprang up in Norwich, London, Gainsborough, Scrooby, and elsewhere in the second half of the 16th century. Many out of these had difficult times. Little bands of Biblical Christians, "harried" out of the land, fled to Holland, where they enjoyed complete religious freedom. But they were not happy there because of the difference in culture. They wished their children to grow up as Englishmen. For this reason they looked to the New World for their future home.

In 1620 the first shipload of these English Separatist immigrants, known as Pilgrims, landed in Plymouth Colony in Massachusetts. They were followed year after year by Puritans from the homeland, who though not Separatists, preferred to leave England to be free to build the church establishment according to their convictions and to create a state church in New England. Large colonies of them, beginning with Massachusetts Bay Colony at Boston, were established here. Meanwhile the Civil Wars were raging between Parliament and the King of England, which stimulated emigration to the New World still more. Puritans of all types flocked to New England. Here there was no civil authority and no church except what the colonists themselves established. By the town meeting they formed a democratic government, and by the congregational meeting they organized a democratic church. Here American democracy and congregational church government were born out of necessity and the practical application of New Testament teaching. Both the earlier Pilgrim Separatists of Plymouth Colony and Puritans of strong Anglican leanings found this government of church and state so satisfactory that they soon all accepted and heartily co-operated in it. The unified state church which they created came to be called the Congregational Church, which was "established" in Massachusetts until 1833.

While these events were taking place in New England the Reformation in England was going forward rapidly. Under the leadership and protection of Cromwell, himself an Independent who granted full religious freedom, the Independent congregations grew steadily in numbers and influence. They came to be called "Congregationalists" because they held to a congregational autonomy in church government.

The first century of the Congregational Church in America was largely the history of New England, especially of Massachusetts and Connecticut. Not until the Mississippi Valley began to attract settlers from the seaboard states did the church spread west, southwest, and south. Congregational churches are today found in nearly every section of the United States.

The genius of the Congregational Church is clearly stated in its declaration on church polity and wider fellowship: "We believe in the freedom and responsibility of the individual soul and the right of private judgment. We hold to the autonomy of the local church and its independence of all ecclesiastical control. We cherish the fellowship of all the churches united in district, state, and national bodies, for counsel and co-operation in matters of common concern. While affirming the liberty of our churches, and the validity of our ministry, we hold to the unity and catholicity of the church of Christ and will unite with all its branches in hearty co-operation; and will earnestly seek, so far as in us lies, that the prayer of our Lord for His disciples may be answered, that they all may be one."

The foregoing statement of polity and recognition of other Christian bodies as also the Church of Christ has numerous parallels in Mennonite teaching and practice. Mennonite polity, except in some of the conservative groups in North America, such as the Mennonite Church (MC), is congregational. The local church is autonomous. District and general conferences are, or originally were, purely advisory. They are the instruments through which the local churches co-operate in tasks too large for a single congregation. These similar traditions and practices, continued over the centuries, are not merely coincidental. They indicate, as historical documents show, a common heritage in the formative years of the Reformation.

The Congregationalists were the pioneers among the American churches in foreign mission work. The American Board of Commissioners for Foreign Missions, organized in 1810, maintains missions in Southwest and West Africa, in Turkey, Syria, India, Ceylon, China, Japan, the Philippines, the Pacific Islands, Mexico, Spain, Bulgaria, and Czechoslovakia. The Board of Home Missions, continuing the work of the American Missionary Association, the Congregational Church Building Society, and the Home Missionary Society, does a similar work in the homeland.

In 1931 the Congregational Church and General Convention of the Christian Church united to form one body, assuming the name Congregational Christian Church. At the time of the merger the Christian Church had 112,326 members while the Congregational Church had a membership of 939,130 in the United States, including Alaska and Hawaii. A further merger between the Congregational Christian Church and the Evangelical Reformed Church of the United States was halted by the courts in 1950.

In 1952 there were 5,626 Congregational Christian churches in the United States, with a total membership of 1,241,477. The Congregationalists in 1928 in England had 438,000 members. Unfortunately the exact relation between continental Anabaptism and English Anabaptism and Congregationalism has not been established.   P.E.W.

W. Walker, *The Creeds and Platforms of Congregationalism* (1893); idem, *The Congregationalists* (1894); A. W. Dale, *The History of English Congregationalism* (1907); G. G. Atkins and F. L. Fagler, *History of American Congregationalism* (1942).

Congregational Mennonite Church, Marietta, Pa., an unaffiliated congregation organized in 1951 by dissident members who had withdrawn from the Lancaster Mennonite Conference (MC) because of dissatisfaction with certain aspects of the conference discipline. In fact, the entire membership of the Marietta Mission (40), including its minister John Histand but not its deacon, withdrew to reorganize in the new congregation. Many dissidents from neighboring congregations have joined the group until the present (1953) membership is about 150.   H.S.B.

Conrad, the Shoemaker (Konrad Schuhmacher), was according to van Braght's *Martyrs' Mirror* a native of Swabia, Germany. He was apprehended at Stein on the Donau and imprisoned in Vienna in 1558. After some time he was brought before Emperor Ferdinand of Austria, to whom he freely confessed his faith. Later on after much suffering in prison he was set free by Emperor Maximilian, and could return to his relatives and his congregation. He is said to have been a young man. (*Mart. Mir.* D 190-91; E 574.)   vDZ.

Conscientious Objector. Although the origin of the term "conscientious objector" remains obscure, it was used during World War I to designate persons whose conscience forbade them to perform military service. Since then the term has remained in common usage.

From their earliest history the Anabaptist-Mennonites have given a Christian testimony against participation in war and military service. In 1524 Conrad Grebel said: "True believing Christians . . . use neither the worldly sword nor engage in war, since among them taking human life has ceased entirely . . . ." Menno Simons said: "The regenerated do not go to war, nor engage in strife. They are the children of peace who have beaten their swords into plowshares and their spears into pruning hooks, and know of no war . . . ." The early Mennonite confessions held the same position.

For more than two centuries service in the armed forces was practically unknown among the Mennonites of all countries. But since military service was voluntary during this period, nonresistance was not usually the immediate cause of conflict between Mennonites and the state. Persecution in this period was usually due to the entire religious position of the Mennonites (a voluntary church, separation of church and state, adult baptism, etc.), of which nonresistance was only one aspect. Following the time of Napoleon, however, when compulsory military service was generally first introduced, the conflict between Mennonites and the state more often than not has converged on the issue of nonresistance. This continued long after the achievement of general toleration.

Following the introduction of universal military service in the 19th century, the Mennonites of western Europe experienced a gradual decline in adherence to their nonresistant principles. During the Napoleonic wars a number of Dutch Mennonites served in the army. As late as 1850, however, when it was possible for conscientious objectors to secure exemption from service by hiring a substitute, most of the Dutch church leaders were opposed to voluntary service in the army. When the new Dutch military law of 1898 was enacted, without exemption for Mennonites, even the leaders failed to offer any objections. Among the Dutch Mennonites called up for military service during World War I, only one was a conscientious objector. He served a term in prison for taking this stand.

The 19th century witnessed a similar decline in nonresistance among the German Mennonites. In the last quarter of the 18th century the Mennonites of Prussia proper were required to give financial support to a military academy and suffered other forms of oppression, causing large numbers to emigrate to Russia. When the Prussian universal military training law was passed in 1814 the Mennonites were granted exemption, but only on condition that they continue to pay a tax instead of personal service. In 1867, following the founding of the North German Confederation, when a new universal military law with no exemption for Mennonites was enacted, the Mennonites appealed to Berlin. The only concession they received, however, was a cabinet order permitting noncombatant military service for those who had scruples against full service. As a result of this legislation Mennonites with strong nonresistant convictions emigrated to America. Those who remained at first accepted only noncombatant service. The difference between noncombatant and regular service was so slight, however, that the German Mennonites gradually accepted the latter. Thus the nonresistant position was gradually abandoned until in 1937 the *Mennonitische Blätter* (1854 ff., published at Elbing), the organ of the *Vereinigung* (Union of Mennonite Churches in Germany), asserted the loyalty of the German churches to the National Socialist regime, and declared that during World War I few if any German Mennonites had taken advantage of the legal provision for noncombatant service, and that there were no conscientious objectors refusing both combatant and noncombatant service. In 1935 the constitution adopted by the reorganized *Vereinigung* contained a statement declaring that the Mennonites had surrendered the principle of nonresistance and no longer claimed any special privileges in regard to military service.

The French Mennonites had a similar experience. Following 1870 French military law made no provision whatever for conscientious objectors. As in the case of Germany, many of the French Mennonites emigrated to America for the sake of their nonresistant faith, and among those who remained the doctrine of nonresistance seemed all but lost by the time of World War I, though it was still believed in a vague and general way. Many of the French Mennonites (especially in Alsace) retained their Swiss citizenship (most of them are of Swiss origin or background) for the specific purpose of evading military service, since as Swiss citizens resident in France, they are not called up for service. To retain their Swiss citizenship, however, and to be eligible to carry a Swiss passport, they must pay an annual Swiss military tax. No doubt many French Mennonites felt that this course kept them somewhat in line with the true Mennonite tradition. On the other hand, there was for several generations no teaching on the subject. For those who were not protected by Swiss citizenship, military service was taken as a matter of course, and during World War II many of the men were in the service, a considerable number losing their lives. This situation is emphasized by the fact that in 1949 a Paris attorney, whose specialty was legal assistance to CO's, and who was well informed about Mennonites as CO's generally, was unaware that any Mennonites resided in France.

In the 17th and 18th centuries the military system of Switzerland approached the methods of modern conscription more nearly than did that of any other country. The Swiss cantons not only recruited soldiers for their own defense, but autocratic noblemen recruited mercenary armies to be hired out to foreign governments. Refusal of the Mennonites to serve in these two capacities was therefore a genuine obstacle to the policies of the authorities, and helps to explain why the Mennonites of Switzerland were persecuted more severely and longer than in any other country. In the 18th century the Mennonites enjoyed military exemption under practically every other government, whereas in Switzerland they were being imprisoned, exiled, and sentenced to the galleys for refusing military service. Not until toward the end of the century was even partial toleration granted them, and not until 1815 were they given complete toleration. Even then they were excused from military service only by furnishing some form of substitute, usually by the payment of a special tax or commutation fee. In 1874, moreover, the administration of Swiss military service was transferred from the jurisdiction of the cantons to that of the confederation, and the controls became increasingly rigid. The law of 1874, however, still provided that CO's could serve in the *Sanitätsdienst* (*q.v.*) (medical corps), which was considered noncombatant service. Mennonites, apparently feeling that the new law providing noncombatant service was the solution of their problem, accepted its terms. Since then the Swiss Mennonites have been in uniform, and although most of them during the next 75 years accepted only noncombatant service, a few entered the regular service. During the first half of the 20th century, therefore, the Mennonites have had no part in the cause of full conscientious objection in Switzerland. Among the 67 cases of conscientious objectors brought to trial in Switzerland in 1939-45, there were no Mennonites. As medical corpsmen, however, the Swiss Mennonites did constitute a conscientious objector group.

Thus, following the adoption of universal compulsory military service by the governments of western Europe, those Mennonites who took their nonresistance most seriously emigrated, while those who remained gradually lost their nonresistance; during the two world wars there were few Mennonite CO's in western Europe. It was rather the Russian, Canadian, and American Mennonites that furnished the conscientious objectors during this period.

In Russia the Mennonites were not included in the national conscription system from the time of their settlement in the 18th century until 1880. After 1880, though they were conscripted, their position as conscientious objectors was recognized by granting them the privilege of alternative service in the Russian government forests. A program was set up in which the forestry service (*q.v.*) was under the direction of the state's technical service, which provided the tools and paid the men a small daily wage. The life of the men, apart from this, was under the direction of the Mennonite Forestry Service Commission, which housed, clothed, and fed the men, and provided them with a spiritual ministry. The term of service was four years. For some years after 1880 the average enrollment in the camps was about 400, with an annual maintenance cost to the church of 70,000 rubles, not counting the original cost of the buildings. Later enrollment increased until in 1913, the year before the beginning of World War I, the Mennonite CO's in the Russian forestry service numbered about 1,000 with an annual expense of 350,000 rubles. When the war began, the demands for service increased, and during the course of the war some 12,000 Mennonite CO's were engaged in government service. About 6,000 were in the forestry, and another 6,000 in the

Mennonite hospital and medical corps. The latter organized and financed complete hospital units of its own, who gathered soldiers from the battlefields and took them back to hospitals on hospital trains manned by Mennonites. During 1917 alone the Mennonites contributed over $1,500,000 for the support of their men in these two forms of service. The action of some Mennonites of the Ukraine in organizing a Self-Defense Corps (*Selbstschutz*, *q.v.*) in 1918 with the help of officers of the German army of occupation, followed by some actual fighting between armed Mennonites and groups of Russian bandits, no doubt increased the difficulties for Mennonite CO's.

The Soviet government, however, continued recognition of Mennonite CO's in principle until about 1935, and granted some form of alternative state service to eligible CO's on individual application quite regularly down to 1925. Thereafter it was made increasingly difficult, but a few cases were reported as late as 1935 by Mennonite refugees reaching Germany in 1943-45. The treatment varied from one case to another. In some cases the CO's were reported to have been shot, and in others the alternative service was practically the same as the forced labor of the concentration camps. The policy of the Soviet government in World War II of not conscripting German colonists because of their political unreliability, which enabled many Mennonites to escape military service, was something quite different.

The traditional policy of the Canadian government with respect to conscientious objectors has been a very liberal one. From 1808 to 1855 members of the Historic Peace Churches were recognized as conscientious objectors, and were excused from military service; but they were required to pay a twenty-shilling tax in peacetime, and four pounds in wartime. From 1855 to 1867 Canadian conscientious objectors were unconditionally exempted from military service. In 1868 the newly organized Dominion government provided for the exemption of CO's, "upon such conditions and such regulations as the Governor or Council may from time to time prescribe." In 1873 an Order in Council of the Dominion government promised complete exemption from all military service to those Mennonites about to immigrate from Russia. When conscription was introduced in 1917 there was some confusion in the application of the various laws and Orders in Council, resulting in prison sentences for a number of CO's. Eventually, however, a uniform policy was arrived at whereby all religious conscientious objectors called by the draft were given indefinite "leaves of absence" from military service.

During World War II the Canadian government provided a program of alternative service for conscientious objectors. When a conscientious objector was called up for service· he was required to file with the Mobilization Board an application for "postponement" of his military service. After he was passed by the Board as a CO, the man was referred to the alternative service officer of one of the Dominion's 13 mobilization districts, who then assigned him to alternative service work; under this system the man was assigned ·either to a government camp or to work for private individuals on farms or in factories. The men in the camps worked on the highways, engaged in forestry service and similar tasks, for which they received board, lodging, medical service, and 50 cents per day. Men working on farms received board and lodging and $25.00 per month for themselves. Earnings beyond this point were withheld and given to the Canadian Red Cross. Men assigned to industrial work paid their own board and lodging and then made payments to the Red Cross on a graduated scale depending on the amount of their monthly earnings. By 1946, when conscription came to an end, more than 5,000 Canadian Mennonites had been classified as CO's and had served in camps or in private agriculture or industry under the conscription system. Manitoba, the home of thousands of Russian Mennonites, had a larger number of CO's than any other Canadian province.

In the last year of World War II the Canadian government organized a "C.O. Medical Corps." Several hundred Mennonites, chiefly from the General Conference Mennonites and Mennonite Brethren, became members of the corps, receiving their training in the military camp at Peterborough in Ontario, and were sent to the military hospitals near the battlefields. For additional information on Canadian conscientious objectors during World War II see **Alternative Service Work Camps.** See also the map of Alternative Service Camps in Canada, page 606.

In the United States the government has always maintained a reasonably liberal policy with respect to conscientious objectors, although not as liberal as that of Canada. In the 18th century Mennonites were found only in the colonies of Pennsylvania, Maryland, and Virginia. During the American Revolution there was something approaching modern conscription in these three colonies. Citizens were required to attend military musters and join companies of soldiers called associations which were organized to fight the British. In all three colonies, however, it was possible to remain a nonassociator, because of religious objections or for other reasons, by paying a fine or furnishing a substitute. In Virginia, in 1777 a law was actually passed exempting Mennonites from military service when called, but putting them under obligation to furnish a substitute who was to be paid for by a levy on the entire church. The public was sometimes less tolerant of the CO than was the government. Frequently a great amount of popular pressure was brought to bear upon citizens to become associators. When nonresistant men refused to enroll, considerable feeling was aroused against them. In Pennsylvania there were actual cases of mob violence, so that the civil authorities had to warn the public to respect the consciences of these people.

During the American Civil War a permanent conscription policy in the North was not completed until late in the war. At the beginning of the war, when conscription was administered by the states, and even after the federal government first assumed the administration of conscription in 1863, it was possible for conscientious objectors and others to obtain exemption from military service by hiring a substitute, or by paying a commutation fee of several hundred dollars to pay for this purpose. But since the Mennonites as well as other conscientious objectors were opposed to the hiring of substitutes, a new federal draft act, passed in February 1864, provided that the commutation fee of $300 be applied to the benefit of sick and wounded soldiers. This fee was generally paid by Mennonite CO's.

The Mennonites of Virginia, located as they were in Southern territory where there was no provision for CO's before the enactment of the Confederate law of October 1862, suffered considerable persecution during the first 18 months of the war. A few weakened under the test and joined the army. Some hid in the mountains and came home to visit their families from time to time at night. Others when drafted went into the army under protest, with the understanding among themselves that they would not shoot. A Confederate general later testified, "There lives a people in the Valley of Virginia, that are not hard to bring to the army. While there they are obedient to their officers. Nor is it difficult to have them take aim, but it is impossible to have them take correct aim. I, therefore, think it better to leave them at their homes that they may produce supplies for the army." In the spring of 1862 a group of Mennonite and Dunker draftees attempting to escape to the North were captured and imprisoned.

The Confederate Conscription Act of October 1862 brought a measure of relief to the Virginia Mennonites. This law made specific reference to conscientious objectors, and provided two methods whereby they might obtain exemption from military service; viz., by finding a substitute, or by paying a tax of $500 into the public treasury. The Mennonites approved the second means of exemption. The new law led to the release of the men in prison, and also to the return of "such as were in the army and such as were in hiding near their homes." It is important to note that the Virginia Mennonites came to the assistance of the imprisoned men and of those in the army, helping them to raise the commutation money, and to pay the price to the authorities to secure their release.

During the last year of the war, when the Confederacy was sorely in need of men, and some of the fighting took place in the territory where the Mennonites lived, it seemed for a time as if the privileges of the law of 1862 would be lost. In spite of the law, attempts were made to impress young Mennonites into the army, with the result that many went into hiding in the mountains, some of them being hunted by army scouts who had orders to shoot them at sight.

During the Civil War the Mennonites in both the North and the South were severely tested. Unfortunately there are no statistics showing how many men were drafted, how many took a clear stand as conscientious objectors, and how many compromised their nonresistant position in one way or another. It is clear, however, that while many

met their test, there were others who did not. It is also clear that the American Mennonite Church in the 1860's did not teach its nonresistant doctrine aggressively and that it was not fully awake to the opportunities and obligations of the time. At the close of the war, for example, Secretary of War Stanton said that he and President Lincoln had "felt that unless we recognized conscientious religious scruples, we could not expect the blessing of heaven," and in the administration of the draft, Stanton went further than Congress in giving consideration to conscientious objectors. When he discovered that some Quakers had scruples against paying the commutation fee he ordered such paroled from the army. It seems probable that if the Mennonites had conceived and promoted a constructive program of alternative service it would have been granted them.

The conscription act of World War I provided for the exemption of CO's, with the further provision that "no person shall be exempted from service in any capacity that the President shall declare to be noncombatant." Although the act was passed on May 18, 1917, and actual conscription began in the late summer of 1917, the President did not define noncombatant service until March 20, 1918, and when he did so he defined it as noncombatant military service, which meant membership in the armed forces and the wearing of the military uniform. As early as 1915, and again after the United States entered the war in April 1917, various Mennonite conferences repeatedly declared themselves unable to accept military service in any form, whether combatant or noncombatant. When the first Mennonite men were called to the military camps the War Department informed them and the church that they would be offered noncombatant military service. If they could not conscientiously accept such service, however, they had the privilege of declining it, in which event they would be segregated until their cases could be officially disposed of. As the weeks passed by, a steadily growing number of Mennonite and other CO's who declined all military service accumulated in the various army camps. Although it was the intention of the War Department that these men should receive fair treatment, and that the conscience of all sincere objectors be respected, officials in the army corps were often lacking in understanding and sympathy. As a result, many CO's were mistreated, and some were court-martialed and sent to federal prison. Several men died as a result of mistreatment while in prison.

In June 1918 the Department of War took two actions which brought relief. The first was to apply to CO's a recently enacted law authorizing furloughs to men in the army "to engage in civil occupations and pursuits." The second was the establishment of a civilian Board of Inquiry to visit the military camps and review all cases of conscientious objectors. Those found sincere were to be granted furloughs, either for farm service or to engage in relief work with the American Friends Service Committee, then operating in France. When the war came to a close in November 1918, the

Board of Inquiry, though it had not yet completed its work, had succeeded in sifting out 1,300 sincere conscientious objectors of various religious beliefs, who accepted either farm service or reconstruction work in France, upon recommendation of the Board.

No complete analytical study has been made of the Mennonites who were conscripted in World War I. The number in camp was apparently nearly 2,000. The various Mennonite groups demonstrated varying degrees of loyalty to the principle of nonresistance; but the majority of the conscripted Mennonites refused service of any kind under the military. A substantial minority accepted noncombatant service, while a few accepted combatant service. Limited records of the Mennonite majority who declined all service under the military indicate that approximately 10 per cent (a total of 138) were court-martialed and sent to prison, chiefly at Leavenworth; 60 per cent accepted alternative service, either farm or reconstruction work; and 30 per cent remained in the camps until the close of the war, most of these not having had an opportunity to appear before the Board of Inquiry.

The experience of World War I had two very important results. First, it clarified the issues of noncombatant service, making it clear both to the Mennonites and to the War Department that no form of service under the military arm of the government was suitable for Mennonite CO's. Second, the farm furlough and the reconstruction program under the American Friends Service Committee pointed the way to the system of alternative service which was used during World War II. When the Conscription Act of 1940 was being written, army officials and representatives of the Historic Peace Churches agreed that this time men with conscientious scruples against both combatant and noncombatant military service should not be taken to the army camps. Consequently the law as passed provided that all persons "who by reason of religious training and belief" were conscientiously opposed to all forms of military service, should, if conscripted, "be assigned to work of national importance under civilian direction."

This provision in the law led to the establishment of the well-known Civilian Public Service system (q.v.) of World War II. The administration of CPS was a co-operative arrangement in which the government assumed responsibility for the work projects, while the church agencies (chiefly of the Historic Peace Churches) assumed responsibility for camp life and the nonworking time of the men. On the government's side, ultimate responsibility was vested in the Director of Selective Service. Under the Director of Selective Service, in immediate charge of the CPS program, was Camp Operations, whose duty it was to locate, equip, maintain, and supervise the CPS camps and special projects. It assigned, transferred, and discharged men from CPS, and reviewed their classifications. It initiated policies and administrative action having to do with the entire CPS system, and dealt directly with technical agencies and project superintendents having to do with CPS.

On the side of the church agencies, the National Service Board for Religious Objectors (q.v.) was organized to serve as liaison between Selective Service and these agencies. Normally Selective Service dealt with the church agencies indirectly through the NSBRO. The church agencies were consulted by Camp Operations in the formulation of its policies and, in the beginning at least, they had a genuine share in developing the program. In the matters of camp regulations, leaves, transfers, and discipline they had a considerable degree of freedom.

The church agency responsible for Mennonite CPS camps was the Mennonite Central Committee. The MCC operated a total of 23 base camps, 10 of which were under the Soil Conservation Service, 6 under the Forestry Service, 4 under the National Park Service, 2 under the Bureau of Reclamation, and 1 under the Federal Security Administration. Beginning in 1942 a large number of CPS units were organized for work in general and mental hospitals, and in public health and related services. No type of CPS service was held in higher esteem, either by the general public or by the men themselves, than were these various types of health service. Altogether, the MCC operated 25 mental hospital and 5 training school units. By the end of 1945, over 1,500 men had given service in such units, and even after the close of CPS some men continued in the hospital jobs to which CPS had assigned them.

The first CPS camps were opened in May 1941, and the program officially came to a close in March 1947. During this time approximately 12,000 conscientious objectors were drafted and assigned to "work of national importance." Of this number, 4,665, or 38 per cent of the total, were Mennonites, most of them serving in MCC camps or units. The Church of the Brethren and related groups had 1,540 men in CPS; the Friends (or Quakers) had 951; the Methodists, 673; the Jehovah's Witnesses, 409; Disciples groups, 227; Baptist groups, 223; the Congregational Christian Church, 209; the Presbyterian, 204; Roman Catholics, 149; Christadelphians, 127; Lutherans, 108; Evangelical and Reformed, 101; numerous other groups had less than 100 members each in CPS.

While the Mennonites furnished more CO's than any other denominational group, and while all of the American Mennonite groups were officially committed to the nonresistant and conscientious objector position, not all Mennonites called by the draft followed this course. In the case of the Old Order Mennonites, all men drafted were given a IV-E (CPS) classification. Two additional small groups had a 100 per cent record. The Old Order Amish and the Church of God in Christ Mennonite each had 93.5 per cent of their drafted men in CPS, and the Hutterian Brethren 90.6 per cent. At the other extreme, however, were the Mennonite Brethren in Christ and the Defenseless Mennonite Church with 4.8 per cent and 10.2 per cent respectively of their drafted men in CPS. The Mennonite Church (MC), the largest Mennonite group, had 59.5 per cent of its drafted men in CPS, the

Mennonite Brethren, 36.4 per cent, and the General Conference Mennonite Church, 26.6 per cent. The average for all American Mennonite groups was 46.2 per cent in CPS, 14.2 per cent classified I-A-O (noncombatant military service), and 39.5 per cent I-A (regular army service). While all Mennonite groups were officially committed to the CO position, not all groups dealt in the same manner with members who accepted military service. As a general rule those groups with a high percentage of men in the armed forces were also more lenient in their attitude toward men who accepted such service. In some cases military service did not affect their church standing whatever. In the more conservative groups, enlistment in the armed forces meant immediate severance of church relationship. The Mennonite Church (MC) represents a more or less middle position. Men who accepted military service were under church censure, but in many instances their cases were not disposed of until after the man returned from service. A census showed that in 1949, three and one-half years after the close of the war, approximately 32 per cent of the members of this group who had accepted military service were restored as members of the church after confession, whereas about 68 per cent had not been restored to fellowship. Since the number of men who joined the armed forces was about 1,300, this means that through the war experience the Mennonite Church (MC) lost approximately 900 young men. No comparable statistics are available for other Mennonite groups.

Although the administration of Selective Service was generally fair, a number of local boards were unsympathetic, and caused much difficulty for the drafted CO's. Some were denied CO classification, several of whom were given prison sentences when they refused induction into the army. From the various Mennonite groups more than 40 men were sentenced to prison, about 20 of whom were Old Order Mennonites who received CO classifications and then refused to serve in CPS. The number of imprisoned Mennonites is small, however, as compared with World War I, when 138 Mennonites were imprisoned in a war of much shorter duration.

During the war it was not only the nonresistance of the drafted men that was under test. It was rather that of the entire brotherhood, which was confronted with a variety of difficult questions related to the war program. In respect to the Red Cross, many Mennonites made contributions with the specific stipulation that they should not be used for military purposes, but that they be allocated to the disaster relief fund. Official attention was given to possible civilian defense activities, and the brotherhood was advised not to participate in any such activities as would contribute to the war effort. Disaster relief and similar activity, when not tied in with support of the war effort, were regarded as consistent, and out of this came constructive proposals which made their contribution to the voluntary service program which continued to grow following the war. Church leaders testified against work in war industries. One public-school teacher is known to have lost her position for refusing to participate in the sale of war stamps. Strong opposition was maintained against the purchase of war bonds, with the result that both the Canadian and the American governments approved plans whereby conscientious objectors to war could lend their money to the government for relief and civilian purposes, instead of for war purposes. Mennonites of the United States and Canada subscribed nearly $10,000,000 for these purposes.

The concern of the entire brotherhood for the cause of nonresistance is seen in the manner in which it supported the CPS program. The church-administered camps were financed by the churches. Although most of the housing and some equipment in the base camps was obtained from the government rent-free, maintenance and heating of the buildings, feeding and maintenace of the men, and general administration costs were met at church expense. Further, since the men received no wages, the church found it necessary to contribute something to their personal needs, and especially for the support of dependents. The total contributions received by the MCC for the operation of CPS, 1941-47, amounted to considerably more than $3,000,000. Since the support of CPS dependents was administered only in part through the MCC, and personal financial support of CPS men was administered almost altogether by local conferences and congregations, it is impossible to determine the total amount of such support. It is known, however, that the MCC spent over $47,000 for dependency aid; that the Mennonite Relief Committee of Elkhart, Ind., spent over $130,000; and that various local conferences and congregations spent from $2,000 to $6,000 each for these purposes. Hence it seems likely that the church contributed between $200,000 and $300,000, and perhaps more, for dependency support; it is impossible to determine the amount of personal contributions for support of individual CPS men. In addition to the above support, some of the Mennonite groups assisted CPS men in their occupational rehabilitation after discharge from camp. Educational grants-in-aid were also provided for men who desired to continue their education after discharge from CPS, the cost of the grants to be shared by the Mennonite colleges and the MCC or its constituent bodies. Closely related to the CPS program as supported by the church were the extensive Mennonite foreign relief and voluntary service programs, as developed during the war and which have continued indefinitely. Hundreds of Mennonite young men and women, many of them discharged young men, served in this work during and after the war.

The wartime experience made a great impact upon the CPS men themselves, and upon the American Mennonite churches as a whole. For the men it was an enriching spiritual experience, giving them a deepened understanding of the Christian life, a new appreciation of the Mennonite heritage, and a strengthening of their nonresistant conviction. While many weaknesses were discovered in the church as a whole, as revealed by the number of drafted men who did not take the CO position, and by numerous illustrations of inconsistency with that position by many church members, the wartime experience did have the helpful effect of making the American Mennonite churches conscious, as never before, of their place in the world and of the contribution they were being called upon to make. Following are some major results:

1. They acquired a new awareness of the Mennonite contribution to theology, and developed a deepened conviction that the Christian Gospel, and the message of love and nonresistance which according to the New Testament is an integral part of it, was sorely needed in their world.

2. They received an enlarged vision of their place in the mission field.

3. The experiences of the war helped to develop among the Mennonites a new social consciousness, and a new sense of social responsibility.

4. The churches came to see more clearly than ever before the place of the youth in the work of the church.

As to the CPS program itself, it was commonly agreed by the Mennonites that under it the opportunities for consistent Christian service were far more satisfactory than under the conditions of World War I. On the other hand, it was also agreed that in some ways CPS was not the most satisfactory solution of the CO problem. In some cases the work program was not as satisfactory as might have been desired. There was also much disappointment when foreign relief service was not permitted as part of the CPS program. Another undesirable feature was the lack of remuneration for the work which the men did. Then there was the question of how far the church should become involved in the enforcement of government regulations in a system such as CPS was. The Mennonite Church as a whole and the great majority of the men in CPS agreed that the decision to operate the camps was a wise one. On the other hand, there was also a general feeling that in case of future conscription some improvements on the wartime plan would be desirable.

Wartime conscription came to an end in March 1947. In 1948, however, a new draft law was passed, which became inactive in 1949. It was extended in July 1950, for one year, then reactivated in August 1950. This law provided for the deferment of all conscientious objectors. Then in June 1951, the law was amended to provide that the CO registrant should "be ordered by his local board, subject to such regulations as the President may prescribe, to perform for a period equal to the period prescribed . . . [for conscripted men in the armed forces], such civilian work contributing to the maintenance of the national health, safety, or interest as the local board may deem appropriate. . . ." It was the definite intention of this law that there should be no CPS system, but that conscripted CO's should give their service in some other manner.

The new program was inaugurated in the summer of 1952 and provided for the assignment of drafted CO's to approved government and private agencies for work which would contribute to the "national health, safety, or interest." The term

of service was fixed at two years, equal to that of men drafted into the army, and the CO's were to be remunerated at the prevailing wage rate of the employing agency. Once the man was assigned to a government or private agency for alternative service he was responsible to that agency until the assignment was completed. The agency would then report the completion of the assignment to Selective Service, and the latter would then certify the man's draft obligations as having been completed. By Sept. 26, 1952, Selective Service had approved the United States Public Health Service throughout the United States and territories as a federal agency to which CO's might be assigned. On the Selective Service list, as of the same date, were no less than 155 specific public and private agencies in 29 states which had been approved for the assignment of CO's. A high percentage of these agencies were hospitals and welfare agencies of various types. On the list of nonprofit private agencies nationally approved for the employment of CO's, were the Mennonite Central Committee, the Brethren Service Committee, and the Near East Foundation. Seventeen domestic and 32 foreign projects of the Mennonite Central Committee had been placed on the approved list. The foreign projects consisted of work in relief and voluntary service units in Europe, the Middle East, the Far East, and Latin America. The domestic projects included service in Mennonite hospitals, homes and charitable institutions, service units among Indians, migrant laborers, and similar services, including two units in Puerto Rico.

Thus in the summer of 1952 the Mennonites of the United States were entering a new era with respect to conscription. Obviously the new law was more liberal in its provisions for conscientious objectors than any previous law had been. A gratifying feature was the approval of foreign relief and service as meeting the requirements of alternative service, a recognition which was not granted during World War II. The absence of CPS camps, and the provision for remuneration for the men avoided certain administrative and financial problems for the church, although it seemed certain that the new program would also bring many new and unforeseen problems. It was confidently hoped, however, that the new program would be an improvement over all previous programs for the conscription of CO's, with greater opportunities for a consistent witness and service for peace.

In October 1953 Selective Service reported 6,964 registrants classified I-O (CO's not yet drafted), or I-W (CO's assigned to work projects and those released). Of these men, 3,712 were in I-W. By January 1954 the number of Mennonites in I-W had reached 2,411. By that month the Mennonite I-W men were serving in 32 states and the District of Columbia and in 18 foreign countries. The largest number of employees were working in mental and general hospitals.

As stated earlier in this article, the early persecution of the European Mennonites was directed primarily against their general religious nonconformity, rather than against nonresistance as such, since in that time there was no military conscription. After conscription was introduced the Mennonites of western Europe either solved the military issue through emigration, or through the process of gradual compromise and accommodation they eventually succumbed to the military requirements of the state. The result of this was that through the time of World War I, among the Mennonites of western Europe there had never been more than an insignificant number of conscientious objectors to war, in the technical, legal meaning of the term, as it was understood among the Mennonites of Russia, the United States, and Canada. As pointed out earlier, there was only one CO among the Dutch Mennonites called up for service during World War I.

It is significant to observe, however, that the period following World War I witnessed a significant revival of nonresistance, first in Holland, and then elsewhere in Europe. The *Gemeentedag* movement, founded among the Dutch Mennonites in 1917, had as its aim 'the bringing of the church to a more thoroughly Biblical faith. Included in its emphasis was nonresistance. During the 1920's and 1930's there gradually developed among the Dutch Mennonites a vigorous body of opinion opposing military service. In 1925 this led to the formation of the Dutch Mennonite Committee Against Military Service. After the war this organization was replaced by the Mennonite Peace Group. This new organization symbolized a changing emphasis in the peace teaching and peace work of the Dutch Mennonites. The earlier emphasis tended to be that of antimilitarism, whereas the later emphasis was increasingly that of Biblical nonresistance, so that by 1954 the Biblical position was dominant. By that time also about two fifths of the Dutch Mennonite ministers were members of the Peace Group.

While this movement was developing among the Mennonites of Holland other Dutch churches were having a similar experience, and shortly before the beginning of World War II the Dutch government recognized the new situation to the extent of liberalizing its military laws so as again to give some recognition to CO's. Following the war a program of alternative service was inaugurated, with civilian public service camps for CO's similar to those in the United States during the war. In 1952 several hundred Dutch CO's were engaged in this service, about 30 of them being Mennonites. These Dutch camps were government camps, however, like those of Canada; and the men also received pay from the government. Most of the men were engaged in soil conservation work, with some serving in mental hospitals. In 1952 also two Dutch Mennonites whose CO position was not recognized by the government were serving prison sentences.

Elsewhere in Europe there was also a revival of interest in nonresistance, although in 1954 this had not gone as far as in the case of Holland. In Germany the constitution of the new West German Republic provided that no one should be compelled against his conscience to perform military service. When the question of remilitarization arose, the German parliament took steps to enact legislation to implement this constitutional provision, the German churches were given the opportunity of stating their position on conscientious objection. In 1950 the German Mennonite conferences then went on record as supporting the position of the conscientious objector. This did not mean that the great body of German Mennonites had come to accept nonresistance in faith and practice once more. It did mean, however, that those who took that position would have the support of the church. In 1954 conscription had not yet been implemented in Germany, hence it was too early to know how many young German Mennonites, if any, would actually take the CO position.

In 1954 the Swiss and French military laws were essentially the same as at the time of World War I. In Switzerland noncombatant service in the medical corps was available, and most young Mennonites accepted this. There were signs of reviving interest in nonresistance, and some were happy for a medical discharge or some other technical means of exemption from military service. But so far none had refused all military service when actually called. French law in 1954 gave no consideration for CO's whatever, but a number of Mennonites who had formerly served in the army had now notified the government that they could not do so again. In 1951 the French Mennonite conferences also took official action requesting the government to provide alternative civilian service for CO's. By 1954 no such action had been taken by the government. Only one man from a Mennonite family had refused to serve when called, and he had disclaimed membership in the Mennonite Church. Thus while there was a growing interest in nonresistance among the Mennonites in Germany, Switzerland, and France, actual conscientious objection to conscription as found in the United States and Holland had not yet developed.   G.F.H.

C. H. Smith, *The Story of the Mennonites* (Newton, Kan., 1950); G. F. Hershberger, *War, Peace, and Nonresistance* (Scottdale, 1944); M. Gingerich, *Service for Peace: A History of Mennonite Civilian Public Service* (Akron, Pa., 1949); G. F. Hershberger, *The Mennonite Church in the Second World War* (Scottdale, 1951); J. S. Hartzler, *Mennonites in the World War, or Nonresistance Under Test* (Scottdale, 1921).

Consecration of Children, an old, though not universally observed custom among the Mennonites, which is based on Matt. 19:13-15; Mark 10:13-16; and Luke 18:15-17. The first mention of this ceremony is found in the letter written by Balthasar Hubmaier (*q.v.*) to Oecolampadius in Basel, on Jan. 16, 1525: "Instead of baptism, I have the congregation assemble, introduce the child, and in German explain Matt. 19:13-15. Then the child is named; the entire church prays with bent knees for it and commends it to Christ, that He may be gracious to it and intercede for it." Pilgram Marpeck (*q.v.*) also mentions the ceremony in his *Confession of Faith* of 1531 (*MQR* XII, 1938, 195).

In Ottius, *Annales Anabaptistici*, p. 35, the statement is made that in Nördlingen in Swabia some of those who left the Catholic Church favored infant baptism, while others opposed it. They reached an agreement by which those who believed in adult baptism should bring their infants to church, where they would be commended to Christ, our Mediator and Redeemer, by the laying on of hands and prayer.

In the *Christliches Handbüchlein* (1661), written in German at Berlin and then translated into Dutch, the non-Mennonite Jeremias Felbinger (*q.v.*) expressed the opinion that infants must be brought to church; the preacher, after a brief address to the congregation on the love of Christ to children, on the obligation of believers to live a childlike life, etc., takes the child into his hands, commends it to the Lord in prayer, and having returned it to the parents, lays his hands on it with a blessing.

Jeme Deknatel (*q.v.*), a Dutch Mennonite preacher, says in his book, *Menno Simons in 't Kleine* (1753, 196), "My brethren, since we do not baptize our infants, because Jesus did not do it or command it, and because they do not have the necessary qualifications, would it not be good to bless them by the laying on of hands, as Jesus taught us by His example? For we do nothing for our infants. If we truly believe these words of Jesus, would it not be good to do as Jesus did? Or if we do not do this would it not be right, when the mother comes back to church with her newborn child, to present the child with her to the Lord and bless them with believing prayer by the preacher and the church?"

Pieter Beets (*q.v.*), a Mennonite preacher of Hamburg-Altona (d. 1771), discusses the consecration of infants in an address delivered when he performed this ceremony in the home of the van der Smissen family. He warmly advocates the consecration of the child in church with thanksgiving for the mother's recovery; he also sponsors the consecration of the child by the preacher in the parental home. This was a practice in the Hamburg-Altona church (*Menn. Bl.,* 1900, 51, 58, 75); in Switzerland and in the Palatinate the practice is also encountered.

At the preachers' conference of the Palatinate and Hesse churches in session on May 9, 1830, it was decided that children should be consecrated the first time the mother comes back to church. On Oct. 8, 1843, this question was again discussed at Sembach and unanimously passed as a resolution. In the Palatine formulary (Worms, 1852, 28 f.) and in the Baden *Leitfaden zum Gebrauch bei gottesdienstlichen Handlungen* (Sinsheim, 1921, 131) infant consecration and the blessing of the mother is considered a church ceremony. The same is true of the *Handbuch zum Gebrauch bei gottesdienstlichen Handlungen* (Berne, 1893, 61), where the reason for the ceremony is explained at length.

The Mennonite Church at Gnadenfeld, Ukraine (1835 ff.), as well as the Mennonite Brethren Church (1860 ff.) there, consecrated their children in a ceremony before the assembled congregation (Friesen, *Brüderschaft,* 83 and p. 331; he derives the custom from Moravian influence).

Thus the consecration of infants is a customary practice in many Mennonite communities; some have both mother and child blessed in the church, in others the child is consecrated at home by the laying on of hands. Some Dutch Mennonite ministers consecrate the children in the home.

In the more conservative Mennonite groups in North America, among them, the large Mennonite Church (MC), the ceremony is relatively infrequent and is often opposed as smacking of infant baptism. In most of the General Conference Mennonite congregations the consecration of children takes place at regular intervals several times a year in connection with the regular Sunday morning service. The parents are asked to bring their children to the front where the minister leads in the consecration service, mostly using the *Ministers Manual.*

NEFF, H.S.B.

Gbl., 1886, 27; 1887, 52 and 60; *Menn. Bl.,* 1887, 41 and 67; 1900, 51, 58, 66, 75, 86; Abr. Hunzinger, *Das Religions-, Kirchen- und Schulwesen der Mennoniten* (Speyer, 1830) III, 113; W. Köhler in Schiele's *Handwörterbuch; ML* II, 487.

Conservative Amish Mennonite Conference was brought into being in 1910, at the invitation of the ministers of the Pigeon River congregation, near Pigeon, Mich., who invited ministers of other similar churches to gather with them in a ministers' meeting. The meeting was held Nov. 24-25, 1910. (An error in the official report of this meeting sets the date as Nov. 24-25, 1911.)

At this preliminary meeting, five ordained men were present: Bishop S. J. Swartzendruber and M. S. Zehr of the hostess congregation; Bishop Joshua King, Hartville, Ohio; Bishop John L. Mast, and Jonas D. Yoder of the Locust Grove congregation, near Belleville, Pa.

The purpose of the meeting was set forth in the first resolution: "That we stand more closely together in the work of the Lord, to maintain peace and unity in the so-called Conservative Amish Mennonite churches."

The name Conservative Amish Mennonite had been brought into use at the turn of the century by M. S. Steiner, compiler of Mennonite statistics, to distinguish these churches from the more progressive Amish Mennonite conferences on the one hand, and the more conservative Old Order Amish churches on the other.

The second meeting was held with the Maple Glen congregation, near Grantsville, Md., May 27-28, 1912. With this session the meeting became established as an annual conference, which it continues to be at this writing. Attending were 16 ordained men from Maryland, Pennsylvania, Ohio, Indiana, Michigan, Iowa, and Missouri. For the most part, those participating in this conference session represented congregations which, as the name of the conference indicates, felt that the established conferences of that day came short of certain Scriptural requirements, and that a more conservative emphasis was needed in the application of the Word of God than these afforded. On the other hand, it was felt that the Old Order Amish churches left certain things to be desired in the way of an aggressive church program. Most of the congregations interested in this new conference

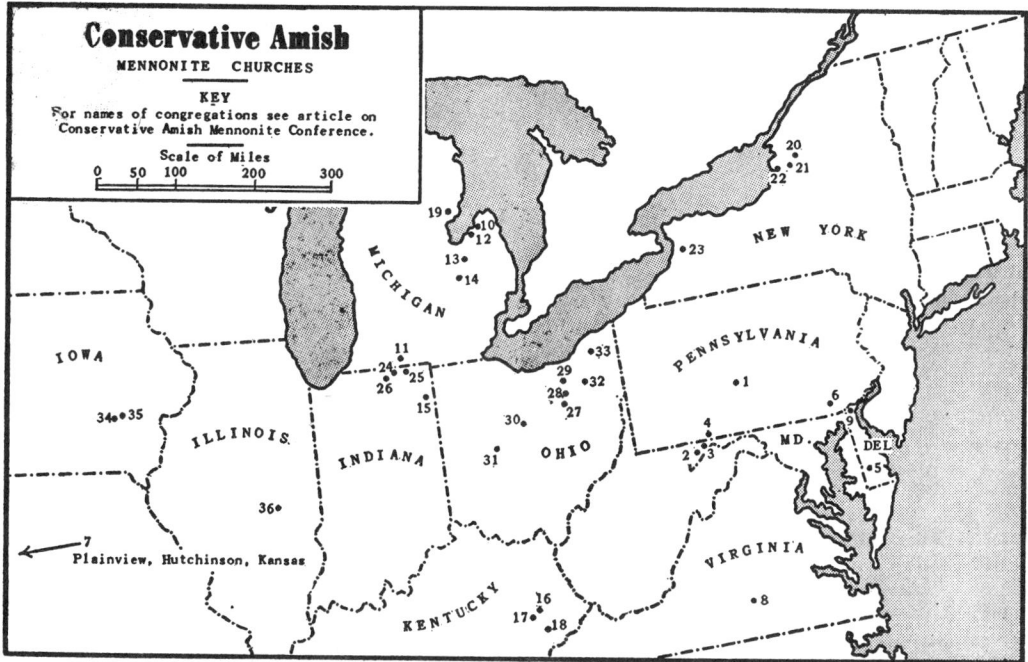

Conservative Amish
MENNONITE CHURCHES

KEY

For names of congregations see article on Conservative Amish Mennonite Conference.

Scale of Miles
0   50   100   200   300

movement stemmed from this latter group and had never been affiliated with any conference, while in several cases their background included contacts with the district Amish Mennonite conferences.

As the conference met year after year and its policies became more clearly outlined, other congregations applied for membership, while a few which had been represented at the first meetings withdrew. In this early stage of development, the conference functioned in a very informal way. It had no written constitution and by-laws to guide it in its work. In fact it did not adopt one until 1945. (Complete text of constitution and by-laws appears in conference report of that year.)

From its beginning, the conference has accepted the 18 articles of the Dordrecht Confession of Faith (q.v.) as an official statement of its belief. It has insisted on separation from the world for its membership in personal, social, and economic life, including such details as fashionable attire, use of tobacco and intoxicants, participation in war in any form, worldly business associations, secret societies, life insurance, and holding of government offices. Correspondingly it has sought to promote a positive Christian testimony through evangelism, benevolence, and personal sanctification.

At its second meeting, in 1912, the conference took steps toward establishing an orphans' home, which plans materialized by 1914 in the A.M. Children's Home, near Grantsville, Md., an institution which cared for many destitute children until it was closed in 1938 because of state restrictions, which among other things made interstate placement of children impossible.

At this same 1912 session a Sunday-school conference followed the church conference sessions and has remained an annual feature for the promotion

Key to Map of Conservative Amish Mennonite Congregations

1. Locust Grove, Belleville, Pa.; 2. Cherry Glade, Bittinger, Md.; 3. Maple Glen, Grantsville, Md.; 4. Oak Dale, West Salisbury, Pa.; 5. Greenwood, Del.; 6. Bart Chapel, Bart, Pa.; 7. Plainview, Hutchinson, Kan.; 8. Gladys, Va.; 9. Wilmington Mission, Del.; 10. Pigeon River, Pigeon, Mich.; 11. Riverview, White Pigeon, Mich.; 12. Fairhaven, Sebewaing, Mich.; 13. Vassar, Mich.; 14. Flint Mission, Mich.; 15. Cuba, Grabill, Ind.; 16. Turners Creek, Talbert, Ky.; 17. Bowlings Creek, Beech, Ky.; 18. Gays Creek, Ky.; 19. Riverside, Twining, Mich.; 20. Croghan, N.Y.; 21. Black River, Lowville, N.Y.; 22. Woodville, N.Y.; 23. Alden, N.Y.; 24. Griners, Middlebury, Ind.; 25. Town Line, Shipshewana, Ind.; 26. Pleasant Grove, Goshen, Ind.; 27. Pleasant View, Berlin, Ohio; 28. Maysville, Ohio; 29. East Union, Ohio; 30. Mt. Gilead, Fredrickstown, Ohio; 31. United Bethel, Plain City, Ohio; 32. Maple Grove, Hartville, Ohio; 33. Maple View, Middlefield, Ohio; 34. Upper Deer Creek, Wellman, Iowa; 35. Fairview, Kalona, Iowa; 36. Arthur, Ill.

of Sunday-school work throughout the congregations.

In 1912 the conference approved a plan for systematic, yearly visitation of all its congregations by ministers appointed for that purpose, who were to preach a number of sermons for each congregation. By 1918, through conference sanction, some of these efforts took on the form of Bible instruction meetings, which have been carried on in varied form and frequency since, in most of the congregations.

In 1917 the conference assumed joint responsibility for the publication of the *Herold der Wahrheit*, a German-English semimonthly periodical, launched in 1912 by a number of interested persons in the Old Order Amish churches.

In the same year the first definite action was taken in mission work, when it was decided that M. S. Zehr should go to the Ozark Mountains of Missouri to preach there if opportunity afforded and investigate the possibility of opening mission work. By 1919 a mission board was appointed by the conference. Besides numerous missionary efforts carried on locally by individual congregations, the conference established under its general mission board in 1929 a city mission at 2124 E. Williamson St., Flint, Mich., and in 1946 a rural mission on Turner's Creek, near Talbert, Ky., with a branch station on Bowling's Creek, near Beech, Ky., about one year later. In 1948 the Mennonite Board of Missions and Charities invited the conference to appoint representatives to its board, and since that time it has had two representatives on this board. In 1950 the conference appointed its first foreign missionaries, a couple to serve under the Eastern (Lancaster) Mennonite Board in Luxembourg, and established its own work in Espelkamp (q.v.), Germany. Since 1950 the following additional home missions have been established: Austin, Ind., Gays Creek, Ky., Mount Morris, Mich., and Blountstown, Fla.

In 1937 the conference elected a representative on the Peace Problems Committee of the Mennonite General Conference (MC). In 1941 it appointed a representative on the Mennonite Central Committee. In co-operation with this committee it contributed material aid and personnel for relief after World War I and during and after the last war, as well as participating in the Civilian Public Service program.

In 1948 a ministers' Bible study-discussion meeting was held which is now a regular annual feature.

Not officially affiliated with the conference, but working with it in matters of mutual interest such as relief and the recent CPS program, are a number of congregations generally known as "Conservative Amish Mennonite—Not under Conference," which are usually listed with this conference in Mennonite statistics. These congregations in 1954 numbered 1,664 members.

The conference ministers are almost always drawn from among the brotherhood of the congregations which they are to serve. Most of the ministers have been ordained through the lot, but this practice has changed considerably in recent years.

Among the founders and earliest supporters of the conference, the following bishops may be named: S. J. Swartzendruber of Pigeon, Mich., who proposed and guided the first meeting; Joel J. Miller of Grantsville, Md., in whose congregation the first general public conference was held, as a result of the preliminary meeting in Michigan; C. M. Nafziger of Lowville, N.Y.; Jonathan Troyer of Indiana; John L. Mast of Belleville, Pa.; Joshua King of Ohio; and the ministers, M. S. Zehr of Pigeon, Mich.; Jacob S. Miller and Jonas B. Miller of Grantsville, Md.; Jonas D. Yoder of Pennsylvania, and Gideon A. Yoder of Iowa.

Among those who later entered the service of the conference only a few may be named here: Elmer G. Swartzendruber and Amos Swartzendruber of Iowa; Emanuel Swartzendruber, Peter Swartz, and Earl Maust of Michigan; Sam T. Eash and Edwin Albrecht of Indiana; Roman Miller, Harry Stutzman, John Swartzentruber, and M. J. Swartzentruber of Ohio; Christian Roggie, Joseph Lehman,

and Joseph J. Zehr of New York; C. W. Bender, Emanuel B. Peachey, Sam T. Yoder, and Shem Peachey of Pennsylvania; Noah Brenneman of Maryland; and Nevin Bender and Eli Swartzentruber of Delaware.

In 1954 the total membership of the conference was 4,259. There were 36 congregations, of which five were in Pennsylvania and Maryland, two in Delaware, four in New York, one in Virginia, three in Kentucky, six in Michigan, seven in Ohio, four in Indiana, one in Illinois, two in Iowa, and one in Kansas. Fourteen bishops, 42 ministers, and 8 deacons were serving in these congregations. In 1954 Amish was dropped from the Conference name.

I.J.M.

Constance (*Konstanz*), a city (population 42,200) on the Bodensee, Baden, Germany, a Roman Catholic bishop's seat until 1817, when it was suppressed. Here John Huss was burned at the stake in 1415. Anabaptism appeared here very early. Already in 1524 Urban Rhegius wrote to Thomas Blaurer (Schiess, *Briefwechsel der Brüder Ambrosius und Thomas Blaurer* I, 94) warning him of it. Let Johann Wanner, the new cathedral preacher, "close their (the Anabaptists') mouths with the hammer of the Scriptures." Wanner wrote to Vadian (*Briefsammlung* III, No. 117, p. 281): "I wish all Anabaptists were wiped out." Hubmaier (q.v.) stopped briefly in Constance in 1526 en route to Nikolsburg. Egli (*Die Züricher Wiedertäufer*, 74) mentions an Anabaptist preacher by the name of Mumprat of Constance in Zürich, of whom hardly anything else is known.

In 1527 the Anabaptists Hans Bulstein of Augsburg and Hans Zurzacher of Zurzach came into the city. "But as soon as it was discovered that they were preaching their doctrine, they were laid in the tower, kept there several days, and were released on Monday, Oct. 7, 1527, and banished from the city upon an oath not to return, but allowed to remain until Sunday; but they should talk to no one about doctrine except in the presence of the regular preacher." "Citizens adhering to the Anabaptist error were warned and threatened with imprisonment" (E. Issel, *Die Ref. in Konstanz*).

In 1528 Ludwig Haetzer (q.v.) came to Constance. He was arrested and executed on Feb. 4, 1529. His execution caused great excitement in the city, revealing how much sympathy there was among the citizenry with Haetzer and the Anabaptists. Thomas Blaurer (q.v.) called the Anabaptists a "pious and calm people in all temporal matters." Johann Zwick, the Protestant pastor in Constance, and the most outstanding co-reformer with Ambrosius Blaurer (q.v.), also expressed himself very favorably concerning them.

But urged by Zwingli the council at first expelled them from the city. Christoph Schultheiss (*Collektaneen* IV, 14) wrote, "On July 12, 1529, Achatius Frömbd of Constance and Steffan Müller of Urach were seized on account of Anabaptism; they have sworn to leave the city."

On April 9, 1530, Urban Mennel was warned by the council that he should not permit an Anabaptist to enter his house, and report to the council any who came. On June 12, 1530, the council warned Marx Seidensticker that he should refrain from rebaptizing on penalty of prosecution. And on June 25, Ulrich Eigenmann, Jos. Peter, and his daughters Barbara and Anna, as well as Frau von Friberg of Bavaria, were ordered not to shelter Anabaptists and not to get mixed up with that faith. On Nov. 11, 1532, Brother Hans was banished from the city "on account of Anabaptism." On Nov. 18 Frau von Friberg met the same fate. In April 1538 Urban Mennel was again warned and threatened with expulsion. The last mention of Anabaptists contained in the council records of Constance was dated May 23, 1579. The daughters of the deceased *Altbürgermeister,* who had openly confessed Anabaptism, were deprived of their citizenship, and "although they had forfeited their life and goods to the imperial recesses and written laws, the council out of love and honor to their dear parents and relatives, has granted them a month to leave the city." Gradually the movement was completely suppressed in Constance. NEFF.

Konrad Gröber, "Die Reformation in Konstanz 1517-1532," in the *Freiburger Diözesan-Archiv* (n.p., 1919) 215, 252, 286; Ph. Ruppert, *Konstanzer geschichtl. Beiträge* V. 36; E. Issel, *Die Ref. in Konstanz* (1898); M. Krebs, *Baden und Pfalz, Quellen zur Geschichte der Täufer* IV (Gütersloh, 1951) 451-71, gives the Anabaptist documents for Constance and also "Thomas Blarers Bericht an Wilhelm Zell über das Ende Ludwig Hetzers" (Constance, 1529); *ML* II, 544.

Constantinople (now Istanbul), former capital of Turkey, served immediately after the Russian Revolution as a gateway of escape for Mennonites from Russia and of entry to Russia for the American Mennonite Relief (*q.v.*) (MCC). From Sept. 27, 1920, to July 1, 1922, an AMR unit administered relief in Constantinople to Russian refugees, particularly Mennonites. The first members of the unit were Orie O. Miller, Clayton Kratz (*q.v.*), and Arthur Slagel. Kratz never returned to Constantinople from his first trip to Halbstadt, from where he disappeared, probably arrested.

During November 1920, over 100,000 Russian refugees, former members of the White Army, arrived in Constantinople. Various American relief organizations, including the AMR, co-operated in helping these desperately needy people. Heinrich Schroeder of Halbstadt, Russia, who arrived on Nov. 19, informed the unit that there were a number of Mennonites among the refugees, who were then gathered in the Mennonite Home, located in the city. In February 1921 the home was moved to Yeni Kuey, six miles north of the city. It was managed by Frank Stoltzfus and later by J. E. Brunk, and had a hospital connected with it. Other workers were Vesta Zook (later Slagel) and Vinora Weaver (later Salzman). The population of the home varied from 100 to 200, of whom usually two thirds were Mennonites. In all, between 250 and 300 Mennonite refugees from Russia spent some time in the home. This included also the "group of sixty-two" men who had been serving in the White Army. Most of the Mennonites went to the United States, Germany, and Canada (for their experiences see "Konstantinopel," *Bote,* Nov. 26, Dec. 3 and 10, 1952). The home was closed in the spring of 1922.

Other activities of the AMR conducted in Constantinople centered around a children's shelter, a Russian women's home, the distribution of clothing, loans for transportation, etc., always keeping in mind the greater need in Russia. During its operation from October 1920 to July 1922, the total expenditure of the Constantinople unit was $200,738.

The AMR was closing its relief activities in Constantinople when 217 Mennonite refugees, stranded in the port of Batum on the eastern shore of the Black Sea in Caucasus, tried to get to Constantinople in order to proceed to the United States. They had come to Batum from the Molotschna and Crimea via Feodosiya. The first group arrived in Feodosiya late in 1921. A second and third group followed in January and February 1922. The last two groups of over 60 left Feodosiya Feb. 12, 1922, and arrived in Batum five days later. Over 70, mostly children and old people, lost their lives through undernourishment, disease, and congested living quarters. Through AMR and Near East Relief, the refugees received some food—flour, condensed milk, rice, beans, and sugar; this food saved the lives of many of the 217 Mennonite refugees. Finally the doors opened and one after another they left for Constantinople where they were cared for in the Mennonite Home until they could emigrate to America. J.K.S.

P. C. Hiebert and O. O. Miller, *Feeding the Hungry, Russia Famine 1919-1925* (Scottdale, 1929) 90-110.

Contenius, Samuel: see Kontenius, Samuel.

Continuation Committee of the Historic Peace Churches was created at the 1935 Conference of Historic Peace Churches (Mennonites, Brethren, and Friends) held at Newton, Kan., to consider ways and means to strengthen and co-ordinate the peace position and testimony of the three groups in the face of approaching World War II. This committee, composed of three representatives, one chosen by the Mennonite Central Committee, one by the Brethren Service Committee, and one informally by the Friends, has been the channel for calling occasional leader-conferences of 25-100 persons representing the three groups to continue the type of effort begun in the 1935 conference. These conferences have been held about once per year, usually in the Chicago area. Orie O. Miller has been the continuous MCC representative; the Brethren representative is now Harold Row, preceded by M. R. Zigler, and initially C. Ray Keim. The first Friends representative was Robert W. Balderston, followed by Errol Elliott.

In 1947 a similar Continuation Committee was set up in Europe under the initiation of M. R. Zigler, also composed of one from the MCC European staff (Robert Kreider, H. S. Bender, G. F. Hershberger, Irvin Horst, J. H. Yoder in order), one English Friend (Eric Tucker), and one from the Brethren Service Committee European staff (M. R. Zigler). This committee has held conferences annually or oftener, the annual conferences meeting in Heerewegen (Zeist), Holland. Recently the International Fellowship of Reconciliation (Percy Bartlett) has joined this group.

Neither committee has any official status or

authority, but both have served frequently to stimulate thinking and action either for the groups individually or together. The European committee was the channel for the formulation of a co-ordinated parallel statement of the four groups to the World Council of Churches, giving their peace testimony under the title *War is Contrary to the Will of God,* printed in 1951, German edition in 1952. It also provided a similar but integrated statement, *Peace Is the Will of God* (1953), prepared for the World Council meeting of 1954 at Evanston, Ill.

H.S.B.

Contra-Huiskoopers (Anti-Housebuyers), the name of a party of Flemish Mennonites in Friesland, who in 1586 became involved in a quarrel with the *Huiskoopers* (house-buyers) concerning the purchase of a house by Thomas Bintgens (*q.v.*) in Franeker. The *Huiskoopers* were also called the "Thomas Bintgens group," and the *Contra-Huiskoopers* were called "Jacob Keest group" after their preacher Jacob Reiningen or Keest. The better-known Claes Ganglofs also belonged to the *Contra-Huiskoopers.* In 1632 and even in 1646 the Flemish Mennonites in Holland were sometimes officially called *Contra-Huiskoopers,* but soon afterward they were known as the *"Sachte* (Gentle) Flemish," or simply "Flemish," the name *Contra-Huiskoopers* falling into disuse.   J.L.

Blaupot t. C., *Friesland,* 112, 163; *idem, Groningen* I, 57, 271-77; *DB* 1875, 30; *Inv. Arch. Amst.* II, Nos. 117, 120-22; *ML* I, 369.

Conversion, from the Latin *com,* together, and *vertere,* to turn, means primarily a turning toward. Theologically, conversion is the changing of purpose, direction, and spirit of life from one of self-seeking and enmity toward God to one of love toward God and man (*Century Dictionary*).

In the English Bible the word "convert" is used seldom but the idea is very common and usually expressed by "turn" in a situation indicating religious connotation, such as, "And if thy people . . . shall *turn again* and confess thy name . . ." (II Chron. 6:24). In the New Testament this turning or conversion, commonly coupled with repentance, becomes a chief end of preaching and involves turning from darkness to light (I Pet. 2:9), from vanities to the living God (Acts 14:15), from death to life (John 5:24). It is the beginning of a new life with all interests and powers of the being centered in Christ. Such a revolutionary and significant change is only conceived of as taking place by divine power, God alone creating the new heart and new spirit. "Regeneration" is employed, strictly speaking, to designate this act from the divine side, while "conversion" refers specifically to the voluntary act of the individual in turning from sin and seeking forgiveness and the new life. However, the distinction is not always maintained and the two words are often used interchangeably.

In the definitive expressions of Anabaptist-Mennonite faith and practice conversion has always occupied a key position. This is clear in 16th-century writings, testimonies, and confessions, and is reiterated in later representative writings. In all such discussions the approach is practical rather than theological and adheres closely to Biblical terms, expressions, and quotations.

Conversion-regeneration was fundamental. Early Anabaptist writers for practical purposes identify conversion with regeneration. In the same breath Menno Simons speaks of the heart "renewed, converted, justified, made pious" (*Works* I, 24), and also "Regeneration . . . is an inward change which converts a man by the power of God" (*Works* I, 27). Furthermore, this single event, whether viewed from the divine or human side or from both together, was so important that it was basic to all else in the Christian life. Menno writes in his chapter on the new birth:

"We must be born from above, must be changed and renewed in our hearts, transplanted from the unrighteous and evil nature of Adam, into the true and good nature of Christ, or we can never be saved by any means, whether human or divine" (*Works* I, 169).

So also Dirk Philips: "Here the kingdom of God is absolutely denied to all who are not born again of God, and who are not created by Him anew after the inner man in His image . . ." (*Enchiridion,* 376).

Conversion was a prerequisite for baptism. The place of the conversion-regeneration experience in the early Anabaptist thinking was delineated clearly in contrast to other prevalent conceptions and was brought to focus in the matter of baptism. For the Catholic mind conversion consisted essentially in the acceptance of a creed and the authority of the church. The Reformers broke with this idea in principle and taught rebirth through faith as necessary to true conversion. In practice they were unable to carry it out in the indiscriminate membership of the state church. As a result regeneration became separated in thought from moral change, with infant baptism serving as the occasion for an inner spiritual regeneration which sometime later would produce the moral fruits of conversion. The Anabaptist-Mennonite fathers broke with the reformers at this point, insisting on the application of rebirth to all members of the visible church. They refused to see regeneration, conversion, and amendment of life as anything but a single transaction essential for all true believers. It was therefore essential for baptism, since only true believers could compose the church. The *Schleitheim Confession* in its first article expresses the position which was repeatedly reaffirmed: "Baptism shall be given to all those who have learned repentance and amendment of life, and who truly believe that their sins are taken away by Christ, and to all those who walk in the resurrection of Jesus Christ . . . and to all those who with this significance request it . . . for themselves. This excludes all infant baptism . . ." (*MQR* XIX, 1945, 248). Thus, through baptism, conversion became the key to voluntary church membership and the Anabaptist brotherhood, a pattern for free churches to follow.

A further point to be noted is that conversion-regeneration marked the entrance into a New Covenant of which baptism was the external sign and seal. The authority of God and God's word was always in the background and the believer entered the new life with a sense of absolute responsibility to obey. This became the foundation of Anabaptist piety; hence amendment of life and obedience to the word of Christ was a necessary concomitant of conversion. Thomas von Imbroich wrote (1558): "Penitent faith is confessed, and so to speak, sealed with Christian baptism. For, after baptism, a constantly good and godly life should follow" (*Mart. Mir.*, 356). This "good and godly life" was part of the expression of a deeper obligation to obedience under suffering which was well expressed by the Hutterite Peter Walpot in writing to the Polish apothecary Simon (1571). Simon had written that "so far everything has been easy and lovely." Peter replies, "It may be that you will suffer martyrdom, my Simon . . ." and then recounts the Hutterite sufferings—wanderings, imprisonment, bonds, death—and continues: "If you should be alone in such an experience, . . . then things will look otherwise. Then you will be for once pushed into the furnace of testing and it will become known what is in your heart. If you desire to become a true disciple and follower of Christ and a member of his church, then you must certainly prepare yourself for such experiences" (Zieglschmid, *Chronik*, 456; *MQR* XIX, 1945, 35). This emphasis in thought on godly living and obedience in suffering was not based on the idea of performing good works and obtaining merit, which the Anabaptists were careful to disclaim, but on the necessary association of faith and love and the identification of the believer with the living Lord. Conversion was an integral part of the life that was to follow which they saw as "nothing but pure dying and suffering" (*Mart. Mir.* 355).

It would be misleading to assume that the ideals and practice of the 16th-century church have been uniformly maintained throughout the intervening centuries. Deviations have been brought about in three ways. First, with the cessation of persecution and with acceptance by society, the ideal of the suffering church became less distinct. Mennonites entered the world in a way impossible for their forefathers with consequent distraction from religious ideals. Conversion became less vital though the form of voluntary decision with adult baptism was always retained. Secondly, where the attempt was made to retain separation from the world on a racial, linguistic, or other formal basis the place of group membership by birth practically beclouded the importance of church membership by rebirth. Thirdly, there came the pietist-revivalist movement which tended to re-emphasize the place of conversion with its spiritual significance. New Mennonite movements arose based on spiritual experience and even cataclysmic conversion. These provided a needed corrective to formalism and secularism but often carried a subjective emphasis on conversion as an experience for its own sake, and by itself, disconnected from the life of suffering and obedience of the martyr days. In some modern Mennonite groups considerable weight is laid on a personal confession of a definite and precise momentary conversion experience as a prerequisite for baptism and church membership. This is particularly true of the Mennonite Brethren Church and related groups and the United Missionary-Mennonite Brethren in Christ Church. The course of these deviations can be traced in Mennonite histories and is well discussed in Robert Friedmann's *Mennonite Piety Through the Centuries*. S.F.P.

"The Schleitheim Confession of Faith," English translation by J. C. Wenger, *MQR* XIX (1945) 243-53; *The Complete Works* of Menno Simons (Elkhart, 1871); Dirk Philips, *Enchiridion or Hand Book of the Christian Doctrine and Religion* (Elkhart, 1910): Zieglschmid, *Chronik* (Carl Schurz Memorial Foundation, 1943); *Mart. Mir.*; R. Friedmann, *Menn. Piety Through the Centuries* (Goshen, 1949); J. C. Wenger, *The Doctrines of the Mennonites* (Scottdale, 1950), where appendices contain in conveniently accessible form English translations of five early confessions and catechisms, with their statements regarding conversion and regeneration.

Cookery, Mennonite (American). Cookery is inextricably interwoven with the family—its housing, its daily routines, its celebrations, its traditions. Geographic and climatic conditions, and the possibilities or difficulties of gardening further contribute to differences in the table fare of the family.

Until recent times, cooking equipment was quite primitive. Among eastern Mennonites "refrigeration" in summer was provided by cool springs; in the west, wells and storm cellars were used. For winter, root vegetables were stored in sand, cabbage in a barrel underground, potatoes and apples in bins. Fruits were frequently dried or pickled. Barrels of sauerkraut, jars of sorghum and apple butter promised variety. A barrel of "boughten" soft white sugar was expected to last throughout the winter.

The hub of warm weather activity for many Mennonite homes was the summer house, which served to keep the heat of the extra cooking during the threshing and preserving seasons out of the house. The Low Germans built *Spoaheat* (brick ovens) into one corner of their kitchens or summer kitchens. Twisted straw or dried dung was used for fuel. The Pennsylvania Dutch built large brick ovens outdoors. On baking day a roaring wood fire was started in the oven. When the heat was great enough, the coals were raked out and a dozen or so loaves of bread were set in to bake. After the bread came 16 to 20 pies, then perhaps trays of fruit to dry. In both East and West, into one corner of the basement, the summer house, or a separate outbuilding, was built what the Low Germans called a *Miagrope*—a bricked-in kettle. Here water was heated for washing or butchering. In it lard was rendered, apple butter cooked down, or soap manufactured. An important piece of equipment among the Pennsylvania Dutch was the doughtray (a rectangular box on legs) in which flour was stored, and dough was mixed, then set near the hearth to rise.

Breadstuff in its various forms indeed served as the staff of life for Mennonites, at times providing the main course. French toast, served with jelly, syrup, or brown sugar, came to be known as Mennonite toast; many a family made a meal of corn bread and milk, or corn-meal mush with milk or fried and served with syrup, apple butter, or creamed tomatoes. Buckwheat, corn, or wheat pancakes were general favorites. The Westerners relished a very thin, large pancake, which sometimes enclosed cherries or cottage cheese. It is reported that when times were hard some Kansas families had only pancakes to eat—breakfast, dinner, and supper. Combinations of flour products and other foods were popular—"rivels" (tiny lumps of egg and flour simmered in milk); fruit soups (bread, milk, and fruit—usually berries); noodles or a variety of dumplings steamed in soup, stew, hot milk or water. *Vareniki* was a dumpling enclosing cottage cheese. It was boiled in water or fried in deep fat. Apple dumplings were usually baked—the Low Germans called them *Piroshki*. They also enjoyed *Bobbat*—a batter in which sausage or salt pork was baked. It was also sometimes used as stuffing for duck.

Breads and cakes were almost indistinguishable, for the German word *Kuchen* applied to much of baking. Coffee cake in varying forms was a universal favorite. Certain other "cakes" were traditional in the various groups—the Pennsylvania Dutch prepared *Fastnachts* (raised doughnuts) for Shrove Tuesday; Swiss weddings or holidays were not complete without "nothings" or "kneepatches" (a very thin, plate-size, fried cruller). The Russian Mennonites considered *Portzelki* (raisin fritters) essential for New Year's Day, and *Rollkuchen* (a rectangular light cruller) a necessary accompaniment to watermelon. *Paskha* (raisin bread) appears at Easter; *Zwieback* still enlivens Christmas, Easter Pentecostal, and even Saturday suppers and Sunday meals. These rich two-layered rolls are often served with *Plumemoos,* and ham. *Plumemoos* was a fruit soup usually made of raisins and prunes, served either hot or cold. Other favorites of the Russian Mennonites are rye bread, poppyseed rolls, and *Schnetke* (a biscuit).

At Christmas the Prussians and the Low Germans fill jars with *Pfeffernüsse, Springerle,* and other hard cookies. Springerle are formed by rolling with a pin which has pictures carved in its surface. Among Mennonites in general, sugar cookies and soft ginger cookies have always been favorites. Cake recipes are found in multitudinous variety in the old handwritten recipe books of the Pennsylvania Dutch but always with vague quantities and directions. One needed to be an artist, indeed, to use them. Early favorites were poundcake without icing, marble cake (the dark part made with brown sugar and molasses), coconut cake, hickory-nut cake, ribbon cakes, and jelly rolls.

Pie was served three times a day by the Pennsylvanians. The "shoofly" pie is a molasses crumb pie; other favorites still appreciated are vanilla tart pies, open-faced custard fruit pies, milk and buttermilk pies, elderberry and green tomato pies. The Amish prepared half-moon dried apple pies which were called "preaching pies" because their dryness allowed them to be carried to church to keep the children pacified during the long services. They were also customarily served at the meal following preaching. Pies were usually stored on swinging shelves in basement or springhouse or later in "safes" (cupboards with pierced tin doors).

In order to fill out the "seven sweets" traditional among the Pennsylvania Dutch, various puddings were developed—"pap" and other milk puddings, fruit puddings, steamed puddings (*Dampf-Knepp*), and the famous *Schnitz und Knepp*. This latter was a dish of dumplings steamed over dried apples and sometimes a ham bone.

Soups were more than another dish; they were a way of life—simple, economical, conserving of precious foodstuffs. Favorites were potato, onion, ham and green bean, chicken and corn, bean, and *Borscht*. The Mennonites of Russian background prepare summer *Borscht* with ham bone and greens; the winter variety with beef, mutton, or chicken and root vegetables and cabbage. An important ingredient is sour cream, added just before serving.

Butchering day was a great event in Mennonite families. It meant hams, bacons, and sausage in the smokehouse—perhaps dried beef and beef sausages too. It meant scrapple, liverwurst, pickled pigs' feet, and jars of lard in the cellar. It provided fats for homemade soap.

Chicken was "for company" and for holidays. But ducks, geese, and turkeys were holiday foods too. Dressings were varied. Since most Mennonites in America were inlanders, their consumption of fish was limited.

Salads are conspicuously absent from early Mennonite menus, except for lettuce, cabbage, and cucumbers served with sour cream dressings. Vegetables were varied but were simply served. In the East the "seven sours" included many relishes, such as piccalilli, corn salad, mixed pickle and pickled fruits, besides the usual cucumber pickles. Pickled beets and eggs are distinctively Pennsylvania Dutch. Russian Mennonites like pickled watermelon.

Beverages were usually simple herb teas; cheeses were either cup, ball, or cottage cheese except among the Swiss; confections were limited to taffy made of sorghum, or to popcorn balls or sugar cubes.

Most of the foods mentioned above are still cherished today, particularly for family holidays; but the fried cakes and steamed dumplings are giving way to more easily digested foods. The use of salads is increasing—gelatine salads are being substituted for the puddings. Other American dishes such as ice cream, hamburgers, and "hot dogs" are being increasingly incorporated into Mennonite diets. Some traditional dishes have become almost a lost art. But the Mennonites continue to be justly renowned for their ability to make plain substantial foods into very palatable ones. It should be said of course that Mennonite cookery has not been uniquely Mennonite but largely an integral part of the culture of the country in the regions of which they are a part, although immigrants coming to America brought with them from the "Old Country" the cookery of their native lands, some of which has persisted in the descendants of the original immigrants for several generations. Eva H.

B. S. Epp, "Typical Low German Foods" (paper, Bethel College); R. Hutchison, *The Pennsylvania Dutch Cook Book* (New York, 1948); *Pennsylvania Dutch Cook Book* (Reading, 1936); M. E. Showalter, *Mennonite Community Cookbook* (Philadelphia, 1950). This last title has sold over 50,000 copies, and is the only available large-size cookbook giving historic and current recipes used by Mennonite women, who furnished most of the recipes in the book. Recently a number of local community cookbooks have been prepared by Mennonite women, sometimes actually published by the local congregation or a subdivision of it. Katie Burkhart, *Lancaster County Cook Book* (2d ed., East Earl, Pa., n.d.); *Mennonite Cook Book* (Danvers, Ill., 1931); *The Sunshine Cook Book* (Peoria, 1952); *The Walnut Creek Cook Book* (Walnut Creek, Ohio, 1949); Mrs. Elmer Lehman, *The Kidron-Orrville Community Cook Book* (Kidron, Ohio, n.d.); *Off the Mountain Lake Range* (Mountain Lake, 1949).

Cool, a Mennonite family in the Netherlands, a branch of which is found in the Dutch province of Groningen. The first known ancestor of this branch was Geert Jans Cool (*ca.* 1725-96) who died in Appingedam. The Cool family was connected by marriage with other Mennonite families such as Blaupot. Some members of the Cool family in the 19th century served their country in high military ranks.

Besides a number of deacons two members of this family were Mennonite pastors: Pieter Cool (*q.v.*) and his son Gerrit Cool (1840-1902), who served the congregation of Wormerveer op het Noord from 1866 until he retired in 1899.

A Cool family, which may not be related to the Groningen branch, is found in Amsterdam; members of a Cool family belonged to the congregation *bij't Lam* as early as 1646.   vDZ.

Inv. Arch. Amst. II, 126; *Ned. Patriciaat* XVII (1927) 129-40.

Cool, Pieter, b. Oct. 31, 1807, at Amsterdam, educated at the seminary in Amsterdam and the university of Leiden, became the Mennonite minister at Purmurend in 1832, and at Harlingen in 1836; he retired in 1872. He died Sept. 12, 1891; in 1838 he married Catharina Fontein (1808-71), of an old Mennonite family at Harlingen. Their son Gerrit was pastor of the Wormerveer op het Noord congregation in 1866-99. Cool was, as his works indicate, a modernist in theology and a total abstainer from the use of alcohol. Collaborating with D. Harting, the Mennonite minister at Enkhuizen, he founded the *Doopsgezinde Bijdragen* (*q.v.*) in 1861, and served as its editor until 1869. In 1870 he published in this yearbook an article (1-15), "De hoogste roeping der Friesche Doopsgezinde Sociëteit en soortgelijke vereenigingen," and in 1877 (101-32), 1878 (78-97), and 1880 (I-41), "Iets over en uit het archief der Doopsgezinde gemeente te Harlingen." Besides a work on Arabic linguistics, the following of his works (all published in Harlingen) should be mentioned: *Redevoering bij het 25jarig bestaan van het Nederlandsch Bijbelgenootschap* (1839); *Gesprekken over het leven van Jesus door Strauss* (1840); *Een woord van opwekking om lid te worden van de vereeniging tot afschaffing van sterken drank* (1854); *Waarheid in beelden* (1857 and 1867); *Is byzondere liefde tot zijn kerkgemeenschap een Christelijk beginsel?* (1857); *De stichting der nieuwe Doopsgezinde kerk te Harlingen* (1858); *Lezen-eten* (1859); *De afschaffing der afschaffingsgenootschappen* (1860); *De feestmorgen van Zondag 13. Oct. 1861 herdacht* (1861); *Een levensrecept* (1869). He and P. Feenstra, Jr., together published

Gedenkschrift van het Menno-Simons monument (Zwolle, 1879). In addition to these works he published a number of articles in the magazines, *De Gids* and *Licht, liefde, leven.* (*Biogr. Wb.* II, 198; *DB* 1892, 139; *ML* I, 370.)   J.L.

Coolman, a Dutch Mennonite family of mostly farmers. This family goes back, as far as is known, to Fiepke Fokkes, who is said to have been born in 1630, and who was a farmer at de Meeden (*q.v.*) in the Dutch province of Groningen. From the third generation on their descendants spread all over the province of Groningen, and are found as members of nearly all Mennonite congregations of this province. The name of Coolman does not appear, it seems, before 1790; in this year the records of the Mennonite congregation of Noordbroek (*q.v.*) mention the name of Fiepke Olferts Coolman, who seems to have assumed this name, which henceforth regularly was used by his sons and his further descendants.

The members of this family nearly all belonged to the Groninger Old Flemish Mennonites. Fiepke Olferts (1692-1729) of Midwolda (*q.v.*) married (1717) the great-granddaughter of the well-known Old Flemish Elder Uco Walles (*q.v.*). Many members of the family have served as deacons, and Fiepke Harms (b. 1690, d. 1759), a farmer of de Meeden, was chosen as a preacher of the Meeden congregation in 1725.

In the course of time the Coolman family, which is known for its outstanding farming (agriculture), has become allied by marriage to other Mennonite families living in this province of Groningen, like Boer, van Calcar, ten Cate, van Cingel, Hesselink, Huizinga, Meihuizen, and others.

A collateral branch of the Coolman family (the name is in the 18th century also spelled Koolman) is the ten Doornkaat Koolman family.

Fiepke Olferts Koolman, first a farmer at Midwolda, then a distiller of brandy at Pekela (*q.v.*), married (1771) Annegien ten Doornkaat, who was a daughter of Jan ten Doornkaat. (This Jan ten Doornkaat was originally from Hengelo, *q.v.*, in the province of Overijssel, where his family is found from about 1650; he settled as a wood-dealer in Noordbroek, province of Groningen.) The son of Fiepke Olferts Koolman and Annegien ten Doornkaat was called Jan ten Doornkaat Koolman. He moved to Norden, East Friesland, Germany, where he married Antje Doedes Cremer (see **Cremer** family) and founded the still existing world-famed distillery.   vDZ.

J. Huizinga, *Stamboek . . . van Fiepke Foppes en Diever Olferts* (Groningen, 1887); *DB* 1902, 113.

Cooman, Joris, an Anabaptist martyr: see **Goris Cooman.**

Co-operatives. The practice of co-operation in human history is as old as is the practice of competition. Both co-operation and competition describe aspects of the human social process. They are expressions of behavior with contrasting characteristics. Co-operation is the act of two or more individuals or agencies working together to obtain common objectives, while competition is the act of two or more individuals or agencies striving against one another, each to attain for himself the same objective.

Co-operation in the form of an organized socio-economic movement with clearly stated principles and permanent organizational structure is, however, only a little more than 100 years old. The origin of the present-day co-operative movement dates back to 1844. In the little industrial town of Rochdale, England, a group of textile weavers developed a set of operating principles which have since served as the basic premises of the world-wide co-operative movement. These principles call for economic organization which provides that all profits be distributed to the patrons on the basis of their respective patronage; it provides that each member have only one vote in the business affairs of the organization regardless of the number of shares held or the amount of money invested; it demands that all capital invested earn a fixed rate of interest rather than a fluctuating rate, depending on the profitableness of the enterprises; it requires political and religious neutrality and an open membership; and it insists that a portion of the earnings be spent for educational purposes to promote the understanding of the co-operative technique.

Mennonites have practiced a form of co-operation much older than the Rochdale co-operative system. Their co-operation has traditionally been called mutual aid. This has been characterized by its basic religious motivation and is a type of brotherhood economics. It has generally been more spontaneous and informal in organization than the present-day systemized and organized co-operative movement. Mennonite communities have been significantly affected by the modern co-operative movement, but there has been great variation according to geographical locality and official church attitudes. In some communities Mennonites have remained completely aloof from all co-operative organizations. In other communities they have participated in patronizing co-operative organizations but have refrained from holding membership and from accepting offices; and in still other communities they have been active promoters of the co-operatives and have taken the lead in organizing new co-operative ventures and in enthusiastically promoting the growth of co-operatives.

The reasons for opposition to co-operatives are primarily two. First from a religious angle, church members are urged to refrain from joining co-operatives because it is feared that to join such an organization would mean becoming unequally yoked with unbelievers (II Cor. 6:14). The second basic objection sometimes offered is that co-operatives seem to be a threat to such basic tenets of capitalism as freedom of individual enterprise and the profit motive. However, those who are attracted to the co-operative movement see in this economic method an ethical ideal superior to the prevailing ethics of competition under capitalism. They feel the co-operative principles are more nearly commensurate with basic Christian ethics than is the unregulated competition of capitalism.

Co-operatives have significantly affected the economic life of many American Mennonite communities, and the growth of co-operatives is everywhere apparent according to recent trends. The co-operative movement in America is strongest among farmers, and Mennonites, being predominantly agricultural, find themselves directly affected by both local and national economic currents. The most common types of co-operative organization in Mennonite communities are grain elevators, oil service stations, creameries, groceries, and credit unions. In most areas where Mennonites engage in specialized farming, such as orange growing in California, potato growing in Idaho and Ohio, poultry and dairying in Indiana and Pennsylvania, fruit growing in British Columbia and Ontario, raising sugar beets in Alberta, wheat in Kansas, and sunflower seeds in southern Manitoba, Mennonite farmers tend to join marketing co-operatives to dispose of their products to the best possible economic advantage. Many Mennonites join the Farm Bureau Co-operative.

In Canada, especially, there are numerous illustrations of co-operative health prepayment plans and a number of co-operative burial societies. The latter are generally carry-overs from the older mutual aid organizations, and are not properly classed as co-operatives.

Organized co-operatives are found much more frequently in the United States and Canada among the Mennonites of Russian origin than among those of Swiss and South German or Alsatian origin. The explanation in part probably lies in the fact that the Mennonites in Russia and in Prussia developed an extensive system of mutual aid organizations (see **Mutual Aid**) to which modern co-operative organizations are a natural appendage. In at least some of the Mennonite communities studied, it was found that the leaders of mutual aid organizations were also the leaders in establishing the more modern co-operatives. There is therefore something of a continuous chain between the older mutual aid organizations and practices of the Mennonites and the modern co-operative organizations in Mennonite communities.

Among Mennonite colonists in Paraguay the co-operative is the most important economic organization. It is a legally incorporated entity chartered by the national government in the country where it is located. Its primary and original function in each colony is to serve as a store. However, the co-operative performs a much wider scope of functions. It not only serves as the buying and selling agency for the ordinary consumer goods of the colonists but it serves also as the chief, and in many cases the only, marketing agency for all salable commodities. In addition the co-operative serves as a colony bank. Since very little cash is handled many colonies have their only liquid assets as credit on the books of the colony co-operative.

Almost all Paraguay family heads belong to a co-operative. It resembles a farmers' co-operative in the United States and Canada except that it does not operate on the Rochdale principles, under which dividends are paid to the members in proportion to their savings which have been determined by the amount of business done. In South America the co-operatives are operated solely for the benefit of the entire colony somewhat on the order of a company store. Members are paid interest rates on balances due on their accounts and adjustments are made between time for withdrawals. Colony members may borrow money from the co-operative as well as make loans to it.

The co-operatives have been so essential to the welfare of the colonies that it is doubtful if the colonization efforts could have succeeded without them. The extreme isolation of the colonies from markets, the lack of transportation, and the poverty of the colonists make it impossible for individuals to market their produce or to journey to the markets to make their purchases in person. (See **Fernheim** *Agricultural Co-operative* and **Friesland** *Agricultural Co-operative.*) J.W.F.

C. A. Dawson, *Group Settlement: Ethnic Communities in Western Canada* (Toronto, 1936) Part II; J. W. Fretz, "Mutual Aid Among Mennonites," *MQR* XIII, 28-58 (January 1939); 187-209 (July 1939); *idem*, "Mennonite Mutual Aid: A Contribution Toward the Development of a Christian Community" (Ph.D. Thesis, Univ. of Chicago, 1941); *idem*, *Pilgrims in Paraguay* (Scottdale, 1953); *idem*, "Recent Community Building in Canada," *MQR* XVIII, 5-21 (January 1944); M. Gingerich, *The Mennonites in Iowa* (Iowa City, 1939) Chapter 20; D. Paul Miller, "Co-operative Transforms Rural Economy," *Menn. Life* IV, 18-20 (April 1949); J. J. Siemens, "Sunflower Rebuilds Community," *Menn. Life* IV, 28-31, July 1949).

Coopersburg, called Freyburg from 1818 to 1832, is located at the southern tip of Lehigh Co., Pa., and has a population of 1,462. The original white settlers of this place were mostly Mennonites who immigrated from the Palatinate between 1725 and 1737. George Bachman was one of these early settlers. About 1738 the Saucon Mennonite Meetinghouse was built. Preacher Michael Landis built a house here in 1808, which is well preserved. The Calvary Mennonite (MBC) Church is also located here. The Mennonite population of the area is 250. W.W.S.

Coopersburg, an Old People's Home at Akkrum, Dutch province of Friesland, founded 1900 by Folkert H. Cooper. This Folkert was a son of Willem Harmens Kuiper and IJtje Rommerts de Vries, both loyal members of the Mennonite congregation of Akkrum. They were rather poor and had a large family. So their son Folkert Harmens Kuiper at the age of 23 decided to emigrate to America, as did many in Friesland in the second half of the 19th century. In the United States he first had some very difficult years, but then made a fortune in business, owning at first a drugstore in Peoria, Ill., and then managing large stores in Chicago and New York, of which in the course of time he became the private owner. He changed his name to Cooper. Before long he was well-to-do, and about 1890 even a very wealthy man. He did not forget his parents. As soon as he could earn money he sent some to his parents and relatives, first a little, and soon more. He also visited his father, who died in 1897 at the age of 94, many times. His mother had died shortly after he emigrated. Cooper himself spent his last years in his native country, dying at Akkrum on Dec. 31, 1904.

In 1900 he founded the Coopersburg Old People's Home to the memory of his parents, as the Frisian inscription in the cornerstone states. The home contains 22 small houses, which are intended particularly for married couples at least 60 years of age. They have their own living quarters and also a small kitchen to prepare their meals. The inmates also receive a certain sum of money. The home is not limited to Mennonites, though Mennonites have priority. The foundation is administered by a board, of which the Mennonite minister of Akkrum is a member (*DJ* 1911, 68-81, with picture.) vDZ.

Coopmans (Koopmans), a Dutch Mennonite family, originally living at Grouw, province of Friesland. A known ancestor of this family was Rinse Coopmans, b. at Grouw about 1650. He was a butter merchant. His great-grandson Claas Rinses Coopmans, b. 1739 at Grouw, d. 1793 at Leeuwarden, was for some time also a butter merchant and exporter, but in 1772 he disposed of this trade, because he thought that a true Christian could not be a merchant. Then he became a preacher of the Mennonite congregation of Leeuwarden, capital of Friesland. His son Rinse Coopmans, who like his descendants spelled the name "Koopmans" (*q.v.*), was a Mennonite minister and professor at the Amsterdam Mennonite Seminary. vDZ.

Ned. Patriciaat XI, 1920, 124-32; F. H. Pasma, *De Doopsgezinden te Grouw* (Grouw, 1930) 16.

Coornhert, Dirk Volkertsz, b. 1522 at Amsterdam, d. Oct. 29, 1590, at Gouda, was a Dutch scholar versed in many fields of science and art, an outstanding figure of the Renaissance in Holland, versatile and talented. Though he never actually left the Catholic Church, he nevertheless opposed it and went his own independent way. It was his aim to hold to "the clear meaning of Christ"; the center of evangelical doctrine is love to God and one's neighbor. Man must strive to be perfect as Christ of the Gospels and he is able to achieve this (perfectionism). Coornhert was a typical individualist. No one church can be the true church. Church reform, dogma, and confessions of faith are the work of men; if one has Christ in one's heart one does not need these things. Kühler called him the "Sebastian Franck of the Netherlands." This Coornhert, who found violent opponents among the Calvinists and was severely attacked by Calvin himself, had considerable influence on the Dutch Mennonites, especially on the Waterlander branch, who like Coornhert laid much stress on uprightness of life and were inclined "to have no assurance that their church was the visible church of God." During the time when Coornhert was notary and city secretary of Haarlem (1577-88) he had many contacts with the Waterlanders.

Coornhert was a close friend of Hans de Ries (*q.v.*), the great Waterlander leader, who followed Coornhert in the doctrine of perfectionism. The regenerated person is able through the power of God in Christ living within him, to keep the commands of the Gospel perfectly. In 1580 Coornhert sent to "de Ries and his friends" a booklet on *'t Overheyds Ampt* (The Office of Government). He set a beautiful monument to the friendship which bound him "to God-loving Hans de Rijcke" (Ries) in the booklet, *Opperste goedts nasporinghe.*

When in 1587 dissension broke out in the Waterlander congregation in Haarlem, Coornhert, who was probably present at the meeting, managed to subdue it and prevent a division. Soon afterward, in November 1587, at a conference in Alkmaar, Coornhert had a debate with Jacob Jansz Scheedemaker (*q.v.*), the elder of the Haarlem Waterlander congregation, in which, under Coornhert's influence, the audience came to the conclusion that persons who live a Christian life (keep God's commands) must also be considered as "dear fellow members of their congregations even though they have had neither baptism nor communion or other customary forms of worship." Of great significance was Coornhert's opposition to David Joris. He wrote against Joris the booklet, *Kleyn-Munster, Des groot-roemigen David Jorisens roemrijke en wonder bare schriften elckerlyck tot een proeve gestelt* (1590).   vdZ.

Of the copious literature on Coornhert we will mention only: Kühler, *Geschiedenis* I, *passim*; *Biogr. Wb.* II, 212-49; J. Lindeboom, *Stiefkinderen van het Christendom* (The Hague, 1929) 264-74; B. Beeker, "Coornhert," in *N.N.B.Wb.* X (1927); H. Bonger, *D. V. Coornhert* (1941); *Inv. Arch. Amst.* I, Nos. 2311 f.; *ML* I, 370.

Cop Heyne, of Couwerve near Reimers-Wool, Dutch province of Zeeland, a linen weaver, an Anabaptist who recanted but was nevertheless executed at Middelburg, capital of Zeeland. During his trial he gave some very remarkable information about the life and practices of the congregation.   vdZ.

Pekelharing, "Bijdrage van de Gesch. der Herv. in Zeeland," *Archief Zeeuwsch Genootschap* VI (1806) 26-29; *DB* 1908, 8; Mellink, *Wederdopers*, see Index.

Copenhagen, the capital of Denmark. During the War of the American Revolution, in which both England and France were involved, Mennonites repeatedly requested citizenship in Copenhagen, as, for instance, did Peter Ackerman of Ameland in 1782. Refusal to take the oath of loyalty prevented the granting of the requests. The Danish government sent an inquiry on this matter to the Danish German chancellery, which controlled the German-speaking duchies and understood conditions at Altona, and received the information that it was "a foregone conclusion that no Mennonite would swear a formal oath, but could promise with his Christian yea and nay." But no congregation was ever built up in Copenhagen. The MCC headquarters for its relief service to the West Prussian Mennonite refugees in Denmark was located in Copenhagen from April 1946 to January 1949. (*ML* II, 548.)   R.Do.

Coppenol, now **Coppenaal,** a former Mennonite family. Willem Jansz (van) Coppenol, b. about 1525, fled in 1579 with his family from Thielt in Flanders, Belgium, to Haarlem, Dutch province of North Holland. He was a Mennonite and likely a cloth merchant. His son Pieter, b. about 1550, who was a tailor, was a member of the Waterlander congregation at Haarlem; another son, Willem, b. about 1571 at Thielt, was also a member of this church and later at Leiden, where he ran a school, which was attended by Mennonite children. A son of Willem was Lieven Willemsz van Coppenol, b. about 1599 at Leiden and after about 1617 living in Amsterdam. He was also a schoolteacher; besides this he was a poet and a well-known calligrapher. He seems to have been a rather rough man; about 1650 he lost his mind. He was well acquainted with

Rembrandt (*q.v.*), who made three portraits of him (an oil painting of about 1632, now in Kassel, Germany, and of 1658, now in London, and an etching of 1658). (*Jaarb. Amstelodamum* XXX, 1933, 93-187.) On the Dutch island of Goeree-Overflakkee, province of South Holland, the family name Coppenaal is still very common. At the present time all the bearers of this name belong to the Reformed Church. They are of Flemish descent; during the 17th and 18th centuries their forefathers were mostly Mennonites.   vdZ.

Cops: see **Kops.**

Corbachius, Johannes, a Jesuit, author of the book, *Contra Anabaptistas unici baptismatis assertio* (Cologne, 1535), written entirely in the traditional line of historiography, with no understanding of the nature and significance of the Anabaptist movement. (*ML* I, 370.)   NEFF.

Cordell, Washita Co., Okla., is a Mennonite trading center of 3,500 population, located in the west-central part of the state. Mennonites (GCM and MB) occupy nearly one third of the county adjoining the city on the northeast. Wheat farming is predominant. There are 65 Mennonites living in Cordell, and 2,000 within shopping distance of the city. In the area there are four churches from 8 to 18 miles from the city with 1,250 members, Herold and Bergtal of the General Conference Mennonites, and Bessie and Corn of the Mennonite Brethren. P.D.

Corn, Okla., located in the northeast corner of Washita County, owes its start to the Mennonite Church (GCM), built that the growing number of Mennonite members might have a common place to worship. Today a large Mennonite church (GCM) stands at Corn.

In 1894 Peter Bergman donated part of his land for a Mennonite church. A sod church was built, a dugout with a low sloping roof and sides made of sod. Benches were made of cottonwood from local trees.

The name Korn, as it was spelled originally, was given to the town by a government agent who came out to select a site for a post office. Because a patch of corn was located in the vicinity, the town was named Korn. During World War I the spelling was changed to Corn, and has remained that way to this day.

Corn is the center for four Mennonite communities of which two are M.B. and two General Conference Mennonite. Wheat raising is the major industry, though along the Washita River, four miles to the west, feed and cotton are grown extensively. Corn has a public school and high school, and also the Corn Bible Academy under the auspices of the M.B. Church.   H.H.

Corn Bible Academy was established by the Corn M.B. Church in 1902 at Corn, Okla., as a Bible and language school, under the name of "Washita Gemeinde Schule." From 1902 to 1906 it had a children's and also a young people's department with separate instruction. Then until 1919 it was conducted only for young people with one instructor and a three-year course. In 1920 the curriculum was expanded and two teachers employed until 1934, when it was fully accredited with the state of Oklahoma and more instructors were added to the staff. Since then there has been a normal but steady growth until today (1954) the school has six full-time instructors and one part-time instructor. Each student is required to take a Bible subject each semester plus the four units of high-school work. The new building (the third building since its founding) erected in 1945-48 includes a 300-seat auditorium, a 1,750-volume library, and a study hall. Present building plans call for the erection of another wing, thus adding four more classrooms. The 95 students enrolled come from the local church and the M.B. churches of Oklahoma, Texas, and Kansas. J. W. Vogt is superintendent. The superintendents who have served the school, with their lengths of service, are here given: D. J. Klassen, 1902-4; D. L. Schellenberg, 1904-5; J. F. Duerksen, 1905-11; D. F. Straus, 1916-18; H. D. Wiebe, 1919-37; L. S. Wiebe, 1937-41; H. R. Wiens, 1941-46; B. P. Pauls, 1946-47; J. P. Kliewer, 1947-48; Leo Goentzel, 1948-49; and J. W. Vogt, 1949- . During the years 1911-12 and 1918-19 the school did not operate, the first time because of lack of funds, and the second time because of the World War I situation.   J.W.V.

Corn (Okla.) Mennonite Brethren Church, with a baptized membership of 680, is a member of the Southern District Conference of that body. It was organized Nov. 2, 1893, by 16 Russian Mennonite families coming here from Goessel and Buhler, Kan., early in the same year. At first services were held in homes; in 1894 a dugout church was built which gave way to a frame building in 1898, to which two wings were added in 1905. A new and larger sanctuary was built in 1918, which was destroyed by fire Jan. 16, 1949. On March 3, 1949, work was begun on a new brick building with a seating capacity of 1000. A special church project is the Bible School begun in 1902 in a new two-story frame building, which was superseded by a new brick structure in 1919. Begun in 1947 and now complete, the Bible School and Academy has adequate classrooms and auditorium, a faculty of six and a student body (1954) of 95, and has a fully accredited high school. In 1947 a Home for the Aged was completed with a capacity of 20 rooms.

Pastors serving the church were Abraham Richert, Peter Neufeld, Isaac Harms, H. H. Flaming, J. J. Wiebe, J. K. Warkentin, and J. P. Kliewer, the last three salaried. With them have served 21 associate ministers and 15 deacons. Twenty-eight missionaries have gone to the foreign field. The church has a Sunday-school department, Christian Endeavor (*Jugendverein*), Christian fellowship, midweek Bible school, YMCA, YWCA (local only), choir, Gospel team, sewing circle, junior mission circle, conducts a daily vacation Bible school, a weekly radio broadcast, and several organizations do extension work.

Members of the extinct Mennonite Brethren churches of Gotebo, Okla., and Caddo Co., Okla., joined the Corn congregation between 1910 and 1920. Members of the extinct Krimmer Mennonite Brethren Church of Weatherford joined in the late 30's.   J.P.K.

Cornelia, an Anabaptist martyr who was executed by drowning at Zutphen, Holland, on March 30, 1549. She was the widow of Claes van Leeuwen (*q.v.*), the rector of the school at Zutphen, who had also been baptized upon confession of his faith. When it became known after his death that he had been rebaptized the government had his corpse exhumed and buried in unconsecrated earth. But Cornelia was arrested and subjected to a severe cross-examination. She at first refused to render the oath, referring to Matt. 5. But at the end, probably forced to it by terrible torture, she gave the oath "with upraised fingers." She denounced infant baptism, Mass for souls, prayer to the saints, and the Catholic doctrine of purgatory and the sacrament of the altar with appropriate Scriptures. She had been baptized by Adam Pastor.   NEFF.

DB 1881, 42, note; 1909, 112 ff.; *ML* I, 370; *Kerkhistorisch Archief* I (Amsterdam, 1857) 116-18, contains a letter written by Cornelia; *ML* I, 370.

Cornelia Wouters, wife of Jan Pieters, of Middelburg, Dutch province of Zeeland, was put to death by beheading on Oct. 15, 1535, because she had lodged Anabaptist preachers and read heretical books. Her husband was banished from the territory of Holland, Zeeland, and Friesland for 50 years. (Te Water, *Reformatie van Zeeland,* 1766, 14.)
                                                        VDZ.

Cornelis of Culemborg (Kulenborg), a Dutch city south-of Utrecht, whose official name was Cornelis Aertsz de Man, an Anabaptist martyr, unmarried, who was held a prisoner at Culemborg for three years, tormented by all sorts of attempts to convert him by priests, monks, and prominent clergymen; and then, remaining steadfast, was burned on Aug. 13, 1552 (or perhaps 1562). Van Braght (*Mart. Mir.*) closes the account with a reference to a song about his death, which has, however, not been found. The *Veelderhande Liedekens* (1569) contains a song concerning his death, "Het is wel te beclagen" (It is a pity). (*Mart. Mir.* D 147, E 151; *Bibliographie,* No. 436; *ML* I, 370.) NEFF, VDZ.

Cornelis Adriaensz (Brother Cornelis) was a Franciscan monk. His father, Adriaen Corneliszoon, was the Catholic priest of the Nieuwe Kerk at Dordrecht, Holland. Both father and son had a bad reputation as to their moral conduct. In 1566 Cornelis began to preach in Brugge, and incited the populace against the Mennonites. At least two martyrs debated with him: Jacob de Rore or Keersgieter (*q.v.*) and Herman van Vleckwijk (*q.v.*). These debates are recorded in the *Martyrs' Mirror* (D 425-52, E 785-98). Cornelis is the author of the cruel statement that with the Anabaptists one must "debate with the executioner." It is a moot question whether the *Historie en Sermoonen van Broeder Cornelis Adriaensz* (Part I printed in 1569, second part 1578; there were several reprints) is genuine. S. Cramer thought it was not (*DB* 1899, 94 f., 145; 1900, 191). R. Fruin (*Verspreide geschriften* . . . The Hague, 1900, 387) took the opposite view, as after him Kühler did also (*Geschiedenis* I, 289, 405, 446).   VDZ.

Studiën en Bijdr. op 't gebied der hist. Theol. I (Amsterdam, 1870) 16 vv., p. 80; *Kerkhist. Archief* II

(Amsterdam, 1860) 325-36; *Ned. Archief v. Kerkgesch.* VII (1908) 325-36.

Cornelis Aelbrechts, an Anabaptist martyr of Leiden, Dutch province of South Holland, was beheaded at Amsterdam on Jan. 16, 1553, according to the recorded sentence. He confessed that he had been rebaptized, and admitted that he had attended many *conventikelen* (meetings) at which Gillis van Aken preached. (K. Vos, *Antwerpen,* 387; Grosheide, *Bijdrage,* 309.)   vpZ.

Cornelis van den Bosch, of the territory of Münster, was seized May 25, 1539, when a meeting of Anabaptists was surprised in the house of Lambrecht Duppijns (*q.v.*) at Haarlem, Dutch province of North Holland. Cornelis, who is supposed to have been a follower of David Joris (*q.v.*), after repeated torture was beheaded on June 2, 1539, at Haarlem. (*Bijdrage en Mededelingen van het Hist. Genootschap, Utrecht* XLI, 1920, 199-201, 208, 210, 218.)   vpZ.

Cornelis wt den Briel (Pietersz), a Dutch Anabaptist, a well-to-do shoemaker, one of the 12 apostles sent out by Jan Matthys in 1533. He preached and baptized in various places, including Leiden. Like Jacob van Campen (*q.v.*) he believed that armed attacks were wrong; but that did not prevent him from being an emissary of the revolutionary Jan van Geelen (*q.v.*), and as such going to Leiden early in January 1534 to incite the brethren to buy weapons for the expedition to Münster. It seems that Cornelis left the Catholic Church before 1530, before the rise of Anabaptism in the Netherlands; with this group he united wholeheartedly. He was beheaded in The Hague in 1535. (*Inv. Arch. Amst.* I, Nos. 113, 288; *DB* 1917, 98, 101-104, 105, 108-10; Kühler, *Geschiedenis* I, 152-54; Mellink, *Wederdopers,* Index.)   vpZ.

Cornelis Claesz, an Anabaptist martyr of Beverwijk, Dutch province of North Holland, was beheaded at Alkmaar, on June 24, 1538, because he admitted having been rebaptized. (*DB* 1909, 20.)

Cornelis Claesz (Claessens), an Anabaptist martyr, a native of Gent, Belgium, was burned at the stake with three companions, Christiaen Janssens Langedul, Mattheus de Vik, and Hans Symonsz, in Antwerp, Sept. 13, 1567, after terrible torture. By trade he was a shoemaker. From prison he wrote his wife a moving letter, comforting her and encouraging her in the faith. (*Mart. Mir.* D 345 f., E 704; *Antw. Arch.-Bl.* IX, 459, 461; X, 65; XIV, 46-47, No. 521.)   vpZ.

Cornelis (Cornille) Claissone, an Anabaptist martyr of Leiden, Holland, was burned at the stake at Gent, Belgium, on Feb. 17, 1553, because he had baptized a number of persons at Gent and elsewhere. (Verheyden, *Gent,* 18, No. 35.)   vpZ.

Cornelis Cornelisz (Cornelis de Gijselaer in *Mart. Mir.*), an Anabaptist martyr. He was arrested when a meeting of many Mennonites at Klundert (*q.v.*) was surprised on Aug. 5, 1571 (not 1572, as *Mart. Mir.* states). He was a well-to-do citizen of Dordrecht (Dutch province of South Holland), 40 years old, and a cloth shearer by trade. He had married the widow of the martyr Valerius de Schoolmeester

(*q.v.*). Some years previously he had been rebaptized near Emden in East Friesland by a preacher called "Leenaertsoen" (perhaps Leenaert Bouwens). Several times he was tortured, but he remained true to his faith and was executed, apparently in October 1571. (*Mart. Mir.* D 603-5, E 929-31; *DB* 1912, 35, 39, 42-43; *ML* II, 213.)   vpZ.

Cornelis Cornelisz Kelder, a Dutch Anabaptist martyr, who was put to death on Oct. 11, 1536, at The Hague, although there was no evidence against him except that he had been baptized on Nov. 2, 1534, by Meindert (*q.v.*) of Delft. In May 1535 he had been in Amsterdam. The martyr Jan Evertsz (*q.v.*) declared in his trial at Middelburg, March 27, 1534, that Kelder was a weaver of wool and lived in Speyestrate in The Hague. (*Inv. Arch. Amst.* I, No. 175; *DB* 1896, 40; *ML* II, 478.)   vpZ.

Cornelis Cuyper of Delft, Netherlands, an otherwise unknown Anabaptist leader, who was a follower of David Joris. (*DB* 1909, 30; 1917, 119, No. 95.)   vpZ.

Cornelis Dircxs, an otherwise unknown Dutch Anabaptist martyr, whose name is found in a list of martyrs (*Inv. Arch. Amst.* I, 745) and who was burned at the stake on Dec. 22, 1568. Place of execution was likely The Hague. According to the charge made against him, he had attended a wedding at Brielle (*q.v.*), performed by Jan Willems "in accord with the teaching of Menno." (*Inv. Arch. Amst.* I, No. 417.)   vpZ.

Cornelis Evertsz, an Anabaptist martyr, a shoemaker by trade, b. at Deventer, Dutch province of Overijssel. He had been baptized by Obbe Philips (*q.v.*) at Delft, province of South Holland, in the fall of 1534. When a persecution arose in Delft in March 1535 Cornelis left this town and settled in England. He was beheaded at Utrecht on June 11, 1539, because he had been (re)baptized. He was likely a brother of the martyr Jan Evertsz (*q.v.*). (*Berigten Hist. Genootschap, Utrecht* IV, 1851, 139; Mellink, *Wederdopers,* Index.)   vpZ.

Cornelis Geryts, an Anabaptist (preacher) of Westzaan, Dutch province of North Holland, who was beheaded at The Hague on April 10, 1534.   vpZ.

Inv. Arch. Amst. I, 745; *DB* 1905, 173; 1917, 115, No. 50; J. G. de Hoop Scheffer, *Gesch. der Kerkherv. in Nederland* (1873) 569.

Cornelis Gysbrechtsz, Anabaptist martyr of Beverwijk, Dutch province of North Holland, burned at the stake on July 1, 1535, in The Hague. Particulars are lacking. (*Inv. Arch. Amst.* I, 745.)   vpZ.

Cornelis Jan Oliviers Appelman, originally of Leiden, Dutch province of South Holland, an Anabaptist leader who, after the death of Jan van Batenburg (*q.v.*) in 1538, led the revolutionary activity of the Münsterites. He was very active, especially in the eastern provinces of the Netherlands and brought much loss upon the peaceful and defenseless Mennonites. Appelman was taken prisoner in May 1544 and burned at the stake at Utrecht on Feb. 7, 1545. (*Inv. Arch. Amst.* I, Nos. 265-67, 301, 307, 310; *DB* 1917, 138 ff., 174 ff.)   vpZ.

Cornelis Jansz, an Anabaptist martyr, burned at the

stake at Amsterdam on March 12, 1569 (see also **Clement Hendricksz**). He was a seaman of Haarlem, Dutch province of North Holland. He had not yet been baptized, and in spite of admonition and torture, remained "stubborn" and was put to death along with Jan Quirijnsz (*q.v.*) and Willem Jansz (*q.v.*). (*Mart. Mir.* D 492, E 833; Grosheide, *Bijdrage*, 181, 310; *ML* II, 390.)   vDZ.

Cornelis Jansz Bommer, a Dutch Anabaptist martyr, living at Delft, province of South Holland, was sentenced to death by the Court of Holland on Nov. 8, 1544, and then beheaded. He was a follower of David Joris (*q.v.*). (*Inv. Arch. Amst.* I, Nos. 297, 744, 745.)   vDZ.

Cornelis int Kerckhof (also Kershof), who together with Harmen Schoemaker (*q.v.*) was the center of an unsound fanatical Anabaptist movement at 't Zand in the Dutch province of Groningen in February 1535. Cornelis was arrested but was soon released. (P. G. Bos, "De Groningsche Wederdooperswoelingen in 1534 en 1535," in *Ned. Archief v. Kerkgesch.* VII, 1900, 1-47; Kühler, *Geschiedenis* I, 145 ff.)   vDZ.

Cornelis Luytsz (or Luytgensz), an Anabaptist martyr of "Krommenieërdijk in Waterlandt," Dutch province of North Holland, was put to death in The Hague on April 15, 1534, with unusual brutality, along with Jan Dirksz (also called Jan Walen, *q.v.*) and Dirk Gerritsz (*q.v.*). These three brethren had traveled together to Bergklooster (*q.v.*) en route to Münster, but were arrested on their way. This execution is placed erroneously by van Braght (*Mart. Mir.*) in the year 1542 and also in another place in 1527, without mentioning the place of execution. (*Mart. Mir.* D 62, 13; E 464; Kühler, *Geschiedenis* I, 108; *ML* II, 709.)   vDZ.

Cornelis (also called Jacob) **van Middeldonck**, an Anabaptist martyr, a tinsmith (*tingieter*), was beheaded at Antwerp, Belgium, on May 19, 1537. It is not clear whether he remained loyal to his faith or recanted. (*Antw. Arch.-Bl.* VII, 432-33; XIV, 14-15, No. 156.)   vDZ.

Cornelis Pietersz: see **Cornelis wt den Briel**.

Cornelis Polderman (Polterman), also called Polderman de Zeeuw because he was a native of the Dutch province of Zeeland, was a very active Anabaptist of the Münsterite wing. During 1533 he preached in Middelburg, Dutch province of Zeeland, from which he escaped in 1534. At this time he was a disciple of Melchior Hofmann (*q.v.*). While Hofmann was the Elijah, Polderman was looked upon by the believers (or thought himself to be) Enoch, the two celestial messengers who should precede the coming Lord; from Münster he came to Strasbourg to find Melchior Hofmann, was arrested and cross-examined on Nov. 22, 1535, and again on Dec. 3, this time in the presence of Bucer (*q.v.*) and Capito (*q.v.*). Of some significance is his letter, which was read to the council on Nov. 26, 1533 (printed in Röhrich, 74; Cornelius II, 373).   NEFF, vDZ.

BRN VII, 115 f., 126; C. A. Cornelius, *Gesch. des Münsterischen Aufruhrs* II (Leipzig, 1860); W. I. Leendertz, *Melchior Hofmann* (Haarlem, 1883) 281, 293, 298 ff., 364 f., 308, 318; F. O. zur Linden, *Melchior Hof-*

mann . . . (Haarlem, 1885) 340 ff.: T. W. Röhrich, "Zur Gesch. der Strassburger Wiedertäufer," in *Ztscht f. d. Hist. Theol.*, 1860; Kühler, *Geschiedenis* I, 66, 71; *ML* III, 381.

Cornelis de Schoenmaker (Shoemaker), an Anabaptist martyr, is identical with Cornelis Claesz (*q.v.*).

Cornelis Simons, a Dutch Anabaptist martyr of Delft, province of South Holland, was beheaded in September or October 1538. He was likely a follower of David Joris (*q.v.*). Particulars are lacking. (*Inv. Arch. Amst.* I, No. 744.)   vDZ.

Cornelis Stevensz, an Anabaptist martyr, b. at Montfoort, Dutch province of Utrecht, was baptized at Gorinchem, Dutch province of South Holland, was married in an Anabaptist meeting at Haarlem, lived for some years in Rotterdam, where he presided at meetings and taught from the Scripture. He was beheaded at Rotterdam on March 4, 1535. According to Vos he was a Münsterite. He had been baptized at Gorinchem by Lenart Boekbinder.   vDZ.

DB 1905, 171; 1917, 118, No. 83; Mellink, *Wederdopers*, 182, 223 ff., 228.

Cornelis de Vlaminck, an Anabaptist martyr, was beheaded at Zwolle, Dutch province of Overijssel in March 1535. He was born in 1491 in Amsterdam of a patrician family. His father, Cornelis van Handtshoorne, had been a sheriff of the city of Amsterdam in 1500 and a burgomaster in 1510. Cornelis himself, who was a grain merchant like his father, was in 1525 also a sheriff. Soon after 1530 he joined the Anabaptists. He had participated in the journey (March 1534) of the Anabaptists from Amsterdam to Bergklooster (*q.v.*) en route to Münster, and the next year, when arrested at Zwolle, was accused of having planned an attack on the city of Deventer. During the persecution he seems to have temporarily abandoned his faith, but soon after he felt repentant and henceforth remained loyal to his faith until his death. He was a very active man, who gave Jan Paeuw and the other deacons of the church considerable amounts of money. (Grosheide, *Verhooren*, 10, 49; *DB* 1917, 112, No. 26; Mellink, *Wederdopers*, Index.)   vDZ.

Cornelis Willemsz (Willemsse), an Anabaptist martyr of Haarlem, Dutch province of North Holland, by trade a trunk-maker or maker of rush bottoms for chairs, was beheaded at Amsterdam on March 6, 1534, with eight brethren. He was rebaptized, but did not repent of it, "because one should not act contrary to the Scriptures of God." (*Mart. Mir.* D 412, E 673; Grosheide, *Verhooren*, 52-53.)   vDZ.

Cornelis Wolfartsz, a cooper of Hoogeveen, Dutch province of Drenthe, an Anabaptist martyr, was beheaded at Delft, Jan. 10, 1539, together with three other martyrs. Cornelis presumably was an adherent of David Joris. (*Inv. Arch. Amst.* I, 749; *DB* 1899, 158-60; 1917, 160-63.)   vDZ.

Cornelisz, Adriaan, an elder of the Flemish congregation at Dordrecht (1626-32), the actual author of the *Dordrecht Confession* (*q.v.*), died on Nov. 6, 1632, at the age of 51 years. K.V.

Inv. Arch Amst. I, Nos. 569, 583-85, 592, 598; II, 1694-96; *ML* I, 371.

Cornelisz, Claes, author of *Een klare vertooninghe vant verschael ende onderscheyt datter is tusschen die ghenaemde vereenichde Ghemeente ende die Evangelische leeringhe Christi ende sijn Apostelen* (Amsterdam, 1616). In this book Cornelisz, who was a member and presumably a deacon of the Waterlander congregation of Amsterdam, combats the conservative views of a United Frisian and High German branch of the Mennonites called the *Afgedeelden* (*q.v.*); he particularly takes his stand against the interdiction of *buitentrouw* (outside marriage). His son Cornelis Claesz was a preacher of the Waterlander church in Amsterdam in the first half of the 17th century. (*DB* 1864, 64, 67, 71.)

vDZ.

Cornelisz, Jacob, a preacher at Amsterdam: see **Dalen, Jacob Cornelisz van.**

Cornelisz, Jan, elder at Warns in Holland, 1716-50. He was born in Warns, moved to Bakhuizen (*q.v.*) with his wife Oak Sibles in 1702, where he was chosen preacher in 1710. When he was made elder in 1716 he returned to Warns. He was the first preacher in the congregation to receive a fixed salary, which was 150 florins annually. It was his duty to preach half the sermons; in addition he managed a small farm. Very faithfully and zealously he served the numerous congregations around Warns with preaching, baptism, and communion. He kept detailed notes, which are now a valuable source for the history of these Dutch Mennonite churches. (*DB* 1874, 87, 110 f.; 1900, 47; 1901, 83 ff.; *ML* I, 371.) NEFF.

Cornelisz, Pieter, preacher of the Reformed Church at Alkmaar (Holland), opponent of Hans de Ries (*q.v.*), with whom he disputed for two days in 1592 on infant baptism in the house of Arent Claesz. On Aug. 10, 1591, he had sent a compilation of 26 arguments proving that it is a Christian's duty to bear government office, to Jacob Jansz Scheedemaker, the coelder of Hans de Ries. Aided by de Ries, Scheedemaker presented a refutation on Sept. 21, 1594, *Nootwendige Verantwoordinge*. When these booklets were published against the wish of Cornelisz, he published a reply in 1597, *Grondige Wederlegginghe,* etc., which closed the argument. (*Biogr. Wb.* II, 252-57; *DB* 1864, 32, 34; 1891, 1; 1909, 34-46; *ML* I, 372.) NEFF.

Cornelisz, Zacharias, a Mennonite printer and book dealer in Hoorn, Holland, published many Mennonite works in the first half of the 17th century, including some of Menno Simons'. He published the first issue of Menno's book against Jan van Leyden (written in 1535) without a name. He also published in 1627 P. J. Twisck's *Kleyn Liedtboecxken* and other theological works of this author, and some Mennonite songbooks, as well as two editions of the martyrbooks: *Historie der warachtige getuygen J.C.,* in 1617, and *Historie van de vrome Getuygen J.C. . . . ,* 1626.

Probably he belonged to the Old Frisian church at Hoorn, of which P. J. Twisck was an elder.

He must have died before 1640. (*Catalogus Amst.,* 15, 84, 213, 214, 270, 271; *ML* I, 372.) vDZ.

Cornelius, an otherwise unknown Dutch Mennonite preacher, had a dispute with the Reformed pastor Henricus Antonides (*q.v.*) at Loosdrecht in 1567. Particulars about this disputation were not available. (*DB* 1873, 83-84.) vDZ.

Cornelius, Carl Adolf (1819-1903), the historiographer of the Münster revolt, the eldest son of the actors Carl and Friederike Cornelius, was born March 12, 1819, at Würzburg, Germany, growing up in Mainz and Wiesbaden. To attend the gymnasium he lived with his uncle, the *Provinzialschulrat* Brüggemann, first in Coblenz and later in Berlin. The strict Catholic piety of this home in contrast with the freer atmosphere of his own home made a lasting impression on him. From 1836 on he devoted himself to the study of history and philology in Bonn and Berlin, especially under Ranke.

Cornelius began to teach in 1841, but not until his appointment as professor of history at the Lyceum in Braunsberg in 1846 was it possible for him to devote himself to scholarship. Always active in politics as well as scholarship, in 1848 he became the Braunsberg delegate to the Frankfurt parliament. His experience here during the revolution of 1849 stirred his interest in writing on the Münster rebellion.

Since his account of the origin of the book on Münster prepared for his publisher (June 1845) may be of interest to the reader, it is herewith presented:

"When in the spring of 1849 at Frankfurt I experienced the beginnings of a serious revolution, I formed the idea of writing a history of the Münster revolt, the only real and complete revolution on German soil. This vivid experience aided me in giving a clear picture of that movement. . . .

"Careful examination of extant works and a comparison of these with the known sources soon convinced me that the lazy use of accessible aids would not be adequate in carrying out my intention. My predecessors had neither exploited the sources with sufficient thoroughness, nor discriminated between the relative value of the individual reporters. Then it turned out that the sources they had used were themselves for the most part not original but secondary, and that the true source materials were still to be discovered. I therefore had to change my original plan for a historical and political sketch into a really scholarly work. I . . . have ever since been occupied with this subject, at first fully without interruption, then in the time I could spare from my teaching duties. Rarely has so much time and effort been expended on so limited a topic.

"The result of my investigations in libraries and archives was (1) the use of the hitherto neglected but extensive account of the only eyewitness, Meister Gresbeck; (2) the discovery of the chief writings of the Münster Anabaptists; (3) the discovery of several minor writings in printed and manuscript form and over 1,000 authentic documents.

"The result of my critical efforts was a thorough

reworking of the material from the ground up. I owe nothing to any of my predecessors; almost every stroke of my historical picture deviates to some extent at least from the traditional presentations.

"Since I have by way of introduction published two preliminary smaller works, *Die Münsterischen Humanisten und ihr Verhältnis zur Reformation. Ein historischer Versuch* (Münster, 1851); and *Der Anteil Ostfrieslands an der Reformation bis zum Jahr 1535* (Münster, 1852), and had published a part of my new sources and a detailed critique of the total supply of sources, *Berichte der Augenzeugen über das Münsterische Wiedertäuferreich. 2. Teil der Geschichtsquellen des Bistums Münster* (Münster, 1853), I now intend to publish the principal work, *Geschichte des Münsterischen Aufruhrs*, in three books.

"The third book, *Neu-Jerusalem*, describes the kingdom of Jan van Leyden, the doctrinal system of the sect, the ecclesiastical and political institutions and the life of the congregation, the struggle of the imperial forces against Münster and the outcome."

Cornelius did not return to Braunsberg when his term in Frankfurt was finished, but devoted all his time in the following years to archival research and working over the unexpected treasures he found. In 1850 he took his doctor's degree in Münster with the dissertation, *De fontibus, quibus in historia seditionis Monasteriensis Anabaptisticae narranda viri docti huc usque usi sunt*, in which he demonstrates the inadequacy of the sources hitherto used. The monograph, *Die Münsterischen Humanisten und ihr Verhältnis zur Reformation*, which he worked out at the same time, followed. He then acquired the *venia legendi* in Breslau in 1852 with a third work, *Ostfrieslands Anteil an der Reformation*. His scholarly achievements found immediate recognition. Early in 1854 he was made associate professor at the university of Breslau, and in the same year full professor at Bonn. In 1855 appeared the first volume of his history of the Münster revolt. In the autumn of 1856 he was called to a professorship at the university of Munich, and remained there until his death.

With the establishing of the Bavarian Historical Commission in 1858 a new field was opened to him and his students. The publication of the Wittelsbach correspondence ordered by the king delayed his work on the third volume of his history of the Münster revolt, the second volume of which had appeared in 1860. Later he returned to this work and published a part of his studies in *Münchener Akademische Abhandlungen*, 1869; *Historisches Taschenbuch*, 1872; and *Zeitschrift des Bergischen Geschichtsvereins* X and XIV. But he never concluded his Münster studies, for he waited in vain for the recovery of a document which he thought was hidden in a peasant house in Westphalia.

The scholarly work of his later years was concerned almost exclusively with the history of Calvin. After he resigned from active teaching at the age of 70, partly in consequence of the attitude of the Munich Ministry of Religious Affairs toward his ecclesiastical position, he devoted himself to this new task until a cerebral hemorrhage in 1897 disabled him. On Feb. 10, 1903, he died.

When the dogma of papal infallibility was decreed by the Vatican Council of 1870, Cornelius left the Roman Catholic fold to become a leader (until his death) of the Old Catholic Church.

His sketch of his father's personality (in *ADB*), is a most striking description of his own character: "In daily conduct amiable, sociable, and cheerful, in all his obligations faithful, helpful, unselfish, of highest integrity and purity of heart, the foe of all falsehood and all pretense; at once possessed by a sense of dignity as a man of God's grace and personal honor and by childlike modesty toward all foreign outside recognition."　　H.C.

Carl Adolf Cornelius rendered the greatest service to the historiography of the Anabaptists. He broke completely with the traditional, prejudiced, state-church treatment of the subject. In untiring and thorough research he pursued the sources and with marvelous lucidity in a noble zeal for the truth he uncovered and exposed all the malice and bias of previous presentations. With amazement we see in his writings his gradual growth into the tremendous material and regret that he was unable to carry the great work to completion. In classically beautiful language, in concentrated brevity, with the most thorough familiarity with and fullest use of the sources, which he notes carefully and in part reproduces, in benevolent kindly judgment which endeavors to secure justice to the Anabaptist movement, this meritorious historian has produced an epoch-making presentation of one of the phases of Anabaptist history and obligated us to lasting gratitude. (*ML* I, 372 ff.)　　NEFF.

Cornelsen (Kornelsen, Knels, Cornies, Cornelius, Cornelis, Cornelieszen, Cornels, Knelsen, Korniesz), a West Prussian Mennonite family name not clearly distinguishable in its variants in the past centuries. The origin of all the forms of the name is the personal name Cornelis (Cornelius, Knels). The first mention of the name is in 1595 at Schönsee (Sosnovka), in 1611 at Freienhuben, and in 1678 in the Danzig Mennonite Church record. It appeared in Frisian, Flemish, and Old Flemish congregations. The families in the Vistula Valley and their descendants mostly adopted the form Knels. In 1776, 20 families of this name lived in West Prussia (without Danzig), and in 1935 (including Elbing) 44 persons. Members of these families moved to Poland, Russia, and America. The name appears principally among the Mennonite Brethren in Kansas, Alberta, Saskatchewan, Oklahoma, and among the Mennonites of Mexico.

Johann Cornies (*q.v.*) of South Russia was the most outstanding representative of the family. Another outstanding leader and educator was Philip Cornies of the same territory. Abraham Cornelsen (*q.v.*) was one of the founders of the Mennonite Brethren Church in Russia. The Cornelsen form of the name is today the most common. (G. E. Reimer, *Familiennamen . . .* , 105.)　　C.K.

Cornelsen, Abraham (1826-84), an outstanding elder in the Mennonite Brethren Church, was born in

Grossweide, Molotschna settlement, Ukraine, South Russia, on Aug. 11, 1826, the oldest son of Abraham and Aganetha Cornelsen. His parents had at least one other son, John, who taught school in Russia and later emigrated to the United States and farmed. Abraham married Agnetha Gaede on Feb. 1, 1849, and taught school in Elisabethtal. Ten sons and three daughters were born to them; three sons are still living.

Abraham Cornelsen pioneered for the cause of evangelical Christianity in the Molotschna settlement, showing warm interest in the Bible studies and missionary rallies conducted by Edward Wüst (*q.v.*). He is reportedly the one who administered the Lord's Supper as a layman to a small group who had gathered in a private home in Elisabethtal in December 1859, and later drew up the document of secession signed by the 18 charter members of the Mennonite Brethren Church, Jan. 6, 1860, with his signature as the first. At the same meeting on Jan. 6 he was elected as one of the three who were to represent the new group before ecclesiastical as well as governmental agencies. Under pressure of the colonial inspector of the Russian government he and the other two representatives of the new group signed a promise not to separate themselves from the established Mennonite Church, nor to engage in any religious activity in opposition to the elders, without first obtaining permission of the Russian government. This signature prevented him from taking any further leading part in the establishment of the M.B. Church until after it had been recognized by the government. Because of his association with the new group, he had to withdraw from teaching in the Molotschna and settled in the Don region (*q.v.*), where he was elected to the ministry and later ordained elder of a group which later joined the Baptists. From here he emigrated to America in 1879 and settled at Ebenfeld, Marion Co., Kan., and became elder of the Ebenfeld M.B. Church. He traveled through many of the M.B. churches in Russia as well as in America, winning the hearts of his hearers by his fervent yet loving pulpit ministry.

He died in Ebenfeld on Sept. 24, 1884, and was buried in the M.B. cemetery at Ebenfeld. J.J.T.

Friesen, *Brüderschaft;* J. F. Harms, *Gesch. der Menn. Brüdergem.* (Hillsboro, 1924); P. Regier, *Kurzgefaszte Gesch. der Menn. Brüdergem.* (Berne, 1901); Franz Isaak, *Die Molotschnaer Mennoniten* (Halbstadt, 1908); J. H. Lohrenz, *The Mennonite Brethren Church* (Hillsboro, 1950).

Cornelye Andries, an Anabaptist martyr, a native of Dordrecht, was baptized in 1534, came to Brugge and was captured there and burned at the stake on Aug. 21, 1538. She is not mentionel in the *Martyrs' Mirror.* (Verheyden, *Brugge,* 33, No. 8)

vᴅZ.

Cornies family: see **Cornelsen.**

Cornies, Johann (1789-1848), who was born June 20, 1789, at Baerwalde near Danzig, migrated to Russia with his parents in 1804. After a two-year sojourn at Chortitza, the Cornies family joined the new colony on the banks of the Molotschna, where they took over a homestead of 175 acres in the newly settled village of Ohrloff. Here father Cornies became the settlement "doctor" until his death in 1814, using healing herbs found in the steppes.

Johann Cornies, the oldest of the four sons, worked first for a year as a laborer for a miller at Ohrloff. Then for three years he marketed farm produce from the settlement in the near-by cities of Simferopol, Feodosiya, and Sevastopol.

In 1811 Cornies married Agnes Klassen and the following year bought a homestead at Ohrloff and erected buildings. But his plans reached far beyond the boundaries of his own village. He soon recognized the favorable opportunities which the steppes presented for cattle-breeding, and began to breed sheep, renting the fallow-lying government lands for grazing.

In 1830 Cornies leased 9,000 acres of government land along the Yushanlee River, where he had until then maintained a small sheep ranch. Six years later Czar Nicholas I gave him 1,350 acres of this land as a reward for his services in the improvement of agriculture. Here Cornies first raised cattle, but soon began gradually to cultivate 729 acres of the land, using 16 acres to start a large nursery to furnish the colonists with tree seedlings. He also began to plant a forest which in a few years numbered 68,000 trees.

As early as 1816, Cornies undertook his first successful attempts with horse-breeding, and about the same time improvement of the cattle by the use of imported bulls, whose progeny he gave to the colonists. By 1847 his own livestock consisted of 500 horses, 8,000 sheep, and 200 head of cattle of Dutch stock.

Two years after the establishment of Yushanlee, Cornies purchased Tashchenak, an estate of 9,450 acres near Melitopol, and ten years later another estate, Verigin, bordering on it, so that he was finally cultivating about 25,000 acres. His own brickyard produced the bricks necessary for his many buildings, while the tile works yielded worthwhile profits.

The government soon took note of Cornies' large-scale activities. By 1817 it had made the 28-year-old Cornies lifelong chairman of the Society for the Effective Promotion of Afforestation, Horticulture, Silk-Industry, and Vine-Culture, later called Agricultural Association (*q.v.*), which was founded on the suggestion of the *Fürsorgekomitee* (*q.v.*). The settlers of Chortitza also founded an agricultural society in which Cornies became influential by virtue of his position as authorized (governmental) agent over all the Mennonites.

Cornies was tireless in opening up new industrial possibilities for the settlers. For a long time, the silk industry was his special concern. To develop this industry on a large scale, he built a school in Ohrloff to instruct the girls of the colony in the art of silk-reeling. But in the end it proved impossible to reel the silk with the available help, and in addition the silkworm plague and strong Italian and French competition injured this industry. The tobacco industry met a similar fate. Also the culture of corn made slow progress; the colonists valued summer fallow more highly than the profit from growing corn. Growing of flax also made little headway at the Molotschna. Grain production thus became the most important enterprise of the immigrants.

With tireless zeal and at his own expense Cornies experimented to find the methods of farming best suited to the locality. For example, he recognized that it was essential to preserve the moisture in the soil during the winter because of the lack of summer rainfall. As early as 1835 he began the practice of summer fallowing in the Molotschna. Three years later the colony began the system of four-crop rotation. By damming up the streams of the steppes, which in summer were largely dry, Cornies irrigated the meadows, tremendously improving both pasture land and the hay crop.

Cornies exercised special care in the planting of forests. He understood their significance for treeless steppes, and, when necessary, promoted his long-range purpose with ruthless force. In 1845 over a half-million fruit and forest trees were found in the Molotschna alone, to which 300,000 mulberry trees were added. Six years later there were over five million trees in 47 villages. Fruit trees were planted on the comparatively wide space betweet the street and house, and hedges and rows of trees were planted on the back of the long lot, thus giving the villages a more inviting appearance. Cornies also instructed the settlers in raising vegetables and flowers.

The confidence of the government in Cornies' educational abilities is shown by the fact that it placed a number of young Russians in his hands every year for instruction in practical agriculture. In 1839 Cornies accepted 16 boys, while his wife took four Russian girls into the house to instruct them in the domestic arts. Later these Russians established special model villages. The value of such training was soon clear. For example, potatoes were unknown in South Russia until the Mennonites introduced them. Many Russian and Ukrainian farmers were sent to the Mennonite settlements to learn how to raise potatoes. Cornies' aid also was given to the Dukhobors and the Molokans, and he was made responsible for placing model Mennonite farmers in the newly established Jewish settlements in the province of Kherson.

Under Cornies' leadership 50 Hutterite families emigrated from Radichev, Chernigov province, near Melitopol in 1842 and founded the villages Huttertal (*q.v.*) and Johannesruh. Cornies founded Neuhalbstadt (*q.v.*), a business and handicraft village, to provide the Molotschna settlement with an industrial and trade center.

Cornies was also instrumental in settling the nomadic Nogais, 17,000 of whom were made sessile after 1835 because of Cornies' efforts, although later they emigrated to Turkey. At the wish of the government, Cornies traveled to the distant Kalmuck steppes to advise these nomadic tribes there in settling.

Cornies particularly insisted that the educational system of the Mennonites was in need of reform. In 1818 he founded the Society for Christian Education (*q.v.*), which built its first secondary school

in Ohrloff in 1820. He also began a library and created a reading circle. Until 1843 the schools of the Mennonites in Russia were controlled by the church. As there were no trained teachers, farmer-teachers instructed the children. That year the schools were placed under the Society for Christian Education which was to co-operate with the church leaders. Cornies divided the Molotschna settlement into six school districts, planned for the improvement of the school buildings, dismissed a number of the most incompetent teachers, and insisted upon regular school attendance.

The curriculum itself, however, was in need of a thoroughgoing reform. The only sources of instruction were the ABC-book, Bible, catechism, and hymnbook. Among the major written contributions of Cornies in the field of education are his "General Rules Concerning Instruction and Treatment of School Children," which reveal the understanding and vision with which he sought to improve the system. Although Cornies was able to serve as chairman of the Society for Christian Education for only five years (1843-48), his long-range work constituted a real reform. It was Cornies who laid the foundation for the later development of the school system of the Mennonites in Russia. A year before his death the Department of Crownlands also placed the Chortitza schools under his control.

On March 13, 1848, Cornies died at the early age of 59 years. A huge crowd attended his funeral, among whom were many Ukrainians, Russians, Nogais, Molokans, and Tatars. His people placed a memorial for him in the cemetery at Ohrloff which, according to the wishes of the deceased, was a broken marble column. His wife had preceded him in death on March 30, 1847. Two children, Johann and Agnes, survived.

That Cornies' influence and activities spread beyond the limits of the settlement is shown by the esteem in which he was held by the South Russian authorities and by the government at St. Petersburg. The governor of New Russia and Bessarabia, Count Vorontsov, was a frequent guest at the Cornies home and sought his advice on problems concerning agriculture and cattle-breeding. Ten years before his death the Committee of Scholars of the Department of Crownlands asked him to become an honorary member. Here also Cornies did exemplary work; he sent countless reports and charts regarding his work to the Committee and stimulated and advised the authorities at St. Petersburg.

The officials of Russia showed their appreciation of the great Mennonite pioneer by various honors. In 1825 Alexander I as well as the Crown Prince visited him. In 1837 he was received by Nicholas I at Simferopol. He refused honors and medals which were offered him on various occasions, accepting only a simple gold commemorative medal.

Cornies achieved more than anybody else in the realm of cultural and economic advancement among the Mennonites of Russia. In dealing with the opposition of religious leaders, ignorant conservative farmers, or personal opponents he could be ruthless. That he was able to carry through his mighty reforms in spite of great opposition was due to the fact that as representative of the authorities, he was endowed with almost unlimited powers and that he was self-sacrificing and upright in his dealings. A warm feeling of good will and a superb calmness marked his relationships with people. In spite of his great wealth and influence Cornies remained a plain Mennonite farmer.†

W.Q.

D. H. Epp, *Johann Cornies, Züge aus seinem Leben und Wirken* (Berdyansk, 1909); Friesen, *Brüderschaft*, 75 ff.; Chr. Neff, "Was aus einem einfachen Bauersmann werden kann," *Gem.-Kal.* 1914, 83-95; W. Quiring, "Johann Cornies—A Great Pioneer," *Menn. Life*, July 1948 (III) 30-34, 38; M. S. Harder, "Johann Cornies—Pioneer Educator," *Menn. Life*, Oct. 1948 (III) 5-7, 44; B. H. Unruh, "Johann Cornies zum hundertjährigen Todestag," *Der Mennonit* I (1948) 54-55; E. Crous in *NDB; ML* I, 347.

Cornies, Philipp David, son of David Cornies, and grandson of David, an older brother of the noted Johann Cornies (*q.v.*), born in Spat, Crimea 1884 or 1885, last seen alive about 1942 in northern Russia, an outstanding educator and leader of the Russian Mennonites. He attended school in Ohrloff, then spent two years in the normal school in Halbstadt. He taught elementary school in Klubnikovo, Neu-Samara, 1902-05, where he married Luise Penner, then in Rosenort in the Molotchna 1905 to 1923 until forced out by the Bolsheviks. He served on the Executive Committee of the Molotchna Mennonite Teachers Association. He was also a poet of some ability. He refused ordination as a preacher, although he preached occasionally, and was a master of the Russian language. After 1922 he served with B. B. Janz in the leadership of the *Verein Bürger Holländischer Herkunft.* In one of his several imprisonments through torture he was forced to promise to stay in Russia and help build up the country, which promise he kept, serving several places as a technician in agriculture, also in the latter years as director of a dairy cattle breeding project in the concentration camp region of Ukhta-Pechorski Kray where he was last seen by Jacob A. Neufeld (now in Canada) in 1942. Earlier he had spent five and a half years in the concentration camp in North Russia on the Solovetski Islands. (A. Töws, *Mennonitische Märtyrer,* Winnipeg, 1949, 271-275.)

H.S.B.

Cornille Marins, an Anabaptist martyr who was imprisoned in Brugge, Belgium, and burned there at the stake between April 13 and July 28, 1568. Particulars are lacking. (Verheyden, *Brugge* 56, No. 60.)

vDZ.

Corning Mennonite Church (MC), now extinct, located north of Sacramento, Cal., the center of a small Mennonite settlement established in 1907. E. Stahley, formerly of Nampa, Idaho, served as deacon and in 1911 was ordained minister. Services were held in an old Methodist church in Corning, the building having been purchased by Stahley. The first family moved away in 1910; others followed so that in several years no members remained there.

M.G.

Corporación Paraguaya. When some Canadian Mennonites moved to Paraguay in the 1920's, several corporations were formed to help dispose of their land and equipment in Canada and to secure land for them in the Paraguayan Chaco. The Intercontinental Company, Limited (*q.v.*), was organized to handle the Canadian transactions, and the Corporación Paraguaya was organized to handle the Paraguayan transactions. Incorporated in Asunción in April 1926, with a capitalization of $750,000, Corporación Paraguaya specifically was to arrange for the purchase of Chaco land from the Carlos Casado Company, which owned three million acres of land between the Paraguay River and the Bolivian border west of Puerto Casado. The corporation was then to sell the lands to the Mennonites from Canada and to help manage the details of actual settlement of the Canadians on their lands. The leading spirit in this organization, as well as in the Intercontinental Company, Limited, was General (retired) Samuel McRoberts, a prominent financier who was president of the Chatham-Phoenix National Bank of New York and vice-president of the National City Bank.

Already in 1919 a delegation of Old Colony Mennonites from Canada had made contact with McRoberts through Fred Engen (*q.v.*) and asked him to help them find a new home. On board ship en route to Argentina in 1920, McRoberts met Manuel Gondra, president-elect of Paraguay, and Eusebio Ayala, his foreign minister, later the president of Paraguay and also of the newly organized Corporación Paraguaya. These men persuaded McRoberts to investigate Paraguay as a possible future home for Mennonites. McRoberts hired Fred Engen, experienced and once wealthy land agent, to help explore the possibilities of the Paraguayan Chaco. Though the group of Canadian Mennonites that was originally interested in Paraguay decided to settle in Mexico, another Mennonite group from Canada took advantage of the aid extended by McRoberts and established Menno Colony in the Chaco. Since the sums involved in buying the Canadian lands of the Mennonites and selling them to others, and in buying and selling the Chaco lands to the Mennonites, were quite large, McRoberts took on a partner in the operations, Edward B. Robinette, head of the investment banking firm of Stroud and Company in Philadelphia.

Corporación Paraguaya purchased from the Casado Company 100 square leagues of land, over 100 miles west of the Paraguay River, for $733,950, in American gold. This was approximately 720 square miles, or 463,387½ acres. Of this amount the Canadian Mennonites purchased 30 square leagues, or 138,990 acres. Smaller additional amounts were purchased later. Buying the land at $1.50 per acre from Casado, Corporación Paraguaya sold it at $5.00 per acre to the Mennonites.

The corporation also helped with the arrangements for housing the Canadians in Puerto Casado in wooden barracks and tents, until they could settle on their lands. Repeated delays in the land surveys which the corporation had agreed to undertake caused a great deal of discontent among the Mennonites, 16 months elapsing after the arrival of the first colonists before they were able to make the

first settlements. After Menno Colony was organized, the corporation lent a helping hand to the needy in the colony by lending over $10,000 for an indefinite period without interest, and by extending credit in the two stores it established in and near the colony. At its Chaco headquarters at Hoffnungsfeld, near Menno Colony, the corporation operated, in addition to a store, a sawmill, a workshop, and an agricultural experiment station. After a few years, however, these were abandoned, and the corporation gradually withdrew from the enterprise, leaving the colony on its own. In 1937 the Mennonite Central Committee purchased Corporación Paraguaya for $57,500 and thus inherited its financial arrangements with Menno Colony, as well as with the more recently established Fernheim, a colony of Mennonites from Russia. It liquidated the remaining assets of the corporation in 1952. Though the corporation was the subject of much complaint, and though those in the enterprise did not have the qualifications of skill which such an undertaking required, it appears that the mistakes made were those of inexperience and ignorance, and not necessarily fraud and sharp practice. (J. E. Bender, "Paraguay Calling," Part II, mimeographed ms. in the MCC files, Akron, Pa.) The complete records of the C.P. are in the Archives of the Mennonite Church at Goshen College, Goshen, Ind.
W.H.S.

Corte Belijdenisse des Geloofs ende der Voornaemster Stucken der Christenlijcke Leere (Short Confession of Faith and of the Principal Points of Doctrine) is a Dutch confession, drawn up by Hans de Ries (*q.v.*) and Lubbert Gerritsz (*q.v.*) in 1610. This confession usually is called the Waterlander Confession. Already in 1577 Hans de Ries in co-operation with Jacob Jansz and some others had drawn up a confession of 25 articles (published in *DB* 1904, 145-56). The particular purpose of this 1610 confession was to accomplish a union between the Waterlanders and a group of English Brownists living at Amsterdam and led by John Smyth (*q.v.*). To this end de Ries and Gerritsz composed a confession of 38 articles, to which later two more articles were added. This confession like that of 1577 is a typical Waterlander confession. "It is founded on the Scriptures as the revelation of God; it is Biblical without being dogmatic; it presents faith and no theology" (Kühler, *Geschiedenis* II, 95). It did not mean to prescribe what had to be believed, but to define the creed. For the rest it is very moderate: shunning (avoidance) is not inserted and concerning *buitentrouw* (intermarriage) it takes a broad stand. This confession of 40 articles was first printed in 1618 (Hoorn). It was reprinted at De Rijp 1624, Hoorn 1643, de Rijp 1658, de Rijp 1681, Amsterdam 1716, Rotterdam 1740, Amsterdam 1741, and besides this published in H. Schijn, *Geschiedenis der Protestantsche Christenen in't Vereenigde Nederland genoemd Mennoniten, . . .* (Amsterdam-Utrecht, 1727) 153-90. There is also a German translation by J. C. Schmellentin, published 1741 in Amsterdam, entitled: *Ein kurz Bekäntnusz der fürnämsten Hauptstückken des Christlichen Glaubens . . . .* A Latin translation was published in 1723 in Amsterdam: Joannes Resius et Lubbertus Gerardi, *Praecipuorum Christianae fidei articulorum brevis confessio . . . .* vdZ.

Kühler, *Geschiedenis* I, 355 ff.; *idem*, II, 95; Blaupot t. C., *Holland* I, 119, 385-88; *DB* 1904, 138-59; N. van der Zijpp, *Gesch. der Doopsgez. in Nederland* (Arnhem, 1952) 88-89; *Catalogus Amst.,* 169-70.

Cortébert-Berg (also called Cortébert-Matte), a Mennonite congregation on Cortébert Mountain in the Bernese Jura of Switzerland. Details of its early history are lacking. It was apparently founded in the 18th century by emigrants from the eastern part of the canton of Bern, who found refuge from persecution on the lonely farms of the Bernese Jura. Their religious services had to be held secretly at first; they chose for this purpose a remote ravine, which is still called the "Täufergraben." Later on the congregation met twice a month in rotation in the homes of its members. The membership has declined through emigration. In 1888 it had 50 baptized members. In 1917 there were 82 souls who lived in six villages on Cortébert and in the neighboring villages, engaged in agriculture. A church record has been kept since 1897. All members may vote. Since the end of the 19th century the church has had a Sunday school during the summer, which is attended by children of the non-Mennonite parents. Since 1893 the catechetical booklet issued by the *Badischer Verband* has been used for baptismal instruction. The church has a poor fund of 34,800 francs, acquired from the disbanded Büdrichgraben congregation in 1869, which fund is used to aid the poor of other Mennonite churches and also of non-Mennonites. The present (1952) pastor and elder is David Lerch, Jr., and the membership (1948) 28. The congregation has no meetinghouse. It continues to use the German language. HEGE.

Müller, *Berner Täufer,* 249; Delbert Gratz, *Bernese Anabaptists* (Goshen, 1953) see Index; *ML* I, 375.

Cortenbosch, Dirk Jansz and **Jacob Fredriks,** two Dutch Mennonites, having visited the churches on the Rhine in Germany in April 1572, paid a visit to Prince William of Orange, then staying at Dillenburg, Germany, to ask him if they could be of service to him upon their return to Holland. The Prince asked them to collect money for "the common Christian cause." With these words he meant the fight for freedom from the Spanish and Roman Catholic yoke, the War of Liberation (80 Years' War) of the Dutch begun in 1568. Since Jacob Fredriks was not able to carry out the plan, Pieter W. Bogaert (*q.v.*) was asked by Prince William to take the place of Fredriks, and Cortenbosch and Bogaert, as a result of their endeavor, could hand to the Prince on July 22, 1572, an amount of 1,060 guilders. Nothing further is known about Cortenbosch. (Blaupot t. C., *Holland* I, 84-85, 381-82; *DB* 1873, 4-5, 8-9; *Inv. Arch. Amst.* I, Nos. 421 f.) vdZ.

Cortoys, a cabinetmaker (joiner) of Hainault, Belgium, was beheaded in Utrecht on June 11, 1539, because he had been an active Anabaptist. Nothing further is known about him nor about the nature of his activities. (*Berigten Hist. Genootschap, Utrecht* IV, 2, 1851, p. 139; *DB* 1917, 118, No. 89.) vdZ.

Corver, a Mennonite family originally living at Zaandam, Dutch province of North Holland. Dirk Corver, b. about 1590, was a well-to-do lumber merchant, as were also most of his descendants. Gerrit Jacobsz Corver was about 1600 a preacher of the Frisian congregation of Westzaan and Westzaandam *Oude Huys;* his son Jacob Gerritsz Corver was a preacher here from 1608 until his death in 1660. From 1709 to 1870, nine members of this family were also found in Amsterdam, where Adriaan Corver and Cornelis Corver served as deacons in the *Zon* (*q.v.*) congregation.

C. Corver, a member of this family, was a Mennonite minister, serving the congregation of Pingjum and Witmarsum, 1859-63, Grouw, 1863-66, and Groningen, 1866-67. Here he took leave on Dec. 15, 1867, and resigned together with his colleague J. W. Straatman (*q.v.*) because they, having become adherents of radical modernism, had proposed to the church board to abolish baptism and communion services, and the Bible. When the congregation did not accede to their views and wishes, both ministers resigned. On this question Corver published *Woord aan de Broederschap* (Groningen, n.d.—1868). Corver later lived in Paris; here he died in 1903 in poverty and misery. vDZ.

A. M. van de Waal, *Geslachtslijst van de familie Corver 1590-1847* (n.p., n.d.); S. Lootsma, *Het Niuwe Huys* (Zaandam, 1937) 189-95; *DB* 1868, 167-79; H. Dassel Sr., *Menno's volk in Groningen* (Groningen, n.d.—1952) 55-57.

Corvinus (Rabe), **Antonius,** a Lutheran divine (1501-53), one of the most important reformers of North Germany, organizing the Lutheran church at Goslar am Harz 1528-31, and Hildesheim in 1544. In 1536 Landgrave Philip of Hesse (*q.v.*) sent to him some Münsterite Anabaptists who had been taken prisoner, in order to convert them, but Corvinus did not succeed in "converting those stubborn *Widertouffer."* Corvinus wrote much about the Münsterite Anabaptists: *Acta*: *Handlungen*: *Legation und schriffte . . . Inn der Münsterschen sache geschehen. . . . Item. Gespreche und disputation Antonij Coruini und Joannis Kymei mit dem Münsterschen König . . . MDXXXVI* (Wittenberg, n.d.) (a copy is in the Goshen College Library); *De miserabili Monasteriensium Anabaptistarum obsidione* (The Miserable Occupation of the Anabaptists of Münster), which was a letter to the Lutheran divine G. Spalatinus (published 1536, n.p.). The *Waarachtige Historie,* which has been attributed to Corvinus, was not written by him, but is a Dutch translation of *Warhafftige Historie,* attributed to Cornelius (*Berichte der Augenzeugen über das Münsterische Wiedertäuferreich*) to joint authorship by Heinrich Dorpius (named in the title) and Dietrich Fabricius von Anhalt. (*HRE* IV, 3d ed., 302-5; *Catalogus Amst.,* 52, 349; *ML* I, 375.) vDZ.

Cosquín Mennonite Church (MC) is located in the city of Cosquín, pop. 7,000, on the Córdoba-Cruz del Eje branch of the Northern Argentine Railroad, seat of the county of Cosquín, in the Province of Córdoba, Argentina. The work here was begun by D. P. and Lillie Lantz under the Mennonite Board of Missions and Charities in 1935. The property was bought in 1939 and by July 9, 1940, the new church building was ready for dedication.

The membership fluctuates considerably because Cosquín is a health resort and people remain there only long enough to regain their strength and vitality. The 1954 membership was 14. The Lantzes served this congregation during the years 1935-37 and 1939-47; the L. S. Webers in 1937-38; and the J. L. Rutts, 1947- . (J. W. Shank *et al., The Gospel Under the Southern Cross,* Scottdale, 1943.)

E.V.S.

Coster, a Dutch Mennonite family found especially at Almelo, province of Overijssel, where a number of this family lived as linen weavers and later as textile manufacturers. Gerrit Coster, a descendant of a non-Mennonite family from Westphalia, Germany, living in Almelo, is said to have been the first of this family to join the Mennonite Church.

In course of time the Coster family, which soon became closely related by marriage with other Mennonite families in Almelo, such as ten Cate and Willink, was very loyal to the congregation; many of them served as deacons. In the 18th century the family is also found in other congregations.

At least two members of the Coster family served as pastors: Herman Gerrit Coster of Almelo (1801-69) was pastor of Noordzijpe (Oudesluis) 1831-36 and Winterswijk 1836-66; Lambertus ten Cate Coster, also of Almelo (d. 1877), served at Zwolle 1833-58. vDZ.

Coster, Pieter, an Anabaptist martyr: see **Pieter Claesz van Zaandam.**

Coster(us), Franciscus, a Jesuit priest, author of *Toetsteen van de versierde Apostolische Successie eens wederdoopers Jacob Pieterssen van der Molen* (Antwerp, 1603). Jacob P. van der Meulen (*q.v.*) had published a theological work on the Apostolic Succession (*q.v.*), in which he had written that not the Roman Catholics, but the Mennonites possessed the true apostolic succession, because they maintained the doctrine of the apostles. Coster tried to refute the thesis of van der Meulen in his *Toetsteen,* and was answered by van der Meulen, who wrote *Vertoogh aen de Successoirs des Jesuijts,* 1604.

vDZ.

Cotswold Bruderhof, Ashton Keynes, Wiltshire, England. Early in 1936 a Hutterite community was founded here by members of the brotherhood organized by Eberhard Arnold in Germany in 1920. The connections with England, which had existed from the beginning, were cultivated and deepened by lectures and visits, so that from 1934 an increasing number of seekers in England came to the Bruderhofs in Germany and Liechtenstein. Thereby the stage was set for active work in England. As an initial step, the brotherhood leased some buildings and lands of the Ashton Fields Farm, and in 1936 purchased the entire estate, gradually increasing it to 500 acres. From the first, an intensive program of agriculture was practiced. Around the meeting hall and the dwelling houses in the center of the court there were groups of other buildings for schools, children's houses, farm buildings, and workshops. Agriculture with gardening, farming, poultry raising, dairying, and beekeeping formed the foundation of the economic life, supplemented by other activities like cabinetmaking, publication, printing, and bookbinding. The educational work and school system grew through the influx of new families and the admission of needy children from England and Austria. The rise and growth of the Hutterite communal living stirred the spirits of seeking pacifist circles in England; many united with the brotherhood. The task of propagating the witness of the brotherhood by book and periodical literature was served by the output of the Plough Publishing House, Ashton Keynes, especially by the periodical *The Plough* and its German version, *Der Pflug*. The most important publication was a new edition (1938) of the *Rechenschaft unserer Religion, Lehr und Glaubens* by Peter Riedemann, and an English translation in 1950. Besides missionary journeys within the country, the Brethren also traveled through Holland, Sweden, and Switzerland. The inner structure of the brotherhood with respect to community of goods, the training of children, sharing of work, inward composure, and the testimony to the outer world were carried out in complete agreement with the traditional Hutterite practices and principles as they were established in the Rhönbruderhof (*q.v.*) and the Almbruderhof (*q.v.*). Connections with the Hutterian Brethren in America were strengthened through the visit of the elders David Hofer of Manitoba and Michael Waldner of South Dakota. With the increase of the size of the colony caused by the compulsory abandonment of the Rhönbruderhof in Germany and the transfer of the Almbruderhof, the membership of the Cotswold Bruderhof grew to 250 by the end of 1938, so that steps had to be taken in 1939 to establish another Bruderhof at Oaksey, four miles east of Ashton Keynes. The name "Society of Brothers" was chosen as the name for the entire brotherhood.

The further growth of the brotherhood was interrupted by World War II, and the entire colony migrated to Paraguay. Although the British members were released from military duty by the current tribunal, and the restrictions originally placed upon them as Germans were also removed, since they were regarded as refugees from National Socialist oppression, nevertheless a strong popular feeling of antipathy arose among the neighbors of the colonies because of their German background. This feeling became stronger after the collapse of France in 1940, assuming increasingly unpleasant forms. Questions were raised in both houses of Parliament; the answers given were favorable to the colonists. But when the popular boycott made the sale of their produce more and more difficult, and the government, yielding to popular pressure, was about to intern the German members, the brotherhood decided to emigrate in order to preserve community with people of the various nations. They sent two Brethren to the United States and Canada to secure permission for the entire body to immigrate to one or the other of the two countries, hoping to be able to settle in the neighborhood of the American Hutterite colonies. This attempt failed in spite of the

affidavit of the American Hutterian Brethren in Washington and their intervention in Ottawa. Finally through the mediation of the Mennonite Central Committee, the colony was able to settle in Paraguay in 1940 and 1941, where they founded the Primavera colony. Since a small number had to remain behind in England to finish the business of closing the Cotswold Bruderhof, and this group at once began to increase in size through the admission of new members, the Wheathill Bruderhof was organized in England in 1942 to take the place of the Cotswold Bruderhof. E.C.H.A.

Der Pflug and its English version *The Plough*, 1938-40, contain reports of the rise and growth of the new Hutterian Brotherhood in England and articles by Eberhard Arnold on Hutterite history, such as Claus Felbinger's *Rechenschaft vor dem Rat zu Landshut von 1560* (II, Nos. 1, 2, and 4), Johannes Waldner's short sketch of Hutterian history from a letter in the Moravian (Herrnhut) archives of 1811, brought up-to-date to 1938 (I, No. 1), David Hofer's report of the dissolution of the Rhön Bruderhof (I, No. 3), J. G. Ewert's account of the sufferings of the Hutterian Brethren in World War I (II, No. 2), besides some references to the relations of the Quakers with the Hutterian Brethren in Hungary in 1663 (I, No. 4 and II, No. 1). The Plough Publishing House, Ashton Keynes, published the series of Eberhard Arnold's Lectures and Writings in the following booklets: (1) *The Early Christians;* (2) *The Individual and World Need;* (3) *God and Anti-God;* (4) *The Peace of God;* (5) *The Hutterian Brothers: Four Centuries of Common Life and Work.* A supplement of *The Plough* was issued in 1938 with the title, *Children in Community;* it contains articles and reports on the education and schoolwork of the children in the Cotswold Bruderhof.

Cottage City (Md.) Mennonite Suburban Mission (MC) was founded by young Mennonite carpenters, mostly from Denbigh, Va., working in Washington, D.C., in the fall of 1922. They started a church under the Virginia Conference; but since October 1927, the mission has been under the mission board of the Lancaster Conference. Ray J. Shenk is the minister and mission superintendent. The membership in 1954 was 38. I.D.L.

Cottonwood County is located in southwestern Minnesota, the third county east of the South Dakota line in the second tier of counties north of the Iowa border. Russian Mennonites selected it as a site for settlement upon the recommendation of William Seeger, the State Treasurer and Secretary of the Board of Immigration, who urged them to come to Minnesota when they arrived in Elkhart, Ind., and later at Yankton, S.D., in 1873. Thirteen families, including 80 persons, took Seeger's advice and settled in the southeastern part of Cottonwood County in the vicinity of Mountain Lake in October of the same year. This settlement was augmented by the arrival of about 1,700 additional Mennonite immigrants between 1874-80. Most of these settled in the Mountain Lake vicinity; others, near Butterfield in adjoining Watonwan County; a later group of Galician Mennonites, also near Butterfield and in the vicinity of Westbrook in the northwestern part of Cottonwood County.

After enduring pioneer hardships, the settlement prospered with Mennonites engaging mainly in agriculture while a few set up business establishments. By 1950 the community had two modern hospitals, a large new Home for the Aged, and a

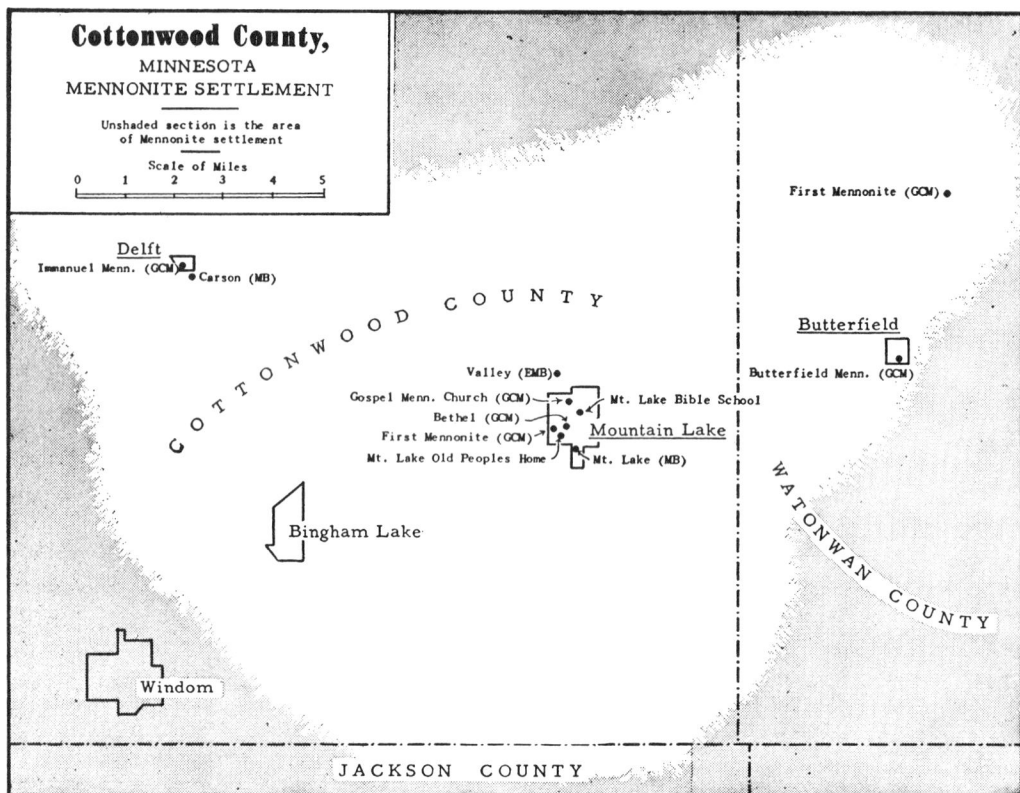

Cottonwood County,
MINNESOTA
MENNONITE SETTLEMENT

Unshaded section is the area
of Mennonite settlement

Scale of Miles
0   1   2   3   4   5

First Mennonite (GCM)●

Delft
Immanuel Menn. (GCM)● ●Carson (MB)

COTTONWOOD COUNTY

Butterfield
Butterfield Menn. (GCM)

Valley (EMB)●
Gospel Menn. Church (GCM)
Bethel (GCM)
First Mennonite (GCM)
Mt. Lake Old Peoples Home

Mt. Lake Bible School
Mountain Lake
Mt. Lake (MB)

WATONWAN COUNTY

Bingham Lake

Windom

JACKSON COUNTY

Bible School, all operated by Mennonites. Numbering approximately 1,800, they worship in ten Mennonite churches, eight of which are in Cottonwood
and two in Watonwan County: the Evangelical
Mennonite Brethren, the Mennonite Brethren, the
First Mennonite (GCM), the Bethel Mennonite
(GCM), and the Gospel Mennonite (GCM) churches of Mountain Lake; the Carson Mennonite Brethren and the Immanuel Mennonite (GCM) churches
of Delft; the New Home Mennonite (GCM) Church
of Westbrook (now disbanded); and the First Mennonite Church (GCM) and the Mennonite Church
(GCM) of Butterfield.   E.W.

Council Bluffs (Pottawattamie Co., Iowa) United
Missionary Church was organized in May 1944. In
1948 the congregation had 11 members and Fanny
Overholt served as pastor.   F.O.

Council of Boards is an annual union meeting of all
boards and elected committees of the General Conference Mennonite Church (*q.v.*) to provide clear-
ance for common problems, to review the work of
the Conference, and to decide on budgets of the
various boards and committees. This Council includes, in addition to the members of the boards
and committees, the officers of the General Conference and the presidents of the District Conferences.
The Council convenes annually for a number of
days, before the end of the fiscal year.   C.K.

Council of Mennonite and Affiliated Colleges met
for the first time in August 1942, at Winona Lake,

Ind. E. E. Miller, president of Goshen College, took
the initiative in calling the conference, which was
attended by seven colleges. The primary purpose
of the meeting was to discuss immediate problems
confronting the Mennonite colleges as a result of
the war. Known as the Conference for Administrators of Mennonite Colleges, it later was called the
Committee of Mennonite and Affiliated College Administrators, but since 1945 is called the Council
of Mennonite and Affiliated Colleges. Members of
the council include these colleges: Bethel, Bluffton,
Eastern Mennonite, Freeman, Goshen, Hesston,
Messiah, Tabor, and Upland.

Among the activities of the council is the sponsoring of a biennial program on Mennonite educational problems. The Conference on Mennonite
Cultural Problems (*q.v.*), sponsored by the council,
meets conjointly with the conference on educational
problems.

In the fall of 1946 the council in co-operation with
the MCC launched a student exchange program that
in its first five years brought 119 young people from
Europe for a year of study in the Mennonite colleges
of America. Related to this undertaking was the
European voluntary service program, in which
American young people, selected by the council,
toured Europe and spent four to six weeks working
in service projects. These annual tours have been
sponsored since the summer of 1947. During the
first five years approximately 150 Mennonite young
people from North America have participated in

these programs. Meeting several times each year, the representatives of the participating colleges share experiences, discuss their common problems, and take up matters of business related to the student exchange program and other projects of mutual interest to the group.   M.G.

Counsel Meeting (Inquiry Meeting or Examination Meeting), the name given in the Mennonite (MC) and Amish Mennonite churches of North America to the meeting of the congregation held prior to the communion service to determine whether the membership is ready to proceed with the service. In the Old Order Amish group the service is called *Ordnungsgemeinde*. It is to be distinguished from the Preparatory Service (*q.v.*), which is held in some Mennonite (MC) congregations on a weekday afternoon (Saturday) or evening or on the preceding Sunday morning to help the participants to be spiritually prepared for the communion.

Although there is some variation in the details of the procedure, the intent of the counsel meeting is always the same. After an appropriate sermon the bishop either reads the entire conference discipline and current regulations or, in case of the Amish, reads the particular items of conduct which are subject to discipline (*Abstellungen*) or currently at issue, taking the liberty as he sees fit to admonish the congregation or discuss any particular weakness or shortcoming he has observed. He then, with the assistance of the other ministers, "takes the counsel" of the congregation to determine whether the members are "at peace with God, with fellow men, and with the church" and are willing to proceed with the appointed communion service. In the Old Order Amish and more conservative Amish Mennonite congregations the bishop, with the deacon, proceeds down the aisle from bench to bench, asking each individual member to indicate either by a nod of the head or an audible "yes" to confess peace and readiness. If any member wishes he may raise concerns and objections on the spot and discuss them with the bishop. Sometimes the bishop appoints two ministers to take the counsel. The Amish counsel meeting sermon is always based on Matthew 18 and I Corinthians 5, both chapters being read entire before the sermon.

Among the Mennonite (MC) congregations the procedure varies slightly. In the Franconia Conference the bishop with the preachers and deacons take seats in the "amen corner" (alternately on the men's side and the women's side) or immediately in front of the pulpit at the center aisle where they remain seated while the members file past one by one and shake hands with each of the ordained men in order of seniority, beginning with the bishop, but speaking no word. In the Lancaster Conference (*q.v.*) the bishop with the preachers and deacons retires to the anteroom (or they separate into two anterooms depending upon the size of the congregation), where they await seated the entrance of the members in groups of 20-25 (large enough to fill the anteroom), to whom they address the questions regarding peace and readiness, which are to be audibly answered, but add a further question, "Are you satisfied with the housekeeping of the congregation?" This ques-

tion gives opportunity to the members to comment on or criticize the manner in which the bishop and ministers have been handling the discipline of the congregation or to criticize the state of the congregation in general. In the other Mennonite conferences it was formerly quite customary to invite the members to come to the anteroom singly or by families to "give counsel" and express peace. More recently the above lengthy and often tedious procedure (occasionally lengthened unduly by a critical member who occupied much time in the anteroom) has frequently been abandoned and instead a rising vote is taken of the congregation at the conclusion of the counsel meeting sermon. In some cases the meeting takes on the character of a testimony meeting with members rising at their seats one after the other to express peace with God and men.

The practice of having members vote on "peace" and "readiness" is a very real part of democratic church government and participation of the laity. It is actually possible, though it seldom happens, that the members can block a communion service and compel the bishop to pay attention to their concerns and criticisms. They can also review the "housekeeping" of the bishop and the ministers, who in effect submit themselves to the critique of the laity. The shift to a more or less routine mass vote, with no privilege of discussion, in effect cancels out a part of the lay participation.

The entire counsel meeting concept and procedure has deep roots in tradition and undoubtedly goes back to the very beginning of the Anabaptist movement. Similar practices were formerly common among the Dutch, German, Swiss, Russian, and Hutterite groups and are still maintained in the more conservative bodies such as the Old Colony, Kleine Gemeinde, and Church of God in Christ. The third article of the Schleitheim Confession of 1527 clearly implies that unity in the congregation is a necessary prerequisite to participation in the communion. Only a close communion practice with strict discipline of course could logically require the above preliminary counsel meeting, but all Anabaptist and Mennonite groups officially practiced both close communion and strict group discipline.

In the *Badischer Verband* the counsel meeting (*Umfrage*) is still regularly held preceding each communion service, although the practice of questioning each member privately in the anteroom was discontinued in 1907.

There is a divergence in the exact name and significance of the counsel meeting. Some prefer to call it council meeting, meaning a meeting of the congregation in council. The *Mennonite Church Polity* (MC) uses the term "council meeting."

In the other larger North American Mennonite branches both the counsel meeting and Preparatory Service are practically unknown. However, in the Eastern District, as well as the Swiss churches of the General Conference (GCM) counsel meeting was formerly held and has died out in the last fifty years, but Preparatory Service is still held on the Sunday preceding communion. In the Mennonite Brethren Church the announcement of the communion service, usually made several weeks in advance, is accompanied by an admonition to self-examination and reconciliation of any outstanding disputes among the brethren. A preparatory sermon is sometimes preached on the Sunday preceding communion. H.S.B.

Counter Reformation, today more often called the Catholic Reformation, from about 1550 to 1620 or 1650. The term originated with the great German historian Leopold von Ranke and was first used by him in 1843 to denote the purposeful activities of the Roman Catholic Church (RCC) against the Protestants in order to regain the countries lost to them and to win their people back to the Church of Rome. It was, strictly speaking, a twofold activity: (1) a counter movement against the Protestants of all shades, a fight, and (2) an internal reform toward improving and lifting the standards of the church itself, by which reforms more permanent results were expected (as the previous decline of standards was generally blamed for the fateful split in Western Christianity). The medieval unity of the Western church was to be restored by all means, moral as well as political ones, by persuasion and if need be by force and compulsion. The attempts toward real internal reforms begin as early as 1534, but the Counter Reformation proper is usually reckoned between the pontificates of Paul IV (beginning 1555) and Sixtus V (d. 1590). In Central Europe the climax of the Counter Reformation came between 1600 and 1620, fateful years for all non-Catholics but above all for the Anabaptists. Under the relentless impact of these church activities (aided naturally by the secular governments) the once powerful Anabaptist movement steadily declined until it almost disappeared in Catholic countries save for a few remnants.

Traditionally three agencies are named as instrumental in carrying out the purposes of the Counter Reformation. They are: the Council of Trent (1545-63), the Society of Jesus (S.J.), commonly called Jesuits (approved by the pope in 1540), and the renewed Inquisition together with the Index of prohibited books. On this list of forbidden books one finds, incidentally, also the works of Balthasar Hubmaier. Of these three agencies the Jesuits (q.v.) were by far most efficient, considering the achievement of their ends. They dominated both the schools (from the elementary grades up to the university) and the confessionals. Hence they dominated both the youth and the conscience of all participants. That the Counter Reformation had such tremendous success is at least partly due to the disunity of the Protestant parties and national churches and their unwillingness to co-operate among themselves. Since the Anabaptists were hated by both Protestants and Catholics, they naturally had to suffer most.

The Counter Reformation was at times very strong, indicating a revived spirit of crusading within the church, determined and not hesitating even before thrones. Inasmuch as the princes yielded to the church's demands (and ideas of toleration or liberty of conscience did not exist in effect during the 16th and 17th centuries), the "subjects" had little chance of resisting. First attacked were the lower masses of peasants and small craftsmen, then came the commercial middle classes, and eventually also the old nobility. Only in Hungary could conditions persevere for another hundred years; here the Counter Reformation did not become effective until the middle of the 18th century, the time of the Hutterite exodus to Russia.

The most thorough success of the Counter Reformation was achieved in Spain and Italy; even rudiments of Protestantism were made impossible in these countries, mainly due to the work of the Inquisition. Elsewhere, however, this Inquisition did not exist; hence the field was taken over by the Jesuits. Since Anabaptism flourished only in central and northwestern Europe (Netherlands), the present article restricts itself to a discussion of these countries. The Netherlands, to be sure, was the only country which managed to break away altogether from Roman influence, experiencing a total change and thus creating an island of free atmosphere where also Mennonites could unmolestedly develop.

Yet also in the Netherlands the influence of the Counter Reformation was clearly perceptible, especially after 1620. Though the Reformed Church was the state church in the Netherlands, and both the Catholic Church and Mennonites as well as Remonstrants were merely tolerated and could meet only in their hidden churches, the Jesuit missionaries worked secretly, but very actively. Particularly in Amsterdam they succeeded in winning many for their church including some Mennonites, among whom Joost van den Vondel (q.v.), who had been a deacon of the Waterlander congregation, and joined the Catholic Church about 1641, is the most striking example of such "conversions."

Germany and Austria (the Habsburg domain) felt the impact of the Counter Reformation strongly, and in the 17th century also Poland, heretofore a refuge for all nonconformist church groups. In 1551 the Jesuits appeared for the first time in Vienna, Austria; here worked later the Father Canisius, the author of a famous Catholic catechism which came into wide use all over Europe. Another center was Munich, Bavaria, facetiously called the "second Rome," mainly under the Duke Albrecht V (q.v.). Also the Rhineland bishoprics such as Mainz, Cologne, and Treves became centers of aggressive re-Catholization, and only Crefeld was able to retain a certain amount of independence and liberty. In Switzerland, Carl Borromeo, archbishop of Milan, became active in the seven Catholic cantons and even beyond, and his impact was heavily felt by the Swiss Brethren. In 1576 Jesuits were in Lucerne and in 1580 they were in Neuchâtel.

Very interesting are the conditions in the Habsburg countries (see **Habsburg and Austria**). While Ferdinand I (q.v.) was an ardent champion of Catholicism and a supporter of the Counter Reformation by all means, the Anabaptists could still carry on, at least in a clandestine way, in Tirol, and in an open way in Moravia, which belonged to the kingdom of Bohemia. Then followed Emperor Maximilian II (1564-76), of whom it is said that he himself leaned strongly toward Protestantism. Under him began the "golden age" of the Hutterites in Moravia, protected to be sure by the nobles of the land. Then with Emperor Rudolphus II (1576-1612) a radical change set in, the militant restoration of Catholicism everywhere. For instance, Nikolsburg and Olmütz (Olomouc) now become centers of Catholic aggression in Moravia. While up to this time the lords of Nikolsburg were fairly lenient toward the Hutterites (they needed them as workers), conditions changed within a few years under the Cardinal Franz Dietrichstein (q.v.), who pressed the brethren so hard that the settlements declined very rapidly (around 1600).

The Thirty Years' War (1618-48) represented finally the concluding battle between the two camps, ending in a tie and settling for the future the relation and distribution of the churches in Europe. At its beginning was the fateful battle of White Mountain (Weissenberg) near Prague in 1620, where Protestantism received one of its severest defeats. Bohemia and Moravia were now thoroughly made Catholic by often most brutal means, and in 1622 the Hutterites were finally and almost completely driven out from Moravia, only to settle down in adjoining Hungary.

In Poland conditions changed under Sigismund III (1587-1632), derisively called "the king of the Jesuits." Under him the former toleration ceased, and the golden days of the nonconformists were terminated. The Bohemian Brethren (now called Moravians) slowly declined, while the Socinians, the Little Polish Church, migrated to liberal Netherlands. Evangelical Anabaptism (of which a few groups had settled in Poland during the 16th century) had long before disappeared.

In the 18th century eventually also Hungary saw the working of the Jesuits. About 1700 the Turks had been driven out, and a stronger centralized bureaucracy receiving its orders from Vienna now supported the Jesuits. True, many nobles still remained Calvinists, but for the Anabaptists there remained no chance any longer, neither in Slovakia, where the newly converted Hutterites now came to be called "Habaner" (q.v.), nor in Transylvania where Lutherans were tolerated but no Anabaptists. The Jesuit Delpini worked successfully in Transylvania around 1750 to make life for the Brethren unbearable. The great trek to Walachia and then to Russia set in. (See Toleration, Jesuits, and Dietrichstein.) R.F., vDZ.

G. Loesche, Gesch. des Protestantismus in Österreich (1930); L. von Ranke, History of the Popes (1896); L. von Pastor, History of the Popes (1891 ff., mainly XIV-XXI); B. J. Kidd, The Counter-Reformation 1550-1600 (1933); P. Janelle, The Catholic Reformation (1949); L. Keller, Die Gegenreformation in Westfalen und am Niederrhein 3v (Leipzig, 1891-95); ML II, 42-47.

Countess, Alta., settlement: see Rosemary.

County Line Old Order Mennonite Church, now extinct, was located approximately four miles northwest of Wakarusa, Ind. It had its origin in the Wisler schism of 1871 (see Jacob Wisler). About 1877 a church was built on the county line of Elkhart and St. Joseph counties for those members of the group living in the area. Services were held

there every third Sunday, alternating with Blosser's Church (q.v.) and Yellow Creek (q.v.) Church. By 1900 the membership of the three may have reached 200. Bishops that have served at County Line include Jacob Wisler, Christian Shaum, John Martin, and Joseph Martin. Schisms in the congregation in 1907 on issues such as the use of telephones and in 1947 on the use of chewing tobacco and rubber-tired tractors plus the moving away of members decreased the membership of the congregation so that its building was closed in 1950 and sold the following year. M.G.

County Line Old Order (Wisler) Mennonite Church located near Dalton, Wayne Co., Ohio, is a meeting place of a congregation belonging to the Ohio and Indiana Conference. The congregation also worshiped in the Chestnut Ridge Mennonite Church (q.v.). The present church was built in 1891, when the Pleasant View Mennonite Church (with whom they alternated services) began to build a new building, on which project they could not agree.

In the spring of 1953 a group withdrew from the Chestnut Ridge-County Line congregation because the congregation refused to begin Sunday school, prayer meetings, and mission work. This withdrawing group now worships every Sunday at the Chestnut Ridge meetinghouse, while the continuing Chestnut Ridge-County Line Old Order (Wisler) congregation now worships every Sunday at the County Line meetinghouse. The withdrawing group has been received into the Virginia Mennonite Conference (MC). H.B.

Courgenay (German Jennsdorf), a village near Porrentruy (German Pruntrut) in the northwest corner of the canton of Bern, Switzerland, where an Amish congregation was formed around 1900, largely of families coming from the Seigne (q.v.) congregation in France. Elder Pierre Ramseyer (ordained 1896) moved from Seigne to near Courgenay in 1903. Members lived on both sides of the Swiss-Alsatian border and the congregation was affiliated with the Alsatian conference. In 1916 the congregation numbered 55 souls, all farmers and scattered in six villages. Services were held in German, biweekly until the death of Elder Ramseyer in 1933. At that time the congregation ceased to exist, remaining members attaching themselves to the neighboring Swiss Mennonite congregations of Lucelle or Porrentruy (see below).

In the same area and the same period as the formation of the Amish Mennonite congregation of Courgenay, there took place an immigration of Swiss Mennonites from the Jura region into the Porrentruy area. Meetings were held monthly in homes, beginning in 1893. Between 1919 and 1939 a hall was rented in Porrentruy; since 1939 the congregation has its own chapel in the near-by village of Courgenay, and thus carries the name Courgenay without being directly related to the earlier congregation of the same name. Elders in the early period were Samuel Gerber (later moved to La Paturatte, q.v.) and Henri Schmutz; the elder in 1952 is Christian Schmutz. Services are held in both French and German, the congregation belonging however to the (German-language) Swiss conference. The baptized membership in 1948 was about 70. (*ML* I, 376.)   J.H.Y.

Courtrai: see Kortrijk.

Couwenhoven (in Prussia usually Kauenhoven, *q.v.*), a family of Flemish emigrees who left Flanders about 1600 and moved to the Netherlands, where they were found in Brielle and Haarlem. The Brielle branch of this family, which was very numerous in the 17th century and some members of which moved to Rotterdam, belonged to the Reformed Church. It is not clear whether they were Reformed from the beginning, or had turned from Mennonitism to the Reformed Church.

The Haarlem branch was Mennonite and belonged to the (Old) Flemish branch. From the Netherlands some members of the Couwenhoven family emigrated to Danzig, where they are found since 1661. Cornelis Couwenhoven became a preacher of the Danzig Old Flemish congregation in 1720.
                                                       vDZ.

Couwenhoven, Johannes, b. December 1731 at Haarlem, d. Feb. 25, 1806, at Amsterdam, was one of the last two preachers of the Amsterdam Mennonite congregation which met in "de Zon." He was trained for the ministry by Petrus Smidt (*q.v.*), was made assistant preacher in 1752 by the church council of this congregation, and two years later preacher. He served in this office until 1801, when the Zonists merged with the Lamists to form the present congregation. Until his death Couwenhoven received an annual pension of 1,000 florins. One of his sermons has been published, *Het orgelspel. Rede by het eerste gebruik van het orgel in de kerk De Zon* (Amsterdam, 1786).   J.L.

DB 1898, 13, 16, 21, 22, 37; *Catalogus Amst.,* 147; *Naamlijst* 1806, 63; *ML* I, 376.

Cove Mennonite (rural) Mission Church (MC), east of Mathias, W. Va., under the Virginia Conference, probably started in 1876 or earlier as an outgrowth of the work at Powder Spring, five miles east in Shenandoah Co., Va. Early work in connection with this station was carried on at the Basore and Hinegardner schoolhouses located two and six miles respectively north of the Whitmer schoolhouse, where services are now held once a month. The 1948 membership was eight.   T.S.

Covenant Theology, also known as "Federal Theology." This formulation of Calvinism arose in various places, both on the continent and in the British Isles, in the 16th century, and was greatly furthered in the 17th century by theologians like Johannes Cocceius (1603-69), H. Witsius (1636-1708), and Francis Turretin (1623-87). According to this theology, God has dealt with man in essentially two ways: the Covenant of Works, made with Adam, and the Covenant of Grace, by which men receive salvation on the basis of faith. The Covenant of Works, it is said, offers salvation on the ground of obedience, although no man is able thus to merit eternal life since the Fall of man. It should also be pointed out that the Covenant of Grace did not begin with Calvary or Pentecost; God also began its unfolding in the Garden of Eden. God has administered the Covenant of Grace in three dispensations: from Abraham to Moses, with circumcision as its sign; from Moses to Christ, with the Passover added; and from Christ to the end of the world, during which the two signs are baptism and the Lord's Supper.

According to the Covenant Theology, this Covenant of Grace extends to the children of believers. One believing parent has the right to regard his or her children as participants in the Covenant of Grace. Hence such children are to be baptized. Just as the Abrahamic Covenant was with the patriarch "and his seed after him," so the Covenant of Grace now includes the children of the "elect."

It is thus evident that the Reformed theologians as well as the Lutherans emphasized the continuity of the Old Testament and the New, the Mosaic and the New covenants. The Anabaptists, on the other hand, stressed the change, and the fulfillment of the first by the second. The symbol of the struggle between the Protestants and the Anabaptists was baptism. For the former, baptism was the successor to circumcision, and was therefore to be administered to the children of the Covenant. For the Anabaptists, baptism was the symbol of one's personal covenant with God to take up the cross of Christian discipleship and to live a holy life of obedience. Not to be forgotten was the fortunate rendering of I Peter 3:21 in the German Bible, where the apostle calls baptism the "covenant" of a good conscience with God (*Bund eines guten Gewissens mit Gott*). Actually, the rather obscure word employed in this classic passage for the Anabaptists is perhaps best rendered "appeal," but it served the Brethren well in their contention that baptism was the symbol of a commitment which no infant could make. As a matter of fact, it should also be mentioned that the Anabaptists believed in the salvation of their children without baptism. They relied, they said, not on water, but on the blood of Christ. That is, they rejected all sacramentalism and took their stand on the universal atonement made by Jesus.

The Anabaptist view that at baptism the individual believer makes a voluntary covenant with God, of which baptism is the symbol, and that the church is actually a brotherhood of such "covenanters" cannot properly be called a covenant theology. It is worth while noting, however, that the term "covenanter" (*Bondgenooten*) was much used in the early days of the Anabaptist movement in Northwest Germany and Holland. C. Krahn (*Menno Simons,* 1936, "Die Taufe der Bundgenossen," 22-23) points out that the idea was transplanted from Strasbourg to the North by Melchior Hofmann, 1530 ff., and that the new groups of Melchiorites called themselves "Covenanters." Krahn quotes a petition of Jakob Kautz and Wilhelm Reublin of 1529 to the Strasbourg Council (taken from Hulshof's *Geschiedenis van de Doopsgezinden te Straatsburg,* 1905), as saying: "When the merciful God called us by His grace to His marvelous light, we did not reject the heavenly message but made a covenant with God in our hearts, to serve Him henceforth in holiness all our days, by His power, and to report our purpose to the covenanters (*Bundgenossen*)."

Even in Reformed and Presbyterian circles the covenant theology is much less stressed than formerly. And some modern theologians, notably Karl Barth, are now beginning to recognize that infant baptism is inconsistent with that which the New Testament binds the baptized one to follow.

It is not clear whether the Anabaptist idea of the covenant had any influence on the rise of the covenant idea and theology among the Reformed theologians, in spite of the negative judgment on this point by such a scholar as L. J. Trinterud in "The Origins of Puritanism," *Church History* XX (1951) p. 56, footnote 28, which reads as follows: "The attempt to trace the origins of the church covenant idea in English Puritanism to an Anabaptist source, as in C. Burrage, *The Church Covenant Idea*, 1904, fails to take account of the indisputable, widespread interest, in both the Rhineland and England, in the social contract theory of the state, and in the covenant theology, prior to any possible influence from Anabaptist sources. Moreover, Burrage grants that the first clear, explicit use of the covenant notion in Anabaptist theology came in 1530, by Melchior Hofmann. Burrage believed that Hofmann had gotten these initial covenant notions (regarding baptism and the covenant) from other Anabaptists in Strassburg, *ibid.*, pp. 19 ff. Yet it was in Strassburg that Capito, Bucer, and others in the Rhineland cities had sponsored this idea apart from, and independent of, Anabaptist influences. Much more likely the Anabaptists in Strassburg got the idea from Capito (who was for a time very friendly to them) and from other Rhineland reformers through personal contact, or through books; or they also may have gotten at least elements of it from common late medieval notion. But, dependence of the English advocates of the church covenant idea upon Anabaptist sources cannot be maintained."

Walter Hollweg, in an article on Bernhard Buwo, a moderate opponent of Anabaptism, upholds the view, based on Buwo, Rembert, and Schrenk, that "very likely the Anabaptists gave the Reformers the idea of the 'covenant' and caused them to formulate their own thoughts along these lines. It is well known that the Anabaptists called themselves 'covenanters' (*Bundgenossen*) . . . . What was more logical for the Zürich Reformers than to investigate the Biblical content of the concept of the covenant in their struggle against the Anabaptists! In doing so they found a highly welcome starting point in their opposition and struggle" (p. 83). The origin of the Anabaptist concept of the covenant and its relationship to that of the Reformers still needs a thorough investigation. J.C.W.

The most comprehensive study of the continental covenant theology (*Bund-* or *Föderaltheologie*) is Gottlob Schrenk, *Gottesreich und Bund im älteren Protestantismus* (Gütersloh, 1923); a complete bibliography on this subject is found in Schrenk's article, *RGG* I (2nd ed.) col. 1364-67; W. Hollweg, "Bernhard Buwo, ein ostfriesischer Theologe aus dem Reformationsjahrhundert," *Jb. der Ges. f. bildende Kunst und vaterländische Altertümer zu Emden*, 1923, 71-90; Champlin Burrage, *The Church Covenant Idea, Its Origin and Its Development* (Philadelphia, 1904); the otherwise thorough study by F. Littell, *The Anabaptist View of the Church* (Am. Soc. of Church Hist., 1952), does not discuss the covenant concept.

Coventry, England. An Anabaptist congregation existed here, of which no particulars are known except that together with Anabaptist congregations at London, Sarum, Lincoln, and Tyverton, it sent a letter to Hans de Ries (*q.v.*) and Reinier Wybrands (*q.v.*) and their congregations in Holland on Nov. 12, 1626, pleading for a union between these English congregations and the Dutch Waterlander churches. This letter had been preceded by correspondence between Elias Tookey (*q.v.*) and his followers of London and de Ries in 1624. The letter of Nov. 12, 1626, was personally delivered to Amsterdam by two English Anabaptists, who are said to have been persons of high rank, and who were representatives of a group of about 150 adherents.

The English churches stated in this letter that they had read the confession of de Ries; they were much pleased with this confession, and asked for further information. In the name of the Dutch elders de Ries replied that the Waterlander Mennonites of Holland could not agree to the proposal of the English congregations because of the differences between the two groups: the English Anabaptists did not absolutely reject the oath, desired to have a communion service each week, permitted baptism and communion to be administered not only by the ministers of the church, but by any member if there was no minister present, and also permitted their members to hold government offices and to bear arms. Thus the union did not come about. (*Inv. Arch. Amst.* II, Nos. 1368-77.) vdZ.

Coventry Mennonite Church (MC), now extinct, located in East Coventry Twp., Chester Co., Pa., was the first Mennonite congregation in this area. Mennonite settlers came into the Coventry community as early as 1739, and probably conducted their religious services in private homes prior to the erection of the first meetinghouse (1751). The second Coventry meetinghouse was built in 1798 at the present location. The present building was erected in 1890.

Church services at Coventry were conducted by the ministers of the near-by Vincent congregation, though Coventry was originally a larger congregation. However, by 1890 its membership had dwindled to about 20. In 1882 a Sunday school was organized at Coventry as a union school with the Church of the Brethren. This, however, led to some difficulties resulting in the discontinuance of the Sunday school and gradual loss of members to other churches. By 1914 services at Coventry were discontinued.

The maintenance of the German language in the services and its location on the outer fringe of the Franconia Mennonite Conference were probably the causes for the rapid decline and final extinction of the congregation. The cemetery is now completely in the control of non-Mennonites. Q.L.

Cowissehoppin: see **Goshenhoppen.**

Cowley County, Kan. Several Mennonites (MC), among whom was Abram Means of Arkansas City, were living in this county in the 1890's.

Craandijk, a Dutch Mennonite family of German origin. Dirck Jansz Craandijk, b. about 1634, came from Vreden in Westphalia to Amsterdam, where he was baptized in the Mennonite Church *bij't Lam* on July 2, 1664. He was a linen weaver and died before October 1690. His sons were also weavers. Later on the family grew rather wealthy; in the 18th century many members of the Craandijk family were owners of a feed mill at Amsterdam; and later some of them also at Amsterdam, were brokers, especially ship brokers, wood dealers, and shipowners. Jacobus Craandijk (1834-1912, *q.v.*) was a Mennonite pastor. Herman Craandijk, b. Jan. 12, 1897, at Leeuwarden, a well-known lawyer at Amsterdam and since 1951 president of the General Conference of the Dutch Mennonites (A.D.S.), is a descendant of this family. (*Ned. Patriciaat* XXXVI, 1950, 91-103.)　　　　　　　　　　　　　　　　　　vDZ.

Craandijk, Jacobus, b. Sept. 7, 1834, at Amsterdam, d. June 3, 1912, at Haarlem, of an old Mennonite family, the son of Pieter Hendrik Craandijk, a wood dealer and shipowner at Amsterdam, and Maria van Coppenaal, studied at the Mennonite Seminary at Amsterdam, after which he served the following congregations as a pastor: Borne 1859-62, Rotterdam 1862-84, and Haarlem 1884-1900. Craandijk was very influential in the Dutch Brotherhood. He was the organizer and president of an important conference of prominent Dutch Mennonite leaders held at Amsterdam in 1879, where the questions were discussed whether a member of a non-Mennonite church, desiring to be a member of a Mennonite congregation, should be baptized or not, and if persons could be admitted as members of the church without having received baptism on their confession. (*DB* 1880, 97-132.)

Craandijk's activities were not limited to the Mennonites. From 1864 to 1911 he was a member of the board of the (General) *Nederlandsch Zendelings Genootschap* (Dutch Mission Society), and in 1897 as its president he held an address at the centennial celebration of this mission society.

Craandijk wrote a large number of (mostly literary) articles in many Dutch periodicals. His popular booklets, *Wandelingen door Nederland* (Rambles Through the Netherlands), show Craandijk as a man who knew and loved the beauties of his fatherland, both in the towns and in the country.

Craandijk was married 1861 to Anna Geertruida Ballot, of Borne.　　　　　　　　　　　　　　　　vDZ.

Levensberichten, Maatschappij v. Ned. Letterkunde (Leiden, 1916) 37-66; *DJ* 1915, 21-29, with portrait.

Crabapple Mennonite Mission (MC) holds regular Sunday morning services in the Crabapple schoolhouse, Richland Twp., Belmont Co., near Fairpoint, Ohio. This work was envisioned by Dan B. Raber, Aurora, Ohio, begun by Alfred L. Brenner, Rittman, Ohio, in the spring of 1939, and was assumed by the Mission Board of the Ohio Mennonite and Eastern A.M. Conference in early 1941. The membership is eight.　　　　　　　　　　　　　　　G.Mu.

Craen, Huig, martyr: see **Huyge Jacobsz Kraen.**

Crafts of the Hutterian Brethren. Anyone who carries on research in the archives of Austria, Moravia, and Hungary, finds notices of the industrial activity of the Hutterian Brethren, and one who roams through the museums of those countries finds products of their industry which even today attract attention, as did the pottery in the exhibition at Troppau in 1924. The catalogs list precious "Hutterian knives," and the old manuscript hymnals are not only written in fine penmanship, but are also distinguished by the solidity of their binding.

From the specimens of these and other trades it is clear that the crafts of the Hutterian Brethren were for a long time on a high level, recognized by their friends and foes. When the Hutterian Brethren arrived in this "Promised Land" uninvited, they had to suffer the envy and persecution of the native populace, and to establish themselves and prove their good points. Wherever a patron offered them a place of refuge they settled, struggling with want and misery and subjected to manifold inner conflicts.

The Hutterites could not develop successful trades until the great persecution diminished, and first the "good age" (1554-65), then the "golden age" (1565-92) of the brotherhood dawned, and they were able to find a market for their products among the populace and especially the landed patrons. Those are the times in which laudatory reports were made. In fairness we must give their own report the preference, i.e., the report found in their *Geschichtsbuch,* and shall supplement it with some citations of court records.

It sounds like a hymn of rejoicing when the Anabaptist chronicler describes the life of the Hutterian brotherhood in the last three decades of the 16th century, when God had provided "rest for his people," and they were living in the land that He had ordained especially for them, where they observed the true Christian community of goods, as Christ taught it and the ancient church observed it. Swords and spears were turned into pruning knives, saws, and other useful articles. . . . Patience was the only defense in any strife.

"To the temporal government they obediently paid their dues and . . . taxes and tithes, . . . and gave them honor for their God-ordained office. In brief, all twelve articles of the Christian faith were practiced. There were deacons and teachers for their schools. They sustained themselves with all kinds of manual labor in fields, meadows, and vineyards. There were not a few carpenters, especially in Moravia, but also in Austria, Hungary, and Bohemia, many beautiful and useful mills, breweries, and other buildings which they built for the barons, the noblemen, and the citizens. For every trade special Brethren were appointed who took over the work, gave directions, and settled disputes. There were also not a few millers and mills in the land taken over from the lords to manage them. They also managed the dairies and farms for the lords for a good salary, as was reasonably agreed upon by both sides.

"Nobody was idle. The brotherhood maintained all kinds of useful crafts; there were masons, blacksmiths, coppersmiths, locksmiths, clockmakers, knifesmiths, tinsmiths, tanners, furriers, cobblers and saddlers, . . . weavers, tailors, . . . glaziers, . . . barbers and physicians." Each of these trades had an overseer who took charge of the work, arranged it, paid the bills, sold the products and put the proceeds into the brotherhood treasury. "All of them, wherever they were, worked for the common welfare and helped each other wherever there was occasion. It was like a perfect body, that has only real and living members, each needing the other. Or it was like a clock, where one wheel drives and aids another." This brotherhood, says the chronicle in conclusion, became known in the world. Everyone wanted them for their faithfulness. Only in the eyes of some there were too many of them in the land "because of their religion."

What the chronicle relates about the "golden age" of Hutterite crafts is confirmed by contemporary reports. From their workshops the landlords of Moravia and beyond procured the best scythes, the most beautiful pottery, the most expensive knives, the finest hair-sieves and millers' pouches. Hence the great demand for their products. Unwittingly and unwillingly their greatest adversary, the Catholic priest Christoph Andreas Fischer (*q.v.*), sings their praise: "Do I not see on every Sunday and holiday, especially in the morning, the people come to you in droves and purchase their necessities of you? And this is the case not only here in Feldsberg, but throughout the land." The Catholic population soon began to complain that they were unable to compete with the Hutterites, who were taking their bread away before their very mouths. Therefore on March 23, 1601, a decree was issued to the barons in Upper and Lower Austria, that they remove all Anabaptists occupied in mills or otherwise. But the decree was not generally obeyed; in Moravia it was not even proclaimed.

The principal reason for the high value placed on Hutterite products was the fine quality of their work at reasonable prices. "We desire," said Klaus Braidl, "to satisfy everybody for his money, and if the people were not satisfied they would not come to us." . . . "Blades that are seen to be defective shall not be sold, and imperfect work shall be sold for less than perfect work. Those responsible for the work shall, in accord with the principles and regulations of the brotherhood, see to it that good wares only are given out, so that the good and honorable name of the brotherhood be not lost or maligned and that the people be not cheated." "Cutters shall insist on good workmanship, so that people will get something decent for their money, as the price of knives is high. Hungarian and Silesian iron shall not be offered for sale in the place of Styrian iron, for defamation would follow, and it would not be right. One also ruins business thereby." The regulations for other trades are similar.

Thus each craft or trade had its own regulations (*Ordnungen*), which were occasionally read to the artisans, who then gave a pledge to follow them faithfully. To be sure, we are acquainted only with the rules of the later period, but there is evidence that they were observed in earlier times. Thus we find in the manuscripts the following statements: "Anno 1561, on Dec. 9, the cobblers' regulations were recognized by the elders and deacons and were renewed in 1570." In 1571 there were rules for millers, in 1574 for carpenters. In 1591 the remark is made, "On January 8 all the overseers assembled at Neumühl; in the presence of all the preachers a discussion was held on what the cobblers, cutters, menders and buyers should not permit." From time to time reforms were necessary, and revisions became necessary and were carried through. Andreas Ehrenpreis (*q.v.*), the leader who died in Sobotiste in 1662, did valuable work in collecting all these regulations, preserved today in one codex only of the archiepiscopal library of Gran (*q.v.*). It contains the regulations for the separate trades. For many, however, including several very successful ones like wool-weaving, no regulations have been preserved. It is important to note that the approval of the leaders of the church was required for the economic regulations.

After these general statements some details on specific crafts are in order. Not all crafts and occupations were permitted, several were indeed prohibited, others permitted conditionally. On these points Riedemann's *Rechenschaft* gives some information: "Merchandizing and shopkeeping we allow to none among us, for it is a sinful trade, as the wise man says 'A merchant or trader can hardly keep himself from sinning, and as a nail penetrates between a door and hinge, so sin enters between buying and selling.' Therefore we permit no one to buy anything for the purpose of selling it, as merchants are accustomed to do. But one who sells to provide for the needs of the household or to obtain material for his trade, and sells the article he has made we regard not as doing wrong, but as doing right. But we consider it wrong (Sir. 20) if one buys an article and then sells the same article and takes his gain, thereby making the article more expensive to the poor and taking the bread from their mouth, and thus the poor man must become nothing more than the servant of the rich man."

Conditionally permitted was tailoring. "Christians shall not apply their industry on outward ornamentation to please the world. Whatever tends to create pride, haughtiness, and vanity, . . . we permit no one to make, in order that our conscience may be served spotless before God." Sword and knife making were similarly restricted. "It serves mostly only for killing, injuring and ruining human beings: therefore we make no swords, spears, guns, or similar weapons or arms. But what is made for the daily use of men, as breadknives, axes, hoes, etc., we may and do make. But if one would say one might possibly injure another with them, they are nevertheless not made for this purpose."

The wool-weaving craft was on a high plane with the Hutterian Brethren; their products were so highly prized, that after the expulsion of the Anabaptists the government sought to fill their place by skilled Belgians. In the crafts permitted, native trade had sharp competition, which it was naturally not capable of meeting because, aside from the much simpler living conditions and customs of the Hutterites, their methods of production in the individual trades were much simpler and the great profits of the middlemen were eliminated. For here the individual trades were co-ordinated to aid each other. It was strictly forbidden to get raw materials outside the Bruderhofs if they were available there. Thus from the slaughterhouses the hides were sent to the tanners and from them to the saddlers, harness makers, and cobblers. A similar relationship existed between the production of wool, weaving, and tailoring. Only a few raw products, like iron and fine oils, were bought from the outside. The miller's trade had an excellent reputation. We know from an epistle that millers were sent into Switzerland to learn various methods of milling. On the other hand, in 1560 millers came to the Brethren from Bellinzona (Italy) to get the plan for an ox-power mill.

Great stress was laid on proper training for a trade. Young people were to be led to industry, honesty, piety, and manual skill. They should not be beaten nor treated rudely. The overseer must see to it that they did not forget how to read and write, and that they did not dawdle. "The young smiths shall be trained to work well and skillfully and to learn to do all kinds of neat work, so that the smith's craft may not deteriorate."

This was the character of the handicrafts of the Hutterite brotherhood in its best days. Unfortunately it could not remain so. At the end of the 1570's the terrible Counter Reformation set in in the West, and took possession of a good part of western, southern, and southeast Germany, and was also victorious in the country that had previously been considered a mighty fortress of religious tolerance, Moravia. There the "recurrence of sorrow" took place, the Bocskay forces came, then the events of the Bohemian War, the outbreak of the Bohemian revolt which brought on the Thirty Years' War; all the tribulations that fell on the beautiful Bruderhofs, as the attack on Pribitz, the arson of wild war hordes, and finally the expulsion of the Brethren from Moravia in 1622. It was inevitable that all of this would affect the inner life of the Brethren, thus having a harmful effect on the development of Hutterite craftsmanship. The old zeal of the brotherhood was cooling, the old, strict rules were disregarded if not forgotten; economic deterioration followed in its wake, which the capable Ehrenpreis tried in vain to stem. (See **Habaner**.)

J. LOSERTH.

Peter Rideman, *Account of our Religion* . . . (1950); Wolkan, *Geschicht-Buch*; R. Friedmann, *Die Habaner in der Slowakei* (1927); Beck, *Geschichtsbücher*; J. Loserth, *Kommunismus*; L. Müller, *Der Communismus der mährischen Wiedertäufer* (Leipzig, 1927); F. Hruby, *Die Wiedertäufer in Mähren* (Leipzig, 1935); E. Correl, *Das schweizerische Täufer-Mennonitentum* (Tübingen, 1925); ML II, 105.

CRALOG, Council of Relief Agencies Licensed for Operation in Germany, was the joint organization co-ordinating private relief importations to Germany following World War II. The Mennonite Central Committee was numbered among the eleven American agencies initially organizing CRALOG on Jan. 14, 1946. CRALOG was planned at the instigation of the President's War Relief Control Board. General Lucius D. Clay signed on Jan. 29, 1946, the first contract with CRALOG which permitted the importation of relief supplies into the American Zone of Occupation in Germany. CRALOG was officially established on Feb. 19, 1946, when President Truman issued a directive concerning relief contributions to Germany. Contracts with the respective military governments followed: for the British Zone on July 12, 1946, the French Zone on July 30, 1946, and Berlin in April 1947. MCC staff serving as CRALOG representatives in Germany during the period of 1946-48 included Robert Kreider, Walter Eicher, Cornelius Dyck, and Delbert Gratz. J. N. Byler was elected treasurer of the original executive committee of CRALOG and served later as vice-chairman. CRALOG's primary function was that of a centralized shipping channel for bulk relief contributions to Germany. In the first two years of operation the MCC was the largest contributor of private relief supplies to Germany through CRALOG.   R.K.

Cramer Family: see **Cremer.**

Cramer, Alle Meenderts, a Dutch Mennonite preacher and historian, b. March 25, 1805, at Norden, East Friesland, Germany, d. Dec. 14, 1894, at Haarlem, the son of Meendert Alle Cramer and Geertje Cremer, both parents being of old Mennonite families. One of his ancestors fled from Antwerp because of his faith and settled in Norden and set up a mercantile establishment there. Alle Meenderts Cramer attended the German school in Norden. He was permitted to use the German language when he took the entrance examination in Amsterdam in 1828. As a student he made a highly favorable impression on his two professors, W. Cnoop Koopmans and Samuel Muller. He married Muller's daughter Elisabeth; the marriage lasted 45 years and was a happy one. To them were born nine children; one of the sons, Samuel Cramer (*q.v.*), became professor at the Mennonite seminary in Amsterdam, while another, Hendrik, distinguished himself as the captain of a ship in a Dutch shipping company.

In 1829 Alle entered the preaching service in the Huizinge in the Dutch province of Groningen, now Middelstum, and in 1832 he accepted a call to Middelburg, which was at that time combined with Vlissingen. In 1849 his health made it necessary to have an assistant appointed, and later Klaas Rutger Pekelharing was made his colleague. They worked together until 1871, when Cramer retired. He lived in Lochem until 1890, and then in Haarlem, where he died in his ninetieth year.

Though his career was not externally particularly rich or brilliant, it was inwardly rich and beautiful. All who knew him agreed that he was a simple, modest, friendly and kindly person; as a preacher he did not make a striking impression, for his manner lacked oratory and figurative language. But his sermons are always logically developed, even when they deal with emotional subjects. This economy of language, however, had its charms. "The Gospel does not require ornamentation," he was accustomed to say.

Partisanship was foreign to him: he preferred to call himself a follower of simple Biblical Christianity. He had an open mind for modern theology, but he also had his doubts about it. He collaborated with J. Boeke (*q.v.*) in a reply to J. Halbertsma (*q.v.*), who in his book *De Doopsgezinden en hunne herkomst* (Deventer, 1843) pleaded for a liberal philosophy instead of Biblical theology. In his scholarly work he was frequently occupied with matters of dogma, but his strength lay first of all in his historical studies, as is shown in his published works. He is the author of *Het leven en de verrigtingen van Menno Simons* (Amsterdam, 1837) and of a biography of David Joris, which was published in parts V and VI of the *Nederl. Archief voor Kerkgeschiedenis*. Though these books are now antiquated, they offered building stones for later historiographers of the Mennonite brotherhood, Cramer having been a pioneer in the difficult path of Mennonite historiography. Further historical works by Cramer were "De twee acten van Prins Willem I betreffende de Doopsgezinden" (*Vaderl. Letteroefeningen* 1836), "Aanteekeningen van eene rondreis in alle Oud-Vlaamsche gemeenten in 1754" (*DJ* 1844), "Het eigenaardige der Doopsgezinden, vooral hier te lande" (*DB* 1873). He belonged to a number of learned societies.

Cramer's interest in the practical was also apparent in his work for social welfare. In this field he accomplished much that has been of lasting value. He was one of the first to think of creating work for the unemployed for the cold winter months. In recognition of his services the government bestowed on him the Order of the Dutch Lion.   H.W.

B. Cuperus, "Levensbericht van Alle Meenderts Cramer," in *M. v. Ned. Letterkunde* (Leiden, 1895) 351-402; *Biogr. Wb.* II, 287-90 lists Cramer's numerous publications; *ML* I, 376.

Cramer, Samuel, a Mennonite minister and theologian, professor at the Amsterdam municipal university and the Mennonite seminary, b. July 3, 1842, at Middelburg (capital of the Dutch province of Zeeland), d. at Amsterdam, Jan. 30, 1913. His father was Alle Meenderts Cramer (*q.v.*), his mother a daughter of Samuel Muller (*q.v.*). In his home the boy received the deep religious impressions and the outstanding character education of which he gave evidence throughout his life.

His education began in the elementary and Latin schools of his home town. In 1861 he attended the Athenaeum in Amsterdam, which later became the Amsterdam university, and the seminary where Willem Moll, S. Hoekstra, J. G. de Hoop Scheffer, P. J. Veth, and other capable teachers initiated him into the mysteries of church history, the problems of philosophy, and the manifold questions of theology. His independence was early apparent in an article he published in the student almanac in cooperation with his friend H. D. Tjeenk Willink, in which they sharply criticized the seminary. This naturally evoked some disapproval on the part of the professors and the board of directors. But his untiring and thorough theological work protected him from any adverse consequences of this bold critique. He was most attracted by S. Hoekstra, his professor of ethics and dogmatics. Though Cramer was a thorough liberal, he was also permanently influenced by his maternal grandfather,

who was in his advanced years a genuinely pious, sincere, and rather conservative person.

On April 16, 1866, Cramer acquired his doctor's degree with a *summa cum laude* at the university of Utrecht, since the Athenaeum was not yet giving the degree, with a treatise on Zwingli's theology (*Zwingli's Leer van het Godsdienstig Geloof*, Middelburg, 1866). His professional adviser in his graduation was Prof. J. J. van Oosterzee, who was noted as a theologian and preacher and who was a competent co-worker on Lange's Bible commentary.

With the consent of the seminary board Cramer had spent a semester at the universities of Heidelberg and Zürich. On Nov. 18, 1866, he entered the Mennonite ministry at Zijldijk in the province of Groningen. He was introduced by his father with a sermon on I Cor. 4:1 and 2, which he himself followed with a sermon on II Cor. 5:20. True to the thought of the text, Cramer was untiring in preaching, religious instruction, pastoral visits, and studies. He devoted all his time and his extraordinary strength to his congregation and the brotherhood in the wider sense, then as always consuming himself in the service of his office. The first fruits were reaped by the *Doopsgezinden Bijdragen* (*q.v.*). The first issue of the new series under Harting and Cool was opened with an article by Cramer, "Verdraagzaam of bekrompen? (Tolerant or narrowminded?) This article is evidence of his wide reading and of his comprehensive interest in Mennonite history and the objectives arising from that history. The second issue also began with an article by Cramer, this time a genial account of his visits to Mennonites in other countries. He also wrote articles for scholarly journals.

On Sept. 18, 1870, Cramer left Zijldijk and went to Emden, taking charge of the small congregation on Sept. 25. Here he became the good friend of Anna Brons (*q.v.*), the wife of the outstanding Isaak Brons (*q.v.*), who was currently the deacon of the Emden congregation and filled an important place in national affairs. In intimate association with this family he received inspiration and information. His own contribution is indicated by the words Mrs. Brons wrote to me nearly 25 years later (1893): "I am very happy to know that a man so zealous and so filled with a high calling as Professor Cramer is your teacher."

Cramer was not long in Emden. In 1872 he accepted a call to Enschede, preaching as his farewell sermon at Emden "Ons Koninkrijk" (Harlingen, 1872) on Oct. 13. In Enschede he found a challenging field. For more than 12 years he served this congregation, constantly developing his talents. Though he apparently devoted all his time to theological study, his actual interest lay only in the building and strengthening of his brotherhood, his congregation being merely the small portion of total Christendom entrusted to his care by divine Providence. When in 1877 dissension broke out in the Reformed congregation in Enschede he did not hesitate to speak words of admonition to both sides; his interest was valued as the Christian advice of a dear brother. When Cramer transferred to Zwolle in 1885 the Reformed congregation of Enschede also presented him with gifts. In Enschede Cramer continued his literary work. One of his books was *Konservatief Modernisme, Godgeleerdheid en Volksleven* (Leyden, 1882). In addition he published many articles in Dutch and German periodicals: *Doopsgezinde Bijdragen, De Hervorming, Het Theologisch Tijdschrift, Volksalmanak, Protestantische Kirchenzeitung für das evangelische Deutschland, Mennonitische Blätter, Schweizerische Reformblätter*, etc.

In 1883 Cramer was delegated by the Dutch *Protestantenbond* to attend the German *Protestantentag* at Neustadt a.d. Hardt. On this occasion he visited the congregations of the Palatinate and the school at the Weierhof. On his journeys he made as many contacts as possible with like-minded persons. At Neustadt he made the acquaintance of C. H. Zimmermann and his wife of Danzig, a member of the city council. The dilapidated state of the Weierhof school, information received from his Danzig friends, and his experiences among the Palatine Mennonites led him to undertake an extended journey among the German Mennonites, including also those in Polish Prussia. On this journey he persuaded the Danzig church council to call the meeting held in Berlin on Oct. 2 and 3, 1884, which resulted in the organization of the *Vereinigung der Mennonitengemeinden im Deutschen Reich* (*q.v.*). Thus this institution, so fraught with importance to the future development of the Mennonite brotherhood in Germany, owes its existence partly to Cramer. The account of his visits to the German, French, and Swiss congregations in 1883 and 1884 is found in *DB* 1885, 1-53 (East Friesland, Hamburg, along the Rhine, the Palatinate, Alsace, Switzerland, Baden, etc., Danzig, East and West Prussia); *DB* 1886, 1-72 (East and West Prussia and Poland).

While at Enschede Cramer married Maria Charlotte de Clercq, who was also descended from an old Mennonite family. This union was blessed with a daughter and two sons. Maria died on March 18, 1898, after a long illness.

In his last year at Enschede Cramer published *Christengodsvrucht in Doopsgezind gemeenteleven* (Enschede, 1885). Soon afterward he was called to Zwolle, and served there from March 15, 1885, to April 20, 1890. Then he succeeded J. G. de Hoop Scheffer (*q.v.*) as professor at the Amsterdam seminary and university. The topic of his inaugural address was "Beschrijvende en Toegepaste Godgeleerdheid in haar verschil en onderling verband" (published in Amsterdam, 1890). In 1894, upon the sudden death of de Hoop Scheffer, he also assumed the editorship of the *Doopsgezinde Bijdragen*, a large part of the obligations indirectly connected with the professorship having already fallen to his lot.

At that time he could hardly have been called a man of outstanding scholarship. After the dissertation with which he earned his degree, no really scholarly work had appeared from his pen. He was not a pioneer, nor did he represent any particular theological view which would have attracted general attention to himself. He was only a man of scholarly education who devoted his leisure hours to study, and in addition worked in various intellectual fields at the same time. He later warned his students against making a similar error. Nevertheless he was a successful teacher and in 1900 served with honor as the head of the rectorship of the Amsterdam university. Before 1899 no works of outstanding merit were published by him. In that year he published in the *Doopsgezinde Bijdragen* an extensive study of the dependability of van Braght's *Martyrs' Mirror* (*q.v.*). The next volume of the *Bijdragen* contained his conclusion of the above study and an article on the history of Mennonite church music. After that his productions followed in rather rapid succession, especially in the *Bijdragen*. Most of these dealt with Mennonite history; he was also the author of the sketch on the Mennonites in the third edition of Herzog's *Realenzyklopaedie*. But his principal work, a *monumentum aere perennius*, did not appear until 1904-12. This was the *Bibliotheca Reformatoria Neerlandica* (*q.v.*), which he edited in co-operation with Dr. F. Pijper, professor of theology at the university of Leiden. It is a collection of writings from the period of the Reformation in Holland, published in the original with minute exactness and provided with introductions and notes based on modern scholarly research. Cramer worked through four stately volumes, the last of which was published posthumously by Dr. Pijper. A history of the *Algemene Doopsgezinde Sociëteit* which he had planned to write in collaboration with the author of this biographical sketch and for which much material had been gathered, was interrupted by the failing of Cramer's strength and his death.

But Cramer's significance cannot be measured by a merely scholarly standard. His aim was rather to produce capable preachers and faithful shepherds for their future flocks. In this he was outstandingly successful. His influence consequently increased, so that the celebration of the centennial of the A.D.S. in 1911 became as a matter of course a tribute to Cramer. To the congregations he was like a father; not always a gentle father, and in the beginning of his professorship his too personal regulation of the management of some rural congregation produced some displeasure on the part of the deacons. But he won their hearts by his frank acknowledgment that he had erred.

He entered his second happy marriage with Maria A. Stuart in 1900, and was privileged to spend his last years in a blessed family life. On the occasion of the commemoration of the centennial of the founding of the A.D.S. on Sept. 28, 1911, where he delivered an address, he was not in the best of health. In June 1912, he gave his last lecture at the university, and on Jan. 30, 1913, his suffering came to an end.†   F.C.F.

W. J. Kühler, "Levensbericht van S. Cramer," in *DB* 1916, 1-32, where the stately list of Cramer's publications is also given; *DJ* 1914, 21-35, with portrait; *ML* I, 377-81.

Crautwald, Valentin (1470-1545), canon and lector of theology at Liegnitz in Silesia, Germany. He was not an Anabaptist (as Keller erroneously supposed), but was a close friend of Schwenckfeld, as well as his teacher of Greek and theological counselor. He is the source of the systematic presentation and foundation of the Schwenckfeldian doctrine of communion, which involved both of them in conflict with Luther. Of Crautwald's work, mention should be made of *Von bereytunge zum sterben* (Breslau, 1524) and *Der neue Mensch* (1543). NEFF.

ADB IV, 570; C. A. Salig, *Vollständige Historie der Augsburgischen Confession* (1734) III; L. Keller, *Die Waldenser und die deutschen Bibelübersetzungen* (Leipzig, 1886) 30; ML I, 381.

Crawford County, in northwestern Pennsylvania, received its first Mennonites when a family settled near Spartansburg in 1917. Others came in 1931 and later. Britton Run Church (MC) was started in 1932, by Mennonite families from Nebraska and Ohio. The Meadville mission (MC) began in 1935. Sunnyside Church (MC), near Conneaut Lake, was built in 1938 to accommodate settlers from Iowa and other states, while Meadville continued as a mission point. The combined Mennonite membership of approximately 224 (1954) included a few residing in Erie County. A few residents attended Beaver Dam Church, Erie County, which was started in 1940. In 1949 a colony of Old Order Amish resided near Atlantic and a few Conservative Amish attended church in near-by Mercer County. J.A.S.

Crawford-Richland Counties, Ohio, Mennonite (MC) community, now extinct. In 1818 Samuel Pletcher, a Palatine emigrant who had stopped briefly in Lancaster Co., Pa., moved to Richland (then Ashland County), Ohio. The next year he moved across the line into Crawford County near Galion. His children married into the following families: Imhof, Kilmer, Hibschman, Nesselrodt, Seiler, and Null. The small congregation worshiped in their homes and in the union meetinghouse in Ontario, Richland County, with Joseph Freed as minister, and disintegrated after Freed's death in 1872. A number of the families moved to Elkhart Co., Ind. The few who remained were visited occasionally by Mennonite ministers. Their children united with other denominations. J.S.U.

Crechtingsvolk, after Berend Krechting (*q.v.*). The name Crechtingsvolk is found in a sentence of death, pronounced at Deventer, Dutch province of Overijssel, on May 18, 1542, to indicate the revolutionary Münster Anabaptists (*q.v.*). (*Inv. Arch. Amst.* I, 246.) vDZ.

Credit Unions may be described as co-operative banks. They may be small organizations consisting of one or two dozen members with a few hundred dollars as loan capital, or they may consist of several hundred members with loan capital amounting to thousands of dollars. Credit unions as such are seldom found in Mennonite communities. Most Mennonites use the regularly established bank facilities for depositing funds and as a source of loan credit.

The credit union idea, which is widespread in Europe and America today, originated in Germany during a depression in 1846-47. The leaders were non-Mennonites named Raiffeisen and Schulze-Delitsch. The Mennonites in Russia became familiar with the idea before World War I, founding mutual credit societies, although little information is available about their operations. In Canada and United States credit unions have frequently been organized in conjunction with co-operatives especially among Mennonite farmers. Most of these, however, are not confined to Mennonites, but are opened to all who join the co-operative. In 1944 the Crosstown Credit Union (*q.v.*), organized in Winnipeg for Mennonites, had over 1,000 members by 1952. There are no other known credit unions among Mennonites exclusively for church members. A few individual congregations in America have loan funds raised by members of the congregation which are available to members of this congregation at nominal rates of interest. In such cases members might borrow several hundred dollars to establish homes, and buy cars or equipment to aid them in earning their livelihood.

In 1945 the two largest Mennonite bodies in America established mutual aid services in which a primary function is to provide financial assistance to members of their own conferences. This money was raised from members interested in helping the brethren. These organizations, while serving some of the same purposes as credit unions, are operated differently from the normal credit unions. Mennonite Mutual Aid (MC) was organized in 1945 under the authorization of the Mennonite General Conference as a separate incorporated body with headquarters at Goshen, Ind. The General Conference Mennonite Church, on the other hand, made its mutual aid program an integral part of the conference service program. These mutual aid activities are still in their infancy, with a combined total of less than one-half million dollars in their revolving funds. J.W.F.

Crefeld (or Krefeld), a city (population 170,000) of Germany on the left side of the Lower Rhine, officially called Krefeld-Uerdingen am Rhein. Though it received the status of a town in 1373, it nevertheless remained for 300 years a walled village of poor peasants and weavers. Here, as all along the Lower Rhine, the temperament of the people reflects the admixture of cheerfulness and gloom in the landscape. Religious life has always been active here, though not explosive in nature. Here Dr. Johannes Weyer (1515-88) at Cleve attacked witchhunting; Mennonites, Labadists, and Quakers found refuge here, and here Gerhard Tersteegen, for the only time in his life, entered the Mennonite pulpit.

The town, belonging to the counts of Moers, but surrounded by the territory of Electoral Cologne, suffered unspeakably in the dynastic wars. In the 16th century it was twice reduced to ashes. Not until the rule of the house of Orange (1600-1702) and the Hohenzollerns (after 1702) did it begin to thrive. Toleration and industry, combined with government protection, brought prosperity and rapid growth; by 1786 its population had increased to 7,500, and 100 years later to 100,000.

When the first Mennonites came to Crefeld cannot be ascertained; but there was a Mennonite congregation here before the middle of the 17th century, perhaps even at the end of the 16th. The first Mennonites known to have settled in Crefeld were the op den Graeffs, who came in 1609 or soon after from Aldekerk (*q.v.*). According to the family chronicles of Hubert Rahr ("Familie Königs-Konings," in *Heimat* V, 268), the Kempen Protestants were permitted to hold their services in the city hall by 1536, whereas the 100 Mennonites living there held theirs in Weyer's barn and buried their dead behind the barn. (This family tradition was probably the basis of the painting *Die Gehetzten, Mennonitenpredigt in einer Scheune*, by F. ter Meer, 1845, of Crefeld.)

The head of the Crefeld Mennonites was Hermann op den Graeff (*q.v.*, 1585-1642). To the annoyance of the Reformed pastor Holtmann (Xylander), op den Graeff was not molested by the Orange government, though Holtmann complained to the government that the Mennonites were holding regular conventicles and luring the simple. By 1634 the Mennonites ventured to preach openly and to consider themselves a congregation. In 1632 Hermann op den Graeff and Weylen Kreynen signed the Dordrecht Confession. The records of the Reformed Church of 1636 report 22 talers contributed by the Reformed Church, and 25 talers by "Hermann uff den Graff" in the name of the Mennonites, for the support of some widows and orphans of Reformed clergymen. This indicates the tolerable situation of the congregation. In 1646 the Reformed preacher Mathias Kolhagen complained to the synod that the Mennonites were bold, that their offensive public meetings were noticeably harming the Reformed Church. Repeated complaints had little influence on the Orange government. Refugees from Jülich (*q.v.*) augmented the congregation, especially about 1678 (*Inv. Arch. Amst.* I, No. 1419). The Catholics remaining in Crefeld were permitted to use only the convent church and had to pay baptismal, marriage, and death fees to the Reformed Church. The Mennonites fared better.

In the middle of the 17th century renewed persecution set in, in Jülich and Cologne (Rembert, "*Wiedertäufer*," 625). The archives of the Amsterdam Mennonite Church contain valuable records on the Mennonites driven out of Jülich, causing a new influx of Mennonites into Crefeld, large numbers coming from Gladbach (1654). Not all of them found room in the city, and some had to seek refuge on farms. In 1694 refugees from severe persecution in Rheydt (*q.v.*) increased the Mennonite population again (see **Instrumentum Publicum**). The support of these refugees and their final relief from persecution by the Mennonites of Crefeld and Holland are a monument of Christian charity.

Upon renewed complaints by the Reformed clergy the government in The Hague in 1657 sent a committee to Crefeld to investigate the situation; it was decided that the Mennonites should continue to live in Crefeld and worship as they liked; but in the matter of military service a study should be made to determine whether they should be charged a fee to pay for substitutes.

Not only were civil protection and freedom of conscience assured the Mennonites, but also freedom of worship. But since the Reformed Church should predominate, the Mennonites must meet "quietly and modestly, without offensive character, one hour after the service in the parish church." Renewed complaints made by the Reformed in 1670, that the Mennonites were planning to build a church, were fruitless; the Orange government now gave the Mennonites the right of full citizenship, and 29 families at once applied.

In 1683, 13 families of Crefeld weavers, all until the 1670's members of the Mennonite Church, emigrated to America, "in order to live an active and God-fearing life with complete religious liberty." They were for the most part related to each other, and most had become Quakers before they left for America, through the influence of Quaker missionaries. They founded Germantown (*q.v.*) and by their industry and thrift contributed to the development of the country. Abraham and Derick op den Graeff there signed the first American protest against slavery in 1688. In 1920 a monument was erected in Germantown to these Crefeld emigrants, a bronze copy of which is found in the museum in Crefeld. In later years some additional Mennonites from Crefeld and vicinity joined them.

The influx of many victims of persecution contributed greatly to the prosperity of Crefeld. The circumstance that from 1689 Crefeld, together with Holland and Great Britain, was under the sovereignty of the House of Orange, was also of benefit to the city. In 1695 the Mennonites built a church in a new addition to the city. The first marriage was solemnized here on Jan. 19, 1696. The church was remodeled and enlarged in 1843, but the old baroque gate was saved. In 1943 the church was partly destroyed by bombing, but was rebuilt in 1950.

In the years 1695-1715 the Crefeld congregation co-operated with the Amsterdam committee (later called *Commissie voor Buitenlandsche Nooden, q.v.*) on behalf of the persecuted brethren in the Palatinate and Switzerland; Wilhelm von der Leyen and Gosen Goyen intermediated between the Palatinate and Amsterdam.

To the Mennonite silk firm of F. and H. von der Leyen (*q.v.*) Crefeld owes its good competition with Lyons. What would Crefeld be without this determined and cautiously creative Mennonite family, which in its first official year of business (1669) began Crefeld's rise "with the blessing of God"? (The Heinrich van Leyen or Leien, who was granted citizenship in 1668 was Reformed, and was of a different family.) Adolf and Heinrich von der Leyen became citizens of Crefeld in 1679, William in 1681. They came from Rade vorm Wald in the duchy of Berg. For generations the Mennonites were permitted to develop unmolested. A city with a planned network of streets came into being. Members of the von der Leyen family became officials in commerce and were very prominent, entertaining nobility and royalty at their country home, Alt-

Leyenthal. Six additions were made to the city at their urging before they lost their prominence.

As early as 1725 it was officially reported, "Crefeld is carrying on a very heavy foreign trade . . . so that it has the reputation of almost being Germany's greatest trade city." "The flowering of this city is to be ascribed to the linen trade of the Mennonites; there are besides the linen trade also silk, ribbons, hosiery, needles, and other factories, which the Mennonites and the (Amish) . . . have industriously promoted and continued" (*Heimat* IV, 89, 94). Against the reactionary economic and guild politics of Cologne, the old German silk center, the young competitor was protected by the policies of economic liberty by the kings of Prussia.

The Mennonites were given specific protection by Frederick William I of Prussia, who visited the silk mills and inquired at length of one of the officials about their economic activity and religious life. He asked whether they were more like the Reformed, but sang more psalms and their preachers had no collars. They were paying double fees to the Reformed for church services which they performed for themselves. The king granted their request to be absolved from these fees, and agreed that "they are good Christians and fine people." (See **Dompelaars** for a poem describing toleration in Crefeld.)

The *Acta Borussica* (*Denkmäler der preussischen Staatsverwaltung im 18. Jahrhundert, Seidenindustrie* II; *Heimat* VI, 90, 101) show that the king gave the young silk center every encouragement by reducing their taxes. Because of their initiative, industry, and progressiveness they were to be assured of absolute religious freedom, lest they emigrate (*Heimat* V, 133).

Constantly renewed complaints by the Reformed inform us that in the last quarter of the 17th century other Separatists, like the Labadists and Quakers, many of whom came from England, found asylum and preached here. In 1692 the once Reformed Pastor Reiner Copper of Moers was ordered to stop his sharp sermons to large Labadist audiences.

It must not be forgotten that Crefeld, in particular the Mennonite church there, was for a century (1650-1750) a focal point for awakened Christians and mystics. Goebel (*Gesch. des christlichen Lebens* II, 197) says, "When the Quaker, Labadist, Separatist, Baptist, Mystic and Herrnhuter movements began, Crefeld became a place of refuge and the Mennonite church and pulpit a sure support." Among those prominent in religious life who had active contacts here were Gottfried Arnold (*q.v.*), Hochmann von Hohenau (*q.v.*), Charles Hector, Marquis of Marsay, and especially Gerhard Tersteegen (*q.v.*), born 1697 in Moers. Mrs. von der Leyen corresponded with Tersteegen; when he was in Crefeld he preached in the Mennonite church. A faithful admirer of Tersteegen was Arnold Goyen (*q.v.*, the son of the Mennonite preacher at Crefeld), who in 1727 married Susanna von der Leyen, and became the father-in-law of Johann von der Leyen. After the death of his wife in 1735 Arnold Goyen retired to Moers and lived in Tersteegen's house (Keussen, *Geschichte*, 376).

Especial protection was enjoyed by the firm of von der Leyen. In the 1760's, it had in operation besides the thread and ribbon mills about 500 looms for silk, velvet, silk handkerchiefs, ribbons, and East Indian materials. Of its 4,000-5,000 hand weavers most lived outside the city. Its monopoly even excluded other Mennonite firms like Floh, Preyers, von Beckerath, etc., until the French Revolution. The growth of the city is therefore parallel with the development of the firm of von der Leyen (*Acta Borussica* II, 585, 647; *Heimat* XI, 57).

Visitors also drew a glowing picture of the city with its industrial grounds, thriving trade, and the social provisions for the city. Most of the important merchants were Mennonites: Floh, Heydweiller, Lingen, von Wyk, von Beckerath, Helgers, Rahr, Scheuten, Stetius, etc. When a tax was levied it was unloaded on the wealthier citizens. Crefeld was at that time (1789) as before known as the "center of trade and industry of the entire region."

In his will (May 1, 1790) Heinrich von der Leyen with justifiable pride points out that if by the grace of God he was able to achieve his ambition to build factories, it was for the interest and welfare of the city (Keussen, *Geschichte*, 486; *Heimat* XI, 57). The greatest benefactor of his native city was Friedrich von der Leyen, who during the French occupation most unselfishly used his energy and influence to ward off all hard measures and oppressive levies. Under Napoleon I he was made mayor and first president of the Board of Trade. Probably no important visitor to the Lower Rhine neglected to pay a visit to the hospitable house of the von der Leyens. In 1789 J. H. Campe (*Reise von Braunschweig nach Paris*) with the young Wilhelm von Humboldt appeared here. Both are extravagant in their praise of the charm of the house, the culture of the family, the unusual liberty and toleration of the city. Campe writes: "Mr. von der Leyen once invited to his house people of all creeds and sects who were accustomed to combating each other, and saw to it that they were heartily happy and merry. The consequence was friendship and understanding" (*Heimat* IV, 105).

There were, of course, voices raised in protest against the too progressive and luxurious life of the merchants and in criticism of the business and social life of the Mennonites. On the other hand, as Engelbert von Bruck admits, the citizens of Crefeld were distinguished for their morality, charitable gifts, and frugality, and even the populace showed less rudeness than in the outlying villages; daily contact with the Mennonites resulted in Mennonite simplicity of manner becoming a trait in the Crefeld character.

It was due to the influence of the von der Leyens that trained ministers were employed as soon as finances permitted. The first lay preacher, who preached in Low German, was Adam Scheuten, 1639-68. He left a very valuable family register of the church, which, continued by the families themselves, is a genealogical treasure-trove. Other lay preachers were Johannes Ewalds (d. 1697), Nicolaus ter Meer (d. 1698), Leonhard Paulsen (d. 1701), Jan Crous (preacher 1716-24), and Gosen (or

Goswin) Goyen (b. 1667, d. 1737). The names of the last two are connected with the controversy on the form of baptism (1710-30), from which the Dompelaars (*q.v.*) arose. Gosen Goyen (*q.v.*) had himself baptized by immersion, while Jan Crous was strictly opposed (*Heimat* IV, 94). An agreement was finally reached, recognizing both forms. Shortly after Goyen's death immersion disappeared. Other preachers were Leonhard Ewalds together with David Köters (b. 1699, preacher 1730-55), Winand Winands (1727-77), and Johann Remkes (b. 1714, preacher 1752-70). In 1764 a birth registry was begun.

On April 4, 1766, the brothers Friedrich and Heinrich von der Leyen set aside an endowment for the church, from which "a well-educated and capable preacher should be paid 100 talers annually." The first trained ministers came from Holland, and had been trained at the Dutch Mennonite Seminary of Amsterdam: Wopko Molenaar (1739-94), serving 1770-94, Zino van Abbema (d. 1787) 1771-87, Assuerus Doyer 1788-93, Hidde Wybius van der Ploeg 1793-1818, Isaac Molenaar, son of Wopko, 1818-34; they were followed by Leonhard Weydmann and his son Ernst, under whom the membership rose to 1,125. Leonhard Weydmann, born at Crefeld, was the first German-trained preacher called, after a series from Holland.

Little by little the Crefeld Mennonites yielded the point of nonresistance. In 1810 the decision was left to the individual members. Only a few refused military service. Adaptation to the established church led not only to pleasant relations, but also to intermarriage and the loss of several families to the church. The continued existence of the church rested upon family tradition rather than an awareness of any valuable peculiar belief or trait, and church attendance declined. Gustav Kraemer, a former minister of the Lutherans, was chosen (1937) preacher of the Crefeld Mennonites. Gradually interest in the congregational life increased, and many members of the state church now joined the Mennonites.

Following the death of Isaac Molenaar (*q.v.*), during whose time some members of the congregation (a de Greiff, a Hermes, and a Winkelmann) once more fought through the questions of nonresistance and the oath all the way up to the king, the following pastors served the congregation: 1836-66, Leonhard Weydmann (1793-1868); 1866-1903, Ernst Weydmann (1837-1903); 1903-36, Gustav Kraemer (1863-1948); 1937-50, Dirk Cattepoel (b. 1912); Daniel Reuter, 1951- .

The two Weydmanns (*q.v.*), father and son, were natives of Crefeld; Kraemer came from Wissen on the Sieg; Cattepoel, born in Middelburg (Holland), stemmed from Neuwied. The two Weydmanns were educated at the Mennonite Seminary in Amsterdam, Kraemer in Jena and Bonn, Cattepoel at Berlin and **Vienna.**

Leonhard Weydmann (*q.v.*), who had already proved himself as a preacher in Monsheim, also took his work at Crefeld seriously, lecturing on Dante and writing on Luther, thus extending his sphere of influence beyond the confines of the denomina-

tion. He introduced the use of the catechism in Crefeld, and reduced the age of baptism from 19 to 16. But like many others he was unable to cope with the decline in church interest. It was therefore decided to give him a young assistant after he had passed the age of 70. Among the candidates were two Dutch Mennonites, G. E. Frerichs (*q.v.*) and J. P. Müller (*q.v.*), Karl Harder (*q.v.*) of Neuwied, and a second Isaac Molenaar (*q.v.*). The choice fell on Ernst Weydmann (*q.v.*). His contract of employment reveals that the congregation observed baptism on Palm Sunday, and communion at Easter and on the Sunday after Michaelmas, and placed importance on a thorough instruction and regular visits in the home of the poor and ill; the salary was to be 1,000 talers (Prussian currency) and parsonage, and some reduction in taxes. His duties and rights were to correspond with those of the Protestant pastors. There is in general an unmistakable trend toward adaptation to the Protestant Church. The times were such that Ernst Weydmann was also deprived of the proper fruits of his labors.

It is probably not a mere accident that Johannes Brahms, the musician, maintained live contacts with the Mennonites of Crefeld from 1880 to his death in 1897. Hans Joachim Moser, an authority on music, sees in him the master who is the most worthy representative of middle-class "educated" Protestantism in the second half of the 19th century in the field of German music. The *Deutsches Requiem* (1868) avoids "all that is actually Christian, in order to move the eternally human into the foreground." "Also his preludes to the chorals (*Choralvorspiele*) and the *Vier ernste Gesänge* (Op. 121, Biblical texts) are not the fruit of ecclesiastical thought, but are very personal, though highly worthy, treatments of the idea of death." Rudolf von der Leyen and Alwin von Beckerath, G. Ophüls, and the artist Willy von Beckerath were his close friends, and the Biblical texts that he set to music lived long after his death among his friends in the Crefeld Mennonite Church.

At the beginning of the 20th century a German Protestant pastor was chosen in preference to four Dutch Mennonite candidates. He was Gustav Kraemer. He had obtained his education in the outspokenly liberal universities of Jena and Bonn, and as a modernist he would have nothing to do with a blood theology. On the other hand, he was probably attracted by Anabaptism at a time when Hans Denk (*q.v.*) was actually proclaimed to be a forerunner of the newer theology (Haake, *Hans Denk,* 1897). From the history of his term in Crefeld—among his co-workers was Elder Otto Crous (1876-1936)—he himself related the following in 1937: "The orphanage was for want of orphans turned into a home for the aged. A new expensive organ was installed and used by master musicians; concerts were given even after the beginning of the war. The church and other church-owned buildings were remodeled, beautified, and enlarged at great expense. Central heating, electric lights, and new pews were installed in the church. In 1911 the first general German *Mennonitentag* was duly celebrated in Crefeld; in 1912 a new constitution was adopted which made the women eligible for places on the church council. Numerous transfers of membership into the Mennonite Church testify to its life. The vacation periods spent at the Hülserberg every summer until near the end of the war are an unforgettable experience for the youth of the period. The 'war kitchen' aided many persons of all creeds." In an impressive evaluation Kurt von Beckerath said of him, "And Gustav Kraemer was an awakener. A lively religious movement passed through the congregation, which retroactively also strengthened him."

But there was also difficulty and that of the severest kind. Old, respected families died out, not only through the war which prevented many a hope for the future of the congregation from returning home. Inflation made great inroads into the savings of decades. Decline in the birth rate and emigration lowered the membership. "The hereditary good spirit overcame all the difficulties."

Nothing else can characterize this time and the change in the times as the "General Principles" of 1912, especially in comparison with the Dordrecht Confession of 1632 (q.v.), which the founder of this congregation signed:

"The Mennonite congregation of Crefeld counts itself as one of the brotherhood of old-evangelical Mennonite congregations, a brotherhood existing in many lands.

"As members it admits, as a matter of principle, only those who enter voluntarily and consciously. It therefore rejects the baptism of small children. Baptism is considered as the covenant of a good conscience with God. No obligation to any dogmatic creed is connected with admission into the congregation.

"It holds fast to the complete freedom of the congregation in its affairs as well as the religious liberty of each member. 'To his own master he standeth or falleth' (Rom. 14:4); each person is responsible for himself alone before God.

"It advocates the goals of life which Christ set, recognizing the marks of Christian communities in pure intentions and active love.

"Requiring truthfulness as the basis of all morality, it considers the swearing of an oath as unchristian and unpermissible.

"Faith is for it a purely inward possession, the courage to hold fast to God and the good. Externally it shall be shown only in a moral frame of mind and responsible personal life.

"It considers itself bound to strict obedience toward the laws of the state and expects the same of all its members; but it repudiates all compulsory measures on the part of the state in its religious and congregational affairs."

Also from the "Congregational constitution," chapter on church institutions:

"Baptism is as a rule not administered before the age of fifteen years, and usually on Palm Sunday in a public ceremony in the church.

"Communion is celebrated, in repudiation of any sacramental concept, as a sign of the Christian unity among the members."

48

During World War I the Crefeld Mennonites supported a kitchen which fed a large number of Reformed and Catholic children free of charge. The ensuing inflation wiped out the endowments of the church, and many of the wealthy were completely impoverished. Nevertheless there was a will to master the difficulties with self-sacrifice. The orphanage, for want of orphans, became a home for aged women. The membership suffered through war casualties, expulsion of the completely indifferent, emigration, outside marriages, and a decline in the birth rate, so that in 1934 there were only 760 on the roll.

In 1939 Crefeld was host to the last German *Mennonitentag* before the war. In 1941 Cattepoel did not hesitate to take a Christian position against the program of euthanasia promoted by the state. For the rest of the war he was then a soldier, so that the care of the congregation fell upon Kraemer again and Elder Kurt von Beckerath, the successor of Otto Crous. On June 22, 1943, a large part of the town was destroyed by an air attack, including the church, parsonage, and the Mennonite home for the aged.

The congregation did not despair. In 1946 it published a small hymnal, and Cattepoel was one of the leaders in a petition (*Bittgang*) of all creeds. In 1948, while Cattepoel was attending the Mennonite World Conference held at Goshen and Newton, the congregation was served by his wife. Services for young people and children (12 to 15 years) were instituted in addition to the regular services. A group of young people carries on handicrafts, and another discusses important books. Besides choir practice and sewing circle meetings a reading hour unites something like a core congregation. Many a non-Mennonite joined the congregation; a large number of Mennonite refugees from West Prussia also added to the congregation a group that the Cattepoels served with exemplary devotion. At the end of 1949 the congregation had a membership of 836 baptized persons and 256 children. At the end of 1953 the total number of souls in the congregation was 1230, of whom 870 were refugees. On May 21, 1950, the rebuilt church was dedicated (until then the congregation had worshiped in the Protestant church with sincere participation by all the creeds represented in the city. A few months later the congregation received the greatest blow of its entire recent existence. Because of personal affairs of the pastor, who resigned from his office, opposition flared up between the representatives of the older modernistic Kraemer tradition and those who were more attracted by Cattepoel's more evangelical manner. Again a pastor was chosen from the state church, Daniel Reuter. Heinz von Beckerath succeeded Kurt von Beckerath as elder.

In February 1947, the Mennonite Central Committee established a relief unit in Crefeld, which continued until the summer of 1949, with Peter Bartel in charge until December 1948. A child-feeding program was the chief work in Crefeld with up to 7,000 children receiving daily supplementary feeding. Old people were also helped and much clothing was distributed. From Crefeld also other relief projects were developed in the North Rhine-

Westphalia area. There was close co-operation between the MCC unit and the Crefeld congregation, Pastor Cattepoel serving as the general director of the Crefeld relief kitchens. Regular weekly fellowship meetings were held for some months at the MCC center, with considerable attendance of Crefeld Mennonites.   K.R., E.C.

H. Keussen, *Die Stadt und Herrlichkeit Crefeld* (Crefeld, 1859-65); *idem, Beiträge zur Geschichte Crefelds und des Niederrheins* (Cologne, 1898); Rembert, *Wiedertäufer; Die Heimat, Mitteilungen des Vereins für Heimatkunde in Krefeld,* ed. Rembert, I-XI (Crefeld, 1921-); C. Henry Smith, *The Mennonite Immigration to Pennsylvania* (Norristown, 1929); Diary of Claas ter Meer in Crefeld (1732-58), ms. in the possession of the Crefeld Historical Association; G. von Beckerath, "Die wirtschaftliche Bedeutung der Krefelder Mennoniten und ihrer Vorfahren im 17. und 18. Jahrhundert" (diss. Bonn, 1951); D. Cattepoel, *Die academisch vorgebildeten Prediger der der Krefelder Mennonitengemeinde* (Schriftenreihe des Menn. Geschichtsvereins No. 2, Weierhof, 1939); E. Crous, *Mennoniten im alten Reich und Staat* (Crefeld, *Heimat,* 1939); W. Fellmann, "Johannes Brahms und seine Beziehungen zu Krefelder Mennoniten," in *Gem.-Kal.,* 1939, 82-85; F. Nieper, *Die ersten deutschen Auswanderer von Krefeld nach Pennsylvanien* (Neukirchen, 1940); Kraemer, *Gedenkschrift* (Crefeld, 1948); *RGG* I 2d ed., Col. 1213 ("Brahms" by Moser); Constitution of the Crefeld Mennonite congregation (Crefeld, 1912); *Inv. Arch. Amst.* I, Nos. 1164, 1372, 1376, 1378, 1380, 1402, 1419, 1427; II, 2616-23; II, 2, No. 858; *ML* II, 558-65.

Cremer (Kremer, Kreemer, Cramer, Kramer), a very common Dutch family name. The word *kramer* or *cremer* means simply a traveling merchant or peddler, and thus originally only indicated a business. For this reason it is impossible to trace the relationship of all who bear this name. It is not even clear whether the several families with the name of Cremer and Cramer are related.

In East Friesland, Germany, there is a Mennonite Cremer family. A Lubbert Kremer is said to have been a refugee from Brabant, and have resided at Neustadt-Gödens (*q.v.*) about 1524. One of his descendants was Lubbert Jansz Cremer (Kremer, *q.v.*), b. 1711 at Neustadt-Gödens and d. there 1781, who was a preacher of the Old Flemish congregation in his native town 1737-81. Other descendants were Albert Tobias Cramer (Kramer), b. 1702, likewise a preacher of the Neustadt-Gödens Old Flemish church 1729-56; Harmen Allerts Cremer, preacher of the Old Flemish congregation of Norden (*q.v.*) 1755-ca. 68. Antje Doedes Cremer, b. 1778 at Norden, d. there 1810, was married to Jan ten Doornkaat Koolman. Their daughter Antje Cremer ten Doornkaat, b. 1810 at Norden, d. 1902 at Emden, was married to Isaak Brons (*q.v.*). The Cremer family is still found in Norden.

To this family also belonged Alle Meendertz Cramer (*q.v.*), b. Norden 1805 (grandson of Lubbert Jansz Kremer mentioned before), and his son Samuel Cramer (*q.v.*). A collateral branch of this family is found in Groningen and Deventer in the Netherlands. In Deventer we find Abraham Willemsz Cremer (*q.v.*). b. 1631, d. 1690, who was elder of the Old Flemish congregation there from 1657 until his death in 1690. Berent (or Bernard) Cremer, b. about 1768 at Groningen, was a Mennonite minister of Maastricht 1792-95, Cleve 1795-1801, where he married Anna Leendertz, and Frane-

ker 1801-11. In 1811 he left the ministry to become a schoolteacher at Vollenhove, Overijssel. Herman C. Cremer of Norden studied at the Mennonite Seminary in Amsterdam in 1850-55 and served the congregations of Huizinge in 1856-57, Gorredijk-Lippenhuizen 1857-66, and Westzaan-Zuid 1866, in which year he retired.   vDZ.

J. Huizinga, *Stamboek . . . van Fiepke Foppes en Diever Olferts* (Groningen, 1887) 15, 32; *DJ* 1840, list of p. 52; *Naamlijst* 1731 ff.; *Nederl. Patriciaat* XIX (1930) 136; *Deutsches Geschlechterbuch* XXVI, 1913.

Cremer, Abraham Willemsz, an important elder of the Groninger Old Flemish in Deventer, Holland, d. July 15, 1690, "a man very famous and of great understanding, experienced and mighty in the Scripture" (*DB* 1879, 10), was in 1669 summoned with his colleague Jan Lambertsz ten Cate, preacher of the United Flemish and High German congregation at Deventer, by the city government to give an account on several questions concerning their attitude toward the Socinians (*q.v.*) and the state. These questions and answers were published in two booklets (*Remonstrantie en deductie over de leere, en conventiculen der Mennisten der stede Deventer uyt name des Kerckenraets geexhibeert aen de Ed. Achtb. magistraet derselver stede den 17. October 1670,* and *Antwoorde op het Boeckjen geintituleert: Remonstrantie . . . 1670* found in the library at Amsterdam. In 1670 another book was published, *Redenen waerom de Ed. Achtb. Magistraet den Mennisten tot Deventer niet magh toelaten Conventiculen te houden: door een Liefhebber van Waerheyt en van rechte vryheyt,* which raised very severe charges of a theological and political nature against the Mennonites. A. W. Cremer countered with a *Nootwendige ontschuldinge . . .* (1670), in which he skillfully refuted the charges. His opponent composed a violent answer, *Rechtmatige bestraffinge aan A. W. Cremer over zijn boekje . . . genaemt Nootwendige Ontschuldinge,* to which Cremer replied in a similar vein with *Wederlegginge op de onrechtmatighe Bestraffinge.* The magistrate obviously sided with the opponents of the Mennonites and prohibited their meetings on Nov. 17, 1670. Two other pamphlets against the Mennonites appeared in 1671, but Cremer did not trouble to reply to them. Among his brethren A. W. Cremer stood in high regard. He was repeatedly summoned to settle difficulties among them. (*DB* 1870, 17-31, 115; 1879, 12 f.; 1883, 75; 1919, 48-60; *Catalogus Amst.,* 148; *Biog. Wb.,* 301-2; *ML* I, 381.)

         NEFF, vDZ.

Cremer, Lubbert Jansz (or Kremer), b. 1702 at Neustadt-Gödens, East Friesland, d. there 1781, was a preacher of the Groninger Old Flemish congregation of Neustadt-Gödens 1737-81. In 1754 being appointed a candidate for elder, he made a tour of the congregations in the Netherlands and East Friesland to introduce himself. Eight candidates had to make such a preaching tour. After all of them had finished their trip the votes of all congregations were sent to Groningen as the central point. Four elders were chosen; Wolter ten Cate (*q.v.*) had obtained most votes (397). Cremer was not chosen; he had polled only 189 votes, the lowest number except one. Cremer wrote an account of his tour which lasted from June 12 to Sept. 31, 1754.

During his trip he visited 34 Groninger Old Flemish congregations, of which he gives particulars (number of members in 1710, 1733, and 1754, names of preachers and deacons, place where he preached —it often was still a private home—and number of people present at his preaching). This remarkable and important document was published by A. M. Cramer with an introduction in *DJ* 1840, 33-52.

vdZ.

Cremer, Steven Abrahams (the name is also spelled Kremer, or Cramer), was a son of Abraham Willemsz Cremer (*q.v.*). He lived in Deventer, Dutch province of Overijssel, b. 1660 (date of death unknown), was a member of the Old Flemish Mennonite congregation and a brewer. He is known as a member of the Dutch Committee of Foreign Needs. As such he provided for the Swiss refugees who had come to Amsterdam on Aug. 3, 1711. While a considerable number of the Swiss Brethren were migrating to Groningen, Cremer conducted 81 Mennonites from Amsterdam to Kampen, and 106 to Deventer, both in the province of Overijssel. In both places the Swiss Mennonites were welcomed and sheltered by the Dutch congregations and gradually settled on the farms which Cremer had bought or rented for them.

vdZ.

J. Huizinga, *Stamboek van Samuel Peter (Meihuizen) en Barbara Frij* (Groningen, 1890) 44-45, 117, 121; Müller, *Berner Täufer*, 321, 324, 325; *Inv. Arch. Amst.* I, Nos. 1016, 1212, 1216, 1224, 1299, 1323, 1329.

Cremona (Alta.) United Missionary Church was organized in 1932, when a meetinghouse was built with a seating capacity of 100. The membership in 1953 was 17.

M.G.

Crespin, Jean, b. at Arras, France, d. 1572 at Geneva of the plague. A lawyer by profession, he lived in Paris, Arras (banished from there in 1545), Strasbourg, and Geneva. Crespin is the author and publisher of *Le Livre des Martyrs*, an account in the French language of the life and suffering of the Protestant martyrs, beginning with Jean Hus. The first edition appeared 1554 at Geneva (687 pages). There are five editions of 1554, all with slight differences; during the life of Crespin the book of martyrs was reprinted several times, the titles being somewhat changed; the last edition, revised and printed by the author himself, is dated 1570 (1,424 pages). The martyrbook of Crespin was very popular among the Calvinists. After the death of Crespin some new editions were issued by Simon Goulart, a Reformed preacher of Geneva, the last of which was published in 1619. This version was published about 1920 in a new edition at Toulouse (by D. Benoit). There are also Latin, German, and Italian translations. Besides Calvinist martyrs Crespin also gave place to Waldenses and Albigenses as well as to Wycliffites; but Anabaptists and Mennonites are intentionally excluded. According to his preface he thought it terrible to believe that Anabaptists could be martyrs for the truth. Crespin's book is interesting and important for the study of religious conditions and church history of the 16th century, especially in France.

vdZ.

Bibliographie II, 87-252; C. Sepp, *Geschiedkundige Nasporingen* (Leiden, 1873) II, 20-44; F. Pijper, *Martelaarsboeken* (The Hague, 1924) 5-33.

Cressman, a Mennonite family name found principally in Waterloo Co., Ont. The progenitor of this family was Nicholas Cressman, who immigrated from Switzerland to Pennsylvania before the American Revolution. His son Nicholas II was born in Pennsylvania about 1727 and his grandson Nicholas III in 1751. John Cressman, son of Nicholas II, came to Waterloo County in 1807; and Abraham Cressman, grandson of Nicholas II, in 1806. Bishop Amos Cressman (b. 1836), the eighth son of Abraham, served in Wilmot Township. Bishop Curtis Cressman, in the same family line, now serves this district. For many years Silas Cressman, a great-grandson of Abraham, served as an elder in the Mennonite Brethren in Christ (now United Missionary) Church, and his son Lloyd has recently been appointed president of Friends University at Wichita, Kan. Menno C. Cressman, a grandson of Abraham, was for many years a leading layman in the Ontario Conference (MC) of Mennonites. The Cressmans are most numerous today at the Cressman Mennonite Church (Breslau), the Biehn Mennonite Church (near New Hamburg), and the First Mennonite Church of Kitchener, Ont. J.B.C.

Cressman, Menno Cressman (1861-1953), was born on Nov. 5, 1861, near New Dundee in Waterloo Co., Ont., the son of Samuel and Barbara Cressman. His grandfather Abraham Cressman came to Waterloo County in 1806 from Chester Co., Pa. In 1887 M. C. Cressman was married to Mary Ann Nahrgang of New Hamburg, Ont., daughter of Joseph Nahrgang, a Mennonite preacher. She died in 1948. There are two children of this marriage, Grace (Mrs. M. L. Shuh) and Joseph Boyd. After several years' experience in Hanover and New Hamburg, M. C. Cressman came to Berlin, now Kitchener, in 1892 and conducted his dry-goods business there until he retired in 1927. Both he and his wife were active workers in First Mennonite Church (MC) of Kitchener and in the Ontario Conference of Mennonites (MC). From 1910 to 1929 he served as financial representative in Ontario for the Mennonite Board of Missions and Charities of Elkhart. Later he served a 5-year term on the executive committee of this board. J.B.C.

Cressman Mennonite Church (MC) is located one-half mile from Breslau, Waterloo Co., Ont. The congregation, organized in 1826, is affiliated with the Ontario Conference and in 1954 had a membership of 155. The first meetinghouse was moved from Kitchener to the present site in 1834. The second building, of brick, was erected in 1856 and the third, also of brick, in 1908. Early family names included Brech, Snyder, Cressman, Weber, Clemmer, Clemens, Shoemaker, and Gole. Pennsylvania German is spoken in about half of the homes of the congregation although the national backgrounds of the members include five nations. One of the earliest Sunday schools in this area of the church was organized here in 1872. Oscar Burkholder, ordained bishop in 1949, was the pastor of the congregation 1912-54, followed by Carl Rudy. Earlier prominent bishops who served the church were Joseph Hagey and Elias Weber.   O.B.

Crest Hill (rural) Mission Church (MC), three miles north of Wardensville, W. Va., is under the Virginia Conference. The church is a frame building purchased from the Presbyterians in 1924. Services had been held in Wardensville and near-by places by Virginia ministers 1905-24. The Washington Co., Md., Mennonites took over the work. They ordained a minister and deacon from among the sons of Thomas Heishman, who had moved here in 1905, thus organizing a congregation. A few years later the oversight was returned to the Virginia Conference. Most of the members are descendants of Thomas Heishman. The 1953 membership was 28.   T.S.

Creutz, a village near Göding in Moravia, where the last adherents of the Anabaptist Gabriel Ascherham (*q.v.*) lived. They united with the Hutterian Brethren in 1565 and established a Bruderhof, which was plundered and burned down by soldiers on June 12, 1605. (Beck, *Geschichts-Bücher,* 248 and 351; *ML* I, 381.)   HEGE.

Crichton, Wilhelm, b. 1732 at Königsberg, d. 1805 as a Reformed chaplain. In addition to various writings on theological subjects, he published two collections of *Urkunden und Beiträge zur Preussischen Geschichte aus handschriftlichen Nachrichten.* From the second part of the above he republished a section as a separate booklet of 44 pages under the title, *Zur Geschichte der Mennoniten* (Königsberg, 1786). It contains a list of works previously published about the Mennonites, and expresses the author's opinion "that most of the information comes from men who were possessed by prejudices against them, and were probably also filled with passion, hate, and bitter envy." Then follows a listing of events and regulations concerning the Mennonites in East and West Prussia from 1545 to 1780, for the most part taken from older works. (*ML* I, 382.)   **A.S.**

Criders Schoolhouse is located nine miles northwest of Bergton, Hardy Co., W. Va., just outside of the northwest corner of Rockingham Co., Va. Here work was begun about 1910 under the leadership of the Virginia (MC) Mennonite Conference. The 1953 membership was 16.   T.S.

Crimea (Krim), a peninsula on the north coast of the Black Sea, connected with the mainland by the Isthmus of Perekop (3 miles wide), with a great variety of landscape and topography: prairies in the north, mountains with meadows (the Yaila) and woods in the center, the Riviera-like south shore with resorts (Yalta), military harbors (Sevastopol, Kerch), an area of slightly more than 9,000 sq. mi., and a population of 741,081 of several races: Russians, Tatars, Jews, and Germans, including 4,817 Mennonites (1926).

Mennonites began to settle here soon after the Crimean War (1854-56); probably they became acquainted with it in the course of their transportation duties for the government and preferred it to the other lands under consideration for settlement situated on the Amur in Siberia. In 1860 Mennonite land seekers looked over several possible sites, and in 1862 four villages were established, which were later followed by others. Settlement was made on purchased as well as on leased land, in several large villages, but mostly in small ones, on scattered farms, and a few large estates owned by single families, the largest comprising some 20,000 acres. Before World War I there were 25 villages and many separate ranches. In 1926 there were 70 villages with 892 families and 4,817 persons, besides those on larger estates. After the difficulties of beginning had been conquered, the Crimean colony developed fast. In 1926 it covered 108,000 acres. Agriculture, cattle raising, and fruit culture were the chief occupations.

The Mennonite settlers of the Crimea originally came from the Molotschna settlement. They lived mostly in small villages or on estates, which were located in the following districts: Kerch, Theodosia (Feodosiya), Simferopol (in which the larger Mennonite villages and centers such as Karassan and Spat were located), Dzhankoi, Eupatoria (Yevpatoriya), and Perekop (with Tchongrav where the Bible school was located).

Intellectual progress kept pace with the material. Schools were taken for granted; in Karassan and Spat there were secondary schools; in 1918 a Bible school was opened in Tchongrav (*q.v.*), which was later transplanted to Winkler, Man. To promote spiritual life a publishing company was opened in Spat in 1897 by Abraham and Jakob Kroeker (*q.v.*), which published the Christlicher *Familien-Kalender,* and later the *Christlicher Abreisskalender;* in 1902 they began the first Mennonite weekly, the *Friedensstimme,* which was later (1905) transferred to Halbstadt on the Molotschna, in northern Taurida. These publications and Herman A. Rempel's *Evangelische Mennonitische Brüderschaft* group gave voice to the strongly pietistic tendencies of the Crimean Mennonites.

Before World War I the Crimea was also the center of the *Phyloxera Commandos* (*q.v.*), a group of Mennonite young men who performed their alternative service, not in the usual forestry, but in finding and destroying the dangerous *phyloxera* vine louse in the state vineyards. As a rule the commandos worked only in summer. During the war there were a good dozen Mennonite commandos here with 1,000-1,500 men in road-building and forestry; they were demobilized in 1917 and 1918.

Thanks to its favorable strategic situation the Crimea was protected from Bolshevik and anarchist invasion during the Revolution 1917 ff. It therefore served as a refuge for persons fleeing the mainland. Hence the number of Mennonites increased. In 1910 there were 3,500 souls; in 1926 over 5,000, because here the Revolution with its shooting, deportations, etc., and its consequence, emigration, did not diminish the population. In 1921, which was a severe famine year, the Crimea, through Sevastopol, became the gate of entry for American Mennonite Relief.

The oldest and largest Mennonite congregation was the Karassan Mennonite Church (*q.v.*), which was founded in 1862 and had branches in Spat (since 1882), Dyurmen (since 1884), and Pasha-Tchakmak (since 1890). In 1905 it had a total membership of 846 and a total Mennonite population of 1,928. The elder at that time was Abraham Friesen. The Busau Mennonite Church (*q.v.*) was founded in 1882 and located in the district of Eupatoria. In 1905 the congregation had a membership of 272 and a total population of 632. In 1913 P. G. Friedrichsen was the elder. The Spat-Schöntal (M.B.) Church (*q.v.*) was established in 1885 and in 1903 had a membership of 301 and a total population of 847 with David Dürksen as elder. Hermann Peters and his group from the Molotschna settled at Eupatoria for a while, and from here later moved to Siberia (see **Apostolische Brüdergemeinde**). In 1921 Hermann A. Rempel, the elder of the Karassan Mennonite Church, founded a new congregation called the *Evangelische Mennonitische Brüderschaft* (*q.v.*). By the following year he had gained a following of seven ministers and 136 members. Rempel stressed specially repentance, conversion, prayer, confession of sins, and baptism by immersion. The Crimea was also the place of the origin of the Krimmer Mennonite Brethren Church (*q.v.*), which emigrated as a body to America in 1874.

During the Soviet era the Mennonites of the Crimea suffered just as much as at other places. Many were sent to the north and east into exile even before 1930. At this time worship services became impossible. When in 1941 the Germans occupied the Ukraine most of the Crimean Mennonites were evacuated by the Soviets to the Far East. Some of those that remained have found their way to Canada and South America. (For further information see articles: **Ukraine, Russia,** and **Concentration Camps.**) TH.B., C.K.

Friesen, *Brüderschaft;* K. Lindemann, *Von den deutschen Kolonisten in Russland* (Stuttgart, 1924); J. Quiring, *Die Mundart von Chortitza in Süd-Russland* (München, 1928); A. Ehrt, *Das Mennonitentum in Russland* (Langensalza, 1932); H. H. Friedrichsen, "Die Geschichte der Busaer Menn.-Gem.," *Unser Blatt* II (1927) 236-38; *idem,* "Aus der Gesch. der Krimmer Menn.-Brüdergem." (H.K.), *ibid.,* 327-28.

Crocius, Paul, translated the martyrbook of Jean Crespin (*q.v.*) from the French into German (editions of Hanau, 1606, 1617; Bremen, 1682, 1722). Because the name of the French author is not mentioned in these editions, the impression is given that *Das Grosse Martyr-Buch und Kirchen-Historien . . .* is the product of Crocius. VDZ.

Crockett Mennonite Mission (MC), Crockett, Ken., is sponsored by the Virginia Mennonite District Mission Board. It was established in 1949 and in 1954 had seven members. M.G.

Croghan, N.Y., a town of about 850 population, is located in the northeastern part of the state, about 50 miles east of the mouth of the St. Lawrence River, in the western foothills of the Adirondack Mountains. The town is located on the east side of the Black River which divides Lewis County almost exactly in half.

About 1833 the first Amish and Mennonite settlers arrived in the Croghan community, then called French Settlement. About 1849 the major portion of the church membership left to form a new church called at first the New Amish but later changed to the Evangelical Baptist (Apostolic Christian). On Nov. 11, 1941, 68 members of the Conservative Amish Church withdrew and formed a new congregation now known as the New Bremen First Mennonite Church, independent of any conference. The churches in the community are the Croghan Conservative Amish Mennonite Church and the Lowville (Dadville) Conservative Amish Mennonite Church, with a combined membership of about 600, and the New Bremen First Mennonite Church with a membership of 142.

In 1909 three families sold their farms near Croghan and moved to the west side of the river. Now there are nearly as many families living west of the Black River as east of it. In 1928 a new church was built just west of the river called the River Church or the Dadville Church. Lowville, the county seat, then became the trading center for these families.

The two towns, Croghan and Lowville, located about 10 miles apart, share the trading of these people, about half of the total number living within shopping distance of each town. The Mennonites and Amish Mennonites are scattered in all directions from the two towns with no particular concentration. Only about 20 Mennonite families reside in the village of Croghan and about 15 in the village of Lowville.

The community is very isolated from other Mennonite and Amish communities. The nearest group is located in western New York—250 miles west. It has survived the blow of the first major split and has developed into a large and growing Mennonite and Amish settlement. R.S.L.

Croix, André du, b. Oct. 13, 1910, at Amsterdam, studied theology at the University of Amsterdam and the Mennonite Seminary at the same place. He became a ministerial candidate in 1936, and served the congregations at IJlst (1936-39) and Winschoten (1939-45). At the time of the occupation of the Netherlands by the German National Socialists, André du Croix was district leader of the *Nederlandsche Unie* (Dutch Union, an organization which tried to prevent the Germanization of the Netherlands), and when this organization was forbidden by the occupying powers, he continued his work in secret. Along with others, he founded a secret organization to forestall the murder of and revenge on Germans when the time would come for them to return to their home country. Because of this illegal work he was arrested in January 1944 in the evening while conducting a catechism class, but was released after a few days. On May 14, 1944, he was again imprisoned by the Germans and was taken from one prison to another (Groningen, Amersfoort, Vught), and on Sept. 6, 1944, along with many others, taken to Germany, where he endured much distress. On account of his courage and loyalty, his charity and strong faith, he was able to be a support to many in prisons and concentration camps. The certainty that Christ remains victor gave him strength, and in his religious life the cross of Christ occupied a continually greater place. When André daily saw people about him dying or brought to death, he prepared himself "to expect from the Lord deliverance from sin and the forgiveness of human guilt, and in this manner to mount up into the light of God's eternal grace and to go forth from strength to strength, in the body still on this earth, yet spiritually already living from the Reality in which time and space no longer exist" (Mesdag). This martyr of our own time died on March 10, 1945, in the notorious camp of Bergen-Belsen. (W. Mesdag, *In dit Teeken . . . . Aan de nagedachtenis van Ds. A. du Croix,* Amsterdam, 1946.)   vDZ.

CROP (Christian Rural Overseas Program) began its operation in August 1947 under the sponsorship of Church World Service. A year later Lutheran World Service and the Catholic Rural Life Conference became co-sponsors, but withdrew in 1952.

CROP was organized to solicit and receive bulk gifts-in-kind from American farmers during the harvest season for needy people overseas. Each cooperating state has its own director and committee who in turn work through county and local committees. Active solicitation and collection is carried on by local church representatives on the principle of American Christians sharing with their needy brethren overseas. Gifts received are distributed through church agencies abroad among the most needy regardless of race, creed, or color.

The first large project was the Abraham Lincoln Friendship Train in 1948 which consisted of 4 sections and total of 283 cars. During the first two years of its operation, CROP collected approximately 118,000,000 pounds of farm products.

Although the Mennonite Central Committee, the official Mennonite foreign relief agency, is not a member of CROP, Mennonites in many rural areas have contributed liberally to CROP collections. Most of these contributions have been designated for the MCC. In this indirect way MCC has received considerable support in its foreign relief program.   J.N.B.

Crosshill Amish Mennonite Church is located six miles north of the Wellesley Mapleview Amish Church in Waterloo Co., Ont. The two places of meeting serve the membership of the one congregation, known as the Wellesley congregation. It began in an unused church, in which they held summer Bible school in 1948. Two years later the congregation bought the building and began Sunday school. More than 100 worship here regularly. The ministers of Mapleview share in preaching at this place.   J.C.F.

Crossroads Mennonite Church (MC), Juniata Co., Pa., is a member of the Lancaster Conference. Bishop John Graybill's home was the place of worship for the Richfield community until 1854 when a large stone church was built near Richfield, but in Snyder County. In 1930 a new brick meetinghouse known as Crossroads was erected in Juniata County. This church with the Lauver church has a joint membership of 165. W. W. Graybill and Donald Lauver are the bishops, with Menno B. Brubaker and J. Walter Graybill as ministers.   ·   I.D.L.

Crossroads Mennonite (rural) Mission Church (MC) at Timberville, Rockingham Co., Va., under the Virginia Conference, meets in a community church that was built by popular subscription, and was formerly used by a number of groups, principally by the Baptists. For a number of years, however, it was rarely used except for singings. The Northern District of the Virginia Conference took up the work about 1933, holding Sunday school, preaching services, singings, and in 1948 prayer meetings. The 1954 membership was 39.   T.S.

Crosstown Credit Union is a co-operative society operated for and by members of the Mennonite churches in and around Winnipeg, Man. It is incorporated under the Companies Act of Manitoba, under date of April 4, 1944. It is an outgrowth of the credit union idea started in Germany by Raiffeisen and Schultz-Delitzsch in the 19th century. It found its way into popularity among the Mennonites in Canada in the 1930's and later. At present there are ten credit unions among the southern Manitoba Mennonites. The Crosstown Union restricts its membership to Mennonites within a radius of 40 miles from Winnipeg. On Aug. 1, 1954, it had 1,046 paid-up shares and a membership of over 1,000.

The board consists of seven directors elected by the members at general meetings. A supervisory committee of three members inspects the books once a month and a credit committee of five members considers all requests for loans and has sole authority for granting them. N. J. Neufeld was one of the prime movers to have the credit union organized and has been its president from the beginning.
J.W.F.

Crous (Kroes, Krus, Kraus), **Jan** (1670-1729), of Reformed origin, the son-in-law of Klas ter Meer (1650-98), who was the preacher of the Crefeld Mennonite Church. Jan Crous was also a preacher of this congregation. He is said to have dedicated the new church on Königsstrasse on Jan. 19, 1696, with a marriage; beyond this there is no evidence that he was a preacher except 1716-24. Two of his sermons have been preserved: Palm Sunday, April 5, 1716, and one for 1721. These sermons breathe the spirit of "the traditional Mennonite manner of faith; simple, sober, remote from all speculation, practical" (Cattepoel), with a rationalistic cast. The Dompelaar movement of the time also struck Crefeld and its Mennonite congregation; the preacher Gosen Goyen (1667-1737), whose marriage on Jan. 19, 1696, was the first to be solemnized in the new church, had himself baptized by immersion in the Rhine Jan Crous opposed this movement, maintaining the method of sprinkling, on the ground that the principle was more important than the method. He, however, was tolerant and did his best (which was not the case in Hamburg) to prevent a schism. "We will gladly bear with those who advocate immersion, and hope for the same attitude in the others." The Dompelaars of Solingen who were imprisoned in Jülich from the end of 1717 to the end of 1720 were visited by Crous and other Crefeld Mennonites; they finally emigrated to Pennsylvania via Crefeld.

A number of Jan Crous's descendants have been of importance in the history of Crefeld and its Mennonite congregation as well as the Mennonite brotherhood in general. E.C.

D. Cattepoel in *Beiträge zur Gesch. rheinischer Menn.* (*Schriftenreihe des Menn. Gesch.-Vereins*, No. 2, Weierhof, 1939) 13, 14, 18, 19; E. Crous in *loc. cit.*, 35; *Gem.-Kal.*, 1935, 64 ff.; Max Goebel, *Gesch. des christl. Lebens in der rhein.-westph. evangelischen Kirche* 3 vv. (Coblenz, 1849-60; *Die Heimat*, Krefeld IV (1924) 197 ff. (Crous); XXII (1951) 62 (Niepoth); *Menn. Gesch.-Bl.* IV (1939) 32 (Niepoth); *ML* I, 459 (Neff); II, 563 (Rembert); Fr. Nieper, *Die ersten deutschen Auswanderer von Krefeld nach Pennsylvanien* (Neukirchen, 1940) 273 f.; *Das Scheuten'sche Stammbuch*, copy in the Mennonite research center in Göttingen, "Tafel 20."

Crown Hill Mennonite Church (MC), Wayne Co., Ohio, founded by settlers from Switzerland and Upper Alsace in 1825, was first known as Chippewa. It was organized between 1825 and 1834 with Peter Steiner and Daniel Steiner as ministers. This congregation in the earlier years was a part of the Sonnenberg congregation in southern Wayne County. Although the Sonnenberg congregation erected a log meetinghouse in 1834, the Crown Hill group had no separate meetinghouse until 1850. This was erected on the Christian Steiner farm approximately one mile northwest of the present Crown Hill Church. The first church at Crown Hill was erected in 1883. The Sunday school, organized in 1874, at first met violent opposition from the older members because they felt it would mean losing the German language. Among those active in the congregation were C. D. Steiner, D. C. Amstutz, John Amstutz, and Fred Amstutz. The first lay Sunday-school superintendents, John Ulrich and Daniel Steiner, were elected in 1883. On Aug. 4, 1936, the Crown Hill meetinghouse built in 1883 was destroyed by storm. The work on the new building began on Aug. 27 of the same year. The Crown Hill congregation now occupies a modern well-equipped up-to-date church building. Its membership in 1954 was 149. Ministers in 1954 were Noah Hilty and John Drescher. J.S.U.

D. Gratz, *Bernese Anabaptist* (Scottdale, 1953) *passim.*

Crown Hill Mennonite School (MC), Marshallville, Ohio, was founded in September 1944, after the Crown Hill congregation had studied the possibilities in several meetings. The first term of school for grades one through eight was opened on Sept. 18, 1944, with Alma Maust as teacher. During the 1946-47 term, 22 pupils were received from the Sonnenberg congregation, bringing the enrollment up to 52, of whom ten were taking first-year high-school work. With the opening of a school by the Sonnenberg congregation in the following year, the attendance dropped, ten being enrolled for 1952-53. E.O.H.

Cruciger (also Creuziger and Creutzinger), **Kaspar** (1504-48), the reformer of Leipzig, Germany, professor of theology in Wittenberg and co-worker with Luther, followed Melanchthon in his views on the Anabaptists, and together with him, Luther and Bugenhagen signed the opinion of June 5, 1536, that Landgrave Philip of Hesse had requested of the Wittenberg theologians and which advocated capital punishment for Anabaptists. (See **Punishment** of Anabaptists.) **NEFF.**

W. H. Hochhuth, "Mitteilungen aus der protestantischen Sekten-Geschichte in der hessischen Kirche," in *Ztscht für die hist. Theol.*, 1858, 560-65; *ML* I, 382.

Cruels, Srijnken (Joosynken), an Anabaptist martyr: see **Sijntgen van Gelder.**

Crumstown Mennonite Church (MC), located southwest of South Bend, in St. Joseph Co., Ind., met at first in an abandoned schoolhouse which had been used as a church by the Methodists and was deeded to the Olive Mennonite Church in May 1933, when they started services at this place. In 1947 the work was transferred to the Indiana-Michigan Mennonite Mission Board. A new church building was completed in 1948, when the church was organized. Membership in 1954 was 52, with William Miller as pastor. C.A.S.

Cruysere (Kruisheer), **Joose de,** an Anabaptist martyr: see **Joost Verbeeck.**

Crystal Springs is a village in Harper Co., south-central Kansas, on the southern branch of the Santa Fe Railroad, in the heart of a Mennonite (MC) community, one-fourth mile west and one mile north of the church. The village was composed of 15 families with a population of 50 in 1950. The Mennonites began the Crystal Springs settlement in 1904. Since the population of the village is largely composed of Mennonites, its businesses are also largely owned or operated by Mennonites. G.G.Y.

Crystal Springs Hutterite Bruderhof, founded near Magrath, Alta., in 1930 by members of the New Elmspring Bruderhof. Their preachers were Peter Entz and Peter J. Entz. In 1947 the Bruderhof had 40 baptized members in a total of 104 souls. D.D.

Crystal Springs (Kan.) Mennonite Church (MC), located in Harper County, originated as an Amish Mennonite Church in western McPherson Co., Kan. Amish settlers from Iowa, Nebraska, and Ohio came to McPherson County 1872-84. The first minister, John Zimmerman, arrived from Iowa in 1887. The congregation was probably organized in 1878, and the first church was built in 1886. Five families who did not favor building a church withdrew, and organized an Old Order Amish congregation. Seeking cheaper land, the Amish Mennonites moved to Harper Co., Kan., near Crystal Springs, in 1904, dismantling their church and rebuilding it in Harper County. The present church was built in 1928. A severe loss was suffered in 1910 when 19 members withdrew, and moved to Shelbyville, Ill., to become members of the John D. Kauffman group. Crystal Springs is the only Amish Mennonite congregation out of 12 to survive in Kansas as an individual congregation. It is a member of the South Central Conference (MC). The 1954 membership was 125. G.G.Y.

Cuauhtemoc, a town located 75 miles west of the city of Chihuahua in the state of Chihuahua, Mexico, pop. 2,826, composed almost entirely of Mexicans with the exception of foreign-born people who have come there as traders. The town of Cuauhtemoc has developed since the coming of the Mennonites in the 1920's although very few Mennonites live in town, for it is the Mennonite shopping center. A railroad, a highway, and a bus line connect Cuauhtemoc with Chihuahua.

The Mennonites are settled in the San Antonio Valley, as far as 75 miles to the north of the town. There are no improved roads leading from the hinterland into Cuauhtemoc. There is a General Conference Mennonite church in the town composed almost entirely of Mennonite refugees who came to Mexico after World War I. The growth of the Mennonite population due to natural increase and to additional immigration from Canada in recent years has stimulated its economic activities. A small cereal factory has been established by non-Mennonites, while a large cheese factory, slaughterhouse, and ice plant have been erected by Mennonites (the Redekops) in the town. In 1947 the Mennonite Central Committee established a service unit in Cuauhtemoc to provide health services, recreational direction, and assistance in educational activities of German-speaking children.   J.W.F.

Cuauhtemoc settlement of Old Colony Mennonites in Mexico. The Manitoba colony and the Swift Current colony, with a joint population of approximately 10,000, compose the Old Colony Mennonite settlement in the San Antonio Valley near the city of Cuauhtemoc in the state of Chihuahua, Mexico. These colonies, named after their respective places of origin in western Canada, resemble each other in pattern but are under separate leadership. The Swift Current group is the smaller of the two and borders the Manitoba colony to the northwest. These settlements, established between 1922 and 1927, are located about 230 miles south of El Paso, Texas, and 75 miles west of the capital city of Chihuahua.

The Mennonites went to Mexico because the Canadian government withdrew the educational privileges which it had granted the first Mennonite immigrants from Russia in 1874. They felt that a nationalization of their schools was a direct threat to their beliefs. President Obregon of Mexico assured them the educational and religious liberties which they desired, and steps were immediately taken to dispose of real estate in Canada and move to Mexico as rapidly as possible.

The first purchase of land consisted of 155,000 acres. The price, eight dollars per acre, was reasonable compared with prices in Canada, but was far above prevailing prices in Mexico. This land was surveyed and laid out in villages, following the same pattern they had used in Russia and in Canada. In 1950 there were about 45 villages in the Manitoba colony and 16 in the Swift Current colony. An additional 12 villages compose a daughter colony at the northern end. The latter are situated on a separate 7,200-acre tract of land purchased in 1945 for the purpose of settling landless young married couples from both colonies. Each village is provided with enough land for 10 to 30 farm families. The farmyards are arranged on either side of a broad main street, with the various fields in the background. The average farm is about 160 acres, parceled out so that each farmer has to take his share of unproductive land along with his fields of fertile land. Each village also reserves a specified acreage for the common pasture. Technically, the farmers do not own their land. They have no titles or deeds, and cannot mortgage their land or sell to outsiders. Usually the Oberschulze (general manager) and another person in the colony have these documents for a large parcel, and from them the individual farmer makes his purchase. A record of payments is kept by the Oberschulze, and, in practice, when all the payments are made, a farmer is considered owner, although he has no legal documents to prove this. Apparently the integrity of the Oberschulze is never doubted.

The Mennonites in Mexico are farmers. Farming methods and types of crops, partly limited by climatic conditions, are invariably the same in all settlements. Due to the semiarid conditions, crops are seeded when the rains begin in June or July. Irrigation is used only on a small scale for gardens and orchards, and for the occasional small patch of alfalfa. Oats, corn, and beans are the principal crops. Corn and beans are the staple food of the Mexican, and have a ready home market, but the price of the oats fluctuates according to the law of supply and demand. Wheat cannot be grown successfully because of unfavorable climatic conditions.

During the first five years farmers met with bitter disappointment because they tried to apply the same crops and methods they had used in Canada. However, they have now become adjusted to their environment and are superior farmers compared to the Mexicans. Power machinery is becoming increasingly popular; farmyards are neat and orderly; buildings, although of mud-brick construction and simply furnished, are comfortable and adequate. Livestock, especially horses, is far superior to that of the Mexican. Gardens and orchards are productive and form an attractive background to the farmyard. Some of the shrubs have been brought directly from Canada.

Business and industry, although frowned upon by the church, have developed in certain areas, partly out of necessity. Although trading is done mostly in Cuauhtemoc and occasionally in Chihuahua, 75 miles to the east, many stores are found in the villages. Cheese factories are scattered throughout the colonies. They not only provide a market for the milk, but also give employment to a few landless men. There are blacksmith and machine shops, and there is a drugstore and a print shop. In this print shop several books have been printed, the type being set by hand by three or four adolescent employees. There are several self-educated dentists and doctors serving the colonies, but medical and health practices are many years outmoded by American standards. Since Old Colony Mennonites prohibit their members from living in towns, it is obvious that industrial opportunities are limited.

The strongest organization in the community is the church. Church membership and citizenship in the community are synonymous. To step outside the church regulations means ostracism and loss of social status. The Manitoba Colony has eight churches served by one bishop and several preachers, who have ultimate authority in matters pertaining to life and conduct in the colony. Discipline is maintained by the threat of excommunication.

Worship services, two or three hours in length, are conducted in plain meetinghouses furnished with backless wooden benches. The *Vorsänger* (choristers) who select the hymns and set the pitch for the congregation, have a place beside the pulpit next to the ministers. The melodies and singing resemble those used by the Amish in the *Ausbund* of several centuries ago. The use of harmony or musical instruments does not occur. The sermon is read in High German and expository comments are made in Low German. Young people are baptized in their early twenties, usually just before marriage. It is reported that there are approximately one hundred marriages a year in the colony. Intermarriage with Mexicans occurs but rarely. Concerning the moral and ethical status of the colony there are differences of opinion; some colony leaders express fear that contact with the natives is having a detrimental effect on the colony's original high moral reputation. The writer's observation, although not conclusive, indicated evidence of moral laxity, intellectual stagnation, and perhaps spiritual dormancy.

The Old Colony Church attempts to keep its parochial schools. It is on this issue that they migrated to Mexico. The church and the school are closely bound together. Each village has its own school, which is usually in session from November to April or May. The teacher is selected from the male church membership without special training. The schools are under the supervision of the ministers. The *Fibel*, Catechism, Bible, and *Gesangbuch* constitute the main study materials. Instruction is by rote and in the High German language, although all of the children speak Low German at play, and many teachers have but a poor knowledge of the High German. Reading material is scarce, even in the home. The *Steinbach Post* is frequently the only source of reading. Some of the more alert members of the community are dissatisfied with the condition of their schools, but the general philosophy is to prevent people from learning too much so that they will be content to remain tillers of the soil within the colony. It is true, however, that very few of the young people have left the colony, but the tendency for the landless and unattached to drift away is increasing with an increase in population. A long-continued drought caused the return of several hundred to Canada in 1954.

The government of Mexico is friendly toward the Mennonites. They are looked up to as model farmers. Social intercourse between Mennonites and Mexicans is restricted mainly to business transactions. The Mennonites are glad for their freedom in religious, educational, and agricultural matters, but they have not yet become Mexican citizens. (See **Mexico,** and **Old Colony** Mennonites.) J.E.

J. W. Fretz, *Mennonite Colonization in Mexico* (Akron, Pa., 1945); *idem*, "Mennonites in Mexico," in *Menn. Life,* April 1947; W. Schmiedehaus, "Mennonite Life in Mexico," in *Menn. Life,* April 1947; *idem, Ein Feste Burg ist Unser Gott* (Cuauhtemoc, Mexico, 1948).

Cuba Conservative Amish Mennonite Church is located 12 miles east of Fort Wayne, near Harlan in Allen Co., Ind. The congregation was organized with the assistance of S. J. Swartzendruber of Pigeon, Mich., in 1924. Ministers who have served

the congregation are Menno D. Miller, Menno Coblentz, Noah Zehr, and Edwin Albrecht, the present pastor (1952). The present meetinghouse, built in 1949, accommodates a membership of 160.
E.A.

Culbertson (Neb.) Mennonite Brethren Church dates back to 1879 when several Mennonite Brethren families settled in western Nebraska. For some time it flourished and increased to a membership of 60. At present, however, it has only 18 members. Ministers who have served this church are Adam Ross, David Hooge, R. C. Seibel, A. A. Loewen, G. H. Janzen, Karl Dick, Raymond Laird, Dave Plett, and P. P. Balzer, who was serving in. 1954. At present Raymond Laird leads this group.
H.E.W.

Cullers Run Schoolhouse (rural) Mission Church (MC), five miles southwest of Mathias, W. Va., is under the Virginia Conference. Work was started at this place in 1932 with Sunday school and church services under the care of the ministers of the Northern District of the Virginia Conference. The membership in 1954 was 21. T.S.

Cullom Mennonite Church (MC) is located in the town of Cullom, Livingston County, near Pontiac, Ill. The congregation belongs to the Illinois Conference. It was first organized as a congregation about 1860. The church was built in 1882 and remodeled in 1914. The 1954 baptized membership was approximately 16. A.H.L.

Culm (also Kulm, Polish *Chelmno*), in former West Prussia, in the Marienwerder district, on the right bank of the Vistula, 24 miles northwest of Thorn (Torun). Its population of 50,069 (1910) included 276 Mennonites who belonged to the Schönsee (*q.v.*) congregation. They were partly of Dutch and partly of High German origin. Dutch Mennonites settled here as early as the middle of the 16th century; the High Germans probably came from Moravia during the first persecutions. These latter retained the old peasant coat with hooks and eyes until the first decades of the 19th century. On Aug. 22, 1553, King Sigismund of Poland granted the Mennonites permission to settle here (F. Schultz, 12). About 1590 a union took place between the Frisians, who were for the most part immigrants from Holland, and the High Germans. In the lowlands of Culm and Schwetz there were two other congregations of the strict Groninger Old Flemish (*q.v.*). Under the jurisdiction of the Culm bishops and several noblemen who valued the Mennonites as colonists all the groups enjoyed considerable liberty. On June 17, 1689, Bishop Casimir Opalinski gave them a charter of religious freedom and toleration. In 1728 the Bishop of Culm defended them against oppression by the clergy and gave them a written guarantee on this point. Because they had received several Lutherans and Catholics into their membership they were to be expelled from the district of the city of Culm by the episcopal edicts of June 16 and July 9, 1732. But by April 6, 1733, this edict was revoked, after they had been forced to pay 10,000 florins. They were assisted in raising this sum by their brethren in Holland (Brons, 257; *Inv. Arch. Amst.* I, No. 1091). August III of Poland extended all the earlier privileges (granted by the kings John Casimir and John Sobieski) by a government rescript of Sept. 9, 1750 (W. Mannhardt, 93-95), to the Mennonites of the Culm lowlands. In 1768 the Mennonites were expelled from several villages they had been living in since 1588, whereupon they settled to the northwest in Brenkenhofswalde (*q.v.*) in the province of Brandenburg. At the time of the first emigration to Russia (1789) the following Mennonites were living in the Culm region (Reisswitz, 321).

Place	M.	W.	S.	D.	Servants M.	W.
Schönsee	13	11	22	18	2	6
Dorposch	3	10	20	12	..	1
Crenz	4	3	6	5	..	..
Schwetzer Kampen	10	9	15	17	..	..
Nieder-Ausmass	11	11	17	17	2	1
Ober-Ausmass	2	2	6	5	..	..
Klein-Lunau	20	21	20	21	1	..
Gross-Lunau	14	12	13	15	8	2
Jamrau	10	10	12	9	4	..
Schöneck (Schöneich)	12	12	9	19	3	2
Rossgarten	1	2	4	2	..	..
Steinwage	2	2	6	1	2	..
Gogolin	4	4	6	8	3	2
Horst	3	3	12	5	..	2
	109	112	168	154	25	16

Total 584

M—Men, W—Women, S—Sons, D—Daughters.

In the following years the number of Mennonites decreased steadily. Census statistics show: 1861, 580; 1871, 505; 1880, 407; 1890, 385; 1900, 342; and 1910, 276. In 1945-48 the German-speaking population of this area, including the Mennonite settlement, was completely wiped out either by flight or by deportation by the Polish government, as a result of the victory of Russia over the German armies.   NEFF.

W. Mannhardt, *Die Wehrfreiheit der Altpreussischen Mennoniten* (Danzig, 1863); Reisswitz and Wadzeck, *Beiträge zur Kenntnis der Mennonite-Gemeinden* (Berlin, 1821); J. A. Starck, *Gesch. der Taufe und Taufgesinnten* (Leipzig, 1789); F. Schultz, *Gesch. der Stadt Kulm in skizzierter Darstellung* (1872); A. Brons, *Ursprung . . . der Mennoniten* (Emden, 1912); *Inv. Arch. Amst.* I, Nos. 1091, 1367, 1574, 1647, 1648, 1702; II, 2, No. 779; H. Wiebe, *Das Siedlungswerk niederländischer Mennoniten im Weichseltal zwischen Fordon und Weissenberg bis zum Ausgang des 18. Jahrhunderts* (Marburg, 1952); *ML* I, 382 f.

Culm Military Academy, a building and institution in the city of Culm, then in West Prussia, built in 1778 by King Frederick the Great, which is closely associated with the history of the Mennonites of West Prussia. For its support the Mennonites had to contribute 5,000 talers annually, thereby purchasing their continued exemption from military conscription. The building, a large barracks-like structure, was burned on Aug. 18, 1912. Until April 1, 1884, it was used to train officers for the army. Then it became the barracks of a battalion of sharpshooters. On June 20, 1774, a mandate was issued ordering the Mennonites in West Prussia and Lithuania to pay 5,000 talers annually as of June 1, 1773, for the benefit of the Culm academy. But not until

the *Gnadenprivilegium* of Frederick the Great of March 29, 1780, did they receive an express guarantee of freedom from military duty. The sum had to be paid until the revocation of the privilege of military freedom on Nov. 9, 1867.   NEFF.

Menn. Bl., 1912, 66 f.; Mannhardt, *Die Wehrfreiheit der Altpreussischen Mennoniten* (Marienburg, 1863); Anna Brons, *Ursprung, Entwicklung und Schicksale der Altevangelischen Taufgesinnten oder Mennoniten* (Emden, 1912); *ML* II, 383.

Culross Township Mennonite Church: see **Bruce County, Ont.**

Cumberland County, Pa., located southwest of Harrisburg, was carved out of Lancaster County on Jan. 27, 1750. In 1755 the Proprietary Government suggested that the Irish settle in here, leaving Lancaster for the Mennonites. Consequently the Mennonites did not move in before the late 1780's and '90's, and their first house of worship was Slate Hill, built in 1820. Today (1950) there are three Mennonite churches in the county: Slate Hill, Churchtown, and Diller. William M. Strong is the bishop of these churches.   I.D.L.

Cuperus (Cuperius), Andries Scheltes, originally of Blessum, Friesland, b. about 1750, d. 1812 at Zijldijk, Groningen, was a Dutch Mennonite pastor, serving the congregations of Terschelling, 1782-90; Knijpe (Nieuw Brongerga), 1790-1804; and Zijldijk, 1804-12. Through his influence the two congregations of Terschelling (*q.v.*) decided to unite (*DB* 1861, 89). During his pastorate at Knijpe he was interested in politics and since the dissenters, including the Mennonites, had obtained equal political rights with the members of the Reformed Church in 1796, Cuperus was for a few years a member of the Frisian provincial government, which was, however, not much appreciated by a large part of his congregation. (P. H. Veen, *De Doopsgezinden in Schoterland,* Leeuwarden, 1869, 78-98.)   vDZ.

Cuperus, Bartholomeus, b. Amsterdam 1836, d. 1914, a Dutch Mennonite pastor. After finishing his theological studies at the University and the Mennonite Theological Seminary at Amsterdam, he served the congregations of Rottevalle-Witveen 1861-63, Borne 1863-71, IJlst 1871-73, and Zutphen 1873-90. He wrote *Afscheidsrede te Zutphen* (Zutphen, 1890); *Godsdienst een maatschappelijke kracht* (Zutphen, 1890), and *Levensbericht van Alle Meenderts Cramer* (Leiden, 1895).

He was the power behind the recently established congregation of Wageningen (*q.v.*), which owes its existence both spiritually and financially to a large extent to Cuperus. Even before the congregation was founded Cuperus gave catechetic instruction to Mennonite children here, starting on May 23, 1895, and from October 1895 he often conducted a service for the Mennonites residing here. He dedicated the first church of Wageningen on May 24, 1901. In 1904 and again in 1905 he presented the church with a considerable gift of money for a pipe organ. Until the first minister of Wageningen preached his induction sermon (A. J. van Loghum Slaterus, Nov. 22, 1908), Cuperus acted as temporary pastor of the congregation. (*DB* 1895, 183; 1896, 209; 1901, 214; *DJ* 1927, 58-65, 68.)   vDZ.

Cuperus, Johannes, a Dutch Mennonite preacher, b. March 10, 1725, at Deinum, acquired a thorough education at Franeker and the Mennonite Seminary in Amsterdam, was called to den Hoorn on Texel, delivering his first sermon there in February 1753. In October of the same year he transferred to Vlissingen, and in 1758 to Utrecht (first sermon on Nov. 26), where he served until his death on April 17, 1777. He was a colleague of Martin Schagen (*q.v.*), whose funeral sermon he preached in 1770, which was later published. On Nov. 7, 1773, he had charge of the dedicatory service for the new Mennonite church in Utrecht (*Kerkrede*). He is praised for his excellent catechetical instruction. He must have had some contacts with the American Mennonites in the region of Philadelphia (see the letter to Crefeld and to Cuperus, *MQR* III, 1929, No. 4, 226-32). The Amsterdam Mennonite Library contains a valuable manuscript of 335 pages from his pen on the origin and divisions of the Dutch Mennonites, some of which was published in the *Doopsgezinde Bijdragen*. C. de Vries (*q.v.*), a colleague of Cuperus and successor of Schagen, delivered his funeral sermon: *De onderscheidene en uitsteken der Geluksaligheid* . . . (Amsterdam, 1777).

NEFF, vDZ.

J. Cuperus, *Kerkrede* (Utrecht-Amsterdam, 1773); *Inv. Arch. Amst.* I, Nos. 1545, 1954, 2341; *DB* 1868, 85 ff.; *Biogr. Wb.* II, 330-32; *ML* I, 383.

Curitiba, Brazil, is the capital of the state of Parana. It is situated about 40 miles from the Atlantic Ocean (the harbor is Paranagua) and has an elevation of about 3,300 ft. The climate is therefore favorable for settlers coming from northern Europe. The (1950) population is about 160,000. Its most important industry is its trade in lumber and yerba-mate.

The Mennonites of the near-by settlement of Bouqueirao (*q.v.*) furnish about three fourths of the total milk supply of the city. Mennonites are also living in the city and on its fringes, most of them employed as skilled laborers and in factories.

P.K.

Curitiba (Brazil) Mennonite Brethren Church had its beginning in 1936. The constituents forming this church were a group of settlers of this denomination who together with other Mennonites had moved for economic reasons from the Stoltz Plateau, Santa Catharina Province, to Parana Province, establishing the village Bouqueirao near the city of Curitiba. Here dairying became the means of livelihood because of the profitable market in Curitiba. With the group had also come Elder Jacob F. Huebert who became their leader by common consent. The group has increased to a membership of around 400 (1952). Because of the advancing age of Elder Huebert, the congregation has called Minister Peter Hamm into the responsibility of leadership.

The larger part of the Mennonite Brethren membership is located at Bouqueirao. Some of the members living at a distance from this location have since 1949 been gathering at Guaratuba for worship services under the leadership of Minister Peter Janzen. For larger festivities and for communion services the two groups unite at Bouqueirao.

It should be inserted here that during the initial years following 1936 the three Mennonite groups represented in this area, namely, the Mennonite Brethren, the General Conference, and the Evangelical Mennonites, met in union services for several Sundays during each month. The small and newer group of settlers at Vila Guaira even now conduct their services unitedly regardless of church affiliation, which has been a common practice in South America when settlements were started containing families from the various Mennonite groups.   A.E.J.

Curitiba (Brazil) Mennonite Brethren Mission. In November 1945 the Board of Foreign Missions appointed the Jacob D. Unruhs, who had worked for several years among homeless children in Brazil, to start a home for unfortunate children near Curitiba. The mission accepts Brazilian homeless children below four years of age to feed, house, and clothe, gives them an elementary education, teaches them habits of cleanliness and industry, and, above all, imparts to them the way of eternal life through Bible instruction.

The mission maintains a school on the compound, operates a 50-acre farm to furnish employment for the children, and has a staff of ten workers to look after the medical, physical, and spiritual needs of the children. The supervision of the orphanage is in the hands of the Erven A. Thiesens and Linda Banman. The mission now has three buildings on the main compound, and a residence, barn, and sheds on the farmyard. The present capacity is around 60 children. This number is being kept somewhat lower until the program has become more stabilized.

A feature of this project resides in the opportunity it furnishes the Mennonite churches of Brazil to share in its support as well as to enable those of their young people who feel a call to missions to serve at this place. Opportunities for evangelization are opening in neighboring villages and cities.   A.E.J.

Curitiba (Brazil) Mennonite Church was formed by members of the Witmarsum and Stoltz Plateau congregations, who left those settlements and gradually found their homes in and near Curitiba, in Bouqueirao (*q.v.*). The leader of the congregation, Elder David Koop, settled here in 1935, and since that time there has been a Mennonite congregation here. It was at first quite small, but made a rapid growth since 1947. For regular services the Mennonite Church and Mennonite Brethren met together, and also shared their Sunday school. The monthly business meetings, communion services, and youth work were held separately.

In 1946 the two groups conjointly built two churches, the largest in Bouqueirao with a seating capacity of about 700, the smaller in Vila Guaira, a suburb of Curitiba. The Mennonite Church had in 1950, 130 baptized members. It had two ordained ministers and three others not ordained, Elder David Koop, Peter Klassen, Heinrich Loewen, Willi Berg, and Jakob Wiebe. In the church services as in all the church work the German language was used. During the last war, Portuguese and Low

German were used. Several hymnals were in use; the most used were the new Canadian *Gesangbuch,* and a collection of familiar hymns assembled in Curitiba. *Evangeliumslieder* (Gospel Hymns) was also used. The congregation is a member of the General Conference Mennonite Church.   P.K.

Curits, Claudis K. (1850-1943), served as presiding elder in several conferences of the Mennonite Brethren in Christ Church. He was born in Waterloo Co., Ont., was ordained in the Indiana and Ohio Conference in 1886, and held pastorates in Indiana and Michigan.   M.G.

Custer County (Okla.) Amish Mennonite settlement. The Amish located in western Oklahoma in 1892. They originally came from Pennsylvania, Ohio, and Indiana. The first group included Benjamin B. Miller, Moses K. Yoder, Rudy Z. Yoder, and Jacob E. Miller. All except the last secured homestead grants. The next group, arriving in 1896, were John J. E. Miller, Joseph C. Bontrager, and David D. Nissley.

The first minister to arrive was Jacob Yoder (1845-1911) of Pennsylvania, in 1898. Other families following were Solomon Detweiler and Peter Thomas in 1899, Daniel D. Miller in 1901, Moses T. Yoder, David S. Yoder, and Edward F. Bontrager in 1902. Then later families carrying the following names moved in: Bontrager, Schlabach, Miller, Eash, Mast, Yoder, Gingerich, Bender, Stutzman, and Hostetler.

Sixty years after the original settlement the group numbered only about 90 baptized members. This congregation never had a major schism, but like many other similar groups it has endured much internal strife in its effort to maintain a strict "no-change" policy and a number of concessions have been made in recent years. In the meantime, however, some of the more progressive members transferred to Pleasant View Mennonite Church (MC) north of Hydro. Still others moved to other states for various reasons.

The Amish are located between Thomas and Weatherford, but when they first arrived neither of these towns existed and their nearest railroad station was at El Reno, about 65 miles east of the settlement. There were no bridges and a trip to town involved the crossing of two rivers and a number of creeks and canyons and required about three days of hard driving with a team and wagon. In the fall of 1898, the town site of Weatherford was laid out and the Rock Island track was built to it from El Reno. These early settlers experienced the hardships of pioneering at first hand, living in roughly constructed log houses and even dugouts.

The first Amish church service was held in a dugout in 1898 on a farm now owned by Joseph J. Miller. Services were conducted by Bishop Jonas Bontrager of Reno Co., Kan., and the formerly mentioned Jacob Yoder. In 1903 a Sunday school was organized and a meetinghouse was built which still serves for Sunday school and Bible school meetings.

Upon the arrival of Bishop Samuel W. Bender, the congregation was divided and the south district was committed to his charge. In 1930 Ira Nissley

(1890-   ) was ordained bishop for the north district to relieve the aged bishop, Tobias T. Yoder, of these duties. In 1933 Moses W. Yoder (1895-   ) was ordained to the ministry in the south district. In 1948 the ministers serving both districts were John A. Yoder (1879-   ), ordained as minister in 1916 and as bishop in 1941; Benedict T. Yoder (1896-   ), ordained minister in 1915; Joel P. Beachy (1900-   ), ordained as deacon in 1929; David A. Miller (1910-   ), ordained minister in 1938 and bishop in 1953; and Clarence S. Wingard (1908-   ), ordained minister in 1938.

In October 1940 a young people's meeting, at which both young and old participate, was organized under the appointed leadership of Joni A. Yoder and Henry J. Yoder. The leaders for these meetings are now elected by a majority vote every two years. These meetings are held every Sunday evening. The larger part of the service is devoted to the singing of Gospel hymns. A pre-selected chapter of Scripture is read and expounded, and following a prayer and a parting hymn the meeting is closed. While a minority of the congregation did not approve of the idea of a young people's meeting, they later unanimously conceded that the system was far superior to the earlier so-called "singings," and that by co-operation of young and old, the moral standards of youths had been raised to higher levels.

By such weekly Bible study some realized the need of Christian evangelism and have ventured into a mission program, but as yet the effort is mostly confined to evangelizing the Amish body itself. In the summer of 1952 David A. Miller preached the full Gospel to the Amish in Lancaster County, Pa., with the result that some of the congregations there broke fellowship with the western Amish churches and completely closed the door to his teaching. In 1953 he preached every day for two weeks to the Amish in Holmes County, Ohio, in spite of severe opposition. The past three winters (1952-54) he preached at the village of Pinecraft, near Sarasota, Fla., where many Amish from the north resort in their winter homes. With the intensification of this program it is hoped that the Amish will ultimately be revived and bear a living testimony to their risen Lord with their distinct way of life.   J.B.M.

Cuyck, Jan Wouters van, an Anabaptist martyr: see **Jan Wouters.**

Cuyper, Frans de, a Dutch Mennonite elder: see **Frans de Cuyper.**

Cyprian, the well-known Catholic Church Father and Bishop of Carthage, North Africa, who died a martyr in 258. He was the originator of the idea of the one exclusive, true saving church, well expressed in his oft-quoted dicta: "Outside the church [that is the external Catholic Church represented by the bishops] there is no salvation," and "He who does not have the Church as his mother cannot have God as his Father." Proceeding from this idea he rejected the baptism of heretics and schismatics (those who separated from the Catholic Church) and demanded a repetition of baptism when such returned to the Catholic Church, who had been baptized by them. He was sharply opposed by Pope Stephen of Rome, who declared only that baptism to be invalid that was not performed in the name of the Trinity or in the name of Christ, and would have nothing to do with a repetition of baptism. The consequence of this difference was the fateful controversy over baptism by heretics, which ended in the victory of the Roman practice. The Donatists (q.v.) followed Cyprian's views. Menno Simons frequently referred to Cyprian in defense of the validity and necessity of rebaptism, meaning of those baptized in infancy, which is, of course, not what Cyprian meant at all. (Vos, *Menno Simons,* Leiden, 1914; *ML* I, 384.) NEFF.

Contents

1

Explanation of Illustrations

The illustrations in the MENNONITE ENCYCLOPEDIA appear as pictorial supplements at the end of each of the four volumes. They are grouped according to the topics they illustrate. For instance, pictures of Mennonite colleges are grouped under the heading "Colleges," and appear in Volume I, since this volume includes the letter "C." In the case of portraits, however, pictures are presented only for those persons for whom articles appear within the volume. An alphabetical index indicates the location of the pictures by pages in the supplement. In the text of the volume itself, the symbol (†) at the end of the article indicates that an illustration for the article appears in the pictorial supplement of that volume. The choice of illustrations has been limited by availability.

The co-operation of the many individuals and institutions who have secured or contributed pictures is here gratefully acknowledged, even though individual recognition is not given. The larger number of illustrations have been drawn from two chief sources: the Bethel College Historical Library, North Newton, Kan. (Cornelius Krahn, director) and the Goshen College Mennonite Historical Library, Goshen, Ind. (Nelson Springer, curator). In addition the Archives of the Mennonite Church at Goshen College (Melvin Gingerich, custodian), the Library of the United Mennonite Church at Amsterdam, Netherlands (N. van der Zijpp, director) and the Library of the Mennonite Research Center at Göttingen, Germany (Ernst Crous, director), deserve recognition for their contributions. The following periodicals kindly granted us the use of pictures which they had published: *Mennonite Life,* North Newton, Kan., and *Der Mennonit,* Frankfurt a.M., Germany.

The principle of selection of pictures has varied according to the type of matter to be illustrated. Thus, only a few typical dwellings were chosen, in cases where the dwelling represents a distinct type. But in the case of meetinghouses, age, historic importance, style, and regional and denominational representation, have all played a part in the decision, along with the availability of good photographs. Under "Art" only works of genuine merit, and artists of established reputation, have been chosen. For title-pages of Bibles, catechisms, and confessions of faith only first editions, where available, of titles of historic significance have been used. All North American Mennonite colleges were included in the college group. The costume selections have been chosen to illustrate as wide as possible a range of Mennonite costume (but only when it differs from the common national or regional costume, with a few exceptions) in all countries and times; but the choice has been seriously limited by lack of extant costume sketches of earlier periods. Of historic church records only a few specimens have been used.

I. Architecture: Typical Dwellings

1. Switzerland, Emmental; 2. Netherlands, Friesland (not Mennonite); 3. Germany, West Prussia; 4. Russia, Chortitza, Ukraine; 5. Canada, Manitoba; 6. Colonial Pennsylvania near Lancaster, Christian Herr House, built in 1719, also used as meetinghouse.

II. Architecture: Meetinghouses: Netherlands

1. Witmarsum, *ca.* 1650; 2. Zijldijk, 1791; 3. Vlissingen, 1949; 4. Leeuwarden, 17th century; 5. Singel Church, Amsterdam, *ca.* 1630, organ 1777; 6. Rotterdam, 1951.

6

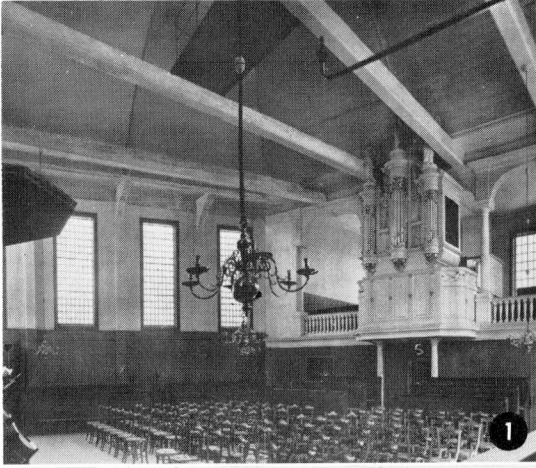

III. Meetinghouses: Netherlands and Germany

1. Netherlands: Westzaan-Zuid, 1731; 2. Netherlands: Pingjum, *ca.* 1575, restored in 1950; 3. Germany: Hamburg, 1915; 4. Germany: Crefeld, 1693, 1952; 5. Germany: Norden, 1796; 6. Germany: Danzig, 1819.

IV. Meetinghouses: West Prussia

1. Pr.-Rosengart, 1891; 2. Ellerwald; 3. Schönsee (Culm),
1618; 4. Fürstenwerder, 1768; 5. Elbing, 1900; 6. Heubuden, 1768.

8

V. Meetinghouses: Germany, Switzerland, and France

1. Palatinate, Sembach, 1777, 1853; 2. Palatinate, Deutsch-hof, 1950; 3. Palatinate, Friedelsheim, 1838; 4. Bavaria, Ingolstadt, 1950; 5. Switzerland: Langnau (Emmental), 1888; 6. Switzerland: Sonnenberg-Jeangisboden (Jura) 1930; 7. France: Alsace, Pfastatt; 8. France: Montbéliard, 1930.

VI. Meetinghouses: Russia and Poland

1. Chortitza (Menn.), *ca.* 1835 from the painting by J. Sudermann; 2. Schönsee (Menn.), Molotschna, 1909; 3. Einlage (MB), Molotschna, 1904; 4. Rückenau (MB), Molotschna, 1883; 5. Schönsee (Menn.), Molotschna; 6. Nikolaifeld (Menn.), Zagradovka, 1891; 7. Lemberg (Menn.), Poland, 1911.

10

VII. Meetinghouses: United States

1. Germantown, Pa. (GCM), 1770; 2. Franconia, Pa. (MC), 1892, 1917; 3. Landisville, Lancaster, Pa. (MC), 1790; 4. Mellinger's (MC), Lancaster, Pa., 1914; 5. Groffdale (MC), Lancaster, Pa., 1910; 6. Weaver's (MC), Harrisonburg, Va.; 7. First, Berne, Ind. (GCM), 1912.

11

VIII. Meetinghouses: United States

1. First of Christian (GCM), Moundridge, Kan., 1950;
2. Corn, Okla. (MB), 1951; 3. Ebenezer (EMB), Henderson, Neb., 1883, 1915; 4. Grace (CGC), Halstead, Kan., 1939; 5. Springfield (KMB), Lehigh, Kan., 1894; 6. Alexanderwohl (GCM), Goessel, Kan., 1886, 1928.

IX. Meetinghouses: United States
1. Metamora, Ill. (MC), 1952; 2. Reedley, Cal. (MB),
1952; 3. Menno (GCM), Ritzville, Wash., 1950.

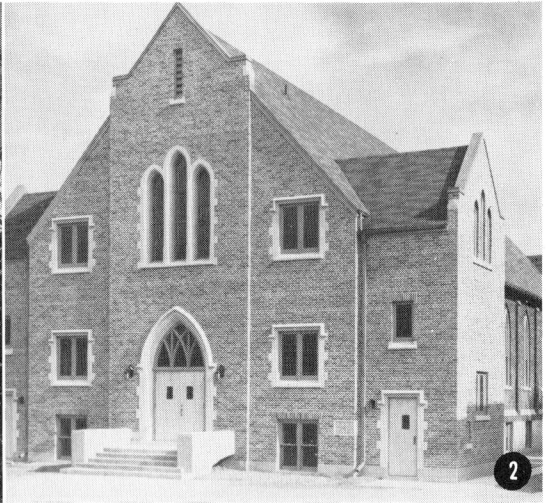

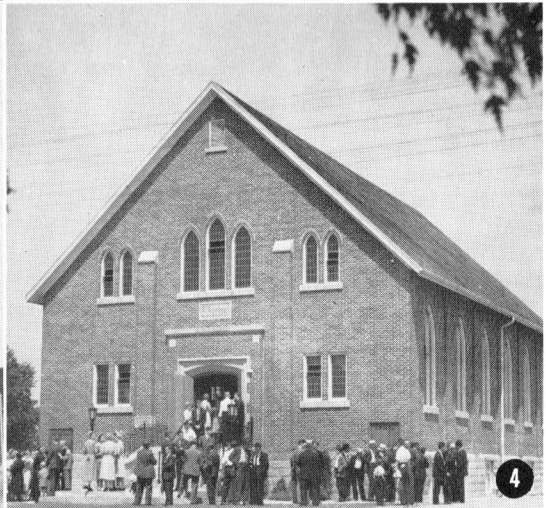

X. Meetinghouses: Ontario, Canada

1. First (MC), Kitchener, 1902, 1928, 1950; 2. Stirling Ave. (GCM), Kitchener, 1925, 1952; 3. Kitchener (MB), 1953; 4. Steinman (AM), Baden, 1948; 5. Almira (MC), Markham, 1860; 6. Martin's (OOM), St. Jacobs, 1848, 1900.

Photos by David L. Hunsberger

14

XI. Meetinghouses: Western Canada

1. Elmwood (MB), Winnipeg, Man., 1955; 2. First (Schönsee, GCM), Winnipeg, Man., 1950; 3. Coaldale, Alberta (MB), 1939; 4. Yarrow, B.C. (MB), 1938, 1953; 5. Rosenort Mennonite (GCM), Rosthern, Sask., 1912, 1948; 6. Altona, Man. (Bergthal, GCM), 1952; 7. Morris Evangelical (Kleine Gemeinde), Morris, Man.; 8. Winkler (MB), Man., 1947.

XII. Meetinghouses: Latin America

1. Filadelfia (GCM), Fernheim, Paraguay; 2. Karlsruhe (MB and GCM), Fernheim, Par.; 3. Gnadenfeld Old Colony Mennonite, near Cuauhtemoc, Mex., 1926; 4. Calvary (MC) La Plata, Puerto Rico; 5. Bragado (MC), F.C.O., Argentina, 1935; 6. Pehuajo (MC), F.C.O., Argentina; 7. Bouqueirao (GCM), Curitiba, Parana, Brazil; 8. Witmarsum (GCM), Santa Catarina, Brazil.

16

XIII. Meetinghouses: Asia and Africa

1. Korba (GCM), India; 2. Telugu (MB), South India;
3. Shantipur (MC), M.P., India, 1925; 4. Donorodjo, Java,
Indonesia; 5. Kai Chow (GCM), Hopei, China; 6. Chinese
Mennonite Church, Kudus, Java, 1941; 7. Matshi, Belgian
Congo, Africa; 8. Shirati (MC), Tanganyika, Africa, 1939.

17

XIV. Art: Mennonite Themes

1. *Christopher Dock* by O. W. Schenck (1930); 2. *Hans de Ries* by M. J. van Mierevelt (*ca.* 1630); 3. *Menno Simons* by C. van Sichem (1605); 4. *Menno Simons* by Arend Hendriks (1948).

XV. Art: Mennonite Themes
1. *C. C. Anslo and Wife* by Rembrandt (1641); 2.
Gozewijn Centen Family by C. Lubienietzki (1721).

19

XVI. Art: Mennonite Themes

1. *The Martyrs David and Levina* by Jan Luiken, from the Dutch *Martyrs' Mirror* (1685); 2. *The Arrest of the Martyr Anneken Jans,* from the Dutch *Martyrs' Mirror* (1685).

XVII. Art: Mennonite Themes

1. *Bernese Farm* by Aurele Robert (*ca.* 1850); 2. *A Martyr Scene* by Jan Luiken, from the Dutch *Martyrs' Mirror* (1685).

21

XVIII. Mennonite Artists: Netherlands

1. Jacob van Ruisdael (1628-82), *The Mill of Wijk near Durstade;* 2. Salomon van Ruysdael (1605-70), *The Ferry-Boat.*

22

XIX. Mennonite Artists: Netherlands

1. Jacob Backer (1608-51), *Luke the Evangelist;* 2. Lambert Jacobsz (*ca.* 1598-1636), *Paul;* 3. Govert Flinck (1614-60), *Isaak Blesses Jacob.*

XX. Mennonite Artists: Germany

1. Balthasar Denner (1685-1749), *Küchenfrau;* 2. Enoch Seemann, Jr. (1644-1744), *Self-Portrait;* 3. Daniel Wohlge- muth (1875-   ), *Christian Neff;* 4. Marie Birckholtz-Bestvater (1888-   ), *Johann Penner.*

XXI. Mennonite Artists: Russia, Brazil, and United States

1. Russia: Johann H. Janzen (1844-1904), *Peace on the Molotschna;* 2. Brazil: Johannes Janzen, *Witmarsum School* (1939); 3. United States: J. P. Klassen (1888-   ), *Famine in Russia;* 4. United States: Arthur Sprunger (1897-   ), *Amish Family.*

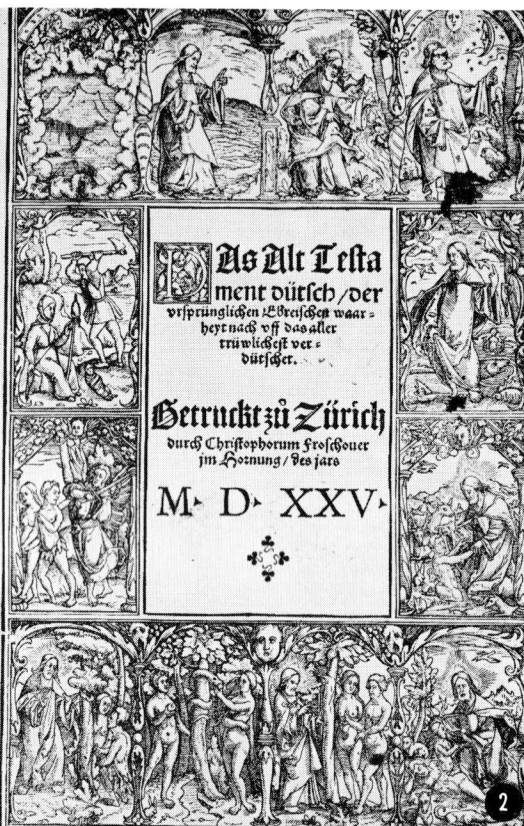

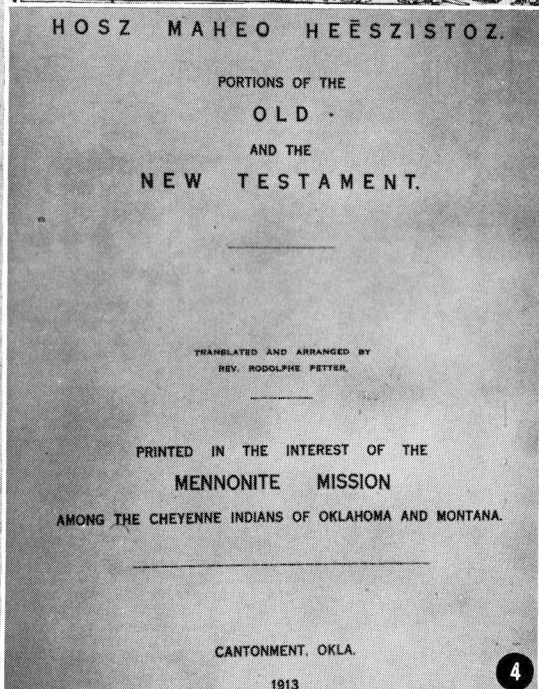

XXII. Bibles

1. H. Denk-L. Haetzer, *The Prophets* in German (Worms, 1527); 2. *Froschauer Bible* in German (1st ed., Zurich, 1525); 3. *Biestkens Bible* in Dutch (1st ed., Emden, 1560); 4. *Cheyenne* (Indian) *Bible* (portions, 1913).

XXIII. Catechisms

1. B. C. Roosen, Hamburg-Altona, Germany (1st ed., 1727); 2. T. J. van Braght, Dordrecht, Netherlands (1st ed., 1657); 3. Elbing, West Prussia (1st ed., 1778); 4. Christian Burkholder, First American catechism (first two editions, Ephrata, 1804).

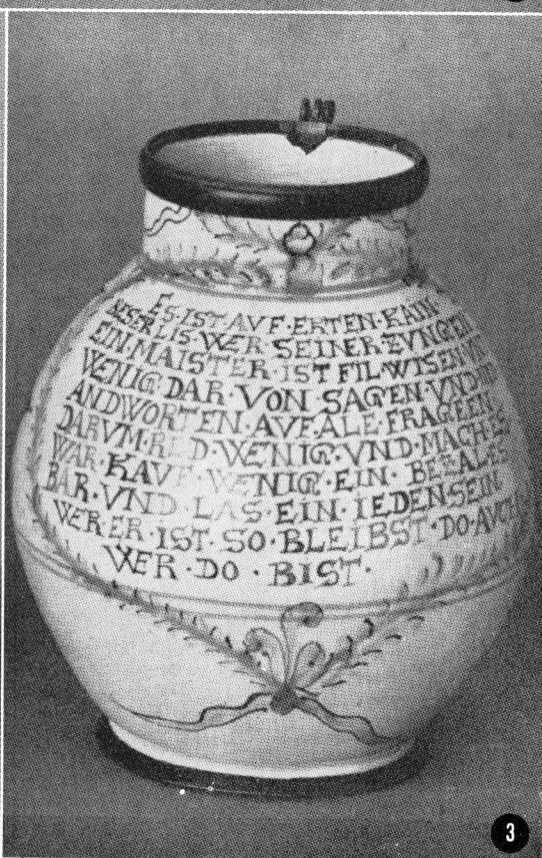

XXIV. Ceramics: Hutterite

1. Jar of 1609, plate of 1687 and jug of 1654; 2. Jug of
the 17th century; 3. Jug of the 17th century.

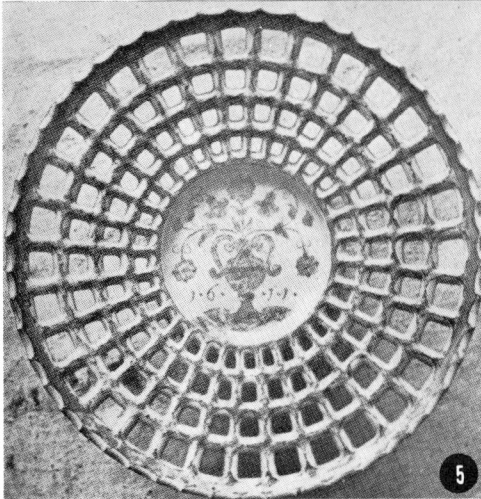

XXV. Ceramics: Dutch and Hutterite

1. Makkum, Netherlands: Mennonite Central Committee Plate (1948); 2. Makkum, Dutch Mennonite Motto Plate (*ca.* 1940); 3. Makkum, Plate of Menno Simons Church at Witmarsum (1936); 4. Hutterite Plate of 1602; 5. Hutterite Plate of 1611; 6. Hutterite Plate of 1634.

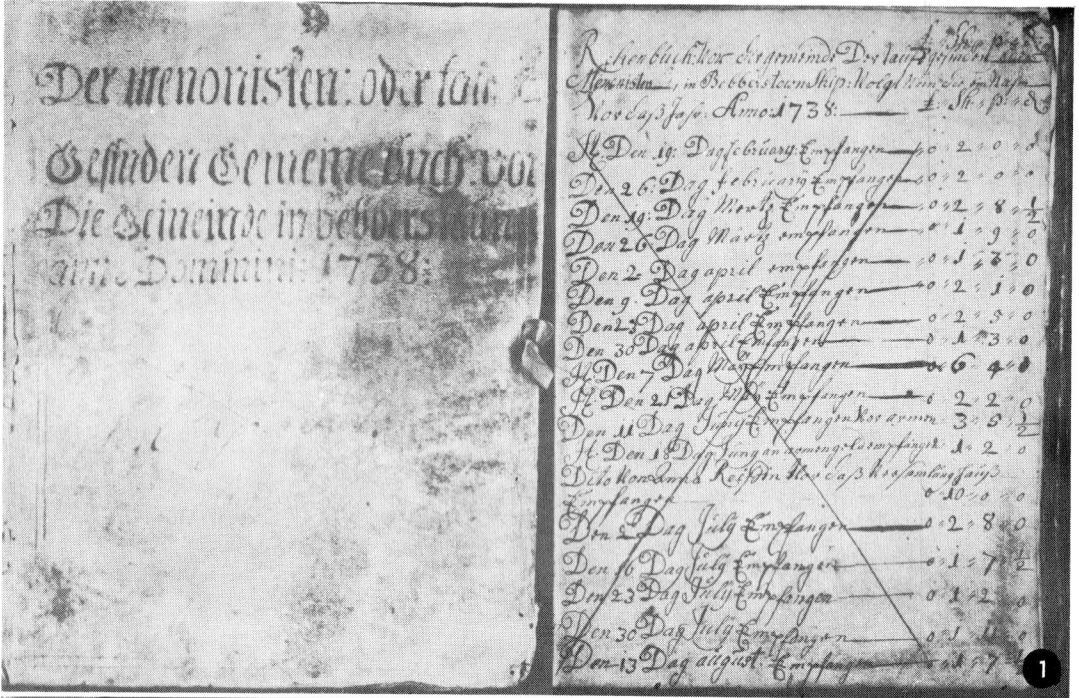

XXVI. Church Record Books and Seals

1. Almsbook of the Skippack (Bebberstown), Pa., congregation (MC), begun in 1738; 2. Typical Church Seals of Mennonite congregations in West Prussia, Russia, and Kansas.

XXVII. Church Record Books

1. Church Record of the Alexanderwohl congregation (GCM), Goessel, Kan., begun in Prussia in the 17th century; 2-3. Church Records of the Danzig, Germany, congregation, begun in the early 17th century.

XXVIII. Colleges: United States
1. Bluffton College (GCM), Bluffton, Ohio; 2. Bethel
College (GCM), North Newton, Kan.

XXIX. Colleges: United States
1. Eastern Mennonite College (MC), Harrisonburg, Va.;
2. Goshen College (MC), Goshen, Ind.

33

XXX. Colleges: United States and Canada

1. Tabor College (MB), Hillsboro, Kan.; 2. Pacific Bible College (MB), Fresno, Cal.; 3. Mennonite Brethren Bible College (MB), Winnipeg, Man.; 4. Canadian Mennonite Bible College (GCM), Winnipeg, Man.

XXXI. Junior Colleges: United States and Canada

1. Freeman Junior College (GCM), Freeman, S. D.; 2. Hesston College and Bible School (MC), Hesston, Kan.; 3. Mennonite Collegiate Institute (GCM), Gretna, Man.; 4. Rosthern Junior College (GCM), Rosthern, Sask.

35

Brüderliche vereyni=
gung etzlicher kinder Gottes /
siben Artickel betreffend.

Item / Eyn sendtbrieff Michel sat=
lers / an eyn gemeyn Gottes / sampt kurtz=
em / doch warhafftigem anzeyg / wie
er seine leer zu Rottenburg am
Necker / mitt seinem blut
bezeuget hat.

M. D. XXvij.

1

... Glaubens / Von den Brü=
der: so man die Hutterisch
en nent außgangen /
Durch
Peter Ryedeman.

Seit alle zeit vrbütig ye
derman zur verantwortung / dem
der grund fodert der hoffnüg
die inn euch ist.
1. Pet. 3.

2

CONCEPT
Van
CEULEN,

Van den eersten Mey,
ANNO 1591.

Te VLISSINGHE;
Voor Geleyn Jansz, Boeck-verkooper achter de groote Kerck. ANNO 1666.

3

Corte
Belijdenisse des
Geloofs / ende der voor=
naemster stucken der
Christelijcke
leere.

2. Corinth. 4. 13.
Maer aenghesien dat wy den selven
Gheest des Geloofs hebben / (na
datter gheschreven is: Ick hebbe
ghelooft / daerom hebbe ick ghe-
sproken) so hebben wy oock ghelooft / daerom spreken wy oock.

Matth. 10. 32.
So Wie my belijden sal voor den Menschen,
dien sal ick oock belijden voor mijnen
Vader die in de Hemelen is : maer so wie
my verloochenen sal voor dē Menschen,
dien sal ick oock verloochenen voor mijnen Vader die in de Hemelen is.

1. Pet. 3. 15.
Zijt altijt bereyt ter verantwoordinghe eenen ye-
ghelijcken / die daer gront eysschet des hoops
die in u is / ende dat met sachtmoedicheyt ende
vreese.

Tot Hoorn,
Gedruckt by Jan Jochimsz. Bywranck /
woonende op't Noort / in't blau Lam van
Haerlem. Anno 1618.

4

XXXII. Confessions of Faith

1. First Anabaptist confession, *Schleitheim Articles* (1527, ed. of *ca.* 1560); 2. First Hutterite confession, Peter Riede-mann's *Rechenschaft* (1545) (1st ed. 1565); 3. *Concept of Cologne*, Germany (1591) first printed in 1666 at Vlissingen, Netherlands, with *Handelinghe Der Ver-eenigde Vlaemse, en Duytse Doops-gesinde Gemeynten;* 4. Waterlander Confession of Hans de Ries and Lubbert Gerrits (1618).

1.

Chriſtliche

Glaubens-

BEKENTNVS

Der waffenloſen/ und fürnehmlich in den Niederländern (unter dem nah-men der Mennoniſten) wohlbekan-ten Chriſten;

Wie auch

Etliche Chriſtliche Gebähte eben derſelben Glaubens-bekenner:

Wobei gefügt ſieben geiſtliche Lob- und andere Ge-ſänge/ aus einer anzahl von 400 eines Gottſeeli-gen Lehrers ſelbiger Bekentnüs gezogen/ und zur probe anher geſtellet;

Als auch noch ein Anhang zum unwiderſprech-lichen beweiſe/ daß gemelte Glaubens-bekenner ſich im leben und lehren/ viel anders befinden/ als man bis anher/ durch unkunde/ von ihnen urteilen wollen.

T. T. V. S.

In AMSTERDAM/ Bey Iohan. Paſkovium, im Jahr 1664.

2.

The

Chriſtian

CONFESSION

Of the Faith of the harmleſs Chriſtians, in the Nor-therlands, known by the name of

MENNONISTS.

AMSTERDAM. Printed, and Re-printed and Sold by Andrew Bradford in Philadelphia, in the Year, 1727.

3.

CONFESSION

Oder

Kurtze und Einfältige

Glaubens-

Bekentnis

derer/ ſo man nennet/

Die vereinigte Flämiſche/ Frie-ſiſche und Hochdeutſche Tauffs-ge-ſinnete/ oder Mennoniſten in Preuſſen.

Außgegeben von denen obigen Gemei-nen daſelbſten;

Gedruckt im Jahr CHRISTI.

1660

4.

DE

GELOOFSLEERE

DER WAARE

MENNONITEN

OF

DOOPSGEZINDEN;

By aanvang ontworpen

TEN DIENSTE, EN OP VERZOEK, VAN DE VEREENIG-DE VRIESSE EN WATERLANDSE DOOPSGEZIN-DE GEMEENTE TE HOORN.

Doch vervolgens, en meer byzonder

Ten grondſlag eener algemeene vereeniging aller Doops-gezinde Gemeenten, en Societeiten, in de ver-eenigde Nederlanden, en daar buiten.

TER PROEVE AANGEBODEN

Aan de Eerw. Societeit der Mennoniten, haare Jaarlykſe Verga-dering houdende in de Kerk de Zon te Amſterdam, en nu op verzoek derzelve aan de byzondere Leden toegezonden, om nader onderzogt en overwoogen te konnen worden.

Met een OPDRAGT aan de genoemde SOCIETEIT; als mede, eene AANSPRAAK aan de Gemeente te Hoorn: vervolgens aan alle Doopsgezinden in 't gemeen, en eindelyk aan alle heil-begeerige Leezers hoe genaamt.

DOOR

CORNELIS RIS.

Leeraar der Mennoniten te Hoorn.

Te Hoorn, by T. TJALLINGIUS, Boekverkooper. MDCCLXVI.

XXXIII. Confessions of Faith

1. Dordrecht Confession (1632, 1st German ed., 1664); 2. Dordrecht Confession (1st American ed., 1727); 3. First Prussian confession (Danzig, 1660); 4. Cornelis Ris Confes-sion (1st ed., Hoorn, Netherlands, 1766).

37

XXXIV. Costume: Netherlands

1. Man and Woman of *ca.* 1730, from Picard, *Ceremonies and Religious Customs* (London, 1733-37); 2. Amsterdam Anabaptist, from Picard; 3. Baptism in the Amsterdam Singel Church, from Picard; 4. The Jacob Bierens family of Amsterdam (1663) by Hendrik Sorgh (1611-70).

XXXV. Costume: Netherlands, Switzerland, France

1. Woman of Aalsmeer, Netherlands, *ca.* 1880; 2. Woman of Friesland taking Communion, *ca.* 1700; 3. Basel Swiss couple, *ca.* 1824, by Joseph Reinhard (1749-1829); 4. Alsatian Amish couple, *ca.* 1815, by Lewicki.

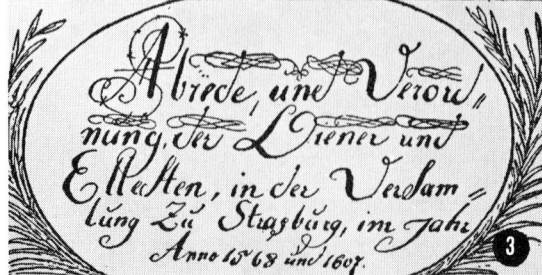

XXXVI. Costume: Switzerland

1. Anabaptist man, *ca.* 1750; 2. Anabaptist woman, *ca.* 1750; 3. Anabaptist group, *ca.* 1750; 4. Anabaptist preacher, *ca.* 1750.

40

XXXVII. Costume: Germany, United States, Canada

1. Maria van der Smissen of Hamburg-Altona, *ca.* 1750, by D. van der Smissen (1705-60); 2. Mrs. Isaac Eby of Kitchener, Ont., *ca.* 1900; 3. Magdalene (van Kampen) Zimmermann of Danzig (1797-1872) by Heinrich Zimmermann (1805-45); 4. Lancaster Mennonite woman, *ca.* 1830, by Jacob Eichholtz (1776-1842).

41

XXXVIII. Costume: Old Colony and Hutterite

1. Old Colony preacher with boots, Mexico, 1950; 2. Old Colony woman, Mexico, 1950; 3. Old Colony women, Mexico, 1950; 4. Hutterite girl and child, South Dakota, 1950; 5. Hutterite family and house, from C. Erhard's *Historia* (Munich, 1588); 6. Hutterite bishop, Manitoba, 1950.

XXXIX. Costume: Amish

1. Two Amish men, *ca.* 1950; 2. Amish man and woman, *ca.* 1950.

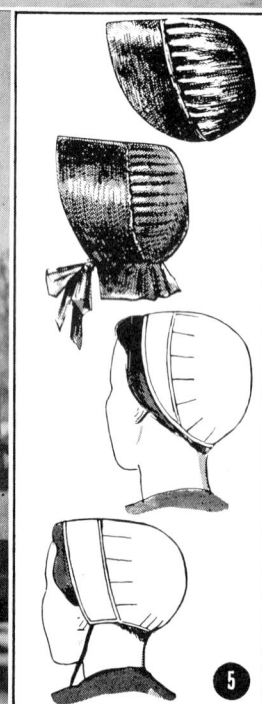

XL. Costume: Conservative U.S.A.

1, 2, 5, Illustrations of Eastern Pennsylvania conservative Mennonite costume, taken from the 1954 catalog of the Hager Co. of Lancaster, Pa.; 3 and 4, Costume groups at Elkhart, Ind., *ca.* 1895; 5. Displays of several types of bonnets and prayer veilings.

44

XLI. Portraits

1. Samuel Cramer, Amsterdam, Netherlands (1842-1913);
2. S. B. ten Cate, Hoogesand, Netherlands (1807-84); 3.
T. J. van Braght (1625-64), Dordrecht, Netherlands; 4. J.
Cornies (1789-1848), Molotschna, Ukraine, Russia; 5. A.
Binnerts (1865-1932), Haarlem, Netherlands; 6. Daniel Bren-
neman (MBC) (1834-1919), Goshen, Ind.; 7. J. S. Coffman
(MC) (1848-99), Elkhart, Ind.; 8. S. F. Coffman (MC)
(1872-1954), Vineland, Ont. (Photo by Belair); 9. Heinrich
Adrian (MB) (1851-1936), Buhler, Kan.

45

Index of Illustrations

Asterisk (*) indicates meetinghouse; P, portrait; *italics,* a book or manuscript; A, art.